# 新和英大辞典プラス

渡邉敏郎
Stephen Boyd ほか
［編］

研究社

まえがき

　2003 年 7 月，収載項目約 48 万を以て刊行された『新和英大辞典 第 5 版』は，その約 1 年後の 2004 年春に開始された研究社オンライン辞書検索サービス (Kenkyusha Online Dictionary, KOD) に『KOD 和英』として加わり，爾来そこを舞台として寸時も休むことなく新語・新用例の採集・追加の作業が続けられて来ました．2008 年 2 月，研究社創業 100 年記念事業の一環として『電子版 研究社英語大辞典』(DVD-ROM 版) が刊行されましたが，『新和英大辞典 第 5 版』も『KOD 和英』への追加語彙約 3 万 5,000 項目を加えた『新和英大辞典 電子増補版』としてそこに収録されました．その後も増補作業は続けられ，更に追加語彙約 5,000 を加えて，KOD 上の『新和英大辞典』の総収録語彙は今や 52 万項目に達しています．

　このたび，5 年前に第 5 版を購入された方々の便に供するため，その後に追加された語彙約 4 万項目を冊子にまとめ『新和英大辞典・プラス』のタイトルで刊行することになりました．90 年に及ぶ『新和英大辞典』の歴史の中で追加語をまとめて出版するのは今回が 2 度目で，1931 年(昭和 6 年)刊の第 2 版の増補版が戦後の混乱いまだ鎮まらぬ 1949 年(昭和 24 年)に出版されています．それは第 2 版の冒頭に 68 ページ分の追加語を付け足した形のもので，追加語のみが一冊にまとめて出版されるのは今回が初めてです．1949 年の増補版と比べ追加語彙数は段違いに大量のものとなりました．そうならざるを得なかった原因は二つあります．その一つは科学技術・医学・政治・経済・軍事・環境など社会のあらゆる分野において世界的規模で現在起こりつつある急激な進歩・変化と，それに伴う新語の増加です．もう一つの原因はインターネットを含む様々な情報媒体の急速な発達により，かつては各分野において純然たる専門語であった多くの語彙が今や一般人のものとなりつつあるという現実です．たとえば，少し前までは医学専門誌にしか見られなかったような病名や治療法，薬剤名が一般新聞の健康記事にごく自然に登場するようになっており，他の分野においても全く同じことが起こっています．一般向けの辞書である『新和英大辞典』は，このように著しく拡大した一般人の知識量，関心の範囲に見合うものでなくてはなりません．また次々に生産される流行語の氾濫も無

視できません．言葉の世界で起こっているこれらの現象に遅滞なく対応するためには 24 時間作動する防犯カメラのような態勢が必要ですが，辞書出版の事業をとりまく今の厳しい環境の中ではコンピューターの威力を借りてもそれは楽な仕事ではありません．

　追加語収集の方法は第 5 版本体のそれを踏襲しました．具体的には，新聞・雑誌・テレビ・ラジオなどから新語・新語義を採集し，その意味の理解に必要と思われる説明を付したものが英米人スタッフに回され，英訳が付けられたあと再び日本人スタッフに戻されて元の日本語と英語訳の整合性がチェックされ，必要な場合にはもう一回英米人スタッフに戻され訳が修正されました．しかし防犯カメラに死角があるように，編集陣の力不足もあって重要な新語の採集洩れも少なくないと思われます．既に利用者からこれまでに寄せられた数々のご指摘・ご意見に深く感謝するとともに，これからも皆さまからの叱咤・叱正を頂きながら増改訂の作業を継続し，時代の要請に応えるべく努力を重ねてまいります．下に掲げるのは『研究社・新和英大辞典』の初版である『武信和英大辞典』(1918 年) に付された武信由太郎先生の序文の末尾部分です．

　　　著手以來實に二十餘名の友人助手を煩はし，編者自ら公職の一部を辭し，拮据數年，渾身の心血を注ぎ，更に著書，辭典，雜誌を渉獵して普く内外學者の研究に参し，悉く其珠玉を收め，以て遺漏なからんことを期す．唯，紙數に限りありて解義或は精細に亘るを許さざるものあり，加ふるに時日切迫して研究尚徹せざるものあり，和英辭典として吾人の理想を去る尚遠しと雖も，凡そ明治大正英語界の進歩は略ぼ此一卷に結晶し得たるに庶幾からんか．参照せる所の著書，譯書，辭典，雜誌は一々茲に舉ぐるに遑あらず．今や刻成りて之を江湖に薦めんとするに際し，謹んで感謝の意を表し，功は之を現代學界の進歩に歸し，罪は編者自ら之を負ひ，徐ろに他日の大成を期せんのみ．

　最後の「罪は編者自ら之を負ひ，徐ろに他日の大成を期せんのみ」はそのまま，90 年後の現在『新和英大辞典』の増改訂作業に参加している私たちの思いでもあります．この『新和英大辞典・プラス』を併せた『研究社・新和英大辞典 第 5 版』が様々な分野で活躍される方々のお役に立ち，世界に向けて日本を発信する上でいささかの貢献をなすであろうことを心から念願いたします．

2008 年 7 月

『新和英大辞典』編者

# 目　次

まえがき …………………………………… iii

編集組織 …………………………………… vi

凡例 ………………………………………… vii

略語一覧 …………………………………… x

新和英大辞典・プラス ……………………… 1

付属 CD-ROM について …………………… 453

## 『新和英大辞典・プラス』『KOD和英』編集組織

### 編集委員

| | |
|---|---|
| 渡邉 敏郎 | Watanabe Toshirō |
| 沢村 灌 | Sawamura Kan |
| 須部 宗生 | Sube Muneo |
| 石井 みち江 | Ishii Michie |
| 井上 清 | Inoue Kiyoshi |
| スティーブン・ボイド | Stephen Boyd |
| トム・ガリー | Tom Gally |
| ポール・スノードン | Paul Snowden |
| ロジャー・ノースリッジ | Roger Northridge |
| ローレル・シコード | Laurel Seacord |
| ジョン・ブレナン | John Brennan |

編集部　逸見一好　松原悟　小倉宏子　佐々木則子　黒澤孝一

編集協力　大竹由美　北川弘子　根本保行　不動悦子　菅田晶子　鈴木亜紀子

# 凡　例

## 『新和英大辞典』第 5 版との関係

本辞典は『新和英大辞典』第 5 版(以下,『和大 5』)の補遺として刊行するもので,記述方式は原則として同辞典の方式を踏襲している.本辞典の利用者の多くは『和大 5』の利用者でもあることが想定されるので,本凡例では特に必要と思われる事項をのぞき,簡略化して記述した.

記述方式についての詳細な説明が必要なときは,『和大 5』もしくは,付属 CD-ROM を用いることで利用できる「研究社オンラインディクショナリー」(KOD)『和大 5』の「メニュー」にある「凡例」を参照されたい.

なお『和大 5』との関係という点では,特に以下に留意されたい.

i) 本辞典と『和大 5』で同一の見出しが立てられている場合,本辞典の記述はあくまでも『和大 5』を補足するものであり,例外を除き,『和大 5』にある情報は採録しなかった.

ii) 『和大 5』で採録されている見出し語が,同辞典で「同一表記の見出しを区別する右肩の番号」が付されている場合は,その番号をそのまま採用した.なお『和大 5』に 1, 2, 3 ... と肩番号がある見出し語でも,本辞典で必ずしもそのすべてを採録しているわけではないため,本辞典のみを見たときには,その通番が完備されていない場合がある.

iii) 『和大 5』に既存の見出し語と同一表記の見出し語を新たに採録する場合,また『和大 5』に既存の見出し語に新たに語義を追加する場合,「同一表記の見出しを区別する右肩の番号」ならびに「語義を区分する番号」は『和大 5』からの通し番号とした.そのため通番の点では,上記 ii) と同様,本辞典のみで完備していない場合がある.

**あいしょう[1]【相性】**...

※ 本辞典ではこの見出し語のみに対する補遺情報を採録しているが,『和大 5』には上記のほか,「あいしょう[2], あいしょう[3] ... あいしょう[8]」が見出し語として立てられている.

**かせい[2]【化成】**...
**かせい[9]【仮性】**...
**かせい[18]【華西】**...

※『和大 5』には,「かせい[1], かせい[2] ... かせい[17]」が見出し語として立てられている.「かせい[18]」は本辞典で追加された見出し語である.

**アイ・ピー【IP】**
3 〔知的資産〕IP; intellectual property.

※『和大 5』「アイ・ピー」の項に,語義 1, 2 がある.なお,本辞典の番号が 2 から始まる場合は,本辞典で記述が加えられたことにより番号が発生したもので,『和大 5』の該当項目には通し番号がふられていない.

**アーヴィング[2]**

※『和大 5』の見出し語「アーヴィング」には,通し番号がふられていない.

**サイクロン**
2 〔遠心分離方式の集塵装置〕a cyclone.

※『和大 5』「サイクロン」の語義には,通し番号がふられていない.

## 1　見出し語

(1) **見出しの表記**　かな書きで五十音順に配列した.配列の詳細は後出の (5) 以下に.

外国の人名・地名に現れる v の音の表記には「ヴ」の文字を採用したが,検索の便のために「ヴ」による表記を採らない見出しを重複して設けてあることも多い.

なお,英語アルファベットの読みの表記について,後出「英語アルファベットとかたかなの対応一覧」参照.

(2) **中国語圏および朝鮮半島の人名・地名**　現在,日本で一般的に行われている表記のしかたにならった.つまり,中国語圏の人名・地名については,「ペキン」「シャンハイ」など一部の都市名を除いて,漢字の音読みのひらがな表記を見出しとし,朝鮮半島の人名・地名については,原語での発音に近づけたかたかな表記を主たる見出しとした.

(3) **漢字表記**
i) 漢字を当てることができる語については,原則として,かな表記の次に【　】の中で漢字表記を示した.
ii) 常用漢字による表記を基本とし,常用漢字だけでは表記しきれない語については非常用漢字も挙げた.

(4) **「作品名」の見出しの表記**　「　」(かぎかっこ) にくるみ,かな書き・漢字表記の両方があるものは漢字表記のほうを見出しとした.

(5) **配列**
i) 清音,濁音,半濁音の順に.
ii) 促音,拗音,および (かたかな表記で用いられる) 小さい母音字は直音の次に.
iii) 音引き(—)は直前のかなの母音に読み替えて置き場所を決定した.

(6) **同音語の配列**　見出しの表記パターンにより 3 つに区分し,漢字表記を伴うもの,ひらがな表記だけのもの,かたかな表記だけのものの順に配列した.

(7) **見出しの表記が同一の語の配列**　自立語どうしは基本的に名詞,代名詞,動詞,形容詞・形容動詞,副詞,擬声語・擬態語,接続詞,感動詞,句の順に配列することとしてある.そして品詞ごとに順次,以下の要領で区分して配列した.

i) 漢字表記を伴うものどうしで,漢字の字数に違いがあるときは字数の少ないものから多いものへの順に.

ii) 漢字の字数が同一の場合は，まず1字めの画数の少ないものから多いものへの順に．1字めの画数が同一のときは2字めの画数による．
iii) 固有名詞(見出し自体が漢字を含む形で表記される「作品名」を含む)は普通名詞の次に．

## 2 本　文

（1）**用例の配列**
i) 見出し語が名詞(句)のとき：動詞化の用例と形容詞化の用例以外は，次のパターンに分類し，この順序に配列した．
1 見出し語の前に，見出し語を修飾する語や句がつく用例．
2 見出し語に接尾語などがつく用例．
3 見出し語に原則として「は」を除く助詞がつく用例．助詞ごとにグループ化し，各グループは助詞の五十音順に配列した．
4 見出し語に助詞「は」がつく文例．そのほか以上のいずれにも分類されない文例．
ii) 名詞(句)以外：基本的に，句の形の用例(以下「句例」)を先に集め，それから文の形の用例(以下「文例」)を挙げる．

（2）**準見出し**　用例の下に，ゴシック体・漢字交じりで，頭から読み下したときの五十音順に配列した．準見出しで扱うのは次の語句である．
i) 〜な があるとき：見出し語に「に」が続く形容動詞の連用形．連用形に「する」および「なる」がついてできる動詞．また，見出し語の派生語として，見出し語(語幹)に「さ」「げ」「がる」がつく形．
ii) 見出し語が形容詞のとき：見出し語の語幹に「く」がついた連用形．以下 i) に同じ．
iii) 慣用句の類．
ただし，本文全体が小規模な語については，上記の区分に当てはまる語句であっても準見出しを設けない場合がある．

（3）**複合語**　最後に，見出し語の前後に別の語がつく複合語を挙げた．見出し語が後に来るパターンを▢▣，前に来るパターンを▣▢，という記号のもとに，それぞれ見出し語につく語の五十音順に配列した．

**えき**⁵【駅】
▣▢ 橋上駅(舎)… 高架下駅(舎)… 地下駅(舎)…
▢▣ 駅スタンプ… 駅売店… 駅貼り… 駅メロ…

（4）**語義の区分**　見出し(準見出しを含む)の語句に語義(また用法)が複数あるときは，**1**, **2**, **3**, …で区分し，番号の次に〔　〕でそれぞれの語義を説明するようにした．番号で区分するほどではないが意味の区別が必要なときは，やはり〔　〕または（　）で説明し分けた．
注：見出しの表記が同一となる姓の人名が複数あるときは，1つの見出しのもと，姓名のアルファベット表記のABC順に番号で区分して配列し，また個々の人物についての説明では，例外的に姓名の表記の後に置いた．

（5）**語義による漢字表記の区分**　番号の次，語義の説明の前に，その語義に対応する漢字表記を見出しと同様【　】の中に示した．

**ごくわせ**【極早稲・極早生】
**1**【極早稲】〔稲〕
**2**【極早生】〔一般に作物の〕…

（6）**本文中での漢字の使用について**　用例等においては見出しで示されている漢字を必ずしも使っていない．

**かかと**【踵】
▢▣ かかと落とし〔格闘技のわざ〕…

（7）**動植物名の表記**　見出しはひらがなで表記する動植物名も，本文中では(かな書きとするときは)原則としてかたかな表記を採る．

**かいみじんこ**【貝微塵子】
〖動〗〔カイミジンコ科の甲殻類の総称〗…

## 3 英　語　訳

（1）**訳の間の区切り**　1つの日本語に訳が複数あるときの区切りには
i) 訳語 (words)・句 (phrases) についてはセミコロン (;) を用いた．
ii) 訳文 (sentences) については | の記号を用いた．なお，センテンスどうしが必ずしも同意義を表さない場合があるが，これらはいわゆる直訳と意訳，および日本文の語感から来る解釈の相違とご承知ありたい．
ただし，[ ] ( ) 《 》の各記号の内部では，原則としてコンマ (,) を用いた．

（2）**名詞の冠詞について**　可算名詞には a, an をつけ，可算・不可算両方ある場合には (a), (an) のように ( ) を用いた．

（3）**スペリングとシラビケーションについて**
基本的に米国式スペリングを優先させた．スペリングとシラビケーションの基準はだいたい米国 Merriam-Webster 社の辞典によった．なお，米・英で著しくつづりの違うものは *(=米国式), "(=英国式) の記号表示で断ってある．

（4）**訳の中のイタリック体**
i) 英語以外の言語(日本語を含む)に由来する語句で(まだ完全には)英語化していないことを意味する．
ii) 特に動植物の学名や，用例で「作品名」を持ち出した場合のその訳の表記に用いる．

（5）**日本語のローマ字書き**　訳の中で日本語の語句(固有名詞を含む)をそのままローマ字化するとき，書体の違いなどは以下に述べる原則にのっとった．
i) 米国の辞典複数の見出しを照合して，それらの辞典に共通して収録されている語は英語化したものと見なし，その見出しのつづり(ローマン体)を採用した．
ii) 上の条件に当てはまらない普通名詞は，イタリック体で表記した．
iii) 固有名詞は原則ローマン体とした．また，人名はローマ字書きでも姓，名の順を採用した．

（6）**[ ] による訳語句の言い換えについて**　下に注記する場合を除き，[ ] 内の語句と置き換え可能な語句(語が複数のときは最初の語)の左肩に「という記号

を付し，言い換えの対象範囲が明確になるようにした．

**はんこう**[4]【犯行】
犯行時間帯 the period during which「a crime [an offense] occurred．

次のケースでは「の記号は用いていない．
　i) 言い換えの対象範囲が訳の最初からであるとき．
　ii) 同一訳中に[ ]を複数含む場合で，後の[ ]の対象範囲がその前の[ ]の直後からであるとき．

**アスペルガーしょうがい**【-障害】
〘精神医〙Asperger [Asperger's] disorder．

**アイ・エイチ**【IH】
▣▢ IH クッキングヒーター〔電磁波調理器〕an「induction [IH] cooktop [cooker]．

iii) ハイフンを含む語の内部の言い換えで，次のように対象となる部分が自明のとき．

**げつめん**【月面】
▣▢ 月面探査衛星　a moon-probing[-probe] satellite．

（7）**動植物名について**　本邦産の動植物は外国のそれと完全には一致しないものが多いので，そのような場合は最も近似の種と考えられるものの英語名，またはその種を含む属あるいは科の動[植]物を総称する英語名を挙げ，英語名が得られない場合は学名だけを示すにとどめた．

（8）**作品名，法律名，機関・団体名について**
　i) 作品名の見出し語訳はイタリック体ではなくローマン体で表記した．
　ii) 日本の国内法の名称については，英語訳が公式には特に定められていないという事情があり，本辞典では一般に英語訳として使われることが多い英語を基本的に利用した．
　iii) 英語圏以外の国・地域の機関・団体については，その機関[団体]が自ら使用している英語名称があれば，それをそのまま採用した．

## 各種記号一覧表

（1）*sb*, *sth*
　i) *sb*, *sb's*（=*sb* の所有格）：自分以外．訳が動詞句のときに，主語となる人物以外の者．
　ii) *sth*：人間以外の事物．
　iii) *one*, *one's*（=*one* の所有格），*one*self（=*one* の再帰代名詞形）：自分．訳が動詞句のときに，主語と同一の人物．
　iv) *do*：動詞．*doing* で動名詞を表す．

*sb*, *sb's* を，同一の訳において代名詞で受ける必要が生じた場合には，それに準ずる記号として *he* というイタリック体表記を用いた．この *he* は，置き場所に応じて *his*, *him*, *him*self と格変化する．同様に，センテンス以外の訳で用いられた a person などの単数の人間を指す語についても，*he* という代名詞を用いることとした．

（2）〔　〕日本語の語義等の区別，見出し語の解説，用例のコンテクストの補足説明．

（3）[　]　直前の語句の言い換えを示す．下記（4）を参照．

（4）「　」英文中 [　] 内の語句と言い換えられる語句の始まりを示す．凡例 3 英語訳（6）参照．

（5）（　）
　i) 省略可能な部分を表す．
　ii) 人物，参照先等の補足説明，また前出（2）の下位の補足的説明．

（6）《　》
　i) 訳語句のコロケーションの例示．
　ii) 訳のスピーチ・ラベル．後出 略語表 参照．
　iii) *pl*. *sing*. とともに不規則な複数形・単数形を表す．

（7）〈　〉訳の英語についての文法上の注記．

（8）〘　〙専門語の分野を示す．分野名の略語については後出 略語表 参照．

（9）=, ⇨　参照項目を示す．
　i) = は基本的に，異形の同義・類義語句[表現]を表す．
　ii) ⇨ は「その方を(も)見よ」の意．
　iii) 他項目中の異形の語句・表現を参照させる場合には，( ) により補足する．

（10）◆ 用例の始まりを示す．1 つの見出し語について用例がいくつかの「ブロック」に分かれているときは（凡例 2 本文（1）参照）各ブロックの始まりごとにこの記号を繰り返した．

（11）〖　〗etymology を示す．凡例 3 英語訳（4）i)，また後出 略語表 外国語 欄を参照．

（12）<　上の記号の中で用いて日本語の語源を示す．

（13）/　用例の区切りを示す．下の（14）との違いに留意されたい．

（14）|　同一の日本文に対して複数の英語の訳文があるときの区切りを示す．（凡例 3 英語訳（1）ii)）．

（15）▣▢, ▢▣　凡例 2 本文（3）参照．

（16）〜
　i) 見出し語が代入可能なことを表す．
　ii) 訳語の複数形の表示で，単数形の代用を示す．

（17）"　"
　i) 訳語にやむなく日本語そのもの(をローマ字表記したもの)を用いたとき．
　ii) 原意を示すため日本語を直訳したとき．
　iii) 対話文形式の用例の訳で．

（18）▶　付加的情報・注記を示す．

（19）▷　派生的な情報を示す．

（20）（略：）英語の略称を示す．

（21）*　米国語法（Americanism）を表す．

（22）‖　英国語法（Briticism）を表す．

# 略　語　表

## スピーチ・ラベル

《口》 口語　　《文》 文語　　《俗》 俗語　　《卑》 卑語　　《詩》 詩語　　《雅》 雅語　　《古》 古語
《戯言》 戯言的 (jocular) な表現
注: *《口》, *《俗》 は，それぞれ米国語法での口語，英国語法での俗語，の意.

## 分　野　名

| | | | | | |
|---|---|---|---|---|---|
| 〖医〗 | 医学 | 〖建〗 | 建築(学) | 〖彫〗 | 彫刻 |
| 〖遺〗 | 遺伝学 | 〖言〗 | 言語(学) | 〖哲〗 | 哲学 |
| 〖印〗 | 印刷 | 〖工〗 | 工学, 工業 | 〖天〗 | 天文(学) |
| 〖宇〗 | 宇宙 | 〖光〗 | 光学 | 〖電〗 | 電気(工学) |
| 〖英〗 | 英国 | 〖鉱〗 | 鉱物(学), 鉱山 | 〖動〗 | 動物(学) |
| 〖映〗 | 映画 | 〖古生〗 | 古生物(学) | 〖農〗 | 農業, 農学 |
| 〖園〗 | 園芸 | 〖昆〗 | 昆虫 | 〖美〗 | 美術, 美学 |
| 〖化〗 | 化学 | 〖史〗 | 歴史(学) | 〖物〗 | 物理(学) |
| 〖解〗 | 解剖学 | 〖詩〗 | 詩学 | 〖米〗 | 米国 |
| 〖海〗 | 航海, 海洋(学) | 〖社〗 | 社会学 | 〖簿〗 | 簿記 |
| 〖海保〗 | 海上保険 | 〖狩〗 | 狩猟 | 〖法〗 | 法律, 法学 |
| 〖幾〗 | 幾何(学) | 〖宗〗 | 宗教(学) | 〖冶〗 | 冶金(学) |
| 〖機〗 | 機械(工学) | 〖修〗 | 修辞学 | 〖薬〗 | 薬学, 薬物 |
| 〖ギ〗 | (古代)ギリシャ | 〖商〗 | 商業 | 〖理〗 | 理学 |
| 〖ギ神話〗 | ギリシャ神話 | 〖植〗 | 植物(学) | 〖倫〗 | 倫理学 |
| 〖菌〗 | 菌類 | 〖織〗 | 織機, 織物 | 〖ロ〗 | (古代)ローマ |
| 〖空〗 | 航空 | 〖数〗 | 数学 | 〖ロ神話〗 | ローマ神話 |
| 〖軍〗 | 軍隊, 軍事 | 〖生化〗 | 生化学 | 〖労〗 | 労働(法) |
| 〖経〗 | 経済(学) | 〖聖〗 | 聖書 | 〖論〗 | 論理学 |
| 〖劇〗 | 演劇 | 〖地〗 | 地学 | | |

注: 〖英〗 と 〖米〗 は，例えば 〖英史〗 (=英国史) や 〖米法〗 (=米国法) のようにして用いる. 〖ギ〗 と 〖ロ〗 も同様.

## 外　国　語

| | | | |
|---|---|---|---|
| Chin | 中国語 (Chinese) | Kor | 韓国・朝鮮語 (Korean) |
| Du | オランダ語 (Dutch) | L | ラテン語 (Latin) |
| F | フランス語 (French) | Port | ポルトガル語 (Portuguese) |
| G | ドイツ語 (German) | Russ | ロシア語 (Russian) |
| Gk | ギリシャ語 (Greek) | Skt | サンスクリット語, 梵語 (Sanskrit) |
| It | イタリア語 (Italian) | Sp | スペイン語 (Spanish) |

## 英語アルファベットとかたかなの対応一覧

| | | | | | | | | | | | |
|---|---|---|---|---|---|---|---|---|---|---|---|
| A | エー | F | エフ | K | ケー | P | ピー | U | ユー | Z | ゼッド |
| B | ビー | G | ジー | L | エル | Q | キュー | V | ブイ, ヴィー | | |
| C | シー | H | エイチ | M | エム | R | アール | W | ダブリュー | | |
| D | ディー | I | アイ | N | エヌ | S | エス | X | エックス | | |
| E | イー | J | ジェー | O | オー | T | ティー | Y | ワイ | | |

# あ

アーヴィング[2]〔米国テキサス州北東部の市〕Irving.
アーキン Arkin, Alan (1934– ；米国の映画俳優；本名 Alan Wolf Arki).
アークエット Arquette, Patricia (1968– ；米国の映画女優).
アークコサイン〖数〗〔逆余弦〕an arccosine.
アークコセカント〖数〗〔逆余割〕an arccosecant.
アークコタンジェント〖数〗〔逆余接〕an arccotangent.
アークサイン〖数〗〔逆正弦〕an arcsine.
アークセカント〖数〗〔逆正割〕an arcsecant.
アークタンジェント〖数〗〔逆正接〕an arctangent.
アーケード ▫️ アーケード・ゲーム機 an arcade game machine.
アースウォッチ〔1971年設立の国際的 NGO；本部はボストン〕the Earthwatch Institute.
アース・コンシャス〔地球を意識した；地球環境・自然を考慮した〕earth-conscious 《consumers, products, businesses, etc.》. ▷ earth-consciousness n.
アースポリシーけんきゅうじょ【-研究所】〔環境政策を提言する米国の NPO〕the Earth Policy Institute（略：EPI）.
アーチ ▫️ 特大アーチ〖野球〗a towering home run. ◐ 特大~を放つ hit [launch, smash] a towering home run. メモリアルアーチ〖野球〗〔記念となるホームラン〕(hit) a 「memorable [historic, landmark] home run [homer].
▫️ アーチ雲〖気象〗an arcus.
「アーチーでなくっちゃ!」〔米国の、学園コメディーのテレビアニメ〕The Archie Show.
アーツプラン21〔文化庁の芸術創造推進事業〕Arts Plan 21.
アート ▫️ アートフラワー〔布で作った造花〕a fabric flower；〖技法〗fabric flower making. アート・マップ an art map；a guide map showing the location of artworks. アート・マネジメント arts management. アート・メーキング〖美容〗〔(眉など)メイクが落ちないように皮膚を染色する化粧法〕(application of) permanent make-up.
アート・セラピー〖精神医〗〖芸術療法〗(arts) arts therapy.
アートメーク〖美容〗〔表皮に色素を注入する美容術〕(semi) permanent make-up；micropigmentation；beauty treatment by applying coloration to the epidermis.
アーネムランド〔オーストラリア、ノーザン・テリトリー北部の地域〕Arnhem Land.
アーノルド・パーマー〖商標〗〔傘のマークの米国ブランド製衣料品〕Arnold Palmer.
アーバン ▫️ アーバン・コンプレックス〔都市型の大規模複合建築群〕an urban complex. アーバン・ツーリズム〔都市観光〕urban [city] tourism. アーバン・デザイン〔都市設計〕urban [city] design. アーバン・リゾート〔都市近郊のリゾート〕an urban [a city] resort.
アービトラージ〖商〗〔裁定取引〕arbitrage.
アービトラージャー〖証券〗〔裁定取引を行う投資家〕an arbitrager.
アーフェルカンプ Avercamp, Hendrick (1585–1634；オランダの画家).
アー・ベー・セー【ABC】〔スペインの日刊紙〕ABC.
アーミー・ルック〖服飾〗an army look.
アーミッシュ〔キリスト教の一派〕the Amish；〔アーミッシュの人〕an Amish man；an Amish woman.
アーミテージ Armitage, Richard (Lee) (1945– ；米国の政治家；国務副長官 [2001-05]).
アーム ▫️ アーム・ウォーマー〖服飾〗〔筒状に腕をおおう防寒具〕(a pair of) arm warmers. アーム・ロボット ⇨ ロボット.
アームストロング Armstrong, Gillian (1950– ；オースト ラリア生まれの映画監督).
アーモンド ▫️ アーモンド・オイル almond oil.
アーリントン1〔米国テキサス州北部の都市〕Arlington.
2〔米国マサチューセッツ州東部の町〕Arlington.
3〔米国ヴァージニア州北東部の郡〕Arlington.
アール・アンド・アイ【R&I】〔格付投資情報センター〕R&I；Rating and Investment Information, Inc.
アール・エー・エー【RAA】〖日本史〗〔特殊慰安施設協会；太平洋戦争後、進駐軍のために設立された〕the Recreation and Amusement Association.
アール・エス・アイ【RSI】〖医〗〔反復運動過多損傷〕an RSI；a repetitive strain injury.
アール・エス・ウイルス【RS-】〖菌〗〔風邪の原因となるウイルスの1つ〕respiratory syncytial virus (略：RSV). ▫️ RSウイルス感染症〖医〗(a) respiratory syncytial virus infection.
アール・エス・エー【RSA】〔公開鍵暗号方式の1つ〕the RSA cryptosystem. ▶ RSA は開発者、Ronald Rivest, Adi Shamir, Leonard Adleman の頭文字から.
アール・エス・エス【RSS】〖電算〗〔ウェブサイトの内容の要約や更新情報を配信するための規格の総称〕RSS. ▶ RDF (= Resource Description Framework) Site Summary, Rich Site Summary, Really Simple Syndication いずれかの略. 開発の経緯により以上3つの規格が存在する. ▫️ RSS リーダー〔ウェブサイトを巡回してサイトの RSS を読み込んで内容や更新状況を知らせるソフトウェア〕an RSS reader.
アール・エヌ・エー【RNA】 ▫️ 一本鎖 RNA (a) single-strand(ed) RNA (略：ssRNA). 二本鎖 RNA (a) double-strand(ed) RNA (略：dsRNA). ▫️ RNAウイルス an RNA virus. ▷ プラス鎖~ウイルス a positive-strand RNA virus / マイナス鎖~ウイルス a negative-strand RNA virus. RNA干渉〔RNA で遺伝子の発現を抑制する現象〕RNA interference (略：RNAi).
アール・エフ・アイ・ディー【RFID】〔電波で情報を読み取れる超小型無線 IC チップを用いた電子タグ技術；電波方式認識〕RFID；radio frequency identification. ▫️ RFIDシステム an RFID system. RFIDタグ〔チップ〕an RFID「tag [chip].
アール・エフ・エムぶんせき【RFM 分析】〔企業の顧客管理手法の1つ〕RFM analysis. ▶ Recency (最近の購買日), Frequency (購買頻度), Monetary (累計の購買金額) の3点から顧客を分析するもの.
アール・オーすい【RO 水】〔逆浸透法で処理した水〕RO water. ▶ RO は reverse osmosis (逆浸透法) の略.
アール・ディー・エックス【RDX】〖化〗〔軍事用に研究開発された高性能爆薬〕RDX. ▶ Research (and) Development Explosive の略. サイクロナイト cyclonite, ヘキソゲン hexogen ともいう.
アール・ディー・エフ【RDF】〔ごみ固形燃料〕RDF. ▶ refuse-derived fuel の略. ▫️ RDF発電 RDF (power) generation. ◐ ~発電所 an RDF power plant.
アール・ディー・ディーほう【RDD 法】〖統計〗〔すべての電話番号から無作為に番号を選ぶ乱数ダイヤル調査；random digit dialing. ◐ ~による電話世論調査 (conduct) 「an RDD [a random digit dialing] telephone survey.
アール・ピー・エスほう【RPS 法】〖法〗the RPS Law. ▶ 「新エネルギー利用特別措置法」の通称；RPS は Renewables Portfolio Standard (代替エネルギー使用割合の基準) の略.
アール・ピー・エフ【RPF】〔古紙や廃プラスチックを原料とす る固形燃料〕refuse paper and plastic fuel；RPF.

アール・ブリュット 〖<F〗〔自らの行為をアートと認識することのない者によって営まれる美術活動およびその作品〕art brut; outsider art.

アール・マーク【R -】〔本・雑誌の無断複写禁止のマーク〕an R mark. ▶ R は reprography と right から.

アール・ユー・エス・アイ【RUSI】〔英国の王立統合軍事研究所〕the RUSI; the Royal United Services Institute for Defence and Security.

アール・ユー・エフ【RUF】〔革命統一戦線; シエラレオネの反政府勢力〕the RUF; the Revolutionary United Front.

アール・ユーよんはちろく【RU486】〖薬〗〔フランスで開発された経口中絶薬〕RU486. ▶ RU は開発したフランスの製薬会社名 Roussel-Uclaf から; 一般名はミフェプリストン.

アーレイ・バークきゅうちくかん【-級駆逐艦】〖軍〗〔米国のミサイル駆逐艦〕an Arleigh Burke-class destroyer.

アーレフ〔旧オウム真理教名〕Aleph.

アーンスト・アンド・ヤング〔米国の国際会計事務所〕Ernst & Young〔略: E&Y〕.

アーン・トーン〔タイ中部の県; その県都〕Ang Thong.

アイ・アール・エル【IRL】〔自動車のフォーミュラカーレース主催団体〕(the) IRL; the Indy Racing League.

アイ・アール・オー【IRO】〔国連の国際難民機関〕IRO; the International Refugee Organization.

アイ・アール・シー【IRC】1〔国際赤十字〕the IRC; the International Red Cross. 2〔国際救援[救済]委員会〕the IRC; the International Rescue Committee. 3〖電算〗〔インターネットリレーチャット〕IRC; Internet Relay Chat.

アイ・アール・ディー・エー【IrDA】〖電算〗〔赤外線通信協会 (the Infrared Data Association) の規格〕IrDA. ▫️ IrDA ポート an IrDA port.

アイ・アール・ビー【IRB】1〔研究所・病院などの施設内倫理委員会〕an IRB; an institutional review board. 2〔国際ラグビー評議会〕the IRB; the International Rugby Board.

アイ・アイ・ピー【IIP】〔鉱工業生産指数〕IIP; an index of industrial production.

アイアナ【IANA】〖電算〗〔1998 年までドメイン名などを管理していた組織; ICANN (アイキャン) の前身〕IANA. ▶ Internet Assigned Number Authority の略.

「I am Sam アイ・アム・サム」〔映画〕I Am Sam.

「アイ・アム・レジェンド」〔映画〕I Am Legend.

「アイアン・ジャイアント」〔アニメ映画〕The Iron Giant.

アイアン・ハンマー〔2003 年イラク戦争の米国による掃討作戦の作戦名〕Operation Iron Hammer.

アイアンマン ▫️ ハワイ・アイアンマン・トライアスロン〔ハワイで行われる世界一過酷といわれるレース〕the Hawaii Ironman Triathlon.

アイ・イー・エル・ティー・エス【IELTS】=アイエルツ.

アイ・イー・ディー【IED】〔即席爆発装置〕an IED; an improvised explosive device.

アイ・イー・ティー・シー【IETC】〔国際環境技術センター〕IETC; the International Environmental Technology Centre.

アイ・エイチ【IH】 ▫️ IH クッキングヒーター〔電磁波調理器〕an「induction [IH] cooktop [cooker].

アイ・エイチ・エヌ【IHN】〔動物病理〕〔伝染性造血器壊死症; 魚の伝染病〕IHN; infectious hematopoietic necrosis.

アイ・エー・イー・エー【IAEA】 ▫️ IAEA 追加議定書 the IAEA Additional Protocol.

アイ・エー・ディー・エル【IADL】〖医〗〔手段的日常生活動作〕an IADL; an instrumental「activity of daily living [ADL].

アイ・エス・エー【ISA】〔自動車〕〔速度制御支援システム〕ISA. ▶ intelligent speed adaptation の略.

アイ・エス・エム【ISM】〔全米供給管理協会〕ISM; the Institute for Supply Management. ▫️ ISM 指数〖経〗〔全米供給管理協会が発表する景気総合指数〕the ISM index. ISM 製造業景気[景況]指数〖経〗the ISM manufacturing index. [=ISM 指数] ISM 非製造業景気[景況]指数〖経〗the ISM non-manufacturing index.

アイ・エス・エム・エス【ISMS】〔情報セキュリティー・マネジメントシステム〕an ISMS; an information security management system. ▫️ ISMS 適合性評価制度 an ISMS compatibility evaluation system.

アイ・エスち【Is 値】〖地震〗〔構造耐震指標〕a seismic index of structure; Is.

アイ・エス・バランス【IS -】〖金融〗〔投資貯蓄バランス〕IS balance; the investment-saving(s) balance.

アイ・エス・ピー・エス・コード【ISPS -】〖海法〗〔船舶と港湾施設の保安のための国際コード〕the ISPS Code; the International Ship and Port Facility Security Code.

アイ・エス・ブイ【ISV】〔独立系ソフトウエアベンダー〕an independent software vendor〔略: ISV〕.

アイ・エックス【IX】〖電算〗〔プロバイダー間でネットを相互接続する機能〕IX; an Internet Exchange.

アイ・エヌ・アール【INR】〖医〗〔血液凝固能の国際標準比〕an INR; an international normalized ratio.

アイ・エヌ・エス【INS】〔NTT の高度情報通信システム〕INS; an [the] Information Network System.

アイ・エヌ・エス・ピー・エー・エス・エス【INSPASS】〔入国審査の迅速化のために米国の空港などで採用されている方式〕INSPASS; the「Immigration and Naturalization Service's [INS] Passenger Accelerated Service System.

アイ・エフ・アール・エス【IFRS】〔国際財務報告基準〕IFRS; International Financial Reporting Standards.

アイ・エフ・エー【IFA】〔独立系ファイナンシャル・アドバイザー〕an IFA; an independent financial advisor.

アイ・エム【IM】〖電算〗IM; instant messaging. [=インスタント・メッセージング (⇒インスタント)]

アイ・エム・アール・ティー【IMRT】〖医〗〔強度変調放射線治療〕IMRT; intensity modulated radiation therapy.

アイ・エム・エス【IMS】〔知的生産システム〕IMS; an intelligent manufacturing system.

アイ・エム・エム【IMM】〔シカゴ・マーカンタイル取引所の通貨先物市場〕the IMM; the International Monetary Market (of Chicago Mercantile Exchange).

アイ・エム・シー【IMC】〔国際通貨会議〕the IMC; the International Monetary Conference.

アイ・エム・ディー【IMD】⇨こくさいけいえいかいはつけんきゅうじょ.

アイ・エム・ティーにせん【IMT-2000】〖通信〗IMT-2000. ▶ International Mobile Telecommunications-2000 の略.

アイ・エム・ブイ【IMV】〔トヨタ自動車の世界戦略車種のシリーズ〕IMV. ▶ IMV は innovative international multi-purpose vehicle の略.

アイ・エム・ユー【IMU】〔ウズベキスタン・イスラム運動; ウズベキスタンの反政府武装組織〕the IMU; the Islamic Movement of Uzbekistan.

アイエルツ【IELTS】〔商標〕〔英国圏の留学生向け英語力テスト〕IELTS; the International English Language Testing System. ▫️ アイエルツ【IELTS】テスト the [an] IELTS「test [exam].

アイ・オー・シー【IOC】 ▫️ IOC 倫理委員会 the IOC Ethics Commission.

アイ・オー・ディー・ピー【IODP】〔統合国際深海掘削計画〕the IODP; the Integrated Ocean Drilling Program.

アイオライト〔宝石; 菫青(きんせい)石〕an iolite; 〖鉱〗cordierite; dichroite.

アイオリ【料理】〔マヨネーズに似たスペインのソース〕aioli; aïoli.
あいかぎ【合い鍵】▭ 合い鍵屋 a key cutter; a key maker; a keysmith.
アイカラー〔化粧品の〕colored eye shadow.
あいがん²【愛玩】▭ 愛玩動物飼養管理士 a pet care adviser [advisor]. 愛玩(用)ロボット a pet robot.
あいき³【愛輝】〔中国黒竜江省北部の県〕Aihui.
アイギストス【ギ神話】Aegisthus.
アイキャン【ICANN】〖電算〗〔ドメイン名などを管理する非営利組織〕ICANN. ▶ Internet Corporation for Assigned Names and Numbers の略.
アイ・キュー・エス【IQS】〔米国のコンサルティング会社 J.D. Power 社が発表する自動車の初期品質調査〕the IQS; the Initial Quality Study.
あいくぎ【間釘・合釘】a double-pointed nail.
あいこく²【愛国】▭ 愛国教育 teaching (of) patriotism; patriotic education. 愛国主義教育基地〔中国国民の愛国主義教育のために利用される施設など〕a base for "patriotic education"; a "patriotic education" base; an institution for inculcating patriotism. 愛国無罪〔2005年の中国における反日デモに際して叫ばれたスローガン〕"Patriotism (Is) No Crime."
あいこくしゃほう【愛国者法】〖米法〗=パトリオットほう.
あいことう【愛国党】〔タイの政党〕タイあいことう.
あいこくのひ【愛国の日】〔米国の同時多発テロ事件を追悼する日; 9月11日〕Patriot Day.
アイザフ, アイサフ【ISAF】〔アフガニスタンの国際治安支援部隊〕(the) ISAF; the International Security Assistance Force.
アイ・シー【IC】▭ IC チップ an IC chip.
アイ・シー・イー【ICE】〔ドイツの超高速列車〕an ICE; an Inter-City Express.
アイ・ジー・イー【IgE】〖生化〗〔免疫グロブリン E〕IgE; immunoglobulin E. ▭ 高 IgE 症候群〖医〗hyperimmunoglobulin-E [hyper-IgE] syndrome (略: HIES). ▭ IgE 抗体 an IgE antibody.
アイ・ジー・エフ・シー【IGFC】〔石炭ガス化燃料電池複合発電〕IGFC; integrated coal gasification fuel cell combined cycle.
アイ・シー・シー【ICC】〔国際刑事裁判所〕the ICC; the International Criminal Court.
アイ・ジー・シー・シー【IGCC】〔石炭ガス化複合発電〕IGCC; an integrated coal gasification combined cycle.
アイ・シー・ティー【ICT】〔情報コミュニケーション技術〕ICT; information and communication(s) technology. ▭ ICT 教育 ICT education.
アイ・シー・ディー【ICD】〔WHO による国際疾病分類〕the ICD; the International Classification of Diseases.
アイ・ジー・ディー【IgD】〖生化〗〔免疫グロブリン D〕IgD; immunoglobulin D.
アイ・シー・ブイ・ティー【i-CVT】〖自動車〗〔フル電子制御自動無段変速機〕i-CVT; intelligent continuously variable transmission.
アイ・シー・ユー【ICU】▭ アイ・シー・ユー症候群 ICU syndrome [psychosis].
あいしょう¹【相性】▭ 相性交換〔パソコン関連製品などが相性により使えなかった場合に販売店が交換に応じること〕a 《guarantee of》 exchange in case of incompatibility. 相性保証〔パソコン関連製品などで相性により使えなかった場合に何らかの補償をすること〕a compatibility guarantee.
アイシン・コード【ISIN-】〖金融〗=国際証券コード(⇨ しょけん⁵).
「愛人/ラマン」〔映画〕The Lover; 〔原題〕L'Amant.
アイス ▭ アイス・クラッシャー〔砕氷機〕an ice crusher.
「アイス・エイジ」〔アニメ映画〕Ice Age.
アイス・コア【地質】〔氷盤からドリルで円柱状に掘り出した古い氷〕an ice core. ▭ アイスコア分析 (an) ice core analysis.
アイス・スレッジ・ホッケー〖スポーツ〗ice sledge hockey.
「アイ・スパイ」〔米国の, スパイ活劇の TV アクション・コメディ〕I Spy.
アイスバイン【料理】〔豚のすね肉の料理〕Eisbein; eisbein.
「アイズワイドシャット」〔映画〕Eyes Wide Shut.
アイセーフ〖光学〗〔レーザー光などが目の網膜を傷つけない〕eye-safe. ▭ アイセーフ・レーザー an eye-safe laser.
アイゼンメンゲルしょうこうぐん【-症候群】〖医〗Eisenmenger('s) syndrome.
あいぞう¹【愛憎】▭ 愛憎劇 a love-hate「struggle [battle, conflict]《with [between] …》.
あいぞう²【愛蔵】▭ 愛蔵版 a bibliophile edition.
アイソタイプ【ISOTYPE】〔国際的な絵言葉・絵表示のシステム〕ISOTYPE. ▶ international system of typographic picture education の略.
アイソメトリックス〖生理〗〔等尺性運動〕isometrics; (an) isometric [(a) static] exercise.
アイソレーター〔ウイルス・振動・騒音などから隔離する装置〕an isolator; 〖電〗〔絶縁体〕an insulator; an isolator.
あいたい【相対】▭ 相対売買〖証券〗a negotiated transaction.
あいちゃく【愛着】▭ 愛着形成〖心理〗attachment formation [building]. ◐ ~形成不全 incomplete attachment. 愛着行動〖心理〗attachment behavior. 愛着障害〖心理〗(an) attachment disorder.
あいちょう³【愛聴】▭ 愛聴者〔特定のラジオ放送の〕a regular (shortwave) listener; a regular listener 《to a shortwave broadcast》.
アイ・ティー【IT】▭ IT 音痴 hopelessness with「information technology [IT, computers]; IT illiteracy; 〔人〕an IT illiterate. IT 革命 the IT Revolution. IT ケイパビリティ〔企業の IT 活用能力〕IT capability. IT 講習会 an IT course. IT コーディネーター an「IT [information technology] coordinator. IT 国家戦略 a national IT strategy. IT 時代 the information technology age. IT 社会 an IT society. IT 弱者〈集合的に〉the IT-deprived; people without access to information technology. IT スキル標準 IT skills standards (略: ITSS). IT 戦略 an IT strategy. IT 大国 an IT superpower. IT 投資促進税制 the IT investment promotion tax (incentive) system. IT ナイフ〖医〗an IT knife; an electrosurgical「knife [scalpel]. IT 入試〔インターネットを利用した入学試験〕a university entrance exam conducted over the Internet; an IT exam for university entrance. IT 不況 an IT recession.
アイ・ティー・アイ・エル【ITIL】〖商標〗〔各国の有力企業で採用されている情報技術運用の規格・認定資格〕ITIL; Information Technology Infrastructure Library.
アイ・ティー・イー・アール【ITER】〔国際熱核融合実験炉〕ITER; the International Thermonuclear Experimental Reactor.
アイ・ティー・エス【ITS】〖自動車〗〔高度道路交通システム〕ITS. ▶ intelligent transportation system の略.
アイ・ティー・エフ【ITF】〔国際運輸労働者連盟〕ITF; the International Transport Workers' Federation.
アイ・ティーがんしょう【IT 眼症】〖医〗computer vision syndrome (略: CVS).
アイ・ティー・シー【ITC】〔インドのコングロマリット〕ITC Limited. ▶ 旧社名は the Imperial Tobacco Company of India Limited.
アイ・ディー・シー【IDC】〖電算〗=データ・センター (⇨データ).
アイ・ティーしょめんいっかつほう【IT 書面一括法】〖法〗the Comprehensive IT Document Law. ▶ 正式名称は「書面の交付等に関する情報通信の技術の利用のための関係法律の整備に関する法律」.

## アイディーりろん

**アイ・ディーりろん**【ID 理論】the 「ID [intelligent design] theory [＝インテリジェント・デザイン理論 (⇨インテリジェント)]
**アイディタロッド**〔アラスカで毎年行われる国際そり長距離レース〕the Iditarod; the Iditarod Trail Sled Dog Race.
**あいてさき**【相手先】▣ 相手先ブランド[相手先商標製品]製造業者 an original equipment manufacturer (略: OEM).
**アイテム** ▣ レア・アイテム a rare [an unusual] item.
**あいとう**【哀悼】▣ 哀悼談話 an 「unofficial [informal] expression of 「regret at (the news of) *sb*'s death [mourning for *sb*].
**アイドリング** ▣ アイドリングストップ宣言車 a vehicle that is taking part in an "idling stop" campaign; 〔揭示〕This Vehicle Shuts Off Its Engine When Stopped.
**アイドル** ▣ アイドル・ファンド〖証券〗〔新人アイドルに投資する金融商品〕the (Pinup) Idol Fund; a fund investing in the career of selected aspiring media stars.
**アイヌぶんかしんこうほう**【─文化振興法】〖法〗the Law for the Promotion of the Ainu Culture; the Ainu Culture Promotion Law.
**「愛のエチュード」**〔映画〕The Luzhin Defence.
**あいはぎ**【相剝】〔修復・複製などのために和紙を 2 枚に剝ぐ技法〕duplicating an ink painting by paring the paper into two sheets. ▣ 相剝本〔相剝で作った裏側の画〕a duplicate produced by paring off the underside of an ink painting.
**アイ・ピー**【IP】
3〔知的資産〕IP; intellectual property. ▣ **IP** ネットワーク, **IP** 網〖電算〗an IP network.
**アイ・ピー・エー**【IBA】1〔英国の独立放送公社〕the IBA; the Independent Broadcasting Authority.
2〔イスラエル公共放送〕the IBA; the Israel Broadcasting Authority.
**アイ・ピー・エー**【IPA】1〔情報処理振興事業協会〕IPA; the Information-Technology Promotion Agency.
2〔国際音声記号[音声文字]〕IPA; the International Phonetic Alphabet.
3〔子どもの遊ぶ権利のための国際協会〕IPA; the International Association for the Child's Right to Play. ▶ IPA はこの団体の旧称 International Playground Association (国際遊び場協会) の略.
**アイ・ピー・エス**【IPS】〔電子工学〕〔横電界方式の TFT 液晶駆動方式〕IPS; in-plane switching. ▣ **IPS 液晶** an IPS 「liquid crystal display [LCD]. **IPS 方式** an 「in-place switching [IPS] mode.
**アイ・ピー・エフ**【IBF】＝こくさいボクシングれんめい.
**アイ・ピー・オー**【IPO】〔新規株式公開〕an IPO; an initial public offering. ▣ **IPO 株価** an IPO stock price 《of $50 per share》.
**アイ・ピー・ディー・エル**【IPDL】＝とっきょでんしとしょかん.
**アイ・ピー・ピー**【IPP】〔一般電気事業者に電力を供給する独立発電事業者〕an IPP; an independent power producer.
**アイ・ピー・ブイ・シックス**【IPv6】＝インターネット・プロトコル・バージョン・シックス (⇨プロトコル).
**あいびょう**【愛猫】▣ 愛猫家 a person who loves cats; a cat lover.
**アイ・ピロー**〔目の上にのせて目の疲れをとる道具〕an eye pillow.
**アイ・ブイ・アール**〔音声自動応答〕IVR; 〔音声自動応答装置〕〖システム〗an IVRS. ▶ IVR は interactive voice response, IVRS は interactive voice response system の略.
**アイフォン**〖商標〗〔アイポッド (iPod) に携帯電話機能を加わったもの〕iPhone; 〔1 台の〕an iPhone.

**アイベリー**〔イチゴの品種の 1 つ〕an Eyeberry.
**アイボ**〖商標〗〔ソニー製犬型ロボット〕AIBO.
**アイポイント**〔自動車運転時などの目の位置〕an 「eyepoint [eye point, eye-point].
**アイポッド**【iPod】〖商標〗〔アップルコンピューター社製の携帯音楽・ビデオプレーヤー〕an iPod.
**アイマックス**【IMAX】〖*image* ＋ *maximum*〗〖商標・映〗〔カナダで開発された大画面映画・立体映画の撮影機; その上映システム〗IMAX. ▣ アイマックス・シアター an IMAX theater.
**アイメート**〔盲導犬〕an eyemate; a guide dog.
**アイ・ユー・ディー**【IUD】〔子宮内避妊器具〕an intrauterine device; an IUD.
**「I love ペッカー」**〔映画〕Pecker.
**「アイ・ラブ・ルーシー」**〔米国のどたばた TV ホームコメディー〕I Love Lucy. ▶ 主演 ルシール・ボール (Lucille Ball).
**アイリス・チャン** ⇨チャン².
**アイレンベルク** Eilenberg, Richard (1848–1925; ドイツの作曲家).
**「アイ, ロボット」**〔映画〕I, Robot.
**アインシュタイン** ▣ アインシュタイン・ポドルスキー・ローゼン相関〖物〗the 「Einstein-Podolsky-Rosen [EPR] correlations. アインシュタイン・ポドルスキー・ローゼンのパラドックス〖物〗the 「Einstein-Podolsky-Rosen [EPR] paradox.
**アウグスト** August, Bille (1948– ; デンマークの映画監督).
**アウシュヴィッツきょうせいしゅうようじょ**【─強制収容所】〔第二次大戦中ポーランドのオシフィエンチム (アウシュヴィッツ) 市の郊外にあったナチスドイツの強制収容所〕the Auschwitz Concentration Camp. (⇨アウシュヴィッツ・ビルケナウ ナチスドイツきょうせい・ぜつめつしゅうようじょ)
**アウシュヴィッツ・ビルケナウ ナチスドイツきょうせい・ぜつめつしゅうようじょ**【─強制・絶滅収容所】Auschwitz Birkenau, German Nazi Concentration and Extermination Camp (1940–1945). ▶ 「アウシュビッツ強制収容所」(the Auschwitz Concentration Camp) のユネスコによる新しい正式名称; 2007 年「アウシュビッツ・ビルケナウ強制収容所」(the Auschwitz-Birkenau Concentration Camp) から改称.
**アウストラロピテクス** ▣ アウストラロピテクス・アファレンシス *Australopithecus afarensis*. アウストラロピテクス・アフリカヌス *Australopithecus africanus*.
**アウスレーゼ**〔完熟したブドウで造るドイツワイン〕Auslese. ▣ トロッケンベーレンアウスレーゼ Trockenbeerenauslese (略: TBA).
**「アウター・リミッツ」**〔米国の, SF の TV ドラマ〕The Outer Limits. ▶「ウルトラゾーン」の邦題でも放映.
**アウト** ▣ アウトスタート〖ゴルフ〗starting from the first (tee); 〔トラック競技で〕setting off in the outside lane; starting on the outside lane.
**「アウト・オブ・タウナーズ」**〔映画〕The Out-of-Towners.
**アウトサイダー** ▣ アウトサイダー・アート〔自らの行為をアートと認識することのない者によって営まれる美術活動およびその作品〕outsider art;《F》art brut.
**アウトバウンド**〔外部へ出ていく; 海外への〕outbound《travelers》. ▣ アウトバウンド業務〔見込み顧客への電話営業〕outbound services. アウトバウンド・データ〖電算〗〔システムやネットの外への送信データ〕outbound data.
**「アウトブレイク」**〔映画〕Outbreak.
**アウトプレースメント**〔人員整理予定者に対する他社への再就職支援〕outplacement.
**アウトポール**〖建〗〔柱を室内に出っ張らせない工法; 外柱工法〕an external beam method.
**アウトライトとりひき**【─取引】〖証券〗〔無条件売買〕an outright transaction.
**「アウトランド」**〔映画〕Outland.
**アウトリーチ**〔専門技能を有する個人や組織が市民に向けて

行う普及・啓蒙活動〕(public) outreach. ▷ アウトリーチ活動 outreach activities.

**アウトレンジ** ▷ アウトレンジ攻撃〔軍〕〔敵の射程外からの攻撃〕an attack in which one army's guns outrange the others. アウトレンジ戦法〔軍〕〔敵の射程外から攻撃する戦術〕outranging tactics.

**アヴネット** ＝アブネット.

**アエタぞく**【-族】〔フィリピン諸島の先住民族〕the Aeta;〔1人〕an Aeta《pl. ～, ～s》.

**あえんめっき**【亜鉛鍍金】 ▷ 溶融亜鉛めっき hot-dip galvanizing. ▷ 溶融～鋼板 a hot-dip zinc-coated steel sheet.

**あおあしかつおどり**【青足鰹鳥】〔鳥〕a blue-footed booby; *Sula nebouxii*.

**あおいろしんこく**【青色申告】 ▷ 青色申告特別控除 a special allowance for filing a blue tax return.

**あおかけす**【青懸巣】〔鳥〕〔北米産のカラス科の鳥〕a blue jay; *Cyanocitta cristata*.

**あおぎす**【青鱚】〔魚〕〔キス科の魚〕a small-scale sillago; *Sillago parvisquamis*.

**あおくびだいこん**【青首大根】a green-neck(ed) daikon.

**あおしお**【青潮】〔低酸素水塊の上昇による海面の変色〕(a) blue tide.

**アオスタ**〔イタリア北西部の都市〕Aosta.

**あおぞら**【青空】 ▷ 青空議会 an open-air assembly. 〔⇨ランツゲマインデ〕

**あおのどうくつ**【青の洞窟】〔イタリア,カプリ島にある洞窟〕the Blue Grotto;《It》Grotta Azzurra.

**あおまつむし**【青松虫】〔昆〕〔マツムシ科〕a green tree cricket; *Calyptotrypus hibinonis*; *Truljalia hibinonis*.

**あおみみびょう**【青耳病】〔獣医〕blue-eared pig disease. 〔＝ぶたはんしょく・こきゅうきしょうがいしょうこうぐん〕

**あかいすいしょう**【赤い水晶】〔イスラエルの赤十字運動組織〕the Red Crystal.

**あかいよあけさくせん**【赤い夜明け作戦】〔イラク戦争での米国による〕Operation Red Dawn.

**あかいれ**【赤入れ】〔校正;赤字での字句の修正〕marking proofs; proofreading ～する mark [correct] proofs; proofread.

**アカウント** ▷ アカウント情報 one's account information; information about one's account.

**アカウント・アグリゲーション**〔金融〕〔顧客が持つ複数の金融機関の口座情報などを一覧表示するサービス〕account aggregation; an account aggregation service.

**アカウント・エグゼクティブ**〔広告代理店などの営業係〕an account executive (略: AE).

**あかえりかいつぶり**【赤襟かいつぶり】〔鳥〕〔カイツブリ科の鳥〕a red-necked grebe; *Podiceps grisegena*.

**あかおざる**【赤尾猿】〔動〕a 〔redtail [coppertail] monkey〕; a Schmidt's guenon; *Cercopithecus ascanius*.

**あかがしらからすばと**【赤頭烏鳩】〔鳥〕a Japanese wood pigeon; *Columba janthina nitens*.

**あかかびびょう**【赤黴病】〔植物病理〕scab.

**あかかみあり**【赤噛み蟻】〔昆〕〔米国南部・中米原産のアリ〕a tropical fire ant; *Solenopsis geminata*.

**あかカンガルー**【赤-】〔動〕a red kangaroo; *Macropus rufus*.

**あかぐすり**【赤釉】〔製陶〕(a) red glaze.

**あかくびワラビー**【赤首-】〔動〕a red-necked wallaby; a Bennett's wallaby; *Macropus rufogriseus*.

**あかげのエリック**【赤毛の-】Erik the Red (950–c.1003). 〔ノルウェーのバイキング;グリーンランドの最初の入植者〕

**あかじ**【赤字】 ▷ 文化赤字 a cultural deficit. 赤字球団 a loss-making (baseball) team. 赤字決算 a deficit settlement; a final loss 《for the year》. 赤字地方債 a 〔local [prefectural, municipal] deficit(-financing) bond. 赤字ローカル線〔鉄道などの〕a money-losing local railway line; 〔航空の〕a money-losing

feeder route.

**アカシジア**【精神医】〔着座不能〕akathisia.

**あかしたびらめ**【赤舌平目】〔魚〕〔ウシノシタ科の海産魚〕a red tongue sole; *Cynoglossus joyneri*.

**あかじゅうたん**【赤絨毯】〔映画祭・国会などの花道〕a red carpet. ▷ ～を敷く roll out the red carpet (for sb).

**あかせん**【赤線】〔売春公認地域〕a 〔an officially sanctioned〕 red-light district. ▶ 1956年,売春防止法施行に伴い廃止.

**アカぞく**【-族】〔中国・タイ・ミャンマー・ラオスなどに住む少数民族〕the Akha;〔1人〕an Akha《pl. ～(s)》.

**あかたまねぎ**【赤玉葱】〔植〕a red onion.

**アガチス**【植】〔ナンヨウスギ科の針葉樹;東南アジア・太平洋諸島産;加工容易で木目は緻密〕agathis; kauri.

**あかちゃん**【赤ちゃん】 ▷ 赤ちゃんポスト〔さまざまな事情で子育てができない親が新生児を匿名で託す設備〕a baby post (box); a baby 〔hatch [drop-off]〕; a foundling wheel.

**あかてがに**【赤手蟹】〔動〕〔イワガニ科のカニ〕a red clawed crab; *Sesarma haematocheir*.

**アカデミーしょう**【-賞】 ▷ アカデミー賞授賞式 the《78 th》Academy Awards ceremony; the Oscar ceremony.

**アカデミック** ▷ アカデミック・ガウン〔大学の学生・教員が卒業式などで着用するガウン〕an academic gown;〔帽子を含む〕a cap and gown.

**アカデムゴロドク**〔ロシア,ノヴォシビルスク近郊の学術都市〕Akademgorodok.

**あかねあわび**【茜鮑】〔貝〕〔北米産のアワビ〕a red abalone; *Haliotis rufescens*.

**あかバイ**【赤-】〔消防活動二輪車〕a fire 〔motorcycle [bike]〕.

**あかはじろ**【赤羽白】〔鳥〕〔カモ科の鳥〕a Baer's pochard; *Aythya baeri*.

**あかはた²**【赤羽太】〔魚〕〔ハタ科の海産魚〕a blacktip grouper; *Epinephelus fasciatus*.

**あかひげ**【赤髭】 ▷ 赤ひげ先生〔患者中心の自己犠牲的な医師〕Doctor Red Beard; the altruistic Edo-period doctor, featured in the novel by Yamamoto Shūgorō and the film by Kurosawa Akira, who devotes his life to treating the poor.

**あかほしびょう, あかぼしびょう**【赤星病】〔植物病理〕brown spot disease.

**あかほん**【赤本】 3〔ミシュラン・ガイドの,食事と宿泊の案内版〕the (Michelin) Red Guide.

**あかまい**【赤米】〔古代米の一種〕red rice.

**あかまるかいがらむし**【赤丸貝殻虫】〔昆〕〔柑橘類の病害虫〕California red scale; *Aonidiella aurantii*.

**あかみみがめ**【赤耳亀】〔動〕a red-eared slider (turtle); *Trachemys scripta*.

**あかめやなぎ**【赤芽柳】〔植〕〔ヤナギ科の落葉高木〕a Japanese pussy willow; *Salix chaenomeloides*.

**あかやしお**【赤八染】〔植〕〔日本原産,ツツジ科の落葉低木〕*Rhododendron pentaphyllum*.

**あかやまあり**【赤山蟻】〔昆〕a warrior ant; *Formica sanguinea*.

**あかゆう**【赤釉】〔製陶〕(a) red glaze.

**あがりしょう**【上がり症】(a) social phobia; chronic [extreme] shyness [stage fright];〔医〕social anxiety disorder.

**あかワラルー**【赤-】〔動〕an antilopine wallaroo; *Macropus antilopinus*.

**あかんたい**【亜寒帯】 ▷ 亜寒帯系[産](の) subarctic; subpolar;〔森林〕subarctic-[subpolar-]zone; boreal.

**アカントアメーバ**〔動〕〔角膜炎などを引き起こす病原性アメーバ〕acanthamoeba.

**あかんぴょうき**【亜間氷期】〔地質〕an interstadial (period); an interstade.

## あ

**あき**¹【秋】▶秋採用 autumn [fall] recruitment.
「秋」〔芥川龍之介作の小説〕Autumn.
**あきいろ**【秋色】〔秋らしい色〕an autumn(al) color; *a fall color. ◆~にすっかり染まった山〔紅葉しているさま〕mountains「dyed [ablaze, decked out] in「autumnal [*fall] colors. ◆秋色メーク cosmetics in「autumn [*fall] colors
**あきかん**【空き缶】▶空き缶回収 empty can collection.
**あきこうばん**【空き交番】an [a temporarily] unmanned police box; a police box with nobody on duty. ◆~の解消 solving the problem of unmanned police boxes; making sure that police boxes always have somebody on duty.
**アキ・コミュノテール**〔EUの法規の総体; EU加盟の際に受け入れが必要〕the acquis communautaire; the accumulated body of EU law.
**あきたいぬ**【秋田犬】〔犬〕＝あきたけん.
**あきたいふう**【秋台風】an autumn [*a fall] typhoon.
**あきたけん**【秋田犬】〔犬〕an Akita (dog); an Akita inu.
**あきてんぽ**【空き店舗】an「abandoned [empty, unoccupied, untenanted] store [shop]. ◆近gosta駅前に~が目立つようになった. One can't help noticing the number of empty stores around the station recently. ▶There are more and more abandoned shops in front of the station. ◆市は~を活用した保育所の設置に力を入れている. The municipality is encouraging the use of empty stores as nursery schools. ▶空き店舗対策 a policy for [measures for] (dealing with) abandoned stores.
「秋の童話 オータム・イン・マイ・ハート」〔韓国のテレビドラマ〕Autumn Fairy Tale.
**アキバけい**【-系】〔秋葉原に集まるアニメ・ゲーム・パソコンなどのオタク〕《anime》geeks frequenting Akihabara in Tokyo; "Akihabara geeks."
**あきゅうせい**【亜急性】▶亜急性期 a subacute「stage [phase]. ▶亜急性硬化性全脳炎〔医〕subacute sclerosing panencephalitis (略: SSPE).
**アキュテイン**〔商標・薬〕〔米国の皮膚薬; ビタミンAの一種〕Accutane. ▶一般名は isotretinoin.
**アキレギア**〔植〕〔キンポウゲ科オダマキ属の総称〕an aquilegia.
**アクア** ▶アクアミネラル〔鉱泉水〕mineral water.
**アクアヴィット**〔北欧の蒸留酒〕aquavit; akvavit.
**アクアサイズ**〔＜ aqua ＋ exercise〕〔水中での運動〕aquacise.
**アクアセラピー**〔医〕〔飲泉・温冷水浴・水中運動などによる治療〕aquatherapy; aquatic therapy; hydrotherapy.
**アクアチント**〔美〕〔銅板画の技法〕aquatint;〔作品〕an aquatint (print).
**アクアパーク**〔水上スポーツ関連の設備を備えた施設〕an aqua park; a water park.
**アクアビクス**〔水中での運動〕aquabics; aerobic exercise(s) performed in water.
**アクシスじか**【-鹿】〔動〕an axis deer; a chital; *Axis axis*.
**あくしつ**²【悪質】▶悪質業者 an underhand(ed) trader; a crooked operator.
「アクシデンタル・スパイ」〔映画〕The Accidental Spy.〔中国語タイトル〕特務迷城.
**あくしゅ**³【握手】▶握手会〔アイドルなどとファンの〕a handshake session.
**アクス**【阿克蘇】〔中国, 新疆ウイグル自治区内の地区・市〕Aksu.
**アクスム**〔エチオピア北部の町〕Aksum; Axum.
**あくせい**²【悪性】▶悪性コード〔電算〕a malicious code. ▶悪性線維性組織球腫〔医〕a malignant fibrous histiocytoma (略: MFH).
**アクセシビリティー**〔交通機関・建築物・電気通信機器などをすべての人が自由に利用できる状態〕accessibility.

**アクセシブル・デザイン**〔高齢者・身障者が使いやすいように配慮した設計〕accessible design.
**アクセス** ▶アクセス記録〔電算〕an access record; an access log.
**アクセルロッド** Axelrod, Julius (1912-2004;〔米国の生化学者〕.
**あくだま**【悪玉】 ▶超悪玉 a supervillain; a super-villain; an arch villain; an arch-villain. ▶悪玉菌 pathogenic bacteria; bad bacteria; harmful bacteria.
**アクチグラフ**〔身体活動量の連続測定装置〕an actigraph.
**アクチニジン**〔化〕〔マタタビに含まれるアルカロイドの一種〕actinidine.
**アクチビン**〔生化〕〔ペプチド性ホルモンの1つ〕activin.
**アクチュアリー**〔保険数理士〕an actuary.
**アクチン** ▶アクチン・フィラメント〔線維〕an actin filament.
**アクティビスト・ファンド**〔株を買い集め積極的に企業に経営改善を要求してゆく投資会社〕an activist fund.
**アクティブ** ▶アクティブ運用〔株式〕⇒うんよう. ▶アクティブ・サスペンション〔自動車〕active suspension; an active suspension system. ▶アクティブ試験〔核燃料再処理工場で本物の使用済み核燃料を再処理する試験〕an active test. ▶アクティブ・シニア〔社会への参加意欲や消費意欲が強いとされる, 団塊の世代を中心とした高齢者〕an active senior (citizen). ▶アクティブ・ファンド〔金融〕an active fund.
**アクトス**〔商標・薬〕〔糖尿病治療薬〕Actos.
**アクトネル**〔商標・薬〕〔骨粗鬆症治療薬〕Actonel. ▶成分名はリセドロン酸ナトリウム水和物 (risedronate sodium hydrate), 一般名は risedronate.
**-あぐねる** ＝あぐむ.
「悪魔のいけにえ」〔映画〕The Texas Chainsaw Massacre.
「悪魔のくちづけ」**1**〔1967年の映画〕Games. **2**〔1997年の映画〕The Serpent's Kiss.
「悪魔の棲む家」〔映画〕The Amityville Horror.
**あくむ**【悪夢】▶悪夢障害〔医〕nightmare disorder.
**-あぐむ**【-倦む】 ◆ゆるいカーブを打ち~ try to hit slow curves without success; be unable to hit slow curves / 将来のことを一人で考え~ think about the future by *oneself* and get nowhere; ponder over the future with no success; have no idea about *one's* future.
**アクリル** ▶アクリルパネル an acrylic panel. ▶アクリル板 an acrylic「sheet [plate, board].
**アグレ** Agre, Peter (1949- ;〔米国の化学者〕.
**アクロシン**〔生化〕acrosin.
**アグロバクテリウム**〔菌〕〔植物に遺伝子を組み込む土壌微生物アグロバクテリウム属の総称〕an agrobacterium (*pl.* -ria).
**アグロフォレストリー**〔農業・林業両用の土地利用〕agroforestry. ▶agroforester *n*.
**アクロマイシン**〔商標・薬〕〔テトラサイクリン製剤〕Achromycin.
**アクロン**〔米国オハイオ州北東部の都市〕Akron.
**あけい**²【亜型】a subtype; a variant.
**あげしお**【上げ潮】 ▶上げ潮政策〔経〕the "rising tide policy."
**あげつらう**【論う】criticizing; finding fault《with…》; quibbling《over details》; splitting hairs.
**あげどまり**【上げ止まり】a halt in the rise (of…); hitting [reaching] a ceiling. ◆ダウ平均株価が1万ドルの大台を突破し, 市場の~感が強まっている. With the Dow-Jones industrial average having broken through the 10,000-point benchmark, there's a growing feeling that the market has "hit a ceiling [topped out].
**あげどまる**【上げ止まる】stop「rising [increasing]; top out; hit a ceiling. ◆株価が上げ止まって下落に転じる気配を見せている. Stock prices have topped out and are now showing signs of retreat.
**あげどり**【揚げ鶏】〔料理〕fried chicken.

あげまきがい【揚巻貝】〖貝〗a (species of) razor clam; *Sinonovacula constricta*.

アゲラタム〖植〗〔キク科の1年草〕an ageratum 《*pl.* ~s》; *Ageratum houstonianum*.

あげんしりゅうし【亜原子粒子】〖物〗a subatomic particle.

あこうそく【亜光速】《travel at》near light speed.

あごつき【顎付き】〔食事代付き〕 ▶ ～で日給 8,000 円の仕事 work that pays 8,000 yen a day including meals.

アコンカグアさん【-山】〔アンデス山脈中にある西半球の最高峰〕Mount Aconcagua; Cerro Aconcagua.

アサーション・トレーニング〔自分と相手の両方を尊重した自己表現訓練〕assertiveness [assertion] training. [=アサーティブ(ネス)・トレーニング]

「アザーズ」〖映画〗The Others.

アサーティブネス〔自己主張の積極性〕assertiveness.

アサーティブ(ネス)・トレーニング〔自分と相手の両方を尊重した自己表現訓練〕assertiveness training.

アサード〖料理〗〔アルゼンチンなどで作られる牛肉の塊（かたまり）の網焼き〕asado.

アザーン〖イスラム教〗〔祈りの時刻の告知〕azan; adhan; 《call》《an [the]》'azan [adhan].

あさいり【浅煎り】〔コーヒー豆の〕light roast.

「アサインメント」〖映画〗The Assignment.

あさがお【朝顔】 ▶ 変化朝顔〔突然変異系統の朝顔〕a varied Japanese morning glory. ▶ 朝顔症候群〖眼科〗morning glory syndrome.

あさだき【浅炊き】〖料理〗〔素材の味を生かすように薄味で野菜・魚介類などを軽く煮ること〕light flavoring and simmering. ▶ 浅炊き佃煮 lightly flavored and simmered *tsukudani*.

アサダバード〔アフガニスタン東部, クナール州の州都〕Asadabad.

アサド 1 al-Assad, Bashar (1965– ；シリアの政治家；大統領〔2000– 〕；2 の子). 2 al-Assad, Hafiz (1928?–2000；シリアの軍人・政治家；大統領〔1971–2000〕；1 の父).

あさドラ【朝-】the (NHK) morning drama serial(s); the morning serial TV novel (on NHK).

あさどり【朝採り】〔野菜などを早朝に収穫すること〕(a) morning harvest; picking [harvesting]《vegetables》in the morning. ▶ ～のトマトが午後には店頭に並んでいた. Tomatoes picked that morning were in the store by the afternoon.

あさひひょうもん【旭豹紋】〖昆〗〔タテハチョウ科のチョウ〕a zigzag fritillary; *Clossiana freija*.

あさむし【浅蒸し】light steaming. ▶ 浅蒸し茶 light-steamed tea.

アサルト・ライフル〔突撃銃〕an assault rifle.

あし¹【足・脚】 ▶ 足運び the movements of 'sb's [the] feet; *sb*'s foot movements; how [the way] *sb* moves 'sb feet; 〖スポーツ〗footwork.

アジア ▶ アジア・カー〔アジア市場向けの低価格自動車〕an Asian car. ▶ アジア風邪〖医〗Asian 'flu [influenza]. ▶ アジア麺（southeast）Asian noodles.

アジアあんぜんほしょうかいぎ【-安全保障会議】〔英国の国際戦略研究所の主催で毎年行われているもの〕the Asia Security Summit. ▶ 2002 年, 最初の開催場所となったシンガポールのホテルの名前から "the Shangri-la Dialogue" とも呼ばれる.

アジアいしれんらくきょうぎかい【-医師連絡協議会】the Association of Medical Doctors of Asia (略：AMDA). [=アムダ]

アジアオリンピックひょうぎかい【-評議会】the Olympic Council of Asia (略：OCA).

アジアかいぞくたいさくちいききょうりょくてい【-海賊対策地域協力協定】the Regional Cooperation Agreement on Anti-Piracy in Asia (略：ReCAAP).

アジアかいはつききん【-開発基金】the Asian Development Fund (略：ADF).

アジアカップ〖サッカー〗the Asian Cup.

アジアきょうりょくたいわ【-協力対話】Asia(n) Cooperation Dialogue (略：ACD). ▶ アジア協力対話外相会議 the 《fourth》'Asia(n) Cooperation Dialogue [ACD] Foreign Ministers' Meeting.

アジア・クリーン・エネルギーききん【-基金】the Asian Clean Energy Fund (略：ACEF).

アジアけいざいけんきゅうじょ【-経済研究所】〔JETRO の研究機関〕the Institute of Developing Economies (略：IDE(-JETRO)).

アジアサッカーれんめい【-連盟】〖サッカー〗the Asian Football Confederation (略：AFC).

アジアシリーズ〖野球〗〔日本・韓国・中華台北・中国の各リーグ優勝チームによる選手権試合；2005 年から〕the Asia Series.

アジアせいとうこくさいかいぎ【-政党国際会議】the 《Third》International Conference of Asian Political Parties (略：ICAPP).

アジアだいとしネットワークにじゅういち【-大都市-21】〔アジアにおける都市問題解決のための国際組織〕the Asian Network of Major Cities 21 (略：ANMC21).

アジアたいへいようあんぜんほしょうきょうりょくかいぎ【-太平洋安全保障協力会議】the Council for Security Cooperation in the Asia Pacific (略：CSCAP).

アジアたいへいよううちゅうきょうりょくきこう【-太平洋宇宙協力機構】the Asia-Pacific Space Cooperation Organization (略：APSCO).

アジアたいへいようじゆうぼうえきけん【-太平洋自由貿易圏】〔2004 年の APEC 首脳会議で出された構想〕a Free Trade Area of the Asia Pacific (略：FTAAP).

アジアたいへいようしりょうセンター【-太平洋資料-】the Pacific Asia Resource Center (略：PARC).

アジアたいへいようちいきうちゅうきかんかいぎ【-太平洋地域宇宙機関会議】the Asia-Pacific Regional Space Agency Forum (略：APRSAF).

アジアたいへいようちいきエイズこくさいかいぎ【-太平洋地域-国際会議】the International Congress on AIDS in Asia and the Pacific (略：ICAAP).

アジアたいへいようちいきそしき【-太平洋地域組織】〔国際自由労連 (ICFTU) の〕the Asian and Pacific Regional Organisation (略：APRO).

アジアたいへいようでんきつうしんきょうどうたい【-太平洋電気通信共同体】the Asia-Pacific Telecommunity (略：APT).

アジアたいへいようとうごうモデル【-太平洋統合-】〖環境〗the Asian-Pacific Integrated Model (略：AIM).

アジアたいへいようほうそうれんごう【-太平洋放送連合】the Asia-Pacific Broadcasting Union (略：ABU).

アジアたいへいようマネーロンダリングたいさくグループ【-太平洋-対策-】the Asia/Pacific Group on Money Laundering (略：APG).

アジアのろば【-野驢馬】〖動〗an Asiatic (wild) ass; *Equus hemionus*.

アジア・ハイウェイ〔東アジアとトルコを結ぶ国際道路網〕the Asian Highway (略：AH).

アジアパラリンピックいいんかい【-委員会】the Asian Paralympic Committee (略：APC). ▶ 2002 年発足.

アジアパラリンピックきょうぎたいかい【-競技大会】〔アジアパラリンピック委員会主催の〕the Asian Paralympic Games; the Asian Paralympics. ▶ 2010 年から開催予定.

アジア・バレーボールれんめい【-連盟】the Asian Volleyball Confederation (略：AVC).

アジアふかくさんきょうぎ【-不拡散協議】the Asian Senior-Level Talks on Non-Proliferation (略：ASTOP).

アジア・ブロードバンドけいかく【-計画】the Asia

## あ

アジアぼうさいセンター Broadband Program.
アジアぼうさいセンター【防災-】the Asian Disaster Reduction Center (略: ADRC).
アジアやきゅうれんめい【-野球連盟】〔国際野球連盟の加盟組織; 本部は韓国〕the Baseball Federation of Asia (略: BFA).
アジアラグビーきょうかい【-協会】the Asian Rugby Football Union (略: ARFU).
アシール〔サウジアラビア南西部の州〕Asir.
あしいれ【足入れ】〔履き物などに足を入れること〕◐ この靴は〜がスムーズだ。These shoes slip on smoothly. ◑ 足入れおんぶ紐 an on-the-back baby sling with foot holes. 足入れ感 ◐ 〜感のよいテニスシューズ tennis shoes that slip on comfortably. 足入れ布団[毛布] a 「quilt [blanket] with a foot pocket.
あしうら【足裏】《足裏健康法 sole therapy; reflexology (on the soles of the feet). 足裏マッサージ (a) sole massage.
あじかん【阿字観】《仏教》ajikan (meditation); a method of meditation in Shingon Esoteric Buddhism.
あしくち【足口】〔靴下の上端〕a foot opening; 〔ショーツなどの下端〕a leg opening. ◑ 足口ゴム ◐ 〜ゴム入りの靴下 socks with elastic bands around the tops. 足口レース ◐ 〜レースショーツ panties with lace-trimmed leg openings.
あしくび【足首】◑ 足首固め〔格闘技の技〕an ankle 「hold [lock].
アシコ《楽器》〔アフリカやラテン音楽の太鼓〕an ashiko.
あしこし【足腰】◑ 足腰年齢 《test》「one's age as judged by the state of one's legs and lower back muscles.
アジズ Aziz, Tariq (1936-   ; イラクの政治家).
アシスタント ◑ アシスタント・ドッグ〔身体障害者補助犬〕a service [an assistance, a helper, an aid] dog.
アシスト ◑ アシスト機能 assist(ance) function. ◐ 電動〜機能 power [electric] assist(ance) 《bicycles》.
アシスト・グリップ〔自動車〕〔乗降時や、揺れるときにつかまる取っ手〕an assist 「handle [grip].
アシタレ【脚[足]-】〔靴の広告写真などで足だけを写されるタレント〕a 「leg [foot] model.
あしちりょう【足治療】*podiatry; "chiropody. ◑ 足治療医 *a podiatrist; "a chiropodist.
あしどり【足取り】◑ 足取り捜査 a tracking investigation; investigative tracking.
あしなか【足半】〔かかと部分のない短いわらじ〕half-soled straw sandals; straw sandals which are designed only for the front half of the foot.
あしながきあり【足長黄蟻】〔虫〕a yellow crazy ant; Anoplolepis gracilipes.
あしながこうか【脚長効果】the effect of making one's legs look longer (of clothing or footwear). ◐ このジーパンには〜がある。These jeans will make your legs look longer.
あしはば【足幅】〔靴のサイズで、上から見た足の横幅〕one's foot width.
あしはら【葦原】a field of reeds; a reedy 「field [plain]; a wilderness of reeds.
あしぶみ【足踏み】◑ 足踏み洗濯 washing [cleaning] sth by treading on it with bare feet.
アシモ【商標】〔ホンダ製二足歩行ロボット〕ASIMO.
あしもととう【足下灯、足元灯】a steplight; a step light; a light at floor level.
アジャスタブル 〜な〔調節可能な〕adjustable. ◑ アジャスタブル・カフ(ス)〔服飾〕〔ボタンが2つ並んでいて袖口の寸法が調整できる〕adjustable cuffs.
「アジヤデ」〔P·ロティ作の小説〕Aziyade.
アジャリア〔グルジアの、黒海に接する自治共和国〕Ajaria. 〔公式名〕アジャリア自治共和国 the Autonomous Re-

public of Ajaria. ▷ Ajarian adj., n.; 〔住民〕an Ajarian; 〔首都〕バトゥーミ Batumi.
あしゅくにょらい【阿閦如来】《仏教》《<Skt》Aks(h)obhya Tathagata.
アシュケロン〔イスラエル、地中海沿岸の町〕Ashqelon; Ashkelon. ▶ 古称 アスカロン (Ascalon).
アシュラ〔イスラム教シーア派の宗教行事〕the 「Ashura [Ashoura].
あしゅらどう【阿修羅道】《仏教》〔六道の1つ〕the (Buddhist) world where Asura (demons) live; the world of permanent strife.
アシロマかいぎ【-会議】〔1975年米国カリフォルニア州アシロマ (Asilomar) で開催されたバイオハザードについての国際会議〕the Asilomar Conference; 〔公式名称〕the International Congress on Recombinant DNA Molecules.
あずかりしさん【預かり資産】client assets in custody. 預かり保証金 guaranty「money [deposits] received. ◐ 〜保証金制度〔新規参入球団に対する〕a deposit system.
あずけいれ【預け入れ】◑ 預け入れ限度額 a maximum deposit.
アスター³【ASTER】〔宇宙〕〔地球観測センサー〕ASTER. ▶ Advanced Spaceborne Thermal Emission and Reflection Radiometer の略.
アスタキサンチン《化》〔カロテノイドの一種〕astaxanthin.
アスチルベ【楮】〔ユキノシタ科アスチルベ属の総称〕an astilbe.
アスティン Astin, Sean (1971-   ; 米国の映画俳優).
アストゥリアス²〔スペイン北西部の自治州〕Asturias.
アストミン【商標·薬】〔燐(2)酸ジメモルファン; 鎮咳去痰剤〕Astomin.
アストラゼネカ〔英国の医薬品会社〕AstraZeneca plc.
アストロ〔魚〕〔南米原産のシクリッド科の淡水魚〕an astronot; an oscar; a velvet cichlid; Astronotus ocellatus.
アスナール Aznar, José María (1953-   ; スペインの政治家; 首相 [1996-2004]).
あすのかい【あすの会】〔全国犯罪被害者の会の通称〕⇒ぜんこくはんざいひがいしゃのかい.
アズハルだいがく【-大学】〔エジプト、カイロの〕Al-Azhar (Al-Shareef) University; 〔パレスチナ、ガザ地区の〕Al-Azhar University-Gaza.
アスプラ【ASPLA】ASPLA. ▶ 次世代半導体製造技術を開発する国内大手十社の共同出資会社「先端 SoC 基盤技術開発」(Advanced SoC Platform Corp.) の略称.
アスベスト ◑ アスベスト関連企業 an asbestos-related company. アスベスト被害[被曝]《suffer from》「asbestos exposure [exposure to asbestos]. ◐ 〜被害者 an asbestos exposure victim.
アスベストしんぽう【-新法】《法》=せきめんけんこうひがいきゅうさいほう.
アスペリティ〔地質〕an asperity.
アスペルガーしょうがい【-障害】《精神医》Asperger [Asperger's] disorder.
アスペルガーしょうこうぐん【-症候群】《精神医》Asperger [Asperger's] syndrome (略: AS).
アスペルギルス ◑ アスペルギルス肺炎〔医〕aspergillus pneumonia.
アスポリン《生化》〔たんぱく質の一種〕aspolin.
アスレチック ◑ アスレチック・トレーナー an athletic trainer; 〔資格を持った人〕a certified athletic trainer.
アセアン【ASEAN】
ASEAN 安全保障共同体 the 「ASEAN Security Community (略: ASC). ▶ 2015年創立予定. ASEAN 共同体 the ASEAN Community. ▶ ASEAN 安全保障共同体、ASEAN 経済共同体、ASEAN 社会·文化共同体の3つの共同体から構成される; 2015年創立予定.
ASEAN 経済共同体 the ASEAN Economic Community (略: AEC). ▶ 2015年創立予定. アセアン産業協力スキーム, アセアン産業協力計画 the ASEAN Industrial Cooperation [AICO] Scheme. ASEAN 社会·文

化共同体 the ASEAN Socio-Cultural Community (略: ASCC). ▶ 2015 年創立予定.
アセアン・ビジネス・インベストメント・サミット the ASEAN Business and Investment Summit.
あせかき【汗かき】 ▣ 汗かき指数〔天気予報の〕a [the] heat and humidity index.
アセチルカルニチン〖生化〗〔脳の神経細胞の表面に存在し神経細胞の再生に必要な物質〕acetylcarnitine.
アセット〔資産・財産〕an asset. ▣ アセット・マネージメント〔資産管理〕資産運用〕asset management.
アセトアルデヒド ▣ アセトアルデヒド脱水素酵素〖生化〗 aldehyde dehydrogenase (略: ALDH).
アセトン ▣ アセトン血性嘔吐症〖医〗 acetonemic vomiting.
アセトンシアンヒドリン〖化〗 acetone cyanohydrin.
アセボチン〖化〗〔馬酔木(あせび)の有毒成分〕asebotin.
アセボトキシン〖化〗〔馬酔木(あせび)の有毒成分〕asebotoxin.
アゼライン さん【-酸】〖化〗azelaic acid. ▣ アゼライン酸エステル[塩] azelate. アゼライン酸ジオクチル dioctyl azelate.
アセロラ〖植〗〔キントラノオ科の常緑低木; その果実〕(an) acerola; *Malpighia glabra*.
アソート(メント)〔各種取り合わせ・詰め合わせ〕an assortment. ▣ アソート・クッキー assorted ['cookies [''biscuits]; an assortment of ['cookies [''biscuits]. アソート・ボックス a box of 'assorted [miscellaneous]《toys》.
アソシエイト〖電算〗〔インターネット上のウェブサイトに掲載した広告を経由してユーザーが商品を購入した場合にウェブサイトの管理者に報酬が支払われる仕組み; 成果報酬型広告〕associate marketing. [=アフィリエイト] ▣ アソシエイト・サイト an associate (Web) site. アソシエイト・プログラム an associate program. アソシエイト・リンク an associate link.
あそびぐい【遊び食い】〔幼児が食事に集中せず, 食べ物で遊んだりすること〕(just) playing with *one*'s food.
あそびだま【遊び球】〖野球〗a wasted pitch.
アゾラ〖植〗〔アカウキクサ科の水生シダ〕azolla;〔属名〕*Azolla*.
アダーミ Fenech-Adami, Edward [Eddie] (1934- ; マルタの政治家; 大統領〔2004- 〕).
あだうち【仇討ち】 ▣ 仇討ち禁止令〔日本史〕＝復讐禁止令 (⇨ふくしゅう2).
アタカマおおがたミリはサブミリはかんしょうけい【-大型-波-波干渉計】〖天〗 the Atacama Large Millimeter(/submillimeter) Array (略: ALMA).
あたたかいガス【温かい-】〖天〗warm gas.
アダナ〔トルコ南部の州・都市〕Adana.
アダプトせいど【-制度】〔公共の施設・地域の一部を「養子」とみなして, 住民・団体などが「里親」となり「養子」となった部分を責任をもって保守管理する制度〕an [the] "adoption system"; a system whereby citizens or groups "adopt" an area and commit themselves to maintaining it.
アダミ ＝アダーミ.
アダミヤ〔イラク, バグダッド北西部の地区〕Adhamiya.
アダム・ウォルシュどうほごほう【-児童保護法】〔米法〕the Adam Walsh Child Protection and Safety Act of 2006. ▶ 名称は 1981 年に起きた誘拐殺人事件の被害児童の名から.
アダムクス Adamkus, Valdas (1926- ; リトアニアの政治家; 大統領〔1998-2003, 2004- 〕).
アダムス・ストークスしょうこうぐん【-症候群】〖医〗 Adams-Stokes syndrome.
アダムス・ストークスほっさ【-発作】〖医〗an Adams-Stokes attack.
「アダムスのお化け一家」〔米国で, ブラックユーモア的な TV ホームコメディ〕The Addams Family.
「アダムス・ファミリー」〔映画〕The Addams Family. ▶ 続編は「アダムス・ファミリー 2」(Addams Family Values).

アタムバエフ Atambayev, Almazbek Sharshenovich (1956- ; キルギスの政治家; 首相〔2007〕).
アタヤルぞく【-族】＝タイヤルぞく.
あたらしい【新しい】 ▣ 新しい物好き ＝あたらしものずき.
あたらしいにほんをつくるこくみんかいぎ【新しい日本をつくる国民会議】the National Congress on 21st Century Japan. [=にじゅういっせいきりんちょう]
あたらしいれきしきょうかしょをつくるかい【新しい歴史教科書をつくる会】the Japanese Society for History Textbook Reform.
あたらしものずき【新し物好き】〔事〕novelty seeking;〔人〕a novelty seeker;〔新発売の商品などをすぐ買う人〕an early adopter. ◆ 〜が高じてロボット犬を買ってしまった. Overcome by my love of new things, I ended up buying a 「robotic [robot] dog. ◆ 彼は〜なので携帯に新機能付きの製品が出るたびに買い換えている. He's an early adopter, so he buys a new cellphone every time one comes out with new functions.
あたりまけ【当たり負け】getting knocked aside. 〜する get knocked 「aside [out of the way]. ◆ 大柄な選手に〜しない体を作るために筋力トレーニングに励む do muscle training to develop the sort of body that won't get knocked aside by heavily-built players.
アダルト ▣ アダルト・ゲーム an adult game. アダルト・コンテンツ〔ウェブサイトなどの〕adult [pink] content. アダルト・サイト an adult (Web) site. アダルト番組〔ネットや電話での〕adult entertainment 「service [(テレビ) program]. ◆〈ネット上などでの〉有料〜番組 paid adult entertainment content.
アタワルパ Atahual(l)pa (1502?-33; インカ帝国最後の皇帝).
アチェ ⇨ナングロ・アチェ・ダルサラムしゅう.
アチェ・ジャヤ〔インドネシア, アチェ州の県〕Aceh Jaya.
アチェ・シンキル〔インドネシア, アチェ州の県〕Aceh Singkil.
アチェ・セラタン[スラタン]〔県〕⇨みなみアチェ.
アチェ・タミアン〔インドネシア, アチェ州の県〕Aceh Tamiang.
アチェ・バラ(ット) ⇨にしアチェ.
アチェ・ブサール ⇨だいアチェ.
アチソン・ライン〖史〗〔1950 年米国が発表した北東アジア軍事防衛線〕the Acheson line. ▶ トルーマン大統領の下で国務長官を務めた Dean (Gooderham) Acheson (1893-1971) より.
アチャラ〔未熟なパパイアなどを甘酢に漬けたフィリピンの漬物〕(an) 'achara [atchara, atsara]; (a) pickled unripe papaya.
あっかいしけん【圧壊試験】〖工〗a 'crush [crushing, collapse] test.
あっこん【圧痕】〔くぼみ〕(an) indentation. ◆ ダイヤ型の〜 a diamond-shaped indentation. ◆ 圧子によってきた〜を計測する measure the indentations made by the indenter.
アッコン〔パレスチナ地方の海港〕Acre; 'Akko; Saint-Jean-d'Acre.
アッサムード〖軍〗〔イラクのミサイル〕an Al-Samoud (missile).
アッサムとういつかいほうせんせん【-統一解放戦線】〔インド北東部アッサム州の独立をめざす武装組織〕the United Liberation Front of 'Asom [Assam] (略: ULFA).
アッサンブラージュ〖＜F〗〖美術〗〔既製品や素材を寄せ集め組み合わせたりして作品化する技法〕assemblage;〔その作品〕an assemblage.
アッシャルク・アルアウサト〔英国ロンドン発行のアラビア語紙〕Asharq Al-Awsat.
あっしゅく【圧縮】 ▣ 圧縮強度試験 a compressive strength test 《of concrete》.
アッシュトレイ〔灰皿〕an ashtray.
あっせい[2]【圧政】 ▣ 圧政国家 a tyranny; a tyrannical

あっせん

state;〔米国の政治家コンドリーザ・ライスが国務長官就任前の2006年1月、北朝鮮など6か国を非難して使った言葉〕outposts of tyranny.
**あっせん**【斡旋】▫▫ 斡旋利得 profits made from (illegal) influence peddling. ◐ ～利得罪【法】(the crime of) making profits from (illegal) influence peddling.
**あっそう**【圧送】〔水や生コンクリートなどの流体をポンプ・圧力タンクなどで加圧して送ること〕(a) pressure feed; (a) force feed; pumping.
～する pressure-feed; force-feed; pump. ▫▫ 圧送車〔流体を加圧して送る機械を積んだ車〕a pump truck.
**あっちむいてほい**〔日本の遊びの１つ〕*atchi muite hoi*; a "look that way" game; a game in which two people play a round of「rock-paper-scissors (*janken*), the winner points at the loser's face and moves his or her finger quickly up, down, left or right while saying "atchi muite hoi," and the loser simultaneously moves his or her face in one of those four directions, losing again if the winner's finger and the loser's face move in the same direction.
**アッドール, アッドウル**＝ダウル.
**あつにゅう**【圧入】▫▫ 圧入装置〔$CO_2$を地中に封じ込めるための〕an injection plant.
**アッバ(ー)ス** Abbas, Mahmoud (1935-　 ；パレスチナの政治家；自治政府首相〔2003年4月-9月〕；自治政府議長〔2004-05〕；大統領〔2005-　 〕).
**アップデーター**【電算】〔更新を行うデータ〕an updater.
**アップルゲイト**＝アップルゲート.
**アップルゲート** Applegate, Christina (1971-　 ；米国の映画女優).
**あつりょく**【圧力】▫▫ 圧力販売〔企業が自己の優越的地位を利用して下位企業などに商品を半強制的に売りつけること〕high-pressure sales. 圧力抑制室【原子力】a pressure suppression chamber.
**アディポサイトカイン**【生化】〔脂肪細胞から分泌される生理活性物質〕adipocytokine.
**アディポネクチン**【生化】〔脂肪細胞から分泌される生理活性ホルモンの一種〕adiponectin. ▫▫ アディポネクチン受容体 an adiponectin receptor.
**アディロンダック**〔火星の岩石〕Adirondack. ▶ 米国のアディロンダック山地にちなんで名付けられた.
**あてがき**【当て書き】〔脚本家が演者を想定して書くこと〕writing with a「certain [particular] actor in mind.
～する write for a certain actor. ◐ 森光子に～した脚本 a script written (specially) for Mori Mitsuko.
**アデコ**〔人材派遣会社〕Adecco.
**アデ・タポンツァン** Adhe Tapontsang (1932-　 ；チベットの女性抵抗運動家).
**アテネ・オリンピック** the Athens (2004)「Olympics [Olympic Games].
**アテネこくさいくうこう**【―国際空港】〔ギリシャ、アテネの国際空港〕Athens International Airport.
**アデノイド**▫▫ アデノイド増殖症[肥大症]【医】adenoid vegetation.
**アデノシン**▫▫ アデノシン・デアミナーゼ adenosine deaminase (略：ADA). ◐ ～デアミナーゼ欠損症【医】adenosine deaminase deficiency; ADA deficiency.
**アテモヤ**【植】〔バンレイシ科の小高木；チェリモヤとバンレイシの交配種；果樹〕an atemoya; a custard apple; *Annona atemoya*; *Annona cherimoya × A. squamosa*;〔果実〕an atemoya; a custard apple.
**アテレクトミー**【医】〔粥腫(じょう)切除術〕(an) atherectomy.
**アテローム**▫▫ アテローム血栓性脳梗塞(an) atherothrombotic brain infarction (略：ABI); (an) atherothrombotic (cerebral) infarction.
**アト**- [$10^{-18}$] atto-（略：a）. ▫▫ アト秒 an attosecond（略：as）.
**アドウェア**【電算】〔無料で利用できるかわりにユーザーの画面に強制的に広告が表示されるソフトウェア〕adware.

**あとおい**[1]【後追い】▫▫ 後追い型 ◐ 実際に被害が出るまで対策を講じなかった市の～型の対応に市民は強く抗議した. Citizens protested strongly at the way the city's response fell behind and its failure to take action until「damage [injuries] actually occurred. 後追い記事 a follow-up story. 後追い報道 follow-up reporting.
**あとおい**[2]【後追い】▫▫ 後追い商品 an imitation [a copycat] product.
**アトキンソン** Atkinson, Rowan (1955-　 ；英国生まれの俳優；本名 Rowan Sebastian Atkinson).
**あとしょり**【後処理】▫▫ 後処理費用 aftertreatment [recovery, cleanup] expenses;〔核燃料サイクルの〕＝バックエンドコスト.
**あとだし**【後出し】〔じゃんけんの〕a late play (at *janken*).
～する〔じゃんけんで〕make *one's* play later than the other player(s) when doing *janken*; cheat at *janken*;〔はじめに提示しておくべきことを故意に伏せて自分の利益を図る〕wait until the other person has revealed his hand before making *one's* conditions; show [reveal, declare] *one's* hand late (in the day). ◐ 大臣は国会での審議に不利になると判断して、議論の前提となるデータを審議終了後に～したのである. Judging that it would put him in a weak position in the Diet, he deliberately「failed to reveal [held back] the data necessary for the debate until after it was over.
**あとつけ**【後付け】▫▫ 後付け装置 a post-purchase「accessory [add-on].
**アドバイザリーけいやく**【―契約】〔投資・経営などに関して助言を与える契約〕an (investment) advisory contract.
**アドバイザリー・ボード**〔諮問委員会〕an advisory board.
**アドバトリアル**〔*advert*isement ＋ edi*torial*〕〔記事体広告；広告とタイアップで編集した記事〕an advertorial.
**アドバンスト・フォト・システム**【写】〔1995年にサービスが開始された写真システム〕the Advanced Photo System（略：APS）.
**アドプトせいど**【―制度】＝アダプトせいど.
**アドベント**【キリスト教】〔待降節・降臨節；クリスマス前の約4週間〕Advent. ▫▫ アドベント・カレンダー〔12月1日から24日までの日めくりカレンダーでクリスマスまでのカウントダウンを楽しむもの〕an Advent calendar. アドベント・クランツ〔リース〕《＜G *Adventskranz*》〔もみの木で輪になり4本のろうそくを立てたもの〕an Advent wreath.
**アドボカシー**〔権利の代弁・擁護；政策の提言〕advocacy.
**アトムエネルゴプロム**〔ロシアの政府系原子力独占企業、アトムプロムの正式名称〕Atomenergoprom.
**アトムプロム**〔ロシアの政府系原子力独占企業〕Atomprom. ▶ 正式名称はアトムエネルゴプロム (Atomenergoprom).
**アトラスおおかぶとむし**【―大兜虫】【昆】〔コガネムシ科の昆虫；東南アジア原産〕an Atlas beetle; *Chalcosoma atlas*.
**「アトランティスから来た男」**〔記憶を喪失した海底人が悪の科学者と闘う、米国のTVドラマ〕The Man from Atlantis.
**「アトランティスのこころ」**〔S・キング作の小説・その映画化〕Hearts in Atlantis.
**「アトランティック・マンスリー」**〔米国の月刊総合誌〕The Atlantic Monthly.
**あとりよう**【後利用】an after use. ◐ オリンピック施設の～ the post-Olympics use of the facilities.
**アドルノ** Adorno, Theodor Wiesengrund (1903-69；ドイツの思想家・音楽批評家).
**アドレール**【商標】〔エスカレーターの手すりベルトを広告媒体とするもの〕ADRail.
**アドレス**▫▫ アドレス変更【電算】address modification. ◐ ～変更(を)する modify「an [*one's*] address.
**アトロベント**〔商標・薬〕〔喘息治療薬〕Atrovent.
**あなあき**【穴開き】〔穴の開いた〕pierced; drilled; having a hole (in it). ▫▫ 穴あきお玉 a slotted spoon. 穴あき靴

下〔はき古して穴があいたもの〕a holey sock; socks with holes in them. 穴あき硬貨〔五円玉など〕a perforated coin; a coin with a hole in the middle.
**アナアナへんかん**【-変換】analog-to-analog conversion.
**アナール**(がく)**は**【-(学)派】《F L'école des Annales》〔フランス歴史学派〕the Annales school.
**あなうま**【穴馬】▫▫ 穴馬券 a ticket for a 「dark horse [long shot].
**アナウンサー** ▫▫ フリー・アナウンサー a freelance announcer. メイン・アナウンサー the main announcer 《of a TV program》.
**あなじゃこ**【穴蝦蛄】【動】a mud shrimp; *Upogebia major*. ▷ アナジャコ科 Upogebiidae.
**アナ・スイ** Anna Sui (1955/64?- ; 米国のファッションデザイナー).
**アナストロゾール**【薬】〔乳がん治療薬〕anastrozole.
**「あなたが寝てる間に…」**【映画】While You Were Sleeping.
**「あなたが欲しい」**〔エリック・サティ作曲の楽曲〕Je Te Veux (=I Want You).
**「あなたのために」**【映画】Where the Heart Is.
**「あなたは目撃者」**〔米国の、セミドキュメンタリーTVドラマ〕You Are There.
**アナトーしきそ**【-色素】【化】〔ベニノキの種子から抽出した色素〕annatto extract.
**アナトリアつうしん**【-通信】〔トルコの通信社〕the Anatolian News Agency.
**アナハイム**〔米国カリフォルニア州南西部の都市〕Anaheim.
**アナハイム・スタジアム**〔米国、アナハイムにある競技場〕Anaheim Stadium.
**アナフラニール**【商標・薬】〔抗鬱薬・遺尿症治療剤〕Anafranil. ▶ 一般名は塩酸クロミプラミン (clomipramine hydrochloride).
**「アナライズ・ミー」**【映画】Analyze This.
**アナログ** ▫▫ アナログ回路【電冥】an analog(ue) circuit. アナログ世代 the analog generation. アナログテレビ (an) analog(ue) 「television [TV]. アナログ文化 (an [the]) analog culture; (a [the]) pre-digital culture.
**アニストン** Aniston, Jennifer (1969- ; 米国の女優).
**アニタ・ムイ** Anita Mui (1963-2003; 香港の歌手・女優; 中国語名 梅艷芳 Mui Yim-Fong).
**アニマティクス**【映】〔撮影用のた目安として絵コンテを動画にしたもの; 簡単な手描きのアニメや低解像度のCGで作る〕an animatic; 《その技法》animatics.
**アニマル** ▫▫ アニマル柄 (an) animal 「pattern [motif]. ~柄のセーター an animal 「pattern [motif] sweater. アニマル・スピリット〔旺盛な事業意欲〕animal spirits. ▶ 経済学者J・M・ケインズの用語. アニマル・トラッキング〔動物の足跡などを調べたこと〕(animal) tracking. アニマル・ライト[ライツ]〔動物の権利〕animal rights.
**アニメ** ▫▫ アニメ制作会社 an 「animation [anime] production company.
**アニメーター**〔アニメーション作家〕an animator.
**アニヤ・ハインドマーチ**【商標】〔イギリス製のバッグなどのブランド〕Anya Hindmarch.
**アヌシー**〔フランス東部の都市〕Annecy.
**アヌシーこ**【-湖】〔フランス東部の湖〕Lake Annecy.
**アヌビス**〔エジプト神話〕〔黒犬の頭をした半人半獣の神〕Anubis.
**アヌビスひひ**【-狒狒】【動】〔オナガザル科のサル〕an 「olive [anubis] baboon; *Papio anubis*.
**あねったい**【亜熱帯】▫▫ 亜熱帯系【産】(の) subtropical; subtropic.
**「姉のいた夏、いない夏」**【映画】The Invisible Circus.
**アノー** Arnaud, Jean-Jacques (1943- ; フランス生まれの映画監督).
**「あの頃ペニー・レインと」**【映画】Almost Famous.
**「あのころ僕らは」**【映画】Don's Plum.

**「あの子を探して」**【映画】Not One Less; 〔中国語タイトル〕一個都不能少.
**アノマロカリス**《古生物》〔古生代カンブリア紀に海に棲息していた節足動物〕an anomalocarid; (属名) *Anomalocaris*.
**アノマロスコープ**【眼科】〔色覚異常検査装置〕an anomaloscope.
**アノミー**【社会】〔無規範・没価値状況〕anomie. ▷ anomic *adj*.
**アハーン** Ahern, Bertie (1951- ; アイルランドの政治家; 首相〔1997-2008〕; 本名 Bartholomew Patrick Ahern).
**「アバウト・ア・ボーイ」**【映画】About a Boy.
**「アバウト・シュミット」**【映画】About Schmidt.
**アバガイトう**【-島】〔ボリショイ島の別名〕Abagaitu Islet.
**アバカン**〔ロシア連邦、ハカシア共和国の首都〕Abakan.
**アバスチン**【商標・薬】〔がん治療薬ベバシズマブの商品名〕Avastin.
**アバター**〔インターネットのコミュニケーションツールで自分の分身となるキャラクター〕an avatar.
**アハたいけん**【-体験】〔それまでわからなかったことがわかった瞬間、脳が活性化し発達するという理論に基づく〕an aha experience.
**アパチャー・グリル**《テレビ》〔CRTディスプレーの表示方式の1つ〕an aperture grille.
**アパッチ**〔米陸軍の対地攻撃ヘリコプター〕an Apache (helicopter).
**アバット**(メント)〔土木〕〔橋台(きょうだい)〕an abutment; 〔歯科〕〔人工歯根の支台部分〕an abutment.
**アバネロ** ≒ ハバネロ.
**アハマディネジャド** = アフマディネジャ(ー)ド.
**あばれうち**【暴れ打ち】〔太鼓の〕vigorous and energetic beating of drums.
**あばれつゆ、あばれづゆ**【暴れ梅雨】a heavy local downpour towards the close of the rainy season.
**アピール** ▫▫ アピール度 a degree of appeal. ▫▫ 面接官の印象に残るように~度の高い履歴書を作成した. I wrote a CV that would 「make as much impression as possible on [make me seem highly attractive to] the interviewer. アピール・ポイント (an attraction; a charm; a good thing. ▫▫ 低燃費のよさがハイブリッド車の~ポイントだ. Fuel efficiency is 「the chief attraction of the hybrid car [what makes the hybrid car attractive].
**「アビエイター」**【映画】The Aviator.
**アビエーション・アート**【美】〔航空絵画〕aviation art.
**アピオス**【植】〔マメ科の蔓性多年草〕(an) apios; (a) groundnut; a groundnut vine; a potato bean; *Apios tuberosa*.
**アビシニア・ジャッカル**【動】a Simien jackal; *Canis simensis*. [=エチオピアおおかみ]
**「アビス」**【映画】The Abyss.
**アビトゥ(ー)**(ー)〔<G *Abiturientenexamen* (=leavers' examination)の短縮形〕〔ドイツの高校卒業試験・大学入学資格試験〕Abitur.
**アビリンピック**〔全国障害者技能競技大会〕Abilympics; the Olympics of Abilities.
**アビルドセン** Avildsen, John G. (1935- ; 米国の映画監督).
**アフィリエイター**〔アフィリエイト広告で収入を得ている人〕an affiliate earner.
**アフィリエイト**【電算】〔インターネット上のウェブサイトに掲載される広告を経由してユーザーが商品を購入した場合に、そのウェブサイトの管理者に報酬が支払われる仕組み; 成果報酬型広告〕affiliate marketing. ▫▫ アフィリエイト・サービス an affiliate service. ◯ ~サービス・プロバイダー an affiliate service provider (=ASP). アフィリエイト・サイト an affiliate (Web) site. アフィリエイト・プログラム an affiliate program. アフィリエイト・リンク an affiliate link.
**アフヴァ(ー)ズ** = アフワ(ー)ズ.
**アフォーダンス**【心理】〔環境世界が知覚者に対して与えるも

の〕(an) affordance. ◆アフォーダンス理論〔米国の心理学者 J. J. Gibson が提唱した認知心理学における概念〕the theory of affordances; affordance theory.

**アフガニ**〔アフガニスタンの通貨単位〕an afghani.

**アフガニスタンふっこうしえんかいぎ**【-復興支援会議】the International Conference on Reconstruction Assistance to Afghanistan.

**アフガン** ◆アフガン帽 an Afghan cap.

**アフガン・イスラムつうしん**【-通信】the Afghan Islamic Press (略: AIP).

**アブグレイブ**〔イラク, バグダッド郊外の地区〕Abu Ghraib.

**アブグレイブけいむしょ**【-刑務所】〔イラク, バグダッド郊外の刑務所〕the Abu Ghraib prison.

**アブサヤフ**〔フィリピンのイスラム過激派組織〕the Abu Sayyaf Group (略: ASG).

**アプサラス**〔ヒンドゥー神話〕〔天界の水の精・踊り子〕an apsara; an apsaras 《*pl.* apsaras, apsarases》.

**アブシンベルしんでん**【-神殿】〔エジプト, ナイル河畔にある古代遺跡〕Abu Simbel; the Temple(s) of Abu Simbel.

**アフタ**[2]〔AFTA〕〔ASEAN 自由貿易地域〕AFTA; the ASEAN Free Trade Area.

**アフター・サポート** after support; an after-support service.

**アフターパーツ**〔自動車や自転車などの, 個別の調整用に単品で販売されている部品〕aftermarket 《car》 parts.

**アブ・ディス**〔イスラエル, 東エルサレム近郊の町〕Abu Dis.

**アプテッド** Apted, Michael (1941-   ; 英国生まれの映画監督).

**アフテンポステン**〔ノルウェーの日刊紙〕Aftenposten.

**アブドラ 1** Abdullah Ahmad Badawi (1939-   ; マレーシアの政治家; 首相〔2003-   〕).
**2** Abdullah bin Abdulaziz Al-Saud (1924-   ; サウジアラビア国王〔2005-   〕).

**アブネット** Avnet, Jon (1949-   ; 米国の映画監督・製作者; 本名 Jonathan Michael Avnet).

**アブハー**〔サウジアラビア, アシール州の州都〕Abha.

**アブハジア**〔グルジア共和国内の, 黒海に臨む自治共和国〕Abkhazia;〔公式名〕アブハジア自治共和国 the Republic of Abkhazia. ▷ Abkhazian *adj.*, *n.*;〔住民〕an Abkhaz 《*pl.* ~》;〔言語〕Abkhaz;〔首都〕スフミ Sukhumi.

**アブハフス・アルマスリりょだん**【-旅団】〔イスラム過激派組織〕the Brigades of (the Martyr) Abu Hafzu al-Masri.

**アプフェルシュトルーデル**〔リンゴやシナモンなどを薄いパイ生地でロール状に包んで焼き, バニラアイスや生クリームを添えて食べるオーストリアの伝統的な菓子〕(an) apfelstrudel.

**アフマディネジャ(ー)ド** Ahmadinejad, Mahmoud (1956-   ; イランの政治家; 大統領〔2005-   〕).

**アフラ**〔イスラエル北部の町〕Afula.

**あぶら**[1]【油】◆流出 an oil spill. ◇~流出事故 an oil spill accident.

**あぶらぶん**【油分・脂分】(an) oil content. ◇スナック菓子の~が肥満の原因になります。 The oil in snack food causes obesity. ◇皮膚の余分な~を吸い取る紙 paper that absorbs the skin's excess oiliness.

**アフリカーナー**〔南アフリカ共和国のオランダ系白人〕an Afrikaner.

**アフリカかいはつかいぎ**【-開発会議】the Tokyo International Conference on African Development (略: TICAD).

**アフリカこうどうけいかく**【-行動計画】〔2002年 G8 サミットで採択された〕the G8 Africa Action Plan; the G8 Action Plan for Africa.

**アフリカすいぎゅう**【-水牛】〘動〙an African buffalo; *Syncerus caffer*.

**アフリカせんしゅけん**【-選手権】〘サッカー〙the 《24th》 African Cup of Nations.

**アフリカつめがえる**【-爪蛙】〘動〙an African clawed frog; a platanna (frog); *Xenopus laevis*.

**アフリカにほんきょうぎかい**【-日本協議会】the Africa-Japan Forum (略: AJF).

**アフリカまいまい**【-舞舞】〘動〙〔アフリカ原産の大型の陸産貝類; 沖縄にも生息〕an giant African snail; *Achatina fulica*.

**アブリコソフ** Abrikosov, Alexei A. (1928-   ; ロシア出身の米国の物理学者).

**アプルーブド・カー**〔正規ディーラーで扱う高品質の中古車; 認定中古車〕an approved (used) car.

**アフルエンザ**〔*afflu*ence 〔*affluent*〕+ in*fluenza*〕〔過剰な豊かさから生じる漠然とした罪悪感・倦怠・無関心など; 消費伝染病〕affluenza.

**アフレック 1** Affleck, Ben (1972-   ; 米国の映画俳優; 本名 Benjamin Geza Affleck; 2 の兄).
**2** Affleck, Casey (1975-   ; 米国の映画俳優; 本名 Caleb Casey Affleck; 1 の弟).

**アフワ(ー)ズ**〔イラン南西部, フーゼスターン州の州都〕Ahvaz.

**アペールしょうこうぐん**【-症候群】〘医〙Apert syndrome.

**アペル** Appel, Karel (1921-2006; オランダの画家).

**アベルトしょうこうぐん**【-症候群】〘医〙=アペールしょうこうぐん.

**アベンティス**〔フランスの医薬品会社〕Aventis.

**アポイント(メント)** ◆アポイントメント商法〔セールス〕〔電話・手紙などで指定場所に客を呼び出して商品を売りつける商法〕"appointment sales"; high-pressure selling by appointment.

**アポジ・モーター**〘宇宙〙〔人工衛星を静止軌道に乗せるために遠地点で点火する固体燃料ロケット〕an apogee motor.

**アポトーシス** ◆アポトーシス誘導剤 an apoptosis inducer; an inducer of「apoptosis〔programmed cell death〕.

**アポプレキシー**〘医〙〔脳卒中〕a stroke; (cerebral) apoplexy.

**アポリポたんぱく**【-蛋白】〘生化〙apolipoprotein.

**アポロ, アポロン** ◆アポロキャップ 《アポロ宇宙船の乗組員がかぶっていた帽子から》 a baseball-style cap (often with a laurel design along the brim). アポロ(ン)神殿 a Temple of Apollo.

**「アポロ 13」**〔映画〕Apollo 13.

**アマ**[2]〔以前, 東アジア, 主として中国に居住する欧米人の家庭に雇われた現地人の女中〕an amah.

**あまあがり**【天上がり】〔民間企業の社員が中央官庁に出向し公務員として働くこと〕the practice of former private sector employees finding employment in central government ministries.

**アマ・アデ**〔アデ・タポンツァンの愛称〕⇒アデ・タポンツァン.

**あまぎしゃくなげ**【天城石楠花】〘植〙*Rhododendron degronianum* var. *amagianum*.

**あまくだり**【天下り】 ◆天下り規制 regulations on the「parachuting〔appointment〕of retired government officials「into〔to〕private sector posts. 天下り的〔式〕〔説明なしに結論を与える〕 ◇~的に結論を与える state one's conclusion without「offering reasons〔showing the reasoning〕.

**あますじ**【雨筋】〔降る雨が空中に描く線〕streaks of rain; rain streaks;〔建物の壁などに雨水によって生じる筋状の汚れ〕rain streak marks.

**アマゾナイト**〔宝石の一種; 天河(ﾃﾝｶﾞ)石〕〘鉱〙an amazonite; an amazonstone.

**アマゾン・コム**〔米国に本社があるインターネット上の通信販売会社〕Amazon.com.

**アマチュア** ◆ハイ・アマチュア〔上級アマチュア〕a high amateur (level, standard). ◆アマ(チュア)棋士 an amateur「go〔*shōgi*〕player. アマチュア資格 amateur status. アマチュア時代〔プロになる前の〕one's time as an amateur; the period「when *one* was an amateur〔be-

fore *one* turned pro]. アマチュア横綱 an amateur「*yo-kozuna* [grand champion].
アマプロ〔アマチュアとプロフェッショナル〕⇨プロアマ.
あまみ【甘味】▫甘味処 a sweet parlor.
あまみぐんとうしんこうかいはつききん【奄美群島振興開発基金】〔独立行政法人〕the Fund for the Promotion and Development of the Amami Islands.
あまみぐんとうしんこうかいはつとくべつそちほう【奄美群島振興開発特別措置法】〔法〕the Special Measures Law for the Promotion and Development of the Amami Islands.
あまめしば【天芽芝】〔植〕〔トウダイグサ科の常緑低木・小高木; 東南アジア原産〕a sweet leaf bush; katuk; *Sauropus androgynus*.
あまやか【甘やか】〜な 《in》 sweet [honeyed] 《tones》. ▶〜な香り a sweet fragrance.
甘やかに sweetly; in a「sweet [honeyed] voice. / 恋human を〜に歌う sing「sweetly [in a sweet voice] of *one's* love. 甘やかさ sweetness.
アマラ〔イラク南東部の都市〕Amarah; Amara.
アマランサス〔植〕〔ヒユ科ヒユ属の各種の総称〕an amaranth.
アマルテア〔ギ神話〕Amalthea;〔天〕〔木星の衛星〕Amalthea.
アマルテイア〔ギ神話〕=アマルテア.
アマレット《<It》〔アーモンド風味のイタリアのリキュール〕amaretto.
アミエル Amiel, Jon (1948- ; 英国生まれの映画監督).
あみき【編み機】▫自動編み機 an automatic knitting machine.
「アミスタッド」〔映画〕Amistad.
アミぞく【〜族】〔台湾の先住民族〕the Ami(s);〔1人〕an Ami 《*pl*. 〜(s)》.
あみてん【網点】〔印刷〕a halftone dot;〈集合的に〉a halftone screen.
アミノカルボンさん【〜酸】〔化〕an aminocarboxylic acid.
アミノさん【〜酸】▫アミノ酸コンディショニング〔アスリートの体調管理法の一種〕amino acid conditioning. アミノ酸スコア〔生化〕〔たんぱく質の性能を表す数字〕an amino acid score 《of 100》. アミノ酸製剤〕an amino acid preparation. アミノ酸配合飲料 an amino acid supplement drink. アミノ酸輸液 amino acid infusion.
あみめきりん【網目麒麟】〔動〕a reticulated giraffe; *Giraffa camelopardalis reticulata*.
アミューズメント ▫アミューズメント産業 the「entertainment [amusement] industry;〔1つ〕an「entertainment [amusement] enterprise. アミューズメント施設 an「entertainment [amusement] facility. アミューズメント・センター〔娯楽街〕an「entertainment [amusement] quarter;〔ゲームセンター〕an「entertainment [amusement] center; a *game [「an amusement] arcade; *a video arcade. アミューズメントスペース〔遊園地などの総合娯楽施設〕an amusement park;〔デパート内などの娯楽施設・ゲームセンター〕an amusement center. アミューズメント・パーク an amusement park.
アミュレット〔装身具的なお守り〕an amulet.
アミロイド ▫ベータ・アミロイド〔たんぱく質〕beta-amyloid. ▫アミロイド前駆体たんぱく質〔生化〕amyloid precursor protein（略: APP). アミロイド・ベータ(たんぱく質)〔生化〕〔ベータ・アミロイド〕amyloid beta (protein)（略: Aβ, A beta).
アミロース〔生化〕amylose. ▫酵素合成アミロース an enzymatically synthesized amylose（略: ESA). 低アミロース米 low-amylose rice.
アムールひょう【〜豹】〔動〕an Amur leopard; *Panthera pardus orientalis*.
アムスラー・グリッド〔眼科〕〔黄斑変性の検査に用いる図〕an Amsler grid.

アムダ〔アジア医師連絡協議会〕AMDA; the Association of Medical Doctors of Asia.
アムダリアがわ【〜川】〔パミール高原に発しアラル海に注ぐ川〕the Amu Darya River; the Amu Darya.
アムナート・チャルーン〔タイ東北部の県; 同県の県都〕Amnat Charoen.
アムラーム【AMRAAM】〔米軍〕〔アクティブ電波ホーミング式の中距離空対空ミサイル AIM-120 の通称〕AMRAAM. ▶ advanced medium-range air-to-air missile の略.
アムラプラ〔インドネシア, バリ島東部の町〕Amlapura.
アムリッツァ(ル)〔インド北部パンジャブ州の都市〕Amritsar.
アムリトサル =アムリッツァ(ル).
アムロジン〔商標・薬〕〔高血圧症・狭心症治療薬, ベシル酸アムロジピンの商品名〕Amlodin.
あめ[1]【雨】▫雨マーク〔天気予報図の雨天のしるし〕an umbrella「icon [sign]; a picture of an umbrella.
あめかぜ【雨風】▫雨風食堂〔食事・酒・甘味など何でも出す食堂〕an all-round restaurant (serving meals, alcohol, cakes, etc.).
アメコミ〔米国の漫画〕an American comic (book); American comics.
あめざいく【飴細工】▫飴細工師 an artisan who produces wheat-gluten figures.
アメしゃ【〜車】〔アメリカ製自動車〕an American(-made) car; a US car.
アメしょん〔戦後の日本人の短期アメリカ旅行〕going to America just long enough for a pee; a derogatory word for a short trip to the USA after the Second World War in order to boost *one's* credentials.
あめそうろ【雨走路】〔オートレース・競輪など〕a「rainy [wet] track.
アメナーバル Amenábar, Alejandro (1972- ; チリ生まれの映画監督・脚本家).
アメナバール =アメナーバル.
アメノフィス〔古代エジプトの王〕Amenophis.
「アメリ」〔映画〕Amelie From Montmartre;〔原題〕Le Fabuleux Destin d'Amélie Poulain.
アメリカあかおおかみ【〜赤狼】〔動〕a red wolf; *Canis rufus*.
アメリカあかりす【〜赤栗鼠】〔動〕an American red squirrel; *Tamiasciurus hudsonicus*.
アメリカいしかい【〜医師会】the American Medical Association（略: AMA).
アメリカ・イスラエルこうほういいんかい【〜広報委員会】〔アメリカの親イスラエルロビー団体〕the American Israel Public Affairs Committee（略: AIPAC).
アメリカいわなんてん【〜岩南天】〔植〕〔ツツジ科の常緑低木〕a drooping leucothoe; *Leucothoe walteri*.
アメリカえいがきょうかい【〜映画協会】=べいこくえいがきょうかい.
「アメリカ, 家族のいる風景」〔映画〕Don't Come Knocking.
アメリカこうくううちゅうがっかい【〜航空宇宙学会】=べいこくこうくううちゅうがっかい.
アメリカこうしゅうえいせいきょうかい【〜公衆衛生協会】the American Public Health Association（略: APHA).
アメリカこがも【〜小鴨】〔鳥〕〔カモ科の鳥, コガモの亜種〕a green-winged teal; *Anas crecca carolinensis*.
アメリカ・ジャスミン〔植〕=においばんまつり.
アメリカせいしんいがくかい【〜精神医学会】=べいこくせいしんいがくかい.
アメリカたんていさっかクラブ【〜探偵作家-】the Mystery Writers of America（略: MWA).
アメリカなきうさぎ【〜啼き兎】〔動〕an American pika; *Ochotona princeps*.
アメリカはなずおう【〜花蘇芳】〔植〕〔マメ科の落葉小高木〕

アメリカビーバー

アメリカビーバー a redbud; a Judas tree; *Cercis canadensis*.
アメリカビーバー 〖動〗 an [a North] American beaver; *Castor canadensis*.
アメリカひどり【─緋鳥】〖鳥〗〔ガンカモ科の鳥〕 an American wigeon; *Anas americana*.
アメリカふよう【─芙蓉】〖植〗〔アオイ科の多年草〕a common rose mallow; a marshmallow; *Hibiscus moscheutos*.
アメリカほどいも【─塊芋】〖植〗a hog peanut; a potato bean; a groundnut; *Apios americana*.
アメリカ・マナティー 〖動〗a West Indian manatee; *Trichechus manatus*.
アメリカミンク 〖動〗〔イタチ科の哺乳類〕an American mink; *Mustela vison*.
アメリカモーターサイクルきょうかい【─協会】=ぜんべいモーターサイクルきょうかい.
アメリカン・エンタープライズけんきゅうじょ【─研究所】〔米国の調査研究機関〕the American Enterprise Institute (for Public Policy Research) (略: AEI).
アメリカン・カンファレンス〔米国のナショナルフットボールリーグNFLの2つあるカンファレンスの1つ〕the American Football Conference (略: AFC).
アメリカン・コッカー・スパニエル〖犬〗an American cocker spaniel.
アメリカン・コミックス =アメコミ.
アメリカンしょうけんとりひきじょ【─証券取引所】〔ニューヨーク市にある全米第2の取引所〕the American Stock Exchange; the Amex.
「アメリカン・パイ」〖映画〗American Pie.
「アメリカン・ヒーロー」〔米国の、高校教師が宇宙人から空飛ぶスーツをもらい悪人をたおすTVドラマ〕The Greatest American Hero.
「アメリカン・ヒストリーX」〖映画〗American History X.
「アメリカン・ビューティー」〖映画〗American Beauty.
アメリカン・レモネード〔カクテル〕a cocktail made of red wine and lemonade; "American lemonade."
アモサイト〖鉱〗〔茶石綿〕発がん性の強い石綿〕amosite.
アモバン〖商標・薬〗〖睡眠薬〗Amoban. ▶ 一般名 ゾピクロン (zopiclone).
アモルフォファルス・ギガス〖植〗〔インドネシア、スマトラ島原産サトイモ科の希少植物〕*Amorphophallus gigas*.
あやかりしょうひん【あやかり商品】goods (sold by being) linked to something famous or popular. ◐ 町のオリンピックの〜であふれていた. The town was flooded with Olympic-related goods.
アユタヤ〔タイ中部の県; その県都〕Ayutthaya.
アヨ（─）ディヤ〔インド北部ウッタル・プラデシュ州の町; ヒンズー教の聖地〕Ayodhya. ▶ 別称 アウド Oudh.
アラー ◐ アラー・アクバル〔アラビア語で、アラーは偉大なり〕Allahu akbar; God is great.
アラーク =アラク.
アラート〖電算〗〔不正操作・異常などを知らせる警報音・警告文〕an alert.
あらいがえ【洗い替え】1〔洗濯の際、代わりに着る衣類など〕a 「spare [second]」 (t-shirt) to 「use [wear] while the other one is in the wash.
2〔古い木製家具などを洗い、(削り直して)再生させること〕cleaning or planing wooden furniture to revive it.
あらいだし【洗い出し】〔調べて明らかにすること〕bringing (the facts) to light 《by investigation》; 〖建〗〔壁・土間などの塗り仕上げの1つ〕a wash and brush technique. ◐ 現行の選挙制度の問題点の〜を行う investigate and shed light on the problems in the current election system / 警察は被害者の交友関係を中心に不審人物の〜を進めた. Centering their investigation on the victim's friends and acquaintances, the police proceeded with their attempts to flush out the suspect.
あらいなおし【洗い直し】1〔もう一度洗うこと〕(a) rewashing;《give it》「another [a second]」wash. ◐ 地面に落としてしまった洗濯物の〜は憂鬱だ. It's depressing having to rewash laundry that has fallen on the ground.
2〔調べ直すこと〕(a) reinvestigation; 《take, have》 another look《at…》. ◐ 問題点の〜 a reinvestigation of [another look at] the issues. ◐ 警視庁はこの未解決事件の〜を始めた. The Metropolitan Police Department has started reinvestigating this unsolved case.

アラウ Arau, Alfonso (1932– ; メキシコ生まれの映画俳優・監督).
アラク〔イラン中部、マルカジ州の州都〕Arak.
アラクノフォビア〖医〗〔クモ恐怖症〕arachnophobia.
「アラクノフォビア」〖映画〗Arachnophobia.
-あらし【-荒らし】◐ 学校荒らし a school burglary; a school burglar.
アラスカはくとうわし【─白頭鷲】〖鳥〗a northern (American) bald eagle; *Haliaeetus leucocephalus alascensis*. ▶ 2004年、国際希少野生動植物種から削除.
アラスカン・マラミュート〖犬〗an Alaskan malamute.
アラバ〖商標・薬〗〔レフルノミド; 抗リウマチ薬〕Arava. [=レフルノミド]
アラビア・オリックス〖動〗〔オマーン産レイヨウの一種〕an Arabian oryx; *Oryx leucoryx*.
アラブ ◐ アラブ首脳会議 the《16th》[an] Arab League summit. アラブ・ボイコット〔アラブ諸国のイスラエルに対する経済ボイコット〕the Arab boycott (of Israel).
アラブふっこうしゃかいとう【─復興社会党】〔バース党の正式名〕the Baath Arab Socialist Party.
あらりえき【安良里海豚】◐ 〜まだいるか.
あらりえき【粗利益】◐ 粗利益率 a gross margin ratio.
アラル〔サウジアラビア、北部国境州の州都〕Arar.
アラルダイト〖商標〗〔エポキシ樹脂系接着剤〕Araldite.
アラン・スミシー〖映〗〔実名表記を好まない監督やプロデューサーが用いる映画のクレジット中の仮名〕Alan Smithee.
あり[1]【有】1〔ある〕◐ はじめに結論〜きの審議会 a meeting to rubberstamp conclusions already reached. [⇨ ありき]
2〔許容される〕◐ 彼ならそれも〜かもしれない. In his case even that is possible.
アリアス Arias Sánchez, Oscar (1940– ; コスタリカの政治家; 大統領〔1986–90, 2006– 〕).
アリアンス・フランセーズ〔パリに本部を置くフランス語・フランス文化を世界に広めることを目的とする組織〕the Alliance Française.
アリーシュ〔エジプト、シナイ半島北部の都市〕Arish.
アリ（─）リ【─廟】=イマーム・アリ（─）びょう.
アリウム〖植〗〔ユリ科ネギ属の総称〕Allium.
アリエス Ariès, Philippe (1914–84; フランスの歴史家).
アリエフ 1 Aliyev, Heydar (1923–2003; アゼルバイジャンの政治家; 大統領〔1993–2003〕; 2の父).
2 Aliyev, Ilham (1961– ; アゼルバイジャンの政治家; 大統領〔2003– 〕).
アリエル〖天〗〔天王星の衛星〕Ariel.
アリオリ〖料理〗=アイオリ.
ありき ◐ はじめに民営化〜の政府案 a government proposal based on the assumption of privatization. ◐ はじめに言葉〜. In the beginning was the Word. / 弁明の機会も与えずに解任〜では私は承服できない. We cannot accept the decision to dismiss him without giving him the chance to explain, then I cannot resign myself to it.
アリス・スプリングス〔オーストラリア、ノーザン・テリトリーの町〕Alice Springs.
アリスティド Aristide, Jean-Bertrand (1953– ; ハイチの政治家; 大統領〔1990–2004〕).
アリセプト〖商標・薬〗〔アルツハイマー型認知症治療薬〕Aricept. [= 塩酸ドネペジル（⇨えんさん）]
アリミデックス〖商標・薬〗〔乳がん治療薬〕Arimidex. ▶ 一

般名：アナストロゾール].
**アリムタ**〖商標・薬〗〔悪性胸膜中皮腫治療薬ペメトレキセドの米国での商品名〕Alimta.
**アリランこうえん**〖-公演〗＝アリランさい.
**アリランさい**〖-祭〗〔北朝鮮の祭典〕the Arirang Festival.
**アリルイソプロピルアセチルにょうそ**〖-尿素〗〖化〗〔催眠・鎮静作用物質〕allylisopropylacetylurea.
**ありんかい**〖亜臨界〗〖物〗〜の subcritical. ⇨亜臨界状態 a subcritical state. 亜臨界水 subcritical water.
**アル・アイヤーム**〔パレスチナの日刊紙〕Al-Ayyam.
**アル・アクサ・インティファーダ**〔2000年9月に始まったパレスチナ人の民衆蜂起〕the al-Aqsa intifada; the second intifada.
**アル・アクサじいん**〖-寺院〗〔エルサレムの〕the al-Aqsa Mosque.
**アルアクサじゅんきょうしゃりょだん**〖-殉教者旅団〗〔PLOの最大組織ファタハの軍事部門〕the al-Aksa Martyrs Brigade.
**アル・アサド**〔イラク中西部、アンバル州の町〕Al Assad.
**アルアハラム**〔エジプトの有力日刊紙〕Al-Ahram.
**アルアラビア**＝アルアラビーヤ.
**アルアラビーヤ**〔アラブ首長国連邦の衛星テレビ局〕Al Arabia.
**アル・イラキーヤ**〔イラクの国営テレビ局〕Al-Iraqiya.
**アルカイム**＝カイム.
**アルカティリ** Alkatiri, Mari Bin Amude (1949- ; 東ティモール初代首相〔2002-06〕).
**アルガトロバン**〖薬〗〔抗血栓薬〕argatroban.
**アルガムベイ**〔スリランカ南東部のリゾート地〕Arugambay.
**アルカラ・デ・エナーレス**〔スペイン中部の都市〕Alcalá de Henares.
**アルカリ** ⇨アルカリ体質 ＝アルカリ性体質 (⇨アルカリい).
**アルカリせい**〖-性〗 ⇨アルカリ性体質 an alkaline body; alkaline blood; alkalosis.
**アルカリフォスファターゼ**〖生化〗〔肝臓・骨などに含まれる酵素〕alkaline phosphatase (略：ALP).
**アルカリホスファターゼ**〖生化〗＝アルカリフォスファターゼ.
**アルキ**〔アルジェリア戦争でフランス側についたアルジェリア人補充兵〕a harki.
**あるきぐい**〖歩き食い〗eating while walking. 〜する eat while walking; walk and eat (at the same time). ◐ 〜はやめなさい. Stop eating while you're walking.
**アルキニル**〖化〗alkynyl.
**アルギンさん**〖-酸〗 ⇨アルギン酸カリウム potassium alginate.
**アルクッズ・アルアラビ**〔英国ロンドン発行のアラビア語紙〕Al-Quds Al-Arabi.
**アルクラッド**〖金属〗〔ジュラルミン板の表裏にアルミの薄板を圧着して耐食性を増したもの；航空機などに使用〕alclad.
**アルグンがわ**〖-川〗〔中国とロシアの国境の川、アムール川〔黒竜江〕の支流〕the Argun River; the Argun.
**アルゲ・バム**〔イランの要塞都市遺跡〕Bam Citadel; Arg-e Bam.
**アルコール** ⇨アルコール製剤 (an) alcohol-based 「disinfectant 「disinfection agent」. アルコール脱水素酵素〖生化〗alcohol dehydrogenase (略：ADH). アルコール漬け〔標本の〕being preserved in alcohol;〔酒浸り〕being pickled (in alcohol). ◐ 〜漬けの標本 a specimen (preserved) in 「alcohol [spirits] / 忘年会続きで〜漬けだ. With one end-of-year party after another, I am pickled all the time. アルコール・ハラスメント〔飲酒を無理強いすること〕alcohol harassment.
**アルコールやくぶつもんだいぜんこくしみんきょうかい**〖-薬物問題全国市民協会〗Japan Specified Nonprofit Corporation to Prevent Alcohol and Drug Problems (略：ASK). ▶ 略語のASKは "*A*lcohol *Y*akubutsu Mondai Zenkoku *S*himin *K*yokai" より.

**アルコキシグリセロール**〖化〗alkoxyglycerol.
**アルコバール**〔サウジアラビア東部の都市〕Al Khobar.
**アルゴン** ⇨アルゴン・ガス argon (gas); gaseous argon.
**アルサムード**〖軍〗＝アッサムード.
**アルジェント** 1 Argento, Asia (1975- ; イタリア生まれの映画俳優；2の子). 2 Argento, Dario (1940/43- ; イタリアの映画監督；1の父).
**アルジネート** ⇨アルジネート印象材〔歯科〕(an) alginate impression material.
**アル・ジャウフ**〔サウジアラビア北部の州；イエメンの州〕Al Jawf.
**アルジャジーラ**〔カタールの衛星テレビ局〕Al-Jazeera.
**アル・ジャウフ**＝アル・ジャウフ.
**アルジュベール**〔サウジアラビアの東海岸の工業地区〕Al-Jubail.
**アル・ジョウフ**＝アル・ジャウフ.
**アルジルリン**〖美容〗〔しわの改善に有効とされる化粧品成分〕argireline.
**アルスターとういつとう**〖-統一党〗〔アイルランドのプロテスタント政党〕the Ulster Unionist Party (略：UUP).
**アルストム**〔フランスに本社を持つ多国籍企業；電力・原子力発電機器・鉄道車両・船舶などを製造〕Alstom.
**アルセーニエフ** Arsenyev, Vladimir (1872-1930; ロシアの極東地域探検家).
**アルセロール**〔ルクセンブルクの世界大手鉄鋼メーカー〕Arcelor.
**アルゼンチンあり**〖-蟻〗〖昆〗〔南米原産のアリ〕an Argentine ant; *Linepithema humile*.
**アルダビ(ー)ル**＝アルデビル.
**アルダン** Ardant, Fanny (1949- ; フランスの映画女優；本名 Fanny Marguerite Judith Ardant).
**アルチムボルド** Arcimboldo, Giuseppe (1527-93; イタリアの画家).
**アルディピテクス・カダバ**〖人類〗〔エチオピアに生息していた初期の猿人〕*Ardipithecus kadabba*. [＝カダバえんじん].
**アルデビール**＝アルデビル.
**アルデヒド** ⇨アルデヒド脱水素酵素〖生化〗aldehyde dehydrogenase (略：ALDH).
**アルデビル**〔イラン北西部、アゼルバイジャンと国境を接する州；その州都〕Ardabil; Ardebil.
**アルテルナンテラ**〖植〗〔ヒユ科アルテルナンテラ属の総称〕an alternanthera.
**アルトドルファー** Altdorfer, Albrecht (1480-1538; ドイツの画家・版画家).
**アルトマン** Altman, Robert (1925-2006; 米国の映画監督).
**アルトリア**〔世界第1位のたばこ会社である米国 Philip Morris を所有する企業グループ〕Altria Group, Inc.
**アルドリーノ** Ardolino, Emile (1943-93; 米国の映画監督).
**アルバ** Alba, Jessica (1981- ; 米国の映画女優).
**アルパ**〖楽器〗〔中南米のハープ〕a llanera [plains] harp.
**アルバイン**〔イスラム教シーア派の宗教行事〕Arba'een.
**アルバカーキ**〔米国ニューメキシコ州中部の都市〕Albuquerque.
**アルハダル**〔イラク、ムサンナ州の都市；イラク、ジカール州の町〕Al Khadr.
**アルハノフ** Alkhanov, Alu (1957- ; チェチェン共和国大統領〔2004-07〕).
**アルハヤト**〔アラブ圏の日刊紙〕Al-Hayat.
**アルハラ**＝アルコール・ハラスメント (⇨アルコール).
**アルハンゲリスク**〔ロシア北西部の州・都市〕Arkhangelsk; Archangel.
**アルビノ**〖白色変種〗an albino 《*pl.* 〜s》. ▷ albino, albinotic *adj*.
**アルビル**〔イラク北部の都市〕Irbil; Arbil; Erbil.
**アルファ** ⇨α遮断薬〖薬〗〔交感神経α遮断薬〕an alpha-[α-]sympatholytic agent. アルファリポ酸, αリポ酸〖生化〗

## アルプス

alpha-lipoic acid; α-lipoic acid (略: ALA).
**アルプス** ⇨ アルプス越え crossing [traversing] the Alps.
**アルフラ** 〔アラビア語衛星テレビ〕Alhurra. ►「アルフラ」はアラビア語で「自由なるもの」(The Free One) の意.
**アルブミン** ⇨ アルブミン値 an albumin value.
**アルフレッド・チョン** Alfred Cheung (1955- ; 中国の映画俳優・監督・脚本家; 中国語名 張堅庭 Cheung Kin-Ting).
**あるへいぼう**【有平棒】〔床屋の三色の回転看板〕a barber('s) pole.
**アルホバル** ＝アルコバール.
**アルマ**【ALMA】〔天〕＝アタカマおおがたミリはサブミリはかんしょうけい.
**「アルマゲドン」**〔映画〕Armageddon.
**アル・マジド** al-Majid, Ali Hassan (1941- ; イラクの軍人; ⇒ケミカル・アリ).
**「アルマジャラ」**〔英国ロンドン発行のアラビア語週刊誌〕Al-Majallah.
**アルマナール**〔レバノンのニューステレビ局; イスラム教急進派組織ヒズボラが運営〕Almanarre.
**アルマニャック**〔南フランス産の辛口ブランデー〕Armagnac.
**アルミ** ⇨ アルミ(ニウム)地金 aluminium [*aluminum] metal. アルミ二次合金 secondary [*aluminium] alloy. アルミパック [柔らかいアルミ製の容器] an aluminum foil bag.
**アルミニウム** ⇨ アルミニウム・イオン 〔化〕(an) [*aluminum [*aluminium] ion.
**アルメニアじんぎゃくさつ**【人虐殺】〔史〕[19 世紀末から第 1 次大戦期にかけての, トルコ政府による国内アルメニア人の大虐殺] the Armenian Genocide.
**アルモドバル** Almodóvar, Pedro (1951- ; スペインの映画監督・脚本家・製作者).
**アル・ラス**〔サウジアラビア中北部, カシム州の町〕Al-Ras; Ar-Rass.
**アルロン**〔ベルギー南東部の都市〕Arlon.
**アレカやし**【-椰子】〔植〕＝やまどりやし.
**アレキサンドラとりばねあげは**【-鳥羽揚羽】〔昆〕〔アゲハチョウ科のチョウ; ニューギニア産; 世界最大のチョウ〕a Queen Alexandra's birdwing; Ornithoptera alexandrae.
**アレクサンドル** Alexandre, Boniface (1936- ; ハイチの政治家; 大統領〔2004-06〕).
**アレクシーにせい**【-2 世】Alexy [Alexis, Aleksei] II (1929- ; ロシア正教会のモスクワ総主教〔1990- 〕; 本名 Aleksey Mikhailovich Ridiger).
**アレグラ**〔商標・薬〕〔塩酸フェキソフェナジンの商品名〕Allegra.
**アレッチひょうが**【-氷河】〔スイスアルプスにあるヨーロッパ最大の氷河〕the Aletsch Glacier.
**アレッポ**〔シリア北部の都市〕Aleppo.
**アレバ**〔フランスの大手原子力企業〕AREVA.
**アレフ** ＝アーレフ.
**アレルギー**
⇨ 蕎麦(そば)アレルギー an allergy to buckwheat; a soba allergy. 猫[犬, 鳥など]アレルギー (an) allergy to [cats [dogs, birds, etc.]; (a) cat [dog, bird, etc.] allergy.
⇨ アレルギー原因物質 ＝アレルギー物質. アレルギー対応食 food (suitable) for a person with [a food allergy [food allergies]; meals for people with food allergies. アレルギー物質 an allergen; an allergenic substance. ◆〜物質表示 [食品などに表示すること] labeling of allergens; allergen labeling; [そのラベル] an allergen label. ◆〜物質を含む食品 foods containing [allergenic substances [allergens]. アレルギー誘発性 allergenicity. ▷ allergenic adj.
**アレルゲン** ⇨ アレルゲン性〔アレルギー誘発性〕allergenicity. ▷ allergenic adj.
**アレロパシー**〔生態〕〔他感作用; 植物の出す化学物質が他の植物に影響を与える現象〕allelopathy. ▷ allelopathic adj.
**アレン** Allen, Nancy (1950- ; 米国の映画女優).
**アロー** Arrow, Kenneth Joseph (1921- ; 米国の経済学者).
**アローカシア**〔植〕＝アロカシア.
**アロカシア**〔植〕〔サトイモ科クワズイモ属の各種常緑多年草〕an alocasia.
**アロノフスキー** Aronofsky, Darren (1969- ; 米国の映画監督).
**アロマ** ⇨ アロマ・オイル (an) [aroma [aromatic, aromatherapy] oil. アロマ・コーディネーター an [aroma [aromatherapy] coordinator; an aromatherapist.
**アロマコロジー**《aroma + psychology》〔芳香心理学〕aromachology.
**アロマシン**〔商標・薬〕〔抗がん剤〕Aromasin. ► 一般名 エキセメスタン.
**アロマセラピスト** ＝アロマテラピスト.
**アロマターゼ**〔生化〕〔酵素の一種〕aromatase. ⇨ アロマターゼ阻害剤〔薬〕〔薬〕an aromatase inhibitor.
**アロマテラピスト**〔芳香療法家〕an aromatherapist.
**アロマ・ホップ**〔植〕〔香りのよいビール用ホップ〕an aroma hop.
**アロマ・マッサージ** aroma [aromatic] massage.
**アロヨ** Arroyo, Gloria Macapagal (1947- ; フィリピンの政治家; 大統領〔2001- 〕).
**あわ[1]**【泡】⇨ 泡消火剤 a foam extinguishing agent.
**あわおどり**【阿波踊り】〔徳島を本場とする盆踊り〕(the) Awa Odori; (the) Awa Dance.
**あわび**【鮑】⇨ 干しあわび (a) dried abalone.
**アワミれんめい**【-連盟】〔バングラデシュの主要政党の 1 つ〕the (Bangladesh) Awami League (略: BAL).
**あわよとう**【粟夜盗】〔昆〕〔ヤガ科のガ〕a common armyworm; a rice armyworm; Pseudaletia separata.
**アンカー** ⇨ アンカー・テナント〔経営〕〔商業施設の集客力の核となる大型店舗〕an anchor tenant; a draw tenant.
**アンカップリング・プロテイン**〔化〕〔脱共役たんぱく質〕an uncoupling protein (略: UCP).
**アンカリング** anchoring;《アーチェリー》〔弦を引いて顔に当て矢を固定すること〕anchoring;《心理》〔初めに得た情報によってその後の判断に偏りが生じること〕anchoring.
**アンガルスク**〔ロシア, 東シベリアの都市〕Angarsk.
**あんしゃ[1]**【行脚】⇨ 謝罪[お詫び]行脚 ◇ 警察は情報漏洩事件の被害者への謝罪〜を始めた. The police have started visiting all those affected by the leak to express their apologies.
**あんきんたん**【安近短】〔安い費用で近場の観光地に短い日程で旅行すること〕taking a short, inexpensive trip to a nearby location.
**アングラー**〔釣り人〕a sport fisherman; an angler.
**アングラード** Anglade, Jean-Hugues (1955- ; フランスの映画俳優).
**アンクル・ホールド**〔格闘技の技〕an ankle hold.
**アンクル・ロック**〔格闘技の技〕an ankle lock.
**アンクルン**〔楽器〕〔インドネシアを発祥の地とする竹製楽器〕an anklung.
**あんごう[1]**【暗号】⇨ 暗号解読機 a decryption [device [machine]; a [code-breaking [deciphering] machine; cryptanalysis [cryptanalytic] equipment. 暗号作成 code-[cipher-]making; the [making [creation] of a code; [暗号化] encoding; encryption; encipherment; coding. ◇〜作成者 a code-[cipher-]maker. 暗号電文 a coded telegraph.
**あんごうか**【暗号化】⇨ 暗号化技術 encryption technology; an encryption technique.
**あんこく**【暗黒】⇨ 暗黒小説〔ジャンル〕noir fiction; hardboiled fiction; 〔作品〕a (roman) noir; a hard-boiled novel; a " black [dark] novel."
**アンゴラぜんめんどくりつみんぞくどうめい**【-全面独

立民族同盟】the National Union for the Total Independence of Angola（略：UNITA）．

アンサ【ANSA】〔イタリアの通信社〕ANSA．▶ *Agenzia Nazionale Stampa Associata* の略．

アンサール・（アル）イスラム〔クルド人のスンニ派系イスラム原理主義組織〕Ansar al-Islam．

アンサール・（アル）スンナ〔アラブ人のイスラム教スンニ派系の武装組織〕Ansar al-Sunna．

アンサリ・エックス・プライズ【-X-】『宇宙』the [an] Ansari X Prize．[＝エックス・プライズ]

アンザン〔ベトナム南部，メコンデルタ地帯の省〕An Giang．

あんざんがん【安山岩】▯▯ 輝石安山岩 pyroxene andesite．

あんし【暗視】▯▯ 暗視ゴーグル night-vision goggles．

「アンジェラの灰」〔米国の作家フランク・マコート（Frank McCourt）作の小説・その映画化〕Angela's Ashes．

アンジオテンシン，アンギオテンシン『生化』angiotensin．▯▯ アンジオテンシン受容体拮抗薬〔降圧剤〕an angiotensin receptor blocker（略：ARB）．アンジオテンシン変換酵素 an angiotensin converting enzyme（略：ACE）．アンジオテンシン変換酵素阻害薬〔降圧剤〕an angiotensin converting enzyme inhibitor; an ACE inhibitor．アンジオテンシンI[II, III] angiotensin I[II, III]．

アンジャン ⇨アンザン．

アンジュレーション『ゴルフ』〔コース上の起伏〕(an) undulation．◐ このゴルフコースはどのホールも自然の〜を生かした設計になっている．Every hole on this golf course was designed to preserve the natural undulations．

アンス【ANS】〔米国国家規格〕ANS．▶ the American National Standards の略．

あんぜん【安全】▯▯ 安全確認《do, carry out》a safety check．◐ 〜確認を怠る fail [neglect] to do a safety check．安全確保命令〔事故などを起こした運送業者などに国土交通省が出す〕an order [instructions] to improve safety standards．安全祈願 a prayer for safety．◐ 交通〜祈願 ⇨こうつうあんぜん／〜祈願祭〔工事開始時などに行う〕a ceremony (prayer) for safety《before construction work begins》．安全技術 safety technology．安全評価 (a) safety「assessment [evaluation]．安全評価委員会 a safety assessment committee．安全評価報告書〔原発などの〕a safety assessment report．安全棒〔原子力〕a safety rod．

あんぜんうんてん【安全運転】▯▯ 安全運転管理者 a driving safety manager．安全運転支援システム〔路上の危険情報などを車内のナビゲーションに伝えるシステム〕a [the] Driving Safety Support System（略：DSSS）．安全運転宣言車〔輸送トラックなどに貼ったステッカー表示〕a safe-driving declaration vehicle．

あんぜんかつよういなかいがいとこうイニシアチブ【安全かつ容易な海外渡航-】〔2004 年のサミットで合意された文書；航空・海上交通テロ対策の行動計画〕the Secure and Facilitated International Travel Initiative（略：SAFTI）．

あんぜんせい【安全性】▯▯ 安全性評価指針 a《food》safety assessment guideline；〔厚生労働省が定める，組み換え DNA 技術応用食品・食品添加物の安全性評価指針〕the Guideline for Safety Assessment of Foods and Food Additives Produced by Recombinant DNA Techniques．

あんぜんほしょう【安全保障】▯▯ 安全保障政策 a security policy．

あんぜんほしょうかいぎせっちほう【安全保障会議設置法】〔法〕the Law on the Establishment of the Security Council of Japan．

アンソール Ensor, James (Sydney) (1860-1949；ベルギーの画家・版画家)．

アンダーウッド Underwood, Ron (1953- ；米国の映画監督)．

アンダークロス¹ 〜する〔立体交差で他の道路[線路]の下をくぐる〕cross under 《another train line》．

アンダークロス²〔テーブルクロスの下に敷く布〕an undercloth；〔厚手のフェルトやビニール製の〕a table pad．

アンダー・セブンティーン【U-17】〖サッカー〗〔大会〕the Under-17 World Cup (Soccer) Championship；Under-17；U(-)17．▶ 17歳未満の選手のみ出場可能．▯▯ U-17 日本代表〔チーム〕the Japan Under-17 National Team；〔選手〕a Japanese Under-17 player；a member of the Japan Under-17 National Team．

アンダーソン 1 Anderson, Gillian (1968- ；米国の女優)．2 Anderson, Paul Thomas (1970- ；米国の映画監督)．3 Anderson, Paul W. S. (1965- ；英国の映画監督)．

アンダー・トゥエンティー【U-20】〖サッカー〗Under-20；U(-)20；〔ワールド・ユース選手権〕the World Youth (Soccer) Championship；a world youth (soccer) tournament．▯▯ U-20 日本代表〔チーム〕the Japan Under-20 National Team；〔選手〕a Japanese Under-20 player；a member of the Japan Under-20 National Team．

アンダー・トゥエンティースリー【U-23】〖サッカー〗〔オリンピックのサッカー大会〕Under-23；U(-)23．▶ 23歳未満の選手のみ出場可能．▯▯ U-23 日本代表〔チーム〕the Japan Under-23 National Team；〔選手〕a Japanese Under-23 player；a member of the Japan Under-23 National Team．

アンダーヘア〔陰毛〕pubic hair．

「アンタッチャブル」〔米国の，ギャングと財務省特別捜査官の闘いを描いた TV ドラマ・映画〕The Untouchables．

「アンダルシアのロマンス」〔サラサーテ作曲のバイオリン曲〕Romanza Andaluza（＝Andalusian Romance）．

「アンダンテ・カンタービレ」〖音楽〗〔ゆっくりと歌うように〕andante cantabile．

「アンダンテ・カンタービレ」〔チャイコフスキー作曲の弦楽四重奏曲〕Andante Cantabile．

アンチウイルス アンチウイルス・ソフト(ウェア)『電算』antivirus software．

アンチエイジング〔抗老化・抗加齢〕antiaging．▯▯ アンチエイジング医療 (an) antiaging「therapy [treatment]．アンチエイジング・ケア ＝エイジングケア(⇨エイジング)．

アンチセンス・アール・エヌ・エー【-RNA】『遺伝』antisense RNA．

アンチセンスりょうほう【-療法】『医』antisense therapy．

アンチモン アンチモン化合物『化』an antimony compound．

あんてい【安定】▯▯ 安定株式 ＝安定保有株．安定保有株 non-floating「shares [stock]；(company-held) shares unlikely to fluctuate in value．

「アンディー・ウィリアムス・ショー」〔米国の，歌謡バラエティー TV 番組〕The Andy Williams Show．

アンティーク アンティーク家電 antique electric(al) appliances．

あんていか【安定化】▯▯ 安定化軍〔軍〕a stabilizing force（略：SFOR）．

アンディジャン〔ウズベキスタン東部の都市〕Andijan；Andijon．

あんていせい【安定性】▯▯ 安定性試験 a stability test．

あんていせいちょうきょうてい【安定成長協定】〔EU の〕the Stability and Growth Pact（略：SGP）．

アンティパスト〘＜It〙〔イタリア料理で，前菜〕antipasto；an antipasto 《*pl*. -ti, ～s》．

アンデスきょうどうたい【-共同体】〔1996 年創設〕the Andean Community (of Nations)（略：CAN）．▶ CAN はスペイン語 *Comunidad Andina de Naciones*

## アンテナ

より。
アンテナ　▣スロット・アンテナ a slot antenna.　▣アンテナ社員〔街を歩いて消費動向を探る社員〕an employee who monitors consumer trends「on the street [firsthand]; an "antenna" staff member. アンテナ素子 an antenna element.
アンデパンダンてん【-展】《<F Le Salon des Indépendants》〔美術〕〔フランスの美術展〕The Salon des Independants.
あんてん[1]【暗点】　▣閃輝(性)暗点 a fortification spectrum; a scintillating scotoma.　▣閃輝～症 teichopsia.
アン・トーン ＝アーン・トーン．
「アンドリュ−NDR114」〔映画〕The Bicentennial Man.
アンドリュースくうぐんきち【-空軍基地】〔米国ワシントンDC郊外にある米空軍基地〕Andrews Air Force Base.
アンドル〔フランス中部の県〕Indre.
アンドルーズくうぐんきち【-空軍基地】＝アンドリュースくうぐんきち．
アンドル・エ・ロワール〔フランス中西部の県〕Indre-et-Loire.
アンドロゲン　▣アンドロゲン受容体 an androgen receptor (略: AR).
アンドロステノン〔生理〕〔男性の体臭の原因物質〕androstenone.
アンドロステンジオン〔生化〕〔男性ホルモンの一種〕androstenedione.
アン・トン ＝アーン・トーン．
あんどん【行灯】　▣掛け行灯 a wall-mounted paper-covered lamp; a wall lamp. 軒行灯 a lamp hanging from the eaves《of a shop》; an eaves lamp.
あんない【案内】　▣案内ロボット ⇨ロボット．
「アンナと王様」〔映画〕Anna and the King.
アンバール ＝アンパル．
アンバサダー【大使】an ambassador.
アンバラットかいいき【-海域】〔セレベス海にある海域〕the Ambalat area.

アンバル〔イラク西部の州〕Anbar. ▶州都はラマディ.
アンパンマン〔商標〕〔アニメキャラクター〕Anpanman.
あんぴ【安否】　▣安否確認 ascertainment [confirmation] of sb's safety.　◯～確認をする ascertain [make sure of, confirm] sb's safety; check「whether [that] sb is alright. 安否確認システム〔災害時などの〕a system for checking whether people are safe. 安否情報〔災害時などの〕victim [survivor] information. 安否不明 unaccounted for; of unknown safety status. 安否不明者 a person whose safety is unknown; an unaccounted-for person;〈集合的に〉the unaccounted for.
アンファ(ー)ルさくせん【-作戦】〔イラクのフセイン政権によるクルド人掃討作戦〕the Anfal Campaign.
「アンブレイカブル」〔映画〕Unbreakable.
アンブレラしゅ【-種】〔生態〕〔地域の生態ピラミッドの頂点に位置し、個体群維持のために広い生息地を必要とする動物〕an umbrella species.
アンペイド・ワーク〔無償労働〕unpaid work.
アンホ[アンフォ]〔ばくやく〕【-(-爆薬)】〔硝安油剤爆薬〕ANFO. ▶ANFO は ammonium nitrate fuel oil explosive の略.
あんぽり【安保理】　▣安保理拡大 an increase in the membership of the (UN) Security Council; (UN) Security Council expansion.　◯～拡大決議案 a [the] resolution「to expand the (UN) Security Council [for (UN) Security Council expansion]. 安保理付託 submission to the (United Nations) Security Council.
アンボン〔インドネシアの島・市〕Ambon. ▷Ambonese, Amboinese adj., n.
あんもく【暗黙】　▣暗黙知 tacit knowledge.
アンモニア　▣アンモニア濃度 ammonia concentration; an ammonia level.
アンラプラ ＝アムラプラ．
アン・リー Ang Lee (1954- ；台湾生まれの映画監督；中国語名 李安).
アンリ・ムオ ⇨ムオ．
アンワル・イブラヒム Anwar Ibrahim (1947- ；マレーシアの政治家).

## い

い[2]【亥】　▣亥固まる 〔相場〕〔亥年は堅調である, の意〕In the year of the Boar, the market tends to be「strong [bullish]. [⇨たつみてんじょう]
イアペトゥス〔ギ神話〕Iapetus;〔天〕〔土星の衛星〕Iapetus.
「ER 緊急救命室」〔米国の 病院ものの TV ドラマ〕ER.
イー・アール・ピー【ERP】〔統合基幹業務システム〕ERP; enterprise resource planning.
イー・アイ・エー【EIA】〔経済統合協定〕an EIA; an economic integration agreement.
イー・イー・ゼット【EEZ】〔排他的経済水域〕an EEZ; an exclusive economic zone.
イーウー【義鳥】〔中国中部の市〕⇨う．
イー・エー【EA】〔軍〕＝電子攻撃〔⇨でんし〕．
イー・エー・ディー・エス【EADS】〔欧州の大手航空宇宙会社〕the European Aeronautical Defence and Space Company (略: EADS).
イー・エー・ピー【EAP】＝従業員支援プログラム〔⇨じゅうぎょういん〕．
イー・エス【ES】＝従業員満足(度)〔⇨じゅうぎょういん〕．
イー・エス・エル【ESL】〔第二言語としての英語〕English as a second language.
イー・エス・シー[2]【ESC】〔自動車〕〔横滑り防止装置〕ESC; electronic stability control.
イー・エス・ピー【ESP】〔エネルギー・サービス・プロバイダー〕

an ESP; an energy service provider.
イー・エヌ・ジー【ENG】〔テレビ〕〔電子機器を用いたニュース取材〕ENG; electronic news gathering.
イー・エル・ブイ【ELV】〔使用済み自動車；廃車〕an ELV; an end-of-life vehicle.
イーキン・チェン Ekin Cheng (1967- ；香港の映画俳優；中国語名 鄭伊健 Cheng Yee-Kin).
イーグル　▣イーグル・パット 〔ゴルフ〕an eagle putt.　◯～パットを沈める sink an eagle putt.
イーコム【ECOM】〔次世代電子商取引推進協議会〕ECOM; the Next Generation Electronic Commerce Promotion Council of Japan.
イー・シー・アール【ECR】〔商〕〔効率的消費者対応〕ECR; efficient consumer response.
イー・ジー・アール【EGR】〔自動車〕〔排気ガス再循環〕EGR; exhaust gas recirculation.　▣クールドEGR cooled「EGR [exhaust gas recirculation].
イー・シー・エヌ【ECN】〔取引〕〔電子証券取引ネットワーク〕an ECN. ▶Electronic Communications Network の略.
イー・シー・オー【ECO】〔イラン・パキスタン・トルコの経済協力機構〕(the) ECO; the Economic Cooperation Organization.
イー・ジーさいぼう【EG 細胞】〔解〕〔胚性生殖幹細胞〕an

embryonic germ cell; an EG cell.
イー・シー・ショップ【EC -】〔電子商取引を行う仮想商店〕an electronic commerce shop; an E-shop.
イージーボール〘球技〙〔処理しやすい打球など〕an easy ball.
イー・シー・ユー[2]【ECU】〘機・自動車〙an ECU;〔電子制御装置〕an electronic control unit;〔エンジン制御装置〕an engine control unit.
イージスくちくかん【-駆逐艦】〘軍〙an Aegis destroyer.
イージスごえいかん【-護衛艦】〘軍〙an Aegis escort.
イージスじゅんようかん【-巡洋艦】〘軍〙an Aegis cruiser.
イー・シネマ【e -】〘映画〙e-cinema; electronic cinema.〔=デジタル・シネマ(⇨デジタル)〕
いいじまむしくい【飯島虫喰】〘鳥〙〔ヒタキ科ウグイス亜科の鳥〕an Ijima's ﬁleaf-warbler [willow warbler]; Phylloscopus ijimae.
イー・ジャパンじゅうてんけいかく【e-Japan 重点計画】the e-Japan Priority Policy Program.
イー・ジャパンせんりゃく【e-Japan 戦略】〔国民が情報通信技術の恩恵を最大限に享受できる社会の実現に向けて 2001 年に決定された政府の基本戦略〕an [the] e-Japan strategy.
イースター ▫ イースター・エッグ an Easter egg.
イースタン・ケープ ⇨ ひがしケープ.
イー・スリーねんりょう【E3 燃料】〔エタノール 3% 混合燃料〕E3 fuel.
イータス【ETAS】〔オーストラリア政府の発行する電子ビザ〕an ETA; an electronic travel authority; an electronic visa. ▶ ETAS は Electronic Travel Authority System (電子入国許可システム) の略.
イータックス〔国税の電子申告・納税システム〕(an) "e-Tax".
いいたて【言い立て】〔芝居・落語などで物事の由来・効能などを節をつけて並べ立てる長ぜりふ〕a long enumerative recitation accompanied by a tune.
イー・ティー・シー【ETC】 ▫ ETC カード an ETC card. ETC 車載器 an on-board ﬁelectronic toll collection [ETC] unit; ETC on-board equipment (略: ETC OBE).
イー・ティー・ビー・イー【ETBE】〘化〙⇨エチル・ターシャリー・ブチル・エーテル.
イー・テンねんりょう【E10 燃料】〔エタノール 10% 混合燃料〕E10 fuel.
イード〔イスラムの大祭〕Id; Eid.
イー・ばくだん【E 爆弾】〘軍〙〔電磁パルスを発生させ精密機械を破壊する非殺傷兵器〕an e-bomb.
イー・ビー【EB】〔他社株転換債〕an EB; an exchangeable bond.
イー・ビー・アール【EPR】〔拡大生産者責任〕EPR; extended producer responsibility.
イー・ビー・アールそうかん【EPR 相関】〘物〙the EPR correlations. ▶ EPR は 3 人の物理学者, Einstein, Podolsky, Rosen の頭文字.
イー・ビー・アール・パラドックス【EPR -】〘物〙the EPR paradox. ▶ EPR は 3 人の物理学者, Einstein, Podolsky, Rosen の頭文字.
イー・ビー・エム【EBM】〘医〙〔科学的根拠に基づく医療〕EBM; evidence-based medicine.
イー・ビー・オー【EBO】〘経営〙〔一般従業員を買い手とした企業譲渡〕an EBO; an employee buyout.
イー・ピー・ジー【EPG】〘テレビ〙〔電子番組表〕EPG. ▶ electronic program guide の略.
イー・ビー・ディー【EBD】〘自動車〙〔電子制御動力分配システム〕EBD; electronic brake-force distribution.
イー・ビット・ディー・エー, イー・ビット・ダー【EBITDA】〘経〙〔金利, 税金, 償却前利益〕EBITDA. ▶ earnings before interest, taxes, depreciation and amortization の略.
イー・ブイ[2]【EV】〘保険〙(an) embedded value.〔⇨エンベデッド・バリュー〕
イー・ブイ / イー・ビット・ディー・エーばいりつ【EV/EBITDA 倍率】〘株〙〔企業価値 (EV) を償却前営業利益 (EVITDA) で割ったもの〕(an) EV/EBITDA ratio.
イー・ぶんしょほう【e-文書法】〘法〙the e-Document Law. ▶〔民間事業者等が行う書面の保存における情報通信の技術の利用に関する法律〕と〔民間事業者等が行う書面の保存等における情報通信の技術の利用に関する法律の施行に伴う関係法律の整備等に関する法律〕の総称.
イーベイ〔米国のインターネット競売会社〕eBay Inc.
イー・マーケットプレース【e -】〔企業間の電子取引市場〕an [the] e-marketplace.
イー・ユー【EU】 ▫ 拡大 EU an expanded EU. ▫ EU 拡大 EU expansion. EU 旗 the ﬁEuropean Union [EU] flag. EU 指令〔EU の全加盟国に対してある目標を達成することを義務づける EU 理事会の指令; 達成の方法や形式は各加盟国に任せられる〕an EU [a European Union] directive.
イー・ユーけんぽうじょうやく【EU 憲法条約】〔2004 年の〕the Treaty establishing a Constitution for Europe (略: TCE).
イー・ユー・シー【EUC】〘電算〙〔企業内のコンピューター実務者がシステムの構築・運用・管理に携わること〕EUC; end-user computing.
イー・ユーしゅのうかいぎ【EU 首脳会議】〔欧州理事会会合の通称〕an EU Summit.
イー・ユーぼうえいちょう【EU 防衛庁】the EU Defence Agency.
イー・ラーニング【e -】〔IT 技術を活用した遠隔学習・教育〕e-learning.
イーラム〔イラン西部の州; その州都〕Ilam.
イーラム〔イランの地名〕=イーラーム.
イーリント【ERINT】〘米陸軍〙〔戦術ミサイル迎撃用の地対空ミサイルの一種〕ERINT; an extended range interceptor.
イールド〘金融〙〔利回り〕a yield. ▫ 逆イールド(カーブ) an inverted [a negative] yield curve. 順イールド(カーブ) a ﬁforward [positive] yield curve. イールド・カーブ〔利回り曲線〕a yield curve. イールド・スプレッド〘株〙〔株式相場の割安・割高を判断する指標〕(a) yield spread.
イールド・レシオ〘株〙〔株式相場の割安・割高を判断する指標〕a yield ratio.
いいんかい【委員会】 ▫ 製作[制作]委員会〔映画などの〕a consortium for producing ﬁ(a movie); a 《movie》 consortium. ▫ 委員会設置会社〔2003 年 4 月より施行された改正商法に基づく〕a committee-system company.
いえ[1]【家】 ▫ 家墓 a single grave in which bones of the dead of one family are buried.
イェ(ー)イ〔"やったぞ" という意の発声〕Yeah! | Done it! | Olé!
イェーキン Yakin, Boaz (1966- ; 米国の映画監督・脚本家・製作者).
イエス[3]【YES】〘金融〙=ワイ・イー・エス.
イェドヴァブネじけん【-事件】〘史〙〔1941 年, ポーランド北東部のイェドヴァブネ村でユダヤ人多数が虐殺された事件〕the Jedwabne tragedy.
イエロー ▫ イエロー・フラッグ〔自動車レースで, 注意走行を促すために振る黄旗〕a yellow flag.
イェンバイ〔ベトナム北東部の省; その省都〕Yen Bai.
「硫黄島からの手紙」〔映画〕Red Sun, Black Sand;〔別タイトル〕Letters from Iwo Jima.
イオニクス〔イオン工学〕ionics. ▫ 固体イオニクス solid state ionics.
イオネン〘化〙ionene.
イオン ▫ 銀イオン a silver ion; ionic silver. ▫ イオン飲料 an isotonic drink. イオン液体 (an) ionic fluid. イオン基 an ionic group. イオン工学 ion engineering. イオン推進〘宇宙〙ion propulsion. イオン導入 ionto-

phoresis. ◯ ~導入器〘美容〙an iontophoresis device.
いか[5]【烏賊】◯◻ イカ刺し squid sashimi.
イカ〘ペルー南部の州・州都〙Ica.
いがく[1]【医学】◻ 医学モデル =医療体系 (⇨いりょう[3]).
いがくぶつりし【医学物理士】〘医〙a physicist in medicine; a medical physicist.
いかしきる【生かしきる, 活かしきる】apply fully; make full use of…. ◯ 彼女は持って生まれた才能をまだ生かし切っていない。She still isn't making use of all of her natural talent. / 水俣病の教訓を生かし切れず, またしてもこのような悲劇を防げなかった厚生労働省の責任は大きい。By not having learned all of the lessons of Minamata disease, the Ministry of Health, Labour and Welfare bears heavy responsibility for not being able to prevent this similar tragedy.
イカットおり【-織り】〘紡織〙〔インドネシアなどのくくり染め〕ikat.
イカリット〘カナダ, ヌナヴト準州の州都〙Iqaluit.
イカルイト =イカリット.
いかん[4]【胃管】◻ 胃管栄養(法)〘医〙◯ 経鼻~栄養(法) nasogastric (tube) feeding.
いき[6]【閾】◻ 閾刺激〘生理〙a 「threshold [liminal] stimulus (《pl.》-li). 閾下刺激〘生理〙a 「suprathreshold [supraliminal] stimulus.
いき[10]【遺棄】◻ 遺棄化学兵器 an abandoned chemical weapon (略: ACW). ◯ 中国~化学兵器 abandoned chemical weapons in China.
いきさいてき【域際的】interregional; transregional. ◯ 人・物・金の~交換 (the) 「interregional [transregional] exchange of persons, goods, and money.
「生きてこそ」〘映画〙Alive.
いきない【域内】◻ 域内経済 a regional economy. 域内通信網〘電算〙an intranet.
イギリス ◻ イギリス(陸軍)特殊空挺部隊 =特殊空挺部隊 (⇨とくしゅ[1]).
「イギリスから来た男」〘映画〙The Limey.
「活きる」〘映画〙Lifetimes;〘別タイトル〙Living; To Live;〘中国語タイトル〙活着.
イグエイ〘ドミニカ共和国東部の都市〙Higuey.
いくじ[1]【育児】◻ 育児期 the child-rearing period. 育児教室 a 「childcare [child-rearing] class (for young mothers). 育児経験者 =子育て経験者 (⇨こそだて). 育児語〔母親などが幼児に話しかける言葉〕baby talk; motherese; child-directed speech. 育児支援 childcare 「support [assistance]. 育児ストレス parenting stress. 育児放棄 child neglect. ◯ ~放棄する neglect 「one's child. 育児有給休暇 paid childcare leave.
いくじきゅうぎょう【育児休業】◻ 育児休業取得率 a childcare-leave utilization rate.
「イグジステンズ」〘映画〙eXistenZ.
いくすう【育雛】◻ 自然[人工]育雛 natural [artificial] brooding (of chicks).
いくせい【育成】◻ 育成者権〘農・園芸〙〔植物品種の〕plant breeders' (intellectual property) rights; plant variety rights (略: PVR). 育成礁〘海洋〙a breeding reef.
イグノーベルしょう【-賞】〔最初は笑わせて次に考え込ませるような研究に対して贈られる賞; ノーベル賞のパロディー版〕(win) an Ig Nobel Prize. ▶「Ig Nobel」は ignoble と Nobel をかけたもの。
いくもう【育毛】◻ 育毛促進剤 a hair-growth promoter.
イグレシア Iglesia, Alex de la (1965- ; スペインの映画監督).
いけいけ【行け行け】〔2つの部屋などが内部で通行可能になっている状態〕◯ 寝室とバスルームがドア一枚で~になっている。You can go back and forth between the bedroom and bathroom through a single door. | The bedroom and bathroom are accessible to each other through a single door. | Just one door separates the bedroom and bathroom.
イケイケ〔慎重さを欠いた積極性・抑制のきかない奔放性〕◯ ~ムード a go-go mood / ~ギャル a go-go girl / ~ドンドンの拡大路線 go-go expansionism.
いけいせい(しょう)【異形成(症)】◻◻ 高度[中等度, 軽度]異形成 severe [moderate, mild] dysplasia. 線維筋性異形成(症)〘医〙fibromuscular dysplasia (略: FMD).
イケメン a 「handsome [good-looking] man [《口》guy];《口》a hunk.
イケヤ・セキすいせい【-彗星】〘天〙Comet Ikeya-Seki.
いけん[3]【意見】
◻◻ 監査意見〔財務諸表監査における監査人の〕an opinion; an 「accountant's [auditor] opinion. 限定付適正意見〔財務諸表監査における監査人の〕a qualified opinion. 不適正意見〔財務諸表監査における監査人の〕an adverse opinion. 無限定適正意見〔財務諸表監査における監査人の〕a clean opinion; an unqualified opinion. 意見具申 offering 「one's opinion 《on sth》(to 「one's superior). 意見公募〔パブリック・コメント〕public comment. 意見集約 a compilation of opinions. 意見聴取 a (public) hearing. ◯ ~聴取する [を行う] undertake 「(oral) research [an oral survey, a hearing] to 「find out what 《people》think [establish the state of opinion] / ~聴取対象(者) persons asked for their views; the target(s) of an investigation into the state of opinion 《about a proposal》. 意見調整 (the) coordination of 「views [opinions]; reconciliation of [reconciling] (conflicting) views. 意見陳述〔裁判・議会などでの〕a position statement; a brief. 意見提出権〔内閣・国会に対する地方団体の〕the right (of local municipalities) to submit opinions 《on 「concerning the allocation of taxes to local government》. 意見募集 solicitation [soliciting] of opinions.
いこう[9]【意向】◻ 意向表明書〔株式取得などに関する〕a letter of intent (略: LOI).
いこうかくにんしょめん【意向確認書面】〔保険商品の販売時に作成し顧客に提示することが義務化されている書類の1つ〕a form for customers to confirm in writing that an insurance proposal meets their needs; an doublecheck form for potential insurance customers.
イコール ◻ ニアリー・イコール〔ほぼ同じ〕(a) near equivalence;《be》nearly equal 《to…》. ◯ 彼は脳死と死はニアリー~だと考えている。He believes that brain death and death are practically the same thing. ◻ イコール・フッティング〔公平な競争条件〕《be on》an equal footing 《with…》.
いこつ【遺骨】◻ 遺骨箱〔骨壷を入れる箱〕a case for an urn; an urn box;〔遺骨を入れる箱〕a box for the 「ashes [bones] of a dead person.
いごん【遺言】◻ 自筆証書遺言 a holograph(ic) will. 公正証書遺言 a 「notarial [notarized] will.
イサーン〘タイの東北地方〙I-san. ◻◻ イサーン料理 I-san cuisine [food].
いさはやわんかんたくじぎょう【諫早湾干拓事業】=こくえいいさはやわんかんたくじぎょう.
いさん[5]【遺産】◻ 複合遺産 ⇨せかいふくごういさん. ◻ 遺産整理業務 legacy [estate] 「planning [management] (services).
いし[2]【医師】◻ 医師国家資格 a nationally recognized qualification as a 「doctor [medical practitioner]; certification by the state as a doctor. 医師主導(型)治験 physician-led clinical 「trials [testing]. 医師紹介会社 a doctor agency. 医師免許更新制度 a 「re-licensing [revalidation] system for doctors.
いし[6]【意思】◻◻ 意思伝達装置〔言語障害者用の〕a 「speech [speaking] aid.

いじ[5]【遺児】　⇨ 自死[自殺]遺児　a suicide-bereaved child.
いしいるか【石海豚】〘動〙a Dall's porpoise; *Phocoenoides dalli*.
いしうちけい【石打ち刑】〘イスラム教〙〔囚人を土中に半ば埋め、死ぬまで石を投げ続ける刑罰〕(the punishment of) death by stoning; stoning *sb* to death.
いしがきふぐ【石垣河豚】〘魚〙〔ハリセンボン科の海産硬骨魚〕a spotfin burrfish; *Chilomycterus reticulatus*.
いしき【意識】
　⇨ 辺縁意識　peripheral consciousness; the「state [area]」between consciousness and unconsciousness.
　⊙ 意識改革　a change in (mental) attitude; a new way of thinking. 意識転換 a「change [turnabout] of」awareness [consciousness]. ◯～転換を図る　aim [strive] for a change in awareness / 深刻な環境汚染を前にわれわれは～転換を迫られている。Faced with serious environmental pollution, there is a pressing need for a change in awareness on our part. 意識レベル〘医〙a「level [degree] of consciousness;〔あることについての関心の度合い〕a「level [degree] of awareness《about [regarding]…》. ◯ 患者の～レベルは今朝になってから急激に低下した。The patient's level of consciousness dropped sharply this morning. / 廃棄物の不法投棄は環境に対する国民の～レベルの低さを物語っている。Illegal waste dumping shows how little people are aware of the environment.
いしきり[2]【石錐】〘考古〙a chipped-stone drill.
いしはらひょう【石原表】〘眼科〙〔石原式色覚異常検査表〕the Ishihara (color) test plates.
いしやり【石槍】〘考古〙＝せきそう[3].
いしゅ[1]【異種】　⇨ 異種(間)感染〘医〙〔細菌・ウイルスの〕(an) interspecies infection;〔異種移植による〕(a) xenogeneic infection. 異種混交(性)《文化人類》heterogeneity; hybridity.
いしょ[2]【異所】　⇨ 異所開口尿管〘医〙an ectopic ureteral orifice.
いしょう[1]【衣装・衣裳】　⇨ 衣装ケース　a set of drawers (for clothes). 衣装[衣裳]倒錯　transvestism;《口》cross-dressing.
いしょう[3]【意匠】　⇨ 意匠権侵害 (a) design「right [copyright] infringement; (an) infringement of design right. ◯～権侵害訴訟　a suit against an infringement of (a) design right.
いじょう[3]【委譲・移譲】　⇨ 税源移譲　the transfer of tax revenue sources to local governments.
いじょう[3]【異状】　⇨ 異状死　an abnormal death. 異状死体　the body of a person who died an abnormal death.
いじょう[3]【異常】　⇨ 異常死 ⇒異状死(⇒いじょう[4]). 異常死体 ⇒異状死体 (⇒いじょう[4]). 異常繁殖　abnormally rapid reproduction; rampant [unchecked] growth. 異常卵〔複黄卵や肉球卵など〕an abnormal egg;《口》a freak egg.〔⇒ふくおうらん〕
いじょう[6]【移乗】　⇨ 強行移乗〔密輸船などへの〕(a) forced boarding《of (a) ship》. / 移乗機器〔身体不自由者の〕a transfer device; transfer equipment.
いしょく[2]【委嘱】　⇨ 委嘱状　a letter of「appointment [nomination]. ◯ 親善大使の～状を手渡す〔受け取る〕deliver [receive] a letter of appointment as a goodwill ambassador.
いしょく[4]【移植】
　⇨ 顔面移植〘医〙a「face [full-face] transplant. 病(気)腎移植〘医〙transplantation [donation] of a「sick [diseased] kidney.
　⊙ 移植医　a transplant「surgeon [physician, doctor]. 移植医療　transplant(ation) surgery; medical transplantation. 移植希望者　a prospective《liver》transplant「candidate [patient, recipient]. 移植前処置〔骨髄移植の〕(pre-transplant) conditioning chemotherapy; a (transplant) conditioning regimen. 移植治療 transplant(ation) therapy. 移植胚〘生物〙an embryo transplant; a transplanted embryo.
いしわた【石綿】　⇨ 石綿症〘医〙(pulmonary) asbestosis. 石綿肺〘医〙asbestos lung; pulmonary [lung] asbestosis.
いずおおしまきんかいじしん【伊豆大島近海地震】〔1978年1月14日の〕the Izu-Oshima-Kinkai Earthquake (of January 14, 1978).
イスカンダリヤ〔イラク中部の町〕Iskandariya.
いずしちとう【伊豆七島】the Izu Seven Islands.
いずしょとう【伊豆諸島】the Izu Islands.
イスタリフ〔アフガニスタン、カブール郊外の村〕Istalif.
イストミアさい【-祭】〔古代ギリシャの競技祭〕the Isthmian Games.
イスバス〘スポーツ〙〔車椅子バスケットボール〕wheelchair basketball.
イスムス【ISMS】＝アイ・エス・エム・エス.
イスラエル　イスラエル・ボイコット〔アラブ諸国のイスラエルに対する経済ボイコット〕the Boycott Israel Campaign.〔＝アラブ・ボイコット(⇒アラブ)〕イスラエル・ロビー〔米国での親イスラエル圧力団体〕the「Israel [pro-Israel] lobby.
イスラエルこくぼうぐん【-国防軍】the Israel Defense Forces (略: IDF).
イスラム　⇨ イスラム途上国8か国　the Group of Eight Developing Islamic Countries (略: D-8); the Developing Eight Economic Cooperation Group; the D-8 Group.
イスラムかいほうとう【-解放党】＝ヒズブ・タフリール.
イスラムかくめいぼうえいたい【-革命防衛隊】〔イラン革命(1979)後に、反革命勢力に対抗するために編成された非正規軍〕the Islamic Revolutionary Guard(s) Corps (略: IRGC).
イスラムきょうわこくつうしん【-共和国通信】〔イランの国営通信社〕the Islamic Republic News Agency (略: IRNA).
イスラムしゅうきょうしゃいいんかい【-宗教者委員会】＝イスラムせいしょくしゃきょうかい.
イスラムしゅうだん【-集団】〔エジプトの過激派組織〕the Islamic Group (略: IG).
イスラムせいしょくしゃきょうかい【-聖職者協会】〔イラクの〕the Islamic Clerics Committee.
イスラムだいとうほうこうげきたい・せんせん【-大東方攻撃隊・戦線】〔イスラム過激派組織〕the Great Eastern Islamic Raiders' Front (略: IBDA-C).
イスラムだん【-団】〔エジプトのイスラム過激派組織〕al-Gama'a al-Islamiyya. ► アラビア語で"the Islamic Group"の意.
イスラムぼうえいせんせん【-防衛戦線】〔インドネシアのイスラム過激派組織〕the Islamic Defenders Front (略: FPI). ► FPIは *Front Pembela Islam* より.
イスラムほうてい【-法廷】〔ソマリアのイスラム教原理主義者の武装組織〕the Islamic Court Union (略: ICU).
イスラム・マグレブしょこくのアルカ(ー)イダそしき【-諸国の-組織】〔アルジェリアを拠点とするイスラム過激派〕Al-Qaeda in the Islamic Maghreb.
イスランブリりょだん【-旅団】〔イスラム過激派組織〕the Islambouli Brigade.
イズリントン〔英国、ロンドン北部の住宅街〕Islington.
イ・スンヨプ【李承燁】Lee Seung-yeop (1976-　; 韓国の野球選手).
いせい[5]【異性】　⇨ 異性恐怖症《精神医》heterophobia; sexophobia.
いせいか【異性化】　⇨ 異性化(液)糖　isomerized liquid sugar; high fructose corn syrup (略: HFCS).
いせいそう【異性装】〔異性の衣類を身につけること〕cross-dressing; transvestism. ⇨ 異性装者　a cross-dresser; a transvestite.

いせき³【移籍】▷◁ 移籍市場〔プロスポーツ選手などの〕a ˈtransfer [trade] market. 移籍話〔プロスポーツ選手などの〕talk [mention, discussion] of a ˈtransfer [trade].
イソ【ISO】▷◁ 環境 ISO environmental ISO. ▶ ISO 14001 のこと.
いそう⁵【移送】▷◁ 移送サービス〔高齢者・障害者の〕《provide》 transportation services 《to senior citizens and people with disabilities》.
いぞく²【遺族】
▷◁ 自死[自殺]遺族 suicide-bereaved family members.
▷◁ 遺族外来〔喪失感に苦しむ遺族のための外来診療〕outpatient counselling for bereaved relatives. 遺族感情〔殺人事件などの〕the ˈfeelings [emotions, emotional state, emotional suffering] of the bereaved. ◐ 裁判長は被告に反省の態度が見えないこと,犯行の態様や被害者の～感情などを考慮して死刑を選択した. The judge acknowledged the accused's remorse, but in consideration of the nature of the crime and the emotional suffering caused to the bereaved, chose the death penalty.
いそざい【異素材】different materials. ◐ ～を組み合わせたソファー a sofa ˈcombining [made of a combination of] different materials. ▷◁ 異素材使い〔レザーとニットの〕使いのジャケット a jacket incorporating leather and ˈknitted material [knitwear].
イソプロピル ▷◁ イソプロピル・メチルフェノール《化》 isopropyl methylphenol (略: IPMP).
いそべやき【磯辺焼き】a grilled 《rice cake》 wrapped in nori.
イソベん【-弁】〔経営者弁護士の事務所に所属して実務経験を積む弁護士〕a "lodger [freeloader] lawyer"; a dependent lawyer (attached to a firm that is not his own).
いそやけ【磯焼け】《海洋》〔コンブ・テングサなどの有用な海藻が沿岸岩礁地域で一斉に枯死する現象〕rocky-shore denudation.
いそん, いぞん【依存】▷◁ 依存効果〔消費者の需要が企業の宣伝などによって喚起される現象〕the dependence effect. ▶ ガルブレイス (John Kenneth Galbraith) の用語. 依存率 a dependency ˈratio [rate]; a dependence ˈratio [rate]; a [the] rate [ratio] of dependency. ◐ 食糧の輸入～率 a [the] ratio of dependence on imported food; the ratio of imported food to total food consumption / わが国の食糧の輸入～率を今の半分に落としたい. We want to reduce Japan's dependence on imported food to half its present level.
いた【板】▷◁ 板割り〔空手の演技の〕board breaking.
いたい³【遺体】▷◁ 遺体保全 embalming; embalmment. 遺体回収 corpse ˈrecovery [retrieval]; the recovery of corpses. 遺体確認 identification of a 《dead》 body. ◐ ～確認を行う identify a 《dead》 body. 遺体損壊(罪)〔死体損壊〕mutilation of a dead body. 遺体発見現場 the site where 《the missing girl's》 body was found. 遺体袋 a body bag. 遺体防腐処理 《an》 embalming; embalmment.
いだい³【遺題】〔和算家が著書の最後に解答無しで載せた難問〕a difficult unsolved problem which a mathematician of the traditional Japanese *wasan* school placed at the end of a book.
いたく²【委託】▷◁ 委託業者 a subcontractor; a subcontracting business. 委託生産 contract manufacturing; outsourcing.
いたじてんしゃ【痛自転車】＝いたチャリ.
いたしゃ【痛車】〔アニメやゲームのキャラクターのシールやイラストを貼り付け,あるいは塗装した自動車〕a car ˈdecorated with [covered in] 《illustrations of》 anime characters.
いたチャリ【痛-】〔アニメやゲームのキャラクターのシールやイラストを貼り付け,あるいは塗装した自転車〕a bicycle ˈdecorated with [covered in] 《illustrations of》 anime characters.
いたとびこみ【板飛び込み】a springboard dive; springboard diving. ◐ 男子 3 メートル～ the men's three-meter springboard 《diving》. ◐ ～の選手 a springboard diver.
イタリアン・パセリ《植》〔パセリの一種〕Italian parsley; flat-leaved [flat, flat-leaf] parsley.
イタル・タスつうしん【-通信】〔ロシアの通信社〕the ITAR-TASS News Agency. ▶ ITAR-TASS は Information Telegraphic Agency of Russia—Telegrafneye Agentstvo Suverennykh Stran の略.
いたんしゃ【痛単車】〔アニメやゲームのキャラクターのシールやイラストを貼り付け,あるいは塗装した単車〕a 《motor》bike ˈdecorated with [covered in] 《illustrations of》 anime characters.
いち³【位置】▷◁ 位置情報 ⇨いちじょうほう.
いちう【一宇】〔一棟の建物〕one ˈhouse [building]; 〔屋根を同じくすること〕《under》 one roof.
いちえん【一円】
▷◁ 一円会社〔資本金 1 円から設立できる会社〕a one-yen company; a company established with capital of at least one yen under a special government program to promote start-up enterprises. 一円起業 starting [establishing, launching] a ˈone-yen company [company capitalized at one yen] 《utilizing an exemption to the minimum-capital requirement》. 一円入札〔競争を排除する一種の不正入札〕a one-yen ˈbid [tender] 《for a construction contract》. 一円パチンコ〔パチンコ玉 1 個の値段が 1 円のパチンコ〕one-yen pachinko; pachinko for which each ball costs one yen. 一円落札 a successful one-yen ˈbid [tender].
いちおく【一億】▷◁ 一億総中流社会 the Japanese society of the 1970's and '80s, in which most people saw themselves as being middle class. 一億総中流時代 the period when most Japanese saw themselves as being middle class.
いちぎょう【一行】▷◁ 一行詩 a one-[single-]line poem. 一行ニュース one-line news; a single-line news ˈfeed [ticker].
いちぐん¹【一軍】▷◁ 一軍登録〔プロ野球などで〕putting 《a player》 [being put] on the 《official》 《team》 roster; activating 《a player》 [being activated]. ◐ ～登録を抹消する be removed from the 《official》 《team》 roster; be deactivated.
いちごうぶんけん【一号文書】〔中国共産党中央委員会で年頭に発表される最重要政策〕the No. 1 Document.
いちじ²【一次】▷◁ 一次情報 direct [firsthand] information. 一次責任 《have, bear》 primary responsibility 《for payment》. 一次予防 primary prevention.
いちじていし【一時停止】▷◁ 一時停止義務〔道路での〕an obligation to stop.
いちじひごじょうりくきょか【一時庇護上陸許可】《法》〔難民認定基準に該当すると思われる者への〕landing permission for temporary refuge.
いちじふていし【一時不停止】〔交差点などでの〕failure to stop 《at a stop sign》.
いちじゅんめ【一巡目】the first round. ▷◁ 一巡目指名《スポーツ》〔ドラフト制での〕a first-round ˈselection [pick].
いちじょうほう【位置情報】《通信》 positional information. ▷◁ 位置情報サービス a positional information service.
いちぞく【一族】▷◁ 一族支配 control by ˈone [a single] family.
いちにち【一日】▷◁ 一日花〔アサガオなど,開花した日にしぼんでしまう花〕an ephemeral flower.
いちばんしょうぶ【一番勝負】〔将棋・囲碁などの〕a contest decided by a single ˈround [game].

いちぶ[2]【一部】 ▶□ 一部通行止め a partial stoppage (of traffic). ◐ 国道44号のA町-B町間が道路陥没により～通行止めになっている。 Due to subsidence, Route 44 is 「partially [partly] closed to traffic between A chō and B chō.

いちぶじむくみあい【一部事務組合】 a wide-area federation of cities and villages for the performance of selective functions such as waste disposal, fire fighting, management of crematoriums, etc.

いちぶそん【一部損】《保険》 partial loss.

いちや【一夜】 ▶□ 一夜干し〔魚の〕lightly dried fish; fish that has been dipped in dilute salted water and dried in the shade for a day and a night.

イ・チャンドン【李滄東】 Lee Chang-dong (1954- ; 韓国の映画監督・脚本家).

いちょう[6]【銀杏】 ▶□ イチョウ葉 (a) ginkgo (biloba) leaf. イチョウ葉エキス (a) ginkgo biloba extract.

いちらん【一覧】 ▶□ 一覧性〔一度に多くの情報を伝えられる性質〕the ability to be 「seen [viewed, read] all at once (at a glance); at-a-glance 「visibility [readability]. ◐ ～性の高い画面 a screen that can be easily seen in its entirety / 新聞はネットよりも～性の点ですぐれている。 Newspapers are superior to the Internet because their pages can be viewed all at once.

いちらんせい【一卵性】 ▶□ 一卵性親子〔非常に仲のよい親子；多くは母娘〕a 「parent [mother] and child who have a very close relationship. ◐ 彼女と母親は～親子みたいだ。 She and her mother are (as) thick as thieves.

いつか[1]【五日】 ▶□ 5日移動平均線〘株式〙 a five-day moving average.

いっかつ[1]【一括】 ▶□ 一括合意 (a) comprehensive [(an) all-inclusive] agreement. 一括採決 an omnibus vote. 一括下請け a blanket subcontract. 一括受注〔鉄道輸送システムなど〕 「a package [an all-in package]. ◐ その企業連合はアラブ首長国連邦の旅客鉄道システムを約3,600億円で～受注した。 The cartel accepted an all-in order for a passenger railway system for the United Arab Emirates for about ¥360,000,000,000. 一括消去〘電算〙 simultaneous deletion (of a block of text); one-stroke deletion. 一括送信〘電算〙〔電子メールなどの〕(a) simultaneous transmission. 一括変換〘電算〙simultaneous conversion 《of one word into another》; one-stroke 《word [phrase]》 replacement; changing all the instances of 《a word》 at once. 一括売却 a bulk sale; selling in bulk.

「いつか晴れた日に」〘映画〙Sense and Sensibility.

いっかんこう【一貫校】 ▶□ 小中[中高]一貫校 a combined 「elementary and junior high [junior and senior high] school.

いっき[1]【一気】 ▶□ 一気コール a call to drink up; "Bottoms up!"

いっきゃく[2]【一脚】《写真》〔撮影時にカメラを支え、ぶれを防ぐ棒状物〕a monopod; a unipod.

いっきょく[3]【一極】 ▶□ ～の unipolar. ▶□ 一極化 unipolarization 《of the world economy around the US》. ▷ unipolarize v. 一極支配 unipolar 「dominance [hegemony] 《over the EU market by France and Germany》. 一極主義《the age of US》 unipolarism.

いっけつ[3]【溢血】 ▶□ 溢血点 a petechia 《pl. -chiae》. ▷ petechial adj. 溢血斑 an ecchymosis 《pl. -ses》. ▷ ecchymotic adj.

いっこく[1]【一国】 ▶□ 一国治安主義 (a policy of) dealing with security issues 「internally [within the borders of one country]. 一国繁栄主義 concern for [interest in] the prosperity of only one country; the belief that the interests of 「one [one's own] country override those of others; the principle of putting one's own country's interests above those of all others. ◐ グローバリゼーションとは、もはや～繁栄主義ではやって行けないという意味だ。 Globalization means that we can no longer work on the assumption that the interests of one country 「override those of all others [are paramount].

いっこくまいり【一国参り】〔四国巡礼で県ごとに区切ってまわること〕《making》a pilgrimage to the designated temples in a single prefecture of Shikoku, (to complete the pilgrimage of 88 temples in four stages).

いっしょうびん【一升瓶】 a 1.8 liter bottle; a bottle with a capacity of 1.8 liters 《traditionally used for sake》.

いっせい[3]【一斉】 ▶□ 一斉下校〔全校または同学年の児童が同時刻に下校すること〕going home from school in a group at the same time. 一斉攻撃 a general [an all-out, a comprehensive] attack; an attack on all fronts; an assault; an onslaught;〔一斉射撃〕a fusillade. ◐ 軍はゲリラ部隊に～攻撃を仕掛けた。 The army commenced 「an all-out [a general] attack on the guerrillas. | The army mobilized all its forces against the guerrillas. / 不正が発覚し、彼はマスコミから～攻撃を受けた。 When his misconduct became known, all the media 「opened fire [came down] on him. / ウイルスに感染したパソコンがA社のサイトを～攻撃した。 All the infected computers attacked the A company site 「at once [simultaneously]. 一斉清掃 a group clean-up; cleaning up in a group. 一斉捜査 a 「simultaneous [coordinated] investigation. ◐ 警察はその誘拐事件に関連して3県5か所の～捜査を実施した。 The police carried out a simultaneous investigation of five locations in three prefectures in connection with the kidnapping. 一斉送信〘電算〙〔電子メールなどの〕(a) simultaneous transmission. 一斉調査 a 「survey [investigation, check-up]. ◐ 北海道でタンチョウの個体数の～調査が行われた。 A simultaneous survey was carried out all over Hokkaidō to establish how many Japanese cranes there are. / 先週、政府はダイオキシン汚染の全国～調査を実施した。 Last week the government carried out an all-Japan survey of dioxin pollution. 一斉摘発 a simultaneous raid. ◐ 警察は海賊版DVDの～摘発を行った。 The police conducted a simultaneous raid on DVD pirate operations. | In simultaneous raids on several locations, the police 「brought DVD pirates to justice [uncovered several DVD operations]. 一斉点検 (a) comprehensive [an overall] (simultaneous) inspection. ◐ その地震後、鉄道会社はトンネルの～点検を行った。 After the earthquake the railway company carried out a comprehensive inspection of all the tunnels. 一斉値上げ[値下げ] a comprehensive [an all-round] price 「rise [cut]. ◐ 原油価格の上昇により、石油会社は小売価格を一斉に値上げした。 With the rise in crude oil prices, all the oil companies raised 「*gas [「petrol] prices 「in unison [simultaneously]. / 冬物の～値下げ〔掲示〕All winter clothing reduced. 一斉配信〘電算〙〔電子メールなどの〕(a) simultaneous distribution. 一斉発売 putting 《a car》 on sale simultaneously 《all over the world》; marketing 《a new product》 everywhere at the same time. ◐ この新車は来週、全世界で～発売される。 Sales of the new car are to start next week, at the same time throughout the world.

いっせんきゅう【一線級】 ◐ ～の top-class; top-level; top-rank; first-grade / ～の選手をそろえる line up (a team of) top-rank players. ◐ 不運にも予選で～と当たってしまった。 Unfortunately I was drawn against a top-class player in a preliminary round.

いったい[1]【一体】

いつだつ

▢ 一体運営〔経営〕〔複数の事業の〕unified [seamless] management. 一体関係 an inseparable connection; an integral relationship. ◯ 暴力団と〜関係にある企業 a firm integrally linked to organized crime; a business with indissoluble ties to a gangster organization. 一体性 oneness; unity; integrity. ◯ 夫婦別姓は家族の〜性を損なうものだという根強い反対論がある。There is a deep-seated opposition to the concept of husband and wife having different family names on the grounds that it would destroy the integrity of the family. / 新しい建物のデザインは周囲の環境との〜性を持つものにしたい。I'd like the design of the new building to form an integrated whole with its surroundings.

いつだつ【逸脱】 ▢ 逸脱行為〔行動〕deviant behavior. 逸脱行動〔社会〕deviant behavior. 逸脱防止ガード〔鉄道〕= 脱線防止ガード（⇨だっせん²）.

いっち【一致】 ▢ 一致遅行比率〔経〕the coincident to lagging index ratio; the ratio of the coincident index to the lagging index.

いっちょう¹【一丁】 ▢ 一丁締め an abbreviated form of "ippon jime"; a single collective clap at a gathering after everybody has said yohhh!

いつづけ【居続け・流連】staying in a brothel without going home.

イッテン Itten, Johannes (1888–1967; スイスの画家).

いってんごせい【1.5 世】〔幼時に親とともに移民した人を指す言葉〕a 1.5(th) generation immigrant.

いっとう⁷【一棟】a whole「*apartment building [¹¹block of flats]. ▢ 一棟売り selling [(a) sale of] a whole「*apartment building [¹¹block of flats]. ～売りマンション〔アパート〕an 「*apartment building [¹¹block of flats] sold [for sale] as a whole. 一棟買い purchasing [(a) purchase of] an 「*apartment building [¹¹block of flats] as a whole.

いっぱく²【一泊】 ▢ 一泊手術 surgery [an operation] involving a one-night stay in hospital.

いっぱつ【一発】 ▢ 一発攻勢〔野球〕a home-run「attack [onslaught, barrage]. ◯ 〜攻勢をかける launch [mount] a home-run「attack [onslaught]; unleash a barrage of homers. 一発退場〔サッカーの試合などで〕a [an immediate] sending off. ◯ 彼は乱暴行為で〜退場になった。He was sent off (immediately) for violent behavior. 一発録り〔音楽〕〔最初から最後まで通しで 1 回で録音すること〕(a) one-take recording; (a) live recording; 〔すべてのパートを同時に 1 回で録音すること〕live tracking; (a) one-take recording; (a) live recording.

いっぱつげい【一発芸】a quick trick.

いっぱん²【一般】 ▢ 一般形鋼 general [general-purpose, non-specific] steel; steel for general purposes. 一般家庭ごみ〔家庭ごみ〕household「waste(s) [refuse, *garbage, ¹¹rubbish]. 一般車両〔特殊用途の車両に対して〕a regular vehicle; 〔関係者以外の車両が〕an unauthorized vehicle. ◯ 〜車両進入禁止。〔掲示〕Authorized Vehicles Only. 一般貿易〔加工貿易に対して〕general trade; trade in non-manufactured goods. 一般有料道路 an ordinary toll road. 一般旅券 an ordinary passport.

いっぱんかいけい【一般会計】a general account; general accounts. ▢ 一般会計歳出 general account expenditure. 一般会計予算 a general account budget.

いっぱんじむ【一般事務】general clerking (duties). ▢ 一般事務職 (general) administration (duties); 《口》admin; 〔人〕an 「administrative [admin] assistant.

いっぱんしょうぎょうがいしゃ【一般商法会社】a general commercial company.

いっぴ²【一日】the first day of a month; the first of the month. ◯ 来月の〜付けでお送りします。I'll send it on the first of next month.

いっぷく¹【一服】 ▢ 一服感〔相場など〕a sense of a lull. ◯ 景気回復の動きに〜感が見られる。There is a sense of a lull in the trend to economic recovery.

イップス《スポーツ》〔極度の緊張で身体が思うように動かなくなる症状〕(have, get) the yips.

いっぺんいっこく【一辺一国】〔中国と台湾はそれぞれ別の国だという陳水扁 台湾元総統の発言〕one country on each side (of the Taiwan Strait).

いっぽんさ【一本鎖】〔生化〕a single strand. ▢ 一本鎖 DNA single-stranded DNA.

イディオト・アハロノト〔イスラエルの日刊紙〕Yediot Aharonot.

いてだき【凍滝】a frozen waterfall; an icefall.

いでん【遺伝】 ▢ 隔世遺伝 atavism 〔▷ atavistic adj.〕; (a) reversion; (a) throwback. ◯ 遺伝資源 genetic resources. ◯ 植物～資源 plant genetic resources. 遺伝疾患 (a) genetic disease; a genetic disorder. 遺伝毒性 genotoxicity; genetic toxicity. ◯ ～毒性試験 a genotoxicity「test [assay] / 〜毒性物質 a genotoxin.

いでんし【遺伝子】 ▢ 青色遺伝子〔園芸など〕the "blue gene." 色素遺伝子 a pigment gene. ▢ 遺伝子汚染 genetic「pollution [contamination]. 遺伝子解析 genetic analysis; (a) gene analysis. 遺伝子技術 gene [genetic] technology. 遺伝子検査「genetic [gene] test. 遺伝子構造 genetic「structure [makeup]. 遺伝子再集合〔医〕genetic reassortment. 遺伝子多型〔生物〕〔DNA の配列の個体差〕genetic [DNA] polymorphism. 遺伝子特許 a gene patent. 遺伝子配列 gene「sequence [arrangement]. 遺伝子非組み換え non-GM (crops); non-genetically modified (products). ◯ 〜非組み換え大豆 non-GM [non-genetically modified] soybeans. 遺伝子変異 (a)「gene [genetic] mutation. 遺伝子密度 gene density. 遺伝子模型 a gene model; a DNA model; a model of the DNA molecule. 遺伝子レベル a genetic level. ◯ ダイオキシンなどの有害物質が人間にどういう影響を与えるかを〜レベルで研究する study the effects of dioxin and other harmful substances on human beings at the genetic level; study the genetic effects on humans of harmful substances such as dioxin.

いでんしくみかえ【遺伝子組み換え】 ▢ 非遺伝子組み換え non-genetically modified (rice); non-GMO (soybeans). ▶ GMO は genetically modified organism (遺伝子組み換え体) の略。 ▢ 遺伝子組み換え作物 (a)「transgenic [genetically modified, genetically engineered] crop; (a) GM crop. 遺伝子組み換え大豆 genetically「modified [engineered, altered] soybeans; GM soybeans. 遺伝子組み換え品種 a genetically modified variety.

いと¹【糸】 ▢ 糸ようじ〔商標〕dental floss; a dental floss pick.

いとあやつり【糸操り】 ▢ 糸あやつり人形 a string「puppet [marionette].

いどう⁴【異動】 ▢ 異動届〔年金受給者などが提出する〕《submit》a notification of a change in one's「status [circumstances].

いどう⁵【移動】 ▢ 移動期間 a「transit [travel] period. 移動基地局〔通信〕a mobile base station. 移動距離 the distance covered (in a day). 移動禁止(措置)〔家畜伝染病が発生した際の家畜〕a ban on moving (poultry across prefectural borders); an (animal) movement ban. 移動交番 a mobile police box. ◯ 〜交番車 a police car serving as a mobile police box. 移動時間 a「transit [travel] time; (the) time (spent) in transit. 移動式発電機 a mobile (power) generator. 移動式トイレ a portable toilet. 移動(式)発射台〔ミサイルなどの〕a mobile launcher. 移動制限 (a) movement restriction; (a) restriction of movement; a restriction

on the movement 《of 「people [poultry]》. ◐ ～制限
区域 a (movement-)restricted area. 移動中 ◐ 彼女
は～中にも書類に目を通している. She looks over documents even while 「in transit [on the move, going from place to place]. 移動電源車 a mobile power 「generator [generating] car [truck]. 移動入浴車〔介 助用の〕a mobile bath 「car [vehicle]. 移動日 a 「travel [transit] day. 移動盲腸【医】(a) mobile c(a)ecum; c(a)ecum mobile.
いどうたい【移動体】【通信】a mobile unit. ◯◻ 移動体衛星通信 mobile satellite communication. 移動体向け放送 mobile broadcasting; broadcasting to mobile devices.
イトゥリ〔コンゴ民主共和国北東部の地方〕Ituri.
イドゥル・アダ〔イスラムの犠牲祭〕Id al-Adha; Idul Adha.
イドゥル・フィトリ〔イスラムの断食明けの祭り〕Idul Fitri; Id al-Fitr.
「糸車の聖母」〔ダ・ヴィンチ作の油絵〕Madonna of the Yarnwinder.
いどころ【居所】 ◯◻ 居所不明者 a person whose whereabouts 「are [is] unknown. [⇨住所不明者(⇨じゅうしょ)]
「愛しのローズマリー」〔映画〕Shallow Hal.
イナーシャ〔慣性〕inertia, 〔空〕〔慣性始動機〕an inertia starter.
いなし【相撲】〔いなすこと〕sweeping 《one's opponent》after stepping 「to one side [out of the line of attack]. ◐ 大関の右からの～が効果的に決した. The bout was effectively decided by the Ozeki's sidestep and sweep from the right.
イナバウアー〔フィギュア〕《do》an Ina Bauer. ▶ Ina Bauer (1941-   ; ドイツのフィギュアスケート選手)より.
いなわら【稲藁】(a) rice straw; straw from rice.
イニシャル ◯◻ イニシャル・トーク〔話題に上る人物の名前を頭文字だけで語る座談〕a discussion in which other people are referred to only by their initials.
イニャリトゥ Iñárritu, Alejandro González (1963-    ; メキシコ生まれの映画監督).
いにん【委任】 ◯◻ 委任契約 a 「delegation [authorization] contract; a contract of 「delegation [authorization]; 〔高齢者・精神障害者などに対する任意後見の〕a contract delegating legal authority 《to a guardian》.
いぬ¹【犬】 ◯◻ 犬型ロボット a robot(ic) dog; a dog(-shaped) robot.
いぬ²【戌】 ◯◻ 戌(は)笑う《相場》〔戌年はよい相場になる、の意〕In the year of the Dog, the market tends to prosper. [⇨たつみてんじょう]
イヌイットしゅうきょくかいぎ【-周極会議】the Inuit Circumpolar Conference (略: ICC).
イヌクティトゥットご【-語】〔カナダ極北地域で話されるイヌイットの一方言〕Inuktitut.
いぬぶし【櫟】=じぞうかんば.
いねむり【居眠り】 ◯◻ 居眠り警報装置【自動車】a drowsiness warning system. 居眠り病 =かみん(しょう).
いねわら【稲藁】=いなわら.
いのこり【居残り】 ◯◻ 居残り練習 (an)「extended [overtime] practice [rehearsal].
イノベーター〔革新者〕an innovator.
イバイとう【-島】〔マーシャル諸島、クワジェリン環礁の島〕Ebeye Island.
いはくざい【威迫罪】【法】〔他人に対し言語・動作で気勢を示し、不安・困惑の念を生じさせる罪〕the crime of intimidation. ◯◻ 裁判員等威迫罪 intimidation of a 「lay [citizen] judge. 証人等威迫罪 intimidation of a witness. 地位利用威迫罪 intimidation through abuse of one's status; power harassment. 利害関係利用威迫罪 intimidation by 「applying [exploiting] commercial leverage [exploiting business interests].

いばしょ【居場所】 ◯◻ 居場所情報〔GPS 携帯電話などを利用した〕one's location information; one's personal coordinates.
いはなつ【射放つ】shoot off [release, let fly]《an arrow》.
イ・ビョンホン【李炳憲】Lee Byung-hun (1970-   ; 韓国の映画俳優).
イフォマイド〔商標・薬〕〔抗悪性腫瘍薬〕Ifomide. ▶ イフォスファミドの商品名.
イフス【EIFS】【建】〔外断熱外壁仕上げシステム〕EIFS. ▶ exterior insulation and finish system の略.
イフタール〔イスラム〕〔断食明けの食事〕an iftar.
イブニング・スタンダード〔英国の夕刊紙〕The Evening Standard.
イプラトロピウム ⇨しゅうかイプラトロピウム.
イブレア〔イタリア北部の町〕Ivrea. ▶ オレンジを投げ合うカーニバルで有名.
イベリコハム〔食品〕〔イベリコ豚から作られる高級ハム〕(an) 「Iberian [Iberico] ham; Jamón Ibérico.
イベリコぶた【-豚】〔スペイン西部産のイベリア種の黒豚〕an 「a black] Iberian pig; a cerdo negro; 〔その肉〕Iberian 「pig [pork]; 〔それを原料とする高級ハム〕⇨イベリコハム.
イベルメクチン【薬】〔寄生虫駆除薬〕ivermectin.
イベロアメリカしゅのうかいぎ【-首脳会議】〔イベリア半島と中南米諸国の首脳会議〕the Ibero-American Summit.
イベント ◯◻ スポーツ・イベント a sport(s) event. 文化イベント a cultural event. イベント業者 an event 「organizer [planner, company]. イベントくじ an event lottery. イベントサークル a special-event club. イベント・スペース〔種々の催し物が開催できる空間・広場〕an event(s) space; a space for events.
いほう⁵【違法】 ◯◻ 違法意識 a sense [an awareness] of 《without》criminal intent. 違法サイト〔インターネット上の〕《visit》an illegal (Web) site. 違法操業〔engage in〕illegal《fishing》operations. ◐ ～操業船 an illegal《fishing》vessel; a vessel engaged in illegal《driftnet》fishing activities; IUU vessel [▶ IUU is illegal, unreported and unregulated (fishing) の略]. 違法表示〔行為〕illegal [prohibited] labeling;〔1つの〕an illegal label. 違法薬物 an 「illegal [illicit] drug.
いほうどうでんフィルム〔異方導電〕【電】an anisotropic conductive film (略: ACF).
イマーム・アリ(ー)びょう【-廟】〔イラク、ナジャフにある、シーア派初代指導者アリ(ー)の墓所〕the Imam Ali mosque.
いまカノ【今-】one's current girlfriend.
いまカレ【今-】one's current boyfriend.
いまげんざい【今現在】just now; at this moment. ◐ 容疑者は～どこに隠れているのか. Where is the suspect hiding at this moment?
いまさっき【今さっき】〔つい今しがた〕only [just] a moment ago; just now.
イマチニブ【薬】〔白血病治療薬〕imatinib.
いみ²【意味】 ◯◻ 意味不明 ◐ ～不明の記号 a meaningless 「sign [symbol]; a sign which 「has no meaning [means nothing]; an incomprehensible sign / 彼は～不明な言動を繰り返すようになった. He started gabbling and behaving incomprehensibly.
イ・ミョンバク【李明博】Lee Myung-bak (1941-   ; 韓国の政治家, 大統領 [2008-   ]).
いみん【移民】 ◯◻ 移民暴動 a riot [rioting] by immigrants.
いみんきかきょく【移民帰化局】〔米国の〕the Immigration and Naturalization Service (略: INS).
いむ⁵【医務】 ◯◻ 医務官 a medical officer;〔軍人〕a military medical officer.
イメージ

イメージングプレート

い

国際(的)イメージ an international image; international perceptions《of France》; the way《China》is「seen [perceived] by the (outside) world. ◎そんなになれば日本の国際的～は大きく損なわれることになるだろう. If that happens it will「greatly damage Japan's international image [sully the image of Japan in the world]」.
イメージ映像 a video「image [clip] giving an impression of something (rather than showing the thing itself); an illustrative video「image [clip]. イメージ回復 the repair of sb's image. ◎～回復を図る try to repair one's image. イメージ図[画] a conceptual「drawing [diagram, illustration]. イメージスケッチ〔頭に思い描いたことを絵にしたもの〕an image sketch; a conceptual sketch. イメージセッター〔印画紙・フィルム等にレーザー光熱で感光印字する高解像度出力機〕an imagesetter. イメージ戦略 an image strategy. ◎CMによる～戦略が功を奏して, この商品は大いに売れた. The image strategy of their commercials paid off, and the product sold very well. イメージソング an "image song"; a song composed or chosen for a public event or for a particular area, etc. イメージ・ハンプ〔路面の塗装や材質を変えて障害物があると錯覚させ, 車の運転者に減速をうながす方法〕an image hump. イメージ・ファイバー〔電子工学〕(an) image fiber. イメージ野[脳]〔解〕〔大脳の〕the (visual) imaging「area [part] of the brain.
イメージング・プレート〔蛍光フィルムの一種〕an imaging plate.
いも【芋】 芋けんぴ〔けんぴに似たさつまいもが原料の菓子〕fried and sugared sweet-potato strips.
いもあらいこうどう【芋洗い行動】〔ニホンザルの〕sweet potato washing.
いもあらいじょうたい【芋洗い状態】overcrowding; a crush (of people).
いもづけ【芋付け】〔金属加工〕〔パイプや棒を突き合わせて断面のみを溶接すること〕butt welding.
イモビライザー〔自動車〕an (engine) immobilizer.
いもん【慰問】 慰問活動 activities undertaken to comfort or entertain 《hospital patients, soldiers in the field, etc.》.
いやく[1]【医薬】 医薬食品局〔厚生労働省の〕the Pharmaceutical and Food Safety Bureau. ► 医薬局から改称. 医薬中間体【薬】pharmaceutical intermediates.
いやくばんけんきゅうじょ【医薬基盤研究所】the National Institute of Biomedical Innovation (略: Ni-Bio).
いやくこうぎょうきょうかい【医薬工業協議会】the Japan Generic Pharmaceutical Manufacturers Association (略: JGPMA); ► 2008年4月, 日本ジェネリック製薬協会 (the Japan Generic Medicines Association; 略: JGA) に名称変更.
いやくひん【医薬品】 未承認医薬品 an unapproved drug; a medicinal product that has not yet been approved. 医薬品候補物質 candidate substances for (new) medications. 医薬品成分 a pharmaceutical ingredient. ◎外国製のダイエット食品から～成分が検出された. Pharmaceutical ingredients were detected in foreign-manufactured diet foods.
いやくひんいりょうききそうごうきこう【医薬品医療機器総合機構】〔独立行政法人〕the Pharmaceuticals and Medical Devices Agency (略: PMDA).
いやちこ【灼然】〔神仏の利益(?)・霊験が著しい〕manifest [indubitable, conspicuous]《miracle》.
イヤホン, イヤホーン ◎イヤホン・マイク〔携帯電話などで手を使わずに通話するための器具〕a hands-free headset; a handsfree.
いようせい【胃溶性】【薬】◎～の gastrosoluble.
イ・ヨンエ【李英愛】Lee Yeong-ae (1971- ; 韓国の女

26

優).
イライザほう【ELISA 法】【医】=エライザほう.
「依頼人」〔映画〕The Client.
イラクあんていかかいぎ【-安定化会議】〔2007年3, 5月の〕the Iraq stabilization conference.
イラク・イスラムかくめいさいこうひょうぎかい【-革命最高評議会】the Supreme Council for the Islamic Revolution in Iraq (略: SCIRI).
イラク・イスラムとう【-党】〔イラクのスンニ派政党〕the Iraqi Islamic Party (略: IIP).
イラクきほんほう【-基本法】【法】the Iraqi Transitional Administrative Law. ► 正式名称は the Law of Administration for the State of Iraq for the Transitional Period.
イラクけんきゅうグループ【-研究-】〔超党派の有識者で構成する米国の〕the Iraq Study Group (略: ISG).
イラクこうとうほうてい【-高等法廷】the Iraqi High Tribunal.
イラクこくみんかいぎ【-国民会議】1〔イラクの政治勢力〕the Iraqi National Congress (略: INC). 2〔イラク戦争後の新政府の諮問評議会を選出した〕the Iraqi national conference; Iraq's national conference.
イラクこくみんぎかい【-国民議会】the Iraqi National Assembly.
イラクこくみんごうい【-国民合意】〔イラクの政党〕the Iraqi National Accord (略: INA).
イラクこくみんリスト【-国民-】〔2005年12月のイラク国民議会選挙における政治勢力の1つ〕the Iraqi National List.
イラクせかいほうてい【-世界法廷】the World Tribunal on Iraq (略: WTI).
イラクとうちひょうぎかい【-統治評議会】〔イラク戦争後のイラクの〕the Iraqi Governing Council.
イラクとくそほう【-特措法】【法】the Law Concerning the Special Measures on Humanitarian and Reconstruction Assistance in Iraq. ►「イラクにおける人道復興支援活動及び安全確保支援活動の実施に関する特別措置法」の通称.
イラクとくべつほうてい【-特別法廷】〔イラク高等法廷の旧称〕the Iraqi Special Tribunal.
イラクのじゆうさくせん【-の自由作戦】〔2003年のイラク戦争の米英軍などによる作戦名〕Operation Iraqi Freedom.
イラクのせいせんアルカイダそしき【-の聖戦-組織】〔イスラム教スンニ派の過激なテロ組織〕the Al-'Qaida [Qaeda] of Jihad in Iraq.
イラクふっこうしえんぐん【-復興支援群】〔イラク復興支援特別措置法に基づいて組織された自衛隊部隊〕the Iraqi Reconstruction Support Group.
イラクふっこうしえんこくかいぎ【-復興支援国会議】an Iraqi reconstruction conference.
イラクふっこうしえんとくべつそちほう【-復興支援特別措置法】【法】the Law Concerning the Special Measures on Humanitarian and Reconstruction Assistance in Iraq. ►「イラクにおける人道復興支援活動及び安全確保支援活動の実施に関する特別措置法」の通称.
イラクふっこうしんたくききん【-復興信託基金】the International Reconstruction Fund Facility for Iraq (略: IRFFI).
イラム =イーラーム.
イランふかくさんほう【-不拡散法】【米法】the Iran Nonproliferation Act (略: INA).
イラン・リビアせいさいほう【-制裁法】【米法】〔1996年の〕the Iran-Libya Sanctions Act (ILSA). ► 提案者の上院議員 Alfonse D'Amato の名を取って ダマト法 (the D'Amato Act) ともいう.
いりゅう[3]【遺留】 遺留微物 trace evidence. 遺留物〔犯行現場などでの〕specimens《of blood, semen, etc.》.

left at the scene of a crime.
いりょう³【医療】
　□◉ 育成医療 special (medical and surgical) care for disabled minors. 要医療〔医〕〔診断書や健康診断報告書などに書き入れる指示〕Requiring [In Need of] Treatment.
　◉ 医療安全 medical safety;〔患者の安全〕patient safety. ◯～安全管理 medical safety management;〔患者の安全管理〕patient safety management. 医療援助 medical「assistance [help]. 医療格差〔医療を受ける機会の〕inequality of medical「provision [treatment];〔医療技術の〕=治療(成績)格差(⇨ちりょう). 医療過誤 a shortage of medical「staff [services]《in a rural area》. ◯～過疎地域 a medically underserved area; an area with a shortage of medical「staff [services]. 医療監視 a medical audit. 医療関連死 (a) (medical) treatment-related death. 医療現場 a health care site; the front lines of health care. ◯ 耐性菌の出現は各地の～現場で深刻な問題になっている. The appearance of resistant bacteria is a serious problem「on the front lines of health care [where health care is provided, for health care providers] in many locations. 医療行為発生時点情報管理システム the Point of Act System (略: POAS). 医療コーディネーター a medical coordinator. 医療支援 medical assistance. 医療システム a「medical care [health-services, health-care] system; a system「of [for] medical care. 医療システム学〔科目名〕Medical Care [Health-services, Health-care] Systems; Health Services「Management [Policy]. 医療ジャーナリスト a medical journalist. 医療従事者 a person in「medicine [the medical profession]; a person engaged in medical work; a medical「worker [professional];《口》a medic;〈集合的に〉people in「medicine [the medical profession]. ◯ 非―従事者 a person who is not a medical「worker [professional]; a non-medical professional;《口》a non-medic;〈集合的に〉people not in「medicine [the medical profession]; people outside the medical field;〔医療の素人〕a layman. 医療受給者証 a medical care identification card. 医療訴訟 medical malpractice litigation; a medical malpractice suit. 医療体系 a medical「system [model]. 医療提供者 a medical care provider. 医療被害 (a) medical injury; medical damage; damage or injury arising from (medical) mistreatment. 医療不信 distrust of medical「care [practitioners]. 医療不審死 = 医療関連死. 医療部隊 a medical corps. 医療放射線 medical radiation. 医療報酬 remuneration by a health insurance society for medical treatment carried out by a doctor or hospital. 医療補助 medical support. 医療補助者〔救急救命士・救急隊員・看護師・助産婦など〕a paramedic. 医療モール〔複数の診療所をーか所に集めた施設〕a medical mall. 医療モデル =医療体系. 医療(用)ロボット a medical robot.
いりょう⁴【遺領】〔領主などの死後に遺された土地〕land left by《the deceased》(after *his* death); land in a deceased person's estate; bequeathed land.
いりょうひん【衣料品】□◉ 衣料品スーパー(マーケット) a clothing(-based) supermarket.
いりょうほけん【医療保険】□◉ 終身医療保険 whole life medical insurance; medical insurance for life. 積立型医療保険 medical insurance that pays a premium on maturity; savings-type medical insurance. 無選択型医療保険〔医師の診査や健康状態等の告知なしで加入できる〕simplified health insurance [a simplified health insurance policy] designed for people in their fifties and over, for which no medical examination is necessary.
いるい²【異類】□◉ 異類婚《社会》heterogamy.
いるか【海豚】□◉ イルカ・セラピー〔介在療法〕〔心理療法〕

dolphin(-assisted) therapy (略: DAT).
イルカンジ【動】〔オーストラリア産の猛毒クラゲ〕an Irukandji jellyfish; *Carukua barnesi*.
イルクーツクせいめい【―声明】〔2001年の〕the Irkutsk Statement. ▶ 正式名称は「平和条約問題に関する交渉の今後の継続に関する日本国総理大臣及びロシア連邦大統領のイルクーツク声明」(the Irkutsk Statement by the Prime Minister of Japan and the President of the Russian Federation on the Continuation of Future Negotiations on the Issue of a Peace Treaty).
イルベス Ilves, Toomas Hendrik (1953-　；エストニアの政治家; 大統領[2006-　]).
「イル・ポスティーノ」〔映画〕Il Postino (=The Postman).
「イルマーレ」〔韓国映画〕Il Mare;〔その米国リメーク版〕The Lake House.
いれい³【慰霊】□◉ 慰霊式《hold》a spirit-consoling service. 慰霊巡拝 a visit to sites where people died to console their spirits. 慰霊登山 climbing a mountain to console the spirits of people who died there.
「イレイザー」〔映画〕Eraser.
イレッサ〔商標・薬〕〔抗がん剤ゲフィチニブの商品名〕Iressa.
イレブン・ナイン〔電子工学〕〔集積回路等に使われるシリコンの純度; 99.999999999%〕eleven nines.
いろ【色】□◉ 色校正〔印刷〕color proofing.
いろう¹【胃瘻】□◉ 胃瘻栄養(法) gastrostogavage.
いろえおおざら【色絵大皿】a large dish or plate decorated in color after glazing.
いろぐすみ【色ぐすみ】discoloration; discoloring.
いろけづく【色気づく】become interested in the opposite sex; become sexually awakened; have one's coming of age; arrive at [reach] the age of) puberty; begin to feel the sex urge. ◯ 私の娘はこのごろ色気づいて化粧を始めた. Lately my daughter has gotten to that age where she's started using makeup.
いろぞろえ【色揃え】a range of colors.
いろみ【色味】【色調】a (color) tone;〔美〕tonality;〔色合い〕coloring; coloration; a「shade [tone, hue, tint] (of color). ◯ 写真の～を調整する adjust the「hue [tint] of a photograph.
いろゆう【色釉】【製陶】(a) color glaze; (a) colored glaze.
いわい【祝い】□◉ お祝い返し a gift made in return for a present given for a wedding or other celebratory event. 祝い肴(¹⁷ᶦ)〔新春・婚礼などを祝う料理〕celebratory「dishes [food].
いわえん【頤和園】〔中国, 北京市にある公園〕Yiheyuan; the Summer Palace.
いわとびペンギン【岩跳び―】〔鳥〕〔ペンギンの一種〕a rockhopper penguin; *Eudyptes chrysocome*.
いんあつ【陰圧】□◉ 陰圧室〔病院などの〕a negative pressure room.
いんがい²【院外】□◉ 院外処方〔調剤〕〔薬〕extramural dispensing.
インカム²〔商標〕〔現場スタッフが装着する無線トランシーバー〕Incom; a microphone headset.
インキュベーション〔起業〔創業〕支援〕(business) incubation. □◉ インキュベーション事業 an incubation business. インキュベーション施設 an incubation facility.
いんきょ³【允許】〔認めて許すこと〕permission; approval. □◉ 允許状 a「letter [certificate] of approval.
インクジェット □◉ インクジェット・ペーパー〔紙〕ink-jet paper.
イングランド(サッカー)きょうかい【―協会】〔サッカー〕the Football Association (略: FA). □◉ イングランド(サッカー)協会カップ the「FA [Football Association] Cup.
「イングリッシュ・ペイシェント」〔映画〕The English Patient.
イングリッシュ・ポインター〔犬〕an English pointer; a pointer.

**イングリングきゅう**

い　イングリングきゅう【—級】〖ヨット〗the Yngling class.
インクルージョン《教育》▫️ソーシャル・インクルージョン〔社会で暮らすすべての人々を孤立や孤独・排除・摩擦から援護し、社会の一員として包み、支え合うこと〕social inclusion. ▫️インクルージョン教育 inclusive education.
いんけい【陰茎】▫️陰茎折症〘医〙penile fracture; rupture of the erect penis.
いんごのうよう【咽後膿瘍】〘医〙retropharyngeal abscess (略: RPA).
「インサイダー」〘映画〙The Insider.
「インサイド・マン」〘映画〙Inside Man.
「イン・ザ・カット」〘映画〙In the Cut.
インジェクター【自動車】〔燃料噴射装置〕a (fuel) injector. ▫️パルス・インジェクター a pulse injector.
いんしつ【陰湿】▫️陰湿化 becoming more underhand. ◯いじめがますます〜化する傾向が見られる。Bullying is showing a tendency to become more and more underhand.
いんしゅうんてん【飲酒運転】▫️飲酒運転幇助〘法〙aiding and abetting drunk driving.
インシュレーション・ボード【建】〔耐熱防音性にすぐれた植物繊維の圧縮集成板〕an insulation board.
いんしょう⁴【印象】▫️印象形成〘心理〙impression formation. 印象材〘歯科〙(an) impression material.
いんしょうろん【印象論】an argument based on one's impressions.
インショップ〔大型店の店内で独立店形態で運営している店〕a shop-in-shop《pl.》〜s, shops-in-shop, shops-in-shops》; 〘販売方式〙shop-in-shop「marketing [retailing].
インシリコ〘＜L〙〘電算〙〔シリコンチップ内で; コンピューター(シミュレーション) による〕in silico.
いんすい【引水】〔取水すること〕drawing [channeling, taking] water《from a reservoir》; 〔引いた水〕water drawn《from a river》.
〜を draw [take] water《from a stream》.
インスタント ▫️インスタント・メッセージ〘電算〙〔インターネットに接続したパソコン同士で直接やりとりするメッセージ〕an instant message. インスタント・メッセージング〘電算〙〔パソコン同士のメッセージ交換〕instant messaging (略: IM).
インスト 1【機器などの取り扱いや組み立ての説明書】an instruction「manual [pamphlet, sheet]. 2〘音楽〙〔インストルメンタル〕instrumental music; an instrumental. 3〔インストール〕installation (of software).
インスリン ▫️インスリン抵抗性症候群〘医〙insulin-resistance syndrome.
いんせい³【陰性】▫️陰性症状〘精神分析〙〔統合失調症で、正常な心理状態に及ばない不活発な状態〕a negative symptom. 陰性率〘医〙〔感染検査やがん検診などの〕a negative rate.
いんぜい【印税】▫️印税生活者 a person who「earns his」living from [lives off] copyright royalties.
インセスト・タブー〔近親相姦禁忌〕(an [the]) incest taboo.
いんせん¹【陰線】〘株式〙〔ローソク足チャートで、下げ相場を表す黒塗り四角〕a black body.
いんせん²【飲泉】drinking spring water; 《文》taking the waters. ▫️飲泉療法 treatment by drinking spring water.
インセンティブ ▫️インセンティブ方式 an incentive method.
いんそつ【引率】▫️引率教師〘教師〙an accompanying teacher. 引率責任者 an accompanying「person [adult] responsible《for children's safety》.
インターアクション・カウンシル〔元国家元首・首相経験者による国際会議〕the InterAction Council.
インターカラー〔国際流行色委員会の通称〕こくさいりゅうこうしょくいいんかい.
インター・シティ・エクスプレス〔ドイツの超高速列車〕an Inter-City Express (略: ICE).
インターシャ ▫️インターシャ編み〘手芸〙intarsia knitting.
インターナショナル ▫️インターナショナル・スクール an international school.
インターナショナル・バカロレア ＝こくさいバカロレア.
インターネット
▫️インターネット・アンケート an Internet「poll [questionnaire, survey]; a poll on the Internet. インターネット依存症 Internet addiction disorder (略: IAD). インターネット占い online fortune-telling. インターネット絵本 an Internet picture book; an illustrated book on the Net. インターネット・オークション an「Internet [online] auction. インターネット・カジノ an「Internet [online] casino. インターネット家電 networked home appliances. インターネット関連企業 a dot.com company. インターネット教育 Internet education. インターネット・ギャンブル ＝ネット・ギャンブル (⇨ネット). インターネット求人広告 advertisement on the Internet for a job opening; Internet job vacancy advertising. インターネット競売サイト an Internet auction site; a Net auction site. インターネット銀行 an「Internet [online] bank. インターネット金融 Internet [online] financing [lending]. インターネット警察 the「Internet [Net] police. インターネット掲示板〘電算〙a [an electronic] bulletin board. インターネット決済 an「Internet [online] settlement. インターネット検定 an Internet proficiency test. インターネット広告 Internet advertising; advertising on the Internet. インターネット・サーファー〔インターネットサーフィンをする人〕an Internet surfer; a netsurfer. インターネット詐欺 (an) Internet fraud; an Internet scam. インターネット証券会社 an Internet securities company. インターネット商談 an「Internet [online] business「negotiation [deal]. インターネット書店 an Internet「bookshop [bookstore]; an online「bookshop [bookstore]. インターネット人口 the Internet population《of Japan》. インターネット人口《female》Internet users. インターネット申請 (an)「Internet [online] application. インターネット・セキュリティ Internet security. インターネット接続網 an Internet connection network. インターネット専業銀行 ＝ネット専業銀行 (⇨ネット). インターネット専業証券会社 ＝ネット専業証券会社 (⇨ネット). インターネット端末 an Internet terminal. インターネット通信 Internet communication(s); communication(s)「on [through, via] the Internet. インターネット通信料 Internet (communication) fees; fees for using the Internet. インターネット通販 Internet [online] shopping. インターネット通話 calling [phoning, telephoning] over the Internet; using the Internet for telephoning. インターネット・データセンター ＝データ・センター (⇨データ). インターネット・ニュース Internet [online] news. インターネット・バー an Internet [a net] bar; a cyberbar. インターネット配信 ＝ネット配信 (⇨ネット). インターネット白書 a white paper on the Internet. インターネット博覧会 an Internet「exhibition [fair]. インターネット・バブル an Internet bubble. インターネット・ビジネス (an)「Internet [online] business. インターネット放送 Internet broadcasting; broadcasting「over [through, via] the Internet; [1回の] an Internet broadcast; a broadcast on the Internet. ◯〜放送局 an Internet broadcast(ing) station. インターネット・ミーティング an「Internet [online] meeting [conference]. インターネット・ムービー ＝ネット・ムービー (⇨ネット). インターネット予約 an Internet reservation;《make》a reservation「over [via] the Internet. インターネット世論 Internet (public) opinion. インターネット世論調査 an Internet (public) opinion poll; Internet (public) opinion research. インターネット・ラジオ Internet radio. インターネット・リレー・チャット〔インターネットを使った文字による会話システム〕Internet Relay Chat (略: IRC). インターネット・ワーム

an Internet worm.
インターバル ▫ インターバル走法 interval running. インターバル・レック ＝間欠記録 (⇨かんけつ²).
インターファクス ⇨インタファクス.
インターフェロン ▫ インターフェロン注射 (an) interferon injection.
インターブランド [英国のコンサルティング会社] Interbrand (Corporation).
インタービュー ＝インタービュー.
インターブリュー [ベルギーのビールメーカー] Interbrew.
インターリージョナル interregional. [＝いきさいてき]
インターロック（システム）[機][機器の安全運転・誤作動防止のための関連装置連携システム] an interlock. ▫ アルコール・イグニション・インターロック [飲酒運転防止のための] an alcohol ignition interlock (device).
いんたい¹ [引退] ▫ 引退会見 a retirement interview. ～会見を行う[開く] conduct [hold] a retirement interview. 引退届 (submit) a written retirement notification. 引退レース [競走馬などの] a retirement race.
「インタビュー・ウィズ・ヴァンパイア」[映画] Interview with the Vampire: The Vampire Chronicles.
インタファクス [ロシアの通信社] the Interfax News Agency.
インタラクティブ ▫ インタラクティブ・ドラマ [視聴者参加型のテレビドラマ] (an) interactive drama; an interactive play.
インタレスト ▫ インタレスト・カバレッジ・レシオ 《金融》[金利負担能力を計る財務指標の1つ] an interest coverage ratio (of 1.5).
インディアンきょく [-局] 《米》 the Bureau of Indian Affairs (略: BIA).
インディアン・パシフィック [オーストラリア東部のシドニーと西部パース間を結ぶ鉄道] the Indian-Pacific.
インディカー・シリーズ [米国の自動車レースシリーズ] the Indycar Series.
インディ・ジャパンさんびゃくマイル [-300-] [日本で行われるレーシングカーの300マイルレース] the Indy Japan 300.
インディペンデント・スピリットしょう [-賞] [映] an Independent Spirit Award.
インテグラル・タンク [空] [主翼が航空機の構造部自体を燃料容器とするもの] an integral tank.
インデックス ▫ インデックス運用 [株式] ⇨うんよう.
「インデペンデンス・デイ」 [映画] Independence Day.
インテリジェント ▫ インテリジェント・カー [カーナビ・種々の自動安全設備などを備えた自動車] an intelligent [car automobile]. インテリジェント触媒 [自動車] an intelligent catalyst. インテリジェント・スクール [情報機器の設備が充実している学校] an 'intelligent ["intellligent"] school. インテリジェント・デザイン [宗教] [反進化論的な仮説の] intelligent design (略: ID). ～デザイン理論 the intelligent design theory. インテリジェント・ネットワーク [通信] an intelligent network (略: IN); a smart network.
インテル² ▫ インテル互換 [電算] [インテル社製のCPUへの適応性] Intel compatibility. ▷ Intel-compatible adj.
いんてん² [陰転] [相場] a 'change [return] to a fall. ～する start going down (again).
インド ▫ インド人学校 a Global Indian International School (略: GIIS).
インドア ▫ インドア・グリーン [屋内に置いた観葉植物など] <集合的に> indoor 'greenery [plants].
いんとう¹ [引湯] ▫ 引湯権 the right to pipe in hot water (from a source).
インドきょうさんとうもうたくとうしゅぎは [-共産党毛沢東主義派] the Communist Party of India-Maoist (略: CPI-Maoist).

いんとく¹ [陰徳] ▫ 陰徳善事 doing good 'in secret [anonymously, without others knowing]; doing secret acts of 'kindness [charity].
「インドシナ」 [映画] Indochine.
インドシナとうざいかいろう [-東西回廊] ＝とうざいけいざいかいろう.
インドじんみんとう [-人民党] [インドの政党] the Bharatiya Janata Party (略: BJP).
インドネシアこくみんきょうぎかい [-国民協議会] the 'People's Consultative Assembly [MPR] of the Republic of Indonesia. ▶ MPR は Majelis Permusyawaratan Rakyat の略.
インドネシア・ラヤ [インドネシアの国歌] Indonesia Raya.
インドよう（おお）つなみ [-洋(大)津波] [2004年12月の] the (2004) Indian Ocean Tsunami. [⇨スマトラ(とう)おきじしん]
イントルーダー [米軍] [米海軍・海兵隊がベトナム戦争および以降に使用した攻撃機 A-6 の愛称] an Intruder.
インナー・シティ ▫ インナー・シティ問題 an inner-city problem.
インナー・マッスル [解] [深層筋] (an) inner muscle.
いんない [院内] ▫ 院内学級[学校] an in-hospital 'class [school]. 院内死亡率 an in-hospital [a nosocomial] mortality rate.
「イン・ハー・シューズ」 [映画] In Her Shoes.
インバース・マニュファクチャリング [資源循環工程を組み込んだ生産システム; 逆生産] inverse manufacturing.
インバウンド [外部から入ってくる; 海外からの] inbound (tourism). [⇨アウトバウンド] ▫ インバウンド業務 [顧客からの電話に応対する業務] inbound services.
インパク ＝インターネット博覧会 (⇨インターネット).
インパクト ▫ インパクト・ゾーン [ゴルフ・テニスなど] an impact zone.
インパルス ▫ インパルス銃 [圧縮した水を発射する, 携行用消火装備] an IFEX impulse gun. ▶ IFEX は impulse fire extinguishing system の略.
インビトロ 《<L》 [生物] [試験管内で(の)・生体外で(の)] in vitro.
インビボ 《<L》 [生物] [生体内で(の)] in vivo.
「インファナル・アフェア」 [映画] Infernal Affairs; [中国語タイトル] 無間道.
インフィオラータ [イタリアの, 花を敷きつめて絵模様を描く祭り] the Infiorata.
インフィル [建物の設備・内装部分] the nonstructural components of a newly constructed domicile.
インフォーマル ▫ インフォーマル・グループ [会社・工場などにおいて従業員間に自然発生的にできるグループ; 非公式グループ] an informal group. インフォーマル・ケア [公的なサービスに対して, 地域住民のボランティア活動などは非公式な介護] (provide) informal care.
インフォームド・チョイス [医] [医師から十分な説明を受けた上で患者自身が治療方法を選択すること] (an) informed choice.
インフォシス [インドの IT コンサルティング企業] Infosys Technologies Ltd.
インフォマイカ [商標・電算] [NTT が開発した次世代メモリー] info-MICA.
インプライド・ボラティリティー [取引] [予想変動率] implied volatility (略: IV).
インフラ（ストラクチャー） ▫ 交通インフラ（ストラクチャー） a 'transportation [transport, traffic] infrastructure.
インプラント [歯] [人工歯根] a dental [an] implant; [施術] (dental) implantation; [研究・治療] (dental) implantology. ▫ インプラント治療 (dental) implant treatment.
インフリキシマブ [薬] [関節リウマチ治療薬] infliximab.
インフルエンザ ▫ インフルエンザ脳症 [医] influenza-associated encephalopathy.

インフルエンサー・マーケティング〖宣伝〗〔社会的に影響力のある人を宣伝に利用する手法〕influencer marketing.
インフレ(ーション) ▭ インフレ参照値 〖経〗an inflation reference value.
インフレーター〖自動車〗〔エアバッグを急激に膨らませる装置；自転車の空気入れ〕an inflator.
いんぺい【隠蔽】▭ 隠蔽配管〖建〗concealed piping.
「インベーダー」〖米国の、地球人になりすました宇宙人との闘いを描く TV ドラマ〗The Invaders.
インベスター【投資家】an investor. ▭ インベスター・リレーションズ〔投資家への広報活動；財務広報〕investor relations（略: IR）.
インペラー〖機〗〖羽根車〗an impeller.
インホイール・モーター〖自動車など〗〔個々の車輪に組み込まれたモーター〕an in-wheel motor.

いんぼう【陰謀】▭ 陰謀史観 a [the] conspiratorial [conspiracy] view [theory] of history; history as conspiracy. 陰謀説 (a) conspiracy theory.
「陰謀のセオリー」〖映画〗Conspiracy Theory.
いんよう¹【引用】▭ (被)引用度〔論文の〕a citation frequency.
いんよう⁴【飲用】▭ 飲用酢 (a) drinking vinegar; (a) vinegar for drinking.
インライン・ホッケー〔インラインスケートをはいて行うアイスホッケーに似たゲーム〕inline hockey.
いんりょう【飲料】▭ 冷凍飲料 frozen drinks. 冷凍ペット飲料 frozen bottled drinks.
インレーこ【−湖】〔ミャンマー中北部にある〕Inle Lake; Lake Inle.

# う

う¹【卯】▭ 卯(う)(は)跳ねる〔相場〕〔卯年は相場が上昇する、の意〕In the year of the Rabbit, the market tends to leap.〔⇨たつみてんじょう〕
ヴァージニア・ビーチ〔米国ヴァージニア州東部の都市〕Virginia Beach.
「ヴァージン・スーサイズ」〖映画〗The Virgin Suicides.
「ヴァージン・ハンド」〖映画〗Picking Up the Pieces.
ヴァーホーヴェン Verhoeven, Paul (1937- ；オランダ生まれの映画監督).
ヴァイツェン〔ビールの種類〕weizen.
ヴァヴェルじょう【−城】=バベルじょう.
ヴァザーリ Vasari, Giorgio (1511-74; イタリアの画家・建築家).
ヴァチカンこうかいぎ【−公会議】〔キリスト教〕a Vatican Council. ▭ 第 1 ヴァチカン公会議〔1869-70年の〕the First Vatican Council. 第 2 ヴァチカン公会議〔1962-65年の〕the Second Vatican Council.
ヴァルダク =ワルダック.
ヴァレラ Varela, Francisco J. (1946-2001; チリの神経生理学者).
ヴァンクリーフ・アーペル〖商標〗〔フランスの宝飾品ブランド〕Van Cleef & Arpels.
ヴァン・サント Van Sant, Gus (1952- ；米国の映画監督).
ヴァンダム Van Damme, Jean-Claude (1960- ；ベルギー生まれの映画俳優；本名 Jean-Claude Camille François Van Varenburg).
ヴァンデンバーグくうぐんきち【−空軍基地】〔米国カリフォルニア州の〕Vandenberg Air Force Base.
ヴァンハネン Vanhanen, Matti Taneli (1955- ；フィンランドの政治家；首相〔2003- 〕).
ウィアー Weir, Peter (1944- ；オーストラリア生まれの映画監督).
ヴィーガン【<vegetarian】〔完全菜食主義者〕a vegan.
ウィースト Wiest, Dianne (1948- ；米国の映画女優).
ヴィーノ・ノヴェッロ〖<It = new wine〗〔イタリア産のその年の新酒〕vino novello.
ウィーンじょうやく²【−条約】〔オゾン層保護のための；1985年〕the Vienna Convention for the Protection of the Ozone Layer.
ヴィエケスとう【−島】〔プエルトリコ東部の島〕Vieques Island.
ヴィエンチャンこうどうけいかく【−行動計画】〔2004年にASEANの首脳会議で採択された〕the Vientiane Action Program（略: VAP）.
ウィキペディア〔ウェブ上の百科事典〕Wikipedia.
ヴィクトリアこうえん【−公園】〔香港にある公園〕Victoria Park.

ヴィクトリア・ピーク〔香港島にある山〕Victoria Peak.
ウィクラマシンハ Wickremesinghe, Ranil (1949- ；スリランカの政治家；首相〔1993-94, 2001-04〕).
ウィザースプーン Witherspoon, Reese (1976- ；米国の映画女優；本名 Laura Jean Reese Witherspoon).
ウィジェ〔アンゴラ北西部の州；その州都〕Uíge.
ヴィシェグラード・グループ〔スロバキア・ハンガリー・ポーランド・チェコの 4 か国による域内協力のための国家グループ〕the Visegrad Group. ▶ 通称 ヴィシェグラード 4 (the Visegrad Four; 略: V4).
ヴィスタ =ビスタ².
ウィスラー²〔カナダ西部の観光都市〕Whistler.
ウィチェフレイベルガ =ビケフレイベルガ.
ウィッシュ・リスト〔欲しいものの表〕a wish list.
ウィット Witt, Alicia (1975- ；米国の映画女優).
ウィテカー Whitaker, Forest (1961- ；米国の映画俳優).
「ヴィドック」〖映画〗Vidocq.
ウィニー〖電算〗〔ファイル交換ソフト〕Winny.
ウィリアムズ Williams, Ted (1918-2002; 米国の野球選手；本名 Theodore Samuel Williams).
ウィリスどうみゃくりん【−動脈輪】▭ ウィリス動脈輪閉塞症〖医〗occlusion of the circle of Willis.
ウイルス ▭ 鳥(インフルエンザ・)ウイルス ⇨とりインフルエンザ. ▭ ウイルス感染メール〖電算〗(a)「virus [virus-infected] mail. ウイルス駆除ツール〖ソフト〗〖電算〗a virus [disinfection [eradication] tool; virus [eradication] software. ウイルス性胃腸炎〖医〗viral gastroenteritis. ウイルス対策会社〖電算〗an antivirus company. ウイルス分離検査 a virus isolation test.
ウイルタ〔サハリンの原住民族〕the Uilta; [1 人] an Uilta (pl. ~). ▶ オロッコ (Orok) ともいう.
ウィンウィン〔どちらにとっても有利な〕win-win (situations).
ウィンウィンウィン〔三者とも有利な〕win-win-win (situations).
ウィンガー Winger, Debra (1955- ；米国の映画女優).
ウィンクラー Winkler, Irwin (1931- ；米国の映画製作者・監督).
ウィンサー Wincer, Simon (1943- ；オーストラリア生まれの映画監督).
ウィンズ〖WINDS〗〔日本の超高速インターネット衛星の愛称〕WINDS; the Wideband Inter-Networking Engineering Test and Demonstration Satellite.
ウインズ〖WINS〗〔日本中央競馬会の場外馬券発売所の愛称〕WINS; an ["off-track ["off-course] betting shop.
ウィンスレット Winslet, Kate (1975- ；英国生まれの映

画俳優).
ヴィンソン Vinson, Carl (1883-1981; 米国の政治家).
ヴィンソン・マッシフ (Mount) Vinson Massif.
「ウィンター・ゲスト」[映画] The Winter Guest.
ウィンターズ Winters, Shelley (1920-2006; 米国の映画女優).
ウィンターボトム Winterbottom, Michael (1961- ; 英国生まれの映画監督).
ウインドミル [風車] a windmill. ▯ ウインドミル投法 [ソフトボール] the windmill pitch. ▷ windmill pitcher n.
ウィンブルドン ▯ ウィンブルドン現象 [経] [市場が外資系金融機関に独占される状態] Wimbledonization; the Wimbledon phenomenon.
ウィンルーズ [一方が勝って一方が負ける] win-lose 《situations》.
ヴィンロン [ベトナム南部, メコンデルタ地帯の省; その省都] Vinh Long.
ウヴァ 1 [スリランカ南東部の州] Uva.
2 [紅茶] Uva (tea).
ヴーヴ・クリコ [商標] [シャンパンの銘柄] Veuve Clicquot.
ウージ [沖縄方言で, さとうきび] a sugar cane. ▯ ウージ染め *uuji* [sugar cane] dyeing.
ウーファ [ドイツの映画会社] Ufa; die Universum-Film AG.
「ウーマン・オン・トップ」[映画] Woman on Top.
ウーリーくもざる【-蜘蛛猿】[動] a wooly spider monkey; *Brachyteles arachnoides*.
ウーロンちゃ【烏龍茶】▯ 鉄観音烏龍茶 tie guan yin; iron goddess of mercy oolong (tea). 凍頂烏龍茶 dong ding oolong (tea).
ウェアハウス ▯ ウェアハウス・ストア [倉庫のような簡素な店舗でサービスなしで割引価格で販売する小売店] a warehouse store.
ウェアラブル [身体に装着可能な] wearable. ▯ ウェアラブル・コンピューター [電算] a wearable computer.
ウェイツ Weitz, Paul (1966- ; 米国の映画監督・脚本家・製作者).
ウェイバック・マシン [ネット上の情報をデータベースとして蓄積し, 利用者が過去にさかのぼって検索できるシステムやサービス] a wayback machine.
ウェイン・ワン Wayne Wang (1949- ; 香港生まれの米国の映画監督).
ウェーゲナー² =ヴェゲナー.
ウェーバー¹ ▯ ウェーバー公示 [野球選手が退団する際にチームが保有権を他の球団に示す公示] notification of a waiver. ウェーバー指名 [野球] [野球のドラフト会議で指名順に下位球団から行う] a waiver claim. (完投) ウェーバー制 [方式] [野球] [日本プロ野球ドラフト方式の1つ] a system under which teams with relatively worse win-loss records select new players before teams with better records do. 逆ウェーバー方式 [ドラフト制で, 上位の球団から指名していく方式] (a system of) reverse waivers.
ウェーブ・セーリング [ウインドサーフィンの競技種目の１つ] wave sailing.
「ウェールズの山」[映画] The Englishman Who Went Up a Hill, But Came Down a Mountain.
ウェゲナー Wegener, Alfred Lothar (1880-1930; ドイツの地球物理学者・気象学者; 大陸移動説を発表).
ウェザー・マーチャンダイジング [天気に応じた商品管理] weather merchandising.
ウェザリング [模型の汚し塗装] weathering; 《give a model》 a weathered effect.
ウェスタン・ケープ =にしケープ.
ウェスタン・ブロットほう [-法] [生化] Western blotting.
ウェステージ [原子力] [損耗] wastage.
ウエスト² [野球] [ウエスト・ボール] a waste pitch. ～する waste a pitch.

ウエスト³ West, Simon (1961- ; 英国生まれの映画監督).
ウエストしょうこうぐん【-症候群】[医] West syndrome; [点頭癲癇] infantile [nodding, salaam] spasm; infantile myoclonic seizure.
ウエスト・テキサス・インターミディエイト [原油価格の世界の指標になっている米国産油種] West Texas Intermediate (略: WTI).
ウエスト・フランス [フランスの有力地方紙] Ouest-France.
うえつけ【植え付け】▯ 植え付け時期 [シーズン] the planting 「season [period].
ウエッジ ▯ サンド・ウエッジ a sand wedge. ピッチング・ウエッジ a pitching wedge.
ウエット ▯ ウエット・クリーニング wet cleaning. ウエット・タオル a wet towel.
ウエディング ▯ ウエディング・プランナー a wedding planner.
「ウェディング・シンガー」[映画] The Wedding Singer.
「ウェディング・プランナー」[映画] The Wedding Planner.
ウェブ
▯ ウェブ・アドレス a Web address. ウェブ絵本 an illustrated Web book. ウェブ会議 a 「web [net] conferencing; [方式] web [net] conferencing. ウェブ検索 《do》 a Web search. ウェブ広告 Web advertising; advertising on the Web; [1件の] a Web advertisement; an advertisement on the Web. ウェブコミック a webcomic; an online comic; an Internet comic. ウェブ・サーバー a Web server. ウェブ・サーファー [ウェブサーフィンをする人] a Web surfer. ウェブ・サーフィン [ウェブページを次々と渡り歩くこと] Web surfing. ウェブ通帳 [インターネット上の預金通帳] a Web passbook. ウェブ・デザイナー a Web designer. ウェブ・デザイン Web design. ウェブマスター [ウェブサイトの管理者] a webmaster.
ウエファ【UEFA】[欧州サッカー連盟] UEFA; the Union of European Football Associations. ▯ UEFAカップ the UEFA Cup. UEFA チャンピオンズリーグ the UEFA Champions League.
うえぶれ【上振れ】=うわぶれ.
ヴェブレン Veblen, Thorstein (Bunde) (1857-1929; 米国の政治経済学者・社会学者). ▷ Veblenian *adj*.
ウェブログ [電算] a Web log; a blog.
ヴェリズモ [リアリズム] ▯ ヴェリズモ・オペラ [音楽] (a) verismo opera.
ヴェリブ =ベリブ.
ウェルカム・トラスト [英国の財団] the Wellcome Trust.
ウェルシュきん【-菌】[菌] *Clostridium perfringens*.
ウェルシュ・コーギー [犬] a Welsh corgi.
ウェルシュ・コーギー・ペンブローク [犬] a Welsh corgi Pembroke.
ウェルシュ・テリア [犬] a Welsh terrier; a Welshie.
ウェルズ Wells, Simon (1961- ; 英国生まれの映画監督).
ウェルス・マネ(ー)ジメント [金融] [富裕層向けの財産管理] wealth management.
ウェルチア [コンピュータ-ウイルスの１つ] Welchia.
ヴェルデンスガング [ノルウェーの日刊紙] Verdens Gang; VG.
ヴェルホフスタット =フェルホフスタット.
ヴォイト Voight, Jon (1938- ; 米国の映画俳優; 本名 Jonathan Voight; 女優アンジェリーナ・ジョリーの父).
ウォーカー Walker, Paul (1973- ; 米国の映画俳優).
ウォーカーじゅんかん【-循環】[気象] [大気大循環の一種] the Walker circulation.
ウォーキング ▯ ウォーキング・マップ [ウォーキングに適したコースを記した地図; 散策地図] a 《Kyoto》 walking map.
「ウォーク・ザ・ライン/君につづく道」[映画] Walk the Line.

う

「ウォーク・トゥ・リメンバー」〔映画〕A Walk to Remember.

ウォーター・ガーデニング〔水生植物園芸〕water gardening.

ウォーター・カッター〔機〕〔高圧水流によって金属板などを切断する機械〕a「water jet [waterjet] cutter; a water cutter.

ウォーター・クーラー〔冷水器〕a water cooler.

ウォータージャンプ〔スキージャンプ用のスロープとプールを組み合わせた施設〕a water ramp.

ウォーターズ Waters, John (1946– ; 米国の映画監督・脚本家・製作者).

ウォーター・ハンマー〔水撃(さよう)(作用)〕a water hammer; water-hammering.

ウォーターフォール・モデル〔システム開発手順のモデルの1つ〕a [the] waterfall (lifecycle) model.

ウォーター・レタス〔植〕〔サトイモ科の浮遊性の水草で常緑多年草；牡丹浮草〕(a) water lettuce; (a) water cabbage; Pistia stratiotes.

「ウォーターワールド」〔映画〕Waterworld.

ウォード Ward, Vincent (1956– ; ニュージーランド生まれの映画監督).

ウォーリー〔多くの人々の絵の中から主人公を探し出す英国の絵本 "Where's Wally?" の主人公〕Wally; (米国では) Waldo.

ウォールバーグ Wahlberg, Mark (1971– ; 米国の映画俳優; 本名 Mark Robert Michael Wahlberg).

ヴォカリーズ〔音楽〕〔母音唱法〕vocalise;〔その曲〕a vocalise.

ウォシャウスキー 1 Wachowski, Andy (1967– ; 米国の映画監督・製作者・脚本家; 2の弟). 2 Wachowski, Larry (1965– ; 米国の映画監督・製作者・脚本家; 1の兄). ●〜兄弟 the Wachowski brothers.

ウォッチャー □ 日銀ウォッチャー〔日本銀行の金融政策を分析する専門家〕a BOJ watcher; a specialist who analyzes the Bank of Japan's financial policies.

ウォルシュ Walsh, Raoul (1887–1980; 米国の映画監督・脚本家).

ウォルバーグ =ウォールバーグ.

ウォルフしょう【—賞】〔イスラエルのウォルフ財団が, 物理・化学・医学・農学・数学などに功績があった人に授与する賞〕a Wolf Prize;〔個々の賞をまとめて〕the Wolf Prizes.

ウォルマート〔米国のディスカウントストア・チェーン〕Wal-Mart.

「ウォレスとグルミット 野菜畑で大ピンチ」〔アニメ映画〕Wallace & Gromit: The Curse of the Were-Rabbit.

ウォレマイ・パイン〔植〕〔ナヨウスギ科の針葉樹; 世界最古の種子植物; オーストラリア原産〕a Wollemi pine; Wollemia nobilis. ▶日本での愛称は ジュラシック・ツリー (Jurassic Tree).

ヴォロニン, ヴォロニン Voronin, Vladimir (1941– ; モルドヴァの政治家; 大統領 2001– ]).

ウォン・カーウァイ〔王家衛〕Wong Kar-Wai (1958– ; 中国の映画監督).

ウォンビン【元斌】Wonbin (1977– ; 韓国の映画俳優).

うかい[1]【迂回】□ 迂回献金 an indirect (political) 「contribution [donation]. 迂回送金 (an) indirect remittance; [代金の] (a) roundabout payment 迂回輸出 indirect export(ation).

うがじん【宇賀神】〔日本神道古来の水神で, 農業の神; 人頭蛇身の女神〕Ugajin; the God of Grain and Happiness (often depicted as a white snake or celestial nymph).

うかのかみ【宇賀の神】=うがじん.

うからやから【親族】one's family and relatives.

うきかわ【浮皮】〔柑橘類の果実の中身と皮の間が離れ, 皮が浮いた状態になること〕a loose skin.

うきこぼれ【浮きこぼれ】〔学校の授業内容よりも進んでいる子供が授業を物足りなく感じ, クラスの中で疎外される状態〕estrangement [isolation] for being too far ahead of one's「class [peers]; overachievement;〔人〕an overachiever.

うきだま【浮き球】〔サッカー〕a ball in flight. □ 浮き球シュート〔バス〕a loop「shoot [pass].

うきやね【浮き屋根】〔貯蔵タンクなどの〕a floating roof.

うけざら【受け皿】□ 受け皿会社 a「receptor [receiving] company (for a failed enterprise).

うけとり【受(け)取(り)】□ 受取配当金 dividends received.

うし[1]【丑】□ 丑はつまづく《相場》〔丑年には下落する, の意〕In the year of the Ox, the market tends to stall. [⇨つみてんじょう]

うし[2]【牛】□ 牛柄 a cow-skin pattern.

うじ[2]【蛆】□ 蛆治療 maggot [larval] (debridement) therapy.

うしえび【牛海老】〔動〕〔クルマエビ科のエビ〕a black tiger prawn; a giant tiger prawn; Penaeus monodon.

うしこたいしきべつじょうほうかんりとくそほう【牛個体識別情報管理特措法】〔法〕=きゅうにくトレーサビリティーほう.

うしつき【牛突き】〔闘牛; 島根県隠岐などの伝統行事〕bullfighting; traditional bullfighting held at Oki in Tottori Prefecture, in which two bulls fight each other.

うしのつのつき【牛の角突き】〔新潟県小千谷市・旧山古志村の伝統行事〕bullfighting; traditional bullfighting held in Niigata Prefecture, in which two bulls fight each other.

ウジミナス〔ブラジルの大手鉄鋼メーカー〕Usiminas.

うしろだおし【後ろ倒し】〔実施の時期を先延ばしすること〕moving back; postponing. ●〜する delay; move back; postpone; put off. □ 地価の上昇を見込んで業者たちその造成地の発売時期を半年ほど〜(に)するらしい. It seems that the company is delaying sale of the housing site for six months in the hope that the price of the land will go up.

うすい[1]【雨水】□ 雨水タンク a rainwater tank. 雨水ます〔桝〕 a rainwater pit. 雨水利用ビル a building (equipped) with a rainwater utilization system.

うすいろひょうもんどき【薄色豹紋蜻】〔昆〕〔タテハチョウ科のチョウ〕Melitaea protomedia; Melitaea regama.

うすがた【薄型】□ 薄型化〔テレビなどの〕slimming down (of electronic products).

うすこうはん【薄鋼板】□ 冷延【熱延】薄鋼板 cold-rolled [hot-rolled] sheet steel.

うすずみ【薄墨】□ 薄墨桜 an usuzumi zakura; a cherry tree with grayish white blossoms.

うすちゃ【薄茶】□ 薄茶器 a vessel designed to hold powdered weak green tea.

うすで【薄手】3〔貧弱なこと〕weakness; meagerness; thinness. ●〜の守備 (a) weak [(an) inadequate] defense. ●彼の論文は内容が〜だ. The content of his thesis is rather meager. / His thesis isn't very meaty.

ウズベキスタン・イスラムうんどう【—運動】〔ウズベキスタンの反政府武装組織〕the Islamic Movement of Uzbekistan (略: IMU).

うすめえき【薄め液】thinner. ●この塗料は〜で薄めないと塗りにくいです. This paint is hard to apply unless you dilute it with thinner.

うすめばる【薄眼鮋】〔魚〕〔フサカサゴ科の魚〕a goldeye rockfish; Sebastes thompsoni.

うせつ【右折】□ 右折車線【レーン】a right-turn lane.

うそくさい【嘘臭い】unlikely; improbable; doubtful; fishy.

ウタイ・タ(ー)ニ(ー)〔タイ北部の県; その県都〕Uthai

Thani.
「歌え!フィッシャーマン」〔映画〕Cool & Crazy;〔原題〕Heftig og Begeistret.
うたせぶね【打瀬船】a sailing trawler.
「歌に生き, 恋に生き」〔プッチーニ作曲のオペラ『トスカ』中のアリア〕Vissi d'arte, vissi d'amore (＝I lived for art, I lived for love).
ウタラディット〔タイ北部の県; その県都〕Uttaradit.
うちあそび【内遊び】〔子供の, 外遊びに対して〕(遊ぶこと) playing 「indoors [inside]; (具体的な遊び) an indoor game.
うちこみ【打ち込み】□打ち込み音楽 music created on a computer; desktop music (略: DTM).
うちぞめ【打ち初め】□〔囲碁・将棋などの〕the first [opening] game of the year;〔太鼓などの〕the first [opening] session of the year; the first performance of the year;〔新硬貨などの〕the start of minting 〔of a coin〕; the first minting. □ 打ち初め式〔囲碁・将棋などの〕the ceremonial first game of the year;〔太鼓などの〕the ceremonial first「session [performance] of the year;〔新硬貨などの〕the ceremonial minting of a new coin.
うちざりがに【内田蜊蛄】【動】a signal crayfish; Pacifastacus leniusculus.
うちだんねつ【内断熱】【建】「internal [interior] insulation. □ 内断熱住宅 a house with internal [interior] insulation; an internally insulated house.
「うちのママは世界一」〔米国の, 平和な家庭の TV ホームドラマ〕The Donna Reed Show.
うちのり【内法】□内法面積〔建物などの〕the internal floor area; the area enclosed by the interior faces of the walls; the net floor area.
うちはもの【打刃物】a hammer-forged「cutting tool [blade].
「うちへ帰ろう」〔映画〕The Autumn Heart.
うちゅう¹【宇宙】
□ 宇宙往還機〔地球と低・中軌道宇宙間の輸送システム〕a space plane. 宇宙観光 space tourism. ○～観光客 a space tourist. 宇宙機関会議〔国際宇宙ステーション計画による国際会議〕the Heads of Agency (略: HOA). 宇宙軍拡 the militarization of space. 宇宙ステーション補給機〔宇宙航空研究開発機構 (JAXA) の〕an H-II Transfer Vehicle (略: HTV);〔欧州宇宙機関 (ESA) の〕an Automated Transfer Vehicle (略: ATV). 宇宙赤外線望遠鏡(装置)〔米国 NASA の〕the Space Infrared Telescope Facility (略: SIRTF). [⇨スピッツァー] 宇宙天気〔太陽風・磁気嵐などの地球周辺環境〕space weather. 宇宙背景放射観測衛星 the「Cosmic Background Explorer [COBE] satellite. 宇宙望遠鏡 a space telescope. 宇宙輸送機 a space transporter; a launch vehicle (略: LV). ○再使用型～輸送機 a space shuttle; a reusable launch vehicle (略: RLV).
「宇宙怪人ゴースト」〔米国の, 宇宙ヒーローものの TV ギャグアニメ〕Space Ghost.
「宇宙家族ジェットソン」〔米国の, 未来社会が舞台のホームコメディーのアニメ〕The Jetsons.
「宇宙家族ロビンソン」〔米国の, 宇宙冒険ものの TV ドラマ〕Lost in Space.
うちゅうかんきょうしんらいせいじっしょうシステム【宇宙環境信頼性実証-】the Space Environment Reliability Verification Integrated System (略: SERVIS).
うちゅうきょういくセンター【宇宙教育-】〔日本の宇宙航空研究開発機構が運営する教育機関〕the Space Education Center.
「宇宙空母ギャラクチカ」〔米国の, 宇宙冒険ものの TV ドラマ〕Battlestar Galactica.
うちゅうこうくうけんきゅうかいはつきこう【宇宙航空研究開発機構】the Japan Aerospace Exploration

Agency (略: JAXA). ▶ 2003 年に文部科学省宇宙科学研究所, 航空宇宙技術研究所, 宇宙開発事業団が統合して発足。
うちゅうこうくうけんきゅうかいはつきこうほう【宇宙航空研究開発機構法】【法】the Japan Aerospace Exploration Agency Law.
うちゅうじっしょうえいせい【宇宙実証衛星】＝うちゅうかんきょうしんらいせいじっしょうシステム.
うちゅうせいぶつがくけんきゅうじょ【宇宙生物学研究所】〔米国 NASA の〕the NASA Astrobiology Institute (略: NAI).
うちゅうせん²【宇宙線】□宇宙線被曝 cosmic ray exposure.
「宇宙大作戦」〔米国の, 宇宙冒険ものの TV ドラマ〕Star Trek. ▶「宇宙パトロール」の邦題でも放映。
「宇宙探検」〔米国の, 宇宙開拓者 McCauley 大佐の TV ドラマ〕Men into Space.
「宇宙パトロール」⇨「宇宙大作戦」。
「宇宙ライダーエンゼル」⇨「キャプテン・ゼロ」。
「美しい人」〔映画〕Nine Lives.
「美しき諍い女」〔映画〕The Beautiful Troublemaker;〔原題〕La Belle Noiseuse.
「美しき日々」〔韓国のテレビドラマ〕Beautiful Days.
うづくり【宇造り】【木工】〔家具製造技法の 1 つで, 表面をこすることで木目を際だたせる方法〕grain「texturing [enhancement].
ウッズ Woods, James (1947－ ); 米国の映画俳優; 本名 James Howard Woods.
ウッズホールかいようけんきゅうじょ【-海洋研究所】〔米国マサチューセッツ州の〕the Woods Hole Oceanographic Institution (略: WHOI).
ウッズホールかいようせいぶつがくけんきゅうじょ【-海洋生物学研究所】the Marine Biological Laboratories (at Woods Hole) (略: MBL).
ウッタラディット＝ウタラディット.
ウッド Wood, Elijah (1981－ ); 米国の映画俳優; 本名 Elijah Jordan Wood.
ウッドデッキ〔屋外に付設された木製の床〕a wooden「deck [floor, platform].
ウッドパネル〔自動車部品・建築・家具などに用いられる木目調パネル〕a wood-grain panel; wood-grain paneling.
ウッド・プラスチック (a) wood-plastic composite (略: WPC).
「ウッドペッカー」〔米国の, キツツキが主人公の TV ギャグアニメ〕Woody Woodpecker.
うつびょう【鬱病】□季節性鬱病 seasonal depression. 産後鬱病【医】postpartum [postnatal] depression. 遷延(せんえん)性鬱病 protracted [prolonged] depression. 単極性鬱病 unipolar depression. 荷下ろし鬱病【医】postcompletion depression. 反応性鬱病【医】reactive depression.
うど【独活】□軟化【軟白】うど〔地下の穴ぐらで栽培したうど〕blanched udos (cultivated in an underground dugout). 山うど〔畑で栽培された〕cultivated udos;〔天然ものの〕wild udos.
ウドムサイ〔ラオス北部の県〕Oudomxay; Udomxai; Oudomsai;〔同県・県都〕サイ².
ウトリックかんしょう【-環礁】〔マーシャル諸島にある環礁〕Utirik Atoll.
ウドン・タニ〔タイ北東部, ラオスとの国境近くの県・市〕Udon Thani.
ウドン・メンチェイ〔カンボジア北部の州〕Otdar Meanchey.
ウノ〔トランプ〕〔カードゲームの一種〕Uno.
うのはな【卯の花】□卯の花腐(くたし) a long period of rainy weather in late spring.
ウバ＝ウヴァ.
ウバイディ〔イラク西部の村〕Ubaydi.
ウプサラひょうが【-氷河】〔アルゼンチン南部の氷河〕the

ウブド(ゥ)〔インドネシア, バリ島の町〕Ubud.
Upsala Glacier.
ウポポ〔アイヌの伝統的な歌〕upopo; the upopo style of traditional Ainu singing.
ウボン・ラーチャターニー〔タイ東部の県〕Ubon Ratchathani.
うま¹【午】 ▯ 午尻下がり〔相場〕〔午年は値が下がる, の意〕In the year of the Horse, the market tends to fall. [⇨たつみトレンド]
ウマイヤド・モスク〔シリア, ダマスカスにあるモスク〕the Umayyad Mosque.
うまインフルエンザ【馬—】〔獣医〕equine influenza; horse flu.
うみあけ【海明け】〔春, 接岸していた流氷が沖に去ること〕the day on which the ice floes start thinning out (and navigation becomes possible again).
うみじろ【海城】a seaside 「castle [fortress].
「海の上のピアニスト」〔映画〕The Legend of 1900.
うみぶどう【海葡萄】〔植〕〔緑藻類イワヅタ科の海藻, 小球が連なる様がブドウを思わせる〕sea grapes; *Caulerpa lentillifera*.
「海辺の家」〔映画〕Life as a House.
うみわれ【海割れ】〔潮が引いて人間が渡れる砂州(ﾇ)が現れる現象〕a parting of the sea.
ウムカスル〔イラク南部の都市〕Umm Qasr.
ウムラ〔メッカ小巡礼; 巡礼月以外に行われる〕umra; 'umrah; (the) lesser hajj.
うめ【梅】〔料理〕(a) plum (dipping) sauce; a dip made with *umeboshi* concentrate. 梅だれ = 梅ソース.
うめばか【埋(め)墓】〔両墓制で, 遺体を土葬する墓〕a grave where the bodies of the dead are actually buried (as opposed to the "memorial grave", where prayers and services are held for them).
うめもどし【埋め戻し】〔掘り出した物に〕reburial; 〔掘った跡に〕refilling. ◆修理した水道管の〜作業はまだ終わっていない. The reburial of the repaired water pipe has not yet finished. / 掘削した箇所の〜が完了した. The refilling of the excavated site was completed.
うめもどす【埋め戻す】〔掘り出した物に〕rebury; 〔掘った跡を〕refill. ◆犬が掘り返してしまった球根を埋め戻した. I reburied the bulbs that the dog had dug up. / その遺跡は調査が終わった段階で埋め戻されることになっている. That archaeological site is to be 「reburied [returned to the earth] after the survey has finished. / 廃坑を建設残土で埋め戻した. The abandoned mine was 「refilled [filled in] with surplus soil from a construction site.
うら-【裏-】〔陰の; 正式にその地位にあるわけではないが実際にはその仕事をすること〕behind-the-scenes (leadership). ▯ 裏合意 (a) 「secret [behind-the-scenes] agreement. 裏社長 the behind-the-scenes president; the person who 「controls the company from behind the scenes [pulls the president's strings]; the real boss of the company. 裏番長 a 「hidden [secret] boss [leader].
うらがね【裏金】 ▯ 裏金疑惑〔賄賂の〕a 「bribery [payoff] scandal; 〔簿外金作りの〕an off-the-book(s) scandal.
うらがみ【裏紙】1〔剥離紙; シール・両面テープなどの台紙〕(sticker) release paper. ◆これは〜をはがして軽く押さえるだけだからだれでも簡単に貼れる壁紙です. Anybody can hang this wallpaper. All you have to do is peel off the backing and then press it on lightly.
2〔片面は使用済みだが裏がまだ使える用紙〕(a sheet of) paper 「used [printed] on one side.
うらけん【裏拳】〔空手〕〔手の甲での打撃〕a backhand 「chop [blow].
うらさんどう【裏参道】〔神社・仏閣への参道で「裏」にあたるもの〕the back approach to a 「shrine [temple].

うらしゃかい【裏社会】the underside of society; the underworld.
うらせってい【裏設定】〔ゲーム・物語などの, 表には出てこない設定・背景など〕a backstory.
うらせんたい【裏選対】a secret headquarters for an election campaign.
うらづけ【裏付け】 ▯ 裏付け取材 corroborative [follow-up] reporting.
うらない【占い】 ▯ 相性占い (a) compatibility reading. 運勢占い fortune-telling; predicting *one's* fate. コーヒー占い (a) coffee-ground reading; coffee divination; (coffee) tasseography. 動物占い fortune-telling based on the characteristics of 12 animal characters; animal fortune-telling. 花占い (a) flower reading. 恋愛占い love [romance] fortune-telling.
うらぬけ【裏抜け】〔印刷〕bleed-through.
うらネタ【裏—】information [news, a report] from 「an unverified [a dubious] source.
うらばん【裏番】1〔裏番長〕⇨うら-.
2〔テレビ〕〔裏番組〕a program in the same time slot on a different channel.
3〔競馬〕〔外枠から数えた番号〕a post position counting from the outside.
うらぶたい【裏舞台】 ◆〜で暗躍する operate behind the scenes.
ウラマー〔イスラム〕〔宗教法・イスラム神学の指導者〕an 「ulama [ulema] (*pl.* 〜, 〜s).
ウラマひょうぎかい【—評議会】〔インドネシアのイスラム指導者団体〕the Indonesian Ulemas Council (略: MUI). ▶ MUI は Majelis Ulama Indonesia の略.
うらやき【裏焼き】〔印刷・映画〕〔誤って裏返しにプリントしてしまうこと〕〔写真を〕wrong-reading; 《口》flopping; 〔映画のフィルムを〕inversion.
ウラン
▯ 加工ウラン processed uranium.
ウラン化合物〔化〕a uranium compound. ウラン型〔核の〕a 「uranium-based [uranium-fueled] 《nuclear bomb》. ウラン鉱石 uranium ore. ウラン酸ナトリウム sodium uranate. ◆重—酸ウラン sodium diuranate. ウラン残土 waste from uranium ore. ウラン試験〔核燃料再処理施設での〕uranium testing; a uranium test. ウラン転換 uranium conversion. ◆—転換施設〔工場〕a uranium conversion 「facility [plant]. ウラン235〔化〕uranium-235; U(-)235 (記号: ²³⁵U). ウラン238〔化〕uranium-238; U(-)238 (記号: ²³⁸U).
うり²【売り】 ▯ 大口[小口]売り〔相場〕bulk [small-scale] selling; a 「bulk [small-scale] sale.
うりあげ【売り上げ】 ▯ 売り上げ実績[成績] sales results. 売り上げ総利益率 (a) gross profit 「margin [percentage]. 売り上げ伸び率 a sales growth rate; a growth rate for sales. 売り上げ倍増 a doubling of sales. 売り上げ割り戻し引当金 a 「provision [reserve] for sales rebates.
うりあげだか【売り上げ高】
▯ 売り上げ高営業利益率 the ratio of operating profit to net sales. 売り上げ高経常利益率 the ratio of ordinary profit to sales. 売り上げ高原価率 the cost to sales ratio. 売り上げ高広告宣伝費率〔経営〕the ratio of advertising expenses to (net) sales. 売り上げ高収益率[利益率] a return on sales 《of 2.5%》(略: ROS). 売り上げ高純利益率〔経営〕a net profit 「margin [ratio]. 売り上げ高人件費(比)率 the ratio of labor costs to sales. 売り上げ高ランキング (a) sales (volume) ranking. ◆その会社は世界の製薬会社の〜ランキングで5位に入っている. That company ranks fifth in sales among the world's pharmaceutical companies.
うりこし【売り越し】 ▯ 売り越し額 the amount of net selling.
うりこみ【売り込み】 ▯ 売り込み攻勢 = 販売攻勢 (⇨は

んぱい).

うりせん【売り専】〔男性同性愛者相手の売春宿〕a gay whorehouse; a gay brothel;〔男娼〕a male prostitute; a (male) hustler; a rentboy.

ウリツカヤ Ulitskaya, Lyudmila (1943-　 ;〔ロシアの女性作家〕.

ウリとう【ウリ党】〔韓国の政党〕the Uri Party. ▶ Uri は韓国語で「わが」の意.

ウリベ Uribe Vélez, Álvaro (1952-　 ;〔コロンビアの政治家〕大統領〔2002-　 〕).

うるうどし【閏年】 ▫▪ 閏年問題〔電算〕〔閏年のシステム障害問題〕the leap-year「bug [problem].

うるささしすう【うるささ指数】〔航空機騒音指数〕an aircraft noise index;〔加重等価平均感覚騒音レベル〕(a) weighted equivalent continuous perceived noise level (略: WECPNL).

ウルズガン〔アフガニスタン南部の州〕Oruzgan.

「ウルトラゾーン」「アウター・リミッツ」.

ウルトラ・ディープ・フィールド〔天〕〔超深宇宙の領域〕an ultra deep field (略: UDF). ▫▪ ハッブル・ウルトラ・ディープ・フィールド ⇨ハッブル.

「ウルトラ二等兵」〔米陸軍のお人よしの二等兵によるどたばた TV コメディー〕No Time for Sergeants.

ウルビ・エト・オルビ〔クリスマスに読み上げられるローマ教皇の全世界に向けたメッセージ〕Urbi et Orbi. ▶ Urbi et Orbi は"to the city and the world"（ローマおよび世界に; 全世界に）の意.

ウルンディ〔南アフリカ共和国南東部, クワズール（－）・ナタール州の州都〕Ulundi.

ウレタン ▫▪ ウレタン素材 urethane; a urethane material. ウレタン・ビーズ a urethane bead.

うれつ【雨裂】〔雨水による土壌浸食の溝〕a gully.

うろこ【鱗】 ▫▪ 鱗取り〔うろこを取ること〕scaling (fish);〔うろこを取り除く金属製の道具〕a (fish) scaler.

うわうけ【上請け】〔中小の業者が注文を受注し, 上位業者の業務に下請けすること〕a practice whereby a relatively small firm, having been contracted to do a job that exceeds its capabilities, contracts a larger firm to perform the work.

うわき【浮気】 ▫▪ 浮気相手 an [sb's] illicit lover; a [sb's] partner in an adulterous love affair. 浮気調査 an infidelity investigation.

「ウワサの真相/ワグ・ザ・ドッグ」〔映画〕Wag the Dog.

うわね【上値】 ▫▪ 上値追い (share prices are on)「the up [an upward trend]. 上値抵抗線〔株〕an upper resistance line.

うわのせ【上乗せ】 ▫▪ 上乗せ価格 an「additional [extra, added] price; an addition to the price. 上乗せ条例 a stiffer regulation; an addition to the rules. 上乗せ幅〔金利などの〕a range of mark-up.

うわぶれ【上振れ】〔経〕〔数値の上方変動〕an (economic) upturn; an upturn ((in the market)); an upward swing ((of commodity prices)). ▫～する turn upward(s); show [make] an upturn. ▫ 原油価格は予測値以上に～する可能性がある. There is a possibility that crude oil prices may turn upward beyond expectations.

うわもの【上物】 ▫▪ 上物法人〔上下分離方式での〕a higher (management) company.

うんき²【運気】【運勢】one's stars; fortune; luck;〔自然界に現れる人の運勢〕a sign [an indication] (of good [bad]) fortune; an omen. ▫～が下がる [上がる] the indications for sb「worsen [improve]. ▫ 運気好転 a「turn [stroke] of good fortune.

うんこう¹【運行】 ▫▪ 運行供用者〔法〕〔車両などの〕party responsible for the use of a vehicle. 運行司令室 [部, 所]〔交通機関の〕an operation control「room [office]; an operation headquarters.

うんこう⁴【運航】service; operation;〔飛行機の〕flight;〔船の〕navigation.

～する operate; ply; run;〔飛行機を〕fly;〔船を〕sail. ▫ 東京・釧路間を～しているフェリー a ferry(boat) that 「operates [runs] between Tokyo and Kushiro / 日本とアメリカの間を定期的に～しているジャンボジェット機 a jumbo jet that flies regularly between Japan and the United States. ▫▪ 運航規程〔空〕an operations manual. 運航乗務員〔空〕a member of「a flight crew [an aircrew]; a flight crew [an aircrew] member;〈集合的に〉a flight crew.

うんしん【運針】 ▫▪ 運針縫い＝並縫い（⇨なみ²）.

うんせい【運勢】 ▫▪ 運勢占い ⇨うらない.

うんちく【蘊蓄】 ▫▪ 蘊蓄本 a book「covering [on] every aspect of (tea).

うんてん【運転】
▫▪ 回復運転〔電車などが遅れを取り戻すための〕((insist on))「catching up with the timetable [getting back on schedule] after a delay. 管制運転〔エレベーターなどの〕automated [(automatically) controlled] operation. ▷ 地震時管制－装置 earthquake control equipment; an earthquake unit; a seismic switch (unit). 定時運転〔電車・バスなどの〕running「punctually [to schedule, on time, without delays]. ▷～運転よりも安全運転を優先させるべきだ. Priority should be given to safety rather than punctuality. | It is more important for trains to run safely than punctually. 無謀運転 reckless driving. 連続運転 continuous「operation [running].
▫▪ 運転意識低下警報システム〔自動車〕〔居眠り運転防止用〕a driver alertness warning system. 運転時分〔鉄道〕〔駅間の〕the journey time「between stations [from one station to another];〔路線の起点から終点までの〕(a) total journey time (between two terminuses). 運転速度〔自動車などの〕a driving speed;〔機械の〕an operating [a running] speed. 運転代行 substitute driving. ▷～代行業 a substitute-driver service. 運転適性検査[診断] a driving aptitude test; driving aptitude assessment. 運転日誌〔電車・バス・タクシーなどの〕a driver's log〔book [sheet]〕;〔機械の〕a (machine's) usage log. 運転マナー motoring [driving] manners; driving etiquette.

うんてんだいこうぎょうほう【運転代行業法】〔法〕the Substitute Driving Business Law. ▶ 正式名称は「自動車運転代行業の業務の適正化に関する法律」.

うんてんめんきょ【運転免許】 ▫▪ 運転免許試験 a driver's license test. 運転免許取得可能年齢 the minimum legal driving age. 運転免許センター a drivers' license center.

うんてんれき【運転歴】the length of time one has driven; how long one has driven. ▷～30 年のベテラン・ドライバー a veteran driver with 30 years「of driving experience [(of experience) on the road].

うんどう【運動】 ▫▪ 運動機能 the (one's) motor functions. ▷～の低下 (a) motor-function disorder. 運動強度〔生理〕(an) exercise intensity. 運動発作〔医〕a motor「seizure [epilepsy]. 運動マシン an exercise machine. 運動免疫学 exercise immunology. 運動浴〔水中運動〕(swimming) pool exercise(s); fitness training in「water [a pool]. 運動連鎖〔生理〕〔筋肉間の〕kinetic chain.

「運動靴と赤い金魚」〔映画〕Children Of Heaven;〔原題〕Bacheha-Ye aseman.

うんぷ【運否】〔運不運〕good and bad luck.

ウンブリエル〔天〕〔天王星の衛星〕Umbriel.

ウンムカスル〔イラク南部の, ペルシャ湾に面した港湾都市〕Umm Qasr.

うんゆ【運輸】 ▫▪ 運輸多目的衛星 a multifunctional transport satellite (略: MTSAT).

うんゆしせつせいびじぎょうだん【運輸施設整備事業団】the Corporation for Advanced Transport &

うんゆほあんきょく

Technology (略: CATT). ▶ 2003年に日本鉄道建設公団と統合して鉄道建設・運輸施設整備支援機構となる。

**うんゆほあんきょく【運輸保安局】**〔米国国土安全保障省の一部局〕the Transportation Security Administration (略: TSA).

**うんよう【運用】** ▢🔲 アクティブ運用〔株式〕active management. インデックス運用〔株式〕〔パッシブ運用の一種〕index management. 長期[短期]運用〔資産の〕(a)「long-term [short-term] investment. パッシブ運用〔株式〕passive management. ▢🔲 運用改善〔条約・協定などの〕improved implementation 《of an agreement》. ◯ 日米両政府は日米地位協定の〜改善に合意し、起訴前even でも日本側が被疑者を米国軍人の身柄を拘束できるようになった。The Japanese and US governments agreed to improve the implementation of their Status of Forces Agreement so that Japanese authorities can take custody of American military suspects even before they have been indicted. 運用環境〔資産などの〕a management environment;《電算》〔コンピューターシステムなどの〕an operating environment. 運用規則〔規程〕application [operating] rules [regulations]; rules [regulations] for the「application [operation]《of…》. ◯ 情報ネットワーク〜規則 operating rules for a data network / NPO法〜規程 regulations governing the implementation of the NPO Law. 運用効率〔資産などの〕((asset)) management「efficiency [effectiveness]. 運用(収)益 investment [asset management] profit. 運用損(失) investment [asset management] loss. 運用費〔機材・システムなどの〕operational costs; running costs. 運用報酬〔ファンドの運用に対してファンドを運用する会社に支払われる費用〕a management fee.

**うんりゅうやなぎ【雲竜柳】**《植》〔ヤナギ科の落葉高木; 中国原産〕a corkscrew willow; *Salix matsudana* var. *tortuosa*.

**うんりん【雲林】** ⇨ユンリン。

# え

**エア** ▢🔲 エア・クッション・カー an air-cushion vehicle (略: ACV); a hovercraft. エアクッション型揚陸艇《軍》a landing craft air cushion (略: LCAC). エア・シャワー〔食品工場などの出入り口にある、衣服などに付着した埃や粉塵などを吹き飛ばす装置〕an air shower room. エアソフト・ガン an airsoft gun. エアソフト剣〔スポーツ・チャンバラで用いる武器〕a foam sword. エア・マーシャル〔ハイジャック防止などのため航空機に搭乗する航空保安官〕an air marshal. [=スカイ・マーシャル] エアライン・スタッフ〔航空会社の〕《a member of the》airline staff.
「**エアーウルフ**」=「超音速攻撃ヘリ・エアーウルフ」。
**エア(ー)・プランツ**《植》〔パイナップル科ティランジア属 (*Tillandsia*) に属する植物の総称〕an air plant.
**エアコン** ▢🔲 自動車用エアコン an automobile [a car] air conditioner; air-conditioning [an air conditioner] for a car.
**エア・ダム**《自動車》〔空気抵抗を減らし安定性を増す目的で車体前面下部に取り付ける装置〕an air dam.
**エア・バッグ** ▢🔲 カーテン・エアバッグ a curtain air bag. ニー・エアバッグ a knee air bag.
**エアバンド**《空》airband;〔航空無線〕aeronautical [aircraft] radio. ▢🔲 エアバンド・レシーバー〔航空無線受信機〕an airband receiver.
「**エアフォース・ワン**」〔映画〕Air Force One.
**エアロパーツ**〔自動車・バイクなどの、空力性能改善のための部品〕aerodynamic ((auto)) parts.
**エアロバイク**〔エクササイズ・マシン〕an exercise「bicycle [bike]; 《商標》Aerobike.
**エアロボクシング**〔ボクシングの動作を組み合わせたエアロビクス〕aeroboxing.
**エイ・アール・ブイ・ディー【ARVD】**《医》〔不整脈源性右室心筋変性症〕ARVD; arrhythmogenic right ventricular dysplasia.
**えいが[1]【映画】** ▢🔲 劇場用映画 a theater movie; a made-for-(the-)theater movie. 低予算映画 a low-budget movie. 独立系映画 an independent「film [movie]; 《口》an indie「film [movie]. ▢🔲 映画教室 a movie course 《for parents and children》. 映画ソフト movie [film] software.
**えいかいわ【英会話】** ▢🔲 英会話教室 an English conversation class.
**えいがげいじゅつかがくアカデミー【映画芸術科学—】**〔米国の〕the Academy of Motion Picture Arts and Sciences (略: AMPAS).
**えいがとうさつぼうしほう【映画盗撮防止法】**《法》the Anti-Camcording Law; the law「prohibiting [criminalizing] video-camera piracy in cinemas. ▶ 正式名称は「映画の盗撮の防止に関する法律」(the Law Concerning Prevention of the Unauthorized Recording of Cinematographic Works).
**えいがはいゆうくみあい【映画俳優組合】**〔米国の〕the Screen Actors Guild (略: SAG). ▢🔲 映画俳優組合賞 a Screen Actors Guild [a SAG] Award;〔個々の賞をまとめて〕the 《11th》Annual Screen Actors Guild Awards; the SAG Awards.
**えいきゅう【永久】** ▢🔲 永久カレンダー〔時計などの〕a perpetual calendar. 永久失格 permanent [lifetime] disqualification. ◯ 〜失格処分を受ける receive permanent disqualification; be permanently disqualified; be disqualified for the rest of *one's* life. 永久挿入《医》〔がん治療用の放射線小線源の〕permanent「implantation [insertion]. 永久氷〔地質〕〔極地などの〕permanent ice. 永久氷冠 a permanent ice cap.
**えいきゅうついほう【永久追放】**a permanent ban. 〜する ban *sb* for life. ◯ 彼は球界から〜になった。He was banned for life from professional baseball. ▢🔲 永久追放処分 punishment by banning 《a player》for life.
**えいきゅうほぞん【永久保存】** ▢🔲 永久保存版 ⇨ほぞんばん。永久保存品 an article preserved in perpetuity; a work in the permanent collection 《of the Museum of Modern Arts, New York》.
**えいぎょう【営業】** ▢🔲 営業赤字[黒字] an operating「loss [surplus]. 営業運転《begin》commercial operation. 営業禁止命令 an order to cease business; an order prohibiting business. 営業車 a commercial vehicle. 営業譲渡益 gains on《income from》(a) transfer of business. 営業職員〔生命保険会社などの〕(the) sales staff; a sales staff member; a sales staffer. 営業損益 operating income or loss. 営業損益ベース an operating level. ◯ 〜損益ベースでは30億円の赤字である。There is an operating loss of 3 billion yen. 営業停止命令 an order to suspend business. ◯ そのレストランは本日東京都知事から〜停止命令を受けた。the restaurant was today ordered to close by the Governor of Tokyo.
**エイクロイド** Aykroyd, Dan (1952– ; カナダ生まれの映画俳優; 本名 Daniel Edward Aykroyd).
**えいご[1]【英語】** ▢🔲 英語指導助手 an assistant English teacher (略: AET).

えいこう¹【曳航】 ㊀ 曳航索〔海〕a towline; a towrope; a tow cable; a towing 「line [rope, cable].
えいこく【英国】 ㊀ 英国(陸軍)特殊空挺部隊 ＝特殊空挺部隊 (⇨とくしゅ¹).
えいこくイスラムひょうぎかい【英国-評議会】〔英国内のイスラム系組織〕the Muslim Council of Britain (略: MCB).
えいこくおうりつこくさいもんだいけんきゅうじょ【英国王立国際問題研究所】⇨おうりつこくさいもんだいけんきゅうじょ.
えいこくかくねんりょうがいしゃ【英国核燃料会社】British Nuclear Fuels (略: BNFL).
えいこくきかくきょうかい【英国規格協会】the British Standards Institution (略: BSI).
「英国万歳!」〔映画〕The Madness of King George.
えいこくムスリムきょうかい【英国-協会】＝えいこくイスラムひょうぎかい.
エイサー¹〔沖縄本島の盆おどり〕a Bon Festival dance performed on Okinawa Island.
エイサー²〔台湾のコンピューター企業〕Acer (Inc).
エイサット【ASAT】＝エーサット.
えいじゅう【永住】 ㊀ 永住型マンション an apartment [a condominium] for lifelong residence.
えいしょう²【泳鐘】【動】〔クラゲの遊泳器官〕a swimming bell; an umbrella; a nectocalyx.
エイジレス ㊀ エイジレス社会〔高齢者が充実した生活を送ることができる社会〕a society for all ages; an ageless society.
エイジング〔老齢化; 経年変化〕aging; ageing.
〜する age. ㊀ エイジングケア【美容】antiaging care.
エイズ〔いきなりエイズ〕【発症してはじめてHIVの感染に気づく症例〕the onset of AIDS symptoms without a previous diagnosis of HIV infection; "sudden AIDS." ㊀ エイズ孤児 an AIDS orphan.
エイズよぼうきしだん【-予防財団】the Japanese Foundation for AIDS Prevention.
えいせい³【衛生】 ㊀ 衛生サック〔コンドーム〕a (prophylactic) condom.
えいせい⁴【衛星】 ㊀ 親(主)衛星〔人工衛星の〕a main satellite. 子(副)衛星〔人工衛星の〕a subsatellite; a sub-satellite. 地震(観測)衛星 an earthquake satellite. 月周回衛星【宇】a lunar 「orbiter [satellite]; a moon orbiter; a circumlunar 「orbiter [satellite].
㊀ 衛星インターネット satellite Internet (access [service]). 衛星攻撃兵器 an anti-satellite weapon (略: ASAT). 衛星電話 a satellite phone; 〔サービス〕satellite phone service. 〜電話回線 a satellite phone line. 衛星破壊実験 a satellite destruction test. 衛星誘導 satellite guidance. 〜誘導システム a satellite guidance system / 〜誘導弾「ミサイル」a satellite-guided 「bomb [missile].
えいせいこうぞくせい【永世皇族制】the system of unending imperial descent.
えいせいほうそう【衛星放送】 ㊀ 衛星放送事業者 a satellite broadcasting company.
えいぞう¹【映像】
㊀ 未編集映像 unedited footage; an unedited take.
㊀ 映像エンジン『電算』an 「imaging [image] engine. 映像化 (an) adaptation for the screen; production for the screen; production as a 「film [movie, video];【医】visualization. 〜〜化する adapt (a novel) for the screen; produce 《an idea》「as a video [for the screen, in a visual medium]; visualize 〜〜《この作品は〜化は不可能だと言われてきた. This work has always been said to be impossible to adapt for the screen. 映像周波数〔テレビ〕(a) video frequency. 映像ソフト visual software. 映像美 visual beauty. 映像配信 video distribution. 映像表現 expression through 「images [imagery]. 映

37　エイチティービブ

像編集〔動画の〕video editing;〔写真の〕image [photograph(y)] editing. 映像メディア (the) 「video [film] media.
えいたい¹【永代】 ㊀ 永代使用〔墓地などの〕the use in perpetuity《of a gravesite》. ㊀ 〜使用料 a fee for use in perpetuity《of a gravesite》. 永代墓 ＝永代供養墓 (⇨えいたいくよう).
えいたいくよう【永代供養】 ㊀ 永代供養墓 a grave attended to in perpetuity (by a temple on sb's behalf). 永代供養料 a fee to have services performed in perpetuity for the repose of sb's soul.
エイチ・アイ・ディー・(ヘッド)ランプ【HID-】〔自動車〕〔高電圧放電型の前照灯〕an HID 「headlamp [head-light]. ▶ HID is high-intensity discharge の略.
エイチ・アイ・ブイ【HIV】 ㊀ 抗HIV薬[剤] an anti-HIV drug.
エイチ・エー・エム【HAM】【医】⇨ハム⁴.
エイチ・エー・ディー・エス【HADS】【医】〔患者が病院で感じる抑うつ・不安についての調査票〕HADS; the Hospital Anxiety Depression Scale.
エイチ・エー・ブイ・アイ【HAVi】〔家庭用AV機器・情報家電の相互接続のための規格〕HAVi. ▶ Home Audio /Video interoperability の略.
エイチ・エス・エス・ティー【HSST】〔常電導磁気浮上式リニアモーターカーのシステム名〕HSST; High Speed Surface Transport.
エイチ・エス・ビー・シー【HSBC】〔英国の銀行グループ〕HSBC; HSBC Holdings plc.
エイチ・エフ・シー【HFC】〔化〕＝ハイドロフルオロカーボン.
エイチ・エム・アール【HMR】〔家庭料理の代用となる調理済み食品や総菜〕(an) HMR;〔その販売所〕an HMR shop.
エイチ・エム・オー【HMO】〔米国の医療組織〕an HMO; a health maintenance organization.
エイチ・エム・ディー【HMD】〔ヘッド・マウント・ディスプレー〕an HMD; a head-mounted display.
エイチかぶ【H株】＝香港H株 (⇨ホンコン).
エイチかぶしすう【H株指数】〔証券〕〔香港の株式市場におけるハンセン中国企業指数〕the H-share Index (略: HSI); the Hang Seng China Enterprises Index (略: HSCEI).
エイチ・ツー・エー・ロケット【H2A-】〔日本製ロケット〕an H-2A rocket; an H-II A.
エイチ・ツー・ロケット【H2-】〔日本製ロケット〕an H-II launch vehicle.
エイチ・ディー【HD】1〔電算〕〔ハードディスク〕a hard disk. 2〔過酷な使用に耐えうる〕heavy-duty. ㊀ HD車 a heavy-duty vehicle.
エイチ・ディー・アール【HDR】〔人道援助用保存食〕humanitarian daily rations (略: HDRs).
エイチ・ディー・アイ【HDI】＝人間開発指数 (⇨にんげん).
エイチ・ディー・エム・アイ【HDMI】〔商標〕〔高精細映像等の機器の接続規格〕HDMI; High-Definition Multi-media Interface.
エイチ・ティー・エム・エル【HTML】 ㊀ HTML言語 the HTML language. HTMLメール (an) HTML e-mail.
エイチ・ディー・ディー【HDD】 ㊀ HDD内蔵 〜内蔵DVD レコーダー a DVD recorder with a built-in hard disk. HDDナビ〔自動車〕an HDD car navigation system.
エイチ・ディー・ティー・ブイ【HDTV】〔テレビ〕〔高品位テレビ〕HDTV; high-definition 「television [TV].
エイチ・ディー・ディー・ブイ・ディー【HDDVD】〔商標〕〔DVDの次世代の光ディスク〕HDDVD;〔1枚の〕an HDDVD. ▶ high-definition DVD の略.
エイチ・ティー・ブイ【HTV】〔宇宙〕〔宇宙航空研究開発機構 (JAXA) の宇宙ステーション補給機〕an HTV; an

エイチビーエスこうたい

H-II Transfer Vehicle.
エイチ・ビー・エスこうたい【HBs抗体】《生化》〔B型肝炎表面抗体〕hepatitis B surface antigen; HBsAg.
エイチ・ビー・シー【HBc】《生化》〔B型肝炎ウイルスコアたんぱく質〕HBc; hepatitis B core. ⇨ **HBc抗原** hepatitis B core antigen; HBcAg.
エイチ・ピー・ブイ【HPV】《医》〔ヒト・パピローマ・ウイルス〕HPV; human papilloma virus.
エイチ・ユー・エス【HUS】《医》〔溶血性尿毒症症候群〕HUS; hemolytic [haemolytic] uremic syndrome.
エイド[2]【AID】《医》〔非配偶者間人工受精〕AID; artificial insemination by donor. ⇨ **AID児、エイド児** an AID child.
えいびん【鋭敏】 ⇨ 鋭敏化《医・心理・金属加工》sensitization. ▷ sensitize v.
エイブラハムズ Abrahams, Jim (1944– ; 米国の映画監督・脚本家).
エイブラムズ《米軍》〔米軍の主力戦車 M1 の愛称〕an Abrams.
えいゆう[1]【英雄】 ⇨ 英雄視 〇 ~視する regard (sb) as a hero / ~視されて be regarded as a hero.
「英雄の条件」〔映画〕Rules of Engagement.
えいよう[1]【栄養】 ⇨ 経管栄養《医》tube [enteral] feeding. 〇 栄養アドバイザー a nutrition advisor. 〇 スポーツ~アドバイザー a certified sports nutrition advisor (略: CSNA). 栄養管理 nutrition(al) management. 栄養情報担当者〔栄養に関する正確な情報・知識を有し、それを消費者に提供・伝達することを業務とする人〕a nutritional representative (略: NR).
えいようサポートチーム【栄養-】〔病院の〕a nutrition support team (略: NST).
えいようしほう【栄養士法】《法》the Nutritionists Law.
えいようほじょしょくひんけんこうきょういくほう【栄養補助食品健康教育法】《米法》the Dietary Supplement Health and Education Act (略: DSHEA).
えいり[2]【営利】 ⇨ 営利目的 《for》commercial purposes. 〇 ~目的でのご利用はご遠慮ください。Please refrain from using 《this product》for commercial purposes. 営利目的所持〔麻薬・覚醒剤などの〕possession 《of drugs》for commercial use. 営利目的密輸入〔麻薬・覚醒剤などの〕smuggling [illegal importation] 《of contraband goods》for「commercial purposes [profit]. 営利(目的)略取 abduction [kidnapping] for profit.
エイロス【ALOS】⇨りくいきかんそくぎじゅつえいせい.
エインズレイ《商標》〔英国の陶磁器ブランド〕Aynsley.
「A.I.」〔映画〕Artificial Intelligence: AI.
エー・アイ・エス【AIS】〔船舶自動識別装置〕an AIS. ▶ automatic identification system の略.
エー・アイ・シー・オー【AICO】〔ASEAN 産業協力スキーム〕the ASEAN Industrial Cooperation Scheme.
エー・アイ・ビー・しょくひんあんぜんとうごうきじゅん【AIB 食品安全統合基準】〔米国 AIB による食品工場の食品安全管理基準〕the AIB Consolidated Standards for Food Safety. ▶ AIB is American Institute of Baking (米国製パン研究所) の略; 現在は AIB International という.
ええい 〇 ~, こうなりゃもうなるようになれ. Well, that's that, and I don't care what happens next. / ~, 一か八かでやってみよう. Okay, let's give it a shot like this.
エー・イー・ディー【AED】〔自動体外式除細動器〕an AED; an automated external defibrillator.
エー・エー・アール・ピー【AARP】〔米国の高齢者団体〕AARP. ▶ 本来の名称は the American Association of Retired Persons (アメリカ [全米] 退職者協会) であるが、50 歳以上を対象とする会員総数に占める退職者の比率減少に伴い, 1999年に略称を正式名称とした.
エー・エス・アール【ASR】 1【精神医】〔急性災害症候群ストレス反応〕ASR; acute stress reaction. 2〔自動車〕〔タイヤのスリップを防ぐ装置〕ASR; anti-slip regulation.
エー・エス・ディー【ASD】《医》〔急性ストレス障害〕(an) ASD; (an) acute stress disorder.
エー・エス・ピー【ASP】〔ネット経由のソフトの提供〕ASP; application service provision;〔提供業者〕an ASP; an application service provider.
エー・エス・ブイ【ASV】〔先進安全自動車〕an ASV. ▶ advanced safety vehicle の略.
エー・エフ・シー【AFC】〔アメリカン・カンファレンス〕.
エー・エフ・シー・チャンピオンズリーグ【AFC-】〔サッカー〕the AFC Champions League (略: ACL). ▶ AFC は Asian Football Confederation (アジアサッカー連盟) の略.
エー・エフ・ティー・エー【AFTA】〔ASEAN 自由貿易地域〕AFTA; the ASEAN Free Trade Area.
エー・エフ・ディー・ビー【AfDB】〔アフリカ開発銀行〕the AfDB; the African Development Bank.
エー・エム・エスたんねんだいそくてい【AMS 炭素年代測定】《考古》⇨エー・エム・エスほう.
エー・エム・エスほう【AMS 法】《考古》〔加速器質量分析法; 放射性炭素年代測定の1つ〕AMS; accelerator mass spectrometry.
エー・エム・オー・エル・イー・ディー【AMOLED】〔電子工学〕〔アクティブマトリックス式有機発光ダイオード〕an AMOLED; an active-matrix organic light-emitting diode; an active-matrix OLED.
エー・エム・ディー・エー【AMDA】=アムダ.
エー・エル・エム【ALM】《金融》〔資産負債管理〕ALM; asset-liability management.
エー・エル・ティー【ALT】〔外国語指導助手〕an ALT; an assistant language teacher.
エー・オー・アール【AOR】 1〔大人向けのロック〕AOR; adult-oriented rock. 2〔レコードアルバム放送中心のロック〕AOR; album-oriented rock.
エー・オー・シー【AOC】〔フランスワインの原産地統制呼称〕AOC. ▶ AOC は フランス語 *appellation d'origine contrôlée* (=controlled name of origin) の略.
エー・かぶ【A株】an A-share. [=上海 A 株 (⇨シャンハイ), 深圳 A 株 (⇨しんせん)]
エー・ケー・ティー【Akt】《生化》〔たんぱく質燐酸化酵素〕Akt. ▶ PKB とも呼ばれる 〇 ~47【AK(-)47】《軍》〔ソ連製の突撃銃〕an AK-47. ▶ 設計者の名から カラシニコフ Kalashnikov とも呼ばれる.
エーサット【ASAT】〔衛星攻撃兵器〕an ASAT; an anti-satellite weapon.
エー・シー・イーそがいやく【ACE 阻害薬】《薬》=アンジオテンシン変換酵素阻害薬 (⇨アンジオテンシン).
エー・ジー・エフ【AGF】《生化》〔肝臓から分泌されるたんぱく質〕AGF; angiopoietin-related growth factor.
エー・シー・ジーゆでん【ACG 油田】〔アゼルバイジャンのカスピ海沿岸にある海底油田〕the ACG oil field. ▶ Azeri (アゼリ), Chirag (チラグ), Gunashli (グナシリ) の3つの油田から成る.
エース 〇 エース・ショット an ace (shot).
エースそがいやく【ACE 阻害薬】《薬》=アンジオテンシン変換酵素阻害薬 (⇨アンジオテンシン).
エーストップ【ASTOP】〔アジア不拡散協議〕the Asian Senior-Level Talks on Non-Proliferation.
エー・ソれんがた【A-連型】《医》〔インフルエンザ・ウイルスの〕the type-A Russian「flu [influenza] virus.
エー・ディー・アイ【ADI】〔許容1日 [一日] 摂取量〕ADI; an [the] acceptable daily intake.
エー・ティー・アンド・ティー【AT&T】〔米国の電気通信会社〕AT&T Corp.
エー・ディー・エー【ADA】《化》〔アデノシン・デアミナーゼ〕ADA; adenosine deaminase.
エー・ディー・エーけっそんしょう【ADA 欠損症】《医》

〔アデノシンデアミナーゼ欠損症〕ADA deficiency; adenosine deaminase deficiency.

エー・ティー・エス・ピー【ATS-P】〘鉄道〙〔改良型自動列車停止装置〕ATS-P. ▶ automatic train stop-pattern の略.

エー・ディー・エル【ADL】〘医〙〔日常生活動作〕an ADL; an activity of daily living.

エー・ティー・シー・シー【ATCC】〘商標〙〔米国の微生物系統保存機関〕ATCC; American Type Culture Collection.

エー・ティー(しゃ)げんていめんきょ【AT(車)限定免許】〔自動車・オートバイの〕a「*driver's license [''driving licence] limited to vehicles with automatic transmissions.

エー・ティー・ピー【ATP】 □▶ ATP ランキング 《テニス》(an) ATP ranking.

エー・ディー・ピー【ADP】 □▶ ADP リボース 《生化》ADP(-)ribose. ◯ ポリ〜リボース poly(ADP-ribose). ▶ 括弧が必要. ADP リボシル化 ADP(-)ribosylation.

エー・ティー・ブイ【ATV】〘宇宙〙〔欧州宇宙機関 (ESA) の宇宙ステーション補給機〕an ATV; an Automated Transfer Vehicle.

エー・ビー・アイ【ABI】〘医〙〔上腕と足首の血圧比〕an ABI; an ankle brachial index.

エー・ピー・アイ【API】 □▶ API 度〔米国石油協会の原油比重指標〕the API degree; an API degree《of 32》.

エー・ビー・エー【ABA】〘心理〙〔応用行動分析〕ABA; applied behavior analysis.

エー・ビー・エヌ・アムロ【ABN AMRO】〔オランダの銀行〕ABN AMRO Bank.

エー・ピー・エフ・エス【APFS】〔在日外国人の相互扶助・自立支援を目的とする国際交流団体〕APFS; the Asian People's Friendship Society.

エー・ビー・エル【ABL】〘動産担保融資〙ABL; asset-based lending.

エー・ピー・テスト【AP-】〘教育〙〔米国で, 高校生対象の〕an「AP [Advanced Placement] Exam.

エー・ブイ【AV】 □▶ AV 男優 a male video porn star; a porno actor; an actor in X-rated videos.

エー・ブイ・シー・エス【AVCS】〘自動車〙〔可変バルブタイミング機構の一種〕AVCS; active valve control system.

エーペック【APEC】 □▶ APEC 閣僚会議 an APEC ministerial conference. APEC 財務相〔財務大臣〕会議 an APEC finance ministers meeting. APEC 首脳会議 an APEC summit meeting. APEC ビジネス諮問委員会 the APEC Business Advisory Council《略: ABAC》. APEC 貿易相〔貿易担当大臣〕会議 an APEC trade ministers meeting.

エー・ホンコンがた【A 香港型】〘医〙〔インフルエンザ・ウイルスの〕(influenza virus) type A Hong Kong [A/Hong Kong] (H3N2).

エーメック・スリー【AMEC3】〔高度救命救急センター〕an Advanced Medical Emergency Critical Care Center.

エール[1] □▶ リアル・エール〔伝統的製法で樽の中で発酵させてのままで生ビール〕real ale.

エオリアしょとう【-諸島】〔イタリア南部, シチリア島近くの諸島〕the Aeolian Islands.

エカーズリー Eckersley, Dennis (1954– ; 米国の野球選手).

えがすり【絵絣】figured *kasuri* weave.

えき[4]〘液〙 □▶ 液density (a) liquid density.

えき[5]〘駅〙

□▶ 橋上駅(舎) an elevated station (building). 高架駅(舎) a station (building) under an elevated「*railroad [''railway]. 地下駅(舎) an underground [a subterranean] station (building); an underground station. 駅スタンプ〔駅に置かれた記念スタンプ〕a station stamp; a commemorative rubber stamp issued by a train station. 駅売店 a (railway) station kiosk. 駅貼り〘広告〙〔ホームなどに有料でポスターを貼る宣伝〕in-station advertising. 駅メロ「station (platform) [departure] melody; the melody sounded on a station platform just before the doors of a train are closed.

えぎ, エギ【餌木】〘釣り〙〔アオリイカ釣りのためのルアー〕an oval-squid lure; a bigfin reef squid lure. □▶ エギロッド〔エギを付ける釣り竿〕a fishing rod for use with「oval-squid [bigfin reef squid] lures; a squid-lure (fishing) rod.

えきがく[2]〘疫学〙 □▶ 運動疫学 exercise epidemiology. 分子疫学〘医〙molecular epidemiology. 民族疫学〘医〙ethno-epidemiology. □▶ 疫学(的)研究 epidemiological research; 〔1 件の〕an epidemiological「study [investigation].

えきしょう【液晶】 □▶ 液晶駆動(用)IC〔電子工学〕a liquid crystal driver IC. 液晶ドライバー〔電子工学〕a liquid crystal driver. 液晶フィルム liquid crystal film. 液晶プロジェクター an LCD [a liquid-crystal-display] projector. 液晶モニター a liquid crystal monitor.

エキストラ □▶ エキストラ登録〔フィルム・コミッションなどへの〕(movie) extra registration.

エキセメスタン〘薬〙〔乳がん治療薬〕exemestane. ▶ 商品名 アロマシン.

えきたい【液体】 □▶ 液体火薬〘爆薬〙(a) liquid explosive. 液体物検査装置〔空港などで, 瓶内の液体の引火性などを調べる装置〕a bottled liquid checker.

えきだし【益出し】〘株式〙realizing current profits by selling stocks in hand.

えきちゅうかんそうほう【液中乾燥法】〘化・工〙in-liquid drying.

えきでん【駅伝】 □▶ 出雲駅伝 the Izumo *ekiden*. ▶ 正式名称は 出雲全日本大学選抜駅伝競走.

えきナカ【駅-】〔駅の構内〕the interior of a station;《retail shops》'inside [within] a station. □▶ 駅ナカ店 a retail shop inside a station; an in-station「store [shop]. 駅ナカビジネス (an) in-station business.

えきべん【駅弁】 □▶ 駅弁フェア〘祭り〙an "ekiben" fair; a special sale of famous kinds of "ekiben" from around the country.

えきまえ【駅前】 □▶ 駅前集積〘商業施設などの〙concentration [accumulation]《of commercial facilities》around a railroad station.

えぎんぐ, エギング【餌木-】〘釣り〙〔エギを使ったアオリイカ釣り〕squid-lure fishing.

エクイティー □▶ 擬似エクイティー〘金融〙quasi-equity.

エクエーターげんそく【-原則】〔途上国での開発プロジェクト融資に金融機関が環境・社会配慮を組み込んだもの〕the Equator Principles.

エクササイズ □▶ エクササイズ・ボール ＝バランス・ボール. エクササイズ・マシ(ー)ン an exercise machine; a training machine.

エクステ〔付け毛〕a hair extension; extension hair.

エクストリーム・アイロニング〔野外の極限状況においてアイロンをかけるスポーツ〕extreme ironing.

エクストリーム・スポーツ〔インラインスケート・スケートボード・BMX などのスポーツの総称〕extreme sports.

エクスパンション・ドラフト〘野球〙＝拡張ドラフト (⇨かくちょう[1]).

エクスペリエンス・カーブ〘経〙〔経験曲線〕the experience curve.

エクスマウス〔ウェスタン・オーストラリア州北西部の町〕Exmouth.

「エグゼクティブ・デシジョン」〘映画〙Executive Decision.

エクソン・フロリオじょうこう【-条項】〔外国企業による国家安全保障を損なうような企業買収などを阻止しうる権限を大統領に与え, 米国包括通商法の規定〕the Exon-Florio「amendment [provision].

## え

**エクパット・インターナショナル**【ECPAT-】=こくさいエクパット.

**エクリチュール**〖<F écriture〗〖書くこと〗writing;〔書かれたもの; 文書〕writing; written work.

**エクルストン** Eccleston, Christopher (1964- ; 英国の映画俳優).

**エケベリア**〖植〗〔ベンケイソウ科エケベリア属 (*Echeveria*) の各種の草本〕an Echeveria.

**エコ**
　**エコ効率** eco-efficiency. **エコシティー**〔環境共生都市〕an ʳeco(-)city [Eco(-)city]. **エコセメント** ecocement; ecoconcrete. **エコテクノロジー**〔地球環境の保護に役立ち経済効用もある科学技術〕ecotechnology. **エコトイレ**〔環境に負荷をかけない〕an ecological toilet; an environment(ally) friendly toilet. **エコドライブ**〔環境に配慮した車の運転方法〕eco-friendly driving (techniques). **エコハウス**〔環境共生住宅〕environmentally friendly housing. **エコバッグ**〔ごみになるスーパーのレジ袋の代わりに持参する買い物袋〕an ecological (shopping) bag; a reusable (cotton or canvas) shopping bag. **エコファーマー**〔環境保全型農業に取り組む生産者〕an ecofarmer. ▷ ecofarming *n*. **エコマテリアル**〔環境〕〔環境負荷が少ない素材〕an environmentally-friendly material; an eco-material; a green ⦅building⦆ material. **エコミュージアム**〔生活環境博物館〕an ecomuseum.

**エコーネット**【ECHONET】〔日本の大手電機メーカーなどが提唱する家庭内の電灯線や無線を利用したネットワーク規格〕ECHONET. ▶ ECHONET は Energy Conservation and Homecare Network の略.

**エゴグラム**〖心理〗〔性格分析法の1つ〕an egogram.

**エコブリッジ**〔森林を切り開いて道路を作る場合に, 動物が道路を越えて渡れるようにする橋〕an "ecobridge"; an animal overpass.

**エコマネー**〔様々なボランティア活動に対して支払われる地域通貨〕a ʳlocal [community] currency. ▫ **電子エコマネー** local e-money.

**エコライト**〔温室効果ガス排出権〕an [a carbon] emission(s) credit; a carbon credit; the right to emit greenhouse gases.

**エコリーフかんきょうラベル**【-環境-】〔環境ラベルの一種〕an EcoLeaf environmental label.

**エコロジー**　▫ **エコロジー住宅** an eco-house; an ecological house; an eco-friendly house.

**エコロジカル・フットプリント**〔人間が生態系に与える悪影響〕an ecological footprint.

**えさ**【餌】▫ **餌釣り** =えづり. **餌やり** feeding; provisioning. ◐ 旅行中の猫の～やりを隣の人に頼んだ. I asked my neighbor to feed my cat while I was traveling.

**エジプト・マングース**〖動〗an ichneumon; an Egyptian mongoose; *Herpestes ichneumon*.

**えず**【絵図】▫ **切〔切り〕絵図**〔全体図の一部分の絵図〕a sectional map.

**エス・アール・アイ**【SRI】▫ **SRI インデックス**〔社会的責任投資指数〕an SRI index.

**エス・アール・エス**【SRS】〖自動車〗an SRS air bag. ▶ SRS は supplemental restraint system (補助的拘束装置) の略.

**エス・アイ・エス**【SIS】〔英国の諜報機関〕the Special Intelligence Service. 〔⇨エム・アイ・シックス〕

**エス・アイち**【SI 値】〖地震〗〔揺れが建物に与える影響を数値化したもの〕an ʳSI [spectral intensity] value.

**エス・イー・ディー**【SED】〔電子工学〕〔表面伝導型電子放出素子ディスプレー〕an SED; a surface-conduction electron-emitter display. ▫ **SED テレビ** an SED ʳtelevision [TV].

**エス・エー・アール**【SAR】**1**〔携帯電話端末が発する電波の比吸収率〕an SAR; a specific absorption rate. **2**〔宇宙・空〕〔合成開口レーダー; 飛行機・衛星に搭載〕(an)

SAR; (a) synthetic-aperture radar.

**エス・エー・エー・エス**【SaaS】〔ネット経由でソフトの中から自分に必要な機能だけを選択して利用できるサービス〕SaaS; Software as a Service.

**エス・エー・エス**【SAS】〔英国陸軍の特殊挺部隊〕the SAS; the Special Air Service.

**エス・エー・シー・ディー**【SACD】〖音響〗〔スーパーオーディオ CD〕an SACD. ▶ Super Audio CD の略. ▫ **SACD プレーヤー** an SACD player.

**エス・エー・ビー・ミラー**【SAB-】〔英国に本社があり, 米国 Miller 社などを傘下に持つビール会社〕SABMiller plc.

**エス・エス・アール・アイ**【SSRI】〖薬〗〔選択的セロトニン再取り込み阻害薬; 抗うつ薬〕SSRI; a selective serotonin reuptake inhibitor.

**エス・エスつうしん**【SS 通信】〖通信〗=スペクトラムかくさんつうしん.

**エス・エス・ディー・エス**【SSDS】〔社会・人口統計体系〕SSDS; a system of social and demographic statistics.

**エス・エヌ・エス**【SNS】〖電算〗〔ソーシャル・ネットワーキング・サービス〕an SNS; a social networking service.

**エス・エヌ・ピー**【SNP】〖生物〗〔一塩基多型〕SNP; single nucleotide polymorphism. 〔=スニップ〕

**エス・エム・エー**【SMA】=セパレートリー・マネージド・アカウント.

**エス・エム・エス**【SMS】〖通信〗=ショート・メッセージ・サービス〔⇨ショート[3]〕. ▫ **SMS 拒否機能** an SMS rejection function. **SMS 送信通数制限** an SMS message limit.

**エス・エム・オー**【SMO】〔治験施設支援機関〕an SMO; a site management organization.

**エス・エム・スリー**【SM-3】〖軍〗〔迎撃ミサイル〕a SM-3. ▶ Standard Missile-3 の略.

**エス・エム・ワイ・ディーさん**【SMYD3】〖遺伝〗〔メチル基転移酵素〕the SET and MYND domain protein (SMYD).

**エス・エル・シー**【SLC】〖電算〗〔高密度配線基板〕an SLC; a surface laminar circuit.

**エス・オー・エフ**【SOF】〖化〗〔可溶性有機成分〕SOF; (a) soluble organic fraction.

**エス・オー・シー**【SoC】〖電算〗SoC; system-on-chip.

**エス・キュー・エル**【SQL】▫ **SQL インジェクション**〔データベースを不正に操作するプログラムの1つ〕(an) SQL injection. **SQL スラマー**〔コンピューターウイルスの1つ〕SQL Slammer.

**エスきゅうライセンス**【S 級-】〖サッカー〗〔日本サッカー協会 (JSA) 公認の指導者免許〕the JFA's Grade S license.

**えずく**【嘔吐く】〔吐く〕vomit; disgorge; 〔吐きそうになる〕feel ʳnauseous [nauseated, nausea, queasy, sick]; retch.

**エスクロー**　▫ **エスクロー・サービス**〔インターネット上の取引の個人向け仲介サービス〕an escrow service.

**エス・ケー・ユー**【SKU】〖商〗〔在庫管理〔保管〕単位〕SKU. ▶ stockkeeping unit の略.

**エスコ**【ESCO】〔企業に対して省エネルギー診断やエネルギー効率の改善提案を行うこと〕ESCO. ▶ energy service company の略.

**エス・ジー・マーク**【SG-】〔日本の製品安全マーク〕an SG mark. ▶ SG は和製英語 safety goods の略.

**エス・シー・ユー**【SCU】〖医〗〔専門別集中治療病棟〕(an) SCU; a special care unit; 〔脳卒中集中治療室〕(an) SCU; a stroke care unit.

**エスじょうけっちょう**【S 状結腸】▫ **S 状結腸がん**〖医〗(a) cancer of the sigmoid colon; (a) sigmoid colon cancer.

**エス・ティー・エス**【STS】〔科学技術社会論〕STS; science, technology, (and) society.

**エス・ディー・エス・エスけいかく**【SDSS 計画】〔日米共同の宇宙地図作成計画〕the Sloan Digital Sky Survey Project.

エス・ティー・エヌ【STN】 ◻ STN 液晶 (an) STN liquid crystal.
エス・ディー・エム・アイ【SDMI】〔オンライン音楽配信における著作権保護計画〕the SDMI; the Secure Digital Music Initiative.
エス・ティーしすう【ST 指数】〖証券〗＝ストレーツ・タイムズしすう.
エス・ティー・ディー【STD】 ◻ STD 感染 (an) STD infection.
エス・ディー・ティー・ブイ【SDTV】〖テレビ〗〔高品位テレビ(HDTV)に対して標準テレビ〕SDTV; standard-definition「television [TV].
エス・ディー・ラム【SDRAM】〖電算〗〔同期型随時書き込み読み出しメモリー〕SDRAM; synchronous DRAM; synchronous dynamic random access memory.
エスティ・ローダー〖商標〗〔米国の化粧品ブランド〕Estée Lauder.
エステヴェス Estevez, Emilio (1962- ; 米国の映画俳優; マーティン・シーンの子).
エステベス ＝エステヴェス.
エストラ(ー)ダ Estrada, Joseph (1937- ; フィリピンの政治家; 大統領 [1998-2001]).
エストラサイト〖商標・薬〗〔女性ホルモン剤・抗腫瘍薬〕Estracyt.
エスバンド【S-】〖通信〗〔周波数帯域の１つ〕the S-band.
エス・ビー・アイ・アール【SBIR】〔中小企業技術革新制度〕SBIR; the Small Business Innovation Research program.
エス・ピー・イーぶた【SPE 豚】〔特定病原菌不在豚〕a specific pathogen free pig.
エス・ピー・エー【SPA】〔アパレル製造小売り専門業者〕an SPA; a specialty store retailer of private label apparel.
エス・ピー・ティー【SPT】〔空港での渡航手続きの簡素化〕SPT; Simplifying Passenger Travel; Simplified Passenger Travel.
えぞばふんうに【蝦夷馬糞胆】〖動〗〔オオバフンウニ科のウニ〕a species of short-spined sea urchin.
えぞひぐま【蝦夷羆】〖動〗a Hokkaido (brown) bear; *Ursus arctos yesoensis*.
えぞむしくい【蝦夷虫喰】〖鳥〗〔ヒタキ科ウグイス亜科の鳥〕a pale-legged「leaf-warbler [willow warbler]; *Phylloscopus tenellipes*.
えぞももんが【蝦夷鼯鼠】〖動〗〔リス科の動物, タイリクモモンガの亜種〕a Russian flying squirrel; *Pteromys volans orii*.
エタネルセプト〖薬〗〔関節リウマチ治療薬〕etanercept.
エタノール ◻ セルロース・エタノール cellulosic ethanol. ◻ エタノール混合ガソリン ethanol-blended gasoline. エタノール混合燃料 ethanol-blended fuel.
えだみどりいし【枝みどり石】〖動〗〔ミドリイシ科のサンゴ〕*Acropora tumida*.
エチオピアおおかみ【-狼】〖動〗an Ethiopian wolf; *Canis simensis*. [＝アビシニア・ジャッカル]
エチオピアじんみんかくめいみんしゅせんせん【-人民革命民主戦線】〔エチオピアの政党連合〕the Ethiopian People's Revolutionary Democratic Front (略: EPRDF).
えちぜんくらげ【越前水母】〖動〗〔ビゼンクラゲ科の大型クラゲ〕an Echizen jellyfish; a Nomura's jellyfish; *Stomolophus nomurai*.
エチニルエストラジオール〖薬〗〔女性ホルモン剤・抗腫瘍薬〕ethinylestradiol; ethinyl estradiol (略: EE).
エチル・ターシャリー・ブチル・エーテル〖化〗〔ガソリン混入剤〕ethyl tertiary-butyl ether (略: ETBE).
えっきょう【越境】 ◻ 越境汚染〔越境公害〕trans-boundary [cross-border, transborder] pollution. 越境酸性雨〔国境を越えて降る酸性雨〕cross-border [transborder] acid rain. 越境者 an illegal immigrant;

a border jumper. 越境テロ cross-border terrorism.
えっきょう[2]【越僑】〔海外在住ベトナム人〕an overseas Vietnamese; a Viet kieu.
エックス【X】 ◻ X 理論〖経営〗Theory X.
エックス・エー・エフ・エス【XAFS】〖化〗〔X 線吸収微細構造〕XAFS; X-ray absorption fine structure.
エックス・エス【XS】〔物品のサイズ〕XS.
エックス・エム・エム・ニュートン【XMM-】〖宇宙〗〔欧州宇宙機関の X 線観測衛星〕the XMM-Newton (X-ray Observatory).
エックス・エル【XL】〔物品のサイズ〕XL.
エックス・ゲームズ【X-】〖スポーツ〗〔スケートボードなどの競技大会〕(the) X Games. ◻ エクストリーム・スポーツ.
エックス・ジー・エー【XGA】〖電算〗〔画面規格〕XGA. ▶ 1024×768 ドット; extended graphics array の略.
エックスせん【X 線】
◻ X 線画像診断 (an) x-ray (image) diagnosis. ◻ デジタル～画像診断 digital x-ray diagnosis. X 線吸収微細構造〖化〗X-ray absorption fine structure (略: XAFS). マイクロ X 線 CT ⇨ マイクロ・シー・ティー. X 線自由電子レーザー an X-ray free electron laser (略: XFEL). X 線センサー〖電子工学〗an X-ray sensor. X 線断層撮影〖医〗X-ray「computed tomography [CT]. X 線探知器 an X-ray detector. X 線透視 (X-ray) fluoroscopy. ◻ ～透視画像 (a) [(an) X-ray] fluoroscopic image / ～透視検査 (a) [(an) X-ray] fluoroscopic examination. X 線微少熱量計〖天〗a high-resolution X-ray spectrometer (略: XRS). X 線フラッシュ〖天・物〗an X-ray flash (略: XRF). X 線分光(法)〖物〗X-ray「spectrometry [spectroscopy].
エックス・プライズ【X-】〖宇宙〗〔民間による宇宙開発促進のための賞金〕the [an] X Prize. ▶ 2004 年, スペースシップワン (SpaceShipOne) が初めて獲得.
「X-メン」〖映画〗X-Men.
エックスリーグ【X-】〔日本の, アメリカンフットボール社会人リーグ〕the X-league.
エッグ・タイマー〔ゆで卵用のタイマー〕an egg timer.
エッグノッグ〔卵・牛乳・砂糖などをかきまぜてつくる飲み物; しばしばラム酒・ブランデーなどを加える〕eggnog.
えつけ【絵付け】 ◻ 絵付け職人 a ceramics painter.
えっけんがっぺい【越県合併】⇨がっぺい.
エッジワース・カイパー・ベルト〖天〗the Edgeworth-Kuiper Belt (略: EKB). [＝カイパー・ベルト] ◻ エッジワース・カイパー・ベルト天体 an Edgeworth-Kuiper Belt object (略: EKBO).
エッセイ〔随筆・小論文〕an essay.
えっそ【越訴】＝おっそ.
えっとう【越冬】 ◻ 越冬蛹〖昆〗an overwintering [a wintering, a hibernating] pupa. 越冬燕 an overwintering swallow.
えっぽくしゃ【越北者】a border crosser to the North; an intruder into the North; a South Korean who crosses the border into North Korea.
えつらん【閲覧】
◻ 閲覧(回)数〖電算〗〔インターネットのページの閲覧回数〕(the number of)「page views [hits]. 閲覧禁止 (a)「prohibition [denial] of access;〖表示〗Access「Forbidden [Prohibited]; No Access (Allowed); 〔インターネット上の〕Access Forbidden; Permission Denied. 閲覧請求 a consultation application; an application to「consult [peruse]《a register》. 閲覧制限 restrictions [limitations] on access; access restrictions; 〔図書館などでの〕restricted [limited] access《shelves》;〖表示〗Access「Restricted [Limited]. ◻ 閲覧制ソフト〖電算〗〔インターネット上の有害サイトを閲覧させないようにするソフト〕web [content] filtering software. 閲覧制度 a system of public「access [viewing]. ◻ 住民基本台帳の～制度 a system of public「access to [viewing of] the basic resident register.

えづり【餌釣り】〔釣り〕bait fishing.
エディトリアル・デザイン〔出版物における視覚表現技術〕editorial design.
エデン・プロジェクト〔英国, コーンウォールの植物園〕the Eden Project.
えど[1]〔江戸〕▣ 江戸しぐさ〔江戸町民の互いを気遣うしぐさ〕Edo「gestures [mannerisms, etiquette]. 江戸簾〔竹などの天然素材の味わいを生かすように編んだ簾〕Edo-style bamboo blinds. 江戸太神楽 one variant of a traditional performance art that features juggling and other physical stunts as well as dancing.
エドガーしょう【-賞】〔アメリカ探偵作家クラブによる推理小説・短篇小説賞〕an Edgar Allan Poe Award; an Edgar (Award);〔個々の賞をまとめて〕the Edgar Allan Poe Awards; the Edgars.
エトキシ-《化》ethoxy-.
「エド・サリバン・ショー」〔米国の, 歌謡ショー TV 番組〕The Ed Sullivan Show. ▶ 助演のネズミのトッポ・ジージョ (Topo Gigio) も人気を得た.
「エド tv」〔映画〕Ed tv.
エトポシド〔薬〕〔抗悪性腫瘍薬〕etoposide.
エドモントサウルス〔古生物〕〔草食恐竜〕an Edmontosaurus;〔属〕Edmontosaurus.
エトルタ〔フランス, ノルマンディー地方の保養地〕Etretat.
エトロ〔商標〕〔イタリアの服飾ブランド〕Etro.
エドワーズしょうこうぐん【-症候群】《医》＝エドワードしょうこうぐん.
エドワードしょうこうぐん【-症候群】《医》Edwards' syndrome.〔⇨じゅうはちトリソミー〕
エナルク〔<F〕〔フランス国立行政学院 (ENA) の卒業生〕an "enarque." 〔⇨こくりつぎょうせいがくいん〕
エナン・アーデン Henin-Hardenne, Justine (1982– ; ベルギーのテニス選手).
エナンティオルニスるい【-類】〔古生物〕〔白亜紀の鳥類〕the Enantiornithes.
エニアグラム〔実用的な性格心理学の1つ〕(the) Enneagram.
「エニイ・ギブン・サンデー」〔映画〕Any Given Sunday.
エヌ・アール・エス・アール・オー【NRSRO】〔証券〕〔米国の公認格付け機関〕an NRSRO; a nationally recognized statistical rating organization.
エヌ・アール・オー【NRO】〔国家偵察局〕米国国防省の偵察衛星情報分析機関〕the NRO; the National Reconnaissance Office.
エヌ・アイ・エイチ【NIH】〔米国の国立衛生研究所〕NIH; the (US) National Institutes of Health.
エヌ・アイ・エス・ディー・エヌ【N-ISDN】〔狭帯域ISDN〕N-ISDN; narrowband ISDN.
エヌ-アセチルグルコサミン【N-】《化》N-acetylglucosamine (略: NAG).
エヌ・イー・オー【NEO】〔天〕＝地球近傍小天体〔⇨ちきゅう[1]〕.
エヌ・イー・ピー【NEP】〔米〕＝こっかエネルギーせいさく.
エヌ・エイチ・エル【NHL】〔北米プロアイスホッケーリーグ〕the NHL; the National Hockey League.
エヌ・エイチ・ケーほうそうぎじゅつけんきゅうじょ〔NHK 放送技術研究所〕the NHK Science & Research Laboratories (略: NHK STRL).
エヌ・エー・ピー・エム【NAPM】〔全米購買部協会〕NAPM; the National Association of Purchasing Management. ▶ 全米供給管理協会 (the Institute for Supply Management, ISM) の旧称.〔⇨アイ・エス・エム〕
エヌ・エス・エフ【NSF】1《生化》〔たんぱく質〕NSF. ▶ N-ethylmaleimide-sensitive factor の略.
2〔全米科学財団〕the NSF; the National Science Foundation.
エヌ・エス・エフ・インターナショナル【NSF-】〔米国にある国際衛生財団; 公衆衛生の評価・認定を行う機関〕NSF International. ▶ NSF は National Sanitation Foundation の略. ▣ NSF 基準 an NSF standard;(one of) the NSF standards. NSF マーク〔NSF の認証マーク〕an [the] NSF mark.
エヌ・エス・ジー【NSG】〔原子力供給国グループ〕the NSG; the Nuclear Suppliers Group.
エヌ・エス・ティー【NST】〔病院の栄養サポートチーム〕NST; a nutrition support team.
エヌ・エヌ・エス・エー【NNSA】〔米国エネルギー省の核安全保障局〕NNSA; the National Nuclear Security Administration.
エヌ・エフ・エー・ティー【NFAT】《生化》〔細胞増殖に関係するたんぱく質の一種〕NFAT; the nuclear factor of activated T cells.
エヌ・エフ・エル【NFL】〔米国のナショナルフットボールリーグ〕the NFL; the National Football League. ▣ NFL ヨーロッパリーグ the NFL Europe League; NFL Europe; the NFLE; the NFLEL.
エヌ・エフ・シー【NFC】⇨ナショナル・カンファレンス.
エヌ・エム・ユー【NMU】《生化》＝ニューロメジン・ユー.
エヌ・エル・ディー【NLD】〔国民民主連盟; ミャンマーの政党〕the NLD; the National League for Democracy.
エヌ・キャップ【NCAP】〔自動車〕＝自動車アセスメント〔⇨じどうしゃ〕.
エヌ・キュー【NQ】〔思いやり指数; 共存指数〕an NQ; a network quotient. ▶ 韓国の大学教授 金武坤 (キム・ムゴン, Kim Moo-kon) の著書『NQ 人間を幸福にする「思いやり」指数』(Live by Your NQ (Network Quotient)) から.
エヌ・ケー・ティーさいぼう【NKT 細胞】《免疫》a natural killer T cell; an NKT cell.
エヌ・シー【NC】〔数値制御〕NC; numerical control. ▣ NC 工作機械〔機〕a numerically controlled [an NC, a computer-controlled] machine tool. NC 旋盤 a numerically controlled [an NC, a computer-controlled] lathe. NC プログラミング NC programming.
エヌ・ジー・オー きょうどうセンター【NGO 協働-】the NGO Collaboration Center.
エヌ・シー・ビー・エー【NCBA】〔全米肉牛生産者協会〕NCBA; the National Cattlemen's Beef Association.
エヌ・システム【N-】〔警察の自動車ナンバー自動読取り装置〕the "N-System"; an automatic vehicle license-number detection system.
エヌ・ディー・エー【NDA】〔非開示契約〕an NDA; a nondisclosure agreement. ◐〜に縛られている be bound by an NDA.
エヌ・ディー・ティー・ブイ【NDTV】〔インドのニュース専門のテレビ局〕NDTV; New Delhi Television Ltd.
エヌ・ティーばいりつ【NT 倍率】〔証券〕〔日経平均株価を東証平均株価で割った値; 市場の動向を見る指標〕the NT index; the ratio of the Nikkei average divided by the TOPIX index.
エヌ・ピー・アール【NPR】1 ＝ナショナル・パブリック・ラジオ.
2〔2002年1月に公表された米国ブッシュ政権の核態勢見直し〕the NPR; the Nuclear Posture Review.
エヌ・ビー・エム【NBM】《医》〔患者が自身について語る物語に基づく治療法〕NBM; narrative-based medicine.
エヌ・ピー・エム【NPM】〔行政・経〕〔新公共経営〕NPM; new public management.
エヌ・ピー・オー【NPO】 ▣ NPO 学校 an NPO school. NPO 銀行〔バンク〕a nonprofit bank (for NPO's). NPO 支援税制 the NPO「preferential tax [tax support] system.
エヌ・ビー・シー[2]【NBC】〔核・生物・化学〕nuclear, biological and chemical. ▣ NBC テロ NBC terrorism. NBC 兵器 NBC weapons; nuclear, biological and chemical weapons.
エヌ・ピー・ビー【NPB】＝にほんやきゅうこう.

「エネミー・オブ・アメリカ」〔映画〕Enemy of the State.
「エネミー・ライン」〔映画〕Behind Enemy Lines.
エネルギア〔旧ソ連スペースシャトル用の大型宇宙ロケット〕(the) Energia; the Energia launcher.
エネルギー
　▫ エネルギー管理士 a certified energy manager. エネルギー企業 an energy corporation. エネルギー起源(の) 〜起源 $CO_2$〔二酸化炭素〕$CO_2$ [carbon dioxide] emissions from fuel combustion; energy-derived [fossil fuel-derived] $CO_2$ / 非〜起源 $CO_2$〔二酸化炭素〕non-energy derived $CO_2$. エネルギー効率化 making 《homes》 more energy-efficient; increasing the energy-efficiency 《of homes》. エネルギー・サービス・プロバイダー〔電力・ガスなどエネルギーを一括供給・管理する業者〕an energy service provider (略: ESP). エネルギー・サイクル an energy cycle. エネルギー支援 energy「aid [assistance]《to North Korea》. エネルギー植物 plants (grown [suitable]) for bioethanol. エネルギー自給率《Japan's》 energy self-sufficiency rate. エネルギー自由化 energy deregulation. エネルギー消費効率 energy consumption efficiency;〔消費電力当たりの冷却・加熱能力を表す数値, COP〕the [a] coefficient of performance (略: COP). エネルギー多消費型産業 an energy-intensive industry. エネルギー白書 a white paper on energy;〔経済産業省資源エネルギー庁の〕Energy in Japan (2005). エネルギー変換効率 energy conversion efficiency. エネルギー利用効率《improve》energy utilization efficiency. エネルギー林 trees (grown [suitable]) for bioethanol.
エネルギーせいさくきほんほう〔-政策基本法〕〔法〕the Basic Law on Energy Policy.
「エバー・アフター」〔映画〕Ever After.
エバディ Ebadi, Shirin (1947- ；イランの弁護士・人権活動家).
エバンジェリスト 1〔福音伝道者〕an evangelist.
　2〔ある製品の心酔者で他人にそのよさを説いて回る人〕an evangelist 《for Linux》.
エピエーション・アート ＝アビエーション・アート.
エピカテキン〔化〕〔ポリフェノールの一種〕epicatechin.
エピカテキン・ガレート〔化〕〔ポリフェノールの一種〕epicatechin gallate.
エピガロカテキン〔化〕〔ポリフェノールの一種〕epigallocatechin.
エピガロカテキン・ガレート〔化〕〔ポリフェノールの一種〕epigallocatechin gallate.
えびこうりょう〔海老虹梁〕〔建〕a curved beam.
エピジェネティクス〔遺伝〕〔DNAの配列変化を伴わずに子孫や娘細胞に伝達される遺伝子機能についての研究; 後成遺伝学〕epigenetics. ▷ epigeneticist $n$.
エビデンス〔根拠・証拠〕evidence.
エビデンス・ベースト・メディスン〔医〕〔科学的根拠に基づいた医療〕evidence-based medicine (略: EBM).
エビデンドラム〔植〕〔ラン科エピデンドラム属 (Epidendrum) の植物の総称〕an epidendrum.
エピトープ〔生化〕〔抗原決定基〕an epitope.
エピネフリン ▫ エピネフリン自己注射 a self-injection of epinephrine; (an) epinephrine self-injection.
エピメテウス〔ギ神話〕Epimetheus;〔天〕〔土星の衛星〕Epimetheus.
エフ・アール・ヌ【FRN】〔変動利付債〕an FRN; a floating-rate note.
エフ・アイ・ブイ【FIV】〔獣医〕〔猫免疫不全ウイルス〕FIV; feline immunodeficiency virus.
エフ・アイ・ユー【FIU】〔金融〕〔マネー・ロンダリングなどの金融犯罪の監視を行う政府の金融情報機関〕an FIU; a financial intelligence unit. ▶ 日本では金融庁の特定金融情報室に相当.
エフ・イー・ディー【FED】〔電子工学〕〔電界放出ディスプレー〕an FED; a field emission display.

えふうとう〔絵封筒〕an *efūtō*; an envelope illustrated with a drawing by the sender.
エフ・エー【FA】 ▫ FA機器 FA equipment. FA部品 FA「components [parts].
エフ・エー・エー【FAA】〔米国の連邦航空局〕FAA; the Federal Aviation Administration.
エフ・エー・エス【FAS】〔医〕〔胎児(性)アルコール症候群〕FAS; fetal alcohol syndrome.
エフ・エス【FS】〔連邦規格; 米国政府が調達する物品の規格〕FS. ▶ Federal Standards の略.
エフ・エス・ケー【FSK】〔通信〕〔周波数偏移符号化(方式)〕FSK; frequency shift keying.
エフ・エス・ピー【FSP】〔優良顧客対応プログラム; 顧客の会員化・特典供与により頻繁な来店を促すシステムなど〕a frequent shoppers program.
エフェドラ〔生薬〕ephedra.
エフ・エフ・ピー【FFP】1〔薬〕〔新鮮凍結血漿〕FFP; fresh frozen plasma.
　2〔利用回数の多い旅客を優遇する制度〕a frequent 「flyers [fliers] program (略: FFP).
エフ・エム【FM】 ▫ FM文字多重放送 FM multiplex「broadcasting [telecasting].
エフ・エムけいやく【FM契約】＝フルメンテナンスけいやく.
エフ・エムざい【FM剤】〔摩擦調整剤〕a friction modifier.
エフ・エム・シー【FMC】〔通信〕〔固定・携帯融合〕FMC; fixed mobile convergence.
エフ・エム・ディー【FMD】〔医〕〔線維筋性異形成(症)〕FMD; fibromuscular dysplasia.
エフ・オー・イー・ジャパン【FoE Japan】〔環境NGO〕FoE Japan. ▶ FoE は Friends of the Earth の略.
エフ・オー・エム・シー【FOMC】〔米国の連邦公開市場委員会〕the FOMC; the Federal (Reserve) Open Market Committee.
エフ・ケー【FK】〔サッカー〕〔フリー・キック〕an FK; a free kick.
エフ・シー【FC】〔フランチャイズ・チェーン〕an FC; a franchise chain.
エフ・シー・エス【FCS】〔軍〕〔火器管制装置〕FCS; a fire control system.
エフ・ジー・シー【FGC】〔女性性器切除〕FGC; female genital cutting.
エフじこう【f字孔】〔楽器〕〔バイオリンなどの〕an f-hole.
エフ・ティー【FT】〔医〕〔卵管鏡下卵管形成術〕FT; falloposcopic tuboplasty.
エフ・ティー・エー【FTA】〔自由貿易協定〕an FTA; a free trade agreement. 二国間[地域]FTA a「bilateral [regional] free trade agreement.
エフ・ティー・エー・エー【FTAA】〔米州自由貿易地域〕the FTAA; the Free Trade Area of the Americas.
エフ・ティー・エス・イー【FTSE】〔英国の経済紙 The Financial Times とロンドン証券取引所の合弁会社〕FTSE; FTSE International Ltd.; (通称) Footsie. ▶ FTSE は the Financial Times and the Stock Exchange の略. ▫ **FTSE4** グッド・グローバル・インデックス〔投資家向けに, 企業の社会的責任を評価した指標〕the FTSE4Good Global Index.
エフ・ティー・エス・イー・ひゃくしゅそうごうかぶかしすう【FTSE100 種総合株価指数】＝エフ・ティーひゃくしゅへいきんかぶかしすう.
エフ・ディー・エム【FDM】〔通信〕〔周波数分割多重方式〕FDM; frequency-division multiplexing.
エフ・ティーごうせい【FT合成】〔化〕〔一酸化炭素と水素から炭化水素燃料を合成する技術〕the Fischer-Tropsch synthesis.
エフ・ディー・ジー【FDG】〔生化〕〔フルオロデオキシグルコース〕FDG; fluorodeoxyglucose.
エフ・ディー・ディー【FDD】〔通信〕〔周波数分割複信〕FDD; frequency division duplex. ▫ **FDD** 方式 an

エフティーティーエイチ

FDD [a frequency division duplex] system.
エフ・ティー・ティー・エイチ【FTTH】《通信》〔光ファイバーを家の中まで引き込むインターネットを利用すること〕FTTH. ▶ fiber to the home の略.
エフ・ディー・ビー【FDB】《機》〔流体動圧軸受け〕an FDB; a fluid-dynamic bearing. ▭ **FDB モーター** an FDB [a fluid-dynamic-bearing] motor.
エフ・ティーひゃくしゅへいきんかぶかしすう【FT100種平均株価指数】〔ロンドン証券取引所の代表的指数〕the Financial Times Stock Exchange 100 Index; the FTSE 100 index.
「**FBIアメリカ連邦警察**」〔実話に基づいてFBIの活動を描いた社会派TVドラマ〕The F.B.I. ▶ 邦題は後に「FBIアメリカ連邦捜査局」に変更.
エフ・ピー・シー【FPC】《電子工学》〔フレキシブルプリント基板〕an FPC; a flexible printed circuit.
エブリデー・ロー・プライス《経営》an everyday low price (略: EDLP); everyday low pricing (略: EDLP).
エフリン《生化》〔血管形成・発毛促進にかかわるたんぱく質〕ephrin.
エフロン Ephron, Nora (1941-    ; 米国の映画監督・脚本家).
エフワンそう【F1層】《テレビ・広告》〔20–34歳の女性の層〕the female 20–34 age group; women in the prime target group for advertising.
えほう【恵方】▭ 恵方巻 a "lucky direction sushi roll"; a thick sushi roll eaten on the night of *setsubun* while facing the year's lucky direction and making a wish (for *one's* health, luck or prosperity).
えぼしどり【烏帽子鳥】〔鳥〕〔エボシドリ科の鳥〕a t(o)uraco 《*pl.* ~s》. ▭ エボシドリ科 Musophagidae.
エボデボ【進化発生生物学】evolutionary developmental biology; evolution of development; 《口》evo-devo.
エマージングしじょう【-市場】《経》=エマージング・マーケット.
エマージングしょこく【-諸国】〔急速な経済成長が期待できる発展途上国〕emerging 'countries [nations].
エマージング・マーケット《経》〔アジア・中南米・東欧などの新興成長市場〕an emerging market.
エム・アール【MR】 1《電算》〔複合現実感; 現実世界と仮想世界を融合する技術〕MR; mixed reality.
**2**《医》〔はしかと風疹の混合ワクチン〕MR. ▶ measles (はしか), rubella (風疹) の略.
エム・アール・アイ【MRI】▭ **機能的 MRI**〔撮影法〕fMRI; functional magnetic resonance imaging; 〔装置〕an fMRI; a functional magnetic resonance imager.
エム・アール・エー【MRA】《医》〔磁気共鳴血管撮影[造影(法)]〕MRA; magnetic resonance angiography.
エム・アール・ピー【MRP】《経営》=資材所要量計画 (⇒しざい[7]).
エム・アール・ワクチン【MR-】《医》〔新二種混合ワクチン〕the MR vaccine. ▶ MR は, measles (はしか), rubella (風疹) の略.
エム・アイ・エー【MIA】《軍》〔戦闘中行方不明者〕MIA; missing in action.
エム・アイ・エス【MIS】《軍》〔米国の陸軍情報部〕the MIS; the Military Intelligence Service.
エム・アイ・シックス【MI6】〔英国の諜報機関; SIS の通称; 国外活動を担当〕the Special Intelligence Service. ▶ MI6 は前身の Military Intelligence section 6 (軍事情報部第六課) の略.
エム・アイ・ピー【MIP】〔各種スポーツで最も印象に残った選手〕an [the] MIP; the most impressive player (of the year).
エム・アイ・ファイブ【MI5】〔英国の諜報機関; 国内・英連邦を担当〕the Security Service. ▶ MI5 は前身の Military Intelligence section 5 (軍事情報部第五課) の略.
エム・アンド・エー【M&A】▭ **M&A レシオ**《経》〔M&

A の対象企業を選別する指標の1つ〕M&A ratio.
エム・アンド・エム・カンファレンス【M&M-】《医》〔病院内における重症症例および死亡症例検討会〕a morbidity and mortality [an M & M] conference.
エム・エー・ジー・ティー・エフ【MAGTF】《米軍》〔海兵空陸機動部隊〕MAGTF; a Marine Air-Ground Task Force.
エム・エス・エヌ・ビー・シー【MSNBC】〔米国の24時間放送の報道ケーブルテレビ局〕MSNBC. ▶ Microsoft 社と NBC 放送が共同出資.
エム・エス・シー【MSC】〔海洋管理協議会〕the MSC; the Marine Stewardship Council.
エム・エス・シー・アイ（せかいかぶか）しすう【MSCI (世界株価)指数】《証券》the MSCI World Index. ▶ MSCI は Morgan Stanley Capital International の略.
エム・エス・シー・ビー【MSCB】《証券》〔転換価格の修正条項付き転換社債型新株予約権付き社債; ムービング・ストライク転換社債〕an MSCB; a moving strike convertible bond.
エム・エス・ダブリュー【MSW】《医療ソーシャルワーカー》an MSW; a medical social worker.
エム・エス・ディー・エス【MSDS】〔製品安全データシート〕an MSDS; a material safety data sheet.
エム・エス・ブラスト【MS-】〔コンピューターウイルスの1つ〕the Blaster (computer) worm; Blaster.
エム・エヌ・エヌ・ジー【MNNG】⇒ニトロソグアニジン.
エム・エム・シー[2]【MMC】《工》〔金属基複合材〕an MMC; a metal matrix composite.
エム・エムほう【MM砲】《野球》〔1960年代の米大リーグ, ヤンキースの強打者ミッキー・マントル (Mickey Mantle) とロジャー・マリス (Roger Maris) を指して言った呼び名〕the M &M Boys.
エム・エムりろん[てい]【MM 理論[定理]】《経》〔経営理論の1つ〕the Modigliani-Miller theory [theorem]. ▶ 米国の経済学者 Franco Modigliani と Merton Miller より.
エム・エル・アール・エス【MLRS】《米軍》〔多連装ロケットシステム〕(an) MLRS. ▶ multiple launch rocket system の略.
エム・オー・ティー【MOT】〔技術経営〕management of technology.
エムきょうし【M 教師】〔問題教師〕⇒もんだい. ▶ M は mondai (問題) の M.
エム・ケーこう【MK 鋼】《冶金》〔永久磁石の一種〕MK steel. ▶ MK はこの金属の開発者の姓「三島」とその旧姓「喜住」の頭文字を並べたもの.
エム・コマース〔移動体通信を利用した電子商取引〕m-commerce; mobile commerce. [=モバイル・コマース (⇒モバイル)]
エム・ジー・エスさいぼう【mGS 細胞】《生物》〔多能性生殖幹細胞〕an mGS cell; a multipotent germline stem cell.
エム・ジェー・オー【MJO】《気象》〔マッデン・ジュリアン振動〕the MJO; the Madden-Julian Oscillation.
エムじゅうろく【M-16】〔米国製の自動小銃〕an M16 (rifle).
エム・ツー【M₂, M-2】▭ **M₂** **[M-2]+CD**《経》M₂ plus CDs.
エム・ディー・アール・ピー【MDRP】《菌》〔多剤耐性緑膿菌〕MDRP; multidrug-resistant *Pseudomonas aeruginosa*.
エム・ディー・エー【MDA】《薬》〔合成麻薬の一種〕MDA; 3,4-methylenedioxyamphetamine. ▶ 通称 ラブ・ドラッグ (the love drug).
エム・ディー・エス【MDS】《医》〔骨髄異形成症候群〕MDS; myelodysplastic syndrome.
エム・ディー・エフざい[ばん]【MDF 材[板]】〔中質繊維板〕(an) MDF board; (a) medium-density fiberboard.

エム・ディー・シー【MDC】=ちゅうしんこく.
エム・ティー・ビー【MTB】1〔マウンテン・バイク〕an MTB; a mountain bike.
2〔軍〕〔高速魚雷艇〕an MTB; a motor torpedo boat.
エム・ティー・ビー・イー【MTBE】〔化〕=メチル・ターシャリー・ブチル・エーテル.
エムバックりょうほう【M-VAC 療法】〔医〕〔4 種類の抗がん剤を併用する治療法〕M-VAC chemotherapy. ▶ M-VAC は, methotrexate (メトレキサート) と vinblastine (ビンブラスチン), adriamycin (アドリアマイシン), cisplatin (シスプラチン)
エム・ピー・オー【MPO】〔証券〕〔随時転換促進型の第三者割当増資〕MPO. ▶ multiple private offering の略.
エム・ビー・ピー【MBP】〔化〕〔ミエリン塩基性たんぱく質〕MBP; myelin basic protein.
エム・ブイ・エヌ・オー【MVNO】〔仮想移動体通信事業者〕an MVNO; a mobile virtual network operator.
エムワンそう【M1 層】〔テレビ・広告〕〔20-34 歳の男性の層〕the male 20-34 age group; men in the prime target group for advertising.
エメリッヒ Emmerich, Roland (1955- ; ドイツ生まれの映画監督・脚本家).
エメンタール〔スイス産の硬質チーズ〕Emmental; Emmentaler cheese.
エヤデマ Eyadema, Gnassingbe (1935-2005; トーゴの政治家; 大統領〔1967-2005〕).
エライザけんさ【ELISA 検査】〔医〕〔血液抗体検査の1つ〕an ELISA test. ▶ ELISA は enzyme linked immunosorbent assay の略.
エライザほう【ELISA 法】〔医〕the ELISA method. ▶ ELISA は enzyme linked immunosorbent assay の略.
エリア ◻ エリア・カバー ◯ A 社の光ファイバー網は全国の 90% を〜カバーしている. Company A's fiber optic network covers 90% of the country. エリア・カバー率 area coverage. ◯ 〜カバー 100% を達成する achieve「100% [full] coverage; achieve a 100% coverage rate. エリア・マーケティング〔地域の市場特性を反映したマーケティング〕area marketing.
エリクソン[2]〔スウェーデンの通信企業〕Ericsson.
えりぐち【襟口】the neck. ◯ 〜レースをあしらったブラウス a blouse with a lace neck; a lace-neck(ed) blouse.
えりさき【襟先】collar「points [ends].
エリザベス Elizabeth, Shannon (1973- ; 米国の映画女優; 本名 Shannon Elizabeth Fadal).
「エリザベス」〔映画〕Elizabeth.
エリザベスアーデン〔商標〕〔米国の化粧品ブランド〕Elizabeth Arden.
エリザベスきゅうひんほう【-救貧法】〔英法〕〔1601 年制定の〕the Elizabethan Poor Law.
「エリザベスタウン」〔映画〕Elizabethtown.
エリシター〔生化〕〔生体の防御反応を誘導する化学物質群〕an elicitor.
エリスポット〔舞台〕〔楕円形の反射鏡を使ったスポットライト〕an ellipsoidal spotlight; an ellipsoidal.
エリスリトール〔化〕erythritol.
エリセ Erice, Victor (1940- ; スペインの映画監督).
エリトリアじんみんかいほうせんせん【-人民解放戦線】the Eritrean People's Liberation Front (略: EPLP).
エリナシン〔化〕erinacine.
えりまききつねざる【襟巻狐猿】〔動〕a ruffed lemur; Varecia variegata.
「エリン・ブロコビッチ」〔映画〕Erin Brockovich.
エル・アール・エー【LRA】=かみのていこうくん.
エル・アール・ティー【LRT】〔次世代路面電車; ライトレール〕LRT; light-rail transit.
エル・イー・ディー【LED】 ◻ 青色[白色, フルカラー] LED a「blue [white, full-color] LED. (超)高輝度 LED a (super) high-brightness LED. 有機 LED an organic「light-emitting diode [LED] (略: OLED).
◻ LED 照明 LED「lighting [illumination]. LED 素子 an LED device. LED バックライト an LED backlight; LED backlighting.
エル・イー・ピー【LEP】〔セルン (CERN) の大型電子・陽電子衝突型加速器〕LEP; the Large Electron-Positron Collider.
エル・エイチ・シー【LHC】〔欧州合同原子核研究機関 (CERN) が建設した大型ハドロン衝突型加速器〕an LHC; a large hadron collider.
エル・エー・エム【LAM】〔医〕〔リンパ脈管筋腫症〕LAM; lymphangioleiomyomatosis.
エル・エー・ケーりょうほう【LAK 療法】〔医〕〔リンフォカイン活性化キラー細胞療法〕LAK [lymphokine-activated killer] therapy.
「L.A.コンフィデンシャル」〔映画〕L.A. Confidential.
エル・エス・アイ【LSI】 ◻ システム LSI〔多機能大規模集積回路〕a system LSI.
エル・エス・イー【LSE】〔金融〕〔ロンドン証券取引所〕the LSE; the London Stock Exchange.
エル・エル・シー【LLC】〔有限(責任)会社〕an LLC; a limited liability company.
エル・エル・ピー【LLP】〔有限責任事業組合〕an LLP; a limited liability partnership.
エル・エル・ピーほう【LLP 法】〔法〕the LLP Law. [=ゆうげんせきにんじぎょうくみあいほう]
エル・オー・シー【LOC】〔インド・パキスタン間の停戦ライン〕=実効支配線 (⇨じっこう[2]).
エルキャック【LCAC】〔軍〕〔エアクッション型揚陸艇〕an LCAC; a landing craft air cushion.
エルク・テスト〔自動車〕〔危険回避性能テスト〕an elk [a moose] test.
エルゴノミクス ◻ エルゴノミクス・キーボード〔電算〕=エルゴノミック・キーボード (⇨エルゴノミック). エルゴノミクス・デザイン (an) ergonomic design.
エルゴノミック〔人間工学に基づいた〕ergonomic. ◻ エルゴノミック・キーボード〔電算〕an ergonomic keyboard. エルゴノミック設計[デザイン] ergonomic design.
エルゴノミックス =エルゴノミクス.
エル・コス・エス【LCoS】〔反射型液晶〕an LCoS. ▶ liquid crystal on silicon の略.
エル・ジー・ビー・ティー【LGBT】〔性的少数者〕LGBT. ▶ lesbians, gays (同性愛者), bisexuals (両性愛者), transgender persons (性転換者) の略.
エルシニア・エンテロコリチカ〔菌〕Yersinia enterocolitica.
エルズバーグ Ellsberg, Daniel (1931- ; 米国の元官吏・政治活動家).
エルタックス〔地方税のポータルシステム〕"eL TAX."
エルダップ【LDAP】〔電算〕LDAP. ▶ Lightweight Directory Access Protocol の略.
エル・ディー・アール【LDR】〔陣痛・分娩・回復期すべてが同室の出産室〕an LDR room; a labor-delivery-recovery room.
エル・ディー・エル【LDL】〔生化〕〔低密度リポたんぱく質〕LDL. ▶ low-density lipoprotein の略. ◻ 小型 LDL (a) small dense LDL. ▶ 通称,「超悪玉コレステロール」.
エル・ティーぼうえき【LT 貿易】〔日中国交正常化前の貿易〕the "L-T" Trade. ▶ LT は中国 (Liao Chengzhi 廖承志) と日本 (高碕達之助) の代表者の頭文字から.
エルドアン Erdogan, Recep Tayyip (1954- ; トルコの政治家; 首相〔2003- 〕).
エル・ドーパ【L-】〔薬〕〔ドーパミン補充薬〕L-dopa.
エルパイス〔スペインの日刊紙〕El Pais.
エルバラダイ ElBaradei, Mohamed (1942- ; エジプト出身の国際原子力機関事務局長〔1997- 〕).
エルバンド【L-】〔通信〕〔周波数帯域の1つ〕the L-band.
エル・ビー・オー【LBO】〔経〕〔借入金をてこにした買収〕an

エルビービー

LBO; a leveraged buyout.
エル・ビー・ビー【LBB】〚原子力〛〔配管などの破断前漏洩(るえい)〕LBB; leak before break.
エルビタックス〚商標・薬〛〔がん治療薬セツキシマブの商品名〕Erbitux.
エルベグドルジ Elbegdorj, Tsakhiagiin (1963-   ; モンゴルの政治家).
エル・ムンド〔スペインの日刊紙〕El Mundo.
エル・モード【L-】〚商標〛L-mode.
エルリーグ【L-】〔日本女子サッカーリーグの通称〕the L-League.
エルロン〚空〛〔飛行機・グライダーの補助翼〕an aileron.
エレガント・ワラビー〚動〛a whiptail wallaby; *Macropus parryi*.
エレクトロクロミックそし【-素子】〚電子工学〛an electrochromic device.
エレクトロニック   エレクトロニック・アート〔電子芸術〕electronic art.
エレベーター    エレベーター・ガール *an elevator「girl [woman]; "a lift「girl [woman]. エレベーター・ボーイ *an elevator「boy [man]; "a lift「boy [man].
エレボン〚空〛〔昇降舵と補助翼の役割を兼ね備えた舵面〕an elevon. ▶ elevator (エレベーター) と aileron (エルロン; 補助翼) の合成語.
エロ    エロ親爺 a dirty old man; an old goat.
エロージョン・コロージョン〚金属〛〔金属の腐食が加速する現象; 機械的作用による侵食と化学的作用による腐食との相互作用で起きる〕erosion-corrosion (略: EC).
えんあん²【延安】    延安精神〔中国共産党の革命思想の原点〕the Yanan「Way [Spirit].
エンヴィサット〔<*env*ironmental + *sat*ellite〕〔欧州宇宙機関の地球観測衛星〕Envisat; the Envisat satellite.
えんか⁹【塩化】    塩化カリウム potassium chloride. 塩化セチルピリジニウム cetylpyridinium chloride.
えんか⁹【演歌】    ど演歌〔古くさい典型的な演歌〕a traditional-style [an old-fashioned] Japanese popular song.
えんかい²【沿海】    沿海域戦闘艦〚米軍〛=沿岸戦闘艦 (⇨えんがん¹).
えんかく³【遠隔】    遠隔画像診断 remote image diagnosis. 遠隔監視 remote surveillance.  ～監視システム a remote surveillance system. 遠隔講義 a remote lecture. 遠隔診断 telediagnosis. 遠隔実験 a remote experiment. 遠隔病理診断 telepathology. 遠隔放射線診断 teleradiology.
えんかつ【円滑】    円滑化 facilitation; streamlining.  ～化する facilitate; streamline; make *sth* go more smoothly.
えんかぶつ【塩化物】    塩化物泉 a chloride spring.
エンカレッジ・スクール a remedial school for students needing extra motivation; a motivational school; an "encourage school."
えんがん¹【沿岸】    沿岸戦闘艦〚米軍〛a littoral combat ship (略: LCS).
えんぎ⁴【縁起】    縁起(えん)ぎ superstitiousness; a belief in omens or superstitions.
えんぎ⁵【燕岐】=ヨンギ.
えんぎ(ぎゃく)しき【延喜(格)式】〔三代格式の 1 つ〕the Engi Shiki, the Rule of the Engi Era. [⇨さんだい(きゃ)しき, こうにん(きゃく)しき, じょうがん(きゃく)しき]
えんきょり【遠距離】    遠距離結婚 a long-distance marriage. 遠距離大量送水車〔消防車の一種〕a super pumper.
エングル Engle, Robert F. (1942-   ; 米国の経済学者).
えんけい【円-】=クロスえん.
えんげい¹【園芸】    園芸種 a cultivated species (of ...).
エンケラド(ゥ)ス〚天文〛=エンセラダス.
えんけんしりょく【遠見視力】〚眼科〛distance [distant]

vision.
えんこ³【縁故】    縁故資本主義 =クローニー・キャピタリズム. 縁故人事 personnel「changes [management] through「personal [family] connections.
えんさん【塩酸】
   塩酸アンブロキソール〚薬〛〔去痰薬〕ambroxol hydrochloride. 塩酸エピルビシン〚薬〛〔抗がん剤〕epirubicin hydrochloride. 塩酸ゲムシタビン〚薬〛〔抗がん剤〕gemcitabine hydrochloride. 塩酸セルトラリン〚薬〛〔抗鬱剤〕sertraline hydrochloride. 塩酸タムスロシン〚薬〛〔前立腺肥大による排尿障害の改善薬〕tamsulosin hydrochloride. 塩酸テトラヒドロゾリン〚薬〛〔血管収縮薬〕tetrahydrozoline hydrochloride. 塩酸ドネペジル〚薬〛〔アセチルコリンの分解抑制物質, アルツハイマー型認知症治療剤〕donepezil hydrochloride. 塩酸パロキセチン〚薬〛〔抗うつ剤〕paroxetine hydrochloride. 塩酸フェキソフェナジン〚薬〛〔アレルギー性疾患治療薬〕fexofenadine hydrochloride. 塩酸フェニルプロパノールアミン〚薬〛〔交感神経刺激薬〕phenylpropanolamine hydrochloride (略: PPA). 塩酸プソイドエフェドリン〚薬〛〔鼻炎治療の医薬品成分〕pseudoephedrine hydrochloride. 塩酸ブテナフィン〚薬〛〔抗真菌薬〕butenafine hydrochloride. 塩酸フルスルチアミン〚薬〛〔ビタミン B1 誘導体〕fursultiamine hydrochloride. 塩酸ベラパミル〚薬〛〔血管拡張薬〕verapamil hydrochloride. 塩酸ロキサチジン・アセタート〚薬〛〔$H_2$ ブロッカーの一種〕roxatidine acetate hydrochloride.
えんざん²【演算】    演算機能〚電算〛an「arithmetic [operational] function. 演算処理装置〚電算〛a processing unit (略: PU)    数値～処理装置〚電算〛a numerical processing unit (略: NPU) / 中央～処理装置〚電算〛a central processing unit (略: CPU) / 超小型～処理装置〚電算〛a microprocessor unit (略: MPU).
えんし⁴【偃師】〔中国河南省の県・市〕Yanshi.
エンシエロ〚<Sp〛〔スペインのサンフェルミン祭りで行われる牛追いのイベント〕the Encierro; the Running of the Bulls.
エンジニアード・ウッド =エンジニアリング・ウッド (⇨エンジニアリング).
エンジニアリング    エンジニアリング・ウッド〔強度・耐久性などを強化した木材; 集成材など〕engineered wood.
えんしゅう²【演習】    演習場〚軍〛a maneuvering ground.  東富士～場 the Fuji maneuvering ground.
えんじょ【援助】    援助協調 coordinated assistance. 援助行動〚心理〛helping behavior.
えんしょうせい【炎症性】〚医〛～の inflammatory.    炎症性大腸炎 inflammatory colitis. 炎症性腸疾患 (an) inflammatory bowel disease (略: IBD). 炎症性乳がん inflammatory breast cancer (略: IBC). 炎症性ポリープ an inflammatory polyp.
エンジン
   水平対向エンジン〚自動車・空〛a horizontally opposed engine; a boxer engine; a flat engine. ボクサー・エンジン a boxer engine. [=水平対向エンジン]
   エンジン音 the sound of an engine; engine noise.  キーンという甲高い～音 the high-pitched whine of an engine. エンジン効率 engine efficiency. エンジン・キー〚自動車〛an engine key. エンジン車〔バッテリー車に対して〕an engine-driven「car [vehicle]. エンジン制御装置 an engine control unit (略: ECU). エンジン燃焼実験〔ミサイル・ロケットなどの〕an engine「combustion [ignition] experiment.
エンジン・カッター〚機〛〔鋼材などの切断に用いられるガソリンエンジン駆動の機械〕an engine cutter.
えんすい¹【円錐】    円錐切除(術)〚医〛〔子宮頸部の病変に対する処置の 1 つ〕(a) conization.
えんすい¹【遠水】〔遠くにある水〕distant water; water from far away.  ～は近火を救わず. Distant water will not quench a nearby fire. | A local crisis cannot be dealt with from far away.

エンセラダス 〖天文〗〔土星の衛星〕Enceladus.
エンゼル ▫️ エンゼル・プラン〔少子化対策〕the "Angel Plan"; Basic Orientations to Assist Child-Raising, a Japanese government plan to create a better environment for working mothers.
えんそ[2]【塩素】▫️ 塩素系漂白剤 (a) chlorine bleach.
エンターテイ(ン)メント ▫️ エンターテイ(ン)メント・ロボット an entertainment robot.
えんたい【延滞】▫️ 延滞債権 a delinquent [a non-performing, an overdue] loan.
えんたいごう【掩体壕】〖軍〗〔空襲から軍用機を守る格納庫〕an aircraft bunker.
えんだか【円高】▫️ 円高ショック〖経〗a (high, strong) yen shock; the 《1995》yen shock.
えんだん[3]【鉛弾】▫️ 非鉛弾 lead-free ammunition. ▫️ 鉛弾使用禁止区域 a no-lead-ammunition area.
えんちじしん【遠地地震】a teleseismic earthquake; a distant earthquake; (an) earthquake by a teleseism. ▫️ 遠地地震学 teleseismology. 遠地地震波 a teleseismic wave. 遠地地震波形 a teleseismic waveform.
えんちょう[2]【延長】▫️ 延長幅〔会期などの〕the length of [an extension [a prolongation]. ◐ 会期の〜幅をめぐって与野党が激しく争っている。The Governing and Opposition parties are battling fiercely about 「how long the session should be extended [how long to continue sitting after the end of the current session].
エンディング ▫️ エンディング曲〔歌〕an ending song; a closing song; 〔番組の最後に流れる曲〕the closing theme (music)《of a TV show》.
エンデバー〔米国のスペースシャトル〕Endeavor.
エンデューロ〔自動車・オートバイなどの耐久レース〕an enduro《pl. ~s》.
エンテロウイルス 〖菌〗〔腸管で増殖するウイルス〕an enterovirus.
えんでん【塩田】▫️ 揚浜式塩田 a salt production facility in which brine is pumped up out of the ocean and spread on sand, from which salt is then recovered. 入浜式塩田 a salt production facility in which brine is brought through tidal action into salt beds, from which salt is then recovered. 流下式塩田 a salt production facility in which brine is poured down a sandy slope, from which salt is then recovered.
えんとう[3]【遠投】▫️ 遠投釣り〔釣り〕long casting.
えんどう【豌豆】▫️ エンドウたんぱく pea protein.
「エンド・オブ・デイズ」〔映画〕End of Days.
「エンド・オブ・バイオレンス」〔映画〕The End of Violence.
エンドニエストルきょうわこく【沿=共和国】〔モルドヴァ東部, 分離独立を宣言している地域の自称〕Pridnestrovie. [⇨トランスニエストル]
エンドユーザー・コンピューティング〖電算〗〔企業内のコンピューター実務者がシステムの構築・運用・保守に携わること〕end-user computing. (略: EUC).
えんば【円馬】〖体操〗〔鞍馬の練習用具〕a training mushroom (for the pommel horse). [=ポック]
エンバーマー〔エンバーミングを施す人〕an embalmer.
エンバーミング〔遺体衛生保全・遺体防腐処理〕embalming; embalmment.
エンパワーメント〔能力開化・権限付与〕empowerment.
えんぴつ【鉛筆】▫️ 鉛筆補助軸 a pencil 「lengthener [extender].
エンフォースメント〔法執行・強制〕enforcement.
エンフバヤル Enkhbayar, Nambaryn (1958– ; モンゴルの政治家).
エンフボルド Enkhbold, Miyeegombyn (1964– ; モンゴルの政治家).
エンブレム ▫️ 公式エンブレム〔スポーツ大会などの〕an official emblem.
エンブレル〔商標・薬〕〔エタネルセプト; 関節リウマチ治療薬〕Enbrel. [⇨エタネルセプト]
エンプロイアビリティ〔雇用条件にかなっていること〕employability.
エンプロイー・バイアウト〖経営〗〔従業員による自社買収〕an employee buyout (略: EBO).
えんぶん[3]【塩分】▫️ 塩分摂取量 (a) salt intake; (an) intake of salt. ◐ 〜摂取量を減らす reduce [lower] one's salt intake; take less salt.
エンベッドしゅざい【-取材】〔従軍取材〕embedded 「reporting [coverage].
エンベデッド・バリュー〖保険〗〔生命保険会社の純資産価値, 将来もたらされる利益の現在価値を加えたもの; 潜在(的)価値〕(an) embedded value.
えんぺん【縁辺】▫️ 縁辺海域《Japanese waters and》adjacent seas; the seas adjacent《to the archipelago》.
えんぽう【遠方】〖天〗a distant galaxy. 遠方展開〖軍〗long-distance [remote] deployment. ▫️ 〜展開能力 (a) 「long-distance [remote] deployment capability.
えんま【閻魔】▫️ 閻魔大王 the Great Enma.
えんまく【煙幕】▫️ 煙幕弾 a smoke ball; 〔発煙弾〕a smoke 「shell [bomb].
えんまん【円満】▫️ 円満解決 an outcome [a solution] acceptable to 「all [both] parties; a mutually acceptable 「outcome [solution]; 《come to, reach》an amicable [a peaceful] settlement. ◐ その件は先方が陳謝することで〜解決した。The matter was resolved amicably when the other party apologized.
えんめい【延命】▫️ 延命効果《have》a life-prolonging effect. 延命治療〔医療〕life-prolonging treatment; 《refuse》treatment to 「keep one alive [prolong one's life].
えんゆう[2]【鉛釉】〔製陶〕(a) lead glaze.
エンライト Enright, Anne (1962– ; アイルランドの小説家).
えんりえど【厭離穢土】〖仏教〗〔汚れたこの世を嫌って離れること〕an abhorrence of [a disgust at] (living in) this corrupt world.
えんれん【遠恋】〔遠距離恋愛〕a long-distance 「romance [relationship, love affair]; love across the miles.
エンロフロキサシン〔薬〕〔合成抗菌剤の1つ〕enrofloxacin.
エンロン〔米国の総合エネルギー企業; 2001年倒産〕Enron Corp.

# お

おい[1]【老い】▫️ 老い支度[仕度]《ﾞ》preparation(s) for old age. ◐ 〜支度をする prepare (oneself) [get ready] for old age.
おいがわ【負い革】a shoulder 「strap [belt]; 〔弾薬帯〕a bandolier.
おいきり【追い切り】▫️ 最終追い切り a final trial.
おいこみ【追い込み】▫️ 追い込み漁 drive 「fishing [hunting]. ◐ イルカ〜漁 dolphin drive 「fishing [hunting].
「おいしい生活」〔映画〕Small Time Crooks.
オイスカ〔国際産業精神文化促進機構〕OISCA(-International); the Organization for Industrial,

**オイスター**

Spiritual and Cultural Advancement International. ▶1961 年日本で設立の民間の援助機関.
**オイスター** □□ オイスター・チャウダー (an) oyster chowder.
**オイセッツ【OICETS】**〔光衛星間通信実験衛星〕OICETS; the Optical Inter-Orbit Communications Engineering Test Satellite.
**オイリュトミー**〔シュタイナーの提唱した教育法;音楽・言葉のリズムに合わせた身体表現を行う〕eurythmy.
**オイル** □□ オイル・マッサージ (an) oil massage. オイル・ルート〔石油輸送ルートである海路〕an oil route.
**オイル・ワンド**〔いろいろな形・色の粒と油を詰めたガラスの管;管を動かした時の粒の動きをみて楽しむ〕an oil wand.
**-おう【-央】**〔地理的・時間的に中ほどであること〕the center 《of a city》; the middle 《of a month》. ◎月〜 《in, around, about》the middle of a month / 年〜 《in, around, about》the middle of a year [midyear] / 1980 年代〜《in, around, about》the mid-1980's / 18 世紀〜《in》the mid-18th century / 県〜 the「center [heart] of a prefecture; central 《Kanagawa》(Prefecture).
**おうあつ【横圧】**〔鉄道〕a lateral force.
**おうえん¹【応援】** □□ 応援メッセージ a message of support; a support message.
**おうかくまく【横隔膜】** □□ 横隔膜神経麻痺〔医〕phrenic nerve「palsy [paralysis] (略: PNP).
**おうかしょう²【黄化症】**〔植物病理〕chlorosis.
**おうきさん【王岐山】**Wang Qishan (1948- ;中国北京市長〔2004- 〕).
**おうきゅう²【応急】** □□ 応急危険度判定〔被災建築物の〕(a)「quick [stopgap] inspection of post—earthquake damage to buildings; (an) emergency safety assessment. 応急危険度判定士 an analyst「of [specializing in] tentative inspection of post—earthquake building damage; an emergency safety assessor. 応急救護処置〔応急処置〕「give [administer] emergency「care [treatment]; 《administer》first aid (treatment).
**おうごん¹【黄金】** □□ 黄金コンビ a golden [an ideal, a splendid] combination [pair, pairing]. ◎ジョン・フォード監督とジョン・ウェインの〜コンビによる名作『駅馬車』Stagecoach, the Masterpiece by the perfect combination of director John Ford with John Wayne.
**おうごんのみかづきちたい【黄金の三日月地帯】**〔アヘンの生産地であるアフガニスタン・イラン・パキスタンの国境地帯〕the Golden Crescent.
**「黄金のロバ」**〔アプレイウス作の小説〕The Golden Ass; 〔原題〕Metamorphoses.
**おうさつ¹【応札】** □□ 応札者 a bidder; a tenderer. 応札倍率 a bid-to-cover ratio.
**おうしゅう²【押収】** □□ 押収書類 seized [impounded] documents; papers [a document] seized [impounded] (by the police). 押収品 an amount「seized [confiscated]; a (drugs) haul. ◎昨年中の成田空港における麻薬の〜量は過去最高を記録した. Last year's haul of drugs at Narita airport broke all records.
**おうしゅう³【欧州】** □□ 欧州憲法 the European Constitution; the EU Constitution. 欧州人 a European.
**おうしゅうアルカイダきこうひみつそしき【欧州—機構秘密組織】**〔2005 年 7 月 7 日ロンドンで同時多発テロを行ったとされる過激派組織〕the Secret Organization Group of al-Qaeda of Jihad Organization in Europe.
**おうしゅうエネルギーとりひきじょ【欧州—取引所】**〔ドイツにある〕the European Energy Exchange (略: EEX).
**おうしゅうきょうそうほう【欧州競争法】**European competition law.
**おうしゅう（けいじ）けいさつきこう【欧州（刑事）警察機構】**=ユーロポール.

**おうしゅうけんぽうじょうやく【欧州憲法条約】**=イー・ユーけんぽうじょうやく.
**おうしゅうこうくうぼうえいうちゅうがいしゃ【欧州航空防衛宇宙会社】**the European Aeronautic Defence and Space Company (略: EADS).
**おうしゅうサッカーれんめい【欧州—連盟】**the Union of European Football Associations (略: UEFA).
**おうしゅうじどうしゃこうぎょうかい【欧州自動車工業会】**〔ブリュッセルに本部を置く〕the European Automobile Manufacturers Association (略: ACEA). ▶ACEA は《F》*Association des Constructeurs Européens d'Automobiles* の略.
**おうしゅう（しほう）さいばんしょ【欧州（司法）裁判所】**the European Court of Justice (略: ECJ);〔正式名称〕the Court of Justice of the European Communities.
**おうしゅうしょくひんあんぜんきかん【欧州食品安全機関】**the European Food Safety Authority (略: EFSA).
**おうしゅうせいやくだんたいれんごうかい【欧州製薬団体連合会】**the European Federation of Pharmaceutical Industries and Associations (略: EFPIA).
**おうしゅうなんてんてんもんだい【欧州南天天文台】**〔天〕=ヨーロッパなんてんてんもんだい.
**おうしゅうのせいせんアルカイダそしき【欧州の聖戦—組織】**Al-Qaida's Jihad in Europe.
**おうしゅうふうりょくエネルギーきょうかい【欧州風力—協会】**the European Wind Energy Association (略: EWEA).
**おうしゅうぶんかしゅと【欧州文化首都】**the European Capital of Culture 《for 2008》.
**おうしゅうみなみてんもんだい【欧州南天文台】**〔天〕=ヨーロッパなんてんてんもんだい.
**おうしょう²【応召】** □□ 応召義務〔医師・予備自衛官・消防士などの〕an obligation to respond.
**「往生要集」**〔源信著の仏教書〕The Essentials of Rebirth (in the Pure Land).
**おうしん³【往診】** □□ 往診かばん a doctor's bag.
**おうだん²【横断】** □□ 横断検索 =けんさく³. 横断組織 a cross-sectional organization. 横断歩行者妨害 the obstruction of a pedestrian.
**おうちょう【王朝】** □□ 王朝絵巻 a (picture) scroll depicting court life in the Nara and Heian periods. ◎5 月 15 日は葵祭で, 雅やかな〜絵巻が都大路に繰り広げられた. May 15th was the Aoi Matsuri, when a graceful and elegant parade proceeded along the main thoroughfare of Kyoto, like something out of a scroll of court life in the Heian period.
**おうとう³【応答】** □□ 応答速度〔電算〕(a) response speed.
**「王の男」**〔映画〕The King and the Clown.
**おうはん²【黄斑】** □□ 黄斑上膜(形成症)〔眼科〕epiretinal membrane (略: ERM); macular pucker. 黄斑変性(症)〔眼科〕macular degeneration. ◎加齢〜変性(症) age-related macular degeneration (略: ARMD, AMD) / 老人性〜変性(症) senile macular degeneration (略: SMD).
**おうふく【往復】** □□ 往復航空券 *a round-trip airline ticket;「a return airline ticket.
**おうへん【黄変】**yellowing.
**〜する** yellow; turn yellow.
**おうぼ【応募】** □□ 応募倍率 the「applicant [response] rate. 応募方法 (the) method of application 《for…》; how to apply 《for…》.
**オウムしんりきょう【-真理教】**Aum Shinrikyo.
**おうよう²【応用】** □□ 応用倫理学 applied ethics.
**おうようりょく【応用力】**practical skills. ◎実社会で必要な基礎学力と〜を身につけることが義務教育の目的の 1 つである. One of the purposes of compulsory education is to provide the basic academic knowledge and

practical skills required for the real world.
**おうらい【往来】** ▫ 往来危険罪〖法〗(be indicted for) endangerment of traffic.
**おうりつこくさいもんだいけんきゅうじょ【王立国際問題研究所】**〔英国の〕the Royal Institute of International Affairs (略: RIIA).
**おうりつとうごうぐんじけんきゅうじょ【王立統合軍事研究所】**〔英国の〕the Royal United Services Institute for Defence and Security (略: RUSI; the RUSI.
**おうりつとうごうぼうえいあんぽけんきゅうじょ【王立統合防衛安保研究所】**〔英国の〕the Royal United Services Institute for Defence and Security Studies (略: RUSI).
**おうりょう²【押領】** seizure [takeover] of 《sb's》 land; 《口》 a land grab.
**おうりょく【応力】** ▫ 応力解析 (a) stress analysis. ◆〜解析装置 a stress analyzer. 応力測定 (a) stress measurement. ◆〜測定装置 a stress meter. 応力値〖機械工学〗a stress value. 応力腐食割れ〖原子力〗stress corrosion cracking (略: SCC). 応力分析 stress analysis. ◆〜分析装置 a stress analyzer. 応力誘発〖地震〗stress triggering.
**オー・アイ・イー【OIE】**〖国際獣疫事務局〗the OIE; the World Organization for Animal Health. ▶ OIE はフランス語 *l'Office international des épizooties* の略.
**オー・アイ・シー・イー・ティー・エス【OICETS】** =オイセッツ.
**おおあめ【大雨】** ▫ 大雨被害 heavy rain damage; damage from heavy rain(fall). ◆梅雨前線による〜(の)被害 heavy rain damage due to the rainy season front.
**おおイタビ【大─】**〖植〗〔クワ科の常緑つる性低木〕a creeping fig; *Ficus pumila*.
**オーウェル** ▫ オーウェル的(な) Orwellian 《dystopia》.
**オー・エイチ・アール【OHR】**〖経営〗〔経費を業務粗利益で割った値〕an overhead ratio.
**オー・エー・ブイ【OAV】**〔オリジナル・アニメーション・ビデオ〕(an) original 「animation [anime] video; (an) 「animation [anime] released directly to video.
**オー・エス・シー・イー【OSCE】**〖医〗〔客観的臨床能力試験〕OSCE; an objective structured clinical examination.
**オー・エヌ・エー【ONA】**〖電算〗〔異なるネットの端末同士でも通信ができるネットの仕組み〕(an) ONA; (an) open network architecture.
**オー・エヌほう【ON 砲】**〖野球〗〔読売ジャイアンツの主力打者 王貞治と長嶋茂雄を指して言った呼び名〕the O-N Cannon.
**オー・エフ・ディー・エム【OFDM】**〖通信〗〔直交周波数分割多重方式〕OFDM; orthogonal frequency-division multiplexing.
**オー・エム・エー【OMA】** =しじょうつうじょいじきょうてい.
**オー・エム・グループ【OM ─】**〔ストックホルム証券取引所の持ち株会社〕(the) OM Group.
**オー・エル・イー・ディー【OLED】**〖電子工学〗〔有機発光ダイオード〕an OLED; an organic light-emitting diode.
**オーガスタ 1**〔米国メイン州の州都〕Augusta.
**2**〔米国ジョージア州中東部の市〕Augusta.
**おおがた【大型・大形】** ▫ 大型化 ◆〜化する make *sth* 「big(ger) [large(r)]; 〈物や主題を〉get [become] big(ger) [large(r)] / 近年, 台風が〜化する傾向が見られる. Typhoons are becoming increasingly bigger in recent years. 大型機〖空〗a large passenger 「plane [aircraft]. ◆超〜 a jumbo jet. 大型固体補助ロケット a large solid 「rocket [strap-on] booster. 大型ジェット機〖空〗a large passenger jet; a jumbo jet. 大型汎用機〖電算〗a general-purpose mainframe (computer). 大型ビジョン〔ビルの外壁などに設置した巨大スクリーン〕a 「large [giant, jumbo] (TV) screen. 大型輸送ヘリ a 「large [heavy] transport helicopter. 大型連休 a long holiday period; a period with several (national) holidays in a row; a (very) long weekend.

**おおがち【大勝ち】** a great victory; 《口》a big win; 〔大儲け〕a huge profit; 《口》a killing.
〜する win a great victory; make a 「big win [huge profit]. ◆競馬で〜する win a large amount betting on horses; make a killing at the track.
**オーガニック** ▫ オーガニック・コットン〔無農薬栽培された綿花で作られたコットン〕organic cotton.
**おおかわちしゃ【大川萵苣】**〖植〗〔ゴマノハグサ科の植物〕a water speedwell; *Veronica anagallis-aquatica*.
**おおかんばん【大看板】**〔大きな看板〕a large signboard; a billboard; 〔一座の中心的な役者・芸人〕the 「main [leading] star (attraction).
**おおきんけいぎく【大金鶏菊】**〖植〗〔キク科の多年草〕a lanceleaf coreopsis; *Coreopsis lanceolata*.
**オークショニア【競売人】**an auctioneer.
**オークション** ▫ 中古車オークション, オート・オークション a used car auction. ◆オークション会場 an auction venue.
**おおぐち, おおくち【大口】** ▫ 大口契約 a major contract; 《口》a megadeal. 大口〔取引〕価格 a large lot price; the price for a large 「amount [quantity, lot]. 大口配送 large cargo delivery. 大口割り引 a 「quantity [bulk (purchase)] discount.
**おおぐちでんりょくカーブ【大口電力─】**〔景気判断指標の１つ〕a large industrial (electrical power) user curve.
**おおぐちでんりょくしようりょう【大口電力使用量】**〖経〗〔景気判断指標の１つ〕large industrial electrical power use.
**おおくらしょう【大蔵省】** ▫ 大蔵省証券 a Finance Ministry note; a treasury bill.
**オーケー** ▫ オーケー・サイン, **OK サイン** an OK sign.
**オーサー・ビジット**〔人気作家などが学校に出向いて授業を行うこと〕(arrange, plan) an author visit.
**おおさかアメニティパーク【大阪─】**Osaka Amenity Park (略: OAP).
**おおさかかがくぎじゅつセンター【大阪科学技術─】**〔1960 年設立の財団法人〕the Osaka Science & Technology Center (略: TSTEC).
**おおさかしょうけんとりひきじょ【大阪証券取引所】**the Osaka Securities Exchange (略: OSE).
**おおさしがめ【大刺椿象】**〖昆〗〔サシガメ科の吸血昆虫〕a kissing bug; *Triatoma rubrofasciata*.
**おおさわくずれ【大沢崩れ】**〔富士山の〕the Ōsawa Collapse; the large gully on the south-west of Mt Fuji created by landslide activity.
**オー・シー・エイチ・エー【OCHA】** ⇒じんどうもんだいちょうせいじむしょ.
**オー・シー・エヌ【OCN】**〔NTT のインターネット通信サービス〕OCN. ◆ open computer network から.
**オー・ジー・シー【OGC】** ⇒せいようこうちょう.
**オー・ジー・ティー・ティー【OGTT】**〖医〗〔経口ぶどう糖負荷試験〕an OGTT; an oral glucose tolerance test.
**おおしまつむぎ【大島紬】**Ōshima tsumugi weave; traditional splash-patterned silk cloth from the Japanese island of Amami Ōshima.
**「オーシャン・オブ・ファイヤー」**〔映画〕Hidalgo.
**「オーシャンズ 11」**〔映画〕Ocean's Eleven.
**おおすじ【大筋】** ▫ 大筋一致 ◆〜一致する agree in general; reach [come to] a general agreement. 大筋合意 (a) general agreement; 〔there is〕substantial agreement 《between [among]》… 》. ◆〜合意に至る come to [reach] a general agreement; agree in general.
**「オースティン・パワーズ」**〔映画〕Austin Powers: Inter-

オーステナイト

national Man of Mystery. ▶ 続編は「オースティン・パワーズ:デラックス」(Austin Powers: The Spy Who Shagged Me) と「オースティン・パワーズ ゴールドメンバー」(Austin Powers in Goldmember).
オーステナイト 〘□〙 オーステナイト鋼 austenitic steel.
オーストラリアあしか〘-海驢〙〘動〙an Australian sea lion; *Neophoca cinerea*.
オーストラリア・グループ〔生物・化学兵器の輸出管理のに関する国際的枠組み〕the Australia Group (略: AG).
オーストラリアン〔オーストラリアの日刊紙〕The Australian.
オーストラリアン・フットボール〘スポーツ〙Australian Rules (football); Australian football; Aussie Rules.
オーストンやまがら〖-山雀〗〘鳥〙〔シジュウカラ科の鳥〕an Owston's varied tit; *Parus varius owstoni*.
おおせぐろかもめ〖大背黒鷗〗〘鳥〙〔カモメ科の鳥〕a slaty-backed gull; *Larus schistisagus*.
「オーソン・ウェルズ劇場」〔俳優オーソン・ウェルズの解説によ，恐怖と怪奇の TV ドラマ〕Orson Welles' Great Mysteries.
オーダー・エントリー・システム〘医〙a computerized physician order entry system.
オーダーメード 〘□〙 オーダーメード医療〔遺伝子情報の個人差に基づいた医療〕tailored (medical) treatment. オーダーメード薬〘薬〙〔個人の体質に合わせて処方する薬〕a tailored drug; a「custom-made [custom-tailored] drug. オーダーメード・ワクチン a custom-made[-tailored] vaccine; a [an individually] tailored vaccine.
おおたぼはん〖太田母斑〗〘医〙a n(a)evus of Ota; an Ota('s) nevus; blue sclera; oculodermal [ocular] melanosis.
おおだま〖大玉〗〔野菜や果実の〕(of) large size; a giant; a giant《strawberry》.
「オータム・イン・ニューヨーク」〔映画〕Autumn In New York.
おおて〖大手〗 〘□〙大手行 a「major [leading] bank.
オー・ディー・アイ〖ODI〗〘医〙〔血中の酸素飽和度が 3%以上低下した回数の1時間当たり平均回数〕an ODI《of 5 per hour》; an oxygen desaturation index.
オー・ディー・エー〖ODA〗 〘□〙 ODA 白書 =政府開発援助白書〘⇨せい⁵〙. ODA 民間モニター a civilian ODA monitor; an aid monitor (for ODA).
オー・ディー・エム〖ODM〗〔相手先が要求する商品を自ら設計し，相手先ブランドで製造・供給すること〕original design manufacturing;〔その製造業者〕an original design manufacturer.
オー・ティー・オー〖OTO〗〔内閣府に本部がある市場開放問題苦情処理推本部〕the OTO; the Office of the Trade and Investment Ombudsman.
オーデカーク Oedekerk, Steve (1961- ; 米国の映画監督・脚本家).
オートゥイユ Auteuil, Daniel (1950- ; アルジェリア生まれの映画俳優).
オートバイ 〘□〙 オートバイ・タクシー〔東南アジア等で見られる〕a motorcycle taxi. オートバイ・トライアル〔オートバイ競技〕a motorcycle trial.
オートファジー〘生理〙〔自食作用〕autophagy. ▷ autophagic *adj*.
オートポイエーシス〔自己創出・自己形成〕autopoiesis. ▷ autopoietic *adj*. 〘□〙オートポイエーシス理論 the theory of autopoiesis; autopoietic [autopoietic] theory.
オートマチック(しゃ)げんていめんきょ〖-(車)限定免許〗 =エー・ティー・(しゃ)げんていめんきょ.
オートリキシャ 〘□〙 = リキシャ.
おおとりもの〖大捕(り)物〗a roundup〔of「criminals [escaped animals]〙; a (large-scale) manhunt. ◆ 静かな住宅街にサルが現れ，パトカーが出動して〜が演じられた。A monkey appeared in a quiet residential area and a major operation, with police cars in attendance, got

under way to catch it.
オートローテーション〘空〙〔ヘリコプターが降下する際の〕autorotation.
オート・ログイン〘電算〙〔コンピューターネットワークへの自動ログイン〕auto(matic) log-in.
オートロック 〘□〙 オートロック・マンション *an apartment building [「a block of flats」] with a locked entrance.
オーナー
〘□〙 オーナー企業〔経営者が自社株の大半を保有している企業〕a private「company [enterprise]; a company [an enterprise] in which the owner holds a majority of the shares;〔スポーツチームなどの〕the company that owns《a professional baseball team》. オーナー・シェフ an owner chef《of a restaurant》; a restaurant owner-chef. オーナーシップ社会〔米国のジョージ・W・ブッシュ大統領が推進した国内政策のスローガン〕an ownership society. オーナー制度 an ownership [a private ownership] system. ◆ 棚田〜制度 to introduce a system to encourage private ownership of terraced「paddy [rice] fields. オーナー店長〔コンビニなどの〕an owner manager《of a convenience store》; a store owner-manager.
オーハ〖ORHA〗〔復興人道支援局〔室〕; 米国国家安全保障会議の一機関〕ORHA. ▶ Office of Reconstruction and Humanitarian Assistance の略.
オーバー 〘□〙 制限時間オーバー 《go》「over [beyond] a time limit.
オーバーエージ 〘□〙 オーバーエージ枠〔サッカー代表チームなどの〕a quota of overage players; overage「exemptions [slots].
オーバークロス 〜する〔立体交差で他の道路〔線路〕の上を越える〕cross over《a street》.
オーバーサイト〔監視・監督〕oversight.
オーバースイング〔ゴルフ・野球などで〕(an) overswing; overswinging. 〜する overswing.
オーバースペック〔機器の性能の(一部)が利用する側から見て過剰であること〕 〜な over-spec(')ed; with higher specs than *one* needs.
オーバーダビング〔録音済みのテープなどに別の音声をかぶせて録音すること〕overdubbing. 〜する overdub.
オーバーツ〔考古学上そこにあるはずのない場違いな遺物〕an oopart. ▶ out-of-place artifact の略.
オーバートレーニングしょうこうぐん〖-症候群〗〔激しいトレーニングをした後，疲労を回復しないままトレーニングを継続することによって起こる慢性疲労状態〕《develop》overtraining syndrome (略: OTS).
オーバーバンキング〔銀行過剰; 銀行数が多すぎる状態〕overbanking.
おおはば〖大幅〗 〘□〙大幅増 a「significant [huge] increase. ◆ 彼は国防費の〜増を提案した。He proposed a significant increase in defense spending.
おおばひるぎ〖大葉蛭木〗〘植〙〔ヒルギ科の常緑小高木; マングローブ構成種〕*Rhizophora mucronata*.
おおばまほう〖大浜槿〗〘植〙〔アオイ科の常緑小高木〕a sea hibiscus; *Hibiscus tiliaceus*.
おおはんごんそう〖大反魂草〗〘植〙〔キク科の多年草〕a cutleaf coneflower; *Rudbeckia laciniata*.
オー・ビー〖OB〗 〘□〙 OB サミット =インターアクション・カウンシル.
オー・ピー・アール・シーじょうやく〖OPRC 条約〗= だくしたいさくきょうりょくじょうやく.
オー・ピー・ピー〖OPP〗〘化〙=オルソフェニルフェノール.
おおひきがえる〖大蟇蛙〗〘動〙a cane toad; *Bufo marinus*.
オービス〘商標〙〔速度違反車自動撮影装置〕Orbis.
おおひらたけ〖大平茸〗〘菌〙〔食用キノコ〕an abalone mushroom; *Pleurotus cystidiosus*.
オー・ブイ・エー〖OVA〗〔オリジナル・ビデオ・アニメーション〕(an) original video「animation [anime]; (an)「anima-

tion [anime] released directly to video.
**おおふさも**【大房藻】〖植〗〔熱帯アメリカ原産の多年生抽水植物〕(a) parrot feather (watermilfoil); (a) parrot's feather; *Myriophyllum aquaticum*.
**オープニング** ▣ オープニング曲〔歌〕an opening song; 〔番組の最初に流れる曲〕the opening theme (music) 《of a TV drama》; 〔コンサートなどで最初に演奏される曲〕an opening number; a first piece. オープニング・スタッフ〔新規開店に際しての〕the opening staff 《of a new restaurant》. オープニング・セール〔開店セール〕an opening sale.
**「オー・ブラザー!」**〔映画〕O Brother, Where Art Thou?
**オープン**
▣ オープン・アンサー〔アンケートなどでの自由回答〕an open-ended answer; a free answer. オープン・ウォーター・スイミング [スイム]《スポーツ》〔海、川、湖などで行う水泳競技〕open water swimming; an open water swim. オープン化〔情報などを公開すること〕making 《information》 freely available; 《スポーツ》〔プロ・アマの区別をなくすこと〕making 《a competition》 open to 「all [both amateur and professional]. ▶ 携帯電話のソフトウェア開発の分野で〜化が急速に進んでいる. The field of cell phone software development is rapidly becoming more open. / アジア選手権予選会の出場資格を〜化する open up 「the qualifications [eligibility] for participation in the preliminary round of the Asian championships. オープン攻撃〔球技〕open offense. オープン参加〔open [non-member] participation. ▶ 〜参加する participate「freely [as a non-member]. オープン・スクール〔無料の公開講座〕an open school. オープン・ソース〔電算〕〔プログラムを無償で配布し、ソースコードも添付して改変・再配布なども自由とする考え〕open source. ▶ 〜ソースのソフトウェア open-source software (略: OSS).
**オープン・スカイ**〔空〕〔航空機の国際線運航の自由化〕
▣ オープンスカイ協定 an "open skies" agreement. オープンスカイ政策 an "open skies" policy.
**オープン・スカイズじょうやく**【-条約】〔空〕〔当条約加盟国が相互に軍事活動・施設などを非武装の偵察機によって監視できるとと定めた〕the Open Skies Treaty; the Treaty on Open Skies.
**オープン・デスク**〔「オープン・キャンパス」などに倣った造語〕〔設計事務所などでの研修〕(an) internship.
**オープン・プラン**〔建〕〔間仕切りをなくすか最小限にとどめた空間〕open plan ▷ open-plan *adj.*;〔教育〕〔1つの空間で複数の学級が学ぶ〕an open-plan「school [classroom].
**おおみみぎつね**【大耳狐】〖動〗(a) bat-eared fox; *Otocyon megalotis*.
**おおむぎわかば**【大麦若葉】green barley. ▶ 〜の青汁 green barley juice.
**オーラソーマ**〔カラーセラピーの一種〕Aura-Soma.
**オーラル** ▣ オーラル・ケア〔口腔の手入れ〕oral care. ▶ 〜ケア用品 an oral-care item; oral-care supplies.
**「オール・アバウト・マイ・マザー」**〔映画〕All About My Mother;〔原題〕Todo Sobre Mi Madre.
**オールでんかじゅうたく**【-電化住宅】an all-electric home;〈集合的に〉all-electric housing.
**オールでんかわりびき**【-電化割引】〔電力料金の〕a deduction for an all-electric home.
**オールドカマー**〔戦前日本に移住した永住外国人〕a permanent foreign resident who entered Japan before the end of World War II; a long-term foreign resident.
**オールドマン** Oldman, Gary (1958- ;英国生まれの映画俳優).
**オールにっぽんスーパーマーケットきょうかい**【-日本-協会】the All Japan Supermarket Association (略: AJS).
**オールラウンダー**〔オールラウンドな人〕a versatile [well-rounded] person [individual]; 「an all-rounder.
**おおるりしじみ**【大瑠璃小灰蝶】〖昆〗〔シジミチョウ科の

チョウ〕*Shijimiaeoides divinus* (*asonis*). ▶ 絶滅危惧種.
**オーロラ**[2] **1**〔米国コロラド州中部の都市〕Aurora. **2**〔米国イリノイ州北東部の都市〕Aurora.
**「オーロラの彼方へ」**〔映画〕Frequency.
**オーロラ・ビジョン**〔商標〕〔三菱電機製の大型映像情報装置〕Aurora Vision; a large video screen.
**おおわく**【大枠】▣ 大枠合意 ＝大筋合意 (⇨おおすじ).
**オカヴァンゴがわ**【-川】〔アンゴラで〕the「Kubango [Cubango] (River);〔ボツワナで〕the Okavango (River).
**オカヴァンゴ・デルタ**〔ボツワナ北部の湿地帯〕the Okavango「Delta [Swamp].
**おがさわらがびちょう**【小笠原画眉鳥】〖鳥〗〔ヒタキ科ツグミ亜科の鳥〕a Bonin Islands thrush; *Turdus terrestris*.
**おがさわらからすばと**【小笠原烏鳩】〖鳥〗〔ハト科の鳥〕a Bonin wood pigeon; *Columba versicolor*.
**おがさわらしじみ**【小笠原小灰蜆】〖昆〗〔シジミチョウ科のチョウ〕*Celastrina ogasawaraensis*.
**おがさわらしょとうしんこうかいはつとくべつそちほう**【小笠原諸島振興開発特別措置法】〔法〕the Special Measures Law for the Promotion and Development of the Ogasawara Islands.
**おがさわらとかげ**【小笠原蜥蜴】〖動〗an Ogasawara snake-eyed skink; *Cryptoblepharus boutonii (nigropunctatus)*.
**おがさわらとんぼ**【小笠原蜻蛉】〖昆〗*Hemicordulia ogasawarensis*.
**おがさわらましこ**【小笠原猿子】〖鳥〗〔アトリ科の鳥、絶滅種〕a Bonin (Islands) grosbeak; *Chaunoproctus ferreorostris*.
**オガたん**【-炭】sawdust charcoal; sawdust briquettes.
**オガデン**〔エチオピア東部の地域〕(the) Ogaden.
**オガデンせんそう**【-戦争】〔1977-78 年にエチオピアとソマリアの間で起こった戦争〕the Ogaden War.
**オガデンみんぞくかいほうせんせん**【-民族解放戦線】〔エチオピアのイスラム系武装反政府組織〕the Ogaden National Liberation Front (略: ONLF).
**オカバンゴがわ**【-川】＝オカヴァンゴがわ.
**オカバンゴ・デルタ**＝オカヴァンゴ・デルタ.
**おかまっぽい**【お釜っぽい】gay;〔口〕*swishy; faggoty; "poofy.
**おかみ**[2]【御上】▣ 御上意識 arrogance; 《have》 delusions of grandeur. ▶ 一部の公務員の頭からはいまだに〜意識が抜け切れていない. Among public officials there are some who「have not even now got rid of the feeling that their position places them above criticism [still feel themselves too good for the rest of society].
**おかめこおろぎ**【お亀蟋蟀】〖昆〗(ハラオカメコオロギ) *Loxoblemmus arietulus*; (タイワンオカメコオロギ) *Loxoblemmus aomoriensis*; (モリオカメコオロギ) *Loxoblemmus sylvestris*; (ミツカドコオロギ) *Loxoblemmus doenitzi*.
**おかわり**【お代わり】▣ お代わり自由.〔掲示〕Eat [Drink, Help yourself to] all [as much as] you like. ▶ あの店はコーヒーの〜は自由だ. You can drink all the coffee you like at that place. | They let you help yourself to coffee as often as you like there.
**おかん**[1]【悪寒】▣ 悪寒期〖医〗〔マラリアの〕the cold stage.
**おきいそ**【沖磯】offshore rocks. ▣ 沖磯釣り fishing from the rocks offshore.
**オキサイド・パン** Oxide Pang (Chun) (1967- ;香港生まれの映画監督;中国語名 彭順;ダニー・パンの双子の兄).
**オキサリプラチン**〖薬〗〔抗がん剤〕oxaliplatin.
**オキソリニックさん**【-酸】〖化〗〔抗菌剤〕oxolinic acid.
**おきてい**【沖堤】an offshore breakwater.
**おきなわイニシアチブ**【沖縄-】〔より豊かで安全な太平洋のための地域開発戦略及び共同行動計画〕the Okinawa Initiative.
**おきなわいれいのひ**【沖縄慰霊の日】〔沖縄戦終戦記念

**おきなわしんこうとくべつそちほう** 日；6月23日〕Okinawa Memorial Day.

**おきなわしんこうとくべつそちほう**【沖縄振興特別措置法】《法》the Special Measures Law for the Promotion and Development of Okinawa.

**おきなわトラフ**〔沖縄-〕〔地質〕the Okinawa Trough.

**おきなわにかんするとくべつこうどういいんかい**【沖縄に関する特別行動委員会】the Special Action Committee on Okinawa (略：SACO).

**おきなわ(ほんど)ふっききねんび**【沖縄(本土)復帰記念日】〔5月15日〕the ⟨30th⟩ Anniversary of Okinawa's Reversion to Japan.

**おきば**【置き場】▶置き場渡し〔商〕〔鉄鋼・金属などの取引で買い手が運賃を負担する場合の価格〕an ex-works price; an ex-warehouse price.

**おきゅうと**《食品》〔海草加工食品〕okyūto; a low-calorie jelly made from species of seaweed, famous as a breakfast food in Hakata.

**おくえり**【奥襟】〔柔道〕the collar at the back of the neck. ◆彼は右手で相手の～をつかんだ。He gripped the back of his opponent's collar with his right hand.

**おくがい**【屋外】▶屋外看板〔広告のための〕⁺a billboard [ˈa hoarding]; 〔案内標識など〕an outdoor [exterior] sign;〈集合的に〉ˈoutdoor [exterior] signage. 屋外球場 an outdoor stadium ⟨for ˈbaseball [football, soccer]⟩. 屋外競技場 an outdoor ˈstadium [arena, sports ground] ⟨⟨for track and field events⟩⟩. 屋外広告 outdoor [out-of-home] advertising;〔個々の〕(an) outdoor advertisement;〔看板〕*(a) billboard [ˈ(a) hoarding] advertisement. 屋外撮影〔写真の〕outdoor photography;〔動画の〕an outdoor ˈshoot [filming]. 屋外席〔野外の観覧席〕bleacher seats; bleachers;〔レストラン・カフェなどの〕terrace [outdoor] seats. 屋外設置 outdoor installation ⟨of ˈan antenna [sculptures]⟩. ◆～設置型給湯器 an outdoor-type boiler. 屋外装飾 exterior ˈdecoration [design]. 屋外テニスコート an outdoor tennis court. 屋外展示 outdoor ˈexhibition [exhibit, display];〔展示物〕an outdoor ˈexhibition [exhibit, display]. 屋外排気 outdoor ventilation. 屋外プール an outdoor pool. 屋外リンク an outdoor rink.

**「奥様は魔女」**〔米国のテレビドラマ〕Bewitched.

**おくじょう**【屋上】▶屋上園芸 rooftop [roof] gardening.

**オクタコサノール**〔米や小麦の胚芽に極微量に含まれる運動能力増強成分〕octacosanol.

**オクチルフェノール**〔化〕octylphenol. ▶**4-オクチルフェノール**〔抗酸化剤；樹脂中間体；内分泌攪乱物質とされる〕4-octylphenol.

**おくない**【屋内】▶屋内スポーツ indoor sports. 屋内装飾 interior ˈdecoration [design]. 屋内プール an indoor pool. 屋内緑化 indoor ˈgreenery [greening]; decorating indoors with ˈgreenery [plants]; displaying ˈgreenery [plants] indoors.

**おくりび**【送り火】▶〔京都〕大文字送り火 ＝ごさんのおくりび.

**おぐろヌー**【尾黒-】《動》a blue wildebeest; a brindled gnu; *Connochaetes taurinus*.

**おぐろプレーリードッグ**【尾黒-】《動》a black-tailed prairie dog; *Cynomys ludovicianus*.

**おけはざまのたたかい**【桶狭間の戦い】〔日本史〕the Battle of Okehazama.

**-おこし**【-興し・-起こし】▶地域興し local [regional] revitalization [development]; 町[村]興し town [village] revitalization; a ˈtown [village] development project.

**おこしことば**【起こし言葉】〔手紙の本題に入ることを示す言葉〕a transitional word or phrase indicating the start of the body of a letter.

**オコナー 1** O'Connor, Donald (1925-2003；米国の映画俳優).
**2** O'Connor, Pat (1943- ；アイルランド生まれの映画監督).

**おサイフケータイ**〔商標〕an "O-saifu Keitai"; a wallet cell phone; a mobile wallet.

**おざしき**【お座敷】▶お座敷遊び a (private) geisha entertainment; an entertainment session in a private room for a small number of customers, involving several geisha and other entertainers. お座敷料〔日本料理屋の座敷の使用料〕a (tatami) room ˈcharge [fee]; the ˈcharge [fee] for a reserved (tatami) room.

**おさわがせ**【お騒がせ】▶～芸能人 an entertainer who is always in the news; an attention-grabbing entertainer. ◆結局、電源コードが抜けていただけとわかった。とんだ～だった。It just turned out that the plug had been pulled out. It was all a big fuss over nothing.

**おさん**【お産】▶お産椅子〔座位分娩のための〕a birthing ˈchair [stool]. お産難民 an expectant mother desperately searching for a maternity hospital.

**オシ**〔キルギス南部の州；その州都〕Osh.

**おしあげこうか**【押し上げ効果】a ˈstimulating [positive, boosting] effect. ◆これによるGDFは～は2兆円ほどになると見込まれる。It is anticipated that ˈthe positive effect of this on GDF will be in the region of [this will raise GDF by some] two thousand million yen.

**おしあるき**【押し歩き】〔自転車・バイクなどの〕walking and pushing. ～する walk and push ⟨a bicycle⟩. ◆自転車の～中の事故が意外に多い。A surprising number of accidents occur while people are pushing their bicycles on foot.

**おしがし**【押し貸し】〔闇金融業者が無断で現金を入金し、数か月後に法外な利息の取り立てを行う、詐欺の手口〕a high-interest loan fraudulently imposed on a borrower.

**おしき**【折敷】〔食器用の四角い盆〕a tray; a wooden placemat with raised edges.

**オシキャット**《猫》〔アメリカ産の人工種〕an ocicat.

**おしぐま**【押し隈】〔歌舞伎〕〔役者の隈取りを紙や布に押しつしたもの〕an imprint of a Kabuki player's *kumadori* makeup; an *oshiguma*.

**おしさげこうか**【押し下げ効果】a ˈdepressant [negative] effect. ◆ハリケーン〔カトリーナ〕による米国経済成長の～は0.5％程度にとどまると見込まれる。It looks as if ˈthe negative effect of Katrina on American growth rates will be in the region of 0.5% [Katrina will push down growth in the US economy by something like 0.5%].

**オジサン**《魚》〔スズキ目の海洋魚〕a manybar goatfish; *Parupeneus multifasciatus*.

**おしつけあい**【押し付け合い】〔なすりあい〕(mutual) recrimination; blaming each other.

**おしなみ**【押し波】〔津波の〕(a) (tsunami) run-up; (an) uprush; a swash.

**おしょく**【汚職】▶汚職疑惑 a corruption scandal. 汚職政治家 a corrupt politician.

**オショロコマ**《魚》〔サケ科イワナ属の淡水魚〕a Dolly Varden (trout); a bull trout; a red-spotted trout; *Salvelinus malma*.

**オズ 1** Oz, Amos (1939- ；イスラエルの作家).
**2** Oz, Frank (1944- ；英国生まれの米国の人形師・映画監督).

**おすい**【汚水】▶汚水浄化装置 sewage treatment equipment.

**オスカー** ▶オスカー・ファッション〔アカデミー賞授賞式参列者たちのファッション〕Oscar fashion.

**オスカー²**《魚》＝アストロ.

**オストミー**〔医〕〔人工排泄口造設術〕(an) ostomy;〔人工排泄口〕a stoma;〔人工排泄口装用者〕an ostomate.

**オストメイト**〔医〕〔人工排泄口装用者〕an ostomate.

**オスメント** Osment, Haley Joel (1988- ；米国の映画俳

オスロごうい【-合意】〔1993年のパレスチナ暫定自治に関する合意〕the Oslo Accords.
オセアニア・サッカーれんめい【-連盟】the Oceania Football Confederation (略: OFC).
オセダックス【動】〔ゴカイの仲間の環形動物の属名〕Osedax.
オゼッラしょう【-賞】【映】〔ヴェネツィア国際映画祭の賞〕the Osella「Award [Prize].
オセルタミビル【薬】〔インフルエンザ治療薬〕oseltamivir. ▶ 薬品名 タミフル.
オセロ ▸◂ オセロ・ゲーム《play》Othello.
おせん【汚染】▸◂ 金属汚染 metal pollution. 景観汚染 scenic destruction; destruction of (the) scenery; scenic pollution. 視覚汚染 visual pollution. 重金属汚染 heavy metal pollution. 騒音汚染 noise pollution. ▸◂ 汚染原因 a cause of pollution. ◐ 〜原因企業 a polluting company; a polluter. 汚染濃度 [the] degree of pollution; pollution [contamination] concentrations.
おそじも【遅霜】▸◂ 遅霜注意報 a late frost advisory.
おそばちたい【遅場地帯】=遅場米地帯 (⇒おそばまい).
おそばまい【遅場米】▸◂ 遅場米地帯 a late rice harvest area; a region with a late rice harvest.
オゾン ▸◂ オゾン脱臭機[器, 装置] an ozone deodorizer. オゾンそうほごじょうやく【-層保護条約】〔1985年の〕the Vienna Convention for the Protection of the Ozone Layer. [=ウィーンじょうやく²]
オダー・ミンチェイ =ウドン・ミンチェイ.
オダイン【商標・薬】〔抗男性ホルモン剤・抗腫瘍薬〕Odyne.
おたから【お宝】▸◂ お宝グッズ a treasured article.
おたきあげ【お焚き上げ】〔神事・仏事に用いられた品を祈禱(きとう)をしながら燃やすこと〕the ceremonial burning of sacred objects; a burnt offering.
おたま【お玉】 ▸◂ 穴あきお玉 a slotted spoon.
オタリ Naji al-Otari, Muhammad (1944- ; シリアの政治家).
オタリア【動】〔アシカ科の海産動物〕a South American sea lion; a Southern sea lion; Otaria flavescens; Otaria byronia.
オタワじょうやく【-条約】the Ottawa「Convention [Treaty].
おちかん【落ち感】【服飾】 ◐ 〜のあるスカート a skirt that drapes well.
おちこぼれぼうしほう【落ちこぼれ防止法】【米法】the No Child Left Behind Act (略: NCLB).
オックスナード〔米国カリフォルニア州南西部の都市〕Oxnard.
おっそ【越訴】《日本史》〔正規の手続きを経ない違法訴訟〕a direct appeal (to a senior official without going through the normal formalities).
オッドー・ミアンチェイ =ウドン・ミアンチェイ.
オッド・ジャケット【服飾】〔ズボンと柄違いの替え上着〕a non-matching jacket.
オッド・ベスト【服飾】〔ジャケットと柄違いのチョッキ〕a non-matching 「*vest [waistcoat].
おでい【汚泥】▸◂ 汚泥乾燥処理 sludge drying (treatment). ◐ 〜乾燥処理施設[装置] a sludge drying 「facility [unit]. 汚泥減容化技術[減量化技術] sludge reduction technology.
「オテサーネク 妄想の子供」【映画】Little Otik; 〔原題〕Otesanek.
おてつだいロボット【お手伝い-】a helper robot; a robot 「helper [assistant].
おとくかん【お得感】a 「money-saving [bargain] feeling.
おとこがお【男顔】〔男性的な顔〕(女性の) the face of a man; a mannish face; masculine features; (男性の) a masculine face; manly [virile] features.
おとしいた【落とし板】【建】(a wall formed of) boards inserted horizontally between two grooved uprights.

おとしぬし【落とし主】▸◂ 落とし主不明の unclaimed 《bags》. ◐ 道で拾ったお金を交番に届けたが、半年後、〜不明で私のものになった. I took the money I'd found on the road to a police box, but half a year later 「it was still unclaimed [nobody had claimed it], so 「I got it [it became my property].
おとな【大人】 ▸◂ 大人買い purchasing (of collectibles) by adults.
おとない【訪い】〔訪問〕a call; a visit. ◐ 〜をいれる announce oneself (at the door).
おとなこども【大人子供】〔成人しても心が大人になりきらない〕a kidadult; a kiddult.
オドネル O'Donnell, Chris (1970- ; 米国の映画俳優).
「乙女の祈り」【映画】Heavenly Creatures.
おとも【お供】▸◂ お供本 a book to take along 《to the beach, on a trip》.
おともれ【音漏れ】〔ヘッドホンなどからの〕sound leakage.
おとり【囮】▸◂ おとりアユ a (live) decoy ayu. おとりミサイル[弾] 【軍】a decoy 「missile [bomb].
おどりて【踊り手】a dancer; 〔女性〕 *a dance girl; "a dancing girl; 《口》a hoofer. ◐ フラメンコの〜 a flamenco dancer.
「踊れトスカーナ!」【映画】Il Ciclone.
おとわれ【音割れ】crackling (noise). ◐ 〜する crackle. ◐ このスピーカーは〜する. This speaker crackles. ◐ このスピーカーは〜がひどい. This speaker makes a terrible crackling noise.
おなかいっぱい【おなか一杯】〔腹一杯〕heartily; 〔思う存分〕to one's heart's content. ◐ 安くて〜になる店 a cheap restaurant where 「you can eat your fill [the food will fill you up] ◐ 〜だ. I'm full. | I feel stuffed.
おながいぬわし【尾長犬鷲】【鳥】〔ワシタカ科の鳥〕a wedge-tailed eagle; Aquila audax.
おなら ▸◂ おなら恐怖症【精神医】a pathological fear of passing wind; 《俗》flatuphobia.
おにいとまきえい【鬼糸巻-】【魚】〔大型のマンタ〕a giant manta; a manta ray; Manta birostris.
オニール O'Neill, Jennifer (1948- ; ブラジル生まれの映画女優).
おにかさご【鬼笠子】【魚】〔フサカサゴ科の海産魚〕a hairy stingfish; a weedy stingfish; a raggy scorpionfish; Scorpaenopsis cirrhosa.
「鬼警部アイアンサイド」〔米国の、車いすの警部が主人公のTVドラマ〕Ironside.
おにごっこ【鬼ごっこ】▸◂ 逆鬼ごっこ〔1人の鬼をみんなが追いかける〕《play》reverse tag.
「オネーギンの恋文」【映画】Onegin.
おねば【御粘】〔米を炊くときにできる半液体状の澱粉(でんぷん)〕a starchy solution formed during rice cooking.
おばか ◐ こんな〜な質問してみません. Sorry for asking such a 「silly [ridiculous] question. ◐ 〜な探偵の珍道中 the adventurous journey of a 「dopey [goofy, ditzy] detective.
おばかさん a silly person; a dope. ◐ これがわからないとしたら〜なのだ. You're pretty stupid if you don't understand this. / 健太の〜[健太ったら〜ねえ], お母さんがあなたのこと見捨てるはずがないじゃない. Don't be silly, Kenta. You don't think I would just leave you, do you?
オパビニア【古生物】〔頭部に長い触手と5つのセンサーをもつ海生動物〕an opabinia; Opabinia regalis.
オビーじょうこう【-条項】【米法】〔米国製の戦闘機F-22を海外に輸出することを禁止する条項〕the "Obey" amendment. ▶ Obey は米国の共和党下院議員 David Obey (1938- ) の名より.
オピオイド【薬】〔麻薬系鎮痛剤〕an opioid.
おびぶん【帯文】〔本の〕the blurb (on the strip around a

おひょうもも【おひょう桃】『バラ科の小低木；中国原産』a flowering almond; *Prunus triloba*.

おひるぎ【雄蛭木】『ヒルギ科の常緑樹；マングローブ構成樹』a Burma mangrove; *Bruguiera gymnorrhiza*.

おひろめ【お披露目】▷お披露目会 an opening [an unveiling] ceremony;〔新メンバーなどを〕a party to introduce《the bride, newcomers》.

オフィシャル[2] ▷オフィシャル・グッズ〔選手・タレントなどの所属団体や大会の主催者が販売を公認した商品〕an official licensed product; a licensed product. オフィシャル・サプライヤー契約 a contract as (an) official supplier. オフィシャル・ショップ〔公認店〕an official shop. オフィシャル・スポンサー〔あるスポーツ大会から生じる権利を独占的に活用できる大会公式スポンサー〕an official sponsor. オフィシャル・パートナー〔スポーツ大会などの公式協賛企業〕an official partner《at the「Olympic Games [World Cup]》. ◉JOC〜パートナー an official partner of the Japan Olympic Committee; a JOC official partner. オフィシャル・パートナーシップ〔オリンピックなどで公式のパートナー[協賛企業]であること〕an official partnership. ◉〜パートナーシップ契約《sign》an official partnership agreement.

オフィス ▷オフィス家具 office furniture. オフィス空室率 an office vacancy rate. オフィス・プランニング〔快適で機能的な事務所の設計〕office environment planning. オフィス文書 an office document.

オフサイド ▷オフサイド・トラップ《サッカー》an offside trap. オフサイド・ライン《サッカー・ラグビーなど》the offside line.

オフショアかいはつ【-開発】『経営』〔システム開発やプログラミングなどを海外の会社に任せること〕offshore development; offshoring.

オフショアリング〔開発・生産の海外移転〕offshoring. [⇨オフショアかいはつ]

オプション ▷オプション契約〔金融・法〕an option contract. オプション評価理論〔証券〕option valuation theory.

オプティマル・ヘルス〔その年齢での最高の健康状態〕optimal health.

オプトアウト〔電子ダイレクトメールなどの未承諾配信〕▷オプトアウト・メール〔配信承諾がないままユーザーから中止を求めない限り送られてくる電子ダイレクトメール〕(an) opt-out mail.

オプトイン〔電子ダイレクトメールなどの配信承諾〕▷ダブル・オプトイン〔電子ダイレクトメールの送信に先立ちいったんメールをユーザー宛に送付し、ユーザーが配信承諾のメールを返送した場合に送信が開始する方式〕(a) double opt-in mail; (a) double confirmation mail. ▷オプトイン・メール〔配信を承諾した結果送られてくる電子ダイレクトメール〕(an) opt-in mail.

オフトークつうしん【-通信】『通信』〔電話回線の空き時間に地域情報などを流すシステム〕"off-talk communication service", a service offered by some Japanese providers which allows information such as local news to be distributed through telephone lines when they are not being used.

オプトメカトロニクス〔光学・機械工学・電子工学を合わせた技術〕optomechatronics.

オプトロニクス〔光電子工学〕optronics.

おふないり【お舟入り】(the ceremony of) placing a member of the Japanese Imperial Family in a coffin; the "encoffining" of《an Emperor》.

オフバランス(シート)〔会計〕『貸借対照表に計上されないこと』オフバランス化 off-balance sheet accounting. ▷オフバランス化 off-balancing. オフバランス資産 off-balance-sheet assets. オフバランス取引 off-balance sheet transaction.

オフ・プライス〔値引き(の)・ディスカウント(の)〕*off-price. ◉当店では一流ブランド品を〜で提供しております。At our store we offer top brands at 'off-store ["discount] prices. ▷オフプライス・ショップ *an off-price ["a discount] store.

オフポンプしゅじゅつ【-手術】『医』〔心臓バイパス手術など〕off-pump (coronary) bypass surgery; an off-pump (coronary) bypass (operation).

オフレコ ▷オフレコ取材 off-the-record news gathering.

オブローモフしゅぎ【-主義】〔無気力・懶惰( )・無為徒食〕Oblomovism. ▶ロシアの作家ゴンチャロフの小説 *Oblomov* の主人公から。

オペ ▷オペ室〔医〕an operating 'room [theater].

オペック【OPEC】 ▷オペック・バスケット〔OPECが価格の指標とする主要原油の一括名称〕the OPEC basket. ◉〜バスケット価格 an OPEC basket price; the price of OPEC's basket.

オペラント〔心理〕〔自発的・操作的〕operant. ▷オペラント学習 operant learning. オペラント行動 operant behavior. オペラント条件付け operant conditioning.

オペレーション ▷オペボイス[音声]オペレーション〔音声による入力操作〕voice operation. ▷オペレーション・ソフト〔電算〕operation software.

オホーツクぶんか【-文化】『考古』〔北海道北部・東部などオホーツク海沿岸を中心に8-15世紀ごろ栄えた文化〕the Okhotsk culture.

オマ(ー)ル Omar, Mohammad (1959?- ;アフガニスタンの旧政権タリバンの最高指導者).

オマーンかい【-海】the Sea of Oman; the Oman Sea.

オマーンげんゆ【-原油】〔ドバイ原油とともにアジア原油市場での指標となる銘柄〕Oman crude oil.

「おまえが欲しい」=「あなたが欲しい」。

おまぬけ【お間抜け】 ▷〜コメディー a ['screwball [wacky] comedy.

おみぬぐい【御身拭い】 ritual cleaning of Buddhist images in a temple with a white silk cloth.

おみわたり【御神渡り】〔主に諏訪湖で起き、結氷した湖面が帯状に盛り上がる現象〕*omiwatari* (the god's crossing); the phenomenon of broken ice moving across Lake Suwako, supposedly when the male god of the Kami Suwa shrine crosses it to meet the female god at the Shimo Suwa shrine.

オムそば〔料理〕〔オムライスのように卵でくるんだ焼きそば〕fried noodles wrapped in an omelette.

おむつ ▷おむつ替え a change of 'diapers [nappies]; a 'diaper [nappy] change. おむつ替えシート〔おむつ替えの時、赤ちゃんの下に敷く防水布〕a diaper-changing 'pad [sheet];〔公衆トイレなどに設置されているおむつ替え用の台〕a diaper-changing table.

オムニキン〔キンボールの試合で球を打つ前に発する掛け声〕Omnikin.

オムニバス ▷オムニバス調査〔総合一括〕調査〕《conduct》an omnibus survey.

オムバーグ『料理』〔オムライスのように卵でくるんだハンバーグ〕a hamburger patty wrapped in an omelette.

オメガ[3]〔海・航空〕〔電波航法の1つ〕Omega. ▷オメガ航法 Omega navigation.

おもいやり【思い遣り】 ▷思いやり指数 an NQ; a network quotient. [⇨エヌ・キュー]

おもちゃえほん【おもちゃ絵本】〔仕掛けのある玩具を兼ねた絵本〕a 'toy and picture [toy/picture] book; a picture book which has pop-up pictures and the like.

おもてかいどう【表街道】〔裏街道に対して〕a 'main [trunk] road; a major route; a highway; a highroad;〔人生の〕life's highway; the thoroughfare of life; the bright pathway(s) of life.

おもみづけ【重み付け】weighting.

おやがく【親学】〔親になるために必要な知識と努力〕the skills and effort necessary for parenthood; "parentology"; parenting《courses》. ◉〜が必要な時代になった。Nowadays people need to learn how to be parents.

おやくしょたいしつ【お役所体質】a bureaucratic「character [disposition, makeup].

おやこ【親子】▭ 親子ドア a wide and narrow double door; a door with an opening sidelight.

おやばれ【親ばれ】〔よくない行動が親にばれること〕one's parents finding out. ▶万引きでも何でも平気でする。～以外こわいものはない。They don't mind shoplifting or anything else. The only thing they're afraid of is their parents finding out.

おやまりんどう【御山竜胆】【植】〔リンドウ科の多年草；日本特産〕Gentiana makinoi.

おやゆび【親指】▭ 親指族〔携帯電話などを親指で器用に操作する人〕the thumb tribe.

おら【己】【私】I; me.

オランダびょう【-病】【経】〔為替レート高騰がもたらす経済危機〕the Dutch Disease.

オリーブ ▭ オリーブ・ドラブ〔緑褐色〕olive drab.

オリーブきょうしょうのういしゅくしょう【-橋小脳萎縮症】【医】olivopontocerebellar atrophy (略：OPCA).

オリヴェイラ Oliveira, Manoel de (1908- ；ポルトガルの映画監督).

オリガーキー =オリガルヒ.

おりかた、おりがた【折形】a「method [technique] of folding paper (to wrap gifts).

オリガルヒ〔ソ連邦解体後に財を成したロシアの新興財閥〕the oligarchs;〔1 人〕an oligarch.

オリゴとう【-糖】▭ 乳化オリゴ糖 lactosucrose. [=ラクトスクロース] 大豆オリゴ糖 ⇨だいず.

おりこみ【折り込み】▭ 新聞折り込み inserting folded advertisements and leaflets into newspapers;〔折り込み広告〕an「ad insert [advertising circular]; *a flyer; "an inset. ▶チラシを新聞～に配布する distribute leaflets「folded and inserted [by folding them and inserting them] in newspapers.

オリジナル ▭ オリジナル曲〔ソング〕original music;〔歌〕an original song; a song written for a specific occasion. オリジナル作品 an original work. オリジナル商品 an「original [own-brand] product. ▶その店は～商品の開発や販売に力を入れている。The store is making strong efforts to develop and market original products.

おりたたみ【折り畳み】▭ 折り畳み自転車 a「folding [collapsible] bicycle.

おりたたみしき【折り畳み式】▭ 折り畳み式携帯電話 a folding cellular phone.

オリンピック ▭ オリンピック・イヤー an Olympic year.

オルヴィエート〔イタリア中部の都市〕Orvieto.

オルソフェニルフェノール【化】〔柑橘類の白かび防止剤〕orthophenyl phenol (略：OPP).

オルテガ Ortega, Daniel (1945- ；ニカラグアの革命指導者；大統領〔1985-90, 2007- 〕).

オルトけいさんテトラメチル【-酸-】【化】tetramethyl orthosilicate (略：TMOS). [=テトラメトキシシラン]

オルドバイきょうこく【-峡谷】〔タンザニア北部の〕Oldvai Gorge. ▶アウストラロピテクスの骨が発見された地.

オルメカぶんめい【-文明】the Olmeca civilization.

オルメルト Olmert, Ehud (1945- ；イスラエルの政治家；首相〔2006- 〕).

おれ【俺】▭ オレ流 one's own (independent)「way of thinking [approach].

オレキシン【生化】〔覚醒維持・睡眠制御の働きをする脳内たんぱく質〕orexin.

「俺たち賞金稼ぎフォールガイ」〔スタントマンが副業に懸賞金付きの悪人を追う、米国の TV ドラマ〕The Fall Guy.

オレフィン ▭ オレフィン化合物 an「olefinic [olefin] compound.

オレンジかくめい【-革命】〔2004年ウクライナで起こった政治活動〕the Orange Revolution. ▶大統領選挙結果に対する抗議運動。オレンジ色がシンボルカラーだったことから。

オレンジ・ブック【医】〔医療用医薬品品質情報集〕the [an] Orange Book;【電算】the [an] Orange Book.

オレンジ・ペコー〔紅茶の茶葉のサイズと形を示す等級名〕orange pekoe.

オレンジ・ボウル【アメフト】〔米国の大学対抗4大フットボール試合の1つ〕the Cotton Bowl.

おろし[2]【卸し】▭ 鬼おろし a coarse grater (made of bamboo and wood).

-おろし【-下ろし】〔要職にある人をその地位から引きずり下ろすこと〕an ouster [(a) removal, (a) deposition]《of sb from office》.

オロッコ〔サハリンの原住民族〕the Orok;〔1人〕an Orok《pl. ～》. [⇨ウィルタ]

オロリンえんじん【-猿人】【人類】Orrorin tugenensis.

オロリン・ツゲネンシス【人類】=オロリンえんじん.

おわらい【お笑い】▭ お笑い芸人 a comedian; a comic. ▶若い～芸人 a young「comedian [comic].

おわらかぜのぼん【おわら風の盆】〔富山県八尾(やつお)町の伝統行事；台風被害が起こらないことや五穀豊穣を祈願する〕the Owara Kaze-no-bon Festival; a harvest festival with traditional music and dancing, held in Yatsuomachi, Toyama Prefecture.

おわりね【終り値】▭ 終値取引 a closing price transaction. 終値比(で)【株式】compared with the closing price. ▶前日終値比(で) compared with (the)「previous [last] close.

オン ▭ ツー[2]オン【ゴルフ】reaching the green in two shots. ▶ツー～する reach the green in two shots.

おんあつ【音圧】▭ 瞬間音圧 instantaneous sound pressure;〔そのレベル〕an instantaneous sound pressure level. ▭ 音圧センサー a sound-pressure sensor.

おんがく【音楽】▭ 映像音楽 (the) music accompanying an image;〔映画などに合わせて作られた音楽〕film music. ▭ 音楽再生機 a music player;〔録音機〕a music「recorder [recording device, recording machine]. ▶デジタル～再生機 a digital music player. 音楽配信〔インターネットによる音楽データ販売〕online music「distribution [sales]. ▶～配信サービス an online music「distribution [sales] service ／ ～配信サイト a music distribution site. 音楽表現 expression through music; musical expression.

おんかほう【温家宝】Wen Jiabao (1942- ；中国の政治家；首相〔2003- 〕).

おんきゅう[1]【恩給】▭ 恩給欠格者 a person「disqualified from receiving [not qualified to receive] a public service pension.

おんきょう【音響】▭ 音響工学 acoustic engineering; sonics. 音響測定 (an) acoustic measurement; acoustic measuring. ▭ ～測定艦 an acoustic ocean-surveillance「vessel [ship] (略：AOS). 音響調整卓〔ホールなどで、音響の分配・合成・制御する操作盤〕a sound [an audio] control console; a sound mixing console; a mixing desk; a soundboard. 音響ビデオ・カメラ an acoustic video camera.

オングルとう【-島】〔南極の〕the Ongul Islands. ▶東オングル島 (East Ongul Island) と西オングル島 (West Ongul Island) から成る.

おんげん【音源】▭ 音源分離 sound source separation. ▶～分離アルゴリズム (a) sound source separation algorithm ／ ～分離技術 (a) sound source separation technology ／ ～分離装置 a sound source separation system.

オンコセルカしょう【-症】【医】onchocerciasis.

オンコロジー【医】〔腫瘍学〕oncology.

オンサイト ▭ オンサイト電源 an on-site generator. オンサイト発電 on-site power generation.

おんしつこうかガス【温室効果-】▭ 温室効果ガス観測技術衛星〔宇宙航空研究開発機構 (JAXA) の〕the

**おんしつこうかガスしゅよう** Greenhouse Gas Observing Satellite (略: GOSAT).
**おんしつこうかガスしゅようはいしゅつこくかいぎ**【温室効果-主要排出国会議】the Major Economies Meeting on Energy Security and Climate Change.
**おんしつつやこばち**【温室艶小蜂】〔昆〕⇨つやこばち.
**おんしつどけい**【温湿度計】a hygrothermometer.
**おんしゃ**[1]【恩赦】▣ 個別恩赦〔政令恩赦に対して〕an individual amnesty. 常時恩赦〔特別恩赦に対して〕a regular amnesty.
**おんじょう**[4]【温情】▣ 温情判決 a lenient「sentence [decision, judgment, adjudication]. 温情論 leniency; an「argument [appeal] for「leniency [clemency]. ◐ 党規違反者に対して〜論と厳罰論が交錯している. Toward those who have infringed party rules there is a complex mix of arguments for leniency and for strict punishment.
**おんすい**【温水】▣ 温水床暖房「hot-water [hydronic] floor heating 《system》.
**おんせい**【音声】▣ 音声圧縮〔電算〕voice compression. ◐ 〜圧縮技術 (a) voice compression technology. 音声技術 (a)「speech [voice] technology. 音声記録 a voice recording. 音声外科 phonosurgery;〔病院の診療科〕the phonosurgery department; the department of phonosurgery. 音声工学 speech [voice] engineering. 音声自動応答 interactive voice response (略: IVR). 音声自動応答装置〔システム〕interactive voice response system (略: IVRS). 音声電子辞書 a speaking (electronic) dictionary. 音声認証 voice [speech] authentication. 音声メモ a voice memo. ◐ 〜メモ機能 a voice memo function. 音声メモリー (a) voice memory.
**おんせん**[2]【温泉】▣ 掘削温泉 a hot spring resulting from「boring [drilling]; an *onsen* using subterranean water. 汲み上げ温泉 = 掘削温泉. 地下温泉 an underground hot spring. 天然温泉 a natural hot spring. ◐ 天然〜表示マーク the symbol for a natural hot spring; the natural hot spring symbol.〔天然〕自噴温泉 a naturally occurring hot spring; a hot spring which「comes up [breaks through, has erupted] naturally. ▣ 温泉掘削業者 a hot spring drilling company. 温泉分析書 a hot spring analysis table. 温泉脈 a hydrothermal vein; a vein of hot water. 温泉療養 convalescence at a hot spring; balneotherapy.
**おんぞん**【温存】▣ 温存手術 conservative surgery. ◐ 乳房〜手術 breast-conserving surgery (略: BCS); (a) lumpectomy.
**おんたい**[1]【温帯】▣ 温帯系〔産〕(の) temperate-zone (plant, agriculture).
**おんだん**【温暖】▣ 温暖期〔地球の〕a warm period.
**おんだんか**【温暖化】▣ 脱温暖化 prevention of [taking measures against] global warming. ◐ 脱〜社会 a「society [world] which「combats [takes measures against, faces up to] global warming. ▣ 温暖化対策 a global warming tax. 温暖化ビジネス〔温室効果ガス削減の必要から生まれた新事業〕global warming businesses.
**おんち**【音痴】▣ 経済音痴 being「no good [hopeless] at economics; not understanding economic affairs;〔人〕a person who has no understanding of economics. 政治音痴 being「no good [hopeless] at politics; not understanding political affairs;〔人〕a person who has no understanding of politics.

**オン・デマンド** ▣ オン・デマンド出版 on-demand publishing.
**おんど**[2]【温度】▣ 周辺(部)温度 (a) peripheral temperature; (the) temperature at the periphery. 暖房温度〔エアコンなどの〕a「warm [high] temperature [setting]; a heating setting. ◐ (エアコンの)暖房〜を26度に設定する (with the air conditioner on 'warm',) set the temperature to 26 degrees. 中心温度 (a)「central [core] temperature; (the) temperature at the「center [core]. 冷房温度〔エアコンなどの〕a「cool [low] temperature [setting]; a cooling setting. ◐ (エアコンの)冷房〜を26度に設定する (with the air conditioner on 'cool',) set the temperature to 26 degrees. ▣ 温度依存的性決定機構〔生物〕=温度性決定. 温度性決定〔生物〕temperature-dependent sex determination (略: TSD). 温度設定 setting the temperature《on an air conditioner》. 温度センサー a temperature sensor; a thermosensor.
**おんどく**【音読】▣ 音読サービス a reading service (for the blind and visually impaired).
**おんどけい**【温度計】▣ 中心温度計 a core temperature thermometer.
**おんながお**【女顔】〔女性的な顔〕(男性の) the face of a woman; feminine features;〔女性の〕a feminine face.
**おんぱ**【音波】▣ 音波探査〔海底などの〕(an) acoustic exploration.
**おんばしらまつり**【御柱祭】〔6年ごとに開かれる長野・諏訪大社の大祭〕*Onbashira* Festival; Sacred Pillars Festival, held every six years at the Grand Shrine of Suwa, Nagano Prefecture.
**おんぷう**【温風】▣ 温風扇 a warm air fan.
**オンブズマン** ▣ オンブズマン・ネットワーク an ombudsman network; a network of ombudsmen.
**おんもん**[2]【音紋】〔潜水艦などが発する音の〕a soundprint; a sound print.
**おんやく**【音訳】▣ 音訳 CD a CD for the blind.
**おんよく**【温浴】▣ 温浴効果 the (medicinal) effect of a「warm [hot] bath. ◐ 菖蒲(しょうぶ)には〜効果を高める作用がある. Irises can heighten the (medicinal) effects of a「warm [hot] bath.
**オンライン** ▣ オンライン・オークション〔ネット・オークション〕an online [an Internet, a Net] auction. オンライン献金 (an) online donation. オンライン・コミック an online comic. [=ウェブコミック (⇨ウェブ)] オンライン・コミュニティー〔インターネット上で意見交換ができる電子掲示板や電子会議室など〕an online community. オンライン辞書 an online dictionary. ◐ 〜辞書検索サービス an online dictionary「search [look-up] service. オンライン商店街 =オンライン・モール. オンライン・ショッピング online shopping. ▷ online shopper *n*. オンライン・ショップ an online shop. オンライン・ストア an online「store [shop]. オンライン・ストレージ・サービス〔電算〕(provide) an online storage service. オンライン専業証券 an online stock broker. オンライン・テスト〔インターネットなどで行われる試験〕an online test; a test on line. オンライン・ポルノ「online [Internet] porn [pornography]. オンライン・ミュージック〔インターネット上などで提供[配信]される音楽〕online music. オンライン・モール an online (shopping) mall.
**オンライン・トラストマーク**〔ネット通信販売者への認証〕an online trustmark.
**「オンリー・ザ・ロンリー」**〔映画〕*Only the Lonely*.

# か

**カー¹** 🔲 カー・シェアリング〔車の共同利用〕car sharing.
**カー・オブ・ザ・イヤー**〔年間を通じて最も優秀な車に与えられる賞〕the Car of the Year.
**カーカス**〘自動車〙〔タイヤの骨格をなす部分〕a (tire) carcass.
**カーギル**〔米国の穀物商社〕Cargill.
**カークパトリックさん**【-山】〔南極大陸中央部の山〕Mount Kirkpatrick.
**カーゴ** 🔲 カーゴ・パンツ〘服飾〙(a pair of) cargo pants; cargoes.
**ガーション** Gershon, Gina (1962- ; 米国の映画女優).
**カーター** Carter, Helena Bonham (1966- ; 英国生まれの映画女優).
**ガーダシル**〘商標・医〙〔子宮頸がんワクチン〕Gardasil.
**カーディシーヤ** ＝カディシャ.
**カーティス** Curtis, Jamie Lee (1958- ; 米国の映画女優).
**ガーディン**〘生化〙〔がん転移誘導たんぱく質〕Girdin.
**カート²**【CART】〘自動車〙〔米国のフォーミュラカーレース主催団体; 2003年倒産〕CART; the Championship Auto Racing Teams;〔そのレース〕the CART race.
**カード** 🔲 サブカード〔主として用いるカードとは別のクレジットカード〕a secondary [back-up] credit card. メーン[メイン]カード〔主として用いるクレジットカード〕a primary credit card. 🔲 カード情報 information on a ⟨credit⟩ card; magnetic card information. ◯そのクレジット会社で200万件の～情報流出事件があった. More than 2,000,000 card information leaks occurred at that credit card company.
**カートかん**【-缶】a carton can.
**ガード・ランナー**〔マラソンで他選手との接触を防ぐため伴走するランナー〕a guard (runner).
**カーニー** Carney, Art (1918-2003; 米国の俳優; 本名 Arthur Wiliam Matthew Carney).
**カーニボー**〔FBIの電子メール傍受システム〕Carnivore.
**カーネギーきょうかい**【けんきゅうじょ】【-協会[研究所]】＝ワシントン・カーネギーきょうかい.
**カービング** 🔲 カービング・スキー〔ターンを容易にするためにトップとテールが太くサイドカーブがきつくなっているスキー板〕(a pair of) carving skis.
**カーブ²** 🔲 **S字カーブ** an S bend; an S-bend. 右[左]カーブ a ｢right-[left-](hand) ｢bend [curve].
**カーペンター** Carpenter, John (1948- ; 米国の映画監督・脚本家; 本名 John Howard Carpenter).
**ガーボロジー** ＝ガボロジー.
**カーボン** 🔲 カーボン・ナノホーン〘化〙〔一方が円錐状に開いたカーボンナノチューブ〕(a) carbon nanohorn. カーボン・マイクロコイル〘化〙〔コイル状炭素繊維〕a carbon microcoil (略: CMC).
**カーボン・ディスクロージャー・プロジェクト**〔世界の大企業500社に対して金融機関が温暖化対策や$CO_2$排出などの情報開示を求める, 炭素情報開示制度〕the Carbon Disclosure Project.
**カーマウ** ⇨カマウ.
**カーミング・シグナル**〔相手との緊張関係を緩和し, 自分の安全を図るための犬のボディーランゲージ〕a calming signal.
**ガーメント・ケース**〘バッグ〙〔旅行用衣料かばん〕a garment ｢case [bag].
**カーライル** Carlyle, Robert (1961- ; スコットランド生まれの映画俳優).
**カーライル・グループ**〔米国に本社がある世界最大級の投資会社〕the Carlyle Group.
**カーラシン**〔タイ東北部の県; 同県の県都〕Kalasin.
**｢カーラの結婚宣言｣**〔映画〕The Other Sister.

**ガーリック** 🔲 ガーリック・ライス garlic rice.
**カール¹** 🔲 カール・コード〘電気〙〔螺旋(らせん)状になった伸縮自在のコード〕a curly cord.
**カーン 1** Kahn, Cédric (1966- ; フランスの映画監督).
**2** Kahn, Madeline (1942-99; 米国の女優; 本名 Madeline Gail Wolfson).
**ガーン** 🔲 ザ・ガーン.
**かい⁵**【貝】 見むき〔貝の殻から身を出すこと〕shelling;〔その道具〕a shell knife.
**かい⁹**【解】 🔲 解の公式〘数〙〔二次方程式の〕a solution formula ⟨for a quadratic equation⟩.
**かい¹⁷**【買い】 🔲 大口[小口]買い〘相場〙bulk [small-scale] buying; a ｢bulk [small-scale] purchase.
**がい⁶**【臥位】a reclining position;〘医〙decubitus.
**がい⁷**【垓】one hundred quintillion; ten to the twentieth power; one followed by twenty zeros.
**ガイア** 🔲 ガイア理論 (the) Gaia theory.
**かいいぬ²**【甲斐犬】〘犬〙＝かいけん⁵.
**かいいん¹**【会員】 🔲 会員割引 (offer) a membership discount. ◯ ～割引価格 a ⟨25％⟩ membership discount price.
**がいいん¹**【外因】 🔲 外因死 (a) death by (an) external cause; (an) external death; (an) exogenous death.
**かいうん¹**【海運】 🔲 海運自由の原則 the principle of freedom of ｢the seas [shipping].
**かいうん²**【開運】 🔲 開運厄除け ◯ ～厄除けを願う pray for ｢good [better] luck and against ｢evil [misfortune] / ～厄除けのお守り a talisman [a charm, an amulet] to bring luck and ward off evil.
**がいえき**【外役】〔囚人が刑務所の外でする作業〕(prisoners') outside work.
**かいか³**【開花】 🔲 開花情報 information on ⟨cherry tree⟩ ｢flowering [blossoming] times. 開花宣言〔主に桜の〕a declaration that ⟨cherry trees⟩ are in bloom; a declaration of ⟨cherry⟩ blossoms. 開花予想日 the day ⟨cherry trees⟩ are expected to (come into) ｢bloom [flower, blossom].
**かいが²**【絵画】 🔲 絵画修復家[士] a picture restorer. 絵画主義〔写真の〕pictorialism. ◯ ～主義的写真 pictorialist(ic) photography;〔1枚の〕a pictorialist photograph.
**がいか¹**【外貨】 🔲 外貨兌換券 a foreign exchange certificate (略: FEC). 外貨定期預金 a foreign currency ｢time [｢time] deposit. 外貨取引 foreign currency trading.
**かいがい²**【海外】 🔲 海外安全情報 overseas safety information;〔外務省の〕海外危険情報. 海外移籍〘スポーツ〙〔選手の〕the transfer of a player to an overseas team. 海外委託〘業務などの〕overseas outsourcing; outsourcing ⟨work⟩ overseas. 海外売上高 sales volume [turnover]. ◯ ～売上高比率〔売上総額に占める〕the overseas sales ratio. 海外危険情報〔外務省の〕overseas risk information; an overseas danger warning. 海外挙式 an overseas wedding. 海外拠点〔企業などの〕an overseas base; a base ｢abroad [overseas]. 海外県〔フランスの行政区〕an overseas department (略: DOM). ▶ DOM はフランス語の *Département d'outre-mer* より. 海外権益 overseas interests. 海外公演 an overseas performance. 海外在留邦人 a Japanese person living overseas; an overseas Japanese; a Japanese expatriate. 海外先物取引〔海外商品先物取引の〕overseas commodity futures trading. 海外取材 covering [cover-

age of]《(a story)》「outside Japan [abroad]; overseas 「reporting [journalism].  海外情勢白書  a white paper on 「overseas conditions [the foreign situation].  海外生産拠点  an 「overseas [foreign, offshore] production base.  海外戦略  (an) overseas (production [manufacturing]) strategy; a strategy for [of] moving production 「overseas [abroad].  海外展開  (an) overseas deployment 《(of the Self-Defense Forces)》; (an) overseas expansion 《(of business operations)》.  ▶あの製薬会社は積極的に～展開を進めている.  That pharmaceutical company is aggressively expanding (its operations) overseas.  海外転出届  notification [notice] of moving [overseas [abroad].  海外渡航  ▶～渡航情報〔外務省の〕 Overseas Travel Information / ～渡航歴  one's overseas travel 「record [history].  海外ドラマ  an overseas [a foreign] 《TV, radio, stage》drama.  海外療養費  overseas medical treatment 「costs [expenses].  ▶～療養費(支給)制度〔国民健康保険の〕an overseas medical treatment benefit system.  海外ローミング〔通信〕overseas [global, international] roaming.

**かいがいきんむけんこうかんりセンター**【海外勤務健康管理～】the Japan Overseas Health Administration Center (略: JOHAC).

**かいがいこうりゅうしんぎかい**【海外交流審議会】〔外務大臣の諮問機関〕the Council on the Movement of People Across Borders.

**かいがいしじょう**【海外市場】 ▷▶ 海外市場調査  overseas market research.

**かいがいしじょきょういくしんこうざいだん**【海外子女教育振興財団】Japan Overseas Educational Services (略: JOES).

**かいがいとこうイニシアチブこうどうけいかく**【海外渡航-行動計画】＝あんぜんかつようかいがいとこうイニシアチブ.

**かいがいとこうしゃのためのかんせんしょうじょうほう**【海外渡航者のための感染症情報】〔厚生労働省検疫所が発する〕For Traveler's Health (略: FORTH); information on infectious diseases overseas (provided by the Japanese Ministry of Health, Labour and Welfare).

**かいがいふはいこういぼうしほう**【海外腐敗行為防止法】〔米法〕the Foreign Corrupt Practices Act (略: FCPA).

**かいかく**[1]【改革】 ▷▶ 改革派  a reformist faction; reformists.  ▶穏健～派  a moderate reformist faction; moderate reformists / 急進～派  a radical [an extreme] reformist faction; radical [extreme] reformists.

**がいかく**[1]【外角】 ▷▶ 外角速球〔野球〕a fastball on the outside corner of the plate].

**かいかけ**【買い掛け】 ▷▶ 買掛債務  an account payable 《pl. accounts payable》.

**がいかだて**【外貨建て】〔金融〕foreign-currency(-denominated) [non-yen] (deposits).  ▷▶ 外貨建て MMF  a foreign-currency「MMF [money-market fund].  外貨建て外国債券  a foreign bond denominated in a foreign currency.  外貨建て債  a foreign-currency(-denominated) bond.  外貨建て債券  a foreign-currency issue.  外貨建て債権  a foreign-currency 「receivable [claim].  外貨建て債務  a foreign-currency 「obligation [debt].  外貨建て[非円]資産  foreign-currency [non-yen] assets.  外貨建て証券  a 「foreign-currency [non-yen] security.  外貨建て相場  the (exchange) rate in a foreign currency.  外貨建て取引  a foreign-currency(-denominated) transaction.

**がいかぶ**【外株】〔外国株式〕foreign 「stock(s) [shares].

**かいぎ**[1]【会議】 ▷▶ 会議外交〔国際会議の場での外交活動〕conference diplomacy.

**かいぎ**[2]【海技】 ▷▶ 海技士  a ship's officer.  海技(士)資格  a ship officer's certification.

**がいき**【外気】 ▷▶ 外気温  (an) outside (air) temperature; the temperature outside; (an) ambient [(a) surrounding, (an) atmospheric] temperature.

**かいきゃく**[2]【開脚】 ▷▶ 開脚ジャンプ  a straddle jump.

**かいきゅう**[2]【階級】 ▷▶ 階級分化  class [caste] differentiation.

**かいきょう**[6]【開胸】〔医〕 ▷▶ 開胸心マッサージ  open-chest cardiac massage.

**かいきょうこうりゅうききんかい**【海峡交流基金会】〔中国・台湾の両岸関係を扱う台湾側の機関〕the Strait Exchange Foundation (略: SEF). [⇨かいきょうりょうがんかんけいきょうかい]

**かいきょうりょうがんかんけいきょうかい**【海峡両岸関係協会】〔中国・台湾の両岸関係を扱う中国側の機関〕the Association for Relations across the Taiwan Strait (略: ARATS).  [⇨かいきょうりゅうききんかい]

**かいきん**[4]【解禁】 ▷▶ 解禁日  the first day 《of the ayu fishing season》.  ▶今年のボージョレ・ヌーボー～日は11月15日だ. The Beaujolais Nouveau release day this year is November 15. | This year's Beaujolais Nouveau goes on sale on November 15.

**かいぐ**【戒具】〔拘禁した人の身体を拘束するための器具〕a restraining device; a restraint.

**かいぐん**【海軍】 ▷▶ 沿岸海軍  a 「green-water [coastal] navy.  外洋[大洋]海軍  a blue-water [an ocean-going, an oceanic] navy.

**かいけい**[2]【会計】 ▷▶ 会計参与  an accounting counselor.  ▶～参与制度  (a system of) accounting counseling.  会計専門職大学院  a graduate school of professional accountancy.  会計操作  manipulation of accounts.  〈口〉cooking the books.  会計帳簿  an account(s) book; a ledger; 〔その記録〕a book of account(s); 《keep》the books; *a financial book. ▶～帳簿閲覧権〔株主の〕the right to inspect 「accounts [the books].

**かいけいだいがくいんきょうかい**【会計大学院協会】the Japan Association of Graduate Schools for Professional Accountancy.

**かいけいちょう**【海警庁】〔韓国の〕＝かいようけいさつちょう.

**かいけつ**[2]【解決】 ▷▶ 解決金〔金銭解決制度のもとで支払われる〕a monetary settlement (in a case of disputed dismissal).  解決率〔犯罪捜査などの〕a 《high》《crime》solution rate.

**かいけん**[5]【甲斐犬】〔犬〕a Kai (dog); 〔異称〕a tiger dog.

**かいげんぶたい**【戒厳部隊】martial law (enforcement) troops.

**かいこ**[4]【懐古】 ▷▶ 懐古調(の)  nostalgic; antique; antiquarian.  ▶～調のデザインの車  a car with 「an antiquarian design [a design that appeals to nostalgia].

**かいご**[1]【介護】 ▷▶ 遠距離介護  long-distance 「care [care-giving] 《(for the elderly)》; looking after (an elderly parent) from 「a distance [far away].  多重介護  caring [having to care] for a lot of relatives; multiple caring.  要介護  requiring nursing care.  ▶～機器  nursing care equipment.  介護給付  nursing-care benefit (disbursement); a disbursement made for a service under the nursing-care insurance system.  介護給付費  payment for nursing care issued by a nursing-care organization under the nursing-care insurance system.  介護犬  a care dog.  介護講習 《take》a caregiver course; 《receive》caregiver training.  介護支援専門員  a care manager.  介護事業「care [caregiving] business; the business of care.  介護事業者  a (nursing) care provider.  介護食士  a certified nursing-food cook.  介護疲れ  ▶母は祖母の～疲れがもとで倒れてしまった. My mother's collapse arose from the exhaustion of nursing my grandmother. | It

was the strain of looking after my grandmother that made my mother fall ill. 介護認定審査会 a care needs assessment committee. 介護ヘルパー a 「home care [home-care] helper; 《口》a helper. 介護報酬単価 a unit price for care. 介護放棄 failure to provide (proper) care《for the elderly》; neglect. 介護浴槽 an invalid (bath)tub. 介護予防〔高齢者の〕preventive 「health care for the elderly [geriatric care]. ◐ ～予防運動指導員 an instructor in preventive health care for the elderly. / ～予防教室 a class [classes] in preventive health care for the elderly. / ～予防サービス preventive health care services for the elderly. / ～予防事業 a business promoting preventive health care for the elderly. / ～予防システム a preventive health care system for the elderly. / ～予防プラン a preventive health care plan for the elderly. / ～予防ヘルパー a preventive health care helper for the elderly / ～予防マネ(ー)ジャー the manager of a preventive health care project for the elderly; a case manager for preventive geriatric care. 介護ロボット a home care robot.
**がいこう¹【外交】** ◐ ヴァチカン[法王]外交〔ローマ教皇による外交活動〕Vatican [papal] diplomacy. 屈辱外交 humiliating diplomacy. 広報外交〔文化交流などを通じて外国の世論に働きかける外交活動〕public diplomacy. 盃外交〔やくざ同士の〕diplomacy by ritual exchange of sake《to seal an alliance》. 市民外交 citizen diplomacy. 対市民外交〔相手国の政府だけでなく国民に直接・間接に働きかける外交〕public diplomacy. 謝罪外交〔アジア諸国などに対する戦後日本の〕"apology diplomacy"; the diplomacy of apology. 追随外交 diplomacy that (simply) 「follows [conforms with, follows in the footsteps of] 《America's》. ◐ 外交演説〔国会開会時の〕the speech on foreign affairs (given by the Minister for Foreign Affairs at the opening of a Diet session). 外交慣例 diplomatic practice; (a) diplomatic 「custom [convention]. ◐ それは～に慣例に反する. This 「is [goes] against normal diplomatic practice. 外交工作 diplomatic maneuvering. 外交戦略 a ~「foreign policy [diplomatic] strategy. ◐ 対北朝鮮～戦略を見直す reconsider [rethink] strategy towards North Korea. 外交戦略家 a 「foreign policy [diplomatic] strategist. 外交評論家 a diplomatic 「commentator [analyst].
**がいこう³【外航】** ◐ 外航海運会社 an 「ocean(-going) [overseas] shipping company. 外航海運(業) ocean(-going) [overseas] shipping
**がいこう⁷【外構】**【建】the exterior; the outdoor 「area [facilities]. ◐ 外構工事 exterior construction.
**がいこうしりょうかん【外交史料館】**〔外務省の〕the Diplomatic Record Office of the Ministry of Foreign Affairs of Japan.
**がいこうしりょうかんほう【外交史料館報】**〔外務省刊行の〕Journal of the Diplomatic Record Office.
**がいこうせいさくセンター【外交政策-】**〔英国の, 外交問題についてのシンクタンク〕the Foreign Policy Centre (略: FPC).
**がいこく【外国】** ◐ 外国会社 a foreign 「corporation [company]. 外国株指数 a foreign stock index. 外国軍用品審判所〔防衛庁所管の〕a foreign military equipment inspectorate; an inspectorate of foreign military 「equipment [vessels]. 外国船舶監督官〔国土交通省所属の〕a port state control officer. 外国投資〔外国からの投資〕foreign investment; 〔外国への投資〕overseas investment; investment overseas. 外国弁護士〔外国での弁護士資格を持つ弁護士〕a lawyer qualified to practice abroad.
**がいこくかわせ【外国為替】** ◐ 外国為替保証金[証拠金]取引 foreign exchange margin trading (略:

FEMT).
**がいこくかわせおよびがいこくぼうえきほう【外国為替及び外国貿易法】**【法】the Foreign Exchange and Foreign Trade Law. ► 外国為替及び外国貿易管理法を改称・改正.
**がいこくこうむいんぞうわいぼうしじょうやく【外国公務員贈賄防止条約】**〔OECDの〕the OECD Anti-Bribery Convention. ► 公式名称は「国際商取引における外国公務員に対する贈賄の防止に関する条約」(the OECD Convention on Combating Bribery of Foreign Public Officials in International Business Transactions).
**がいこくしゅけんめんじょほう【外国主権免除法】**〔米法〕the Foreign Sovereign Immunities Act (略: FSIA).
**がいこくじん【外国人】** ◐ 外国人株主 a foreign 「stockholder [shareholder]. ◐ ～株主比率 a foreign 「shareholders [shareholders'] ratio. 外国人集住都市会議 the Conference of Cities with 「Concentrated Populations of Immigrants [Large Numbers of Non-Japanese Residents]. 外国人登録者 a registered alien. 外国人犯罪 crimes committed by foreigners. 外国人保有(比)率〔株式〕a [the] percentage of shares held by foreigners. 外国人力士 a foreign sumo wrestler; a sumo wrestler from a foreign country. 外国人労働 foreign labor. 外国人労働力 a foreign workforce. 外国人枠〔プロスポーツで〕a quota on foreign players.
**がいこくせいねんしょうちじぎょう【外国青年招致事業】**＝ジェット・プログラム.
**がいこくとうしいいんかい【外国投資委員会】**〔米国の〕＝たいべいがいこくとうしいいんかい.
**がいこくぼうえきしょうへきほうこく【外国貿易障壁報告】**〔米国通商代表部の〕the《2006》National Trade Estimate Report on Foreign Trade Barriers (略: NTE).
**がいこくほうじむべんごし【外国法事務弁護士】**〔外国での弁護士資格を持ち, 日本の法律に基づき法務大臣の承認を受けて日本で法律業務を行うことを認められた弁護士〕a foreign lawyer qualified to practice in Japan.
**カイコ・ゲノム【蚕-】**【生物】the silkworm genome.
**かいこし【買い越し】** ◐ 買い越し額 the amount of net buying.
**かいごほけんほう【介護保険法】**【法】the Public Nursing Care Insurance Law.
**かいごろうどうあんていセンター【介護労働安定-】**the Care Work Foundation.
**かいこん⁴【開梱】** unpacking. ～する unpack.
**カイザースラウテルン**〔ドイツ西部, ラインラントプファルツ州の都市〕Kaiserslautern.
**かいさつ¹【改札】** ◐ 改札機 an automatic ticket gate. 改札前＝改札口前 (⇨かいさつぐち).
**かいさつぐち【改札口】** ◐ 改札口前 ◐ 明日は新宿駅南口～前に集合してください. Tomorrow, please assemble outside the ticket barrier at the South Exit of Shinjuku Station.
**かいさん⁴【解散】** ◐ 解散価値〔株式〕liquidation value. 解散詔書 the emperor's dissolution rescript; the imperial order to dissolve the Diet. 解散請求 a demand for the 「dissolution《of the Prefectural Assembly》 [liquidation《of the company》]; a 「demand [request] that《the sect》be dissolved.
**がいさん【概算】** ◐ 概算医療費 approximate annual national medical expenditures.
**かいじ⁶【開示】** ◐ 開示資料 disclosed material(s)《about a company's performance》. 開示注意銘柄〔証券〕a stock whose issuing company has received a disclosure warning. ◐ 株式を～注意銘柄に指定する put《a company's》stock on the watch list (for inade-

がいし

quate disclosure).
**がいし**[5]**【外資】** ▭ 外資規制 restrictions on [the regulations controlling] foreign ownership. 外資系《の》foreign-owned 《firms》; foreign affiliated 《companies》. ◐ 〜系ホテル a foreign-owned hotel / 〜系保険会社 a foreign-owned insurance company. 外資警戒論 ⇨警戒論 (⇨けいかい[4]). 外資参入 an 「inflow [influx]」 of foreign 「capital [investment]」. ◐ 〜参入による競争の激化 increased competition from foreign 「capital [investors, companies]」. 外資支配 《come under》 foreign control.
**かいじせいきゅう【開示請求】** a disclosure request. 〜する request the disclosure 《of information》. ▭ 開示請求権 the right to request the disclosure 《of information》.
**がいじつリズム【概日―】** ▭ 概日リズム睡眠障害 〔医〕 a circadian rhythm sleep disorder.
**かいしゃ**[1]**【会社】** ▭ 会社解散 (the) 「dissolution [liquidation, winding up]」 of a company.
**かいしゃく**[2]**【解釈】** ▭ 弾力的解釈 a flexible interpretation.
**がいしゃし【外斜視】** ▭ 間欠性外斜視 (an) intermittent exotropia. 恒常性外斜視 (a) constant exotropia. 調節性外斜視 (an) accommodative exotropia.
**かいしゃほう【会社法】**〔法〕the Company Law.
**がいしゅ【外需】** ▭ 外需関連株〔銘柄〕an overseas-demand-related 「stock [issue]」. 外需主導 ◐ 〜主導の景気回復 foreign demand-led economic recovery.
**かいしゅう**[2]**【回収】** ▭ 回収可能な recoverable 《cost》; collectible 《loan》; recoverable [retrievable] 《spaceship》; returnable 《bottles》.
**がいしゅう【外周】** ▭ 外周規制線〔米軍機などが事故を起こした際に二重に設けられる立ち入り規制線のうち外側の規制線〕an outer cordon.
**がいしゅつ【外出】** ▭ 外出恐怖(症) 〔精神医〕agoraphobia; a fear of (open [public]) 「spaces [situations] that cause anxiety.
**かいしゅん**[3]**【買春】** ▭ 買春ツアー 《go on》 a sex tour.
**かいじょ**[1]**【介助】**
▭ 介助車 a transport chair; 〔車いす〕a wheelchair. 介助バー〔ベッド・いすなどに取り付け、起き上がったりする際につかまる用具〕a support 「rail [bar]」. 介助法 a method of assistance. ◐ 入浴―法 how to help sb take a bath. 介助ボランティア volunteer work 「for [with]」《the handicapped》; volunteer caregiving; 《do》 work as a volunteer caregiver; 〔人〕a volunteer caregiver. 介助用 (designed) 「for [to aid] care 《of the elderly》. ◐ 〜用車椅子 a wheelchair for care 《of the handicapped》 / 〜用食器 tableware designed for care 《of the elderly》 / 〜用浴室 a bathroom designed for care 《of the handicapped》. 介助浴 assisted bathing.
**かいじょ**[3]**【解除】** ▭ 解除ボタン 〔機〕〔機能設定を取り消すための〕an 《alarm》 release button; a reset button.
**かいじょう**[4]**【海上】**
▭ 海上安全保障 ＝海洋安全保障 (⇨かいよう[1]). 海上給油 maritime refueling; refueling at sea. 海上警察 (the) 「marine [maritime]」police. 海上事前集積船〔軍〕〔装備・補給品の〕a maritime prepositioning ship (略: MPS). 海上阻止訓練〔軍〕〔PSI(大量破壊兵器拡散防止構想)に基づく〕a Maritime Interdiction Exercise. 海上テロ maritime terrorism; terrorism at sea; 〔1回の攻撃〕a maritime terrorist 「attack [act]」; an act of terrorism at sea. 海上特殊無線技師 a special maritime radio operator, 《category I, category II, category III》. ◐ 第一級から第三級まである. 海上濃霧警報 〔issue〕a dense (marine) fog warning. 海上配備 〔軍〕 maritime deployment (of nuclear weaponry). 海上配備型迎撃ミサイル 〔軍〕 a 「sea-to-air [sea-based] interceptor missile. 海上風力発電所〔電〕an

offshore wind power 「plant [station]」. 海上輸出 seaborne export(s); exports [exporting] by sea. 海上油田 an offshore oil field.
**かいじょう**[11]**【解錠】** ▭ 解錠業者 a locksmith.
**かいしょう**[3]**【外傷】** ▭ 外傷初期診療ガイドライン(日本版)〔医〕Japan Advanced Trauma Evaluation and Care; JATEC. 外傷病院前救護ガイドライン(日本版)〔医〕the Japan Prehospital Trauma Evaluation and Care guidelines; the JPTEC guidelines.
**がいしょう**[5]**【街商】** a street vendor; a peddler; a hawker.
**かいじょうぎじゅつあんぜんけんきゅうじょ【海上技術安全研究所】**〔独立行政法人〕the National Maritime Research Institute (略: NMRI).
**がいしょうしゃ【外照射】**〔医〕＝外部照射 (⇨がいぶ). ▭ 外照射治療 ＝外部照射治療 (⇨かいぶ).
**がいしょうせい【外傷性】** ▭ 外傷性ショック死 death from traumatic shock; (a case of) fatal traumatic shock. 外傷性窒息〔医〕traumatic asphyxiation. 外傷性脳内出血〔医〕a traumatic 「brain [intracerebral]」hemorrhage.
**かいじょうそしかつどう【海上阻止活動】**〔「不朽の自由作戦」に基づく〕the Operation Enduring Freedom-Maritime Interdiction Operation (略: OEF-MIO).
**かいじょうほあん【海上保安】** ▭ 海上保安レポート〔海上保安庁の〕the Japan Coast Guard Annual Report 《2005》.
**かいしょく**[1]**【会食】** ▭ 会食恐怖症 a (pathological) fear of dinner (parties [conversation]); 〔精神医〕deipnophobia.
**がいしょく【外食】** ▭ 外食恐怖症〔精神医〕＝会食恐怖症 (⇨かいしょく[1]).
**かいすい【海水】** ▭ 海水温 (an) ocean temperature. 海水面 sea level. ◐ 〜面上昇 a rise in sea level.
**かいすいよく【海水浴】** ▭ 海水浴シーズン the (seaside) 「swimming [bathing] season; the beach season.
**かいせい**[1]**【回生】** ▭ 回生エネルギー〔電〕regenerated energy.
**かいせき**[4]**【解析】** ▭ 解析コード an analysis code.
**かいせき【懐石】** ▭ 洋風懐石 western cuisine served in the kaiseki style. 和風懐石 a traditional Japanese multi-course meal.
**かいせじょう【解施錠】**〔解錠と施錠〕locking and unlocking.
**かいせん**[2]**【回旋】** ▭ 回旋腱板〔解〕a rotator cuff.
**かいせん**[4]**【回線】** ▭ 一般回線 a conventional [an ordinary] (telephone) 「circuit [line]」. 警察〔消防〕回線 a dedicated (telephone) 「circuit [line] for 「police [firefighting]」 services. ▭ 回線相互接続 interconnection of (telephone) lines.
**かいせん**[5]**【改選】** ▭ 改選議席 a seat up for election (at completion of a term of office). ◐ 民主党は都市部を中心に順調に得票を重ね、〜議席(38)を大きく上回る50議席を獲得した. The DPJ made healthy gains, especially in urban areas, and obtained fifty seats, a great improvement on the number they held before the election (38).
**かいせん**[8]**【疥癬】** ▭ 角化型疥癬〔医〕＝ノルウェーかいせん.
**かいぜん【改善】**
▭ 改善勧告〔監督官庁の〕(issue) 「advice [instructions] to 「make improvements [improve (operations)]」. 改善計画 an improvement 「plan [project]」; plans for improvement(s); plans [a plan] to 「improve [reform]」《the stock exchange》. 改善策 ＝改善 ⇨きょう / 経営―計画 ⇨けいえい[2] 改善計画書 a draft 「improvement [reform] plan; written plans for improvement(s) 《to …》. 改善効果 《have》 an 「ameliorative [improving] effect 《on …》. 改善指示〔監督官庁の〕(is-

sue》) an improvement advisory. 改善指導〔監督官庁の〕(issue) (a) guidance to ﾌmake improvements [improve 《operations》]. 改善報告書 ＝業務改善報告書(⇨ぎょうむ). 改善命令〔監督官庁の〕(issue) an improvement order. [⇨ぎょうむ (業務改善命令)] 改善薬 an ﾌimprovement [alleviation] drug; a drug to ﾌimprove 《potency》 [alleviate 《symptoms》].

**かいせんぞく**【快閃族】＝フラッシュ・モブ.

**かいそう**[7]【改装】□ 全面[部分]改装 (a) ﾌfull [partial] renovation 《of a shop》. □ 改装工事 redecorating (work); refurbishment.

**かいそう**[15]【階層】□ 階層意識 stratum [status] consciousness. 階層格差 a class ﾌdifference [gap, divide]; a 《widening》 ﾌgap [disparity] between rich and poor. 階層間移動《社会》movement [mobility] between strata; movement (mobility) within a hierarchy; inter-strata movement. 階層帰属意識 stratum ﾌidentification [consciousness]. 階層方式〔関税削減方式などの〕a tiered formula 《for tariff reduction》.

**かいぞう**[1]【改造】□ 改造エア・ガン a converted air gun; an air gun modified to fire metal bullets at high velocity.

**かいぞくじょうほうきょうゆうセンター**【海賊情報共有-】〔アジア海賊対策地域協力協定 (ReCAAP) によって設置された〕the (ReCAAP) Information Sharing Center (略: ISC).

**かいぞくじょうほうセンター**【海賊情報-】＝国際海事局海賊報告[情報]センター(⇨こくさいかいじきょく).

**かいぞくばん**【海賊版】□ 海賊版ソフト pirated [pirate] computer software.

**かいたい**[3]【解体】□ 解体撤去 demolition and removal 《of buildings, etc.》. ○ 撤去費 the cost of demolition and removal. 解体費(用)〔出費〕demolition costs; the cost of demolition; 〔料金〕⇨解体料(金). 解体料(金) a demolition charge; the charge for demolition.

**かいたいてき**【解体的】□ 解体の改革 (a) ﾌreform [reorganization] based on taking the present system apart. 解体の出直し taking things apart and starting again from ﾌthe beginning [scratch].

**かいたし**【買い足し】buying more of an item 《one already has》.

**がいタレ**【外-】〔外国人の(テレビ)タレント〕a foreign (TV [media]) ﾌpersonality [celebrity].

**かいちゅう**[3]【海中】□ 海中水族館 an underwater aquarium.

**がいちゅう**[1]【外注】□ 外注管理 outsourcing management; subcontract control. 外注費 outsourcing expenses; the cost(s) of outsourcing.

**がいちゅう**[2]【害虫】□ 害虫駆除業者[会社] an exterminator (company).

**かいちょう**[2]【回腸】□ 回腸遠位部《獣医》the distal ileum 《of cattle》.

**かいちょう**[8]【開張】□ 開張足《医》(a) splayfoot.

**かいちょう**[9]【階調】□ 階調表現 gradation expression. 階調補正《写真》tone correction.

**かいつけ**[1]【買い付け】□ 買い付け価格 a purchase price; 〔株式公開買い付けなどの〕a bid price.

**かいてい**[3]【海底】□ 海底遺跡 seabed remains; submarine ruins; submerged ruins. 海底崖《地形》a ﾌsubmarine [underwater] escarpment [cliff]. 海底(地形)測量 seabed surveying; 〔1 回の〕a seabed survey. 海底林 an underwater forest.

**かいてい**[5]【開廷】□ 連日[連続]開廷〔判決を早期に出すために公判を可能な限り毎日行うこと〕holding court sessions every day (as far as possible in order to expedite ﾌa [the] verdict).

**「海底大戦争 スティングレイ」**〔英国の, 海底活劇ものの人形劇 TV ドラマ〕Stingray.

**かいていちけいめいしょうしょういいんかい**【海底地形名称小委員会】〔大洋水深総図 (GEBCO) の下部組織〕the Sub-Committee on Undersea Feature Names (略: SCUFN).

**かいてき**【快適】□ 快適性 comfort; pleasantness. ◐ 最新式の空調システムにより, 高い～性を実現しました. The newest-type air conditioning systems have enabled the realization of a high degree of comfort. / 今回発売する新型車は安全性と～性を追求したモデルです. The new car we are now marketing is a model that seeks to maximize safety and comfort.

**かいてん**[2]【回転】□ 回転径《機》a rotation diameter. 回転座席 ＝回転座シート. 回転座シート〔自動車・列車などの〕a bench seat that revolves to face another seat. 回転(式)遊具〔小学校や公園などで〕revolving playground equipment. 回転技《スポーツ》〔フィギュアスケートなどの〕a spin; a turn; 〔スノーボードなどで〕(a 360, a 540) rotation.

**カイト** □ カイトサーフィン kitesurfing. ▷ kitesurfer *n*. [＝カイトボーディング] カイトボーディング kiteboarding. ▷ kiteboarder *n*. [＝カイトサーフィン]

**ガイド** □ 国際山岳ガイド a certified international mountain guide. 山岳[登山]ガイド a ﾌmountain [mountaineering] guide. 登攀(とはん)ガイド a (mountain) climbing guide.

**かいとう**[9]【解答】□ 解答率〔(無解答に対して)解答してあった割合〕a response rate; a [the] percentage of questions ﾌanswered [attempted].

**がいとう**[4]【街頭】□ 街頭アンケート an on-street ['a pavement, *a sidewalk] questionnaire. 街頭活動〔行動, 運動〕street activism; a street campaign. 街頭紙芝居 street storytelling with picture cards. ◐ ～紙芝居師 an itinerant picture-card storyteller. 街頭献血 on-the-street [mobile] blood donation. 街頭詩人 a street poet. 街頭指導 on-the-street guidance 《of juveniles》. 街頭集会 a street rally. 街頭署名活動〔launch〕a street ﾌpetition [signature(-collecting)] campaign. 街頭犯罪 (a) street crime.

**かいどき**【買い時】□ 買い時感 a feeling that now is the time to buy. ◐ 地価の下落に伴い新築住宅の～感は高まっている. With the drop in land prices, more and more people feel that this is the right time to buy a newly built home.

**かいないきん**【回内筋】□ 円回内筋 the pronator teres (muscle). 方形回内筋 the pronator quadratus (muscle).

**かいにゅう**【介入】□ 介入軍《軍》an intervening force.

**カイネティクス**〔動力学; 動態〕kinetics.

**ガイノイド**〔SF などで, 女性のアンドロイド〕a gynoid.

**かいは**【会派】□ 会派届 (a) notification of the formation of a parliamentary group.

**かいば**[1]【海馬】□ 海馬状隆起《解》〔脳の〕the hippocampus.

**カイパー** Kuiper, Gerard Peter (1905-73; オランダ生まれの米国の天文学者).

**カイパー・ベルト** □ カイパー・ベルト天体 a Kuiper Belt object.

**かいはつ**【開発】

□ 開発学 development studies. 開発競争 development competition; competition [a race] to develop 《new technologies》. ◐ 新製品の～競 competition [a race] to develop new products / 核兵器 ～ 競争 a nuclear arms race. 開発区〔中国の〕a development ﾌzone [area]. 開発経済学 development economics; the economics of development. 開発コスト the cost of development. ◐ ～コストを削減する reduce development cost(s). 開発三角地帯〔ラオス・カンボジア・ベトナム三国国境をまたぐ貧困地域〕the

かいばつ

(Cambodia-Laos-Vietnam) Development Triangle. **開発段階**《be at》a〔the〕development stage. ◐～段階にある製品 a product (which is)〔at the development stage〔under development〕/ 彼はこの新車には～段階から関わっている. He was involved with the new model from the development stage. | He was involved with developing the new car from the start. **開発法学** law and development studies.

**かいばつ**[1]【海抜】▣▢ 海抜表示板 a sign indicating height above sea level; an altitude sign.

**かいはつしきんかいぎ**【開発資金会議】〔国連の〕the International Conference on Financing for Development(略: FfD); the International Financing for Development Conference.

**かいひ**[4]【開扉】▣▢ 開扉性《自動車》〔自動車などの安全性能で、事故後のドアの開閉しやすさ〕door openability.

**かいひょう**[4]【開票】▣▢ 開票立会人 a ballot-counting「observer [witness]」; "a scrutineer (at a ballot count).

**がいぶ**【外部】
▣▢ 外部化 outsourcing. ◐～化する outsource / 老人介護の～化は少子高齢化の必然的結果である. Care for the elderly by outside providers is an inevitable result of the declining birthrate and the growing elderly population. **外部監査員**〔企業・法人・自治体など の〕an external auditor. **外部協力者** an「outside [external] cooperator [helper, participant]; a「cooperative [helpful] outsider. **外部照射**【医】〔放射線の〕external「radiation [irradiation]; radiation from outside the body. ◐～照射治療 external「radiation [irradiation] treatment. **外部調査** an「outside (external) investigation. **外部調査委員会** an「external [independent] investigation committee.

**かいふく**[1]【回復】◐治安回復 the restoration of public order. **被害回復** restoration of「a loss [damage]; recompensation in kind. ◐犯罪被害者の救済と被害～制度 a system for aiding and restoring losses to crime victims. ◐回復感 signs of recovery; recovery indicators. ◐景気～感 signs of economic recovery. **回復手術**【医】〔視力や音声の〕restorative surgery (to improve「eyesight [hearing]).

**かいふくき**[1]【回復期】▣▢ 回復期リハビリ(テーション)病棟 a rehabilitation ward (for convalescent patients).

**かいへいえんせいぐん**【海兵遠征軍】【米軍】the《1st, 2nd, 3rd》Marine Expeditionary Force (略: MEF).

**かいへいえんせいたい**【海兵遠征隊】【米軍】the《1st, 2nd, 3rd》Marine Expeditionary Unit (略: MEU).

**かいへいえんせいりょだん**【海兵遠征旅団】【米軍】the《1st, 2nd, 3rd》Marine Expeditionary Brigade (略: MEB).

**かいへき**【界壁】【建】a separation wall;〔特に集合住宅で各住戸間の〕=こざかいへき.

**かいほう**[10]【開放】▣▢ 開放病棟〔患者の出入り自由の〕an open ward.

**かいぼう**[1]【海防】▣▢ 海防艦〔旧日本海軍の〕a coast(al) defense vessel.

**かいほうにっぽう**【解放日報】〔中国の新聞〕上海市の共産党機関紙〕the Liberation Daily; Jiefang Ribao.

**かいまく**【開幕】▣▢ 開幕演説[スピーチ]《make》an opening speech. **開幕試合** the opening game《of the season》; a season opener. ◐松坂は～試合に先発で登板した. Matsuzaka was the first to take the mound in the season opener.

**かいまけ**【買い負け】〔競りや買い付け競争で負けること〕losing out (to a higher bidder).

**かいまける**【買い負ける】lose out (to a higher bidder). ◐日本の水産物輸入業者が中国の業者に～ケースが増えてきている. There is a growing number of cases of Japanese importers of marine products losing out to Chinese companies.

**かいまし**【買い増し】〔株などを買って保有量を増やすこと〕the「buying [purchase] of more《shares》;〔機器などを買って保有台数を増やすこと〕the「buying [purchase] of more《equipment》.
～する〔株などを〕buy [purchase] more《shares》;〔機器などを〕buy [purchase] more《equipment》.

**かいます**【買い増す】〔株などを買って保有量を増やす〕buy [purchase] more《shares》; increasing *one's* holdings.

**かいみじんこ**【貝微塵子-】【動】〔カイミジンコ科の甲殻類の総称〕(a) cypris (*pl.* cyprides).

**かいみん**【快眠】▣▢ 快眠ビジネス the sleep business.

**かいみんかつぎょ**【快眠活魚】【商標】〔魚の脳に針を刺して眠らせ鮮度を保つ方法〕*Kaimin Katsugyo*; an acupuncture-type method of keeping fish in suspended animation to ensure freshness.

**カイム**〔イラク西部の村〕(al-)Qaim.

**がいむ**【外務】▣▢ 外務審議官 a deputy foreign minister. **外務報道官**〔外務省の〕the Director-General for Press and Public Relations; the Press Secretary.

**かいめん**[2]【海綿】▣▢ 海綿骨【解】spongy [cancellous] bone.

**かいもの**[2]【買い物】▣▢ 買い物履歴 =購買履歴 (⇒こうばい[4]).

**がいや**【外野】▣▢ 外野守備コーチ an outfield defense coach.

**かいやく**[2]【解約】▣▢ 解約還付金《保険》a policy cancellation refund.

**かいよう**[1]【海洋】▣▢ 海洋安全保障 maritime [marine] security. **海洋汚染物質** a marine pollutant. **海洋環境学** marine environmental「studies [science]. **海洋権益**《the country's》maritime interests《in the East China Sea》. **海洋国家** a maritime「state [country, nation]. **海洋戦略**〔一国の〕(a) maritime strategy. **海洋保護区**〔海洋生態系を保護するための〕a marine protected area (略: MPA). **海洋民族** a maritime「people [《文》nation]. **海洋リザーバー効果**〔考古〕〔年代測定に使われる〕an [the] ocean reservoir effect.

**がいよう**[1]【概要】▣▢ 概要調査〔高レベル放射性廃棄物の最終処分地選定のための〕⇒文献調査 (⇒ぶんけん[5]).

**かいようおせんぼうしじょうやく**【海洋汚染防止条約】the International Convention for the Prevention of Pollution from Ships. ▶ 1973 年に制定後、78 年に改定. 現在の正式名称は「1973 年の船舶による汚染の防止のための国際条約に関する 1978 年の議定書」(the International Convention for the Prevention of Pollution from Ships, 1973, as modified by the protocol of 1978 relating thereto (略: MARPOL 73/78)). [=マルポールじょうやく]

**かいようかいはつけんきゅうきこう**【海洋開発研究機構】the Japan Agency for Marine-Earth Science and Technology (略: JAMSTEC).

**かいようがくいいんかい**【海洋学委員会】⇒ユネスコせいふかんかいようがくいいんかい.

**かいようかんりきょうぎかい**【海洋管理協議会】〔ロンドンに本部を置く国際機関〕the Marine Stewardship Council (略: MSC).

**かいようきほんほう**【海洋基本法】【法】the Basic Law on the Oceans.

**かいようけいさつちょう**【海洋警察庁】〔韓国の〕the Korea Coast Guard (略: KCG).

**かいようけんきゅうかいはつきこう**【海洋研究開発機構】the Japan Agency for Marine-Earth Science and Technology (略: JAMSTEC).

**かいようせいさくけんきゅうざいだん**【海洋政策研究財団】the Ocean Policy Research Foundation (略: OPRF).

**がいらい**【外来】▣▢ 外来動物[植物] an alien [a non-native] species of「animal [plant]; an animal [a plant] from abroad; an exotic;〔導入種〕an introduced spe-

cies;〔定着種〕a colonist. **外来河川**〔地質〕an exotic 「river [stream].  **外来魚** a non-native fish; a fish from abroad; an exotic;〔導入種〕an introduced species;〔定着種〕a colonist.  **外来診療** outpatient 「treatment [care].  **外来診療記録** an outpatient 「medical [treatment] record (略: OMR, OTR).
**がいらいしゅひがいぼうしほう**【外来種被害防止法】《法》=がいらいせいぶつほう.
**がいらいせいぶつ**【外来生物】an alien [a non-native] organism.  ▶ **特定外来生物** an invasive alien species (略: IAS).  **未判定外来生物** an uncategorized alien species (略: UAS).  **要注意外来生物** a potentially (dangerous) invasive species.
**がいらいせいぶつほう**【外来生物法】《法》the Invasive Alien Species Law. ▶ 正式名称は「特定外来生物による生態系等に係る被害の防止に関する法律」.
**カイラン**【芥藍】〔植〕〔中国野菜〕Chinese kale.
**カイロこうどうけいかく**【-行動計画】〔1994年、国連の国際人口開発会議で採択された〕the Cairo Programme of Action. ▶ 正式名称は「国際人口開発会議行動計画」(the Programme of Action of the United Nations International Conference on Population & Development).
**カイロプラクター** a chiropractor.
**かいわ**[1]【会話】▶ **会話ロボット** a conversational robot.
**カイン** ▶ **カイン・コンプレックス**《精神分析》a Cain complex.
**カイン**[2]〔地震〕〔SI 単位を表す速度の単位〕a kine.
**カインホア** ⇨カンホア.
**カヴィーゼル** Caviezel, James [Jim] (1968- ; 米国の映画俳優; 本名 James Patrick Caviezel).
**カウカがわ**【-川】〔コロンビアの川〕the Cauca River; the Cauca.
**カウキャッチャー**《放送・広告》〔番組が始まる直前の CM〕a cowcatcher.
**ガウテン** =ハウテン.
**カウプしすう**【-指数】〔乳幼児の肥満度指数〕the Kaup index.
**カウフマン** Kaufman, Philip (1936- ; 米国の映画監督).
**カウフマン・スタジアム**〔米国, ミズーリ州カンザス・シティーにある野球場〕Kauffman Stadium.
**カウラ**〔オーストラリア, ニューサウスウェールズ州の町〕Cowra.  ▶ **カウラ事件**《史》〔1944年8月5日、オーストラリアのカウラで起きた日本兵捕虜集団脱走事件〕the Cowra Breakout.
**ガウリ**《軍》〔パキスタンが北朝鮮の協力を得て開発した核弾頭搭載可能な中距離弾道ミサイル〕a Ghauri missile.
**カウリスマキ 1** Kaurismäki, Aki (1957- ; フィンランドの映画監督・脚本家; 2 の弟).  **2** Kaurismäki, Mika (1955- ; フィンランドの映画監督・脚本家; 1 の兄).
**かうん**【家運】▶ **家運隆昌**《pray for》the prosperity of a family.
**カウンセリング** ▶ **心理的カウンセリング** psychological counseling.  ▶ **カウンセリング心理学** counseling psychology. ◐ ~**心理学者** a counseling psychologist.
**カウンター**[2] ▶ **カウンター越し** 《バーテンが~越しに話しかけてきた.》The bartender spoke to me 「from behind [across] the bar.  **カウンター商品** counter 「goods [items].
**カウンター**[3] ▶ **カウンター狙い**《playing》a counterattack 「game [style]; a counterattack strategy.
**カウンターパート**〔交渉などを進める際の、一方と対等な地位にある相手〕one's 「counterpart [opposite number]. ◐ 《この会議の米国側の~は農務長官である.》His American counterpart at the conference is the Secretary of Agriculture.
**カウントダウン** ▶ **カウントダウン時計** a countdown clock.  **カウントダウン・ボード**〔残り日数などの表示盤〕a countdown board.
**かえい**[2]【火映】〔火山火口部の噴煙などが赤く照らし出される現象〕(a) volcanic glow.
**かえりづゆ**【返り[帰り]梅雨】rainy days [wet weather] after the apparent end of the rainy season.
**かえりばな**【返り[帰り]花】second blooms in the same year.
**かえるあんこう**【蛙鮟鱇】〔魚〕a frogfish; *Antennarius striatus*.
**かお**【顔】▶ **顔画像** a facial image.  **顔認証** face 「recognition [authentication].
**かおけんしゅつきのう**【顔検出機能】〔写真〕〔カメラの〕a face recognition function.
**かおじゃしん**【顔写真】▶ **顔写真入り[付き]身分証明書** a photo ID card; an ID with photo.
**かおだに**【顔だに】〔動〕〔顔面の毛穴などに巣くうダニ〕=にきびだに.
**かおパス**【顔-】▶ **顔パスシステム**〔顔認証による〕a security system using face「recognition [authentication];《商標》FacePass.
**カオバン**〔ベトナム北東部の省; その省都〕Cao Bang.
**カオラック**〔タイ南部, パンガー県の都市〕Khao Lak.
**かがい**[1]【加害】▶ **加害少年** a juvenile 「assailant [attacker, murderer].
**かかく**[2]【価格】
▶ **サンプル価格** a sample price.
▶ **価格インセンティブ** a price incentive.  **価格競争入札** a price competitive auction. ◐ **非~競争入札** a non-price competitive auction.  **価格下落率** the rate of price decline.  **価格交渉** price 「negotiations [talks]; bargaining;《口》haggling (over the price).  ◐ ~**に入る** enter into price negotiations 《with…》.  **価格交渉力**《have》price bargaining power.  **価格攻勢** a price 「offensive [assault]. ◐《わが社の製品はアジア諸国による厳しい~攻勢にさらされている.》Our company's products are being subjected to a fierce price offensive by Asian countries.  **価格訴求力** the appeal of low price(s); low-price appeal; the ability of low prices to attract customers.  **価格弾力性**《経》price elasticity.  **価格転嫁** price pass-through (of petroleum products).  **価格転嫁率** the percent of price pass-through.  **価格動向** price trends; a trend in (oil) prices; how [the way] prices move.  **価格バンド制**〔OPEC の石油価格安定化のための制度〕the [OPEC's] price band system.  **価格比較サイト**〔インターネット上の〕a price comparison (Web)site.  **価格変動リスク** the risk of price changes.
**かがく**[1]【下顎】▶ **下顎前突**〔歯科〕mandibular protrusion.
**かがく**[2]【化学】▶ **化学攻撃** a chemical (weapons) attack.  **化学合成細菌** chemosynthetic bacteria.  **化学合成独立栄養**〔生物〕chemoautotrophy. ▷ **chemoautotrophic** *adj.* ◐ ~**合成独立栄養生物** chemoautotroph.  **化学試験**〔原子力〕〔再処理施設の〕《carry out》a chemical test.  **化学飼料** chemical feed.  **化学戦争** chemical warfare.  **化学物質等安全データシート** =製品安全データシート(=データシート).  **化学防護服** a chemical-proof suit.  **化学放射線療法**〔医〕chemoradiotherapy.
**かがく**[4]【科学】▶ **科学研究費** ◐ ~**研究費補助金**〔文部科学省の助成金〕a government subsidy [government funding, a grant-in-aid (*pl.* grants-in-aid)] for scientific research.  **科学コミュニケーター** a science communicator.  **科学捜査研究所**〔各都道府県警察の〕a criminal investigation laboratory.  **科学発展観** =科学的発展観(⇨かがくてき[2]).  **科学リテラシー** science [scientific] literacy.
**かがくおよびけっせいりょうほうけんきゅうじょ**【化学

及血清療法研究所】the Chemo-Sero-Therapeutic Research Institute.
**かがくぎじゅつ**【科学技術】▶□ 科学技術関係経費 science and technology-related expenditures. 科学技術研究費 expenditure for scientific and technical research; science and technology research costs. 科学技術振興調整費 special coordination funds for promoting science and technology. 科学技術振興費 science and technology promotion expenditures. 科学技術創造立国 ＝科学技術立国. 科学技術白書 a white paper on science and technology;〔文部科学省の〕the White Paper on Science and Technology《2004》. 科学技術立国 a national commitment to science and technology; national development based on science and technology.
**かがくぎじゅつえいぞうさい**【科学技術映像祭】〔日本の〕the《47th》Science and Technology Film/Video Festival.
**かがくぎじゅつきほんけいかく**【科学技術基本計画】〔日本政府が5年に1度策定する〕the《Third》Science and Technology Basic Plan.
**かがくぎじゅつきょういくきょうかい**【科学技術教育協会】the Foundation for Education of Science and Technology（略：FEST）.
**かがくぎじゅつしゅうかん**【科学技術週間】〔発明記念日(4月18日)を含む1週間〕Science and Technology Week.
**かがくぎじゅつしんこうきこう**【科学技術振興機構】the Japan Science and Technology Agency（略：JST）. ▶ 2003年に科学技術振興事業団より移行.
**かがく・こくさいあんぜんほしょうけんきゅうじょ**【科学・国際安全保障研究所】〔米国ワシントンに本部を置く民間機関〕the Institute for Science and International Security（略：ISIS）.
**かかくたい**【価格帯】a price「range [spectrum].◆ 最も売れている〜 the best-selling price range／10万から20万円の〜の商品 a commodity (selling) in the ¥100,000 to 200,000 price range. □ 最多価格帯 the largest price range; the price range of the largest number of《apartments》. 中心価格帯 the median price range.
**かがくてき**[2]【科学的】▶□ 科学的発展観〔中国政府の指導思想〕the "scientific concept of development."
**かがくぶっしつかんりセンター**【化学物質管理―】〔製品評価技術基盤機構の〕the Chemical Management Center.
**かがくぶっしつしんさきせいほう**【化学物質審査規制法】〔法〕〔化学物質の審査及び製造等の規制に関する法律の通称〕the Law Concerning the Examination and Regulation of Manufacture, etc., of Chemical Substances.
**かがくへいき**【化学兵器】▶□ 化学兵器物質 a chemical warfare agent（略：CWA）.
**かかけん**【花架拳】〔中国武術の流派の1つ〕Hua Jia Quan; Huaquan; flower(-style) boxing; flower [blossom] fist.
**かかつどう**【過活動】〔医〕〔発達障害・精神病などの一症状〕hyperactivity.
**かかつどうぼうこう**【過活動膀胱】〔医〕an overactive bladder（略：OAB）; a hyperactive bladder.
**かかと**【踵】▶□ かかと落とし〔格闘技のわざ〕a heel drop-kick. かかと蹴り〔格闘技のわざ〕an ax kick.
**かがぶた**【鏡蓋】〔植〕〔ミツガシワ科の浮葉植物〕a water snowflake; a floating heart; *Nymphoides indica.*
**かがみ**[1]【鏡】▶□ 鏡越しに ◆《化粧室などで》隣に立った女性が〜越しに話しかけてきた。The woman standing next to me spoke to me in the mirror.
**カガメ** Kagame, Paul（1957- ; ルワンダの政治家; 大統領〔2000- 〕）.

**かかりつけ**【掛かり付け】▶□ 掛かりつけ歯科医初診料 an initial fee for regular dental treatment.
**かき**[5]【火器】▶□ 火器管制レーダー〔軍〕a fire control radar.
**かき**[9]【牡蠣】▶□ 殻付きカキ〔料理〕an oyster on the (half) shell.
**かき**[12]【掻き】〔水泳〕a [an arm] stroke. ◆ 平泳ぎは〜と蹴りのタイミングが命だ。For the breast stroke the timing of the arm stroke and the kick is crucial.
**かぎあな**【鍵穴】▶□ 鍵穴手術〔医〕〔切開部を極力小さくして行う脳などの手術〕keyhole surgery; a keyhole operation.
**かきおとし**[2]【掻き落とし】**1**〔建〕sgraffito.
**2**〔製陶〕sgraffito; scraping away an outer layer to form a pattern.
**かきおろし**[2]【描きおろし】painting pictures for a volume at the request of a publisher;〔作品〕pictures painted for a volume at the request of a publisher; a new [an original] drawing [picture, painting].
**カキコ**〔インターネットの掲示板などに書き込まれた文章〕a post; a posting; a message.
**〜する**〔掲示板などに書き込む〕post《a message on a BBS》.
**かきごおり**【欠き氷】▶□ かき氷機[器] an ice shaver; an ice shaving machine.
**かきごりんこくさいきょうぎれんめいれんごう**【夏季五輪国際競技連盟連合】the Association of Summer Olympic International Federations（略：ASOIF）.
**かきどう**【下気道】〔解〕the lower respiratory tract.
**がきどう**【餓鬼道】〔六道の1つ〕(Buddhist) realm of starvation;《fall into》the world of hunger.
**かきのはずし**【柿の葉寿司】persimmon leaf sushi; a variety of sushi (from Nara), shaped into a cube, topped with salmon or mackerel, and wrapped in a persimmon leaf.
**かきゅう**[1]【下級】▶□ 下級武士 a low-ranking samurai.
**かきゅう**[4]【加給】▶□ 加給年金 an additional pension.
**かく**[3]【核】▶□ 核オプション〔状況によっては核兵器の保持または使用が可能であるとする考え方〕the nuclear option. 核カード (play) the nuclear card. ◆ 北朝鮮は〜カードを巧みに使いながら日米韓に揺さぶりをかけているように見える。North Korea seems to be using its nuclear card cleverly to put pressure on Japan, the US and South Korea. 核拡散防止構想 the Proliferation Security Initiative（略：PSI）. 核関連物質 nuclear-related materials. 核災害 a nuclear disaster. 核事故 a nuclear accident. 核使用 the use of nuclear weapons. ◆ 米大統領は地域紛争での〜使用に含みを残した。The US president did not rule out「using nuclear weapons [the nuclear option] in regional conflicts. 核都市〔核兵器の開発・製造のための都市〕a nuclear city. 核都市イニシアチブ〔ロシアの核都市で働いていた科学者・技術者の平和的雇用を確保するための米・ロ共同プロジェクト〕the Nuclear City Initiative（略：NCI）. 核(兵器)保有宣言《North Korea's》declaration [announcement] that《it》has nuclear weapons;《North Korea's》declaration of possession of nuclear weapons. 核閉鎖都市〔周辺地域から遮断された核都市〕a closed nuclear city. 核放棄 relinquishing [getting rid of] nuclear capabilities; giving up [dropping] a nuclear program. ◆ 完全[段階的]〜放棄 the「complete [gradual] abandonment of nuclear programs／完全で検証可能かつ後戻りできない〜放棄 (a) complete, verifiable and irreversible dismantlement of《North Korea's》nuclear programs（略：CVID）.
**かくあんぜんほしょうきょく**【核安全保障局】〔米国エネルギー省の〕the National Nuclear Security Administration（略：NNSA）.

**がくい**【学位】□▶ 共同[二重]学位〔2つの大学[大学院]の学位を最短4年[2年]で同時に取得できる制度〕a「dual [double] degree program (略: DDP). □▶ 学位詐称 faking [misrepresenting, lying about] one's academic degree(s). 学位工場 ＝ディプロマ・ミル. 学位商法 a「diploma [degree] mill scam. 学位証明書 a degree certificate; a certificate of (a) degree.

**かくう**【架空】
□▶ 架空出品〔ネットオークションなどでの詐欺行為の一種〕putting up a nonexistent item (for Internet auction). 架空請求 fraudulent [phony] billing. 架空請求業者 a「fraudulent [phony] billing「company [operation]. 架空請求詐欺 a「fraudulent [phony] billing「scheme [scam]. 架空請求メール[葉書] a fraudulent「e-mail [postcard] demanding money. 架空伝票〔支出を装うための〕a fictional slip. 架空投資(話) a「bogus [false, fraudulent] investment scheme. 架空予算 earmarking money (from a budget) for bogus《traveling expenses》.

**かくかい**³【角界】□▶ 角界入り entry [induction] into the sumo world. ◯ ～入りする enter [be inducted into] the sumo world; become a professional sumo wrestler.

**がくかんせつ**【顎関節】□▶ 顎関節炎〔医〕arthritis of the temporomandibular joint; temporomandibular arthritis.

**がくがんめんげか**【顎顔面外科】〔医〕maxillofacial surgery.

**がくがんめんほてつ**【顎顔面補綴】〔医〕maxillofacial prosthetics.

**がくぎょう**【学業】□▶ 学業成就《pray for, a prayer for》successful school results.

**かくきんかいぎ**【核禁会議】⇨かくへいききんしへいかんせつこくみんかいぎ.

**かくげんりょうぶっしつ, かくねんりょうぶっしつおよびげんしろのきせいにかんするほうりつ**【核原料物質, 核燃料物質及び原子炉の規制に関する法律】〔法〕the Law for the Regulation of Nuclear Source Material, Nuclear Fuel Material and Reactors. ▶「原子炉等規制法」(the Nuclear Reactor Regulation Law) の正式名称.

**かくさ**¹【格差】□▶ 医療格差 ⇨いりょう³. 地域(間)格差 regional disparities (in income). □▶ 格差拡大 a widening gap. 格差給 (a system of) differential [differentiated] pay; differential「salaries [wages]. 格差社会 an economically stratified society; a society with「a wide gap between rich and poor [wide disparities of wealth]; a society in which wealth is unequally distributed. 格差是正 correction [rectification] of an「imbalance [inequality].

**がくさい**⁴【学祭】〔学園祭〕a「school [campus] festival.

**かくさん**¹【拡散】□▶ 拡散板〔電〕a diffuser.

**かくさん**²【核酸】□▶ 核酸増幅検査〔医〕a nucleic acid amplification test (略: NAT).

**かくさんスペクトラムつうしん**【拡散－通信】〔通信〕＝スペクトラムかくさんつうしん.

**がくし**¹【学士】□▶ 学士力〔大学を卒業するまでに学生が最低限身につけなければならない能力〕minimum standards (to be met) for「graduation (from a four-year university) [a bachelor's degree]; the knowledge, skills and abilities required of graduates.

**がくしきしゃ**【学識者】an academic; an expert [a specialist]《from X university》.

**かくしつ**¹【角質】□▶ 角質細胞 a corneocyte; a cornified cell.

**かくじつ**²【確実】□▶ 確実視 ◯ ～視される be regarded as「certain [《口》a sure thing] / 石田氏は総選挙後, 衆議院議員就任が～視されている. Ishida is seen as「certain [*《口》a shoo-in] to be appointed Speaker of the House of Representatives after the general election.

**かくじっけん**【核実験】□▶ 核実験監視施設 a nuclear test monitoring facility.

**がくしゃ**²【学者】□▶ 学者ばか a fool [an ignoramus] except in one's own (academic) field.

**かくしゅ**²【核種】□▶ 超ウラン核種 a transuranic nuclide. TRU 核種 ＝超ウラン核種.

**がくしゅう**【学習】□▶ 学習学 "learnology"; (the science of) learner-centered learning. 学習到達度 a level of「educational [scholastic] achievement. 学習到達度調査〔OECD による〕the Programme for International Student Assessment (略: PISA); 〔IEA による〕the Trends in International Mathematics and Science Study (略: TIMSS). 学習漫画 an「educational [instructional] comic book [manga]. 学習療法〔商標〕〔認知症高齢者のための〕learning therapy.

**がくしゅう**【鄂州】〔中国, 湖北省の市〕Ezhou.

**がくじゅつ**【学術】□▶ 学術研究都市 a scientific research city. 学術交流 academic「exchange [interchange];《develop》academic links《with...》. ◯ 国内外の大学との～交流を深める deepen (academic) exchange [develop stronger academic links] with universities at home and abroad. 学術創成研究費 ＝科学研究費補助金 (⇨かがく⁴). 学術探検《the members of》a scientific expedition. 学術探査 scientific exploration. ◯ ～探査隊 a scientific exploration party.

**かくせい**¹【覚醒】□▶ 早朝覚醒〔医〕early morning「awakening [arousal] (insomnia). 中途覚醒〔医〕sleep maintenance insomnia. □▶ 覚醒(下)手術〔脳〕awake surgery; an awake operation. 覚醒度 (the) degree of arousal.

**かくせい**³【廓清】□▶ リンパ節廓清〔医〕(a) lymphadenectomy; (a) lymph node「dissection [excision].

**がくせい**¹【学生】□▶ 学生委員会〔学生を構成員とする〕a「student [students'] committee;〔学生の生活指導のための〕a student「life [welfare] committee. 学生納付特例制度〔国民年金保険料の〕student exemption from payment of「contributions [premiums].

**がくぜつこつきん**【顎舌骨筋】〔解〕a mylohyoid (muscle).

**かくせん**²【角栓】〔毛穴の中で皮脂などが固まったもの; コメド〕a comedo (pl. -dones).

**がくそつ**【学卒】□▶ 学卒未就職者 an unemployed《high school, university》graduate.

**かくだい**¹【拡大】□▶ 拡大自殺〔他者を道連れにした自殺〕extended suicide. 拡大中東地域〔北アフリカからアフガニスタンに至るイスラム地域〕the Greater Middle East. 拡大読書器 a video magnifier.

**かくたいきょう**【額帯鏡】〔医〕〔耳鼻咽喉科医などが額に装着する円形凹面鏡〕a head mirror.

**かくだいちゅうとうこうそう**【拡大中東構想】〔米国提唱の中東諸国の民主化と安定化をめざす改革〕the Broader Middle East Initiative.

**かくだいよぼうせっしゅけいかく**【拡大予防接種計画】〔世界保健機関の〕the Expanded Program on Immunization (略: EPI).

**かくたん**【喀痰】□▶ 喀痰吸引器 a phlegm suction unit. 喀痰細胞診〔医〕(a) sputum cytology.

**かくだんとう**【核弾頭】□▶ 核弾頭搭載可能な nuclear-capable《missiles》.

**かくちょう**¹【拡張】□▶ 拡張員 ＝新聞拡張員 (⇨しんぶん). 拡張現実感〔電算〕augmented reality, (略: AR). 拡張ドラフト〔野球〕〔新規参入球団に既存の球団の選手を振り分けるためのドラフト〕an expansion draft.

**がくちょう**¹【学長】□▶ 学長室 the「president's [chancellor's] office.

**かくづけ【格付け】** ▶ 勝手格付け〘証券〙〔債務者からの依頼のない格付け〕(an) unsolicited rating. ▷日本の国債については、格付け会社によって勝手な〜がなされている. Unsolicited ratings have been issued by rating agencies for Japanese government bonds.

**かくづけとうしじょうほうセンター【格付投資情報-】**〔日本の格付け会社〕Rating and Investment Information, Inc. (略: R&I).

**かくていきゅうふきぎょうねんきんほう【確定給付企業年金法】**〘法〙the Defined-Benefit Corporate Pension Law.

**かくていきょしゅつねんきんほう【確定拠出年金法】**〘法〙the Defined Contribution Pension Law.

**かくていてき【確定的】** ▶ 確定的(な)殺意 a definite intent to murder.

**カクテキ**〘料理〙〔大根のキムチ〕kkakdugi; diced radish kimchi.

**カクテル** ▶ カクテル・パーティー効果〘心理〙〔複数の音源から来る音の混合の中から、特定の音源の音だけを抽出して聴くことができる現象〕the cocktail party effect. カクテル・ピン〔カクテルグラスの中に入れるオリーブやチェリーなどに刺すつまようじ状のピン〕a cocktail pick. カクテル療法〘医〙〔多剤併用療法〕(a) combined therapy; (a) "cocktail" therapy. カクテルリング〔色の違う石を組み合わせたデザインの指輪〕〔大きめの色石を使った指輪〕a cocktail ring.

**かくとう²【格闘】** ▶ 格闘家 a martial artist. 格闘ゲーム〔コンピューターやオンライン上の〕a 'fighting [beat-'em-up] game.

**がくどう【学童】** ▶ 学童記録 a junior record《for the 400-meter hurdles》.

**がくどうほいく【学童保育】** ▶ 学童保育所 an after-school child-care center.

**かくとく【獲得】** ▶ 獲得席 (the number of) seats won. 獲得競争 a competition to acquire《sth》. ▷ブロードバンドなど顧客の〜競争が激化している. The 'competition [fight] for broadband customers is heating up. / ヤンキースはその大物選手の〜競争に名乗りを上げた. The Yankees entered the bidding war for that star player.

**がくない【学内】** ▶ 学内保育施設〔教職員の子弟のため〕a school 'nursery [crèche].

**がくにふくきん【顎二腹筋】**〘解〙a digastric (muscle).

**かくにん【確認】** ▶ 確認標章 = 放置車両確認標章 (⇒ほうり¹). 確認(有限)会社 a (limited liability) company established with capital of at least one yen under a special government program to promote start-up enterprises. [⇒一円会社 (⇒いちえん)]

**かくねん【隔年】** ▶ 隔年春闘 a biennial spring wage offensive. 隔年展〔It〕a biennale; a biennial exhibition.

**がくねん【学年】** ▶ 学年(雑)誌〔学年別の学習雑誌〕a magazine for children in a particular school year. 学年集会 a meeting [an assembly] of [for] all the students in one '*grade* [¹year]. ▷3年生の〜集会を開く hold a meeting for all the students in the third '*grade* [¹year].

**かくねんりょう【核燃料】** ▶ 核燃料サイクル施設 a nuclear fuel cycle 'facility [complex, plant].

**かくのう【格納】** ▶ 格納扉〘空〙〔車輪の〕a landing-gear door; (the) landing-gear doors.

**かくへいききんしへいわけんせつこくみんかいぎ【核兵器禁止平和建設国民会議】**the National Council for Peace and Against Nuclear Weapons.

**かくへいきようかくぶんれつせいぶっしつせいさんきんしじょうやく【核兵器用核分裂性物質生産禁止条約】**the Fissile Material Cut-off Treaty (略: FMCT). ▶ 通称 カットオフ条約. 構想段階の条約.

**がくへんしょう【顎偏位症】**〘歯科〙mandibular displacement.

**がくへんけいしょう【顎変形症】**〘医〙a jaw deformity.

**かくほう³【閣法】**〔内閣提出の法案〕a bill introduced by the Cabinet. [⇒内閣立法 (⇒ないかく⁵)]

**かくまく¹【角膜】** ▶ 円錐角膜〘眼科〙keratoconus. ▶ 角膜再生 corneal regeneration; regeneration of the cornea. 角膜症〘眼科〙keratopathy. 角膜内皮〘解〙(the) corneal endothelium. 角膜乱視〘眼科〙(a) corneal astigmatism.

**かくマルは【革-派】**〔日本革命的共産主義者同盟革命的マルクス主義派〕the Japan Revolutionary Communist League (Revolutionary Marxist Faction) (略: JCRL (-RMF).

**かくめいじんみんかいほうとうせんせん【革命人民解放党戦線】**〔トルコの極左過激派組織〕the Revolutionary People's Liberation Party/Front (略: DHKP/C).

**かくめいとういつせんせん【革命統一戦線】**〔シエラレオネの反政府勢力〕the Revolutionary United Front (略: RUF).

**かくめいぼうえいたい【革命防衛隊】**〔イランの〕⇒イスラムかくめいぼうえいたい.

**かくやす【格安】** ▶ 格安航空会社 a 'low-cost [low cost] airline. 格安ルート〔旅行運賃の安い経路〕a 'cheap [cut-price, discount] route;〔商品流通の〕cheap [discount] channels.

**かくゆうごう【核融合】** ▶ 核融合発電 (nuclear) fusion power generation.

**かぐらこうもり【神楽蝙蝠】**〘動〙〔西表島などにすむ小型のコウモリ〕a 'Bang's [lesser great] leaf-nosed bat; a lesser roundleaf bat; *Hipposideros turpis*.

**かくらん²【攪乱】** ▶ 攪乱工作 harassment 'tactics [activities]. 攪乱戦法 (a strategy of) harassment; harassing《the enemy》.

**かくりつ³【確率】** ▶ 確率統計 probability and statistics.

**かくりょう²【閣僚】** ▶ 閣僚懇談会 a round-table discussion of cabinet ministers; an informal ministerial conference. 閣僚経験者 an ex-cabinet member. 閣僚席〔国会の議場などでの〕the 'government [cabinet] benches. 閣僚レベル折衝 ministerial-level negotiations.

**がくりょく【学力】** ▶ 学力向上フロンティアスクール〔文部科学省が2002年度から2004年度まで行った学習指導方法研究事業〕"the Frontier School Project (for Academic Ability Development)";〔その学校〕a "Frontier school"; an "Academic Ability Development Frontier school". 学力重視 attaching too much importance to [(an) overemphasis on] academic ability.

**かくれ【隠れ】** ▶ 隠れ信者 a secret [a clandestine, an underground, a hidden] believer.

**がくれき【学歴】** ▶ 学歴汚染 the proliferation of 'diploma [degree] mills. 学歴逆詐称 faking [misrepresenting, lying about] one's academic record in order to make it appear that one's qualifications are lower than they really are; faking [misrepresenting, lying about] one's academic record in order to apply for a job limited to high school graduate applicants. 学歴商法 a 'diploma [degree] mill scam.

**かけい⁹【家計】** ▶ 家計支出 household spending. 家計消費状況調査 a survey of 'family [household] expenditure;〔総務省統計局が行う〕the Survey of Household Economy. 家計所得 household income.

**かけい¹¹【科刑】**〔刑罰を科すること〕sentencing; (the) imposition of a 'penalty [punishment]. ~する punish; impose a punishment《on sb》; sentence sb《to three years in prison》; carry out sentencing.

**かけいけいざいけんきゅうじょ【家計経済研究所】**the Institute for Research on Household Economics (略: IRHE).

かけきん¹【掛け金】⇨ 掛け金建て年金 ＝拠出建て年金 (⇨きょしゅつ).
かけごえだおれ【掛け声倒れ】◯〜に終わる end up as mere sloganeering / 政治家のスローガンは〜に終わることも多い. Many are the political slogans that start with a roar and end with a whimper. / 教育改革を〜に終わらせてはならない. We must not allow educational reform to end up as mere sloganeering.
かけこみ【駆け込み】⇨ 駆け込み合併〔合併特例法による市町村の〕amalgamation [a merger] of municipalities undertaken in haste (in order to make use of the preferential treatment before the deadline). 駆け込み購入〔値上げ前など の〕a last-minute purchase. ◯ 消費税引き上げ前の自動車の〜購入 a last-minute car purchase before a rise in the consumption tax; buying a car just before the consumption tax goes up. 駆け込み事件〔〔脱北者など の〕外国公館への〕a rush for sanctuary; an incident in which〔refugees〕「rush [force their way] into《an embassy》seeking sanctuary. 駆け込み者〔〔脱北者など の〕外国公館への〕a「refugee [fugitive, defector] seeking「shelter [asylum] (in a foreign embassy or consulate).
かけつけん【化血研】＝かがくおよびけっせいりょうほうけんきゅうじょ.
かけながし【掛け流し】〔温泉で源泉を浴槽に流しっぱなしにしていること〕free-flowing (hot-spring water).
かけにげ【掛け逃げ】〔柔道など〕a「mock [false] attack; pretending to attack while avoiding contact《with one's opponent》.
かけひき【駆け引き】⇨ 駆け引き材料〔use sth as〕a bargaining chip.
かげれん【陰練】〔こっそりと練習すること〕＝みれん.
かけん²【加憲】addition to the Constitution.
かげん²【下限】⇨ 下限割れ〔数量や値段などの下の限界を割ること〕dropping [falling] below the「lower limit [minimum]，〔日本銀行の当座預金残高の〕falling below [failing to meet] the liquidity target.
かけんしすう【加権指数】〔証券〕〔台湾の株価指数〕the Taiwan capitalization-weighted stock index.
かこう⁴【加工】⇨ 加工用米 rice for processing.
かこうせい【加工性】〔素材物質の〕processability; workability. ◯ 〜に優れた《an alloy》「with [of, having] excellent「workability [processability]. ◯ 〜の悪い with poor「workability [processability]. ⇨ 成形加工性 formability; moldability; formable [moldable] properties. 熱加工性 thermoformability; thermal「processability [moldability]. プレス加工性 press formability. 曲げ加工性《have excellent》bending workability.
かこししんそうきゅうめいいいんかい【過去史真相究明委員会】〔韓国の〕a "historical truth" committee set up in Korea in May 2005. ▶ 2005年5月発足.
かこしせいりきほんほう【過去史整理基本法】〔韓国の法律〕the Basic Law on the Review of Past History for Truth and Reconciliation.
かこしほう【過去史法】〔韓国の法律〕＝かこしせいりきほんほう.
かこみ【囲み】⇨ 囲み会見 ＝囲み取材. 囲み取材 an on-the-spot interview by「surrounding [a scrum of] reporters.
かさ³【傘】⇨ 傘美人 a beauty with an umbrella; a woman who looks beautiful carrying an umbrella.
カザア【電算】〔ソフトの無料ダウンロードのためのファイル共有ソフト〕KaZaA; Kazaa.
かさい【火災】⇨ 収斂⦅しゅうれん⦆火災〔思わぬ日常生活用品が凸レンズや反射鏡となって一点に集中した太陽光で可燃物を発火させることにより発生する火災〕a lens-effect fire; a fire caused by《a bottle》acting as a lens.
かさいサージ【火砕サージ】〔火山噴火に伴って発生する土砂流りの高温の爆風で火砕流より低密度〕(a) pyroclastic surge.
かさいまいぞうりょう【可採埋蔵量】〔石油資源などの〕recoverable reserves.
かさかし【傘かしげ】〔狭い道で人とすれ違うとき、反対側に傘を傾けて相手が通りやすくすること〕(politely) tilting one's umbrella away from the path of another person approaching with an umbrella.
かざきりおん【風切り音】＝かぜきりおん.
かさだか【嵩高】⇨ 嵩高紙〔製紙〕high bulk paper. 嵩高性〔繊維・羽毛などの〕loft.
かさだかい【嵩高い】bulky. ⇨ 嵩高い置換基〔化〕a bulky substituent.
かさつき【かさつくこと】being dry and rough; desiccation; roughening; parching;〔特に寒さによる〕chapping. ◯ この化粧水はお肌の〜を抑えます. This toilet lotion prevents「your skin from getting dry and rough [desiccation and roughening of the skin].
カザトムプロム〔カザフスタンの国営ウラン開発会社〕Kazatomprom.
かさねどり【重ね撮り[録り]】〔ビデオテープなどの〕recording over《another program》. ◯ 〜する record over《onto the same tape》. ◯ このテープは〜しても画質の劣化が少ない. This tape can be recorded on again and again with little loss of picture quality.
かさねばし【重ね箸】〔食事の時、特定の料理ばかり食べること〕eating only one kind of food at a time at meals (instead of the traditional Japanese way of alternating between rice and the various other foods on the table), which is considered rude.
かざりぼうちょう【飾り包丁】〔見た目をよくするために食材に切れ目を入れること〕(a) decorative scoring. ◯ 〜を入れる give《eggplant》a decorative scoring.
かざん¹【火山】⇨ 火山観測情報〔気象庁が発表する〕a volcanic observation report.
かさんか¹【過酸化】⇨ 過酸化アセトン acetone peroxide. 過酸化水素水 (a) hydrogen peroxide solution.
かざんかつどう【火山活動】⇨ 火山活動レベル a volcanic activity level. ◯ 気象庁は浅間山の〜レベルを2から3に引き上げた. The Meteorological Agency raised the level of volcanic activity for Mt. Asama from 2 to 3.
かざんせい【火山性】⇨ 火山性ガス volcanic gases. 火山性堆積物〔地質〕a volcanic deposit.
かし²【貸し】⇨ 貸し倉庫 a rental warehouse;〔トランクルーム〕a rental storage「unit [room].
かし⁴【下肢】⇨ 下肢障害 (a)「lower-limb [leg] impairment. ◯ 〜障害者 a person with (a)「lower-limb [leg] impairment. 下肢静脈血栓症〔医〕venous thrombosis of the「lower extremities [legs, lower limbs]. 下肢静脈瘤〔医〕a varicose vein [varicosis] of the lower extremities.
かし⁶【可視】⇨ 可視外飛行〔無人ヘリコプターなどの〕flight [flying] beyond (the operator's) visual range. 可視通信 visible light communication(s). 可視光望遠鏡 a solar optical telescope《略：SOT》.
かし¹⁶【瑕疵】⇨ 瑕疵保証保険〔住宅の〕a warranty「against [for] defects; a defects「warranty [guarantee]; insurance against defects.
かじ¹【舵】⇨ 舵付きフォア〔ボート〕〔競技〕＝舵手付きフォア（⇨だしゅ）. 舵無しフォア〔ボート〕〔競技〕＝舵手無しフォア（⇨だしゅ）.
かじ⁴【家事】⇨ 家事援助〔支援〕〔在宅介護の〕support [assistance] with「housework [domestic tasks]. 家事代行サービス homemaker services; (a) homemaker service. 家事分担 housework sharing; sharing [splitting (up), dividing (up)] the housework《with one's spouse》. 家事ロボット ＝おてつだいロボット.

カシーム =カシム.
「ガシェ博士の肖像」〔ゴッホ作の絵画〕Portrait of Dr. Gachet.
「華氏911」〔映画〕Fahrenheit 9/11.
かしきんぎょうほう【貸金業法】〖法〗〔貸金業規制法〕the Moneylending Control Law.
かしこうつうしんコンソーシアム【可視光通信-】the Visible Light Communications Consortium（略：VLCC）.
かしこむ【貸し込む】〔融資する〕lend 《sb 3 million yen》; loan 《sb the money to set up a business》; provide a loan 《of 3 million yen》;（過大な金額を）fix [set] sb up with a (huge, massive) loan 《of $3 million》.
かしだおれ【貸し倒れ】▭ 貸し倒れ償却費 the ˈexpense [cost] of ˈcovering [making up, writing off] bad debts.　貸し倒れ引当金［準備金］a bad debt ˈreserve (fund) [allowance] / a provision [reserve] for ˈloan losses [bad debts].　貸し倒れ率 a bad-debt ratio.
かしだし【貸し出し】▭ 貸し出し（金）残高 a [the] balance of ˈloans outstanding [outstanding loans].　貸し出し・資金吸収動向〔日銀の〕the principal figures of financial institutions.
かしたんぽ【瑕疵担保】▭ 瑕疵担保責任 defect liability.　瑕疵担保特約 a defect warranty (clause).
かしつけ【貸し付け】▭ 過剰貸し付け excessive lending; overlending;〔1回に〕an excessive loan.
カシニョール Cassigneul, Jean-Pierre (1935- ; フランスの画家).
カジノ ▭ カジノ産業 a [the] casino industry.　カジノ資本主義 casino capitalism.
かしビル【貸し-】▭ 貸しビル業 the (office) building rental business.
かしますさぎ【貸します詐欺】〔低利融資をもちかけて保証金をだまし取る詐欺〕a low-interest loan fraud. [＝融資保証金詐欺〈ゆうし¹²〉]
カシム〔サウジアラビア中部の州〕Qasim. ▶州都 ブライダ.
カシャガンゆでん【-油田】〔カスピ海の〕the Kashagan oil field.
カシヤノフ Kasyanov, Mikhail Mikhailovich (1957- ；ロシアの政治家; 首相〔2000-04〕).
ガシャモク〘植〙〔ヒルムシロ科の水草; 日本・中国原産〕Potamogeton dentatus.
カジュアル ▭ カジュアル・ダウン〔よりカジュアルな服装をすること〕dressing down. ▷ ～ダウンする dress ˈdown [more casually].
かじゅう¹【加重】▭ 加重収賄〖法〗〔公務員について〕aggravated acceptance of a bribe.
カシュクール《＜F cache coeur》〘服飾〙〔セーターなどの左右の襟⁽ぇ⁾の身ごろのように重ね合わせたデザイン〕a crossover 《sweater, cardigan, etc.》.
かしょう³【火傷】▭ 火傷死 (a) death from burning.
かしょう¹²【過少】▭ 過少支払い underpayment.
かしょう⁵【過剰】▭ 過剰敬語 an excessive honorific.　過剰収容〔刑務所などの〕《prison》overcrowding.　過剰照射〔放射線治療における〕excessive irradiation; over-irradiation.　過剰摂取 excessive intake. ▷ 糖分の～摂取には気をつけましょう. Be careful about ˈexcessive intake of sugar [eating too much sugar].　過剰徴収〔税・料金などの〕(mistakenly) charging [collecting] too much 《(a) tax》; overcollection 《of taxes》.　過剰流動性相場 a liquidity-driven market.
かしょく¹⁰【可食】▭ 可食期間〔食料品の〕an edibility period.　可食期限 (the) ˈuse-by [eat-by] date.　可食(性)インク edible ink.　可食[部分]〔魚・家畜など〕an edible part. ▷ 非～[部分] an inedible part / ～部率 an edible ˈ(pro)portion [ratio] / パッションフルーツの～部率は43％だ. The edible portion of a passion fruit is 43%.
かじん³【華人】▭ 華人経済圏 the economic area

comprising China and the various overseas Chinese communities.
かしんき【加振機[器]】〘機〙a vibration exciter; a shaker.
かしんしゃ【華晨汽車】〔中国の自動車メーカー〕Brilliance China Automotive Holdings (Limited).
かしんほう【化審法】〖法〗〔化学物質の審査及び製造等の規制に関する法律の通称〕the Law Concerning the Examination and Regulation of Manufacture, etc., of Chemical Substances.
ガス　▭ ガスエンジン・コジェネ（レーション）［コージェネ（レーション）］gas engine cogeneration; a gas engine cogeneration system.　ガス・カートリッジ〔携帯用ガスコンロなどに使う〕a gas ˈcartridge [canister].　ガス給湯器 a gas water heater.　ガス・クロマトグラフ〘化〙a gas chromatograph.　ガス・ハイドレート〘化〙(a) gas hydrate.　ガス発電 gas-powered electricity generation. ▷ ～発電所 a gas-powered electric(-power) plant; a gas-powered generating ˈplant [station].　ガス比重〘化〙gas specific gravity.
かすいぶんかい【加水分解】▭ 加水分解プロテイン (a) hydrolyzed protein.
ガズヴィ(ー)ン〔イラン北西部の州；その州都〕Qazvin.
ガスか【-化】▭ ガス化溶融炉 a gasification melting furnace.
カスタマー ▭ カスタマーセントリック〘商〙〔顧客中心主義の〕customer-centric. ▷ customer centricity n.　カスタマー・リレーションシップ・マネ(ー)ジメント〖経営〗〔顧客関係管理〕customer ˈrelationship [relations] management（略：CRM）.
カスダン Kasdan, Lawrence (1949- ；米国の映画監督・脚本家・製作者).
かずつり【数釣り】mass fishing; fishing for quantity.
カスティーリャ・イ・レオン ⇨カスティーリャ・レオン.
カスティーリャ・ラ・マンチャ〔スペイン中部の自治州〕Castilla-La Mancha.
カスティーリャ・レオン〔スペイン北部の自治州〕Castilla y Leon.
ガス・トゥー・リキッド〔天然ガスを液体燃料化すること〕gas to liquid(s). [⇨ジー・ティー・エル]
カストディアン〘証券〙〔有価証券を保管する金融機関〕a custodian.
ガズニ〔アフガニスタン東部の州；同州の州都〕Ghazni.
カスパーゼ〘生化〙〔たんぱく質分解酵素〕caspase.
カスバートソニー〘植〙〔ラン科の草本〕a cuthbertsonii; Dendrobium cuthbertsonii.
かずはごんどう【数歯巨頭】〘動〙〔マイルカ科の哺乳類〕a melon-headed whale; Peponocephala electra.
ガスパンあそび【-遊び】〔シンナーの代わりにライターガス・カセットコンロ用のガスなどを吸引する危険な遊び〕gas-sniffing; sniffing butane.
ガスプロム〔天然ガス生産で世界最大のロシアの準国営企業〕Gazprom.
ガスしゅつこくフォーラム【-輸出国-】the Gas Exporting Countries Forum（略：GECF）.
かすり¹【絣・飛白】▭ 絣くくり ikat [tie-dyeing of the yarn] for producing kasuri patterns in textiles.
かぜ²【風邪】▭ 集団風邪 a mass outbreak of flu; a (major) flu epidemic.　風邪症候群〖医〗(the) common cold syndrome.
かせい²【化成】▭ 化成品 a chemical product.
かせい⁹【仮性】▭ 仮性認知症〖精神医〗pseudodementia.
かせい¹⁸【華西】1〔中国、江蘇省の村〕Huaxi.　2〔台湾、台北市内の街区〕Huashi; Huaxi.
かぜい²【課税】▭ 一体課税〔複数の金融商品による所得を通算し1つの所得として課税すること〕(an) integrated tax.　居住地国課税 residence-country taxation; residence-based taxation.　源泉地国課税 source-country taxation; source-based taxation. ▭ 課税遺産額 a

taxable estate 《of $1,000,000》. 課税遺産総額　a total taxable estate 《of several billion yen》; the total taxable value of an estate. 課税逃れ　tax evasion; evading taxes. 課税標準額　a standard taxable value; 〔所得の〕taxable income.
かせいぎ【火星儀】a Martian globe; a globe of Mars.
かせいさばくけんきゅうきち【火星砂漠研究基地】『宇宙』〔米国ユタ州の〕the Mars Desert Research Station (略: MDRS).
かせき[1]【化石】▷□ 化石試料〔古生物〕a fossil sample. 化石人間〔完全に時代の流れに取り残された人〕a fossil.
かぜきりおん【風切り音】〔走行する自動車などの〕wind noise. ～エンジンは静かだが、時速110 km/hを超えたあたりから～がやや気になった. It has a quiet engine, but at speeds over 110 km/h wind noise became slightly irritating.
「風の谷のナウシカ」〔アニメ映画〕Nausicaa of the Valley of the Wind.
かぜまち【風待ち】▷□ 風待ち港　a「harbor [port] where ships wait for a wind.
かせん【河川】▷□ 河川維持流量　river maintenance flow. 河川整備計画　a river development project.
かせん[9]【寡占】▷□ 寡占化　oligopolization 《of a market》; increasing「domination 《of a market》[market domination]《by a few large companies》. ～薄型テレビの分野では上位メーカーによる～化が進んでいる. In the flat-screen TV sector, the market is becoming increasingly dominated by the top (few) manufacturers. 寡占度　the degree of「oligopoly [market control, market dominance]. ～度指数　an oligopoly index; the Herfindahl index; the Herfindahl-Hirschman index (略: HHI).
かせんかんきょうかんりざいだん【河川環境管理財団】the Foundation of River & Watershed Environment Management.
かそ[2]【過疎】▷□ 過疎債　＝過疎対策事業債. 過疎集落　a depopulated「settlement [community]. 過疎対策事業債　a government bond for a project in a depopulated area.
かそう[2]【火葬】▷□ 火葬許可申請書　an application for a cremation permit. (移動)火葬車〔ペット用の〕a mobile (pet) crematory.
かそう[3]【仮想】▷□ 仮想空間 (a) virtual space. 仮想私設通信網〔電算〕a virtual private network (略: VPN). 仮想内視鏡検査(法)〔医〕virtual endoscopy. 仮想評価法[市場法]　a contingent valuation method (略: CVM). 仮想閉域網 ⇨ブイ・ピー・エヌ. 仮想ペット ＝バーチャル・ペット (⇨バーチャル).
かそう[6]【家相】▷□ 家相学　divination based on the position and form of a house; house divination.
がぞう【画像】
▷□ 可視画像〔気象衛星の〕a visible 《satellite》 image; visible imagery. 合成画像　a composite image. 赤外(線)画像〔気象衛星の〕an infrared image; infrared imagery. 熱画像　a thermal image. ▷熱～直視装置〔救助用などの〕a forward-looking infrared imager (略: FLIR). ▷□ 画像圧縮〔電算〕image [video] compression. ▷～圧縮技術 (an) image [(a) video] compression technology / ～圧縮方式　an image [a video] compression method / ～圧縮率　an image [a video] compression ratio. 画像解析 (an) image analysis. ▷～解析システム　an image analysis system. 画像解像度　image resolution. 画像管理〔電算〕image management. ▷～管理ソフト　image management software. 画像合成・image compositing. 画像資料　image data. 画像診断医　a diagnostic radiologist. 画像ディスプレー〔電算〕an image display. ▷三次元〔立体〕ディスプレー　a「3-D [three-dimensional] image display. 画像認証〔電算〕image authentication. 画像補正　image「correction

[compensation].
カソヴィッツ　Kassovitz, Mathieu (1967-　；フランスの映画監督・俳優).
かそうどうたいつうしんじぎょうしゃ【仮想移動体通信事業者】〔携帯電話などの無線通信で、自社回線を持たず他社から借りてサービスを行う事業者〕a mobile virtual network operator (略: MVNO).
かそうけん【科捜研】＝科学捜査研究所 (⇨かがく[4]).
カソドルミネ(ッ)センス〔物〕cathodoluminescence (略: CL).
かぞく[1]【加速】▷□ 加速感　a「sense [feeling] of acceleration.
かぞく[1]【家族】▷□ 家族アセスメント〔心理〕family assessment. 家族会　a family association; an association of the families 《of victims of…》. 家族神話〔心理〕family mythology. 家族葬　a (family) household. 家族葬　a family funeral (service); a funeral (service) attended only by close family members. 家族相談士　a licensed family counselor.
かぞくき【加速器】▷□ 超伝導加速器　a superconducting accelerator.
かぞくけいかくこくさいきょうりょくざいだん【家族計画国際協力財団】the Japanese Organization for International Cooperation in Family Planning (略: JOICFP). [＝ジョイセフ]
かぞくせい【家族性】▷□ 家族性アミロイドーニューロパチー　familial amyloidotic polyneuropathy (略: FAP). 家族性高脂血症〔医〕familial hyperlipemia. 家族性腫瘍　a familial tumor.
かそちいきかっせいかとくべつそちほう【過疎地域活性化特別措置法】〔法〕the Law for Special Measures for Revitalizing Depopulated Areas.
かそちいきじりつそくしんとくべつそちほう【過疎地域自立促進特別措置法】〔法〕the Law for Special Measures for Promoting Self-reliance of Depopulated Areas.
カソデックス〔商標・薬〕〔抗男性ホルモン剤・抗腫瘍剤〕Casodex.
カソビッツ　＝カソヴィッツ.
ガソリン　▷□ ガソリンエンジン車　a gasoline(-engine) car. ガソリン添加剤　a gasoline additive.
かた[3]【肩】▷□ 肩出し〔服飾〕off-shoulder 《blouse》.
がたい〔《大きな》体つき〕a (large)「body [frame]. ▷～がいい〔体つきが大きくてがっしりしている〕well built; husky; big and brawny.
かたいじゅう【過体重】overweight.
かたいみ【方忌み】〔易占〕avoiding going in an ill-starred direction.
かたうちしき【肩撃ち式】▷～の　shoulder-mounted 《missiles》.
かたおや【片親】▷□ 片親世帯　a single parent household. ▷～世帯の85％は母と子供で生活しています. Eighty-five percent of single parent households consist of a mother and child (living together).
「ガタカ」〔映画〕Gattaca.
かたかな【片仮名】▷□ カタカナ職業　a newly-emerging occupation expressed by (a foreign word transcribed into) katakana.
かたがわ【片側】▷□ 片側交互通行　two-way traffic alternating along a single lane. 片側歩行、片側空け〔エスカレーターの〕stepping aside on an escalator to allow others to get past one.
かたたすき【片襷】holding one kimono sleeve out of the way with a cord crossing from one shoulder to the opposite armpit.
かたたたき【肩叩き】▷□ 肩たたき券　a coupon for a free shoulder massage.
かたつう【肩痛】shoulder pain; (a) pain in the shoulder; (a) shoulder ache; an aching shoulder; 〔医〕om-

odynia.
かたて【片手】 ▫ 片手打ち〘テニスなど〙one-handed [single-handed]《play》;〔携帯メールなどを打つときの〕texting with one hand. 片手運転〔自動車の〕one-handed driving;〔自動車・自転車の〕one-handed steering;〔自転車の〕one-handed riding.
かたはい【片肺】 ▫ 片肺着陸《make》a「one-engine [single engine] landing.
カダバえんじん【-猿人】〘人類〙*Ardipithecus kadabba*.
かたばたらき【片働き】 ▫ 片働き世帯 a household in which only one spouse works; a single-income「family [household]; a one-income「family [household]. 片働き夫婦 a single-income couple; a one-income couple.
かたひき【肩引き】〔狭い道で人とすれ違うとき、片方の肩を引き体をななめにして相手が通りやすくすること〕(politely) pulling in *one's* right shoulder in order to make it easier for an approaching person to pass.
カタプレキシー〘医〙〔情動性脱力発作〕cataplexy;〔1 回に〕a cataplectic「attack [seizure]; an attack of cataplexy. ▷ cataplectic *adj.*
かためうち【固め打ち】〘野球〙hot hitting;《have, swing》a hot bat. ◐ 彼は 2 試合連続 5 安打の〜で打率首位に浮上した. His hot hitting with five hits in two consecutive games made him the batting leader.
カダラッシュ〔フランス南部の都市〕Cadarache.
かたり2【騙り】 ▫ かたり商法 a fraudulent business practice;《口》a scam.
かたりおろし【語りおろし】dictating a piece at the request of a publisher;〔作品〕a literary work specially dictated at the request of a publisher.
カダロール ＝カッダロール.
カタログ ▫ カタログ通(信)販(売) a mail-order (catalog) business; a catalog business.
かたわく【型枠】 ▫ 型枠大工 a「shuttering [concrete form] carpenter; a「shuttering [formwork] joiner.
カタンガ〔アフリカ中部, コンゴ民主共和国南部の州〕Katanga.
かち3【勝ち】 ▫ 勝ち運〔勝運〕luck at winning. 勝ち札〔トランプ・ゲームでの〕a「winning [trump] card;〔開運護符〕a talisman.
かち4【価値】 ▫ 感性(的)価値 (an) aesthetic [(a sensual, (a) sensation] value. 機能(的)価値 (a) function (al) value.
かちがしら【勝ち頭】a top scorer; *a breadwinner《of a team》. ◐ 彼は現在 13 勝で, チームの〜だ. With thirteen wins (to his credit), he is currently the team's top scorer.
かちかん【価値観】 ▫ 世界価値観調査 the World Values Survey (略: WVS).
かちく【家畜】 ▫ 家畜病 (a) livestock disease. 家畜防疫 control of communicable livestock disease(s); livestock epidemic prevention. 家畜防疫員 an animal quarantine officer (略: AQO). 家畜防疫官〔動物検疫所の〕an animal quarantine officer (略: AQO); an animal quarantine inspector.
かちくかいりょうセンター【家畜改良-】the National Livestock Breeding Center (略: NLBC).
かちくはいせつぶつ(しょり)ほう【家畜排泄物(処理)法】▶正式名称は「家畜排泄物の管理の適正化及び利用の促進に関する法律」(the Law Concerning Appropriate Management and Promotion of the Use of Livestock Waste).
かちこし【勝ち越し】 ▫ 連続勝ち越し〔阪神は 5 カード連続〜を決めた.〘野球〙The Hanshin Tigers have won five series in a row. / 彼は 2 場所連続〜を決めた.〘相撲〙He (has) succeeded in winning two successive tournaments. 連続勝ち越し記録〘相撲〙a record for consecutive winning tournaments;〘野球〙a record for consecutive winning series. ▫ 勝ち越し打〘野球〙a「lead-taking [go-ahead] hit.
かちどけい【勝ち時計】〘競馬〙〔1 位になった馬の走破時間〕the winning time.
かちのこり【勝ち残り】 1〔試合などに勝って優勝圏内に残ること〕winning a「match [game] to remain in contention (for a championship). 2〔相撲〕〔勝った力士が(次の取組の力士に力水と力紙を手渡すために)土俵下にとどまること〕remaining at ringside after winning a match.
カチャーシー〔沖縄の古典舞踊〕*kachasi*; a lively Okinawan folk dance performed with hand gestures to samisen accompaniment.
ガチャガチャ〔玩具入りカプセル自動販売機〕a capsuled-toy vending machine; a capsule machine.
ガチャポン〔ガチャガチャ〕a capsuled-toy vending machine; a capsule machine.
カチューシャ2〔旧ソ連製の多連装ロケットランチャー〕a Katyusha multiple rocket launcher.
かちょうきん【課徴金】 ▫ 課徴金減免制度〔独占禁止法違反を自主申告した場合, その先着 3 社までに対する〕a system of reduction of or exemption from penal charges. 課徴金算定率〔国家が国民から徴収する租税以外の金銭についての〕the relative proportion of non-tax charges to taxation;〔独占禁止法に違反した企業から徴収する金銭についての〕the proportion of charges levied under the Antimonopoly Law. 課徴金制度〔インサイダー取引などの証券取引法違反や, 独占禁止法違反についての〕a system of penal charges.
かちょうふうえい【花鳥諷詠】composing haiku poems on「flowers and birds [nature] with detached objectivity. ▶ 高浜虚子の作句理念.
カチン〔ミャンマー北部の州〕Kachin.
ガチンコ, がちんこ〘相撲〙〔手加減をしない本気のぶつかり合い〕◐ 相手がお前の親友であることを忘れろ. 〜でやれ. (Don't hold back.) Forget「he's [she's] a friend and give it everything you've got. | Forget that your opponent is a friend and「be merciless [put your whole heart and soul into the fight]. ▫ ガチンコ勝負[対決] a do-or-die contest; a face-off you put「your heart and soul [everything you've got] into.
カチンスキ(ー) 1 Kachinski [Kaczynski], Jaroslaw (1949- ; ポーランドの政治家; 首相[2006-07]; 2 の双子の兄).
2 Kachinski [Kaczynski], Lekh [Lech] (1949- ; ポーランドの政治家; 大統領[2005- ]).
カツァブ Katsav, Moshe (1945- ; イスラエルの政治家; 大統領[2000-07]).
カツヴィン ＝ガスヴィ(ー)ン.
がっき3【楽器】 ▫ 生楽器 ⇒なま.
がっきゅう2【学級】 ▫ 学級通信 a class newsletter.
かつぎわざ【担ぎ技】〘柔道〙a shoulder「carry [throw].
がっけんとし【学研都市】=学術研究都市 (⇒がくじゅつ).
がっこう【学校】 ▫ 学校安全ボランティア a school safety volunteer; a volunteer who protects children at, or on the way to and from, school. 学校外学習 study outside of school; extracurricular learning. 学校間格差〔学校差〕(a) disparity (in academic standards) among schools. 学校経営学 school administration. 学校歯科医 a school dentist. 学校(週)五日制 a [the] five-day school week. ◐ 完全〜(週)五日制 a [the] complete [fully-implemented] five-day school week. 学校(自由)選択制 a system that allows parents to send their children to public schools outside their school zones. 学校税〔米国の〕a school tax. 学校葬〔校葬〕a school funeral; a funeral performed at school expense. 学校相談員 a school counselor. 学校机 a school desk. 学校納付金 a「school [tuition] fee;

school [tuition] fees [expenses]. 学校保健統計調査 a school health statistical survey. 学校任せ dependence on the school. ◐(親の)しつけを～任せにする leave teaching manners up to the school. 学校薬剤師会 a school pharmacists' association.

がっこううんえいきょうぎかい【学校運営協議会】〔地域社会が運営する学校（コミュニティー・スクール）の〕a school management committee.

かっこくオリンピックいいんかいれんごう【各国=委員会連合】the Association of National Olympic Committees（略：ANOC）.

カッサム〔イスラム原理主義組織ハマスが開発したロケット弾〕a Qassam [Kassam] (rocket).

カッサムたい【-隊】〔イスラム原理主義組織ハマスの軍事部門〕the Izzedine al Qassam Brigades; the Izz Al-Din Al-Qassam Brigades.

がっさん【合算】 合算対象期間〔国民年金未加入期間で受給資格期間に算入できる期間〕a period during which a person is not enrolled in a pension program but that can be counted as part of *his* eligibility period for the pension. 合算タイム〔自動車レース〕(a) total time.

カッシーニ[2]〔米国の土星探査機〕Cassini.

カッシム =カシム.

かつしゅうきょく【活褶曲】〔地質〕an active fold; active folding. 活褶曲帯 an active folding 「zone [area]; a zone [an area] of active folding.

がっしゅく【合宿】 合宿免許 ＝合宿教習（⇨きょうしゅう[2]）.

かっしょくハイエナ〔褐色-〕〔動〕a brown hyena; *Hyaena brunnea*.

かっすい[2]【渇水】 渇水被害 drought damage; damage from drought.

カッスラー Cussler, Clive (1931- ；米国の冒険小説作家).

かっせい【活性】 活性酸素除去酵素〔生化〕〔スーパーオキシド・ジスムターゼ〕superoxide dismutase. 活性酸素除去作用 action [effectiveness] in removing active oxygen. 活性酸素除去能力 (an) ability to remove active oxygen. 活性水素水 water containing active hydrogen.

かっせいか【活性化】 活性化リンパ球療法〔医〕activated lymphocyte cell therapy.

かっせん[1]【合戦】 猿蟹合戦〔民話〕the battle between the monkey and the crab.

カッター カッターヘッド〔機〕〔掘削機の頭部〕a cutter-head.

カッタネオ Cattaneo, Peter (1964- ；英国生まれの映画監督).

カッダロール〔インド南部、タミルナードゥ州の県・都市〕Cuddalore.

かつだんそう【活断層】 海底活断層 an active submarine fault.

がっち【合致】 合致度 a degree of 「matching [agreement]; how much [the degree to which]《A》 matches [agrees with]《B》.

かっちゅうそう【褐虫藻】〔植〕〔サンゴなどの体内に共生する単細胞藻類の総称〕a zooxanthella (*pl.* -lae).

ガッツ[2]【GATS】〔サービスの貿易に関する一般協定〕GATS; the General Agreement on Trade in Services; the GATS.

かって【勝手】 勝手サイト〔NTTドコモのiモードサービスで閲覧可能なウェブサイトのうちの非公式サイト〕an i-mode (Web) site not officially sponsored by NTT; a voluntary site.

かつどう[1]【活動】 活動周期〔火山・地震などの〕an active cycle; a cycle of activity; 〔太陽の〕a [an active] solar cycle; a (solar) cycle of activity.

カットボール〔野球〕a cut fastball; a cutter.

カット・モデル〔髪型カットのモデル〕a 「haircut [hairstyling] model.

カツどん【-丼】 ソースカツ丼 a bowl of rice topped with breaded pork cutlets soaked in sauce. 味噌カツ丼 a bowl of rice topped with breaded pork cutlets covered with miso.

かつのうしょう【滑脳症】〔医〕smooth brain; lissencephaly. ▷ lissencephalic *adj*.

かっぷ【割賦】 個品(☆)割賦〔クレジットカードによる総割賦に対して、各商品ごとに消費者と信販会社が契約する決済法〕(a) retail installment purchase. 割賦手数料 the (extra) costs 「of [involved in] installment purchase.

カップ カップ酒 sake sold in a 180 ml glass tumbler.

がっぺい【合併】 越県合併 a cross-prefectural 「annexation [merger]. 救済合併 a relief merger; a failing firm 「*defense* [*defence*]（略：FFD）. 自治体合併 a 「local-government [municipal] merger; a merger [an amalgamation] of local authorities. 飛び地合併〔市町村の〕a merger between non-contiguous municipalities. 合併関係市町村〔合併予定の市町村〕municipalities which are considering 「consolidation [amalgamation]. 合併協定書〔市町村合併の〕a 「merger [unification] agreement《between neighboring municipalities》. 合併市町村〔市町村合併で生まれた自治体〕a municipality created by 「consolidation [amalgamation]. 合併市町村補助金 a municipality consolidation [amalgamation, merger, annexation] grant [subsidy]. 合併対価〔合併に際し、消滅する会社の株主に存続会社が支払う対価〕merger money; expenses to cover a merger. 合併特別区〔市町村合併における〕a post-merger special area. 合併ラッシュ〔市町村の〕a rush toward 「consolidation [amalgamation] of municipalities; a rush by municipalities to amalgamate;〔銀行・企業などの〕a rush of mergers.

がっぺいとくれいほう【合併特例法】〔法〕〔市町村合併特例法〕the Special Law on the Merger of Municipalities.

かつまく【滑膜】〔解〕a synovial membrane; a synovium. 滑膜切除術〔医〕a synovectomy. 滑膜ひだ〔解〕a synovial fold.

かつよう[1]【活用】 活用能力《Internet》literacy.

かつれつ【割裂】〔石材・木材・竹などの〕splitting; cracking; cleaving; fissuring. ～する split; crack. 割裂性 splitting [cracking, cleavage] properties. 割裂破壊〔コンクリート・岩石などの〕cleavage [cracking] failure.

かてい[3]【家庭】 家庭排水［廃水］〔台所・浴室などの〕domestic 「drainage [waste water];〔水洗便所の〕domestic sewage. 家庭復帰〔児童養護施設や介護施設などからの〕(a) return to 「the [*one's*] family; returning [being returned, being restored] to 「the [*one's*] family. 家庭部門 the 「household [domestic]《consumption》 sector. 家庭訪問 residential [home] sales [selling].

かてい[6]【下底】〔幾何〕〔台形の〕a lower base.

カディシヤ〔イラク中南部の州〕Qadisiyah.

かていない【家庭内】 家庭内ストックホルム・シンドローム[症候群]〔心理〕(the) Domestic Stockholm Syndrome（略：DSS）.

カディマ〔2005年、シャロン・イスラエル首相がリクードを離党して結成した新党；意味は「前進」〕Kadima; Kadimah.

カディミヤ ＝カミヤ.

かていよう【家庭用】 家庭用ゲーム a home-use game; a home video game. 家庭用電源 a 「home [household] power source. 家庭用生ごみ処理機 a household garbage disposal. 家庭用燃料電池 a 「home [household] fuel cell《power system, unit》.

カディロフ 1 Kadyrov, Akhmad (1951-2004; チェチェンの政治家; 大統領 [2003-04]).
2 Kadyrov, Ramzan (1976- ; チェチェンの政治家; 1の子; 首相 [2006-07]; 大統領 [2007- ]).

カテーテル ▫ カテーテル検査 〖医〗a 《cardiac》 catheter 「test [examination, investigation]; catheterization.

ガデス Gades, Antonio (1936-2004; スペインのフラメンコ舞踊家・振り付け師).

かてん【加点】 ▫ 加点法〔競技の審査や試験に〕a 「point-addition [plus-points] system; assessment based on giving positive points (in various categories).

かでん[7]【架電】〔電話をかけること〕calling; dialing.  ◐ 先日の件についてご返事お待ちしております。 I await your response to what we discussed on the phone the other day.  ▫ (不正)自動架電〔インターネットのダイヤルアップ接続の設定を勝手に変更し, 後に高額の利用料を請求する詐欺〕an automatic dialing scam;〔そのプログラム〕an automatic dialer.

ガテンけい【一系】〔肉体労働・現業職〕"Gaten"-type work; manual labor of the kind advertised [the sort of job they advertise] in the magazine "Gaten";〔人〕a "Gaten"-type worker; a manual laborer. ▶ 主に現業職を扱う就職雑誌『ガテン』より.

かとう[5]【果糖】 ▫ 果糖ぶどう糖液糖 high fructose corn syrup (略: HFCS).

かどう[2]【可動】 ▫ 可動域 〖医〗〔関節の〕= 関節可動域 (⇒かんせつ).

かどう[3]【河道】 ▫ 河道閉塞〔土砂などが河川をせき止める現象〕(a) channel blockage.

かどう[7]【稼働】 ▫ 再稼働 restarting [a restart]《of operation》. ◐ 状況によっては核施設の再～もあり得ることを大使は示唆した. The ambassador suggested that, under certain conditions, the nuclear facilities might be 「restarted [put back into operation].

かどうぎん【華道吟】 Chinese poetry recitation accompanied by flower arrangement.

かどうちじゅう【角撃ち銃】〖軍〗= コーナー・ショット.

カトーけんきゅうじょ【―研究所】= ケイトーけんきゅうじょ.

カドミヤ〔イラク, バグダッド北部の地区〕Khadimiya.

カトラン Cathelin, Bernard (1919-2004; フランスの画家).

カトリーナ〔2005年8月末, 米国南部に壊滅的な打撃を与えた巨大ハリケーン〕Hurricane Katrina.

カナ〔レバノン南部の村〕Qana.

かなあみ【金網】 ▫ 金網デスマッチ 〖プロレス〗〔リングを金網で囲った時間無制限一本勝負〕a steel-cage death match.

かながた【金型】 ▫ 精密金型 a precision 「die [mold]. ◐ プレス金型 a press 「die [mold]. ▫ 金型加工 die [mold] machining. 金型技術 die [mold] technology. 金型材(料) die [mold] material. 金型産業 the 「die [mold] industry. 金型製作 [製造] die [mold] making. 金型設計 die [mold] design. 金型部品 a 「die [mold] component [part]. 金型メーカー a moldmaker; a 「die [mold] manufacturer.

かなざら【金皿】a compact-pan; a godet.

「悲しき恋歌」〔韓国のテレビドラマ〕Sad Love Story.

カナダがたじゅうすいろ【―型重水炉】〔原子力〕a 「CANDU [Canadian deuterium uranium] (reactor).

カナダかわうそ【―川獺】〖動〗a North American river otter; a Canadian otter; Lutra canadensis.

カナダやまあらし【―山荒し】〖動〗a North American porcupine; Erethizon dorsatum.

ガナッシュ〔菓子〕〔チョコレートをベースに生クリーム・バター・牛乳などの乳製品を混ぜ合わせたもの〕ganache.

カナナスキス〔カナダ西部アルバータ州の観光地〕Kananaskis.

カナル・プリュス〔フランスの有料テレビ会社〕Canal Plus.

かなん[3]【華南】 ▫ 華南経済圏 the south China economic zone.

かにゅう【加入】 ▫ 加入手続き admission [membership application] procedure(s) [formalities]. 加入率 percentage of 《union》 members; percentage of 《cell phone》 owners.

カニンガム Cunningham, Sean S. (1941- ; 米国の映画監督・製作者).

カヌレ〖<F〗〔フランス, ボルドー地方の焼菓子〕canneles de Bordeaux.

かねあまり【金余り】 ▫ 金余り現象 〖経〗(a phenomenon of) excess liquidity; a monetary surplus; a money glut.

かねつ[3]【過熱】 ▫ 過熱報道 excessive (news) coverage.

かねもうけ【金儲け】 ▫ 金儲け優先 priority to making money; a money-first approach. ◐ ～優先の病院経営 money-first hospital management.

かねんせい【可燃性】 ▫ 可燃性ガス濃度制御系〔原子炉の〕a flammability control system (略: FCS).

かのうは【狩野派】〔日本画の一派〕the Kanō school (of Japanese painting).

「彼女を見ればわかること」〔映画〕Things You Can Tell Just By Looking at Her.

カバー 5〔カバー・バージョン〕〖音楽〗a cover (version). ～する cover. ◐ 明菜が聖子の昔の曲を～した. Akina 「covered [redid] one of Seiko's old songs.  ▫ セルフカバー〔同じ人による再録音〕a new version of one's own song; a remake. ◐ カバー曲 a cover (version). ◐ 今度の彼女のアルバムは～曲ばかりで独自の新曲がない. Her latest album is all 「cover songs [cover tracks, covers]; it doesn't have any new originals. カバー・プランツ[クロップ] = グラウンドカバー・プランツ (⇒グラウンド).

かはい【加配】 ▫ 加配教員 extra [additional] teaching staff [teachers].

かばいあい【庇い合い】mutual protection. ▫ かばい合い体質〔業界団体などの〕a culture of mutual protection.

かばきこまちぐも【樺黄小町蜘蛛】〖動〗〔フクログモ科のクモ〕a Japanese foliage spider; Chiracanthium japonicum.

カバコシルバ Cavaco Silva, Aníbal (1939- ; ポルトガルの政治家; 首相 [1985-95]; 大統領 [2006- ]).

かばた【川端】〔わき水を利用した洗い場〕a river spring used for washing; a washing place on a river or stream.

かばっさい【過伐採】〖林業〗overcutting; overharvesting; overlumbering.

かばつねんれい【可罰年齢】the minimum age for criminal punishment.

かばのあなたけ【樺の穴茸】〖菌〗〔担子菌類タバコウロタケ科の薬用キノコ〕Fuscoporia obliqua. ▶ 別名 チャーガ, チャガ (-) (chaga).

かはん【可搬】～の[な] portable. ▫ 可搬型[式]の 「portable-type 《air conditioners》. 可搬式発電機 a portable (power) generator. 可搬ポンプ〔消防用などの〕a portable pump.

かはんしん【下半身】 ▫ 下半身強化〔スポーツ選手などが腰から下の筋力を鍛えること〕strengthening the lower half of one's body. 下半身スキャンダル (a) 「sex [sexual] scandal. 下半身でぶ 《have》 a fat bottom and legs; 《be》 pear-shaped. 下半身麻痺 paralysis [numbness, anesthesia] from the waist down; 〖医〗paraplegia. ▷ paraplegic adj. ～麻痺患者 a paraplegic.

かび[1]【黴】 ▫ カビ胞子 a mold spore.

がびちょう【画眉鳥】〖鳥〗〔ヒタキ科チメドリ亜科の鳥〕a melodious laughing thrush; a hwamei; Garrulax canorus.

カビラ 1 Kabila, Joseph (1972- ; コンゴ民主共和国の政治家; 大統領 [2001- ]; 2の子).

**2 Kabila, Laurent** (1939–2001；コンゴ民主共和国の軍人・政治家；大統領〔1997–2001〕；1 の父).

**カビラヴァストゥ**〔古代インド（現ネパール）の都市名；釈迦の生誕地〕Kapilavastu.

**かぶ**[7]【寡婦】▷▶ 寡婦福祉資金 a (low interest) welfare loan for a widow.

**かぶ**[1]【株】▷▶ 小売株 retail shares; shares of retail companies. 材料株 incentive-backed shares. ⊖仕手系～株 speculative, incentive-backed shares / 低位～株 low-priced, incentive-backed shares. 種類株〔議決権や利益配当などの権利内容が普通株式と異なる株式〕classified stock. 流行株〔医〕〔インフルエンザなどの〕an epidemic strain.

**かぶ**[2]【下部】▷▶ 下部気道〔解〕=かきどう.

**カブア**[2] ⇨ディ・カブア.

**カフィーヤ** =カフィエ.

**カフィエ**〔一部のアラブ諸国で用いられる頭巾〕a kaffiyeh.

**カプール** Kapur, Shekhar (1945– ；インド生まれの映画監督).

**カフェ** ▷▶ カフェ・オ・レ斑（は）〔医〕〔薄茶色のしみ状の皮膚疾患〕café-au-lait spots.

**カフェ・マロン**【植】〔アカネ科の植物；モーリシャスのロドリゲス島で発見された〕Café Marron; *Ramosmania rodriguesii*.

**かぶか**【株価】▷▶ 株価上昇率 the rate of increase in stock prices. 株価動向 stock [share] price movements; stock [share] price trends. 株価崩壊 a stock-price collapse. 株価リターン stock price returns.

**かぶけん**【株券】▷▶ 株券(の)電子化 computerization of (stock) trading; computerization of the stock market. 株券不発行制度〔株主権が株券でなく、株主名簿によって管理される制度〕a stock certificate nonissuance system. ▶ 2004 年 6 月成立公布.

**カプサイシノイド**〔化〕〔唐辛子に含まれる辛味成分カプサイシンとその類似化合物の総称〕capsaicinoid.

**カプシエイト**〔化〕〔辛くないトウガラシの成分の 1 つ〕capsiate.

**かぶしき**【株式】
▷▶ 完全議決権株式 full voting ⌈stock [shares]⌋. 議決権制限株式 limited voting ⌈stock [shares]⌋. 種類株式〔⇨かぶ[1]〕. 複数議決権株式 multiple [super] voting ⌈shares [stock]⌋.
▷▶ 株式移転比率 a percentage of shares transferred; a ⌈stock [share]⌋ transfer ratio. 株式運用益 stock trading profit(s). 株式オプション取引 dealing [trading] in share options; making a share option ⌈transaction [deal]⌋. 株式交換契約 an agreement ⌈a contract⌋ for the exchange of ⌈stock(s) [shares]⌋. 株式交換比率 a stock exchange ratio. 株式時価総額 the aggregate market value ⌈of ExxonMobil shares⌋. 株式資産額 a stock asset value; an assessed stock value. 株式譲渡契約 a stock transfer agreement. ⊖～譲渡契約書 a ⌈written agreement [contract]⌋ for the transfer of ⌈stocks [shares]⌋. 株式譲渡制限会社〔閉鎖会社〕a ⌈close [closed] corporation⌋; ⌈a proprietary company⌋. 株式新規公開 an initial public offering（略: IPO). 株式大量保有報告書〔証券〕a substantial shareholding report; a 5% report. 株式売却益 the ⌈gain [profit] on the sale of ⌈stock [shares]⌋. 株式評価損 a loss from stock revaluation. 株式含み益 (a) latent [(an) unrealized, (a) paper] profit on shares; hidden stock profits. 株式含み損 (a) latent [(an) unrealized, (a) paper] loss on shares; hidden stock losses. 株式分割(予定)銘柄 a stock scheduled to split. 株式分布状況（略）the distribution of shareholdings（as at 8 February 2007）; distribution of shares held by different shareholders. ⊖～分布状況表 a table showing the distribution of ⌈shareholdings [shares held by different shareholders] / ～分布状況調査 an investigation (by the Tokyo Stock Exchange) into the distribution of shares held

by different shareholders. 株式保有 stockholding; shareholding; the holding of ⌈stocks [shares]⌋. 株式保有(比)率 a [the] percentage [ratio] of ⌈shares [stock]⌋ held. 株式値上がり益 capital gain(s) on ⌈stock(s) [shares]⌋. 株式ミニ投資 "mini-stock investment"; a system making it possible for investors to purchase one tenth of the normally permitted number of shares. 株式累積投資(制度) an accumulating fixed-sum monthly stock purchase system.

**かぶしきがいしゃ**【株式会社】▷▶ 株式会社学校 a corporation-managed school. 株式会社病院 a for-profit [an investor-owned] hospital. 株式会社(立)大学 a ⌈for-profit [corporate-owned]⌋ university.

**カプセル** ▷▶ カプセル化〔暗電算〕〔暗号の鍵が仕込まれた再生ソフト以外では音楽や映像を鑑賞することができないというコピーガード対策〕encapsulation. ▷ encapsulate *v*. カプセル玩具〔プラスチックのカプセルに入った小型玩具〕a capsule(d) toy. カプセル内視鏡〔医〕a capsule endoscope.

**かぶぬし**【株主】▷▶ 株主価値 shareholder value. 株主資本比率〔自己資本比率〕(the) capital (adequacy) ratio; (the) equity ratio; (the) net worth ratio. 株主平等原則 (the principle of) equal ⌈rights for [treatment of]⌋ shareholders.

**かぶぬしオンブズマン**【株主—】〔株主として企業活動を監視する NPO 組織〕the Kabunushi (Shareholders) Ombudsman.

**カプラン** Kaplan, Jonathan (1947– ；フランス生まれの米国の映画監督).

**かぶり**[2]【被り】▷▶ 青[赤, 緑]かぶり〔写真〕blue [red, green] tint [color bias].

**ガブリエル**[2]【天】〔ゼナの衛星〕Gabrielle.

**かふん**【花粉】▷▶ ひのき花粉 Japanese cypress [*hinoki*] pollen. 花粉荷（か）〔ミツバチが花粉を蜜で固めたもの〕bee pollen. 花粉計数器 a pollen counter. 花粉飛散量 an atmospheric pollen count; the amount of pollen in the air.

**がぶんしゅう**【画文集】a ⌈collection [book]⌋ of pictures and prose.

**かふんじょうほうきょうかい**【花粉情報協会】the Pollen Information Association.

**かへい**[3]【貨幣】▷▶ 貨幣状湿疹〔医〕nummular [discoid] eczema; nummular (eczematous) dermatitis. 貨幣試験〔造幣局が行う〕the annual testing of coin weights (carried out at the Osaka Mint Bureau).

**かへいそんしょうとうとりしまりほう**【貨幣損傷等取締法】〔法〕the Law against the Debasement of Coinage.

**かへいはくぶつかん**【貨幣博物館】〔日本銀行分館内の〕the Currency Museum.

**かべんもうそうるい**【渦鞭毛藻類】【生物】〔渦巻状の鞭毛で遊泳する微生物〕dinoflagellate.

**かほう**[1]【下方】▷▶ 下方圧力〔力学・相場〕(a) downward pressure.

**かほうしゅうせい**【下方修正】▷▶ 下方修正条項付(き) CB〔転換社債〕〔証券〕a moving strike convertible bond [an MSCB] with a downward adjustment.〔⇨エム・エス・シー・ビー〕.

**カポエイラ**〔ブラジルの格闘技ダンス〕capoeira.

**カポエラ** =カポエイラ.

**カボタージュ**〔航空機・船舶などによる国内 2 地点間の運輸〕cabotage.

**かぼちゃ**[1]【南瓜】▷▶ おもちゃカボチャ =ペポカボチャ.

**ガボロジー**【garbage + -logy】〔ゴミ学〕garbology.

**カボンバ**【植】〔ハゴロモモ科の水草；房藻菜（ふさもくさ）〕cabomba; fanwort; *Cabomba caroliniana*. ▶ 金魚の水槽用に用いられるので金魚藻（も）とも呼ばれる.

**かま**[1]【釜】▷▶ 回転釜〔調理用の〕a rotary ⌈pan [cooker]⌋; 〔ミシンの〕a rotary hook. 水平(全)回転釜〔ミシンの〕a horizontal rotary hook.

かまあげ【釜揚げ】〔釜でしたあとそのまま供される食べ物〕《udon》straight from the pot;〔釜揚げうどん〕⇒釜揚げうどん. 釜揚げうどん straight-from-the-pot udon; a dish in which freshly boiled udon is transferred right from the pot to a bowl containing hot water or light broth. 釜揚げしらす boiled young sardines; young sardines boiled in brine.

カマウ〔ベトナム南部, メコンデルタ地帯の省;その省都〕Ca Mau.

かました【かま下】〔マグロの"かま"の下側の部分で, 大とろなどがとれる〕the neck of the tuna.

かみ[4]【紙】▫▫ 紙パック〔飲料などの〕a paper carton;〔掃除機の〕a paper (dust) bag. 紙パックマーク〔環境ラベルの一種〕a paper carton (recycling) mark. 紙パンツ〔使い捨て下着で〕disposable paper underwear;〔紙おむつ〕disposable paper [*diapers [*nappies].

かみ[5]【髪】▫▫ 髪年齢 (a [one's]) hair age.

かみがかり【神がかり】▫▫ 神がかりの enchanted; entranced; …as if possessed. ◐ ～的手腕 (a) supernatural [(an) inhuman] ability / ～的勝利 a spellbinding victory.

かみがた[1]【上方】▫▫ 上方落語 kamigata rakugo; (the style of) rakugo performed in the Kansai.

かみジャケ【紙-】〔CDの紙製ジャケット〕a paper sleeve;〔紙製ジャケット付きのCD〕a paper-sleeved CD.

かみつ[2]【過密】▫▫ 過密日程 an overcrowded [a packed, a hectic] schedule. ◐ そんな～日程を消化するには人並み外れた体力と精神力が必要だ. Coping with such a packed schedule requires extraordinary physical and mental strength.

かみのあいのせんきょうしゃかい【神の愛の宣教者会】〔マザー・テレサが設立したインド, カルカッタのカトリック修道会〕the Missionaries of Charity.

かみのけざ【髪座】▫▫ かみのけ座銀河団 the Coma Cluster of Galaxies. かみのけ星雲【星団】the Coma Star Cluster.

かみのていこうぐん【神の抵抗軍】〔ウガンダの反政府武装勢力〕the Lord's Resistance Army (略: LRA).

かみばいたい【紙媒体】(the) print media;《in, through》the medium of print.

かみやき【紙焼き】〔写真〕〔印画紙に写真を焼き付けること〕printing (on paper);〔画像を焼き付けた印画紙〕a (paper) print.
～する print 《a photograph》(on paper).

かみん[1]【仮眠】▫▫ 仮眠室 a nap room.

かみん[3]【過眠】〔日中に過剰な眠気が起きる状態〕excessive sleepiness; =過眠症. ▫▫ 過眠症〔医〕hypersomnia; somnolence; excessive daytime sleepiness (略: EDS). ◐ 周期性[反復性]～症 periodic [recurrent] hypersomnia [somnolence] / 特発性～症 idiopathic hypersomnia.

カミング Cumming, Alan (1965– ; 英国の映画俳優).

カミンスキー Kaminski, Janusz (1959– ; ポーランド生まれの米国の撮影監督・製作者).

ガム ▫▫ ガム・テスト〔医〕〔唾液分泌機能テスト〕a gum test.

カムカム【樹】〔フトモモ科の果樹, ペルー, アマゾン原産〕a camu-camu; Myrciaria dubia.

カムタイ Khamtai Siphandon (1924– ; ラオスの政治家, 大統領 [1998-2006]).

ガムたばこ【ガム状のたばこ】gum-based chewing tobacco; tobacco (chewing) gum.

カムチャツカ〔ロシア極東の州〕Kamchatka.

カムペーン・ペット〔タイ北部の県;その県都〕Kamphaeng Phet.

ガムペン・ペット =カムペーン・ペット.

ガムラン ▫▫ ガムラン音楽 gamelan music.

カムランド〔岐阜県神岡鉱山の地下にあるニュートリノの観測装置〕KamLAND. ▶ Kamioka Liquid Scintillator Anti-Neutrino Detector (神岡液体シンチレータ反ニュートリノ検出器)の略.

かめい[3]【加盟】▫▫ 準加盟 preliminary accession《to the European Union》; associate [half] membership; semi-membership. 正加盟 formal accession《to the European Union》; full membership. ▫▫ 加盟金〔フランチャイズへの〕a franchise fee;〔連盟への〕an affiliation fee; a membership fee. 加盟条件[基準] a 「condition [criterion] for membership. ◐ EUの～条件 conditions for membership in the EU; the Copenhagen criteria. ▶ 1993年, コペンハーゲン欧州理事会で決定された. 加盟率〔連盟・連合団体などへの〕the percentage of 《stores》'belonging to [that have joined]《a neighborhood store association》. 加盟料 a 《baseball organization》'membership [affiliation] fee.

かめい[4]【仮名】▫▫ 仮名報道 a news report 「with [under] a pseudonym [a made-up name]; reporting without using a real name.

カメラ ▫▫ カメラ機材 camera 「equipment [apparatus, gear]. カメラ・テスト〔写真機のテスト〕a camera test 《on a new model》;〔テスト撮影〕a camera test《on an aspiring actress》.

カメラえいぞうききこうぎょうかい【-映像機器工業会】the Camera & Imaging Products Association (略: CIPA).

かめん[3]【仮面】▫▫ 仮面就職 taking a job in an easy-to-enter company, really intending to find a better job.

かもく[1]【科目・課目】▫▫ 得意科目 one's strong subject. 不得意科目 one's weak subject. ▫▫ 科目等履修生 a specially registered (non-degree) student.

かもつ[2]【貨物】▫▫ 貨物検査 (an) inspection of (a) cargo; (a) cargo inspection. 貨物利用運送事業者 a (freight) forwarder.

かもつじどうしゃうんそうじぎょうほう【貨物自動車運送事業法】〔法〕the Trucking Business Law.

かもつりよううんそうじぎょうほう【貨物利用運送事業法】〔法〕the Freight Forwarding Business Law. ▶「貨物運送取扱事業法」から改正.

カモフラージュ ▫▫ カモフラージュメイク camouflage cosmetics.

かもん[3]【家紋】▫▫ 家紋瓦 a tile with a family crest on it.

ガユーム Gayoom, Maumoon Abdul (1937– ; モルディブの政治家; 大統領 [1978– ]).

かゆうらない【粥占い】〔吉凶占いの1つ〕a method of divination in which three bamboo tubes are placed in rice gruel before cooking and, after cooking, the distribution of rice grains in each is used for prediction.

がよう【瓦窯】a tile kiln. ▫▫ 瓦窯跡 the 「remains [site] of a tile kiln.

「花様年華」〔映画〕In the Mood for Love.

ガヨ・ルス〔インドネシア, アチェ州の県〕Gayo Lues.

から[1]【空】▫▫ 空期間〔国民年金の〕a period during which a person is not enrolled in a pension program but that can be counted as part of his eligibility period for the pension. 空財源〔予算に計上された, 財源の裏付けのない収入〕non-performing assets; imaginary 「fictitious」 assets. 空請求 = 架空請求 (⇒かくう). 空メール〔応募などでメールアドレスを伝えるために送る, 内容がブランクのメール〕(a) blank mail.

カラー[1] ▫▫ カラー・ピアス〔襟先に付けるアクセサリー〕a collar pin.

カラー[2] ▫▫ カラー・コーディネーション color coordination. カラー・コーディネート =カラー・コーディネーション. ◐ テーブルクロスやナプキンを取り替えることで何通りもの～コーディネートが楽し

めます。 You can enjoy a number of different color coordinations by ⌈changing the [substituting different] tablecloths and napkins. カラー・セラピスト〔色彩療法士〕a color therapist; a chromotherapist. カラー・バリエーション a variety of colors. ▶その製品は～バリエーションが豊富です。 This product comes in a wide variety of colors. カラー・フィルター〔写真〕a color filter. カラー・マッチング color matching.
「カラー・オブ・ハート」〔映画〕Pleasantville.
カライナウ〔アフガニスタン西部、バドギス州の州都〕Qala-I-Naw; Qala-I-Now.
**からうり**【空売り】□ 空売り株〔株式〕a ⌈short sale [shorted] stock.
カラオケ □ カラオケ教室 a karaoke class.
カラカウア (King) Kalakaua (1836–91) 〔ハワイ王国国王 〔1874–91〕).
**からがし**【空貸し】〔架空の貸借契約を装い不法に返済を迫ること〕a fraudulent [an unsubstantiated] demand for loan repayment. □ 空貸し電報 a phony dunning telegram.
**がらくた** □ がらくたDNA〔遺伝〕=ジャンクDNA (⇨ジャンク2).
**からくち**【辛口】□ 辛口トーク cruel [bitter, vicious, scathing] talk.
**からしよう**【空雇用】fictitious employment.
**からしし, からじし**【唐獅子】□ 唐獅子牡丹〔絵柄〕a lion and peony ⌈design [pattern].
カラシン =カーラシン.
ガラス【硝子】□ 強化ガラス tempered [toughened] glass. セルフクリーニング・ガラス self-cleaning glass. 低反射ガラス low-reflection glass. 特殊ガラス special glass. 防汚ガラス セルフクリーニング・ガラス. □ ガラス基板〔電子工学〕a glass substrate.
カラス(ウ)〔ウズベキスタン東部、キルギスとの国境の町〕Kara-Suu; Korasuv.
**ガラスかほう**【-化法】〔生化〕〔卵子凍結法〕vitrification.
ガラセ Qarase, Laisenia (1941– ;フィジー諸島共和国の政治家;首相〔2000–06〕).
**からたねおがたま**【唐種招霊】〔植〕〔モクレン科の常緑小高木; 中国原産〕a banana shrub; Michelia figo; Michelia fuscata.
**からだねんれい**【体年齢】〔筋肉や脂肪の量、基礎代謝などからみた体の年齢〕body age. ▶まだ40代には～は60歳と言われてショックを受けた。 It was a shock to be told that he had ⌈a body age of 60 [the body of a 60 year-old] when he was still in his 40s.
**からちょうず**【空手水】purifying oneself at a temple or shrine when no water or salt is available by making the symbolic gesture of washing one's hands.
カラックス Carax, Leos (1960/61– ;フランスの映画監督).
ガラばこ【-箱】〔部品を再利用するために壊れた機械類を貯めておく箱〕a ⌈scrap [junk] box.
**からばし**【空箸】a breach of etiquette consisting of touching food with one's chopsticks and then withdrawing them without eating.
カラビニエリ〔< It〕〔イタリア警察軍〕the Carabinieri.
カラビラ〔イラク西部の村〕Karabila.
カラフ =カラフェ.
カラフェ〔卓上用の水差し〕a carafe.
**からふとるりしじみ**【樺太瑠璃小灰[蜆]】〔昆〕〔シジミチョウ科のチョウ〕a cranberry blue; Vacciniina optilete.
**からふとわし**【樺太鷲】〔鳥〕〔タカ科の鳥〕a greater spotted eagle; Aquila clanga.
**からぶり**【空振り】□ 空振り率〔野球など〕a swing and miss rate;〔天気予報などの〕a false alarm rate.
カラボボ〔ベネズエラ中北部の州〕Carabobo.
カラマンリス Karamanlis [Caramanlis], Costas (1956– ;ギリシャの政治家;首相〔2004–    〕).

**からみ**[1]【辛味】□ 辛味成分 a ⌈pungent [spicy, sharp, hot] component [ingredient]. 辛味大根 a ⌈hot [strong, sharp, pungent] daikon [radish]. 辛味調味料 a hot [spicy, sharp, pungent] seasoning [flavoring].
**からみ**[3]【絡み】
3〔からまること〕tangling; entanglement. ▶衣類の～ tangled clothes.
カラム[1]【電算】〔列〕a column;【化】〔分離管〕a column.
カラム[2] Kalam, A.P.J. Abdul (1931–  ;インドの政治家;大統領〔2002–07〕).
**からやき**【空焼き】1【料理】〔中に何も入れず鍋などを加熱すること〕(調理準備として) preheating;(不注意で) empty heating; heating an empty 《pot》.
2【料理】〔パイに詰め物をせず生地だけ焼くこと〕cooking [baking] only the crust.
**カラヤンくいな**【-水鶏】〔鳥〕〔クイナ科の鳥〕a Calayan rail; Gallirallus calayaensis.
カランク《<F calanque》〔断崖の入り江〕a rocky inlet.
カランバ〔フィリピン、ラグナ州の都市〕Calamba.
**かりあげ**[2]【借り上げ】□ 借り上げ社宅 housing rented 《by a company》 for employee accommodation; company-rented employee accommodation.
ガリ(一)【地質】〔雨による土壌浸食の溝〕a gully. □ ガリ(一)浸食 gully erosion.
カリーモフ =カリモフ.
ガリヴァー □ ガリヴァー企業 a mammoth enterprise.
**ガリウムひそ**【-砒素】□ ガリウム砒素(系)太陽電池 a ⌈GaAs [gallium arsenide] solar cell.
カリエス □ カリエス・リスク検査[テスト]〔歯科〕〔虫歯になる危険度を測る唾液検査〕a caries risk test (略: CRT).
カリオフィレン □ アルファ[ベータ]カリオフィレン alpha-[beta-]caryophyllene.
**かりかんじょう**【仮勘定】□ 建設仮勘定 a construction-in-progress account.
**かりけってい**【仮決定】a provisional ⌈ruling [decision]. ～する rule [decide] provisionally; issue a provisional ⌈ruling [decision]. ▶～を下す =～する.
**かりしょぶん**【仮処分】□ 仮処分決定 a provisional disposition ruling. 仮処分手続き (a) provisional disposition procedure.
カリスマ □ カリスマ美容師〔モデル、主婦、バイヤー、シェフ、教師〕a charismatic ⌈hairdresser [fashion model, homemaker, buyer, chef, teacher].
**かりたいいん**【仮退院】(a) provisional discharge from (the) hospital;〔少年院などからの〕(a) ⌈provisional [probationary] release (from 《a reformatory》).
～する be discharged provisionally from (the) hospital;〔少年院などから〕be released on probation.
カリフ □ カリフ制 the [a] caliphate system.
**カリフォルニアあしか**【-海驢】〔動〕a California sea lion; Zalophus californianus.
**カリフォルニアしゅうきょうしょくいんたいしょくねんきんききん**【-州教職員退職年金基金】=カルスターズ.
**カリフォルニアしゅうしょくいんたいしょくねんきんきん**【-州職員退職年金基金】=カルパース.
**カリフォルニアしゅうりつだいがく**【-州立大学】California State University (略: CSU); Cal State.
**カリフォルニアたいきしげんきょく**【-大気資源局】the California Air Resources Board (略: CARB).
**カリフォルニアねんりょうでんちパートナーシップ**【-燃料電池-】the California Fuel Cell Partnership (略: CaFCP).
カリモフ Karimov, Islam (1938–  ;ウズベキスタンの政治家;大統領〔1991–    〕).
**かりゅう**[1]【下流】□ 下流課税〔石油などの小売段階の課税〕downstream taxation.
**かりゅう**[7]【顆粒】□ 顆粒スティック a (little) packet of 《sugar, etc.》.
**かりょうはんばい**【過量販売】forcing too many goods

カリンバ

on customers; forcing customers to buy too much.
**カリンバ**〔楽器〕〔アフリカの小型鍵盤楽器;親指ピアノ〕a kalimba; a thumb piano.
**「カル」**〔映画〕Tell Me Something.
**カルカ**〔先込め銃で銃身に弾や火薬を込めるのに用いる細長い棒〕a ramrod; a scouring stick.
**カルキリヤ**〔ヨルダン川西岸のパレスチナ自治区の市〕Qalqilya; Qalqiliya.
**カルギル**〔インド領カシミールの町〕Kargil. ▭ カルギル紛争〔1999年のインド・パキスタン間の〕the Kargil conflict.
**カルキン 1** Culkin, Kieran (1982- ;米国の映画俳優;2の弟).
**2** Culkin, Macaulay (1980- ;米国の映画俳優;1の兄).
**カルザイ** Karzai, Hamid (1957- ;アフガニスタンの政治家;大統領〔2002- 〕).
**ガルシア 1** García, Alan (1949- ;ペルーの政治家;大統領〔1985-90, 2006- 〕;フルネーム Alan Gabriel Ludwig García Pérez).
**2** Garcia, Andy (1956- ;キューバ生まれの米国の映画俳優;本名 Andres Arturo Garcia-Menendez).
**カルシウム** ▭ カルシウム・イオン a calcium ion.
**カルスターズ** CalSTRS. ▶ 正式名称は カリフォルニア州教職員退職年金基金 (the California State Teachers' Retirement System).
**かるた** ▭ 競技かるた a "Concentration-["Pelmanism-]-like game in which two players memorize the positions of 50 cards on which the fourth and fifth lines of tanka poems are written and compete at touching the cards as the poems' first three lines are read aloud; *kyōgi karuta*.
**カルチュラル・スタディーズ**〔宗教・芸術・政治・経済・技術など人間研究の諸分野を包含する学際的研究〕cultural studies.
**カルテ** ▭ カルテ改竄(かいざん) falsification [improper alteration] of a patient's ⌈chart [medical record(s)].
**カルティエ**〔商標〕〔フランスの宝飾品ブランド〕Cartier.
**カルデロン** Calderón, Felipe de Jesus (1962- ;メキシコの政治家;大統領〔2006- 〕).
**カルト** ▭ カルト犯罪 (a) cult crime.
**カルトナージュ**〔<F>〕〔フランスの伝統的な厚紙手工芸品〕cartonnage.
**カルネアデス** Carneades (214?-?129 BC;古代ギリシャの哲学者). ▭ カルネアデスの板〔他人の生命を犠牲にした緊急避難は許されるのかという命題〕the Plank of Carneades.
**カルパース**〔世界最大の公的年金〕CalPERS. ▶ 正式名称は カリフォルニア州職員退職年金基金 (the California Public Employees' Retirement System).
**カルパイン**〔生化〕〔心筋の中にあるたんぱく質分解酵素〕calpain.
**カルパス**〔ドライソーセージの一種〕kielbasa [kolbasa] (sausage).
**ガルバンソ**〔Sp〕〔植〕〔ひよこ豆のスペイン語名〕a garbanzo (bean).
**ガルバンゾ(ー)**〔植〕=ガルバンソ.
**カルビティス** Kalvitis, Aigars (1966- ;ラトヴィアの実業家・政治家;首相〔2004-07〕).
**カルマ**[2]〔イラク中部, ファルージャ東郊の地区〕Karma.
**カルマパじゅうななせい**〔-17世〕the 17th Karmapa (1985- ;チベット仏教, カギュ派の最高位僧・活仏).
**カルモジュリン** ▭ カルモジュリン・キナーゼ〔生化〕〔破骨細胞内の酵素の一種〕calmodulin kinase (略: CaMK).
**カルローズ**〔商標〕〔米カリフォルニア産の中粒米〕Calrose (rice).
**かれい**[3]〔加齢〕▭ 加齢現象 an aging phenomenon; a phenomenon of aging.
**かれい**[8]〔家例〕〔家の慣習〕a family ⌈custom [tradition].
**かれい**[9]〔下令〕giving an order.

~する give ⌈an order [a command]; order; command. ◐ ただちに防衛出動が~された. The Self-Defense Forces were ordered to mobilize immediately.
**「カレイジャス・キャット」**〔米国の, 猫が主人公の変身ヒーローものの TV アニメ〕Courageous Cat.
**「華麗な探偵ピート&マック」**〔米国の, 探偵コンビの TV ドラマ〕Switch.
**カレッジ・ボード**〔SAT 等を運営する米国の大学入学試験委員会〕the College Board; the College Entrance Examination Board.
**「カレリア」**〔シベリウス作曲の管弦楽曲〕the Karelia Suite; Karelia.
**カレリアけん**〔-犬〕〔犬〕〔北欧カレリア地方産の熊猟犬〕a Karelian bear dog.
**「カレン」**〔米国の, 女子高校生 Karen がヒロインの TV ホームドラマ〕Karen.
**カレンシー** ▭ カレンシー・ボード制〔経〕a currency board system (略: CBS).
**カレンじけん**〔-事件〕〔医〕〔1976 年, 米国で植物状態に陥った女性の両親が尊厳死を認めるよう求めた事件〕the (Karen Ann) Quinlan case.
**カレンニーぞく**〔-族〕〔ミャンマー北部の山岳民族〕the Karenni(s); 〔1 人〕a Karenni.
**カレンニーみんぞくかいはつ[しんぽ]とう**〔-民族開発 [進歩]党〕〔ミャンマーの反政府武装勢力〕the Karenni National Progressive Party (略: KNPP).
**カレンみんぞくどうめい**〔-民族同盟〕〔ミャンマーの少数民族カレン族の組織〕the Karen National Union (略: KNU).
**カレン・モク** Karen Mok (1970- ;香港の映画女優;中国語名 莫文蔚 Mok Man-Wai).
**かろうと, かろうど**〔屍櫃〕〔墓石の下の納骨用石室〕a stone vault [box] for the bones of the deceased; a stone ossuary (under a grave).
**カロート** =かろうと.
**ガロカテキン**〔化〕〔ポリフェノールの一種〕gallocatechin.
**カロリー** ▭ 消費カロリー (the number of) ⌈calories consumed [used]. ▭ カロリー消費量 calorie consumption; (a) calorie expenditure. カロリー・ベース(で)〔食料自給率算出法の1つ〕(a 40% self-sufficiency rate) in terms of calorie supply.
**カロリンスカけんきゅうじょ**〔-研究所〕〔スウェーデンの医科大学〕the Karolinska Institute.
**かわあるき**〔川歩き〕〔渓流に沿って歩くこと〕river [stream] trekking.
~する go ⌈river [stream] trekking; go on a ⌈river [stream] trek.
**「かわいい魔女ジニー」**〔米国の TV ホームコメディー〕I Dream of Jeannie. ▶ 原案・脚本は シドニー・シェルダン (Sidney Sheldon).
**がわじ**〔側地〕=側生地 (⇨きじ[3]).
**かわせ**[2]〔為替〕▭ 為替介入 (a) foreign exchange intervention. 為替差損益 foreign exchange gain(s) or loss(es). 為替水準 foreign exchange [an exchange rate, a currency] level. 為替操作国 a currency manipulator. ◐ ~操作国と認定する designate ⟨a country⟩ as a currency manipulator.
**かわちばんかん**〔河内晩柑〕〔柑橘類の一種〕a *kawachi-bankan* ⌈pomelo [pummelo].
**かわづざくら**〔河津桜〕〔バラ科の落葉高木〕a Kawazu cherry (tree); *Prunus lannesiana* cv. *Kawazu-zakura*.
**かわどこ**〔川床〕▭ 川床料理 Kyoto cuisine designed to be eaten on a *kawadoko*.
**かわなかじまのかっせん**〔川中島の合戦〕〔日本史〕the battles of Kawanakajima.
**「河の上の夏の夜」**〔ディーリアス作曲の楽曲〕Summer Night on the River.
**かわパン, かわパンツ**〔革-, 革-〕leather pants.

かわひばりがい【河雲雀貝】〖貝〗〔イガイ科カワヒバリガイ科に属する貝〕a golden mussel; *Limnoperma fortunei*.
かわほととぎすがい【河時鳥貝】〖貝〗a zebra mussel; *Dreissena polymorpha*.
かわまき【革巻き】🔲 革巻きステアリングホイール[ハンドル]〖自動車〗a leather-wrapped steering wheel.
かわら¹【瓦】🔲 瓦割り〔空手の演技の〕tile breaking.
かわりざき【変わり咲き】◐〜の variant blossoming / 〜のチューリップ a variant blossom(ing) tulip. ◐ この花はダリアで〜です. This flower is a variant blossom of the dahlia.
かん⁵【缶・罐】🔲 缶チューハイ (a) canned *shōchū* cocktail; a can of *shōchū* mixed with soda water or soda pop. 缶バッジ[バッチ]〔通例ブリキ製で円盤型のバッジ〕a tin badge.
かん⁸【官】🔲 官から民へ〔公的サービスの民営化〕(a) transfer from the public to the private sector; privatization.
かん²⁰【管】🔲 管工事 plumbing work; piping work. 管工事施工管理技士 a licensed [certified] plumbing supervisor.
-かん²【-感】a sense 《of speed》; a 《lethargic》feeling. ◐ 新しい洗剤を使ったら洗濯物のごわごわ〜がなくなった. When I used a new detergent, the clothes didn't feel stiff anymore. / 胸の底のざわざわ〜がなくならない. I can't get rid of the uneasy feeling at the pit of my stomach. / そのバーの適度なざわざわ〜が気に入った. I liked the nice level of hubbub in that bar.
がん³【癌】🔲 デノボがん〔正常粘膜から発生したがん〕(a) de novo cancer; a de novo carcinoma [tumor]. ポリープがん〔良性のポリープから転化したがん〕(a) polyp carcinoma [cancer]. がん専門薬剤師 an oncology [a cancer] pharmacist. がん難民〔がんに関する情報や納得できる治療を求めて病院を転々とするがん患者〕a cancer patient who goes from hospital to hospital seeking information and care; a "cancer refugee." がんワクチン〔(an) anti-cancer〕vaccine. ◐ 自家〜ワクチン (an) autologous cancer vaccine.
ガン¹ ガン・カメラ〖軍〗〔機銃を撃つのに連動して撮影できる航空機搭載カメラ; 射撃の成果が記録できる〕a gun camera.
ガン³ Gunn, Thom (1929–2004; 英国生まれの詩人; 本名 Thomson William Gunn).
かんい⁵【簡易】🔲 簡易包装 simplified packaging; (a) simplified wrapping.
かんインドよう【環-洋】the Indian Ocean Rim; the rim of the Indian Ocean. 環インド洋経済圏 the Indian Ocean economic zone.
かんえん【肝炎】🔲 脂肪性肝炎 steatohepatitis; fatty liver. アルコール性肝炎〜 alcoholic fatty liver (略: ASH); alcoholic fatty liver / 非アルコール性脂肪性〜 nonalcoholic steatohepatitis (略: NASH); nonalcoholic fatty liver.
かんおう³【陥凹】〖医〗〔落ちくぼんでいること〕vallecula; indentation. 🔲 陥凹型大腸[胃]がん depressed(-type) colorectal [gastric] cancer.
かんか⁸【感化】🔲 感化力 the ability to influence 《affect, inspire, move》《people》.
かんか¹²【患家】〖患者のいる家庭〕the family of a patient; a patient's family.
がんか⁷【眼窩】🔲 眼窩底〖解〗the orbital floor. ◐ 〜底骨折〖医〗〔吹き抜け骨折〕a blowout fracture.
かんがい⁶【灌漑】🔲 点滴灌漑〖農〗drip irrigation; trickle irrigation.
かんがいたんかんがん【肝外胆管癌】〖医〗(an) extrahepatic cholangiocarcinoma.
かんかく¹【間隔】🔲 間隔尺度〖統計〗an interval scale.
かんかく²【感覚】🔲 肌感覚〔肌を通じての〕a skin feel [sensation]; touch; the feel of (*one's*) skin; how *sth* feels 「on [to] the skin; 〔肌のような〕a [the] feel of skin; a skin-like feel [touch, texture]; a feeling [texture] like skin. ◐ ブランドに惑わされず化粧品は肌〜で選びましょう. Don't worry about the brand; choose your cosmetics by how they feel on the skin. / 肌〜で治安の悪化を知る have [get] a direct intuition of the decline in law and order; really feel (for *oneself*) how the situation is worsening / 肌〜のシリコン製ブラジャーパッド a silicone bra pad which feels like *one's* own skin [as soft as skin].
🔲 感覚学〖医〗esthesiology; aesthesiology. 感覚公害〔騒音・悪臭など〕sensory pollution.
カンガルー【-金貨】〔オーストラリア政府発行の〕a Kangaroo gold coin; an Australian Kangaroo nugget (coin).
かんきせん【換気扇】a ventilation [ventilating] fan; an extractor fan. ◐ 〜の羽根 an extractor fan blade. ◐ 〜を回す turn on [start] an extractor fan / 〜を止める turn off [stop] an extractor fan.
かんきのう【肝機能】🔲 肝機能値 a liver count; hepatic function values.
かんきゃく²【観客】🔲 観客いじり〔芸人が観客に話しかけて笑いを取ろうとすること〕playing to the audience. 観客参加型 audience participation. ◐ 〜参加型演劇 audience-participation theater.
かんきゃくどういんりつ【観客動員率】percentage of seats filled [sold]《in a theater, auditorium, stadium, or other venue》.
かんきゅう⁵【緩急】🔲 緩急自在 ◐ 〜自在の攻撃 an attack of (skillfully) varied pace; a well-paced [skillfully paced] attack.
かんきゅう⁷【漢級】〖軍〗＝はんきゅう⁵.
がんきゅう【眼球】🔲 眼球運動障害〖医〗an ocular motility disorder. 眼球結膜 the bulbar [ocular] conjunctiva.
かんきゅうじほう【環球時報】〔中国の国際時事新聞; 週3回刊〕the Global Times.
かんきょう²【環境】
🔲 音環境 a sound environment; an acoustic environment; an aural environment. ◐ 音〜デザイナー a sound environment designer / 私たちは静けさを含めた心地よい音〜作りを心がけています. We strive to create environments of soothing sounds, including silence.
🔲 環境開発サミット〔環境サミット〕an environment(al) summit;〔持続可能な開発に関する世界首脳会議 (2002)〕the World Summit on Sustainable Development (略: WSSD). 環境学 environmental science; environmentology. 環境格付け (an) eco-rating. ◐ 〜格付け融資 financing at preferential terms for a company with a good eco-rating. 環境危機時計〔環境悪化による人類滅亡までの残り時間を表す時計〕the environmental doomsday clock. 環境技術 (an) environmental technology. 環境基準値 an environmental standard value. 環境共生(型)社会 an environment(ally)-friendly society. 環境共生住宅部品 environmentally-friendly housing components. 環境共生都市〔エコシティ〕an eco(-)city [Eco(-)city]. 環境経営 environmental management; green management. 環境計画学 environmental planning (studies). 環境考古学 environmental archaeology. 環境効率 eco-efficiency. ◐ 製品〜効率 product environmental efficiency; the environmental efficiency of a product. 環境サンプル〔環境汚染調査のための採取物質〕an environmental sample. ◐ 〜サンプル調査 environmental sampling. 環境 JIS Environmental JIS. 環境車 ＝環境対応車. 環境社会学 environmental sociology. 環境譲与税〔国が地方公共団体の地球温暖化対策に充てる税〕environment tax income transferred (from the

Central Government) to local government(s). 環境スワップ〔債務環境スワップ〕a debt-for-nature swap. 環境生命医学 environmental life science(s). 環境測定 (an) ambient measurement. 環境対応技術 (an)「environmentally friendly [eco-friendly, environment-friendly] technology. 環境対応車 a green「vehicle [car]; an environmentally friendly「vehicle [car]. 環境中毒学 ecotoxicology; environmental toxicology; (medical) ecotoxicology. 環境調査衛星 an environmental survey satellite. 環境調整〔行政〕environmental coordination; 〔精神医〕providing [provision of] a suitable environment 《for a patient》; adjusting 《a patient's》environment. 環境適応能(力) environmental adaptability. 環境(的)正義 environmental justice. 環境トイレ〔環境に負荷をかけないトイレ〕an ecological toilet; an environment(ally) friendly toilet. 環境配慮 care [concern] for the environment. 環境配慮(型)住宅 an「environmentally friendly [eco-friendly] house. 環境配慮(型)製品 an「environmentally friendly [eco-friendly] product. 環境配慮(型)融資 environmentally friendly「financing [credit]. 環境発がん environmental carcinogenesis. 環境美化 improving the appearance of the environment; making the environment more attractive; creating a more attractive environment. 環境付加価値 environmental value added (略: EnVA); environmental added value. 環境予防医学 environmental (and) preventive medicine. 環境リスク an environmental risk. 環境リスク評価 (an) environmental risk assessment.
**かんきょうかくほじょうれい**【環境確保条例】〔東京都の〕the Ordinance on Environmental Preservation. ▶「都民の健康と安全を確保する環境に関する条例 (the Ordinance on Environmental Preservation to Secure the Health and Safety of Tokyoites)」の略称.
**かんきょうけいえいかくづけきこう**【環境経営格付機構】the Sustainable Management Rating Institute (略: SMRI).
**かんきょうけいえいがっかい**【環境経営学会】the Sustainable Management Forum of Japan (略: SMF).
**かんきょうけいえいそくしんほう**【環境経営促進法】〔法〕the Green Management Promotion Law.
**かんきょうさいせいほぜんきこう**【環境再生保全機構】the Environmental Restoration and Conservation Agency (略: ERCA).
**かんきょうじしゅこうどうけいかく**【環境自主行動計画】=けいだんれんかんきょうじしゅこうどうけいかく.
**かんきょうじちたいかいぎかんきょうせいさくけんきゅうじょ**【環境自治体会議環境政策研究所】the Research Institute for Local Initiative of Environmental Policies (略: RELIEP).
**かんきょうとかいはつにかんするせかいいんかい**【環境と開発に関する世界委員会】〔国連〕the World Committee on Environment and Development (略: WCED).
**かんきょうのひ**【環境の日】=せかいかんきょうデー.
**かんきん**[5]【監禁】□□ 監禁傷害罪〔法〕(a charge of) unlawful confinement resulting in injury. 監禁場所 a place of captivity; a location where sb is held (captive).
**がんぐ**[1]【玩具】□□ 浴玩[入浴]玩具 a bath toy. □□ 玩具療法 toy therapy.
**カンクンかくりょうかいぎ**〔-閣僚会議〕[2003年9月の] the (WTO) Cancún summit.
**かんけい**[4]【関係】□□ 関係強化 (a [the])「strengthening of relations [ties]《between Japan and the USA》. ▶首相は日米同盟関係を基軸としたうえで、中国、ロシア、韓国など周辺諸国との―強化を図る考えである. The Prime Minister aims to strengthen ties with regional nations such as China, Russia and South Korea, while maintaining its fundamental alliance with the United States. 関係構築 relationship [relation] building; building [forging] relations 《with…》.
**かんけいしゃ**[1]【関係者】□□ 業界関係者 people「in [involved in, connected to] the《entertainment》industry.
**かんけつ**[2]【間欠】□□ 間欠記録〔一定の間隔で映像を断続的に記録できるビデオカメラなどの機能〕(an) interval recording. 間欠性爆発性障害〔精神医〕an intermittent explosive disorder (略: IED).
**かんげん**[6]【還元】□□ 社会還元 donating part [donation of part] of the proceeds to the community; plowing [ploughing] back part of the profits into society. 還元麦芽糖 reduced maltose; maltitol. 還元麦芽糖水飴 reduced maltose (starch) syrup; maltitol syrup. 還元水飴 reduced syrup.
**がんけん**[2]【眼瞼】□□ 眼瞼結膜〔解〕the palpebral conjunctiva. 眼瞼結膜炎〔医〕blepharoconjunctivitis. 眼瞼ミオキミア〔医〕eyelid myokymia.
**かんこう**[3]【完工】□□ 完工検査 =竣工検査 (⇨しゅんこう[2]).
**かんこう**[9]【慣行】□□ 人事慣行 personnel management practices; the way personnel matters are carried out.
**かんこう**[15]【観光】□□ 周遊(型)観光 tourism [going on a tour] without stopping long at any one place; roundabout tourism. 体験(型)観光 "real-experience" tourism;《go on》a real-experience tour. 滞在型観光 long-stay tourism. 観光英語 English for「tourism [tourists]; tourist English; tourism English. 観光学 tourism studies. 観光白書 a white paper on tourism; the《2005》 White Paper on Tourism. 観光物産品 a (local)「tourism [tourist] product; a product for tourists. 観光立国 a national commitment to tourism. ○ ～立国構想 a national tourism promotion plan.
**かんこう**[22]【汗孔】〔解〕a sweat pore.
**かんこう**[3]【嵌合】〔機〕fit; fitting. ～する fit; engage 《with…》. ○ このナットに～するボルトが必要だ. We need a bolt that will fit this nut.
**がんこう**[3]【雁行】□□ 雁行陣〔テニス〕〔ダブルスで〕an up-and-back formation; a one-up one-back formation.
**かんこうき**【緩降機】〔高い階からの避難用具〕a slow-descent「machine [device].
**かんこうじゅほう**【官公需法】〔法〕the Law on Ensuring the Receipt of Orders from the Government and Other Public Agencies by Small and Medium Enterprises. ▶ 正式名称は「官公需についての中小企業者の受注の確保に関する法律」.
**かんこうせい**[2]【緩効性】〔ゆっくりと長時間にわたって効果があること〕slow [gradual] effectiveness;《have》a slow [gradual] effect. □□ 緩効性肥料〔園芸・農〕(a) slow-acting fertilizer.
**かんこうとし**【環濠都市】a city surrounded by a moat; a moated city.
**かんこうへん(しょう)**【肝硬変(症)】□□ 脂肪性肝硬変(症) fatty cirrhosis. 胆汁性肝硬変(症) biliary cirrhosis.
**かんこくこうそくてつどう**【韓国高速鉄道】the Korean Train Express (略: KTX).
**かんこくこくさいぼうえききょうかい**【韓国国際貿易協会】the Korea International Trade Association (略: KITA).
**かんこくじんけんセンター**【監獄人権―】〔NPO法人〕the Center for Prisoners' Rights Japan (略: CPR).
**かんこくそうごう(かぶか)しすう**【韓国総合(株価)指数】the Korea Composite Stock Price Index (略: KOSPI).
**かんこくとりひきじょ**【韓国取引所】the Korea Ex-

change〔略: KRX〕.
かんこくやきゅういいんかい【韓国野球委員会】〔韓国のプロ野球団体〕the Korean Baseball Organization〔略: KBO〕.
かんごし【看護師】 ▷■ 潜在看護師〔看護師免許を持っているが実務に就いていない人〕a qualified but non-practicing nurse.
かんごそち【観護措置】〔法〕〔少年鑑別所への送致〕placing〔a child〕under protective detention; imposing a care and custody order; sending〔a child〕to a juvenile classification home [detention home, remand home].
「看護婦物語」〔看護婦の生活をシリアスに描いた，米国のTVドラマ〕The Nurses.
かんこんそうさい【冠婚葬祭】 ▷■ 冠婚葬祭費 ceremonial expenses.
かんさ² 【監査】 ▷■ 監査委員会〔委員会等設置会社の〕an internal audit committee. 監査証跡〔電算〕an audit trail.
かんさい¹ 【完済】 ▷■ 早期［繰り上げ］完済 early repayment in full.
かんざい³ 【管財】 ▷■ 小額管財〔法〕a small-remuneration receivership; a receivership in which the administrator is paid a relatively low sum in compensation. ▷■ 管財手続き〔法〕〔倒産・破産の際の〕a receivership proceeding [procedure].
がんさい³ 【岩彩・顔彩】(natural) mineral pigments.
かんさいぼう¹ 【肝細胞】 ▷■ 肝細胞増殖因子 (a) hepatocyte growth factor（略: HGF）.
かんさいぼう³ 【幹細胞】
▷■ 間葉系幹細胞 a mesenchymal stem cell（略: MSC）. 骨格筋幹細胞 a skeletal muscle stem cell. 心筋幹細胞 a cardiac stem cell. 組織幹細胞 a tissue stem cell. 胎児由来幹細胞 an embryonic stem cell（略: ESC）. 多能性幹細胞 a multipotent stem cell. ◑ 成体多能性〜 a multipotent adult progenitor cell（略: MAPC）／誘導多能性〜 an induced pluripotent stem cell. 多能性生殖幹細胞〔生物〕＝エム・ジー・エスさいぼう. 胚性生殖細胞〔生物〕〔EG細胞〕an embryonic germ cell; an EG cell（略: EGC）.
かんさいみなまたびょうそしょう【関西水俣病訴訟】the Chisso Minamata Disease Kansai Lawsuit.
かんさつ² 【観察】 ▷■ 試験観察〔法〕〔少年に対する〕juvenile probation. ◑ 在宅試験〜 home juvenile probation. ▷■ 観察小屋〔野生動物などの〕an observation hut [shelter].
かんさついむいん【監察医務院】〔東京都の〕the (Tokyo) Medical Examiner's Office.
かんし⁶ 【監視】
▷■ 街頭監視 street surveillance. ◑ 街頭〜カメラ a street surveillance camera. 社会監視 social surveillance; (the) surveillance of society. 相互監視 mutual surveillance. ◑ 相互〜社会 a mutual surveillance society. ▷■ 監視化学物質〔化審法（化学物質の審査及び製造等の規制に関する法律）による分類〕a monitored chemical. ◑ 第1種[第2種，第3種]〜化学物質 a type 1 [2, 3] monitored chemical. 監視機能〔電算〕a monitoring function. 監視国〔米国の知的財産権保護に関する対外制裁条項で，3番目のレベルの〕the Watch List. 監視小屋 an observation hut〔shelter〕; *a watch hut; *a blind; ''a hide. 監視サイト〔インターネット上の〕a surveillance (Web) site. 監視社会 the [a] surveillance society. 監視対象国 a watch list country; a country on a watch list〔for human-rights violations〕. ◑ 優先〜対象国 a priority watch list country（略: PWL）. 監視態勢 surveillance (readiness);《go on》(the) alert;《be on》the watch [lookout]《for eruptions》. ◑ 浅間山の噴火活動に対し〜態勢に入る start surveillance

of〔go on the watch for〕volcanic activity at Mount Asama／過激派の〜態勢を強める strengthen surveillance of extremist groups. 監視盤〔中央制御室などにある〕a monitoring panel [board].
かんじ⁴ 【幹事】 ▷■ 代表幹事〔業界団体などの〕a chairman.
かんじ⁵ 【漢字】 ▷■ 漢字Tシャツ a kanji T-shirt.
カン・ジェギュ【姜帝圭】Kang Je-gyu (1962–  ；韓国の映画監督).
かんしき³ 【鑑識】 ▷■ 鑑識技術〔警察の〕criminal identification technology; crime-scene investigation technology.
がんじく【眼軸】《解》〔角膜と網膜を結ぶ線〕the geometrical axis (of the eye). ▷■ 眼軸長 the axial length (of the eye).
ガンジスかわいるか【―河海豚】《動》〔カワイルカ科のハクジラの一種〕a Ganges river dolphin; a susu; *Platanista gangetica*.
かんじたい【簡字体】〔中国語の〕the simplified form of a Chinese character.
かんじゃ² 【患者】 ▷■ 患者団体 a patient's [patients'(s)] group.
「ガンシャイ」〔映画〕Gun Shy.
かんじゃがく【患者学】〔良質な医療を受けるための患者としてのノウハウ〕how to be a smart patient.
かんしゅ⁸ 【緩手】〔囲碁・将棋〕a weak move; a wasted move; a meaningless move. ◑ 相手の〜をとがめる punish [pounce on, take advantage of] one's opponent's weak move.
かんしゅう² 【監修】 ▷■ 監修料 a [an editorial] supervision fee [charge].
かんじゅく¹ 【完熟】 ▷■ 完熟度 the degree of ripeness.
かんじゅく² 【慣熟】 ▷■ 慣熟走行〔自動車レースなどの，コースに慣れるために実際にコース上を走ること〕driving practice laps. 慣熟飛行 a training [trial, practice] flight.
かんじょう⁷ 【感情】 ▷■ 感情価《心理》emotional [emotive] value [valence]. ◑ 〜の高い言葉 a word with high emotional value; a highly emotive word. 感情指数《心理》＝情動指数（⇒じょうどうしすう）. 感情労働 emotional labor. 感情論理 emotional logic [reasoning].
がんじょうがたえんじん【頑丈型猿人】《人類》Paranthropus.
かん(じょう)どうみゃく【冠(状)動脈】 ▷■ 経皮的冠(状)動脈インターベンション〔医〕percutaneous coronary intervention（略: PCI）. 冠(状)動脈血栓〔医〕a coronary thrombus（*pl.* -bi）. ◑ 経皮的〜血栓溶解療法 percutaneous transluminal coronary recanalization（略: PTCR）. 冠(状)動脈血栓症〔医〕coronary thrombosis.
かんしょく⁷ 【完食】eating *sth* completely;《口》eating every last scrap (of a meal). 〜する finish eating《a huge portion of food》;《口》eat every last scrap《on one's plate》.
がんしん² 【眼振】 ▷■ 眼振検査〔医〕a nystagmus test.
ガンズ Gans, Christophe (1960–  ；フランス生まれの映画監督).
かんすい² 【冠水】 ▷■ 冠水被害 submergence [flood] damage; damage from submergence [flooding]. ◑ 大雨で農作物が〜被害を受けた. Crops suffered damage from submergence due to the heavy rain.
かんすいへいアーク【環水平―】《気象》a circumzenithal [circumhorizon(tal)] arc.
「ガンスモーク」〔法と秩序のために町の住民が闘うTV西部劇；20年間続いた〕Gunsmoke.
かんずり【寒作里】〔トウガラシを雪にさらして作られる香辛料〕*kanzuri*; a spice made from red peppers that have been set out on snow and then mixed with salt and

other flavorings.

**かんせい**[2]【完成】□□ 完成稿 a [the] final [finished] draft. ○ ～稿に至るまで6回書き直した。He rewrote it six times before completing the final draft.

**かんせい**[5]【官製】□□ 官製金融 state [governmental, non-private] credit. 官製報道 government「news (media)」information, reporting.

**かんせい**[16]【管制】□□ 管制指示〔空〕an「air traffic control [ATC] instruction. ○ ～指示違反 (a) violation of [violating] an ATC instruction.

**かんぜい**[2]【関税】□□ 関税撤廃 elimination [abolition] of tariffs; removing [lifting] the tariff「on…」. 関税撤廃率 the percentage of imports on which tariffs「have been [are to be] abolished.

**かんせいだんごうぼうしほう**【官製談合防止法】〔法〕the Public Sector Bid-Rigging Prevention Law. ▶ 正式名称は、「入札談合等関与行為の排除及び防止に関する法律 (the Law Concerning Elimination and Prevention of Involvement in Bid Rigging, etc.)」.

**がんせき**【岩石】□□ 岩石惑星〔天〕a rocky planet.

**かんせつ**[3]【間接】□□ 間接規制〔法〕indirect regulation;〔事項〕indirect regulations. 間接支配《have, exercise》indirect control 《over…, of…》. 間接出資 (an) indirect investment.

**かんせつ**[4]【関節】□□ 関節液〔解〕synovial fluid. 関節円板〔解〕an articular「disc [disk]. 関節可動域〔医〕(a) range of motion (略: ROM). ○ ～可動域訓練 a「range-of-motion [ROM] exercise. 関節鏡検査 (an) arthroscopy. 関節造影〔法〕〔医〕(an) arthrography.

**ガンゼルしょうこうぐん**【—症候群】〔精神医〕Ganser('s) syndrome.

**かんせん**[7]【感染】
□□ 医療関連感染 (a) healthcare-associated infection (略: HAI). 家庭内感染 (a)「domestic [household, home] infection; infection occuring in the home. 環境感染 (an) environmental infection;〔院内感染〕hospital infection; nosocomial infection; hospital-acquired infection. 血液感染 infection「through [by, via] blood. 体液感染 infection「through [by, via] body fluids.
□□ 感染拡大 the spread of an infection. ○ ～拡大を食い止める stop the spread of an infection / ～拡大を. The infection is spreading. 感染検査[テスト] an infection「test [check]. 感染制御学 infection control science. 感染対策マニュアル an infectious diseases control manual. ○ 院内～対策マニュアル a manual for the control and treatment of hospital-acquired infections / ノロウイルス～対策マニュアル a control manual for norovirus outbreaks. 感染地域 an infected「area [zone]. 感染爆発 an explosion of 《bird flu》cases. 感染被害 infection damage; damage from infection. ○ 鳥インフルエンザウイルスによる～被害が拡大している。Damage from infection with the bird flu virus is spreading. 感染被害救済制度 ＝生物由来製品感染等被害救済制度 (⇒せいぶつ[1]). 感染予防 prevention of infection spread. ○ インフルエンザの流行を防ぐには～予防対策の徹底が重要だ。To prevent an epidemic of influenza, thoroughgoing prevention measures are required. 感染率〔病気が感染した人などの割合〕an infection rate. ○ その国のエイズ～率〔人口の何パーセントが感染しているか〕the AIDS infection rate in that country; that country's rate of infection with AIDS / 新しいコンピューターウイルスの～率〔コンピューターの何パーセントが感染しているか〕the infection rate of a new computer virus; the percentage of computers infected by a new computer virus. 感染ルート an infection route; the route of an infection. ○ ～ルートの解明を急がなくてはならない。We must urgently establish the route of (the) infection.

**かんせん**[8]【観戦】□□ (平穏)観戦権〔スポーツ試合などの〕the right to enjoy 《games》「undisturbed [in tranquility]; the personal rights of spectators. 観戦チケット a match ticket; a spectator ticket. 観戦ツアー a spectator tour. ○ ワールドカップ～ツアーでフランスに行ったが、肝腎の～チケットが手に入らなかった。I went to France on a World Cup spectator tour, but couldn't get the all-important match ticket(s).

**かんぜん**[1]【完全】□□ 完全栄養食 a perfect form of nutrition; a perfect food. 完全包装 full formal wrapping; (a) formal (double) wrapping. 完全保存版 ⇒ほぞんばん. 完全優勝 (an) overall victory; victory [winning] in all「categories [classes]. 完全予約制 a reservation(s)-only system;〔広告・看板で〕Reservations Only.

**かんせんいしょう**【肝線維症】〔医〕hepatic fibrosis.

**かんせんしょう**【感染症】□□ 一[二, 三, 四]類感染症 a category「I [II, III, IV] infectious disease. 新感染症 a new [an emerging] infectious disease. 指定感染症〔1年間に限って政令で指定された感染症〕an infectious disease designated by government ordinance; a designated infectious disease.

**かんせんしょうほう**【感染症法】〔法〕the Infectious Diseases Control Law. ▶ 正式名は「感染症の予防及び感染症の患者に対する医療に関する法律」(the Law Concerning the Prevention of Infectious Diseases and Medical Care for Patients with Infections).

**かんせんしょうよぼう・いりょうほう**【感染症予防・医療法】〔法〕the Law Concerning Prevention of Infectious Diseases and Medical Treatment for Patients Suffering Infectious Diseases.

**かんせんしょうよぼうほう**【感染症予防法】〔法〕the Infectious Diseases Control Law. ▶ 正式名称は「感染症の予防及び感染症の患者に対する医療に関する法律」. 1998年、伝染病予防法を廃止し制定.

**かんせんせい**【感染性】□□ 感染性胃腸炎〔医〕infectious gastroenteritis. 感染性スポンジ(状)脳症〔医〕infectious spongiform encephalopathy.

**「完全犯罪クラブ」**〔映画〕Murder by Numbers.

**かんそう**[4]【乾燥】□□ 乾燥機能付き洗濯機 a washing machine with drying「function [capability]. 乾燥大麻 dried [marijuana [hemp].

**かんそう**[12]【換装】□□〔製品にあらかじめ搭載されている部品等を使用者が別のものに交換すること〕replacement of「parts [equipment].
～する replace「parts [equipment]. ○ ハードディスクを～する replace the hard disk 《in a personal computer》.

**かんぞう**[2]【肝臓】□□ 肝臓細胞 a liver cell. 肝臓値〔医〕a liver count. ○ ～値が高い have a high liver count.

**かんそく**[5]【観測】□□ 観測ヘリ〔軍〕an observation helicopter.

**カンダール**〔カンボジア南部の州〕Kandal.

**かんたい**[1]【寒帯】□□ 寒帯系[産](の) polar; polar region.

**かんたい**[4]【艦隊】□□ 東海艦隊〔中国海軍の〕the East Sea Fleet. 南海艦隊〔中国海軍の〕the South Sea Fleet. 北海艦隊〔中国海軍の〕the North Sea Fleet.

**かんたい**[6]【桿体】〔網膜にある視細胞の一種; 桿状体〕a rod. □□ 桿体細胞〔解〕a rod (cell).

**がんたい**[2]【岩体】〔地質〕a rock body; solid rock; dry rock. □□ ナピア岩体〔南極の〕the Napier Complex.

**かんたいかんミサイル**【艦対艦—】〔軍〕a ship-to-ship missile (略: SSM).

**かんたいくうミサイル**【艦対空—】〔軍〕a ship-to-air missile (略: SAM).

**がんたいさくきほんほう**【がん対策基本法】〔法〕the Basic Law on Cancer.

**がんたいさくじょうほうセンター**【がん対策情報—】〔国

立がんセンターの〕the Center for Cancer Control and Information Services.
**かんたいちミサイル**【艦対地-】〖軍〗a ﾞsea-to-surface [ship-to-surface] missileˮ(略: SSM).
**かんだちめ**【寒立馬】〔厳冬期の放牧馬〕a horse on winter pasture.
**カンダハル**〔アフガニスタン南部の州〕Kandahar; Qandahar.
**カンタブリア**〔スペイン北部の自治州〕Cantabria.
**ガンダム**〖商標〗〔アニメ・キャラクター〕Gundam.
**カンダル**＝カンダール.
**カンタロープ**〖植〗〔メロンの一種〕a cantaloupe (melon).
**かんたんすいげか**【肝胆膵外科】〖医〗surgery of the liver, biliary tract, and pancreas.
**かんち**[7]【感知】▢▯感知センサー a sensor; a detector; a ﾞsensing [detection] deviceˮ. ◯侵入～センサー an ﾞintrusion [intruder] sensor [detector]ˮ/人体～センサー＝じんかんセンサー.
**かんちく**[2]【患畜】〔家畜伝染病にかかっている家畜〕an infected animal;〈集合的に〉infected livestock. ▢▯擬似患畜 a ﾞBSE-suspect animalˮ;〈集合的に〉BSE-suspect livestock. **BSE 患畜** a ﾞBSE-infected animalˮ;〈集合的に〉BSE-infected livestock.
**カンチプーラム**〔インド, タミルナドゥ州の観光地〕Kanchipuram.
**かんちゃく**【緩着】〖囲碁・将棋〗＝かんしゅ[8].
**カンチャナブリ 1**〔タイ中西部の県〕Kanchanaburi. **2**〔タイ中西部の都市, カンチャナブリ県の県都〕Kanchanaburi.
**カンチレバー**〖物〗〔片持ち梁様の探針〕a cantilever.
**かんてい**[1]【官邸】▢▯官邸主導 prime minister-led (initiative); (implement political reform) on the initiative of the prime minister. ◯～主導で構造改革を進める advance [promote] structural reforms on the prime minister's initiative /～主導の政治体制 a prime minister-led political system.
**かんてい**[5]【鑑定】▢▯私(的)鑑定〔裁判所によらない〕a private [an unofficial] evaluation. 写真鑑定 ⇨しゃしん. 鑑定サイト〔インターネット上の〕a "we'll assess you" site. 鑑定士 a certified appraiser. 鑑定試料 a ﾞsample [specimen] for (DNA) ﾞanalysis [examination, testing]ˮ. 鑑定入院〔法〕〔精神鑑定のために医療機関に入院させること〕hospitalization for psychiatric ﾞexamination [evaluation].
**カンデサルタン**〖薬〗〔血圧降下剤〕candesartan.
**かんてつ**[3]【完徹】〔完全な徹夜〕a ﾞcomplete [total] all-nighter.
～する stay up all through the night; pull a ﾞcomplete [total] all-nighter.
**かんでん**[1]【乾田】▢▯乾田化〔水田の〕conversion of a rice paddy into a (dry) field. ◯～化する convert a rice paddy into a (dry) field /～化事業 the process of converting a rice paddy into a (dry) field.
**かんてんじ**【漢点字】kanji braille; Chinese characters in braille.
**かんてんちょうアーク**【環天頂-】〖気象〗＝かんすいへいアーク.
**かんとう**[3]【巻頭】▢▯巻頭インタビュー〔雑誌などの〕a prefatory [an opening] interview. 巻頭論説〔雑誌などの〕a prefatory [an opening] editorial.
**かんどうひん**【感動品】a fully-operational ﾞproduct [unit].
**かんとうまつり**【竿灯祭り・竿燈祭り】the *Kantō* Festival; originally a harvest festival in Akita Prefecture, now a parade in which dancers balance dozens of lighted lanterns, representing rice bales, on long bamboo poles.
**かんとく**【監督】▢▯監督会議〔プロ野球などの〕a man-

agers' ﾞconference [meeting]ˮ. 監督義務 an obligation [a responsibility] to supervise. 監督兼選手 a ﾞplayer [playing] managerˮ. 監督推薦〔野球〕〔オールスターゲーム出場選手の〕referral [recommendation] by the (team) manager.
**かんどく**【完読】～する read《a book》ﾞto the end [from cover to cover]ˮ.
**かんどくせい**【肝毒性】〖医〗hepatotoxicity. ▷ hepatotoxic *adj*.
**かんない**[2]【館内】▢▯館内電話 an ﾞinternal [inside] (tele)phoneˮ.
**かんないたんかんがん**【肝内胆管癌】〖医〗(an) intrahepatic cholangiocarcinoma.
**かんなぎ**【巫・覡】〔神意を世俗の人々に伝える役割の人〕a medium (between the gods and mortals); a shaman; an oracle.
**かんなめさい**【神嘗祭】〔伊勢神宮の祭儀〕a (Shinto) rice harvest festival.
**がんねんまく**【眼粘膜】〖解〗the mucous membrane of the eye.
**かんのう**[7]【感応】▢▯感応式信号〔交通信号の一種〕a vehicle-actuated signal. 感応度 (a degree of) sensitivity; responsiveness, responsivity; a response level.
**かんのうほう**【肝嚢胞】〖医〗a liver cyst.
**カンバス** ▢▯シェイプ・カンバス〖美術〗〔変形カンバス〕(a) shaped canvas.
**かんぱちぐも**【環八雲】〔東京の環状八号線上空に出現する積雲類〕a cloud belt over Metropolitan Loop Road No. 8; Kanpachi (street) clouds.
**かんばつし**【間伐紙】▢▯間伐紙 paper made from forest thinnings.
**カンパニー・カラー**〔その会社のシンボルカラー〕a company color.
**かんばん**【看板】▢▯大〖看〗看板 ⇨おおかんばん. 壁(掛け)看板 a wall-mounted sign. 突き出し[袖]看板 a projecting sign (board). 吊り[吊るし]看板 a hanging sign(board). ▢▯看板候補〔ある政党の〕a ﾞstar [leading, celebrity] candidateˮ. 看板車種〖自動車〗(a company's) trademark [representative] model. 看板商品 a ﾞtrademark [hallmark, showcase] productˮ. 看板選手 a star player. 看板番組〔テレビ局などの〕a ﾞTV channel'sˮ ﾞtop-rated [popular, flagship] programˮ. 看板メニュー[料理]〔レストランなどの〕a ﾞspecialty [representative] dishˮ.
**かんばん**【岩盤】▢▯岩盤強度 bedrock strength 岩盤浴 "bedrock bathing"; a "bedrock bath"; a health and beauty treatment in which people lie on heated rock slabs.
**カンピオン** Campion, Jane (1954- ; ニュージーランド生まれの映画監督・脚本家).
**かんびしょう**[2]【乾皮症】▢▯色素性乾皮症 xeroderma pigmentosum (略: XP).
**かんぴん**【完品】a ﾞproduct [unit] with no missing parts.
**カンプ**【広告】〔広告原稿の最終レイアウト〕a comprehensive; a comp; a final layout.
**カンフー**【功夫】▢▯カンフー・シューズ 《a pair of》kung fu shoes.
**かんぷう**[1]【完封】▢▯完封リレー〖野球〗〔1 試合に複数のピッチャーが投げて完封すること〕a combined shutout.
**カンブリア 1**〔英国, ウェールズの古称〕Cambria. **2**〔米国, カリフォルニア州の都市〕Cambria.
**カンペーン・ペット** ＝カムペーン.
**カンポ**[3]【簡保】▢▯かんぽの宿〔簡易保険加入者福祉施設の 1〕a ﾞKampo [post office life insurance] innˮ; a resort facility for post office life insurance subscribers.
**カンホア**〔ベトナム中南部の省〕Khanh Hoa.

かんぼう²【感冒】▯▯ 普通感冒 a common cold.
がんぼう²【願望】▯▯ 結婚願望 a desire to get married; a yearning for marriage. 自殺願望 a suicidal tendency. シンデレラ願望 a Cinderella complex. 痩身願望 a desire to slim; an obsession with slimming. 変身願望 an obsession with changing one's appearance; an Adonis Complex.
がんぼう³【顔貌】a [one's] face; a [one's] facial appearance; (one's) features. ▯〜がそっくりだと言っても彼を犯人と特定することはできない。 Even if [his facial appearance is identical [he has the same face], he cannot be identified as the perpetrator. ▯彼女は逃亡中に整形で〜を変えた。 While she was on the run, she had her features altered by plastic surgery. / 患者はその病気に特有の〜を呈していた。 The patient had the distinctive look of that disease. ▯顔貌認証＝顔認証 (⇨ん).
ガンボ(ー) 〔アメリカ南部の料理; いろいろな野菜に魚介類などを加え、オクラでとろみをつける〕gumbo.
カンポート ＝カンポット.
かんぽせいめいほけん【かんぽ生命保険】Japan Post Insurance Co., Ltd (略: JP Insurance).
カンポット 〔カンボジア南部の州; 同州の州都〕Kampot.
がんぽん【元本】▯▯ 元本割れリスク (the) risk of principal loss.
ガンマ-オリザノール〔γ-〕《化》gamma-oryzanol.
ガンマせん【-線、γ線】▯▯ 空間ガンマ線 environmental gamma-rays.
かんみん【官民】▯▯ 官民格差 the ʳdifference [gap] between (the《pensions》of) government officials and ordinary people. 官民競争入札制度 (a system of) competitive bidding between the public and private sectors. [⇨しじょうかテスト] 官民パートナーシップ〔協働、提携、連携〕(a) public private partnership (略: PPP).
かんむり【冠】▯▯ 冠番組 a namesake ʳprogram [show].
がんめん²【顔面】▯▯ 顔面再建《医》facial reconstruction. 顔面ミオキミア《医》〔眼輪筋の痙攣(ﾋ)〕facial myokymia.
かんもう²【換毛】▯▯ 季節換毛 seasonal mo(u)lting; a seasonal mo(u)lt.
かんもんはた【関門斑太・関門籏】《魚》〔ハタ科の海水魚〕a honeycomb grouper; a honeycomb rock cod; *Epinephelus merra*.
かんゆう³【勧誘】▯▯ 不招請勧誘〔押し売り〕unsolicited ʳsales [selling].
かんよう⁶【慣用】▯▯ 慣用暗号方式〔秘密鍵暗号方式〕a conventional encryption system.
かんらん¹【甘藍】▯▯ 紫甘藍 (a) red cabbage.
かんり³【管理】▯▯ 〜地. 〔地.〕 Managed Property; Property Managed 《by XYZ Realty》.
▯▯ 管理委託費 charges for management and upkeep entrusted to《a management company》. 管理型信託業 trust asset management services; managed trust services. 管理基準 a ʳmanagement [control] standard. ▯危険物〜基準 a management standard for hazardous materials. 管理規約〔共同住宅などの〕《condominium》ʳrules [*bylaws]. 管理区域〔放射線などによる被爆から防護するための〕a controlled area. ▯汚染〜区域 a contamination controlled area / 放射線〜区域 a radiation controlled area. 管理使用〔危険物質などの、厳重な管理の下での使用〕controlled use 《of asbestos》; (strictly)ʳcontrolled [supervised] use; use under control [supervision, surveillance]. 管理釣り場 a managed site for fishing; a《local-gorvernment》administered place for fishing. 管理ライン ＝実効支配線 (⇨じっこう²).

かんり⁴【監理】▯▯ 監理ポスト《証券》〔上場廃止の可能性ある株式に割り当てられる取引の場〕the supervision post. ▯(株券を)〜ポストに移す assign《a listed stock》to the supervision post.
かんりしょく【管理職】▯▯ 管理職試験 an [a promotion] examination for administrators;《口》an admin exam. 管理職登用 appointment to an administrative position. ▯女性の〜登用を促進する encourage the appointment of women to administrative positions.
かんりにん【管理人】▯▯ (ウェブ)サイト管理人 a (Web) site ʳmanager [operator].
かんりゅう⁵【還流】▯▯ 還流資金 capital reflux.
かんりゅう⁸【韓流】＝はんりゅう³.
がんりゅうアミノさん【含硫-酸】《生化》a sulfur-containing amino acid.
かんりょう²【官僚】▯▯ 官僚OB a former government official.
がんりょう²【顔料】▯▯ 顔料インク (a) pigment ink.
がんりょう³【岩稜】a rocky ridge.
かんれい¹【寒冷】 cooling of the earth; global cooling; the ʳstart [onset] of an ice age. ▯〜化する cool (down); grow [get] cooler. 寒冷期〔地球の〕a cold period; 〔1年のうちの〕the [ʳcold season.
かんれい²【慣例】▯▯ 慣例化 routinization; making *sth* (a matter of) routine. ▯〜化する routinize; make *sth* (a matter of routine); make *sth* ʳthe norm [customary, general usage] / 半ば〜化している市議会議員の視察名目の観光旅行は廃止すべきだ。 Sightseeing trips under the pretext of inspection tours that councilors have almost turned into a routine practice should be abolished.
かんれん【関連】▯▯ 関連法案 related bills. ▯有事〜法案 an emergency(-related) [a contingency(-related)] bill.
かんろくがち【貫禄勝ち】an effortless win; a victory demonstrating consummate ʳmastery [skill]. ▯〜する win effortlessly; overcome [beat, defeat] (an) opponent with effortless ease; demonstrate imperturbable mastery in *one's* victory.
かんわ⁴【緩和】▯▯ 緩和医療[治療] palliative ʳmedicine [treatment].

# き

き⁴【忌】▯▯ 桜桃忌 an anniversary of Osamu Dazai's death (19 June), named after his short story "Cherries." 利休忌 an anniversary of Rikyū's death (27 or 28 March).
キア Kier, Udo (1944– ; ドイツ生まれの映画俳優.
キアー ＝キア.
きあい²【気合】▯▯ 気合十分 ▯彼らは「絶対優勝するんだ」と〜十分である。 Full of spirit, they say that they're confident of winning.

キアじどうしゃ【起亜自動車】〔韓国の自動車メーカー〕Kia Motors.
きあん【起案】▯▯ 起案者 an author of a ʳproposal [draft]; an original author; a drafter.
キー¹ ▯▯ キー・テナント《経営》〔商業施設の集客力の核となる大型店舗〕a key tenant. [⇨アンカー・テナント (⇨アンカー)] キー・デバイス〔製品などの最重要部品〕a key [an essential] device. キーロガー〔電算〕〔キーボードからの入力を監視・記録するソフト〕a keylogger.

キーア〖鳥〗＝ケア³.
キーストーン　⬜ キーストーン・コンビ〖野球〗〖二塁手と遊撃手の間の連携プレー〗a keystone combination.
キーストーンしゅ【―種】〖生態〗〖個体数は少ないがその種が属する生物群や生態系に大きな影響を及ぼす種〗a keystone species.
キートセラス〖植〗〖浮遊珪藻; エビ・カニなどの幼生期の餌となる〗*Chaetoceros*. ⬜ キートセラス・カルシトランス *Chaetoceros calcitrans*.
キートセラス〖植〗＝キートセラス.
キートン Keaton, Michael (1951-   ; 米国の映画俳優; 本名 Michael John Douglas).
キープ　⬜ キープカ〖サッカーなど〗ball-holding ability; 〖整髪料など〗〖hair-〗holding power.
キーファー Kiefer, Anselm (1945-   ; ドイツの画家).
キーラ(ー)ン ＝ギラン.
キーレス・エントリー〖自動車などの, リモコンドアロック開閉機構〗remote keyless entry (略: RKE).
きいろい【黄色い】⬜ 黄色い血〖頻繁な売血のため赤血球が減り, 黄色味を呈している血液〗"yellow" blood; anemic blood from frequent blood donors.
きいろいハンカチうんどう【黄色い―運動】〖イラクに赴く自衛隊員の無事を祈る運動〗the Yellow Handkerchief Campaign.
キーロフ・オペラ〖ロシアの歌劇団〗the Kirov Opera.
キーロフ・バレエ〖ロシアの舞踊団〗the Kirov Ballet.
キーワード　⬜ キーワード検索〖do〗a keyword search.
ぎいん³【議員】⬜ 議員年金 a legislators' pension; 〖国会議員の〗＝国会議員互助年金 (⇨こっかいぎいん). 議員連盟〖国会議員の有志で作る〗a Diet members' league. ◐ 死刑廃止～連盟 the Diet Members' League for the Abolition of the Death Penalty / 超党派～連盟 a suprapartisan [a non-party] league of Diet members.
ぎいんせい【偽陰性】〖医〗〖検査で陰性と判定された陽性〗a false negative.
ぎう【義烏】〖中国浙江省の県・市〗Yiwu.
きうま【木馬】〖山中での木材運搬用の木ぞり〗a (wooden) [log [lumber] sled. ⬜ 木馬道 a log sled trail (with sleepers).
キエンザン〖ベトナム南部, メコンデルタ地帯の省〗Kien Giang.
キエンジャン ＝キエンザン.
「きおく・せきにん・みらい」ききん【「記憶・責任・未来」基金】〖ドイツ政府および企業の出資による, 強制労働に対する補償基金〗the Foundation "Remembrance, Responsibility and the Future."
きか⁶【幾何】⬜ 幾何解析学 geometric analysis. ◐ 離散～解析学 discrete geometric analysis.
きが³【飢餓】⬜ 飢餓人口 a starving population. 飢餓撲滅大使〖国連世界食糧計画の〗an Ambassador Against Hunger.
きかい⁷【機械】⬜ 機械受注統計 a statistical survey of orders received for machinery;〖内閣府発表の〗the Statistical Survey of Orders Received for Machinery. 機械漉き〖製紙〗machine paper-making. 機械弁〖医〗〖人工の素材でできている弁〗a mechanical valve. 機械浴〖身障者介護の〗mechanical [assisted] bathing. 機械読み取り式 machine-readable 《passports》.
きがい¹【危害】⬜ 危害射撃 a shot (intended) to injure.
ぎかいよさんきょく【議会予算局】〖米国の〗the Congressional Budget Office (略: CBO).
きかく¹【企画】⬜ 企画会議 a 「planning [project]」 meeting. ◐ ～に企画にかける consider [take up] ～ at a planning meeting. 企画会社 a planning 「firm [company]」. 企画展〖企画テーマに関する資料・作品などの展示会〗a 「planned [theme(d), special」 exhibition;〖借り集めた展示品による〗a loan exhibition.

きかく²【規格】⬜ 統一規格 a 「consistent [unified]」 standard. 規格争い【戦争】〖ビデオ機器などの〗a format war. 規格大量生産 standardized mass production. 規格統一 standardization (of specifications); unification of standards.
きかくだおれ【企画倒れ】a failure 「of design [from the design stage]」. ◐ 志は高かったのだが, 結局～に終わった. Their aim was high, but in the end it was a failure from the design stage.
きかん³【気管】⬜ 気管孔〖医〗〖のどに造設する人工的な呼吸孔〗a tracheal stoma. 気管食道瘻〖医〗a tracheoesophageal fistula (略: TEF).
きかん¹⁰【帰還】⬜ 帰還事業〖1959年から84年にかけて行われた, 日本から北朝鮮への朝鮮人の〗the repatriation program for North Koreans.
きかん¹²【基幹】⬜ 基幹通信網 a 「basic [key]」 communications 「network [system]」. 基幹電源 a major power source.
きかん¹⁴【期間】⬜ 期間工 a fixed-term (factory) worker; a fixed-term employee (in a factory). 期間雇用 fixed-term employment. ◐ ～雇用労働者 a fixed-term employee. 期間社員 ⇨しゃいん². 期間従業員 ⇨じゅうぎょういん.
きかん¹⁶【旗艦】⬜ 旗艦機種[車種]〖機器・自動車などの〗a flagship model. 旗艦車〖その自動車メーカーの代表的な車種〗an automaker's flagship model.
きかん¹⁸【機関】⬜ 受け入れ機関〖留学生・移民・天下りなどの〗receiving organization;〖an [the] organization [a body, an institution] that 「takes *sb* in [accepts *sb*, takes *sb* on]」. 送り出し機関〖留学生・移民などの〗a [the] sending organization; an [the] organization [a body, an institution] that 「sends [dispatches]」 *sb*. ⬜ 機関音〖船などの〗engine sound; the sound of an engine. 機関決定〖組織としての決定〗an 「organizational [organization's]」 decision; the decision of 「an [a whole]」 organization; a decision by an organization.
きかんげんてい【期間限定】(a) time limitation; a time limit. ◐ ～で無料にする make (admission) free of charge for a limited period ◐ ～のビール a limited-edition beer ◐ このセールは8月1日から15日までの～です. This sale is (on) for a limited period, from August 1st to 15th. / このデパートの屋上は9月までので ビヤガーデンがオープンしています. On the roof of this department store, a beer garden will be open for a limited time, until September.
⬜ 期間限定価格 a time-limited price 《offer, reduction》. 期間限定(商)品 a product [an item] on sale for a limited 「time [period]」 (only). 期間限定販売[発売] (a) time-limited sale. 期間限定割引 a time-limited 「discount [price reduction]」.
きかん¹【気管支】⬜ 気管支切開〖医〗(a) bronchotomy. 気管支挿管〖医〗bronchial intubation.
きかんじゅう【機関銃】⬜ 短期関銃 a submachine gun.
きかんてき【基幹的】⬜～な basic; key; fundamental. ◐ ～道路の整備 construction of major [roads [thoroughfares]」. ⬜ 基幹的農業従事者〖統計〗people forming the nucleus [core members] of those engaged mainly in farming.
きかんのほう【帰還の法】〖イスラエルの法律; すべてのユダヤ人にイスラエルへの移住を認めるもの〗the Law of Return.
きき¹【危機】⬜ 危機遺産リスト〖緊急の保全策が必要な世界遺産のリスト〗the List of World Heritage in Danger; the World Heritage in Danger list. ◐ ユネスコはガラパゴス諸島を～遺産リストに登録することに決した. UNESCO has decided to include the Galapagos on its List of World Heritage in Danger. 危機介入〖精神医・心理〗crisis intervention. 危機対応勘定〖金融〗〖預金保険機構の〗the crisis management account. 危機リス

ト＝危機遺産リスト．**危機理論**〖精神医・心理〗crisis theory.

**ぎぎ**[2]【疑義】▫️ 疑義照会〖薬〗〔調剤に際しての薬剤師から医師への疑問点の問い合わせ〕prescription verification (by a pharmacist) with the prescribing doctor.

**ききおくしょうこうぐん**【偽記憶症候群】〖精神医〗false memory syndrome (略：FMS).

**ききかんり**【危機管理】▫️ 危機管理官 a crisis management「officer [manager]．◯ 空港・港湾〜官 a crisis management「officer [manager] for airports and harbors. 危機管理規定 crisis management procedures. 危機管理広報 crisis [risk-management] communication. 危機管理センター〔首相官邸内の〕Crisis Management Center.

**ききくらべ**【聞き比べ】listening and comparing; comparing by listening. 〜する＝ききくらべる．◯ ヘッドホンを購入する前にすべきことは〜だ．Before buying a pair of headphones you should listen through them and compare them with others.

**ききくらべる**【聞き比べる】listen to《two things or more》and compare; compare《different versions of a musical work》after hearing《them》．◯ 二人の演奏を〜 hear performances by the two and compare them / 候補者の主張を〜 listen to the「arguments [assertions] of the candidates and compare them / 同じ曲をCDとMDで聞き比べてみた．I tried listening to the CD and MD versions of the same song and comparing them.

**ききこみ**【聞き込み】▫️ 聞き込み情報 information gathered「through interviews《with local residents》[by questioning《bystanders》]．

**ききざけ**【利き酒】▫️ 利き酒師 a certified sake taster.

**ききちょく**【利き猪口】a sake tasting cup, usually made of white porcelain with a pattern of two concentric blue circles on the inside bottom.

**きぎょう**[1]【企業】
▫️ 企業意識 corporate「attitude(s) [consciousness, awareness]．企業会計基準委員会 the Accounting Standards Board of Japan (略：ASBJ). 企業価値 (a) corporate value. 企業健診 ＝企業健康診断 (⇨けんこうしんだん). 企業行動委員会〔企業内に設けられる〕a committee on corporate behavior; a corporate compliance committee. 企業広報 corporate communications. 企業コンサルタント〔企業を顧客とする〕a business consultant;〔企業内の〕an in-house consultant; an internal company consultant. 企業実習 corporate [workplace] training. 企業色 a corporate feel; a company-affiliated[-dominated, -dedicated] feeling. ◯ あのチームは〜色が強い．It's very much a company team. 企業人 a business person; a member of the business community. 企業心理 (a) corporate psychology. 企業スポーツ company-[corporate-]sponsored sports. 企業説明会〔会社説明会〕a company explanation meeting; an orientation meeting for prospective employees; a preliminary introduction to a company. ◯ 合同〜説明会 a job fair. 企業存続計画 ＝緊急時事業継続計画 (⇨きんきゅうじ). 企業体質 corporate character; corporate idiosyncrasy. 企業チーム〔企業スポーツの〕a company team. 企業通貨〔商品券・ポイントカードなど〕(a) corporate currency. 企業統合 ＝企業合併 company [corporate] integration. 企業淘汰 (a)「weeding out [shake-out] of businesses (by a process of survival of the fittest). 企業内〜研究者 a company [an in-house] researcher. 企業内大学 a corporate [an in-company, an in-house] university. 企業内勤務ビザ an intra-company transfer visa; an L-1A visa. 企業内保育所 an「internal [in-company] day nursery; a company childcare facility. 企業内貿易 intra-firm trade.

企業ファイナンス〔企業に対する融資〕corporate financing;〔企業の財務状況〕corporate finances. 企業文化《build》a corporate culture. 企業防衛 corporate defense (against hostile takeovers). 企業〜防衛策 corporate defense measures. 企業防災 disaster prevention in private companies. 企業向けサービス価格指数〔日本銀行発表の〕a corporate service price index; the Corporate Service Price Index (略：CSPI). 企業メセナ corporate support of the arts. 企業理念 a corporate「ideology [vision]．企業論理 corporate logic; the reasoning behind a company; the rationale for a corporate enterprise.

**きぎょう**[2]【起業】▫️ 起業教育 entrepreneurship「education [training]．起業支援 (business) incubation. [＝インキュベーション]．

**きぎょうかいかくほう**【企業改革法】〖米法〗〔サーベンス・オクスレー法〕the Sarbanes-Oxley Act (略：SOA, SarbOx). ▶ 正式名称は 上場企業会計改革および投資家保護法 (the Public Company Accounting Reform and Investor Protection Act of 2002).

**きぎょうかちけんきゅうかい**【企業価値研究会】〔経済産業省の〕the Corporate Value Study Group.

**きぎょうねんきんれんごうかい**【企業年金連合会】the Pension Fund Association. ▶ 2004年，厚生年金基金連合会を改組．

**きぎょうメセナきょうぎかい**【企業－協議会】the Association for Corporate Support of the Arts, Japan; Kigyo Mecenat Kyogikai (略：KMK).

**ききん**[1]【飢饉】▫️ 嫁飢饉 a bride shortage; a shortage of brides.

**ききんぞく**[2]【貴金属】▫️ 貴金属店 a「jewelry [ⁿjewellery] store.

**きく**[3]【規矩】▫️ 規矩術〖建〗(the「art [technique] of) marking timber for building with *sumi* and a carpenter's square.

**きぐ**[3]【棋具】〔囲碁・将棋の道具〕go [*shōgi*] equipment; a「go [*shōgi*] board, pieces and accessories.

**きく**【疑懼・危懼】doubt and fear.

**きぐすみ**【黄ぐすみ】becoming [turning] yellow(ish); yellowing.

**ぎけい**[1]【偽計】▫️ 偽計取引〖法〗stock market manipulation;《口》rigging the stock market. 偽計入札妨害（罪）〖法〗interference with fair bidding.

**ぎけつ**【議決】▫️ 再議決〔参議院で否決された法案の衆議院での〕passage of [passing] a (rejected) bill by resubmitting it《to the Lower House》．◯ 再〜する pass a (rejected) bill by resubmitting it《to the Lower House》．

**ぎけつけん**【議決権】▫️ 議決権行使書〔株主総会での〕a voting right exercise form. 議決権〔付き〕株式 a voting「stock [share]．議決権比率 a percentage of voting rights. 議決権ベース《株式》《on》a voting-rights basis. ◯ A社の発行済み株式を〜ベースで10％ 保有する own 10 percent of A. company's outstanding shares in terms of voting rights.

**きけん**[1]【危険】▫️ 危険球退場〖野球〗the expulsion (of a pitcher) from [throwing (a pitcher) out of] a game for throwing a dangerous pitch. 危険分担 risk sharing.

**きけん**[4]【棄権】▫️ 途中棄権 ⇨とちゅう[2].

**きけんうんてん**【危険運転】▫️ 危険運転致死傷罪〖法〗dangerous driving resulting in death or injury. 危険運転致傷罪〖法〗dangerous driving resulting in injury.

**きげんつき**【期限付き】▫️ 期限付き移籍〔プロスポーツ選手などの〕the loan of a player《to…》．◯ 田中選手はイタリアのチームに〜移籍することが決まった．It has been decided to loan Tanaka (temporarily [for a fixed term]) to an Italian team.

きけんぶつ【危険物】 危険物一般取扱所〔消防法に基づく施設〕a facility handling general hazardous materials. 危険物処理ロボット an explosives [an explosive ordnance, a bomb] disposal robot.

きこう³【気候】 気候感度〔気象〕〔大気中の二酸化炭素の上昇に応じた気温上昇の程度〕climate sensitivity. 気候政策 a climate policy. 気候取引所〔環境〕温室効果ガス排出権取引所〕a climate exchange. [＝排出権取引所(⇒はいしゅつけん)] 気候変動税〔英国の〕a climate change levy (略：CCL). 気候モデル a climate model. 〜モデル計算 a climate model calculation.

きこう¹⁵【寄港・寄航】 寄航地〔航空機の〕an airport of call.

きこく²【帰国】
  帰国事業 ＝帰還事業(⇒きかん¹⁰). 帰国者 a returnee (from abroad); a homecomer. 帰国のための渡航書〔旅券を紛失した場合などに発給される書類〕a passport replacement document for travel back to one's country; temporary travel papers for return to one's home country. 帰国報告 a homecoming report. 東ティモールの住民投票監視のため日本から派遣されていた文民警察官らが総理官邸を訪ね、小渕総理に〜報告をした The civilian police officers dispatched from Japan to observe the East Timor referendum called at Prime Minister Obuchi's official residence and made a homecoming report.

きさい⁵【起債】 起債制限比率 a debt-to-income ratio restriction 〔on a local government's right to issue new bonds〕.

きざい¹【基材】a matrix; a substrate; a base material.

きさきもの【期先物】〔先物取引〕a「distant [deferred] (futures) contract.

きさせんにん【期差選任】〔買収者が改選期に取締役会を支配するのを防ぐため、取締役の任期を分散すること〕a staggered board system.

きさにんき【期差任期】〔経営〕staggered terms of office. 期差任期制(度) a system of staggered terms of office.

キサラタン〔商標・薬〕〔緑内障治療薬〕Xalatan.

きじ³【生地】 側(が)生地〔ふとん［マットレス］用の布地〕the outer cover of a「futon [mattress].

きじ⁴【記事】 記事体広告 アドバトリアル.

ぎじ¹【疑似・擬似】 擬似外国会社〔法〕a「pseudo-foreign [quasi-foreign] company. 擬似パート ＝フルタイムパート (⇒フルタイム).

ぎしき【儀式】 儀式化 ritualization. 国会での党首討論はもはや〜化していて内容きわめて空疎である。The party-leaders' debate in the Diet 「has turned into a mere ritual [is now merely a matter of form], totally lacking in substance.

きしつせい【器質性】 器質性便秘〔医〕organic constipation.

きじつまえ【期日前】before [in advance of] the (specified) day. 期日前投票〔投票日前に選挙人名簿登録地で行う投票〕pre-election-day voting.

きしねんりょ【希死念慮】〔精神医〕death ideation.

きじはた【雉子羽太】〔魚〕〔ハタ科の海産魚〕a redspotted grouper; a Hong Kong grouper; Epinephelus akaara.

きしめじ【黄占地・黄湿地】〔菌〕〔担子菌類キシメジ科の食用キノコ〕yellow knight (fungus); man on horseback; Tricholoma equestre; Tricholoma flavovirens. キシメジ科 Tricholomataceae.

きしゃ²【記者】 記者発表 a「media [press] announcement. その会社は警備ロボットを開発し、大々的に〜発表を行った。That company developed a security robot, which they announced at a major press conference.

きしゃかいけん【記者会見】 記者会見資料 a press kit.

きしゅ⁸【機種】 高級［低価格］機種 a「high-end [low-end] model. 最新機種 the「latest [newest, most recent] model. 対応機種 a compatible model. ボーダフォン〜機種 a model compatible with Vodafone; a Vodafone-compatible model. 機種変更〔携帯電話の〕a model change. 〜変更する change the model 《of one's mobile phone》; 《口》get a new (type of) 《mobile phone》.

きじゅう⁴【帰住】 帰住先〔刑務所出所者・長期入院後の退院者などが最初に身を寄せる住居〕accommodation for a「released 《reformatory》 inmate [discharged patient]; a place to stay (after 「leaving jail [leaving an institution,《口》getting out]). 帰住地〔刑務所出所者・長期入院後の退院者などの最初の居住地〕a place of residence for a「released 《reformatory》 inmate [discharged patient].

きしゅういぬ【紀州犬】〔犬〕＝きしゅうけん.

きしゅうけん【紀州犬】〔犬〕a Kishu (dog).

ぎじゅつ【技術】 要素技術〔ある製品の製造の基盤となる技術〕the underlying technology; the technology behind 《environmentally friendly cars》. 技術開発力 technology [technological] development capability. 技術経営「technology [engineering] management; management of technology (略：MOT). 技術職〔地位・職〕a career in technology [engineering];〔人〕a technician; an engineer. 技術提案書〔入札する業者が発注者に提出する〕a technical proposal. 技術伝承[継承] inheriting「(a) technology [know-how]; handing [passing] down [on]「(technological skills). 技術評価 technology assessment (略：TA); technology evaluation. 技術兵〔米軍〕an army [a navy, an air force] specialist. 技術力 (a) technological [technical] capability [ability]; technological [technical] strength;《the level of one's》technology.

ぎじゅつしほう【技術士法】〔法〕the Professional Engineer Law.

ぎじゅつてき【技術的】 技術的助言 technical advice.

きじゅん²【基準・規準】 採点基準 grading criteria; criteria for「grading [marking]. 判断基準 standards「for judging [of judgment]; a yardstick (for measuring 《research productivity》); criteria (for a loan). 基準緩和 relaxation of a「standard [requirement]. 基準地〔地価調査の〕benchmark land. 基準地価格〔基準地〕benchmark land values; land prices used to assess fixed-property taxes. 基準・認証制度〔安全確保や経済取引の適正化のため、製品や施設に基準を設け、それが満たされているかを検査・証明するシステム〕a standardization and certification system. 基準木 ＝標準木 (⇒ひょうじゅん²).

きじょ²【機序】 発症機序 an onset mechanism.

キショイ〔気色悪い〕《俗》be grossed out《by…》;〈物が主語〉gross.

きしょう³【希少】 希少疾病〔医〕〔発症者数が非常に少ない疾病〕a rare [an orphan] disease. 希少疾病用医薬品《薬》an orphan drug.

きじょう¹【机上】 机上演習 simulated [theoretical] practice; a war game. 机上計算 desktop calculations; calculations done on paper (but not tested in the field). 机上出版〔デスクトップ・パブリッシング〕desktop publishing (略：DTP).

きしょうきねんび【気象記念日】〔6月1日〕Meteorological Day (Japan).

きしょうぎょうむしえんセンター【気象業務支援−】the Japan Meteorological Business Support Center (略：

きしょうとう JMBSC).
きしょうとう【希少糖】《化》a rare sugar.
きしょく⁵【奇食】〔奇抜な食べ合わせの食事〕an unusual [a strange] food combination.
キシリトール ▢ キシリトール・ガム xylitol gum.
きしんごう【黄信号】an amber [a yellow] traffic 「light [*signal]. ◐ 日本の国連常任理事国入りに〜がともった. The chances of Japan getting a seat on the UN Security Council began to look less promising. | A shadow fell on Japan's hopes of getting a Security Council seat. ◐ 〜に出くわして停止するか，スピードをあげて通過するかでドライバーの人柄がわかる. You can judge what a driver is like by whether he stops or accelerates 「at [when he comes to] a yellow light. ◐ 便秘は大腸がんの〜だ. Constipation is a warning sign for colon cancer.
きずいきしゃ【奇瑞汽車】〔中国の自動車メーカー〕Qirui Qiche; Chery Automobile.
きすいぶんりき【気水分離器】〔原子力〕a steam separator.
きせい¹¹【規制】
 ▢ 事後規制〔事業の認可後にその運営に関して制限を加えること〕ex post regulation. 事前規制〔事業の認可に先立ってその運営に関して制限を加えること〕ex ante regulation.
 ▢ 規制改革 regulatory reform. 規制強化 (a) tightening of regulations. 規制権限 (the) authority to control ⟨over…⟩. ◐ (の)不行使 failure to exercise the authority to control. 規制値 a 「regulated [regulatory, regulation] value; a limit value; a limit. 規制標識 a regulatory [an instructional] sign; a sign giving orders. 規制品 a 「controlled [restricted] item; controlled [restricted] goods. ◐ 輸入〜品 an 「import-controlled [import-restricted] item; import-controlled [import-restricted] goods.
ぎせい⁶【犠牲】▢ 犠牲祭〔イスラム教の〕the Feast of Sacrifice; 'Id al-Adha; Eid al-Adha.
きせいかいかく・みんかんかいほうすいしんかいぎ【規制改革・民間開放推進会議】the Council for the Promotion of Regulatory Reform (略: CPRR). ▶ 2004年4月発足.
きせいかいかく・みんかんかいほうすいしんほんぶ【規制改革・民間開放推進本部】the Headquarters for the Promotion of Regulatory Reform.
ぎせいしゃ【犠牲者】▢ 遠因犠牲者 an indirect [a secondary, a long-term] victim.
「奇跡の海」〔映画〕Breaking the Waves.
「奇蹟の輝き」〔映画〕What Dreams May Come.
きせつ³【季節】▢ 季節限定商品 ＝季節限定品. 季節限定品 a product on sale only during the season; a seasonal product. 季節調整指数《経》a seasonal adjustment index. 季節列車 a seasonal train.
キセノン キセノン・ガス xenon gas.
きせのはぜ【煙管沙魚】〔魚〕Gymnogobius cylindricus.
きそ⁶【起訴】▢ 起訴事実 the facts presented in an indictment. ◐ 〜事実を全面的に認める[否認する] admit [deny] all the facts presented in the indictment. 起訴相当《法》〔検察審査会での議決の１つ〕a determination that prosecution is appropriate. 起訴率 a prosecution rate.
きそ²【基礎】▢ 浮き基礎《建》a floating foundation. 布基礎《建》continuous footing. ラフト〔筏⁽いかだ⁾〕基礎《建》a raft foundation. ▢ 基礎化学品 a basic chemical. 基礎自治体 a basic municipality. 基礎データ (a patient's) basal data; basic ⟨seismic⟩ data. ◐ 体温，脈拍，血圧などといった患者の〜データ the patient's basal data such as body temperature, pulse and blood pressure. 基礎パッキング，基礎パッキン《建》foundation packing. 基礎パッキング工法《建》a foundation packing

construction method. 基礎利益〔生命保険会社の〕a base profit.
きそう⁵【起草】▢ 起草作業 (the process of) drafting. ◐ 議案の〜作業に入る start drafting a bill.
きそう¹¹【奇相】〔珍しい人相〕a strange physiognomy; 〔珍しいほどにすぐれた人相〕a unique physiognomy.
きそう¹²【機捜】＝機動捜査隊（⇨そうさ²).
きそう¹【偽装】
 ▢ 牛肉偽装事件〔2001年，BSE対策事業の一環としての国産牛肉買い取り事業を悪用し，食肉業者が輸入牛肉を国産牛肉と偽り補助金を詐取した詐欺事件〕the fraudulent beef-labelling case.
 ▢ 偽装請負 employment contract fraud; a fraudulent contract. 偽装心中 ⇨しんじゅう¹. 偽装売買《法》〔仮装売買〕a fake(d) transaction;《証》〔実際には成立していない株の売買〕fake selling; a faked sale; 〔損失控除額を増やそうとする同一人による同一株の短期間売買〕selling ⟨stock⟩ and repurchasing it (illegally) immediately or within a short period (in order to reduce tax); *washing; *a wash sale. 偽装名義株 shares [stock] (registered) under a fictitious name. 偽装メール (a) spoof(ed) e-mail.
ぎぞう【偽造】▢ 偽造ナンバープレート a fake 「"license [*number] plate.
ぎぞう・とうなんカードよちょきんしゃほごほう【偽造・盗難・預貯金者保護法】《法》the Law Concerning the Protection of Depositors from Illicit Deposit Withdrawals Using Counterfeit or Stolen Cash Card through ATMs. ▶ 正式名称は「偽造カード等及び盗難カード等を用いて行われる不正な機械式預貯金払戻し等からの預貯金者の保護等に関する法律」.
きぞく¹【帰属】▢ 帰属欲求《心理》"belonging needs"; the need to belong.
きぞくいん【貴族院】▢ 貴族院議員〔旧憲法下の〕a member of the House of Peers.
きそねんきん【基礎年金】▢ 基礎年金拠出金〔厚生年金・共済年金などが基礎年金の財源として拠出する金〕basic pension contributions; contributions 「to [toward(s)] the basic pension. 基礎年金番号 a basic pension number. ◐ 〜番号制度 a [the] basic pension number system / 〜番号通知書《receive》a notification of one's basic pension number.
きそん¹，きぞん【既存】▢ 既存株主 existing shareholders. 既存店 an [the] existing 「store [shop, branch, restaurant]; a [the] present store.
ぎだ【犠打】▢ 犠打成功率 a successful sacrifice hitting average.
きたアイルランドふんそう【北-紛争】《史》the Northern Ireland conflict.
きたアチェ【北-】〔インドネシア，アチェ州の県〕Aceh Utara.
「ギター弾きの恋」〔映画〕Sweet and Lowdown.
きたい⁵【期待】▢ 期待インフレ率《経》an expected inflation rate. 期待収益〔投資・事業などから予想される収益〕an [the] expected return. ◐ 〜率 an [the] expected rate of return. 期待族〔暴走族の暴走行為を見物に集まり声援を送っておる連中〕car gang 「fans [supporters]. 期待利益〔発明や特許により見込まれる利益〕an expected profit; expected earnings.
ぎだい【議題】▢ 議題設定 agenda-setting; the setting of an agenda. ◐ 〜設定機能〔マスコミの〕the agenda-setting function of the media.
きたオセチア【北-】North Ossetia(-Alania).《公式名》北オセチア共和国 the Republic of North Ossetia-Alania. ▢ 《首都》ウラジカフカス Vladikavkaz.
きたキプロス【北-】Northern Cyprus;《公式名》北キプロス・トルコ共和国 the Turkish Republic of Northern Cyprus (略: TRNC). ▶ 1983年，キプロスから一方的に独立を宣言. 独立を承認しているのはトルコのみ.
きたく¹【帰宅】▢ 帰宅支援マップ ＝震災時帰宅支援

マップ（⇨しんさい²）. **帰宅部**〔放課後すぐ帰宅してしまいクラブ活動をしないことを戯言的に言って〕a "going-straight-home" club. ● あいつは～一部だから、3時以降は学校にいないよ. The only activity that interests him is going home [He's the sort with no outside interests], so he's never in school after the three.

**きたケープ**【北－】〔南アフリカ共和国中部の州〕Northern Cape; (アフリカーンス語名) Noord-Kaap. ▶ 州都はキンバリー.

**きたごよう**【北五葉】〔植〕〔マツ科の常緑高木; ゴヨウマツの変種〕Pinus parviflora var. pentaphylla.

**きたしろさい**【北白犀】〔動〕a northern white rhinoceros; Ceratotherium simum cottoni.

**きたスマトラ**【北－】〔インドネシアの州〕North「Sumatra [Sumatera]; (インドネシア語名) Sumatera Utara. ▶ 州都はメダン.

**きたたいせいよう**【北大西洋】 ◯ 北大西洋振動《気象》the North Atlantic Oscillation (略: NAO).

**きたたいせいようかいさんほにゅういいんかい**【北大西洋海産哺乳動物委員会】the North Atlantic Marine Mammal Commission (略: NAMMCO).

**きたたいせいようりじかい**【北大西洋理事会】〔北大西洋条約機構の最高意思決定機関〕the North Atlantic Council (略: NAC).

**きたちょうせんじんけんほう**【北朝鮮人権法】**1**〔米国〕〔2004年制定の〕the North Korea Human Rights Act (略: NKHRA).

**2**〔法〕〔2006年制定の〕the North Korea Human Rights Law.

**きたちょうせんなんみんきゅうえんききん**【北朝鮮難民救援基金】the Life Funds for North Korean Refugees (略: LFNKR).

**きたちょうせんによるらちひがいしゃかぞくれんらくかい**【北朝鮮による拉致被害者家族連絡会】the Association of the Families of Victims Kidnapped by North Korea (略: AFVKN).

**きたちょうせんにらちされたにほんじんをきゅうしゅつするためのぜんこくきょうぎかい**【北朝鮮に拉致された日本人を救出するための全国協議会】the National Association for the Rescue of Japanese Kidnapped by North Korea (略: NARKN).

**きたホラサン**【北－】〔イラン北東部の州〕North Khorasan; (ペルシャ語名の音訳) Khorasan-e Shomali.

**きたまえぶね**【北前船】〔史〕a boat that carried goods from Hokkaido to the Osaka area by the Japan Sea route, calling in at Tsuruga, Obama and Shimonoseki.

**きたマルクしゅう**【北─州】〔インドネシアの州〕North Maluku (Province).

**きたむらさきうに**【北紫海胆】〔動〕〔オオバフンウニ科のウニ〕Strongylocentrotus nudus.

**きたりす**【北栗鼠】〔動〕a Eurasian red squirrel; Sciurus vulgaris.

**きたん³**【綺譚・奇譚】〔ありそうもない不思議な話〕a strange tale.

**きだん⁴**【基壇】〔建物の重量を支える石または突き固めた盛り土〕a foundation「floor [platform, layer]; a supporting「platform [floor, layer].

**きちかもの**【期近物】〔先物取引〕a nearby (futures) contract.

**きちく**【鬼畜】 ◯ 鬼畜米英〔日本史〕〔太平洋戦争下の標語〕American and British devils.

**きちっとかん**【きちっと感】=きちんとかん.

**きちゅう³**【忌中】 ◯ 忌中札 a mourning sign.

**きちょう²**【記帳】 ◯ 記帳所 a「registration [registry] site.

**きちょう⁵**【基調】 ◯ 円高[円安]基調 a trend toward a「stronger [weaker] yen; (signs of)「strength [weakness] in the yen. 回復基調〔景気などの〕(be on) the road to recovery; 《show》signs of recovery. プラス[マイナス]基調《経》a「positive [negative] state [trend]; 「strengthening [weakening]. ◯ 基調判断〔景気の〕(an) assessment of underlying trends (in the economy).

**ぎちょう**【議長】 ◯ 議長総括〔国際会議などの〕a chair's summary.

**キチンじゅんかん**【-循環】《経》〔在庫投資による、ほぼ3年半の景気循環〕the Kitchin cycle. ▶ 米国の経済学者Joseph Kitchinが発見.

**きちんとかん**【きちんと感】 ◯ 就職の面接には～のある服装を心がけなさい. When you go to a job interview, take care to wear clothes which are a good fit and feel suitable.

**キチンのなみ**【-の波】=キチンじゅんかん.

**きつえん**【喫煙】 ◯ 喫煙対策 an antismoking measure. ● 職場における～ measures (taken) against smoking in the workplace.

**きつおん**【吃音】 ◯ 吃音者 a stammerer; a stutterer.

**きっきん**【喫緊】〔さしせまって大切なこと〕 ◯ ～の課題 an urgent [a pressing] issue.

**ギック**【GIC】《保険》〔利率保証契約〕a GIC; a guaranteed interest contract.

**キックオフ** ◯ キックオフ・パーティー〔開始を祝うパーティー〕(have) a kickoff party. キックオフ・ミーティング〔企画や事業の発会式〕a《project》kickoff meeting.

**キックスケーター**〔スポーツ遊具の1つ〕a scooter.

**きっこう¹**【拮抗】 ◯ 拮抗ホルモン an antagonistic hormone. ● インスリン～ホルモン an insulin-antagonistic hormone.

**キッシュとう**【-島】〔イランの島〕Kish Island.

**きっしょう**【吉祥】 ◯ 吉祥図 an auspicious picture. 吉祥日 a lucky day. 吉祥紋 an auspicious design.

**きっしょうてん**【吉祥天】〔植〕〔リュウゼツラン科の多肉植物〕Agave parryi var. huachucensis.

**きっそう²**【吉左右】〔good [happy] news.

**きつだいよくりゅう**【吉大翼龍】〔古生物〕Jidapterus edentus.

**キッダルト**〔おとなこども〕a kidadult; a kiddult.

**きってぼん**【切手盆】a rectangular lacquer tray for holding monetary offerings and gifts.

**キ(ッ)テリョン**【旗対嶺】〔北朝鮮、江原道（カンウォン）の峠; ミサイル基地がある〕Kittaeryong.

**きつね**【狐】 ◯ 狐狩り fox hunting. ● ～狩り禁止法 a law banning fox hunting. 狐目 narrow, slanted eyes.

**きつねあめ**【狐雨】(a) light rain while the sun「shines [is shining]; a sun-shower.

**キッパ**〔ユダヤ教徒がかぶる皿状の帽子〕a kippa; a kipa; a kipah; a kippah.

**きつぶす**【着潰す】wear out《a jacket》. ◯ スーツはワンシーズンで～つもりで安物を買うことにしている. Since I intend to wear a suit out in a single season, I make a point of buying cheap ones.

**きてい³**【基底】 ◯ 基底細胞がん〔医〕(a) basal cell「carcinoma [cancer]; (略: BCC); (a) basal cell epithelioma.

**きてい⁴**【規定】 ◯ 規定打数〔ゴルフ〕par.

**キティたいふう**【-台風】〔1949年関東地方を襲った〕Typhoon Kitty.

**きとう**【祈禱】 ◯ 祈禱殿 a building for prayers in a shrine or temple; a prayer hall.

**きどう²**【軌道】 ◯ 周回軌道〔宇宙〕〔人工衛星などの〕a circling orbit. 低軌道〔宇宙〕〔人工衛星などの〕a low earth orbit (略: LEO). ◯ 軌道系交通機関 a rail transportation system. 軌道飛行 (an) orbital flight. 軌道陸上兼用作業車〔鉄道〕〔線路上も道路上も走れる保線用車両〕a road-rail (service) vehicle (for inspecting the tracks).

きどう³【起動】
▣ 起動音〚電算〛〔電源を入れた時に鳴る効果音〕a ˈstartup [start-up] sound; [パソコンの] a boot-up sound. 起動項目〚電算〛[パソコンの電源を入れた時、自動的に起動するファイルなど] a startup item. 起動時間〚電算〛[起動するまでにかかる時間] (a) ˈloading [startup] time; [電源を入れてから経過した時間] elapsed time (from startup). 起動速度〚電算〛a start-up speed. 起動中〚電算〛◎ ～中である[ソフトウェアなどが] (now) loading; [コンピューターが] booting / パソコンの～中にエラーが発生する。A booting error occurs. | There is a booting error. | I get an error message when booting.

きどう⁴【機動】 ▣ 機動的(な) agile; flexible; nimble; light-footed; quick to respond 《to changes》. ◎ 資産の～的な運用 flexible management of assets.

キトラこふん【—古墳】〚考古〛[奈良県明日香村にある古墳] the Kitora ˈtomb [tumulus]. ▣ キトラ古墳壁画 the Kitora tomb paintings.

きどるい【希土類】 ▣ 希土類磁石 a rare-earth magnet.

キナバタンガンがわ【—川】[マレーシア、ボルネオ島北部の川] the Kinabatangan River; the Kinabatangan.

きなり【生成り】 ▣ 生成り砂糖 unrefined sugar.

きにら【黄韮】〚植〛[野菜] yellow garlic chives; *gau wong*.

ぎにんちしょう【偽認症】〚精神医〛pseudodementia; depressive dementia.

きぬぎぬのわかれ【衣々[後朝]の別れ】[一夜の逢瀬の翌朝の] (a) parting in the morning after a (single) night together.

ギネスブック ▣ ギネスブック認定 ◎ ～認定の世界最大の花時計 a flower clock recognized by the *Guinness Book* as the largest in the world.
ギネス・ワールド・レコーズ Guinness World Records. [＝ギネスブック]

キネティックだんとう【—弾頭】〚軍〛a kinetic warhead.

きねん²【記念】
▣ 記念建造物 a monument; a commemorative structure; 《文》an edifice raised to commemorate 《*sb's* victory》. 記念公演 a commemorative performance. ◎『蝶々夫人』の初演百周年を祝って～公演が行われた。There was a commemorative performance of *Madam Butterfly* to celebrate the hundredth anniversary of 〈the [its] first performance〉. 記念セール a celebration sale; a sale to ˈmark [celebrate] 《the store's 20th anniversary》. ◎ ロッテ・マリーンズ優勝～セール a sale to celebrate the Nihon Series victory of the Lotte Marines. 記念配(当)〚株式〛(pay) a commemorative dividend 《of 100 yen》; a special dividend 《to mark the 50th Anniversary of the Foundation》.

きねんび【記念日】 ▣ 記念日症候群〚精神医〛anniversary syndrome.

きのう⁵【機能】 ▣ 高[低]機能 ◎ こうきのう、ていきのう. 機能横断(型)チーム〚経営〛a cross-functional team. 機能訓練士 a functional trainer. 機能生物学 functional biology. 機能廃絶〚生理〛[臓器の] (organ) function loss; functional loss; loss of a function. 機能不全家庭 a dysfunctional family.

ぎのう【技能】 ▣ 技能講習 (take) a skills course; (receive) skills training. 技能職 skilled work. 技能職員 a skilled nonclerical employee;〈集合的に〉the skilled nonclerical staff 《of a university》. 技能伝承[継承]〚熟練工などの〛inheriting a skill; handing [passing] down [on] 《traditional skills》. 技能労務職員〚学校や地方自治体などの〛〈集合的に〉the skilled nonclerical and labor workforce 《of a university》.

ぎのうごりんこくさいたいかい【技能五輪国際大会】 ＝こくさいぎのうきょうぎたいかい.

きのうせい【機能性】 ▣ 機能性胃腸障害, 機能性胃腸症〚医〛a functional gastrointestinal disorder (略: FGID). 機能性ガム (a) functional chewing gum. 機能性牛乳 (a) functional milk. 機能性化粧品 functional cosmetics. 機能性樹脂〚化〛a functional resin. 機能性便秘〚医〛functional constipation. 機能性野菜[栄養面での付加価値を高めた野菜] "functionally enhanced" vegetables. 機能性油脂 functional lipids.

ぎのうボランティアかいがいはけんきょうかい【技能—海外派遣協会】the Nippon Skilled Volunteers Association (略: NISVA).

キバキ Kibaki, Mwai (1931-　; ケニアの政治家; 大統領[2002-　]).

きばく【起爆】 ▣ 起爆実験 a test explosion 《of ˈa nuclear weapon [dynamite]》. 起爆力 detonating power; [活動・変革などをスタートさせる力] impetus 《to initiate a reform》; driving force; thrust.

きばしおおらいちょう【黄嘴大雷鳥】〚鳥〛＝ヨーロッパおおらいちょう.

きばた【黄旗】[自動車レースで、注意走行を促すために振る黄色い旗] a yellow flag.

きはつ【揮発】 ▣ 揮発性有機塩素化合物〚化〛a volatile organochlorine compound.

きはつばい【既発売】
～の (already) on ˈsale [the market]. ▣ 既発売商品 an ˈitem [article] (already) on ˈsale [the market].

きはっぴょう【既発表】
～の already [previously] published. ▣ 既発表論文 a (previously) published ˈpaper [article, thesis].

きばなコスモス【黄花—】〚植〛[キク科の 1 年草; メキシコ原産] (an) orange [(a) yellow, (a) sulphur] cosmos; *Cosmos sulphureus*.

きばん¹【基板】 ▣ 液晶基板 a liquid crystal substrate. シリコン[セラミック]基板 a ˈsilicon [ceramic] substrate. 多層基板 a multilayer substrate. 電子回路基板 an electronic circuit board. 配線基板 a circuit board. プリント(配線)基板 a printed-circuit board; a PC board.

きばん²【基盤】 ▣ 法的基盤〚要件〛a legal infrastructure; 〚根拠〛a legal basis 《for military action against Iraq》. 基盤技術[先端技術に対して] basic [fundamental] technology. 基盤人材 key personnel; essential staff.

きばんごう【記番号】〚紙幣の〛a serial number.

きばんてきぼうえいりょくこうそう【基盤的防衛力構想】a concept for fundamental defense capabilities.

きびとう【きび糖】(a) cane sugar.

きふ³【寄付】 ▣ 寄付税制 a donation tax (system). 寄付促進税制 a tax ˈsystem for encouraging [to promote] philanthropy.

きふきん²【貴腐菌】〚＜F *pourriture noble* ＝noble rot〛noble rot; grey mould; (botrytis) bunch rot; *Botrytis cinerea*.

ギブソン Gibson, Don (1928-2003; 米国のカントリー歌手・作曲家).

キプロスふんそう【—紛争】〚史〛(1964, 1974年、ギリシャ・トルコ間の) the Cyprus conflicts.

きぶん【気分】 ▣ 気分変調性障害, 気分変調症〚医〛dysthymia; (a) dysthymic disorder.

キプンジ〚動〛[オナガザル科のサル; 2005年にタンザニア南西部で発見された新種のサル] a kipunji; *Rungwecebus kipunji*.

ぎべん【擬娩・偽娩】〚民俗〛[妻の出産の際にその夫も床についたり、時には苦しんだりして、いろいろな禁忌に従う習俗] couvade. ▣ 擬娩症候群 couvade syndrome.

きほう¹【気泡】 ▣ 気泡緩衝材 bubble wrap; air bubble sheet. 気泡シート ＝気泡緩衝材.

きぼう⁵【希望】 ▣ 希望卸売価格 a suggested wholesale price (略: SWP). 希望降任[降格]制度 a system of ˈdemotion [reclassification] by request.

きほん【基本】 基本使用料 a basic「usage [rental] fee [charge]. 基本設計図〘建〙a「basic [draft, preliminary] drawing. 基本特許 a basic patent.

きみがよ【君が代】 君が代斉唱 singing the「national anthem [*Kimigayo*] in「chorus [unison].

「きみに読む物語」〘映画〙The Notebook.

ぎむ【義務】 義務化 making [rendering]《an activity》compulsory. ◆兵役を～化する make [render] military service compulsory; impose [introduce] conscription. 義務投票制〘選挙投票を有権者に義務づける制度〙compulsory [mandatory] voting.

キム・イルソン【金日成】 金日成バッジ a Kim Il-sung badge.

キム・ギドク【金基徳】Kim Ki-duk (1960- ; 韓国の映画監督).

ぎむきょういく【義務教育】 義務教育学校〘9年制の小中一貫校〙a (nine-year) compulsory education school; a combined elementary and junior high school.

ぎむきょういくひょうじゅんほう【義務教育標準法】〘法〙the Law Concerning Class Size and Numbers of Educational Personnel in Public Compulsory Schools. ▶ 正式名称は「公立義務教育諸学校の学級編制および教職員定数の標準に関する法」.

キム・ジョンナム【金正男】Kim Jong-nam (1971- ; 北朝鮮の指導者キム・ジョンイルの長男).

キムチ キムチ鍋[チゲ] *kimchi chige*; *kimchi nabe*.

ギムナジウム〘ドイツの大学予備校〙a gymnasium《*pl.* ～s, -sia*》. gymnasial *adj*.

キム・ヒソン【金喜善】Kim Hee-sun (1977- ; 韓国の女優).

キム・ヨンスン【金容淳】Kim Yong-sun (1934-2003; 北朝鮮の朝鮮労働党書記; 対韓国・日本関係担当).

きめい³【貴名】your name.

きめうち【決め打ち】〘野球〙selective hitting. ～する swing only at certain (types of) pitches. ◆彼はインコースのストレートを～した. He only went after inside fastballs.

キメラ キメラ抗体【免疫】a chimeric antibody.

キモい〘気持ち悪い〙《俗》feel yucky [gross];〈物が主語〉「yucky; gross.

きもったま【肝っ玉】 肝っ玉母さん a tough「*mom [*mum].

きもやき【肝焼き】broiled liver.

ぎゃく【逆】 逆上陸〘逆輸入〙reimport(ation); reverse import(ation); import back《into…》. 逆バネ〘反発の原動力〙reverse spring motion; rebound. ◆安倍氏の圧勝ムードが～バネになり, 対立候補が予想以上の票を得た. The general feeling that Abe would win by a landslide worked against him, with other candidates getting more votes than expected.

ぎゃくあし【逆足】〘利き足でないほうの足〙one's「weaker [subordinate] leg.

ぎゃくうち【逆打ち】〘四国巡礼で霊場を八十八番札所から一番札所まで逆の順番でまわること〙《completing》a pilgrimage around the 88 designated temples in Shikoku, in reverse order starting from no. 88. [⇨じゅんうち]

ぎゃくさし【逆指し】〘商〙=逆指し値注文《⇨きゃくさしね》.

ぎゃくさしね【逆指し値】〘商〙a stop price. 逆指し値注文 a stop order.

ぎゃくさば【逆さば】 逆さばを読む〘年齢を多めにいうなど通常とは逆の方向に数字を偽る〙◆彼女は酒屋で高校生なのに～を読んで二十歳だと言った. Although she was a high school student, at the liquor shop she exaggerated her age and said she was 20.

ぎゃくしさんこうか【逆資産効果】〘経〙an adverse「wealth [assets] effect.

ぎゃくしょう【逆唱】〘一連の数字などを聞いたあとそれを逆に暗誦すること〙reverse repetition; repetition《of a string of numbers》in reverse (order). ～する repeat [recite]《a string of numbers》in reverse (order).

ぎゃくしん【逆進】 逆進課税 regressive taxation.

ぎゃくせいかつ【逆正接】〘数〙an arcsecant.

ぎゃくせいげん【逆正弦】〘数〙an arcsine.

ぎゃくせいさん【逆生産】＝インバース・マニュファクチャリング.

ぎゃくせいせつ【逆正接】〘数〙an arctangent.

きゃくせん【客船】 大型客船 a large「passenger [cruise] ship. 豪華客船 a luxury「cruise ship [(ocean) liner].

ぎゃくせんのう【逆洗脳】deprogramming; reverse brainwashing. ～する deprogram. ◆カルト宗教の信者を～するのは難しい. It's hard to deprogram cult members.

ぎゃくそう¹【逆走】 逆走事故 an accident caused by driving in the wrong direction《on an expressway》. 逆走車 a「car [vehicle] travelling in the wrong direction.

ぎゃくそう²【逆層】〘地質〙〘岩壁などの〙a reverse fault. ◆あの岩尾根は～で登りにくい. That ridge is a reverse fault, and hard to climb.

ぎゃくたい【虐待】 経済的虐待 economic abuse. 身体的虐待 physical abuse. 虐待死 abuse resulting in death; death by abuse. 死させる cause《a child's》death by abuse. 虐待防止 abuse prevention. ◆～防止ネットワーク an abuse prevention network; a network for preventing cruelty《to children [the elderly]》.

ぎゃくだま【逆球】〘野球〙a pitch opposite to the catcher's sign.

きゃくちゅう³【客注】〘顧客の注文〙a customer's order; an order from a customer. 客注品 an item ordered by a customer; a customer-ordered item.

ぎゃくデイ【逆–】 逆デイ・サービス《⇨デイ・サービス》.

ぎゃくていとうゆうし【逆抵当融資】a reverse mortgage.

ぎゃくてん【逆転】 逆転現象 a reversal phenomenon; an opposite phenomenon. ◆年功序列神話が崩壊した今, 職場における上司と部下の年齢の～現象はそれほど珍しくなくなってきた. Now that the myth of the seniority system has collapsed, it is no longer so unusual in workplaces for the relative ages of bosses and subordinates to be reversed. 逆転敗訴 a (judicial) reversal (against *one*). 逆転満塁ホームラン〘野球〙a come-from-behind grand slam. 逆転有罪判決 a sentence of guilty which reverses a lower court's judgment.

ぎゃくてんしゃこうそそがいざい【逆転写酵素阻害剤】〘薬〙〘HIVの増殖抑制薬〙a reverse transcriptase inhibitor. 核酸系逆転写酵素阻害剤 a nucleoside reverse transcriptase inhibitor (略: NRTI). 非核酸系逆転写酵素阻害剤 a nonnucleoside reverse transcriptase inhibitor (略: NNRTI). ヌクレオチド系逆転写酵素阻害剤 a nucleotide reverse transcriptase inhibitor (略: NtRTI).

ぎゃくとっく【逆特区】〘特別に保護を残す地区〙a reverse special economic zone; an economic zone still subject to protection.

ぎゃくナン【逆–】〘女性が男性に声をかけて誘惑すること〙《a man》being approached by a woman (and asked for a date); picking up a guy.

きゃくばなれ【客離れ】a decrease in customers; customer loss. ◆公営ギャンブルの世界では全体的に～が進んでいる. Public gambling generally is「losing more and more customers [suffering an increasing loss of

ぎゃくばりこうほう

customers]. ～を食い止める put an end to [stop any further] loss of customers.
**ぎゃくばりこうほう【逆梁工法】**〖建〗〖梁を室内に出っ張らせない工法〗a「reverse [recessed] beam method.
**ぎゃくはん【逆版】**〖印刷〗〖左右または上下逆にしてしまった印刷〗inverted printing; inversion.
**ぎゃくふんしゃ【逆噴射】** □□ 逆噴射レバー〔航空機など の〕a thrust reverser lever; a reverse thrust lever.
**ぎゃくほうい【逆包囲】**(a) counterencirclement.  ～する counterencircle 《the enemy's forces》.
**ぎゃくまわり【逆回り】**〖逆回転すること〗turning backwards; 〖順路を逆に行くこと〗going the opposite way.  ～する 〖逆回転する〗rotate [turn] the other way; 〖順路を逆に行く〗go the opposite way. ◐ 南半球では排水口に吸い込まれる水の渦は北半球とは～するそうだ. I hear that in the southern hemisphere, water spins down the drain the opposite way from in the northern hemisphere. / いつもの散歩コースを～する walk a path the opposite way from the usual. ◐ 彼は前回の～で2度目の世界一周ヨット単独航海に成功した. He succeeded in sailing solo around the world a second time, going in the opposite direction from the first time. ◐ ハンドルを時計と～に 90 度まわす turn the steering wheel 90 degrees counterclockwise.
**ぎゃくゆうしょう【逆有償】**〖廃棄物などを処分する際に売却でなく逆に料金を支払うこと〗an inverse onerous contract. ◐ これらの業者は～で回収した古紙を外国に安く売っている. These dealers sell the wastepaper they have collected at low prices overseas, under an inverse onerous contract.
**ぎゃくよかつ【逆余割】**〖数〗an arccosecant.
**ぎゃくよげん【逆余弦】**〖数〗an arccosine.
**ぎゃくよせつ【逆余接】**〖数〗an arccotangent.
「**キャスト・アウェイ**」〖映画〗Cast Away.
**キャスビー【CASBEE】**〖建築物総合環境性能評価システム〗CASBEE; the Comprehensive Assessment System for Building Environmental Efficiency.
**きゃっかん【客観】** □□ 客観視 ◐ 自分自身を～視する能力を持たなくてはいけない. One needs to be able to see oneself objectively. / 彼は夢ばかり追い求め, 現実を～視できない人間だ. He's always chasing his dreams and is unable to face reality head-on.
**きゃっかんてき【客観的】** □□ 客観的臨床能力試験〖医〗an objective structured clinical examination (略: OSCE).
**ぎゃっこう²【逆行】** □□ 逆行催眠〖精神医〗= 退行催眠 (⇨たいこう¹⁴).
**キャッシュ¹**
□□ キャッシュ・アウト〔現金支払い; カジノなどでのチップの換金〕(a) cash-out; (a) cash-back. キャッシュアウト・リファイナンス〖金融〗〖ローンを借り増して一部を現金化すること〗cash-out refinancing. キャッシュ・アンド・キャリー〔現金払い持ち帰り〕cash-and-carry. キャッシュバック 《earn》 a「cash-back [cash] rebate. キャッシュ型年金〔企業年金の一種〕a cash balance (略: CB) pension (plan). キャッシュ・ポジション〔正味資産総額に対する現金の割合〕a 《strong》 cash position. キャッシュ・マネジメント・システム〖会計〗a cash management system (略: CMS). キャッシュリッチ(な)〔潤沢な現金ないしは即時現金化可能な預金などを有している〕cash-rich. ◐ ～リッチ企業〖ファンド〗a cash-rich「company [fund].
**キャッシュ²** □□ キャッシュ・サーバー〖電算〗a cache server.
**キャッスルマンびょう【一病】**〖医〗Castleman's disease.
**キャッチオールきせい【一規制】**〖貿易〗〖大量破壊兵器等の不拡散のための輸出管理〗a catch-all control.
「**キャッチ・ミー・イフ・ユー・キャン**」〖映画〗Catch Me If You Can.
**キャッチ・ライト** 1 〖写真〗〖瞳に映った光源の光〗catch light.

2〔特定の所にだけ光を当てるピンスポットライト〕a pin spotlight.
**キャッツクロー**〖植〗〖南米産のアカネ科の薬用植物〗(a) cat's claw; *Uncaria tomentosa*.
「**キャットウーマン**」〖映画〗Catwoman.
**キャットテール**〖植〗〖トウダイグサ科の多年草〗a red cat's tail; *Acalypha reptans*.
**キャップ²【CAP】**〔子供への暴力防止〕child assault prevention.
**ギャップ¹** □□ ギャップ・イヤー(制度)〖教育〗〖大学入学あるいは就職が決まった後に取る, 進学[入社]前の通常 1 年間の休学[休職]期間〗《take, do》 a gap year. ギャップ結合〖生理〗〖細胞間の〗a gap junction.
**ギャップ²【GAP】**= ジー・エー・ピー.
**ギャップ³**〖商標〗〖米国の衣料品専門店〗Gap.
**キャップ・アンド・トレード**〖環境〗〖温室効果ガスの排出量取引方式〗cap and trade; a cap-and-trade system.
**キャップシール**〔鉛合金の薄板製の, ワインの瓶の封〕a capsule.
**ギャップ・フィラー**〖通信〗a gap filler (略: GF).
**キャップ・ロック**〖地質〗〖不浸透性の岩盤〗cap rock.
**キャド【CAD】** □□ 3 次元 CAD 3D CAD.
**キャドカム, キャドキャム【CAD/CAM】** □□ 3 次元 CAD/CAM 3D [three-dimensional] CAD/CAM.  □□ CAD/CAM システム a CAD/CAM system.
**キャトラル** Cattrall, Kim (1956- ; 英国生まれの映画女優).
**キャニオニング**〖渓流下り〗canyoning.
**ギャネンドラ** Gyanendra Bir Bikram Shah Dev (1947- ; ネパール国王 [2001-08]).
**キャバクラ** a cabaret club; a bar with female companions for male customers.
**キャパシター**〖電〗〖コンデンサーの一種〗a capacitor. □□ ナノゲート・キャパシター a nanogate capacitor.
**キャパシティー** □□ キャパシティー・ビルディング〔能力開発〕capacity building (略: CB).
**キャバリア・キング・チャールズ・スパニエル**〖犬〗a Cavalier King Charles spaniel; an English toy spaniel.
**キャバリエ**〖犬〗= キャバリア・キング・チャールズ・スパニエル.
**キャプショー** Capshaw, Kate (1953- ; 米国の映画女優).
**キャプチャ**〖電算〗〖画像認証技術の 1 つ〗CAPTCHA; Captcha. ► Completely Automated Public Turing Test to Tell Computers and Humans Apart (コンピューターと人間を区別する完全に自動化された公開チューリングテスト) の略から.
**キャプチャー**〖映〗パフォーマンス・キャプチャー〔アニメーション製作の新手法の 1 つ〕performance capture. ビデオ・キャプチャー〔映像機器から映像と音声をデジタルデータとしてコンピューターの中に取り込むこと〕video capture.
「**キャプテン・スカーレット**」〔英国の人形劇 TV ドラマ, 特殊機関員 Scarlet が, 敵 Mysterons と闘う〕Captain Scarlet and the Mysterons.
「**キャプテン・ゼロ**」〔米国の, 変身ヒーローものの TV アニメ, 口だけが実写〕Space Angel. ► 「宇宙ライダーエンゼル」の邦題でも放映.
「**キャプテン・ドレーク**」〔実在した英国の海賊船長を元にした冒険活劇 TV ドラマ〕Sir Francis Drake.
「**ギャベ**」〖映画〗Gabbeh.
**キャベツ** □□ 新キャベツ = 春キャベツ. 春[夏, 冬]キャベツ a「spring [summer, winter] cabbage.
**キャミソールトップ, キャミトップ**〔キャミソール様の上身衣〕a camisole top.
**キャメロン** 1 Cameron, David (1966- ; イギリスの政治家; 保守党党首 [2005- ].
  2 Cameron, James (1954- ; カナダ生まれの映画監督・脚本家・製作者; 本名 James Francis Cameron).
「**ギャラクシー・クエスト**」〖映画〗Galaxy Quest.
**キャラメライザー**〔ケーキに振りかけた粉糖を一気に加熱しる

ラメル状にする鏝(à)] a caramelizer.
**ギャラリスト** [画廊経営者] a gallery「owner [operator]; a gallerist.
**「ギャラントメン」** [米国の, イタリア戦線の従軍記者のTVドラマ] The Gallant Men.
**キャリア**[1]
⊡ キャリア・ガイダンス〔職業説明会〕a career counseling session. キャリア・カウンセラー〔個人のキャリア形成に関する相談員〕a career counselor. キャリア・カウンセリング career counseling. キャリア・コンサルタント a career「consultant [counselor, advisor]. キャリア・ショック〔自分の職業上の実績や将来像が, 環境や状況の変化により, 急激に崩壊してしまうこと] career shock. キャリア・デザイン〔職業設計〕planning [designing] a career; planning for a long-term career. キャリア・デベロップメント〔キャリア開発〕career development. キャリア・パス〔職業についてたどる進む道筋〕a career path.
**キャリア**[2] ⊡ 無発症キャリア〔医〕a「latent [symptomless] carrier.
**キャリア・カー**〔車両運搬車〕a car carrier; an auto transport truck; a (multiple) car transporter.
**キャリアこうりゅうプラザ**〔-交流-〕〔中高年管理職向け就職支援施設〕a "Career Exchange Plaza"; a facility providing job-seeking support for middle-aged and older employees in the administrative or managerial sector.
**キャリー**[2] Carrey, Jim (1962- ;カナダ生まれの映画俳優; 本名 James Eugene Carrey).
**キャリー**[3] 〔ペット・手荷物などの運搬具〕a carrier.
**キャリーバッグ** a carrying bag.
**「キャリントン」** 〔映画〕Carrington.
**ギャル** ⊡ ギャル系 "gal-type"; describing a fashion adopted by young Japanese teenage girls, characterised by dyed hair, dark sunburnt skin and flashily matched clothing. ◯ 〜系ファッション (a) "gal-type" fashion. ギャル文字 "gal characters"; a writing system using unconventional kanji and symbols in place of similar-looking standard characters.
**ギャルゲー** a (video) game featuring young girls.
**ガロ** Gallo, Vincent (1962- ;米国の映画俳優・監督).
**キャロム** キャロム・ビリヤード carom; carom billiards.
**「ギャング・オブ・ニューヨーク」** 〔映画〕Gangs of New York.
**キャンバス** ⊡ キャンバス地〔厚地の粗布〕canvas. ◯ 〜地のトートバッグ a canvas tote (bag). キャンバス・トップ〔自動車〕〔キャンバス地でできた屋根〕a canvas top.
**キャンプ** ⊡ 訓練キャンプ a training camp. ◯ テロリスト訓練〜 a terrorist training camp. デイ・キャンプ〔日帰りキャンプ〕a day camp. ⊡ キャンプ・ツーリング〔キャンプをしながらバイクでツーリング旅行をすること〕motorcycle camping.
**キャンプイン** 〔スポーツ〕the「start [opening] of training camp. 〜する start [begin] training camp.
**キャンプ・ペンドルトン** 〔米国, カリフォルニア州南西部にある米海兵隊基地〕Camp Pendleton.
**ギャンブル** ⊡ ギャンブルスタート〔野球〕the act (performed by a base runner in baseball) of breaking for the next base immediately before or just as the hitter's bat makes contact with the ball.
**キャンペーン** ⊡ 防止キャンペーン a campaign「to prevent [against]〔child abuse〕. ◯ 薬物乱用防止〜 an anti-drug abuse campaign / 未成年者喫煙防止〜 a campaign to stop underage smoking.
**キャンベル** Campbell, Neve (Adrianne) (1973- ;カナダ生まれの映画女優).
**キュアロン** = クアロン.
**キュー・アール・コード**【QR -】〔商標〕QR Code. ▶ QR は quick response の略. バーコードより情報圧縮度が高い2次元コード.
**きゅうえん**[0]【救援】⊡ 救援外交 disaster relief diplomacy.
**キュー・オー・エス**【QoS】〔電算〕〔サービスの質〕quality of service; QoS.
**きゅうか**[2]【休暇】⊡ 特別休暇 an extraordinary [a special] leave. 分散休暇《take》staggered vacations.
**きゅうかい**[2]【球界】⊡ 球界再編 a reorganization of the baseball world; a reorganization of baseball.
**きゅうがいけいせいふぜん**【臼蓋形成不全】〔医〕acetabular dysplasia.
**きゅうかく**[2]【嗅覚】⊡ 嗅覚中枢〔生理〕the olfactory center.
**きゅうかそく**【急加速】(a) sudden「acceleration [increase in speed]. 〜する suddenly「accelerate [pick up speed, speed up].
**きゅうかん**[9]【吸汗】sweat absorption. ⊡ 吸汗加工 rendering《cloth》sweat absorbent. 吸汗性 sweat absorbency. ◯ 〜性に優れた素材 (a) highly sweat-absorbent material / 〜性のある sweat absorbent. 吸汗素材 (a) sweat-absorbent material.
**きゅうき**[2]【吸気】⊡ 吸気バルブ〔機〕〔エンジンの〕an intake valve.
**きゅうきゅう**[2]【救急】⊡ 救急外来 emergency outpatient「treatment [care]. ◯ 夜間〜外来 nighttime emergency outpatient「treatment [care]. 救急救命 first aid and lifesaving; emergency medical care.
**きゅうきゅうきゅうめいしほう**【救急救命士法】〔法〕the Emergency Medical Technician Law.
**きゅうきゅうのひ**【救急の日】〔9月9日〕First-Aid Day.
**きゅうけい**[2]【休憩】⊡ 休憩動議 a motion to recess.
**きゅうけつまく**【球結膜】〔解〕= 眼球結膜 (⇒がんきゅう).
**きゅうご**[2]【救護】⊡ 救護義務〔交通事故を起こした際の〕a [the] (driver's) duty to aid the injured. ◯ 〜義務違反 (a) violation of the duty to aid the injured. 救護措置義務 = 救護義務.
**きゅうご**[2]【球後】⊡ 球後視神経炎〔眼科〕retrobulbar neuritis.
**きゅうこう**[13]【救荒】⊡ 救荒食 (a) famine food.
**きゅうこん**[4]【球根】⊡ 春〔秋〕植え球根 a「spring [autumn] planted bulb.
**きゅうさい**[3]【救済】⊡ 救済宗教 a salvation(ist) religion.
**きゅうさいこう**【九寨溝】〔中国四川省にある自然保護区〕Jiuzhaigou (Valley); Jiǔzhàigōu.
**キューザック** 1 Cusack, Joan (1962- ;米国の映画女優; 2の姉). 2 Cusack, John (1966- ;米国の映画俳優; 1の弟).
**きゅうざん**【休山】〔鉱山の操業休止〕temporary closure of a mine; temporarily closing (down) a mine; suspension of mining operations.〔操業休止になった鉱山〕a temporarily closed (down) mine. 〜する temporarily close (down) a mine; suspend mining operations. ◯ その鉱山は不況のため〜となった. The mine「was temporarily closed down [suspended operations] due to the recession.
**きゅうし**[12]【吸脂】sebum [oil] absorption. ⊡ 吸脂力 sebum [oil] absorptivity.
**きゅうじつ**[2]【休日】⊡ 休日価格 (a [the]) price on weekends and national holidays; a [the] weekend and holiday price. 休日緊急診療 emergency medical care on Sundays and holidays. ◯ 〜緊急診療所 an emergency clinic open on Sundays and holidays. 休日緊急(当番)医 an emergency physician on duty on Sundays and holidays. 休日(勤務)手当 an allowance for working on a holiday; a holiday allowance. 休日診療所 a clinic open on weekends and national holidays.
**きゅうしゅう**[2]【吸収】⊡ 吸収分割〔会社分割の1つ〕

きゅうしゅつ

(a) division-merger.
きゅうしゅつ【救出】□■救出性《自動車》〔自動車などの安全性能で、事故後の乗員の救出しやすさ〕rescuability.
きゅうしゅん²【球春】◯〜の到来 arrival of the baseball season. ◯〜を告げるプロ野球オープン戦が各地で始まった. Exhibition games started up all over the country signaling the start of the pro baseball season.
きゅうじょ【救助】□■救助訓練《carry out, conduct》a rescue drill. 救助工作車 a rescue truck. 救助ヘリ(コプター) 〔救難ヘリコプター〕a rescue 'helicopter [《口》chopper]. 救助ロボット〔災害救助ロボット〕a rescue robot.
きゅうじょう¹【弓状】□■弓状紋〔指紋の〕an arch (pattern).
きゅうじょう⁴【休場】□■休場届〔相撲〕a notice of absence 《from a 'bout [tournament]》.
きゅうじょう⁶【球状】□■球状太陽電池 a spherical solar cell. 球状変性《医》〔細胞が変性により著明し膨潤すること〕ballooning degeneration.
きゅうじょうひ【嗅上皮】《解》the olfactory epithelium 《pl. 〜s, -lia》.
きゅうしょく²【求職】□■求職サイト〔インターネット上の〕a 'job-hunting [job-hunter] site; a job site.
きゅうしょく³【給食】□■(学校)給食センター a school 'lunch [meal] center. 給食センター方式〔数校分の給食をまとめて一か所で調理する〕the multi-school lunch center style.
キューしょくぶつえん【—植物園】〔英国, ロンドンにある王立植物園〕the Royal Botanic Gardens, Kew; Kew Gardens.
きゅうじょけんくんれんしきょうかい【救助犬訓練士協会】the Rescue Dog Trainers' Association 《略: RDTA》.
きゅうじょたい【救助隊】□■高度救助隊〔全国の中核市等に配備予定の〕an 'advanced [elite] rescue team. 特別高度救助隊〔全国の政令指定都市に配備予定の〕a special 'advanced [elite] rescue team.
きゅうじん⁴【求人】□■求人開拓〔公共職業安定所(ハローワーク)が行う〕(new) job offer development. 求人サイト〔インターネット上の〕a job 'offer [information, listings] site; a help-wanted site.
きゅうしんけい【嗅神経】□■嗅神経鞘グリア細胞《略》an olfactory ensheathing glial cell 《略: OEG》.
きゅうじんるい【旧人類】【人類】〔旧人〕an archaic human (species); early *Homo sapiens*; 〔古いタイプの人; 時代に取り残されている人〕a person who is 'outdated [antediluvian]; 《口》a Neanderthal 《when it comes to computers》.
きゅうせい⁴【急性】□■急性冠症候群《医》acute coronary syndrome 《略: ACS》. 急性期《医》⇒きゅうせいき. 急性吸入毒性 acute inhalation toxicity. 急性経口毒性 acute oral toxicity. 急性硬膜下血腫 (an) acute subdural hematoma. 急性呼吸不全 acute respiratory 'failure [insufficiency]. 急性死亡 (an) acute death. 急性循環不全《医》acute circulatory failure 《略: ACF》; shock. 急性ストレス障害《医》(an) acute stress disorder 《略: ASD》.
きゅうせいき【急性期】《医》an [the] acute 'phase [stage]. □■超急性期 a [the] hyperacute 'period [phase, stage]. 超急性期管理 management of 'the hyperacute phase [the hyperacute (patient), hyperacute patients]. 急性期医療 acute medical care. 急性期管理 management 'of [during] the acute phase; acute phase management. 急性期治療 acute treatment. 急性期病院 an acute hospital; a hospital for acute care.
きゅうせいさいがいしょうこうぐんストレスはんのう【急性災害症候群-反応】《精神医》(post-disaster) acute stress reaction 《略: ASR》.

きゅうせっきん【急接近】〔急に近づくこと〕a 'fast [quick] approach;〔急速に親密の度を深めること〕(a) quick intimacy.
〜する〔急に近づく〕approach quickly; make a fast approach 《to…》;〔急速に親密の度を深める〕form a quick intimacy 《with…》; get to know 《sb》 quickly. ◯中国がアメリカに〜した. China rapidly formed close ties with the United States. / このところ敬介と洋子が〜している. Recently Keisuke and Yōko have suddenly become close. | Things have heated up quickly between Keisuke and Yōko lately.
きゅうそ³【嗅素】【化】an odorous substance.
きゅうたん³【吸痰】phlegm suction.
きゅうだん¹【糾弾】□■糾弾(集)会 a "denunciation meeting"; a 'meeting [gathering] to denounce 《a person, a policy》.
きゅうだん²【球団】□■球団運営会社 a (baseball) team management company. 球団記録〔野球〕a team record. 球団スコアラー a team 'scorer [scorekeeper]. 球団統合 a team merger.
きゅうちせいど【級地制度】〔地域における生活様式や物価差による生活水準の差を生活保護基準に反映させる制度〕a system for adjusting 'livelihood protection [*welfare, 'social security'] standards based on regional lifestyles and prices; a region-based rating system.
きゅうちゃく【吸着】□■吸着マット an absorbent mat; absorbent matting.
きゅうちゅう【宮中】□■宮中行事 an event at the Imperial Court; a [an] Imperial Court function. 宮中祭祀 a rite at the Imperial Court; (imperial) Court rites.
きゅうてい²【宮廷】□■宮廷舞踊 court dancing; a court dance. 宮廷料理 (Imperial) court cuisine.
キュー・ディー・アイ・アイ【QDII】《株》〔適格国内機関投資家〕a QDII. ▶ qualified domestic institutional investor の略.
「宮廷女官 チャングムの誓い」〔韓国のテレビドラマ〕Dae Jang Gum;（漢字表記では）大長今.
「キューティ・ブロンド」〔映画〕Legally Blonde.
「宮廷料理人ヴァテル」〔映画〕Vatel.
きゅうてきこくじょうこう【旧敵国条項】=敵国条項 《⇒てきこく》.
きゅうてんいちいちいいんかい【9.11 委員会】〔米国で 2001 年 9 月 11 日に起こった同時多発テロに関する独立調査委員会の通称〕the '9-11 [9/11] Commission. ▶ 正式名称は the National Commission on Terrorist Attacks Upon the United States.
ぎゅうとうじんしん【牛頭人身】a human body with the head of a bull; a minotaur.
きゅうなん²【救難】□■救難捜索機 a search-and-rescue plane. 救難飛行艇 a rescue flying boat.
ぎゅうにくトレーサビリティーほう【牛肉-法】【法】the Beef Traceability Law. ▶ 正式名称は、「牛の個体識別情報の管理と伝達に関する特別措置法」(the Law for Special Measures Concerning the Management and Relay of Information for Individual Identification of Cattle).
ぎゅうにくりれきかんりほう【牛肉履歴管理法】【法】=ぎゅうにくトレーサビリティーほう.
ぎゅうにゅう【牛乳】□■(紙)パック牛乳 a carton of milk; milk in a carton. 成分調整牛乳 homogenized milk. 牛乳紙パック a milk carton.
ぎゅうにゅうふきゅうきょうかい【牛乳普及協会】a 《prefectural》 Dairy Promotion and Research Association. □■全国牛乳普及協会 the National Dairy Promotion and Research Association.
きゅうねんまく【嗅粘膜】《解》the olfactory mucosa 《pl. -sae, 〜(s)》.
きゅうば²【急場】□■急場しのぎ〔行為〕tiding over

[surviving] a difficult situation;〔その手段・策〕a stopgap; a quick fix. ◐～しのぎの策《take》stopgap measures《to check inflation》;《do… as》a stopgap measure.
キューバあまがえる【雨蛙】【動】＝キューバずつきがえる.
きゅうはいき【給排気】ventilation. ◐◐ 自然給排気式〔暖房器具などの〕balanced flue. 給排気設備 ventilation equipment. 給排気筒 a ventilation duct.
キューバずつきがえる【ずつき蛙】【動】a Cuban tree frog; *Osteopilus septentrionalis*.
きゅうはちかべ【98 両価格】〔切りよく千円などとせずに 980 円として客に割安感を与える価格づけ〕psychological pricing;〔その価格〕a psychological price.
きゅうばつ【救抜】salvation.
～する save《*sb* [*sth*] from…》.
キューバ・リバー〔カクテル〕a Cuba libre.
キューバ・リブレ ＝キューバ・リバー.
きゅうびょう【急病】◐◐ 急病死 death from (an) acute 「disease [illness]; sudden death from disease. ◐～死する die (suddenly) from an acute disease.
きゅうふ[2]【給付】◐◐ 給付建て年金 a ʻdefined [fixed] benefit(s) pension plan.
キューフィー【QFII】【株式】〔適格海外機関投資家〕a QFII. ▶ qualified foreign institutional investor の略.
きゅうふじょう【急浮上】a sudden appearance (of a submarine); a sudden increase (in public interest); a fast rise (in rank).
～する〔潜水艦が〕surface quickly;〔問題などが急に人々の関心の対象となる〕arise (appear, come up) suddenly;〔順位などが急上昇する〕rise quickly; shoot up. ◐ 大統領の兵役逃れ疑惑が～してきた. Suspicion arose suddenly that the president had avoided military service. /〔ゴルフで〕昨日の 40 位から一気に 3 位へ～した. She shot up from 40th place yesterday to 3rd today.
キューブラーロス Köbler-Ross, Elisabeth (1926-2004; スイス生まれの米国の精神科医・著述家).
きゅうへん【急変】◐◐ 急変事態〔突然の体制崩壊など〕an (sudden) emergency; a (sudden) crisis; an upheaval; trouble.
きゅうほうしつ【吸放湿】moisture absorption and release. ◐◐ 吸放湿性 moisture absorption and release properties. ◐ 珪藻土は～性にすぐれている. Diatomite absorbs and releases moisture extremely well.
きゅうみん[1]【休眠】◐◐ 休眠打破【生物】〔休眠状態を終わらせること〕dormancy breaking. 休眠誘導【生物】〔休眠状態に入らせること〕dormancy induction. (がん)休眠療法【医】tumor dormancy therapy.
きゅうめい[4]【救命】◐◐ 救命救急医 an emergency physician. 救命講習《take》a lifesaving course;《receive》lifesaving training. ◐ 普通[上級]～講習 a regular [an advanced] lifesaving course. 救命処置〔措置〕《provide, receive》lifesaving treatment. ◐ 緊急～処置 immediate life support (略: ILS). 救命率 a survival rate. ◐ 心停止後, 1 分経過するごとに～率が 7 ％から 10 ％低下する. The survival rate decreases by seven to ten percent with each passing minute following cardiac arrest.
きゅうやく[4]【休薬】〔薬の服用を一時やめること〕(a) temporary cessation of (anti-cancer) medication.
きゅうゆ[1]【吸油】◐◐ 吸油紙 oil-absorbent paper. 吸油性 oil ʻabsorptivity [absorption capacity], absorbing capacity. ◐ 吸油マット〔海面に流出した重油などを処理するための〕an oil-absorbing [-absorption] mat. 吸油力 oil-absorbing[-absorption] power.
きゅうゆ[2]【給油】◐◐ 給油缶 a fuel can. 給油機〔ガソリンスタンドの〕*a gasoline pump;〔a petrol pump;《fill up at》the pump;〔空中給油機〕an airborne refueling aircraft; an in-the-air fueling craft; an air tanker (plane). 給油キャップ a fuel cap; *a gas cap;〔a petrol

93　　　　　　　　　　　　　　　　きょういく

cap. 給油パイプ〔管〕a fuel (supply) pipe.
きゅうよ[1]【給与】◐◐ 無償給与〔教科書などの〕free supply《of school textbooks》; supplying《textbooks》ʻfree (of charge) [gratis]. 給与カット a salary cut; a cut in salary. 給与税 (a) payroll tax. 給与天引き salary deduction; the deduction of 《insurance premiums》 from *one's* salary.
きゅうよう[1]【休養】◐◐ 積極的[消極的]休養〔体を軽く動かして[安静にして]疲れを取る休養法〕(an) active [(a) passive] rest.
きゅうりょう[6]【給料】◐◐ 給料生活者〔俸給生活者〕a salaried worker; a salary earner; a white-collar worker;〈集合的に〉the salaried class.
キュー・レシオ【Q－】〔証券〕〔実質株価純資産倍率〕the 「Tobin's] Q ratio.
キュクロプス【ギ神話】〔巨人族〕the Cyclopes; [1 人] a Cyclops.
キュニコスがくは【－学派】〔犬儒(けんじゅ)学派〕the Cynics; [1 人] a Cynic.
キュリオ【商標】〔ソニー製二足歩行ロボット〕QRIO.
ギュル Göl, Abdullah (1950-　;トルコの政治家; 首相 [2002-03]; 大統領 [2007-　]).
きよ[1]【寄与】
◐◐ プラス[マイナス](の)寄与【経】a ʻpositive [negative] contribution.
寄与分【法】the portion of an estate to which somebody has a prior legal claim under inheritance tax law if he or she has provided special care or services during the deceased's lifetime. 寄与度〔割合〕〔統計〕a degree of contribution; a contribution (degree). ◐ 設備投資の GDP 成長率への～度は 1.2％と予想されている. The contribution of capital investment to the GDP growth rate is estimated at 1.2％. | Capital investment is estimated to account for 1.2% of the growth in GDP. 寄与率〔統計〕a contribution ratio; a contribution coefficient.
ぎょいこう【御衣黄】【植】〔バラ科の落葉高木〕*Prunus lannesiana* cv. *Gioiko*.
きょうあく【凶悪】◐◐ 凶悪化 ◐ 少年犯罪の～化は憂うべき問題だ. The problem of juvenile crime becoming increasingly vicious is deeply deplorable. | Deplorably, crimes committed by young people are growing more and more brutal. 凶悪事件 a ʻheinous [vicious] crime; a brutal [an atrocious] incident.
きょうい[2]【脅威】◐◐ 外部[内部](からの)脅威 an ʻexternal [internal] threat.
きょういく【教育】
◐◐ 教育格差 an educational gap; a gap in education. 教育観 (one's) views ʻon [about] education; a (one's) view of education; the way *one* thinks ʻabout [of] education. 教育機会 (an) educational opportunity; (an) opportunity for ʻeducation [schooling]. 教育基準〔国・大学などの〕academic [education(al)] standards; the standards of education《at a college, in a country》. 教育訓練 education and training. 教育訓練費〔企業などが支出する〕education and training expenses; the cost(s) of education and training. 教育雑誌 an education(al) magazine. 教育書 a book ʻon [about] education [pedagogy]. 教育投資 investment in education; educational investment. 教育特区〔構造改革特区の１つ〕a special educational district; a special structural-reform zone for deregulated educational services. ◐ 英語[外国語]～特区 a special district for English-[foreign-]language education / 言語～特区〔日本語・外国語を問わず言葉の教育に力を入れる〕a special district for language education. 教育病院〔研修医を教育する病院〕a teaching hospital. 教育プログラム an educational program. 教育法学 teaching [education(al)] methodology;《study》ʻteaching

methods [methods of education]. 教育目標〔学校などの〕educational 「aims[objectives]. 教育理念 (a) [one's] 「philosophy [idea, concept] of education.
**きょういくかいかくこくみんかいぎ**【教育改革国民会議】the National Commission on Educational Reform.
**きょういくぎじゅつほうそくかうんどう**【教育技術法則化運動】the Teachers' Organization for Skill Sharing (略：TOSS).
**きょういくさいせいかいぎ**【教育再生会議】〔安倍晋三内閣の諮問機関〕the Education Revitalization Council.
**きょういろん**【脅威論】◐東南アジア諸国の間には根強い中国〜がある。There 「is long-standing concern [are deep-seated fears] in the countries of South-East Asia about the threat from China. | People in South-East Asia view China with deep-seated concern. ◐北方脅威論 discussions [theories] about the threat 「from North of Japan [lying to the North of Japan].
**きょういん**【教員】◐教員免許更新制 a teacher's licence recertification system; a renewable teacher's license system.
**きょうえい**¹【共栄】◐共栄植物〖生態・園芸〗〔生育を助け合う、種類の異なる植物〕a companion plant. [=コンパニオン・プランツ]
**きょうえき**【共益】◐共益権〔株主の〕collective benefit-rights. 共益団体 a group organized for the mutual benefit of the members.
**きょうか**³【強化】◐強化委員会〔スポーツなどの〕a training committee. 強化液〔消火器用の〕an alkali-metal salt solution. ◐〜液消火器 a wet chemical fire extinguisher. 強化子〖心理〗a reinforcer. ◐正［負］の〜子 a 「positive [negative] reinforcer. 強化炭素繊維 reinforced carbon fiber. 強化費〔スポーツ選手の強化トレーニング経費〕training costs; a payment for (intensive) training (in a sport, for an event).
**きょうか**⁵【教科】◐教科指導〔教師の評価の一基準として〕teaching efficiency.
**ぎょうが**【仰臥】◐仰臥位分娩 (a) supine delivery; giving birth 「in a supine position [lying down].
**きょうかい**³【教会】◐地下［家庭］教会〔キリスト教の信仰が政府に統制されている国の非公認信者組織〕an underground [a home] church. ◐教会離れ〔教会通いの回数が減ること〕decreasing [a decrease in] church-going;《文》estrangement from [disaffection with] the 「church [Church].
**きょうかい**⁵【境界】◐境界型糖尿病〖医〗borderline diabetes. 境界潤滑 boundary lubrication.
**きょうかい**¹【業界】◐業界地図 a market (share) map; a map of the market. ◐米国の大手スーパーマーケット・チェーンの日本参入により国内スーパーの〜地図が塗り変えられることは必至と見られる。With the entry of large-scale American supermarket chains into Japan, domestic supermarkets face drastic changes to market share. 業界初 the first in the industry. ◐〜初の製品 the first product of its 「kind [type] in the industry;《announce》an industry first. 業界風土 a business culture; the culture《of the construction industry》.
**きょうかく**³【胸郭】◐胸郭出口症候群〖医〗thoracic outlet syndrome (略：TOS).
**きょうがく**¹【共学】◐男女共学化〔男女別教育制の廃止〕abolition of single-sex 「schools [education];〔ある学校を共学校にすること〕changing [a change] to co-education; going co-educational.
**きょうがし**【京菓子】(traditional) Kyoto-style 「confectionery [cakes].
**きょうかしょ**【教科書】◐教科書訴訟〔検定をめぐっての〕a [the] school textbook screening suit.

**きょうかしょむしょうそちほう**【教科書無償措置法】〖法〗⇒むしょうそちほう。
**きょうかようとしょけんていきそく**【教科用図書検定規則】the regulations 「for [governing] the authorization of textbooks.
**きょうかようとしょけんていちょうさしんぎかい**【教科用図書検定調査審議会】〔1950年に旧文部省(現文部科学省)のもとに設置〕the Textbook Authorization and Research Council.
**きょうかん**²【共感】◐共感能力 an [the] ability [capacity] to sympathize《with other people》; a capacity for sympathy.
**きょうかんざい**【強肝剤】a liver strengthener.
**きょうぎ**¹【協議】◐個別協議 independent [separate] negotiations; one-on-one-talks. 全体協議 all-party talks; negotiations involving all (the) parties. ◐協議機関 a 「consulting [consultative] organization [organ].
**きょうぎ**⁵【競技】◐競技人口 the number of people who 「do [take part in] a type of sport or competitive game. ◐日本における馬術の〜人口 the number of people in Japan who take part in riding events; the horsemanship population of Japan. / サッカーの〜人口は年々ふえている。More and more people are playing soccer. | The soccer(-playing) population is growing year by year.
**きょうきゅう**【供給】◐供給調整 (a) supply adjustment; (an) adjustment of supply.（資金）供給予定額〔日銀の資金供給オペにおける〕the planned amount (of funds) to be supplied.
**きょうきゅうかんりきょうかい**【供給管理協会】〔米国の〕⇒ぜんべいきょうきゅうかんりきょうかい。
**きょうぎょう**²【競業】business competition. ◐競業会社［企業］a 「competing [rival] company [corporation]. 競業避止〖労〗non-competition. ◐〜避止義務 a (contractual) duty [an obligation] not to compete; a duty of fidelity / 〜避止条項 a non-competitive[-compete] clause; a covenant not to compete.
**ぎょうきょう**【業況】business conditions; the business climate. ◐業況感 business sentiment. 業況判断 (an) assessment of business conditions.
**ぎょうけいしせつ**【行刑施設】〔刑務所・少年刑務所・拘置所の総称〕a penal institution.
**ぎょうけいしょく**【行刑食】a prison meal.
**きょうけん**⁷【強権】◐強権発動 adoption of a strong official measure; imposition of state power.
**きょうげん**【狂言】◐狂言方(かた) a kyōgen actor.
**きょうけんてき**【強権的】〜な high-handed; overbearing; pushy. ◐〜な政治手法 high-handed political tactics / 行政改革を〜に推し進める push administrative reform through in a high-handed manner.
**ぎょうこ**【凝固】◐凝固止血 coagulation [coagulative] hemostasis. 凝固能〖医〗〔血液の〕coagulability (of the blood).
**きょうこう**²【恐慌】◐恐慌性障害〖精神医〗〔パニック障害〕panic disorder.
**きょうこう**⁵【強行】◐強行突入 (a) forced entry; a raid. ◐特殊部隊がハイジャックされた旅客機に〜した。The special forces 「forced their way [charged] onto the hijacked aircraft.
**きょうこう**⁷【強硬】◐強硬カード〔交渉を有利に運ぶ手段としての〕a tough card. ◐日本に対し〜カードを切る play the tough card with respect to Japan. 強硬戦略 a 「tough [hardline, hawkish] strategy. ◐〜戦術を adopt a hardline strategy. 強硬措置 strong [extreme] measures; drastic 「action [measures].
**きょうこうしば**【強光子場】〖物〗an intense laser field.

⊡ 強光子場科学 intense laser science.
きょうこうはん【強行犯】(a) crime involving the use of force; (a) violent crime; crimes of violence.
ぎょうさい【業際】 ⊡ 業際的な interindustry; inter-industrial; cross-industry; multi-industry. 業際ビジネス (a) 「cross-industry [multi-industry]」business.
「恐妻天国」〔米国の、原始時代の家族によるホームコメディーのTVアニメ〕The Flintstones. ▶ 邦題は「原始家族フリントストーン」「行け行けバンバン恐竜天国」ともされた。
きょうさく³【狭窄】 ⊡ 再狭窄《医》restenosis.
きょうさつ【挟殺】 ⊡ 挟殺プレー《野球》a rundown play.
きょうさん²【協賛】 ⊡ 協賛企業 a supporting 「company [corporation]; a supporting sponsor (company). 協賛金《pay》a supporting sponsorship fee; financial sponsorship (contributed by a supporting company).
きょうさんとう【共産党】 ⊡ 共産党中央委員会〔日本共産党の〕the Central Committee of the Japanese Communist Party; the Japanese Communist Party Central Committee. ◐～中央委員会総会 a general meeting of the Central Committee of the Japanese Communist Party.
きょうじ⁶【挟持】〔両側から挟んで固定すること〕clamping. ～する secure (from both sides); clamp; grapple.
ぎょうしゃ【業者】 ⊡ 無登録業者 ⊡〔闇金融業者など〕an 「unregistered [unauthorized]《lender》. ⊡ 業者委託 outsourcing《to another company》; contracting (work) to an outside company.
きょうしゅう²【教習】 ⊡ 合宿[泊]教習〔運転免許を取得するための〕(intensive) driving instruction on a residential course; 《take》a residential driving course. 技能教習〔自動車教習所での〕driving practice (at a driving school); in-car 「training [instruction]」 (at a driving school). 学科教習〔自動車教習所での〕theoretical [classroom] instruction (for the driving test). ⊡ 教習射撃 shooting instruction (for obtaining a gun license). 教習生 a person undergoing 「instruction [training]」; a trainee; a learner.
ぎょうしゅう【凝集】 ⊡ 凝集体《化》an aggregate.
ぎょうしゅく【凝縮】 ⊡ 凝縮水 condensed [condensate] water.
きょうしょう³【狭小】 ⊡ 狭小住宅 a compact 「residence [home]」《集合的に》compact housing.
きょうしょう⁷【競翔】pigeon racing. ⊡ 競翔鳩 a racing pigeon; a racer.
きょうしょきょうふしょう【狭所恐怖症】《精神医》stenophobia; a (pathological) fear of narrow spaces.
きょうしょく【教職】 ⊡ 教職大学院 a 「graduate [post-graduate]」teacher training school.
きょうしょく²【共食】〔孤食に対して〕eating together [sharing meals] with others. ～する eat together [share meals] with others.
きょうしん¹【共振】 ⊡ 共振現象《物》〔地震時の巨大構造物の〕building resonance.
きょうしんしゅう【強侵襲】《医》high invasiveness. ⊡ 強侵襲手術[医療] (a) highly invasive 「surgery [medical treatment]」.
きょうしんしょう【狭心症】 ◐ 微小血管(性)狭心症 microvascular angina.
きょうしんどう【強震動】《地震》strong (ground) motion. ⊡ 強震動地震学 strong motion seismology. 強震動予測 (a) strong motion prediction.
きょうすい【胸水】 ⊡ 人工胸水《医》artificial pleural effusion.
きょうせい【共生】 ⊡ 共生(細)菌 a symbiotic bacterium《pl. -ria》.
きょうせい³【強制】 ⊡ 強制執行妨害罪《法》obstruction of compulsory execution. 強制退去者〔集合住宅などからの〕an evictee;〔国外への〕a deportee. ◐～退去者リスト〔入国管理局の〕a list of deportees. ⊡《法》〔主に、児童虐待家庭への警察の〕(the right of) forcible entry. 強制立ち退き (a) 「forced [mandatory]」expulsion [eviction, evacuation]. 強制調査〔税務当局による〕(a) compulsory inspection; a compulsory search. ◐～調査権 the right to make a compulsory inspection. 強制売春 forced prostitution. 強制排除 forced [enforced, compulsory] expulsion. 準強制猥褻罪《法》(an) indecent 「(a) sexual」assault against a person who cannot offer resistance (due to sleep, inebriation, etc.).
きょうせい⁹【矯正】
⊡ O脚矯正 correction of bowlegs. 小顔矯正 facial correction to reduce the size of the face. 骨盤矯正 pelvic correction. 美容矯正 cosmetic correction. ⊡ 矯正行政 correctional administration. 矯正処遇〔受刑者に対する〕correctional treatment. ◐～処遇官 a correctional treatment officer. 矯正展〔受刑者の矯正状況を紹介する広報的催し〕an exhibition of prison life and articles made by prisoners (as part of a campaign to encourage understanding and reform). 矯正不能, 矯正不可能 incorrigibility; incurability; irredeemability. ◐～不(可)能な〔犯罪者などが〕incorrigible;〔歯列などが〕incorrectable. 矯正労働〔be sentenced to〕corrective labor.
ぎょうせい¹【行政】 ⊡ 後追い行政 follow-up [catch-up] administration. 予防(的)行政 proactive administration. ⊡ 行政規則 an administrative regulation. 行政経費〔一般行政事務に必要な人件費及び事務費の合計〕administrative expenses. 行政コスト administration [administrative] costs; the cost(s) of《local government》administration. ◐～コスト(の)削減 (a) reduction of administration costs; reducing the costs of《local government》administration. 行政コスト計算書 a (written) statement of《local government》administration costs. 行政職〔地位・職種〕《work in》administration; an administrative 「post [position, job, career]」; administrative work. ◐一般～職 an ordinary administrative post / 専門～職 an administrative post (in a Japanese Ministry, etc.) for a person with specialist skills. 行政制裁《法》an administrative sanction. 行政対象暴力 intimidation [coercion] of public officials. 行政手続き《法》(an) administrative procedure. 行政(の)不作為《法》(an) administrative omission. 行政評価 (an) 「administration [administrative]」evaluation. 行政文書 an administrative document.
ぎょうせいかいかくすいしんほう【行政改革推進法】《法》the Administrative Reform Promotion Law. ▶ 正式名称は「簡素で効率的な政府を実現するための行政改革の推進に関する法律」(the Law Concerning Promotion of Administrative Reform to Bring about a Simple and Efficient Government).
ぎょうせいかんりよさんきょく【行政管理予算局】《米》〔大統領直属の補佐機関〕the Office of Management and Budget (略: OMB).
ぎょうせいしゃかい【共生社会】a tolerant pluralistic society. ⊡ 多文化共生社会 a multicultural society. 多民族共生社会 a tolerant, multi-ethnic society; a society in which different ethnic groups can live peacefully together. 男女共生社会 a gender-equal society.
ぎょうせいてきしっそうぼうしじょうやく【強制的失踪防止条約】〔国連の〕the Convention for the Protection of All Persons from Enforced Disappearances.
ぎょうせいてつづきオンラインかかんけいさんぽう【行政手続-化関係三法】《法》the three laws for provid-

## ぎょうせいてつづきオンライン

ing online administrative procedures. ► 正式には次の三法をいう:「行政手続等における情報通信の技術の利用に関する法律」(the Law Concerning the Use of Information and Telecommunications Technology on Administrative Procedures); 通称「行政手続オンライン化法」(the Online Administrative Procedures Law), 「行政手続等における情報通信の技術の利用に関する法律の施行に伴う関係法律の整備等に関する法律」(the Law Concerning Preparation of Related Laws for Enforcing Online Administrative Procedures Law); 通称「整備法」(Preparation Law), 「電子署名に係る地方公共団体の認証業務に関する法律」(the Law Concerning Digital Signature Certification of Local Public Entity); 通称「公的個人認証法」(the Public Individual Certification Law).

**ぎょうせいてつづきオンラインかほう**【行政手続−化法】〘法〙⇨ぎょうせいてつづきオンラインかかんりさんぽう.

**ぎょうせいひょうかほう**【行政評価法】〘法〙=せいさくひょうかほう.

**ぎょうせき**[2]【業績】 ▫️ 業績開示〔企業の〕disclosure of [business [performance]] results 《for the current year》. 業績改善 (a) business performance [an earnings] improvement; (an) improvement in [business performance [(business) results, earnings]. ●社長は来年度の−改善に自信を見せた. The president expressed confidence that business performance would improve in the coming year. 業績回復 (an) improvement in [results [performance]; a (business) recovery (in results). ●自動車業界の最近の−回復はめざましい. Business results have been recovering dramatically in the car industry recently. 業績向上 improvement in (business) performance. 業績説明会〔経営者側による株主などへの〕a results briefing. 業績低迷 (a) poor (business) performance; 《get, show》poor (business) results; a [slump [prolonged downturn] in business performance. ●彼は−低迷の責任を取って社長を辞任した. He resigned as president to take responsibility for the company's sluggish business performance. 業績目標 《set, achieve》a business performance [an earnings] target. 業績連動(型)賞与 a 《company》productivity-linked bonus (for employees); a 《company》results-related bonus. 業績連動(型)配当 a performance-linked dividend; a dividend linked to 《company》[productivity [performance]. 業績連動(型)報酬 productivity-linked remuneration; remuneration linked to [productivity [《company》performance]. ●連動(型)役員報酬 productivity-linked remuneration for [directors [executives, board members].

**きょうそ**【教祖】 ▫️ 教祖的(な) guru-like; founding 《father》. ●彼は若い登山家の−的存在だ. He is a founding-father figure for young mountaineers.

**きょうそう**[4]【競争】 ▫️ 競争的研究資金 the competitive research fund. 競争入札妨害 《be charged with》obstructing competitive bidding.

**きょうそう**[7]【協奏】〘音楽〙playing together. 〜する play together in [harmony [concert] (with…).

**きょうぞう**[3]【鏡像】 ▫️ 鏡像印刷〘印刷〙mirror-image printing. [=左右反転印刷〘⇨さゆう〙].

**きょうそうほう**【競争法】〘法〙competition law.

**きょうそうりょくひょうぎかい**【競争力評価会】〔米国の〕the Council on Competitiveness.

**きょうそく**[4]【京速】=けいそく[2].

**きょうぞく**[2]【共属】 ▫️ 共属意識 a shared sense of belonging; a consciousness of belonging to the same group. 共属感(情) shared emotions of belonging; a feeling of belonging to the same group.

**きょうそん, きょうぞん**【共存】 ▫️ 共存指数 an NQ; a network quotient. [⇨エヌ・キュー] 共存形態 (a system of) coexistence; a coexistence regime. ●平和〜体制 (a system of) peaceful coexistence / 民放と NHK との〜体制 a system of coexistence between NHK and commercial broadcasting companies.

**ぎょうたい**【業態】 ▫️ 業態転換 converting a business to a different type; 《carry out》a (business) conversion.

**きょうちょう**[2]【協調】 ▫️ 協調行動 (a) concerted action. ●市場を安定させるために日米欧が〜行動を取らなくてはだめだ. Japan, the United States and Europe must take concerted action to stabilize the market.

**きょうちょく**【強直】 ▫️ 強直間代発作〘医〙a [tonic-clonic [grand mal] seizure.

**きょうつう**[1]【共通】 ▫️ 共通効果特恵関税 a common effective preferential tariff (略: CEPT). 共通重心〘天〙a barycenter; the center of mass. 共通逮捕状〔EU 内の〕a European arrest warrant. 共通認識 《reach, have》a [common [shared] understanding 《about…》;《have》a [common [shared] awareness 《of…》. 共通理解 《reach》a [common [shared] understanding 《of [about] sth》. ●行政と住民はこの件に関しての〜を図るために話し合いを重ねる必要がある. The government and local residents need to hold frequent talks in order to reach a common understanding about this matter.

**きょうづくえ**【経机】a sutra desk; a sutra table.

**きょうど**[2]【強度】 ▫️ 強度偽装〘機械・建築物などの〙(a) fraudulent description of the strength (of a building). 強度計算〘構造物などの〙intensity [strength] calculation. 強度実験 a strength experiment. 強度変調放射線治療〘医〙intensity modulated radiation therapy (略: IMRT).

**きょうど**[4]【郷土】 ▫️ 郷土意識 local [consciousness [awareness]; a sense of one's local roots.

**きょうどう**[1]【共同】 ▫️ 共同危険行為〘法〙dangerous driving in tandem with [another vehicle [other vehicles]. 共同漁業水域 a joint [fishing [fishery] zone; a common fishing zone. 共同訓練 《hold》a joint military exercise. 共同実施〔京都メカニズムの 1 つ〕joint implementation (略: JI). ●〜実施活動 activities implemented jointly (略: AIJ). 共同推薦 a joint recommendation. ●〜推薦する recommend sb [jointly [together] / 入会には会員 2 名の〜推薦が必要です. To join, you must [receive a joint recommendation from [be recommended by] two members. 共同調達〔商品・原材などの〕joint procurement. 共同統合運用調整所〔在日米軍と自衛隊との〕the (Bilateral) Joint Operations Coordination Center (略: BJOCC). 共同配送 (a) joint delivery; joint distribution. 共同文書〔外交上などの〕a joint [document [statement].

**きょうどう**[5]【教導】 ▫️ 教導隊〘自衛隊〙a training group. ●飛行〜隊 a fighter training group.

**きょうどう**[8]【協働】collaboration; cooperation; (joint) participation. ▫️ 市民協働 citizen participation 《in local planning》; participation by citizens 《in local planning》. 協働契約栽培 contract cultivation as a collaborative venture. 協働事業 a [collaborative [cooperative] project.

**きょうどうくみあいによるきんゆうじぎょうにかんするほうりつ**【協同組合による金融事業に関する法律】〘法〙the Law Concerning Financial Business by Co-operatives.

**きょうどうけっていほう**【共同決定法】〘ドイツ法〙[1976 年制定の, 従業員の企業経営参加を定めた法律] the Co-determination Law.

**きょうどうさいこうけいえいせきにんしゃ**【共同最高経営責任者】a Co-Chief Executive Officer; a Co-

CEO.
きょうどうしゅっし【共同出資】(a) joint investment; a joint contribution; pooling of funds. 〜する make a joint 「investment (in…) [contribution 《to…》]; pool funds 《for…》. ◨ 共同出資会社 a joint venture (company, corporation).
きょうとうしょう【狭頭症】【医】leptocephalia; leptocephaly. ▷ leptocephalous adj.
きょうとぎていしょ【京都議定書】◨ 京都議定書目標達成計画 the Kyoto Protocol Target Achievement Plan.
きょうどく【強毒】【医】〔ウイルスなどの〕strong [high] virulence; 〔毒液などの〕strong [high] toxicity. ◯ マフグの皮や腸は〜だ. The purple puffer's skin and intestines are strongly toxic. ◨ 強毒ウイルス a highly virulent virus. 強毒化 ◯ 〜化する become highly 「virulent [toxic]. 強毒型の highly 「virulent [toxic]. ◯ 〜型の鳥インフルエンザ 《an outbreak of》 highly virulent avian influenza.
きょうどくせい【強毒性】acute [high] toxicity. ◯ 〜の highly [acutely] toxic; highly poisonous.
きょうとしょう【京都賞】〔世界の科学, 文明の発展に貢献した人に贈られる〕the 《2005》 Kyoto Prize.
きょうとだいがくかがくけんきゅうじょ【京都大学化学研究所】the Institute for Chemical Research, Kyoto University.
きょうとだいがくこくさいゆうごうそうぞうセンター【京都大学国際融合創造-】(the) Kyoto University International Innovation Center (略: KU-IIC).
きょうとだいがくれいちょうるいけんきゅうじょ【京都大学霊長類研究所】⇒れいちょうるいけんきゅうじょ.
きょうどほうえいぎゆうぐん【郷土防衛義勇軍】【史】〔日本占領下で日本軍が創設した, インドネシア人だけの軍事組織〕the Sukarela Tentara Pembela Tanah Air. ▶ 通称は ペタ (the PETA).
きょうとメカニズム【京都-】【国連気候変動枠組み条約の京都議定書で定めた, 温室効果ガス削減のために各国間で行う社会的仕組み〕the Kyoto Mechanism.
きょうばい【競売】◨ 競売入札妨害(罪)【法】interference with [obstruction of] a public auction or tender. ◯ 威力〜 入札妨害(罪) forcible interference with a public auction or tender; intimidation of bidders at a public auction or tender. 競売物件 (a) property sold at auction; auctioned 《houses》.
きょうはく¹【脅迫】◨ 脅迫メール (a) threatening e-mail.
きょうはく³【強迫】◨ 強迫性障害【精神医】〔強迫観念・強迫行為の反復・持続を特徴とする精神障害〕an obsessive-compulsive disorder (略: OCD).
きょうふ¹【恐怖】◨ 恐怖スポット〔心霊スポット〕⇒しんれい. 恐怖体験 a 「frightening [horrific] experience.
きょうふ³【胸部】◨ 胸部圧迫感 a feeling of pressure in the chest.
きょうふう¹【強風】◨ 強風波浪高潮注意報 a gale, high-waves and storm surge advisory.
きょうふしょう【恐怖症】◨ 音恐怖症 phonophobia.
きょうほう³【僑胞】〔中国語・朝鮮語で「国外に住む同胞」の意〕a Chinese [Korean] resident abroad; an overseas 「Chinese [Korean].
きょうぼう¹【共謀】◨ 共謀罪【法】the [a] crime of conspiracy.
きょうまく¹【胸膜】◨ 胸膜がん【医】(a) pleural cancer; (a) cancer of the pleura. 胸膜肥厚【医】pleural thickening. ◯ びまん性〜肥厚【医】diffuse pleural thickening.
きょうまく²【強膜・鞏膜】◨ 強膜内陥術【眼科】scleral burkling surgery; a scleral buckling procedure.
きょうむ【教務】◨ 教務委員会 an academic affairs committee; a committee 「on [for] academic affairs.

ぎょうむ【業務】
◨ 業務粗利益 gross operating profit(s) (略: GOP). 業務委託 outsourcing; subcontracting. ◯ 〜委託契約 an outsourcing [a subcontracting] contract / 〜委託費 outsourcing [subcontracting] costs / 運用〜委託 outsourcing [subcontracting] management fee. 業務請負 undertaking [taking on] outsourced [contracted] work. 業務請負会社 an outsourcing company. 業務概況 the business outlook; (general) business conditions; the (general) business situation. 業務概況書 a report on 「the business outlook [business conditions]. 業務改善 business improvement. 業務改善勧告〔監督官庁の〕business improvement 「advice [instructions]. 業務改善計画〔銀行が金融庁へ提出する〕(submit) a business improvement 「program [plan]. 業務改善指示〔監督官庁の〕business improvement advisory. 業務改善報告書〔業務改善命令を受けた団体が, その命令を実行した結果を監督官庁に報告する書類〕a report on improvements implemented (in a business). 業務改善命令〔監督官庁が出す指導の一種〕a business improvement order. 業務拡大 (a) business expansion. 業務核都市〔東京への産業や人口の集中を防ぐために都市機能を強化整備された首都圏の中核的な都市〕a core business city. 業務協力協定 a business cooperation agreement. 業務継続計画 = 緊急時事業継続計画 (⇒きんきゅうじ). 業務形態 a form of business; a mode of business operations; a way of doing business. 業務効率《improve》business efficiency. 業務効率化 improving business efficiency. 業務災害 (an) occupational sickness, injury or death. 業務従事命令〔有事の際に自衛隊や医師・鉄道事業者などに出す協力要請〕an emergency mobilization order. 業務上過失往来妨害罪【法】obstruction of traffic through negligent conduct in breach of duty of care. 業務上失火罪【法】(be accused of) allowing a fire to break out through professional negligence; professional negligence leading to a fire. 業務職 special [specialist] work; a specialist 「job [position]. 業務遂行能力〔an employee's〕business ability. 業務ソフト【電算】business software (programs). 業務提供誘引販売取引〔仕事を斡旋するとしてそれに必要な機器などを売りつける商法〕a business offer soliciting sales transaction. 業務提携 ◨ 包括(的)〜提携 a comprehensive business 「alliance [tie-up]. 業務用ゲーム〔家庭用ゲームに対して, アーケードゲーム〕a commercial game; an arcade game. ◯ 〜用ゲーム機 a commercial game machine. 業務(用)販売 selling [sales] to businesses. ◯ 〜(用)販売店 an outlet for businesses.
ぎょうむばいしょうせきにんほけん【業務賠償責任保険】business liability insurance. ◨ IT 業務賠償責任保険 liability insurance for IT companies. 医療業務賠償責任保険 liability insurance for the medical profession.
きょうめい¹【共鳴】◨ 共鳴弦〔楽器の〕a sympathetic string.
きょうめつ【共滅】coextinction. ◯ 核兵器の使用による人類〜 the annihilation of the human race through the use of nuclear weapons.
きょうめん²【鏡面】◨ 鏡面加工【金属加工】mirror (surface) finishing. 鏡面仕上げ a mirror finish.
きょうやく²【共役・共軛】◨ 共役断層【地質】⇒だんそう³.
きょうやさい【京野菜】Kyoto vegetables; vegetables traditionally grown in and around Kyoto.
きょうゆう¹【共有】◨「共有地の悲劇」【環境】〔米国の生物学者 G・ハーディンが 1986 年『サイエンス』誌に発表した論文; 共有の資源は濫用されがちで, その濫用が資源を枯渇させてしまうと説いている〕The Tragedy of Commons.

◐反～地の悲劇〔共有されるべき資源なのに，所有権者が他者に使わせないことによって生じる悲劇〕the tragedy of the anticommons. ▶G・ハーディンの「共有地の悲劇」と対称的な概念.

きょうゆうでん【強誘電】▫️▫️強誘電体メモリー (a) ferroelectric memory.

きょうよう¹【共用】▫️▫️共用機〔複数の波長などに対応できる機械〕a「multipurpose [multifunction, multistandard] machine [device];〔職場などで個人専用でなく多数の人が使える機械〕a shared machine.

きょうよう²【供用】▫️▫️供用性〔道路などの〕performance.

きょうよう⁴【教養】▫️▫️教養娯楽〔家計簿の費目名など〕culture and entertainment.

ぎょうよう【業容】▫️▫️業容拡大 an increase in the scale and activities of「a business [an undertaking].

きょうようひんしんこうきこう【共用品推進機構】the Kyoyo-hin Foundation(, a foundation for the promotion of common use goods).

きょうりしょう【教理省】〖カトリック〗〔教皇庁の〕the Congregation for the Doctrine of the Faith;（一般に）the Holy Office.

「恐竜家族」〔米国の，擬人化された恐竜によるTVホームコメディ〕Dinosaurs.

きょうりょく¹【協力】▫️▫️協力協定 a cooperation agreement 《on drug trafficking》.

きょうろう²【経楼】a tower for housing Buddhist scriptures.

きょうわとう【共和党】▫️▫️共和党大会〔米国の〕the Republican National Convention.

きょうわぶん【共和文】〘経〙cointegration.

きょか¹【炬火】▫️▫️炬火台〔競技場の〕a flame platform.

きょか²【許可】▫️▫️許可事業 a government-licensed「business [enterprise].

ぎょかい【魚介】▫️▫️魚介類感染症 infections in aquatic animals.

ぎょかく【漁獲】▫️▫️漁獲可能量 a total allowable catch（略: TAC）．漁獲規制 a「fishing [catch] restriction．漁獲枠＝漁獲可能量．

きょぎ【虚偽】▫️▫️虚偽記載[記入]forging [faking] an entry《in a statement》; a「forged [fake, counterfeit] entry《in a report》. 政治資金収支報告書の～記載は政治資金規正法違反となる．Forging an entry in a political funding report constitutes an infringement of the Political Funds Control Law. 虚偽報告 a「false [mendacious] report. 虚偽有印公文書作成〘法〙〔有印公文書偽造〕forgery of an official document with signature or seal.

ぎょぎょう【漁業】▫️▫️漁業管轄権 fisheries [fishery] jurisdiction; jurisdiction of fishing《for crab》．漁業共済保険 Fishery Mutual Aid Insurance. 漁業振興 fishery「promotion [development]．～振興費 the cost of「promoting [developing] fishing; fishery promotion costs. 漁業調整 fisheries coordination. ◐～調整規則 rules [regulations] for fisheries coordination / ～調整規則ライン〔北海道近海の日ロの〕a line defined by「rules [regulations] for fisheries coordination / ～調整事務所 a fisheries coordination office. 漁業被害 damage to「fishery [fishing]．漁業補償 compensation to「fishermen [the (local) fishing industry]; fisheries compensation. ◐～補償交渉 negotiations on compensation to fishermen / ～補償 money for [the cost of, expenses for] compensation to fishermen.

きょく³【極】▫️▫️極循環〘気象〙〔大気大循環の一種〕the Polar cell.

ぎょく¹【玉】▫️▫️見せ玉〖取引〗＝みせたま．

ぎょくい【玉衣】〔古代中国の貴人の葬服〕a shroud of jade plates sewn together.

きょくげん³【極限】▫️▫️極限環境 an extreme environment. 極限環境生物圏 an [the] extreme biosphere. 極限環境微生物 an extremophilic microorganism.

きょくしゃ²【局舎】an office;〔電話会社の〕an exchange.

きょくしょ【局所】▫️▫️局所所見〘医〙local [regional, topographical] findings. 局所治療〔局所療法〕a「local [topical] remedy.

きょくしょう¹【極小】▫️▫️極小モデル〘数〙a minimal model.

きょくすい【曲水】＝ごくすい．

きょくせん¹【曲線】▫️▫️右[左]曲線〘鉄道〙〔右[左]にカーブする線路〕a「right-[left-]turning curve; a「right [left] bend．平面曲線〘数〙a plane curve．▫️▫️曲線半径〔土木・鉄道〕a curve radius.

きょくせん³【曲先】〘音楽〙〔先に曲ができて後から歌詞をはめこむ製作方法〕(composing) music first (and lyrics second).

きょくだい【極大】▫️▫️極大地震動 (the) maximum seismic intensity.

きょくち¹【局地】▫️▫️局地激甚災害 a devastating「localized [local] disaster; a devastating disaster in a restricted locality. 局地戦 localized fighting; a localized battle. 局地的豪雨 torrential rain(s) in a restricted area; torrential local(ized) rain.

きょくち²【極地】▫️▫️極地研究 polar research.

きょくちょう²【局長】▫️▫️局長級会談[協議]a conference [discussions] at (the) directorial level; a director-level conference. ◐日米～級会談 Japan-US bureau-chief-level talks / 3カ国外務省～級協議 a three-nation foreign ministry conference at the bureau-chief level

きょくとう¹【極東】▫️▫️極東条項〔日米安全保障条約第6条の通称〕the Far East clause.

きょくとうさいばん【極東裁判】〔極東国際軍事裁判〕the International Military Tribunal for the Far East.

きょくとうさそり【極東蠍】〘動〙a Chinese scorpion; Buthus martensii. ▫️▫️キョクトウサソリ科 Buthidae.

きょくめん²【局面】▫️▫️拡大[縮小]局面〘経〙〔景気・生産・雇用・投資などの〕an expansionary [a reduction] phase. 後退局面〘経〙〔景気などの〕a sluggish phase.

きょけつ【虚血】▫️▫️虚血性腸炎 ischemic enteritis.

ぎょこうぎょじょうせいびほう【漁港漁場整備法】〘法〙the Law for the Upkeep and Maintenance of Fishing Ports and Fishing Grounds.

きょこん¹【巨根】▫️▫️巨根信仰〔崇拝〕(the) worship of large phalluses.

きょさいぼう【巨細胞】〖生物〗a giant cell. ▫️▫️巨細胞性動脈炎〘医〙giant cell arteritis.〔=側頭動脈炎（⇨そくと う⁴）〕巨細胞性肺炎〘医〙giant cell pneumonia. 巨細胞肉芽腫〘医〙a giant cell granuloma（pl. ～s, -mata）．

きょじゅう²【居住】▫️▫️居住確認 confirmation of residence [that sb lives《in [at]…》]．居住費〔介護施設利用者の〕a「residential [residence] fee.

ぎょしゅこうたい【魚種交替[交代]】〔ある海域に生息する魚の種類が入れ替わり増減すること〕fish species replacement; (1回の現象) a fish species replacement.

きょしゅつ【拠出】▫️▫️拠出金 donated money; a monetary donation. ◐国連～金《Japan's》contribution to the UN [UN contribution]．拠出建て年金 a「defined [fixed] contribution(s) pension plan.

ぎょしょう²【魚礁】▫️▫️浮(き)魚礁 a fish aggregating device（略: FAD）．

ぎょじょう【漁場】▫️▫️好漁場 a good fishing「place [spot]．◐ワタリガニの好～ a good place to catch swimming crab.

ぎょしょく¹【魚食】▫️▫️魚食性鳥類 a「fish-eating [piscivorous] bird.

きょじん・たいほう・たまごやき【巨人・大鵬・卵焼き】〔1960年代，子供の好きなもの・あこがれの代名詞〕the Gi-

ants, Taihō, and omelette loaf; the Giants baseball team, sumo wrestler Taihō, and omelette loaf, representing the favorite items of children in the 1960s.
「巨人の惑星」〔宇宙船が巨人の住む星に不時着する，米国のTVドラマ〕Land of the Giants.
きょせい² 【去勢】 □□ 化学的[薬物]去勢 〔ホルモン投与などにより一時的に去勢する；主にヨーロッパや米国での性犯罪者に対する刑罰〕chemical castration.
ぎょせん 【漁船】 □□ 漁船再保険 fishing「vessel [boat]」reinsurance.
ぎょそう² 【魚倉】 a 〔ship's〕 fish hold.
ぎょそう³ 【魚巣】 〔魚の産卵・繁殖をうながすための装置〕an artificial spawning ground 《for herring》.
きょだい 【巨大】 □□ 巨大児 〔出生体重が4,000g以上の〕an excessively large「baby [infant]」; a newborn weighing over 4,000 grams; 〖医〗a (case of) macrosomia; a macrosomic baby. 巨大衝突説 〖天〗〔月の起源についての〕the giant impact theory.
きょだいか 【巨大化】 growth to「great [huge, immense]」size; huge [immense] growth.
〜する grow huge; expand to immense size. ● 中国経済の〜 the immense growth of the Chinese economy; China's expansion into an economic giant. □□ 巨大化傾向 a tendency toward great size; 〖医〗giantism; gigantism.
きょたく 【居宅】
□□ 居宅介護 home(-based) [in-home, at-home] care; care [nursing] in「the [one's own] home」; care [nursing] at (one's) home. 居宅介護支援事業 a home-care support「service [business, scheme]」. ● 〜介護支援事業者 a home-care support (service) provider. 居宅サービス介護事業 a home care service provider. 居宅生活支援事業 a「home help [domestic support]」service (operation). ● 精神障害者〜生活支援事業 a home help service for the mentally handicapped / 難病患者〜生活支援事業 a home help service for people with serious diseases / 老人〜生活支援事業 a home health care service for the old. 居宅療養管理指導 at-home health care management and guidance.
キョッポ 【僑胞】〔朝鮮語で「国外に住む同胞」の意〕a Korean resident abroad; an overseas Korean.
きょてん 【拠点】 □□ 国際拠点 an international「stronghold [hub]」《of research and development》. □□ 拠点集約 base [location] consolidation.
きょにんか 【許認可】 □□ 許認可事業 a business [an undertaking, an enterprise, an activity] requiring「recognition [permission]」and a license from the government.
キョポ ⇨キョッポ.
きょよう 【許容】 □□ 許容応力度(等)計算 〖建〗〔耐震強度計算法〕allowable stress calculation. 許容応力度設計 〖建〗allowable stress design; working stress design. 許容字体 〔人名用漢字の〕a permitted character variant.
「距離の暴虐」〔G・ブレイニー著のオーストラリア史論〕The Tyranny of Distance.
キョンヒグン 【慶熙宮】〔韓国，ソウルにある宮殿；史跡〕the Gyeonghui Palace; Gyeonghuigung.
キョンボックン 【景福宮】〔韓国，ソウルにある李朝の王宮〕the「Gyeonbok [Kyongbok] Palace; Gyeongbokgung.
キラー □□ キラー海藻 〖植〗〔温帯で大量発生して生態系を破壊する熱帯・亜熱帯の海藻〕(a) killer「seaweed [weed]」. キラー・パルス 〖地震〗〔地震に伴う長周期パルス波〕a「killer pulse」; a seismic wave with a frequency of two to three seconds which renders structures more vulnerable to subsequent longer-frequency waves.
ギラーミン Guillermin, John (1925- ；英国生まれの映画監督).

ギラーン =ギラン.
ギラファのこぎりくわがた 【-鋸鍬形】 〖昆〗〔東南アジアに広く分布する，大型のノコギリクワガタ〕a giraffe stag beetle; *Prosopocoilus giraffa*.
キラル □□ キラル高分子 a chiral polymer. キラル・テクノロジー 〖化〗chiral technology.
ギラン 〔イラン北西部，カスピ海沿岸の州〕Guilan.
ギラン・バレーしょうこうぐん 【-症候群】 〖医〗the Guillain-Barré syndrome.
ぎり 【義理】 □□ 義理返し giving a present「in exchange for [by way of thanks for]」a present one has received; giving sb a return gift. ● 隣人がしょっちゅういろいろなものをくれるので，一返しに何かあげなければ気が済まなくなってしまったのだ。The people next door keep giving us things, so we felt we「really had to [were duty-bound to]」give them something in return.
ギリアム Gilliam, Terry (1940- ；米国の映画監督・俳優；本名 Terry Vance Gilliam).
きりえ 【切り絵】 □□ 切り絵画家[作家] a paper-cutting artist.
きりかね，きりがね 【截金・切金】 1 〔金銀を伸ばした薄い板〕gold [silver] foil.
2 〔金銀箔を糸状や三角・四角・眉形などの細片に切って工芸品に貼り，文様を表す技法〕gold [silver] foil craft; gold [silver] overlaying; decoration (of lacquerware) with shapes cut out of「gold [silver] foil. □□ 截金師 a gold foil worker; a *kirikane* craftsman.
きりがみ 【切り紙】 □□ 切り紙絵 〔色紙を切り抜き紙に貼りつけて表現するもの〕a (cut-out) collage.
「ギリガン君SOS」〔米国の，無人島漂着者たちのどたばたTVコメディー〕Gilligan's Island.
きりくしゃ 【軌陸車】 〖鉄道〗=軌道道路兼用作業車 (⇨きどう²).
キリシタン □□ キリシタン大名 〖日本史〗a Christian「daimyo [feudal lord]」.
きりしまみどりしじみ 【霧島緑蜆】 〖昆〗〔シジミチョウ科のチョウ〕*Chrysozephyrus ataxus*.
キリストきょう 【-教】 □□ キリスト教右派 〈集合的に〉the Christian Right. キリスト教右派 the Christian Right.
キリストきょうしゃかいどうめい 【-教社会同盟】 〔ドイツの政党，バイエルン州が拠点〕the Christian Social Union (in Bavaria); Christlich-Soziale Union (in Bayern) (略：CSU).
キリストきょう(と)れんごう 【-教(徒)連合】〔米国のキリスト教団体〕the Christian Coalition.
キリストきょうほうそうもう 【-教放送網】〔米国に本部を置くケーブルテレビの番組提供組織〕the Christian Broadcasting Network (略：CBN).
キリストしゃれんごう 【-者連合】 =キリストきょう(と)れんごう.
きりつ² 【規律】 □□ 規律委員会 a disciplinary committee.
キリノッチ 〔スリランカ北部の都市〕Kilinochchi.
キリム 〔中央アジア・中近東などの遊牧民に伝わる平織りの織物〕a「kilim [kelim]」(rug [carpet]).
きりよけ (びさし) 【霧除け(庇)】〔雨などを防ぐために窓や出入口の上に張り出した小さい庇〕a「window [door] hood [awning]」.
「キリング・ミー・ソフトリー」〔映画〕Killing Me Softly.
キルギスこくみんうんどう 【-国民運動】〔キルギスのバキエフ氏を党首とする野党連合〕the National Movement of Kyrgyzstan.
キルキラス Kirkilas, Gediminas (1951- ；リトアニアの政治家；首相〔2006- 〕).
キルクディクディク 〖動〗〔アフリカ産レイヨウの一種〕a Kirk's dik-dik; *Madoqua kirkii*.
キルスイッチ 〖機・自動車〗〔機械[機関]の作動を停止させるスイッチ〕an engine kill switch; (自動車の) an ignition

キルター cut-off switch.
キルター [キルトの作り手] a quilter.
キルチネル Kirchner, Néstor (Carlos) (1950-    ; アルゼンチンの政治家；大統領 [2003-   ]).
キルト² [2枚の布の間に綿・毛・羽などをはさんで刺し縫いしたもの] a quilt. ◐ ～の壁掛け a hanging quilt.
ギルバート Gilbert, Lewis (1920-    ; 英国の映画監督).
キルパトリック Kilpatrick, William Heard (1871-1965; 米国の教育学者).
キルビーとっきょ【—特許】〖電気〗〖半導体集積回路に関する特許〗 a [the] Kilby patent. ▶ 米国の物理学者 Jack St. Clair Kilby (1923-2005) にちなむ.
「キル・ビル」［映画］Kill Bill. ▶ 続編は「キル・ビル Vol.2」(Kill Bill: VOL. 2).
キルマー Kilmer, Val (1959-    ; 米国の映画俳優; 本名 Val Edward Kilmer).
きれ【切れ】
6 [さらっとして後に残らない口あたり] dryness; (a) lack of aftertaste. ◐ このビールはコクがあり、～もよい. This beer is full-bodied and has little aftertaste.
7 [付着しているもののとれ具合] ◐ この洗剤は泡の～がよい. This detergent loses its suds quickly. ◐ 痰(たん)の～をよくする飴 candy that improves phlegm removal.
8 [目尻の切れ込み] the outside「slit [end] (of an eye).
きれい² 【機齢】[航空機や機械の稼動年数] the age of「an aircraft [a machine]. ◻□ 平均機齢 [航空会社1社が保有する全航空機の] the average aircraft age.
きれいいろ【きれい色】[華やかな感じの色][引き立てる色] one's best color.
「きれいなおかあさん」［映画］Breaking the Silence; [中国語タイトル] 漂亮媽媽.
キレート 【—療法】〖医〗chelation therapy.
きれこ【切れ子】[たらこの] broken [split(-sac)] cod roe; cod roe with split sacs.
ぎれん【議連】= 議員連盟 (⇨ぎいん²).
きろう² 【棄老】taking old people considered a burden to a mountainous area and abandoning them.
キロきゅうせんすいかん【—級潜水艦】〖軍〗[ロシアの潜水艦] a Kilo-class submarine.
きろく【記録】
◻□ 記録更新 the「establishment [setting] of a new record. ◐ 日本～更新 the「establishment [setting] of a new Japanese record (for the long jump) / ～更新は時間の問題だ. It's only a matter of time until someone sets a new record. 記録選択無形民俗文化財 [記録作成等の措置を講ずべき無形民俗文化財] an intangible folk-culture asset designated for recording on tape or video etc. lest it should die out; a folk [an ethnic] tradition or activity registered as being a cultural treasure which should be preserved on tape or film. 記録簿〖電算〗[CD, DVD などの] a recording layer.
ギロチン【切断】◻□ ギロチン破断 [原子力] a guillotine break.
きわ【際】◻□ 際剃り [頭髪の生えぎわ部分を剃ること] shaving [cutting back] the hairline.
-ぎわ【-際】1 [―のすぐそば] (immediately) adjacent to…; in close proximity to…; in the physical vicinity of…; (very) close to…; (right) beside….
2 [―しようとしたちょうどそのとき] on the (very) point of doing; (just) about to do.
キワニス・クラブ [米国発祥の社会奉仕団体] Kiwanis; the [a] Kiwanis Club.
キワニス・ドール [小児科医が患者に説明するときなどに用いる人形] a Kiwanis doll.
キワノ [ウリ科の植物 Cucumis metuliferous の果実] a kiwano (pl. ~s); a horned [melon; an African horned melon [cucumber]; a jelly melon.
きん² 【金】◻□ 金先物相場 a gold futures quote.
きん⁵ 【筋】◻□ 筋生理学 muscle physiology. 筋年齢

(a [one's]) muscle age.
ぎん² 【銀】◻□ 銀食器 silver; silverware. 銀マット [キャンプ用などの] a silver [sleeping] mat [groundsheet].
きんいろジャッカル【金色—】〖動〗a golden jackal; Canis aureus.
きんえん⁴ 【禁煙】◻□ 禁煙ガム stop-smoking gum; quit-smoking gum; [ニコチンを含む] nicotine gum. 禁煙週間 a no-smoking week. 禁煙先進国 an advanced country in terms of its non-smoking policies; an advanced anti-smoking nation. 禁煙ゾーン a [no-smoking [nonsmoking] zone [area]. 禁煙タクシー a no-smoking taxi.
きんかくわん【金角湾】[トルコ、イスタンブールの湾] the Golden Horn.
ぎんがめあじ【銀河目鯵】〖魚〗a bigeye trevally; Caranx sexfasciatus.
きんきゅう² 【緊急】
◻□ 緊急決議 an emergency resolution. 緊急交通路 [大災害時などの] a road [a route, an exclusive access route] for emergency vehicles. 緊急雇用創出特別基金 the Special Emergency Fund for Job Creation. 緊急処置 [緊急措置]《take》 urgent measures; 《adopt》 emergency measures; [病気・けがなどの] emergency「care [treatment]; first aid (treatment). 緊急対処事態 [武力攻撃事態対処法などの規定に基づく] a situation in which there is a likelihood of an imminent military attack endangering a large number of lives; [一般的に] a「situation [crisis] requiring urgent attention. 緊急脱出訓練 emergency「evacuation [escape] training. 緊急脱出用スライド [航空機の] an (inflatable) emergency evacuation slide. 緊急治療 emergency [urgent] medical care. 緊急道路 = 緊急交通路. 緊急搬送 [急病人・負傷者などの] emergency「transportation [transport, transfer] to a hospital. ◐ 救急車は急病人や怪我人を医療機関に～搬送する車両である. An ambulance is a vehicle for taking emergency cases or the injured to a medical facility. 緊急浮上 [潜水艦などの] emergency surfacing; an emergency ascent. 緊急物資 (the distribution of) emergency supplies. 緊急部隊 an emergency unit. 緊急輸血 (perform, receive) an emergency blood transfusion. 緊急輸送 emergency「shipment [transportation] (of food and medical supplies).
きんきゅうじ【緊急時】◻□ 緊急時事業継続計画 business continuity planning (略: BCP); a business continuity plan (略: BCP).
きんきゅうしょうぼうえんじょたい【緊急消防援助隊】an emergency firefighting「unit [team].
きんぎょはなだい【金魚花鯛】〖魚〗[ハタ科の魚; 雄の数が減ると雌が雄に性転換する] a fairy basslet; a「scalefin [lyretail] anthias, a sea goldie; Pseudanthias squamipinnis.
キング・ウィリアムズ・タウン [南アフリカ共和国南部、東ケープ州の州都] King Williams Town.
キングス・パーク [オーストラリア、パースにある公園] Kings Park.
キングスレー Kingsley, Ben (1943-    ; 英国の映画俳優; 本名 Krishna Bhanji).
キングズレー = キングスレー.
きんけんしりょく【近見視力】〖眼科〗near vision.
きんこ² 【金庫】◻□ 金庫番 the person in charge of a cash depository.
きんこう² 【近郊】◻□ (大都市)近郊区間 [鉄道・高速道路における] the greater (Fukuoka) area.
ぎんこう² 【銀行】◻□ 民間銀行 [市中銀行] a private bank. 銀行保有株式 bank-owned stock; bank shareholdings. 銀行マン [銀行員][1人] a bank「clerk [employee]; [集合的に] the staff of a bank.
ぎんこう⁴ 【吟行】a poetry-writing excursion to a scenic

or historic location. **〜する** go on a poetry-writing excursion; take a trip to get ⌈ideas [inspiration]⌉ for poems. ◐ **〜に出かける** = **〜する**. ▣ 吟行句会 a haiku excursion.

**ぎんこうとうほゆうかぶしきとくしゅこう**【銀行等保有株式取得機構】〔銀行の持ち合い株解消の受け皿機構〕the Banks' Shareholdings Purchase Corporation (略：BSPC).

**きんし**¹【近視】▣ 単純近視 simple myopia. 変性[病的]近視 pathological [degenerative] myopia; high degree myopia.

**きんじししょう**【金獅子賞】〔ヴェネツィア国際映画祭の大賞〕the Golden Lion (Award); 〖<It.〗 Leone d'Oro.

**きんしゃ**⁵【菌舎】〔食用キノコの菌を育成する小屋〕a mushroom shed.

**きんしゅう**³【錦秋】autumn, richly arrayed in colored 《maple》 leaves; the autumnal ⌈array [brocade] of crimson foliage.

**ぎんしょうぶんり**【銀証分離】prohibiting banks from dealing in securities; the separation of banking and securities business. 「う.

**きんしょうほう**【金商法】〖法〗＝きんゆうしょうひんとりひきほ **きんしん**³【近親】▣ 近親愛〖心理〗incest. 近親関係 ◐ 彼とは〜関係にある. I am closely related to him. ｜ He is a close relative of mine. 近親憎悪 (mutual) hatred ⌈between kin [within a family]⌉.

**きんしんしゃ**【近親者】a close ⌈relative [relation]⌉. ◐ 最〜 one's nearest relative; one's next of kin. ◐ 〜以外の人々 people outside ⌈one's [the] immediate family⌉ / 〜以外は知らない醜聞 a scandal known only within the family circle. ◐ 葬儀は〜のみですませました. The funeral was attended only by the immediate family. ｜ We only had close relatives to the funeral. / 彼は私の〜だ. He's a ⌈close relative [member of my immediate family]⌉. / 彼らはみな〜同士です. They are all ⌈closely related [close relatives, 《文》 close kin]⌉.

**キンスキー** 1 Kinski, Klaus (1926–91; ドイツの俳優; 本名 Nikolaus Nakszynski; 2 の父).
2 Kinski, Nastassja (1961– ; ドイツ出身の映画女優; 本名 Nastassja Nakszynski; 1 の子).

**きんせつ**¹【近接】▣ 近接学 proxemics. ▷ proxemic adj.

**きんせん**²【金銭】
▣ 金銭汚職 monetary corruption; corruption involving money. 金銭解決制度〔解決金を支払うことで被解雇者の雇用解消する制度〕a [the] system for monetary settlement in cases of disputed dismissal. 金銭供与 bribing sb (to get favorable treatment). 金銭授受 a ⌈transfer [flow] of money⌉. ◐ 警察の捜査は, 業者と政治家の間に不適切な〜授受はなかったと結論づけた. The police investigation concluded that there had been no inappropriate ⌈transfer [flow] of money from the company to the politician. 金銭消費貸借契約書 a loan contract. 金銭哲学 a philosophy of money; one's attitude to cash. 金銭トラブル money trouble; a problem with ⌈money [cash]⌉. ◐ 離婚のもとは〜トラブルだった. It was money troubles that led to the couple's divorce.

**ぎんせん**²【銀線】▣ 銀線細工 filigree.

**きんせんいしもち**【金線石持】〔魚〕〔テンジクダイ科の体側に鮮やかな線がある人魚; 雌が産んだ卵を雄が口の中で保護する習性がある〕a ⌈yellowstriped [goldstriped] cardinalfish; an orangestriped cardinalfish; a striped colored cardinal; *Apogon cyanosoma*.

**きんせんうん**【金銭運】【金運】luck with money.

**きんそう**【筋層】〖解〗a muscular ⌈coat [layer]⌉. ▣ 固有筋層 the proper muscle (layer) [coat]. ▣ 筋層浸潤 〖医〗〔がんの〕muscle invasion. ▷ muscle-invasive adj.

**きんぞく**¹【金属】▣ スクラップ金属 scrap metal. ▣

金属錯体 a metal complex. 金属加工油(剤)(a) metalworking ⌈fluid [lubricant]⌉. 金属基複合材〖工〗a metal matrix composite (略: MMC). 金属材料 metallic materials. ◐ 〜材料学 metallic materials science. 金属スクラップ metal scrap. 金属たわし a metal ⌈pot scrubber [scrubbing brush]⌉. 金属窒化物〖化〗a ⌈metal [metallic] nitride. 金属プレス金型 a metal press die. 金属粒 a metal pellet.

**きんぞくるいかいしゅうれい**【金属類回収令】〖日本史〗[1941(昭和 16)年の] the "Metal Collection Order"; the Government order ⌈for the surrender to the authorities [authorizing the requisitioning] of metals.

**「キンダーガートン・コップ」**〔映画〕Kindergarten Cop.

**きんちじしん**【近地地震】a regional earthquake.

**きんちゃく**¹【巾着】▣ 卵[餡入り]巾着〖料理〗a deep-fried tofu pouch with ⌈an egg [*mochi*]⌉ inside. ◐ 巾着寿司〖料理〗a kind of sushi consisting of a pouch of paper-thin omelette containing vinegared rice and other ingredients. 巾着煮〖料理〗a deep-fried tofu pouch which has been simmered in a broth.

**きんちょう**³【緊張】▣ 緊張型(性)頭痛〖医〗a tension headache.

**ギンツブルク** Ginzburg, Vitaly L. (1916– ; ロシアの物理学者).

**きんてん**¹【均霑】▣ 均てん化 ◐ 医療水準の〜化 providing (access to) [making it possible for everybody to have] equal standards of medical care.

**きんとうか**【均等化】equalization.
**〜する** equalize; make equal. ◐ 日本社会はまだ男女雇用機会の〜には消極的. Japanese society is still not committed to creating equal employment opportunities for men and women. ◐ 一票の格差を是正するために選挙区間の人口の〜を図ることが必要だ. In order to eliminate the disparity in the relative weights of votes, the populations of voting districts must be made the same.

**きんとりほう**【金取法】〖法〗＝きんゆうしょうひんとりひきほう.

**きんトレ**【筋トレ】〜ニング〗muscle training.

**キン・ニュン** Khin Nyunt (1939– ; ミャンマーの軍人・政治家; 首相 [2003–04]).

**きんばく**¹【緊縛】▣ 緊縛強盗 ⇨ ごうとう¹.

**きんぱく**¹【金箔】▣ 金箔打紙〔金箔を打ち延ばすときに使用する薄い和紙〕ultrathin Japanese paper used for manufacturing gold leaf.

**きんぱくか**【緊迫化】(an) increase in [(a) tightening of] tension.
**〜する** become tense; become strained. ◐ 中国が台湾海峡での軍事演習を繰り返したために中台関係は著しく〜した. Relations between China and Taiwan became severely strained due to China's repeated military exercises in the Taiwan Strait. ◐ 朝鮮半島情勢の〜 growing tensions on the Korean Peninsula.

**きんひべん**【筋皮弁】〖医〗〔皮膚・皮下組織ごと切り取られた筋肉片〕a myocutaneous flap. ▣ 腹直筋皮弁〖医〗a rectus abdominis myocutaneous flap. ▣ 筋皮弁法〖医〗〔乳房切除後の再建法の 1 つ〕背中・腹の皮・筋肉を移植する〗myocutaneous flap reconstruction.

**きんぴん**【金品】▣ 金品授受 giving and receiving money [and or] valuables. ◐ 彼らに職務に関して〜授受があった場合, 収賄罪や贈賄罪の適用を受ける. If they have exchanged money or valuables in connection with their official duties they will be charged with (the offense of) giving or receiving bribes.

**きんべん**【勤勉】▣ 勤勉手当 a "diligence allowance"; 〔勤務状況がよかった者に追加支給される金〕a salary supplement paid to hard-working employees.

**きんへんせい**【筋変性】〖医〗myodegeneration; muscle ⌈mutation [degeneration, deterioration]⌉; deteriora-

tion of a muscle.
**キンボール**〖商標〗〔カナダ発祥の, 風船状の巨大なボールを打ち合うスポーツ〕(a) Kin-ball.
**きんま**【木馬】＝きうま.
**きんまくえん**【筋膜炎】〖医〗fasci(i)tis.
**きんみらい**【近未来】near-future《technologies》. ▶〜型の車[携帯端末, オフィス] a car [a mobile phone, an office] likely to be seen in the near future.
**きんむ**【勤務】
▫️ 勤務延長制度 an extended employment system. 勤務時間短縮 (a) reduction [a cut] in working hours; making working hours shorter; shorter working hours. 勤務実態 one's actual work status. ▶大学医学部の医師が, 〜実態のない病院に名義だけ貸している問題が新聞で取り上げられた. Newspapers reported the issue of doctors at university medical schools letting hospitals use their names even though the doctors did not actually work there. 勤務ダイヤ a [one's] shift schedule. 勤務地限定採用 employment with a guarantee that the employee will not be transferred out of the region; region-specific employment. 勤務日誌 a [duty [shift] logbook.
**きんゆう**【金融】
▫️ 金融NPO a nonprofit [financial organization [lender, bank] (for NPO's). 金融学 monetary economics. 金融経済 〔実物経済に対して〕monetary economy. 金融経済統計月報 〔日本銀行の〕the Financial and Economic Statistics Monthly; (その1号) a Financial and Economic Statistics Monthly. 金融コングロマリット 〔銀行, 証券, 保険など複数の異なる金融機関で構成される複合企業体〕a financial conglomerate; a financial supermarket. 金融コンサルタント a financial consultant. 金融コンサルタント会社 a financial consulting [firm [company]; a financial consultancy. 金融市場動向 financial market trends. 金融弱者 a person who is [financially vulnerable [in a weak position vis a vis banks, etc.]; 〈集合的に〉the financially [vulnerable [disadvantaged, weak]. 金融収益 financial earnings. 金融収支 the financial [account [balance]. 金融所得 financial income. ▶〜所得課税 taxation on financial income. 金融政策決定会合 〔日本銀行の〕a Bank of Japan monetary policy meeting. 金融特区 a "special financial zone"; an economic zone which tries to attract investment by providing reduced corporate taxation terms and the like. 金融不況 a financial recession. 金融マン a finance man. 金融リテラシー financial literacy.
**きんゆうイノベーションかいぎ**【金融-会議】the Council for Financial Innovation.
**きんゆうかつどうさぎょうぶかい**【金融活動作業部会】〔マネーロンダリング対策の推進を目的とする国際的な枠組み〕the Financial Action Task Force on Money Laundering (略: FATF).
**きんゆうきこうきょく**【金融機構局】〔日本銀行の〕the Financial Systems and Bank Examination Department.
**きんゆうきのうあんていかきんきゅうそちほう**【金融機能安定化緊急措置法】〖法〗the Financial Function Stabilization Law. ▶ 正式名称は,「金融機能の安定化のための緊急措置に関する法律」(the Law of Emergency Measures to Stabilize Financial Functions). 1998年制定, 同年廃止.
**きんゆうきのうきょうかほう**【金融機能強化法】〖法〗〔金融機能の強化のための特別措置に関する法律の通称〕the Financial Function Reinforcement Law. ▶ 2004年8月1日施行.
**きんゆうこうどかセンター**【金融高度化-】〔日本銀行の金融機構局内の〕the Center for Advanced Financial Technology.
**きんゆうサービスきこう**【金融-機構】〖英国の〗the Financial Services Authority (略: FSA).
**きんゆうサービスしじょうほう**【金融-市場法】〖英法〗〔2001年施行〕the Financial Services and Markets Act (略: FSMA).
**きんゆうサービスほう**【金融-法】〖法〗〔英国の〕Financial Services Act (1986) (略: FSA); 〔日本の金融商品販売法〕the Financial Products Sales Law; (現在 制定が議論されている) a financial services law.
**きんゆうさいせいプログラム**【金融再生-】〔2002年に金融庁が主要銀行に対して公表したもの〕the Program for Financial Revival.
**きんゆうさいへんそくしんほう**【金融再編促進法】〔金融機関等の組織再編の促進に関する特別措置法の通称〕〖法〗the Financial Reorganization Promotion Law.
**きんゆうさきものとりひきぎょうきょうかい**【金融先物取引業協会】the Financial Futures Association of Japan (略: FFAJ).
**きんゆうさきものとりひきほう**【金融先物取引法】〖法〗the Financial Futures Trading Law.
**きんゆうシステムかいかくほう**【金融-改革法】〖法〗the Financial System Reform Law.
**きんゆうしょうひんとりひきほう**【金融商品取引法】〖法〗the Financial Instruments (and) Exchange Law (略: FIEL).
**きんゆうしょうひんはんばいほう**【金融商品販売法】〖法〗the Financial Products Sales Law.
**きんゆうしんぎかい**【金融審議会】the Financial System Council.
**きんゆうせいどかいかくほう**【金融制度改革法】〖法〗the Financial Systems Reform Law.
**きんり**【金利】
▫️ グレーゾーン金利 〔利息制限法の上限金利と出資法の上限金利との間の金利〕gray-area interest (rates); interest rates falling between the maximum rates permitted by the Interest Restriction Law on the one hand and the Capital Subscription Law on the other. 灰色金利 ＝グレーゾーン金利. 誘導金利 ➡ゆうどう.
▫️ 金利感応度 〖金融〗〔金利の変動に対する株価などの〕interest rate sensitivity. 金利固定期間 a fixed interest rate term. 長短金利差 the difference in yield between short- and long-term (treasury bonds). 金利先物 interest rate futures. 金利先物取引 trading in interest rate futures. 金利引き上げ a rise in interest rates; an interest rate rise. 金利引き下げ a cut in interest rates; an interest rate cut. 金利誘導目標 an interest rate target. ▶短期〜誘導目標 a short-term interest rate target.
**きんりん**【近隣】 ▫️ 近隣住区 〔人口に応じた生活関連施設を備えた, まとまりある住宅地域〕a residential area with a full range of social services; an integrated residential neighborhood. 近隣住民 neighboring residents 《of a US army base》. 近隣諸国条項 〔社会科教科書の検定基準の一条項〕the neighboring-countries clause.
**きんるぎょくい**【金縷玉衣】〔古代中国の貴人の葬服〕a shroud of jade plates sewn together with gold silk.
**きんレフ**【銀-】〖写真〗〔表面に銀紙を張ったレフ板〕a silver reflector.
**きんろう**【勤労】 ▫️ 勤労青少年ホーム a working youth center.
**きんろうしゃざいさんけいせいそくしんほう**【勤労者財産形成促進法】〖法〗the Law for the Promotion of Workers' Property Accumulation.
**きんろうしゃたいしょくきんきょうさいきこう**【勤労者退職金共済機構】the Organization for Workers' Retirement Allowance Mutual Aid.
**きんろうせいしょうねんのひ**【勤労青少年の日】〔7月の第3土曜日〕Working Youth Day.

# く

**クアッガ**〘動〙〔南アフリカ産のシマウマに似た動物; 19世紀に絶滅〕a quagga; *Equus quagga*.
**グアヤコール** ◯□ グアヤコール法〔米の鮮度判定法〕the guaiacol method.
**クアラ・シンパン**〔インドネシア, アチェ州, アチェタミアン県の県都〕Kuala Simpang.
**クアラ・トレンガヌ**〔マレーシア, トレンガヌ州の州都〕Kuala Terengganu.
**クアロン** Cuarón, Alfonso (1961- ; メキシコ生まれの映画監督).
**クアンタン**〔マレーシア, パハン州の州都〕Kuantan.
**クアンチ**〔ベトナム中北部の省〕Quang Tri.
**クアンナム**〔ベトナム中南部の省〕Quang Nam. ▶省都はダナン.
**クアンニン**〔ベトナム北東部の省〕Quang Ninh.
**クアンビン**〔ベトナム中北部の省〕Quang Binh.
**クイーカ**〔楽器〕〔サンバなどのブラジル音楽で使われる太鼓〕a cuica.
**クイーン・メリーにせいごう**〔-2世号〕〔世界最大の豪華客船; 2004年就航〕Queen Mary 2; QM2.
**クイズ** ◯□ クイズ大会 a quizz contest.
「**クイズ・ショウ**」〔映画〕Quiz Show.
「**クイック&デッド**」〔映画〕The Quick and the Dead.
**クイックバード**〘商標〙〔米国の, 商用高性能観測衛星〕QuickBird.
**クイティ(ア)オ**〔タイの麺料理〕kwaytiow.
**クイニ(ー)アマン**〔フランス, ブルターニュ地方の焼き菓子〕(a) kouign amann.
「**クイルズ**」〔映画〕Quills.
**クインケふしゅ**〔-浮腫〕〘医〙Quincke's edema. [ = 血管神経性浮腫 (⇨けっしょう[3])]
**くいき**〔空域〕◯□ 空域封鎖 an airspace blockade; a blockade of 《Lebanon's》airspace.
**くうかん**〔空間〕◯□ 空間演出〔室内などの空間を魅力的なものにするための工夫〕space [spatial] design [coordination]. 空間経済学〘経〙spatial economics. 空間情報 spatial information. ◯ ~情報分析〔テロ対策などの〕spatial information analysis. 空間生態学 spatial ecology. 空間デザイナー a 'space [spatial] designer. 空間認識 space [spatial] perception. ◯ ~認識能力 spatial perception ability. 空間認知 spatial cognition. ◯ ~認知能力 spatial 'cognitive [cognition] ability.
**くうき**〔空気〕◯□ 空気極〔燃料電池の〕an air pole; a cathode electrode. 空気ジャッキ an air jack. 空気清浄フィルター an air (purifying) filter. 空気漏れ《have》an air leak; (an) air leakage.
**くうきちょうわ・えいせいこうがくかい**〔空気調和・衛生工学会〕the Society of Heating, Air-Conditioning and Sanitary Engineers of Japan (略: SHASE).
**くうこう**[1]〔空港〕◯□ 空港会社 an airport company. 空港保安検査員 an airport security 'inspector [guard]. 空港整備特別会計 an airport improvement special account. 空港島〔空港建設のために造成した人工島〕an airport island. 空港ラウンジ an airport lounge.
**くうこうかんきょうせいびきょうかい**〔空港環境整備協会〕the Airport Environment Improvement Foundation (略: AEIF).
**くうこうしゅうへんせいびきこう**〔空港周辺整備機構〕the Osaka Airport Periphery Redevelopment Organization.
**くうしょう**〔空床〕〔病院の〕(the number of) unoccupied hospital beds. ◯□ 空床率 a non-occupancy rate for hospital beds.
「**グース**」〔映画〕Fly Away Home.
**くうせき**〔空席〕◯□ 空席照会 an inquiry about [a search for] available seats [seat availability].
「**偶然の恋人**」〔映画〕Bounce.
**ぐうぞう**〔偶像〕◯□ 偶像化 idolization. ◯ ~化する make [turn] 《sb》into an idol.
**くうちゅう**〔空中〕◯□ 空中消火 aerial firefighting; fighting fires [firefighting] from the air.
**くうてい**〔空挺〕◯□ 空挺団 an airborne brigade.
**クート**〔イラク東部の都市〕Kut.
**くうない**〔腔内〕〘医〙the 'inside [interior] of a cavity. ◯ ~の intracavitary. ◯□ 腔内照射〔放射線の〕intracavitary 'radiation [irradiation].
**クーパー** Cooper, Chris (1951- ; 米国の映画俳優).
**クーバース**〘犬〙a kuvasz.
**クーパーズタウン**〔米国ニューヨーク州の町; 野球の殿堂博物館がある〕Cooperstown.
**くうはく**〔空白〕◯□ 空白区〔選挙である政党の立候補者がいない選挙区〕a vacant constituency.
**クーハン**〘<F *couffin*〙〔新生児を寝かせる持ち運びカゴ〕a portable bassinet.
**クーファ**〔イラク中部の都市〕Kufa.
**クーファン** =クーハン.
**くうふく**〔空腹〕◯□ 空腹感 an empty stomach [a hungry] feeling; a feeling of 'emptiness in the stomach [hunger]. 空腹時高血糖〘医〙fasting hyperglycemia. 空腹時低血糖〘医〙fasting hypoglycemia.
**クーベルチュール**〔菓子〕〔製菓用チョコレート〕couverture (chocolate); chocolate couverture.
**くうぼ**〔空母〕◯□ 原子力空母 a nuclear (aircraft) carrier. 通常型空母 a 'conventional [non-nuclear] (aircraft) carrier.
**クーポン** ◯□ クーポン誌 =クーポン・マガジン. クーポン・マガジン〔割引クーポン券を綴じ込んだ情報誌〕a coupon magazine.
**くうまんじょうほう**〔空満情報〕=まんくうじょうほう.
**くうやむし**〔空也蒸し〕〔料理〕〔豆腐入りの茶碗蒸し〕steamed egg custard with tofu.
**くうりき**〔空力〕◯□ 空力性能 aerodynamic performance.
**クーリング・オフ** ◯□ クーリングオフ対象外商品 = 政令指定消耗品 (⇨せいれい[3]). クーリングオフ対象商品 = 政令指定商品 (⇨せいれい[3]).
**クールー**〔仏領ギアナの北部の町; 欧州宇宙機関の基地がある〕Kourou.
**クールマイヨール**〔イタリア北西部のスキーリゾート地〕Courmayeur.
**クーロン**[1] ◯□ クーロン爆発〘物〙a coulomb explosion.
**クエイド 1** Quaid, Dennis (1954- ; 米国の映画俳優; 2の弟). **2** Quaid, Randy (1950- ; 米国の映画俳優; 1の兄).
**クエゼリンかんしょう**〔-環礁〕=クワジェリンかんしょう.
**クエゼリンとう**〔-島〕=クワジェリンとう.
「**グエムル-漢江の怪物-**」〔映画〕The Host;〔漢字タイトル〕怪物.
**クエルダ** Cuerda, José Luis (1947- ; スペインの映画監督・製作者).
**クエンさん**〔-酸〕◯□ クエン酸タモキシフェン〘薬〙〔抗がん剤〕tamoxifen citrate.
**グエン・タン・ズン** Nguyen Tan Dung (1949- ; ベトナム

の政治家; 首相〔2006- 〕).
**クエンチ** ◨◨ クエンチ現象 quenching phenomenon.
**クエンチング**〖物〗＝クエンチ.
**グエン・ミン・チェット** Nguyen Minh Triet (1942- ; ベトナムの政治家; 国家主席〔2006- 〕).
**クオーク** ◨◨ クオーク凝縮 quark condensation.
**クオカード**【QUO-】〔プリペイドカードの一種〕a QUO Card; a Quo card.
**クォドルプル**【ボート】〔スカルの 4 人漕ぎ〕a quadruple scull. ◨◨ 舵[舵手]付きクォドルプル a coxed quadruple scull. 舵[舵手]無しクォドルプル a coxless quadruple scull.
**クォリファイング・トーナメント**〖ゴルフなど〗〔ツアー参加資格を決定するために行われるトーナメント〕a qualifying tournament (略: QT).
**グォン・サンウ, クォン・サンウ**〔權相佑〕Kwon Sang-woo (1976- ; 韓国の俳優).
**くがみらくづめ**【苦髪楽爪】long hair of the distressed, long nails of the idle.
**くかん**[1]【区間】◨◨ 区間エントリー(リスト)〔駅伝〕the 'entry list [list of runners entered] for one leg of a 'relay [ekiden] (race).
**くぎりうち**【区切り打ち】〔四国巡礼で八十八か所の霊場を何回かの旅行に区切ってまわること〕《breaking up》a pilgrimage around the 88 designated temples in Shikoku, completing each section on a different occasion.〔⇒とおしうち〕
**くぐりもん**【潜り門】〔小さい門〕a small gate; 〔大きな門扉の脇などについている小さな扉〕a side door at a gate.
**ククリンスキ** Kuklinski, Ryszard Jerzy (1930-2004; ポーランドの軍人; 冷戦期にワルシャワ条約機構の秘密文書を米 CIA に流した).
**クグロフ**【菓子】〔型に入れて焼くフルーツケーキ〕a gugelhupf; a kugelhopf; a kouglof.
**ぐざい**【具材】〔料理の具〕a main ingredient; a solid piece (of food in a stew, soup, etc.).
**くさサッカー**【草-】grassroots soccer.
**くさり**[1]【鎖】◨◨ 鎖場〔取り付けられている鎖につかまりながら登る険しい登山道〕a chain-assisted 'trail [route].
**くし**[1]【串】◨◨ 串打ち sticking a 'spit [skewer] in (a fish); skewering 《an eel》.
**くし**[2]【櫛】◨◨ 櫛切り cutting 《a tomato》 into wedges.
**しがた**【櫛形】◨◨ 櫛切り 〔櫛切り〕(⇒くし[2]).
**くじごじ**【九時五時】〔午前 9 時から午後 5 時までの勤務時間〕nine-to-five. ◯～の会社に勤めたい. I'd like to get a job in a company 'where I can work from nine to five [with a nine-to-five working day]. ◯ わが社は～です. The working day at our company is from nine to five.
**クシナガラ**〔インド, ウッタルプラデシュ州の村; 釈迦入滅の地〕Kushinagar.
**クシャダス, クシャダシ**〔トルコ西部, エーゲ海沿岸のリゾート地〕Kusadasi.
**くしゅくしゅ**【しわが寄ったような感じの】wrinkled 《boots》; baggy 《pants》.
**くしゅプレス**【服飾】crinkle-pressed 《fabric》. ◨◨ くしゅプレスタンクトップ a 'crinkle-pressed [wrinkled-fabric] tank top.
**くじょ**【駆除】◨◨ 駆除対象動物 harmful 'animals [beasts] for killing. 駆除ツール[ソフト]〔電算〕〔ウイルスの〕a virus 'disinfection [eradication] tool; virus 'disinfection [eradication] software. 駆除動物 harmful 'animals [beasts] which have been killed; animals killed because they 'are harmful [damage the crops].
**くじょう**【苦情】◨◨ 苦情請願〔行政の怠慢などによって被る権利侵害の訴え; 参議院の行政監視委員会が審査する〕a petition on an administrative complaint. 苦情電話[メール] a complaining 'phone call [e-mail].
**くずいも**【葛芋】〖植〗〔マメ科の食用植物〕a yam bean; a jicama; *Pachyrhizus erosus*.

**クスコ**[2]〖医〗〔膣鏡〕a Cusco's speculum.
**クストリッツァ** Kusturica, Emir (1954- ; ユーゴスラヴィア生まれの映画監督).
**くせだま**【くせ球】**1**〖野球〗〔微妙に打ちにくい球〕a tricky pitch (to hit). **2**〔(比喩的に)対応しにくい主張・提案〕a curve; a curveball. ◯ 政府側は野党が次々に投げてくる～の対応に追われた. The government was forced to respond to a series of 'curveballs [unexpected challenges] thrown at it by the opposition.
**グセフ・クレーター**〖天〗〔火星の赤道近くにあるクレーター〕Gusev Crater.
**くそ**-〔強意〕この～忙しいときに！ Just when I'm so 'damn [《卑》fucking] busy!
**クソン**〔亀城〕〔北朝鮮の都市〕Kusong.
**クタ**〔インドネシア, バリ島の繁華街〕Kuta.
**くたい**【躯体】〖建〗〔建築物の構造部体部分; 建具・造作・仕上げ・設備などを除く〕a frame; (a) framework; a skeleton. ◨◨ 躯体工事 frame construction.
**クタチャネ**〔インドネシア, アチェ州, 東南アチェ県の県都〕Kutacane.
**くだもの**【果物】◨◨ 果物アレルギー 《have》a fruit allergy.
**くだもの**[2]【管物】〖園芸〗〔菊花の〕a flower with tubular petals.
**くちうら**【口裏】◨◨ 口裏合わせ arranging what to say (to 《other people》); coordinating *one*'s stories. ◯ ～合わせ工作 a strategy to tell the same story.
**くちきき**【口利き】◨◨ 口利きビジネス the use of *one*'s political power in return for favors and contributions; influence-peddling.
**くちこ**〔なまこの卵巣の干物〕dried sea-cucumber eggs.
**くちこきゅう**【口呼吸】mouth breathing; breathing through the mouth; mouth [oral] respiration.
**くちコミ**【口-】◨◨ 口コミ情報 word-of-mouth information. 口コミマーケティング〖宣伝〗word-of-mouth marketing.
**くちさけおんな**【口裂け女】〔都市伝説の, 口が耳まで裂けた怪女〕a supernatural woman with her mouth sliced open from ear to ear.
**くちだて**【口立て】〖劇〗〔口頭による演技指導〕oral [word-of-mouth] directing (of an unscripted play); 〔決まった筋書・台詞はなくその場の思いつきで演じる芝居〕an impromptu 'play [drama]. ◯ 台本なしで～でせりふを伝え'立て稽古 an impromptu [extemporary] rehearsal, carried out without a script after the leading actor, acting as director, has allotted roles and situation, etc. by word of mouth.
**くちづくり**【口造り】〔陶器などの口の部分〕the 'rim [lip] 《of a tea bowl》.
**クチマ** Kuchma, Leonid (1938- ; ウクライナの政治家; 大統領〔1994-2005〕).
**クチュール**〔高級婦人服仕立て〕couture.
**クッキング** クッキング・シート〔料理やケーキを焼く時に下に敷く耐熱性の紙〕a cooking sheet. クッキング・ペーパー〔水切り, 油切りなどに使うやわらかい不織紙〕cooking paper.
**クック** Cook, Rachael Leigh (1979- ; 米国の映画女優).
**くっけんえん**【屈腱炎】〖獣医〗〔馬の〕a bowed tendon. ◨◨ 浅屈腱炎 tendinitis of the 'superficial digital flexor tendon [SDFT]. 深屈腱炎 tendinitis of the 'deep digital flexor tendon [DDFT].
**くっさく**【掘削】◨◨ 掘削孔 a borehole; a drill hole. 掘削(口)径 a 'borehole [boring] diameter. 掘削深度[深さ] a 'drilling [drill, bore, borehole] depth. 掘削船 a drillship; a drilling 'ship [vessel]. 掘削高さ, 掘削高 (a) cutting height. 掘削(土)量 the volume of material removed in 'boring [drilling]. 掘削幅 a cutting

width; an excavation width; a digging width. 掘削ロボット an excavation [a digging] robot; a robotic excavator.
くつじゅう【屈従】▶︎ 屈従外交 servile diplomacy; flunkeyism《toward the United States》.
クッション ▶︎ サイド・クッション〔座席などの〕a side cushion.
くっしん² 【掘進】▶︎ 掘進機〔土木〕a tunneling machine. ▶︎ シールド〜機 a shield machine.
くっしん³ 【屈身】〔体操〕〔体操の技などで、身体を折り曲げた状態〕a waist bend; bending at the waist. ▶︎ 後方屈身2回宙返り〔体操〕a double back somersault in pike position.
グッズ ▶︎ 応援グッズ cheering paraphernalia. パーティー・グッズ party goods; toys and things for a party; party accessories. 防災グッズ emergency [disaster] preparation supplies. ポケモングッズ Pokémon 'merchandise [goods]. 旅行グッズ travel goods.
くっせつ【屈折】▶︎ 屈折検査〔眼科〕refractometry.
クッツェー Coetzee, J(ohn) M(ichael) (1940-  ; 南アフリカ生まれの小説家).
グッディング Gooding, Cuba, Jr. (1968-  ; 米国の映画俳優).
「グッド・ウィル・ハンティング/旅立ち」〔映画〕Good Will Hunting.
グッドウィン Goodwin, Doris Kearns (1943-  ; 米国の伝記作家; リンドン・ジョンソン大統領の補佐官).
グドール Goodall, Jane (1934-  ; 英国の動物行動学者).
グッドデザインしょう【—賞】a "Good Design" award.
グッドデザインたいしょう【—大賞】a "Good Design" Grand Prix award.
「グッドナイト&グッドラック」〔映画〕Good Night, and Good Luck.
「グッドナイト・ムーン」〔映画〕Stepmom.
グッドマン Goodman, John (1952-  ; 米国の映画俳優).
「グッドモーニング・アメリカ」〔米国 ABC テレビのニュースショー番組〕Good Morning America.
クドロー Kudrow, Lisa (1963-  ; 米国の映画女優).
クナ(ー)ル〔アフガニスタン東部の州〕Kunar; Konar. ▶︎ 州都はアサダバード.
くにおやしそう【国親思想】〔親の適切な養育・保護を受けられない児童に対しては国がそれを行う責務があるとする考え方〕the parens patriae doctrine; the doctrine that the state has an obligation to protect children who do not receive adequate parental care.
クニッツ〔植〕〔インドネシア産のウコン〕kunyit.
グヌーテラ〔電算〕〔インターネットを通じて個人間でファイル交換を行うソフト〕Gnutella.
グヌンシトリ〔インドネシア、北スマトラ州、ニアス島の中心都市〕Gunungsitoli.
クネイトラ〔シリア南西部ゴラン高原にある町〕Quneitra.
クノップ〔米国の出版社〕Alfred A. Knopf(, Inc.).
くびさ【首差・頸差】〔競馬〕◐〜で《win》by a neck.
くびれづた【括れ蔦】〔植〕=うみぶどう.
くびれみどろ【括れ味泥】〔植〕〔フシナシミドロ科の黄緑藻類; 沖縄県絶滅危惧種〕a species of marine algae; Pseudodichotomosiphon constricta.
くびわおおこうもり【首輪大蝙蝠】〔動〕=だいとうおおこうもり.
クフォー Kufuor, John Agyekum (1938-  ; ガーナの政治家; 大統領 [2001-  )).
くま² 【熊】▶︎ 熊犬, 熊猟犬 a bear-hunting dog; a dog which is used to chase bears.
「クマゴロー」〔米国の、食いしん坊のクマと国立公園管理人の争いを描いた TV ギャグアニメ〕Yogi Bear.
クマラトゥンガ Kumaratunga, Chandrika Bandaranaike (1945-  ; スリランカの政治家; 大統領〔1994-2005〕).

くみ¹ 【組】▶︎ 組事務所〔暴力団の〕the 'office [headquarters] of a crime syndicate.
くみあい【組合】▶︎ 組合課税 =パス・スルー課税 (⇨パス・スルー).
くみおどり【組踊】kumiodori; 〔数人による踊り〕a group dance; 〔数種の踊りの組み合わせ〕a medley of dances; 〔沖縄の古典芸能〕a performing art native to Okinawa Prefecture combining spoken lines, with song and dance. ▶︎ 組踊立方(たちかた) a kumiodori dancer.
くみかつ【組み勝つ】〔柔道・相撲などで〕get [grapple] one's opponent into a position which is favorable to one.
くみこみ【組み込み】▶︎ 組み込みソフト(ウェア)〔電算〕embedded software.
くみまける【組み負ける】〔柔道・相撲などで〕fail to grapple with one's opponent in a way which is favorable to one.
クムチャンリ【金倉里】〔北朝鮮の都市〕Kumchangri.
くものすがめ【蜘蛛巣亀】〔動〕〔リクガメ科の亀〕a Madagascan spider tortoise; Pyxis arachnoides. ▶︎ 国際希少野生動植物種.
くよう² 【供養】▶︎ 供養祭〔亡くなった人のための〕a service for the repose of a dead person's soul; 〔死んだペットや実験動物、こわれた道具などのための〕a ceremony of thanksgiving (for broken utensils, for dead experimental animals, etc.). 供養札〔供養のために死者の名前を書いて寺に納める紙片あるいは細板〕a slip of paper or wooden tablet with a dead person's name on it, given as an offering at a temple for the repose of the person's soul. 供養料 the fee (paid to the priest) for a memorial service.
クラーク 1 Clark, Helen (1950-  ; ニュージーランドの政治家; 首相〔1999-  〕).
2 Clark, Larry (1943-  ; 米国の映画監督).
クライアント ▶︎ クライアント企業[会社] a client company.
クライシス ▶︎ クライシス・コミュニケーション〔危機管理広報〕crisis communication.
クライシュテルス Clijsters, Kim (1983-  ; ベルギーのテニス選手).
グライド《水泳》glide. ▶︎ グライド・キック kick glide.
クライフ Cruyff, Johan (1947-  ; オランダのサッカー選手).
「クライム&ダイヤモンド」〔映画〕Who is Cletis Tout?
クライン Kline, Kevin (1947-  ; 米国の映画俳優).
「クライング・ゲーム」〔映画〕The Crying Game.
クラウジック =クラヴジック.
クラウチク Krawczyk, Gérard (1953-  ; フランス生まれの映画監督).
クラウス Klaus, Václav (1941-  ; チェコの政治家; 大統領〔2003-  〕).
グラウビュンデン〔スイス東部の州; 美しい渓谷で有名〕Graubünden.
クラウン ▶︎ クラウン化合物〔化〕a crown compound. クラウン・ゴール〔植物病理〕crown gall.
クラウン² 〔道化師〕a clown. ▶︎ クラウン・ドクター〔医〕a clown doctor. [= 臨床道化師 (⇨りんしょう²)]
クラウン・ジュエル〔被買収会社の最も価値がある部門〕a crown jewel.
グラウンド ▶︎ グラウンドカバー・プランツ〔園芸〕〔グラウンドカバー用の[に適した]植物〕a ground cover plant. グラウンド整備〔競技場などの〕groundskeeping.
グラウンドワーク〔英国起源の市民・行政・企業が連携した地域環境の整備活動〕Groundwork.
くらおきば【蔵置場】=そうじょう.
くらがえ【鞍替え】▶︎ 鞍替え上場〔株式〕moving one's listing《from the Osaka to the Tokyo Stock Exchange》.
グラクソ・スミスクライン〔英国の大手医薬品会社〕GlaxoSmithKline plc.
クラコウ 1 〔ポーランドの都市クラクフ〕Kraków; Cracow.

**クラシカル**

**2**〔ドライソーセージの一種〕(a) Cracow sausage.
**クラシカル** ▣ クラシカル競技〘スキー〙a classical race. クラシカル走法〘スキー〙classical skiing.
**クラス** ▣ クラス・サポーター〔児童, 生徒, 学生の学習面・生活面の支援をするためクラスごとに置かれる〕a classroom supporter for students.
**グラスグラヴァー**〘<G Glasglaveur, Glasglaveurin〙〔グラスリッツェンをする人〕a glass graver.
**クラス・スイッチ**〘医・生理〙〔抗原の種類により抗体が変化する現象〕a class switch; class switching. ▣ クラススイッチ組み換え a class switch recombination.
**クラスター** ▣ クラスター構成〘電算〙a cluster configuration.
**クラスタリング**〘電算〙〔複数のコンピューターを組み合わせて一体として利用すること〕clustering. ▣ クラスタリング技術 (a) clustering technology.
**グラスフェッド**〘畜産〙〔牧草肥育の〕grass-fed [pasture-fed] (cattle, beef). 〔⇨グレインフェッド〕
**グラスリッツェン**〘<G Glasritzen〙〔ダイヤモンドポイント・ガラス工芸〕glass etching.
**くらだし【蔵出し】** ▣ 蔵出し税 an excise tax imposed when a product is shipped.
**クラチエ**〔カンボジア東部の州; 同州の州都〕Kratie; Kracheh.
**クラッシャブルゾーン**〘自動車〙〔衝突時にぐしゃっとつぶれて衝撃を吸収する車体の部位〕a crumple zone.
**クラッシュ** ▣ クラッシュ症候群, クラッシュ・シンドローム〘医〙〔挫滅症候群〕crush syndrome.
**クラッチ**[1] ▣ 乾式単板クラッチ〘自動車〙a dry(-type) single-plate clutch. 湿式多板クラッチ〘自動車〙a wet (-type) multi-plate clutch.
**グラッパ**〔ブドウしぼり器の残滓から蒸留したイタリアのブランデー〕grappa.
**クラティエ** ＝クラチエ.
**「グラディエーター」**〔映画〕Gladiator.
**グラナディラ**〘植〙＝グレナディラ.
**グラニテ**〔砂糖シロップと果汁をかきまぜて固めた粒状シャーベット〕granité.
**クラバー**〔クラブによく通う人〕a regular at a club music disco.
**グラハム** Graham, Heather (1970– ; 米国の映画女優).
**グラハムこ【—粉】**〔全粒粉〕graham flour.
**クラビ** **1**〔タイ南部の県〕Krabi.
**2**〔タイ南部の都市, クラビ県の県都〕Krabi.
**グラビア(ばん)** ▣ グラビア雑誌 a (photo)gravure magazine.
**クラビット**〘商標・薬〙〔合成抗菌剤〕Cravit.
**くらびと【蔵人】**〔酒造り職人〕a skilled worker at a sake brewery.
**クラブ**[5]〔クラブミュージックを流すディスコ〕a disco with club music. ▣ クラブ・ミュージック club music.
**グラフィック** ▣ グラフィック・ノベル〔漫画の一種〕a graphic novel.
**クラフォードしょう【—賞】**〔スウェーデン王立科学アカデミーが生物学・数学・天文学などの分野における優れた業績に対して授与する賞(個々の賞)〕a Crafoord Prize; (個々の賞をまとめて) the Crafoord Prize.
**クラフチュク** Kravchuk, Leonid Makarovich (1934– ; ウクライナの政治家; 初代大統領〔1991–94〕).
**グラベル**〘砂利〙gravel. ▣ グラベル・ラリー〔未舗装路での自動車ラリー〕a gravel rally.
**グラベル・ベッド**〔自動車レースのコース脇の小石を敷き詰めた退避エリア〕a gravel bed.
**クラミジア** ▣ 肺炎クラミジア〘医〙chlamydia pneumonia(e).
**クラミドモナス**〔緑藻綱の単細胞鞭毛虫均類〕chlamydomonas.
**グラミンぎんこう【—銀行】**〔バングラデシュの銀行〕the Grameen Bank. ▶ 低金利・無担保の少額融資で女性や貧困層の自立を助けた. 創設者(ムハマド・ユヌス)は2006年ノーベル平和賞受賞.
**クラムシェル** ▣ クラムシェル・バケット a clamshell bucket.
**グラモキソン**〘商標・薬〙〔除草剤パラコートの商品名〕Gramoxone.
**くらもと【蔵元】**〔酒・醤油などの醸造所〕a (sake) brewery.
**クラランス**〘商標〙〔フランスの化粧品ブランド〕Clarins.
**クラリチン**〘商標・薬〙〔花粉症治療薬〕Claritin.
**クラン**[2]〔マレーシア, マレー半島西岸の港市〕Kelang.
**グラント** Grant, Hugh (1960– ; 英国の映画俳優; 本名 Hugh John Mungo Grant).
**グランド・クロス**〔惑星が太陽を頂点にして地球を中心に巨大な十字を描く状態〕a grand cross.
**グランドソフトボール**〔視覚障害者のためのソフトボール〕ground softball.
**グランド・デザイン**〔全体構想〕a grand design.
**グランド・ナショナル**〔英国最大の障害競馬レース〕the Grand National.
**クランベリー** ▣ クランベリー・ジュース cranberry juice. クランベリー・ソース cranberry sauce.
**グランマ**〔キューバ共産党機関紙〕Granma.
**グランマ(ル)ニエ**〘商標〙〔コニャックベースのオレンジキュール〕Grand Marnier.
**クリア** ▣ クリア・ボール〘球技〙a cleared ball. クリア・ラッカー〔透明塗料〕clear lacquer.
**クリアウォーター**〔米国フロリダ半島西部の都市〕Clearwater.
**くりあげ【繰り上げ】** ▣ 繰り上げスタート〔駅伝の〕an advance start. 繰り上げ投票 early voting. 繰り上げ優勝〔優勝選手の失格による〕a「win [victory] awarded to a losing competitor due to 《disqualification of the winner》; a「win [victory] by default.
**クリア・ファイル** a「clear [transparent] file.
**クリアランス** ▣ クリアランス・レベル〔原発などからの廃棄物のうち放射性物質として扱う必要のない基準値〕a clearance level.
**クリアリングハウス**〔手形交換所〕a clearinghouse.
**クリース** Cleese, John (1939– ; 英国生まれの映画俳優; 本名 John Marwood Cleese).
**クリーナー・プロダクション**〔環境低負荷型の生産システム〕cleaner production (略: CP).
**グリーナウェイ** Greenaway, Peter (1942– ; 英国生まれの映画監督).
**グリーフ・ケア**〔遺族の悲嘆の精神的介助〕grief [bereavement] care [counseling].
**クリーブランド・クリニックざいだん【—財団】**〔米オハイオ州クリーブランドにある医療・研究機関〕the Cleveland Clinic Foundation (略: CCF).
**クリーム** ▣ クリーム・スキミング〔通信・運輸などの公共サービス部門で, 規制緩和により参入した新規事業者が収益性の高い分野にのみサービスを集中させて利益を上げること〕cream skimming; cherry picking. クリーム・ブリュレ〔菓子〕＝クレーム・ブリュレ.
**クリールしょとう【—諸島】**＝ちしまれっとう.
**クリーン** ▣ クリーン・コール・テクノロジー〔環境低負荷型の石炭利用技術〕clean coal technology (略: CCT). クリーン・ディーゼルエンジン a clean diesel engine. クリーン燃料 (a) clean fuel.
**グリーン**[1] ▣ グリーン・インベスター〔環境対策に積極的に取り組む企業に優先的に投資する投資家〕a green investor. グリーン・エイド・プラン〔途上国の公害防止のためにエネルギー環境技術の支援を行う協力プログラム〕the Green Aid Plan (略: GAP). グリーン・エネルギー〔太陽エネルギー・地熱・風力・水力など, 汚染物質を出さないエネルギー〕green energy. グリーン購入 ＝グリーン調達. グリーン・コーディネーター〔観葉植物などを使って室内空間を演出する人〕an interior foliage designer. グリーンGDP〔環境汚染被害・自然資源

の消耗などによる経済的損失を考慮して算出する GDP〕the green GDP. **グリーン証書**〔環境〕〔再生可能なエネルギー源による政府が発行する証明書〕a green certificate;〔正式名称〕a tradable renewable energy certificate（略：TREC）. ▶ a tradable green certificate（略：TGC）, a tradable renewable certificate（略：TRC）ともいう. **グリーンセンター**〔ゴルフ〕〔グリーンの中央〕the center of the green. **グリーン調達**〔環境に配慮した部品や材料を調達すること〕green「purchasing [procurement]; environmentally「friendly [responsible] purchasing [procurement]; environmentally preferable「purchasing [procurement]（略：EPP）. **グリーン・ツーリズム**〔農村などで休暇を過ごすこと〕green tourism. ▷ green tourist *n*. **グリーン・テクノロジー**〔環境配慮型技術〕green technology. **グリーン電力**〔太陽光・風力など環境に悪影響を与えないエネルギーによる電力〕green power. **グリーン・パートナーシップ**〔大企業が仕入れ業者などと連携して環境負荷の低減をめざす活動〕a green partnership. **グリーン・フラッグ**〔自動車レースで, 障害物がコースから排除されたことを知らせる再スタートの合図〕a green flag. **グリーン・プラ**〔生分解性プラスチック〕(a) biodegradable plastic; (a) "green" plastic. **グリーン物流**〔環境に優しい物流システム〕green logistics. **グリーン物流総合プログラム**〔グリーン物流の構築を目指す施策〕the Green Logistics Comprehensive Program(s). **グリーン包装**〔環境に配慮した包装のしかた〕green packaging. **グリーンメーラー**〔証券〕〔グリーンメールのために株を買い集める業者〕a greenmailer.
**グリーン**[2] Green, Seth (1974- ; 米国の映画俳優).
**グリーン・アノール**〔動〕〔米国東部・西インド諸島原産のトカゲ〕a green anole; *Anolis carolinensis*.
**グリーン・イグアナ**〔動〕a green iguana; *Iguana iguana*.
**グリーンウッド** Greenwood, Bruce (1956- ; カナダ生まれの映画俳優).
「**グリーン・カード**」〔映画〕Green Card.
**クリーンかいはつメカニズム**【-開発-】〔国連〕〔京都議定書に定められた温暖化ガス削減措置の1つ〕the Clean Development Mechanism（略：CDM）.
**グリーンこうにゅうほう**【-購入法】〔法〕the Green Purchasing Law.〔国等による環境物品等の調達の推進等に関する法律〕(the Law Concerning the Promotion of Procurement of Eco-Friendly Goods and Services by the State and Other Entities) の通称.
**グリーンシートしじょう**【-市場】〔株式〕〔日本証券業協会が未上場企業のために開設した証券市場〕a green-sheet market.
**グリーンスパン** Greenspan, Alan (1926- ; 米国の連邦準備制度理事会議長 [1987-2005]).
**グリーン・ゾーン**〔バグダッド中心部の米軍管理区域〕the Green Zone.
「**グリーン・デスティニー**」〔映画〕Crouching Tiger, Hidden Dragon.
「**グリーンフィンガーズ**」〔映画〕Greenfingers.
**グリーンベルトうんどう**【-運動】〔ケニアの環境活動家, ワンガリ・マータイが創始した環境保護運動〕the Green Belt Movement（略：GBM）.
「**グリーン・ホーネット**」〔米国の, 勧善懲悪アクション TV ドラマ〕The Green Hornet. ▶ ブルース・リー (Bruce Lee) が助演.
**グリーンマーク**〔環境ラベル; 古紙利用製品に表示される〕a "green mark"; a recycled-paper「mark [logo].
「**グリーンマイル**」〔S・キング作の小説；その映画化〕The Green Mile.
**グリーン・ライン** 1〔イスラエルとパレスチナの境界線〕the Green Line. 2〔キプロス共和国と北キプロス・トルコ共和国を分ける, 国連が定めた境界線〕the Green Line.
**グリヴナ**〔ウクライナの通貨単位〕a hryvnia (*pl.* ~(s)); a hryvna; a grivna.
**クリオ(-)ロ**〔植〕〔カカオの一品種〕criollo.

**グリオブラストーマ**〔医〕〔神経膠芽腫〕a glioblastoma (*pl.* ~s, -mata); a spongioblastoma (*pl.* ~s, -mata).
**くりかえし**【繰り返し】 ▣ **繰り返しゲーム**〔ゲーム理論の〕repeated game theory; repeated games.
**グリコーゲン** ▣ **グリコーゲン・ローディング**〔スポーツ〕glycogen loading;〔カーボ・ローディング〕carbohydrate loading;《口》carbo-loading.
**くりこし**【繰り越し】 ▣ **繰り越し額** a [the] amount carried over《from the previous「year [period]》. **繰り越し欠損** loss(es)〔carried [brought] forward; loss(es) carried over. **繰り越し欠損金** (a) deficit carried forward. **繰り越し控除**〔損失の〕a (loss) carryover deduction.
**グリコヘモグロビン**〔生化〕〔糖化ヘモグロビン〕glycohemoglobin.
**クリスタル**[1] ▣ **クリスタル・インテリジェンス**〔結晶性知能〕crystal intelligence.
**クリスチャン・コアリション** ⇨キリストきょう(と)れんごう.
**クリスチャンれんごう**【-連合】=キリストきょう(と)れんごう.
**クリステンセン** Christensen, Hayden (1981- ; カナダ生まれの映画俳優).
**クリストファー** Cristofer, Michael (1945- ; 米国の映画監督・脚本家).
**クリスマス** ▣ **クリスマス・スピーチ** a Christmas speech. **クリスマス・レクチャー**〔英国王立研究所がクリスマスに子供を対象に開催する科学実験講座〕the Christmas Lectures.
**クリソタイル**〔鉱〕〔温石綿〕chrysotile.
**グリゾン** =グラウビュンデン.
**クリック**[1] ▣ **クリック・アンド・モルタル**〔インターネット上の店舗と実際の店舗を組み合わせたビジネス手法〕clicks and mortar. ▷ click-and-mortar *adj*. **クリック募金**〔ウェブ上でクリックするだけで寄付ができるシステム〕(a) one-click donation. **クリック保証型広告**〔インターネット広告で, ユーザーのクリック回数に応じて広告掲載者に報酬が支払われるもの〕pay-per-click [PPC] advertising. **クリック・ラップ契約**〔インターネット上の契約で, 画面上の同意ボタンをクリックすることで成立する契約〕a click-wrap agreement.
**グリッシーニ**〔イタリア風の細長い棒状の乾パン〕grissini.
**グリッド・コンピューティング**〔電算〕〔複数のコンピューターをインターネットを通じて接続し, 1台の高性能コンピューターとして利用する技術〕grid computing.
**クリッピング(しゅ)じゅつ**【-(手)術】〔医〕〔動脈瘤の手術法〕a clipping operation.
**クリップスプリンガー**〔動〕〔アフリカ産レイヨウの一種〕a klipspringer; *Oreotragus oreotragus*.
**クリニカル・パス**〔医〕〔疾患別・医療行為別ケアのフローチャートを用いる医療の質管理の一手法〕a clinical path.
**クリニクラウン**〔医〕=臨床道化師 (⇨りんしょう[2]).
**くりのべ**【繰り延べ】 ▣ **繰り延べ税金資産** deferred tax asset.
**グリフィス** Griffith, Melanie (1957- ; 米国の映画女優;ティッピ・ヘドレンの娘).
「**グリフターズ／詐欺師たち**」〔映画〕The Grifters.
**クリプトン** ▣ **クリプトン 85**〔化〕〔原子炉の核生成物の1つである放射性ガス〕krypton 85.
**グリブナ** =グリヴナ.
「**クリフハンガー**」〔映画〕Cliffhanger.
**グリベック**〔商標・薬〕〔白血病治療薬イマチニブの商品名〕Gleevec.
**くりまゆ**【栗繭】〔養蚕〕〔樟蚕(くすさん)の繭からとる栗色の生糸〕chestnut silk.
「**クリムゾン・タイド**」〔映画〕The Crimson Tide.
「**クリムゾン・リバー**」〔映画〕The Crimson Rivers;〔原題〕Les Rivières Pourpres. ▶ 続編は「クリムゾン・リバー2 黙示録の天使たち」(Crimson Rivers 2: Angels of the Apocalypse;〔原題〕Les Rivières Pourpres 2-Les Anges De L'Apocalypse).
**くりもどし**【繰り戻し】〔税〕〔欠損金などの〕a carryback. ▣ **繰り戻し還付** a loss-carryback refund.
**クリュグ** =クリュッグ.

クリュッグ〔シャンパンの一種〕Krug.
クリュティエ(一)〔ギ神話〕Clytie.
クリルしょとう【―諸島】=ちしまれっとう.
「グリンチ」〔映画〕How the Grinch Stole Christmas.
グリント Grint, Rupert (1988-　; 英国生まれの映画俳優).
クリンプ〔ひだ・縮み・波形〕crimping. ▫▪ クリンプ加工 a crimping process; crimping. クリンプ金網 (a) crimped metal mesh; crimp weave.
クリンリネス =クレンリネス.
グルー² 〔GRU〕《<Russ. *Glavnoe Razvedyvatel'noe Upravlenie* (=Main Intelligence Directorate)》〔旧ソ連邦軍およびロシア連邦軍の参謀本部情報総局〕the GRU.
「クルーエル・インテンションズ」〔映画〕Cruel Intentions.
クルーガーこくりつこうえん【―国立公園】〔南アフリカ北東部にある野生動物公園〕the Kruger National Park.
クルーソー〔商標・電算〕〔米国製の低消費電力 CPU〕Crusoe.
クルーゾンしょうこうぐん【―症候群】〔医〕=クルーゾンびょう.
クルーゾンびょう【―病】〔医〕Crouzon's 「syndrome [disease].
クルーニー Clooney, George (1961-　; 米国の映画俳優; 本名 George Timothy Clooney).
クループ ▫▪ クループ症候群 croup syndrome.
グループ ▫▪ グループ・アプローチ〔心理・教育〕a group approach. グループ・インタビュー〔市場調査などのための〕a group interview; a focus-group interview; a group discussion. グループ送迎〔幼稚園児などの〕=集団送迎 (⇨しゅうだん²). グループハウス a group-living home. グループ・リビング〔高齢者の〕〔その建物〕=グループ・ハウス. グループ・ワーク〔人間関係の体験学習法の1つ; 集団作業〕group work.
グルおん【―音】〔医〕〔蠕動(ﾜﾀﾞﾌ)運動の音〕a gurgle.
グルガオン〔インド北部の都市〕Gurgaon.
グルカン ▫▪ βグルカン〔医〕〔免疫活性物質の1つ〕β-[beta-]glucan.
グルココルチコステロイド〔生化〕〔副腎皮質ステロイド〕a glucocorticosteroid.
グルコシダーゼ〔生化〕glucosidase. ▫▪ アルファ[ベータ]グルコシダーゼ α-[β-]glucosidase; alpha-[beta-]glucosidase. ▪α―阻害薬〔剤〕〔薬〕an α-[alpha-]glucosidase inhibitor.
グルコバイ〔商標・薬〕〔アカルボースの商品名〕Glucobay.
グルジアぐんようどうろ【―軍用道路】〔トビリシとロシアを結ぶ道路〕the Georgian Military Highway.
クルス Cruz, Penélope (1974-　; スペイン生まれの映画俳優; 本名 Penélope Cruz Sánchez).
クルドあいこくどうめい【―愛国同盟】〔イラクの〕the Patriotic Union of Kurdistan (略: PUK).
クルドじん【―人[族]】▫▪ クルド人自治区 the Kurdish autonomous region.
クルドどうめい【―同盟】the Democratic Patriotic Alliance of Kurdistan.
クルドみんしゅとう【―民主党】〔イラクの〕the Kurdistan Democratic Party (略: KDP).
クルドろうどうしゃとう【―労働者党】〔トルコの過激派組織〕the Kurdistan Workers' Party; 〔クルド語〕Partiya Karkeren Kurdistan (略: PKK).
グルニエ¹ 《<F *grenier*》〔建〕〔屋根裏部屋〕an attic; a garret.
クルバン・バイラム〔イスラムの犠牲祭〕Kurban Bayram; the Feast of Sacrifice.
くるぶし【踝】 ▫▪ 外踝 the outer ankle; 〔解〕the lateral malleolus.
くるまいす【車椅子】 ▫▪ 足こぎ車いす a 「pedal-driven [foot-driven] wheelchair; a cycling chair. 競技用車いす a racing wheelchair. 手こぎ車いす a 「hand-operated [hand-driven, hand-propelled] wheelchair. ▫▪ 車いす移動車 a wheelchair accessible vehicle (略: WAV); a wheelchair accessible car. 車いすスポーツ wheelchair sports. 車いすダンス wheelchair dancing; a wheelchair dance. 車いす用トイレ a wheelchair (accessible) toilet. 車いすランナー a wheelchair competitor 《in a marathon》.
クレアチン・キナーゼ〔生化〕creatine kinase (略: CK).
くれい【句例】〔俳句の例〕a haiku example; 〔句の例〕a phrase example.
クレイ² ▫▪ クレイ・モデル〔粘土で作ったデザイン原型〕a clay model.
クレイ³ 1 Cray, Seymour Roger (1925-96; 米国の電気工学者).
2 Qurei(a), Ahmed (1937-　; パレスチナ自治政府首相 [2003-06]).
クレイヴン Craven, Wes (1939-　; 米国の映画監督・俳優).
クレイザー Kleiser, Randal (1946-　; 米国の映画監督).
グレイシーじゅうじゅつ【―柔術】〔ブラジルのグレイシー家が創始した格闘技〕Gracie Jujutsu.
クレイブン =クレイヴン.
グレインフェド〔畜産〕〔穀物肥育の〕grain-fed 《cattle, beef》. ▫▪ グラスフェッド
「グレースと公爵」〔映画〕The Lady and The Duke; 〔原題〕L'Anglaise et le Duc.
グレーター〔おろし器〕a grater. ▫▪ チーズ・グレーター a cheese grater.
グレーター・サンライズ〔ティモール海にある油田・ガス田〕the Greater Sunrise.
グレート・ウォール〔天〕〔銀河の壁〕the Great Wall.
グレート・ジンバブエ〔ジンバブエの石造建築遺跡群〕Great Zimbabwe.
グレープシード・オイル〔ブドウの種から抽出する食用油〕grapeseed oil.
クレーム・ブリュレ〔カスタードクリームの表面にグラニュー糖をまぶし, バーナーで焦げ目をつけた菓子〕crème brûlée 《pl. crème brûlées, crèmes brûlées》.
クレーン ▫▪ クレーン・ゲーム〔ゲームセンターなどのゲームの一種〕a crane game.
クレジット ▫▪ クレジット・デフォルト・スワップ〔金融〕〔クレジット・デリバティブの一種〕a credit default swap (略: CDS).
クレティエン Chrétien, Jean (1934-　; カナダの政治家; 首相 [1993-2003]).
グレナディラ〔植〕〔オーボエ・クラリネットなどの木管楽器の素材となるアフリカ産のマメ科の黒色の木〕African blackwood; mpingo; grenadilla; *Dalbergia melanoxylon*.
クレプトクラシー〔収奪政治〕kleptocracy; 〔収奪国家〕a kleptocracy.
クレメンタイン〔植〕〔南米産の小型オレンジ〕a Clementine orange; *Citrus reticulata* var. *clementine*.
グレリン〔生化〕〔成長ホルモンの分泌を促進するたんぱく質〕ghrelin.
グレン 1 Glen, John (1932-　; 英国生まれの映画監督).
2 Glenn, Scott (1942-　; 米国の映画俳優).
グレンイーグルズ〔英国スコットランドのリゾート地〕Gleneagles.
グレンコー〔スコットランド, ハイランド州の渓谷〕Glencoe.
グレンジャー Granger, Clive W.J. (1934-　; 米国の経済学者).
グレンデール 1〔米国アリゾナ州中部の都市〕Glendale.
2〔米国カリフォルニア州南西部の都市〕Glendale.
クレンリネス〔清潔度〕cleanliness.
くろあかこうもり【黒赤蝙蝠】〔動〕the Hodgson's bat; the Copper-winged bat; the Korean orange-whiskered bat; *Myotis formosus*.
くろあしいたち【黒足鼬】〔動〕a black-footed ferret; *Mustela nigripes*.

くろあしねこ【黒足猫】〖動〗〔アフリカ南部産の小型のネコ〕a black-footed cat; *Felis nigripes*.
クロアチアみんしゅどうめい【-民主同盟】〔クロアチアの政党〕the Croatian Democratic Union (略: HDZ). ▶略称の HDZ は *Hrvatska Demokratska Zajednica* より.
くろあわび【黒鮑】〖貝〗*Haliotis discus discus*.
くろいあめ【黒い雨】〔原爆投下後に広島・長崎の爆心地周辺に降った泥やすすなどを含む放射能を帯びた雨〕black rain.
クロイツフェルト・ヤコブびょう【-病】〖病〗家族性クロイツフェルト・ヤコブ病 familial Creutzfeldt-Jakob disease; familial CJD. 孤発性[孤発型]クロイツフェルト・ヤコブ病 sporadic Creutzfeldt-Jakob disease; sporadic CJD. 散発性[散発型]クロイツフェルト・ヤコブ病 = 孤発性[孤発型]クロイツフェルト・ヤコブ病. 変異型クロイツフェルト・ヤコブ病 variant Creutzfeldt Jakob disease; vCJD.
くろいもり【黒い森】〔ドイツ南西部の森林地帯〕the Black Forest; Schwarzwald.
クロウ 1 Crowe, Cameron (1957- ; 米国の映画監督・脚本家).
2 Crowe, Russell (1964- ; ニュージーランド生まれの映画俳優).
くろえりはくちょう【黒襟白鳥】〖鳥〗a black-necked swan; *Cygnus melancoryphus*.
グローヴァー Glover, Danny (1947- ; 米国の映画俳優; 本名 Danny Lebern Glover).
クローザー 〖野球〗〔抑え投手〕a closer.
「クローサー・ユー・ゲット」〖映画〗The Closer You Get.
クローズ 1 Close, Glenn (1947- ; 米国の映画女優).
2 Clouse, Robert (1928-97; 米国生まれの映画監督).
グロース[3] 〖成長〗growth. グロース株〖株〗〖成長株〗a growth stock. グロース(株)ファンド a growth (stock) fund.
クローニー・キャピタリズム〔政治権力者が血縁者や親しい仲間に意図的に利権を配分して利益を独占すること; 縁故資本主義〕crony capitalism.
クローネンバーグ Cronenberg, David (1943- ; カナダ生まれの映画監督・俳優).
クローネンブルグ 〖商標〗〔フランスのビール〕Kronenbourg.
グローバー ＝グローヴァー.
グローバリゼーション ⇨ 反グローバリゼーション anti-globalization.
グローバル ⇨ グローバル・ガバナンス〔国家を超えた問題解決への取り組み〕global governance. グローバル競争 global competition. グローバル契約 a global contract. グローバル採用 global recruiting. グローバル・テロ〔地球規模で展開されるテロ〕global terrorism. グローバル・リテラシー〔国際的対話能力〕global literacy; ability to communicate anywhere in the world.
グローバル・ホーク〔米軍〕〔高々度長距離無人偵察機 RQ-4A の愛称〕a Global Hawk.
グローブ・アンド・メール〔カナダ最大の日刊全国紙〕The Globe and Mail.
クローン ⇨ クローン ES 細胞〖生物〗a cloned embryonic stem cell. クローン携帯〔不正使用を目的として他人の携帯電話の内部記憶装置などに複製したもの〕a cloned ["cellphone ['mobile]. クローン・ペット〔クローンの愛玩動物〕a pet clone; a cloned pet.
クローンぎじゅつきせいほう【-技術規制法】〖法〗the Human Cloning Techniques Regulation Law. ▶ 正式名称は「ヒトに関するクローン技術等の規制に関する法律」(the Law Concerning Regulation Relating to Human Cloning Techniques and Other Similar Techniques).
クローンきせいほう【-規制法】〖法〗=クローンぎじゅつきせいほう.
「クローンズ」〖映画〗Multiplicity.
クローンほう【-法】〖法〗=クローンぎじゅつきせいほう.

くろぐすり【黒釉】〖製陶〗(a) black glaze.
くろくもざる【黒蜘蛛猿】〖動〗〔オマキザル科のサル〕a black spider monkey; *Ateles paniscus*.
くろさび【黒錆】〔赤錆に対し、表面にできるマグネタイト組成の酸化鉄〕(black) magnetite; black rust.
クロザピン 〖薬〗⇨ 向精神薬〗clozapine.
クロザリル 〖商標・薬〗⇨ 向精神薬〗Clozaril.
くろじ[2]【黒字】⇨ 黒字決算 a surplus settlement; a final profit 《for the year》. 黒字転換 returning to [going back into] the black [profit, a surplus]. ⇨ ～転換する return to [go back into] the black [profit, a surplus].
くろしお【黒潮】⇨ 黒潮大蛇行 ⇨だこう.
くろしゃかい【黒社会】〔中国・台湾で暴力団を表す言葉〕a criminal syndicate; a "black society."
くろしろえりまききつねざる【黒白襟巻狐猿】〖動〗〔マダガスカル産のキツネザルの一種〕a black and white ruffed lemur; a ruffed lemur; *Varecia variegata*.
くろず【黒酢】black (rice) vinegar.
グロス[2] 〖艶(つや)〗〔艶だし化粧品〕gloss. ▷ glossy *adj*.
「黒水仙」〖映画〗Last Witness.
クロスえん【-円】〔米ドル以外の外国通貨の対円為替レート〕(the euro/)yen cross rate.
クロス・カップリング 〖化〗cross coupling. ⇨ クロス・カップリング反応 a cross-coupling reaction.
クロスサイト・スクリプティング 〖電算〗cross-site scripting (略: CSS, XSS).
クロス・シート〔列車の進行方向と直角をなす座席〕a cross seat. ⇨ 回転式クロスシート a reversible (carriage) seat.
クロスしゅうけい【-集計】〖統計〗cross-tabulation. ⇨ クロス集計表 a cross-tabulation table.
クロス・ドッキング〔入荷した商品を在庫させず、ただちに仕分けして出荷する方法〕cross docking.
クロスドレッサー〔異性の衣類を身につける人; 異性装者〕a cross-dresser; a transvestite.
グロスバード Grosbard, Ulu (1929- ; ベルギー生まれの映画監督).
クロスファンクショナル・チーム〖経営〗〔企業などが課題解決のため、業務部門の枠にとらわれず適材を集めて結成したチーム〕a cross-functional team (略: CFT).
クロスボール〖サッカー〗a cross; a crossing pass.
クロス・マーチャンダイジング〖商〗〔種類の異なる商品を一箇所に集めて同時に販売促進させること〕cross merchandising.
くろずみ[2]【黒炭】〔やわらかずみ〕soft black charcoal.
クロスメディア〔マスメディアとインターネットを関連させた情報提供方式〕cross media.
くろせいたかしぎ【黒背高鴫】〖鳥〗a black stilt; *Himantopus novaezealandiae*.
くろぞめ【黒染め】〖金属加工〗〔鉄製部品の錆止め表面仕上げ; 四酸化鉄の被膜を作ること〕black oxide finishing; 〔その表面〕black oxide finish.
くろだま【黒玉】〖宝石〗＝ジェット[2].
グロタンディーク Grothendieck, Alexander (1928- ; ドイツ生まれのフランスの数学者).
グロック〖商標・銃砲〗〔オーストリアの拳銃のメーカー〕Glock; 〔その製品〕ボディにプラスチックを多用する独創的な設計で知られる〕a Glock.
くろつぶれ【黒潰れ】〖写真〗〔露出不足で画像が黒くなってしまうこと〕black crushing; loss of dark detail.
くろつらへらさぎ【黒面箆鷺】〖鳥〗〔トキ科の水鳥〕a black-faced spoonbill; *Platalea minor*.
クロトー 〖生化〗〔老化抑制ホルモン〕Klotho.
グロナス【GLONASS】〔ロシアの衛星航法システム〕GLONASS; the Global Navigation Satellite System.
クロノグラフ ⇨ スプリットセコンド・クロノグラフ〔計測専用秒針を2本そなえたクロノグラフ〕a split-second chrono-

graph. ▫ クロノグラフ針 the chronograph (stopwatch) hand.
クロノテラピー 〖医・薬〗〔時間治療〕chronotherapy.
くろばクローバー【黒葉-】〖植〗=くろばつめくさ.
くろばつめくさ【黒葉詰草】〖植〗〔マメ科の常緑多年草；シロツメクサの変種；葉は紫色で緑色の縁取りがある〕(a) black clover; (a) dark dancer; *Trifolium repens* var. *nigricans*.
くろひきふりそで【黒引き振り袖】〔婚礼の正装としても着用される、黒地に模様が描かれた振り袖〕a black「*furisode*［long-sleeved kimono］.
クロピドグレル 〖薬〗〔抗血小板薬〕clopidogrel.
くろふねつつじ【黒船躑躅】〖植〗〔ツツジ科の落葉低木〕a royal azalea; *Rhododendron schlippenbachii*.
くろまい【黒米】〔古代米の一種〕black rice.
クロム ▫ クロム酵母 chromium yeast.
クロムウェル Cromwell, James (1940-  ；米国の映画俳優).
くろむつ【黒鯥】〖魚〗〔ムツ科の海産魚〕*Scombrops gilberti*.
クロモグラニン・エー【-A】〖生化〗〔唾液に含まれる糖たんぱく・精神ストレスマーカー〕chromogranin A (略: CgA).
クロモソーム, クロモゾーム 〖生物〗〔染色体〕a chromosome. ▷ chromosomal *adj*.
くろゆう【黒釉】〖陶〗(a) black glaze.
くろよんもんだい【九六四問題】the problem of "nine-six-four" taxation.
「グロリア」〔1980年の映画；その1999年のリメーク〕Gloria.
クロルピリホス 〖化〗〔農薬〕chlorpyrifos.
くろロム【黒-】〔白ロムに対し、通常の使用可能な状態の携帯電話端末〕a programmed cellphone.
クワ（ー）オワー〔冥王星より外側を公転する太陽系の小惑星〕Quaoar. ▶ 命名は、北米原住民の伝説に登場する創造の神から.
クワジェリンかんしょう【-環礁】〔マーシャル諸島にある世界最大の環礁〕Kwajalein Atoll.
クワジェリンとう【-島】〔マーシャル諸島中の島〕Kwajalein Island.
クワシニエフスキ Kwasniewski, Aleksander (1954-  ；ポーランドの政治家；大統領［1995-2005］).
クワジャリンとう【-島】=クワジェリンとう.
クワズール（ー）・ナタール〔南アフリカ共和国南東部の州〕KwaZulu-Natal (略: KZN). ▶ 州都はピーターマリッツバーグならびにウルンディ.
グワダル〔パキスタン南西部の港町〕Gwadar; Gawadar.
クワ（ッ）チャ〔ザンビア・マラウィの通貨単位〕a kwacha (*pl.* ~).
クワン Kwan, Michelle (1980-  ；米国の女子フィギュアスケート選手).
くんえん²【燻煙】▫ 燻煙加工 smoking process.
「軍艦マーチ」〔曲名〕Warship March.
ぐんき¹【軍紀】▫ 軍紀粛正 strict enforcement of military discipline.
ぐんこ【軍鼓】〔行進時の小太鼓〕a marching drum;〔いくさの合図に使う太鼓；陣太鼓〕a war drum.
くんこう³【君侯】a lord.

ぐんこく【軍国】▫ 軍国少年 a boy indoctrinated with militant patriotism; a military-minded boy.
ぐんこん【群婚】〖文化人類〗〔一群の男子と一群の女子との共同的婚姻関係；集団婚〕(a) group marriage.
ぐんじ【軍事】
▫ 軍事会談 military talks 《between the two Koreas, with the US》. 軍事拡大 military expansion. 軍事学校 a military school. 軍事訓練《receive》military training. 軍事攻勢 a military offensive. 軍事交流 a military exchange. 軍事情報 military information;〔敵国などについて収集した秘密情報〕military intelligence. 軍事侵略 military aggression; a military invasion. 軍事制裁 military sanctions. 軍事占領 (a) military occupation. 軍事対決 a military confrontation. 軍事展開 =軍事プレゼンス. 軍事動員 (a) military mobilization. 軍事ドクトリン a military doctrine. 軍事バランス (a) military balance. 軍事部門〔急進派組織などの〕a military wing. 軍事プレゼンス《maintain》a military presence. 軍事ロボット a military robot.
ぐんじかがくいん【軍事科学院】〔中国人民解放軍の〕the Academy of Military Sciences (略: AMS).
ぐんじじょうほうにかんするいっぱんてきほぜんきょうてい【軍事情報に関する一般的保全協定】〔同盟国間の〕a general security of military information agreement (略: GSOMIA).
ぐんじじょうほうほぜんきょうてい【軍事情報保全協定】=ぐんじじょうほうにかんするいっぱんてきほぜんきょうてい.
ぐんじてき【軍事的】▫ 軍事的脅威 a military threat《to Japan》. 軍事的緊張《amidst heightening》military tension(s). 軍事的攻勢 =軍事攻勢 (⇒ぐんじ). 軍事的勝利 a military victory. 軍事的侵略 =軍事侵略 (⇒ぐんじ). 軍事的占領 =軍事占領 (⇒ぐんじ). 軍事的対決 =軍事対決 (⇒ぐんじ). 軍事的能力 military capability. 軍事的プレゼンス =軍事プレゼンス (⇒ぐんじ).
ぐんしゅう¹【群衆】▫ 群衆雪崩 〖俗〗the「domino-effect [incremental] collapse of a crowd; an accident in which more and more people fall down and are crushed by the pressure of a crowd.
ぐんしょく²【群植】〖園芸〗〔花壇などに同じ種類の植物をまとめて数多く植えること〕cluster planting of a single species of「flowers [plants].
ぐんどく【群読】▫ 群読劇 a group recitation drama.
ぐんみん【軍民】▫ 軍民共用［共同使用］〔飛行場などの〕joint military/civilian use 《of an airfield》. 軍民共用空港 a joint-use airport (for military and civil planes).
ぐんみん²【郡民】an inhabitant of a county;〈集合的に〉county「folk [people].
ぐんよう¹【軍用】▫ 軍用ヘリコプター a military helicopter.
くんれん【訓練】▫ 訓練施設 a training「facility [center]. ▷ 盲導犬→施設 a guide dog training「school [facility] / 都市型→施設〔軍・警察〕an urban (military) training facility.

# け

ケア¹ ▫ ケア・クラーク〔介護保険事務専門員〕a nursing care clerk. ケア・マネージメント〔介護が必要な高齢者・障害者が社会を暮らしていけるようなサービスを計画・管理すること〕care management.
ケア³〖鳥〗〔ニュージーランド産のオウム科の鳥〕a kea; *Nestor notabilis*.
けあな【毛穴】▫ 毛穴ケア pore care.

ケアハラ =ケア・ハラスメント.
ケア・ハラスメント〔介護ヘルパーなどに対するいやがらせや暴力〕abuse [harassment] of caregivers.
ケアリング・クラウン〔病院その他の施設に出向いて笑いと心の癒しを提供する道化師〕a caring clown; a therapeutic clown;〔クリニクラウン〕=臨床道化師 (⇒りんしょう²).
ゲアン〔ベトナム中北部の省〕Nghe An. ▶ 省都 ヴィン

(Vinh).
けい¹【経緯】 ▫️ 経緯説明〔事情説明〕⇨じじょう³;〔経過説明〕⇨けいか³.
けいいんさつ【軽印刷】《印刷》〔ろう原紙に原稿をタイプしたものを直接印刷機にかけて刷る簡単な印刷〕 mimeography. ▫️ 軽印刷機 a mimeograph (machine).
けいえい²【経営】
▫️▫️ 無借金経営 debt-free management; no-debt management.
▫️▫️ 経営アナリスト a management analyst. 経営安定資金〔中小企業に対する〕management stabilization funding. 経営委員会 a「managerial [management] committee; an administrative committee. 経営改善 management「improvement(s) [reform(s)]; improving the「management [running] (of expressways). 経営改善計画 a plan for management「improvement(s) [reform(s)]; plans for improving [a plan to improve]「management [running] (of city transport). 経営感覚 a「feeling [sense] for business; business [management] talents; the sort of personality for「business [management]. ◐ 新社長の〜感覚を疑わざるを得ない. We cannot but have doubts about the new president's business talents. | It is difficult not to have doubts about whether the new president is suited to run a business. 経営環境 a「business [management] environment. ◐ 電気事業をめぐる〜環境は現在かなり厳しい. The business environment for the electrical industry at present is pretty harsh. 経営形態 a「form [style] of (business) management. 経営効率化 development of「managerial [business] efficiency; making「management [business] efficient. 経営再建〔立て直し〕 business「reconstruction [rehabilitation]; a corporate turnaround. 経営収支 (the) income and expenditure (of a business). 経営責任 management [administrative] responsibility. ◐ 〜責任を取って辞任するtake responsibility as「manager [administrator] and resign. 経営団体〔ある事業を経営する団体〕 a「management [managerial] organization;〔事業経営者たちが組織する団体〕a business「organization [federation]. 経営内容 management [operational] details. ◐ 経営〜を改善する improve「(a company's) management [the way (a company) is run]; make (a company) more profitable. 経営ノウハウ business (management) [managerial] know-how.
けいえいかいはつこくさいけんきゅうじょ【経営開発国際研究所】＝こくさいけいえいかいはつけんきゅうじょ.
けいおんき【警音器】《自動車》 a horn.
けいか³【経過】 ▫️▫️ 経過説明 an interim explanation; a status update. ◐ 夫を劇症肝炎で亡くした妻は医師から〜説明を2回受けたが, 専門用語ばかりで理解できなかった. The wife who lost her husband to fulminant hepatitis had been updated twice on his condition, but she didn't understand the explanations because of all the technical terminology.
けいかい⁴【警戒】 ▫️▫️ 警戒論 ◐ 最近, 外資〜が高まってきた. There has been increasing discussion recently about the possible dangers of investment from abroad. | Recently people have increasingly been arguing the need for caution with regard to investment from overseas.
けいがいわくせい【系外惑星】〔太陽系外惑星〕a planet outside the solar system;〔天〕an extrasolar planet.
けいかく²【計画】 ▫️▫️ 計画停止〔発電所などの〕a planned shutdown. 計画犯〔計画的な犯罪〕a premeditated crime;〔実行犯に対し〕a planner of a crime; a mastermind (of [behind] a crime);《口》the brains behind a crime.
けいかじほう【京華時報】〔中国の新聞〕The Beijing Times.

けいかもつ【軽貨物】light freight. ▫️▫️ 軽貨物運送 light freight「transportation [transport]. ◐ 〜運送会社 a light freight「transportation [forwarding] company.
けいかん⁴【桂冠】 ▫️▫️ 桂冠指揮者〔特定のオーケストラなどの〕a conductor laureate.
けいかん⁶【景観】 ▫️▫️ 景観アセスメント (a)「landscape [scenery] assessment. 景観規制 aesthetic zoning (regulations). 景観工学 landscape engineering. 景観(の)利益 the benefits of a view. 景観破壊 scenic destruction; destruction of (the) scenery. 景観まちづくり条例 an urban landscape ordinance.
けいかんほう【景観法】《法》the Landscape Law.
けいかんみどりさんぽう【景観緑三法】《法》the three laws concerning the conservation of green space and landscapes.
けいき⁵【景気】 ▫️▫️ 景気総合指数 a composite economic index. 景気浮揚感 a sense of economic recovery.
けいきかいふく【景気回復】 ▫️▫️ 景気回復基調 (be on) the road to economic recovery;(show) signs of economic recovery. 景気回復局面 a「phase [stage] of economic recovery.
けいきょう【景況】 ▫️▫️ 景況判断指数 a business「survey [sentiment] index (略: BSI).
けいくうぼ【軽空母】a light (aircraft) carrier.
けいけつ²【経血】《医》menstrual blood. ▫️▫️ 経血量 menstrual blood loss.
けいけん¹【経験】 ▫️▫️ 経験工学 empirical engineering; engineering based on experience. 経験知 knowledge from experience; heuristic knowledge.
けいご²【警護】 ▫️▫️ 警護官〔要人の〕a bodyguard《for the Prime Minister》; a《Presidential》bodyguard. 警護対象者 a person who needs「guarding [a guard]; a person under「guard [protection, escort].
けいこう¹【経口】 ▫️▫️ 経口挿管《医》oral intubation. 経口中絶薬 an abortion drug; abortion medication; an [the] abortion pill. 経口補水液《医》oral rehydration solution (略: ORS). 経口ポリオワクチン (an) oral polio vaccine (略: OPV). 経口輸液〔行為〕oral rehydration;〔液体〕an oral rehydration solution (略: ORS).
けいこう³【傾向】 ▫️▫️ 暖冬傾向 ◐ 世界的な暖冬〜がここ数年続いている. A worldwide trend toward warmer winters has continued for some years. | For some time now winters have tended to be warmer. / まだ冬に入ったばかりだが, 今年も暖冬〜が顕著である. Though the winter has just started, it promises to be another warm one.
けいこう⁵【蛍光】
▫️▫️ 蛍光眼底造影《眼科》fundus fluorescein angiography (略: FFA). 蛍光気管支鏡(検査)《医》autofluorescence bronchoscopy (略: AFB). 蛍光球＝電球型蛍光灯(⇨けいこうとう). 蛍光クラックボール〔銀行強盗などの乗った逃走車両などに投げつけるための〕a paintball. 蛍光撮影(法)〔X 線による〕photofluorography. 蛍光色 a fluorescent color;《商標》a Day-Glo color. 蛍光診《医》fluorescent diagnosis (of colon cancer). 蛍光フィルム (a) fluorescent film. 蛍光プローブ《医・生物》a fluorescent probe.
けいこうとう【蛍光灯】 ▫️▫️ 直管型蛍光灯 a linear fluorescent「lamp [light]. 電球型蛍光灯 a neon light bulb; a bulb-shaped neon light. 丸型〔丸管, リング, サークル〕蛍光灯 a round fluorescent「lamp [light]; a neon (light) ring.
けいこく⁴【警告】 ▫️▫️ 警告看板 a warning「sign [placard, signboard]. 警告表示 a warning (label, notice);〔家電製品の〕a warning label;〔たばこの箱などの〕＝健

警告表示 《⇨けんこう[4]》. 警告票 a warning (ticket). 指導～票〔危険な自転車運転に対して警察が出す〕a (police) warning ticket for cyclists; a slip of paper warning cyclists to go carefully / 駐車違反の～票 an illegal parking warning (slip). 警告ブロック〔視覚障害者用の〕a (braille) warning block. [=点状ブロック 《⇨てんじょう[4]》]. 警告累積〔サッカー〕= 累積警告 《⇨るいせき》.

**けいさい**[1]【掲載】 ▫ 掲載記事 an article published 《in The New York Times》. ◐ ～記事の無断転載を禁じます。〔掲示〕Reproduction without permission (is) prohibited. | No Reproduction Without Permission. 掲載作(品) ◐ ～作品の著作権は作者に帰属します。〔掲示〕Copyright for works published 《in this magazine, in The Times》 belongs to the 「author [artist].

**けいざい**[1]【経済】 ◐ ～の自由化 economic liberalization.
▫ 経済演説 the speech on 「economic policy [the state of the economy] (given by the Economic and Fiscal Policy Minister). 経済格差 an economic 「disparity [gap, imbalance, inequality, gulf]. ◐ ～格差を是正する correct [rectify] an economic 「imbalance [inequality] / ～格差を縮小する reduce [narrow] the economic gap 《between nations》. 経済活性化 improvement 「of [in] the economy; 〔活発にすること〕stimulation of the economy; economic stimulation. 経済技術開発区〔中国各地の〕an economic-technological development area. 経済競争力《strengthen》 economic competitiveness. 経済交流 economic exchange(s) 《between…》. 経済財政白書 a white paper on the economy and public finance;〔内閣府の〕the Annual Report on the Japanese Economy and Public Finance. 経済3団体 the three major economic organizations of Japan, (the Japan Chamber of Commerce, the Japan Business Federation, the Japan Association of Corporate Executives). ▶ 日本商工会議所, 日本経済団体連合会(日本経団連), 経済同友会の3団体。 ◐ ～3団体首脳 (the) leaders of the three major economic organizations of Japan. 経済至上主義 the belief that the economy 「should come first [is more important than anything else]; an [the] "economy-first" principle. 経済指数 an economic index. 経済諮問委員会〔米国の〕the Council of Economic Advisors 《略: CEA》. 経済酒 = ぞうじょうしゅ. 経済自由度 (the degree of) economic freedom. 経済状況 the economic situation 《in Japan》; economic conditions; the economy. 経済対策 economic measures. 経済データ economic data. 経済統合協定 an economic integration agreement 《略: EIA》. 経済犯〔人〕an economic criminal;〔罪〕(an) economic crime. 経済犯罪 (an) economic crime. 経済ファンダメンタルズ (the country's) economic fundamentals. 経済付加価値 economic value added 《略: EVA》. 経済分析 an economic 「analysis [assessment]. 経済崩壊《cause》 an economic collapse.

**けいざいがく**【経済学】 ▫ 数量経済学 quantitative economics. 地域経済学 regional economics; regional economic studies 都市経済学 urban economics; urban economic studies.

**けいざいきょうりょくすいしんいいんかい**【経済協力推進委員会】〔韓国と北朝鮮の〕the Inter-Korean Economic Cooperation Promotion Committee.

**けいざいざいせいうんえいとこうぞうかいかくにかんするきほんほうしん**【経済財政運営と構造改革に関する基本方針】 the Basic Policies for Economic and Fiscal Policy Management and Structural Reform. ▶「骨太の方針」(2002年) の正式名称.

**けいざいさんぎょうけんきゅうじょ**【経済産業研究所】〔独立行政法人〕the Research Institute of Economy, Trade and Industry 《略: RIETI》.

**けいざいしゃかいそうごうけんきゅうじょ**【経済社会総合研究所】= ないかくふけいざいしゃかいそうごうけんきゅうじょ.

**けいざいスパイほう**【経済-法】【米法】〔1996年制定〕the Economic Espionage Act.

**けいざいせいさいほう**【経済制裁法】 economic sanctions laws.

**けいざいせいさくけんきゅうじょ**【経済政策研究所】〔米国の〕the Economic Policy Institute 《略: EPI》.

**けいざいてき**【経済的】 ▫ 経済的暴力〔DVの一形態としての〕economic [financial] violence.

**けいざい・ぶっかじょうせいのてんぼう**【経済・物価情勢の展望】〔日本銀行が年に2回発行する報告書〕the Outlook for Economic Activity and Prices.

**けいざいれんけいきょうてい**【経済連携協定】 an economic partnership agreement 《略: EPA》. ◐ 日・タイ～ the Japan-Thailand Economic Partnership Agreement 《略: JTEPA》 / 日・ASEAN 包括的～ the Japan-ASEAN Comprehensive Economic Partnership Agreement.

**けいさつ**【警察】 ▫ 警察車両 a police 「vehicle [car]. 警察通訳 police interpreting; interpreting for the police;〔人〕a police interpreter. 警察比例の原則 the principle of proportionate police response 《to 「violence [a level of threat]》.

**けいさん**[2]【計算】 ▫ 計算式 a (mathematical) formula. 計算プログラム a calculation program. ◐ 住宅ローン～プログラム a home mortgage 「calculation program [calculator].

**けいし**[2]【刑死】 ▫ 刑死者 an executed person.

**けいし**[9]【係止】【機】 locking;【船舶】 mooring. ～する【機】 lock;【船舶】 moor. ▫ 係止部【機】 a locking part.

**けいじ**[2]【刑事】 a penal institution; a prison. ▶ 刑務所・少年刑務所・拘置所の総称. 刑事共助条約 a mutual legal assistance treaty 《略: MLAT》. 刑事処分可能年齢 the minimum age for criminal punishment. ◐ ～処分可能年齢を16歳から14歳に引き下げる lower the minimum age for criminal punishment from sixteen to fourteen (years of age). 刑事手続き criminal 「proceedings [procedures]. 刑事補償請求権【法】【憲法第40条の規定】the right to sue the state for wrongful detention. 刑事免責【法】criminal immunity; immunity from criminal liability; exemption from criminal prosecution.

**けいじ**[3]【計時】 ▫ 公式計時〔オリンピック競技などの〕official timekeeping. 手動計時 timing 《a race》 with a stopwatch; stopwatch timing.

**けいじ**[9]【鮭児】【魚】〔卵巣・精巣が未成熟な鮭〕sexually immature salmon.

**ケイジ** Cage, Nicolas (1964- ; 米国の映画俳優; 本名 Nicholas Kim Coppola).

**けいしき**[1]【形式】 ▫ 形式知 explicit [formal] knowledge. 形式犯(罪)【法】a formal crime.

「刑事コジャック」〔米国の, 刑事もののTVドラマ〕Kojak. ▶ 主演はテリー・サヴァラス (Telly Savalas).

**けいじしせつ・じゅけいしゃしょぐうほう**【刑事施設・受刑者処遇法】【法】the Law Concerning Penal Institutions and the Treatment of Prisoners.

**けいじしほうきょうじょうやく**【刑事司法共助条約】 a treaty on mutual legal assistance in criminal matters.

「刑事スタスキー&ハッチ」〔米国の, 刑事コンビのTVドラマ〕Starsky & Hutch.

**けいしちょう**[1]【警視庁】 ▫ 警視庁副総監 the Deputy 「Superintendent-General [Chief] of the (Tokyo) Metropolitan Police Department.

**けいしつ**[1]【形質】 ▫ 形質発現【遺伝】(a) phenotypic

expression.
けいじばん【掲示板】 ⇨ 掲示板管理人[管理者]〔インターネット上の〕a bulletin board manager. 掲示板サイト〔インターネット上の〕a bulletin board site.
けいしゃ²【傾斜】 ⇨ 傾斜掘削〔土木〕slant drilling. 傾斜地 a slope; sloping ground; 〔小区画の〕a sloping 「lot [plot].
けいしゃりょう【軽車両】【法】〔道路交通法で，自転車・車いす・荷車・人力車・馬車・牛馬など〕a light vehicle.
けいじょう²【形状】 ⇨ 形状認識 shape recognition.
けいじょう⁴【計上】 ⇨ 二重計上 doubling an entry [counting an entry twice] (in order fraudulently to increase the total).
けいじょう⁶【経常】 ⇨ 経常利益率 ◯ 売上高〜利益率 the ratio of ordinary profit to sales / 総資産〜利益率 the ratio of ordinary profit to total assets.
けいしょく²【軽食】 ⇨ 軽食喫茶〔看板に〕Snacks & Beverages.
けいしょくどうエコー(けんさ)ほう【経食道ー(検査)法】【医】＝けいしょくどうしんエコー(けんさ)ほう.
けいしょくどうエコーず【経食道ー図】【医】＝けいしょくどうしんエコーず.
けいしょくどうしんエコー(けんさ)ほう【経食道心ー(検査)法】【医】transesophageal echocardiography (略：TEE). ▷ transesophageal echocardiography *adj*.
けいしょくどうしんエコーず【経食道心ー図】【医】a transesophageal echocardiogram (略：TEE).
けいずい【頸髄】〔脊椎の首の部分〕the cervical spine. 頸髄損傷【医】cervical spine injury.
けいすいろ【軽水炉】 ⇨ 加圧水型軽水炉 a pressurized light-water reactor (略：PLWR). 沸騰水型軽水炉 a boiling light-water reactor (略：BLWR). ⇨ 軽水炉発電 light water reactor power generation.
けいせい¹⁰【鶏西】〔中国黒竜江省南東部の都市〕Jixi; Chihsi.
けいせいしんけいきんしょうこうぐん【頸性神経筋症候群】【医】cervical neuro muscular syndrome.
けいそう²【係争】 ⇨ 係争海域 disputed territorial waters. 係争水域 disputed waters. 係争地域，係争地〔a〕disputed territory; an area [a territory, land] which is the subject of a dispute.
けいそうこうきどうしゃ【軽装甲機動車】【軍】a light armored vehicle.
けいそく【計測】 ⇨ 計測震度〔地震〕measured seismic intensity. ◯ 〜震度計〔地震〕a seismic intensity meter. 計測制御工学 instrumentation and control engineering (略：ICE); measurement and control engineering (略：MCE).
けいそく²【京速】【電算】〔1秒間に1京回の計算能力〕a speed of 10 petaflops.
けいぞく²【継続】
⇨ 継続企業【会計】a going concern. ◯ 〜企業の前提【会計】the assumption of going concern. 継続協議 continued [consultation [deliberation, discussion]. ◯ 〜協議する continue to 「confer [deliberate, discuss] (at a future session); carry over 「discussion [deliberation]」(to a future session). 継続ケア〔退院後の〕continued care. 継続審議 a continued「discussion [debate]. ◯ 法案を〜審議にする carry a bill over to the next 「Diet」session. 継続性 continuity. ◯ あの会社は経営方針に〜性を欠いている. That company lacks continuity in its business policy.
けいたい²【携帯】
⇨ お財布携帯 ⇨おサイフケータイ.
⇨ 携帯依存症 (a) 「*cellphone [「mobile (phone)」addiction; (an) addiction to 「*cellphones [「mobile phones]. 携帯(音楽)プレーヤー a portable music player. 携帯ゲーム機 a portable (video) game 「console

[machine]. 携帯小説 a 「*cellphone [「mobile-phone] novel. 携帯(電話)用充電器 a 「cellphone [「mobile-phone] battery charger. 携帯トイレ a portable toilet. 携帯ナビゲーション〔GPS機能搭載の携帯機器によって歩行者を誘導すること〕portable navigation. ◯ 〜ナビゲーション機器〔システム〕a portable navigation 「device [system]. 携帯発固定着料金 a rate for calls from mobile to fixed phones. 携帯用 portable; mobile; handy (to carry);〔携帯電話用〕*cellphone [「mobile-phone]. 携帯用ゲーム機 a portable game machine. 携帯用サイト a 「*cellphone [「cellular, 「mobile-phone] (Web) site. 携帯用ストラップ a 「*cellphone [「mobile-phone] strap. 携帯用テレビ a mini-TV. 携帯用灰皿 a pocket ashtray.
けいたいでんわ【携帯電話】 ⇨ 携帯電話依存症 ＝携帯依存症 (⇨けいたい²).
けいだんれんかんきょうじしゅこうどうけいかく【経団連環境自主行動計画】〔経団連が1997年に発表〕the Keidanren Voluntary Action Plan on the Environment.
けいだんれんちきゅうかんきょうけんしょう【経団連地球環境憲章】〔経団連が1991年に発表〕the Keidanren Global Environment Charter.
けいちょう⁴【傾聴】 ⇨ 傾聴技術 active listening 「skills [techniques]. 傾聴法 active listening
けいちょう⁵【慶弔】 ⇨ 慶弔花 congratulatory and sympathy flowers. 慶弔花環 congratulatory and sympathy wreaths.
けいちょう⁷【経腸】【薬】〜の enteral. ⇨ 経腸栄養(剤)【医】《deliver》enteral nutrition. 経腸栄養法【医】《use》enteral nutrition.
けいちょうけんおうしせつ【慶長遣欧使節】〔日本史〕the Keichō mission to Europe (of 1613).
ケイツ Cates, Phoebe (1963‒ ) 米国の映画女優; 本名 Phoebe Belle Katz).
けいつい【頸椎】 ⇨ 頸椎症性脊髄症【医】spondylotic cervical myelopathy. 頸椎捻挫(ねんざ)【医】(a) cervical sprain.
ゲイツききん【‒基金】＝ビル・アンド・メリンダ・ゲイツききん.
けいとう¹【系統】 ⇨ 系統電力【電】〔自家発電などの分散型電源による電力に対し，電力会社の電力〕publicly 「distributed [supplied] electricity; public electricity; grid electricity; transmission line power; 「line power; 」「mains 「electricity [power]. 系統連系(型)システム【電】a grid-connected 《photovoltaic》system.
けいどうみゃく【頸動脈】 ⇨ 頸動脈エコー【医】carotid 「ultrasound [ultrasonography]. 頸動脈狭窄(症)【医】carotid artery stenosis. 頸動脈(血栓)内膜剥離術【医】carotid endarterectomy (略：CEA). 頸動脈ステント留置術【医】carotid artery stenting.
ケイトーけんきゅうじょ【‒研究所】〔米国のシンクタンク〕the Cato Institute.
ケイトン・ジョーンズ Caton-Jones, Michael (1958‒ )〔スコットランド生まれの映画監督〕.
げいにん【芸人】 ⇨ 若手芸人 a young entertainer;〈集合的に〉young talent.
けいねん【経年】 ⇨ 経年調査 a chronological survey; a survey (made) over time;〔年ごとの〕a yearly survey. 経年的に over time; with the passage of time. ◯ 侵食が〜的に進んだ. The erosion progressed over time. | The erosion gradually got worse.
げいのう【芸能】 ⇨ 芸能プロダクション an entertainment 「production company [agency]. 芸能欄〔新聞などの〕an entertainment 「column [section].
げいのうじん【芸能人】 ⇨ 芸能人証明書〔興業資格で在留するための〕a certificate stating that the holder is an entertainer.
けいばがっこう【競馬学校】〔中央競馬会が主催する，騎手・調教師を育成する機関〕the Horse Racing School.

けいはつ【啓発】 ▶ 啓発グッズ〔社会的運動などへの関心喚起のために無料配布する品物〕an educational giveaway; free gifts designed to 「enlighten the public [improve public behavior]. 啓発ビデオ an educational video; a public awareness video.

けいひ²【経皮】 ▶ 経皮的 percutaneous; transcutaneous. ～的冠動脈形成術 percutaneous transluminal coronary angioplasty (略: PTCA) / ～的血管形成術 percutaneous transluminal angioplasty (略: PTA). 経皮薬 a percutaneous drug.

けいひ³【経費】 ▶ 経費率〔商〕〔事業の経費総額の総収入に対する割合〕an expense ratio.

けいび¹【経鼻】 ▶ 経鼻胃管〔鼻孔を経由して胃に挿入さるチューブ〕a nasogastric [an NG] tube. 経鼻挿管 nasal intubation.

けいび³【警備】 ▶ 警備犬 a security dog. 警備封鎖〔会場などの〕a security lockdown. 警備当局 the security authorities. 警備ロボット a security robot; a security guard robot.

けいびぎょうほう【警備業法】〖法〗the Security Industry Law.

けいひろうじんホーム【軽費老人ーム】a low-cost home for the elderly.

けいぶ²【頸部】 ▶ 頸部エコー〖医〗〔頚動脈の〕carotid 「ultrasound [ultrasonography];〔子宮頸部の〕cervical 「ultrasound [ultrasonography]. 頸部血管超音波検査〖医〗=頸動脈エコー (⇨けいどうみゃく).

「警部マクロード」〔米国の, 警察もの TV ドラマ〕McCloud.

けいへいき²【軽兵器】a light weapon;〈集合的に〉light weaponry.

けいべつ【軽蔑】 ▶ 軽蔑語 an insulting [a contemptuous, prejudicial] word.

けいぼう³【警棒】 ▶ 特殊警棒 a steel baton; *〔口〕a billy club; a slapper. ◐ 高圧特殊～ a stun baton / 三段特殊～ a three-stage telescopic (collapsible) baton.

けいほうき【警報器・警報機】 ▶ 音声警報器 a voice 「alarm [warning] (device).

けいむ¹【刑務】 ▶ 刑務作業品 prisoner-produced goods;（handicraft）articles [things, items] made by prisoners (for sale to the public).

けいむ²【警務】 ▶ 警務員[士] a security officer; a guard. 警務隊〔自衛隊の〕the Military Police (Corps)（略: MP).

ケイメン Kamen, Michael (1948-2003; 米国の作曲家).

けいもう¹【啓蒙】 ▶ 啓蒙活動《conduct, be engaged in》enlightenment activities; activities to promote understanding.

けいやく【契約】 ▶ 契約慣行 contract practice(s). 契約義務 contractual obligations;〖法〗an obligation of contract. ◐ ～義務違反 a breach [(a) violation] of contractual obligations. 契約更改 contract revision;〖法〗a novation. ◐ ～更改交渉 contract revision negotiations. 契約農家[農場] a contract(ed) farm. 契約プロ a《company》sponsored professional (「player [athlete]》); a professional (「player [athlete]》) with a sponsorship contract《with a company》. 契約率〔新築マンションなど の〕a contract completion rate; the sales ratio《on condominiums》.

けいようどうし【形容動詞】〖文法〗an adjectival noun; a nominal adjective; a quasi-adjective; a na(-type) adjective.

けいよじしん【芸予地震】〔2001 年 3 月の〕the Geiyo earthquake (of 2001).

けいしゃ【刑余者】an ex-convict; a person who has done time (in jail, in prison).

けいら²【警邏】 ▶ 警邏隊 a patrol squad.

ゲイラ・カイト〖商標〗〔米国製の三角凧〕a Gayla kite.

けいり²【経理】 ▶ 経理操作 manipulating 「an account [the accounts]; 〔口〕creative accounting.

けいりゅう²【渓流】 ▶ 渓流魚 a mountain stream fish.

けいりょう¹【計量】 ▶ 計量言語学 mathematical [quantitative] linguistics. 計量国語学 mathematical [quantitative] linguistics for Japanese.

けいりょうきねんび【計量記念日】〔11 月 1 日〕Metrology Day.

けいりょうこくごがっかい【計量国語学会】the Mathematical Linguistic Society of Japan.

ゲイリン Geyelin, Philip (1923-2004; 米国の新聞記者).

けいれき【経歴】 ▶ 経歴放送〔選挙で, 候補者についての〕a《TV, radio》broadcast introducing the 「career [record, background] of an election candidate.

けいれつ【系列】 ▶ 系列局〖テレビ・ラジオ〗an affiliated station; an affiliate. ◐ TBS の～局 a TBS-affiliated station; a TBS affiliate. 系列工場 an affiliated factory.

けいれん【痙攣】 ▶ 痙攣性イレウス〖医〗spastic ileus.

けいろ²【経路】 ▶ 経路情報〖電算〗〔インターネットの〕routing information. 経路ハイジャック〖電算〗〔インターネットの〕route hijacking.

げうお【下魚】an inferior [a low-grade] fish [shellfish, food fish].

ケー・エスこう【KS 鋼】〖冶金〗〔永久磁石として優れた〕KS steel. ▶ KS はこの金属の開発を資金援助した住友吉左右衛門の頭文字.

ケー・オー・イレブン【KO11】〔遺伝子組み換え大腸菌〕E. coli KO11. ▶ E. coli は Escherichia coli の略.

ケー・ジェーほう【KJ 法】〔文化人類学者 川喜田二郎が考案した問題解決法〕the KJ method.

ケース ▶ ケース・マネージメント〔介護が必要な高齢者・障害者が社会で暮らしていけるようなサービスを計画・管理すること〕(health [geriatric]) case management. ケース・マネージャー a (health [geriatric]) case manager.

ケータイ ▶ お財布ケータイ ⇨おサイフケータイ.

ケー・ダブリューにゅうさんきん【KW 乳酸菌】〖菌〗the Lactobacillus KW;〔学名〕Lactobacillus paracasei, KW3110 strain.

ケーち【K 値】〔魚肉・食肉などの鮮度指標〕the K-value.

ゲーティッド・コミュニティー〔治安のため入口をゲートで遮断し, 周囲にフェンスを巡らせた米国の高級住宅地〕a gated community.

ゲーテ・インスティテュート〔ドイツのミュンヘンに本部を置くドイツ語・ドイツ文化を世界に広めることを目的とする組織〕the Goethe Institute; the Goethe-Institut.

ゲート ▶ ゲート・コミュニティー ⇨ゲーティッド・コミュニティー.

ゲートウェイ〔米国のパソコンメーカー〕Gateway.

ゲート・トレーナー〔障害者のための歩行補助器〕a gait trainer.

ケードロ【警泥】〔遊技〕=ドロケイ.

ケー・ピー・シー【KPC】〖生化〗〔たんぱく質の一種〕KPC; Kip1 ubiquitylation-promoting complex.

ケープきりん【-麒麟】〖動〗a southern giraffe; Giraffa camelopardalis giraffa.

ケープ・ハイラックス〖動〗a 「rock [cape] hyrax; Procavia capensis.

「ケープ・フィアー」〔映画〕Cape Fear.

ケーブル ▶ ケーブル・モデム〔ケーブルテレビ用に開設されたケーブル網を用いてデータ通信を行うためのモデム〕a cable modem.

ゲーム ▶ 1 点差ゲーム a game 「won [lost] by one 「point [goal, run, etc.]; a match in which there is only one 「point [goal, run] difference in the final score;〔野球〕a one-run game. 開幕[最終]ゲーム an opening [a closing] game. 個人ゲーム a solo game; a game for one

player. 対戦(型)ゲーム a multiplayer game; 《(play)》 a game「against [with]《(a computer)》. ◐ネットワーク[オンライン]対戦〜 a multiplayer online game; 《(play)》 an online game「against [with]《(a computer)》.
◻ ゲーム・オン・デマンド game [gaming] on demand (略: GoD). ◻ (〜)に対する感覚〕=試合勘 (⇨しあい). ◐この本では〜感覚で英単語を覚えられる。 With this book you can learn English vocabulary as if it were a game. / ゲーム〜をペットを飼ってはいけない。 You can't treat pets as though they were video games. ▎Keeping pets isn't just something you can treat like a videogame. / ゲーム〜の犯罪 a game-like crime; a game carried out as if it were a game. ゲーム・クリエーター[作家] a game creator. ゲーム脳 "game brain"; dementia caused by prolonged use of electronic (video) games. ゲーム配信〔インターネットによるゲーム配信〕online game「distribution [sales]; distribution [sales] of games online. ゲーム・プラン〔試合の作戦〕a game plan. ゲーム・プログラマー a game programmer.

**ケーラー** Köhler, Horst (1942- ; ドイツの政治家; 大統領 (2004- )).

**ケー・ワン【K-1】**〔格闘技〕K-1. ◻ **K-1 格闘家** a K-1 fighter.

**「外科医ガノン」**〔米国の, 病院もののTVドラマ〕Medical Center.

**けかり【毛刈り】**〔羊の〕(sheep)shearing.

**げきから【激辛】** ◐〜 fiery hot [super-spicy, extra-spicy]《(curry)》. ◻ 激辛食品 super-spicy food. 激辛ブーム a「boom [fad] for super-spicy food.

**げきしゃ【激写】** a「powerful [intense] photo(graph). 〜する take a「powerful [intense] photo(graph)《(of...)》.

**げきしょう[1]【劇症】** ◻ 劇症化【医】fulmination. ◐〜化する become「fulminant [hyperacute].

**げきしょう[2]【劇場】** ◻ 劇場型選挙 a「sensational [thrilling] election; an election which has the voters on tenterhooks.

**げきじん【激甚】** ◻ 激甚災害指定 (a) designation as a「devastating [severe] disaster.

**げきそう【激走】** a flat-out run.

**げきたい【撃退】** ◻ 撃退法 a method of「combating [fighting off]《(an annoyance)》. ◐〜無言電話の〜 a method of eliminating silent phone calls / 肩こり[腰痛]〜法 a method of combating「stiff shoulders [backache].

**げきはく【激白】**〔激しい告白〕a「frank [shocking] confession [revelation, disclosure]. 〜する reveal completely; admit plainly. / 彼女は離婚の理由は夫の浮気だと〜した。She「made the shocking disclosure [came right out and admitted] that the reason she got divorced was that her husband had been cheating on her.

**げきはつ[2]【激発】** ◻ 激発物破裂【法】detonating an explosive「substance [object]; causing an explosion.

**げきひょう[2]【激評】** a frank [an honest, a no-holds-barred] evaluation [review]. 〜する evaluate [review]《(sth)》「frankly [honestly], without pulling any punches].

**げきやせ【激痩せ】** extreme「thinning [weight loss]. 〜する lose a great deal of weight. ◐彼女は拒食症になって〜した。She got anorexia and became rail thin.

**「激流」**〔映画〕The River Wild.

**げきれい【激励】** ◻ 激励慰労費〔警察の〕an incentive and reward fund. 激励会 a pep rally. 激励パーティー〔山田候補〜会を開く〕hold [give, organize] an encouragement party for candidate Yamada / 高校野球に出場する野球部のために〜会を催した。We held a support party for our baseball club which was entering the High School Championship. 激励

文 a「letter [statement] of encouragement. 激励メッセージ a message of encouragement.

**げこく【下刻】**〔昔の時刻で〕the third third of「a *koku* [a two-hour period].

**ケサランパサラン【民俗】** a kesaran pasaran; an imaginary creature like a ball of fluff, said to bring good fortune if kept in a chest of drawers and fed with white makeup powder.

**けし【芥子・罌粟】** ◻ 芥子パール[真珠] a keshi (pearl).

**けしょう[2]【化粧】** ◻ 化粧筆 a makeup brush. 化粧療法 cosmetic therapy.

**げすい【下水】** ◻ 下水消化ガス sewage [wastewater] digester gas.

**げだい【下代】**〔問屋やメーカーから小売店への納入価格; 仕入れ値段〕a「wholesale [purchase, cost, buying] price.

**げだい【外題】** ◻ 外題役 a title role.

**けだくそ【卦体糞】** ◻ もうきょう.

**けだま【毛玉】** ◻ 毛玉詰まり【獣医】=毛球症 (⇨もうきゅう).

**けつあつ【血圧】** ◻ 血圧脈波検査【医】(an) examination「combining ABI and PWV testing [using an ABI/PWV device]. 血圧脈波検査装置 an ABI/PWV device.

**けつえき【血液】** ◻ 血液運搬車 a blood transport(-ation) vehicle. 血液剤〔血液製剤〕a blood「product [derivative]; 〔化学兵器の〕a blood agent. 血液細胞 a blood cell;〔特に無脊椎動物の〕a hemocyte. 血液事業報告〔厚生労働省の〕the Report on Blood Operations. 血液内科〔病院の〕a department of hematology. ◐〜内医 a hematologist. 血液白書 a white paper on「blood safety [the blood supply]. (⇨血液事業報告). 血液病理学 hematopathology; hemopathology.

**けつえきせいざい【血液製剤】** ◻ 濃縮血液製剤 a concentrated blood product.

**けつえん【血縁】** ◻ 血縁家族 a consanguine family; a family related by blood. 血縁結婚 (a) consanguineous marriage.

**けっか[3]【結果】** ◻ 結果回避可能性 avoidability of consequences. 結果予見可能性 foreseeability of consequences.

**けっかく[1]【欠格】** ◻ 欠格期間〔運転免許などの〕a disqualification period; the period of disqualification. ◐飲酒運転に対する〜期間は何年ですか。How long does a driver get disqualified for for drinking and driving?

**けっかく[2]【結核】** ◻ 多剤耐性結核 multidrug-resistant tuberculosis (略: MDR-TB). ◻ 多剤耐性〜菌 multidrug-resistant tubercle bacilli. 超多剤耐性〜 extensively drug-resistant tuberculosis (略: XDR). ◐ 超多剤耐性〜菌 extensively drug-resistant tubercle bacilli. 薬剤耐性結核 drug-resistant tuberculosis (略: DRTB). ◐広範囲薬剤耐性〜 = 薬剤耐性結核 / 超多剤耐性〜 extensively drug-resistant tuberculosis (略: XDR-TB).

**けっかくよぼう【結核予防】** ◻ 結核予防週間〔9月24日から1週間〕Tuberculosis Prevention Week.

**ケツカッチン【放送】**〔予定時間帯の最後が次の予定時間帯とつながっているため, 前の仕事の終わりの時間が決められてしまう〕a fixed「ending time [deadline].

**けっかん[2]【欠陥】** ◻ 欠陥隠し〔メーカーなどによる〕concealment of「concealing defects. 欠陥建築(物) a defective [(口) jerry-built] building [construction, structure]. 欠陥住宅保険 construction-[building-] defect(s) insurance for private housing]. 欠陥人間 a「defective [flawed] human being [person]; a failure; a loser.

**けっかん[3]【血管】** ◻ 血管音 blood vessel noise. 血管奇形【医】(a) vascular malformation; (a) blood vessel malformation. 血管外科 vascular surgery; angiosurgery. 血管神経性浮腫 〚医〛angioneurotic edema. 血管内治療 〚医〛intravascular treatment. 血管吻合(術) 〚医〛(a) 「vascular [vessel]」anastomosis. 血管迷走神経反応[反射] 〚生理〛a vasovagal 「reaction [reflex]」(略：VVR).

**げっかん**[2]【月間】 ▯ 月間賞 a monthly prize; the prize for《player》of the month. 月間天気予報 a weather forecast for the 「month [coming month, month ahead]」; a monthly weather forecast.

**けっかんしゅ**【血管腫】〚医〛a hemangioma《pl. ～s, -mata》; an angioma《pl. ～s, -mata》. ▯ いちご状血管腫 a strawberry 「mark [nevus]」. 肝血管腫 a liver 「hemangioma [angioma]」. 静脈(性)血管腫 a venous 「angioma [hemangioma]」. 脊髄血管腫 a spinal 「hemangioma [angioma]」. 老人性血管腫 a senile 「angioma [hemangioma]」.

**けつぎ**【決議】 ▯ 書面決議〔取締役会などの〕a 「written [round-robin] resolution. 非難決議 a resolution of 「criticism [condemnation]」; a resolution 「criticizing [condemning]」《the country for its human rights record》.

**けつぎあん**【決議案】 ▯ 非難決議案 a《UN》draft resolution condemning《North Korea for testing a nuclear weapon》.

**げっきゅうぎ**【月球儀】a lunar globe; a globe of the moon.

**けっきゅうどんしょくしょうこうぐん**【血球貪食症候群】〚医〛(a) hemophagocytic syndrome (略：HPS, HS).

**けつぎょ**【桂魚】〚魚〛[魚食性の淡水魚] a Chinese perch; a《species of》Mandarin fish; *Siniperca chuatsi*.

**ケックてんもんだい**【-天文台】〔米国ハワイ島の天文台〕the (W. M.) Keck Observatory.

**ケックぼうえんきょう**【-望遠鏡】〔天〕〔米国ハワイ島のケック天文台にある反射望遠鏡〕the (W. M.) Keck Telescopes.

**けっこう**[3]【血行】 ▯ 血行促進 improvement [stimulation] of blood circulation. 血行不良 poor 「circulation [blood flow]」.

**けつごう**[2]【結合】 ▯ 結合アミノ酸〔たんぱく質を構成しているアミノ酸〕combined amino acids.

**げっこうぞく**【月光族】〔中国で，月給を残さず使って気ままに暮らす若者たち〕yuèguāngzú; young people who live a carefree life and use up all of their paycheck by the end of the month.

**げっこうめがみ**[じょろう]【月光女神[女郎]】〔中国で，月給を残さず使って気ままに暮らす若い女性〕a Chinese girl who lives a carefree life and uses up all of her paycheck by the end of the month.《⇨げっこうぞく》

**げっこうよく**【月光浴】moonbathing; a moonbath.

**けっこん**[2]【結婚】 ▯ 結婚コンサルタント a marriage consultant. 結婚市場 a [the] marriage market. 結婚情報誌 a bridal magazine. 結婚立会人 a marriage witness;《be》a witness to a marriage. 結婚難 difficulty in finding [the difficulty of finding] a marriage partner.

**けっさい**[2]【決済】 ▯ 強制決済《証券》a forced (cash) settlement. ▯ 決済業務 a settlement service. 決済性預金 a checkable deposit. 決済専門銀行 a bank that provides only payment services. 決済短信《経営》a summary financial statement; a financial summary. 決済用預金 ＝決済性預金《⇨けっさい[2]》.

**けっさいきこうきょく**【決済機構局】〔日本銀行に〕the Payment and Settlement Systems Department.

**けっさん**【決算】 ▯ 好決算《show》a healthy profit. ▯ 決算型 ◐毎月[3か月，1年]～型《投資信託など》a monthly [a 3-monthly, an annual] dividend payment type《fund》. 決算検査報告 an auditors' report on the accounts. 決算書 a statement of accounts; a

balance statement. 決算短信〔上場企業の決算内容の要点をまとめた報告書〕summary of accounts.

**げっしょ**【月初】[月初め] the beginning of the month.

**けっしょう**[2]【決勝】 ▯ 決勝進出 reaching [making, advancing to] the finals. ◐～進出を果たす[決める] reach [make, advance to, move into] the finals. 決勝打《野球》a winning hit.

**けっしょう**[3]【結晶】 ▯ 結晶系(シリコン)太陽電池 a crystalline (silicon) solar cell. 結晶性知能[知性] crystal intelligence.

**けっせい**【血清】 ▯ 血清コリンエステラーゼ《生化》serum cholinesterase. 血清自己抗体《医》(a) serum autoantibody. 血清鉄 serum iron (略：SI). 血清尿酸値《医》a serum uric acid level.

**けっせいえきしょう**【血精液症】〚医〛hematospermia; hemospermia.

**けっせん**[1]【血栓】 ▯ 血栓吸引療法《catheter》thrombus aspiration. 血栓止血 thrombosis and hemostasis. ◐～止血学 (the study of) thrombosis and hemostasis. 血栓内膜剥離術《医》＝頸動脈(血栓)内膜剥離術《⇨けいどうみゃく》.

**けっそく**【結束】 ▯ 結束バンド〔電気コードなどを束ねる締め付け具〕a cable tie.

**けったくそ**【卦体糞】 ◐～(が)悪い〔著しく不愉快である〕disgusting; nasty; obnoxious《person》.

**けっちゅう**【血中】 ▯ 血中酸素濃度《医》(a) blood oxygen 「level [content]」. 血中たんぱく blood [serum] proteins; protein(s) in the blood. 血中中性脂肪(値) 《医》a blood triglyceride level.

**けっちょう**【結腸】 ▯ 結腸過長症《医》(an) elongated colon; dolichocolon.

**けってい**[1]【決定】 ▯ 決定機《サッカー》(miss) the chance of a goal; a chance at goal;《get》a goal-scoring opportunity. ◐彼は再三の～機にシュートをはずした. He repeatedly missed opportunities to shoot a goal. 決定事項 a decision; an agreement; something [an article] agreed 「on [upon]」; a settled matter. ◐株主総会での～事項をただちに実行に移す immediately implement 「the agreement reached [the decision taken]」at the general meeting of stockholders.

**けっていりょく**【決定力】[決断力] decision-making ability; the ability to make up *one's* own mind; decisiveness; [サッカーなどのスポーツでの得点力] scoring ability. ◐両チームともに～を欠き，引き分けた. Both teams lacking in scoring ability, the match ended in a draw. ▯ 自己決定力 self-determination [self-determining] ability. ▯ 決定力不足〔サッカーなどのスポーツで〕inadequate scoring ability.

「ゲット・ア・チャンス！」《映画》Where the Money Is.

**けっとう**[5]【血闘】a bloody fight.

**けっとうち**【血糖値】 ▯ 空腹時血糖値 (a) fasting blood sugar level. 食後血糖値 (an) after-meal [(a) postprandial] blood sugar level. ▯ 血糖値管理 blood sugar control.

**ゲット** ▯ ゲット化〔差別的な囲い込み〕ghettoization; turning into [becoming] a ghetto. ◐低所得層向けの集合住宅の多くが～化しつつある. Most of the collective housing for low income earners is in the process of turning into a ghetto.

**げっぱん**【月販】[1か月の販売量] monthly sales; monthly turnover.

**けっぴん**【欠品】[品切れ] stockout. ◐～する ～している be out of stock. ▯ 欠品率 a stockout [an out-of-stock] rate.

**けつびん**【欠便】[交通機関の運行停止] suspension [cancellation] of a transportation service.

**ケップ**〔カンボジア南部の都市(特別市)〕Kep.

**げつぼつ**【月没】[月が沈むこと] moonset. ▯ 月没帯食 a (lunar) eclipse at moonset.

げつめん【月面】 ◉◻ 月面探査衛星 a moon-probing [-probe] satellite.
ケツもち【-持ち】〔集団走行のしんがりを務める車〕a 「last [tail] driver [rider]; 《俗》a tail gunner; 〔トラブルを起こしたとき面倒をみてくれる暴力団員など〕a fixer.
けつらく【欠落】 ◉◻ 欠落部分〔記録などの〕a 「gap [missing part, lacuna] 《in the historical record》.
けつりゅう¹【血流】 ◉◻ 血流障害 a 「circulatory [blood flow] disorder.
げつれい²【月齢】
3〔牛の〕◐ 牛の〜 a (cow's) calving age (in months); a cow's age in months. ◉◻ 月齢判別〔牛の〕cattle month-age identification; assessment of a cow's age in months.
けつろ²【結露】 ◉◻ 結露防止 prevention of 「sweating [condensation]; prevention of 《a car window》 「fogging [misting (up [over])]; dew condensation prevention.
けとう【毛唐】〔西洋人に対する軽蔑語〕a 「damn [hairy] Westerner [foreigner, *gaijin*].
「ゲド戦記」〔米国の女性SF作家、ル・グイン作のEarthseaを舞台にした一連の小説〕the Earthsea series. ▶「ゲド戦記」は日本での呼び名.
ケトン ケトン性昏睡 〖医〗(a) ketotic coma. ◐ 非ケトン性昏睡 (a) nonketotic coma / 高浸透圧性非〜性昏睡 (a) hyperosmolar nonketotic coma (略: HONK).
ケネイラ = ジェネイラ.
ケネディ Kennedy, Paul M. (1945- ;英国の歴史学者).
けねん【懸念】
◉◻ 懸念国〔核拡散などに関する〕a 「state [country] of 《proliferation》 concern; a state that is a cause for (particular) concern 《to the world community》; a country of particular concern (略: CPC). 懸念先〔経営破綻などに関する〕an object [a target] of concern 《as to bankruptcy》. ◐ これらの〜先への融資は早急に回収する必要がある. Loans to such vulnerable debtors should be recovered as a matter of urgency. 懸念対象 an object of concern; (a) cause for concern. ◐ の銀行をマネーロンダリング〜対象に指定する designate the bank as a money-laundering 「suspect [concern]; say that the bank is suspected of money-laundering / 鳥インフルエンザ感染の〜対象者 people it is feared may have (been infected with) avian flu; (human) bird flu suspects.
ゲノム ◉◻ ゲノム疫学〔遺伝子情報を取り入れた疫学〕genome epidemiology. ゲノム解析 genome [genomic] analysis. ゲノム機能学 functional genomics. ゲノム情報 genome [genomic] information. ゲノム地図 a genome map. ゲノム・リプログラミング genome [genomic] reprogramming.
ゲノム・ネット〔京都大学化学研究所のデータベース〕GenomeNet.
ケバブ 〖料理〗〔カバブ〕(a) (shish) kebab; (a) kabob; (a) kebob; (a) cabob.
ゲフィチニブ 〖薬〗〔肺がん治療薬〕gefitinib.
ゲブーザ Guebuza, Armando Emilio (1943- ;モザンビークの政治家; 大統領〔2005- 〕).
ゲブザ = ゲブーザ.
げほげほ(と)〔咳の音〕(the sound of) 「a wet cough [wet coughing]. ◐ 先ほどから風邪をひきはなしで、〜咳をし続けている. I've had a cold with a wet cough ever since last month.
ケマリズム〔トルコ革命においてケマル・アタチュルクが行った政治路線〕Kemalism.
ケミカル・アリ〔イラクの元国防相アル・マジドのあだ名〕Chemical Ali. ▶ クルド人弾圧のために毒ガス使用を命じたことから.
ゲムツズマブ 〖薬〗〔抗がん剤〕gemtuzumab.

けむり【煙】 ◉◻ 煙体験室〔火災訓練用の〕a smoke simulation room. 煙ハウス〔火災による煙を疑似体験する設備〕a smoking fire simulation house.
ケメロボ〔ロシア、西シベリアの州〕Kemerovo Oblast; 〔ロシア語名〕Kemerovskaya Oblast'; 〔その州内の都市〕Kemorovo.
ゲラー 1 Gellar, Sarah Michelle (1977- ;米国の映画女優).
2 Geller, Uri (1946- ;イスラエル生まれの自称超能力者; スプーン曲げで有名).
げらく【下落】 ◉◻ 株価〔物価〕下落 a fall in 「share [commodity] prices. 地価下落 a 「fall [decline] in land prices. ◉◻ 下落幅 an 「extent [amount, degree] of 「decrease [reduction, decline, fall]. 下落率 a rate of 「decrease [reduction, decline, fall].
ケラトメーター〔眼科〕〔角膜計〕a keratometer.
ゲラン〔商標〕〔フランスの化粧品ブランド〕Guerlain.
ケランタン〔マレーシア北東部の州〕Kelantan.
-けり〔過去を表現する文語の助動詞〕◐ 奥山道に春は来に〜. Spring has come to these paths deep in the mountains. / 明治は遠くなりに〜. The Meiji era has now receded into the distant past.
ケリー・チャン Kelly Chen (1973- ;香港の映画俳優; 中国語名 陳慧琳 Chén Wai-Lam).
ゲル²〔モンゴルの移動式住居〕a ger.
ゲルストマン・ストロイスラー・シャインカーびょう【-病】〖医〗Gerstmann-Sträussler-Scheinker disease (略: GSS).
ケルソ Kelso, Louis O. (1913-91;米国のエコノミスト).
ケルテース Kertész Imre (1929- ;ハンガリーの作家).
ケルマーン = ケルマン.
ケルマン〔イラン南東部の州; 同州の州都〕Kerman.
ケルマンシャー〔イラン西部、イラクと国境を接する州; その州都〕Kermanshah. ▶ 旧称 バフタラン.
ケルンテン〔オーストリア南部の州〕Carinthia; 〔ドイツ語名〕Kärnten.
けんあい【兼愛】〔中国の思想家、墨子(ぼくし)が説いた普遍的な愛〕universal love; love and care for all human beings regardless of their relationship to *one*.
げんあつ【減圧】 ◉◻ 減圧給水〔給水を制限する方法の1つ〕water pressure reduction; reducing [reduction of] water pressure. 減圧装置 a (gas [water]) pressure regulator; pressure reducing equipment.
けんあん¹【検案】 ◉◻ 検案医 a medical examiner.
けんいん²【牽引】 ◉◻ 牽引治療〔療法〕〖医〗〔整形外科における〕traction [extension] therapy.
げんいん¹【原因】 ◉◻ 原因因子 a causative 「agent [factor]; a 《common》 factor that causes 《cancer》. 原因解明 clarification of the cause 《of an accident》; making clear why 《an accident》 occurred. 原因確率 (a) probability of causation (略: POC). 原因企業〔公害などの〕a company that causes 《pollution》; a company to blame (for emitting pollution); a source (of pollution). 原因菌 a pathogen. ◐ 歯周病の〜 a periodontal pathogen. 原因物質 a causative agent. ◐ アレルギーの〜物質 〖医〗 an allergen.
けんえき¹【検疫】 ◉◻ 輸入〔輸出〕検疫 an 「import [export] quarantine. ◉◻ 検疫(探知)犬 a 「customs [quarantine] dog.
けんえき²【権益】 ◉◻ 経済(的)権益 economic (rights and) interests.
げんえき²【現役】
◉◻ 現役引退 ◐ 〜を表明する〔スポーツ選手などが〕announce one's 「intention [decision] to retire 「from active participation in the game [as a player] / 彼女は〜引退後コーチとしてチームに残った. She retired from the team and stayed on as a coach. 現役教師 a working teacher. 現役合格 passing 《an exam》 while still a student. 現役時代 (the time) when *one* had an active

career; (the time) when *one* was「a working《firefighter》[an active《athlete》];*one's* days《as an active politician》. 現役生 a student「still [currently] in school. 現役生活 an active life《as a professional baseball player》; a career《as a politician》. ▶15年間の〜生活にピリオドを打つ bring *one's* 15-year career to an end; say goodbye to *one's* life as《a competitor》after 15 years. 現役世代 the working generation; people who are now「working [employed]. 現役選手 an active player; a player「on the active list [in active competition]. 現役復帰《艦船などの》demothballing;〔人の〕returning to active「service [work]. ▶長い療養生活の後、〜復帰を果たす return to work after a long period of medical treatment.

**けんえつ**【検閲】▣ 検閲国家 a censorship state; a state with strict censorship.

**けんおうしせつ**【遣欧使節】『日本史』《send》a mission to Europe. ▣ 慶長遣欧使節 ⇨けいちょうけんおうしせつ.

**けんか**⁵【献花】▣ 献花者 a「flower [wreath] donor. 献花料[代] a cash offering for flowers《at a shrine》.

**げんか**²【原価】▣ 原価配分 cost allocation.

**けんかい**³【狷介】▣ 狷介孤高 a determined aloof indifference to the ways of the world. 狷介固陋(ろう)(a) narrow-minded, self-righteous obstinacy.

**げんかい**²【限界】▣ 限界削減費用《環境》〔環境汚染物質の〕(a) marginal abatement cost (略: MAC). 限界集落 a rural community at the limit of viability due to aging and depopulation; a barely viable community. 限界耐力計算《建》〔耐震強度計算法〕limit strength calculation.

**げんかいつつじ**【玄海躑躅】『植』〔ツツジ科の落葉低木〕 *Rhododendron mucronulatum* var. *ciliatum*.

**けんがく**¹【見学】▣ 社会見学 a (social studies)「field trip. 自由見学〔案内人のつかない〕a free [an unrestricted, an unescorted] tour《of the museum》; going around《an exhibition》「on *one's* own [at *one's* own pace]. ▣ 見学会《a factory》「visit [tour]. ▶現地〜会〔不動産物件などの〕an on-site visit; a visit to the site《of a new house》; 県内史跡〜会 a tour of historical sites in the prefecture / 国会議事堂〜会 a「visit to [tour of] the Diet Building.

**げんかしょうきゃく**【減価償却】▣ 減価償却資産 a depreciable asset. ▶小額〜資産 a「small [petty] sum depreciable asset; a depreciable asset of between 200,000 and 100,000 yen.

**げんかほう**【原価法】《商》the (historical) cost method. ▣ 最終仕入原価法 the last「purchase price [purchase, cost] method.

**ケンガリ**【小鉦】『楽器』〔朝鮮の伝統打楽器〕a Kwanggari.

**げんかん**¹【玄関】▣ 玄関飾り〔正月の〕New Year *genkan* decorations;〔飾りつけること〕decorating the front door (area) for the New Year. 玄関収納 *genkan* storage; making space to store《things》in the *genkan*.

**げんかんさりょうほう**【減感作療法】▣ 舌下減感作療法 sublingual immunotherapy (略: SLIT).

**けんかんろん**【遣韓論】『日本史』〔朝鮮に使節を派遣し外交関係を樹立すべきだという西郷隆盛の主張〕the debate over sending a diplomatic mission to Korea (as advocated by Saigō Takamori).

**けんき**³【建機】〔建設機械〕construction「equipment [machinery]. ▣ 建機レンタル業 construction equipment rental. ▶〜レンタル業者 a construction equipment rental company.

**けんきゅう**²【研究】▣ 研究委託 entrusting [farming out] research《to a laboratory》. 研究委託費 fees for research《into the peaceful use of atomic energy》commissioned from《various universities》. 研究業績 research results; a research record. 研究拠点 a center of research. ▶国際〜拠点 an international center of research. 研究書《write》a study《of Leonard da Vinci》. 研究試料 a research「sample [specimen];《genetic》material(s). 研究主任 a person in charge of research; a「chief [administrator]. 研究職〔地位・職種〕a career in research; a research position;〔人〕a researcher. 研究段階《in, at》the research stage. ▶その技術はまだ〜段階にある. The technology is still「in [at] the research stage. 研究調査費 research and survey「funds [expenses]. 研究倫理 research ethics. 研究炉〔原子力〕a research reactor.

**けんきゅういん**【研究員】▣ 上席[上級]研究員〔研究所などの〕a senior「fellow [researcher]《at the ABC Institute》.

**けんきゅうかいはつせんりゃくセンター**【研究開発戦略〜】〔科学技術振興機構の1部門〕the Center for Research and Development Strategy (略: CRDS).

**げんきょく**²【限局】▣ 限局がん『医』(a) localized「cancer [carcinoma].

**げんきょくせい**【限局性】〜の『医』localized; circumscribed. ▣ 限局性がん (a) localized「cancer [carcinoma]. 限局性強皮症 localized [circumscribed] scleroderma. 限局性前立腺がん localized prostate cancer.

**けんきん**²【献金】▣ 迂回献金 ⇨うかい¹. 大口[小口]献金 a「large [small] contribution.

**げんきん**¹【現金】▣ 現金給与総額 total cash wages. 純現金収支〔フリーキャッシュフロー〕free cash flow (略: FCF). 現金(収支)割引法 discounted cash flow method. 現金持ち帰り〔購入品の配達や分割払いに対して〕cash-and-carry《store, system》.

**げんけい**³【原型】▣ 原型炉『原子力』a prototype reactor.

**げんけい**⁵【減刑】▣ 減刑判決 a「reduced [commuted] sentence.

**けんけつ**²【欠缺】『法』▶意思の〜〔意思表示が意図と異なること〕lack of intent.

**げんげつ**³【限月】▶中心限月〔最も取引高が多い限月のこと〕the most active contract month; the active month.

**けんてつまく**【瞼結膜】『解』= 眼瞼結膜(⇨がんけん²).

**げんご**¹【言語】▣ 異言語〔母語以外の〕another [a foreign, a different] language;〔相異なる〕different languages. 言語外言語 (a) non-verbal language. 言語発達遅滞『精神医』delayed speech development; language [speech] delay. 言語文化 language and culture; linguistics and culture(s);《a》language [linguistic] culture; the culture of《a》language; the language of a culture. 言語野〔脳〕『解』〔大脳の〕the「language [speech] area [part] of the brain. ▶ブローカ中枢(言語理解領野, Broca's area)とウェルニッケ中枢(言語運動領野, Wernicke's area)とがある. ▶非〜脳〔大脳の〕non-language「area [part] of the brain. 言語力 language ability; ability at a language. ▶学校教育で〜力の涵養を図る aim to develop「language [linguistic] ability at school.

**けんこう**⁴【健康】▶*one's* health「luck [fortune]. 健康オタク = 健康マニア. 健康管理士 a certified health care manager. 健康管理手帳〔危険有害業務に従事した労働者に交付される〕a health care handbook. 健康グッズ[用品] health「products [goods]. 健康警告表示〔たばこの箱の〕a《cigarette》health warning (message). 健康サンダル health sandals. 健康志向 health consciousness; health awareness. ▶最近、年齢・性別を問わず〜志向が高まっている. Recently health awareness has been increasing among both sexes and all age groups. / 〜

志向商品[食品] health-oriented 「products [foods]. 健康寿命 (an) average healthy life expectancy. ◐平均~寿命 (of 70 years for children born in 1999). 健康検査 a 「health [medical] check-up [examination]. 健康線 [手相] the 「health [Health] line; the 「line of health [Line of Health]. 健康茶 health tea. 健康ノイローゼ (a) health neurosis [obsession]; (a) 「neurosis about [(an) obsession with] (one's). ◐~被害救済制度 a system to assist people whose health has been damaged ⟪by pollution⟫. 健康病 ＝健康ノイローゼ. 健康マニア a health nut; a health freak. ◐~マニアの彼は毎日走って通勤している. He's such a health nut he runs to work every day. 健康余命 healthy life expectancy (略：HLE). 健康ランド〔大浴場を中心に健康増進や保養のための設備を備えた施設〕a health resort; a health spa with public baths and other health-promoting and recreational facilities.

けんごう1【剣豪】 ▫ 剣豪小説 a 「swordfighting [swashbuckling] novel;〔ジャンル〕swashbuckling fiction.

げんごう3【現合】〔加工作業の現場合わせ〕＝現場合わせ（⇨げんば）.

けんこういじきこう[そしき]【健康維持機構[組織]】＝エイチ・エム・オー.

けんこううんどうしどうし【健康運動指導士】a certified health and athletic trainer.

けんこうしんだん【健康診断】 ▫ 企業健康診断 a company medical examination.

げんごがく【言語学】 ▫ 神経言語学 neurolinguistics. ◐ neurolinguistic adj.

けんこく4【献穀】offering [an offering of] newly harvested 「grain [rice, millet] to the gods. ~する offer [make an offering of] newly harvested 「grain [rice, millet] to the gods. ▫ 献穀祭 a grain-offering ceremony; a Shinto ceremony where newly harvested grain is offered to the gods.

けんさ【検査】 ▫ 検査忌避〔監督官庁の検査に対する非協力や妨害〕evasion of inspection; evading an inspection. 検査商法〔悪質商法の一種〕an inspection scam; the method of making sales by posing as inspectors and declaring the need for replacement items. 検査データ inspection data. 検査被曝 diagnostic radiation exposure. 検査妨害 obstruction of [interference with] inspection; obstructing [interfering with] an inspection. 検査ライン〔製造工場などの〕an inspection line. 検査率〔輸入食品などに対する〕the inspection rate (for imported beef).

げんさい3【減災】natural disaster (damage) reduction. ▫ 減災社会 a society in which damage from natural disasters can be kept to a minimum. 減災目標 a target for reducing damage from natural disasters; a natural disaster damage reduction target.

げんざい2【現在】 ▫ 現在価値〔会計〕(a) present value (略：PV). ◐ 正味~価値〔会計〕(a) net present value (略：NPV).

けんさく3【検索】 ▫ 横断検索〔複数の検索対象を一挙に検索すること〕cross-searching. ◐ 横断~可能な cross-searchable. ▫ 検索広告 ＝検索連動型広告. 検索窓, 検索ウインドー〔電算〕〔検索ソフトなどで検索する文字列を入力する場所〕a search window. 検索漏れ (a search failure; failure to retrieve an item. ◐ 完全一致で検索すると比較的~漏れが少なくて済む. If you do a search with an initial match you will be 「less likely to miss an item [more likely to find all the relevant items]. | Searching with a wildcard at the end of a string will reduce the chance of missing items. 検索連動型広告〔インターネット上の〕pay-per-click advertising.

けんさつ2【検察】 ▫ 検察側冒頭陳述 an [the] opening statement by the prosecutor; the prosecutor's [a prosecution] opening statement.

けんさにんしょうせいど【検査認証制度】〔有機農産物及び有機農産物加工食品の〕the Inspection and Certification System for Organic Agricultural Products and Organic Processed Foods.

けんさん4【硯山】〔中国雲南省の県〕Yanshan.

げんさん3【原産地】 ▫ 原産地表示〔食品などの〕an indication of (the place of) origin. ◐ 原料~表示〔加工食品の〕an indication of (the place of) origin of ingredients.

けん5【検視】 ▫ 検視調書 a 「medical [forensic] examiner's report.

げんし9【嫌子】【心理】⟪act as⟫ 「(a) negative reinforcement [a negative reinforcer].

げんし3【原子】 ▫ 原子燃料サイクル〔核燃料サイクル〕the nuclear fuel cycle. 原子メモリー〔電算〕atomic memory. 原子野〔原爆が落ちた後の焼け野原〕an atomic 「wasteland [desert, wilderness].

げん6【原始】 ▫ 原始海洋 the primordial ocean. 原始資本主義 primitive capitalism. 原始生物 a primitive 「organism [form of life]; ⟨集合的⟩ primitive life. 原始生命 primitive life. 原始反射【医】〔乳児の〕an infantile [a primitive] reflex. 原始反応【精神医】a primitive reaction. 原始微生物 a primitive 「microbe [microorganism].

げんし9【原資】 ▫ 配当原資 a dividend payment fund.

げんしかく【原子核】 ▫ 原子核変換【物】(a) nuclear 「transformation [transmutation].

「原始家族フリントストーン」⇨「恐妻天国」.

げんじつ2【現実】 ▫ 現実問題 a practical problem;〔副詞的に〕in 「practice (actuality); as a matter of fact. ◐~問題として, この企画を進めるには人数が足りない. The fact of the matter is that we do not have the manpower to carry out this plan. / ~問題, この収入で生活していくのは難しいんですよ. In practice, trying to live on this level of income is difficult.

げんしほうしゃせんのえいきょうにかんするこくれんかがくいいんかい【原子放射線の影響に関する国連科学委員会】the United Nations Scientific Committee on the Effects of Atomic Radiation (略：UNSCEAR).

けんじゃせいしょう【検邪聖省】〔カトリック〕〔教理省の旧名〕the Supreme Sacred Congregation of the Holy Office.

けんしゅ【犬種】a breed of dog.

けんしゅう1【研修】 ▫ 校外研修 out-of-school 「training [education]; an out-of-school course;〔大学の〕*off-campus [「extramural] training [education]. 校内研修 in-school 「training [education]; an in-school course;〔大学の〕*on-campus [「intramural] training [education]. 宿泊研修 a training camp; a residential course 「away from school [off campus];⟪going on⟫ a residential study trip. 新人[新入社員]研修 training [a training course] for 「newcomers [new members, new employees]. 洋上研修 training at sea.

けんじゅう5【拳銃】 ▫ 二丁拳銃 two 「guns [pistols]; ⟪a man with⟫ a 「gun [pistol] in each hand. ▫ 拳銃自殺 killing [shooting] oneself with a 「pistol [handgun]. 拳銃使用 the use of firearms. ◐ 適正な~使用 the appropriate use of firearms. 拳銃使用基準〔警官などの〕regulations on [rules on, standards for] the use of firearms.

「拳銃無宿」〔銃を腰に旅をする賞金稼ぎの TV 西部劇〕Wanted: Dead or Alive. ▶ スティーブ・マックイーン

けんしょう

(Steve McQueen)の出世作.

けんしょう⁴【検証】 ▭ 検証記事 a report on the results of an internal inquiry (into the accuracy of 《an article》); an internal inquiry report. 検証番組 a program announcing the results of an internal inquiry (into the accuracy of 《a documentary》); an internal inquiry program.

けんしょう⁸【顕彰】 ▭ 顕彰運動 a campaign to publicly honor 《the late Mr. Yamada》. ◐ 戦没者～運動 a campaign to publicly honor the war dead.

けんしょう¹⁰【懸賞】 ▭ オープン懸賞〔応募に制限がなく, はがきやネットでだれでも応募できる懸賞〕an open contest. クローズド懸賞〔あらかじめ商品を買って規定の応募券などを入手して応募する懸賞〕a closed contest. ▭ 懸賞マニア a person who is obsessed with entering prize contests; a rabid contest enterer. 懸賞幕〔相撲〕【懸賞金を出すスポンサー名入りの小型の旗〕a small flag presented to a sumo wrestler by a financial sponsor.

けんじょう⁴【謙譲】 ▭ 謙譲表現 a deferential「expression [phrase, choice of words]; a phrase indicating「deference [humility].

げんしょう⁴【現症】〔医〕〔現在の症状〕《a patient's》current condition; the status 《of an illness》.

げんしょう²【現状】

▭ 現状追認 acceptance of the status quo. 現状認識 recognition [understanding, perception] of the「status quo [present situation]. ◐ 老後は国が面倒を見てくれるだなんて, 君の～認識は甘すぎるよ. If you think the government will look after you in your old age, your understanding of the status quo leaves something to be desired. 現状判断指数〔経〕〔内閣府が行う景気ウォッチャー調査の〕an index of current economic indicators; an economic diffusion index. 現状分析 (an) analysis of the「status quo [present situation]. 現状変更 (an) alteration [(a) modification] of the status quo. ◐ 市は歴史的な町並みを保存するため, 建造物の～変更の規制を定めた. To preserve the historic townscape, the city enacted restrictions on changes in the condition of buildings. 現状渡し〔中古物件などの〕handing *sth* over in its present state.

げんしょうせつ【元宵節】〔中国の祭り; 旧暦1月15日〕the Lantern Festival; Yuan xiao jie.

げんしょく⁴【検食】1〔責任者による給食品の検査・試食〕(a) food inspection.

2〔食中毒発生に備えて給食品ごとに2週間以上冷凍保存される少量の検体〕a「stored [reserve] sample.

げんしりょく【原子力】 ▭ 原子力白書〔内閣府〕the White Paper on Nuclear Energy 《2004》.

げんしりょくあんぜんきばんこう【原子力安全基盤機構】〔独立行政法人〕the Japan Nuclear Energy Safety Organization (略: JNES).

げんしりょくあんぜんはくしょ【原子力安全白書】〔内閣府〕the 《2004》White Paper on Nuclear Safety.

げんしりょくきょうきゅうこくグループ【原子力供給国-】the Nuclear Suppliers Group (略: NSG).

げんしりょくせいさくたいこう【原子力政策大綱】〔原子力委員会が2005年に策定〕the Framework for Nuclear Energy Policy.

「原子力潜水艦シービュー号海底科学作戦」〔米国の, 海底冒険ものの TV ドラマ〕Voyage to the Bottom of the Sea.

げんしりょくのひ【原子力の日】〔10月26日〕Atomic Energy Day.

げんしりょくはつでんかんきょうせいびきこう【原子力発電環境整備機構】the Nuclear Waste Management Organization of Japan (略: NUMO).

げんしりょくはつでんぎじゅつきこう【原子力発電技術機構】the Nuclear Power Engineering Corporation (略: NUPEC).

げんしりょくはつでんしょのたいしんせっけいしんさしん【原子力発電所の耐震設計審査指針】=耐震指針 (⇒たいしん⁶).

げんしりょくほう【原子力法】【米法】the Atomic Energy Act.

げんしろ【原子炉】 ▭ 原子炉格納容器 a (nuclear) reactor containment vessel. 原子炉隔離冷却系〔原子炉の給水系停止時に炉心に給水を行う設備〕a reactor core isolation cooling system (略: RCIC). 原子炉出力 reactor power.

けんしん²【健診・検診】 ▭ 企業健診=企業健康診断 (⇒けんこうしんだん).

けんしん⁴【検針】 ▭ 検針器〔水道・ガス・電気などの〕a meter reading device; meter reading equipment;〔縫製品などの〕a device for inspecting clothing to ensure that no needles etc. remain in the material. 検針票〔水道・ガス・電気などの〕a slip of paper showing a meter reading; a meter-reading slip.

けんすい⁴【懸垂】 ▭ 懸垂幕〔垂れ幕〕a (vertical) banner.

げんすいばくきんしにほんきょうぎかい【原水爆禁止日本協議会】the Japan Council against Atomic and Hydrogen Bombs.

げんすいばくきんしにほんこくみんかいぎ【原水爆禁止日本国民会議】the Japan Congress against A- and H-Bombs.

ゲンズブール Gainsbourg, Serge (1928-91; フランスの歌手・作曲家; 本名 Lucien Ginsbury).

けんせい⁸【県西】〔宮崎〕the western (part of the) prefecture; western《Miyazaki Prefecture》. ◐ ～《a fishing port》in western《Ehime》.

げんぜい【減税】 ▭ 減税補填債 a tax-income reduction compensation bond.

けんせいじゅん【建制順】〔組織内の部局などの設置順〕(in) chronological order of「establishment [incorporation, founding].

けんせいだい【顕生代】【地質】the Phanerozoic (eon). ▷ Phanerozoic *adj*.

けんせつ¹【建設】 ▭ 建設協力金〔会計〕〔集合住宅・ビルなどの建築開始前に入居予定者から建て主に出資される建設金〕a construction cooperation fee; upfront construction money. 建設資材 construction materials. 建設投資循環〔経〕the construction investment cycle. 建設副産物〔建設工事に伴い発生する再生資源と廃棄物〕construction by-products. 建設用運搬船 a construction barge.

けんせつこうじふんそうしんさかい【建設工事紛争審査会】〔各都道府県に1つずつ設置〕a [the] Committee for Investigation of Construction Disputes. ▭ 中央建設工事紛争審査会〔国土交通省に設置〕the Central Committee for Investigation of Construction Disputes. 都道府県建設工事紛争審査会 Prefectural Committees for Investigation of Construction Disputes.

けんぜん¹【健全】 ▭ 健全経営 sound management. 健全性指標〔経営の〕an economic health index;〔河川・土壌などの〕an environmental health index.

けんぞうぶつ【建造物】 ▭ 建造物侵入【法】illegal [unlawful] entry into a building or other structure; trespass(ing)「in [on] a building. 建造物等放火罪【法】the crime of setting fire to buildings or other structures. 建造物緑化 making buildings green; the greening of buildings; decorating buildings with greenery.

げんそく¹【原則】 ▭ 原則合意 an agreement「in principle [on principle(s)]. 原則論 a theory [an argument] based on principle(s). ◐ 米朝は互いに～論を繰り返すばかりで, 歩み寄ろうとする姿勢を見せなかった. The United States and North Korea just repeated their hardline arguments and showed no willingness to

compromise.
**げんそく**[3]【減速】　▣　減速感〔景気などの〕a「sense [feeling] of slowdown《in the economy》.
**げんそん**[3]【減損】　▣　減損処理《会計》book value depreciation of a fixed asset; an accounting system requiring firms to record valuation losses on fixed assets.
**けんたい**[5]【検体】　▣　保管検体〔献血された血液の〕a stored sample.
**けんたい**[6]【献体】　献体者　a whole body donor.
**けんたい**[4]【減胎】《医》selective reduction; fetal reduction.　減胎手術　a selective reduction operation.
**げんだい**[2]【現代】　現代国語《教科名》modern Japanese.　現代美術[芸術]　contemporary art.
**げんだい**[3]【現代】＝ヒュンダイ.
**げんたいしょうしゃ**【原体照射】《医》〔放射線療法の1つ〕conformation radiotherapy.
**げんだいてききょういくニーズとりくみしえんプログラム**【現代的教育-取組支援-】《教育》〔文部科学省が社会的要請の強い課題に対応した優れた教育的取り組みを公募で選び予算を重点配分した〕the Support Program for Contemporary Educational Needs.
**けんたん**[2]【検反】fabric inspection.
**げんたんい**【原単位】《経営》a「basic [standard] unit《of output》.
**けんち**[4]【検知】　▣　検知機能 a「recognition [detection] function.　◐インク残量～機能〔プリンターなどの〕a remaining ink level detection function; ink level detection / 顔～機能〔デジタルカメラなどの〕a face recognition function.
**げんち**[2]【現地】　▣　現地音 a [the] local「reading [pronunciation]《of a place name》.　◐外国地名は～音に準じて表記する. We follow the local reading(s) of foreign place names.｜Foreign place names are given their local readings.　現地解散　breaking up [dispersing, saying goodbye] on the spot.　現地価格　local price; price at point of origin.　現地現物主義《insist on》the principle of the actual article in its own location. [⇒現場主義《⇨げんば》]　現地集合　meeting [getting together] on the spot; gathering at the venue.　現地取材《carry out》「on-location [on-the-spot] research;《do》an assignment on (the) site.　現地食　local [regional] food.　現地通貨建て債券　a local currency denominated bond.　現地保存　local preservation.
**けんちく**[0]【建築】　▣　建築構造学　structural engineering (for architects); architectural structure(s).　建築残材　waste (products) from construction; building waste.　建築廃材[廃棄物]《illegal dumping of》construction debris.　建築防災学　disaster prevention engineering.
**けんちくかんきょう・しょうエネルギーきこう**【建築環境・省-機構】〔財団法人〕the Institute for Building Environment and Energy Conservation (略: IBEC).
**けんちくけんきゅうじょ**【建築研究所】〔独立行政法人〕the Building Research Institute (略: BRI).
**けんちくぶつ**[0]【建築物】　▣　建築物環境衛生管理基準〔ビル衛生管理法に定める〕standards for the environmentally hygienic management of buildings.　建築物緑化　making buildings green; the greening of buildings.
**けんちくぶつそうごうかんきょうせいのうひょうかシステム**【建築物総合環境性能評価-】the Comprehensive Assessment System for Building Environmental Efficiency (略: CASBEE). [＝キャスビー]
**げんちょう**[3]【弦長】《空》〔翼の前後の幅〕a chord.　▣　翼弦長　the chord of a wing; a wing chord.　付根弦長 a chord at root; a wing root chord; a root chord.　翼端弦長　a chord at tip; a wing tip chord; a tip chord.

**けんてい**[1]【検定】　▣　片側検定《統計》a one-tail(ed) test.　色彩(能力)検定 a color coordination test.　▶「文部科学省認定 ファッションコーディネート色彩能力検定」の通称.　両側検定《統計》a two-tail(ed) test.　▣　検定外教科書　an unauthorized textbook; a textbook not authorized by the Japanese Ministry of Education, Culture, Sports, Science and Technology.　検定球 ＝公式(試合)球 (⇨こうしき[1]).
**げんてい**[1]【限定】　▣　限定生産　limited production.
**ケント**[2]　Kent, Stacey (1968-　; 米国出身の女性ジャズ歌手).
**げんど**【限度】　▣　限度額 a limit; the「most [least] one is prepared to accept; the「highest [lowest] acceptable「sum [amount]; a「maximum [minimum] (sum).　◐最高[最低]～額　an [the] absolute limit; the (very)「highest [lowest] acceptable sum; one's utmost / 借入～額　a borrowing limit; the maximum one can borrow.
**けんとう**[5]【検討】　▣　検討課題　an issue for examination.　検討事項[項目]　an item「for consideration [to be considered].
**けんとう**[7]【県東】the eastern (part of the) prefecture; eastern《Saitama Prefecture》.　◐～の《the industrial zone》in eastern《Kanagawa》.
**けんとう**[7]【玄冬】〔冬の異称〕(the) winter.
**けんとうし**【遣唐使】　▣　遣唐使船　(one of) the ships conveying Japanese missions to Tang-dynasty China.
**けんとうしき**【見当識】　▣　現実見当識訓練〔認知症対処療法の1つ〕reality orientation (略: RO).　▣　見当識障害　(an) orientation disturbance; impaired orientation; disorientation.
**けんどじょう**【検土杖】《地質》〔土壌検査用の〕a soil [an earth] auger [sampler]; a soil sampling「auger [rod].
**けんなん**[1]【県南】the southern (part of the) prefecture; southern《Fukushima Prefecture》.　◐～の《the forests》in southern《Wakayama》.
**げんにく**【減肉】《金属》〔金属の厚みが腐食や摩耗によって薄くなること〕thinning; wastage.　～する　become thin(ner).　▣　減肉現象[事象] a「thinning [wastage] phenomenon.　減肉摩耗　corrosion wastage.
**げんにん**[2]【現認】＝現場確認 (⇨げんば).　～する　conduct an on-the-spot check; confirm《what has happened》by going to check (for oneself).
**げんねんりょう**【原燃料】〔原料・材料および燃料〕raw materials and fuel(s).　▣　原燃料価格[費]　raw material and fuel「prices [costs]; costs [prices] of raw materials and fuels.　原燃料費調整制度〔原油・天然ガスなどの輸入価格と為替相場の変動を3か月ごとに電気・ガス料金に反映させる制度〕the system whereby changes in the price of fuels, resulting from exchange-rate fluctuations or import-price changes, are reflected after three months in consumer prices for electricity and gas.
**けんのう**[2]【権能】　▣　国家権能 a function of the state.
**げんば**【現場】　▣　現場合わせ〔図面とか数値に頼るのではなく, 現場で現物を合わせてみて加工すること〕an on-site [an on-the-spot, a field] adjustment [modification].　現場海域[水域]〔海難事故などの〕the「neighboring [adjacent] waters; the waters where《the accident》took place; the area of《the incident》.　◐不審船発見の報告を受けて海上保安庁は警備艇3隻を～海域に急行させた. Informed that a mystery ship had been discovered, the Japan Coast Guard rushed three patrol boats to the area.　現場確認《現場における状況の確認》an on-site check; (an) on-site confirmation;〔現場がどこであるかの確認〕＝現場特定.　現場指揮　on-the-spot「supervision [control, command]; responsibility at the site.　◐～指揮官[者]

げんばく

the「official [person] in charge on the spot; the「official [person] in charge at a site; a local [an on-site] superintendent / ～指揮本部 (a) local [(an) on-site, (an) on-the-spot] headquarters; (a) headquarters at the site. 現場主義 a focus [an emphasis] on「on-the-spot activities [the workplace, where the action is]. 現場責任者 the person in charge of a《building》site; a site「foreman [supervisor]. 現場第一主義 treating what happens on location as a priority; giving priority to the people actually involved. 現場特定 specification [confirmation] of a location; establishing the site《of a crash》. ◐墜落現場はこの海域と思われるが、夜間のため～特定が遅れている。The crash is thought to have taken place in this part of the sea, but since it is night time it has not yet been possible to confirm the location. | The plane is thought to have crashed in this area of the sea, but it is still dark, so there is being a delay in establishing the actual spot. 現場復帰 a return《to the scene》;《make》a comeback.

げんばく² 【原爆】 ◐ 原爆忌 the《60th》anniversary of the atomic bombing of「Hiroshima [Nagasaki]. ▶ 広島は8月6日、長崎は8月9日。原爆死没者慰霊式 a memorial service for the atomic bomb victims. ◐ 広島市～死没者慰霊式並びに平和祈念式 the Hiroshima Peace Memorial Ceremony. 原爆小頭症〔医〕microcephaly caused by A-bomb radiation. 原爆症認定 official「registration [certification] of a person as suffering from an A-bomb disease. ◐ ～症認定患者 a「registered [certified] victim of an A-bomb disease.

げんばつ 【厳罰】 ◐ 厳罰化 toughening [stiffening, strengthening] a penalty; making a punishment「more stringent [harsher]. ◐ 飲酒運転の～化を求める声が大きくなってきている。Calls for stronger penalties for drinking and driving are growing. | There is an increasing demand for stiffer penalties for drink-driving. 厳罰論 an argument for strict punishment.

げんばつ 【原発】 ◐ 原発アレルギー an aversion to nuclear power. 原発ジプシー〔原子力発電所を渡り歩く労働者〕a nuclear「gypsy [nomad]; a nuclear power worker who moves from job to job. 原発耐震指針 耐震指針(⇨たいしん⁶). 原発不明がん〔医〕〔原発巣が不明ながん〕(a) cancer of unknown primary (略: CUP).

げんぱつせい 【原発性】 ◐ 原発性アルドステロン症〔医〕primary aldosteronism. 原発性硬化性胆管炎〔医〕primary sclerosing cholangitis (略: PSC).

げんばん² 【鍵盤】 ◐ 足鍵盤 a pedalboard.

げんばん² 【原盤】 ◐ 原盤権〔著作隣接権の一つで、原盤制作者の権利〕master recording rights.

げんぱん 【原版】〔複製・翻訳などの元となるもの〕a master; an original.

げんび² 【巻餅】《菓子》〔小麦粉を練り細切りにして焼いたもの〕baked dough strips. ◐ 芋けんぴ ⇨いも.

けんびきょう 【顕微鏡】 ◐ 形状測定顕微鏡 a (3D) profile (measuring) microscope. ◐ 顕微鏡カメラ a microscope camera.

げんぶつ² 【現物】 ◐ 現物債 a physical bond. ◐ ～債市場 the physical bond market. 現物投資 a spot investment. ◐《金(*き*)の》～投資 a spot gold investment.

けんぼう 【健忘】 ◐ 全生活史健忘〔医〕generalized amnesia.

けんぽう⁴ 【憲法】 ◐ 恒久[暫定]憲法 a「permanent [provisional] constitution. 憲法解釈 the「interpretation [construction] of the Constitution; constitutional interpretation. 憲法解釈権 the right to interpret the constitution. 憲法起草委員会 a constitution(al) drafting committee. 憲法裁判所 a constitutional court. 憲法尊重擁護義務〔日本国憲法の第99条の規定〕《have》the obligation to respect and uphold the Constitution.

けんぽうちょうさすいしんぎいんれんめい 【憲法調査推進議員連盟】 the Federation of Diet Members for the Promotion of Research on the Constitution.

けんぽうちょうさとくべついいんかい 【憲法調査特別委員会】〔衆議院と参議院にそれぞれ設置される〕the Special Investigative Committee on the Constitution. ▶正式名称は「日本国憲法に関する調査特別委員会」.

けんぽく 【県北】 the northern (part of the) prefecture; northern《Kumamoto Prefecture》. ◐ ～の《the farming area》in northern《Kagoshima》.

げんまい 【玄米】 ◐□ 玄米ご飯 (cooked) brown rice.

けんみん 【県民】 ◐□ 県民栄誉賞 a prefectural prize of honor.

げんめつ 【幻滅】 ◐□ 幻滅感 a sense of「disillusionment [disenchantment]《with politics》.

けんやく 【倹約】 ◐□ 倹約遺伝子〔遺伝〕a thrifty gene.

げんゆ 【原油】 ◐□ 原油先物価格 a crude oil futures price. 原油先物市場 a crude oil futures market. 原油スポット価格 spot oil prices. 原油スポット市場 the spot market for crude oil. 原油調達 crude oil procurement. ◐ ～調達コスト the cost of crude oil procurement.

げんよきん 【現預金】〔現金および預金など〕cash and cash equivalents.

けんり 【権利】 ◐□ 権利意識 (an) awareness [(a) consciousness] of one's rights. ◐ 株主の～意識が高い米国では、機関投資家が経営陣に注文を付けることは日常茶飯事である。In the USA, where people are highly conscious of their rights, it is perfectly ordinary for institutional investors to make demands of the management. / ～意識に目覚める become aware of one's rights; realize that one has rights. 権利関係 (a matter related to) rights. ◐ 過去のテレビ番組をインターネットで流すのは～関係が複雑で簡単にはいかない。With complex problems of rights involved, it is not easy to show old TV programs on the Internet. 権利行使価格〔取引〕an exercise [a strike] price. 権利床〔再開発事業によって建設されたビルの〕(land and) floor space allocated to the original landowner; landholder space. [⇨保留床 (⇨ほりゅう¹)]. 権利の行使〔法〕exercise (of a right). 権利(の)喪失〔法〕(a) forfeit(ure) of「a right [sb's right]《to appeal》.

げんりしゅぎ 【原理主義】 ◐□ キリスト教原理主義 Christian fundamentalism.

けんりつ 【県立】 ◐□ 県立公園 (be designated) a prefectural park.

げんりょう¹ 【原料】 ◐□ 主原料 a main ingredient. ◐ バーボンウイスキーはトウモロコシを主～とする。Bourbon has corn as its main ingredient. 副原料 a「secondary [subsidiary] ingredient. ◐ 日本のビールは、主な原料は麦芽だが、副～として米やトウモロコシが用いられることが多い。In Japanese beer, the main ingredient is barley malt, but often such things as rice or corn can be used as secondary ingredients. ◐□ 原料コスト the cost of raw materials; raw material costs. 原料価格 raw material(s) prices; the price of raw materials. 原料調達ルート a「procurement [supply] route for raw materials; the「route [channels] through which raw materials are procured. 原料費調整制度〔ガス料金の〕a pricing system indexed to raw material costs.

けんりょく 【権力】 ◐□ 権力中枢 a center of power. 権力犯罪 criminal abuse of power.

げんろん¹ 【言論】 ◐□ 言論弾圧 (the) suppression of free speech.

# こ

**コア** コア・インフレ率〔エネルギーと食料品を除いた物価上昇率〕a core inflation rate. コア技術〔他社にはない自社独自の技術〕a [one's] core technology; a 《firm's》 unique area of expertise. コア業務〔中核となる業務〕a core business.
**ゴア**[2] Gore, Al(bert Arnold), Jr. (1948- ;米国の政治家；クリントン政権の副大統領〔1993-2001〕).
**こあがり**【小上がり】a raised tatami-floored seating area in a Japanese restaurant.
**コア・ネットワーク**〔電算〕a core network.
**コア・ビジネス**〔中核事業〕a core business.
**ごアミノサリチルさん**【5-酸】〔化〕5-aminosalicylic acid (略：5-ASA). 5-アミノサリチル酸製剤 a 5-aminosalicylic acid product.
**ゴアレーベン**〔ドイツ，ニーダーザクセン州の町〕Gorleben.
**こい**[1]【恋】 恋占い romantic fortune-telling. ヒナゲシの花の花びらで〜占いをしてみた. I plucked the petals from a red poppy to find out my romantic fate.
**こい**[4]【故意】 確定的(な)故意〔法〕(a) definite intent.
**こいくちシャツ**【鯉口〜】〔服飾〕a Japanese-style round-necked loose T-shirt (for festivals).
「**恋する遺伝子**」〔映画〕Someone Like You.
「**恋する神父**」〔映画〕Love So Divine.
「**恋する惑星**」〔映画〕Chungking Express；〔中国語タイトル〕重慶森林.
「**恋に落ちたら…**」〔映画〕Mad Dog and Glory.
「**恋におぼれて**」〔映画〕Addicted to Love.
「**恋は嵐のように**」〔映画〕Forces of Nature.
**こいびとみさき**【恋人岬】〔グアム島の岬〕Two Lovers Point.
**こいまり**【古伊万里】old Imari (ware).
**コイララ** Koirala, Girija Prasad (1925- ;ネパールの政治家；首相〔1991-94, 1998-99, 2000-01, 2006- 〕).
**コイル** コイル塞栓術〔医〕〔血管内治療〕(a) coil embolization.
**コイン** コイン精米機 a coin-operated rice-milling [-polishing, -cleaning] machine. コイン・パーキング〔コイン式の有料駐車場〕a coin-operated parking; a coin-operated parking lot.
**コインき**【COIN 機】〔軍〕〔対ゲリラ戦専用機〕a COIN aircraft; a counterinsurgency aircraft.
**コインテグレーション**〔経〕＝きょうぶん.
**こう**[14]【香】 コーン香〔円錐型の香〕cone incense. 香皿 an incense 「tray [holder, stand]. 香立て an incense 「stand [holder].
**こうあつ**[4]【高圧】 高圧給水加熱器 a high-pressure feedwater heater. 高圧水素タンク a high-pressure hydrogen tank. 高圧電力〔電〕high-voltage [high-tension] power [electricity].
**こうあつガスほあんほう**【高圧-保安法】〔法〕the High Pressure Gas Safety Law.
**こうあん**[1]【公安】 公安車両 a public security vehicle. 公安省〔中国の〕the Ministry of Public Security (of the People's Republic of China) (略：MPS).
**コウアンドロゲン**【抗-】〔生化〕an antiandrogen.
**こうい**[3]【行為】 行為規範〔職責の持つあるべき姿を示す規則〕a code of behavior 《for legislators》.
**こうい**[6]【皇位】 皇位継承資格 qualification for the Imperial succession; a [the] right to succeed to the Imperial Throne. 〜継承資格者 a person 「qualified [entitled] to succeed to the Imperial Throne.
**こうい**[8]【高位】 高位推計 a high 「estimate [projection]. 高位発熱量〔物〕a high 「heating [heat] value (略：HHV).

**ごうい**【合意】 三党[四党]合意〔与党三党[四党]間などの〕a 「three party [four party] agreement. 合意形成 consensus-building. 合意事項 agreed items. 合意政治 consensus politics.
**こういき**【広域】 広域応援〔災害時の〕broad(er) regional aid. 広域合併〔市町村などの〕a「wide-area [regional] merger. 広域基幹林道 an arterial forestry road. 広域緊急援助隊 a regional emergency rescue team. 広域航法〔空〕area navigation (略：RNAV). 広域災害 a disaster covering a wide region; an [a geographically] extensive disaster. 〜災害救急医療情報システム a medical information system for use in geographically extensive disasters. 広域自治体〔構想中の道州制における〕a wide-area municipality. 広域市町村圏 a greater city area (consisting of a major city and smaller surrounding municipalities). 広域停電 a wide area [an extensive] power outage [blackout, power cut]. 広域搬送〔災害時の〕transportation 《of victims to medical facilities》in geographically extensive disasters. 広域被害〔公害などの〕extensive [wide-area] damage; damage over a wide area. 広域連携〔複数の自治体間などの〕cooperation (between neighboring municipalities) over a wide area.
**こういき**[2]【高域】〔音〕the 「high-frequency [treble] range；《at》high frequencies. 高域音 (a) high-frequency sound. 超～音 (an) ultrahigh-frequency sound. 高域再生 reproduction of high frequencies; treble reproduction.
**こういんしょう**【好印象】a 「favorable [good] impression. 〜を持つ have a good impression《of…》/ 〜を与える make a good impression《on…》.
**ごうう**【豪雨】 豪雨被害 torrential rain damage; damage from torrential rain(fall). 全国各地で〜被害が相次いでいる. All over the country, one area after another is suffering damage from torrential rainfall.
**こうウイルス**【抗-】 抗ウイルス薬治療[療法]〔医〕＝こうレトロウイルスりょうほう.
**こうえい**[1]【公営】 公営競技 government-controlled competitive sports events.
**こうエイチ・ビー・エス・(ヒト)めんえきグロブリン**【抗HBs(人)免疫-】〔薬〕anti-HBs immunoglobulin.
**こうえき**[1]【公益】 公益性 public 「benefit [welfare, interest]. そのダムは〜性が低いと判断され、建設が見送られた. The dam was judged to have little public benefit, and construction was put off. 公益法人白書 a white paper on nonprofit corporations;〔総務省の〕the Annual Report on Public Interest Corporations.
**こうえきじぎょうもちかぶがいしゃほう**【公益事業持株会社法】〔米法〕the Public Utility Holding Company Act (略：PUHCA).
**こうえきつうほうしゃほごほう**【公益通報者保護法】〔法〕the Whistleblower Protection Law. ▶ 2006年施行.
**こうエネルギーかそくきけんきゅうきこう**【高-加速器研究機構】the High Energy Accelerator Research Organization (略：KEK).
**こうえん**[1]【口演】 口演記 a transcription of a《comic storyteller's》spoken performance.
**こうえん**[3]【公演】 旗揚げ公演 a debut [an inaugural] performance (by a theatrical company).
**こうえん**[17]【口縁】〔器(う)などの口の部分〕the 「rim [lip]《of a bowl or vessel》.

こうえんちょう【高遠長】〔高い費用はかかるが遠距離の目的地に長期日程で旅行すること〕taking an expensive trip to a distant location; going (on a trip) to a distant place in spite of the price.〔⇨あんきんたん〕

こうえんりょくちかんりざいだん【公園緑地管理財団】the Parks and Recreation Foundation.

こうおん⁶【高温】▷ 高温岩体発電 hot dry rock [HDR] geothermal power generation. 高温期〔基礎体温の〕a [the] high-temperature 「phase [period];〔気温の〕a 「hot [high-temperature] period; a period of high temperature (s). 高温工学試験研究炉〔原子力〕a high-temperature engineering test reactor (略: HTTR). 高温処理 high-temperature [treatment]. 高温プラズマ【物】(a) high-temperature plasma. 高温ポリシリコン TFT 液晶パネル a high-temperature 「polysilicon [poly-Si, PolySi] TFT-LCD panel; a HTPS TFT-LCD panel. 高温ラプチャ〔原子力〕(a) high-temperature rupture.

こうおんしつ【高音質】high [superior] sound quality. ▷〜の high sound quality《recording》. ▷ このテレビは高性能スピーカーを搭載し〜を実現しました. This television is equipped with high performance speakers and has realized superior sound quality. 高音質再生 high sound quality 「reproduction [playback]. 高音質録音 (a) high sound quality recording.

こうか⁷【効果】▷ ウラシマ効果【物】〔亜光速運動を長時間行うことを行った物体の時間が周囲に対して遅れるという現象〕time dilation.

こうか¹¹【降下】▷ 降下訓練〔ロープでの〕(a) descent practice; a practice descent;〔パラシュートでの〕a practice jump.

こうか¹³【高価】▷ 高価買い取り purchasing at high prices;〔掲示〕High Prices Paid.

こうか¹⁴【高架】▷ 高架化〔鉄道など〕elevating [raising](railway tracks). ▷ 中央線の〜化工事 construction work to raise the Chūō Line. 高架水槽 an elevated water tank.

こうかん¹²【公開】▷ 公開計量〔ボクシング〕〔ボクサーが試合に先立って関係者立ち会いのもとで行う体重測定〕an official weigh-in. 公開スパーリング〔ボクシング〕〔ボクサーが試合に先立って報道陣などに見せる模擬試合〕an open [a public] sparring session. 公開生放送 a live broadcast in front of an audience; a live public broadcast. 公開弁論〔韓国の法廷での〕public oral proceedings; a public 「pleading [argument]. 公開法廷〔be tried in〕open court.

こうがい¹【光害】▷ 光害防止条例 a light-pollution 「control [prevention] ordinance.

こうがい¹⁰【郊外】▷ 郊外集積〔大型小売店などの〕concentration 《accumulation》《of superstores》in suburban areas.

こうがい⁷【校外】▷ 校外行事 an out-of-school event. 校外授業 an 「out-of-school [extra-mural] class.

こうかいがいしゃ【きぎょう】かいけいかんしいいんかい【公開会社【企業】会計監査委員会】〔米国の〕the Public Company Accounting Oversight Board (略: PCAOB).

こうかいかぎ【公開鍵】▷ 公開鍵(暗号)基盤 (a) public key infrastructure (略: PKI).

こうかいくんれんじょ【航海訓練所】〔独立行政法人〕the National Institute for Sea Training (略: NIST).

こうかいけい【公会計】public-sector accounting.

こうかいようざい【抗潰瘍剤】【薬】an antiulcer 「drug [agent].

こうかく⁸【降格】▷ 降格圏〔下位リーグなどへ〕a relegation zone. ▷ 自動〜圏〔サッカー〕〔be in, go out of〕the automatic relegation zone.

こうがく²【光学】▷ 光学衛星 an optical satellite. 光学エンジン〔電算〕〔プロジェクターなどの〕an optical engine. 光学ズーム〔写真〕〔デジタルカメラの〕optical zooming;〔そのレンズ〕an optical zoom (lens). ▷ 10倍〜ズーム a 10x optical zoom (lens). 光学素子 an optical device; an optical element.

こうがく⁵【高額】▷ 高額納税者番付 a list of 「high [top] (income) taxpayers.

こうがくれき【高学歴】▷ 高学歴化 an increase in the level of academic achievement. ▷ 女性の〜化と本格的な社会進出は1960年代から顕著になった. Higher levels of academic achievement by women, and their full-scale engagement with society, became noticeable from the 1960s.

こうがさいぼうしゅ【膠芽細胞腫】＝こうがしゅ.

こうがしつ【高画質】▷ 高画質撮影〔写真の〕high-resolution photography;〔動画の〕high-definition filming. 高画質テレビ (a) high-definition 「television [TV]; a high-definition 「television [TV] set; an HDTV (set). 高画質放送 a high-definition [an HDTV] broadcast; high-definition [HDTV] broadcasting. 高画質録画 (a) high-definition [(an) HDTV] recording.

こうがしゅ【膠芽腫】【医】(a) glioblastoma《pl. 〜s, -mata》.

こうかっせいこうレトロウイルスりょうほう【高活性抗－療法】【医】highly active antiretroviral therapy (略: HAART).

こうかび【抗黴】▷ 抗カビ剤 an antifungal agent; (a) fungicide.

こうがもの【甲賀者】【甲賀忍者】a Kōga ninja; a samurai retainer from Kōga, famed for skill at guerrilla tactics.

こうかれい【抗加齢】antiaging. ▷ 抗加齢医学 antiaging medicine.

こうカロリーじょうみゃくえいよう【高-静脈栄養】【医】intravenous hyperalimentation (略: IVH).

こうかん⁴【交換】▷ 列車交換〔鉄道〕〔単線区間において両方向から来る列車のすれ違いを行うこと〕passing (of trains going in opposite directions along a single-track line). ▷ 交換駅【鉄道】〔単線区間において両方向からの列車がすれ違う駅〕a passing station. 交換婚【社会】marriage by exchange. 交換生体腎移植 a liver transplant between two living couples.

こうかん¹⁸【鋼管】▷ 角形鋼管 a rectangular steel tube;〈集合的に〉rectangular steel tubing. 電縫(鋼)管 an 「electric resistance welded [ERW] (steel) pipe. 溶接(鋼)管 a welded (steel) pipe.

こうがん³【睾丸】▷ 停留睾丸【医】a retained [an undescended] testicle [testis]; cryptorchi(di)sm. ▷ 停留〜が自然に降りてくることはほとんどない. A retained testicle will almost never descend 「naturally [on its own].

こうがん⁴【後願】【特許】〔同一の発明について2つ以上の出願があった場合の二番手以降の出願〕a later 「application [filing]. ▷ 後願者 a later applicant;〔特許訴訟などで〕the junior party.

こうがんざい【抗癌剤】▷ 抗癌剤感受性試験 an anticancer agent 「susceptibility [sensitivity] test. 抗癌剤治療 treatment with anticancer drugs; (an) anticancer drug treatment.

こうかんじゅせい【高感受性】(a) high susceptibility《to infection》. ▷〜の highly susceptible《to antibiotics》. ▷ 高感受性者 a person who is highly susceptible《to infection》;〔免疫力が低下した患者〕a compromised patient.

こうかんしょく【好感触】a positive impression. ▷ 彼に監督就任を要請したところ, 受諾してくれそうな〜を得た. When we asked him to serve as manager, 「we got a

positive impression [it seemed likely] that he would accept.
こうかんど2【高感度】▣ 高感度撮影 high-sensitivity photography.
こうき10【後期】▣ 後期日程〔入学試験などの〕a late schedule (for entrance examinations).
こうき20【綱紀】▣ 綱紀弛緩 (a) slackening of official discipline.
こうぎ5【抗議】▣ 厳重抗議 a stiff protest. ◐相手国政府に厳重~する convey a stiff protest to the other government. ▣ 抗議船 a protest boat. 抗議電話 a complaint call; a (tele)phone complaint. 抗議 FAX [メール] a complaint 「fax [e-mail]; a faxed [an e-mailed] complaint. ◐…に~FAX[メール]を送る send a complaint by 「fax [e-mail] to…. 抗議文書 a (written) protest; a note of protest; a letter of protest.
こうきあつ【高気圧】▣ 高気圧エアチェンバー ＝高気圧カプセル. 高気圧カプセル a hyperbaric 「chamber [capsule].
こうきじょう【好騎乗】〖競馬〗skillful riding; (superior) riding skill. ◐今回のレースは佐藤騎手の~が光った. Expert riding by the jockey Satō was on display in this race.
こうきでんりょく【光起電力】▣ 光起電力素子[セル] a photovoltaic cell.
こうきどうしゃ【高機動車】〖自衛隊〗a highly maneuverable vehicle (略: HMV).
こうきどこうかがくけんきゅうセンター【高輝度光科学研究~】the Japan Synchrotron Radiation Research Institute (略: JASRI).
こうきのう【高機能】high functionality; advanced [sophisticated] functions [performance]. ◐~の highly functional; high-performance; advanced; sophisticated. ◐このソフトは~だから初心者には使いづらい. This software is so advanced that it's hard for beginners to use.
▣ 高機能化 the 「adoption [implementation] of 「higher functionality [more advanced functions]. ◐~化する raise the functionality 《of sth》; make sth more advanced. 高機能携帯電話 a smart mobile phone. 高機能化粧品 advanced cosmetics. 高機能自閉症〖精神医〗⇨こうきのうじへいしょう. 高機能樹脂 (a) high-performance resin. 高機能商品 high-functionality [advanced, sophisticated] products. 高機能繊維 (a) high-performance fiber. 高機能ソフト high-performance software. 高機能ロボット a high-performance robot; a (highly) sophisticated robot.
こうきのうこうはんせいはったつしょうがい【高機能広汎性発達障害】〖医〗a high-functioning pervasive developmental disorder (略: HFPDD).
こうきのうじへいしょう【高機能自閉症】〖精神医〗high-functioning autism.
こうきみつ【高気密】high [good] airtightness. 〔⇨こうきねつ〕〖高気密〗high [good] airtightness 《of a building》.
こうきゅう9【高級】▣ 高級腕時計 a luxury [a (high) quality, an expensive] (wrist)watch. 高級鋼[材] high-grade steel. 高級食材 (high) quality [luxury, expensive] foods [foodstuffs]. 高級セダン[スポーツカー] a 「luxury [deluxe, high class] sedan [sports car]. 高級ブランド a 「luxury [high-class, (high) quality] brand. ◐~ブランド店 a 「luxury [high-class, (high) quality] brand store / ~ブランド品 a 「luxury [high-class, (high) quality] brand 「item [product]. 高級マンション a luxury 「apartment [「flat].
こうきゅうじむレベルかいごう【高級事務~会合】〔APEC〕a senior officials(') meeting (略: SOM).
こうきょう2【公共】▣ 公共車両優先システム a Public Transportation Priority System (略: PTPS). 公共マナー public manners.
こうぎょう1【工業】▣ 工業生産指数 an industrial production index. 工業統計調査 a census of manufactures. 工業統計表〔経済産業省が刊行する〕Tables of Industrial Statistics.
こうぎょう4【興行】▣ 興行ビザ an entertainment visa.
こうきょうこうじひんかくほう【公共工事品確法】〖法〗the Public Works Quality Assurance Law. ▶正式名称は「公共工事の品質確保の促進に関する法律」(the Law for Ensuring the Quality of Public Works).
こうきょうじぎょうコストこうぞうかいかくプログラム【公共事業~構造改革~】the Program for Cost Structure Reform in Public Works Projects.
こうぎょうしょゆうけんほう【工業所有権法】〖法〗the Industrial Property Law. [＝さんぎょうざいさんけんほう]
こうきょうとうし【公共投資】▣ 公共投資関係費 expenses related to public works.
こうきん2【公金】▣ 公金納付 (the) payment of funds to a public entity.
こうきん4【抗菌】▣ 抗菌活性 antimicrobial [antibacterial] activity. ◐~活性物質 an antimicrobially active substance. 抗菌繊維 (an) 「antimicrobial [antibacterial] fiber.
こうくう1【口腔】▣ 口腔ケア oral care.
こうくう2【航空】▣ 航空絵画 ＝アビエーション・アート. 航空コンテナ an air cargo container. 航空障害灯〖空〗〔地表・水面から60メートル以上の建築物などに付ける赤色の点滅灯〕an obstruction light. 航空情報 aeronautical information. 航空政策 an air traffic policy. 航空性中耳炎〖医〗aerotitis (media). 航空阻止〖軍〗〔攻撃機などが敵地域に進入しての後方連絡線などを絶つ活動〕(an) air interdiction. 航空灯火 an aviation light. 航空保安官 ＝スカイ・マーシャル. 航空輸出 airborne export(s); exports [exporting] by air. 航空連合〔複数の航空会社の連合体〕an airline alliance; 〔日本の複数の航空会社の労働組合連合体〕the Japan Federation of Aviation Industry Unions (略: JFAIU). 航空路線 ＝こうくうろ.
こうくうアレルギーしょうこうぐん【口腔~症候群】〖医〗〔食後に口腔などでアレルギー反応〕oral allergy syndrome (略: OAS).
こうくうき【航空機】▣ 航空機リース aircraft leasing.
こうくうききけんこういしょばつほう【航空危険行為に処罰法】〖法〗the Law against Dangerous Aviation Practices.
こうくうきせいぞうじぎょうほう【航空機製造事業法】〖法〗the Aircraft Manufacturing Industry Law.
こうくうろ【航空路】▣ 航空路レーダー情報処理システム a radar data processing system (略: RDPS).
こうくうろし【航空路誌】〔国土交通省航空局が発行する〕an aeronautical information publication (略: AIP). ▣ 航空路誌アメンドメント[改訂版] an AIP amendment. 航空路誌サプリメント[補足版] an AIP supplement.
こうくうろずし【航空路図誌】〔防衛省が自衛隊機用に発行する〕a flight information publication (略: FIP).
こうくり【高句麗】▣ 高句麗古墳群〔北朝鮮にある高句麗後期の古墳群〕the (complex of) Koguryo tombs. 高句麗論争〔古代朝鮮の高句麗をめぐる韓国と中国の歴史論争〕the Koguryo issue.
こうけい6【後継】▣ 後継指名 the 「appointment [designation] of a successor. ◐首相の~指名 the 「appointment [designation] of a successor by the prime minister 「himself [herself].
こうけい9【絞頸】ligature strangulation; strangulation with a cord; 〖強盗による〗garroting.
こうげい【工芸】▣ 工芸官〔紙幣等の原図・原板の製作者〕a craftsman [an artisan] employed by the Na-

こうげいが

tional Printing Bureau; an official bank-note artisan. 工芸職人 a craftsman; an artisan.
こうげいが【巧芸画】〖複製画の一種〗a photogravure reproduction of an ink painting or print.
こうけいきん【広頸筋】〖解〗〔首の周辺の筋肉〕(a) platysma 《pl. ~s, -mata》.
こうけいこつきん【後脛骨筋】〖解〗the tibialis posterior (muscle).
こうけいしゃ【後継者】▣ 後継者争い a succession struggle; a struggle for the succession; a struggle to succeed sb. 後継者探し a search for a successor《to sb》.
こうけいぶ【後頸部】〖解〗▣ the nape; the back of the neck. ◐ ~の nuchal. ▣ 後頸部浮腫〖医〗nuchal translucency〖略: NT〗. ◐ ~浮腫検査 nuchal translucency「screening [scanning]; a nuchal translucency「scan [screening test].
こうげき【攻撃】▣ 予防攻撃 a「preemptive [preventive] attack [strike]. 攻撃陣〔スポーツで〕attacking [attack] players; (the) attackers. 攻撃的布陣〔スポーツなどで〕(take) an「offensive [aggressive] stance [position]. 攻撃本能 an aggressive instinct.
こうげき[2]【口撃】a verbal attack;《口》bashing; trashing;《give sb》a tongue-lashing.
 ◐ ~する attack《sb》verbally;《口》slam; bash; trash.
こうけつ[3]【硬結】〖医〗(an) induration.
こうけつあつ【高血圧】▣ 仮面高血圧 masked hypertension. 逆白衣高血圧 reverse white-coat hypertension; masked hypertension. 軽症[中等症, 重症]高血圧 mild [moderate, severe] hypertension. 職場高血圧 workplace hypertension. 早朝高血圧 morning hypertension. 二次性[続発性]高血圧〖医〗secondary hypertension. 夜間高血圧 nocturnal hypertension. ▣ 高血圧症 high blood pressure; (a) hypertensive condition. ◐ ~症治療薬[剤] a drug for high blood pressure; an anti-hypertensive drug.
こうげん[8]【高原】▣ 高原鉄道 a highland railway.
こうけんけん【後見権】guardianship.
こうげんすい【高減衰】high damping. ▣ 高減衰ゴム high-damping rubber. ◐ ~ゴム・ダンパー a high-damping rubber damper.
こうご[1]【口語】▣ 口語化 colloquialization; putting (the Civil Law) into colloquial language.
こうごいし【神籠石】〖考古〗a stone wall fortification (encircling a hill or valley).
こうこう[10]【航行】▣ 航行禁止海域 prohibited waters; an area prohibited to navigation. 航行警報〔海上保安庁が出す〕(issue) a「navigational [navigation] warning.
こうごう[2]【咬合】▣ 咬合(異常)関連症候群〖歯科〗disturbance of functional occlusion syndrome〖略: DOFOS〗. 咬合紙 (an)「articulating [articulation, occluding] paper. 咬合調整 (an) occlusal adjustment. 咬合治療 treatment for malocclusion; occlusal「therapy [treatment]. 咬合誘導 occlusal guidance.
こうこうぎょう【鉱工業】▣ 鉱工業生産財 industrial produce; industrial production goods. ◐ ~生産額出荷指数 an [the] industrial production index.
こうこく[1]【公告】▣ 電子公告〔インターネット上で行う新株発行などの公告〕an「online [internet] ad (for…); online [internet]《stock》「promotion [advertising].
こうこく[3]【広告】▣ 広告協賛金 an advertising sponsorship fee. 広告掲載料〔広告〕advertisement [ad] rates; advertising「rates [charges]. 広告作家 an ad-artist. 広告制作会社 an advertising agency. 広告募集 solicitation of advertising; 〔募集文句〕Advertise with us. 広告メール (an)「advertisement [advertising] e-mail; an e-mail advertisement.
こうこく[4]【抗告】▣ 許可抗告 a permitted「complaint

[appeal]. ▣ 抗告棄却 dismissal of an appeal.
こうこじゅうたくゆうしほしょうきょうかい【公庫住宅融資保証協会】the Housing Loan Guarantee Corporation.
こうこつ[2]【恍惚】▣ 恍惚体験 an ecstatic experience; an experience of ecstasy.
こうコレステロールやく【抗-薬】〖薬〗an anti-cholesterol drug.
こうさ[2]【交差・交叉】▣ 交差[交叉]汚染〖医〗cross contamination.
こうざ[1]【口座】▣ 仮名口座 a fictitious account. ▣ 口座管理料〔口座維持手数料〕an account maintenance fee. 口座屋〔架空口座の開設・売買で利益を得る業者〕a dealer in fictitious bank accounts (for online remittance scams).
こうざ[3]【高座】▣ 高座着〔落語家などの〕《a rakugo artist's》(traditional) stage attire.
こうざい[5]【鋼材】▣ 自動車用鋼材 steel for automobiles. 汎用鋼材 general-purpose steel.
こうさいさんひん【高[好]採算品】〔儲り率の高い品〕a「well-selling [fast-moving] item; a「good [quick] seller.
こうさく[1]【工作】▣ 説得工作《try, use》persuasion. ◐ 説得~を行う use [attempt] persuasion; try to persuade sb to do; urge sb to do; appeal to sb to do; use [exert] one's influence (to make sb do); put (moral) pressure on sb (to do) / 説得~を強める put stronger (moral) pressure on sb (to do). ▣ 工作部隊 a military intelligence「unit [corps]; special forces.
こうさく[3]【耕作】▣ 耕作放棄地 agricultural land left fallow for a year or more; uncultivated farmland.
こうさてん【交差点】▣ 交差点事故 an intersection accident.
こうさんか[2]【抗酸化】▣ 抗酸化酵素 an antioxidant enzyme.
こうさんきん[2]【好酸菌】〖生物〗an acidophilic bacterium《pl. -ria》.
こうし[7]【光子】▣ 光子場 a「photon [light] field.
こうし[16]【格子】▣ 格子状角膜変性症〖眼科〗〖網膜の〗lattice corneal dystrophy.
こうし[25]【好子-】〖心理〗《act as》「(a) positive reinforcement [a positive reinforcer].
こうじ[2]【工事】▣ 工事車両 a construction vehicle. ◐ ~車両出入口.〔掲示〕Gate for Construction Vehicles. 工事渋滞 a traffic jam [traffic congestion] caused by roadworks. 工事代金〔建造の〕construction fees;〔修理の〕repair fees; fees for repair(s). 工事単価 a work unit price; (a) price per「task [job]; (an) item price《for construction》.
こうじ[4]【公示】▣ 公示日 (the) announcement of an election. 公示日 the announcement day for an election. 公示前勢力〔選挙公示前の各政党の勢力〕《a political party's》strength before the announce of an election.
こうしえん【甲子園】1〔甲子園球場〕the Kōshien Stadium.
2〔(硬式)の全国高校野球大会〕the National High-School Baseball Tournament. ◐ 春の~〔選抜高等学校野球大会の通称〕the Spring「Kōshien [High-School Baseball] Tournament / 夏の~〔全国高等学校野球選手権大会の通称〕the Summer「Kōshien [High-School Baseball] Tournament. ◐ ~に出る appear [play] at Kōshien; represent one's prefecture at the National High-School Baseball Tournament. 3〔高校生対象の全国大会につける愛称〕the National High-School《Haiku》Competition.
こうしがくいん【孔子-学院】〔北京に本部を置く中国語・中国文化を世界に広めることを目的とする機関〕the Confucius Institute.

こうしき¹【公式】◧▸ 公式グッズ ＝オフィシャル・グッズ (⇨オフィシャル²). 公式サイト[ホームページ] an official Web site. 公式試合 ◯〜(試合)球〔球技〕an official game ball. 公式種目〔競技大会などの〕an official event. 公式スポンサー ＝オフィシャル・スポンサー (⇨オフィシャル²). 公式ファンクラブ an official fan club. 公式文書 an official document. 公式マスコット〔チームや競技大会などの〕an official mascot. 公式ルート〔交渉・命令伝達などの〕official channels; an official route. 公式練習〔スポーツ〕official training; an official training session.

こうしし【皇次子】〔天皇の次子〕the「second [next] child of an emperor;〔天皇の次男〕the second son of an emperor.

こうしつ²【皇室】◧▸ 皇室ジャーナリスト an Imperial Family journalist.

こうしつてんぱんにかんするゆうしきしゃかいぎ【皇室典範に関する有識者会議】〔首相の私的諮問機関;2004年設置〕the Advisory Council on the Imperial House Law.

こうしぼう【高脂肪】◯〜の high-fat. ◧▸ 高脂肪食 a high-fat diet. 高脂肪食品[乳] high-fat「food(s) [milk].

こうしゃかいてきこうどう【向社会的行動】《社会・心理》prosocial behavior.

こうしゃさい【公社債】◧▸ 公社債店頭売買参考統計値〔日本証券業協会の調べによる〕statistics on trading volumes of over-the-counter bonds.

こうじゅ¹【皇寿】one's one hundred and eleventh birthday.

こうしゅう²【口臭】◧▸ 口臭防止剤 a breath freshener;〔液体の〕a mouthwash.

こうしゅう⁴【公衆】◧▸ 公衆送信権《法》〔著作権法上の〕the right of public transmission. 公衆無線 LAN〔電算〕a public wireless LAN (略: PWLAN).

ごうしゅうしょくにくかちくせいさんしゃじぎょうだん【豪州食肉家畜生産者事業団】Meat & Livestock Australia (略: MLA).

こうしゅうにっぽう【広州日報】〔中国の新聞〕(The) GuangZhou Daily.

こうしゅうは【高周波】◧▸ 高周波電流 a high-frequency current. 高周波変圧器〔電〕a high-frequency transformer.

こうじゅうりょくきん【抗重力筋】《解》(an) antigravity muscle.

こうしゅつりょく【高出力】high power;〔電〕high output. ◧▸ 高出力エンジン a high-pow-er(ed) engine. 高出力半導体レーザー〔電子工学〕a high-power semiconductor laser. 高出力マイクロ波〔電子工学〕high-power(ed) microwaves (略: HPM). ◯〜マイクロ波兵器 a high-power(ed) microwave [an HPM] weapon. 高出力レーザー〔電子工学〕a high-power(ed) laser (略: HPL).

こうじゅほうしょう【紅綬褒章】a Red Ribbon Medal (awarded for lifesaving).

こうじょ⁴【控除】◧▸ 定額控除 a fixed deduction. 特定支出控除〔給与所得者の〕(a) deduction for specified expenditure. 老年者控除 a「deduction [allowance, exemption] for seniors [the elderly].

こうじょ⁵【公助】〔公的援助〕public [government] aid [help, assistance].

こうしょう¹【口承】◧▸ 口承文化 (an) oral culture.

こうしょう⁹【公傷】◧▸ 公傷制度〔相撲・野球など〕a system for exempting players injured in an official「match [game] from demotion or pay reduction; an official injury exemption system.

こうしょう¹⁰【交渉】◧▸ 裏交渉 backstage negotiations. 補償交渉〔民事裁判の〕negotiations on [negotiating] compensation; compensation negotiations;〔国家間の〕negotiations on reparations; reparation(s) negotiations. ◧▸ 交渉決裂 a「breakdown [rupture] in negotiations. 交渉ルート[チャンネル] a「negotiation [negotiating] channel《with…》.

こうしょう¹⁶【咬傷】◧▸ 咬傷事故 an animal-bite case; a biting;〔犬による〕a dog-bite case.

こうじょう¹【口上】◧▸〔外交〕〔無署名親書〕a verbal note;〔F〕a note verbale《pl. notes verbales》.

こうじょう²【工場】◧▸ 工場景観 an industrial landscape; industrial scenery; a factory-scape. 工場出荷価格 an ex-factory price.

こうじょう⁷【恒常】◧▸ 恒常化 normalization. ◯〜その国では政治犯に対する拷問が〜化している。Torture for political crimes has become normal (practice) in the country.

こうじょうせん【甲状腺】◧▸ 甲状腺髄様がん medullary thyroid「cancer [carcinoma]. 甲状腺乳頭がん papillary thyroid「cancer [carcinoma]. 甲状腺未分化がん anaplastic thyroid「cancer [carcinoma]. 甲状腺濾胞がん follicular thyroid「cancer [carcinoma].

「交渉人」〔映画〕The Negotiator.

こうじょうはいすいきせいほう【工場排水規制法】《法》the Factory Waste Water Control Law.

こうしょうひん【香粧品】cosmetics.

こうしょへいしょう【高所平気症】《have》no fear of heights.

こうしん⁴【交信】◧▸ 交信記録 a record of communications《between…, with…》. ◯〜事故調査委員会は墜落機の機長と管制塔との〜を記録を公開した。The accident investigation committee「have [has] released a record of communications between the pilot of the downed aircraft and the control tower.

こうしん²¹【香信】《菌》〔笠(⁶)がほとんど開いた肉薄のシイタケ〕a thin fleshed shiitake mushroom of which the cap is almost completely open; a koushin shiitake.

こうず⁵【香醋】aromatic vinegar.

こうすい⁴【降水】◧▸ 降水予報 precipitation forecasting;〔個々の〕a forecast of precipitation.

こうずい【洪水】◧▸ 洪水被害 flood damage; damage from flooding. ◯〜東南アジア諸国が〜被害に見舞われている。Southeast Asian countries have been hit by flood damage.

こうスタート【好〜】a「good [strong] start. ◯〜を切る get off to a「good [strong] start.

こうせい⁷【攻勢】◧▸ 反転攻勢 a「switch [change] to「an attack [the offensive].

こうせい⁸【更正】◧▸ 更正処分《impose》a (punitive) retrospective tax adjustment.

こうせい⁹【更生】◧▸ 更生教育 rehabilitation education.

こうせい¹⁰【厚生】◧▸ 厚生保険 welfare insurance. 厚生保険特別会計 the welfare insurance special account; the Special Account for Employees' Insurance. 厚生労働白書〔厚生労働省の〕the White Paper on Welfare and Labour.

こうせい¹⁶【校正】◧▸ 校正士〔資格の一種〕a certified proofreader.

こうせい¹⁹【構成】◧▸ 構成員課税 ＝パス・スルー課税 (⇨パス・スルー). 構成作家 ＝放送作家 (⇨ほうそう⁴). 構成表〔人員表〕a (hierarchical)「membership [personnel] chart;〔組織図〕an organizational「diagram [chart]; an organogram.

こうせい²¹【合成】◧▸ 合成開口レーダー〔宇宙・空〕(a) synthetic-aperture radar (略: SAR). 合成軽油 a synthetic (diesel) oil. 合成指標〔複数の経済指標を組み合わせたもの〕a composite index《pl. 〜es, indices》(略: CI).

こうせいかがくしんぎかい【厚生科学審議会】〔厚生労働省の諮問機関〕the Scientific Council.

ごうせいこうそ【合成酵素】◧▸ 合成酵素連鎖反応《生

こうせいさいがぞう[えいぞう]【高精細画像[映像]】a high-definition image. ▷▷ 高精細画像[映像]化 high-definition imaging.

ごうせいじゅし【合成樹脂】▷▷ 合成樹脂シート a synthetic resin sheet; a plastic sheet; plastic sheeting.

こうせいはってんとう【公正発展党】[トルコのイスラム政党] the Justice and Development Party (略: AKP). ▶ AKP はトルコ語 Adalet ve Kalkinma Partisi の略.

こうせいほごほう【更生保護法】【法】the Offenders Rehabilitation Law. ▶「犯罪者予防更生法」と「執行猶予者保護観察法」を統合したもの.

こうせつ¹【公設】▷▷ 公営公設 ~公設施設[病院] a「facility [hospital] set up [established] and「managed [run] by「the public sector [local government]. 公設民営 (the) private management of publicly-owned「services [facilities]. ▷ ~民営化 (the) privatization of publicly-owned「services [facilities] / ~民営学校 a privately managed「*public [「state] school / ~民営の保育所 a privately「run [managed] public「nursery school [day care center, preschool].

こうせつ⁷【降雪】▷▷ 終降雪 the last snow(fall) of the season. 初降雪 the first snow(fall) of the season. ▷▷ 降雪機 =人工降雪機.

ごうせつ¹【豪雪】▷▷ 豪雪地仕様 ⇨しよう⁴. 豪雪被害 heavy snow damage; damage from heavy snow. ▷ 日本海側は~(の)被害が多い. Regions along the Japan Sea coast frequently suffer heavy snow damage.

こうせつりょうり【江浙料理】[中国, 上海周辺の料理] Jiangzhe cuisine.

こうせん¹⁴【鉱泉】▷▷ 鉱泉水 mineral water.

こうせん¹⁷【公船】[国家の公権を行使する船舶] a public vessel.

こうせんこうせつぞく【公専公接続】【通信】connection of public networks through a private network.

こうせんせつぞく【公専接続】【通信】connection of a public network to a private network.

こうせんりきがく(てき)りょうほう【光線力学(的)療法】【医】[加齢黄斑変性の治療法] photodynamic therapy (略: PDT).

こうそ²【公訴】▷▷ 公訴参加(制度)【犯罪被害者等の】participation in trials by crime victims or members of their families.

こうそ⁸【酵素】▷▷ 酵素遺伝子 an enzyme gene. 酵素ジュース enzyme juice.

こうそう¹⁴【高層】▷▷ 高層住居誘導地区〔都市の〕an urban zone in which regulations are relaxed in order to encourage the construction of high-rise buildings; a high-rise building zone.

こうそう¹⁸【構想】▷▷ 構想段階《still in》the「conceptual [planning] stage. ▷ アジア共通通貨はまだ~段階だ. A common Asian currency is still on the drawing board. 構想メモ a rough draft; an outline; notes.

こうそう¹⁹【咬創】a bite; a wound caused by a bite; a bite wound.

こうぞう【構造】▷▷ 構造躯体【建】a (structural) skeleton. 構造計画【建】structural planning. 構造計画書【建】a structural plan. 構造計算【建】structural calculation. 構造計算書【建】a structural calculation sheet. 構造材(料)【建】structural material. ▷ 航空機の~として炭素繊維の需要が伸びている. Demand is growing for carbon fiber as a structural material for aircraft. 構造性能【建】structural performance. 構造耐力【建】structural resistance. 構造部【建】a structural part; a supporting structure. 構造部材【建】a structural (support) member; a structural「component [element]. ▷ 非~部材 a non-structural「component [element].

こうぞうかいかくとっくほう【構造改革特区

区域法】【法】the Law on Special Zones for Structural Reform.

こうぞうかいかくとっくほう【構造改革特区法】【法】the Law on Special Zones for Structural Reform.

こうぞうしょく【構造色】【光】a structural color.

こうそく⁶【高速】▷▷ 高速技術 high-speed technology. 高速魚雷艇〔軍〕a motor torpedo boat (略: MTB). 高速券〔高速道路の回数券〕an expressway ticket. 高速スライダー〔野球〕a cut fastball; a cutter. 高速大量輸送 high-speed mass [*transportation [*transport]. ▷ ~大量輸送システム a high speed mass [*transportation [*transport] system. 高速通信 high-speed communications. ▷ ~通信回線 high-speed communications line. 高速電子【物】a fast electron. 高速連写【写真】high-speed consecutive「shooting [shots]. ▷ ~連写で take (a series of) high-speed consecutive shots.

こうぞく¹【後続】▷▷ 後続車 the car behind (one).

こうそくか【高速化】speeding up; a speedup; acceleration. ~する speed up; accelerate. ▷ アプリケーションの起動を~する方法 a method for「speeding up the launching of applications [making applications launch faster]. ▷ 鉄道の~ the speeding up of railway operations; faster train speeds.

こうそくどうろ【高速道路】▷▷ 高速道路回数券 an expressway coupon ticket. 高速道路整備計画〔国土開発幹線自動車道建設会議が決定する〕the roadmanagement plan for expressways (established by the National Development Arterial Expressway Committee).

こうそくどうろかぶしきがいしゃほう【高速道路株式会社法】【法】the Highway Corporation Law.

こうそくどうろこうだん【高速道路公団】the expressway public corporations.

こうそつ【高卒】▷▷ 高卒人口 =高校卒業人口 (⇨じんこう¹). 高卒認定試験 a high school equivalency examination.

こうたい¹【交代・交替】▷▷ 交代勤務 (rotating) shift work. ▷ この工場は, 3~勤務の24時間体制で稼働している. This factory operates「24 hours a day [round the clock] on a three-shift system.

こうたい³【抗体】▷▷ 抗体医薬 an antibody drug.

こうだい⁶【高台】▷▷〔陶器の〕a foot. ▷▷ 切り高台 a cut foot.

こうたいいき【広帯域】▷▷ 広帯域 ISDN【通信】broadband ISDN (略: B-ISDN). [=ビー・アイ・エス・ディー・エヌ] 広帯域地震計 a broadband seismometer.

こうだいれんけい【高大連携】〔高校と大学の連携教育〕an alliance between a high school and university (allowing high school students to take university classes for credit).

こうだんねつ【高断熱】high [good] (thermal) insulation. ▷▷ 高断熱高気密 good insulation and airtightness. ▷ ~高気密住宅 well-insulated airtight housing.

こうたんぱく(しつ)しょく【高蛋白(質)食】a high-protein diet.

こうち⁵【拘置】▷▷ 拘置延長【法】(an) extension of detention; (a) detention extension. 拘置停止【法】(a) suspension of detention. ▷ ~理由開示 disclosure of reasons for detention. / ~理由開示法廷 hearing [court session] for disclosure of reasons for detention.

こうちょう⁵【校長】▷▷ 民間(人)校長 a school principal brought in from the business world.

こうちょうかい【公聴会】▷▷ 地方公聴会〔地方に委員を派遣して行う〕a「local [regional] public hearing attended by (officials) from (the central government). 中央公聴会〔国会内で行う〕a public hearing (held) in the Diet.

**こうちょうし**【皇長子】〔天皇の長子〕the first child of an emperor;〔天皇の長男〕the eldest son of an emperor.

**こうちょうそん**【皇長孫】〔天皇の初孫〕the first grandchild of an emperor;〔天皇の一番年長の男孫〕the eldest grandson of an emperor.

**こうちょうは**【高調波】▷ 高調波障害 harmonic interference.

**こうつう**【交通】
▷ 交通監視カメラ a traffic(-monitoring) camera. 交通機動隊〔警察の〕a mobile traffic unit. 交通業過〔交通関係の業務上過失致死傷罪〕professional negligence on the road resulting in injury and/or death. 交通教室 (a series of) road safety lessons. ▷ 移動〜教室 police visits to give road safety lessons. 交通システム工学 transportation system(s) [transport system(s)] engineering. 交通死亡事故 a fatal traffic accident; a traffic accident resulting in death. 交通死亡事故多発警報 a warning about (frequent) road「deaths [fatalities]. 交通誘導〔工事現場付近などでの〕traffic control; directing traffic; flagging. ▷ 〜誘導する direct traffic; flag. 交通誘導員 a traffic control person; a flagger. 交通誘導灯 an illuminated traffic control baton.

**こうつうあんぜん**【交通安全】▷ 交通安全祈願 a prayer for road safety. 交通安全教室 a traffic safety class. 交通安全講習《take》a traffic safety course;《receive》traffic safety training. 交通安全白書〔内閣府の〕the White Paper on Traffic Safety in Japan (2005).

**こうつうじこ**【交通事故】▷ 交通事故遺族 the families of people killed in traffic accidents; people bereaved in traffic accidents. 交通事故多発地域 an accident blackspot;〔掲示〕Caution! Accident Black Spot. 交通事故発生マップ a traffic accident map.

**こうつうせいり**【交通整理】▷ 交通整理員 a traffic control guard; a person who guides pedestrians and traffic《at a building site》.

**こうつうバリアフリーほう**【交通-法】【法】the Barrier-Free Transportation Law. ▶「高齢者・身体障害者等の公共交通機関を利用した移動の円滑化の促進に関する法律」の通称. 2000年に施行. 2006年に バリアフリー新法(高齢者・障害者等の移動の円滑化の促進に関する法律)に改正.

**こうディーこうたい**【抗D抗体】【生理】an anti-D antibody.

**こうディー(ヒト)めんえきグロブリン**【抗D(人)免疫—】【薬】〔新生児溶血性疾患の予防剤〕anti-D immunoglobulin.

**こうてき**[1]【公的】▷ 公的援助 public [government] aid [help, assistance]. 公的企業 a public corporation. 公的固定資本形成 public fixed capital formation. 公的年金(等)控除 a《tax》deduction for public pensions. 公的標準 =デジュール・スタンダード. 公的補助 government support; support from public funds; a government subsidy《to an ailing company》.

**こうてきけんしょうきんせいど**【公的懸賞金制度】〔凶悪事件の解決に結びつく情報を提供した人に懸賞金を出す制度〕an official reward system for information leading to the resolution of criminal cases.

**こうてきこじんにんしょうサービス**【公的個人認証-サービス】the Public Certification Service for Individuals; the Japanese public key infrastructure (略: JPKI).

**こうてきこじんにんしょうほう**【公的個人認証法】【法】
▷つかってつづきオンラインかかんけいんぽう》

**こうてきしきんしんほう**【公的資金新法】【法】=きんゆうきのうきょうかほう.

**こうてきしんようほしょうせいど**【公的信用保証制度】a public credit guarantee system.

**こうてきつきそいにんせいど**【公的付添人制度】【法】〔少年審判の〕a [the] system for) provision from public funds of defense lawyers for juveniles accused of serious crimes.

**こうてきべんごせいど**【公的弁護制度】〔2006年4月からの〕the public defense system.

**こうてん**[8]【荒天】▷ 荒天時 times of「rough [foul, heavy] weather. ▷ フェリーは〜時には運行中止になる. The ferry doesn't run in rough weather. 荒天準備〔船舶〕preparation(s) for stormy weather. ▷ 〜準備をする prepare [get ready, clear the decks] for a storm;〔海〕snug (down). 荒天中止〔荒天による中止〕cancellation because of stormy weather;〔荒天の場合は中止〕To be cancelled in case of stormy weather. 雨天決行、〜中止. To be cancelled in case of storms but not in case of rain.

**こうてん**[2]【光電】▷ 光電変換効率【物】photoelectric conversion efficiency.

**こうでん**[3]【香典・香奠】▷ 香典泥棒 a thief who steals offerings made at a funeral; an "incense money" thief.

**こうでんあつ**【高電圧】(a) high voltage. ▷ 〜をかける apply a high voltage《to…》. ▷ 〜危険.〔掲示〕Danger! High Voltage. 高電圧工学 high-voltage engineering. 高電圧電源装置 a high-voltage「generator [generating device]. 高電圧パルス a high-voltage pulse. ▷ 〜パルス発生器 a high-voltage pulse generator.

**こうど**[5]【高度】▷ 高度医療施設 an advanced medical care facility; a high-level health care facility. 高度救命救急センター〔厚生労働省が一定の基準を満たした医療施設]〕an Advanced Medical Emergency and Critical Care Center (略: AMEC3). 高度文明社会 a highly civilized society.

**こうとう**[2]【口頭】▷ 口頭指導 verbal「guidance [counseling]. 口頭注意〔懲戒処分の1つ〕an [a verbal] admonition.

**こうとう**[7]【皇統】▷ 皇統譜〔歴代の天皇・皇族の身分に関する事項を登録する帳簿〕the Record of Imperial Lineage; the Imperial Family Register.

**こうとう**[11]【後頭】▷ 後頭連合野 the occipital association area.

**こうとう**[16]【喉頭】▷ 喉頭軟化症【医】laryngomalacia.

**こうどう**[1]【公道】▷ 公道レース a「highway [road] race;〔違法な〕an illegal road race;《口》a cannonball run.

**こうどう**[2]【行動】
▷▷ 生得的[獲得性]行動 innate [acquired] behavior; an「innate [acquired] form of behavior.
▷ 行動遺伝学 behavioral genetics; the genetics of behavior. 行動海域〔艦船などの〕a「zone [sphere] of action. 行動基準 a「procedural [behavioral] standard; a rule of conduct. 行動規範 a code [rules] of conduct. 行動経済学 behavioral economics. 行動制限〔患者・仮釈放者などに対する〕《place》restrictions on the movements《of patients》. 行動的環境【心理】a [the] behavioral environment. 行動分析 behavior analysis. 応用〜分析 applied behavior analysis (略: ABA) / 実験的〜分析 the experimental analysis of behavior (略: EAB). 行動変容【心理】(a) behavior modification. 行動理論【心理】behavior theory.

**こうどう**[9]【皇道】(a) government led by the Emperor; Imperial rule. 皇道派〔日本史〕〔旧陸軍内の一派閥〕the Kōdōha; the "Imperial Way Faction"; a faction of the former Japanese Imperial Army that opposed the Tōseiha and advocated Imperial rule.

**ごうとう**[1]【強盗】▷ 緊縛強盗 (a) tie-up robbery; tying up and robbing《sb》. コンビニ強盗〔犯人〕a con-

ごうどう

venience store robber; 〔行為〕a convenience store robbery.
**ごうどう**【合同】▶︎ 合同海上訓練《carry out》a joint maritime drill. 合同墓〔合葬墓〕a shared grave; one grave for《husband and wife, a family》.
**こうとうがっこうそつぎょうていどにんていしけん**【高等学校卒業程度認定試験】〔大学入学資格検定（大検）に代わる制度〕the Upper Secondary School Equivalency Examination.
**こうどうせいりがく**【行動生理学】behavioral physiology. ▶︎ 行動生理学者 a behavioral physiologist.
**こうどじょうほうつうしんネットワークしゃかいすいしんせんりゃくほんぶ**【高度情報通信・社会推進戦略本部】the Strategic Headquarters for the Promotion of an Advanced Information and Telecommunications Network Society. ▶ IT 戦略本部の正式名称.
**こうない**[1]【口内】▶︎ 口内性交《engage in》oral 「intercourse [sex].
**こうない**[5]【構内】▶︎ 構内運搬車 a「warehouse [factory] truck.
**こうなん**[2]【硬軟】▶︎ 硬軟両様 both hard and soft《approaches》. ▶︎ 〜両様の構えを取る adopt a carrot-and-stick stance; combine [mix] toughness with tenderness.
**こうにち**【抗日】▶︎ 抗日戦争〔史〕〔中国から見た日中戦争の呼称〕the [China's] war of resistance against Japan.
**こうにちせんそうきねんかん**【抗日戦争記念館】〔中国北京の, 盧溝橋(ろこうきょう)近くにある博物館〕the Memorial Hall of the War of Resistance Against Japan.
**こうにゅう**【購入】▶︎ 購入価格 a purchase price; the sum paid for a purchase. 購入先 a supplier; the source of a purchase;《a company》from which sth is 「bought [purchased]. 購入年齢層 a「buyer [consumer] age group; the age group of《motorcycle》purchasers. 購入比率 a purchase ratio. ▶︎ この車は女性の〜比率が他車に比べて著しく高い. The percentage of women who buy this car is far higher than the percentage of men. | Far more women than men buy this model. 購入履歴 a purchase history.
**こうにん**[2]【後任】▶︎ 後任人事 (a)《staff [personnel]》replacement; deciding new「staff [personnel]. ▶︎ 辞表を提出したパウエル国務長官の〜人事についてブッシュ大統領はライス大統領補佐官に就任要請をした. President Bush demanded that Rice, his Presidential aide, be appointed to「replace [succeed to] Powell as Secretary of State, who had tendered his resignation.
**こうにんかいけいし**【公認会計士】▶︎ 公認会計士・監査審査会 the CPA and Auditing Oversight Board（略: CPAAOB）.
**こうにん(きゃく)しき**【弘仁(格)式】〔三代格式の１つで最初のもの〕the Kōnin Rule; the Kōnin(kyaku) Shiki.〔こうにん(きゃく)しき, じょうがん(きゃく)しき, えんぎ(きゃく)しき〕
**こうねつ**[2]【高熱】▶︎ 高熱処理 high-temperature「processing [treatment].
**こうねつきん**【好熱菌】〔生物〕a thermophilic bacterium《pl. -ria》. ▶︎ 超好熱菌 a hyperthermophilic bacterium《pl. -ria》.
**こうねつすいひ**【光熱水費】fuel「heating], lighting, and water「expenses [charges, costs].
**こうねつすいりょう**【光熱水料】＝こうねつすいひ.
**こうねんれいきゅうしょくしゃきゅうふきん**【高年齢求職者給付金】benefits for older persons seeking employment.
**こうねんれいこようけいぞくきほんきゅうふきん**【高年齢雇用継続基本給付金】continued basic employment benefits for older workers.
**こうねんれいこようけいぞくきゅうふ**【高年齢雇用継続給付】continued employment benefits for older workers.
**こうねんれいさいしゅうしょくきゅうふきん**【高年齢再就職給付金】employment benefits for older workers who have been rehired.
**こうねんれいしゃこようあんていほう**【高年齢者雇用安定法】〔法〕the Law Concerning Stabilization of Employment of Older Persons.
**こうねんれいしゃこようかいはつきょうかい**【高年齢雇用開発協会】the Association of Employment Development for Senior Citizens.
**こうのう**[2]【効能】▶︎ 効能本 an authoritative book (on the effectiveness of a product);《口》a users' bible.
**こうはい**[10]【皇配】〔女性天皇の配偶者〕a prince consort.
**こうばい**[1]【公売】▶︎《インター》ネット公売 an「online [Internet] public auction.
**こうばい**[4]【購買】▶︎ 購買習慣 buying habits. 購買履歴〔クレジットカードなどの〕a [one's] shopping history.
**こうはく**[1]【紅白】▶︎ 紅白幕 a (celebratory) curtain with red and white stripes; a red and white striped curtain.
**こうはん**[1]【公判】▶︎ 公判停止 the「suspension [halting] of a trial.
**こうはん**[6]【紅斑】▶︎ 持久性隆起性紅斑〔医〕erythema elevatum diutinum.
**こうはんせきちゅうかんきょうさくしょう**【広範脊柱管狭窄症】〔医〕diffuse spinal canal stenosis.
**こうはんまえせいりてつづき**【公判前整理手続】〔法〕(a) pretrial procedure.
**こうひ**[5]【公費】▶︎ 公費天国 a publicly funded paradise; living high on the public purse. 公費負担 expenditure from public funds; the burden on public finances; the public financial burden. ▶︎ 結核患者医療費の〜負担 the public share of the medical treatment costs of TB patients. 公費乱用 misappropriation of public「funds [money].
**こうひょう**[2]【好評】▶︎ 好評開催中 open [in session, being held] to a「good reception [positive response];〔掲示〕Now Open to Rave Reviews. 好評発売中 being sold [selling] to a good response;〔宣伝文句〕Now Selling with Great Popularity. 好評分譲中（lots, apartments）「being sold [selling] to a good response;〔宣伝文句〕《Lots, Apartments》Now Selling with Great Popularity. 好評連載中 serialized to good reviews;〔宣伝文句〕Now「Being Published [Running] to Great Reviews; A Popular Series.
**こうびょうげんせい**【高病原性】〔医〕highly pathogenic《virus》. ▶︎ 高病原性鳥インフルエンザ ⇨とりインフルエンザ.
**こうびろう**【後鼻漏】〔医〕postnasal drip.
**こうひんしつ**【高品質】▶︎ 高品質結晶 a high quality crystal. 高品質単結晶 a high quality single crystal.
**こうふ**[3]【交付】▶︎ 交付機 a《certificate-, document-》issuing machine (in a government office). ▶︎ 自動〜機〔証明書などの〕an automatic issuing machine (for《identification certificates》) / 住民票〜機 a residence-certificate (issuing) machine. 交付式 an issuance [a certification] ceremony.
**こうぶ**[4]【項部】the posterior「cervical [neck] region; the nuchal region; the nape.
**こうふきん**【交付金】▶︎ 運営費交付金〔政府から独立行政法人への〕an official [a public] grant [subsidy] for operating expenses.
**こうふくし**【高福祉】high-quality welfare services. ▶︎ 〜高負担 high-quality, high-fee welfare services. ▶︎ 高福祉国家 a high-quality welfare state. 高福祉社会 a high-quality welfare society.
**こうぶしょうしたいはくり**【後部硝子体剥離】〔眼科〕(a) posterior vitreous detachment (略: PVD).

こうふちょう【好不調】variation(s) in「performance [condition]. ◐〜の波 ups and downs [upswings and downswings, peaks and troughs] in「performance [condition] / あいつは〜の波が激しい。 He swings widely between performing well and performing poorly. | When he's hot he's hot, and when he's「cold he's really cold [not he's not].
こうぶつ³【鉱物】◐◨ 鉱物組成 mineral composition.
こうプレー【好〜】a good「play [move, shot, stroke].
こうぶんし【高分子】◐◨ 高分子吸収体〔高吸収性樹脂〕a「super(-)absorbent [superabsorbent] polymer (略: SAP). 高分子有機物 high molecular weight [HMW] organic matter.
こうぶんれん【高文連】=ぜんこくこうとうがっこうぶんかれんめい.
ごうべん【合弁】◐◨ 合弁相手 a partner in a joint「venture [enterprise].
こうほ²【候補】◐◨ 花嫁[花婿]候補 a prospective「bride [groom]. 候補擁立 fielding [putting up] a candidate《for mayor》. ◐〜擁立を見送る[断念する] decide not to field [give up the idea of fielding] a candidate.
こうぼ¹【公募】◐◨ 公募候補〔選挙で〕an openly recruited candidate. 公募制〔教員などの〕a system of recruitment by (public) advertisement; an open「recruitment [hiring] system;〔政党公認立候補者の〕an open candidacy system. 公募増資《株式・債券》(making) a public「offering [issue] (of new「shares [bonds]). 公募地方債 (public) regional bonds. 公募入札 public「bidding [tender]. 公募ファンド a (public) subscription fund.
こうぼ²【公簿】◐◨ 公簿面積〔土地の〕the area《of a plot》as recorded in a land register.
こうぼ³【酵母】◐◨ 泡あり酵母 foaming yeast. 泡なし酵母 non-foaming yeast. 天然[自然]酵母 natural yeast. ◐〜酵母パン natural yeast bread. パン酵母 bakers'[bakers] yeast.
こうほう⁴【広報・弘報】◐◨ 広報委員会 a public relations committee. 広報外交〔文化交流などを通じて外国の世論に働きかける外交活動〕public diplomacy. 広報番組 a「public relations [PR] program [broadcast]. ◐政府〜番組 a government information「program [broadcast]. 広報ビデオ an informational video. 広報マン a PR man.
こうほう⁵【後方】◐◨ 後方地域〔軍〕a rear area; the rear. 後方宙返り〔体操〕(turn) a backward somersault;《do》a「backflip [flip-flop].
こうぼう⁵【攻防】◐◨ 攻防ライン〔戦い・競争などでの〕the line of attack and defense.
ごうほう【合法】◐◨ 合法性〔行為の〕legality;〔正統性〕orthodoxy; legitimacy. 合法ドラッグ a legal [an unregulated] drug [narcotic].
こうほしゃ【候補者】◐◨ 候補者登録 registration「as a candidate [of candidates]. 候補者討論会〔選挙の〕a candidates' debate; a「debate [discussion] between [among] candidates. 候補者擁立 =候補擁立 (⇨こうほ²).
こうまく【硬膜】◐◨ 硬膜移植〔医〕《receive》a dura mater transplant. 硬膜外腔〔解〕the epidural space. 硬膜外無痛分娩〔医〕(a) painless delivery under epidural anesthesia. 硬膜動静脈奇形〔医〕dural arteriovenous malformation; dural AVM (略: DAVM). 硬膜動静脈瘻〔医〕(a) dural arteriovenous fistula.
こうまる【甲丸】◐◨ 甲丸指輪 a ring with a D cross-section.
こうまわり【甲回り】〔足の〕one's foot circumference;〔手の〕one's hand circumference.
こうみ【香味】◐◨ 香味焼き《pork》roast with「spices [herbs]. ◐豚肉の〜焼き spicy [spiced] roast pork.

こうみつど【高密度】◐◨ 高密度集積回路〔電子工学〕a large-scale integrated circuit; an LSIC. ◐超〜集積回路 a very large-scale integrated circuit; a VLSIC.
こうみんけんいいんかい【公民権委員会】〔米国の〕the Commission on Civil Rights (略: CCR).
こうむ²【公務】◐◨ 公務外災害 an accident sustained when「not at work [not on duty, off the job].
こうむいん【公務員】◐◨ 公務員制度 a civil service system. ◐〜制度改革 reform of the civil service (system); civil service reform(s) / 〜制度改革関連法案 a civil service reform bill.
こうむこうきょうサービスろうどうくみあいきょうぎかい【公務公共−労働組合協議会】the Alliance of Public Services Workers Unions (略: APU).
こうむろうきょう【公務労協】=こうむこうきょうサービスろうどうくみあいきょうぎかい.
こうもく¹【項目】◐◨ 記入[入力]項目 a section [an item] to be「filled in [typed in].
こうもん⁴【肛門】◐◨ 肛門温存手術〔医〕〔直腸がんなどの〕sphincter-preserving surgery. [⇨温存手術 (⇨おんぞん)]
ごうもんきんしいいんかい【拷問禁止委員会】=こくれんごうもんきんしいいんかい.
こうゆ²【鉱油】◐◨ 無鉱油(の)〔化粧品など〕oil-free; without mineral oil.
こうゆうすいめんうめたてほう【公有水面埋立法】〔法〕the Publicly-Owned Surface Water Reclamation Law.
こうゆうちん【高優賃】=高齢者向け優良賃貸住宅 (⇨こうれいしゃ).
こうよう¹【公用】◐◨ 公用旅券 an official passport.
こうよう⁵【紅葉・黄葉】◐◨ 紅葉シーズン the best time to see「autumnal colors [the turning leaves].
こうようりょう【高用量】〔薬〕a high「dose [dosage]《of epinephrine》. ◐この薬を用いると発がんのリスクがある。 This drug can be carcinogenic when used in high doses. ◐◨ 高用量ピル ⇨ピル.
こうらいつぎょ【高麗桂魚】〔魚〕〔魚食性の淡水魚〕a (species of) Mandarin fish; Siniperca scherzeri.
こうらぼし【甲羅干し】◐〜(を)する sunbathe lying on one's stomach; lie on one's stomach to get a suntan on one's back.
こうり²【小売り】◐◨ 小売価格調査 a retail price survey. 小売り表示規約〔家電製品についての〕(voluntary) labeling rules (under the Fair Competition Code).
こうりつがっこうきょうさいくみあい【公立学校共済組合】the Japan Mutual Aid Association of Public School Teachers.
こうりっち【好立地】a「good [favorable, convenient] location. ◐この地区は、北 1 キロのところに鉄道駅があり、国道 246 号線にも近く、東名高速道路も利用できる〜にある。 With a railroad one kilometer to the north, Route 246 nearby and access to the Tōmei Expressway, the district is「conveniently located [well placed].
ごうりてき【合理的】◐◨ 合理的理由[根拠]〔法〕reasonable grounds《for…》; a reasonable ground《for…》. ►この意味では ground は複数形で用いるほうが多い. ◐医師の処置には〜はなく、死なせるために行った処置ではない。There were reasonable grounds for the doctor's (choice of) treatment, and it was not intended to bring about (the patient's) death.
こうりゃく¹【攻略】◐◨ 攻略法 a strategy to「beat [defeat]《one's opponent》. ◐オーストラリアチームは日本チーム〜法を徹底研究していたに違いない。 The Australian team must have thoroughly researched how to「beat [defeat] the Japanese team. / 新しいパチンコ台の〜法がネットで話題になっている。 Strategies for beating the new-style pachinko machines are being discussed on the Internet.

こうりゅう

こうりゅう² 【交流】
⇨ 交流イベント an event promoting interaction ((between newcomers and longtime residents)). ◆ 国際～イベント an event promoting international interaction; an international exchange event. 交流会 a party [a meeting, an assembly] to get to know each other; a social gathering; (口) a social; a get-together. 交流戦, 交流試合 〔野球などリーグ間の〕an interleague 《baseball》game. ◆ セ・パ～戦 〔野球〕an interleague game between Central and Pacific League teams ／ 日中親善～試合 a friendly (game [match]) between Japan and China; a Japan-China international friendly (game [match]).

こうりゅう⁴ 【拘留】 ⇨ 拘留請求 〔法〕〔検察庁が裁判所に対して行う〕a request for detention.

こうりゅうきょうかい 【交流協会】⇨にほんこうりゅうきょうかい.

こうりょ² 【行旅】 ⇨ 行旅死亡人 〔旅行中に死亡し, 引取人がいない者〕an unclaimed dead traveler; 〔身元不明の死体で引取人がいない者〕an unidentified and unclaimed ˹dead person [dead body, corpse]. 行旅病人 a person who has fallen ill while traveling; an ill traveler.

こうりんきん 【口輪筋】〔解〕the orbicularis oris (muscle).

こうりんは 【光琳派】＝りんぱ.

こうれい¹ 【高齢】 ⇨ 高齢運転者[ドライバー] an elderly driver. 高齢社会白書 〔内閣府の〕the Annual Report on the Aging Society 《2005》. 高齢歩行者 an elderly pedestrian.

こうれいか 【高齢化】 ⇨ 高齢化率 the ˹elderly [aging] ratio; the percentage of the population aged 65 or older.

こうれいきん 【好冷菌】〔生物〕a psychrophilic bacterium 《pl. -ria》.

こうれいしゃ 【高齢者】
⇨ 超高齢者 a very old person; 〈集合的に〉the very old. 特定高齢者 〔介護や支援が必要となるおそれのある高齢者〕an elderly person ˹who may need care or support [with potential care and support needs].
⇨ 高齢者医療 medical ˹treatment [care] for the elderly. 高齢者医療制度 a medical ˹care [treatment] system for the elderly. ◆ 前期～医療制度 〔65 歳から 74 歳に適用する〕a medical care system for people aged sixty-five to seventy-four ／ 後期～医療制度 〔75 歳以上に適用する〕a medical care system for people over seventy-four years old. 高齢者医療費 ＝老人医療費 (⇨ろうじんいりょう). 高齢者傾聴技能士 a qualified ˹listener [companion (aide)] for the elderly. 高齢者事故 an accident involving an elderly person. 高齢者マンション an apartment (block) for the elderly; "a block of flats for senior citizens. 高齢者(向け)住宅 〔高齢者用住宅〕a house (designed) for elderly people. 高齢者向け優良賃貸住宅 a subsidized high-grade rental apartment for the elderly; "a subsidized high-quality residence let to senior citizens. 高齢者労働 elderly labor.

こうれいしゃかいエヌ・ジー・オーれんけいきょうぎかい 【高齢社会 NGO 連携協議会】the Japan NGO Council on Ag(e)ing (略：JANCA).

こうれいしゃきょじゅうほう 【高齢者居住法】〔法〕the Law on Provision of Housing for the Elderly. ▶ 正式名称は「高齢者の居住の安定確保に関する法律」.

こうれいしゃじゅうたくざいだん 【高齢者住宅財団】the Foundation for Senior Citizens' Housing.

こうれい・しょうがいしゃこようしえんきこう 【高齢・障害者雇用支援機構】the Japan Organization for Employment of the Elderly and Persons with Disabilities (略：JEED).

こうレトロウイルスやく 【抗-薬】〔薬〕an antiretroviral ˹drug [agent].

こうレトロウイルスりょうほう 【抗-療法】〔医〕antiretroviral therapy (略：ART).

こうレベルほうしゃせいはいきぶつ 【高-放射性廃棄物】 ⇨ 高レベル放射性廃棄物管理施設 a high-level radioactive waste management facility. 高レベル放射性廃棄物処分場 a high-level radioactive waste disposal site.

こうろ⁵ 【航路】 ⇨ 航路帯 〔船舶の〕a sea lane; 〔航空機の〕an air lane.

こうろ⁶ 【高炉】 ⇨ 高炉メーカー 〔鉄鉱石を原料として高炉で鉄鋼を生産する企業〕a blast-furnace steel maker; an integrated steel manufacturer.

こうろうか 【抗老化】antiaging. ⇨ 抗老化医学 〔抗加齢医学〕antiaging medicine. 抗老化粧品 antiaging cosmetics.

こうろひょうしきほう 【航路標識法】〔法〕the Aids to Navigation Law.

こうわ¹ 【口話】 ⇨ 口話教育 education through (the medium of) lipreading.

こうわん 【港湾】 ⇨ 港湾整備特別会計 a special account for harbor improvement.

こうわんくうこうぎじゅつけんきゅうじょ 【港湾空港技術研究所】〔独立行政法人〕the Port and Airport Research Institute (略：PARI).

こえかけ 【声掛け】 ◆ 学童への不審な～が相次いでいる. There has been a series of suspicious (persons making) approaches to school children. ◆ 下校時の児童に～をする greet [say something to] children on their way home after school.
⇨ 声かけ運動 a friendly-greeting campaign; a campaign for people to exchange greetings.

ゴエフ・ユー 【5(-)FU】〔薬〕〔抗がん剤; 5-フルオロウラシル〕5(-)FU; 5-fluorouracil.

ゴーイング・コンサーン 〔会計〕〔継続企業〕a going concern. ◆ ～の前提 〔会計〕the assumption of going concern.

コーエン 1 Coen, Ethan (1957- ； 米国の映画監督・脚本家・製作者; 2 の弟).
2 Coen, Joel (1954- ； 米国の映画監督・脚本家; 1 の兄).
3 Cohen, Rob (1949- ； 米国の映画監督・製作者).

コーカサスおおかぶとむし 【大兜虫】〔昆〕〔コガネムシ科の昆虫; 東南アジア原産〕a Caucasus beetle; Chalcosoma caucasus.

コーカンちく 【-地区】〔中国系のコーカン族が住むミャンマー東部の特別区; 世界有数のケシの栽培地だったが, 2003 年に全面禁止〕the Kokang region.

コーギー 〔犬〕a corgi.

コー・ケー 〔カンボジアの遺跡〕Koh Ker.

コース¹ ⇨ コース・マネ(ー)ジメント 〔ゴルフ〕〔各コースの攻め方を決めること〕course management. コース料理 a ˹full-course [multicourse] meal. コース・レーシング 〔ウインドサーフィンの競技種目の 1 つ〕course racing. コース・レコード 〔ゴルフ・マラソン・モータースポーツなどの〕a course record.

ゴーズ² 【GOES】〔米国の地球観測衛星〕GOES; a Geostationary Operational Environmental Satellite. ◆ ～12 号 GOES-12.

コースウェア 〔教育用ソフトウェア〕courseware.

コーズウェイ・ベイ 〔香港の一地区〕Causeway Bay.

「ゴースト・オブ・マーズ」〔映画〕Ghosts of Mars.

コーズ・リレーテッド・マーケティング 〔商〕〔NPO 活動支援を謳った販売促進〕cause-related marketing (略：CRM).

コーチ² 〔商標〕〔米国の服飾ブランド〕Coach.

ゴー・チョクトン 【呉作棟】Goh Chok Tong (1941- ； シンガポールの政治家; 首相 [1990-2004]).

コーチング 〔経営〕coaching.

コーチング・スタッフ〔コーチ陣〕(a) coaching staff.
コーデックスいいんかい【-委員会】〔国連食糧農業機関(FAO)と世界保健機構(WHO)が合同で設置した国際食品規格委員会〕the Codex Alimentarius Commission.
コーデックスきかく【-規格】〔コーデックス委員会の定めた国際食品規格〕(meet) Codex Standards.
コード[4]〔空〕=げんちょう[3].
ゴードセー Godse, Nathuram (1910–49; マハトマ・ガンジーを暗殺したヒンズー教至上主義者).
コートネイ Courtenay, Tom (1937–  ; 英国の俳優; 本名 Thomas Daniel Courtenay).
コード・ハーモニカ〔楽器〕a chord harmonica.
コード・プロジェクト〔国連児童基金等による観光地での児童買春防止のためのプロジェクト. 実際にはこのプロジェクトにより世界全体で遵守が呼びかけられている「旅行と観光における性的搾取からの子供たちの保護のための」行動規範を指す〕the Code of Conduct (for the Protection of Children from Sexual Exploitation in Travel and Tourism).
ゴードン・セッター〔犬〕a Gordon setter; a Scottish setter; a black and tan setter.
ゴードン・チャン Gordon Chan (1960–  ; 香港の映画監督; 中国語名 陳嘉上 Chan Ka-Seung).
ゴードン・ベルしょう【-賞】〔米国の並列計算技術推進のための賞〕the Gordon Bell Prize.
コーナー ▷ S字コーナー =S字カーブ (⇒カーブ[2]).
コーナー・フラッグ〔サッカーなど〕a corner flag. ▷〜フラッグ・ポスト a corner flag post.
コーナー・ショット〔商標・軍〕〔米国製の銃; 射手が身を隠して敵の銃火を避けながら銃撃できる〕a Corner Shot.
コーパイン ⇒コーピン.
コーピン the COPINE Project. ▶ COPINE は Combating Paedophile Information Networks in Europe (欧州における小児性愛者情報ネットワークとの闘い) の略.
コープレイ【動】〔インド・インドシナ産のウシ科の動物〕a kouprey; *Bos sauveli*.
コーホート ▷ コーホート分析 (a) cohort analysis.
コーポラティブじゅうたく【-住宅】=コーポラティブ・ハウス.
コーポラティブ・ハウス〔入居希望者が建設組合を作って共同で建設する住宅〕a cooperative house; 〈集合的に〉cooperative housing.
コーポレート・カラー〔その企業のシンボルカラー〕a corporate color.
コーポレート・メッセージ〔企業が自社の経営理念を端的に伝える文言〕a corporate 'message [statement].
ゴーモーション〔商標・映〕〔人形アニメーションの撮影技法の1つ; 人形はコンピュータ制御の動く棒に取り付けられ, 動く写体として撮影される〕GoMotion.
ゴーモン〔フランスの発明家, レオン・ゴーモン (Léon Gaumont, 1864–1946) が設立した映画スタジオ〕Gaumont; Gaumont Pictures.
こおりあられ【氷霰】〔気象〕ice pellets; small hail.
こおりちくねつ【氷蓄熱】▷ 氷蓄熱式空調システム ice thermal storage air-conditioning. 氷蓄熱システム an ice thermal storage system.
コーリャン【高粱】〔植〕〔中国産モロコシ〕kaoliang.
ゴール[1] ▷ ゴール・ゲッター〔サッカーなど〕a goal 'scorer [getter]. ゴール・ネット〔スポーツ〕a goal net. ▷〜ネットを揺らす〔サッカーで, 得点する〕score a goal; hit the back of the net. ゴールマウス〔サッカー・ホッケー〕〔ゴール前面のエリア〕the goalmouth.
ゴールデン・アローしょう【-賞】〔その年の芸能界で活躍した人に与えられる賞〕a Golden Arrow Prize.
ゴールデン・グローブしょう【-賞】〔その年の映画・テレビの優秀作品に与えられる賞〕a Golden Globe Award.

ゴールデン・ゴール〔サッカー〕〔延長戦の一方式; 前後半15分ずつの延長戦を行い, 先に1点を入れたチームがその時点で勝ちとなる〕the golden goal rule; sudden death;〔その方式に基づいたゴール〕a golden goal.
ゴールデン・スコア〔柔道〕〔延長戦での勝負の決め方〕golden score; the golden score 'rule [system]. ▷ 試合は〜に突入した. The match went into golden score (time).
ゴールデン・ターキン【動】〔中国産ウシ科の哺乳類〕a golden takin; *Budorcas taxicolor bedfordi*.
ゴールデン・ハムスター【動】〔小アジア原産のキヌゲネズミ〕a golden hamster; a Syrian hamster; *Mesocricetus auratus*.
ゴールデン・パラシュート〔経営〕〔解任される取締役への多額の退職金〕a golden parachute.
「ゴールデンボーイ」〔映画〕Apt Pupil.
ゴールデン・ホーン〔地名〕きんかくわん.
ゴールドウィン Goldwyn, Tony (1960–  ; 米国の映画俳優・監督; 本名 Anthony Goldwyn).
ゴールドかち【-勝ち】〔野球〕a called victory. 〜する win a called game. ▷ ジャガーズはパイレーツに15対0で7回に〜した. The Jaguars defeated the Pirates 15 to 0 in a game called in the seventh inning.
ゴールドブラム Goldblum, Jeff (1952–  ; 米国の映画俳優; 本名 Jeff Lynn Goldblum).
「コールド マウンテン」〔映画〕Cold Mountain.
コールドまけ【-負け】〔野球〕a called defeat. 〜する lose a called game.
ゴールドマン・サックス〔米国の投資銀行〕Goldman Sachs.
ゴールドマンしやけい【-視野計】〔眼科〕a Goldmann perimeter.
コーン[3] ▷ コーン油[オイル] corn [maize] oil.
「コーンウォールの森へ」〔映画〕All the Little Animals.
コーン・ケー〔-ケー〕=コンケン.
こがいしゃ【子会社】 ▷ 完全子会社 a wholly-owned subsidiary. 事業子会社 a nonfinancial subsidiary. 専門子会社 a dedicated subsidiary. 戦略子会社 a strategic 「affiliate [subsidiary]. ▷ 子会社連動株式〔証券〕subsidiary tracking stock.
こかいよう【古海洋】〔地質〕〔かつて地球上に存在した海洋〕an ancient ocean; a paleocean. ▷ 古海洋学 paleoceanography. ▷ palaeoceanographic *adj*.
こがお【小顔】〔小さな顔〕a small face;〔化粧などで小さく見せた顔〕a 'little [tiny, petite] face. ▷ 小顔整形〔美容〕face [size; jaw] reduction surgery; cosmetic surgery to reduce the size of the face.
ごがくしどうとうをおこなうがいこくせいねんしょうちじぎょう〔語学指導等を行う外国青年招致事業〕=ジェット・プログラム.
こがた【小型・小形】 ▷ 小型犬 a small (breed of) dog. 小型船舶操縦士 a licensed small 「boat('s) [ship('s)] pilot. 小型動力ポンプ〔消防用〕a portable motor pump. 小型旅客機〔ジェット機〕〔空〕a small passenger 「plane [jet].
こかつ【枯渇】 ▷ 枯渇資源 exhaustible [non-renewable] resources. ▷ 非〜資源 inexhaustible [renewable] resources.
こがねたけやし【黄金竹椰子】〔植〕=やまどりやし.
こかみあり【小噛み蟻】〔昆〕a little fire ant; *Wasmannia auropunctata*.
コカリナ〔商標〕〔「サクラの木でできたオカリナ」と呼ばれるハンガリーの楽器をもとに日本で考案された木製楽器〕a Kocarina.
こかんきょうがく【古環境学】paleoenvironmental 「studies [sciences]; paleoenvironmentology.
こかんせつ【股関節】 ▷ 股関節臼蓋形成不全〔医〕きゅうがいけいせいふぜん. 股関節形成不全〔医〕hip dysplasia. ▷〔獣医〕(canine, feline) hip dysplasia.
コキーこやすがえる【-子安蛙】【動】〔プエルトリコ原産の両

こきこうがく

生類〕a coqui; *Eleutherodactylus coqui*.
**こきこうがく**【古気候学】paleoclimatology. ▷ paleoclimatological *adj*. ◐▯ 古気候学者 a paleoclimatologist.
**こきしょうがく**【古気象学】paleometeorology. ▷ paleometeorological *adj*. ◐▯ 古気象学者 a paleometeorologist.
**こぎって**【小切手】◐▯ 小切手外交〔金に物を言わせる強引な外交〕checkbook diplomacy.
**こきゃく**【顧客】
◐▯ 顧客開拓 finding「new [potential] customers; prospecting for customers. 顧客獲得 customer acquisition; obtaining「customers [custom]. ◐ 〜獲得競争 competition to「acquire [get] customers; competing for custom. 顧客関係管理 customer「relationship (relation(s)] management (略: CRM). 顧客心理 customer psychology; customer attitudes. 顧客層〔客層〕a customer stratum. 顧客争奪戦 a scramble for customers; a customer war. 顧客単価〔客単価〕(the) per-customer spending; the (average) amount spent by each customer. 顧客中心主義 customer centricity. ▷ customer-centric *adj*. 顧客離れ customer erosion; the erosion of《a company's》customer base. ◐ 〜離れを食い止める stop [prevent] customer erosion.
**こきゅう**[1]【呼吸】◐▯ 呼吸療法〔医〕respiratory therapy. ◐ 〜療法士 a respiratory therapist / 〜療法認定士 a certified respiratory therapist
**ごぎょうか**【五行歌】a five-line (Japanese) poem.
**こくい**[1]【国威】◐▯ 国威発揚 the「promotion [enhancement] of national prestige. ◐ オリンピックが〜発揚の場と考えられたのは過去のことだ. In the past, the Olympics was considered a venue for enhancing national prestige.
**こくえいいさはやわんかんたくじぎょう**【国営諫早湾干拓事業】the Isahaya Bay reclamation project.
**こくえいイランつうしん**【国営−通信】the Islamic Republic News Agency (略: IRNA).
**こくえき**[2]【黒液】〔化〕〔パルプを製造する際にできる黒色の廃液〕black liquor.
**こくえん**[1]【黒煙】◐▯ 黒煙濃度〔ディーゼルエンジンから排出された黒煙の〕black smoke density; density of black smoke.
**こくえん**[2]【黒鉛】◐▯ 黒鉛ナノチューブ〔化〕a graphite nanotube.
**こくがい**【国外】◐▯ 国外移送目的略取〔誘拐, 拐取〕(罪)〔法〕(the crime of)「kidnapping [abducting] people for the purpose of transporting them to another country. 国外退避 evacuation from [fleeing] a country. ◐ テロ発生に備えて外務省はその国に滞在している邦人が〜退避を勧告した. As a precaution against terror attacks, the Ministry of Foreign Affairs warned Japanese to leave that country.
**こくかつしとう**【黒瞎子島】〔大ウスリー島の中国名〕Heixiazi Island.
**こくぎょく**【黒玉】『宝石』=ジェット[2].
**こくご**【国語】◐▯ 国語力 (Japanese speakers') Japanese language ability. ◐ 音読は児童の〜力の向上に効果があります. Reading aloud is effective in improving Japanese children's language ability.
**こくさい**[2]【国債】◐▯ 10年物国債 a 10-year government bond. ◐▯ 国債買い切りオペ a buy-up operation targeting government bonds. ◐ 短期〜買い切りオペ a buy-up operation targeting short-term government bonds. 国債貸し出し制度 = しながし. 国債先物取引 government bond futures trading. 国債市場特別参加者 a specially chartered dealer in the Japanese bond market. 国債発行残高〔国債残高〕(the amount of) government「bonds [securities] outstanding. 国債流

通利回り a government bond yield.
**こくさい**[3]【国際】
◐▯ 国際移動者〔国外への出稼ぎ労働者など〕an international migrant; a foreign worker; a migrant worker;〈集合的に〉migrant labor. 国際映像 an international video feed. 国際NGO an international NGO. 国際学力調査 an international academic ability survey;＝学習到達度調査 (⇨がくしゅう). 国際貨物 international cargo. ◐ 〜貨物ターミナル an international cargo terminal / 〜貨物便 an international cargo flight / 〜貨物輸送 international cargo transportation. 国際関係論〔講座名・書名など〕International Relations (略: IR). 国際監視制度〔包括的核実験禁止条約 (CTBT) にもとづく〕the International Monitoring System (略: IMS). 国際感染症 an international infectious disease. 国際急送便 an international express service. 国際協調 ◐ 〜協調主義 the「principle [spirit] of international harmony / 〜協調路線 a policy of international harmony. 国際協力活動 international「cooperation [collaboration] activities; international assistance. 国際軍 an international (military) force. 国際合意 (an) international agreement. 国際航空貨物混載(業) international air freight forwarding. 国際(公認)球〔球技の〕an official「game [match] ball for an international game. 国際交流 ◐ 〜交流委員会 an international exchange committee. 国際交流員 a coordinator for international relations (略: CIR). ◐ スポーツ〜交流員 ⇨スポーツ. 国際人権法 international human rights law. 国際スピード郵便〔郵便〕Express Mail Service (略: EMS). 国際生産 global [international] production;〔海外生産〕overseas production. 国際チャーター便〔飛行機の〕an international charter(ed) flight. 国際定期便 a regular international flight. ◐ 米子-ソウル〜定期便 a regular (international) flight between Yonago and Seoul. 国際難民法 international refugee law. 国際年〔テーマ〕an international「year [day]; the International「Year [Day]《of Education》. 国際俳優 an international (movie) star. 国際標準 an international [a global] standard (for …). 国際標準規格 an international standard; (an) international standard specification. 国際部隊 an international brigade. 国際報道官〔外務省の〕the Director of the International Press Division; the Assistant Press Secretary. 国際メール便 an international mail service. 国際郵便〔send *sth* by〕international [overseas] mail. ◐ 〜郵便物 an item of, some) international [overseas] mail. 国際理解 international understanding. ◐ 〜理解教育 education for international understanding (略: EIU). 国際離婚 (an) international divorce. 国際ルール international rules《of [for] air transportation》. 国際連帯税〔フランスの提唱による〕an international solidarity tax. 国際(連帯)航空券税〔国際連帯税の手始めとしての〕an international airline ticket tax. 国際ローミング〔通信〕international [global, overseas] roaming.
**こくさいあかちゃんがっかい**【国際赤ちゃん学会】the International Society on Infant Studies (略: ISIS).
**こくさいあくしつせいひんしょう**【国際悪質製品賞】〔消費者団体の国際組織コンシューマーズ・インターナショナルが発表する, 社会的責任を欠いた商品を発表する"賞"とまとめて) the International Bad Products Award;《個々の賞をまとめて》the International Bad Products Awards.
**こくさいアグリバイオじぎょうだん**【国際−事業団】the International Service for the Acquisition of Agri-biotech Applications (略: ISAAA).
**こくさいアビリンピック**【国際−】the International Abilympics.
**こくさいアメリカンフットボールれんめい**【国際−連盟】the International Federation of American Football

(略: IFAF).
**こくさいあやとりきょうかい**【国際あやとり協会】the International String Figure Association (略: ISFA).
**こくさいアルツハイマーびょうきょうかい**【国際-病協会】Alzheimer's Disease International (略: ADI).
**こくさいアロマセラピストれんめい**【国際-連盟】the International Federation of Aromatherapists (略: IFA).
**こくさいあんぜんほしょうかんきょう**【国際安全保障環境】the global security environment (in the 21st century).
**こくさいうんゆろうどうしゃれんめい**【国際運輸労働者連盟】the International Transport Workers' Federation (略: ITF).
**こくさいうんゆろうれん**【国際運輸労連】=こくさいうんゆろうどうしゃれんめい.
**こくさいえいきょうひょうかがっかい**【国際影響評価学会】the International Association for Impact Assessment (略: IAIA).
**こくさいエイズワクチンすいしんこうそう**【国際-推進構想】〔エイズ予防ワクチンの開発・普及を目的とする国際組織〕the International AIDS Vaccine Initiative (略: IAVI).
**こくさいエクパット**【国際 ECPAT】〔児童の商業的性的搾取に反対する国際 NGO; 世界 30 か国にネットワークを広げる〕the ECPAT International. ▶ ECPAT は End Child Prostitution, Child Pornography And Trafficking in Children for Sexual Purposes の略.
**こくさいエネルギースタープログラム**【国際-】the International Energy Star Program.
**こくさいか**【国際化】 国際化戦略 an internationalization strategy.
**こくさいかいじきょく**【国際海事局】〔国際商業会議所の〕the International Maritime Bureau (略: IMB).  国際海事局海賊報告[情報]センター the IMB Piracy Reporting Centre.
**こくさいかいはつちょう**【国際開発庁】〔米国の〕the United States Agency for International Development (略: USAID).
**こくさいかいようおせんぼうしじょうやく**【国際海洋汚染防止条約】=かいようおせんぼうしじょうやく.
**こくさいかがくオリンピック**【国際化学-】the International Chemistry Olympiad (略: IChO).
**こくさいかがくオリンピック**[2]【国際科学-】the International Science Olympiads.
**こくさいかがくぎじゅつざいだん**【国際科学技術財団】the Science and Technology Foundation of Japan (略: JSTF).
**こくさいがくしゅうとうたつどちょうさ**【国際学習到達度調査】=学習到達度調査 (⇨がくしゅう).
**こくさいがくせいかがくぎじゅつはくらんかい**【国際学生科学技術博覧会】=こくさいがくせいかがくフェア.
**こくさいがくせいかがくフェア**【国際学生科学-】the (Intel) International Science and Engineering Fair (略: (Intel) ISEF). ▶ Intel 社主催の高校生のための科学技術コンテスト.
**こくさいかぞくデー**【国家家族-】〔5 月 15 日; 国連制定〕the International Day of Families.
**こくさいかでんショー**【国際家電-】the International Consumer Electronics Show (略: ICES).
**こくさいカヌーれんめい**【国際-連盟】the International Canoe Federation (略: ICF).
**こくさいかんきょうぎじゅつセンター**【国際環境技術-】〔国連環境計画 (UNEP) の〕the International Environmental Technology Centre (略: IETC).
**こくさいかんこうしんこうきこう**【国際観光振興機構】the Japan National Tourist Organization (略: JNTO).
**こくさいかんこうホテルせいびほう**【国際観光-整備

法】《法》the Law for Improvement of International Tourist Hotel Facilities.
**こくさいかんせんしょうがっかい**【国際感染症学会】the International Society for Infectious Diseases (略: ISID).
**こくさいかんようデー**【国際寛容-】〔11 月 16 日; 国連制定〕the International Day for Tolerance.
**こくさいきしょうやせいどうしょくぶつしゅ**【国際希少野生動植物種】International Endangered Species of Wild Fauna and Flora.
**こくさいきねんぶつついせきかいぎ**【国際記念物遺跡会議】the International Council on Monuments and Sites (略: ICOMOS).
**こくさいぎのうきょうぎたいかい**【国際技能競技大会】〔国際技能オリンピック〕the WorldSkills Competition.
**こくさいきゅうえんいいんかい**【国際救援委員会】〔米国の難民支援 NGO〕the International Rescue Committee (略: IRC).
**こくさいきゅうさいいいんかい**【国際救済委員会】=こくさいきゅうえんいいんかい.
**こくさいきゅうじょたい**【国際救助隊】〔TV 番組『サンダーバード』の〕International Rescue.
**こくさいきょういくとうたつどひょうかがっかい**【国際教育到達度評価学会】the International Association for the Evaluation of Educational Achievement (略: IEA). ▶ 本部はオランダ, アムステルダム.
**こくさいきょうぎだんたいれんごう**【国際競技団体連合】the General Association of International Sports Federations (略: GAISF).
**こくさいきょうぎれんめいれんごう**【国際競技連盟連合】the General Association of International Sports Federations (略: GAISF).
**こくさいきょうそうりょくねんかん**【国際競争力年鑑】=せかいきょうそうりょくねんかん.
**こくさいきょうそうりょくランキング**【国際競争力-】〔世界経済フォーラムが毎年発表する〕the Global Competitiveness Rankings.
**こくさいきょくねん**【国際極年】〔1882-83, 1932-33〕the International Polar Year (略: IPY).
**こくさいきんせいがっかい**【国際禁制学会】the International Continence Society (略: ICS).
**こくさいきんゆうじょうほうセンター**【国際金融情報-】the Japan Center for International Finance (略: JCIF).
**こくさいクマかいぎ**【国際-会議】the (17th) International Conference on Bear Research and Management (2006).
**こくさいけいえいかいはつけんきゅうじょ**【国際経営開発研究所】〔スイスのローザンヌにある国際的な経営学研究所〕the International Institute for Management Development (略: IMD).
**こくさいけいざいけんきゅうじょ**【国際経済研究所】〔米国の〕the Institute for International Economics (略: IIE).
**こくさいけいじさいばんしょ**【国際刑事裁判所】  国際刑事裁判所設立条約 the Rome Statute of the International Criminal Court.
**こくさいけいばとうかつきかんれんめい**【国際競馬統括機関連盟】the International Federation of Horseracing Authorities (略: IFHA).
**こくさいげんごがくオリンピック**【国際言語学-】the International Linguistic(s) Olympiad (略: ILO).
**こくさいけんしゅうきょうりょくきこう**【国際研修協力機構】the Japan International Training Cooperation Organization (略: JITCO).
**こくさいげんしりょくパートナーシップ**【国際原子力-】〔米国が 2006 年発表した新しい原子力政策の構想〕the Global Nuclear Energy Partnership (略: GNEP).
**こくさいこうどうがっかい**【国際行動学会】the Asso-

こくさいこうどうセンター　136

ciation of International Behavioral Studies.
こくさいこうどうセンター【国際行動-】〔米国の反американ権利団体〕the International Action Center (略：IAC).
こくさいこうれいしゃデー【国際高齢者-】〔10月1日；国連制定〕the International Day of Older Persons.
こくさいコメねん【国際-年】〔国連制定；2004年〕the International Year of Rice (略：IYR).
こくさいざいむほうこくきじゅん【国際財務報告基準】International Financial Reporting Standards (略：IFRS).
こくさいサッカーひょうぎかい【国際-評議会】the International Football Association Board (略：IFAB).
こくさいさばくさばくかねん【国際砂漠・砂漠化年】the International Year of Deserts and Desertification. ▶ 2006年.
こくさいサンゴしょうねん【国際-礁年】〔1997年, 2008年〕the International Year of the Reef.
こくさいしきじデー【国際識字-】〔9月8日；国連制定〕International Literacy Day.
こくさいしぜんほごれんめい【国際自然保護連盟】the International Union for Conservation of Nature and Natural Resources (略：IUCN).
こくさいじてんしゃきょうぎれんごう【国際自転車競技連合】the International Cycling Union (略：UCI). ▶ UCIはフランス語の l'Union Cycliste Internationale の略.
こくさいじどうしゃこうぎょうかい【国際自動車工業会】〔米国の〕the Association of International Automobile Manufactures (略：AIAM).
こくさいみんスポーツれんめい【国際市民-連盟】〈＜G＞〉Internationaler Volkssportverband (＝Internationale Federation of Popular Sports) (略：IVV).
こくさいしゃかいけいざいけんきゅうじょ【国際社会経済研究所】the Institute for International Socio-Economic Studies (略：IISE).
こくさいしゃげきれんめい【国際射撃連盟】the International Shooting Sport Federation (略：ISSF). ▶ 1998年 Union Internationale de Tir (略：UIT) から改称.
こくさいじゅうえきじむきょく【国際獣疫事務局】the World Organization for Animal Health; the OIE. ▶ OIEはフランス語の l'Office international des épizooties の略.
こくさいしょうけんとりひきじょれんごう【国際証券取引所連合】＝くさいとりひきじょれんごう.
こくさいしょうひしゃきこう【国際消費者機構】Consumers International (略：CI). ▶ 1995年, IOCU (International Organization of Consumers Unions) から名称変更.
こくさいしょうひょうきょうかい【国際商標協会】the International Trademark Association (略：INTA).
こくさいじょうほうオリンピック【国際情報学-】the International Olympiad in Informatics (略：IOI).
こくさいしょくぎょうくんれんきこう【国際職業訓練機構】the WorldSkills Organisation. ▶ 2003年改名，旧名 the International Vocational Training Organisation (略：IVTO).
こくさいじょせいデー【国際女性-】〔3月8日〕International Women's Day (略：IWD).
こくさいショッピングセンターきょうかい【国際-協会】the International Council of Shopping Centers (略：ICSC).
こくさいじんけんエーきやく【国際人権A規約】＝しゃかいけんきやく.
こくさいしんぜん【国際親善】▢▫国際親善デー〔の日〕International Friendship Day.
こくさいすうがくしゃかいぎ【国際数学者会議】the International Congress of Mathematicians (略：ICM).

こくさいずつうがっかい【国際頭痛学会】the International Headache Society (略：IHS).
こくさいすもうれんめい【国際相撲連盟】the International Sumo Federation.
こくさいせいぶつがくオリンピック【国際生物学-】the International Biology Olympiad (略：IBO).
こくさいせいやくだんたいれんごうかい【国際製薬団体連合会】the International Federation of Pharmaceutical Industries and Associations (略：IFPIA).
こくさいせいりききんとくべつかいけい【国債整理基金特別会計】the special account for consolidation of the national debt; the National Debt Consolidation Fund Special Account.
こくさいせきじゅうじ・せきしんげつしゃれんめい【国際赤十字・赤新月社連盟】the International Federation of Red Cross and Red Crescent Societies (略：IFRC).
こくさいせきゆこうりゅうセンター【国際石油交流-】the Japan Cooperation Center, Petroleum (略：JCCP).
こくさいせきゆとうしこうしゃ【国際石油投資公社】〔アラブ首長国連邦のアブダビ首長国の〕the International Petroleum Investment Company (略：IPIC).
こくさいせんくどうほう【国際先駆導報】〔中国, 新華社発行の週刊紙〕The International Herald Leader.
こくさいそしきはんざいとう・こくさいテロたいさくすいしんほんぶ【国際組織犯罪等・国際-対策推進本部】(Japan) Headquarters for Promotion of Response to International Organized Crime and International Terrorism.
こくさいそしきはんざい（ぼうし）じょうやく【国際組織犯罪（防止）条約】the (United Nations) Convention against Transnational Organized Crime. ▶ 正式名称は, 国際的な組織犯罪の防止に関する国際連合条約.
こくさいソフトボールれんめい【国際-連盟】the International Softball Federation (略：ISF).
こくさいたいそうれんめい【国際体操連盟】the Fédération Internationale de Gymnastique (略：FIG).
こくさいたっきゅうれんめい【国際卓球連盟】the International Table Tennis Federation (略：ITTF).
こくさいちあんしえんぶたい【国際治安支援部隊】〔アフガニスタンの〕the International Security Assistance Force (略：ISAF).
こくさいつうかきんゆういいんかい【国際通貨金融委員会】〔国際通貨基金 (IMF) の機関〕the International Monetary and Financial Committee (略：IMFC).
こくさいつなみじょうほうセンター【国際津波情報-】the International Tsunami Information Centre (略：ITIC).
こくさいティー・エーきょうかい【国際 TA 協会】the International Transactional Analysis Association.
こくさいてき【国際的】▢▫国際的スター【女優】an international 「star 「actress」. 国際的発言権 the right to 「speak [express oneself, give one's views] internationally [to other countries]; 《have, acquire》 a voice on the international stage. 国際的枠組みへのintertional framework. ◇気候変動問題に関する~枠組みとして京都議定書が1997年に合意された. The Kyoto Protocol was agreed to in 1997 as an international framework on the issue of climate change.
こくさいテニスれんめい【国際-連盟】the International Tennis Federation (略：ITF).
こくさいテロきんきゅうてんかいチーム【国際-緊急展開-】〔警察庁の〕the Terrorism Response Team (略：TRT).
こくさいでんきつうしんきそぎじゅつけんきゅうじょ【国際電気通信基礎技術研究所】the Advanced Telecommunications Research Institute International (略：ATR).

こくさいでんきつうしんれんごう【国際電気通信連合】 ▫️ 国際電気通信連合憲章 the Constitution and Convention of the International Telecommunication Union; the ITU Constitution and Convention.
こくさいてんもんがくオリンピック【国際天文学-】the International Astronomy Olympiad (略: IAO).
こくさいとうにょうびょうれんごう【国際糖尿病連合】the International Diabetes Federation (略: IDF).
こくさいとっきょほう【国際特許法】〘法〙〔分野としての〕international patent law.
こくさいとりひきじょれんごう【国際取引所連合】the World Federation of Exchanges (略: WFE).
こくさいなぎなたれんめい【国際なぎなた連盟】the International Naginata Federation (略: INF).
こくさいのうぎょうこうりゅう・しょくりょうしえんききん【国際農業交流・食糧支援基金】the Japan International Agricultural Council (略: JIAC).
こくさいは【国際派】a person with an international outlook; an internationally active person; a cosmopolitan; a world citizen. ▫️ 国際派スター[女優] an internationally active [a cosmopolitan] star [actress].
こくさいバカロレア【国際-】〔国際的な大学入学資格試験〕International Baccalaureate (略: IB). ▫️ 国際バカロレア資格証書 an International Baccalaureate Diploma. 国際バカロレア事務局 the International Baccalaureate Organization (略: IBO).
こくさいはくぶつかんかいぎ【国際博物館会議】〔UNESCO の専門機関〕the International Council of Museums (略: ICOM).
こくさいはくぶつかんのひ【国際博物館の日】〔5 月 18 日〕International Museum Day.
こくさいはくらんかいじむきょく【国際博覧会事務局】=はくらんかいこくさいじむきょく.
こくさいはくらんかいじょうやく【国際博覧会条約】the Convention on International Exhibitions.
こくさいばじゅつれんめい【国際馬術連盟】the International Equestrian Federation (略: FEI). ▶ FEI はフランス語の Fédération Équestre Internationale の略.
こくさいハップマップけいかく【国際-計画】〔遺伝〕〔アジア人・アフリカ人・欧米人などについてハプロタイプ地図の作成を目指す国際プロジェクト〕the International HapMap Project.
こくさいバドミントンれんめい【国際-連盟】the International Badminton Federation (略: IBF).
こくさいバレーボールれんめい【国際-連盟】the International Volleyball Federation (略: FIVB). ▶ FIVB はフランス語の Fédération Internationale de Volleyball の略.
こくさいはんどうたいせいぞうそうちざいりょうきょうかい【国際半導体製造装置材料協会】the Semiconductor Equipment and Materials International (略: SEMI).
こくさいビフレンダーズ【国際-】〔自殺防止団体〕Befrienders International.
こくさいひまんがっかい【国際肥満学会】〔団体名〕the International Association for the Study of Obesity (略: IASO); 〔会合名〕《10th》International Congress on Obesity 《2006》(略: ICO).
こくさいフィルム・アーカイブれんめい【国際-連盟】the International Federation of Film Archives (略: FIAF). ▶ FIAF はフランス語の Fédération Internationale des Archives du Film の略.
こくさいフェンシングれんめい【国際-連盟】the International Fencing Federation (略: FIE). ▶ FIE はフランス語の Fédération internationale d'escrime の略.
こくさいぶつりオリンピック【国際物理-】the International Physics Olympiad (略: IPhO).
こくさいぶつりがくねん【国際物理学年】the International Year of Physics. ▶ 日本では「世界物理年」と呼称.

こくさいぶんつうしゅうかん【国際文通週間】International Letter-Writing Week.
こくさいへいわ【国際平和】▫️ 国際平和協力活動 international peace cooperation activities. 国際平和貢献《Japan's》contribution to international peace.
こくさいへいわかつどうきょうかい【国際平和活動協会】the International Peace Operations Association (略: IPOA).
こくさいほう【国際法】▫️ 国際法上 ◯…することは〜上認められている. Doing is 'recognized [accepted] under international law.
こくさいぼうさいせんりゃく【国際防災戦略】〔国連の〕the (United Nations) International Strategy for Disaster Reduction (略: ISDR).
こくさいぼうさいのひ【国際防災の日】〔10 月第 2 水曜; 国連制定〕the International Day for Natural Disaster Reduction.
こくさいほうしゃせんぼうごがっかい【国際放射線防護学会】the International Radiation Protection Association (略: IRPA).
こくさいほうりつかいいんかい【国際法律家委員会】〔「法の支配」の確立を目的として設立された非政府機関〕the International Commission of Jurists (略: ICJ).
こくさいボートれんめい【国際-連盟】the International Rowing Federation; the International Federation of Rowing Associations (略: FISA). ▶ FISA はフランス語の Fédération Internationale des Sociétés d'Aviron の略.
こくさいボクシングれんめい【国際-連盟】the International Boxing Federation (略: IBF).
こくさいほっきょくけんけんきゅうセンター【国際北極圏研究-】〔アラスカ大学の〕the International Arctic Research Center (略: IARC).
こくさいまやくとうせいいいんかい【国際麻薬統制委員会】〔国連の〕the International Narcotics Control Board (略: INCB).
こくさいみずきょうかい【国際水協会】the International Water Association (略: IWA).
こくさいやきゅうれんめい【国際野球連盟】the International Baseball Federation (略: IBAF).
こくさいゆうごうそうぞうセンター【国際融合創造-】⇒こくさいかくこくさいゆうごうそうぞうセンター.
こくさいユニヴァーサルデザインきょうかい【国際-協議会】the International Association for Universal Design (略: IAUD).
こくさいようじきょういくがっかい【国際幼児教育学会】the International Association of Early Childhood Education (略: IAECE).
こくさいラグビーきこう【国際-機構】=こくさいラグビーひょうぎかい.
こくさいラグビーひょうぎかい【国際-評議会】the International Rugby Board (略: IRB).
こくさいラグビーボード【国際-】=こくさいラグビーひょうぎかい.
こくさいりくじょうかがくくっさくけいかく【国際陸上科学掘削計画】the International Continental Scientific Drilling Program (略: ICDP).
こくさいりゅうこうしょくいいんかい【国際流行色委員会】the International Commission for Fashion and Textile Colors; 〔通称〕Intercolor.
こくさいりんかいかいはつけんきゅうセンター【国際臨海開発研究-】〔財団法人〕the Overseas Coastal Area Development Institute of Japan (略: OCDI).
こくさいレコードさんぎょうれんめい【国際-産業連盟】the International Federation of the Phonographic Industry (略: IFPI).
こくさいレスリングれんめい【国際-連盟】the International Federation of Associated Wrestling Styles (略:

こくさいろうしゃスポーツ

FILA). ► FILA はフランス語の *Fédération Internationale des Luttes Associées* の略.

**こくさいろうしゃスポーツいいんかい**【国際ろう者委員会】the International Committee of Sports for the Deaf (略: CISS). ► CISS はフランス語の *Comité International des Sports des Sourds* の略.

**こくさく**【国策】⦿ 国策捜査〔政府の意思・方針によって行われる刑事事件の捜査〕a government-instigated criminal investigation; a criminal investigation instigated at the behest of the government.

**こくじ**[7]【刻字】〔文字を彫りつけること〕inscription; 〔彫りけた文字〕an inscription.
〜する inscribe [engrave]《*sb*'s initials on a ring》.

**こくしつ**[2]【黒質】〖解〗〔中脳にある神経核〕the substantia nigra (略: SN).

**こくしょ**[3]【酷暑】⦿ 酷暑害〔気象〕damage《to crops》resulting from extremely high temperatures. 酷暑日 =もうしょび.

**こくしょ**[4]【刻書】engraved「writing [calligraphy]; 〔作品〕an engraved text.

**ごくしょう**【極小】⦿ 極小カプセル a microcapsule. 極小未熟児 =ごくていしゅっせいたいじゅうじ.

**こくじょういん**【国情院】=こっかじょうほういん.

**こくじょく**【国辱】⦿ 国辱者 a disgrace to one's「country [nation]; a national disgrace.

**こくじんちいこうじょうきょうかい**【黒人地位向上協会】〔米国の〕⇨ぜんべいこくじんちいこうじょうきょうかい.

**ごくすい**【曲水】〔庭園や樹林を蛇行して流れる細い水路〕a winding stream (in a Japanese garden or wood). ⦿ 〜の宴 a drinking party for Heian period nobles at which cups of sake were floated down a winding stream and participants seated on the bank had to improvise a「tanka [verse] before taking a sip.

**こくぜい**【国税】⦿ 国税五税 the "five national taxes"; income tax, corporation tax, liquor tax, consumption tax and tobacco tax. ► 所得税, 法人税, 酒税, 消費税, たばこ税をいう. 国税収納金整理資金 the Adjustment Fund of National Tax Receipts.

**こくせき**【国籍】⦿ 国籍不明者 a person「of unknown nationality [whose nationality is not known].

**こくたに**【古九谷】old Kutani (ware).

**こくたん**[2]【黒炭】〔やわらかずみ〕soft black charcoal; 〔石炭の一種, 瀝青炭〕bituminous [pitch, soft] coal.

**こくち**【告知】⦿ 病名告知 announcing《to a patient》[informing《a patient of》] the name of his disease; a diagnosis (to the patient).

**こくち**[1]【小口】⦿ 小口化〔株式などの〕subdivision《of shares》.

**こくちバス**【小口—】〔魚〕〔サンフィッシュ科の淡水魚〕a smallmouth bass; *Micropterus dolomieu*.

**「獄中記」**[2]〔ジェフリー・アーチャーの著作〕A Prison Diary. ►「地獄篇」(Hell), 「煉獄篇」(Wayland-Purgatory), 「天国篇」(Heaven) の三部作.

**ごくちゅうし**【獄中死】(a) death [dying] in prison; a prison death.
〜する die in prison.

**ごくていしゅっせいたいじゅうじ**【極低出生体重児】〖医〗a very low birth weight infant.

**こくど**[1]【国土】⦿ 国土形成計画 the Plan for「Sustainable National Land Development [the Sustainable Development of National Land]. ► 2005 年, 全国総合開発計画から改称. 国土緑化 national (land) afforestation; greening the nation;《the campaign for》a greener nation.

**こくどあんぜんほしょうほう**【国土安全保障法】〖米法〗the Homeland Security Act.

**こくどう**【国道】⦿ 直轄国道 a「road [highway] maintained by the national government.《⇨一[二]桁国道, 補助国道》一[二, 三]桁国道 a single-[double-, triple-] digit numbered national「road [highway]. ► 路線番号の桁数により直轄国道を一[二]桁国道, 補助国道を三桁国道とも呼ぶ.《⇨直轄国道, 補助国道》補助国道 a「road [highway] maintained by the prefectural government; a prefecture-maintained national「road [highway].《⇨三桁国道, 直轄国道》

**こくどかいはつかんせんじどうしゃどうけんせつかいぎ**【国土開発幹線自動車道建設会議】the National Development Arterial Expressway Committee.

**こくどけいせいけいかくほう**【国土形成計画法】〖法〗the Law for「Sustainable National Land Development [the Sustainable Development of National Land]. ► 2005 年, 国土総合開発法から改正.

**こくどこうつうはくしょ**【国土交通白書】〔国土交通省の〕the White Paper on Land, Infrastructure, Transport and Tourism in Japan《2008》.

**こくどじく**【国土軸】〔国土開発のための地域連携軸〕a national axis.

**こくどりょくかすいしんきこう**【国土緑化推進機構】the National Land Afforestation Promotion Organization (略: NLAPO). ► 農林水産省所管の社団法人.

**こくない**【国内】⦿ 国内企業物価 domestic corporate goods prices. ◎ 〜企業物価指数 the domestic corporate goods price index (略: DCGPI). 国内材〔木材〕domestic [domestically produced] lumber [timber, building materials]; 〔石材〕domestic [domestically quarried] rock [stone].

**こくないきしょうやぜいしょくぶつしゅ**【国内希少野生動植物種】the National Endangered Species of Wild Fauna and Flora.

**こくないそうししゅつ**【国内総支出】〖経〗gross domestic expenditure (略: GDE).

**こくはつ**【告発】⦿ 告発サイト〔インターネット上の〕a Website devoted to airing accusations or grievances against a specific person or organization. 告発本 a whistle-blowing book; a book that「reveals [takes the lid off, uncovers]《corruption》.

**こくはつもんだいきょうぎかい**【告発問題協議会】〔公正取引委員会と検察当局とで構成する〕a consultative meeting for criminal prosecutions (consisting of representatives from the Fair Trade Commission of Japan and from a prosecutors office).

**こくひ**【極秘】⦿ 極秘通話 a top secret (tele)phone「call [conversation].

**こくべん**【黒便】black tarry feces.

**こくぼう**【国防】⦿ 国防政策見直し構想〔日米の〕a [the] Defense Policy Review Initiative (略: DPRI). 国防白書 a white paper on national defense.

**こくぼうこうとうけんきゅうけいかくちょう**【国防高等研究計画庁】〔米国国総省〕the Defense Advanced Research Projects Agency (略: DARPA).

**こくぼうじょうほうきょく**【国防情報局】〔米国国総省の〕the Defense Intelligence Agency (略: DIA).

**こくぼうじょうほうセンター**【国防情報—】〔米国の反戦市民派のシンクタンク〕the Center for Defense Information (略: CDI).

**こくぼうしょうこうとうけんきゅうけいかくきょく**【国防総省高等研究計画局】=こくぼうこうとうけんきゅうけいかくちょう.

**ごくぼそ**【極細】⦿ 超極細 super-fine; ultra-fine. ◎ 超〜ペン a super-fine [an ultra-fine] pen; a pen with「a super-fine [an ultra-fine] point [nib].

**こくまざさ**【小熊笹】〖植〗〔イネ科の多年草〕*Sasaella kogasensis* var. *gracillimia*.

**こくみん**【国民】
⦿ 国民意識〔ある事柄に関する〕a「national [popular] attitude [feeling]《toward…》; 〔国民であるという自覚〕awareness [consciousness] of being [that *one* is] a citizen of《Japan》. 国民受け ◎ あの政党は選挙の時に

だけ～受けする政策を掲げる．It is only at election time that the party sets out policies with popular appeal. **国民協議会**〔インドネシアの〕＝インドネシアこくみんきょうぎかい．**国民食** a standard dish; (a) popular food; a [the] national food. **国民保護基本指針** (the) Basic Guidelines for (the) Protection of the People. **国民保護計画**〔有事の際の〕a plan to protect people in case of a national emergency; a national protection plan.

**こくみんあんぜんのひ**【国民安全の日】〔7月1日〕National Safety Day.

**こくみんうんどうれんごう**【国民運動連合】〔フランスの連合政党〕the Union for a Popular Movement (略: UMP). ▶ UMP はフランス語の *Union pour un Mouvement Populaire* の略.

**こくみんけんこう・えいようちょうさ**【国民健康・栄養調査】a national health and nutrition survey; 〔日本の〕the National Health and Nutrition Survey (略: NHNS);〔米国の〕the National Health and Nutrition Examination Survey (略: NHANES).

**こくみんしょとく**【国民所得】 🔲 国民所得統計 national income statistics. ○～統計速報 an [a quick] estimate of national income.

**こくみんしんとう**【国民新党】the People's New Party (略: PNP). ▶ 2005年に結成.

**こくみんせいかつ**【国民生活】 🔲 国民生活基礎調査 the Comprehensive Survey of the Living Conditions, Health and Welfare of the People. **国民生活選好度調査**〔内閣府が行う〕the National Survey on Lifestyle Preferences. **国民生活動向調査**〔国民生活センターが毎年実施する〕the Survey of Trends in People's Livelihood, an annual survey of consumer attitudes.

**こくみんそうこうふくりょう**【国民総幸福量】gross national happiness (略: GNH). ▶ ブータン国王が提唱した概念.

**こくみんだいかいぎ**【国民大会議】〔イスラム教国の〕a [the] National Assembly; 〔イラクの〕a [the] loya jirga.

**こくみんねんきん**【国民年金】 🔲 国民年金推進員 a "national pension promoting worker"; a part-time worker who visits private homes to「collect [urge the payment of] national pension contributions. **国民年金特別会計** the national pension(s) special account; the Special Account for National Pensions.

**こくみんほごほう**【国民保護法】(法) the Civilian Protection Law. ▶〔武力攻撃事態における国民の保護のための措置に関する法律〕(the) Law Concerning Measures for Protection of the Civilian Population in an Armed Attack Situation) の略.

**こくみんみんしゅとう**【国民民主党】〔ドイツ・エジプトなどの政党〕the National Democratic Party. ▶ 略称 NDP;ドイツの政党はドイツ語で *Nationaldemokratische Partei Deutschlands* の略.

**こくみんれんめい**【国民連盟】〔ミャンマーの政党〕the National League for Democracy (略: NLD).

**こくめい**³【刻銘】〔石仏・石碑・陶器などに刻んだ文章・言葉〕an inscription; words [writing] inscribed 《on a monument》;〔刀剣などに刻んだ製作者名〕an inscription giving the name of the「maker [artist]. ～する inscribe 《a name》[make an inscription] 《on a monument》.

**こくもつ**【穀物】 🔲 食用穀物〔小麦・米など〕(a) food grain. **粗粒穀物**〔トウモロコシ・大麦など〕(a) coarse grain. **穀物在庫率** a grain stock-to-use ratio. **穀物飼料**〔家畜用の〕(a) cereal feed. **穀物自給率**〔a [the] grain self-sufficiency「rate [ratio]. **穀物酢** grain vinegar. **穀物肥育**〔畜〕grain feeding. ○～肥育牛〔牛肉〕grain-fed「cattle [beef].

**こくゆうか**【国有化】 🔲 一時国有化 temporary nationalization 《of a regional bank》.

## 139　こくりつスポーツかがくセンター

**こくゆうしさんかんとくかんりいいんかい**【国有資産監督管理委員会】〔中国・国務院内に設置の〕the Commission of the State-owned Assets Supervision and Administration.

**こくようせき**【黒曜石】 🔲 黒曜石石器〔考古〕an obsidian tool.

**こくついんさつきょく**【国立印刷局】the National Printing Bureau.

**こくりつうちゅうけんきゅうセンター**【国立宇宙研究―】〔フランスの〕⇨フランスこくりつうちゅうけんきゅうセンター.

**こくりつえいせいいがくけんきゅうじょ**【国立衛生医学研究所】〔フランスの〕the French National Institute for Health and Medical Research (略: Inserm). ▶ Inserm はフランス語の *Institut national de la santé et de la recherche médicale* の略.

**こくりつえいせいけんきゅうじょ**【国立衛生研究所】〔米国メリーランド州にある医学研究所〕the (US) National Institutes of Health (略: NIH).

**こくりつおきなわせんぼつしゃぼえん**【国立沖縄戦没者墓苑】the National Okinawa War Dead「Mausoleum [Cemetery].

**こくりつオリンピックきねんせいしょうねんそうごうセンター**【国立―記念青少年総合―】the National Olympics Memorial Youth Center (略: NYC).

**こくりつがんけんきゅうじょ**【国立癌研究所】〔米国の〕the National Cancer Institute (略: NCI).

**こくりつきょういくせいさくけんきゅうじょ**【国立教育政策研究所】the National Institute for Educational Policy Research.

**こくりつぎょうせいがくいん**【国立行政学院】〔フランスの〕the *École Nationale d'Administration* (略: ENA); (英語名) the French National School of Public Administration.

**こくりつきょくちけんきゅうじょ**【国立極地研究所】the National Institute of Polar Research (略: NIPR).

**こくりつこうどせんもんいりょうセンター**【国立高度専門医療―】the National Center for Advanced and Specialized Medical Care.

**こくりつこうぶんしょかんほう**【国立公文書館法】(法) the National Archives Law.

**こくりつこうぶんしょろくかんりきょく**【国立公文書記録管理局】〔米国の〕the (US) National Archives and Records Administration (略: NARA).

**こくりつきゅうこはくぶついん**【國立故宮博物院】〔台湾，台北の大博物館〕the National Palace Museum (略: NPM); Guoli Gugong Bowuyuan.

**こくりつこくさいいりょうセンター**【国立国際医療―】 🔲 国立国際医療センターエイズ治療・研究開発センター the International Medical Center of Japan's AIDS Clinical Center (略: ACC).

**こくりつこっかいとしょかんほう**【国立国会図書館法】(法) the National Diet Library Law.

**こくりつしゃかいほしょう・じんこうもんだいけんきゅうじょ**【国立社会保障・人口問題研究所】the National Institute of Population and Social Research.

**こくりつじゅういかがくけんえきいん**【国立獣医科学検疫院】〔韓国の動物検疫機関〕the National Veterinary Research and Quarantine Service (略: NVRQS).

**こくりつじゅうどちてきしょうがいしゃそうごうしせつのぞみのその**【国立重度知的障害者総合施設のぞみの園】Nozominosono, the National Center for Persons with Severe Intellectual Disabilities.

**こくりつしょうにほけんはついくけんきゅうじょ**【国立小児保健発育研究所】the National Institute of Child Health and Human Development (略: NICHD).

**こくりつスポーツかがくセンター**【国立―科学―】the Japan Institute of Sports Sciences (略: JISS).

こくりつだいがくほうじんほう【国立大学法人法】《法》 the National University Corporation Law.

こくりつちょうじゅいりょうセンター【国立長寿医療-】the National Center for Geriatrics and Gerontology (略: NCGG). ▯ 国立長寿医療センター研究所 the National Institute for Longevity Sciences, NCGG. 国立長寿医療センター病院 the National Hospital for Geriatric Medicine, NCGG.

こくりつとくしゅきょういくそうごうけんきゅうじょ【国立特殊教育総合研究所】〔独立行政法人〕the National Institute 「for [of] Special Education.

こくりつながさきげんばくしぼつしゃついとうへいわきねんかん【国立長崎原爆死没者追悼平和記念館】the Nagasaki National Peace Memorial Hall for (the) Atomic Bomb Victims.

こくりつハリケーンセンター【国立-】〔米国, フロリダ州マイアミにある〕the National Hurricane Center (略: NHC). ▶ 他にハワイのホノルルに「中部太平洋ハリケーンセンター the Central Pacific Hurricane Center (略: CPHC)」がある.

こくりつハンセンびょうりょうようじょ【国立-病療養所】a national leprosarium.

こくりつびょういんきこう【国立病院機構】the National Hospital Organization (略: NHO).

こくりつびょういんきこうさいがいいりょうセンター【国立病院機構災害医療-】〔国立病院機構に属する病院の1つ〕the National Disaster Medical Center.

こくりつひろしまげんばくしぼつしゃついとうへいわきねんかん【国立広島原爆死没者追悼平和祈念館】the Hiroshima National Peace Memorial Hall for the Atomic Bomb Victims.

こくれん【国連】
▯ 国連改革 United Nations [UN] reform. 国連視軍 a 「United Nations [UN] observer force. 国連軍事監視団 a United Nations military observer group. 国連査察 a 「United Nations [UN] inspection. 国連察団 a 「United Nations [UN] inspection team. 国連首脳会合[会議] a 「United Nations [UN] summit. 国連中心主義 UN-centrism. 国連ハイレベル会合 a United Nations High-Level Meeting 《on「Iraq [AIDS]》. 国連平和大使 a United Nations Messenger of Peace. 国連平和の日〔9月21日〕the 「United Nations [UN] Day of Peace. 国連予算分担金 ＝予算分担金 (⇨よさん).

こくれんアフガニスタン[アフガン]しえんだん【国連-[-]支援団】the United Nations Assistance Mission in Afghanistan (略: UNAMA).

こくれんイラクしえんだん【国連-支援団】the United Nations Assistance Mission for Iraq (略: UNAMI).

こくれんかがくいいんかい【国連科学委員会】the United Nations Scientific Committee (略: UNSC). [=げんしほうしゃせんのえいきょうにかんするこくれんかがくいいんかい]

こくれんかんきょうけいかく【国連環境計画】▯ 国連環境計画金融イニシアティブ the UNEP Finance Initiatives (略: UNEP FI).

こくれんぐんしゅくきょく【国連軍縮局】the United Nations) Office for Disarmament Affairs (略: (UN) ODA).

こくれんくんれんちょうさけんきゅうじょ【国連訓練調査研究所】the United Nations Institute for Training and Research (略: UNITAR).

こくれんけいざいてきしゃかいてきぶんかてきけんりいいんかい【国連経済的社会的文化的権利委員会】〔経済社会理事会の常設委員会の1つ〕the UN Committee on Economic, Social and Cultural Rights (略: CESCR).

こくれんごうもんきんしいいんかい【国連拷問禁止委員会】the United Nations Committee against Torture.

こくれんこくさいそしきはんざい(ぼうし)じょうやく【国連国際組織犯罪(防止)条約】⇨ こくさいそしきはんざい(ぼうし)じょうやく.

こくれんこくさいぼうさいせんりゃく【国連国際防災戦略】the United Nations International Strategy for Disaster Reduction (略: UNISDR).

こくれんこどもとくべつそうかい【国連子ども特別総会】the United Nations General Assembly Special Session on Children.

こくれんコンゴかんしだん【国連-監視団】＝こくれんコンゴみんしゅきょうわこくミッション.

こくれんコンゴみんしゅきょうわこくミッション【国連-民主共和国-】the United Nations Organization Mission in the Democratic Republic of the Congo (略: MONUC). ▶ MONUC は Mission de l'Organisation des Nations Unies en République Démocratique du Congo の略.

こくれんじぞくかのうなかいはつのためのきょういくのじゅうねん【国連持続可能な開発のための教育の10年】⇨ じぞくかのうなかいはつのためのきょういくのじゅうねん.

こくれんしょうがいしゃのけんりじょうやく【国連障害者の権利条約】the United Nations Treaty on the Rights of Persons with Disabilities.

こくれんじょうほうぎじゅつサービス【国連情報技術-】the United Nations Information Technology Service (略: UNITeS).

こくれんじょせいのちいいいんかい【国連女性の地位委員会】the United Nations Commission on the Status of Women (略: UNCSW).

こくれんじらいたいさくちょうせいセンター【国連地雷対策調整-】a UN Mine Action Coordination 「Center [Centre].

こくれんじんけんりじかい【国連人権理事会】the United Nations Human Rights Council.

こくれんじんどうもんだいちょうせいじむしょ【国連人道問題調整事務所】the United Nations Office for the Coordination of Humanitarian Affairs (略: UNOCHA).

こくれんスーダンはけんだん【国連-派遣団】the United Nations Mission in (the) Sudan (略: UNMIS).

こくれんスーダンミッション【国連-】＝こくれんスーダンはけんだん.

こくれんソマリアかつどう【国連-活動】the United Nations Operation in Somalia (略: UNOSOM).

こくれんたいきせいど【国連待機制度】the United Nations Stand-by Arrangements System (略: UNSAS).

こくれんたいきぶたい【国連待機部隊】a United Nations reserve force.

こくれんたいりくだなげんかいいいんかい【国連大陸棚限界委員会】the Commission on the Limits of the Continental Shelf (略: CLCS).

こくれんちめいひょうじゅんかかいぎ【国連地名標準化会議】the United Nations Conference on the Standardization of Geographical Names (略: UNCSGN).

こくれんデー【国連-】〔10月24日〕United Nations Day.

こくれんにんげんきょじゅういいんかい【国連人間居住委員会】the (United Nations) Commission on Human Settlements. ▶ 2002年に「国連人間居住計画」となった.

こくれんにんげんきょじゅうけいかく【国連人間居住計画】the United Nations Human Settlements Programme; 〔通称〕UN-Habitat.

こくれんにんげんきょじゅうセンター【国連人間居住-】the United Nations Centre for Human Settlements (略: UNCHS). ▶ 2002年に「国連人間居住計画」となった.

こくれんネパールしえんだん【国連-支援団】the United Nations Mission in Nepal (略: UNMIN).
こくれんハビタット【国連-】⇨ハビタット.
こくれんひがいしゃじんけんせんげん【国連被害者人権宣言】the Declaration of Basic Principles of Justice for Victims (of Crime and Abuse of Power).
こくれんひがしチモールしえんだん【国連東-支援団】＝こくれんひがしティモールしえんだん.
こくれんひがしティモールざんていぎょうせいきこう【国連東-暫定行政機構】the United Nations Transitional Administration in East Timor (略: UNTAET).
こくれんひがしティモールしえんだん【国連東-支援団】the United Nations Mission of Support in East Timor (略: UNMISET).
こくれんひがしティモールじむしょ【国連東-事務所】the United Nations Office in Timor-Leste (略: UNOTIL). ▶ 2005年5月20日から1年間活動.
こくれんひがしティモールとうごうはけんだん【国連東-統合派遣団】the United Nations Integrated Mission in Timor-Leste (略: UNMIT).
こくれんふじんかいはつききん【国連婦人開発基金】the United Nations Development Fund for Women (略: UNIFEM).
こくれんふはいぼうしじょうやく【国連腐敗防止条約】the United Nations Convention against Corruption.
こくれんへいわこうちくいいんかい【国連平和構築委員会】the United Nations [UN] Peacebuilding Commission.
こくれんぼうさいせかいかいぎ【国連防災世界会議】the United Nations World Conference on Disaster Reduction.
こくれんまやくいいんかい【国連麻薬委員会】＝まやくいいんかい.
こくれんみずのひ【国連水の日】〔3月22日〕World Day for Water.
こくれんミレニアムせんげん【国連-宣言】〔2000年9月, 国連首脳会議での〕the United Nations Millennium Declaration.
こくれんやくぶつとうせいけいかく【国連薬物統制計画】the United Nations International Drug Control Programme (略: UNDCP).
こくれんやくぶつはんざいじむしょ【国連薬物犯罪事務所】the United Nations Office on Drugs and Crime (略: UNODC).
こくれんリベリアしえんだん【国連-支援団】the United Nations Mission in Liberia (略: UNMIL).
こくれんルワンダしえんだん【国連-支援団】the United Nations Assistance Mission for Rwanda (略: UNAMIR).
ごくわせ【極早稲・極早生】1 【極早稲】〔稲〕very [extra] early ripening. ◐〜のコシヒカリ a very [an extra] early ripening (variety of) *Koshihikari* 〔rice〕. 2 【早生】〔一般に作物に〕very [extra] early ripening. ◐〜の果物[野菜] very [extra] early ripening 「fruit [vegetables].
こけだま【苔玉】〔園芸〕a moss ball.
ここ【古語】▯ 古語辞典 a dictionary of archaic words.
ここいち【午後一】〔午後一番先〕(the) first thing in the afternoon. ◐〜で伺います. では1時にお会いしましょう. I'll come by 「(the) first thing in the afternoon [just after lunch]. See you at one o'clock.
ココスやし【-椰子】〔植〕＝ヤタイやし.
ココやし【-椰子】1 〔コスタリカの〕Cocos [Coco] Island. 2 〔ミャンマーの〕the Coco Islands. ▶ 大ココ島 (Great Coco Island) と小ココ島 (Little Coco Island) とがある.
ここのおびアルマジロ【九帯-】〔動〕a nine-banded armadillo; *Dasypus novemcinctus*.

141　　　　　　　ごしゅうぎそうば

「地上(ミ)より何処(ｽﾞ)かで」〔映画〕Anywhere But Here.
こころきいた, こころきく【心利いた, 心利く】considerate; thoughtful. ◐〜もてなしを受ける be given a very considerate reception ◐彼には〜側近がいない. He has no aides who really consider his needs.
「心の指紋」〔映画〕The Sunchaser.
コ・コン〔カンボジア南西部の州; 同州の州都〕Koh Kong.
コ・ゴン【高建】Goh Kun (1938- ; 韓国の政治家; 首相 2003-04).
ごごん【五言】▯ 五言古詩 a five-character-line poem in an ancient style.
ごさ【誤差】▯ 非標本誤差〔統計〕(a) nonsampling error. 標本誤差〔統計〕(a) sampling error. 予測誤差 prediction error. ▯ 誤差幅 (an) error span.
こさいきん【古細菌】▯ 超好熱古細菌 a hyperthermophilic archaebacterium.
こざかい【戸境壁】〔建〕a party wall.
コサックぎつね【-狐】〔動〕a corsac fox; *Vulpes corsac*.
コサックダンス a Cossack dance.
ござんのおくりび【五山の送り火】〔8月16日に京都で行われる送り火〕the Kyoto Great Bonfire Festival; a festival in which bonfires spelling out Chinese characters are lit on the sides of five hills around Kyoto to guide the spirits of the dead back to the underworld on the last day of Obon.
こし¹【腰】▯ 腰浮かせ, 腰浮かし ＝拳腰浮かせ (⇨こぶし). 腰手拭い wearing a hand towel tucked in at one's waist; 〔その手拭い〕a hand towel tucked in at the waist.
こし³【古紙・故紙】▯ 雑誌古紙 old magazine paper (略: OMG). 段ボール古紙 old corrugated cardboard (略: OCC).
ごしうんどう【五・四運動】〔史〕1919年5月4日, 中国の北京に始まった反帝国主義民族運動〕the May Fourth Movement.
コジェネレーション ▯ 家庭用コジェネ(レ)ション home cogeneration; a home cogeneration system.
「ゴシカ」〔映画〕Gothika.
こしかべ【腰壁】〔建〕〔内・外壁の腰の高さまでの部分とは異なる建材で仕上げた〕a dado; a wainscot; wainscoting; 〔バルコニーなどの, 腰の高さの壁〕a 「waist-high [low] wall. ▯ 腰壁パネル a 「dado [wainscot] panel; dado [wainscot] paneling.
こしじろやまどり【腰白山鳥】〔鳥〕〔キジ科の鳥; ヤマドリの亜種〕an Ijima copper pheasant; *Phasianus soemmerringii ijimae*.
こしつ²【個室】▯ 個室ビデオ〔風俗店〕a private-room video shop.
ゴシック・ロリータ〔服飾〕"Gothic Lolita" (fashion); a fashion style combining Rococo- and Victorian-style girls' clothing with a Gothic sensibility.
こしのこばいも【越乃小貝母】〔植〕〔日本原産のユリ科の多年草〕*Fritillaria japonica* var. *koidzumiana*.
こしばい【小芝居】〔歌舞伎〕Kabuki performed in a small theater; small-scale Kabuki.
こしばき【腰穿き】〔ズボンを腰骨あたりまで下げてはくこと〕wearing 「baggy [loose, lowrider] 《pants》; wearing one's 《pants》 low.
こしばた【腰機】＝じばた.
こしぶくろ【腰袋】〔大工などが腰に下げる工具入れの袋〕a waist apron; a carpenter's apron.
コジャエリ〔トルコ北西部の県; その県都イズミットの別称〕Kocaeli.
こじゃれた²【小じゃれた】〔ふざけた〕jokey; joky.
こしゅ¹【戸主】▯ 戸主制〔韓国の〕the family headship system.
ごしゅうぎそうば【ご祝儀相場】〔相場〕a buoyant market (on a festive occasion); 〔季節商品の初切りなどを祝って付ける高値〕a 《season-opening》 festive market.

ごじゅうごさいしょうきゅうていしせいど【55歳昇給停止制度】〔1998年の人事院勧告による〕the system of freezing wages (of public officials) at age 55.
こしゅく【固縮】〖医〗〔筋肉の〕rigidity.
こしょう⁴【故障】▣▶故障上がり just after recovery from 《a sports》injury. ◉彼は〜上がりで、まだ十分練習していない。He's just back from injury and hasn't done enough training yet.
ごしよう【誤使用】misuse; abuse; improper [incorrect] use; mishandling.
〜する misuse; abuse; use 《a machine》 ˈwrongly [incorrectly]; mishandle. ◉製品の〜による事故が増えている。There has been an increase in accidents arising from ˈmisuse [mishandling] of products. | More and more accidents are being caused by people using products in the wrong way.
▣▶誤使用事故 an accident caused by misuse; an accident arising from mishandling. 誤使用防止 prevention of ˈmisuse [abuse, mishandling]; preventing 《machinery》 being wrongly used. ◉薬品の〜防止を図る try to prevent a drug being wrongly used / 〜防止ストッパー〔スプレー剤などの〕a protective catch.
こしょく¹【古色】▣▶古色付け making 《a ˈpainting [statue]》 look old.
こしょく²【個食】
▣▶個食化〔食事のときに家族がめいめい別のものを食べる傾向〕a [the] tendency for each member of the family to eat different things (at family meals);《孤食化とも書く》〔食事をひとりでとる傾向〕a tendency (for members of the family) to eat alone. ◉料理の好みがみんなバラバラなのでわが家の食事は〜化している。The whole family like(s) different kinds of food, so each of us is increasingly eating different things at meals. / 日本では家族が各自べつべつに食事をとる〜化が進んでいる。There is an increasing tendency in Japan for members of the family to ˈeat on their own [take meals by themselves].
こしょく³【孤食】《個食とも》〔ひとりでとる食事〕eating alone (as opposed to eating in one's family).
ごしょく²【誤食】eating sth ˈaccidentally [by mistake]; accidental ingestion.
〜する eat sth ˈaccidentally [by mistake]; accidentally ingest sth. ◉食用キノコに似た毒キノコがあるので〜しないよう注意が必要だ。Since some poisonous mushrooms resemble edible mushrooms, care is required so as not to eat them accidentally.
こしわり【腰割り】〔両脚を開いて立ち、腰を落とす運動〕《do》 squats (with knees wide apart).
こじん³【個人】
▣▶個人（営業）店〔個人商店〕a privately-run ˈstore [shop]; a one-man business; an independently-owned business. 個人企業経済調査〔総務省統計局行う〕the Unincorporated Enterprise Survey. 個人記録〔スポーツなどの〕a personal record;〔個人に関する記録〕a personal (private) record. 個人広告 a personal ad. ◉〜広告欄 personals. 個人再生〖法〗〔破産に際しての〕《file for》individual rehabilitation. ◉〜手続き《commence》individual rehabilitation proceedings. 個人サイト〖電算〗〔ウェブサイトの〕a personal Web site. 個人資格 (a) qualification as an individual; 《in》 an individual capacity. 個人事業主 an individual owner-manager. 個人住民税 (a) ˈresidential [residence, residents] tax (raised on the individual). ◉〜住民税率 the percentage of individual income on which residential taxation is based. 個人成績〔スポーツなどの〕an individual's [sb's individual] results [score, record, performance]. ◉彼は今シーズン打率3割2分の〜を残した。His ˈindividual [personal] batting average this season was .320. 個人貯蓄率 a [the] personal

savings rate. 個人データ data on ˈan individual [individuals]; personal [private] data [information]. ◉〜データの流出 a leak [an unauthorized release] of personal data. 個人認証 personal ˈidentification [verification, authentication]. 個人墓 an individual grave; a grave for one person. 個人保険 personal [individual] insurance. 個人名義株 privately ˈheld [owned] shares [stock]. 個人預金 a ˈpersonal [private] deposit; personal [private] savings.
ごしん⁵【護身】▣▶護身ビクス self-defense aerobics. 護身（用）スプレー (a) self-protection spray.
こじんさいせいほう【個人再生法】〖法〗〔民事再生法に追加された個人再生の規定〕individual rehabilitation procedures.
こじんしょうひ【個人消費】▣▶個人消費支出物価指数 the personal consumption expenditures price index (略: PCEPI); the PCE price index.
こじんじょうほう【個人情報】▣▶個人情報取扱事業者 an enterprise that handles personal information. 個人情報保護士 a personal data protection officer; an expert in protection of personal data. 個人情報保護条例〖法〗 a personal-data-protection ordinance; a local ˈprivacy-protection [private-information-protection] law. 個人情報流出 a leak of personal information; a personal data leak; (an) unauthorized release of ˈpersonal [private] information.
こじんたいしょく（ねんきん）かんじょう【個人退職（年金）勘定】〔米国の個人年金積立制度〕an individual retirement account (略: IRA).
こじんてき【個人的】▣▶個人的無意識〖心理〗〔ユングの学説〕a [the] personal unconscious.
こじんほうかつりょこうわりびきうんちん【個人包括旅行割引運賃】〖空〗an IIT fare. ▶ IIT は Individual Inclusive Tour の略.
こじんむけ【個人向け】▣▶個人向け金融商品 a financial product for individuals; a personal financial product. 個人向け国債 a government bond for individual investors. 個人向けサービス (a) service for individuals; (an) individual [(a) personal, (a) private] service. 個人向け投資信託 personal investment trusts. 個人向け保険 personal [individual] insurance. 個人向け利付国庫債券 =個人向け国債. 個人向けローン〖融資〗 a personal loan.
コスト ▣▶高コスト体質 high-cost [cost-intensive] tendencies. ▣▶コスト構造 a cost structure. ◉高〜構造 a high cost structure / 〜構造を見直す revise a cost structure. コスト効率 cost-effectiveness. ▷ cost-effective adj. コスト試算 a trial cost calculation. コスト・センター〖経営〗〔原価中心点〕企業の中で直接的な利益を生み出さない部門〕a cost center. コスト力 cost efficiency.
コスとう【—島】〔ギリシャの島〕Kos [Cos] Island. ▷ Koan; Coan adj.
コストカッター〔経費を削減する人・方式〕a cost-cutter.
ゴズネル Gosnell, Raja (1968- ; 米国の映画監督).
コスピ【KOSPI】=かんこくそうごうかぶかしすう.
「ゴスフォード・パーク」〔映画〕Gosford Park.
コスプレ ▣▶コスプレ喫茶 a cosplay cafe.
コスメル〔メキシコ、ユカタン半島東部の島〕Cozumel Island.
「コスモス/宇宙」〔カール・セーガン (Carl Sagan) 博士が宇宙の解説をする米国のTV番組〕Cosmos.
ゴスロリ【服飾】〔「ゴシック・ロリータ」の略〕"GothLoli." 〔⇒ゴシック・ロリータ〕
こせい¹【個性】▣▶個性化教育 individualized education. 個性派 a unique type; a distinctive kind. ◉〜の一人 a one-off. ◉〜派俳優 a ˈunique [distinctive kind of] actor; an actor who is ˈone of a kind [like nobody else].
こそう²【個装】▣▶個装箱 an individual [a separate]

**こっかかくあんぜんほしょうきょく**

box.
**こそう**³【古筝】〖楽器〗〔琴に似た中国の撥弦楽器〕a zheng; a guzheng.
**ごそう**³【護送】▷ 護送機 an escort.
**ごそうさ**【誤操作】a mistake [an error] in「operating [handling]《a machine》; an operating [an operational, a handling] error [mistake]. 大事なファイルを～で削除してしまった。I「deleted [erased] an essential file by mistake. | I mistakenly「deleted [erased] an essential file. ▷ 機械の～による事故が多発している。A lot of accidents are occurring due to mistakes in operating machinery. ▷ ～を防ぐ guard against [protect from] operational errors. ▷ 誤操作防止機能 an operating error protection function.
**ごそうしん**【誤送信】〔メール・FAX など〕missending; mistransmitting; sending [transmitting]《a fax》in error;（間違った相手に送信すること）sending《a message》to the wrong「person [number, address];（間違ったものを送信すること）sending the wrong《message》(to sb). ～する〔間違った相手に送信する〕send《an e-mail》to the wrong「person [number, address];〔間違ったものを送信する〕send the wrong《e-mail》(to sb);〔書きかけの内容などを誤って送信してしまう〕accidentally「send [transmit]《a fax》; send《an e-mail》in error.
**ごそく**【五速】〖自動車〗〔変速機の前進第 5 段〕fifth; fifth gear. ▷ ギヤを～に入れる put the car into fifth /～にシフトアップする shift up to fifth (gear). ▷ 五速自動変速機 a「five-speed [5-speed] automatic transmission.
**こそだて**【子育て】▷ 子育て経験者 a person with experience raising children;〔親〕an experienced「parent [father, mother]. 子育てサロン〔乳幼児とその親たちの交流の場〕a child-rearing salon. 子育て世代 the generation that's raising children.
**こそん**【呼損】〖通信〗〔接続できないこと〕call「failure [loss]. ▶ 電話をかけても通じないことなど。▷ 呼損率 probability of call「failure [loss].
**コタールしょうこうぐん**【-症候群】〖精神医〗Cotard's syndrome. ▶ フランスの精神医 Jules Cotard〔1840–89〕にちなむ。
**こたい**¹【固体】▷ 固体ロケットブースター a solid rocket booster (略: SRB).
**こたい**²【個体】▷ 個体識別番号〔牛肉などの〕an individual identification number. 個体数調査 a population survey; a survey of《surviving》numbers. ▷ ジャイアントパンダの～数調査を行う conduct [carry out] a survey of「the giant panda population [numbers of giant pandas]《surviving in the wild》.
**こだい**¹【古代】▷ 古代湖〔十万年以上存在している湖〕a lake a hundred thousand years old or more. 古代船〔考古〕a ship (of a kind) used in「ancient times [antiquity, the distant past].
**コタバト**〔フィリピン, ミンダナオ島の州〕Cotabato.
**ごダブリューいちエイチ**【5W1H】〔ニュース記事などの必須要素〕the five Ws and one H. ▶ who, what, when, where, why and how の意。
**こだま**【小玉】〔野菜や果実の〕《of》small size; a dwarf; a dwarf《cabbage》.
**こちゃく**【固着】▷ 固着帯〖地質〗〔2 つの地球プレートが特にしっかり噛み合っている部分〕an asperity.
**コチャン**【高敞】〔韓国, 全羅北道の郡; 世界遺産の支石墓群がある〕Gochang.
**ごちゅうもん**【誤注文】=ごはっちゅう。
**コチュジャン**【韓国料理の調味料】gochujang; kochujan.
「**こちらブルームーン探偵社**」〔米国の, 探偵ものの TV ドラマ〕Moonlighting. ▶ ブルース・ウィリス (Bruce Willis) の出世作。
**こつ**¹【骨】▷ 骨生検〖医〗a bone biopsy. 骨接合材料〖医〗

143　こっかかくあんぜんほしょうきょく

osteosynthetic material(s). 骨転移〖医〗〔腫瘍など の〕bone「metastasis [《口》mets].
**こっか**³【国家】
▷ 国家内国家 a state within a state. 失敗国家〔政府が統治能力をまったく欠いている国家〕a failed state. 宗教国家 a religious「state [nation, country]. 新国家《the「birth [creation] of》a new nation. 人治国家〔権力者の意向が法令に優先する国家〕a nation (which is) under the rule of powerful men. 世俗国家 a secular「state [nation, country]. 創新型国家〔中国が国家目標とする〕an innovative country.
▷ 国家行政施設 a national government facility. 国家情報長官〔米国の〕the Director of National Intelligence (略: DNI). ▷ 情報・諜報活動を統轄する大統領直属の閣僚級役職。国家像〔国のあるべき姿〕the way a country should be; an ideal [a vision] for the nation (to aspire to). 国家転覆扇動罪〔中国の〕《be charged with》incitement to overthrow the state. 国家侮辱罪 (the crime of) insulting the state. 国家無答責〔国により個人が損害を受けても国は個人に対し責任を負わないとする立場; 明治憲法下の考え方〕exemption of the state from responsibility to individuals.
**こっか**⁴【国歌】▷ 国歌斉唱 singing (of) the national anthem. ▷ ～斉唱. 〔式典の司会者の言葉〕Let us [We shall] now sing the national anthem (together). / 英国～斉唱および国旗の掲揚を行いますので, みなさまご起立いただき, 国旗にご注目ねがいます。Ladies and gentlemen, please rise and face the flag for the British national anthem and the raising of the Union Jack.
**こっか**⁶【骨化】〖生理〗(an) ossification. ～する ossify.
**こっかあんぜんほしょうきほんほう**【国家安全保障基本法】〖米〗the National Security Act.
**こっかあんぜんほしょうしょかん**【国家安全保障書簡】〖米〗FBI その他の政府機関が捜査に必要と判断した個人情報の提出を裁判所の令状なしに金融機関・通信業者などに命じる文書〕a National Security Letter (略: NSL).
**こっかあんぜんほしょうせんりゃく**【国家安全保障戦略】a national security strategy.
**こっかい**²【国会】▷ 国会対策費 Diet strategy expenses. 国会特別手当〔通称, 乱闘手当〕a special allowance paid to Diet staff. [⇨乱闘手当 (⇨らんとう)].
**こっかいいてんほう**【国会移転法】〖法〗=こっかとうのいてんにかんするほうりつ.
**こっかいぎいん**【国会議員】▷ 国会議員候補者 a candidate for the Diet. 国会議員互助年金 a mutual-aid pension for Diet members.
**こっかいぎいんさいひほう**【国会議員歳費法】〖法〗the Law Concerning Allowances for Diet Members.
**こっかいぎいんしさんこうかいほう**【国会議員資産公開法】〖法〗the Parliamentarians Assets Disclosure Law.
**こっかいけいざいきょうりょくきこう**【黒海経済協力機構】the Black Sea Economic Cooperation (略: BSEC).
**こっかいしんぎかっせいかほう**【国会審議活性化法】〖法〗the Diet Deliberations Vitalization Law. ▶ 正式名称は, 「国会審議の活性化及び政治主導の政策決定システムの確立に関する法律」the Law Concerning the Vitalization of Diet Deliberations and the Establishment of a Policy-making System with Political Leadership).
**こっかいとうのいてんにかんするほうりつ**【国会等の移転に関する法律】〖法〗the Law for the Relocation of the Diet and Other Organizations.
**こっかエネルギーせいさく**【国家-政策】〔米ブッシュ大統領が 2001 年に発表したもので, 原子力発電の拡大などが盛り込まれている〕the National Energy Policy (略: NEP).
**こっかかくあんぜんほしょうきょく**【国家核安全保障局】=かくあんぜんほしょうきょく.

こっかかんり【国家管理】 ▭ 国家管理色 ○〜色が強い be under the strict control of the government.
こっかくきん【骨格筋】 ▭ 骨格筋細胞 a skeletal muscle cell; a skeletal myocyte.
こっかこうむいんりんりしんさかい【国家公務員倫理審査会】 the National Public Service Ethics Board.
こっかさいがいひじょうじたい【国家災害非常事態】a state of national disaster. ○〜を宣言する declare a state of national disaster. ▭ 国家災害非常事態宣言 the declaration of a state of national disaster.
こっかじょうほういん【国家情報院】〔韓国の情報機関〕the National Intelligence Service (略: NIS). ▶ 1981年, 韓国中央情報部 (KCIA) から 国家安全企画部 (ANSP) に改称, 1998年, 国家情報院 に改称.
こっかじょうほうかいぎ【国家情報会議】〔米国の〕the National Intelligence Council (略: NIC).
こっかじょうほうセンター【国家情報−】〔中国政府のシンクタンク〕the State Information Center (略: SIC).
こっかじょうほうひょうか【国家情報評価】〔米国の国家情報会議が作成する報告〕National Intelligence Estimates (略: NIE).
こっかだいげきいん【国家大劇院】〔北京にある国立劇場〕the National Grand Theater; the Grand National Theater; (愛称) the Egg.
こっかていさつきょく【国家偵察局】〔米国国防省の偵察衛星情報分析機関〕the National Reconnaissance Office (略: NRO).
こっかとういついいんかい【国家統一委員会】〔国家統一綱領を定めた台湾総督府の組織〕the National Unification Council.
こっかとういつこうりょう【国家統一綱領】〔台湾の中国との統一の条件・手続などについて定めたもの; 1991年制定〕the Guidelines for National Unification.
こっかナノテクノロジー・イニシアティブ【国家−】〔米国の〕the National Nanotechnology Initiative (略: NNI).
こっかナノテクノロジーせんりゃく【国家−計画】=こっかナノテクノロジー・イニシアティブ.
こっかはってんかいかくいいんかい【国家発展改革委員会】〔中国の国務院の一機関〕the National Development and Reform Commission (略: NDRC).
こっかひじょうじたい【国家非常事態】 ▭ 国家非常事態宣言 a "state-of-national-emergency" declaration.
こっかへいわはってんひょうぎかい【国家平和発展評議会】〔ミャンマーの軍事政権〕the State Peace and Development Council (略: SPDC). ▶ スローク (SLORC, 国家法秩序回復評議会) の後身.
こっかほあんほう【国家保安法】〔法〕〔韓国の〕the National Security Law.
こっかみんしゅとう【国民民主党】〔ドイツの〕the National Democratic Party of Germany (略: NPD). ▶ NPD は, ドイツ語の Nationaldemokratische Partei Deutschlands の略.
こっかんかいぎ【国幹会議】=こくどかいはつかんせんじどうしゃどうけんせつかいぎ.
こっきのぎ【告期の儀】〔皇室儀礼〕the Rite of Announcing the Date; the ceremony of announcing the date of the wedding ceremony.
こっきょう² 【国境】 ▭ 国境管理 border 「control [administration]; control of 「borders [a border]. 国境警備 border security; guarding 「borders [a border]. 国境措置〔貿易に関する〕a border measure. 国境閉鎖 (a) border closure.
こっきょうなきがくせい【国境なき学生】〔国境なき医師団を支援する学生団体〕Étudiants sans frontières (= Students Without Borders) (略: ESF).
こっきょうなきぎしだん【国境なき技師団】Engineers without Borders (略: EWB).

こっきょうなききしゃだん【国境なき記者団】〔弾圧されている記者の支援団体〕Reporters sans frontières (= Reporters Without Borders) (略: RSF).
こっきょく【骨棘】〔医〕an osteophyte (▷ osteophytic adj.); a (bone) spur.
こつきりじゅつ【骨切り術】〔医〕osteotomy.
こっきん² 【黒金】〔台湾で暴力団と金権を表す言葉〕organized crime and political corruption; "black gold." ▭ 黒金政治 "black-gold" politics.
コック¹ ▭ コック帽 a chef's hat (pl. chefs' hats).
コックス Cox, Alex (1954− ; 英国生まれの映画監督・脚本家).
コックス・ツーそがいざい【COX2 阻害剤】〔薬〕〔消炎鎮痛剤〕a COX-2 inhibitor.
こっこ【国庫】 ▭ 国庫納付金〔日銀が利益の一部を国に納めるもの〕payments to the national treasury. 国庫補助率 a [the] Treasury subsidy rate; rates of support from the central government for 《*welfare ["social security]》.
こつごもり【小晦(日)】〔大晦日の前日〕the day before New Year's Eve. ▶ 旧暦では 12 月 29 日.
こつざけ【骨酒】fish-bone sake; warm sake「flavored with [poured on] roasted fish or fish bones.
こっし【骨子】 ▭ 骨子案 an outline [a rough] plan [proposal, draft].
こつずい【骨髄】 ▭ 骨髄間質細胞 a bone marrow stromal cell. 骨髄不全〔医〕(a) bone marrow failure.
こつずいいしょくすいしんざいだん【骨髄移植推進財団】the Japan Marrow Donor Program (略: JMDP).
こつそしょうしょう【骨粗鬆症】 ▭ 閉経後骨粗鬆症 postmenopausal osteoporosis. 老人性骨粗鬆症 senile osteoporosis.
ごっつんとう【ごっつん盗】〔わざと前の車に追突し, 前の車の運転者が外に出てきたすきにその車を盗む自動車盗〕a "bump-and-run" (car theft).
コッテージ ▭ コッテージ・パイ〔料理〕=コテージ・パイ (⇨コテージ).
こつでんどう【骨伝導】bone conduction; osteophony. ▭ 骨伝導スピーカー a bone conduction speaker. 骨伝導受話器 a bone conduction receiver. 骨伝導補聴器 a bone conduction hearing aid.
「ゴッド・アンド・モンスター」〔映画〕Gods and Monsters.
こっとう(ひん)【骨董(品)】 ▭ 骨董的価値, 骨董(品)的価値 antique value; value as an antique. ○〜的価値はあるかもしれないね. This may have some 「antique value [value as an antique].
ゴッドホープ〔グリーンランドの政庁所在地〕Godthaab. [⇨ヌーク]
こつばん【骨盤】 ▭ 骨盤矯正[調整] pelvic correction. 骨盤臓器脱〔医〕(a) pelvic organ prolapse. 骨盤底 pelvic floor. 骨盤底筋 the pelvic floor muscles. 骨盤底筋体操《do》pelvic floor exercises.
「コップランド」〔映画〕Copland.
コッポラ Coppola, Sofia (1971− ; 米国の映画監督・俳優; フランシス・フォード・コッポラの娘).
こつめかわうそ【小爪川獺】〔動〕〔イタチ科の哺乳類〕an Asian small-clawed otter; Aonyx cinerea.
こてい² 【固定】 ▭ 固定金利(型)住宅ローン a fixed rate mortgage (略: FRM). 固定金利(型)ローン a fixed interest loan. 固定金利期間選択型ローン a fixed-to-adjustable-rate mortgage. 固定制 a 「fixed [flat]《charge, rate》 system. ○料金は月額〜制です. There is a 「monthly fixed charge [flat monthly rate]. 〜だとアクセスしても, まったくアクセスしなくても, 課金は完全〜制です. However much you access the system, and even if you don't, the charge is an absolutely fixed amount. 固定通信〔移動(体)通信に対して〕fixed telecommunications. 固定通信網 a

fixed telecommunications network. 固定発携帯着料金 a rate for calls from fixed to mobile phones.
こていけいたいゆうごう(サービス)【固定・携帯融合(−)】〘通信〙fixed mobile convergence (略：FMC); a fixed mobile convergence service.
こていしさん【固定資産】 ▯▯ 固定資産税課税標準額 the standard taxable value of 'fixed property [real estate]. 固定資産投資 (a) fixed assets investment; (an) investment in fixed assets. ◉ 〜投資総額 the total amount invested in fixed asset. 固定資産売却 (a) 'sale [disposal] of a fixed asset; selling [disposing of] a fixed asset. 固定資産売却益 (a) profit on the 'sale [disposal] of a fixed asset. 固定資産売却損 (a) loss on the 'sale [disposal] of a fixed asset. 固定資産評価証明書 a fixed assets evaluation certificate. 固定資産評価審査委員会 a fixed assets assessment commission.
コテージ ▯▯ コテージ・パイ 〘料理〙(a) cottage pie. [＝シェパーズ・パイ]
こてんせき【古典籍】an old and respected [a venerable] classic.
ゴド(ゥ)ノフ Godunov, Boris (Fyodorovich) (1551–1605; ロシア皇帝).
ゴトし【−師】〘器具等を使用し, パチンコ店等で不正に出玉を獲得する人〙a 〘pachinko〙cheater; a person who secretly rigs gambling machines to earn a high payout.
「ことの終わり」〘映画〙The End of the Affair.
こども【子供】 ▯▯ 子供看護休暇 (a) sick-child leave. 子ども 110 番の家 an emergency (place) of refuge for children threatened with molestation.
こどもうん【子供運】luck with (one's) children. ◉ 彼は〜がよかった[悪かった]. He had 'good [bad] luck with (his) children. | He was 'lucky [unlucky] with (his) children.
こども・こそだておうえんプラン【子ども・子育て応援−】〔少子化対策の1つ〕a plan to support children and child rearing; the New Angel Plan.
こどものじこよぼうこうがくカウンシル【子どもの事故予防工学−】〔産業技術総合研究所の〕the Childhood Injury Prevention Engineering Council (略：CIPEC).
こどものしょうぎょうてきせいてきさくしゅ【子どもの商業的性的搾取】the commercial sexual exploitation of children (略：CSEC).
こどものしょうぎょうてきせいてきさくしゅにはんたいするせかいかいぎ【子どもの商業的性的搾取に反対する世界会議】the World Congress Against Commercial Sexual Exploitation of Children.
こども(の)どくしょかつどうすいしんけいかく【子ども(の)読書活動推進計画】the Project for the Promotion of Children's Reading Activities.
こども(の)どくしょかつどうすいしんほう【子ども(の)読書活動推進法】〘法〙the Law for the Promotion of Children's Reading Activities. ▶ 正式名称は「子どもの読書活動の推進に関する法律」.
こどもはくしょ【子ども白書】a white paper on children.
こどもみらいざいだん【こども未来財団】the Foundation for Children's Future.
ゴナイーヴ〔ハイチ西部, カリブ海沿岸の都市〕Gonaïves.
コナル〔アフガニスタン東部の州〕Konar.
コニファー〘植〙〔園芸品種の針葉樹の総称〕a (garden) conifer.
ごにゅうりょく【誤入力】inputting 《data》by mistake; an inputting error.
〜する input sth 'by mistake [in error]. ◉ メールアドレスの〜があると確認メールが届きませんのでご注意ください. Take care not to make any mistakes in inputting your mail address, otherwise you will not receive a confirmation e-mail.

ごにん【誤認】 ▯▯ 優良[有利]誤認 ⇨ゆうりょう³, ゆうり¹. ▯▯ 誤認発射〔狩猟などで〕a mistaken shooting; a shooting accident.
こねぎ【小葱】〔若いうちに収穫した葉ねぎ〕young welsh onion leaves (gathered when about 5 cm tall).
コネキシン〘生理〙〔ギャップ結合たんぱく〕a connexin. ▯▯ コネキシン遺伝子 a connexin gene.
コネクチン〘化〙connectin.
コネリー Connelly, Jennifer (1970– ; 米国の映画俳優).
このかんごきゅうかせいど【子の看護休暇制度】a childcare leave system.
「この森で, 天使はバスを降りた」〘映画〙The Spitfire Grill.
ごパーセントルール【5% −】〘株式〙〔株券等の大量保有の状況に関する開示制度〕the five-percent rule.
こばえ【小蝿】a small-sized fly; 〔ショウジョウバエ〕a drosophila 《pl. -lae》; a 'fruit [vinegar] fly; 〔ノミバエ〕⇨みはえ.
こはくさん【琥珀酸】 ▯▯ コハク酸スマトリプタン sumatriptan succinate.
こばしうみすずめ【小嘴海雀】〘鳥〙a Kittlitz's murrelet; Brachyramphus brevirostris.
こばた【小旗】a 'small [little] flag. ◉ 〜の波が選手団を迎えた. The team was greeted with the fluttering of small flags. ◉ 〜を振って迎える welcome 《sb》by waving small flags; wave little flags 'in welcome [to welcome 《sb》]. ▯▯ 応援小旗 a little flag waved 'in support of [to cheer on] 《marathon runners》; a small rooting flag.
こはつ【孤発】 ▯▯ 孤発性〘医・遺伝〙sporadic occurrence; sporadicity. 孤発例〘医・遺伝〙a sporadic case 《of Alzheimer's disease》.
ごはっちゅう【誤発注】an erroneous order; making a mistake when placing an order; a misorder; a misplaced order.
〜する place an erroneous 《sell》order.
こはば【小幅】 ▯▯ 小幅続伸〘株式〙(a) 'continuous [continued] small 'slight] rise [gain]. ◉ 今日も円は対ドルで〜続伸した. Today, too, the yen continued to rise slightly against the dollar. 小幅高[安]〘相場〙a slight 'rise [fall] (in prices). ◉ 27日のニューヨーク証券取引所は〜安で始まった. The New York Stock Exchange opened slightly higher on the 27th.
ごばらい²【誤払い】(a) payment in error; a payment error; paying the wrong 'sum [person]; paying by mistake.
コバル ＝アルコパール.
こばん¹【小判】 ▯▯ 小判皿〔小判型の皿〕an 'oval [elliptical] paste [dish].
「湖畔のひと月」〘映画〙A Month by the Lake.
ごび²【語尾】 ▯▯ 語尾上げ[下げ] rising [falling] inflection at the end of a 'word [phrase, sentence].
コピー ▯▯ 孫[二次]コピー recopying; 〔再複製物〕a copy of a copy; a second-generation copy. ▯▯ コピー商品 a copycat 〔an imitation, a counterfeit〕product. ◉ ルイ・ヴィトンの〜商品 a fake Louis Vuitton 《product》. コピー・ワンス〘電算〙〔デジタルコンテンツの著作権保護のため録画などのコピーを1回に制限すること〕copy once; one-time copying. ◉ 〜ワンス規制[制限] a "copy once" restriction. コピーコントロール・シー・ディー【−CD】〔音楽著作権を守るため複製防止策を施したCD〕a copy-control(led) CD; a copy-protected CD.
コピーすうたけい【−数多型】〘遺伝〙copy number polymorphism.
こひき【粉引】〘陶芸〙〔素地面を白泥に浸し透明釉をかけた陶器〕kohiki; pottery with clear glaze over white slip.
こびじゅつ【古美術】 ▯▯ 古美術鑑定家 a (good) judge

**ゴピチャンド** of antiques; an antique(s) expert; a connoisseur of antiques; an antiquarian.

**ゴピチャンド**【楽器】〔インドの一絃琴〕a gopicand; an ektara.

**こひつ**【古筆】◻ 古筆切れ a scrap of ancient writing; a sample of classical calligraphy.

**ごひょうじ**【誤表示】mistaken labelling;〔その文字・記号など〕a「mistaken [wrong] label; an erroneous display. 〜する label [display] sth「mistakenly [wrongly, in error]. ◯〜の〜 an erroneous display on a「meter [gauge]. ◯ コンビニの弁当の賞味期限に〜があった。The「best-before [expiry] date on the convenience store lunch box was mistakenly displayed. | There was a mistake in the「best-before [expiry] date displayed on the convenience store lunch box. ◯ ネット通販の商品価格が〜だったために混乱が起きた。Confusion [Chaos] arose due to the fact that the prices of products sold over the Internet were wrongly displayed.

**こびれごんどう**【小鰭巨鯨】【動】a short-finned pilot whale; *Globicephala macrorhynchus*.

**こふき**【粉吹き】◻ 粉吹き芋「料理」peeled, boiled and drained potatoes. 粉吹き乾燥肌 dry flaky skin. 粉吹き肌 flaky skin.

**コフギールーイェ(オ)・ブーイェルアフマド**〔イラン南部の州〕Kohkiluyeh and Buyer Ahmad;〔ペルシャ語名の音訳〕Kohgiluyeh va Buyer Ahmad.

**こぶし**[1]【拳】◻ 拳腰浮かせ, 拳腰浮かし〔江戸しぐさの一種; 腰を浮かせてこぶしひとつ分座席を詰めること〕moving over a bit (to make room for another to sit).

**こぶはくじら**【瘤歯鯨】【動】a Blainville's beaked whale; *Mesoplodon densirostris*.

**コブラ・ゴールド**〔タイ軍, 米軍などの多国間合同軍事演習〕Exercise Cobra Gold.

**コプラナー** ◻ コプラナーPCB【化】〔毒性が強いポリ塩化ビフェニール〕a coplanar PCB.

**コブラボール**【軍】〔米空軍の弾道ミサイル追跡機〕a Cobra Ball (aircraft).

**コフレ**《〈F〉》〔化粧品をバッグなどに詰め合わせた限定品〕a (Christmas) coffret.

**ごぶん**[1]【五分】◻ 五分五乗方式〔住宅資金などの贈与の特例として, 金額が550万-1500万円までの場合に適応される贈与税軽減のための計算方法〕a "divided by 5 times 5" taxation system; a system allowing certain monetary gifts to be taxed in five equal installments over five years.

**こべつ**[1]【戸別】◻ 戸別収集〔ごみの〕house-to-house「waste [*garbage, "rubbish] collection. 戸別配布 house-to-house distribution (of census forms).

**こべつ**[2]【個別】◻ 個別学力試験〔センター試験などの統一試験に対して, 大学が個別に行う試験〕an individual university academic achievement test. 個別協定 a separate agreement. 個別対応 (an) individualized「service [treatment, response]; (a) personalized service; (a) service for individual《customers》; a tailor-made「service [response]. ◯ 特殊な注文についても〜対応いたします。We can also「meet requests [take orders] for individually tailored items. | We also provide tailor-made「items [services, etc.] for the individual customer. / 現在の教師数では生徒のさまざまな問題に〜できない。It is not possible, with current teacher numbers, to deal with the students' various problems on an individual basis. 個別的労使関係 individual labor(-management) relations. 個別法【会計】the specific identification method. 個別リサイクル法 a law governing one designated area of recycling.

**こべつろうどうふんそうかいけつそくしんほう**【個別労働紛争解決促進法】【法】the Individual Labor Disputes Resolution Law. ▶ 正式名称は「個別労働関係紛争の解決の促進に関する法律」(the Law on the Promotion of Solutions Associated with Labor Disputes Between Individuals and Businesses).

**ごほうこく**【呉邦国】Wu Bangguo (1941– ; 中国の政治家).

**ごぼうせい**【五芒星】〔神秘的図形とされる一筆書きの五線星形〕a pentagram; a pentacle.

**コホート** ◻ コホート研究 a cohort study.

**こほめじょうれい**【子ほめ条例】a local ordinance promoting the official commendation of children; a child-praising ordinance.

**コポリマー**【化】〔共重合体〕a copolymer.

**ごほんだいこくこがね**【五本大黒黄金】【昆】〔コガネムシ科の昆虫, 絶滅危惧種〕*Copris acutidens*.

**こま**[1]【駒】◻ 駒不足〔戦力となる選手などの不足〕a「shortage [lack] of strong players.

**ごま**[3]〔渋柿の渋みがとれると果肉に生じる褐斑〕a dark brown spot appearing in the flesh of a persimmon after the astringency has been removed. ◯〜が入っているのは渋が抜けた甘い柿だ。When there are brown spots on a persimmon it has lost its astringency and is good and sweet.

**ゴマ**〔コンゴ民主共和国東部, ルワンダとの国境近くの市〕Goma.

**こまおち**【齣落ち】〔動画の〕frame「dropping [skipping].

**こませ**【漁業・釣り】〔撒き餌〕*chum;"groundbait. ◻ こませ釣り《釣り》*chumming;"groundbaiting.

**ごみ**[1]【塵・芥】◻ 日常ごみ household「garbage [rubbish, trash, refuse]; domestic garbage; everyday garbage. 漂着ごみ beach「waste [rubbish, garbage]; waste washed「ashore [on shore]. ◻ ごみ収集カレンダー a「garbage [rubbish, trash, refuse] (collection) calendar. ごみ焼却灰 refuse incineration ash. ごみ戦争 a [the] garbage [rubbish] war. ごみ挟み garbage [refuse, rubbish] tongs. ごみ拾い ⇨ごみひろい. ごみ減らし waste [garbage, rubbish, trash] reduction.

**ゴミがく**【-学】garbology.

**ごみゼロ** zero「waste [garbage, rubbish]. ◯〜の zero-waste《communities》. ◻ ごみゼロ運動 a zero-waste campaign.

**コミットメント** ◻ コミットメント・ライン【金融】〔企業が金融機関との間であらかじめ設定する融資枠〕a commitment line. 〜ライン契約 a commitment line「agreement [contract].

**こみばし**【込み箸】〔口いっぱいの食べ物を箸で奥に押し込むこと〕stuffing food into *one's* mouth with *one's* chopsticks.

**ごみひろい**【ごみ拾い】garbage [rubbish, refuse, waste, litter] collecting; garbage collection; picking up garbage; collection of garbage;〔清掃〕cleaning up; a clean-up. ◯〜をする collect [pick up] garbage; clean up.

**コミューター** ◻ コミューター空港 a commuter airport.

**コミュニケーション** ◻ コミュニケーション・サーバー【電算】a communication server (略: CS). コミュニケーション(の)理論〔社会・心理〕communication(s) theory.

**コミュニタリアン** ◻ コミュニタリアン運動〔共同体主義の〕a communitarian movement.

**コミュニティー** ◻ コミュニティーFM〔局〕a community FM radio station;〔放送〕community FM (broadcasting). コミュニティー・オーガニゼーション〔地域組織活動〕community organization. コミュニティー・カレッジ〔米国・カナダの公立大学; 主に2年制〕a community college. コミュニティー・ガーデン〔地域の公共用地や空き地などにつくり出された緑地空間〕a community garden. コミュニティー・スクール〔地域社会が運営に参画する学校〕a community school. コミュニティー道路 a community road. コミュニティー・バス〔地域社会の需要に合わせて運行されるバス路線〕(a) community bus service;［1 台のバス］a community bus. コミュニティー・ビジネス［地域社会の要求に応え, 地域の利益を重視する事業］a community business. コミュニティー・ホテル［結婚式場など地域社会の様々な需要を満たすホテル］a community hotel. コミュニティー・ワーク［社会福祉の援助方法の1つ; 地域援助技術］community work.

コミュニティー・アクション・ネットワーク［英国の NPO］the Community Action Network（略: CAN).

ゴム ▭ ゴム銃 ＝ゴム鉄砲. ゴム段 ＝ゴム跳び. ゴム弾銃 a rubber bullet gun. ゴム鉄砲［輪ゴムを飛ばす玩具］a rubber [an elastic] band gun. ゴム跳び, ゴム飛び［輪にしたひも状のゴムをぴんと張り, 歌に合わせて跳び越す遊び］Chinese jump rope.

ゴム² ［イラン中部の州; その州都］Qom.

コムキャスト［米国のケーブルテレビ会社］Comcast Corp.

コムスタット 《computer [comparative] + statistics》［コンピューターを活用した米国ニューヨーク市警察の犯罪統計システム］CompStat.

ゴムわ【-輪】 ▭ ゴム輪結紮療法［医］［痔（じ）の］(a) rubber [(an) elastic] band ligation.

こめ【米】 ▭ 米券 a rice ｢*gift certificate [｢voucher]. 米焼酎 shōchū made from rice; rice (shōchū) spirits. 米離れ the trend away from (eating) rice.

コメかかくセンター【-価格-】［全国米穀取引・価格形成センターの通称］the National Rice Trade and Price Formation Center.

コメディー ▭ コメディー・タッチ［喜劇的な表現の仕方］a comic(al) touch; a touch of comedy. 〜タッチのホームドラマ a family drama with a comic(al) touch to it.

コメディカル・スタッフ［医師以外の医療従事者; 看護師・薬剤師・臨床検査技師など］《集合的に》(a) paramedical staff;〈1人の〉a paramedical staff member.

こめひゃっぴょう【米百俵】 "One Hundred Sacks of Rice"; an emergency gift of rice, intended to relieve hunger in Nagaoka after the Meiji Restoration, but instead sold to finance the building of a school. 〜の精神 the idea of going without in the short term for the sake of ｢creating future wealth [benefiting future generations].

コメルサント［ロシアの日刊紙］Kommersant.

こもの【小物】 ▭ 紳士小物 men's accessories. ▭ 小物遣い use [handling] of small ｢items [articles]. 彼女はネックレスやベルトなどの〜遣いがうまい. She's very skillful about choosing and wearing accessories like necklaces and belts.

こもん³【顧問】 ▭ 上級顧問 a senior ｢advisor [adviser]. ▭ 大統領〜顧問 a senior presidential ｢advisor [adviser]; a senior ｢advisor [adviser] to the President. 名誉顧問 an honorary ｢advisor [adviser]. ▭ 顧問税理士 an ｢accounting [accountancy] advisor;［個人の］a personal accountant. 顧問税理士 a ｢tax [fiscal] advisor;［個人の］a personal tax accountant.

「コモンズの悲劇」＝「共有地の悲劇」(⇨こゆうち).

コモンレール【機・自動車】［燃料噴射用の蓄圧器］a common rail. ▭ コモンレール式燃料噴射 common-rail fuel injection.

こやじ［口にオヤジじみた男性］a young geezer.

コヤン【高陽】［韓国, ソウル郊外の都市］Koyang.

こよう³【雇用】
▭ 雇用維持 employment maintenance; job preservation. 雇用環境 the ｢job [employment] environment. 雇用管理調査［厚生労働省］an employment management survey. 雇用均等室［各都道府県労働局の］an equal employment office. 雇用市場 the ｢job [employment] market. 雇用失業率 an [the] unemployment rate. 雇用人員判断 DI [指数] the employment ｢DI [diffusion index]; the diffusion index of "excessive employment" minus "insufficient employment." 雇用促進住宅 employment promotion

housing. 雇用 DI［企業の新規雇用の動向を表す数値］an employment ｢DI [diffusion index]. 雇用破壊 ｢雇用状況を急激に悪化させること］job destruction. 雇用判断 DI [指数] ⇨雇用人員判断 DI [指数]. 雇用福祉 employees' welfare. 雇用（保険）三事業 the three aspects of unemployment insurance. 雇用保険被保険者証 an unemployment insurance card. 雇用保険料 an unemployment insurance premium. ▭ 〜保険料率 an unemployment insurance premium rate.

ごよう¹【御用】 ▭ 御用機関 a body [an organization] that ｢follows the government line [curries favor with the government]. 御用大工［幕府・藩の］an official ｢carpenter [builder] to the government.

こようそくしんじぎょうだん【雇用促進事業団】the Employment Promotion Corporation. ▶ 雇用・能力開発機構の前身.

「コヨーテ・アグリー」［映画］Coyote Ugly.

コラーゲン ▭ I [II, III, IV（など）型 collagen「I [II, III, IV, etc.] collagen. 魚［フィッシュ］コラーゲン (a) fish collagen. ベビー・コラーゲン baby collagen. 変性コラーゲン (a) modified collagen.

コラート［タイ東北部の都市］Korat.

ごらく【娯楽】 ▭ 娯楽費 recreation ｢expenses [spending, expenditure]; expenditure [spending] on recreation.

コラチ Coraci, Frank (1966–  ; 米国の映画監督).

「コラテラル」［映画］Collateral.

「コラテラル・ダメージ」［映画］Collateral Damage.

コラボレーション
〜する collaborate. ▭ A 社と B 社が〜した商品 a ｢collaborative [joint] Company A-Company B product; a product ｢developed [designed, marketed, etc.] collaboratively [jointly] by Company A and Company B / 日産は家具メーカーと〜した自動車を販売している. Nissan is selling an automobile developed together with a furniture manufacturer. ▭ ピアノと三味線の〜 a duet for piano and samisen; (a) piano-samisen fusion. ▭ コラボレーション企画 a ｢collaborative [joint] project. ▭ 〜商品［モデル］a ｢collaborative [joint] product [model].

コラボレート［共同作業］(a) collaboration.
〜する collaborate.［＝コラボレーションする（⇨コラボレーション)］

コリアゲート《史》［1976年, 韓国人実業家による米議会買収工作事件］Koreagate.

コリエレ・デラ・セラ［イタリアの日刊紙］Corriere della Sera.

コリジョン・コース［衝突進路］《on》a collision course.

こりつ【孤立】 ▭ 国際的孤立 《avoid》international isolation.

コリネきん【-菌】［生物］コリネバクテリウム (Corynebacterium). 属に属する細菌 a corynebacterium.

コリネバクテリウム［生物］［真正細菌の一属］Corynebacterium.

ごりん²【五輪】 ▭ 五輪停戦 the Olympic Truce; an Olympic cease-fire: a ｢truce [cease-fire] during the Olympics.

コリンエステラーゼ ▭ 血清コリンエステラーゼ ⇨けっせい¹.

ゴルカ［ネパール中部の町］Gorkha.

ゴルガ（ー）ン［イラン北部, ゴレスタン州の州都］Gorgan.

ゴルカルとう【-党】［インドネシアの政党］Golkar. ▶ インドネシア語で Sekber Golongan Karya より.

コルコバード［ブラジル, リオデジャネイロの山］Corcovado.

コルデスタ（ー）ン［イラン西部, イラクと国境を接する州］Kordestan. ▶ 州都はサナンダジ.

「コルト 45」［コルト拳銃の発明者の息子が主人公の TV 西部劇］Colt .45.

ゴルフ ▭ ゴルフ場農薬 pesticides used on golf

ゴルファー 148

courses. ゴルフ肘〖医〗golfer's elbow; golf elbow. ゴルフ保険 ＝ゴルファー保険（⇨ゴルファー）.
**ゴルファーほけん** ▭ゴルファー保険 golf insurance.
**ゴルマール**〔フランスのアルザス地方の都市〕Colmar.
**ゴルムド**【格爾木】〔中国青海省中西部の都市〕Golmud.
**コレア** Correa, Rafael (1963- ; エクアドルの政治家; 大統領〔2007- 〕).
**コレウス・フォルスコリ**〘植〙〔ヒマラヤ原産のシソ科の食用植物〕Coleus forskohlii.
**コレーズ**〔フランス中南部の県〕Corrèze.
**コレクター** ▭ コレクターズ・アイテム〔収集欲をそそる品〕a ˈcollector's [collectors] item.
**ゴレスタ(ー)ン**〔イラン北部の州〕Golestan.
**コレット** Collette, Toni (1972- ; オーストラリア生まれの映画女優).
**コレッリ** Corelli, Franco (1921-2003; イタリアのオペラ歌手).
**コロケーション** ▭ コロケーション・サービス〔電算〕〔顧客のサーバーなどを預かるサービス〕(a) collocation service.
**コロ(ッ)セウム**〔ローマの円形大競技場〕the Colosseum.
**コロナ**〔コロナ・ガス〔太陽の〕coronal gas.
**コロンバス** Columbus, Chris (1958- ; 米国の映画監督・脚本家).
**コロンビアかくめいぐん**【-革命軍】the Revolutionary Armed Forces of Colombia（略：FARC）.▶ FARC はスペイン語の Fuerzas Armadas Revolucionarias Colombianas の略.
**コロンビアじけいぐんれんごう**【-自警軍連合】〔コロンビアの極右武装集団〕the United Self-Defense Forces of Colombia（略：AUC）.▶ AUC はスペイン語の Autodefensas Unidas de Colombia の略.
**コロンビアじりす**【-地栗鼠】〘動〙a Columbian ground squirrel; Spermophilus columbianus.
**コロンビア・メモリアルきち**【-基地】〘宇宙〙〔NASA の火星探査車スピリットの着陸地点〕the Columbia Memorial Station.
**こわけ**【小分け】 ▭ 小分け業者 a repackaging company.
**こわしや**【壊し屋】〔既存のものを破壊しようとする人〕a wrecker; a smasher; a crusher; a destroyer.
**「こわれゆく世界の中で」**〔映画〕Breaking and Entering.
**こん**³【紺】 ▭ 紺ブレ〔紺色のブレザー〕a ˈdark-blue [navy-blue] blazer.
**こんいん**【婚姻】 ▭ 婚姻費用分担請求〖法〗a ˈclaim [demand] for the sharing of marriage expenses.
**「コン・エアー」**〔映画〕Con Air.
**こんきょ**【根拠】 ▭ 根拠法 a base law; the law on which a regulation is based. ◐ 交通違反点数制の～法は道路交通法である. The law on which the system of points for traffic violations is based is the Road Traffic Law.
**「ゴング・ショー」**〔米国の, 素人一芸披露 TV 番組; つまらないとゴングを鳴らされつまみ出される〕The Gong Show.
**コンクリート** ▭ ALC コンクリート〔軽量気泡コンクリート〕ALC; autoclaved lightweight concrete. ▭ コンクリート固化 ＝セメント固化. コンクリート爆弾 a concrete bomb. コンクリート破砕器〔爆破装置〕a concrete cracker. コンクリート破砕機〖機械〗a concrete crusher.
**こんけい**²【根茎】 ▭ 根茎類 rhizomatous plants.
**コン・ケーン** ＝コン・ケン.
**こんけん**【根圏】〘生態〙〔土壌中で植物の根の影響が及ぶ範囲〕a rhizosphere. ◐ 水稲〔タマネギ〕の～ the rhizosphere of ˈa rice-paddy plant [an onion]. ▭ 根圏細菌〘農〙rhizosphere [rhizospheric] bacteria. 根圏微生物 a ˈrhizosphere [rhizospheric] microorganism [microbe].
**コン・ケン**〔タイ東北部の県; 同県の県都〕Khon Kaen.

**こんごう**²【混合】 ▭ 混合飼料〔家畜用の〕(a) mixed feed. 混合水域〘海洋〙〔黒潮(暖水塊)と親潮(冷水塊)が混ざって存在する場所〕the Mixed Water Region（略：MWR）.
**こんごうせいけつごうそしきびょう**【混合性結合組織病】〖医〗mixed connective tissue disease（略：MCTD）.
**コンコルドきょうてい**【-協定】〔F1 レースの運営に関する協定書〕the Concorde Agreement.
**コンサータ**〔商標・薬〕〔注意欠陥多動性障害の治療薬〕Concerta. ▶ メチルフェニデート徐放剤の商品名.
**コンサート** ▭ ミニ・コンサート a mini-concert.
**コンサバ**〔保守的〕conservative. ◐ ～系スーツ a conservative suit.
**コンサバティブ** ＝コンサバ.
**コンサベーション・インターナショナル**〔米国の環境保護団体〕Conservation International（略：CI）.
**コンサルタント** ▭ 建設コンサルタント a construction consultant.
**コンサルティング** ▭ コンサルティング契約 a ˈconsulting [consultancy] contract. ◐ 技術～契約 a technical consulting contract.
**コンシーラー**〔肌のしみ, くすみ, 荒れなどを隠すための基礎化粧品〕▭ a concealer.
**コンシューマー** ▭ コンシューマー・ゲーム〔家庭・個人用ゲーム〕a consumer game; a home video game. ◐ ～ゲーム機 a ˈconsumer [home video] game console.
**コンスタンシア**〔南アフリカ共和国, ケープ・タウン南方のワイン生産地域; 同地域産のワイン〕Constantia.
**コンセイエ**〘＜F conseiller〙〔店頭でワインに関する助言を行いつつ販売することを認定された人〕a wine advisor.
**こんせいじん**【金精神・金勢神】〔石製や木製の男根をまつった神〕a phallic god; Priapus.
**コンセプト** ▭ コンセプト・ウイルス〔電算〕〔新しい技術や感染方法を検証するための実験的なウイルス〕a concept virus.
**コンセルタ**〔商標・薬〕〔向精神薬〕Concerta.
**こんせん**¹【混戦】 ▭ 混戦模様 ◐ 優勝争いは～模様だ. The championship race appears tight.
**コンタクティー**〔宇宙人から接触を受けたと自称する人〕a contactee.
**コンタクト** ▭ コンタクト・センター a (customer) contact center.
**コンタクト・レンズ** ▭ コンタクトレンズ装着液 contact lens comfort drops.
**こんだんかい**【懇談会】 ▭ 朝食[昼食, 夕食]懇談会 a ˈbreakfast [lunch, dinner] meeting.
**コンチネンス**〔排泄抑制能力〕continence. ▭ コンチネンス・ケア continence [incontinence] care.
**こんちゅう**【昆虫】 ▭ 昆虫テクノロジー insect technology.
**コンテ**² Conte, Lansana (1934- ; ギニアの政治家; 大統領〔1993- 〕).
**コンディショナリティー**〔IMF などの国際金融機関が途上国援助の融資を行う際の条件〕(IMF) conditionality.
**コンディショニング** ▭ コンディショニング・コーチ〔スポーツチームで選手の体調管理・トレーニング指導を行う人〕a strength and conditioning coach.
**コンテインメント**〔国際政治〕〔封じ込め〕containment.
**コンテナ** ▭ セミコンテナ船〔コンテナと一般貨物の両方を運ぶ貨物船〕a semi-container ship. フルコンテナ船〔コンテナ専用貨物船〕a full-container ship. コンテナボックス〔収納箱〕a container (box),〔コンテナ式の貸倉庫〕a storage container.
**コンテナリゼーション** containerization.
**コンデンサ** ▭ 大容量コンデンサー a ˈhigh [large] capacity capacitor.
**コンデンセート**〔化〕〔天然ガスの採取精製の過程で得られる液体の炭化水素〕(a) natural gas condensate; (a) (gas) condensate.

コンテンツ ▭ コンテンツ産業 the content industry. コンテンツ・ターゲット広告 content-targeted advertising. コンテンツ・デリバリー・サービス a content delivery service (略: CDS). コンテンツ・デリバリー・ネットワーク〔コンテンツ配信用のネットワーク〕a content delivery network (略: CDN). コンテンツ・マッチ〔電算〕＝コンテンツ連動(型)広告. コンテンツ連動(型)広告〔電算〕a「content-targeted [contextual] advertisement.

コンテンツかいがいりゅうつうそくしんきこう【─海外流通促進機構】〔日本の映画･音楽ソフトなどの海外での著作権保護を扱う専門組織〕the Content Overseas Distribution Association (略: CODA).

コンテンツほう【─法】〔法〕the Content Law. ▶ 正式名称は「コンテンツの創造、保護及び活用の促進に関する法律」(the Law Concerning the Promotion of the Creation, Protection and Utilization of Content).

コンテンポラリー ▭ コンテンポラリー・アート〔現代美術〕contemporary art. ▷ contemporary artist n. コンテンポラリー・ダンス〔既成のジャンルにとらわれない新しい創造的ダンス〕contemporary dance.

コントゥム〔ベトナム中央高地の省; その省都〕Kon [Con] Tum.

ゴンドリー Gondry, Michel (1963– ; フランスの映画監督).

コントロールド・デリバリー〔密輸ルート全体を摘発するために麻薬などの移動を阻止せずに監視を続けること〕a controlled delivery (略: CD).

こんない【婚内】 〜の intramarital. ▭ 婚内子 a legitimate child; a child born「in lawful wedlock [to (legally) married parents].

こんなん【困難】 ▭ (教育)困難校〔生徒の中退などの問題が多い〕a problem school.

こんにゃく【蒟蒻】 ▭ 赤コンニャク red konnyaku. 板コンニャク block konnyaku; a block of konnyaku. 黒コンニャク black konnyaku; konnyaku with powdered seaweed added (and colored by the seaweed). 刺身コンニャク sashimi(-style) konnyaku; soft konnyaku to be sliced and eaten uncooked. 白コンニャク white plain konnyaku. 玉コンニャク ball-shaped konnyaku.

コンバインド・ローラー〔地固め機の一種〕a combination roller.

コンパクト ▭ コンパクト版 a compact edition. コンパクト・マンション a compact condominium.

コンパクト・シティー〔都市･商業機能を中心区域に集中させた都市〕the [a] compact city.

コンパクトフラッシュ〔商標･電算〕〔記憶媒体カードの１つ〕a CompactFlash (card).

コンパチ(ブル)・プレーヤー〔DVDとCDなど、複数のメディアを再生できるプレーヤー〕a compatible 《DVD/CD》player.

コンバット ▭ コンバット・ストレス〔軍〕〔戦場の極限状態で兵士などが受けるストレス〕combat stress.

コンバット・タロン〔米軍〕〔空軍特殊戦集団の侵攻作戦用輸送機 MC-130 シリーズの愛称〕a Combat Talon.

コンパニオン・プランツ〔生態･園芸〕〔生育を助け合う、種類の異なる植物〕a companion plant.

コンバラトキシン〔薬〕〔スズランに含まれる毒; 強心配糖体〕convallatoxin.

コンパラブル・ワース〔労〕〔同等価値･同一価値労働同一賃金〕comparable worth.

コンピテンシー〔成果や業績につながる社員の能力〕competency.

コンビニ ▭ コンビニ ATM an「automated teller machine [ATM] at a convenience store. コンビニ決済 paying bills at a convenience store.

コンビネゾン〔＜F combinaison ＝combination〕〔服similar〕〔ジャンプスーツ〕a jumpsuit.

コンピューター ▭ コンピューター援用[利用]設計 computer-aided design (略: CAD). コンピューター科学 computer science. コンピューター画像 a「computer [computer-generated] image. コンピューター教育 computer education. コンピューター工学 computer engineering. コンピューター・ペスト〔電算〕〔ウイルス以外の不正プログラム〕a computer pest. コンピューター倫理, コンピューター・エシックス computer ethics.

コンピュータ・エンターテインメントきょうかい【─協会】the Computer Entertainment Supplier's Association (略: CESA).

コンピュータ・エンターテインメントレーティングきこう【─機構】the Computer Entertainment Rating Organization (略: CERO).

コンピュータソフトウェアちょさくけんきょうかい【─著作権協会】the Association of Copyright for Computer Software (略: ACCS).

コンピレーション ▭ コンピレーション CD〔企画物のCD〕a compilation CD.

コンプ〔カジノの上客などに対する、ホテル側の判断による支払いの一部の無料化や割引き〕a comp; a complimentary service.

コンフェデレーションズ・カップ〔サッカー〕the Confederations Cup.

コンフォート・シューズ〔履きやすさを優先した靴〕《a pair of》comfort shoes.

コンフォート・バイク〔マウンテン・バイクをベースに道路走行用にアレンジした自転車〕a comfort bike.

コンフォメーションびょう【─病】〔医〕〔たんぱく質の変形によって起こる病気の総称〕a (protein) conformation disease.

コンプライアンス ▭ 企業コンプライアンス corporate compliance. コンプライアンス管理 compliance management. コンプライアンス条例 corporate compliance regulations; a corporate compliance ordinance.

コンベア〔機〕a conveyor; a conveyer. ▭ 垂直[水平]コンベア a「vertical [horizontal] conveyor. ねじコンベア a screw conveyor. ベルト・コンベア a belt conveyor. ローラー・コンベア a roller conveyor. ▭ コンベア・システム a conveyer system. コンベア・ベルト a conveyor belt.

コンベクション〔対流〕convection. ▭ コンベクション・オーブン a convection oven.

コンベンション ▭ コンベンション・ホール〔大会議場〕a convention hall.

こんぼう[2]【棍棒】 ▭ 棍棒投げ〔競技〕〔パラリンピックの種目の１つ〕the club throw.

コンポスト ▭ コンポスト・トイレ a compost toilet.〔＝バイオトイレ〕

コンポン・スプー〔カンボジア南部の州; 同州の州都〕Kampong [Kompong] Speu [Spoe].

コンポン・チャム〔カンボジア中南部の州; 同州の州都〕Kampong [Kompong] Cham.

コンポン・チュナン〔カンボジア中南部の州; 同州の州都〕Kampong [Kompong] Chhnang.

コンポン・トム〔カンボジア中北部の州; 同州の州都〕Kompong [Kampong] Thom.

こんめい[3]【混迷】 ▭ 混迷期 a period of confusion 《after a war》.

コンヤ〔トルコ南西部の都市〕Konya.

こんやさい【根野菜】〔根菜類〕root crops; roots grown for food.

コン・リー Gong Li (1965– ; 中国の映画女優; 中国語名鞏俐).

コンレン【混練】mixing; kneading. 〜する mix; knead. ▭ 混練機 a「mixing [kneading] machine; a mixer; a kneader.

こんろ【焜炉】 ▭ 簡易こんろ a portable stove; a camp stove.

# さ

-さ[2] 〔接尾辞〕(性質) -ness; (その程度) (the)「degree [amount, extent] of…. ◐ 静か～ quietness; quiet / 自然～ naturalness / セクシー～ sexiness / 眠～ sleepiness / 重～ weight / 困難～ the degree of difficulty / スポーティーなデザインで商品の新しさを表現する express the product's「newness [novelty] through its sporty design / あまりのとんでもなさに読むのをやめた。It was so ridiculous I quit reading it.
**サーカシビリ** Saakashvili, Mikhail (1967- ; グルジアの政治家; 大統領〔2004- 〕).
**サーカス** ◐□ サーカス小屋 a circus tent.
**サーキス** Serkis, Andy (1964- ; 英国生まれの映画俳優).
**サーキット** ◐□ サーキット・レース circuit racing; 〔1回の〕 a circuit race.
**サーク** Sirk, Douglas (1900-87; ドイツ生まれの映画監督; 本名 Claus Detlef Sierck).
「**サークル・オブ・フレンズ**」〔映画〕Circle of Friends.
**サース**〔SaaS〕〔ネット経由でソフトの中から自分に必要な機能だけを選択して利用できるサービス〕SaaS; Software as a Service.
**サーズ**〔SARS〕◐□ **SARS** コロナウイルス the SARS coronavirus.
**サーズ**[2]〔SaaS〕=サース.
**サーチナ**〔商標〕〔インターネット上の中国情報サイト〕Searchina. ▶ Searchina は search と China からの造語.
「**13デイズ**」〔映画〕Thirteen Days.
**サードゥー**〔ヒンズー教〕=サドゥー.
**サードパーティー・ロジスティクス**〔荷主に対して物流業務に関する改革案を提案し、物流業務を包括して外部委託する方法〕third-party logistics (略: 3PL).
**サーバー**[1] ◐□ ルート・サーバー〔電算〕⇒ルート[2]. ◐□ サーバー型放送 server-type broadcasting. サーバー・コンピュータ a server computer.
**サーバー・ベース・コンピューティング**〔電算〕server-based computing.
**サービサー**〔債権回収会社〕a loan servicer.
**サービス**
◐□ 顧客サービス customer service. ◐ 顧客～の一環として… as part of our service to our customers…. 読者サービス reader benefits. ファン・サービス fan benefits. ◐ あの歌手はファン～もおろそかにしない。That singer is conscientious about serving his fans.
◐□ サービス介助士 a helper for the elderly and disabled; a "care fitter". サービス基盤 a service infrastructure. ◐ 介護事業の～基盤を早急に整える必要がある。There is an urgent need to put in place a service infrastructure for the caregiving business. サービス収支〔経〕〔国際収支の〕the services account; the balance on services. サービス出勤 working「without pay [off the clock]; unpaid work. サービス担当者会議〔介護に関する〕a nursing care conference. サービス提供事業者〔介護サービス提供〕a nursing care agency. サービス提供責任者〔介護サービスの現場を管理する〕a person in charge of nursing care service providers. サービス内容 (a「description [list] of the) services (offered). サービス品質保証制度 a service (quality) assurance system.
**サービス力** the「power [capacity] to serve (customers).
**サービスざんぎょうこんぜつ(の)つうたつ**〔-残業根絶(の)通達〕〔労働〕a notification issued by the Ministry of Health, Labour and Welfare, aimed at abolishing unpaid overtime work. [=よんろくつうたつ]
**サービスじゅぎょういんこくさい(ろうどう)くみあい**〔-従業員国際(労働)組合〕〔米国・カナダ・プエルトリコに

組織をもつ〕the Service Employees International Union (略: SEIU).
**サーブ** ◐□ アンダーハンド・サーブ《バレーボール・テニス》an underhand serve. スパイク・サーブ《ジャンプ・サーブ》a jump serve. スピン・サーブ《テニス》a spin serve. スライス・サーブ《テニス》a slice serve. ドライブサーブ〔バレーボールなどの球技で〕a spin serve. ▶「ドライブサーブ」は和製英語. 投げ上げサーブ〔卓球〕a high-toss serve. フラット・サーブ《テニス》a flat serve. ◐□ サーブカット《バレーボール》delivering a serve to the setter. サーブミス《バレーボールなど》〔サーブの失敗〕a service error.
「**サーフサイド6**」〔マイアミが舞台の、探偵ものの青春TVドラマ〕Surfside 6.
**サーベイランス** ◐□ サーベイランス委員会 a surveillance committee.
**ザーヘダーン** =ザヘダン.
**サーベンス・オクスレーほう**〔-法〕〔米法〕=きぎょうかいかくほう.
**サーマクール**〔商標〕〔皮膚のたるみをとる高周波治療器〕thermaCool.
**サーマン** Thurman, Uma (1970- ; 米国の映画女優; 本名 Uma Karuna Thurman).
**サーメ**〔ラップランドの先住民〕a Sami.
**サーモバリックばくだん**〔-爆弾〕〔軍〕〔殺傷能力の高い熱圧爆弾〕a thermobaric bomb.
**サーモン・パッチ**〔医〕〔母斑の一種〕a salmon patch.
**ザーライ** ⇒ザライ.
**サーリーフ** Johnson-Sirleaf, Ellen (1939- ; リベリアの経済学者・政治家; 大統領〔2005- 〕). ▶ アフリカ初の女性大統領.
**サーレハ** =サレハ.
**サイ**[2]〔ラオス、ウドムサイ県の郡・県都〕Xay.
**サイアム・セメント**〔タイの複合企業体〕Siam Cement「Public Company Limited [PCL] (略: SCC).
**ざいいん**〔在院〕〔医〕hospital stay. ◐□ 平均在院日数〔病院の〕the average length of hospital stays.
**サイエンス** ◐□ サイエンス・ライター〔科学・技術系の記事を書く人〕a science writer. サイエンス・レンジャー a science ranger.
「**サイエンス**」〔米国科学振興協会発行の科学誌〕Science; the journal *Science*.
「**サイエンティフィック・アメリカン**」〔米国の月刊科学雑誌〕Scientific American.
**サイエントロジー**〔商標〕〔米国人 L. Ron Hubbard によって 1952 年に創設された応用宗教哲学〕Scientology. ▷ Scientologist *n*.
**さいおう**[2]〔斎王〕〔日本史〕〔天皇の代理として伊勢神宮に仕えていた未婚の皇女〕an unmarried Imperial Princess serving at the Ise Shrine in place of the Emperor; a *saiō*.
**さいおおて**〔最大手〕largest《company》; the《industry》leader. ◐□ ～の旅行会社 the「largest [industry-leading] travel company.
**サイオン・パーク**〔英国の由緒ある公園〕Syon Park.
**さい**[8]〔才華〕genius; brilliance. ◐ 詩歌の～を咲かせる display one's「brilliant talent for [brilliance at] poetry.
**さいか**[9]〔差異化〕differentiation. ◐ ～する differentiate. ◐□ 差異化技術 a「differentiation [differentiating] technology.
**さいかい**[5]〔最下位〕◐□ 最下位争い〔揶揄($)的な表現〕a race for「the bottom《of the league》[last place, *the cellar*]. ◐ ～争いを演じる be in a race for last place. 最下位脱出 escaping from [breaking out of] bottom

place [the bottom ((of the league)), last place, *the cellar]. 最下位転落 a「drop [fall] to「bottom place [the bottom ((of the league)), last place, *the cellar].
さいがい¹【災害】
◑ 災害医療 disaster medicine. 災害医療センター a medical center for disasters; a disaster medical center. [⇨こくりつびょういんきこうさいがいいりょうセンター] 災害医療派遣チーム〔日本の〕a Disaster Medical Assistance Team (略: DMAT). 災害援助金 a disaster aid fund. 災害援助協定〔自治体間の〕an agreement「on mutual support [to help each other] in case of a disaster. 災害看護 disaster nursing. ◑ ～看護学 disaster nursing studies. 災害監視衛星 a disaster observation satellite. 災害関連死 (a) disaster-related death. 災害拠点病院 a「hub [coordinating, pivotal] hospital for disaster「relief [response]. 災害ごみ disaster garbage; garbage generated by a disaster. 災害時帰宅支援ステーション〔地震などの災害で交通が途絶したときに、通勤・通学者などの徒歩帰宅者に水道水・トイレ・道路情報などの提供を行うコンビニエンスストアなど〕shops used as convenience stores equipped to support people making their way home on foot after a natural disaster by providing drinking water, toilets and maps, etc. 災害社会学 the sociology of disaster; disaster sociology. 災害弱者 a person (especially) vulnerable in case of a (natural) disaster;〈集合的に〉《protect》the vulnerable (if there is an earthquake). 災害出動〔自衛隊・消防隊などの〕(a) (natural) disaster mobilization; going into「action [operation] in a disaster. ◑ 今回の大地震で県知事は自衛隊に～出動を要請した. The Prefectural Governor has requested the Self-Defense Forces to「go into operation [help] in the earthquake-stricken area. 災害準備金〔保険〕〔災害に備えて保険会社などが積み立てる資金〕a disaster reserve fund. 災害時要援護者 a person [people] requiring support in times of disaster. ◑ ～時要援護者台帳 a register of people requiring support in times of disaster ／ ～時要援護者名簿 a「list of names [roster] of people requiring support in times of disaster. 災害情報 disaster information. 災害情報学〔論〕disaster information (studies). ◑ ～情報学の講座[コース] a course on disaster information. 災害心理学 disaster psychology. ▷ disaster psychologist *n*. 災害弔慰金〔地方自治体などの〕disaster condolence money. 災害廃棄物 disaster waste; waste generated by a disaster. 災害派遣〔自衛隊の〕disaster-relief duty; dispatch (of Self-Defense Forces) for disaster relief [on disaster-relief duty]. ◑ ～派遣手当 an allowance for disaster-relief duty. 災害復興住宅融資 disaster reconstruction housing loan; a housing loan for post-disaster reconstruction; finance for rebuilding homes after a disaster. 災害ボランティア〔活動〕disaster (-relief) volunteering;〔人〕a disaster(-relief) volunteer. 災害用伝言ダイヤル〔電話会社の〕a disaster messaging service. 災害用伝言板サービス ＝災害用伝言ダイヤル.

ざいかい【財界】◑ 財界3団体 ＝経済3団体 (⇨けいざい¹).

ざいがい【在外】◑ 在外選挙制度 the overseas election system; the system enabling Japanese citizens abroad to vote in elections to the Diet. 在外米軍 American forces overseas.

さいがいきゅうじょ【災害救助】◑ 災害救助基金 a disaster relief fund. 災害救助隊 a disaster relief「team [unit].

ざいがいこうかんいむかんじょうほう【在外公館医務官情報】〔外務省が発する〕information from medical officers attached to embassies abroad on local health conditions; Foreign Ministry Health Reports ((from Canada)).

さいがいじんどういりょうしえんかい【災害人道医療支援会】〔NPOの1つ〕the Humanitarian Medical Assistance (略: HuMA).

さいがいたいさく【災害対策】◑ 災害対策会議 a disaster (response)「conference [meeting]; a meeting to discuss measures to deal with a natural disaster. 災害対策室 a disaster response office.

さいかいはつ【再開発】◑ 再開発会社 a redevelopment company. 再開発等促進区 a redevelopment promotion district.

さいかきこみ【再書き込み】〔電算〕rewriting; reprogramming. ◑ ～可能な読み出し専用メモリー (a)「rewritable [reprogrammable] read-only memory; (a)「flash ROM.

さいぎゃくてん【再逆転】a second reversal; regaining the lead;〔自分側の〕turning the tables on *sb* again;〔相手側が〕having the tables turned on *one* again. ～する regain the lead; turn the tables on ((one's opponent)) again. ◑ ～を許す have the tables turned on *one* again; suffer a setback after once gaining the lead.

さいきん²【細菌】◑ 細菌基準〔食品の〕standards for bacteria; the standard for permissible levels of potentially harmful bacteria. ◑ その店は～基準の2倍を超えるケーキを売っていたことが判明した. It became clear that the shop had sold cakes containing more than twice the permissible「number [amount] of potentially harmful bacteria.

さいきんせい【細菌性】◑ 細菌性髄膜炎〔医〕bacterial meningitis.

さいくつ【採掘】◑ 採掘可能埋蔵量 ＝かさいまいぞうりょう.

サイクル ◑ サイクル・トレイン〔自転車を持ち込める列車〕a train on which passengers are allowed to take their bicycles;〔自転車専用の車両を備えた列車〕a train with a「*car [*carriage] for bicycles.

サイクロフィリン〔生化〕＝シクロフィリン.

サイクロン² 〔遠心分離方式の集塵装置〕a cyclone. ◑ デュアル・サイクロン〔商標〕〔二重竜巻構造の集塵装置〕Dual Cyclone. ◑ サイクロン掃除機 a「cyclone [cyclonic] vacuum cleaner.

ざいけ【在家】◑ 在家信者〔在俗の信徒〕(男性) a layman; (女性) a laywoman; a layperson; a member of the laity, a lay believer;〈集合的に〉the laity.

ざいけい²【財形】◑ 財形住宅貯蓄 asset-formation housing savings.

さいけいやく【再契約】a contract extension; a new contract; (a) renewal of a contract. ～する renew [extend] a contract; sign a new contract. ◑ 彼はカージナルスと3年間3,000万ドルで～した. He signed a new three-year contract with the Cardinals for 30 million dollars. ◑ 再契約金 contract extension money.

さいけつ¹【採血】◑ 採血針 a blood (collection) needle.

さいけっしょう【再結晶】◑ 再結晶宝石 a recrystallized gemstone.

さいけん¹【再建】◑ 会社再建 restructuring [the restructuring of] a company; putting a company back on its feet. ◑ 再建医療〔医〕reconstructive medicine. 再建支援 reorganization assistance. ◑ ～支援ビジネス a reorganization-assistance business.

さいけん²【債券】◑ ユーロ豪ドル建て債券 a bond denominated in Australian dollars traded in「the Euromarket [markets outside Australia]. ◑ 債券先物オプション〔取引〕a bond futures option. 債券先物相場 a bond futures price. 債券トレーダー a bond(s) trader.

さいけん

債券標準価格〖日本経済新聞社,金融工学研究所,野村證券,野村総合研究所の4者が共同で評価する〗(the) Japan Standard Bond Price; (the) JS Price.
さいけん[3]【債権】▫▫ 債権回収会社 a loan servicer. 債権回収業《be in》the debt collection business. ◯▪ 回収業者《個人》a「debt [bill] collector;《企業》a「debt [bill] collection agency. 債権流動化 securitization of receivables.
さいげん[1]【再現】▫▫ 再現実験〔事故などの〕a reproducibility test. 再現写真 a reenactment photo 《of …》. 再現ドラマ a dramatic reenactment.
ざいげん【財源】▫▫ 財源確保 establishment of a source of「revenue [financing].
さいけんしゃ【債権者】▫▫ 債権者破産〘法〙〔債権者の申し立てによって破産手続きが開始される〕a third-party bankruptcy (whereby a creditor requests to have an insolvent company declared bankrupt).
ざいこ【在庫】
▫▫ 市場在庫 market inventory. 店頭在庫 store [shop] inventory.
▫▫ 在庫圧縮[削減] (an) inventory reduction. 在庫確認 confirmation that an item is in stock. 在庫管理システム an inventory「control [management] system. 在庫期間 an inventory period. 在庫コスト[管理費] inventory costs. 在庫指数〘経〙an inventory index. 在庫循環〘経〙the inventory cycle.[⇨キチンじゅんかん] 在庫情報 inventory information; information on (an) inventory. 在庫廃棄損[ロス] loss on disposal of inventory. 在庫評価 〘会計〙(an) inventory valuation.
在庫評価益〘会計〙(an) inventory valuation gain. 在庫評価損〘会計〙(an) inventory valuation loss. 在庫(保管)費 ＝在庫コスト[管理費]. 在庫リスク the (financial) risk of stocking 《a book》 (for a long time). 在庫率 an inventory-sales[-shipment] ratio; a stock-to-sales ratio. 在庫率指数〘経〙an inventory ratio index.
さいこう[5]【採光】▫▫ 採光部 a natural light source; an opening that allows sunlight into 《a building》. ◯▪ 居間は〜部を広くとりたい. We want to allow as much light as possible into the living room. | We want the living room to be as open as possible to natural light.
さいこう[8]【最高】▫▫ 最高指揮監督権 the《prime minister's》supreme authority to command 《the SDF》. 最高出力〔エンジンの〕a maximum power output.
さいこうぎじゅつせきにんしゃ【最高技術責任者】〔企業の〕a chief technical officer (略: CTO).
さいこうじょうほうせきにんしゃ【最高情報責任者】〔企業の〕a chief information officer (略: CIO).
さいこうじょうほうセキュリティーせきにんしゃ【最高情報セキュリティ責任者】〔企業の〕a chief information security officer (略: CISO).
さいこうじんみんけんさついん【最高人民検察院】〔中国の最上級検察機関〕the Supreme People's Procuratorate.
さいこうじんみんほういん【最高人民法院】〔中国の最上級裁判所〕the Supreme People's Court.
さいこうセキュリティーせきにんしゃ【最高セキュリティ責任者】〔企業の〕a chief security officer (略: CSO).
さいこうせんりゃくせきにんしゃ【最高戦略責任者】〔企業の〕a chief「strategy [strategic] officer (略: CSO).
さいこうちしきかんりせきにんしゃ【最高知識管理責任者】〔企業の〕a chief knowledge officer (略: CKO).
さいこうとうしせきにんしゃ【最高投資責任者】〔企業の〕a chief investment officer (略: CIO).
さいこうにゅう[0]【再購入】repeat purchasing. 〜する buy [purchase] 《a product》again. ▫▫ 再購入率〔顧客が次回も同じ製品を買う割合〕a repeat purchase「rate [ratio].
さいこうマーケティングせきにんしゃ【最高マーケティング責任者】〔企業の〕a chief marketing officer (略: CMO).

サイコダイナミクス《心理・精神医》〔精神力動・精神力学〕psychodynamics.
サイコパス〔精神病質者; 反社会的人格障害者〕a psychopath. ▫▫ サイコパス的人格(者) (a) psychopathic personality.
さいころ【賽子・骰子】▫▫ さいころステーキ diced steak.
サイゴン ▫▫ サイゴン解放〔1975年; ベトナム戦争終結時の〕the liberation of Saigon.
さいさいはつ【再々発】〔がんなどの〕a second recurrence.
さいさん[2]【採算】▫▫ 採算面 ◯▪ この美術館は一面ではここ数年きびしい状態が続いている. Profit-wise [From a profit point of view, From the point of view of profitability], this museum has「been in difficulties for the last few years [had a few difficult years]. 採算レート〔相場〕〔輸出企業の損益が均衡する為替レート〕the break-even exchange rate.
ざいさん【財産】▫▫ 財産三分法ファンド〔資産を株式・債券・不動産に分散投資する投資信託〕an asset allocation fund; a fund which distributes holdings between stocks, bonds and real estate. 財産犯〘法〙a property offense.
さいじ[1]【採餌】▫▫ 水面採餌〔水鳥の〕surface feeding. 潜水採餌〔水鳥〕sub-surface feeding; feeding under the surface; (空から突入しての) diving for food; (首から上だけを水面下に潜らせての) dabbling.
さいしき[2]【彩色】▫▫ 復元彩色 restoring 《a work of art》by replacing the「coloring [paint]. 補修彩色 restoring the color 《of a sculpture》; restoring 《a work of art》by replacing missing paint.
さいしげんか【再資源化】▫▫ 再資源化率 a recycling rate.
さいしゅ【罪種】types [categories] of crimes.
さいしゅう[2]【最終】
▫▫ 最終学歴 the final stage「of [in] one's education. 最終需要財〘経〙final demand goods. 最終選考会 a final qualifying「round [competition]. 最終損益〘経〙a [the] bottom line. 最終地位交渉 final status talks 《on Jerusalem》. 最終調整 final「coordination [adjustment(s), modulation]. ◯▪ その二つの会社は合併に向けての〜調整に入った. The two companies have entered the final coordination stage of their merger negotiations. 最終テスト a final test. 最終文書 a final document. 最終報告書 a final report. 最終ラウンド《ボクシング・ゴルフなど》the「final [last] round.
さいしゅうしょく【再就職】▫▫ 再就職先 the place of reemployment. 再就職者 a person returning to「work [the work force]; a person who starts working again; a reentrant to the labor force.
「最終絶叫計画」〖映画〗Scary Movie.
さいじゅうよう【最重要】〜の[な]《a matter》of (the) utmost importance. ▫▫ 最重要課題 an issue of (the) utmost importance; a vitally important issue. 最重要視 ◯▪ わが社は常に品質を〜視している. Our company always regards quality as being more important than anything else. | We always give top priority to quality.
さいじゅんかん【再循環】▫▫ 排気[排出]ガス再循環, 排気再循環〔自動車〕exhaust gas recirculation (略: EGR).
さいしょ[2]【彩書】decorative calligraphy; illuminated lettering.
さいしょう[3]【最少】▫▫ 最少失点 the fewest「points [runs, goals] allowed. ◯▪ 彼はこのピンチを〜失点で切り抜けた. He managed to get through the tough spot giving up only one run.
さいしょう[4]【妻妾】one's [a] wife and「one's [a] mistress. ▫▫ 妻妾同居 one's [a] wife and「one's [a] mistress living (not in different houses but) in the same house.
さいしよう【再使用】reuse; reusage; further [repeated]

⌈use [usage]．~する reuse; use《cans》again; make ⌈further [repeated] use of《a container》; recycle《materials, cans》． ▫ 再使用料 a fee for reuse．

ざいしょう¹【罪証】 ▫ 罪証隠滅 destruction [concealing] of evidence．

ざいじょう【罪状】 ▫ 罪状認否留保 withholding [postponing] a plea on arraignment．

さいじょうじょう【再上場】《株式》refloatation [reflotation]《of the company on the stock market》．~する refloat《the company on the stock market》． ◆3 年以内の~を目指す aim to ⌈refloat the company [list the company's shares again] within three years．

さいじょうりく【再上陸】〔台風などの〕a second landfall．~する make a second landfall《on the Hokkaidō coast》; hit [strike] land again． ◆台風 21 号は九州に上陸後，四国を横断して，大阪に~した．After coming ashore in Kyūshū, typhoon no. 21 cut across Shikoku and struck land again in Osaka Prefecture．

ざいしょく【在職】 ▫ 在職証明書 a certificate of employment．

さいしん¹【再診】 ▫ 再診料 an additional fee charged for a patient's subsequent medical visit．

さいしん²【再審】 ▫ 再審公判 a retrial．

サイズ¹ ▫ ワンサイズ one size． ▫ ワン~小さい one size smaller． ▫ サイズ切れ〔あるサイズの商品の在庫がないこと〕being [running] out of a size． ◆~の際はお届けまで 2 週間程度かかります．〔通信販売で〕If we are out of your size, deliveries will take about two weeks．／気に入ったのがあったと思ったら~切れだった．There was one I liked, but they had run out of my size． サイズ制〔運送費などの〕a system of pricing by size; a size-based system．

サイズモア Sizemore, Tom (1964- ; 米国の映画俳優; 本名 Thomas Edward Sizemore Jr.).

さいせい¹【再生】 ▫ 追いかけ再生〔録画映像の〕chase playback; playback of a video from the start even while it is still recording． ▫ 早聞き再生〔録音の〕slow [fast] playback． スロー再生 = 遅聞き再生． ▫ 再生時間〔携帯映像/音声/機器などの〕《maximum》video playback time． ◆連続~時間 continuous video playback time． 再生樹脂 reprocessed resin． ◆ペットボトル~樹脂 recycled PET (bottle) resin． 再生水〔下水を高度に浄化処理した水〕recycled [reclaimed] water． 再生ソフト【電算】playback software; a playback ⌈application [program]; a player． ◆音楽[映像]~ソフト a ⌈music [video] playback ⌈application [program]; a ⌈music [video] player． 再生銘柄〔証券〕reborn ⌈stocks [securities]．

ざいせい²【財政】 ▫ 拡大財政 an expansionary fiscal policy． ▫ 財政健全化 restoring the finances to health; putting the finances on a ⌈healthy [sound] footing． 財政措置〔take〕a financial measure． 財政調整基金 a financial adjustment fund． 財政破綻〔の〕financial ⌈collapse [failure]; (a) bankruptcy． 財政優遇措置 measures to ease funding． 財政融資資金 the Fiscal Loan Fund． 財政力指数 financial strength index; index of financial potential．

ざいせいあんてい(せいちょう)きょうてい【財政安定(成長)協定】〔法〕あんていせいちょうきょうてい．

さいせいしげんりようそくしんほう【再生資源利用促進法】〔法〕the Law for Promotion of Utilization of Recyclable Resources．

ざいせき²【在籍】 ▫ 在籍記録〔大学などでの〕a record of ⌈enrollment [having been enrolled]．

さいせきじん【細石刃】〔考古〕a microblade．

さいぜんれつ【最前列】 ▫ 最前列スタート〔レースなどの〕《secure》a front-row start．

さ

さいた【最多】 ▫ 最多安打〔野球〕the most hits． ◆シーズン~安打記録 the record for most hits in a season． 最多セーブ〔野球〕《have the record for》most saves． ◆~セーブポイント most relief wins plus saves／~セーブ投手賞 the prize for the pitcher with the most saves． ◆最多得点 the most ⌈points [runs, goals] scored． ◆FIFA ワールドカップの~得点は 1954 年ハンガリーチームが記録した 27 だ．The most goals scored in a FIFA World Cup were the 27 recorded by the Hungarian team in 1954．

さいだい【最大】 ▫ 最大エネルギー積【物】a maximum energy product． 最大使用電力 maximum power consumption．

さいたいけん【再体験】〔もう一度体験すること〕experiencing sth again; reexperiencing; going through sth again;〔心の中で思い出すこと〕reliving《one's past》; (a) reliving《of the past》; (a) reexperiencing《of trauma》．~する〔もう一度体験する〕go through《an experience》again; reexperience;〔心の中で思い出す〕relive《the past》． ◆患者は抑圧していた感情を~することで快方へ向かうことがある．Reexperiencing [Reliving] emotions that have been suppressed sometimes puts patients on the route to recovery．| It can help patients to go back ⌈through [over] repressed emotions．

さいたく²【採拓】〔拓本の〕stone rubbing;〔魚拓の〕fish rubbing．~する〔拓本を〕make a rubbing《of…》; rub《an inscribed stone》;〔魚拓を〕make [take] a fish ⌈print [rubbing]; take a fish impression．

ざいたく【在宅】 ▫ 在宅医療廃棄物 home care medical waste． 在宅確認〔宅配業者などが配達時に行う〕confirmation [checking, making sure] that sb is at home;〔消費者金融などが事前に行う居住確認〕⇒きょじゅう². 在宅患者 a home [an at-home] patient． 在宅起訴 at-home ⌈indictment [prosecution]; indictment without arrest． ◆彼は公職選挙法違反で~起訴された．He was indicted but not arrested for infringing the Public Offices Election Law． 在宅高齢者 an elderly person living at home;〈集合的に〉the living-at-home elderly． 在宅死 dying at home; (a) home death． 在宅児 a preschool child not attending a kindergarten or day nursery． 在宅重度障害者 a severely handicapped person living at home． 在宅就労者＝在宅ワーカー． 在宅復帰率 the《patient》return home rate． 在宅保育 taking care of a preschool child at home (in combination with a home visitor service)． 在宅率〔住民の〕the at-home rate;〔集合的に〕at home;〔重症患者などの〕the treatment-at-home rate; the ratio《of patients》receiving treatment at home． ◆このマンションの~率がもっとも高いのは午前 3 時，もっとも低いのは午前 11 時だ．In this apartment block the at-home rate is highest at 3AM and lowest at 11AM．／認知症の要介護度が高いほど~率が低い．With dementia (patients), the higher the level of care required, the lower the treatment-at-home rate． 在宅療育 home-based care and education ⌈of [for] a disabled child． 在宅ワーカー an at-home worker; a home worker;〔コンピューターによる〕a telecommuter; a teleworker; a remote worker． ◆パソコンの普及で~ワーカーが増えている．Due to the spread of computers, ⌈the number of telecommuters is increasing [an increasing number of people are working ⌈at [from] home]．

さいたん¹【採炭】 ▫ 採炭夫 a coal miner; a coal mining worker．

さいチャレンジ【再-】＝さいちょうせん． ▫ 再チャレンジ社会 a society in which people can ⌈get another chance

さいチャレンジすいしんかいぎ [get back on the rails, make a fresh start].

さいチャレンジすいしんかいぎ【再-推進会議】the Cabinet committee entrusted with considering how to increase opportunities for citizens to make a fresh start in life.

さいちょうせん【再挑戦】a「repeated [second] attempt [try]; a reattempt; a retry; a comeback attempt;〔人への〕a renewed challenge 《to sb》.
～する attempt [try] again; reattempt; retry;〔人に〕rechallenge; challenge again.

さいていしほんきんきせい【最低資本金規制】minimum capital regulations. ▶最低資本金規制(の)特例〔設立後５年までは資本金１円でよいとする特例〕an exception to minimum capital regulations.

さいていちんぎん【最低賃金】▶法定最低賃金 the [a] (legal) minimum wage.

サイディヤ〔イラク,バグダッド市内の地名〕Sayidiya.

さいてき【最適】▶最適解〔数〕an optimal solution.

ざいテク【財-】▶財テクブーム a financial management boom.

さいてん2【採点】▶採点作業【業務】〔入試などの〕marking work. 採点ルール〔採点競技における〕(the) scoring rules.

サイト ▶地下サイト〔電算〕〔非合法のインターネットサイト〕an「illegal [underground]「Internet] site;〔軍〕〔地下ミサイル発射基地〕an underground missile site. 偽サイト〔電算〕a「fake [bogus] (Web) site. ▶サイト運営者【主催者】〔電算〕a (Web) site operator. サイト訪問率〔電算〕〔ウェブサイトへの〕a site visitors rate.

サイド ▶左[右]サイド〔サッカー〕the「left [right] side. ▶サイド攻撃【アタック】〔サッカーなどで〕a side attack.

ざいとうきかんさい【財投機関債】〔特殊法人が資金を調達するための債券〕a FILP bond. ▶ FILP は Fiscal Investment and Loan Program の略.

サイドスティック(・コントローラー)〔空〕〔操縦士の座席横にある操縦桿〕a side stick; a side-stick controller.

サイド・ステッパー〔足踏み式のトレーニングマシン〕a side stepper.

サイド・ストーリー〔アニメ・漫画などの外伝〕a side story.

サイドスピン〔球技〕〔ボールの横回転〕sidespin.

サイドゾル〔生化〕〔細胞質ゾル〕cytosol.

サイドハンド〔競技〕sidearm 《pitching》. ▶サイドハンド・スロー a sidearm throw; sidearm throwing.

サイトラ〔視訳〕＝しゃく3.

ざいにちべいこくしょうこうかいぎしょ【在日米国商工会議所】the American Chamber of Commerce in Japan 《略: ACCJ》.

さいにゅうこく【再入国】▶再入国許可申請 application for reentry permit. ○～許可申請書 an application for reentry permit.

さいにょう【採尿】▶採尿室 a room (in a hospital) where urine samples are taken; a urine-sampling [-collecting] room.

ざいにん1【在任】▶在任期間 a [sb's] term of「office [service]; the period of a posting.

さいにんほう【再認法】〔心理〕〔記憶力測定法の１つ〕a recognition method.

さいにんよう【再任用】〔管理職など高い役職への〕reappointment;〔一般的な職への; 再雇用〕reemployment; rehiring.
～する〔管理職など高い役職に〕reappoint 《a director》;〔一般的な職に〕reemploy [rehire] 《an employee》.

さいねん【再燃】▶(自然)再燃現象〔精神医〕〔薬物乱用などによる〕a flashback.

さいねんしょう【最年少】▶最年少記録 a [the] record for being the youngest 《world champion》. ○彼女はオリンピック金メダルの～記録を塗り替えた。She set a new record as the youngest ever winner of an Olympic Gold.

さいねんちょう【最年長】▶最年長記録 a [the] record for being the oldest 《person to climb Everest》. ○ホームラン王の～は45歳だ。The record for the oldest home run king is 45. | Forty-five is the oldest anyone has ever become a home run king.

さいは【砕波】〔海洋〕a breaker; breakers; a broken sea. ▶砕波高 breaking height. 砕波水深 depth of breaking. 砕波帯 a breaker zone.

サイバー ▶サイバー空間 cyberspace. サイバー攻撃 a cyber attack. サイバー・コート〔別々の場所にいる関係者をコンピューターネットワークで結んで行う裁判〕a cyber court. ▶構想段階の裁判形式. サイバーストーカー a cyberstalker. ▷ cyberstalking をする. サイバー戦争, サイバーウォー a cyberwar. サイバー大学〔講義をインターネット上で行う大学〕a cyber university. サイバーナイフ〔商標・医〕a Cyber-Knife. サイバー・パトロール〔警察などによるネット上の違法情報の監視〕cyber patrol. サイバー反体制派 a cyberdissident.

さいばい【栽培】▶人工栽培 artificial cultivation 《of edible mushrooms》. ▶栽培キット a 《mushroom》 growing kit. 栽培農家 a cropping farm; a 《tomato-》 growing farm. 栽培面積 the area of (the) land under cultivation 《with tomatoes》.

さいはいたつ【再配達】〔郵便物などの〕redelivery. ～する redeliver; deliver again.

さいはつ【再発】▶局所再発〔医〕〔がんの〕(a) local recurrence. 転移性再発〔医〕〔がんの〕(a) metastatic recurrence. [＝遠隔転移 《⇒てんい6》] 再発防止 recurrence prevention;〔病気の〕relapse prevention. 再発防止策 recurrence prevention measures; measures to keep 《an accident》 from「occurring [happening] again;〔病気の〕antirelapse「measures [treatment, therapy]. 再発抑制療法〔医〕suppressive therapy for recurrent 《genital herpes》.

サイババ Sathya Sai Baba (1926- ;世界中に信奉者を持つインドの宗教指導者).

さいはん1【再犯】▶再犯防止 prevention of「reoffending [repeat offending, reoffense]. ○性犯罪受刑者の～防止策を講じる work out [devise] a method of preventing repeat offenses by sex offenders.

さいばん1【裁判】▶裁判心理学 forensic psychology. さいばんいんほう【裁判員法】〔法〕the Lay Judge Law.

さいばんがいふんそうかいけつ【裁判外紛争解決】〔処理〕〔法〕(an) alternative dispute resolution 《略: ADR》. ▶裁判外紛争解決手続 alternative dispute resolution 《ADR》 procedures; the ADR process.

さいばんじんそくほう【裁判迅速化法】〔法〕the Law for the Expediting of Trials; the Speedy Trial Law.

さいひょうか【再評価】▶再評価率〔年金支給額の算定に用いる〕a reassessment rate.

さいふ【財布】▶(お)財布機能〔携帯電話などの〕a「wallet [payment] function.

ざいぶつ【財物】▶財物犯〔法〕(a) property crime;〔人〕the perpetrator of a property crime.

さいぶんぱい【再分配】▶所得再分配〔経〕redistribution of income; income redistribution. ○所得～調査 an income redistribution survey. ▶再分配所得〔経〕redistributed income.

サイペック【CIPEC】〔子供の事故予防工学カウンシル〕CIPEC; the Childhood Injury Prevention Engineering Council.

さいへん2【再編】▶米軍再編 the [a] reorganization of the US military. 米軍基地再編 the reorganization of US military bases. ○在日米軍基地～問題 the「issue [question] of the reorganization of US military bases in Japan. ▶再編淘汰〔企業などの〕restructuring and weeding out 《in the steel industry》; a shake-out and reorganization 《in retailing》.

**さいほ**【再捕】〔放流した稚魚などの成長後の捕獲〕catching adult fish, etc. which have been released after being caught when young; 〔標識を付けて放した鳥獣・魚類・昆虫などの再捕獲〕recapture of a tagged 《bird》. ▶ 再捕率〔放流魚などの〕the recapture rate of adult fish which have matured from released fry; 〔標識を付けて放した鳥獣・魚類・昆虫などの〕the recapture rate of tagged 《turtles》.

**さいぼう**【細胞】▶ 細胞イメージング〔医〕cell [cellular, intracellular] imaging. 細胞外液 extracellular fluid. 細胞外マトリックス〔生物〕an extracellular matrix（略: ECM）. 細胞間脂質〔医〕an intercellular lipid. 細胞凝集 cell agglutination. 細胞シート〔医〕〔再生医療に用いられる〕a cell sheet; a sheet of cells. ◎ ～シート工学 cell-sheet engineering. 細胞接着分子〔生理〕a cell adhesion molecule. 細胞操作 cell manipulation. 細胞増殖 cell proliferation. ◎ ～増殖因子 (a) cell growth factor. 細胞増殖阻害剤〔薬〕〔がん治療の〕a cell proliferation inhibitor. 細胞治療 cell therapy. 細胞内液 intracellular fluid. 細胞内共生説〔生物〕〔ミトコンドリアなどの〕the antisemitic theory. 細胞内脂質〔医〕an intracellular lipid.

**さいほうえい**【再放映】rebroadcasting; a「rerun [rebroadcast]《of a program》. ～する rerun [rebroadcast]《a movie》; do a rerun. ▶ 再放映権 = 再放送権（⇨さいほうそう）.

**さいほうそう**【再放送】▶ 再放送権 rebroadcast(ing) [rerun] rights. 再放送料 a「rebroadcasting [rerun] fee.

**さいほうもんりつ**【再訪問率】【電算】〔ウェブサイトへの〕a visitor retention rate; a 《high》revisit rate.

「**サイボーグ危機一髪!!**」 ⇨「600 万ドルの男」.

**さいまつ**[2]【歳末】▶ 歳末助け合い募金 year-end fund-raising for charity.

**さいみん**[2]【催眠】▶ 催眠鎮静剤〔薬〕〔薬〕a sedative-hypnotic drug.

**さいむ**【債務】▶ 借入債務 a debt. 後発債務〔運用環境などの想定外の悪化によって生じる債務〕subsequent liabilities. ▶ 債務担保証券〔証券〕a collateralized debt obligation（略: CDO）. ◎ 合成～担保証券 a synthetic CDO. 債務帳消し writing off [canceling] a debt; (a) debt「cancellation [write-off]; debt relief. 債務不存在確認 confirmation of the「nonexistence [absence] of (a) debt. 債務不履行リスク a default risk. 債務保証損失引当金 a reserve [an allowance, a provision] for loss on guarantees. 債務免除益〔債権放棄を受けて生じる帳簿上の利益〕(a) gain on debt forgiveness.

**ざいむ**【財務】▶ 財務基盤 a 《solid》financial basis. ◎ ～基盤を強化[確立]する strengthen [establish]《a company's》financial footing. 財務原案 a budget draft prepared by the Ministry of Finance. 財務コンサルタント[アドバイザー] a financial「consultant [advisor]. 財務体力 《a company's》financial strength. 財務内容《assess, analyze》the financial condition《of a company》. 財務リストラ financial restructuring. 財務レバレッジ financial leverage.

**ざいむかいけいじゅんしんぎかい**【財務会計基準審議会】〔米国の〕the Financial Accounting Standards Board（略: FASB）.

**さいむしゃ**【債務者】▶ 主債務者 a [the] main debtor; a [the] principal obligor.

**ざいむしょう**[2]【財務省】▶ 財務省証券〔米国の〕a treasury「bond [bill, note].

「**サイモン・ヴィーゼンタール・センター**」〔米国ロサンジェルスに本部を置くユダヤ人人権擁護団体〕the Simon Wiesenthal Center（略: SWC）.

**サイモントンりょうほう**【-療法】〔医〕〔がんの心理療法〕the Simonton method (of cancer therapy).

「**サイモン・バーチ**」〔映画〕Simon Birch.

**さいゆう**[3]【彩釉】a colored overglaze. ▶ 彩釉磁器 colored overglazed porcelain.

**さいゆうしゅう**【最優秀】▶ 最優秀歌唱賞 a best「singer [singing] award.

**さいゆうせん**【最優先】▶ 最優先課題 a question of the highest priority; a top-priority issue.

**さいよう**[1]【採用】▶ 採用選考 screening (of candidates) for employment. 採用取り消し cancellation of a hiring agreement; cancellation of a job offer. 採用銘柄〔証券〕〔各種の平均株価算出のための〕representative stocks. ◎ 日経平均～銘柄 the NIKKEI-225. 採用面接 a job interview.

**ざいらい**【在来】▶ 在来工法〔建〕the [a] traditional method of construction.

**さいらん**【採卵】▶ 採卵農家 an egg farmer. 採卵日 a laying date.

**ザイリアン** Zaillian, Steven (1953- ; 米国の映画監督・脚本家).

**サイリウム**〔化〕〔食物繊維の 1 つ〕psyllium.

**ざいりゅう**【在留】▶ 在留証明書 a「residence [residential] certificate.

**さいりょう**[4]【裁量】▶ 裁量行政 discretionary administration.

**ざいりょう**【材料】▶ 株価材料 a stock price factor; a factor affecting stock prices. 下支え材料〔相場・景気などの〕a supporting [an underpinning] factor. 新規材料〔株式〕a new「element [factor]. 説得材料 an argument; a persuasive argument; (the) means to persuade sb;《文》artillery. ◎ 強硬派への説得～が乏しく、ストライキ中止は困難な状況だ. Few arguments are available to「dissuade the hard-liners [bring the hard core around], so it's doubtful that the strike can be called off. 発奮材料 sth that「rouses one [spurs one on] to「work [try, fight] harder; a spur to action. ◎ 前回あのチームに負けたことが発奮～になって猛練習を重ね、今度は勝つことができた. Losing to that team in the last game spurred us on to do a lot of hard training, and this time we managed to win. ▶ 材料工学 material(s) engineering.

**さいりょうてきししゅつ**【裁量的支出】discretionary spending.

**サイレース**〔商標・薬〕〔催眠鎮静剤・抗不安剤; 日本の商品〕Silece. ▶ 一般名はフルニトラゼパム（flunitrazepam）.

**さいわ**【再話】(a) retelling. ～する retell. ◎ 谷崎氏の～による日本昔話 old tales of Japan (as) retold by Mr. Tanizaki.

「**ザ・インターネット**」〔映画〕The Net.

**サヴァンしょうこうぐん**【-症候群】〔医〕〔知能程度は低いが、ある一点に関してのみ突出した能力をもつ症状〕savant syndrome.

**サウジ・アラムコ**〔サウジの国営石油会社〕Saudi Aramco.

**サウス・チャイナ・モーニング・ポスト**〔香港の英字新聞〕The South China Morning Post（略: SCMP）.

**サウゼドゥルクス**〔イタリア北西部、ピエモンテ州の町〕Sauze d'Oulx.

**サウラ** Saura, Carlos (1932- ; スペインの映画監督・脚本家).

**サウロパス・アンドロジナス**〔植〕= あまめしば.

**サウンドデモ**〔大音量の音楽に合わせて踊りながら練り歩くデモ行進〕a street protest featuring dancing to loud music; a "sound demo."

「**ザ・エージェント**」〔映画〕Jerry Maguire.

**サエレト・マトカル**〔イスラエル軍の精鋭特殊部隊〕the Sayeret Matkal.

**さえん**[2]【差延】〔哲〕différance. ▶ デリダの造語.

さおだけ【竿竹】 ▷ 竿竹売り, 竿竹屋 a (bamboo) pole seller.
サカ Saca, Elías Antonio (1965– ; エルサルバドルの政治家; 大統領〔2004– 〕; 通称 Tony Saca).
サカーカ ＝サカカ.
ザ・ガーン〔オーストラリア南部のアデレードと中部のアリス・スプリングス間を走る列車〕the Ghan.
サカカ〔サウジアラビア北部, アルジャウフ州の州都〕Sakakah.
ざがく【座学】desk work; desk study.
さかしお[2]【逆潮】a reverse「tide [current].
さかしょう【酒匠】a licensed sake taster.
さかずき【杯】 ▷ 杯細胞〔解〕a goblet cell.
サカテカス〔メキシコ中部の州・その州都〕Zacatecas.
さかのぼりろくおん【さかのぼり録音】〔専用ボタンを押した時点からさかのぼって録音する機能〕retroactive recording 《device》.
さかばりこうほう【逆梁工法】〔建〕＝ぎゃくばりこうほう.
さかまい【酒米】rice for (brewing) sake; sake rice.
さかみち【坂道】 ▷ 坂道ダッシュ〔トレーニングで〕sprinting up a slope (to strengthen one's legs).
さがみトラフ【相模─】〔地質〕the Sagami Trough.
さがらぶ【相良布】〔植〕〔褐藻類コンブ科の海藻〕a southern sea palm; Eisenia arborea.
さがりかべ【下がり壁】〔建〕a suspended wall.
ザカルパチア〔ウクライナ西部の州〕Zakarpattya.
サガルマータ〔エヴェレスト山のネパール語名〕Sagarmatha.
サガルマータこくりつこうえん【─国立公園】〔ネパールの, エヴェレスト山がある国立公園〕Sagarmatha National Park.
ザガワぞく【─族】〔スーダンの1部族〕the Zagawa;〔1人〕a Zagawa. 《pl. ～, ～s》.
ザ・ガン ＝ザ・ガーン.
さぎ[2]【詐欺】 ▷ 詐欺商法 a fraudulent business practice;《口》a scam (operation). 詐偽登録 ＝不正登録 (⇒とうろく[2]). 詐欺メール (a)「scam [fraudulent] (e-) mail; (a) phish(ing) mail.
さきおくり【先送り】 ▷ 決裁先送り postponing [putting off, delaying] settling a matter; postponing [putting off, delaying] a decision; putting things off. 先送り決裁 settling a matter for the time being by putting it off; postponing settling an issue.
さきおり【裂織】cloth woven from heavy threads in the warp and strips of old cloth in the woof; sakiori.
さきゆき【先行き】 ▷ 先行き懸念〔景気〕concern [anxiety] about future prospects.
サキュレント〔植〕〔多肉植物〕a succulent (plant).
さぎょう[1]【作業】 ▷ 作業車 a「work [utility] vehicle. 作業船〔浚渫(しゅんせつ)・海底油田掘削などのための〕a workboat. 作業チーム a working group. 作業要員 (the) personnel [workers, workforce] necessary [required] for 《a job》.
さぎょうけん【作業犬】〔警察犬・盲導犬などのほか麻薬探知・災害救助等の活動に従事する犬〕a working dog.
さきわたし【先渡し】 ▷ 先渡し取引 a forward trade; forward trading.
さくあがり【作上がり】〔園芸〕increased「flowering [fruiting].
さくい[1]【作為】 ▷ 作為義務〔法〕〔特定の行為が法によって強制されている場合に人が負う義務〕a duty of commission; an obligation.
さくおち【作落ち】〔園芸〕diminished「flowering [fruiting].  ～する show diminished「flowering [fruiting]. ▷ チューリップは球根を植え替えないと翌年～する. If tulip bulbs are not replanted, flower production falls off (in the following year).
さくげん【削減】 ▷ 削減幅 a「reduction [shrinkage, cut-off] (rate) 《of 4.2%》.
さくこう【索溝】〔ひも状のもので頸部が絞められた場合に生じる溝状の陥没〕a strangulation groove.
さくこん【索痕】〔ひも状のものの圧迫・擦過等によって生じた表皮剝脱など〕a「ligature [strangulation] mark. [＝索条痕 (⇒さくじょう[2])]
さくさん[2]【酢酸】 ▷ 酢酸ウラニル uranyl acetate. 酢酸ゴセレリン【薬】〔乳がん治療薬〕goserelin acetate. 酢酸リュープロレリン【薬】〔がん治療薬〕leuprorelin acetate.
さくじょう[2]【索条】 ▷ 索条痕〔縊死・絞死の〕a strangulation mark. ◆遺体の頸部には一痕が認められた. The body had strangulation marks around the neck.
さくせん[1]【作戦】 ▷ 作戦空間〔軍〕an operational area. 作戦統制権〔軍〕operational control. ◆戦時～統制権 wartime operational control.
さくっと〔手早く; 短時間で〕quickly; snappily; with alacrity. ◆この仕事は～済ませちゃいましょうよ. Let's snap to it and finish the job quickly.
さくてい[2]【削蹄】hoof trimming. ▷ 牛削蹄師 a cattle hoof trimmer.
さくひん【作品】 ▷ 作品番号 a work number;〔音楽〕an opus 《pl. ～es, opera》《略: op.》. ◆ソナタ第10番ト長調―番号96 Sonata No. 10 in G major,「Opus [Op.] 96.
さくほう[2]【冊封】〔皇帝の命令によって封爵を授けること〕investiture (by the Chinese court) as a tributary (state). ▷ 冊封関係《東洋史》〔中国周辺諸国の支配者が中国王朝に臣従する代わりに支配権を認知してもらう関係〕recognition 《of a sovereign by Imperial China》 under the tributary system; relations of peripheral countries with (Imperial) China (under a seal of investiture). 冊封体制 the tributary (states) system (in Imperial China); the system under which sovereigns of peripheral states were recognized《by Imperial China》under a seal of investiture.
さくもん【作問】〔問題作成〕the creation of exam questions. ◆入試の～を委嘱される be commissioned to create exam questions.
さくゆ【搾油】 ▷ 搾油(効)率 an oil (extraction) yield; an oil extraction rate.
さくら【桜】 ▷ 桜茶 cherry-blossom [sakura] tea.
さくらんぼ【桜ん坊】 ▷ さくらんぼ狩り cherry picking.
さぐりばし【探り箸】〔汁物の椀を箸でかき回して中身を探ること〕searching around in soup with one's chopsticks.
さけ[2]【鮭】 ▷ 鮭とば, 鮭冬葉〔うす塩の鮭の切り身を熟成乾燥したもの〕salmon jerky; (strips of) cured salmon.
サゲーウ ＝サ・ケ(─)オ.
サ・ケ(─)オ〔タイ中部の県; その県都〕Sa Kaeo [Sakaeo]; Sa Kaew [Sakaew]; Sa Keo [Sakeo].
さけがしら【鮭頭】〔魚〕〔フリソデウオ科の深海魚〕Trachipterus ishikawae.
さげどまり【下げ止まり】(a) bottoming out;《reach》a floor;《hit》rock bottom. ◆東京圏や名古屋圏の地価は～傾向にあるが, 大阪圏では～感はまだまだ薄い. Land prices in the Tokyo and Nagoya areas are「bottoming out [reaching a floor], but in the Osaka area there is little sign that they have hit rock bottom yet. / 景気は～状態にあり, 鉱工業生産など一部の指標には明るさが見られる. The economic decline has stopped [economy has halted its slide], and positive signs can be seen in some indicators, including mining and industrial production.
ざこう【座高】 ▷ 座高計 a sitting-height measuring device; a seated stadiometer.
ザコパネ〔ポーランド南部の市〕Zakopane.
サコン・ナコ(─)ン〔タイ東北部の県; 同県の県都〕Sakon Nakhon.
サザーランド Sutherland, Kiefer (1966– ; 英国生まれの映画俳優;〔ドナルド・サザーランドの子〕.
ささつ【査察】 ▷ 強制査察 (a) compulsory inspection; a compulsory search. ▷ 査察飛行〔領空の〕an

inspection flight; 〔パイロットの能力検査のための〕a flying test; a pilot flight test; a test for pilot competence.
ささなり【笹鳴り】a 〔the〕rustle of bamboo leaves in a gentle breeze.
ササラでんしゃ【簓電車・-電車】〔除雪用の路面電車〕a streetcar with rotary (bamboo) snow broom attached.
サザンウッド【植】〔キク科の多年草；南欧原産〕a southernwood; *Artemisia abrotanum*.
さしあぶら【差し油】〖料理〗replenishing deep-fry oil; 〔その油〕replenished deep-fry oil; cooking oil added to replace that absorbed by fried foods.
さしいろ【差し色】〔インテリアやファッションなどで、アクセントとして地色に添える目立つ色〕a highlight color; color highlights.
さじき【桟敷】◧ 桟敷席 a box seat.
ざしき【座敷】◧ 座敷料〔日本料理屋の使用料〕a (tatami) room「charge [fee]; the「charge [fee] for a reserved (tatami) room (at a traditional Japanese restaurant).
さしきりがち【差し切り勝ち】〖競馬〗coming from behind to win (at the end of a race); pipping 《another horse》 at the post.
さしこむ【差し込む】
4 〖野球〗 ◯ 差し込まれる〔打者が速球などに〕get jammed 《by a fastball》◯ 打者は内角の直球に差し込まれ、ほてゴロを打った．The hitter got jammed by a fastball over the inside corner and hit a slow grounder.
さしちがえ[1]【刺し違え】stabbing each other (to death); dying on each other's swords.
さしとめ【差し止め】 ◧ 工事差し止め an order to stop construction; a construction ban. ◯ 工事〜処分 a「provisional disposition [temporary restraining order] against construction．事前差し止め〔出版の〕a prior ban (on publication).
さしばし[1]【刺し箸】〔料理に箸を突き刺して食べること〕(eating by) sticking one's chopsticks into food.
さしばし[2]【指し箸】〔箸で人や物を指し示すこと〕(a breach of etiquette consisting of) pointing 《at *sb*》 with one's chopsticks.
さしもどし【差し戻し】◧ 差し戻し控訴審 a trial of a case「sent [referred] back from the Supreme Court.
さしょう[3]【査証】◧ 査証免除 ＝ビザ免除 〔⇨ビザ〕．
さしょう【詐称】◧ 経歴〔履歴〕詐称 a false statement of one's (past)「career [record]; falsification [misrepresentation] of one's personal history.
さしりょう【差料】a *sashiryō* (sword); a (samurai's) belted sword. ◯ これは坂本龍馬の〜だ．This is「Sakamoto Ryōma's sword [the sword Sakamoto Ryōma wore at his belt].
さしんていけいせいしょうこうぐん【左心低形成症候群】〖医〗hypoplastic left heart syndrome (略: HLHS).
「ザスーラ」〔映画〕Zathura: A Space Adventure.
さずかりごん【授かり婚】a「wedding [marriage] with「the bride (already) pregnant [a baby on the way]; a「wedding [marriage] where the bride is (already) pregnant; an enforced [a hurried] wedding [marriage] (because a baby is on the way).
サスツルギ〖< Russ *zastrugi*〗〔南極などで、強風によって形成された硬い雪面のうねり〕a sastruga 《*pl.* sastrugi》; a zastruga 《*pl.* zastrugi》.
サステナビリティー〔持続可能性〕sustainability.
ざする【座する】
座して doing nothing; taking no action; (just) sitting (here); sitting on one's hands．◯ 座して食う live a life of idleness〔座して死を待つより打って出たほうがよい．Let's go out and meet them; it's [it would be] better than just sitting「here [on our hands] waiting to die．◯ 座して食らえば山も空し．Idleness will eat away a mountain of wealth.

ざせき【座席】◧ ◯ 座席間隔〔前後の〕＝シート・ピッチ 〔⇨シート[2]〕．座席決め ＝せきぎめ．
ざせん【左折】◧ 左折車線〔レーン〕a left-lane.
ざぜん【座禅・坐禅】◧ 座禅会 a collective Zen session.
「ザ・ダイバー」〔映画〕Men of Honor.
「サタデー・ナイト・ライブ」〔米国の、生放送の音楽バラエティー TV 番組〕Saturday Night Live.
さつえい【撮影】◧ 撮影現場〔映画などの〕a「movie [filming] location; 〔撮影所内の〕a (movie, film) set．撮影隊 a「camera [film] crew．撮影ポイント〔スポット〕〔撮影するのに適した場所〕a scenic「spot [location] for photographs; a photogenic「spot [location].
ざつおん【雑音】◧ 低〔高〕雑音 low [high] noise. ◯ 低-増幅器〔アンプ〕 a low-noise amplifier (略: LNA).
ざっか【雑貨】◧ 雑貨デザイナー a household goods designer.
サッカー[1] ◧ サッカー学校 a soccer (training) school．サッカー(競技)場 a soccer field; 〔観覧席がある〕a soccer stadium．サッカー大国 a「major [leading] soccer nation; a soccer giant.
ザッカー 1 Zucker, David (1947- ; 米国の映画監督・脚本家・製作者; 2 の兄).
2 Zucker, Jerry (1950- ; 米国の映画監督・脚本家・製作者; 1 の弟).
さっかこん【擦過痕】〖医〗an abrasion scar.
さつかん【札勘】〔金融機関などで手作業で紙幣を数える方法〕(manual) banknote counting.
さっき[4]【削器】〖考古〗a scraper.
ざっき[2]【雑器】〔道具〕miscellaneous utensils; 〔うつわもの〕miscellaneous「bowls and dishes [chinaware]. ◧ 生活雑器 (everyday) household utensils; ordinary [everyday] tableware.
さっきん【殺菌】◧ 加熱殺菌 heat sterilization. ◯ 殺菌効果 a「disinfectant [disinfection] effect. ◯ アルコール製剤のほうが石鹸をつかった手洗いより〜効果が高い．An alcohol-based hand rub「is more effective than soap as a disinfectant [disinfects the hands more effectively than soap].
サックス・フィフス・アベニュー〔米国ニューヨーク市にある高級デパート〕Saks Fifth Avenue (略: SFA).
ざっこたい【雑固体】〔原子力発電所から出る種々の固体廃棄物〕miscellaneous solid (radioactive) waste.
サッサー〔コンピューターウイルスの 1 つ〕Sasser.
さつしょぶん【殺処分】〔動物の〕slaughter(ing); euthanasia.
〜する〔家畜を〕slaughter; destroy; 〔ペットなどを〕euthanize; 《口》put down; put to sleep.
さっしん【刷新】◧ 経営刷新〔経営陣の交代による〕a management「reorganization [shake-up]; 〔経営方針の転換による〕a new management approach. ◯ 刷新可能性調査 an innovation feasibility study.
さつじん[1]【殺人】◧ 間接殺人 (an) indirect murder. ◯ 殺人ウイルス a killer virus．殺人請負サイト〔インターネット上の〕a contract murder (Web) site．殺人教唆 incitement to murder．殺人サイト〔インターネット上の〕a murder (Web) site．殺人幇助〈ホウジョ〉〖法〗⇨さつじんほうじょ．
さつじんほうじょ【殺人幇助】〖法〗aiding and abetting (a) murder; being an accessory to (a) murder. ◧ 殺人幇助罪 the crime of aiding and abetting (a) murder.
さっそう[2]【擦奏】rubbing; scraping; playing.
〜する play 《a musical saw》; rub [scrape] 《a gourd》. ◧ 擦奏楽器 a「friction [rubbed, scraped] (musical) instrument; a friction idiophone.
さつぞう【撮像】imaging.
〜する image 《a molecule, the surface of Pluto》. ◧ 撮像装置 an imaging device; imaging equipment．撮

像素子【電子工学】an image sensor; an image sensing device.
さつたば【札束】▷ 札束外交〔金に物を言わせる強引な外交〕checkbook diplomacy.
ざっとう【雑踏】▷ 雑踏警備 crowd control.
サットン・フー〔イングランドの遺跡〕Sutton Hoo. ▷ サットン・フーの兜〔考古〕the Sutton Hoo helmet.
ザッパ Zappa, Frank (1940-93; 米国のロックミュージシャン).
さっぱん【刷版】〖印刷〗〔印刷機に直接取り付けて印刷を行う版〕a printing plate.
サッポロようウイルス【-様-】〖医〗(a) sapporo-like virus (略: SLV). ▶ 現在は サポウイルス が正式名.
ざつみ【雑味】〔ワインの味や香りの濁りやしつこさ〕an odd [a strange] taste [flavor].
さつもん【擦文】▷ 擦文(式)土器 Satsumon「ware [pottery]; scratch-pattern pottery. 擦文時代 the Satsumon period. 擦文文化 (the) Satsumon culture.
さつりょう【刷了】〖印刷〗〔印刷作業の終了〕the end of printing; the completion of a printing job.
さてい【査定】▷ 給与査定 (a) performance-based」salary assessment. 減額査定 (a) downward assessment ((of value)); (a) recommendation of ((a lower salary)). ▷ 査定昇進 a「salary [pay] raise [「rise」] by assessment; a performance-based pay「raise [「rise」]. ◐ わが社は来年度より勤務実績に基づく～昇給を導入する. From next (fiscal) year our company is introducing a pay raise system based on work performance. 査定資料 assessment「documentation [materials]; material evidence for (an) assessment ((of salary)).
サテライト ▷ サテライト会場〔本会場に対して〕a satellite venue.
サテライト・デイ(サービス) =逆デイ・サービス (⇨デイ・サービス).
サデラトぎんこう【-銀行】〔イランの国営銀行〕Bank Saderat (Iran) (略: BSI).
サドい sadistic; hard on others.
サドゥー〔ヒンズー教〕〔行者〕a sadhu; a saddhu.
サトゥ(ーン)〔タイ南部の県、その県都〕Satun.
さとおや【里親】▷ 里親登録 foster parent registration. ◐ ～登録する register ((oneself)) as a foster parent / ～登録者 a registered foster parent.
さとがえり【里帰り】〖印刷〗〔里帰り出産〕childbirth「after returning to [at] one's parents' home. ◐ ～出産をする return to one's parents' home to have a baby.
さとちさとやまほぜんさいせいモデルじぎょう【里地里山保全再生-事業】a model project for regenerating mountain villages and the woodland around them.
さどトキほごセンター【佐渡-保護-】the Sado Japanese Crested Ibis Conservation Center.
サドル[2] al-Sadr, Muqtada (1974?-  ; イスラム教シーア派の指導者の1人).
サドルシティー〔バグダッド北東部のシーア派居住地区〕Sadr City. ▶ 旧名は サダムシティー (Saddam City).
「ザ・トレンチ 塹壕」〔映画〕The Trench.
サナーデル Sanader, Ivo (1953-  ; クロアチアの政治家; 首相 ((2003-  )).
ザナミビル〖薬〗〔インフルエンザ用吸入薬〕zanamivir.
サナムルアン〔タイ, バンコクの王宮前広場〕Sanam Luang.
サノフィ・サンテラボ〔フランスの製薬会社〕Sanofi-Synthelabo.
さば【鯖】▷ サバ寿司 (pickled, marinated) mackerel sushi. ◐ 焼き～寿司 baked [grilled] mackerel sushi.
サバイバー〔生存者〕a survivor. ▷ サバイバーズ・ギルト〔精神医〕〔事故や災害を生き延びた人が抱く罪悪感〕survivor's guilt.
サバイバル ▷ サバイバルウォーク〔自然災害時の交通網寸断に備えた, 徒歩による帰宅訓練〕a disaster [an earthquake] survival walk; a walk home from「work

[school] without using public transportation as a disaster drill.
サバイビン【生化】survivin.
-さばき【-捌き】▷ 箸捌き one's「use [handling] of chopsticks; the way one uses chopsticks. ◐ 彼は箸～がへたで豆粒をはさめない. He's too clumsy with chopsticks to pick up beans one by one. ボール[球]捌き ball control. ◐〔サッカーで〕観客の視線は彼の華麗なボール～に釘付けだった. The spectators were transfixed by「his sparkling ball control [the brilliant way he controlled the ball].
さばく[2]【砂漠】▷ 砂漠の船〔ラクダのこと〕the ship of the desert. ◐ ラクダは～の船と呼ばれる. The camel is called the "ship of the desert."
「砂漠鬼部隊」⇨「ラット・パトロール」.
サパテロ Zapatero, Jóse Luis Rodríguez (1960-  ; スペインの政治家; 首相 ((2004-  )).
「サハラ 死の砂漠を脱出せよ」〔映画〕Sahara.
「サハラに舞う羽根」〔映画〕The Four Feathers.
さはり【響銅・砂張・佐波里】〔銅・鉛などとの合金〕sahari (alloy); a copper alloy; an alloy of copper with a little tin (and small amounts of lead, zinc and silver).
「ザ・ハリケーン」〔映画〕The Hurricane.
サバンしょうこうぐん【サバン症候群】〖医〗=サヴァンしょうこうぐん.
サバンナ・ダイカー〖動〗〔アフリカ産レイヨウの一種〕a common duiker; Sylvicapra grimmia.
サバンナ・モンキー〖動〗〔オナガザル科のサル〕a vervet (monkey); an African green monkey; Cercopithecus aethiops.
さび[4] ▷ さび頭(がしら)〔音楽〕〔サビを頭にもってくる曲づくり〕beginning a song with the catchy part.
「ザ・ビーチ」〔映画〕The Beach.
さびきん【銹菌】〖植〗〔さび病を起こす担子菌〕rust; a rust fungus.
さびくぎ【錆釘】a rusty nail. ◐ 黒豆を煮るときに～を入れると色よく仕上がる. You'll get a nice color when boiling black soybeans if you add a rusty nail.
サブ ▷ サブ球場 a secondary stadium. サブグラ(ウ)ンド a subsidiary ground.
「ザ・ファーム/法律事務所」〔映画〕The Firm.
サファイア ▷ サファイア・ブルー〔色〕sapphire blue.
サフィリン【鉱】sapphirine.
ザブール〔アフガニスタン南部の州〕Zabul.
サブジ〔料理〕〔インド料理; 野菜の蒸し煮・炒め煮〕sabzi.
サブダ Sabuda, Robert (1965-  ; アメリカの絵本作家; "飛び出す絵本"の作家).
サブバッグ a「small [second] handbag.
サブプライム・ローン〔米国の低所得者向けローン〕a subprime loan.
サブマシンガン〔軽機関銃〕a submachine gun.
サブマリン ▷ サブマリン特許〔特許〕a submarine patent.
サブミリは【-波】〖電〗a submillimeter wave. ▷ サブミリ波望遠鏡〖天〗a submillimeter-wave telescope.
サプライ・サイド ▷ サプライサイド経済学〔エコノミックス〕〔供給側重視の経済理論〕supply-side economics.
サプライ・チェーン〔経〕〔供給連鎖〕a supply chain.
サブラタ〔リビア北西部の古代都市〕Sabratha.
サフラン ▷ サフラン・ライス saffron rice.
サブリース〔転貸〕a sublease. ▷ サブリース契約 a sublease contract.
サフルランド〔氷河時代に東南アジアからミクロネシアにかけて存在した広大な陸地〕Sahulland.
「サベイランス-監視-」〔映画〕Antitrust.
ザヘダン〔イラン南東部, シスターン・バルチスタン州の州都〕Zahedan.
さべつ【差別】▷ 差別(的)表現 a discriminatory expression; 〔人種差別の〕a racist expression; 〔性差別の〕

a sexist expression. 差別犯罪 (a) hate crime; illegal [criminal] discrimination; (a) discrimination「crime [offense].
**サヘラントロプス・チャデンシス**〖人類〗〔アフリカ, チャドで発見された猿人化石〕Sahelanthropus tchadensis. ▶ 愛称は, 現地語で「トゥーマイ」(Toumai).
**サボイ・キャベツ**〖植〗〔アブラナ科の1-2年草; ヨーロッパ原産の野菜〕a savoy (cabbage); Brassica oleracea var. sabauda.
**さぼう**[1]【砂防】 ▫ 砂防学 erosion control engineering.
**サボウイルス**【医】〔冬季, 嘔吐下痢症の原因となるウイルス〕(a) sapovirus (略: SaV). ▶ 以前はサッポロ様ウイルス と呼ばれていた.
**サポート** ▫ サポート業務 support services. ◎ 彼は1年間, 人材派遣会社から当社に派遣されて, コンピューターシステムの〜業務をおこなった. He was assigned to our company by a temp agency for one year and「provided support services [did support] for our computer systems.
**サボン** Savon, Felix (1967- ;キューバのボクサー).
**「サマー・オブ・サム」**〔映画〕Summer of Sam.
**サマーワ**〔イラク南部の都市〕=サマワ.
**サマワ**〔イラク南部の都市〕Samawa(h).
**サマンサ**〔「奥様は魔女」の登場人物〕Samantha Stevens.
**さみどり**【早緑】〔若草や若葉の緑色〕(a) fresh green.
**サムイとう**【-島】〔タイ南部の島〕Samui Island.
**サムサコ(ー)ン** =サムット・サ(ー)コ(ー)ン.
**サムスン**【三星】〔韓国の企業グループ〕Samsung.
**サムソンクラム** =サムット・ソンクラ(ー)ム.
**サムターン**〔ドア内側の鍵を開閉するつまみ〕a thumbturn. ▫ サムターン回し 〔不正開錠の手口〕opening [forcing open] a thumbturn (from the other side of the door).
**サムチョク**【三陟】〔韓国東海岸, 江原道の都市〕Samch(e)ok.
**サムット・サ(ー)コ(ー)ン**〔タイ中部の県; その郡都〕Samut Sakhon.
**サムット・ソンクラ(ー)ム**〔タイ中部の県; その郡都〕Samut Songkhram.
**サムット・プラ(ー)カ(ー)ン**〔タイ中部の県; その郡都〕Samut Prakan.
**サムプラカーン** =サムット・プラ(ー)カ(ー)ン.
**さむらい**【侍】 ▫ サムライ映画 a samurai「movie [film].
**サムラオン**〔カンボジア北部, ウドンメンチェイ州の州都〕Samraong.
**サム・ランシーとう**【-党】〔カンボジアの政党〕the Sam Rainsy Party (略: SRP).
**サムロー**〔タイなどの三輪タクシー〕a samlor.
**「ザ・メキシカン」**〔映画〕The Mexican.
**ざめつ**【挫滅】【医】a crushing injury; crushing. ▫ 全身挫滅 (a) crushing of the whole body; total (body) crushing. 脳挫滅 crushing of the brain. ▫ 挫滅損傷, 挫滅創 a crush injury.
**さめはだ**【鮫肌】 ▫ 鮫肌水着〔水の抵抗を減らすために鮫肌を模した競技用水着〕sharkskin swimwear.
**サモサ**〖料理〗〔インド料理; 春巻きに似た三角形の揚げ物〕a samosa.
**サモ・ハン・キンポー** Sammo Hung Kam-bo (1952- ;香港の映画俳優; 中国語名 洪金寶).
**さもん**[2]【砂紋】ripple marks; a wavy pattern;〔枯れ山水の〕a raked pattern (of sand [gravel]). ◎〔石庭に〕〜を描く [引く] rake wavy patterns (in「sand [gravel]).
**「ザ・モンキーズ」**〔米国のアイドルポップスグループによるTVコメディー〕The Monkees.
**さや**[2]【鞘】 ▫ 鞘尻 the tip of a sheath; the point of a scabbard; a chape.
**さゆう**【左右】 ▫ 左右打ち〖野球〗=りょううち. 左右反転印刷【印刷】reverse printing.
**「SAYURI」**〔映画〕Memoirs of a Geisha. ▶ 原作は米国作家アーサー・ゴールデン (Arthur Golden) 作の小説 Memoirs of a Geisha (邦題『さゆり』).
**さよう**[1]【作用】 ▫ 作用型 ▫ 短時間[長時間]〜型の薬剤 a「short-term [long-term] effective (type of) drug.
**さようなら, さよなら** ▫ さよなら満塁ホームラン〖野球〗a walk-off grand slam.
**サラーハッディーン** =サラハ(ッ)ディン.
**ザライ**〔ベトナム中央高地の省〕Gia Lai.
**サラウンド** ▫ 5.1ch〔チャンネル〕サラウンド 5.1-surround. ▫ サラウンド音声 surround sound. ◎ 臨場感のある〜音声が楽しめるホームシアター a home theater system that enables you to enjoy surround sound in a realistic ambience. サラウンド・ステレオ surround stereo [sound]. サラウンド(ステレオ)放送 surround(-sound) broadcasting;〔1回の放送〕a surround(-sound) broadcast.
**サラきん**【-金】 ▫ サラ金地獄 loan-shark hell; the plight of people in debt to loan sharks.
**さらさうつぎ**【更紗空木】〖植〗〔ユキノシタ科の落葉低木〕Deutzia crenata.
**サラソタ**〔米国フロリダ州西部の都市〕Sarasota. ▷ Sarasotan adj., n.
**ざらっと** 〜した音色(ね) a「rough [rasping, grating] tone. 〜する手ざわり a「rough [coarse, grainy] feel.
**サラハ(ッ)ディン**〔イラク中北部の州〕Salah ad-Din. ▶ 州都 ティクリート.
**サラフ(ッ)ディン**〔イラクの州名サラハ(ッ)ディンの異形〕Salahuddin.
**サラブリ**〔タイ中部の県; その郡都〕Saraburi.
**サラマンカせんげん**【-宣言】〔1994年に国連が出した, スペシャルニーズ教育に関する宣言〕the Salamanca Statement on Principles, Policy and Practice in Special Needs Education. ▶ サラマンカはスペシャルニーズ教育に関する世界会議が行われたスペインの地名.
**サラヤ・アル・ムジャヒディン**〔イラクの武装グループ〕the Saraya al-Mujahideen; the Mujahideen Brigades.
**ザランド**〔イラン南東部の都市〕Zarand.
**「サリエラ」**〔チェリーニ作の金細工〕Saliera.
**サリックス**〖植〗〔ヤナギ科の落葉低木〕(an) Elaeagnus willow; (a) hoary willow; (a) rosemary willow; (an) olive willow; Salix elaeagnos.
**サリプル**〔アフガニスタン北部の州〕Saripul.
**サリンひがいぼうしほう**【-被害防止法】【法】〔サリン等による人身被害の防止に関する法律の通称〕the Law on the Prevention of Personal Injury Caused by Sarin, etc.
**さる**[1]【申】 ▫ 申酉騒ぐ〔相場〕〔申年と酉年は変動が激しい, の意〕In the years of the Monkey and the Rooster, the market tends to be turbulent. 〔⇨たつみてんじょう〕
**ザルカウィ, ザルカウイ** al-Zarqawi, Abu Musab (1966- ;イスラム過激派の幹部).
**サルガド** Salgado, Sebastião (1944- ; ブラジルの報道写真家).
**サルコジ** Sarkozy, Nicolas (1955- ; フランスの政治家; 大統領 [2007- ]).
**サルファーフリー**〔ガソリン・軽油に含まれる硫黄分が10 ppm以下の〕sulfur-free (gasoline).
**サルマン・パク [パック]**〔イラク, バグダッド南郊の町〕Salman Pak.
**サルモネラ** ▫ サルモネラ属菌 bacteria of the salmonella group.
**サレハ** Saleh, Ali Abdullah (1942- ; イエメンの軍人・政治家; 大統領 [1978- ]).
**「ザ・ロイヤル・テネンバウムズ」**〔映画〕The Royal Tenenbaums.
**サロド**〖楽器〗〔インドの撥弦楽器〕a sarod.
**「ザ・ロック」**〔映画〕The Rock.
**サロッド**〖楽器〗=サロード.
**さわ**【沢】 ▫ 沢下り canyoning.
**ザワヒリ** (Al-)Zawahiri, Ayman (1951- ; エジプト生まれ

さわむらしょう

のイスラム過激派指導者).
**さわむらしょう**【沢村賞】〖野球〗〔プロ野球でそのシーズンの最優秀投手に与えられる賞〕a [the] Sawamura Award. ▶プロ野球草創期の名投手 沢村栄治 [1917-44] にちなむ.
**さんアール**【3R】=スリー・アール.
**さんアール・イニシアティブかくりょうかいぎ**【3R-閣僚会議】=スリー・アール・イニシアティブかくりょうかいぎ.
**サンアンジェロ**〖米国,テキサス州中西部の市〗San Angelo.
**さんいちせつ**【三一節】〔韓国の独立運動記念日;3月1日〕Independence Movement Day; Samil Jeol.
**さんいん**[2]【参院】 〇□ 参院先議 prior consideration by the House of Councillors.
**さんエル**【3L】〔3リットルの略〕3 l.; 3 lit.;〔物品のサイズが〕3 L.
**さんおうらん**【三黄卵】〔1つの卵に黄身が3つ入っているもの〕a triple-yolk(ed) egg.(⇨ふくおうらん, におうらん)
**さんか**[7]【参加】 〇□ 参加型学習 participatory learning. 参加費[料] an entry fee. ●～費[料]無料 no charge「to participate [for participation]; free admittance.
**さんか**[9]【産科】 〇□ 産科瘻孔=産科フィスチュラ(⇨フィスチュラ).
**さんか**[11]【酸化】 〇□ 酸化亜鉛薄膜 (a) zinc oxide thin film. 酸化インジウムスズ indium tin oxide (略: ITO). 酸化鉱 (an) oxide ore. 酸化触媒 an oxidation catalyst. 酸化ストレス〖医〗oxidative stress. 酸化熱 heat generated by oxidation. 酸化分解〖化〗oxidative decomposition. 酸化力 oxidizing power. ●抗～力 antioxidizing power.
**ザンガーいいんかい**【-委員会】〔核不拡散条約に基づき核物質・設備・資材の範囲を協議する核保有国の会議〕the Zangger Committee; the NPT Exporters Committee.
**サンガーけんきゅうじょ**【-研究所】〔英国の医学研究機関〕the (Wellcome Trust) Sanger Institute. ▶Wellcome Trust (ウェルカム・トラスト) は英国の財団.
**さんかい**[4]【散会】 〇□ 散会動議 a motion to adjourn.
**さんかく**[1]【三角】 〇□ 三角折り〔トイレットペーパーの先端の〕folding of the tip of a roll of toilet paper into a triangle. 三角債〖商〗〔中国で, 売り掛け債権の回収がスムーズに進まない状態〕(an) interfirm debt; a "triangle [triangular] debt." 三角座り crouching holding one's knees in one's arms. 三角地〖三角形の敷地〗a triangular lot. 三角停止板=三角表示板. 三角頭蓋〖医〗trigonocephaly; metopic synostosis. 三角表示板〖自動車〗〖非常用停止表示板〗an (auto) emergency warning triangle.
**さんかく**[2]【参画】 〇□ 社会参画 social participation (of women) in planning; (women) taking part in social「planning [projects];〖社会参加〗social participation; participation in society.
**さんがく**[2]【山岳】 〇□ 山岳ガイド a mountain guide. 山岳救助隊 a mountain rescue「team [unit].●～救助隊員 a member of a mountain rescue team; a mountain rescue team member. 山岳協会 a mountaineering association. 山岳警備隊 a mountain security team; mountain rangers.●～警備隊員 a mountain ranger. 山岳工法〖土木〗the mountain tunneling method. 山岳寺院 a mountain temple. 山岳宗教 a "mountain religion"; a religion or sect that worships in the mountains. 山岳戦 mountain「warfare [fighting]; a mountain battle. 山岳仏教 mountain Buddhism. 山岳文明 (a) mountain culture. 山岳民族 a mountain route「people [〖文〗nation]. 山岳ルート a mountain route.
**さんがく**[4]【算額】〔和算家が神社仏閣に奉納した絵馬〕a votive horse tablet offering presented to a shrine or temple by a mathematician of the traditional wasan school (by way of thanks).

**さんがくかん**【産学官】〔産業界・大学等の教育機関・行政機関〕industry, government and「academia [universities]. 〇□ 産学官連携 cooperation [a tie-up, a partnership, a consortium] among industry, government and「academia [universities].
**さんかくたべ**【三角食べ】〔食事の時, 主食＞おかず＞汁物などと順番に食べること〕"triangle eating"; taking something alternately from each dish on the table.
**さんかくばアカシア**【三角葉-】〖植〗〔マメ科の落葉中低木; オーストラリア東部原産〕a knife-leaf wattle; a knife acacia; *Acacia cultriformis*.
**さんがくれんけい**【産学連携】〔産学協同〕cooperation between industrial enterprises and universities; industry-university cooperation.
**さんかてき**【酸化的】 〇□ 酸化的ストレス〖医〗=酸化ストレス(⇨さんか[11]).
**さんぎょう**[2]【産業】 〇□ 産業間貿易 intra-industry trade. 産業競争力 industrial competitiveness. ●～競争力を強化する[高める] strengthen [improve] industrial competitiveness. 産業クラスター〖経〗〔特定分野の企業・関連機関が地理的に集中し, 協力, 競争する形態〕an industrial cluster. 産業景観 an industrial landscape; industrial scenery; a factory-scape. 産業財産権〔特許権, 実用新案権, 意匠権, 商標権の4つ〕industrial property rights. 産業事故 an industrial accident. 産業動向調査 an industry trends survey. 産業美術 industrial art. ●～美術家 an industrial artist. 産業福祉 industrial welfare. 産業部門 the industrial sector. 産業ベルト an industrial belt. ●ハイテク技術～ベルト地帯 a hi-tech industrial belt. 産業保護 industrial「protection [preservation]; the protection of《local》industries. 産業(用)車両 an industrial vehicle.
**さんぎょういがくそうごうけんきゅうじょ**【産業医学総合研究所】the National Institute of Industrial Health (略: NIIH).
**さんぎょうかんきょうかんりきょうかい**【産業環境管理協会】the Japan Environmental Management Association for Industry (略: JEMAI).
**さんぎょうぎじゅつそうごうけんきゅうじょ**【産業技術総合研究所】〖独立行政法人〗the National Institute「of [for] Advanced Industrial Science and Technology (略: AIST).
**さんぎょうこようあんていセンター**【産業雇用安定-】the Industrial Employment Stabilization Center of Japan; SANKO.
**さんぎょうざいさんけんほう**【産業財産権法】〖法〗the Industrial Property Law. [=こうぎょうしょゆうけんほう]
**さんぎょうさいせいきこう**【産業再生機構】the Industrial Revitalization Corporation of Japan (略: IRCJ). 〇□ 産業再生機構送り referring《a failing company》to the IRCJ《for a bailout》. 産業再生機構担当大臣 the Minister of State for the Industrial Revitalization Corporation of Japan.
**さんぎょうさいせいきこうほう**【産業再生機構法】〖法〗the Law for the Industrial Revitalization Corporation (of Japan).
**さんけい**[4]【参詣】 〇□ 参詣道 a pilgrimage route.
**ざんけいきかん**【残刑期間】〖法〗〔仮釈放者の〕time remaining to be served; the remainder of《a convict's》prison sentence.
**「惨劇の週末」**〖映画〗The Art of Dying;〔原題〕El Arte de Morir.
**さんご**[2]【珊瑚】 〇□ 珊瑚環礁 an [a coral] atoll.
**さんこう**[7]【参考】 〇□ 参考意見 an advisory [an outside, a second] opinion;〖法〗an amicus curiae brief. 参考価格 a [the] reference price. 参考市場価格 a [the] reference market price. 参考相場圏〔為替相場など〕a reference range.

さんごう【三合】〔中国吉林省龍井市の行政区画，豆満江沿いにある〕Sanhe.

さんこうしょうそく【参考消息】〔中国の新華社通信傘下の日刊国際情報紙〕the Reference News.

ざんこうせい【残効性】residual ｢activity [effectiveness]; a residual ｢characteristic [property]. ○ これらの農薬は速効性にすぐれているが～は期待できない．These agrichemicals are strikingly effective in the short term but ｢they don't offer much promise of working in the long term [their residual effectiveness is doubtful].

さんこうにん【参考人】○■ 参考人制度 the unsworn witness system.

ざんさ【残渣】残渣油〔石油蒸留塔の底部から採取する重質油〕residual oil; residue; residuum.

さんさい[3]【山菜】○■ 山菜採り edible wild plant gathering.

さんさく【散策】○■ 散策地図［マップ］a walking map. 散策路 a foot path; a ｢walking [hiking] course.

さんさんか【三酸化】○■ 三酸化モリブデン molybdenum trioxide (略: MoO3).

さんさんななびょうし【三三七拍子】a rhythmic three-three-seven clapping pattern.

さんじ[1]【三次】○■ 三次医療〔医〕tertiary (medical) care. 三次責任 〈have, bear〉 tertiary responsibility 《for payment》. 三次予防 tertiary prevention.

サンシェード〔日除け〕a sunshade.

サン・シカリオ〔イタリア北西部，ピエモンテ州の町〕San Sicario.

さんじかん【参事官】a counsel(l)or; a councillor; a secretary; an attaché. ○■ 経済参事官 an economic ｢counsel(l)or [councillor, attaché]. 公使参事官 a minister-｢counsel(l)or [councillor]. 大使館参事官 an embassy ｢attaché [counsel(l)or, councillor].

さんじげん【三次元】○■ 三次元映像 a ｢three-dimensional [3D] image. 三次元照射〔医〕〔放射線の〕three-dimensional [3D] irradiation. 三次元測定器〔機〕a three-dimensional measuring device; three-dimensional measuring equipment.

さんじゃくだま【三尺玉】〔打ち上げ花火の〕a ball-shaped firework (with a shell ｢three *shaku* [about 90cm] in diameter].

ザンジャン〔イラン北西部の州; その州都〕Zanjan.

さんしゅ[3]【散種】〔哲学〕dissemination. ▶ デリダの造語．

さんしゅう[2]【参集】○■ 参集訓練 ＝集合訓練 (⇨しゅう[3]).

さんじゅうとび【三重跳び】〔縄跳びの〕triple ｢jumping [skipping]; (a) triple under. ○～をする triple-jump; triple-skip; do a triple under.

さんじゅうれん【三重連】〔鉄道〕〔機関車を3両連結して車両を牽引すること〕triple-heading; 〔その列車〕a triple-headed (steam) train. [⇨じゅうれん]

さんしゅつ[3]【算出】○■ 算出基準 a calculation basis; a basis for calculating 《salaries》. 算出[方]法 〔数値の〕a calculation method; a method of calculation; a way of calculating 《crime rates》.

ざんしょうぶつ【残焼物】〔火災現場などの〕the remains of a fire; (evidence retrieved from) the ｢ashes [embers].

さんじょく【産褥】○■ 産褥シッター［ヘルパー］a postnatal assistant; a new-mother's helper.

さんしょくがたしきかく【三色型色覚】〔眼科〕trichromatism; trichromatopsia. ▷ trichromatic, trichromic *adj*. ◁ 異常三色型色覚 anomalous trichromatism.

サン・ジョルディ【聖】〔スペイン，カタルニャ地方の守護聖人〕Saint George. ▶ 祝日 サン・ジョルディの日 (Saint George's Day) は 4 月 23 日．

サンズ Sands, Julian〈1958-  ; 英国生まれの映画俳優〉．

さんせい[3]【山西】○■ 山西料理 Shanxi cuisine.

さんせい[6]【酸性】○■ 酸性雪 acid snow. 酸性体質 an acidic body; acidic blood; acidosis.

さんせい[8]【三星】＝サムスン．

さんせい[9]【産生】〔生化〕production. ～する produce. ○ メタン～菌 methane-producing bacteria ／ ベロ毒素～性大腸菌 verotoxin-producing *E. coli* ／ ボツリヌス菌による毒素～ toxin production by *Clostridium botulinum*. ○ 抗体～を抑制する suppress the production of antibodies. ○■ エネルギー産生〔生理〕energy production (in the body).

「サンセット 77」〔ロサンゼルスのサンセット通りに住む探偵たちの TV ドラマ〕77 Sunset Strip.

さんせん[4]【酸洗】○■ 酸洗鋼板 (a) pickled steel sheet.

さんせんべん【三尖弁】○■ 三尖弁閉鎖(症)〔医〕tricuspid atresia (略: TA).

さんそ【酸素】○■ 純粋酸素 pure oxygen. ○■ 酸素系漂白剤 (an) oxygen bleach. 酸素水 "oxygen water"; water containing dissolved oxygen. 酸素チューブ〔医療用の〕an oxygen tube. 酸素透過性〔コンタクトレンズの〕oxygen permeability. ○ ～透過性の oxygen-permeable 《contact lenses》. 酸素透過率 an oxygen transmission rate. 酸素燃焼法〔CO2 回収技術の1つ〕the oxygen combustion method. 酸素濃縮器 an oxygen concentrator. 酸素バー〔酸素の吸入サービスを提供する店〕an oxygen bar. 酸素不足 (a) ｢shortage [lack] of oxygen; oxygen deprivation; insufficient oxygen. 酸素浴 oxygen bathing.

ざんぞう【残像】○■ 残像感〔液晶テレビなどの〕image ｢retention [sticking].

さんそん[1]【山村】○■ 山村集落 a mountain ｢settlement [community].

ざんそん【残存】○■ 残存視力 residual sight. 残存勢力〔旧政権などの〕residual ｢forces [elements]; loyalists 《to the former regime》. 残存聴力 residual hearing.

さんそんしんこうほう【山村振興法】〔法〕the Mountain Village Promotion Law.

サンタ・アナ ○■ サンタ・アナ風〔気象〕〔米国カリフォルニア州南部のサンタ・アナ山脈の斜面を吹き下ろす乾いた熱風〕(the) Santa Ana winds.

「サンダーバード」〔英国の人形劇 TV ドラマ; 5人の兄弟が災害や事故の救難活動を行う〕Thunderbirds.

サンダーボルト〔米軍〕〔第二次大戦の米陸軍航空隊の戦闘機 P-47 の愛称〕a Thunderbolt.

さんだい(きゃく)しき【三代(格)式】〔平安時代にまとめられた法典，弘仁(ミネ)，貞観(ミネ)，延喜(ミネ)〕the Rules of Three Generations; the Sandai(kyaku) Shiki. [⇨こうにん(きゃく)しき, じょうがん(きゃく)しき, えんぎ(きゃく)しき]

さんだいこくさいえいがさい【三大国際映画祭】the three major international film festivals. ▶ ヴェネツィア国際映画祭 (the Venice International Film Festival)，カンヌ国際映画祭 (the Cannes Film Festival)，ベルリン国際映画祭 (the Berlin International Film Festival) の3つをさす．

ざんだか【残高】○■ 残高証明書〔預金の〕a bank balance certificate; a bank statement (showing the current balance in *one*'s account).

さんたく[1]【三択】○■ 三択クイズ a ｢test [quiz] consisting of ｢three-choice [three-item multiple choice] questions.

サンタ・クラリタ〔米国カリフォルニア州の都市〕Santa Clarita.

さんだんかざり【三段飾り】〔ひな人形の〕a three-tiered display 《of *hina-ningyo*》.

サンタンジェロじょう【～城】〔イタリア，ローマにある城〕St. Angel('s) Castle; 〔イタリア語では〕Castel Sant'Angelo.

サンダンスえいがさい【～映画祭】〔米国ユタ州で毎年開催される独立系映画の映画祭〕the Sundance Film Festival.

さんち²【産地】▯ 産地偽装 fraudulently claiming that 《produce, vegetables, fruit, etc.》 comes from a particular area or country. 産地呼称 naming a product after the place where it is produced; giving a product an appellation of origin. 産地廃棄〔豊作による値崩れを防ぐための、野菜などを〕throwing out「produce [vegetables, fruit]」(in order to keep up the price). 産地銘柄 a local brand (name).
サンチェス Sánchez de Lozada, Gonzalo (1930-  ; ボリビアの政治家; 大統領〔2002-03〕).
サンチュ〔レタスの一種; 韓国料理の食材〕sangchu; Korean lettuce.
さんちゅうぜんかい【三中全会】〔中国共産党中央委員会第3回全体会議〕the Third Plenary Session (of the Central Committee of the Communist Party of China).
さんちょく²【三陸】= サムチョク.
さんつう²【三通】〔中国・台湾間の通商・通信・通信〕the three (direct) links (commerce, navigation and postal service) between China and Taiwan. ▯ 三通問題 the "three links" issue.
さんづけ【さん付け】▯ さん付け運動〔組織内で名前に肩書をつけて呼んだり呼び捨てにするのをやめ、平等に「さん」付けで呼ぶ運動〕a movement advocating the use of the courtesy title -san among employees of the same organization, regardless of position.
ざんてい【暫定】▯ 暫定首位《have》a provisional lead. ◐ 土曜日の時点で宮里は7アンダー〜首位に立っていた。 On Saturday Miyazato was leading provisionally with a score of 7 under par. 暫定統治〔行政〕機構〔政権崩壊や内戦終結などの後の〕an interim [a transitional] administration [authority]. 暫定投票〔米国の選挙制度での〕provisional balloting. ◐ 〜投票制度 the provisional ballot system. 暫定票〔米国の選挙制度での〕《cast》a provisional ballot.
サンディアこくりつけんきゅうじょ【-国立研究所】〔米国の核研究施設〕(the) Sandia National Laboratory (略: SNL).
サンディニスタみんぞくかいほうせんせん【-民族解放戦線】〔ニカラグアの左翼政党〕the Sandinista National Liberation Front (略: FSLN). ▶ FSLNはスペイン語のFrente Sandinista de Liberación Nacionalの略.
サンデー¹ ▯ サンデー・ドライバー〔休日にしか車に乗らないため運転がへたな人〕a Sunday driver;〔週末にしか運転しない人〕a weekend driver.
サンデー・タイムズ〔英国の高級日曜紙〕The Sunday Times.
サンデー・テレグラフ〔英国の高級日曜紙〕The Sunday Telegraph.
サンデー・ミラー〔英国の日曜大衆紙〕the Sunday Mirror.
サンテラ〔サンテリアの女性聖職者〕a Santera.
サンテリア²〔アフリカ起源のキューバの宗教〕Santeria.
サンテロ〔サンテリアの男性聖職者〕a Santero《pl. 〜s》.
サンド³〔砂; 砂色〕sand. ▯ サンドブラスト〔ガラス加工などの砂吹き〕sandblasting; a sandblast.
ざんど【残土】▯ 残土処理〔処分〕場 a surplus soil disposal site; a surplus soil dump.
サンドイッチ ▯ サンドイッチ症候群〔2つのものの間で板挟みになったことによって生じる諸症状〕sandwich syndrome.
さんとうへい【三等兵】〔軍〕a third-class private;〔口〕a buck private.
サンド・トラップ 1〔自動車レースのコース脇の砂が敷き詰めてある退避エリア〕a sand trap. 2〔ゴルフ場のバンカー〕a sand trap; a bunker.
サントメール〔フランス北部の町〕Saint-Omer.
サンドラー Sandler, Adam (1966-  ; 米国の映画俳優).
さんねつ【産熱】〔生理〕thermogenesis.

さんのうもんだい【三農問題】〔中国の農業の低生産性、農村の疲弊、農民の低所得の3つの問題〕the "three agriculture-related problems."
さんぱい¹【参拝】▯ 参拝の儀 the ceremony of paying a visit to《the main shrine》;〔皇室儀礼〕the ceremony of「worshiping [bidding farewell to] the imperial ancestors.
さんぱい³【産廃】▯ 産廃運搬車(両)〔産業廃棄物運搬車両〕an industrial waste truck. 産廃銀座〔産業廃棄物処理場などが密集している地域〕an area with many industrial waste processing and disposal sites; a「haven [mecca] for industrial waste.
サンパイオ Sampaio, Jorge (Fernando Branco de) (1939-  ; ポルトガルの政治家; 大統領〔1996-2006〕).
さんばいぞうじょうしゅ【三倍増醸酒】= ぞうじょうしゅ.
さんぱいとくそほう【産廃特措法】〔法〕the Law on Special Measures against Industrial Waste. ▶ 正式名称は、特定産業廃棄物に起因する支障の除去等に関する特別措置法 (the Law Concerning Special Measures for the Removal of Obstacles Caused by Specified Industrial Waste).
「三ばか大将」〔米国のどたばた短編映画シリーズ〕The Three Stooges.
さんばし【桟橋】▯ 桟橋工法〔土木〕〔多数の杭の上に建設する工法〕the method of building《a runway》on piles (driven into the seabed).
サン・ピエトロひろば【-広場】〔ヴァチカン市国の〕St. Peter's Square;〔the〕Piazza San Pietro; (the) Vatican Square;〔イタリア語〕la Piazza San Pietro.
サンフェルミンまつり【-祭り】〔スペインのパンプローナ市で毎年7月に催される〕San Fermín.
さんぷせいさく【三不政策】〔1998年、クリントン米大統領が訪中の際に述べた台湾に対する3つの不支持〕the "three noes" policy. ▶ 二つの中国を支持しない、台湾の独立を支持しない、台湾の国連参加を支持しない、の3つの不支持.
サンフランシスコ(おお)じしん【-(大)地震】〔1906年の〕the (Great) San Francisco earthquake of 1906.
ざんべんかん【残便感】a feeling「of constipation [that one's bowels have not emptied properly].
さんぽう¹【三方】▯ 三方活栓〔医〕a three-way stopcock. 三方よし〔経営〕〔商売上の理念で〕"all three parties doing well"; everybody「doing well [making a profit]; purchaser, buyer and society all benefitting.
サンボール・プレイ・クック〔カンボジアの遺跡〕Sambor Prei Kuk.
さんめいがく【算命学】〔道教を源とする占星術〕(Chinese-style) numerology; "sanmeigaku"; "Counting Life."
さんもん¹【三文】▯ 三文役者 a hack actor; a ham actor.
さんゆりょう【産油量】volume of「oil [petroleum] produced; oil [petroleum] production [output]. ◐ ロシアはサウジアラビアに次いで世界第2位の〜を誇る。 Russia boasts the world's second largest oil output, after Saudi Arabia.
サンヨン【双龍】〔韓国の自動車メーカー〕Ssangyong Motor Co.
さんらん²【産卵】▯ 産卵礁〔海洋〕a spawning reef. 産卵地 a spawning ground. ◐ アカウミガメの〜地 the spawning grounds of the loggerhead turtle.
さんらん³【散乱】▯ 散乱理論〔物〕scattering theory.
さんりげん【三利源】〔生命保険〕〔死差益・利差益・費差益〕three major profit sources (of mortality, interest and operating gains).
ざんりゅう¹【残留】▯ 残留争い〔スポーツリーグで所属クラス最下位付近にいるチーム同士の〕a battle to avoid relegation《to a lower division》. 残留応力〔冶金〕(a) residual stress. 残留思念〔超心理〕〔物や場所に残っている強い思念〕residual「thoughts [consciousness]. 残留性

〖化〗〔有機汚染物などの〕persistency; persistence. ▷ ～性の(ある) persistent. **残留洗剤** residual detergent. **残留濃度**〔農薬などの〕a「residual [residue] concentration. **残留農薬基準** agrochemical residue standards.
**サン・ルイス・オビスポ**〔米国, カリフォルニア州太平洋岸の都市〕San Luis Obispo.
**サン・ルイとう**【―島】〔パリのセーヌ川の中の島〕the Île Saint-Louis.
**さんろスイッチ**【三路―】〖電〗〔照明器具を2か所でオン・オフできるスイッチ〕a three-way switch.
**さんわりルール**【三割―】〖経〗〔公的資金投入を受けた銀行の収益が経営健全化計画の利益目標を2期連続で3割以上下回った場合トップに辞任を求めるなどの規定〕the "thirty-percent rule"; the rule requiring banks in receipt of public funds not to fall more than 30% below target earnings. ▣ **三割ルール適用** application of the "thirty percent rule."

# し

**し**[7]【死】 ▷ ～の四重奏〖医〗〔肥満・糖尿病・高血圧・高脂血症を併せ持った状態のこと〕the deadly quartet (of obesity, diabetes, high blood pressure, and high triglyceride levels).
**し**[10]【師】 2〔軍隊〕an army; troops;〔戦争〕a war; a campaign. ▷ 無名の～ an unjustified war. ▷ ～を起こす start [wage] (a) war 《against…》.
**ジア, Khaleda** (1945- ) 〔バングラデシュの政治家; 首相 [1991-96, 2001-06]〕.
**しあい**【試合】 ▷ **無観客試合**〔サッカーなどの〕a「match [game] without spectators. ▣ **試合勘** match sense; sense for a game. ▷ ～勘を取り戻す recover one's sense for a game. **試合間隔** an interval [the time] between one「game [match, tournament] and the next. ▷ ～間隔が開きすぎると選手のコンディションの調整が難しくなる. If there is too much time between games it is difficult to keep the players in condition.
**じあい**[4]【時合】〔釣り〕the time frame when the fish are striking.
**しあげる**【仕上げる】〔仕事などを完了させる〕finish (off, up); complete; perfect; get sth「finished [done]; get through with 《one's work》;〔木材などを〕trim;〔石材などを〕face;〔皮革などを〕dress;〔スポーツ選手がコンディションをベストに持っていく〕get in「shape [「trim」]. ▷ 研究論文を～ complete a research paper / 依頼されていた絵を～ finish a painting one was commissioned to paint /〔投手が〕肩を～ get one's「shoulder [arm] (back) in shape /〔彫刻などを〕なめらかに美しく～ give a beautiful smooth finish to 《a sculpture》/〔クリーニングで〕防汚加工で～ apply a soil-resistant finish to 《a jacket》. ▷ 1週間以内に仕上げてもらいたい. I want (to have) it「finished [ready] within a week. / 今回『ピノキオ』を親子で楽しめるミュージカルに仕上げました. We've now made "Pinocchio" into musical that can be enjoyed by both parents and children. / サトイモを白く仕上げたい場合は薄口しょう油で煮るとよい. If you want the taro to come out white, you should boil it with light-colored soy sauce. /〔壁塗りで〕最後はローラーをかけて仕上げます. Finish it off with a roller. / 今は風邪ぎみですが, 試合当日までにはきっちり～自信があります. I have a slight cold now, but I'm confident that I will be in top condition by the day of the fight.
**ジアシルグリセロール**〖化〗〔体に脂肪がつきにくい食用油の原料〕diacylglycerol (略: DAG).
**ジアゾキサイド, ジアゾキシド**〖薬〗〔低血糖症改善薬〕diazoxide.
**シアター** ▣ **シアター・ルーム**〔映画・ビデオ視聴のための部屋〕a theater room.
**シアチェンひょうが**【―氷河】〔カシミール地方北部にある〕the Siachen Glacier.
**シアトル・タイムズ**〔米国シアトルの日刊紙〕The Seattle Times.
**シアヌークヴィル** ⇒プレア・シアヌーク.

**シアノバクテリア**〖菌〗a cyanobacterium 《pl. -ria》;〔藍藻〕a blue-green alga 《pl. blue-green algae》. ▷ cyanobacterial adj.
**ジアリールエテン**〖化〗〔光により可逆的に異性化する有機化合物〕a diarylethene.
**シアリス**〖商標・薬〗〔勃起不全治療薬〕Cialis.
**ジアルジアしょう**【―症】〖医〗giardiasis.
「**しあわせ色のルビー**」〔映画〕A Price Above Rubies.
**シアンス・ポ** ⇒パリせいじがくいん.
**ジー**[G, g] ▣ **縦 G**〔加速時・減速時にかかる重力加速度〕longitudinal g-force;〔鉛直方向にかかる重力加速度〕vertical g-force. **横 G**〔進行方向に対して横向きの重力加速度〕lateral g-force;〔水平方向の重力加速度〕horizontal g-force.
**シー・アール・エス**【CRS】〖電算〗〔コンピューター利用の航空座席やホテルの予約システム〕CRS; a「computerized [computer] reservation system.
**シー・アール・エム**【CRM】〔顧客関係管理〕CRM. ▶ customer「relationship [relation] management の略.
**ジー・アール・ピー**【GRP】〔延べ視聴率〕a GRP; a gross rating point.
**シー・アール・ビーしすう**【CRB 指数】〔米国 CRB 社による, ニューヨーク先物取引所 (NYFE) で取引が行われている商品先物指数〕the CRB index. ▶ CRB は Commodity Research Bureau の略; 現在は ロイター・ジェフリーズ CRB 指数 という.
**ジー・アール・ユー**【GRU】⇨ロシアれんぽうぐんさんぼうほんぶじょうほうそうきょく.
**ジー・アイ・エス**【GIS】〔地域情報システム〕GIS; a geographic information system. ▣ **防災 GIS** an emergency GIS; a disaster prevention GIS.
**シー・アイ・エス・オー**【CISO】〔企業の最高情報セキュリティー責任者〕a CISO; a chief information security officer.
**シー・アイ・エスたいようでんち**【CIS 太陽電池】a CIS solar cell. ▶ CIS は copper (銅), indium (インジウム), selenium (セレン) の略.
**シー・アイ・エル・ピー**【CILP】〖生化〗〔軟骨細胞間の基質に存在するたんぱく質〕CILP. ▶ = cartilage intermediate layer protein の略. ▣ **CILP 遺伝子**〖医〗a CILP gene.
**シー・アイ・ジー・エスたいようでんち**【CIGS 太陽電池】a CIGS solar cell. ▶ CIGS は copper (銅), indium (インジウム), gallium (ガリウム), selenium (セレン) の略.
**ジー・アイち**【GI 値】〔ある食品に含まれる炭水化物が消化されて血中に入っていくるまでの時間を示す指標; 食パンの基準食品を 100 とする〕the GI; the glycemic index.
**シー・アイ・ディー・ピー**【CIDP】〖医〗=慢性炎症性脱髄性多発根神経炎 (⇨しんけいえん).
**シー・アイランド**〔ジョージア州の大西洋岸沿いにある島; 保養地・別荘地〕Sea Island.
**ジー・イー・エム**【GEM】1〔香港証券取引所のベンチャー企業市場〕GEM. ▶ Growth Enterprise Market の略.
2〔女性が積極的に経済や政治などに参画しているかどうかを

シーイーピーティー

示すもの；国連開発計画の人間開発指数の調査基準の1つ〕GEM; the gender empowerment measure.

シー・イー・ピー・ティー【CEPT】〔共通効果特恵関税〕CEPT; a common effective preferential tariff.

シー・イー・ブイ【CEV】〔宇宙〕〔スペースシャトルの後継として計画されている宇宙往還機〕a CEV. ▶ crew exploration vehicle の略.

シー・イー・マーキング, シー・イー・マーク【CE-, CE-】〔EU で販売される指定製品に貼付が義務づけられている安全マーク〕a CE marking; a CE mark. ▶ CE は フランス語 Conformité Européene (= European Conformity) の略.

ジー・エイチ【GH】〔生化〕〔成長ホルモン〕GH; growth hormone. ▣ GH 検査〔ドーピング検査の1つ〕a GH test.

ジー・エイチ・ジー【GHG】〔環境〕〔温室効果ガス〕GHG. ▶ greenhouse gas(es) の略.

ジー・エイチ・ビー【GHB】〔薬〕〔気分高揚剤〕GHB. ▶ gamma-hydroxy butyrate の略.

ジー・エイト【G8】〔主要8か国首脳会議〕the Group of Eight; the G8. ▶ 1998 年より英国・ドイツ・英国・フランス・イタリア・カナダ・ロシアと日本の主要8か国で構成. ▣ G8 サミット a「Group of Eight [G8] summit (meeting)」.

シー・エー・ティー・ブイ【CATV】 ▣ CATV インターネット〔電算〕〔ケーブルテレビ回線を利用したインターネット〕CATV Internet.

ジー・エー・ピー【GAP】〔適正農業規範；農作物の生産および供給の管理に関する基準〕GAP; good agricultural practice(s).

シー・エー・ピー・ディー【CAPD】〔医〕〔腎不全の持続的携帯型腹膜透析(法)〕CAPD; continuous ambulatory peritoneal dialysis.

シー・エス【CS】1〔通信衛星〕a CS; a communications satellite. 2〔顧客満足度〕CS; customer satisfaction. ▣ CS 放送 CS broadcasting. ◉ アナログ〔デジタル〕放送 analog [digital] CS broadcasting / 110 度〜 110-degree CS (digital) broadcasting.

シー・エス・アール【CSR】〔企業の社会的責任〕CSR; corporate social responsibility.

ジー・エス・エー【GSA】〔米国政府資材調達局〕GSA; the (US) General Services Administration.

ジー・エス・エム【GSM】〔通信〕〔汎ヨーロッパデジタル移動通信システム〕GSM. ▶ global system for mobile communication(s) の略.

シー・エス・オー【CSO】1〔市民社会組織〕a CSO; a civil society organization. 2〔企業の最高セキュリティー責任者〕a CSO; a chief security officer. 3〔企業の最高戦略責任者〕a CSO; a cheif「strategy [strategic] officer.

シー・エス・ピー・アイ【CSPI】〔企業向けサービス価格指数〕CSPI; a corporate service price index.

ジー・エヌ・エイチ【GNH】〔国民総幸福量〕GNH; gross national happiness.

シー・エヌ・シー【CNC】〔電算〕〔コンピューターによる数値制御〕CNC; computer [computerized] numerical control; computer numerically controlled《machine》.

シー・エヌ・ジー【CNG】 ▣ CNG 車〔圧縮天然ガス車〕a CNG car.

ジー・エヌ・ピー【GNP】 ▣ GNP 1% 枠〔日本の国家予算の1% を防衛費に当てるという枠〕a defense expenditure limit of 1% of GNP; the spending cap on defense of 1% of GNP.

シー・エフ・アール・ピー【CFRP】〔炭素繊維強化プラスチック〕(a) CFRP; (a) carbon-fiber reinforced plastic.

ジー・エフ・アール・ピー【GFRP】〔ガラス繊維強化プラスチック〕(a) GFRP; (a)「glass fiber [glass-fiber, glass fibre] reinforced plastic.

シー・エフ・アイ・ユー・エス【CFIUS】〔米国の対米外国投資委員会〕the CFIUS; the Committee on Foreign Investments in the United States.

シー・エフ・オー【CFO】〔企業の最高財務責任者〕a CFO; a chief financial officer.

シー・エフ・ティー・シー【CFTC】〔米国の商品先物取引委員会〕the CFTC; the Commodity Futures Trading Commission.

ジー・エフ・ピーいでんし【GFP 遺伝子】a GFP gene. ▶ GFP is green fluorescent protein (緑色蛍光たんぱく質) の略.

シー・エム【CM】 ▣ CM 撮影 shooting [filming] (television) commercials; CM filming. CM スキップ〔飛ばし〕〔CM を飛ばして再生するビデオレコーダーの機能〕commercial skipping (replay). CM ディレクター a「commercials [CM] director.

ジー・エム【GM】 3〔遺伝子組み換え〕genetic modification. ▣ GM 食品〔遺伝子組み換え食品〕(a) GM food; (a) genetically「modified [engineered, altered] food. GM 大豆 genetically「modified [engineered, altered] soybeans; GM soybeans.

シー・エム・エス【CMS】1〔自動車〕〔追突軽減ブレーキ〕CMS. ▶ collision mitigation brake system の略. 2〔会計〕〔キャッシュ・マネジメント・システム〕CMS. ▶ cash management system の略.

ジー・エム・エス【GMS】1〔静止気象衛星〕a GMS; a geostationary meteorological satellite. 2〔総合スーパー〕⇒総合スーパー (⇒そうごう³).

シー・エム・エム・アイ【CMMI】〔企業等でのソフトウェア開発能力の成熟度を示す指標〕(the) CMMI; (the) Capability Maturity Model Integration. ▶ レベル1 (Level 1) からレベル5 (Level 5) まである.

シー・エム・オー【CMO】〔企業の最高マーケティング責任者〕a CMO; a chief marketing officer.

ジー・エム・オー【GMO】 ▣ GMO フリーゾーン〔遺伝子組み換え作物の栽培を拒否している地域〕a GMO-free zone.

ジー・エム・ディー・エス・エス【GMDSS】〔海〕〔海上での遭難・安全に関する世界的制度〕GMDSS. ▶ Global Maritime Distress and Safety System の略.

ジー・エム・ピー【GMP】 ▣ GMP レベル〔薬〕GMP level; 《meet》 GMP standards. ◉ 〜レベル(で)の〔基準を満たした[に従った]〕(facilities) meeting GMP standards; (production) according to GMP standards.

シー・エル・エー【CLA】〔化〕〔共役リノール酸〕CLA; (a) conjugated linoleic acid.

シー・オー・イーきょてん【COE 拠点】〔中核的研究拠点〕a COE; a Center of Excellence.

シー・オー・シーにんしょう【COC 認証】〔森林管理協議会による製品認証〕qhain-of-custody certification.

シー・オー・ツー【CO₂】 ▣ CO₂ 回収 CO₂ recovery. ◉ 〜回収技術 CO₂ recovery technology. CO₂ 排出量《reduce》 CO₂ emissions; emissions of CO₂.

ジー・オー・ティー²【GOT】〔商〕〔発注端末の1つ〕a GOT; a graphic order terminal.

シー・オー・ピー【COP】〔物〕〔消費電力当たりの冷却・加熱能力を表す数値〕a COP (of 3); the coefficient of performance 《of a heat pump》.

シー・オー・ピー・ディー【COPD】〔医〕〔慢性閉塞性肺疾患〕chronic obstructive pulmonary disease.

ジーカール = ジカール.

シー・カヤック a sea kayak; 〔スポーツ〕sea kayaking.

しいく【飼育】 ▣ 屋外[室外]飼育 outdoor (pet) ownership; keeping (a pet) outdoors. 屋内[室内]飼育 indoor (pet) ownership; keeping (a pet) indoors. ▣ 飼育キット a (cricket) breeding kit. 飼育小屋〔学校など〕a pen (for rabbits); a small animal enclosure. 飼育(容)器〔昆虫・爬虫類などの〕a rearing container.

ジークレー〖＜F giclée〗〘美術〙〔コンピューターを使った版画技法〕giclee printing; (その版画) a giclee (print).
シークヮーサー〖植〗〔ミカン科の常緑低木; ヒラミレモン〕a shekwasha; a flat lemon; Citrus depressa.
シー・ケー【CK】〖サッカー〗〔コーナーキック〕CK; a corner kick.
シー・ケー・オー【CKO】〔企業の最高知識管理責任者〕a CKO; a chief knowledge officer.
ジーコ Zico (1953- ; ブラジルのサッカー選手; 本名 Arthur Antunes Coimbra).
シーサー〔沖縄で魔除けのシンボルとされる獅子の像〕Shisa; a mythical lion-dog.
シーザーあんごう【—暗号】〔アルファベットを一定の数だけアルファベット順にずらして得られる暗号〕a Caesar cipher.
シーザー・サラダ〘料理〙〔イタリア人シェフ Caesar Cardini がメキシコのレストランで供したのが起源といわれる、レタスを主材とするサラダ〕(a) Caesar salad.
ジーザーン =ジザン.
シーサケート =シーサケット.
シーサケット〔タイ東北部の県; 同県の県都〕Sisaket.
シー・ジー【CG】 ▷ CG デザイナー a「computer graphics [CG] designer.
シー・ジー・アイ【CGI】〘電算〙〔ウェブサーバーがプログラムを利用する規格〕CGI. ▶ Common Gateway Interface の略. ▷ CGI プログラム a CGI program.
ジー・シー・エイチ・キュー【GCHQ】〔英国の情報機関(政府通信本部)〕GCHQ; the Government Communications Headquarters.
シー・ジー・エル【CGL】〘製鋼〙〔溶融亜鉛めっき鋼板製造ライン〕CGL; a continuous galvanizing line.
シー・シー・オー【CCO】 1〔企業の最高違法責任者; 最高倫理担当役員〕a CCO. ▶ chief compliance officer の略. 2〔最高コミュニケーション責任者〕a CCO. ▶ chief communication officer の略.
シー・シー・シー【CCC】〔中国強制認証マーク〕a CCC mark; a China Compulsory Certification mark.
シー・シー・シー・ディー【CCCD】〔複製防止対策を施したCD〕a CCCD; a copy control(led) CD.
シー・ジー・シリコン【CG-】〘電子工学〙〔連続粒界結晶シリコン〕CG silicon; continuous-grain silicon. ▷ CG シリコン液晶 a CG silicon LCD. CG シリコン技術 CG silicon technology.
シー・シー・ディー【CCD】 ▷ CCD スキャナー〔バーコード読み取り装置〕a CCD scanner. CCD センサー a CCD sensor; a charge-coupled device sensor.
シー・ジェー・ディー【CJD】〘医〙〔クロイツフェルト・ヤコブ病〕CJD. ▶ Creutzfeldt-Jakob disease の略. ▷ 家族性 CJD familial CJD. [=家族性クロイツフェルト・ヤコブ病 (⇨クロイツフェルトヤコブびょう)] 孤発性 CJD sporadic CJD. [=孤発性クロイツフェルト・ヤコブ病 (⇨クロイツフェルトヤコブびょう)] 変異型 CJD variant CJD; vCJD. [=変異型クロイツフェルト・ヤコブ病 (⇨クロイツフェルトヤコブびょう)]
シース ▷ シース・ナイフ〔さや入りのナイフ〕a sheath knife.
シーズ〔メーカーの所有する技術・材料・アイデアなど〕new「ideas [products, services] proposed by a company to consumers; producer-driven solutions.
「シーズ・オール・ザット」〘映画〙She's All That.
「シーズ・ソー・ラブリー」〘映画〙She's So Lovely.
シースルー ▷ シースルー階段〘建〙a see-through staircase. シースルー・バック〘時計〙a see-through back.
シーズン ▷ シーズン最多安打記録〘野球〙the record for most hits in a season.
じいそ【地磯】a rocky shore. ▷ 地磯釣り fishing off the rocks.
シータ ▷ シータ波〘脳波〙the theta rhythm; a theta wave.
シー・ダブリュー・ディー【CWD】〘獣医〙〔慢性消耗病〕CWD; chronic wasting disease.
シー・ティー【CT】 ▷ CT 画像診断 CT diagnostic imaging.
シー・ディー【CD】 ▷ CD エクストラ〔音楽の他に映像も記録できるCD〕CD Extra.
シー・ティー・アイ【CTI】〘電算〙〔コンピューターと電話を連係させた仕組み〕CTI; computer telephony integration.
シー・ティー・エー【CTA】〔商品〔先物〕取引顧問業者〕a CTA; a commodity trading advisor.
シー・ディー・エス【CDS】 1〘電算〙〔コンテンツ配信サービス〕a CDS; a content delivery service. 2〘電算〙〔コンテンツ配信システム〕a CDS; a content delivery system. 3〘金融〙〔クレジット・デフォルト・スワップ〕a CDS; a credit default swap.
シー・ディー・エヌ【CDN】〘電算〙〔コンテンツ配信用のネットワーク〕a CDN; a content delivery network. ▷ CDN 事業 a CDN project.
シー・ディー・エム【CDM】=クリーンかいはつメカニズム.
ジー・ティー・エル【GTL】〘化〙〔天然ガスを分解・液化して軽油・灯油・ナフサを得る技術〕GTL; GtL; gas to liquid(s).
シー・ティー・オー【CTO】〔企業の最高技術責任者〕a CTO; a chief technical officer.
シー・ディー・オー【CDO】〘証券〙〔債務担保証券〕a CDO; a collateralized debt obligation. ▷ シンセティック CDO〔合成債務担保証券〕a synthetic CDO.
シー・ディー・シー【CDC】〔米国疾病対策センター〕the CDC; the Centers for Disease Control and Prevention.
ジー・ティー・ティー【GTT】〘医〙〔ぶどう糖負荷試験〕GTT; a glucose tolerance test.
シー・ティー・ビー【CTB】〘ラグビー〙〔センター〕a centre three-quarter.
シー・ティー・ピー【CTP】〘印刷〙〔コンピューターから直接製版する方式〕CTP; computer-to-plate《printing》.
ジー・ディー・ピー【GDP】 ▷ 高齢化修正 GDP (a [the]) GDP adjusted for the aging of the population; (an [the]) aging-adjusted GDP. 実質 GDP (a [the]) real GDP (略: RGDP). ◐ 実質〜伸び率 a [the] real GDP growth rate《of 1.7%》. 名目 GDP (a [the]) nominal GDP (略: NGDP). ◐ 名目〜伸び率 a [the] growth rate of nominal GDP; a nominal GDP growth rate《of 7%》. ▷ GDP ギャップ a GDP gap. GDP 弾性値〘経〙GDP elasticity. ◐ エネルギー需要〘消費〙の〜弾性値 the GDP elasticity of energy「demand [consumption]」.
シート[2] ▷ シート・ピッチ〔乗り物の前後の座席間隔〕(a) seat pitch. ◐ ビジネスクラスの〜ピッチを拡大する increase the「seat pitch [distance between seats, legroom]」in business class.
シー・トゥー・シー【C to C】〔消費者間商取引〕C2C [consumer-to-consumer] commerce.
ジー・トゥー・シー【G to C】〔行政機関・市民間の情報伝達の電子化〕G to C; government to citizen(s); 〔行政機関・消費者間の情報交換の電子化〕G to C; government to consumer(s).
ジー・トゥー・ジー【G to G】〔行政機関間の情報交換の電子化〕G to G; government to government.
シー・トゥー・ビー【C to B】〔インターネットなどを利用して消費者が自らの欲するものの情報を企業に伝えること〕C to B; consumer to business.
ジー・トゥー・ビー【G to B】〔行政機関・企業間の情報伝達の電子化〕G to B; government to business.
シート・コンピューター〘電算〙〔液晶画面に組み込まれた超薄型コンピューター; 現在開発中〕a sheet computer.
シート・シャッター〔ポリエステル製などの自動開閉シャッター〕

シートベルト a sheet shutter.
シートベルト ▷ シートベルト・コンビンサー〔シートベルト装着時の衝撃体験装置〕a seatbelt convincer. シートベルト体験車 ＝シートベルト・コンビンサー. シートベルト・リマインダー〔自動車〕〔シートベルト非着用で発進すると警告音が鳴る警報装置〕a seat-belt reminder.
シード・ペレット〔農〕〔種子と肥料などを固めて団塊にしたもの〕(a) seed pellet. ▷ マクロ・シード・ペレット〔肥料を固めて団塊にしたものに種子をまぶしつけたもの〕macroseed pellets (containing grass seeds, suitable for sowing on uneven terrain).
シーニガマ〔スリランカ南西部の村〕Sinigama.
ジーにじゅう【G20】〔有力途上国グループ〕the G20; the Group of Twenty.
ジーにじゅうに【G22】〔22か国蔵相・中央銀行総裁会議〕the G-22.
シーバンド【C –】〔通信〕〔周波数帯域の1つ〕the C-band.
シー・ビー【CB】〔証券〕〔転換社債型新株予約権付社債〕a CB; a convertible bond.
シー・ビー【CP】▷ CP 対称性【物】CP symmetry. CP 対称性の破れ【物】CP violation.
シー・ビー・アール・エヌ【CBRN】〔化学・生物・放射能・核兵器の〕CBRN; chemical, biological, radiological and nuclear. ▷ CBRN テロ CBRN terrorism.
シー・ピー・エー【CPA】〔イラクの連合国暫定当局〕the CPA; the Coalition Provisional Authority.
ジー・ピー・エーせいど【GPA 制度】〔教育〕〔大学の成績評価制度の1つ〕a GPA system. ▶ GPA は grade point average(学業平均値)の略.
ジー・ピー・エーひょうか【GPA 評価】〔教育〕〔成績などの〕a ranking [evaluation] based on a grade point average.
ジー・ピー・エス【GPS】▷ GPS 携帯電話 a GPS 「cellular [mobile] phone. GPS 端末 a GPS terminal. GPS 津波計 a GPS tsunami gauge.
シー・ビー・ティー【CBT】1〔電算〕〔コンピューターを使った試験〕CBT. ▶ computer-based testing の略. 2〔電算〕〔コンピューターで学習活動を助けるシステム〕CBT. ▶ computer-based training の略.
シー・ピー・ユー【CPU】▷ CPU 基板 a CPU board.
「シービスケット」〔映画〕Seabiscuit.
シー・ブイ・アイ・ディー【CVID】〔完全で検証可能かつ後戻りできない核放棄〕CVID; (a) complete, verifiable and irreversible dismantlement of 《North Korea's》 nuclear programs (略: CVID).
シー・ブイ・エス【CVS】1〔交通〕〔コンピューター制御自動運転輸送システム〕a computer-controlled vehicle system.
2〔コンビニエンス・ストア〕a CVS; a convenience store.
シー・ブイ・エム【CVM】〔仮想評価法〕CVM. ▶ CVM は contingent valuation method の略.
シー・ブイ・シー・エフ【CVCF】〔電気〕〔定電圧定周波数電源装置；交流出力の無停電電源装置〕a「constant-voltage constant-frequency [CVCF] power supply; an AC 「uninterruptible power supply [UPS].
シー・ブイ・ディー【CVD】〔物・化〕〔化学蒸着(法)〕CVD; chemical vapor deposition. ▷ 低温 CVD low-temperature CVD.
ジー・フォー【G4】〔国連の非常任理事国のうち 2006 年に常任理事国入りを意図した4か国のグループ〔日本・ドイツ・インド・ブラジル〕〕the G4 (nations); the Group of Four.
シー・フォー・アイ【C4I】〔軍〕〔指揮・統制・通信・コンピューター・情報〕C4I; command, control, communication, computers, and intelligence. ▷ C4I システム a C4I system.
シー・ブリーズ 1〔商標〕〔米国製の薬用ローション〕Sea Breeze.
2〔カクテル〕a sea breeze.
ジーマージャン【芝麻醤】＝チーマージャン.

ジーム Ziem, Félix (François Georges Philibert) (1821–1911; フランスの画家).
シーモス【CMOS】▷ CMOS (イメージ)センサー a CMOS (image) sensor.
シー・モンキー〔商標・動〕〔アルテミア科のミジンコの一種；幼生は熱帯魚の稚魚の餌とされる〕a Sea-Monkey; *Artemia salina*. ▶ 一般名は brine shrimp.
ジー・ユー・エー・エム【GUAM】〔独立国家共同体の4か国で 1996 年結成した協力体〕GUAM. ▶ 構成国 (Georgia, Ukraine, Azerbaijan, Moldova) の頭文字から. 1997-2005 年は Uzbekistan を加え GUUAM と呼ぶだ.
ジー・ユー・ユー・エー・エム【GUUAM】〔独立国家共同体の5か国で結成の協力体〕GUUAM. ▶ 構成国 (Georgia, Ukraine, Uzbekistan, Azerbaijan, Moldova) の頭文字から. 2005 年のウズベキスタン脱退により GUAM に戻る.
ジーリーきしゃ【吉利汽車】〔中国の自動車メーカー〕Geely Automobile.
シール[1] ▷ シール容器 a (re)sealable (plastic) container. シール・リング 【機】a seal(ing) ring.
シール[3]【SEAL】〔米軍〕〔米海軍の特殊作戦部隊〕SEAL；〔その1人〕a (Navy) SEAL. ▶ *sea*, *air*, *land* の略.
シールド ▷ シールド・マシン〔土木〕〔トンネル掘削機の一種〕a shield (tunnelling) machine.
シー・ワイ・ピー・ワン・エー・ツー【CYP1A2】〔生化〕〔肝薬物代謝酵素〕CYP1A2. ▶ cytochrome P450, family 1, subfamily A, polypeptide 2 の略.
ジー・ワン〔競馬の最上級レース 16〕【G1】G1; Grade 1.
シーン 1 Sheen, Charlie (1965–; 米国の映画俳優；本名 Carlos Irwin Estevez; 2の子).
2 Sheen, Martin (1940–; 米国の映画俳優；本名 Ramon Estevez; 1の父).
しうんてん【試運転】▷ 試運転車 a test vehicle.
シェア ▷ 国内[世界]シェア the 「domestic [world] (market) share.
じえい[2]【自衛】▷ 自衛艦旗 a [the] Maritime Self-Defense Force flag. 自衛軍 a self-defense army. 自衛消防隊〔企業などの〕a private 「fire prevention [fire-fighting] team. 自衛戦争 a defensive war; a war in self-defense.
「JSA」〔映画〕JSA-Joint Security Area.
ジェイキャップ【JCAP】＝ジェーキャップ.
シェイク[2]〔(アラビア語で)長老〕a sheik(h); a shaykh.
「ジェイコブス・ラダー」〔映画〕Jacob's ladder.
シェイ・スタジアム〔米国ニューヨーク市にある競技場〕Shea Stadium.
ジェイセック【JSEC】JSEC; the Japan Science and Engineering Challenge. ▶ 朝日新聞社主催の高校生のための科学技術コンテスト.
ジェイゾロフト〔商標・薬〕〔抗鬱剤〕(日本での名称) J-Zoloft;〔米国などでの名称〕Zoloft. ▶ 一般名は 塩酸セルトラリン.
ジェイ・ターン【J–】〔出身地から都会に進学や就職した後、出身地近くの地域に戻ること〕the return of people from the provinces to places near their hometowns after studying or working in big cities.
ジェイハン〔トルコ南部, 地中海沿岸の都市〕Ceyhan.
ジェイ・ピー・モルガン・チェース【JP–】〔米国の銀行〕J. P. Morgan Chase & Co.
ジェイ・ロック【J–】J-rock; Japanese rock music.
「ジェヴォーダンの獣」〔映画〕Brotherhood of the Wolf;〔原題〕Le Pacte des Loups.
ジェー・アイ・シー【JIC】〔英国の情報機関〕統合情報委員会〕the JIC; the Joint Intelligence Committee.
ジェー・エー【JA】▷ JA 共済〔全国共済農業協同組合連合会〕the National Mutual Insurance Federation of Agricultural Cooperatives (略: Zenkyoren).
ジェー・エフ・エル【JFL】〔日本フットボールリーグ〕JFL; the Japan Football League.

「**JFK**」〔映画〕JFK.
「**JLG/自画像**」〔映画〕JLG/JLG – Self-Portrait in December;〔原題〕JLG/JLG – autoportrait de decembre.
**ジェーキャップ**〖JCAP〗〔大気改善のための自動車および燃料技術開発事業〕JCAP; the Japan Clean Air Program.
**ジェー・シー・エー・ピー**〖JCAP〗＝ジェーキャップ.
**ジェー・パワー**〖J –〗〔電源開発株式会社の略称〕J-POWER. ▶ 正式名称は Electric Power Development Co., Ltd.
**ジェー・ピー・エー・ピー**〖JPAP〗⇨ジャパン・パートナーズ・アゲンスト・ペイン.
**ジェームズ・ロスとう**〖–島〗〔南極半島北端の島〕James Ross Island.
**ジェー・リーガー**〖J –〗〔J リーグに属している選手〕a J. Leaguer.
**ジェー・ワン**〖J1〗 ▫ J1 昇格 ◐ ～昇格を目指す〔決める〕aim at [win] promotion to J1.
「**ジェーンズ・ディフェンス・ウイークリー**」〔英国の軍事情報週刊誌〕Jane's Defence Weekly.
**じえき**² 〖自益〗(an) individual [a personal] benefit; (an) individual [a personal] profit. ▫ 自益権〖株主の～〗one's personal profit rights as a shareholder. 自益信託 a personal trust.
**シェケル**〔イスラエルの通貨単位〕a shekel 《pl. ～s》.
**シェケル・バイラム**〔イスラムの断食明けの祭り；砂糖祭〕Seker Bayram; the Sugar Holiday.
**ジェゴグ**〖楽器〗〔インドネシア，バリ島の竹製の打楽器〕a jegog.
「**ジェシカおばさんの事件簿**」〔米国の、元教師の作家 Jessica の推理劇 TV ドラマ〕Murder, She Wrote.
**ジエチルトルアミド**〖化〗〔防虫剤〕diethyltoluamide; *〘俗〙DEET.
**ジェット** ▫ ジェット風船 a rocket balloon. ジェット・ヘリコプター〖空〗〔ターボシャフトエンジン装備のヘリコプター〕a jet helicopter. ジェット・ミル〖機〗a jet mill.
**ジェット**² 〖宝石〗〖黒玉〗a jet.
**ジェットき**〖–機〗 ▫ 自家用ジェット機 a private jet.
「**ジェットジャクソン**」〔ジェット機を駆って悪に挑む元米空軍パイロットの TV ドラマ〕Jet Jackson, Flying Commando. ▶ 当初のタイトルは Captain Midnight.
「**ジェット・パイロット**」〔米海軍の曲技飛行チームの TV ドラマ〕The Blue Angels.
「**ジェット・ファイター**」〔米空軍中佐 Steve Canyon が新鋭機開発に尽力する TV ドラマ〕Steve Canyon.
**ジェット・プログラム**〖JET –〗〔語学指導等を行う外国青年招致事業〕the JET Programme; the Japan Exchange and Teaching Programme.
**ジェット・リー** Jet Li (1963– ; 中国の映画俳優; 中国語名 李連杰 Li Lian-Jie).
「**シェナンドー**」〔記憶喪失の男が南北戦争直後の西部をさまよう TV ドラマ〕A Man Called Shenandoah.
**ジェニン**〔ヨルダン川西岸北部のパレスチナ自治区の市〕Jenin.
**ジェネイナ**〔スーダン，西ダルフール州の州都〕Geneina.
**ジェネシス**〔米国の太陽探査機〕Genesis.
**ジェネラル・サントス**〔フィリピン、ミンダナオ島南部の都市〕General Santos.
**ジェネラル・パートナー**＝ゼネラル・パートナー.
**ジェノヴァ** ▫ ジェノヴァ・ソース Geno(v)ese sauce;《It》*salsa genovese*. ジェノヴァ・ペースト〖スパゲティソースの1種〗《It》*pesto (genovese)*.
**シェパーズ・パイ**〖料理〗〔挽き肉とマッシュ・ポテトで作るイギリスの家庭料理〕(a) shepherd's pie.
**ジェフロイくもざる**〖–蜘蛛猿〗〖動〗a Geoffroy's spider monkey; *Ateles geoffroyi*.
**シェブロンテキサコ**〔米国の石油会社〕ChevronTexaco.

**ジェマー・イスラミア**〔東南アジアのテロ組織〕Jemaah Islami(y)ah; Jamaah Islami(y)ah (略: JI).
**ジェミニてんもんだい**〖–天文台〗〖天〗the Gemini Observatory;〔ハワイの〕the Gemini North Observatory;〔チリの〕the Gemini South Observatory.
**ジェミニぼうえんきょう**〖–望遠鏡〗〖天〗a Gemini telescope;〔ハワイの〕the Gemini North telescope;〔チリの〕the Gemini South telescope.
**ジェムザール**〖商標・薬〗〔抗がん剤 塩酸ゲムシタビンの商品名〕Gemzar.
**シェム・リアップ**＝シエム・レアプ.
**シエム・レアプ**〔カンボジア北西部の州；同州の州都〕Siem Reap.
**ジェリー・バッグ**〖服飾〗a jelly bag.
**シェルター** ▫ ▫ 民間シェルター〔DV 被害者などの〕a privately operated shelter《for domestic violence victims》.
**シェルティ**〖犬〗a sheltie.
**シェルトン** Shelton, Ron (1945– ；米国の映画監督・脚本家).
**シェロー** Chéreau, Patrice (1944– ；フランスの映画監督).
**しえん**¹ 〖支援〗 ▫ ▫ 支援活動 assistance [support] activities. 支援材料 an encouraging [a favorable] factor. ◐ 堅調に推移する日本株が円の～材料となっている. The strengthening of Japanese stocks is supporting [favorable to] the Yen. 支援センター a support center《for earthquake victims》. 支援費制度〖障害者のため〗an assistance funding system《for the handicapped》.
**ジェンダー** ▫ ▫ ジェンダー・エンパワーメント指数 ＝ジェンダー・エンパワーメントそくてい. ジェンダー・エンパワーメント測定〖女性が積極的に経済や政治などに参画しているかどうかを示すもの；国連開発計画の人間開発指数の調査基準の1つ〗the gender empowerment measure（略: GEM）. ジェンダー主流化〖男女間に不平等が存在することを認識し、その解消を目指して努力すること〗gender mainstreaming.
**ジェンツァーノ**〔イタリア、ローマ郊外の都市〕Genzano.
**ジェンベ**〖楽器〗a ジャンベ.
**しおどおし**〖潮通し〗tide flow. ◐ ～がよい〔悪い〕 the tide flow is good [poor]; it has a strong [weak] tide flow / この場所は～がよく、魚がたくさん集まっている. The tide flow is good in this spot, and a lot of fish have gathered.
**しか**¹¹ 〖歯科〗 ▫ ▫ 法歯科(学) forensic dentistry [odontology]; dentistry used in the identification of bodies. ◐ 法～医 a forensic dentist [odontologist]. ▫ ▫ 歯科医師国家資格 a nationally recognized qualification as a dentist [dental license]; certification by the state as a dental practitioner. 歯科医師国家試験 the National Examination for Dentists. 歯科カルテ ＝歯科記録. 歯科記録 a dental chart.
**しが**² 〖歯牙〗歯牙腫〖医〗odontoma.
**しが**³ 〖自家〗 ▫ ▫ 自家感作性皮膚炎〖医〗(an) id reaction; autosensitization dermatitis; autoeczematization.
**じか**⁵ 〖時価〗 ▫ ▫ 時価評価損〔益〕mark-to-market loss [gain]. 時価ベース《on》a market value basis.
**じか**⁷ 〖磁化〗 ▫ ▫ 磁化水 ＝磁気活性水（⇨じき⁷）.
**シガー** ▫ ▫ シガー・ボックス〖大道芸のジャグリングの演目で、木製の箱3個で演じる〗cigar boxes；〔その箱〕a cigar box.
**ジカール**〔イラク南部の州〕Dhi Qar. ▶ 州都 ナシリヤ.
**しがい**¹ 〖市外〗 ▫ ▫ 市外通話 a long-distance call; a toll [an out-of-town] call. ◐ 県外～通話 an out-of-prefecture long-distance call / 県内～通話 an in-prefecture long-distance call; an intraprefectural call.
**しがい**⁴ 〖紫外〗 ▫ ▫ 紫外光 ultraviolet light.
**しがいせん**〖紫外線〗 ▫ ▫ **A** 紫外線〖長波長紫外線〗ultraviolet-A (略: UVA). **B** 紫外線〖中波長紫外線〗ul-

traviolet-B〔略：UVB〕．**C** 紫外線〔短波長紫外線〕ultraviolet-C〔略：UVC〕．深紫外線〔物〕deep ultraviolet [DUV] light [rays]．　□▶ 紫外線ランプ[ライト] an ultraviolet lamp.

**しがいち**【市街地】　□▶ 既成市街地〔法〕an existing urban area．□▶ 市街地価格指数 the urban land price index（略：ULPI）．　□▶ 六大都市～価格指数 the urban land price index in six major cities．市街地再開発促進区域 an urban redevelopment promotion area．市街地（戦闘）訓練場〔自衛隊の〕an urban military exercise area (for the Ground Self-Defense Force).

**しかいりょうじょうほうすいしんきこう**【歯科医療情報推進機構】the Institute of Dental Information（略：IDI）.

**しかく**[6]【視覚】　□▶ 視覚化 visualization．視覚センサー〔ロボットなどの〕a visual sensor.

**しかく**[7]【資格】　□▶ 資格外活動〔在留外国人の〕activities other than those permitted under *one's* status of residence．資格外活動許可申請書 an [a written] application for permission to engage in an activity other than those permitted under *one's* status of residence．資格取得 getting [obtaining] a qualification; qualification．資格停止 (a) suspension; suspension of qualification; suspension of a license．　□▶ ～停止処分になる[を受ける] be [get] suspended; (免許)have *one's* license suspended; get a suspension.

**しがくきょうさい**【私学共済】＝しりつがっこうきょうしょくいんきょうさいくみあい．

**しがくじょせいほう**【私学助成法】〔法〕＝しりつがっこうしんこうじょせいほう．

**「シカゴ特捜隊M」**〔米国，殺人担当刑事集団の TV ドラマ〕M Squad．▶M は murder の頭文字．

**シカゴ・トリビューン**〔米国シカゴの朝刊紙〕The Chicago Tribune.

**しがしゅう**【詩画集】a collection of poems and illustrations; an illustrated [illuminated] poetry collection.

**しかつ**【死活】　□▶ 死活的 life-and-death [life-or-death]（issues）．　□▶ これはこれからの日本にとって～的な意味を持つ大問題だ．This is a matter of huge importance which will be a life-and-death issue for Japan's future. | This is an issue with the most vital implications for Japan's future.

**「四月の雪」**〔映画〕April Snow.

**シガトキシン**〔生化〕〔魚類中に含まれ，神経をおかす毒の1つ〕(a) ciguatoxin.

**じがね**【地金】　□▶ 亜鉛[銅]地金 zinc [copper] metal.

**じかばし**【直箸】　□▶ 料理を盛った大皿を5人で囲み、～で食べた．The five of us gathered around the platter of food and helped ourselves, all eating off the same plate.

**しかぼん**【私家本】a privately printed book.

**しがん**[3]【志願】　□▶ 志願状況 the current number of 「applicants [candidates]（for the law department of Waseda University）．　□▶ 千葉県は県内の私立高校入試の～状況を発表した．Chiba Prefecture announced the number of applicants per place at private high schools in the prefecture．志願倍率〔入試の〕the [a] ratio of 「applicants [candidates] to places; a [the] ratio of 「applicants [candidates] per place; 〔就職試験などの〕the [a] ratio of job applicants to jobs; an applicant to job ratio.

**じかん**[3]【耳管】　□▶ 耳管扁桃〔解〕a tubal tonsil; the tubal tonsils.

**じかん**[4]【時間】　□▶ 時間軸〔グラフで時間の経過を示す横軸〕a 「time [temporal] axis; a time base．　□▶ 核燃料サイクル技術の研究開発はもう少し～軸を長くとり、安全面に進めるべきだ．It would be better to adopt a slightly longer time base for R & D on the technology for the nuclear fuel cycle, and proceed with safety as the first priority．時間軸効果〔金融〕a policy duration effect．時間軸政策〔日本銀行の〕(a) time-axis policy．時間短縮勤務 shorter working hours．時間通貨〔互助的なサービスの交換単位としての時間〕a time(-based) currency; a time currency system.

**じかんさ**【時間差】　□▶ 一人時間差〔バレーボール〕a delayed (solo) spike; a solo fake-and-spike play.

**じかんたい**【時間帯】　□▶ 時間帯お届け〔宅配便・郵便などの〕time-period delivery; delivery《of a parcel》during a specified time period．　□▶ ～お届けサービス a time-period delivery service．時間帯割引 an off-peak time discount.

**しき**[11]【指揮】　□▶ 指揮船〔集団遠泳・海難救助などの〕a command boat.

**じき**[7]【磁気】　□▶ 磁気活性水 magnetic water; magnetized water．磁気記録〔電子工学〕(a) magnetic recording．　□▶ 面内[水平]～記録方式 longitudinal magnetic recording．磁気シールド a magnetic shield; magnetic shielding．磁気水 ＝磁気活性水．磁気ストライプ〔クレジットカードなどの裏側の黒い磁気テープ〕a magnetic 「stripe [strip]．磁気センサー a magnetic sensor．磁気治療器 a magnetic 「healing product [healer]．磁気データ magnetic data．磁気変態点〔冶〕a magnetic transition point; a magnetic transformation point．磁気冷凍 magnetic refrigeration．　□▶ ～冷凍材料 a magnetic refrigerant.

**じき**[8]【磁器】　□▶ 強化磁器 strengthened [high-strength] porcelain.

**しきかく**【色覚】　□▶ 色覚特性〔眼科〕color-vision characteristics.

**しきかん**【指揮官】　□▶ 指揮官旗 a [the] commander's banner.

**しきかんとく**【指揮監督】　□▶ 指揮監督権 《give the prime minister》the right of command《over the Self-Defense Forces》;《give the president》the authority to command《the armed forces》.

**じききょうめい**【磁気共鳴】　□▶ 磁気共鳴血管撮影[影]〔法〕〔医〕magnetic resonance angiography（略：MRA）; MR angiography．磁気共鳴断層撮影 magnetic resonance imaging（略：MRI）.

**しきさ**【色差】(a) color difference; (a) difference in colors.

**しきさい**【色彩】　□▶ 色彩セラピスト a color therapist; a chromotherapist．色彩療法士 a color therapist; a chromotherapist.

**しきざい**[2]【資機材】〔材料・部品および機器の総称〕mechanical equipment and materials.

**しきそ**【色素】　□▶ 色素増感(型)太陽電池 a dye-sensitized solar cell（略：DSSC）.

**しきち**【敷地】　□▶ 敷地境界基準〔法〕〔大気汚染防止法で定められたアスベスト等の発生についての環境保全基準〕the standards on the border line between the grounds of a factory or business establishment and a neighboring property.

**しきひき**【敷引】　□▶〔賃貸住居から退去する際、次の入居のための補修費用などを敷金から差し引くこと〕money withheld from a deposit (after a renter has moved out, to cover repairs prior to renting again).

**しきべつ**【識別】　□▶ 識別マーク〔紙幣の〕tactile marks.

**じきぼうぎょそうち**【自機防御装置】〔軍〕〔戦闘機・輸送機などをミサイル攻撃から守る〕defensive countermeasures.

**じきみや**【直宮】　□▶ 直宮家 the house of a prince 「in a direct line from an emperor [of the imperial blood].

**しきゅう**[1]【子宮】　□▶ 子宮腺筋症〔医〕uterine adenomyosis; adenomyosis of the uterus.

**じきゅう**[2]【持久】　□▶ 持久系　□▶ ～系スポーツ an en-

しきゅうないまく【子宮内膜】▷ 子宮内膜がん (a) ⌈carcinoma [cancer] of the endometrium; endometrial ⌈carcinoma [cancer]. 子宮内膜増殖症 〖医〗 endometrial hyperplasia. 子宮内膜剥離術[アブレーション] 〖医〗 endometrial ablation.
しぎょ【仔魚】a larva 《*pl.* larvae, 〜s》; (fish) larva; larval fish. ▷ 孵化仔魚 a larval fish; fish larvae. ▷ 仔魚期 the larval stage 《of salmon》.
しきょう³【市況】▷ 国際商品市況 the international commodity market.
じぎょう³【事業】
▷ 事業運営 business ⌈management [operations]. 事業運営安定資金 government funding designed to stabilize business ⌈management [operations]. 事業改善命令 a business improvement order. 事業継続計画 ＝緊急時事業継続計画 (略: BC). 事業承継 (a) business succession; succession of a business. ◐ 〜承継税制 the business succession tax system. 事業譲渡 transfer of a business 《to new ownership》. 事業スポンサー a corporate sponsor. 事業体 a business entity. 事業停止命令 an order to ⌈stop [cease] operations [(doing) business]. 事業認可 project ⌈approval [authorization].
じぎょうさいせいじつむかきょうかい【事業再生実務家協会】the Japanese Association of Turnaround Professionals.
じぎょうしょ【事業所】▷ 事業所内託児[保育]施設 a ⌈workplace [company] nursery [⌈crèche]. 事業所内託児施設設助成金 a subsidy for a workplace nursery.
じきょく²【時局】▷ 時局詠 a tanka on the current situation of the state.
しきり¹【仕切り】▷ 仕切り時間 〖相撲〗the (allotted) time for the warming-up ritual. ▷ 仕切り時間制 time limit for the warming-up ritual; 《口》time to get to grips. 仕切り役 a coordinator; a moderator; a facilitator.
しきん⁵【資金】
▷ 資金援助方式〔金融機関破綻の際の預金者保護方式〕the formula by which the Deposit Insurance Organization of Japan allocates funding support to bridge banks. 資金回収 recovery of invested capital. 資金供給 providing [provision of] capital [funds]; funding. 資金吸収オペ(レーション)〔日銀の〕fund-absorbing operations. 資金供給オペ(レーション)〔日銀の〕fund-supplying operations. 資金拠出 funding; (making) a contribution; contribution 《to a cause》. 資金循環 (the) circulation of money; a [the] flow of ⌈funds [capital]; (a) money flow; (a) funds flow. 資金循環統計 flow-of-funds ⌈account(s) [accounting]; 〔日銀の〕flow-of-funds statistics. 資金調達力 (a) fund-raising ⌈ability [capacity]. 資金提供 a funding offer; an offer of ⌈capital [funding]. ◐ 〜提供の offer ⌈capital [funding]; make ⌈funding [capital] available; put up capital; fund / 〜提供国 a funding ⌈country [nation]; a donor ⌈country [nation]; a contributing ⌈country [nation]; a financial contributor / 〜提供者 a financial contributor; a contributor of ⌈capital [money, funding]; a financial supporter; a financial backer; a funder. 資金利益 〖金融〗〔貸出・預金の利息収支を示す〕interest income; income from interest.
しきんうんよう【資金運用】▷ 資金運用収支〔銀行などの〕a balance from ⌈fund administration [administrating a fund].
しきんぐり【資金繰り】▷ 資金繰り指標 ＝資金繰り判断 DI[指数]; 資金繰り判断 DI[指数] the financial position ⌈DI [diffusion index]; the diffusion index of "easy" minus "tight."

じく²【字句】▷ 字句修正 (an) alteration [(an) amendment, (a) change, (a) modification] to the wording; (a) re-wording. ◐ 条文に若干の〜修正を施す make minor changes to the wording; alter the wording slightly.
ジグザグ ▷ ジグザグ打線 〖野球〗〔右打者と左打者を交互に並べた打線〕an alternating (lefty-righty) lineup; a lefty-righty lineup.
シグナル ▷ シグナル効果 〖金融〗a signal effect; an announcement effect. シグナル分子 〖生化〗a signal molecule.
しくみ【仕組み】▷ 仕組み債 〖金融〗structured bonds.
シグリ〔インドネシア・アチェ州、ビドィ県の県都〕Sigli.
しぐれ【時雨】▷ 秋時雨 (autumnal [*fall]) shower. 片時雨 a local(ized) shower; localized showers; showers in places. 春時雨 a spring shower. 雪時雨 a sleet shower; a shower of sleet.
シクロサリン 〖化〗〔有機リン系神経ガス〕cyclosarin.
シクロフィリン 〖生化〗〔細胞質たんぱく質の一種〕cyclophilin (略: CyP).
しけい²【死刑】▷ 死刑確定者, 死刑確定囚〔死刑囚〕a condemned ⌈convict [criminal, prisoner]; a convict ⌈under sentence of death [on death row]; a death-row convict. 死刑求刑 demand for the death ⌈penalty [sentence]. 死刑存置国 a country which ⌈retains [still has] the death penalty. 死刑廃止国 a country which ⌈has abolished [no longer has] the death penalty.
しけいはいしをすいしんするぎいんれんめい【死刑廃止を推進する議員連盟】the Diet Members' League for the Abolition of the Death Penalty.
じけいれつ【時系列】▷ 時系列調査 a time-series survey.
しげき²【刺激】▷ 刺激頂 〖生理〗a terminal ⌈threshold [stimulus].
しけつ【止血】▷ 直接圧迫止血(法) the direct pressure method.
しけん³【試験】▷ 試験運用 trial [test] operation; a ⌈trial [test] run. ◐ 〜運用する do a ⌈trial [test] run 《on [of]…》. 試験営業 trial operation; a test run. 試験範囲 the ⌈coverage [scope] of an exam; what an exam covers.
しげん⁴【資源】▷ 非在来型[在来型]資源 unconventional [conventional] resources. ▷ 資源株 a ⌈resources [resource] stock. 資源工学 resources [resource] engineering. 資源節約型 resource(s)-saving (society). 資源多消費型 resource-guzzling (industry, society). 資源探査 resource exploration. 資源摩擦 friction over resources.
じけん¹【事件】▷ 事件屋 a fixer.
じげん²【時限】▷ 時限(式)発火装置 a timing ignition device. 時限措置 a limited-time measure. ◐ この減税は 3 年間の〜措置だ. The tax reduction is ⌈a three-year, limited-time measure [limited to three years].
「事件記者コルチャック」〔米国の，超常現象や怪物を追う記者の TV ドラマ〕Kolchak: The Night Stalker.
しげん・そざいがっかい【資源・素材学会】the Mining and Material Processing Institute of Japan (略: MMIJ).
しげんゆうこうりようそくしんほう【資源有効利用促進法】〖法〗the Law for Promotion of Effective Utilization of Resources.
しご²【死後】▷ 死後出産〔母体の死後の出産〕(a) ⌈postmortem [perimortem] delivery; posthumous birth; 〔夫の死後，冷凍保存精子による〕posthumous (conception and) birth from the dead father's preserved sperm. 死後生殖 〖医〗〔夫の凍結精子による生殖〕posthumous reproduction. 死後妊娠〔懐胎〕〔冷凍保存精子による〕postmortem conception.
じこ¹【自己】

## じこ

自己アピール personal appeal; 《good》 self-presentation. 自己開示〖心理〗 self-disclosure. 自己管理能力 self-control「ability [capacity]; capacity for self-control[-discipline]. 自己記録 〔陸上競技など〕a personal record. ▶ ～記録更新〔set〕a new personal record / ～記録を更新する extend [improve on] one's personal record. 自己(血)貯血 banking blood before surgery; (an) autologous (blood) donation. 自己検査キット〖医〗a self-diagnosis kit. 自己研鑽(さん) advancing one's knowledge; self-development; self-improvement. ▶ ～研鑽する advance one's knowledge; develop [improve] oneself. 自己検証 self-examination; self-reflection. 自己肯定 self-approval. 自己臭(恐怖)症〖精神医〗olfactory reference syndrome (略: ORS). 自己受容 self-acceptance. 自己情報 information about oneself; one's (own) personal 「information [data]. 自己情報コントロール権 the right to control「one's personal information [how one's personal information is used]. 自己信託〖法〗〔家族などは受益者として財産権を自分に信託すること〕a self-administered trust. 自己推薦入試 admission [(university) entrance] based on self-recommendation. 自己増殖 self-reproduction; self-propagation. ▶ ～増殖する self-reproduce; self-propagate / ～増殖型の self-replicating; self-propagating; self-reproducing / ～増殖型ウイルス〖電算〗a self-propagating virus. 自己鍛造弾〔車両などの装甲を貫通する威力を持つ〕a self-forging fragment (略: SFF). ▶ 爆発成形弾 ともいう. 自己投影 self-projection; projecting oneself 《on the characters in one's novels》. 自己投入 ＝自己投影;〔没頭〕self-immersion. 自己売買〔証券〕buying and selling on one's own account; dealing 《in stocks》. 自己判断 judging by oneself; deciding on one's own; using one's own judgment; making up one's own mind. ▶ 胃炎と似た症状を示す重大な病気もあるので～判断は禁物だ. Since there are serious diseases with symptoms similar to gastritis, never「decide for yourself [make your own diagnosis]. 自己判定 self-assessment; self-adjudication. 自己変革 self-reform. 自己PR self-advertisement; self-publicity; self-PR. ▶ ～PRする advertise [publicize] oneself; do one's own「PR [publicity]. 自己評価委員会 a 《university》 self-assessment[-evaluation] committee. 自己表現能力 capacity for self-expression; self-expression ability. 自己複製 self-replication. ▶ ～複製する self-replicate.

**じこ**[2]【事故】 ▣ 受傷事故 an injury accident. 対人事故 an [a car, an automobile] accident resulting in injury or death to a person or people not in「the [one's] vehicle. 対歩行者事故〔自動車などの〕an [a car, an automobile] accident resulting in pedestrian injury or death. 多重事故 a multiple (car) accident. 非接触事故 a no-contact accident. 誘因事故〔衝突回避装置によって発生した交通事故〕a secondary [an avoidance] accident (resulting from taking evasive action). ▣ 事故学 accidentology. 事故機 an airplane involved in an accident. 事故渋滞 a traffic jam caused by an accident. 事故状況報告書 an「accident [incident] report; 〔保険の〕an insurance「accident [incident] report. 事故情報 (car, product) accident information. 事故申告 notification [notice] 《of an accident》; notifying [informing] 《the post office》 that (mail has not arrived). ▶ 自転車の事故では～申告がなされないケースが多い. People often don't「notify the police of bicycle accidents [report bicycle accidents (to the police)]. 事故(発生)確率〔事故が起こる可能性についての〕(high, low) accident probability. 事故不申告〔交通事故などの〕failure to「notify [inform, tell] 《the authorities》 《of an accident, that there has been an accident》. 事故論 ＝事故学.

**じこ**[2]【事後】 ▣ 事後収賄〖法〗〔過去に公務員であった人に関して〕acceptance of a bribe after leaving office. 事後対応 (a) subsequent response; (an) after-the-fact response. 事後通告 retrospective「notification [notice]; ex post facto「notification [notice]. 事後テスト〔教育指導の成果を試すための〕a posttest. 事後買収〖法〗〔選挙終了後などの金品の提供〕bribery ex post facto.

**しこう**[10]【思考】 ▣ 思考停止 the coming of thought to a standstill; an inability to think; going blank. ▶ ～停止状態に陥る become unable to think; go blank.

**しこう**[18]【嗜好】 ▣ 嗜好性 a taste 《for wine》; a「liking [fondness]; a personal preference. ▶ 甘いものは～性が強いから控えたほうがいい. It's easy to become overly fond of sweets, so you should cut back on them.

**しこう**[20]【試行】 ▣ 試行期間 a trial period 《for a new system》.

**しこう**[21]【趾行・指行】【動】 ▣ 趾行性(の) digitigrade. 趾行動物 a digitigrade.

**じこう**[3]【耳垢】 ▣ 耳垢栓塞[塞栓]〖医〗impacted cerumen; impacted earwax.

**じこう**[4]【事項】 ▣ 所管事項 an area of responsibility 《of the Budget Bureau》; a responsibility 《of family courts》.

しごういん【四合院】〔中央の庭を四棟の建物で囲む, 中国の伝統的な建築様式〕si he yuan; the si he yuan traditional Chinese style of residential building.

じこうがた【持効型】【薬】sustained-effect 《drugs》 ▣ 持効型インスリン sustained-effect insulin.

しこうさじょうかく【視交叉上核】〖解〗the suprachiasmatic nucleus (略: SCN).

じこうせい【持効性】【薬】＝じこうがた.

じこうていかんけつ【自工程完結】〖生産工学〗〔各工程ごとに製造の不備を発見して対処し, 後工程に影響を及ぼさないようにするシステム〕"defect-free process completion" at every stage of production; (the system of) ensuring that each component is defect-free before it moves on to the next stage of assembly.

じこうほうしき【自校方式】〔学校内で調理する給食方式〕the system of preparing school lunches on site.

じこかぶしき【自己株式】 ▣ 自己株式取得枠 the amount of treasury stock that may be「acquired [purchased].

じこかんけつ【自己完結】self-sufficiency. ▣ 自己完結型の[的な] self-sufficient 《organizations》.

じごくどう【地獄道】〖仏教〗〔六道の1つ〕the (Buddhist) hell.

しこくはちじゅうはっかしょ【四国八十八箇所】 ▣ 四国八十八箇所巡り (a) pilgrimage to the Eighty-eight Buddhist temples in Shikoku.

じこしほん【自己資本】 ▣ 中核的自己資本 Tier 1 capital; core capital.

じこしょくばい【自己触媒】【化】autocatalysis. ▣ 不斉自己触媒反応 asymmetric autocatalysis.

したんたん【色丹島】〔北海道東部, 根室半島沖合にある島〕(the island of) Shikotan.

しごと【仕事】 ▣ 仕事運 one's「work [career] luck [fortune]. 仕事漬け working constantly; being snowed under with work. ▶ ここのところ～漬けの毎日を送っている. Recently I've been snowed under with work every day. 仕事人間 a person who「lives for his work [always puts his work first]; a「work-oriented [career-oriented, career-minded] person.

じこはさん【自己破産】 ▣ 準自己破産〖法〗a quasi-voluntary bankruptcy 《whereby a director of an insolvent company requests to have the company declared bankrupt》.

**じこふたん【自己負担】** 〘 〙 自己負担分＝〔自己負担額〕the amount「paid [to be paid] individually [by an individual]; each individual's contribution; the amount of personal payment; ＝自己負担率. 自己負担率 the individual「contribution [payment] rate.

**じこめんえき【自己免疫】** 略〉自己免疫性肝炎 〘医〙 autoimmune hepatitis (略: AIH).

**しさ[3]【視差】** 〘 〙 視差バリア〔立体画像を表示するために液晶ディスプレーに配置するスリット〕a parallax barrier.

**じさ[3]【時差】** 〘 〙 時差式信号〔交通信号の一種〕a delayed signal. 時差症候群 desynchronization syndrome; jet lag.

**「シザーハンズ」**〘映画〙Edward Scissorhands.

**しざい[7]【資材】** 〘 〙 資材置き場 a storage「site [area, yard]. 資材所要量計画〘経営〙material requirements planning (略: MRP).

**しさえき【死差益】**〘生命保険〙〔予定死亡率と実際の死亡率の差によって生じる利益〕mortality「profits [gains].

**しさく[5]【試作】** 〘 〙 試作エンジン an experimental engine. 試作機〔飛行機の〕an experimental [a test] airplane;〔バイクの〕an experimental [a test] motorcycle;〔機械の〕an experimental machine. 試作車両〔鉄道の〕experimental rolling stock.

**しさそん【死差損】**〘生命保険〙〔予定死亡率と実際の死亡率の差によって生じる損〕mortality losses.

**しさそんえき【死差損益】**〘生命保険〙〔予定死亡率と実際の死亡率の差によって生じる損益〕a mortality profit or loss.

**じさつ[2]【自殺】** 〘 〙 偽装自殺〔自殺を装った他殺〕(a) murder disguised as (a) suicide;〔自殺と見せかけて行方をくらますこと〕a fake suicide. グループ自殺 (a) group suicide. 〘 〙 自殺遺族 ⇨いぞく[2]. 自殺願望 (a) suicide wish; (a) suicidal「desire [inclination, feeling]. ◇ ～願望者 a suicidal person; a potential suicide. 自殺関連サイト a suicide-related site (on the Web). 自殺(系)サイト〔インターネット上の〕a suicide Web site. 自殺予防〘learn, study〙suicide prevention; how to prevent suicide(s).

**じさつたいさくきほんほう【自殺対策基本法】**〘法〙the Basic Law on Measures to Discourage Suicide.

**じさつたいさくしえんセンター・ライフリンク【自殺対策支援–】**the Lifelink Suicide Prevention Action Network.

**しさん[4]【試算】** 〘 〙 試算値 an estimated value; an estimate.

**しさん[5]【資産】** 〘 〙 資産課税〘経〙estate taxation; real estate taxation. 資産管理会社 an asset management company (略: AMC). 資産効率 asset efficiency. 資産等報告書〔政治家・自治体首長などの〕an asset disclosure statement. 資産評価額 the「appraised [estimated, assessed] value of assets. 資産評価益〘会計〙(a) gain on revaluation of assets. 資産評価損〘会計〙(a) loss on revaluation of assets. 資産負債管理〘金融〙asset-liability management (略: ALM). 資産報告書 ＝資産等報告書.

**しざん【死産】** 〘 〙 死産届 reporting a「stillbirth [fetal death] (to the local government).

**じさん[2]【持参】** 〘 〙 持参薬〔入院時に患者が病院に持ち込む薬〕(a patient's own)「medicines [medication] brought into hospital.

**ジザン**〔サウジアラビア南西部, 紅海沿岸の州; その州都〕Jizan.

**しざんけつが【屍山血河】**mountains of dead (bodies) and rivers of blood (after a battle). ◇ ～を築く cause mountains of dead and rivers of blood.

**じざんこう【自山鉱】**〔鉱工業の会社が自ら所有する鉱山〕(a) mining company('s) mine.

**じじ[4]【時事】** 〘 〙 時事漫画 a topical cartoon.

**シシケバブ**〘料理〙〔トルコなど中近東の(おもに)羊の串焼き肉〕shish「kebab [kabob].

**ししつ[3]【脂質】** 〘 〙 脂質異常 dyslipidemia; lipid abnormalities. 脂質代謝〘生理〙lipid metabolism. 脂質代謝異常 abnormal [an error of] lipid metabolism. 脂質メディエーター〘生理〙〘生理活性脂質〙a lipid mediator. ◇ ～メディエーター受容体 a lipid mediator receptor.

**じじつ[1]【事実】** 〘 〙 事実確認 confirming [verifying, ascertaining] the facts《regarding an accident》. ◇ 航空機ハイジャックの発生に伴い, 政府は情報の収集と～確認を急いでいる. In the wake of the aircraft hijacking, the government is urgently gathering information to determine what actually happened. 事実審理〘法〙a hearing; a trial. 事実認識 (an) awareness [(a) recognition, (an) apprehension, (an) understanding] of the facts. ◇ 双方の～認識には大きなへだたりがある. There is a big gap in the way the two sides「understand [apprehend] the facts. | The two sides have widely different views of the true situation.

**ししとう(がらし)【獅子唐(辛子)】**a *shishito* pepper; a sweet Japanese「chile [chili] pepper.

**じしゃ[2]【自社】** 〘 〙 自社技術 (an) in-house technology;《our company's》own technology. 自社買収〘経営〙a management buyout (略: MBO). 自社利用 internal [in-house] use. ◇ ～利用目的のソフトウェア software for「internal [in-house] use.

**じしゅ[1]【自主】** 〘 〙 自主開発〔共同開発などに対して〕independent development. ◇ 人工衛星を～開発する develop (artificial) satellites「independently [on one's own]; develop one's own (artificial) satellites. 自主開発原油〔石油〕independently developed (crude) oil. ◇ ～開発石油比率 the percentage of independently developed (crude) oil. 自主開発油田 an independently developed oil field. 自主開発車 an independently developed automobile. 自主企画 independent [autonomous, private] planning;〔催し物・事業など〕an independently [a privately] planned「event [enterprise]. ◇ ～企画事業 an independently planned「project [enterprise] / ～企画商品 ＝PB商品 (⇨ピー・ビー). 自主決定権 the right of self-determination. 自主再建 self-managed rehabilitation. ◇ 銀行が～再建を断念し, 更生特例法の適用を申請した. The bank gave up trying to「recover on its own [save itself] and applied for a bailout under the Special Corporate Rehabilitation Law. 自主(的)判断〘exercise〙independent judgment. 自主返還〔過払い金・横領金などの〕(a) voluntary reimbursement;〔免許・特権などの〕returning [relinquishing] sth「of one's own free will [on one's own initiative]. ◇ 当該行員は着服の事実を認めて, 着服した金額をすでに～返還し懲戒免職処分を受けているので, 告訴はしなかった. Since the clerk in question confessed and has already returned the money she pocketed and has been dismissed, we have not pressed charges. / 彼は70歳の誕生日に運転免許証を～返還した. On his 70th birthday he「voluntarily relinquished his driver's license [took the initiative and turned in his driver's license]. 自主防災 locally managed disaster「prevention [relief]. ◇ ～防災組織〘会〙a locally managed disaster「prevention [relief] organization. 自主ルール self-determined rules;〘play by, devise〙one's own rules. 自主練習 self-managed [self-organized]《sports》「practice [training]; voluntary「training [practice].

**じしゅ[2]【自首】** 〘 〙 自首減軽〘法〙(a) reduction in sentence for an offender who voluntarily turns「himself [herself] in.

**じしゅトレ(ーニング)【自主-】** 〘 〙 合同自主トレ voluntary group training.

シシュマレフ〔米国アラスカ州西部の村〕Shishmaref.
ししゅんき【思春期】 ▫思春期外来 adolescents' outpatient ˹services [treatment]˼.
じしょ⁵【辞書】 ▫内蔵辞書 a built-in dictionary.
▫辞書ソフト〘電算〙〔英和・和英・国語辞典など〕dictionary software.
ししょう¹【支障】 ▫支障木〔交通・送電などの障害となる立木〕an interfering tree; a tree ˹blocking [in the way of]˼《a planned road》.
ししょう¹³【視床】 ▫視床下核 a subthalamic nucleus.
しじょう³【市場】
▫国際市場 the international market. 米市場 the rice market. 有望市場 a promising market《for Japanese products》.
▫市場外流通 distribution ˹outside [bypassing]˼ wholesale ˹markets [channels]˼; direct distribution. 市場寡占度 ＝寡占度《⇨かせん⁹》. 市場型間接金融 market-oriented indirect financing. 市場関係者 people in the market. ◐～関係者によると[よれば] according to people in the market. 市場規模 market ˹size [scale]˼; the ˹size [scale]˼ of a market. ◐北欧における携帯電話の～規模は非常に大きい. The ˹mobile [cell]˼ phone market in Northern Europe is ˹very large [huge]˼. 市場金利連動型融資 spread lending. 市場経済国〔政府貿易機関（WTO）協定上の〕a market economy ˹country [nation]˼. ◐～経済国の地位《grant a country》market economy ˹country [nation]˼ status / 非～経済国 a ˹non market economy [NME]˼ country [nation]. 市場公募地方債 a publicly-marketed ˹municipal [local government]˼ bond. 市場心理 market psychology. 市場推定価格 an estimated market ˹price [value]˼. 市場動向 a market trend. ◐われわれはビールと発泡酒の～動向を分析している. We are analyzing trends in the market for beer and low-malt beer. 市場動向調査《conduct》a market trend survey. 乗用車～動向調査 a passenger car market trend survey / マンション～動向調査 a survey of trends in the market for apartments. 市場統治 ＝マーケット・ガバナンス《⇨マーケット》. 市場内[市場外]取引《証券》《株》on-market [off-market] trading. 市場予想価格 an anticipated market price《of $45》.
しじょう⁴【矢状】 ▫矢状稜〘動〙〔猿人・類人猿などの頭蓋骨にある突起〕a sagittal crest.
しじょう⁶【至上】 ▫至上命題 ◐次の選挙で過半数の議席を確保することが～命題だ. In the next election the absolute priority must be to obtain an overall majority.
しじょう¹⁰【紙上】 ▫紙上大会 ◐全国川柳～大会 a nationwide newspaper *senryū* contest.
しじょう¹¹【歯状】 ▫歯状回〘解〙the dentate gyrus. 歯状線〘解〙〔直腸と肛門の境〕the dentate line.
しじょう¹⁵【施条】 ▫施条〘銃砲〙〔弾丸に回転を与えるために何本もの螺旋(ｾﾝ)状の溝を銃身に刻むこと〕rifling. 施条痕〔発射された銃弾の銃腔面が付けた溝の痕〕rifling marks; land and groove impressions.
じじょう²【自浄】 ▫自浄作用 ⇨じじょうきのう.
じじょう³【事情】 ▫事情説明 an explanation《of the situation》; an account; an elucidation. ◐党は当該議員を党本部に呼び～説明を求めた. The party has summoned the member concerned to party headquarters to ˹explain the circumstances˼ [give an account of what happened].
しじょうかテスト【市場化-】〔官民競争入札制度〕a system of》competitive bidding between the public and private sectors; a competitive bid in which public and private sectors take part.
じじょうきのう【自浄機能】a 《self-》rectification function; the ability to self-correct; a purgative function;

a ˹correction [corrective]˼ function; the ability to return to an normal state. ◐この会社では～が有効に働いていなかった. The company proved incapable of ˹cleaning up its act [purging itself]˼ on its own. ◐この病気は体の～の加齢減退によるものだ. This disease is the result of a decline in the ageing body's ability to ˹repair itself [get rid of unwanted substances]˼.
しじょうげんり【市場原理】 ▫市場原理主義 free market [laissez-faire] principles; the belief that the market should be ˹left alone [allowed to determine the economy]˼. ◐～主義者 ˹believer in [proponent of]˼ the free market; a free marketeer.
しじょうちつじょいじきょうてい【市場秩序維持協定】〔米国〕an orderly marketing agreement《略: OMA》.
ししょく¹【試食】 ▫試食コーナー〔デパート・スーパーの食品売り場などの〕a food ˹sample [sampling]˼ corner [counter, booth]. 試食販売 sampling《selling》; a tasting; selling food or drinks by letting customers ˹taste [try, sample]˼ them. ◐～販売を行う hold a ˹tasting [《food》sampling]˼ campaign《to sell《a product》》.
ししょく³【屍食】 ▫屍食 necrophagia; necrophagy. ▫屍食性(の) necrophagous《insects》.
じしょく《さよう》【自食《作用》】〘生理〙autophagy. ▷ autophagic *adj*.
ししょくしん【視触診】〘医〙〔乳がん検診などの〕visual inspection and palpation. ～する visually inspect and palpate《the breasts》.
じしょく【自触媒】〘化〙＝じしょくばい.
しじらおり【しじら織り】〘紡織〙a traditional Japanese weaving technique which uses different tension or different widths for the warp and the weft, producing a light woven cotton fabric, used typically for *yukata*;〔その布地〕*shijira* cloth.
しじりつ【支持率】 ▫政党支持率 an approval ˹rating [rate]˼ for each《political》party.
ジジ・リョン Gigi Leung（1976-  ；香港の映画女優・歌手；中国語名 梁詠琪 Leung Wing-Kei; Liang Yong Qi）.
じしん¹【地震】
▫海溝（型）地震 a trench earthquake. 五百年間隔地震〔北海道東方沖で起こると予想される〕a five hundred year earthquake; an earthquake occurring at intervals of five hundred years. 連続地震 a ˹series [succession]˼ of earthquakes; earthquakes occurring one after another.
▫地震火災費用保険金 earthquake fire expense insurance. 地震恐怖症 (a)《pathological》fear of earthquakes;《an》earthquake ˹phobia [neurosis]˼. 地震雲 an earthquake cloud. ◐～雲が出ていた次の日に強い地震があった. The day after the earthquake cloud appeared there was a powerful earthquake. 地震警報 an earthquake ˹warning [alert]˼. 早期地震《検知》警報システム an earthquake alert system《略: EAS》. 地震再保険 earthquake reinsurance. ◐～再保険特別会計 the Special Account for Earthquake Reinsurance. 地震対応 earthquake [seismic] preparedness [readiness]. 地震防災学 disaster mitigation seismology; the prevention of earthquake damage. 地震防災情報システム an earthquake disaster information system. 地震防災戦略〔2005年に中央防災会議で策定された〕the strategy for dealing with earthquake ˹damage [disasters]˼. 地震補償《保険》earthquake coverage.
じしん³【自信】 ▫自信力《have》the strength of self-confidence.
ししんけい¹【視神経】 ▫視神経交叉上核〘解〙＝しこうさじょうかく. 視神経乳頭〘解〙an optic disc.
じしんちょうさいいんかい【地震調査委員会】〔政府の〕the Earthquake Research Committee.
じしんちょうさけんきゅうすいしんほんぶ【地震調査

**研究推進本部】** the Headquarters for Earthquake Research Promotion.

**じしんつなみかんしか【地震津波監視課】**〔気象庁の〕the Earthquake and Tsunami Observations Division.

**じしんぼうさいたいさくきょうかちいきはんていかい【地震防災対策強化地域判定会】**〔気象庁の〕the Prediction Council for the Area under Intensified Measures against Earthquake Disaster.

**しすい¹【止水】** ▣ 止水域〔湖・沼・池など〕a dead water region. 止水板〔地下への入口などに設置する〕a watertight barrier.

**しすう¹【指数】** ▣ 指数治安〔犯罪統計上の治安度〕public security as established from「crime statistics [the crime index]; how safe (an area) is according to crime statistics.

**シスターニ** ＝シスタニ.

**シスターン・バルチスタ(ー)ン**〔イラン南東部, パキスタン・アフガニスタンと国境を接する州〕Sistan and Baluchistan; (ペルシャ語名の音訳) Sistan va Baluchestan.

**シスタニ** al-Sistani, Ali (1930- ; イスラム教シーア派の指導者).

**シスタン・バルチスタン** ＝シスターン・バルチスタ(ー)ン.

**システム**
▣ システム・インテグレーター〔電算〕a system integrator (略：SI). システム・オン・チップ〔電算〕a system-on-chip (略：SoC). システム管理者〔電算〕a system(s) administrator. システム障害 a system「malfunction [glitch]; a glitch in the system. ◎ ～障害のためメール受信ができなかった. There was a glitch in the system and I couldn't get my mail. | A system malfunction prevented the delivery of mail. システム情報工学 systems and information engineering. システム生物学 systems biology. システム・バス〔浴槽・蛇口・鏡など浴室に必要な部品を自由に組み合わせて選べるセット設備〕a bathroom system. システム・リスク〔金融〕systemic risk. システム理論 systems theory. ◎ 一般～理論 general systems theory.

**システムあんぜんがく【-安全学】**system(s)「safety [security] (studies).

**ジストニア**〔医〕〔異緊張症・筋失調症〕dystonia. ▷ dystonic *adj*. ▣ 頸部ジストニア ＝痙性斜頸(⇒しゃけい²). 捻転ジストニア torsion dystonia.

**ジストロフィー** ▣ 筋強直性[筋緊張性]ジストロフィー〔医〕myotonic dystrophy (略：MD).

**ジストロフィン**〔生化〕〔筋肉の細胞膜を形成するたんぱく質の1つ〕dystrophin.

**シズルかん【-感】**〔広告〕〔食べ物の絵や写真が鮮やかで, みずみずしい素材感やおいしさ感に溢れているさま〕sizzle; dazzle; excitement; a draw; a reach.

**しせい⁵【市井】** ▣ 市井小説〔時代小説の1分野〕a novel of townsmen.

**しせい¹⁴【姿勢】** ▣ 企業姿勢 a corporate stance; a company's position. ◎ それがわが社の創業以来一貫した企業～である. That has been our company's stance ever since we were established. | Our company has been committed to that as long as we have been in business. | 姿勢反射異常〔医〕abnormal postural reflex.

**じせい¹【自生】** ▣ 自生林 a natural「woods [grove]. ◎ シャクナゲの～林 a natural rhododendron「grove [thicket].

**じせい¹⁰【磁性】** ▣ 磁性細菌〔生物〕a magnetic bacterium.

**しせき¹【史跡】** ▣ 史跡指定 designation as a historic site.

**じせき⁷【磁石】** porcelain stone.

**じせきき【耳石器】**〔解〕an otolith organ.

**じせだい【次世代】** ▣ 次世代省エネ基準〔建〕"next-generation energy-saving standards". 次世代ロボット a next-generation robot.

**じせだいいくせいしえんたいさくすいしんほう【次世代育成支援対策推進法】**〔法〕the Law to Promote Measures to Support Fostering Next-Generation Youths.

**じせだいでんししょうとりひきすいしんきょうぎかい【次世代電子商取引推進協議会】** the Next Generation Electronic Commerce Promotion Council of Japan (略：ECOM).

**じせだいロボットビジョンこんだんかい【次世代-懇談会】**〔経済産業省の〕the Study Group on the Vision of Robots in the Future.

**しせつ¹【私設】** ▣ 私設私書箱 a private post-box. 私設取引システム〔証券〕a private trading system (略：PTS).

**しせつ⁴【施設】**
▣ 嫌悪施設 ＝迷惑施設. 迷惑施設 a「nuisance [NIMBY] facility [⇒ニンビー]; an eyesore.
▣ 施設科〔陸上自衛隊〕the Corps of Engineers. 施設基準 facility standards;〔医療機関の〕〔医療実績に関する〕health facility standards「for [of] performance;〔設備に関する〕health facility standards for equipment;〔人員数などに関する〕health facility standards for staffing. 施設整備費 the cost of「building [setting up] a facility. 施設設置負担金〔固定電話加入時の〕an installation charge. 施設内倫理委員会〔研究所・病院などの〕an institutional review board (略：IRB).

**じせっき【耳石器】** ＝じせきき.

**しせん⁶【視線】** ▣ 視線恐怖症〔精神医〕(a) pathological fear of being stared at; scopophobia; ophthalmophobia.

**しせん¹⁰【脂腺】**〔解〕a sebaceous gland; an oil gland.
▣ 脂腺母斑〔医〕nevus sebaceus; (a) sebaceous nevus.

**しせん¹¹【詞先】**〔音楽〕〔先に歌詞ができて後から曲をつける製作方法〕(writing) lyrics first (and music second).

**しぜん¹【自然】**
▣ 自然育雛 natural brooding (of chicks). 自然海塩 natural sea salt. 自然回帰 going back [a return] to nature. ◎ ここ数年, 若者の間で自然～の傾向が強まっている. In recent years there has been something of a return to nature among young people. 自然環境学 natural environment(al)「studies [science]; study of the natural environment. 自然享受権〔他人の私有地を自由に散策できる権利〕public access rights; a [the] right of public access. 自然交配〔動植物の〕natural「hybridization [cross-breeding, cross-fertilization];〔動物の〕natural mating. ◎ 大島桜と緋寒桜が～交配して河津桜が生まれた. The Kawazu cherry is a natural hybrid of the Oshima and Taiwan cherries. 自然酵母 ⇒こうぼ³. 自然コース〔ゴルフ〕a natural golf course. 自然再生型公共事業 a natural restoration-type public works project. 自然散策 a nature walk. ◎ ～を策する take a nature walk. 自然志向 a desire for「nature [the natural]. ◎ 都市部では～志向が高まっている. In urban areas「there is an increasing desire for the natural [people are increasingly nature-oriented]. 自然渋滞 normal traffic congestion; a normal traffic jam. 自然条件 natural features; an [a natural] environment; environmental conditions. ◎ 彼らはわずかな降雨量という厳しい～条件の中で生活している土地で. They live in a harsh environment of poor soil and little rain. | Conditions are harsh and they subsist on poor soil with little precipitation. / 日本は米の栽培に適した～条件を備えている. Japan has [possesses, is endowed with] the right conditions for rice cultivation. | Japan possesses a suitable environment for growing rice. 自然増加数〔人口の〕(a) natural increase. 自然体

じせん

験《children's》experience of nature. 自然体験型観光 nature (experience) tourism. 自然繁殖 natural「breeding [propagation, reproduction]; propagation in nature. 自然孵化(ふ) natural incubation 《of eggs》. ◐自然～した鮭の稚魚 naturally incubated salmon fry. 自然劣化 natural deterioration. ◐屋外の展示物の～劣化を完全に食い止めるのは困難だ。It is difficult fully to prevent the natural deterioration of outdoor exhibits.

じせん³【次戦】【次の試合】the next「game [match]. ◐彼は～には出場できない。He won't be able to play in the「next [upcoming] game.

じぜん²【事前】◨ 事前許可（get, obtain）prior permission. ◐輸入の～許可制 a system of importing with prior permission / 書面による～を得ない無断転載を一切禁ずる Unauthorized reproduction strictly prohibited without (prior)「permission in writing [written permission]. 事前交渉《participate in》pre-negotiations; prior negotiation. 事前質問票〔株主総会などの〕a list of issues. 事前集積船 ＝海上事前集積船（⇒かいじょう⁴）. 事前承諾《with》prior「consent [assent]. 事前審査制〔法案の、与党による〕the system for advance screening of legislation (by the ruling party). 事前審理〔法案などの〕a「preliminary [prior] hearing. 事前対応 (a) prior response. 事前調整《make》'advance arrangements [arrangements in advance];《lay》the groundwork;《make》preparations. 事前避難 (an) advance [(a) prior] evacuation; an evacuation in advance of《an eruption》. 事前復興計画 an advance [a predisaster] reconstruction plan. 事前予約 an advance「appointment [arrangement, reservation, order]; an appointment made「in advance [ahead of time]. ◐破傷風の予防接種には～予約が必要です。It is necessary to make an (advance) appointment for tetanus injections. 事前旅客情報システム〘空〙the Advance Passenger Information System（略: APIS）.

しぜんかがくけんきゅうきこう【自然科学研究機構】the National Institutes of Natural Sciences（略: NINS）.

しぜんげんご【自然言語】◨ 自然言語検索〘電算〙a natural language search; natural language searching.

しぜんさいせいすいしんほう【自然再生推進法】〘法〙the Nature Regeneration Promotion Law.

しぜんのけんりそしょう【自然の権利訴訟】〘法〙〔動物など人間以外の自然を原告として起こす訴訟〕a nonhuman rights lawsuit.

しぜんほご【自然保護】◨ 自然保護官 a「forest [(nature) conservation] ranger; a ranger (in a national park); a (national) park ranger. 自然保護佐 ＝アクティブレンジャー（⇒レンジャー）. 自然保護監視員 a nature conservation「guard [inspector]. 自然保護条例 a nature conservation ordinance; an ordinance for nature conservation.

しぜんゆう【自然釉】〘製陶〙(a) natural ash glaze.

しそ²【紫蘇】◨ シソエキス perilla extract.

しそ⁴【私訴】〘法〙a private「action [lawsuit].

しそう⁷【思想】◨ 指導思想 a guiding「philosophy [idea, ideology].

じぞうかんば【地蔵樺】〘植〙〔カバノキ科の落葉高木〕Betula globispica.

じぞくかのうなかいはつのためのきょういくのじゅうねん【持続可能な開発のための教育の10年】〔国連の〕the United Nations Decade of Education for Sustainable Development（=UNDESD）. ▶ 2002年に決議された2005年から2014年までの10年計画.

シソポン〔カンボジア北西部、バンテイ・メンチェイ州の州都〕Sisophon.

シゾン〘植〙〔原始的な単細胞紅藻〕Cyanidioschyzon merolae.

じそん²【自尊】◨ 自尊感情（feelings of）self-respect;《文》(a sense of) self-esteem.

じそん³【自損】◨ 自損事故保険 self-caused-injury accident insurance.

シダーウッド〔香油〕cedarwood (essential) oil;（モロッコ産サイプ; ホワイト）atlas cedarwood (essential) oil;（北米産ヒノキ科、レッド）red cedarwood (essential) oil.

したい⁴【死体・屍体】◨ 永久死体 a permanent corpse. 死体「屍体」愛好「嗜好」(症) necrophilia; necrophilism. 死体遺棄幇助〘法〙aiding and abetting in the disposal of a corpse. 死体袋 a body bag. 死体防腐処理 embalming《a corpse》; embalmment《of a corpse》.

じたい³【事態】◨ 事態収拾 restoration of normal conditions;《regain》control of a situation. ◐～収拾のめどは立っていない。There is no indication that the situation is coming under control. / ～収拾を図る try to bring a situation under control.

じだい⁵【時代】◨ 時代仕上げ〘技法〙giving《a table》an antique finish; antiquing《furniture》. 時代認識 an awareness [a perception, a sense] of the times. ◐政治家は的確な～認識を持って行動しなくてはならない。A politician has to take action based on an accurate perception of the times.

したいかいぼうほぞんほう【死体解剖保存法】〘法〙the Law Governing the Preservation of Cadavers for Anatomical Purposes.

したうけ【下請け】◨ 下請け会社 a subcontractor (company); a「subcontracting [subcontracted] company. ◐一次[二次]～会社 a「primary [secondary] subcontractor.

したうけだいきんしはらいちえんとうぼうしほう【下請代金支払遅延等防止法】〘法〙the Law on the Prevention of Delay in the Payment of Subcontracting Charges and Related Matters.

したうけほう【下請法】〘法〙the Subcontracting Law. ▶ 正式名称は「下請代金支払遅延等防止法」(the Law on the Prevention of Delay in the Payment of Subcontracting Charges and Related Matters).

じたく¹【自宅】◨ 自宅外生〔自宅以外のアパートなどから学校に通う学生生徒〕a student who commutes from lodgings. 自宅隔離〘医〙(be placed under)「home quarantine; quarantine「in the [at] home. 自宅死〘医〙dying at home; (a) home death. 自宅生〔自宅から学校に通う学生生徒〕a student who commutes from home; a「commuting [commuting] student. 自宅通学 commuting to school from home. ◐～通学する commute to school from home. 自宅通勤 commuting to work from home. ◐～通勤する commute to work from home. 自宅復帰〔病院からの〕returning home (after hospitalization).

したささえ【下支え】◨ 下支え材料 ⇒ざいりょう.

シタツンガ〘動〙〔アフリカ産ウシ科の哺乳類〕a sitatunga; Tragelaphus spekei.

したね【下値】◨ 下値支持線〘株式〙a lower support line.

したぶれ【下振れ】〘経〙〔数値の下方変動〕a [an economic] downturn; a downturn (in the market); a downward swing (of commodity prices). ～する turn downward(s); show [make] a downturn. ◐株式市場ではこの会社の収益が今期～するとの懸念が消えない。Fears persist on the stock market that the company's profits will show a downturn this quarter.

したみ【下見】◨ 下見会〘公売名〙a viewing; an inspection.

したものほうじん【下物法人】〔下上分離方式での〕a lower (construction or operating) company.

しだれうめ【枝垂れ梅】〖植〗〔バラ科の落葉高木〕a weeping plum; *Prunus mume* f. *pendula*.

じだん【示談】 ▢□ 示談交渉サービス〔自動車保険などの〕negotiation services for out-of-court settlements.

ジダン Zidane, Zinedine (1972– ；フランスのサッカー選手).

じち[2]【自治】 ▢□ 自治会館 a self-government hall;〔地域の自治会の集会所〕a neighborhood association hall. 自治政府 an autonomous government;〔パレスチナの〕＝パレスチナ暫定自治政府 (⇨パレスチナ).

しちきょ【七去】〔儒教で，妻を離縁できるとする 7 つの理由〕seven reasons for which a man is permitted to divorce his wife in Confucian tradition.

しちぎょ【仔稚魚】a 「juvenile [larval] fish.

じちたい【自治体】 ▢□ 自治体 CIO〔自治体の情報統括役員〕a 「municipal [「council] CIO [chief information officer]. 自治体破綻 (the) financial collapse of a local government; (a) local government bankruptcy. 自治体病院 a municipal hospital.

しちとうめじろ【七島目白】〖鳥〗〔メジロ科の鳥〕*Zosterops japonicus stejnegeri*.

しちやえいぎょうほう【質屋営業法】〖法〗the Pawnshop Law.

しちゅう[4]【市中】 ▢□ 市中価格 an open-market price; the open-market value《of steel》.

しちょう[9]【視聴】 ▢□ 視聴時間〔テレビの〕(total) television [TV] viewing (time). 視聴質〔量的視聴率に対して〕audience quality. 視聴履歴〔あるテレビ視聴者がいつの時刻にどの番組を見たかに関する記録〕《a viewer's》TV viewing history.

じちょう[2]【自重】 ▢□ 自重自愛 being sensible and taking good care of *one*self. ◎ ご退院をお祝いし，一層の～自愛をお祈りします．Congratulations on your discharge from hospital(, with prayers for your ever greater good health).

しちょうしゃ[2]【視聴者】 ▢□ 視聴者受け ◎ 近頃は～受けを狙っただけの番組が多い．Recently there have been a lot of programs aimed only at garnering popularity with viewers.

しちょうりつ【視聴率】
▢□ 高視聴率 high 「TV [television] ratings; high television viewership; a high 「viewer [audience] rating. 瞬間最高視聴率 a maximum instantaneous audience rating《of 75%》. ◎ 瞬間最高～60％を記録する record a maximum instantaneous audience rating of 60 %. 世帯視聴率 a households-using-television [a homes-using-television, an HUT] rating. テレビ視聴率 TV [television] ratings; TV [television] viewership.

じつえん【実演】 ▢□ 実演家 a live performer.

じつえんかちょさくりんせつけんセンター【実演家著作隣接権–】the Center for Performers' Rights Administration (略：CPRA).

しっかい【悉皆】 ▢□ 悉皆調査〖統計〗〔全数調査〕《conduct》a complete 「survey [count]; a 100% inspection; a census survey. 悉皆屋〔江戸時代の染め直し屋〕a redyer (of old clothes).

しつがいなんこつなんかしょう【膝蓋軟骨軟化症】〖医〗chondromalacia patella; cartilage softening in the knee. [⇨ランナー膝 (⇨ランナー)].

しっかん[1]【疾患】 ▢□ 原因疾患 a causative disease 《of hypotension》.

しつかんせつ【膝関節】 ▢□ 変形性 膝関節症〖医〗gonarthrosis; osteoarthritis of the knee.

しつぎ【質疑】 ▢□ 一般質疑〔予算委員会の〕a general interpellation (with the Minister of Finance and other relevant ministers in attendance). 基本的質疑〔予算委員会の〕an overall interpellation (with the full cabinet in attendance). 参考人質疑〔国会の〕an inter-

pellation of an unsworn witness (before the Diet). 総括質疑〔予算委員会の〕＝基本的質疑. ◎ 締めくくり総括～〔予算委員会の〕a concluding overall interpellation (with the full cabinet in attendance).

じつぎ【実技】 ▢□ 実技指導〔運転の〕practical driving (skills) instruction;〔スポーツの〕skills 「coaching [instruction]; coaching [instruction] in technique.

じつぎょうだん【実業団】 ▢□ 実業団チーム a 「corporate [company] team. 実業団リーグ a 「corporate [company] league.

シック・カー〔体調不良を引き起こす化学物質が内装に使われている自動車〕a sick car.

シック・カーしょうこうぐん【–症候群】〔自動車の内装に使われている化学物質による体調不良〕the sick car syndrome.

シックス ▢□ シックス・ポケット〔両親と祖父母の合計 6 つのポケット（＝財布）から潤沢に子供のために支出されること〕"six pockets"; the support of one child by two parents and four grandparents.

シック・スクール〔体調不良を引き起こす化学物質を建材に含んだ校舎〕a sick school.

シック・スクールしょうこうぐん【–症候群】〖医〗〔校舎の建材に含まれる化学物質により引き起こされる体調不良〕sick school syndrome.

シックス・シグマ【6σ】〖経〗〔品質管理手法の 1 つ〕six sigma.

「シックス・センス」〖映画〗The Sixth Sense.
「シックス・デイ」〖映画〗The 6th Day.
「60 セカンズ」〖映画〗Gone in 60 Seconds.

シック・ハウス〔体調不良を引き起こす化学物質を建材に含んだ住宅〕a sick house. ▢□ シック・ハウス症候群〖医〗sick house syndrome (略：SHS). シック・ハウス対策 sick house countermeasures; measures to prevent sick house syndrome. シック・ハウス問題 the sick house problem.

しつけ[1]【躾】 ▢□ しつけ教育 education in appropriate social behavior; instruction in basic etiquette.

しっけつ【失血】 ▢□ 失血性ショック死 death from hemorrhagic shock; (a case of) fatal hemorrhagic shock.

じっけん[4]【実験】 ▢□ 実験音楽 experimental music. 実験系 an experimental 「setup [arrangement, configuration]. 実験社会心理学 experimental social psychology.

じつげん【実現】 ▢□ 実現可能性 feasibility; practicability; realizability; implementability.

じつげんど【実現度】a [the] degree 「of realization [that *sth* was realized]. ◎ 市長が選挙戦中に公約した政策の～を検証する evaluate what percentage of the policies promised by the mayor during the campaign have been implemented.

ジツコ【JITCO】〔国際研修協力機構〕JITCO; the Japan International Training Cooperation Organization.

しっこう[2]【執行】 ▢□ 執行官〔地方裁判所の〕a court executive (officer); a sheriff; "a bailiff. 執行役員制度 an executive system.

じっこう[1]【実行】 ▢□ 実行可能解〖数〗a feasible solution. 実行機能障害〖医〗disorders of procedural memory; executive dysfunction; apraxia. 実行役〔犯罪の〕the 「actual [〖法〗material] perpetrator (of a crime).

じっこう[2]【実効】 ▢□ 実効支配線〔係争中の国境地帯の〕the line of actual control (略：LAC);〔インド・パキスタン間の停戦ライン〕the Line of Control (略：LOC).

じっさい【実際】 ▢□ 実際原価 the actual cost.

じっし[4]【実施】 ▢□ 実施主体〔事業などの〕the 「developer [promoter]《of a project》. 実施設計〖建〗〔基本設計に対して〕a working design.

じっしつ【実質】 ▢□ 実質原油価格 real crude-oil

prices. 実質倍率〔入学試験などの〕an actual pass rate. 実質本位 substance; quality. ◯結婚祝いには～本位の品を選んだ. As a present for their wedding I chose ｢something which would really be useful [substance rather than flim-flam]｣.
じっしつしはいりょくきじゅん【実質支配力基準】〖経営〗the standards ｢defining [determining] actual ｢control [power]《over a company》｣.
じっしゃ¹【実写】▯ 実写動画 stop-motion [stop-action] animation.
じっしゃ²【実車】▯ 実車試験《自動車》a (real) vehicle test.
じっしゅう²【実習】▯ 実習助手〖教育〗a teacher's assistant.
じつじゅう【実銃】〔模造の銃に対し, 本物の銃〕a real gun.
しつじゅん【湿潤】▯ 湿潤療法〖医〗〔擦過傷・熱傷の〕moist wound healing.
じっしょう²【実証】▯ 実証実験 a ｢demonstration [verification] experiment [test]. ◯公道～実験〔燃料電池車など新種の車両や新しい交通システムなどの, 公道を使っての実験〕a verification test for [verification testing of]《fuel cell electric vehicles》on public roads. 実証(的)研究 an empirical research. 実証プラント a《water recycling》demonstration plant.
じっしょうけん【実証試験】〔新しい方式・製品などについての〕a ｢verification [proof] test; verification [proof] testing. ▯ 焼却実証試験〔廃プラスチックなどの〕an incinerator test [incinerator testing] (for《toxic emissions》); testing and monitoring of waste incineration. 耐震実証試験 a seismic simulation test; a seismic vibration test; seismic ｢vibration [simulation]｣ testing.
しっしん²【湿疹】▯ 異汗性[発汗異常性]湿疹 dyshidrotic eczema; pompholyx. 貨幣状湿疹 nummular [discoid] eczema; nummular dermatitis, nummular eczematous dermatitis. 乾燥性湿疹 dry eczema.
じっせい【実勢】▯ 実勢地価 the ｢actual [market]｣ price of land; actual land prices.
じっせき³【実績】▯ 治療実績〔病院・医師などの〕(the number of) cases treated; 〔治癒率〕a ｢recovery [cure]｣ rate.
じっせん¹【実戦】
▯ 実戦感覚〔スポーツ選手の〕the feeling of a real ｢game [match]｣. ◯この練習試合は～感覚を取り戻すためのものだ. This practice (game) is ｢so that we can recover the feelings of a real game [to remember what a real match is like]｣. 実戦訓練 live-fire training; training ｢under fire [in battle conditions]｣. 実戦論 a ｢practical [realistic, concrete] strategy; a step-by-step ｢guide [approach]; a 「the how-to《of home-publishing》}. ◯企業合併～論 a ｢practical [step-by-step] guide to mergers; "How to Carry Out a Merger."
じっせん²【実践】 ▯ 実践的理想主義 practical idealism. 実践例 a practical example. ◯この療法は欧米では盛んだが, 国内での～例はまだあまり多くない. This treatment is common in Europe and North America, but ｢there have been few cases of its implementation [it has not yet been widely applied]｣ in Japan. 実践論 practice; practical guidance. ◯在宅介護～論 practical [a practical guide to] home-care nursing; the how-to of home-care nursing.
しっそう¹【失踪】▯ 強制的失踪 (an) enforced [involuntary] disappearance.
しっそう²【疾走】 疾走感 a feeling of ｢speed [rapid motion, velocity]｣. ◯この映画には『スピード』のような～感がある. This movie has a feeling of velocity like "Speed." ▶『スピード』は映画のタイトル.
じっそう²【実装】▯ 実装技術〔電子工学〕〔電子部品や半導体を基板に取り付ける技術〕mounting technology.
じっそく【実測】▯ 実測面積〔不動産などの〕the measured (land, floor) area.
じったい¹【実体】▯ 実体波〖地震〗〔地球の内部に侵入して進む地震波〕a (seismic) body wave.
じったい²【実態】 ▯ 実態解明 (a) clarification of the real situation. ◯警視庁はその教団の～解明に乗り出した. The Metropolitan Police Department began to clarify the actual situation of that religious group. / 警察はその密輸組織の～解明を急いでいる. The police are hurrying to clarify the real situation of that smuggling organization. 実態把握《have》a grasp of actual conditions. ◯～把握に努める endeavor to grasp actual conditions / ～把握に乗り出す begin to grasp actual conditions.
じつだいさんじげんしんどうはかいじっけんしせつ【実大三次元震動破壊実験施設】〔防災科学技術研究所が兵庫県に設置〕E-Defense(, a full size three-dimensional vibration destruction facility).
しっち¹【失地】▯ 失地農民〔中国の〕a farmer who has lost his land; a dispossessed ｢farmer [peasant]｣.
じっち【実地】▯ 実地監査《conduct》a field audit. 実地検査 an on-the-spot inspection; 〔会計検査の〕a field audit.
しっちゅうい【膝肘位】〔両膝と両肘を床につけた姿勢〕 ◯～で on one's knees and elbows.
しっちょう²【失聴】▯ 中途失聴 loss of hearing occurring after childhood.
シット[SIT]〔警察の特殊犯捜査係〕SIT. ▶ special investigation team の略.
しつない【室内】▯ 室内園芸 indoor gardening. 室内高〔自動車の〕an interior height. 室内長〔自動車の〕an interior length. 室内幅〔自動車の〕an interior width. 室内練習場〔スポーツ〕an indoor ｢training [practice]｣ area.
しつにんしょう【失認症】▯ 相貌失認症 recognition disorder; prosopagnosia.
しっぱい【失敗】▯ 失敗学 error studies; error theory. 失敗事例〔失敗例〕a failure; an instance of failure.
じつばい【実売】▯ 実売価格 an actual [a retail] selling [sales] price.
じっぴ²【実費】▯ 実費負担 covering actual ｢expenses [costs]｣; paying for expenses incurred.
しっぴつ【執筆】▯ 執筆陣 a group of ｢writers [authors]｣; the writers for《The New Yorker》. ◯豪華～陣 a group of ｢outstanding [stellar] writers [authors]｣.
「シッピング・ニュース」〔映画〕The Shipping News.
じつぶつ【実物】▯ 実物経済《金融》〔金融経済に対して〕object economy.
しっぺい【疾病】▯ 疾病分類〖医〗a diagnosis-related group (略: DRG).
しっぺいかんりセンター【疾病管理-】＝しっぺいたいさくセンター.
しっぺいたいさくセンター【疾病対策-】〔米国の〕the Centers for Disease Control and Prevention (略: CDC).
しっぺいたいさくよぼうセンター【米国疾病対策予防-】＝しっぺいたいさくセンター.
じつむ【実務】▯ 実務家教員〔専門職大学院などの〕a teacher [an instructor] with a career in the subject he or she teaches. 実務協議 ＝実務者協議《⇨じつむしゃ》. 実務担当者〔実務者〕a person doing ｢business [the actual work]｣.
じつむしゃ【実務者】▯ 実務者協議 working-level talks. ◯日朝～協議《⇨にっちょう》.
しつめい²【失明】▯ 中途失明 loss of sight [blindness] occurring after childhood.

じつよう¹【実用】▢ 実用段階 the practical ⌈application [use] stage. ◐ ～段階に入った技術 a technology in the practical application stage / 燃料電池車はすでに～段階に達している. Fuel cell vehicles are now ready for practical use. 実用炉〘原子力〙＝商業炉（⇨しょうぎょう）.
じつりょうぶんせきそうち【質量分析装置】a mass spectrometer. ▢ 液体クロマトグラフ質量分析装置 a liquid chromatograph mass spectrometer (略: LCMS); a liquid chromatograph/mass spectrometer (略: LC/MS); a liquid chromatograph-mass spectrometer (略: LC-MS). ガス・クロマトグラフ質量分析装置 a gas chromatograph mass spectrometer (略: GCMS); a gas chromatograph/mass spectrometer (略: GC/MS); a gas chromatograph-mass spectrometer (略: GC-MS). 2次イオン質量分析装置 a secondary ion mass spectrometer (略: SIMS). 飛行時間型質量分析装置 a ⌈time-of-flight [time of flight] mass spectrometer (略: TOFMS, TOF-MS).
じつりょく【実力】▢ 実力勝負 defeat or victory being decided by pure skill; success depending purely on ability. ◐ 将棋の世界は～勝負の世界だ. 強さに年齢や性別は関係ない. In the world of *shōgi* ⌈what decides the outcome is ability alone [it is winning that counts]. Age or gender have nothing to do with it.
してい⁴【指定】▢ 指定解除 removal of the designation ⟪of North Korea as a terrorist-supporting state⟫; delisting of ⟪North Korea (as a state sponsor of terrorism)⟫. 指定可燃物 designated ⌈combustibles [burnables]. 指定管理者制度〔公共施設の管理を民間に委託する〕the Designated Manager System. 指定公共機関 a designated public organization. 指定ごみ袋 designated garbage bags; rubbish bags of a type specified ⟪by the local government⟫. 指定職俸給表 a compensation table for specially designated high-level government posts. 指定袋〔ごみの〕＝指定ごみ袋. 指定法人 a designated corporation.
してい⁵【師弟】▢ 師弟対決 a ⌈confrontation [showdown] between teacher and student.
シティー・ホテル a city(-type) hotel.
「シティ・オブ・エンジェル」〔映画〕City of Angels.
していりゅうつうきこう〔指定流通機構〕〔不動産の〕a designated real estate distribution organization.
してき³【私的】▢ 私的参拝 visiting ⟪a shrine⟫ ⌈in a private capacity [as a private individual]. 私的整理〔倒産に際しての〕voluntary liquidation. ◐ ～整理に関するガイドライン guidelines for voluntary liquidation. 私的複製〔著作権法で容認されている私用のコピー〕private copying ⟪of copyright-protected material⟫.
してきろくおん・ろくがほしょうきんせいど〔私的録音・録画補償金制度〕〔著作権法上の〕the Compensation System for Digital Private Recording.
シテ・ソレイユ〔ハイチ, ポルトープランスにある貧民地区；"太陽の街"〕Cite Soleil.
しではらがいこう〔幣原外交〕〘日本史〙〔幣原喜重郎外相による国際協調外交〕Shidehara diplomacy.
じてんしゃ【自転車】▢ 自転車安全整備士 a bicycle-safety maintenance mechanic. 自転車組み立て整備士 a bicycle assembly and maintenance mechanic. 自転車利用環境整備モデル都市〔国土交通省指定の〕a model bicycle-friendly city.
じてんしゃきょうかい【自転車協会】the Bicycle Association (Japan). ▢ 自転車協会認証〔安全基準〕Bicycle Association (Japan) Approved (略: BAA).
じてんしゃさんぎょうしんこうきょうかい【自転車産業振興協会】the Japan Bicycle Promotion Institute (略: JBPI).
じてんしゃほう【自転車法】〘法〙the Bicycle Law. ▶ 正式名称は「自転車の安全利用の促進及び自転車等の駐車対策の総合的推進に関する法律」.
しと⁵【使途】▢ 使途報告書〔助成金などの〕a statement of use; a report explaining how ⟪a grant⟫ has been used. ◐ 政党交付金～報告書 a report on the uses to which an official subsidy to a political party has been put.
しどう⁴【始動】▢ 始動性〘自動〙startability; start-up performance.
しどう⁵【指導】▢ 指導医〔研修医を指導する〕a preceptor. 指導監督 guidance and supervision. ◐ ～監督する guide and supervise / ～監督を怠る neglect ⟪one's obligation⟫ to guide and supervise. 指導監督基準 guidance and supervision standards; standards for guidance and supervision. 指導監督義務 an obligation [a responsibility] to guide and supervise. 指導基準 guidance standards. 指導義務 an obligation [a responsibility] to guide.
じどう¹【自動】
▢ 自動演奏 automatic playing. ◐ ～演奏楽器 an automatic musical instrument 自動音声 an automated voice. 自動音声応答装置〔システム〕＝音声自動応答装置〔システム〕（⇨おんせい）. 自動鑑査機〔偽造紙幣を見分けるための機器〕a counterfeit ⌈(bank)note [currency, money] detector. 自動血圧計 an automatic ⌈sphygmomanometer [blood pressure gauge]. 自動消火装置 an automatic fire-extinguishing system. 自動進路制御装置〘鉄道〙a programmed route control system; a PRC system. 自動通報装置〔エレベーターなどの〕an automatic reporting device. 自動認識システム an ⌈automatic [automated] identification system. 自動搬送車 an ⌈automatic [automated] guided vehicle (略: AGV). 自動判定 automatic [automated] judgment; automatic decision(-making); automatic evaluation. ◐ ⟪サッカーでボールが⟫ゴールしたか[メールがスパムメールか]どうか～判定する judge [decide] automatically whether ⌈a goal has been scored [an e-mail is spam]. 自動引受機〔旅行保険などの〕a ⌈flight [travel] insurance machine.
じどう²【児童】▢ 児童育成手当 a ⌈childcare [child support] allowance payable to a household with a child or children (under 18) lacking one or both parents because of death or divorce. 児童性愛 pedophilia. ◐ ～性愛者 a pedophile. 児童売買 child trafficking; trafficking in children. 児童福祉士 a child-welfare worker. 児童保育 childcare; (day) care for children. 児童保護費 childcare costs. ◐ ～保護費等負担金 the ⟪central government, local authority⟫ share of childcare costs.
じどうしゃ【自動車】
▢ 自動車アセスメント〔自動車安全性能評価〕the New Car Assessment Program(me) (略: NCAP);〔日本の〕the Japan New Car Assessment Program(me) (略: JNCAP);〔欧州の〕the European New Car Assessment Program(me) (略: Euro NCAP). 自動車運転代行＝運転代行（⇨うんてん）. 自動車関連製品 automobile-related products. 自動車警邏隊〔警察の〕a police-car squad; a squad of police cars. 自動車検査登録特別会計 a special account for car inspection and registration. 自動車工学 automobile engineering. 自動車ジーメン〔東京都などの自動車公害監察員〕⟪Tokyo Metropolitan Government⟫ diesel vehicle inspectors; automobile "G-men." 自動車シュレッダー・ダスト〘環境〙an automobile shredder residue (略: ASR). 自動車衝突防止装置 the Car Collision Avoidance System (略: CCAS). 自動車船〔自動車運搬船〕a car carrier ship. 自動車損害賠償責任再保険特別会計 special accounting for compulsory automobile liability reinsurance. ▶ 2002年度より自動車損害賠償保

じどうしゃうんてんだいこう

事業特別会計に引き継がれた。**自動車損害賠償保障事業特別会計** special accounting for automobile liability security operations. **自動車破砕屑**〔残渣〕〔環境〕＝自動車シュレッダー・ダスト。**自動車フロン券**〔廃車のエアコンフロンの回収破壊費用払込済み券〕an automobile CFC coupon. **自動車保有率** a car-ownership rate. **自動車(用)鋼板** automobile steel; (galvanised) steel for automobiles.

**じどうしゃうんてんだいこうぎょうほう**【自動車運転代行業法】〔法〕＝じどうしゃうんてんだいこうぎょう。

**じどうしゃけんさとうろくきょうりょくかい**【自動車検査登録協力会】the (Japan) Automobile Inspection & Registration Association (略: AIRA).

**じどうしゃけんさどくりつぎょうせいほうじん**【自動車検査独立行政法人】the National Agency of Vehicle Inspection.

**じどうしゃけんさほうじん**【自動車検査法人】⇒じどうしゃけんさどくりつぎょうせいほうじん。

**じどうしゃじこたいさくきこう**【自動車事故対策機構】the National Agency for Automotive Safety & Victims' Aid (略: NASVA). ▶ 2003年自動車事故対策センターより移行。

**じどうしゃそうれん**【自動車総連】the Confederation of Japan Automobile Workers' Unions (略: JAW). ▶ 正式名称: 全日本自動車産業労働組合総連合会。

**じどうしゃノックス・ピーエムほう**【自動車 NOx・PM 法】〔法〕〔改正自動車 NOx 法〕the Automobile NOx/PM Reduction Law.

**じどうしゃぼうえきせいさくかいぎ**【自動車貿易政策会議】〔米国の〕the Automotive Trade Policy Council (略: ATPC).

**じどうそくどとりしまりき**【自動速度取締機】an automatic speed camera. ○~設置路線。〔掲示〕Speed Cameras Installed on This Road.

**じどうチェックインき**【自動-機】an「automated [automatic] check-in machine.

**じどうはんばいき**【自動販売機】 ▭ 募金型自動販売機 a "charity vending machine"; a vending machine which gives a purchaser the option of making a donation to (a) charity. ▭ 自動販売機荒らし ＝自販機荒らし (⇒じはんき)。

**じどうふくし**【児童福祉】 ▭ 児童福祉学 child welfare (studies).

**じどり**【地取り】 ▭ 地取り捜査〔調査〕〔事件現場周辺での聞き込みや遺留品捜索など〕a police investigation carried out in the immediate vicinity of a crime site.

**シトルリン** ▭ シトルリン化 citrullination.

**しなうす**【品薄】 ▭ 品薄感 a feeling of scarcity. **品薄 an** item in short supply; a scarce item.

**しながし**【品貸し】〔金融〕〔貸与料とともに債権を貸し出すと〕the lending of securities; securities lending;〔日銀が保有する国債を金融機関に貸し出す国債供給制度〕the lending of「Japanese government bonds [JGBs]; JGB lending. ▭ 品貸し料 a securities lending fee.

**しなさがる**【品下がる】lose one's dignity; go downhill. ○ 長い貧乏暮らしであの男もついに品下がった。That guy really went downhill after living for a long time in poverty.

**シナジー** ▭ グループ・シナジー〔経営〕〔グループ結成がもたらす相乗効果〕group synergy.

**しなだし**【品出し】〔店頭への商品補充〕shelf stocking;〔人〕a stock person.

**シナバン**〔インドネシア, アチェ州, シムル県の県都〕Sinabang.

**しなまんさく**【支那満作】〔植〕〔マンサク科の落葉小高木; 中国原産〕a Chinese witch hazel; *Hamamelis mollis*.

**しなもくずがに**【支那藻屑蟹】〔動〕＝ちゅうごくもくずがに。

**シナリオさっかきょうかい**【-作家協会】the Association of Scenario Writers Japan.

**ジニ** Gini, Corrado (1884-1965)〔イタリアの統計学者;

178

ジニ係数の考案者〕.

**シニア** ▭ シニア海外ボランティア a senior overseas volunteer. シニアドライバー an elderly [a senior] driver. シニア・ビジネス (a) business targeted at seniors. シニア料金 a fee for senior citizens; a「special [reduced] fee for the elderly. シニアローン〔金融〕〔優先ローン〕a senior loan.

**シニアカー**〔高齢者向け電動三輪〔四輪〕車〕a mobility [an electric] scooter (for seniors).

**シニーズ** Sinise, Gary (1955- ; 米国の映画俳優).

**シニオラ** Siniora, Fouad (1943- ; レバノンの政治家; 首相〔2005- 〕).

**しにく**[2]【歯肉】 ▭ 歯肉溝 the gingival「sulcus [crevice].

**しにすじ**【死に筋】 ▭ 死に筋商品 a poor seller; a product that doesn't sell; a flop; a dud;〔市場にだぶついている〕a drug on the market.

**しにせき**【死に席】〔劇場で舞台がよく見えない「音がよく聞こえない」席〕a seat「with a bad view (of the stage) [you can't hear properly from].

**しにょう**【屎尿】 ▭ 屎尿溜(だ)め a cesspool.

**シネクティ(ッ)クス**〔創造工学〕synectics. ▷ synectic *adj*.

**シノア**〔＜F *chinois*〕〔金属製のスープ漉(こ)し器〕a chinois; a fine, conical soup strainer. ○~でコンソメスープを漉す strain the consomme through a chinois.

**シノーペ**〔天〕〔木星の衛星〕Sinope.

**シノギ**〔暴力団が資金を得る手段〕a「source of income [moneymaker]《for a gang》.

**「しのけんり」きょうかいせかいれんごう**【「死の権利」協会世界連合】the World Federation of Right to Die Societies (略: WFRTDS).

**シノドス** ⇒せかいだいひょうしきょうかいぎ.

**しのびこみ**【忍び込み】〔夜間, 就寝時に住宅に侵入し盗みをすること〕sneak theft;〔人〕a sneak thief; a cat burglar.

**シノプト**【眼科】＝シノプトフォア.

**シノプトフォア**【眼科】〔斜視矯正訓練用機器〕a synoptophore.

**シノペック** ＝ちゅうごくせきゆかこうしゅうだん.

**ジノリ**〔商標〕⇒リチャード・ジノリ.

**しば**[1]【芝】 ▭ 芝コース〔競馬〕a turf「course [track].

**しば**[2]【磁場】 ▭ 磁場変動 variation(s)「of [in] a magnetic field; magnetic field variation(s).

**ジハーディスト**〔聖戦主義者; イスラム原理主義の勢力のメンバー〕a jihadist.

**ジハードだん**【-団】〔エジプトの非合法組織〕the Jihad Group.

**じばいせき**【自賠責】 ▭ 自賠責特会 ＝自動車損害賠償責任再保険特別会計 (⇒じどうしゃ).

**じはく**【自白】 ▭ 自白上申書〔法〕a written confession submitted (by the defendant) to the「police [prosecution]. 自白調書 a written statement of a confession; a written (and signed) confession. 自白偏重 (an) overreliance on confessions. ○~偏重捜査 an investigation overly reliant on (extracting) confessions《from suspects》.

**じばく**[2]【自爆】 ▭ 自爆テロリスト ＝自爆犯. 自爆犯〔自爆テロの実行者〕a suicide bomber.

**じばた**【地機】a loom with a backstrap for pulling warps tight. ▭ 地機織り backstrap loom weaving.

**シパダンとう**【-島】〔セレベス海の島〕Sipadan Island.

**じはっこう**【自発光】 ▭ 自発光式標識 a self-luminous sign. 自発光塗料 self-luminous paint.

**じはつつう**【自発痛】【医】(a) pain without apparent cause; spontaneous pain.

**しばはり**【芝張り】turf-laying; turfing.

**しはらい**【支払い】 ▭ 支払査定時照会制度〔生命保険の〕the Data Inquiry System for Assessment of Claims. 支払い督促〔監督官庁による〕an order to pay;

〔当事者による〕a demand for payment. 支払い余力 (a) solvency margin.
**しはん**[2]【市販】▫▫ 市販車 a commercially sold car; a car for sale on the market.
**しはん**[7]【紫斑】▫▫ 紫斑病〔医〕purpura; peliosis.
**じばん**【地盤】▫▫ 地盤陥没 ground subsidence. 地盤基礎工学 geotechnical (and) foundation engineering; geotechnical engineering. 地盤補強〔土木〕〔ビル・建物などの〕foundation reinforcement.
**しはんき**【四半期】▫▫ 四半期開示〔経営〕〔企業の〕quarterly disclosure《of financial information》.
**じはんき**【自販機】▫▫ 自販機荒らし〔行為〕robbing [stealing from] a vending machine;〔人〕a vending machine thief.
**じはんれん**【自販連】＝にほんじどうしゃはんばいきょうかいれんごうかい.
**じビール**【地-】▫▫ 地ビール・メーカー a microbrewery.
**ジビエ**《<F *gibier*》〔野生の鳥獣肉〕game.
**しびじん**【死美人】a dead beauty; a beautiful corpse.
**じひつ**【自筆】▫▫ 自筆署名 a handwritten signature.
**ジヒドロカプサイシン**【化】〔唐辛子の辛味成分の１つ〕dihydrocapsaicin.
**しひょう**[2]【指標】▫▫ 環境指標 an environment(al) indicator. 目安指標 target criteria 〔for health spending〕. ▫▫ 指標価格 a「target [reference, benchmark] price. 指標銘柄〔証券〕a bellwether issue; a benchmark security.
「**シビル・アクション**」〔映画〕A Civil Action.
**シビル・ユニオン**〔同性婚を異性婚と区別するための呼称〕a civil union. ▫▫ シビル・ユニオン法 a civil「partnership [union] law
**シフェール** Sieffert, René (1923-2004; フランスの日本研究家; 日本文学などの仏訳者).
**ジフェニルアルシンさん**【-酸】《化》〔有機砒素化合物の１つ〕diphenylarsinic acid (略: DPAA).
**しぶカジ**【渋-】《<「渋谷カジュアル」の略》〔服飾〕〔1980 年代末期のカジュアルファッション〕the "casual Shibuya look" (of the late eighties).
**しぶかわつつじ**【渋川躑躅】〔植〕＝じんぐうつつじ.
「**至福のとき**」〔映画〕Happy Times;〔中国語タイトル〕幸福時光.
**ジプシー・ローズ・リー** Gypsy Rose Lee (1913-70; 米国のバーレスク・ダンサー).
**ジブ・セール**〔ヨット〕〔船首三角帆〕a jib (sail).
**じふだ**【字札】〔カルタの, 字が書かれた札〕a card with writing on it.
**シフト** ▫▫ 守備シフト〔野球など〕a defensive shift.
**シブトラミン**【化】〔食欲抑制剤〕sibutramine.
**シプリ**{SIPRI}＝ストックホルムこくさいへいわけんきゅうじょ.
**じぶんかつ**【時分割】▫▫ 時分割複信〔通信〕＝ティー・ディー・ディー.
**しぶんけん**【支分権】〔著作権を構成する個々の権利; 複製権, 公衆送信権, 上映権, 録音権, 演奏権, 貸与権, 出版権, 翻案権など〕copyright and related rights.
**しへい**[2]【紙幣】▫▫ 紙幣鑑別機〔偽造紙幣発見機〕a counterfeit bill detector.
**じへいしょう**【自閉症】▫▫ 自閉症スペクトラム the autistic spectrum.
**じへいしょう・はったつしょうがいしえんセンター**【自閉症・発達障害支援-】a support center for persons with autism or developmental disability.
「**シベリアの理髪師**」〔映画〕The Barber of Siberia.
**しぼ**[1]【私募】▫▫ 私募ファンド a private fund.
**しほう**[3]【司法】▫▫ 司法過疎 a shortage of judicial services (in a rural area). ▫ ▫ 過疎地域 a judicially underserved area; an area with a shortage of judicial「officers [services]. 司法手続き (a) legal procedure. 司法闘争 a legal「dispute [《口》tussle]; (a) legal conflict; legal strife. 司法判断 a judicial decision.

**しぼう**[2]【死亡】▫▫ 死亡報告書〔公文書〕a report of a death. 死亡報道 (the) news [a report]「of *sb*'s death [that *sb* has died, that *sb* is dead]; (the) news reporting *sb*'s death. 死亡見舞金 a gift of money on 「*sb*'s death [bereavement].
**しぼう**[3]【志望】▫▫ 志望先 one's first choice《for a university》; one's desired《employer》.
**しぼう**[5]【脂肪】▫▫ 脂肪吸引器 a liposuction device. 脂肪注入肉 meat injected with beef tallow (to make it look marbled and tender). 脂肪燃焼 fat「burning [oxidation]; (the) oxidation of fat. ▶ ～燃焼ダイエット a fat-burning diet / ～燃焼量 an amount of fat burned.
**じほう**[2]【次鋒】〔武道の団体戦で２番目に出場する選手〕(a) *jihō*; the *jihō* position.
**しほうせいどかいかくしんぎかい**【司法制度改革審議会】the Judicial Reform Council (略: JRC). ▶ 内閣に設置. ▫▫ 司法制度改革審議会意見書 the《2001》Recommendations of the Judicial Reform Council.
**しぼうりつ**【死亡率】▫▫ 粗死亡率《総人口に対する死亡数の比率》a crude death rate《of 8.1 deaths per 1000 population》(略: CDR). 年齢別死亡率 an age-specific death rate (略: ASDR). 標準死亡率〔過去の統計に基づいて１年間に死亡する人の割合を男女別・年齢別に予測した数値〕a standard death rate.
**しぼり**【絞り】▫▫ 全絞り〔散弾銃銃口部の; フルチョーク〕a full choke. 絞り口〔チューブ入りマヨネーズなどの〕the mouth《of a tube》. 絞り袋〔ケーキの飾りのクリームなどを絞り出すための口金のついた袋〕a pastry bag.
**シボルガ**〔インドネシア・北スマトラ州, スマトラ島西岸の港町〕Sibolga.
**しほん**【資本】▫▫ 資本移動 (a) movement of capital; capital movement(s); (a) capital flow. ▶ ～移動の自由化 liberalizing [the liberalization of] capital movements. 資本拘束条項〔ライセンス契約などにおいて, 買収などで一方の会社の支配権が変わった場合はもう一方の会社が契約を破棄できるとする条項〕a change-of-control clause. [＝チェンジ・オブ・コントロール] 資本効率 capital efficiency. 資本集約財 capital-intensive「goods [products]. 資本増強 an increase in capital; (a) capital build-up.
**しほんしゅぎ**【資本主義】▫▫ 縁故資本主義 ＝クローニー・キャピタリズム.
**しまい**[3]【姉妹】▫▫ 姉妹提携 twinning; affiliation as 「twin [sister]《cities》. 姉妹都市協定 a sister city agreement.
**しまうた**【島唄】〔沖縄歌謡〕an Okinawan folk song.
**じまえ**【自前】▫▫ 自前主義〔経営〕〔技術・人材・ノウハウのすべてを自社内にそろえる経営方針〕(totally) independent management《model》; in-company management.
**しまく**【風巻く】rage; blow hard; lash《at *one*'s face》.
**じまく**【字幕】▫▫ 字幕装置〔劇場などの〕a subtitle device. 字幕版 a subtitled version《of a movie》.
**しましま**【縞々】▫▫ 縞々パンツ striped [stripey, stripy] pants [「underpants].
**しまスカンク**【縞-】〔動〕a striped skunk; *Mephitis mephitis*.
**しますずき**【縞鱸】〔魚〕＝ストライプト・バス.
**じまど**【地窓】〔建〕〔床面に接している窓〕a floor-level window (in a tea-ceremony room).
**しまハイエナ**【縞-】〔動〕〔ハイエナ科の動物〕a striped hyena; *Hyaena hyaena*.
**シマンテック**〔米国のコンピュータウイルス対策ソフト会社〕Symantec.
**シミック**{CIMIC}〔民軍協力〕CIMIC. ▶ civil-military cooperation の略.
**シミュラークル**〔文化人類〕〔似て非なるもの・まがいもの〕a simulacrum《*pl*. -lacra, ~s》.
**シミランしょとう**【-諸島】〔タイ南部の〕(the) Similan Is-

しみん

lands.

**しみん**[3]【市民】 ◻️ 市民感覚[感情] popular [local] feeling(s) [sentiment]. 市民救命士 a certified citizen lifesaver. 市民社会組織 a civil society organization (略: CSO). 市民葬 *a welfare funeral; "a civil funeral (ceremony). 市民ランナー〔マラソンの〕a citizen [an amateur, a regular] runner.

**しみんきょう**【市民協】⇨しみんふくしだんたいぜんこくきょうぎかい.

**しみんさんか**【市民参加】 ◻️ 市民参加型行政 participatory「government [administration].

**じみんとう**【自民党】 ◻️ 自民党(議)院議員会長 (the) Chairman of the General Assembly of LDP Members in the House of Councillors. 自民党役員連絡会 an extraordinary meeting of the Liberal Democratic Party board.

**しみんのじゆうほう**【市民の自由法】〔米法〕〔第 2 次大戦中に強制収容された日系米国人に対して補償金を払うことを定めた 1988 年の法律〕the Civil Liberties Act (of 1988).

**しみんパートナーほう**【市民~法】〔英法〕the Civil Partnership「Act [Law]. ▶ 同性結婚を認める法律.

**しみんふくしだんたいぜんこくきょうぎかい**【市民福祉団体全国協議会】the Network Center for Human Service Association.

**じむ**[2]【事務】 ◻️ 事務負担 a「clerical [paperwork] burden. ◯ われわれは徴税に伴う~負担の半減を目指している. We aim to halve the amount of paperwork involved in tax collection. 事務レベル会合 a working-level meeting. 事務レベル協議 (hold) working-level「talks [negotiations, discussions].

**シム・ウナ**【沈銀河】Shim Eun-ha (1972-　; 韓国の映画女優).

**じむしょ**[2]【事務所】 ◻️ 設計事務所 an architectural design firm. ◯ 機械設計~ a「machine [mechanical engineering] design firm. デザイン事務所 a design「office [firm].

**じむそうちょう**【事務総長】 ◻️ 事務総長特別顧問〔国連の〕Special Adviser to the Secretary-General.

**シムル**(-)〔インドネシア, アチェ州の県・島〕Simeulue.

**しめい**[4]【指名】 ◻️ 指名争い a battle for nomination. ◯ 大統領候補の~争いが過熱している. The battle for the nomination of the presidential candidate(s) is heating up. 指名委員会〔委員会等設置会社の〕a nominating committee. 指名買い preferential buying. 指名業者 a designated「company [dealer, business, supplier]. 指名停止〔業者に対する〕⇨指名停止措置. ◯ ~停止期間 a period of suspension of designated contractor status / ~停止措置〔処分〕punishment by suspension of [measures to suspend] designated contractor status. 指名ドライバー ＝ハンドルキーパー〔⇨ハンドル〕.

**シメイ**《商標》〔ベルギーのビール〕Chimay.

**しめいてはい**【指名手配】 ◻️ 重要指名手配被疑者 a most wanted suspect. 特別指名手配 most wanted (suspect). ◻️ 指名手配被疑者[容疑者] a wanted suspect. 指名手配リスト a wanted list.

**シメウルエ** ＝シムル(-).

**じめん**[2]【地面】 ◻️ 地面現象警報 a「ground phenomenon [landslide] warning. 地面現象注意報 a「ground phenomenon [landslide] advisory. 地面効果《流体力学》〔航空機が地面近くを飛ぶとき抵抗が減少し揚力が増加する現象〕the wing-in-ground effect (略: WIG).

**しも**[2]【霜】 ◻️ 霜注意報 a frost advisory.

**しもつけこうほね**【下野河骨】〔スイレン科の水生多年草〕Nuphar submersa. ▶ 2006 年発見の新種.

**じもと**【地元】 ◻️ 地元開催 ◯ 知事の努力にもかかわらず~開催は実現しなかった. The Governor failed in「his [her] efforts to bring the Olympics to「his [her] Prefecture. | In spite of the Governor's efforts, the attempt to turn the Olympics into a local event was not successful. 地元学 study of「a local area [the area where *one* lives]; local area studies. 地元企業 a local「business [company, corporation]. 地元出身 ◯ ~出身の相撲力士 a sumo wrestler (who comes) from 《this》area; a sumo wrestler of local origin(s). 地元出身者 a person (who comes) from 《that》area; a person of local origin(s). 地元商店街 a local shopping「street [arcade]. 地元自治体 ◯ その原発は~自治体の反対によって建設工事が中断している. Due to opposition by the local government, work on the atomic power station has been put on hold. 地元振興策 a local revitalization plan. 地元密着型の locally oriented 《businesses》; community-based 《organizations》.

**しものく**【下の句】the「second half [fourth and fifth lines] (of a tanka poem).

**しもわれ**【霜割れ】 ＝とうれつ.

**しもん**[1]【指紋】 ◻️ 遺留指紋 a fingerprint left on the scene (of a crime); a latent fingerprint. ◻️ 指紋鑑定 fingerprint analysis. 指紋検出 fingerprint detection. 指紋採取 fingerprinting; fingerprint taking. ◯ ~採取器 a「fingerprinting [fingerprint-taking] kit [set]. 指紋スキャン fingerprint scanning; fingerscanning. 指紋センサー a fingerprint sensor. 指紋(認証)錠 a fingerprint《door》lock; a fingerprint recognition《door》lock.

**シモンいも**【~芋】〔ブラジル原産の白サツマイモの一種〕a white sweet potato; *Ipomoea batatas* cv. *Simon*.

**しや**【視野】 ◻️ 視野障害《医》visual field disorders.

**ジャー** ◯ ジャー炊飯器 a rice cooker and warmer.

**シャーガステン**《医》＝シャウカステン.

**シャーガスびょう**【~病】《医》Chagas disease.

**ジャージー・シティ**〔ニュージャージー州北東部の都市〕Jersey City. ▷ Jersey Cityite n.

**ジャージャーめん**【~麺, 炸醤麺】《料理》「麺に肉味噌をかけた中華料理」Chinese noodles topped with a paste of minced meat and sweetened miso.

**ジャーナリストほごいいんかい**【~保護委員会】〔ニューヨークに本部を置く非営利組織〕the Committee to Protect Journalists (略: CPJ).

**ジャーヘッド**〔映画〕Jarhead.

**シャーロット・グレイ**〔映画〕Charlotte Gray.

**シャイアン**〔北米先住民に育てられた白人が悪と闘う TV 西部劇〕Cheyenne.

**ジャイアント・ロベリア**《植》〔キキョウ科の植物〕a giant lobelia; *Lobelia telekii*.

**シャイダー** Scheider, Roy (1932-2008; 米国の映画俳優).

**しゃいん**[2]【社員】 ◻️ 外勤社員 an employee working「outside [away from] the company; an external employee. 期間社員 a fixed-term employee. 準社員 a quasi-employee; an associate staff member 内勤社員 an employee working「inside [at] the company; an internal employee; an office [a desk] worker. 非正規社員 an irregular [a non-regular] employee (of a company). ◻️ 社員教育 employee「training [education]; (company) training for employees. 社員章 an employee's [a company, a staff] badge. 社員割引価格 a staff [an employee's] discount(ed) price.

**ジャウォック**【JAWOC】《サッカー》〔2002 年 FIFA ワールドカップ日本組織委員会〕JAWOC; the Japan Organising Committee for the 2002 FIFA World Cup Korea /Japan.

**シャウカステン**《<G Schaukasten》《医》〔X 線写真の読影装置〕an X-ray film viewer.

**ジャウフ** ⇨アル・ジャウフ.

**しゃえん**【社縁】〔会社での職場仲間や仕事で付き合いのある人たちとの人間関係〕(social) relations within a com-

pany and with business partners outside.
**しゃ**³【卸下】〔積み荷の〕unloading. 〜する unload.
**しゃかい**²【社会】
▶ ムラ社会〔閉鎖性, 共同性, 対外排斥性の強い集団〕a tight-knit, consensus-based 「group [society] which excludes outsiders; a 「closed [self-contained] society [world]; a "*mura shakai*."
▶ 社会移動《社会》〔社会において人がある社会階層から他の社会階層へ移動すること〕social mobility. 社会インフラ＝社会基盤. 社会疫学《社会・医》socio-epidemiology. 社会格差 ＝社会的格差（⇨しゃかいてき）. 社会慣行 a social practice. 社会技術 (a) sociotechnology. 社会技術論〔学問分野〕(the theory of) sociotechnology. 社会機能 the functioning of 「a community [(a) society]; a 「community [social] function. ▷ 〜機能維持者 personnel who keep a community functioning; a person who is necessary for the maintenance of primary community functions. 社会基盤 a social infrastructure. 社会恐怖症《精神医》(a) social phobia; sociophobia; (a) social anxiety disorder（略: SAD）.〔＝社会不安障害（⇨ふあんしょうがい）〕社会経験 experience of 「life [society]; experience of working with other people. ▷ 〜経験が豊富な高齢者 old people with plenty of experience of life / 就職して 〜経験を積む get a job and accumulate experience (of 「life [the real world]). 社会システム論 social systems studies. 社会常識 social 「awareness [common sense]; (awareness of) what is socially acceptable. ▷ 彼には〜常識というものが欠けている. He is lacking in 「social awareness [an awareness of what is socially acceptable]. 社会実験 a 「field [consumer] test. 社会進出 engagement with society; entering 「employment [the job market]; entry into the (real) world. 社会進出度 a rate of 《women》 entering employment. 社会診断《社会》〔ケースワークの手法の1つ〕social diagnosis. 社会成層 social stratification. 社会体験〔学習〕work experience; practical studies in the real world. 社会適応 social adaptation. 社会病理現象《社会》a sociopathological phenomenon. 社会不安症《精神医》＝社会恐怖症. 社会風潮 a social trend. 社会モデル《社会》a social model. 社会予防医学 social (and) preventive medicine. 社会類型《社会》a social type.
**しゃがい**¹【社外】▶ 社外委員 an outside member of a committee.
**しゃかいかがくこうとうけんきゅういん**【社会科学高等研究院】〔フランスの〕the School for Advanced Studies in the Social Sciences;（フランス語名）École des Hautes Études en Sciences Sociales（略: EHESS）.
**しゃかいがく**【社会学】▶ 労働社会学 the sociology of 「labor [work].
**しゃかいぎじゅつけんきゅうかいはつセンター**【社会技術研究開発-】〔科学技術振興機構の1部門〕the Research Institute of Science and Technology for Society（略: RISTEX）.
**しゃかいきばんがく**【社会基盤学】the study of social infrastructure.
**しゃかいけんやく**【社会権規約】〔国連の「経済的, 社会的及び文化的権利に関する国際規約」の通称; A規約〕the International Covenant on Economic, Social, and Cultural Rights（略: ICESCR）.
**しゃかいこうけん**【社会貢献】▶ 社会貢献度 the (degree of) social contribution 《made by a company toward energy saving》; how far [the degree to which]《a company》 contributes to society.
**しゃかいしほんせいびしんぎかい**【社会資本整備審議会】〔国土交通省の〕the Council for Social Infrastructure.
**しゃかいしゅぎ**【社会主義】▶ 官僚社会主義 bureaucratic socialism.

**しゃかいじん**【社会人】▶ 社会人講師〔小中高も大学にも〕a lecturer from the outside world. 社会人大学院 a graduate school for working students. 社会人チーム a company 《soccer》 team; (an in-company) citizens' (sports) team.
**しゃかいせいかつ**【社会生活】▶ 社会生活力〔社会で自己の要求を満たすことができるようにする力〕social functioning ability（略: SFA）.
**しゃかいてき**【社会的】
▶ 社会的圧力 social pressure(s). 社会的格差 disparities [a disparity] 「of [in] wealth; a [the] gap between the haves and (the) have-nots. ▷ 〜格差を是正する rectify disparities of wealth; reduce [get rid of] the gap between the haves and (the) have-nots. 社会的学習理論《社会》(a [the]) social learning theory. 社会的基盤 ＝社会基盤（⇨しゃかい²）. 社会的儀礼 a matter of 「social form [accepted social protocol]. 社会的合意 the [a] social consensus. 社会的性格《心理》social character. 社会的責任投資株価指数〔インデックス〕a socially responsible investing [an SRI] index. 社会的相当性 social 「acceptability [appropriateness, suitability]. ▷ それは〜相当性を逸脱した行為である. Such behavior is socially unacceptable. 社会的促進《社会・心理》social facilitation. 社会的動機《社会・心理》a social motive. 社会的動機づけ《社会・心理》social motivation. 社会的認知《社会・心理》social cognition. 社会(的)背景 (a) social 「background [context]. 社会的評価 (a) social evaluation.
**しゃかいふくし・いりょうじぎょうだん**【社会福祉・医療事業団】the Social Welfare and Medical Service Corporation（略: WAM）. ▶ 2003年に福祉医療機構となる.
**しゃかいふっき**【社会復帰】▶ 社会復帰調整官〔保護観察所の〕a social rehabilitation coordinator.
**しゃかいほうし**【社会奉仕】▶ 社会奉仕刑 compulsory community service.
**しゃかいほけんぎょうむセンター**【社会保険業務-】the Social Insurance Operation Center.
**しゃかいほけんじむしょ**【社会保険事務所】a social insurance office.
**しゃかいほしょう**【社会保障】▶ 社会保障協定 a social security agreement. ▷ 日米〜協定 the Japan-US Social Security Agreement. 社会保障個人会計 a unified "account" for the management of the individual's social security. 社会保障税〔米国の〕social security taxes. 社会保障番号〔米国の〕a Social Security number（略: SSN）.
**しゃかいほしょう・じんこうもんだいけんきゅうじょ**【社会保障・人口問題研究所】⇨こくりつしゃかいほしょう・じんこうもんだいけんきゅうじょ.
**しゃかく**⁵【社格】the status of a Shinto shrine.
**しゃがみぐい**【しゃがみ食い】eating while squatting (down). 〜する squat (down) and eat.
**しゃかんきょり**【車間距離】▶ 車間距離制御システム〔自動車の〕an 「adaptive cruise control [ACC] system.
**しゃかんじどうせいぎょシステム**【車間自動制御-】《自動車》an 「adaptive cruise control [ACC] system.
**しやく**²【試薬】▶ 細菌[ウイルス]検査試薬 a 「bacterial [viral] reagent.
**しやく**³【視訳】sight translation. 〜する translate at sight.
**じゃくがい**【若害】a juvenile problem; a problem caused by (inexperienced) young people.
**じゃくし**²【弱視】▶ 屈折異常(性)弱視 ametropic amblyopia. 経線弱視 meridional amblyopia. 視性刺激遮断弱視 stimulus deprivation amblyopia. 斜視弱視 strabismic amblyopia. 不同視弱視 anisometropic amblyopia.
**じゃくしゃ**【弱者】▶ 災害弱者 a person (especially)

ジャクソン vulnerable in case of a (natural) disaster;〈集合的に〉(protect) the vulnerable 《if there is an earthquake》.
**ジャクソン** 1 Jackson, Janet (1966-　；米国の歌手；Michael Jackson の妹).
2 Jackson, Mick (1960-　；英国生まれの映画監督).
3 Jackson, Peter (1961-　；ニュージーランドの映画監督・脚本家・製作者).
4 Jackson, Samuel L. (1948-　；米国の映画俳優；本名 Samuel Leroy Jackson).
**しゃくちけん**【借地権】⇨　建物譲渡特約付借地権〔定期借地権の一種〕land leasehold with a special agreement that after thirty or more years the landowner will purchase the building.
**ジャグデオ** Jagdeo, Bharrat (1964-　；ガイアナの政治家；大統領〔1999-　〕).
**しゃくとり**²【酌取り】a sake server; a person who serves sake at a Japanese restaurant.
**しゃくねつ**【灼熱】⇨　灼熱期【医】〔マラリアの〕the hot stage.
**じゃくねん**¹【若年】
⇨　若年結婚 (an) early marriage. 若年雇用 employment of young people; youth employment. 若年失業〔15-24歳の〕youth unemployment. 若年失業率 the youth unemployment rate. 若年者 a young person;〈集合的に〉the young. 若年者就職基礎能力支援事業　the Youth Employability Support Program (略: YES Program). ▶ 2004年、厚生労働省が創設。若年者就職基礎能力修得証明書 a certificate of a young person's employability. 若年無業者 a young unemployed person;〔ニート〕a NEET (⇨ニート).
**じゃくねん(せい)**【若年(性)】
〜の【医】juvenile. ⇨　若年(性)健忘症 early-onset memory loss. 若年(性)認知症【医】presenile [early-onset] dementia. 若年性パーキンソン病【医】early-onset Parkinson's disease.
**しゃくほう**【釈放】⇨　釈放指揮書〔検察官が刑事施設の長に対して被収容者の釈放を命じる文書〕a written release order.
**しゃくや**【借家】⇨　借家契約 a rental contract (for a house); a contract to rent 「a house [accommodation]. ◎定期〜契約 a fixed-term rental contract.
**じゃくれいぼうしゃ**【弱冷房車】a railway 「*car [˺carriage] with the air conditioning 「turned down [set to a higher temperature].
**しゃけい**²【斜頸】⇨　痙性斜頸【医】spasmodic torticollis; cervical dystonia.
**ジャケがい**【〜買い】〔ジャケットが気に入っただけで CD[レコード]を買ってしまうこと〕buying [purchasing] 《a CD》 only because of the ˹jacket [cover, sleeve].
**しゃけん**²【車検】⇨　車検場 a (motor) vehicle ˹inspection [testing] station [garage]. ◎民間〜場 a privately operated vehicle inspection station.
**しゃこ**¹【車庫】⇨　車庫入れ parking the car in the garage. ◎私は〜入れが苦手だ. I have trouble putting the car in the garage.
**しゃこう**¹¹【遮光】⇨　遮光膜【電子工学】a light-shielding film. 遮光眼鏡 light-shielding [glare-reducing] glasses;〔溶接用の〕welding ˹goggles [glasses].
**シャコタン**【車高短】〔暴走族の車などで車高を低く改造したもの〕a lowered car; a lowrider.
「**シャザーン**」⇨「大魔王シャザーン」.
**しゃさい**¹【社債】⇨　社債管理会社 a bond management company.
**しゃさい**¹【車載】⇨　車載工具【自動車】car [automobile] tools; a ˹car [automobile] tool set. 車載情報機器〔カーナビなど〕an ˹onboard [in-car] information system. 車載情報システム【通信】= テレマティクス. 車載(用)テレビ car [an in-car] television [TV].

**しゃざい**²【謝罪】⇨　謝罪会見《hold》a press conference to apologize《for an accident》. 謝罪記事《publish》˹an apology [an article of apology, an article to apologize《for unethical behavior》]. 謝罪番組《broadcast》˹an apology [a program to apologize《for a reporter's actions》].
**しゃさいとうふりかえほう**【社債等振替法】【法】〔社債等の振替に関する法律の通称〕the Law Concerning the Transfer and Settlement of Debentures.
**しゃし**³【斜視】⇨　下斜視 hypotropia; cataphoria. 回旋斜視 cyclotropia. 仮性(偽)斜視 pseudostrabismus; pseudoesotropia; false strabismus. 上斜視 hypertropia; anatropia. 上下斜視 vertical strabismus.
**ジャジコフ** Zyazikov, Murat (1957-　；イングーシ共和国の政治家；大統領〔2002-　〕).
「**じゃじゃ馬億万長者**」〔米国の、田舎者の石油成金一家が高級住宅地に移り住む TV コメディー〕The Beverly Hillbillies.
**しゃしゃかんつうしん**【車車間通信】vehicle-to-vehicle [intervehicle] communication.
**しゃしゅ**²【車種】⇨　最量販車種 a [the] best selling model《worldwide》.
**しゃじょう**²【車上】⇨　車上生活者[ホームレス] a (homeless) person living in an automobile.
**しゃじょうし**【車上子】【鉄道】ATS システムなどで地上子との情報の送受信に用いるコイル〕a pickup coil.
**しゃしょく**²【社食】〔社員食堂〕a ˹staff [company] canteen [cafeteria, dining hall].
**しゃしん**¹【写真】
⇨　写真愛好家 a photography enthusiast; a keen (amateur) photographer. 写真鑑定 (an) analysis [evaluation] of a photograph. 写真記者 a photojournalist; a ˹photo [photographic] journalist. 写真工学 photographic engineering. 写真付きカード〔住基カードなど〕a (" Jūki Net ") card with an ID photograph on it; a 《local resident's》 ID card with a photograph of the possessor on it. 写真付き切手 a (postage) stamp with a photograph; a photo stamp. 写真文集 = しゃしんしゅう. 写真用印画紙 photographic printing paper. 写真用年賀はがき a New Year's card for photographic printing; a photo-printable New Year's card. 写真療法 phototherapy.
**しゃしんかんこうざいりょうこうぎょうかい**【写真感光材料工業会】the Photo-Sensitized Materials Manufacturers' Association (略: PMMA).
**しゃじんけん**【社人研】= こくりつしゃかいほしょう・じんこうもんだいけんきゅうじょ.
**しゃしんのひ**【写真の日】〔6月1日〕Photography Day.
**ジャズ**⇨　ジャズ・エイジ[時代] the Jazz Age. ジャズ・ピアノ[ギター、トランペット(など)] jazz ˹piano [guitar, trumpet, etc.].
**しゃすい**【遮水】water ˹interception [insulation]; seepage control.
〜する intercept water; control seepage. ⇨　遮水工【土木】seepage control work. 遮水材(料) an [a water] impermeable material; (a) seepage control material. 遮水シート a ˹water-impermeable [seepage control, liner] sheet. 遮水性 (water) impermeability; imperviousness (to water). 遮水性舗装 (water) impervious paving. 遮水壁 an impermeable wall; (a watertight) bulkhead. 遮水膜 an impermeable membrane.
**ジャスダック**【JASDAQ】⇨　ジャスダック株価指数 the JASDAQ index.
「**ジャスティス**」【映画】Hart's War.
**ジャスほう**【JAS 法】【法】= にほんのうりんきかくほう.
**しゃせいどう**【社青同】= にほんしゃかいしゅぎせいねんどうめい.
**しゃせん**²【車線】⇨　右[左]車線 the ˹right(-hand) [left(-hand)] lane. 車線維持装置【自動車】a lane-

keeping [assistance [assist] system.
しゃせん[3]【斜線】 ▫️ 斜線部分 a shaded area.
ジャタ【JATA】〔日本旅行業協会〕JATA; the Japan Association of Travel Agents.
しゃたい[1]【車体】 ▫️ 車体傾斜システム〔鉄道〕〔列車〕a body tilting system. 車体傾斜装置〔鉄道〕〔列車〕body tilting equipment. 車体番号〔車台番号〕the vehicle identification number (略: VIN).
しゃちがわら【鯱瓦】= しゃちほこ瓦 (⇨しゃちほこ).
しゃちぶり【魚】〔シャチブリ科の深海魚〕a jellynose fish; *Ateleopus japonicus*.
しゃちほこ【鯱】 ▫️ しゃちほこ瓦 ornamental *shachihoko* at each end of a roof-ridge.
しゃちょう[1]【社長】 ▫️ 社長決済 a [payment [settlement] made by the head of a company. ◐〜決済を要する多額の出費 a large expenditure that has to be made by the head of the company.
しゃちょう[2]【車長】 1〔軍〕〔戦車長〕a tank commander. 2〔車の長さ〕(a) vehicle length.
しゃっか【借家】 ▫️ 借家契約 a rental contract (for a house); a contract to rent [a house [accommodation]. ◐ 定期〜契約 a fixed-term rental contract.
しゃっかん【借款】
▫️ エンジニアリング・サービス借款〔調査・設計などのための円借款〕an engineering service (yen) loan. 開発金融借款〔相手国の金融機関を介した円借款〕a development finance loan; a financial sector intermediation (yen) loan (略: FSIL); a development (yen) loan through the local banking system; a "two-step" (yen) loan. 通称 ツー・ステップ・ローン. 構造調整借款〔経済構造の再建・調整のための資金援助〕a structural adjustment loan (略: SAL). 商品借款〔決められた商品輸入のための円借款〕a commodity (yen) loan. セクター・プログラム借款〔相手国産業の特定セクター発展のための円借款〕a (forestry) sector program loan. プロジェクト借款〔特定プロジェクト向けの円借款〕a project (yen) loan.
「ジャッキー・ブラウン」〔映画〕Jackie Brown.
しゃっきん【借金】
▫️ 借金苦 the pain of (being in) debt. 借金癖 (have) [a [the] habit of borrowing money. ◐ 彼は〜癖がなかなか直らない. He just won't stop borrowing money. 借金財政 debt-based finance. 借金地獄 (fall into) (a) debt hell. 借金生活 a debt-filled life; (live one's) life in debt. 借金体質 the institutionalization of debt; a state of indebtedness which has become the norm. ◐ 新財務大臣に課せられた任務は〜体質からの脱却だ. The task of the new Finance Minister is to free the country from a condition in which debt is the normal state of affairs. 借金漬け being up to one's [eyes [ears] in debt. ◐ 〜漬けになる [buried [mired] in debt / 彼はギャンブルにはまり〜漬けになった. He became addicted to gambling and got up to his eyes in debt.
しゃっきんどけい【借金時計】〔国などの借金額をリアルタイムで表示する時計〕a debt clock.
ジャック[2] 〜する〔乗っ取る・占拠する〕take over; monopolize. ◐ 広告で渋谷を〜する fill [cover] Shibuya with advertisements.
ジャックフルーツ〔植〕〔クワ科の果物; 食用となるその実〕a jackfruit; *Artocarpus heterophyllus*.
ジャックマン Jackman, Hugh (1968– ; オーストラリア生まれの映画俳優).
しゃっこつ【尺骨】 ▫️ 尺骨神経炎〔医〕(an) inflammation of the ulnar nerve; (an) ulnar nerve inflammation.
「ジャッジ・ドレッド」〔映画〕Judge Dredd.
ジャッズ【JAHDS】= じんどうもくてきのじらいじょきょしえんのかい.
シャッター ▫️ シャッター街〔通り〕〔シャッター商店街〕a shuttered shopping mall; a street with many closed [*stores [*shops].
ジャッド Judd, Ashley (1968– ; 米国の映画女優).
シャットネラ【生物】〔赤潮を発生させる藻類〕*Chattonella*.
しゃてい[2]【射程】 ▫️ 射程圏 = 射程範囲. 射程範囲 a range.
しゃていきょり【射程距離】 ▫️ 有効射程距離 an effective range.
ジャド = ジャッド.
「シャドウ・オブ・ヴァンパイア」〔映画〕Shadow of the Vampire.
シャドー[1] ▫️ シャドー・ピッチング〔野球〕shadow pitching. シャドー・ロール〔気の小さい馬の目の影におびえないよう目と鼻の間に取り付ける馬具; 毛付き鼻勒(びろく)〕a shadow roll.
シャトールー〔フランス中部, アンドル県の県都〕Châteauroux.
シャドヤック Shadyac, Tom (1960– ; 米国の映画監督).
シャトヤンシーこうか【-効果】〔宝石〕〔宝石の表面に猫の目のような光の帯が現れる現象〕a chatoyancy effect; a cat's-eye effect
ジャドリヤ〔イラク, バグダッド市内の地名〕Jadriyah.
シャトル ▫️ シャトル・ラン〔体力測定の一種で, 短距離の往復持久走〕a shuttle run; shuttle running.
ジャトロファ〔植〕〔トウダイグサ科ナンヨウアブラギリ属の低木の総称〕*Jatropha*. ▫️ ジャトロファ油 jatropha oil.
しゃない[1]【社内】 ▫️ 社内いじめ workplace bullying. 社内 FA 制 an in-house free agent system. 社内カンパニー, 社内分社 an in-house company; a strategic business unit (略: SBU). ◐ 〜カンパニー[分社]制 an in-house company system. 社内金融 in-house financing. 社内コンペ an in-house (design) competition. 社内処分 (a) company [(an) internal company] punishment; (in-house) disciplinary measures. ◐ 3 か月間 10%減給の〜処分を受ける have one's salary cut by 10% for three months as a company punishment; be disciplined by having one's salary by 10% for three months. 社内大学 a corporate [an in-company, an in-house] university. 社内弁護士 an in-house [lawyer [attorney, counsel]. 社内風土 a corporate [an in-house] climate [atmosphere, culture]. 社内不祥事 an in-house scandal. 社内リサイクル[再利用] in-house recycling (system). 社内倫理委員会 《a firm's》in-house ethics committee. 社内倫理規定 《a firm's》in-house code of ethics.
シャニダールどうくつ【-洞窟】〔イラク北部の洞窟; ネアンデルタール人の骨が発見された〕the Shanidar Cave.
しゃねつ【遮熱】 heat-blocking.
〜する block heat. ▫️ 遮熱ガラス (a) low-emissivity glass; (a) low-e glass. 遮熱材 heat-blocking material. 遮熱性(の) heat-blocking. 〜性舗装 heat-blocking pavement. 遮熱塗料 insulating [heat-blocking] paint; (a) heat-blocking coating.
じゃのめエリカ【蛇の目-】〔植〕〔ツツジ科の常緑低木; 南アフリカ原産〕*Erica canaliculata*.
シャハーダ〔イスラム世界で, 証言・証拠・殉教などの意〕(the) shahadat; (the) Shahadat.
シャバク〔イスラエルの国内防諜保安機関〕the Shabak. ▶〔シンベト〕(the Shin Bet) も参照.
ジャパニーズ・スマイル the Japanese smile.
しゃはば【車幅】 ▫️ 車幅感覚 a [feeling for [sense of] the width of one's car. ◐ 〜感覚を身につける get used to [the width of one's car [how wide one's car is].
シャハブ〔軍〕〔イランが北朝鮮の協力を得て開発した中距離弾道ミサイル〕a Shahab missile.
ジャバリヤ〔パレスチナ, ガザ地区北部の難民キャンプ地〕the [Jabalya [Jabalia] refugee camp.

ジャパン・ソサエティー〔各国にある日本協会〕a Japan Society; the Japan Society《of the UK, of Boston》.
ジャパン・パートナーズ・アゲインスト・ペイン the Japan Partners Against Pain (略: JPAP). ▶ がん性疼痛緩和治療の重要性や社会的意義の啓発を目的とする団体.
ジャパン・プラットフォーム〔日本の国際人道支援機関〕the Japan Platform (略: JPF).
ジャパン・ラグビー・トップリーグ the Japan Rugby Top League.
シャヒード《イスラム教》〔殉教者〕a shahid; a shaheed; a martyr.
シャヒーン《軍》〔パキスタンが中国の協力を得て開発した核弾頭搭載可能な弾道ミサイル〕a Shaheen missile.
ジャファ・マーク【JHFA-】〔健康補助食品の審査合格マーク〕a JHFA mark. ▶ Japan Health Food Authorization の略. 日本健康・栄養食品協会 (Japan Health Food & Nutrition Food Association (JHNFA)) が認定.
ジャファリ (Al-)Jaffari, Ibrahim (1947- ; イラクの政治家; 移行政府首相 [2005-06]).
しゃぶつ〔写仏〕(the ritual of) copying [tracing] an image [a portrait] of the Buddha; 〔写した絵〕a copied portrait of the Buddha.
シャフト ⇨ シャフト・ドライブ《機》〔二輪車・自転車などの〕a shaft drive.
シャフナー Schaffner, Franklin J. (1920-89; 米国の映画監督).
しゃふりほう〔社振法〕《法》＝しゃさいとうふりかえほう.
シャフレ・コルド〔イラン中南部, チャハールマハール・バフティヤーリー州の州都〕Shahr-e Kord.
しゃぶんしゅう〔写文集〕〔写真とエッセーで編集した本〕a photo essay; a photo journal.
しゃへい〔遮蔽〕 □ 遮蔽板〔熱・音・放射線などの〕a protective「screen [shield]; 〔刑務所内の面会室の〕a dividing screen; a (glass) partition.
しゃべりたおす〔しゃべり倒す〕〔しゃべりまくる〕jabber away; babble on;〔相手を圧倒する勢いでしゃべる〕talk sb's ear off; rattle on. ◐ たまの休日は女友達とおしゃべり〜のが私の息抜き. On my rare days off I let off steam by just jabbering away with my girl friends. / 彼はシンポジウムに呼ばれて, 2時間しゃべり倒した. He was invited to the symposium and rattled on unstoppably for two solid hours.
ジャボチカバ《植》〔ブラジル原産のフトモモ科の常緑小高木〕a jaboticaba; *Myrciaria cauliflora*.
シャボンだまのき〔-玉の木〕《植》〔トウダイグサ科の落葉低木; 熱帯アメリカ原産〕a physic nut; *Jatropha curcas*.
シャマラン Shyamalan, M. Night (1970- ; インド生まれの米国の映画監督・脚本家).
ジャマリ Jamali, Zafarullah Khan (1944- ; パキスタンの政治家; 首相 [2002-04]).
シャミール Shāmil (1797?-1871; 北カフカスの政治・宗教指導者; 反ロシア解放運動家).
ジャムステック【JAMSTEC】〔海洋研究開発機構〕JAMSTEC; the Japan Agency for Marine-Earth Science and Technology.
しゃよう[2]〔斜陽〕 □ 斜陽化〔特定の産業などの〕the decline《of the movie industry》.
シャラーモフ Shalamov, Varlam (1907-82; ロシアの反体制作家).
ジャライ ⇨ ザライ.
シャラポワ Sharapova, Maria (1987- ; ロシア生まれのテニス選手).
ジャラルアバド〔キルギス西部の州; その州都〕Jalal-Abad.
シャリフ[2] Sharif, Nawaz (1949- ; パキスタンの政治家; 首相 [1990-93, 97-99]).
しゃりょう[2]〔車両〕 □ 最後尾車両〔列車の〕the last *car [ˈcarriage, coach]. 先頭車両〔列車の〕the first [front] *car [ˈcarriage, coach]. □ 車両運搬車 ＝キャ

リア・カー. 車両基地〔鉄道の〕a rail yard; a train yard. 車両工学 vehicle engineering. 車両センター〔JR など鉄道の〕a train [car] depot. 車両保険 vehicle damage insurance. 車両モニター〔鉄道車両・トラックなどに搭載した〕an event recorder.
シャルドネ[1] ⇨ ピエモンテ・シャルドネ〔イタリア北部ピエモンテ州産の白ワイン〕(a)「Piemonte [Piedmont] Chardonnay.
シャルム・エル・シェイク〔エジプト, 紅海沿岸のリゾート地〕Sharm el-Sheikh.
シャルル・ジョルダン《商標》〔フランスの服飾ブランド〕Charles Jourdan.
シャルルロワ〔ベルギー南西部の都市〕Charleroi.
しゃれい[2]〔車齢〕the age of an automobile; a car's age. ◐ 〜10年の中古車 a 10-year-old used car.
しゃろうし〔社労士〕〔社会保険労務士〕a licensed social insurance consultant.
ジャロザイ〔パキスタン北西部のアフガニスタン難民キャンプ〕the Jalozai (refugee) camp.
シャワー □ シャワー・キャップ a shower cap. シャワー効果〔デパートなどの最上階での催しに集まった客が下の階の売り場に売り上げをもたらすこと〕the shower effect; increased sales on the lower floors of a multistory retail venue as a result of significant attendance at an event or attraction on a higher floor.
ジャワ・マングース《動》a small Indian mongoose; a Javan mongoose; *Herpestes javanicus*.
シャン[2]〔ミャンマー東北部, 中国・ラオス・タイと国境を接する州〕Shan.
ジャンガリアン・ハムスター《動》a Djungarian hamster; a Russian dwarf hamster; *Phodopus sungorus*.
ジャンク[2] □ ジャンク DNA《遺伝》〔がらくた DNA; なんら機能を果たしていないとされる DNA 領域〕junk DNA.
ジャン・コード【JAN-】〔日本の商品コード〕a JAN code. ▶ JAN は Japanese Article Number の略. 〔⇨しょうひんコード〕
ジャンジャウィード〔スーダン西部の武装した遊牧民からなるアラブ人民兵組織〕the「Janjaweed [Janjawid, Jingaweit].
しゃんしゃん[1] □ シャンシャン大会 a rigged convention.
シャンソニエ《＜F *chansonnier*》〔シャンソンのライブハウス〕a chanson bar.
シャンツァイ〔香菜〕《＜Chin》xiang cai;〔コリアンダー〕coriander.
シャンディガフ〔カクテル〕a shandygaff.
シャント《医》〔血管バイパスの形成〕a shunt. □ 内 [外] シャント an 「internal [external] shunt. □ シャント手術 shunt surgery; a shunt operation.
ジャンドゥーヤ〔菓子〕〔ヘーゼルナッツペースト入りチョコレート〕gianduja.
「シャンドライの恋」〔映画〕Besieged.
「シャンヌのパリ, そしてアメリカ」〔映画〕A Soldier's Daughter Never Cries.
ジャンパー □ ジャンパー膝《医》jumper's knee. [＝ランナー膝〔⇨ランナー〕]
シャンハイ □ 上海 A 株 [B 株]〔上海市場上場銘柄〕a Shanghai「A-share [B-share]. 上海語 Shanghainese; the Shanghai dialect.
シャンハイがに〔上海蟹〕《動》＝ちゅうごくもくずがに;〔食材としては〕Shanghai crab.
シャンハイきしゃ〔こうぎょうしゅうだん〕【上海汽車〔工業集団〕】〔中国の自動車メーカー〕Shanghai Automotive Industry Corporation (Group) (略: SAIC).
シャンハイきょうりょくきこう【上海協力機構】〔中国・ロシア・カザフスタン・キルギス・タジキスタン・ウズベキスタンの6か国首脳会議〕the Shanghai Cooperation Organization (略: SCO).
シャンハイさきものとりひきじょ【上海先物取引所】

the Shanghai Futures Exchange (略: SHFE).
**シャンハイそうごう(かぶか)しすう**【上海総合(株価)指数】《証券》the Shanghai Stock Exchange composite index (略: SSEC).
**シャンハイにっぽう**【上海日報】〔中国, 上海の英字日刊紙〕Shanghai Daily.
**シャンハイ・ファイブ**【上海-】〔中国周辺5か国による首脳会議〕the "Shanghai「Five [5]」summit. ▶中国, ロシア, カザフスタン, キルギス, タジキスタンの5か国.
**シャンハイほうこうしゅうだん**【上海宝鋼集団】〔中国の国有鉄鋼メーカー〕Shanghai Baosteel Group Corporation.
**シャンパン** ◳ シャンパン・ファイト〔自動車レース終了後に上位入賞者らがシャンパンをかけあうこと〕a champagne fight.
**シャンピニオン, シャンピニョン**〔マッシュルームのフランス語名〕a champignon.
**ジャンプ** ◳ 3回転半ジャンプ《フィギュア》《land》a three and a half axel; a three and a half revolution jump. ◳ ジャンプトス《バレーボール》a jump set; jump setting. ◳〜トスを上げる make a jump set; jump set.
**シャンプー** ◳ シャンプーハット shampoo shield.
「**シャンプー台のむこうに**」《映画》Blow Dry.
**ジャンベ**《楽器》〔西アフリカの打楽器〕a djembe.
**ジャンボ** ◳ ジャンボ・タクシー a van taxi; a "jumbo taxi."
**ジャン・ポール・ゴルチエ**《商標》〔フランスの服飾ブランド〕Jean Paul Gaultier.
**しゅい**[3]【首位】 ◳ 首位奪還[奪回] recapturing「first place [the lead].
**ジュイソン** Jewison, Norman (1926–　; カナダ生まれの米国の映画監督; 本名 Norman Frederick Jewison).
**しゅう**[2]【州】 ◳ 赤[青い]州《米》〔大統領選挙で共和党[民主党]が制した(あるいは優勢な)州〕a「red [blue] state. ▶選挙報道でしばしば赤[青]色で示される.
**シュー** Shue, Elisabeth (1963–　; 米国の映画女優).
**シュー**[2]【<F chou】 ◳ シュー皮 choux [cream puff] pastry. シュー生地 pâte à choux; choux [cream puff] paste.
**じゆう**[1]【自由】 ◳ 自由席回数券 a set of discounted tickets for non-reserved seats; 〔1枚〕a discounted non-reserved seat ticket (from a set). 自由席特急券 a ticket for a non-reserved seat on a limited express; a limited express non-reserved seat ticket. 自由標榜(制)《医》〔医師の診療科目についての〕(the) freedom to advertise 《a medical practice》.
**じゅう**[6]【銃】 ◳ 空気銃 an air「gun [rifle]. 自動銃 an automatic「gun [weapon]; an automatic; 〈集合的に〉automatic「weaponry [firearms]. 特殊銃 a special「firearm [gun]. 元折れ銃 a folding gun. 銃社会 an armed「populace [society]; a gun-toting society. 銃犯罪 (a) gun crime; 《commit》a crime with a gun. ◳ アメリカでは少年たちによる〜犯罪が多発している. Juvenile gun crimes occur frequently in the United States. 銃保管庫 a gun locker. 銃乱射事件 a random shooting incident.
**じゆうアジアほうそう**【自由-放送】〔米国のアジア向け放送〕the Radio Free Asia (略: RFA).
**シュヴァスマン・ヴァハマンだいさんすいせい**【-第3彗星】《天》the Comet 73P/Schwassmann-Wachmann (3) (略: SW 3).
**じゆうアチェうんどう**【自由-運動】〔インドネシアの武装組織〕the Free Aceh Movement (略: GAM). ▶GAM は Gerakan Aceh Merdeka の略.
**しゅういん**【衆院】 ◳ 衆院議会制度協議会 the (House of Representatives) Council on the Parliamentary System.
**しゅうえき**[2]【収益】 ◳ 収益還元法〔不動産鑑定評価法の1つ〕the income approach 《to property valuation》. 収益配分 revenue [profit] sharing; a share of「proceeds [earnings, revenue].
**しゅうか**[3]【臭化】 ◳ 臭化ベクロニウム《薬》〔筋弛緩剤〕vecuronium bromide.
**しゅうかい**[1]【周回】 ◳ 周回機《宇宙》an orbiter.
**しゅうかいイプラトロピウム**【臭化-】《薬》〔呼吸困難を緩和する薬〕ipratropium bromide.
**しゅうがく**[3]【修学】 schooling. ◳ 修学支援[援助] schooling assistance. 修学資金[学費] school expenses;〔資金〕an education fund.
**しゅうがくてき**【集学的】 〜な multidisciplinary. ◳ 社会学に対する〜なアプローチ a multidisciplinary approach to sociology. 集学的に multidisciplinarily. ◳ 集学的治療《医》〔様々な治療法を組み合わせる〕multidisciplinary treatment.
**じゆうかくとく**【自由獲得】《野球》 ◳ 自由獲得選手 a freely selected player; a free pick. 自由獲得枠 a free-selection quota.
**じゅうかしつ**【重過失】 ◳ 重過失失火《法》a fire resulting from gross negligence.
**じゅうがつざくら**【十月桜】《植》〔コヒガンザクラの園芸品種〕an "October cherry (tree)"; *Prunus × subhirtella* cv. *Autumnalis*.
**しゅうかん**[1]【収監】 ◳ 収監者 a prisoner; a detainee; a detained person. 収監命令 a detention order.
**しゅうき**[2]【周期】 ◳ 固有周期《地震》〔建造物などの振動の〕a 《structure's》natural period 《of vibration》. 卓越周期《地震》《地盤》a predominant period 《of 0.06s》; the predominant period 《of the soil》.
**しゅうき**[3]【銃器】 ◳ 銃器情報 information [a tip] on illegal firearms. ◳〜情報提供者 a person providing information [an informant] on illegal firearms. 銃器犯罪 =銃犯罪 (⇨じゅう[6]).
**シューキーパー**〔靴の型崩れを防ぐために, はかないときに入れておく木製などの靴型〕a shoe tree.
**しゅうぎいん**【衆議院】 ◳ 衆議院議会制度協議会 =衆院議会制度協議会 (⇨しゅういん). 衆議院規則 the Rules for the House of Representatives.
**しゅうぎいん(ぎいん)せんきょくかくていしんぎかい**【衆議院(議員)選挙区画定審議会】the Council for the Demarcation of Constituency Boundaries for Elections to the House of Representatives.
**しゅうぎいん(ぎいん)せんきょくかくていしんぎかいせっちほう**【衆議院(議員)選挙区画定審議会設置法】《法》the Law on the Establishment of the Council for the Demarcation of Constituency Boundaries for Elections to the House of Representatives.
**しゅうぎいんテロぼうしとくべついいんかい**【衆議院-防止特別委員会】⇨テロぼうしとくべついいんかい.
**しゅうきせい**【周期性】 ◳ 周期性四肢運動障害《医》a periodic limb movement disorder (略: PLMD).
**しゅうきぜみ**【周期蟬】《昆》〔13年・17年などの周期で大量発生するセミ〕a periodical [13-year, 17-year] cicada [locust]; *Magicicada septendecim*.
**しゅうきゃく**【集客】 ◳ 集客〔《be》a draw; effectiveness in attracting customers. ◳ 集客効果 ◳ DVD はビデオより小さいので, 同じレンタル店の面積で3倍以上の本数が置け, 〜効果も期待できる. Since DVDs are smaller than video tapes it is possible to keep more than three times as many in the same rental store and it should be possible to「attract [bring in] more customers. 集客作戦 a strategy for attracting customers. 集客施設 a customer-attracting facility; 《口》a customer draw. 集客法 a「method for attracting [way to attract] customers.
**じゅうきょ**【住居】 ◳ 住居学 housing studies.
**しゅうきょう**[3]【宗教】 ◳ 宗教右派〈集合的に〉the religious right. 宗教観 one's religious「views [outlook];

しゅうぎょう

*one's* attitude toward religion; how *one* views religion. 宗教行事 a religious ⌜ceremony [event]⌟. 宗教的情操 (a) religious sentiment; religious sentiments.

**しゅうぎょう³【就業】** ▯▮ 正規[非正規]就業 formal [informal] employment. ▯▮ 就業機会 a job [an employment] opportunity. 就業教育 career(s) ⌜guidance [counselling, advice]. 就業体験 (an) internship. 就業対策〔高齢者やニートに対する〕an employment measure《for older people》. 就業達成度 the extent to which ⌜employment has been achieved [jobs have been created]; an employment level. 就業年齢〔就職年齢〕the age of (first) employment; the age at which ⌜people start [*one* starts] working;〔生産年齢〕the working age. 就業年齢人口 the working age population; the population of working age. 就業能力 employability. 就業比率 a labor-force participation rate. ▯▮ 第三次産業〜比率 the labor-force participation rate in the service sector.

**じゅうぎょういん【従業員】** ▯▮ 期間従業員 a fixed-term employee. ▯▮ 従業員支援[援助]プログラム an employee assistance program(略: EAP). 従業員満足(度) employee satisfaction(略: ES). 従業員持ち株会 a group ⌜of [for] employee stock owners; staff ⌜participating in [belonging to] an ESOP.

**しゅうきん²【集金】** ▯▮ 訪問集金 door-to-door collection《of payment》. ▯▮ 集金袋〔集金人が携帯する〕a ⌜money [cash] bag;〔子供に授業料・給食費などを持たせるための〕a ⌜money [cash] (collection) envelope.

**じゅうぐん【従軍】** ▯▮ 従軍画家 a military artist. 従軍カメラマン〔写真家〕a ⌜military [war, combat] photographer;〔ある部隊と行動を共にする〕an embedded ⌜photographer; a photographer embedded ⌜with the Marines〕;〔撮影技師〕a ⌜military [war, combat] cameraman;〔ある部隊と行動を共にする〕an embedded cameraman. 従軍作家 a war writer.

**しゅうけい³【集計】** ▯▮ 集計漏れ (a) failure to include 《a figure》 in the total. ▮ 今回の選挙で約200票の〜漏れがあった. In this election some 200 votes ⌜were omitted from the total [failed to appear in the final count].

**しゅうけい⁴【周径】** a circumference; a measurement around《the base, the waist》; a ⌜length [distance] around《a pond》; a girth of《a thigh》. ▮ 〜約5メートルの巨木 an immense tree, nearly five meters in circumference; a huge tree with a girth of nearly five meters.

**しゅうけいしょうがい【醜形障害】**〖精神医〗＝しんたいしゅうけいしょうがい.

**しゅうこう¹⁰【収公】**〔政府による没収〕expropriation; confiscation.
〜する expropriate [confiscate]《property》.

**しゅうごう³【集合】** ▯▮ 集合訓練〔災害・非常事態などに備えて自衛隊員・公務員などに対して行う訓練〕《have, hold》an emergency muster drill; emergency assembly practice. 集合知 collective intelligence; collective wisdom; the wisdom of ⌜crowds [groups]. 集合的記憶〖社会〗(a) collective memory.

**じゅうこう⁴【重厚】** ▯▮ 重厚感 a feeling of ⌜solidity [substance]. ▮ 〜感あふれる外観デザイン an exterior design imbued with an aura of solidity.

**じゅうこん²【重婚】** ▯▮ 重婚的内縁関係《be involved in》a bigamous common-law marriage.

**しゅうさい²【秀才】** ▯▮ 秀才タイプ ▮ 〜タイプの人 the type of person who is touched with genius.

**じゅうさいむこく【重債務国】**〔世界銀行が認定する〕a highly indebted country.

**じゅうさん【十三】** ▯▮ 十三参り a traditional ritual where 13 year olds visit ⌜the *Gokuzo Bosastsu* at Hōrinji Temple in Kyoto [a temple or a shrine] to pray for good luck, wisdom, and health on March 13 th of the lunar calendar.

**しゅうさんき【周産期】** ▯▮ 周産期医療 perinatal care. 周産期医療ネットワーク a perinatal care network.

**じゅうさんぶつ, じゅうさんぼとけ【十三仏】**〖仏教〗the thirteen ⌜Buddhas [images of Buddha or Buddhist saints]《each representing one of the 13 memorial services held after *sb's* death》.

**しゅうし¹【収支】** ▯▮ 所得収支〔国際収支の〕the income account; the balance on income. 投資収支〔国際収支の〕the financial account; the balance on investment income.

**じゅうじ¹【十字】** ▯▮ 十字靭帯〖解〗a cruciate ligament. ▮ 前〜靭帯 an anterior cruciate ligament(略: ACL) / 後〜靭帯 a posterior cruciate ligament(略: PCL).

**じゅうしちねんぜみ【十七年蝉】**〖昆〗a seventeen-year ⌜locust [cicada]; *Magicicada septendecim*.

**じゅうしつゆ【重質油】** heavy oil.

**しゅうじふく【周恩復】** Zhou Erfu (1914–2004; 中国の作家・書家).

**しゅうしゅう¹【収拾】** ▯▮ 収拾策[案] plans for a ⌜solution [settlement, resolution]; measures to ⌜settle [solve, resolve, put right] a problem.

**しゅうじゅう【集住】**〔一か所に集まって居住すること〕living together in a (concentrated) community. 〜する gather [concentrate] in one area and live ⌜together [with other《immigrants》]; live in a concentrated community. ▯▮ 外国人集住地域 an area with a concentrated population of ⌜immigrants [non-Japanese residents].

**じゅうしゅう²【自由州】**〔南アフリカ共和国中東部の州〕Free State;《アフリカーンス語名》Vrystaat. ► 旧オレンジ自由州. 州都はブルームフォンテイン.

**しゅうじゅく【習熟】** ▯▮ 習熟給 an ⌜achievement-based [ability-based] salary.

**しゅうしゅくき【収縮期】**〖医〗〔心臓の〕the systolic phase. ▯▮ 収縮期(血)圧〖生理〗systolic (blood) pressure; maximum blood pressure.

**じゅうしょ【住所】** ▯▮ 住所地特例〔介護保険上の〕an exception《to normal procedure》concerning the locality of residence; a system in which the municipality where a resident of a nursing home originally lived bears the nursing care expenses. 住所不明者 a person whose ⌜address [residence] is unknown.

**じゅうしょう²【重症】** ▯▮ 重症化 aggravation; worsening. ▮ アトピー性皮膚炎はステロイド剤の副作用で〜化することがある. Atopic dermatitis can be ⌜aggravated [worsened] as a side effect of (taking) steroids. 重症度〔疾患の〕the (degree of) severity《of a complaint》.

**しゅうしょく⁴【就職】** ▯▮ 就職委員会〔大学などの〕a careers committee. 就職支援 employment ⌜support [assistance]; helping《women》to obtain employment. ▮ 〜支援を行う provide employment assistance; help《young people》to obtain employment / 〜支援講座 a ⌜lecture [class, course] for people ⌜seeking employment [looking for a job] / 〜支援セミナー a job-hunting seminar. 就職商法 selling through deceptive job advertisements; a job (advertisement) scam. 就職情報サイト〔ウェブ上の〕a job information site. 就職仲介 a job [an employment] brokerage service. 就職年齢〔初めて職業に就く年齢〕the age of (first) employment; the age at which ⌜people start [*one* starts] working. 就職白書 a white paper on ⌜finding employment [job seeking]. 就職面接 a job interview.

**しゅうしょく⁶【襲職】** succession to《a post》.

**しゅうしん³【終身】** ▯▮ 身比例1位〔選挙に際して, 政党の比例候補者リストでの〕a lifelong top position (on

the proportional representation ballot). 終身名誉監督 a lifetime honorary manager 《of the Yomiuri Giants》.
**しゅうじん**[1]【囚人】 ▷□ 囚人食 prison food; a prison meal. 囚人のジレンマ〔ゲーム理論の１つ〕the prisoner's dilemma.
**じゅうしん**[1]【重心】 ▷□ 重心移動 (a) weight shift; a center-of-gravity shift; a shift「in [of] the center of gravity. ◐ 右半身から左半身へのスムースな〜移動 a smooth shift in center of gravity from the left of the body to the right / これからの社会には生産性から持続可能性への〜移動が必要だ. Modern society is going to need to shift its weight from productivity to sustainability.
**じゅうすい**[2]【重水】 ▷□ 重水漏れ〔原子力発電所の事故〕 a heavy water leak.
**しゅうせい**[2]【修正】
▷□ 修正画像〔写真〕 a modified [an edited] image [photograph];〔肖像写真などの〕an enhanced [a retouched, a touched-up] image [photograph];〔画像に部分的削除・追加・差し替えの改変を施した〕 an altered「image [photograph]; an "improved"「image [photograph]; an image [a photograph] edited 《to make the view look better》;〔ヌードなどの〕an image [a photograph] of a nude with the genitalia「airbrushed (out) [edited out]; an airbrushed nude. ◐ 無〜画像〔写真〕 an「unmodified [unedited] image [photograph];〔肖像写真などの〕 an「unenhanced [unretouched] image [photograph];〔画像に削除・追加・差し替えなどの改変を施してない〕an unaltered「image [photograph]; a true「image [photograph];〔ヌードなどの〕an image [a photograph] of a nude with the genitalia not airbrushed (out); an uncensored nude (image [photograph]). 修正協議〔法案などの〕a meeting for「amendment of [negotiating changes to] legislation. ◐ 野党が〜協議に応じない構えなので, この法案の今国会成立は困難な情勢だ. Since the stance of the opposition parties is to refuse to take part in discussions to amend the bill, it seems unlikely to be passed in the current Diet session. 修正条項〔法律の条文などについての〕an amendment 《to [of] a law》;〔米国憲法の〕the Amendments. 修正漏れ (a) failure to correct《an error》. ◐ そのコンピュータープログラムには〜漏れがあった. An error in the computer program「had been missed [hadn't been put right]. | There was an uncorrected error in the computer program.
**じゅうせいかつ**【住生活】 ▷□ 住生活学〔科目名などとして〕(the study of) home(s) [housing] and lifestyle(s); domestic arrangements and ways of life; life and the home.
**しゅうせき**[3]【集積】 ▷□ 集積効果〔同系の施設の〕the (industrial) agglomeration effect. 集積度〔電算〕(the) degree of integration. 集積促進〔農地の〕cooperativization (of agricultural land); land pooling;〔関連産業の〕industrial agglomeration; agglomeration of industries.
**しゅうせき**[4]【就籍】〔日本人で戸籍に記載されていない者が戸籍をつくる〕establishment of a family register (for a Japanese citizen who did not have one).
**しゅうせつ**【終雪】 the last snow(fall) of the season.
**しゅうぜん**[1]【修繕】 ▷□ 修繕ドック〔船舶の〕a repair dock. 修繕引当金 a reserve [an allowance, a provision] for repairs. ◐ 特別〜引当金 a reserve [an allowance, a provision] for special repairs.
**じゆうせんたく**[2]【自由選択】 ▷□ 自由選択制〔公立学校の〕a system in which students may seek to enroll in any school in the entire district.
**しゅうそ**[2]【臭素】 ▷□ 臭素化ダイオキシン〔化〕〔臭素系難燃剤を燃やすと発生する有害物質〕brominated dioxin. 臭素系難燃剤〔化〕a brominated flame retardant.
**じゅうそう**[7]【縦走】 ▷□ 縦走筋〔解〕a longitudinal muscle. 縦走路 a traverse (route)《through a mountain range》.
**しゅうぞく**【習俗】 ▷□ 民間習俗 folk manners and customs.
**じゅうたい**[2]【渋滞】 ▷□ 渋滞学 congestion studies. 渋滞緩和 (the) alleviation of (traffic) congestion. 渋滞情報 traffic jam information; information on congestion.
**じゅうだい**[2]【重大】 ▷□ 重大インシデント〔航空・鉄道〕〔事故につながりかねない事態〕a serious incident.
**じゅうだいそしきはんざいちょう**【重大組織犯罪庁】〔英国の〕the Serious Organised Crime Agency (略: SOCA).
**しゅうたいほう**【臭袋法】〔におい測定法〕the odor bag method. ◐ 三点比較式臭袋法 the triangular odor bag method.
**じゅうたく**【住宅】
▷□ 住宅火災 a residential [house] fire. 住宅火災保険 residential [house] fire insurance. 住宅再建共済制度〔災害時に備える兵庫県独自の〕the Housing Reconstruction Mutual Aid System. 住宅市場 the housing market. ◐ 新築〜市場 the housebuilding [housing construction] market. 住宅性能 housing performance. ◐ 〜性能表示制度 a housing performance assessment system; a system for grading the reliability, performance, and efficiency of a residential building, covering nine categories / 〜性能評価 a housing performance assessment / 〜性能評価機関 an organization authorized to carry out housing performance assessment / 〜性能評価書 a housing performance assessment certificate / 〜性能保証制度 a housing「quality [performance] guarantee system. 住宅補修費 the cost of「repairing [repairs to] a house. 住宅密集地 an area dense with housing; a (densely) built-up residential area. 住宅模型 a scale-model「house [home].
**じゅうたくきんゆうしえんきこう**【住宅金融支援機構】 the Japan Housing Finance Agency (略: JHF). ▶ 2007 年 住宅金融公庫から改称.
**じゅうたくひんしつかくほすいしんほう**【住宅品質確保促進法】〔法〕the Housing Quality Assurance Law.
**じゅうたくほしょうきこう**【住宅保証機構】〔財団法人〕the Organization for Housing Warranty (略: OHW).
**じゅうたくリフォーム・ふんそうしょりしえんセンター**【住宅-紛争処理支援-】 the Center for Housing Renovation and Dispute Settlement Support (略: CHORD).
**しゅうだん**[2]【集団】
▷□ 集団営巣地 a (nesting) colony;〔カラス・ペンギンなどの〕a rookery. 集団越冬 mass wintering. ◐ 〜越冬 (over-)winter「en masse [in large groups]. 集団化〜化する少年非行 the increasingly group-oriented nature of juvenile crime; the increasing tendency for young criminals to form gangs / 地場産業の〜化 congregation [concentration] of local industries in one area. 集団感染 a mass「infection [outbreak]《of tuberculosis》. 集団カンニング(事件) (a case of) mass cheating. 集団協定 a collective agreement. 集団結婚式 a「mass [group] wedding. 集団決定 (a) group decision. 集団自決 mass「group [communal] suicide. 集団心理療法〔医〕〔集団精神療法〕group psychotherapy. 集団送迎〔生徒の〕taking one's children to and from school in (large) groups; accompanying [taking] children to and from school in a group. ◐ 最近, ほとんどの幼稚園が〜送迎を実施している. Recently, most kindergartens have adopted the policy of having adults accompany children in both directions. 集団

提訴 filing [the filing of] a class action lawsuit. 集団(による)犯行 (a) 「collective [group] crime; a crime carried out by a group. 集団(の)凝集性《社会》group 「cohesiveness [cohesion]. 集団暴走(行為) speeding [biking, hot-rodding] in gangs. 集団(お)見合い a 「mass meeting with [collective party for] prospective marriage partners. 集団暴力 mob [mass] violence. 集団密航 mass smuggling 《(of Chinese into Japan)》; mass people smuggling. 集団密航助長(罪)《法》the furtherance of [(the crime of) encouraging] mass people smuggling. 集団予防接種 mass vaccination(s). ◆インフルエンザの〜予防接種を受ける be given [receive] mass influenza vaccination(s). 集団力学《心理》group dynamics. 集団レイプ〔輪姦〕a gang rape. ◆〜レイプする gang-rape 《a girl》.

じゅうだん【十段】〔囲碁・将棋の称号〕Jūdan; a holder of the tenth 「dan [rank] in 「go [shōgi]. ◆〜十段位 the Jūdan title. 十段戦 the Jūdan tournament.

じゅうだん²【縦断】◆□ 縦断曲線〔土木・鉄道〕a vertical curve.

しゅうだんごうかんざい【集団強姦罪】《法》《be charged with》 gang rape.

じゅうたんさん【重炭酸】◆□ 重炭酸土類泉 a calcium bicarbonate or magnesium bicarbonate spring.

じゅうたんぞう【自由鍛造】《冶金》free forging.

じゅうだんちょうさ【縦断調査】〔同じ対象者に対する継続的調査〕a longitudinal study [survey]. ◆□ 中高年者縦断調査 a longitudinal study of middle-aged and elderly adults. 21世紀出生児縦断調査〔厚生労働省〕the 《Third》 Longitudinal Survey of Babies Born in the 21st Century. 21世紀成年者縦断調査〔厚生労働省〕the Longitudinal Survey of Adults in the 21st Century.

しゅうだんてき【集団的】◆□ 集団的過熱取材〔メディア・スクラム〕news gathering by 「a crowd of reporters [″media scrum]. 集団的無意識《心理》「集合的無意識」the collective unconscious (of 「the human race [the individual]). 集団的労使交渉 collective labor(-management) relations; collective bargaining.

しゅうちしん【羞恥心】◆□ 性的羞恥心 (a sense of) sexual 「modesty [decency, propriety].

しゅうちゅう³【集中】〔春闘〕the day when most companies respond to labor union demands. 集中打〔野球〕a bunch [a cluster, a barrage, an avalanche] of hits; bunched hits. 集中討議 intensive discussion(s); intensive [concentrated] talks.

しゅうちゅうちりょう【集中治療】◆□ 新生児集中治療室[部] a neonatal intensive care unit (略: NICU).

シュー・ツリー a shoe tree. ◆〜シューキーパー.

シューティング・ガード〔バスケット〕a shooting guard.

「シューティング・フィッシュ」〔映画〕Shooting Fish.

じゅうてん²【重点】◆□ 重点区〔選挙区での〕a constituency viewed as a priority (by the LDP); a critical constituency (to which a party gives priority in an election). 重点(的)投資 (a) priority investment.

じゅうでん¹【充電】◆□ 急速[高速]充電〔電〕a 「fast [rapid, high-speed] charge; fast [rapid, high-speed] charging. ◆急速〜器 a 「fast [rapid, high-speed] charger. 緊急充電 a 「boost [boosting] charge; boost charging. ◆緊急〜器 a booster; a boost(ing) charger / 携帯電話(用)緊急〜器 a boost(ing) charger for a cellphone. ◆□ 充電切れ run-down [depleted, dead] 《batteries》. 充電スタンド〔携帯電話などの〕a 「charge [charging] cradle (for a cellular phone); 〔電気自動車の充電用〕a 「charging [charge] station.

じゅうでんち【充電池】a rechargeable battery; a storage battery. ◆□ ニッケル水素充電池 a nickel-metal hydride [an NiMH] rechargeable battery.

シュート¹ ◆□ シュート数《サッカー》the number of shots at goal. ◆〜数はうちのチームのほうが勝っていたのに試合に負けてしまった. Our team was ahead on number of shots at goal, but we ended up losing the game.

じゅうど²【重度】◆□ 重度後遺障害 severe residual 「damage [difficulties]; a serious residual disorder. 重度重複障害 severe (and) multiple 「handicaps [disabilities]. ◆〜重複障害者 a person with severe (and) multiple 「handicaps [disabilities].

じゅうどう【柔道】◆□ 柔道畳 a judo 「mat [tatami].

じゅうとうじんしん【獣頭人身】a human body with the head of an animal. ◆□ 獣頭人身像 an animal-headed human figure.

シュートオフ〔射撃〕〔同点の場合の勝者決定戦〕《(have)》 a shoot-off.

しゅうとく¹【拾得】◆□ 拾得物横領(罪)《法》《(be charged with)》 misappropriation of lost property [failing to report a find].

しゅうとく²【習得・修得】◆□ 習得観念〔哲〕an acquired idea.

じゆうとはんえいのこ【自由と繁栄の弧】〔日本が中東から北東アジアにかけて期待する未来像〕the "Arc of Freedom and Prosperity"; a new basis for Japanese diplomacy, proposed by Foreign Minister Asō Tarō in November 2006, designed to extend support to the new democracies on the periphery of Eurasia.

シュートボクシング〔立ち技格闘技の1つ〕shootboxing.

「17歳のカルテ」〔映画〕Girl, Interrupted.

じゅうにしちょう【十二指腸】◆□ 十二指腸がん《医》(a) duodenal cancer; (a) cancer of the duodenum; (a) duodenal carcinoma; (a) carcinoma of the duodenum. 十二指腸狭窄(症)《医》duodenal stenosis. 十二指腸閉鎖(症)《医》duodenal atresia. 十二指腸閉塞(症)《医》duodenal 「obstruction [ileus].

しゅうにゅう【収入】◆□ 手数料収入 (a) commission income.

しゅうにん【就任】◆□ 就任会見 a press conference (given) on taking office; 〔米大統領の〕a post-inaugural press conference. 就任宣誓 an oath of office. ◆大統領の〜宣誓をする take the presidential oath / 〜宣誓式 a swearing-in ceremony.

しゅうのう³【就農】◆□ 就農者 a new farmer.

じゆうのかべ【自由の壁】〔米国ワシントンD.C.にある第二次大戦記念碑〕(the National World War II Memorial) 〜の一部〕the Freedom Wall.

しゅうは²【宗派】◆□ 宗派抗争 (a) sectarian conflict; sectarian strife. 宗派対立 (a) sectarian confrontation.

しゅうはすう【周波数】◆□ 周波数オークション a frequency auction. 周波数分割複信《通信》〔=エフ・ディー・ディー〕. 周波数変動《電》(a) frequency 「variation [fluctuation].

しゅうはちトリソミー(しょうこうぐん)【18-(症候群)】《医》〔染色体起因障害の1つ〕trisomy 18 (syndrome).

しゅうはん【週販】〔1週間の販売量〕weekly sales; weekly turnover.

じゅうはん²【重版】◆□ 重版出来(しゅったい). 〔広告などで〕Now in second printing.

しゅうびしょう【臭鼻症】《医》ozena.

ジューフ〔アル・ジャウフ〕.

じゅうぶん²【十分・充分】◆□ 十分注意〔外務省が出す海外渡航情報の「危険情報」の第一段階〕a travel caution.

じゅうへいき【重兵器】a heavy weapon; 〈集合的に〉heavy weaponry.

しゅうへん【周辺】◆□ 周辺校 neighboring [nearby] schools. 周辺取材 investigating nearby sources. ◆〜取材を行う do an investigation into [collect materials on] people close to 《the victim》.

**しゅうほう**⁴【襲封】succession to a fief. **〜する** succeed to ((one's father's)) fief.

**じゆうほっかんほうそう**【自由北韓放送】〔脱北者が韓国で発足したインターネットラジオ放送局〕Freedom North Korea Broadcast (略: FNK); Free NK Radio.

**シューマカー** Schumacher, Joel (1939– ; 米国の映画監督).

**しゅうまつ**²【週末】 ▫▫ 週末婚〔夫婦が週末だけ一緒に生活をする結婚形態の1つ〕a weekend marriage; weekend wedlock. 週末ドライバー〔週末にしか運転しない人〕a weekend driver.

**じゅうみん**【住民】
▫▫ 住民アンケート((do)) a ⌈survey of residents [residential survey], ((carry out)) a questionnaire (survey) of residents ((to find out what they feel)). 住民異動届 a resident relocation or change-of-circumstances notification. 住民監視 ⌈住民による⌉ surveillance by local residents ((of illegal dumping)); a neighborhood ((crime)) watch; 〔住民に対する〕surveillance of local residents. 住民管理組合〔集合住宅の〕a (condominium) residents' ((management)) association. 住民基本台帳カード a Basic Resident Registration Card; a Jūki Card. 住民情報系システム〔自治体の〕a resident-information system; a system for recording information about residents. 住民説明会 ((hold)) an explanatory meeting for local residents, ((organize)) a meeting to inform local people ((about the projected expressway)). 住民発議 a ⌈citizens' [residents'] initiative. ▶ 〜発議制度 a ⌈citizens' [residents'] initiative system.

**じゅうみんひょう**【住民票】▫▫ 住民票コード〔個人の住民票に付せられた11桁の数字〕a resident ⌈identification [ID] number.

**シューメーカー・レビーだいきゅうすいせい**〔—第9彗星〕〔天〕Comet Shoemaker-Levy 9.

**しゅうやく**【集約】▫▫ 集約化 concentration; intensification. ▶ 中核病院への産科医師の〜化 a concentration of obstetricians at ⌈central [major] hospitals / 当社は全国に10あった製造工場をいわき工場と横浜工場に〜化した. Our company, which used to have 10 manufacturing plants nationwide, has concentrated its operations at the two plants of Iwaki and Yokohama.

**じゅうよう**³【重要】▫▫ 重要証人 a material witness. 重要防護施設〔テロなどの攻撃を受けた際, 陸上自衛隊が最優先で防護する施設〕a key defense facility.

**じゅうらい**【従来】▫▫ 従来路線〔交通機関の在来のルート〕an existing ⌈route [line]; 〔経営などのこれまでの方向性〕an established [a conventional] business ⌈policy [line]. ▶ この企画はわが社の〜路線から脱していない. This plan does not deviate from the course the company has always followed.

**しゅうらく**【集落】▫▫ 集落営農 cooperative community farming. 集落営農組織 a cooperative community farming organization; a community farming cooperative.

**しゅうり**【修理】▫▫ 修理記録 a record of repairs ((to a car)); a repair record. 修理歴 a history of repairs ((to a car)); a ((used car)) repair history.

**じゅうりゅうし**【重粒子】▫▫ 重粒子線治療 heavy charged particle therapy.

**じゅうりょう**²【重量】▫▫ 重量制〔運送費などの〕a system of pricing by weight; a weight-based system.

**じゅうりょう(かきん)せい**【従量(課金)制】〔料金の〕a meter-rate system; a measured rate system; a pay-for-use system; a variable fee system. ▶ 〜の料金 a variable fee ((depending on…)); 〔電写〕〔接続時間に応じた〕a connection-time fee; 〔通信量に応じた〕a ⌈traffic [usage] fee; 〔1時間単位での〕an hourly fee.

**じゅうりょうでんとう**【従量電灯】meter-rate [metered] lighting.

**じゅうりょく**【重力】▫▫ 重力探査衛星 a gravity probe. ▶ 〜探査衛星 B Gravity Probe B (略: GP-B). 重力波天文学 gravitational wave astronomy. 重力波天文台 a gravitational-wave observatory.

**じゅうれん**²【修練】▫▫ 修練院〖キリスト教〗a seminary. 修練者〖キリスト教〗a seminarian; a novice. 修練長〖キリスト教〗the ⌈*principal [⌈head] of a seminary.

**じゅうれん**【重連】〔鉄道〕〔機関車を2両連結して車両を牽引すること〕double-heading; 〔その列車〕a double-headed (steam) train. [⇨さんじゅうれん] ▫▫ 重連運転 double-headed operation.

**しゅうろう**³【就労】
▫▫ 就労意欲〔労働意欲〕a will to work; 〔(失業者・病人など現在仕事に就いていない人の)就職したいという意欲〕(a) willingness to find ⌈a job [employment]. 就労機会 = 就業機会 (⇨しゅうぎょう³). 就労期間 a period of employment; (the length of) the period during which sb is employed; ((depend on)) how long sb has been employed. 就労許可証 a work permit. 就労形態 a type of employment; a job type. 就労支援 employment ⌈support [assistance]; helping ((women)) to obtain employment. 就労資格証明書〔在留外国人の〕((apply for)) a ⌈work qualification certificate [certificate of authorized employment]. 就労者 a worker; 〈集合的に〉labor. 就労所得 (a) ⌈salary [salaried] income. 就労年齢 = 就業年齢 (⇨しゅうぎょう³).

**ジュエリー** ▫▫ ジュエリーニット〖服飾〗knitwear ⌈decorated [fringed] with beads or rhinestones.

**「THE JUON / 呪怨」**〔映画〕The Grudge.

**しゅか**³【朱夏】〔夏の異称〕(the) summer.

**しゅか**¹【儒家】▫▫ 儒家思想 Confucian ⌈thought [ideology].

**シュガー** ▫▫ シュガークラフト〔砂糖で加工して造花などを作る工芸〕sugarcraft.

**じゅかい**【珠海】〔中国広東省の都市〕Zhuhai.

**しゅがき**【朱書き】writing in red (ink). **〜する** write in red (ink).

**しゅかん**¹【主幹】▫▫ 主幹制御器〔鉄道〕〔列車の速度を制御する機器〕a master controller.

**しゅかんしょうけん(がいしゃ)**【主幹事証券(会社)】〖証券〗〔ある会社の証券の発行を扱う証券会社のうち中心となる会社〕a lead manager; a lead managing underwriter; a lead underwriter.

**しゅき**¹【手記】▫▫ 特別手記 a special note; a personal memorandum.

**しゅぎ**²【手技】(a) (manual) skill; skill with one's ⌈hands [fingers]; (a) (manual) technique.

**シュキー**【主—】〔電算〕〔データベースの〕a primary key.

**じゅきゅう**【受給】▫▫ 不正受給〔保険金・補助金などの〕unfair [unjustified] receipt ((of an insurance payment)). 受給条件 a condition for payment ((of an allowance)); a qualification ((for financial assistance)).

**じゅきゅう**²【需給】▫▫ 需給動向 supply and demand [demand and supply] trends ((for LCDs)). 需給の逼迫 a tight demand-supply situation. 需給の不均衡 a ⌈supply-demand [supply / demand] imbalance; an imbalance between supply and demand.

**じゅぎょう**【授業】▫▫ 授業助手 a teaching assistant (略: TA). 授業評価〔学生・生徒による授業内容の評価〕course [class] evaluation. ▶ 〜評価アンケート a ⌈course [class] evaluation questionnaire.

**じゅぎょうりょう**【授業料】▫▫ 授業料標準額 standard ((university)) fees.

**しゅきん**【種菌】=たねきん.

**じゅく**【塾】▫▫ 個別指導塾 a one-on-one tutoring school. 集団指導塾 a group-class tutoring school. 補習塾 a supplementary school.

しゅくい²【宿意】〔年来の志望〕a long-cherished desire;〔かねてからの恨み〕a long-standing grudge.
しゅくが【祝賀】⇨▯ 祝賀行事 celebratory「functions [events].
しゅくげん【縮減】⇨▯ 縮減率 a「reduction [shrinkage] (rate)《of 6.7%》.
しゅくしゅ【宿主】⇨▯ 自然宿主 a natural host. ⇨▯ 宿主細胞《生物》a host cell.
しゅくしょう²【縮小】⇨▯ 縮小効果〔がん治療などの〕(have) a 'reducing [shrinking] effect《on a tumor》. 縮小手術《医》(volume) reduction surgery.
じゅくせい²【熟成】⇨▯ 熟成(貯蔵)庫〔ワイン・チーズなどの〕an ag(e)ing [a maturing] cellar (cave, room); a 《wine, cheese》「cave [cellar].
じゅくせん(しんじ)【粥占(神事)】=かゆうらない.
じゅくたつ【熟達】⇨▯ 熟達者 a「practiced [skilled] hand; an experienced and skillful person; an expert; a veteran; a past master《at [with]…》.
じゅくねん【熟年】⇨▯ 熟年結婚 getting married late in life; marrying when one is 「middle aged [elderly]. 熟年再婚 getting married again late in life; marrying again when one is 「middle aged [elderly].
しゅくはく【宿泊】⇨▯ 宿泊拒否 refusal of accommodation; refusal to accommodate sb. ⇨▯〜拒否される be refused accommodation; be turned away《from a hotel》. 宿泊券, 宿泊クーポン〔ホテル・旅館などの〕a「hotel [lodging] voucher [coupon]; an accommodation ticket. ⇨▯ ご応募の方の中から抽選で20名様にペア一券を差し上げます. We will present two-person accommodation tickets to 20 applicants, to be selected by lottery. 宿泊特化型ホテル a no-frills hotel. 宿泊予約 a (lodging) 「booking [reservation].
じゅくみん【熟眠】⇨▯ 熟眠感 a [the] sensation of 「having slept well [being refreshed by a good sleep]; a [the] feeling that one has slept well. 熟眠感欠如《医》not feeling refreshed by sleep; lack of refreshment from sleep. 熟眠障害〔困難〕《医》sleep maintenance insomnia.
じゅくれん【熟練】⇨▯ 熟練職人 an experienced [a skilled, an expert] craftsman.
しゅげい【手芸】⇨▯ 手芸作家 a craftsperson; a handicraft artist.
じゅけいしゃいそうじょうやく【受刑者移送条約】the (Council of Europe) Convention on the Transfer of Sentenced Persons; the Strasbourg Convention. ▶正式名称は「刑を言い渡された者の移送に関する条約」.
じゅけいしゃしょぐうほう【受刑者処遇法】《法》⇨けいじしせつじゅけいしゃしょぐうほう.
しゅけん【主権】⇨▯ 主権譲渡 transfer of sovereignty. 主権侵害[侵犯]《法》(a) violation of sovereignty. 主権的権利〔自国の天然資源などに対する〕(have) a sovereign right. 主権的民主主義〔ロシアのプーチン政権が唱える〕sovereign democracy. 主権独立国家 an independent sovereign [a sovereign independent] state.
じゅけん³【授権】⇨▯ 授権株式(数) (the number of) authorized「shares [stocks]. 授権資本枠 the number of authorized capital stock.
じゅけんほう【授権法】《法》=ぜんけんにんほう.
しゅこうデルタけいざいけん【珠江一経済圏】〔中国の〕the 「Pearl River Delta [PRD] economic zone.
しゅこん²【手根】⇨▯ 手根管 a carpal [canal [tunnel]. 手根管症候群《医》carpal tunnel syndrome (略: CTS).
しゅざい³【取材】⇨▯ 取材相手 an interviewee; the person one is interviewing; the subject of an interview. 取材合戦 competition among 「the media [news reporters]. ⇨▯ 激しい〜合戦が展開された. Fierce competition developed among the media (to get the scoop). 取材規制 restrictions on media coverage. 取材競争 competition in news 「gathering [coverage]; competitive (news) coverage. 取材経費 information-gathering [news-gathering, reporting] expenses. 取材攻勢 a media frenzy; intensive media coverage; a media blitz. 取材陣 a group of reporters; (members [representatives] of) the press. 取材申請 =取材申し込み. 取材制限 restrictions on news gathering. 取材テーマ a topic of 「investigation [research]: a topic for 「investigation [research]; the topic one is looking into. 取材ノート a reporter's notebook. 取材班 a reporting team; a team of reporters. 取材費 =取材経費. 取材ヘリ(コプター) a news helicopter. 取材メモ interview notes. 取材網 a news-gathering [-collection] network; a reporting network. 取材申し込み an interview request.
じゅし³【樹脂】⇨▯ プラスチック樹脂 plastic resin.
じゅしゅ【樹種】〔樹木の種類〕a tree species; a「species [variety] of tree.
しゅしゅう²【酒臭】a smell of 「alcohol [liquor]; the reek of 「alcohol [liquor]《on his breath》.
しゅじゅつ【手術】⇨▯ 開頭手術 craniotomy. 難手術 major surgery; a major (surgical) operation. 手術跡, 手術痕 an operation scar; a scar from an operation. 手術合併症〔術後合併症〕postoperative complications. 手術給付金〔保険〕a surgery benefit. 手術支援ロボット ⇨ロボット. 手術適応 operability. ⇨▯ 本症例は〜適応がある[ない]. This condition is 「operable [inoperable]. 手術針 a surgical (suture) needle.
しゅじゅつしき【手術式】《医》=しゅじゅつ.
しゅしょう⁴【首相】⇨▯ 首相公選法 the argument for direct election of the prime minister; the view that the prime minister should be elected directly.
じゅしょう²【受賞】⇨▯ 共同受賞〔2人以上の人あるいは2つ以上の組織などが共同で1つの賞を受けること〕receiving [getting, winning] a shared 「prize [award]; sharing a 「prize [award]. ⇨▯ 小平邦彦博士は1954年, フィールズ賞をジャン・ピエール・セール教授と共に〜した. In 1954, Kodaira Kunihiko shared (the award of) the Fields Medal with Jean-Pierre Sere. ダブル受賞 ⇨▯ その作品は江戸川乱歩賞と直木賞をダブル〜した. The work was awarded both the Edogawa Rampo and the Naoki Prizes. / ノーベル賞物理学賞の小柴昌俊氏と化学賞の田中耕一氏のダブル〜が日本を沸かせた. Japan was excited by the award of double Nobel Prizes, to Koshiba Masatoshi for Physics and to Tanaka Kōichi for Chemistry.
じゅじょう【樹状】⇨▯ 樹状細胞ワクチン《医》(a) dendritic cell vaccine.
じゅじょう³【儒城】=ユソン¹.
しゅしん²【主審】⇨▯ プロ主審《サッカー》=スペシャル・レフェリー《⇨スペシャル》.
しゅしん¹【受信】⇨▯ 受信拒否〔携帯電話などの〕message rejection. 受信契約〔放送会社との〕a reception contract. 受信障害〔テレビ・ラジオなどの〕interference with《TV》reception;《television》reception interference. 受信速度〔電算〕(a) data 「receiving [reception] speed.
じゅしん²【受診】⇨▯ 受診率〔集団検診などの〕an examination rate. ⇨▯ 集団検診の〜率を高める increase the participation rate in group medical examinations. 受診歴《a patient's》medical (consultation) history. ⇨▯ 彼にはこの病院での〜歴はない. He has never been treated at this hospital.
しゅすい【取水】⇨▯ 取水施設 a water intake facility.
しゅせきさん【酒石酸】⇨▯ 酒石酸ゾルビデム《薬》《睡眠薬》zolpidem tartrate. 酒石酸ビノレルビン《薬》《抗がん剤》vinorelbine tartrate.
しゅせんえいせいはっしゃセンター【酒泉衛星発射~】〔中国の〕the Jiuquan Satellite Launch Center.
シュタージ〔旧東ドイツの秘密警察〕the Stasi.

しゅたい【主体】 ▷ 主体思想〔チュチェ〕juche; self-reliance.
シュタイナー ▷ シュタイナー教育 Steiner education.
シュタウフェンベルク Stauffenberg, Claus von (1907–44; 第二次大戦中のドイツ陸軍大佐; ヒトラー暗殺計画実行者の1人).
じゅたく【受託】 ▷ 受託開発 entrusted development 《of computer systems》. 受託研究〔企業からの委託を受けて大学教員が行う研究〕sponsored [commissioned, contracted] research. ▷ 〜研究員〔企業から大学に派遣される大学院レベルの研究を行う人〕a 「sponsored [contracted] researcher. 受託責任 fiduciary responsibility. 受託生産会社 a commissioned manufacturer; 〔半導体製造などの〕a foundry; a fabrication plant; a fab.
じゅちゅう【受注】 ▷ 受注価格 an agreed price; an order price; a contract price; a [the] price 「agreed upon [contracted for]. 受注側 the recipient of the order; the party receiving the order; the person to whom the order is made. 受注業者[企業] the recipient of the order; the company receiving the order; the company to whom the order is made. 受注競争 competition to get 「orders [business]. 受注契約 an order contract; a [the] contract for an order. 受注先 an order-source; the source of an order. 受注者 a supplier; the recipient of an order; a person to whom an order is made. 受注情報 information on [the status of] orders received; 〔公共工事の〕information on the current status of public works orders received. 受注増 an increase in orders. ▷ この製品は、大幅な〜増が見込まれている. We expect a major increase in orders for this product. | This product is likely to see a major increase in orders. 受注調整 (a) bid-winner adjustment; adjusting [sharing out] the orders received. 受注配分 allocation (distribution) of orders; allocation of ordering.
しゅついん【出院】〔少年院を出ること〕release from a juvenile reformatory. 〜する be 「released from [let out of, discharged from] a juvenile reformatory. ▷ 出院者 a released (reformatory) inmate. 出院準備教育 an educational program required for probation.
しゅつえん²【出捐】〔寄付〕(a) donation; (a) disbursement; 〔法〕(economic, monetary) expenditure. 〜する〔寄付する〕donate 《money》; make a donation; 〔法〕expend 《money》.
しゅっか¹【出火】 ▷ 出火原因 (determine) the cause of a fire.
しゅっか²【出荷】 ▷ 出荷価格 an ex-《warehouse》 price; a price to wholesalers; 〔医薬品の〕a wholesale acquisition price (略: WAC). ▷ 工場〜価格 an ex-factory price. 出荷作業 the work of 「shipping [consigning, despatching] 《produce, goods》.
しゅつが【出芽】 ▷ 出芽酵母 budding yeast; Saccharomyces cerevisiae.
しゅつがん【出願】 ▷ 出願取り下げ〔特許などの〕withdrawal of an application 《for a patent》.
しゅっきん²【出勤】 ▷ 出勤停止 (a) suspension from 「work [one's duties]. ▷ 5 日間の〜停止を命じられる be suspended from work for five days; be ordered to stay at home for five days (as a punishment).
しゅっけつ²【出血】 ▷ 出血死 bleeding to death. ▷ 〜死 bleed to death. 出血部位 a [the] site of 「bleeding [a hemorrhage]; a bleeding 「site [source]. ▷ 〜部位を特定する identify the site of bleeding.
しゅつご²【術後】 ▷ 術後患者 a postoperative patient. 術後管理 postoperative 「management [care]. 術後補助化学療法 〔がんの〕postoperative adjuvant chemotherapy. 術後補助療法 postoperative adjuvant therapy.
しゅっこう¹【出向】 ▷ 出向先 one's 「place [post] of assignment. 出向元 one's original place of work.
しゅっこう⁵【出稿】 ▷ 広告出稿 publicity submission; submission of (advertising) copy to the media. ▷ 広告〜量 advertising volume; volume of advertising 《placed in a paper》.
しゅっこく【出国】 ▷ 出国命令制度《法》〔不法滞在者に対する〕the [a] (voluntary) deportation order system; a [the] system whereby an illegal resident may be deported without being charged with a criminal offense.
しゅっさん【出産】 ▷ 高リスク出産 (a) high-risk delivery. ▷ 出産育児一時金 a lump-sum maternity allowance. 出産帰省 returning to one's parents' home to have a baby. 出産時 the time of (giving) birth. 出産時外傷《医》a birth trauma. 出産時障害《医》a birth defect. 出産準備品 childbirth [birth] supplies. 出産適齢期 a suitable age for childbirth; the best age to have babies. 出産届〔出生届〕(a) registration of a birth; registering a birth. 出産難民 ＝お産難民 (⇨おさん).
しゅっし²【出資】 ▷ 出資比率〔経営〕the percentage of 《a company's》 「stake [share] 《in a business》. ▷ あの企業へのわが社の〜比率を高める[下げる]必要がある. We need to 「increase [reduce] our share in that company.
しゅっしき【術式】《医》〔手術の方式〕a surgical [an operative] technique [method].
しゅっしゃ¹【出社】 ▷ 出社停止 (a) suspension from one's (company) duties.
しゅっしょ【出所】 ▷ 満期出所 (a) full-term release 《from prison》; release on completion of a sentence. ▷ 出所者情報《法》post-release information; information on the location of a criminal after release from prison.
しゅっしょう【出生】 ▷ 出生コーホート〔社会〕a birth cohort. 出生時 the time of 「birth [being born]. 出生時外傷 a birth trauma. 出生時障害《医》a birth defect. 出生性比 the sex ratio of births.
しゅつじょう【出場】 ▷ 出場権《earn》 the right to appear 《in the Olympics》. 出場枠〔試合などへの〕the number of entries 《for an Olympic event》. 出場枠数 the number of 「players [teams] scheduled to appear.
しゅっしん【出身】 ▷ 出身高校[大学] the 「high school [college, university] one 「graduated from [went to, was at].
しゅっしんこく【出身国】〔移民などの〕a country of origin. ▷ フランスの〜別移民数 the number of immigrants to France by country of origin.
しゅっすい¹【出水】 ▷ 出水率〔ある期間の河川の水量をこれまでの同じ期間の平均水量と比較した割合〕a water flow rate.
シュッセル Schüssel, Wolfgang (1945– ; オーストリアの政治家; 首相 [2000–06]).
じゅつぜん【術前】 ▷ 術前化学療法《医》〔がん治療における〕neoadjuvant chemotherapy (略: NACT). 術前診断 preoperative diagnosis.
しゅっそう【出走】 ▷ 出走権〔競馬のレース出場権〕a right of entry 《for a horse race》; a 《horse》 entry right. ▷ 優先〜権 a priority 「right of entry [entry right] 《for a horse race》.
しゅつだい【出題】 ▷ 出題ミス〔試験の〕a mistake in 「preparing [setting] an exam question; 〔間違った問題〕an incorrect 「question [problem]; 〔範囲外からの出題〕an off-topic 「question [problem].
じゅっちゅう【術中】 ▷ 術中死《医》(a) death during 「surgery [an operation]; (an) intraoperative death. 術中迅速診断《医》(an) intraoperative diagnosis; (a)

しゅっちょう

rapid intraoperative diagnosis. 術中(迅速)病理診断〖医〗=術中迅速診断. 術中放射線療法[治療] intraoperative radiotherapy (略: IORT).
しゅっちょう¹【出張】 ▢▶出張校正〖出版〗〔編集部員などが製版所に出かけて行って校正作業を行うこと〕on-site proofreading; proofreading at the printing plant. 出張授業 =出前授業(⇨でまえ). 出張復命書 a report of an official trip.
しゅってん²【出店】 ▢▶過剰出店 a superfluity of branches; ((have)) too many branches. ▢▶出店競争 competition in setting up new branches. 出店コンサルタント a consultant who assists at the opening of a new franchise branch. 出店料〔電子商店街・フリーマーケットなどへの〕a set-up fee; a space rental (fee, charge); a site charge.
しゅっとう【出頭】 ▢▶身代わり出頭 turning oneself in (to the police) in place of (one's husband). ▢▶出頭在延命令[法] a subpoena requiring attendance throughout a trial. 出頭要請 a request to appear ((in court)). 出頭率〔出頭命令などに応じての〕an appearance rate; the percentage of people obeying a summons.
しゅつどう【出動】 ▢▶出動待機 ((put the Self-Defense Forces on)) alert.
しゅつにゅうこく【出入国】 ▢▶出入国管理記録 emigration and immigration [embarkation and disembarkation] records.
しゅつにゅうこくかんりなんみんにんていほう【出入国管理難民認定法】[法] the Immigration Control and Refugee Recognition Law.
しゅっぱつ【出発】 ▢▶出発ゲート〖空港〗 a departure gate. 出発(ゲート)ラウンジ a departure gate lounge.
しゅっぱん²【出版】 ▢▶共同出版 publishing jointly funded by the author and publisher; subsidy [sponsored] publishing. ▢▶出版禁止命令 a publication ban; an injunction [a restraining order] banning publication (of a magazine).
しゅっぱんぶんかさんぎょうしんこうざいだん【出版文化産業振興財団】the Japan Publishing Industry Foundation for Culture (略: JPIC).
じゅっぺい【恤兵】war relief; comfort for the troops ((at the front)). 恤兵金 a war relief fund; money for the troops.
しゅつぼつ【出没】 ▢▶出没情報〔不審者・野生動物などの〕(report) a sighting.
しゅつりょく【出力】 ▢▶出力密度 (a) power [(an) output] density.
「シュテルン」〔ドイツの代表的ニュース週刊誌〕Stern.
しゅと²【首都】 ▢▶首都(圏)直下(型)地震 an earthquake occurring below the Tokyo metropolitan region.
しゅどう¹【手動】 ▢▶手動操作 manual「handling [operation]. ▢〜操作の manually operated [hand-operated]《convertible top》; operated by hand. 手動装置 a「manual [manually operated, hand-operated] device; manually operated [hand-operated] equipment.
しゅどう²【主導】 ▢▶主導性 leadership; initiative. 主導力 (a) leadership ability.
じゅどう³【樹洞】a tree hollow. ▢▶樹洞性の hollow-dwelling《animals》; hollow-nesting《birds》.
しゅとく²【取得】 ▢▶取得価格〔資産・株式などの〕an acquisition price. ▢平均〜価格 an average acquisition price / みなし〜価格 an acquisition price for tax purposes. 取得率〔有給休暇などの〕a《paid vacation》utilization rate.
しゅとけん【首都圏】 ▢▶首都圏防衛 metropolitan defense; defense of the《Tokyo》Metropolitan area.
しゅとけんディーゼルしゃきせいじょうれい【首都圏車規制条例】the Regulations for Diesel-Powered Vehicles in the Environmental Security Ordinance.
しゅとこう【首都高】〖首都高速道路〗the Tokyo Metropolitan Expressway.
しゅとこうそくどうろかぶしきがいしゃ【首都高速道路株式会社】the Metropolitan Expressway Company Limited.
シュトラウス Strauss, Leo (1899–1973; ドイツ生まれの米国の哲学者).
シュトルーデル〔果物・チーズなどを薄い生地に巻いて焼いたデザート用菓子〕(a) strudel.
シュトロイゼル〖菓子〗〔クッキー・ケーキなどにかけるバター・小麦粉などで作ったそぼろ〕streusel.
ジュニア ▢▶ジュニア議員 a second-generation Diet member. ジュニア・ローン〖金融〗〔後順位抵当権による貸付〕a junior loan.
ジュニア・アチーブメント〔世界最大の非営利経済教育団体; 1919 年に発足〕Junior Achievement.
じゅにゅう【授乳】 ▢▶授乳障害〖医〗lactation disorder(s); (a) disturbance「of [in] lactation. 授乳服 breastfeeding「clothes [wear, apparel].
じゅにん²【受忍】 ▢▶受忍義務 an obligation to「accept [put up with]《noise from one's neighbors》.
ジュネ Jeunet, Jean-Pierre (1953– ; フランス生まれの映画監督・脚本家).
シュノーケリング〔シュノーケルを装着しての潜水〕snorkeling.
しゅばしこう【朱嘴鸛】〖鳥〗〔欧州産コウノトリ科の鳥〕a white stork; Ciconia ciconia.
じゅはっちゅう【受発注】ordering (and supplying).
シュビ²【守備】 ▢▶守備練習〖野球〗fielding practice.
じゅひ【樹皮】 ▢▶樹皮堆肥 =バークたい肥.
しゅひぎむ【守秘義務】 ▢▶守秘義務規定 confidentiality「provisions [rules, regulations]. 守秘義務契約〔非開示契約〕a nondisclosure agreement (略: NDA).
しゅひけいやく【守秘契約】=守秘義務契約(⇨しゅひぎむ).
シュピドラ Špidla, Vladimír (1951– ; チェコの政治家; 首相 [2002–04]).
しゅびょう²【種苗】 ▢▶種苗放流 releasing eggs and fry ((into the sea)); distributing《oyster》spat ((on the seabed)).
しゅびょうかんりセンター【種苗管理―】〔農業水産省管の〕the National Center for Seeds and Seedlings (略: NCSS).
しゅびょうほう【種苗法】[法]〔種苗の開発者の権利を守る法律〕the Plant Variety Protection Law; the Plant Breeders Rights Law.
シュふ²【主婦】 ▢▶有職主婦 a working housewife.
シュプレーがわ【―川】〔ドイツ,ベルリンを流れる川〕the Spree River; the Spree.
じゅふん【受粉】 ▢▶受粉樹〖植〗〔他の樹に受粉するために使われる樹〕a pollinating tree; a pollinator tree.
しゅぼう【首謀】 ▢〜する mastermind. ▢テロ事件を〜する mastermind a terrorist attack.
ジュマイエル Gemayel, Pierre Amine (1972–2006; レバノンの政治家).
シュマイザー〔ドイツ製の短機関銃〕Schmeisser.
シュマッカー =シューマーカー.
シュマッチャー =シューマーカー.
「ジュマンジ」〖映画〗Jumanji.
しゅみ【趣味】 ▢▶趣味嗜好 preferences [interests] and tastes. 趣味人 a person with many「interests [hobbies]; 〔軽蔑的に〕a dilettante. 趣味性 a particular interest; a fondness 《for crime fiction》. ▢服飾やオーディオなどといった〜性の高い商品 products geared toward wants (rather than needs), such as clothes and audio equipment / コンバチブルというのは非常に〜性の高い[強い]自動車である. A convertible is an automobile

the appeal of which is ˈheavily [strongly] determined by personal interest.
**じゅみょう**【寿命】 ▯ 寿命計算〔器物・構造物などの〕calculating [a calculation of] the lifespan《of a building》.
**しゅもく**[1]【種目】 ▯ 種目別《a record for》a single event. 種目別優勝 (a)ˈvictory [win] in a single event.
**じゅもく**【樹木】 ▯ 樹木葬 a woodland burial. ▷〜葬墓地 a woodland burial ground.
**しゅよう**[2]【主要】 ▯ 主要株主〔major [principal] stockholder [shareholder]. 主要紙 aˈmajor [leading] newspaper.
**しゅよう**[4]【腫瘍】 ▯ 腫瘍内科〔病院の〕a department of oncology. ▷〜内科医 a medical oncologist.
**じゅよう**[3]【需要】
▯ 宴会需要 demand for receptions. 最大需要 maximum [highest] demand. ▷最大〜電力 maximum [highest] electricity demand; maximum [highest] demand for electricity. 個人需要 (individual) consumer demand. 法人需要 corporate demand. ▯ 需要家[者, 先] aˈuser [consumer]《of electrical power》. 需要期 a demand season; a season of (high) demand《for air-conditioners》. 需要実績 (a record of) past demand. 需要喚起 demandˈstimulation [creation];《create》a boost in demand. 需要積み上げ方式〔株式〕〔ブックビルディング方式〕book building.
**しゅようぎんこうかしだしどうこうアンケートちょうさ**【主要銀行貸出動向―調査】〔日本銀行が実施・発表する〕a Senior Loan Officer Opinion Survey on Bank Lending Practices at Large Japanese Banks.
**じゅようたい**【受容体】 ▯ トリ型ヒト型受容体〔生理〕〔鳥インフルエンザウイルスに対する動物細胞の表面の〕aˈbird [human] receptor. ▯ 受容体作動薬〔刺激薬, 作用薬〕〔薬〕a receptor agonist. ▷ドーパミン〜刺激薬 a dopamine receptor agonist.
**しゅようはいしゅつこくかいぎ**【主要排出国会議】⇨おんしつこうかガスしゅようはいしゅつこくかいぎ.
**ジュラ**〔スイス北西部の州〕Jura.
**シュラウド**〔原子炉〕〔炉心隔離〕a reactor core shroud. ▯ シュラウド・サポート・リング〔原子炉〕a shroud support ring.
**ジュラシック・ツリー**【植】⇨ウォレマイ・パイン.
**ジュラム**〔インドネシア・アチェ州, ナガンラヤ県の県都〕Jeuram.
**「シュリ」**【映画】Shuri.
**ジュリー**〔競技〕〔審査員団〕a jury. [⇨プレジデント・ジュリー（プレジデント）]
**シュリーヴ** Shreve, Anita (1946– ; 米国の女性小説家).
**しゅりょう**[1]【狩猟】 ▯ 狩猟採集時代〔文化人類〕a hunter-gatherer period.
**しゅりょく**【主力】 ▯ 主力機種〔車種〕aˈmain [staple, leading, key] model. 主力工場 a [the]ˈmain [key] factory《of a company》.
**シュリンクパック**〔シュリンク包装〕shrink-wrap[-wrapping].
**シュリンクラップけいやく**【―契約】〔シュリンク包装を破ることで成立する契約〕a shrink-wrap agreement; (使用許諾) a shrink-wrap license.
**しゅるいそうごうけんきゅうじょ**【酒類総合研究所】〔独立行政法人〕the National Research Institute of Brewing(略: NRIB).
**ジュルチャーニ** Gyurcsány, Ferenc (1961– ; ハンガリーの政治家; 首相〔2004– 〕).
**じゅれいき**【受令機】a (radio) receiver.
**「シュレック」**〔アニメ映画〕Shrek.
**シュレッダー** ▯ シュレッダー鋏 shredding scissors.
**しゅろがやつり**【棕櫚蚊帳吊り】〔植〕〔カヤツリグサ科の水辺植物〕an umbrella plant; an umbrella palm; *Cyperus alternifolius*.

**しゅわ**【手話】 ▯ 手話教育 education through (the medium of)ˈsign language [signing]. 手話ソング a signed song. 手話通訳士 a licensed sign-language interpreter.
**シュワスマン・ワハマンだいさんすいせい**【―第3彗星】〔天〕＝シュヴァスマン・ヴァハマンすいせい.
**「シュワルツェネッガー / プレデター」**【映画】Predator.
**じゅんあい**【純愛】 ▯ 純愛小説 a novel of pure love.
**「純愛中毒」**【映画】Addicted.
**じゅんうち**【順打ち】〔四国巡礼で霊場を一番札所から八十八番札所まで順番にまわること〕《completing》a pilgrimage around the 88 designated temples in Shikoku, in numerical order from no. 1 to no. 88. [⇨ぎゃくうち]
**じゅんか**[2]【順化・馴化】 ▯ 高所順化〔高所順応〕adaptation to high altitude(s); altitudeˈaccommodation [adaptation]. 野生順化 adaptation [rehabilitation]《of a species》to the wild.
**じゅんかい**【巡回】 ▯ 巡回キャラバン aˈtraveling [touring] exhibition. 巡回相談 (a) peripatetic consultation;《medical》visiting.
**じゅんかつゆ**【潤滑油】 ▯ 潤滑油圧力計 an oil pressure indicator.
**しゅんかん**[3]【瞬間】 ▯ 瞬間移動〔心霊〕〔人体・物体が消え, 次の瞬間に離れた場所に出現する超常現象〕teleportation.
**じゅんかん**[4]【循環】 ▯ キチン循環 ⇨キチンじゅんかん. ▯ 循環呼吸(法)〔音楽〕circular breathing. 循環処理〔温泉〕safe recirculation《of hot-spring water》; a system which disinfects《hot-spring water》and renders it safe before recirculating it. 循環ポンプ a circulation pump. 循環利用〔廃棄物などの〕recycling; recirculation. 循環濾過 filtering circulation; circulation filtering.
**じゅんかんがた**【循環型】 ▯ 循環型社会白書〔環境省の〕the White Paper on the Recycling-Based Society.
**じゅんかんがたしゃかいけいせいすいしんきほんほう**【循環型社会形成推進基本法】〔法〕the Basic Law for Establishing a Recycling-based Society.
**じゅんきっさ**【純喫茶】aˈregular [plain] tearoom [coffeehouse]; a tearoom [coffeehouse] that does not serve alcohol.
**じゅんきょ**【準拠】 ▯ 国公準拠〔地方公務員の給与は国家公務員の給与を基準にして決めるとする原則〕the principle that local government officials' pay should be proportionate to that of national public service personnel. 民間準拠〔公務員の給与は民間企業の従業員の給与を基準にして決めるとする原則〕the principle of basing public officials' pay on salaries paid in industry.
**しゅんぎょうガスでん**【春暁―田】〔東シナ海にあるガス田〕the Chunxiao gas field.
**じゅんきょうしゃひろば**【殉教者広場】〔ベイルート〕(the) Martyrs' Square.
**じゅんけん**[2]【巡検】 ▯ 巡検ラッパ〔旧海軍の消灯ラッパ〕a bugle call signalling the end of the day.
**じゅんげん**【純減】 ▯ 公務員純減 (a) net reductionˈof public servants [in public service personnel]. ▯ 純減目標〔公務員の定員の〕a [the] target for net reduction of public servants.
**しゅんこう**[2]【竣工】 ▯ 竣工検査 a (construction) completion inspection.
**じゅんごうかんざい**【準強姦罪】〔法〕〔準婦女暴行罪〕(a) sexual assault against a person who cannot offer resistance (due to sleep, inebriation, etc.).
**「春香伝」**【映画】Chunhyang.
**春秋**〔儒教の経書; 五経《の1つ》〕The Spring and Autumn Annals; Chunqiu; Ch'un-ch'iu. ▷〜の筆法をもってすれば as the ancient Spring and Autumn Annals would say.
**じゅんじょ**【順序】 ▯ 順序尺度〔統計〕an ordinal

scale.
じゅんしょう³【順唱】〔一連の数字などを聞いたあとその まま暗誦すること〕accurate repetition; repetition 《of a string of numbers》 in the correct order.
～する repeat [recite] 《a string of numbers》「accurately [in the correct order].
じゅんすい²【純粋】 ▭▭ 純粋殺人 murder for 「its own [murder's] sake; pure murder.
じゅんすいけい【準水系】semiaqueous. ▭▭ 準水系溶剤 a semiaqueous solvent.
しゅんせつ²【浚渫】 ▭▭ 浚渫ポンプ a 「dredge [dredging] pump.
しゅんせつ³【春節】〔中国の旧正月〕the Chinese New Year.
じゅんてんちょうえいせい【準天頂衛星】〔宇宙〕a quasi-zenith satellite. ▭▭ 準天頂衛星システム a quasi-zenith satellite system.
じゅんび²【準備】 ▭▭ 準備中.〔開店前であることを示す飲食店などの掲示〕Open Soon.
じゅんびきん【準備金】 ▭▭ 異常危険準備金【保険】 a contingency reserve. 支払い準備金【保険・銀行】(payment) reserves.
じゅんふじょぼうこうざい【準婦女暴行罪】【法】=じゅんごうかん.
じゅんぽう²【遵法・順法】 ▭▭ 遵法[順法]意識 a sense of respect for [consciousness of] the law. ◐～意識が高い[低い]. They have 「great [little] respect for the law.
じゅんミリは【準ミリ波】〔通信〕a submillimeter wave.
しゅんりん【春霖】〔春の長雨〕a long spell of spring rain.
ジョアノー Joanou, Phil (1961- ；米国の映画監督).
ジョアン・チェン Joan Chen (1961- ；中国生まれの映画女優・監督；中国語名 陳冲).
ジョイセフ【JOICFP】〔家族計画国際協力財団〕JOICFP. ► the Japanese Organization for International Cooperation in Family Planning の略から.
しよう⁴【仕様】 ▭▭ 豪雪地仕様〔住宅など〕(meet) (building) specifications for heavy snowfall. 新仕様 new specifications.
しよう⁸【使用】 ▭▭ 使用協定 a usage agreement. ◐国と市の間で結ばれている基地～協定を見直す必要がある. It is necessary to reconsider the agreement reached between the government and the city on the use of the base. 使用実績 instances of actual 「use [usage]. 使用説明書 an instruction manual; 《read》the instructions 《for…》.
-しょう【-床】 ▭▭ 380～の病院 a 380-bed hospital; a hospital with 380 beds.
ジョヴァンニ Giovanni, José (1923-2004；フランスの映画監督・作家).
じょうい²【上位】 ▭▭ 上位陣 the top-ranked 《players》; the leaders; the frontrunners. 上位進出 getting a placing (in the top three); doing very well (in the semi-finals); emerging near the top. ◐今回彼女は豊富なレース経験を生かした走りで～進出を狙っている. On this occasion she plans to put all her experience in races to good use in her running and to 「get a really good placing [end up near the front].
じょういうち【上意討ち】 assassination [execution] (on the command of a feudal lord).
じょういんとう【上咽頭】【解】the epiglottis. ▷ epiglottal, epiglottic adj. ▭▭ 上咽頭がん【医】epiglottic [epiglottal] carcinoma [cancer]; cancer of the epiglottis.
じょううお【上魚】a prize fish [shellfish, food fish].
じょうえい【上映】 ▭▭ 上映禁止 prohibition of the showing of a 「movie ["film"]; a movie ban. ◐マニラ市議会は『ダ・ヴィンチ・コード』の～禁止を決議した. The Manila City Council voted to ban the showing of "The Da Vinci Code."

しょうえき¹【漿液】 ▭▭ 漿液性腺がん【医】serous adenocarcinoma (略：SAC).
しょうえき³【省益】the interests of a 「ministry [department]; ministerial [departmental] interests. ◐～を国益に優先させる put the interests of a ministry before those of the nation.
しょうエネほう【省-法】【法】the Energy Saving Law. ► 正式名は「エネルギーの使用の合理化に関する法律」(the Law Concerning the Rational Use of Energy).
しょうエネ【省エネ(ルギー)】【省-】 ▭▭ 省エネ家電 an energy-saving home appliance. 省エネ(ルギー)基準 an energy conservation standard. ◐～基準達成率 an energy conservation standard achievement rate. 省エネ効果 (an) energy-saving effect. 省エネ(ルギー)支援〔企業などに対する〕support [a subsidy] for energy conservation. 省エネ性 energy-saving effectiveness; efficiency in saving energy. 省エネ表示 energy-efficiency labelling; an energy-efficiency label. 省エネマーク[ラベル]〔環境ラベルの一種〕an energy conservation mark. 省エネラベリング制度 an energy conservation labeling system. 省エネルック an energy-saving look.
しょうエネルギーセンター【省-】〔財団法人〕the Energy Conservation Center, Japan (略：ECCJ).
しょうえん⁷【松煙】〔松材の煤から作る黒色顔料〕black pigment made from pine soot;〔たいまつの煙〕smoke of a pine torch;〔松材の煤から作る墨・松煙墨〕a stick of ink made from pine soot. ▭▭ 松煙墨 (a stick of) pine-soot ink.
じょうえん¹【上演】 ▭▭ 上演禁止 prohibition of the performance of a play. ◐オスカー・ワイルドの『サロメ』はイギリスでは～禁止になった. Performance of Oscar Wilde's "Salome" was 「prohibited [forbidden, banned] in England. | Wilde's "Salome" was banned from the stage in England.
ジョヴォヴィッチ Jovovich, Milla (1975- ；ウクライナ生まれの映画俳優；本名 Milla Natasha Jovovich).
しょうおん²【昇温】(a) temperature increase; (a) rise in temperature;〔加熱による〕heating.
しょうおん²【常温】 ▭▭ 常温倉庫 a non-refrigerated [an unrefrigerated] warehouse. 常温輸送 non-refrigerated [unrefrigerated] transport.
しょう⁵【消化】 ▭▭ 消化仕入れ【商】backdating of payment [retrospective payment] to suppliers for the proportion of goods actually sold《by a department store》. 消化態 ▭▭ 態栄養剤 a predigested nutrition; a predigested (nutritional) supplement / 半-態栄養剤〔自然食品が人工的に処理されていて腸で多少消化されてから吸収される経腸栄養剤〕a partially predigested (nutritional) supplement.
しょうか⁶【消火】 ▭▭ 初期消火 ⇨しょき¹.
しょうか⁷【生姜】 ▭▭ ginger juice.
しょうか⁸【錠菓】〔粒状の菓子〕〈集合的に〉tablet candy;〈その1個〉a candy tablet.
しょうかい²【哨戒】 ▭▭ 哨戒所 a guard post (略：GP). 哨戒ヘリ(コプター) a patrol helicopter.
しょうかい²【紹介】 ▭▭ 紹介予定派遣〔就職することを前提として一定期間「派遣」という雇用形態でその企業で働くこと〕temp-to-hire placement.
しょうがい¹【生涯】 ▭▭ 生涯学習 lifelong learning (studies). 生涯学習社会 a lifelong learning society. 生涯現役 lifelong activity; remaining active (staying on the job) for one's entire life. 生涯現役社会 a society in which people 「remain active [stay on the job] throughout their lives. 生涯青春 lifelong youth(fulness); staying young at heart throughout one's life. 生涯スポーツ continuing to enjoy [keeping up] sports throughout

*one's* life. 生涯設計 a lifelong plan; planning for *one's* whole life. 生涯未婚率〔50歳時点で一度も結婚したことのない人の割合〕the「proportion [share, percentage] of people remaining single for life; the percentage of people not yet married at the age of fifty.

**しょうがい**[4]【障害】 ▷ 400 [110]メートル障害〔競技〕the「400-meter [110-meter] hurdles. 障害学 disability studies. 障害灯〔空〕= 航空障害灯 (⇨こうくう[2]).

**じょうがい**[2]【場外】 ▷ 場外戦〔競技場の外での争い〕a fight outside the stadium. 場外舟券〔競艇の〕an off-course (motor)boat-race ticket. 場外舟券売り場〔競艇の〕an off-course (motor)boat-racing betting「office [parlor, facility, "shop]. 場外流通 = 市場外流通 (⇨しじょう[3]).

**しょうがいがくしゅうしんこうほう**【生涯学習振興法】〖法〗the Lifelong Learning Promotion Law.

**しょうがいじ**【障害児】 ▷ 障害児福祉手当〔国の〕a welfare allowance for「disabled children [a disabled child].

**しょうがいしゃ**【障害者】 ▷〖 〗障害者加算〔生活保護費への〕a welfare supplement for「a handicapped person [the disabled]. 障害者雇用率〔労働〕the「disabled [handicapped] employee ratio; the percentage of「disabled [handicapped] people in the workforce. 障害者(雇用)枠 a (legally prescribed) employment quota of handicapped persons ((in private companies)); a「disabled [handicapped] quota. 障害者支援費制度 ⇨支援費制度 (⇨しえん[1]). 障害者週間〔12月3日-9日〕Disabled Week. 障害者スポーツ sports for「the disabled [people with disabilities]; disability sports. 障害者手帳 =〔身体障害者手帳〕a physical disability handbook; a handbook for the physically handicapped;〔精神障害者保健福祉手帳〕a mental disability handbook. 障害者白書 a white paper on people with disabilities;〔内閣府の〕the Annual Report on Government Measures for Persons with Disabilities. 障害者福祉 welfare [help] for「handicapped people [the handicapped]. 障害者プラン〔1995年政府策定の〕the Government Action Plan for Persons with Disabilities.

**しょうがいしゃインターナショナル**【障害者-】 ▷ 障害者インターナショナル日本会議 the Japan National Assembly of Disabled Peoples' International.

**しょうがいしゃさべつきんしほう**【障害者差別禁止法】〖米法〗the Americans with Disabilities Act (略：ADA);〖英法〗the Disability Discrimination Act (略：DDA).

**しょうがいしゃじりつしえんほう**【障害者自立支援法】〖法〗the Law to Encourage Self-Reliance Among the Handicapped.

**しょうがいしゃ(の)けんりじょうやく**【障害者(の)権利条約】〔国連の〕= 国連障害者の権利条約.

**しょうがいそう**【障害走】〖競技〗a hurdle race; the hurdles;〖競馬・競技〗a steeplechase.

**しょうがいぶつ**【障害物】 ▷ 障害物検知装置 an obstruction detector; an obstruction detection device;〔踏切障害物検知装置〕an automatic「*railroad ["level] crossing obstruction detection device.

**しょうがいをもつアメリカじんほう**【障害を持つ-人法】〖米法〗the Americans with Disabilities Act (略：ADA). [=しょうがいしゃさべつきんしほう]

**ショウガオール**〔ショウガの辛味成分の1つ〕shogaol.

**しょうかき**[2]【消化器】 ▷ 消化器外科 digestive [gastroenterological] surgery. 消化器疾患 a digestive「disease [disorder]. 消化器内科 gastroenterology; digestive medicine.

**じょうがく**【上顎】 ▷ 上顎前突〔歯科〕maxillary protrusion.

**しょうがくきん**【奨学金】 ▷ 奨学金制度 a scholar-

ship system.

**しょうがくたんきほけん**【少額短期保険】small-amount short-term insurance. 少額短期保険業者 a small-amount short-term insurance provider.

**しょうがつ**【正月】 ▷ 正月太り New Year's waist. ◇～太りする put on weight at New Year's.

**しょうかどうべんとう**【松花堂弁当】a Shōkadō lunch box; a lunch box divided into square compartments for various kinds of food.

**しょうがプロジェクト**【嫦娥-】〖宇〗〔中国の月探査計画〕the Chang'e「Program [Project].

**しょうかん**【使用感】1〔使ってみての感想〕one's「feeling [impressions] after use ((of a product)). ◇製品の～を開発者に報告 report to the developers how *one* felt after trying a product.
2〔使う上での感触〕feel. ◇製品開発において機能だけではなく～も重視する emphasize not only functionality but also feel when developing products.

**しょうかん**[10]【償還】 ▷〖 〗5 [10, 60] 年償還 《government bonds》 redeemable in「five [ten, sixty] years. ◇60年～ルール〖国債の〗the "sixty-year rule", which specifies that government bonds issued to finance a public works project must be redeemed within sixty years.
▷ 償還主義〖経〗〔高速道路などの〕the full cost recovery principle. 償還能力指標 an indicator of redemption「ability [capacity]. 償還払い〔医療機関などの窓口で支払った料金のうち限度額を超えた分が、本人の申請により払い戻される〕(a) refund for overpayment.

**じょうがん**【情願】〖法〗〔受刑者が刑務所内の人権侵害などについて法務大臣などに対し書面をもって行う嘆願〕a「complaint [protest] sent by a prisoner directly to ((the Minister of Justice)); a prisoner's「complaint [protest].

**じょうがん(きゃく)しき**【貞観(格)式】〔三代格式の1つ〕the Jōgan Rule; the Jōgan(-kyaku) Shiki. ◇さんだい(きゃく)しき, こうにん(きゃく)しき, えんぎ(きゃく)しき

**じょうがんけんきょきん**【上眼瞼挙筋】〖眼科〗the elevator muscle of the upper eyelid; musculus levator palpebrae superioris.

**じょうがんけんしかんしょう**【上眼瞼弛緩症】〖医〗blepharochalasis.

**しょうかんのん**【聖観音・正観音】the Sacred Avalokiteśvara.

**しょうき**[6]【笑気】 ▷ 笑気鎮静法〖医〗nitrous oxide sedation.

**じょうき**[7]【蒸気】 ▷ 蒸気井(せい)〔地熱発電などの〕a steam well.

**じょうき**[8]【乗機】an aircraft manned by ((*sb*)). ◇その空戦で少尉の～は F-14 だった. The aircraft manned by the second lieutenant was an F-14. | The second lieutenant flew an F-14 during that air battle.

**しょうききょうとうけいえいかいぜんしきんゆうせいど**【小企業等経営改善資金融資制度】⇨マルけいゆうし.

**しょうぎたい**【彰義隊】〖日本史〗Brigade of Righteousness (formed to defend the Shogunate in 1868).

**しょうきぼ**【小規模】 ▷ 小規模化 downscaling (▷ downscale *v*.); downsizing (▷ downsize *v*.). 小規模校 a small(-scale) school. 小規模作業所〔福祉作業所の一種〕a small(-scale) workshop. 小規模・多機能型小規模多機能(型)居宅介護 care [nursing] in a small-scale multi-functional facility. 小規模多機能施設 a small-scale multi-functional facility.

**しょうきゃく**[4]【償却】 ▷ 償却前営業利益〔営業利益と減価償却費の合計；キャッシュフロー〕(adjusted)「EBITDA [earnings before interest, taxes, deprecia-

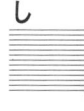

じょうきゃくじぜんしきべつコンピューターシステム〖乗客事前識別-〗〘航空〙CAPPS; the Computer Assisted Passenger Prescreening System.〘乗客事前識別コンピューターシステム1[2] CAPPS Ⅰ [Ⅱ].

しょうきゅう[4]【昇給】▶昇給制度 a pay-raise system.

しょうきゅうしゃ【消救車】〔消防車と救急車の機能を併せ持つ車両〕a combined fire engine and ambulance; an ambulance-fire engine; a fire engine-ambulance.

しょうきょ【消去】▶遠隔消去〘電算〙remote deletion《of data》.▶盗難にあったパソコンのデータを遠隔~する remotely delete data on a stolen computer.

しょうきょ【譲許】〔関税率交渉などでの譲歩・その約束〕concessions (and commitments).▶非譲許▶非~の品目 a no-concession item; an item not covered by a country's concessions.譲許税率 a concession tariff.譲許表〔譲許の結果の税率を示す〕a schedule of concessions and commitments.譲許品目 a concession item.

しょうぎょう【商業】▶商業施設 a commercial institution.▶複合(型)~施設⇨ふくごう[3].商業犯罪 (a) commercial crime.商業販売額 the value of commercial sales.商業販売統計 statistics on [figures for] the value of commercial sales.商業利用 (the) commercial use (of atomic energy).▶~利用する make commercial use of (atomic energy) / 宇宙の~利用 (the) commercial 'use [exploitation] of space / われわれは今回開発したシステムの5年後の~利用を目指しています.We are aiming to put our newly developed system to commercial use in five years' time.商業炉〘原子力〙a commercial reactor.

じょうきょう[2]【状況・情況】▶状況説明 a briefing; an explanation of the situation.▶~説明を受ける get [receive] a briefing; have the situation explained (to one).状況把握 a grasp [an understanding] of the situation; an awareness of how matters stand.▶鉄道事故の~把握に手間取り、対策が後手に回った.It took time to understand what had happened in the train accident, and the response was delayed.

しょうきょうせい【床矯正】〘歯科〙orthodontic jaw correction.

しょうきょくてき【消極的】▶消極的支持 passive [negative, muted, unenthusiastic] support; support by default.▶この政党を支持している理由には、他に支持したい政党がないからという~支持が多い.People's main reason for supporting the party is a negative one: they don't want to support any of the other parties.

しょうきん[4]【賞金】▶生涯獲得賞金〔プロゴルフほかで〕career prize 'winnings [earnings].▶賞金額 a sum [an amount] of prize money; (the) prize money.賞金シード(権)〘ゴルフ〙the right to be seeded based on a player's earnings in a season.賞金女王〔女子プロゴルフ界などで〕the women's 'top prizewinner [leading money winner].

じょうきん【常勤】▶常勤医(師)〔病院などの〕a full-time 'physician [doctor].

しょうぎんが【小銀河】〘天〙a small galaxy.

じょうげ【上下】▶上下分離方式〔空港・鉄道などの土木構造物を整備する下物法人と、施設を管理運営する上物法人の二つに分けて業務を行うやり方〕vertical separation (of the construction and operating companies from the management companies).

しょうけい[1]【小径】▶小径材 small-diameter timber.小径木 a small-diameter tree.

しょうけい[5]【承継】▶承継会社 a successor company.

しょうけい[11]【掌形】〔てのひらの形〕the shape of a palm;

palm geometry;〔指を含む〕the shape of a hand; hand geometry.▶掌形認証 palm [hand] recognition.掌形判別機 a 'palm [hand] geometry [recognition] system.

じょうけい[2]【情景】▶情景描写 (a) description of scenery; (a) delineation of nature.

しょうげき[2]【衝撃】▶衝撃吸収ボディー〘自動車〙an impact-absorbing body.衝撃砕波圧 impulsive breaking wave force(s).

しょうけん[5]【証券】▶地場証券 a local securities company.▶証券化 securitization.▶~化する convert into securities; securitize /~化ローン a securitized loan.証券コード〘金融〙〔銘柄識別番号〕a securities code.▶国際~コード〘金融〙an ISIN code.▶ISINはInternational Securities Identification Numberの略.証券子会社 a securities subsidiary.証券詐欺 (a) securities fraud.証券税制 a securities taxation system; the taxation of securities.証券仲介業 securities intermediation; (a) securities intermediary business.証券取引 securities trading; trading in securities.証券不況 a securities 'slump [recession].証券マン a securities man; a securities firm employee.

じょうけん【条件】▶条件緩和 the 'relaxation [relaxing, easing, lowering] of requirements '(for certification).条件検索〘電算〙a conditional search.条件整備 the creation of favorable conditions; (lay) the groundwork (for…).▶高齢者の雇用を促進するための~整備を図る work to create conditions favorable for promoting the employment of senior citizens.条件提示 a statement of conditions; (make) an offer (of conditions).

じょうげん[2]【上限】▶上限関税 a ceiling tariff rate (of 40 percent).上限金利 a maximum legal interest rate; a ceiling interest rate.

しょうけんか【証券化】〘金融〙securitization.▶~する convert (bad loans) into securities; securitize 《sb's assets》.▶不動産の~ real estate securitization / 不動産の小口~ small denomination real estate securitization /債務の~ debt securitization / 不良債権の~ bad-loan securitization.

しょうけんとうししゃほごききん【証券投資者保護基金】the Securities Investor Protection Fund (Japan) (略: SIPF(J)).

しょうこ[4]【証拠】▶消極的証拠〔間接証拠〕indirect evidence;〘法〙〔犯罪の存在を否定するような〕negative evidence.積極的証拠〔直接証拠〕direct evidence;〘法〙〔犯罪の存在を証明する証拠〕positive evidence.▶証拠集め collection of [collecting] evidence; evidence collection.開示[未開示]証拠 disclosed [undisclosed] evidence; evidence 'disclosed [not disclosed]《to the defense》.証拠金率〘証券〙a margin rate; a margin requirement; a down payment.証拠捏造[偽造] production [submission] of evidence.証拠捏造[偽造] fabricating [fabrication of] evidence; concocting evidence.証拠(の)散逸 dispersal [scattering] of evidence.

じょうこう[3]【乗降】▶乗降介助〔身障者・高齢者などがタクシーなどに乗降する際の介助〕assistance with 'getting into and out of (taxis) [boarding and dismounting from (trains), getting on and off (trains)].乗降時間〔電車などの〕(a) (passenger) boarding and alighting time; the time it takes for passengers to get on and off (a train).

しょうこうき【昇降機】▶階段昇降機 a stair lift.

じょうざい[3]【商材】a product; a commodity; merchandise; goods.

じょうざいきん【常在菌】〘医〙indigenous [resident] bacteria [microbiota, microbes]. ▶□ 口腔常在菌 indigenous [resident] oral「bacteria [microbiota]. 皮膚常在菌 indigenous [resident] dermal [skin] bacteria [microbiota].

**じょうざいせんじょう**【常在戦場】◇君たちには～の心がけが必要だ. It's like a battlefield, and you must be constantly alert for hidden dangers.

**しょうさん**[5]【硝酸】▶□ 硝酸性窒素《化》nitrate-nitrogen.

**じょうさんかきょううんどう**【上山下郷運動】〔1960年代から70年代にかけての中国の文化大革命時代の〕the "(Up to the Mountains and) Down to the Countryside Movement"; the sending of young city people to rural areas during the Cultural Revolution.

**しょうし**[13]【硝子】▶□ 硝子体網膜症《医》vitreoretinopathy.

**しょうじ**[9]【障子】▶□ 内障子〔ガラス窓の内側に設けた障子〕(an) inner shoji; (a) shoji placed over the inside of a window.

**じょうし**[5]【上肢】▶□ 上肢障害 (an)「upper-limb [arm] impairment. ◇～障害者 a person with (an)「upper-limb [arm] impairment. 上肢帯《解》the「shoulder [pectoral] girdle. 上肢帯筋《解》the shoulder girdle muscles.

**しょうしか**【少子化】▶□ 少子化現象 (the phenomenon of) a declining birth rate. 少子化社会対策大綱〔厚生労働省の〕the Basic Guidelines for Measures to Halt the Declining Birthrate. 少子化社会白書〔内閣府の〕(2004) White Paper on the Declining Birthrate.

**しょうしかしゃかいたいさくきほんほう**【少子化社会対策基本法】《法》the Basic Law on Measures to Counteract the Falling Birthrate.

**じょうしき**[2]【常識】▶□ 国際常識 generally accepted behavior in international relations; what is taken for granted「internationally [all over the world].

**じょうせい**【常磁性】▶□ 常磁性金属 a paramagnetic metal (略: PM). 常磁性絶縁体 a paramagnetic insulator (略: PI).

**じょうじつ**【情実】▶□ 情実融資 loans made on the basis of personal acquaintance with customers and inadequately assessed for risk.

**じょうしてん**【上死点】▶□《機》〔エンジンの燃焼室の容積が最小になる時のピストンの位置〕a top dead center.

**しょうしゃ**[5]【勝者】▶□ 勝者総取り〔米国大統領選挙における各州選挙人の配分法など〕winner-take-all 《primaries》.

**じょうしゃ**[1]【乗車】▶□ 乗車位置〔プラットホーム上の〕a (platform) boarding position;〔事故被害者などが乗っていた場合〕(a passenger's) position on a「train [bus, etc.]; where (a passenger) was (at the time of the accident). 乗車マナー passenger etiquette. ◇～マナーの乱れを嘆く deplore「the worsening manners of passengers [how badly people have come to behave on (trains)]. 乗車密度 passenger density. ◇平均～密度 the average passenger density / 路線別～密度 the passenger density by rail line.

**しょうしゃく**[3]【昇爵】an elevation in rank; a promotion. ～する be raised in the peerage. ◇公爵に～する be「elevated [promoted] to duke.

**しょうしゅう**[3]【消臭】▶□ 消臭ゲル (a) deodorant gel. 消臭効果 a deodorant effect.

**しょうしゅう**[3]【常襲】▶□ 常襲地帯 an area frequently hit (by storms); a susceptible area. ◇台風[水害]～地帯 a「typhoon-prone [flood-prone] area.

**しょうじゅつきん**【賞恤金】a sum of money given by the state to soldiers, police, and other public officials, or their survivors, in compensation for injury or death suffered in the line of duty.

**じょうしょう**[2]【上昇】▶□ 上昇幅 an「extent [amount, degree] of increase. 上昇率 a rate of increase. ◇前年比～率 a (slightly lower) rate of increase (as) compared to「last [the previous] year / 物価[地価, 賃金]～率 the rate of increase in「commodity prices [land prices, wages].

**じょうしょう**[2]【上場】▶□ 新規上場 an initial public offering (略: IPO); a new「listing [issue]. ◇新規～株 a newly「listed [issued] stock; newly listed shares. ▶□ 上場以来 ⇒上場来. 上場商品《取引》an exchange-traded commodity. 上場審査〔証券取引所への〕a listing review. ◇～審査基準 standards for listing reviews. 上場投資信託 an exchange-traded fund (略: ETF). 上場不動産投資信託〔不動産投資信託〕a real estate investment trust (略: REIT). 上場来 ◇今期わが社は～来初の黒字を達成いたしました. This term we have made a profit for the first time since we have been listed. 上場来(最)高値 a record [an all-time] high. 上場来(最)安値 a record [an all-time] low.

**じょうじょう**[4]【情状】▶□ 情状鑑定 (an) assessment of the《perpetrator's》psychological state; a psychological「assessment [evaluation]. 情状鑑定書《法》an [a written] assessment of sb's psychological state; a psychological assessment report. 情状証人《法》a witness who gives evidence of extenuating or mitigating circumstances.

**しょうしょく**[2]【小職】〔官職にあるものが自分を指して言う謙譲語〕I. ◇～には判断いたしかねます. I am afraid I cannot make a decision on the matter. | It is not for me, as a public servant, to decide.

**しょうしん**[3]【昇進】▶□ 昇進試験 a promotion「examination [exam, test]; an examination for promotion.

**しょうじん**[6]【省人】▶□ 省人化 manpower [personnel, labor] reduction [savings]. ◇ビル管理を～化する reduce the manpower required for building management.

**しょうじんがに**【精進蟹】《動》〔イワガニ科のカニ〕a brachyuran crab; Plagusia dentipes.

**しょうすう**[2]【少数】▶□ 少数者 a minority ◇死刑廃止論者は, 残念ながら日本では～者だ. Opponents of capital punishment are unfortunately in「a [the] minority in Japan. 少数者調査〔野党などの少数者に与えられた行政調査権〕the right of a「parliamentary [Diet] minority to obtain official information.

**しょうスペース**【省-】◇～の space-saving.

**しようずみ**【使用済み】▶□ 使用済み自動車〔廃車〕an end-of-life vehicle (略: ELV).

**じょうせい**[3]【情勢】▶□ 情勢判断 an assessment [a grasp] of a situation. ◇～判断が甘い be overly optimistic in one's assessment of the situation. 情勢分析 an analysis of the situation.

**じょうせいこっぷん**【蒸製骨粉】〔家畜の飼料〕steamed bone meal.

**しょうせき**[2]【掌蹠】▶□ 掌蹠多汗症《医》palmoplantar hyperhidrosis; excessive sweating from the palms of the hands and soles of the feet.

**じょうせき**[2]【定石・定跡】▶□ 定石書, 定石本〔囲碁・将棋〕a book of「set moves [established tactics] (in「go [shogi]).

**しょうせつ**[3]【小説】▶□ 企業小説 a corporate novel; 〔ジャンル〕the corporate novel; corporate novel-writing.

**しょうせつ**[4]【消雪】▶□ 消雪パイプ a snow-melting pipe.

**しょうせっかい**[2]【小切開】▶□《医》(a) small incision. ▶□ 小切開(創)白内障手術 (a) small-incision cataract surgery.

「**小説家を見つけたら**」〔映画〕Finding Forrester.

しょうせんきょく【小選挙区】▶ 小選挙区選挙〔衆議院〕a single-seat constituency election.

しょうせんげんちりょう【小線源治療】〚医〛brachytherapy.

しょうぞう²【肖像】▶ 肖像彫刻 (a) portrait sculpture.

じょうそう²【上層】▶ 上層階〔ビルなどの〕the upper「floors [stories]《of a building》.

じょうだ【嫋娜】litheness; lissomeness; slender grace.

しょうたい【小帯】▶ 上唇[下唇]小帯〔唇の裏側と歯茎をつなぐ粘膜のひだ〕the frenulum of the「upper [lower] lip; the「upper [lower] lip frenulum; the frenulum labii「superioris [inferioris].

しょうたい⁴【招待】▶ 招待講演 an invited talk; an invited lecture. 招待所〔北朝鮮の拉致被害者収容施設〕a "guest house"; a holding facility for abductees. 招待論文 an invited paper.

しょうたい¹【上体】▶ 上体起こし〔脚を押さえられた状態で上半身を起こし、腹筋を鍛える運動〕a sit-up; a curl-up; a trunk curl.

じょうたい⁴【常態】▶ 常態化 ◐〜化する become the norm; become institutionalized /わが社ではサービス残業が〜化している At our company, unpaid overtime has become institutionalized.

しょうだん³【商談】▶ 商談相手 a negotiating partner; a partner「in [for] business negotiations. 商談会 a「business [sales] fair. 商談成立 closing [the closing of] a (business) deal. ◐〜話し合いの後に〕これで〜成立ね！ Right; it's a deal!

しょうち³【招致】▶ 招致運動[活動] a campaign to「bring《the Olympics to Osaka》[host《the World Cup》]. 招致決議 a resolution to (try and)「bring [attract]《the Olympics to Tokyo》. ◐〜決議書 a written record of a resolution to (try and hold)「an event in one's town》; 《dispatch》a formal bid (for the Olympics). 招致レース a [the] race to get《the Olympics》. ◐ 五輪〜レースはニューヨーク、マドリード、モスクワ3都市の間で繰り広げられている。The race is on between New York, Madrid and Moscow to bag the Olympics.

じょうちゅう²【常駐】▶ 常駐警備員 a guard on permanent duty (at a particular location).

しょうちょう¹【小腸】▶ 小腸閉鎖(症)〚医〛small「intestinal [bowel, intestine] atresia; atresia of small「intestine [bowel]. 小腸閉塞(症)〚医〛small「intestinal [bowel, intestine] obstruction; obstruction of the small「intestine [bowel].

しょうちょう²【省庁】▶ 省庁横断型 inter-government agency type; cross-government agency type. ◐〜横断型の作業部会 an inter-government agency type「task force [working committee].

しょうちょう⁴【象徴】▶ 象徴暴力〔ニュース性を高めるために行う、市民的不服従の延長線上としての暴力〕symbolic violence.

じょうちょう²【冗長】▶ 冗長化〔情報機器などの故障の際に機能を引き継ぐ設備を別に用意しておくこと〕backup redundancy. 冗長性〔冗長さ〕prolixity; diffuseness; verbosity; tediousness; redundancy.〚電算〛〚情報機器〕redundancy.

じょうちょくきん【上直筋】〚眼科〕the superior rectus muscle; musculus rectus superior.

じょうてい³【上底】〔幾何〕〔台形の〕an upper base.

しょうてん⁵【掌典】▶ 掌典職 the job of [being] a ritualist.

しょうでん¹【昇殿】▶ 昇殿参拝 worshipping [praying] at an inner(most) shrine.

しょうてんし【小転子】〚解〕〔大腿骨頸と大腿骨体との結合部の後下部から内後方へ突出する部分〕the「lesser [minor] trochanter; the trochanter minor.

じょうでんどうじきふじょうしきリニアモーターカー【常電導磁気浮上式-】a normal-conducting maglev.

しょうど²【焦土】▶ 焦土化経営〔企業を買収した後、その企業が持っている資産を買収者側に根こそぎ移すこと〕a scorched-earth management policy.

しょうど³【照度】▶ 照度センサー a light intensity sensor; a photosensor.

じょうと【譲渡】▶ 譲渡益課税 (a) capital gains tax. 譲渡制限株式 transfer-restricted「stock [shares]. 譲渡制限会社〔閉鎖会社〕a「close [closed] corporation; "a proprietary company."

しょうどう⁷【衝動】▶ 衝動殺人 (an) impulsive「murder [homicide, killing, slaying]. 衝動制御障害〚精神医〕an impulse control disorder（略：ICD).

じょうとう⁵【常套】▶ 常套表現 a "conventional [trite, stock] expression.

じょうどう⁴【情動】▶ 情動指数〚心理〕an EQ; an emotional quotient. 情動失禁〚医〕〔感情失禁〕emotional [affective] incontinence. 情動性脱力発作〚医〕＝カタプレキシー.

しょうどうてき【衝動的】▶ 衝動的犯行 an impulsive [an unpremeditated] criminal act.

しょうどうぶつ【小動物】small animals; smaller animals.

しょうとつ【衝突】
▶ 全面衝突 an all-out (military)「conflict [clash]. 二次衝突〔自動車〕〔衝突直後に起こった他の自動車との衝突〕a secondary collision;〔自動車の車内での人と物の衝突〕a secondary collision《of the car occupants》. ▶ 衝突安全性能試験〔自動車などの〕a collision safety performance test. 衝突回避 collision avoidance. 衝突回避義務〔船舶・航空機などの〕collision avoidance「duties [responsibility]; duty [responsibility] to avoid collision. 衝突回避システム a collision avoidance system. 衝突回避装置 a collision avoidance system（略：CAS). 衝突実験〔自動車などの〕a「collision [crash] experiment. 衝突シミュレーション〔隕石などの〕a collision simulation;〔自動車などの〕a (car) crash simulation. 衝突時の impactor. 衝突予防 collision prevention; prevention of collision.

しょうないざお【庄内竿】〔釣り〕〔庄内地方で作られる和竿の一つ〕a Shōnai fishing rod.〔⇨わざお〕

しょうに【小児】▶ 小児救急 pediatric emergency care. ◐〜救急医療 pediatric emergency medicine. 小児保健 child health. 小児慢性特定疾患〚医〕a specified chronic pediatric disease.

しょうにん³【承認】
▶ 承認国 ◐台湾〜国 a country that recognizes Taiwan /がん治療薬イレッサの最初の〜国は日本だった。 Japan was the first country to approve the anticancer drug Iressa. /国連〜国は現在192である。 One hundred ninety-two countries are currently recognized by the United Nations. 承認申請 (an) application for approval;〔医薬品の〕(新薬製造承認申請) application for approval of manufacturing a new drug. 承認薬 an approved [a Government-approved] drug. 承認欲求〔他人から無視されず、認識・評価・尊重されたいと思う欲求; 社会的な認識欲求〕(a) need for (social)「approval [esteem]; esteem needs.

しょうにん⁶【証人】▶ 証人申請〚法〕an application [a request] for a subpoena. ◐〜申請する apply for [request] a subpoena. 証人陳述〚法〕a witness('s)「deposition [statement].

しょうねんいん【少年院】▶ 少年院送致 sentencing [sending]《(a juvenile)》to「*a reformatory ["an approved school]; *a reformatory sentence; a custodial sentence [custodial sentencing]《for a juvenile offender》.

しょうねんいんほう【少年院法】〚法〕the Reformatory

Law.
しょうねんけいさつボランティア【少年警察-】a volunteer youth officer.
じょうば【乗馬】▣ 乗馬療法 hippotherapy; therapeutic (horse) riding.
しょうはい¹【勝敗】▣ 勝敗ライン 〔選挙の〕a level of victory; a victory line. ▶(政党の)〜ラインを250議席に設定する set 《a party's》 level of victory at 250 seats; decide that 《a party》 has won if it captures 250 seats.
しょうひ【消費】
▣ 基礎的消費〔経〕basic consumption; spending on basics. 選択的消費〔経〕optional consumption; spending on non-essentials.
▣ 消費意欲 consumer ⌈confidence [motivation]; (the) motivation to spend; a desire to buy. 消費意欲指数〔経〕a [the] consumer confidence index; an [the] index of consumer confidence. 消費拡大 growth [(an) increase] in ⌈consumption [spending]; consumption growth; increased spending. 消費需要 consumption demand; 〔消費者需要〕consumer demand. 消費低迷 a continuing consumer slump. 消費動向 consumer behavior; a consumer trend; a trend in consumption. ▶〜動向調査 a consumer behavior survey; a survey of consumer trends. 消費不況〔経〕a consumer recession; a recession caused by ⌈depressed [sluggish, slack] consumption. 消費予測 consumption forecasting; a consumption forecast.
しょうひ¹【上皮】▣ 上皮成長因子受容体〔生理〕an epidermal growth factor receptor; 〔略: EGFR〕.
じょうび【常備】▣ 常備灯 an emergency ⌈*flashlight [*torch] (that lights when pulled off the wall).
しょうひしゃ【消費者】▣ 消費者行動論 consumer behavior (studies). ▶〜行動論の講座〔コース〕a course on consumer behavior. 消費者信用団体生命保険 a consumer financing firm if the insured should die before repaying a loan. 消費者信頼感指数〔米国などの〕the Consumer Confidence Index. ▶ミシガン大学〜信頼感指数 the University of Michigan Consumer Sentiment Index. 消費者生成メディア 〔インターネット上のブログなど〕consumer-generated media (略: CGM). 消費者相談室 a customer consultation center; 〔自治体などの〕a consumer counselling center. 消費者態度指数〔経〕a consumer attitude index. 消費者調査〔商〕a consumer survey; consumer research. 消費者パネル a consumer panel. 消費者物価地域差指数 an index of ⌈comparative regional consumer prices [consumer prices by region].
しょうひしゃきこうにっぽん【消費者機構日本】the Consumers Organization of Japan (略: COJ). ▶2004年9月設立.
しょうひしゃしえんききん【消費者支援基金】the Consumer Rights Protection Fund.
しょうひしゃせいひんあんぜんいいんかい【消費者製品安全委員会】〔米国の〕the (US) Consumer Product Safety Commission (略: CPSC).
しょうひぜい【消費税】
▣ 消費税課税【免税】事業者 a business operator who is ⌈liable to [exempt from] consumption tax payment. 消費税課税事業者届出書 a certificate for registration as a business operator liable to consumption tax payment. 消費税簡易課税制度 the simplified (tax) system of consumption tax. ▶〜簡易課税制度選択届出書 a reporting form to elect the simplified (tax) system of consumption tax / 〜簡易課税制度選択不適用届出書 a reporting form used when one does not elect to apply the simplified (tax) system of consumption tax. 消費税率 a consumption tax rate; *a sales tax rate; ⌈a VAT rate. ▶〜率の引き上げ an increase in consumption tax rates; increasing [putting up, raising] consumption tax rates; a consumption tax ⌈increase [rise, hike].
しょうひせいかつ【消費生活】▣ 消費生活コンサルタント a consumer consultant. 消費生活専門相談員〔国民生活センターが資格認定する〕a consumer ⌈counselor [advisor]. 消費生活相談 consumer counseling; consumer advice on consumer affairs. 消費生活相談員〔消費生活アドバイザー〕a consumer ⌈adviser [advisor].
しょうひょう¹【商標】▣ 地域団体商標 the trademark of a local producers' association.
しょうひん²【商品】
▣ 最終商品〔開発段階の商品に対して〕a final product; a finished consumer product; an end item.
▣ 商品企画 product planning. 商品開発力 product development capability. 商品指数〔投資〕a commodity index (pl. commodity ⌈indices [indexes]). 商品寿命〔ライフサイクル〕〔製品ライフサイクル〕a ⌈product [product's] life cycle (略: PLC). 商品政策 merchandising. 商品設計 product ⌈design [planning]. 商品説明 a product explanation. 商品説明能力 the ability to explain a product. 商品調達 (a) merchandise procurement; (a) procurement of merchandise. 商品調達力 ability to procure merchandise. 商品陳列 (a) product display. 商品力 product ⌈salability [sales power].
しょうひんか【商品化】▣ 再商品化〔廃品などの〕recycling materials into ⌈saleable products [commodities]. ▶〜再〜する turn recycled materials into ⌈saleable products [commodities].
しょうひんコード【商品-】〔米国・カナダの〕a Universal Product Code (略: UPC); 〔欧州の〕a European Article Number (略: EAN); 〔日本の〕a Japanese Article Number (略: JAN). ▶ 日本のJANは欧州のEANに含まれる.
しょうひんさきものとりひきいいんかい【商品先物取引委員会】〔米国の〕the Commodity Futures Trading Commission (略: CFTC).
しょうぶ³【勝負】▣ 勝負運 one's luck at ⌈gambling [betting, etc.]. 勝負カラー【色】〔ここ一番というときに身につける服や色の〕one's lucky color. 勝負度胸 the courage to win.
ジョウフ⇨アル・ジャウフ.
しょうふく⁴【慴伏・慴伏】〔恐れてその人の前に平伏すること〕prostration.
〜する prostrate oneself 《before sb》.
しょうふく³【条幅】〔縦長の書画の軸物〕a hanging scroll made from a half-length piece of Chinese drawing paper.
「娼婦ベロニカ」〔映画〕A Destiny of Her Own.
じょうぶん²【条文】▣ 条文化 (a) stipulation. ▶〜化する stipulate / 公務員の飲酒運転に懲戒免職とすることが多くの自治体で〜化されている. Many local authorities stipulate that public servants who drive while under the influence of alcohol will be dismissed.
じょうぼう²【消防】▣ 消防学校 a firefighting school. 消防服＝防火服 (⇨ぼうか). 消防ロボット a firefighting robot.
じょうあつ¹【上方】▣ 上方圧力〔力学・相場〕(an) upward pressure.
じょうほう²【情報】
▣ 観測〔注意, 予知〕情報〔東海地震に関して〕earthquake ⌈observation [alert, prediction] information. 有力情報 (highly) ⌈reliable [dependable] information; information which can be relied on. ▣ 情報アクセシビリティー〔情報を自由に入手できる状態〕information accessibility. 情報隠蔽＝情報隠し. 情報開示請求 an information disclosure request. ▶

しょうぼうきねんび

~開示請求権 the right to request the disclosure of information. 情報(科)学 information science; informatics. 情報隠し concealing [hiding] information; information concealment; an information cover-up. ▶国交省では,その自動車会社により意図的な~隠しが行われたと確認されれば刑事告発の対象になるとしている. The Ministry of Land, Infrastructure and Transport regards that auto maker as a target for criminal charges if the company is confirmed to have intentionally covered up information. 情報隔壁〔情報漏れを防ぐための〕a [an information] wall; a [an information] fence. 情報教育 information [data] education. 情報掲載料〔情報誌・ウェブサイトなどへの〕a (data) display fee. 公然情報〔公開資料やメディアなどから得られる情報〕open source intelligence (略: OSINT). 情報サービス会社 an information service company; an information agency. ▶金融~サービス会社 a financial information「service company [vendor, supplier, agency]; a company providing financial information / 結婚~サービス会社 a marriage agency. 情報サイト〔インターネット上の〕an information site. 情報錯綜 [contending, irreconcilable] information; conflicting reports; a conflict of information. 情報共有センター an information-sharing center. 情報共有 sharing [pooling] (of) information. 情報資本主義 information capitalism. 情報遮断 blocking (out)《harmful》 information; cutting off information《from overseas》. 情報収集能力 (an) information-gathering「ability [capability, capacity]; an [the] ability to 「collect [gather, obtain, get] information; 〔軍事関係などの〕intelligence-gathering capabilities; an [the] ability to obtain intelligence. 情報受領者 a recipient of information. ▶第一次[第二次]~受領者 a 「primary [secondary] recipient of information. 情報商材[商品]an information product. 情報提供 providing information; information provision. 情報帝国〔マスメディアの〕an information empire;〔諜報活動の〕an intelligence empire. 情報デザイン〔情報を視覚化しわかりやすく伝達するための各種手法〕information design. 情報伝達 information transmission. 情報伝達訓練〔災害時などを想定しての〕an information transmission drill; a drill to「ensure that [check whether] information gets passed on properly. 情報伝達コスト information transmission costs; the cost of「transmitting information [information transmission]. 情報伝達物質〔生理〕〔脳内細胞間の〕an intercellular messenger. 情報統括役員 a chief information officer (略: CIO). 情報統制 information control; control of information. 情報発信地 an information「source [resource]. ▶このホームページは韓国についての~発信基地として知られている. This Web site is well known as a source of information on South Korea. 情報発信者 an information provider; a provider of information. 情報バリアフリー〔情報入手に関して高齢者・障害者が不利を被らない状態〕information barrier-free 《environment》. 情報評価分析〔情報の〕information analysis. ▶北朝鮮の核兵器保有数について~分析を行う conduct information analysis of the number of nuclear weapons held by North Korea. 情報保護システム an information「protection [security] system. 情報モラル information ethics; information morals. 情報流出 an information leak; informunauthorized「release [disclosure] of information. ▶顧客情報~ a leak of customer information [data]. 情報倫理 information ethics. 情報漏洩〔情報を(意図的に)外部に漏らすこと〕leaking [divulging, disclosing] information;〔情報が(悪意もしくは事故によって)外部に流出してしまうこと〕⇒情報流出. ▶~漏洩リスク a [the] risk that information will be「leaked [divulged]; a

[the] danger that (secret) information will get out. しょうぼうきねんび【消防記念日】〔3月7日〕Fire Prevention Day; Fire Fighting Day. しょうぼうけんきゅうじょ【消防研究所】〔独立行政法人〕the National Research Institute of Fire and Disaster (略: NRIFD). じょうほうこうかい【情報公開】▷□ 情報公開請求 an information disclosure request. ▶~請求を行う request the disclosure of《personal》information. じょうほうこうかいクリアリングハウス【情報公開-】〔NPO法人〕the Information Clearinghouse Japan (略: ICJ). じょうほうさんぎょうろうどうくみあいれんごうかい【情報産業労働組合連合会】the Japan Federation of Telecommunications, Electronic Information and Allied Workers. じょうほうしゅうせい【上方修正】▷□ 上方修正条項付(き)CB[転換社債]《証券》a moving strike convertible bond [an MSCB] with an upward adjustment. [⇨エム・エス・シー・ビー] じょうほうしょり【情報処理】▷□ 情報処理会社 a data [an information] processing company. 情報処理能力 (an) information processing「capacity [ability]; (the) ability to process information. じょうほうしょりすいしんきこう【情報処理推進機構】〔独立行政法人〕the Information-technology Promotion Agency, Japan (略: IPA). じょうほうせいめいかがく【情報生命科学】bioinformatics. じょうほうセキュリティー・マネジメントシステム【情報-】⇨アイ・エス・エム・エス. じょうほうそう【省包装】minimal「wrapping [packaging]. ▶~の野菜 minimally wrapped vegetables. じょうほうつうしんけんきゅうきこう【情報通信研究機構】〔独立行政法人〕the National Institute of Information and Communications Technology (略: NICT). じょうほうつうしんしんぎかい【情報通信審議会】the Telecommunications Council. じょうほうつうしんネットワークさんぎょうきょうかい【情報通信-産業協会】the Communications and Information Network Association of Japan (略: CIAJ). じょうほうとくれいほう【商法特例法】《法》the Commercial Code Special Exemption Law. ▶ 正式名称は「株式会社の監査等に関する商法の特例に関する法律」(the Law for Special Provisions for the Commercial Code Concerning Audits, etc., of Joint-Stock Companies). じょうほうろうれん【情報労連】=じょうほうさんぎょうろうどうくみあいれんごうかい. しょうまく【漿膜】▷□ 漿膜下層《解》a subserous layer. じょうみゃく【静脈】▷□ 静脈認証〔てのひらまたは指の〕vein authentication. ▶てのひら~認証 palm vein authentication / 非接触型てのひら~認証 contactless palm vein authentication / 指~認証 finger vein authentication / 非接触型指~認証 contactless finger vein authentication. ~認証技術 vein authentication technology / ~認証システム a vein authentication system. 静脈パターン〔生体認証に用いる〕a vein pattern. じょうむ[1]【乗務】▷□ 乗務時間(数) time [hours] on board; operating hours;〔客室乗務員などの〕flying「hours [time]; hours [time] in the air;〔タクシー運転手などの〕hours at the wheel;〔操縦士などの〕hours at the controls. しょうめい[5]【照明】▷□ 照明技術者[技師] a lighting「director [technician]. 照明デザイナー a lighting designer. 照明デザイン lighting design. しょうめん【正面】▷□ 正面突破〔攻撃や問題解決に際

しての〕a frontal breakthrough.
**しょうもう**[2]【消耗】 消耗部品 nondurable parts; parts that will in time require replacement.
**しょうもうないはん**【睫毛内反】《医》〔逆さまつげ〕ingrowing eyelashes;〔症状〕trichiasis.
**しょうもん**[2]【掌紋】 掌紋識別機〔識別装置〕a palm print recognition system. 掌紋認証 palm print recognition.
**じょうもんすぎ**【縄文杉】《植》〔鹿児島県屋久島のスギのうち、特に樹齢の高いスギ〕the Jōmon「sugi [cedar].
**じょうやく**【条約】 条約締結 (the) conclusion of a treaty. 条約締結国〔条約加盟国〕a signatory (country).
**しょうゆ**【醤油】 醤油洗い〔ゆでた野菜などを薄めた醤油にひたすこと〕washing [rinsing, soaking, dipping] 《boiled green vegetables》in diluted soy sauce and then squeezing out the liquid.
**しょうよ**【賞与】 賞与引当金 a reserve [an allowance, a provision] for bonus payments; a bonus payment reserve.
**じょうよう**[2]【常用】 常用雇用 regular [full-time] employment. 常用雇用指数 the「regular [full-time] employment index. 常用雇用者〔労働者〕a full-time「employee [worker]; a person in「full-time [regular] employment. 常用ブレーキ〔鉄道〕〔非常ブレーキに対して〕a service brake.
**しょうようか**【商用化】commercialization.
～する commercialize; develop 《a product》for the market. ● 燃料電池車の～をめざす aim to make fuel cell vehicles a commercial proposition; plan to develop fuel cell vehicles for the market.
**しょうようしゃ**【商用車】〔自動車〕a commercial vehicle.
**しょうらい**[3]【将来】 将来価値〔会計〕(a) future value (略: FV).
**しょうり**[3]【勝利】 初勝利 a [one's] first victory. 勝利演説 a victory speech. 勝利至上主義 the belief that winning「should come first [is more important than anything else]; (the belief that) nothing matters except winning. 勝利宣言 a victory declaration; a declaration of victory;〔選挙での〕a victory speech. ● ～宣言をする declare one's 《election》victory; make a victory speech.
**じょうりく**【上陸】 上陸記録 ● 年間最多～記録〔台風〕a record number of annual landings; a record number of typhoons 《hitting Japan》in one year. 上陸訓練《hold》a landing drill. 上陸台風 a typhoon that「comes ashore [hits《Honshū》].
**じょうりせい**【条里制】〔古代の土地区画制度〕the jōri system; the system of land subdivision (in ancient Japan).
**しょうりゅう**[3]【商流】〔商売の流れ〕(a)「business [transaction] flow.
**じょうりゅう**[1]【上流】 上流課税〔石油などに対する出荷段階での課税〕upstream taxation.
**しょうりんカンフー**【少林-】Shaolin kung fu.
「**少林サッカー**」〔映画〕Shaolin Soccer;〔中国語タイトル〕少林足球.
**じょうれい**[2]【条例】 条例制定権 the right to enact an ordinance.
**じょうれん**【常連】 常連客 a regular (customer).
**しょうわくせい**【小惑星】 小惑星探査機 an asteroid probe.
**しょうわけんぽう**【昭和憲法】〔昭和21年 (1946年) 発布の日本国憲法のこと〕the Shōwa Constitution.
**しょうわとうなんかいじしん**【昭和東南海地震】〔1944年のの〕(1944) Shōwa Tōnankai Earthquake.
**しょうわなんかいじしん**【昭和南海地震】〔1946年の〕the (1946) Shōwa Nankai Earthquake.
**しょうわのひ**【昭和の日】〔4月29日〕Shōwa Day. ▶ 2007年より. 4月29日は2006年までは「みどりの日」だった.
**じょうわん**【上腕】 上腕骨内(側)上顆炎《医》medial epicondylitis. 上腕骨外(側)上顆炎《医》lateral epicondylitis.
**ショーヴェどうくつ**【-洞窟】〔フランス南東部の洞窟遺跡〕the Chauvet Cave.
**ショー・カー**〔自動車ショーに展示する出品車〕a show car.
**ジョーダン** Jordan, Neil (1950- ; アイルランド生まれの映画監督).
**ショート**[3] ショート・コント〔お笑いの寸劇〕a short sketch. ショート・パスタ《料理》〔マカロニなど、短いイタリア麺類〕short pasta. ショート・メッセージ・サービス《通信》〔携帯電話の〕a short message service (略: SMS). ショート・オーバル〔自動車レースで、一周1マイルの楕円形コース〕a short oval. ショートオーバル競技 short oval racing.
**ショート・コーナー**《サッカー》〔コーナーキックで近くにいる味方にパスすること〕《play, receive [take]》a short corner (kick).
**ショーメ**《商標》〔フランスの宝飾品ブランド〕Chaumet.
「**ショーン・オブ・ザ・デッド**」〔映画〕Shaun of the Dead.
**ジョーンズ 1** Jones, Elvin (Ray) (1927-2004; 米国のジャズドラマー).
**2** Jones, Norah (1979- ; 米国の歌手; ラビ・シャンカールの娘).
**3** Jones, Orlando (1968- ; 米国の映画俳優).
**4** Jones, Tommy Lee (1946- ; 米国の映画俳優).
**5** Jonze, Spike (1969- ; 米国の映画監督・監督; 本名 Adam Spiegel).
**しょかい**[2]【初回】 初回限定生産 once only [one-off, not-to-be-repeated] production. 初回出荷〔新製品などの第1回発売〕an initial shipment;〔その量〕the amount of an initial shipment.
**しょかん**[3]【所管】 所管官庁 the government office(s) responsible; the「competent [appropriate, proper] authority [authorities]; the authorities concerned.
**しょき**[1]【初期】 初期医療 initial (medical) care. 初期故障〔機械などの〕an initial malfunction; initial malfunctioning. 初期消火《a delay in》initial firefighting. 初期対応 an initial response. 初期負荷〔運動・機〕an initial load. 初期不良〔機械などの〕an initial defect.
**じょきゃく**【除却】 除却命令〔違法建築などに対する〕a demolition order.
**じょきょう**【助教】〔2007年の学校教育法改正によって大学に設けられた職制〕an assistant professorship;〔人〕an assistant professor.
**じょきょしょく**【除去食】〔アレルゲンを含む食材を使わない献立〕food [a diet] from which allergens have been removed. 完全除去食 an allergy-free [an allergen-free, a nonallergenic] diet. 除去食療法 therapy [treatment] based on removing allergens from the diet.
**じょきょしょくひん**【除去食品】〔アレルゲンを含む食材を使わない食品〕allergy-free [allergen-free, nonallergenic] food.
**じょきん**【除菌】 除菌イオン antimicrobial ions.
● イオン発生装置 an antimicrobial-ion generator. 除菌フィルター a sterilization filter.
**しょくいき**【職域】 職域加算〔共済年金の〕an occupational supplementary payment. 職域相当部分〔共済年金の〕the occupational element (in a government employee's pension). 職域団体 an interest group. 職域年金制度〔共済年金の〕an occupational pension plan;「an occupational pension scheme.
**しょくいく**[1]【食育】〔栄養教育〕nutrition education;〔正しい食生活を通じて心身を育むこと〕diet [dietary]

education.
しょくいく²【職育】1〔職業教育〕vocational 「education [training]」.
2〔職業と育児〕(women's) work and child-rearing; working and raising children. ▶職育近接 having one's workplace near 「somewhere to leave one's children [a kindergarten or nursery]」.
しょくいくきほんほう【食育基本法】〖法〗the Basic Law for Food Education.
しょくいくすいしんかいぎ【食育推進会議】〔食育の推進を図るために内閣府に設置された組織〕the (Cabinet Office) Council for Food Education Promotion.
しょくいくすいしんきほんけいかく【食育推進基本計画】〔食育推進会議が策定する〕the Basic Plan for the Promotion of Food Education.
しょぐう【処遇】▶処遇類型別指導〔受刑者に対する〕treating convicts through guidance according to type of crime.
しょくえん【食塩】▶食塩感受性〖医〗salt sensitivity. 食塩泉 a (common) salt spring (containing at least 1 gram of salt per liter of water). ▶含石膏重曹～泉 an alkaline salt spring containing calcium sulfate / 含石膏ホウ酸～泉 a salt spring containing calcium sulfate and boric acid.
しょくえん²【職縁】〔職場で付き合いのある人たちとの人間関係〕(social) relations in the workplace. ▶職縁社会 a society that 「sees workplace relations as important [values relations in the workplace]」.
しょくぎょう【職業】▶職業観 an [one's] opinion of [view of, outlook on] one's job [a job, work]. 職業差別 prejudice against a certain job. 職業設計 career design. 職業適性 vocational aptitude. ▶～適性診断 a vocational aptitude test. 職業不詳 ▶～不詳の男 a man of 「no known [unknown]」occupation /「警察は殺人の疑いで指名手配していた住所不定、～不詳の山田太郎容疑者(34)を東京都内で逮捕した。Police have arrested a man on the wanted list as a murder suspect; Yamada Tarō, aged 35, of no fixed abode and no known occupation. | Yamada Tarō, aged 35, a man of no fixed abode or known occupation and on the wanted list for murder, has been arrested by police in Tokyo.
しょくぎょうけん【職業犬】=さぎょうけん.
しょくご【食後】▶食後高血糖 high blood sugar after eating; 〖医〗postprandial hyperglycemia.
しょくざい【贖罪】▶贖罪教育〔刑務所など矯正施設での〕restitution education.
しょくじ¹【食事】
▶(お)食事会〔朝食〕a breakfast meeting;〔昼食〕a lunch meeting;〔夕食〕a dinner meeting.〔食事券・〕「meal [food] ticket [voucher]」. 食事性アレルギー〖医〗an alimentary allergy. 食事指導〔栄養指導の〕dietary instructions.（お）食事処 a「restaurant [cafeteria] (featuring Japanese food). 食事バランスガイド〔2005年、農水省と厚労省が作成、一日に何をどれだけ食べたらよいかをイラストで示したもの〕Japanese Food Guide; a guide to a balanced diet (produced by the Japanese Ministries of Agriculture and Health). 食事療養費〔入院患者の食当たりの〕a [the] charge per meal payable by hospitalized patients. 食事療養標準負担額〔被保険者の入院患者が負担する一食当たりの金額〕a [the] standard charge per meal payable by hospitalized patients.
しょくしゅ³【職種】▶職種転換 a change in one's line of work; reassignment 《of an employee》to a different type of work.
しょくじゅういったい【いったい】【職住一体[一致]】living and working in the same place; combined living and working《space》. ▶職住一体型住宅 a combined living and working housing unit.

しょくじゅうきんせつ【職住近接】▶職住近接型～型の都市 a city with housing near workplaces.
しょくじゅうせっきん【職住接近】〔職住近接〕having one's workplace near one's home.
しょくじゅうぶんり【職住分離】living and working in separate places.
しょくず【触図】〖図法〗tactile graphics;〔その図〕a tactile 「picture [diagram, graphic]」; a tactile.
しょくたく²【嘱託】▶嘱託警察犬 a privately trained dog registered as a police dog.
しょくちゅうしゅ【食中酒】drinking at mealtimes; 《have》a drink with one's meal(s).
しょくどう²【食道】▶食道静脈瘤破裂〖医〗rupture of esophageal varices. 食道挿管〖医〗esophageal intubation. 食道閉鎖(症)〖医〗esophageal atresia. 食道裂孔ヘルニア〖医〗an esophageal hiatal hernia.
しょくにく²【食肉】▶食肉衛生検査所 a meat inspection 「office [station]」.
しょくにん【職人】▶職人魂 the artisan spirit.
しょくにんわざ【職人技】a craftsman's 「technique [skill]」; (an example of) craftsmanship; fine craftsmanship;〔専門家の技〕professional 「skill [technique(s)]」. ▶この漆器は～が光る逸品だ。This piece is a consummate example of the lacquer maker's craftsmanship. ▶この見事な透かし彫りはまさに～だ。This magnificent openwork is 「an example of consummate craftsmanship [a wonderful piece of craftsmanship]」. | This wonderful openwork demonstrates the craftsman's 「exquisite skill [consummate mastery of her craft]」. / 彼のギターテクニックは～だ。He plays the guitar like a professional. | He has the guitar technique of a master.
しょくのう【職能】▶職能格 a competency 「level [category]」. 職能集団〔プロの集まり〕a professional group. 職能等級〔職務遂行能力レベルによる従業員の区分〕(a) performance rating.
しょくのう²【食農】diet and agriculture. ▶食農教育 dietary and agricultural education.
しょくば【職場】
▶職場進出〔特に女性の〕entry 《of women》to 「employment [the workplace, the job market]」. ▶女性の～進出は着実に進行している。The number of women entering the job market is increasing steadily. 職場ストレス stress in the workplace; workplace [occupational, job] stress. 職場体験 workplace experience; a temporary job placement (for students to experience a job). ▶学生のうちに～体験をする have [get] workplace experience while one is (still) a student. 職場適応〔障害者・中高齢者などの〕workplace adaptation 《for people with disabilities》. 職場適応援助者 =ジョブ・コーチ. 職場適応訓練〔障害者などの〕workplace adaptation training.
しょくばい【触媒】▶触媒被毒 catalyst poisoning.
しょくひん【食品】
▶食品安全部〔厚生労働省の〕the Department of Food Safety. ▶食品保健部 から改称。食品汚染 food contamination; food pollution. ▶～汚染物質 a food contaminant; a food pollutant. 食品工場 a food (-processing) factory. 食品スーパー(マーケット) a food (-based) supermarket. 食品廃棄率〔賞味期限切れ、食べ残などによる〕the rate [percentage] of food discarded. 食品照射〔放射線による〕food irradiation. 食品表示 a food label;〈集合的に〉food labeling. 食品表示ウォッチャー〔農林水産省の〕a food labeling 「watcher [monitor]」. 食品リコール〔メーカーによる不良食品の自主回収〕《initiate》a food recall. ▶～リコール(費用)保険 food recall insurance.
しょくひんあんぜんいいんかい【食品安全委員会】〔食品安全基本法に基づく〕the Food Safety Commission

(略: FSC).
**しょくひんあんぜんきほんほう**【食品安全基本法】〖法〗 the Food Safety Basic Law.
**しょくひんあんぜんけんさきょく**【食品安全検査局】〔米国農務省の〕the Food Safety Inspection Service (略: FSIS).
**しょくひんそうごうけんきゅうじょ**【食品総合研究所】the National Food Research Institute (略: NFRI).
**しょくひんはいきぶつリサイクルほう**【食品廃棄物リサイクル法】〖法〗 the Food Waste Recycling Law.
**しょくぶつ**【植物】 ▭ 植物育種学 plant breeding. 植物遺伝学 plant genetics. 植物エキス a plant extract. 植物ステロール〔フィトステロール〕phytosterol. ◐〜ステロール・エステル a plant sterol ester; a phytosterol ester. 植物生態雁 ⇨せいたい⁴. 植物プラスチック ＝バイオマス・プラスチック (⇨バイオマス). 植物由来成分[物質] a vegetable(-derived)「ingredient [substance].
**しょくぶつしんひんしゅほごこくさいどうめい**【植物新品種保護国際同盟】the International Union for the Protection of New Varieties of Plants (略: UPOV).
▶ UPOV はフランス語の Union internationale pour la protection des obtentions végétales の略.
**しょくぶつせい**【植物性】 ▭ 純植物性 ◐純〜の 100-percent [100%] vegetable (oil).
**しょくぶつのしんひんしゅのほごにかんするこくさいじょうやく**【植物の新品種の保護に関する国際条約】＝UPOV条約 (⇨ユー・ピー・オー・ブイ).
**しょくふん**【食糞】 〜する feed on dung; eat feces. ▭ 食糞行動 scatophagous [scatophagic] behavior. 食糞性(の) scatophagous [scatophagic, dung-eating] 《insects》.
**しょくほうしんしんがいしゃ**【触法精神障害者】〖法〗 a mentally ill offender.
**しょくむ**【職務】
▭ 職務経歴 one's 「working [professional, business] career [experience]. 職務経歴書 a professional CV (▶ CV は curriculum vitae の略); a record of one's working career; *a résumé. 職務行為 an「act [action] in the line of duty. 職務遂行能力 one's ability 「in the workplace [to carry out one's job]; one's effectiveness as a worker. 職務専念義務 the duty to「concentrate on [give one's undivided attention to] one's job. ◐〜違反 an infringement of one's duty to concentrate on one's job / 〜免除 being excused from [(an) exemption] from one's duty to concentrate on one's job. 職務犯罪 (an) occupational crime. 職務放棄 dereliction [abandonment, forsaking] of (one's) duty. 職務満足《経営》job [work] satisfaction.
**しょくもう**¹【植毛】 ▭ 植毛手術《美容》 a hair transplant (procedure).
**しょくよう**【食用】 ▭ 食用インク edible ink.
**しょくようほおずき**【食用酸漿】《植》〔ナス科の多年草〕a dwarf Cape gooseberry; a strawberry tomato; *Physalis pruinosa*.
**しょくよく**【食欲】 ▭ 食欲抑制ホルモン an appetite-suppressing hormone; an anorectic hormone.
**しょくりょう**¹【食料】 ▭ 食料需給表 a food balance sheet (略: FBS).
**しょくりょう**²【食糧】 ▭ (世界)食糧安全保障委員会〔国連の食糧農業機関(FAO)の〕the Committee on World Food Security. 食糧証券 a food financing bill.
**しょくりょうのうぎょうのうそんきほんけいかく**【食料・農業・農村基本計画】〔農林水産省の〕the Basic Plan on Food, Agriculture and Rural Areas.
**しょくりょうのうぎょうのうそんきほんほう**【食料・農業・農村基本法】〖法〗 the Basic Law on Food, Agriculture and Rural Areas.

**しょくりょう・のうぎょう・のうそんせいさくしんぎかい**【食料・農業・農村政策審議会】the Council of Food, Agriculture and Rural Area Policies. ▶ 2001年設置.
**しょくりょう・のうぎょう・のうそんはくしょ**【食料・農業・農村白書】〔農林水産省の〕the Annual Report on Food, Agriculture and Rural Areas in Japan 《2004》.
**しょくりょうひん**【食料品】 ▭ 食料品スーパー(マーケット) ＝食品スーパー(マーケット) (⇨しょくひん).
**しょくりん**【植林】 ▭ 植林ボランティア〔活動〕volunteer tree-planting (activities);〔人〕a tree-planting volunteer; a volunteer tree-planter.
**じょくん**²【叙勲】 ▭ 危険業務従事者叙勲〔警察官などの〕a decoration for people in high-risk occupations. 高齢者叙勲 a senior citizen's order of merit (awarded at the age of 88). 死亡叙勲 a posthumous「award [decoration]. 春秋叙勲 the spring and autumn decorations; awards「made [conferred] in the spring and autumn.
**じょけい**¹【女系】 ▭ 女系天皇 a female-line emperor (of Japan); a Japanese emperor from the female line.
**しょこう**⁴【諸侯】 ▭ 諸侯経済〔中国の〕《China's》little empire economies.
**しょこう**⁶【蹠行】《動》 ▭ 蹠行(の) plantigrade. 蹠行動物 a plantigrade.
**しょこう**⁷【初交】 first (sexual) intercourse; loss of virginity. ▭ (平均)初交年齢 the (average) age of first (sexual) intercourse; average age of losing virginity.
**しょこう**⁸【初稿】a [the] first draft. ◐その作家は〜を一気に書き上げた. The writer dashed off the first draft 「without a break [in a single sitting].
**しょごう**【初号】 ▭ 初号試写《映》the first (test [preview]) screening 《of a film》.
**じょこう**⁴【除睾】《医》〔睾丸摘出手術〕(an) orchiectomy; (an) orchidectomy.
〜する perform an「orchiectomy [orchidectomy]《on sb》.
「**ショコラ**」〔映画〕Chocolat.
**ショコラティエ**〔チョコレート職人[販売店]〕a chocolatier 《pl. 〜》.
**しょこん**【初婚】 ▭ 初婚率 the first marriage rate.
**しょざい**【所在】 ▭ 所在表示〔図〕a location「map [guide];〔一覧表〕a location list. 所在不明 ◐現在の書類は〜のままだ. The「location [whereabouts] of the document is currently unknown. | The document cannot be found at present. / 〜不明株主 an unlocatable shareholder; a stockholder of no known address; a stockholder whose whereabouts「is [are] unknown.
**じょさい**²【除災】 driving「off [away] misfortune; getting rid of bad luck. ▭ 除災招福 getting rid of misfortune and bringing good luck.
**じょさん**¹【助産】 ▭ 助産学 tocology; tokology; obstetrics. 助産行為 midwifery [obstetric] practice.
**じょしテニスきょうかい**【女子テニス協会】the Women's Tennis Association (略: WTA).
**しょじょ**²【処女】 ▭ 処女膜閉鎖(症)《医》(an) imperforate hymen; hymenal atresia.
**じょじょう**²【抒情・叙情】 ▭ 抒情画 lyricism;〔1枚の〕a lyric(al) painting.
**しょしん**²【初診】 ▭ 初診時特定療養費〔初診時に保険外負担分に追加される料金〕a special additional fee (not covered by insurance) for an initial「consultation [examination].
**じょせい**²【女性】
▭ 女性管理職比率 the ratio of women「in management [at management level]. 女性議員比率 the [a] ratio of women in the Diet. 女性就業率[有業率] a [the] female employment rate; the percentage of

women over fifteen in employment. 女性仕様車 a car 「designed with women in mind [for women]. 女性(専門)外来 【医】women's outpatient 「services [treatment]. 女性天皇 a female (Japanese) emperor; an empress (in her own right). 女性度 【心理】femininity. 女性法学 (a) feminist jurisprudence. 女性労働白書 a white paper on 「women's labor [working women]; the 《2005》White Paper on Women's Labor.

**じょせい**[5] 【助勢】 現場助勢罪 【法】= 傷害(現場)助勢罪. 傷害(現場)助勢罪【法】(aiding and) abetting [encouraging the commission of] bodily harm at the scene of the crime.

**じょせいき**【女性器】【解】the female genitalia; the female genital organs;《口》the female genitals. ▫️ 女性器切除〔主にアフリカなどで行われている慣習〕female genital 「mutilation [cutting] (略: FGM, FGC).

**じょせいざい**【除錆剤】(a) rust remover; a rust-removing agent.

**じょせいさべつてっぱいいいんかい**【女性差別撤廃委員会】[国連の] the Committee on the Elimination of Discrimination against Women (略: CEDAW).

**じょせいのじんけんホットライン**【女性の人権-】[法務省が各地に設置した電話相談機関] the Women's Rights Hotline.

**じょせいのためのアジアへいわこくみんききん**【女性のための平和国民基金】the Asian Women's Fund (略: AWF).

**じょせいのちいいいんかい**【女性の地位委員会】[国連の] = こくれんじょせいのちいいいんかい.

**じょせいのひ**【女性の日】[4月10日; 厚生労働省による] Women's Day (▶ 1998年に「婦人の日」から改称); [国際女性デー; 3月8日] International Women's Day.

**しょせき**【書籍】 ▫️ 書籍化 turning (a blog) into a book; publishing 《a blog》as a book.

**じょせき**【除籍】 ▫️ 除籍処分〔団体からの〕expulsion《from…》. ▫️ 彼は学費を払えず、大学を～処分となった. He was expelled from university because he could not pay his fees. / 彼女は党から～処分を受けた. She was expelled from her (political) party.

**じょせつ**[3]【除雪】 ▫️ 除雪ボランティア a snow removal volunteer.

**しょぞう**【所蔵】 ▫️ 所蔵家〔美術品などの〕an owner [a possessor]《of valuable paintings》. 所蔵作品 works in a collection. ▫️ ～作品目録 a catalog of works in a collection.

**じょそう**[5]【除草】 ▫️ 除草剤耐性 【農・化】herbicide tolerance. ▫️ ～剤耐性作物 a herbicide-tolerant crop.

**じょぞく**[3]【除族】 deprivation of a samurai's status; demotion to commoner status.

**ショタコン**〔少年に性的関心を抱くこと〕a sexual 「interest in [preference for] young boys; boy love.

**しょだん**[1]【処断】 ▫️ 処断刑 a discretionary 「sentence [penalty].

**しょち**【処置】 ▫️ 処置請求【法】a demand by a court for punitive measures to be taken against 「lawyers [prosecutors] who fail to follow due procedure.

**しょち**[2]【暑地】a hot region. ▫️ 暑地訓練 training in a hot 「region [environment]; hot-climate [hot-weather] training.

**「署長マクミラン」**〔米国の, 警察署長とその妻のTVドラマ〕McMillan and Wife.

**しょっかく**[3]【触覚】 ▫️ 触覚ディスプレー〔視覚障害者用の〕a 「tactile [haptic] display.

**しょっき**[1]【食器】 ▫️ 食器洗い乾燥機 a dish-washer and drier; a dish-washer/drier. 食器乾燥(器)【器】 a dish drier. 食器洗浄機 a dishwasher;「a washing-up machine. 食器洗浄乾燥機 = 食器洗い乾燥機. 食器用洗剤 (a) dish(-washing) detergent; dish-washing liquid.

**ショック** ▫️ ショックパンツ【医】〔加圧して血圧を維持するための上げるためのズボン〕medical antishock trousers (略: MAST).

**しょっこん**【食痕】signs of feeding;〔化石に残る〕feeding traces. ▫️ 木の幹に残る～からみて、この山には約300頭の鹿が生息していると推定できる. The eating marks left on the tree trunks suggest that some 300 deer live on this mountain.

**ショット** ▫️ スーパー・ショット〔ゴルフ・テニスなどで見事なショット〕a 「super [magnificent, superlative] shot.

**ショット・ピーニング**【金属加工】shot peening. ▫️ ショットピーニング機 a shot-peening machine; a shot peener.

**ショットブラスト**【金属加工】〔砥粒を吹きかけて表面処理を行う方法〕shot blasting; shotblasting. ▫️ ショットブラスト機 a shot-blasting machine; a shot blaster. ショットブラスト仕上げ a shot-blasted finish.

**ショッピング** ▫️ ショッピング・サイト〔インターネット上の〕[an Internet] shopping site. ショッピング番組 = テレビショッピング番組 (⇨テレビ). ショッピング・ローン = 個品割賦 (⇨かっぷ).

**ショップ** ▫️ ショップ袋〔店が宣伝を兼ねて買い物客に提供する〕a shop bag; a bag from a famous store.

**しょどう**[2]【書道】 ▫️ 書道教室〔学校〕a calligraphy school; a school that teaches calligraphy;〔授業〕a calligraphy 「class [course]; calligraphy lessons; lessons [a course, a class] in calligraphy. 書道塾 a calligraphy school.

**しょどうぎん**【書道吟】Chinese poetry recitation accompanied by calligraphy.

**しょとく**【所得】 ▫️ 所得移転 income transfer. ▫️ 世代間～移転 (an) intergenerational income transfer; passing on income from one generation to the next. 所得譲与税 an locally transferred income tax. 所得代替率〔現役時の手取り賃金と定年退職後に受け取る年金額の比〕an income replacement 「ratio [rate]. 所得弾力性 【経】income elasticity. 所得等報告書〔政治家・公職者などの〕an income 「statement [declaration]; a statement of income. 所得番付 income rankings; (a list of) the top《100》earners. ▫️ その年, 彼は～番付の作家部門で第1位になった. That year he came first in the income rankings for writers. 所得分布 personal income distribution (略: PID). 所得分布曲線 a graph of personal income distribution. 所得補償保険 income protection insurance.

**しょとくぜいほう**【所得税法】【法】the Income Tax Law. ▫️ 所得税法違反 (a) violation [(an) infringement] of the Income Tax Law; an income tax offense; (an) income tax violation; income tax irregularities. ▫️ ～違反で起訴される be prosecuted for an income tax violation.

**ジョニー・クエスト**〔アニメの主人公〕Jonny Quest. [⇨「冒険少年 JQ」]

**ショパール**〔商標〕〔スイスの宝飾品ブランド〕Chopard.

**じょはすいみん**【徐波睡眠】〔ノンレム睡眠の第3, 4段階〕slow-wave sleep (略: SWS).

**しょはつ**【初発】 ▫️ 初発患者【医】the 「first [initial, index] patient 《suffering from avian influenza in Japan》[case《of avian influenza in Japan》].

**しょばつ**【処罰】 ▫️ 処罰感情〔加害者の処罰を求める被害者の感情〕the desire of the victim of a crime, or of his or her relatives, for the perpetrator to be punished harshly. ▫️ 被告人の改悛(かいしゅん)の情が顕著なので, 被害者側の～感情もやわらいでいると思われる. Since the defendant shows strong signs of remorse, 「the victim has [the victim's family have] ceased to demand the maximum sentence. 処罰規定 punishment [penalty] regulations.

しょひ[2]【書皮】〔買った客に本を手渡す前にかける紙製ブックカバー〕an outer wrapper for a book (put on by a bookseller before being handed to a customer).

じょびかん【鋤鼻器官】〖解〗〔副嗅覚器で、性フェロモンの受容器〕the vomeronasal organ; Jacobson's organ.

ジョフィ Joffé, Roland (1945- ; 英国生まれの映画監督).

ジョブカフェ〔若者向け就職支援センター〕a "job café"; an employment information and consulting center for young people.

ショぶくろ【−袋】=ショップ袋 (⇨ショップ).

ジョブ・コーチ〔障害者のための職場適応支援員〕a job coach《for the disabled》.

ジョブズ Jobs, Steven Paul (1955- ; 米国の企業家).

ジョブレス・リカバリー〖経〗〔雇用なき景気回復〕(a) jobless recovery. ▶ 景気が回復しているにもかかわらず、雇用の回復が見られない状態。

しょぶん【処分】 ▫▫ 内部処分〔社内・学内など〕an internal 「punishment [disciplinary action]. ▫▫ 処分価格 a clearance price. ◐ 在庫〜価格 a stock clearance price / 最終〜価格 a final clearance price. 処分取り消し cancellation of a punishment. 処分保留 a suspended indictment. ◐ 逮捕された男性は、その後〜保留で釈放された. The man who was arrested was later released with a suspended indictment. 処分量定〔処罰の〕determination of punishment.

しょほう[1]【処方】 ▫▫ 処方ミス[過誤]〖薬〗a prescribing error.

じょほう[3]【徐放】 ▫▫ 徐放性〔薬の成分の〕sustained [controlled, delayed, extended, timed] release. 徐放(性)カプセル a sustained-[extended-]release capsule. 徐放(製)剤, 徐放薬 a sustained-release drug. 徐放錠 an extended-release tablet.

しょほうせん【処方箋】 ▫▫ 処方箋医薬品 a 「prescription [prescription-only] drug; an ethical drug. ▶ 「要指示医薬品」から改称.

しょみん【庶民】 ▫▫ 庶民文化 popular culture; culture of the common people.

しょめい[2]【署名】 ▫▫ 反対署名 a signature against sth. ◐ 3,000人の反対〜を取り付ける raise 3,000 signatures against (sth). ▫▫ 署名集め[活動] 〔署名運動〕a signature(-collecting) campaign; a petition drive. 署名式 a ceremony of signing; a signing ceremony.

じょめい[2]【除名】 ▫▫ 除名処分 ◐ 規則に違反した会員を〜処分にする expel a member who has violated the rules / 〜処分を受ける be expelled.

しょめん【書面】 ▫▫ 書面審査〔書類審査〕screening of documents; 〔書類選考〕selection [screening] of candidates by examining their 「report cards [personal histories] (before further examination); 《fail》a document screening. 書面審査員 《a test, an application》document 「screener [referee].

ジョモ・ケニヤッタこくさいくうこう【−国際空港】〔ケニア、ナイロビの国際空港〕Jomo Kenyatta International Airport.

しょゆう[2]【所有】 ▫▫ 所有代名詞 a possessive pronoun.

しょゆうけん【所有権】 ▫▫ 所有権移転登記〔移転登記〕registration of a (land) transfer; registration of a transfer《of sb's estate to one》. 所有権放棄 relinquishment [abandonment] of ownership rights.

しょゆうしゃ【所有者】 ▫▫ 所有者不明土地 land of unknown ownership.

しょよう[2]【所要】 ▫▫ 所要資金 necessary funds.

ジョリー Jolie, Angelina (1975- ; 米国の映画女優; 本名 Angelina Jolie Voight; ジョン・ヴォイトの子).

しょりょうび【初猟日】 the opening day of hunting season; the hunting opener.

ジョル Joll, James (1918-94; 英国の政治・歴史学者).

じょれい[3]【除霊】(an) exorcism; spirit banishment.

じょれつ【序列】 ▫▫ 序列化 ranking. ◐ 最近、公立高校の〜化が進行している. There is an increasing tendency for public high schools to be 「arranged in a hierarchy [ranged hierarchically].

ジョン〖料理〗〔韓国料理; 衣をつけた焼き物〕jeon.

ジョン・ウー John Woo (1946- ; 中国生まれの映画監督・脚本家・製作者; 中国語名 呉宇森).

ジョンストン Johnston, Joe (1950- ; 米国の映画監督).

ジョンソン Johnson, Mark Steven (1964- ; 米国の映画監督).

シラー[2]〖植〗〔ユリ科シラー属〔ツルボ属〕の総称〕a scilla.

じらい[1]【地雷】 ▫▫ ちょうちょ地雷 =バタフライ地雷. バタフライ地雷〔空中散布式の地雷〕a butterfly mine. 地雷処理 demining. 〜処理機 demining equipment; a demining machine. 地雷除去作業 a 「mine clearance [mine-clearing] operation.

じらいたいさくちょうせいセンター【地雷対策調整−】〔国連〕a UN Mine Action Coordination 「Center [Centre].

しらかばたけ【白樺茸】〖菌〗〔南〕=かばのあなたけ.

しらさぎかやつり【白鷺蚊帳吊り】〖植〗〔カヤツリグサ科の水辺植物〕a star rush; star grass; white-top [white topped] sedge; *Dichromena colorata*; *Rhynchospora colorata*.

じらし【焦らし】〔じらすこと〕needling; teasing; irritation. ▫▫ じらし戦法〔戦術〕a teaser strategy; a strategy of needling (sb into doing).

しらすうなぎ【幼鰻・白子鰻】〖魚〗〔ウナギの稚魚〕an elver; a young eel.

シリカライト〖化〗silicalite.

じりき[2]【自力】 ▫▫ 自力再建〔企業の〕reconstruction 「under one's own power [without outside help]; independent reconstruction. 自力走行 running under its own 「power《口》steam》. ◐ 〜走行する run under its own 「power《口》steam》/ 東京発博多行きの「のぞみ9号」が、名古屋駅の1キロ手前で突然止まり、〜走行ができなくなった. Nozomi No. 9 from Tokyo bound for Hakata stopped suddenly one kilometer before Nagoya Station and was unable to proceed under its own power. 自力優勝 (a) victory through one's own exertions; an unaided 「win [victory]. ◐ この負けで、チームの〜優勝の望みはなくなった. This defeat means that the team won't be able to win the series even if they win all the remaining games.

シリマンガン〔合金鉄の一種〕silicomanganese.

シリコン ▫▫ シリコン太陽電池 a silicon solar cell. シリコン・チューブ〖化〗a silicone tube; 〈集合的に〉silicone tubing. シリコン半導体 a silicon semiconductor. シリコン・メモリー〖電算〗(a) silicon memory.

しりたたき【尻叩き】(a) spanking; 〔強い働きかけ〕strong 「encouragement [urging].

じりつ[2]【自立】 ▫▫ 自立支援 self-reliance support. ◐ 〜支援施設 a self-reliance support facility. 自立支援プログラム a program to support self-reliance.

じりつ[3]【自律】 ▫▫ 自律航法〔外部からの信号に頼らず正しい進路を選択するシステム〕dead reckoning.

じりついどうしえんプロジェクト【自立移動支援−】〔障害者・外国人などに対する国土交通省の〕the autonomous mobility support project.

しりつがっこうきょうしょくいんきょうさいくみあい【私立学校教職員共済組合】the Mutual Aid Association of Private School Personnel.

しりつがっこうしんこうじょせいほう【私立学校振興助成法】〖法〗the Private 「School [Educational Institution] Promotion Subsidy Law.

しりつがっこうほう【私立学校法】〖法〗the Private School Law.

じりつほこう【自立歩行】unassisted [unaided] walk-

ing; walking without「help [assistance]; walking on one's own;〖医〗unassisted ambulation.
〜する walk without「help [assistance, support]; walk on one's own;〖医〗ambulate unassisted. ◨自立歩行型ロボット a robot that can walk unassisted.
ジリノフスキー Zhirinovsky, Vladimir Volfovich (1946− ;ロシアの政治家).
しりょう[6]【資料】 ◨資料館 a museum: a library; an archive; a record office. 資料集〖教科書の副読本の一種〗a collection of materials; a set of (compiled) materials.
しりょう[7]【飼料】 ◨化学[合成]飼料 chemical [synthetic] feed. ◨飼料汚染〖家畜の〗feed contamination.
しりょく[2]【視力】 ◨中心外視力 =〖周辺視力〗peripheral vision. 低視力 ⇨ていしりょく.
シリンガレシノール〖化〗〖抗酸化物質〗syringaresinol.
シリンダー ◨シリンダー・フィン〖機〗〖エンジンの〗a cylinder fin. シリンダー・ブロック〖機〗〖エンジンの〗a cylinder block.
シルヴァーストーン Silverstone, Alicia (1976− ;米国の映画女優).
ジルガ〖アフガニスタンの伝統的長老会議〗a jirga.
ジルコニウム ◨炭化ジルコニウム zirconium carbide (記号: ZrC).
ジル・ド・レ Gilles de Rais (1404–40; フランスの軍人; 悪魔主義・誘拐・幼児殺害の罪で刑死; 聖なる怪物 (the Pious Monster) と呼ばれた).
シルバー[1] ◨シルバー・ゴール《サッカー》〖延長戦の一方式〗前半 15 分を終えた時点で得点差がなければ、後半 15 分を戦う. 1 点が入った時点で試合終了ではない〗the silver goal rule;〖その方式に基づいたゴール〗a silver goal. シルバーワー the power of the elderly; old people's「energy [vigor]. シルバー110 番〖高齢者とその家族への相談サービス〗a「helpline [telephone counselling service] for the elderly and their families.
シルバーストーン =シルヴァーストーン.
シルバーリング Silberling, Brad (1963− ;米国の映画監督).
シルミド【実尾島】〖韓国の島〗Silmido; Silmi Island.
「シルミド」〖映画〗Silmido.
シルム〖韓国相撲〗ssireum; traditional Korean wrestling.
シレット〖バングラデシュ北東部の町〗Sylhet.
しれとこすみれ【知床菫】〖植〗〖スミレ科の多年草〗Viola kitamiana.
しろあごがえる【動】a white-lipped tree frog; Polypedates leucomystax.
しろあじさし【白鯵刺】〖鳥〗〖カモメ科の海鳥〗a white tern; Gygis alba.
シロアムのトンネル〖エルサレムにある古代地下水路〗the Siloam Tunnel.
しろあり【白蟻】 ◨シロアリ商法〖点検商法の1つ〗"termite scam"; a scam in which a door-to-door caller pretends to find termites and persuades the homeowner to sign an expensive contract to exterminate them, or to ventilate and dry out the area beneath the floors. 白蟻塚 a termite mound.
しろいんげん(まめ)【白隠元(豆)】〖植〗a white kidney bean.
しろう[2]【脂漏】 ◨脂漏性角化症〖医〗(a) seborrheic keratosis. 脂漏性皮膚炎〖医〗seborrheic dermatitis.
じろうがき【次郎柿】〖植〗〖カキの一品種; 静岡県原産〗a Jiro persimmon.
じろうかじゃ【次郎冠者】Jirōkaja; a common name for a manservant in「kyōgen [Noh farce].
しろオリックス【白−】〖動〗〖アフリカ産レイヨウの一種〗a scimitar-horned oryx; Oryx dammah.
しろがおザキ【白顔−】〖動〗〖オマキザル科のサル〗a white-faced saki; Pithecia pithecia.
シロガネーゼ〖東京・白金周辺に住む金持ちの主婦〗a wealthy woman who lives in Shirogane, Tokyo; a "Shiroganese."
しろきじ[2]【白木地】plain (unlacquered) wood;〖製品〗unlacquered woodwork.
しろぐすり【白釉】〖製陶〗(a) white glaze.
しろじ【白地】 ◨白地地域〖線引き都市の市街化調整区域〗a no land-use「zoning [regulation] area;〖非線引き都市で用途地域の指定がない区域〗an outside of「city [urban] planning area; an outside of zoning area.
しろしょうぞく【白装束】 ◨白装束団〖パナウェーブ研究所の〗the white-clad group.
しろずみ【白炭】〖かたずみ〗hard white charcoal.
ジロ・デ・イタリア〖イタリアの長距離自転車レース〗Giro d'Italia.
しろとび【白飛び】〖写真〗〖露出オーバーで画像が白くなってしまうこと〗whiteout; overexposure; blooming; blocked-up whites.
しろぬけ【白抜け】〖印刷〗(a) solid black [a black background] with white microdots.
「白バイ野郎ジョン&パンチ」〖米国の、白バイ警官の TV ドラマ〗CHiPs. ▶ CHiPs は California Highway Patrol の頭文字.
しろはらくいな【白腹水鶏】〖鳥〗a white-breasted water hen; Amaurornis phoenicurus.
しろはらぐんかんどり【白腹軍艦鳥】〖鳥〗a Christmas Island frigate bird; Fregata andrewsi.
シロビキ〖旧ソ連の軍部・KGB・警察出身の政治家〗the siloviki;〖1 人〗a silovik.
しろびょうし(ぼん)【白表紙(本)】〖文部科学省による教科書検定のために作られた、書名・発行者名・著者名などの書いていない教科書原本〗a plain-cover draft edition of a school textbook (submitted to the Ministry of Education for approval).
しろぼし【白星】 ◨白星スタート 〜スタートを切る start 《the season》with a win.
しろホリ(ゾン)【白−】〖撮影のための真っ白の背景〗a white「background [backdrop].
シロリムス〖薬〗〖免疫抑制剤〗sirolimus.
しろロム【白−】〖電話番号がまだ設定されていない携帯電話端末〗an unprogrammed cellphone.
しろわに【白鰐】〖魚〗〖オオワニザメ科のサメ〗a sand tiger (shark); a gray nurse shark; Carcharias taurus.
しわけ[2]【仕訳】〖簿〗journalizing.
〜する enter [record] in a journal; journalize. ◨仕訳帳 a journal. 〜帳に記入する enter [record] in a journal; journalize.
しわすのおおはらえ【師走大祓】〖12 月 31 日に行われる大祓〗a winter purification rite; a traditional Shinto purification ceremony held on December 31.
シン Singh, Manmohan (1932− ; インドの政治家; 首相 (2004− )).
じん[4]【陣】 ◨女性陣 the female「staff [participants, members]; the women in the 《office》. 男性陣 the male「staff [participants, members]; the men in the 《office》.
じん[5]【尽】 ◨晦日(みそか)〗the last day of the month. ◨七月〜 the last day of July.
しんアジェンダれんごう【新−連合】〖1998 年に結成されたブラジル・エジプト・アイルランド・メキシコ・ニュージーランド・南アフリカ・スウェーデン・スロベニアの 8 か国からなる非核保有国連合〗the New Agenda Coalition (略: NAC). ▶ スロベニアはのちに離脱.
じんい[1]【人為】 ◨人為ミス (a) human error.
しんイラクぐん【新−軍】〖連合国暫定当局 (CPA) が創設したイラク治安維持のための軍隊〗the new Iraqi army.
じんいん【人員】 ◨人員過剰 a personnel surplus; surplus personnel; overstaffing; too many「workers

[employees, staff]. 人員配置 (a) personnel [assignment [placement, deployment]]. 人員不足 a personnel shortfall; insufficient personnel; undermanning; understaffing; not enough [too few] workers [employees, staff].
じんう【腎盂】 ◻ 腎盂がん 〖医〗(a) cancer [carcinoma] of the renal pelvis; (a) renal pelvis cancer.
しんうちゅう【深宇宙】 ◻ 深宇宙港〔宇宙航空研究開発機構が構想中の〕the Deep Space Harbor; the Gateway to Space.
じんえい²【陣営】 ◻ 対立[ライバル]陣営 an opposing [a rival] camp.
しんエネルギーとうでんきりようほう【新-等電気利用法】〖法〗=しんエネルギーりようとくそちほう.
しんエネルギーりようとくべつそちほう【新-利用特別措置法】〖法〗the Special Measures Law for Promoting the Use of New Energy. [⇨アール・ピー・エスほう]
しんえんど【真円度】circularity; roundness. ◻ 真円度測定 roundness measurement. 真円度測定器 a roundness measuring [instrument [system, machine, tester]; roundness measurement equipment.
しんか⁸【進化】 ◻ 進化発生生物学 evolutionary developmental biology; evolution of development; evo-devo.
シンガー Singer, Bryan (1966- ; 米国の映画監督).
しんかい【深海】 ◻ 深海探査 deep-sea exploration. 深海油田 a deep-sea oil field.
しんがい⁵【侵害】 ◻ 侵害受容性疼痛〖医〗nociceptive pain. 侵害責任〔著作権の〕copyright infringement liability; liability for [copyright infringement [infringement of copyright]. ◻ 寄与~責任〖米法〗liability for contributory infringement / 代位~責任〖米法〗vicarious infringement liability.
しんがい⁴【震害】damage [caused by [from] an earthquake; earthquake [seismic] damage. ◻ 震害調査 an earthquake [a seismic] damage survey; (an) earthquake damage assessment.
じんかくほう【人確法】〖法〗=じんざいかくほほう.
じんがん【腎癌】〖医〗〔腎臓がんの一種〕a nephroblastoma 《pl. ~s, -mata》.
しんがた【新型】 ◻ 新型インフルエンザ a new type of [influenza [flu]. 新型肺炎〔サーズ; 重症急性呼吸器症候群〕SARS; severe acute respiratory syndrome.
しんかぶ¹【新株】 ◻ 新株発行 a new [share [stock] issue; the issuance of new shares. 新株予約権〔転換社債権・新株引受権・ストックオプションの総称〕a call option.
シンガポール・スリング〔カクテル〕a Singapore sling.
しんがん³【真贋】 ◻ 真贋問題 the question of 《a painting's》authenticity.
しんかんせん【新幹線】 ◻ フル規格新幹線 the [full [full-standard, full-gauge] Shinkansen. ミニ新幹線 the mini-Shinkansen; the narrow-gauge Shinkansen. ◻ 新幹線電気軌道総合試験車 a Shinkansen electric and track inspection train; a Shinkansen high-speed test train. 新幹線ホテル〔事故などによる列車不通時にホテル代わりに使用される新幹線車両〕a Shinkansen car used for sleeping in (when services are stopped).
じんかんセンサー【人感~】〔人などの動きを感知するセンサー〕a human sensor. ◻ 人感センサー付き照明 a motion [sensor [detector] light.
しんかんせんとくれいほう【新幹線特例法】〖法〗the (Special) [Law [Ordinance, Regulations] on Threats to Safety on the Shinkansen [Bullet Train]. ▶ 正式名称は「新幹線鉄道における列車の安全を妨げる行為の処罰に関する特例法」.
しんき⁶【新規】 ◻ 新規株式公開 an initial public offering (略: IPO). 新規契約 a new contract.
しんぎ⁹【審議】 ◻ 審議委員会 a review committee.

審議官級協議 deputy minister-level talks. 審議日程 a discussion schedule; a [timetable [schedule] for [discussion [deliberation].
ジンキー【<zebra + donkey》〖動〗〔オスのシマウマとメスのロバから生まれた動物〕a zenkey.
〘新規航空会社〙a new airline.
しんきゅう¹【鍼灸・針灸】 ◻ 鍼灸マッサージ acupuncture, moxibustion and massage. ◯ ~マッサージ師 an acupuncture, moxibustion and massage therapist.
シンギュラー・ワイヤレス〔米国の携帯電話会社〕Cingular Wireless.
しんきょうほう【新京報】〔中国の日刊紙〕the Beijing News.
シンキル〔インドネシア, アチェ州, アチェ・シンキル県の県都〕Singkil.
しんきん¹【心筋】 ◻ 心筋焼灼術〔カテーテルによる不整脈の根治療法の1つ〕catheter ablation. ◯ 経皮的中隔心筋~焼灼術 percutaneous transluminal septal myocardial ablation (略: PTSMA).
しんくう【真空】 ◻ 真空容器 a vacuum [vessel [chamber].
じんぐうつつじ【神宮躑躅】〖植〗〔ツツジ科の落葉低木〕Rhododendron sanctum.
シン・クライアント【電算】〔サーバーにその機能の多くを依拠する, ハードディスクなしのコンピューター〕a thin client.
シングリッシュ〔シンガポール英語〕Singapore English; Singlish.
シングル¹ ◻ シングル志向〔独身志向〕a preference to stay single. シングル率 =独身率 (⇨どくしん³).
「ジングル・オール・ザ・ウェイ」〔映画〕Jingle All the Way.
シングルトン Singleton, John (1968- ; 米国の映画監督・俳優).
シンクロトロン ◻ シンクロトロン加速器 a synchrotron accelerator.
シンクロ(ナイズド)いたとびこみ【-板飛び込み】synchronized springboard diving. ◯ 女子 3 メートル~ the women's three-meter synchronized springboard diving.
シンクロ(ナイズド)たかとびこみ【-高飛び込み】synchronized platform diving. ◯ 男子 10 メートル~ the men's ten-meter synchronized platform diving.
シンクロニシティー〔共時性〕synchronicity.
しんけい¹【神経】
◻ 神経因性疼痛〖医〗neuropathic pain. 神経温存手術〖医〗nerve-preserving surgery. 神経回路機能 a neural network function. 神経芽腫〖医〗〔神経芽細胞腫〕neuroblastoma. 神経管閉鎖障害〖医〗a neural tube defect (略: NTD). 神経言語プログラミング〖心理〗neuro-linguistic programming (略: NLP). 神経工学 neural engineering; neuro-engineering. 神経鞘腫（しょう）〖医〗neurilemoma; neurinoma. 神経線維腫〖医〗neurofibromatosis. 神経線維腫症〖医〗[=レックリングハウゼンびょう]. 神経年齢 (a [one's]) neural age. 神経変性疾患〖医〗a neurodegenerative disease.
しんけいえん【神経炎】 ◻ 慢性炎症性脱髄性多発根神経炎 chronic inflammatory demyelinating polyneuropathy (略: CIDP).
しんけいげん【神経原】 ◻ 神経原性疼痛〖医〗neurogenic [neuropathic] pain.
しんけいこう¹【神経膠】 ◻ 神経膠芽腫 glioblastoma.
しんけいすいじゃく【神経衰弱】 ◻ 神経衰弱状態 (be in) a state of nervous breakdown.
しんけっかん【心血管】 ◻ 心血管障害 a cardiovascular disorder. 心血管病, 心血管疾患 (a) cardiovascular disease.
ジンゲロール〖化〗〔ショウガの辛味成分の1つ〕gingerol.
しんけん⁵【親権】 ◻ 共同親権 joint parental authority. 単独親権 sole parental authority. ◻ 親権争い

a 《bitter》 custody fight. 親権終了 termination of parental authority. 親権喪失 〖法〗loss of parental authority. ◐ ~喪失宣告〖法〗a declaration of loss of parental authority. 親権代行者〖法〗a representative of a legal guardian (of a minor). 親権停止〖法〗suspension of parental authority.

**しんげん**[5]【震源】◐ 震源断層〖地質〗a seismogenic [an earthquake-producing, an earthquake source] fault.

**じんけん**[3]【人権】◐ 新しい人権〔日本国憲法で新たに保障すべきだと言われている権利；プライバシー権、環境権など〕new human rights (proposed for inclusion in the Constitution). ◐▯ 人権委員会 a human rights「commission [committee]；〔国連の〕the United Nations Commission on Human Rights. ▶ 2006 年、国連人権理事会に改組. 人権意識 (an) awareness of human rights; human rights awareness. 人権活動 human rights activities. ◐ ~活動家 a human rights activist. 人権救済 human rights「relief [redress]. ◐ ~救済を申し立てる demand「relief [redress] for a human rights violation / ~救済制度 a human rights relief system. 人権軽視 (a) lack of respect for human rights; (a) contempt for human rights; not taking human rights seriously. 人権啓発企業連絡会 the Industrial Federation for Human Rights, 《Tokyo》. 人権賞 a human rights award. 人権団体 a human rights organization; an organization for human rights. 人権担当大使〔国際会議などに派遣される人権問題専任の〕a human rights ambassador; an ambassador in charge of human rights. 人権無視 (a) disregard for human rights.

**しんけんぽうきそういいんかい**【新憲法起草委員会】〔自民党の〕the constitution drafting committee (of the Liberal Democratic Party).

**じんけんりじかい**【人権理事会】〔国連の〕the (United Nations) Human Rights Council (略: UNHRC).

**しんこう**[2]【侵攻】◐▯ 全面侵攻《launch》an all-out invasion.

**しんこう**[8]【進行】◐▯ 進行がん〖医〗advanced cancer.

**しんこう**[15]【新興】◐▯ 新興経済圏 an emerging economic bloc. 新興独立国 a newly independent state.

**しんごう**【信号】◐▯ 感応式信号 ⇨かんのう[7]. 信号エラー an errant [a false] signal; a false alarm. 信号故障〔鉄道などの〕(a) signal(ing)「failure [breakdown]. 信号冒進〖鉄道〗proceeding through a red light.

**じんこう**[1]【人口】◐▯ 高校卒業人口 the「'high-school-graduate ['school-leaving] population; the population of 「'high-school graduates ['school leavers]. 十八歳人口 the 18-year-old population; the population of 18-year-olds. 生産人口 the [a] productive population; 〔生産年齢人口〕the「working-age [productive] population; the (total) number of people of working age. 非生産人口 the [a] nonproductive population; the nonproductive part of the population. ◐▯ 人口カバー率 a population coverage rate. 人口減少時代 a period of population decrease. 人口減(少)社会 a society with a decreasing population. 人口集中 population concentration; concentration of the population (in urban areas). 人口置換水準〖置換率〗〖社会・統計〗a [the] population replacement「level [rate]. 人口普及率 a population penetration rate.

**じんこう**[2]【人工】◐▯ 人工育雛 artificial brooding 《of chicks》. 人工関節置換術〖医〗implant arthroplasty; artificial joint replacement (surgery); an artificial joint replacement. 人工肝臓 an artificial liver. 人工観葉植物 an artificial「leafy [decorative] plant. 人工降雪機 a snowmaker; a snowmaking machine. 人工酵素〖生化〗

a synthetic enzyme. 人工股関節 an artificial hip joint. 人工栽培 artificial cultivation 《of *matsutake*》. 人工増殖 artificial breeding. 人工知能システム an「artificial intelligence [AI] system. 人工知能ロボット an「artificial intelligence [AI] robot. 人工知能ソフト《ウェア》artificial intelligence [AI] software. 人工内耳 a cochlear implant. 人工肺 an artificial lung. 人工干渇 artificial [man-made] wetlands. 人工微生物 a synthetic microbe. 人工網膜〖眼科〗an artificial retina; an AR. 人工網膜チップ〖眼科〗an artificial (silicon) retina chip; an AR chip; an ATC; an ASRC.

**しんごううん**【信号運】◐ 今日はどうも ~ が悪い. 〔赤信号が多い〕I've been「having bad luck with [missing all] the signals today. | I've been hitting a lot of red lights today.

**しんこうきょうけいえい**【新公共経営】〖行政・経〗new public management (略: NPM).

**しんこうせい**【進行性】◐▯ 進行性核上性麻痺〖医〗progressive supranuclear palsy (略: PSP). 進行性化骨筋炎〖医〗progressive ossifying myositis. ▶ 人名「進行性骨化性線維異形成症」これのラテン語名 fibrodysplasia ossificans progressiva の頭文字を取って FOP と略されることもある. 進行性骨化性線維異形成症〖医〗＝進行性化骨炎. 進行性認知症〖医〗progressive dementia.

**しんこうせん**【新合繊】a new synthetic fiber.

**しんこうどうしゅぎ**【新行動主義】〖心理〗neobehaviorism. ◐▯ 新行動主義心理学 neobehaviorism; neobehavioristic psychology.

**じんこうはまく**【人工破膜】〖医〗〔卵膜の切開〕(an) amniotomy; (an) artificial rupture of (the) membranes; (an)「ARM [AROM].

**しんごうむし**【信号無視】ignoring a「(traffic) signal [red light].
~(を)する ignore a (traffic) signal; *(口)* run a red light; "(口) jump the lights; 〔歩行者が〕jaywalk. ◐ 彼は ~ で警官に制止された. He was stopped by a police officer for going through a red light.

**しんこほん**【新古本】〔出版社から流れた新品の処分本〕a new book sold at a marked-down price.

**シンコロブエこうざん**【-鉱山】〔コンゴ民主共和国南東部の鉱山〕the Shinkolobwe Mine.

**しんごん**【真言】◐ 真言密教 Shingon esoteric teachings; esoteric Buddhist teachings of the Shingon sect.

**しんごんしゅう**【真言宗】the *Shingon* sect of Buddhism; *Shingon* Buddhism.

**しんさ**[2]【審査】◐▯ 審査員特別賞 a「judges [judges'] special award. 審査ミス a screening「error [failure].

**しんさい**[2]【震災】◐▯ 震災関連死 an earthquake-related「death [fatality]. 震災時帰宅支援マップ a "returning home in times of disaster" support map; a post-disaster escape route map.

**じんざい**【人材】◐▯ 人材確保 personnel procurement. 人材教育 personnel「training [education]. 人材供給 a supply of personnel. ◐ ~供給源 a source of personnel. 人材交流 personnel exchange. ◐ ~交流プログラム a personnel exchange program. 人材情報誌 a job seeker's information magazine. 人材争奪戦 (a) headhunting competition. 震災対策用救助車 a earthquake disaster response rescue vehicle. 人材投資 investment in human resources. ◐ ~投資促進税制 a tax system「favoring [promoting] human resource(s) investment.

**じんざいかくほほう**【人材確保法】〖法〗the Educational Personnel Procurement Law. ▶ 正式名称は「学校教育の水準の維持向上のための義務教育諸学校の教育職員の人材確保に関する特別措置法」(the Special Measures Law Concerning the Securing of Capable Educational Personnel in Compulsory Education Schools

for the Maintenance and Enhancement of School Education Standards.
しんさんぎょうとし【新産業都市】〔1962年施行の新産業都市建設促進法により指定された都市〕a new industrial city.
しんさんしき【晋山式】〖仏教〗〔新しく任命された住職の着任式〕the inauguration ceremony for the head priest of a temple.
しんし[8]【震死】〔落雷で死ぬこと〕(a) death by lightning. 〔=落雷死 (⇨らくらい)〕
しんじ[5]【神事】▫ 神事芸能 an entertainment performed at a Shinto ritual.
じんじ[1]【人事】▫ 人事案件 a plan for (a) personnel change; 《propose》a change of personnel. 人事畑 the「human resources [personnel] field. ▶ 彼はその会社で一貫して～畑を歩んできた。He has worked in human resources for his entire time at that company.
じんじいん【人事院】▫ 人事院規則 (the) National Personnel Authority Regulations.
しんじぎょうそうしゅつそくしんほう【新事業創出促進法】〖法〗the Law for the Promotion of New Business Creation.
しんしこう【新思考】▫ 新思考外交 new-thinking diplomacy.
しんしっかん【心疾患】〖医〗a heart「disorder [problem, ailment]; (a) heart disease; heart trouble. ▫ 心疾患集中治療室 a「cardiac [(冠疾患) coronary] care unit (略: CCU).
「真実の行方」〔映画〕Primal Fear.
「シン・シティ」〔映画〕Sin City.
しんしゃ[3]【新車】▫ 新車販売実績 new car sales; sales of new cars.
ジンジャー〔セグウェイの開発中の名称〕Ginger. 〔⇨セグウェイ〕
ジンジャー・クッキー〔ショウガ入りクッキー〕*a ginger (bread) cookie; "a ginger biscuit; (特に人形などの形をした) *a gingerbread man; (薄焼きの) *a gingersnap; "a ginger nut.
しんジャガ【新-】a new potato.
しんじゅ[2]【真珠】▫ 本真珠 a「genuine [true] pearl. 無核真珠 a seedless pearl. 〔⇨芥子パール (⇨けし)〕▫ 真珠腫性中耳炎〖医〗cholesteatoma otitis media.
じんしゅ【人種】▫ 人種ハラスメント racial harassment.
しんじゅう[1]【心中】▫ 偽装心中 a murder disguised as a「double-suicide [suicide pact].
しんじゅうごごう【神舟5号】〔中国初の有人宇宙船; 2003年10月に打ち上げ成功〕Shenzhou V.
しんじゅうじぐん【新十字軍】a new crusade; new crusaders.
しんしゅく[1]【伸縮】▫ 伸縮素材〔衣服などの〕(a) stretchable「material [fabric].
しんしゅくせい【伸縮性】▫ 伸縮性素材 ＝伸縮素材 (⇨しんしゅく[1]).
しんしゅつ[2]【浸出】▫ 浸水 seeping water; 〖環境〗〔産業廃棄物の埋め立て処分場からの〕seeping leachate. ▶ ～水処理 seeping leachate treatment / ～水処理施設 a seeping leachate treatment facility.
しんしゅつ[3]【滲出】exudation; effusion. ～する exude; seep (out). ▫ 滲出液〔物〕(an) exudate. 滲出性 weeping; exudative. 滲出性胸膜炎〖医〗exudative pleurisy; pleurisy with effusion. 滲出性湿疹〖医〗weeping [exudative] eczema. 滲出性体質〖医〗exudative diathesis. 滲出性中耳炎〖医〗otitis media with effusion (略: OME); secretory otitis media (略: SOM); glue ear.
「真珠の耳飾りの少女」〔フェルメール作の絵画〕Girl with a Pearl Earring.
しんじょ[3]【糝薯】〖料理〗a kind of fish-cake made from ground fish or prawn combined with grated yam, flavored and steamed or boiled; *shinjo*. ▫ 海老しんじょ shrimp [prawn, lobster] *shinjo*. ▫ しんじょ揚げ deep-fried *shinjo*.

しんしょう[1]【心証】▫ 心証形成〔裁判官の〕establishing [assessing, forming an assessment as to] the degree of culpability 《of a defendant》.
しんしょう[7]【親称】〔親しみをこめた二人称代名詞〕an informal [a familiar] second person pronoun.
しんじょう[2]【身上】▫ 身上把握《have》a command of the facts about *sb's* personal background.
しんじょう[8]【真蒸】〖料理〗＝しんじょ[3].
しんじょうせい【尋常性】▫ 尋常性乾癬〖医〗psoriasis vulgaris.
じんじょうせいはくはん【尋常性白斑】〖医〗vitiligo vulgare; vitiligo; leucoderma.
しんしょびん【信書便】▫ 信書便 correspondence delivery. ▫ 信書便事業 (a) delivery service for letters and postcards. ▶ 一般～事業 (a) delivery service for ordinary letters and postcards / 特定～事業〔配達物の重量や配達時間を限定して信書を集配する信書便事業〕a delivery service for types of correspondence specified according to weight, delivery time, etc.
しんしょびんほう【信書便法】〖法〗the Correspondence Delivery Law. ▶ 正式名称は「民間事業者による信書の送達に関する法律」.
しんしりょく【深視力】〖眼科〗depth perception.
しんしろく【紳士録】▫ 紳士録商法〔悪徳商法の一種〕a Who's Who scam; charging large sums for listing names in a social register.
しんしん[9]【伸身】〖体操〗〔体を伸ばした状態〕▫ 伸身宙返り a layout「flip [somersault].
じんしん[3]【人身】▫ 人身傷害補償保険 personal injury「protection [compensation] insurance. 人身取引 human trafficking; trafficking in human beings.
しんしんしょうがいがく【心身障害学】disability sciences.
しんしんそうしつしゃいりょうかんさつほう【心神喪失者医療観察法】〖法〗the Mental Illness Treatment and Observation Law. ▶ 正式名称は「心神喪失等の状態で重大な他害行為を行った者の医療及び観察等に関する法律」(the Law Concerning the Medical Treatment and Observation of Individuals Who Have Committed Grave Acts against Others while in a State of Insanity).
じんしんとりひきたいさくこうどうけいかく【人身取引対策行動計画】Action Plan against Human Trafficking.
じんしんとりひき(ほそく)ぎていしょ【人身取引(補足)議定書】the Protocol to Prevent, Suppress and Punish Trafficking in Persons; (パレルモ議定書) the Palermo Protocol. ▶ 正式名称は「国際的な組織犯罪の防止に関する国際連合条約を補足する、特に女性及び児童の取引を防止し、抑止し及び処罰するための議定書」(the Protocol to Prevent, Suppress and Punish Trafficking in Persons, Especially Women and Children, supplementing the United Nations Convention against Transnational Organized Crime).
じんしんばいばい【人身売買】▫ 人身売買ブローカー a middleman [a broker, an agent] in human trafficking.
じんしんばいばいきんしネットワーク【人身売買禁止-】the Japan Network Against Trafficking in Persons (略: JNATIP).
しんすい[2]【浸水】▫ 浸水被害 inundation [flood] damage; damage from「inundation [flooding]. ▶ 多くの住宅が～被害を受けた。 Many homes「suffered inundation damage [were damaged by inundation]. 浸水林 a flooded forest.
しんすい[6]【親水】▫ 親水効果 a hydrophilic effect.

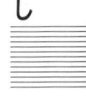

しんぜい【新税】《introduce》a new tax.
じんせい¹【人生】 □ 人生ゲーム 〔商標〕〔ボードゲームの一種〕the Game of Life.
しんせいじ【新生児】 □ 仮死新生児 an asphyxiated newborn (baby, infant). □ 新生児破傷風 〔医〕neonatal tetanus (略：NT). 新生児溶血性疾患 〔医〕hemolytic disease of the newborn (略：HDN).
しんせつ⁴【新設】 □ 新設分割 〔経営〕〔会社分割の1つ；1部門を切り離して新設の企業に譲渡すること〕an independent merger.
「親切なクムジャさん」〔映画〕Sympathy for Lady Vengeance.
しんせん⁹【深圳】 □ 深圳A株[B株] 〔深圳市場上場銘柄〕a Shenzhen「A-share [B-share].
しんそ³【心礎】〔木造の塔の中心柱(しん)を支える礎石〕the [a] base stone for the central pillar.
しんそう²【真相】 □ 真相究明 an「inquiry into [investigation of] the「truth [facts]《of a matter》.  ◐ ～究明に当たる  begin an investigation of the true facts《of a case》.
しんそう⁴【深層】 □ 深層筋 〔解〕(an) inner muscle. 深層循環〔深海における地球の規模での海水循環〕deep water circulation；〔海洋〕abyssal circulation.
しんぞう²【心臓】
 □ 心臓核医学 〔医〕nuclear cardiology. 心臓血管外科  cardiovascular surgery；〔病院の〕a department of cardiovascular surgery. ◐ ～血管外科専門医  a cardiovascular surgeon. 心臓再同期療法 〔医〕cardiac resynchronization therapy (略：CRT). 心臓糸状虫 〔動〕〔フィラリア原虫〕a filaria (pl. -riae)；a heartworm. 心臓震盪(とう) 〔医〕cardiac concussion；concussion of the heart；commotio cordis. 心臓突然死 〔医〕sudden cardiac death (略：SCD). 心臓バイパス手術 〔医〕heart [coronary] bypass surgery；a「heart [coronary] bypass (operation). 心臓リハビリテーション  cardiac rehabilitation.
しんぞく²【親族】 □ 親族企業  a family enterprise.
じんそく【迅速】 □ 迅速検査 〔医〕a rapid test (for HIV). 迅速病理診断 〔医〕= 術中迅速診断 (⇨じゅつちゅう).
しんたい¹【身体】
 □ 身体依存 〔医〕physical dependence. 身体運動科学  kinesiology；kinesiological science；the science of body movement. 身体活動レベル (one's) physical activity level (略：PAL). 身体言語  body language. 身体拘束  physical restraint. 身体醜形障害〔精神医〕body dysmorphic disorder (略：BDD). 身体愁訴  physical complaint. 身体知〔身体を鍛え、使い込んでゆく中で獲得する知能〕「intelligence [knowledge]. 身体髪膚(ぱっぷ) ◐ ～を父母に受く.  You receive your body from your parents (and therefore should value it). 身体犯 〔法〕assault；(a) crime against the person；〔人〕a person who commits assault；the perpetrator of a crime against the person. 身体表現性障害〔精神医〕a somatoform disorder.
じんたい¹【人体】 □ 人体装着型ロボット  a wearable robot；a robot suit. 人体浮揚〔マジックなどでの〕levitation.
じんたい²【靱帯】 □ 十字靱帯 ⇨じゅうじ¹. 側副靱帯 ⇨そくふく¹. 膝～損傷  a knee ligament injury. 靱帯断裂 〔医〕rupture of a ligament；(a) ligament rupture；a ruptured ligament. ◐ 十字～断裂 《anterior》cruciate ligament rupture / ～形成手術  plastic surgery for a ruptured ligament.
しんたいか【身体化】〔精神医〕〔不安やストレスが身体の症状となって現れること〕somatization.  ～する  somatize；somaticize. □ 身体化障害  a somatization disorder. ◐ ～障害患者  a somatizer.

しんたいしょうがいしゃ【身体障害者】 □□ 身体障害者認定  recognition [designation] as a「disabled person [person who has a disability]. 身体障害者用  for (the use of) the physically handicapped. 身体障害者用自動車  a「car [vehicle] for the physically handicapped. 身体障害者用駐車場 (specifically designated) parking spaces for the physically handicapped. 身体障害者用トイレ  a toilet for the physically handicapped.
しんたいしんせっけいほう【新耐震設計法】〔1981年施行の〕the New Seismic Design Code.
しんたかくてきぼうえきこうしょう【新多角的貿易交渉】〔WTOの〕a new round of multilateral trade「negotiations [talks]；a new round. [＝ドーハ・ラウンド]
しんたく¹【信託】 □ 一括支払信託  a lump-sum accounts-payable trust system. □ 信託契約代理業  trust agreement agency business. 信託受益権  the [a]「right to benefit from a trust. 信託受益権販売業  trading in (trust) beneficiary rights. 信託報酬  a trust fee.
しんたくきょうかい【信託協会】the Trust Companies Association of Japan.
しんたくぎょうほう【信託業法】〔法〕the Trust Business Law.
シンタグマひろば【—広場】〔ギリシャ, アテネの中心部にある〕Syntagma Square.
しんだん【診断】 □ 発症前診断 〔医〕⇨はっしょう. 診断群分類 〔医〕diagnosis procedure combination (略：DPC). 診断被曝  diagnostic radiation exposure. 診断率 a「diagnosis [detection] rate.
じんちゃく【人着】〔白黒の写真や映画に人工的に着色すること〕colorizing.  ～する  colorize《old black-and-white movies》.
じんちゅう³【陣中】 □ 陣中食  a「combat [military] ration《for Takeda Shingen's army》.
しんちゅうは【親中派】supporters of China (in the Diet)；〔politicians〕sympathetic to「China [Chinese policy]；(the) pro-Chinese；the China lobby.
しんちょう¹【伸長・伸張】 □ 黒伸張[伸長] 〔写真〕
しんちょう²【身長】 □ 身長差 (a) height difference [differential]；(a) difference in height. ◐ 平均～差  an [the] average height difference；the average difference in height《between boys and girls》.
しんちょう⁴【慎重】 □ 慎重家  a「careful [cautious, prudent] person. 慎重居士  Mr.「Careful [Cautious, Prudent].
しんちょく²【進捗】 □ 進捗率〔工事などの〕a construction progress rate《of 15%》；the degree of completion；how much of《the construction》has been completed.
しんちょっかつほうしき【新直轄方式】〔高速道路整備方式〕a new system for direct government control of highway construction；a new direct-control method.
じんてい【人定】 □ 人定尋問 〔法〕〔裁判で行われる、証人・鑑定人など被告以外の人の氏名・住所・年齢を確認するための尋問〕questions put to a witness or person other than a defendant to establish his or her identity；identification questions (for a nondefendant).
シンディア〔経済発展の著しい中国とインドをまとめて言い表す造語〕Chindia. ▶ Chindia は China + India の合成語.
しんていし【心停止】 □ 突然の心停止 (a) sudden cardiac arrest (略：SCA). □ 心停止状態 (in) a state of cardiac arrest. ◐ 彼は～状態で病院に搬送され, 到着後死亡が確認された.  He was taken to 《the》hospital with cardiac arrest and was confirmed dead on arrival.
しんてき²【心的】 □ 心的外傷ケア  post-traumatic care. 心的外傷〔精神医〕a「mental [psychological, psy-

chic] disorder [disability, disturbance].
**じんてき【人的】** ▫ 人的基盤 a 《strong》「human resources [personnel] base [foundation]. ◐〜基盤の充実を図る seek to enhance 《a company's》 human resources base. 人的情報(収集)〔スパイを使っての諜報活動〕human intelligence (略：HUMINT). 人的被害〔人的損害〕(a) human loss; a casualty. 人的ミス (a) human error.
**「シンデレラマン」**〔映画〕Cinderella Man.
**しんでんず【心電図】** ▫ 心電図モニター an「electrocardiogram [ECG] monitor;〔モニターすること〕electrocardiogram [ECG] monitoring.
**しんでんのおか【神殿の丘】**〔エルサレム旧市街にあるユダヤ・イスラム両宗教の聖地〕the Temple Mount;〔ヘブライ語名〕Har Habayit;〔アラビア語名〕Haram esh-Sharif.
**しんど[5]【震度】** ▫ アンケート震度 (an) (earthquake) intensity as established through questionnaire; a subjective reaction-survey intensity. 計測震度 measured seismic intensity. 体感震度 (a) subjective intensity; the intensity of an earthquake as established by subjective human reaction. ▫ 震度分布図 a seismic intensity distribution map; a distribution map of seismic intensity.
**しんとう[4]【浸透】** ▫ 浸透度〔普及度〕〔周知度〕the degree to which *sth* is commonly known;《遺伝》〔ある遺伝子を持つ個体群の中で、予想される形質を一定条件下で発現する個体の割合〕penetrance. 浸透度調査〔普及度〕a (market) penetration survey;〔周知度〕an awareness survey; a survey「of awareness of《digital broadcasting》[to establish how much the public knows about《nuclear energy》].
**しんどう[1]【伸銅】** ▫ 伸銅品 wrought copper and copper alloy products.
**しんどう[5]【振動】** ▫ 振動吸収 vibration(al) absorption. 振動吸収ゴム vibration-absorbent rubber. 振動吸収材 a vibration-absorbing material; a vibration absorber. 振動吸収シート a vibration-absorbing sheet. 振動吸収性 vibration absorbency; (a) vibration-absorbing capacity. ◐この車のシートには〜吸収性に優れている。The seats in this car have an outstanding capacity to absorb vibrations. 振動吸収装置 a vibration absorber; vibration absorbing equipment. 振動モーター a vibration motor.
**しんどう[7]【震動】** ▫ 震動台〔耐震実験などを行う装置〕a shaking table; a seismic simulator.
**じんどう【人道】** ▫ 人道援助物資 humanitarian aid supplies. 人道団体 a humanitarian organization. 人道復興支援活動 activities for humanitarian and reconstruction assistance.
**じんどうてき【人道的】** ▫ 人道的活動 humanitarian「activities [efforts]; a humanitarian operation. 人道的配慮 humanitarian considerations. ◐〜配慮を求める call for [demand] humanitarian considerations [a humanitarian response].
**じんどうもくてきのじらいじょきょしえんのかい【人道目的の地雷除去支援の会】**the Japan Alliance for Humanitarian Demining Support (略：JAHDS).
**じんどうもんだいちょうせいじむしょ【人道問題調整事務所】**〔国連の〕the (United Nations) Office for Coordination of Humanitarian Affairs (略：OCHA).
**じんどくせい【腎毒性】**〘医〙renal toxicity; nephrotoxicity. ◐〜の nephrotoxic.
**じんどくそ【腎毒素】**〘医〙a nephrotoxin.
**しんとだん【神徒壇】**a「household [family] Shinto altar.
**しんない【新内】**＝しんないぶし.
**しんないぶし【新内節】**〔浄瑠璃の一派〕the Shinnai style of singing.

**しんにち【親日】** ▫ 親日感情 pro-Japanese feelings; (a) pro-Japanese sentiment.
**しんにちはんみんぞくとくべつほう【親日反民族特別法】**〔韓国の法律〕the Special Law to Probe into the Truth behind Pro-Japanese and Anti-Korean Acts. ▸ 正式名称は「日帝強制占領下反民族行為の真相糾明に関する特別法」.
**しんにっちゅうゆうこうにじゅういっせいきいいんかい【新日中友好21世紀委員会】**the New Japan-China Friendship Committee for the 21st Century. ▸ 両国政府の諮問機関. 2004年設立.
**しんにゅう[2]【侵入】** ▫ 侵入盗 a burglar; a thief; a break-in「artist [thief]. 侵入用具〔空き巣狙いなどの〕a「breaking-and-entering [breaking-in] tool.
**しんにゅうまく【新入幕】**〔相撲〕rising to the「*makuuchi* [*maegashira*] division (in sumo). ◐〜を果たす achieve promotion to the senior grade (of sumo wrestling).
**しんねん[2]【新年】** ▫ 新年互礼会〔賀詞交換会〕a meeting to exchange New Year's greetings.
**しんのアイ・アール・エー【真のIRA】**〔IRAの分派組織〕the Real IRA (略：RIRA).
**しんのう[2]【親王】** ▫ 親王妃 the wife of a prince; a princess. ◐文仁〜妃 紀子 Her Imperial Highness Princess Akishino; Princess Kiko.
**じんのうほう【腎嚢胞】**〘医〙a renal cyst; a kidney cyst.
**シンハー**〔商標〕〔タイのビール〕Singha.
**しんぱい[1]【心肺】** ▫ 心肺運動負荷試験 a cardiopulmonary exercise test (略：CPET).
**じんぱい【塵肺】** ▫ トンネル塵肺 pneumoconiosis in tunnel workers. ▫ 塵肺訴訟 a pneumoconiosis「case [(law)suit].
**しんぱく【心拍】** ▫ 心拍計 a heart rate monitor. 心拍動下 off-pump《bypass surgery》. ◐〜動下手術する perform off-pump heart surgery; operate off-pump /〜動下冠(状)動脈バイパス手術 beating heart coronary artery bypass grafting; off-pump coronary artery bypass grafting (略：OPCAB); off-pump CABG.
**しんぱつさい【新発債】**〔証券〕a「new [fresh] issue 《of shares》.
**しんはつねつりょう【真発熱量】**〘物〙a net heating value (略：NHV).
**ジンバラン**〔インドネシア、バリ島の高級リゾート地〕Jimbaran.
**しんぱん[2]【侵犯】** ▫ 領海侵犯船 a vessel encroaching on 《a country's》 territorial waters; an encroaching vessel. 領空侵犯機 an aircraft encroaching on 《a country's》 territorial airspace; an encroaching aircraft.
**しんぱん[4]【審判】** ▫ 審判官〔準司法的機能を有する行政機関の〕a judge; an administrative law judge. ◐〜官制度 a judge [an administrative law judge] system. 審判記録〘法〙a record of (official) proceedings. 審判長 a chief「umpire [referee, judge].
**しんぴ[5]【秦皮】**〘生薬〙〔トネリコの樹皮〕ash bark.
**シンビン**〔アイスホッケー・ラグビーなど〕〔ラフプレーなどによる一時退場〕sin-binning; temporary dismissal (for foul play);〔そのつどるペナルティーボックス〕a sin bin. ◐試合開始早々〜を食らった。He was sin-binned immediately after the game started.
**しんぶ【深部】** ▫ 深部静脈〘解〙a deep vein. 深部脳刺激《療法》a deep brain stimulation (略：DBS).
**しんふじん【新富人】**〔中国の新興富裕階級〕the new(ly) rich in China.
**しんふぜん【心不全】** ▫ 虚血性心不全 *ischemic [ischaemic] heart failure.
**シンプソン・ミラー** Simpson-Miller, Portia (1945-　; ジャマイカの政治家; 首相 [2006-07]).
**しんぶっしつ【芯物質】**〔マイクロカプセル内の〕a core substance.

シンプティ

**シンプティ**【SMPTE】〔全米映画テレビ技術者協会; 同協会が制定した映像と音声を同期させるための規格〕SMPTE. ▶ Society of Motion Picture and Television Engineers の略.

**シンブリ**〔タイ中部の県; その県都〕Singburi.

**「シンプル・プラン」**〔映画〕A Simple Plan.

**しんフロイトは**【新–派】【心理】the neo-Freudians;〔1人〕a neo-Freudian. ▷ neo-Freudian *adj*.

**しんぶん**【新聞】 ▣ 新聞拡張員 a newspaper salesman. 新聞拡張団 a newspaper sales team. 新聞配達員 a newspaper delivery「man [woman]; *a (newspaper) carrier.

**じんぶんちりがっかい**【人文地理学会】the Human Geographical Society of Japan (略: HGSJ).

**ジンベ**【楽器】＝ジャンベ.

**シンベト**〔イスラエルの国内防諜保安機関〕the Shin Bet. ▶「シャバク」(the Shabak) ともいう.

**しんぺん**[1]【身辺】 ▣ 身辺警護官 a personal bodyguard. 身辺整理 tidying things up; putting *one's* affairs in order; ordering *one's* affairs《in preparation for *one's* death》. 身辺捜査 a police investigation into a suspect's private life;《run》a background check on a suspect. 身辺調査 a background check on *sb*; a check(up) on *sb*.

**しんぼう**[1]【心房】 ▣ 心房内血流転換手術【医】an (intra-)atrial switch「procedure [operation]. [⇨マスタードしゅじゅつ, セニングしゅじゅつ].

**シンボル** ▣ シンボル・アスリート〔日本オリンピック委員会(JOC)に肖像権を預けた選手〕a "symbol athlete"; a「top [high-profile]athlete whose image is used by corporate sponsors.

**しんまい**【新米】 ▣ 新米ママ[パパ] a new「mom [dad].

**しんみつ**【親密】 ▣ 親密性 intimacy《with [between]…》; closeness《between [to]…》.

**「親密すぎるうちあけ話」**〔映画〕Confidences Trop Intimes;〔英語タイトル〕Intimate Strangers.

**じんみゃく**【人脈】 ▣ 人脈構築 building a network of contacts. 人脈社会 a society which functions through personal connections.

**じんみんかいほうせんせん**【人民解放戦線】〔スリランカの過激派組織〕the Janatha Vimukthi Peramuna (略: JVP); the People's Liberation Front of Sri Lanka.

**じんみんげん**【人民元】 ▣ 人民元レート the renminbi exchange rate.

**じんみんけんさついん**【人民検察院】〔中国の検察機関〕a people's procuratorate.

**じんみんしゅぎとう**【新民主主義党】〔ギリシャの政党〕the New Democratic Party (略: ND).

**しんみんとう**【親民党】〔台湾の政党〕the People First Party (略: PFP).

**しんみんばんぽう**【新民晩報】〔中国, 上海の夕刊紙〕the Xinmin Evening News.

**じんみんほういん**【人民法院】〔中国の裁判所〕a people's court.

**しんみんろせん**【親民路線】〔近年の中国政府の〕a people-first policy.

**じんめい**[2]【人命】 ▣ 人命軽視 disregard [disdain] for human life. 人命最優先 giving top priority to human life; putting human life first. ◐ ～最優先で人質の救出に当たりたい. Our first priority when rescuing hostages is to bring them back alive. 人命探査装置 a life-detection「system [device]. 人命被害 harm [damage] to human life; human loss(es). ◐ この台風による～被害は死者23人, 行方不明者30人. The human cost of this typhoon has been 23 dead and 30 missing.

**シンメトレル**〔商標・薬〕〔パーキンソン病・A型インフルエンザ治療薬〕Symmetrel.

**しんもの**【新物】〔その季節の最初に出回る農産物・海産物・加工食品〕the first (crop [fruit, seafood, produce]) of the season; something which has just come on the market. ◐ ～の new《vegetables》; newly harvested《beans》; freshly caught《fish》/ ～の梅干し new [this year's] *umeboshi*. ◐ ズワイガニの～入荷.〔掲示〕Fresh [Freshly delivered] Snow Crabs. | Tanner Crabs: Just In.

**しんもん**[3]【唇紋】a lip print.

**しんもん**[4]【神門】〔神社の門〕a shrine gate; the entrance to a shrine; the entrance gate of a shrine.

**しんや**【深夜】 ▣ 深夜外出 going out late at night; a midnight outing. ◐ 青少年の～外出を禁止する条例 an ordinance forbidding minors from being out late at night; a late-night curfew for minors. 深夜スーパー a late-night supermarket. 深夜帯〔放送・交通〕an after-midnight (time) slot. 深夜徘徊〔未成年などの〕late-night prowling; prowling around「late at night [in the middle of the night];〔認知症老人などの〕late-night wandering; wandering about「late at night [in the middle of the night]. 深夜便 a late-night「flight [service, departure].

**しんやく**[3]【新薬】 ▣ 新薬(開発)競争 pharmaceutical competition; competition to produce new drugs.

**しんよう**[1]【信用】 ▣ 信用拡大【金融】(a) credit expansion; (an) expansion of credit. 信用失墜 (a) loss of credibility; forfeiting public trust. ◐ 最近の教育界で相次ぐ教職員の～失墜行為は, 憂慮に堪えないものがある. It is「much to be deplored [deeply regrettable]that there have recently been so many cases of people in education forfeiting the trust of the public by their activities. | Deplorably, there has recently been one case after another of teachers behaving in a way which forfeits public trust in education. 信用情報 credit information. ◐ ～情報機関 a credit information agency. 信用デリバティブ【金融】credit derivatives. 信用倍率〔証券〕a margin ratio.

**しんようとりひき**【信用取引】 ▣ 一般信用取引 a "negotiable margin transaction." 制度信用取引 a "standardized margin transaction." 無期限信用取引 ＝一般信用取引.

**しんらい**[1]【信頼】 ▣ 信頼回復 recovering *one's* good name; regaining《*sb's* [public]》trust. ◐ ひたすら～回復に努める do *one's* (very) best to recover *one's* good name; do everything in *one's* power to「regain [get back]《a friend's [public]》trust. 信頼失墜 (a)「loss [failure]of「trust [credibility, confidence].

**しんらいせい**【信頼性】 ▣ 信頼性試験〔製品の品質についての〕reliability testing;〔1回の〕a reliability test.

**しんラウンド**【新–】＝しんたかくてきぼうえきこうしょう.

**しんり**[1]【心理】 ▣ 心理カウンセラー a (psychological) counselor. 心理鑑定《undergo》a psychological「evaluation [examination]. 心理判定員〔児童相談所・福祉施設などの〕a (certified) psychological diagnostician. 心理分析 psychoanalysis.

**しんり**[2]【審理】 ▣ 形式審理【法】(legal) proceedings of form. 実体審理 substantive (legal) proceedings. ◐ 審理期間〔裁判などの〕《shorten》the length of (court) deliberations.

**しんりがく**【心理学】 ▣ 身体心理学〔科目などとして〕somatic psychology. 対人心理学 interpersonal psychology. 悲嘆心理学 grief psychology.

**じんりき**【人力】 ▣ 人力タクシー a human-powered taxi; a Velotaxi;〔東南アジアなどの〕a pedicab.

**ジン・リッキー**〔カクテル〕a gin rickey.

**しんりてき**【心理的】 ▣ 心理的依存 psychological dependence《on alcohol》. 心理的強制 psychological duress. ◐ ～強制下

すいこう

にあって under psychological duress. 心理的負荷〔業務などによる〕(a) psychological load. 心理的負荷評価表 a tabulated 「assessment 「evaluation」of psychological load. 心理的負担 a psychological burden; (psychological) stress. ◎働きながらの育児は肉体的，～負担が大きい。Bringing up children while working is「both a physical and a psychological burden [stressful both physically and psychologically]. 心理的リアクタンス〖心理〗〔自由の拘束に対する抵抗感〕psychological reactance. 心理的離乳〖心理〗psychological weaning.

**しんりょう**² 【診療】
🔲 自費診療 treatment payable by the「individual [patient]; ＝保険外診療 (⇨ほけん¹). 🔲 診療ガイドライン a clinical practice guideline. 診療記録 a medical record. 診療情報 health information. 診療情報管理士 a certified medical information manager. 診療情報提供書〔医療機関間の〕an authorization to transfer《a patient's》medical「information [records]. ▶「紹介状」の正式名称. 診療日〔病院の〕days when a「hospital [clinic] is open; 〔患者の〕the day one regularly receives medical「care [treatment]. 診療報酬債権 credit for remuneration for medical treatment. 診療報酬請求 a request (to a health insurance society) for remuneration for medical treatment. 診療報酬請求書 a bill for remuneration for medical treatment (sent to a health insurance society). 診療報酬単価 a unit of remuneration for medical treatment. 診療報酬点数 (a number of) points for medical service remuneration. ◎医科[歯科, 調剤]～報酬点数表 a table of points for「medical [dental, pharmaceutical] service remuneration.

**しんりょうしか**【心療歯科】〔歯と心の病気の関連を扱う医学分野〕(a department of) psychosomatic dentistry.

**しんりん**² 【森林】
🔲 森林環境税 (a) forest environment tax. 森林吸収源〖環境〗〔温室効果ガスの吸収体としての森林〕a forest sink. 森林吸収量〔二酸化炭素の〕the amount of「carbon dioxide [$CO_2$] absorption by forests; the amount of forest $CO_2$ absorption. 森林税 ＝森林環境税. 森林整備 forest management. 森林整備法人 a forest management corporation. 森林被害 forest damage;

tree damage; damage to「forests [trees]. ◎台風[酸性雨]による～害 forest damage due to「typhoons [acid rain]. 森林保険 forest insurance. 森林保養地 a forest area for health and recuperation; a forest resort. 森林・林業白書 a white paper on forests and forestry;〔林野庁の〕the Annual Report on Trends of Forest and Forestry《2005》.

**しんりんかんりきょうぎかい**〔森林管理協議会〕〔メキシコに本部を置く世界的な森林認証団体〕the Forest Stewardship Council (略: FSC).

**しんりん・りんぎょうきほんほう**〔森林・林業基本法〕〖法〗the Basic Law for Forests and Forestry. ▶ 2001年, 林業基本法を改正.

**じんるいがく**【人類学】 🔲 環境人類学 environmental anthropology. ▷ environmental anthropologist n. 社会人類学 social anthropology. ▷ social anthropologist n. 生理人類学 physiological anthropology.

**じんるいのこうしょうおよびむけいいさんのけっさく**【人類の口承及び無形遺産の傑作】〔ユネスコの〕a Masterpiece of the Oral and Intangible Heritage of Humanity.

**しんれい**¹【心霊】 🔲 心霊スポット〔超常現象などがよく起こるとされている場所〕a「psychic [haunted] spot.

「シン・レッド・ライン」《映画》The Thin Red Line.

**しんろ**²【進路】
🔲 進路指導室〔中学校などの〕an academic and career「counseling [guidance] office. 進路指導主事〔中学校などの〕an academic and career「counseling [guidance] administrator. 進路変更〔学業の方向転換〕a change of course; changing「one's field of study [course, direction];〔車線変更〕a lane change; changing lanes. 進路予想[予測]〔台風・ハリケーンなどの〕(hurricane) path prediction; a《typhoon》path forecast; predicting [forecasting] the「path [course] of a hurricane [typhoon]. ◎～予想図 a projected path map《for a hurricane》; a map of the projected path《of a typhoon》.

**しんろうじん**【新老人】〔75歳以上で, 心身ともに自立し, 社会に寄与する能力をもつ人〕a new elder citizen. ▶ 聖路加国際病院名誉院長 日野原重明氏が提唱した言葉.

**しんわ**¹【神話】 🔲 成長神話 the myth of ever-increasing (economic) growth.

# す

**す**⁴【酢】 🔲 酢油漬け《料理》pickling in oil and vinegar. ◎ナスの～油漬け eggplant pickled in oil and vinegar. 酢洗い〔野菜や魚肉片を酢水にひたすこと〕washing [rinsing, soaking, dipping]《sliced fish》in diluted vinegar before cooking it.

**ずあかあおばと**【頭赤青鳩】《鳥》〔ハト科の鳥〕a whistling green pigeon; *Treron formosae*.

**すいあつ**¹【水圧】 🔲 水圧破砕(法)〖工〗〔岩盤掘削などのための〕hydraulic fracturing.

**すいいき**【水域】 🔲 危険水域〔海の〕dangerous waters; a dangerous area (of「the sea [a river, etc.]); a dangerous stretch of water;〔憂慮すべき段階〕a dangerous stretch; a「risky [dangerous, hazardous] area;《enter on, tread on》dangerous ground(s); dangerous waters. ◎原油価格は日本経済にとって今が危険～に入りつつある。Oil prices could endanger the Japanese economy at any time. | With oil prices rising, Japan's economy is on the point of entering「a dangerous stretch [dangerous waters].

**スイーツ** sweets. ◎彼は～には目がない He has a sweet tooth.

**スイート・エリア**《スポーツ》〔スイートスポットの周辺〕a sweet area.

**すいか**⁴【西瓜】 🔲 大玉すいか a「large [large-size(d)] watermelon; a giant watermelon. 黄肉すいか a yellow watermelon. 黄皮[黒皮]すいか a yellow-[black-]rind watermelon with a「yellow [black] skin [rind]. 小玉すいか a「small [small-size(d)] watermelon; a dwarf watermelon.

**すいか**¹【水塊】《海洋》a「warm [cold] water mass.

**ずいがさいぼうしゅ**【髄芽細胞腫】〖医〗＝ずいがしゅ.

**ずいがしゅ**【髄芽腫】〖医〗a medulloblastoma (*pl.* ～s, -mata).

**すいけい**³【推計】 🔲 高位[中位, 低位]推計 ⇨こうい⁸, ちゅうい¹, ていい¹. 🔲 推計人口 an estimated population.

**すいこう**⁷【推考】inference; conjecture; reasoning; deliberation.

～する infer; conjecture; reason; deliberate. 🔲 容易推考性〖法〗conceivability; ease of「conception [invention]《of a patent》. 非容易推考性〖法〗inconceiv-

すいさん

ability; difficulty of「conception [invention]《of a patent》.
**すいさん**[1]【水産】 ☐☐ 水産白書 a white paper on fisheries;〔農林水産省の〕the Annual Report on Developments in the Fisheries Industry in《2005》.
**すいさんきほんほう**【水産基本法】【法】the Basic Law on Fisheries.
**すいさんそうごうけんきゅうセンター**【水産総合研究-】the Fisheries Research Agency (略: FRA).
**すいし**[1]【水死】 ☐☐ 水死人 a drowned person.
**すいじ**【炊事】 ☐☐ 炊事車〔災害地救援用などの〕a mobile kitchen (vehicle);〔軍〕a field kitchen vehicle.
**ずいじ**【随時】 ☐☐ 随時調整契約〔電力などの需給が逼迫〕した時に事前連絡の上で使用量の抑制を電力会社が顧客企業に要請できる契約〕a contract with major industrial consumers permitting power companies to undertake emergency load-adjustment measures.
**すいしつ**【水質】 ☐☐ 水質階級 a water quality class. 水質調査《carry out》a water quality survey.
**すいじゃく**【衰弱】 ☐☐ 衰弱死 (a) death due to「prostration [emaciation].  ◯ ～死する die from「prostration [emaciation].
**すいしょう**[3]【水晶】 ☐☐ 赤水晶 red quartz. 煙水晶 smoky quartz. 茶水晶 brown quartz.
**すいじょう**[1]【水上】 ☐☐ 水上安全 water safety. 水上タクシー a water taxi.
**すいしょく**[4]【水色】〔お茶を淹れたときの色〕the color of tea when poured.
**すいしん**[3]【推進】 ☐☐ 推進員《payment》"promoting worker."  ◯ 求人開拓～員〔ハローワークの〕a "job-offer development promoter"/健康～員 a "health-promoting worker"/電波適正利用～員 a worker responsible for promoting efficient use of the radio spectrum.
**スイスほうしき**【-方式】〔税削減方式の1つ〕the Swiss Formula. ▶ 高関税ほど削減幅を大きくする方式.
**すいせい**[3]【水性】 ☐☐ 水性ゲルインク a water-based [an aqueous] gel ink.
**すいせい**[0]【水星】 ☐☐ 水星探査機《launch》a Mercury probe.
**すいせい**[0]【彗星】 ☐☐ 彗星探査機《launch》a comet probe.
**すいせん**[2]【水洗】 ☐☐ 水洗化〔トイレの〕conversion to flush toilets.  ◯ ～化率 the percentage (of households) converted to flush toilets.
**すいせん**[0]【推薦】 ☐☐ 共同推薦 joint endorsement《by [from] the Democratic Party and the Liberal Democratic Party》. 単独推薦 solo endorsement《by [from] the Liberal Democratic Party》. ☐☐ 推薦枠 a quota for「recommendations [《students》] recommended for《admission》].
**すいそ**【水素】 ☐☐ 水素(エネルギー)社会 a「hydrogen-based [hydrogen energy] society; a society in which hydrogen「is [replaces fossil fuels as] a primary form of energy. 水素エンジン車 a hydrogen-engine vehicle; a hydrogen car. 水素ステーション〔燃料電池車に水素を供給する施設〕a hydrogen《filling》station. 水素電池 a hydrogen「battery [cell]. 水素内燃機関〔エンジン〕a hydrogen internal combustion engine (略: ICE, HICE). 水素燃料電池 a hydrogen fuel cell. 水素ハイブリッド車 a hydrogen hybrid「vehicle [car].
**すいそう**[5]【水層】 a water layer;〔解〕〔角膜表面の涙液の〕water(y) layer; a lacrimal layer.
**すいたい**[0]【衰退】 ☐☐ 衰退産業〔経〕a「declining [failing] industry.
**すいたいぶ**[3]【膵体部】〔解〕the body of the pancreas; the pancreatic body. ☐☐ 膵体部がん〔医〕(a) pancreatic body cancer; (a) cancer of the pancreatic body; (a) pancreatic body carcinoma; (a) carcinoma of the pancreatic body.
**すいちゅう**[1]【水中】 ☐☐ 水中運動 (under)water [aquatic] exercise; aquabics.
**スイッチ** ☐☐ スイッチ・プレー《サッカー》a switch play.  ◯ ～プレーをする switch play《from left to right》.
**スイッチグラス**〔植〕〔米国産イネ科の植物〕switchgrass; *Panicum virgatum*.
**すいてい**[0]【推定】 ☐☐ 推定意思〔意思表示できない終末期患者などの〕(a) presumptive will. 推定樹齢 the estimated age of a tree. 推定飛距離〔ホームランの〕(a home run hit with) an estimated distance《of 643 feet》;〔ゴルフでドライブの〕(a drive with) an estimated distance《of 225 feet》. 推定埋蔵量〔石油資源などの〕probable [estimated] reserves.
「**推定無罪**」〔映画〕Presumed Innocent.
**すいとう**[3]【水稲】 ☐☐ 水稲共済金 mutual aid money paid to paddy(-rice) farmers (in years of poor crop yields).
**すいとうしょう**【水頭症】 ☐☐ 正常圧水頭症 normal-pressure hydrocephalus.
**すいとうぶ**【膵頭部】〔解〕the head of the pancreas; the pancreatic head. ☐☐ 膵頭部がん〔医〕(a) pancreatic head cancer; (a) cancer of the pancreatic head; (a) pancreatic head carcinoma; (a) carcinoma of the pancreatic head.
**すいのうほう**【膵嚢胞】〔医〕a pancreatic cyst.
**すいはんき**【炊飯器】 ☐☐ 圧力炊飯器 a pressure rice cooker.
**すいびぶ**【膵尾部】〔解〕the tail of the pancreas; the pancreatic tail. ☐☐ 膵尾部がん〔医〕(a) pancreatic tail cancer; (a) cancer of the pancreatic tail; (a) pancreatic tail carcinoma; (a) carcinoma of the pancreatic tail.
**すいふよう**【酔芙蓉】〔植〕〔フヨウの園芸品種〕*Hibiscus mutabilis* cv. *vercicolor*.
**すいぶん**【水分】 ☐☐ 水分活性〔生物〕water activity (略: Aw).
**すいふんが**【綏芬河】〔中国黒竜江省東南部の工業都市〕Suifenhe.
**すいへい**[1]【水平】 ☐☐ 水平射撃〔撃ち〕level shooting;〔1回の〕a level shot.
**すいへいかん**【水平環】〔気象〕＝かんすいへいアーク.
**すいへいこ**【水平弧】〔気象〕＝かんすいへいアーク.
**すいぼつ**【水没】 ☐☐ 水没林〔雨期に発生する〕a flooded forest;〔水底の枯木群〕a submerged forest.
**すいみん**【睡眠】
☐☐ 睡眠医学 sleep medicine; the medicine of sleep. 睡眠改善薬〔薬〕a sleep improver. 睡眠科学 sleep science; the science of sleep. 睡眠細胞〔テロ組織などの秘密活動グループ；指令が下るまでは目立たぬよう"休眠"している〕a sleeper cell. 睡眠時随伴症〔医〕(a) parasomnia. 睡眠習慣《one's》sleeping habits. 睡眠時遊行症〔医〕somnambulism; sleepwalking; (a) sleepwalking disorder. 睡眠発作〔医〕(an attack of) narcolepsy; a narcoleptic attack. 睡眠麻痺〔医〕〔金縛り〕sleep [hypnogogic, hypnopompic] paralysis; old hag syndrome.
**すいようせい**[0]【水溶性】 ☐☐ 水溶性酸化チタン aqueous titanium oxide. 水溶性食物繊維 water-soluble dietary fiber.
**すいり**[1]【水利】 ☐☐ 水利使用 utilization [use] of water《for irrigation》; water「use [usage].  ◯ ～使用許可 permission [a permit] to utilize water.
**すいれん**[2]【睡蓮】 ☐☐ 睡蓮鉢 a lotus flower basin.
**すいれん**[3]【垂簾】 ☐☐ 垂簾政治〔中国史で〕regency government. 垂簾の政(まつりごと)＝垂簾政治.
**すいろん**【推論】 ☐☐ 後方〔後ろ向き〕推論 backward reasoning. 前方〔前向き〕推論 forward reasoning. ☐☐ 推論エンジン〔電算〕an inference engine.

スイング 🔲 スイング・サービス〔普通預金と貯蓄預金の口座間で資金を移動できる仕組み〕a swing service. スイング・トレーダー〖株式〗〔数日から一週間程度で売買をする投機家〕a swing trader.
スヴァーリ Suvari, Mena (1979- ；米国の映画女優).
スヴァイ・リエン〔カンボジア南部の州；同州の州都〕Svay Rieng.
スウィーツ ＝スイーツ.
「スウィート・ノベンバー」〔映画〕Sweet November.
「スウィーニー・トッド フリート街の悪魔の理髪師」〔映画〕Sweeney Todd: The Demon Barber of Fleet Street.
ズウィック Zwick, Edward (1952- ；米国の映画監督・製作者).
スウェイジ Swayze, Patrick (1954- ；米国の映画俳優).
スウェイラ〔イラク，バグダッド南方の町〕Suwayra.
スウェイン Swain, Dominique (1980- ；米国の映画女優).
スウェーデン 🔲 スウェーデン方式〔公的年金制度で〕the Swedish (pension) system.
スウェーデンおうりつかがくアカデミー【-王立科学-】the Royal Swedish Academy of Sciences.
スーサイド・クリフ〔サイパン島北部の崖；第二次大戦末期，追い詰められた多くの日本人が投身自殺をした断崖〕Suicide Cliff.
すうじ[1]【数字】 🔲 洋数字 Western numerals. 🔲 数字恐怖症〖精神医〗arithmophobia; numerophobia; (pathological) fear of numbers. 数字選択式宝くじ〔通称ナンバーズ〕a number-selection lottery.
スーダン 🔲 スーダン（南北）内戦〔1983-2005 年の〕Sudan's (north-south) civil war.
スーダンかいほうぐん【-解放軍】〔黒人主体の反政府勢力の 1 つ〕「Sudan [Sudanese] Liberation Army (略：SLA).
スーダンじんみんかいほううんどう【-人民解放運動】the Sudan People's Liberation Movement (略：SPLM).
スーダンじんみんかいほうぐん【-人民解放軍】the 「Sudan [Sudanese] People's Liberation Army (略：SPLA).
ス(一)ダンレッド〖化〗〔工業用着色剤〕Sudan Red.
すうち【数値】 🔲 数値改竄〖法〗falsifying figures; numerical falsification; tampering with 「figures [numbers].
すうちか【数値化】numerical expression 《of information》; representation 《of the result》in numbers. 〜する express 《the result》「numerically [in numbers]; put 《a problem》into numbers.
すうどく【数独】〖商標〗〔数字パズルの 1 つ〕sudoku; a sudoku puzzle; SuDoku; SUDOKU; Number Place.
スーパー 🔲 深夜スーパー a late-night supermarket. 都市型スーパー〔駅に近く，24 時間営業のところもある〕a city type supermarket. 24 時間スーパー a 24-hour [an all-night] supermarket.
スーパーオーディオ・シー・ディー【-CD】〖音響〗a Super Audio CD (略：SACD).
スーパー・キャッシュ〖商標〗〔電子マネーの一種〕Super-Cash.
スーパーこうげん【-抗原】〖免疫〗a superantigen.
スーパー・サイエンス・ハイスクール〔文部科学省が指定する，理系教育に重点を置く高校〕a "Super Science High School"(, a designation awarded by the Ministry of Education, Culture, Sports, Science and Technology to an upper-secondary school prioritizing science, technology, and mathematics education).
「スーパーサイズ・ミー」〔映画〕Super Size Me.
スーパーざっそう【-雑草】〖植〗〔厳しい環境や除草剤にも耐性をもつ雑草〕a superweed.

スーパー・スプレッダー〔多くの人への感染拡大の感染源となった患者〕a superspreader.
「スーパースリー」〔米国の，スパイもののTVアニメ；主役の3人の表の顔は超人気アイドルグループ〕The Impossibles.
スーパーセル〖気象〗〔竜巻などの原因となる巨大積乱雲〕a supercell;〔それが引き起こす暴風〕a supercell「storm [thunderstorm].
スーパーせんい【-繊維】〔高性能の人工繊維〕a (synthetic) superfiber.
スーパーセンター〔複合大型ショッピングセンター〕a supercenter.
スーパーせんとう【-銭湯】a deluxe public bath; a super sentō.
スーパーちゅうすうこうわん【-中枢港湾】a super hub port.
スーパーていき【-定期】a special fixed-term deposit account.
スーパーていぼう【-堤防】〔高規格堤防〕an embankment engineered to the highest specifications; a "super-embankment."
スーパーノート〔超精密偽造ドル紙幣〕a supernote; a superdollar.
スーパー・ヒートポンプ〖機〗〔超高性能のヒートポンプ〕a super heat pump.
スーパー・フェニックス〔フランスの高速増殖炉〕Superphenix (略：SPX).
スーパーマウス〔遺伝子操作でつくられた，発がん物質に対する抵抗力がきわめて強いマウス〕a supermouse 《pl. supermice》.
スーパー・リーグ〔バスケットボールの〕the 《Japanese basketball》Superleague.
スーピマ〖商標・紡績〗〔超長繊維の高級綿(%)〕Supima. 🔲 スーピマ綿 Supima cotton.
スーフィー〔イスラム神秘主義者〕a Sufi. ▷ Sufi, Sufic adj.
スーフィズム〔イスラム神秘主義〕Sufism.
スープレックス〔レスリング〕〔逆(%)落とし押さえ込み〕a suplex (hold). 🔲 ジャーマン・スープレックス(ホールド) a German suplex hold.
「ズーランダー」〔映画〕Zoolander.
すうり【数理】 🔲 数理生物学 mathematical biology. ▷ ～生物学者 a mathematical biologist. 数理モデル a mathematical model; mathematical modeling.
すうりょう【数量】 🔲 数量限定 a limit on 「quantity [numbers]; a 「quantity [numerical] limit; (in) limited numbers. ▷ このカメラは～限定 100 台です．お早めにご注文ください．Production of this camera has been limited to 100 [This camera is a limited edition of 100]. Place your order now! 数量限定《商品 a limited production 「item [product]; a 「limited edition [quantity limited] product [item]. 数量限定特価 a limited edition price. 数量限定販売[発売] limited 「volume [production, edition] sales.
スオメリンナとう【-島】〔フィンランド〕the Suomenlinna Island.
「スカートの翼ひろげて」〔映画〕The Land Girls.
「スカーフェイス」〔映画〕Scarface.
スカーフきんしほう【-禁止法】〔イスラム教徒の女生徒のスカーフ着用を禁止する法律〕legislation outlawing the wearing of the headscarf; 《impose》a headscarf ban.
スカーボロかんしょう【-環礁】〔南沙諸島の〕Scarborough Reef.
スカーリット Skerrit, Roosevelt (1972- ；ドミニカの政治家；首相〔2004- 〕).
スカーリング[1]〖水泳〗〔水をとらえるための腕の動作〕sculling. 〜する scull. [2]〔カヌーなどの幅寄せ〕sculling《to the right》. 〜する scull《to the right》.

スカイキャプテン

「スカイキャプテン ワールド・オブ・トゥモロー」〔映画〕Sky Captain and the World of Tomorrow.
スカイチーム〔商標・空〕〔航空会社提携グループの1つ；航空貨物輸送では世界最大〕the SkyTeam Airline Alliance; SkyTeam.
スカイプ〔商標・電算〕〔音声通話ソフト〕Skype. ～する Skype sb. ◐ 昨晩，アメリカの友人と～した．I Skyped my friend in America last night. ▣ スカイプ携帯〔電話〕＝スカイプ・フォン．スカイプ通話 a Skype call. スカイプ・フォン a Skype phone.
スカイ・マーシャル〔ハイジャック防止などのため航空機に搭乗する航空保安官〕a sky marshal.
スカウト ▣ スカウト人事 headhunting (recruitment); headhunting sb《from another company》.
スカッチ Skutch, Alexander F(rank) (1904–2004; 米国の鳥類学者，コスタリカで研究生活を送った).
スカパン〔短いスカートとパンツが一体化した女性の水着〕a skirt 「pants [bathing suit].
スカベンジャー ▣ スカベンジャー受容体《生化》a scavenger receptor. ◐ マクロファージ～受容体 a macrophage scavenger receptor.
スカルブスネス〔南極大陸の沿岸地域〕Skarvsnes.
すぎ[2]〔須義〕〔魚〕〔スズキ目の硬骨魚〕a cobia; a sergeant fish; Rachycentron canadum.
すぎあや〔杉綾〕 ▣ 杉綾織り〔織〕herringbone weave; 〔その布地〕herringbone cloth.
スキー ▣ 山スキー，山岳スキー backcountry skiing; ski touring; off-piste skiing; mountain skiing. ▣ スキー指導員〔インストラクター〕a ski(ing) instructor.
スキークロス〔競技〕skicross.
すきいれ〔漉き入れ〕〔漉き入れバーパターン〔紙幣の〕a watermark bar pattern.
すぎかくめい〔杉革命〕〔2005年レバノンの〕the Cedar Revolution.
すきこむ[1]〔鋤き込む〕*plow [ˈplough]《dead leaves》(back) in. ◐ 畑の土に枯れ草を～ plow dead vegetation (back) into the soil of a field.
すきこむ[2]〔漉き込む〕〔紙に透かし模様や文字を〕create [insert, leave] a watermark; 〔和紙に他の素材を〕add《hemp fibers》to washi paper; mix [put]《hemp fibers》into washi paper.
「過ぎた春」〔グリーグ作曲の弦楽曲〕The Last Spring.
スキットル〔ズボンの尻ポケットなどに入れる平たい携帯用酒ボトル〕a hip flask.
すきばさみ〔梳き鋏〕〔散髪用の〕(a pair of) thinning scissors.
すぎひらたけ〔杉平茸〕〔菌〕〔担子菌類キシメジ科のキノコ〕angel's wings; Pleurocybella porrigens. ▣ スギヒラタケ脳症〔医〕acute encephalopathy apparently associated with the ingestion of angel's wings.
スキポールくうこう〔-空港〕〔オランダ，アムステルダムの国際空港〕Schiphol Airport.
すきま〔透き間・隙間〕 ▣ 隙間家具 (a piece of) furniture for restricted space(s). 隙間商品 a niche 「product [article, item]. 隙間用ノズル〔狭いところを掃除するための電気掃除機付属の吸い口〕a crevice nozzle.
スキマー〔クレジットカードの情報を不正に読み取るスキミング用の機械〕a skimmer.
スキミング 1〔特殊な端末機器を使用してクレジットカードの磁気情報を読み取り，偽造カードにそれをコピーして使用するカード犯罪〕(credit card) skimming. 2〔速読法の1つ；飛ばし読み〕skimming.
「スキヤキソング」〔『上を向いて歩こう』の米国版タイトル〕Sukiyaki.
スキル ▣ ポータブル・スキル〔会社や業界を変わっても役立つ汎用性の高い専門的知識〕(develop) a 「transferable [portable] skill.
スクイーク〔電算〕〔子供向け学習用プラットフォームソフト〕Squeak.

スクーター ▣ 三輪スクーター a 3-wheel(ed) scooter.
スクービードゥー〔アニメの犬〕Scooby-Doo. [⇨「弱虫クルッパー」]
スクール ▣ スクール・ソーシャルワーカー a school social worker.
スクデット《It》《サッカー》〔セリエAのリーグ優勝〕Scudetto. ◐ ～を獲得する win the Scudetto.
スクラムジェット・エンジン〔燃焼器内部を超音速に保ったまま燃焼を行う極超音速用の次世代航空機エンジン〕a scramjet engine. ▶ scramjet は supersonic combustion ramjet の略.
スクラロース《化》〔人工甘味料〕sucralose.
スクランブル ▣ スクランブル発進 a scramble.
スクリーントーン〔白黒印刷の原稿に陰影や模様を付けるのためのシール〕a screentone sheet; screentone.
スクリプト ▣ スクリプト・ライター〔撮影台本作家〕a script writer.
スクレイピー〔獣医〕〔伝達性海綿状脳症〕scrapie.
スクロール ▣ スクロール・ホイール〔マウスの左右ボタンにある小さな回転部で，回すと画面が上下に動く〕a scroll wheel.
ずぐろかもめ〔頭黒鷗〕《鳥》〔カモメ科の鳥〕a Saunders' gull; Larus saundersi.
すけかん〔透け感〕 ◐ ～がある sheer; gauzy; diaphanous.
すけこまし〔女をだましてもてあそぶこと〕taking advantage of women; philandering; womanizing; (人) a man who takes advantage of women; a philanderer; a womanizer; a betrayer; a deceiver; 〔女性をだまして売りとばすこと〕pandering [pimping] for an unsuspecting woman; (人) a deceitful 「pander [pimp].
スケリット Skerritt, Tom (1933– ; 米国の映画俳優).
スケルトン[1] ▣ 裏スケルトン〔時計〕＝シースルー・バック〔⇨シースルー〕. ▣ スケルトン・インフィル住宅〔骨格と内装設備を分けた住宅設計〕skeleton infill [SI] housing; 〔その住宅〕a skeleton infill [an SI] house [dwelling]. スケルトン階段〔建〕＝シースルー階段〔⇨シースルー〕. スケルトン賃《賃貸ビルの〕leasing of an unfinished building. スケルトン図〔配管などの〕a 「piping [plumbing, wiring] diagram. スケルトンリフォーム〔建〕〔マンションなどの構造躯体以外の全面的改装〕a complete condominium renovation involving the removal of fixtures and exposure of concrete walls and floors; a "skeleton" renovation.
すけろく〔ずし〕【助六(寿司)】〔稲荷ずしと巻きずしのセット〕inarizushi and makizushi served together.
スコア ▣ 好スコア a good score. トータル・スコア one's total score. ハイ・スコア one's high score. ベスト・スコア one's best score.
スコアリング・モデル〔金融〕a scoring model.
スコアレス・ドロー〔スポーツの試合で双方無得点の引き分け〕a 「scoreless [goalless] draw [tie].
スコヴィル〔トウガラシの辛さの単位〕a Scoville 「scale [unit].
スコーカー〔オーディオの中音用スピーカー〕a squawker.
スコータイ〔タイ西部の古都〕Sukhothai.
スコッツデール〔アリゾナ州中南部の市〕Scottsdale.
スコット 1 Scott, George C(ampbell) (1927–99; 米国の映画俳優). 2 Scott, Tony (1944– ; 米国の映画監督; Ridley の弟).
スコット・トーマス Scott-Thomas, Kristin (1960– ; 英国の映画女優).
スコラ Scola, Ettore (1931– ; イタリアの映画監督).
スコリア ▣ スコリア丘 a scoria cone. スコリア質〔の〕scoriaceous. スコリア層 a scoria 「bed [layer].
「スコルピオンの恋まじない」〔映画〕The Curse of the Jade Scorpion.
すさのおのみこと【素戔嗚尊・須佐之男命】Susanoo-

no-mikoto; the son of Izanagi-no-mikoto and Izanami-no-mikoto, and younger brother to Amaterasu-oomikami, the Sun Goddess.
すし【鮨・寿司】⦿寿司職人 a sushi chef. 寿司ネタ seafood ingredients for sushi. 寿司ロボット a sushi(-making) robot.
すじあおのり【筋青海苔】〖植〗〔緑藻類アオサ科の海藻〕*Enteromorpha prolifera*.
すじぐろかばまだら【筋黒樺斑】〖昆〗〔沖縄産のマダラチョウ科の蝶〕*Salatura genutia*.
すじぐろしろちょう【条黒白蝶】〖昆〗〔シロチョウ科のチョウ〕a black-veined white.
すじぼり【筋彫り】〔線で表わした彫刻〕(a) line-carving; 〔輪郭を彫った刺青〕a line tattoo; line tattooing.
すす【煤】⦿煤粒子 a soot particle.
すすびょう【煤病】〖植物病理〗sooty mold; meliola.
すすめたけ【進茸】〔菌科の発光性のキノコ〕*Dictyopanus gloeocystidiatus*.
すずり【硯】⦿硯(彫り)師 an inkstone carver. ▷ inkstone carving *n*.
すそぐち【裾口】a (bottom) hem. ❹このズボンは～がひもで絞れるようになっています。These slacks can be bunched around the ankles with drawstrings. / このズボンは～が若干広がっている。These slacks have slightly flared bottoms.
すそまわり【裾回り】a (bottom) hem. ❹～210センチのスカート a skirt 210 centimeters around at the hem; a skirt with a 210-centimeter hem. ❹～にパイピングをあしらったジャケット a jacket with piping around the bottom.
スター[1] ⦿スター街道 the road to stardom. ❹この映画に出演後, 彼はスター～をまっしぐらに突き進んだ。His appearance in this movie put him on the high road to stardom.
スター・アライアンス〖空〗〔世界的な航空企業連合の１つ〕Star Alliance.
スターク Stark, Ray (1915-2004; 米国の映画プロデューサー).
「スターシップ・トゥルーパーズ」〖映画〗Starship Troopers.
スタージョンのほうそく【-の法則】Sturgeon's law. ▶「世の中のあらゆるものの90％はクズである。」(Ninety percent of everything is「crud [crap].) という SF 作家 Theodore Sturgeon の言葉から.
スターズ・アンド・ストライプス ＝せいじょうきしんぶん.
スターチス・シヌアータ〖植〗〔イソマツ科の１年草〕a notchleaf sea lavender; *Limonium sinuatum*.
スターティング ⦿スターティング・ゲート〔競馬・スキー競技など〕a starting gate.
スターティング・グリッド〔自動車レースの出走車のスタート位置の表示〕a starting grid.
スタート[1] ⦿スタート順〔レースなどの〕a「starting [start]」order.
「スタートレック」⇨「宇宙大作戦」.
スターバックス〔コーヒーチェーン店〕Starbucks.
「スターリングラード」〖映画〗Enemy at the Gates.
スターンマン〖カヌー など〕〔船尾担当員〕a coxswain.
スタイ〔よだれかけ〕a (baby) bib. ▶ 米国のメーカー名に由来するとされる和製英語.
スタイルズ Stiles, Julia (1981- ; 米国の映画女優).
スタインボック〖動〗〔アフリカ産レイヨウの一種〕a steenbok; a steinbok; *Raphicerus campestris*.
スタチン〖薬〗〔抗高脂血症薬〕a statin. ⦿スタチン系薬剤 a statin drug.
スタッガード・ボード〖経営〗〔取締役の任期を分散すること; 敵対的買収への時間対応策などに〕staggered boards.
スタッブス Stubbs, Imogen (1961- ; 英国の映画女優).
スタテル〔古代ギリシャの貨幣〕a stater.

スタニシェフ Stanishev, Sergei (1966- ; ブルガリア政治家; 首相〔2005- 〕).
ずたぼろ ⦿～に〔ずたずた・ぼろぼろ〕into「pieces [shreds]」. ❹～にされる be wiped out《by an opponent》; be torn up《over a divorce》/ 私は彼とかかわったために身も心も～にされてしまった。My involvement with him left me 「wiped out [in tatters]」both physically and mentally.
スタメン ⦿スタメン出場 an appearance as a「starting player [starter]」. ❹～出場する appear as a「starting player [starter]」; start. スタメンマスク〖野球〗❹～マスクをかぶる〔捕手が〕be the starting catcher; start (a game) as catcher.
スタリ・モスト〔ボスニア・ヘルツェゴビナの石橋〕Stari Most; the Old Bridge in Mostar; the Old Mostar Bridge.
スタンダード・アンド・プアーズ〔米国の格付け機関〕Standard & Poor's (略: S&P).
スタンド ⦿両立〔一本, 片側〕スタンド〔自転車などの〕a「double-legged kickstand [(single-legged) kickstand, prop stand]」. ⦿スタンド灰皿 a (floor) stand ashtray.
スタントン Stanton, Harry Dean (1926- ; 米国の映画俳優).
スタンパ ＝ラ・スタンパ.
スタンプ ⦿スタンプ・カード a stamp card.
スタンプ[2] Stamp, Terence (1939- ; 英国生まれの映画俳優).
スチール[1] ⦿スチール弦〔ギターなどの〕a steel string. スチール・ハウス〔枠組みに鋼材を使用した住宅〕a steel house.
スチグマ〖カトリック〗＝スティグマ.
「スチュアート・リトル」〖映画〗Stuart Little.
スチュワート Stewart, Patrick (1940- ; 英国生まれの映画俳優).
ずつう【頭痛】⦿筋収縮性頭痛 (a) muscle contraction headache. 緊張性〔型〕頭痛 (a) tension-type headache. 群発(性)頭痛 (a) cluster headache. 症候性頭痛 (a) symptomatic headache. 新規発症持続性連日性頭痛 (a) new daily-persistent headache. 非器質性頭痛 (a) nonorganic headache.
すっとこどっこい〔人を罵る言葉〕a stupid「idiot [fool, moron]」.
ステアリング ⦿逆ステアリング〔クレーン車の機能の逆方向反応〕reverse steering.
スティーブンス Stevens, George (1904-75; 米国の映画監督).
スティーンバーゲン Steenbergen, Mary (1953- ; 米国の映画女優).
スティグマ〖カトリック〗〔聖痕〕stigmata.
「スティグマータ / 聖痕」〖映画〗Stigmata.
スティグリッツ Stiglitz, Joseph E. (1943- ; 米国の経済学者).
スティック・バルーン〔棒の先に風船がついたもの〕a balloon on a stick;〔棒状の風船〕a stick-shaped balloon.
スティラー Stiller, Ben (1965- ; 米国の映画俳優).
スティング Sting (1951- ; 英国のロックシンガー・ソングライター; 本名 Gordon Matthew Sumner).
ステークホルダー〔利害関係者〕a stakeholder. ⦿ステークホルダー・ダイアローグ〔利害関係者間の意見交換〕a dialogue「between [among]」stakeholders.
ステーター〖機〗〔モーターの固定子〕a stator.
ステガノグラフィ〔秘密情報を通常データの中に埋め込んで, 秘密の存在自体を隠す技術〕steganography. ▷ steganographic *adj*.
すてごま【捨て駒】〖将棋〗〔取られるのを承知で作戦として打つ駒〕a sacrificed piece;〈比喩的に〉(be used as) a sacrificial pawn.
ステッパー １〔足踏み式健康運動具〕a stepping machine. ２〖電子工学〗〔半導体素子製造装置の一種〕a stepper.
ステップ[1] ⦿ステップアップ死亡保障〖保険〗〔生命保険の〕a stepped-up benefit.

ステップ³【STEP】〔製品データ交換のための国際標準規格〕STEP; standard for the exchange of product model data.
ステップファミリー〔再婚家族〕a stepfamily.
すてゆ【捨て湯】waste [discarded, unused] (hot) water; 〔温泉の〕hot spa water which is「not made use of [discarded, allowed to drain off].
ステルス ▷ ステルス機〖軍〗a stealth aircraft 《pl. 〜》. ステルス性 《a missile with》stealth characteristics.
ステレオグラム〔立体的に見える平面画像〕a stereogram.
ステロイド ▷ ステロイド治療[療法]〖医〗steroid「therapy [treatment]. ステロイド点眼薬[点鼻薬]〖薬〗steroid「eye [nose] drops.
スデロット〔パレスチナ, ガザ地区近郊のイスラエルの町〕Sderot.
ステンカ・ラージンのらん【〜の乱】〖史〗〔1670-71年に起きたロシアの農民反乱〕the Revolt of Stenka Razin.
ステント〖医〗〔血管・食道・尿道などを広げるための網目状の金属製パイプ〕a stent. ▷ 薬剤溶出性ステント a drug-eluting stent. ステント留置(術)stenting.
ステンレス ▷ ステンレス鋼板 a stainless steel sheet.
スト ▷ スト決行 going ahead with a strike; taking strike action. ◐ 〜決行を決議する decide [vote, pass a resolution] to take strike action / 〜決行中. The strike is on. スト突入 rushing into a strike. ◐ 組合は賃金未払いを理由に来週から〜突入の構えを見せている. The union shows signs of rushing into a strike from next week on the grounds of non-payment of wages.
ストア¹ ▷ ストア・ブランド〖商〗a「store [house] brand.
ストゥン・トレン〔カンボジア北東部の州; 同州の州都〕Stung Treng.
ストーカー¹ ▷ ストーカー殺人 (a)「stalking [stalker] murder. ◐ 〜殺人犯 a stalker-murderer. ストーカー保険 stalking [stalker, anti-stalker] insurance.
ストーブ ▷ ペレット・ストーブ a pellet stove. ストーブ列車 a (railroad) train with (coal- or wood-burning) stoves; a stove-heated (railroad) train.
ストーマ〖医〗〔人工排泄口〕a stoma. ▷ ストーマ・ケア stoma care.
すどおり【素通り】▷ 素通り客 a passer-through. ◐ 高速道路が開通してから〜客が増え, この町のホテルの半分が廃業した. Since the expressway opened, an increasing number of tourists just by-pass the town, and half the hotels have closed.
「ストーリー・オブ・ラブ」〔映画〕The Story of Us.
ストッカー〔店頭用陳列棚〕a display case; a showcase; 〔収納棚〕a (storage) cabinet; 〔引き出しがある〕a chest (of drawers). ▶ ストッカーは和製英語. ▷ 冷凍ストッカー a chest freezer; a freezer chest.
ストッキング ▷ 圧迫[弾力, 弾性, 着圧]ストッキング compression stockings. サポート(タイプ)・ストッキング〔着圧により脚の血行・スタイルを改善する〕support stockings. シアー(タイプ)・ストッキング〔薄地のストッキング〕sheer stockings.
ストック ▷ ストック型経営〖経営〗stock-type「business operations [management].
ストックホルムこくさいへいわけんきゅうじょ【〜国際平和研究所】the Stockholm International Peace Research Institute (略: SIPRI).
ストップオーバー〔飛行機の乗り継ぎ地に滞在すること〕a stopover. 〜する stop over 《in [at] Bangkok》.
ストライカー²〖米軍〗〔高速戦闘車両〕a Stryker.
ストライカーりょだんせんとうチーム【〜旅団戦闘〜】〖米軍〗a Stryker brigade combat team (略: SBCT).
ストライプト・バス〔魚〕〔魚食性の淡水魚〕a striped bass; Morone saxatilis.
ストラップ ▷ ネック[リスト]・ストラップ a「neck [wrist] strap.

ストラテジスト〔経済活動の戦略を立てて顧客に提供する専門家〕an investment [a sales, an M & A, etc.] strategist.
ストランディング〔クジラなどが座礁したり, その死体が岸に漂着すること〕(a) stranding.
ストリート ▷ ストリート・フード〔路上で供される料理〕street food.
ストリッピング〖医〗〔表在静脈を皮下で抜去すること〕stripping; venous stripping.
ストリップスさい【〜債】〔米国の元本利子分離債〕STRIPS. ▶ Separate Trading of Registered Interest and Principal of Securities の略.
ストルテンベルグ Stoltenberg, Jens (1959- ; ノルウェーの政治家; 首相〔2000-01, 05- 〕).
「ストレイト・ストーリー」〔映画〕The Straight Story.
ストレージ〖電算〗〔記憶媒体〕a storage medium; a data carrier. ▷ ストレージ・サービス〖電算〗=オンライン・ストレージ・サービス(⇨オンライン).
ストレーツ・タイムズ〔シンガポールの日刊紙〕The Straits Times.
ストレーツ・タイムズしすう【〜指数】〖証券〗〔シンガポールの株価指数〕the Straits Times Index (略: STI). ▶ ストレーツ・タイムズ (The Straits Times) はシンガポールの日刊紙.
ストレス
▷ 快ストレス〖精神医〗eustress. 不快ストレス〖精神医〗distress.
▷ ストレス死 (a) death from stress; (a) stress-related death. ストレス心筋症〖医〗stress cardiomyopathy. ストレス対処行動〖心理〗stress-coping behavior. ストレス耐性 stress「resistance [tolerance] (gene). ▷ stress-resistant[-tolerant] adj. ストレス適応 stress adaptation; adaptation to stress. ストレス・ドック〖医〗a stress checkup. ストレス・ホルモン a stress hormone. 抗ストレス・ホルモン an anti-stress hormone. ストレス要因[原因]a cause of stress; a stressor; a stress builder. ストレス理論 stress theory.
ストローク ▷ ストローク数〔水泳などで〕a stroke count; the number of strokes 《required to swim 50 meters》.
「スナイパー」〔映画〕Liberty Stands Still.
スナイプス Snipes, Wesley (1962- ; 米国の映画俳優).
すないろワラビー【砂色〜】〔動〕an agile wallaby; Macropus agilis.
すなだし【砂出し】=すなぬき.
スナックえんどう【〜豌豆】〔植〕=スナップえんどう.
スナッグゴルフ〔商標・スポーツ〕SNAG golf. ▶ SNAG は Starting New At Golf の略.
スナップ ▷ スナップ・ボタン〔服飾〕a snap button.
スナップえんどう【〜豌豆】〔植〕〔マメ科エンドウの一品種〕a sugar「snap [pea]; a sugar snap pea; "a mangetout (pl. 〜, 〜s).
スナップル〔商標〕〔米国製の清涼飲料〕Snapple.
すなぬき【砂抜き】〔貝類を水に浸けて砂を吐き出させること〕sand removal (by immersion in water).
スニーカー ▷ スニーカー・ソックス 《a pair of》sneaker socks.
スニップ【SNP】〔遺伝〕SNP. ▶ single-nucleotide polymorphism (一塩基多型) の略.
スヌーカー〔ビリヤードのゲームの一種〕snooker (pool).
「スネーク・アイズ」〔映画〕Snake Eyes.
ずのう【頭脳】▷ 頭脳集約型 brain-intensive 《industries》. 頭脳循環〔頭脳流出と頭脳流入の連鎖〕brain circulation. 頭脳戦 a battle of wits 《between the criminal and the police》; a psychological「battle [struggle]; a battle of wills. 頭脳派 a brainy [an intellectual] type. ◐ 古田は〜派のキャッチャーだという定評がある. Furuta is generally thought to be a brainy-type catcher. 頭脳流入 a brain gain; an inflow of talent.

スノー² 1 〔雪〕snow.
2 《自動車レース》〔雪路面〕snowy surface conditions.
▫ スノーホワイト 〔真っ白〕snow-white; (as) white as snow.
スノーケリング ＝シュノーケリング.
スノーシュー 〔かんじき〕《wear》snowshoes.
スノーシューイング 《スポーツ》snowshoeing.
スノーバー 〔登山〕〔雪壁登攀用の器具〕a snow fluke.
スノーボードクロス 《競技》snowboardcross (略: SBX).
スノーボール・アース ＝全球凍結 (⇨ とうけつ).
スノッドグレス Snodgrass, Carrie (1946–2004; 米国の映画女優).
スパ 〔温泉〕a hot spring. ▫ スパ・リゾート 〔温泉保養地〕a spa resort; a hot-spring(s) resort.
スパーク¹ ▫ スパーク・プラグ 〔内燃機関の点火プラグ〕a spark plug; "a sparking plug.
スパーリ ＝スヴァーリ.
スパイ ▫ スパイウェア 〔電算〕〔パソコンに侵入し、ユーザーの個人情報などを外部に漏洩するソフトウェア〕spyware.
「スパイキッズ」〔映画〕Spy Kids.
スパイク ▫ スパイクミス 〔バレーボール〕an attack error.
「スパイ・ゲーム」〔映画〕Spy Game.
「スパイダー」〔映画〕Along Came a Spider.
「スパイダーパニック！」〔映画〕Eight Legged Freaks.
「スパイ大作戦」〔米国の、スパイものの TV ドラマ・映画〕Mission: Impossible.
「スパイのライセンス」〔米国の、釈放を条件に諜報員となった元泥棒の TV ドラマ〕It Takes a Thief. ▶ 初回放映時の邦題は「プロ・スパイ」.
スパイラル ▫ スパイラル・モデル 〔システム開発手順のモデルの１つ〕a [the] spiral (lifecycle) model.
スパイ・リエン ＝スヴァイ・リエン.
スパイロメーター 〔肺機能検査装置〕a spirometer.
スパウト・キャップ a spout cap.
スパゲ(ッ)ティー ▫ スパゲ(ッ)ティー症候群 (the) spaghetti syndrome.
すはだ【素肌・素膚】 ▫ 素肌美人 a woman who is beautiful without makeup; an unadorned [a natural] beauty.
「スパニッシュ・アパートメント」〔映画〕The Spanish Apartment; 〔原題〕L'Auberge Espagnole.
「素晴らしき日」〔映画〕One Fine Day.
「素晴らしき日々」〔60 年代末期の激動の米国社会の中学・高校生活を描いた TV ドラマ〕The Wonder Years.
スパロー 〔米軍〕〔セミアクティブ電波ホーミング式の中距離空対空ミサイル AIM-7 の愛称〕a Sparrow.
スパンブリ 1 〔タイ中部の県〕Suphanburi.
2 〔タイ中部の都市, スパンブリ県の県都〕Suphanburi.
スピアーズ Spears, Britney (1981– ; 米国のポップス歌手).
スピーカー ▫ 波動スピーカー a wave speaker; a vibrational speaker; a vibration speaker. フロント・スピーカー 〔サラウンド再生用の前方スピーカー〕a front speaker. リア・スピーカー 〔サラウンド再生用の後方スピーカー〕a rear speaker.
「スピーシーズ／種の起源」〔映画〕Species.
スピーチ a speech. ▫ スピーチ・セラピスト 〔言語療法士〕a speech therapist (略: ST). スピーチライター a speech-writer (for the president).
スピーディ【SPEEDI】〔緊急時迅速放射能影響予測 (ネットワーク) システム〕SPEEDI; the System for Prediction of Environmental Emergency Dose Information.
スピード ▫ スピード仕上げ fast [quick] finishing. ▫ カラープリント、～仕上げ 〔掲示板〕Fast Color Prints. スピード・バッグ 〔ボクシング〕〔パンチング・ボール〕a speed bag.
「スピード」〔映画〕Speed. ▶ 続編は「スピード 2」(Speed 2: Cruise Control).
スピッツァー 〔天〕〔米国 NASA の宇宙赤外線望遠鏡〕the

Spitzer Space Telescope.
スピナー 〔釣り〕〔回転式の擬餌針〕a spinner.
スピネーカー 《ヨット》＝スピンネーカー.
スピリーバ 〔商標・薬〕〔気管支拡張剤〕Spiriva.
スピルオーバー ▫ スピルオーバー効果 〔経〕〔公共支出による間接的経済効果〕a spillover effect.
スピルリナ 〔植〕〔ラセン藻〕spirulina.
スピン ▫ 低スピン 〔ゴルフ〕〔ドライバーの〕(a) low spin. ▫ スピン量 〔ゴルフ〕〔ボールの〕a spin rate (of 7,500 RPM).
スピン² 〔製本〕〔ひも状のしおり〕a 'ribbon [tassel] bookmark(er). ▶ 和製英語.
スピント 《＜It》〔音楽〕〔オペラ歌手の声質を表現する言葉の、強〈鋭い声〉spinto.
スピン・ドクター 〔政治家の報道対策アドバイザー〕a spin doctor.
スピンドル ▫ スピンドル・モーター 〔機〕a spindle motor.
スピンネーカー 〔ヨット〕〔レース用ヨットの大マストに張る大三角帆; 追い風用〕a spinnaker.
スピンホールこうか【～効果】〔物〕the spin Hall effect.
スフィア 〔幾何〕Sphere.
スフィンクス² 〔猫〕〔1966 年に生まれた突然変異に由来する無毛猫〕a Sphynx (cat); a Canadian hairless (cat).
スフィンゴミエリナーゼ 〔化〕sphingomyelinase.
スプーフィング 〔通信〕〔なりすまし詐欺〕spoofing.
ズブコフ Zubkov, Viktor (1941– ; ロシアの政治家; 首相 [2007–08]).
ズブコフ ＝ズブコフ.
スプマンテ 〔イタリア産発泡性ワイン〕spumante.
スプモーニ 〔カクテル〕a spumoni; a cocktail made from Campari, grapefruit juice and tonic water.
スプラウト 〔芽野菜〕a sprout.
スプラット・ファースじょうこう【～条項】〔低威力核兵器の研究開発を禁じた米国の国防歳出権限法〕the Spratt-Furse 'provision [amendment, law]. ▶ 名称はこれを提案した二人の下院議員の姓から.
スプリング ▫ スプリング効果 〔ゴルフ〕〔クラブフェースの反発力〕a spring-like effect.
スプリングエイト【～-8】〔兵庫県にある大型放射光施設〕SPring-8; Super Photon ring-8 GeV.
スプリント² 〔医〕a splint. ▫ スリープ・スプリント 〔睡眠時無呼吸症候群治療用の口腔内装具〕a sleep splint.
スプルーアンスきゅうくちくかん【～級駆逐艦】〔軍〕〔米国の駆逐艦〕a Spruance-class destroyer.
スプレー ▫ カラー・スプレー 〔噴霧式着色料〕a color spray. ▫ スプレー式殺虫剤 (a) spray insecticide. スプレー式消火器 a 《foam-, water-》spray fire extinguisher.
スプレーぎく【～菊】〔植〕a spray chrysanthemum.
スペイダー Spader, James (1960– ; 米国の映画俳優).
スペインおおやまねこ【～大山猫】〔動〕a Spanish lynx; Felis pardina.
スペース ▫ スペース・ケーブルネット 〔通信衛星を利用してテレビ番組を伝送するネットワーク〕a space cable network. スペース・ハブ 〔宇〕a Spacehab (research) module; a Spacehab laboratory.
スペース 1999 〔英国の、宇宙冒険ものの TV ドラマ〕Space: 1999.
「スペース・カウボーイ」〔映画〕Space Cowboys.
スペースシップワン 〔世界初の民間開発による有人小型宇宙船〕《米》SpaceShipOne.
スペキュラ 〔医〕〔検鏡〕a speculum 《pl. -la, ~s》.
スペクター 〔米軍〕〔対地射撃専用の攻撃機 AC-130 の愛称〕a Spectre.
スペクト【SPECT】〔医〕〔単光子放出断層撮影(法)〕〔装置〕SPECT. ▶ Single Photon Emission Computed Tomography [Tomograph] の略.
スペクトラムかくさんつうしん【～拡散通信】〔通信〕spread spectrum communication.

スペシャル ▣ スペシャル・レフェリー《サッカー》〔日本サッカー協会が認定したプロの審判員〕a special referee (略: SR).
スペシャル・オリンピックス〔知的障害者にスポーツの機会を提供する国際組織〕the Special Olympics;〔その大会〕a Special Olympics; the Special Olympics《Summer》Games.
スペシャルさんびゃくいちじょう【-301 条】《米法》〔通商法における知的財産権保護に関する条項の通称〕the "Special 301" provisions (of the Trade Act of 1974).
スペシャル・ニーズ〔教育面などで障害者がかかえる特殊な必要性〕a special need. ▣ スペシャル・ニーズ教育 special needs education.
スペツナズ《＜Russ spetsialnoe naznachenie special purpose》〔ロシア軍の特殊部隊〕SPETSNAZ.
すべらか ～な smooth; slippery; slick.
すべりどめ【滑り止め】▣ 滑り止め付き手袋 gloves with nonslip palms. 滑り止め塗料〔プラットホームなどの〕nonslip paint.
スホイ《軍》＝スホーイ.
スポイラー ▣ チン・スポイラー《自動車》〔車の前面下部に取り付ける空力部品〕a chin spoiler.
スホイ・ログ〔ロシア,クラスノヤルスク地方にある金鉱床〕Sukhoi Log.
スホーイ〔旧ソ連・ロシア製の戦闘機・曲技スポーツ機など〕a Sukhoi.
スポーカン ＝スポケーン.
スポーケン ＝スポケーン.
スポーツ
▣ 競技スポーツ a competitive sport.
▣ スポーツ・アナウンサー a sports announcer. スポーツ医科学 sports medical science. スポーツ・インストラクター a sports instructor. スポーツ運動学 sports [studies [science, kinesiology]; physical education. スポーツ・カフェ a sports café. スポーツ刈り a [sports [crew] cut. ▷ ～刈りにする[している] get [have] a [sports [crew] cut. スポーツ教室 a sports class. スポーツ経営学 sports management [studies [science]. スポーツ・クラブ a sports [an athletic] club. ▷ 総合型～クラブ a comprehensive sports club. スポーツ国際交流員 a sports exchange advisor (略: SEA). スポーツ紙 a sports newspaper;〔日刊の〕a sports daily. スポーツ指導員 a sports [an athletics] instructor. スポーツ社会学 sport(s) sociology. スポーツ・ジャーナリスト a sports journalist. スポーツ塾 a sports training [center [program]. スポーツ狩猟 sport hunting; hunting for sport;〔鳥獣を殺すという意味で〕a blood sport. スポーツ振興くじ a sports promotion lottery. スポーツ整形外科 sports [orthopedics [orthopedic surgery]. スポーツ・ターフ〔スポーツ競技用の芝生〕sports turf. スポーツダイニング・バー a sports/dining bar. スポーツ・チャンバラ sports chanbara. 反スポーツ的行為 unsportsmanlike conduct; unsporting behavior. スポーツ・トレーナー a sports trainer;〔資格を持った人〕a certified sports trainer. スポーツ・バー〔スポーツ番組をテレビ観戦できるバー〕a sports bar. スポーツ・ビジネス the sports business. スポーツ・プログラマー a certified (recreational) sports programmer. スポーツ・ヘルニア《医》a sports hernia. スポーツ・マーケティング sports marketing. スポーツ(用)多目的車 ⇒スポーツ・ユーティリティー・ビークル.
スポーツあんぜんきょうかい【-安全協会】the Sports Safety Association.
スポーツしんこうきほんけいかく【-振興基本計画】〔文部科学省策定の〕the Basic Plan for the Promotion of Sports.
スポーツ・ユーティリティー・トラック〔ピックアップトラックでスポーツ仕様の〕a sport-utility truck (略: SUT).
スポーツ・ユーティリティー・ビークル〔スポーツタイプの多目的車〕a sport-utility vehicle (略: SUV).
スポーケン〔米国ワシントン州東部の市〕Spokane.
スポッター〔フーリガンなどの顔を識別する警備対策専門の警察官〕a (hooligan) spotter. ▷ (hooligan) spotting n.
スポット ▣ スポット情報〔特定の地域に関する情報〕information on a specific [location [travel destination];〔外務省が出す渡航関連情報〕spot information.
ずぼっと〔物が狭いところに一気にはまりこんだり, きっちりはまった所から勢いよく抜けるさま〕▣ 雪道を歩いていて道から一歩わきに踏み外したら, ～膝まで雪に埋まってしまった. When I was walking along a snow-covered road, I stepped off the road by mistake and sank with a crunch up to my knee in snow. ／泥から突き出ている杭を引っぱると～抜けた. When I pulled on the pole sticking out of the mud, it came out with a [squelch [squirt, slurp].
スポティスウッド Spottiswoode, Roger (1945-   ; 英国生まれの映画監督).
スポレート〔イタリア中部の都市〕Spoleto.
スポンサー ▣ スポンサー企業 a sponsoring [company [corporation]; a corporate sponsor. スポンサー契約 [sign] a sponsorship contract. スポンサー権ship rights. スポンサー(権)料 a (corporate) [sponsorship [sponsor, sponsor's] fee; a fee for sponsorship rights.
スマート
▣ スマート IC ＝スマートインターチェンジ. スマート・インターチェンジ〔自動車専用道路のパーキング・エリアやサービス・エリアに設けた, ETC専用のインターチェンジ〕a "smart interchange"; an entry/exit at a parking or service area, accessible to vehicles with ETC onboard equipment. スマート・カー a smart car. スマート地雷 a smart mine. スマート・ドラッグ〔脳・精神機能を高めるための合法の薬物〕a smart drug;〔多幸感・快感を高めるための合法の薬物〕⇒合法ドラッグ(ごうほう). スマート・ビル〔情報機器などの設備が充実しているオフィスビル〕an intelligent [a smart] building. スマート・プレート《自動車》〔電子ナンバープレート〕a SMART plate. ▶ SMARTは国土交通省が命名したSystem of Multifunctional Integration of Automobiles and Roads in Transport in the 21st Century の略.
スマート・グロース〔米国の都市計画の１つ〕Smart Growth.
スマドラ ＝スマート・ドラッグ (⇒スマート).
スマトラさい【-犀】《動》a Sumatran rhinoceros; Dicerorhinus sumatrensis.
スマトラ(とう)おきじしん【-島)沖地震】〔2004年12月の〕the (2004) Great Sumatra Earthquake. [⇒インドよう(おお)つなみ]
スマトリプタン《薬》〔偏頭痛治療薬〕sumatriptan.
すみ[1]【炭】▣ 炭電池 a charcoal battery.
すみいか【墨烏賊】《動》〔コウイカ〕a cuttlefish; Sepia esculenta.
すみうち【墨打ち】＝すみつけ.
すみおこし【炭熾し】〔炭をおこすこと〕starting [lighting] charcoal;〔道具〕a charcoal starter.
すみかえ【住み替え】▣ 高齢者住み替え支援 assistance to elderly people moving house.
スミシー ⇒アラン・スミシー.
スミス 1 Smith, Alexis (1921-93; カナダ生まれの映画女優; 本名 Gladys Smith).
2 Smith, Kevin (1970-   ; 米国の映画監督・俳優).
3 Smith, Will (1968-   ; 米国の映画俳優).
スミソニアンきょうてい【-協定】＝スミソニアンごうい.
スミソニアンごうい【-合意】〔1971年の〕the Smithsonian Agreement.
スミソニアンこうくうちゅうはくぶつかん【-航空宇宙博物館】the Smithsonian National Air and Space Museum.
すみだし【墨出し】＝すみつけ.
すみつけ【墨付け】《建》〔木材などに墨で線や印をつけること〕carpenter's marking《device》.
すみに【墨煮】《料理》▷ イカの～ squid in ink sauce;

calamari neri.
すみび【炭火】 ▯ 炭火アイロン a charcoal iron.
すみやき【炭焼き】 ▯ 炭焼き職人 a charcoal burner.
スムージング ▯ スムージング・オペレーション〘金融〙〔急激な為替相場の変動を調整するための市場介入〕a smoothing operation; an intervention to moderate market volatility.
スムート・ホーリー（かんぜい）ほう【-（関税）法】〘法〙＝スムート・ホーレー（かんぜい）ほう.
スムート・ホーレー（かんぜい）ほう【-（関税）法】〘米法〙〔1930年制定〕the Smoot-Hawley Tariff Act.
すもう【相撲】 ▯ 相撲解説者 a sumo commentator.
相撲教習所 the Sumo Training School.
すもうはくぶつかん【相撲博物館】〔両国国技館内の〕the Sumo Museum.
スモーカーズ・フェース〔喫煙により老化した顔〕smoker's face.
スモーキー・マウンテン〔フィリピン,マニラ郊外のごみ山〕Smoky Mountain.
スモール・ビジネス〔小規模の企業〕a small「business [enterprise].
スモール・（ベース）ボール〘野球〙〔機動力や小技を特に重視する野球〕small ball.
スモール・ライト〘自動車〙〔車幅灯〕sidelights; side marker [position] lights [lamps].
スモンそしょう【-訴訟】〔1970年代の〕the SMON「case [suit].
スラータニー ＝スラタニ.
スラーヤ〔衛星携帯電話サービスの1つ〕Thuraya.
スライム〔ゲル状の物体の玩具〕slime.
スラタニ 1〔タイ南部の県〕Surat Thani.
2〔タイ南部の都市, スラタニ県の県都〕Surat Thani.
スラッグしゃげき【-射撃】〔射撃競技の1つ〕slug shooting.
スラッシャーえいが【-映画】〘映〙〔刃物で斬りつける殺人犯が主人公の映画〕a slasher「movie [film].
スラット〔ブラインドの小割り板〕a slat;〘空〙〔離着陸時に使う翼前面の高揚力装置〕a slat.
スラブ[1]〔スラブ軌道〘鉄道〙〔道床の一種〕a slab track.
スラムダンク〘バスケット〙a slam dunk.
スラユット Surayud Chulanont (1943- ; タイの軍人・枢密院議員; 首相〔2006-08〕).
スランプ ▯ スランプ気味〔あの選手は最近～気味だ。That player has「been in something [shown signs] of a slump recently.
すり[2]【掏摸】 ▯ 断ぎり【ナイフでバッグなどを切り裂き,中のものを奪うスリ〕cutting and picking; sb's《bag》).
武装すり団 a gang of armed muggers; an armed gang of thieves.
スリー・アール【3R】〔循環型社会構築のための3要素〕the three Rs; the 3Rs. ▶ 3R は reduce（廃棄物の発生抑制）, reuse（再使用）, recycle（再資源化）の意. ▯ 3R政策 a "3R" policy; a "reduce, reuse and recycle" policy.
スリー・アール・イニシアティブかくりょうかいぎ【3R-閣僚会議】the Ministerial Conference on the 3R Initiative. ▶ 2005年東京で開かれた循環型社会の実現をめざす国際会議. 3R は reduce, reuse, recycle の意.
スリーエックス・エル【XXXL】〔物品のサイズ〕XXXL.
「スリー・キングス」〔映画〕Three Kings.
スリー・チャイナ〔中国・台湾・香港を合わせた呼称〕the three Chinas.
スリートップ〘サッカー〙〔前線にフォワード3人を配置する攻撃態勢〕a「three-forward [three-striker] attack [formation].
スリーパー・セル ＝睡眠細胞（⇨すいみん）.
スリーバック〘サッカー〙〔ディフェンダー3人を配置する戦術〕a「three-back [three-defender] formation.
「スリーピー・ホロウ」〔映画〕Sleepy Hollow.

「スリーピーホローの伝説」〔ワシントン・アーヴィング作の短篇集『スケッチ・ブック』中の一篇〕The Legend of Sleepy Hollow.
スリープ ▯ スリープ機能〘電算〙〔節電用の休止機能〕a sleep function.
スリーボックス・カー【-[3]-】〘自動車〙*a sedan; "a saloon.
スリック・タイヤ〔溝のないタイヤ〕a slick tire.
スリミング・コスメ〔塗った部分が痩せると称する塗布剤〕(a) slimming「treatment [lotion, gel].
スリランカ ▯ スリランカ内戦〔1980年代以降の〕(the) civil war in Sri Lanka; the Sri Lanka(n) civil war.
スリン 1〔タイ東北部の県〕Surin.
2〔タイ東北部の町, 同名の県の県都〕Surin.
スリング〔赤ちゃんをだっこするための袋状の吊り帯〕a baby sling.
スルー・パス〘サッカー〙a through pass.
するがトラフ【駿河-】〘地質〙the Suruga Trough.
スルファジミジン〘化〙〔合成抗菌剤〕sulfadimidine.
スルファメサジン〘化〙〔合成抗菌剤〕sulfamethazine. [= スルファジミジン]
スルフォラファン〘化〙〔抗がん物質〕sulforaphane.
ずるむけ【ずる剥け】〔皮膚がベロリとむけたさま〕 ▯ 皮膚が～になった焼死体 horribly burned bodies「with no skin on them [from which the skin had peeled off].
スレイマニア〔イラク北東部の州;その州都〕Sulaymaniyah.
スレイマン・ベイク〔イラク中北部,サラハディン州の都市〕Sulayman Beg.
スレーター Slater, Christian (1969- ; 米国の映画俳優; 本名 Christian Hawkins).
スレッジ・ホッケー〔そりに乗って行う身障者向け（アイス）ホッケー〕sledge hockey.
スレブレニツァ〔ボスニア東部の町〕Srebrenica.
スレブレニツァぎゃくさつじけん【-虐殺事件】〔1995年7月セルビア人勢力によりボスニア・ヘルツェゴヴィナのスレブレニツァにおいてイスラム教徒の男性7,000人以上を虐殺した事件〕the Srebrenica Massacre; Srebrenica Genocide.
すろうにん【素浪人】a common「rōnin [masterless samurai].
スロー[2] ▯ スロー・トレーニング slow training. ▯ スロー走行〘自動車レースで〕slow driving. スロー・ツーリズム slow tourism. スロー・ライフ (a) slow life. ▯ ～ライフを送る live a slow life.
スローク【SLORC】〔ミャンマーの国家法秩序回復評議会〕SLORC, the State Law and Order Restoration Council. ▶ 1997年, 国家平和発展評議会と改称.
スロースリップ〘地質〙＝ゆっくりすべり.
スローピッチ・ソフトボール〘スポーツ〙〔ソフトボールの一種〕slow-pitch softball.
スローフードきょうかい【-協会】〔本部はイタリア〕Slow Food.
スロー・モーション ▯ スロー・モーション撮影 a slow-motion shot.
スロッシング〔容器の揺れに伴って液体表面が大きく共振する現象〕sloshing (phenomenon).
～する slosh.
スロトレ ＝スロー・トレーニング（⇨スロー[2]）.
すわかれ【巣分かれ・巣別れ】〔蜜蜂の分封〕swarming.
スワップ ▯ スワップ金利 swap interest; interest on a swap transaction.
スワデシ, スワデーシー〔インドの国産品愛用/英国品排斥］運動〕Swadeshi.
スワポ【SWAPO】〔南西アフリカ人民機構〕SWAPO; the South-West African People's Organization.
スワヤンブナート〔ネパール,カトマンズ西部のチベット仏教寺院〕Swayambhunath Stupa.
すわりづくえ【座り机】a low desk (used in a Japanese-style room).

すわりばた【座り機】＝じばた．
スワロフスキー〖商標〗〔オーストリアのクリスタルブランド〕Swarovski．
スワンク Swank, Hilary (1974–　；米国の映画女優；本名 Hilary Ann Swank).
スワンナブーム〔タイ，バンコク郊外に 2006 年開港の国際空港名〕Suvarnabhumi Airport．
スンアン【順安】〔北朝鮮平壌の地区〕Sunan．
スンウ【星宇】〔韓国，江原道のスキーリゾート地〕Sungwoo．

スンガイコ(ー)ロク〔タイ南部，マレーシア国境の町〕Sungai Kolok．
スンダランド〔東南アジアの古大陸〕Sundaland．
スンチョン【順川】〔北朝鮮，平安南道の都市〕Sunchon．
スンニ・トライアングル〔イラクのバグダッド・ラマディ・ティクリートを結ぶ三角地帯；イスラム教スンニ派の住民が多い〕the Sunni triangle．
スンニはさんかくちたい【－派三角地帯】〔スンニ・トライアングル〕the Sunni triangle．

# せ

# せ

せあかはなどり【背赤花鳥】〖鳥〗〔ハナドリ科の小鳥〕a scarlet-backed flowerpecker; *Dicaeum cruentatum*.
せい⁵【性】▱ 性依存症 (a) sexual addiction. 性嗜好異常〖精神医〗paraphilia. ▷ paraphiliac *adj*. ◐ ～嗜好異常者 a paraphiliac; a paraphile. 性衝動 ⇨せいしょうどう. 性自認〖心理〗gender identity. 性情報 information about sex. ◐ ～情報の氾濫 a「deluge [flood] of information about sex. 性産業 a [the] sex industry. 性描写 (a)「description [depiction] of sex; (a) sexual「description [depiction]. 性風俗店 a sex establishment.
-せい⁴【-性】〔性質・程度などを表す〕-ty; -ity; -ness. ◐ 残虐～ cruelty / 可能～ possibility / 排他～ exclusiveness / 作家～ writerliness; *one's* characteristics as a writer.
ぜい¹【税】▱ 税財政 tax finances.
-ぜい【-勢】◐ 日本～ Japanese (players, companies, etc.) / ベテラン～と新顔～監督による作品 works by experienced and new directors / 弊社のシェア低下の原因はアジア～の進出にある．The reason for the drop in our market share is the entry of competitors from Asia. / 全国大会で地元～にがんばってほしい．I hope the locals will try hard in the national tournament.
せいあつ【制圧】◐ 制圧国〔ハンセン病などの〕a country where the prevalence of《leprosy》is less than one per 10,000 people. ◐ 未～国 a country where the prevalence of《leprosy》is more than one per 10,000 people. 制圧作戦 a suppression「operation [campaign]; an operation [a campaign] to subdue 《rebels》; a suppression strategy.
「ゼイ・イート・ドッグス」〔映画〕In China They Eat Dogs.
せいいく¹【生育】▱ 生育条件 growth conditions. 生育不足〖動植物の〗insufficient growth. 生育歴〔(a baby's)〕growth history; the history of《a baby's》development.
せいいく²【成育】〔育ち，成長すること〕growth (into maturity).
～する grow (up); be「brought up [raised]. ▱ 成育医療 pediatric and parental health care. 成育歴 a record of growth; a development record.
せいう³【星宇】＝スンウ．
せいおん⁵【静音】▱ 静音化 noise [sound] reduction; muting; damping; muffling. 静音性〖機〗〔モーター音などがしないこと〕quietness; silence. 静音冷却 quiet [silent] cooling.
せいか⁶【成果】▱ 成果主義人事 performance-based staffing; a performance-based personnel policy. 成果主義 resultism. 成果報酬型広告〔インターネット広告の一種〕pay-per-performance advertising. 〔⇨アフィリエイト〕成果目標 a targeted result.
せいか¹⁷【製菓】▱ 製菓衛生師 a confectionery hygienist.
せいかい¹【正解】▱ 正解率 a《high》percentage of correct answers.

せいかい⁴【政界】▱ 政界地図 a map of the political world; a [the] political map《of Japan》. 政界復帰 returning [a return] to politics《after serving a prison sentence》. ◐ 彼は次の総選挙で～復帰をめざしている．He is aiming to「make a political comeback [get back into politics] at the next general election.
せいかいチベットてつどう【青海-鉄道】＝せいぞうてつどう．
せいがいふ【聖骸布】〖キリスト教〗〔キリストの遺骸を包んだ布〕Christ's shroud.
せいかく⁴【性格】▱ 性格分析 character [personality] analysis. 性格分類 personality [character] typing [classification]. 血液型〔体型〕による～分類 personality classification according to「blood type [somatotype, type of physique].
せいかつ²【生活】
▱ 生活音 household「noises [sounds]; the「noises [sounds] of daily domestic life. 生活学 daily living skills; life skills; "daily life studies." 生活家電 household electric appliances. 生活幹線道路 a main road serving a community; an arterial community lifeline road. 生活拠点 a [*one's*] (domestic) base. ◐ 彼は退職後，都内のマンションから海辺の町に～拠点を移した．After he retired he moved from his city apartment and「established a new base [started a new life] in a town by the sea. 生活訓練〔障害者・受刑者などに対する〕rehabilitation training. 生活ごみ household「garbage [rubbish, trash, refuse]; domestic garbage; everyday garbage. 生活痕 traces [vestiges] of human life《in a cave》. 生活雑貨 goods [things] for everyday life. 生活弱者 a disadvantaged person; a person for whom life is difficult;〈集合的に〉the weak; the disadvantaged. 生活相談 counseling concerning matters of daily life; life counseling. 生活体力 sufficient (physical) strength for an independent life. 生活パターン a lifestyle pattern. ◐ 毎朝 7 時に起床して，夜は 11 時には就寝というのが，今の私の基本的な～パターンです．Right now my basic lifestyle pattern consists of getting up at seven o'clock every morning and going to bed at eleven o'clock at night. 生活福祉資金 a (low interest) welfare loan. 生活保障（financial [economic]）security; security of livelihood(s). 生活密着型《a convenience store》closely geared to daily living. 生活モデル〔社会福祉などにおける〕a possible life style《for a handicapped person》; a model for living. 生活用水 water for daily life; a domestic water supply;〔地域の〕a community water supply. 生活リズム *one's* life rhythm; the rhythm of《*one's*》daily life;〔生体リズム〕a biorhythm. 生活リハビリ a rehabilitation program designed to enable patients to maintain and improve physical functions so that they can carry on a normal daily life. 生活歴〔患者の〕《a patient's》background; the background《of a patient》.

せいかつかんきょうせいびほう【生活環境整備法】〖法〗 the Living Environment Maintenance Law. ▶ 正式名称は「防衛施設周辺の生活環境の整備等に関する法律」(the Law Concerning Adjustment, etc. of the Living Environment in the Environs of Defense Facilities).

せいかつクラブせいきょうれんごうかい【生活＝生協連合会】the Seikatsu Club Consumers' Co-operative Union (略: SC(CU)).

せいかつしえん【生活支援】 ▭ 生活支援ロボット a home-help robot; a home life support robot.

せいかつふかっぱつびょう【生活不活発病】〖医〗〔廃用症候群〕disuse syndrome.

せいかつほご【生活保護】 ▭ 生活保護家庭 a family on「*welfare [ᵁmoulding]benefit(s)」. ▭ 生活保護費「*welfare [ᵁsocial security] benefits. 生活保護費自己負担の the「central government, local authority」share of「*welfare [ᵁsocial security] costs.

せいかん⁹【製缶】 ▭ 製缶会社 a can「manufacturer [manufacturing company].

せいがん³【西岸】 ▭ 西岸入植地〔パレスチナのヨルダン川西岸のイスラエル人入植地〕a West Bank settlement.

せいがん⁵【請願】 ▭ 請願駅〖鉄道〗a railway station constructed at the request of a municipal government or local residents or businesses.

せいかんせんしょう【性感染症】 ▭ 性感染症検査 an STD test; STD testing; a test [testing] for sexually transmitted diseases. ◯ 〜検査キット an [a home] STD testing kit.

ぜいかんそうごしえんきょうてい【税関相互支援協定】a customs mutual assistance agreement (略: CMAA).

せいがんふ【聖顔布】〖キリスト教〗〔十字架を背負ったイエスの顔をぬぐった布〕the mandylion.

せいがんほう【請願法】〖法〗〔日本の〕the Petition Law.

せいかんろん【征韓論】〖日本史〗〔幕末から明治初期にかけての, 武力で朝鮮を開国しようとする主張〕the debate over sending a military expedition to Korea; (the) seikanron.

せいき⁷【性器】 ▭ 性器脱〖医〗genital prolapse. 性器露出 indecent exposure (of one's genitals); exhibition [display] of the genitals.

せいぎ¹【正義】 ▭ 正義論 a theory of justice.

せいきざん【正規産】〖医〗〔妊娠 37−41 週での出産〕(a) full-term delivery. ▭ 正期産児 a full-term「baby [infant].

せいぎとびょうどううんどう【正義と平等運動】〔スーダンの反政府武装勢力〕the Justice and Equality Movement (略: JEM).

せいぎょ³【制御】 ▭ 集中制御 centralized control (略: CC). ▭ 制御音〔騒音を低減するための逆位相の音波〕a (noise)「control [cancellation] wave. 制御素子 a control「device [element]. 制御ソフト〖電算〗control software. 制御不能 out of control; uncontrollable. ◯ 〜不能になる〔陥る〕〈人が主語〉become unable to control sth; lose control 《of one's car》; 〈物が主語〉get out of control; become uncontrollable.

せいきょう³【政教】 ▭ 政教分離規定〖憲法〗a (constitutional) provision for the separation of「religion and politics [church and state].

せいぎょう²【生業】 ▭ 生業支援〔生活福祉資金の 1 つ〕financial support to reintegrate a welfare recipient into the workforce.

せいきょうぶんりほう【政教分離法】〖フランス法〗the (1905) Law of Separation (of Church and State); 〔フランス語〕La loi de séparation de l'Eglise et de l'Etat (de 1905).

ぜいきん【税金】 ▭ 税金逃れ tax evasion; evading taxes. 税金避難地 a tax haven.

せいきんは【星菫派】 the「Seikin [stars and violets] school of romantic poets of the late Meiji era.

せいけい³【成形・成型】 ▭ 一体成型 solid casting. ▭ 成形技術 (a)「molding [ᵁmoulding, forming] technology.

せいけん⁶【政権】 ▭ 本格政権 a「formal [proper, regular] government. ▭ 政権運営 management [the running] of「an administration [a cabinet]. ◯ 国民の高い支持率に支えられて首相は安定した〜運営ができるだろう。With high poll ratings the Prime Minister should be able to run a stable administration. 政権協力〔政権を取るための政党間の〕(inter-)party cooperation (to gain power [for election purposes]). 政権公約〔政党の〕an election platform;「an election manifesto. 政権奪還〔奪回〕a return to power. 政権奪取 seizing [《口》 grabbing] power; taking over 《from the Liberal Democratic Party》; (a) seizure of power; taking over the reins of government. 政権転覆 the「overthrow [overturn, subversion] of「a government [regime]. 政権離脱 withdrawal from [quitting] the「ruling coalition [government].

せいけん⁸【精検】 ▭ 要精検〖医〗〔健康診断後の指示〕Needs Follow-Up; Detailed Examination Required.

せいげん³【制限】 ▭ 収入制限 ＝所得制限. 所得制限 an income limit; a limit on (permitted) income; a maximum income. ▭ 児童手当には所得〜がある。There is「an income limit [a maximum permitted income] for child benefits. 持ち込み制限 restrictions [limit] on objects that may be brought in. ◯ 機内持ち込み〜品 objects one may not bring on board an airplane. ▭ 制限付き株式 ＝譲渡制限株式 (⇒じょうと).

せいげん¹【税源】 ▭ 税源移譲 ⇨いじょう³.

せいこう⁴【成功】 ▭ 成功(事)例 an example [a case] of success; a successful「example [case]. 成功体験 (a)「successful [success] experience; (an [the]) experience of success. 成功報酬型広告 ＝成果報酬型広告 (⇒せいか⁶). 成功モデル a「successful [success] model. 成功裏, 成功裡 ◯ 〜裏に終わる end in success; be a success / 超小型人工衛星の打ち上げ実験は〜に終了した。The experimental launch of the ultra-small artificial satellite was「successfully concluded [brought to a successful conclusion].

せいこう⁹【性交】 ▭ 性交死 《sudden》death during (or after)「sexual intercourse [sex]. 性交障害 an impediment to intercourse; sexual dysfunction. 性交体験〔経験〕率 a rate of「sex [sexual] experience 《among college students》.

せいこん¹【成婚】 ▭ 成婚率〔結婚相談所などの〕a「rate [percentage] of「marriages [marriage unions] concluded.

せいさ¹【性差】 ▭ 社会的性差 (social) gender. 生物学的性差 (biological) sex. ▭ 性差医療〖医〗gender-specific medicine.

せいさ⁴【聖座】〖カトリック〗〔教皇・教皇庁〕the Holy See. ▭ 空飛ぶ聖座〔積極的な外交活動を展開したヨハネ・パウロ 2 世について使われた言葉〕the Flying Pope.

せいさい²【制裁】 ▭ 制裁解除 lifting [removal] of sanctions. 制裁課税 punitive taxation; a punitive tax. 制裁減免制度 a「punishment [penalty, sanction] reduction and exemption system; a leniency system. 制裁対象国 a sanctioned country. 制裁の慰謝料 punitive compensation. 制裁品目〔経済制裁の〕embargoed [sanctioned] goods [items, products]; items subject to「embargo [sanctions].

せいざい¹【製材】 ▭ 製材残material ＝製材廃材. 製材材 wood [lumber] scraps.

せいざいかい【政財界】the political and business「world [communities]; political and business circles. ◯ 〜の大物 leading figures in politics and business /

**せいさく** ～の癒着 collusion between 「the political and business worlds [politicians and business leaders]. ◆ 政財界人 politicians and businesspeople.

**せいさく**[1]【制作】 ◆ 制作ドキュメンタリー〔映画などの作品の制作過程を記録した映像〕a "making-of" documentary; a (behind-the-scenes) documentary on the making of 《a feature film》. 制作番号〔リトグラフなどの〕a print number; a copy number;〔製品の〕a production number; a serial number;〔工場の〕a factory number.

**せいさく**[2]【政策】 ◆ 政策課題 a policy issue. 政策活動費 political activity funding from political parties to Diet members. 政策通 a policy expert;《口》a policy wonk. 政策統括官 a policy director-general. 政策目標 a policy 「goal [target]; the goal of a policy.

**せいさくけんきゅうだいがくいんだいがく**【政策研究大学院大学】the National Graduate Institute for Policy Studies (略: GRIPS).

**せいさくひょうかほう**【政策評価法】【法】the Law on Assessment of Policies. ▶ 正式名称は「行政機関が行う政策の評価に関する法律」(the Law Concerning Assessment of Policies Carried Out by Administrative Agencies).

**せいさん**[2]【生産】 ◆ 限定生産 limited production. ◆ 初回限定～ once only [one-off, not-to-be-repeated] production / 予約限定～ production only to meet advance orders; production on a limited advance-order basis. ◆ 生産請負制〔各農家が生産を請け負い、一定の生産物を上納すれば残りは市場で販売できる今日の中国の制度〕the household responsibility contract system (of agricultural production); the (agricultural) production contract system. 生産効率〔生産能率〕(increase) (production) efficiency. 生産時点情報管理システム a 「point-of-production [POP] system. 生産情報 production information. ◆ ～情報公表 JAS 規格のJapanese Agricultural Standard on the disclosure of production information. 生産動態統計〔経済産業省発表の〕current production statistics. 生産補完 complementary production of different types of vehicle by the companies in an alliance. 生産履歴 a production history. 生産枠 a production quota. ◆ OPEC の国別～枠 OPEC production quotas by 「country [nation].

**せいさん**[6]【清算】 ◆ 清算市場 a clearing market. 清算取引《商》a clearing contract.

**せいさんしゃ**【生産者】 ◆ 生産者責任 producer responsibility (略: PR). ◆ 拡大～責任〔生産者・輸入業者は製品のライフサイクルを通じてそれが環境に及ぼす影響に関して応分の責任を負うという考え方〕extended producer responsibility (略: EPR). 生産者番号〔manufacturer('s) [producer('s)] identification number.

**せいさんぶつぶんよきょうてい**【生産物分与協定】〔事業の当事国とその事業に投資している外国企業との間の利益配分に関する取り決め〕a production sharing agreement (略: PSA).

**せいじ**[3]【政治】 ◆ 政治アナリスト a political analyst. 政治カード《use sth as》a political bargaining chip. ◆ 中国政府は靖国問題を～カードとして利用していると彼は主張した. He claimed the Chinese government was using the Yasukuni Shrine issue as a political bargaining chip. 政治介入 (a) political intervention. 政治活動費 political (activity) expenses. 政治コンサルタント a political consultant. ◆ ～コンサルタント会社 a political consultancy. 政治雑誌 a political magazine. 政治手法 a certain 「politician's [political party's] way of dealing with things. 政治心理学 political psychology. 政治体質 a political 「framework [set-up];（escape from the traditional）kind of politics. 政治（的）手腕 political 「skill(s) [《口》 savvy, "nous"]. ◆ ～手腕を発揮する display one's political skills / 新大統領の～手腕は未知数だ. The new president's political skills are an unknown quantity. 政治難民 a political refugee. 政治犯罪 a political offense. 政治文書 a political document. 政治マター a political matter; a matter for the politicians (to handle). 政治漫画〔ひとこま漫画の〕a political cartoon. 政治理念 one's political ideal(s).

**せいしき**[1]【正式】 ◆ 正式種目【競技】〔オリンピックなどの〕an official 《sports》event.

**せいししょう**【青視症】【医】cyanopsia; blue vision.

**せいじてき**【政治的】 ◆ 政治的意図 political intentions; a political intent(ion). 政治の賭け a political gamble. 政治の駆け引き political bargaining. 政治的緊張 political tension(s)《in the Middle East》. 政治的けじめ ◆ ～けじめをつけて辞職する take responsibility as a politician and resign; resign to take political responsibility. 政治的混乱〔create, invite〕political 「confusion [turmoil, chaos]. 政治の弾圧 political oppression.

**せいしぼさつ**【勢至菩薩】【仏教】《<Skt》Mahasthamaprapta Bodhisattva.

**せいしゃいん**【正社員】 ◆ 短時間正社員 a regular (company) employee working (temporarily) reduced hours; a regular member of staff whose working hours are temporarily reduced《for childcare》. 地域限定正社員 a regular employee who cannot be reassigned to a position requiring a change of residence. 非正社員 a non-regular employee; a temp(orary) worker.

**せいしゅ**【清酒】 ◆ 清酒酵母 (a) sake yeast.

**せいじゅう**【聖獣】〔神聖視されている動物〕a sacred 「beast [creature].

**ぜいしゅう**【税収】 ◆ 税収弾性値【経】elasticity of tax revenue.

**せいしゅん**【青春】 ◆ 青春小説 a novel 「of youth [about young people]; a youth novel. 青春ドラマ a (TV) drama 「of youth [centered on young people]; a youth drama. ◆ その韓国ドラマは20年ほど前の日本の～ドラマを見るようだった. Watching the Korean TV drama was like watching a Japanese youth drama of about twenty years ago.

**せいしょう**[8]【星章】 ◆ 銀星章《米軍》a Silver Star (Medal). 青銅星章《米軍》a Bronze Star (Medal).

**せいじょう**[3]【星状】 ◆ 星状細胞腫【医】an astrocytoma《pl. ～s, -mata》; an astrocytic tumor.

**せいじょうえいせいはっしゃセンター**【西昌衛星発射-】〔中国の〕the Xichang Satellite Launch Center.

**せいじょうきしんぶん**【星条旗新聞】〔米軍の準機関誌〕Stars and Stripes.

**せいしょうどう**【性衝動】(the) sex drive; the [a] sexual urge;【医・心理】(the) libido. ◆ その瞬間彼は強い～に駆られ、少女に襲いかかった. At that instant he was overcome by 「sexual passion [(an attack of) lust] and threw himself on her. ◆ この薬には～を抑える効果がある. This 「drug [medicine] has the effect of reducing 「libido [the sex drive].

**せいしょうねん**【青少年】 ◆ 青少年育成施策大綱 the Guidelines for Measures on the Cultivation of Youth. 青少年育成指導員 a youth guidance 「counselor [officer]. 青少年育成推進本部〔政府の〕the Headquarters for Promotion of Cultivation of Youth. 青少年健全育成条例 a healthy youth development ordinance; an ordinance on healthy youth development. 青少年白書 a white paper on youth;〔内閣府の〕the 《2004》White Paper on Youth in Japan. 青少年問題協議会 a Juvenile Problems Council.

**せいしょく**[3]【生殖】 ◆ 卵生殖【生物】〔異形配偶子の接

合による〕oogamy. ▷ oogamous adj. 🔲 生殖医学 reproductive [reproduction] medicine. [⇨生殖医療] 生殖医療〚医〛reproductive [reproduction] treatment;〔生殖補助医療〕assisted reproductive technology (略: ART);〔不妊治療〕infertility [fertility] treatment; treatment for「infertility [sterility]. 生殖群泳〚生物〛〔魚の〕reproductive swarming. 生殖生物学 reproductive biology.

**せいしょく**[5]【青色】🔲 青色巨星〚天〛a blue giant (star). 青色超巨星〚天〛a blue supergiant.

**せいしょくがく**【生殖学】〚生物〛reproductive [reproduction] biology; the biology of reproduction;〔遺伝〕genesiology. 🔲 環境生殖学 environmental reproductive biology. 動物生殖学 animal reproductive biology.

**せいしん**[4]【制振・制震】🔲 アクティブ[パッシブ]制振 active [passive] vibration damping. 🔲 制震技術 seismic engineering. 制震装置 a seismic [an antiseismic] device.

**せいしん**[8]【精神】🔲 精神活性物質 a psychoactive substance. 精神生理性不眠症〚医〛psychophysiological insomnia. 精神発達遅滞〚医〛〔精神遅滞〕mental retardation.

**せいじん**[1]【成人】🔲 新成人 "new adults"; 20 year-olds who have just「come of age [attended a coming-of-age ceremony]. 🔲 成人識別 (IC) カード〔たばこなどの自動販売機に使う〕an adult identification card (with an integrated circuit). 成人識別機能〔酒・たばこなどの自動販売機の〕the ability to recognize an adult; an adult recognition device. ◯ ～識別機能付き自動販売機 a vending machine that can「recognize an adult [distinguish adults from minors].

**せいしんかんてい**【精神鑑定】🔲 精神鑑定書 a psychiatric「report [evaluation].

**せいしんしょうがいのしんだん・とうけいマニュアル**【精神障害の診断・統計】〔米国精神医学会による精神障害の診断・統計マニュアル〕the Diagnostic and Statistical Manual of Mental Disorders (略: DSM).

**せいしんてき**【精神的】🔲 精神的圧力〔put〕psychological pressure (on sb). 精神的虐待〔暴力〕psychological [mental] abuse [violence]. 精神的支柱〔柱〕(a)「psychological [spiritual, moral] support; a psychological [an emotional] prop [mainstay]; the [one's] chief psychological support. 精神的指導者 a spiritual「leader [teacher, mentor, guide].

**せいじんびょう**【成人病】🔲 三大成人病〔がん・心疾患・脳血管疾患〕the three major adult diseases; cancer, heart disease and stroke.

**せいしんほけん**【精神保健】🔲 精神保健福祉手帳 a handbook for the welfare of the mentally disordered.

**せいすいべん**【制水弁】a water control valve;〔堰などの〕a sluice valve.

**せいせい**[4]【精製】🔲 精製度 a (high) degree of refinement; (a) purity. ◯ ～度 99.9% の砂糖 sugar of a purity of 99.9%.

**ぜいせい**[2]【税制】🔲 税制適格年金〔適格退職年金〕the Qualified Employee Retirement Pension (Plan); the Retirement Annuity for Qualified Personnel. 税制優遇措置 a tax preference;〔口〕a tax break.

**せいせき**[1]【成績】🔲 成績係数〚物〛〔消費電力当たりの冷却・加熱能力を表す数値〕a coefficient of performance (略: COP, CP); a performance coefficient. 成績分布 (a) test [(an) exam] results distribution; the distribution of results.

**せいせん**[4]【聖戦】🔲 聖戦機構〔イスラム諸国などの〕a ji-had organization.

**せいぜん**[1]【生前】🔲 生前意思(表示) a living will. 生前給付〔生命保険の〕a living benefit; an accelerated death benefit. 生前保険 living benefit insur-

ance. 生前同意 consent given「during one's life [before one dies]; lifetime consent.

**せいせんし**【聖戦士】a holy warrior; a crusader;〔イスラム世界の〕a jihadi; a jehadi.

**せいそう**[9]【清掃】🔲 清掃登山 a 《Mount Fuji》 cleanup climb; a 《Mount Everest》 cleanup expedition.

**せいそう**[13]【世宗】=セジョン 1.

**せいぞう**[3]【製造】🔲 製造基盤白書 =ものづくり白書 (⇨ものづくり). 製造小売り〔衣料〕〔製造から販売までの一括管理〕SPA. ▶ SPA は specialty store retailer of private label apparel (アパレル製造小売り専門業者) の意;〔小売り業者〕a manufacturing retailer. 製造者責任〔欠陥製品などに対する〕(a) manufacturer's responsibility;〔製品が環境に及ぼす影響に対する〕⇨せいさんしゃ〔生産者責任〕.

**せいぞうてつどう**【青蔵鉄道】〔中国の青海省とチベットを結ぶ、世界で最も標高の高い区間を含む鉄道〕the Qinghai-Tibet Railway.

**せいぞうはんばいごあんぜんかんりきじゅん**【製造販売後安全管理基準】〚薬〛〔医療用医薬品製造販売業の許可要件となる市販後管理の実施基準を定めた省令〕(a) good-vigilance practice (略: GVP).

**せいぞうはんばいひんしつほしょうきじゅん**【製造販売品質保証基準】〚薬〛〔医療用医薬品製造販売業の許可要件となる品質保証の実施基準を定めた省令〕(a) good-quality practice (略: GQP).

**せいそく**[2]【生息】🔲 生息域 a habitat; a range; a territory. 生息状況〔野生生物などの〕the state of survival 《of a species》. 生息数 the number 《of tigers》 in the wild; (the size of) a population;〔希少動物などの〕the number of individuals surviving. ◯ 野生のトラの楽園といわれるインドでトラの～数が激減している. In India, said to be a paradise for wild tigers, the number of surviving individuals has declined dramatically. 生息調査〔野生生物などの〕a population survey. 生息範囲 (the「range [extent, size] of) a habitat; a range. ◯ 地球温暖化のせいで, 熱帯生物の～範囲が北に広がっている. With global warming, tropical organisms are extending their habitats north(wards). 生息分布 the population distribution 《of a species》. 生息密度 (a) population density.

**せいぞん**【生存】🔲 生存確認 confirmation that sb is (still) alive. 生存空間〔列車・自動車・航空機などの衝突時の破壊・変形に対して内部の人間の生存を確保できるだけの空間〕;〔動植物が生存できる空間〕a survival zone. 生存時間解析〚統計〛survival analysis. 生存情報《receive》information that sb is still alive. 生存分析〚統計〛survival analysis. 生存欲求〚心理〛the need to survive;〔生理的欲求〕physiological needs.

**せいたい**[3]【生体】🔲 生体確認〔生体認証〕biometrics; biometric「authentication [verification]. 生体情報 biological information;〔パスポートなどで使う〕biometric information;〚医〛〔生命徴候〕(a patient's) vital signs. 生体試料 a biological specimen. 生体弁〚医〛〔人工弁の一種, ブタやウシの組織から作る〕a tissue valve. 生体防御 biodefense; biophylaxis. ◯ ～防御機能 a biodefense「function [mechanism].

**せいたい**[4]【生態】🔲 生態画 an「ecology [ecological, ecosystem] picture; an ecopicture. ◯ 動物[植物]～画 a picture of「animal [plant] life. 生態機能〔環境への対応機能〕(an) ecological function. 生態研究 ecological research;《study》ecology. ◯ 日本猿の～研究を行う do research on the ecology of the Japanese monkey; carry out an ecological study on the Japanese macaque. 生態の展示 =生態展示 (⇨てんじ[3]).

**せいたい**[6]【声帯】🔲 声帯結節〚医〛a vocal (cord) nodule.

せいたい[10]【静態】▶□ 静態保存〔不可動状態での車両・機械などの保存〕conservation of 《a vehicle》 in a non-driv(e)able condition. ▷ ~保存する conserve 《a vehicle》 in a non-driv(e)able condition.

せいたいがく【生態学】▶□ 数理生態学 mathematical ecology. ▷ ~学者 a mathematical ecologist.

せいたいしょう【正対称】perfect symmetry.

せいたいでんじかんきょうけんきゅうすいしんいいんかい【生体電磁環境研究推進委員会】〔総務省の〕the Committee to Promote Research on the Possible Biological Effects of Electromagnetic Fields.

せいたかユーカリ【背高-】〔植〕〔フトモモ科の巨木; オーストラリア原産〕a mountain ash; *Eucalyptus regnans*.

せいたく【請託】▶□ 請託罪〔法〕〔裁判員への〕jury tampering.

せいたんきょうかい【聖誕教会】〔ベツレヘムにある, イエスが誕生したとされる場所に建てられた教会〕the Church of the Nativity.

せいちゃ【製茶】▶□ 製茶機械 a 「tea-making [tea-manufacturing] machine.

せいちゅう[1]【正中】▶□ 正中歯〔歯科〕〔前歯の間に生える過剰歯〕a mesiodens 《*pl. -dentes*》.

せいちゅうい【精中委】＝マンモグラフィーけんしんせいどかんりちょういいんかい.

せいちょう[2]【成長】▶□ 成長性 growth 「characteristics [potential]. ▷ ~性の高い high-growth 《companies, businesses》 / ~性評価 (a) growth potential assessment. 成長(第一)主義 a growth-first 「approach [strategy, ideology]; growthism. 成長余力 《have enormous》 growth potential. 成長路線 《on》 a 「path [route] to growth. ▷ 日本経済を再活性化し, ~路線に復帰させる reinvigorate the Japanese economy and 「get it growing again [put it back on the path to growth].

せいちょうかいちょう【政調会長】〔政務調査会長〕(the) Chairman [Chairperson] of the 「Policy Research Council [Political Affairs Research Committee].

せいちょうしんぎかい【政調審議会】〔自由民主党の〕the Policy Deliberation Commission.

せいちょうホルモン【成長-】▶□ 成長ホルモン分泌不全症〔医〕growth hormone deficiency (略: GHD).

せいちょうよくせい【成長抑制】growth 「inhibition [suppression]. ▷ 成長抑制因子〔生化〕a growth 「inhibitory [inhibiting] factor. 成長抑制剤 a growth 「inhibitory [inhibiting] agent. 成長抑制手術〔医〕a growth-stunt(ing) operation; an operation to stunt growth.

せいてき[1]【性的】▶□ 性的快感 sexual 「pleasure [enjoyment, gratification, satisfaction, arousal]; a (sexual) thrill; 《口》 《find high heels》 a turn-on; 《get》 a (sexual) kick 《from…》. ▷ ~快感を得る obtain [get] sexual pleasure 《from…》; be [get] (sexually) aroused 《by…》; 《口》 get a sexual kick 《from…》 / ~快感を覚える experience [feel] sexual pleasure. 性的搾取 sexual exploitation 《of teenage girls》. 性的指向[志向] sexual orientation. 性的嗜好 sexual preference. 性的嗜癖〔性依存症〕(an) addiction to sex. 性的少数者 a member of a sexual minority; an LGBT person 《⇨エル・ジー・ビー・ティー》. 性的自己決定権 the right of sexual self-determination. 性的自由 sexual 「freedom [liberty]. 性的尊厳 《women's》 sexual dignity.

せいてきとうさつきんしほう【性的盗撮禁止法】〔法〕the Law Against Taking Secret Indecent 「Photographs [Videos] of Women; the Anti-"upskirting" Law.

せいてつ[3]【製鉄】▶□ 製鉄遺跡〔考古〕ironmaking remains; the remains of an ironmaking site.

せいとう[4]【政党】▶□ 政党間協議 an interparty discussion; interparty talks; talks between parties. 政党交付金[助成金] an official [a public] subsidy [grant] to a political party; a party subsidy. 政党要件 the 「necessary conditions [requisites] for a (political) party.

せいとう[8]【正当】▶□ 正当事由〔法〕a legitimate reason. ▷ ~事由制度 a system requiring a landlord to have a legitimate reason to evict a tenant.

せいどう[2]【制動】▶□ 制動灯〔自動車〕a brake light; a stoplight; "a stop lamp.

せいどういつせい【性同一性】▶□ 性同一性障害者 a person with a gender identity disorder.

せいどういつせいしょうがいしゃせいべつとくれいほう【性同一性障害者性別特例法】〔法〕⇨せいどういつせいしょうがいしゃのせいべつのとりあつかいのとくれいにかんするほうりつ.

せいどういつせいしょうがいしゃのせいべつのとりあつかいのとくれいにかんするほうりつ【性同一性障害者の性別の取扱いの特例に関する法律】〔法〕the Law Concerning Special Cases in Handling Gender for People with Gender Identity Disorder. ▶ 略称は「性同一性障害者性別特例法」.

せいどういつせいしょうがいとくれいほう【性同一性障害特例法】〔法〕the Gender Identity Disorder Special Law. [＝せいどういつせいしょうがいしゃのせいべつのとりあつかいのとくれいにかんするほうりつ]

せいとく[1]【生得】▶□ 生得的(な) natural; inborn; innate; inherent. / ~的開発機構〔生物〕an innate releasing mechanism / ~的行動〔生物〕(an) innate behavior / 肌の色や身長といった~的な特徴で人を差別してはならない. People must not be discriminated against because of innate characteristics such as skin color and height.

せいどけんさ【性度検査】〔心理〕〔男性度・女性度検査〕a 「masculinity-femininity [masculinity/femininity] test.

「聖なる嘘つき/その名はジェイコブ」〔映画〕Jakob the Liar.

せいなんアチェ【西南-】〔インドネシア, アチェ州の県〕Aceh Barat Daya.

せいねん[2]【成年】▶□ 成年被後見人 an adult ward.

せいねんこくさいこうりゅうじぎょう【青年国際交流事業】〔内閣府などの〕International Youth Exchange.

せいは[1]【制覇】▶□ 全国制覇 ⇨ぜんこく. 2階級制覇〔階級のあるスポーツで〕winning a championship with two divisions. ▷ 彼は無差別, 100キロ超級の2階級~を果たした. 〔柔道で〕He won in two categories, both the open-weight and the over 100 kg.

セイバー《米軍》〔米空軍が朝鮮戦争などに使用したジェット戦闘機 F-86 の愛称〕a Sabre.

せいはんいったい【製販一体】〔製造・販売の両部門が一体化した体制〕integrated manufacturing and sales. ▶□ 製販一体化 integration of manufacturing and sales.

せいはんざい【性犯罪】▶□ 性犯罪者処遇プログラム〔法務省の〕a sex offender treatment program.

せいはんぶんり【製販分離】〔製造・販売の両部門が分離している体制〕separation of manufacturing and sales.

せいび[3]【整備】▶□ 整備記録 maintenance records 《for an aircraft》. 整備ミス〔整備不良〕a maintenance record. 整備ミス a fault [an error] of maintenance; a maintenance 「fault [error]. ▷ 警視庁は事故原因について, 機長の判断ミス, 機体の老朽化, ~ミ, の観点から捜査中. The Metropolitan Police Department is investigating possible causes of the accident: pilot error, metal fatigue in the airframe, or a fault of maintenance.

ぜいびき【税引き】▶□ 税引き後赤字 《show》 an after-[a post-]tax 「loss [deficit] 《of a million yen》. 税引き後黒字 《record》 an after-[a post-]tax 「gain [surplus] 《of a million yen》.

せいびょう[3]【成猫】an adult [a fully-grown, a mature]

cat.

せいひん³【製品】
□ 製品アセスメント product assessment. 製品安全データシート〔指定された化学物質を含む化学製品の毒性や安全な取り扱いに関する説明書〕a material safety data sheet (略: MSDS). 製品安全マーク ＝エス・ジー・マーク. 製品化 development《of a model》into a product. ○ ～化する develop [turn]《research results》into「a product [manufactured goods]. 製品回収〔不良品・欠陥品などの〕(a) product recall. ○ 使用済み～回収 product「return [collection]; the collection of《used containers》. 製品競争力 product competitiveness; the competitiveness of「a product [an article, (manu-facture) goods]. 製品保証引当金 a「provision [re-serve] for product warranties; a product warranty reserve. 製品ライフサイクル管理 product lifecycle man-agement (略: PLM].
せいひんあんぜんきょうかい【製品安全協会】〔経済産業省所管の〕the Consumer Product Safety Associa-tion (略: CPSA).
せいひんひょうかぎじゅつきばんきこう【製品評価技術基盤機構】the National Institute of Technology and Evaluation (略: NITE).
せいふ²【政府】
□ 政府開発援助白書〔外務省の〕the Japan's「Official Development Assistance [ODA] White Paper《2005》. 政府公約 a government「commitment [promise]. 政府最終消費支出 government final con-sumption expenditure. 政府債務 (a) government debt. 政府債務残高 outstanding government debt(s). 政府借款 a government(al) loan. 政府出資法人 a government-funded corporation. 政府主導 ○ ～主導で進められた業界再編 a government-led reor-ganization of an industry. 政府代表団 a「govern-ment [governmental] delegation [mission]; a perma-nent mission《to the United Nations》. 政府答弁「Government's [Cabinet's] reply [answer]. ○ ～答弁書 a Cabinet's written answer《to a question sub-mitted by a Diet member》. 政府保証〔債券の元本や利子の支払いに対する〕a government guarantee《for the redemption of a bond》. 政府・与党協議会 a confer-ence between the Government and the ruling「party [parties]; a Government-《LDP》conference. 政府立法 government [cabinet](-initiated) legislation.
せいふインターネットテレビ【政府―】Government Internet TV.
せいふかんかいようがくいいんかい【政府間海洋学委員会】⇒ユネスコせいふかんかいようがくいいんかい.
せいふかんさいん【政府監査院】〔米国の〕the (US) Gov-ernment Accountability Office (略: GAO). ▶ 2004 年に the General Accounting Office (会計検査院) から改称.
せいふちょうたつちょう【政府調達庁】〔英国の〕the Office of Government Commerce (略: OGC).
せいぶつ¹【生物】
□ 生物海洋学 biological oceanography. ○ ～海洋学者 a biological oceanographer. 生物科学 biosci-ence. ▷ bioscientific adj.; bioscientist n. 生物化学的酸素要求量〔生態〕biochemical oxygen demand (略: BOD). 生物(学的)療法 biotherapy. 生物環境 ○ [the] bioenvironment. ▷ bioenvironmental adj. 生物剤〔軍〕[生物兵器用の] a biological agent. 生物製剤〔生物材料を起源とする医薬品〕biologics. 生物フォトン〔生物〕[生物微弱発光] a biophoton. 生物由来製品〔医薬品の〕a「biologically derived [bio-derived] product. ○ 特定～由来製品 a specified bio-derived product / ～由来製品感染等被害救済制度 a system to protect victims of infection arising from biologically derived products.

せいぶつついでんしげんぶもん【生物遺伝資源部門】〔製品評価技術基盤機構 (NITE) の〕the NITE Biological Resource Center (略: NBRC).
せいぶつがく【生物学】 □ 生物学的多様性〔生物〕bio-logical diversity.
せいぶつたようせいこっかせんりゃく【生物多様性国家戦略】〔生物多様性条約締結国政府がそれぞれ策定する戦略〕a national biodiversity strategy. □ 新・生物多様性国家戦略〔日本政府が 2002 年に改定したもの〕the New National Biodiversity Strategy (of Japan).
「西部の男パラディン」＝「西部のパラディン」.
「西部のパラディン」〔義侠心の強い主人公の TV 西部劇〕Have Gun-Will Travel.
せいぶん²【成分】 □ 記載成分〔医薬品・食品などに添付表示されている〕listed ingredients.
せいぶんかいせい【生分解性】 □ 生分解性樹脂 bio-degradable resin. 生分解性素材 (a) biodegradable material. 生分解性ポリマー a biodegradable polymer.
せいふんぼきょうかい【聖墳墓教会】〔エルサレムの教会〕the Church of the Holy Sepulcher.
せいべつ²【性別】 □ 社会的性別《one's》(socially de-termined) gender. 生物学的性別《one's》(biological) sex. □ 性別適合[再指定, 再判定]手術〔医〕sex reas-signment surgery (略: SRS); gender reassignment surgery (略: GRS). 性別変更〔戸籍への〕a registered gender change; a change in one's registered gender. 性別欄〔提出書類などの〕the gender「field [space]《on an application form》.
せいほ【生保】 □ 生保離れ a [the] turning-away from life insurance; a decrease in the taking out of life insurance policies. 生保レディー a life insurance sales-woman.
せいみつ【精密】 □ 精密器機 a precision instrument. 精密機器 precision「equipment [machinery]. 精密機器メーカー a precision equipment maker. 精密司法 precise justice. 精密成型 precision「casting [mold-ing]. 精密測定 precise measurement. 精密調査〔高レベル放射性廃棄物の最終処分地選定のための〕⇒文献調査《⇒ぶんけん⁵》. 精密爆弾 a「smart [precision] bomb. 精密誘導弾 a precision-guided missile.
せいむ³【政務】 □ 政務調査費〔地方自治体から議員に対して支払われる補助金〕a political affairs research al-lowance; an additional stipend paid by local govern-ment bodies to council members.
ぜいむ【税務】 □ 税務査察 a tax investigation. 税務処理 tax processing; dealing with taxes; handling taxes. ○ 当社の～処理に不適切な点があったことを認めます. We admit that there have been irregularities in the way we have dealt with our taxes. 税務申告 a 《company》tax return.
せいめい【声明】 □ 緊急声明 an emergency「declara-tion [statement]; an urgent statement. ○ 緊急～を発表する issue an emergency declaration.
せいめいせつ【清明節】〔中国の祭日; 4 月 5 日頃〕the Qingming Festival; the Ching Ming Festival; Qing ming jie.
せいめいほけん【生命保険】 □ 生命保険料 a life in-surance premium. 生命保険料控除証明書 a cer-tificate of life insurance premiums paid.
せいめいりんり【生命倫理】 □ 生命倫理評議会〔ブッシュ大統領の諮問機関〕the Bioethics Council; the (President's) Council on Bioethics.
せいめいりんりせんもんちょうさかい【生命倫理専門調査会】〔内閣府, 総合科学技術会議の〕⇒そうごうかくぎじゅつかいぎ.
せいもん²【声紋】 □ 声紋鑑定 voiceprinting; voice-print identification.
せいやく¹【成約】 □ 成約率 a [the] percentage of「successful sales [sales completed, contracts con-

せいよういわなんてん【西洋岩南天】⦅植⦆＝アメリカいわなんてん.
せいようおおまるはなばち【西洋大丸花蜂】⦅昆⦆〔ヨーロッパ原産のミツバチ科のハチ〕a buff-tailed bumblebee; *Bombus terrestris*.
せいようおとぎりそう【西洋弟切草】⦅植⦆〔オトギリソウ科の多年草〕a St. John's wort; *Hypericum perforatum*.
せいようしゃくなげ【西洋石楠花】⦅植⦆〔ツツジ科ツツジ属 (*Rhododendron*) の交配品種の1つ〕a rhododendron.
せいようしろやなぎ【西洋白柳】⦅植⦆a white willow; *Salix alba*.
せいようばいかうつぎ【西洋梅花空木】⦅植⦆〔ユキノシタ科の落葉低木〕a large-flowered mock orange; *Philadelphus grandiflorus*.
せいよく³【静翼】⦅機⦆a stationary「blade [vane]; a stator「blade [vane].
せいらんし【正乱視】⦅眼科⦆regular astigmatism.
せいり¹【生理】⇨ 生理活性脂質 ⦅生理⦆a lipid mediator.
せいり²【整理】⇨ 財産整理〔贈与・売却など〕(deciding) the disposition of *one's* property; settling「one's [sb's] estate. 私的[法的]整理〔倒産に際しての〕voluntary [legal] liquidation. 整理ポスト⦅証券⦆〔上場廃止が決定した株が上場廃止までの期間に割り当てられる取引の場〕the liquidation post. ⇨ （株券を～ポストに移す) assign (「a listed stock」) to the liquidation post.
せいり³【清吏】an「incorruptible [honest] (public) official [civil servant, bureaucrat].
ぜいりしほう【税理士法】⦅法⦆the Certified (Public) Tax Accountant Law.
ぜいりつ【税率】⇨ 基本税率 a basic tax rate. 暫定税率 a provisional tax rate. 複数税率〔消費税の〕a multiple tax rate; multiple tax rates.
せいれい³【政令】⇨ 政令指定商品〔クーリングオフ対象商品〕goods specified as returnable within the cooling-off period. 政令指定消耗品〔クーリングオフ対象外の商品〕non-returnable disposable goods.
せいれいけいねつ【政冷経熱】〔日本・中国間の，"政治は冷え，経済は熱い"状態〕hot economic, (but) cold political「ties [relationships] (between Japan and China).
せいれいしていとし【政令指定都市】⇨ 政令指定都市市長会 a designated major city mayors'「conference [meeting].
「精霊の踊り」〔グルック作曲のオペラ『オルフェオとエウリディーチェ』から〕Dance of the Blessed Spirits.
セヴィニー Sevigny, Chloë (1974- ; 米国の映画女優).
セウェルス Severus, (Lucius) Septimius (146-211; ローマ皇帝 [193-211]).
ゼウス ⇨ ゼウス神殿 a Temple of Zeus.
ゼーグロッテ〔オーストリアにあるヨーロッパ最大の地底湖〕the Seegrotte.
セーフティー ⇨ セーフティー・スクイズ⦅野球⦆「打者がバントを成功させたのを見届けてから三塁走者が走りはじめるスクイズ〕a safety squeeze (play).
セーラム・ラン〔アラスカの犬ぞり大会〕the Serum Run.
ゼーリック Zoellick, Robert B. (1953- ; 米国通商代表 [2001- ]).
セールス ⇨ セールス・スタッフ (the) sales staff; a sales staff member; a sales staffer. セールスドライバー a delivery service driver; *a route sales driver. セールス・フォース・オートメーション〔IT などにより営業活動を効率よく管理し，営業力の強化を図るシステム〕sales force automation (略: SFA).
セール・ドリル⦅海⦆〔マストに帆を張る訓練〕a sail drill.
セガール Seagal, Steven (1951- ; 米国の映画俳優).
せかい【世界】
⇨ 世界株価指数 a world index of stock prices. 世界企業番付〔米国の経済誌『フォーチュン』の〕the Fortune Global 500. 世界戦略車〔自動車〕a world car. 世界展開 worldwide [global] expansion [development]. ⇨ ～展開する expand [develop] worldwide [globally] / Visa は米国で生まれ～展開しているクレジットカードです. Visa is a credit card that was born in the United States and has expanded all over the world. 世界殿堂 a「World [an International] Hall of Fame. ⇨ 彼女はゴルフの～殿堂入りを果たした. She succeeded in entering the World Golf Hall of Fame. 世界特許 a world (wide) [an international, a global] patent. 世界の工場〔かつては日本が，今では中国がこう呼ばれている〕the world's factory. 世界標準規格 a「world [global] standard; (a)「world [global] standard specification. 世界ブランド a「world [worldwide, global] brand.
せかいアンチ・ドーピングきこう【世界–機構】the World Anti-Doping Agency (略: WADA).
せかいいしかい【世界医師会】the World Medical Association (略: WMA).
せかいウイグルせいねんかいぎ【世界–青年会議】〔新疆ウイグル自治区の過激派組織〕the World Uighur Youth Congress (略: WUYC).
せかいエイズ・けっかく・マラリアたいさくききん【世界–結核・対策基金】〔WHO が提唱し，2002 年設立〕the Global Fund to Fight AIDS, Tuberculosis and Malaria (略: GFATM).
せかいエイズデー【世界–】〔12 月 1 日〕World AIDS Day.
せかいエネルギーかいぎ【世界–会議】the World Energy Council (略: WEC).
せかいかいはつきんゆう【世界開発金融】〔世界銀行が毎年発行する報告書〕Global Development Finance《2006》(略: GDF).
せかいかいはつじょうほうのひ【世界開発情報の日】〔10 月 24 日; 国連制定〕World Development Information Day.
せかいかしょうたいかい【世界華商大会】the World Chinese Entrepreneurs Convention (略: WCEC).
せかいかんきょうデー【世界環境–】〔6 月 5 日; 国連制定〕World Environment Day.
せかいききん【世界基金】＝せかいエイズ・けっかく・マラリたいさくききん.
せかいきしょうのひ【世界気象の日】〔3 月 23 日; 国連制定〕World Meteorological Day.
せかいきょうそうりょくねんかん【世界競争力年鑑】〔国際経営開発研究所 (IMD) が発行する〕the World Competitiveness Yearbook (略: WCY).
せかいきょりべつせんしゅけん(たいかい)【世界距離別選手権(大会)】〔スピードスケートの〕the World Single Distances (Speed Skating) Championships.
せかいきろくいさん【世界記録遺産】〔ユネスコの指定する〕a Memory of the World (略: MOW).
せかいぎんこう【世界銀行】⇨ 世界銀行債 a World Bank bond.
せかいけいざいこくさいかんけいけんきゅうじょ【世界経済国際関係研究所】〔ロシア科学アカデミーの〕the Institute of Global Economics and International Relations (略: IMEMO).
せかいけいざいみとおし【世界経済見通し】〔IMF による〕the World Economic Outlook (略: WEO).
せかいけいりょうきねんび【世界計量記念日】〔5 月 20 日〕World Metrology Day.
せかいけっかくデー【世界結核–】〔3 月 24 日; 世界保健機関制定〕World TB Day.
せかいげんしりょくきょうかい【世界原子力協会】the World Nuclear Association (略: WNA).
せかいげんしりょくはつでんじぎょうしゃきょうかい【世界原子力発電事業者協会】the World Association of Nuclear Operators (略: WANO).

せかいこうこがくかいぎ【世界考古学会議】the World Archaeological Congress (略: WAC).

せかいこしょうかいぎ【世界湖沼会議】the International Conference on the Conservation and Management of Lakes.

せかいこどものひ【世界子供[子供]の日】〔11月20日; 国連制定〕Universal Children's Day.

せかいシオニストきこう【世界−機構】the World Zionist Organization (略: WZO).

せかいじさつぼうしのひ【世界自殺防止の日】=せかいじさつよほうデー.

せかいじさつよぼうデー【世界自殺予防−】〔9月10日〕World Suicide Prevention Day.

せかいしぜんほごききん【世界自然保護基金】□□ 世界自然保護基金ジャパン〔日本支部〕the World Wide Fund for Nature Japan (略: WWF Japan).

せかいじどうしゃこうぎょうかい【世界自動車工業会】〔パリに本部を置く〕the International Organization of Motor Vehicle Manufacturers (略: OICA). ▶ OICA はフランス語の Organisation Internationale des Constructeurs d'Automobiles の略.

「世界中がアイ・ラブ・ユー」〔映画〕Everyone Says I Love You.

せかいしゅうきょうがくしゅうきょうしかいぎ【世界宗教学宗教史会議】the International Association for the History of Religions (略: IAHR).

せかいじょうほうしゃかいサミット【世界情報社会−】〔2003年, 2005年に国連が開催〕the World Summit on the Information Society (略: WSIS).

せかいじょせいスポーツかいぎ【世界女性−会議】an [the 《Fourth》] International Conference on Women and Sport.

せかいじんこうデー【世界人口−】〔7月11日; 国連制定〕World Population Day.

せかいスプリントせんしゅけん【世界−選手権】【スケート】the World Sprint Championships.

せかいせいしょうねんこうりゅうきょうかい【世界青少年交流協会】the World Youth Visit Exchange Association.

せかいせいしんいがくかい【世界精神医学会】the World Psychiatric Association (略: WPA).

せかいだいしきょうしゅきょうかい【世界代表司教会議】the 《12th》Ordinary General Assembly of the Synod of Bishops. ▶ シノドス (Synodus Episcoporum) ともいう.

せかいだんじょかくさほうこく【世界男女格差報告】〔世界経済フォーラムが発表する〕the Global Gender Gap Report.

せかいテコンドーれんめい【世界−連盟】the World Taekwondo Federation (略: WTF).

せかいてつどうひょうぎかい【世界鉄道評議会】〔国際鉄道連合〕the World Executive Council (略: WEC).

せかいテレビ・デー【世界−】〔11月21日; 国連制定〕World Television Day.

せかいでんきつうしんのひ【世界電気通信の日】〔5月17日; 国連制定〕World Telecommunication Day.

せかいとしょ・ちょさくけんデー【世界図書・著作権−】〔4月23日; 国連制定〕World Book and Copyright Day.

せかいなんみんのひ【世界難民の日】〔6月20日〕World Refugee Day.

「世界の料理ショー」〔米国の、料理バラエティーTV番組〕The Galloping Gourmet. ▶ 司会は Graham Kerr.

せかいはんどうたいじょうとうけい【世界半導体市場統計】〔世界の半導体メーカーが加盟する統計機関〕World Semiconductor Trade Statistics (略: WSTS).

せかいはんドーピングきかん【世界反−機関】the World Anti-Doping Agency (略: WADA).

せかいひがいしゃがっかい【世界被害者学会】the World Society of Victimology (略: WSV).

せかいひょうじゅんのひ【世界標準の日】〔10月14日; 国連制定〕World Standards Day.

せかいヒンズーひょうぎかい【世界−評議会】the Vishwa Hindu Parishad (略: VHP); the World Hindu Council.

せかいふくごういさん【世界複合遺産】〔自然・文化の両面から世界遺産に登録されているもの〕a mixed World Heritage (site).

せかいぶつりねん【世界物理年】the World Year of Physics (略: WYP).

せかいふにんがっかい【世界不妊学会】〔組織名〕the International Federation of Fertility Societies (略: IFFS); 〔この学会の催す会議〕the 《19th》World Congress on Fertility and Sterility.

せかいぶんかいさん【世界文化遺産】〔世界遺産条約で指定された〕a World Cultural Heritage site.

せかいぶんかしょう【世界文化賞】⇒たかまつのみやでんかきねんせかいぶんかしょう.

せかいへいわきねんび【世界平和記念日】〔11月11日〕World Peace Day. ▶ 第一次大戦の停戦協定調印日.

せかいへいわけんきゅうじょ【世界平和研究所】〔財団法人〕the Institute for International Policy Studies (略: IIPS).

せかいほうどうのじゆうのひ【世界報道の自由の日】〔5月3日; 国連制定〕World Press Freedom Day.

せかいボクシングきこう【世界−機構】the World Boxing Organization (略: WBO).

せかいほけんデー【世界保健−】〔4月7日; 国連制定〕World Health Day.

せかいみずかいぎ【世界水会議】the World Water Council (略: WWC).

せかいゆうびんデー【世界郵便−】〔10月9日; 国連制定〕World Post Day.

せかいユダヤじんかいぎ【世界−人会議】the World Jewish Congress (略: WJC).

せかいりょくちゃきょうかい【世界緑茶協会】the World Green Tea Association.

セカンド □□ セカンド・ラベル〔高級ワインのB級品〕a second label.

セカンド・ソース〔他社の開発した製品と同一または互換性のある製品を供給する会社〕a second source.

セカンド・レイプ〔性犯罪被害者がこうむる精神的二次被害〕the second rape.

せき¹【咳】 □□ 咳中枢〔解〕the cough center.

せきう【積雨】〔長雨〕continuous rain; a 「long [continuous] spell [period] of rain.

せきがい【赤外】 □□ 赤外光 infrared light; an infrared ray. ◐ 遠〜光 far-infrared light; a far-infrared ray / 近〜光 near-infrared light; a near-infrared ray.

せきがいせん【赤外線】 □□ 中間赤外線 intermediate-infrared radiation. 熱赤外線 thermal infrared radiation. ◐ 熱〜カメラ a thermal infrared (imaging) camera. □□ 赤外線感知器 an infrared sensor. 赤外線撮影 infrared「imaging [photography]. 赤外線通信 infrared「communication [transmission]. 赤外線通信機能 《equipped with》an infrared communication function. 赤外線分光器 an infrared spectroscope. ◐ 近〜分光器 a near-infrared spectroscope.

せきぎめ【席決め】placement; deciding the seating (arrangement) 《at an event》; deciding who sits where. ◐ 披露宴の客の〜は大変だ. The placement of [Deciding the seating (arrangement) for] guests at a wedding reception is a difficult task.

せきさい【積載】 □□ 積載効率 load-carrying [cargo-carrying] efficiency.

せきさん【積算】 □□ 積算計 a 「device [meter] to measure amounts 《of time elapsed, power consumed, dis-

tance covered, etc.』;〔時計の〕a stopwatch; a chronograph;〔車の〕an odometer. 積算ソフト〔電算〕quantity surveyor software. 積算単価〔土木工事などの〕the accumulated「cost(s) [price(s)] (for a building project).
**せきじ**²【席次】 ⇨ 席次表〔宴会・会合などの〕a seating「chart [plan].
**せきししょう**【赤視症】【医】erythropsia; red vision.
**せきじゅん**²【席順】 ⇨ 席順表〔宴会・会合などの〕a seating「chart [plan].
**せきしょく**【赤色】 ⇨ 赤色点滅灯 a flashing red light. 赤色発光ダイオード〔電子工学〕a red LED.
**せきすい**【石錐】【考古】=いしきり².
**せきずい**【脊髄】 ⇨ 脊髄形成異常(症), 脊髄異形成【医】(a) myelodysplasia. ⇨〜形成異常[異形成]症候群 (a) myelodysplastic syndrome (略: MDS). 脊髄硬膜外[硬膜下]膿瘍【医】spinal「epidural [subdural] abscess. 脊髄変性症【医】degeneration of the spinal cord; spinal cord degeneration.
**せきせつ**²【積雪】 ⇨ 初積雪 the first「accumulation of [accumulated] snow. 終積雪 the last「accumulation of [accumulated] snow.
**せきそう**²【積層】 ⇨ 積層技術 (a) stacking technology. 積層ゴム〔免震建物用の〕a laminated rubber bearing (略: LRB). ⇨〜・ゴム・アイソレーター a laminated rubber isolator.
**せきそう**³【石槍】【考古】a stone spear point.
**せきたい**【石帯】〔宮廷服の束帯に締める, 玉(ぎょく)の飾りが付いた革製の帯〕a bejewelled leather belt forming part of the formal attire of a court nobleman.
**せきたん**【石炭】 ⇨ 石炭ガス(製造)工場 a coal gasification plant. 石炭火力発電所 a「coal-fired [coal-burning] power plant.
**せきたんエネルギーセンター**【石炭-】〔財団法人〕the Japan Coal Energy Center (略: JCOAL).
**せきちゅう**²【脊柱】 ⇨ 脊柱起立筋【解】the erector spinae (muscle [muscles]); the sacrospinalis. 脊柱靱帯骨化症【医】ossification of the spinal ligament.
**せきつい**【脊椎】 ⇨ 脊椎管狭窄(症)【医】spinal canal stenosis. ⇨ 腰部〜管狭窄症 lumbar spinal canal stenosis.
**せきどめ**【咳止め】 ⇨ 咳止めシロップ cough syrup.
**せきにん**【責任】
⇨ 一次[二次, 三次]責任 ⇨いちじ², にじ², さんじ¹. 過去[未来]責任 responsibility for the「past [future]. 背後責任 (an) indirect responsibility for (the) consequences. 歴史責任 (a) historical responsibility;《take》responsibility for history.
⇨ 責任回数〔野球〕〔投手の〕(a pitcher's)「required [expected] number of innings. ⇨ 彼は先発投手として〜回数を投げ抜くことができずに降板した. He left the mound after failing to pitch the number of innings expected of him as starting pitcher. 責任系統 a「chain [line] of responsibility; a hierarchy of responsibility. 責任追及制〔中国の政府幹部などの過失責任を問う制度〕a responsibility investigation system.
**せきにんあるまぐろぎょぎょうすいしんきこう**【責任-るまぐろ漁業推進機構】the Organization for the Promotion of Responsible Tuna Fisheries (略: OPRT).
**せきめん**¹【石綿】
⇨ 白石綿〔温石綿(おんじゃくめん)〕chrysotile. 茶石綿 brown [amosite, gray] asbestos; amosite.〔=アモサイト〕飛散性石綿 airborne asbestos. 非飛散性石綿 non-airborne asbestos. 吹き付け石綿 sprayed asbestos.
⇨ 石綿胸水【医】asbestos pleural effusion.〔良性〜胸水〕benign asbestos pleural effusion (略: BAPE). [=石綿胸膜炎] 石綿関連疾病 (an) asbestos-related disease. 石綿胸膜炎 asbestos pleurisy. 石綿小体 an asbestos body. 石綿肺【医】asbestos lung; pulmonary [lung] asbestosis. 石綿パイプ (an) asbestos cement pipe.
**せきめん**²【赤面】 ⇨ 赤面症 blushing; a tendency to blush (easily);【精神医】erythrophobia; ereuthophobia..
**せきめんけんこうひがいきゅうさいほう**【石綿健康被害救済法】the Asbestos Health Damage Compensation Law; the Law for Compensation of Patients with Asbestos-Related Diseases. ▶ 正式名称は「石綿による健康被害の救済に関する法律」.
**せきめんじょうやく**【石綿条約】the Asbestos Convention. ▶ 正式名称は「石綿の使用における安全に関する条約」(the Convention Concerning Safety in the Use of Asbestos).
**せきゆ**【石油】
⇨ 石油安定化基金 a petroleum stabilization fund. 石油卸売手 a major oil wholesaler. 石油温風機〔器〕an oil fan heater; an oil「(space) heater [stove]. 石油価格 the price of oil;《a huge drop in》oil prices. ⇨ 国際〜価格 international oil prices. 石油系鉱物油 petroleum mineral oil. 石油鉱区 an oil field; an oil drilling area; an oil exploration block. 石油国家〔経済力を石油生産に依存する国家〕a petro-state. 石油証券 petroleum securities. 石油製品価格 prices of petroleum products; petroleum product prices. 石油製品市況動向調査〔財団法人石油情報センターによる〕the survey of「market conditions for oil products [oil and gasoline prices] at service stations. 石油石炭税 (a) petroleum and coal tax. 石油・石炭製品 petroleum and coal products. 石油代替エネルギー an「energy alternative [alternative energy] to oil. 石油代替燃料 an alternative fuel to oil. 石油トレーダー[ブローカー] an oil「trader [broker]. 石油販売権 the right to sell oil;〔国連の対イラク人道支援事業における〕a right to buy「oil [petroleum] (under the UN Iraq program Oil-for-Food).
**せきゅう**【施灸】〔灸をすえること〕(a) moxa treatment; the application of moxa《on a point》. ⇨ 施灸点 a moxibustion point.
**せきゆじょうほうセンター**【石油情報-】〔財団法人;日本エネルギー経済研究所の付属機関〕the Oil Information Center.
**せきゆしょくりょうこうかんプログラム**【石油食糧交換-】〔国連管理の下に行われてきたイラクでの〕the (United Nations) Oil-for-Food Program.
**せきゆだいたいエネルギーほう**【石油代替-法】【法】〔石油代替エネルギーの開発及び導入に関する法律の通称〕the Law Concerning Promotion of the Development and Introduction of Alternative Energy.
**せきゆてんねんガス・きんぞくこうぶつしげんきこう**【石油天然-金属鉱物資源機構】the Japan Oil, Gas and Metals National Corporation (略: JOGMEC).
**セキュリティー** ⇨ セキュリティー機能〔電算〕〔パソコンなどの〕a security feature. セキュリティー・ゲート〔商店での万引き防止用の〕a (store) security gate; a shoplifting gate. セキュリティー対策 security measures《against hackers》. セキュリティー・ポリシー〔企業などの情報セキュリティーに関する基本方針〕a security policy. セキュリティー・リスク〔安全管理上のリスク〕a risk to security.
**せきりょう**³【寂寥】 ⇨ 寂寥感 a「lonely [desolate] feeling.
**せきわん**【隻腕】one arm. ⇨〜の one-armed /〜の人 a one-armed person.
**せぎんさい**【世銀債】=世界銀行債 (⇨せかいぎんこう).
**セグウェイ**【商標】〔充電式二輪車〕a Segway; a Segway Human Transporter.
**セクター** ⇨ 公共[民間]セクター the「public [private] sector.
**セクハラ** ⇨ 逆セクハラ reverse sexual harassment. ⇨ セクハラ疑惑 an allegation [a suspicion] of sexual

harassment.
セクフレ =セックスフレンド (⇒セックス).
セクメト〖エジプト神話〗〔ライオンの頭部をもつ女神〕Sekhmet.
せぐろジャッカル【背黒-】〖動〗a black-backed jackal; *Canis mesomelas*.
せけんち【世間知・世間智】knowledge of [familiarity with] the ways of the world. ◐ 〜にうとい be 「unschooled in [ignorant of] the ways of the world / 〜に長(ﾀｹ)けている be 「wise [experienced] in the ways of the world; be worldly.
せこう¹【施工】◑▶ 施工管理 construction management. 施工状況[結果]報告書 a report to be submitted 「during [after the completion of] construction work.
せしゅう【世襲】◑▶ 世襲候補 a hereditary candidate.
せじゅつ【施術】〔手術・催眠術・灸治療などを施すこと〕performing ⦅surgery⦆; administering ⦅hypnosis, moxa therapy⦆.
セジョン【世宗】**1** Sejong (1397-1450; 朝鮮 李朝第4代の王 [1418-50]). **2**〔韓国が忠清南道(チュンチョンナムド)に計画中の新行政中心複合都市〕Sejong.
せすう【世数】the number of generations.
セストリエール, セストリエーレ〔イタリア北西部, ピエモンテ州の町〕Sestriere.
ぜせい【是正】◑▶ 是正勧告〔監督官庁の〕notification of a need for improvement.
セゼル Sezer, Ahmet Necdet (1941- ; トルコの政治家; 大統領 [2000-07]).
せたい¹【世帯】◑▶ 家族世帯 a (family) household. サラリーマン世帯 a salaried-worker household. ◐ 〜リーマン〜の平均貯蓄残高 the average savings balance of salaried-worker households. ◑▶ 世帯所得 (a) family income 世帯動態調査〔厚生労働省の〕(a) household dynamics survey. 世帯普及率 the penetration rate per household; ownership per household. ◐ わが国のテレビの〜普及率はほぼ100%に達している. TV ownership per household has reached almost 100 percent in Japan.
せだい【世代】◑▶ 世代間 ⇒せだいかん. 世代論 characterizing a generation; a theory about what distinguishes a generation.
せだいかん【世代間】intergenerational ⦅equity⦆. ◐ 調査の結果, 憲法改正については〜で認識に大きな差があることが判明した. The survey revealed a wide gap in attitudes toward revision of the constitution among different generations. / あの監督については選手たちの〜で極端に評価が異なる. That coach is viewed very differently by players of different ages. ◐ 〜のずれ[差, 断絶] a [the] generation gap / 〜の公平 intergenerational [intragenerational] equity. ◑▶ 世代間格差 a difference ⦅in pension benefits⦆ between generations. 世代間ギャップ a [the] generation gap. 世代間交流 (an) intergenerational exchange; intergenerational contacts. 世代間対立 a generational confrontation; (a) conflict between generations; (a) generation conflict 世代間扶養〔年金などによる〕intergenerational support. 世代間倫理 intergenerational ethics. 世代連鎖〔行動パターンなどの〕(inter-)generational transmission; transmission ⦅of values⦆ from generation to generation. 世代間連帯 ⇒れんたい².
ゼタ・ジョーンズ Zeta-Jones, Catherine (1969- ; 英国生まれの映画女優).
セチ【SETI】〔地球外知的生命探査計画〕SETI. ▶ Search for Extraterrestrial Intelligence の略.
せつ⁴【説】◑▶ 死亡説 a 「rumor [theory] of *sb's* death. ◐ 大統領の死亡〜が流れた. There was a rumor going around

231

せつげん

that the president had died. 破局[離婚]説 a 「rumor [theory] of a 「breakup [split, divorce]. ◐ 大物カップルの破局[離婚]〜が浮上している. There is a rumor being floated that the famous couple 「have broken up [are getting divorced]. 不仲説 a 「rumor [theory] of discord; a rumor that *sb* is on bad terms with *sb*. ◐ あの人気バンドはメンバーの不仲〜がささやかれている. It is being whispered that the members of the popular band are on bad terms with one another.
ぜつえん²【絶縁】◑▶ 絶縁不良 poor [faulty] insulation.
せっか³【赤化】◑▶ 赤化統一〔北朝鮮による朝鮮半島の〕red unification. ◐ 武力〜統一 red unification by force.
せっかい¹【切開】◑▶ 切開剥離法〖医〗〔内視鏡的粘膜下層切開剥離法〕endoscopic submucosal dissection (略: ESD).
せっかい²【石灰】◑▶ 石灰化上皮腫〖医〗(a) calcifying epithelioma. 石灰泥 lime mud.
せっかん³【折檻】◑▶ 折檻死 a death by 「whipping [castigation]. ◐ 父親が2歳の幼児を〜死させた事件 the incident in which a father killed his two-year old child by whipping.
せっき⁴【炻器】〖陶芸〗〔焼き物の一種〕stoneware (pottery).
セツキシマブ〖薬〗〔がん治療薬〕cetuximab.
せっきゃく【接客】◑▶ 接客能力 customer skills. 接客マナー〔店での〕etiquette in serving customers; 〔自宅などの〕etiquette toward guests. 接客ロボット a receptionist robot; a "hospitality" robot.
せっきょう²【説教】◑▶ 説教癖 a habit of lecturing people; a tendency to lecture (people). ◐ 彼女には〜癖がある. She has a habit of lecturing people. | She's always lecturing people. 説教調 a lecturing [a preachy, an admonishing] tone (of voice). ◐ 彼に対しては, つい〜調になってしまう. I can't help adopting 「a lecturing [an admonishing] tone with him. | Something makes me get preachy with him.
ぜっきょう¹【絶叫】◑▶ 絶叫調 ◐ 〜調のスポーツ中継 a sports broadcast in 「a wild [an (over-)excited] voice.
せっきょくてき【積極的】◑▶ 積極的改善措置〔男女共同参画推進のための措置〕positive action; 〔アメリカの少数者優遇措置〕affirmative action.
せっきん【接近】◑▶ 接近禁止命令 ⦅win, be given⦆ a restraining order. 接近遭遇〔宇宙人などとの〕a close encounter ⦅with an extraterrestrial⦆. 接近ブザー〖鉄道〗(a train) approach alarm.
せっきん²【赤筋】〖解〗(a) red muscle.
セックス ◑▶ セックス恐怖症 (a) fear of sex; (a) (pathological) fear of 「(sexual) intercourse [coitus]; 〖精神医〗 erotophobia; genophobia; coitophobia. セックスフレンド a bed mate; a friend for sex; a sex(ual) partner.
せっけい³【設計】◑▶ 将来設計 *one's* plans for the future; *one's* future. 設計価格 a planning price. 設計資産〖電算〗design assets; 〔知的資産〕intellectual property (略: IP). 設計自由度 the scope for (the skills of) a designer. 設計寿命 a design service life.
ぜっけい【絶景】◑▶ 絶景マンション an apartment ["a condominium] with a ⦅breathtaking, splendid⦆ view 「(of the harbor).
せっけん³【接見】◑▶ 秘密接見〔拘置所などでの〕(the right to) a private interview. 面会接見〖法〗〔秘密交通権が保障されていない状況での弁護士と被疑者・被告人との短時間の面会〕a brief 「nonconfidential [nonprivileged] meeting ⦅between a lawyer and *his* client⦆. ◑▶ 接見室〔引見室〕an audience 「chamber [room]; 〔拘置所の〕a meeting [an interview] room.
せつげん⁶【接舷】◑▶ 強行接舷 forcing *one's* vessel 「alongside [alongside another].

**ぜっこうき**【絶好機】a「golden [perfect, rare] opportunity (for…[to *do*]); an excellent [a rare] chance; the chance of a lifetime;*《俗》a bang-up opportunity.

**ぜっこん**【舌根】◨◨ 舌根沈下《医》glossoptosis. 舌根扁桃《解》=ぜつへんとう.

**せっさく**[1]【切削】◨◨ 切削加工《金属加工》machining;《metal-》cutting.

**せっし**[3]【窃視】〔のぞき見〕voyeurism; peeping. ～する peep [peek]《at [in, into]…》. ◨◨ 窃視者 a voyeur; a peeper. [⇨窃視症者（⇨せっししょう）]

**せっししょう**【窃視症】◨◨ 窃視症者 a voyeur; a Peeping Tom; a scoptophiliac.

**せっしゅ**[4]【接種】◨◨ 接種率〔予防接種の〕a vaccination rate.

**せつじゅ**【接受】◨◨ 接受国支援〔駐留軍に対する受入れ国の支援〕host nation support（略: HNS）.

**せっしょう**[1]【折衝】◨◨《対〜》折衝力 negotiation skills.

**せっしょく**[1]【接触】◨◨ 接触者率〔電算・テレビなど〕〔インターネット全利用者のうちで特定のサイトにアクセスした人や、全テレビ視聴者のうちで特定の番組を視聴した人などの割合〕an active reach《of 25%》; a percentage of users. 接触障害《電》(a) contact failure; a bad contact.

**せっすい**【節水】◨◨ 節水対策 water conservation measures.

**せっせん**[2]【接戦】◨◨ 大接戦 a really close game;《口》 a nail-biter. ◨◨ 接戦区〔選挙戦での〕a closely「contested [fought] election district [constituency].

**せつぞく**【接続】◨◨ 接続業者, 接続事業者〔インターネットプロバイダー〕an Internet service provider（略: ISP）. 接続障害《電算》(a) connection failure; a bad connection. 接続容量 connection capacity;《電算》〔バックボーンなどへの〕access capacity.

**せったい**【接待】◨◨ 接待汚職 corruption by [bribery through] the provision of "entertainment."接待漬け constant [nonstop] entertaining. ◯ 当時、企業は官僚を～漬けにして見返りを求めた. At the time, corporations sought favors from government officials by constantly entertaining them.

**ぜったい**[2]【絶対】◨◨ 絶対国防圏《日本史》〔第二次世界大戦時に、日本が本土防衛のため不可欠と設定した地域〕the "Absolute National Defense「Sphere [Zone]"; the area defined as vital for Japan's mainland defense (during World War II). 絶対防衛圏 an area that must be defended. 絶対防衛線〔ライン〕a last line of defense.

**せつだん**【切断】◨◨ 切断事故 (an) accidental amputation. ◯ 指→事故 (an) accidental「finger [toe] amputation.

**せっち**[1]【接地】◨◨ 接地圧〔車両・建物などが接地面に加える単位面積あたりの圧力〕(ground) contact pressure. 接地部分〔機械・装置などの〕the ground contact area《of a tire》. 接地面〔車輪・タイヤなどの〕(a) tread.

**せっち**[2]【設置】◨◨ 設置認可〔教育機関・施設等の〕《apply for》authorization 《from the Ministry of Education, Culture, Sports, Science and Technology》to "establish [set up]《a college》.

**セット**[1]
◨◨ セット性〔インクなどが乾いて固化する性質〕hardening [curing, drying, fixing] properties;〔布などに型を付けられること〕formability;〔整髪剤などの〕=セット力;〔機器に用紙・材料などをセットする際の性質〕settability; loading performance. ◯ 高速～性〔インクなどが早く乾く性質〕quick-drying properties. 高温～性〔熱を加えると形ができる性質〕heat-setting [heat-curing] properties. 低温～性のあるプラスチック〔低温で成形できる〕plastic that cures at low temperatures / 用紙の～性を改善する improve the paper loading. セット率〔バレーボールの試合などで、勝ちセット数を全セット数で割った値、または勝ちセット数を負けセット数で割った値〕the ratio of sets won to sets「played [lost]. セット力〔整髪料が髪の形を整える力〕setting [holding] power [strength]. ◯ ～力の高いスタイリング剤 a hairstyling agent that「sets [holds] well.

**セットアッパー**《野球》〔リードしているときの中継ぎ投手〕a setup man.

**セットアップマン**《野球》=セットアッパー.

**せっとう**【窃盗】◨◨ 窃盗教唆 incitement to theft. 窃盗団〔グループ〕a group of thieves;《car》theft ring.

**セットしすう**【SET 指数】《証券》〔タイの株価指数〕the SET Index. ▶ SET は the Stock Exchange of Thailand（タイ証券取引所）の略.

**ゼッド, ゼット**【Z】◨◨ Z 理論《経営》Theory Z.

**セット・トップ・ボックス**〔テレビに接続して種々のサービスを受けられるようにする小型補助装置〕a set-top box（略: STB）.

**セットバック** ◨◨ セットバック済み〔不動産広告で、建築基準に合わせた敷地後退の工事が完了していること〕setback completed; fully set back;《The building has been》set back to fulfill zoning regulations.

**セット・プレー**《スポーツ》a set play; a restart play.

**せっぱく**[1]【切迫】
3〔呼吸や脈拍が小刻みに速くなること〕acceleration; quickening; accelerated《respiration, pulse》. ～する accelerate; quicken; speed up. ◨◨ 切迫感 a sense of urgency; feeling under「threat [pressure]; a sense that《an earthquake》is imminent. ◯ 東海地方に比べて関東は大地震に対する～感が薄いような気がする. It seems to me that in the Kantō there is less sense of urgency about the imminence of a major earthquake than there is in the Tōkai.

**せっぱりいるか**【背張海豚】《動》a Hector's dolphin; *Cephalorhynchus hectori*.

**せっぱん**【折半】◨◨ 折半出資 sharing the financing《of a venture》equally; going halves on an investment; making equal contributions. ◯ A 社と B 社は～出資で新会社を設立した. Company A and company B set up a new company by contributing equal shares of capital.

**せっぱん**[2]【接伴】attendance《on *sb*》; service《to *sb*》. ～する attend [serve, wait on]《a guest》.

**せつび**【設備】◨◨ 設備投資循環《経》the capital investment cycle; the (plant and) equipment investment cycle. 設備投資動向 changes in「capital investment [investment in plant and equipment].

**せっぴ**【雪庇】◨◨ 雪庇雪崩 a cornice avalanche.

**せつびょうデータセンター**【雪氷-】《米国の》the National Snow and Ice Data Center（略: NSIDC）.

**ぜつへんとう**【舌扁桃】《解》a lingual tonsil; the lingual tonsils.

**ぜつぼう**【絶望】◨◨ 絶望視 ◯ 患者はもう～視されている. The patient's life is despaired of. | There is no hope (for the patient). | The doctors have given up hope (for the patient).

**せつめい**【説明】
◨◨ 事後説明 a post facto explanation; an explanation after the fact. 事前説明 an explanation before the fact; an advance explanation.
◨◨ 説明資料 explanatory material. 説明調〔物事を順序立てて丁寧に説明する調子〕(in) an explanatory「style [tone];〔単調で平板な硬い説明口調・文章〕(in) a「dull [monotonous, wooden] tone [style]. ◯ 登場人物の台詞がことごとく～調で、生き生きした会話になっていないのがシナリオの難点だった. The weakness for [in] the scenario was that the characters' lines were completely monotonous in tone, and never came to life as real conversation.

**セデーション**《医》〔苦痛緩和のための〕鎮静《put *sb* under》sedation.

せとじ【背綴じ】〖製本〗(a)「spine [back] binding.
セドナ〖天〗［冥王星軌道の小惑星〛Sedna.
せどり¹【瀬取り】［海上での荷物の積み替え］(an) offshore delivery ⟨of drugs⟩; (a) delivery at sea.
せどり²【競取り・背取り】［売買の仲介をし手数料を取ること］jobbing; buying and selling; dealing (in used books); ［その人］a jobber; a dealer. ◐▭ 競取り屋 a jobber; a dealer.
セナ Sena, Dominic (1949- ; 米国の映画監督).
ゼナ〖天〗［海王星より外側に位置する天体の1つ 2003 UB₁₃ の通称］Xena.
せなげ【背毛】［肩から背中にかけて生えている体毛］(upper) back hair.
セニアカー〖商標〗［高齢者向け電動三輪［四輪］車］a Senior Car. [⇨シニアカー]
セニオラ ＝シニオラ.
ぜにたむし【銭田虫】〖医〗［体部白癬］body ringworm; *tinea corporis*.
ぜにん【是認】 ◐▭ 自己是認欲求 ＝しょうにんよっきゅう. 申告是認 ［税務申告などの］approval of ⟨a tax return⟩.
セニングしゅじゅつ【—手術】〖医〗［心房内の血流を転換させるための］a Senning operation; the Senning procedure.
せぬき【背抜き】 ◐▭ 背抜き座椅子 an open-backed legless chair.
ゼネラル・パートナー〖米経営〗［リミテッド・パートナーシップにおける資産の運用・管理責任者］a general partner (略: GP).
ゼネラル・ユニオン〖労働〗［雇用形態・職種・性別・国籍などにかかわらずだれでも一人から入れる労働組合］the General Union.
せのり【背糊】〖製本〗bookbinding [binding, spine] glue.
セパレートリー・マネージド・アカウント〖証券〗［株式の売買注文のみならず資産の運用や管理に関するアドバイスなども提供するサービス；ラップ口座］a separately managed account (略: SMA).
ぜひ【是非】 ◐▭ 是非善悪 ⟨distinguish between⟩ right and wrong.
セフゾン〖商標・薬〗［抗生物質］Cefzon.
セフタジジム〖薬〗［抗生物質］ceftazidime.
ゼプト-　◐▭ ゼプト秒 a zeptosecond (略: zs).
ゼブラ　◐▭ ゼブラ柄 a zebra(-skin) pattern.
セフレ ＝セックスフレンド (⇨セックス).
「セブン」〖映画〗Se7en.
「セブン・イヤーズ・イン・チベット」〖映画〗Seven Years in Tibet.
セポン［ラオス，サヴァンナケット県の郡］Xepon; Sepon(e).
セミオーダー(メード)
～の semi-order-made; semi-custom-made; semi-tailor-made; semi-tailored. ◐～で服を作る buy a suit「semi-order-made [semi-custom-made, semi-tailor-made, semi-tailored]; have a suit made to order without a fitting. ◐▭ セミオーダー絵本 a personalized picture book. セミオーダー家具 a semi-custom-made furniture. セミオーダー・システム a semi-custom system. セミオーダー品 a semi-custom product.
セミリンガル［2つ［以上］の言語のいずれにおいても母語話者のレベルに達していない状態］semilingualism; distractive bilingualism. ◐～の semilingual / ～の人 a semilingual (person).
セムナ(—) ［イラン中北部の州；その州都］Semnan.
セメスター〖米〗［セメスター制［前期・後期の2学期制］a [the] semester system.
セメント　◐▭ セメント固化［放射性廃棄物などの］cement solidification. セメント固化体［放射性廃棄物などの］cement-solidified (radioactive) waste.
セモリナ［硬質小麦の胚乳部から製する粒状澱粉］semolina.
せゆう【施釉】〖製陶〗glazing;［その製品］glazed ware.

セラーノ〖植〗［メキシコ産の唐辛子の一品種］(a) serrano (pepper).
ゼラチン　◐▭ ゼラチン質 gelatin; (a) gelatinous material.
ゼラニウム　◐▭ センテ(ィ)ッド[ニオイ]・ゼラニウム a scented geranium. ローズ・ゼラニウム a rose geranium.
セラピー　◐▭ セラピー・アニマル［動物療法に用いられる］a therapy animal.
セラミス〖商標・園芸〗［ドイツ製の栽培用土］Seramis.
セラミック　◐▭ セラミック・レーザー a ceramic laser.
せり³【競り】 ◐▭ 競り人［競売の仲立ちをする］an auctioneer; an auction broker.
ゼリー　◐▭ ゼリー飲料 a jelly drink.
ゼルウィガー Zellweger, Renée (1969- ; 米国の映画女優; 本名 Renée Kathleen Zellweger).
セルこうかんこうりつ【—変換効率】［太陽光発電装置の］(a) cell conversion efficiency.
セルシン²〖商標・薬〗［催眠・鎮静剤；日本の商品名］Cercine. ▶ 一般名はジアゼパム (diazepam).
セルせいさん【—生産】［一人ないし数人の作業員がある製品の製作に必要なすべての部品を自分たちの手元に置いて製作の全行程を受け持つ生産方式］cell [cellular] production [manufacturing];［a「cell [cellular] production [manufacturing] system.
セルトラリン〖薬〗［抗鬱剤］sertraline. [＝塩酸セルトラリン (⇨えんさん)]
セルビー Selby, Hubert, Jr. (1928-2004; 米国の作家).
セルフ　◐▭ セルフチェックアウト・システム［購入者が自分で料金を精算する仕組み］a self-checkout system.
セルフィーユ〘＜F *cerfeuil*〙〖植〗［セリ科の香草；チャービル］(a) chervil; *Anthriscus cerefolium*.
セル・フレーム［めがねの］an acetate [a plastic] frame [rim]. ◐～のめがね acetate [plastic] frame glasses.
セルライト［皮膚の表面に現れる脂肪分などの塊］cellulite.
セレウスきん【—菌】〖菌〗Bacillus cereus.
セレス³ [CERES]〖環境〗［米国の，環境に責任を持つ経済機構のための協議会］CERES; the Coalition for Environmentally Responsible Economies.
セレックスほう【SEREX 法】〖医〗［がん抗原同定法］the SEREX method. ▶ SEREX は serological expression cloning の略.
セレニカ(アール)【—(R)】〖商標・薬〗［抗てんかん薬］Selenica (R).
セレブる［有名人を気取る］behave as though *one* is a celebrity;［有名人の生活を味わう］experience the life of a celebrity.
セレモニー　◐▭ セレモニー・ホール［葬祭場・結婚式場］a hall for「funerals [ceremonies, weddings]; a ceremony hall.
「セレンディピティ」〖映画〗Serendipity.
ゼロ・エミッション　◐▭ ゼロ・エミッション事業 a zero-emission(s)「project [enterprise].
セローム〖植〗［サトイモ科の常緑多年草；南米原産］a tree philodendron; a cut-leaf philodendron; *Philodendron bipinnatifidum*; *Philodendron selloum*.
ゼロきゅうゼロきんゆう【090 金融】［携帯電話を使う無店舗営業］"090"［cellphone] financing.
「0011／ナポレオン・ソロ」［米国の，コメディーがかったスパイものの TV ドラマ］The Man from U.N.C.L.E. ▶ U.N.C.L.E. は米国の秘密機関で，United Network Command for Law and Enforcement の略とされる.
ゼロハン［排気量 50cc のバイク］a 50 cc motorbike.
セロン Theron, Charlize (1975- ; 南アフリカ生まれの映画女優).
せわたしぶね【瀬渡し船】a coast(al) boat; a coastal vessel.
せんい²【戦意】 ◐▭ 戦意高揚映画 a「morale-boosting [morale-raising] movie.
せんい³【遷移】 ◐▭ バイオ繊維 biofiber. ◐▭ 遷移領域

せい

a transition「zone [region, area]; a zone of transition.
**せんい**[4]【繊維・線維】□ 線維筋痛症〔医〕(▷ fibrositic *adj*.); fibromyalgia. 繊維材〔繊維状に分解した木材を圧縮成形したもの〕*(a) fiberboard; "(a) fibre-board. 繊維片 a fiber fragment; a fragment of fiber. ▷ 容疑者が事件当日着用していたマフラーの繊維が、現場に残されていた〜片と一致した. Fibers from the muffler worn by the suspect on the day of the incident matched fiber fragments left at the (crime) scene.
**ぜんい**[2]【善意】□ 善意取得〔法〕〔動産を占有している無権利者を真の権利者と過失なく誤信して取引をした者が、その動産について完全な権利〔所有権または質権〕を取得させる制度〕good-faith [bone-fide, innocent] purchase [acquisition].
**ぜんいん**【全員】□ 全員集合〔掛け声〕Come [Everybody come] ((over) here))! | Go [Everybody go] ((to the reception area))! | Get together! | Assemble (in front of the building). 全員野球 ▷ タイガースは〜野球でジャイアンツに勝った. With every member of the team doing his bit [Thanks to contributions from every player], the Tigers beat the Giants.
**ぜんおし**【全押し】〖写真〗(a) full press. 〜する fully press ((the shutter button)). ▷ シャッターボタンを〜する press the shutter button all the way down.
**せんか**[14]【泉下】〔死後の世界〕the next world; the other world.
**せんかい**[4]【旋回】□ 旋回計〔空〕〔航空機の旋回の速度を示す計器〕a turn indicator; a turn coordinator; 〔旋回の角速度と横滑りを示す計器〕a turn and slip indicator; 〔旋回の角速度と傾斜角を示す計器〕a turn and bank indicator.
「戦火の勇気」〔映画〕Courage Under Fire.
**せんかん**[1]【専管】□ 専管事項 one's exclusive「responsibility [authority]; ((口)) one's bailiwick; one's turf. ▷ 公定歩合の操作は日銀の〜事項である. Managing the official discount rate is the sole responsibility of the Bank of Japan. | It's up to the BOJ to set the official discount rate.
**せんがん**[4]【腺癌】□ 分化型腺がん〔医〕(a) differentiated adenocarcinoma.
**せんがん**[5]【先願】〔特許〕〔同一の発明について2つ以上の出願があった場合の一番早い出願〕the「first [earliest] application [filing]; 〔他の出願より早い出願〕a prior [an earlier] application [filing]. ▷ 〜を調べる search for「prior [earlier] applications [filings]. 先願権〔先に特許を出願することで発生する権利〕a first-to-file right. 先願者 the first applicant; 〔特許訴訟などで〕the senior party. 先願主義 a first-to-file system. 先願調査 a prior application search. 先願特許 the first-filed patent. 先願発明 the first-filed invention.
**ぜんかんむ**【善管義務】=ぜんかんちゅういぎむ.
**ぜんかんちゅういぎむ**【善管注意義務】【法】〔善良なる管理者としての注意義務〕a duty of care; due「diligence [care].
**ぜんき**[3]【前期】□ 前期日程〔入学試験などの〕an early schedule (for entrance examinations). 前期比〔その期との〕the ratio to the previous term; 〔昨期との〕the ratio to last term. ▷ 〜比 15% の減益 a 15% decline in profits compared to「the preceding term [last term].
**せんきょ**[3]【選挙】□ 選挙啓発ポスター an election promotion poster; a voter education poster. 選挙 CM an election「advertisement [ad, advert, announcement, message]. 選挙集会 a campaign rally. 選挙情勢調査 a tracking poll. 選挙セール 〔an "election sale"〕 a system where local stores offer discounts to citizens who vote. 選挙前勢力《(the Democratic Party's)》pre-election strength《(of 250 seats)》.

**せんぎょ**【鮮魚】□ 鮮魚店 a fresh fish retailer; "a fishmonger's (shop).
**せんぎょう**[1]【専業】□ 専業主夫 a househusband; a stay-at-home husband.
**せんきょく**[4]【選挙区】□ 海外選挙区 an overseas [a foreign] electoral district. 重点選挙区 a constituency on which《the LDP》places particular importance. 重要選挙区 an important constituency. ▷ 最重要〜 the most important constituency; a「key [vital, critical] constituency. 都市型〔農村型〕選挙区 an urban [a rural] electoral district [constituency]. □□ 選挙区選挙〔参議院での〕a district election. 選挙区選出議員 a Diet member elected from an electoral district.
**せんきょにん**【選挙人】□ 選挙人制度〔米国の〕the elector system.
**せんきょにんめいぼ**【選挙人名簿】□ 選挙人名簿登録者数 the number of voters registered on the electoral「register [roll]; the number of registered voters. 選挙人名簿登録証明書〔洋上投票をする船員に交付される〕a (seaman's) certificate of「voter ["electoral] registration.
**ぜんギリシャしゃかいしゅぎうんどう**【全一社会主義運動】〔ギリシャの政党〕the Panhellenic Socialist Movement (略：PASOK). ► PASOK は *Panellinio Sosialistiko Kinima* の略.
**ぜんきれん**【全基連】=ぜんこくろうどうきじゅんかんけいだんたいれんごうかい.
**せんく**[1]【先駆】□ 先駆性 pioneering「traits [characteristics]; a pioneering spirit. 先駆体、先駆物質〔前駆体、前駆物質〕a precursor.
**せんくつ**【洗掘】〖地質〗〔川の流れや潮汐が堤防などを侵食すること〕scouring; scour.
**ぜんくつ**【前屈】□ 長座体前屈〔体力測定としての〕(the) sit-and-reach (test).
**せんぐんせいじ**【先軍政治】〔北朝鮮の〕the military-first policy《(of North Korea)》.
**ぜんけいこつきん**【前脛骨筋】〖解〗the tibialis anterior (muscle).
**せんけつ**[2]【専決】□ 専決事項 a discretionary matter《(for the prime minister)》; a matter decided at the discretion《(of the managing director)》.
**せんげつ**【先月】□ 先月比 the ratio compared to「last month [a month ago].
**せんげん**[3]【線源】□ シード線源〖医〗a seed radiation source.
**ぜんけんいにんほう**【全権委任法】〖法〗an enabling act; 〔史〕〔1933 年 ドイツの〕the Enabling Act of 1933; *Ermächtigungsgesetz*.
**ぜんけんつきそいにんせいど**【全件付添人制度】=当番付き添い人制度《(⇒とうばん)》.
**せんご**[2]【戦後】□ 戦後処理 (a) postwar settlement; settling matters after a war. 戦後統治 a post-war administration. ▷ イラクの〜統治 the post-war administration of Iraq. 戦後 60 年決議〔2005 年 8 月衆議院で採択された決議〕the Resolution Commemorating the 60th Anniversary of the End of World War II. ► 正式名称は「国連創設およびわが国の終戦・被爆 60 周年に当たり、さらなる国際平和の構築への貢献を誓約する決議」(the Resolution Pledging Further Contributions to the Creation of World Peace on the Occasion of the 60th Anniversary of the Founding of the United Nations, the End of World War II and the Atomic Bombings of Japan).
**せんこう**[1]【先行】□ 先行企業〔製品開発などの〕a pioneering company; a pioneer (company). 先行特許 a prior patent. ▷ 〜特許調査をしないで特許を出願してはいけません. You shouldn't put in a patent application without re-

searching whether a prior patent exists. 先行逃げ切り〔競馬などで〕leading all the way (and winning). 先行発売〔販売〕〔一般販売に先立って売ること〕(a) presale; (an) advance sale. ◇当劇場のファンクラブ会員の方には,上演会のチケットを~販売いたします. Members of the theater's fan club can buy「tickets ahead of the general public [advance tickets]」. /その新型車は日本発売に先駆け,今春米国で~発売されることになった. The new model is to go on sale in the US this spring,「before going on in the Japanese market [ahead of selling in Japan]」 Initial sales of the new model in the US this spring will precede sales in Japan. 先行薬 ＝先発(医薬)品 (⇨せんぱつ[1]). 先行予約 an advance「reservation [order]」; a prereservation; a preorder. ◇~予約受付中.〔広告〕Now accepting advance「reservations [orders]」.

せんこう[7]【穿孔】 ▣▣ 大腸穿孔《医》(a) perforation of the large「intestine [bowel]」;〔結腸の〕(a) colonic perforation;〔直腸の〕(a) perforation of the rectum; (a) rectal perforation. 腸穿孔《医》(an) intestinal [(a) bowel] perforation.

せんこう[8]【閃光】 ▣▣ 閃光弾 a flash bomb.

せんこう[13]【潜航】 ▣▣ 潜航試験 a submergence test; submergence testing. 潜航深度 (a) submerged depth.

せんこう[16]【選考】 ▣▣ 選考漏れ (a) failure to be chosen; (a) rejection of an「application [applicant]」 ◇第一志望の会社から~漏れの連絡があった. The company which was my first choice contacted me to tell me「I'd been rejected [they wouldn't take me on]」 /I got a rejection from the company which was my top choice.

せんこう[20]【先公】 1〔先代の君主〕the「last [previous]」lord; the late lord. 2〔先生に対する軽蔑語〕a damn teacher;《口》a teach.

ぜんごうオープン【全豪-】〔テニス〕the Australian Open Tennis Championships; the Australian Open (Tennis).

せんこうしゃメリット【先行者-】＝せんこうしゃりえき.

せんこうしゃりえき【先行者利益】〔経〕〔先駆けとなった企業がその市場において優位性を持つこと〕(a) first-mover advantage.

ぜんこうスイッチ【全光-】〔通信〕〔光の信号を光によって制御する素子〕an all-optical switch.

せんこく[5]【線刻】line「carving [engraving]」 ~する carve [engrave, etch]〔a line figure〕. ▣▣ 線刻画〔考古・美〕a line「carving [engraving]」

せんこく【戦国】 ▣▣ 戦国絵巻〔戦国時代の合戦・武将などを描いた絵巻物〕a picture scroll of battles and warriors in the Warring States period. 戦国大会〔参加チームの実力が拮抗している競技の〕a fiercely competitive contest. 戦国武将《日本史》a「military commander [general]」in the Warring States period.

ぜんこく【全国】 ▣▣ 全国一斉学力テスト a nationwide「scholastic [academic] achievement test. 全国均一サービス a uniform nation-wide service; a universal (national) service. 全国制覇 a nationwide「victory [championship]」 ◇~制覇する win the national championship; be the nationwide winner. 全国総合指数〔消費者物価指数から生鮮食品を除いたもの〕the "nationwide core CPI"; the Consumer Price Index after excluding「fresh foods [perishable foodstuffs]」 全国総合消費者物価指数 ＝全国総合指数.

ぜんこくあんぜんセンター【全国安全-】＝ぜんこくろうどうあんぜんえいせいセンターれんらくきょうぎかい.

ぜんこくいがくぶちょうびょういんちょうかいぎ【全国医学部長病院長会議】the Association of Japanese Medical Colleges (略: AJMC).

ぜんこくかいごじぎょうしゃきょうぎかい【全国介護事業者協議会】the Japan Home Care Service Providers Association.

ぜんこくかしきんぎょうきょうかいれんごうかい【全国貸金業協会連合会】the Federation of Moneylenders Association of Japan.

ぜんこくがっこうえいようしきょうぎかい【全国学校栄養士協議会】the National Association of School Nutritionists.

ぜんこくきけんぶつあんぜんきょうかい【全国危険物安全協会】the Japan Association for Safety of Hazardous Materials.

ぜんこくキャッシュサービス【全国-】〔金融機関共用のオンラインネットワークシステム〕the Multi Integrated Cash Service (略: MICS); the Japanese nationwide multi-integrated cashing service.

ぜんこくく【全国区】〔選挙〕a「national [nationwide]」constituency (district);〔知名度〕nationwide publicity. ◇~から出馬する run (for election) from the nationwide district. ◇~になる〔全国的に知られるようになる〕become nationally「famous [well-known]」/彼女の歌のおかげでこの町は一躍~になった Thanks to her song, this town suddenly became known「nationwide [throughout the country]」 ▣▣ 全国区制 the national constituency system.

ぜんこくけいじどうしゃきょうかいれんごうかい【全国軽自動車協会連合会】the Japan Mini Vehicles Association. (略: JMVA).

ぜんこくけんこうふくしさい【全国健康福祉祭】an [the] All-Japan Health and Welfare Festival.

ぜんこくけんせつぎょうきょうかい【全国建設業協会】the Associated General Constructors of Japan.

ぜんこくけんせつろうどうくみあいそうれんごう【全国建設労働組合総連合】the National Federation of Construction Workers' Unions.

ぜんこくこうとうがっこうぶんかれんめい【全国高等学校文化連盟】the All Japan Senior High School Cultural Federation.

ぜんこくこうりしゅはんくみあいちゅうおうかい【全国小売酒販組合中央会】the All-Japan Liquor Merchants Association.

ぜんこくしぎかいぎちょうかい【全国市議会議長会】the National Association of Chairpersons of City Councils.

ぜんこくしちょうかい【全国市長会】the Japan Association of City Mayors.

ぜんこくしみんオンブズマンれんらくかいぎ【全国市民-連絡会議】the Japan Citizen's Ombudsman Association.

ぜんこくしゃかいふくしきょうぎかい【全国社会福祉協議会】the Japan National Council of Social Welfare.

ぜんこくしゃかいほけんろうむしかいれんごうかい【全国社会保険労務士会連合会】the All Japan Federation of Certified Social Insurance Labour Consultant Associations.

ぜんこくしゅんじけいほうシステム【全国瞬時警報-】〔地震の発生・津波の到達や海外からの武力攻撃などが急迫した事態に備えて開発されているもの〕the Japanese instantaneous alert system; the J-ALERT system; Japan's satellite-based disaster warning system.

ぜんこくしょうがいしゃぎのうきょうぎたいかい【全国障害者技能競技大会】＝アビリンピック.

ぜんこくしょうねんほどういんきょうかい【全国少年補導員協会】the National Association of Juvenile Guidance Counselors.

ぜんこくしょうひじったいちょうさ【全国消費実態調査】the National Survey of Family Income and Expenditure.

ぜんこくしょうひせいかつそうだんいんきょうぎかい【全国消費生活相談員協議会】the Japan Association of

## ぜんこくじょうほうこうかいど

Consumer Affairs Specialists (略: JACAS).

**ぜんこくじょうほうこうかいどランキング**【全国情報公開度−】〔各都道府県の〕a national information 「disclosure [transparency] ranking.

**ぜんこくしょくにくじぎょうきょうどうくみあいれんごうかい**【全国食肉事業協同組合連合会】the All Japan Meat Industry Co-operative Associations (略: AJMIC).

**ぜんこくじんけんようごいいんれんごうかい**【全国人権擁護委員連合会】the National Federation of Civil Rights Commissioners.

**ぜんこくしんようじょうほうセンターれんごうかい**【全国信用情報センター連合会】the Federation of Credit Bureaus of Japan (略: FCBJ).

**ぜんこくしんりんくみあいれんごうかい**【全国森林組合連合会】the National Federation of Forestry Associations.

**ぜんこくせいしょうねんけんぜんいくせいきょうちょうげっかん**【全国青少年健全育成強調月間】National 「Healthy [Sound] Youth Development Month.

**ぜんこくせいしんしょうがいしゃかぞくかいれんごうかい**【全国精神障害者家族会連合会】the National Federation of Families with the Mentally Ill in Japan.

**ぜんこくせきずいそんしょうしゃれんごうかい**【全国脊髄損傷者連合会】Spinal Injuries Japan (略: SIJ).

**ぜんこくだいがくせいかつきょうどうくみあいれんごうかい**【全国大学生活協同組合連合会】the National Federation of University Co-operative Associations (略: NFUCA).

**ぜんこくちいきあんぜんうんどう**【全国地域安全運動】the National Community Safety Campaign.

**ぜんこくちきゅうおんだんかぼうしかつどうすいしんセンター**【全国地球温暖化防止活動推進−】the Japan Center for Climate Change Action (略: JCCCA).

**ぜんこくちじかい**【全国知事会】the National Governors' Association (of Japan).

**ぜんこくちょうそんかい**【全国町村会】the National Association of Towns & Villages.

**ぜんこくちょうそんぎかいちょうかい**【全国町村議会議長会】the National Association of Chairmen of Town and Village Assemblies.

**ぜんこくとしせいそうかいぎ**【全国都市清掃会議】the Japan Waste Management Association (略: JWMA).

**ぜんこくとどうふけんぎかいぎちょうかい**【全国都道府県議会議長会】the National Association of Chairpersons of Prefectural Assemblies.

**ぜんこくなんみんべんごだんれんらくかいぎ**【全国難民弁護団連絡会議】the Japan Lawyers' Network for Refugees (略: JLNR).

**ぜんこくはんざいひがいしゃしえんネットワーク**【全国犯罪被害者支援−】＝ぜんこくひがいしゃしえんネットワーク.

**ぜんこくひがいしゃしえんのかい**【全国犯罪被害者の会】the National Association of Crime Victims and Surviving Families (略: NAVS).

**ぜんこくひがいしゃしえんネットワーク**【全国被害者支援−】〔犯罪被害者のための組織〕the National Network for Victim Support (略: NNVS).

**ぜんこくべいこくとりひき・かかくけいせいセンター**【全国米穀取引・価格形成−】⇒コメかセンター.

**ぜんこくぼうはんきょうかいれんごうかい**【全国防犯協会連合会】the Japan Crime Prevention Association.

**ぜんこくぼうりょくついほううんどうすいしんセンター**【全国暴力追放運動推進−】the National Center for the Elimination of Boryokudan.

**ぜんこくほけんセンターれんごうかい**【全国保健−連合会】the All Japan Federation of Municipal Health Centers.

**ぜんこくもうどうけんしせつれんごうかい**【全国盲導犬施設連合会】the National Federation of All Japan Guide Dog Training Institutions (略: NFGD).

**ぜんこくもくざいくみあいれんごうかい**【全国木材組合連合会】the Japan Federation of Wood-Industry Associations (略: JFWIA).

**ぜんこくやきゅうしんこうかい**【全国野球振興会】the All Japan Baseball Foundation (略: ABF).

**ぜんこくりんぎょうかいりょうふきゅうきょうかい**【全国林業改良普及協会】the National Forestry Extension Association in Japan.

**ぜんこくろうじんふくししせつきょうぎかい**【全国老人福祉施設協議会】the Japanese Council of Senior Citizens Welfare Service (略: JS).

**ぜんこくろうじんほけんしせつきょうかい**【全国老人保健施設協会】the Japan Association of Geriatric Health Service Facilities.

**ぜんこくろうどうあんぜんえいせいセンターれんらくかいぎ**【全国労働安全衛生−連絡会議】the Japan Occupational Safety and Health Resource Center (略: JOSHRC).

**ぜんこくろうどうかんけいきょく**【全国労働関係局】〔米国の〕the National Labor Relations Board (略: NLRB).

**ぜんこくろうどうきじゅんかんけいだんたいれんごうかい**【全国労働基準関係団体連合会】the National Federation of Labour Standards Associations.

**ぜんこくろうどうしゃきょうさいせいかつきょうどうくみあいれんごうかい**【全国労働者共済生活協同組合連合会】〔全労済〕the National Federation of Workers and Consumers Insurance Cooperatives (略: Zenrosai).

**せんこつ**²【仙骨】◪ 仙骨神経  a sacral nerve.

**ぜんざ**【前座】◪ 前座歌手  a singer who is not the main attraction; a singer whose function is to open a show; an opening singer; a 「second [secondary] singer.

**センサー**◪ センサー・ライト〔人などが近づくと自動的に点灯する照明〕⇒じんかんセンサー.

**せんさい**³【戦災】◪（一般）戦災死没者  a person killed in a war;〈集合的に〉(the) war dead.

**せんざい**³【洗剤】◪ 粉洗剤 (a) detergent powder; (a) powdered detergent.

**せんざい**⁶【潜在】◪ 潜在化 ◯ −化する  become latent / 児童虐待や女性に対する暴力は〜化していることが多く、実体の把握がなかなか困難である。 So much tends to 「remain [be kept] hidden about child cruelty and violence against women that it's pretty hard to grasp the true situation. 潜在学習【心理】latent learning. 潜在競争力 potential competitiveness. 潜在睾丸【医】undescended 「testicle [testis]; cryptorchi(di)sm. 潜在構造分析 latent structure analysis. 潜在顧客 a 「potential [prospective] customer; a (sales) prospect. 潜在 GDP【経】(the) potential GDP. 潜在成長力【経】growth potential. 潜在(的)価値【保険】＝エンベデッド・バリュー.

**ぜんさんぎょうかつどうしすう**【全産業活動指数】〔経済産業省が発表する〕the Indices of All Industrial Activity.

**せんし**⁷【戦死】◪ 戦死公報 (a) notification of death in action; 「(receive) (a) notification that sb has been killed on active duty.

**せんじ**²【戦時】◪ 戦時死亡宣告〔旧厚生省による〕pronouncement of death in action (of one who did not return from the Pacific War). 戦時援護演習 ＝連合戦時増援演習(⇒れんごう¹). 戦時動員令 a wartime mobilization order.

**せんじかさん**【戦時加算】〔対日講和条約で課された著作権保護期間の〕an additional copyright protection period to compensate for insufficient protection during wartime; a wartime extension.

**せんしつ**²【泉質】 ▯▭ the water quality of a hot spring; spring quality.

**ぜんじつだん**【前日談[譚]】〔ある事件が起こった後に、それ以前の状況・出来事を振り返って語ること〕a retrospective《on the events》; retrospective talk; (a) retrospection; 〔映画などの公開後に、その中で扱われた事件に先行する状況・出来事をテーマとして作られる作品〕a prequel《to …》.

**ぜんじどう**【全自動】 ▯▭ 全自動血圧計 a fully automatic sphygmomanometer.

**せんしゃ**¹【洗車】 ▯▭ 撥水洗車 (a) car wash and water-repellent treatment. ポリマー洗車 (a) car wash and polymer treatment. 水洗い洗車 (a) car wash with water. ワックス洗車 (a) car wash and wax.

**せんしゅ**⁵【腺腫】 ▯▭ 線維腺腫〔医〕a fibrous adenoma.

**せんしゅ**⁷【選手】 ▯▭ 選手会長〔スポーツチームなどの〕a team captain. 選手兼監督 a「player [playing] manager. 選手寿命 (the span of) a player's career; a sporting career span. ◯ ボクサーの～寿命は平均して他のスポーツよりも短い。A boxer's career (in the ring) is on average shorter than for any other sport.

**せんじゅ**【川寿】 one's one hundred and eleventh birthday.

**せんしゅう**⁴【専修】 ▯▭ 専修免許 an Advanced Teacher's Certificate for MA Graduates.

**せんじゅう**¹【先住】 ▯▭ 先住民居住区 a reservation for the「original inhabitants [natives, native peoples]. 先住民保護区 a reservation for the protection of the「original inhabitants [natives, native peoples].

**せんじゅう**²【専従】 ▯▭ ヤミ専従〔雇用主から給与を受け取りながら組合活動に専従する者〕a person illegitimately engaging in full-time union activities while receiving a salary from《a local government》.

**せんじゅうみんぞくのけんりにかんするせんげん**【先住民族の権利に関する宣言】〔国連〕the United Nations Declaration on the Rights of Indigenous Peoples.

**せんじゅつ**²【戦術】 ▯▭ 戦術航空士〔軍〕a tactical coordinator（略: TACCO）.

**せんしょう**³【戦勝】 ▯▭ 戦勝報告 a victory report. ◯ ～報告(を)する report one's victory《to …》/ ～報告会 a victory announcement「session [party]; 〔戦勝祝賀会〕a victory celebration.

**せんじょう**³【洗浄】 ▯▭ 洗浄保存液〔コンタクトレンズの〕a rinsing and「storing [storage] solution. 洗浄力〔洗濯機・洗剤などの〕detergency.

**せんじょう**⁷【戦場】 ▯▭ 戦場カメラマン a「war [combat] photographer [cameraman]. 戦場ジャーナリスト a「combat [war] journalist.

**せんじょう**¹⁰【線状】 ▯▭ 線状ブロック〔点字ブロックの 1 つ〕a lined「paving [guide] block.

**せんしようけん**【先使用権】〔特許〕〔先願の特許出願より前に同様の発明をなした者がそれを製造・販売する権利〕(the) right of「first [prior] use.

**せんしようしゅぎ**【先使用主義】〔特許〕〔商標〕a first-to-use「system [principle].

**せんじょうたいくしつへんせいしょう**【線条体黒質変性症】〔医〕striatonigral degeneration（略: SND）.

**ぜんしょうとう**【前照灯】 ▯▭ すれ違い用前照灯 low beam. 走行用前照灯 high beam.

**「戦場のアリア」**〔映画〕Merry Christmas;〔フランス語タイトル〕Joyeux Noel.

**「戦場のピアニスト」**〔映画〕The Pianist.

**ぜんしょうれん**【全商連】＝ぜんこくしょうこうちゅうきょうれんごうかい.

**せんしょく**¹【染色】 ▯▭ 染色性〔繊維などの〕dyeability;〔細胞・組織などの〕stainability. ◯ 易[難]～性〔fabrics〕easy-to-dye [hard-to-dye]《fabrics》.

**せんしょく**²【染織】 ▯▭ 染織(作)家 a dyer and weaver.

**せんしょくたい**【染色体】 ▯▭ チンパンジー22 番染色体 chimpanzee chromosome 22. ヒト 21 番染色体 human chromosome 21. ▯▭ 染色体転座〔遺伝〕(a)「chromosomal [gene] translocation.

**ぜんしょち**【前処置】〔医〕〔骨髄移植の際の移植前に行う処置〕(pre-transplant) conditioning chemotherapy; a (transplant) conditioning regimen. ▯▭ 前処置薬剤〔検査・手術などの前に投与する〕a pre-treatment「medication [drug].

**ぜんしん**¹【全身】 ▯▭ 全身鏡, 全身ミラー a full-length mirror.

**ぜんしん**³【前進】 ▯▭ 前進翼〔空〕a forward swept wing.

**ぜんじん**¹【全人】 ▯▭ 全人(的)医療 whole-person medicine.

**センシング** ▯▭ 画像センシング vision sensing. ▯▭ センシング技術 (a) sensing technology. センシング・システム〔自動検知装置〕a (gas) sensing system.

**せんしんこく**【先進国】 ▯▭ 高度先進国 a more developed country.

**せんしんてきしょくにくかいしゅう**【先進的食肉回収】〔骨に付着している肉を, 骨を破壊せずに除去する方法〕advanced meat recovery（略: AMR）. ▯▭ 先進的食肉回収システム an advanced meat recovery system.

**せんすい**²【潜水】 ▯▭ 潜水航行 ＝せんこう¹³. 潜水士免許 a diving license; a diver's license.

**せんすいかん**【潜水艦】 ▯▭ 原子力潜水艦 a nuclear (-powered) submarine; an N-sub(marine). 原子力弾道ミサイル潜水艦 a ballistic missile nuclear submarine; an SSBN. 原子力潜水艦〔米・旧ソ連など〕a guided missile nuclear submarine（略: SSGN）. 巡航ミサイル潜水艦 a guided missile submarine（略: SSG）. 弾道ミサイル潜水艦 a ballistic missile submarine（略: SSB）. ▯▭ 潜水艦探知能力 (a) submarine detection capability.

**せんすいきょう**【潜水橋】＝沈下橋《⇨ちんか¹》.

**ぜんせ**【前世】 ▯▭ 前世体験 (a) past-life regression;「past-life [previous-life] experience. 前世療法 past life regression [PLR] therapy.

**せんせい**¹²【先制】 ▯▭ 先制ゴール ＝先制弾. 先制使用〔核兵器など〕first use of nuclear weapons. 先制打 a first「scoring [go-ahead] hit. 先制弾〔野球〕a home run scoring the first run(s) of the game;〔サッカーなど〕the first goal (scored). 先制的自衛 preemptive self-defense. ◯ ～の自衛攻撃 a preemptive attack (made in self-defense). 先制パンチ a first「blow [punch];〔相手の出鼻をくじく言葉・行動〕《draw》first blood; a preemptive strike. ◯ 阪神は初回に 2 連続ホームランで強烈な～パンチを浴びせた. The Hanshin Tigers hit the Chunichi Dragons with a powerful first blow when they scored two successive homeruns in the first inning. / 第 1 回目の講義からまったく理解できず, いきなり～パンチを食らった気分だった. Right from the first lecture I couldn't understand a thing. I felt I'd been dealt a body-blow before I could find my feet. 先制不使用〔核兵器の〕(the principle of) No-First-Use ["no first use"] of nuclear weapons. 先制ホームラン〔野球〕＝先制弾.

**せんせい**³【宣誓】 ▯▭ 宣誓台 a podium. 宣誓文 an oath.

**ぜんせき**¹【全席】 ▯▭ 全席優先席 the designation of all seats as priority seating; all-seat priority seating.

**せんぞ**【先祖】 ▯▭ 先祖供養 a memorial service for the repose of one's ancestors. 先祖木 the original stock《of Kawazu cherry》; the tree from which all other specimens「are derived [have been cloned].

**せんそう**⁴【戦争】 ▯▭ 戦争請負会社 ＝民間軍事会社《⇨みんかん》. 戦争協力者 a (war) collaborator; a (pro-

せんぞう

war) sympathizer. 戦争史 a history of war. ▶世界～史〔戦争の世界史〕a world history of war;〔世界戦争の歴史〕a history of the world wars.

**せんぞう**【潜像】▶□ 潜像模様〔紙幣などの〕a latent image.

**ぜんそうとどけ**【全喪届】《社会保険》〔休業・廃業により全従業員が社会保険から脱退する際に社会保険事務所に出す届〕a notification by a business establishment of withdrawal from the social insurance system due to bankruptcy, suspension of business, etc.; a social-insurance withdrawal notification.

**せんぞく**【専属】▶□ 専属作家〔劇団などの〕a playwright in residence;〔画廊などの〕an in-house artist;〔レコード会社などの〕a contract「songwriter [composer]. 専属秘書 one's own secretary; a dedicated secretary.

**ぜんそく**[1]【全速】▶□ 全速走行〔自動車レースなどで〕top [full] speed driving; driving at「top [full] speed.

**ぜんそく**[2]【喘息】▶□ 咳喘息 cough (variant) asthma; coughing asthma.

**せんだ**【潜舵】《海》〔潜水艦の〕a diving plane.

**センター**
　▶□ センター化 concentration of《the facilities in an area》. ▶医療の～化〔医師の負担を軽減し診療の効率化をはかるため医師を中核的な病院に集めること〕concentrating doctors at a「medical center [central hospital] (in order to alleviate overwork and improve efficiency). センター返し《野球》hitting the ball to center (field);〔その打球〕a ball hit to center (field). センター・メーター〔自動車〕〔計器類をダッシュボード中央部にまとめて配置する方式〕a center meter cluster. センター利用入試 ＝センター試験利用入試〈⇨センターしけん〉.
**センターしけん**【～試験】▶□ センター試験利用入試〔大学入試センター試験結果を利用する入試〕a university entrance exam using the results of the「(National) Center Test [standardized preliminary examination].
「**センターステージ**」〔映画〕Center Stage.
**センターファイア・ピストル**〔射撃〕a center-fire pistol;〔競技種目〕center-fire pistol.

**せんたく**[1]【洗濯】▶□ 洗濯乾燥機 a washing/drying machine; a (combination) washer/dryer. ▶縦型～乾燥機 a top-loading washer/dryer / ドラム式〔横型〕～乾燥機 a front-loading washer/dryer. 洗濯ネット a laundry net; a mesh laundry bag.

**せんたく**[2]【選択】▶□ 選択バイアス《医》selection bias.

**せんたくかんげんしょくばい**【選択還元触媒】〔自動車が排出する窒素酸化物を減らす方式〕a [the] selective catalytic reduction (system) (略: SCR).

**せんたくき**【洗濯機】▶□ 乾燥機能付き洗濯機 ⇨かんそう[4]. 縦型洗濯機 a top-loading washing machine. 横型〔ドラム式〕洗濯機 a front-loading washing machine.

**せんたくてき**【選択的】▶□ 選択的抗トロンビン剤《薬》a selective thrombin inhibitor; a selective antithrombin agent. 選択的セロトニン再取り込み阻害薬《薬》〔抗うつ薬〕a selective serotonin reuptake inhibitor (略: SSRI). 選択的農薬 a selective insecticide.

**せんたん**[2]【先端・尖端】▶□ 先端研究 advanced research. 先端兵器 an advanced [a state-of-the-art] weapon;〔集合的に〕advanced [state-of-the-art] weaponry.

**せんだん**[3]【剪断】▶□ 剪断力《機》shearing force.

**せんたんエス・オー・シーきばんぎじゅつかいはつ**【先端SoC 基盤技術開発】＝アスプラ.

**ぜんだんかい**【前段階】an「early [initial] stage; the previous stage. ▶認知症の～にある患者 a patient「in the early stages of [with incipient] dementia.

**ぜんちきゅうそくいシステム**【全地球測位～】▶□ 全地球測位システム衛星 a global positioning satellite; a GPS satellite.

**ぜんちたいばん**【前置胎盤】《医》placenta previa.

▶□ 全前置胎盤 total placenta previa. 部分前置胎盤 partial placenta previa.

**ぜんちっそ**【全窒素】〔水中に含まれる窒素化合物の総量; 環境基準の1つ〕total nitrogen (略: TN).

**センチネル・リンパせつ**【～節】《解》a sentinel lymph node. センチネル・リンパ節検索 a sentinel (lymph) node search. センチネル・リンパ節生検《医》(a) sentinel lymph node biopsy.

**センチュリー・ハウジング・システム** the "Century Housing System" (略: CHS), a system set up by the Japanese Ministry of Construction to encourage the development of durable and easily maintained housing, with provisions for certification. ▶ 1980年, 旧建設省が策定した住構性能高度化推進プロジェクトの一環.

**せんてい**[3]【剪定】▶□ 剪定ゴミ 《dispose of》prunings.

**ぜんてい**[3]【前庭】▶□ 前庭神経炎《医》vestibular neuronitis.

**ぜんてき**[2]【全摘】▶□ 全摘(手)術 an operation to remove all of the《thyroid》; (a) total《thyroidectomy》.

**せんでん**【宣伝】▶□ 宣伝広告費 publicity and advertising expenses.

**ぜんてんきゅう**【全天球】▶□ 全天球型映像〔システム〕a full 360-degree spherical image (system). 全天球パノラマ a full 360-degree spherical panorama「view [picture].

**せんてんせい**【先天性】▶□ 先天性巨大結腸症《医》congenital megacolon; Hirschsprung's disease. [＝ヒルシュスプルングびょう] 先天性障害 a congenital handicap. 先天性胆道拡張症 congenital biliary dilatation (略: CBD). 先天性肥厚性幽門狭窄症《医》congenital hypertrophic pyloric stenosis. 先天性副腎低形成(症) congenital adrenal hypoplasia. 先天性無汗症《医》＝むつうむかんしょう.

**せんてんてき**【先天的】▶□ 先天的障害 ＝先天性障害〈⇨せんてんせい〉.

**せんでんひ**【宣伝費】▶□ 広告宣伝費 advertising and publicity expenses.

**ぜんと**[3]【全塗】〔自動車などの塗装をすっかり塗り替えること〕an overall paint job; a complete respraying.

**せんとう**[5]【戦闘】▶□ 戦闘海域 battle waters. 戦闘群《米軍》a battle group. ▶空母～群 a carrier battle group. 戦闘指揮所《軍》a combat information center (略: CIC). 戦闘司令部《軍》(a) warfighting headquarters (略: WFHQ). 戦闘年齢 《males of》combat(ant) age. 戦闘ヘリ a combat helicopter. 戦闘用糧食 combat rations.

**せんとう**[6]【銭湯】▶□ 銭湯絵師 a bathhouse muralist.

**ぜんとう**[1]【全党】▶□ 全党大会 a full party conference. 全党的 concerning [covering] a whole (political) party; full-party. ▶政治資金の改革に～的に取り組む tackle reform of political funding at the full party level.

**ぜんとう**[6]【前頭】▶□ 前頭側頭葉 the「frontotemporal [front-temporal] lobe. 前頭側頭葉型認知症 (a)「frontotemporal [fronto-temporal] dementia (略: FTD). 前頭側頭葉変性症《医》frontotemporal [fronto-temporal] lobar [lobe] degeneration (略: FTLD). 前頭洞《解》a frontal sinus. 前頭連合野《解》the frontal association area.

**せんとうき**【戦闘機】▶□ 重戦闘機 a heavy fighter. 統合攻撃戦闘機《軍》a joint strike fighter (略: JSF).

**ぜんとうけんさ**【全頭検査】〔狂牛病などの〕blanket testing; testing of all《cattle》.

**せんとうこ**【千島湖】〔中国浙江(セッ)省にある人造湖〕Qiandao Lake.

「**セント・オブ・ウーマン／夢の香り**」〔映画〕Scent of a Woman.

「**千と千尋の神隠し**」〔映画〕Spirited Away.

**ぜんとっかえ**【全取っ替え】〔総入れ替え〕a「complete [to-

tal, full] replacement; a full changeover.
「**セントラル・ステーション**」〔映画〕Central Station;〔原題〕Central do Brasil.
**セントラル・ロケーション・テスト**《広告》〔会場集合試験〕a central location test (略: CLT).
**セントレア** ⇨ちゅうぶこくさいくうこう.
**ぜんにほん**【全日本】🔲 全日本学生選手権〔種々の競技の〕an All-Japan Student Championship.
**ぜんにほんアーチェリーれんめい**【全日本-連盟】the All Japan Archery Federation (略: AJAF).
**ぜんにほんからてどうれんめい**【全日本空手道連盟】the Japan Karatedo Federation (略: JKF).
**ぜんにほんこうつううんゆさんぎょうろうどうくみあいきょうぎかい**【全日本交通運輸産業労働組合協議会】the Japanese Council of Transport Workers' Unions.
**ぜんにほんコーヒーきょうかい**【全日本-協会】the All Japan Coffee Association (略: AJCA).
**ぜんにほんじつぎょうだんたいこうえきでん**【全日本実業団対抗駅伝】the 《50th》 All Japan Corporate Team *Ekiden* Championships.
**ぜんにほんしりつようちえんれんごうかい**【全日本私立幼稚園連合会】the All-Japan Private Kindergarten Federation.
**ぜんにほんしんきゅうがっかい**【全日本鍼灸学会】the Japan Society of Acupuncture and Moxibustion (略: JSAM).
**ぜんにほんだいがくサッカーれんめい**【全日本大学-連盟】the Japan University Football Association (略: JUFA).
**ぜんにほんつりだんたいきょうぎかい**【全日本釣り団体協議会】the All Japan Fishing Association.
**ぜんにほんてをつなぐいくせいかい**【全日本手をつなぐ育成会】Inclusion Japan; the Japanese Association 「of [for] People with Intellectual Disabilities.
**ぜんにほんなんしきやきゅうれんめい**【全日本軟式野球連盟】the Japan Rubber Baseball Association.
**ぜんにほんはくぶつかんがっかい**【全日本博物館学会】the Museological Society of Japan.
**ぜんにほんびょういんきょうかい**【全日本病院協会】the All Japan Hospital Association (略: AJHA).
**ぜんにほんぶんぐきょうかい**【全日本文具協会】the All Japan Stationery Association (略: AJSA).
**ぜんにほんゆうえんしせつきょうかい**【全日本遊園施設協会】the Japan Amusement Park Equipment Association (略: JAPEA).
**ぜんにほんゆうせいろうどうくみあい**【全日本郵政労働組合】the All Japan Postal Labour Union. ▶ 2007年10月に 日本郵政公社労働組合と統合して 日本郵政グループ労働組合 となった.
**せんにゅう**[3]【潜入】🔲 潜入工作〔スパイなどによる〕infiltration activities. 潜入捜査 an (inside) undercover investigation.
**せんにん**[3]【専任】🔲 専任教員[教授] a full-time 「teacher [professor]; a career 「teacher [professor].
**ぜんねん**【前年】🔲 前年実績 last [the previous] year's 「results [performance]. 7月の平均消費支出は8か月連続で~実績を下回り, 消費低迷は深刻である. The slackening in consumption is severe, with average consumer spending in July down on the previous year for the eighth month in succession. 前年並み ⇨ ぜんねんなみ.
**ぜんねんどうき**【前年同期】🔲 前年同期割れ ◯ 今年に入ってからのわが国のパソコン売上高は3か月連続で~割れだ. Since the start of this year, sales of computers have been lower than for the equivalent periods last year for three months running.
**ぜんねんなみ**【前年並み】the same as [equal to] last [the previous] year. ◯ 2004年の四輪車販売台数はほぼ~だった. Sales of four-wheeled vehicles in 2004 「nearly matched [were in line with] the previous year's.
**ぜんねんひ**【前年比】〔その前の年との〕the ratio to 「a year earlier [the previous year];〔去年との〕the ratio to 「a year ago [last year]. ◯ ~ 24.5% 増[減] a 24.5% 「increase [decrease] from 「a year earlier [the previous year].
**せんのう**[3]【洗脳】🔲 洗脳工作《be subjected to》(a program of) 「brainwashing [indoctrination].
**せんぱく**[2]【船舶】🔲 船舶安全(性)検査 a ship safety inspection《under Port State Control》. 船舶・航空機用ビーコン a 「nautical [shipping] and 「airway [aviation, aerial] beacon. 船舶通信 shipping communications. ◯ ~通信士 a ship's radio operator.
**ぜんぱく**【前泊】〔前の日に現地に到着して宿泊すること〕~する stay 《in a hotel》the night before; spend the night before《in a hotel》.
**せんぱくけんさほう**【船舶検査法】〔法〕the Ship Inspection Law.
**せんぱくゆだくそんがいばいしょうほしょうほう**【船舶油濁損害賠償保障法】〔法〕the Law on Liability for Oil Pollution Damage.
**せんぱつ**[1]【先発】🔲 先発(医薬)品〔薬〕originator drugs. 先発企業 a 「pioneering [pioneer] company (in 《pharmaceuticals》); an early entrant 《in the high-tech market》. 先発起用 ◯ ジーコ監督はワールドカップ第一戦に中田を~起用した. Coach Zico headed up his team for the first World Cup match with Nakata. 先発出場 playing from the start《of a game》. ◯ ~出場する be the first to play《in a tournament》. 先発メーカー a pioneering producer; a (production) pioneer; an early entrant 《in this area of production》. 先発薬 = 先発(医薬)品.
**せんはっぴょうしゅぎ**【先発表主義】〔特許〕a "first-to-publish" system.
**せんぱん**[2]【戦犯】🔲 戦犯裁判 a war crimes trial.
**ぜんはんかい**【全半壊】complete or partial 「destruction [collapse]; destruction of or serious damage to 《private houses》. ~する be completely or partially destroyed; completely or partially collapse; be destroyed or seriously damaged. ◯ 今回の災害で住宅 160 戸が~した. 160 homes were either totally destroyed or suffered serious damage in the recent disaster. 🔲 全半壊家屋 completely or partially destroyed 「houses [buildings]. 全半壊世帯 a completely or partially destroyed household.
**ぜんはんしょう**【全半焼】complete destruction or serious damage by fire. ~する be completely or partially 「burned out [destroyed by fire]; be totally destroyed or seriously damaged by fire. ◯ 山田さん方から出火, 木造2階建て住宅と隣接する住宅3棟が~した. Breaking out in the home of Mr. Yamada, the fire destroyed or seriously damaged the two-storey wooden house and three other neighboring homes.
**せんぴ**[3]【戦費】🔲 戦費調達 raising war funds; obtaining the finance for a war; financing a war.
**せんびき**【線引き】🔲 線引き都市〔市街化区域と市街化調整区域との区分を定めた都市〕a city with distinct zones for the encouragement and for the control of urbanization. ◯ 非~都市〔市街化区域と市街化調整区域との区分を定めない都市〕a city without distinct zones for the encouragement and for the control of urbanization.
**ぜんひてい**【全否定】total negation. ~する totally [completely] negate [deny]. ◯ 恋愛に二度も三度も失敗したからといって自分を~する必要はない. Just because you have failed in love two or three

せんぶつ

times, there is no need to completely「negate yourself [despair of yourself].
せんぶつ【甎仏】a Buddhist「deity [motif] molded in relief on a clay tile.
ぜんふつオープン【全仏-】『テニス』the French Open Tennis Championships; the French Open (Tennis).
ぜんぶろん【先富論】〖経〗〔鄧小平の〕the [Deng Xiaoping's] theory of allowing some people to get rich「first [before others].
ぜんぶん²【前文】 □▷ 憲法前文 the preamble of the constitution.
ぜんべいえいがきょうかい【全米映画協会】=べいこくえいがきょうかい.
ぜんべいかがくアカデミー【全米科学-】=べいこくかがくアカデミー.
ぜんべいかでんきょうかい【全米家電協会】the Consumer Electronics Association (略: CEA).
ぜんべいきぎょうエコノミストきょうかい【全米企業-協会】the National Association of Business Economists (略: NABE).
ぜんべいきょうきゅうかんりきょうかい【全米供給管理協会】the (US) Institute for Supply Management (略: ISM).
ぜんべいこくじんちいこうじょうきょうかい【全米黒人地位向上協会】the National Association for the Advancement of Colored People (略: NAACP).
ぜんべいこつずいバンク【全米骨髄-】the National Marrow Donor Program (略: NMDP).
ぜんべいしょうけんぎょうきょうかい【全米証券業協会】the National Association of Securities Dealers (略: NASD).
ぜんべいしょくひんしょうぎょうろうどうくみあい【全米食品商業労働組合】the United Food and Commercial Workers (Union) (略: UFCW). ▶ カナダも含まれるので the United Food and Commercial Workers International Union (北米合同食品商業労働組合) が正式名.
ぜんべいせいぞうぎょうしゃきょうかい【全米製造業者協会】the National Association of Manufacturers (略: NAM).
ぜんべいぞうきぶんぱい[はいぶん]ネットワーク【全米臓器分配[配分]-】the United Network for Organ Sharing (略: UNOS).
ぜんべいちりがくきょうかい【全米地理学協会】= ナショナル・ジオグラフィックきょうかい.
(ぜん)べいていとうきんゆうきょうかい【(全)米抵当金融協会】the Mortgage Bankers Association (略: MBA).
ぜんべいにくぎゅうせいさんしゃきょうかい【全米肉牛生産者協会】the National Cattlemen's Beef Association (略: NCBA).
ぜんべいモーターサイクルきょうかい【全米-協会】the American Motorcyclist Association (略: AMA).
ぜんべいやきゅうきしゃきょうかい【全米野球記者会】the Baseball Writers' Association of America (略: BBWAA).
ぜんべいレコードきょうかい【全米-協会】the Recording Industry Association of America (略: RIAA).
ぜんべいレコードこうぎょうかい【全米-工業会】= ぜんべいレコードきょうかい.
センペルセコイア【植】〔スギ科の大高木〕a coast redwood; a Californian redwood; *Sequoia sempervirens*.
ぜんほうい【全方位】 □▷ 全方位戦略 a comprehensive strategy; an omnidirectional strategy.
ぜんほうこう【全方向】 □▷ 全方向カメラ an omnidirectional camera.
せんぼつ²【潜没】 □▷ 潜没航行 =せんこう¹³.
せんぼつしゃ【戦没者】 □▷ 戦没者墓苑 a cemetery for the war dead.

せんぼつしょうへいきねんび【戦没将兵記念日】〔米国の〕5月最終月曜日〕Memorial Day.
せんぼんごうし【千本格子】〖建〗vertical lattice; lattice of vertical slats set close together.
せんまいだ【千枚田】〔棚田〕terraced「paddy [rice] fields.
ぜんマレーシア・イスラムとう【全-党】〔マレーシアの政党〕the Parti Islam Se-Malaysia (略: PAS).
せんめい¹【宣明】 □▷ 宣明書 a written declaration.
せんめん¹【洗面】 □▷ 洗面カウンター a bathroom counter;〔その天板〕a bathroom countertop.
ぜんめん¹【全面】 □▷ 全面解禁 a complete「removal [lifting] of「a ban [an embargo] (on…). ▶解禁する lift [remove] a ban [an embargo] completely ((on …))/ 一部の保険商品については銀行での販売がすでに始まっているが、政府はその規制を～解禁する方針だ. Some insurance products have already begun to be sold by banks, and the government plans to eliminate all remaining restrictions. 全面提携〔企業同士などの〕(form) a「comprehensive [full] tie-up.
ぜんめん²【前面】 □▷ 前面衝突 a frontal collision.
センモノロム〔カンボジア東部, モンドル・キリ州の州都〕Senmonorom.
せんもん¹【専門】 □▷ 専門量販店 a「mass [large-scale] retailer of specialist products. ▶パソコン～量販店 a「mass [large-scale] computer retailer.
せんもんい【専門医】 □▷ 専門医認定制度 a system for certifying medical specialists.
ぜんや²【前夜】 □▷ 前夜式〔キリスト教の葬儀における通夜〕a wake.
せんゆう¹【占有】 □▷ 占有離脱 loss of possession. 占有離脱物(罪) lost [unclaimed] property. ▶離脱物横領(罪) misappropriation [embezzlement] of「lost [unclaimed] property.
せんゆう²【専有】 □▷ 専有面積〔集合住宅内の住居などの〕the area of (the area for) exclusive (private) use.
せんよう³【専用】
□▷ 専用狭域通信技術 dedicated short range communications (略: DSRC). 専用使用権〔商標・マンションの特定共用部分などに関する〕(an [the]) exclusive right of use. 専用チューナー〔衛星放送用などの〕a dedicated tuner. 専用デスク〔専門の担当部署〕a dedicated contact (person). 専用電話 ▶カード～電話 a public telephone that accepts only prepaid cards; a cardonly phone / ガスもれ通報～電話 a telephone line reserved for reporting gas leaks; a (dedicated) gasleak line / 警察相談～電話 a telephone line reserved for use by people seeking advice from the police; a police [*help line [ˮadvice line] / 消費生活相談～電話 a consumer「hotline [*help line, ˮadvice line] / チケット～電話〔演劇・観戦などの〕a ticket hotline / 着信～電話 a telephone line reserved for incoming calls / 予約～電話〔航空会社・ホテルなどの〕a reservation (hot)line. 専用フリーダイヤル〔サービス〕a dedicated toll-free service;〔電話番号〕a dedicated toll-free number. 専用列車 a special train;〔団体専用列車〕a train reserved for groups; a group train.
ぜんよう¹【全容】 □▷ 全容解明 elucidation [clarification] of the overall picture. ▶捜査本部は事件の～解明に全力を挙げている. The investigation center is doing all it can to「get [gain] an overall picture of「the incident [what happened]./ 事件の～解明が待たれる. Clarification of what happened in the incident is awaited.
ぜんようそせいさんせい【全要素生産性】〖経〗total factor productivity (略: TFP).
せんようのほうがん【腺様嚢胞癌】〖医〗(an) adenoid cystic carcinoma (略: ACC, AdCC).
「1492・コロンブス」〔映画〕1492: Conquest of Para-

dise.

ぜんりつせん【前立腺】⇨ 前立腺液〖解〗prostatic 「fluid [juice].

せんりゃく【戦略】⇨ 戦略眼《have》a strategic vision. 戦略拠点 a strategic foothold. 戦略経営 strategic management. 戦略資源 strategic resources. 戦略対話 a strategic dialogue《with…, between…》. 戦略パートナー a strategic partner. 戦略目標〔狙い〕a strategic objective;〔標的〕a strategic target. ◯ 共通～目標 common strategic objectives.

せんりゃくこうげきせんりょくさくげんじょうやく【戦略攻撃戦力削減条約】〔米口間の; 2002年締結〕the Strategic Offensive Reductions Treaty（略: SORT）. ▶ モスクワ条約 (the Moscow Treaty) ともいう.

せんりゃくこくさいけんきゅうセンター【戦略国際研究―】＝せんりゃくこくさいもんだいけんきゅうじょ.

せんりゃくこくさいもんだいけんきゅうじょ【戦略国際問題研究所】〖米国のシンクタンク〗the Center for Strategic and International Studies（略: CSIS）.

せんりゃくてき【戦略的】⇨ 戦略的の外交 strategic diplomacy. 戦略的の開発同盟 a strategic development alliance《between Japan and the US》. 戦略的の拠点 a strategic hub《for「the US military [business]」》. 戦略的互恵（関係）strategic reciprocity; a strategic, mutually beneficial relationship. 戦略的中心市街地商業等活性化支援事業 a strategic assistance project for revitalization of commerce in city center areas.

ぜんりゅうこくもつ【全粒穀物】〔精白度が低く, 健康によい成分を保持した穀物〕whole grain(s).

ぜんりゅうふん【全粒粉】〔小麦の粒を丸ごと製粉したもの〕whole wheat flour.

せんりょう³【染料】⇨ 染色インク (a) dye ink.

せんりょう⁴【線量】⇨ 線量レベル ＝放射線量レベル（⇨ほうしゃせん）.

せんりょう⁵【全量】⇨ 全量転換〔ガソリンの国内全需要量をバイオエタノール混合ガソリンに転換すること〕conversion to gasohol.

ぜんりん²【善隣】⇨ 善隣友好協力 good-neighborly cooperation.

ぜんりん³【全燐】〔水中に含まれるリン化合物の総量; 環境基準の1つ〕total phosphorus（略: TP）.

ぜんれい²【前例】⇨ 前例主義 reliance on precedent. 前例踏襲 following [observing] precedent.

ぜんれき【前歴】⇨ 前歴者 a previous offender; a person with a black mark against him. ◯ 凶悪犯罪～者 a person「with a record for violent crime [who has previously committed a vicious crime]」/ 性犯罪～者の住居情報 information about the addresses of sexual offenders.

ぜんろうけん【全老健】＝ぜんこくろうじんほけんしせつきょうかい.

ぜんろうさい【全労済】Zenrosai. [＝ぜんこくろうどうしゃきょうさいせいかつきょうどうくみあいれんごうかい]

そ

# そ

そあく【粗悪】⇨ 粗悪紙 low-quality paper.

そいん³【訴因】⇨ 訴因変更 a change in the「charge [indictment]」; a change of charge.

そう⁴【相】⇨ 相変化メモリー〖電算〗phase-change memory（略: PCM）.

そう⁷【層】
4〔共通の意識・様式などをもつ集団〕a type; a group; a segment; a demographic. ◯ ハイエンドユーザー～ high-end users /初心者～《sell to》the beginner market /ファミリー～ the family 「demographic [market segment]」/年齢～ without consideration of age group /男女問わず幅広い～に受け入られる popular with all types of people, including both men and woman. ⇨ 層崩壊[破壊]〖建〗〔破壊により建物の特定の階がすべて無くなること〕a "story ["storey] collapse.

そう¹⁴【躁】〔躁病〕mania. ▷ manic adj. ⇨ 躁状態〖医〗(be in) a manic state;《have》a manic episode;《口》(be on) a high.

そう-【総-】⇨ 総コレステロール total cholesterol（略: TC）. ◯ ～コレステロール値 a total cholesterol level. 総出演 ◯ 有名俳優の～出演 a performance [an appearance] by a complete cast of famous actors. 総発熱量〖物〗a gross heating value（略: GHV）.

ぞうあく【増悪】⇨ 増悪因子〔肥満, 運動・睡眠不足など〕an aggravating [an exacerbating] factor.

ぞうあつ【増圧】⇨ 増圧直結方式〔集合住宅における給水方式の1つ〕(a) direct water-supply system with booster pump.

そうあんせい【操安性】＝操縦安定性（⇨そうじゅう）.

そうい⁷【葬衣】＝そうふく³.

ぞうえん¹【造園】⇨ 造園技能士 a certified landscape gardener. 造園施工管理技士 a certified landscape gardening supervisor.

そうおどり【総踊り】mass [large-group] dancing; a dance in which everyone participates.

そうおん【騒音】⇨ 騒音対策《traffic》noise control measures. 騒音被害 noise damage; damage due to noise. ◯ 大阪空港の発着機の増便と大型化に伴って～被害が深刻化している. With more planes taking off and landing at Osaka airport, and aircraft getting larger, the noise damage is becoming serious.

そうか¹⁰【層化】⇨ 層化二段無作為抽出法〖統計〗stratified two-stage random sampling.

そうかい²【爽快】⇨ 爽快感 a feeling of「refreshment [release, exhilaration, invigoration]」. ◯ あの映画の終わり方には～感が感じられなかった. There was something「unsatisfying [frustrating]」about the way the film ended. | I felt let down by the way the movie ended.

そうかい³【掃海】⇨ 掃海母艦 a minesweeper tender（略: MST）.

そうかい⁵【総会】⇨（株主）総会検査役〔株主総会の手続き・進行などの公正性をチェックする人; 会社が裁判所に選任申請する〕an auditor of a general shareholders meeting.

そうかがっかい【創価学会】(the) Soka Gakkai, a Buddhistic religious organization of Japanese origin.

そうがく²【総額】⇨ 総額裁量制〔義務教育における教職員給与などに関し都道府県が国庫負担金の範囲内で自由に決められる制度〕the total budget discretion system; the system permitting local authorities to allocate their education budgets at their own discretion. 総額表示〔価格の〕《mark items with》the total price including tax.

そうかつ¹【総括】⇨ 総括原価主義 ＝総括原価方式. 総括原価方式 a [the] general-cost method. 総括判断〔日銀の金融経済月報における景況判断〕an overall assessment of economic conditions.

そうかん⁵【相関】⇨ 偏相関〖統計〗a partial correlation.

そうかんぶんり【総幹分離】〔総裁と幹事長を異なる派閥から出すという自民党の慣例〕the practice in the Liberal Democratic Party of selecting party president and

secretary-general from different factions.
そうき¹【早期】
▣ 早期英語教育 early English(-language) education. 早期化 making earlier; advancing; moving up. ◐ 連結決算発表の〜化 earlier announcement of consolidated financial results. 早期解約〔保険などの〕(an) early cancellation. 早期示談 an early [a prompt] settlement 《of a dispute》. 和解による〜決着 an early settlement 《of a court case》 by reconciliation. 早期警戒管制機〔軍〕an 〔airborne〕 early-warning and control [AEW&C] aircraft. 早期警戒レーダー〔軍〕early-warning radar. ◐ 移動式〜警戒レーダー mobile early-warning radar. ◐ 早期退職優遇制度 a system of preferential treatment for employees who choose early retirement. 早期発見率 a [the] rate of early detection. 早期米〔早場米〕rice from an early harvest area; (an) early rice. 早期離職 leaving a ⌈job [company]⌋ after a short period of employment. ◐ 〜離職する leave a ⌈job [company]⌋ after a short period of employment / 〜離職者 a person who leaves a ⌈job [company]⌋ after a short period of employment / 〜離職率 the percentage of people who ⌈do not stay long in a job [quit after a brief period of employment]⌋. 早期留学 early study abroad; overseas study by young students.
そうき⁴【想起】 ▣ 純粋想起(法)〔広告〕unaided recall. 助成想起(法)〔広告〕aided recall; prompted recall.
そうき⁶【搔器】《考古》=さっき⁴.
そうぎ³【葬儀】 ▣ 葬儀業者 a funeral ⌈company [agency]⌋.
ぞうき³【臓器】 ▣ 臓器保存 organ preservation; preservation of (donor) organs. ◐ 〜保存液 (an) organ preservation solution.
そうきゅう⁴【宋級】〔軍〕=そんきゅう.
そうぎょう²【創業】 ▣ 創業者(ʳ)⁽ˢ⁾ a ⌈founding [founder's]⌋ family. ◐ 彼は〜家出身の最後の社長だった。He was the last president from the founding family. 創業祭 commemoration of the founding of a business. 〜祭開催中 Founder's Sale Now in Progress / 第9回〜大大売り出し〔広告〕Ninth Anniversary Sale. 創業支援 (business) incubation. [＝インキュベーション] 創業者社長 (the) founder and president 《of the company》.
そうぎょう⁴【操業】 ▣ 本格操業 a ⌈regular [full-scale]⌋ operation.
そうきょくせい【双極性】bipolarity; dipolarity. ▣ 双極性うつ病《精神医》＝双極性障害. 双極性感情《気分》障害《精神医》＝双極性障害. 双極性障害《精神医》(a) bipolar [manic-depressive] disorder.
そうきん【送金】 ▣ 送金業務 a remittance service; remittance business. ◐ 国際〜業務 an international remittance service; international remittance business. 送金停止〔外国への〕《impose》an embargo on money transfers.
ぞうきん【雑巾】 ▣ 化学[科学]雑巾 a chemically treated dustcloth.
そうげい【送迎】 ▣ 送迎保育ステーション a childcare staging facility; a childcare transit station.
ぞうけい¹【造形・造型】 ▣ 造形感覚 a sense of ⌈form [shape]⌋. 造形美 beauty of form.
そうけいちゅう【双係柱】《海》〔桟橋などにある2つ一組の係船柱〕a bollard.
ぞうけつ¹【造血】 ▣ 造血細胞 a hematopoietic cell.
ぞうけつ³【増血】increasing [improving] the blood supply; an ⌈increase [improvement]⌋ in the blood supply; supplementing the blood. ▣ 増血剤 a blood supplement; an anti-anemia agent. 増血作用《have》the ⌈effect [function]⌋ of ⌈increasing [improving]⌋ the blood supply.

「宋家の三姉妹」〔映画〕The Soong Sisters; 〔中国語タイトル〕宋家皇朝.
そうけん⁸【創憲】creation of the Constitution.
そうご¹【倉庫】 ▣ 倉庫稼働率 (a) warehouse occupancy rate. 倉庫型店舗 a warehouse store.
そうご²【相互】 ▣ 相互応援協定 a mutual ⌈aid [support]⌋ agreement. 相互汚染《医》mutual contamination. 相互補完 mutual complementation. ◐ 〜補完的 mutually complementary / 〜補完的な役割を果たす complement [reinforce, supplement] each other's functions.
そうこう¹【爪甲】 ▣ 厚硬爪甲 pachyonychia; thickening of the nails. 爪甲鉤彎(ゎん)(ゎん)症 onychogryposis; ram's horn (nail). 爪甲層状裂症《医》onychoschizia. [＝二枚爪 (⇨にまい)]
そうこう³【走行】
▣ 快適走行 comfortable [pleasant] driving. スポーツ走行 performance driving. 注意走行〔掲示〕driving with caution; 〔カーレースで〕running under a yellow flag. 片輪(かた)(りん)走行 going [driving] on two wheels; 〔アクロバティックな自動車運転〕two-wheel tilt driving.
▣ 走行安定性《自動車》(running) stability. 走行支援道路システム an 〔the〕Advanced Cruise-Assist Highway System. 走行試験〔テスト〕〔車両などの〕(give a vehicle) a 〔test [trial]〕run. ◐ 公道〜試験〔テスト〕a test run on ordinary ⌈roads [tracks]⌋. 走行中 ◐ 〜中の事故 a driving accident; an accident (ocurring) while ⌈driving [in motion, moving]⌋ / 〜中に居眠りをする fall asleep [nod off] when driving [at the wheel] / 〜中は運転手に話しかけないでください。〔掲示〕Please do not speak to the driver unnecessarily ⌈when [while]⌋ the bus is ⌈in motion [running]⌋.
そうごう³【総合】 ▣ 総合エネルギー企業 a comprehensive energy ⌈company [corporation]⌋. 総合外来 a general outpatients department; 〔病院の掲示で〕General Outpatients. 総合週刊誌 a ⌈general [general-interest]⌋ weekly (magazine). 総合スーパー a general merchandise store (略: GMS). 総合デパート a general department store. 総合評価(落札)方式 a comprehensive evaluation bid(ding) system.
そうごうかがくぎじゅつかいぎ【総合科学技術会議】 ▣ 総合科学技術会議生命倫理専門調査会 the Bioethics Committee of the Council for Science and Technology Policy.
そうごうかぶかしすう【総合株価指数】〔証券〕〔韓国の〕⇨かんこくそうごうかぶかしすう.
そうごうきせいかいかくかいぎ【総合規制改革会議】 ▣ the Council for Regulatory Reform (略: CRR). ▶ 2004年4月に「規制改革・民間開放推進会議」に移行.
そうごうぎょうせいネットワーク【総合行政-】a comprehensive administrative network; 〔日本の〕the Local Government Wide Area Network (略: LGWAN).
そうごうしげんエネルギーちょうさかい【総合資源-調査会】the Advisory Committee for Natural Resources and Energy.
そうごうしゅうさんきぼしいりょうセンター【総合周産期母子医療-】a comprehensive perinatal care center for mothers and infants.
そうごうのうせいちょうさかい【総合農政調査会】〔自民党の〕the Research Commission on Comprehensive Agricultural Administration.
そうごうほうりつしえんほう【総合法律支援法】〔法〕the Comprehensive Legal Aid Law.
ぞうこく²【増石】1〔酒の生産量を増やすこと〕an increase in the quantity brewed.
〜する increase the quantity brewed; brew more 《liquor》.

**ぞうせつ**

2 《日本史》〔俸禄が増えること〕a stipend increase. 〜する〔俸禄を〕increase [raise] 《a retainer's》 stipend; 〔俸禄が〕increase; rise.

**そうさ**[1]【走査】 ▷ 走査線数〔電子工学〕the number of 「scanning [scan] lines. ▷ 有効〜線数 the number of effective scanning lines.

**そうさ**[2]【捜査】
▷ 合同捜査 (a) joint investigation. ▷ 合同〜本部 《set up》a joint investigation headquarters. 特殊(犯)捜査係[班]〔都道府県の警察の〕a special investigation team. ▷ 捜査共助 (interagency [intergovernmental]) cooperation with an investigation. 捜査協力 cooperation with an investigation. ▷ 中国の警察当局に〜協力を申し入れる ask the Chinese police authorities to assist in an investigation / 〜協力者 a collaborator in an investigation; 〔情報提供者〕an informant. 捜査権 investigatory power(s). ▷ 犯人の女児は13歳なので警察の〜権に及ばない。Since the girl who committed the crime is 13 years old, the police have no power to investigate the case. 捜査権限 the right 「of [to] investigation; 《police》 search rights; the authority to conduct 「a search [an investigation]. 捜査隊 an investigation team. ▷ 機動〜隊〔警察の〕a mobile investigation team / 特別〜隊〔警察の〕a special investigation team. 捜査通訳 police interpreting; interpreting for the police; 〔人〕a police interpreter. 捜査手続き (criminal) investigation procedure(s). 捜査特別報奨金 a special reward for information leading to the arrest of 《the suspect》. 捜査報告書 an investigation report. 捜査方針 an investigation policy; a policy on investigations. ▷ 県警は〜方針の変更を迫られた。The prefectural police were 「pressured [under pressure] to change their investigation policies. 捜査ミス an investigation error; an error in investigation. ▷ 警察は〜ミスを認め、彼に謝罪した。The police admitted the error in their investigation(s) and offered him an apology.

**そうさ**[3]【操作】 ▷ 無人[有人]操作 unmanned [manned] operation. ▷ 操作スピード〔パソコンなどの作動〕(an) operation speed; (a) speed of operation; 〔機器類を操作する人の〕(an) operating speed. 操作パネル〔小型機器の〕a control panel; 〔工場などの〕a control 「board [panel]; a console. 操作ボタン an 「operation [operating] button.

**そうさい**[2]【葬祭】 ▷ 葬祭業 undertaking; the funeral business. 葬祭業者 a funeral director; an undertaker; *a mortician.

**そうさく**[2]【創作】 ▷ 創作劇 an original play. 創作詩 an original poem. 創作ノート〔小説家などの〕an author's notebook.

**ぞうさく**【造作】 ▷ 造作家具 built-in furniture.

**そうさくてい**【装削蹄】hoof trimming and fitting of horseshoes. ▷ 装削蹄師 a hoof trimmer and fitter of horseshoes.

**そうし**[8]【草姿】〔園芸〕the shape of a plant. ▷ この植物は〜が美しい。This plant forms a beautiful shape.

**そうじ**[4]【掃除】 ▷ 掃除サービス a cleaning service. ▷ お墓の〜サービス a grave cleaning service.

**ぞうし**[1]【増資】 ▷ 架空増資 a fictitious increase of stock. 公募増資 ⇨ こうぼ[1].

**そうじき**【掃除機】 ▷ 水フィルター掃除機 a water-filter(ed) vacuum cleaner.

**そうしさん**【総資産】 ▷ 総資産回転率 total asset turnover.

**そうしは**【走資派】《中国》〔毛沢東時代に資本主義化路線を主張する者を非難した呼称〕a capitalist roader.

**そうじほう**【双耳峰】〔頂上が二つ並んでいる山〕a twin-peaked mountain; twin peaks.

**ぞうしゅ**[2]【像主】〔肖像画や彫像のモデルとなった人〕the model 《for a sculpture》; the person depicted 《in a portrait》.

**そうじゅう**[0]【操縦】 ▷ 操縦安定性〔自動車〕controllability.

**そうしゅつ**[3]【送出】《放送》(a) transmission. 〜する transmit; send (off [out]). ▷ 番組送出 (a) transmission of a program; (a) program transmission.

**そうしゅつきょ**【走出去】〔中国の国家戦略としての産業の海外進出〕zouchuqu; overseas expansion; "Go Overseas" 《policy》.

**そうしょう**[5]【創傷】 ▷ 慢性創傷 (a) chronic trauma.

**そうしょう**【爪床】〔解〕a nail bed.

**そうしょう**[8]【争訟】a (legal) dispute. ▷ 両議院は、各々その議員の資格に関する〜を裁判する。〔日本国憲法 第55条〕Each House shall judge disputes related to qualifications of its members.

**そうしょう**[2]【増床】〔売り場の床面積を増やすこと〕an increase in (sales) floor space; 〔病院のベッド数を増やすこと〕an increase in hospital beds.

**そうしょう**[3]【贈賞】prize-giving; giving [awarding] a prize [an award] 《to sb》; 《文》 conferring [conferral of] a prize 《on…, upon…》.
〜する give [award] a prize 《to sb, for an achievement》. ▷ 贈賞式 a 「prize-giving [an award-giving] ceremony; a prize-giving. 贈賞理由 the reason for 「a prize [an award]; what a prize is 「given [awarded] for.

**そうじょうしきゅうたいこうかしょう**【巣状糸球体硬化症】〔医〕focal glomerulosclerosis; focal glomerular sclerosis (略: FGS).

**そうじょうしきゅうたいじんえん**【巣状糸球体腎炎】〔医〕focal glomerulonephritis.

**ぞうじょうしゅ**【増醸酒】〔清酒に糖類、酸味料、調味料などをくわえたもの〕sake to which saccharide, acidulant, flavorings, etc. have been added during production.

**そうじょうぶんせつせいしきゅうたいこうかしょう**【巣状分節性糸球体硬化症】〔医〕focal segmental glomerulosclerosis; focal segmental glomerular sclerosis (略: FSGS).

**そうしょく**[2]【装飾】 ▷ 装飾板〔建築用の〕a decorative board.

**ぞうしょく**【増殖】 ▷ 増殖礁〔海洋〕a propagation reef.

**そうしん**[1]【送信】 ▷ 送信済みメール sent items; e-mail(s) [mail(s)] sent. ▷ 夫の携帯電話に愛人宛ての〜済みメールがたくさん残っていて、それが理由で彼女は離婚した。There were a lot of e-mails to her husband's girlfriend in the "sent (items)" folder on his mobile phone, and for this reason she divorced him. 送信速度〔電算〕(a) transmission speed. 送信日時〔メールなどの〕the date and time 「sent [transmitted]. 未送信メール〔電算〕e-mail(s) for sending; unsent 「e-mail [mail].

**そうしん**[4]【痩身】 ▷ 痩身エステ(ティック)〔美容術〕(a) slimming treatment; 〔施設〕a slimming 「salon [clinic]. 痩身効果 《have》 a slimming effect. ▷ 〜効果を謳(う)た)う食品 foods which are 「claimed to have [advertised as having] a slimming effect.

**そうすいぎん**【総水銀】〔環境基準の1つ〕total mercury.

**そうせい**[14]【創生】〔初めて作りだすこと〕creation; formation; origination; 〔新しく生まれること〕birth; formation. ▷ 持続可能な社会の〜 the creation of 「a sustainable society / 太陽系の〜 the birth of the solar system.

**そうせい**【造成】 ▷ 造成工事〔土地の〕creation [clearing] of land. ▷ 宅地〜工事 creation [clearing] of land for residential purposes.

**そうせいじゅ**【早成樹】a fast-growing (species of) tree.

**ぞうせつ**[2]【造設】construction.
〜する construct. ▷ 人工肛門造設(術)〔医〕《per-

ぞうせつ

form》(a) colostomy; construction of「a stoma [an artificial anus]《after resection of the rectum》; stoma construction; proctostomy; rectostomy.

ぞうせつ³【造雪】snow making. ▣（人工）造雪機[装置]（artificial）snow-making equipment; a [an artificial] snow-making「machine [device]; a snow maker; a snow cannon; a snow fan.

そうそう⁴【葬送】▣ 葬送曲 funeral music; a funeral piece.

そうぞう²【創造】▣ 創造工学 creative engineering.

そうそうたる【錚々たる】prominent; eminent; outstanding; conspicuous; distinguished; foremost; leading; first-rate;《口》crack.▶その雑誌には一寄稿者が名をつらねて. The magazine had a long list of prominent contributors.

そうそうぶんり【総総分離】〔自民党総裁と内閣総理大臣は別々の人間が就任すべきだという主張〕the view that the positions of Liberal Democratic Party President and Prime Minister should be occupied by different people.

そうぞく²【相続】▣ 相続時精算課税制度 an integrated gift and inheritance tax system (under which previously paid gift taxes are deducted from inheritance taxes). 相続税評価額 an [the] assessed sum on which inheritance tax is payable.

そうたい¹【双胎】▣ 一絨毛膜(性)双胎 monochorionic [MC] twins. 二絨毛膜(性)双胎 dichorionic [DC] twins. ▣ 双胎間輸血症候群【医】twin-(to-) twin transfusion syndrome (略: TTTS).

そうたい³【相対】▣ 相対得票率〔有効投票数に占めるその候補者の得票の割合〕a comparative proportion of votes (cast)《for sb》.

そうたつ【送達】▣ 特別送達（郵便）〔裁判所から特別の手続きによって関係者に送達され、配達された事実を差出人に報告するか郵便〕special delivery (of legal documents).

そうだん¹【相談】▣ 相談罪 =共謀罪（⇒きょうぼう］. 相談登録弁護士制度 a free legal aid service system. 相談窓口〔対面式〕a consultation [an advice] desk [center];〔電話による〕a「consumer」hotline.

そうたんかん【総胆管】▣ 総胆管がん【医】(a) common bile duct cancer; (a) cancer of the common bile duct; (a) common bile duct carcinoma; (a) carcinoma of the common bile duct.

そうち¹【草地】▣ 草地学 grassland science. 草地学者 a grassland scientist.

ぞうちょう【蔵置場】a depository; a storehouse. ▣ 保税蔵置場⇒ほぜい.

そうちゃく²【装着】▣ 装着液 ＝コンタクトレンズ装着液（⇒コンタクト・レンズ）. 装着感 a feel (when fitted); ＝装用感（⇒そうようカン³）.

そうつい【双対】▣ 双対尺度法【統計】dual scaling.

そうてい⁶【想定】▣ 想定元本〔デリバティブ取引の〕a notional principal amount. 想定図〔イメージ図〕a conceptual「drawing (diagram, illustration). 想定被害〔大規模災害などによる〕predicted [forecast] damage.

そうてい⁸【装蹄】horseshoe fitting; shoeing a horse; horseshoeing. ▣ 装蹄師 a farrier; a horseshoe fitter.

そうてん²【争点】▣ 争点化 taking up (the Okinawa military base problem) as an issue. ▶政治的な～化を避けるため、歴代首相の多くは「在任中は改憲しない」と宣言してきた. In order to prevent it becoming a political issue, most previous Prime Ministers have stated that they will not attempt constitutional revision during their period of office. 争点整理【法】〔裁判における〕mutual disclosure (by prosecutors and defense lawyers) and discussion of the points of contention in advance of a trial.

そうでん²【送電】▣ 送電会社 a power [an electricity]

transmission company. ▶送電専門の会社で、日本には存在しない. 送電線使用料 a power line rental charge. [＝託送料金（⇒たくそう²）] 送電鉄塔〔送電塔〕a (power) transmission tower.

そうとう⁶【総統】▣ 総統府〔台湾などの〕the Presidential Office.

ぞうとう【贈答】▣ 贈答文化 a gift-giving culture.

そうとうせい【相当性】【法】appropriateness; suitability. ◆社会的～ ⇒しゃかいてき. ▶被告人の行為が、情緒障害児を更生させようという目的であったとしても、～を欠いていると言わざるを得ない. Even if designed to rehabilitate an emotionally disturbed child, the behavior of the defendant can only be considered (socially)「unacceptable [inappropriate].

そうとく【総督】▣ カナダ総督 the Governor General of Canada.

そうどり（ほうしき）【総取り（方式）】〔選挙〕winner-takes-all《system》.

そうなん【遭難】▣ 遭難死 (a) death [dying] in「an accident [a disaster]; (an) accidental death.

そうにゅう【挿入】▣ 挿入歌 a song that is sung between parts of a drama. 挿入音 interval music;〔歌〕an interval song.

ぞうのおり【象の檻】〔沖縄本島にある米軍の通信施設の通称〕the "Elephant Cage."

そうば【相場】▣ 相場展開 stock price development(s); developments in the stock market. ◆来週も激しい～展開が予想される. Next week is likely to see violent developments in the stock market. | Next week is likely to be a stormy one for stock markets. 相場転換 a change in market direction; a market turnaround.

そうはいじょうみゃくかんりゅういじょうしょう【総肺静脈還流異常症】【医】total anomalous pulmonary venous drainage (略: TAPVD).

そうはき【造波機】【機】＝ぞうはそうち.

そうはそうち【造波装置】【機】a wave-maker. ▣ 多方向不規則波造波装置 a multi-directional irregular wave-maker.

そうばつせい【双罰性】【法】double criminality.

そうはん³【窓販】▣ 銀行窓販〔銀行の窓口での保険販売〕over-the-counter insurance sales by banks.

そうはん¹【造反】▣ 造反議員 a rebel「legislator [Diet member]《of the Liberal Democratic Party》.

そうひょう³【総評】▣【give】「a general [an overall] assessment《of...》;（make）a general comment《on...》. ▶〔コンクールの審査委員長などに対して、司会が〕お願いします. Please give your general assessment. | How would you rate this overall?

そうびょう²【躁病】▣ 単極性躁病 unipolar mania.

そうふく³【葬服】〔被葬者に着せる衣〕a shroud; grave-clothes.

そうふんしゃ【送粉者】【生物】a pollinator.

そうへいきんほう【総平均法】【会計】the periodic average method.

そうほ【相補】▣ 相補医療【医】complementary medicine. 相補代替医療【医】complementary and alternative medicine.

そうむ²【総務】▣ 総務懇談会〔自由民主党の〕an informal meeting of the General Council.

ぞうもう【増毛】〔補毛〕hair restoration; hair replacement;〔育毛〕the「promotion [encouragement] of hair growth; hair restoration.
〜する restore one's hair. ▣ 増毛法 a hair「restoration [replacement] method.

そうやく¹【創薬】▣ 創薬競争 pharmaceutical competition; competition to produce new drugs. 創薬スクリーニング drug screening.

ぞうよ【贈与】▣ 贈与金 a monetary gift.

そよう³【装用】wearing; using; use. 〜する wear; use. ▷ 連続装用 continuous「wearing [use]」. ◎1週間連続〜使い捨てコンタクトレンズ disposable contact lenses that can be worn continuously for one week. ▷ 装用感 a feel (when being worn). ◎ ソフトコンタクトレンズはハードレンズよりも薄いので〜感がよい. Since soft contact lenses are thinner than hard ones, they have a better feel when they are being worn. 装用者 a user ⦅of a hearing aid⦆

そようか【相容化】〖化〗compatibilization. ▷ 相容化剤 a compatibilizing agent; a compatibilizer.

そようせい【相容性】〖化〗compatibility.

そうらん⁵【騒乱】▷ 騒乱状態 a state of「rebellion [disturbance]; rioting.

ぞうり【草履】▷ 竹皮草履 zori made with the outer sheath of bamboo. 布草履 zori [sandals] made with twisted cloth. わら草履 ⇨ わら.

ぞうりゅう【造粒】▷ 造粒炭 granulated carbon.

そうりょう¹【送料】▷ 送料お客様負担. Shipping charges paid by the customer. | You pay the shipping charges. | Shipping not included (in the price). 送料当社負担. 〔宣伝文句〕We pay the shipping charges. | Shipping included (in the price). 送料無料〔掲示〕Free shipping. | Free delivery. ◎ 市内〜無料〔掲示〕Free delivery within the city. | Free local delivery.

そうりょく²【総力】▷ 総力取材 full [unremitting] coverage. ◎ 本誌は臓器売買の衝撃の実態を〜取材しました. We gave 'full [unremitting]' coverage to the shocking reality of the buying and selling of human organs. 総力態勢 all one's 'power [strength]'. ◎ 次の試合には〜態勢で臨みます. We are approaching the coming game with all our strength.

ぞうりん【造林】▷ 造林公社 an afforestation corporation.

そうりんそうこうしゃ【装輪装甲車】〖軍〗a wheeled armored vehicle.

「ソウル・トレイン」〔米国,ソウル音楽ショーの TV 番組〕Soul Train.

「壮烈! 第七騎兵隊」〔南北戦争の勇士カスター将軍の TV 西部劇〕Custer.

そうわそく【総和則】〖物〗the sum rule.

ソーシャル ▷ ソーシャル・グループワーク = グループ・ワーク (⇨ グループ). ソーシャル・ネットワーキング・サービス〖電算〗a social networking service (略: SNS).

ソース¹ ▷ フルーツ・ソース (a) fruit sauce. ブルーベリー・ソース blueberry sauce.

ソーズドゥ = サウザンドゥルクス.

「ソードフィッシュ」〔映画〕Swordfish.

ソー・ビッグ・エフ【-F】〔コンピューターウイルスの1つ〕So-big.F.

「ソープ」〔米国の,姉妹の日常を描く辛口 TV ホームドラマ〕Soap.

ソーマチン〖化〗〖甘味料〗(a) thaumatin.

ソーラー ▷ ソーラー照明灯 solar lighting. ソーラー・セール〖宇〗〔太陽光の圧力を利用して航行するための宇宙船の帆〕a solar sail; 〔太陽光の圧力を利用して航行するための宇宙船〕a solar sail spacecraft. ソーラー電卓 a solar calculator. ソーラーボート a solar-powered boat.

ゾーン・ダイエット〔ホルモンのバランスを整え体脂肪が燃えやすい体をつくるダイエット法〕the Zone diet.

ソーントン Thornton, Billy Bob (1955-     ; 米国の映画俳優).

そきゅう²【遡及】▷ 遡及処罰 retroactive punishment. ◎〜処罰の禁止〔憲法第39条の規定〕the ban on retroactive punishment.

そくあつ²【足圧】〖医〗〔足の裏が床にかける圧力〕foot pressure. ▷ 足圧計 an instrument to measure foot pressure; a pedobarograph. 足圧分布 foot-pressure distribution. ◎〜分布測定 foot-pressure mapping.

そくい¹【即位】▷ 即位礼正殿の儀 the enthronement ceremony of the emperor held in the State Room of the Imperial Palace.

そくい³【測位】〖測位〗measurement of positions. ▷ 衛星測位〔人工衛星を用いた測位〕satellite positioning. ▷ 測位衛星 a positioning satellite. 測位情報 positioning information.

そくい⁴【足囲】〔靴のサイズで,足の親指と小指の付け根にある骨の出ている部分の周囲〕one's foot circumference.

そくがい【即買い】〔商品を見てその場で買うこと〕an on-the-spot purchase; 〔衝動買い〕an impulse purchase; impulse buying.

ぞくがいこん【族外婚】〖社会〗〔外婚〕exogamy. ▷ exogamous, exogamic adj.

ぞくぎいん【族議員】▷ 農水族議員 a farming or fisheries「special-interest [lobby] diet member [politician]; a「diet member [politician] who「lobbies for [represents] farming or fisheries interests. 郵政族議員 a postal service special interest「diet member [politician]; a diet member who「lobbies for [represents] postal service interests.

そくじつ【即日】▷ 即日オペ〔経〕〔日本銀行による公開市場操作の1つ〕a same-day fund-supplying operation.

そくしん¹【促進】▷ 促進作用 promotion; encouragement.

そくせき²【即席】▷ 即席カレー〔具入りのレトルトカレー〕(an) instant curry; (a) ready-made curry; 〔ルー〕(an) instant curry roux. 即席爆発装置〔あり合わせの爆発物と起爆装置で作った簡易手製爆弾の総称〕an improvised explosive device (略: IED).

そくせん⁴【塞栓】▷ 子宮動脈塞栓術〖医〗〔子宮筋腫の治療法の1つ〕uterine artery embolization (略: UAE).

ソクチャン〔ベトナム南部,メコンデルタ地帯の省〕Soc Trang.

そくちょう²【足長】〔靴のサイズで,足底の長さ〕one's foot length.

そくてい¹【足底】▷ 足底筋膜炎[腱膜炎]〖医〗plantar fasciitis.

そくてい²【測定】▷ 測定不能(の) impossible to measure; unmeasurable.

そくど¹【速度】▷ 速度違反自動監視装置 an automatic speeding infringement「surveillance [monitoring] system. 速度照査〖鉄道〗a speed check. 速度超過 exceeding the speed limit.

そくとう⁴【側頭】▷ 側頭動脈炎〖医〗temporal arteritis. [=巨細胞性動脈炎 (⇨ きょさいぼう)] 側頭連合野 the temporal association area.

ぞくないこん【族内婚】〖社会〗〔内婚〕endogamy. ▷ endogamous, endogamic adj.

ゾグビー〔米国の世論調査機関〕Zogby International.

そくびょうい【足病医】*a podiatrist; "a chiropodist.

そくふく【側副】▷ 側副靱帯〖解〗a collateral ligament. ◎ 内側〜靱帯 a medial collateral ligament (略: MCL) / 外側〜靱帯 a lateral collateral ligament (略: LCL).

そくほう【速報】▷ 速報性 the「promptness [speed] of (news) reporting. ◎ 新聞は〜性ではテレビにかなわない. Newspapers cannot match television in the promptness of their news reports. | Newspapers are unable to report news as quickly as television can.

そくほう²【速崩】〔すぐに崩れること〕rapid disintegration. ▷ 口腔内速崩錠〖薬〗an [a rapid] oral disintegrant.

そくめん【側面】▷ 側面支援 indirect support.

そけいざい【素形材】materials that have been molded or pressed into almost the shape of the finished product; near-net-shape products; semifinished materials; sokeizai.

そげき【狙撃】▫□ 狙撃犯 a (criminal) sniper.
そこうち【底打ち】▫□ 底打ち感 a [the] feeling [sentiment] that ｢(the market) has [(prices) have] reached bottom. ◆ようやく景気の〜感が出てきた。The economy is at last showing signs of bottoming out.
そこざさえ【底支え】
〜する underpin; keep ｢up [sth going]. ◆低金利が日本の景気を〜していると言える。It can be said that low interest rates are keeping the Japanese economy booming.
そこち【底地】〔借地権を持つ人が居住している宅地〕leased land;〔底地権〕ownership of leased land.
そこね【底値】▫□ 底値感 a sense that a price has hit bottom. ◆先月あたりから〜感が強まりはじめている。The feeling has been growing stronger since last month that prices have bottomed out.
そざい【素材】【フリー素材】【電算】free resources. ▫□ 素材インフレ (raw) material(s) inflation. 素材価格 material(s) prices; the price of materials. 素材サイト《電算》a resource(s) site; a site for resources.
ソシオエステティシャン〔＜F socio-esthéticien(ne)〕〔病院・福祉施設・老人ホームなどで働く美容師〕a socio-esthetician; a social/cosmetic therapist.
ソシオエステティック〔＜F socio-esthétique〕〔病院・福祉施設・老人ホームなどで働くエステティック〕socio-esthetics; social/cosmetic therapy.
そしき【組織】
□ 末端組織 a branch; a subsidiary ｢organization [body]; an end organization.
▫□ 組織改革 (an) organizational reform. 組織改編 (a) reorganization; (a) restructuring. 組織拡張器【医】〔乳房再建術などに用いられる〕a tissue expander. 組織固め strengthening the solidarity of an organization; increasing solidarity (within an organization). ◆後援会の〜固めを進める promote solidarity within a supporters' association. 組織検査【医】(a) tissue examination. 組織再生 revitalization of an organization; 〔生物〕〔元通りの組織を形成すること〕tissue regeneration. 組織修復〔生物〕tissue repair. 組織内照射【医】interstitial irradiation. 組織培養ワクチン a tissue culture vaccine (略: TCV). 組織風土〔組織成員の行動に影響すると考えられるその組織全体の特性〕an organizational climate. 組織文化 the culture of an organization; an ｢organizational [organization's] culture. 組織防衛 (rearguard action in) defense of a system; defensive action to protect a system. ◆改革を避けて〜防衛に走る avoid reform by taking defensive action; take rearguard action to avoid reform.
そしきてき【組織的】▫□ 組織的詐欺罪【法】《be arrested for》organized fraud. 組織的選挙運動管理者 an organized election-campaign manager. 組織的犯行 an organization crime; a crime carried out by ｢an organization [a group]. ◆それが大統領の命を狙った計画的・〜犯行であることは明らかだ。It is clear that the attempt on the President's life was a planned attack, carried out by a criminal group.
そしきはんざい【組織犯罪】【広域組織犯罪】organized crime across a large geographical area; regional organized crime. ▫□ 組織犯罪対策課〔警察の〕an ｢organized [anti-organized] crime department; an organized crime section.
そしきはんざいしょばつほう【組織犯罪処罰法】【法】the Organized Crime Punishment Law. ► 正式名称は「組織的な犯罪の処罰及び犯罪収益の規制等に関する法律」(the Law for Punishment of Organized Crimes, Control of Crime Proceeds and Other Matters).
そしきはんざいたいさくほう【組織犯罪対策法】【法】the Anti-Organized Crime Law.
そしゃく【咀嚼】▫□ 片側咀嚼【医】unilateral ｢mastication [chewing]. 自由咀嚼【医】free mastication. ▫□ 咀嚼機能障害【医】impaired mastication; mastication dysfunction.
そしょう【訴訟】▫□ 訴訟指揮 conduct of legal proceedings. ◆裁判長の〜指揮は著しく被告寄りだった。The judge's conduct of the proceedings was clearly prejudiced toward the defense. 訴訟社会 a (highly) litigious society. 訴訟取り下げ withdrawal of ｢an action [a suit].
そせい¹【粗製】▫□ 粗製ガソリン［半精製のガソリン］raw gasoline.
そせい⁴【蘇生】▫□ 蘇生学【医】resuscitation science; resuscitology. 蘇生室〔救急病棟の〕a trauma room. 蘇生術 resuscitation [resuscitative] techniques [skills]. 蘇生措置 resuscitative [resuscitation] measures.
そせいごのうしょう【蘇生後脳症】【医】encephalopathy following resuscitation.
そせん【祖先】▫□ 祖先神 an ancestral deity.
そそぎぞめ【注ぎ染め】＝ちゅうせん³.
ソダーバーグ Soderbergh, Steven (1963–　; 米国の映画監督・脚本家・製作者).
そち【措置】▫□ 措置命令 an order [instructions] to take measures (to do). ◆原状回復の〜命令 an order to restore《the site》to its original condition.
そつい【訴追】▫□ 訴追停止【法】(a) suspension of prosecution.
そつえん²【卒煙】giving up smoking (permanently); breaking the smoking habit; smoking cessation.
そっかん¹【速乾・即乾】quick [fast, rapid] drying. ▫□ 速乾加工 a quick-drying process. 速乾シーツ a quick-drying sheet. 速乾性 quick-drying characteristics. ◆〜性インク[ペンキ, ワニス] (a) quick-drying ｢ink [paint, varnish] / このマーカーは〜性である。This is a quick-drying marker pen. | This marker is quick-drying. 速乾ペイント ＝〜性ペンキ.
ぞっかん⁴【続巻】the next volume.
そっき【速記】▫□ 機械速記 mechanical ｢stenography [shorthand (writing)]. 手書き速記 manual ｢stenography [shorthand (writing)].
そつぎょう【卒業】▫□ 卒業単位(数) the number of credits required for graduation. 卒業展示会【展覧会】a ｢graduation [graduating] exhibition; an exhibition of graduating students' work(s). 卒業認定 《obtain, grant》authorization to graduate. 卒業見込み ◆〜見込みの an expected graduate / 〜見込み証明書 a certificate of expected graduation.
そっきょてん【測距点】〖写真〗a focus point.
そっきん²【側近】▫□ 側近中の側近 a member of 《the President's》innermost circle; sb's closest advisor; an intimate ｢associate [aide]; somebody extremely close 《to the King》.
そっきん³【速筋】〖生理〗(a) fast muscle. ▫□ 速筋線維 (a) fast muscle fiber.
ソックスほう [SOX 法]〖米法〗the SOX Act; the Sarbanes-Oxley Act. ► 名称はこの法案の提出者である Paul Sarbanes 上院議員と Michael G. Oxley 下院議員の名前から.［＝きぎょうかいかくほう］
ソックチャン ⇨ソクチャン.
ソックラム【石窟庵】〔韓国, 慶州の石寺院; 世界遺産〕Sŏkkuram; Seogguram.
そっくり ▫□ そっくり食品 mock food.
そっこん¹【足根】▫□ 足根管 the tarsal tunnel. ◆〜管症候群【医】tarsal tunnel syndrome (略: TTS).
そつてん【卒展】＝卒業展示会【展覧会】(⇨そつぎょう).
そでぐろづる【袖黒鶴】〖鳥〗〔ツル科の鳥〕a Siberian crane; Grus leucogeranus.
そでやま【袖山】〔袖を肩口に縫いつける部分〕a sleeve cap; a sleeve head seam;〔和服の〕the creased upper part

(of a kimono sleeve).
ゾド〔モンゴルの雪害〕a zud.
そとあそび【外遊び】〔子供の〕(遊ぶこと) playing 「outdoors [outside];〔具体的な遊び〕an outdoor game. ◖〜をする　play「outdoors [outside].
そとがま【外釜】〔屋外設置用のボイラー〕an outdoor (bath) boiler;〔料理器の〕the outer pot 《of a rice cooker》.
そとだんねつ【外断熱】◻️ 湿式外断熱工法　an exterior insulation and finish system (略: EIFS).
ソナチアン〔韓国ドラマ『冬のソナタ』のファン〕a "Winter Sonata" fan.
「ソニー号空飛ぶ冒険」〔米国の, ヘリコプターでの救難活動を描く TV ドラマ〕Whirlybirds.
ソネンフェルド　Sonnenfeld, Barry (1953- ；米国の映画監督).
「その名にちなんで」〔映画〕The Namesake.
そばずし【蕎麦寿司】a sushi roll made with soba (instead of rice).
そばたしきどき【曽畑式土器】〖考古〗〔縄文式前期の, 九州で発掘される〕Sobata(-type) pottery.
ソバリエ【蕎麦(師) ＋ ソムリエ】〔蕎麦の専門家〕a "sobalier"; a certified soba specialist.
そはんほう【組犯法】〖法〗＝そしきはんざいしょばつほう.
ソビエスキー　Sobieski, Leelee (1982- ；米国の映画女優; 本名 Liliane Rudabet Gloria Elsveta Sobieski).
ソフト　◻️ ソフト産業　the software industry. ソフトシャツ〔服飾〕a "soft shirt"; a shirt with soft collar and cuffs. ソフト面　◖市は住みよい街作りのために施設整備といったハード面ばかりでなく教育や福祉など一面の充実も図るべきだ. To create a comfortable living environment, the city (authorities) should seek not just to improve the hard infrastructure, in terms of facilities, but also to upgrade the soft infrastructure, such as education and welfare.
ソフトウェア　◻️ ソフトウェア・エンジニアリング　software engineering. ソフトウェア特許　a software patent.
ソフトエアガン＝エアソフト・ガン(⇨エア).
ソフト・カレンシー〖経〗〔その国の国際収支が不安定なため国際通貨と自由に交換できない通貨〕(a) soft currency.
ソフト・グッズ〔繊維製品などの非耐久財〕soft goods.
ソフト・ターゲット〔防備が薄く狙いやすい標的〕a soft target.
ソフト・ドラッグ〔マリファナなど中毒性の弱い薬物〕a soft drug.
ソフトボール　◻️ ソフトボール投げ〔体力[運動]能力調査の項目の 1 つ〕softball throwing; a softball throw;〔スペシャル・オリンピックスの種目として〕the Softball Throw.
ソプラニスタ〖音楽〗〔男性ソプラノ〕a sopranista.
ソブリンかくづけ【-格づけ】〖証券〗a sovereign credit rating.
ソブリンさい【-債】〖金融〗〔国債や政府機関債〕a sovereign bond.
ソブレメンヌイきゅうちくかん【-級駆逐艦】〖軍〗〔ロシアのミサイル駆逐艦〕a Sovremenny-class destroyer.
ソポアンガ　Sopoanga, Saufatu (1952- ；ツバルの政治家; 首相 2002-04〕.
そぼう² 【粗暴】◻️ 粗暴犯〖警察〗〔犯罪〕a violent crime; a crime of violence;〔犯罪者〕a violent criminal.
ソマーズ　Sommers, Stephen (1962- ；米国の映画監督・脚本家).
ソマリアないせん【-内戦】〔1990 年代の〕the Somalian civil war.
ソムリエール〔女性ソムリエ〕a female sommelier; a sommeliere.
ゾメタ〔商標・薬〕〔がん治療薬〕Zometa.
そらし【空師】〔巨木の手入れをする植木職人〕a tree-climbing arborist; an arborist specializing in the pruning of tree-tops inaccessible to cranes or ladders.
ゾラデックス〔商標・薬〕〔乳がん治療薬〕Zoladex. ▶ 一般名は酢酸ゴセレリン.
「空飛ぶモンティ・パイソン」〔英国の, ギャグのバラエティーTV 番組〕Monty Python's Flying Circus.
「空飛ぶロッキー君」〔米国の, ムササビとヘラジカがソ連のスパイと闘う TV アニメ〕Rocky and Bullwinkle.
そらのひ【空の日】〔9 月 20 日〕Sky Day. ▶ 1992 年「航空の日」を改称.
そらべん【空弁】〔空港で売っている弁当〕a 「packed meal [box lunch, packed lunch] sold at airports.
ソラレン〖生化〗〔紫外線吸収剤〕psoralen.
そりきず【剃り傷】〈get〉a shaving cut.
ソリダゴ〖植〗〔キク科アキノキリンソウ属の総称; 北米原産〕a solidago《pl. ~s》.
そりのこし【剃り残し】missed [unshaven] hairs [whiskers].
ソリューション　◻️ ソリューション会社〔コンサルティングからシステム構築, アフターサービスを含んだ総合サービスを提供する会社〕a solution「company [firm].
ゾリラ〖動〗〔南アフリカ産のイタチ科の哺乳類〕a zorilla; a striped polecat; Ictonyx striatus.
ソルヴィーノ　Sorvino, Mira (1967- ；米国の映画女優).
ソルガム〖植〗〔イネ科の 1 年草; 食用〕sorghum. ◻️ ホワイト・ソルガム　white sorghum.
ゾルドロネート〔薬〕〔がん治療薬〕zoledronate
ソルビーノ ＝ソルヴィーノ.
ソルビノ ＝ソルヴィーノ.
ソルビンさんカリウム【-酸-】〔食品添加物の一種〕potassium sorbate.
ソルベンシー・マージン　◻️ ソルベンシー・マージン比率　a《high》solvency margin ratio.
それっぽい …like《that》. ◖インターネットで知り合った人を駅で探したが, 〜人はいなかった. I searched at the station for the person I had met online, but there was nobody who 「seemed to look like that [met the description].
それっぽさ　reality; genuineness; typicalness. ◖CG の〜に感動した. I was struck by 「the realism of the computer graphics [how real the computer graphics looked].
ソレノイド　◻️ ソレノイド・コイル　a solenoid coil. ◖中心〜コイル　a central solenoid coil. ソレノイド(方)式[型] solenoid(-type) 《magnets》.
「それ行けスマート」〔米国の, スパイもののパロディーの TV コメディー〕Get Smart.
それん【-連】〔ソ連風邪 (1977 年の)〕(the) Russian 「influenza [flu].
そろいうち【揃い打ち】〔太鼓の〕drumming in unison; drumming in time.
ソロクト【小鹿島】〔韓国, 全羅南道の島〕Sorok Island.
ソロス　Soros, George (1930- ；ハンガリー生まれの世界的投機家).
ゾロフト〔商標・薬〕〔抗鬱剤〕Zoloft. ▶ 一般名は 塩酸セルトラリン.
ソロンズ　Solondz, Todd (1959- ；米国の映画監督).
ソン・イェジン【孫芸珍】Son Ye-jin (1982- ；韓国の女優).
そんえき【損益】◻️ 損益分岐点比率　a break-even point ratio.
そんかい² 【損壊】◻️ 一部損壊　partial destruction. 道路 [橋梁, 軌道] 損壊　destruction of [damage to] roads [bridges, railroad tracks]. ◖県内の道路〜は 12 か所. Roads were 「destroyed [damaged] at 12 locations in the prefecture. ◻️ 損壊住宅　destroyed [damaged] houses [homes].
そんがいばいしょう【損害賠償】◻️ 損害賠償限度額　a limit on compensation for 「damage [loss, reparation for injury, indemnity (for damage done)]. 損害賠償

そんがいほけん

スク the (degree of) risk of being sued for damages 《for exposure to asbestos》. ◐ 〜リスク評価 (an) assessment of the risk(s) of being sued for damages.

そんがいほけん【損害保険】 ◐ 損害保険料 a nonlife insurance premium. 損害保険料控除証明書 a certificate of nonlife insurance premiums paid.

そんがいほけんりょうりつさんしゅつきこう【損害保険料率算出機構】the Non-Life Insurance Rating Organization of Japan (略: NLIRO).

そんがいほけんりょうりつさんしゅつだんたいにかんするほうりつ【損害保険料率算出団体に関する法律】〘法〙the Law Concerning Non-Life Insurance Rating Organizations.

ソン・ガンホ【宋康昊】Song ˈKang-ho [Gang-ho] (1967– ; 韓国の映画俳優).

そんきゅう【宋級】〘軍〙〔中国の原子力潜水艦のクラス〕the Song class. ◐ 宋級潜水艦 a Song-class submarine.

そんきん【損金】 ◐ 損金処理〘会計〙writing off 《leasing costs》as a loss.

ソンクラー〔タイ南部の県; その県都〕Songkhla.

ソンクラ(ー)ン〔タイの旧正月を祝う水掛け祭り〕Songkran; the Songkran festival.

そんけい【尊敬】 ◐ 尊敬表現 an honorific ˈexpression [phrase, choice of words]; a phrase indicating respect (for the addressee).

そんげんし【尊厳死】 ◐ 尊厳死法 a ˈright-to-die [death-with-dignity] law.

そんげんしきょうかい【尊厳死協会】the Japan Society for Dying with Dignity.

そんしつ【損失】 ◐ 損失引当金 a loss reserve fund.

そんしょう² 【損傷】 ◐ 多発性損傷〘医〙multiple injuries.

ゾンビ ◐ ゾンビ・グラス〔背の高いタンブラー〕a zombie glass.

ソン・ヘギョ【宋慧喬】Song Hye-gyo (1982– ; 韓国の女優).

ソン・ミ〔ベトナム南部の村〕Son My. [⇨ミ・ライ]

ソン・ラ〔ベトナム北西部の省; その省都〕Son La.

# た

**ダーウィン・フィンチ**〖鳥〗〔ガラパゴス諸島のホオジロ科の鳥の総称〕Darwin's finches.
**ダーカウ**〔シャトルコックを足でけり合うベトナムの遊戯〕Da Cau.
**ターク** =タク.
**ダーク・ピット**〔米国作家 クライブ・カッスラー作の一連の冒険小説の主人公〕Dirk Pitt.
**ターゲスツァイトゥング**〔ドイツ,ベルリンの日刊紙〕die tageszeitung.
**ターゲット** ▣ ターゲット広告 targeted advertising. ターゲット・マーケット〖商〗a target market.
**ターサイ**〔中国原産の野菜〕Tah Tsai; Tatsoi.
**ターセム** Tarsem Singh (1962- ; インド生まれの映画監督)
**ダーチャ**〔ロシアの家庭菜園付きセカンドハウス〕a dacha.
**ダート**[3]【DART】〖宇宙〗〔自動操縦ランデブー技術テストのためにNASAが開発中の宇宙船〕DART. ▶ Demonstration for Autonomous Rendezvous Technology の頭文字から.
**タートゥーロ** =タトゥーロ.
**ダートトライアル**〖カーレース〗dirt(-track) racing; a dirt (-track) race.
**ダートラ** =ダートトライアル.
**ターナー** Turner, Kathleen (1954- ; 米国の映画女優; 本名 Mary Kathleen Turner).
**ダーパ**〔米国の国防総省高等研究計画局〕DARPA; the Defense Advanced Research Projects Agency.
**ダービー・マッチ**〔サッカーなど〕〔同地区のチーム同士の試合〕a derby match.
**ターピオン** =トゥールビヨン.
**タービン** ▣ タービン建屋 a turbine building (略: TB).
**タープ** ▣ タープ・シェルター〔簡易テント〕a tarp shelter.
**ダーベポエチン**〖薬〗〔抗貧血薬〕darbepoetin.
**ターボ** ▣ ターボシャフト・エンジン〖空〗〔ヘリコプター用ガスタービンエンジン〕a turboshaft engine.
**ターマック**〔タールマカダム舗装した走路〕the tarmac. ▣ ターマック・ラリー〔舗装路での自動車ラリー〕a tarmac rally.
**ターミナル** ▣ ターミナル使用料〔空港などの〕a terminal 「fee [charge].
「**ターミナル**」〔映画〕The Terminal.
「**ターミナル・ベロシティ**」〔映画〕Terminal Velocity.
**ターミネーション・ショック**〖天〗〔末端衝撃波面〕the termination shock.
**ダームスタチウム**〖化〗darmstadtium. ▶ 原子番号110, 元素記号 Ds.
**ダーモスコープ**〖医〗〔皮膚疾患診断用の拡大光学機器〕a dermoscope.
**ダーモスコピー**〖医〗〔ダーモスコープを利用した皮膚疾患診断〕dermoscopy.
**ダーラン**〔サウジアラビア南東部の町〕Dhahran.
**ダーリン**[2]〔「奥様は魔女」の登場人物〕Darrin Stevens.
**ダール** Dahl, John (1956- ; 米国の映画監督).
**ターレット・トラック**〖商標〗〔構内運搬車〕a Turret Truck.
**ダワワとう**【一党】〔イラクのイスラム教シーア派政党〕the Islamic Dawa Party (略: IDP).
**ダーン** 1 Dern, Bruce (1936- ; 米国の映画俳優; 本名 Bruce MacLeish Dern; 2 の父).
2 Dern, Laura (1967- ; 米国の映画女優; 本名 Laura Elizabeth Dern; 1 の子).
**ターンアラウンド・マネ(ー)ジャー**〔企業再生の指揮を執る人〕a turnaround manager.

**タイ**[1] ▣ 1位[首位, トップ]タイ a tie for first (place). 最多タイ ◐ 彼は昨夜, リーグ最多〜の8勝目を挙げた. He got his eighth win last night, putting him in a tie for the league lead.
**タイ**[2] ▣ タイ式マッサージ Thai massage. ◐ 〜式マッサージ師 a Thai 「masseur [masseuse].
**タイあいこくとう**【-愛国党】〔タイの政党〕the Thai Rak Thai Party (略: TRT).
**ダイアジノン**〖薬〗〔有機リン系殺虫剤〕diazinon.
**だいアチェ**【大-】〔インドネシア, アチェ州の県, アチェブサール〕Aceh Besar.
**たいあつ**[2]【耐圧】▣ 耐圧殻〔深海調査船などの〕a pressure-resistant shell; a pressure hull 《for a deep submergence research vehicle》. 耐圧構造 a pressure-resistant structure; (a) pressure-resistant construction. 耐圧試験 pressure testing; [1回の] a pressure test. 耐圧服 a pressure-resistant suit; an atmospheric (diving) suit.
**ダイアナ・モンキー**〖動〗〔オナガザル科のサル〕a Diana monkey; *Cercopithecus diana*.
**だいアヤトラ**【大-】〔イスラム教シーア派で最高位の称号〕a grand ayatollah.
**たいいく**【体育】▣ 体育座り, 体育の座り方 ◐ 〜座りをする sit on the ground with one's arms around one's knees.
**だいいち**【第一】▣ 第一分野〖保険〗〔生命保険〕the first sector.
**だいいちきしゃしゅうだん**【第一汽車集団】〔中国の自動車会社〕First Auto Works (略: FAW). ▶ 正式名称は中国第一汽車集団公司 (China First Auto Works Group Corporation).
**だいいちせんたくやく**【第一選択薬】〖薬〗〔最初に投与すべき治療薬〕a 「first-line [first-choice] drug; a drug of first choice.
**だいいちれっとうせん**【第一列島線】〔中国の軍事戦略上のライン; 日本列島から台湾, フィリピンに至る〕the first island chain. ▶〖だいにれっとうせん〗
**たいいんせい**【耐陰性】〖植〗〔植物の日照不足に耐えられる性質〕shade tolerance. ▷ shade-tolerant *adj*.
**ダイウスリー(-スキー)とう**【大-島】〔ロシア, ハバロフスクそば, 中国とロシアの国境の島〕(ロシア名) Ostrov Bol'shoy Ussuriyskiy. ▶ 中国名は黒瞎子（ヘイシャーズ）島.
**だいうつびょうせいしょうがい**【大鬱病性障害】〖医〗a major depressive disorder; clinical depression.
**だいエネほう**【-代-法】〖法〗=せきゆだいたいエネルギーほう.
**だいえり**【台襟】a neckband.
**たいえん**[3]【退園】〔保育期間の中途の強制的な〕expulsion from preschool; 〔保育期間の中途の自発的な〕withdrawal from preschool; 〔その日の保育時間が終わった後の〕leave [getting out of] preschool (at the end of the day). 〜する〔保育期間の中途で強制されて〕be 「expelled from [asked to leave] preschool; 〔保育期間の中途で自発的に〕withdraw [leave] preschool; 〔保育期間が終わり〕graduate from [finish] preschool; 〔その日の保育時間が終わって〕leave [get out of] preschool (at the end of the day). ◐ 彼女は入園して5日後に〜させられた. She was asked to leave preschool after 5 days. ▣ 退園時間 preschool closing time.
**たいおう**[1]【対応】▣ 対応措置 a countermeasure; 〔対策〕a measure; a step. ◐ 警察は秘密情報がインターネットを通じて外部に流出した事件について〜措置を検討しである. The police are considering taking countermea-

sures in an incident where secret information leaked to the outside through the Internet.

**-たいおうがた**【-対応型】 ◐ 場面→指導事例集 (a manual of) instructional case-studies / 短期入所＝施設 a short-term stay facility (for the elderly) / インターネット～マンション an Internet apartment; an apartment with pre-installed Internet access facilities.

**ダイオキシンるいたいさくとくべつそちほう**【-類対策特別措置法】〔法〕the Law Concerning Special Measures against Dioxins.

**たいおん**【体温】 ▣ 腋窩体温 (an) armpit temperature;《take「one's [sb's]》temperature under the armpit. 口内[口中]体温 (an) oral temperature; (a) mouth temperature;《take「one's [sb's]》temperature orally. 深部体温 (a) deep-body temperature (略: DBT). 舌下体温 (a) sublingual temperature;《take「one's [sb's]》temperature under the tongue. 中心体温 ＝直腸体温. 直腸体温 (a) rectal temperature; (a) temperature per rectum;《take「one's [sb's]》temperature rectally. ▣ 体温調節 thermoregulation; (body) temperature regulation.

**たいか**[7]【耐火】 ▣ 耐火服 ＝防火服(⇨ほうか).

**タイガー・スタジアム**〔米国, デトロイトにある野球場〕Tiger Stadium.

**たいがい**[3]【体外】 ▣ 体外離脱 ＝幽体離脱(⇨ゆうたい[5]).

**たいがい**[4]【対外】 ▣ 対外資産〔対外債権〕foreign [external] credit. 対外資産負債残高（Japan's) international investment position (略: IIP). 対外証券投資 outward portfolio investment. 対外直接投資 outward「foreign direct investment [FDI]. 対外負債〔対外債務〕foreign [external] liabilities [debt, indebtedness].

**たいがいちあんそうきょく**【対外治安総局】〔フランスの情報機関〕the General Directorate for External Security (略: DGSE). ▶ DGSE はフランスの Direction Générale de la Sécurité Extérieure の略.

**たいがいれんらくぶ**【対外連絡部】〔中国・北朝鮮の〕the External Liaison Department.

**たいかく**[2]【体格】 ▣ 体格差 a size difference; a difference in「size (build, physique). ◐ 彼らには大人と子供ほどの～の差がある. They are as different in size as an adult and a child.

**だいがく**【大学】 ▣ 大学人 a university person; an academic.

**「大学」**〔儒教の経書; 四書(しょ)の1つ〕The Great Learning; Daxue; Ta-Hsöeh.

**だいがくきじゅんきょうかい**【大学基準協会】the Japan University Accreditation Association (略: JUAA).

**だいがくぎょうせいかんりがっかい**【大学行政管理学会】the Japan Association of University Administrative Management.

**だいがくとうぎじゅついてんそくしんほう**【大学等技術移転促進法】〔法〕the Law for Promotion of University-Industry Technology Transfer.

**だいがくはつベンチャー**【大学発-】〔大学の教官や学生による研究成果の事業化〕a 「university-led [university-initiated] venture (business).

**だいがくひょうか・がくいじゅよきこう**【大学評価・学位授与機構】the National Institution for Academic Degrees and University Evaluation (略: NIAD-UE).

**たいかん**[7]【体感】 ▣ 体感治安 perceived security. ◐ 国民の～治安は急速に悪化している. There has been a drastic decline in public perceptions of security. 体感的 ◐ ～的学習 learning through the「senses [body] / 気温が高くても湿度が低いと～的にはさほど暑さを感じない. Even when air temperature is high, if humidity is low it doesn't feel that hot to「the [one's]

body. 体感(テレビ[ビデオ])ゲーム a video game involving bodily sensation.

**たいがんじっかねんそうごうせんりゃく**【対がん十か年総合戦略】the 《Third Term》Comprehensive 10-Year Strategy for Cancer Control.

**だいかんせん**【大感染】an epidemic《of foot-and-mouth disease》; a《bird-flu》epidemic; a massive outbreak《of a disease》; 〔コンピューターウイルスの〕a「major [massive] infection《of a computer virus》.

**たいき**[1]【大気】 ▣ 大気揺らぎ〔天〕atmospheric blurring.

**たいき**[4]【待機】 ▣ 待機場所 a waiting area. 待機部隊 a reserve force;〈集合的に〉the reserves; 〔国連の〕⇨くれたいきぶたい. 待機要請 a request to stand by.

**たいき**[5]【隊旗】 ▣ 隊旗授与式 the (ceremonial) presentation of the colors (to a unit). 隊旗返還式 the (ceremonial) return of the colors (by a unit).

**だいきぼ**【大規模】 ▣ 大規模校 a large(-scale) school. 大規模災害〔地震・台風など〕a「large-scale [major] disaster. 大規模半壊 partial but extensive damage; (serious) damage extending to at least 50% but not more than 70% of the surface area of building. ▶ 延べ床面積の 20% 以上 50% 未満の損壊を「半壊」, 50% 以上 70% 未満の損壊を「大規模半壊」という. ◐ ～半壊世帯 a household whose dwelling has been partially but extensively damaged.

**たいきょく**[3]【対局】 ▣ 対局場 a「go [shōgi] room [center, club]. 対局料〔各種のタイトル戦・棋戦への出場棋士に主催者が提供する対戦料〕a tournament participation fee paid by a sponsoring organization to a professional go or shōgi player. ◐ 指導～料〔プロ棋士と対局するためにアマチュアが払う指導料〕a tutorial fee paid by an amateur for a match with a professional go or shōgi player.

**たいきょり**(**りょうきん**)**せい**【対距離(料金)制】〔有料道路の〕a「per-kilometer [distance-based] (road toll) system.

**だいぎんが**【大銀河】〔天〕a「large [big] galaxy.

**たいくうけんさ**【耐空検査】〔空〕an airworthiness inspection. 耐空検査員 an airworthiness inspector.

**たいくうせい**【耐空性】 ▣ 耐空性改善通報〔空〕〔国土交通省航空局が発行する〕a technical circular directive (略: TCD). 耐空性改善命令〔空〕〔米国の連邦航空局やその他の国の民間航空局が発行する〕an airworthiness directive (略: AD).

**タイグエン**〔ベトナム北東部の省; その省都〕Thai Nguyen.

**だいくんい**【大勲位】 ▣ 大勲位菊花章〔総称〕Supreme Orders of the Chrysanthemum.

**だいけい**[2]【大慶】 ▣ 大慶油田 the Daqing oil field.

**だいけい**[3]【大径】〔長い直径〕a「large [major] diameter. ▣ 大径材 large-diameter timber. 大径木 a large-diameter tree.

**たいけつ**【対決】 ▣ 対決法案 a controversial bill; controversial legislation.

**だいけっかんてんいしょう**【大血管転位症】〔医〕transposition of the great vessels. 完全大血管転位症 complete transposition of the great vessels.

**たいけん**[3]【体験】 ▣ 快体験〔快感の〕a pleasant experience; 〔恍惚感の〕＝恍惚体験(⇨こうこつ[2]). 体験教育 a hands-on class. 体験学習 ＝ワーク ショップ. ◐ 一日～教室 a one-day「hands-on class [workshop]. 体験ツアー[旅行] a "real-experience" tour; an adventure tour. 体験博物館 ＝体験型博物館(⇨たいけんがた). 体験発表 an experience「report [presentation]; a report on one's experience《of⋯》. ◐ 高齢者介護の～発表を行う present a report on one's experience of caring for elderly people. 体験飛行《have, experience》a real flight.

たいけんがた【体験型】◐〜の practical; working 《holiday》; 《volunteer work》for experience; hands-on 《experience》. ◰ 体験型学習〔体験型学習〕learning through practical experience; hands-on experience. 体験型観光 ⇨かんこう15. 体験型テーマパーク a theme park where「you can try things out [visitors can have "real" experience]. 体験型博物館 a "hands-on" museum; a museum where visitors can experience using the exhibits.

たいこ3【太鼓】◰ 太鼓椅子 a barrel(-shaped) stool.

たいこう11【対向】◰ 対向列車 an oncoming train; a train on the「oncoming [opposite] track.

たいこう12【対抗】◰ 対抗心 a feeling of「rivalry [antagonism, competition]. ◐〜…に対する〜心をむき出しにする bare [openly reveal, openly betray] feelings of「rivalry [antagonism] toward(s)….

たいこう14【退行】◰ 退行現象〖心理〗regression; 〔幼児の〕infantile regression. 退行催眠 〖精神医〗regressive「hypnosis [hypnotherapy].

だいこう1【代行】◰ 代行運転〔運転した交通機関の代わりに運行すること〕=代行輸送〔飲酒後などに車の運転を他人に代行してもらうこと〕=運転代行 (⇨うんてん). 代行手数料 an agency fee. 代行輸送〔運転した交通機関の代わりの〕《provide》「substitute transportation [a substitute service]. 代行輸入 proxy importing.

たいこうかんりん【退耕還林】〔傾斜地の耕地を森林や草地に戻すこと; 中国の政策〕restoration of hill farmland as forest or grassland.

たいこうさんみゃく【太行山脈】〔中国, 山西・河北両省の境をなす山脈〕the Taihang Mountains.

だいこうへんじょう【代行返上】〔公的年金業務のうち, 企業が国に代わって行ってきた部分を国の所管に戻すこと〕transfer of the management of a public pension fund back to the government. ◰ 代行返上益 profit(s) on public pension funds returned to the government (by a firm which has been managing them).

だいごきょうわせい【第五共和政】〖史〗〔フランスの〕the Fifth Republic.

だいこくこがね【大黒黄金】〖昆〗〔コガネムシ科の昆虫; 準絶滅危惧種〕a species of dung beetle; *Copris ochus.*

たいさ3【堆砂】〔ダムの貯水池の底に土砂が溜まること〕siltation; sedimentation; 〔その土砂〕silt; sediment. 〜する sediment; accumulate.

だいさいしょう【大宰相】a great prime minister.

たいさいぼう【体細胞】◰ クローン技術 somatic cell cloning technology.

たいさく3【対策】◰ 直前対策〔入試などの〕last-minute「measures [steps, actions]. ◰ 対策室 a 《disaster》countermeasures office.

だいさん2【第三】◰ 第三の新人〔戦後の日本文学の〕the "Third Generation" of new writers; "Daisan no shinjin." 第三のビール a "third beer"; a beer-like (alcoholic) beverage.

だいさんごくじん【第三国人】〖日本史〗a colloquial term for persons from Korea and Taiwan residing in Japan at the end of World War II.

だいさんじさんぎょう【第三次産業】◰ 第三次産業活動指数 a tertiary industry activity index.

だいさんしゃ【第三者】◰ 第三者委員会 a [an independent] third-party「committee [commission]. 第三者機関 third-party organization (略: TPO). 第三者の供与〖法〗〔斡旋収賄における〕the offering of「profits [benefits] to a person or persons connected to the politician in question. 第三者承継〔事業をその経営者の親族以外の者が引き継ぐこと〕passing [handing over]「management of a business」to a third party. 第三者認証ラベル〔日本環境協会が発行する〕a third-party certification label. 第三者評価 a third-party [an outside, an impartial, a neutral] evaluation [assessment].

◐〜評価機関 a third-party evaluation organization.

だいさんせだい【第三世代】◰ 第三世代携帯電話 a third-generation cellular phone.

たいし5【胎仔】〖生物〗an embryo (*pl.* 〜s).

たいし6【隊士】a team member.

たいじ2【胎児】◰ 胎児医療 fetal [prenatal] treatment. 胎児手術〖医〗fetal surgery.

たいしつ1【体質】◰ 隠蔽体質〔官庁などの〕a penchant for secrecy; an obsession with secrecy. ◰ 体質強化〔企業・組織などの〕improvement [strengthening] of the「makeup [character]「of「a business [an organization, etc.].」

たいしつりょう【大質量】〜の〖天〗great mass. ◐〜のブラックホール = 大質量ブラックホール (⇨ブラック・ホール). ◰ 大質量星 a massive star.

たいしゃ4【代謝】◰ 代謝症候群〖医〗〔メタボリックシンドローム〕metabolic syndrome. 代謝当量〖生理〗a metabolic equivalent (of task) (略: MET).

たいしゃ7【堆砂】= たいさ3.

たいしゅ4【退守】a retreat into a defensive posture; a defensive withdrawal. 〜する retreat and shore up *one's* defenses; make a defensive withdrawal.

たいしゅう1【大衆】◰ 大衆迎合的 populistic; populistic; catering to [accommodating] the public. ◐〜迎合的な選挙公約 a populist campaign pledge / 今日の首相の演説は〜迎合的で格調に欠けるものだった. The Prime Minister's speech today was「an undignified populist performance [a cheap appeal to public prejudices].

たいしゅう2【体臭】◰ 体臭恐怖症〖精神医〗bromidrosiphobia; bromidrophobia; (a) (pathological) fear of body odors.

たいじゅう【体重】◰ 体重移動 moving [shifting] *one's* weight. ◐ ハンググライダーは〜移動で操縦します. You「steer [pilot] a hang glider by shifting your「weight [center of gravity]. 体重差 (a) weight「difference [differential]; (a) difference in weight. ◐二人の力士の〜差は 30 キロあった. There was a difference in weight between the two wrestlers of 30 kilograms. 体重無差別〔柔道などで〕open weight; 《under》the open-weight system.

たいしゅく【退縮】◰ 自然退縮〖生理〗〔腫瘍などの〕spontaneous regression (of cancer).

たいしょ5【対処】◰ 対処機制〖心理〗a coping mechanism. [=適応機制 (⇨てきおう)] 対処行動〖心理〗coping behavior.

たいしょう1【大正】◰ 大正ロマン Taishō romanticism.

たいしょう2【大将】◰ 大将旗 a [the] general's banner.

たいしょう10【対象】◰ 対象関係〖精神分析〗object relations; an object relationship. 対象関係(理)論〖精神医〗(an) object relations theory. 対象魚〖釣り〗a fisherman's (favorite) target(-fish); a game fish. 対象月齢〔おもちゃ・肉牛の BSE 検査などの〕a target age group [the relevant age group] in months. 対象年齢 a target age (group); the age (group) concerned; the relevant age group. ◐〜年齢 3 歳以上〔おもちゃなどの表示〕(Designed) for Children of 3 and Upward(s). / 老人保健の〜年齢が引き上げられた. The age for old people's public health programs was raised. They put up the age at which old people qualify for public health「services [care].

たいしょう1【退場】◰ 退場処分 expulsion from 《a game》. ◐〜処分を受ける be「expelled from [thrown out of] 《a game》.

だいしょう3【代償】◰ 代償機能〖生理〗a compensatory function. 代償性発汗〖医〗compensatory sweating.

だいじょうしけん【台上試験】〖自動車〗a bench test.
だいしょうヘラクレスしすう【大証-指数】〖証券〗=ヘラクレス指数（⇨ヘラクレス）.
たいしょく⁴【退職】　◯▶ 退職勧告 advice [encouragement] to resign. 退職給付会計 retirement benefit accounting. 退職給付金 a retirement benefit. 退職給付債務 a pension benefit obligation（略：PBO）. 退職給付信託 a retirement allowance trust. 退職給付制度〔一時金〕a retirement lump-sum benefit;〔年金〕a retirement pension benefit. 退職給付引当金 a「reserve (fund) [provision] for employees' retirement benefits; a retirement reserve (fund). 退職所得控除 a tax deduction on retirement income.
たいしょくきん【退職金】　◯▶ 前払い退職金 prepaid retirement benefits;〔制度〕a prepaid retirement benefit plan.
たいしょほう【対処法】a「way [means] of「coping [dealing] with (stress); a coping method; an approach to 《a problem》. ◯ ぜんそく発作の〜 a way of dealing with asthma attacks. ◯ わが社の製品に関して顧客から寄せられるクレームへの〜を社内で統一する必要がある. We need to develop a standard in-house method of dealing with complaints from customers about our products. / 緊急事態の〜をあらためて確認しよう. Let's double-check our methods for coping with an emergency.
たいしん⁶【耐震】◯▶ 耐震安全性 seismic safety. 耐震化〜たいしんか. 耐震強度〔耐震性[力]〕resistance to「earthquakes [seismic shocks]; ability to withstand earthquakes. 耐震強度偽装 fake earthquake-proofing; falsification of data to make it appear that a building is more earthquake resistant than is actually the case. 耐震工事 earthquake-proofing (work). 耐震指針〔原子力発電所の〕the Seismic Safety Guidelines on the Design of Nuclear Power Plants. 構造耐震指標 a seismic index of structure（略：Is）. 耐震設計指針 earthquake-resistant design guidelines. 耐震設計審査指針〔原子力発電所の〕=耐震指針.
たいじん²【対人】　◯▶ 対人行動〖心理〗interpersonal behavior. 対人能力 skill with people; social [interpersonal] skills; human relations skills;《口》people skills. 対人暴力 violence (directed) against people. 対人魅力〖心理〗interpersonal attraction.
だいじん²【大臣】　◯▶ 大臣規範 a code for (cabinet [government]) ministers; a ministerial code;〔英国の〕the Ministerial Code. 大臣折衝〔財務大臣と各省庁の大臣による〕budget negotiations between the Minister of Finance and other Ministers; Ministerial-level budget negotiations.
たいしんか【耐震化】〔建物・構造物などの〕earthquake-proofing; strengthening《a building》against earthquakes. 〜する earthquake-proof《a school building》. ◯▶ 耐震化住宅 an earthquake-proof(ed) house. 耐震化率 an earthquake-proofing rate; the percentage 《of schools》which have been earthquake-proofed.
たいしんかいしゅうそくしんほう【耐震改修促進法】〖法〗the Law for Promotion of Seismic Retrofitting.
ダイシング・ソー〖機〗〔半導体に使うシリコンウェハーなどのチップ分割を行う精密切断装置〕a dicing saw.
だいしんど【大深度】　◯▶ 大深度核実験 nuclear testing deep「underground;［1 回］a「deep underground nuclear test. 大深度トンネル a deep (underground) tunnel.
だいしんどちかほう【大深度地下法】〖法〗the Law for the Public Use of the Deep Underground.
たいじんりょく【対人力】〔良好な人間関係を築く能力〕sociability; personableness; skill at interpersonal communication.

ダイス² Deiss, Joseph (1946-　　；スイスの政治家；大統領〔2004〕.
だいず【大豆】　◯▶ 酢大豆〔ダイエット食品〕vinegared soybeans. ◯▶ 大豆イソフラボン〔化〕soy isoflavone. 大豆イソフラボン・アグリコン〔化〕soy isoflavone aglycone. 大豆オリゴ糖 (a) soybean oligosaccharide. 大豆サポニン (a) soybean saponin. 大豆食品 soybean food; a soybean foodstuff. 大豆たんぱく (a) soybean protein. 大豆胚芽 soybean germ. 大豆ペプチド (a) soybean peptide. 大豆ミール soybean meal.
たいすいあつ【耐水圧】water resistance. ◯ 〜 2 m の水中カメラ a camera that is water-resistant to a depth of two meters.
たいせい⁷【体制】　◯▶ 体制内改革 internal reform(s); reform(s) within an organization. 体制批判 criticism of the (current)「system [regime]. 体制変革[変更] (a) regime change. 体制崩壊〖政治〗(a) regime collapse; the collapse of a regime.
たいせい¹¹【耐性】　◯▶ 除草剤耐性 ⇒じょうす⁵. ◯▶ 耐性ウイルス a drug-resistant virus.
たいせい¹⁴【態勢】　◯▶ 観測態勢《establish》a monitoring [an observation] program [system]. 初動態勢 an initial response; (an) action priority. ◯ 緊急時の初動〜作りが急務である. It is a matter of urgency to establish「action priorities [what should be done first] in an emergency. 戦闘態勢 combat readiness; readiness for「combat [battle]. ◯ 戦闘〜を取る prepare [get ready] for「combat [battle]; go on combat alert / 戦闘〜を整えている be「ready [prepared] for action; be ready to go into action; be combat-ready; be in combat readiness. 臨戦態勢 a state of war readiness; readiness for war. ◯ 臨戦〜に入る prepare《oneself》for war; get ready [make preparations] for war; get into a state of war readiness.
たいせいよう【大西洋】　◯▶ 大西洋同盟〔西欧と米国の結束〕an [the] Atlantic alliance. 大西洋無着陸横断飛行 a nonstop transatlantic flight.
だいせっきん【大接近】a close approach;〔天〕〔地球から見た天体同士の〕conjunction. 〜する make a close approach《to…》;〔天〕〔地球から見た天体同士が〕come into [make a] conjunction《with…》. ◯ 木星と金星が〜している. Jupiter and Venus are in conjunction. ◯ 火星の〜 a close approach of Mars《to Earth》/ 月と火星の〜 a conjunction of the moon and Mars.
だいせつたかねひかげ【大雪高嶺日陰】〖昆〗〔ジャノメチョウ科のチョウ〕Oeneis melissa (daisetsuzana).
たいせん³【対戦】　◯▶ 対戦カード the (team [player]) pairings; the match-ups.
たいせん⁴【対潜】　◯▶ 対潜能力 (an) antisubmarine capability.
だいせん²【台船】a barge. ◯▶ クレーン台船 a floating crane; a「boat [ship] equipped with a crane.
たいぜんき【対前期】compared with the previous「period [quarter].
たいせんしゃ【対戦車】　◯▶ 個人携帯対戦車弾 a shoulder-mounted antitank「shell [rocket].
たいせんすいかん【対潜水艦】　◯▶ 対潜水艦戦 antisubmarine warfare（略：ASW）. 対潜水艦戦闘能力 antisubmarine「capability [capabilities].
たいぜんねんど【対前年度】compared with the previous fiscal year.
たいそう⁷【体操】　◯▶ 整理体操 (a)「cool-down [cooling-down] exercise.
たいそせい【体組成】〔筋肉, 脂肪などから成る体の構成〕body composition. ◯▶ 体組成計 a body composition monitor; a body composition analyzer. ◯ 体重〜計〔体組成計に体重計を組み込んだ計器〕a body composition「monitor [analyzer] with (a)「scale [weighing machine].

たいそん【退村】〔村という名称が付いている施設からの〕leaving《a camping, an Olympic》village. ▭ 退村式〔オリンピック選手村からの〕a ceremony to commemorate leaving an Olympic village.
タイソン・フーズ〔米国の食品会社〕Tyson Foods.
だいたい[3]【大腿】▭ 大腿骨頸部 the neck of the femur; the femoral neck. ◉ 〜骨頸部骨折《医》(a) fracture of the 「neck of the femur [femoral neck]. 大腿骨頭壊死(┊)《医》avascular necrosis of the femoral head. 大腿動脈閉塞《医》femoral artery occlusive disease. ◉ 浅〜動脈閉塞 superficial femoral artery occlusive disease.
だいたい[4]【代替】▭ 代替作物《農》an alternative [a substitute, a replacement] crop. ◉ ケシの〜作物 an alternative (crop) to [a substitute for] the opium poppy. 代替試合 a makeup game. 代替資産 a replacement (property); a different 《plot of land》 as a replacement. 代替食 (a) substitute [(an) alternative] food. 代替着陸 ⇨だいたいちゃくりく. 代替調剤《薬》alternative prescription. 代替燃料車 an alternative-fuel vehicle (略: AFV). 代替要員 a 「substitute [replacement]《worker》; a substitute; a replacement;〈集合的に〉substitute [replacement] personnel. 代替療法《医》alternative therapy.
だいたいちゃくりく【代替着陸】〔着陸予定の空港以外への〕(an) alternative landing. ◉ 私が乗った飛行機はエンジン不調のため福岡空港に〜した. The plane I was travelling in 「made an alternative landing at [was diverted to] Fukuoka airport due to engine trouble. ▭ 代替着陸地 an alternative landing site.
だいだく【代諾】《法》〔判断できない状態の人に代わって承諾すること〕(代理же) proxy consent; consent on sb's behalf. 〜する give proxy consent; (give) consent on behalf of sb; (give) consent on sb's behalf. ▭ 代諾者 a proxy for consent 《to medical treatment》. 代諾養子《人》a child adopted by proxy; a proxy adoptee;〔縁組み〕=代諾(養子)縁組. 代諾(養子)縁組 (a) proxy adoption; (an) adoption by proxy.
タイタニア《天》〔天王星の衛星〕Titania.
「タイタンズを忘れない」〔映画〕Remember the Titans.
たいだんせい【耐弾性】《軍》bulletproofness; bullet resistance. ◉ 〜にすぐれた装甲 highly [extremely] bulletproof armor; armor with excellent bullet resistance.
たいち[2]【対地】▭ 対地接近警報装置〔航空機の〕a ground proximity warning system (略: GPWS).
だいちこうたい【大地溝帯】〔アフリカ大陸東部を南北に走る世界最大の地溝帯〕the Great Rift Valley.
たいちゅう【対中】▭ 対中貿易赤字《Japan's》trade deficit with China.
たいちゅう[2]【台中】⇨タイチョン.
だいちゅうとうこうそう【大中東構想】〔米国提唱のアラブ諸国民主化支援策〕the Greater Middle East Initiative.
たいちょう[2]【体調】▭ 体調管理 control [management] of one's physical condition. ◉ 〜管理に気をつかう control [manage] one's physical condition carefully; watch one's 「physical condition [health]. 体調不良 a health problem; poor [bad] health. ◉ 〜不良のため欠席いたします. I will have to 「be absent today on grounds of health. | I'm not well, so I won't be able to come today.
たいちょう[4]【退潮】▭ 退潮傾向 a declining tendency; a downhill tendency; a downward 「path [trend]; a decline. ◉ 労働党は明らかに〜傾向にある. The Labour Party is clearly on a 「decline [downward path].
だいちょう[1]【大腸】▭ 大腸憩室《医》a colonic diverticulum《pl. -la》. ◉ 〜憩室炎 colonic diverticulitis

/ 〜憩室症 colonic diverticulosis. 大腸内視鏡 a colonoscope.
だいちょうきん【大腸菌】▭ 大腸菌数 a coliform count.
タイチョン【台中】〔台湾中部の都市・県〕Taichung; Taizhong.
だいてんし【大転子】《解》〔大腿骨外側上部にある脚と胴の骨のつなぎ目〕the 「greater [major] trochanter; the trochanter major.
たいど[3]【態度】▭ 態度測定《心理》attitude measurement. 態度変容《心理》(an) attitude change.
たいとう[8]【台東】⇨タイトン.
たいどう[2]【帯同】▭ 帯同経験 ◉ 日本代表チームへの〜経験が豊富なスポーツドクター a sports doctor highly experienced in accompanying Japanese national teams.
だいとうおおこうもり【大東大蝙蝠】《動》〔オオコウモリ科のコウモリ; 南・北大東島に生息; 絶滅危惧種〕a Daito fruit bat; a Ryukyu flying fox; Pteropus dasymallus daitoensis.
たいとうのう【耐糖能】▭ 耐糖能障害 impaired glucose tolerance (略: IGT).
だいとうほうイスラムせんし【とつげき】せんせん【大東方・戦士【突撃】戦線】=イスラムだいとうほうこうげきたい・せんせん.
だいどうみゃく【大動脈】▭ 大動脈破裂《医》(an) aortic rupture.
だいとうりょう【大統領】▭ 暫定大統領 an interim [a provisional] president. ▭ 大統領経済諮問委員会〔米国の〕the Council of Economic 「Advisors [Advisers] (略: CEA). 大統領首席補佐官 a [the] chief assistant to the President. 大統領特別補佐官 (a) Special 「Advisor [Adviser] to the President; the President's Special 「Advisor [Adviser]《on cybersecurity》. 大統領報道官 a [the] (Presidential) Press Secretary. 大統領補佐官 a presidential assistant. ◉ 国家安全保障担当〜補佐官〔米国の〕the Assistant to the President for National Security Affairs;《通例》the National Security Advisor.
だいとうりょうせいめいりんりひょうぎかい【大統領生命倫理評議会】=生命倫理評議会 (⇨せいめいりんり).
だいどころ【台所】▭ 台所用洗剤 (a) kitchen detergent.
だいとし【大都市】▭ 大都市部 metro(politan) areas.
タイトン【台東】〔台湾南東部の都市・県〕Taitung; Taidong.
たいない[1]【体内】▭ 体内温度 (an) internal body temperature. 体内年齢 (a 《one's》) 「body [biological] age. 体内リズム an 《one's》 internal (body, biological) rhythm.
たいない[2]【対内】▭ 対内証券投資 inward portfolio investment. 対内直接投資 inward 「foreign direct investment [FDI]. 対内直接投資規制 restrictions on inward 「foreign direct investment [FDI]. 対内投資規制 restrictions on inward foreign investment.
たいない[3]【胎内】▭ 胎内記憶 (a) fetal memory. 胎内経 a sutra (found) inside a 「Buddha [Buddhist statue]. 胎内死 (a) fetal death; a death in utero. 胎内仏 a small Buddhist image inside a larger one.
たいないてき【対内的】〜な〔内部に向けた〕internal; inside; intramural;〔対外に対し〕internal; ...at home. ◉ 大統領は対外的には国際協調を標榜しながら, 〜には軍備拡張に努めた. While advocating international cooperation abroad, the president worked to bolster military preparedness 「domestically [at home]. / 社長は進歩的経済人として著名だが, 〜にはまぎれもない独裁者だ. The president is widely known as a progressive business leader, but inside the company he's an absolute dictator.

**ダイナミック** ⇨ ダイナミック・パッケージ ＝組み立て旅行 (⇨りょこう).

**タイナン**〖台南〗〔台湾南西部の都市〕Tainan.

**だいに**〖第二〗⇨ 第二稿 a [the] second draft. 第二分野〖保険〗〔損害保険〕the second sector.

**だいにせんたくやく**〖第二選択薬〗〖薬〗〔第一選択薬で効果がなかった場合に使用される治療薬〕a second-line drug; a drug of second choice.

**たいにち**[1]〖対日〗⇨ 対日強硬派 an anti-Japan hard-line group. ⇨ 米国民主党内の～強硬派 anti-Japan hardliners within the Democratic Party. 対日強硬論《take》a tough anti-Japan「attitude [stance]; an argument [arguing] for strong measures vis-à-vis Japan. ⇨ ～強硬論を唱える advocate「strong measures vis-à-vis Japan [being tough with Japan]. 対日工作活動 secret [underground] activities vis-à-vis Japan. 対日交渉 negotiations [negotiating] with Japan. 対日債務 indebtedness [debt(s)] (owed) to Japan; money「owed [owing] to Japan. ⇨ インドネシアの～債務 Indonesia's debt(s) to Japan. 対日姿勢 an attitude [a stance] toward [vis-à-vis] Japan. ⇨ 米国の～姿勢の変化 changes in US attitudes to Japan; a change in the American stance toward Japan. 対日制裁 sanctions「against [on] Japan. ⇨ ～制裁に踏み切る (decide to) impose sanctions against Japan; embark on the imposition of sanctions against Japan. 対日政策 (a) policy toward Japan; (a) Japan policy. ⇨ ～政策を見直す re-think [have another look at] policy towards Japan. 対日投資 investment [investing] in Japan. 対日批判 criticism(s) of Japan. ⇨ 首相の靖国神社参拝をめぐって韓国内で～批判が高まって[強まって]いる. Criticism of Japan is growing in South Korea in connection with the Prime Minister's visits to Yasukuni. 対日不信 distrust of Japan. ⇨ 首相の最近の言動が近隣諸国の～不信を招いている. By his words and actions the Prime Minister is inviting increasing distrust of Japan among neighboring nations. 対日輸出 exports [exporting] to Japan. ⇨ 牛肉の～輸出の拡大 an increase in beef exports to Japan.

**たいにちぼうえきとうしこうりゅうそくしんきょうかい**〖対日貿易投資交流促進協会〗the Manufactured Imports and Investment Promotion Organization (略: MIPRO).

**だいにれっとうせん**〖第二列島線〗〔中国の軍事戦略上のライン; 小笠原諸島からグアム・サイパン, オーストラリア西海岸に至る〕the second island chain. (⇨だいいちれっとうせん)

**たいにん**[3]〖退任〗⇨ 退任会見《give, hold》a「retirement press-conference [press-conference to mark one's retirement].

**タイニン**〔ベトナム南部の省; その省都〕Tay Ninh.

**ダイニング** ⇨ ダイニング・バー a dining bar.

**たいねつ**[1]〖体熱〗⇨ 体熱産生 thermogenesis. [＝熱産生(⇨ねつ)] 運動誘発性～産生 exercise-induced thermogenesis / 寒冷誘発性～産生 cold-induced thermogenesis / 食事誘発性～産生 diet-induced thermogenesis.

**たいねつ**[2]〖耐熱〗⇨ 耐熱手袋 a「heat-resistant [heat-proof] glove. 耐熱ボウル〔調理器具〕a「heatproof [heat-resistant] bowl.

**だいのう**[1]〖大脳〗⇨ 大脳死〖医〗〔死の判定基準の１つ〕cerebral death. 大脳白質 cerebral white matter. 大脳白質病変 a cerebral white matter lesion; a lesion of the cerebral white matter.

**ダイバーター**〖電〗〔分流加減器〕a (flow) diverter.

**たいばくスーツ**〖対爆〗〔爆発物処理業務に着用する防護服〕a bomb disposal suit.

**たいはくレーダー**〖対迫〗〔軍〕〔迫撃砲陣地を発見するための装置〕(a) counter-mortar radar.

「**第八救助隊**」〔米国の, 消防ものの TV ドラマ〕Rescue 8.

**たいばん**〖胎盤〗⇨ 共有胎盤〖医〗a shared placenta. 癒着胎盤〖医〗placenta accreta. 胎盤エキス placenta extract. 胎盤共有児〔共有児〕〔二絨毛膜(性)双胎〕twins sharing a single placenta; ＝一絨毛膜(性)双胎 (⇨そうたい). ⇨ 二卵性～共有双子 fraternal twins sharing a single placenta; uniplacental dizygotic twins. 胎盤癒着〖医〗＝癒着胎盤.

**だいびき**〖代引き〗〔代金引き換え〕cash on delivery (略: COD).

**たいひょう**[1]〖体表〗⇨ 体表温度 (a) body surface temperature.

**だいひょう**[2]〖代表〗⇨ 代表選(挙)《hold》an election to choose a「representative [leader, delegate]. ⇨ 民主党～選 an [the] election to chose the President of the Democratic Party of Japan. 代表復帰〖スポーツ〗⇨ ～復帰する rejoin the national 《soccer》team. ⇨ 代表部〗a representative office; 〔国連などへの〕a (permanent) mission 《of Japan to the United Sates》; 〔EU などへの〕a (permanent) representation.

**タイビン**〔ベトナム北部ホン河デルタ地帯の省; その省都〕Thai Binh.

**ダイビング** ⇨ ダイビング・インストラクター a diving instructor.

**タイプーサム**〔ヒンズー教の祭り〕Thaipusam.

**だいふく**〖大福〗⇨ イチゴ[豆]大福 a「strawberry [pea] daifuku; a daifuku containing「strawberry [sweetened browned peas].

**タイフごうい**〖－合意〗〔レバノン内戦終結時の; 1989 年〕the Taif Agreement.

**たいぶんきょう**〖対文協〗⇨ちょうせんたいがいぶんかれんらくきょうかい.

**たいべい**[1]〖対米〗⇨ 対米追従 servility [blind obedience] to the United States. 対米武器技術供与 the transfer of Japanese military technology to the US.

**たいべいがいこくとうしいいんかい**〖対米外国投資委員会〗〔米国の〕the Committee on Foreign Investments in the United States (略: CFIUS).

**たいへいよう**〖太平洋〗⇨ 太平洋ルート〔東シベリアからの石油パイプライン〕a northern (pipeline) route.

**たいへいようがっかい**〖太平洋学会〗the Pacific Society.

**たいへいようけいざいいいんかい**〖太平洋経済委員会〗the Pacific Basin Economic Council (略: PBEC).

**たいへいよう・しまサミット**〖太平洋・島－〗⇨にほんたいへいようしょとうフォーラムしゅのうかいぎ.

**たいへいようしょとうフォーラム**〖太平洋諸島－〗the Pacific Islands Forum (略: RIF).

**たいへいようせんそうひがいしゃほしょうすいしんきょうぎかい**〖太平洋戦争被害者補償推進協議会〗〔韓国の団体〕the (Korean) Association for the Promotion of Reparations for Victims of the Pacific War.

**たいへいようつなみけいほうセンター**〖太平洋津波警報－〗〔米国の〕the Pacific Tsunami Warning Center (略: PTWC).

**たいへいようてんもんがっかい**〖太平洋天文学会〗〔米国サンフランシスコに本部を置く〕the Astronomical Society of the Pacific (略: ASP).

**たいへいようとうしょこくフォーラム**〖太平洋島嶼国－〗＝たいへいようしょとうフォーラム.

**たいほ**[2]〖逮捕〗⇨ 逮捕致死(罪)〖法〗illegal confinement resulting in death. 逮捕容疑 the charge on which one「is [has been] arrested. ⇨ ～容疑を否認する〔認める〕〔容疑者が〕deny [admit] the charge on which one「is [has been] arrested.

**たいぼう**[4]〖待望〗⇨ 待望論 (the idea of) pinning one's hopes on the advent of 《a strong leader》; expectation of (future) 《high economic growth》. ⇨ 小沢首相～論 pinning one's hopes on Ozawa becoming prime minister / 激動の時代には決まって英雄～論が出

る．In a turbulent age「there are always calls for a savior [people always pin their hopes on a savior].
**タイボー【TIBOR】**〖東京銀行間取引金利〗TIBOR; the Tokyo Interbank Offered Rate.
**ダイポールモード・イベント**〖気象〗＝ダイポールモードげんしょう．
**ダイポールモードげんしょう【-現象】**〖気象〗a Dipole Mode Event (略: DME); a Dipole Mode Phenomenon. ▶ インド洋ダイポールモード現象 the Indian Ocean Dipole (Mode Event) (略: IOD).
**ダイホルタン**〖商標・農薬〗Difolatan. ▶ カプタホール (captafol) の商品名．
**タイマー** ▭ タイマー・リモコン〖空調機などの，タイマー設定機能の付いたリモコン〗a remote control with a timer.
**「大魔王シャザーン」**〖米国の，魔法を使う巨人が活躍する冒険 TV アニメ〗Shazzan.
**たいまもう【耐摩耗】** ▭ 耐摩耗試験 an abrasion test; abrasion testing. 耐摩耗性 abrasion [wear] resistance. ▯ 〜性にすぐれたタイヤ wear-resistant tires; tires with (a) high resistance to abrasion.
**たいまん[2]【対激】**〖1 対 1 の殴り合いのけんか〗a one-on-one「fight [argument]; a grudge match.
**だいまんぞく【大満足】**being「greatly [completely] satisfied. ▯ 男の子は欲しかったおもちゃをもらって〜だった．That boy was completely satisfied at receiving the toy he wanted.
**タイム[1]** ▭ タイム・ダラー〖互助的サービスの交換単位としての時間〗time dollars. タイム・パラドックス a time paradox; a paradox in time travel.
**「タイムズ文芸付録」**〖英国の文芸週刊誌〗the Times Literary Supplement (略: TLS). [⇨ティー・エル・エス]
**「タイムトラベラー／きのうから来た恋人」**〖映画〗Blast from the Past.
**「タイム・トンネル」**〖米国の，タイムトラベルものの TV ドラマ〗The Time Tunnel.
**タイム・ハニー**〖ハーブ蜂蜜の一種〗thyme honey.
**だいムフティー【大-】**〖イスラム法学の最高権威者〗a grand mufti.
**ダイムラー・クライスラー**〖ドイツの自動車メーカー〗DaimlerChrysler.
**「タイムライン」**〖映画〗Timeline.
**タイムレス** 〜な〖時代を超えた；不変の〗timeless. ▯ 〜な名曲 a timeless「song [melody] / 〜なデザインの腕時計 a wristwatch of timeless design.
**タイムワーナー**〖米国のメディア会社〗Time Warner.
**だいメコンけん【大-圏】**〖メコン川流域の中国(雲南省)・ミャンマー・ラオス・タイ・カンボジア・ベトナムの 6 か国を指す語〗the Greater Mekong Subregion (略: GMS).
**たいめん[2]【対面】** ▭ 対面営業 dealing《with customers》face-to-face; (a) face-to-face business. 対面調査 a face-to-face [an in-person] examination; an interview survey.
**タイもじ【-文字】**a Thai character.
**ダイモス** ＝デイモス．
**だいもん[2]【大問】**〖試験問題中の大きな問題〗a main question (in an exam); one of the main questions.
**だいもんじ【大文字】**＝ごさんのおくりび．
**タイヤ** ▭ 雨用タイヤ〖主にレース用の〗a rain tire. ▭ タイヤ・ゲージ〖タイヤの空気圧の測定器〗a tire gauge. タイヤ脱落事故 an accident caused by a wheel「coming off [coming off]《a truck》. タイヤ・バリア〖自動車レースのコース脇の，古タイヤを積み上げた障壁〗a tire barrier; a tire wall.
**ダイヤ(モンド)** ▭ 遺灰[遺骨]ダイヤ(モンド) a life gem; a diamond made with the carbon from a deceased loved one. テーパー(ド)・ダイヤ〖先細形の〗a tapered diamond. マーキス・ダイヤ〖ボート形の〗a marquise (brilliant) diamond. メレ(-)・ダイヤ〖小粒の〗a melee (diamond). ▭ ダイヤモンド状炭素 diamond-like carbon

(略: DLC). ▭ 〜状炭素素膜 (a) diamond-like carbon film. ダイヤモンド薄膜〖電子工学〗(a) diamond thin film. ダイヤモンド富士 "Diamond Fuji"; a view of Mt. Fuji with the sun aligned with the summit. ダイヤモンド惑星〖天文〗〖高圧のため内部がダイヤモンド化している仮想タイプの〗a diamond planet.
**ダイヤル** ▭ ダイヤル回線〖電話の〗a pulse line.
**タイヤルぞく【-族】**〖台湾の先住民族〗the Atayal; 〖1 人〗an Atayal.
**たいよ【貸与】** ▭ 貸与権〖法〗〖1984 年の著作権法改正で認められた権利〗(a) lending right.
**たいよう[3]【太陽】** ▭ 太陽(線)吸収率 solar absorptance. 太陽(線)透過率 solar transmittance. 太陽光(線)反射率 an albedo value; a solar reflectance. 太陽光発電衛星 a solar power satellite (略: SPS). 太陽信仰〖太陽崇拝〗heliolatry; sun worship; the cult of the sun. 太陽線〖手相〗the line [Sun, Apollo] line; the line of「the sun [the Sun, Apollo]. 太陽族 the Sun Tribe; lotus-eating young people who appear in Ishihara Shintarō's novel the Season of the Sun. 太陽発電衛星 ＝太陽光発電衛星．
**だいよう【代用】** ▭ 代用乳〖子牛用の〗a milk substitute.
**たいようけい【太陽系】** ▭ 太陽系外縁天体 a「transneptunian [trans-Neptunian] object (略: TNO). 太陽系外縁部 the「outer edge [outskirts] of the solar system. [⇨エッジワース・カイパー・ベルト] 太陽系外惑星 a planet outside the solar system; 〖天〗an extrasolar planet.
**たいようすいしんそうず【大洋水深総図】**〖組織〗the General Bathymetric Chart of the Oceans (略: GEBCO); 〖海図〗a chart produced by GEBCO.
**「太陽の雫」**〖映画〗Sunshine.
**たいようのとう【太陽の塔】**〖岡本太郎作の建造物; 1970 年の大阪万博のシンボル〗Sun Tower.
**たいようほう【太陽報】**〖香港の日刊紙〗The Sun.
**だいよくじょう【大浴場】**〖旅館などの〗a [the] main [large] bath(room).
**だいよんせだいげんしりょくシステム【第 4 世代原子力-】**Generation IV Nuclear Energy Systems.
**だいよんせだいげんしりょくシステムにかんするこくさいフォーラム【第 4 世代原子力に関する国際-】**Generation IV International Forum (略: GIF).
**だいよんせだいげんしろ【第 4 世代原子炉】**a Generation IV reactor.
**「第四の核」**〖フレデリック・フォーサイス作の小説・その映画化〗The Fourth Protocol.
**タイラー** 1 Tyler, Liv (1977- ; 米国の映画俳優; 2 の子). 2 Tyler, Steven (1948- ; 米国のロックミュージシャン; 1 の父).
**だいり[2]【代理】** ▭ 代理懐胎, 代理妊娠 (a) surrogate pregnancy. 代理記載〖郵便投票などの〗filling in 《a ballot paper》by proxy. ▯ 〜記載制度 a proxy ballot filling-in system / 〜記載人 a proxy appointed to fill in a ballot paper. 代理購買 proxy purchasing; a proxy purchase; purchasing on sb's behalf. 代理出産契約 ＝代理母契約 (⇨だいりは). 代理処罰(制度)〖法〗〖他国で犯罪を犯して帰国した者に，その犯罪が行われた国に代わって本国が処罰すること〗a system permitting punishment to be carried out under the laws of a country to which a perpetrator has escaped after committing a crime in another country (with which it has no extradition treaty). 代理署名〖署名すること〗signing [instead of, on behalf of] a proxy (for sb); signing 〖その署名〗a proxy signature. ▯ 〜署名する sign 《a document》as a proxy; sign「for [instead of, on behalf of]《one's husband》.
**だいリーグ【大-】** ▭ 大リーグ公認球 an official major-

league baseball.
だいリーグせんしゅかい【大-選手会】〖野球〗the Major League Baseball Players Association (略: MLBPA).
たいりく【大陸】 ▶□ 超大陸〖地質〗a supercontinent. ▶□ 大陸貿易〔日本の対中国貿易〕《Japan's》 trade with China;〔台湾の対中国貿易〕《Taiwan's》 trade with mainland China.
たいりくだな【大陸棚】〖地質〗a continental shelf. ▶□ 大陸棚延長 extension to the edge of the continental shelf. 大陸棚開発 continental shelf development. 大陸棚資源 continental shelf resources. 大陸棚調査 a continental shelf survey.
たいりくだなげんかいいいんかい【大陸棚限界委員会】〔国連の〕the Commission on the Limits of the Continental Shelf (略: CLCS).
たいりくだなしぜんえんちょうろん【大陸棚自然延長論】〔東シナ海における日中の境界線に関する中国側の主張;中国大陸から沖縄トラフまで大陸棚は続いているとする〕China's claims concerning the boundary between 「China and Japan [Chinese and Japanese waters]; the view that the border between China and Japan lies along the eastern extension of the continental shelf (and extends to the Okinawa Trough).
たいりくだなじょうやく【大陸棚条約】〔1958年の〕the Convention on the Continental Shelf.
たいりくももんが【大陸鼯鼠】〖動〗〔フィンランド・ロシア・中国などに棲息するモモンガ〕a Siberian flying squirrel; Pteromys volans.
たいりつ【対立】 ▶□ 対立仮説〖統計〗an alternative hypothesis. 対立状態 a confrontational situation 《between…》; a state of confrontation 《between…》.
だいりにん【代理人】 ▶□ 代理人交渉〔プロスポーツ選手の移籍についての〕negotiation by an agent. 代理人弁護士 a lawyer as agent; an attorney. ▶ 訴訟〜弁護士 a law-suit attorney.
だいりはは【代理母】 ▶□ 代理母契約 a surrogacy contract; a surrogate mother contract.
たいりょう²【大量】 ▶□ 大量供給 a 「huge [large-scale] supply; massive supply (of crude oil). 大量高速輸送＝高速大量輸送(⇨こうそく³). 大量在庫 (have) a deep stock; a large quantity of stock; a huge stock. 大量採用 mass [large-scale] employment 《of staff》; taking on large numbers 《of workers》. 大量失点 many 「points [runs] given up. ▶ チーム上, 序盤の〜失点が響いて完敗した.〔野球で〕The team suffered a crushing defeat due to the large number of runs they gave up in the early innings. 大量取得〔株式の〕(a) 「mass [massive, large-scale] acquisition. 大量使用 mass [massive, large-scale, extensive] use; use 《of asbestos》 on a large scale. 大量消費(型)社会 a [the] mass 「consumption [consumer] society. 大量処分 mass [large-scale, major, sweeping] disposal 《of 「dead animals [infected birds, equipment, ammunition]》. 大量処理 mass [large-scale] processing 《of garbage》. 大量摂取 (a) massive intake 《of alcohol》. 大量絶滅〖生物〗a mass extinction; an extinction event. 大量増殖 mass propagation;〔植物などの微細繁殖〕micropropagation. 大量退職 mass [en-masse] retirement 《of the baby boom generation》. 大量逮捕 (a) mass arrest 《of gang members》. 大量発行〔国債・株式などの〕issuing 《bonds》 on a large scale;〔1回の〕a large [an extensive] issue 《of bonds》. 大量発注〔place〕a bulk order 《for materials》. ▶ 〜発注する order 《materials》 in bulk. 大量放出 (a) 「mass [massive] discharge 《of waste water》; (a) massive release 《of radiation into the atmosphere》; mass emission 《of hydrocarbons》; releasing massive amounts 《of $CO_2$ into the atmosphere》. 大量保有報告書〖証券〗〖株式の〕a substantial shareholding report. 大量リード〔野球などのスポーツで〕a massive lead. ▶ 〜リードを許す concede a 「huge [massive] lead 《to the opposition》; allow 《the opposing team》 to gain a 「huge [massive] lead / 〜リードを奪う gain [capture] a 「huge [massive] lead 《over …》. 大量流出 a mass exodus 《of peasants to the city》; (a) massive loss 《of blood》; a hemorrhage 《of funds》; a massive outflow 《of gold》.
たいりょう³【大漁】 ▶□ 大漁祈願 a prayer for a good catch.
たいりょく¹【体力】 ▶□ 体力仕事 work requiring strength and staying power; physically tough work.
たいりょく²【耐力】 ▶□ 保有耐力〖建〗(a) 「load-carrying [load-bearing] capacity. 保有水平耐力〖建〗(a) horizontal 「load-carrying [load-bearing] capacity; (an) ultimate lateral strength.
タイル ▶□ 色[模様]タイル an encaustic tile. 化粧タイル a decorative tile. 陶製タイル a ceramic tile. 舗装用タイル a paving tile.
たいれいせい【耐冷性】cold [chill] tolerance; psychrotolerance. ▶〜のある cold [chill] tolerant; psychrotolerant.
ダイレクト ▶□ ダイレクトキャッチ〔直接捕球〕a catch of a 「fly ball [line drive]. ダイレクトセール〔直接販売〕direct sales; B2C [B to C] sales. ▶ B2C [B to C] は business to consumer の略. ダイレクト送球〖野球〗a direct throw 《to home plate》. ダイレクトパス〖サッカー〗a direct pass (made without stopping the ball). ダイレクトプリント〔写真〕a direct print (from film). ダイレクトプレー〖サッカー〗a solo play on goal. ダイレクトメール業者 a direct mail company; a direct-mailer. ダイレクトメール発送代行業 a direct mail service.
タイレノール〖商標・薬〗〔アセトアミノフェン系の頭痛薬〕Tylenol.
たいれん【台連】＝たいわんだんけつれんめい.
だいれん【大連】〔中国, 遼寧省の都市〕Dalian; Talien.
だいれんしょうひんこうえきじょ【大連商品交易所】the Dalian Commodity Exchange (略: DCE).
だいれんしょうひんとりひきじょ【大連商品取引所】＝だいれんしょうひんこうえきじょ.
タイ・ロッド〖自動車・建〗a tie rod. ▶ タイロッド工法〔原子力〕〔シュラウド補強のための〕the mounted tie rods method.
たいわ【対話】 ▶□ 対話環境 an interactive atmosphere 《between doctors and patients》. 対話と圧力〔外交戦術としての〕《combine》 dialogue and pressure. 対話能力 the ability to 「conduct a dialogue [exchange opinions].
たいわんおおじしん【台湾大地震】〔1999年の〕the (Taiwan) 「Ji-Ji [Chi-Chi] Earthquake.
たいわんかんけいほう【台湾関係法】〖米法〗the Taiwan Relations Act (略: TRA).
たいわんじんこうきょうじむかい【台湾人公共事務会】〔台湾民進党系の対米ロビー団体〕the Formosan Association for Public Affairs (略: FAPA).
たいわんすじお【台湾筋尾】〖動〗〔台湾・東南アジア原産のナミヘビ科の無毒蛇〕a Taiwanese beauty snake; Elaphe taeniura.
たいわんせきたいでんろせいぞう【台湾積体電路製造】〔台湾の半導体大手メーカー〕Taiwan Semiconductor Manufacturing Company (略: TSMC).
たいわんだんけつれんめい【台湾団結連盟】〔台湾の政党〕the Taiwan Solidarity Union (略: TSU).
たいわんつばめしじみ【台湾燕小灰】〖昆〗〔シジミチョウ科の〕a tailed cupid; Everes lacturnus.
タインホア〔ベトナム中北部の省; その省都〕Thanh Hoa.
ダウ〖証券〗⇨ダウ・ジョーンズ.
「ダ・ヴィンチ・コード」〖米国作家ダン・ブラウン (Dan Brown) 作の小説〗The Da Vinci Code.
ダウ・ケミカル〖米国の総合化学薬品メーカー〗the Dow

Chemical Company; Dow Chemical.
**ダウ・ジョーンズ**〔米国の通信・出版社〕Dow Jones & Co., Inc. ⇨ **ダウ・ジョーンズ工業平均株価**〔証券〕the Dow(-Jones) 「industrial average [industrials]」. **ダウ・ジョーンズ平均(株価)[指数]**〔証券〕the Dow-Jones 「average [index]」.
**ダウジング**〔水脈探査作業・水脈占い〕dowsing. ◐ ~で水脈を掘り当てる find a water vein by dowsing; dowse a water vein.
**ダウナーぎゅう**【-牛】=へたり牛 (⇨へたり).
**ダウニー** Downey, Robert, Jr. (1965- ; 米国の映画俳優).
**タウヒード**〔イスラム〕〔神の唯一性; イスラム教の世界観〕tawhid; tauhid.
**ダウル**〔イラク北部の都市ティクリート郊外の村〕Adwar; Ad Dawr.
**タウンジー**〔ミャンマー中北部に位置するシャン州の州都〕Taunggyi.
**タウンゼント** Townsend, Stuart (1972- ; アイルランド生まれの映画俳優).
**ダウンゾーニング**〔地域の用途指定を再検討して開発を制限すること〕*downzoning. ▷ downzone *v*.
**タウンヂー** =タウンジー.
**ダウンフォース**〔流体力学〕〔自動車レースで, 空気の流れを利用してマシンを下方に押えつける力〕downforce.
**タウン・マネージメントきかん**【-機関】〔中心市街地の活性化を策定する機関〕a town management organization (略: TMO).
**ダウンリンク**〔通信〕a downlink.
**ダウンロード** ⇨ **ダウンロード・サービス**〔インターネットなどを利用しての〕a download service. ◐ 音楽の~(launch) a music download service. **ダウンロード販売**〔ソフトウェアの購入者がオンライン上で購入契約を行いダウンロードする販売方法〕download sales.
**だえき**【唾液】 ⇨ **唾液検査** a saliva test; 〔歯科〕**虫歯になる危険度を測る** a caries risk test (略: CRT).
**-たおす**【-倒す】〔徹底的にする〕*do* to the fullest; *do* completely; *do* thoroughly; 《口》 *do* to the max. ◐ 遊び倒す enjoy oneself to the fullest. ◐ 私は夫と南の島で 2 週間を遊び~のが夢である. I always wanted to go to an island in the south with my husband and have our fill of fun for two weeks. 聞き倒す listen to all 《of a recording》. ◐ 英語の朗読 CD を聞き倒したおかげでリスニングに強くなった. Because I listened to everything on some English spoken-word CDs, my listening skills improved. しゃべり倒す 〔しゃべりまくる〕 jabber away; babble on; 〔相手を圧倒する勢いでしゃべる〕 talk *sb*'s ear off; rattle on. 使い倒す 〔機能を徹底的に活用する〕 apply all the functions 《of a device》. 寝倒す sleep until the cows come home; sleep for a long time. ぼけ倒す keep acting like 「an idiot [a fool]. 誉め倒す praise *sb* to the skies.
**タオユワン**【桃園】〔台湾北西部の都市・県〕Taoyuan.
**タオル** ⇨ **濡れタオル** a 「wet [damp, moistened] towel. **ミニタオル** a mini-towel.
**だおんばち**【駄温鉢】〔園芸〕a type of hard-fired, unglazed, reddish-brown ceramic flowerpot.
**たがい**[2]【他害】〔法〕harming others.
**たがく**【多額】 ⇨ **多額盗難[窃盗]事件** a case of grand 「theft [larceny].
**たかくてき**【多角的】 ⇨ **多角的視点** a multi-angled view.
**たかどまり**【高止まり】〔経〕~**する** be stuck at a high level. ◐ 原油価格の~. ◐ 失業率は 10% 台の~が続いている. The unemployment rate is still soaring above the 10-percent level.
**たかな**【高菜】 ⇨ **高菜漬け**〔高菜の葉を塩漬けして乳酸発酵させた物〕pickled mustard leaves.

**たかね**[2]【高値】 ⇨ **高値維持** continuation [maintenance] of high(er) prices. ◐ OPEC は原油生産を抑制し, 原油価格の~維持を図っている. OPEC has imposed restraints on oil production in an effort to maintain high prices for oil. **高値圏**〔株価などの〕 a zone of high prices; a 「high [the] high price zone. ◐ ~圏で推移する〔株価などが〕 remain [stabilize] in the high price zone.
**タカフル**〔保険〕〔イスラム諸国での互助・保険の基本理念〕Takaful (insurance).
**たかまつのみやでんかきねんせかいぶんかしょう**【高松宮殿下記念世界文化賞】the Praemium Imperiale.
**たかやすどうみゃくえん**【高安動脈炎】〔医〕〔大動脈起始部・大動脈弓の慢性動脈炎〕Takayasu's aortitis. ▶ 1908 年, 高安右人(うじん)博士が初めて報告したことに因む.
**たからくじ**【宝籤】 ◐ **サマージャンボ~** the Summer Jumbo Lottery.
**タカラジェンヌ**〔宝塚歌劇の団員〕a Takarazuka Revue 「girl [performer].
**タギグ**〔フィリピン, マニラ首都圏の都市〕Taguig.
**タキサンけい**【-系】〔薬〕〔抗がん剤〕the taxanes.
**タキシング**〔空〕〔航空機の地上自力走行〕taxiing. ◐ ~**する** taxi 《toward the runway》.
**タキソイドけい**【-系】〔薬〕〔抗がん剤〕the taxoids. [=タキサンけい]
**タキソテール**〔商標・薬〕〔抗がん剤〕Taxotere.
**たきのう**【多機能】 ⇨ **多機能化** ◐ **ゲーム機[携帯電話]の~化** adding multiple functions to 「game machines [cell phones]; making 「game machines [cell phones] multifunctional. **多機能トイレ** a 「multifunctional [multipurpose, barrier-free] toilet.
**だきゅう**【打球】 ⇨ **打球音** the sound of a ball 「on [hitting] a 「bat [racket]. **打球処理** fielding a 「batted [hit] ball. **打球方向** the 「batted [hit] ball direction; the direction of a batted ball.
**たきょくぶんさんがたこくどけいせいそくしんほう**【多極分散型国土形成促進法】〔法〕the Multi-Polar Patterns National Land Formation Promotion Law.
**タク**〔タイ北部の県; その県都〕Tak.
**だく**[4]【抱く】 ⇨ **抱かれたい男** a sexually 「desirable [attractive] man. ◐ **あの俳優はある女性誌のアンケートで抱かれたい男 No.1 だった.** That actor came in number one in a women's magazine poll rating the men that women would most want to have sex with.
**たくじしせつ**【託児施設】a day-care facility for children; a nursery; a crèche.
**たくじしつ**【託児室】a baby-care room; a room where you can leave your baby.
**たくじしょ**【託児所】 ⇨ **事業所内託児施設** ⇨ じぎょうしょ.
**たくじょう**【卓上】 ⇨ **卓上電話** a desk (tele)phone. **卓上ベル** a desk bell.
**タクシン** Thaksin Shinawatra (1949- ; タイの首相 [2001-06]).
**タクシング**〔空〕=タキシング.
**たくそう**[2]【託送】 ⇨ **託送料金**〔電力小売り会社が電力会社に支払う〕a transmission charge (paid by power retailers to power suppliers).
**たくち**【宅地】 ⇨ **宅地見込地** land suitable for (conversion to) residential use; prospective residential land.
**たくちたてものとりひきしゅにんしゃ**【宅地建物取引主任者】a registered real-estate transaction specialist; a person recognized by the state as qualified to engage in real-estate transactions.
**ダクト・テープ**〔粘着テープの一種〕duct tape.
**ダクノン**〔ベトナム中央高地の省〕Dak [Dac] Nong.
**たくはい**【宅配】 ⇨ **宅配サービス** a home delivery service.

**タクマウ**〔カンボジア南部, カンダール州の州都〕Takhmau; Ta Khmau.

**ダクラク**〔ベトナム中央高地の省〕Dak Lak; Dac Lac.

**タグ・ラグビー**〔タックルなどの体のぶつかり合いのないラグビー; 英国発祥〕tag rugby.

**ダグラスありさわのほうそく**【―有沢の法則】〔夫の年収が高いほど妻が仕事を持っている比率は下がるという経験則〕the Douglas-Arisawa law.

**タクリン**〔薬〕〔アルツハイマー型痴呆治療剤〕tacrine.

**たけ**[1]【丈】　□□ 丈詰め　shortening 《pant legs》; raising 《a hem》. 丈直し (a) length adjustment. 丈伸ばし lengthening 《a skirt》; lowering 《a hem》.

**たけ**[2]【竹】　□□ 竹工芸 bamboo craft; bamboo arts. 竹スキー 《a pair of》bamboo skis.

**たけいとういしゅくしょう**【多系統萎縮症】〔医〕multiple system atrophy (略: MSA).

**タケオ**〔カンボジア南部の州, 同州の州都〕Takeo.

**だげき**【打撃】
□□ 打撃好調 good batting; 《口》a hot bat. ◎ ～好調のイチローが今日も 3 安打. Continuing to bat well, Ichiro had three hits again today. / 彼は今シーズンも～好調だ. He has a hot bat again this season. 打撃センス〔野球選手の〕one's feel for hitting. 打撃不振 poor batting; 《口》a cold bat. ◎ ～不振の山田選手はスタメンから外された. Yamada, batting poorly, was taken out of the starting lineup. / 彼は～不振に陥っている. He's fallen into a batting slump. 打撃妨害〔野球〕defensive interference; interfering with a batter. 打撃用手袋〔野球〕batting gloves.

**タケゴン** ＝タケンゴン.

**たけすみ, たけずみ**〔竹炭〕bamboo charcoal.

**たけっしょう**【多結晶】　□□ 多結晶(シリコン)太陽電池 a polycrystalline (silicon) solar cell.

**たけのこ**〔筍・竹の子〕　□□ たけのこ掘り[狩り] bamboo shoot digging [hunting].

**たけのこめばる**〔筍目張〕〔魚〕〔フサカサゴ科の海産魚〕*Sebastes oblongus*.

**たけん**[2]【他県】　□□ 他県ナンバー　◎ ～ナンバーの車 a car 「with [bearing] a license (number) plate from another prefecture.

**だげんがっき**【打弦楽器】a struck stringed-instrument; a stringed instrument struck with 「a plectrum [mallet etc]」.

**タケンゴン**〔インドネシア, アチェ州, 中アチェ県の県都〕Takengon.

**たこ**[1]【凧】　□□ 凧職人 a kitemaker.

**だこう**【蛇行】　□□ 大蛇行(型)〔黒潮などの〕a large 「meander [meandering] (path) 《of the Japan Current》. 非大蛇行(型)〔黒潮などの〕a non-large 「meander [meandering] (path).

**たこうていもち**【多工程持ち】〔一人の作業員が複数の工程を受け持つ生産方式〕multi-process handling.

**だこうどう**【蛇行動】〔鉄道〕〔車体の〕hunting oscillation; hunting.

**タコ**（―）〔軍〕〔戦術航空士〕a TACCO. ▷ tactical coordinator の略.

**たこくかん**【多国間】　□□ 多国間共同訓練〔軍〕multilateral joint exercises. 多国間主義 multilateralism.

**たこくかんせんいきょうてい**【多国間繊維協定】the Multi-Fiber Arrangement (略: MFA).

**たこくせきかいぐんごうどうぶたい**【多国籍海軍合同部隊】〔「不朽の自由作戦」に基づきインド洋で海上阻止行動を行う〕Combined Task Force 150 (略: CTF 150).

**タコチャート**〔自動車〕〔走行記録計の記録(用紙)〕a tachogram; 〔走行記録計〕a tachograph.

**たこつぼ(がた)しんきんしょう[しょうがい]**【たこつぼ(型)心筋症[障害]】〔医〕takotsubo cardiomyopathy.

**たこのまくら**〔蛸の枕・海燕〕〔動〕〔タコノマクラ科の棘皮《棘皮》動物〕*Clypeaster japonicus*.

**たざい**【多剤】　□□ 多剤耐性緑膿菌〔菌〕multidrug-resistant *Pseudomonas aeruginosa* (略: MDRP). 多剤排出トランスポーター〔多剤耐性菌が持つ〕a multidrug efflux transporter.

**タサッウフ**〔イスラム神秘主義〕Tasawwuf.

**たさん**【多産】　□□ 多産少死 a high birth rate and low death rate; many births and 「few deaths [low mortality]. 多産多死 a high birth and high death rate; many births and 「(many) deaths [high mortality].

**タジ**〔イラク, バグダッド北方の町〕Taji.

**だし**【出し】　□□ 粉末だし〔だしの素〕powdered soup stock. □□ だし子〔煮干しなどの小魚〕dried small sardines or other fish used to make soup stock.

**たしあげ**【足し上げ】(a) summation.

**たしあげる**【足し上げる】〔全項目を順次足していく〕add [sum] up.

**たじげん**【多次元】　□□ 多次元尺度解析法〔統計〕＝多次元尺度法. 多次元尺度法〔統計〕multidimensional scaling (略: MDS). □□ 非計量的～尺度法〔統計〕non-metric multidimensional scaling.

**たしぜんがたかわづくり**【多自然型川づくり】neo-natural river reconstruction; a method of river conservation work that avoids, or keeps to a minimum, damage to the natural environment.

**タジッチ** ＝タディッチ.

**たしゃかぶてんかん(しゃ)さい**【他社転換(社)債】〔証券〕an exchangeable bond (略: EB).

**たしゃまたぎ**【他社またぎ】〔保険〕〔1 つの事故に対し加害者と被害者が加入している別々の損害保険会社に保険金の支払い義務が生じるケース〕a situation in which the injured party and the party at fault in a traffic accident are insured against loss by separate insurers.

**たしゆ**【足し湯】〔風呂に熱い湯を加えること〕adding hot water 《to the bath》; 〔湯量を増やすこと〕raising the water level (in the bath).

**だしゅ**[2]【舵手】　□□ 舵手付きフォア〔ボート〕〔競技〕《women's》coxed fours. 舵手無しフォア〔ボート〕〔競技〕《men's》coxless fours.

**たじゅう**[2]【多重】　□□ 多重構造 a multilayer(ed) structure.

**たしょく**[2]【他殖】〔生物〕allogamy; cross-fertilization. □□ 他殖性植物 an allogamous [a cross-fertilizing] plant.

**たしょくしゅきょうどう**【多職種協働】〔介護・看護などの〕multidisciplinary cooperation.

**ダシルヴァ**〔ブラジルの政治家〕＝ルーラ.

**たすうけつ**【多数決】　□□ 二重多数決〔欧州理事会における一国一票と人口比例票の併用〕double majority voting; a double majority (system). □□ 多数決制 a majority rule system.

**たすうこくかんききん**【多数国間基金】〔モントリオール議定書に基づく〕the Multilateral Fund (for the Implementation of the Montreal Protocol) (略: MLF).

**たすうこくかんとうしきん**【多数国間投資基金】〔中南米地域における民間投資促進のため米州開発銀行内に設置された〕the Multilateral Investment Fund (略: MIF).

**タスオミン**〔商標・薬〕〔乳がん治療薬〕Tasuomin. ▶ 一般名 クエン酸タモキシフェン.

**たせん**[2]【多選】　□□ 多選禁止条例〔地方自治体首長の〕a law against frequent re-election; a law against being re-elected more than a certain number of times.

**たそう**[2]【多層】　□□ 多層膜コーティング〔光学〕multilayer coating.

**タタ**〔インドの企業グループ〕the Tata Group.

**ただ**【只・徒】　□□ ただ取り《get》something for nothing; 《get》a free ride. ◎ 駒の～取り〔将棋・チェスなど〕taking [capturing] a piece for free / 仕事もせずに給料を～取りするやつは許せない. I can't stand people who take a

salary without working for it.
たたい【多胎】 ▷ 多胎児 multiple-birth children;〔1人〕a multiple-birth child. 多胎率 the rate of multiple births; a multiple birth rate. ◐ 自然妊娠による～率 the rate of multiple births in natural pregnancies.
たたきあらい【叩き洗い】washing 《clothes》by beating 《them》. ～する wash 《clothes》by beating 《them》.
たたされぼうず【立たされ坊主】〔罰として授業中、教室の外の廊下に立ち続けさせられている生徒〕a student made to stand in the hallway during the class as punishment for misbehavior at school.
タタ・スチール〔インドの大手鉄鋼メーカー〕Tata Steel.
たたみ【畳】▷ 畳ベッド a tatami bed; a bed (made fitted) with tatami matting.
-たたみ, -だたみ【畳み】〔畳むの名詞形〕▷ おむつ畳み folding diapers. 屏風畳み accordion fold; zigzag fold. 本畳み〔和服の正式な畳み方〕the (proper) way to fold a kimono.
たたら【踏鞴】▷ たたら吹き〔砂鉄・木炭を原料とし、たたらを用いて行う日本古来の製鉄法〕(traditional Japanese) tatara steel making method, using a foot-operated bellows.
たちあい[1]【立ち会い】▷ 立会外取引〔取引〕off-hour(s) trading;〔取引が始まる前の〕premarket trading;〔取引終了後の〕after-hours trading. 立会外分売 selling shares in small lots outside trading hours. 立会取引〔取引〕regular-hours trading; trading during 「opening (daytime) hours.
たちあげ【立ち上げ】▷ 店舗立ち上げ a store launch; a store opening.
たちいち【立ち位置】〔出演者が舞台上で立つ位置〕one's standing location; one's position; the place where one stands;〔立場〕one's 「position (status, role)〔in society〕.
たちいり【立ち入り】▷ 立ち入り制限 limited [restricted] access [entry]; access limits. ◐ ～制限区域 a 「restricted-[limited-]access area;〔時間によって〕an area with restricted access times.
たちかた[2]【立方】〔日本舞踊の踊り手〕a performer of (classical) Japanese dance;〔能〕〔囃子方(はやしかた)に対して舞い手〕a Noh actor (as opposed to a musician).
たちぐい【立ち食い】▷ 立ち食い寿司 a stand-up sushi 「bar [restaurant].
たちだい【裁ち台】〔裁縫〕a fabric cutting board.
たちづくえ【立ち机】a 《press-conference》podium.
たチャンネル【多-】〔放送〕multichannel 《satellite broadcasting》. ▷ 多チャンネル時代 a [the] multichannel era.
タッカー Tucker, Chris (1972- ; 米国の映画俳優).
だっき【脱気】〔物〕deaeration; degassing. ～する deaerate; degas. ▷ 脱気器 a deaerator; a degasser.
ダッキー〔カヌーの一種〕a 「ducky [duckie]; an inflatable kayak;〔スポーツ〕duckying; inflatable kayaking.
たっきゅうびん【宅急便】〔商標〕Takkyubin (door-to-door parcel delivery service).
だつきょうやく【脱共役】▷ 脱共役たんぱく質 an uncoupling protein (略: UCP).
タックス ▷ タックス・プランニング〔税務対策〕tax planning.
ダックス(かぶか)しすう【DAX(株価)指数】〔証券〕＝ドイツかぶかしすう【―】.
ダックラック ⇨ダクラク.
ダックワーズ, ダクワーズ〔菓子〕a dacquoise.
たっけん[3]【宅建】▷ 宅建主任者＝たくちたてものひきしゅにんしゃ.
だっけんちゃっかん【脱健着患】〔介護〕〔体が不自由な人の着替えを手伝う際のこつ、脱がせる時は健康な側から脱がせ、着せる時は患っている側から着せるというもの〕starting with the good limb when undressing and the disabled

limb when dressing.
だっさい【獺祭】arranging a catch of fish in a row (as otters do, as if in worship);〔比喩的に〕surrounding oneself with reference books while writing. ▷ 獺祭忌 the anniversary of Masaoka Shiki's death. ▶ 9月19日.
だっしにゅう【脱脂乳】skim [skimmed, nonfat] milk. ▶ 日本では乳脂肪分 0.5% 未満のもの(0.5-3%のものが部分脱脂乳).
だっしゅ[2]【奪首】taking [getting] first place. ～する take first place.
ダッシュ[2]【DASH】〔食事療法による高血圧予防〕DASH; Dietary Approaches to Stop Hypertension.
ダッシュポット〔機・物〕〔緩衝装置・そのモデル〕a dashpot.
だっしょう[1]【脱硝】▷ 脱硝装置〔化〕denitrification [denitration] equipment.
たっせい【達成】▷ 達成度 the degree of achievement; the degree of attainment 《of the goals》; how far one 「achieves [has achieved] one's goals. 達成動機〔経営〕an achievement motive. 達成動機付け〔心理〕achievement motivation. 達成目標 a goal (to achieve); an achievement goal. 達成率 an achievement rate. ◐ 鉄道車両内禁煙化～率 the 「success rate [degree of success] in implementing no-smoking in railway carriages.
だっせん[2]【脱線】▷ 滑り上がり脱線 slide-up derailment. せり上がり脱線 ＝乗り上がり脱線. 飛び上がり脱線 jump-up derailment. 乗り上がり脱線 wheelclimb derailment. ▷ 脱線係数〔鉄道〕a derailment 「coefficient [factor]. 脱線痕〔電車が脱線した時に、レールや枕木にできる傷〕a derailment mark. 脱線防止ガード〔鉄道〕an anti-derailment device. 脱線防止レール〔鉄道〕an anti-derailment (guard)rail; a guardrail; 「a check-rail.
だっそう【脱走】▷ 脱走罪〔軍隊からの〕《be tried for》 desertion.
タッターソール・チェック〔交互に 2 色を配した格子柄〕(a) tattersall check.
だつダムせんげん【脱-宣言】a "no more dams" declaration; a declaration of opposition to further dam construction.
タッチ ▷ ツータッチ. ⇨ツータッチ. ▷ タッチケア maternal cuddling (to encourage stable psychological development); *touch childcare. タッチ数〔キーボードの〕number of keystrokes;〔サッカーなどの競技で〕number of touches 《of the ball》. ◐ なるべく少ない～数で文章を入力したい.〔電算〕I want to input the sentence with as few keystrokes as possible. / 日本は～数の少ないすばやいパス回しで相手チームを翻弄した.《サッカー》Japan ran rings around the other team with just a few touches of the ball and a rapid exchange of passes. タッチ板〔水泳〕〔計時のためにプールのコース両端の水面下に設置する〕a touch pad.
タッチ・アンド・ゴー〔空〕〔連続離着陸訓練〕a touch-and-go 《pl. ～es》.
ダッチほうしき【-方式】〔株式〕〔株式公開初日の価格決定方式の 1 つ〕a Dutch auction.
だつどうちょう【脱同調】〔生物〕〔生体リズムにずれが生じること〕desynchronization. ▷ 外的脱同調 external desynchronization. 内的脱同調 internal desynchronization.
ダッハウ〔ドイツ南部の都市; ナチ強制収容所があった〕Dachau.
だっぽう[2]【脱包】〔薬室・弾倉から実弾を取り出すこと〕unloading. ～する unload《a gun》.
だっぽう[3]【脱泡】〔化〕defoaming. ▷ 脱泡剤 a defoaming agent; (a) defoamer. 脱泡装置 defoaming equipment.
だっぽく【脱北】～する escape from [defect, get out

だっぽくきこくしゃしえんきこう 260

of] North Korea. ▭ 脱北者 a「defector [refugee] from North Korea.
**だっぽくきこくしゃしえんきこう**〖脱北帰国者支援機構〗〔NGO〕the Japan Aid Association for North Korean Returnees.
**だつまく**〖脱膜〗〔皮膜・塗膜の除去〕removal [stripping] of「coating [plating, film].
**たつみてんじょう**〖辰巳天井〗〘相場〙〔辰年と巳年は最高値になりやすい、の意〕In the years of the Dragon and the Snake, the market tends to peak. ▶ 十二支でいう「辰巳天井、午(?)尻下がり、未(?)辛抱、申酉(?)騒ぐ、戌(?)(は)笑い、亥(?)固まる、子(?)は繁栄[繁盛]、丑(?)はつまづき、寅(?)千里を走り、卯(?)(は)跳ねる」という格言から.
**だつもう**〖脱毛〗▭ 光脱毛 (pulsed) light hair removal. ▭ 脱毛作用 《cause》 hair loss; a depilatory「effect [action]; 〔頭の〕《cause》 balding; a balding「effect [action]. ◐ 抗〜作用 / この薬品には抗〜作用があります. This chemical「prevents balding [inhibits hair loss]. 脱毛斑 a bald「patch [area, spot]; a patch of hair loss.
**だつもうしょう**〖脱毛症〗▭ 女性型脱毛症 female-pattern「baldness [hair loss]; female(-pattern) (androgenetic [androgenic]) alopecia.
**タディッチ** Tadić, Boris (1958– ; セルビアの政治家; 大統領〔2004– 〕).
**タティング**〔レース編みの一種〕tatting. ▭ タティング・レース tatting (lace).
**たてがく**〖縦額〗a vertical frame.
**たてかじ**〖縦舵〗〘海〙〔潜水艦の〕a「vertical [steering] rudder.
**たてこもり**〖立て籠もり〗▭ 〔人質〕立て籠もり事件 a "(kidnap-and-)barricade" incident; an incident in which a criminal (takes hostages and)「refuses to come out of [barricades himself into] a building.
**タテノリ**〖縦乗り〗〘音楽〙〔リズムに合わせて体を上下に動かしたり飛び跳ねたりすること〕the pogo; jumping up and down to the beat of the music.
**たてまえ**[3]〖建(て)前・立(て)前〗▭ 建前論 an official announcement; an announcement for public consumption; obfuscation. ◐ それに対する国土交通省の回答は抽象論や〜論の域を出ていない. The Ministry of Land, Infrastructure, Transport and Tourism's response to that fails to go beyond the abstract and mere public obfuscation.
**たてや**〖建屋〗▭ 原子炉建屋 a nuclear reactor building.
**たてやまりんどう**〖立山竜胆〗〘植〙〔リンドウ科の植物〕*Gentiana thunbergii* var. *minor*.
**たてロール**〖縦〜〗〔有閑女性の髪型〕ringlets; ringlet [sausage] curls.
**たてわり**〖縦割り〗▭ 縦割りグループ ◐ 1年生から3年生までを含む〜グループ a group formed from first- through third-year classes. 縦割り組織 a vertical organization.
**たとう**[4]〖多頭〗▭ 多頭飼い〔犬や猫の〕keeping a large number《of「dogs [cats]》.
**たとう**[5]〖多糖〗▭ 増粘多糖類〖化〗〔食品に粘りを付けるための多糖類〕a polysaccharide thickener.
**タトゥーロ** Turturro, John (1957– ; 米国の映画俳優).
**「タトラー」** 1〔ロンドンで R・スティールが週1回刊行した雑誌 (1709–11)〕the Tatler. 2〔社交界人士の話題を集めた英国の月刊誌〕Tatler.
**たな**[2]〖棚〗▭ 棚差し〖出版〗shelving 《a book》 spine-out. 棚割り〖商〗shelf(-space) allocation; allocation of shelf space.
**たなおろし**〖棚卸し・店卸し〗▭ 棚卸し資産回転率〖会計〗*(an) inventory [(a) merchandise] turnover (ratio)*; "(a) stock turnover. 棚卸資産廃棄損〖会計〗loss on disposal of inventories. 棚卸ロス inventory loss.

**たなかじょうそうぶん**〖田中上奏文〗〖日本史〗〔昭和初期に世界に流布した日本の対中国政策に関する怪文書. 偽書とも言われる〕the Tanaka Memorial.
**ダナキャラン・ニューヨーク**〖商標〗〔米国の服飾ブランド〕Donna Karan New York.
**ダナキルさばく**〖—砂漠〗〔エチオピアの〕the Danakil Desert.
**ダナゾール**〖薬〗〔子宮内膜症治療薬〕danazol.
**ダナム** Dunham, Katherine (Mary) (1909–2006; 米国の黒人ダンサー・振付師・人類学者).
**だに**[2]〖壁蝨〗▭ 耳ダニ〖獣医〗an ear mite; *Otodectes cynotis*.
**「ダニー・ケイ・ショー」**〔米国の, 音楽バラエティー TV 番組〕The Danny Kaye Show.
**ダニー・パン** Danny Pang (1965– ; 香港生まれの映画監督; 中国語名 彭發; オキサイド・パンの双子の弟).
**ダニエルズ** Daniels, Jeff ( ; 米国の映画俳優).
**たにけい**〖谷径〗〔ライフル銃の口径の〕a groove diameter.
**たにん**〖他人〗▭ 他人受入率〔生体認証機器などの〕a false-acceptance rate.
**たねきん**〖種菌〗〔シイタケ栽培に用いる〕shiitake mycelia biomass; shiitake spores and mycelia.
**たねつけ**〖種付け〗▭ 種付け権〔種馬・種牛の〕stud rights《to a champion racehorse》.
**たのう**〖多能〗▭ 多能工〖産業〗a multi(-skilled) worker; a multifunctional worker; a cross-trained worker; a worker with multifunctional skills.
**たのみがたい**〖恃みがたい〗 ◐ まことに恃みがたきは人の心だ. What you can't count on at all is the human heart. / すべては恃みがたきを恃んだ私の責任だ. It's all my fault for putting our hopes on something that wouldn't be there when we needed it.
**タバ**〔エジプト・シナイ半島東部, イスラエルとの国境沿いのリゾート地〕Taba.
**ダハウ** =ダッハウ.
**タパクトゥアン** =タパトゥアン.
**たばこ**〖煙草〗▭ たばこ顔 smoker's face; smoker's wrinkles. たばこ病 (a) tobacco disease. ◐ 〜病訴訟 a tobacco lawsuit.
**タパス**〔スペイン語で酒の肴(?)〕tapas.
**たはつ**〖多発〗▭ 多発外傷〖医〗《sustain》 multiple trauma.
**だばつ**〖打罰〗〖ゴルフ〗▭ 1[2]打罰 a「one-stroke [two-stroke] penalty; 《incur》 a penalty of「one stroke [two strokes].
**たはつせい**〖多発性〗〖医〗▭ 多発性骨髄腫 multiple myeloma (略: MM). 多発性脂腺嚢腫 =多発性毛包嚢腫. 多発性毛包嚢腫 multiple follicular cysts.
**タパトゥアン**〔インドネシア・アチェ州, 南アチェ県の県都〕Tapaktuan.
**タバナン**〔インドネシア, バリ島中部の県〕Tabanan.
**ダハブ**〔エジプト, 紅海沿岸のリゾート地〕Dahab.
**ダビデのせきじゅんしゃ**〖—の赤盾社〗〔イスラエルの救急活動組織; 赤十字運動に加盟〕the Red「Shield [Star] of David.
**ダビデのほし**〖—の星〗the Star of David; the David's star; 《<Heb "shield of David" の意》the Magen David. 〔⇨ろくぼうせい〕
**たびばんぐみ**〖旅番組〗〔テレビなどの〕a travel program.
**たひんしゅしょうロットせいさん**〖多品種小—生産〗〔多品種少量生産〕production of multiple models in smaller lots; small-lot production of a wide variety of products; diversified small-quantity production; low-volume diversified production.
**ダフィー** Duffy, Troy (1971– ; 米国の映画監督).
**ダブーク** =タブク.
**ダフーク**〔イラク最北の州; その州都〕Dahuk.
**タブク**〔サウジアラビア北部の州; その州都〕Tabuk.
**タブラオ**《<Sp *tablao*》〔フラメンコのライブハウス〕a fla-

menco cabaret.
**ダブリュー・アール・シー**【WRC】〖自動車〗〔世界ラリー選手権〕WRC; the World Rally Championship.
**ダブリュー・アール・ピー**【WRP】〔米国の、障害をもつ大学生が政府機関で仕事を体験するプログラム〕the WRP. ▶ Workforce Recruitment Program for College Students with Disabilities の略から.
**ダブリュー・アイ・ディー**【WID】〔途上国における開発への女性参加を支援する運動〕WID; women in development.
**ダブリュー・イー・シー・ピー・エヌ・エル**【WECPNL】〔航空機騒音の程度を示す国際単位；うるささ指数〕WECPNL; (a) weighted equivalent continuous perceived noise level.
**ダブリュー・エス・エス・ディー**【WSSD】〔持続可能な開発に関する世界首脳会議〕WSSD; the World Summit on Sustainable Development.
**ダブリュー・エス・ティー・エス**【WSTS】〔世界半導体市場統計〕WSTS; World Semiconductor Trade Statistics.
**ダブリュー・エム・ディー**【WMD】〔大量破壊兵器〕WMD; a weapon of mass destruction.
**ダブリュー・キュー・エー**【WQA】〔米国水質協会の略〕WQA; the Water Quality Association.
**ダブリュー・ティー・エー**【WTA】〔女子プロテニス選手協会〕▷ **WTA** ツアー the WTA Tour. ▶ 2005 年、Sony Ericsson WTA Tour に改称. **WTA** ランキング (a) WTA ranking.
**ダブリュー・ティー・オー**【WTO】〔世界貿易機関〕▷ **WTO** 交渉 WTO negotiations 《on agriculture》. **WTO** 紛争解決機関 the Dispute Settlement Body of the World Trade Organization 《略: (WTO-)DSB》; the WTO Dispute Settlement Body.
**ダブリュー・ティー・ビー**【WTB】〖ラグビー〗〔ウイング〕a wing three-quarter.
**ダブリュー・ビー・オー**【WBO】=せかいボクシングきこう.
**ダブリュー・ビー・ジー・ティー**【WBGT】〖気象〗〔湿球黒球温度；暑熱環境指標；熱中症指標〕WBGT; the wet bulb globe temperature.
**ダブリュー・ピー・ダブリューしょうこうぐん**【WPW 症候群】〖医〗WPW syndrome; Wolff-Parkinson-White syndrome.
**ダブリンきょうてい**【-協定】〔EU 各国間の入国管理と難民問題を定めた協定〕the Dublin Convention.
**ダブル** ▷ ダブルスカル 〖漕艇〗〔2 人乗りスカル競技〕double sculls. ダブル・ダッチ〔両端の 2 人が 2 本のロープを交互に逆回りに回し、別の人がその間をまたぶ縄跳び〕double Dutch.
**ダブル・エックス・エル**【XXL】〔物品のサイズ〕XXL.
**「ダブル・ジョパディー」**〔映画〕Double Jeopardy.
**「ダブルタップ」**〔映画〕Double Tap;〔中国語タイトル〕鎗王.
**ダブル・チェック** ▷ ダブル・チェック体制 a system of double checks; a double-checking system.
**ダブル・トラップ**〔クレー射撃の競技〕double trap.
**ダブルハングまど**【-窓】〔上げ下げ窓〕a ‘double-hung [sash] window.
**ダブル・ペリア**〖ゴルフ〗▷ ダブル・ペリア方式〔ハンディキャップ算出法の 1 つ; 12 ホールから算出〕the double peoria system.
**タブレット** ▷ タブレット化 tableting. ▷ tablet v. タブレット **PC**〔ペン入力のできるパソコン〕a tablet PC.
**たぶんか**【多文化】▷ 多文化共存 coexistence of (many) cultures; multicultural coexistence.
**タペータム**〖動〗=タペタム.
**たべきり**【食べ切り】〔食べきること〕eating at one sitting;〔1 回に食べられる量〕a single helping. ▷ この豆腐は一回~です. This tofu is a single-helping size. ▷ 食べ切りサイズ a single-helping size.

**たべくらべる**【食べ比べる】do food tasting; compare the food 「cooked by different people [served at different places].
**タペストリー** ▷ タペストリー・ガーデン〔多肉植物などを敷きつめて模様を描いた庭〕a tapestry garden.
**タペタム**〖動〗〔猫・サメ・クモなど様々な動物の網膜の裏側にある反射層〕a tapetum 《pl. tapeta》.
**たべづらい**【食べ辛い】unpleasant to eat. ▷ このヨーグルトは酸っぱくて~. This yoghurt is so sour it's almost inedible. ▷ ダイエット中の彼女の前でおいしいケーキを食べづらかった. I had a hard time eating some nice cake in front of her when she was on a diet.
**たべにくい**【食べにくい】hard to eat; difficult to get down; unpalatable. ▷ このハンバーガーは厚すぎて~. This hamburger is so thick it's hard to eat. / 小骨の多い魚は~から嫌いだ. I don't like fish with lots of small bones because they're so hard to eat. / オープンカフェでは通行人の視線があるので~という人もいる. Some people say they don't like to eat at outdoor cafes because they can be seen by passersby.
**たべやすい**【食べやすい】easy to eat; palatable. ▷ ~大きさのチキンナゲット chicken nuggets in an easy-to-eat size; bite-sized chicken nuggets. ▷ このチーズは味がマイルドでとても~. This cheese has a mild flavor and goes down very smoothly.
**食べやすくする** make sth ‘easier to eat [more palatable]. ▷ シチューの具を小さめに切って子供に食べやすくしました. I cut the solid ingredients of the stew into smaller pieces so that they would be easier for the children to eat.
**食べやすくなる** become ‘easier to eat [more palatable]. ▷ 納豆に少量の酢を加えるとあの臭みが消えて食べやすくなる. Fermented soybeans are more palatable if you add a little vinegar to eliminate the odor.
**食べやすさ** palatability. ▷ 食べやすさを考え、このキムチは辛さをおさえてあります. Out of palatability considerations [To make it easier to eat], we have toned downed this kimchi's spiciness.
**ダボ**〖ゴルフ〗▷ 連続ダボ consecutive [back-to-back] double bogeys.
**タポンツァン** ⇨ アデ・タポンツァン.
**たまあじさい**【玉紫陽花】〖植〗〔ユキノシタ科の多年草〕a bracted hydrangea; *Hydrangea involucrata*.
**たまかず**【球数】〖野球〗the number of pitches. ▷ 6 回表で彼は~がすでに 100 球を超えていた. By the bottom of the sixth inning he had already thrown more than 100 pitches.
**たまぎれ**[1]【球切れ】〔電球が切れること〕(a) lightbulb burn-out.
**たまぎれ**[2]【弾切れ】running out of ‘bullets [ammunition]. ▷ ~になる run out of [use up all of *one's*, exhaust *one's*] bullets [ammunition].
**たまぎわ**【球際】▷ ~に強い〔野球・サッカーなど〕(be, stay) focused on the ball [game] / フォールきのボールを捕えようとする~に強い選手 a relentless player who will even foul to try to capture the ball / ~に弱い〔野球・サッカーなど〕not focused on the ball [game] / あのチームの外野選手たちは~に弱く、捕球しかけたフライを落とすことが多い. The outfielders on that team have poor concentration and often miss the fly balls that they put after.
**たまご**【卵】▷ 卵かけご飯 rice with raw egg. 卵料理 an egg dish; egg dishes.
**たまごっち**〖商標〗〔携帯型ペット育成ゲーム機〕Tamagotchi.
**タマサートだいがく**【-大学】〔タイの〕Thammasat University.
**ダマじか**【-鹿】〖動〗a fallow deer; *Dama dama*.
**ダマトほう**【-法】〖米法〗⇨ イラン・リビアせいさいほう.
**たまばなれ**【球離れ】〖野球〗▷ 彼は腕が長く~が遅いので、

打者は非常に打ちにくい．Since his arms are long and he is slow to let go of the ball, his pitches are very hard for batters to hit.

**タマホリ** Tamahori, Lee (1950-　；ニュージーランド生まれの映画監督).

**たまむしのずし**【玉虫厨子】the Beetle Wing Shrine; a miniature shrine decorated with iridescent beetle wings, kept in the Treasure Hall of Hōryūji.

**たまゆら**【玉響】［ほんの少しの間］a (brief) moment. ◎ ～の命を燃やし尽くす live one's brief life to the「limit [fullest].

**たまりせき**【溜まり席】［相撲］［土俵近くの席］a ringside seat (at a sumo tournament).

**タマリロ**［植］［南米原産のナス科の低木］a tamarillo (pl. ~, ~s); a tree tomato; Cyphomandra betacea.

**ダマンスキーとう**【-島】［ウスリー川に浮かぶ島］Damansky Island. ▶ 中国名は珍宝島．

**ダミー** ◻ ダミー・カメラ ［威嚇用の防犯カメラ］a dummy (security, surveillance) camera.

**タミーム**［イラク北部の州］Tamim. ▶ 州都 キルクーク．

**タミフル**［商標・薬］［抗インフルエンザウイルス剤］Tamiflu.

**ダム**[1] ◻ 穴あきダム a flood control dam. 脱ダム宣言 ⇨ だつダムせんげん．◻ ダム湖 a dammed (up) lake; ［地質］［堰止め湖］a dammed lake; a lake formed by the natural damming of a river or stream.

**だめ**【駄目】
**駄目さ**（加減）worthlessness. ◎ 自分の～さ加減がわかってきた．I've come to realize「how worthless [how hopeless, what a loser] I am. ◻ ダメ男［女］a「worthless [lousy] man [woman]; 《俗》a loser.

**ためし**[2]【試し・験し】 ◻ お試し期間 a (free) trial period. お試しキャンペーン a trial campaign. お試し商品 a trial product; a sample (product). お試しセット a trial set. 試し割り ［空手などでの］《(tile-)》breaking test.

**タメル**［ネパール, カトマンズのツーリストの集まる地区］Thamel.

**だめん**【打面】［ドラムなどの, スティックが当たる面］a struck [an impact] face [surface]; ［ゴルフクラブなどの, ボールを打つ面］an impact face; a face.

**だめん**[2]【舵面】［空］the control surface.

**だめんず**［ダメな男たち］worthless [lousy] men; 《俗》male losers.

**たも**［植］［モクセイ科の落葉広葉樹］an ash (tree); Fraxinus mandshurica.

**タモキシフェン**［薬］［女性の乳がん治療薬］tamoxifen.

**たもぎたけ**【たもぎ茸】［菌］［食用キノコ］a golden oyster mushroom; Pleurotus (cornucopiae var.) citrinopileatus.

**たもくてき**【多目的】 ◻ 多目的スペース a multipurpose space. 多目的乗用車 a sport-utility vehicle (略: SUV). 多目的トイレ a multipurpose toilet (unit).

**タヤ** Taya, Maaouya Ould Sid'Ahmed (1941-　；モーリタニアの軍人・政治家; 大統領 [1984-2005]).

**たようと**【多用途】 ◎ ～の general-purpose 《cars》; utility 《vehicles》. ◻ 多用途支援機 ［軍］a utility support aircraft.

**たらいぶね**【盥舟】a tub boat.

**タラウマラぞく**【-族】［メキシコ北部の高地に住むインディオ］the Tarahumara; [1人] a Tarahumara 《pl. ~, ~s》.

**「ダラス」**［米国の, 富と権力を手中にした石油成金一族を描くTVドラマ］Dallas.

**ダラット**［ベトナム南部, ラムドン省の省都］Da Lat.

**タラップ** ◻ タラップ車 ［航空機乗降用車両］a passenger step (vehicle).

**たらのめ**【楤の芽】angelica tree buds; aralia shoots; taranome.

**タラバニ** Talabani, Jalal (1933-　；イラクの政治家; 大統領 [2005-　]).

**タラバロフとう**【-島】［中ロ国境, 大ウスリー島西部の島］Tarabarov Island.

**ダラボン** Darabont, Frank (1959-　；フランス生まれの映画監督・脚本家).

**ダラムサラ**［インド北部の町］Dharamsala. ▶ チベット亡命政府の所在地．

**タラモ**［料理］tarama. [= タラモサラタ]

**タラモサラタ**［料理］［ギリシャ料理でタラコとジャガイモをペースト状にして混ぜ合わせたもの］taramasalata; taramosalata.

**たられば**［仮定］the "if onlies"; the "(would haves, could haves, and) should haves." ◎ 今さら～の話をしてもしょうがない．"If only" stories won't do you any good now.｜It's too late to talk about "should haves."

**ダラン**［インドネシアの影絵芝居ワヤンの演者兼語り手］a dalang.

**タランさん**【-山】［インドネシア, スマトラ島中部の山］Mount Talang; (インドネシア語名) Gunung Talang.

**ダリーご**【-語】= ダリご．

**タリート**［ユダヤ教徒が祈祷の時に着用する肩掛け］a [the]「tallith [tallit, tallis].

**タリー・ランプ**［放送］［放送中であることを示すため, カメラやモニターなどについている赤ランプ; 放送表示灯］a tally lamp.

**ダリご**【-語】［アフガニスタンの公用語の1つ］Dari.

**だりつ**【打率】 ◻ 対左投手［対右投手］打率 a [one's] batting average against「left-[right-]handed pitchers.

**ダリッツ** Dalitz, Richard Henry (1925-2006; オーストリア生まれ英国の物理学者).

**タリル**［イラク南部の地域］Tallil.

**タル・アファル**［イラク北部, ニナワ州の都市］Tall Afar.

**ダルク**［薬物依存者リハビリセンター］a DARC; a drug addiction rehabilitation center; a drug rehab center.

**タルクかん**【-缶】［商標］TULC. ▶ Toyo Ultimate Can の頭文字から．

**ダルこ**【-湖】［インド北部, カシミール地方の湖］Dal Lake.

**たるこう**【樽香】［ワインやウイスキーに含まれる貯蔵樽の香り］barrel [cask] aroma [scent, smell].

**タルトス**［シリア西部, 地中海沿岸の町］Tartus; Tartous.

**タルト・フランベ**［料理］［フランス・アルザス地方の郷土料理］a「tarte [tart] flambé.

**ダルドリー** Daldry, Stephen (1960-　；英国生まれの映画監督).

**ダルトン** Dalton, Timothy (1946-　；英国生まれの映画俳優).

**ダルナビル**［薬］［エイズ治療薬］darunavir. ▶ 商品名はプレジスタ．

**ダルフール**［スーダン西部の地方］Darfur.

**ダルフールふんそう**【-紛争】［スーダン西部ダルフール地方で2003年から行われている民族紛争］the Darfur conflict.

**ダルブッカ, ダラブッカ, ダルブカ**［楽器］［アラブ音楽で使われる酒杯型の片面太鼓］a darbuka.

**タルボサウルス**［古生物］［肉食恐竜］a Tarbosaur; (属名) Tarbosaurus.

**だるま**【達磨】 ◻ だるま市 a daruma fair; a fair at which round red Bodhidharma dolls and other good-luck decorations are sold.

**だるまいんこ**【達磨鸚哥】［鳥］［オウム科の鳥］a red-breasted parakeet; a moustached parakeet; Psittacula alexandri.

**タルミヤ**［イラク, バグダッド近郊の町］Tarmiya(h).

**タルラック**［フィリピン, ルソン島の州］Tarlac.

**ダレスこくさいくうこう**【-国際空港】［米国ワシントンD.C. にある国際空港］Washington Dulles International Airport.

**「誰にでも秘密がある」**［映画］Everybody Has Secrets.

**だれば**【だれ場】［芝居などで盛り上がりに欠け, 客が退屈するような場面］a「slow [dull] part [scene]; ［観客の緊張をいったんゆるめるため, 意図的にドラマの展開を中断する場面］a

「slower [quieter] part [scene]; a breather. ◐ この映画は～がなく, 内容が濃い. This is a tightly woven film with never a dull moment. ◐ 3 時間にわたる長丁場の舞台では見せ場と～の巧妙な配合が必要だ. A long, three-hour play requires an adept mixture of highlight scenes and slower sections.
「誰も寝てはならぬ」〔プッチーニ作曲のオペラ『トゥーランドット』中のアリア〕Nessun dorma.
タレント ▭ タレント養成所 a training facility for (TV) entertainers.
タロコぞく【-族】〔台湾の先住民族〕the Taroko;〔1 人〕a Taroko《pl. ～》.
タワー ▭ タワー・マンション a high-rise [*apartment building [*condominium, "block (of flats)]; *an apartment [a condominium] tower; "a tower block.
ダン Dunne, Griffin (1955- ; 米国の映画俳優・監督).
だんあつ【弾圧】 ▭ 宗教弾圧 oppression [suppression] of religion; religious「oppression [suppression]. 政治弾圧 political oppression.
たんい²【単位】 ▭ 単位型投資信託〔ユニット型投資信託〕a unit-type investment trust; a unit trust; a unit investment trust. 単位互換履修生 a credit-exchange student; a student on a (joint) credit-recognition program. 単位料金区域〖電話〗a (single unit charge) message area（略: MA）.
たんいつ【単一】 ▭ 単一電子メモリー〖電算〗a single-electron memory（略: SEM）.
たんいはっせい【単為発生】〖生物〗〖単為生殖〗parthenogenesis. ▷ parthenogenetic adj.; parthenogenetically adv.
だんえん【断煙】〔喫煙をやめること〕smoking cessation.
だんか⁵【炭化】 ▭ 炭化水素化合物 a hydrocarbon compound. 炭化水素油 (a) hydrocarbon oil. 炭化米〖考古〗carbonized rice.
だんか²【檀家】 ▭ 檀家制度 the 《Buddhist temple》lay supporter system.
だんかい¹【団塊】 ▭ 団塊マネー baby-boomers' money; the retirement wealth of the generation born immediately after World War II.
だんかい²【段階】 ▭ 途中[中途]段階 an intermediate stage. ▭ 段階金利 tiered interest rates; a tiered interest rate system.
たんかく¹【単核】 ▭ 単核球 a mononuclear cell. 単核細胞 a mononuclear cell.
たんかん²【胆管】 ▭ 胆管細胞がん〖医〗cholangiocellular carcinoma（略: CCC）.
たんかん³【単館】 ▭ 単館系映画 an art-house film. 単館公開〖映画などの〕(a) single-theater [(an) art-house] release. 単館上映〖映画などの〕(a) single-theater [(an) art-house] screening [showing].
ダンカン Duncan, Michael Clarke (1957- ; 米国の映画俳優).
たんき⁵【短期】 ▭ 短期公社債投信 a「short-term [limited-term] bond investment trust. 短期工法〖建〗a「rapid [quick] construction method. 短期就労者 a short-term worker; a person in short-term employment. 短期滞在 (make) a short stay. 短期地価動向調査〔国土交通省の発表する〕the survey of short-term land-price trends. 短期離職＝早期離職（⇨そうしょく）.
「単騎, 千里を走る」〔映画〕Riding Alone for Thousands of Miles;〔中国語タイトル〕千里走単騎.
たんきだいがくきじゅんきょうかい【短期大学基準協会】the Japan Association for College Accreditation（略: JACA）.
たんきんぞく【単金属】〖化〗a single metal.
タングステン ▭ タングステン鉱〖鉱〗tungsten ore.
たんぐつした【短靴下】(a pair of) socks.
タンクバン・プラフ〔インドネシア, ジャワ島西部の活火山名〕Tangkuban Prahu.

タングラとうげ【-峠】〔中国の青海省とチベットを結ぶ峠〕the Tanggula Mountain Pass.
だんけい【男系】 ▭ 男系男子 a male descendant in the male line《of Imperial Ancestors》.
たんげつ【単月】a single month. ◐ 円高ドル安を食い止めるための日銀による 1 月の介入は, ～で過去最高だった昨年 9 月の 5 兆円をすでにはるかに上回っている. The Bank of Japan's intervention in January to hold down the yen's rise against the dollar has already far outpaced last September's「monthly record [record for a single month] of 5 trillion yen. ◐ 9 月の米貿易赤字は～として過去最大の赤字額を更新した. The US trade deficit for September was the highest for any month on record. ▭ 単月増加額[数, 量] a monthly increase.
たんけっしょう【単結晶】 ▭ 単結晶（シリコン）太陽電池 a single crystal (silicon) solar cell.
たんげん【単元】 ▭ 単元株〖証券〗stock shares constituting one「trading unit [round lot] (and conferring the right to one vote). ◐ ～株数設定[変更] the establishment of [a change in] the number of stock shares constituting a「trading unit [round lot]. 単元株制度〖証券〗the unit stock system. 単元未満株〖証券〗an odd-lot share.
たんこう³【探鉱】 ▭ 探鉱権 mineral (and oil) exploration rights.
だんごう【談合】 ▭ 官製談合 government-led bid-rigging. ▭ 談合事件 a bid-rigging「scandal [case]. 談合情報 information about bid-rigging《provided to the authorities》. 談合政治 politics conducted through behind-the-scenes collusion. 談合組織 a bid-rigging「ring [group].
たんごせつ【端午節】〔中国の祭日; 旧暦 5 月 5 日〕the Dragon Boat Festival; the Tuen Ng Festival; Duan wu jie.
たんこん【単婚】monogamy. ▭ 単婚家族〖形態〗the monogamous family;〔1 つの〕a monogamous family.
たんさ【探査】 ▭ 探査船〖海洋・宇宙などへの〕an「exploration [exploratory] ship [vessel].
「ダンサー・イン・ザ・ダーク」〔映画〕Dancer in the Dark.
たんざい【単剤】〖薬〗a single agent. ▭ 単剤療法〔治療〕(a) single-agent「therapy [treatment].
タンザナイト〖宝石〕a tanzanite;〖鉱〕tanzanite.
たんし⁷【端子】 ▭ AUX 端子 an AUX terminal. ▶ AUX は auxiliary の略. 外部(接続)端子 an external (connection [connecting]) terminal.
たんじ²【担持】(a) support. ～する support《a catalyst》. ◐ ～パラジウム触媒 a supported palladium catalyst / シリカ～白金触媒 a silica-supported platinum catalyst; platinum loaded on silica. ▭ 金属担持触媒 a metal-supported catalyst.
たんじかん【短時間】 ▭ 短時間勤務制度 a「shortened [shorter] work-hour system.
たんじくびりゅうし【単磁区微粒子】〖物〗a single-domain magnetic particle.
だんしプロテニスきょうかい【男子-協会】the Association of Tennis Professionals（略: ATP）.
タンジャ Tandja, Mamadou (1938- ; ニジェールの政治家; 大統領《1999- 》).
たんじゅう¹【胆汁】 ▭ 胆汁酸ミセル〖生化〗bile acid micelle.
たんしゅうき【短周期】 ▭ 短周期地震動 a short-period (seismic) tremor. 短周期波〖地震〗a short-period (seismic) wave;〖海洋〗a short-period wave.
たんじゅん【単純】 ▭ 単純作業 simple work; a repetitive job;〔不熟練作業〕unskilled work. 単純写真〖医〗〖造影剤を使用しないで撮影された X 線フィルム〕plain film. ◐ 胸部[腹部]～写真 chest [abdominal] plain film. 単純所持〖法〗〔覚醒剤・猥褻物などの〕simple pos-

session 《of child pornography》.
**たんじゅんせいけっかんしゅ**【単純性血管腫】〖医〗hemangioma simplex.
**だんじょ**【男女】▫▫ 男女格差指数 a [the] gender gap index (略：GGI); 〔社会進出の〕a [the] gender-related development index (略：GDI). 男女共同参画白書〔内閣府の〕the White Paper on Gender Equality 《2005》. 男女混合チーム a mixed male and female team.
**たんじょう**【誕生】▫▫ 誕生死 being born dead; (a) death (of a baby) before, during or at birth.
**だんじょきょうどうさんかくすいしんほんぶ**【男女共同参画推進本部】the Headquarters for the Promotion of Gender Equality.
**ダンジョン**〔地下牢〕a dungeon.
**だんじり**【檀尻・楽車】▫▫ だんじり祭り a *danjiri* festival.
**たんしん**³【単身】▫▫ 単身赴任手当 an allowance [paid to] employees on unaccompanied postings.
**だんしん**【弾芯】〖銃砲〗a bullet core.
**だんしん**【弾信】＝しょうひしゃしんようだんたいせいめいほけん.
**たんしんしつ(しょう)**【単心室(症)】〖医〗single ventricle; univentricular heart.
**たんす**【箪笥】▫▫ 箪笥株券 a stock certificate held by the stockholder; a hoarded stock certificate.
**「箪笥」**〔映画〕A Tale of Two Sisters.
**ダンス** ▫▫ ダンス・ムーブメント・セラピー dance/movement therapy. ダンス・ユニット a dance 'unit [team, group].
**たんすい**³【湛水】▫▫ 冬期湛水〔田に冬場も水を張っておくこと〕winter flooding (of rice fields).
**ダンスト** Dunst, Kirsten (1982– ; 米国の映画女優).
**ダンス・ドリル**〔米国で球技系スポーツのハーフタイムなどに行われるリズムダンス〕dance/drill.
**だんせい**²【男性】▫▫ 男性原理 〖心理〗the masculine principle. 男性終止 〖音楽〗a masculine cadence. 男性度 〖心理〗masculinity.
**だんせい**³【弾性】▫▫ 弾性表面波 〖物〗a surface acoustic wave. 弾性流体潤滑 〖物〗elastohydrodynamic lubrication (略：EHL).
**だんせいき**【男性器】〖解〗〔陰茎, 精巣などの総称〕the male genitalia; the male genital organs; 〔(1) the male genitals; 〔特に陰茎〕the male genital organ.
**だんせいきのう**【男性機能】male potency; virility. ▫～の低下[強化] a decline [an increase] in 'male potency [virility].
**だんせいち**【弾性値】〖経〗elasticity; a value of elasticity. ▫▫ 価格弾性値 ＝価格弾力性 (⇨かかく²). 所得弾性値 ＝所得弾力性 (⇨しょとく).
**「断絶の時代」**〔P・F・ドラッカーの著作〕The Age of Discontinuity.
**たんそ**²【炭素】▫▫ 炭素原単位 carbon intensity; a carbon intensity 《of…》. 炭素14 〖化〗〔放射性炭素〕carbon(-14); ～14年代測定法〔考古〕carbon(-14) dating. 炭素繊維強化炭素複合材料 (a) 'carboncarbon [C/C] composite.
**だんそう**³【断層】▫▫ 海底断層 a submarine [an underwater] fault; an ocean-floor [a sea-floor] fault. 共役断層 conjugate faults; 〔片方〕a conjugate fault. ▫▫ 断層群 a fault complex; a 'complex [group] of faults.
**たんそかくりリーダーシップ・フォーラム**〔炭素隔離〕〔二酸化炭素を地下に貯留する技術に関する国際会合〕Carbon Sequestration Leadership Forum (略：CSLF).
**だんたい**¹【団体】▫▫ 団体協約締結権 the right to enter into a collective agreement. 団体受験 taking 'a test [an exam] in a group; group testing. 団体信用生命保険 group credit life insurance. 団体展 〖美術協会〗が主催する展覧会〕an exhibition by members of the same group; a group exhibition. 団体優勝 《win》'victory [the championship] in a team event.
**たんたいじ**【単胎児】a single-birth child; a singleton.
**ダンテ** Dante, Joe (1946– ; 米国の映画監督).
**「ダンディ2 華麗な冒険」**〔英国の, しゃれたスパイものの TV ドラマ〕The Persuaders.
**「探偵ハート&ハート」**〔米国の, 富豪夫妻が主人公の探偵ものの TV ドラマ〕Hart to Hart.
**「ダンテズ・ピーク」**〔映画〕Dante's Peak.
**タンデム** ▫▫ タンデム走行 riding in tandem; tandem riding.
**たんとう**²【担当】▫▫ 担当官庁 ＝所管官庁 (⇨しょかん³).
**たんとう**⁷【短答】〔試験問題などの〕a short answer. ▫▫ 短答式試験問題 a short answer type question.
**たんどう**¹【胆道】▫▫ 胆道炎 〖医〗inflammation of the biliary tract; biliary tract inflammation. ▫急性～炎 acute inflammation of the biliary tract. 胆道拡張症 〖医〗biliary dilatation.
**だんとう**²【弾頭】▫▫ 化学弾頭 《a missile equipped with》a chemical warhead. 通常弾頭〔核弾頭でない〕a conventional warhead.
**タン・ドゥン**【譚盾】Tan Dun (1957– ; 中国出身の作曲家・指揮者).
**たんどく**²【単独】▫▫ 単独決算 〖会計〗〔連結決算に対して〕a separate account; an account (for one section) in isolation; separate figures for a single section (of a larger corporation). 単独(行動)主義 a penchant for independent action; 〔国際紛争などに際しての〕unilateralism. ▫～行動主義者 a non-joiner. 単独犯説 the theory that a crime 'was carried out by one person [had a sole perpetrator].
**タンドリー・チキン**〔インド料理の1つ〕tandoori chicken.
**「歎異抄」**〔親鸞の語録〕Passages Deploring Deviations of Faith.
**だんねつ**【断熱】▫▫ 断熱住宅 an insulated house; a house with insulation.
**たんねん**²【単年】a single year. ▫▫ 単年契約 a one-year [an annual] contract.
**たんねんど**【単年度】a single fiscal year. ▫その会社はまだ累積損失が残っているが, ～では2年連続黒字になった. That company still has a cumulative loss, but it has been in the black for two consecutive fiscal years. ▫▫ 単年度方式 a single-(fiscal-)year system. 単年度予算 a one-year budget.
**だんのうらのたたかい[かっせん]**【壇ノ浦の戦い[合戦]】〔日本史〕〔1185年の〕the Battle of 'Dannoura [Dan-noura].
**タンバール**〔写真〕〔ソフトフォーカスレンズ〕Thambar.
**ダンバウ**〖楽器〗〔ベトナムの一弦琴〕dan bau.
**たんぱく**²【蛋白】▫▫ たんぱく同化剤 〖薬〗＝たんぱく同化ステロイド. たんぱく同化ステロイド an anabolic steroid.
**だんばく**【段瀑】a tiered waterfall; a cascade (waterfall).
**タンパクさんぜんプロジェクト**【-3000-】〔2002年度から文部科学省が行っているタンパク質の構造・機能解析プロジェクト〕the National Project on Protein Structural and Functional Analyses.
**たんぱくしつ**【蛋白質】▫▫ 蛍光たんぱく質 (a) fluorescent protein (略：FP). ▫緑色蛍光～ (a) green fluorescent protein (略：GFP). 不凍たんぱく質 (an) antifreeze protein (略：AFP). ▫▫ たんぱく質燐酸化酵素 protein kinase.
**タンパリング**〔野球〕〔選手契約に関する不正な事前取引〕tampering; illicit [unauthorized] negotiations between players, coaches, managers, or umpires of different clubs.
**たんパン**【短-】《a pair of》shorts.
**たんばんよく**【炭盤浴】warming *one*self ["bathing"]

over mildly heated charcoal board.
**たんびへきさん**【短尾碧鵲】⦅鳥⦆〔カラス科の鳥〕a short-tailed green magpie; *Cissa thalassina*.
**ダンピング** ▫ ダンピング競争〔ダンピング合戦〕a dumping war.
**タンブリ**〔フィリピン, マクタン島のリゾート〕Tambuli.
**たんぽ**¹【担保】▫ 追加担保 (an) additional「collateral [security]. ▫ 担保金 security money;《pay ￥1,000,000 as》a security; a deposit. 担保評価額 the appraised value of a security.
**タンホア** ⇨タインホア.
**だんボール**【段-】▫ 段ボール原紙 base paper for corrugated paperboard. 段ボール古紙 ⇨こし³. 段ボールシー

ト〔段ボール原紙を貼り合わせて作る〕(a) corrugated cardboard sheet. 段ボールニット⦅服飾⦆3-layer cotton (knit).
**タンボチェ**〔ネパール, エヴェレスト山麓の村〕Tengboche.
**ダンマーン** ＝ダンマン.
**ダンマン**〔サウジアラビア, 東部州の州都・ペルシャ湾沿岸の都市〕Dammam.
**だんりゅう**¹【断流】▫ 断流現象〔河川の〕(a) drying up《of the Yellow River》.
**だんりょく**【弾力】▫ 弾力化 elasticizing; elasticization. ◎補助金の給付基準を~化する elasticise the standards for payment of subsidies. 弾力条項⦅法⦆〔公的予算の弾力的支出を認める条項〕an elastic clause.
**だんわ**【談話】▫ 談話分析⦅言⦆discourse analysis.

# ち

**ち**²【血】▫ 血の同盟〔盟約〕〔朝鮮戦争時の中国と北朝鮮の〕the "blood alliance" (between China and North Korea).
**「チアーズ!」**〔映画〕Bring It On.
**ちあん**【治安】▫ 治安悪化 a decline in public security;〔犯罪の増加〕an increase in crime; a rising crime rate. ◎外国人労働者の受け入れについては, 労働市場の混乱や~悪化の恐れがあるなどの理由から慎重論を唱える人が多い。Many people advise caution on the admission of foreign workers out of fear that the labor market might suffer and the crime rate might rise. 治安攪乱 (a) disturbance of the public「peace [order]. 治安機関 a security「organization [organ, agency, body]. 治安緊急事態 security emergency; 治安権限 responsibility for security; security responsibilities. 治安状況 a《deteriorating》security situation《in Iraq》. 治安情勢 security (conditions); a security situation; a [the] state of security. ◎その国の~情勢は日に日に悪化している。Security [The security situation] in the country is deteriorating day by day. 治安状態 the state of public order. 治安対策 (public) security measures; measures [steps] to ensure law and order. 治安問題 problems「of [with] public order; public order issues.
**ちあんいじ**【治安維持】▫ 治安維持活動 a public security operation.
**ちい**²【地位】▫ 地位向上 (an) improvement in the status《of women》. 地位利用 abuse [misuse] of *one's*「position [status]. ◎~利用収賄 accepting [taking] a bribe in return for misusing *one's* position.
**ちいき**¹【地域】▫ 緊急調整地域〔ある事業分野で供給過剰などが見られ需給調整の対象となる地域〕an emergency adjustment area. ▫ 地域安全ボランティア a neighborhood watch volunteer; 「local [neighborhood] security volunteer. 地域運営学校 a locally managed school. 地域 FM local FM. 地域興し〔起こし〕local [regional] revitalization [development]. 地域学 local area studies; research on「a [*one's, sb's*] locality. 地域活性化 regional revitalization. ◎観光によって~活性化を図る try to「revitalize [bring life to] an area through tourism. 地域活性化創造技術研究開発補助金 a subsidy for the cost(s) of「R & D [research and development] on creative technology for regional revitalization. 地域がん診療拠点病院 a regional hub hospital for cancer treatment. 地域がん登録 a regional cancer registry; a population-based cancer registry. 地域協定 a regional agreement. 地域計画学 regional planning. 地域経済報告〔日本銀行の〕the Regional Economic Report. 地域限定価格 a region-specific price. 地域限定採用 ＝勤務地限定

採用 (⇨きんむ). 地域限定車 a「region-specific [locally marketed] car (model). 地域高規格道路 a (Japanese) road designated as a regional high-standard highway. 地域貢献 a contribution to a community. ◎~貢献活動 an activity contributing to a community. 地域雇用創造支援事業 a program to help create local employment. 地域再生本部〔内閣に設置された〕the Headquarters for the Regional Revitalization. 地域支援病院 ＝地域医療支援病院 (⇨ちいきいりょう). 地域自治 regional autonomy. ◎~自治区 a regional autonomous area / ~自治組織 an autonomous regional organization. 地域社会学 regional sociology; regional and community studies. 地域住宅交付金 a grant from the central government to local governments to encourage local initiative in developing housing. 地域審議会 a regional council. 地域スタッフ a local staff (member);〔NHK〕a local license fee contracting and collection staff; a local staff (member) who encourages viewers to sign license fee contracts. 地域戦争 regional warfare; a regional war. 地域相関研究〔生態学的研究〕an ecological study. 地域創業助成金 a local business start-up「grant [subsidy]. 地域調整手当 a cost-of-living allowance (略: COLA). 地域特性「distinguishing features [character] of the district. 地域猫 a (stray [homeless])「neighborhood cat. 地域爆撃〔都市への〕area bombing. [＝都市爆撃 (⇨とし⁴)] 地域復興チーム ＝ちほうふっこう(しえん)チーム〔高齢者介護のための〕a comprehensive regional support center (for the elderly). 地域防災計画 a local disaster-damage prevention plan; a「plan [project] for「local [regional] disaster-damage prevention. ◎相互間~防災計画 a mutual local disaster-damage prevention plan. 地域ボランティア〔活動〕local [neighborhood] volunteering;〔人〕a「local [neighborhood] volunteer. 地域密着店⦅商⦆a community-based「office [shop, store]. 地域密着路線〔企業などの活動方針として〕a community-based policy. 地域リスク〔災害・治安悪化などの〕a「local [regional] risk. 地域枠〔地元出身者のための入学・採用枠〕(an enrollment, a job) quota for「locals [local residents].
**ちいきいりょう**【地域医療】▫ 地域医療支援病院 a regional general hospital coordinating community health care.
**ちいきかいぜんたいさくきょうぎかい**【地域改善対策協議会】〔同和問題早期解決のための〕the Consultative Council on Regional Improvement Measures.
**ちいきこうきょうこうつうかっせいかさいせいほう**【地域公共交通活性化再生法】⦅法⦆the Law Concerning the Revitalization of Regional Public Transporta-

ちいきこうようかいはつ

tion. ▶ 正式名称は「地域公共交通の活性化及び再生に関する法律」.
**ちいきこようかいはつそくしんほう**【地域雇用開発促進法】〖法〗 the Law Concerning the Promotion of Local Employment Development.
**ちいきさいせいほう**【地域再生法】〖法〗 the Regional Revitalization Law.
**ちいきさいとうしほう**【地域再投資法】〖米法〗 the Community Reinvestment Act (略: CRA).
**ちいきじゅうたくけいかく**【地域住宅計画】＝ホープけいかく.
**ちいきしょく**【地域色】regional「color [flavor].◐ ～豊かな食文化 a「food culture [cuisine] rich in [full of] regional flavor.◐ お雑煮は～が出る料理だ. Zōni is a dish that exudes regional flavor.◐ ～を強く打ち出した番組 a (TV, radio) program that strongly conveys (a sense of) regional color.
**ちいきしんこうせいびこうだん**【地域振興整備公団】the Japan Regional Development Corporation (略: JRDC). ▶ 2004 年, 都市部門は都市再生機構へ改組, 産業系部門は中小企業基盤整備機構へ改組.
**ちいきテロたいさくきこう**【地域-対策機構】〔上海協力機構がタシケントに設立した機構〕the Regional Anti-Terrorism Structure (略: RATS).
**ちいきほけんほう**【地域保健法】〖法〗 the Regional Health Law.
**「小さな中国のお針子」**〔映画〕Balzac and the Little Chinese Seamstress.
**チーズ** ◻️ ウォッシュ(ド)(・タイプ)チーズ (a) washed-rind cheese. クリームチーズ cream cheese. スモークチーズ (a) smoked cheese. ソフト[ハード]チーズ (a)「soft [hard](-type) cheese. ナチュラルチーズ (a) natural cheese.
**チードル** Cheadle, Don (1964- ; 米国の映画俳優).
**チーパオ**【旗袍】〔服飾〕〔チャイナドレス〕《＜Chin.》a Qipao; a traditional (body-hugging) Chinese dress; a mandarin gown.
**チーマージャン**【芝麻醬】〔調味料〕(Chinese) sesame paste.
**チーママ**〔バーのマダム 2 人のうちの若いほう〕the junior mistress《of a bar》.
**チーム** ◻️ チーム医療 team medicine. チーム・スピリット《develop, build》team spirit. チーム・スプリント《自転車競技》〔種目〕the《men's》team sprint. チーム作り team building; building [forming, putting together] a team. チーム防御率【野球】a team「earned run average [ERA]; a team ERA. チーム力 team strength; team power. チーム・リーダー a team leader.
**チーロイきしゃ**【奇瑞汽車】＝きずいきしゃ.
**チェア** ◻️ チェアウォーカー〔車いす生活者〕a wheelchair user.
**チェイニー** Cheney, Dick (1941- ; 米国の政治家; 副大統領《2001- 》; 本名 Richard Bruce Cheney).
**「チェオクの剣」**〔韓国のテレビドラマ〕The Legendary Police Woman; (別タイトル) Damo; The Undercover Lady Detective; (漢字表記は) 茶母.
**チェザーナ**〔イタリア北西部, ピエモンテ州の村〕Cesana.
**チェサピーク**〔米国ヴァージニア州南東部の都市〕Chesapeake.
**チェ・ジウ**【崔志宇】Choi Ji-woo (1975- ; 韓国の女優).
**チェスト・ガード**〔胸部防護具〕a chest guard.
**チェック¹** ◻️ チェック項目 an item for「checking [「ticking]; a「check [「tick] box. ◐ この本はマンションびの～項目を列挙してあって便利だ. This book has a list of items to「*check [「tick] when choosing an apartment, which makes it convenient. チェック・システム a check system. チェック漏れ〔点検漏れ〕(a) failure to「check [inspect]《a mechanical part》; (確認漏れ) (a) failure to「confirm [check]《a signature》; (質問漏れなど) 該当...に印をつけるのを忘れること (a) failure to「fill in

[complete] an item. ◐ 以下の項目に一つでも～漏れがあると正しい診断ができません. If any of the items below「is blank [has not been filled in], it will be impossible to make a correct diagnosis. | No diagnosis will be possible if there are any gaps in the following fields. / ～漏れで見たい番組を見逃してしまった. I didn't make a note of the program I wanted to see, so I missed it. / チェックリストを作成し～漏れを防ぐ make a check-list to「prevent omissions [make sure nothing is left out].
**チェブラーシカ**〔ロシアのアニメ・キャラクター〕Cheburashka.
**チェ・ミンシク**【崔岷植】Choi Min-sik (1963- ; 韓国の映画俳優).
**チェ・ミンス**【崔民秀】Choi「Min-soo [Min-su] (1962- ; 韓国の映画俳優).
**チェルソム** Chelsom, Peter (1956- ; 英国生まれの映画監督).
**ちえん**【遅延】◻️ 遅延行為〔裁判などでの〕delaying action;〔競技中の〕delaying play. 遅延証明書〔交通機関が発行する〕a delay slip. 遅延戦術 delaying [delay] tactics.
**チェン・カイコー**【陳凱歌】Chen Kaige (1952- ; 中国生まれの映画監督).
**チェンジ・オブ・コントロール**〔ライセンス契約などにおいて, 買収などで一方の会社の支配権が変わった場合はもう一方の会社が契約を破棄できるとする条項; 資本拘束条項〕a change-of-control clause.
**「チェンジング・レーン」**〔映画〕Changing Lanes.
**チェンマイ・イニシアチブ**〔アジア域内における国際金融協力〕the Chiang Mai Initiative (略: CMI).
**チェンライ**〔タイ北部の県〕Chiang Rai.
**チオトロピウム**〖薬〗〔気管支拡張薬〕tiotropium.
**ちか¹**【地下】◐ 地下壕 a bunker; a [an underground] dugout. 地下高速道路 an underground expressway. 地下生物圏 the deep biosphere. 地下貯留〔雨水などの〕underwater storage. ◐ ～貯留槽 an underground storage tank. 地下トンネル an underground [a subterranean] tunnel. 地下発射基地〔ミサイルなどの〕an underground launching site. 地下評論員〔インターネットでは一般市民を装い反政府的な発言を政府の望む方向に導く役割を果たす工作員〕a government undercover online commentator. 地下ルート〔地下を通るルート〕an underground [a subterranean] route;〔非合法の流通経路〕underground channels. ◐ A 駅からの延伸線は～ルートになっている. From A. Station the new extension「goes underground [follows an underground route]. / 彼はそのドラッグを～ルートから手に入れた. He got hold of the drug「through underground channels [illicitly].
**ちか²**【地価】 ◻️ 地価デフレ falling land prices; land price deflation.
**ちがき**【稚牡蠣】a young oyster.
**ちかく³**【地殻】◻️ 地殻内微生物 a subsurface「microorganism [microbe]. 地殻プレート〖地質〗a「tectonic [crustal] plate.
**ちかく⁴**【知覚】◐ 知覚的防衛〖心理〗〔不快なもの, 望まなくないものが無意識的に知覚されにくいこと〕(a) perceptual defense.
**ちかこうじほう**【地価公示法】〖法〗the Public Notice of Land Prices Law.
**ちかしげんほう**【地下資源法】〔ロシア連邦の〕the Underground Resources Law.
**ちかしつ**【地下室】◻️ 地下室マンション a condominium on a slope with residential floors designated as basements in order to get around zoning limits on height; a multibasement condominium.
**ちかてつ**【地下鉄】◐ 地下鉄工事 *subway [「underground, tube] construction (work); a subway [「underground, tube] construction [repair] job; subway [「underground, tube] repair work [repairs]. 地下鉄路

線図[マップ] *a subway ["an underground, a tube] (route) map.
ちかん² 【痴漢】 ▶痴漢被害 suffering [being the victim of] (a) sexual attack; being (sexually) molested; 〔電車内などでの〕being groped; suffering「groping [a groping attack].
ちかん³【置換】 ▶置換療法〔医〕replacement therapy. ◇ニコチン〔ホルモン〕～療法 nicotine [hormone] replacement therapy.
「チキチキマシン猛レース」〔米国の, 自動車レースがテーマのTV ギャグアニメ〕Wacky Races.
ちきゅう¹【地球】 ▶地球観測衛星 an earth observation satellite (略: EOS). 地球球体説 the「spherical-earth [round-earth]」theory. 地球近傍小天体〔天〕a near-earth object (略: NEO). 地球時間 earth time. 地球市民 a global citizen; a citizen of the earth. 地球周回軌道 (an) earth orbit; (a) Clarke orbit. 地球自由振動【地球物理】Earth's free oscillations. ◇常時～自由振動 Earth's continuous free oscillations. 地球深層ガス〔石油生成に関する仮説上の〕(a) deep-earth gas. 地球深部 earth's depths; the depths of the earth; areas [places, regions] deep in the earth. 地球深部探査船 a deep-sea drilling vessel. 地球地図〔日本の提唱による地球環境問題解明のためのプロジェクト〕Global Mapping; the Global Mapping Project; 〔作成された地図〕a global map. ◇～地図国際運営委員会 the International Steering Committee for Global Mapping (略: ISCGM). 地球平和監視時計〔直近の核実験からの日数を表示する時計, 広島市の原爆資料館にある〕the Peace Watch Tower. 地球防衛軍〔SFなどでの〕an [the] Earth Defense Force; a [the] Terrestrial Defense Force. 地球惑星科学 earth and planetary sciences. ▶地球物理の対象が広がりこのように呼ばれるようになってきている.
ちきゅうおんだんか【地球温暖化】 ▶地球温暖化対策(推進)大綱〔環境省の〕Guidelines for Measures to Prevent Global Warming.
ちきゅうおんだんかたいさくすいしんほう【地球温暖化対策推進法】〔法〕the Law for the Promotion of Measures to Deal with Global Warming.
ちきゅうおんだんかたいさく・ヒートアイランドたいさくモデルちいき【地球温暖化対策・対策-地域】a model district for measures against global warming and heat islands.
ちきゅうおんだんかぼうしかいぎ【地球温暖化防止会議】the Conference of Parties of the UN Framework Convention on Climate Change (略: UNFCCC).
ちきゅうがい【地球外】 ▶地球外知性体 =地球外知的生命体. 地球外知的生命体 an intelligent「alien [extraterrestrial being]; extraterrestrial intelligence. 地球外微生物 an extraterrestrial「microorganism [microbe].
ちきゅうかんきょうけんしょう【地球環境憲章】=けいだんれんちきゅうかんきょうけんしょう.
ちきゅうかんきょうこうどうかいぎ【地球環境行動会議】Global Environmental Action (略: GEA).
ちきゅうかんきょうこくさいぎいんれんめい【地球環境国際議員連盟】the Global Legislators Organization for a Balanced Environment (略: GLOBE).
ちきゅうかんきょうさんぎょうぎじゅつけんきゅうきこう【地球環境産業技術研究機構】〔日本の法人〕the Research Institute of Innovative Technology for the Earth (略: RITE).
ちきゅうかんきょうパートナーシッププラザ【地球環境-】the Global Environment Information Centre (略: GEIC).
ちきゅうかんきょうモニタリング・システム【地球環境-】〔国連環境計画の〕the Global Environment Monitoring System (略: GEMS).

ちきゅうかんそくサミット【地球観測-】the 《second》Earth Observation Summit.
ちきゅうきぼせいぶつたようせいがいきょう【地球規模生物多様性概況】the Global Biodiversity Outlook (略: GBO).
ちきゅうシミュレーター【地球-】〔電算〕〔日本製のスーパーコンピューター〕the Earth Simulator.
ちきゅうせいぶつかいぎ【地球生物会議】〔動物愛護団体〕All Life In a Viable Environment (略: ALIVE).
ちきん【遅筋】〔生理〕(a) slow muscle. ▶遅筋線維 (a) slow muscle fiber.
チキン ▶チキンカツ【料理】a deep-fried breaded cutlet of chicken.
チキン・ゲーム (a game of) chicken.
「チキンラン」〔アニメ映画〕Chicken Run.
チキン・レース (a game of) chicken. ◇対向車と～をする play chicken with an oncoming car.
ちく¹【地区】 ▶地区優勝 victory in [winning] a regional tournament; 〔米国のスポーツで〕victory in [winning] a division championship.
ちく³【築】 ▶平成元年～のマンション an apartment building「built in [dating (back) to] 1989. ◇木造家屋は～20年で住宅としてはほとんど無価値になることが多い. Wooden houses built 20 years ago [Twenty-year-old wooden houses] are often almost worthless as homes. ▶築後 ◇～後10年の二階家 a two-story house built 10 years ago; a 10-year-old two-story house. 築年数 the age (in years) 《of a building》.
ちくあさ【築浅】 ▶築浅一戸建て住宅 a recently built detached house.
ちくかん【竹簡】〔考古〕a bamboo writing strip (used in China from the Spring and Autumn and Warring States periods until the Han dynasty).
ちくこう²【蓄光】=ちっこう³.
ちくさく【竹酢(液)】bamboo vinegar.
ちくじ【逐次】 ▶逐次再生【電算】〔インターネットなどでデータの〕streaming.
チクシュルーブ =チチュルブ.
ちくせき【蓄積】 ▶蓄積進行性 ◇～進行性の疾患〔加害行為あるいは有害物質の摂取の終了後かなりの期間が経過してから発症する病気〕a progressive, late-onset disorder (resulting from accumulation of exposure).
ちくぜんに【筑前煮】〔日本料理〕〔鶏肉と根菜類の煮染め〕boiled chicken and vegetables Chikuzen-style.
ちくたん【竹炭】bamboo charcoal.
ちくねつ【蓄熱】 ▶蓄熱システム a thermal storage system. 蓄熱調整契約 a「heat [thermal] storage「rider [discount plan]. ◇業務用～調整契約 a commercial「heat [thermal] storage rider / 産業用～ an industrial「heat [thermal] storage rider / 低圧～調整契約 a low-voltage「heat [thermal] storage rider.
チクル ▶天然チクル natural chicle.
チクングンヤ(ねつ)【-熱】〔医〕〔感染症の1つ〕chikungunya (fever).
チケット ▶チケットショップ[店]〔割引販売の〕a discount ticket shop.
チケットレス〔切符や券の代わりにICカード・携帯電話などを使う方式〕a ticketless system.
ちけん³【治験】 ▶医師[企業]主導(型)治験 physician-[company-]led clinical「trials [testing]. 国際共同治験 an international joint clinical trial (of new drugs). 多施設共同治験 a multi-facility joint clinical trial (of new drugs). ▶治験施設支援機関 エス・エム・オー. 治験者[治験者など]a test subject 《for a new medication》. 治験新薬 an investigational new drug (略: IND). 治験ネットワーク a clinical「trial [testing] network.
ちけん⁴【知見】 ▶新知見 new「information [knowledge]. ◇この発見はアルツハイマー病研究に新～をもたらす

可能性がある。This discovery could provide new insights for research into Alzheimer's.
ちけんそくしんセンター〔治験促進-〕〔日本医師会の〕⇨にほんいしかいちけんそくしんセンター.
ちごがに〔稚児蟹〕〖動〗〔スナガニ科のカニ〕Ilyoplax pusilla.
ちごはやぶさ〔稚児隼〕〔鳥〕〔ハヤブサ科の鳥〕a Eurasian hobby; Falco subbuteo.
ちざい[2]〔知財〕＝ちてきざいさん. ▫▫ 知財研究会 an "intellectual property [IP] study group. 知財戦略本部〔知的財産戦略本部の略〕⇨ちてきざいさんせんりゃくほんぶ. 知財訴訟〔file, bring〕an intellectual property suit 《against…》. 知財ハラスメント power harassment involving intellectual property; using one's power to claim the intellectual property of one's subordinates as one's own. 知財本部〔知的財産戦略本部の略〕⇨ちてきざいさんせんりゃくほんぶ.〔大学内に設置の〕an intellectual property office. 知財立国 a national commitment to intellectual property; national development based on intellectual property.
ちざいこうさい〔知財高裁〕＝ちてきざいさんこうとうさいばんしょ.
ちさん[1]〔治山〕▫▫ 治山治水 forest conservation and "flood control [river improvement].
ちさんぜんしょう〔地産全消〕(the) nationwide consumption of "locally produced goods [local products].
ちし[5]〔致死〕▫▫ 致死性不整脈〖医〗(a) "lethal [fatal] arrhythmia. 致死注射〔死刑囚などへの〕a lethal injection. 致死薬 a lethal "drug [agent];〔特に安楽死のための〕a euthanasia drug.
ちしき[1]〔知識〕▫▫ 知識管理〖経営〗knowledge management（略：KM）.〔＝ナレッジ・マネージメント〕
ちぎょ〔稚仔魚〕＝しちぎょ.
ちしつ[1]〔地質〕▫▫ 地質改良 soil quality improvement.
ちしつちょうさそうごうセンター〔地質調査総合-〕〔産業技術総合研究所の〕the Geological Survey of Japan（略：GSJ）. ▶ 2001 年,「地質調査所」から名称変更.
ちしまかいこう〔千島海溝〕〖地質〗the "Kuril(e) [Kuril-Kamchatka] Trench.
ちしまれっとう〔千島列島〕the Kuril(e) "Islands [Archipelago]; the Kuriles.
ちじょう[1]〔地上〕▫▫ 地上絵 a geoglyph. 最低地上高〔自動車〕the minimum ground clearance. 地上配備型迎撃ミサイル〖軍〗a land-based interceptor missile. 地上放送〔地上波放送〕terrestrial broadcasting. 地上放送事業者 ＝ちじょうはほうそうじぎょうしゃ.
「地上最強の美女バイオニック・ジェミー」〔米国の,サイボーグ美女諜報員の TV ドラマ〕The Bionic Woman.
ちじょうし〔地上子〕〔鉄道〕〔ATS システムなどで車両に取り付けた車上子との情報の送受信に用いるコイル〕a wayside "coil [beacon, balise].
ちじょうデジタルほうそうすいしんきょうかい〔地上-放送推進協会〕the Association for Promotion of Digital Broadcasting（略：D-pa）. ▶ 2007 年, デジタル放送推進協会 に統合.
ちじょうは〔地上波〕▫▫ 地上波 DMB〔移動体向け地上波デジタル放送の規格の一つ〕T-DMB; terrestrial digital multimedia broadcasting. 地上波テレビ〔受像機〕a terrestrial television (set);〔放送〕terrestrial broadcasting. 地上波デジタルテレビ〔受像機〕a "digital terrestrial [terrestrial digital] television (set);〔放送〕digital terrestrial [terrestrial digital] broadcasting. 地上波放送事業者 a terrestrial broadcasting company.
ちしん〔地心〕▫▫ 地心距離〔天〕〔太陽系内の天体の中心と地球中心との距離〕a geocentric distance.
ちず〔地図〕▫▫ 広域[中域, 狭域]地図 a "wide-area [midrange, close-up] map.
ちすい[2]〔治水〕▫▫ 治水対策 flood "control [prevention] measures. 治水ダム a flood-prevention dam. 治水問題 the flood control "problem [issue]. 治水容量〔土木〕〔ダムの洪水調節容量〕a flood control volume. 治水緑地 a greenbelt flood buffer "zone [area].
ちせい[3]〔知性〕▫▫ 知性化〖心理〗〔防衛機制の 1 つ〕intellectualization. ▷ intellectualize v. 知性派 an intellectual; an intellect;〈集合的に〉the intelligentsia. ▷ 彼は自分では一派だと思っている。He thinks of himself as an intellectual.
ちせい[4]〔治政〕administration; government.
ちせき[1]〔地積〕▫▫ 地積測量図 a lot survey map.
ちせき[2]〔地籍〕▫▫ 地籍調査 a land resurvey (to obtain current information on boundaries, areas, property use, etc.).
ちたいかんミサイル〔地対艦-〕〖軍〗a "surface-to-ship [ground-to-ship] missile（略：SSM）.
ちたいくうミサイル〔地対空-〕〔携帯用〔携帯型〕地対空ミサイル a shoulder-fired surface-to-air missile.
チタン ▫▫ チタン鉱石 titanium ore. チタンテープ〔健康製品〕titanium tape.
ちち[2]〔乳〕▫▫ 乳揉み〔授乳期の母親に母乳の分泌を促すマッサージ〕breast massage.
チチ〔カクテル〕a chi-chi.
チチェンイツァ〔メキシコのマヤ文明遺跡〕Chichen Itza; Chichén Itzá.
ちちおや〔父親〕▫▫ 父親不在 absence of a father;〔存在感が薄い〕(a) lack of paternal influence. ▷ 両親は私が幼いころに離婚し, 私は一不在の家庭で育ちました。My parents divorced when I was little and I was brought up in a family without a father. / 父親が仕事に追われて子供と顔を合わせる時間がないという～不在の家庭が多い。There are a lot of families where the father is so occupied with work that he and his children have little time to be together. | Many families have absentee fathers, so busy at work that they rarely see their children.
「父親たちの星条旗」〔映画〕Flags of Our Fathers.
ちちぶこうもり〔秩父蝙蝠〕〖動〗a barbastelle; Barbastella leucomelas.
チヂミ〔料理〕〔韓国のお好み焼きに似た料理〕jijimi; chijimi.
チチュルブ〔メキシコ, ユカタン半島北部の巨大クレーター〕the Chicxulub crater.
ちつ[2]〔膣〕▫▫ 膣狭窄〖医〗vaginal stenosis; stenosis of (the) vagina. 膣脱〖医〗colpocele; colpoptosis; prolapse of the vaginal walls. 膣閉鎖(症)〖医〗vaginal atresia.
ちっか〔窒化〕▫▫ 窒化アルミニウム〖化〗aluminum nitride（略：AlN）. 窒化ガリウム〖化〗gallium nitride（略：GaN）.
チック[2] ▫▫ 運動チック motor tic (disorder);〈have〉a motor tic. 音声チック vocal tic (disorder);〈have〉a vocal tic. 顔面チック〈have〉a facial tic.
チックピー〔植〕a chickpea.
ちっこう[3]〔蓄光〕phosphorescence. ▫▫ 蓄光ガラス luminous [phosphorescent, glow-in-the-dark] glass. 蓄光器 a phosphorescence recharger. 蓄光剤 a "luminous [phosphorescent] agent. 蓄光弾〔夜間のサバイバルゲームで用いられる BB 弾〕a glow-in-the-dark BB. 蓄光テープ luminous [phosphorescent, glow-in-the-dark] tape. 蓄光塗料 luminous [phosphorescent, glow-in-the-dark] paint. 蓄光標識〔避難路などを示す〕a "luminous [neon, fluorescent] sign; a sign which glows in the dark.
ちつじょ〔秩序〕▫▫ 秩序感覚〈have〉a 《good》sense of order.
ちっそ〔窒素〕▫▫ 窒素充填 nitrogen filling.
ちっそく〔窒息〕▫▫ 窒息剤〔化学兵器の〕a choking agent; a pulmonary agent.
チッピング〔塗料〕〔塗装面が衝撃・振動などによってはがれるこ

と〕chipping. ◨ 耐チッピング性 chipping resistance 《of a coating》.
**チップ**[1] ◨ 埋め込み込みチップ〘医〙〔体内への〕a human-implantable「RFID [radio frequency identification] microchip.
**チップとデール**〔ディズニーのアニメに登場する双子のリス〕Chip 'n Dale.
**ちてき**〔知的〕◨ 知的クラスター創成事業 a knowledge cluster creation project. ▶ 文部科学省が 2002 年から推進. cluster は Cooperative Link of Unique Science and Technology for Economy Revitalization の略. 知的権力〔専門知識を持つ者の〕expert [intellectual] authority; the authority of an expert. 知的材料・構造システム〘材料工学〙〔航空機・自動車の部品や高層建築の柱などにひび割れなどができた際、自分でそれを直してしまうシステム〕smart materials and structures. 知的刺激《provide》intellectual stimulation; an intellectual stimulus. ◯ その本は～刺激に富むものであった. The book was「extremely stimulating intellectually [full of stimulating ideas]. 知的資産 intellectual assets; intellectual property. 知的生産システム an intelligent manufacturing system《略: IMS》. 知的生命体 intelligent life. ◯ 地球外～生命体 ⇨ ちきゅうがい. 知的発達障害〔知的障害〕a mental disability; mental retardation.
**ちてきざいさん**【知的財産】intellectual property. ◨ 知的財産権 intellectual property rights. 知的財産権協定《WTO の》=トリップスきょうてい. 知的財産権《file, bring》an intellectual property suit《against…》. 知的財産立国 a national commitment to intellectual property; national development based on intellectual property.
**ちてきざいさんきほんほう**【知的財産基本法】〘法〙the Basic Law on Intellectual Property.
**ちてきざいさんきょういくきょうかい**【知的財産教育協会】the Association of [for] Intellectual Property Education.
**ちてきざいさんこうとうさいばんしょ**【知的財産高等裁判所】an intellectual property high court. ▶ 2005 年創設予定.
**ちてきざいさんすいしんけいかく**【知的財産推進計画】the Intellectual Property Promotion Plan.
**ちてきざいさんせんりゃくかいぎ**【知的財産戦略会議】〔2001 年、小泉首相の提唱によって設置された諮問会議〕the Strategic Council on Intellectual Property.
**ちてきざいさんせんりゃくすいしんじむきょく**【知的財産戦略推進事務局】〔知的財産戦略本部の事務局〕the Secretariat of the Intellectual Property Strategy Headquarters.
**ちてきざいさんせんりゃくたいこう**【知的財産戦略大綱】〔2002 年、知的財産戦略会議において決定〕the Intellectual Property Strategic Program.
**ちてきざいさんせんりゃくほんぶ**【知的財産戦略本部】the Intellectual Property Strategy Headquarters.
**ちデジ**【地-】〔地上デジタル放送〕digital terrestrial [terrestrial digital] broadcasting.
**ちどりがふちせんぼつしゃぼえん**【千鳥ヶ淵戦没者墓苑】the Chidorigafuchi Cemetery for the War Dead.
**ちどりはふ**【千鳥破風】a triangularly shaped decorative roof gable used in Japanese castle architecture; a "plover gable"; a "chidori hafu."
**チヌーク**〔米軍の大型輸送ヘリコプター〕a Chinook.
**ちねつ**【地熱】◨ 地熱井《—せい》a geothermal well.
**チノう**〔中国系フィリピン人〕a Chino.
**ちのう**[1]【知能】◨ 知能情報学 intelligent informatics.
**「ちびっ子ギャング」**〔米国の、子供向けドタバタ短編映画シリーズ〕Our Gang; The Little Rascals.
**「ちびっこ大将」**〔米国の、子供向け TV コメディー; 元は タイレント映画〕The Mischief Makers.
**ちぶさ**【乳鋲】a metal ornament in the shape of a woman's breast, used to decorate a door.
**ちべい**【知米】◨ 知米派 people who are knowledgeable about the United States;《口》(old) America hands.《～派の政治家 a politician familiar with the United States.
**チベットぼうめいせいふ**【-亡命政府】the Tibetan Government in Exile. ▶ 正式名称は、中央チベット行政府 (the Central Tibetan Administration).
**ちほう**[1]【地方】◨ 地方行政改革指針 guidelines for promoting the administrative reform of local government; local administrative reform guidelines. 地方事務官〔地方自治体に勤務する国家公務員〕a public official from the「national bureaucracy [central government] working at a local government office. 地方単独事業 a regional enterprise financed out of non-central government sources. 地方道路譲与税 (a)"local road transfer tax"; a portion of the gasoline consumption tax transferred to local governments for the upkeep of roads. 地方独自課税 taxation determined at local-government level. 地方入試 a regional entrance exam《for a university in Tokyo》. ◯ 本学では次の 5 か所で～入試を行っています. We hold regional entrance exams at the following five locations.
**ちほうきょういくぎょうせいほう**【地方教育行政法】〘法〙the Local Education Administration Law.
**ちほうきょてんほう**【地方拠点法】〘法〙the Regional Hub Development and Relocation Law. ▶ 正式名称は「地方拠点都市地域の整備及び産業業務施設の再配置の促進に関する法律」(the Law for Comprehensive Development of Regional Core Cities with Relocation of Office-Work Functions).
**ちほうけいばぜんこくきょうかい**【地方競馬全国協会】the National Association of Racing《略: NAR》.
**ちほうこうふぜい**【地方交付税】◨ 地方交付税特別会計 a special account for local grant tax.
**ちほうざいせい**【地方財政】◨ 地方財政計画 the Local Finance Plan. 地方財政審議会 the Local Finance Council. 地方財政白書〔総務省の〕the White Paper on Local Public Finance《2004》.
**ちほうさいていちんぎんしんぎかい**【地方最低賃金審議会】〔都道府県が設置する〕a prefectural minimum wage council.
**ちほうじちじょうほうセンター**【地方自治情報-】〔総務省の外郭団体〕the Local Authorities Systems Development Center《略: LASDEC》.
**ちほうじちたいざいせいけんぜんかほう**【地方自治体財政健全化法】〘法〙the Law for「Restoring Local Government Finance to a Healthy Condition [Putting Local Government Finances on a Sound Footing].
**ちほうじゅうたくきょうきゅうこうしゃほう**【地方住宅供給公社法】〘法〙the Law on Regional Housing Corporations.
**ちほうしょうけんとりひきじょ**【地方証券取引所】a「regional [local] stock exchange.
**ちほうふっこう(しえん)チーム**【地方復興(支援)-】〔イラク・アフガニスタンなどでの〕a Provincial Reconstruction Team《略: PRT》.
**ちほうぶんけんいっかつほう**【地方分権一括法】〘法〙the Comprehensive Decentralization Law.
**ちほうろくだんたい**【地方六団体】the six major regional government associations. ▶ 全国知事会、全国市長会、全国町村会、全国都道府県議会議長会、全国市議会議長会、全国町村議会議長会の六団体.
**チマ**〔朝鮮の民族服のスカート〕a ch'ima.
**チミノ** Cimino, Michael《1943- ; 米国の映画監督》.
**チムーおうこく**【-王国】〘史〙《1100-1470 年頃のペルー北部

の王国) the Chimú kingdom.
**ちめいひょうじゅんかかいぎ**〖地名標準化会議〗〔国連の〕⇨こくれんちめいひょうじゅんかかいぎ.
**チモシェンコ** ＝ティモシェンコ.
**ちゃ**【茶】▣ 茶系 a shade [shades] of brown; a brown hue; (in) the brown range; a brown. ● 彼は紺のスーツに〜系のネクタイ姿だった. He was wearing a「dark [navy] blue suit with a (neck)tie in a shade of brown. 茶農家 a tea「grower [farmer].
**チャーヴィン** ⇨チャビン.
**チャーガ**《＜Russ.》〖カバノアナタケ［シラカバタケ］の別名〗a chaga.
**ちゃあざ**〖茶痣〗＝扁平母斑 (⇨ほはん[1]).
**チャージャー**〖充電器〗a (battery) charter.
**チャーター**▣ チャーター直行便〖飛行機〗a direct charter(ed) flight.
**チャーノッカイト**〖鉱〗charnockite.
**「チャーリーズ・エンジェル」** 1〖米国の, 探偵もののTVドラマ〗Charlie は雇い主の大富豪, Angels は3人の美女探偵で元警察官) Charlie's Angels. ▶ ファラ・フォーセット (Farrah Fawcett) が主演.
2〖映画〗Charlie's Angels. ▶ 続編は「チャーリーズ・エンジェル／フルスロットル」(Charlie's Angels: Full Throttle).
**「チャーリーとチョコレート工場」**〖映画〗Charlie and the Chocolate Factory.
**チャイ**〖インドやトルコなどの紅茶〗spiced milk tea; masala chai.
**チャイドル**〖アイドルである子供〗a child「star [entertainer];〖アイドルのようにかわいがられる子供〗a popular child.
**チャイナ** ▣ チャイナ・スクール〖中国重視派の外務官僚などの通称〗the "China school" (in the Ministry of Foreign Affairs). チャイナフリー〖中国産の原材料を使用していない」という食品などの表示〗"China-free" (label). チャイナ・リスク〖中国で外国企業が経済活動を行う際のリスク〗a [the] China risk.
**チャイナート**〖タイ中部の県; その県都〗Chinat.
**チャイナット** ＝チャイナート.
**チャイナ・デイリー**〖中国日報; 中国の全国英字紙〗The China Daily.
**チャイナ・ボーチー**【中国博奇】〖中国の環境関連企業〗China Boqi Environmental Solutions Technology.
**チャイヤプーム**〖タイ東北部の県; 同県の県都〗Chaiyaphum; Chaiyapoom.
**チャイルド**[1] ▣ チャイルド・シッター〖子供の子守〗《find》a child sitter. チャイルド・ソルジャー〖子供の兵士〗a child soldier (*pl.* child soldiers, children soldiers). チャイルドフリー〖子供を持たない〗childfree (couples). チャイルドマインダー〖英国発祥の, 子供を自宅で世話をする保育士〗a childminder. チャイルド・ライフ・スペシャリスト〖入院治療中の子供を精神的に支援する医療専門スタッフ〗a child life specialist (略: CLS). チャイルドライン〖子供が自分の思いを自由に話せる電話サービス〗ChildLine; Childline.
**「チャイルド・プレイ」**〖映画〗Child's Play.
**ちゃいんりょう**〖茶飲料〗a tea drink. ▣ 無糖茶飲料 a sugarless tea drink.
**チャウ・シンチー**【周星馳】Stephen Chow; Chow Sing Chi (1962– ); 香港の映画監督・俳優).
**チャカ**〖ピストル〗a pistol;《口》a gat; *《口》a rod.
**チャー(一)** ＝チャーガ.
**チャガイ**〖パキスタン, バロチスタン州の村; 核実験場がある〗Chagai.
**ちゃきん**【茶巾】▣ 茶巾蒸し〖料理〗tofu and vegetables squeezed into shape in a cloth and steamed.
**ちゃくあつ**【着圧】compression. ▣ 着圧ストッキング［ソックス］ compression「stockings [socks]. ● 段階着圧ストッキング graduated compression stockings
**ちゃくうた**【着歌】〖歌が流れる着メロ〗a ring song.

**ちゃくがんたいきょく・ちゃくしゅしょうきょく**【着眼大局・着手小局】keeping an eye on both the general picture and the details; bearing both strategy and tactics in mind.
**ちゃくごえ**【着声】〖携帯電話の着信音に声を使ったもの〗a voice ringtone.
**ちゃくしゅつ**【嫡出】▣ 推定嫡出 presumed legitimacy. ● 嫡出否認 denying [(a) denial] that *one* is the (biological) father of 《the child》; denying that 《the child》 is *one's* own.
**ちゃくじょうりく**【着上陸】(an) air「and [or] sea landing. ▣ 着上陸侵攻 (an) invasion by air「and [or] sea; a combined airborne and seaborne invasion.
**ちゃくしん**【着信】▣ 着信拒否〖電話で特定の相手からの着信はつながらないようにする機能・サービス〗call「blocking [screening]. 着信ボイス a voice ringtone.
**ちゃくせつ**【着雪】▣ 着雪注意報 a snow accretion advisory.
**ちゃくだん**【着弾】〜する land; strike 《a target》; hit 《the ground》. ● 防衛省は, ミサイルが日本列島を飛び越え三陸東方沖数百キロの太平洋上に着弾した可能性があると発表した. The Ministry of Defense reported that the missiles might have flown over the Japanese Archipelago and landed in international waters in the Pacific Ocean several hundred kilometers east of Sanriku.
**ちゃくち**【着地】▣ 着地ミス〖体操競技などで〗a「bad [poor] landing.
**ちゃくひょう**【着氷】▣ 着氷注意報 an ice accretion advisory.
**ちゃくボイス**【着-】〖携帯電話の〗a voice ringtone.
**チャクマヒヒ**[-狒々]〖動〗〖オナガザル科のヒヒ〗a chacma baboon; *Papio ursinus*.
**ちゃくメロ**【着-】〖携帯電話などの〗▣ 着メロサイト a ringtone (Web) site.
**ちゃくりく**【着陸】▣ 着陸滑走〖空〗a landing run. 着陸滑走距離 (a) runway landing「length [distance]. 着陸機〖着陸しようとしている航空機〗a landing aircraft; an aircraft「coming in to land [approaching the runway];〖着陸した航空機〗an aircraft that has just landed;〖宇宙〗a lander; a landing module; a landing vehicle. 着陸灯 a landing light.
**ちゃくれき**【着歴】〖携帯電話などの着信履歴〗a record of「incoming calls [calls received].
**ちゃけいいんりょう**【茶系飲料】a tea drink.
**ちゃじゅ**【茶寿】*one's* one hundred and eighth birthday.
**チャタム・ハウス**〖英国の国際問題研究機関〗Chatham House. ▶ 2004 年に王立国際問題研究所から改称.
**チャチェンサオ**〖タイ中部の県; その県都〗Chachoengsao.
**チャチャポヤス**〖ペルー北部の町〗Chachapoyas. ● チャチャポヤス文明 the Chachapoyas culture.
**チャチュ(一)ンサオ** ＝チャチェンサオ.
**ちゃっか**【着火】▣ 着火源 the cause of ignition. 着火剤 *a fire starter;「a firelighter.
**ちゃっかん**【着艦】▣ 着艦訓練 deck landing practice (略: DLP). ● 夜間着艦訓練 night landing practice (略: NLP).
**ちゃっかんだっけん**【着艦脱健】〖介護〗＝だっけんちゃっかん.
**ちゃっきょ**【着拒】＝着信拒否 (⇨ちゃくしん).
**ちゃっきん**【着金】▣ 着金日 the date of payment.
**チャット** ▣ チャット占い fortune-telling on a chat site.
**ちゃつみ**【茶摘み】▣ 茶摘み娘 a girl or young woman who picks tea.
**チャトウィン** Chatwin, Bruce (1940–89; 英国の作家).
**チャナッカレ**〖トルコのアジア側にあるダーダネルス海峡に臨む港市; ダーダネルス海峡のトルコ語名〗Canakkale.
**ちゃのこくもんはまき**【茶の小角紋葉巻】〖昆〗[ハマキガ

科の蛾；茶樹の害虫〕the smaller tea tortrix; *Adoxophyes honmai*.
チャハールマハール・バフティヤーリー〔イラン中南部の州〕Chahar「Mahaal [Mahall] and Bakhtiari; (ペルシャ語名の音訳) Chahar Mahall va Bakhtiari.
チャパン〔ウズベク人などの着る外套〕a chapan.
チャビン〔ベトナム南部, メコンデルタ地帯の省；その省都〕Tra Vinh.
ちゃぶうとう〔茶封筒〕a「light-brown [manila] envelope (for everyday use).
チャプチェ〔料理〕〔韓国料理；春雨入り炒め物〕chapchae.
チャベス Chávez, Hugo (1954- ；ベネズエラの政治家；大統領〔1999- 〕).
チャマメ〔アルゼンチンの民俗音楽〕Chamamé.
ちゃむすめ〔茶娘〕=茶摘み娘 (⇨ちゃつみ);〔コンテストなどで選ばれた〕a tea-picking queen.
チャラン〔インドネシア, アチェ州, アチェジャヤ県の県都〕Calang.
チャリティー ▫ チャリティー・マラソン a charity marathon.
チャレンジ ▫ チャレンジ校〔自分の実力よりランクが上だが腕試しに受験してみる学校〕a reach school. チャレンジショップ unoccupied retail space in a shopping arcade leased at a low rent to an enterprising retailer.
チャレンジド〔障害者〕a 《physically, mentally, visually》 challenged person.
チャン[2]〔張緩如〕Chang, Iris Shun-Ru (1968-2004；アメリカのジャーナリスト・著述家・政治活動家).
チャンカイぶんか〔-文化〕〔11-15世紀頃のペルーの文化〕the Chancay culture.
チャンギ(一)〔シンガポール東部の町〕Changi.
チャンギ(一)けいむしょ〔-刑務所〕〔シンガポールの刑務所；日本人の B, C 級戦犯が処刑された刑務所〕Changi Prison.
チャンギョングン〔昌慶宮〕〔韓国, ソウルにある宮殿；史跡〕the Changgyeong Palace; Changgyeonggung.
チャング〔杖鼓〕〔楽器〕〔朝鮮音楽の伝統打楽器〕a changgo.
ちゃんこばん〔ちゃんこ番〕〔相撲部屋での料理当番のこと〕being in charge of [*one's* turn for] the *chankonabe*.
チャンタブリ〔タイ中部の県；その県都〕Chanthaburi; Chantaburi.
チャン・ツィイー〔章子怡〕Zhang Ziyi (1979- ；中国の映画女優).
チャン・ドゥック・ルオン Tran Duc Luong (1937- ；ベトナムの政治家；国家主席〔1997- 〕).
チャンドックン, チャンドッグン〔昌徳宮〕〔韓国, ソウルにある宮殿；史跡〕the Changdeok Palace; Changdeokgung.
チャンドラ・エックスせんかんそくえいせい〔-X 線観測衛星〕〔天〕〔NASA の〕the Chandra X-ray Observatory (略: CXO).
チャン・ドンゴン〔張東健〕Jang Dong-gun (1972- ；韓国の映画俳優).
チャンパ〔2-17世紀のベトナム中部の王国・その遺跡〕Champa.
ちゃんばら ▫ ちゃんばらごっこ playing at「swordfighting [a samurai duel]; a pretend sword-fight.
チャンピ Ciampi, Carlo Azeglio (1920- ；イタリアの政治家；首相〔1993-94〕, 大統領〔1999-2006〕).
チャンピオンズリーグ〔サッカー〕〔各国リーグ戦の優勝チームによって争われる地域選手権〕the Champions League. ▫ アジア・チャンピオンズリーグ = エー・エフ・シー・チャンピオンズリーグ. **UEFA チャンピオンズリーグ**〔サッカー〕⇨ ウエファ. **AFC (アジア)チャンピオンズリーグ** = エー・エフ・シー・チャンピオンズリーグ.
ちゆ〔治癒〕 ▫ 治癒能力 healing power(s); curative properties.
チュイリーきゅう(でん)〔-宮(殿)〕〔フランス, パリの旧王宮〕the Tuileries Palace;〔フランス語名〕Palais des Tuileries.
チュイリーこうえん〔-公園[庭園]〕〔フランス, パリにある公園〕the Tuileries Gardens;〔フランス語名〕Jardins des Tuileries.
ちゅうアチェ〔中-〕〔インドネシア, アチェ州の県〕Aceh Tengah.
ちゅうい[1]〔中位〕 ▫ 中位推計 a medium「estimate [projection].
ちゅうい[3]〔注意〕 ▫ 注意喚起 ⇨ ちゅういかんき. 注意監督 supervision. ● 親は子供を十分に〜監督する義務がある. Parents have a duty to exercise adequate supervision over their children's behavior. 注意義務違反 an infringement of[/the] duty of care. ● 〜義務違反に問われる be held responsible for failure to maintain a duty of care; be charged with taking inadequate care.
ちゅういかんき〔注意喚起〕calling *sb's* attention to 《a fact》; bringing 《a fact》 to *sb's*「attention [notice]; alerting *sb* to 《a fact》. 〜する call *sb's* attention to…; bring 《information》 to *sb's*「attention [notice]; make *sb* aware「that… [of…]; alert *sb* to 《the fact that…》. ▫ 注意喚起情報〔保険商品などの販売時に作成し顧客に提示することが義務化されている情報の１つ〕information which a company is obliged to bring to the attention of potential customers; disclaimer information; a disclaimer;〔公的機関が発する種々の〕a warning. 注意喚起表示〔電気製品などの使用についての〕warning labeling;（そのシールなど）a warning「label [notice].
ちゅういきけん〔中域圏〕a meso-area; a moderately homogeneous geographical region.
ちゅういきょう〔中医協〕= ちゅうおうしゃかいほけんいりょうきょうぎかい.
ちゅういり〔中煎り〕〔コーヒー豆の〕medium roast.
ちゅういんとう〔中咽頭〕〔医〕(an) oropharynx. ▷ oropharyngeal *adj*. ▫ 中咽頭がん〔医〕(an) oropharyngeal cancer; (a) cancer of the oropharynx; (an) oropharyngeal carcinoma; (a) carcinoma of the oropharynx.
ちゅうえつだいしんさい〔中越大震災〕⇨ にいがたけんちゅうえつだいしんさい.
ちゅうおう[1]〔中央〕 ▫ 中央制御室 a central control room. 中央統制 central [centralized] control.
ちゅうおうアジアきょうりょくきこう〔中央-協力機構〕the Central Asia Cooperation Organization (略: CACO).
ちゅうおうぐんじいいんかい〔中央軍事委員会〕〔中国軍の最高指導機関〕the Central Military Commission.
ちゅうおうさいていちんぎんしんぎかい〔中央最低賃金審議会〕〔厚生労働省の〕the Central Advisory Committee on Minimum Wages (略: CACMW).
ちゅうおうしゃかいほけんいりょうきょうぎかい〔中央社会保険医療協議会〕〔厚生労働省の〕the Central Social Insurance Medical Council.
ちゅうおうしょうちょう(とう)かいかくきほんほう〔中央省庁(等)改革基本法〕〔法〕the Basic Law on Reform of Central Government Ministries Etc.
ちゅうおうしょくぎょうのうりょくかいはつきょうかい〔中央職業能力開発協会〕the Japan Vocational Ability Development Association (略: JAVADA).
ちゅうおうそくおうしゅうだん〔中央即応集団〕〔自衛隊の〕a Central Readiness Force (略: CRF). ▫ 中央即応集団司令部 the 《GSDF》 Central Readiness Force Command.
ちゅうおうチベットぎょうせいふ〔中央-行政府〕the Central Tibetan Administration (略: CTA). ▶ ダライ・ラマ法王のチベット亡命政府の正式名称.
ちゅうおうでんしだい〔中央電視台〕〔中国のテレビ局〕China Central Television (略: CCTV).

ちゅうおうとう(がっ)こう【中央党(学)校】〔中国共産党の幹部研修機関〕the Central Party School; 〔正式名称〕the Party School of the Central Committee of the Communist Party of China.

ちゅうおうにっぽう【中央日報】 **1**〔韓国の日刊紙〕The JoongAng Daily; The JoongAng Ilbo. **2**〔台湾・国民党の機関紙〕The Central Daily News.

ちゅうおし【中押し】 ▶ 中押し勝ち〔負け〕a「win〔loss〕by a wide margin; winning〔being beaten〕easily.

ちゅうかい¹【仲介】 ▶ 仲介業者 a broker; an agency. 仲介工作 mediation (activities); attempts to mediate 《between…, in a dispute》.

ちゅうかく¹【中核】 ▶ 中核の研究拠点〔文部科学省のプログラムで〕a Center of Excellence (略: COE).

ちゅうかくてき【中核的】～な core; central; fundamental; basic.

ちゅうかくは【中核派】〔革命的共産主義者同盟全国委員会〕the Japan Revolutionary Communist League (略: JRCL).

ちゅうかしょくぎょうぼうきゅうだいれんめい【中華職業棒球大連盟】〔台湾の〕the Chinese Professional Baseball League (略: CPBL).

ちゅうがた【中型・中形】 ▶ 中型機〔ジェット機〕〔空〕a medium-size(d) passenger「plane〔jet〕. 中型犬 a medium-sized (breed of) dog.

ちゅうかにほんがっかい【中華日本学会】the Chinese Association for Japanese Studies.

ちゅうかん²【中間】 ▶ 中間筋〔生理〕(an) intermediate muscle. ▶ ～筋線維 (an) intermediate muscle fiber. 中間集計 an「intermediate〔in-progress〕total〔aggregate〕. 中間省略登記〔不動産の〕recording a real estate transfer directly under the ultimate purchaser's name (in order to avoid taxation on the intermediary purchaser). 中間線〔排他的経済水域の〕a〔the〕「(dividing) line〔border〕between exclusive economic zones. 中間素材 an intermediate (raw) material; a semi-processed material. 中間値 the median. 中間熱交換器《原子力》an intermediate heat exchanger (略: IHX). 中間発行《株式》(an) issue of shares at prices intermediate between par value and current market value. 中間利息〔金融〕interim interest;〔保険〕〔逸失利益計算の際の〕interim interest as assessed in calculation of the assumed future earnings of a person deprived of income by 《a traffic accident》 resulting in death or disability. 中間利息控除《保険》〔逸失利益計算の際の〕the rate of interest assumed in deducting interim interest when calculating lost income. 中間流通業者 an intermediate distributor.

ちゅうかんしょく²【中間食】〔食事と食事の間の軽食〕a morning〔an afternoon〕snack;〔半調理食材〕《supply》semi-prepared meals.

ちゅうかんしょり【中間処理】〔産業廃棄物の〕intermediate (waste) processing. ～する subject 《waste》to intermediate processing. ▶ 中間処理業者 an intermediate (waste) processing company. 中間処理施設, 中間処理場 an intermediate (waste)「processing plant〔disposal facility〕.

ちゅうかんそん【中関村】〔中国, 北京市内, 北西部の地区〕Zhongguancun.

ちゅうかんほうじんほう【中間法人法】〔法〕the Intermediate Corporation Law.

ちゅうき²【中期】 ▶ 中期財政試算〔国や地方自治体の財政見通しを示す〕a medium-term[-range] financial forecast. 中期日程〔公立大学入試などの〕a mid-term schedule (for entrance examinations). 中期防衛力整備計画 ▶ 次期～防衛力整備計画 the next five-year defense build-up program.

ちゅうきゅう¹【中級】 ▶ 中級医療職〔米国の, 医師以外の医療関係者〕co-medical staff; a co-medical professional.

(ちゅうきょう)ちゅうおうせいじきょく【(中共)中央政治局】＝中国共産党中央政治局 (⇨ちゅうごく).

ちゅうきょり【中距離】 ▶ 中距離拡大防空システム〔米国・ドイツ・イタリア3国の〕the Medium Extended Air Defense System (略: MEADS).

ちゅうけい²【中継】 ▶ 同時中継〔複数地点への〕a simultaneous live broadcast;〔生中継〕a live (on the scene) broadcast; live coverage. ▶ 準同時～ a time-delayed broadcast. 中継施設〔電波などの〕a《radio》relay installation;〔ごみ・廃棄物などの〕a refuse transfer station (略: RTS); a garbage transfer station. 中継塔〔電波の〕a relay tower. 中継プレー〔野球〕a relay.

ちゅうけん¹【中堅】 ▶ 中堅議員 a middle rank member of the Diet; a Diet member of medium standing. 中堅サラリーマン a reliable mid-grade company employee; a mid-career company employee.

ちゅうげん¹【中元】 ▶ お中元商戦 the battle for *ochūgen* sales; the mid-year gift sales war.

ちゅうこうねん(れい)【中高年(齢)】 ▶ 中高年市場 the middle-aged and elderly market; the mature market; the market of「middle-aged and elderly〔older, mature〕consumers. 中高年フリーター middle-aged people「without a permanent job〔who choose to work part-time〕; a middle-aged "freeter."

ちゅうこく²【中刻】〔昔の時刻で〕the second third of 'a *koku* [a two-hour period].

ちゅうごく【中国】 ▶ 中国共産党中央政治局 the Political Bureau of the CPC Central Committee. ▶ CPC は Communist Party of China の略. 中国共産党中央宣伝部 the Chinese Communist Party Central Propaganda Department. 中国ルート〔東シベリアからの石油パイプラインの〕a China route.

ちゅうごくかいようせきゆこうし【中国海洋石油公司】China National Offshore Oil Corporation (略: CNOOC).

ちゅうごくかいようせきゆそうこうし【中国海洋石油総公司】〔中国の国営石油会社〕the China National Offshore Oil Corporation (略: CNOOC).

ちゅうごくカトリックきょうあいこくかい【中国-教愛国会】ちゅうごくてんしゅきょうあいこくかい.

ちゅうごくかわせとりひきセンター【中国為替取引-】〔上海にある中国唯一の為替市場〕the China Foreign Exchange Trade System (略: CFETS).

ちゅうごくきゅういちはちあいこくもう【中国 918 愛国網】〔中国の, 反日を掲げるインターネットサイト〕china918.net. ▶ 918 は, 1931 年 9 月 18 日 (日中が全面戦争に突入するきっかけとなった満州事変) から.

ちゅうごくじどうしゃこうぎょうきょうかい【中国自動車工業協会】the China Association of Automobile Manufacturers (略: CAAM).

ちゅうごくじほう【中国時報】〔台湾の新聞〕the China Times.

ちゅうごくしゃかいかがくいん【中国社会科学院】the Chinese Academy of Social Sciences (略: CASS). ▶ 社会科学研究の最高学術機関; 30 を超す研究機関をもつ. ▶ 中国社会科学院経済研究所 the Institute of Economics,「Chinese Academy of Social Sciences [CASS]. 中国社会科学院世界経済と政治研究所「Institute of World Economics and Politics,「Chinese Academy of Social Sciences [CASS] (略: IWEP, CASS).

ちゅうごくしょうひしゃきょうかい【中国消費者協会】the Chinese Consumers Association.

ちゅうごくじんみんぶそうけいさつ【中国人民武装警察】the (Chinese) People's Armed Police.

ちゅうごくじんみんみんしゅかうんどうじょうほうセンター【中国人権民主化運動情報-】〔香港の人権団体〕

the Information Centre for Human Rights and Democracy.
ちゅうごくせいねんほう【中国青年報】〔中国の日刊紙〕the China Youth Daily.
ちゅうごくせきゆかこう【中国石油化工】〔中国最大規模の石油・石油化学工業集団〕the China Petroleum and Chemical Corporation. ▶ 略称は Sinopec Corp.
ちゅうごくせきゆかこうしゅうだん【中国石油化工集団】the China Petrochemical Corporation. ▶ 略称は (the) SINOPEC Group.
ちゅうごくせきゆてんねんガスしゅうだん【中国石油天然-集団】=ちゅうごくせきゆてんねんき.
ちゅうごくせきゆてんねんき【中国石油天然気】〔中国の石油会社〕the China National Petroleum Corporation (略: CNPC); 通称 PetroChina.
ちゅうごくてんしゅきょうあいこくかい【中国天主教愛国会】〔中国政府公認の宗教団体の１つ; カトリック〕the Chinese Patriotic Catholic Association.
ちゅうごくにっぽう【中国日報】=チャイナ・デイリー.
(ちゅうごく)ほっぽうこうぎょうこうし(中国)北方工業公司】China North Industries Corporation (略: NORINCO).
ちゅうごくホンカーれんめい【中国紅客連盟】〔対外的なサイバー攻撃を行う集団〕the「Honker [Hackers] Union of China (略: HUC).
ちゅうごくみんかんほちょうれんごうかい【中国民間保釣連合会】〔釣魚島(ちょうぎょとう)(=尖閣諸島)の開発等を目的とする中国の会社〕the China Federation of Defending Diaoyudao Islands Limited.
ちゅうごくもくずがに【中国藻屑蟹】〔動〕〔イワガニ科のカニ〕a Chinese mitten crab; Eriocheir sinensis.
ちゅうごくやきゅうリーグ【中国野球-】the China Baseball League (略: CBL).
ちゅうごくれんごうつうしん【中国聯合通信】China United Telecommunications Corporation; China Unicom.
ちゅうざい【駐在】◯ 駐在武官〔大公使館付武官〕a military attaché. ▶ 日本の場合は「防衛駐在官」.
ちゅうさしぼうさん【中鎖脂肪酸】〘化〙a medium-chain fatty acid.
ちゅうさつもうそう【注察妄想】〘精神医〙a delusion of observation; a [the] delusion that one is being watched.
ちゅうさんかんちいき【中山間地域】〔平野と山地の中間地域〕an area intermediary between plain and mountain; low uplands.
ちゅうし¹【中止】◯ 中止命令〘法〙〔不法行為の〕a cease and desist order.
ちゅうじく【中軸】◯ 中軸打者〘野球〙a「key [leading] batter.
ちゅうしてき【中視的】〘物〙〔巨視的と微視的の中間の〕mesoscopic.
ちゅうしゃ²【注射】◯ 動脈注射〘医〙(an) intra-arterial [(an) arterial] injection. ◯ 注射筒 a [an injection] syringe.
ちゅうしゃ³【駐車】◯ 後退駐車 ＝バック駐車. 前進駐車 ＝前向き駐車. バック駐車 backing [reversing] into a (parking) space; *back-in parking;〔掲示〕Back-in Parking Only. 前向き駐車 driving forwards into a (parking) space; *head-in parking;〔掲示〕Head-in Parking Only. 迷惑駐車 nuisance (car) parking. ◯ 駐車監視員 *a parking enforcement officer (略: PEO); "a parking warden. 駐車サービス〔大型店舗などの〕a free parking service. 〇 代理～サービス（係員による）＝バレット・パーキング. 駐車支援システム〘自動車〙〔車載コンピューターシステム〕a parking assistance system; a「parking assist [park-assist] system.
ちゅうしゃじょう¹【駐車場】◯ 専用駐車場 a「special

[dedicated, «motorcycle»)] parking lot. ◯ 駐車場難民 a driver desperately looking for a vacant parking space.
ちゅうしゃじょうせいびすいしんきこう【駐車場整備推進機構】the Japan Parking Facilities Promotion Organization (略: JPO).
ちゅうしゃじょうほう【駐車場法】〘法〙the Parking Place Law.
ちゅうしゅうせつ【中秋節】〔中国の祭日; 旧暦8月15日〕the Mid-Autumn Festival; Zhong qiu jie.
ちゅうしょう²【中傷】◯ 中傷合戦 a mudslinging「contest [battle]; a bout of mutual slander; a smear campaign. ◯ 選挙中は両陣営の下でなりふり構わぬ～合戦が繰り広げられた. The election turned into a shameless mudslinging contest between the two opposing camps. 中傷記事 a defamatory article. 中傷攻撃 a「mudslinging [slander, smear] attack [offensive]. 中傷広告 an attack [a negative] ad. 中傷ビラ a「slanderous [defamatory] leaflet [handout, poster]. 中傷メール (a) defamatory e-mail.
ちゅうしょうきぎょう【中小企業】◯ 中小企業売上高 (value of) sales by small and medium-sized enterprises. 中小企業再生ファンド a turnaround fund for small and medium(-sized)「enterprises [businesses]. 中小企業退職金共済〔制度〕a smaller enterprise retirement allowance mutual aid system. 中小企業倒産防止共済制度 a mutual aid system to prevent bankruptcies of small and medium(-sized)「enterprises [businesses]. 中小企業白書〔中小企業庁の〕the 《2004》White Paper on Small and Medium Enterprises in Japan. 中小企業向け融資 financing for small and medium(-sized)「enterprises [businesses].
ちゅうしょうきぎょうきばんせいびきこう【中小企業基盤整備機構】the Organization for Small & Medium Enterprises and Regional Innovation, JAPAN (略: SMRJ).
ちゅうしょうきぎょうさいせいしえんきょうぎかい【中小企業再生支援協議会】〔中小企業庁が各都道府県に設置〕a small and medium enterprise [an SME] revitalization support council.
ちゅうしょうきぎょうしんじぎょうかつどうそくしんほう【中小企業新事業活動促進法】〘法〙the Law Concerning Measures for the Promotion of Creative Business Activities by Small and Medium Enterprises.
ちゅうしょうきぎょうそうごうけんきゅうきこう【中小企業総合研究機構】〔財団法人〕the Japan Small Business Research Institute (略: JSBRI).
ちゅうしょうてき【抽象的】◯ 抽象的違憲審査〘法〙abstract「constitutional [judicial] review.
ちゅうしょうれいさいきぎょう【中小零細企業】tiny, small and medium enterprises.
ちゅうしょく【昼食】◯ 昼食難民 somebody desperately searching through crowded restaurants for a vacant seat for lunch.
ちゅうしん¹【中心】◯ 中心暗点〘眼科〙(a) central scotoma. 中心価格(帯) a「median price (band). 中心小体〘生物〙〔細胞の〕a centriole. 中心商品 core merchandise; a core product. 中心値 a median value. 中心転換〘心理〙recentering; changing the「center [central focus] of one's thinking.
ちゅうしんこく【中進国】〔先進国と途上国の間の国〕a「medium [middle] developed country (略: MDC).
ちゅうしんし【中心視】〘眼科〙central vision.
ちゅうしんしがいちかっせいかほう【中心市街地活性化法】〘法〙the Town Center Revitalization Law.
ちゅうすい¹【虫垂】◯ 虫垂がん〘医〙appendix [appendiceal] cancer; cancer of the appendix.
ちゅうすうしんけい【中枢神経】◯ 中枢神経興奮薬

[剤] a central nervous stimulant. 中枢神経刺激薬[剤]
＝中枢神経興奮剤. 中枢神経症状〘医〙《represent》
(a)「central nervous system [CNS] manifestation.
**ちゅうスラウェシ**【中―】〔インドネシアの州〕Central Sulawesi;〔インドネシア語名〕Sulawesi Tengah.
**ちゅうせい**[4]【中性】〔言い回し〕gender-neutral language;〔語句〕a gender-neutral word. 中性的な〔男性的でも女性的でもない〕androgynous. ●彼は～の顔立ちをしている. His (facial) features are androgynous. | His face has an androgynous look.
**ちゅうせいし**【中性子】 ●中性子吸収材〔原子炉の〕a neutron absorber; a neutron-absorbing material. 中性子源〔原子力〕a neutron source.
**ちゅうぜつ**【中絶】 ●中絶胎児 an aborted fetus. 中絶胎児細胞〘医〙aborted「fetal [fetus, embryonic] cells.
**ちゅうせん**[2]【抽選・抽籤】 ●抽選制 a lottery system. 抽選販売 lottery「selling [sales]; selling by lottery.
**ちゅうせん**[3]【注染】〔型染めの一種〕a dye pouring method.
**ちゅうせんぶ**【中宣部】＝中国共産党中央宣伝部 (⇨ちゅうごく).
**ちゅうそつ**【中卒】 ●中卒認定試験 a junior high school equivalency examination.
**ちゅうたい**[1]【中退】 ●中退率 the《school》dropout rate.
**ちゅうだま**【中玉】〔野菜や果実の〕《of》medium size; a「medium-size(d) [normal-size(d)]《pear》.
**ちゅうちょう**【注腸】 ●注腸剤 an enema (solution). 注腸(造影)検査〘医〙a barium enema (略：BE).
**ちゅうちょうゆうこうきょうりょくそうごえんじょじょうやく**〔中朝友好相互援助条約〕the Treaty of Friendship, Co-operation and Mutual Assistance Between the People's Republic of China and the Democratic People's Republic of Korea.
**ちゅうと**【中途】 ●中途金〔国債などの〕(an) early encashment; cashing in《an insurance policy》(early). 中途視覚[聴覚]障害者 a person with《an》acquired「visual [hearing] impairment. 中途入社〔年度半ばでの〕entering a company midway through the year (instead of in April);〔就業経験者の〕entering a company in mid-career. ●～入社する〔年度半ばで〕enter a company midway through the year;〔就業経験者が〕enter [join, start working at] a company in mid-career. 中途枠＝中途採用枠 (⇨ちゅうとさいよう).
**ちゅうとうじゆうぼうえきけん**【中東自由貿易圏】〔構想中の〕the Middle East Free Trade Area (略：MEFTA).
**ちゅうとうつうしん**【中東通信】〔エジプトの国営通信社〕the Middle East News Agency (略：MENA).
**ちゅうとうど**【中等度】〔中度〕a moderate degree.
**ちゅうとうぶ**【中東部】the east central region. ●イングランドへにある町 a town in east-central England.
**ちゅうとさいよう**【中途採用】 ●中途採用枠〔年度半ばの採用〕a quota for recruitment in the middle of the year (instead of in April);〔経験者の〕a quota for recruiting people in mid-career.
**チュードル**【商標】〔スイス製の腕時計〕Tudor.
**ちゅうなんかい**【中南海】〔中国, 北京の故宮西側地区〕Zhongnanhai.
**ちゅうなんぶ**【中南部】the south central region. ●ドイツ～を流れる川 a river flowing through south-central Germany.
**ちゅうにゅう**【注入】 ●注入肉〔脂肪注入肉〕⇨しぼう[5].
**ちゅうねん**【中年】 ●中年処女 a middle-aged virgin. 中年童貞 a middle-aged (male) virgin.
**ちゅうはくしょく**【昼白色】〔昼光色・電球色に対し, 蛍光灯の〕the day white. ▶ JIS では色温度 5000 K としている

が, 国際電気標準会議 (IEC) ではこれに相当する規定はない. 昼光色と電球色の中間としては Cool White (色温度 4200 K) がある.
**ちゅうひしゅ**【中皮腫】 ●胸膜中皮腫 (a) pleural mesothelioma. ●悪性胸膜～ (a) malignant pleural mesothelioma. 心膜中皮腫 (a) pericardial mesothelioma. ●悪性心膜～ (a) malignant pericardial mesothelioma. 腹膜中皮腫 (a) peritoneal mesothelioma. ●悪性腹膜～ (a) malignant peritoneal mesothelioma.
**ちゅうびん**【中瓶】〔ビールの大瓶と小瓶の間の大きさの瓶〕a medium(-sized) bottle.
**チュービング**〔タイヤチューブを使って斜面や川を下るスポーツ〕(inner) tubing.
**チューブ** ●栄養チューブ〘医〙a feeding tube. ●チューブ栄養〘医〙tube nutrition. チューブ食〔栄養液〕tube-feeding formula; チューブ食する tube feeding. チューブ・ライト〔電〕〔管状の点滅灯〕a tube light. チューブ留置〘医〙permanent intubation; leaving [keeping] a《feeding》tube「in [in place].
**ちゅうぶこくさいくうこう**【中部国際空港】〔愛知県に2005 年開港〕Central Japan International Airport. ▶愛称は セントレア (Centrair).
**ちゅうぶしょうひんとりひきじょ**【中部商品取引所】the Central Japan Commodity Exchange (略：C-COM).
**ちゅうぶたいへいようハリケーンセンター**【中部太平洋～】=こくりつたいへいようセンター.
**ちゅうべいじゆうぼうえききょうてい**【中米自由貿易協定】the Central American Free Trade Agreement (略：CAFTA).
**ちゅうべいとうごうきこう**【中米統合機構】the Central American Integration System; Sistema de la Integración Centroamericana (略：SICA).
**ちゅうほくぶ**【中北部】the north central region. ●フランスにある都市 a city in north-central France.
**ちゅうもり**【中盛り】〔料理の並盛りと大盛りの中間〕a medium-large「portion [helping, serving].
**ちゅうもん**【注文】 ●注文情報〔オンラインショッピングなどの〕information on orders《placed with a company》. 注文履歴〔オンラインショッピングなどの〕an order history.
**ちゅうや**【昼夜】 ●昼夜逆転 ●～逆転の生活をする sleep all day and stay up all night; live an upside down life.
**「中庸」**〔儒教の経書；四書(ヒﾞ) の 1 つ〕The Doctrine of the Mean; Zhongyong; Chung-yung.
**ちゅうようりょう**【中用量】〘薬〙a medium「dose [dosage]《of a drug》. ●中用量ピル ⇨ピル.
**ちゅうりつ**【中立】 ●中立語 a neutral word.
**チューリップ** ●チューリップ帽 a tulip hat; a kind of soft floppy hat.
**チューリップかくめい**【～革命】〔2005 年キルギスで起きた反政府行動〕the Tulip Revolution.
**ちゅうりゅう**[3]【駐留】 ●駐留経費 stationing costs. 駐留地 (military)「base [camp]. 駐留施設 base [camp] facilities.
**ちゅうりゅうぐんとうろうどうしゃろうむかんりきこう**【駐留軍等労働者労務管理機構】〔独立行政法人〕the Labor Management Organization for USFJ Employees. ▶ USFJ は the United States Forces, Japan (在日米軍) の略.
**チューリン** Thulin, Ingrid (1926-2004;スウェーデンの女優).
**チューリング** ●チューリング・テスト〔電算〕〔あるコンピューターが知性を持つかどうかを判定するためのテスト〕the Turing Test.
**チュール** ●チュール・レース〔糸を六角形の網状に絡み合わせて作つた下布に刺繍を施して作るレース〕tulle lace.
**ちゅうロぜんりんゆうこうじょうやく**【中―露】善隣友

好条約】〔中国とロシア間で, 2001年締結〕the「Sino-Russian [Russo-Chinese, China-Russia] Treaty on Good-Neighborliness, Friendship and Cooperation.
**チュムポーン** =チュンポン.
**チュムポン** =チュンポン.
**チュラ(ー)ロンコ(ー)ンだいがく【ー大学】**〔タイ, バンコクにある大学〕Chulalongkorn University.
**チュンポーン** =チュンポン.
**チュンポン**〔タイ南部の県; その県都〕Chumphon.
**ちょいワル** slightly off; not quite good enough. ◯〜おやじ a roguishly fashionable older guy.
**-ちょう**[3]【-超】◯失業率7%〜 an unemployment rate (of) over 7 percent / 倒産した会社には100億〜の借金があった. The bankrupt company left debts of more than 10 billion yen.
**ちょうあん**[2]【潮安】〔中国, 広東省の district〕Chao'an.
**ちょうあんきしゃ【長安汽車】**〔中国の自動車メーカー〕Chang'an Automotive Group; Chang'an Motors.
**ちょういうんどう【調位運動】**〖植物生理〗photo-orientation movement.
**ちょういきん【弔慰金】** ◯◯特別弔慰金〔戦没者等の遺族に対する〕special condolence money (paid to a survivor of the war-dead).
**ちょうおおがた【超大型】** ◯◯超大型(旅客)機 a super-jumbo (jet [passenger jet, plane, airliner]).
「**超音速攻撃ヘリ・エアーウルフ**」〔米国の, ヘリコプターアクションTVドラマ〕Airwolf.
**ちょうおんぱ【超音波】** ◯◯超音波画像[映像] an ultra-sound image. 超音波気管支鏡(検査)〖医〗endobron-chial ultrasonography (略: EBUS). 超音波手術 ul-trasound surgery. 超音波電動歯ブラシ an ultrasonic electric toothbrush. 超音波導入 sonophoresis.
**ちょうが【蝶画】** a picture made from butterfly wings.
**ちょうかい**[3]【懲戒】 ◯◯懲戒権 a [the] right of disci-pline; the right to「discipline《workers》[impose dis-cipline (on…)];「(have) disciplinary rights 《over…》.
**ちょうかく**[3]【聴覚】 ◯◯聴覚検査 a hearing test. 聴覚口話法 an auditory-verbal approach. 聴覚センサー an auditory sensor.
**ちょうかつひ【調活費】**=調査活動費 (⇨ちょうさ[2]).
**ちょうかん**[3]【腸管】 ◯◯腸管組織侵入性大腸菌〖医〗en-teroinvasive「Escherichia coli [E. coli] (略: EIEC). 腸管付着性大腸菌〖医〗enteroadherent「Escherichia coli [E. coli] (略: EAEC).
**ちょうき**[2]【長期】 ◯◯長期エネルギー需給見通し a long-term prospect of energy「needs [demand, require-ments]. 長期国債利回り interest [yields, returns] on long-term government bonds. 長期債格付け 《(re-ceive)》a long-term bond rating 《of AA》. 長期債務 (a) long-term debt. ◯〜債務残高 (an) outstanding long-term debt. 長期政権 a long-term「government [regime, administration]; a regime which stays in power for a long time. ◯〜安定政権 a stable, long-term regime; (a) settled, long-term「administration [government]. 長期投薬〖薬〗〘長期投与〙prolonged administration; chronic administration. 長期離脱〔負傷などによる, チームなどからの〕being put out of action for a long time; going on the long-term disabled list. ◯4番バッターのけがによる〜離脱は痛い. It's tough to have the cleanup batter「thrown out of action for a long time [put on the long-term disabled list] by an injury.
**ちょうきか【長期化】** protraction; prolongation; lengthening. 〜する be protracted; be prolonged; go on [last] longer than (expected). ◯入院が〜につれて入院費用が家計を圧迫した. The extended hospi-talization and associated fees put a strain on our household budget. ◯不況の〜による業績の悪化 worsened business performance due to a prolonged

recession. ◯紛争の〜を恐れる fear the prolongation of a conflict.
**ちょうきゃくあもく【鳥脚亜目】**〖古生物〗=ちょうきゃくるい.
**ちょうきゃくるい【鳥脚類】**〖古生物〗〘草食恐竜〙Orni-thopoda.
**ちょうぎょだいげいひんかん【釣魚台迎賓館】**〔中国北京の〕the Diaoyutai State Guest House.
**ちょうぎょとう【釣魚島】**〔沖縄県尖閣諸島の中国語名称〕the Diaoyu Islands.
**ちょうきょり【長距離】** ◯◯長距離割引 a long-distance discount; 〔電話の〕a long-distance (call) dis-count; 《offer》a 《20%》discount for long-distance calls; 〖高速道路などの〗a 《10%》discount for long-distance「use [travel].
**ちょうけん**[2]【朝見】 ◯◯朝見の儀〖皇室儀礼〗the cere-mony of having an audience with the Emperor (and Empress).
**ちょうこう**[8]【朝貢】 ◯◯朝貢外交 tributary diplo-macy.
**ちょうこう**[13]【調光】 ◯◯調光レンズ a「photochromic [photochromatic] lens.
**ちょうこうエネルギーりゅうし【超高-粒子】**〖物〗an ul-tra high-energy particle; an ultra-high energy parti-cle.
**ちょうこうかんど【超高感度】** ◯◯超高感度撮影 high sensitivity photography.
**ちょうこうそう【超高層】** ◯◯超高層マンション a sky-scraper apartment「building [block].
**ちょうこうそく**[1]【超光速】 ◯◯超光速粒子〖物〗a super-luminal [a faster-than-light, an FTL] particle; a tachyon.
**ちょうこうそく**[2]【超高速】 ◯◯超高速インターネット衛星 an ultrahigh-speed Internet satellite; the Wideband Inter-Networking Engineering Test and Demonstra-tion Satellite (略: WINDS).
**ちょうさ**[2]【調査】 ◯◯全国調査 a nationwide「survey [investigation]; a survey covering the whole country. ◯◯〜活動費 investigative [investigation] activities. ◯〜活動費 investigative [investigation] expenses; 〔情報提供者に対する報酬〕informant [informer] ex-penses [compensation]. 調査機関《会社》a 《private》 research「organization [group, institute]. 調査企画書 a「survey [research] proposal. 調査研究機関 a survey and research organization. 調査地 a「survey [study, research] location [area, site].
**ちょうさ**[4]【長鎖】 ◯〖化〗a long chain. ◯◯長鎖アルキル《基》a long-chain alkyl (group). 長鎖アルコール a long-chain alcohol.
**ちょうざい**[2]【調剤】 ◯◯調剤報酬請求事務 dispensing-fee billing operations. ◯〜報酬請求事務専門士 a licensed dispensing-fee billing specialist. 調剤ミス〘調剤過誤〙a dispensing error.
**ちょうさんぼし【朝三暮四】**〔(二者の)目先の差異にとらわれて, それらが結局は同じであることに気づかないこと〕being distracted by superficial differences without noticing that "the substance is the same [《the two things are》 essentially the same, there is no real difference 《be-tween the two》]; 〔詐術をもって人をだますこと〕trickery; chicanery; swindling.
**ちょうし【長子・】** 長子優先〔継承順位の〕priority to the first-born (child); primogeniture.
**ちょうじ**[5]【停止】 suspension 《of musical entertainment as a sign of mourning for a prominent person's death》.
**ちょうしつ**[1]【調湿】 humidity control. ◯◯調湿機能 a humidity control function. 調湿効果 humidity-control effect. ◯和紙や炭は〜効果が高い. Hand-made paper and charcoal have a high humidity-

ちょうしつ

control effect. 調湿材 humidity-control material. 調湿性 humidity-control quality.

**ちょうしつ**²【調質】 ◨ modification; adjustment; treatment;〚冶金〛heat treatment; tempering. ～する modify; adjust; treat;〚冶金〛heat-treat; temper. ◨ 非調質鋼〚冶金〛non-heat-treated steel; untempered steel.

**ちょうしゃ**³【聴者】〔聾(ﾛｳ)者に対して〕a non-deaf person; a person with「normal [good] hearing;〈集合的に〉the hearing.

**ちょうじゅ**【長寿】 ◨ 長寿者 a long-lived person;〔百歳以上の〕a centenarian. ◨ ～者名簿 ＝長寿番付. 長寿商品 a long-selling product; a long seller. 長寿大国 a nation with「very high average life expectancy〔百歳以上の高齢者の多い〕a large number of centenarians. 長寿番付〔全国高齢者名簿〕a longevity list.

**ちょうしゅう**¹【徴収】 ◨ 過少徴収 (mistakenly) charging [collecting] too little〔tax〕; undercharging; undercollection《of taxes》. 誤徴収 taxing sb wrongly; mistaxation; mistaken「taxation [tax collection]. 過(剰)徴収 excess「徴収〔税金・各種公金などの〕a〔fee〕collector. 徴収済徴収員〔税金・各種公金などの〕a〔fee〕collector. 徴収済 collected money;《fee》 collections; receipts. 徴収漏れ〔料金・税金などの〕a failure to collect《fares, taxes》;〔その税金などの〕uncollected「fares [taxes].

**ちょうじゅう**³【鳥獣】 ◨ 鳥獣輸入証明書 a「bird and animal [veterinary] import certificate.

**ちょうしゅうき**【長周期】 ◨ ～の long-period; long-cycle[-cycled]. ◨ 長周期地震動〔地震〕a long-period (seismic) tremor. 長周期波〔地震〕a long-period seismic wave;〔海洋〕a long-period wave.

**ちょうじゅうしょうじ**【超重症児】children with extremely severe disabilities.

**ちょうじゅうほごほう**【鳥獣保護法】【法】the Wildlife Protection and Hunting Law. ▶ 正式名称は「鳥獣の保護及び狩猟の適正化に関する法律」.

**ちょうじゅしゃかいぶんかきょうかい**【長寿社会文化協会】the Wonderful Aging Club (略: WAC).

**ちょうしょ**²【調書】 ◨ 検察官調書〔検面調書〕a written statement taken before and by a prosecutor.

**ちょうしょ**³【彫書】⇨こくしょ⁴.

**ちょうしょう**【趙紫陽】Zhao Ziyang (1919–2005; 中国の政治家; 首相〔1980–87〕、共産党総書記〔1987–89〕).

**ちょうじょう**³【頂上】 ◨ 頂上決戦〔対決〕a showdown between the「leading [top] competitors [players].

**ちょうじん**³【釣人】 ◨ 釣人専門官〔水産庁内に設置する〕a civil servant specializing in matters related to「fishermen [anglers].

**ちょうしんうちゅう**【超深宇宙】〚天〛ultra deep space.

**ちょうしんけい**【聴神経】 ◨ 聴神経腫瘍【医】acoustic「neuroma [neurinoma, schwannoma, neurilemoma, nerve tumor];vestibular schwannoma. 聴神経鞘腫(ｼｮｳｼｭ)【医】＝聴神経腫瘍.

**ちょうしんすいせい**【超親水性】superhydrophilicity. ▷ superhydrophilic adj. ◨ 超親水性効果 a superhydrophilic [effect]. 超親水性表面 a superhydrophilic surface.

**ちょうしんせい**【超新星】 ◨ 重力崩壊型超新星 a core-collapse supernova; a collapse-driven supernova. 核熱爆轟型超新星 a thermonuclear supernova.

「超人ハルク」〔米国の、怒ると緑色の巨人に変身する青年のTVドラマ〕The Incredible Hulk.

**ちょうすいへいせんレーダー**【超水平線-】over-the-horizon radar; OTH radar.

**ちょうせい**¹²【調整】 ◨ 調整運転〔原発などの〕conditioning [adjustment] operation(s). 調整遅れ〔スポーツ選手などの〕delayed [late] preparation [training];《get

off to》a slow start. 調整型 ◨ ～型の政治家 a consensus politician; a consensual politician. 調整中〔時計などが正常に作動していないことを示す張り紙で〕Under Repair; Undergoing Repairs; (Temporarily) Out of Service. ◨ 彼は現在二軍で～中だ. He's been put in the second team「to get [while he gets] back into condition. 調整手当〔公務員などに支給される〕an [a salary] adjustment「bonus [allowance]. ◨ 初任給～手当 a "starting salary adjustment allowance." 調整能力〔自分の調子を状況に合わせる能力〕(an) ability to adjust (oneself); the power to adjust; a capacity for「adjustment [regulation]; the capacity《of the body》 for self-regulation;〔対立関係を緩和させる能力〕a capacity to「bring about [effect] conciliation. 調整保管米 rice stored for price「adjustment [stabilization]; price-buffer rice. 調整率〔年金などの〕an adjustment rate.

**ちょうせいのうかんインプラント**【聴性脳幹-】【医】〔難聴治療法の1つ〕an auditory brainstem implant (略: ABI).

**ちょうせん**¹【挑戦】 ◨ 挑戦校 ＝チャレンジ校 (⇨チャレンジ).

**ちょうせん**⁴【腸腺】〚解〛an intestinal gland; the glands of the intestine.

**ちょうせんたいがいぶんかれんらくきょうかい**【朝鮮対外文化連絡協会】〔北朝鮮の〕the Association of External Cultural Liaison.

**ちょうせんちゅうおうつうしん**【朝鮮中央通信】〔北朝鮮の通信社〕the Korean Central News Agency (略: KCNA).

**ちょうせんちゅうおうテレビ**【朝鮮中央-】〔北朝鮮の国営放送〕the Radio and Television Broadcasting Committee of the Democratic People's Republic of Korea; (略称) KRT.

**ちょうせんちゅうおうほうそう**【朝鮮中央放送】〔北朝鮮の国内向けラジオ放送〕the (North) Korean Central Broadcasting Station.

**ちょうせんとくじゅ**【朝鮮特需】〚日本史〛〔朝鮮戦争時の〕the Korean War boom.

**ちょうせんにっぽう**【朝鮮日報】〔韓国の日刊紙〕The Chosun Ilbo.

**ちょうせんのこえ**【朝鮮の声】〔北朝鮮の海外向け各国語ラジオ放送〕Voice of Korea.

**ちょうせんめじろ**【朝鮮目白】【鳥】〔メジロ科の鳥〕a chestnut-flanked white-eye; Zosterops erythropleura.

**ちょうせんれんぎょう**【朝鮮連翹】〚植〛〔モクセイ科の落葉低木〕Forsythia koreana.

**ちょうそう**³【聴奏】〚音楽〛playing back [reproducing]《a melody》by ear.

**ちょうそん**【町村】 ◨ 町村部 town and village areas.

**ちょうたつ**²【調達】 ◨ 調達先 one's supplier(s); one's source(s) of《raw materials》; a「company [country, bank, etc.] from which one procures《raw materials》.

**ちょうだんせい**【超弾性】 ◨ 超弾性合金 a superelastic alloy.

**ちょうちへいせんレーダー**【超地平線-】over-the-horizon radar; OTH radar.

**ちょうちょうき**【超長期】 ◨ 超長期目標 an ultra long-term「objective [aim].

**ちょうちょうきせんでんぱかんしょうほう**【超長基線電波干渉法】〚天〛very long baseline interferometry (略: VLBI).

**ちょうちょうりんかい**【超々臨界】〚物〛 ◨ ～の ultra-supercritical. ◨ 超々臨界圧 (an) ultra-supercritical [USC] pressure. 超々臨界圧技術 ultra-supercritical [USC] technology. 超々臨界圧発電 ultra-supercritical [USC] power generation. 超々臨界圧ボイラー an ultra-supercritical [a USC] boiler.

**ちょうちん**【提灯】 ◨ 鼻提灯 ⇨はなちょうちん. ◨ 提

灯売り[買い]〖相場〗〔仕手筋をまねて株を売る[買う]こと〕following (the lead of) speculators on the stock market.

**ちょうてい**[7]【調停】▫️ 調停団 an arbitration [a mediation] group [mission]. 調停調書〘法〙a written compromise; the record of a mediated compromise.

**ちょうていしゅっせいたいじゅうじ**【超低出生体重児】〘医〙a very low birth weight infant.

**ちょうでんどう**【超伝導】▫️ 超伝導コイル a superconducting coil. 超伝導電線 (a) superconducting power cable. 超伝導量子干渉素子〘物〙a superconducting quantum interference device (略: SQUID). 超伝導リニア(モーターカー) a superconducting maglev train.

**ちょうとしん**【超都心】▫️ (in) the「absolute [very] center of《a metropolis》; (at) the very heart of《Tokyo》; bang in the middle of《London》.

**ちょうない**[1]【町内】▫️ 町内行事 a「local [neighborhood] event [activity].

**ちょうない**[2]【腸内】▫️ 腸内悪玉菌 harmful intestinal bacteria. 腸内温度 (an) intestinal temperature. 腸内環境 the intestinal environment. ◐〜環境を整えるビフィズス菌 bifidobacteria that「improve [have a beneficial effect on] the intestinal environment. 腸内善玉菌 good intestinal bacteria. 腸内バランス the intestinal balance. ◐ 強いストレスは〜バランスを崩すことがある. Severe stress may disturb the intestinal balance.

**ちょうねじれネマチック**【超ねじれ−】▫️ 超ねじれネマチック液晶 (a) supertwisted nematic liquid crystal; (略) STN liquid crystal. 超ねじれネマチック・セル [液晶表示画素] a supertwisted nematic cell; an STN cell.

**ちょうばつ**【懲罰】▫️ 懲罰房〔刑務所の〕a disciplinary cell.

**ちょうばつてき**【懲罰的】▫️ 非懲罰的 nonpunitive. ◐非〜な矯正措置 nonpunitive corrective measures.

**ちょうひ**[2]【庁費】〖公共機関の予算の雑費項目〗a miscellaneous [government [prefectural, municipal] expense.

**ちょうひ**[3]【庁秘】〖防衛庁の秘密文書〗a classified defense document; a Defense Agency classified document.

**ちょうびさい**(かこう)**ぎじゅつ**【超微細(加工)技術】〔ナノテクノロジー〕nanotechnology.

**ちょうふ**[2]【貼付】▫️ 貼付薬 a (medicated) plaster; a patch; a poultice.

**ちょうふく**[1]【重複】▫️ 重複障害 multiple「handicaps [disabilities]. ◐ 障害者 a person with multiple handicaps; a「multiply handicapped [multihandicapped] person. 重複表現 a tautological expression; a tautology. ◐「社長」に「さん」を付けるのは〜表現です. It's「tautological [redundant] to「use " san" with the word " Shachō" [say something like " Mister Director. "]

**ちょうプラ**【長−】〔長期プライムレート〕〘金融〙a long-term prime rate.

**ちょうぼ**[1]【帳簿】▫️ 帳簿閲覧権 =会計帳簿閲覧権(⇨かいけい[1]).

**ちょうほう**[5]【諜報】▫️ 諜報戦 (an) intelligence war.

**ちょうぼう**[1]【眺望】▫️ 眺望保全 preservation of a view; preserving the《hotel's》view《of Mount Fuji》.

**ちょうみ**【調味】▫️ 調味液 (a) liquid seasoning.

**チョウ・ユンファ**【周潤發】Chow Yun-fat (1955- ; 香港の映画俳優).

**ちょうよう**[5]【腸溶】▫️ 腸溶性 ◐〜性の enterosoluble.

**ちょうよう**[6]【徴用】▫️ 徴用兵 a「conscripted [*drafted] soldier; a conscript; a draftee.

**ちょうようきん**【腸腰筋】〘解〙the iliopsoas (muscle).

**ちょうようせつ**【重陽節】〔中国の祭日; 旧暦9月9日〕the Double Ninth Festival; Chong yang jie; (特に香港の) the Chung Yeung Festival.

**ちょうり**【調理】▫️ 半調理 ◐ 半−済み half-cooked; partially prepared; semi-cooked《pizza》; semi-prepared [partially prepared ]《salad》/ 半〜《食》品 (a)「semi-cooked [half-cooked] food; partially cooked food. ▫️ 調理実習 cooking practice. 調理食品 =〜済み食品. ◐ 冷凍〜食品 a frozen「prepared [precooked] meal; frozen prepared food. 調理済み(の) ready-cooked;《a meal》prepared in advance. ◐〜済み食品 ready-cooked food; a ready meal. 調理麺 pre-cooked noodles.

**ちょうわたい**【調和体】〘書道〙a style of calligraphy employing kana mixed with Chinese characters. ◐〜で書く write (calligraphy) in *chōwa* style.

**チョーキング**〔塗装面の白亜化〕chalking.

**ちょくえい**【直営】▫️ 直営化 placing《a company》under direct control. ◐ 全店舗を〜化する put [place] all branches under direct control.

**ちょくがん**【勅願】▫️ a prayer offered by「an [the] emperor; [勅命による祈願] prayers offered at a「temple [shrine] by imperial decree. ▫️ 勅願寺 a「temple erected for national peace and security by imperial decree. 勅願院 a「temple [shrine] erected for [dedicated to] national peace and security by imperial decree.

**ちょくげき**【直撃】▫️ 直撃雷〔誘導雷に対し, 避雷針や近傍への落雷による電圧が屋内に伝わる雷サージ成分〕direct lightning.

**ちょくげん**【直言】▫️ 直言居士 a plainspoken [a freespoken, an outspoken, a candid] guy [" chap].

**ちょくせつ**[1]【直接】▫️ 直接介入 direct intervention. ◐〜介入する intervene directly《in a dispute》. 直接規制〘法〙direct regulation; 〔事項〕 direct regulations. 直接協議 (have, hold) direct [face-to-face] consultations [discussions]《with…》. 直接支配 (have, exercise)「direct [immediate] control《over…, of…》. 直接処分場〔使用済み核燃料の〕a direct disposal「site [facility]. 直接対決 direct confrontation;〔スポーツで, 強豪チーム同士などの〕a showdown《between two teams》. ◐ 同率首位のミランとユベントスが〜対決し, ミランが勝利を収めた. It was a showdown between the two leading teams, Milan and Juventus, and Milan「came away victorious [carried the day]. 直接投資収益率 the rate of return on direct investment. 直接服薬確認療法〘医〙directly observed treatment (略: DOT). 直接服薬支援 =直接服薬確認療法.

**ちょくそう**[2]【直葬】〔火葬・埋葬のみで葬儀を行わない葬送〕a cremation service.

**ちょくつう**【直通】▫️ 直通運転〔目的地まで途中乗り換えなしの〕a「direct [through] service《from Osaka to Tokyo》. ◐ 相互〜運転 direct train service between two railway companies.

**ちょくばく**[1]【直爆】〔原水爆の直撃〕a direct nuclear「hit [strike].

**ちょくばく**[2]【直瀑】a「free-falling [single-stage] waterfall.

**ちょくふん**【直噴】〔機〕〔燃料の直接噴射〕direct fuel injection. ▫️ 直噴エンジン a direct-injection engine. 直噴ガソリンエンジン a direct-injection gasoline engine. 直噴ディーゼルエンジン a direct-injection diesel engine.

**ちょけつ**【貯血】=自己(血)貯血 (⇨じこ[1]).

**チョコレート** ▫️ チョコレート・ソース (a) chocolate sauce.「チョコレート」[映画] Monster's Ball.

**チョコレートのうほう**[のうしゅ]【−嚢胞[嚢腫]】〘医〙a chocolate cyst.

**ちょさくけん**【著作権】▫️ 著作権管理委託契約 a copyright trust contract. 著作権管理事業者 a copyright「agent [manager]. 著作権教育 copyright education. 著作権信託 a copyright trust. 著作権ビジネス a copyright business. 著作権弁護士 a copyright lawyer.

ちょさくけんじょうほうセンター【著作権情報-】the Copyright Research and Information Center (略: CRIC).
ちょさくしゃ【著作者】▫▫ 著作者人格権 an author's personal rights.
ちょしゃ【著者】▫▫ 著者校正〔出版〕author's proofreading; author proofing. 著者略歴 an author 'biography [((口)) bio].
ちょぞう【貯蔵】▫▫ 貯蔵プール〔使用済み核燃料の〕a spent fuel storage pool.
ちょちく【貯蓄】▫▫ 貯蓄額 an amount of savings; 《one's》 savings. ◯ 平均〜額 an average amount of savings; average savings 〔of Japanese middle-class households〕. 貯蓄貸付組合〔米国の〕a savings and loan association (略: S & L); an S & L. 貯蓄関数 a savings function. 貯蓄性 ◯ 〜性の高い保険 savings-type insurance. 貯蓄投資差額 the household savings/investment balance. 貯蓄(型(性))保険 savings-type insurance.
ちょちくのひ【貯蓄の日】〔10月17日〕(National) Savings Day.
ちょっかがたじしん【直下型地震】▫▫ 首都圏直下型地震 an earthquake directly under the (Tokyo) Metropolitan area. 内陸直下型地震 an earthquake (with an epicenter) directly 「under [below] an inland area. 南関東直下型地震 an earthquake directly under the South Kantō region.
ちょっかつ【直轄】▫▫ 直轄地 an area under the direct 「control [jurisdiction] 《of the federal government》. 直轄領 territory under the direct 「control [jurisdiction] 《of the Tokugawa shogunate》; a direct holding.
ちょっきゅう【直球】▫▫ 直球勝負 《野球》a straight-pitch game; 〔策を弄さないやり方〕 playing it straight; 《give sb》 a fair deal. ◯ 首相には財政問題も〜勝負で解決してほしい. I want the prime minister to solve the nation's fiscal problems by tackling them head-on.
ちょっこう[1]【直交】▫▫ 直交周波数分割多重方式 〔通信〕 orthogonal frequency-division multiplexing (略: OFDM).
ちょっこう[2]【直行】▫▫ 直行バス a 「direct [nonstop, through] bus.
ちょっこうちょっき【直行直帰】straight there and back; straight 《to an appointment》 from home and straight (back) home (without going back to one's workplace). 〜する go straight there and back; go straight 《to an appointment》 from home and straight (back) home (without going back to one's workplace).
ちょとう【貯湯】〔湯をたくわえること〕hot water storage; storage of hot water. 〔たくわえた湯〕stored hot water. ▫▫ 貯湯式(の) hot water storage(-type). ◯ 〜式給湯器 a storage(-type) water heater.
ちょひょう【貯氷】【貯氷】ice storage; storage of ice; 〔氷を stored ice. 〜する store ice. ▫▫ 貯氷庫 an ice tank.
ちょへん【著変】【医】a significant 「change [difference].
ちょボラ = プチボラ.
ちょゆ【貯油】oil storage. ▫▫ 貯油施設 an oil storage facility. 貯油タンク an oil storage tank.
ちょりゅう【貯留】▫▫ 貯留層〔原油・天然ガス・地熱など の〕a reservoir. ◯ ガス〜層 a gas reservoir / 〜流体 reservoir fluid.
チョーラピテクス・アビシニクス【人類】〔エチオピアで発見された類人猿化石〕Chororapithecus abyssinicus.
チョン・ドヨン【全度妍】Jeon [Chun] Do-yeon (1973- ; 韓国の女優).
チョン・ブリ(一)〔タイ中部の県; その県都〕Chon Buri.
チョン・ミョンフン【鄭明勲】Chung Myung-whun (1953- ; 韓国生まれの指揮者・ピアニスト).
チョンリマうんどう【-運動, 千里馬運動】〔史〕〔1950年代北朝鮮の社会主義建設運動〕the Chollima movement.
ちり[2]【地理】▫▫ 地理的環境 a [the] geographical environment.
チリじしん【-地震】〔1960年の〕the (1960) great Chile (an) earthquake; the (1960) Valdivia earthquake.
ちりちょうず【塵手水】【相撲】chiri (chōzu); the cleansing ritual (as part of a sumo pre-match warm-up); ritualized gestures indicating that a fight will be clean.
ちりめん【縮緬】▫▫ ちりめん人形 a crepe doll.
ちりょう【治療】▫▫ 保存的治療〔医〕(a) 「conservative [nonsurgical] treatment. 要治療〔医〕〔医師の指示〕 Requiring [In Need of] Treatment; Treatment Required. ▫▫ 治療跡(痕)〔歯や皮膚に残っている治療のあと〕evidence of (medical) treatment. 治療共同体〔精神医〕a therapeutic community; a community for therapy. 治療記録 a (medical) treatment record. 治療(成績)〔実績〕〔治癒率・生存率などの〕a 「recovery [cure] rate. 治療(成績)格差〔病院間などの〕treatment inequality; inequality of treatment. 治療履歴 a record of (sb's) (previous) treatment; (sb's) medical records; a [sb's] treatment history.
ちりょうこうどうキャンペーン【治療行動-】〔エイズ対策の運動を行っている南アフリカの民間団体〕the Treatment Action Campaign (略: TAC).
チルド ▫▫ チルド室〔冷蔵庫の〕a chill(ed) compartment; a chilled room.
チルドレン children. ◯ 田中〜〔政治家田中に追従する若手政治家〕Tanaka's 「Children [Kids]; politicians riding on Tanaka's coattails.
チロシンキナーゼ【生化】a tyrosine kinase. ▫▫ チロシンキナーゼ阻害剤 a tyrosine kinase inhibitor.
ちんあげ【賃上げ】▫▫ 賃上げ率 a rate of pay increase; a pay increase rate. ◯ ここ数年〜率は低下している. For the last few years pay has been rising at a slower rate.
ちんか[1]【沈下】▫▫ 沈下橋〔流木などで橋が壊れるのを防ぐため増水時には水面下に没する高さに造られている欄干のない橋〕a submergible bridge.
ちんぎん[2]【賃金】▫▫ 年功賃金制度 a 「seniority-based [an age-based] wage system. 年齢別賃金 wages by age. 賃金カーブ the [an] age-wage curve. 賃金事情等総合調査〔厚生労働省が行う〕a comprehensive survey on wage conditions. 賃金成長率 a 《real, nominal》 rate of wage growth rate; a 《high》 rate of wage growth. 賃金不払い残業 unpaid overtime (work).
チンゲンサイ【青梗菜】▫▫ ミニチンゲンサイ baby bok choy.
「珍犬ハックル」〔米国の, 多才な青い犬が活躍するTVギャグアニメ〕Huckleberry Hound. ▶ アニメとして初めてエミー賞を受賞.
ちんこん【鎮魂】▫▫ 鎮魂歌 a requiem (song).
チンしたい【-氏帯】【眼科】〔水晶体と毛様体をつないで水晶体を支える繊維〕Zinn's zonule.
ちんじゅ[3]【珍寿】one's one hundred and twelfth birthday (or a later birthday).
ちんすい【沈水】▫▫ 沈水林 a submerged forest. [= 水没林 ⇒すいぼつ]
ちんすいへん【陳水扁】Chen Shui-bian (1951- ; 台湾の政治家; 総統 2000-08)].
ちんせい[2]【鎮静】▫▫ 鎮静房〔暴れる囚人を入れる懲罰用の独房〕a high-security (solitary-confinement) cell; a padded [an isolation] cell (for dangerous or violent prisoners). 鎮静法〔医〕sedation; (a) 「sedative [sedation] treatment. ◯ 吸入〜法 inhalation sedation; 〔笑気ガスによる〕nitrous oxide sedation / 静脈内〜法 intravenous [IV] sedation.
ちんそう【賃走】〔タクシーが客を乗せて走っている状態〕run-

ning「on hire [(while) engaged, while carrying a passenger]. ◐ ~(中).〔掲示〕On Hire. | Engaged. | In Use.

ちんたい² 【賃貸】 ▣ 賃貸事務所[オフィス]〔貸すための〕an office「for rent [" to let]; 〔貸された〕a rented office room; 〔掲示〕(Office)「For rent [" To let]. 賃貸ビル〔貸すための〕a [an office] building for「rent [lease]; 〔貸し出された〕a「rented [leased] (office) building; a [an office] building held on a lease. 賃貸併用住宅 a house with a rental unit; 〔集合的に〕housing with rental units. 賃貸部分 〔マンションの分譲部分に対して〕the rental units.

ちんたら 〔やる気なくだらだらと物事を行うさま〕lazily; sluggishly. ~する dawdle; dillydally; *goof off. ◐ 何を～やってるんだ. さっさとしろ. What are you doing dawdling like that? Get cracking.

チンディア ＝シンディア.

ちんとんしゃん 〔三味線の擬音〕(an onomatopoeic expression for) the sound of a samisen.

ちんプレー 【珍-】 an amusing play.

ちんべん 【陳弁】 explanation and justification. ~する explain and justify《one's actions》. ◐ ひたすら～につとめる strive earnestly to「excuse [explain and defend]《oneself》.

ちんぽうとう 【珍宝島】〔ダマンスキー島の中国名〕Zhenbao Island.

ちんみ 【珍味】 ▣ 日本三大珍味〔カラスミ・コノワタ・ウニ〕the top three delicacies of Japan (dried mullet roe, salted sea-cucumber entrails, sea urchin ovaries.)

ちんもく 【沈黙】 ▣ 沈黙劇 a silent play. 沈黙の螺旋〔社会〕沈黙を恐れて少数派が意見を表明しなくなること〕a spiral of silence.

ちんれつ 【陳列】 ▣ 圧縮陳列〔量販店などでの〕cramped [packed] (store) display.

# つ

ツアー・オブ・ジャパン 〔自転車レース〕the Tour of Japan.

「再見 ツァイツェン また逢う日まで」〔映画〕Roots and Branches;〔中国語タイトル〕我的兄弟姐妹.

ツァイト 〔ドイツの週刊新聞〕Die Zeit.

つい³ 【終】 ◐ ～の住処(,), ～の棲家(,)〔最後に住むところ〕one's「final [permanent] home; a home for the rest of one's life;〔死後に住むところ〕one's home「after death [beyond the grave] / ～の別れ a final parting; a last good-bye.

ついか 【追加】 ▣ 追加合格 additional [supplementary] admission. ◐ 英語の問題にミスがあり, その大学では 6 人の受験生を～合格にした.〔was discovered〕in the English exam,「an additional [a further] six students were admitted to the university. 追加報道 follow-up reporting;〔1 つの〕a follow-up report.

ついきゅう¹ 【追及】 ▣ 追及姿勢 ◐ 年金問題で野党は政府への～姿勢を強めている. The opposition parties「are planning to strengthen their pursuit [intend to intensify their grilling] of the government over the pensions issue.

「追撃者」〔映画〕Get Carter.

ついし 【堆漆】〔漆工芸の一種〕 tsuishitsu lacquerware; relief-carved lacquerware with several layers of lacquer in different colors.

「ツイスター」〔映画〕Twister.

「追跡者」〔映画〕U.S. Marshals.

ついちょう² 【追徴】 ▣ 追徴額 the amount of money (to be) paid in addition.

ツィッペ Zippe, Gernot (1917-   ; オーストリアの物理学者; 遠心分離機の開発で知られる).

ついで¹ 【序で】 ▣ ついで買い unplanned [impulse] buying. ◐ 公共料金を払いにコンビニに行って, いろいろ～買いをしてしまった. I went to a convenience store to pay a utility bill and ended up buying all sorts of things on impulse. / お客様の～買いを誘う商品陳列を心がけましょう. Let's try to display products in ways that encourage unplanned purchases by customers.

ついとう² 【追悼】 ▣ 追悼慰霊式 a memorial ceremony to console the spirits of the dead. 追悼記事 an obituary; a memorial article. 追悼行事 a memorial「event [function]. 追悼公演[コンサート] a memorial「performance [concert]《for…》. a「performance [concert] in memory of《John Smith》. 追悼試合 a memorial「game [match]. 追悼施設 a memorial facility. ◐ 国立(戦没者)～施設 a national memorial facility

for the war dead. 追悼デモ a demonstration to「remember [commemorate]《the victims of the purge》. 追悼番組 a memorial《TV》program.

ついとつ 【追突】 ▣ 追突注意〔掲示〕Keep Clear of Vehicle Ahead! | Maintain Safe Braking Distance.

ツイ・ハーク Tsui Hark (1951-   ; 香港の映画監督; 中国語名 徐克 Chui Hak).

ついらく 【墜落】 ▣ 墜落死 death by falling (from a high place). ◐ ～死する fall [plunge] to one's death.

「ツイン・ピークス」〔米国の, ミステリーと超自然現象の TV ドラマ・映画〕Twin Peaks. ▶ 監督はデーヴィッド・リンチ (David Lynch).

つういん¹ 【通院】 ▣ 通院治療 outpatient「care [treatment]. 通院等乗降介助 assistance to outpatients (with)「getting into and out of《taxis》[boarding and dismounting from《trains》, getting on and off《trains》]. 通院歴 ◐ 逮捕された容疑者には神経科への～歴があった. Hospital records showed that the arrested suspect had been undergoing outpatient treatment at a neurology department.

ツーエックス・エル【XXL】〔物品のサイズ〕XXL.

つうか² 【通貨】 ▣ 疑似通貨〔ポイント・マイレージ・インターネット通貨など〕pseudo-money; a "world's [world] common [unified] currency. ▣ 通貨オプション取引 a currency option「transaction [deal, trade]. 通貨改革 a currency reform. 通貨交換協定 a swap agreement. 通貨先物取引 a currency futures「transaction [deal, trade]. 通貨主権 currency sovereignty. 通貨スワップ取引 a currency swap「transaction [deal, trade]. 通貨の番人〔中央銀行総裁〕a [the] guardian of the currency. 通貨リスク a currency risk.

つうか³ 【通過】 ▣ 通過訪問〔他の国への訪問のついでに〕(pay) a transit visit《to New York》.

つうかん⁴ 【通関】 ▣ 通関検査 (a) customs「inspection [examination].

つうかんじょうほうしょりセンター 【通関情報処理-】 ▣ the Nippon Automated Cargo Clearance System (略: NACCS).

つうきん 【通勤】 ▣ 通勤路 a [one's] commuting route (to and from work).

つうこう³ 【通航】 ▣ 通航権 (a) right of passage.

つうこうどめ 【通行止め】 ▣ 一部通行止め ⇒いち².

つうこく¹ 【通告】 ▣ 通告義務 a [the] duty to report. ◐ 児童虐待の～義務 《have》a duty to report child abuse.

つうさん【通算】▶︎▢ 通算得点 an overall score; overall 「points [runs, goals etc] (scored). ◉ 彼は今大会の〜得点を10に伸ばした. At the tournament he 「brought his total score up [upped his overall score] to ten points. / 〜得点記録 a record overall score.
ツー・シーター〚自動車〛〘2人乗り乗用車〙a two-seater.
ツーシーム(ファストボール)〘野球〙a two-seam fastball; a two-seamer.
つうしょ【通所】〚通所〛▶︎▢ 通所介護〚デイ・ケア〛day care for 「the elderly [invalids, the handicapped]. ◉ 予防〜介護 preventive day care; a preventive day-care (program). ▶︎「通所介護」の新しい名称. 通所看護 care (service) at a visiting nurse station. 通所授産施設 a nonresidential workplace 《for people with disabilities》; a daytime employment facility 《for…》. ◉ 小規模〜授産施設 a small-scale nonresidential employment facility 《for people with disabilities》. 通所リハビリテーション day-care rehabilitation; outpatient rehabilitation. ◉ 予防〜リハビリテーション preventive rehabilitation at a day-care center. ▶︎「通所リハビリテーション」の新しい名称.
つうしょう²【通商】▶︎▢ 通商紛争 trade friction; a trade dispute.
つうしん【通信】▶︎▢ 通信会社 a carrier; a telecommunications company; *〚口〛a telco 《pl. 〜s》. 通信障害 a problem with 「communication(s) [transmission]; a 「transmission [communication(s)] failure. 通信長〚船舶など〛a chief radio operator. 通信ナビ〚自動車〛an online navigation system. 通信傍受 communication(s) monitoring; 〚盗み聞き〛eavesdropping.
つうすい【通水】▶︎▢ 通水カップ〘ラバー・カップ(⇒ラバー²)〙. 通水管 a water pipe. 通水橋 an aqueduct (bridge). 通水検査〚給水管などの〛= 通水試験. 〚医〛〚卵管〛(a) hydrotubation; a hydrotubation test. 通水作動試験〚原子力〛〚再処理施設の〛《carry out》a waterflow test. 通水式 a ceremony marking the opening of a new water 「facility [channel]. 通水試験〚給水管などの〛a flow test.
ツー・ステップ・ローン〚開発金融借款の通称〛a development finance (yen) loan; a financial sector intermediation (yen) loan (略: FSIL); a development (yen) loan through the local banking system; a "two-step" (yen) loan.
つうぜいかん【痛税感】〚税の負担感〛the pain of taxation. ◉ 〜を弱めるのが政府のねらいだ. The government's aim is to 「reduce the pain of taxation [make taxes hurt less].
ツータッチ〚two + touch〛〚二度触れること〛touching 《sth》twice; a double touch. ◉ 〜でパスを出す 《サッカー》make a two-touch pass / 〜で簡単に折り畳みできるベビーカー a baby carriage 「you can fold in two simple steps [featuring simple two-touch folding operation].
つうちょう¹【通帳】▶︎▢ 通帳記帳〚他人の通帳を不正に使用して金をだまし取ること〛stealing money from sb's account using a savings account book.
つうでん【通電】▶︎▢ 通電火災〚震災後の通電再開時に倒れていた電気器具などに発生する火災〛a fire which breaks out when power is restored after a power-cut (and short-circuits occur in domestic appliances).
ツートップ〚サッカー〛〚前線にフォワード2人を配置する攻撃態勢〛a "two-forward [two-striker] attack [formation].
つうほう²【通報】▶︎▢ 通報義務 an [the] obligation to inform 《partners of an HIV-infected patient》; a 「the] duty to report 《theft of firearms》. 通報ボタン a 「notification [report] button. ◉ 緊急〚非常〛〜ボタン an emergency 「notification [report] button / 火災〜ボタン a fire report button.
つうやく²【通訳】▶︎▢ 医療通訳 medical 「interpreting [interpretation]; 〚人〛a medical interpreter. 行政通訳 administrative interpreting; interpreting for official procedures; 〚人〛an administrative interpreter; an interpreter for official procedures. 司法通訳 judicial interpreting; 〚人〛a judicial interpreter. 電話通訳 telephone interpreting; 〚人〛a telephone interpreter. ▢ 通訳案内士 = 通訳ガイド. 通訳ガイド an interpreter-guide; a guide-interpreter. 通訳ボランティア〚人〛a volunteer interpreter; 〚行為〛volunteering as an interpreter; interpreting volunteering.
つうやくあんないしほう【通訳案内士法】〚法〛the Interpreter-Guide Law.
ツーリスト ▶︎▢ ツーリスト・アート tourist art.
ツールビヨン = トゥールビヨン.
つうわ【通話】▶︎▢ 通話エリア〚携帯電話の〛a [the] (voice) service area. 通話規制〚ある地域で通話が集中した場合などに行われる〛controlling [limiting]《cellular》telephone communication. 通話履歴〚通話記録〛a call log; record of (incoming and outgoing) calls.
つえ【杖】▶︎▢ 一本杖 a straight cane. 多脚杖〚4脚〛a quad cane. ロフストランド杖〚前腕固定型杖〛a Lofstrand (fore-arm) crutch.
つかいきり【使い切り】▶︎▢ 使い切りサイズ enough [the right amount, not more than one needs] for one time; a single-use size (packet). ◉ 〜サイズにカットしてある野菜 vegetables cut into the right amount for one time.
つかいたおす【使い倒す】〚機能を徹底的に活用する〛apply all the functions 《of a device》. ◉ 新作ソフトを〜 make full use of a new software / 携帯電話を〜 use all the functions of a cellphone.
つかいほうだい【使い放題】free use; unlimited use; as much use as one likes. ◉ インターネット使い放題 unlimited [unmetered] use of the Internet [Internet access]; as much use of the Internet as one likes. ◉ 月額2,000円でインターネット〜.〚宣伝文句〛Unlimited Internet access for 2,000 yen per month.
つがまつたけ【栂松茸】〚ツガ林に生えるマツタケ〛a matsutake (mushroom) grown in a hemlock grove; a hemlock matsutake.
つがるじゃみせん【津軽三味線】a Tsugaru shamisen.
つき¹【月】▶︎▢ 月探査衛星 a moon probe; a 「moon-probing [moon-probe] satellite.
つぎくち【注ぎ口】〚やかん・水差しなどの〛a spout; an opening (for pouring); a pourer. ◉ 切れのよい〜 a 「drip-free [no-drip] spout. ◉ 〜のついた容器 a vessel with a spout.
つぎつぎ【次々】▶︎▢ 次々販売〚高齢者などに次から次へと〙(複数の)業者が商品を押し売りする〛multivendor high-pressure selling.
つぎきせい【付きぎせい】suitable; appropriate; becoming; fitting; in keeping 《with…》.
つきて²【着き手】〚相撲〛hand contact (with the dohyō).
つきて¹【継ぎ手・接ぎ手】▶︎▢ 伸縮継ぎ手 an expansion joint.
つきのいり【月の入り】〚月が沈むこと〛moonset; the setting of the moon. ◉ 今日の〜は午後11時38分だ. Moonset will be at 11:38 pm today. | The moon will set at 11:38 pm today. | 月の入り時刻 moonset time.
つきので【月の出】moonrise; the rise of the moon. ◉ 〜を待つ wait for 「the moon to rise [moonrise]. ◉ 明日の〜は午後6時20分だ. Moonrise will be at 6:20 pm tomorrow. | The moon will rise at 6:20 pm tomorrow.
つきひざ【着き膝】〚相撲〛knee contact (with the dohyō).
つきめいにち【月命日】the day each month when sb died; the monthly return of the date of sb's death.
-づく 1〚そのような状態になる・そのようなことが頻繁になる〛◉ 最近出張づいててちょっと疲れちゃった. I've had to go on

quite a few business trips recently, so I'm rather exhausted. / 今年に入って急に病気づいてしまって、このところ三日にあげず病院通いだよ. I've been sick so much since the beginning of the year that these days I've been to see the doctor almost one day in three.
2 〔それに深入りする・その状態から離れられなくなる〕 ◐ 彼、すっかりゴルフづいちゃって、傘を持ってはパットの練習をしてるよ. He's become so attached to golf he even practices putting with his umbrella. / 山本教授は最近めっきりテレビづいて、専門と無関係のバラエティー番組にまで出演している. Prof. Yamamoto has recently been on TV all the time, even appearing on variety programs that have nothing at all to do with his work.

**つくしゃくなげ**【筑紫石楠花】〖植〗〔ツツジ科の常緑低木〕*Rhododendron metternichii*.

**つくね**【捏ね】 ◐◻ つくね串 a skewered 《chicken》 meatball; a ball of minced 《chicken》 grilled on a skewer.

**つくばちゅうセンター**【筑波宇宙-】 the Tsukuba Space Center (略: TKSC).

**つくばほうしき**【筑波方式】〔住宅供給方式の1つ〕the Tsukuba system of land lease and house rental.

**ツグリク** =トゥグリク.

**つくりこみ**【作り込み】 ◐ その模型は細部の〜が見事だった. The detailed craftsmanship that went into (making) that model was amazing. | That model was crafted with superb attention to detail. ◐ メルセデスベンツは〜の良さで定評がある. Mercedes-Benz has an established reputation for the quality of its manufacturing.

**つくりこむ**【作り込む】 ◐ 1cm四方の中にトランジスタ数千万個分を〜 assemble tens of millions of transistors within one square centimeter. ◐ 自分で納得できるまで映画を〜には十分な金と時間が必要だ. It takes time and money to craft a film that's up to your own standards.

**つけえり**【付け襟】〖服飾〗a「detachable [removable] collar.

**つけさげ**【付け下げ】〔着物〕a type of formal kimono worn by women on festive occasions, having modest decorative patterns.

**つけだい**【付け台・漬け台】〔鮨屋の〕a counter (in a sushi restaurant).

**つけづめ**【付け爪】〖美容〗an artificial nail.

**つけば**【漬け場】〔鮨などの調理場〕a 《sushi》 preparation area; a kitchen.

**つじばん**【辻番】〖日本史〗a guard(house) in a residential quarter.

**つしまてん**【対馬貂】〖動〗〔イタチ科の動物; テンの亜種〕Tsushima marten; *Martes melampus tsuensis*.

**つち**¹【土】 ◻ 土作り soil preparation.

**つちくらげ**【土水母】〖菌〗〔ノボリリュウタケ科のキノコ〕pine fire fungus; *Rhizina undulata*.

**つちぶえ**【土笛】〖楽器〗a clay「pipe [flute].

**つちむろ**【土室】〔土を塗り固めて造った(む)〕a mud storage mound;〔地中に造った穴蔵〕an hole in the ground used for storage.

**つちゆび**【槌指】〖医〗a「mallet [hammer] finger [toe].

**つつがゆ**【筒粥】〖神事〗=かゆうらない.

**つづきがら**【続き柄】 ◻ 続き柄欄 a column for (filling out) one's family relationship.

**つっぱり**【突っ張り】 ◐ 突っ張り棒 a「pole [rod] with a sprung extension《for creating extra hanging space》.

**つまわり**【筒回り】〔ブーツの〕a calf「size [measurement].

**つづみ**【鼓】 ◐◻ 鼓椅子 an hourglass-shaped (rattan) stool.

**「綴り字」のシーズン**〔映画〕Bee Season.

**つなうち**²【綱打ち】〔相撲〕belt-making for a *yokozuna*.

**つなぎ**【繋ぎ】 ◐◻ つなぎ剤 a binder.

**つなみ**【津波】 ◐◻ 津波危険地域 a tsunami danger area. 津波計 a tsunami gauge. 津波警戒システム a tsunami warning system. 津波工学 tsunami engineering. 津波避難場所 a tsunami evacuation site. 津波避難ビル a tsunami evacuation building. 津波避難路 a tsunami evacuation route. 津波防災訓練 a tsunami evacuation drill.

**つなわたり**【綱渡り】 ◐◻ 綱渡り的 precarious 《business management》.

**つのしまくじら**【角島鯨】〖動〗〔ナガスクジラ科の哺乳類〕*Balaenoptera omurai*.

**つぼ**¹【坪】 ◐◻ 坪効率〔経営〕(the ratio of) sales [profits] per *tsubo*. 坪単価 the price of land per *tsubo* (≒3.3 m²).

**つぼかび**【壷黴】〖菌〗〔鞭毛を有する細胞を生じることを特とする菌類〕a chytrid (fungus). ◐◻ ツボカビ症〖獣医〗〔両生類の新興感染症〕chytridiomycosis; amphibian chytrid fungus disease.

**つまかべ**【妻壁】〖建〗a gable wall.

**つまぐろおおよこばい**【褄黒大横這】〖昆〗〔カメムシ目の昆虫〕*Bothrogonia ferruginea*.

**つまぐろひょうもん**【褄黒豹紋】〖昆〗〔タテハチョウ科のチョウ〕*Argyreus hyperbius*.

**つまみえ**【摘み絵・摘み画】〔小さくたたんだ布を張り合わせてつくる立体的な絵〕a folded-cloth collage formed into a picture.

**つまもの**〖日本料理〗〔紅葉したモミジや梅の一輪の花など、料理に彩りを添える小物〕(flowers or leaves used as) (a) decoration for a dish.

**つみに**【積み荷】 ◐◻ 積み荷検査 (a) cargo inspection.

**つめとぎ**【爪研ぎ】〔猫などが爪を研ぐこと〕claw sharpening;〔猫が爪を研ぐ器具など〕a claw sharpener. ◐ 〜をする sharpen its claws (on a chair leg).

**つやおおずあり**【艶大頭蟻】〖昆〗a coastal brown ant; *Pheidole megacephala*.

**つやこばち**【艶小蜂】〖昆〗〔オンシツコナジラミなどに対する生物農薬〕an aphelinid「wasp [parasite];(オンシツツヤコバチ)*Encarsia formosa*;〔科名〕Aphelinidae.

**つやつやしい**【艶々しい】shiny [glossy, lustrous, silky]《hair, skin》.

**つよぶくむ**【強含む】〖取引〗show「bullish tendencies [a firmer trend].

**つららいし**【氷柱石】〔鍾乳石の俗称〕a stalactite.

**つり**²【釣り】 ◐◻ 釣り客 a visiting angler; fishing visitors. 釣り雑誌 a fishing magazine.

**ツリー** ◐◻ ツリー・クライミング〔ロープとハーネスを使って行う娯楽としての木登り〕(recreational) tree climbing. ツリー・ハウス〔樹上の小屋〕a tree house.

**つりさつ**【釣り札】〔釣り銭としての紙幣〕a「bill [banknote] in [for] change. ◐ 1万円札をご使用の際の〜の取り忘れにご注意ください.〔自動券売機などの注意書き〕If using a 10,000-yen bill, be sure not to forget your change.

**ツルヴェンコフスキー** Crvenkovski, Branko (1962– ; マケドニアの政治家; 大統領〔2004– 〕).

**ツルバキア，ツルバギア**〖植〗〔ユリ科の各種多年草〕(a) tulbaghia.

**ツルベンコフスキ** =ツルヴェンコフスキー.

**ツワネ**〔南アフリカ共和国の首都圏の名称; 首都プレトリアの新称〕Tshwane.

**ツングースカ**〔1908年に小惑星が上空で空中爆発したとみられるシベリアの地域〕Tunguska. ◐◻ ツングースカ(大)爆発〔事件〕the Tunguska「event [explosion].

# て

**て【手】** ▷ 手湿疹〔医〕hand eczema; eczema of the hand(s).
**であい【出会い・出合い】** ▷ 出会い(系)喫茶[カフェ] a dating cafe (where men pay to meet women).
**であいけいサイトきせいほう【出会い系一規制法】〔法〕** the Dating Site Control Law. ► 正式名称は「インターネット異性紹介事業を利用して児童を誘引する行為の規制等に関する法律」.
**てあて¹【手当】** ▷ 宿日直手当 a night duty or day duty allowance. 特別障害者手当〔国の〕an allowance for「special disabled persons [people designated as severely disabled].
**てあてりょうほう【手当(て)療法】〔医〕**hand healing; therapeutic touch.
**「デイ・アフター・トゥモロー」**〔映画〕The Day After Tomorrow.
**ディアボロ**〔2本の棒に付けた糸で回す空中ごま；その遊び〕(a) diabolo《pl.〜s》.
**「ディアボロス／悪魔の扉」**〔映画〕The Devil's Advocate.
**ていアルコール【低—】**low-alcohol. ▷ 低アルコール飲料 a low-alcohol「beverage [drink]. 低アルコール・ビール low-alcohol beer.
**ていあん²【提案】** ▷ 共同提案 (a) joint proposal. ◁ 共同〜する make a joint proposal. ▷ 提案依頼書 (write) a request for proposal (略: RFP).
**ていい¹【低位】** ▷ 低位推計 a low「estimate [projection]. 低位発熱量〔物〕a low「heating [heat] value (略: LHV).
**ていい²【定位】** ▷ 定位放射線治療[療法]〔医〕stereotactic「radiotherapy [radiation therapy] (略: SRT); stereotactic radiosurgery (略: SRS).
**ディー・アール・エム【DRM】**〔デジタル著作権管理〕DRM; digital rights management.
**ティー・アール・ティー【TRT】**《(警察庁の)国際テロ緊急展開チーム》the TRT. ► TRT は Terrorism Response Team の略.
**ティー・アール・ティー・エー【TRTA】**〔貿易関連技術支援〕TRTA; trade-related technical assistance.
**ディー・アイ・エス【DIS】1**〔地震防災情報システム〕DIS. ► disaster information system の略.
**2**〔英国の情報機関；国防省情報部〕the DIS; the Defence Intelligence Service.
**ディー・イー・エス【DES】1**〔生化〕〔合成女性ホルモン；流産防止の目的で米国などで使われていたが、内分泌攪乱化学物質の1つとされる〕DES. ► diethylstilbestrol の略.
**2**〔金融〕〔債務の株式化〕a debt-equity swap.
**ディー・イー・エム【DEM】**〔薬〕=薬剤イベント・モニタリング《⇨やくざい》.
**ディー・イー・レシオ【D/E—】**〔経〕〔負債自己資本比率〕a debt-(to-)equity ratio; a debt/equity ratio; a D/E ratio.
**ディー・エイチ・イー・エー【DHEA】**〔生化〕〔副腎と性腺で作られるステロイドホルモンの1つ〕DHEA; dehydroepiandrosterone.
**ディー・エイチ・エル【DHL】**〔国際宅配便会社〕DHL. ► DHL はこの社の創設者3人 Adrian Dalsey, Larry Hillblom, Robert Lynn の姓の頭文字から.
**ティー・エー【TA】** ▷ TA 制度〔ティーチング・アシスタント制度〕a「teaching assistant [TA] system.
**ディー・エー・エックス【DAX】**〔証券〕=ドイツかぶしきしすう.
**ティー・エー・ジー【TAG】**〔化〕〔トリアシルグリセロール〕

**TAG**; triacylglycerol.
**ディー・エー・ジー【DAG】**〔化〕〔ジアシルグリセロール〕DAG; diacylglycerol.
**ディー・エー・ディー【DAD】**〔PCM 信号を記録した録音盤；CD など；デジタルオーディオ・ディスク〕a DAD; a digital「audiodisk [audiodisc].
**ティー・エー・ティー・ピー【TATP】**〔化〕〔トリアセトン・トリペルオキシドの略称〕TATP; triacetone triperoxide.
**ティー・エス・エー【TSA】**〔米国国土安全保障省の一部局である運輸保安局〕⇨うんゆほあんきょく. ▷ **TSA** ロック〔TSA 職員が持つ特殊機器で開閉可能な錠前；これ以外の施錠がされている荷物は無断・無補償でこじ開けて検査する権限が TSA 職員にある〕a TSA (approved) lock. ◁ 〜ロック付きケースベルト a TSA (approved) luggage strap.
**ディー・エス・エム【DSM】1**〔電力会社などが、商品(電力)の需要量や需要発生のパターンを自社に都合のよいものにするため顧客に働きかける諸活動〕DSM; demand-side management.
**2**〔米国精神医学会による精神障害の診断・統計マニュアル〕the DSM; the Diagnostic and Statistical Manual of Mental Disorders. ► 分類や治療法の指針に用いられる.
**ディー・エス・エム・フォー【DSM-IV】**〔医〕〔米国精神医学会による精神疾患の分類と診断のマニュアル〕the DSM-IV. ► Diagnostic and Statistical Manual of Mental Disorders-IV の略.
**ディー・エス・ジー・エフ【TSGF】**〔医〕〔腫瘍マーカー；がんの進行とともに増加する生体因子〕TSGF; a tumor-specific growth factor.
**ディー・エス・ゼロに【DS02】**〔2002 年に作成された原爆の被曝線量推定方式〕DS02. ► Dosimetry System 2002 の略.
**ディー・エスはちじゅうろく【DS86】**〔1986 年に作成された原爆の被曝線量推定方式〕DS86. ► Dosimetry System 1986 の略.
**ディー・エス・ピー【DSP】**〔電算〕DSP; a digital signal processor.
**ディー・エヌ・アール【DNR】**〔医〕〔心肺蘇生拒否〕DNR. ► do not resuscitate の略.
**ディー・エヌ・エー【DNA】** ▷ **DNA** 修復遺伝子 a DNA-repair gene. **DNA** 捜査 a DNA investigation. **DNA** 登録 DNA registration (of whale meat); **DNA** 分析 (a) DNA analysis. **DNA** マーカー a DNA marker. **DNA** マイクロアレイ[チップ] a「DNA [genome] microarray [chip]. **DNA** 模型 a gene model; a DNA model; a model of the DNA molecule.
**ディー・エヌ・エー・インク【DNA—】**〔人や動植物のDNA 情報を含むインク；認証システムに活用〕DNA ink.
**ディー・エヌ・エス【DNS】**〔電算〕〔インターネット上のドメイン名と IP アドレスを対応させるシステム〕DNS; the domain name system. ▷ **DNS** サーバー a DNS server.
**ディー・エヌ・ジェー【DNJ】**〔生化〕=デオキシノジリマイシン.
**ディー・エフ【DF】**〔ディフェンス〕DF. ▷ **DF** ライン《スポーツ》=ディフェンス・ライン《⇨ディフェンス》.
**ティー・エフ・ティー【TFT】** ▷ **TFT** アレイ〔電子工学〕a TFT array. **TFT** 液晶パネル a TFT liquid crystal (display) panel; a TFT-LCD panel. **TFT** カラー液晶 TFT color liquid crystal. **TFT** カラー液晶ディスプレー a TFT color liquid crystal display; a TFT color LCD.
**ティー・エム・オー【TMO】**〔タウン・マネージメント機関〕a TMO; a town management organization.

ディー・エム・ティー【DMT】〖薬〗DMT; desoxymethyltestosterone. [＝デソキシメチルテストステロン]

ディー・エム・ブイ【DMV】〔道路と線路の両用車〕a DMV; a dual-mode vehicle.

ティー・エル・エス【TLS】〔タイムズ文芸付録; 英国の文芸週刊誌〕the TLS; the Times Literary Supplement.

ティー・エル・オー【TLO】〔大学・研究機関の研究成果を民間企業に橋渡しする組織; 技術移転機関〕a TLO; a technology licensing organization.

ディー・エル・ピー【DLP】〔商標・電子工学〕〔反射投影方式の映像技術〕DLP. ▶ digital light processing の略. ◨ DLP テレビ a DLP 'television [TV]. DLP プロジェクター a DLP projector.

ていおう【低硫黄】◨ 低硫黄ガソリン (a) low-sulfur gasoline (略: LSG). ◯ 超～ガソリン (an) ultra-low-sulfur gasoline (略: ULSG).

ディー・オー・ティー【DOT】〖医〗DOT; directly observed treatment. [＝直接服薬確認療法(⇨ちょくせつ¹)]

ティーカップ・プードル【犬】a teacup poodle.

ていき【低域】〔音の〕the 'low-frequency [bass] range; (at) low frequencies. ◨ 低域音 (a) low-frequency sound. ◯ 超～音 (an) ultralow-frequency sound. 低域再生 reproduction of low frequencies; bass reproduction.

ティー・グループ【T －】〔心理〕〔人間関係トレーニンググループ〕a T-group. ▶ (Sensitivity) Training group の略.

ティー・ケー・オー【TKO】◨ TKO 勝ち 《get, score》a TKO win. TKO 負け 《suffer》a TKO loss.

ティーけんてい【T 検定】〖統計〗a t-test.

ディーこうげん【D 抗原】〖生理〗a D antigen.

ディー・シー【DC】◨ DC モーター〔直流モーター〕a DC motor. ◯ ブラシレス～モーター a brushless DC motor.

ディー・シー・エフ【DCF】〔会計〕〔割引現在価値〕DCF; discounted cash flow.

ディー・シー・オー【TCO】〔総所有コスト; パソコンシステムの導入・維持・運用にかかる総経費〕TCO; the total cost of ownership. ◨ TCO 削減 total ownership cost reduction.

ディー・シー・ブランド【DC-】designer and manufacturer brands.

ティー・シーりょうほう【TC 療法】〖医〗〔パクリタキセルとカルボプラチンを併用する抗がん療法〕paclitaxel-carboplatin therapy.

ディー・ジェー・エーアイジーしょうひんしすう【DJ-AIG 商品指数】〔米国 DJ 社と AIG 社が算出する商品先物指数〕the DJ-AIG Commodity Index. ▶ DJ-AIG is Dow Jones-American International Group の略.

ディーゼル¹ ◨ ディーゼルエンジン車 a diesel(-engine) car. ディーゼル・ターボ車 a turbo diesel car. ディーゼル排気微粒子除去装置 a diesel particulate filter (略: DPF). ディーゼル・ハイブリッド車 a diesel hybrid (car [vehicle]).

ティーチ【TEACCH】〔自閉症児支援プログラム〕TEACCH. ▶ Treatment and Education of Autistic and Related Communication-Handicapped Children 〔自閉症及び関連領域のコミュニケーションに障害をもつ子供たちの治療と教育〕の略.

ティーチング ◨ ティーチング・プロ〔ゴルフ・テニスなどの〕a teaching pro.

ディー・ディー・アール【DDR】〔武装解除・動員解除・社会復帰; 内戦等が終結した国で元兵士に対して行われるプログラム〕DDR; Disarmament, Demobilization and Reintegration.

ティー・ティー・アイ・シー【TTIC】〔米国のテロ情報統合センター〕the TTIC; the Terrorist Threat Integration Center.

ティー・ティー・エス²【TTS】〖金融〗〔電信売相場〕TTS; a telegraphic transfer selling rate.

ディー・ディー・オー・エスこうげき【DDoS 攻撃】〖電算〗〔分散サービス妨害〕a DDoS attack. ▶ DDoS は distributed denial-of-service の略.

ティー・ディー・シー【DTC】〖商〗〔(メーカーから)消費者へ直の〕direct to consumer; DTC. ◨ DTC 広告〔処方薬の消費者向け直接広告〕direct-to-consumer [DTC] advertising; (1 回の) 'direct-to-consumer [DTC] advertisement.

ティー・ディー・ディー【TDD】〖通信〗〔時分割複信〕TDD; time division duplex. ◨ TDD 方式 a 'TDD [time division duplex] system.

ティー・ディー・ネット【TD-】〖株式〗〔東京証券取引所が運営する適時開示情報伝達システム〕TDnet; the Timely Disclosure Network.

ティー・ディー・パス【TD -】〔アメフト〕〔タッチダウン・パス〕《throw》a 'TD [touchdown] pass.

ティー・ティー・ビー【TTB】〖金融〗〔電信為替買相場〕TTB; a telegraphic transfer buying rate.

ディート【DEET】〖化〗〔防虫剤〕*(a) DEET; (a) deet. ▶ DEET は diethyltoluamide の俗称.

ディー・ドスこうげき【DDoS 攻撃】〖電算〗＝ディー・ディー・オー・エスこうげき.

ディバ〔有名女性オペラ歌手; 歌姫〕a diva.

ティー・ビー・エイチ・キュー【TBHQ】〖化〗〔酸化防止剤・t-ブチルヒドロキノン〕TBHQ; tertiary butyl hydroquinone.

ディー・ピー・エー・エー【DPAA】〖化〗〔ジフェニルアルシン酸〕DPAA; diphenylarsinic acid.

ディー・ピー・エフ【DPF】◨ 連続再生式 DPF〔ディーゼル車の〕a continuously regenerating diesel particulate filter (略: CR-DPF). ◨ DPF 装着車 a DPF-equipped vehicle; a vehicle equipped with a 'diesel particulate filter [DPF].

ティー・ピー・エム【TPM】〔全社的な〕〔全員参加の〕生産保全〕TPM; total productive maintenance.

ティー・ピー・ジー【TPG】〔米国の買収ファンド〕TPG. ▶ 旧テキサス・パシフィック・グループ (Texas Pacific Group).

ディー・ピー・シー【DPC】〖医〗〔診断群分類〕DPC. ▶ diagnosis procedure combination の略.

ティー・ビー・ティー・オー【TBTO】〖化〗＝トリブチルスズオキシド(⇨トリブチルスズ).

ティー・ビー・ティーきょうてい【TBT 協定】the TBT Agreement(s). [⇨ぼうえきのぎじゅつてきしょうがいにかんするきょうてい]

ディープ ～な〔奥の深い〕deep;〔秘儀的な〕deep; profound. ◯ ～な趣味 a deep 'interest [hobby] / テレビゲームマニアたちが～な議論を展開していた。Some video game fans were having an 'abstruse [esoteric] discussion.

ディー・ブイ・エイチ・エス【D-VHS】〔ビデオの一仕様〕Digital VHS; D-VHS.

ディー・ブイ・ディー【DVD】◨ DVD 化 conversion [converting] to (a) DVD. ◯ ～化する convert ((a video tape)) to (a) DVD / ～化権 the right to convert ((a movie)) to DVD. DVD(カー)ナビ a DVD (car) navigation system. DVD ブック〔DVD 付きの書籍〕a book (that comes) with a DVD.

ディー・ブイ・ディー・アール・ダブリュー【DVD-R/W】〖電算〗〔書き込み書換え可能な DVD 規格の 1 つ〕DVD-R/W. ▶ R/W は rewritable の略.

ディー・ブイ・ディー・プラス・アール・ダブリュー【DVD＋RW】〖電算〗〔書き込み書換え可能な DVD 規格の 1 つ〕DVD＋RW. ▶ RW は rewritable の略.

ディープ・インパクト〔宇宙〕〔アメリカの彗星探査機〕Deep Impact.

「ディープ・インパクト」〔映画〕Deep Impact.

「ディープ・エンド・オブ・オーシャン」〔映画〕The Deep End of the Ocean.

「ディープ・ブルー」〔映画〕Deep Blue Sea.

ディーラム【DRAM】 ⇨ 同期[シンクロナス]DRAM ＝エス・ディーラム.
ティー・レックス【T-】『古生物』〔ティラノサウルス属の代表種〕 *Tyrannosaurus rex*.
ていインスリン・ダイエット【低-】〔食事療法によって体内のインスリン分泌量を低く抑えることにより, 結果的に体脂肪を減らすことを図るダイエット法〕a low insulin diet (略: LID).
ていえいよう【低栄養】〔健康状態〕undernutrition; undernourishment; malnutrition; subnutrition; 〔食品の質〕low [poor] nutrition. 〜の〔健康状態について〕undernourished [malnourished]《children》; undernutritional [malnutritional]《status》; 〔食品について〕low-[poor-]nutrition; undernourishing. ⇨ たんぱく質・エネルギー低栄養状態 protein-energy malnutrition (略: PEM). ⇨ 低栄養食 food of「low [poor] nutritional「value [quality]; low-[poor-]nutrition food; undernourishing food.
ティエス〔セネガル西部の州・都市〕Thiès.
ティエンザン〔ベトナム南部, メコンデルタ地帯の省〕Tien Giang.
ティエンジャン ＝ティエンザン.
ディエンビエン〔ベトナム北西部の省〕Dien Bien. ▶ 省都はディエンビエンフー.
ディオーネー『ギ神話』＝ディオネ.
ディオネ『ギ神話』Dione; 『天』〔土星の衛星〕Dione.
ていおん[2]【低温】 ⇨ 低温解凍〔冷凍食品の〕low-temperature defrosting. 低温期〔基礎体温の〕a [the] low-temperature「phase [period]; 〔気温の〕a「cool [cold, low-temperature] period; a period of low temperature(s). 低温注意報 a low-temperature advisory. 低温物流 refrigerated [chilled] distribution. 低温冷蔵庫 a「cold [low-temperature] storage facility.
ていかかく【低価格】 ⇨ 低価格戦略《follow》a low-price strategy.
ていかく[1]【定格】 ⇨ 定格出力 (a) rated output; (a) rated power.
ていがく[2]【定額】 ⇨ 定額タクシー a「fixed-price [fixed-fare] taxi. 定額通信料〔インターネットなどの〕a fixed charge《for (unlimited) Internet access》; a flat rate《for Internet access》. 定額年金保険〔生命保険〕fixed annuity insurance; 〔国などの〕pension insurance paid in fixed regular sums. 定額払い〔医〕＝包括払い(⇨ほうかつ). 定額負担 (a)「flat-sum [fixed-sum] liability [payment (system)]. 定額部分〔年金などの〕a fixed portion. 定額保険 fixed benefit insurance.
ティカッド【TICAD】⇨アフリカかいはつかいぎ.
ティカッド・アジア・アフリカぼうえきとうしかいぎ【TICAD –貿易投資会議】the TICAD Asia-Africa Trade and Investment Conference.
ディ・カプア Di Capua, Eduardo (1865–1917;イタリアの作曲家).
ディカプリオ DiCaprio, Leonardo (1974– ;米国の映画俳優; 本名 Leonardo Wilhelm DiCaprio).
ていかん[5]【停刊】〔刊行停止〕(a)「suspension [cessation] of publication. 〜する suspend [cease] (the) publication《of a magazine》.
てき[2]【定期】 ⇨ 定期事業者検査〔原子力〕〔原発設備に対して電力会社が行う〕(a) regular inspection《of a nuclear power station》by a power company. 定期収入 (a) regular income. 定期清掃 (a) regular cleaning. 定期性預金 time and savings deposits. 定期接種〔予防接種の〕(a) routine vaccination. 定期放映 regular broadcasting; broadcasting at fixed intervals.
てき【鄭義】Zheng Yi (1947– ;中国生まれの米国の作家).
ていきこうくうきょうかい【定期航空協会】the Scheduled Airlines Association of Japan.
ていしゃくちけん【定期借地権】 ⇨ 一般定期借地権 an ordinary fixed-term land leasehold (for fifty or more years). 事業用定期借地権 a fixed-term land leasehold for commercial sites (for ten to twenty years).
ていしゃくやほう【定期借家法】『法』the Fixed-Term Rented Housing Law. ▶ 正式名称は「良質な賃貸住宅等の供給の促進に関する特別措置法」.
ていのう【低機能】(a) low function. 〜の low-function.
ていきんり【低金利】 ⇨ 低金利時代 a low interest rate「period [era]; a period [an era] of low interest rates.
テイクアウト ⇨ テイクアウト・フード take-out「food [meals].
ティクヴァ Tykwer, Tom (1965– ;ドイツの映画監督).
ティクリート〔イラク北部の都市〕Tikrit.
ディグリー・ミル〔学位を乱発する教育機関〕『口』a degree mill.
ティクリット ＝ティクリート.
ていけい[4]【提携】 ⇨ 提携交渉《begin》tie-up talks; 《hold》discussions about a prospective (business) tie-up.
ていけつ[2]【締結】 ⇨ 締結国〔条約などの〕a contracting「state [power, party, country]. 国連海洋法条約の〜国 a contracting party to the United Nations Convention on the Law of the Sea.
ていけつあつ【低血圧】 ⇨ 二次性[症候性]低血圧〔医〕secondary [symptomatic] hypotension.
ていけっとう【低血糖】 ⇨ 空腹時低血糖 fasting hypoglycemia. ケトン性低血糖 ketonic hypoglycemia. 新生児低血糖 neonatal hypoglycemia. 無自覚性低血糖 asymptomatic [(clinically) silent] hypoglycemia.
ていこう[2]【抵抗】 ⇨ 回転抵抗〔物〕＝転がり抵抗. 転がり抵抗〔物〕rolling「resistance [friction, drag]. ⇨ 抵抗野党〔与党に反対するだけの野党〕an (exclusively) anti-government opposition party; a party that opposes for the sake of opposition. 抵抗溶接機 a resistance welder.
ていこう[4]【蹄行】『動』 ⇨ 蹄行性(の) unguligrade. 蹄行動物 an unguligrade.
テイコプラニン『薬』〔メチシリン耐性黄色ブドウ球菌用抗菌薬〕teicoplanin.
デイ・サービス ⇨ 逆デイ・サービス the provision of day care in the outside community for「elderly [handicapped] people in institutions.
ていさんそ【低酸素】 〜の hypoxic. ⇨ 低酸素室〔高地順応あるいはアスリートのトレーニングなどのための〕a hypoxic room. 低酸素状態 a [the] hypoxic state. 低酸素(性)虚血性脳症〔医〕hypoxic ischemic encephalopathy (略: HIE). 低酸素脳症〔医〕hypoxic encephalopathy; cerebral hypoxia.
ていし[2]【停止】 ⇨ 刊行停止 ＝ていかん[5]. 判断停止 cessation of judgment; an inability to judge.
ていじ[1]【丁字】 ⇨ 丁字戦法『海戦』〔日本海海戦などでの〕the "crossing the T" maneuver.
ていじ[3]【定時】 ⇨ 定時率〔運行・運航の〕an on-time「percentage [rate]; 〔運行の〕a percentage of on-time runs; 〔航空便の運航の〕a percentage of on-time flights.
ていじほう【定時法】〔不定時法に対し, 時刻を一定にした時間区分法〕the「regular [fixed] time(-measuring) system. ⇨ ふていじほう.
ていしゃ【停車】 ⇨ 停車時分〔鉄道〕〔列車が乗降のために停車している時間〕stopping [standing] time(s) (at stations); how long trains stop (at stations); (a) dwell time.
ていじゅう【定住】 ⇨ 定住型マンション a residential [an ordinary residential] condominium; a non-resort condominium. 定住促進 the promotion of perma-

nent residency. ◐ ~促進策 a plan to promote permanent residency.
ていしゅっしょう[せい]たいじゅうじ【低出生体重児】 ◐❏ 極низ低出生体重児 ⇒ごくていしゅっせいたいじゅうじ, ちょうていしゅっせいたいじゅうじ.
ディジュリドゥ《楽器》〔オーストラリア先住民の管楽器〕a didgeridoo《pl. ~s》.
ていしょう[1]【低床】 ◐❏ 超低床 a super-low floor. ◐ 超~バス a super-low-floor bus. 〖IC〗 低床車いす a 「low-floor [low-seat, low] wheelchair. 低床ベッド a low bed. 低床〔路面〕電車 a low-floor light rail vehicle; an LFLRV; a low-floor「tram [*streetcar]. ◐ 超~電車 an 「ultra [extra] low-floor 「light rail vehicle [LRV]; an ultra low-floor [a ULF] tram.
ていしょう[6]【定床】〔病院の公称ベッド数〕the (official) number of beds.
ていしりょく【低視力】〖医〗 low vision.
ていしんしゅう【低侵襲】 ◐❏ 低侵襲性(の) minimally invasive.
ていしんちょうしょう【低身長症】〖医〗 dwarfism.
ディスインセンティブ〔阻害要因となるもの〕a disincentive《to…》.
「デイズ・オブ・サンダー」〖映画〗 Days of Thunder.
ディスカバリーせいど【-制度】〖米法〗〔証拠開示手続き; 法廷審理を迅速化するための証拠・情報などの事前開示〕discovery.
ディスク ◐❏ ディスク・カッター〔円盤状の刃を用いる裁断機〕a 「rotary [disk] cutter.
ディスクロージャー ◐❏ タイムリー・ディスクロージャー《株式》〔適時開示〕timely disclosure.
「ディスクロージャー」〖映画〗 Disclosure.
ディスチャージヘッドランプ《自動車》〔高性能の放電式前照灯〕an HID [a high-intensity discharge] headlamp [headlight].
ディストピア〔反ユートピア〕a dystopia. ▷ dystopian adj. ◐❏ ディストピア小説 a dystopian novel.
「ディズニーランド」〔米国の, アニメや遊園地映像のパラエティー TV番組〕Disneyland.
ディスノミア〖天〗〔準惑星エリスの衛星〕Dysnomia.
ディスポーザブル〔使い捨ての〕disposable. ◐❏ ディスポーザブル医療器具 disposable medical equipment. ディスポーザブル〖医療〗製品 a disposable medical product.
ディスポぜいひん【-製品】＝ディスポーザブル〖医療〗製品《⇒ディスポーザブル》.
ディスレクシア, ディスレキシア〖医〗〔失読症・読み書き障害〕dyslexia.
ていせい[4]【訂正】 ◐❏ 訂正放送〔修正した〕a broadcast correction;〔取り消しの〕a broadcast retraction.
ていせい[5]【定性】 ◐❏ 定性情報〔データ〕〔数値化可能な定量情報以外の, 文章・画像・音声などによる〕qualitative「information [data]. 定性調査〘広告〙a qualitative survey; qualitative research. 定性分析〖化〗(a) qualitative analysis. 定性濾紙〖化〗qualitative filter paper.
ていせん[3]【停船】 ◐❏ 停船検査 stopping a ship and making an on-board inspection.
ていそ[2]【提訴】 ◐❏ 共同提訴《bring》a joint「action [suit].
ていそうおん【低騒音】low noise. ◐❏ 低騒音化 noise reduction. 低騒音舗装 low-noise pavement.
ていそく[1]【低速】 ◐❏ 低速運転 driving at (a) 「low [slow] speed; low-speed driving.
ディタ《商標》〔ライチリキュール〕Soho. ▶ 日本ではSohoの商標が使用できなかったため Dita としている.
ていたいおん(しょう)【低体温(症)】 ◐❏ 低体温療法〔脳の〕= 脳低体(体)温療法《脳》.
ていたいじゅうしんせいじ【低体重新生児】a low-weight「newborn (baby) [neonate].
ティタノサウルス〖古生物〗a titanosaur; a titanosaurus.
ディッシャー〔アイスクリームなどを大きな容器からすくい取るた

めの半球に柄のついた道具〕a scoop; an ice cream scoop.
ティッシュ ◐❏ 濡れティッシュ a 「pre-moistened [moist] tissue; a (pre-moistened) wipe.
ティッシュ・エンジニアリング〖医〗〔人体組織工学; 人間の組織・器官の機能回復のためその生物的代替を作成する〕tissue engineering.
ティッセン Thiessen, Tiffani-Amber (1974-   ; 米国の映画女優).
ティッピング・バー〔車いすを後ろに傾けるための足踏み式棒状突起〕a tipping bar.
ディップ・ファイナンス【DIP-】〔再建企業向け融資〕DIP financing; debtor-in-possession financing.
ていてん[1]【定点】 ◐❏ 定点撮影〘写真〙fixed point photography. 定点調査 (a) fixed-point「observation [survey, research].
ていでんあつ【定電圧】 ◐❏ 定電圧定周波 constant voltage constant frequency (略: CVCF).
でいど【泥土】 ◐❏ 建設泥土 construction-site mud; earth removed from a construction site. 浚渫(しゅんせつ)泥土 dredged(-up) mud. 廃泥土 waste mud.
ていとう【抵当】 ◐❏ 抵当権設定登記 registration of a mortgage. 抵当権付き(の) mortgaged《property》. 抵当(権)の抹消《apply for》cancellation of a mortgage.
ていとうしょうけん【抵当証券】 ◐❏ 抵当証券会社 a mortgage securities company.
デイトリッパー〔幻覚剤の一種〕AMT; alpha-methyltryptamine.
デイ・トレーダー《株式》〔日計り商いをする投機家〕a day trader. ▷ day-trade v.
デイ・トレード, デイ・トレーディング《株式》=ひばかり(あきない).
デイトン〔米国オハイオ州の工業都市〕Dayton.
デイトンごうい【-合意】〔1992-95年のボスニア紛争を終結させた和平協定〕the Dayton Peace「Agreement [Accord(s)].
「ディナー・ラッシュ」〖映画〗 Dinner Rush.
でいねい【泥濘】 ◐❏ 泥濘戦 fighting in the 「mud [mire]; a 「muddy [mud-splattered] battle;〘スポーツ〙a muddy game.
ていねん[5]【定年】 ◐❏ 定年廃止 doing away with (the system of) requiring people to retire at a given age; abolition of a fixed retirement age.
ていねんぴ【低燃費】 ◐❏ 低燃費走行 fuel-efficient driving.
ていねんれいか【低年齢化】age「lowering [reduction]. ◐ 凶悪犯罪[売春]の~ a reduction in the age of 「vicious crime [prostitution]. ◐ 犯罪の~が進んでいる. Crimes are being committed by younger and younger 「people [children].
ていのうやく【低農薬】 ◐❏ 低農薬栽培 cultivation using small amounts of agricultural chemicals. 低農薬米〔野菜〕rice [vegetables] grown with small amounts of agricultural chemicals.
ていは【停波】〔電波発信の停止〕= 電波停止《⇒でんぱ[2]》.
「ディパーテッド」〖映画〗 The Departed.
ていはい[1]【低背】(a) low 「height [profile]. ◐❏ 低背型トランス a low-profile transformer.
ていはい[2]【低肺】〖医〗〔低肺機能〕low pulmonary function.
ていはいしゅつガスしゃ【低排出-車】a low-emission vehicle (略: LEV). ◐❏ 低排出ガス車認定制度 a certification system for low-emission vehicles; an LEV certification system.
ていひんい【低品位】 ◐❏ 低品位鉱 low-grade ore. 低品位炭 low-grade coal.
ていフィブリノ(ー)ゲンけっしょう【低-血症】〖医〗 hypofibrinogenemia; dysfibrinogenemia. ◐❏ 先天性[後天性]低フィブリノゲン血症 congenital [acquired] hy-

pofibrinogenemia [dysfibrinogenemia].
ディ(ィ)フェンシン《生化》〔内因性抗菌ペプチド〕defensin.
ディフェンス ◻️ ディフェンス・ライン《スポーツ》a defensive line. ◯ 〜ラインが上がる［下がる］ the defensive line moves「forward [back]／〜ラインを上げる［下げる］advance「pull back] the defensive line.
ディフェンディング・チャンピオン《スポーツ》〔前回の優勝者；タイトル防衛者〕a [the] defending champion.
ディプロマ・ミル〔教育を行わずに大学卒業証書や学位を発行する機関〕《口》a diploma mill.
ていぶんし【低分子】《化》a low molecular weight molecule. ◻️ 低分子化合物 a low molecular weight compound. 低分子有機物 low molecular weight organic matter. 低分子量 low molecular weight.
ていへん【底辺】 ◻️ 底辺拡大〔活動的〕(a) widening [(a) broadening, (an) extension] of the base. 底辺校 a low-end school.
ティムス【TIMSS】〔IEAによる学習到達度調査〕TIMSS; the Trends in International Mathematics and Science Study.
ていめい[1]【低迷】 ◻️ 長期低迷〔景気などの〕a long-term「slump [economic downturn]. ◯ 〜低迷からの脱出を図る try to escape from a lingering slump. ◻️ 低迷期 a period of recession; a slump (period); hard times. 低迷外 ◯ 人気〜中のプロ野球 professional baseball, whose popularity is currently floundering／大相撲は横綱不在で人気〜中だ. The popularity of professional sumo is flagging due to the absence of yokozunas.
テイモア Taymor, Julie (1952– ；米国の映画監督).
ティモシェンコ Tymoshenko, Yulia Volodymyrivna (1960– ；ウクライナの女性実業家・政治家；首相〔2005 2-9月, 2007– ］).
ティモシェンコれんごう【-連合】〔ウクライナの政治家 ユリア・ティモシェンコを中心とする政党〕the Yulia Tymoshenko Bloc(k).
デイモス《神話》Deimos;〔天〕〔火星の衛星〕Deimos.
ディモナ〔イスラエル南部の町〕Dimona.
ディモルフォセカ《植》〔キク科ディモルフォセカ属の総称；南アフリカ原産〕a dimorphotheca; an African daisy.
デイモン Damon, Matt (1970– ；米国の映画俳優；本名 Matthew Paige Damon).
ディヤーラー ＝ディヤラ.
ディヤラ〔イラク、バグダッド東方の州〕Diyala. ▶ 州都 バクバ.
ていようりょう【低用量】《薬》a low「dose [dosage]《of vaccine》. ◯ この薬剤は〜でも副作用が強い. This medicine has strong side-effects even at low doses. ◻️ 低用量ピル ⇨ピル.
「テイラー・オブ・パナマ」〔映画〕The Tailor of Panama.
ティラスポリ〔モルドヴァ東部の「沿ドニエストル共和国」の首都とされる都市〕Tiraspol(').
ティリー Tilly, Jennifer (1958– ；米国の映画女優；本名 Jennifer Chan).
ていりつ[4]【定率】 ◻️ 定率削減方式〔関税の削減方式の1つ〕a linear-cut formula. 定率負担 proportionate liability.
ていりょう[1]【定量】 ◻️ 定量調査《広告》a quantitative survey; quantitative research. 定量評価〔数値を用いての評価〕(a) quantitative「evaluation [assessment, judgment].
ティルトローターき【-機】《空》〔両翼機に大型ローターを持つヘリコプターの機種；離陸後にはローターの角度を変えて固定翼機のように飛行できる〕a tilt-rotor plane.
ティロサウルス《古生物》〔大型の水生爬虫類〕a tylosaur; Tylosaurus.
ディロン Dillon, Matt (1964– ；米国の映画俳優).
ディロング・パラドクサス《古生物》〔白亜紀前期に中国に棲息した小型肉食恐竜；皇帝竜；体表に羽毛が見られる〕Dilong paradoxus.
ディワニヤ〔イラク中南部の都市〕Diwaniya.
ディワリ、ディーパバリ〔ヒンズー教〕〔光の祭り〕Diwali; Deepavali.
「ティン・カップ」〔映画〕Tin Cup.
デインズ ＝デーンズ.
ディンブラ 1〔スリランカ南西部の地方〕Dimbula. 2〔紅茶〕Dimbula (tea).
ディンプル[1] ◻️ ディンプル・キー〔側面にくぼみを付けた鍵〕a dimple key.
デヴィート DeVito, Danny (1944– ；米国の映画俳優；本名 Danny Michael DeVito).
てうち[1]【手打ち】 ◻️ 手打ち麺 handmade noodles.
デーヴィス Davis, Andrew (1947– ；米国の映画監督).
テーザー《商標》〔米国製のスタン・ガン〕Taser. ◻️ テーザー銃 a Taser gun.
データ ◻️ データ改ざん data falsification. データ管理 data management. ◯ 〜管理システム a data-management system. データ・クリーニング《電算》〔データの重複の整理や修正〕data cleaning. データ受信［送信］data「reception [transmission]. データ・センター《電算》〔インターネットへの接続や保守・運用を提供する施設〕a data center (略：DC); an Internet data center (略：IDC). データマン《出版》〔記事の基礎となる情報の収集〕a research assistant.
データほごほう【-保護法】《英法》the Data Protection Act (略：DPA).
デート ◻️ デート商法〔相手の恋愛感情を利用して商品を売りつけるアポイントメント商法〕the sale of goods or services under the guise of dating. デート暴力 ＝デート・ディー・ブイ.
デート・ディー・ブイ【-DV】〔若いカップル間の暴力〕dating violence.
テーブル ◻️ テーブル・ゲーム〔トランプなど卓上で行うゲームの総称〕a table game. テーブル・コーディネーター a tableware coordinator. テーブル・コーディネート "table coordination"; the coordination of tableware, tablecloths, etc. (for entertaining guests at home).
テーブルさんご【-珊瑚】《動》(a) table coral.
テーラー Taylor, Don (1920–98；米国の映画俳優・監督).
テーラーメード ◻️ テーラーメード医療《医》＝オーダーメード医療《⇨オーダーメード》. テーラーメード薬《薬》＝オーダーメード薬《⇨オーダーメード》.
テール[2]〔モンゴルの民族衣装〕a del.
テールウインド〔追い風〕a tailwind.
テールコーン〔航空機の円錐状尾部；ジェットエンジン排気口内部の円錐形部品〕a tail cone.
デーンズ Danes, Claire (1979– ；米国の映画俳優；本名 Claire Catherine Danes).
デオキシノジリマイシン《生化》〔桑葉に含まれる血糖値を抑制する成分〕deoxy-nojirimycin (略：DNJ).
デオキシヘモグロビン《生化》deoxyhemoglobin.
テオクラシー〔神政・神権政治〕theocracy;〔神政国〕a theocracy. ▶ theocratic adj.
ておしポンプ【手押し-】 ◻️ 手押しポンプ式(の)井戸 a hand pump well.
テオルボ〔中世の弦楽器〕a theorbo《pl. 〜s》.
でがいちょう、でかいちょう【出開帳】exhibiting [exposition of] a Buddhist「image [icon] outside (the grounds of) a temple.
てがかり【手掛かり】 ◻️ 手がかり材料《相場》market clues.
てかざりりょうほう【手かざし療法】《医》pranic healing; (a) hand-healing therapy which avoids actual physical contact.
テガフール・ウラシル《薬》〔抗がん剤〕tegafur uracil.〔略：ユー・エフ・ティー〕.
てがみ【手紙】 ◻️ 手紙美人 a beautiful woman, to judge by her writing; a woman whose writing en-

courages *one* to believe that she is beautiful.
**テキーラ・サンライズ**〔カクテル〕a tequila sunrise.
**てきおう【適応】**🔲 過(剰)適応 overadaptation; excessive adaptation. 🔲 適応機構〖生物・心理〗an「adaptive [adjustment] mechanism.
🔲 敵国条項〖国連憲章第 107 条のこと〗the enemy-nation clause (of the UN Charter).
**できこん【できちゃった結婚】**〔できちゃった結婚〕a marriage that results from an unplanned pregnancy; a marriage of necessity; (特に未成年の女性が妊娠した場合) a shotgun「wedding [marriage].
**「テキサス・チェーンソー」**〔映画〕The Texas Chainsaw Massacre.
**てきじ【適時】**🔲 適時開示〖株式〗timely disclosure. ▷ 〜開示情報伝達システム the Timely Disclosure Network (略: TDNet, Tdnet).
**できじあい【出来試合】**a「fixed [rigged] match [game].
**てきじょう²【敵情】**🔲 敵情視察 observation [monitoring] of「the enemy [enemy movements]; spying on the enemy. ▷ 〜視察する observe [monitor, spy on] the enemy [enemy movements].
**てきせい¹【適正】**🔲 適正在庫(量) an appropriate amount of stock (inventory). 適正製造規範〖医薬品・食品の製造管理および品質管理に関する基準〗good manufacturing practice(s) (略: GMP). 適正農業規範〔農作物の生産および供給の管理に関する基準〕good agricultural practice(s) (略: GAP).
**てきせい³【敵性】**🔲 敵性(外)国人 a citizen of an enemy country; an enemy alien. 敵性戦闘員 an enemy combatant.
**てきせんとういん【敵戦闘員】**an enemy combatant.
**てきたい【敵対】**🔲 敵対視 ▷ 銀塩カメラの愛好者の中にはデジカメを〜視する人もいる。Some fans of film cameras look upon digital cameras as the enemy. 敵対勢力 hostile forces.
**てきち¹【適地】**🔲 (最)適地生産 production「in [at] an「optimal [optimum] location; optimum-site production.
**でぐち【出口】**🔲 出口戦略〖事業・作戦などの〗an exit strategy.
**テクニカル**🔲 テクニカル指標〖株式〗a technical index. テクニカル・チャート〖株式〗a technical chart. テクニカル・ルーティン〔シンクロナイズド・スイミングの〕a technical routine.
**テクノスケープ**〔近代的な建造物などの景観〕technoscape.
**「テクノロジー・レビュー」**〔米国の技術革新専門誌〕Technology Review.
**てくび【手首】**🔲 手首自傷 ＝リストカット (⇒リスト²). 手首自傷症候群〖医〗wrist-cutting syndrome. [＝リストカット症候群 (⇒リスト²)].
**てけいさん【手計算】**manual calculation.
**テケツ**〔劇場・映画館などのチケット〕a ticket; 〔チケット売り場〕a box office; 〔チケット売り場の係員〕a box-office clerk.
**てこぎ【手漕ぎ】**rowing [paddling] (by hand). ▷ 〜の漁船 a fishing「*rowboat [*rowing boat]. 🔲 手漕ぎボート *a rowboat; *a rowing boat.
**デコでん【-電】**〔ラインストーンなどを張り付けて装飾した携帯電話〕a bling「phone [mobile]. ▶「デコレーション電話」の略.
**デコトラ**〔電飾などを飾りつけたトラック〕a truck gaudily decorated with chrome, air-brushed pictures and colored lights. ▶「デコレーション・トラック」の略.
**デコピン**〔親指で反動をつけて中指や人差し指ではをはじくこと〕a finger flick「to [on] the forehead. ▷ 〜をする give *sb* a finger flick「to [on] the forehead.
**デコる**〔身の回りの品物や車などに装飾をほどこす〕decorate 〔(口) bling (up)〕(a mobile phone).
**デザート²** 1〔砂漠〕(a) desert.

2〔自動車レース〕〔砂地路面〕a sand surface.
**デザイナー**🔲 デザイナー・ドラッグ〔合成麻薬〕a designer drug.
**デザイナーズ・アンド・キャラクターズ・ブランド** ＝ ディー・シー・ブランド.
**デザイン性** design「characteristics [qualities]. ▷ 高い〜性 good design qualities / 〜性に優れた商品 a well-designed product / 〜性を重視する emphasize the design (of a house). 🔲 デザイン・バーコード〖商標〗a Design Barcode.
**デジコミ** ＝デジタル・コミック, デジタル・コミュニケーション (⇒デジタル).
**デジタル**🔲 デジタル・アート〔デジタル技術による芸術〕digital art. デジタル一眼レフカメラ a digital single-lens reflex camera. デジタル・エコノミー〖経・電算〗〔電子商取引や IT 産業のような、コンピュータを介した経済現象〕a digital economy. デジタル音楽プレーヤー a digital music player. デジタル回路〖電算〗a digital circuit. デジタル画像 a digital image. ▷ 〜画像化する digitalize (a picture). デジタル家電 digital home appliances. デジタル切手 a digital stamp; an E-stamp. [＝電子切手 (⇒でん)]. デジタル景気 a digital boom. デジタル権利管理 ＝デジタル著作権管理. デジタル交換機〔電話の〕a digital switching system. デジタル・コミック〔パソコンを使って制作・配信されるマンガ〕web comics; online comics; digital comics; (Inter)net comics. デジタル・コミュニケーション〔インターネットによる情報発信〕digital communication(s); (Inter)net communication(s). デジタル・コンテンツ digital content. デジタル・サラウンド digital surround (sound, speakers). デジタル・サラウンド・システム a digital surround system. デジタル(自動)血圧計 a digital sphygmomanometer. デジタル・シネマ〖映画〗〔フィルムを用いない〕digital「cinema [filmmaking, cinematography].
デジタル修復〔映像・音声などの〕digital restoration. デジタル・ズーム〔写真〕a digital zoom; digital zooming; (そのレンズ〕a digital zoom lens. ▷ 4 倍〜ズーム a 4x digital zoom (lens). デジタル・スチール・カメラ a digital still camera. デジタル世代 the digital generation. デジタル素材 digital materials. デジタル著作権管理 digital rights management (略: DRM). デジタル・ドアロック a digital doorlock. デジタル文化 (a [the]) digital culture. デジタル編集 digital editing. デジタル補正〔画像の〕digital correction. デジタル保存〖文化財・遺跡などの〗digital preservation. デジタル・モバイル放送 digital mobile broadcasting (略: DMB). ▷ 衛星〜モバイル放送 satellite digital mobile broadcasting; satellite DMB. デジタル・ラジオ放送 digital radio broadcasting. デジタル・リマスター〖映・音楽〗〔デジタルでマスターを作り直すこと〕digital remastering; 〔作り直したもの〕a digital remaster. [⇒リマスター].
**デジタルほうそうすいしんきょうかい【-放送推進協会】**the Association for Promotion of Digital Broadcasting (略: DPA). ▶ 2007 年、BS デジタル放送推進協会と地上デジタル推進協会が統合してできた団体.
**てしぼり【手絞り】**〔手作業の絞り染め〕hand tie-dyeing; 〔植物油などの〕hand squeezing. ▷ 〜の振り袖 a long-sleeved kimono tie-dyed by hand / 〜の胡麻油 hand-squeezed sesame oil.
**デジュール・スタンダード**〔公的標準〕a de jure standard.
**デジューレ・スタンダード** ＝デジュール・スタンダード.
**てじゅん【手順】**🔲 手順前後〖囲碁・将棋〗〔指し手の順序を間違えること〕making a mistake in the order of moves; moving (pieces) in the wrong order; 〔間違った順番でものごとをやること〕doing things in the wrong order; getting the order wrong.
**デスクトップ**🔲 デスクトップ検索〔サーチ〕〖電算〗〔パソコン上に保存されている文書などをキーワードを使って検索すること〕a desktop search.

ですたい【です体】the desu/masu「form [mode];《in》polite style;《at》politeness level.
テスト ◻️ テスト券〔新紙幣の〕a test「banknote [*bill, *note];〔不採用になったデザインの〕an essay《of a banknote》. テスト走行 a test run. ◯ 合同～走行〔レース等に行う〕a combined test run. テスト・ライダー〔試走バイクの〕a test rider.
デスバレーげんしょう【-現象】《経営》〔研究開発への投資が製品として結実しない現象〕the「"valley of death" ["Death Valley"] phenomenon.
ですますたい【ちょう】【ですます体[調]】= ですたい.
デス・マッチ ◻️ ランバージャック・デスマッチ《プロレス》〔リング外に落ちた選手をリングに無理矢理押し上げる形式のデスマッチ〕a lumberjack death match.
デソキシメチルテストステロン【薬】〔筋肉増強効果のあるステロイド〕desoxymethyltestosterone（略: DMT）.
テタレ【手-】〔指輪や化粧品の広告写真などで手だけを写されるタレント〕a hand model.
デチューン ～する〔意図的に機械の性能を落としたり楽器の音程をずらしたりする〕detune《an engine》; put《a guitar》out of tune.
テチョン【泰川】〔北朝鮮の都市〕Taechon.
てあかゆう【鉄赤釉】〔製陶〕(an) iron red glaze.
てっかんのん【鉄観音】〔ウーロン茶の一種〕tie guan yin; iron goddess of mercy oolong (tea).
デッキ ◻️ デッキ・ガラス〔建〕〔舗床ガラス〕a glass paving block.
てぐすり【鉄釉】〔製陶〕(an) iron glaze.
てづくり【手作り】 ◻️ 手作りグッズ a handmade item. 手作り弁当 a「handmade [homemade] lunch. 手作り料理 home cooking; handmade「food [meals, dishes].
てっこつ【鉄骨】 ◻️ 鉄骨工法〔建〕the steel-frame construction method. 鉄骨造り ～造りの建物 a steel-frame building. 鉄骨ラーメン構造 rigid-frame steel(-reinforced concrete) construction.
てっさい【鉄滓】iron slag.
てっしゅう²【撤収】 ◻️ 撤収作戦 withdrawal operations.
てつだい【手伝い】 ◻️ 手伝いロボット ◯ おてつだいロボット.
てっちゃん【鉄ちゃん】〔鉄道ファン〕a trainspotter; a railroad「buff [nerd];"a railway anorak."
てつづき【手続き】 ◻️ 手続きミス〔a〕procedural error; (a) processing error. 手続き論〔理論〕procedural theory; a theory of procedure;〔議論〕a discussion of「procedure [procedural matters]. ◯ 1回目の協議は～に終始した. The whole of the first session was spent on discussing matters of procedure.
デット・アイ・アール【-IR】〔経〕〔企業の金融機関向け広報活動〕debt investor relations.
てつどう【鉄道】 ◻️ 鉄道災害 a railway disaster. 鉄道システム工学 railway systems engineering. 鉄道事業者 a「railway [*railroad] operator. 鉄道マン a railroad man; *a railroader.
てつどうけんせつ・うんゆしせつせいびしえんきこう【鉄道建設・運輸施設整備支援機構】the Japan Railway Construction, Transport and Technology Agency (= JRTT). ▶ 2003年に日本鉄道建設公団と運輸施設整備事業団が統合して発足.
「鉄道唱歌」〔曲名〕Railway Songs.
てつどうのひ【鉄道の日】[10月14日] Railway Day.
「デッドマン・ウォーキング」〔映画〕Dead Man Walking.
てつのシルクロード【鉄の-】〔アジアと欧州を結ぶユーラシア大陸横断鉄道〕an "Iron Silk Road."
デップ Depp, Johnny (1963- ; 米国の映画俳優; 本名 John Christopher Depp III).
てっぽうあめ【鉄砲雨】sheets of rain; torrential rain. ◯ 空の底が抜けたような～が降った. The skies opened and the rain came down in torrents.

てづみ【手摘み】～する handpick《cotton》. ◯ ～のお茶 handpicked tea.
てつや【徹夜】 ◻️ 徹夜組〔イベント会場の入口・切符売り場などに前日から徹夜で並ぶ人々〕people who camp out (in line) overnight (for [to get] tickets).
てつゆう【鉄釉】〔製陶〕(an) iron glaze. ◯ 鉄釉陶器 iron-glazed pottery.
「出てこい！キャスパー」〔米国の、かわいいお化けが主人公のTV ギャグアニメ〕Casper the Friendly Ghost.
テテュス【ギ神話】〔ウラノスの娘でオケアノスの妻〕Tethys;【天】〔土星の衛星〕Tethys.
デデリエどうくつ【-洞窟】〔シリアの洞窟〕〔ネアンデルタール人の骨が発見された〕the Dederiyeh Cave.
テト〔ベトナムの旧正月〕Tet.
デトックス〔体内の毒素・老廃物排出を促進するという触れ込みの美容療法〕(a) detox.
テトラハイドロストリノン【化】〔筋肉増強効果のあるステロイド〕tetrahydrostrinone（略: THG）.
テトラミン〔ヒメエゾボラ・ツブガイなどの貝の唾液腺に含まれる貝毒; 頭痛・めまい・吐気などを催させる〕tetramine.
テトラメトキシシラン【化】tetramethoxysilane. [= オルトケイさんテトラメチル]
てどり¹【手取り】 ◻️ 手取り年収 one's「annual [yearly] take-home pay; an annual [a yearly] take-home income《of...》.
てなおし【手直し】 ◻️ 全面[部分]手直し (a) total [partial] correction [alteration].
ながこがね【手長黄金】【昆】〔コガネムシ科テナガコガネ亜科に属する昆虫の総称〕a long-armed chafer.
テナント¹ ◻️ テナント料 a「tenant [tenancy] fee.
テニス ◻️ テニス肘〔エルボー〕 tennis elbow. ◯ バックハンド[フォアハンド]～肘 backhand [forehand] tennis elbow.
てにもつ【手荷物】 ◻️ 手荷物検査 a baggage「inspection [check]. 手荷物検査場 a [an airport] security checkpoint;《go through》airport security.
テネット Tenet, George (1953- ; 米国中央情報局(CIA)長官 1997-2004).
てのひら【手の平・掌】 ◻️ てのひら認証〔本人確認の手段としての〕palm recognition.
デパオク amusement and other facilities on department store rooftops.
デパガ〔デパート＋ガールの略〕〔デパートの売り子〕a department store salesgirl.
デパケン〔商標・薬〕〔抗てんかん薬〕Depaken.
てパス【手-】〔てのひら静脈認証〕palm vein「authentication [recognition].
デパス〔商標・薬〕〔精神安定薬; 鬱病・筋収縮性頭痛・神経症・睡眠障害などの適薬〕Depas. ▶ 一般名はエチゾラム (etizolam).
テバトロン〔米国立フェルミ研究所にある陽子・反陽子衝突型加速器〕the Tevatron.
てばなし【手放し】 ◻️ 手放し技〔体操〕〔鉄棒などでの〕a release move.
デパレス〔デパートのレストラン〕a department store restaurant; a restaurant in a department store.
デビ(一) Déby, Idriss (1952- ; チャドの政治家; 大統領 [1991- ]).
デビート = デヴィート.
デヒドロエピアンドロステロン【生化】〔副腎と性腺で作られるステロイドホルモンの1つ〕dehydroepiandrosterone（略: DHEA）.
デビュー ◻️ 地域デビュー one's local debut; the first time a retired person takes part in local《welfare》activities (to make the acquaintance of the other volunteers).
「デビル」〔映画〕The Devil's Own.
デフォー Dafoe, Willem (1955- ; 米国の映画俳優; 本名 William Dafoe, Jr.).

デフォルト　デフォルト・オプション〖電算〗a default option;〖金融〗a default option.
てふき²【手吹き】～の handblown.　手吹きガラス ＝ふきガラス.
デフリンピック〔国際ろう者スポーツ委員会主催の聴覚障害者オリンピック〕the Deaflympics; the Deaflympic Games.
てぶれ【手ぶれ】　手ぶれ効果 (a) camera shake effect. 手ぶれ防止 camera shake prevention.　～防止機能 a camera shake prevention function.
てぼう(まめ)【手亡(豆)】〖植〗＝しろいんげん(まめ).
てぼまめ【手亡豆】〖植〗＝しろいんげん(まめ).
デ・ボント, Jan (1943-　；オランダ生まれの映画監督・撮影監督).
てま【手間】　ひと手間 ⇨ひとてま.　手間いらず ～いらずのだし入り味噌 trouble-free miso already in broth.
でまえ【出前】　出前授業 a visiting lecture.
デミ Demme, Jonathan (1944-　；米国の映画監督・製作者).
てゆ【手湯】a「hand bath [handbath].
デュアル　デュアル・タイム〔時計で2種類の時間を表示する機能〕a dual-time function.　デュアルモード・ビークル〔道路と線路の両用車〕a dual-mode vehicle (略: DMV).
チュイルリーきゅう(でん)【-宮(殿)】＝チュイルリーきゅう(でん).
チュイルリーこうえん[ていえん]【-公園[庭園]】＝チュイルリーこうえん.
デューガン Dugan, Dennis (1946-　；米国の映画監督・俳優).
デューク Duke, Bill (1943-　；米国の映画俳優・監督).
デュー・デリジェンス, デュー・ディリジェンス〖証券〗〔投資事前調査〕due diligence.
デュカキス Dukakis, Olympia (1931-　；米国の映画女優).
デュシェンヌがたきんジストロフィー【-型筋-】〖医〗Duchenne muscular dystrophy (略: DMD).
デュナリエラ〖植〗〔緑藻類の藻(⁶)〕Dunaliella.
デュバル Duvall, Robert (1931-　；米国の映画俳優).
「デュラス 愛の最終章」〖映画〗Cet Amour-La (＝That Love).
デュラムセモリナ〔デュラム小麦の粗挽き粉〕durum semolina.
テラー² Teller, Edward (1908-2003；ハンガリー生まれの米国の核物理学者；水爆の父 (the father of the hydrogen bomb)と呼ばれた).
テラコッタ　テラコッタ肌 terracotta skin.
テラヘルツ　テラヘルツ波〔電磁波の一種〕a terahertz wave.
デリー・メトロ〔インド, デリーに建設された大量高速輸送システムの通称〕(the) Delhi Metro.
デリケート　デリケートゾーン〔女性の股間・陰部〕a woman's delicate zone; the V-zone.
テリスロマイシン〖薬〗〔抗生物質〕telithromycin.
デリバリー　デリバリー・ヘルス a (massage parlor) call-girl service.
デリヘル ＝デリバリー・ヘルス (⇨デリバリー).
テルガト Tergat, Paul (1969-　；ケニアのマラソン選手).
デルタ・フォース〖米軍〗〔米陸軍の第一特殊作戦分遣隊〕(the) Delta Force.
デル・トロ 1 Del Toro, Benicio (1967-　；プエルトリコ生まれの米国の映画俳優).
2 Del Toro, Guillermo (1964-　；メキシコ生まれの映画監督).
デルフィニジン〖化〗〔植物色素〕delphinidin.
「テルマ＆ルイーズ」〖映画〗Thelma & Louise.
「テルミン」〖映画〗Theremin.
テレコム・エンジニアリング・センター the Telecom Engineering Center (略: TELEC).

テレビ　薄型テレビ a flat-screen TV.　大画面薄型テレビ a 'flat big-screen [big-screen flat] TV.　テレビ受け ◐ 彼は難しい問題も面白おかしく話すので～受けする. He 'is good on TV [has TV appeal] because he talks entertainingly even about difficult issues. / 試合の動きが激しいスポーツは～受けがいい. Sports where the games involve violent action make for good television. / あの議員は～受けを狙った言動が多いので感心しない. I don't「think much [approve] of that Diet member because most of what he says and does is for「the benefit of the TV cameras [the sake of his TV image].　テレビ会議システム a「videoconferencing [video conferencing, videoconference] system; a teleconferencing system.　テレビショッピング ◐ ～ショッピング番組 a TV shopping program.　テレビ政治 telepolitics.　テレビ人間 a heavy TV「viewer [watcher]; a TV addict.　テレビマン a TV man.
テレフタルさん【-酸】　高純度テレフタル酸 pure terephthalic acid (略: PTA).
テレポリティクス〔テレビ(を意識した)政治〕telepolitics.
テレマティクス〖telecommunication ＋ informatics〗〖通信〗〔車載情報システム；インターネットに接続したコンピューターによるドライバー向け情報サービス〕telematics. ▷ telematic adj.
テレラジオロジー〖医〗〔遠隔放射線診断〕teleradiology.
テレルジ〔モンゴルの保養地〕Terelj.
テロ　テロ危険度 a terror threat level.　テロ支援国家指定解除〔米国による〕removal [delisting] (of North Korea) from the list of state sponsors of terrorism.
テロッパー〖放送〗〔テロップを作って画面に入れる機械〕a titler; a title generator.
テロとくそほう【-特措法】〖法〗〔テロ対策特別措置法〕the Antiterrorism Special Measures Law.
テロぼうしとくべついいんかい【-防止特別委員会】〔衆議院の〕the (Lower House) Special Committee on Antiterrorism Measures.
デロリアン DeLorean, John (Zachary) (1925-2005；米国の自動車会社社長).
テロワール〔＜F〕〔ワインの味わいに影響を与えるブドウ生産地の環境〕a terroir.
てろん ◐ テンセルの～とした感触 the velvety feel of Tencel.
-でん【-電】〔電信・電報の略〕◐ 新華社～によると… according to a wire [by wire] from Xinhua.
でんあんほう【電安法】〖法〗＝でんきようひんあんぜんほう.
てんい⁶【転移】　遠隔転移〖医〗〔がんの〕(a) distant metastasis.　～転移性再発 (⇨さいはつ)　転移(病)巣〔腫瘍などが転移した部位〕a metastatic「lesion [focus].
てんか²【点火】　点火順序〔内燃機関の〕a firing [an ignition] order.
でんかいしつ【電解質】　電解質膜 an electrolyte membrane.
てんがいはた【天蓋はた】〖魚〗〔フリソデウオ科の魚〕Trachipterus trachypterus.
てんがせき【天河石】〖鉱〗＝アマゾナイト.
てんかん²【転換】　転換社債型新株予約権付社債〖証券〗a convertible bond (略: CB). ▶ 転換社債の新しい呼び名.
てんかん³【癲癇】　てんかん発作重積状態〖医〗status epilepticus.
てんがん³【点眼】　点眼麻酔〖眼科〗eyedrop anesthesia.
てんかんかかく(の)しゅうせいじょうこうつきてんかんしゃさい【がたしんかぶよやくけんつきしゃさい】【転換価格(の)修正条項付(き)転換社債(型新株予約権付社債)】〖証券〗＝エム・エス・シー・ビー.

**てんき**[1]【天気】 ⇨ お天気マーク〔天気予報図の晴雨などのしるし〕a weather「icon [symbol].〔⇨晴れマーク(⇨はれ[1])〕

**でんき**[3]【電気】 ⇨ 電気浮き〔釣り〕an electric float. 電気街〔東京の秋葉原などの〕《Akihabara》"Electric Town." 電気工作物 an electric(al) facility. ⇨ 自家用~工作物 a non-utility electric(al) facility. 電気工事施工管理技士 an electrical engineering construction supervisor. 電気コード an electric cord. 電気柵 an「electric [electrified] fence. 電気ジャーポット an electric pump pot; an [a combined] electric kettle and thermos; an electric urn. 電気主任技術者 a 「licensed [certified] chief electrical engineer. 電気比抵抗 =電気抵抗率〔⇨でんきていこう〕. 電気牧場 =電気柵. 電気床暖房 《install》electric floor heating.

**でんききねんび**【電気記念日】〔3月25日〕Electricity Day.

**でんきつうしんこじんじょうほうほごすいしんセンター**【電気通信個人情報保護推進~〕〔日本データ通信協会の〕the Telecommunications Personal Information Protection Promotion Center.

**でんきていこう**【電気抵抗】 ⇨ 電気抵抗率 electric(al) resistivity; specific electric(al) resistance.

**でんきでんしぎじゅつしゃきょうかい**【電気電子技術者協会】⇨べいこくでんきでんしぎじゅつしゃきょうかい.

**でんきめっき**【電気鍍金】 ⇨ 電気めっき鋼板 (an) electroplated steel sheet.

**てんきゅう**[4]【転給】〔遺族共済年金の〕(a) transfer of benefits to successive members of the family in case of the death of the main beneficiary or of a subsequent beneficiary (under the Japanese mutual pension fund system); a benefit transferable on the death of the present beneficiary.

**でんきゅうしょく**【電球色】〔昼光色・昼白色より赤みのある蛍光灯の色〕the warm white.

**てんきょ**[2]【転居】 ⇨ 転居先不明者 a person who has moved to an unknown address.

**でんきようひんあんぜんほう**【電気用品安全法】〔法〕the Electrical Appliance(s) and Material(s) Safety Law.

**てんきん**[2]【転勤】 ⇨ 転勤先 a [one's, sb's] new「place of work [office, work address]; the workplace one「has moved to [is moving to]. ⇨ ~先がニューヨークに決まった. It has been decided that my new「workplace [office, job (location)] will be (in) New York. | I've been told I'm going to be「moved [transferred] to New York. 転勤族 a person who is constantly being sent to a different「office [branch] by his or her employers.

**「天空の城ラピュタ」**〔アニメ映画〕Laputa: The Castle in the Sky.

**でんげき**[2]【電撃】 ⇨ 電撃訪問《make》a「surprise visit [an unexpected visit, a visit out of the blue].

**てんけん**[3]【点検】 ⇨ 点検会社 an inspection company. 点検済車両〔鉄道〕a track inspection「car [vehicle]. 点検リスト a checklist《of items》.

**でんげん**【電源】 ⇨⇨ 分散型電源〔ビルや工場などの自家用発電設備〕a dispersed [decentralized] power source. ⇨ 電源開発促進税 an electric power development promotion tax. 電源開発促進対策特別会計 the Special Account for Electric Power Development Promotion. 電源地域 a power supply region. 電源立地地域対策交付金 a government grant for the area where a power plant is located.

**でんげんかいはつかぶしきかいしゃ**【電源開発株式会社】Electric Power Development Co., Ltd.;〔略称〕J-POWER.

**でんげんとっかい**【電源特会】=電源開発促進対策特別会計(⇨でんげん).

**てんこう**[2]【天候】 ⇨ 天候観測機〔空・軍〕a weather ob-

servation (air)plane. 天候被害〔農作物などの〕weather damage《to crops》.

**てんこう**[4]【転校】 ⇨ 転校先 one's new school; the school one has been transferred to. ⇨ ~先の学校に在学証明書を提出する hand in one's certificate of school attendance to one's new school.

**「天国の青い蝶」**〔映画〕The Blue Butterfly.

**「点子ちゃんとアントン」**〔E・ケストナー作の児童読み物〕Punktchen and Anton.

**でんごん**【伝言】 ⇨ 伝言係 a messenger.

**てんじ**[2]【点字】 ⇨ 点字シール[ラベル] a Braille「seal [label]. 点字プリンター a Braille「embosser [printer].

**てんじ**[1]【展示】 ⇨ 形態展示〔動物園の〕exhibiting [displaying]《animals》so that their form can be easily seen. 行動展示〔動物園の〕exhibiting《animals》so that they display natural behavior; allowing《a species》to behave naturally. 生態展示〔動物園の〕(an) ecologically realistic display; exhibiting《a species》in a realistic ecological environment. ⇨ 展示替え〔博物館などの〕(an) exhibit change. ⇨ この美術館では3か月ごとに作品を~替えしている. This art museum「changes exhibits [puts on a new exhibit] every three months. 展示面積〔博物館などの〕an exhibition [a display] area.

**でんし**【電子】 ⇨ 電子あぶり出し =ステガノグラフィー. 電子イオン水 ionized water. 電子オルゴール an electronic music box. 電子壁新聞 an electronic wall (news) paper. 電子玩具 an electronic toy. 電子基板 an electronic「circuit-board [substrate]. 電子キー〔ドアなどの開閉用の〕an electronic key;〔暗号解読などの〕an electronic cipher. 電子切手〔自分のパソコンとプリンターを使って印刷することが可能な切手〕an E-stamp. 電子教育〔IT技術を活用した遠隔学習教育〕e-learning. 電子攻撃〔軍〕an electronic attack (略: EA). 電子ゴミ〔廃棄された高性能電気製品〕electronic waste; e-waste; hi-tech waste. 電子債券〔証券〕an electronic bond. 電子商取引サイト an e-commerce site. 電子情報ボード an interactive whiteboard. 電子申請システム an「electronic [online] application system; an e-application system. 電子制御(式)燃料噴射 electronic fuel injection (略: EFI). ⇨ ~制御(式)燃料噴射装置 an electronic fuel-injection system; an EFI system. 電子制御装置 an electronic control unit (略: ECU). 電子政府構築計画 an e-government construction plan. 電子チップ an electronic chip. 電子調達 e-procurement; electronic procurement. ⇨ ~調達システム an「e-procurement [electronic procurement] system. 電子ディスプレー an electronic display. 電子(的)金融取引 an electronic financial transaction (略: EFT). 電子読書端末 =読書端末(⇨どくしょ). 電子値札 an electronic shelf label. 電子番組表〔テレビ〕an「electric [electronic] program guide (略: EPG). 電子部品 electronic「parts [components]. 電子ペン〔紙への書きがそのままコンピューターに入力できるペン〕an electronic [a digital] pen [stylus]. 電子マネー・システム an「electronic cash [e-cash] system; an「electronic money [e-money] system. 電子迷彩 =ステガノグラフィー. 電子滅菌 =電子線滅菌(⇨でんしせん). 電子立国 a national commitment to「electronics [electronic(s) technology]; electronics-based national development.

**でんしこうがく**【電子工学】 ⇨ 半導体電子工学 semiconductor electronics.

**でんしこうほういんきゅうじょ**【電子航法研究所】〔独立行政法人〕the Electronic Navigation Research Institute (略: ENRI).

**でんししきんいどうほう**【電子資金移動法】《米法》the Electronic Fund Transfer Act.

**でんししょうとりひきじっしょうすいしんきょうかい**

【電子商取引実証推進協議会】the Electronic Commerce Promotion Council of Japan (略：ECOM). ▶ 2000年4月、電子商取引実証推進協議会に名称変更.

でんししょうとりひきすいしんきょうぎかい【電子商取引推進協議会】the Electronic Commerce Promotion Council of Japan (略：ECOM). ▶ 2005年4月、次世代電子商取引推進協議会に名称変更.

でんししょうひしゃけいやくほう【電子消費者契約法】〔法〕the Electronic Consumer Contract Law.

でんしじょうほうぎじゅつさんぎょうきょうかい【電子情報技術産業協会】the Japan Electronics and Information Technology Industries Association (略：JEITA). ▶ 2000年に日本電子工業振興会と日本電子機械工業会が統合してできた.

でんしじょうほうつうしんがっかい【電子情報通信学会】the Institute of Electronics, Information and Communication Engineers (略：IEICE).

でんしせん²【電子線】▫ 電子線描画装置 an electron-beam lithography system. 電子線滅菌 electron beam sterilization. 電子線リソグラフィー electron-beam lithography.

でんしちょうぼぞんほう【電子帳簿保存法】〔法〕the Law for Computerized Maintenance of Account Books (for national taxes).

でんじてき【電磁的】▫ 電磁的公正証書原本不実記録〔法〕falsification of the electromagnetic record of an officially authenticated document.

でんじてききろく【電磁的記録】▫ 不正電磁的記録カード所持(罪)〔法〕(the crime of) possession of a payment card with an unauthorized electromagnetic record. 電磁的記録媒体 electromagnetic media.

「天使と悪魔」〔米国作家ダン・ブラウン作の小説〕Angels & Demons.
「天使の贈りもの」〔映画〕The Preacher's Wife.
「天使のくれた時間」〔映画〕The Family Man.
「天使のセレナード」〔ブラーガ作曲の楽曲〕Angel's Serenade.

でんじは【電磁波】▫ 電磁波(人命)探査装置〔災害救助などに用いる〕a microwave life detector. 電磁波漏れ〔漏出〕leakage [escape] of electromagnetic waves.

でんしばん【電子版】〔新聞・辞書などの〕an electronic edition. ◯ニューヨーク・タイムズ(〜) The New York Times Electronic Edition (略：NYTEE).

でんしビーム【電子ー】▫ 電子ビーム描画装置 an electron-beam lithography system.

でんしぼうがいそうち【電子妨害装置】▫〔軍〕an electronic jamming system. ▫ 航空機搭載型電子妨害装置 an airborne electronic jamming system.

でんしメール【電子ー】▫ 電子メール爆弾 an e-mail bomb. ▷ mail-bomb v. 電子メール傍受 monitoring [interception] of e-mail(s).

でんしゃ²【電車】▫ 電車区 a 「train [car] depot.

「デンジャラス・ビューティー」〔映画〕Miss Congeniality.

てんじゅこくしゅうちょう【天寿国繍帳】＝てんじゅこくまんだら(しゅうちょう).

てんじゅこくまんだら(しゅうちょう)【天寿国曼陀羅(繍帳)】〔刺繍(しゅう)が施された飛鳥時代作の垂れ幕〕the Tenjukoku (Shūchō) Mandara; an Asuka-period hanging embroidered with an image of paradise.

てんしょつ²【転居】▫ 転居証明書 a certificate of change of 「address [residence, domicile].

てんしょう³【転生】▫ 転生活仏〔チベット仏教の〕a reincarnated Living Buddha.

てんじょう²【傾斜天井】〔建〕a slanted ceiling. 舟底[舟形]天井 a ceiling with two sides sloping from the center; a double-sloped ceiling. ▫ 天井感 ◯相場の〜感 the feeling that the market has reached the ceiling / 株価に〜感が出てきた. There is a feeling that stock prices have reached the ceiling. 天井収納 ceiling storage.

てんじょう⁴【点状】▫ 点状ブロック〔点字ブロックの1つ〕a 「studded [bumpy, textured] paving [guide] block.
「天井桟敷のみだらな人々」〔映画〕Illuminata.

てんしょく²【転職】▫ 転職希望者 people [a person] wishing to change jobs; people [a person] seeking 「a new job [a change of job, a change of career]. 転職先 a [one's, sb's] new place of work; a new job. ◯現在〜を探しています. I'm looking for a new job.

てんしょく²【電飾】▫ 電飾広告 an electric billboard.

でんしんでんわきねんび【電信電話記念日】〔10月23日〕Telecommunication(s) Day.

てんすう¹【点数】▫ 点数単価〔診療報酬の〕a unit price; a points value. 点数評価 a ranking [an evaluation] based on a (numerical) grade. ◯〜評価する rank [evaluate] on the basis of a (numerical) grade.

てんすうか【点数化】〜する quantify 《…》 in terms of points; assign a 「point [numerical] rating 《to…》. / 個々の診療行為を〜して、その点数の合計で1回の治療費が決まる. A rating is assigned to each medical procedure, and the cost per treatment is determined from the total number of points.

でんそう¹【伝送】▫ 伝送遅れ〔電算〕a transmission lag.

でんそう²【電送】▫ 電送写真 a telephotograph.

てんそく【天測】▫ 天測実習〔海〕practice in the taking of [practicing making] astronomical observations (to establish the position of one's vessel).

でんたつ【伝達】▫ 伝達性海綿状脳症〔獣医〕transmissible spongiform encephalopathy (略：TSE).

デンタル ▫ デンタル・チャート〔歯型図〕a dental chart.

でんたん²【伝単】〔敵国の兵士・市民の戦闘意欲を失わせるために配布するビラ〕a leaflet intended to demoralize the enemy.

でんちゅうけん【電中研】＝でんりょくちゅうおうけんきゅうじょ.

でんてい【電停】〔路面電車の停留所〕a streetcar 「stop [station].

てんてき²【点滴】▫ 点滴チューブ an 「intravenous [IV] tube.

テンテナ〔インドネシア、中スラウェシ州の町〕Tentena.

てん-, -てん³【天-, -天】▫ 海老天 prawn tempura; a tempura prawn; a deep-fried prawn in batter. ▫ 天かす bits of fried tempura batter. 天むす(び)〔小エビの天ぷらが載っているおにぎり〕a rice ball topped with deep-fried shrimp.

てんとう²【店頭】▫ 店頭業務 over-the-counter operations. 店頭実勢価格 the 「actual retail [in-store] price. 店頭販(売)促(進) an in-store (sales) promotion.

てんとう⁵【転倒】▫ 転倒死 (a) death from falling 「down [over]. ◯〜する die from falling 「down [over]; fall 「down [over] and die. 転倒事故〔自転車・バイクなどの〕a 「fall [spill] 《off one's bicycle》;〔雪道などで滑っての〕a slip (on an icy road);〔つまずいての〕《have, suffer》 a fall. ◯雪の日には〜事故がふえる. More falls are reported during snowy weather. 転倒防止[予防]〔老人などの〕preventing falls; fall prevention;〔家具などの〕preventing 《furniture》 from falling. ◯〜予防教室 a fall prevention class / 〜予防訓練 fall prevention training / 〜予防体操 fall prevention exercises.

でんとう¹【伝統】▫ 伝統楽器 a traditional (musical) instrument. 伝統儀式 a traditional 「ceremony [ritual]. 伝統技術[技法] traditional technique(s). 伝統行事 a traditional 「event [festival, ceremony]. 伝統漁法 a traditional fishing method. 伝統芸術 traditional arts. 伝統校 a traditional school;〔大学〕a traditional「college [university]. 伝統工芸士 a certified traditional「artisan [craftworker]. 伝統宗教 a traditional religion 伝統食 a traditional meal; a traditional diet. 伝統食品[食材] traditional food(s) 伝統美 the beauty of tradition; traditional beauty. 伝統舞踊 traditional「dance [dancing]. 伝統文化 traditional culture. 伝統民具 a traditional (folk)「utensil [tool, implement]. 伝統野菜 traditional vegetables. 伝統料理 traditional「food [cuisine, cooking].

でんとう² 【電灯】 ▭ 電灯線(搬送)通信 《通信》=電力線 (搬送)通信 (⇨でんりょく).

でんどう²【伝道】 ▭ 伝道宗教 a「missionary [proselytizing] religion. ◐ 非〜宗教 a「non-missionary [non-proselytizing] religion.

でんどう⁴【殿堂】 ▭ 〔世界〕ゴルフ殿堂〔米国フロリダ州にある組織・施設〕the World Golf Hall of Fame.

でんどう⁵【電動】 ▭ 電動糸鋸(いと̈のこ) an electric「fretsaw [jigsaw]. 電動ウォーカー〔エクササイズ・マシン〕an electric [a motorized] treadmill. 電動カート〔歩行が不自由な人のための〕an electric cart;〔ゴーカート〕an electric「go-kart [go-cart]. 電動カッター an electric cutter. 電動スクーター an electric scooter. 電動スライドドア〔自動車〕a power sliding door. 電動三輪車〔歩行が困難な人のための〕an electric tricycle. 電動ドアロック〔自動車などの〕power door locks. 電動ベッド an electric [a motorized] bed.

でんとうかぶきほぞんかい【伝統歌舞伎保存会】the Organization for the Preservation of Kabuki (略: OPK).

デンドリマー 《化》〔球状高分子〕a dendrimer.

てんにゅうがく【転入学】 ▭ 転入学試験 an examination for transfer admission(s); an admissions test for transfer students.

でんねつ¹【伝熱】 ▭ 伝熱管 a heat-exchanger tube.

てんねん【天然】 ▭ 天然栄養素 a natural nutrient. 天然化合物 a natural compound. 天然系 ◐ 〜系の人 a naturally spacey character; a natural airhead / 〜系化粧品 cosmetics made of natural ingredients / 原料は 100%〜です. The ingredients are 100% natural. 天然酵母(こうぼ)³. 天然香料 a natural「scent [perfume]. 天然植物油 (a) natural vegetable oil. 天然成分 a natural ingredient. 天然素材〔衣類・家具などの〕a natural material;〔化粧品・食品などの〕a natural ingredient. 天然ダム a natural dam. [=河道閉塞 (⇨かどう³)] 天然調味料 a natural「flavoring [seasoning]. 天然保湿因子〔角質細胞内の〕a natural moisturizing factor (略: NMF).

てんねんガス【天然-】 ▭ 天然ガス・コジェネレーション natural gas cogeneration.

てんねんきねんぶつ【天然記念物】 ▭ 指定天然記念物〔国または地方自治体指定の〕an animal [a bird] designated as a protected species. ◐ 国(県, 市)指定〜 an animal [a bird, a plant] designated as a「nationally [prefecturally, municipally] protected species. ▭ 天然記念物指定区域 a (designated) protected「area [habitat].

てんねんしげんほごひょうぎかい[きょうぎかい]【天然資源保護評議会[協議会]】〔米国の〕the Natural Resources Defense Council (略: NRDC).

てんねんとう【天然痘】 ▭ 天然痘テロ〔天然痘ウイルスを使ったテロ〕smallpox terrorism; a smallpox terrorist attack. 天然痘ワクチン (a) smallpox vaccine.

てんねんぶつゆうきかがく【天然物有機化学】(the) organic chemistry of natural products; natural product(s) organic chemistry.

でんのう【電脳】 ▭ 電脳量刑〔量刑の算定にコンピューターを用いる中国の方法〕a Chinese method of using computers to assess criminal culpability.

でんぱ²【電波】 ▭ (標準)時刻電波 a standard time signal. ▭ 電波ジャック frequency hijacking. 電波修正機能〔電波時計の自動時刻電波修正機能〕a radio control function. 電波情報 radio intelligence. 電波ソーラー時計 a radio-solar clock;〔腕時計〕a radio-solar watch. 電波帯域 a radio wave band. 電波停止〔放送法による電波発信停止処分〕the suspension of broadcasting (operations). 電波天文衛星 a radio astronomy satellite. 電波発信機 a (radio) transmitter. 電波ビーコン〔道路交通情報を提供するために道路に設置された電波を媒体とする通信装置〕a radio beacon. 電波傍受《(radio) signal「monitoring [interception].

てんばい²【転売】 ▭ 転売益 (a) profit on resale. 転売先 a resale customer.

てんばいばい【転売買】resale and repurchase. ▭ 業者間転売買 resale and repurchase between dealers.

でんぱのひ【電波の日】〔6月1日〕Radio Day.

テンパリング【菓子】〔チョコレートの調温作業〕(chocolate) tempering.

テンパる 1【麻雀】〔テンパイする〕begin「fishing [calling]. 2〔せっぱ詰まった状況で興奮状態になる〕become [get] excited [flustered, worked up]; be about to explode (in anger). ◐ 年末はただでさえ忙しいのにパソコンが故障してすっかりテンパってしまった. I was already busy enough with the end of the year when my computer broke down and I flipped out. / 仕事のストレスでテンパっていたので, 彼女の無神経な言葉についにキレてしまった. I was in a tizzy from all the stress at work, so her insensitive comment made me blow my top.

でんぱん【伝搬】 ▭ 伝搬力 the power to propagate (one's ideas);〔病原菌・情報などの〕the power to disseminate. ◐ インターネットの驚異的な情報〜力 the amazing power of the Internet to disseminate information / カラスの鳥インフルエンザウイルス〜力 the ability of crows to spread bird flu.

てんびく【天引き】 ▭ 給与天引き ⇨ きゅうよ¹.

テンピュール《商標》〔低反発素材〕Tempur.

てんびょう【点描】 ▭ 点描画 a pointillistic painting.

でんぴょう【伝票】 ▭ 配送伝票 a delivery slip.

てんぷ³【添付】 ▭ 添付画像〔電子メールへの〕a picture [an image] attached 《to an e-mail》; an attached「picture [image]. 添付文書〔商品などに添付された〕an attached [appended, accompanying] document; an attachment;〔機器・薬品などのメーカーが製品に添える〕an insert.

テン・フィフティーン・モード【10-15-】〔自動車〕〔燃費・排出ガスなどを算定するための走行パターン〕the 10-15 mode cycle. ▭ 10-15 モード燃費 10-15 mode fuel efficiency.

でんぷう【癜風】《医》〔癜風菌による皮膚の感染症〕tinea [pityriasis] versicolor. ▭ 癜風菌【菌】〔皮膚病・ふけの原因となる真菌の一種〕Malassezia furfur.

てんぷく²【転覆】 ▭ 転覆脱線 turning over and getting derailed; overturning and derailment.

てんぷら【天麩羅】 ▭ 天ぷら火災 a tempura fire; a fire caused by ignited tempura cooking oil.

テンプルだいがく【-大学】〔米国ペンシルヴァニア州にある大学〕Temple University.

テンプレート ▭ テンプレート機能《電算》〔ひな形利用機能〕a template function.

テンペ〔インドネシアの大豆発酵食品〕tempeh.

テンペスト・ストーム Tempest Storm (1928- ; 米国のバーレスク・ダンサー; 本名 Annie Blanche Banks).

テンペルだいいちすいせい【-第一彗星】《天》Comet Tempel 1.

てんぽ¹【店舗】 ▭ 店舗コスト《経営》a「store [shop] cost. 店舗販売 in-store「sales [selling, retailing]. 店舗面積 the (surface) area of a「store [shop]; a store floor area.

てんぼう²【展望】 ⇨ 長期[中期, 短期]展望 a long-[mid-, short-]term prospect. ⇨ 展望風呂 a bath with a view.

テンメンジャン【甜麺醬】〔調味料〕(Chinese) sweet bean sauce.

テンモード【10-】〔自動車〕〔燃費・排出ガスなどを算定するための走行パターン〕 the 10 mode cycle. ▶ 現在は 10-15 モードを用いる. ⇨ 10モード燃費 10-mode fuel efficiency.

てんもん【天文】 ⇨ 天文現象 an astronomical phenomenon.

てんやく²【点訳】 ⇨ 点訳図書 a braille「translation [transcription]《of a book》; a「translation [transcription] into braille. 点訳ボランティア a person who does braille transcription on a volunteer basis; a braille transcription volunteer.

てんよう【転用】 ⇨ 転用薬〔処方薬から市販薬に転用された薬〕 an (Rx-to-)OTC switch(ed) drug.

てんらく【転落】 ⇨ 転落死 death by falling;〔1件の〕 a fatal fall; "a fall to the death. ◐ ～死する fall [plunge] to one's death; suffer a fatal fall / 少女 バスから～死!〔新聞記事などのタイトルで〕Girl Falls to Her Death from Bus | Girl in Fatal Fall from Bus / 彼はビルの5階の窓から～死した. He fell to his death from a window on the fifth floor of the building. 転落事故 an accidental fall; a falling accident; a fall《down a stairway, from a ladder, into a ravine, etc.》. ◐ バス～事故 a bus plunge / 尾根からの～事故 a fall from a ridge. 転落防止柵 fall prevention railing;〔屋上の〕(a) rooftop railing.

てんらん¹【天覧】 ⇨ 天覧競馬 a (horse) race held in the presence of the Emperor.

でんりょく【電力】 ⇨ 電力卸売り wholesale (electric) power sales; wholesale sales of (electric) power. 電力卸売事業 a wholesale (electric) power business. 電力小売り事業者 a retail (electric) power supplier. 電力自由化 electric power deregulation. 電力使用 electricity [power] usage [use]. 電力使用量 an amount of「electricity [power] used [consumed]. 電力線(搬送)通信《通信》power line communication(s) (略: PLC). ◐ 高速～線通信 high-speed「power line communication(s) [PLC]. 電力取引所 an electric power exchange.

でんりょくそうれん【電力総連】 the Federation of Electric Power Related Industry Workers' Unions of Japan. ▶ 正式名称: 全国電力関連産業労働組合総連合 (略: Denryoku-Soren).

でんりょくちゅうおうけんきゅうじょ【電力中央研究所】the Central Research Institute of Electric Power Industry (略: CRIEPI).

でんろ²【電炉】 ⇨ 電炉メーカー〔鉄スクラップを原料として電気炉で鉄鋼を生産する企業〕an electric-furnace steel maker.

でんわ【電話】 ⇨ 安心電話〔独居老人などのための〕a reassurance「phone service [helpline]. 黒電話 [an old, an old-type] black (dial) telephone. 警察電話 a police telephone. 鉄道電話 a「railroad [railway] telephone. ⇨ 電話受付代行(サービス) ＝秘書代行サービス (⇨ひしょ¹). 電話会談 telephone talks; (a) discussion「by [on the] telephone; a telephone discussion. 電話勧誘〔選挙事務所・宗教団体などからの〕telephone solicitation. 電話勧誘販売 telephone sales; telemarketing. 電話中診 (a) telephone consultation. ◐ ～再診料 a telephone consultation fee. 電話作戦 (a) telephone strategy; using the telephone 《to do》. ◐ 選挙戦も終盤に入り, 各党は～作戦に力を入れ始めた. With the election entering its final stage, all the parties started using the telephone「as a weapon [to appeal to the electorate]. 電話セールス telephone sales; telemarketing. 電話中継局 a telephone relay station. 電話(秘書)代行(サービス) ＝秘書代行サービス (⇨ひしょ¹). 電話美人 a beautiful woman over the telephone; a woman whose voice on the phone encourages one to believe that she is beautiful.

「電話で抱きしめて」〔映画〕Hanging Up.

# と

ど¹【度】 9〔造語要素として, 度合い〕a degree; an extent. ◐ 難易～ the「degree [level] of difficulty / 重要～ the degree of importance / 不要～ uselessness / 健全～ healthfulness; soundness; wholesomeness.

ドア ⇨ ドア開閉スイッチ〔電車の〕a door open/close「button [switch]; a button for opening and closing「a [the] door. ドア越し 彼女は～越しに彼に話しかけた. She spoke to him「through [from behind] the door. ドア・パッキン〔冷蔵庫や浴室のドアなどのゴム製シール材〕a door gasket. ドア・ビーム〔ドア内の補強材〕a door beam. ドア・ポケット〔冷蔵庫・自動車などの〕a door pocket; a pocket in a door. ドア・ロック〔ドアの錠〕a door lock.

「ドア・イン・ザ・フロア」〔映画〕The Door in the Floor.

どあほ a complete fool; a perfect idiot.

といおとす【問い落とす】〔質問を重ねて相手に本当のことをしゃべらせる〕question sb until he confesses; pry the truth out of sb.

「トイ・ストーリー」〔アニメ映画〕Toy Story.

トイ・セラピー〔医〕〔小児・高齢者などに対する玩具療法〕toy therapy.

「トイ・ソルジャー」〔映画〕Toy Soldiers.

ドイツかぶしき【かぶか】しすう【一株式[株価]指数】《証券》the German stock index (略: DAX). ▶ DAX はドイツ語の Deutscher Aktienindex から.

ドイツこうきょうほうそう【―公共放送】Deutsche Welle (略: DW).

ドイツこっかみんしゅとう【―国家民主党】⇨こっかみん しゅとう.

ドイツ・サッカーきょうかい[れんめい]【―協会[連盟]】the German Football Association (略: DFB). ▶ DFB はドイツ語の Deutscher Fussball-Bund から.

ドイツしょうけんとりひきじょ【―証券取引所】the Deutsche Börse Group; the German Stock Exchange.

ドイツせきぐんは【―赤軍派】the Red Army Faction (略: RAF);〔ドイツ語名〕Rote Armee Fraktion.

ドイツ・ポスト〔ドイツの郵便会社〕Deutsche Post.

トイ・プードル a toy poodle.

トイレ ⇨ 自己処理型トイレ〔汚物を外に出さず内部で処理するトイレ〕a self-treating toilet; a nondischarging toilet. ⇨ トイレ・カー a (mobile) toilet vehicle.

トウ¹【TOW】《米軍》〔発射筒から撃ち出す光学追随式の有線誘導対戦車ミサイル BGM-71 の通称〕a TOW (missile). ▶ tube-launched optically tracked and wire-guided の略.

トウ²【つま先】 a toe. ⇨ プレーン・トウ〔靴などの, 装飾のないつま先〕a plain toe. ⇨ トウ・セパレーター〔ペディキュアを塗るときに足指を離しておくのに使う〕a toe separator. トウ・リング〔足の指にはめる指輪〕a toe ring.

どう⁶【銅】 ⇨ 銅蒸気レーザー〔物〕a copper vapor laser.

ド

**ドウ**〖料理〗〔パンなどの生地〕dough.
**とうあつ²**【踏圧】foot pressure; the「pressure [tread] of feet.
**トゥアティン・フエ**〔ベトナム中北部の省〕Thua Thien-Hue. ▶ 省都はフエ.
**トゥアニッポウ**【東亜日報】〔韓国の日刊紙〕The Dong-A Ilbo.
**ドゥアルテ** Duarte Frutos, Nicanor (1956–　;パラグアイの政治家;大統領 [2003–　]).
**トゥアンクとう**【–島】〔インドネシア, バニャック諸島内の島〕Tuangku Island;(インドネシア語名)Pulau Tuangku.
**とういつ**【統一】◨▣ 統一旗〔韓国・北朝鮮がスポーツ大会などで共同で活動する際に用いる旗〕the Korean Unification flag. 統一相〔韓国〕the Minister of Unification; the Unification Minister. 統一部〔省〕〔韓国〕the Ministry of Unification (略: MOU). 〔衆議院〕参議院〕統一補欠選挙（a House of「Representatives [Councillors]〕simultaneous by(e)-election. 統一問題〔韓国・北朝鮮の〕the unification「question [problem]; 《discuss》unification.
**とういつイラクどうめい**【統一――同盟】〔イスラム教シーア派の連合会派〕the United Iraqi Alliance (略: UIA).
**とういつエネルギーシステム**[きこう]【統一―[機構]】〔ロシアの電力会社〕United Energy Systems of Russia (略: UES).
**とういつおやこかんけいほう**【統一親子関係法】〔米法〕the Uniform Parentage Act.
**とういつぐんじさいばんほう**【統一軍事裁判法】〔米軍〕〔合衆国軍に属する軍の行動を規定する法典〕the Uniform Code of Military Justice (略: UCMJ).
**とういつこうどうひょうぎかい**【統一行動評議会】〔パキスタンの政党〕the United Action Forum; the Muttahida Majlis-e-Amal (略: MMA).
**とういつしょうひんコード**【統一商品–】a Universal Product Code (略: UPC).
**とういつじんみんじゆうれんごう**【統一人民自由連合】〔スリランカの政党連合体〕the United People's Freedom Alliance (略: UPFA).
**トゥイホア**〔ベトナム中部, フーイェン省の省都〕Tuy Hoa.
**ドゥヴィルパン** = ドビルパン.
**とういん¹**【党員】◨▣ 党員資格 party membership. ◐ 〜資格を剥奪する strip sb of his party membership; expel sb from the party / 〜資格を停止する suspend sb's party membership.
**とういん³**【登院】◨▣ 登院停止 prohibition from entering (either House of) the Diet (for up to thirty days).
**どういん¹**【動因】◨▣ 一次的[二次的]動因 a「primary [secondary] drive.
**どういん²**【動員】◨▣ 組織(的)動員 organizational mobilization. ◨▣ 動員力 drawing power
**トゥインクル・レース**〔夜間の競馬〕a night (horse) race; night (horse) racing.
**トゥーヒー** Twohy, David (N.) (1956–　;米国の映画監督・脚本家).
**トゥーマイえんじん**【–猿人】【人類学】〔アフリカ中央部チャドで発見された頭蓋骨の化石から最古の人類ではないかと推測されている猿人〕Toumai; *Sahelanthropus tchadensis*.
**「トゥームレイダー」**〔映画〕Lara Croft: Tomb Raider. ▶ 続編は「トゥームレイダー2」(Lara Croft Tomb Raider: The Cradle of Life).
**トゥールビヨン, トゥールビヨン**〖<F = whirlpool〗〔重力に影響されない調速機〕a tourbillon.
**トゥーレ²** Touré, Amadou Toumani (1948–　;マリの政治家;大統領 [2002–　]).
**とうえん³**【桃園】⇒タオユワン.
**トゥエンアン**〔ベトナム北部の省;その省都〕Tuyen Quang.
**とうおがれい**【唐招霊】〖植〗=からたちばな.

**とうか⁴**【投下】◨▣ 投下資本収益率〖経〗return on invested capital (略: ROIC).
**とうか¹²**【等価】◨▣ 等価エラー率 the equal error rate (略: EER). 等価定理〖経〗=リカードの等価定理 (⇨リカード).
**どうか¹**【同化】◨▣ 同化主義 a「policy of [belief in] assimilation; assimilationism.
**どうが¹**【動画】◨▣ 動画コンテンツ video content. 動画配信 video distribution.
**とうかい⁴**【東海】〔日本海に対する韓国の呼称〕the East Sea.
**とうがいひなん**【島外避難】〔火山の噴火などによる〕(the) evacuation《of the population》from an island.
**とうかひょう**【投開票】〔投票と開票〕voting and vote counting. ◨▣ 電子投開票 electronic voting and vote counting. 投開票速報 (a report of)「early [up-to-the-minute] returns.
**どうかじゅふん**【同花受粉】〖植〗self-pollination. 〜する self-pollinate.
**とうかヘモグロビン**【糖化–】〖生化〗=グリコヘモグロビン.
**どうかん⁹**【東莞】〔中国広東省の都市〕Dongguan; Dongwan.
**とうき⁷**【投機】◨▣ 投機資金 speculative funds. 投機色 ◐ 〜色の強い短期売買 short-term trading of a highly speculative nature. 投機性 (be of) a speculative nature; speculativeness. ◐ 〜性の高い金融派生商品 a highly speculative financial derivative. 投機対象 a target for speculation.
**とうき⁸**【党紀】◨▣ 党紀委員会 a party('s) disciplinary committee.
**とうき¹¹**【登記】◨▣ 登記事項証明書 a document proving registered matters. 登記事項要約書 a document summarizing registered matters. 登記情報 registered information. 登記情報システム〔法務省の〕a registered information system. 登記原因証明情報 information required for proof of grounds for registration. ▶ 2005年, 登記原因証書を登記原因証明情報に改変. 登記手数料 a《land, building》registration fee. 登記簿抄本 a partial copy of a register; an official copy of part of a register. 登記簿謄本 a(n official) copy of an entire register. ▶ 現在の正式名称は ⇨ 登記事項証明書.
**とうき¹³**【党旗】a party flag.
**とうきごりんこくさいきょうぎれんめいれんごう**【冬季五輪国際競技連盟連合】the Association of International Olympic Winter Federations (略: AIOWF).
**とうきゅう²**【投球】◨▣ 投球間隔 a「pitch [throwing] interval; the interval between「pitches [throws]. 投球術〖野球〗the art of pitching. 投球マシン〔ピッチング・マシン〕a pitching machine.
**とうきゅう⁴**【等級】◨▣ 等級別料率制度〖保険〗〔自動車保険の〕an insurance premium rating system.
**「同級生」**〔映画〕Get Real.
**どうきょ**【同居】◨▣ 三世代同居 three generations living「together [in the same house, under the same roof]. ◨▣ 同居離婚 a「live-together [live-in] divorce. 同居率〔三世代などの〕the percentage of households shared by《three》generations;〔未婚の男女など〕=同棲率 (⇨どうせい¹).
**とうきょうかいようだいがく**【東京海洋大学】Tokyo University of Marine Science and Technology. ▶ 2003年10月, 東京商船大学と東京水産大学の統合により発足.
**とうきょうきょうしようせいじゅく**【東京教師養成塾】(the) Tokyo Teachers' Training School.
**とうきょうこくさいてんじじょう**【東京国際展示場】the Tokyo International Exhibition Center. ▶ 通称は東京ビッグサイト (Tokyo Big Sight).
**とうきょうこくもつしょうひんとりひきじょ**【東京穀物

商品取引所】the Tokyo Grain Exchange (略: TGE).
とうきょうこくもつとりひきじょ【東京穀物取引所】⇒とうきょうこくもつしょうひんとりひきじょ.
とうきょうちかてつかぶしきがいしゃ【東京地下鉄株式会社】Tokyo Metro Co., Ltd.;〔愛称〕東京メトロ Tokyo Metro. ▶ 2004年4月, 帝都高速度交通営団から改称.
とうきょうディーマット【東京-[DMAT]】Tokyo-DMAT. ▶ DMAT は Disaster Medical Assistance Team の略.
とうきょうディズニーリゾート【東京-】Tokyo Disney Resort (略: TDR).
とうきょうでんりょく【東京電力】the Tokyo Electric Power Company (略: TEPCO).
とうきょうとがりねずみ【東京尖鼠】〖動〗〔トガリネズミ科の動物〕a least Siberian shrew; *Sorex minutissimus.*
とうきょうとかんさついむいん【東京都監察医務院】⇒かんさついむいん.
とうきょうビッグサイト【東京-】〔東京国際展示場の通称〕Tokyo Big Sight.
とうきょうメトロ【東京-】〔東京地下鉄株式会社の愛称〕Tokyo Metro.
とうきょうりんかいこうそくてつどう【東京臨海高速鉄道】Tokyo Waterfront Area Rapid Transit (略: TWR).
とうくつ【盗掘】▫️ 盗掘坑 a tomb robbers' tunnel.
どうくつ【洞窟】▫️ 洞窟風呂 a 「grotto [cave] bath.
トゥグリク【モンゴルの通貨単位】a tugrik (*pl.* ~, ~s).
とうけい³【統計】▫️ 統計士〔資格の一種〕a certified statistician.
とうけいか【頭頸科】=頭頸部外科 (⇒とうけいぶ).
とうけいすうりけんきゅうじょ【統計数理研究所】the Institute of Statistical Mathematics.
とうけいてき【統計的】▫️ 統計的仮説検定〖統計〗statistical hypothesis testing.
とうけいのひ【統計の日】〔10月18日〕Statistics Day.
とうけいぶ【頭頸部】▫️ 頭頸部外科 head and neck surgery.
とうげこう【登下校】going to and from school. ◐ 子供たちの~時の安全確保に尽力したい. We must do our best to make sure our children are safe on their way to and from school. ▫️ 集団登下校 going to and from school in a group.
とうけつ【凍結】▫️ 全球凍結〖地球の〗global freezing. ミサイル発射凍結 a freeze on missile launches. 凍結乾燥機 a freeze-dryer; a lyophilizer. 凍結乾燥製剤〖薬〗a lyophilized product. 凍結精子〖医〗frozen sperm; cryopreserved sperm.
とうけんか【董建華】Tung Chee-hwa (1937- ;香港特別行政区行政長官〔1997-2005〕).
とうけんがけい【陶犬瓦鶏】ceramic dogs and clay hens;〔外見はよいが役に立たないものの喩え〕a false 「front [show]; a facade; window dressing.
とうげんかんかくほう【等現間隔法】〖心理〗the method of equal-appearing intervals.
とうこう⁵【投稿】▫️ 電子投稿 electronic submission; online submission. ▫️ 投稿受け付け[受理] ◐ その論文誌は~受け付け[受理]から採択[掲載決定]までの日数がかかりすぎる. That journal takes too long from receipt of submissions to acceptance. ▫️ 投稿サイト〖電気〗〔インターネット上の〕a contribution site. ◐ 動画~サイト a video sharing (Web) site. 投稿写真〖ビデオ〗a submitted 「photograph [video].
とうこう⁸【登校】▫️ 登校禁止(措置)（impose) (a) suspension from school. ◐ 彼はクラスメートへの暴力行為を理由に~禁止を言い渡された. He was suspended from school for 「bullying [violence against (one of) his classmates]. | He was given a suspension from school for 「bullying [violence against (one of) his class-mates].
とうごう³【統合】▫️ 統合医療 integrative medicine. 統合基幹業務システム an enterprise resource planning system; an ERP system. 統合攻撃戦闘機〖米軍〗a joint strike fighter (略: JSF). 統合比率〔合併比率〕a merger ratio. 統合メッセージング〖情報〗unified messaging (略: UM).
どうこう³【同行】▫️ 同行記者 an accompanying reporter. ◐ 首相訪米の~記者団 the press corps accompanying the Prime Minister on 「his [her] visit to America. 同行取材 news coverage《(of a celebrity)》by accompanying reporters. ◐ ~取材してみて初めてそのスターの素顔がわかった. Only when he stayed with the star for a period of time did the reporter find out what she was really like.
とうごうがたちりじょうほうシステム【統合型地理情報~】an integrated geographic information system (略: IGIS).
とうごうこくさいしんかいくっさくけいかく【統合国際深海掘削計画】the Integrated Ocean Drilling Program (略: IODP).
とうごうテロぶんせきセンター【統合-分析-】〔MI6, MI5, 警察などで作る英国の対テロ組織〕the Joint Terrorism Analysis Centre (略: JTAC).
とうごうばくりょうかんぶ【統合幕僚監部】〔防衛省の〕the Joint Staff Office (略: JSO). ▶ 2006年新設.
とうごうばくりょうちょう【統合幕僚長】〔統合幕僚監部の〕the Chief of Staff.
どうこうばん【導光板】〖電子工学〗〔液晶画面を後ろから照らすための板〕a light-guiding plate (略: LGP).
とうざ【当座】▫️ 当座預金残高 a current account balance; *a checking account balance.
とうさい³【搭載】▫️ 搭載機能 an in-built function; a function provided; a function (a camera) is equipped with. ◐ 機種により~機能は異なります. Different models 「have [are equipped with] different functions.
とうざいかいろう【東西回廊】〔インドシナ地域に建設中の幹線道路〕the East-West Corridor.
とうざいけいざいかいろう【東西経済回廊】〔インドシナ半島をベトナム中部からラオス・タイを経てミャンマーまで横断する道路〕the East-West Economic Corridor (略: EWEC).
とうさく¹【倒錯】▫️ 倒錯心理 perverted psychology.
とうさつ【盗撮】▫️ スカート(内)盗撮 "upskirting." 性的盗撮 taking secret indecent 「photographs [videos] of women;〔スカート内の〕"upskirting."
どうさつ【洞察】▫️ 洞察学習〖心理〗insight learning.
とうさわとらのお【とうさわ虎の尾】〔サクラソウ科の多年草〕*Lysimachia candida.* ▶ 絶滅危惧種.
とうさん²【倒産】▫️ 倒産件数 the number of bankruptcies. 倒産法〖法〗bankruptcy law.
どうさん【動産】▫️ 動産担保融資 asset-based lending (略: ABL); an asset-based loan; asset-based financing (略: ABF).
とうし¹【投資】▫️ 過剰[過大]投資 overinvestment. 集中投資 concentrated investment. 多重投資〖金融〗=重複投資. 重複投資〖金融〗repeated [redundant] investment. ▫️ 投資一任契約 a discretionary investment (management) contract. 投資一任口座 a wrap account; a separately managed account (略: SMA). 投資額 an investment 「sum [amount]; the 「sum [amount] of an investment. 投資格付け〔(lower)〕investment rating 〔on…〕. 投資協定 an investment agreement. ◐ 日本は現在, 中国, ロシアなど11の国・地域と~協定を結んでいる. Japan has now signed investment agreements with 11 countries and regions including China and Russia. 投資口価格〔不動産投資信託の価格〕a real estate investment trust price. 投資

グループ an investment group. 投資効率 investment efficiency. 投資財 investment goods. ○〜財出荷指数 an index of investment goods shipments. 投資先 an investee; an investment target. ○〜先企業 an investee company. 投資詐欺 (an) investment fraud; 《fall for》an investment scam. 投資事業組合 an investors'「organization [group, union]. 投資自由化 investment liberalization; liberalization of investment. 投資主体別売買動向《証券》investment trends by investor category. 投資情報 investment information 投資税額控除 an investment tax allowance《略: ITA》. 投資総額 the total sum「of investment [invested「(in a new company)]; a total investment (sum). 投資判断《証券》investment judgment. 投資ファンド an investment fund. 投資分析 investment analysis. ○〜分析ツール an investment analysis tool. 投資保護協定 an investment protection agreement. ○二国間〜保護協定《sign》a bilateral investment protection agreement. 投資マネー investment funds. 投資元 an investor《in an enterprise》. 投資立国 a national commitment to (overseas) investment; (overseas) investment-based national development.

**どうじ**[3]【同時】 ▭□ 同時下校〔全校または同学年の児童が同時刻に下校すること〕going home from school in a group at the same time. 同時行動原則〔米国による北朝鮮敵視政策の変更と北朝鮮による核放棄を行うべきだとする北朝鮮の主張〕the principle of simultaneous actions. 同時出生集団《社会》〔出生コーホート〕a birth cohort. 同時爆破テロ simultaneous terrorist bombings;〔2005年ロンドンの〕⇨ロンドンどうじテロ.

**どうじいしょく**【同時移植】《医》〔複数の臓器の〕a「simultaneous [combined]《heart and kidney》transplant; simultaneous《organ》transplantation. ▭□ 肝腎同時移植 a simultaneous liver-kidney transplant. 膵腎同時移植 a simultaneous pancreas-kidney transplant《略: SPK》.

**とうしか**【投資家】 ▭□ 投資家グループ an investor group; a group of investors. 投資家説明会《hold》an investor relations meeting《for individual investors》. 投資家向け広報 investors relations《略: IR》.

**とうしかんきょうせいびききん**【投資環境整備基金】the Investment Climate Facilitation Fund《略: ICFF》.

**とうじこく**【当事国】 ▭□《関連》当事国会議 a「conference [meeting] of the countries involved《in a dispute》.

**とうしサービスほう**【投資-法】《法》〔仮称〕the Investment Service Law. ▶「金融商品取引法」の仮称・通称として用いられた語.

**とうじしゃ**【当事者】 ▭□ 当事者意識 a sense of「involvement [participation]《in environmental problems》. 当事者責任 the responsibility「as [of] the person(s) concerned.

**とうししんたく**【投資信託】 ▭□ 外(国)債投資信託 a foreign bond investment trust. スポット投資信託 a spot investment trust. 追加型投資信託〔オープン型[開放]投資信託〕open-end investment trust「operations [business].

**とうししんたくきょうかい**【投資信託協会】the Investment Trusts Association, Japan.

**とうししんたくほう**【投資信託法】《法》the Investment Trust Law. ▶正式名称は「投資信託及び投資法人に関する法律」.

**とうしつ**[2]【糖質】▭□ 糖質コルチコステロイド《生化》〔副腎皮質ステロイド〕a glucocorticosteroid. 糖質制限食 a low-sugar diet.

**ドゥジャイル**〔イラク中部, バグダッド北方の村〕Al-Dujaile.

**とうしょ**[1]【当初】 ▭□ 当初所得《経》initial income.

**とうしょ**[4]【島嶼】 ▭□ 島嶼(国)家 an island「nation [country]. 島嶼防衛 islands' defense; the defense of islands.

**とうじょ**【倒叙】 ▭□ 倒叙法〔時間の流れとは逆に現在から過去にさかのぼりながら叙述する形式〕inverted「narrative [narration]; telling《a story》「backwards [in reverse (order)].

**とうしょう**[3]【東証】 ▭□ 東証規模別株価指数 the size-based TOPIX sub-indices. 東証 REIT 指数 the「Tokyo Stock Exchange [TSE] REIT index.《⇨リート[2]》

**とうじょう**[3]【搭乗】 ▭□ 搭乗者傷害保険 passenger injury insurance. 搭乗歩行型ロボット a mountable walking robot. 搭乗率保証制度〔地方自治体と航空会社間で交わされる〕an occupancy guarantee「agreement [arrangement].

**とうしょう**[3]【洞簫】〔楽器〕〔尺八に似た中国の管楽器〕a dongxiao.

**とうじょうき**【搭乗機】an aircraft with《sb》on board. ○ 山本長官の〜 the aircraft with Commander Yamamoto on board; the aircraft carrying Commander Yamamoto. ○ 自分の〜のゲートを確認する check the gate for *one's* plane.

**とうすう**[2]【頭数】 ▭□ 頭数管理《animal》numbers「management [control];《家畜の》herd size「management [control].

**とうせい**[0]【統制】 ▭□ 言論統制 controls [restrictions] on「free [(the) freedom of] speech. 情報統制 information control; control of information.

**どうせい**[3]【同棲】 ▭□ 同棲率〔未婚者などの〕a cohabitation rate; a rate of cohabitation.

**どうせいしみんパートナーほう**【同性市民-法】《英法》= しみんパートナーほう.

**とうせいぶん**【党政分離】〔(中国における)党と政府の機能分離〕separation of「party and government [the Party and (the) Government].

**とうせき**[2]【党籍】 ▭□ 党籍剥奪 expulsion from a political party.

**とうせき**[4]【透析】 ▭□ 透析患者 a dialysis patient; a person on《kidney》dialysis.

**とうせつ**[3]【当接】〜する come into contact《with…》; touch.

**とうせん**[2]【当選】 ▭□ 下位当選 one of the lowest victories; victory with among the fewest votes. ○ 下位〜 one of the winners with the least votes. 最下位当選 the lowest victory; victory with the fewest votes. ○ 最下位〜者 the winner with the least votes; the lowest winner. ○ 当選速報 a quick report of the winner(s). 当選ライン〔選挙での〕「victory [winning] line [mark]. 当選枠 the allotted number of winners.

**どうせん**[3]【動線】 ▭□ 家事動線 the「route [path] followed when engaged in household tasks. 生活動線 the normal household traffic path.

**とうせんきょう**【投扇興】a fan-throwing game; fan.

**とうそう**[3]【逃走】 ▭□ 逃走資金 getaway money. ○ 彼は〜資金が底をつき, 空き巣に入ったところを現行犯逮捕された. His getaway money was running out and he was caught in the act trying to burgle an empty house.

**とうそう**[9]【刀装】sword accouterments. ▭□ 刀装師 a maker of sword accouterments.

**どうそうかい**【同窓会】 ▭□ 同窓会名簿 an alumni [a graduates'] association name-list.

**どうそく**[2]【等速】 ▭□ 等速ジョイント《自動車》a constant-velocity joint《略: CVJ》; a CV joint.

**どうぞく**[1]【同族】 ▭□ 同族経営 family「management [operation, ownership, running]《of a business》.

どうたい¹【同体】 ▫ 同体取り直し restarting a sumo bout after both wrestlers hit the ground at the same time.
どうたい²【胴体】 ▫ 胴体燃料タンク〔航空機の〕a fuselage fuel tank.
どうたい³【動体】 ▫ 動体センサー a motion「sensor [detector].
どうたい⁴【動態】 ▫ 動態調査 dynamic research [a dynamic survey]〔on attitudes to mental illness〕. 動態保存〔可動状態での車両・機械などの保存〕conservation《of vehicles》in a driv(e)able condition. ◐〜保存する conserve《a vehicle》in a driv(e)able condition.
とうだいきねんび【灯台記念日】〔11月1日〕Lighthouse Day.
とうち⁵【統治】 ▫ 統治行為論【法】the theory of Act of State.
トウチジャン【豆豉醤】〔調味料〕(Chinese) black bean sauce.
とうちのしんがく【統治の神学】〔キリスト教徒のみが神から世界の統治を託されたとする; 米国のキリスト教組織「プロミスキーパーズ」が提唱〕dominion theology.
どうちゃく⁵【撞着】 ▫ 撞着語法〔意味の矛盾する言葉を結びつける修辞法〕an oxymoron.
どうちゅうりょうほう【動注療法】【医】〔抗がん剤などを動脈から直接患部に向けて注入する治療法〕intra-arterial injection.
とうちょう⁵【頭頂】 ▫ 頭頂連合野 the parietal association area.
とうつう【疼痛】 ▫ 疼痛物質【生化】a pain substance.
どうてん²【同点】 ▫ 同点ゴール〔球技などの〕an equalizing goal; an equalizer. 同点2[3]ラン〔野球〕(hit) a game-tying, two-run [three-run] home run [homer]. 同点満塁ホームラン〔野球〕(hit) a game-tying grand slam.
どうでん²【導電】 ▫ 導電性インク (a) conductive [(an) electrically conductive] ink; (a) conducting [(an) electrically conductive] ink; (an) electroconductive ink. 導電性プラスチック〔化〕(electrically) conductive plastic(s). 導電性膜〔化〕a conductive membrane.
とうど⁴【糖度】 ▫ 糖度計[測定器] a sugar hydrometer. 糖度測定 sugar (「content [concentration]) measurement.
とうない【党内】 ▫ 党内対立 intraparty「discord [rivalry]. 党内調整 internal coordination (of opinions) inside a party. 党内融和 harmony within a party; (a party's) internal harmony; intraparty harmony. 党内世論 opinion inside a (political) party; (intra)party opinion.
ドゥナリエラ =デュナリエラ.
とうなん²【盗難】 ▫ 盗難自転車 a stolen「bicycle [bike]. 盗難証明書〔警察署発行の〕a certificate of theft; a theft certificate; written evidence of theft (issued by the police). 盗難防止装置 an antitheft device. ◐ 自動車[車両]〜防止装置 a「vehicle [car] antitheft device. 盗難保険金 payment [an insurance payment] for theft; theft benefit.
とうなんアジアしょくれんごう【東南-諸国連合】 ▫ 東南アジア諸国連合地域フォーラム the ASEAN Regional Forum (略: ARF).
とうなんアジアゆうこうきょうりょくじょうやく【東南-友好協力条約】〔ASEANの基本条約〕the Treaty of Amity and Cooperation in Southeast Asia (略: TAC).
とうなんアチェ【東南-】〔インドネシア, アチェ州の県〕Aceh Tenggara.
とうにゅう¹【投入】 ▫ 投入口〔コインの〕a coin slot; a slot;〔シュレッダーの〕a feed slot《of a shredder》.
とうにゅう²【豆乳】 ▫ 豆乳ローション soy (milk) lotion.

どうにょう【導尿】 ▫ 自己導尿 self-catheterization.
とうにょうびょう【糖尿病】 ▫ I 型糖尿病 type 1 diabetes; diabetes mellitus type 1; insulin-dependent diabetes; juvenile-onset diabetes. 隠れ糖尿病 hidden diabetes. II 型糖尿病 type 2 diabetes; diabetes mellitus type 2; non-insulin-dependent diabetes; adult-onset diabetes. ▫ 糖尿病性壊疽(だっそ) diabetic gangrene. 糖尿病療養指導士 a certified diabetes educator.
トゥノム〔インドネシア, アチェ州, アチェジャヤ県の町〕Teunom.
トゥバーノ〔楽器〕〔キューバの太鼓〕a tubano.
とうはつ【頭髪】 ▫ 頭髪密度【医】scalp hair density.
ドゥバヤズィット, ドゥバヤジット〔トルコ東部の町〕Dogubayazit.
どうは【導波路】【光】a waveguide. ▫ 導波路構造 a layered waveguide structure.
とうばん¹【当番】 ▫ 当番付き添い人制度【法】〔少年事件の〕a duty「*attorney ["solicitor] allotted to attend a juvenile defendant charged with a serious crime.
とうばん²【登板】 ▫ 登板間隔〔野球〕a period between pitching appearances.
とうばん²【銅板】 ▫ 銅版画家 a copperplate「printer [artist].
とうひ⁸【頭皮】 ▫ 頭皮ケア scalp care. 頭皮マッサージ (a) scalp massage.
とうひょう²【投票】 ▫ ○×式投票 for-or-against voting; a for-or-against「vote [election];〔日本の〕voting [a vote, an election] in which ○ indicates "for" and × "against." 記号式投票 voting by placing a mark against a choice of pre-printed candidates' names. 自書式投票 handwritten voting. タッチパネル式投票 touch-panel voting. ◐ タッチパネル式〜機 a touch-panel voting machine. 重複投票〔1人が2回またはそれ以上票を投ずること〕multiple voting. 二重投票 double voting; voting twice. ▫ 投票速報 a voting「report [up-date, bulletin].
とうびょう³【闘病】 ▫ 闘病日記 a daily record of one's fight against disease.
とうひん【盗品】 ▫ 盗品等有償譲り受け(罪)【法】receiving (stolen goods). 盗品保管(罪)【法】keeping [possession of] stolen goods.
とうふ【豆腐】 ▫ ざる豆腐 tofu [soybean curd] drained in a bamboo colander. 寄せ豆腐 unmolded「tofu [soybean curd].
とうぶしゅう【東部州】〔サウジアラビアの州〕Eastern Province; (現地語名) Ash Sharqiyah.
どうぶつ²【動物】 ▫ 動物遺伝学 animal genetics. 動物慰霊祭 a spirit-consoling service for animals. 動物介在活動〔介護施設などでの〕(an) animal-assisted activity (略: AAA). 動物看護師 an animal health technician (略: AHT). 動物感染症〔動物間の感染症〕= animal infectious disease;〔動物がヒトに媒介する感染症〕= 動物由来感染症. 動物検疫犬 an animal-products sniffer dog; a customs dog trained to sniff out animal products. 動物生態南 (ぜいたい)⁴. 動物占有者【法】the「possessor [owner] of an animal. 動物取扱業者 a business dealing with animals; an animal-related business; an animal dealer. 動物取扱責任者 a person responsible for (dealing with) animals. 動物由来感染症【医】a zoonosis (pl. -ses); an animal-derived infection.
どうぶつのあいごおよびかんりにかんするほうりつ【動物の愛護及び管理に関する法律】the Law for the Humane Treatment and Management of Animals.
とうぶはいいろりす【東部灰色栗鼠】【動】an eastern gray squirrel; *Sciurus carolinensis*.
とうふよう【豆腐餻】〔料理〕〔豆腐を発酵させて作る沖縄の珍

味〕*tōfu-yō*; Okinawan fermented tofu.
**とうべん**【答弁】 ▣ 答弁能力 the ability to「reply [respond]《to questions in the Diet》.
**とうぼう**【逃亡】 ▣ 逃亡先 a place of「refuge [escape]; a hideout. ◑ 彼は~先のフィリピンで地元の警察によって逮捕された. He was arrested by local police in the Philippines, where he had escaped to.
**どうほう**¹【同胞】 ▣ 同胞意識〔同国人意識〕a shared feeling of patriotism; a sense of patriotic fellowship;〔仲間意識〕a sense of「fellowship [camaraderie, brotherhood]. 同胞抗争〔葛藤〕〔心理〕sibling rivalry.
**どうほう**²【同報】 ▣ 同報無線〔防災無線システム〕a community broadcast (disaster warning) system.
「**逃亡者**」〔米国の、殺人の濡れ衣を着せられた男が警察の捜査を逃れつつ真犯人を追うTVドラマ・映画〕The Fugitive.
**どうほうせい**【同報性】〔1回の送信でカバーエリア内すべての地点に同じ情報を届ける性質〕simultaneous transmission of the same information. ▣ 一斉同報性 = どうほう.
**とうほくのうさぎ**【東北野兎】〔動〕a Japanese hare; *Lepus brachyurus angustidens*.
**トゥマイ** = トゥーマイえんじん.
**どうみゃく**【動脈】 ▣ 動脈解離〔乖離〕〔医〕(an)「artery [arterial] dissection; (a) dissection of the artery. ◑ 頸~解離 (a) carotid artery dissection / 椎~解離 (a) vertebral artery dissection / 脳~解離 (a) cerebral artery [arterial] dissection. 動脈注射〔医〕intra-arterial [(an) arterial] injection.
**どうみゃくこうか(しょう)**【動脈硬化(症)】 ▣ 粥状動脈硬化症〔アテローム硬化症〕atherosclerosis.
**どうみゃくりゅう**【動脈瘤】〔医〕an「aneurysm [aneurism]. ▣ 動脈瘤破裂《have》a ruptured aneurysm. ◑ 大~破裂 a ruptured aortic aneurysm / 脳~破裂 a ruptured intracranial aneurysm.
**とうみん**¹【冬眠】 ▣ 疑似冬眠〔動〕pseudohibernation.
**とうめい**³【透明】 ▣ 透明電極 a transparent electrode. 透明導電酸化物 a transparent conductive oxide. 透明導電膜 a transparent conductive film.
**とうめいゆう**【透明釉】〔製陶〕(a)「transparent [clear]」glaze.
**トウモル**【等—】~の〔化〕equimolar.
**とうやく**²【投薬】 ▣ 投薬量〔1回の〕a dose; (a) dosage;〔合計の〕a [the] total dosage《of antidepressant》.
**どうよく**²【動翼】〔機〕a rotor「blade [vane]; a moving「blade [vane].
**どうりゅうたい**【導流帯】〔安全で円滑な通行のため、車が通らないようにしてある場所を示す道路の標示〕a slip lane.
**どうりょく**【動力】 ▣ 動力車操縦者〔鉄道〕an engineer. ◑ ~車操縦者〔運転〕免許 an engineer's (operating) license. 動力飛行機〔初期の〕a powered airplane.
**とうるい**¹【盗塁】 ▣ 盗塁阻止率 an opposition stolen base average (略: OSBA).
**どうるい**【同類】 ▣ 同婚婚〔社会〕homogamy.
「**トゥルー・クライム**」〔映画〕True Crime.
**トゥ・ループ**〔フィギュアスケート〕a toe loop (jump).
**トゥルカレム**〔ヨルダン川西岸のパレスチナ自治区の都市〕Tulkarem.
**とうれい**【動令】〔号令の〕a command of execution.
**とうれつ**【凍裂】〔急激な寒冷のため樹幹に縦に裂け目が生じること〕a frost crack; frost cracking.
**トゥレットしょうこうぐん**【—症候群】〔医〕Tourette('s) syndrome.
**どうろ**【道路】 ▣ 道路陥没 road subsidence. 道路交通情報センター ⇨ にほんどうろこうつうじょうほうセンター. 道路情報 road [traffic] information; (information on)「traffic [road] conditions. 道路損傷 そんしょう². 道路

率〔道路面積の割合〕a road to area ratio; a ratio of paved to total area.
**どうろかんけいよんこうだん**【道路関係四公団】《the privatization of》the four highway-related public corporations.
**どうろかんけいよんこうだんみんえいかすいしんいいんかい**【道路関係四公団民営化推進委員会】the Promotion Committee for the Privatization of the Four Highway-related Public Corporations.
**とうろく**²【登録】 ▣ 不正登録 (voter) registration fraud. ▣ 登録医 a registered medical practitioner. 登録抽選〔チケットの予約などの〕a registration lottery. ▣ 抽選制 a registration lottery system. 登録通知メール〔インターネット上のさまざまサービスにユーザーを登録した人に送られてくる登録確認のメール〕(a) registration notification e-mail. 登録漏れ (a) failure to「record《data》[register《*sb*'s name》]. ◑ 名簿に~漏れがありましたらご連絡ください. If「there is anything missing from [we have left anything out in] the list of names, please get in touch. | If there are any omissions on the name-list, please contact us.
**どうろこうだんみんえいかほう**【道路公団民営化法】〔法〕the Japan Highway Public Corporation Privatization Law.
**どうろシステムこうどかすいしんきこう**【道路—高度化推進機構】the Organization for Road System Enhancement (略: ORSE).
**どうろせいびきんきゅうそちほう**【道路整備緊急措置法】〔法〕the Law on Emergency Measures for Road Improvement.
**どうろせいびとくべつかいけいほう**【道路整備特別会計法】〔法〕the Roadway Development Special Account Law.
**とうろん**²【討論】 ▣ 討論番組〔テレビなどの〕a《TV》debate program.
**トー**² = トウ².
**ドーア** Dore, Ronald (Philip) (1925- ; 英国の社会学者・日本研究家).
「**遠い空の向こうに**」〔映画〕October Sky.
**ドーヴァーくうぐんきち**【—空軍基地】〔米国デラウェア州にある米空軍基地〕Dover Air Force Base.
「**10日間で男を上手にフル方法**」〔映画〕How to Lose a Guy in 10 Days.
**トーキング・エイド**〔商標〕〔ゲーム会社のナムコが開発した身体障害者向け携帯型意思伝達装置〕a Talking Aid (略: TA).
**ドーキンス** Dawkins, Richard (1941- ; 英国の生物学者).
**トーク**¹ ▣ トーク喫茶[カフェ] = 出会い(系)喫茶[カフェ]⇨であい.
**とおしうち**【通し打ち】〔四国巡礼で八十八か所すべての霊場を一度の旅程でまわること〕(completing)「a full [an uninterrupted] pilgrimage around all the 88 designated temples in Shikoku. ⇨ くぎりうち.
**トータル** ▣ トータル・コーディネート total [complete, comprehensive] coordination [management, control]. ◑ ~コーディネートする coordinate [manage, control]《a project》「completely [comprehensively].
**トータル・コスト・リダクション**〔企業内の各部門が一体となって取り組むコスト削減〕(a) total cost reduction (略: TCR).
「**トータル・フィアーズ**」〔映画〕The Sum of All Fears.
「**トータル・リコール**」〔映画〕Total Recall.
**トーチ**〔スペシャル・オリンピックスの聖火リレー〕a《Special Olympics》torch run.
**ドーハかいはつアジェンダ**【—開発—】〔2001年、WTO加盟国がドーハで行われた貿易相会議で合意した事項〕the Doha Development Agenda (略: DDA).
**とおはなび**【遠花火】(the unfolding of) distant fire-

ドーハのひげさ【-の悲劇】『ｻｯｶｰ』the "Tragedy of Doha"; the match that was played between Japan and Iraq in Doha, Qatar, on October 28, 1993, and that ended in a tie, preventing Japan from advancing to the World Cup.

ドーハ・ラウンド〔WTOの新多角的貿易交渉〕the Doha Round (of WTO negotiations).

ドーフマン Dorfman, Ariel (1942- ; チリの小説家・劇作家).

トーマス Thomas, Betty (1948- ; 米国の映画監督・製作者; 本名 Betty Thomas Nienhauser).

「トーマス・クラウン・アフェアー」〔映画〕The Thomas Crown Affair.

ドーラ〔イラク, バグダッド市内の地名〕Dora.

トールペイント『工芸』〔種々の材質の〕薄い板に色付けする手工芸〕tole painting.

「ドーン・オブ・ザ・デッド」〔映画〕Dawn of the Dead.

トーンチャイム〔楽器〕a tone chime.

とか² 〔渡河〕 ▭ 渡河訓練《stage》a river-crossing drill.

ドカエ Decaë, Henri (1915-87; フランスの映画カメラマン).

とかげはぜ〔蜥蜴鯊〕〔魚〕〔沖縄・東南アジア・オセアニア産の, 干潟にすむハゼ; 絶滅危惧種〕a blue mudhopper; a walking goby; a bearded goby; *Scartelaos histophorus*.

とかちおきじしん〔十勝沖地震〕〔2003年9月26日の〕the (2003) Tokachi Offshore Earthquake.

トキシコゲノミクス〔薬〕toxicogenomics. ▷ toxicogenomic *adj.*

トキシホルモン〔医〕〔がん細胞が分泌する毒素〕a toxohormone.

どきどき ▭ どきどき感 a heart-pounding feeling.

ときのきねんび〔時の記念日〕〔6月10日〕Time Day; Time Memorial Day.

どきょう¹【度胸】 ▭ 試合度胸 guts [determination, focus] going into a 「game [match]. ◎ 彼女は試合〜がある. She is a tough competitor in her matches. / ラグビーの日本代表チームにとってこの海外遠征は試合〜をつけるチャンスだ. This overseas trip will be a good opportunity for the Japanese rugby team to gain confidence in its matches.

どきんがん【ど近眼】extreme nearsightedness. ◎ 私は〜だ. I'm 「extremely nearsighted [as blind as a bat].

とくいさき【得意先】 ▭ 得意先回り going [doing] the rounds of *one's* customers; going around [visiting] *one's* customers. ◎ 〜回りをする go the rounds of *one's* customers.

とくうち〔特打ち〕『野球』=とくだ.

どくえい³【読影】 ▭ 遠隔読影 remote X-ray 「reading [interpretation]. ▭ 読影医 an X-ray 「analyst [interpreter]; a radiologist.

どくガス【毒-】 ▭ 毒ガス兵器 a poison gas weapon.

とくがわきねんざいだん〔徳川記念財団〕the Tokugawa Memorial Foundation.

どくげんきん【独弦琴】〔楽器〕〔中国の一絃琴〕a duxianqin.

どくさそり【毒蠍】a poisonous scorpion.

どじ【独自】 ▭ 独自路線 an independent [*one's* own] course [policy]. ◎ 〜路線を貫く stick rigorously to [never deviate from] an independent policy.

とくしゅ²【特殊】 ▭ 特殊印刷 multiple surface printing. ▭ 特殊機関〔軍隊の特殊部隊〕a special unit. ▭ 特殊空挺部隊〔英国陸軍の〕the Special Air Service (略: SAS). ▭ 特殊合金 a special alloy. ▭ 特殊作戦群〔自衛隊の〕the Special Operations Group (略: SOG). ▭ 特殊車両 a special(-purpose) vehicle. ▭ 特殊トラック a special-purpose truck. ▭ 特殊犯捜査係 a special investigation team (略: SIT). ▭ 特殊メーク special makeup.

とくしゅ³【特守】〔野球〕〔通常の練習時間以外に行う守備練習〕extra fielding practice.

とくじゅ【特需】 ▭ 新札特需 extra [special] demand arising from the issue of new bank notes. オリンピック特需 increased demand [higher sales] for the Olympics. 戦争特需 (war-related) special-procurement demand. 中国特需〔中国の好況を受けての〕Chinese special-procurement demand; special demand from China. 復興特需〔震災直後などの〕(a) special procurement for reconstruction. 猛暑特需〔エアコンやビールなどの売り上げが急増すること〕special demand caused by hot weather.

とくしゅいあんしせつきょうかい〔特殊慰安施設協会〕〔日本史〕〔太平洋戦争後, 進駐軍のために設立された〕the Recreation and Amusement Association (略: RAA).

とくしゅほうじんとうかいかくきほんほう【特殊法人等改革基本法】〔法〕the Basic Law on Special Public Institutions Reform.

どくしょ【読書】 ▭ 読書端末〔デジタル形式で提供される書籍を閲覧するための携帯端末〕an e-book reader. 読書離れ (a) 「movement away from [loss of interest in] reading books; a tendency to read books less. 読書歴 *one's* reading history.

とくじょう【特上】 ▭ 特上同盟兄 = メガ・アライ.

とくしょくあるだいがくきょういくしえんプログラム【特色ある大学教育支援】〔教育〕〔文部科学省の〕the Distinctive University Education Support Program.

どくしょすいしんうんどうきょうぎかい〔読書推進運動協議会〕the Reading Promotion Campaign Association.

どくしん³【独身】 ▭ 独身時代《in》*one's* single days. 独身率 the celibacy rate《of women in their thirties, among farmers》.

どくしん⁴【読唇】lipreading. 〜する lip-read; read (*sb's*) lips. ▭ 読唇術〔法〕lipreading techniques.

トクスグン【徳寿宮】〔韓国, ソウルにある宮殿; 史跡〕the Deoksu Palace; Deoksugung.

どくせい【毒性】 ▭ 急性吸入毒性 ⇨ きゅうせい⁴. 急性経口毒性 ⇨ きゅうせい⁴. ▭ 毒性学 toxicology. ▭ 環境〜学 environmental toxicology / 食品化学〜学 food and chemical toxicology.

とくせつ【特設】 ▭ 特設売り場 a special sales counter. 特設コーナー〔店舗・会場などの〕a specially set-up area.

どくせん²【独占】 ▭ 独占営業権 exclusive 「business [trading] rights; the [an] exclusive right to 「do business [trade]. ◎ 〜営業権を獲得する acquire [obtain, be granted] exclusive 「business [trading] rights. 独占禁止協力協定 a cooperation agreement on competition law enforcement. 独占契約〔sign〕an exclusive contract《with…》. 独占交渉権 exclusive negotiation rights. 独占配信 exclusive distribution《of news》. ◎ 〜配信権 exclusive distribution rights; the [an] exclusive right to distribution.

どくぜん【独善】 ▭ 独善性 self-righteousness; self-complacency; self-flattery.

どくそ【毒素】 ▭ 毒素原性大腸菌〔医〕enterotoxigenic *Escherichia coli* [E. coli]《略: ETEC》.

「特捜刑事マイアミ・バイス」〔マイアミの犯罪組織に潜入する刑事のTVドラマ〕Miami Vice.

とくそうたい【特捜隊】=特別捜査隊《⇨そうさ²》.

とくだ【特打】〔野球〕〔通常の練習時間以外に行う打撃練習〕extra batting practice. ▭ 居残り特打 late (extra) batting practice.

ドクター ▭ ドクター・ショッピング comparison shopping for health care (without ever being satisfied). ドクターバンク〔僻地(へきち)の医師確保のための医師登録・派遣制度〕a "doctor bank."

ドクターイエロー〔新幹線電気軌道総合試験車の通称〕a

ドクターキルディア

"Doctor Yellow" (Shinkansen electric and track inspection train).
「ドクター・キルディア」〔米国の, インターン医師の TV ドラマ〕Dr. Kildare.
ドクターズコスメ〔開発に専門医が参加している基礎化粧品〕medical cosmetics; a cosmeceutical.
とくてい【特定】▷▶ 特定化学物質 a ˈspecified [designated] chemical substance. 特定規模需要〔高圧電線路から受電する大規模施設などの大口の電力需要〕specified-scale demand. 特定規模電気事業者 a power producer and supplier (略: PPS). 特定求職者雇用開発助成金〔高齢者・障害者などの就職促進のための〕a subsidy to encourage the employment of special category job-applicants. 特定継続的役務提供〔事業者が特定のサービスを長期にわたって契約者に提供すること〕a ˈspecific [specified] continuous service offer. ▷ ～継続的役務提供契約 a ˈspecific [specified] continuous service offer contract. 特定公益増進法人 a corporate body making special contributions to public welfare (and thus entitled to preferential tax treatment of contributions received). 特定市街化区域 a designated urbanization-promotion ˈarea [zone]. 特定疾病〔介護保険法における〕a condition designated as an intractable disease. 特定疾病保障保険〔3 大成人病などに対する保険〕insurance ˈfor [against] specified ˈdiseases [conditions]. 特定信書便〔配達物の重量や配達時間を限定して信書を集配する信書便事業〕a delivery service for specified types of correspondence. 特定地方交通線〔旧国鉄の赤字ローカル線〕a specific local railway line (of the Japanese National Railways). 特定調停【法】specific arbitration; court-supervised arbitration between a creditor and a debtor. 特定独立行政法人 a specified independent administrative institution. 特定胚【生物】a ˈspecific [specified] embryo. 特定ハロン〔化〕specified halons. 特定有害物質使用制限指令 ≡ ローズ法. 特定用途制限地域〔住環境を損なう可能性のある風俗店・大型店舗などの建設が制限される区域〕a prohibited use (zoning) ˈdistrict [area]. 特定利益〔特定組織的共済〕〔1 団体〕a special interest.
とくていがいらいせいぶつひがいぼうしほう【特定外来生物被害防止法】【法】= がいらいせいぶつほう.
とくていかがくぶっしつとうしょうがいよぼうきそく【特定化学物質等障害予防規則】【法】the Ordinance on the Prevention of ˈDamage Attributable to [Hazards from] Specified Chemical Substances.
とくていきんゆうじょうほうしつ【特定金融情報室】〔金融庁の〕the Japan Financial Intelligence Office (略: JAFIO).
とくていしさんりゅうどうかほう【特定資産流動化法】【法】the Law Concerning Securitization by a Special-Purpose Company of a Specified Asset. ▶ SPC 法 (the SPC Law) と略記.
とくていしっそうしゃ【特定失踪者】〔北朝鮮により拉致されたと思われる行方不明被害者〕missing Japanese probably related to North Korea. ▷▶ 特定失踪者問題調査会 the Investigation Commission on Missing Japanese Probably Related to North Korea（略: COMJAN）.
とくていしょうがいしゃきゅうふきんほう【特定障害者給付金法】【法】the Law to Provide Treatment for Handicapped People Not Covered by National Insurance.
とくていしょうとりひきほう【特定商取引法】【法】the Specified Commercial Transactions Law. ▶ 訪問販売法を改正したもの；正式名称は「特定商取引に関する法律」.
とくていせんぱくにゅうこうきんし（とくべつそち）ほう【特定船舶入港禁止（特別措置）法】【法】the Law Banning the Entry of Specified Foreign Ships into Japanese Ports.
とくていちょうていほう【特定調停法】【法】the Specific Arbitration Law.
とくていでんしメールそうしんてきせいかほう【特定電子メール送信適正化法】【法】〔「特定電子メールの送信の適正化等に関する法律」の通称〕⇒めいわくメールぼうしほう.
とくていでんしメールほう【特定電子メール法】【法】= めいわくメールぼうしほう.
とくていひえいりかつどうほうじん【特定非営利活動法人】a nonprofit ˈcorporation [organization].
とくていひじょうさいがいとくべつそちほう【特定非常災害特別措置法】【法】the Law on Special Measures for a ˈParticular [Specific] Disaster.
とくてん[1]【特典】特典映像〔DVD などの〕a bonus ˈfeature [clip, video].
とくてん[2]【得点】▷▶ 得点機〔得点の機会〕a scoring opportunity; a chance to score. ▷ ～機を逸する squander a scoring opportunity; miss a chance to score. 得点源〔団体競技でよく得点する選手〕a ˈgoal [run, point, etc] scorer;〔試験などで点を取りやすい科目 (など)〕a [oneˈs] strong subject. ▷ 彼はチームの～源として活躍した. He was a (goal-, run-, point-)scorer for the team. / 彼女は英語を～源にして大学入試に合格した. With English as her strong subject she passed the university entrance exam. | Her English got her through the entrance exam. 得点シーン〔スポーツの試合の〕(the scene of) a score. 得点主義〔昇進や選抜の際の評価方法の 1 つ〕（select [promote] sb by using) the merit system. 得点調整〔受験科目間の〕(an) averaging of (subject) scores; inter-subject scaling. 得点力〔能力〕〔スポーツなど〕scoring ability.
とくにん[2]【特任】(a) special appointment. ▷▶ 特任教授〔教員, 助手〕a specially-appointed ˈprofessor [teacher, assistant].
ドクハラ〔医者が言葉の暴力で患者の心を傷つけること〕verbal abuse of a patient (by a doctor).
とくべつ【特別】▷▶ 特別会計【法】a special account law. 特別監査官 a special auditor. 特別企画 a special《Christmas》ˈproject [program]. 特別機動隊〔警察の〕special riot police. 特別教員免許〔社会人を対象とした〕a special teaching certificate. 特別警備隊〔海上自衛隊の〕a special guard team（略: SGT）;〔海上保安庁の〕a special security team（略: SST）. 特別決議〔株主総会の〕a special resolution. 特別検査〔金融庁の大手銀行に対する金融検査〕a special (financial) investigation. 特別公開 (a) special opening (to the public). ▷ 通常は非公開の社寺・庭園がゴールデン・ウイークの間～公開される. Those temples, shrines and gardens that are normally closed to the public are specially opened during Golden Week. 特別攻撃隊 a "special attack" ˈunit [corps]; a ˈsuicide [banzai] unit; a commando unit; commandoes; a kamikaze party. 特別裁判所〔日本国憲法で設置を認めていない, 司法権の及ばない軍法会議などの裁判機関〕an extraordinary tribunal. 特別支援学校〔障害者のための〕a special support school; a special needs school. 特別支援教育〔障害者のための〕special support education; special needs education. 特別障害者 a special disabled person; a person designated as severely disabled. 特別仕様車 a specially built car; a car ˈbuilt to [with] special specifications; a custom-spec car. 特別清算〔法律処理の一形態〕special liquidation. ▷ ～清算手続き special liquidation proceedings. 特別捜査本部《set up》a special investigation ˈteam [squad]. 特別対策本部《set up》a special task force. 特別地域〔国立公園内などの保護区分の 1 つ〕a special zone. 特別認可法人 a specially authorized corporation. 特別認定選手〔日本オリンピック委員会 (JOC) の承認を前提として自己の商業権を使用できる選手〕an athlete granted control over his im-

age rights by the JOC. 特別表彰 a special award. ◎ 彼はスポーツの振興に功績があったとして～表彰を受けた. He received a special award for his contributions to sport. 特別文書〔首脳会議などで採択される〕a special document. ◎ ～文書を採択する adopt a special resolution《on…》; agree on a special document. 特別報奨金 (receive) a special「bonus [reward, bounty]. 特別法廷 a special tribunal. 特別保護地区〔国立公園内などの保護区分の1つ〕a special protection area.
とくべつかいけい【特別会計】a special account; special accounts. ⇨自動車損害賠償責任再保険特別会計 ⇨じどうしゃ. 電源開発促進対策特別会計 ⇨でんげん.
◎ 特別会計予算 a special account budget.
とくべつこうむいんぼうこうりょうぎゃくざい【特別公務員暴行陵虐罪】〔法〕criminal assault or humiliation by a law-enforcement officer.
とくべつこうむいんぼうこうりょうぎゃくちしょうざい【特別公務員暴行陵虐致死傷罪】〔法〕abuse of authority by a law-enforcement officer causing death or injury.
ドグマチール〔商標・薬〕〔胃・十二指腸潰瘍治療薬・精神運動安定剤〕Dogmatil. ▶ 一般名はスルピリド (sulpiride).
どくまんじゅう【毒饅頭】〔比喩的に〕a poison apple.
◎ ～を食う eat a poison apple; be inveigled.
とくめい[1]【匿名】 ◎ 匿名組合契約 an anonymous association contract; a silent partnership agreement. 匿名社会〔個人情報が過度に保護あるいは隠匿され，個人の顔が見えなくなった社会〕an anonymous society. 匿名情報 (receive) anonymous information.
どくりつ【独立】 ◎ 独立会計〔他との金銭の授受のない収支〕independent accounting. 独立行政法人評価委員会 an independent administrative agency evaluation committee. 独立志向 independent mindedness. 独立委員会 an independent「commission [panel]《to investigate …》. 独立調査委員会 an independent inquiry committee《略: IIC》. 独立不羈《に》independence. ◎ ～不羈の精神《possess》a free and independent spirit. 独立峰 an independent [an isolated] peak; a mountain that does not form part of a chain. 独立リーグ〔スポーツ〕an independent league.
どくりつぎょうせいほうじんつうそくほう【独立行政法人通則法】〔法〕the Law for General Rules for Independent Administrative Institutions.
どくりつほうむかん【独立法務官】〔米軍〕〔軍法会議の〕(an) independent military counsel.
とくれい[1]【特例】 ◎ 特例交付金 a special subsidy; a subsidy given in special cases. 特例子会社〔障害者雇用促進のための〕a "special affiliate company"《established to create employment for disabled people》.
◎ ～子会社制度 the "special affiliate company" system. 特例措置 measures for exceptional cases; exceptional measures. ◎ 破綻した金融機関の預金を全額保護する～措置を打ち切る withdraw [wind up] the special measures guaranteeing full cover for deposits in failed financial institutions. 特例地方債 a deficit-funding「prefectural [municipal] bond.
とけい[2]【時計】 ◎ 世界人口時計〔米国商務省国勢調査局がインターネット上で公表している，現在の世界推定人口〕the world population clock; "World POPClock." 盲人用時計〔腕時計〕a Braille watch. ◎ 時計遺伝子〔生物〕a clock gene. 時計職人 a watchmaker; a clockmaker.
「時計交響曲」〔ハイドンの交響曲第101番ニ長調の通称〕The Clock Symphony.
どげざ【土下座】 ◎ 土下座外交 kowtow [prostration] diplomacy.
とげさんご【棘珊瑚】〔動〕〔ハナヤサイサンゴ科の〕(a) needle coral; (a) bird's nest coral; Seriatopora hystrix.
とげぬきじぞう【刺抜き地蔵】〔身体に刺さったとげを抜いてくれるといわれる地蔵〕Togenuki Jizō; the thorn-removing Jizō; a statue of Jizō believed to have the effect of removing thorns from the flesh, or soothing pain.
とけのこり【溶け残り】〔洗濯時の粉石けんなどの〕《a lump of》residual「soap [detergent] powder.
とこう[2]【渡航】 ◎ 観光(海外)渡航 tourist travel abroad; overseas tourism. 業務渡航 (official) business travel [a business trip, an official business trip] abroad. ◎ 渡航許可証 (a document authorizing) permission to「travel [enter a country]; travel papers; a travel permit; papers of passage. 渡航記録 a (written) record of an individual's entries and departures. 渡航証明書 a travel certificate. 渡航歴 experience [a record] of travel《to America, in Pakistan》. ◎ イギリスへの～歴のある人からの献血受け入れは当分のあいだ見合わせることに決定した. It has been decided not to accept blood donations for the time being from people who have「been to [visited] the UK.
とこうし【塗工紙】〔製紙〕coated paper. ◎ 非塗工紙 uncoated paper. 微塗工紙 lightweight coated paper《略: LWC》.
トコトリエノール〔化・薬〕〔ビタミンEの成分の1つ〕tocotrienol.
ところしりがお【所知り顔】 ◎ ～で looking like「one knows one's way around [a local resident]; not looking like a stranger.
-どころで(は)ない ◎ おなかが痛くてコンサートを楽しむどころではなかった. My stomach hurt so much I was in no mood to enjoy the concert. / 今が家がみんなインフルエンザにかかっていて旅行～. With everyone in our family down with the flu, taking a trip is the last thing we can think about.
「閉ざされた森」〔映画〕Basic.
とさしもつけ【土佐下野】〔植〕〔バラ科の落葉低木〕a snow-mound spirea; Spiraea nipponica var. tosaensis.
とざん【登山】 ◎ 登山医学 mountain medicine. 登山計画書〔届〕a「schedule [notification] of one's planned climbing route. 登山ツアー a (mountain) climbing tour; a mountaineering tour. 登山ナイフ〔大型のシース〔さや入り〕ナイフ〕a large sheath knife.
とし[4]【都市】 ◎ 友好〔友情〕都市《be》a friendship city《of …》. 都市型犯罪 (an) urban crime. 都市基盤 the urban infrastructure. 都市景観 a cityscape. ◎ その派手な色のビルは～景観を損ねている. That garishly-colored building「mars the cityscape [spoils the view of the city]. 都市鉱山〔電子機器廃棄物などに含まれる金属類〕an urban mine. 都市再生 urban renewal. 都市再生緊急整備地域〔都市再生特別措置法に基づく〕an urgent urban-renewal area; an area needing urgent urban renewal. 都市再生本部〔内閣に設置された〕the Urban Renaissance Headquarters. 都市震災軽減工学 urban earthquake disaster mitigation engineering. 都市爆撃 urban bombing; the bombing of「cities [urban areas].
としきこう【都市機構】＝としさいせいきこう.
としこし【年越し】 ◎ 年越しライブ a New Year's (Eve) concert.
とじこみ[2]【閉じ込み】 ◎《車内・室内への》キーの～ locking a key《in a「car [room]》.
とじこめ【閉じ込め】 ◎ 閉じ込め事故〔エレベーターなどの〕an《elevator》entrapment accident; accidental confinement《in an elevator》.
としさいせいきこう【都市再生機構】the Urban Renaissance Agency《略: UR》. ▶ 2004年，都市基盤整備公団から改称.
としさいせいとくべつそちほう【都市再生特別措置法】〔法〕the Special Measures for Urban Renewal Law.

としさいせいほう【都市再生法】〖法〗=としさいせいとくべつそちほう.

としのうさんぎょそんこうりゅうかっせいかきこう【都市農山漁村交流活性化機構】the Organization for Urban-Rural Interchange Revitalization.

としぼうはんけんきゅうセンター【都市防犯研究-】the Japan Urban Security Research Institute (略: JUSRI).

どしゃ【土砂】▫️ 土砂(崩れ)ダム an earthen dam; a landslide dam. 土砂災害 a landslide disaster.

ドジャー・スタジアム〔米国, ロサンゼルスにある野球場〕Dodger Stadium.

どしゃさいがいぼうしほう【土砂災害防止法】〖法〗the Sediment-Related Disaster Prevention Law. ▶ 正式名称は「土砂災害警戒区域等における土砂災害防止対策の推進に関する法律」(the Law Concerning the Promotion of Sediment-Related Disaster Prevention in Sediment-Related Disaster Hazard Area).

どしゃりゅう【土砂流】a mudslide; an earth flow.

とじょう¹【途上】▫️ 途上段階〔発展の〕a development stage;〔変化の〕a transition stage.

どじょう¹【土壌】▫️ 土壌環境基準 environmental quality standards for soil〔pollution [contamination]〕. 土壌作り soil preparation; preparing the soil《for…》;〔環境整備〕(laying the) groundwork; preparing the ground. ◎ 彼女は北朝鮮との交渉の~作りのためにアジア各国を歴訪した. She made visits to countries in Asia to prepare the ground for negotiations with North Korea. 土壌病害 (a) soil-borne disease.

どじょうおせんたいさくほう【土壌汚染対策法】〖法〗the Soil Contamination Countermeasures Law.

としん【都心】▫️ 都心回帰 a return to〔city [urban] centers; an urban revival. ◎ 人口の~回帰が進んでいる. The shifting of the population back to urban centers has progressed.

トス ▫️ トス・ワーク 〖バレーボール〗tossing.

どすう【度数】▫️ 残り度数〔テレホンカードの〕the number of units〔remaining [left]〕on a telephone card.

「トスカーナの休日」〔映画〕Under the Tuscan Sun.

DoSこうげき【DoS攻撃】〖電算〗〔特定のサーバーに大量の接続要求を出すハッキング行為〕a DoS attack. ▶ DoS は denial of service の略. ▫️ 分散 DoS 攻撃 =ディー・オー・エスこうげき.

ドスタム Dostum, Abdul Rashid (1954-   ; アフガニスタンの軍人).

トストネット【ToSTNeT】〖取引〗〔東京証券取引所の立会外取引のための電子取引ネットワークシステム〕ToSTNeT; the Tokyo Stock Exchange Trading Network System. ▫️ トストネット・ワン〔単一銘柄取引・バスケット取引を対象とする〕ToSTNeT-1. トストネット・ツー〔終値取引を対象とする〕ToSTNeT-2.

どせい²【土星】▫️ 土星探査機《launch》a Saturn probe.

どせい¹【土製】▫️ 土製構造品〖考古〗funerary or ceremonial copies of implements, made of clay.

とそう【塗装】▫️ 塗装片〔自動車事故現場などの〕a chip of paint from a car (body).

どぞく¹【土俗】▫️ 土俗的 native; local; indigenous; autochthonous; aboriginal; deeply embedded《local customs》. ◎ ~的宗教 a religion native to《the locality》; an〔indigenous [autochthonous]〕religion.

トタール〔フランスの石油会社名〕Total.

とち²【土地】▫️ 土地資産額 an assessed land value. 土地譲渡益課税 taxation on the profit of a land transfer. 土地白書 a white paper on land;〔国土交通省の〕(2005) White Paper on Land. 土地本位制 the "land standard system"; the principle, based on belief in a continued rise in land values, that loans should be secured primarily on land.

とちさいひょうかほう【土地再評価法】〖法〗the Land Revaluation Law.

とちゅう²【途中】▫️ 途中棄権 withdrawing midway《through the race》; abandoning《the race》. 途中集計 an「intermediate [in-progress]」total [aggregate]. 途中出場〔サッカーなどの試合での〕an entry (of a「player [substitute]」) into a《soccer》game in progress. ◎ ~出場の中田がゴールを決めた. Nakata, who entered the game in progress, scored a goal. 途中狙い〔金融機関で金をおろして帰る途中の人を狙って金を盗んだり脅し取ったりする犯罪行為〕robbing a person who has just withdrawn money;〔その犯人〕a robber who targets people who have just withdrawn money.

とっか¹【特化】▫️ 特化係数〖統計〗a coefficient of specialization; a specialization coefficient.

どっか³【毒化】toxification; turning「toxic [poisonous]」. ~する toxify; turn「toxic [poisonous]」. 毒化機構 a toxification mechanism. ◎ フグの肝臓の~は十分には解明されていない. The mechanism which renders fugu liver「poisonous [toxic]」has not been fully clarified.

とっきょ【特許】▫️ 休眠特許〔製品化されていない特許〕a sleeping [an unused, a dormant] patent. 生命特許 a patent on life; a life patent. ▫️ 特許維持費 a patent maintenance fee. 特許切れ patent expiration. ◎ ~切れの薬 a patent-expired drug; a drug whose patent has expired. 特許裁判所 a patent court. 特許収益性 patent profitability. 特許情報 patent application information. 特許情報検索システム〖電算〗a patent search system. 特許生産性 patent productivity. 特許相互承認〔多国間の〕mutual recognition of patents; mutual patent recognition. 特許報酬〔a〕patent compensation. ◎ 社員の職務発明に対する~報酬 compensation for employees' patented inventions. 特許無効審判 a trial for invalidation of a patent; a patent invalidation trial.

どっきょ【独居】▫️ 独居死〔孤独死〕dying「alone [unattended]」; (a) solitary death; death without anybody present.

とっきょけん【特許権】▫️ 特許権侵害訴訟《file》a patent infringement suit《against…》; patent infringement litigation.

とっきょでんしとしょかん【特許電子図書館】〔特許庁運営の特許情報検索データベース〕the Industrial Property Digital Library (略: IPDL).

とっきょほういん【特許法院】〔韓国の〕the Patent Court of Korea.

ドッグ ▫️ ドッグ・イヤー〔犬の寿命が人間よりはるかに短いことから, 情報化社会の急速な変化をたとえる表現〕a dog year. ドッグ・スクール a dog school; an obedience school. ドッグ・ホテル a dog hotel. ドッグ・マラソン〔犬と飼い主が一緒に走り時間を競う競技〕a dog marathon. ドッグ・ラン〔犬専用の運動場〕a dog run.

とっくりきわた【徳利木綿】〖植〗〔パンヤ科の落葉高木〕a silk floss tree; Chorisia speciosa.

とっくりらん【徳利蘭】〖植〗〔リュウケツジュ科の常緑小高木〕a ponytail (palm); Nolina [Beaucarnea] recurvata.

ドッグ・ローズ〖植〗〔バラ科の落葉低木〕a dog rose; a briar bush; Rosa canina;〔果実〕a rose hip.

とっけい【特恵】▫️ 特恵貿易協定 a preferential trading agreement (略: PTA).

とつげき【突撃】▫️ 突撃銃 an assault rifle. 「突撃! マッキーバー」〔米国の, 陸軍幼年学校の生徒と校長による TV コメディー〕McKeever & the Colonel.

とっけん【特権】▫️ 特権的パートナー〔EU の準加盟国〕a privileged partner. 特権的パートナーシップ〔EU の準加盟国の地位〕privileged partnership.

「特攻ギャリソン・ゴリラ」〔ヨーロッパ戦線の米陸軍非正規兵の TV ドラマ〕Garrison's Gorillas.

「特攻野郎Ａチーム」〔米国の, 勧善懲悪アクション TV ドラマ〕The A-Team.
ドッジビー 〔ボールの代わりにフリスビーを使うドッジボール〕dodgebee; dodge ball played with a Frisbee instead of a ball. ▶ *dodge* ball と Frisbee から造った和製英語.
どっちらけ 〔ひどく白けること〕a big turnoff; a major letdown.
トッド Todd, Emmanuel (1951- ; フランスの人口・人類・歴史学者).
ドット ▫ ドット絵 〔コンピューターを使って描く〕a dot ［picture [drawing]. ドット・ペインティング 〔オーストラリアのアボリジニの点描画(法)〕(a) dot painting. ドット・ボタン 〔服飾〕a snap; button [fastener]; a snap.
とっとく 〔取っとく〕 ◐ 釣り銭はとっとけ〔とっときたまえ〕. You may keep [Keep] the change.
とっとりけんせいぶじしん 【鳥取県西部地震】〔2000 年の〕the (2000) Western Tottori Earthquake.
とつにゅう 【突入】 ▫ 突入作戦 〔立てこもり犯などに対する〕a strategy for storming (a building).
とっぱらい 【とっ払い】〔当日現場での給料現金払い〕(a) payment on the spot; (a) same-day [(an) on-the-spot] payment.
トップクロス a top cloth.
トップ・スピード top speed. ◐ ～に乗る reach top speed.
ドップラーほう 【−法】〔物〕the Doppler method.
ドップラー・レーダー ▫ 気象ドップラー・レーダー Doppler weather radar; weather Doppler radar 〔空港の〕Terminal Doppler Weather Radar (略: TDWR).
トップランナー 〔(リレーなどの) 第一走者〕the「starting [leadoff]」runner; 〔(マラソンなどの) 先頭走者〕the「leading [lead]」runner; 〔一流の走者〕a top runner; 〔ある時代や業界・分野の最先端で活躍する人〕a front runner; a leading player. ◐ 彼はこの業界の～だ. He is a leading player in this industry. ▫ トップランナー方式 〔省エネルギー性能が最も優れた現行製品の性能に基づいて省エネ基準を策定する方式〕the top-runner「approach [method, system]」.
トップリーグ 〔ジャパンラグビー・トップリーグの通称〕the Top League.
どっぽだか 【独歩高】〔証券〕a gain by only one (stock); an isolated gain.
どっぽやす 【独歩安】〔証券〕a decline by only one (stock); an isolated decline.
とどうふけん 【都道府県】 ▫ 都道府県立公園 prefectural parks.
とどけいで, とどけで 【届け出で, 届け出】 ▫ 届出印 a registered seal. 届出制 a notification system. ◐ 事前〔事後〕～ 制 a「prior [post] notification system. 届け出漏れ (a) failure to notify (*sb* of *sth*); a notification failure. ◐ 結核患者発生の保健所への～漏れ failure to notify a public health center of a TB case.
どどめいろ 【どどめ色】purplish red; puce.
ドナー ▫ 重合法ドナー 〔プリンター用の〕polymerized toner. 粉砕法ドナー 〔プリンター用の〕pulverized toner.
ドナー ▫ ドナー休暇 (a) donor leave of absence). ◐ 骨髄～休暇 (be granted) (a) bone-marrow donor leave. ドナー登録 〔臓器提供の, また骨髄バンク等への〕(organ, bone marrow) donor registration; (1 回の) a donor registration. ◐ ～登録者 a registered (organ, blood) donor.
ドナー² Donner, Richard (1930- ; 米国の映画監督; 本名 Richard Donald Schwartzberg).
「となりのトトロ」〔アニメ映画〕My Neighbor Totoro.
「隣のナインヤード」〔映画〕The Whole Nine Yards.
ドナルドソン Donaldson, Roger (1943- ; オーストラリア生まれの映画監督).
「ドニー・ダーコ」〔映画〕Donnie Darko.
トニー・レオン Tony Leung (1962- ; 中国生まれの映画俳優; 中国語名 梁朝偉 Leung Chiu-Wai).
ドハーティー Doherty, Shannen (1971- ; 米国の女優; 本名 Shannen Maria Doherty).
ドバイげんゆ 【−原油】〔オマーン原油とともにアジア原油市場での指標となる銘柄〕Dubai crude oil.
ドバイこくさいきんゆうセンター 【−国際金融−】the Dubai International Financial Center (略: DIFC).
とばしや 【飛ばし屋】〔ゴルフ〕a long-ball golfer.
どはで 【ど派手】 ～な extremely gaudy; super flashy. ◐ 彼女は～な衣装が似合う. She looks good in really flamboyant clothing.
とび³ 【飛び】 ◐ このクラブを使うとボールの～が違う. There's quite a difference in (the ball's) carry when you use this club. ◐ 電波の～のよい丘の上にベースキャンプを設営する set up a base camp on a hilltop where radio waves carry well. ◐ 成田からソウルへはほんのひと～だ. It's just a short hop from Narita to Seoul.
トピアリー ▫ アニマル・トピアリー animal topiary.
とびこみ 【飛び込み】 ▫ 板飛び込み a springboard dive; springboard diving. ▫ 飛び込み営業[セールス] cold selling; unsolicited sales activities.
とびだす 【飛び出す】 ▫ 飛び出す絵本 a pop-up (picture) book.
とびら 【扉】 ▫ 扉越し ＝ドア越し (⇨ドア).
ドビルパン de Villepin, Dominique (Marie François René Galouzeau) (1953- ; フランスの政治家; 首相 [2005-07]).
どぶいた 【溝板】boards (laid) across a ditch to cover it; a wooden gutter cover. ▫ どぶ板営業 grassroots [door-to-door] marketing [sales]. どぶ板政治 grassroots politics. どぶ板選挙 a grassroots door-to-door election campaign. どぶ板戦術 a grassroots strategy; grassroots [door-to-door] tactics.
トベン・ミ（エ）ンチェイ 〔カンボジア北部, プレア・ヴィヒア州の州都〕Tbeng Meanchey.
ドホーク ＝ダフーク.
どぼく 【土木】 ▫ 土木施工管理技士 a「certified [licensed]」construction supervisor.
どぼくけんきゅうじょ 【土木研究所】〔独立行政法人〕the Public Works Research Institute (略: PWRI).
トポラーネク Topolánek, Mirek (1956- ; チェコの政治家; 首相〔2006- 〕).
ドボラックほう 【−法】〔気象〕〔衛星画像による熱帯低気圧解析法〕the Dvorak technique.
とまく 【塗膜】a coating (of paint); (a) paint「film [coating]. 塗膜厚 paint film thickness. 塗膜片 〔自動車事故現場などの〕a chip of paint from a car (body).
トマン 〔イランの通貨単位の 1 つ〕a toman.
とみ 【富】 ▫ 富効果 〔経〕a wealth effect.
ドミノ ▫ ドミノ式 ((fall)) like dominoes. ◐ 巨大企業が倒産すると, それに依存する下請け企業が一式に倒産する. When a giant corporation goes bankrupt, the subcontractor firms relying on it topple like dominoes.
トム・コリンズ 〔カクテル〕a Tom Collins.
「トム・ジョーンズ・ショー」〔米国の, 音楽ショー TV 番組〕This Is Tom Jones.
「トムとジェリー」〔米国のアニメに登場する猫とネズミ〕Tom and Jerry.
トメイ Tomei, Marisa (1964- ; 米国の映画女優).
ドメスティック・パートナーシップほう 【−法】〔米国で, 同性愛のカップルに結婚した夫婦に準じる法的保障を与える法律〕a domestic partnership law.
「ドメスティック・フィアー」〔映画〕Domestic Disturbance.
トモセラピー 〔商標・医〕〔CT と放射線照射機を組み合わせた腫瘍治療法〔装置〕〕TomoTherapy.
ともだち 【友達】 ▫ 友達感覚 a relationship like that of friends. ◐ ～感覚で客に話しかける talk to custom-

ers as if they are friends.
ともだて【共立て】〖菓子〗〔卵黄と卵白を一緒に泡立てること〕whipping [beating] whole eggs [eggs without separating the whites and yolks].
「友へ チング」〖映画〗Friend; Chingu.
トヨタせいさんほうしき【-生産方式】〖経営〗the Toyota Production System (略: TPS).
とら² 【寅】 ▶〔寅年を走る〕〖相場〗〔寅年は大きく値を上げる, の意〕In the year of the Tiger, the market tends to be very strong. 〔たつみごよし〕
トラート 〔タイ中部の県; その県都〕Trat.
トライ ◐ 逆転トライ《ラグビー》a try which 「puts《one's team》back in the lead [turns the tables]; a turnaround try. 再トライ another 「attempt [go, try]; a fresh attempt. ◐ 司法試験に再〜する attempt [try] the Bar Examination again; have another go at the bar exams. 先制トライ《ラグビー》(get in with) the first try (of a match). 同点トライ《ラグビー》an 「equalizing try [equalizer]. ノー・トライ《ラグビー》no tries. ◐ 敵をノー〜に封じる hold one's opponent to no tries; keep one's opponent from scoring a try. 初トライ a first 「attempt [try, go]; 《ラグビー》a first try. ◐ 富士登山に初〜する make one's first attempt 「to climb [on] Mt. Fuji; attempt (to climb) Mt. Fuji for the first time.
◐ トライ・ゲッター《ラグビー》a try scorer.
ドライ ◐ ドライ・キッチン 〔飲食店などで, 排水溝を作らず常に床を乾かした状態で使用する厨房〕a (restaurant) kitchen with a floor which is kept dry.
トライアルこようせいど【-雇用制度】a trial employment system (for the young).
ドライ・カッパー〔通信〕〔未使用のメタルケーブル回線〕dry copper.
トライコフスキ Trajkovski, Boris (1956-2004) 〔マケドニアの政治家; 大統領 [1999-2004]〕.
トライショー〔tri- + rikshaw〕〔シンガポールなどの三輪タクシー〕a trishaw.
ドライ・ドランク 〔空(かん)酔い〕〔アルコール依存症者が非飲酒時に, いら立ちや攻撃性が増す飲酒時と同様の症状を呈すること〕dry drunk syndrome; 〔その人〕a dry drunk.
ドライバー ◐ ドライバー・ショット《ゴルフ》a driver shot. ドライバー歴 =うんてんれき.
ドライバー² Driver, Minnie (1971- ; 英国生まれの映画女優; 本名 Amelia Driver).
トライバル・エリア〔アフガニスタンとパキスタンの国境沿いにある部族地域〕a tribal area.
ドライ・バン〔屋根と箱根のある荷台のあるトラック〕a dry van.
ドライブ ◐ ドライブ・シャフト《機》a drive shaft. ドライブ・レコーダー〔自動車〕〔フライトレコーダーの自動車版; 事故の際などの原因究明や新車開発に役立てる〕a drive recorder; an event data recorder (略: EDR); an automobile "black box."
ドライブ・バイ・ワイヤ〖自動車〗〔スロットルの開閉などを電気信号で行う方式〕drive-by-wire (略: DBW).
ドライ・マウス〖医〗〔口腔乾燥症〕dry mouth; xerostomia (▷ xerostomic adj.).
トラウマ ◐ トラウマ・セラピー trauma therapy.
ドラえもん〖商標〗〖キャラクター〗Doraemon.
「ドラグネット」〔ロサンジェルス市警の刑事2人のTVドラマ〕Dragnet; (リメイク版) L.A. Dragnet.
ドラグノフそげきじゅう【-狙撃銃】a Dragunov sniper rifle (略: SVD). ▶ 略はロシア語の Snaiperskaya Vintovka Dragunova から.
トラクリア〖商標・薬〗〔肺動脈性肺高血圧症の治療薬〕Tracleer.
「ドラゴンハート」〖映画〗Dragonheart.
ドラゴン・フルーツ〖植〗〔サボテン科の多年生多肉植物〕dragon fruit; Hylocereus undatus.
ドラゴン・マート〔アラブ首長国連邦, ドバイにある中国製品卸売りセンター〕(the) Dragon Mart.

トラスツズマブ〖薬〗〔乳がん治療薬〕trastuzumab.
トラセカ〔欧州・コーカサス・アジア輸送路; パリ・上海間約2万キロ〕TRACECA; the Transport Corridor Europe-Caucasus-Asia.
ドラッカリアン〔日本のドラッカー理論信奉者〕a (Japanese) follower of Peter Drucker.
トラッキング ◐ トラッキング現象〖電〗〔コンセントに差し込んだままのプラグの両極間に電流路ができて発火する現象〕tracking. トラッキング・ストック〖証券〗a tracking stock.
トラック² ◐ トラック勝負 ◐ レースは〜勝負にもつれ込んだ. 〔マラソンなどで〕The race remained undecided until the last spurt [the runners entered the stadium].
ドラッグスター〖自動車〗〔短距離レース車〕a dragster.
トラックバック〖電算〗〔ブログ間のつながりの仕組み〕a trackback. ◐ トラックバック・スパム trackback spam.
トラットリア〔イタリア料理店〕a trattoria (pl. -rias, -rie).
「ドラ猫大将」〔米国の, 猫が主人公のTVギャグアニメ〕Top Cat. ▶ 英国ではキャットフードに同名の商品があったため, Boss Cat の名で放映していた.
ドラノエ Delanoé, Pierre (1918-2006; フランスのシャンソン作詞家).
とらのお【虎の尾】〖植〗〔リュウゼツラン科の観葉植物〕Laurentii; snake plant; mother-in-law's tongue; Sansevieria trifasciata.
トラバ〖電算〗=トラックバック.
トラフィッキング〔人身売買〕human trafficking; trafficking in 「persons [human beings].
「トラフィック」〖映画〗Traffic.
ドラフト ◐ ドラフト指名 selection in a draft. ドラフト指名選手 a draft 「selection [pick].
トラブル ◐ トラブル隠し concealing [hiding, covering up] problems; a cover-up. ◐ 電力会社による原発の〜隠しの実態が次々に明らかになった. A stream of facts came out regarding the power companies' cover-ups of nuclear power accidents.
トラベクレクトミー〖眼科〗〔線維柱帯切除術〕trabeculectomy.
トラベクロトミー〖眼科〗〔線維柱帯切開術〕trabeculotomy.
トラベル ◐ トラベル・ボランティア help for disabled travellers; 〔人〕a (paid) volunteer assistant for disabled travellers.
ドラム ◐ ドラム・サークル〖音楽〗〔集団で行う打楽器の即興演奏; その集団〕a drum circle. ドラム・マシン〔電子楽器の一種で, ドラムの音から出すリズムを刻むもの〕a drum machine; a rhythm 「machine [box].
トラリー【TRALI】〖医〗〔輸血関連急性肺障害〕TRALI. ▶ transfusion-related acute lung injury の略.
トラン² 〔タイ南部の県; その県都〕Trang.
トランス² ◐ トランス状態 ◐ 〔go [fall] into〕a trance. トランス・パーティー〔参加者が強烈なリズムの音楽に合わせて興奮状態で踊るパーティー〕a trance party. トランスミュージック〖音楽〗trance music; trance.
トランスドニエストル〔モルドバ東部, 分離独立を宣言している地域の国際的な名称〕Trans-Dniester; Transdniester; 〔ルーマニア語による呼称〕Transnistria.
トランスニストリア Transnistria (⇨トランスドニエストル).
トランスネフチ〔ロシアの国営石油パイプライン会社〕Transneft.
トランスペアレンシー・インターナショナル〔各国の政治腐敗・汚職などを監視する非政府組織〕Transparency International (略: TI).
トランポビクス〔トランポリンを使ったエアロビクス〕trampoline [rebound] aerobics.
トランポリン ◐ ミニトランポリン〔家庭用のトレーニング用品〕a mini-trampoline. ◐ トランポリン効果〔跳ね返りの反発力〕a trampoline effect; 《ゴルフ》〔スプリング効果〕a spring-like effect.
トリア Trier, Lars von (1956- ; デンマークの映画監督・

脚本家; 本名 Lars Trier).
トリアー ▯=トリア.
トリアージ ▯▯ トリアージ・ナース〔トリアージを行う看護師〕a triage nurse. トリアージ・ポスト〔ステーション〕〔トリアージを行う場所〕a triage「station [post].
トリアジメノール〔化〕〔農薬・殺菌剤〕triadimenol.
トリアシルグリセロール〔化〕〔一般の食用油の原料〕triacylglycerol (略: TAG).
トリアセトン・トリペルオキシド〔トリパーオキサイド〕〔化〕triacetone triperoxide (略: TATP).
とりい【鳥居】 ▯▯ 大鳥居 a「large [larger than normal] torii.
ドリーム ▯▯ ドリーム・ゲーム〔スター選手を一堂に集めて行う試合〕a dream game.
「ドリームガールズ」〔映画〕Dreamgirls.
とりインフルエンザ【鳥-】 ▯▯ 高病原性インフルエンザザ・ウイルス an avian influenza virus; a bird [an avian] flu virus.
トリウム ▯▯ トリウム化合物〔化〕a thorium compound. トリウム鉱石 thorium ore.
トリオクタノイン〔化〕trioctanoin.
とりおろし【撮り下ろし】 taking photographs for a volume at the request of a publisher;〔作品〕photographs taken for a volume at the request of a publisher.
トリクロサン〔薬〕〔工業用殺菌剤〕triclosan.
ドリコサウルス〔古生物〕〔トカゲからヘビに進化する中間生物〕a dolichosaur; *Dolichosaurus.*
とりこわし【取り壊し】 ▯▯ 取り壊し命令 ＝除却命令 (⇨じょきゃく).
トリシェ Trichet, Jean-Claude (1942- ; 欧州中央銀行総裁〔2003- 〕).
トリジェネレーション〔熱・電力・二酸化炭素の同時産生・供給〕trigeneration.
とりせつ【取説】〔取り扱い説明書〕an owner's [a user's] manual;〔器械類の〕an instruction manual.
トリソミー〔医〕〔2本で対となるべき染色体が3本になること〕trisomy.
とりだめ【撮り溜め・録り溜め】 〜する ＝とりだめる.
とりだめる【撮り溜める・録り溜める】〔写真・ビデオなどを〕take [shoot]《photographs, video》for later use. ▯ この10年間撮り溜めた2万枚の写真の中から200枚を選んで写真展を開催した。She put on a photo exhibition of 200 works chosen from among 20,000 photographs that she had taken the past decade.
とりつけ【取り付け】 ▯▯ 取り付け金具 a metal fitting.
トリップス【TRIPS】〔知的所有権の貿易関連の側面〕TRIPS. ▶ trade-related aspects of intellectual property rights の略.
トリップスきょうてい【TRIPS 協定】the TRIPS Agreement; the Agreement on Trade-Related Aspects of Intellectual Property Rights. ▶ 正式名称は「知的所有権の貿易関連の側面に関する協定」(the Agreement on Trade-Related Aspects of Intellectual Property Rights).
トリニタリオ〔植〕〔カカオの一品種〕trinitario.
とりのす【鳥の巣】〔2008年, 北京オリンピックのメインスタジアムとなる〕国家体育場」(the National Olympic Stadium) の愛称] the "Bird's Nest" (building).
とりひき【取引】 ▯▯〔架空〕循環取引 a circular transaction. 対顧客取引〔銀行取引などに対して〕a customer transaction; a retail transaction. ▯▯ 取引画面〔電子金融取引で, パソコン上の〕a trading screen. 取引参加者負担金〔証券〕a trading participation fee. 取引事例比較法〔不動産鑑定評価法の1〕the sales comparison approach method. 取引信用保険 trade credit insurance. 取引明細書〔表〕a [an account] statement; a statement of account(s). 取引履歴 a transaction history.

トリブチルスズ ▯▯ トリブチルスズオキシド〔船底・漁網防汚剤〕tributyltin oxide (略: TBTO).
ドリフト ▯▯ ドリフト走行 controlled skidding; drift driving.
トリプル ▯▯ トリプル A AAA; Aaa. ▯ 〜Aから一気に2段階格下げされた。It was downgraded two levels from triple A in a single move. トリプル・ダブル〔バスケット〕a triple double.
ドリブル ▯▯ ドリブル・シュート〔球技〕a dribble shot. ▯ 〜シュートする dribble and shoot. ドリブル突破〔球技〕dribbling「through [past]《opposing players》.
トリプルエックス・エル【XXXL】〔物品のサイズ〕XXXL.
トリマー ▯▯ トリマースクール a pet grooming school.
トリマー[2]〔化〕〔三量体〕a trimer. ▯▯ スチレン・トリマー〔食品トレイなどに使う〕a styrene trimer.
とりまき【採り播き】sowing「fresh [freshly harvested] seeds.
トリム[2]【TRMM】〔熱帯降雨観測衛星〕the TRMM. ▶ Tropical Rainfall Measuring Mission の略.
トリムコース〔各種の運動遊具を備えたジョギング用クロスカントリーコース〕a trim trail.
とりゅう【砥粒】 ▯▯ 砥粒加工 abrasive machining. 砥粒研磨 abrasive polishing. ▯ 電解〜研磨 electrolytic abrasive polishing / 固定〜研磨 fixed abrasive polishing.
とりょう【塗料】 ▯▯ 高反射率塗料〔遮熱用の〕high「reflectance [reflectivity] paint. 溶剤(系)塗料 solvent paint.
どりょく【努力】 ▯▯ 努力規定 a stipulation of an obligation to make an effort 《to do》.
ドリラー〔油田などの掘削技能者〕a driller;〔ボウリングの玉に指を入れる孔を開ける技術者〕a (bowling) ball driller; a driller.
ドリンク ▯▯ ドリンク・バー〔ファミリーレストランなどの飲料コーナー〕a beverage bar. ドリンク・ホルダー a drink holder.
ドル ▯▯ アメリカ[米]ドル an [the] American dollar; a [the] US dollar. ▶ 10 米ドルなどと数えるときには普通の計算名詞だが, 通貨の名称としては the を付ける. 以下の複合語では the の形のみを示す. ▯ 米〜が世界の基軸通貨になっている。The US dollar is the key global currency. / 今は1米〜は1.18 カナダ〜だ。The [One] US dollar is currently worth 1.18 Canadian dollars. カナダ・ドル the Canadian dollar. シンガポール・ドル the Singapore dollar. 東カリブ・ドル〔東カリブ諸国で共通に使われている〕the East Caribbean dollar. 香港ドル the Hong Kong dollar. ▯▯ ドル化政策 a dollarization policy.
トルカレム〔ヨルダン川西岸北部のパレスチナ自治区の市〕Tulkarem; Tulkarm.
トルストイ・ユルト〔チェチェン共和国の村〕Tolstoy-Yurt.
ドルチェ[2]〔＜It〕〔イタリア(料理)のデザート〕dolce《pl. dolci》.
ドルチェ・アンド・ガッバーナ〔商標〕〔イタリアの服飾ブランド〕Dolce & Gabbana.
トルテ〔ドイツ風のケーキ〕(a) torte. ▯▯ トルテ・カッター〔丸いケーキを等分に切るために印を付ける器具〕a torte cutter; a round cutter.
トルナトーレ Tornatore, Giuseppe (1956- ; イタリアの映画監督).
ドルノゴビ〔モンゴル東南部の県〕Dornogovi.
ドルばこ【-箱】 ▯▯ ドル箱路線〔航空路などの〕a money-making route;《口》a cash-cow route.
ドルフィン ▯▯ ドルフィン・トレーナー〔イルカの調教師〕a dolphin trainer.
ドルマル Dormael, Jaco Van (1957- ; ベルギー生まれの映画監督).
トルロ〔英国コーンウォール州の州都; カナダ, ノヴァスコシア州の都市; 米国マサチューセッツ州の町〕Truro.

**ドレイファス** Dreyfuss, Richard (1947– ; 米国の映画俳優).
**ドレイミぞく**【-族】〔イラクの部族〕the Dulaimi tribe.
**トレインスポッター**〔線路脇で汽車を見つめるマニア〕a trainspotter. ▷ trainspotting n.
「**トレインスポッティング**」〔映画〕Trainspotting.
**トレーディング・カード**〔子供が集めて交換するスポーツ選手などの写真カード〕a trading card.
**トレード** ▫▫ **無償トレード**〔プロスポーツ選手の〕a 「free [non-cash] trade.
**トレーナビリティー**〔訓練によって期待できる体力・技術などの伸び〕trainability.
**トレーニング** ▫▫ **加圧(式)トレーニング**〔商標〕Kaatu Training. ▫▫ **トレーニング・コーチ** a training coach. **トレーニング・センター** a training center. **トレーニング・マシン** a training machine; an exercise machine. **トレーニング・メニュー** a training menu. ◐ 〜メニューを作成する[組み立てる] draw up [design] a training menu.
「**トレーニング・デイ**」〔映画〕Training Day.
**ドレス** ▫▫ **ドレス・コード**〔服装規定〕a dress code.
**トレセン**〔=トレーニング・センター（⇒トレーニング）〕.
**ドレッドヘア**〔多数の細い三つ編みからなる髪型〕dreadlocks.
**トレド**[2] Toledo, Alejandro (1946– ; ペルーの政治家; 大統領〔2001-06〕).
**トレニア**〔植〕〔ゴマノハグサ科トレニア属の総称〕a torenia.
**トレブリンカ**〔ワルシャワ近くにあった，ナチスドイツの強制収容所〕Treblinka.
**トレリス**〔四つ目格子〕(a) trellis.
**トレンガヌ**〔マレーシアの州〕Terengganu.
**トレンディー** ▫▫ **トレンディー・スポット** a「trendy [fashionable] area [spot].
**トレンド** ▫▫ **トレンド調査**〔動向〔傾向〕調査〕《conduct》a trend survey. **トレンド・リーダー** a trend leader.
**トロイオンス**〔金銀・宝石などに用いる衡量〕a troy ounce (略: oz t; toz).
**トロイカ** ▫▫ **トロイカ体制** a troika system.
**トロイダル** ▫▫ **トロイダル磁場コイル** a toroidal field coil (略: TFC).
**ドロー** ▫▫ **ドローボール**〔ゴルフ〕〔ボールが落下する際ゆるく左に曲がるショット〕a draw (ball [shot]).
**ドローストリング**〔袋や衣服の開口部を締める引き紐〕a drawstring. ▫▫ **ドローストリング・パンツ**〔服飾〕《a pair of》drawstring pants.
**トロオドン**〔古生物〕〔二足歩行の小型肉食恐竜〕(a) troodon; 〔科名〕*Troodontidae*.
**ドロケイ**〔泥警〕〔鬼ごっこの一種; 泥棒と警察〕《play》cops and robbers.
**トロッコ** ▫▫ **トロッコ列車**〔無蓋の〕an open tramcar; 〔観光用の有蓋の〕a tramcar converted for sightseeing.
**ドロップ・シッピング**〔商〕〔在庫や倉庫を持たず，注文を受けた商品をメーカーや卸売業者から直接顧客に発送する販売方法〕drop shipping; drop shipment.
「**ドロップ・ゾーン**」〔映画〕Drop Zone.
**どろぼう**【泥棒】 ▫▫ **泥棒国家** a kleptocracy.
**トロリー** ▫▫ **トロリー・バッグ**〔持ち運び用の車と取っ手が付いた小型スーツケース〕a trolley bag.

**トロント・ピアソンこくさいくうこう**【-国際空港】〔カナダ，オンタリオ州の国際空港〕Toronto Pearson International Airport.
**トロンボモジュリン**〔生化〕〔血液の流動性を保ったんぱく質〕thrombomodulin (略: TM).
「**トワイライトゾーン**」=「ミステリーゾーン」.
「**永遠**(とわ)**の愛に生きて**」〔映画〕Shadowlands.
**トンガスこくゆうりん**【-国有林】〔アラスカ南東部にある米国の国有林〕the Tongass National Forest.
**どんこ**[2]【冬菇】〔菌〕〔笠(かさ)の開きが小さい肉厚のシイタケ〕a thick-fleshed shiitake mushroom of which the cap is only partly opened; a *donko* shiitake.
**とんこつ**【豚骨】 ▫▫ **豚骨ラーメン** Chinese noodles [ramen] in「pork bone [*tonkotsu*] soup [broth].
**トンサイ・ビーチ**〔タイ，ピピ島にある〕Tongsai Beach.
**トンすう**【-数】 ▫▫ **トン数標準税制** the tonnage tax system.
**ドンタップ**〔ベトナム南部, メコンデルタ地帯の省〕Dong Thap.
**どんとうし**【呑刀師】〔奇術の〕a sword-swallower. ▷ sword-swallowing n.
**ドンドルマ**〔餅のように伸びるトルコのアイスクリーム〕dondurma; Turkish sticky ice cream.
**ドンナイ**〔ベトナム南部の省〕Dong Nai.
**トンネル** ▫▫ **トンネル脱出**〔比喩的に〕◐ 昨日まで10連敗のジャイアンツ，今日の試合に勝って，ようやく〜脱出. With today's win, the Giants finally emerged from the tunnel of their ten-game losing streak. **トンネル覆工**〔トンネルの内壁〕tunnel walls. ◐ 〜覆工検査車 a tunnel-wall inspection vehicle.
**ドンハ**〔ベトナム中部，クアンチ省の省都〕Dong Ha.
**トンパきょう**【東巴教】〔中国，麗江に見られる原始宗教〕Dongbaism.
**トンパもじ**【東巴文字】〔中国雲南省の納西(ナシ)族に使われ続けている象形文字〕a「Dongba [Tompa, Naxi] character;〔集合的に〕the「Dongba [Tompa, Naxi] script.
**ドンびき**【-引き】〔突然非常に気まずい雰囲気になること〕◐ 彼女の涙ながらの弁解に一座は〜だった. Her tearful excuses「made everyone terribly uncomfortable [produced an extremely awkward atmosphere].
**どんぴしゃ** ◐ 〜のタイミング 《with》perfect timing.
**とんぷうしゃ**【東風汽車】〔中国の自動車メーカー〕(the) Dongfeng Motor Corporation.
**トンプソン** Thompson, J. Lee (1914-2002; 英国生まれの映画監督).
**トンヘ**【東海】=とうかい[4].
**ドンベア，ドンペヤ**〔植〕〔アフリカ原産アオギリ科ドンベア属の花木の総称〕a Dombeya.
**とんぼ**【蜻蛉】
4〔グラウンド整備用のレーキ〕a (ground) rake.
**トンボだま**【-玉】〔工芸〕〔1個の〕a glass bead;〔それを用いた工芸品〕glass「bead work [beadwork].
「**トンマッコルへようこそ**」〔映画〕Welcome to Dongmakgol.

# な

**ナーガ**〘ヒンズー教神話〙〔蛇神〕Naga.
**ナーシ**〔ロシア大統領府直属の青少年組織〕Nashi. ▶ ロシア語で「友軍」の意.
**ナーシリヤ**〔イラク南部の都市〕Nasiriyah.
**ナース** ▯ ナース・センター〔各都道府県の〕a nurse center.
**ナーダム**〔モンゴルの夏祭り〕Nadam; the Nadam「Festival [Fair]」.
**ナーン²** **1**〔タイ北部の県, その県都〕Nan.
**2**〔ラオス, ルアン・プラバン県の郡〕Nan.
**ないいん**【内因】 ▯ 内因死〘医〙〔外因死に対して〕death from internal causes; intrinsic death.
**ないかく¹**【内角】 ▯ 内角速球〘野球〙a fastball on the inside corner (of the plate).
**ないかく⁵**【内閣】 ▯ 非常事態内閣 an emergency cabinet. ▯ 内閣官房参与 a Cabinet Secretariat「adviser [advisor]」; an「adviser [advisor]」to the Cabinet Secretariat. 内閣広報官 the Cabinet Public Relations Secretary. 内閣法制局 the Cabinet Legislation Bureau. 内閣立法 government[cabinet](-initiated) legislation.
**ないかくかんぼうじょうほうセキュリティセンター**【内閣官房情報-】〔2005年設立〕the National Information Security Center (略: NISC).
**ないかくふけいざいしゃかいそうごうけんきゅうじょ**【内閣府経済社会総合研究所】the Economic and Social Research Institute, Cabinet Office (略: ESRI).
**ないかくふせっちほう**【内閣府設置法】〘法〙the Cabinet Office Establishment Law.
**ないかけいがっかいしゃかいほけんれんごう**【内科系学会社会保険連合】the Social Insurance Union of Societies Related to Internal Medicine.
**ないこ**【内湖】〔琵琶湖周辺にある小さな湖〕a small「satellite [attached]」lake [lagoon] near Lake Biwa; a *naiko*.
**ないざい²**【内材】〔家具・鞄などの内側に用いる素材〕a lining; lining material.
**ナイジェリアないせん**【-内戦】〘史〙〔1967-70年の〕the Nigerian Civil War; the Biafran War. [= ビアフラせんそう]
**ないしきょう**【内視鏡】 ▯ 拡大内視鏡 a magnifying endoscope. ▯ 内視鏡治療〘医〙endoscopic「therapy [treatment]」. 内視鏡の粘膜切除法〘医〙〔胃がんなどの〕(an) endoscopic mucosal resection (略: EMR).
**ないしゃし**【内斜視】 ▯ 間欠性内斜視 (an) intermittent esotropia. 恒常性内斜視 (an) constant esotropia. 調節性内斜視 (an) accommodative esotropia.
**ないじゅ**【内需】 ▯ 内需関連株〘銘柄〕a domestic-demand-related「stock [issue]」. 内需主導型経済, 内需(型)経済 a domestic demand-led economy; an economy driven by domestic demand. 内需デフレーター〘経〙the domestic demand deflator.
**ないしゅう**【内周】 ▯ 内周規制線〔米軍機などが事故を起こした際に二重に設けられる立ち入り規制線のうち現場に近い方の規制線〕an inner cordon.
**ないしょうじん**【内省人】〔台湾の〕a native Taiwanese.
**ないしん³**【内診】 ▯ 内診台〘医〙〔産婦人科の診察台〕a gyn(ecological chair.
**ないすいめん**【内水面】 ▯ 内水面漁場管理委員会 an inland fisheries commission.
**ないせい³**【内政】 ▯ 内政干渉の権利〔人道的理由による〕the right to intervene《in a genocide situation》; right of interference.

**ないせいきん**【内生菌】〘菌〙〔動植物の内部に生息する菌類〕an endophytic fungus 《*pl.* -gi》. ▯ 胃[腎臓]内生菌 a「gastric [renal] microorganism [bacterium, fungus]《*pl.* -ria, -gi》. 植物内生菌 an endophyte.
**ないぞう²**【内臓】 ▯ 内臓脂肪症候群〘医〙visceral fat syndrome. [= メタボリック・シンドローム]
**ないち¹**【内地】 ▯ 内地材 domestic「lumber [building materials]」.
**ないてい²**【内定】 ▯ 内定辞退 (a) withdrawal from acceptance of a tentative job offer. ◎ ～辞退者 a person who withdraws from acceptance of a tentative job offer. 内定通知《receive, get, send》notification of an unofficial decision; 〔職〕notification of「a [a nonbinding, an informal] job offer; advising [informing] *sb* that *he* will be offered a job subject to subsequent confirmation; 《その文面》an (unofficial) offer letter.
**ないてい⁴**【内偵】 ▯ 内偵捜査 an undercover (police) investigation; a secret inquiry.
**ナイトホーク**〘米軍〙〔米空軍のステルス攻撃機F-117の愛称〕a Nighthawk.
**ナイト・マーケット** **1**〔夜市〕a night market.
**2**〔24時間営業などによって生じる夜間の購買需要〕nighttime「sales [business, turnover]」.
**「ナイトライダー」**〔米国の, 元刑事がスポーツカーを駆って悪と闘うTVドラマ〕Knight Rider.
**「ナイトライン」**〔米国ABCテレビの報道番組〕Nightline.
**ないはつ**【内発】 ▯ 内発的発展〔地域住民が主体となった地元の発展〕spontaneous development.
**ないぶ**【内部】 ▯ 内部管理 internal [inside] management. ◎ ～管理体制 an internal management system. 内部規定 internal regulations. 内部資金〔銀行内部の〕internal funds; internally-generated funds. 内部事情 the internal situation; the「situation [state of affairs] inside (an organization); 〔内幕〕the inside story. 内部情報〔組織の内部に関する情報〕inside [internal] information; 〔内部から漏れる情報〕information from an insider; inside information; a leak. 内部調査委員会 an internal investigation committee. 内部調査報告書 a report on an internal investigation. 内部統制監査報告書〘経営〙an internal control audit report. 内部統制システム an internal control system. 内部統制報告書〘経営〙an internal control report. 内部文書 an「internal [in-house] document. 内部矛盾 (an) internal contradiction. 内部リサイクル〔社内などでの〕in-house recycling《system》.
**ないふく**【内服】 ▯ 内服(薬)治療 oral (medicine) treatment.
**ないぶつうほう**【内部通報】notification [reporting] by an insider (to the authorities of illegal activities by *his*《company》); whistle-blowing. ▯ 内部通報者 an inside informant; a whistle-blower. 内部通報制度 a whistle-blowing system. 内部通報窓口 a contact point for reporting internal problems; a whistleblower notification center.
**ないぶんぴ(つ)**【内分泌】 ▯ 内分泌学者 an endocrinologist. 内分泌攪乱作用 endocrine disturbance. 内分泌代謝科〔病院の〕a department of endocrinology and metabolism.
**ないほれん**【内保連】= ないかけいがっかいしゃかいほけんれんごう.
**ないまく²**【内膜】 ▯ 内膜剥離術 ◎ 子宮～剥離術 ⇒ しきゅうないまく / 頸動脈(血栓)～剥離術 ⇒ けいどうみゃく.

ナイム【NIME】〔メディア教育開発センター；文部科学省内の一組織〕NIME. ▶ National Institute of Multimedia Education の略.
ないや【内野】 ▣ 内野守備コーチ an infield defense coach.
ないリンパ【内-】 ▣ 内リンパ水腫【医】〔内耳のリンパ液が増加した状態；メニエール病を引き起こす〕endolymphatic hydrops.
ナイル²【NAIRU】〔経〕〔インフレを加速させない失業率〕the non-accelerating inflation rate of unemployment.
「ナイロビの蜂」〔映画〕The Constant Gardener.
「ナインスゲート」〔映画〕The Ninth Gate.
ナイン・ボール〔ポケットビリヤードの一種〕*nine-ball.
なえ²【萎え】1〔気力・体力が抜けること〕(a) weakening; (a) loss of strength. ◐ 気持ちの~ a depressed feeling; 《口》the blues. ◐ 仕事で失敗が続き、最近気分が~気味だ. Recently I've been feeling a bit down because of some blunders at work.
2〔アニメ・漫画ファンの間で、キャラクターへの興味が冷めること〕a loss of interest; a letdown feeling;〔嫌悪感を抱くこと〕disgust; dislike.
3〔がっかりすること〕disappointment. ◐ 明日は休日出勤しなきゃならなくなっちゃった. 激~だあ. Tomorrow I have to go to work on what was supposed to be my day off.「What a drag [Major bummer]!
▣ 萎え要素 a disappointing「feature [characteristic]. ◐ あのゲームの下手な効果音が~要素だ. That game's lousy sound effects are a real turnoff.
なおらい【直会】drinking [a drinking party] after a Shinto ritual.
ながえつるのげいとう〔植〕〔南アメリカ原産のヒユ科の多年草〕an alligatorweed; *Alternanthera philoxeroides*.
ながおし【長押し】〔電算〕keeping「(a button)「depressed [pressed down]. ~する keep「(a button)「depressed [pressed down]. ◐ 電源ボタンを2、3秒~すると電源が切れます. To switch off, keep the「power [on/off] button「depressed [pressed down] for two or three seconds.
ながさきげんばくしぼつしゃついとうへいわきねんかん【長崎原爆死没者追悼平和記念館】⇨こくりつながさきげんばくしぼつしゃついとうへいわきねんかん.
ながさきへいわすいしんきょうかい【長崎平和推進協会】the Nagasaki Foundation for the Promotion of Peace.
ながしそうめん【流し素麺】*nagashi somen*; flowing noodles.
ながしよみ【流し読み】skimming; reading without worrying about the details. ~する skim (through)《a book》; skip the details; read 《a document》without worrying about the details; give《a contract》a superficial read-through; glance「at (through)《a letter》.
ながぜりふ【長台詞】a long speech.
ながだま【長玉】〔写真〕《(一眼レフ用の)望遠レンズ》a long lens; a tele lens; a telephoto lens.
なかつぎ【中継ぎ・中次ぎ】 ▣ 中継ぎエース〔野球〕an ace middle reliever.
なかづめ【中詰め】〔土木〕(a) concrete filling.
なかなかどうして ◐ あの女は一見うぶそうに見えるが、~世慣れたものだ. She may look naive, but「she is actually very worldly-wise [in fact she has a very good understanding of what is going on]. / あの映画はまったく期待せずに見たが、~感動的な作品だった. I didn't expect the movie to be any good, but「actually [in fact] it was very powerful.
なかにっぽんこうそくどうろかぶしきがいしゃ【中日本高速道路株式会社】the Central Nippon Expressway Company Limited. ▶ 2005年、日本道路公団民営化に伴い設立.
なかぬけ【中抜け】1〔写真〕〔ピントの〕(a) focusing error that occurs when a camera focuses automatically on the space between two things or people.
2〔中途で一時抜け出すこと〕going away for a while; leaving《a meeting》temporarily;《口》〔短時間の退席〕*stepping ["popping] out《to make a phone call》. ~する take a little time off《work》; *step ["pop] out (and come right back). ◐ 仕事を~して歯医者に行った. I took some time off work [I left work for a while] to go to the dentist.
なかの・にしじま・ゲルマンのほうそく【中野・西島・-の法則】〔物〕the Nakano-Nishijima-Gell-Mann rule.
ナガパ(ッ)ティナム〔インド南部、タミル・ナードゥ州の県・都市〕Nagapattinam.
なかま【仲間】 ▣ 仲間教育 peer education; learning from *one's* peers. 仲間集団〔社会〕a peer group.
ながまわし【長回し】〔映〕a long take.
なかよし【仲良し】 ▣ 仲良しクラブ〔緊張感の欠如した馴れ合いムードの集団〕a「chummy [pally] group; (a group of) good pals. ◐ ~クラブでは試合には勝てない. チームのメンバーが互いに競い合うようでなくてはだめだ. Just being「good pals [chummy (with each other)] won't win games. You've got to compete (with each other).
ながらじょうれい【ながら条例】the Nagara Ordinance, permitting public workers to engage in certain union activities during working hours. ▶ 正式名称は「職員団体のための職員の行為の制限の特例に関する条例」.
ナガン・ラヤ〔インドネシア、アチェ州の県〕Nagan Raya.
ナコーン・シー・タマラート ⇒ナコン・シー・タマラート.
なごしのおおはらえ【夏越大祓】〔6月30日に行われる大祓式〕a summer purification rite; a traditional Shinto purification ceremony held on June 30.
なごやおび【名古屋帯】a Nagoya obi; an obi with a half-width waistband and regular-width bow.
なごやしょうけんとりひきじょ【名古屋証券取引所】the Nagoya Stock Exchange (略: NSE).
ナゴルノ・カラバフふんそう【-紛争】the Nagorno-Karabakh conflict.
ナコン・シー・タマラート〔タイ南部の県；その県都〕Nakhon Si Thammarat.
ナコン・ナ(ー)ヨック〔タイ中部の県；その県都〕Nakhon Nayok.
ナコン・パトム〔タイ中部の県；その県都〕Nakhon Pathom.
ナコン・パノム〔タイ東北部の県〕Nakhon Phanom.
ナサうちゅうせいぶつがくけんきゅうじょ【NASA宇宙生物学研究所】⇨うちゅうせいぶつがくけんきゅうじょ.
ナザン、Sellapan Rama (1924- ；シンガポールの政治家；大統領〔1999- 〕)
なし¹【梨】 ▣ 梨狩り pear-picking; picking pears.
ナシゴレン〔料理〕〔インドネシアのチャーハンに似た料理〕nasi goreng; Indonesian fried rice.
ナシぞく【納西族】〔中国の少数民族の1つ〕the「Naxi [Nashi]; (1人) a「Naxi [Nashi] 《*pl.* ~》.
ナジュラ(ー)ン〔サウジアラビア南部の州；その州都〕Najran.
ナショナル・カンファレンス〔米国のナショナルフットボールリーグNFLの2つあるカンファレンスの1つ〕the National Football Conference (略: NFC).
「ナショナル・ジオグラフィック」〔米国の科学雑誌〕National Geographic (Magazine).
ナショナル・ジオグラフィックきょうかい【-協会】〔米国〕the National Geographic Society.
「ナショナル・ジャーナル」〔米国の政治雑誌〕National Journal.
ナショナル・パブリック・ラジオ〔全米公共ラジオ放送網〕National Public Radio (略: NPR).
「ナショナル・レビュー」〔米国の隔週刊誌〕National Review.
ナジラ(ー)ン =ナジュラ(ー)ン.
ナシリヤ〔イラク南部の都市〕Nasiriyah.
ナスカー【NASCAR】〔全米ストックカーレース協会〕NAS-

CAR; Nascar; the National Association for Stock Car Auto Racing.
**ナスダック** ▫️ ナスダック総合(株価)指数 the NASDAQ Composite Index.
**ナスでんち**【NaS 電池】=ナトリウム硫黄電池 (⇨ナトリウム).
**ナスララ** Nasrallah, Hassan (1960- ; イスラム教シーア派の武装組織ヒズボラの指導者).
「**謎の円盤 UFO**」〔英国の，地球を侵略しにきた宇宙人との闘いを描く TV ドラマ〕UFO.
**なぞりがき**【なぞり書き】tracing;〔書いたもの〕a tracing.
**なだれ**【雪崩・傾れ・頽れ】▫️ 雪崩注意報 an avalanche advisory.
**ナタンズ**〔イラン中部，イスファハン州の村〕Natanz.
**ナチ**(ス) ▫️ ナチ(ス)親衛隊 the Nazi *Schutzstaffel*; the SS.
**ナチュラル** ▫️ ナチュラル・ウォーター〔天然水〕natural water.
**ナチョ**〔チーズとチリソースや揚げた豆などを載せて焼いた薄切りのトルティーヤ〕a nacho 《*pl. ~*s》.
「**なつかしき愛の歌**」〔アイルランドの作曲家 James L. Molloy [1837-1909] 作曲の楽曲〕Love's Old Sweet Song.
**ナックス**【NACCS】=つうかんじょうほうしょりセンター.
「**ナッシング・トゥ・ルーズ**」〔映画〕Nothing to Lose.
**なつすみれ**【夏菫】〔楠〕=トレニア.
**なつたいふう**【夏台風】a summer typhoon.
「**なつたいふうプロフェッサー / クランプ教授の場合**」〔映画〕The Nutty Professor. ▶ 続編は「**ナッティ・プロフェッサー2 / クランプ家の面**」(Nutty Professor II: The Klumps).
**なっとう**【納豆】▫️ ひきわり [きざみ] 納豆 ground [cracked] and ˈfermented soybeans [*nattō*]. 藁〈ミ〉納豆 straw-wrapped ˈfermented soybeans [*nattō*]. 〈藁〉苞〈ミ〉(2)納豆 =藁納豆. ▫️ 納豆樹脂 *nattō* resin; resin of fermented soy beans.
**なっとく**【納得】▫️ 納得顔 ▫️ 彼女は怒っているようだったが，私が事情を詳しく説明すると顔で帰っていった。She seemed to be annoyed, but when I explained the situation in detail, she left with a look of understanding (on her face). / 彼は「試合には負けたが，ベストを尽くして負けたので後悔はない」と〜顔で語った。He said with an air of [satisfaction that he may have lost the game, but he had done his best and so he had no regrets. 納得診療〔医〕informed consent.
「**夏の香り**」〔韓国のテレビドラマ〕Summer Scent.
**なつばて**【夏ばて】▫️ 夏ばて解消 relief from [relieving] summer fatigue. ▫️ 僕の〜解消法は激辛カレーを食べることです。My method for getting relief from summer fatigue is to eat fiery hot curry.
**ナップスター**〔米国の有料音楽配信サービス〕Napster.
「**夏物語**」〔映画〕Once in a Summer.
**ナトゥとうげ**【〜峠】〔中印国境の〕the Nathu La Pass.
**ナトー**【NATO】〔北大西洋条約機構〕▫️ 拡大 **NATO** an expanded NATO. ▫️ **NATO** 拡大 NATO expansion.
**ナトリウム** ▫️ ナトリウム硫黄電池 a sodium-sulfur battery; a NaS battery. ナトリウム・イオン a sodium ion. ナトリウム塩化物強塩溶 a sodium chloride strong salt spring. ナトリウム塩化物泉 a sodium chloride spring. ナトリウム水素交換輸送たんぱく質〔生化〕a sodium-hydrogen [an Na/H] exchanger (略: NHE).
**ナナイモ**〔カナダ，ブリティッシュ・コロンビア州の都市〕Nanaimo.
**なたいりく**【七大陸】the seven continents. ▫️ 七大陸最高峰 the seven summits.
**ななだんかざり**【七段飾り】〔ひな人形の〕a seven-tiered display《of *hina-ningyō*》.
**ななななじへん**【七七事変】〔史〕〔盧溝橋〈ロコウキョウ〉事件の中国での呼称〕the July 7 Incident (of 1937).
**ななめ**【斜め】▫️ 斜め掛け ▫️ ショルダーバッグを〜掛けにする wear a shoulder-bag crosswise.
**ななめよみ**【斜め読み】skimming; glancing [skipping] through《a book》. 〜する skim; glance [skip] through《a book》.
「**ナニー・マクフィーの魔法のステッキ**」〔映画〕Nanny McPhee.
**なにいろ**【何色】▫️ あなたの車は〜ですか？ What color is your car? / 好きな色は〜ですか。What colors do you like? | What's your favorite color?
**なにご**【何語】▫️「デジャブって〜？」「フランス語だよ」"What language is *déjà-vu*?" — "It's French." /「イクラは〜から来ましたか？」「ロシア語です」"What language did the word *ikura* come from?" — "Russian."
**なにじん**【何人】▫️「ビートルズは〜ですか？」「イギリス人です」〔国籍〕"What country were the Beatles from?" — "They were British." /「カルタゴを建設したのは〜ですか？」「フェニキア人です」〔民族〕"What people [What was the nationality of the people who] built Carthage?" — "They were Phoenicians."
**なにどし**【何年】▫️ 君は〜 (生まれ) ですか？〔干支を尋ねて〕Which year were you born in in terms of the Oriental zodiac?
**なにをさしおいても**【何を差し措いても】first of all; before (doing)「anything [everything] else;《do it》first thing.
**ナノ** Nano, Fatos (1952- ; アルバニアの政治家; 首相 [1991, 1997-98, 2002-05]).
**ナノ–** ▫️ ナノ医療 nanomedicine. ナノインプリント nanoimprinting. ナノカーボン〔微小炭素材料〕nanocarbon. ナノケミストリー nanochemistry. ナノコーティング (a)「nanocoating [nano-coating]. ナノ材料〔マテリアル〕(a) nanomaterial. ナノスケール《at the》nanoscale. ナノチューブ a nanotube. ナノテキスト〔超微細文字印刷技術〕nanotext printing technology. ナノテク〔ナノテクノロジー〕nanotechnology. ▫️ 〜テク衣料 nanotech [nano] clothing [clothes]. ナノバイオロジー nanobiology. ナノ物質 (a) nanomaterial; (a) nano-material; (a) nanostructured material; (a) nano-structured material. ナノマシン a nano-machine. ナノ粒子 a nanoparticle. ナノ量子 a nano-quantum.
**ナノーグ**【Nanog】〔アイルランド伝説の不老不死の国 Tir na n'Og より〕〔遺伝〕Nanog.
**ナノキューン** NanoQUINE; the Collaborative Institute for Nano Quantum Information Electronics. ▶ 東京大学ナノ量子情報エレクトロニクス研究機構の英語名称.
**ナノコロイド**〔化〕a nanocolloid. ▫️ 白金ナノコロイド a platinum nanocolloid.
**ナノバブル**〔化〕〔極小の空気泡〕a nanobubble.
**ナノホーン**〔化〕〔一方が円錐状に開いた超微細チューブ〕(a) nanohorn. ▫️ カーボン・ナノホーン ⇨カーボン.
**ナノマシニング**〔超微細加工〕nanomachining; nano-machining. ▫️ ナノマシニング技術 (a) nanomachining technology.
**ナパ**〔米国，カリフォルニア州中西部の都市〕Napa.
**ナパ・バレー**〔米国，カリフォルニア州の渓谷〕Napa Valley.
**ナバラ**〔スペイン北部の自治州〕Navarra; Navarre.
**ナハリヤ**〔イスラエル北部の町〕Nahariya.
**ナプキン**〔羽根付きの [なし] ナプキン〕a sanitary napkin「with [without] wings.
**ナフダトゥ(ー)ル・ウラマ**〔インドネシアのイスラム組織〕the Nahdlatul Ulama (略: NU).
**なべしまやき**【鍋島焼】Nabeshima (ware); pottery from the Arita ware Nabeshima kilns in Saga Prefecture.
**なべはだ**【鍋肌】〔の内側〕the inner surface (of a pan);〔鍋の内側で調理中の食材と接していない部分〕the (inner)

edge; the exposed part of (the inner surface of) a pan. ▷醤油を〜から回し入れます。Swirl the soy sauce from the edge (, not directly onto ((the rice),)) in a circular motion. ▷空焼きした鍋に油を入れ〜になじませます。Preheat the empty pan and coat the surface with (the) oil.

**ナベルビン**〖商標・薬〗〔抗がん剤 酒石酸ビノレルビンの商品名〕Navelbine.

**ナポリターノ** Napolitano, Giorgio (1925- ; イタリアの政治家; 大統領〔2006- 〕).

「**ナポレオン・ソロ**」⇨「0011/ナポレオン・ソロ」.

**ナポレオン・フィッシュ**〖魚〗=めがねもちのうお.

**なま**【生】▣ 生カード〖情報未記入の磁気カード〗a blank 「magnetic(-stripe) [plastic, PVC] card; 《俗》white plastic. 生楽器〖音楽〗an acoustic (musical) instrument. 生コン〖生コンクリート〗liquid concrete. ▷〜コン車 a ready-mix truck. 生写真 a real [an original] photograph (printed on photo stock).

**なまごみ**【生ごみ】▣ 生ごみ発電 generating electricity by burning garbage [(raw) waste]; (kitchen) waste incineration power generation. 生ごみリサイクル kitchen waste recycling.

**なまじまく**【生字幕】real-time [live] subtitles. ▣ 生字幕放送 a real-time subtitled broadcast.

**なまめん**【生麺】fresh noodles;〖パスタ〗fresh pasta.

**なまりぐすり**【鉛釉】〖製陶〗(a) lead glaze.

**なまりさんだん**【鉛散弾】a lead shot. ▣ 鉛散弾規制地域 an area where hunting with lead shot is prohibited; a lead-shot-hunting prohibited area.

**なまりゆう**【鉛釉】〖製陶〗(a) lead glaze.

**なみ**²【並(み)】▣ 並縫い a running stitch. 並盛り〔料理の〕a regular 「portion [helping, serving].

**なみいた**【波板】a corrugated (plastic) sheet.

**なみぶと**【並太】〜の medium-thick; medium-weight. ▷〜の毛糸 medium [sport-weight] yarn.

**ナムケム, ナムケン**〔タイ南部, パンガー県の村〕Nam Khem.

**ナムチェ・バザール**〔ネパール, カトマンズ東部の村; エヴェレスト登山の拠点〕Namche Baza(a)r.

**ナムフレル**〔フィリピンの民間選挙監視団体「自由選挙のための国民運動」〕NAMFREL; the National (Citizens) Movement for Free Elections.

**なめたき**【滑滝】a gradual waterfall; a cascade (waterfall).

**なよせ**【名寄せ】〖金融・年金・保険〗〔分散している同一人の複数の記録を一か所に集めること〕(the) aggregation of 「accounts [deposits] held by the same person.

**ナラーティワート** =ナラティワート.

**ならし-**【慣らし-】▣ 慣らし保育 a program for getting children accustomed to childcare.

**ナラティワート** 1〔タイ南部の県〕Narathiwat. 2〔タイ南部の都市, ナラティワート県の県都〕Narathiwat.

**なりすまし**【成り済まし】impersonation (of sb); using a stolen identity;〖電算〗spoofing. ▷なりすまし詐欺 identity [impersonation] fraud; fraud by impersonation; identity theft. なりすまし犯罪 (an) identity (an) identity(-theft) crime. なりすましメール (a) spoof(ed) e-mail.

**なりたこくさいくうこうかぶしきがいしゃ**【成田国際空港株式会社】Narita International Airport Corporation (略: NAA). ▶ 略称の NAA は前身の新東京国際空港 (New Tokyo International Airport Authority) の略称を継承したもの.

**なりもの**²【鳴り物】▣ 鳴り物応援〔野球試合などでの〕cheering [rooting]《for a team》with noisemakers.

**ナリンゲニン・カルコン**〖化〗〔トマトに含まれるポリフェノールの一種〕naringenin chalcone.

**なるとさわぎく**【鳴門沢菊】〖植〗〔キク科の植物〕(a) Madagascar ragwort; (a) Fireweed; Senecio madagascarien-sis.

**ナルとびえい**【-鳶鱏】〖魚〗〔インド洋・東シナ海産のトビエイ科の魚〕a longheaded eagle ray; Aetobatus flagellum.

**なれずし**【熟れ鮨〖寿司〗, 馴れ鮨〖寿司〗】〖発酵鮨〗fermented sushi; narezushi.

**ナレッジ・マネージメント**〖経営〗〔社内蓄積情報の有効利用を図る経営手法; 知識管理〕knowledge management.

**ナロー・バンク**〔決済中心の銀行〕a narrow bank. ▷ narrow banking n.

**ナローバンド**〔狭帯域通信〕narrowband.

**なわ**【縄】▣ 縄縮み〔土地の実測面積が公簿面積より小さいこと〕being smaller than the area recorded in a land register. 縄延び(伸び)〔土地の実測面積が公簿面積より大きいこと〕being larger than the area registered in a land register.

**なわじり**【縄尻】囚人の〜を取る take the end of a rope (tied around a prisoner); 〜を取る take the end of a rope tied around a prisoner; seize a prisoner by the end of a rope.

**なわでんしゃ**【縄電車】〔遊戯〕a "rope train"; a game in which children surround themselves with a long rope and pretend to be in a train.

**なんかい**²【南海】▣ 南海地震 a Nankai earthquake; an undersea earthquake with epicenter south of the Kii Peninsula or Shikoku.

**なんかいほうまつじけん**【南海泡沫事件】〖英史〗〔1720年の株暴落事件〕the South Sea Bubble.

**ナンガルハル** =ナンガルハル.

**ナンガルハル**〔アフガニスタン東部の州〕Nangarhar. ▶ 州都はジャララバード.

**なんかん**【難関】▣ 難関大学 a highly-selective university.

**なんきょく**¹【南極】▣ 南極氷床 the Antarctic ice sheet. ▷〜氷床コア the Antarctic ice core.

**ナンクロ**〔キーなしのクロスパズル〕a crossword (puzzle) without a key.

**ナングロ・アチェ・ダルサラムしゅう**【-州】〔インドネシア, スマトラ島の州〕Nanggroe Aceh Darussalam (Province) (略: NAD).

**なんこつ**【軟骨】▣ 軟骨無形成(症)〖医〗achondroplasia.

**なんしゅうが**【南宗画】〔中国の〕the Southern school of painting.

**なんしょうかせい**【難消化性】〜の hard-to-digest; indigestible. ▣ 難消化性デキストリン〖生化〗indigestible dextrin.

**なんしょく**³【何色】▷その図柄は〜使っていますか? How many colors are used in that pattern? / あなたの国では虹の色は〜ですか? In your country, how many colors are (said to be) in a rainbow? ▶ 英国や日本では虹の連続スペクトルは 7 色ということになっているが, 米国その他では 5 色, 6 色など一定しない.

**なんすいほくちょう**【南水北調】〔中国南部から北部への導水事業; 水量の多い長江の水を水不足の黄河流域へ運河で運ぶ〕nan shui bei diao; south-north water transfer; diverting water from the south to the north (in China).

**なんせいアフリカじんみんきこう**【南西-人民機構】〔ナミビアの政党〕the South-West African People's Organization (略: SWAPO).

**ナンセンス**▣ ナンセンス漫画 a nonsense manga; a nonsense cartoon.

**ナンセンなんみんしょう**【難民賞】the Nansen Refugee Award. ▶ 1954 年創設.

**なんたいなん**【何対何】▷今〜? 〔スポーツ番組を見ている人などに〕Now it's what to what? | What's the score now?

**ナンタケット**〔米国マサチューセッツ州, ケープコッド南方の島〕Nantucket Island.

なんち【難治】hard to cure; almost incurable; refractory. ▭ 難治がん refractory [intractable] cancer; 〔手術不能の〕inoperable cancer. 難治(性)疾患 an intractable「disease [disorder].

なんちせい【難治性】▭ 難治性歯周病 refractory periodontal disease.

なんちゃって ▭ なんちゃって女子高生〔女子高生になりすましているニセモノ〕a girl who pretends to be a high school student; a「fake [phony] high school girl. なんちゃって制服 a school uniform worn by a nonstudent; a faux school uniform.

なんちょう[3]【難聴】◯ 感音性難聴 sensorineural [perceptive, retrocochlear] hearing loss; nerve [perceptive] deafness. 器質性難聴 organic「deafness [hearing loss]. 機能性[心因性]難聴 functional [non-organic, psychogenic] deafness [hearing loss]. 高度難聴(suffer, have) extreme [a high degree of] hearing loss; profound deafness. 中途難聴 hearing loss occurring after childhood.

なんてん[4]【何点】◯ 今タイガーズ〜? What's the Tigers' score? | How many 《points》 do the Tigers have? / 今日の算数のテスト〜だった? What was your score on the arithmetic test today?

ナントウ【南投】〔台湾中央部の都市・県〕Nantou.

なんなんきょうりょく【南南協力】〔開発途上国同士の協力〕South-South cooperation.

ナンバー ▭ 5 ナンバー〔小型乗用車のナンバー〕a 5-series「*license [*number] plate (for smaller passenger「vehicles [cars]); [5 ナンバー車] a「vehicle [car] with a 5-series「*license [*number] plate. 3 ナンバー〔普通乗用車のナンバー〕a 3-series「*license [*number] plate (for larger passenger「vehicles [cars]); [3 ナンバー車] a「vehicle [car] with a 3-series「*license [*number] plate. Y ナンバー〔在日米軍人などの私有車のナンバー〕a "Y"「*license [*number] plate (for「vehicles [cars] owned by US military personnel); [Y ナンバー車] a「vehicle [car] with a "Y"「*license [*number] plate. ▭ ナンバー・ポータビリティー〔同じ電話番号を使い続けられること〕(telephone) number portability; (携帯電話の) mobile number portability;(略: MNP).

ナンバーズ〔数字選択式宝くじ〕a numbers lottery.

ナンバー・プレース =すうどく.

ナンパはしり【あるき】【〜走り[歩き]】〔同側の手と足が同時に前に出る走り方[歩き方]〕nanba「running [walking];

running [walking] with the arm and leg on each side of the body moving in sync.

なんびょう【難病】▭ 難病患者 a「person [patient] afflicted with [suffering from] a serious illness.

ナンプレ〔ナンバープレースの略〕=すうどく.

なんべい(こっか)きょうどうたい【南米(国家)共同体】〔2004年発足〕the South American Community of Nations (略: CSN). ▶ 略はスペイン語の *Comunidad Sudamericana de Naciones* より.

なんべいせんしゅけん【南米選手権】《サッカー》Copa America.

なんぼく[1]【南北】◯ 南北軍事境界線〔北朝鮮・韓国間の〕the Military Demarcation Line (略: MDL). 南北首脳会談〔韓国・北朝鮮間などの〕a North-South summit meeting.

なんぼくかいろう【南北回廊】〔インドシナ地域に建設中の〕幹線道路〕the North-South Corridor.

なんぼくきょうどうせんげん【南北共同宣言】〔2000年6月の, 韓国・北朝鮮の〕the North-South Joint Declaration.

なんぼくけいざいきょうりょくすいしんいいんかい【南北経済協力推進委員会】=けいざいきょうりょくすいしんいいんかい.

なんぼくじゅうだんてつどう【南北縦断鉄道】〔朝鮮半島の〕an inter-Korean「railroad [railway].

なんみん【難民】◯ 条約難民〔難民条約で難民の要件に該当すると判断された人〕a Convention refugee; a refugee「under [as defined by] the Geneva Convention (of 1951). 水難民 water refugees. ▭ 難民帰還 the return of refugees 《to their country》; refugees returning home. 難民帰還事業 a refugee repatriation「operation [program, scheme]; refugee repatriation「operations [activities]. 難民審査参与員制度〔難民認定の異議申し立て審査に第三者を参加させる制度〕the Refugee Adjudication Counselors System. 難民生活 life as a refugee. 難民送還 sending refugees「back [home]; repatriation of a refugee; refugee repatriation. 難民認定基準 criteria for「refugee status [certification as a refugee, recognizing sb as a refugee]. 難民(の)地位《have, seek, be [granted refused]》refugee status.

なんもん【難問】▭ 難問奇問〔試験の〕a very「tough [testing] question.

# に

ニア・ウォーター〔健康飲料の一種〕near water.

にあまりかん【荷余り感】《経》an oversupply 《of stainless steel in the market》.

にいがたけんちゅうえつじしん【新潟県中越地震】=にいがたけんちゅうえつだいしんさい.

にいがたけんちゅうえつだいしんさい【新潟県中越大震災】〔2004年10月の〕the Niigata Prefecture Chūetsu Earthquake.

ニーズ[2]【NIES】〔新興工業経済地域〕▭ アジア NIEs the Asian NIEs.

ニーズ[3]【NEEDS】〔電算〕〔日経経済情報データバンクシステム〕NEEDS; the Nikkei Economic Electronic Databank System.

ニースじょうやく【〜条約】〔2001年調印の EU 新基本条約〕the Nice Treaty.

ニーソン Neeson, Liam (1952- ; 北アイルランド出身の俳優; 本名 William John Neeson).

ニート〔職業を持たず, 就学中でもなく, 職業訓練を受けている〕わけでもない人〕a NEET. ▶ NEET は "not in employment, education or training" の略.

ニートすいせい【〜彗星】〔天〕a NEAT comet. ▶ NEAT は Near Earth Asteroid Tracking の略.

ニー・ドロップ《プロレス》〔膝または脛を相手の体に落とす技〕a knee drop.

にいな【煮菜】〔新潟地方の郷土料理〕pickled greens with the salt removed boiled with flattened soybeans, fried tofu, or other ingredients.

ニーナワー =ニナワ.

ニーハオ・トイレ〔中国式トイレ; 個室の仕切りがない中国のトイレの俗称〕a "Ni-Hao" toilet; a Chinese toilet without individual enclosures.

ニーム[2] =ナイム.

ニーム[3] Neame, Ronald (1911- ; 英国の映画監督).

ニール 1 Neal, Patricia (1926- ; 米国の映画女優). 2 Neill, Sam (1947- ; 北アイルランド生まれの映画俳優).

ニールセン Nielsen, Leslie (1926- ; カナダ生まれの映画俳優).

ニヴフ〔ロシア極東地域の少数民族〕the Nivkh(s); 〔1 人〕a

Nivkh 《pl. ~, ~s, Nivkhi》.　▫=ヴフ語　Nivkh.
**にエル**【2L】〔2リットルの略〕2 l.; 2 lit.;〔物品のサイズ〕2L.
**におい**【匂い・臭い】　▫=におい分子　an odor molecule.
**においばんまつり**【匂い蕃茉莉】〔植〕〔ナス科の植物〕(a) yesterday-today-and-tomorrow; (a) morning-noon-and-night; (a) kiss-me-quick; *Brunfelsia pauciflora*.
**におうらん**【二黄卵】a double-yolked egg.
**ニカ(ー)ブ**〔イスラム教徒の女性が目以外の顔を覆う布〕a niqab.
**にがくさ**【苦草】〔植〕〔シソ科の多年草〕(a Japanese species of) germander; *Teucrium japonicum*.
**にがっきせい**【二学期制】a two-term[-semester] system.
「**ニキータ**」〔映画〕Nikita.
**にきびだに**〔動〕a (human) demodex mite; *Demodex folliculorum*.
**にぎやかし**【賑やかし】(a) livening-up.　◆同窓会の～にポップ歌手を呼ぶ　engage a pop singer to 「liven up [enliven] an alumni reunion.
**にぎやかす**【賑やかす】〔行事などを〕liven up; brighten (up); enliven; animate; give animation 《to the proceedings》;〔紙面などを〕liven up; enliven.　◆獲れたての魚で食卓を～　brighten up the table with a freshly caught fish / 最近、教師の痴漢行為が新聞を賑やかしている.　Recently the newspapers have been enlivened with the sexual misconduct of teachers. | Stories of teachers molesting women have spiced up the newspapers recently.
**にきょくか**【二極化】　▫=一人二極化〔消費の〕bipolarized single-consumer consumption; the purchase of both luxury and discount goods by the same consumers.　▫=二極化現象　a (bi)polarization phenomenon; the polarization 《of rich and poor》.
**にくあつ**【肉厚】〔管壁・板などの厚さ〕thickness.　～な〔の〕thick.　◆～の唇　thick 「fleshy, full〕lips / 中華料理用の～の包丁　a thick cutting knife for Chinese cooking.　▫=配管肉厚　pipe wall thickness.　▫=肉厚検査〔配管の〕a thickness inspection.
**ニクス**〔天〕〔冥王星の衛星〕Nix.
**にくせい**【肉声】　▫=肉声テープ　a tape of *sb*'s actual voice.　◆その博物館にはトルストイの～テープが保管されている.　The museum owns a tape of Tolstoy's actual voice [an actual voice recording of Tolstoy].
**にくたい**【肉体】　▫=肉体訓練　physical training.　肉体年齢　(a [*one*'s]) 「physical [body] age.　肉体派〔男が〕a 'brawny [muscly] type;〔女優など〕a glamorous type.
**にぐん**【二軍】　▫=二軍スタート〔野球〕starting the season in the reserves.
**にげきり**【逃げ切り】leading all the way (and winning); staying in the lead; maintaining *one*'s lead (from start to finish).　◆～を図る　aim to stay in the lead (all the way).
「**逃げろや! 逃げろ**」〔ギャングの密談を聞いてしまい逃げ続ける男の TV コメディー〕Run, Buddy, Run.
**にげん**【二元】　▫=二元外交　two-track [dual-track] diplomacy.
**にこいち**【二個一】〔2台の機器の各々から使える部品を寄せ集めて1台に復元すること〕restoring 《a car》 from parts taken from it and another; cannibalizing 《a car》 for parts for another.
**にこくろん**【二国論】〔中国に対する台湾政府の〕a two-country 「doctrine [model].
**ニコチアナミン**〔化〕nicotianamine.
**ニコチン**　▫=ニコチン切れ　nicotine depletion.　ニコチン代謝物質　nicotine metabolite (in urine).　ニコチン離脱症状〔医〕〔ニコチン切れ症状〕nicotine withdrawal symptoms.
**ニコヨン**〔第二次大戦後の日雇い労働者の俗称〕a day laborer.

**ニコル**　Niccol, Andrew (1964-　; ニュージーランド生まれの映画監督・脚本家).
**にごろぶな**【似五郎鮒】〔魚〕〔琵琶湖に生息するコイ科の魚〕*Carassius auratus grandoculis*.
**にさばき**【荷捌き】　▫=荷捌き場　a 「place [space] for unpacking and sorting goods.　荷捌き駐車場　a parking lot for unloading goods.
**に・さんいれんごう**【2・3位連合】〔政治〕an alliance between the second- and third-strongest candidates on the first ballot to direct votes in the runoff election to the second-strongest candidate.
**にさんかたんそ**【二酸化炭素】　▫=二酸化炭素泉　a carbonated spring.　二酸化炭素排出抑制　carbon dioxide [$CO_2$] emission control.　～排出抑制対策　measures to control 「carbon dioxide [$CO_2$] emissions.　二酸化炭素排出量　(reduce) $CO_2$ emissions; emissions of $CO_2$.
**にじ**[1]【虹】　▫=逆さ虹〔気象〕=かんすいへいアーク.
**にじ**[2]【二次】　▫=二次合併症〔医〕secondary complications.　二次障害〔医〕a secondary 「disorder [impairment].　二次責任〔have, bear〕secondary responsibility 《for payment》.　二次予防　secondary prevention.　二次利用〔著作物などの〕secondary use 《of copyrighted material》.　◆～利用権　secondary-use rights; the right to secondary use 《of health data》.
**にしアゼルバイジャン**【西-】〔イラン北西部の州〕West Azarbaijan;〔ペルシャ語名の音訳〕Azarbayjan-e Gharbi.　▶ 州都はウルミエ.
**にしアチェ**【西-】〔インドネシア、アチェ州の県、アチェ・バラ(ッ)ト〕〕Aceh Barat.
**にしアフリカいねかいはつきょうかい**【西-稲開発協会】the West Africa Rice Development Association (略: WARDA).
**にじいろくわがた**【虹色鍬形】〔昆〕〔クワガタムシ科の昆虫〕*Phalacrognathus mulleri*.
**にじぐち**【二字口】〔相撲〕〔土俵への上がり口〕the east and west entrances to the sumo ring.
**にしクルナゆでん**【西-油田】〔イラク南部の油田〕the West Qurna oil field.
**にしケープ**【西-】〔南アフリカ共和国南西部の州〕Western Cape;〔アフリカーンス語名〕Wes-Kaap.　▶ 州都はケープタウン.
**にじげん**【二次元】　▫=二次元コード〔電算〕〔発達型バーコード〕a two-dimensional bar code.　二次元バーコード　=二次元コード.
**にしじんふくろおび**【西陣袋帯】a two-ply *Nishijin* woven sash.
**にしスマトラ**【西-】〔インドネシアの州〕West 「Sumatra [Sumatera];〔インドネシア語名〕Sumatera Barat.　▶ 州都はパダン.
**にじっかこくざいむしょう・ちゅうおうぎんこうそうさいかいぎ**【20 か国財務相・中央銀行総裁会議】a meeting of finance ministers and central bank governors of the G-20.
**にしナイルねつ**【西-熱】〔医〕West Nile fever.
**にしナイルのうえん**【西-脳炎】〔医〕West Nile encephalitis (略: WNE); West Nile fever.
**にしにっぽんこうそくどうろかぶしきがいしゃ**【西日本高速道路株式会社】the West Nippon Expressway Company Limited.　▶ 2005 年、日本道路公団民営化に伴い設立.
**にしゃくだま**【二尺玉】〔打ち上げ花火の〕a ball-shaped firework (with a shell 「two *shaku* [about 60cm] in diameter).
**にじゅう**[2]【二重】　▫=二重引用符　a double quotation mark (記号: ").　二重音声〔放送〕dual sound (broadcasting).　二重感染　dual [double] infection(s).　二重敬語　double *keigo*; (a) double honorific; exaggerated [excessive] (and incorrect) polite language.　二重契約

a double contract. 二重処罰, 二重処分 〖法〗double punishment; (a) double penalty. 二重徴収 double charging; double receipt 《of a tax》. 二重登録 double registration. ◐彼の名は2つの市の選挙人名簿に~登録されていた. His name had been registered twice, 「on [in] the electoral rolls of two different cities. 二重被爆 experience [being a victim of] the A-bomb at both Hiroshima and Nagasaki. ◐~被爆者 a victim of [a person exposed to radiation at] (A-bombing at) both Hiroshima and Nagasaki. 二重像〔日の出・日没に太陽が富士山の背後にあり, 手前にある薄い雲がスクリーンとなって影をつくると富士山が二重に見える現象〕a double image of Mt. Fuji. 二重包装 (a) full formal (internal) wrapping with an additional outer wrapping paper for delivery. 二重惑星 〖天〗a double planet; a binary planet.

「21グラム」〔映画〕21 Grams.

にじゅういっせいきシー・オー・イー・プログラム【21世紀 COE-】〔大学の優れた研究拠点に重点的に資金を援助する文科省のプログラム〕the 21st Century Center of Excellence Program.

にじゅういっせいきしょくぎょうざいだん【21世紀職業財団】the Japan Institute of Workers' Evolution (略: JIWE).

にじゅういっせいきりんちょう【21世紀臨調】the National Congress on 21st Century Japan. [=あたらしいにほんをつくるこくみんかいぎ]

にじゅういっせいきわく【21世紀枠】〔春の選抜高校野球大会出場枠の〕a "21st century berth"; a category in a national high school baseball tournament for teams that have overcome special challenges, have had a positive impact or have not played in a similar tournament for more than 30 years.

「25年目のキス」〔映画〕Never Been Kissed.

にじゅうごねんルール【25年-】〔公的年金の受給資格期間の〕the "25-year rule" (for Japanese pensions); the rule that a minimum of twenty-five years of contributions are necessary for entitlement to a government-supported pension.

にじゅうよじかん【二十四時間】◐◐二十四時間空港 a 24-hour airport. 二十四時間社会 a [the] 24-hour society. 二十四時間随時訪問介護サービス a twenty-four hour visiting care service. 二十四時間スト(ライキ)《call》a 24-hour strike. 二十四時間対応〔医療・情報サービスなどの〕24-hour availability. 二十四時間耐久レース a 24-hour endurance race. 二十四時間保育 24-hour (around-the-clock) childcare.

にじゅんめ【二巡目】the second round. ◐彼はドラフト~で指名された. He was 「picked [chosen, drafted] in the second round. ◐◐二巡目指名〔スポーツ〕〔ドラフト制での〕a second-round 「selection [pick].

にしんぐもり【鰊曇り】cloudy weather during the herring season (around April in Hokkaidō).

にしんそば【鰊蕎麦】soba with sweetened dried herring.

にせ[1]【偽】◐◐偽ブランド品 a 「counterfeit [fake] (brand-name, branded) product.

にせんにマーズ・オデッセイ【2001-】〔米国 NASA の周回型の火星探査機〕the 2001 Mars Odyssey.

にせんきゅう【二線級】◐~の second-best; second-rank; second-grade; second-class; second-level; second-string. ◐あのチームが相手なら~だけでも勝てるだろう. We should be able to beat that team with our second-stringers. | If we are up against that team we can probably win with our second-best players.

にせんごせんげん【二千語宣言】〔チェコ知識人による1968年の自由化志向宣言〕Two Thousand Words.

にせんてい【二線堤】〔本堤背後の堤内地にさらに築造される堤防〕a secondary 「levee [embankment].

にせんななねんもんだい【2007年問題】1〔2007年から2009年にかけて第2次大戦後の1947-49年に生まれた団塊の世代が大量に定年退職を迎える問題〕the (Year) 2007 Problem; the retirement bubble. 2〔2007年ごろに18歳人口と大学定員が均衡し, 大学全入時代が到来すること〕the problem of the year 2007, when 「the number of eighteen year olds in the population will be the same as the number of places in tertiary education in Japan [all applicants will be able to enter universities].

にせんろくねんもんだい【2006年問題】〔日本の人口が2006年をピークに減少しはじめること〕the Year 2006 Problem; the problem of population decline in Japan since 2006.

にだいせいとうか【二大政党化】the development of a two-party system. ◐~が進んでいる. A two-party system is 「being formed [taking shape].

にち・アセアンほうかつてきけいざいれんけいこうそう【日・ASEAN 包括的経済連携構想】the Initiative for Japan-ASEAN Comprehensive Economic Partnership.

にちいききょじゅう【二地域居住】〔居住地が2か所あり, その間を行き来する生活スタイル〕spending part of one's life in the countryside (after retirement).

にちぎん【日銀】◐◐日銀支店長会議 a 「BOJ [Bank of Japan] branch managers' meeting; a (quarterly) meeting of BOJ branch managers. 日銀当座預金 the 「BOJ [Bank of Japan] current account; the current account at the BOJ. 日銀当座預金残高 the 「BOJ [Bank of Japan] current account balance; the current account balance at the BOJ. 日銀当座預金残高目標 the 「BOJ [Bank of Japan] current account balance target.

にちぎんけん【日銀券】a Bank of Japan note.

にちぎんネット【日銀-】〔日本銀行と金融機関をつなぐ日本銀行金融ネットワークシステムの略称〕the BOJ-Net. ► BOJ is Bank of Japan の略.

にちじょう【日常】◐◐日常化 ◐停電が~化している. Power outages have become a 「daily [regular] occurrence. | Blackouts have become a part of everyday life. 日常業務 daily 「work [business]; routine work; (daily) routine.

にちじょうせいかつ【日常生活】◐◐日常生活音 household 「noises [sounds]; the 「noises [sounds] of daily domestic life. 日常生活動作(活動) 〖医〗an activity of daily living (略: ADL). ◐手段的~動作〖医〗an instrumental 「activity of daily living [ADL] (略: IADL).

にちべい【日米】◐◐日米共同訓練 a Japan-US joint military exercise. 日米軍事同盟 the [a] Japan-US military alliance.

にちべいあんぽきょうどうせんげん【日米安保共同宣言】〔1996年4月の〕the Japan-US Joint Declaration on Security.

にちべいけいじきょうじょじょうやく【日米刑事共助条約】the 「Mutual Legal Assistance Treaty [MLAT] between Japan and the US. ► 正式名称は「刑事に関する共助に関する日本国とアメリカ合衆国との間の条約」(the Treaty between Japan and the United States of America on Mutual Legal Assistance in Criminal Matters).

にちべいじどうしゃきょうぎ【日米自動車協議】〔1981年以降の〕the Japan-US Automotive Framework Talks.

にちべいじどうしゃまさつ【日米自動車摩擦】〔1980年代の〕Japan-US automobile trade friction.

にちべいせんいきょうてい【日米繊維協定】the Japan-US Textile Agreement.

にちべいせんいこうしょう【日米繊維交渉】〔1969-71年

の〕the Japan-US textile negotiations.
**にちべいせんしゅけいやくきょうてい**【日米選手契約協定】〔プロ野球の〕the「Japan-US [US-Japan] Player Agreement.
**にちべいせんりゃくたいわ**【日米戦略対話】the Japan-US Strategic Dialogue (at the Senior Officials' Level).
**にちべいそうごぼうえいえんじょきょうてい**【日米相互防衛援助協定】 ▣ 日米相互防衛援助協定等に伴う秘密保護法〔法〕the Espionage Law Accompanying Agreements between Japan and the United States of America on Mutual Defense Assistance.
**にちべいぜいじょうやく**【日米租税条約】〔1971年締結の〕the Japan-US Income Tax Treaty;〔2003年改定, 2004年発効の新日米租税条約〕the New Japan-US Income Tax Treaty. ▶ 新日米租税条約の正式名称は「所得に対する租税に関する二重課税の回避及び脱税の防止のための日本国政府と合衆国政府との間の条約」(the Convention between the Government of Japan and the Government of the United States of America for the Avoidance of Double Taxation and the Prevention of Fiscal Evasion with Respect to Taxes on Income).
**にちべいとくべつこうどういいんかい**【日米特別行動委員会】the Special Action Committee on Okinawa (略: SACO). ▶「沖縄に関する特別行動委員会」のこと.
**にちべいはんどうたいまさつ**【日米半導体摩擦】〔1980年代の〕friction between Japan and the United States over trade involving semiconductors.
**にちべいほけんきょうぎ**【日米保険協議】〔1990年代の〕the Japan-US Insurance Talks.
**にちべいほけんきょうてい**【日米保険協定】the Japan-US Insurance Agreement.
**にちべんれんほうむけんきゅうざいだん**【日弁連法務研究財団】the Japan Law Foundation (略: JLF).
**にちぼつ**【日没】 ▣ 日没サスペンデッド〔ゴルフ・テニスなど〕suspension (of play) due to darkness;《a match》suspended due to darkness. 日没中断試合 a game suspended because of bad light. 日没引き分け〔試合の〕a 'tie [draw] due to darkness.
**にちれい**【日齢】〔受精・孵化・出生などからの日数〕age in days; how many days old. ◑ 仔牛は90〜で競(せ)りにかける. Calves are sold at auction from their ninetieth day (after birth). ◑ 40〜のひな a forty-day-old chick. ▣ 日齢別死因分類〔乳幼児の〕classification of cause of (infant) death by number of days old.
**にちろ**【日露, 日口】 ▣ 日露[日口]フォーラム the Japan-Russia Forum.
**にちろこうどうけいかくのさいたくにかんするきょうどうせいめい**【日露行動計画の採択に関する共同声明】〔日本国総理大臣及びロシア連邦大統領の〕the Joint Statement by the Prime Minister of Japan and the President of the Russian Federation Concerning the Adoption of a Japan-Russia Action Plan.
**にちろぼうえきとうしそくしんきこう**【日露貿易投資促進機構】the Japan-Russia Trade and Investment Promotion Organization.
**にっかん**[2]【日韓】日韓国交正常化交渉 diplomatic normalization talks between Japan and South Korea.. 日韓友情年〔2005年〕the Japan-Korea Friendship Year (2005).
**にっかんきほんかんけいじょうやく**【日韓基本関係条約】the Treaty on Basic Relations between Japan and the Republic of Korea. ▶ 1965年締結. 正式名称は「日本国と大韓民国との間の基本関係に関する条約」.
**にっかんきょうどうせんげん**【日韓共同宣言】〔1998年の〕the Japan-Republic of Korea Joint Declaration.
**にっかんぎょぎょうこうしょう**【日韓漁業交渉】Japan-Korea Fisheries negotiations.

**にっかんけいじきょうじょじょうやく**【日韓刑事共助条約】the「Mutual Legal Assistance Treaty [MLAT]」between Japan and Korea.
**にっかんたいりくだなきょうてい**【日韓大陸棚協定】agreements between Japan and the Republic of Korea concerning the Asian continental shelf. ▶「日本国と大韓民国との間の両国に隣接する大陸棚の北部の境界画定に関する協定」(the Agreement between Japan and the Republic of Korea concerning the Establishment of Boundary in the Northern Part of the Continental Shelf to the Two Countries) と「日本国と大韓民国との間の両国に隣接する大陸棚の南部の共同開発に関する協定」(the Agreement between Japan and the Republic of Korea concerning Joint Development of the Southern Part of the Continental Shelf Adjacent to the Two Countries) の2つをあわせた呼称.
**にっかんはんざいにんひきわたしじょうやく**【日韓犯罪人引き渡し条約】the Japan-South Korea Extradition Treaty.
**にっかんへいごうじょうやく**【日韓併合条約】〔史〕the Japan-Korea Annexation Treaty.
**にっかんほごじょうやく**【日韓保護条約】〔史〕the (1905) Japan-Korea「Protection [Protectorate] Treaty.
**にっかんれきしきょうどうけんきゅう**【日韓歴史共同研究】〔2001年の日韓首脳会談での合意に基づき, 両国の専門家が2002年より3年間にわたって歴史教科書問題を協議した〕Japan-ROK joint history research; joint research carried out by Japanese and ROK historians on the treatment of history in textbooks.
**にっかんれきしきょうどうけんきゅういいんかい**【日韓歴史共同研究委員会】the Japan-ROK Joint History Research Committee.〔⇨にっかんれきしきょうどうけんきゅう〕
**ニッキ** ▣ ニッキ飴 cinnamon candy.
**にっきん**【日勤】 ▣ 日勤教育〔JRで, 日勤の時間帯に行われる乗務員の懲罰的再教育〕dayshift「training [education]; disciplinary re-education of Japan Railways staff responsible for errors or delays.
**ニック**【NIC】 ▣〔電算〕「LAN接続用の拡張カード〕a network interface card.
**ニック・アダムス**〔ヘミングウェー作の短篇小説の登場人物〕Nick Adams.
**にっけいアメリカじんほしょうほう**【日系人補償法】〔米法〕しみんのじゆうほう.
**にっけい(かぶかしすう)さんびゃく**【日経(株価指数)300】the Nikkei (Stock Index) 300.
**にっけいこくさいじょうひんしすう**【日経国際商品指数】the Nikkei index of international commodities prices.
**にっけいジャスダックへいきん(かぶか)**【日経−平均(株価)】the Nikkei Jasdaq average.
**にっけいしょうひよそくしすう**【日経消費予測指数】the Nikkei Consumption Forecasting Indicator (略: Nikkei CFI).
**にっけいしょうひんしすう**【日経商品指数】the Nikkei Commodity Price Index.
**にっけいちょう**【日経調】=にほんけいざいちょうさきょうぎかい.
**にっけいへいきんさきものとりひき**【日経平均先物取引】〔取引〕Nikkei stock average [Nikkei 225] futures trading.
**ニッケル** ▣ ニッケル鉱石 nickel ore. ニッケル水素二次電池 a nickel-metal hydride secondary「battery [cell]; a secondary nickel-metal hydride battery.
**にっこう**[1]【日光】 ▣ 日光角化症〔医〕(an) actinic [(a) solar] keratosis.
**にっさ**【日差】〔時計等の日ごとの進みあるいは遅れの程度〕daily rate.
**にっしゃ**【日射】 ▣ 日射吸収率《high, low》solar ab-

sorptance. 日射透過率 solar transmittance. 日射反射率 solar reflectance.
にっしょう² 【日商】 ▭ 日商簿記 ＝日本商工会議所簿記検定試験 (⇨にほんしょうこうかいぎしょ).
にっしょう³ 【日照】 ▭ 日照量 the amount of ⌈sunlight [solar radiation, insolation].
にっしょうきん 【日証金】 ＝にほんしょうけんきんゆうがいしゃ.
にっしれん 【日歯連】 ＝にほんしかいしれんめい.
ニッチ ▭ ニッチ商品 ＝隙間商品 (⇨すきま).
ニッチャー 〔市場の隙間 (ニッチ) を見つけてそこから利益を得ようとする企業〕 a niche ⌈player [company].
にっちゅう¹ 【日中】 ▭ 日中傾眠 【医】 daytime ⌈sleepiness [drowiness].
にっちゅう² 【日中】 ▭ 日中強盗団 a Sino-Japanese gang (in which Japanese criminals supply information about potential victims and the Chinese members implement the robberies). 日中対話 (a) dialogue between Japan and China; (a) ⌈Sino-Japanese [Japan-China] dialogue.
にっちゅうとうしほごきょうてい 【日中投資保護協定】 the Japan-China Investment Protection Agreement.
にっちゅうれきしきょうどうけんきゅう 【日中歴史共同研究】 Japan-China joint history research.
にっちょう 【日朝】 ▭ 日朝実務(者)協議 Japan-North Korea working-level talks.
にっちょうピョンヤンせんげん 【日朝平壌宣言】 〔2002年9月17日の〕 the Japan-⌈North Korea [Democratic People's Republic of Korea, DPRK] Pyongyang Declaration.
にってい² 【日程】 ▭ 日程調節[調整] (a) schedule adjustment.
ニット ▭ ニット帽 《wear》 a knit cap.
にっぱい 【日配】 daily delivery. ▭ 日配(食)品 〔スーパーマーケットなどで, 豆腐・卵・牛乳などの生鮮品〕 (food) items [products] delivered daily.
にっぱち 【二八】 〔商取引が不活発とされる2月と8月〕 February and August (when business is supposed to be sluggish); the sluggish months of February and August.
にっぱちしょうほう 【二八商法】 〔株取引などの買い付け資金の2割を出資すれば残りの8割を低利で融資すると持ちかけ, 出資金をだまし取る詐欺〕 a fraudulent investment scheme in which clients are enticed to invest 20 percent up front with the promise that they will be lent the remaining 80 percent at low interest.
にっぱちづき 【二八月】 ＝にっぱち.
にっぱん 【日販】 〔1日の販売量〕 daily sales; daily turnover.
にっぽん 【日本】 ▭ 日本勢 ⇨ーぜい.
にっぽんサッカーでんどう 【日本-殿堂】 the Japanese Soccer Hall of Fame.
にっぽんデータつうしんきょうかい 【日本-通信協会】 the Nippon Information Communications Association (略: NIC).
にっぽんビリヤードきょうかい 【日本-協会】 the Nippon Billiards Association (略: NBA).
にっぽんぼうえきほけん 【日本貿易保険】 Nippon Export and Investment Insurance (略: NEXI).
にとうへんかんろん 【二島返還論】 〔北方領土の〕 the argument for the return of the Habomai island group and the island of Shikotan to Japan.
にどがき 【二度書き】 〔書道〕 〔なぞり書き〕 tracing. ～する trace.
ニトロキノリン 【化】 nitroquinoline.
ニトロソグアニジン 【化】 〔発癌性のある突然変異誘発物質〕 nitrosoguanidine. ▶ 体系名 N-methyl-N'-nitro-N-nitrosoguanidine の methyl, nitro, nitrosoguanidine から MNNG とも呼ばれる.
ニトロフラン 【薬】 〔フラン系合成抗菌薬の総称〕 nitrofuran.

315　にほんいがくほうしゃせんがっかい

▭ ニトロフラン代謝物 a nitrofuran metabolite.
にどわらし 【二度童】 〔認知症の老人〕 a cognitively impaired elderly person who has returned to his childhood; a person in his second childhood.
にない 【担い】 ▭ 担い売り hawking; peddling goods carried on one's shoulders; 〔人〕 a ⌈hawker [peddler] (who goes around carrying goods on his or her shoulders).
ニナワ 〔イラク北部の州〕 Ninawa. ▶ 州都 モスル.
ネヴェ 〔イラク北部の州ニナワの別称〕 Nineveh. 〔⇨ニナワ〕
にはいにはくしゅいっぱい 【二拝二拍手一拝】 〔神道〕 〔神社参礼の〕 two bows, two hand claps and a final bow.
ニパ・ウイルス 【菌】 Nipah virus. ▭ ニパ・ウイルス感染症 【医】 〔脳炎の一種〕 Nipah virus infection; Nipah encephalitis.
にはちそば 【二八蕎麦】 soba made from 20% wheat and 80% buckwheat.
にばん 【二番】 ▭ 二番手 ＝にせんてい.
「200本のたばこ」 〔映画〕 200 Cigarettes.
ニブフ ＝ニヴフ.
にぶん 【二分】 ▭ 二分脊椎(症) 【医】 〔脊椎骨の先天的形成不全のため脊髄が脊柱の外に出て癒着や損傷を生じる様々な神経障害〕 spina bifida.
ニポラジン 〔商標・薬〕 〔メキタジンの商品名〕 Nipolazin.
にほん 【日本】 ▭ 日本買(売)り 【経】 buying [selling] Japan (in the form of currency or stocks). 日本会計基準 Japanese Accounting Standards. ▶ 日本会計基準審議会 (the Japanese Accounting Standards Board; 略: ASBJ) ＝企業会計基準委員会 (⇨きぎょう¹) が定める. 日本食 a Japanese meal; Japanese cuisine. ▭ 一食ブーム fashionability of Japanese cuisine. 日本選抜 (チーム) a Japanese ⌈all-star [representative] team. 日本茶インストラクター a Japanese tea instructor. 日本版スペースシャトル a [the] Japanese version of the Space Shuttle. 日本名 one's Japanese name. ▭ ラフカディオ・ハーン, 〜名, 小泉八雲 Lafcadio Hearn, Japanese name Koizumi Yakumo.
にほんアイ・エフ・エーにんしょうきこう 【日本 IFA 認証機構】 the Association of Certified Independent Financial Advisors.
にほんあいがんどうぶつきょうかい 【日本愛玩動物協会】 the Japan Pet Care Association.
にほんアイスホッケーれんめい 【日本-連盟】 the Japan Ice Hockey Federation (略: JIHF).
にほんアイ・ビー・エムかがくしょう 【日本 IBM 科学賞】 the Japan IBM Science Award.
にほんあかがえる 【日本赤蛙】 【動】 a Japanese brown frog; Rana japonica.
にほんアパレルさんぎょうきょうかい 【日本-産業協会】 the Japan Apparel Industry Council (略: JAIC).
にほんアミューズメントマシンこうぎょうかい 【日本-工業協会】 the Japan Amusement Machinery Manufacturers Association (略: JAMMA).
にほんアルツハイマーびょうきょうかい 【日本-病協会】 ＝にんちしょうのひとぞくのかい.
にほんアレルギーがっかい 【日本-学会】 the Japanese Society of Allergology (略: JSA).
にほんアロマセラピーがっかい 【日本-学会】 the Japanese Society of Aromatherapy.
にほんイー・ユーていきしゅのうきょうぎ 【日本・EU 定期首脳協議】 the 〔13th〕 ⌈Japan-EU [EU-Japan] Summit Meeting.
にほんいがくかい 【日本医学会】 the Japanese Association of Medical Sciences (略: JAMS).
にほんいがくとしょかんきょうかい 【日本医学図書館協会】 the Japan Medical Library Association (略: JMLA).
にほんいがくほうしゃせん 【日本医学放射線

学会】the Japan Radiological Society（略：JRS）．
にほんいしかいちけんそくしんセンター【日本医師会治験促進―】the Center for Clinical Trials, Japan Medical Association（略：JMA CCT）．
にほんいりょうきのうひょうかきこう【日本医療機能評価機構】the Japan Council for Quality Health Care（略：JCQHC）．
にほんいりょうきゅうえんきこう【日本医療救援機構】Medical Relief Unit, Japan（略：MeRU）．
にほんウオーキングきょうかい【日本-協会】the Japan Walking Association．
にほんうまぬしきょうかいれんごうかい【日本馬主協会連合会】the Japan Owners' Association（略：JOA）．
にほんエアロビックれんめい【日本-連盟】the Japan Aerobic Federation（略：JAF）．
にほんエヌ・アイ・イーがっかい【日本 NIE 学会】the Japan Society for Studies in "Newspaper in Education"; the Japan Society for the Study of Newspapers in Education．
にほんエネルギーけいざいけんきゅうじょ【日本-経済研究所】〔財団法人〕the Institute of Energy Economics, Japan（略：IEEJ）．
にほんエフ・ピーきょうかい【日本 FP 協会】=にほんファイナンシャル・プランナーきょうかい．
にほんエマージェンシー・アシスタンス【日本-】〔日本人が海外で遭遇する緊急事態に対して支援業務を行う会社〕Emergency Assistance Japan（略：EAJ）．
にほんエレベータきょうかい【日本-協会】the Japan Elevator Association（略：JEA）．
「日本奥地紀行」〔英国女性 イザベラ・バード（Isabella Lucy Bird; 1831-1904）の日本旅行記〕Unbeaten Tracks in Japan．
にほんオストミーきょうかい【日本-協会】the Japan Ostomy Association（略：JOA）．
にほんおろしでんりょくとりひきじょ【日本卸電力取引所】the Japan Electric Power Exchange（略：JEPX）．
にほんおんがくかきょうかい【日本音楽家協会】the Japan Musicians Association．
にほんおんがくざいだん【日本音楽財団】the Nippon Music Foundation（略：NMF）．
にほんおんがくりょうほうがっかい【日本音楽療法学会】the Japanese Music Therapy Association（略：JMTA）．
にほんおんせんこうぶつりいがっかい【日本温泉気候物理医学会】the Japanese Society of Balneology, Climatology and Physical Medicine（略：BCPM）．
にほんおんだんかガスさくげんききん【日本温暖化-削減基金】the Japan GHG Reduction Fund（略：JGRF）．▶ GHG は greenhouse gas(es)（温室効果ガス）の略．
にほんかいがいツアーオペレーターきょうかい【日本海外-協会】the Overseas Tour Operators Association of Japan（略：OTOA）．
にほんがいしょうがっかい【日本外傷学会】the Japanese Association for the Surgery of Trauma（略：JAST）．
にほんがいしょうデータバンク【日本外傷-】the Japan Trauma Bank．
にほんかいちゅうぶじしん【日本海中部地震】〔1983 年 5 月の〕the Japan-Sea Earthquake (of 1983)．
にほんかいなんぼうしきょうかい【日本海難防止協会】the Japan Association of Marine Safety（略：JAMS）．
にほんかがくえいぞうきょうかい【日本科学映像協会】the Japan Science Film & Video Institution．
にほんかがくぎじゅつしんこうざいだん【日本科学技術振興財団】the Japan Science Foundation（略：JSF）．
にほんかがくぎじゅつれんめい【日本科学技術連盟】

the Union of Japanese Scientists and Engineers（略：JUSE）．
にほんかがくみらいかん【日本科学未来館】the National Museum of Emerging Science and Innovation（略：MeSci; Miraikan）．
にほんがくこうごうがっかい【日本顎咬合学会】the Academy of Gnathology and Occlusion．
にほんがくじゅつしんこうかい【日本学術振興会】▷□ 日本学術振興会賞 the 'Japan Society for the Promotion of Science [JSPS] Prize．
にほんがくせいかがくしょう【日本学生科学賞】〔中高生の科学研究コンテスト〕the Japan Students Science Awards（略：JSSA）．
にほんがくせいしえんきこう【日本学生支援機構】the Japan Student Services Organization（略：JASSO）．
にほんがくせいやきゅうきょうかい【日本学生野球協会】the Japan Student Baseball Association．
にほんがっかいじむセンター【日本学会事務-】〔財団法人〕the Business Center for Academic Societies Japan．▶ 2004 年破産．
にほんがっこうほけんかい【日本学校保健会】the Japanese Society of School Health．
にほんカヌーれんめい【日本-連盟】the Japan Canoe Federation（略：JCF）．
にほんかもつこうくう【日本貨物航空】Nippon Cargo Airlines（略：NCA）．
にほんカラーラボきょうかい【日本-協会】the Japan Colorphoto Finishers' Association（略：JCFA）．
にほんがんがっかい【日本癌学会】the Japanese Cancer Association（略：JCA）．
にほんがんぐきょうかい【日本玩具協会】the Japan Toy Association．
にほんかんごきょうかい【日本看護協会】the Japanese Nursing Association（略：JNA）．
にほんかんごれんめい【日本看護連盟】the Japan Nursing Federation．
にほんがんちりょうがっかい【日本癌治療学会】the Japan Society of Clinical Oncology（略：JSCO）．
にほんきいん【日本棋院】the Nihon Ki-in; the Japan Go Association．
にほんぎしそうぐしかっかい【日本義肢装具士会】the Japanese Academy of Prosthetists and Orthotists．
にほんきしょうがっかい【日本気象学会】the Meteorological Society of Japan（略：MSJ）．
にほんきょういくがっかい【日本教育学会】the Japan Society for the Study of Education（略：JSSE）．
にほんきょういくぎじゅつがっかい【日本教育技術学会】the Teachers Organization of Skill Sharing（略：TOSS）．
にほんきょうかい【日本協会】=ジャパン・ソサェティー．
にほんきょうせいしがっかい【日本矯正歯科学会】the Japanese Orthodontic Society（略：JOS）．
「日本紀略」〔平安時代に書かれた歴史書〕The Abbreviated History of Japan．
にほんくさちちくさんしゅしきょうかい【日本草地畜産種子協会】the Japan Grassland Agriculture and Forage Seed Association（略：GAFSA）．
にほんくるまいすバスケットボールれんめい【日本車椅子-連盟】the Japan Wheelchair Basketball Federation（略：JWBF）．
にほんクレーしゃげききょうかい【日本-射撃協会】the Japan Clay Target Shooting Association（略：JCTSA）．
にほんクレジットカードきょうかい【日本-協会】the Japan Credit Card Association（略：JCCA）．
にほんクレジットさんぎょうきょうかい【日本-産業協会】the Japan Consumer Credit Industry Association（略：JCIA）．

にほんけいざいけんきゅうセンター【日本経済研究-】the Japan Center for Economic Research (略：JCER).

にほんけいざいせいねんきょうぎかい【日本経済青年協議会】the Junior Executive Council of Japan.

にほんけいざいちょうさきょうぎかい【日本経済調査協議会】the Japan Economic Research Institute (略：JERI).

にほんげいじゅつぶんかしんこうかい【日本芸術文化振興会】the Japan Arts Council.

にほんけいせいげかがっかい【日本形成外科学会】the Japan Society of Plastic and Reconstructive Surgery (略：JSPRS).

にほんけいりんがっこう【日本競輪学校】〔修善寺にある競輪選手養成学校〕the Japan Keirin School.

にほんげかがっかい【日本外科学会】the Japan Surgical Society (略：JSS).

にほんけっせんしけつがっかい【日本血栓止血学会】the Japanese Society on Thrombosis and Hemostasis (略：JSTH).

にほんけんこう・えいようしょくひんきょうかい【日本健康・栄養食品協会】the Japan Health Food & Nutrition Food Association (略：JHNFA).

にほんげんしりょくぎじゅつきこう【日本原子力技術協会】the Japan Nuclear Technology Institute (略：JANTI).

にほんげんしりょくけんきゅうかいはつきこう【日本原子力研究開発機構】the Japan Atomic Energy Agency (略：JAEA).

にほんげんしりょくぶんかしんこうざいだん【日本原子力文化振興財団】the Japan Atomic Energy Relations Organization (略：JAERO).

にほんけんちくかきょうかい【日本建築家協会】the Japan Institute of Architects (略：JIA).

にほんけんちくぼうさいきょうかい【日本建築防災協会】the Japan Building Disaster Prevention Association.

にほんご【日本語】 ▯日本語教師 a Japanese-language「teacher [instructor]. 日本語教室 a Japanese language class. 日本語特区 a special zone for Japanese language education. 日本語名称 the [a] Japanese name for《schizophrenia》.

にほんこうえんりょくちきょうかい【日本公園緑地協会】the Parks and Open Space Association of Japan (略：POSA).

にほんこうかれいいがくかい【日本抗加齢医学会】the Japanese Society of Anti-Aging Medicine.

にほんこうくう・いんとうかがっかい【日本口腔・咽頭科学会】the Japan Society of Stomato-Pharyngology.

にほんこううちゅうがっかい【日本航空宇宙学会】the Japan Society for Aeronautical and Space Sciences (略：JSASS).

にほんこううちゅうこうぎょうかい【日本航空宇宙工業会】the Society of Japanese Aerospace Companies (略：SJAC).

にほんこうくうきそうじゅうしきょうかい【日本航空機操縦士協会】the Japan Aircraft Pilot Association (略：JAPA).

にほんこうけつあつがっかい【日本高血圧学会】the Japanese Society of Hypertension (略：JSH).

にほんこうこくぎょうきょうかい【日本広告業協会】the Japan Advertising Agencies Association (略：JAAA).

にほんこうこくぬしきょうかい【日本広告主協会】the Japan Advertisers Association (略：JAA).

にほんこうしゅうえいせいきょうかい【日本公衆衛生協会】the Japan Public Health Association (略：JPHA).

にほんこうそくどうろほゆう・さいむへんさいきこう【日本高速道路保有・債務返済機構】the Japan Expressway Holding and Debt Repayment Agency. ▶2005 年設立.

にほんこうつうあんぜんきょういくふきゅうきょうかい【日本交通安全教育普及協会】the Japan Traffic Safety Education Association.

にほんこうとうきょういくひょうかきこう【日本高等教育評価機構】the Japan Institution for Higher Education Evaluation (略：JIHEE).

にほんこうにんかいけいしきょうかい【日本公認会計士協会】the Japanese Institute of Certified Public Accountants (略：JICPA).

にほんこうりゅうきょうかい【日本交流協会】〔日本・台湾間の〕Interchange Association, Japan (略：IAJ).
▯日本交流協会台北事務所〔台湾における日本大使館に相当する機関〕Interchange Association (Japan), Taipei Office.

にほんゴールドディスクたいしょう【日本-大賞】the Japan Gold Disc Award.

にほんこがたじどうしゃしんこうかい【日本小型自動車振興会】the Japan Motorcycle Racing Organization.

にほんごきょういくしんこうきょうかい【日本語教育振興協会】the Association for the Promotion of Japanese Language Education (略：APJLE).

にほんこくけんぽう【日本国憲法】 ▯日本国憲法前文 the preamble of the Constitution of Japan.

にほんこくさいきがたいさくきこう【日本国際飢餓対策機構】Japan International Food for the Hungry (略：JIFH).

にほんこくさいこうりゅうセンター【日本国際交流-】the Japan Center for International Exchange (略：JCIE).

にほんこくさいじどうとしょひょうぎかい【日本国際児童図書評議会】the Japanese Board on Books for Young People (略：JBBY).

にほんこくさいはくらんかいきょうかい【日本国際博覧会協会】the Japan Association for the (2005) World Exposition.

にほんこくさいフォーラム【日本国際-】the Japan Forum on International Relations (略：JFIR).

にほんこくさいボランティアセンター【日本国際-】the Japan International Volunteer Center (略：JVC).

にほんこくさいみんかんきょうりょくかい【日本国際民間協力会】Nippon International Cooperation for Community Development (略：NICCO).

にほんこくもつけんていきょうかい【日本穀物検定協会】the Japan Grain Inspection Association (略：KOKKEN).

にほんこつずいバンク【日本骨髄-】the Japan Marrow Donor Program (略：JMDP).

にほんこどもかていそうごうけんきゅうじょ【日本子ども家庭総合研究所】the Japan Child and Family Research Institute (略：JCFRI).

にほんごのうりょくけんていしけん【日本語能力検定試験】the Japanese Language Proficiency Test.

にほんコミュニティほうそうきょうかい【日本-放送協会】the Japan Community Broadcasting Association (略：JCBA).

にほんゴルフツアーきこう【日本-機構】the Japan Golf Tour Organization (略：JGTO).

にほんさ【二本鎖】〖生化〗a double strand. ▯二本鎖 DNA double-stranded DNA.

にほんさいがいいりょうしえんきこう【日本災害医療支援機構】the Japan Voluntary Medical Assistance Team (略：JVMAT).

にほんざいがいきぎょうきょうかい【日本在外企業協会】the Japan Overseas Enterprises Association (略：

にほんさいがいじょうほうがっかい

JOEA).

にほんさいがいじょうほうがっかい【日本災害情報学会】the Japan Society for Disaster Information Studies (略: JASDIS).

にほんさいきんがっかい【日本細菌学会】the Japanese Society of [for] Bacteriology (略: JSB).

にほんサイクリングきょうかい【日本—協会】the Japan Cycling Association (略: JCA).

にほんさいたいけつバンクネットワーク【日本さい帯血—】the Japanese Cord Blood Bank Network.

にほんさくらのかい【日本さくらの会】the Japan Cherry Blossom Association.

にほんざっこくきょうかい【日本雑穀協会】the Japan Millet Association.

にほんさんかふじんかがっかい【日本産科婦人科学会】the Japan Society of Obstetrics and Gynecology (略: JSOG).

にほんさんぎょうえいせいがっかい【日本産業衛生学会】the Japan Society for Occupational Health.

にほんさんぎょうきょうかい【日本産業協会】〔財団法人〕the Japan Industrial Association.

にほんさんぎょうストレスがっかい【日本産業—学会】the Japan Association of Job Stress Research.

にほんさんぎょうはいきぶつしょりしんこうセンター【日本産業廃棄物処理振興—】the Japan Industrial Waste Technology Center.

にほんシー・エフ・オーきょうかい【日本 CFO 協会】the Japan Association for Chief Financial Officers (略: JACFO).

にほんシー・エムほうそうれんめい【日本 CM 放送連盟】the All Japan Radio and Television Commercial Confederation (略: ACC).

にほんしかいしかい【日本歯科医師会】the Japan Dental Association (略: JDA).

にほんしかいしれんめい【日本歯科医師連盟】the Japan Dentists Federation (略: JDF).

にほんしきさいがっかい【日本色彩学会】the Color Science Association of Japan (略: CSAJ).

にほんししつえいようがっかい【日本脂質栄養学会】the Japan Society for Lipid Nutrition (略: JSLN).

にほんじしんこうがくかい【日本地震工学会】the Japan Association for Earthquake Engineering (略: JAEE).

にほんしたいふじゆうじきょうかい【日本肢体不自由児協会】the Japanese Society for Disabled Children.

にほんじてんしゃきょうれんめい【日本自転車競技連盟】the Japan Cycling Federation (略: JCF).

にほんじてんしゃしんこうかい【日本自転車振興会】the Japan Keirin Association.

にほんじどうしゃはんばいきょうかいれんごうかい【日本自動車販売協会連合会】the Japan Automobile Dealers Association (略: JADA).

にほんじどうしゅっぱんびじゅつかれんめい【日本児童出版美術家連盟】the Japan Children's Book Artists Society (略: JCBAS).

にほんじどうはんばいきこうぎょうかい【日本自動販売機工業会】the Japan Vending Machine Manufacturers Association (略: JVMA).

にほんじどうはんばいきょうかい【日本自動販売協会】the Japan Automatic Merchandising Association (略: JAMA).

にほんじどうぶんがくしゃきょうかい【日本児童文学者協会】the Japanese Association of Writers for Children (略: JAWC).

にほんシナリオさっかきょうかい【日本—作家協会】the Japan Writers Guild.

にほんじびいんこうがっかい【日本耳鼻咽喉科学会】the Oto-Rhino-Laryngological Society of Japan, Inc.

318

にほんしほうしえんセンター【日本司法支援—】the Japan Legal Support Center.

にほんしほうしょしかいれんごうかい【日本司法書士会連合会】the Japan Federation of Shiho-Shoshi Lawyer's Association.

にほんジャーナリストかいぎ【日本—会議】the Japan Congress of Journalists. (略: JCJ).

にほんしゃかいしゅぎせいねんどうめい【日本社会主義青年同盟】the Japan League of Socialist Youth (略: JLSY).

にほんじゅういがっかい【日本獣医学会】the Japanese Society of Veterinary Science.

にほんじゅういしかい【日本獣医師会】the Japan Veterinary Medical Association.

にほんしゅうがくりょこうきょうかい【日本修学旅行協会】the Japan School Tours Bureau (略: JSTB).

にほんしゅうだんさいがいいがっかい【日本集団災害医学会】the Japanese Association for Disaster Medicine (略: JADM).

にほんじゅせいちゃくしょうがっかい【日本受精着床学会】the Japan Society of Fertilization and Implantation (略: JSFI).

にほんしゅっぱんとりつぎきょうかい【日本出版取次協会】the Japan Publication Wholesalers Association (略: JPWA).

にほんじゅんかんきかんりけんきゅうきょうぎかい【日本循環器管理研究協議会】the Japanese Association for Cerebro-cardiovascular Disease Control (略: JACD).

にほんしょう【日本賞】〔教育番組国際コンクール〕the Japan Prize International Educational Program Contest.

にほんしょうがいしゃきょうぎかい【日本障害者協議会】the Japan Council on Disability (略: JD).

にほんしょうがいしゃスポーツきょうかい【日本障害者—協会】the Japan Sports Association for the Disabled (略: JSAD).

にほんしょうがいしゃリハビリテーションきょうかい【日本障害者—協会】the Japanese Society for Rehabilitation of Persons with Disabilities (略: JSRPD).

にほんしょうがいフォーラム【日本障害—】the Japan Disability Forum (略: JDF).

にほんしょうけんアナリストきょうかい【日本証券—協会】the Security Analysts Association of Japan (略: SAAJ).

にほんしょうけんきんゆうがいしゃ【日本証券金融会社】Japan Securities Finance Co., Ltd.

にほんしょうけんクリアリングきこう【日本証券—機構】the Japan Securities Clearing Corporation (略: JSCC).

にほんしょうこうかいぎしょ【日本商工会議所】日本商工会議所簿記検定試験 the「Nissho [Japan Chamber of Commerce and Industry] Bookkeeping Certification Examination.

にほんしょうじちゅうさいきょうかい【日本商事仲裁協会】the Japan Commercial Arbitration Association (略: JCAA).

にほんしょうどうぶつじゅういしかい【日本小動物獣医師会】the Japan Small Animal Veterinary Association (略: JSAVA).

にほんしょうにかがっかい【日本小児科学会】the Japan Pediatric Society (略: JPS).

にほんしょうにきゅうきゅういがっかい【日本小児救急医学会】the Japanese Society of Emergency Pediatrics (略: JSEP).

にほんしょうにじゅんかんきがっかい【日本小児循環器学会】the Japanese Society of Pediatric Cardiology and Cardiac Surgery (略: JSPCCS).

にほんしょうにしんけいがっかい【日本小児神経学会】

にほんせんきょがっかい

the Japanese Society of Child Neurology (略：JSCN).
にほんしょうにほけんきょうかい【日本小児保健協会】the Japanese Society of Child Health.
にほんしょうねんやきゅうれんめい【日本少年野球連盟】the Japan Boys Baseball League.
にほんしょうひしゃきょうかい【日本消費者協会】the Japan Consumers' Association (略：JCA).
にほんしょうひしゃきんゆうきょうかい【日本消費者金融協会】the Japan Consumer Finance Association (略：JCFA).
にほんしょうひせいかつアドバイザー・コンサルタントきょうかい【日本消費生活一協会】〔社団法人〕the Nippon Association of Consumer Specialists (略：NACS).
にほんしょうひんいたくしゃほごききん【日本商品委託者保護基金】〔商品先物市場での委託者債権保護のための〕the National Futures Protection Fund.
にほんしょうひんさきものしんこうきょうかい【日本商品先物振興協会】the Japan Commodity Futures Industry Association (略：JCFIA).
にほんしょうひんさきものとりひきききょうかい【日本商品先物取引協会】the Commodity Futures Association of Japan.
にほんしょうひんとうしはんばいぎょうきょうかい【日本商品投資販売業協会】the Japan Commodities Fund Association (略：JCFA).
にほんじょうほうしょりかいはつきょうかい【日本情報処理開発協会】the Japan Information Processing Development Corporation (略：JIPDEC).
にほんじょくそうがっかい【日本褥瘡学会】the Japanese Society of Pressure Ulcers.
にほんしょくちょうきょうかい【日本食鳥協会】the Japan Chicken Association (略：JCA).
にほんしょくひんてんかぶつきょうかい【日本食品添加物協会】the Japan Food Additives Association (略：JAFA).
にほんじょしサッカーリーグ【日本女子一】the Japan Women's Football League. ▶ 通称 L リーグ.
にほんじょしテニスれんめい【日本女子一連盟】the Japan Ladies Tennis Federation (略：JLTF).
にほんじょしプロゴルフきょうかい【日本女子一協会】the Ladies Professional Golfers' Association of Japan (略：LPGA).
にほんしょせきしゅっぱんきょうかい【日本書籍出版協会】the Japan Book Publishers Association (略：JBPA).
にほんしょてんしょうぎょうくみあいれんごうかい【日本書店商業組合連合会】the Japan Booksellers Federation.
にほんしりつがっこうしんこう・きょうさいじぎょうだん【日本私立学校振興・共済事業団】the Promotion and Mutual Aid Corporation for Private Schools of Japan.
にほんしんけいかがくがっかい【日本神経科学学会】the Japan Neuroscience Society (略：JNS).
にほんしんけつかんカテーテルちりょうがっかい【日本心血管一治療学会】the Japanese Association of Cardiovascular Catheterization Therapeutics (略：JACCT).
にほんじんこうがっかい【日本人口学会】the Population Association of Japan (略：PAJ).
にほんじんざいしょうかいじぎょうきょうかい【日本人材紹介事業協会】the Japan Executive Search and Recruitment Association (略：JESRA).
にほんじんざいはけんきょうかい【日本人材派遣協会】the Japan Staffing Services Association (略：JASSA).
にほんじんぞうがっかい【日本腎臓学会】the Japanese Society of Nephrology (略：JSN).

にほんしんぞうざいだん【日本心臓財団】〔1970 年設立の財団法人〕the Japan Heart Foundation.
にほんしんぞうびょうがっかい【日本心臓病学会】the Japanese College of Cardiology (略：JCC).
にほんしんどうきょうかい【日本伸銅協会】the Japan Copper and Brass Association (略：JCBA).
にほんしんぶんきょういくぶんかざいだん【日本新聞教育文化財団】the Japan Newspaper Foundation for Education & Culture.
にほんしんぶんはくぶつかん【日本新聞博物館】the Japan Newspaper Museum.
にほんすいみんがっかい【日本睡眠学会】the Japanese Society of Sleep Research (略：JSSR).
にほんスイミングクラブきょうかい【日本一協会】the Japan Swimming Club Association (略：JSCA).
にほんすいりさっかきょうかい【日本推理作家協会】 ・一しょうの Mystery Writers of Japan, Inc. ▣ 日本推理作家協会賞 the Mystery Writers of Japan Award.
にほんスケートれんめい【日本一連盟】the Japan Skating Federation (略：JSF).
にほんスピッツ【日本一】〔犬〕a Japanese spitz (dog).
にほんスポーツしょうねんだん【日本一少年団】the Japan Junior Sports Clubs Association (略：JJSA).
にほんスポーツしんこうセンター【日本一振興一】the National Agency for the Advancement of Sports and Health (略：NAASH). ▶ 2003 年に日本体育・学校健康センターより移行.
にほんスポーツちゅうさいきこう【日本一仲裁機構】the Japan Sports Arbitration Agency (略：JSAA).
にほんせいかつじょうほうしきょうかい【日本生活情報紙協会】the Japan Free Newspapers Association (略：JAFNA).
にほんせいかんせんしょうがっかい【日本性感染症学会】the Japanese Society for Sexually Transmitted Diseases (略：JSSTD).
にほんせいけいげかがっかい【日本整形外科学会】the Japanese Orthopaedic Association (略：JOA).
にほんせいさくきんゆうこうこほう【日本政策金融公庫法】〔法〕the Japan Finance Corporation Law.
にほんせいしょきょうかい【日本聖書協会】the Japan Bible Society (略：JBS).
にほんせいしょくいがくかい【日本生殖医学会】the Japan Society for Reproductive Medicine (略：JSRM).
にほんせいしょくほじょいりょうひょうじゅんかきかん【日本生殖補助医療標準化機関】the Japanese Institution for Standardizing Assisted Reproductive Technology (略：JISART).
にほんせいしんかびょういんきょうかい【日本精神科病院協会】the Japanese Association of Psychiatric Hospitals (略：JAPH).
にほんせいしんしんけいがっかい【日本精神神経学会】the Japanese Society of Psychiatry and Neurology (略：JSPN).
にほんせいたいがっかい【日本生態学会】the Ecological Society of Japan (略：ESJ).
にほんぜいりしかいれんごうかい【日本税理士会連合会】the Japan Federation of Certified Public Tax Accountants' Associations.
にほんせいりじんるいがっかい【日本生理人類学会】the Japan Society of Physiological Anthropology (略：JSPA).
にほんセーリングれんめい【日本一連盟】the Japan Sailing Federation (略：JSAF).
にほんせきめんきょうかい【日本石綿協会】the Japan Asbestos Association (略：JAA).
にほんせっけんせんざいこうぎょうかい【日本石鹸洗剤工業会】the Japan Soap and Detergent Association (略：JSDA).
にほんせんきょがっかい【日本選挙学会】the Japanese

Association of Electoral Studies.
にほんせんぱくかいようこうがく【日本船舶海洋工学会】the Japan Society of Naval Architects and Ocean Engineers (略: JSNAOE).
にほんせんもんいにんていせいきこう【日本専門医認定機構】the Japanese Board of Medical Specialties.
にほんぞうけつさいぼういしょくがっかい【日本造血細胞移植学会】the Japan Society for Hematopoietic Cell Transplantation (略: JSHCT).
にほんソフトボールきょうかい【日本－協会】the Japan Softball Association.
にほんそんがいほけんだいりぎょうきょうかい【日本損害保険代理業協会】the Independent Insurance Agents of Japan, Inc.
にほんたいせきがっかい【日本堆積学会】the Sedimentological Society of Japan (略: SSJ).
にほん・たいへいようしょとうフォーラムしゅのうかいぎ【日本・太平洋諸島－首脳会議】the 《Fourth》 Japan-Pacific Islands Forum Summit Meeting. ► 通称は「太平洋・島サミット」(the Pacific Island Leaders Meeting, PALM).
にほんたいりょくいがくかい【日本体力医学会】the Japanese Society of Physical Fitness and Sports Medicine (略: JSPFSM).
にほんたからくじきょうかい【日本宝くじ協会】the Japan Lottery Association (略: JLA).
にほんたっきゅうきょうかい【日本卓球協会】the Japan Table Tennis Association (略: JTTA).
にほんたばこきょうかい【日本たばこ協会】the Tobacco Institute of Japan (略: TIOJ).
にほんだんせいがっしょうきょうかい【日本男声合唱協会】the Japan Male Chorus Association (略: JAMCA).
にほんチェーンドラッグストアきょうかい【日本－協会】the Japan Association of Chain Drug Stores (略: JACDS).
にほんちきゅうわくせいかがくれんごう【日本地球惑星科学連合】the Japan Geoscience Union (略: JPGU).
にほんちしつがっかい【日本地質学会】the Geological Society of Japan.
にほんちてきざいさんきょうかい【日本知的財産協会】the Japan Intellectual Property Association (略: JIPA).
にほんちてきざいさんちゅうさいセンター【日本知的財産仲裁－】the Japan Intellectual Property Arbitration Center.
にほんちゅうかねん【日本中華年】［2007年］Chinese Year 2007 in Japan.
にほんちゅうどくじょうほうセンター【日本中毒情報－】the Japan Poison Information Center (略: JPIC).
にほんちょうるいごれんめい【日本鳥類保護連盟】the Japanese Society for Preservation of Birds (略: JSPB).
にほんちりがっかい【日本地理学会】the Association of Japanese Geographers (略: AJG).
にほんつうかんぎょうれんごうかい【日本通関業連合会】the Japan Customs Brokers Association (略: JCBA).
にほんつうしんはんばいきょうかい【日本通信販売協会】the Japan Direct Marketing Association (略: JADMA).
にほんつりしんこうかい【日本釣振興会】the Japan Sportsfishing Association (略: JSA).
にほんディー・エヌ・エー・データバンク【日本 DNA －】the DNA Data Bank of Japan (略: DDBJ).
にほんてきごうせいにんていきょうかい【日本適合性認定協会】〔経済産業省および国土交通省所管の〕the Japan Accreditation Board for Conformity Assessment (略: JAB).
にほんてんかんきょうかい【日本てんかん協会】the Japanese Epilepsy Association (略: JEA).
にほんでんきおおがたてんきょうかい【日本電気大型店協会】the Nippon Electric Big-Stores Association (略: NEBA).
にほんでんしこうぎょうしんこうきょうかい【日本電子工業振興協会】the Japan Electronic Industry Development Association (略: JEIDA). ► 2000年に日本電子機械工業会と統合して電子情報技術産業協会となった。
にほんてんじひょうきほう【日本点字表記法】the Japanese braille system.
にほんてんもんがっかい【日本天文学会】the Astronomical Society of Japan (略: ASJ).
にほんとうけいきょうかい【日本統計協会】the Japan Statistical Association (略: JSA).
にほんとうししゃほごききん【日本投資者保護基金】the Japan Investor Protection Fund (略: JIPF).
にほんとうにょうびょうがっかい【日本糖尿病学会】the Japan Diabetes Society (略: JDS).
にほんとうにょうびょうきょうかい【日本糖尿病協会】the Japan Association for Diabetes Education and Care (略: JADEC).
にほんどうぶつあいごきょうかい【日本動物愛護協会】the Japan Society for the Prevention of Cruelty to Animals (略: JSPCA).
にほんどうろこうつうじょうほうセンター【日本道路交通情報－】the Japan Road Traffic Information Center (略: JARTIC).
にほんとくようりんさんしんこうかい【日本特用林産振興会】the Japan Special Forest Product Promotion Association.
にほんとこういがっかい【日本渡航医学会】the Japanese Society of Travel and Health (略: JSTH).
にほんとりしまりやくきょうかい【日本取締役協会】the Japan Association of Corporate Directors (略: JACD).
にほんないしきょうげかっかい【日本内視鏡外科学会】the Japan Society for Endoscopic Surgery (略: JSES).
にほんないぶんぴがっかい【日本内分泌学会】the Japan Endocrine Society (略: JES).
にほんなんびょうかんごがっかい【日本難病看護学会】the Japan Intractable Illness Nursing Society.
にほんにじゅういっせいきビジョン【日本21世紀－】〔政府の経済財政諮問会議がまとめた日本の将来像〕A Vision for Japan in the 21st Century.
にほんにゅうがんがっかい【日本乳癌学会】the Japanese Breast Cancer Society (略: JBCS).
にほんにんちしょうがっかい【日本認知症学会】the Japanese Society of Dementia Research. ► 日本痴呆学会から2005年改称。
にほんにんちしょうケアがっかい【日本認知症ケア学会】the Japanese Society for Dementia Care.
にほんねっしょうがっかい【日本熱傷学会】the Japanese Society for Burn Injuries (略: JSBI).
にほんねったいせいたいがっかい【日本熱帯生態学会】the Japan Society of Tropical Ecology (略: JASTE).
にほんのうぎょうきかいこうぎょうかい【日本農業機械工業会】the Japan Farm Machinery Manufacturers' Association (略: JFMMA).
にほんのうしんけいげかがっかい【日本脳神経外科学会】the Japan Neurosurgical Society (略: JNS).
にほんのうしんけいけっかんないちりょうがっかい【日本脳神経血管内治療学会】the Japanese Society for Neuroendovascular Therapy (略: JSNET).
にほんのうそっちゅうがっかい【日本脳卒中学会】the

Japan Stroke Society.
にほんのうドックがっかい【日本脳-学会】the Japanese Society for Detection of Asymptomatic Brain Diseases.
にほんのうりつきょうかい【日本能率協会】the Japan Management Association (略：JMA).
にほんのうりんきかくほう【日本農林規格法】【法】the 「Japanese Agricultural Standards [JAS] Law. ▶ 正式名称は，農林物資の規格化及び品質表示の適正化に関する法律 (the Law Concerning Standardization and Proper Labelling of Agricultural and Forestry Products).
にほんはいがんがっかい【日本肺癌学会】the Japan Lung Cancer Society (略：JLCS).
にほんパイプラインかいはつきこう【日本-開発機構】the Japan Pipeline Development Organization (略：JPDO).
にほんばじゅつれんめい【日本馬術連盟】the Japan Equestrian Federation (略：JEF).
にほんはとレースきょうかい【日本鳩-協会】the Japan Racing Pigeon Association (略：JRPA).
にほんはなのかい【日本花の会】the Flower Association of Japan.
にほんばぬしきょうかいれんごうかい【日本馬主協会連合会】＝にほんうまぬしきょうかいれんごうかい.
にほんバレーボール・リーグきこう【日本-機構】the Japan Volleyball League Organization (略：JVL).
にほんばんこくはくらんかいきねんきこう【日本万国博覧会記念機構】the Commemorative Organization for the Japan World Exposition '70.
にほんハンセンびょうがっかい【日本-病学会】the Japanese Leprosy Association.
にほんばんソックスほう【日本版 SOX 法】【法】the Japanese (version of the)「SOX [Sarbanes-Oxley] Act.
にほんはんどうたいせいぞうそうちきょうかい【日本半導体製造装置協会】the Semiconductor Equipment Association of Japan (略：SEAJ).
にほんピー・ティー・エーぜんこくきょうぎかい【日本 PTA 全国協議会】the Japan PTA National Council.
にほんひがいしゃがっかい【日本被害者学会】the Japanese Society of Victimology.
にほんビデオりんりきょうかい【日本-倫理協会】the Nihon Ethics of Video Association (略：NEVA).
にほんひにょうきがっかい【日本泌尿器科学会】the Japanese Urological Association (略：JUA).
にほんひふかがっかい【日本皮膚科学会】the Japanese Dermatological Association (略：JDA).
にほんひょうじゅんしょうひんぶんるい【日本標準商品分類】the Japanese Standard Commodity Classification.
にほんひょうじゅんしょくぎょうぶんるい【日本標準職業分類】the Japanese Standard Occupational Classification.
にほんびょうりがっかい【日本病理学会】the Japanese Society of Pathology (略：JSP).
にほんひんしつほしょうきこう【日本品質保証機構】the Japan Quality Assurance Organization (略：JQA).
にほんファイナンシャル・プランナーズきょうかい【日本-協会】the Japan Association for Financial Planners (略：JAFP).
にほんフィットネスヨーガきょうかい【日本-協会】the Japan Fitness Yoga Association.
にほんフィランソロピーきょうかい【日本-協会】the Japan Philanthropic Association.
にほんフードサービスきょうかい【日本-協会】the Japan Food Service Association (略：JF).

にほんふくごうカフェきょうかい【日本複合-協会】the Japan Complex Cafe Association (略：JCCA).
にほんフットボールリーグ【日本-】the Japan Football League (略：JFL).
にほんふどうさんかんていきょうかい【日本不動産鑑定協会】the Japanese Association of Real Estate Appraisal (略：JAREA).
にほんフランチャイズチェーンきょうかい【日本-協会】the Japan Franchise Association (略：JFA).
にほんプロテニスきょうかい【日本-協会】the Japan Professional Tennis Association (略：JPTA).
にほんプロバスケットボールリーグ【日本-】the Basketball Japan League; the BJ League.
にほんプロフェッショナルやきゅうきょうやく【日本-野球協約】＝やきゅうきょうやく.
にほんプロフェッショナルやきゅうそしき【日本-野球組織】Nippon Professional Baseball (略：NPB).
にほんプロボウリングきょうかい【日本-協会】the Japan Professional Bowling Association (略：JPBA).
にほんプロボクシングきょうかい【日本-協会】the Japan Pro Boxing Association (略：JPBA).
にほんぶんせきかがくかい【日本分析化学会】the Japan Society for Analytical Chemistry (略：JSAC).
にほんベジタブル・アンド・フルーツ・マイスターきょうかい【日本-&-協会】the Japan Vegetable & Fruit Meister Association.
にほんべんりしかい【日本弁理士会】the Japan Patent Attorneys Association (略：JPAA).
にほんほいくがっかい【日本保育学会】the Japan Society of Research on Early Childhood Care and Education.
にほんぼうえきしんこうきこう【日本貿易振興機構】the Japan External Trade Organization (略：JETRO). ▶ 2003 年に日本貿易振興会より移行.
にほんぼうきんぼうばいがっかい【日本防菌防黴学会】the Society for Antibacterial and Antifungal Agents, Japan (略：SAAAJ).
にほんぼうさいしきこう【日本防災士機構】Japan Organization of Disaster Relief Specialists.
にほんほうしゃかいがっかい【日本法社会学会】the Japanese Association of Sociology of Law.
にほんほうしゃせんしゅようがっかい【日本放射線腫瘍学会】the Japanese Society for Therapeutic Radiology and Oncology (略：JASTRO).
にほんボートきょうかい【日本-協会】the Japan Rowing Association (略：JARA).
にほんぼんさいきょうかい【日本盆栽協会】the Japan Bonsai Association.
にほんマウンテンバイクきょうかい【日本-協会】the Japan Mountain Bike Association (略：JMA).
にほんますいかがっかい【日本麻酔科学会】the Japanese Society of Anesthesiologists (略：JSA).
にほん・メキシコけいざいれんけいきょうてい【日本-・経済連携協定】the Japan-Mexico Economic Partnership Agreement (略：JMEPA).
にほんめんしんこうぞうきょうかい【日本免震構造協会】the Japan Society of Seismic Isolation (略：JSSI).
にほんもうじんかいれんごう【日本盲人会連合】the Japan Federation of the Blind.
にほんもうじんしょくのうかいはつセンター【日本盲人職能開発-】the Japan Vocational Development Center for the Blind.
にほんモーターサイクルスポーツきょうかい【日本-協会】the Motorcycle Federation of Japan (略：MFJ).
にほんもくぞうじゅうたくたいしんきょうじぎょうしゃきょうどうくみあい【日本木造住宅耐震補強事業者協同組合】the Japan Wooden Housing Earthquake Resistance Enhancement Construction Contractors Association; "Mokutaikyo."

にほんやきゅうきこう【日本野球機構】the Professional Baseball Organization of Japan;〔略称〕Nippon Professional Baseball (略: NPB).
にほんやまね【日本山鼠】〖動〗a (Japanese) dormouse《pl. -mice》; Glirulus japonicus.
にほんゆうせいかぶしきがいしゃ【日本郵政株式会社】Japan Post Holdings Co., Ltd (略: JP).
にほんゆうせいグループろうどうくみあい【日本郵政–労働組合】Japan Postal Group Union (略: JPGU).
にほんゆうせいこうしゃ【日本郵政公社】▭ 日本郵政公社労働組合 the Japan Postal Workers' Union (略: JPU). ▶ 2007年10月に全日本郵政労働組合 と統合して 日本郵政グループ労働組合 となった.
にほんゆうせいこうしゃほう【日本郵政公社法】〖法〗the Japan Post Law.
にほんゆけつがっかい【日本輸血学会】the Japan Society of Blood Transfusion.
にほんようきほうそうリサイクルきょうかい【日本容器包装–協会】〔財団法人〕the Japan Containers and Packaging Recycling Association (略: JCPRA).
にほんようけいきょうかい【日本養鶏協会】the Japan Poultry Association (略: JPA).
にほんライフセービングきょうかい【日本–協会】the Japan Lifesaving Association (略: JLA).
にほんライフルしゃげききょうかい【日本–射撃協会】the National Rifle Association of Japan.
にほんラジオこうこくすいしんきこう【日本–広告推進機構】〖広〗the Radio Advertising Bureau Japan (略: RABJ).
にほんらんぎょうきょうかい【日本卵業協会】the Japan Egg Industry Association.
にほんりす【日本栗鼠】〖動〗a Japanese squirrel; Sciurus lis.
にほんりっちセンター【日本立地–】〔財団法人〕the Japan Industrial Location Center (略: JILC).
にほんリハビリテーションいがくかい【日本–医学会】the Japanese Association of Rehabilitation Medicine (略: JARM).
にほんりょこうぎょうきょうかい【日本旅行業協会】the Japan Association of Travel Agents (略: JATA).
にほんりんしょうえいようきょうかい【日本臨床栄養–協会】the Japanese Clinical Nutrition Association (略: JCNA).
にほんりんしょうけんさいがくかい【日本臨床検査医学会】the Japanese Society of Laboratory Medicine (略: JSLM).
にほんりんしょうこうろうかいがくかい【日本臨床抗老化医学会】the Japanese Society of Clinical Anti-aging Medicine.
にほんりんしょうしゅようがっかい【日本臨床腫瘍学会】the Japanese Society of Medical Oncology (略: JSMO).
にほんりんしょうしゅようけんきゅうグループ【日本臨床腫瘍研究–】the Japan Clinical Oncology Group (略: JCOG).
にほんりんしょうしんりしかい【日本臨床心理士会】the Japan Society of Certified Clinical Psychologists (略: JSCCP).
にほんりんしょうせいしんしんけいやくりがっかい【日本臨床精神神経薬理学会】the Japanese Society of Clinical Neuropsychopharmacology (略: JSCNP).
にほんれいとうくうちょうこうぎょうかい【日本冷凍空調工業会】the Japan Refrigeration and Air Conditioning Industry Association (略: JRAIA).
にほんレコードきょうかい【日本–協会】the Recording Industry Association of Japan (略: RIAJ).
にほんろうどうべんごだん【日本労働弁護団】the Labour Lawyers Association of Japan (略: LLAJ).
にほんろうねんひにょうきかい【日本老年泌尿器科学会】the Japanese Society of Geriatric Urology.
にほんワイナリーきょうかい【日本–協会】the Japan Wineries Association.
にほんわくせいかがくかい【日本惑星科学会】the Japanese Society for Planetary Sciences (略: JSPS).
にほんわくせいきょうかい【日本惑星協会】the Planetary Society of Japan.
にほんワックスマンざいだん【日本–財団】〔文部科学省所管の財団〕the Waksman Foundation of Japan.
にほんわらいがっかい【日本笑い学会】the Japan Society for Laughter and Humour Studies (略: JSLHS).
にまい【二枚】 二枚爪〖医〗a peeling nail;〔症状〕(have) peeling nails.
にまいおち【二枚落ち】〖将棋〗=ひしゃくおち.
にもつ【荷物】 ▭ 荷物検査〔空港などでの〕baggage [luggage] inspection [check].
にやけがお【にやけ顔】a「pretty-boy [foppish, precious, smirking] expression [smile].
ニヤゾフ Nyyazow, Saparmyrat (1940–2006; トルクメニスタンの政治家; 大統領 [1992–2006]).
ニャンザン〔ベトナム共産党機関誌〕Nhân Dân.
にゅういん【入院】 ▭ 教育入院〔罹患している病気に関する知識と自己管理法を習得させるための〕educational hospitalization; hospitalization「for educational purposes [to provide infected patients with education and advice]. ▭ 入院証明書 a hospitalization certificate; proof of hospitalization. 入院診療記録 an inpatient「medical [treatment] record (略: IMR, ITR). 入院歴 ◊ 入院記録によると彼女は心臓発作で3回の〜歴がある. Hospital records show that she has been admitted three times as a result of heart attacks.｜According to admission records, she has a history of three hospitalizations for heart attacks.
にゅういんかんじゃ【入院患者】 ▭ 入院患者専門医 a hospitalist; an in-patient「doctor [physician].
「ニューイングランド・ジャーナル・オブ・メディシン」〔米国の医学専門誌〕the New England Journal of Medicine.
ニュー・エコノミー【経】〖米国経済の〗the New Economy.
「ニューオーリンズ・トライアル」〔映画〕Runaway Jury.
にゅうかあんていざい【乳化安定剤】〖化〗an emulsion stabilizer.
にゅうがく【入学】 ▭ 四月[九月]入学(制度) (a system of) April [September] admission [entrance]; an April [a September] matriculation system. ▭ 入学辞退者 a candidate for university entrance who fails to take up the offer of a place.
ニューカマー【新来者】a「newcomer [new arrival]《from …》;〔初心者〕a beginner;〔口〕a newbie; a rookie;〔近年日本に移住してきた外国人〕a recently arrived foreign resident.
にゅうがん【乳癌】 ▭ 男性[男子]乳がん〖医〗breast cancer in men.
にゅうかんなんみんほう【入管難民法】〖法〗〔出入国管理及び難民認定法の略〕the Immigration Control and Refugee-Recognition Law.
ニューギニアやりがたりくうずむし【–槍形陸渦虫】〖動〗〔陸産の貝類を捕食するプラナリア〕Platydemus manokwari.
にゅうきょ¹【入居】 ▭ 入居(一時)金 a (one-time) residence fee (at a home for the elderly). 入居(者)募集広告 an advertisement for「residents [tenants].
にゅうきょう³【入境】 ▭ 入境する cross a border《into…》. 〜する cross [go over] a border《into…》; enter《foreign territory》.
にゅうこう¹【入行】 ▭ 入行式 a ceremony for new bank employees.
にゅうこくしんさ【入国審査】 ▭ 入国審査ゲート〔空

港などfor] an immigrations inspection gate.
**にゅうこけいぶん**【乳固形分】(a) milk solids content.
**「ニュー・サイエンティスト」**〔英国の科学雑誌〕New Scientist.
**ニュー・サウス・ウェールズだいがく**【-大学】〔オーストラリア, シドニーにある大学〕the University of New South Wales（略: UNSW）.
**にゅうさつ**【入札】▷受注希望型競争入札 an open tender; bidding open to all qualified parties. ▯▯ 入札会 a bidding session. 入札額〔入札価格〕the price tendered; a「bid [bidding] price. 入札監視委員会 a committee to monitor bidding. 入札談合 collusive 「bidding [tendering]; rigged bidding; bid-rigging;〔1件の〕a rigged bid. 入札物件 an item [an article, a property] for auction.
**にゅうさつけいやくてきせいかほう**【入札契約適正化法】《法》the Law for Promoting Proper Tendering and Contracting for Public Works. ▷正式名称は「公共工事の入札及び契約の適正化の促進に関する法律」.
**にゅうさん**【乳酸】▷乳酸脱水素酵素〔生化〕〔臓器の細胞に含まれる酵素〕lactate dehydrogenase（略: LDH）. 乳酸値 (a) lactic acid value. 乳酸濃度 (a)《blood》lactic acid「concentration [level]」.
**にゅうざん**【入山】▷入山規制 limits on access to [limited access rules for] a mountain area. 入山料〔山の〕a fee for access to a「mountain [hill, mountain area]; a「mountain [hill] access fee;〔寺の拝観料〕an 「admission [entrance] fee.
**にゅうさんきん**【乳酸菌】▷腸内乳酸菌 an intestinal lactobacillus (*pl.* -lli). 有胞子(性)乳酸菌 a spore-forming lactic acid bacterium.
**にゅうし**[1]【入試】▷入試委員会 an entrance「examination [exam] committee; a committee for entrance examinations. 入試倍率 the [a] ratio of「applicants [candidates] to places.
**にゅうじ**【乳児】▷乳児嘔吐下痢症〔医〕infantile vomiting and diarrhea.
**にゅうしぜい**【入市税】a city entry tax.
**「ニュー・シネマ・パラダイス」**〔映画〕Nuovo Cinema Paradiso.
**にゅうしょ**【入所】▷入所型福祉施設 a residential welfare facility. 入所者〔刑務所などの〕an inmate;〔種々の施設などの〕a resident.
**にゅうじょう**[3]【入場】▷入場規制 controlling [regulating, imposing a limit on] admission(s); limiting 「entry [access].
**にゅうじょうけん**【入場券】▷全期間入場券〔期間中、何回でも入場可能な券〕an entrance ticket for the duration《of an event》; a full duration entrance ticket.
**にゅうしょく**[3]【入職】▷入職者 a newly-hired employee;〈集合的に〉(new) hires. ▷中途~者 a mid-career recruit; a (newly hired) mid-career「worker [employee] / ~者数 the number of persons entering employment. 入職率〔新卒者などの〕the accession rate; the entered employment rate.
**ニュース**▷ニュース映像 news footage. ニュース・サイト〔インターネット上などの〕a news site. ニュース・テロップ〔ニュース字幕〕news titles;〔画面上を流れる〕a news scroll.
**ニューズデー**〔米国の日刊紙〕Newsday.
**にゅうせん**[4]【乳腺】▷乳腺外科 breast surgery;〔病院の〕a department of breast surgery. 乳腺線維腺腫〔医〕mammary fibroadenoma. 乳腺専門医 a breast surgeon.
**にゅうそん**[1]【入村】〔村という名称が付いている施設への〕entering [taking up residence in]《a camping, an Olympic》village. ▯▯ 入村式〔オリンピック選手村への〕a ceremony to commemorate taking up residence in an Olympic village.

**にゅうたいかんり**【入退管理】〔工場・マンションなどの〕entrance-exit management; access control;〔監視カメラなどによる〕a video entry system.
**にゅうてん**【入店】**1**〔店にはいること〕entering [entrance into] a shop. ◐~時にカードを呈示する show *one's* card when entering a shop. ◐深夜に子供の~を断る refuse admission to children late at night. **2**〔店のスタッフとなること〕~する be hired by [start working at] a shop. ▯▯ 体験入店 trial employment at a shop. ◐レストランに体験~する be hired by [work at] a restaurant on a trial basis. ▯▯ 入店拒否 barring entrance to a shop (by people with guide dogs). ◐~拒否にあう 「refused admittance to [barred from entering] a shop.
**にゅうとう**[5]【乳頭】▯▯ 乳頭がん〔医〕(a) papillary「carcinoma [cancer]. ◐微小~がん (a) micropapillary carcinoma.
**ニュートリゲノミクス**〔栄養ゲノム科学〕nutrigenomics. ▷ nutrigenomic *adj.*
**ニュートリノ**▷原子炉ニュートリノ a reactor neutrino. 地球ニュートリノ a geoneutrino.
**ニュートン**[3] **1** Newton, Helmut (1920-2004; ドイツ出身の写真家). **2** Newton, Thandie (1972- ; ザンビア生まれの映画俳優; 本名 Thandiwe Newton).
**ニュー・パブリック・マネジメント**《行政・経》〔新公共経営〕new public management（略: NPM）.
**ニュー・ビジネス**▷(start) a new business.
**にゅうふ**[3]【乳腐】＝ふにゅう[2].
**ニューベリーしょう**【-賞】〔米国の児童文学賞〕the Newbery Medal.
**にゅうぼう**[1]【乳房】▯▯ 乳房全摘(手)術〔医〕(a) radical mastectomy; (a) total「removal [excision] of the breast.
**にゅうぼうけんこうけんきゅうかい**【乳房健康研究会】the Japan Society of Breast Health.
**にゅうみん**【入眠】▯▯ 入眠儀式〔入眠をスムーズにするため就寝時に行う習慣的行為〕a habitual rite before sleeping.
**にゅうようじ**【乳幼児】▯▯ 乳幼児医療費助成制度 the system for financing infant medical care.
**「ニューヨーカー」**〔米国の週刊誌〕The New Yorker.
**ニューヨークさきものとりひきじょ**【-先物取引所】the New York Futures Exchange（略: NYFE）.
**ニューヨークしょうぎょうとりひきじょ**【-商業取引所】＝ニューヨーク・マーカンタイルとりひきじょ.
**ニューヨークしょうひんとりひきじょ**【-商品取引所】the New York Board of Trade（略: NYBOT）;〔ニューヨークマーカンタイル取引所の一部門〕the Commodity Exchange（略: COMEX）.
**ニューヨーク・デイリー・ニュース**〔米国ニューヨーク市発行のタブロイド版朝刊紙〕the New York Daily News.
**「ニューヨークの恋人」**〔映画〕Kate & Leopold.
**ニューヨーク・ポスト**〔米国の朝刊紙〕The New York Post.
**ニューヨーク・マーカンタイルとりひきじょ**【-取引所】the New York Mercantile Exchange（略: NYMEX）.
**ニューヨークれんぎんせいぞうぎょうけいき**【-連銀製造業景気〔景況〕指数】《経》the Empire State Manufacturing Survey.
**にゅうよく**[3]【入浴】▯▯ 入浴介護〔介助〕bathing assistance; assistance [help] with bathing. 入浴玩具 a bath toy. 入浴着〔乳房切除手術を受けた女性の〕a bath wrap (worn in a hot spring by a breast cancer survivor). 訪問入浴サービス a home [in-home, a visiting] bath(ing) service. 訪問入浴車〔介護用の〕an assisted-bathing vehicle.
**「ニュー・リパブリック」**〔米国の週刊誌〕The New Re-

にゅうりょく

public.
にゅうりょく【入力】 ☐ 入力項目 items for completion; items to be filled in. ○ ~項目はすべて英語で入力してください。Please「complete [fill in] all items in English. 入力漏れ failure to complete an item; an uncompleted item. ○ 必須入力項目に~漏れがないか確認してください。Please check that you have not left any of the necessary items uncompleted. 入力欄 an entry field; a section for completion; a field to be filled in. ○ ~欄に入力する add [type in]《data, one's name》in the section for completion.
にゅうりん【乳輪】 ☐ 乳輪下膿瘍〚医〛a subareolar abscess.
ニューロメジン・ユー【-U】〚生化〛〔アミノ酸が連なったペプチドで，食べ過ぎ抑制作用をもつ脳内物質〕neuromedin U（略：NMU）.
ニュクス〚ギ神話〛〔夜の女神〕Nyx.
ニュルブルクリンク〔ドイツ西部の自動車レースサーキット〕Nörburgring.
にょう【尿】 ☐ 尿毒素〚医〛(a) uremic toxin.
にょうかん[2]【尿管】 ☐ 尿管がん〚医〛(a) ureteral cancer; (a) cancer of the ureter; (a) ureteral carcinoma; (a) carcinoma of the ureter. 尿管狭窄（症）〚医〛ureteral「stricture [stenosis]. 尿管閉鎖（症）〚医〛ureteral atresia. 尿管閉塞（症）〚医〛ureteral「obstruction [occulusion]．
にょうさん【尿酸】 ☐ 尿酸降下薬〚薬〛an antihyperuricemic「drug [agent]. 尿酸合成阻害薬〚薬〛a uric acid synthesis inhibitor; a xanthine oxidase [an XO] inhibitor. 尿酸生成抑制薬〚薬〛＝尿酸合成阻害薬．
にょうそ【尿素】 ☐ 尿素SCRシステム〔ディーゼル車の窒素酸化物低減technologyの1つ〕a urea-SCR system. ► SCR は selective catalytic reduction の略．尿素水〔尿素SCRシステムで用いる〕(a) urea solution.
にょうどう【尿道】 ☐ 尿道括約筋〚解〛the urethral sphincter; the sphincter urethrae. ○ 外尿道～ the external urethral sphincter／内尿道～ the internal urethral sphincter. 尿道がん〚医〛(a) urethral cancer; (a) cancer of the urethra; (a) urethral carcinoma; (a) carcinoma of the urethra.
にょうろ【尿路】 ☐ 尿路結石症〚医〛urolithiasis; urinary tract stone disease; urinary calculus disease.
にらみたおす【睨み倒す】stare sb down.
にリーグせい【二-制】〚野球〛a two-league system.
にりとう【二里頭】〔中国河南省偃師(い)県の村；中国古代文明の遺跡がある〕Erlitou.
にりん【二輪】 ☐ 二輪消防車 a fire fighter's motorbike; a motorbike equipped for fire-fighting.
ニルギリ 1〔インド南部の高原〕the Nilgiri Hills. 2〔紅茶〕Nilgiri (tea).
にわざくら【庭桜】〚植〛〔バラ科の落葉低木；中国原産〕 Prunus glandulosa var. alboplena.
にんい【任意】 ☐ 任意組合 a voluntary partnership. 任意整理〚法〛＝私的整理（⇨せいり[2]）. 任意接種〔予防接種の〕(a) voluntary vaccination. 任意聴取 questioning by police on a voluntary basis.
にんか【認可】 ☐ 認可基準 licensing standards; standards for approval. ○ その施設は国の~基準に合わないので補助金をもらえない. The institution is ineligible for a「subsidy [grant] because it doesn't meet government licensing standards. 認可共済 a regulated「mutual aid (insurance) cooperative [kyosai]. 認可事業 a business [an undertaking, an enterprise, an activity] requiring「government licensing [a government license]. 認可薬 an approved「drug [medication]; a「drug [medication] approved (by the Ministry of Health, Labour and Welfare). ○ 未~薬 an unapproved「drug [medication].
にんがい【人界】〚仏教〛＝にんげんどう．

にんき[1]【人気】 ☐ 人気企業〔就職先としての〕a company popular with new graduates looking for employment. ○ 就職~企業ランキング a popularity ranking of companies by new graduates. 人気機種[車種] a popular model.
にんき[2]【任期】 ☐ 任期付職 a fixed-term「position [post, job]. 任期付職員[研究員] a fixed-term「employee [researcher]. ○ ~付職員[研究員]業績手当 a performance-related bonus for fixed-term「employees [researchers].
「人気家族パートリッジ」〔家族ロックバンドがバスで全米を巡る TV コメディー〕The Partridge Family.
にんぎょうやき【人形焼き】〔人形の形をした和菓子〕a small (doll-shaped) cake with sweet bean jam filling.
にんげん【人間】 ☐ 人間開発指数〔国連開発計画（UNDP）が発表する，平均寿命・教育水準・国民所得から算出した基本的人間能力の伸長指数〕a human development index（略：HDI）. 人間型ロボット a humanoid robot;〔空想科学小説などで〕an android. 人間将棋〔山形県天童市で行われる伝統的な祭り〕"human shōgi"; a traditional event featuring a round of shōgi in which human beings serve as the gaming pieces. 人間ドラマ a human drama. ○ この映画は少年と老人の友情を描いた~ドラマだ. This movie is a human drama portraying the friendship between a boy and an old man. 人間の盾 a human shield. 人間貧困指数〔国連開発計画（UNDP）が発表する〕a human poverty index（略：HPI）.
にんげんかいはつほうこくしょ【人間開発報告書】〔国連開発計画（UNDP）が発行する〕a Human Development Report（略：HDR）.
にんげんかんけい【人間関係】 ☐ 人間関係不全〚心理〛failure in human relationships; (an) inability to form relationships. 人間関係力 skill at developing good (human) relations.
にんげんきょじゅういいんかい【人間居住委員会】⇨こくれんにんげんきょじゅういいんかい．
にんげんせいかつこうがくけんきゅうセンター【人間生活工学研究-】the Research Institute of Human Engineering for Quality Life（略：HQL）.
にんげんどう【人間道】〚仏教〛〔六道の1つ〕the realm of human beings.
にんげんピラミッド【人間-】〚体操などの〛《form, make》a human pyramid. ○ ~が崩れた. The human pyramid collapsed. ○ ~に加わっている be in a human pyramid.
にんげんぶんかけんきゅうきこう【人間文化研究機構】 the National Institutes for the Humanities（略：NIHU）.
にんしき【認識】 ☐ 認識率 a recognition rate;〔生体認証などの〕an acceptance rate.
にんじゃ【忍者】 ☐ 忍者屋敷 a "ninja yashiki"; a secret home for "ninja."
にんしょう[3]【認証】 ☐ 認証アルゴリズム〚電算〛an authentication algorithm. 認証官任命式〔認証式〕an (Imperial) attestation ceremony; an investiture (ceremony). 認証排出削減量〚環境〛〔温室効果ガスの〕Certified Emission Reduction（略：CER(s)）. 認証率〔生体認証などの〕an acceptance rate; a recognition rate.
にんじょう[1]【人情】 ☐ 人情喜劇 (a) comedy of pathos.
にんしん【妊娠】 ☐ 妊娠高血圧症候群〚医〛pregnancy-induced hypertension (syndrome)（略：PIH）. ►「妊娠中毒症」の正式な呼称. ○ 高血圧症候群軽症[重症] mild [severe] pregnancy-induced hypertension. 妊娠促進剤〚薬〛a fertility drug; a pregnancy drug. 妊娠届 (a) notification of pregnancy; informing《the local government》that one is pregnant.

にんじん【人参】 🔲 人参茶 ginseng tea.
にんそう【人相】 🔲 人相着衣〔事件の容疑者などの〕《a suspect's》appearance and clothing. ◐ 目撃者が犯人の～着衣をはっきりと覚えていた. The witness remembered clearly「the appearance and clothing of the criminal [how the perpetrator looked and what he was wearing].
にんち²【認知】 🔲 認知運動療法〔精神医〕cognitive therapeutic exercise(s). 認知機能 (a) cognitive function. ◐ ～機能検査 a cognitive test [cognitive testing]《for elderly drivers》; a mini-mental state examination (略: MMSE). 認知件数〔犯罪の〕the number of cases 《of assault》known to the police. 認知効果〔宣伝〕(an) awareness effect; (a) cognitive effect. 認知行動療法〔精神医〕cognitive behavior therapy. ◐ 集団～行動療法 cognitive-behavioral group therapy. 認知症〔医〕(a) cognitive impairment; a cognitive disorder. ◐ 軽度～障害 (a) mild cognitive impairment (略: MCI). 認知度調査 a (name) recognition survey; a visibility survey. 認知バイアス《心理》(a) cognitive bias. 認知欲求《心理》= 承認欲求 (⇨しょうにん²).
ニンチ(一)【林芝】〔中国チベット自治区東部の県〕Nyingchi.
にんちしょう【認知症】〔医〕cognitive impairment; dementia; senility. ▶ 痴呆症に代わる語. 🔲 アルツハイマー型認知症 Alzheimer(-type) [Alzheimer's (type)] dementia. 外傷後認知症 posttraumatic dementia. 軽度認知障害 mild cognitive impairment (略: MCI); mild dementia. 血管性認知症 vascular dementia. 若年(性)認知症 ⇨じゃくねんせい. 初老期認知症 presenile [early-onset] dementia. 早発(性)認知症 precocious dementia; 〖L〗 dementia pr(a)ecox. 中毒性認知症 toxic dementia. 脳血管性認知症 cerebrovascular dementia. 麻痺性認知症 paralytic dementia; 〖L〗 dementia paralytica. 老人性認知症 senile dementia. 🔲 認知症グループホーム a group home for dementia sufferers. 認知症ケア dementia care; care for dementia patients. ◐ ～ケア専門士 a (certified) dementia care specialist. 認知症高齢者 a cognitively impaired elderly person. 認知症サポーター a dementia advisor. 認知症対応型共同生活介護施設 ＝認知症グループホー

ム.
にんちしょうのひととかぞくのかい【認知症の人と家族の会】the Alzheimer's Association (of) Japan (略: AAJ).
にんちゃく【人着】〔警察用語で人相着衣のこと〕＝人相着衣 (⇨にんそう).
にんてい²【認定】 🔲 認定完成検査 (a) certified completion inspection. ◐ ～完成検査実施者 a certified completion inspector. 認定基準 certification standards; criteria [standards] for accreditation; accreditation criteria. 認定子供園〔厚生労働省認可の〕a certified children's garden. [⇨ようほえん] 認定中古車〔正規ディーラーで扱う高品質の中古車の〕*a certified pre-owned 「car [vehicle] (略: CPO); an approved (used) 「car [vehicle]. 認定農家〔認定農業者〕a designated farmer. 認定被爆者 a designated [an officially recognized] hibakusha. 認定保安基準を満たした高圧ガス使用企業などに認められる自主検査〕(a) safety inspection. ◐ ～保安検査実施者 a certified safety inspector. 認定ホームラン[本塁打]〖野球〗a ground-rule home run. 認定薬〔薬〕an approved drug.
にんどう²【人道】《仏教》＝にんげんどう.
ニントゥアン〔ベトナム南部の省〕Ninh Thuan.
にんにく¹【大蒜】 ◐ にんにく油 garlic oil (obtained by frying garlic in oil).
ニンビー〔原発・刑務所・ごみ処分場など地域環境にとって好ましくないものが《よそにならともかく》近所に設置されることに反対する運動〕NIMBY; NIMBYism;〔人〕a NIMBYist. ▶ NIMBY is "not in my backyard"〔うちの裏庭にできてもらっては困る〕の略.
ニンビン〔ベトナム北部ホン河デルタ地帯の省; その省都〕Ninh Binh.
にんめい【任命】 🔲 任命責任 the responsibility for「appointing [having appointed] an official [sb《chairperson》]; (the) responsibility for an appointment. ◐ 閣僚の収賄スキャンダルに関して野党は首相の～責任を厳しく追及する方針である. It is the opposition party's policy strictly to pursue the prime minister's responsibility for having appointed a cabinet member involved in a bribery scandal.

# ぬ

ヌイイ(・シュル・セーヌ)〔フランス, パリ北西部の町〕Neuilly(-sur-Seine).
ヌイイじょうやく【-条約】〔史〕〔第１次大戦終結に際し連合国とブルガリア間で調印された条約〕the Treaty of Neuilly.
ヌーク〔グリーンランドの政庁所在地〕Nuuk. ▶ ゴッドホーブ(Godthaab) ともいる.
ヌーサン〔商標〕＝ヌードサンダル.
ヌードサンダル〔商標〕〔ストラップのない, 足裏密着型のサンダル〕Nude Sandals.
ヌーブラ〔商標〕〔シリコン製ブラジャー〕NuBra.
ヌーベ〔料理〕〔<Sp nube〕a frothy sauce.
「ヌーベル・オブセルバトゥール」〔フランスの週刊誌〕Le Nouvel Observateur.
ヌーミー〔NUMMI〕〔トヨタ自動車と米国 GM の合弁企業〕NUMMI; New United Motor Manufacturing, Inc.
ヌーリスタン〔アフガニスタン北東部の州〕Nuristan.
ヌエイバ〔エジプト, シナイ半島東部のリゾート地〕Nuweiba.
ぬか【糠】 🔲 赤糠〔精米時に最初に出る糠で玄米の外皮と胚芽の部分; 肥料や味噌などに使われる〕the outer「bran of rice [layer of rice bran]. 化粧糠 ＝白糠. 白糠〔米

の芯に近い部分で糠全体のわずか 5% を占める; 粒子が細かくビタミンが豊富なため化粧用に使われる〕rice polish; "white bran" from rice; the bran (layer) immediately above the kernel. 中糠〔精米時に赤糠の次に出る糠〕bran from the middle layer of rice bran; intermediate (rice) bran.
ヌゲマ ＝ンゲマ.
ヌジョマ Nujoma, Sam (1929- ; ナミビアの政治家; 大統領 1990-2005).
ヌリスタン ＝ヌーリスタン.
ぬるつく〔ぬるぬるする〕be sticky; be slimy. ◐ ぬるつかずさっぱり洗い落とせるシャンプー shampoo that rinses off completely without clamminess. ◐ この温泉の湯は肌にぬ～. The water in this hot spring leaves the skin feeling slimy.
ぬるまゆ〔ぬるま湯〕 🔲 ぬるま湯(的)経営 complacent management.
ヌワラエリア, ヌワラエリヤ 1〔スリランカ中南部の山岳地帯〕Nuwara Eliya.
2〔紅茶〕Nuwara Eliya tea.

# ね

**ね[1]【子】** ⇨ 子は繁栄[繁盛]《相場》〔子年は好調, の意〕In the year of the Rat, the market tends to rise. 〔⇨たつみてんじょう〕

**ねあかよしやんま【根赤葦蜻蜓】**《昆》*Aeschnophlebia anisoptera*.

**ねあがり[1]【値上がり】** ⇨ 値上がり益〔有価証券や資産売却から生じた利益〕capital gain(s).

**ネアズかいきょう【—海峡】**〔カナダ・グリーンランド間の〕Nares Strait.

**「ネイチャー・イムノロジー」**〔米国の免疫学専門誌〕Nature Immunology.

**ネイリスト**〔ネイルアーティスト〕a nail artist.

**ネイル** ⇨ ネイル・サロン a nail salon. ネイル・ファッション nail fashion.

**ねいれ【値入れ】**《商》〔仕入れ原価に利益分をプラスして売値を決めること〕marking up;〔その利幅〕=値入れ高. ⇨ 値入れ高 a markup; a mark-up. 値入れ率〔売価に対する値入れ高の割合〕a「markup [mark-up] rate (relative to the selling price).

**ネヴァダかくじっけんじょう【—核実験場】**the Nevada Test Site (略: NTS).

**ネーブラてんもんばん【—天文盤】**《天》〔ドイツで発見された世界最古の天文盤〕the Sky Disk of Nebra.

**ネーミング** ⇨ ネーミング・ライツ〔命名権〕a naming right.

**ネオフィリン(じょう)【—(錠)】**《商標・薬》〔強心薬・喘息治療薬〕Neophyllin.

**ネオリベラリズム**〔新自由主義〕neoliberalism. ▷ neoliberal *adj, n.*

**ネオン** ⇨ ネオン看板 a neon sign(board).

**ねがけ【根掛け】**《服》〔女子の髷(#)の後ろに付ける飾り〕a hair tassel for a traditional Japanese lady's hairstyle; a hair ornament worn at the base of a chignon.

**ネガティブ** ⇨ ネガティブ広告[アド]〔中傷広告〕a negative ad(vertisement);〔中傷広告法〕negative advertising.

**ねぎだく** ◯~でお願いします.〔牛丼屋で〕Extra onions, please.

**ねぎま【葱間】**yakitori of alternate pieces of chicken and Welsh onion (on a skewer).

**ねぐされ【根腐れ】**《植物病理》root rot. ~する ◯ サボテンは水をやりすぎると~します. The roots of cacti will rot if they are overwatered.

**ネグロポンテ** Negroponte, John D. (1939– ; 米国の外交官; 国連大使 [2001–04]).

**ねこ【猫】** ⇨ 猫まんま, 猫めし〔ご飯にかつおぶしをのせ, みそ汁か少量の醤油をかけただけの食事〕boiled rice and dried bonito flakes with miso soup or a few drops of soy sauce poured on it.

**ねこぎば【猫義歯】**《魚》〔ナマズ目ギギ科の淡水魚〕*Coreobagrus ichikawai*.

**ねこぐさ【猫草】**〔毛玉を吐かせるために猫に与える草〕cat grass.

**ねこだまし【猫騙し】**《相撲》〔立ち会い直後に相手の目の前で両手を打って相手を驚かせる相撲の技〕a distracting clap; a "fool-the-cat" trick.

**ねこのめ【猫の目】**〔その時々の都合でめまぐるしく変わること〕 ⇨ 猫の目行政 (a) changeable [fickle, piecemeal, chameleon-like] administration. 猫の目天気 changeable weather.

**ねこめこうか【猫目効果】**《宝石》=シャトヤンシーこうか.

**ネザーランド・ドワーフ**《動》〔オランダ原産のアナウサギの一種〕a Netherland dwarf; *Oryctolagus cuniculus*.

**ねじり【捩じり】** ⇨ ねじり下げ《空》〔翼の迎え角を付け根から翼端に向かって減少するように変化させること; 翼端失速を防止する手段の１つ〕washout.

**ねじれげんしょう【—現象】**an incongruous situation. ◯ 衆議院では与党が多数だが, 参議院では野党が多数という~現象が起きている. An incongruous situation has arisen in which the ruling party holds a majority in the House of Representatives while the opposition party holds a majority in the House of Councillors. | With the ruling party controlling the lower house and the opposition party controlling the upper house, an anomalous scenario has emerged.

**ネスティング**《電算》〔入れ子構造にすること〕nesting.

**ねずみ【鼠】** ⇨ ねずみ駆除 rat「control [extermination]. ◯ ~駆除業者 a rat exterminator; a rat control company.

**ねずみふぐ【鼠河豚】**《魚》〔ハリセンボン科の海産硬骨魚〕a porcupinefish; *Diodon hystrix*.

**ネタ** ⇨ 裏ネタ ⇨うらネタ. 新ネタ〔話や記事などの〕new material;〔手品の〕a new trick. ⇨ ネタおろし《落語・講談など》〔習い覚えた演目を高座で初めて演じること〕a first-time performance 《of a newly learned *rakugo* piece》.

**ねだん【値段】** ⇨ 値段交渉 price「negotiations [talks]; bargaining;《口》haggling (over the price).

**ねつ【熱】** ⇨ 熱回収〔エネルギー循環のための〕heat recovery. 熱回収効率 heat recovery efficiency. 熱産生《生理》thermogenesis. 熱産生中枢《生理》a heat-promoting center. 熱放散中枢《生理》a heat-losing center.

**ネツァリム**〔パレスチナ, ガザ地区中部のユダヤ人入植地〕Netzarim.

**ねつえん[2]【熱延】**《金属加工》hot rolling. 熱延コイル a hot-rolled coil. 熱延工場 a hot-rolling plant. 熱延工程 a hot-rolling process. 熱延鋼板 (a) hot-rolled steel sheet.

**ねつえんじゅんかん【熱塩循環】**《海洋》(the) thermohaline circulation.

**ねっかく【熱覚】**《生理》the sensory capacity to perceive heat; heat perception; thermoreception.

**ねっかん【熱間】** ⇨ 熱間鍛造《冶金》hot forging.

**ねつき[3]【値付き】**《証券》price finding; market making. ⇨ 値付き率 a pricing ratio; the percentage of stocks for which a market price has been established.

**「ねっきょうのひ」おんがくさい【「熱狂の日」音楽祭】**=ラ・フォル・ジュルネ.

**ネック** ⇨ ネック・カラー〔頸椎保護のために首に装着するもの〕a cervical (neck) collar; a (protective) neck collar. ネック・ピロー〔首を支えるタイプの枕〕a neck pillow. ネックレス ⇨ キャンディー・ネックレス a candy(-like) necklace. ボリュームネックレス〔大きめで重量感のあるネックレス〕a heavy necklace.

**ねつけ[2]【根付け】** ⇨ 根付け師 a netsuke carver.

**ねつさまし【熱冷まし】** ⇨ 熱冷まし(用冷却)シート a cooling plaster; an antifebrile plaster.

**ねっしょう[2]【熱傷】** ⇨ 熱傷(性)ショック burn shock.

**ねったい【熱帯】** ⇨ 熱帯系《産》(の) tropical; tropic. 熱帯(性)高気圧《気象》tropical high pressure 《belt》.

**ねったいしまか【熱帯縞蚊】**《昆》〔デング熱・黄熱病などの媒介昆虫〕a yellow-fever mosquito; *Aedes aegypti*.

**ねっちゅうし【熱中死】**(a) death from「heatstroke [heat]; (a) heatstroke death. ~する die of heatstroke; die from the heat.

**ねっぽく【熱っぽく】**〔情熱的に〕excitedly; enthusiastically; zealously; fervently; warmly. ◐宇宙開発の夢を~語る speak「enthusiastically [in excited tones] of「the dream of space development [(the vision of) exploiting space].

**ネット** ▭ ネット・アイドル an「Internet [online] idol [star]. ネット・アンケ(ート) an Internet「poll [questionnaire, survey]; a poll on the Internet. ネットいじめ〔インターネットサイトへの誹謗中傷の書き込みによるいじめ〕cyberbullying; net bullying. ネット依存症 Internet addiction disorder (略: IAD). ネット占い＝インターネット占い(⇨インターネット). ネット絵本 an Internet picture book; an illustrated book on the Net. ネット家電 networked home appliances. ネット関連企業 a dot.com company. ネット関連ビジネス (the growth of) Internet-related businesses. ネット教育＝インターネット教育(⇨インターネット). ネット競売［オークション］サイト an Internet auction site; a Net auction site. ネット・ギャンブル a Net gambling. ◐~ギャンブラー an Internet gambler. ネット求人広告 an advertisement on the Internet for a job opening; Internet job vacancy advertising. ネット警察 the「Internet [Net] police. ネット掲示板〔電算〕a [an electronic] bulletin board. ネット決済 Internet [online] settlement. ネット献金 an Internet「donation [contribution]; 《making》a「donation [contribution] on [over, via] the Internet. ネット広告 Internet advertising; advertising on the Internet. ネット詐欺〔インターネット上の〕(an) Internet fraud; an Internet scam. ネット(集団)自殺 an Internet suicide pact. ネット証券会社 an Internet securities company. ネット証券取引 Internet securities「trading [dealing]. ネット書店 an Internet「bookshop [bookstore]; an online「bookshop [bookstore]. ネット人口〔インターネット利用者数〕the「Internet [online] population; the number of「Internet users [people online]. ネット申請 (a) Net [(an) online] application. ネット・セキュリティ Net [Internet] security. ネット専業銀行〔実際の店舗を持たず、インターネット上で銀行業務を行う銀行〕an Internet-only bank. ネット専業証券会社〔実際の店舗を持たず、インターネット上で証券取引を行う証券会社〕an Internet-only securities company. ネット端末 an Internet terminal. ネット中継 an Internet relay《of a solar eclipse》; an Internet hookup. ネット中傷 (a)「slander [libel] on the Net. ネット中毒 Internet addiction. ◐~中毒者 a「net-head [Net-head]; a「netaholic [Netaholic]. ネット通信 Internet communication(s); communication(s)「on [through, via] the Internet. ネット通信料 Internet (communication) fees; fees for using the「Internet [Net]. ネット投資家 an Internet investor. ネット・トレード〔ネット取引〕Internet「trading [dealing]; dealing [trading] on the Net. ネット・バー an Internet [a net] bar; a cyberbar. ネット配信 Internet distribution. ◐~配信会社 an Internet distribution company. ネット・バブル an Internet bubble. ◐~バブルがはじけた. The Internet bubble has burst. ネット・プレーヤー〖テニス〗a net player. ネット放送 Internet broadcasting; broadcasting「over [through, via] the Internet;〔1回の〕an Internet broadcast; a broadcast on the Internet. ◐~放送局 an Internet broadcast(ing) station. ネットマナー Internet etiquette. ネット・ムービー an Internet movie. ネットモニター調査 an Internet「monitor [monitoring] survey. ネット予約 Internet reservation;《make》a reservation「over [via] the Internet. ネット・ラジオ Net radio.

**ネットカフェ**〔インターネットカフェ〕an Internet café. ▭ ネットカフェ難民〔住む場所がなく日雇い仕事で生計を立てながら終夜営業のインターネットカフェや漫画喫茶などで寝泊まりする人〕an Internet café refugee; a homeless person who「spends the night [seeks asylum] at Internet cafés.

**ネットスカイ**〔コンピューターウイルスの1つ〕Netsky.
**ネット・デー**〔学校のネット環境整備を目的とする地域住民のボランティア活動〕a Net day.
**ネットロア**〔インターネット上で広がるうわさ〕netlore; an Internet rumor.
**ネットワーク** ▭ 次世代ネットワーク the next generation network (略: NGN). ▭ ネットワーク・エンジニア〖電算〗a network engineer. ネットワーク科学 network science. ネットワーク型 ▭ ~型データベース〖電算〗a net-work-type database / ~型電子マネー〖電算〗network electronic money. ネットワーク端末 a network terminal. ネットワーク認証〖電算〗network authentication (略: NA).
**ねどり【値取り】**〔原油価格などの上昇分を小売価格に転嫁して上乗せすること〕raising retail prices to offset higher wholesale prices.
**ねなおす【寝直す】**〔一度目覚めたあとに〕go back to sleep.
**ネネ**〔鳥〕〔ハワイ産のガチョウ〕a nene (a goose); *Branta sandwicensis*. ► 別名はハワイガン (Hawaiian goose).
**ネネツじちかんく【~自治管区】**〔ロシア北西部、アルハンゲリスク州に属する〕the Nenets Autonomous Region.
「**ネバーランド」**〔映画〕Finding Neverland.
**ネパールガンジ**〔ネパール西部、インド国境近くの都市〕Nepalganj.
**ネパールきょうさんとうもうたくとうしゅぎは【~共産党毛沢東主義派】**the Communist Party of「Nepal-Maoist [Nepal (Maoist)] (略: CPN-M, CPN (Maoist)).
**ネバダかくじっけんじょう【~核実験場】**＝ネヴァダかくじっけんじょう.
**ネパッド【NEPAD】**〔アフリカ開発のための新パートナーシップ〕the NEPAD; the New Partnership for Africa's Development.
**ねはば【値幅】** ▭ 月間［年間］値幅 a monthly [an annual] spread. 制限値幅〔株価の〕a daily trading limit. ▭ 値幅取り〔相場〕profit-taking; short-time speculation.
**ねばりのぎく【粘耳菊】**〖植〗〔キク科の多年草；北アメリカ原産〕a New England aster; *Aster novae-angliae*.
**ねはん【涅槃】** ▭ 涅槃図 a「painting [drawing] of「the Buddha immediately after his death [the supine Buddha, the Buddha entering nirvana].
**ねびき[1]【値引き】** ▭ 値引き幅 a「markdown [price cut, reduction] 《of ¥20》.
**ネピドー**〔地名〕〔ミャンマー中部、ヤンゴンに代わる新首都；軍事政権が遷都〕Nay Pyi「Taw [Daw]. ▭ ピンマナ.
**ねぶかねぎ【根深葱】**〔白色の根の部分が長く、主にそこを食べる長ねぎ〕a scallion whose long white stem is primarily eaten.
**ねぶた[ねぶた]まつり** 〔ねぶた[ねぶた]祭り〕the「Nebuta [Neputa] Festival; a Tōhoku region festival, celebrating Tanabata, with a colorful procession of giant human and animal shaped lanterns.
**ネブラてんもんばん【~天文盤】**〖天文〗＝ネーブラてんもんばん.
**ネプリライシン**〖生化〗〔酵素〕neprilysin.
**ねむけ【眠気】** ▭ 眠気防止剤 an anti-sleep drug.
**ねむりじゅう【眠り銃】**a long-term unused gun.
**ねむりゆすりか【眠り揺すり蚊】**〖昆〗〔アフリカに生息する〕a sleeping chironomid; *Polypedilum vanderplanki*.
**ネメア**〔ギリシャ、ペロポネソス半島北東部の町〕Nemea. ▷ Nemean *adj*. ▭ ネメア祭〔古代ギリシャの競技祭〕the Nemean Games. ネメアのライオン〖ギリシャ神話〗the Nemean lion.
**ネメス**〔古代エジプトの王のかぶるかぶり物〕a nemes.
**ネリカまい【~米】**〔西アフリカで開発された新種のコメ〕NERICA (rice). ► NERICA is New Rice for Africa の略.
**ネリスくうぐんきち【~空軍基地】**〔米国ネヴァダ州にある米

空軍基地〕Nellis Air Force Base.
**ねりまだいこん**【練馬大根】a Nerima daikon; a long radish once widely cultivated in Nerima, Tokyo.
**ネルスプロイト**〔南アフリカ共和国東部, ムプマランガ州の州都〕Nelspruit.
**ネレイド**〔ギ神話〕〔海神ネレウスの娘たちの総称〕Nereids; 〔天〕〔海王星の衛星〕Nereid.
**ネレトヴァがわ**【-川】〔ボスニア・ヘルツェゴヴィナからクロアチアを流れアドリア海に注ぐ川〕the Neretva River; the Neretva.
**ねんがじょう**【年賀状】 ▭ 年賀状(印刷)ソフト 〔電算〕 New Year's card (printing) software.
**ねんかん**[2]【年間】 ▭ 年間配当(金) an annual dividend. 年間貿易黒字 an annual trade surplus.
**ねんかん**[3]【年鑑】 ▭ 宗教年鑑 〔文化庁の〕the Religions Yearbook.
**ねんきん**【年金】 ▭ 確定給付(型)年金 a「defined [fixed] benefit(s) pension plan. 確定拠出(型)年金 a「defined [fixed] contribution(s) pension plan. 最低保障年金 a minimum-guarantee pension. 住宅担保年金 a "reverse mortgage pension." 所得比例年金 an earnings-based pension. ▭ 年金一元化 consolidation of the public pension systems. 年金改定率 a pension revision rate. 年金給付額 a pension amount. 年金財源 a funding source for pensions. 年金週間 〔11月6日-12日〕Pension Week. 年金住宅融資 a pension housing loan. 年金数理人 a (certified) pension actuary. 年金担保融資 a pension collateral loan. 年金積立金 a pension reserve fund; pension insurance funds; accumulated pension insurance premiums; 〔1回の〕a payment into [a contribution to] a pension reserve fund. ◐ ～積立金を運用する make effective use of pension insurance funds; manage a pension fund effectively. 年金不信 distrust of pensions. 年金分割 〔離婚時の〕pension division; a「division of pension「rights [benefits, interests]. 年金ローン a loan on「a [one's] pension; a loan against「a [one's] pension.
**ねんきんかいかくほう**【年金改革法】〔法〕the Pension Reform Law.
**ねんきんきゅうふほしょうこうしゃ**【年金給付保証公社】〔米国の〕the Pension Benefit Guaranty Corporation (略: PBGC).
**ねんきんせいどかいかくきょうぎかい**【年金制度改革協議会】=よとうねんきんせいどかいかくきょうぎかい.
**ねんきんせいどかいかくほう**【年金制度改革法】〔法〕the Pension System Reform Law.
**ねんきんつみたてきんかんりうんようどくりつぎょうせいほうじん**【年金積立金管理運用独立行政法人】the Government Pension Investment Fund (略: GPIF). ▶ 2006年設立.
**ねんきんもくてきしょうひぜい**【年金目的消費税】a consumption tax for funding pensions; a pension-targeted consumption tax.
**ねんこう**[3]【年縞】〔地質〕〔湖底堆積物などに見られる縞模様〕a varve. ◐ ～のある varved〔sediments〕.
**ねんし**[4]【念紙】〔美術〕〔裏面に炭粉や顔料などを付着させた紙; 下絵と本紙の間にはさみ, 下絵をなぞって転写する〕transfer paper; washi used to transfer a design to a surface for painting.
**ねんじ**【年次】 ▭ 年次教書演説〔ロシアの大統領などの〕an annual policy speech.
**ねんしょう**[3]【燃焼】 ▭ 異常燃焼 〔ノッキング〕knocking. 二段燃焼 two-stage combustion. ◐ 二段～方式 a two-stage combustion system. 無炎燃焼 flameless combustion. 無煙燃焼 smokeless combustion. 有炎燃焼 flaming combustion. 燃焼圧力〔エンジンの〕combustion pressure. 燃焼解析〔化〕combustion analysis. 燃焼式給湯器 a combustion(-type) water heater. 燃焼制御システム[方式] a combustion control system.
**ねんしょらい**【年初来】〔証券〕since the beginning of the year; year to date. ▭ 年初来高値[安値] a year-to-date「high [low].
**ねんとう**[1]【年頭】 ▭ 年頭訓示 the《mayor's》New Year speech; the《president's》first speech of the year.
**ねんとう**[3]【粘投】〔野球〕〔粘り強い投球ぶり〕tenacious [stubborn, tough] pitching.
**ねんぱん**【年販】〔1年間の販売量〕annual [yearly] sales [turnover].
**ねんぴ**【燃費】 ▭ 燃費基準〔二酸化炭素排出量抑制のための〕(set, introduce) a fuel-efficiency「standard [target]. 燃費効率 fuel efficiency. ◐ ～効率のよい車 a fuel-efficient car. 燃費性能 fuel efficiency performance.
**ねんぴけい**【燃費計】〔自動車〕a fuel economy meter.
**ねんまく**【粘膜】 ▭ 粘膜下層 the [a] submucosal layer. 粘膜脱〔医〕〔肛門の〕a mucosal prolapse; a partial prolapse. ◐ ～脱症候群 mucosal prolapse syndrome (略: MPS).
**ねんまつ**【年末】 ▭ 年末進行〔出版〕a year-end schedule.
**ねんゆ**【燃油】 ▭ 燃油特別付加運賃[サーチャージ]〔航空燃料価格高騰の際の〕a fuel surcharge. 燃油費〔航空機の〕the cost of aviation fuel.
**ねんりき**【念力】 ▭ 念力放火〔超能力の一種〕pyrokinesis.
**ねんりつ**【年率】 ▭ 年率換算 annualization ((of quarterly growth)).
**ねんりょう**【燃料】 ▭ ケロシン(系)燃料〔航空燃料の一種〕kerosene(-type jet) fuel. 固体酸化物型燃料電池 a solid oxide fuel cell (略: SOFC). ワイドカット(系)燃料〔航空燃料の一種〕wide-cut (jet) fuel. ▭ 燃料極〔燃料電池の〕a fuel pole; an anode pole. 燃料警告灯〔自動車などの〕a (low-)fuel warning light. 燃料注入〔ロケットなどの〕fueling; fuelling. 燃料費比率〔総経費に占める割合〕the ratio of fuel costs to total costs. 燃料噴射装置 a fuel-injection device. 燃料噴射ポンプ〔機〕a fuel-injection pump. 燃料放出装置〔空〕〔航空機の〕a fuel「dump(ing) [jettison] system. 燃料補給船[艦] a fuel supply「vessel [ship, boat]. 燃料油価格変動調整金〔フェリー会社などが, 燃料油価格の高騰に対処するために利用者に求める上乗せ負担金〕a fuel surcharge.
**ねんりょうでんち**【燃料電池】 ▭ 水素燃料電池 a hydrogen fuel cell. ダイレクト[直接]メタノール(型)燃料電池 a direct methanol fuel cell (略: DMFC). 定置用燃料電池 a「residential [stationary] fuel cell. 溶融炭酸塩型燃料電池 a (molten) carbonate fuel cell (略: (M)CFC). 燐酸型燃料電池 a phosphoric acid fuel cell (略: PAFC).
**ねんりんピック**〔全国健康福祉祭の愛称〕⇨ぜんこくけんこうふくしさい.
**ねんれい**[2]【年齢】 ▭ 高年齢 (an) old age; an advanced age. ◐ ～の old; aged; elderly; 〔比較的高い年齢での〕late; delayed / 最近, 結婚の高～化が急速に進んでいる. Recently there has been a rapid shift to late marriage. / 高～出産 late「child-bearing [maternity]. 低年齢 a young age; youth. ◐ ～の young; 〔比較的低い年齢での〕early / 低～結婚 (an) early marriage / 憂うべきは凶悪犯罪の低～化である. It is a lamentable fact that「vicious crimes are being carried out at an increasingly young age [younger and younger people are committing crimes of violence]. ▭ 年齢区分〔年齢によって分けること〕classification according to age; 〔分けられた1つ〕(年齢層) an age「group [bracket]. 年齢詐称 lying about [misrepresenting, not telling the truth about] one's age; 〔法〕(a) false

statement of *one's* age. 年齢指定〔おもちゃ・映画鑑賞などの〕age-specification; assignment of age. ▶ 3 歳以上の〜指定がついている玩具 a toy designated as (suitable) for children of three or older / この映画はアメリカでは〜指定なしで上映された. This movie was「distributed with a G-rating [shown as suitable for all ages] in the United States. 年齢条件〔要件〕 an age requirement 《of 65 for both men and women》. 年齢変化 (an)「age-related [age-dependent] change. ▶ 聴力の〜変化 (an)「age-related [age-dependent] change in hearing;〔聴力損失〕age-related hearing loss.
ねんれいさべつきんしほう【年齢差別禁止法】《米法》〔雇用における年齢差別を禁じた法律〕the Age Discrimination in Employment Act (略: ADEA).

# の

ノイス Noyce, Phillip (1950- ; オーストラリアの映画監督).
ノイズ ▯▯ 信号[映像]ノイズ【電算】image [signal] noise. ▣▯ ノイズキャンセリング[キャンセル]機能 noise-canceling function. ノイズキャンセリング[キャンセル]・ヘッドホン a pair of noise-canceling headphones; a noise-canceling headphone.
「ノイズ」〔映画〕The Astronaut's Wife.
ノイダ〔インド北部の都市〕Noida.
のいぬ【野犬】a「house [domestic] dog that has gone wild; a「wild [feral] dog.
ノイラミニダーゼ ▯▯ ノイラミニダーゼ阻害薬[剤]【薬】〔インフルエンザの治療薬〕a neuraminidase inhibitor.
のう² 【脳】 ▯▯ 脳機能 (a) cerebral function; brain [neurological] function(s). ▶ 〜機能による〜機能の低下 (a) decline in brain function associated with「aging [ageing] / 〜機能障害 cerebral dysfunction. 脳挫滅《医》(a) crushing of the brain. 脳深部刺激療法《医》deep-brain stimulation (略: DBS). 脳生理学 brain physiology. 脳地図 ⇨のうず. 脳低(体)温療法《医》brain hypothermia treatment. 脳トレ(ーニング) brain training. 脳年齢 a brain age《of 40》; the age of *one's* brain. 脳容量 (a) cerebral capacity.
ノヴェッロ ＝ヴィーノ・ノヴェッロ.
のうエム・アール・アイ【脳 MRI】《医》brain MRI; a brain MRI scan. ▶ MRI は magnetic resonance imaging の略.
のうがくせいめいかがく【農学生命科学】agriculture [agricultural] and life sciences.
のうかん³【脳幹】▯▯ 脳幹反射《生理》a brainstem reflex.
のうきぐ【農機具】▯▯ 農機具倉庫 a farm [an agricultural] machinery shed.
ノウきせい【KNOW 規制】〔大量破壊兵器に転用される恐れがある関連汎用品の輸出を禁じる〕the "know"「standard [system].
のうぎょう【農業】▯▯ 農業共済保険 agricultural mutual aid reinsurance. 農業共済再保険特別会計 an agricultural mutual aid reinsurance special account. 農業公社 an [a public] agricultural corporation. 農業指導者 an agricultural leader; a leading agriculturalist. 農業生産性 (increase) agricultural productivity. 農業大国 a「major [leading] agricultural「country [power].
のうぎょういいんかいほう【農業委員会法】《法》the Agricultural Commission Law.
のうぎょうかいりょうじょちょうほう【農業改良助長法】《法》the Agricultural Improvement Promotion Law.
のうぎょうぎじゅつけんきゅうこう【農業技術研究機構】the National Agriculture Research Organization (略: NARO). ▶ 2003 年に生物系特定産業技術研究推進機構と統合されて農業・生物系特定産業技術研究機構となる.
のうぎょうこうがくけんきゅうじょ【農業工学研究所】〔独立行政法人〕the National Institute for Rural Engineering (略: NIRE).
のうぎょうしゃねんきんききん【農業者年金基金】the Farmers' Pension Fund.
のうぎょう・しょくひんさんぎょうぎじゅつそうごうけんきゅうきこう【農業・食品産業技術総合研究機構】the National Agriculture and Food Research Organization (略: NARO).
のうぎょうしんこうちいきせいびほう【農業振興地域整備法】《法》the Law for Improvement of Agricultural Promotion Areas.
のうぎょう・せいぶつけいとくていさんぎょうぎじゅつけんきゅうきこう【農業・生物系特定産業技術研究機構】the National Agriculture and Bio-oriented Research Organization (略: NARO). ▶ 2003 年に農業技術研究機構と生物系特定産業技術研究推進機構が統合して発足.
のうぎょうせいぶつしげんけんきゅうじょ【農業生物資源研究所】the National Institute of Agrobiological Sciences (略: NIAS).
のうけっかん【脳血管】▯▯ 脳血管内治療《医》cerebrovascular treatment.
のうこうそく【脳梗塞】▯▯ 隠れ脳梗塞 ＝微小脳梗塞. 出血性脳梗塞 hemorrhagic「cerebral [brain] infarction. 心原性脳梗塞 cardioembolic「cerebral [brain] infarction. 多発性脳梗塞 multiple「cerebral [brain] infarction(s). 微小脳梗塞 (a)「cerebral [brain] microinfarction;〔ラクナ梗塞〕⇨ラクナ.
のうこうまく【脳硬膜】《解》cerebral dura mater; dura mater of the brain; dura mater encephali.
のうこつ【納骨】▯▯ 納骨室〔納骨堂〕an ossuary; a repository for the bones of the dead; a charnel (house); a cinerarium 《*pl.* -raria》;〔一家の〕a family vault;〔地下の〕a crypt; a vault;〔ころう〕⇨ろう².
のうさんぶつ【農産物】▯▯ 農産物直売所 a direct sales「store [outlet] for agricultural products. 農産物輸入自由化 the liberalization of the import of agricultural products.
のうし【脳死】▯▯ 脳死肝移植 a liver transplant [liver transplantation] from a brain-dead donor.
のうじ²【農事】▯▯ 農事組合法人 a juridical agricultural union.
のうしゃ¹【納車】▯▯ 納車前点検[整備] a predelivery inspection (略: PDI).
のうしゅく【濃縮】▯▯ 濃縮還元 reconstitution《of fruit juice》from concentrate (略: RFC). ▶ 〜還元フルーツジュース fruit juice reconstituted from concentrate.
のうしょ¹【能書】▯▯ 能書家 a (good) calligrapher; a good penman; a person with good handwriting.
のうしょうがい【脳障害】▯▯ 高次脳障害《医》(a) higher「cortical [cerebral] dysfunction. 後天性脳障害《医》(an) acquired brain injury (略: ABI); acquired brain damage (略: ABD). ▶ 後天性〜児 a child with「(an) acquired brain injury [(an) ABI].
のうしょく【濃色】▯▯ 濃色ビール (a) dark beer.
のうしんけい【脳神経】▯▯ 脳神経学 brain [cranial]

のうずいえき

neurology. 脳神経情報学 neuroinformatics.
のうずいえき【脳髄液】〘解〙cerebral fluid.
のうせい[2]【農政】▶ 農政改革 agricultural reform.
のうぜい【納税】▶ 納税意識 〔義務の自覚〕awareness of one's duties as a taxpayer.
のうぜいしゃ【納税者】▶ 納税者意識 taxpayer awareness.
のうぜいしんこく【納税申告】▶ 電子納税申告 electronic [online] tax filing.
のうせきずい【脳脊髄】▶ 脳脊髄液減少症〘医〙cerebrospinal fluid [CSF] hypovelemia.
のうせん【膿栓】〘医〙a tonsillolith; a tonsilith; lacunar debris.
のうそくせんしょう【脳塞栓症】▶ 心原性脳塞栓症 cardiogenic cerebral embolism.
のうそっちゅう【脳卒中】▶ 脳卒中集中治療室 a stroke care unit (略: SCU).
のうそん【農村】▶ 農村部〔都市部に対して〕rural [farming, agricultural] districts [areas].
のうち【農地】▶ 農地価格 the 「price [value] of agricultural land; agricultural land 「prices [values].
のうちくさんぎょうしんこうきこう【農畜産業振興機構】the Agriculture & Livestock Industries Corporation (略: ALIC). ▶ 2003年に農畜産業振興事業団より移行.
のうちず【脳地図】an atlas [a map] of the brain; a brain 「atlas [map]. 〜を作成する map the brain. ▶ 脳地図作製 (a) brain mapping.
のうとう【納刀】〘動作〙sheathing a sword;〔鞘(さや)に納めた刀〕a sheathed sword. 〜する sheath(e) a sword.
のうどうみゃくりゅう【脳動脈瘤】▶ 未破裂脳動脈瘤 (an) unruptured cerebral aneurysm. ▶ 無症候性未破裂〜 (an) asymptomatic unruptured cerebral aneurysm.
ノウハウ　ノウハウ本 a 「how-to [know-how] book.
のうふ[1]【納付】▶ 納付率〔税金などの〕a 《tax》compliance rate.
のうほう[2]【膿疱】▶ 膿疱性乾癬〘医〙pustular psoriasis.
のうみん【農民】▶ 農民市場(いちば)〔北朝鮮のヤミ市〕a farmers' market.
のうみんこう【農民工】=みんこう.
のうやく【農薬】▶ 無登録農薬 an unregistered agricultural chemical. ▶ 農薬使用基準 a standard for the use of 「agricultural chemicals [pesticides].
のうりょく[1]【能力】▶ 能力等級制度 an ability-based ranking system.
のうりんぎょぎょうしんようききん【農林漁業信用基金】the Agriculture, Forestry and Fisheries Credit Foundations.
のうりんすいさんしょうひぎじゅつセンター【農林水産消費技術-】〔独立行政法人〕the Center for Food Quality, Labeling and Consumer Services.
のうりんすいさんぶつとうゆしゅつそくしんぜんこくきょうぎかい【農林水産物等輸出促進全国協議会】the Council for the Promotion of Agricultural, Forestry and Fishery Exports.
のうりんりがく【脳倫理学】neuroethics.
ノウルーズ〔イラン暦の元日〕Norooz; Nowruz; Norouz.
ノエ Noé, Gaspar (1963- ; アルゼンチン生まれのフランスの映画監督・脚本家).
「ノエル」〔映画〕Noel.
ノーアクション・レター〔法・証券〕〔予定事業の合法性に関する事業者からの問い合わせに対して政府機関が特に問題ないする点はないと回答する書状〕a no-action letter. 〔⇨法令適用事前確認手続 (⇨ほうれい)〕
ノーヴァヤ・ガゼータ =ノーバヤ・ガゼータ.
ノーウォーク・ウイルス〘医〙a Norwalk virus (略: NV).
ノーウォークようウイルス【-様-】〘医〙a Norwalk-like virus (略: NLV).
ノーカーうんどう【-運動】〔環境保護運動の一環としての〕a campaign to discourage commuting by car; a non-car commuting campaign.
ノーゴール〔サッカー〕▶ 三浦は開幕以来11試合〜が続いている. Since the start of the season, Miura has failed to score for eleven games running.
ノーザム Northam, Jeremy (1961- ; 英国生まれの映画俳優).
ノーザン・ケープ =きたケープ.
ノーザン・パイク〘魚〙〔カワカマスの一種〕a northern pike; Esox lucius.
ノーズ▶ ノーズ・アート〔軍用機などの機首側面に描かれた絵〕nose-cone art.
ノース・ウェストしゅう【-州】=ほくせいしゅう.
ノースリッジじしん【-地震】〔1994年, 米国ロサンジェルス市ノースリッジ地方に大被害をもたらした地震〕the (1994) Northridge earthquake.
ノーダル・ポイント〘光〙〔レンズ内の焦点中心〕a nodal point.
ノート[2] Note, Kessai (1950- ; マーシャル諸島共和国の政治家; 大統領〔2000-08〕).
ノートン Norton, Edward (1969- ; 米国の映画俳優).
ノーネクタイ▶ ノーネクタイ・ノー上着運動〔夏の軽装化の〕a "No Necktie, No Jacket" campaign.
ノーバヤ・ガゼータ〔ロシアの新聞〕Novaya Gazeta.
ノープリントプライスほうしき【-方式】〔標準小売価格を商品に表示しない方式〕a formula whereby goods are delivered from the maker without price labels and are labelled by the retailer on the basis of a recommended price list.
ノーベルぶつりがくしょうへのだいいっぽ【-物理学賞への第一歩】〔ポーランド科学アカデミー物理学研究所が主催する高校生の論文コンテスト〕the First Step to Nobel Prize in Physics.
ノーボギー〘ゴルフ〙no bogeys. ▶ 宮里は9バーディー, 〜で回り, 首位に立った. Miyazato took the lead, going round with nine birdies and no bogeys.
ノーボスチつうしん【-通信】〔ロシアの国営通信社〕the Novosti Press Agency (略: APN). ▶ 1991年「ロシア・ノーボスチ通信」に改組.
ノーマライゼーション▶ ノーマライゼーション7か年戦略〔1995年政府策定の〕the Seven-Year Normalization Strategy.
ノーミス▶ 〜の演技《put on, stage》a perfect performance.
「ノーラ・ジョイス 或る小説家の妻」〔映画〕Nora.
ノーラン Nolan, Christopher (1970- ; 英国生まれの映画監督).
ノーリーズ =ノウルーズ.
ノーロード〘金融〙〔手数料無料〕no load. ▶ ノーロード・ファンド a no-load fund.
ノーン・ブワ・ラムプー〔タイ東北部の県; 同県の県都〕Nong Bua Lamphu.
のき【軒】▶ 軒花〔祭りの際に家の軒下につり下げる紙製の花飾り〕a paper flower (hung) under the eaves (at a festival).
ノキア〔フィンランドの企業グループ〕Nokia.
のこぎり【鋸】▶ 鋸音楽 saw music.
のこぎりびき【鋸挽き】〔昔の刑罰〕a form of capital punishment in which a prisoner was pilloried in public for two days and passersby were encouraged to cut his neck with a saw.
のこぎりやし【鋸椰子】〘植〙〔ヤシ科の低木; 北米原産〕saw palmetto; Serenoa repens.
のこりじかん【残り時間】(the) time 「remaining [left]; (the) remaining time;〔インターネットオークションなどの掲示で〕time left《to bid》. ▶ 〜がない there is no 「time left [more time]; be out of time / 〜が5分を切る be

[have] less than 5 minutes「left [remaining] / 最近, 気力, 体力がめっきり衰え, 人生の〜が少なくなってきたと感じる. I have lost a lot of my mental and physical energy lately and feel「I may not have much time to live [my days may be numbered].」 ◐〜あとわずか. 日本の勝利は目前だ.〔サッカーなどで〕With「very little time left [seconds to go],」「victory is (now) in sight [Japan is now certain to win].」/ 持ち時間各 3 時間のうち, 〜は山田各人 6 分, 池田名人 5 分.〔囲碁・将棋〕With a time limit of three hours each, Yamada has 6 minutes「left [on the clock] and Ikeda 5 minutes.」/ 彼は〜1 秒で一本勝ちした.〔柔道〕He won the bout by an ippon with only a second「to spare [of time left].」

**のざわな**【野沢菜】 ◐野沢菜漬け〔信州の野沢温泉特産の漬物で, 蕪菜を塩漬けしたもの〕pickled turnip leaves.

**のし**[2]【熨斗】 ◖▭内[外]のし ◐内[外]〜にする attach a *noshi*「inside [on] the wrapping paper.

**のしいた**【延し板・伸し板】【料理】a kneading board.

**のしだい**【延し台・伸し台】【料理】a kneading「board [table, surface].」 ◖▭大理石延し台 a marble kneading slab.

**-のせ**【-乗せ】〔一定値以上になること〕 ◐ 1200 円〜を待って持ち株を売りに出す sell stock after waiting for the price to「exceed [top, move above] 1,200 yen.

**のぞきみ**【覗き見】 ◖▭覗き見趣味 voyeurism. ◐〜趣味の人 a peeping Tom; a voyeur.

**ノックアウト** ◖▭ノックアウト方式〔スキー競技など〕〔勝ち残り方式〕 a knockout format.

**ノックス・ピーエムほう**【NOx・PM 法】【法】=じどうしゃノックス・ピーエムほう.

**ノッティンガムだいがく**【-大学】〔英国の大学〕the University of Nottingham.

**「ノッティングヒルの恋人」**〔映画〕Notting Hill.

**のどつまり**【喉詰まり】getting《a bone》「stuck [lodged] in *one's* throat; choking on《a pretzel》. ◐餅の〜でようよう死ぬところだった. I choked on some *mochi* and nearly died.

**のねこ**【野猫】a「house [domestic] cat that has gone wild; a「wild [feral] cat.

**ノバーグ**〔コンピュータウイルスの 1 つ; マイドゥームの別名〕Novarg.

**のはらなでしこ**【野原撫子】【植】a Deptford pink; *Dianthus armeria*.

**ノバルティス**〔スイスの医薬品会社〕Novartis AG.

**のび**[1]【伸び・延び】 ◖▭伸び率管理〔医療費・社会保障給付など〕control [restriction] of a growth rate.

**のびしろ**【伸び代】〔期待できる成長の余地〕(show) promise;〔スポーツ〕(have) potential; trainability.

**「ノボケイン 局部麻酔の罠」**〔映画〕Novocaine.

**ノボラザレフスカヤきち**【-基地】〔ロシアの南極基地〕Novolazarevskaya Station.

**のぼり**[2]【幟】 ◖▭幟旗 a vertical「flag [banner, standard].」

**のま**【野馬】〔放し飼いの馬〕a pastured horse.

**のみきり**【飲み切り】〔飲みきること〕drink down;〔1 回で飲みきれる量〕a single drink. ◐この牛乳は一回〜の少量パックです. This milk (carton) is a single-helping size. ◖▭飲み切りサイズ a single-helping size.

**のみごろ**【飲み頃】the right time「to drink [for drinking].」 ◐このワインは 5 年ほどするとよく熟成し〜になる. After about five years, this wine fully matures and is ready「to drink [to be drunk, for drinking]. ◐〜の温度 the right temperature for drinking. ◐昼に冷蔵庫に入れたから, 飲み頃でちょうどいい. I put it in the refrigerator at noon, so it should just about be right for drinking.

**のみづらい**【飲み辛い】unpleasant to drink. ◐この薬は苦くて〜. This medicine is so bitter it's difficult to swallow.

**ノミネート** ◖▭ノミネート作品 a nominated work.

**のみばえ**【蚤蠅】【昆】〔ノミバエ科のハエの総称〕a phorid fly. ◖▭ノミバエ科 Phoridae.

**ノモス**《＜Gk》〔古代ギリシャで, 法律・制度・習慣など〕nomos.

**のやぎ**【野山羊】a wild goat.

**のり**[2]【糊】 ◖▭糊伏せ【染色】〔染色工程の 1 つで, 彩色部分を糊で覆って防染する作業〕resist dyeing.

**のり**[3]【乗り】 ◖▭縦乗り【音楽】⇨タテノリ.

**のり**[4]【海苔】 ◖▭乾燥のり「干し海苔」dried「seaweed [nori].」 ◖▭もみのり shredded (finely sliced)「dried seaweed [nori].」

**のりつぎ**【乗り継ぎ】 ◖▭乗り継ぎ駅 a transfer station; a station for changing《trains》; a junction. ◐新宿は毎日ほう大な数の通勤客の〜駅になっている. Shinjuku is a station where vast numbers of commuters change train(s) everyday. ◖▭乗り継ぎ拠点空港 a transit hub; an air-transit hub. ◖▭乗り継ぎ空港 a transit airport.

**ノリナ**【植】=とっくりらん.

**ノリノリ**【ムードに完全に同調している様子】 ◐聴衆は 1 曲目から〜だった. The audience was really into it right from the first song.

**のりめん**【法面】 ◖▭道路[鉄道]法面 a「roadside [railside] bank [slope].」

**ノリンコ**〔中国最大の兵器製造企業〕NORINCO; China North Industries Corporation; China North Industries Group. ▶中国語名は 北方工業公司.

**ノリントン** Norrington, Stephen (1964– ; 英国映画監督).

**ノルウェーかいせん**【-疥癬】【医】Norwegian [crusted] scabies.

**ノルティ** Nolte, Nick (1941– ; 米国の映画俳優; 本名 Nicholas King Nolte).

**ノルディックきょり**【-距離】〔スキー〕long-distance Nordic (skiing).

**ノルディック・ジャンプ**〔スキー〕Nordic jumping; the Nordic jump.

**ノルバスク**【商標・薬】【高血圧症・狭心症治療薬】ベシル酸アムロジピンの商品名〕Norvasc.

**ノルバデックス**【商標・薬】【抗がん剤】クエン酸タモキシフェンの商品名〕Nolvadex.

**ノルマル・ヘキサン** ◖▭ノルマル・ヘキサン抽出物質【化】(a)「normal-hexane [n-hexane] extract.

**のれんこうもり**【暖簾蝙蝠】【動】a Natterer's bat; *Myotis nattereri*.

**ノロウイルス**【医】〔食中毒の原因となるウイルス〕(a) norovirus. ▶以前は小型球形ウイルス, ノーウォーク様ウイルスと呼ばれていた. ◖▭ノロウイルス感染症 norovirus infection.

**ノン・カイ** 1〔タイ東北部, ラオスとの国境の町〕Nong Khai; Nongkhai. 2〔タイ東北部の県〕Nong Khai; Nongkhai.

**ノンケ**【気】〔同性愛嗜好がない人〕a straight (man); a straight arrow;〈集合的で〉straights. ◐一見ゲイ風だが彼は〜だ. He looks gay but he's really straight.

**ノンコン**【眼科】〔非接触眼圧測定装置〕a noncontact tonometer.

**ノンタブリ**〔タイ中部の県; その県都〕Nonthaburi.

**ノンパッケージりゅうつう**【-流通】【電算】〔音楽やソフトウェアなどの商品をインターネットでダウンロード販売すること〕virtual [online] distribution.

**ノンフライ**〔〜の〕〔油で揚げていない〕non-fried. ◖▭ノンフライ麺〔インスタントラーメンなど〕non-fried instant noodles.

**ノンフリート**【保険】 ◖▭ノンフリート契約〔自動車保険で契約自動車が 9 台以下である場合のもの〕a non-fleet contract. ◖▭ノンフリート等級 rates for a clean (driving) record.

**ノンリコース・ローン**【金融】〔非遡及型融資〕a nonrecourse loan.

# は

バー Burr, Raymond (1917-93; カナダ生まれの俳優; テレビでペリー・メイスン役などを演じた).
ハーイル ＝ハイル.
ハーヴァード・ビジネス・スクール〔米国マサチューセッツ州にある経営大学院〕Harvard Business School（略: HBS).
ハーヴェイ・ロードのぜんてい【-の前提】《経》the pre-suppositions of Harvey Road.
パーカー 1 Parker, Alan (1944-　 ; 英国生まれの映画監督・脚本家).
2 Parker, Trey (1969-　 ; 米国の映画監督).
パーカーライジング〖商標・金属加工〗〔鉄製部品の錆止め表面仕上げ; 燐酸塩の被膜を作ること〕Parkerizing. ▷ Parkerize v. ▶ 一般語としては phosphating.
バーキン Birkin, Jane (1946-　 ; 英国生まれの女優・歌手).
パーキンソニズム〖医〗〔パーキンソン病〕Parkinson's disease; paralysis agitans; 〔パーキンソン病に似た症状が出る病気の総称〕Parkinsonism.
ハーグこくさいしほうかいぎ【-国際私法会議】the Hague Conference on Private International Law.
パーク・ゴルフ ▯▯ パークゴルフ場 a park golf course; (a) park golf links.
バークたいひ【-堆肥】(pine) bark compost.
パークトレイン〖商標〗〔レジャー施設や公園内を循環する汽車（型のバス）〕a park train.
「バークにまかせろ」〔億万長者が道楽でロサンジェルスの殺人課警部をやっているという刑事もののTVドラマ〕Burke's Law.
バークレイズぎんこう【-銀行】〔英国の銀行〕Barclays Bank.
バークレーズぎんこう【-銀行】＝バークレイズぎんこう.
「バークレー牧場」〔大牧場を営むバークレー (Barkley) 一家のTVホームドラマ西部劇〕The Big Valley.
パークロロエチレン〖化〗〔有機塩素系溶剤〕perchloroethylene.
バーゲン[1] ▯▯ バーゲン・ハンティング 《証券》〔安値拾い〕bargain hunting.
バーけん【-券】〔パーティー券〕a party ticket.
バーコード ▯▯ バーコード化 bar-coding. ▷ ～化する bar-code《items in inventory》; adopt bar codes《for product identification》/ 医師の処方内容を～化する bar-code doctors' prescriptions.
ハーザン〔ベトナム北東部の省; その省都〕Ha Giang.
バージ〔平底の運搬船〕a barge.
バージニア・ビーチ ＝ヴァージニア・ビーチ.
「バージニアン」〔米国の, 大牧場に住み付いた流れ者のTV 90分ドラマ〕The Virginian.
ハーシムけ【-家】＝ハシムけ.
バージャーびょう【-病】〖医〗Buerger's disease.
パーシャル・バース・アボーション〔部分出産中絶〕(a) partial birth abortion.
バーション Persson, Göran (1949-　 ; スウェーデンの政治家; 首相〔1996-2006〕).
ハースコヴィッツ Herskovits, Marshall (1952-　 ; 米国の映画監督).
ハースコビッツ ＝ハースコヴィッツ.
「バースデイ・ガール」〔映画〕Birthday Girl.
ハーセプチン〖商標・薬〗〔乳がん治療薬トラスツズマブの商品名〕Herceptin.
バーゼルいいんかい【-委員会】the Basel Committee. [＝バーゼルぎんこうかんとくいいんかい]
バーゼルぎんこうかんとくいいんかい【-銀行監督委員会】〖G10諸国の中央銀行総裁会議により, 1975年設立〗 the Basel Committee on Banking Supervision.
バーゼルごうい【-合意】〖金融〗〔BIS規制〕the Basel Capital Accord; the Basel Concordat.
パーセルフォース〔英国郵政公社の小荷物取扱部門〕the Parcelforce.
バーター ▯▯ バーター協力〔選挙などでの政党間の〕vote bartering《between parties》.
バーチ Birch, Thora (1982-　 ; 米国の映画女優).
バーチャル ▯▯ バーチャル体験 (a) virtual experience. バーチャル・ペット a virtual pet. バーチャル・ミュージアム a virtual museum.
パーツ・モデル〔広告写真などで手・足など体の一部だけを写されるモデル〕a part(s) model; a body-part(s) model.〔⇨テタレ, アシタレ〕
バーディー ▯▯ バーディー・ラッシュ a birdie rush.
パーティー ▯▯ パーティー・バッグ〔服飾〕an evening bag; a party bag. パーティー・ルーム〔パーティー用の（貸）部屋〕a party room; a room for parties.
ハーティエン〔ベトナム南部, カンボジアとの国境の町〕Ha Tien.
「バーティカル・リミット」〔映画〕The Vertical Limit.
パーティクル・ガン〖生物〗a particle gun.
パーティクルぶんせき【-分析】〔粒子の分析〕particle analysis.
バーティゴ〖医〗〔航空機操縦中の空間識失調, 水平線を基準としての正しい姿勢感覚が保持できなくなり空中で方向感覚を失うこと〕vertigo.
ハーディン Hardin, Garrett (1915-2003; 米国の生物学者;「共有地の悲劇」を提示).
パーテール・ポジション《F》《レスリング》(be in)「the parterre position [the crouching position].
ハート 1 Hart, Ian (1964-　 ; 英国生まれの映画俳優).
2 Hart, Melissa Joan (1976-　 ; 米国の映画女優).
3 Hurt, John (1940-　 ; 英国生まれの映画俳優; 本名 John Vincent Hurt).
4 Hurt, William (1950-　 ; 米国の映画俳優).
バード Bird, Antonia (1959-　 ; 英国の映画監督).
「ハート・オブ・ウーマン」〔映画〕What Women Want.
「バード・オン・ワイヤー」〔映画〕Bird on a Wire.
バードギース ＝バドギス.
ハード・グッズ〔耐久消費財〕hard goods.
「バードケージ」〔映画〕The Birdcage.
バートコウィアク Bartkowiak, Andrzej (1950-　 ; ポーランド生まれの映画監督).
ハード・ターゲット〔防備堅固な標的〕a hard target.
ハードディスク ▯▯ ハードディスク内蔵 ▯▯ ～内蔵DVDレコーダー＝HDD内蔵DVDレコーダー〔⇨エイチ・ディー・ディー〕. ハードディスク・ナビ〔自動車の〕＝HDDナビ〔⇨エイチ・ディー・ディーナビ〕.
ハートネット Hartnett, Josh (1978-　 ; 米国の映画俳優; 本名 Joshua Daniel Hartnett).
ハートビルほう【-法】〖法〗the "Heart Building" Law. ▶ 正式名称は「高齢者, 身体障害者等が円滑に利用できる特定建築物の建築の促進に関する法律」(the Law on Buildings Accessible and Usable by the Elderly and Physically Handicapped). 2003年施行, 2006年バリアフリー新法の施行に伴い廃止.
バードほう【-法】〖米法〗〔反ダンピング関税分配法〕the Byrd Amendment.
ハートマンやましまうま【-山縞馬】〖動〗〔アフリカ原産ウマ科の動物〕a Hartmann's (mountain) zebra; Equus zebra hartmannae.
ハートヤイ ＝ハジャイ.

ハード・リカー［アルコール度の高い酒］hard liquor.
ハードロックカフェ［アメリカンレストランチェーン］the Hard Rock Cafe.
バートン Burton, Tim (1958- ；米国の映画監督；本名 Timothy William Burton).
バーナンキ Bernanke, Ben S. (1953- ；米国の経済学者；連邦準備理事会議長 [2005- ]).
バーニーズ・ニューヨーク［米国の高級百貨店チェーン］Barneys New York.
バーハ ＝ババ.
ハーパー Harper, Stephen (1959- ；カナダの政治家；首相 [2006- ]).
「バーバー」［映画］The Man Who Wasn't There.
バービル ＝バビル.
ハーブ ▫︎ ハーブ・ウォーター herbal water; herb water. ハーブ・サラダ a herb salad. ハーブ鶏［豚］［生き物］a herb-fed「chicken [pig];［食肉］herb-fed「chicken [pork]. ハーブ・ハニー、ハーブ蜂蜜 a herb(al) honey. ハーブ風呂 ＝ハーブ湯. ハーブ湯 a herb(al) bath. ハーブ療法 herb therapy.
パープ【PARP】［生化］［酵素の一種］PARP; poly(ADP-ribose) polymerase(s). ► poly(ADP-ribose) の表記について ⇨エー・ディー・ピー（ポリ ADP リボース）.
「パーフェクト・カップル」［映画］Primary Colors.
「パーフェクト・ストーム」［映画］The Perfect Storm.
「パーフェクト・ワールド」［映画］A Perfect World.
ハーフパンツ［特に女性向けの膝丈［七分丈］のパンツ［スラックス］］Capri pants; cropped pants; trouser shorts.
パーフルオロカーボン［化］［代替フロンの一種］(a) perfluorocarbon（略: PFC）.
ハーベイ・ロードのぜんてい【―の前提】［経］＝ハーヴェイ・ロードのぜんてい.
バーベキュー ▫︎ バーベキュー味 barbecue flavor. ▫︎ ～味のポテトチップス barbecue-flavored potato chips. バーベキュー・コンロ a barbecue「grill [stove, burner].
パーペチュアル・カレンダー［時計などの］a perpetual calendar.
バーベラ Barbera, Joseph Roland (1911-2006; 米国のアニメ製作者).
バーホーベン ＝ヴァーホーヴェン.
パーマカルチャー ≪＜permanent ＋ agriculture [culture]≫［資源維持・自足を意図した農業生態系の開発］permaculture.
ハーマン Herman, Mark (1954- ；英国の映画監督).
ハーム【HARM】［米軍］［警察管制レーダー破壊用の空対地ミサイル AGM-88 の通称］a HARM. ► high-speed antiradiation missile の略.
パーラメント・スクエア［英国ロンドンにある公園］Parliament Square.
バーリ・トゥード ≪＜Port. ＝ anything goes, no rules (何でもあり)≫［総合格闘技の1つ］vale tudo.
ハーリン Harlin, Renny (1959- ；フィンランド生まれの米国の映画監督；本名 Renny Lauri Mauritz Harjola).
バーリン Berlin, Isaiah (1909-97; 英国のユダヤ系政治哲学者・思想史家).
バール Barr, Jean-marc (1960- ；ドイツ生まれの映画俳優).
パール[1] ▫︎ パール・インク［印刷］pearl ink.
パール[4] Pal, Radha Binod (1886-1967; インドの法学者；極東国際軍事裁判の判事).
「パール・ハーバー」［映画］Pearl Harbor.
パールベック［レバノン東部の遺跡］Baalbeck.
パール・マイカ［染料］pearl mica.
ハーレイ Hurley, Elizabeth (1965- ；英国の映画女優).
ハーレー ＝ハリー[1].
ハーレツ、ハアレツ［イスラエルの新聞］Ha'aretz; Haaretz.
バーン Byrne, Gabriel (1950- ；アイルランド生まれの映画俳優).
バーンズ Burns, Edward (1968- ；米国の映画俳優).

バーンズ・コレクション［A・C・バーンズの美術収集品の総称］the Barnes Collection.
バーンズざいだん【―財団】the Barnes Foundation.
ハーン・ハリーリ［エジプト、カイロ市内の市場・観光地］Khan el-[al-]Khalili.
はい[3]【肺】 ▫︎ 肺疾患 a「lung [pulmonary] disease; lung trouble; a lung complaint;［医］a chest「disorder [disease]. 肺小細胞がん［医］［小細胞がん］small cell carcinoma. 肺がん［医］pulmonary adenocarcinoma. 肺塞栓症［医］［肺塞栓症］pulmonary thromboembolism. 肺動静脈瘻［医］(a) pulmonary arteriovenous fistula. 肺扁平上皮がん［医］(a) squamous cell「carcinoma of the lung [lung cancer].
パイ[2] ▫︎ パイ・カッター a pie cutter;［円形刃つきの］a pastry wheel.
ハイアール【海爾】［中国の電化製品メーカー］Haier. ► 正式名称は 海爾集団公司.
バイアウト［買い占め］a buyout. ▫︎ バイアウト・ファンド［買収ファンド］a buyout fund.
バイコム［米国のメディア企業］Viacom Inc.
バイアス ▫︎ バイアス電極［電］a bias electrode.
はいあつ[2]【排圧】［自動車］［排気圧］(an) exhaust pressure.
ハイアマ ＝ハイ・アマチュア（⇨アマチュア）.
ハイアムズ Hyams, Peter (1943- ；米国の映画監督).
ハイアリア［米国フロリダ州南東部の市］Hialeah.
はいいろ【灰色】 ▫︎ 灰色決着 a "gray" [an ambivalent, an inconclusive] decision. ▫︎ 土地開発をめぐる知事の収賄疑惑は、証拠不十分として～決着することになった. Due to insufficient evidence, no clear decision was reached in the case of the governor suspected of accepting bribes in connection with a land development deal. 灰色無罪 (be declared)「innocent [not guilty] while still under suspicion [with reservations].
はいいろてんとう【灰色天道】［昆］Olla nigrum.
はいいろやぎゅう【灰色野牛】 ＝コーピレ.
「ハイウェイ・パトロール」［米国の TV ドラマ］Highway Patrol.
はいえき[3]【廃駅】［廃止された駅］an abandoned station; a station「where trains no longer stop [which has closed down].
はいえん[1]【肺炎】 ▫︎ 肺炎双球菌［菌］a pneumococcus (pl. -cocci).
バイオイメージング［生体の器官、細胞、分子などを画像で見るための技術］bioimaging.
バイオエタノール［化］［サトウキビやトウモロコシを原料とする燃料］bioethanol.
バイオきぎょう【―企業】a biotech(nology) company.
バイオさんぎょうじょうほうかコンソーシアム【―産業情報化―】the Japan Biological Informatics Consortium（略: JBIC）.
バイオスフェア・ツー【―2】［米国アリゾナ州の砂漠にある生態系実験施設］Biosphere 2.
バイオセーフティー［生物］［遺伝子組み換え動植物の無害性・有害微生物の取り扱い方法の安全性］biosafety. ▫︎ バイオセーフティー・レベル a biosafety level（略: BSL）. ▫︎ ～レベル 1 [2, 3, 4]［病原微生物の危険度］Biosafety Level 1 [2, 3, 4]; BSL1 [2, 3, 4].
バイオセーフティーぎていしょ【―議定書】［遺伝子組み換え生物の国際取引の規制に関する議定書］the Biosafety Protocol.
バイオディーゼルねんりょう【―燃料】［植物油から作られる軽油代替燃料］biodiesel fuel（略: BDF）.
バイオディフェンス［生体防御］biodefense; biophylaxis;［病原体に対する防衛］biodefense.
バイオテクノロジー ▫︎ バイオテクノロジー戦略大綱［2002年、政府が策定］(the Japanese government's) Biotechnology Strategy Guidelines.
バイオトイレ［微生物を利用して尿尿（ふん）を処理するトイレ］

バイオナノサイエンス

a biotoilet.
バイオナノサイエンス〔細胞生物学〕bionanoscience.
バイオナノテクノロジー bionanotechonology.
「バイオニック・ジェミー」⇨「地上最強の美女バイオニック・ジェミー」.
バイオバーデン〖化・医・薬〗〔製品上の生育微生物数〕(a) bioburden.
「バイオハザード」〔映画〕Resident Evil. ▶続編は「バイオハザードⅡ: アポカリプス」Resident Evil: Apocalypse.
バイオバンク〔個人の遺伝情報を集めてデータベース化したもの〕a biobank.
バイオビジネス〔生物工学関連事業〕a biotech(nology) business.
バイオフィードバック 🔊 バイオフィードバック訓練 biofeedback training (略: BFT). バイオフィードバック療法 (a) biofeedback therapy.
バイオフィルム〖生物〗〔微生物が自己防衛のために寄り集まって作るバリア〕a (microbial) biofilm.
バイオフォトン〖生物〗〔生物微弱発光〕a biophoton.
バイオベンチャー〔バイオテクノロジー分野のベンチャー企業〕a bioventure company; a biotechnology venture business.
バイオポリマー〖生化〗〔生体高分子〕a biopolymer.
バイオマーカー〖生物・医〗〔生物[生体]指標〕a biomarker.
バイオマス 🔊 木質(系)バイオマス wood [woody] biomass. 🔊 木質～発電 wood biomass (electricity) generation. バイオマス・ガス化発電 biomass gasification (power) generation. バイオマス発電 biomass (power) generation. バイオマス発電所 a biomass power 「plant [station]. バイオマスプラスチック (an) organic plastic; a biomass plastic; 〔植物プラスチック〕(a) vegetable(-based) plastic.
バイオミュージック〔音楽療法に用いられる音楽〕biomusic.
バイオメトリクス〔生体認証〕biometrics; biometric authentication. 🔊 バイオメトリクス・パスポート〔旅券〕a biometric passport.
バイオリアクター 🔊 マイクロバイオリアクター〔生物機能を利用した超小型反応装置〕a microbioreactor.
バイオリージョン〔環境・生態〕〔生命地域〕a bioregion. ▷ bioregional adj.
ばいか[1]〔売価〕🔊 売価還元法〔会計〕the retail inventory method.
ばいか[5]〔倍化〕〔倍にすること〕(a) doubling. ～する double. 🔊 倍化時間〔細胞などの〕(a) doubling time.
バイカー〔趣味でバイクに乗る人〕a recreational motorcyclist.
はいかい[2]〔徘徊〕🔊 夜間徘徊〔認知症老人などの〕late-night wandering; wandering about 「late at night [in the middle of the night]. 🔊 徘徊高齢者SOSネットワーク〔地域の〕an SOS network for wandering elderly (dementia) patients.
ばいかしもつけ〔梅花下野〕〖植〗=りきゅうばい.
はいがん[2]〔肺癌〕🔊 中心型肺癌 =肺門部肺癌. 肺門部肺癌 hilar [central] lung cancer; cancer of the pulmonary hilum.
はいき[2]〔排気〕排気圧 (an) exhaust pressure. 排気循環(方)式〔掃除機などの空気を吸い込み口のほうに循環させることで排気を減らす方式〕an exhaust recirculation system. 🔊 ～循環(方)式掃除機 a vacuum cleaner with exhaust recirculation. 排気筒 an exhaust pipe; 〔原子力発電所・汽船などの〕a funnel; a chimney. 排気バルブ〔機〕〔エンジンの〕an exhaust valve.
はいき[3]〔廃棄〕🔊 廃棄コスト waste-disposal costs; the cost of waste disposal. 廃棄自転車 a scrap bicycle. 廃棄車両 a scrap vehicle. 🔊 車両引き取り業者 a scrap vehicle dealer. 廃棄二輪車 a scrap motorcycle. 廃棄ロス a loss due to the discarding of unsalable merchandise.

はいきのう〔肺機能〕🔊 低肺機能〖医〗low pulmonary function.
はいきぶつ〔廃棄物〕🔊 実験(系)廃棄物 laboratory waste. 🔊 廃棄物減量(化)(a) reduction in the 「amount [volume] of waste; waste reduction. 廃棄物処理工学 waste「disposal [management, processing, treatment] technology [engineering].
ばいきゃく〔売却〕🔊 売却物件〔不動産〕(売りに出されている) a (real estate) property for sale; (売却済みの) a (real estate) property (already) sold.
はいきゅう[1]〔配球〕🔊 配球パターン〔投手の〕a (pitcher's) pattern of pitches.
はいきゅう[2]〔配給〕🔊 配給権〔映画など〕distribution rights (to [for, on] a movie).
はいぎょう〔廃業〕🔊 自主廃業 voluntary liquidation; voluntary cessation of business (operations). 🔊 自主～する go into voluntary liquidation; voluntarily cease business.
はいきん[2]〔排菌〕〖医〗the release of 《tubercle》 bacilli; infectiousness; contagiousness; an infectious [a contagious] state. 🔊 排菌(患)者 a contagious [an infectious] 〖TB〗 patient.
はいきん[3]〔配筋〕〖建〗〔鉄筋の配置〕a (reinforcing) bar arrangement; a reinforcement layout. 🔊 配筋検査 a bar arrangement inspection. 配筋図 a bar arrangement drawing.
ばいきん〔黴菌〕🔊 ばい菌恐怖症 a germ phobia; a pathological fear of germs.
バイキング 🔊 ケーキバイキング〔ケーキの食べ放題〕an all-you-can-eat cake buffet. ランチバイキング〔昼食メニュー食べ放題〕an all-you-can-eat lunch buffet. 🔊 バイキング料理 buffet-style [smorgasbord-style] food [dishes, cuisine]; a 「buffet-style [smorgasbord-style] meal.
はいく〔俳句〕🔊 英語俳句 (a) haiku in English; (an) English(-language) haiku.
はいぐうし〔配偶子〕🔊 異形[異型]配偶子 a heterogamete; an anisogamete. 同形[同型]配偶子 an isogamete.
はいぐうしゃ〔配偶者〕🔊 外国人配偶者 a [the] non-Japanese spouse of a Japanese national; a [the] spouse of a Japanese national with foreign 「nationality [citizenship]. 配偶者加給年金 an additional pension for a spouse. 配偶者選択 mate selection; choosing [selecting] a mate. 配偶者相続控除 a marital deduction. 配偶者ビザ a spouse visa; a visa for a spouse. 配偶者暴力相談支援センター a spousal violence counseling and support center.
バイクパーチ〔魚〕〔魚食性の淡水魚〕a pikeperch; a pikeperch; Sander lucioperca.
「ハイ・クライムズ」〔映画〕High Crimes.
ハイグル=ヘイグル.
はいけい[2]〔背景〕🔊 政治的背景 a political background; political motivation. 🔊 警察はその爆弾事件に政治的～があるかどうか捜査中である. A police investigation is under way to ascertain whether 「there was a political motivation to the bombing [the bombing was politically motivated]. 🔊 背景解明 clarifying the background 《of [to] the incident》; making clear what 「lies [lay] behind 《the events》. 背景色 a background color. 背景説明 a background briefing. 背景分析 (a) background [context] analysis.
はいごう[2]〔配合〕🔊 配合成分 a component of a blend; an ingredient. 配合比率〔配合比〕a ratio of combination.
ハイサイド〔オートバイでの転倒の一形態〕a highside. ～する highside; do a highside.
はいさく〔廃作〕〔栽培をやめること〕termination of 《tobacco》 cultivation. ～する stop 「growing [raising,

cultivating]《tobacco》.
はいざら【灰皿】 ▯ 携帯灰皿 a portable ashtray.
はいし[7]【俳誌】a haiku magazine.
バイジ〔イラク北部の都市〕Baiji.
ハイジャック ▯ ハイジャック(対応)訓練 anti-hijack (ing) training.
はいしゅう【買収】 ▯ 敵対的買収 a hostile takeover. ▯ 買収企業〔買収する側の企業〕an acquiring company; a buyer-out. ◯ 被〜企業〔買収される側の企業〕an acquired company; a bought-out company. 買収先企業〔被買収企業〕an acquired company; a company acquired (in a buy-out); a bought-out company. ◯ 社長は〜先企業に自社の経営理念を押し付けようとはしなかった. The president did not attempt to force his own managerial philosophy on the「acquired company [company he had bought out]. 買収ファンド〔企業を買収し, 経営を改善した上で株式を売却し利益を得る投資ファンド〕a buyout fund. (敵対的)買収防衛策〔経営〕a defense against a (hostile) takeover (bid); an antitakeover defense.
はいしゅつ【排出】 ▯ 排出源[元]〔廃棄物・排気ガス・汚染物質などの〕an emission source; an emitter; a source (of pollution). 排出削減〔温室効果ガス・ダイオキシンなどの〕(an) emission(s) reduction. ◯ 〜削減対策 an emissions reduction strategy / 〜削減目標 an emissions reduction target / 〜削減量 an emissions reduction (of 5.2%). 排出事業者責任 ＝排出者責任. 排出者責任〔廃棄物を出す人や企業の責任〕waste disposer('s) liability. 排出抑制効果 an effect in emissions. ◯ 高温燃焼はダイオキシンの〜抑制効果がある. Combustion at high temperature is effective in「reducing [curbing] emissions of dioxin. 排出量許可証 an emissions permit. 排出量取引〔京都メカニズムの1つ〕Emissions Trading (略: ET). 排出量取引所 ＝排出権取引所(⇨はいしゅつけん).
はいしゅつけん【排出権】 ▯ 排出権取引所〔温室効果ガス の〕「emissions-trading [emissions] exchange. 排出権取引制度 an emission(s) trading system (略: ETS).
ばいしゅん[1]【売春】 ▯ 強制売春 ⇨ きょうせい[3].
はいしょう[5]【排簫】【楽器】〔長さの異なる竹管を横へ並べた中国の管楽器〕a paixiao.
ばいしょう[2]【賠償】 ▯ 賠償義務 an obligation [a duty] to「compensate sb [pay compensation]《for an accident》; a duty of compensation.
ばいしょうせきにんほけん【賠償責任保険】liability insurance; insurance against liability《for oil pollution》. ▯ 業務賠償責任保険 ⇨ ぎょうばいしょうせきにんほけん. 個人賠償責任保険 personal liability insurance. 受託者賠償責任保険 trustee liability insurance. 使用者賠償責任保険 employer's liability insurance (略: ELI). 生産物[製造物]賠償責任保険 product liability insurance (略: PLI). 損害賠償責任保険 casualty and liability insurance. 店舗賠償責任保険 storekeepers liability insurance.
はいじょうみゃく【肺静脈】 ▯ 肺静脈還流異常【医】anomalous pulmonary venous return. ◯ 部分[総]〜環流異常 partial [total] anomalous pulmonary venous return.
はいしょく[3]【配食】 ▯ 配食サービス a meal delivery service.
はいしょくぶつゆ【廃植物油】waste vegetable oil.
はいしん[2]【配信】 ▯ 配信会社 a distribution company; a distributor.〔⇨ネット配信⇨ネット〕 ◯ 動画〜会社 an animation distribution company. 配信サービス ⇨ distribution [delivery] service. ◯ 音楽〜ビジ ⇨ おんがく. 配信ビジネス a《music》distribution business.
ばいしん[2]【陪審】 ▯ 陪審義務《法》〔米国などで〕jury duty; jury service. ◯ 〜義務を免除される条件 conditions for exemption from jury「duty [service].
「背信の行方」〔映画〕Simpatico.
はいすい[2]【排水】 ▯ 排水能力〔下水道などの〕(a) drainage capacity. ◯ 下水道の〜能力を上回る豪雨 heavy rains that「exceed the drainage capacity of [overload] the sewers.
ハイズオン〔ベトナム北部ホン河デルタ地帯の省; その省都〕Hai Duong.
バイス・プレジデント〔副大統領・副社長〕a vice president. ▯ 法務担当バイス・プレジデント vice president in charge of the Legal Affairs Department; vice president for legal affairs.
はいせつ[2]【排泄】 ▯ 排泄介護[ケア] incontinence [continence] care. 排泄障害 an excretory disorder.
はいせつ[3]【配設】arrangement; placement; installation; disposal. 〜する arrange; place; install; dispose.
ハイセレニン《商標・薬》〔抗てんかん薬〕Hyserenin.
はいせん[10]【廃川】an abandoned [a buried, a filled(-in)] river [stream] (channel). ◯ 今年中にこの川は〜になる予定. This stream is scheduled to be filled in by the end of the year.
はいぞく【配属】 ▯ 配属先 one's assigned post.
はいた[1]【排他】 ▯ 排他(条件付)取引《商》exclusive dealing.
ハイ・ターゲット〔年齢の高い購買層〕older [adult] consumers.
ばいたい【媒体】 ▯ 映像媒体 video media. 音声媒体 audio media. 活字媒体 (the) print media;《in, through》the medium of print. 通信媒体 a「communications [communication] medium; a medium of communication. ▯ 媒体特性 ◯ 新聞とテレビでは, 同じ報道手段といっても, 〜特性が違う. While newspapers and TV are both news channels, they've got different media「features [characteristics].
はいたてき【排他的】 ▯ 排他的経済水域境界線 an EEZ border; the (outer) limits of an exclusive economic zone. 〔2国間での〕a line of demarcation between two exclusive economic zones.
バイタル・エリア《サッカー》〔得失点につながりやすい, 戦術上重要な空間〕a vital area.
はいち[2]【配置】 ▯ 配置基準〔人員の〕standards for the「disposition [placing] (of staff). ◯ この病院は法で定められた看護師〜基準を守っていない. This hospital does not have the legally required number of nurses.
はいち[3]【廃置】abolishing and establishing [abolition and establishment of]《townships》. ▯ 廃置分合〔行政単位の〕abolition and establishment, division and amalgamation (of administrative units).
ハイ・ティー〔夕方の紅茶と軽食〕high tea.
ハイテク ▯ ハイテク株 a high-tech stock. ハイテク・クラスター〔先端技術集積地域〕a high-tech(nology) cluster. ハイテク紙幣 "high-tech「bills [notes]"; paper money incorporating high-tech features (to combat counterfeiting). ハイテク戦争 high-tech warfare; a high-tech war.
はいてん[3]【配点】 ▯ 配点比率 ◯ 短答問題と論文問題の〜比率は1:4である. The ratio of full marks「for [allotted to] the short-answer and essay sections respectively is one to four.「Full marks for the essay section are four times those for the short-answer section. 配点ミス a point allocation error.
ばいでん[2]【買電】〔自家発電力を電力会社が購入すること〕buying electricity (from a private producer).
ハイテン【金属】＝ハイテンション・スチール (⇨ハイテンション).
はいてん[5]【肺転】【医】(a)「lung [pulmonary] metastasis. ▯ 多発性肺転移 multiple lung「metastases [metastasis].

ハイテンション　□❶ ハイテンション・スチール〚金属〛〔高張力鋼〕high-tensile steel.
はいど【廃土】〚土木工事などで排出される土〛waste「soil [earth].
バイト² 　□❶ 片刃バイト a side-cutting tool.
「ハイ アンド シーク 暗闇のかくれんぼ」〚映画〛Hide and Seek.
はいとう²【配当】　□❶ 配当可能利益 distributable profits; profit available for dividend. 配当起算日 a (dividend) record date. 配当通知書 a dividend (payment)「notice [advice]. 配当取り〚決算期間直近に配当金目当てで株式を取得すること〛dividend capture. 配当予想 the prospect of a dividend; 〔予想配当金〕an expected dividend《per share》.
はいとうたい【配糖体】　□❶ アミノ配糖体〚化〛aminoglycoside. ❷ アミノ〜(系)抗生物質〚薬〛an aminoglycoside antibiotic.
はいとうみつ【廃糖蜜】blackstrap molasses; final molasses.
はいどうみゃく²【肺動脈】　□❶ 肺動脈血栓塞栓症〚医〛〔肺動脈血栓塞栓症〕pulmonary thromboembolism. 肺動脈性肺高血圧症〚医〛pulmonary arterial hypertension（略：PAH）. 肺動脈閉鎖症〚医〛pulmonary atresia.
「灰と土」〔A・ラヒーミー作の小説〕Earth and Ashes.
ハイトナー Hytner, Nicholas (1956– ；英国生まれの映画監督).
ハイドロキシアパタイト〚化〛〔人工骨や歯の材料〕hydroxyapatite. □❶ 薬用ハイドロキシアパタイト medicinal hydroxyapatite. ハイドロキシアパタイト粒子 a hydroxyapatite particle.
ハイドロゲル〚化〛a hydrogel. ❷ シリコーン・ハイドロゲル〔酸素透過率の高いコンタクトレンズ用材料〕a silicone hydrogel.
ハイドロジェル〚化〛＝ハイドロゲル.
ハイドロフルオロカーボン〚化〛〔代替フロンの一種〕(a)「hydrofluorocarbon [hydro-fluorocarbon]（略：HFC）.
ハイドロボール〚園芸〛hydroponic「balls [pellets]; nutrient pellets (for growing plants hydroponically).
ハイドロ(リック)・フラクチャリング〚工〛〔水圧破砕法〕hydraulic fracturing.
ばいにく【梅肉】　□❶ 梅肉ソース〚料理〛(a) plum (dipping) sauce; a dip made with umeboshi concentrate. 梅肉だれ ＝梅肉ソース.
はいにょう【排尿】　□❶ 排尿筋〚解〛the detrusor muscle.
はいにん【背任】　□❶ 背任収賄〚法〛breach of trust and accepting a benefit.
はいねつ【廃熱・排熱】　□❶ 排熱回収 ＝熱回収（⇨ねつ）. 排熱回収効率 ＝熱回収効率（⇨ねつ）.
はいのうち【廃農地】disused「abandoned」farmland.
はいのり【背乗り】〔他人の戸籍を乗っ取りその人物になりすます秘密工作員の手口〕identity theft; impersonation; assuming another person's legal identity for espionage purposes.
ハイパーサーミア〚医〛〔がん治療のための温熱療法〕hyperthermia.
ハイパーレスキューたい【-隊】〔消防救助機動部隊〕a hyper-rescue unit.
ばいばい【売買】　□❶ 回転売買〚相場〛〔頻繁な売り買い〕back-to-back transactions. 女性売買 trafficking [traffic] in [of] women (and girls) (for sexual exploitation). 売買婚 marriage to a purchased bride; the buying and selling of women as marriage partners. 売買注文〚取引〛an order to buy or sell; a buy/sell order.
はいばら【灰原】〚考古〛a waster「dump [pile] near an ancient kiln site.
はいばん³【胚盤】　□❶ 胚盤胞 a blastocyst. ❷ 〜胞移植〚医〛a blastocyst transfer.

はいばん⁵【廃番】　□❶ そのバッグはすでに〜になっています. The bag has already been「delisted [discontinued].
ハイパント〚ラグビー〛〔ボールを高く蹴り上げること〕a punt (kick); punting. □❶ ハイパント攻撃 a punting strategy.
ハイビジョン　□❶ アナログ[衛星]ハイビジョン analog [satellite] high definition (television) [Hi-Vision].
パイピング(げんしょう)【-現象】〚地質〛〔地中に浸透した水が地下に水路を形成し、緩んだ土砂と共に地上に吹き出す現象〕a piping phenomenon; piping.
パイプ　□❶ パイプ・スペース〚建〛〔高層住宅の配管スペース〕a pipe「shaft [space]. パイプ・フレーム〔パイプ枠〕a pipe frame.
「ハイ・フィデリティ」〚映画〛High Fidelity.
パイプライン　□❶ 石油パイプライン a [an oil] pipeline.
ハイブリッド　□❶ ハイブリッド加熱〔オーブンレンジなどで、ヒーターとレンジで同時に加熱する方式〕hybrid heating. ハイブリッド個体〚生物〛〔交雑種〕a hybrid individual. ハイブリッド市場〚取引〛〔伝統的な立会場取引と電子証券取引を組み合わせたもの〕a hybrid market. ハイブリッド車〚ハイブリッド自動車〕a hybrid car; a hybrid (electric) vehicle（略：HV）. ハイブリッド胚〚生物〛a hybrid embryo. ハイブリッド・レコーダー〔ハードディスク録画とビデオテープ録画の両方ができる録画装置〕a hybrid recorder.
バイブル　□❶ バイブル本〔ある特定分野の必読書と称する本〕a bible; an authoritative [a widely-read] publication in a particular field; 〔特定の健康食品などの販売促進を目的としてその効能を書き立てた本〕a publication extolling the virtues of a particular product (for sales promotion purposes).
パイプルーフこうほう【-工法】〚土木〛the pipe roof method.
バイブル・ベルト〔米国の南部・中西部の、聖書を絶対視する超保守的な地域〕the Bible Belt.
「パイプを持つ少年」〔ピカソ作の絵画〕Boy with a Pipe.
はいぶん³【配分】　□❶ 配分表 a (task) allocation chart; a《frequency》distribution chart. 配分比率 an allocation rate. ❷ 資産〜比率 an asset allocation ratio; what percentage of one's assets one allocates to different categories.
はいべん【排便】　□❶ 排便痛 defecation pain.
はいぼく【敗北】　□❶ 敗北意識 a「sense [consciousness] of defeat.
はいぼしびょう【灰星病】〚植物病理〛brown rot.
ハイムリックほう【-法】〚医〛〔食物が喉に詰まったときの救護法〕the Heimlich maneuver.
バイメ Beyme, Klaus von (1934– ；ドイツの政治学者).
はいや【肺野(部)】〚解〛a [the] lung field.
はいゆ【廃油】　□❶ 食用廃油 waste cooking oil. ❷ 廃油凝固剤 a used cooking oil「coagulant [coagulating agent, hardener].
はいゆ²【廃湯】overflow from a (free-flowing) hot spring (bath).
はいよう⁴【廃用】　□❶ 廃用性筋萎縮〚医〛disuse muscular atrophy.
ばいよう【培養】　□❶ 培養細胞 a cultured cell; a cell cultured (in vitro). ❷ ヒト〜細胞 a cultured human cell. 培養軟骨〔移植用の〕cultured cartilage.
はいようゆうろ【灰溶融炉】an ash melting furnace.
バイヨン² 〔カンボジアの遺跡、アンコール・トムの中心にある石造寺院跡〕Bayon, the Bayon (temple)「remains [ruins].
ハイライト　□❶ ハイライト映像〚テレビ〛highlight footage; televised highlights.
バイラル・マーケティング〔宣伝〕〔口コミを利用するマーケティング手法〕viral marketing.
はいらん【排卵】　□❶ 排卵チェッカー an ovulation test strip; an ovulation stick.
ハイリー【海狸】〚魚〛＝すぎ².
ハイリゲンダム〔ドイツ北部の都市〕Heiligendamm.

**ハイリスク** ▭ ハイリスク者〔医〕a high-risk individual; a person [an individual] at high risk 《of infection, of developing stomach cancer》.

**はいりょ**【配慮】▭ 過剰配慮 overconsideration 《(for …)》; excessive solicitude 《toward(s)…》.

**パイリン**〔カンボジア西部の都市(特別市)〕Pailin.

**はいリンパみゃくかんきんしゅしょう**【肺-脈管筋腫症】〔医〕lymphangioleiomyomatosis(略: LAM).

**ハイル**〔サウジアラビア中北部の州;その州都〕Hail.

**はいれい**[1]【拝礼】▭ 拝礼式《hold》a (memorial) service 《for the war dead》.

**「パイレーツ・オブ・カリビアン/呪われた海賊たち」**〔映画〕Pirates of the Caribbean: The Curse of the Black Pearl. ▶ 続編は「パイレーツ・オブ・カリビアン/デッドマンズ・チェスト」(Pirates of the Caribbean: Dead Man's Chest),「パイレーツ・オブ・カリビアン/ワールド・エンド」(Pirates of the Caribbean: At World's End).

**ハイレベル** ▭ ハイレベル国際会議 a high-level international conference.

**ハイレベルいいんかい**【-委員会】〔国連〕the High-Level Panel on Threats, Challenges and Change.

**パイロキネシス** =念力放火 (⇨ねんりき).

**はいロム**〔-ROM〕〔白ロムに対し、電話番号は設定されているが解約などのため使えない状態になっている携帯電話端末〕a disabled cellphone.

**パイワン**[1]〔台湾の高砂族の一部族〕the Paiwan;〔1人〕a Paiwan《pl. ~》.

**パイワン**[2]〔医〕PAI-1.(⇨プラスミノーゲン・アクチベーター・インヒビター1 (⇨プラスミノーゲン)].

**パインハースト**〔米国ノースカロライナ州の村;ゴルフリゾートがある〕Pinehurst.

**ハインリッヒのほうそく**【-の法則】〔潜在事故に関する仮説〕Heinrich's law; the Heinrich Law; the 1:29:300 Law. ▶ 米国の損害保険会社の技師 Herbert William Heinrich (1886-1962) の論文に由来. "1:29:300" は one twenty-nine three hundred と読む.

**ハウィジャ**〔イラク中北部,タミーム州の村〕Hawija(h).

**パウサニアス** Pausanias (2 世紀のギリシャの地理学者・旅行家).

**ハウザン**〔ベトナム南部,メコンデルタ地帯の省〕Hau Giang.

**ハウジング** ▭ ハウジング・サービス〔電算〕〔顧客のサーバーなどを預かるサービス〕(a) housing service.

**ハウス** ▭ ハウス・ウエディング a house wedding; a wedding (held) at a special house rented for the occasion. ハウス・シェアリング〔1つの賃貸物件に親族以外の者同士が住むこと〕house sharing. ハウス・ミュージック〔音楽〕house (music). ハウス・メーカー a home builder.

**パウダー** ▭ パウダー・パーツ〔機〕〔極小歯車〕microgears; "powder parts."

**パウチ** a pouch. ▭ アルミ・パウチ an aluminum pouch. 透明パウチ a transparent pouch. レトルト・パウチ a retort pouch. ▭ パウチ加工 pouch packaging. パウチ容器 a (container) pouch.

**ハウテン**〔南アフリカ共和国の首都圏を含む州〕Gauteng. ▶ 州都はヨハネスバーグ.

**バウビオロギー**【建築】〔居住者と建物の相関関係から人間を中心に考える考え方;建築生物学〕baubiology; building biology.

**バウマン**〔ヨット・カヌーなど〕〔船首担当員〕a bowman; a bow.

**ハウ・ユニット**〔卵の鮮度を表す単位〕the Haugh unit (略: HU). ハウ・ユニット値 a Haugh unit 'value [score].

**バウリンガル**〔商標〕〔犬語翻訳機〕Bowlingual.

**「ハウルの動く城」**〔アニメ映画〕Howl's Moving Castle.

**バウンサー**〔折りたたみ式ゆりかご〕a bouncer.

**バウンス**〔写真〕〔ストロボを天井や壁面に向けて発光し反射光を利用する撮影方法;影が柔らかくなる〕(a) bounce flash; bouncing.

**はえとり**【蠅取り】▭ 蠅取り器 a flytrap. 蠅取りリボン a fly ribbon.

**パオ**【包】〔中国の移動式住居〕a bao;〔モンゴルの〕=ゲル[2].

**パオツァイ**【泡菜】〔野菜を塩漬けして乳酸発酵させた中国四川地方の漬物〕pao cai; pow tsai.

**はおり**【羽織】▭ 羽織物〔夜は冷えるから何か~物を持っていったほうがいいよ. The nights are cold, so take something to ｢keep yourself warm [muffle yourself up].

**ハカ**〔マオリ族の出陣の踊り;ニュージーランド代表のラグビーチームが試合前に演じてみせる〕a [the] haka.

**「バガー・ヴァンスの伝説」**〔映画〕The Legend of Bagger Vance.

**はかい**[2]【破壊】▭ 破壊強さ breaking strength.

**ハカシア**〔ロシア連邦の1つでシベリアにある共和国〕Khakassia; the Khakassia Republic. ▷ Khakassian *adj*.;〔首都〕アバカン Abakan.

**バガス**〔サトウキビなどのしぼりかす〕bagasse. ▭ バガス紙 bagasse (paper).

**はがた**[2]【歯形・歯型】▭ 歯形照合 identification from dental ｢record [structure, data, information].

**はかたおび**【博多帯】an *obi* of tightly woven texture, produced in Hakata, Fukuoka Prefecture.

**はかたにんぎょう**【博多人形】(a) Hakata doll; (a) *Hakata ningyō*; traditional painted pottery dolls from Hakata, in Fukuoka Prefecture.

**バカップル**〔ばかなカップル〕〔混雑した電車の中でいちゃついて,第三者の目から見て場所柄をわきまえない不愉快な行動をするカップル〕a "foolish couple"; a couple who smooch or fondle each other in a public place.

**ばかながい**【馬鹿長い】unbelievably long.

**パカパカ**〔映画・テレビ〕〔高輝度映像の急速点滅〕《(television)》 flicker(ing); a flickering image.

**バガバンディ** Bagabandi, Natsagiin (1950- ; モンゴルの政治家; 大統領 [1997-2005]).

**ばかやろう**【馬鹿野郎】▭ ばかやろう解散〔日本史〕〔1953年,吉田茂首相による衆議院の解散〕the *bakayarō* dissolution; the (1953) dissolution of the Lower House after (Prime Minister) Yoshida Shigeru called an opposition member "an idiot." ▶ 予算委員会で首相が「ばかやろう」と発言したことがきっかけになったことから.

**バカラ**[1] ▭ バカラ賭博 baccarat gambling; gambling on baccarat.

**バキーエフ** =バキエフ.

**バキエフ** Bakiyev, Kurmanbek Saliyevich (1949- ; キルギスの政治家; 大統領 [2005- ]).

**はきこみ**【穿きこみ・履き込み】[1]〔服飾〕〔ズボンなどの上部〕(a) ｢rise [cut]. ▭ このパンツは~が深い[浅い]. These pants have a ｢high [low] rise. | These are ｢high-rise [low-rise] pants.

[2]〔靴のくるぶしより上の部分〕(a) ｢rise [cut] (above the ankle). ▭ ~が深い[浅い]バスケットシューズ ｢high-top [low-top] basketball shoes;《口》high-tops [low-tops].

[3]〔ジーンズなどを穿きこなした期間〕▭ ~歴3年のジーンズ jeans that have been worn for three years.

**パキシル**〔商標・薬〕〔抗うつ剤〕Paxil. ▶ 一般名は塩酸パロキセチン.

**パキスタン・イスラムきょうとれんめい**【-教徒連盟】the Pakistan Muslim League (略: PML).

**パキスタンじんみんとう**【-人民党】the Pakistan Peoples Party (略: PPP).

**はきふるす**【履き古す】wear《shoes [socks]》until they are well worn. ▭ 履き古した old; (much) worn 《shoes [socks]》; used;〔すり切れた〕〔ズボン・靴下など〕threadbare;〔ズボンなど〕out at the knees.

**はぎやき**【萩焼】Hagi ware; ceramics [pottery, porcelain] from Hagi (Yamaguchi Pref.).

**ばきゅうひ**【馬厩肥】〔厩舎の敷藁(しきわら)に馬糞が混入した肥料〕(a) horse-manure and straw mulch.

**パキラ**〔植〕〔パンヤ科の常緑小高木〕a French peanut;

## はきりあり

*Pachira aquatica.*

**はきりあり**【葉切蟻】『昆』a 「leaf-cutting [leaf-cutter]」 ant.

**パキン** Paquin, Anna (1982– ; 米国の映画女優; 本名 Anna Helene Paquin).

**ハグ**〔抱きしめること〕a hug; hugging. ～する hug *sb*; give *sb* a hug.

**バグ** ▯▯ バグ修正プログラム a bug-correcting program.

**はくい**【白衣】▯▯ 白衣現象[効果]〖医〗the white-coat effect.

**ばくいん**【爆飲】～する binge drink; binge-drink.

**はくうんさん**【白雲山】〔中国広東省広州市北郊の山〕Baiyun Shan; White Cloud Mountain.

「**爆撃命令**」〔ヨーロッパ戦線での米陸軍爆撃隊のTVドラマ〕Twelve O'Clock High.

**はくごう**²【博鰲】〔中国海南島の保養地〕Boao.

**パクサス** Paksas, Rolandas (1956– ; リトアニアの政治家; 大統領 [2003–2004]).

**パクザン**〔ベトナム北東部の省; その省都〕Bac Giang.

**はくさんぼく**【白山木】〖植〗〔スイカズラ科の常緑低木〕a Japanese viburnum; *Viburnum japonicum.*

**はくしつ**【白質】▯▯ 白質病変〖医〗〔脳の〕leukoaraiosis.

**はくしゅう**【白秋】〔秋の異称〕(the) autumn; *(the) fall.

**はくしゅつ**【拍出】▯▯ 拍出力〖生理〗the pumping ability of the heart.

**はくしょ**【曝書】〔本の虫干し〕airing (out) books; 〖図書館〗〔蔵書点検〕library inventory; general stocktaking.

**はくじょう**³【白杖】〔盲人安全杖〕a white 「cane [stick].

**ばくしょく**【爆食】～する devour; consume voraciously.

**はくしょくぶんり**【泊食分離】〔旅館の〕staying and eating at separate establishments; staying at one inn and eating at another; separate accommodation and eating (arrangements).

**バクスターこうか**【–効果】〔植物が人間や動物の感情に反応するという現象〕the Backster effect. ▶ 命名は提唱者 Cleve Backster から.

**パクストン** Paxton, Bill (1955– ; 米国の映画俳優; 本名 William Paxton).

「**バグズ・ライフ**」〔アニメ映画〕A Bug's Life.

**ばくせつだん**【爆窃団】a gang of thieves using explosives to break into〈jewelry stores〉.

**はくそう**²【博捜】a wide-ranging search; searching [looking] far and wide [everywhere]. ～する search [look] far and wide [everywhere]. ▯ 膨大な資料を～する search [sift, hunt] through a huge quantity of documents.

**バクタラン** ＝バフタラン.

**ばくだん**【爆弾】▯▯ 路肩爆弾〔路肩に仕掛け遠隔操作で爆発させる爆弾〕a roadside bomb.

**ばくだんテロぼうしじょうやく**【爆弾–防止条約】the International Convention for the Suppression of Terrorist Bombings. ▶ 正式名称は「テロリストによる爆弾使用の防止に関する国際条約」.

**パク・チャヌク**【朴贊郁】Park Chan-wook (1963– ; 韓国の映画監督).

**パクティア**〔アフガニスタン東部の州〕Paktia.

**パクティカ**〔アフガニスタン東部の州〕Paktika.

**バクテー**【肉骨茶】〖料理〗〔中国, 東南アジアなどの骨付き豚肉のスープ煮料理〕bak kut teh; bakuteh; pork rib soup.

**バクニン**〔ベトナム北東部の省; その省都〕Bac Ninh.

**バクバ**〔イラク首都バグダッド北方の都市〕Baquba; Baqouba.

**パクパク**〔心臓の高鳴りを表現する擬態語〕pounding; throbbing; 《one's heart goes》「pitter-patter [pit-a-pat].

**ばくはつ**【爆発】▯▯ 拡散爆発〔噴出するガスが引火して起こる爆発〕(an) expanding (vapor) explosion; expansion and explosion. 予混合爆発〔空気に一定濃度まじっ たガスが引火して起こる爆発〕a premixed gas/air explo-sion. ▯▯ 爆発ヘア〔髪型の一種〕explosive [unruly] hair. 爆発成形弾 an explosively formed projectile (略: EFP). ▶ 自己鍛造弾 ともいう.

**ばくはつぶつ**【爆発物】▯▯ 爆発物探知機[装置] an explosive(s) detector.

**はくぶつかん**【博物館】▯▯ 民俗博物館 a museum of ethnography; an ethnographical [a folk] museum. 歴史博物館 a 「history [historical] museum; a museum of history.

**はくへい**【白兵】▯▯ 白兵創 a wound 「received [inflicted] in 「close combat [hand-to-hand] fighting; a 「bayonet [sword] wound.

**はくぼ**【薄暮】▯▯ 薄暮時 〔at〕twilight (hours).

**バグボ** Gbagbo, Laurent (1948– ; コートジボワールの政治家; 大統領 [2000– ]).

**はくまく**²【薄膜】▯▯ 薄膜半導体〖物〗a thin-film semiconductor.

**はくゆう**【白釉】〖製陶〗(a) white glaze.

**パクラ** Pakula, Alan J. (1928–98; 米国の映画監督).

**ハクラニヤ**〔イラク西部, アンバル州の都市〕Haqlaniya.

**バグラン**〔アフガニスタン北東部の州, 同州の州都〕Baghlan.

**はくらんかい**【博覧会】▯▯ 総合博覧会 a general exhibition.

**はくらんかいこくさいじむきょく**【博覧会国際事務局】〔パリに本部を置く国際組織〕the Bureau of International Exhibitions (略: BIE). ▶ BIE はフランス語の *Bureau International des Expositions* の略.

**バクリエウ**〔ベトナム南部, メコンデルタ地帯の省; その省都〕Bac Lieu.

**パクリタキセル**〖薬〗〔抗がん剤〕paclitaxel.

**バグる**〖電算〗〔バグのため不具合が生じる; 機械が狂う〕become [get, act] buggy; act up; behave strangely. ▯ 今日は朝からコンピューターがバグって仕事にならない. My computer has been 「acting up [*on the fritz] since this morning and I haven't been able to do any work.

**ばくろ**【暴露】▯▯ 間接暴露 indirect exposure (to asbestos). ▯▯ 暴露ウイルス〖電算〗a disclosure virus. 暴露療法〖精神医〗(an) exposure therapy.

**ばくろ・リスクひょうかたいきかくさんモデル**【曝露–評価大気拡散–】the Atmospheric Dispersion Model for Exposure and Risk Assessment. (略: ADMER).

**ハゲタカファンド**〔倒産・経営不振の企業を買収して高値で売る投資ファンド〕a vulture fund.

**パケット** ▯▯ パケット代〔通信料〕a (per-)packet charge. パケット定額制 a fixed packet charge service. パケット料(金) ＝パケット代〔通信料〕.

**パゲット・カット** 〔ダイヤモンドなどの長方形のカット〕a baguette cut. ▯▯ テーパー・バゲット・カット〔台形のカット〕a tapered baguette cut.

**はけん**【派遣】▯▯ スポット派遣 ＝日雇い派遣. 日雇い派遣〖事〗dispatching temporary workers on a daily basis; 〔人〕a temporary worker dispatched on a daily basis. ▯▯ 派遣要請〔要員・人材の〕a request to 「dispatch [send]」 《a medical team》.

**はけん**²【覇権】▯▯ 覇権争い (a) 「struggle [competition, fight] for 「hegemony [dominance, supremacy]. 覇権国家 a hegemonic 「nation [country].

**はこ**【箱】▯▯ 箱弁当 a boxed lunch.

**はこう**²【波高】▯▯ 有義波高〖気象〗〔海上の一点を連続通過する100波以上の波のうち高いほうから3分の1を選びこれを平均した波高〕(a) significant wave height (略: SWH).

**はこうま**【箱馬】〔映画・演劇・写真〕an apple 「box [crate].

**はこがい**【箱買い】buying [purchasing] 《toys》「by the box [in bulk]; bulk purchasing.

**はこぜん**【箱膳】a tableware box with a lid used as an eating tray; a box table.

**はこブランコ**【箱–】a box-type swing.

**バサーエフ** Basayev, Shamil (1965–2006; チェチェン独立

派の指導者).
バザーリ =ヴァザーリ.
はさい【破砕】▶▷ 破砕屑 rubble; detritus; residue; shivers; crushed waste; shredder dust; 〖環境〗〔自動車の〕an automobile shredder residue (略: ASR). 破砕療法[治療]〖医〗〔衝撃波によって結石を砕く治療法〕lithotripsy; extracorporeal shock wave lithotripsy (略: ESWL).
ハザラ〔アフガニスタン中部の山岳地帯などに住むモンゴル系民族〕the Hazara; 〔1 人〕a Hazara 《pl. ~, ~s》.
ハサン〔ロシア極東の行政区プリモルスキーの町; 北朝鮮・中国国境の町〕Khasan.
はしい〔端居〕sitting near the veranda.
バシール 1 Ba'asyir, Abu Bakar (1938- ; インドネシアのイスラム法学者; ジェマー・イスラミアの精神的指導者).
2 al-Bashir, Omar Hassan Ahmad (1944- ; スーダンの軍人・政治家; 大統領〔1993- 〕).
バシキリア〔バシコルトスタン共和国の別称〕Bashkiria.
はしご【梯子】▶▷ はしご受診 consulting one doctor after another; going from one 「doctor [hospital, clinic] to another 《for treatment》.
バシコルトスタンきょうわこく【-共和国】〔ウラル山脈南部の, ロシア連邦内の共和国〕the Bashkortostan Republic; 〔首都〕ウファ Ufa.
バシジ〔イランの革命防衛隊傘下の民兵組織〕the Basij.
はしづめ【橋詰】〔橋のたもと〕the foot [the end, one end] of a bridge; the approach to a bridge.
「橋の上の娘」〔映画〕Girl on the Bridge; 〔原題〕La fille sur le pont.
バジパイ Vajpayee, Atal Bihari (1924- ; インドの政治家; 首相〔1996, 98-99, 99-2004〕).
はしぶとがら【嘴太雀】〖鳥〗〔シジュウカラ科の鳥〕a marsh tit; Parus palustris.
はしぶとごい【嘴太五位】〖鳥〗〔サギ科の鳥〕a 「rufous [nankeen] night heron; Nycticorax caledonicus.
ハシムけ【-家】〔イスラム教の預言者マホメットの血筋を引く一門〕the Hashemites.
ハジャイ〔タイ南部, ソンクラー県の都市, ハートヤイ〕Hat Yai.
パジュ〔坡州〕〔韓国の都市〕Paju.
パシュトゥーン〔アフガニスタンの主要民族〕the Pashtun; 〔1 人〕a Pashtun 《pl. ~, ~s》.
ばしょうふ【芭蕉布】〔芭蕉の葉の繊維からとれる糸で織った布; 沖縄・奄美特産〕banana 「cloth [fabric]; bashō cloth; cloth [fabric] made of banana leaf fibers.
パジョン〖料理〗〔韓国の, お好み焼きに似た料理〕pajeon.
はしらだて【柱立て】1〔家屋の建築に最初の柱を立てること〕(a) pillar raising; 〔その儀式〕a pillar-raising ceremony.
2〔基本構想〕an outline; a framework; the main ideas; the key points; 〔その設定〕outlining; deciding [choosing] the main ideas.
バシランとう【-島】〔フィリピン, ミンダナオ島南西部, スールー諸島の島〕Basilan Island.
バシル =バシール.
「走れチェス」〔米国の, 障害レース馬と少女騎手の TV ドラマ〕National Velvet.
バシロサウルス〖古生物〗〔クジラの祖先〕a basilosaur; Basilosaurus.
バス¹ ▶▷ バス・カード a bus card. ●共通~カード a bus card for multiple 「routes [companies, journeys]; a bus card which can be used on more than one 「bus [route]. バス送迎 bus pickup; a shuttle-bus service; transportation there and back by (special) bus.
バス¹ ▶▷ リバースパス〖サッカー〗intercepting [cutting off, stealing] a pass.
バスキア Basquiat, Jean Michel (1960-88; 米国の画家; ニューヨーク市のらくがきアート (graffiti art) で有名).
バスこくみんとう【-国民党】〔スペインの穏健派の政党〕

the Basque Nationalist Party (略: PNV). ▶ PNV はこの政党のスペイン語名 Partido Nacionalista Vasco の略.
バスクじちしゅう【-自治州】〔スペイン北部の〕the Basque Autonomous Community.
バスクそこくとじゆう【-祖国と自由】〔スペインの非合法組織〕ETA; Basque Fatherland and Liberty. ▶ ETA は Euskadi Ta Askatasuna の略.
はすぐち【蓮口】〔じょうろの〕a sprinkler 「head [nozzle]; a rosette.
バスケット ▶▷ バスケット買い[売り]〖証券〗〔複数銘柄の一括取引〕basket 「buying [selling]. バスケット価格〖経〗〔OPEC の原油価格の指標〕the (OPEC) basket price. バスケット通貨建て債券〖金融〗a basket-currency bond; bonds denominated in a basket of currencies. バスケット取引〖証券〗basket trading; 〔1 回の〕a basket trade. バスケット方式〖金融〗〔主要通貨を加重平均する方式〕a [the] basket approach; 〖環境〗〔温室効果ガスの排出量を削減目標に一括して合算する方式〕a [the] basket approach.
バスケットボールじょしにほんリーグきこう【-女子日本-機構】the Women's Japan Basketball League (略: WJBL).
バスケットボールにほんリーグきこう【-日本-機構】the Japan Basketball League (略: JBL).
はずし【外し】1〔人を現在の地位から引き離すこと〕an ouster; (a) removal; (a) deposition. ●田中~ the 「ouster [removal] of Tanaka.
2〔メンバーに加えないこと・仲間から外すこと〕exclusion 《of sb from a group》; keeping 《sb》out 《of a group》.
3〔常識から意識的に離れること〕a 「different [unique, personal] touch [variation].
パス・スルー ▶▷ パス・スルー課税〔有限責任事業組合の出資者に対する課税方式〕pass-through taxation; a pass-through tax.
パス・セッション〔小グループによる討論〕a buzz session.
バスター ▶▷ バスター・エンド・ラン a fake-bunt-and-run (play).
バステト〔エジプト神話〕〔半人半獣の女神〕Bast; Bastet.
パスニ〔パキスタン南西部の都市〕Pasni.
はすばごおり【蓮葉氷】〔結氷直前の海に浮かぶ蓮の葉に似た薄い氷板〕pancake ice.
パスポート ▶▷ 5[10]年パスポート a 「5-year [10-year] passport.
バス・マーケティング〔宣伝〕〔口コミを利用するマーケティング手法〕buzz marketing.
バス・ミツバー〔ユダヤ少女の成人祭式〕a bat mitzvah.
はずればけん【外れ馬券】a losing betting slip (in a horse race).
「バスを待ちながら」〔映画〕The Waiting List; 〔原題〕Lista de Espera.
バセスク Basescu, Traian (1951- ; ルーマニアの政治家; 大統領〔2004- 〕).
ばぜん【馬前】●主君の~に死す die (in battle) 「before [in the presence of] one's sovereign.
バセンジー〖犬〗a basenji; a Congo dog.
バソヒビン〖生化〗vasohibin.
パソ・ロブレス〔米国, カリフォルニア州中部の都市〕Paso Robles.
はた³【旗】▶▷ 旗判定〖柔道〗a decision rendered by judges at the end of a judo match in which the contestants are tied on points.
はだ【肌】▶▷ 実年齢肌 skin normal 「for [at] one's age. 年齢肌〔若々しさを失いつつある肌〕an ageing skin; a skin which is beginning to age; 〔年齢相応の肌〕⇒実年齢肌. 肌ストレス skin stress.
パターソン 1 Patterson, James (1947- ; 米国の小説家).
2 Patterson, Percival James (1935- ; ジャマイカの政治家; 首相〔1992-2006〕).

**3** Patterson, Richard North (1947- ; 米国の小説家).
バターワース〔マレーシア、ペナン島対岸(マレー半島西岸)の港町〕Butterworth.
パターン □ 生活行動パターン a daily activity pattern; one's pattern of daily activities.
ハタイ〔ベトナム北部ホン河デルタ地帯の省〕Ha Tay.
ばたいじゅう【馬体重】《競馬》a (horse's) weight; the weight of a horse.
はだかいし【裸石】〔枠や台にはめこむ前の, カットを施した宝石〕a loose stone; an unset stone.
はだかでばねずみ【裸出歯鼠】《動》〔東アフリカ産の, 地中で集団生活をする全身に毛がないネズミ〕a naked mole rat; *Heterocephalus glaber*.
バダクシャン〔アフガニスタン北東部の州〕Badakhshan.
はたけしめじ【畑湿地[占地]】〔菌〕〔担子菌類キシメジ科の食用キノコ〕a *hatake*(-)*shimeji* mushroom; a genetically engineered oyster mushroom; *Lyophyllum decastes*.
はたざお【旗竿】 □ 旗竿地〔道路から細い通路でしか入れない敷地〕a flag lot.
はたさしもの【旗指物】a small flag on a pole inserted into the back of a warrior's armor, functioning as a banner to guide the troops in battle.
はだしつ【肌質】(a [my]) skin type; a type of skin; the quality of *sb*'s skin. ◐ 自分の〜に合うローションを見つける find a lotion which suits *one*'s skin (type).
はたち[3]【旗地】= 旗竿地 (⇨はたざお).
パタニ〔パタ-〕.
パタニおうこく【-王国】〔14-18 世紀にかけて現在のパタニにあった王国〕the Pattani kingdom.
バダフシャン = バダクシャン.
はたまねぎ【葉玉葱】〔植〕〔葉は伸びているがまだ結球していない時に収穫した玉ねぎ〕an onion harvested when leaves are present but no bulb.
バダム Badham, John (M.) (1939- ; 英国生まれの映画監督).
バタムとう【-島】〔インドネシアの島〕Batam Island.
バターワース = バターウース.
はたん【破綻】 □ 破綻企業 a bankrupt「company [corporation, enterprise]. 破綻懸念先〔経営破綻が心配される融資先企業など〕a borrower at risk of「insolvency [failure]; a borrower of doubtful solvency. 破綻先 a bankrupt borrower. ◐ 〜先債権 loans to bankrupt borrowers. 破綻処理〔銀行・企業などの〕bankruptcy procedures.
パタンパン = パッタンパン.
バチェレ Bachelet, Michelle (1951- ; チリの政治家; 初の女性大統領 [2006- ]).
パチ《楽器》〔アフリカの民族楽器〕小球二つがひもでつながっていて, カスタネットのように打ち鳴らす a *patica*; *paticas*.
「八月のクリスマス」〔映画〕Christmas in August.
ハチこう【-公】"Hachi," the faithful dog; a dog, Hachi, who continued to wait outside Shibuya Station every day for his master, Tokyo University Professor Ueno Hidesaburō, for 10 years after Ueno's death in 1925. ◐ 忠犬ハチ公 "Hachi," the faithful dog. ◐ 忠犬〜像 the statue of the (faithful dog) Hachi (outside Shibuya Station). □ ハチ公前 ◐ 〜前広場 the square in front of the Hachikō statue (at Shibuya Station). ◐ それじゃあ, 12 時に〜前で. Okay, see you at twelve o'clock in front of「Hachikō [the Hachikō statue].
「87分署」〔米国の, 警察ものの TV ドラマ〕87th Precinct. ► エド・マクベイン (Ed McBain) 原作.
バチスタしゅじゅつ【-手術】〔医〕〔左心室縮小形成手術〕the Batista procedure; a Batista operation. ► この手術を始めたブラジル人医師 Randas Batista から.
はちぞこいし【鉢底石】〔植木鉢の底部に敷く石〕crushed stone [gravel] for the bottom of planters.

「8人の女たち」〔映画〕8 Women;〔原題〕8 Femmes.
ばちばち〔火花などの音〕spit; sputter. ◐ 〜写真を撮る take [snap] one photograph after another / 溶接の火花が〜と飛び散った. The welding sparks sputtered as they flew. / 枯れ枝を集めて火をつけると〜音を立てて燃えた. As I set fire to the dead twigs I'd collected, they crackled in the flames.
はちまるにまるうんどう【8020 運動】〔80 歳になっても 20 本は自分の歯を持とうという運動〕the 80-20 movement; an oral-health campaign intended to help people retain at least 20 natural teeth until the age of 80 and beyond.
はちょう[1]【波長】 □ 波長分割多重【通信】wavelength division multiplexing (略: WDM).
ばちる【撥鏤】〔工芸〕〔漆で染めた象牙に細かい模様を彫る技法〕*bachiru*; engraving of lacquer-stained ivory.
はちろぐん【八路軍】〔中国史〕〔人民解放軍の前身〕the Eighth Route Army.
パチンコ □ パチンコカード a prepaid pachinko card.
はつ-【初-】〔初-〕初白星【黒星】(a wrestler's) first win [first loss] (in a tournament); (a team's) first victory [first defeat] (of the season). 初競り the first wholesale market of the year. 初登板〔野球〕one's first appearance on the mound.
ばつ[2]【罰】 □ 罰ゲーム a punishment; a penalty.
はっか【白華】【化】〔コンクリートなどの白色析出物〕efflorescence; bloom.
はっか[4]【発火】 □ 発火事故〔電気器具などの〕(an electrical) fire accident. 発火地点〔火災の〕the (「place [location] of) the origin of a fire; (the place) where a fire starts.
はつが【発芽】 □ 発芽防止〔ジャガイモなどの〕sprout inhibition. ◐ 〜防止処理 treatment for sprout inhibition. 発芽米〔食品〕sprouted rice. 発芽野菜 sprouted [sprouting] vegetables; vegetable sprouts.
はつがお【初顔】[1]〔新顔〕衆議院への〜 newcomer to [new face in] the House of Representatives / 夏の甲子園への〜 a team appearing for the first time in the High-School Baseball Tournament at Kōshien Stadium.
**2**〔初顔合せ〕playing each other for the first time.
ばっかく[2]【幕閣】〔日本史〕〔幕府の閣僚組織〕the「highest-ranking officials [top echelon] of the Tokugawa shogunate.
ばっかりぐい【ばっかり食い】= ばっかりたべ.
ばっかりたべ【ばっかり食べ】= かきはむし.
はつがん【発癌】 □ 発がん遺伝子 an oncogene. 発癌促進物質【医】a cancer accelerator; a (cancer) promoter.
バッカン〔ベトナム北部の省; その省都〕Bac Kan.
パッキーカード〔パチンコ用のプリペイドカード〕a pachinko card.
バッキーボール《化》〔フレーレンを構成する球状分子〕a buckyball; a fullerene molecule.
バッギス = バドギス.
はっきゅう[2]【発給】 □ 発給条件[要件] the conditions for issuing《a permit, a visa》. 発給申請 an issue quota; a quota for「issuing [the issue of]《permits》. ◐ 査証[ビザ]〜枠 a visa quota / 年間〜枠 an annual quota (of visas).
はっきょう[2]【八強】〔ベスト 8〕the「last [final] eight.
はっきん[3]【白筋】【解】(a) white muscle.
バック[1] □ 3[4]バック〔サッカー〕〔自陣のゴール前に 3[4]人のディフェンダーを配置する守備態勢〕three [four] back formation. バックスタンド〔野球場などの〕the back bleachers. バックモニター・カメラ〔自動車〕〔後方の死角を映すためのカメラ〕a rear view camera.
バック[1] □ 少量【小分け】パック a small-quantity package. □ パック商品〔旅行などの〕a package; a pack-

バック⁴【PAC】〔米国の政治活動委員会〕PAC; a political action committee.

バックアップ ▣ バックアップ体制 backup; a backup「facility [system]; backup coverage. ▣ メインコンピューターがダメージを受けた場合の〜体制は十分に整っている。We have a fully functioning backup system in place in case of damage to the main computer. バックアップ発電 backup power generation. ▣ 〜発電機 a backup (power) generator.

バックエンドたいさく【-対策】〔放射性廃棄物の処理処分対策および原子力施設の廃止措置〕management of the back end of the nuclear fuel cycle; back-end management.

バックエンドひよう【-費用】〔核燃料サイクルでの使用済み燃料の再処理・廃棄処理などに要する費用〕back-end costs.

バック・オーダー〔繰り越し注文〕a back order.

バックシーム〔足の後ろに縫い目のあるストッキング「パンスト」〕(a pair of) back seam「stockings [panty hose, "tights].

バック・ステップ 1〔ダンス・運動競技で〕a back step. 〜する step back; take a step「back [backward(s)]. 2〔バイク〕〔通常の位置より後方に取り付けた足載せ〕set-back「footpegs [footrests].

バックストレート〔競技〕〔競争路で、ゴール地点がある側と反対側の直線走路〕the「backstretch [back straight].

バック・スリー【PAC-3】〔軍〕〔迎撃ミサイル〕a PAC-3. ▶ Patriot Advanced Capability-3 の略。

はっくつ【発掘】 ▣ 発掘調査 an (archeological) excavation; a dig. ▣ 〜調査を行う conduct [carry out] an excavation.

バックトス『バレーボール』tossing the ball to the back of one's court without turning around;〔1 回の〕a toss to the back of the court. ▣ 〜を上げる toss the ball to the back of the court without turning around.

バックドライブ〔卓球〕a backhand drive.

「バックドラフト」〔映画〕Backdraft.

バックネット ▣ バックネット裏 the [area [seats] behind the backstop.

バックパッカー〔バックパック「リュックサック」一つで旅する人〕a backpacker.

バックヒール〔サッカー〕〔ボールを後方に蹴ること〕a back heel. ▷ back-heel v.

バックビルディング〔気象〕〔同じ場所で次々に積乱雲が発達する現象〕backbuilding (略: BB).

ハックフォード Hackford, Taylor (1945– ;米国の映画監督).

バックフリップ〔フリースタイルスキーで〕a backflip. 〜する do a backflip; backflip. ▣ 〜を決める do [complete, turn] a (successful) backflip; backflip successfully.

バックホウ〔土木掘削用機械;ユンボ〕a backhoe.

バックりょうほう【VAC 療法】〔医〕〔3 種類の抗がん剤を併用する治療法〕VAC chemotherapy. ▶ VAC は vincristine (ビンクリスチン), actinomycin D (アクチノマイシン D), cyclophosphamide (シクロホスファミド) の略。

はっけつびょう【白血病】 ▣ 急性前骨髄球性白血病〔医〕acute promyelocytic leukemia (略: APL).

はっけん²【発見】 ▣ 発見現場 a「(fossil) discovery site; the site of「(a) discovery [a find]. ▣ 遺体の現場 〜いたい³. がん〜率 a「(cancer) detection rate. 〔⇨早期発見率 (⇨そうき¹)〕

はっけん³【発券】 ▣ 発券機 〔切符など〕a ticket (vending) machine.

はつげん²【発現】 ▣ 発現率〔副作用・奇形・症状などの〕incidence rate.

はつご【発語】 ▣ 発語失行〔医〕apraxia of speech.

「初恋」〔韓国のテレビドラマ〕First Love.

「初恋のきた道」〔映画〕The Road Home;〔中国語タイトル〕我的父親母親.

はっこう⁴【発光】 ▣ 発光インク〔印刷〕(a) luminescent ink.

はっこう⁵【発行】 ▣ 発行可能枠〔株式〕the maximum number of shares (of capital stock) that may be issued; the maximum number of issuable shares. 発行体【発行元】an issuing body. 発行手数料〔証明書・キャッシュカードなど〕an issuance fee. 発行登録〔証券〕〔有価証券の〕shelf registration. ▣ 〜登録制度 a shelf registration system. 発行元 an issuer.

はっこう⁸【発酵】 ▣ 下面発酵〔醸造〕bottom [top] fermentation. ▣ 下面[上面]〜ビール (a) bottom-[top-]fermented beer. ▣ 発酵飲料 a fermented drink. 発酵促進剤 a fermentation accelerator. 発酵茶 fermented tea. ▣ 不〜発酵 non-fermented tea / 半〜茶 semi-fermented tea / 部分〜茶 partly fermented [partially-fermented] tea. 発酵バター〔料理〕fermented butter. 発酵野菜〈集合的に〉fermented vegetables.

はっこん【発根】〔園芸〕rooting; rootage. 〜する root; take root.

ばっさい【伐採】 ▣ 違法伐採 illegal timber-felling; illegal cutting. 過剰伐採〔林業〕overcutting; overharvesting; overlumbering.

ハッジ〔イスラム〕〔イスラム暦 12 月に行われるメッカ大巡礼〕hajj; haj; hadj.

バッジオ = バッジョ.

パッシブ ▣ パッシブ運用〔株式〕⇨うんよう.

パッシベーション〔化〕〔不動態化〕passivation. ▷ passivate v.

はっしゃ²【発射】 ▣ 発射実験〔ロケットなどの〕test launching;〔1 回の〕a test launch.

バッジョ Baggio, Roberto (1967– ;イタリアのサッカー選手).

はっしょう¹【発症】 ▣ 発症菌量〔医〕an infective dose; the number of bacteria required to cause「(a) disease [symptoms]. ▣ 食中毒の〜菌量は菌の種類によって大きく異なる。The infective dose for food poisoning varies greatly depending on the type of bacteria concerned. 発症馬[鶏]a「horse [chicken] which (develops [has developed] (the symptoms of) 《flu》;a「horse [chicken] with 《flu》. 発症前診断〔医〕advance [early] diagnosis 《of Alzheimer's》. 発症メカニズム an onset mechanism. ▣ パーキンソン病の〜メカニズムを解明する clarify the onset mechanism for Parkinson's disease. 発症例 a case《of cholera》; an outbreak;〔症例数〕(an) incidence. ▣ 2006 年の〜例は 350 人で、110 人が死亡している。There were 350 cases of the disease up to 2006, of which 110 were fatal.

はっしょう²【発祥】origination; beginning. ▣ 発祥地 the「birthplace [cradle]《of golf》.

ばつじょう【罰条】〔法〕〔起訴状に罪名を記載するために示される適用法条〕a punitive「article [clause].

「パッション」〔映画〕The Passion of the Christ.

はっしん¹【発信】 ▣ 情報発信 the「emission [dispatching, sending out] of information. ▣ 情報〜ツールとしての和英辞典 a Japanese-English dictionary as a tool for emitting information. ▣ 発信量 the volume of outgoing《calls, mail, etc.》. ▣ 現首相は前任者に比べてマスメディアへの〜量が少ない。The present Prime Minister「is more reticent with [gives less away to] the media than「his [her] predecessor. 発信力 communicativity; the power to make oneself「known [understood]. ▣ 情報〜力 communicativity; the power to disseminate information《about oneself》. 発信履歴〔記録〕〔電話などの〕a record of「outgoing calls [calls made].

はっすい【撥水】 ▣ 超撥水 (a) super water「repellency [repellence]. ▷ super water-repellent adj. ▣ 超〜表面 a super water-repellent surface / 超〜コー

ティング (a) super water-repellent coating. ◯□ 撥水コーティング (a) water-repellent coating. 撥水性 water repellency.
**ばつずい**【抜髄】〖歯科〗〔歯の神経を抜くこと〕(a) pulpectomy; a baby root canal.
**はっせい**¹【発生】 ◯□ 発生医学 medical embryology. 発生工学 development(al) engineering. 発生例 an outbreak; a case; an instance 《of a disease》;〈集合的に〉(an) incidence. ◯ 6〜8月のインフルエンザの集団〜例はきわめて少ない. The incidence of large-scale influenza epidemics is extremely low between June and August.
**はっせいがく**【発生学】 ◯□ 動物[植物]発生学 animal [plant] embryology [developmental biology].
**はっそう**³【発想】 ◯□ 発想力 an ability to ʳcreate [come up with] new ideas; imagination; creativity.
**はっそうとび**【八艘飛び[跳び]】〔源義経の〕Yoshitsune's leap across eight enemy boats at the battle of Dannoura;〔相撲〕〔大きくジャンプをして相手の視界から消え, 相手を翻弄する技〕an upward jump by a sumo wrestler designed to surprise his opponent by disappearing from the field of vision.
**ばっそく**【罰則】 ◯□ 罰則強化 strengthening [stiffening, tightening] penalties 《for…, against…》; strengthening [stiffening] punishments 《for…》. 金融犯罪の〜強化を検討する consider strengthening the penalties for financial crimes / 不法投棄に対する〜強化を盛り込むために廃棄物処理法を改正した. The Waste Disposal Law has been changed to include stiffer punishments for illegal dumping.
**ばった**²〔投げ売り; 不正規流通〕〔投げ売り〕ばった売り〔投げ売り〕selling off goods at ʳvery low prices [a loss] (to obtain cash). ばった物〔正規の流通ルートを経ていない極端に安値の商品〕goods sold off through irregular channels at ʳvery low prices [a loss]. ばった屋〔ばった物を売る店〕a shop ʳselling [dealing in] irregular, low-priced goods;〔人〕a ʳseller of [dealer in] irregular, low-priced goods.
**ばつだ**【罰打】〖ゴルフ〗=だぶつ.
**パッター(ー)ニー**〔タイ南部の県; その県都〕Pattani.
**パッタイ**〔料理〕〔タイの焼きそば〕pad [phad] Thai.
**はったつ**²【発達】 ◯□ 発達遅滞児 a developmentally delayed child. ◯ 言語〜遅滞児 a child with delayed language development. 発達年齢〖心理〗(a) developmental age (略: DA). ◯ あの生徒の〜年齢は6歳だ. That student has a developmental age of 6.
**はったつしょうがいしゃしえんほう**【発達障害者支援法】〖法〗the Law to Support Sufferers of Developmental Disorders.
**パッタルン**〔タイ南部の県; その県都〕Phatthalung.
**はったん**【八端】 ◯□ 八端判〔座布団のサイズ〕 ◯ 〜判の座布団 a large-size (floor) cushion (59×63cm).
**バッタンバン**〔カンボジア北西部の州〕Battambang.
「**パッチ・アダムス**」〔映画〕Patch Adams.
**バッチグー**〖<「バッチリ」+「グー」〗〖申し分ない〗(absolutely) perfect. ◯ 〜なタイミング perfect timing / 最後にバジルの葉をのせると, これで味も香りも〜. Top it off with some basil leaves and it will taste and smell absolutely perfect.
**はっちゃくしん**【発着信】 ◯□ 発着信履歴〔電話などの〕a record of ʳincoming and outgoing calls [calls made and received]; a call log.
**はつチャレンジ**【初−】=はっちょうせん.
**はっちゅう**¹【発注】 ◯□ 発注額 the (monetary) amount of orders (made). 発注側〔元〕the customer; the party ordering; the person who places the order. 発注先 a source (of 《materials》); the ʳperson [party, company] one orders from; the ʳperson [party, company] from whom materials are ordered. 発注書 an order note;

an order in writing. 発注情報 information on (the processing of) orders; the status of orders;〔公共工事の〕information on the current status of public works orders. 発注予定〔工事の〕projected construction orders. ◯ 〜予定工事 construction (work) orders projected 《for the following year》.
**はっちょうせん**【初挑戦】a first ʳattempt [try, go]. 〜する make ʳa [one's] first attempt 《to do》; attempt [try] for the first time;〔人に〕challenge sb for the first time.
**ハッチンソン・ギルフォードしょうこうぐん**【−症候群】〖医〗〔早老症の一種〕Hutchinson-Gilford progeria syndrome.
**バッツ**【VATS】〖医〗〔胸腔鏡下手術〕VATS; video assisted thoracoscopic surgery.
**バッティング**¹ ◯□ バッティング・グローブ, バッティング用手袋〔野球など〕batting gloves.
**ばってき**【抜擢】 ◯□ 抜擢人事 fast tracking; fast-track promotion. ◯ 彼の社長就任は15人抜きの〜人事だった. He was ʳfast-tracked [catapulted] over 15 others into the president's post.
**バッテリー** ◯□ バッテリー・コーチ〔野球〕a battery coach; a pitching/catching coach. バッテリー車 a battery-powered ʳcar [vehicle].
**はつでん**【発電】 ◯□ クリーン石炭発電〔ガス化した石炭を燃料として行う発電〕clean-coal power generation. ◯ クリーン石炭〜所 a clean-coal power ʳplant [station]. 発電効率 power generation efficiency. 発電床〔通る人の震動で発電する〕a "power generation floor"; flooring incorporating piezoelectric materials that converts the tread of pedestrians into usable energy. 発電素子 a power generation device. 発電単価 a power generation cost 《of 6 yen/kWh》.
**はつでんしょ**【発電所】 ◯□ 自流式(水力)発電所 a run-of-the-river power plant. ダム〔貯水池〕式(水力)発電所 a reservoir power plant. 揚水式(水力)発電所 a pumped storage power plant.
**ハッテンじょう**【発展場, ハッテン場】〔同性愛者が集まる場所〕a (gay) cruising ʳsite [place]; a gay venue.
**はってんてき**【発展的】 ◯□ 発展的記述〔教科書で〕the inclusion in school textbooks of advanced material (beyond the requirements of the curriculum).
**バット**¹ ◯□ バット・コントロール〔野球〕bat control. ◯ 彼は巧みな〜コントロールで右に左に打ち分ける. He controls his bat well and can hit to either the right or the left. バット・リング〔野球〕a bat ring; a bat weight.
**パット** ◯□ パー・パット a par putt; a putt for par.
**パッドいんさつ**【−印刷】〖印刷〗pad printing.
**はつとういん**【初登院】one's first appearance at the House. 〜する go to the House for the first time (after being elected).
**バッド・キアリしょうこうぐん**【−症候群】〖医〗Budd-Chiari syndrome (略: BCS).
「**バット・マスターソン**」〔実在の保安官を描くTV西部劇〕Bat Masterson.
「**バットマン ビギンズ**」〔映画〕Batman Begins.
**ハットン**Hutton, Timothy (1960– ; 米国の映画俳優).
**はつねつ**【発熱】 ◯□ 発熱外来 outpatient treatment of ʳfever(s) [febrile patients]; an outpatient service for patients with fevers of unknown origin. 発熱患者 a patient with a ʳfever [high temperature]; a febrile patient. 発熱剤〔化学反応を利用して火を使わず加熱する薬品; 特に非常食に利用〕an FRH; a flameless ration heater. 発熱植物 a heat-producing plant. 発熱(性)疾患〖医〗pyrexia; a ʳfebrile [pyretic] disease; a disease characterized by fever.
**バッハラッハ**〔ドイツ南西部の町; 世界遺産のライン渓谷中流上部にある古い町〕Bacharach.
「**ハッピィブルー**」〔映画〕The Pallbearer.

ハッピー・マンデー〔祝日を月曜に移動させる制度〕(a) "happy Monday"; scheduling (national) holidays on Mondays.

ハップマップけいかく【-計画】⇨こくさいハップマップけいかく.

ハッブル　▣　ハッブル・ウルトラ・ディープ・フィールド〖天〗〔ハッブル宇宙望遠鏡が捉えた超深宇宙〕the Hubble Ultra Deep Field (略: HUDF).　ハッブル・ディープ・フィールド〖天〗〔ハッブル宇宙望遠鏡が捉えた深宇宙〕the Hubble Deep Field (略: HDF).

はっぽう²【発泡】　▣　発泡水 carbonated [soda, seltzer, sparkling] water.　発泡トレイ a polystyrene tray;〚商標〛a Styrofoam tray.　発泡ビーズ expanded polystyrene beads; EPS beads.

はっぽう⁴【発砲】　▣　発砲音 (the sound of) a shot;〔複数の〕(the sound of)「shooting [firing].　◯パンパンパンと～音が 3 回し, 車の走り去る音が聞こえた. I heard three shots and then the sound of a car driving off.　発砲許可〔give, receive, request〕permission to fire.　発砲命令〔give〕the [an] order to fire.

はっぽう⁵【発報】〔非常警報などの作動〕the activation [sounding]〚of an alarm〛.　～する〔警報機器が〕sound; go off; activate.　◯火災報知器が～した. The fire alarm went off.　▣　誤発報 the erroneous「activation [sounding]〚of an alarm〛.

ばっぽんてき【抜本的】　▣　抜本的改正 a radical revision.　◯労働基準法の～改正を進める advocate a radical revision of the Labor Standards Law.

はつめい【発明】　▣　発明対価 compensation for an invention.　発明報奨制度〚a company's〛invention reward system.

はつめいきねんび【発明記念日】〔4 月 18 日〕Invention(s) Day.

はつめいのひ【発明の日】＝はつめいきねんび.

はつもの【初物】　▣　初物好き〔こと〕a liking for「things [foods] which have just come into season;〔人〕a person who likes「things [foods] which have just come into season.

はつりょう¹【初猟】one's first hunting (trip) of the year.　▣　初猟日　＝しょりょうび.

はつりょう²【初漁】one's first fishing (trip) of the year.

はつれい【発令】　▣　発令権 executive「authority [rights, powers]; a [the] authority to「execute〚a law〛[issue〚an ordinance〛].　発令者 a [the] person with executive authority.

はてい【破堤】〔河川の堤の決壊〕a breach of「an embankment [a dike, a levee]; the bursting of a floodwall.　～する〈堤防が主語〉break; burst;〈川などが主語〉breach [burst]〚a riverbank〛.

ハディーサ〔イラク西部, アンバル州の町〕Haditha.

「パティー・デューク・ショー」〔米国の, 女子高校生の TV コメディー〕The Patty Duke Show.

バティスティーナ〖天〗〔火星・木星間の小惑星〕298 Baptistina; the Baptistina asteroid.　▣　バティスティーナ族 the Baptistina (asteroid) family.

パティル Patil, Pratibha (1934-　　; インドの政治家; インド初の女性大統領〔2007-　　〕).

ハティン〔ベトナム中北部の省; その省都〕Ha Tinh.

はでこん【派手婚】a「big [flashy,《口》blow-out] wedding.

パテント　▣　パテント・トロール〔特許訴訟を通じて莫大な利益を得る企業〕a patent troll.

バテン・レース〔テープ状のレースをかがり合わせて作るレース〕Battenberg lace.

はと【鳩】　▣　レース鳩 a racing pigeon; a racer.　▣　鳩レース pigeon racing;〔1 回〕a pigeon race.

はと²【波止】　▣　波止釣り fishing from the breakwater.

はどう¹【波動】　▣　波動エネルギー wave energy.

ばとうじんしん【馬頭人身】a human body with the head of a horse; a horse-headed figure.

パトゥム・タ(ー)ニ(ー)〔タイ中部の県; その県都〕Pathum Thani.

パ・ド・カレー〔フランス北部の県〕Pas-de-Calais.

バドギス〔アフガニスタン西部の州〕Badghis.

ハドソン 1 Hudson, Hugh (1936-　　; 英国の映画監督).　2 Hudson, Kate (1979-　　; 米国の映画女優; 女優ゴールディー・ホーンの娘).

「ハドソン・ホーク」〖映画〗Hudson Hawk.

ハトフ〖軍〗〔パキスタンのミサイル〕a Hatf missile.

ハトホル〔エジプト神話〕〔雌牛の頭部をもつ女神〕Hathor.

ハトラ〔イラクの遺跡〕Hatra.

パトリオット　▣　パトリオット 3 PAC-3.　▶ PAC は Patriot Advanced Capability の略.

「パトリオット」〖映画〗The Patriot.

「パトリオット・ゲーム」〖映画〗Patriot Games.

パトリオットほう【-法】〖米法〗the USA Patriot Act.　▶ 正式名称は the Uniting and Strengthening America by Providing Appropriate Tools Required to Intercept and Obstruct Terrorism Act.

パトリック Patric, Jason (1966-　　; 米国の映画俳優; 本名 Jason Patric Miller).

パトリック・コックス〚商標〛〔英国の服飾ブランド〕Patrick Cox.

パドル¹　▣　パドル・シフト〖自動車〗〔変速装置の一種〕a paddle shift.

バドルりょだん【-旅団】〔イラク・イスラム革命最高評議会 (SCIRI) の民兵組織〕the Badr Organization;〔旧名〕the Badr Brigade.

ハドレーじゅんかん【-循環】〖気象〗〔大気大循環の一種〕the Hadley cell.

ハドロサウルス〔古生物〕〔鳥脚亜目の草食恐竜〕a hadrosaurus;〔科名〕Hadrosaurus.

ハドン² 〔ベトナム北部, ハタイ省の省都〕Ha Dong.

パトン・ビーチ〔タイ, プーケット島にある〕Patong Beach.

はな⁴【鼻】　▣　鼻削ぎ〔刑罰〕slicing off 《a criminal's》 nose.　鼻ぺちゃ〔have〕a「flat [pug] nose.　◯～ぺちゃな顔 a「pug-nosed [flat-nosed] face.

ハナ Hannah, John (1962-　　; スコットランド生まれの映画俳優).

ハナー ＝ハナ.

バナウェーブけんきゅうじょ【-研究所】the Panawave Laboratory.

はなうがい【鼻含嗽】nasal irrigation (by inhaling fluid into the nose and expelling it out the mouth).

はなうめ【花梅】〔実梅に対し, 花を観賞するための梅〕a「blossom [flower] ume (tree).

はなえんじゅ【花槐】〖植〗〔マメ科の植物〕a bristly locust; a rose acacia; *Robinia hispida*.

はながさまつり【花笠祭り】the *Hanagasa* Festival; the Flower Hat Festival of Yamagata, originally a rice-planting festival, now featuring gorgeously decorated floats and thousands of dancers wearing flowered hats.

はながた【花形】　▣　花形職種 a much sought-after [an extremely popular] job.

はなじあい【花試合】〔親善試合〕a「friendly [friendship] game [match];《play》a friendly;〔顔見せ試合〕a celebrity「game [match].

はなしぐれ【花時雨】a cold rain shower in the cherry-blossom season.

はなせん【鼻栓】〔シンクロの選手などが鼻に挟み, 水が入らないようにするもの〕a nose clip.

はなだかとんぼ【鼻高蜻蛉】〖昆〗*Rhinocypha ogasawarensis*.

はなちょうちん【鼻提灯】a bubble from *sb's* nose.　◯赤ちゃんが～を出した. The baby blew a little bubble from its nose. / 彼は～を出して寝ていた.〔比喩的に〕He

was snoring away. | He was 「in (a) profound slumber [lost to the world].
**はなちらし**【花散らし】 ◐〜の雨〔桜が見ごろのときに降る雨〕rain that ruins the cherry blossoms.
**バナナ** ▣□ バナナ・ペーパー〔バナナの茎の繊維から作る紙〕banana paper.
**はなのひ**【鼻の日】〔8月7日〕Nose Day.
**バナバちゃ**【−茶】banaba tea.
**はなび**【花火】 ▣□ 創作〔創造〕花火 creative fireworks 《display》. 手筒花火〔両腕でかかえ持つ花火〕a large handheld fireworks device made of a bamboo tube packed with powder and bound with rope; a fire-spraying tube. 手持ち花火〔片手で持つ花火〕handheld fireworks. 噴出〔噴水〕花火〔噴き上げる式の花火〕a (fire-works) fountain. ▣□ 花火玉〔打ち上げ花火の火薬玉〕a rocket shell; a ball of explosive; a shell.
**はなびらたけ**【花弁茸】【菌】〔担子菌類ハナビラタケ科の食用キノコ〕a cauliflower mushroom; *Sparassis crispa*.
**パナマックス**〔パナマ運河を通行できる最大船型〕Panamax. ▣□ パナマックス船〔パナマ運河を通行できる最大船型〕a Panamax (vessel [ship]).
**はなみょうが**【花茗荷】1【植】〔ショウガ科の常緑多年草〕 (a) Japanese ginger; *Alpinia japonica*. 2〔ミョウガのつぼみの部分;「茗荷の子」ともいう〕(a) *myōga* [*Zingiber mioga*] (flower) bud.
**ハナム**〔ベトナム北部ホン河デルタ地帯の省〕Ha Nam.
**はなむぎ**【花麦】【植】early-harvested barley plants (used for ikebana and for making barley water).
**はなもも**【花桃】〔実桃に対し、花を観賞するための桃〕a 「blossom [flower] peach (tree).
**パナルジン**《商標・薬》〔血小板凝集抑制薬〕Panaldine.
**はなわぎく**【花輪菊】【植】〔キク科の1年草〕a tricolor chrysanthemum; *Chrysanthemum carinatum*.
**ハニーデュー**【植】〔メロンの一種〕(a) honeydew melon.
**ハニートラップ**〔色仕掛けのスパイ活動;そのスパイ〕a 「honeytrap [honeypot].
「**ハニーにおまかせ**」〔米国、女性私立探偵のアクションTVドラマ〕Honey West.
**ハニ**(−)**ヤ** Haniya, Ismail (1963− ;イスラム組織ハマスの幹部;パレスチナ自治政府首相〔2006−07〕)
**ハニぞく**【−族】〔アカ族の中国名〕the Ha Ni; the Hani;〔1人〕a Ha Ni; a Hani 《*pl*. 〜》. 〔⇨アカぞく〕
**パニック** ▣□ パニック心理 a panic psychology. パニック病【医】panic disease.
「**パニック・ルーム**」〔映画〕Panic Room.
**パニツムマブ**【薬】〔転移性大腸がんの治療薬〕panitumumab.
**バニャックしょとう**【−諸島】〔インドネシア、アチェ州、スマトラ島西岸沖にある〕(the) Banyak Islands;〔インドネシア語名〕Pulau(-pulau) Banyak.
「**バニラ・スカイ**」〔映画〕Vanilla Sky.
**はにわ**【埴輪】 ▣□ 家形埴輪 a house-shaped *haniwa*. 船形埴輪 a ship-shaped *haniwa*.
**バヌアレブ**〔フィジー諸島の島〕Vanua Levu Island.
**ハヌマン・ラングール**〔オナガザル科のサル〕a hanuman langur; *Semnopithecus entellus*.
**はね**【羽・羽根・翅】〔羽〕〔羽扇子・羽扇〕a feather fan.
**はねぎ**【葉葱】【植】〔緑色の葉の部分が長く、主にそこを食べる長ねぎ〕a scallion whose long green leaf is primarily eaten.
**はねだし**【撥ね出し】〔規格外の製品を取り除くこと〕rejection; removal;〔その製品〕a reject.
**はねだす**【撥ね出す】〔規格外の製品を取り除く〕reject; remove;〔追い出す〕expel; throw out. ◐傷のあるリンゴをベルトコンベアから〜 remove bruised apples from a conveyor belt / 今年はわがチームに優秀な新人が多く、私はスタメンからはね出されてしまった。There are a lot of talented new people on our team this year, so I was 「pulled from [kicked off] the starting lineup.
**はねのり**【撥ね海苔】a nori reject; substandard nori.

**パネル** ▣□ パネル駆動〔電子工学〕panel drive. パネル写真 a photographic panel.
**はのえいせいしゅうかん**【歯の衛生週間】〔6月4日から1週間〕Dental Hygiene Week.
**バハ** ▣□〔サウジアラビア南西部の州;その州都〕Bahah.
**ばば**[3]【馬場】 ▣□ 馬場状態 track conditions.
**パパイア** ▣□ 青パパイア a green papaya. ◐ パパイア酵素 a papaya enzyme.
「**母が教えてくれた歌**」〔ドヴォルザーク作曲の楽曲〕Songs My Mother Taught Me.
**ははじまめぐろ**【母島目黒】【鳥】a Bonin (Hahajima) honeyeater; *Apalopteron familiare hahasima*.
**ははそ**【柞】〔クヌギ・ナラの総称〕an oak.
「**パパ大好き**」〔米国の、やもめの父親と3人の息子によるTVホームドラマ〕My Three Sons.
**はばつ**【派閥】 ▣□ 派閥総会 a party faction general meeting.
**パパドプロス** Papadopoulos, Tassos (1934− ;キプロスの政治家;大統領〔2003−08〕).
**ハバネロ**《〈Sp.〉激辛唐辛子》habanero (pepper); *Capsicum chinense*.
「**母の眠り**」〔映画〕One True Thing.
「**パパは何でも知っている**」〔1950年代の理想的な米国の家庭を描くTVホームドラマ〕Father Knows Best.
**パパビリ**〔次期法王候補の枢機卿〕a papabile 《*pl*. papabili》.
**パパママ・ストア**〔個人経営の商店〕a mom-and-pop store.
**パパラオ**〔サンテリアの司祭〕a Babalawo 《*pl*. 〜s》.
**パハン**〔マレーシア中部の州〕Pahang.
**ハビ**【HAVi】〔エイチ・エー・ブイ・アイ.〕
**ハビタット**【HABITAT】〔国連人間居住計画の通称〕UN-Habitat.
**バビラ**【動】〔中米・南米産のワニ〕a babilla.
**バビル**〔イラク、バグダッド南方の州〕Babil. ▶ 州都 ヒッラ.
**パピローマ・ウイルス**【医】⇨ ヒト・パピローマ・ウイルス.
**ハブ** ▣□ ハブ＆スポーク方式〔システム〕〔航空〕a hub-and-spoke system. ハブ港〔海〕〔航空が集中している重要港〕a hub port.
**パブ** ▣□ フィリピン・パブ a "Philippine pub"; a bar with Filipino hostesses. ▣□ パブ記事 a publicity article; an article which gets 《a company》 publicity.
**パプア**〔インドネシアの州〕Papua.
**パフィア**【植】〔南米産ヒユ科の植物;根はハーブとなる〕pfaffia; suma; Brazilian ginseng; *Pfaffia paniculata*.
**パフィン**〔鳥〕〔ツノメドリの類〕ツノメドリ〔エトピリカ (tufted puffin) など〕a puffin.
**パプーリアス** Papoulias, Karolos (1929− ;ギリシャの政治家;大統領〔2005− 〕).
**バフェット** Buffett, Warren (1930− ;米国の企業家・投資家).
**はぶくらげ**【波布水母】【動】a habu jellyfish; *Chiropsalmus quadrigatus*.
**パフタバド**〔ウズベキスタン東部の町〕Pakhtabad.
**バフタラン**〔イラン西部の州・都市ケルマンシャーの旧称〕Bakhtaran.
**ハフニウム** ▣□ ハフニウム板型制御棒〔原子力〕a hafnium control rod.
**ハプニング** ▣□ ハプニング性 the unexpected; something happening; eventfulness. ◐ ジャズの演奏では〜性がないとつまらない。Without the unexpected, a jazz performance is boring.
「**パフューム ある人殺しの物語**」〔映画〕Perfume: The Story of a Murderer.
**パブリー 〜な**〔バブルの時代のような発想の;金づかいが荒い〕extravagant; ostentatious. ◐〜な施設 an 「overly [excessively] expensive [extravagant, luxurious] facility.
**パブリック** ▣□ パブリック・コメント〔公募意見〕public

comment. パブリック・ディプロマシー ＝広報外交〔⇨こほう4）〕

**バブル** ▫ バブル景気 a bubble economy.

**ハプロタイプ**〔遺伝〕a haplotype. ▫ ハプロタイプ地図 a haplotype map《of the human genome》.

**バベシア**〔動〕〔バベシア属の原虫；動物の血液に寄生する〕(a) babesia《pl. ~(s), babesiae》. ▫ バベシア症〔獣医〕babesiosis; babesiasis.

**バベルじょう**【−城】〔ポーランドのクラクフにある城；ポーランド王の居城として11世紀に建造された〕Wawel Castle.

**バベルダオブとう**【−島】〔太平洋南西部、パラオ諸島最大の島〕Babeldaob [Babelthuap] Island.

**はまきぎんが**【葉巻銀河】〔天〕〔M82銀河の通称〕the Cigar Galaxy.

**ハマダーン**〔イラン西部の州；その州都〕Hamadan.

**ハミルトン 1** Hamilton, Guy (1922- ；フランス生まれの英国の映画監督).
**2** Hamilton, Linda (1956- ；米国の映画女優).

**ハミルトンうつびょうひょうかしゃくど**【−鬱病評価尺度】〔医〕〔the Hamilton Rating Scale for Depression（略：HRSD; HRS; HAM-D); the Hamilton Depression Scale. ▶ ドイツ生まれの英国の医学博士・精神科医 Max Hamilton〔1912-88〕が考案.

**ハム**[HAM]〔医〕〔歩行障害や排尿障害などを引き起こす脊髄疾患〕HAM. ▶ HTLV-associated myelopathy の略.

**バム**〔イラン南東部の町〕Bam.〔⇨アルゲ・バム〕

**バムク** Pamuk, Orhan (1952- ；トルコの作家).

「**ハムナプトラ / 失われた砂漠の都**」〔映画〕The Mummy.

「**ハムナプトラ 2 / 黄金のピラミッド**」〔映画〕The Mummy Returns.

「**ハムラビ法典**」〔古代バビロニアの法典〕the Code of Hammurabi.

**はめあい**【嵌め合い】〔機〕＝かんごう3.

**はめあう**【嵌め合う】＝かんごう3(～する).

**はもの**2【葉物】▫ 葉物野菜 green vegetables; edible herbs.

**ハモる**〔声で協和音を作る〕harmonize《with…》; sing harmony《with…》.

**ハモン・イベリコ**〔食品〕〔イベリコ豚を原料とする高級ハム〕Jamón Ibérico; Iberian ham.

「**早撃ちマック**」〔米国の、早撃ちの保安官の馬を主人公とするTV ギャグアニメ〕Quick Draw McGraw.

**パヤオ**〔タイ北部の県；その県都〕Phayao.

**はやご**【早碁】〔囲碁〕〔持ち時間を短く制限された碁〕lightning go; speed go.

**はやさい**【葉野菜】green vegetables; edible herbs.

**はやちねうすゆきそう**【早池峰薄雪草】〔植〕〔キク科の多年草〕Leontopodium hayachinense.

**はやばちたい**【早場地帯】＝早場米地帯〔⇨はやばまい〕.

**はやばまい**【早場米】▫ 早場米地帯 an early rice harvest area; a region with an early rice harvest.

**はやびき**2【速弾き】〔ギターなどの楽器を速く弾くこと〕fast《guitar》 playing [picking, fretwork]. ～する play《a [the] guitar》fast. ▶ギターの～が得意だ．He's an expert fast guitar player.

**はやべん**1【早弁】〔学生が昼休み前に弁当を食べること〕eating one's「packed lunch [bento] before the midday break.

**はやべん**2【速弁】〔高速道路のサービスエリアで売っている弁当〕a (locally prepared) 「box lunch [bentō] sold at an expressway service area.

**はやり**【流行り】▫ はやりもの a fashionable object; sth in fashion; 《口》sth that is 「all the rage [the height of fashion].

**はやわり**【早割】〔運賃などの早期予約者割引〕an early booking discount. ▫ 早割航空券 an early-discount airline ticket.

**バユ・ウンダン**〔ティモール海にある油田・ガス田〕Bayu-Undan.

**ばら**1【薔薇】▫ バラ水〔バラの花びらの蒸留水；美肌用・飲用〕rose water.

**バラーム**〔イスラム法が禁止する行為〕haram.

**バラかくめい**【−革命】〔2003年グルジアの〕the Rose Revolution.

**ハラカト・(ウル・)ムジャヒディン**〔パキスタンの過激派組織〕the Harakat ul-Mujahidin（略：HUM).

**バラシュバリ**〔バングラデシュ北西部の町〕Palashbari.

**バラシンガじか**【−鹿】〔動〕a swamp deer; a barasingha《pl. ~》; Cervus duvauceli.

**バラス**(ト) ▫ バラスト軌道〔鉄道〕〔道床の一種〕a ballast track. ▫ バラスト水〔船舶〕ballast water.

**パラソルモン**〔生理〕〔副甲状腺ホルモン〕parathormone; parathyroid hormone（略：PTH).

**バラド**〔イラク中部の都市〕Balad.

**バラとり**【−録り】〔音楽〕〔楽器・ボーカルなどのパートを別々に録音して後で編集する方法〕(a) track-by-track recording.

**バラド・ル(ー)ズ**〔イラク東部の町〕Balad Ruz.

**パラパラ**〔ユーロビートに合わせて曲ごとに決められた手振りをする日本で生まれたディスコダンス〕para para; disco dancing with synchronized arm motions.

**パラフィリア**〔精神医〕〔性倒錯〕paraphilia.

**はらふしぐも**【腹節蜘蛛】〔動〕〔ハラフシグモ科のクモの総称〕a segmented spider. ▫ ハラフシグモ科 Liphistiidae.

**ハラブジャ**〔イラク北部の町〕Halabja.

**ばらまき**【ばら撒き・ばら蒔き】▫ ばらまき公共事業 public works「pork-barrel projects [pork]. ばらまき財政 haphazard [hit-or-miss, hit-and-miss] fiscal policies ばらまき福祉 subsidizing welfare recklessly and indiscriminately; throwing money at social problems.

**パラミクソウイルス**〔菌〕a paramyxovirus.

**パラミツ**【波羅蜜】〔植〕〔インド原産、クワ科の常緑高木〕a jackfruit; Artocarpus heterophyllus.

**ハラム・シャリーフ**〔エルサレム旧市街にあるイスラム教の聖地〕Haram esh-Sharif. ▶ ユダヤ教の聖地でもある．[＝しんでんのおか]

**パラリンピアン**〔パラリンピック(出場)選手〕a Paralympian.

**パラリンピック** ▫ パラリンピック(出場)選手 a Paralympian; a「competitor [participant] in the Paralympics.

**ばらん**【葉蘭】〔寿司桶や弁当箱に仕切り板として入っている葉蘭(ﾊﾗﾝ)や笹の葉、またはそれを模した緑色の合成樹脂の薄板〕a leaf-shaped garnish for sushi, lunch boxes, etc.; a baran.

**バランス** ▫ バランス飲料 a balanced drink.

**バランス**2〔カーテンレールなどを見えなくするおおい；ベッド・テーブルなどのへりに施を掛け吊り下げるひも〕a valance.

**バランスト・スコアカード**〔経〕〔経営管理手法の1つ〕a balanced scorecard（略：BSC).

**バランス・ボール**〔エクササイズ用のゴムボール〕a balance ball; an exercise ball; a fitness ball.

**はり**5【玻璃】▫ 玻璃戸〔ガラス戸〕a glass door.

**バリアフリーしんぽう**【−新法】〔法〕the (New) Barrier-Free Law. ▶ 正式名称は「高齢者・障害者等の移動等の円滑化の促進に関する法律」．2006年施行．

**バリア・ブンタウ**〔ベトナム南部の省〕Ba Ria-Vung Tau.

**ハリー・ウィンストン**〔商標〕〔米国の宝飾品ブランド〕Harry Winston.

**ハリーハウゼン** Harryhausen, Ray (1920- ；米国の映画特殊効果技術者).

**ハリーリー** al-Hariri, Rafik [Rafic] (1944-2005; レバノンの政治家；首相〔1992-98, 2000-05〕).

「**ハリウッド的殺人事件**」〔映画〕Hollywood Homicide.

**バリウム** ▫ バリウム検査〔医〕〔胃や腸の〕a barium X-ray; a GI series.

パリウム 〖カトリック〗〔大司教が身につける帯状の肩衣〕pallium 《pl. ~s, pallia》.
パリエット 〖商標・薬〗〔胃潰瘍治療薬〕Pariet.
バリカン ▫ 手動バリカン manual hair clippers. 電気バリカン electric (hair) clippers; an electric (hair) clipper.
はりぐすり 【貼り薬】a (medicated) plaster; a patch; a poultice.
ハリケーンセンター ⇒こくりつハリケーンセンター.
ハリコンドリン 〖生化〗〔抗がん物質〕halichondrin.
バリさん 【-3】〔携帯電話で電波の受信状況が最も安定していること〕optimal [the best] reception; 〔そのマーク〕three (reception) bars.
ハリス Harris, Ed (1950- ; 米国の映画俳優・監督; 本名 Edward Allen Harris).
バリスタ 〔エスプレッソコーヒーを淹(い)れる人〕a barista.
はりせいけん 【針生検】〖医〗(a) needle biopsy.
パリせいじがくいん 【-政治学院】〔フランスのエリート高等教育機関〕Institut d'Études Politiques de Paris (= Paris Institute of Political Studies); 〔通称〕シアンス・ポ (Sciences Po).
はりせん 【張り扇】a large pleated paper fan designed to produce maximum noise, used by traditional storytellers to provide accompaniment and gesture and also, in various Japanese comedies, as a mock weapon for whacking people on the head.
バリデーションりょうほう 【-療法】〖医〗〔認知症療法の1つ〕validation therapy (略: VT).
はりなしばち 【針なし蜂】〖昆〗〔ミツバチ科の, 針のないハチの総称〕a stingless bee.
はりねずみ 【針鼠】 ▫ ハリネズミ国家〔強力な軍事力をもつ国〕a well-armed country; a porcupine power.
「バリの確率」〔映画〕Peut-Etre.
ハリバートン 〔米国の石油関連サービス会社〕Halliburton.
はりすびき 【針結び器】〔釣り〕a hook tier.
バリュー ▫ バリュー・アップ〔価値の向上〕increasing [enhancing]《corporate》value. バリュー株〔株式〕〔本来の価値よりも大幅に株価が低い株; 割安株〕a value stock. バリュー(株)ファンド a value (stock) fund. バリュー・シェアリング〔価値の共有〕value sharing. バリュー・チェーン〔経営〕〔価値連鎖〕a value chain. バリュー・フォー・マネー〔支出額に見合った価値・効果〕value for money (略: VFM).
ハリリ =ハリーリー.
パリわへいきょうてい 【-和平協定】〔1973年, ベトナム戦争終結のための〕the Paris Peace Agreement.
パル[2] =パール[4].
パルヴァノフ Purvanov, Georgi (1957- ; ブルガリアの政治家; 大統領 〔2002- 〕).
はるうえ 【春植え】spring planting. ▶ ~の球根 a spring planted bulb.
バルーン ▫ バルーン・アート〔風船を使って形を作ったり装飾したりすること〕balloon art. ▷ balloon artist n. バルーン血管形成術〖医〗balloon angioplasty.
「遥かなる大地へ」〔映画〕Far and Away.
はるがや 【春茅・春萱】〖植〗〔イネ科の多年草〕sweet vernal grass; Anthoxanthum odoratum.
ハルキゲニア 〖古生物〗〔カンブリア紀の海生無脊椎動物〕a hallucigenia.
ハルキディキはんとう 【-半島】〔ギリシャ北部の半島〕the 'Halkidiki [Chalkidiki] Peninsula.
ハルク 〔米国の漫画・テレビ・映画の登場人物で, 緑色の体をした巨人〕the Hulk.
バルク ▫ バルク売り〔方式〕bulk selling; selling in bulk; 〔1回の〕a bulk sale. バルク貨物 bulk cargo. バルクセール 〔一括売り〕a bulk sale. バルク分析〔固体の分析方法の1つ〕bulk analysis.
バルケネンデ Balkenende, Jan Peter (1956- ; オランダの政治家; 首相 〔2002- 〕).
バルコニー ▫ バルコニー席〔劇場などの〕(get, reserve) a balcony seat.

バルザニ Barzani, Massoud (1946- ; イラクのクルド自治政府議長 〔2005- 〕).
ハルシオン 〖商標〗〖睡眠薬〗Halcion. ▶ 一般名はトリアゾラム (triazolam).
パルス パルス光 pulsed light. ▷ 超[極]短〜光 ultrashort pulsed light.
ハルストレム Hallström, Lasse (1946- ; スウェーデン生まれの映画監督).
ハルダンゲル・バイオリン〖楽器〗=ハルダンゲル・フィドル.
ハルダンゲル・フィドル〖楽器〗〔ノルウェーの民族楽器〕a Hardanger fiddle.
バルチックかいうんしすう 【-海運指数】=ビー・ディー・アイ.
バルディヤ 〔ネパール西部の, インド国境沿いの地方〕Bardiya.
パルデュー Pardue, Kip (1976- ; 米国の映画俳優).
バルドネッキア 〔イタリア北西部, ピエモンテ州の町〕Bardonecchia.
バルトリ Bartoli, Cecilia (1966- ; イタリアのメゾソプラノ歌手).
バルトルディ Bartholdi, Frédéric Auguste (1834–1904; フランスの彫刻家; 自由の女神像の作者).
パルトロウ Paltrow, Gwyneth (Kate) (1973- ; 米国の映画女優).
ハルナール 〖商標・薬〗〔排尿障害の改善薬〕Harnal. ▶ 塩酸タムスロシンの製品名.
「春の日は過ぎゆく」〔映画〕One Fine Spring Day.
パルバノフ =パルヴァノフ.
バルバリーしゅ 【-種】〖畜〗〔フランス産の鴨の品種〕(a) Barbary (duck).
バルバロイン 〖化〗barbaloin.
ハルポクラテス 〖ギ神話・ロ神話〗〔沈黙の神〕Harpocrates.
パルマ・ワラビー〖動〗a Parma wallaby; Macropus parma.
パルミザーノ・リポート 〔米国の, 競争力評議会から出された報告の通称〕the Palmisano Report. ▶ 2005年, 「米国を革新せよ」(Innovate America) というタイトルでまとめられた政府への提言; IBMの会長兼CEO (当時) Samuel J. Palmisano の名から.
パルミジャーノ・レッジャーノ 〔イタリア産のチーズ〕Parmigiano-Reggiano.
バル・ミツバー 〔ユダヤ少年の成人祭式〕a bar mitzvah.
パルミトオレインさん 【-酸】〖化〗〔脂肪酸の一種〕palmitoleic acid.
はれ 【晴れ】 ▫ 晴れマーク 〔天気予報図の晴天のしるし〕a sunny [fine] weather 「icon [symbol].
パレ Paré, Michael (1959- ; 米国の映画俳優.
パレスチナ ▫ パレスチナ暫定自治政府 the Palestinian National Authority (略: PNA); the Palestinian Authority (略: PA).
パレスチナかいほうじんみんせんせん 【-解放人民戦線】〔パレスチナの過激派組織〕the Popular Front for the Liberation of Palestine (略: PFLP).
パレスチナかいほうじんみんせんせんそうしれいぶは 【-解放人民戦線総司令部派】〔パレスチナの過激派組織〕the Popular Front for the Liberation of Palestine-General Command (略: PFLP-GC).
パレスチナかいほうみんしゅせんせん 【-解放民主戦線】the Democratic Front for the Liberation of Palestine (略: DFLP).
パレスチナ(りっぽう)ひょうぎかい 【-立法】評議会】the Palestinian Legislative Council (略: PLC).
バレット・パーキング〔車にキーを差したままで車庫係に預ける駐車システム〕valet parking.
はれもの 【腫れ物】 ▫ 腫れ物扱い ▷ 彼女は家族の間で〜扱いされている. She is treated gingerly by her family. | People in her family are careful to tiptoe around her.

バレリン〖商標・薬〗〔抗てんかん薬〕Valerin.
ハレルソン Harrelson, Woody (1961- ; 米国の映画俳優; 本名 Woodrow Tracy Harrelson).
バレンタイン Valentine, Bobby (1950- ; 米国の野球選手・監督; 本名 Robert John Valentine).
バレンタイン(ばくだん)どうじテロ【-(爆弾)同時-】〔2005年2月14日、フィリピンで起こった〕the Valentine's Day Bombings (in the Philippines).
パロアルト〔米国カリフォルニア州西部の都市〕Palo Alto.
パロアルトけんきゅうじょ【-研究所】Palo Alto Research Center, Inc (略:PARC).
はろう¹【波浪】□■ 波浪推進船〔波のエネルギーを利用する省エネ船〕a wave-devouring propulsion ship.
「ハロウズの妻」〔映画〕Beat.
パロウベク Paroubek, Jiri (1950- ; チェコの政治家; 首相 [2005-06]).
ハローキティ〖商標〗〔キャラクター〕Hello Kitty.
バローゾ Barroso, José Manuel (1956- ; ポルトガルの政治家; 首相 [2002-04]; 欧州委員会委員長 [2004- ]).
バローチスタ(ー)ン =バロチスタ(ー)ン.
バロー口〔イタリアのピエモンテ州南部の村〕Barolo;〔その地域一帯で生産される赤ワイン〕a Barolo《pl. ~s》.
バロキセチン【薬】=塩酸パロキセチン(⇒えんさん).
バロチスタ(ー)ン 1〔パキスタン南西部の州〕Balochistan. ▷ Baloch(i) adj. ▶ 州都はクエッタ.
2〔イランの州〕=シスターン・バルチスターン.
パロティング〔受け取った情報を理解しないままそれが自分の意見であるかのように他に伝えること〕parroting (back).
ハロハロ〔フィリピンのアイスデザート〕halo-halo.
パロる〔パロディーにする〕parody; mock.
▷ 人気オペラをパロった作品 a「parody [takeoff] of a popular opera.
バロン²〔インドネシア、バリ島で善の象徴とされる神獣〕Barong. □■ バロン・ダンス〔インドネシア、バリ島の伝統舞踊〕a Barong dance.
ハロンわん【-湾】〔ベトナム北部、トンキン湾内の景勝地〕Ha Long Bay. ▶ 世界遺産.
パワーサッカー〔電動車いすサッカー〕power (wheelchair) soccer.
パワー・ストーン〔霊力を持つと信じられている石〕a power stone.
ハワード 1 Howard, Michael (1941- ; 英国の政治家; 保守党党首 [2003-05]).
2 Howard, Ron (1954- ; 米国の映画監督; 本名 Ronald William Howard).
パワード・スーツ【装甲機動服】a powered suit; a robotic exoskeleton.
パワー・トレイン【機】〔動力伝達装置〕a power train.
パワー・ヒッター〔野球〕a power hitter; a big hitter; a slugger.
ハワイアン □■ ハワイアン・キルト〔さまざまな植物の形のアップリケを施したハワイのキルト〕a Hawaiian quilt.
「ハワイアン・アイ」〔ハワイの探偵のTVドラマ〕Hawaiian Eye.
ハワイかいせん【-海戦】〖史〗〔真珠湾攻撃の日本での呼称〕the Battle of Hawaii.
ハワイがん【-雁】〖鳥〗a Hawaiian goose. [⇒ネネ]
「ハワイ5-O」〔ハワイの警察を描くTVドラマ〕Hawaii Five-O. ▶ 5-Oはハワイが米国で50番目の州であることにちなむ.
はん-²【半-】□■ 半ライス〔ラーメン、チャーハン〕a half serving of「rice [ramen, fried rice].
パン¹ □■ パン券〔ホームレスの人々などに配布される〕a bread「coupon [ticket, voucher]. パン・フラワー〔パン種で模造花を作ること〕dough flower making;〔パン種で作った模造花〕a dough flower.
バン・アレン Van Allen, James Alfred (1914-2006; 米国の宇宙科学者; バンアレン帯の発見者).
はんいんよう【半陰陽】□■ 仮性半陰陽 pseudoher-
maphroditism. 真性半陰陽 true hermaphroditism.
はんおし【半押し】〖写真〗(a) half press. 〜する half-press《the shutter button》. □■ シャッターボタンを〜する press the shutter button halfway down.
パンガ =パンガー.
ハンガー¹ □■ 針金ハンガー a wire hanger.
バンガー〔パンカー・ショット〕(hit) a bunker shot.
パンガー 1〔タイ南部の県〕Phang Nga.
2〔タイ南部の都市、パンガー県の県都〕Phang Nga.
バンカー・オイル =バンカー(じゅう)ゆ.
バンカー(じゅう)ゆ【-重(油)】〔船舶用C重油〕bunker (fuel) oil (略:BFO).
パンガーわん【-湾】〔タイ南部の湾〕Phang Nga Bay.
ばんがい【番外】□■ 番外地 an unnumbered「plot [location].
はんかいとう【半解凍】partial defrosting. 〜する partially defrost.
はんかくさい【半可臭い】ridiculous; ludicrous; absurd.
はんかた²【漢型】〖軍〗=はんきゅう⁵.
バンカメ(リカ) =□■ バンク・オブ・アメリカ.
バンカラ【蛮-】□■ 蛮カラ学生 a deliberately「uncouth-looking [loutish-looking] student; a roughly dressed student.
バンカルう【-島】〔インドネシア、バンニャック諸島内の島〕Bangkaru Island;〔インドネシア語名〕Pulau Bangkaru.
はんかん⁴【反間】〔敵同士の仲を裂くこと〕fomenting dissension; divide-and-conquer. □■ 反間苦肉の策 a last-ditch attempt to divide and conquer.
はんかん⁵【繁閑】〔繁忙と閑暇〕relative busyness;〔繁忙期と閑散期〕busy season and slack season; peak season and off season. ▷ この路線は季節的に〜が激しい. This route has a marked peak season and off season. □■ 繁閑差 the difference between「busy and slack periods [peak and off seasons].
ばんかん²【晩柑】〔晩生の柑橘類〕a late-ripening「citrus [pomelo, pummelo].
はんかんひ【販管費】〖会計〗〔販売費および一般管理費〕selling, general and administrative expenses. □■ (売り上げ高)販管費(比)率 the ratio of cost of sales to「net [gross] sales; the ratio of selling, general and administrative expenses to「net [gross] sales.
ばんき²【晩期】□■ 晩期障害〖医〗a delayed side effect.
パンキッシュ〖音楽〗〔パンク的〕〜な punkish; punk-like; punk-style.
パン・ギムン【潘基文】Ban Ki-moon (1944- ; 韓国の政治家; 国連事務総長 [2007- ]).
はんきゅう⁵【漢級】〖軍〗〔中国の原子力潜水艦のクラス〕the Han class. □■ 漢級原子力潜水艦 a Han-class nuclear(-powered) submarine.
はんきゅうほう【犯級法】〖法〗=はんざいけいしょとうしょふきんのしゅうとうにかんするほうりつ.
はんきょうじせい【反強磁性】□■ 反強磁性金属 an antiferromagnetic metal (略:AM, AFM). 反強磁性絶縁体 an antiferromagnetic insulator (略:AI, AFI).
はんきょうそうてきこうい【反競争的行為】〖経〗anti-competitive「practices [actions, activities].
はんぎょじん【半魚人】〖SFなど〕a gill man.
ハンギョレ〔韓国の日刊紙〕The Hankyoreh.
ばんきん²【板金・鈑金】□■ 板金屋〔自動車の凹み・傷などの補修を行う〕a body shop.
バンキング □■ プライベート・バンキング〖金融〗〔私的財産総合管理〕private banking.
ハンギング・バスケット〔植物用の吊り鉢・壁掛け鉢〕a hanging basket.
バンク² □■ バンク角〔航空機の機体/走行中のバイク・自動車〕などが地面となす角度〕a bank angle.
バンク・オブ・アメリカ〔米国最大の預金高と支店数をもつ銀行〕Bank of America.

バンクオブクレジット

バンク・オブ・クレジット・アンド・コマース・インターナショナル〔アラブ系の多国籍銀行〕the Bank of Credit and Commerce International（略：BCCI）.▶1991年に営業停止.

バングサ〔マレーシア，クアラルンプールの高級住宅地〕Bangsar.

ばんぐみ【番組】 ◨番組収録〔テレビ・ラジオ〕《doing [making]》a recording for a「program [broadcast]; a recording session. 番組宣伝[広告] a program「announcement [promotion].

はんクラ【半―】〔自動車など〕=半クラッチ.

パンクラチオン〔古代ギリシャの格闘技〕a [the] pancratium; a [the] pancration.

はんクラッチ【半―】〔自動車など〕〔手動変速機つきの自動車やバイクで，クラッチを中ほどまで踏んだ状態〕riding the clutch. ◨〜を多用するとクラッチが摩耗する. If you ride the clutch too much, it will wear out.

パンクラティオン =パンクラチオン.
パンクラテオン =パンクラチオン.

バングラデシュみんぞくしゅぎとう【―民族主義党】〔バングラデシュの主要政党の１つ〕the Bangladesh Nationalist Party（略：BNP）.

はんグローバリズム【反―】antiglobalism. ▷ antiglobalist adj., n.

はんげき[1]【反撃】 ◨反撃機〔反撃の機会〕an opportunity [a chance] for a counterattack;〔競技の〕a comeback opportunity. ◨彼女は狙いすましたリターンやボレーで３ゲームを先行し，セレスに〜機を与えなかった.〔テニス〕With well-aimed returns and volleys she took a three-game lead, allowing Seles no opportunity to come back. 反撃ムード ◨２点差に追い上げ，一気に〜ムードが高まった. They rallied to within two「points [runs], and then the comeback spirit really kicked in.

はんこう[4]【犯行】 ◨外部犯行 a crime committed by an outsider; an outside job. 計画的犯行 a premeditated crime. 突発的犯行 a crime committed on (an) impulse; a spur-of-the-moment [an impulsive, an impulse] crime. 内部犯行 a crime committed by an insider; an inside job. 犯行グループ the「group of criminals [criminal group]. ◨警察は〜グループに暴力団が関与していると見ている. The police believe that「there are members of an organized criminal group among the perpetrators [the criminal group includes yakuza members]. 犯行時間帯 the period during which「a crime [an offense] occurred. 犯行事実 the facts of a crime. ◨容疑者は〜事実を認めている. The accused admits the facts of the crime. 犯行集団 a criminal group.

ばんごう【番号】 ◨番号灯〔自動車・オートバイなどの後部ナンバープレート用の照明〕a license plate「light [lamp].

バンコク・ポスト〔タイ，バンコクの英字新聞〕Bangkok Post.

はんこっかぶんれつほう【反国家分裂法】【法】〔中国の〕the Anti-Secession Law.

はんこん[2]【瘢痕】traces of「spots [blemishes]《on the skin》.

はんざい【犯罪】 ◨刑事[刑法]犯罪 a criminal offense. 未発覚犯罪 《information on》an「undetected [undiscovered] crime. ◨犯罪傾向〔最近の犯罪の方向性〕《have》criminal tendencies;〔最近の犯罪の方向性〕criminal trends; trends in crime. 犯罪経済学 criminal economics. 犯罪経歴〔歴〕 a criminal record. 犯罪経歴証明書 a criminal record certificate. 犯罪死 (a) wrongful death. 犯罪(者)集団 a criminal gang. 犯罪収益 criminal [crime] proceeds;〔forfeit〕the proceeds of a crime. 犯罪情報 crime information; information about (a) crime. 犯罪情報匿名通報制度〔日本の〕the system for providing (the police with) anonymous information about crime(s).

犯罪精神医学 forensic [criminal] psychiatry. ◨〜精神医学者 a「forensic [criminal] psychiatrist. 犯罪対策閣僚会議 a ministerial conference on anticrime measures. 犯罪手口 a method of committing a crime; a modus operandi《pl. modi operandi》; an MO. 犯罪白書 a white paper on crime;〔法務省の〕the (2004) White Paper on Crime. 犯罪被害者給付制度 a crime victims' compensation「scheme [system]. 犯罪被害財産【法】crime victim property; property obtained from the party injured by a criminal act constituting an offense against property. 犯罪要件【法】the elements of a crime; what constitutes a (particular) crime. 犯罪類型 a crime「type [pattern].

バンザイクリフ〔サイパン島最北端の崖;第二次大戦末期，追い詰められた多くの日本人がバンザイと叫びながら投身自殺をした断崖〕Banzai Cliff.

はんざいひがいしゃ【犯罪被害者】 ◨犯罪被害者遺族 the bereaved family (members) of a crime victim. 犯罪被害者給付金 compensation for crime victims; crime victims' compensation.

はんざいひがいしゃきほんほう【犯罪被害者基本法】【法】=はんざいひがいしゃとうきほんほう.

はんざいひがいしゃしえんきょうかい【犯罪被害者支援協会】〔英国の〕=ひがいしゃしえんきょうかい.

はんざいひがいしゃとうきほんほう【犯罪被害者等基本法】【法】the Basic Law Concerning Victims of Crime.

はんざいひがいしゃとうきゅうふきんしきゅうほう【犯罪被害者等給付金支給法】【法】the Crime Victims' Compensation Law. ▶現在は「犯罪被害者等給付金の支給等に関する法律」と改称.

はんざいひがいしゃとうきゅうふきんのしきゅうとうにかんするほうりつ【犯罪被害者等給付金の支給等に関する法律】【法】the Law Governing Payment of Compensation to Victims of Crime.

ばんさん[2]【晩産】〔女性が子供を産む年齢が高いこと〕(a) late (first) childbirth. ◨晩婚・〜の傾向がますます顕著になってきている. The trend toward later marriage and childbirth is growing stronger. | People are getting married and having children later and later. ◨晩産化 (a) later childbirth; having children later (in life).

はんじ[2]【判示】【法】a (court) ruling (on a point of law); *a holding. 〜する〔裁判所の判示を示す〕rule《that …》; hold《that …》. ◨判示事項 a (court) ruling (on a point of law); *a holding.

「バンジージャンプする」〔映画〕Bungee Jumping of Their Own.

はんたい【繁字体】〔中国語の〕the「original [unsimplified] form of a Chinese character.

はんしゃ【反射】 ◨反射型液晶 liquid crystal on silicon（略：LCoS）. 反射たすき〔夜間，自動車のヘッドライトを反射し着用者を守る〕a reflective band (for protecting pedestrians and cyclists, etc.). 反射防止フィルム (an) anti-reflection film.

はんしゃかいせい【反社会性】antisociality; antisociability; an antisocial nature. ◨反社会性人格障害〔精神〕antisocial personality disorder（略：APD）.

パンジャブ〔インド北西部の州;パキスタン北東部の州〕Punjab. ▶インドの州は別称 Punjabi Suba. また，インドの州都はチャンディガル，パキスタンの州都はラホール.

はんしょく【繁殖】 ◨繁殖(容)器, 繁殖箱 a hatching「container [box].

はんしん[4]【叛臣】a rebellious「retainer [subject].

はんしんこうそくどうろかぶしきがいしゃ【阪神高速道路株式会社】the Hanshin Expressway Company Limited. ▶2005年の阪神高速道路公団の民営化に伴い設立.

はんじんはんじゅう【半人半獣】〜の half-man[-hu-

man], half-beast[-animal]; therianthropic.
はんじんはんば【半人半馬】〜の half-man[-human], half-horse. ◐ケンタウロスは〜の架空の動物である。The centaur is an imaginary beast, half-man, half-horse.
はんしんふずい【半身不随】 ⇨半[下]半身不随 paralysis from the waist「up [down]. 右[左]半身不随 paralysis of the「right [left] side.
はんずい【半随意】◐〜の semi-voluntary. ⇨半随意筋【解】a semi-voluntary muscle.
はんすうわれ【半数割れ】coming to [a decline to] less than half; falling under fifty percent. ◐今回の参院選の投票率は〜になりそうな見込みである。Voter turnout for the Upper House election is expected to「fall to [be] below fifty percent this time.
ハンズオン ⇨ハンズオン(型)投資〔経営関与型[育成型]の投資〕(a) hands-on investment.
ハンスとう【-島】〔ネアズ海峡の〕Hans Island.
ばんせん[2]【番宣】〔番組宣伝〕a program「announcement [promotion].
ハンセンびょうほしょうほう【-病補償法】【法】the Hansen's Disease Compensation Law.
はんそう[3]【搬送】 ⇨搬送時間 transport [transportation] time. 搬送要請〔急病人・負傷者などの〕a call for 〈an ambulance〉; a call for 《a medical helicopter》. 搬送ロボット ⇨ロボット。
ばんそう[1]【伴走】⇨伴走船 an escort「boat [vessel].
ばんそうこう【絆創膏】⇨液体[水]絆創膏 (a) liquid bandage.
はんそく[5]【犯則】⇨犯則調査 (an) investigation under warrant; an investigation into irregularities which can enforce compliance and collect evidence under a court warrant with a view to criminal prosecution.
ハン・ソッキュ【韓石圭】Han Suk-kyu (1964– ; 韓国の映画俳優).
はんそん【半損】〔保険〕half loss.
ハンソン Hanson, Curtis (Lee) (1945– ; 米国の映画監督).
ハンター 1 Hunter, Holly (1958– ; 米国の映画女優). 2 Hunter, Kim (1922–2002; 米国の映画俳優; 本名 Janet Cole).
ハンタウイルス〔菌〕a hantavirus. ⇨ハンタウイルス肺症候群【医】hantavirus pulmonary syndrome (略: HPS).
はんだく【半濁】semiclear《broth》. ⇨半濁スープ a semiclear soup.
「パン・タデウシュ物語」〔映画〕Pan Tadeusz: The Last Foray in Lithuania.
バンダル・ブシェール〔イラン南部, ブシェール州の州都〕Bandar-e Bushehr. ▶ 単にブシェールとも呼ぶ. [⇨ブシェール].
はんダンピング【反-】⇨反ダンピング法【法】an anti-dumping law.
はんダンピングかんぜいぶんぱいほう【反-関税分配法】【米法】the Continued Dumping and Subsidy Offset Act. ▶ 通称 バード法.
パンチング[2] 1〔穿孔すること〕punching. 2〔スポーツ〕〔拳で打つこと〕punching;〔サッカー〕〔ゴールキーパーの〕punching. ⇨パンチング・ボール〔ボクシング〕〔練習用具〕a punch [punching] ball.
パンチング・メタル〔金属加工〕〔連続的に同一径の穴をあける加工をした金属板〕perforated metal; punched metal.
ハンチントン Huntington, Samuel P(hillips) (1927– ; 米国の政治学者).
パンツ ◐クロップド・パンツ, クロップ・パンツ〔くるぶしの少し上あたりまでの長さの女性用パンツ〕cropped [crop] pants. サブリナ・パンツ Sabrina pants.
バンツー〔民族〕the Bantu;〔人〕a Bantu 《pl. 〜, 〜s》;

〔言語〕Bantu languages and dialects. ⇨バンツー系アフリカ人 a Bantu African. バンツー(系)諸語 the Bantu language family; Bantu languages and dialects. バンツー・スタン〔南アフリカ共和国の黒人居住地区; のちにホームランドと呼ばれる〕a Bantustan. [⇨ホームランド] バンツー・ホームランド ＝ホームランド.
ハンツヴィル〔米国アラバマ州の町; NASA の基地がある〕Huntsville.
ばんづけ【番付】⇨高額納税者番付 a list of「high [top] (income) taxpayers. 長寿番付 ⇨ちょうじゅ. ヒット商品番付 a list of (the biggest) hits. ⇨番付上位力士 sumo wrestlers appearing in the upper half of the 《makuuchi》 division on the「rank(ing) chart [banzuke].
バンテアイ・クデイ〔カンボジアの遺跡〕Banteay Kdei.
バンテアイ・スレイ〔カンボジアの遺跡〕Banteay Srei.
バンテアイ・チュマール〔カンボジアの遺跡〕Banteay Chmar.
バンテアイ・ミアンチェイ ＝バンテイ・メンチェイ.
はんてい[2]【藩邸】a han residence. ◐薩摩〜 the residence of the Satsuma domain.
ハンディカム【商標】a Handycam (Camcorder).
バンディクート【動】〔フクロアナグマ〕a bandicoot.
バンテイ・メンチェイ〔カンボジア北西部の州〕Bantey Meanchey.
パンデピス〔フランス菓子〕pain d'epice(s).
パンデミック【医】〔全国[世界]的規模で発生する流行病; 汎流行病〕a pandemic (disease). ⇨パンデミック・ワクチン〔汎流行病のワクチン〕(a) pandemic vaccine. ⇨プレ〜ワクチン〔臨床試験段階のパンデミックワクチン〕(a) pre-pandemic vaccine.
バンデラス Banderas, Antonio (1960– ; スペイン生まれの映画俳優; 本名 José Antonio Domínguez Banderas).
はんテロあいこくほう【反-愛国法】【米法】＝パトリオットほう.
はんでんし【反電子】【物】a positron; an antielectron.
バンデンバーグくうぐんきち【-空軍基地】＝ヴァンデンバーグくうぐんきち.
ハント Hunt, Helen (1963– ; 米国の映画女優; 本名 Helen Elizabeth Hunt).
バンド[1] ⇨バンド活動 band activities. ◐彼は中学時代にハードロックの洗礼を浴び, 高校時代に〜活動を始めた. After getting into hard rock in junior high school, he started playing in bands while in high school.
はんとう[3]【反党】⇨反党活動 antiparty activities. 反党行為 antiparty behavior. 反党分子 an antiparty element.
はんどう[2]【版胴】【印刷】a cylinder (drum).
バントゥー ＝バンツー.
バントゥル ＝バンツゥル.
「パンと植木鉢」〔映画〕A Moment of Innocence;〔別タイトル〕Bread and Flower;〔フランス語タイトル〕Un instant d'innocence.
はんどうたい【半導体】⇨半導体ウエハー (a) semiconductor wafer. 半導体シリコンウエハー (a) semiconductor silicon wafer.
バントゥル〔インドネシア, ジャワ島中南部の県〕Bantul.
ハンドガン【拳銃】a handgun.
ハンドサイクル〔ハンドル駆動型の三輪くるま椅子〕a handcycle.
ハンドボール[1] ⇨ハンドボール投げ〔体力テストの〕handball throwing; throwing a handball.
ハンドル ⇨ハンドルキーパー〔仲間と飲みに行くとき, 帰路の運転役として 1 人だけ酒を飲まない人〕the member of a drinking party who stays sober so that he or she can be the driver on the return journey. ハンドル操作 the「operation [handling] of a steering wheel; steering. ◐吉田さんは〜操作を誤り, 対向車線に飛び出してトラックと衝突した. Yoshida made a steering error, swerved

バンドンせんげん

over into the oncoming lane, and collided with a truck.
バンドンせんげん【-宣言】〔1955年のバンドン会議での〕the Bandung Declaration.
ハンナ 1 Hanna, William (1910-2001; 米国のアニメ製作者).
2 Hannah, Daryl (1960- ; 米国の映画俳優; 本名 Daryl Christine Hannah).
はんなき【半泣き】 〜する be almost「crying [weeping]; be「almost in [on the verge of] tears. ◐〜で half-crying; almost crying; on the verge of tears / 夏休み最後の日に〜で宿題をやった. Almost in tears, I did my homework on the last day of the summer vacation. ◐ 私はその時, 道に迷って〜になっていた. At the time I had lost my way and「felt like bursting into tears [was almost in tears]. ◐ 別れるとき彼女は〜の顔をしていた. When we parted, her face crumpled and she「nearly burst into tears [looked as though she would cry]. ◐ 彼女は〜だった. She was「almost weeping [on the verge of tears]. | She was almost in tears.
はんなま【半生】 semiperishable (food). 〜 半生うどん [そば] semiperishable「udon [soba]. 半生菓子 semiperishable sweets. 半生ケーキ (a) semiperishable cake; (a) cake that will keep for a while.
ハンナラとう【-党】〔韓国の政党〕the Grand National Party (略: GNP); the Hannara「Dang [Party].
はんなり【落ち着いた華やかさ】 ◐〜したおねえさん a serene, elegant girl / 〜と踊る dance in a self-possessed and elegant manner / 〜とした味 a restrained but lively taste.
はんにち[1]【反日】 〜 反日サイト an anti-Japanese Web site. 反日デモ 《stage》an anti-Japanese demonstration.
「ハンニバル」〔T・ハリス作の小説; その映画化〕Hannibal.
「ハンニバル・ライジング」〔T・ハリス作の小説; その映画化〕Hannibal Rising.
はんにん【犯人】 〜 犯人性【法】《sb's》「apparent [presumed, likely] culpability [guilt]. ◐ 被告の〜性にはいくつかの疑問がある. There are some doubts about the defendant's guilt.
はんのう[1]【反応】 〜 反応場【化】a reaction site.
ばんのうさいぼう【万能細胞】【生物】〔神経・筋肉・血管などの体のどんな組織にもなり得る未分化細胞; 幹細胞の異称】a「smart [master, stem] cell.
ばんのうねぎ【万能葱】=こねぎ.
「パンの笛」〔ドビュッシー作曲のフルート曲〕Syrinx; La Flute de Pan (=The Flute of Pan).
はんばい【販売】 〜 販売価格判断 DI the diffusion index for「sales prices [prices paid]. 販売管理費 =はんかんひ. 販売競争 competition [the battle] for sales. ◐〜の激化 escalation [intensification] of「competition [the battle] for sales. 販売拠点 a sales outlet. ◐ 海外に〜拠点 an overseas outlet / 国内および海外に100以上の〜拠点を持つ企業 a「firm [company] that has more than a hundred outlets at home and abroad. 販売攻勢 a sales offensive; an aggressive sales campaign. ◐ 〜攻勢をかける launch a sales offensive; conduct an aggressive sales campaign. 販売時点情報管理 point of sale (略: POS). 販売時点情報管理システム a「point of sale [POS] system. 販売奨励金 a sales incentive (cash award). 販売面積〔新築マンションなどの〕the「sold [deeded] floor area; 〔造成地などの〕the「sold [deeded] land area.
パンパシフィックすいえいせんしゅけん【-水泳選手権】the Pan Pacific Swimming Championships.
パンパスじか【-鹿】【動】a pampas deer; Ozotoceros bezoarticus.
はんぱつ【反発】 〜 小幅[大幅]反発《取引》〔stage〕a「small [big] rally [recovery].

ハンバニサド, ハンバニサアド〔イラク, バグダッド北方の都市〕Khan Bani Saad.
ハンハネン =ヴァンハネン.
バンバラぞく【-族】〔アフリカ, マリの民族〕the Bambara; 〔1人〕a Bambara 《pl. 〜(s)》.
ハン・ハリョン =ハーン・ハリョン.
パンパンガ〔フィリピン, ルソン島の州〕Pampanga.
ハンプ〔車の速度を落とさせるために路面に付ける凸部〕*a speed bump;「a「speed [road] hump.
バンフ 1〔カナダ西部の観光地〕Banff.
2〔スコットランド北東部の旧州; その州都〕Banff; Banffshire.
バンプ[4]【靴の爪革】a vamp.
パンプキン 〜 パンプキン爆弾〔第2次大戦中, 米軍が原爆投下訓練に用いた模擬爆弾の通称〕a pumpkin bomb.
はんぷく【反復】 〜 反復運動 repetitive motion. 反復運動過多損傷【医】a repetitive strain injury (略: RSI). 反復性腹痛【医】recurrent abdominal pain. 反復横跳び〔体力テストの一種〕(repeated) side stepping; a side-step test.
バンフテレビさい【-祭】〔カナダ, バンフで毎年開かれるテレビ番組の国際コンクール〕the Banff World Television Festival.
ハンフリーじどうしやけい【-自動視野計】【眼科】a Humphrey field analyzer (略: HFA).
パンフレット 〜 案内パンフレット an introductory brochure. ◐ 会社案内 a company brochure / 学校案内 a school「prospectus [brochure].
はんべいほけんきかん【汎米保健機関】the Pan American Health Organization (略: PAHO).
バンほう【VAN 法】【地震】〔地電流解析式地震予知法〕the VAN method. ► ギリシャの研究者3名 Varotsos, Alexopoulos, Nomikos の頭文字から.
はんほげいこく【反捕鯨国】an anti-whaling「country [nation].
ハンマー 〜 ハンマー・トウ【医】a hammer toe. ハンマー指【医】=つちゆび.
はんまる【半丸(枝肉)】〔牛・豚などを解体して半分にしたもの〕a side (of beef).
ハン・ミョンスク【韓明淑】Han Myung-sook (1944- ; 韓国初の女性首相 [2006-07]).
バンメトート〔ベトナム南部, ダクラク省の省都〕Ban Me Thuot; Buon Ma Thuot.
はんや[2]【半矢】 1〔狩猟〕〔急所を外したために獲物の死に至らない弾丸〕a nonfatal wound. ◐ 獲物を〜にする injure an animal (without killing it); only injure the game.
2〔弓道〕〔規定の本数のうち半数が的中すること〕a 50-percent hit rate.
ハン・ユニス〔ガザ地区南部の町〕Khan Yunis; Khan Younis.
はんよう[1]【汎用】 〜 汎用化学品 a commodity chemical. 汎用合成樹脂 (a) general-purpose synthetic resin. 汎用部品 general-purpose parts.
はんらく【反落】 〜 小反落 a slight setback; a small reaction.
はんらん[1]【反乱】 〜 反乱警戒宣言 《declare, lift》a state of rebellion.
はんらん[2]【氾濫】 〜 外水氾濫 =河川氾濫. 河川氾濫 river「overflowing [breaching] its levee. 内水氾濫〔堤防で守られている地域内で起こる洪水〕flooding within the confines of a levee.
はんりゅう[1]【反流】 〜 内側(?)反流 an inshore countercurrent. ◐ 黒潮〜反流 the Kuroshio inshore countercurrent.
はんりゅう[2]【韓流】Korean style; Korean 《movies》; Korean-style 《music》. ◐ 韓流映画 a Korean「film [movie]. 韓流ショップ a Korean shop. 韓流スター a Korean movie star. 韓流ブーム a Korean「boom [fad]. ◐ わが国の〜ブームは一向に衰える気配がない. Our coun-

try's fad for all things Korean shows no sign of waning. 韓流料理 Korean(-style) food.
はんりゅうこうびょう【汎流行病】〘医〙〔全国[世界]的規模で発生する流行病〕a pandemic (disease). [＝パンデミック]
はんりょ【伴侶】 ▫ 伴侶動物 a companion animal.
バンルン〔カンボジア北東部, ラタナ・キリ州の州都〕Banlung; Ban Lung.
はんろ【販路】 ▫ 販路開拓 market development; opening (up) new「markets [outlets]《for goods》. ◐ 新製品の～開拓に取り組む work on「the development of markets for new products [new product market development]. 販路拡大 market expansion. ◐ 首都圏[海外市場]への～拡大をねらう aim to expand the market「in the metropolitan area [overseas]. 販路確保 securing [capturing] a market. ◐ この手の商品は～確保が難しい. It's difficult to secure a market for products of this kind.
はんろん¹【反論】 ▫ 反論広告〔意見広告などに対抗する〕a response「advertisement [ad, "advert]. 反論書〘法〙〔弁駁書〕a written「refutation [retort].

# ひ

ピア〘電子工学〙〔多層基盤の貫通孔〕a via. [＝ビア・ホール] ▫ ビア・ホール a via hole. ◐ ブラインド～（ホール）a blind via (hole). / ベリード～（ホール）a buried via (hole).
ピア(一) ▫ ピア・エデュケーション ＝ピア教育. ピア活動〔仲間同士の知識交換など〕(a) peer activity. ピア教育〔仲間教育〕peer education; learning from *one's* peers. ピア・サポート〔同じ立場にある人の相互援助〕peer support. ピア(一)・プレッシャー〔仲間の圧力; 同じ行動・価値観を求める仲間集団から受ける社会的圧力〕peer pressure. ピア・ヘルパー〔仲間の立場で相談にのるカウンセラー〕a peer companion.
ピアース 1 Pearce, Guy (1967– ) 〔英国生まれの映画俳優; 本名 Guy Edward Pearce〕.
2 Pierce, Kimberly (1967– ) 〔米国の映画監督〕.
ピアジェ² 〘商標〙〔スイス製の腕時計〕Piaget.
ピアス ▫ カラー・ピアス〔色つきのピアス〕colored pierced earrings.
ビア・スプリッツァー〔カクテル〕a cocktail made of white wine and beer; a "beer spritzer."
ビアデッド・コリー〘犬〙a bearded collie;《口》a beardie.
ピアニシ(ッ)シモ〘It〙〘音楽〙〔演奏記号の１つ〕pianississimo (*ppp*).
ピアノ ▫ ピアノ教室〔学校内の〕a「room [classroom] for piano lessons;〔個人的にピアノを教える施設〕a (privately run) piano school;〔個人のレッスン〕piano lessons. ◐ ～教室に通う go「to [for] piano lessons《after school》.
ピアフ²【PIAFS】〘通信〙＝ピー・アイ・エー・エフ・エス.
ビアフラせんそう【-戦争】〘史〙〔1967–70 年の〕the Biafran War; the Nigerian Civil War. [＝ナイジェリアないせん]
ひあり【火蟻】〘昆〙〔南米産のアリ〕a red imported fire ant; *Solenopsis geminata*; *Solenopsis invicta*.
ヒアリング ▫ ヒアリング調査 an interview survey.
ピー・アール【PR】 ▫ PR 会社 a「public relations [PR] firm「company, agency」.
ピー・アール・アール・エス【PRRS】〘獣医〙〔豚繁殖・呼吸障害症候群〕PRRS; porcine reproductive and respiratory syndrome.
ピー・アール・エー・シー【BRAC】〘米軍〙〔米国防総省による米国内基地再編閉鎖計画〕BRAC; Base Realignment and Closure.
ピー・アール・オー【BRO】〔放送と人権等権利に関する委員会機構〕the BRO; the Broadcast and Human Rights/Other Related Rights Organization.
ピー・アール・シー【BRC】〔放送と人権等権利に関する委員会〕the BRC; the Broadcast and Human Rights/Other Related Rights Committee.
ピー・アール・ジー・エフ【PRGF】〔貧困削減・成長ファシリティ; IMF の, 貧困国に対する低利子融資制度〕the PRGF; the Poverty Reduction and Growth Facility.
ピー・アイ【PI】〔都市計画などへの市民参加〕PI. ▶ public involvement (パブリック・インボルブメント) の略.
ピー・アイ・エー・エフ・エス【PIAFS】〘通信〙〔携帯高速デジタル通信規格〕PIAFS; (the) PHS Internet Access Forum Standard.
ピー・アイ・エス・ディー・エヌ【B-ISDN】〔テレビなどの動画像を送受信できる広帯域・高速の ISDN〕B-ISDN; broadband ISDN.
ピー・アイ・シー【PIC】〔絵文字による伝達〕PIC; pictogram ideogram communication.
ピー・イー・エー・ピー【PEAP】〘医〙〔高齢認知症患者への専門的環境支援指針〕PEAP; the Professional Environmental Assessment Protocol.
ピー・エイチ・アイ・ピー【PhIP】〘化〙〔発がん物質〕PhIP. ▶ 2-amino-1-methyl-6-phenylimidazo[4,5-b]pyridine の略.
ピー・エイチ・ピー・ビリトン【BHP –】〔豪英系資源大手〕BHP Billiton. ▶ オーストラリアの BHP 社 (Broken Hill Proprietary) とイギリスの Billiton 社が 2001 年合併してできた会社.
ピー・エー【PA】〔A 紫外線に対する防御効果を示す〕(a) PA. ▶ Protection Grade of UVA の略. ▫ PA 表示 [指数] a PA label; PA labelling.
ピー・エー・エー【BAA】＝自転車協会認証 (⇒じてんしゃきょうかい).
ピー・エー・ユー【BAU】〔平常どおり営業〕BAU; business as usual.
ピー・エー・れんけい【PA 連携】〔消防車と救急車を同時に現場に向かわせること〕simultaneous dispatch of a fire engine and ambulance (to the scene of《an accident》). ▶ PA は消防車 (pumper) と 救急車 (ambulance) の頭文字から.
ピー・エス²【BS】〔英国規格協会が定める規格〕BS. ▶ British Standards の略.
ピー・エス【PS】〔追伸〕PS. ▶ postscript の略.
ピー・エス・アイ【BSI】＝えいこくきかくきょうかい.
ピー・エス・アイ【PSI】〔大量破壊兵器拡散阻止構想〕the PSI; the Proliferation Security Initiative.
ピー・エス・イー【BSE】 ▫ 非定型 BSE atypical BSE.
ピー・エス・イー【PSE】〔電気用品安全法の規格に適合するものであることを証するマーク〕PSE. ▶ PSE は Product Safety of Electrical Appliances and Materials の略. ▫ PSE マーク a PSE mark.
ピー・エス・イーほう【PSE 法】〘法〙〔電気用品安全法の通称〕the PSE Law. ▶ PSE は Product Safety of Electrical Appliances and Materials の略.
ピー・エス・エー【PSA】〘医〙〔前立腺特異抗原〕PSA. ▶ prostate specific antigen の略. ▫ PSA 検査 a PSA test. PSA 値 a PSA「value [count].
ピー・エス・エル【BSL】〘生物〙〔病原微生物の危険度〕

ピー・エスじゅし【PS 樹脂】〖化〗=ポリスチレン樹脂 (⇨ポリスチレン).

ピー・エス・ダブリュー【PSW】〔精神科ソーシャルワーカー〕a PSW; a psychiatric social worker.

ピー・エス・デジタルほうそうすいしんきょうかい【BS-放送推進協会】the Association for Promotion of Satellite Broadcasting (略: BPA). ► 2007 年, デジタル放送推進協会 に統合.

ピー・エス・マーク【PS -】〔製品安全基準マークの１つ〕a PS mark; a product safety mark.

ピー・エヌ・エフ・エル【BNFL】〔英国核燃料会社〕BNFL; British Nuclear Fuels.

ピー・エヌてんたい【BN 天体】〔天〕〔オリオン星雲にある大質量星〕the BN object; the Becklin-Neugebauer object (略: BNO). ► 1967 年, 米国のエリック・ベックリン (Eric Becklin) とゲリー・ノイゲバウアー (Gerry Neugebauer) が発見した.

ピー・エフ・アイ【PFI】〖□〗 PFI 方式 a PFI「arrangement [system, method].

ピー・エフ・シー【PFC】1 〔三大栄養素であるたんぱく質・脂肪・炭水化物〕PFC; protein, fat, carbohydrate. 2〖化〗〔パーフルオロカーボン; 代替フロンの一種〕(a) PFC; (a) perfluorocarbon. 〖□〗 PFC バランス〖栄養〗a [the] PFC balance; a 《suitable》 balance of proteins, fats and carbohydrates.

ピー・エム[3]【PM】〔粒子状物質〕PM; particulate matter. 〖□〗 超低 PM〔排出ディーゼル車〕an ultra-low-PM emission (diesel) vehicle. ► 超低 ― 排出ディーゼル車認定制度〔国土交通省の〕an ultra-low-PM emission diesel vehicle certification system. 〖□〗 PM 濃度 PM [particulate matter] concentration; the concentration of「PM [particulate matter]. PM 排出量 the amount of「PM [particulate (matter)] emissions. PM 量 the amount of「PM [particulate matter] 《in gas emissions》.

ピー・エム・アイ【BMI】〔医〕〔体格指数〕BMI. ► a body mass index の略.

ピー・エム・シー【PMC】〔民間軍事会社〕a PMC; a private military company.

ピー・エム・ティー・シー【PMTC】〔歯科〕〔専門家による歯面清掃〕professional mechanical tooth-cleaning.

ピー・エムびょう【PM 病】〔医〕〔ペリツェウス・メルツバッハ病; 進行性家族性の中枢神経疾患〕PMD; Pelizaeus-Merzbacher disease.

ピー・エル・エム【PLM】〔製品ライフサイクル管理〕PLM. ► product lifecycle management の略.

ピー・エル・シー【PLC】〔パレスチナ(立法)評議会〕the PLC; the Palestinian Legislative Council.

ピー・エル・ディー・ディー【PLDD】〔レーザーによる椎間板ヘルニア減圧術〕PLDD; percutaneous laser disc decompression.

ピー・オー・オー【BOO】〔民間が建設した施設を公共に移管せず, 所有し運営する社会資本整備方式〕BOO. ► Build-Own-Operate の略.

ピー・オー・ジーけいやく【POG 契約】〔エレベーターなどの保守の契約方法の１つ; 機器や装置の点検・給油・調整を引き受ける〕a POG contract. ► POG は parts, oil and grease の略. (⇨フルメンテナンスけいやく)

ピー・オー・ダブリュー【POW】〔軍〕〔戦争捕虜〕a POW; a prisoner of war.

ピー・オー・ティー【BOT】〔民間が建設した施設を一定期間運営し, 事業終了後, 公共に移管する社会資本整備方式〕BOT. ► Build-Operate-Transfer の略.

ぴーおん【-音】〔放送〕〔放送禁止語にかぶせる音〕a bleep; a beep.

ピーがたさんかあえん【P 型酸化亜鉛】〖化〗p-type zinc oxide.

ビーかぶ【B 株】a B-share. [= 上海 B 株 (⇨シャンハイ, 深圳 B 株 (⇨しんせん[9])]

ビーガン =ヴィーガン.

ピーカン・ナッツ a pecan nut.

ビーきゅう【B 級】〖□〗 B 級品 a grade-B「product [item]; a product [an item] with「minor [slight] cosmetic「blemishes [defects, irregularities]; a second 《通例複数形で; a scratch-and-dent「product [item].

ひいく【肥育】〖□〗 肥育〔農場〕a fattening farm.

ピーク[1] 〖□〗 ピーク・カット 〔最大需要電力の抑制〕peak cut.

ビークル 〖□〗 ビークル・ダイナミック・コントロール〔自動車〕〔車体の安定性を制御する装置〕vehicle dynamic control (略: VDC); a vehicle dynamic control system.

ビーグル・ツー【-2】〔宇宙〕〔欧州宇宙機関の火星着陸機〕Beagle 2.

ピー・ケー・アイ【PKI】〖電算〗=公開鍵基盤 (⇨こうかいかぎ).

ピー・ケー・ビー【PKB】〔生化〕〔プロテインキナーゼ B; たんぱく質燐酸化酵素〕PKB; protein kinase B. ► Akt とも呼ばれる (⇨エー・ケー・ティー).

ピーごじゅうさん【p53】〔生物〕〖□〗 p53 遺伝子〔がん抑制遺伝子〕a p53 gene. p53 抗体 a p53 antibody.

ピー・シー【PC】〖□〗 PC グリーンラベル〔パソコンの環境ラベル〕a PC green label. PC グリーンラベル制度 the PC green label system. PC リサイクルマーク a PC recycling mark.

ピー・シー・アール【PCR】〔生化〕〔ポリメラーゼ連鎖反応〕PCR. ► polymerase chain reaction の略.

ピー・シー・エー・エーいんりょう【BCAA 飲料】〔健康飲料〕a BCAA「drink [supplement]. ► BCAA は branched-chain amino acid (分岐鎖アミノ酸) の略.

ピー・シー・エル【BCL】〔海外の短波放送聴取者〕a BCL; a「broadcast [broadcasting] listener.

ピー・シー・シー【bcc】〔電算〕〔受信者には同内容のメールが他にも転送されたことが通知されない電子メール〕bcc; BCC; blind carbon copy.

ピー・シー・シー・アイ【BCCI】〔アラブ系の多国籍銀行〕BCCI; the Bank of Credit and Commerce International. ► 1991 年に営業停止.

ビージーズ〔オーストラリアのポップグループ〕the Bee Gees.

ピー・シー・ピー【BCP】〔緊急時事業継続計画〕a BCP; a business continuity plan; business continuity planning.

ピー・シー・リサイクルほう【PC-法】〔法〕the PC Recycling Law. ► PC は personal computer の略.

ピー・ジェー・リーグ【bj -】〔日本プロバスケットボールリーグ〕the BJ League.

ビーズ 〖□〗 ビーズ刺繍 bead embroidery.

ピース[2] 〖□〗 ピースサイクル〔平和を訴えて行う自転車行進〕cycling for peace.

ピースウィンズ・ジャパン〔NGO の１つ〕Peace Winds Japan (略: PWJ).

ビー・スカイ・ビー【BSkyB】〔英国の衛星放送会社〕BSkyB; British Sky Broadcasting Group plc.

「ピーターガン」〔米国の, 探偵ものの TV ドラマ〕Peter Gunn. ► ヘンリー・マンシーニ (Henry Mancini) が作曲のテーマ曲が知られる.

ピーターズバーグ[2] 〔米国アラスカ州南東部, ミトコフ (Mitkof) 島の都市〕Petersburg.

ピーター・チャン Peter Chan (1962- ; 香港の映画監督; 中国語名 陳可辛 Chan Ho-sun).

ピーター・ポール・アンド・マリー〔米国のフォークソング・トリオ〕Peter, Paul & Mary (略: PP&M, PPM).

ピー・ダブリュー・アール・シー【PWRC】〔自動車〕〔プロダクションカー〔市販車〕による世界ラリー選手権〕the PCWRC; the P-WRC; the PWRC; the Production Car World Rally Championship.

ピー・ダブリュー・エイチ【BWH】〔女性のバスト・ウエスト・ヒップの寸法〕a woman's bust, waist and hip measurements. ○富士子の〜は99·55·88センチです。 Fujiko's measurements are 99-55-88 (centimeters).

ピー・ダブリュー・エス【PWS】〖医〗=プラダー・ウィリーしょうこうぐん.

ピー・ティー¹【BT】〔バイオテクノロジー〕BT. ▶ biotechnology の略.

ピー・ティー²【Bt】〖菌〗〔殺虫性毒素たんぱく質生産細菌〕 *Bacillus thuringiensis*. ◨ **Bt** コーン〔Btの遺伝子を組み込んだトウモロコシ〕Bt corn. **Bt 農薬** a Bt-based insecticide.

ピー・ディー【BD】〖商標·電算〗〔青紫色のレーザーを使った次世代の光ディスク〕BD;〔1枚の〕a BD(-disc); a Blu-ray disc. ▶ Blu-ray Disc の略.

ピー・ディー・アイ【BDI】〖海運〗〔バルチック海運指数〕the Baltic Dry Index. ▶ 不定期船運賃指数ともいう. 穀物·石炭などの商品の各船型別の運賃·傭船料などの国際指標となる.

ピー・ティー・アイつうしん【PTI 通信】〔インド最大の通信社〕PTI; the Press Trust of India.

ピー・ディー・エス・エー【PDSA】〔計画·実施·評価·行動; 品質管理の実践手順〕PDSA; plan, do, study, act(ion).〔⇨ピー・ディー・シー・エー〕

ピー・ディー・エヌ・エフ【BDNF】〖生理〗〔脳由来神経栄養因子〕BDNF; (a) brain-derived neurotrophic factor.

ピー・ディー・エフ【BDF】〔バイオディーゼル〕biodiesel (fuel).

ピー・ティー・オー【BTO】**1**〔受注生産方式〕BTO. ▶ Build-[Built-]To-Order Manufacturing の略. **2**〔民間が建設した施設の所有権を、建設後公共に引き渡し、民間が一定期間運営する社会資本整備方式〕BTO. ▶ Build-Transfer-Operate の略.

ピー・ティー・シー・エー【PTCA】〖医〗=経皮的冠動脈形成術〔⇨けい²〕.

ピー・ディー・シー・エー【PDCA】〔計画·実施·点検·行動; 品質管理の実践手順〕PDCA; plan, do, check, act(ion). ◨ **PDCA サイクル** the 「PDCA [plan-do-check-act] cycle.

ピー・ティー・シー・パイプライン【BTC -】〔アゼルバイジャンのカスピ海沿岸からグルジアを経てトルコの地中海沿岸につながる原油の油送管〕the BTC pipeline. ▶ BTC は、アゼルバイジャンのバクー (Baku) 市、グルジアのトビリシ (Tbilisi) 市、トルコのジェイハン (Ceyhan) 市の頭文字から; the Baku-Tbilisi-Ceyhan pipeline.

ピー・ティー・ティー【PTT】**1**〖化〗〔ポリトリメチレン・テレフタレート; 合成繊維原料樹脂〕PTT; polytrimethylene terephthalate. ◨ **PTT 繊維**〖繊維〗PTT fiber. **2**=プッシュ・ツー・トーク.

ヒート〔イラク中西部、アンバル州の町〕Hit.

「ヒート」〔映画〕Heat.

ビー・トゥー・イー【B to E】〖電算〗〔社員向け電子商取引〕B to E; business to employee.

ヒート・ポンプ ◨ **ヒートポンプ給湯器** a heat pump water heater. **ヒート・ポンプ蓄熱**(combined) heat pump/thermal storage.

ヒートポンプ・ちくねつセンター【-蓄熱-】〔財団法人〕the Heat Pump & Thermal Storage Technology Center of Japan (略: HPTCJ).

ピーナッツ ◨ **ピーナッツ・アレルギー**〔have〕(a) peanut allergy.

ビーノ・ノベッロ〔イタリアのワインの新酒〕《It》vino novello.

「ビーバーちゃん」〔米国の、両親と幼い兄弟のTVホームドラマ〕Leave it to Beaver.

ピー・ビー【PB】◨ **PB 商品**〔a「private [store] brand product.

ピー・ピー・エイチほう【PPH 法】〖医〗〔内核痔・脱肛治療法の1つ〕PPH; procedure for prolapse and hemorrhoids.

ピー・ピー・エス【PPS】〔特定規模電気事業者〕a power producer and supplier.

ピー・ピー・エム【BPM】〖音楽〗〔1分間の拍数で、曲の速さの単位〕BPM. ▶ beats per minute の略.

ピー・ピー・エム²【PP&M, PPM】=ピーター・ポール・アンド・マリー.

ピー・ピー・オー【PPO】〔米国の団体健康保険〕a PPO; a preferred-provider organization.

ピーピー・ガン〔玩具銃〕BB Gun. ▶ BB は ball bullet の略.

ピー・ピー・キュー【ppq】〔千兆分率〕ppq; parts per quadrillion.

ピー・ピー・ケー【PPK】=ピンピンコロリ.

ピー・ビー・ジー・シー【PBGC】〔米国の年金給付保証公社〕the PBGC; the Pension Benefit Guaranty Corporation.

ピー・ビー・シー・ワールド【BBC-】〔英国放送協会の子会社〕BBC World.

ピーピーだん【BB弾】〔玩具銃用の弾〕a BB.

ピー・ビー・ティー【PBT】〖化〗PBT. ▶ polybutylene terephthalate の略. ◨ **PBT 樹脂** PBT resin.

ピー・ピー・ティー【ppt】〔一兆分率〕ppt; parts per trillion.

ピー・ピー・バンド【PP -】〔梱包用の帯ひも〕a PP band; a polypropylene band.

ぴーひゃら〔日本の笛の擬音語〕whistling; tooting.

ビーフ ◨ **ビーフカツ**〖料理〗a deep-fried breaded cutlet of beef.

ピー・ファイブ【P5】〔国連安全保障理事会の常任理事国である5か国〕the P5; the five permanent members (of the Security Council).

ビー・ファクトリー【B-】〖物〗〔B中間子を生成する加速器〕the B Factory.

ピー・ブイ・アール【PVR】〔ハードディスク利用の家庭用テレビ録画機〕a PVR; a personal video recorder.

ピー・ブイ・ディー【PVD】〖物·化〗〔物理蒸着(法)〕PVD; physical vapor deposition.

「ピープル」〔米国の雑誌〕People.

ピープルソフト〔米国のソフトウェア会社〕PeopleSoft, Inc.

ピーポー〔救急車のサイレンの音〕the "bee-po" sound of an ambulance siren.

ピーマーク【P-】=プライバシー・マーク〔⇨プライバシー〕.

ピーマイ〔タイ東北部のクメール遺跡〕Phimai.

ピーよんしせつ【P4 施設】〔きわめて危険な病原体や遺伝子組み換え生物を扱う、封じ込め度合いが最も厳しい実験施設〕a P4 facility. ▶ P は physical containment (物理的封じ込め).

ヒーリーズ〖商標〗〔米国製の、かかとにローラーを装着したスニーカー; かかとに重心をかけると滑ることができる〕Heelys.

ビール¹ ◨ **ビールかけ**〔祝勝会の celebratory beer shower. ○〜かけをする shower「each other [sb] with beer. **ビール指数**〔天気予報などの〕a meteorological "beer drinkability" index [scale]; a weather forecast indicating on a scale how good beer will taste in a given location. **ビール風味(アルコール)飲料**〔いわゆる「第三のビール」〕a 「beer-like [beer-flavored] (alcoholic) beverage.

ビールジャンド =ビルジャンド.

ビールス Beals, Jenniffer (1963- ; 米国の映画女優).

ビールマン・スピン〖フィギュアスケート〗〔do〕a Biellmann spin. ▶ スイスのフィギュアスケート選手、ドニーズ・ビールマン (Denise Biellmann; 1962- ) から.

ビーン **1** Bean, Sean (1959- ; 英国生まれの映画俳優). **2** Biehn, Michael (1956- ; 米国の映画俳優; 本名 Michael Connell Biehn).

ビエケスとう【-島】=ヴィエケスとう.

ピエドラス・ネグラス〔メキシコ北東部の都市〕Piedras Negras.

ピエモンキー〖動〗〔中国原産のオナガザル科のサル〕a Yunnan

snub-nosed monkey; *Rhinopithecus bieti*.
**ピエリシン**《化》〔がん細胞増殖を阻害する作用を持つたんぱく質〕pierisin.
**ビエンチャンこうどうけいかく**【-行動計画】＝ヴィエンチャンこうどうけいかく.
**ビエンナーレ** 〘▶ヴェネツィア・ビエンナーレ〙the Venice Biennale.
**ビエンヌ**〔スイス中部の都市ビールのフランス語名〕Bienne.
**ひがい**[2]【被害】〘▶〙経済(的)被害 economic damage; damage to the economy. 建物被害〔地震などによる〕building damage; damage to buildings. 直接[間接]被害 direct [indirect] damage. 農作物被害〔台風・鳥獣などによる〕damage to 「crops [agricultural products]. 報復被害 ⇨ほうふく[2]. 被害回復給付金〔被害回復給付金支給法によって支給される〕compensation to property crime victims based on recovery. 被害感情 a 「feeling [perception] that *one* is being 「treated unfairly [treated wrongly, treated unjustly, mistreated]. 被害算定型影響評価手法〔環境〕the life-cycle impact assessment method based on endpoint modeling (略: LIME). 被害状況 the (amount of) damage; the extent of the damage. ▷ ~状況はまだ判明していない. It is not yet clear 「how much damage there is [how bad the damage is]. 被害想定《earthquake》damage 「estimation [prediction]; prediction of 《earthquake》 damage (and casualties); predicting the damage (*a disaster*》 will cause. 被害地図〔災害範囲を示す〕a damage map; a map of the 「damaged [affected, stricken] area(s); a map of the area(s) 「damaged [affected, stricken] 《by [in] a disaster》. 被害調書〔犯罪・災害などの〕a victim's (written) statement.
**ひがいかいふくきゅうふきんしきゅうほう**【被害回復給付金支給法】〖法〗the Law to Compensate Property Crime Victims based on Recovery. ▶正式名称は「犯罪被害財産等による被害回復給付金の支給に関する法律」(the Law on the Payment of Damages Recovery Based on the Property of Crime Victims, etc.).
**ひがいしゃ**【被害者】〘▶〙犯罪[報道]被害者 a victim of 「(a) crime [reporting by the media]. 〘▶〙被害者意見陳述〖法〗crime victims or their families 「making [being allowed to make] depositions in court proceedings. 被害者学 victimology. ▷ victimologist *n*. 被害者参加制度〖法〗a system which allows participation in trials by crime victims or their families. 被害者支援員〔地方検察庁に配置される〕a victim-support 「worker [specialist]; (a member of) the victim-support staff.
**ひがいしゃしえんきょうかい**【被害者支援協会】〔英国の犯罪被害者のための全国団体〕Victim Support (略: VS).
**ひがいしゃしえんとみんセンター**【被害者支援都民-】the Victim Support Center of Tokyo.
**ひかいようせいしょうかふりょう**【非潰瘍性消化不良】〖医〗nonulcer dyspepsia (略: NUD).
**ひかえ**【控え】
▸控(の)選手 a 「reserve [backup] player; a benchwarmer.
**ひがえり**【日帰り】〘▶〙日帰り温泉 a hot spring (bath) for 「day trippers [guests not staying overnight]. ▷ ~温泉施設 a hot spring bathing facility for day trippers. 日帰り介護 daytime care for 「the elderly [invalids, the handicapped]; day care.
**ひかく**[1]【比較】〘▶〙比較社会学 comparative sociology. 比較文明学 the comparative study of civilizations.
**ひかく**[3]【皮革】〘▶〙皮革職人 a leather 「worker [craftsman].
**ひかく**[5]【非核】〘▶〙非核平和 (a) nuclear-free peace.
▷ ~平和宣言 a nuclear-free peace declaration / ~平和都市 a nuclear-free peace 「municipality [city].
**ひかげすみれ**【日陰菫】〖植〗〔スミレ科の植物〕*Viola yezoensis*.
**「日蔭のふたり」**〔映画〕Jude.
**ひがしアジアきょうどうたい**【東-共同体】〔構想中の〕an East Asian community.
**ひがしアジアじゆうぼうえきく**【東-自由貿易区】＝ひがしアジアじゆうぼうえきちいき.
**ひがしアジアじゆうぼうえきちいき**【東-自由貿易地域】an East Asia Free Trade Area (略: EAFTA); an East Asia 「Free Trade Zone [free(-)trade zone].
**ひがしアジアじゆうぼうえきちたい**【東-自由貿易地帯】＝ひがしアジアじゆうぼうえきちいき.
**ひがしアジアちいきガンカモるいじゅうようせいそくちネットワーク**【東-地域-類重要生息地-】the Anatidae Site Network in the East Asian Flyway.
**ひがしアゼルバイジャン**【東-】〔イラン北西部の州〕East Azarbaijan; (ペルシャ語名の音訳) Azarbayjan-e Sharqi. ▶州都はタブリーズ.
**ひがしアチェ**【東-】〔インドネシア, アチェ州の県〕Aceh Timur.
**ひがしケープ**【東-】〔南アフリカ共和国南部の州〕Eastern Cape; (アフリカーンス語名) Oos-Kaap.
**ひがしティモールさいけんこくみんかいぎ**【東-再建国民会議】〔政党名〕the National Congress for the Reconstruction of East Timor (略: CNRT). ▶CNRT は *Congresso Nacional da Reconstrução de Timor* の略.
**ひがしティモールしえんだん**【東-支援団】＝こくれんひがしティモールしえんだん.
**ひがしティモールとうごうはけんだん**【東-統合派遣団】⇨こくれんひがしティモールとうごうはけんだん.
**ひがしトルキスタン・イスラムうんどう**【東-運動】〔新疆ウイグル自治区の過激派組織〕the East Turkistan Islamic Movement (略: ETIM).
**ひがしトルキスタンかいほうそしき**[かいほうこう]【東-解放組織[解放機構]】〔新疆ウイグル自治区の過激派組織〕the East Turkestan Liberation Organization (略: ETLO).
**ひがしトルキスタンじょうほうセンター**【東-情報-】〔新疆ウイグル自治区の過激派組織〕the East Turkestan Information Center (略: ETIC).
**ひがしにっぽんこうそくどうろかぶしきがいしゃ**【東日本高速道路株式会社】the East Nippon Expressway Company Limited. ▶2005 年, 日本道路公団民営化に伴い設立.
**ひかぜい**【非課税】〘▶〙非課税世帯 a 「tax-exempt [non-tax-paying] household.
**ピカチュウ**〔商標〕〔キャラクター〕Pikachu.
**ひかり**【光】〘▶〙光回線 an optical network. ▷ ~回線サービス an optical-network service. 光コム〘▶〙〖電〗 optical comb. ▷ ~コム発生器 an optical comb generator. 光産業 an [the] optoelectronics industry. 光CT〖電子工学〗optical 「CT [computed tomography]. 光周波数計測〖電〗(an) optical frequency measurement. 光周波数コム〖電〗an optical frequency comb. ▷ ~周波数コム技術 the optical frequency comb technique / ~周波数コム発生器 an optical frequency comb generator (略: OFCG). 光周波数標準〖電〗an optical frequency standard. 光触媒加工 photocatalyst processing. 光触媒物質 (a) photocatalytic material. 光造形装置 stereolithography apparatus (*pl.* ~(es)) (略: SLA). 光トポグラフィー〖医〗optical topography. 光発電 photovoltaic power generation. ▷ ~発電式時計 a photovoltaic wristwatch. 光ビーコン〔媒体とする通信装置〕an infrared beacon. 光ピックアップ〖電〗〔光ディスクドライブでデータを記録・再生するための装置〕an optical pickup. 光プラズマ photoplasma. 光感受性反応〖医〗a photoparoxysmal response (略: PPR). 光

マイク(ロホン) an optical microphone. 光療法 〖医〗phototherapy; light therapy; phototherapeutics; actinotherapy.
ひかり(えいせいかん)つうしんじっけんえいせい【光(衛星間)通信実験衛星】the Optical Inter-Orbit Communications Engineering Test Satellite (略：OICETS).
ひかりしょくばいこうぎょうかい【光触媒工業会】the Photocatalysis Industry Association of Japan (略：PIAJ).
ひかりディスク【光−】 ⟦⟧ 青色光ディスク a Blu-ray Disc. [=ブルーレイ・ディスク].
「光の旅人 **K-PAX**」〔映画〕K-Pax.
「ひかりのまち」〔映画〕Wonderland.
ひかりファイバー【光−】 ⟦⟧ エルビウム添加光ファイバー an erbium-doped optical fiber. ◯ 光ファイバー回線 a fiber-optic circuit; an optical fiber circuit.
ひかりぶつりがく【光物理学】optical physics.
ビカルタミド〖薬〗〖抗男性ホルモン剤・抗腫瘍薬〗bicalutamide.
「光る眼」〔映画〕Village of the Damned.
ひがん²【悲願】 ⟦⟧ 悲願達成 the「achievement [fulfillment] of a long-held dream; achieving *sth* one has long「wished [prayed] for. ◯ その高校は 3 度目の出場で初制覇を狙ったが、〜達成はならなかった。On its third appearance, the high school had prayed for a first victory, but its long-standing dream was not to be fulfilled.
びがん【美顔器】a facial beautifier. ⟦⟧ 超音波美顔器 an ultrasonic facial massager. 低周波美顔器 a low-frequency facial massager.
ひかんしき【非環式】 ⟦⟧ 非環式レチノイド an acyclic retinoid.
ひぎ⁵【非技】〔相撲〕〔一方の自滅によって勝敗が決まること〕a non-technique; deciding 《a sumo match》 by default; winning 《a sumo match》 through the opponent's error.
びあつしんどう【微気圧振動】infrasound. ⟦⟧ 微気圧振動監視 infrasound monitoring.
ひきあてきん【引当金】 ⟦⟧ 引当(金)不足 insufficient reserves.
ひきこもり【引き籠もり】 ⟦⟧ 引きこもり症候群 pathological shyness; (social) introversion.
ひきしめ【引き締め】 ⟦⟧ 量的引き締め〔金融の〕(a) quantitative tightening.
ひきだし【引き出し】 ⟦⟧ 引き出し限度額〔預貯金の〕a maximum withdrawal. ◯ 現行では、ATM での〜限度額は 100 万円だ。Under current rules, the maximum withdrawal permitted at an ATM is ¥1,000,000.
ひきつえんしゃ【非喫煙者】a nonsmoker.
ひきなおす【引き直す】1〔線などを〕redraw; draw 《a line》 over again.
2〔風邪などを〕 ◯ 風邪を〜 catch cold again.
ひきみず【引き水】＝いんすい.
ひきもきらない【引きも切らない】incessant; continuous; continual; unceasing; everlasting; uninterrupted; unbroken. ◯ 〜問い合わせ a constant [an uninterrupted] stream of inquiries. ◯ 電話による注文が毎日〜。We get orders by phone nonstop every day. | Phone orders keep coming in constantly every day.
ひきや【曳家】house relocation. ⟦⟧ 曳家工事 house relocation work.
びきゃく²【美脚】beautiful [sexy, luscious] legs. ⟦⟧ 美脚効果 the effect of making one's legs look beautiful. ◯ 〜効果抜群のジーパン jeans that make the legs look gorgeous. 美脚パンツ sexy pants; pants that show off *sb's* legs (to the full).
ひきゃくばしり【飛脚走り】＝ナンパはしり.
ひきゅう⁵【皮丘】〔皮膚表面の網目状の溝(⁴/₅)に囲まれた部分〕an epidermal [a skin] ridge.
ひきゆび【引き指】〔銃の引き金に掛ける指〕one's trigger finger.
ひきょう⁴【秘境】 ⟦⟧ 秘境駅 an out-of-the-way station; a station off the beaten track.
ひきわたし【引き渡し】 ⟦⟧ 引き渡し訓練〔緊急時に学校で児童を保護者に引き渡すことを想定しての訓練〕a student release drill; a child pickup drill.
びきん【備金】＝じゅんびきん.
ひく¹【引く】 ⟦⟧ 引く辞典〔読む辞典に対して〕a reference dictionary; a dictionary for consultation.
ピクサー〔米国のアニメーション製作会社〕Pixar Animation Studios.
「ビクター/ビクトリア」〔映画〕Victor/Victoria.
ピクトグラム【絵文字】a pictogram; a pictograph.
ピクトブリッジ【電algn】〔デジタルカメラとプリンターを直接接続するための通信規格〕PictBridge.
ビクトリー ⟦⟧ ビクトリー・ロード the victory road; the road to victory. [⇨ブイ¹ (V ロード)].
ビグロー Bigelow, Kathryn (1951−　；米国の映画監督).
ひけっかくせいこうさんきん【非結核性抗酸菌】〖菌〗a nontuberculous mycobacterium (*pl.* -ria) (略：NTM). ⟦⟧ 非結核性抗酸菌症〖医〗nontuberculous mycobacterial「disease [infection]; nontuberculous mycobacteriosis.
ビケフレイベルガ Vike-Freiberga, Vaira (1937−　；ラトヴィアの政治家；大統領 (1999−2007)).
ひげぼそぞうむし【髭細象虫】〖昆〗〔ゾウムシ科のヒゲボソゾウムシ属の甲虫の総称〕*Phyllobiini*.
ひげわし【髭鷲】〖鳥〗〔大型のワシ〕a「lammergeier [lammergeyer]; *Gypaetus barbatus*.
ひけんいんしゃ【被牽引車】〔トレーラー〕a trailer.
ひこう⁶【飛行】 ⟦⟧ 飛行計画情報処理システム〖空〗〔航空機の運航情報を処理する〕a flight data processing system (略：FDPS; FDP system). 飛行差し止め a ban on「(night) flights [planes flying 《during the early morning》]. 飛行情報管理システム〖空〗a flight data management system (略：FDMS). 飛行制限〖impose〗flight restrictions 《over Tokyo's downtown areas》. 飛行制限空域 a restricted flight zone.〖海軍〗飛行予科練習生 a trainee in the Imperial Japanese Navy's pilot training course. 飛行力学 flight dynamics. 飛行ルート a flight route.
ひこう⁹【皮溝】〔皮膚表面の網目状の溝(⁴/₅)〕an epidermal [a skin] depression.
びこう⁹【鼻孔】 ⟦⟧ 鼻腔拡張テープ ＝鼻腔拡張テープ (⇨びこう¹⁰).
びこう¹⁰【鼻腔】 ⟦⟧ 鼻腔拡張テープ a nasal strip.
ひこうき【飛行機】 ⟦⟧ 飛行機発射型「宇宙」〔ロケットの〕air-launched 《rockets》.
ひこうしき【非公式】 ⟦⟧ 非公式サイト an unofficial (Web) site. 非公式ルート〔交渉・命令伝達などの〕unofficial [informal] route. ◯ 〜ルートからの情報 information 《from unofficial sources》 《obtained through unofficial channels》; unofficial [informal, off-the-record] information.
ひこうせい【肥厚性】 ⟦⟧ 肥厚性瘢痕〖医〗a hypertrophic scar.
ひこうどうてき【非行動的】inactive; passive.
ピコリ Piccoli, Michel (1925−　；フランスの映画俳優；本名 Jacques Daniel Michel Piccoli).
ピコルナウイルス〖医〗〔RNA (リボ核酸) を含む小型ウイルス〕a picornavirus.
ひこん【非婚】 ⟦⟧ 非婚カップル a de facto married couple; a committed unmarried couple;〔同居カップル〕a cohabitating couple. 非婚社会 a society with「a low marriage rate [few marriages].
びさ【微差】a razor-thin margin. ◯ 〜で勝つ win by a razor-thin margin.

ビザ　ガーディアン[保護者，付き添い]ビザ〔オーストラリアの〕a student guardian visa. 電子ビザ　an electronic visa; an electronic travel authority (略: ETA). ビザ免除　(a) visa exemption; exemption of visas ((for diplomats)); a visa waiver ▷これらの人々は～免除の対象となりません．Such persons are not entitled to a visa「exemption [waiver]. | These people are not exempt from visa requirements. ビザ免除プログラム〔米国の〕the Visa Waiver Program (略: VWP).

ピサ[2]【PISA】〔OECDによる学習到達度調査〕PISA; the Programme for International Student Assessment.

ピザ　ピザ・カッター　a pizza cutter.

ひさい[2]【被災】　被災家屋　a house or building「affected by [destroyed or damaged in]《an earthquake》; an affected building. 被災国　a disaster-stricken country. 被災者公営住宅　post-disaster public housing; public housing for disaster victims.

びさい【微細】　微細化　miniaturization;〔粒子などの〕micronization. ▷超～化技術　ultraminiaturization technology. 微細機械　a micromachine; a micro machine. 微細藻類〔植〕microalgae.

ひさいしゃせいかつさいけんしえんほう【被災者生活再建支援法】〔法〕the Disaster-Victim Relief Law.

ひさん【費差損】〔生命保険〕〔保険会社の予定事業費と実際にかかった事業費の差によって生じる損〕operating losses.

ひさんえき【費差損益】〔生命保険〕〔保険会社の予定事業費と実際にかかった事業費の差によって生じる損益〕operating profits or losses.

ひざつう【膝痛】knee pain; (a) pain in the knee; an aching knee;〔医〕gonalgia.

ひさべつ【被差別】being discriminated against; suffering discrimination; being a victim of discrimination. 被差別意識　(an) awareness [(a) consciousness] that one is being discriminated against. 被差別感(情)　a [the] feeling [sense] that one is being discriminated against. 被差別者　a victim of discrimination. 被差別住民　a resident who is discriminated against; a group (of citizens) who are the victims of discrimination. 被差別地域　an area [a district] where the residents suffer discrimination.

ひさん[2]【飛散】　飛散開始日〔花粉の〕the start of the pollen season (when there is more than 1 grain of pollen per square centimeter). 飛散量　an amount ((of pollen)) (suspended) in the air.

ひし[2]【皮脂】　皮脂汚れ　sebaceous dirt ((on a shirt collar)). ▷毛穴に詰まった～汚れを取り除く　remove the sebaceous dirt「clogging up [accumulated in] the (sweat) pores.

ビジット・ジャパン・キャンペーン【国土交通省による外国人旅行者の訪日促進企画】the Visit Japan Campaign (略: VJC).

ビジネス　ストック[フロー]・ビジネス〔資産活用型[利益創造型]の事業モデル〕a「stock [flow] business model; a「stock-base(d) [flow-base(d)] business model. ビジネス継続性〔緊急事態・災害時などの〕business continuity; continuity of business (略: COB). ビジネス支援図書館　a business library; a library that supports business. ビジネスパーソン〔実業家〕a businessperson;〔会社員〕a company employee; an office worker. ビジネス・プラン〔事業計画(書)〕a「business [plan] project. ビジネス・マナー　business manners. ビジネス・ユニット〔経営〕〔事業単位〕a business unit (略: BU).

「ビジネスウィーク」〔米国の週刊誌〕BusinessWeek.

ビジネスしえんとしょかんすいしんきょうぎかい【ビジネス支援図書館推進協議会】the Business Library Association.

ヒジャ(ー)ブ→ヘジャブ.

ひしゃかくおち【飛車角落ち】〔将棋〕a game of shōgi in which the better player plays without a *hisha* and a *kaku* as a handicap. ▷あの有能な若手の三浦君と水野君抜きでその企画を実行するなんて～というものだよ．Carrying out the「project [plan] without those capable young men Miura and Mizuno is like starting out with two strikes against us.

ビジュアル　ビジュアル化　visualization. ▷パソコンソフトを用いて統計資料を～化する　visualize statistical data using computer software.

びしゅうせい【微修正】a「slight [very minor, tiny] revision. ～する　revise slightly. ▷県の条例に～を加える　make a「very minor [tiny] revision to a prefectural ordinance; revise a prefectural ordinance slightly.

びじゅつかんれんらくきょうぎかい【美術館連絡協議会】the Japan Association of Art Museums (略: JAAM).

ひじゅん[2]【批准】　批准国　a ratifying country; a ratifier.

ひしょ【秘書】　秘書代行サービス　a (telephone) secretary service.

ビショ〔南アフリカ共和国南部，東ケープ州の州都〕Bisho.

びじょ【美女】　美女軍団〔スポーツ大会などにおける北朝鮮の女性応援団〕(a team of) beautiful cheerleaders.

ひじょう[6]【飛翔】　飛翔体　a flying object. 飛翔弾　a projectile bomb.

ひじょう[1]【非常】　非常権限〔非常事態に際して緊急命令を発し，必要なあらゆる措置をとる権限〕《seek, demand》emergency powers. 非常災害　an emergency disaster. ▷特定～災害　a disaster certified by the authorities as permitting special measures. 非常駐車帯　an emergency parking area. 非常通報装置　emergency notification equipment. 非常停止ボタン　an emergency stop button. ▷列車～停止ボタン〔鉄道〕an emergency train stop button. 非常手配〔緊急手配〕《make》immediate arrangements ((for…));〔犯罪者の指名手配〕《issue》a warrant for immediate arrest; Urgently Wanted. 非常(用)脱出装置　emergency escape equipment. 非常用電源　an emergency power「source [supply].非常呼出ボタン〔エレベーター内などの〕an emergency call button.

びしょう[2]【美粧】　美粧師　a makeup artist.

びしょう[3]【微小】　微小カプセル　a microcapsule; a microsphere. 微小藻類〔医〕=微細藻類 (⇨びさい).

ひじょうきん【非常勤】　非常勤医(師)　a part-time「physician [doctor].

ひしょうさいぼうがん【非小細胞癌】〔医〕non-small cell cancer.

ひしょうさいぼうはいがん【非小細胞肺癌】〔医〕non-small cell lung cancer.

ひじょうじたいしょう【非常事態省】〔ロシアの〕the Emergency Situations Ministry.

ひじょうじょう【非上場】　非上場企業[会社]　a privately「owned [held] company.

ひしりょうけんさじょ【肥飼料検査所】〔独立行政法人〕the Fertilizer and Feed Inspection Service (略: FFIS).

びじん【美人】　着物美人　a kimono beauty; a woman who looks beautiful in a kimono. 化粧美人　a woman who is beautiful with makeup. すっぴん美人＝素肌美人 (⇨すはだ). 性格美人　a woman with a wonderful personality. 浴衣美人　a *yukata* beauty; a woman who looks beautiful in a *yukata*.

びしんこう【鼻唇溝】〔解剖・美容〕nasolabial sulcus.

ひしんじゅん【非浸潤】　非浸潤がん　(a) noninvasive carcinoma. 非浸潤性(の)　noninvasive. ▷～性乳管がん　(a) ductal carcinoma in situ (略: DCIS).

ひず[1]【氷頭】　氷頭膾〔なます〕a dish of thinly-sliced salmon head gristle and daikon marinated and seasoned in vinegar.

ひすいかずら【翡翠蔓】〘植〙〔マメ科のつる性低木〕a jade vine; *Strongylodon macrobotrys*.
ビスキュイ〘菓子〙a biscuit.
ビスク　▭▫▫ビスク・ドール〔白磁の人形〕a bisque doll.
ピスコ　**1**〔ペルー南部の町〕Pisco.
　**2**〔ペルーとチリで生産されるブランデー〕pisco [Pisco] (brandy).
ビスタ[2]【VISTA】〔ポストBRICsと目される、ベトナム・インドネシア・南アフリカ・トルコ・アルゼンチンの5カ国グループを指す言葉〕VISTA. ▶ VISTAはVietnam, Indonesia, South Africa, Turkey, Argentinaの略.
ビスファチン〘生理〙〔内臓脂肪から出るホルモン〕visfatin.
ヒズフォスアハリル＝ヒズブ・タフリール.
ビスフォスフォネート〘薬〙(a) bisphosphonate.
ヒズブ・タフリール〔イスラム原理主義組織；イスラム解放党〕Hizb ut-Tahrir; the Islamic Party of Liberation.
ヘズブル・ムジャヒディン〔インドのイスラム過激派組織〕the Hezb-ul Mujahedeen.
ひずみ【歪み】　歪み集中帯〘地質〙〔地震のエネルギーがたまっている地域〕a high strain rate zone.
ひずみえ【歪み絵】〔変形させた絵；ある位置から見たり、変形鏡に写したりすると正しく見える〕an anamorphosis (*pl.* -phoses).
ひずみシリコン【歪-】〘電子工学〙strained silicon.
びせいぶつ【微生物】　▭▫▫微生物試験〔食品・医薬品・化粧品などの〕microbial [microbiological] testing; (1回の) a microbial [microbiological] test. 微生物たんぱく質〘生化〙a single-cell protein (略: SCP).
ひせっしょく【非接触】～の contactless; noncontact.
　▭▫▫非接触ICチップ a contactless「IC [smart] chip. 非接触(型)ICカード a contactless smart card. 非接触(型)IDタグ a radio frequency「identification [ID] tag; an RF-ID tag.
ひせっとくせい【被説得性】openness to persuasion; persuadability.
ひせんじょう【鼻洗浄】　▭▫▫鼻洗浄器 a nasal irrigator.
ひせんとうちいき【非戦闘地域】a noncombat zone.
ひせんとうぶたい【非戦闘部隊】a noncombat unit; noncombat troops.
ひそう[3]【悲壮】　▭▫▫悲壮美 tragic beauty.
ひそきゅうがたゆうし【非遡及型融資】〘金融〙〔担保になっている資産以外に債権の取り立てが及ばない融資〕a nonrecourse loan.
ビター・ホップ〔苦みのあるビール用ホップ〕bitter hops.
ひたいしょう【非対称】　非対称戦争〔交戦者間の軍事力に差がありすぎる場合、弱い方がテロなどで対抗する戦争〕asymmetric warfare.
ひだかそう【日高草】〘植〙〔キンポウゲ科の草本〕*Callianthemum miyabeanum*.
「陽だまりのグラウンド」〔映画〕Hardball.
ビタミン　ビタミンM vitamin M; folic acid. ビタミンQ vitamin Q; coenzyme Q. ビタミンC誘導体 a vitamin C derivative. ビタミンB群 B vitamins. ビタミンB複合体 B「complex [group]. ビタミン様物質 a vitamin-like substance.
ビタミン・カラー〔果物のような鮮やかな色〕a「vivid [invigorating, bright] color.
ピタヤ〘植〙〔サボテン科の多年生多肉植物〕a pitahaya; a pitaya. [＝ドラゴン・フルーツ]
ひたん[2]【悲嘆】　▭▫▫悲嘆心理学 grief psychology.
びちく【備蓄】　▭▫▫備蓄倉庫 a stockpile warehouse. ◐防災～倉庫 an emergency stockpile warehouse; a disaster supply warehouse.
ピチット〔タイ北部の県；その県都〕Phichit.
ひちゅうかくじぎょう【非中核事業】a noncore business.
びちゅう【媚中】〔媚中派〕people [politicians, circles] sycophantic toward China.
ビチレブ〔フィジー諸島最大の島〕Viti Levu Island.

ひつうち【非通知】　▭▫▫非通知設定 setting one's phone to「withhold [block] one's number from being displayed;「a (calling) number「withhold [withheld] setting.
ヒッカドゥワ〔スリランカ南西部のリゾート地〕Hikkaduwa.
ヒッキングぼうしほう【-防止法】〘法〙the Lock-picking Prevention Law. ▶ 正式名称は「特殊開錠用具の所持の禁止等に関する法律」.
ピック【PIC】＝ピー・アイ・シー.
ヒックス Hicks, Scott (1953－　；オーストラリアの映画監督).
ビッグ・バン　▭▫▫会計ビッグバン〘金融〙the accounting big bang.
ビッグバンうちゅうこくさいけんきゅうセンター【-宇宙国際研究-】〔東京大学の〕the Research Center for the Early Universe (略: RESCEU).
ビッグマックしすう【-指数】〘経〙〔購買力平価の1つ〕the Big Mac index.
びっくり【吃驚】　▭▫▫びっくり水〘料理〙〔差し水〕adding a little water〔to keep a pot from boiling over〕;〔水〕(a small amount of) cold water added〔to a boiling pot〕.
びっくりしょうこうぐん【びっくり症候群】〘医〙hyperexplexia; startle disease.
「ビッグ・リボウスキ」〔映画〕The Big Lebowski.
ピッサヌローク〔タイ北部の県；その県都〕Phitsanulok.
ひつじ【未】　未辛抱〘相場〙〔未年は値動きが少ない、の意〕In the year of the Sheep, the market tends not to move. [⇒たつみてんじょう]
ひっしゅう【必修】　▭▫▫必修化 making *sth*「compulsory [mandatory]. ◐小学校での英語～化が決まった. It was decided to make English at elementary school compulsory.
ひっしょう【必勝】　▭▫▫必勝態勢 a do-or-die posture; being resolved to win (whatever it takes). ◐この試合にはベストメンバーで～態勢で臨むつもりである. We have all our best players on the team and we are absolutely determined to win this match「whatever it takes [if it kills us]. 必勝だるま a victory *daruma* (doll). 必勝鉢巻き a victory headband.
ピッシング〘畜産〙〔牛を解体する際の、中枢神経を破壊する作業〕pithing.
ひっせき【筆跡】　▭▫▫筆跡心理学 handwriting psychology.
ひつだん【筆談】　▭▫▫筆談ボード a writing board (for communicating with people who are deaf or dumb).
「ヒッチコック劇場」〔番組の前後にヒッチコック監督が解説をする、米国のTVサスペンスドラマ〕Alfred Hitchcock Presents. ▶ 続編The Alfred Hitchcock Hourの邦題は、「ヒッチコック・サスペンス」「新ヒッチコック・シリーズ」. さらに監督の死後、Alfred Hitchcock Presentsが作られ、邦題は「新・ヒッチコック劇場」.
ピッチブック〘商〙〔販売資料；提案書〕a pitch book.
ピッチブレンド〘鉱〙〔ウラン・ラジウムの主原鉱；瀝青(せき)ウラン鉱〕pitchblende.
ひっつきむし【ひっつき虫】〘植〙〔動物や人間に付着して散布される種子〕a burr.
ヒット　▭▫▫ヒット・ゾーン〔野球〕the hit zone;〔釣り〕a hit zone; a strike zone.
ビッド〔付け値・入札〕a bid;〔競売〕bidding.
ひっとう[2]【筆頭】　▭▫▫筆頭理事 the [a] lead director.
ひっぱく【逼迫】　▭▫▫逼迫感 general「tightness [pressure, stringency]. ◐労働市場の～感が強まっている. The general tightness in the labor market has strengthened.
ひっぱり【引っ張り】　▭▫▫引っ張り力〘力学〙tension (force); pull (force).
ヒップ・バッグ〔腰部に装着するバッグ〕a hip bag.
ひつまぶし〔ウナギの料理〕a Nagoya dish of strips of

broiled eels on rice.
**ひづめ**【蹄】▫□ 蹄切り〔装削蹄用具〕hoof nippers; a hoof knife.
**ひつよう**【必要】▫□ 必要事項《fill「in [out]》a 「necessary [required] item [point].
**ヒッラ**〔イラク中部の都市〕Hilla; Al Hillah.
**ピディ**〔インドネシア, アチェ州の県〕Pidie.
**ひていけい**【非定型】▫□ 非定型抗酸菌〔菌〕an atypical mycobacterium《*pl.* atypical mycobacteria》. ▶ 現在は 非結核性抗酸菌 と呼ばれる。非定型抗酸菌症〔医〕atypical mycobacteriosis.〔= 非結核性抗酸菌症（⇒ひけっかくせいこうさんきん）〕
**ビデオ**▫□ ビデオ化 conversion [converting] to (a) video. ○〜化する convert《a movie》to (a) video /〜化権 the right to convert《a movie》to video. ビデオ声明 a video statement. ビデオ・チャット (a)  video chat. ビデオ・メッセージ a video message.
**ビデオリンクほうしき**【〜方式】〔犯罪被害者が加害者と法廷で会うことなく別室でモニターを通じて証言ができる方式〕a closed-circuit video link system (allowing victims to testify in a separate room).
**ビデりん**【〜倫】= にほんビデオりんりきょうかい.
**ひでんかくかん**【非電化区間】〔鉄道〕a non-electrified section.
**ひでんかせいひん**【非電化製品】non-electric(al) 「appliances [equipment]; equipment not requiring electricity.
**ひと**[1]【人】▫□ ヒト ES 細胞〔解〕a human embryonic stem cell. ヒト・インフルエンザ〔医〕〔動物のインフルエンザに対して〕human「influenza [flu]. ヒト胚性幹細胞 = ヒト ES 細胞.
**ひどうめいうんどう**【非同盟運動】〔非同盟諸国会議に参加する国を中心とする運動〕the Non-Aligned Movement（略: NAM）.
**ひとがましい**【人がましい】〔一人前の人間らしい〕like a normal person. ○ ああいう詐欺師が〜顔をしているのを見ると本当に腹が立つ。It makes me really angry when I see that「swindler [con man] acting like a normal person. / この村の人々が〜暮らしを送れるようになったのはここ 10 年ぐらいだ。It is only in the last ten years or so that the people of this village have become able to lead normal lives.
**ヒトカラ** ⇒ ひとりカラオケ.
**ひとがわり**【人変わり】becoming [turning into] a different person; (a) personal transformation. 〜する become a different person; undergo a personal transformation. ○ 就職後, 彼は〜したようにまじめになった。After he got a job, he became so serious that he seemed like a completely different person.
**ひとく**【秘匿】▫□ 秘匿電話〔電話機〕a secure (tele)phone;〔通話〕a secure (tele)phone「call [conversation].
**ヒトゲノムかいせきセンター**【〜解析〜】〔東京大学医科学研究所〕the Human Genome Center(, Institute of Medical Science, University of Tokyo)（略: HGC）.
**ひとじちきょうようしょばつほう**【人質強要処罰法】〔法〕the Hostage Extortion Law. ▶ 正式名称は「人質による強要行為等の処罰に関する法律」(the Law for the Punishment of Extortion Involving Hostage-taking).
**ひとたらし**【人誑し】bamboozling《*sb* into *doing*》;〔人〕a bamboozler; a (confidence) trickster.
**ひとづらはりせんぼん**【人面針千本】〔魚〕〔ハリセンボン科の海産硬骨魚〕a black-blotched porcupinefish; *Diodon liturosus*.
**ひとで**[2]【人出】▫□ 人出予想 a forecast of turnout. ○ 警視庁は来年の正月三が日の〜予想を発表した。The Metropolitan Police have brought out a forecast predicting the likely turnout during the first three days of the New Year.

**ひとてま**【一手間】○ レトルトカレーも〜かけるとぐっとおいしくなる。Even curry in a pouch tastes a lot better if you put a little extra effort into preparing it.
**ヒト・パピローマ・ウイルス**〔医〕human papilloma virus（略: HPV）.
**ピトフ** Pitof (1957-  ; フランスの映画監督; 本名 Jean Christoph Comar).
**ヒト・モノ・カネ**〔経営資源〕people, materials and money; human resources, physical assets and capital.
**ビトリア**〔スペイン北部, バスク自治州の州都〕Vitoria.
**ひとりいっしゃせい**【一人一社制】〔高校生の就職活動の慣行〕the "one-company-at-a-time" job application system; the system allowing high-school-students job seekers to apply to only one company at a time.
**ひとりカラオケ**【一人〜】〔一人で楽しむカラオケ〕solo karaoke; karaoke on *one's* own.
**ひとりまけ**【一人負け】〜する be the sole loser; be far behind everyone else; trail the pack. ○ その晩のマージャンは彼の〜に終わった。He was the only one who lost at mah-jongg that night.
**ひとりよこづな**【一人横綱】○ ここ 2 場所は朝青龍が〜で支えてきた。For these past two sumo tournaments Asashōryu has kept things exciting in spite of being the only ranked *yokozuna*.
**ヒドロキシアパタイト**▫□ ヒドロキシアパタイト粒子 a hydroxyapatite particle.
**ヒドロキシル・ラジカル**《化》〔活性酸素の 1 つ〕the [a] hydroxyl radical.
**ビトロネクチン**〔生化〕〔糖たんぱく〕vitronectin.
**ひなざくら**【雛桜】〔植〕〔サクラソウ科の植物〕*Primula nipponica*.
**ひなながし**【雛流し】floating dolls「down a river [out to sea] as part of a Girls' Festival ceremony (on March 3).
**ひなん**[1]【非難・批難】非難語 a rebuking word; a denunciatory word.
**ひなん**[2]【避難】▫□ 島外避難 ⇒ とうがいひなん。▫□ 避難指示 an evacuation「notice [directive]. ○〜指示解除 termination [lifting] of an evacuation「notice [directive]. 避難準備情報〔災害時などの〕information preparatory to an evacuation. 避難生活 living「as an evacuee [the life of an evacuee]. ○ その村の多くの住民がいまだに〜生活を強いられている。Many of the villagers「still have to live in evacuation shelters [are still unable to return to their homes]. 避難マニュアル an evacuation manual. 避難誘導 evacuation guidance. ○ 客室乗務員は緊急時に乗客を〜誘導しなければならない。Cabin staff have to provide passengers with evacuation guidance in an emergency. / 宿泊客に対する適切な〜誘導が行われなかった。The (hotel) guests did not receive appropriate evacuation guidance. /〜誘導灯 an evacuation light. 避難率〔津波警報などに対する住民の〕a proportion of people「evacuated [taking refuge].
**ビニール**▫□ ビニール傘 a「vinyl [plastic] umbrella. ビニール・フィルム (a)「vinyl [plastic] film.
**ピニシ**〔インドネシアの伝統的な帆船〕a pinisi (schooner).
**ビニタイ**〔ビニールで柔らかい針金をくるんだもので, 袋などの結束用〕a twist tie.
**ひにちじょう**【非日常】the extraordinary; the unusual; the out-of-the-ordinary. ○ 芸能界という〜の世界に足を踏み入れる enter the alternate world of the entertainment industry. ○ 旅の楽しみの一つは〜を味わうことができる点だ。One of the pleasures of travel is being able to experience things that are completely different from our everyday lives. ▫□ 非日常的 ○〜的な光景 an unusual [a strange, an unexpected] scene / 戦争という〜的な体験 the extraordinary experience of war.
**ピニャ・コラーダ**〔カクテル〕a piña colada.

びにゅう【美乳】beautiful [lovely] breasts.
ピネローロ〔イタリア北西部、ピエモンテ州の町〕Pinerolo.
「陽のあたる教室」〔映画〕Mr. Holland's Opus.
ピノシュ Binoche, Juliette (1964– ; フランスの女優).
ひのまる【日の丸】 ▯ 日の丸掲揚 raising the「Rising-Sun [Hinomaru]」flag. 日の丸プロジェクト〔日本の国策的事業〕a Japanese national project.
ピパーチ〔沖縄産の香辛料；コショウ科の植物ヒハツモドキの実の粉末〕long pepper.
ひばかり (あきない)【日計り(商い)】〔株式〕day trading. ▷ day trader n. ～をする day-trade.
ひばく²【被曝】 ▯ 低レベル被曝 low-level radiation exposure. 被曝限度 (acceptable, permissible) exposure limits. 被曝量〔医〕〔被曝線量〕an「exposed [exposure] dose; a radioactive dose; a dose of「radiation [radioactivity]」.
ひばく³【被爆】 ▯ 被爆遺構〔広島・長崎の〕structural remains from the (Hiroshima and Nagasaki) atomic bomb blasts. 被爆国 a country that has「endured an atomic bombing [been attacked with atomic bombs]」. ▯ 世界で唯一の国として日本は国際社会の中で核軍縮に強いイニシアチブを発揮していくべきだ. As the only country in the world to have endured atomic bombings, Japan should demonstrate strong initiative within the international community in support of nuclear disarmament. 被爆体験 experience of「the atom bomb [being atom-bombed]」.
ひばくしゃ【被爆者】 ▯ 遠距離被爆者 a person exposed to A-bomb radiation at a distance (of more than 2 kilometers).
びはだ【美肌】 ▯ 美肌作用 skin「enhancement [beautification]」.
ヒハツもどき【-擬】〔植〕〔東南アジア原産のつる性のコショウ科植物；実は沖縄で香辛料とされる〕a Javanese long pepper; Piper retrofractum.
「ビバリーヒルズ高校白書」〔米国の、青春もののTVドラマ〕Beverly Hills, 90210. ▶ 90210は郵便番号. 続編の邦題は「ビバリーヒルズ青春白書」.
ピピとう【-島】〔タイの島〕Phi Phi Island.
びひん²【備品】 ▯ 備品化 ▯ 学習教材の〜化は資源の節約になる. Providing [Supplying] study materials at school will help to save resources.
ひふ¹【皮膚】 ▯ 皮膚生検〔医〕(do, carry out) a skin biopsy. 皮膚線維腫〔医〕(a) dermatofibroma (pl. ～s, -mata). 皮膚線維肉腫〔医〕dermatofibrosarcoma (pl. ～s, -mata).
ビフカツ【料理】=ビーフカツ (⇨ビーフ).
ひふく¹【被服】 ▯ 被服学 couture; clothing (science).
ヒプシサーマル【気象】〔高温期の〕hypsithermal. ▯ ヒプシサーマル期 the Hypsithermal Interval.
ビブス〔スポーツ競技等でチームの区別をつけるためにユニホームなどの上に着るベスト状のもの〕a team vest (worn to indicate which team one is on).
ひふぞくしょいちこく【非附属書Ⅰ国】〔環境〕〔気候変動枠組条約の附属書に記載されていない国；温室効果ガス削減の義務がない国〕a non-Annex I「country [party]」.
ひふたいか【非不胎化】 ▯ 非不胎化介入 (a) nonsterilized intervention. 非不胎化政策 a non-sterilized intervention policy.
ひふねんまくがんしょうこうぐん【皮膚粘膜眼症候群】〔医〕muco-cutaneo-ocular syndrome.
ヒプノセラピー〔催眠療法〕hypnotherapy.
ひぶん²【非文】 ▯ 非文情報〔辞書などの「この言い方は正しくない」という情報〕information [a warning] about incorrect usage.
ひへいわてき【非平和的】 ▯ 非平和的手段 military; non-peaceful 非平和的手段 military measures; non-peaceful means;〔resort to〕force. ▯ 中国は台湾独立を阻止す

るために～手段を行使するかもしれない. China may resort to force [use "non-peaceful means"] to prevent Taiwanese independence.
ひべん【皮弁】〔医〕〔切り取られた皮膚・皮下組織片〕a (「skin [cutaneous]」) flap.
ひべんかつどう【非弁活動】〔無資格者の弁護士活動〕practicing law without a license.
ひべんこうい【非弁行為】=ひべんかつどう.
ビベンディ〔フランスのメディア複合企業〕Vivendi.
ひぼうりょくてききききかいにゅうほう【非暴力的危機介入法】nonviolent crisis-intervention techniques.
ひほけんしゃ【被保険者】 ▯ 任意継続被保険者〔退職後も、加入していた健康保険を継続する人〕a voluntary continuing beneficiary.
ヒマール〔イスラム教徒の女性がかぶる頭巾；顔は出すが、首や肩を覆う〕a khimar.
ピマめん【-綿】〔紡織〕〔綿(わた)の一種〕pima cotton.
「ヒマラヤ杉に降る雪」〔映画〕Snow Falling on Cedars.
ヒマリア〔天〕〔木星の衛星〕Himalia.
ひまん【肥満】 ▯ 肥満遺伝子 the「obesity [obese]」gene. 肥満外来〔病院の〕an obesity outpatient「department [clinic]」; an outpatient department for the treatment of obesity. 肥満危険度 (the level of) obesity risk. 肥満傾向 a tendency to obesity. ▯ ～傾向児 a child [children] tending「to [toward] obesity. 肥満治療 (the treatment of) obesity; obesity treatment.
ひみつ【秘密】 ▯ 秘密交通〔法〕〔弁護士と被疑者・被告人との〕confidential [privileged] communication (between an arrested suspect and a lawyer). 秘密交通権〔法〕〔弁護人と被疑者が立会人なしで接見し、書類等を受け渡しできる権利〕the right to「confidential [privileged]」communication (between lawyers and their clients). 秘密保持契約 a nondisclosure agreement (略：NDA). 秘密裏、秘密裡 ▯ ～裏に準備をする make「secret preparations [preparations in secret]」/ 日本政府はアメリカ側と～裏に交渉を行っていた. The Japanese government was secretly negotiating with the Americans.
「秘密と嘘」〔映画〕Secret and Lies.
ビミニしょとう【-諸島】〔バハマ諸島西端の島群〕the Bimini Islands.
ひめウォンバット【姫-】〔動〕a common wombat; Vombatus ursinus.
ひめきんぎょそう【姫金魚草】〔植〕=リナリア.
ひめしろはらみずなぎどり【姫白腹水薙鳥】〔鳥〕〔ミズナギドリ科の鳥〕a Stejneger's petrel; Pterodroma longirostris.
ヒメタンたんかすいそ【非-炭化水素】〔化〕a non-methane hydrocarbon (略：NMHC).
ひめはなばち【姫花蜂】〔昆〕〔ヒメハナバチ科の各種のハチ〕an andrenid (bee). ▯ ヒメハナバチ科 Andrenidae.
ひめおうぎずいせん【姫檜扇水仙】〔植〕〔アヤメ科の多年草；園芸植物〕a montbretia; Crocosmia × crocosmiiflora.
ひもじ【非文字】 ▯ 非文字情報 non-[extra-]textual information. 非文字資料 nontext「materials [documents]」. 非文字データ〔電算〕nontext data. 非文字文化 an「unwritten [oral]」culture.
ひもつき【紐付き】 ▯ 紐つき契約 a conditional contract; a contract with「conditions [strings]」attached. 紐つき献金 a (political)「contribution [donation]」with strings attached.
びもん²【尾紋】〔動〕〔オマキザルなどの尾の〕"fingerprints" (at the tip of a spider monkey's tail).
ビヤ Biya, Paul (1933– ; カメルーンの政治家；大統領〔1982– 〕).
びゃくごう【白毫】〔仏像の眉間の小突起〕a「precious stone [jewel]」set in the middle of the brow of a

Buddhist statue, representing a curl of white hair.
**ひやとい**【日雇い】 ▷❶ 日雇い労働 day labor.
**ヒヤリたいけん**【−体験】〔日常生活でひやりとした体験〕a terrifying experience.
**ヒヤリ・ハット** ▷❶ ヒヤリ・ハット体験 an experience of a「scary [chilling, potentially dangerous] incident; a near-miss experience; a close call.
**ヒューイット** Hewitt, Jennifer Love (1979– ; 米国の映画女優).
**ヒューストン** Huston, Anjelica (1951– ; 米国の映画女優; 映画監督ジョン・ヒューストンの娘).
**ピューちょうさセンター**【−調査−】〔米国の民間研究調査機関; 大規模な国際的世論調査を行う〕the Pew Research Center (for the People & the Press).
**「ビューティフル・マインド」**〔映画〕A Beautiful Mind.
**ヒュードロドロ**〔幽霊が出現するときの効果音〕▷〜の音 とともに舞台は暗転した。 An eerie wailing sound accompanied by a drumroll was heard as the stage went dark.
**ヒューマン** ▷❶ ヒューマン・ドラマ ＝人間ドラマ (⇨にんげん).
**ヒューマン・ライツ・ウォッチ**〔米国に本部がある国際人権団体〕Human Rights Watch (略: HRW).
**ヒューミント**〔軍〕〔スパイを使った諜報活動; 人的情報〕HUMINT. ▶ human intelligence の略.
**ピューティアさい**【−祭】〔古代ギリシャの競技祭〕the Pythian Games.
**プユマぞく**【−族】〔台湾の先住民族〕the Puyuma;〔1人〕a Puyuma 《pl. 〜》.
**ヒュンダイ**【現代】〔韓国の企業グループ〕Hyundai.
**ひよう**[2]【費用】 ▷❶ 費用弁償 compensation for expenses. 費用負担 defrayal; a cost burden; the burden of an expense. ▷この法律は消費者にリサイクルの〜負担の一部を求めるものである。 This law requires the consumer to「pay [bear, defray] some of the cost of recycling.
**びよう**[2]【微恙】 slight ill health. ▷彼は〜を言い立てて家に引きこもっている。 He's cooping himself up at home claiming to be「a bit unwell [under the weather].
**びょういん**[2]【病院】 ▷❶ 一般病院 a regular hospital. ▷❶ 病院送り putting sb in [sending sb to] (*the) hospital. ▷汚染された川の魚を食べ、30人が〜に送られた。 Thirty people「were taken to *(the) hospital [were hospitalized,《口》 ended up in (*the) hospital] after eating fish from the polluted river. ▷横綱は荒っぽい技で有望な若手を〜に送りした。 The yokozuna's rough handling landed this promising young wrestler in (*the) hospital. 病院機能評価制度 a hospital「accreditation [evaluation] system.
**ひょうか**[2]【評価】 ▷❶ 外部評価 an「external [outside] evaluation. ▷外部−制度 an「external [outside] evaluation system. 数値評価 (a) numerical evaluation. ▷問題の重要性を数値〜して優先順位をつける evaluate the importance of problems numerically and list them in order of precedence. 内部評価 an「internal [inside] evaluation. ▷❶ 評価項目 an「evaluation [assessment] category [item]; a category for assessment. 評価損益【会計】(a) valuation「profit [gain] and [or] loss; profit「and [or] loss from valuation. ▷〜損益 the rate of profit「and [or] loss from valuation. 評価欲求 =しょうにんよっきゅう.
**びょうがい**【病害】 ▷❶ 病害抵抗性〔作物などの〕disease resistance. ▷〜抵抗性遺伝子 a disease resistance gene / 〜抵抗性検定 disease resistance evaluation.
**ひょうがとっきゅう**【氷河特急】〔ツェルマットとサンモリッツを結ぶスイスの鉄道〕the Glacier Express.
**びょうき**【病期】【医】a stage. ▷病〜によって治療法が変わる。 Treatment methods vary depending on the stage of an illness. ▷がんの〜を決める determine the stage of cancer. ▷❶ 病期分類 staging.
**ひょうけつ**[1]【氷結】 ▷❶ 氷結点 the「freezing [freeze] point 《for potatoes》; the temperature at which 《food products》 freeze.
**ひょうけつ**[4]【評決】 ▷❶ 有罪[無罪]評決 a「"guilty" ["not-guilty"] verdict; a verdict of ["guilty" ["not guilty"].
「**評決のとき**」〔映画〕A Time To Kill.
**びょうげん**【病原】 ▷❶ 病原血清型大腸菌【医】enteropathogenic *Escherichia coli* [E. coli] (略: EPEC). 病原性 pathogenicity; a pathogenic「nature [character]; pathogenic characteristics.
**びょうご**【病後】 ▷❶ 〜の子 a convalescent child. ▷〜児保育 convalescent「childcare [child care] / 〜児保育施設 a「facility [home, hospital] for convalescent children; a pediatric convalescent facility.
**ひょうごたいしんこうがくけんきゅうセンター**【兵庫耐震工学研究−】〔防災科学技術研究所の〕the Hyogo Earthquake Engineering Research Center.
**ひょうざい**【表在】 ▷❶ 表在性がん【医】(a) superficial cancer. 表在静脈【解】a superficial vein. 表在性腫瘍【医】a superficial tumor.
**びょうさつ**【秒殺】〔格闘技などで〕a trouncing. ▷〜する trounce sb.
**ひょうじ**[1]【表示】 ▷❶ 表示素子【電算】a display「device [element]. ▷画像〜素子 an image display「device [element]. 表示デバイス【電算】a display device.
**ひょうしき**[2]【標識】 ▷❶ 標識魚〔放流調査の〕a tagged fish.
**ひょうじゅん**[2]【標準】 ▷❶ 標準授業時間 the length of a「standard [regular] class; a standard class time. 標準賞与額 the standard amount of a person's bonus (used as a base for calculating his or her pension annuity) 標準世帯 a [the] standard「family [household]; an [the] average family. ▷夫婦と子供2人の 〜世帯 a standard family「with two parents [of two adults] and two children. 標準地〔地価公示の〕standard land. 標準テレビ〔高品位テレビに対して〕standard-definition「television [TV] (略: SDTV). 標準報酬〔健康保険・年金保険などの基礎となる〕the standard amount of a person's monthly remuneration (used as a base for calculating his or her pension annuity) ▷〜報酬月額 (a) standard monthly remuneration / 平均〜報酬月額 (an) [(the) average standard monthly remuneration / 〜日額 (a) standard daily remuneration. 標準木〔桜の開花宣言をする際などの〕a standard tree (for determining when 《cherry》 trees are in bloom).
**ひょうじょう**[3]【表情】 ▷❶ 表情筋【解】 (facial) expression lines.
**びょうしょう**[1]【病床】 ▷❶ 病床稼働率〔病院の〕a hospital bed occupancy rate.
**ひょうそう**[2]【表層】 ▷❶ 表層海水 surface seawater. 表層角膜症【眼科】superficial keratopathy. ▷点状〜角膜症 superficial punctate keratopathy (略: SPK). 表層魚 (a) surface water fish. 表層静脈【解】a superficial vein.
**ひょうだい**【表題】 ▷❶ 表題曲【音楽】〔アルバムなどのタイトルになっている曲〕a title piece; a title「song [tune].
**びょうたい**[1]【病態】 ▷❶ 病態栄養学 clinical「nutrition [dietetics].
**ひょうてき**【標的】 ▷❶ 標的企業〔買収・合併などの〕a target(ed)「company [corporation, firm]; a company which is the target of (a takeover bid).
**びょうてき**[2]【病的】 ▷❶ 病的賭博【精神医】pathological gambling.
**ひょうでん**[2]【票田】 ▷❶ 大票田 a populous electoral district.
**ひょうてん**(しゅうかん)【氷点(週刊)】〔中国の週刊紙〕

the Freezing Point. ► 2006年1月, 中国当局により停刊.
**ひょうひすいほうしょう**【表皮水疱症】《医》epidermolysis bullosa (略: EB). 栄養障害型表皮水疱症 dystrophic epidermolysis bullosa (略: DEB). 接合部型表皮水疱症 junctional epidermolysis bullosa (略: JEB). 単純型表皮水疱症 epidermolysis bullosa simplex (略: EBS).
**びょうへん**【病変】 ▷ 肝外病変《医》 肝炎の肝外〜 an extrahepatic manifestation of hepatitis. 非触知病変《医》a nonpalpable lesion. (がんの)非触知〜の検査 an examination for nonpalpable lesions. 病変部《医》〜部を除去[切除]する remove [excise] a lesion.
**ひょうほん**【標本】 学術標本 a scientific specimen. 標本木 ＝標準木 (⇨ひょうじゅん²).
**ひょうめん²**【表面】 表面感 (a) surface texture. 絹のような〜感 a silk-like「texture [feeling]. 表面効果《流体力学》〔有翼体が地面・水面近くを滑走するとき抵抗が減少し揚力が増加する現象〕the wing-in-surface effect (略: WISE). 〜効果翼艇 a wing-in-surface-effect ship (略: WISES). 表面税率 a nominal tax rate.
**ひょうめんでんかいディスプレー**【表面電界-】〔電子工学〕〔表面伝導型電子放出素子ディスプレー〕a surface-conduction electron-emitter display (略: SED).
**ひょうめんでんどうがたでんしほうしゅつそしディスプレー**【表面伝導型電子放出素子-】〔電子工学〕a surface-conduction electron-emitter display (略: SED).
**ひょうめんプラズモンきょうめい**【表面-共鳴】《化》surface plasmon resonance (略: SPR).
**ひょうもんだこ**【豹紋蛸】《動》〔フグ毒をもつ小型のタコ〕a blue-ringed octopus; *Hapalochlaena maculosa*.
**びょうり**【病理】 病理医 a pathologist. 病理検査 (a) pathological examination. 〜検査会社 a pathological laboratory company. 病理所見 pathological findings. 病理診断 a pathological diagnosis. 病理スライド a pathology slide. 病理標本 a pathological specimen.
**ビョーク** Björk (1965- ; アイスランド生まれの歌手・映画女優; 本名 Björk Gudmundsdóttir).
**ひよりみ**【日和見】 日和見菌《医》〔条件次第で善玉とも悪玉ともなる菌〕opportunistic bacteria.
**ピョンサン**【平山】〔北朝鮮の都市〕Pyongsan.
**ピョンソン**【平城】〔北朝鮮の都市〕Pyongsong.
**ピョンチャン**【平昌】〔韓国, 江原道 (カンウォンド) の郡〕Pyeongchang.
**ピョンヤンほうそう**【平壌放送】〔北朝鮮の国外向け朝鮮語ラジオ放送〕Radio Pyongyang.
**ビラ¹** ハンドビラ〔商〕〔手渡しのビラ〕a handbill; a hand-distributed「flyer [flier]. ハンド〜を配る hand out「flyers [fliers].
**ヒラー** Hiller, Arthur (1923- ; カナダ生まれの米国の映画監督).
**ピラーティス**〔ヨガに似た身体運動法〕Pilates.
**ひらい**【飛来】 飛来経路〔渡り鳥などの〕a migration route; a route of migration; 〔黄砂・花粉などの〕a dispersion route.
**ひらかれたウリとう**【開かれた-党】the Yeollin Uri Party. ► 韓国の政党,「ウリ党」の正式名称.
**ひらく³**【披く】〔能楽で〕perform (*Tsurigitsune*) for the first time.
**ピラシカバ**〔ブラジル, サンパウロ州の都市〕Piracicaba.
**ひらだい**【平台】 **1**〔平らな台〕a 'flat [level] table [platform]. **2**〔平台印刷機〕a flatbed (press).
**ひらだま**【平玉】〔号砲のピストルに入れる平たい火薬〕a percussion cap; a cap.
**ピラティス** ＝ピラーティス.
**ひらまく**【平幕】 平幕優勝 a「championship [tournament] win (victory) by an ordinary *makuuchi*; a

plain *makuuchi*「championship [tournament] win. 〜優勝する win (a sumo「championship [tournament])as an ordinary *makuuchi*. 平幕力士 an ordinary [a plain] *makuuchi* wrestler.
**ピラミッド** 逆ピラミッド型の inverted-pyramidal; inverted pyramid-shape(d).
**ひらめ**【平目・鮃・比目魚】 ヒラメ型の人間 a person obsessed with what *his* superiors think. ヒラメ社員 a company employee who constantly monitors「what *his* boss is thinking [*his* boss's mood].
**ヒラリーマン**〔平(ヒラ)のサラリーマン〕a rank-and-file「salary-man [salary woman]; a「rank-and-file [lowly] employee.
**ビリンバウ**〔楽器〕〔ブラジルの民族楽器〕a berimbau.
**ひる²**【蛭】 ヒル治療《医》leech therapy.
**ヒル** Hill, Walter (1942- ; 米国の映画監督・脚本家).
**ピル**《薬》 緊急避妊「事後」ピル 《医》a morning-after pill (略: MAP); a [the] day-after pill. 高用量ビル a「high-dose [high-dosage] (oral contraceptive) pill. 中用量ビル a medium-dose (oral contraceptive) pill. 低用量ビル a「low-dose [low-dosage] (oral contraceptive) pill.
**ビル・アンド・メリンダ・ゲイツききん**【-基金】〔米マイクロソフトのビル・ゲイツ会長夫妻が運営する基金〕the Bill and Melinda Gates Foundation.
**びるいかん**【鼻涙管】 鼻涙管閉塞症《医》(a) nasolacrimal duct obstruction; a tear duct blockage.
**ビルえいせいかんりほう**【-衛生管理法】〔法〕the Law for Maintenance of Sanitation in Buildings. ► 正式名称は「建築物における衛生的環境の確保に関する法律」.
**ビル・エネルギー・マネジメント・システム**〔建物の省エネを図る管理システム〕a building energy management system (略: BEMS).
**ビルカバンバ**〔エクアドル, アンデス山中の村; インカ帝国の聖地; 世界屈指の長寿地域として知られる〕Vilcabamba.
**ヒル・サイズ**〔スキー〕〔ジャンプ競技で, そのジャンプ台で安全に着地できる地点までの距離〕a hill size (略: HS). 〜100メートル, K点90メートルのジャンプ台 a K-90 (ski) jump with a hill size of 100 meters.
**ビルジャンド**〔イラン東部, 南ホラサン州の州都〕Birjand.
**ヒルシュスプルングびょう**【-病】《医》Hirschsprung's disease.
**ピルスナー**〔ビールの種類〕Pilsener; Pilsner.
**ビルト**〔ドイツの大衆紙〕Bild-Zeitung.
**ビルト・ツーすいせい**【-2 彗星】〔天〕Comet Wild 2.
**ひるね**【昼寝】 昼寝ビジネス the business of supplying places where people can sleep during the lunch hour.
**ビルベリー**〔植〕〔コケモモの一種〕bilberry.
**ビルマみんしゅのこえ**【-民主の声】〔ミャンマー軍政下における人権と民主主義の擁護を目標に掲げノルウェーに本拠を置くラジオ・衛星テレビ放送〕the Democratic Voice of Burma (略: DVB).
**ビルマれんぽうこくみんひょうぎかい**【-連邦国民評議会】the National Council of the Union of Burma (略: NCUB).
**ビルン**〔インドネシア, アチェ州の県・都市〕Bireuen.
**ひれい¹**【比例】 比例尺度《統計》a ratio scale. 比例選出議員 ＝比例代表選出議員 (⇨ひれいだいひょう). 比例名簿〔政党から選出される比例代表選挙区の候補者名簿〕a「the] list of candidates for proportional representation constituencies.
**ひれいだいひょう**【比例代表】 比例代表選挙〔衆議院・参議院の〕a proportional representation election. 比例代表選出議員 a proportional representation Diet member; a Diet member elected under the proportional representation system.
**ピレス** Pirès, Gérard (1942- ; フランス生まれの映画監督・脚本家).

ひれながごんどう【鰭長巨鯨】〖動〗a long-finned pilot whale; *Globicephala melas*.
ビレンドラ Birendra Bir Bikram Shah Dev (1945–2001; ネパール国王〔1972–2001〕).
ひろう² 【疲労】▣ 疲労破壊〔工〕fatigue failure.
ビロクシー〔米国ミシシッピ州南東部の、メキシコ湾に臨む都市〕Biloxi.
ひろしまげんばくしぼつしゃついとうへいわきねんかん【広島原爆死没者追悼平和祈念館】⇨こくりつひろしまげんばくしぼつしゃついとうへいわきねんかん.
ひろしまげんばくしりょうかん【広島原爆資料館】〔広島平和記念資料館の通称〕the Hiroshima Atomic Bomb Museum.
ひわ² 【秘話】▣ 撮影秘話 a secret [little-known facts] about the filming 《of a movie》. 制作秘話〔映画などの〕a secret [little-known facts] about the production 《of a movie》. ◐『ゴッドファーザー』三部作の制作〜 some little-known facts about the three Godfather films. 戦争秘話 a ⌈private [secret] war story; an unknown war episode. ◐ 太平洋戦争〜 private [secret] stories of the Pacific War; unknown episodes of the Pacific War. 誕生秘話 ◐ ウォークマンの誕生〜を追ったドキュメンタリー番組 a documentary investigating the (unknown) facts behind how the Walkman came into being.
びわ² 【琵琶】▣ 薩摩琵琶 a Satsuma *biwa*; a Satsuma lute; a lute with four strings and four frets. 平家琵琶〔楽器〕a Heike *biwa*; a Heike lute; a lute with four strings and five frets used to play the *Heike Monogatari*;〔平家物語を平家琵琶を弾きながら語るもの〕=へいきょく.
びわこおおなまず【琵琶湖大鯰】〔魚〕*Silurus biwaensis*.
びわひがい【琵琶鰉】〔魚〕〔琵琶湖に生息するコイ科の魚〕*Sarcocheilichthys variegatus* (*microoculus*).
ピン¹ ▣ ピン・フラッグ〔ゴルフ〕a (golf) pin flag.
ひんかくほう【品確法】1【法】〔住宅品質確保促進法〕the Housing Quality Assurance Law.
2 【法】=こうきょうこうじひんかくほう.
ビンガム Bingham, Hiram (1875–1956; 米国の人類学者; 1911年インカの都市遺跡マチュピチュを発見).
びんかん【敏感】▣ 敏感期〔心理〕〔言語習得などについての〕a sensitive period.
ビンギョル〔トルコ東部の県;同県の県都〕Bingöl.
ピンク ▣ ピンク筋〔解〕(a) pink muscle.
ピンクリボンうんどう【−運動】〔乳がん撲滅のための啓発運動〕the Pink Ribbon movement.
ひんこん【貧困】▣ 貧困国 a poor [an impoverished] country [nation];〔重債務貧困国〕a heavily indebted poor country (略: HIPC). 貧困削減・成長ファシリティー〔IMF の、貧困国に対する石融資制度〕the Poverty Reduction and Growth Facility (略: PRGF). 貧困率 a poverty rate 《of 15%》. ◐ 絶対的〜率〔年収が生活できる最低水準を下回る人が全国民に占める割合〕an absolute poverty rate / 相対的〜率〔年収が全国民の年収

の中央値の半分に満たない国民の割合〕a relative poverty rate.
ひんしつ¹ 【品質】▣ 品質管理レビュー〔監査法人が行った監査を他の監査人が点検すること〕(a) quality assurance review. 品質機能展開〔顧客を満足させる品質を設定し、設計の段階から製造工程まで各段階でその意図を展開していく手法〕quality function deployment (略: QFD). 品質表示基準 a quality labeling standard. ◐〜表示基準制度 a quality labeling standard system. 品質保持期間 a shelf life 《of one week》.
ひんしゅ【品種】▣ 品種登録〔農林水産省に対して行う〕(plant) variety registration.
ひんしゅほごジーメン【品種保護 G −】〔種苗管理センター所属の〕a plant variety protection officer.
ヒンズー ▣ ヒンズー至上主義〔インドの〕Hindu supremacism.
ビンズオン〔ベトナム南部の省〕Binh Duong.
ビンソン・マシフ (Mount) Vinson Massif.
ひんたい【品胎】〔三生児〕triplests;〔三生児の妊娠〕=品胎妊娠. ▣ 品胎妊娠〔医〕(a) triplet pregnancy.
びんちょう（まぐろ）【鬢長（鮪）】〔魚〕an albacore; a long-finned ⌈tuna (tunny); *Thunnus alalunga*.
ピンチョス〔料理〕〔スペインの一口大のおつまみ〕pintxos.
ビンディン〔ベトナム中南部の省〕Binh Dinh.
ビントゥアン〔ベトナム南部の省〕Binh Thuan.
「ヒンドゥスタン・タイムズ」〔インドの日刊新聞〕The Hindustan Times.
ヒントン Hinton, William H. (1919–2004; 米国の中国研究家).
ピントン【屏東】〔台湾南部の都市・県〕Pingtung; Ping-dong.
びんなんご【閩南語】〔中国語の方言; 福建省南部、広東省東部、海南島の一部と台湾で使われる〕Minnan.
ひんにゅう【貧乳】small [tiny] breasts; a flat chest.
ひんば【牝馬】▣ 繁殖牝馬 a brood mare.
ピンピンコロリ〔いつも元気でピンピンしていて、死ぬときはコロリと死にたい、という考え〕staying hale and hearty (into old age) and then just popping off painlessly. ◐ 私も祖父のように〜という具合に行きたいものだ。I hope I'll stay in good shape into old age and then when the time comes just ⌈pop off like that [keel over and die], like my grandfather.
ビンフオック〔ベトナム南部の省〕Binh Phuoc.
ビンフック〔ベトナム北東部の省〕Vinh Phuc.
ひんべん【頻便】〔医〕frequent defecation.
ピンポイント ▣ ピンポイント・クロス〔サッカー〕a pinpoint ⌈cross [crossing pass]. ◐ 田中の〜クロスに鈴木が頭で合わせてゴールを決めた。Suzuki headed Tanaka's pinpoint cross into the goal. ピンポイント照射〔腫瘍などに対する放射線の〕pinpoint radiation.
ピンマナ〔ミャンマー中北部、マンダレー管区の都市〕Pyinmana.
ピンロン ⇨ ヴィンロン.

# ふ

「ファーゴ」〔映画〕Fargo.
ファース Firth, Colin (1960– ; 英国の映画俳優).
ファース・スプラットじょうこう【−条項】=スプラット・ファースじょうこう.
ファースト・キス one's first kiss.
ファーストボール〔野球〕=ファストボール.
「ファースト・ワイフ・クラブ」〔映画〕The First Wives Club.

ファーム ▣ ファーム日本一〔野球〕the farm champion of Japan.
ファールス〔イラン南部の州〕Fars. ▶ 州都はシーラーズ.
ファーロング Furlong, Edward (1977– ; 米国の映画俳優).
ファイザー〔米国の大手医薬品・化粧品会社〕Pfizer Inc.
ファイザバード 1 〔アフガニスタン北東部、バダフシャン州の州都〕Faizabad; Feyzabad.

**2**〔インド北部, ウッタルプラデシュ州の町〕Faizabad; Fyzabad.

**「ファイト・クラブ」**〔映画〕Fight Club.

**ファイトケミカル**〘生化〙〔植物性化学物質〕phytochemicals.

**ファイトプラズマ**〘生物〙〔病原性微生物; 植物に感染するマイコプラズマ〕(a) phytoplasma.

**ファイナル** ▫ ファイナル・フォー〔四強〕the final four; 〘米バスケット〙〔全米学生選手権の準決勝・決勝〕the Final Four.

**ファイナンシャル・アドバイザー**〔経〕a financial adviser. ▫ 独立系ファイナンシャル・アドバイザー an independent financial adviser (略: IFA).

**ファイナンシャル・エンジニアリング**〔金融工学〕financial engineering.

**「ファイナンシャル・タイムズ」**＝フィナンシャル・タイムズ.

**ファイナンシャル・プランニング**〔経〕〔財務上の計画・設計〕financial planning.

**ファイナンス** ▫ 行動ファイナンス〘証券〙〔市場参加者の心理的動きを分析した投資理論〕behavioral finance. ▫ ファイナンス理論 finance [financial] theory.

**ファイファー** Pfeiffer, Michelle (1958- ; 米国の映画女優).

**ファイヤード** Fayyad, Salam (1952- ; パレスチナの政治家; 自治政府首相 [2007- ]).

**ファイル** ▫ 一時ファイル〘電算〙a temporary file. ▫ ファイル共有ソフト〘電算〙file-sharing software.

**ファインズ 1** Fiennes, Joseph (Alberic) (1970- ; 英国の俳優; 2の弟).
**2** Fiennes, Ralph (Nathaniel) (1962- ; 英国の俳優; 1の兄).

**「ファインディング・ニモ」**〔アニメ映画〕Finding Nemo.

**ファウンドリ(ー)**〔(半導体製造などの)受託生産会社[工場]〕a foundry; a fabrication plant; a fab.

**ファオはんとう【－半島】**〔イラク南部の半島〕the「(al-)Faw [(al-)Fao] Peninsula.

**ファクター・エックス【－X】**〔環境効率指標〕factor X.

**ファクティバ**〘電算〙〔ニュースやビジネス情報などのオンラインデータベース〕Factiva.

**ブアケ**〔コートジボワール北部の都市〕Bouaké.

**ファサード** ▫ ファサード保存〔歴史的建造物の正面外壁のみの保存〕facade preservation; facadism.

**ファシリテーター**〔進行役・まとめ役など〕a facilitator.

**ファストボール**〘野球〙〔速球〕a fastball; a cutter. ▫ カット・ファストボール a cut fastball. ムービング・ファストボール a moving fastball.

**ファスン**〘和順〙〔韓国, 全羅南道の郡; 世界遺産の支石墓群がある〕Hwasun.

**ファッション** ▫ ファッション感覚 a sense of fashion; (a) fashion sense. ◉ ファッション業界のバイヤーには～感覚と同時に市場についての正確な情報を持ち合わせていることが要求される。A buyer in the fashion world is expected to have not only a sense of fashion but also to combine it with accurate information about the market. ファッション手袋 fashion gloves. ファッション・リーダー a fashion leader.

**ファテプル**〔パキスタン, バロチスタン州の町〕Fatehpur.

**ファニー・メイ**〔米国の連邦住宅抵当金庫の通称〕Fannie Mae.

**ファニング** Fanning, Dakota (1994- ; 米国の映画女優; 本名 Hannah Dakota Fanning).

**ファフィアこうぼ【－酵母】**Phaffia yeast; Phaffia rhodozyma.

**ファブリーびょう【－病】**〘医〙Fabry's disease.

**ファブレス** ▫ ファブレス企業 a fabless company.

**ブアマン** Boorman, John (1933- ; 英国生まれの映画監督).

**ファミリー** ▫ ファミリー・ハウス〔自宅から遠い病院で治療中の難病患者とその家族のための滞在施設〕a family house. ファミリー・フレンドリー企業 a family-friendly company.

**「ファミリータイズ」**〔米国中北部に住む家族の絆を描くTVホームコメディー〕Family Ties. ▶ マイケル・J・フォックス (Michael J. Fox) の出世作.

**ファム・ファタール**〘＜F〙〔男性の運命を翻弄する女〕a femme fatale. 《pl. femmes fatales》

**ファルージャ**〔イラク中部の都市〕Fallujah.

**ファルス²**＝ファールス.

**ファルスつうしん【－通信】**〔イランの通信社〕the Fars News Agency.

**ファルモルビシン**〔商標・薬〕〔抗がん剤〕Farmorubicin. ▶ 一般名 塩酸エピルビシン.

**ファレス²**〔メキシコ北部の都市〕Juárez.

**ファレリー 1** Farrelly, Bobby (1958- ; 米国の映画監督; 2の弟).
**2** Farrelly, Peter (1956- ; 米国の映画監督; 1の兄).

**ファレル** Farrell, Colin (1976- ; アイルランド生まれの映画俳優).

**ファン²** ▫ ファン・モーター〘機〙a fan motor; a motor fan.

**ふあん【不安】** ▫ 分離不安〘心理〙〔子供が主たる養育者から離れることに対して示す不安反応〕separation anxiety. ◉ 分離～障害 separation anxiety disorder. 予期不安〘精神医〙〔(パニック障害などの)発作があるのではないかという不安〕anticipatory anxiety. ▫ 不要素 grounds [(a) cause] for「concern [anxiety]; 《have》qualms; material for concern.

**ファンゴ**〘＜It〙〔温泉泥; 治療・美容用〕fango.

**ファン・ジャンヨプ**〔黄長燁〕Hwang Jang-yop (1923- ; 北朝鮮の政治家; 1997年韓国に亡命).

**ふあんしょうがい【不安障害】**〘精神医〙(an) anxiety disorder. ▫ 過剰不安障害 overanxious [excessive anxiety] disorder. 社会不安障害 (a) social anxiety disorder (略: SAD). 全般性不安障害 (a) generalized anxiety disorder (略: GAD). 分離不安障害 separation anxiety disorder.

**ファンタジー** ▫ ファンタジー小説〔一編〕a fantasy「novel [story]; 〔ジャンル〕fantasy (fiction). ファンタジー・スポーツ〔実在するスポーツ選手で架空のチームを作り勝敗を競うオンラインゲーム〕a fantasy sport.

**ファンダメンタルズ** ▫ ファンダメンタルズ分析 fundamentals analysis.

**ふあんてい【不安定】** ▫ 不安定階級 an「unstable [insecure] class; ＝プレカリアート. 不安定材料 a destabilizing factor; a cause for concern. 不安定就労 unstable [irregular] employment. ～就労者 an irregular worker / 住居喪失～就労者 an irregular worker「who has lost his [with no] permanent residence. 不安定膀胱 (an) unstable bladder.

**ファンティエット**〔ベトナム南部, ビントゥアン省の省都〕Phan Thiet.

**ふあんていのこ, ふあんていなこ【不安定の弧, 不安定な弧】**〔中東から北東アジアにかけて広がる, テロ発生などの危険が大きいとされる地域〕the Arc of Instability.

**ファンテール**〘鳥〙〔南アジア・オーストラレーシア産の小鳥〕a grey fantail; *Rhipidura fuliginosa*.

**ファンド・オブ・ファンズ**〔金融〕〔投資信託の運用機関が複数の投資信託をまとめて売り出すもの〕a fund of funds.

**ファン・バステン** van Basten, Marco (1964- ; オランダのサッカー選手).

**ファン・バン・カイ** Phan Van Khai (1933- ; ベトナムの政治家; 首相 [1997-2002]).

**ぶい²【部位】** ▫ 手術部位〘医〙a surgical site. ◉ 手術～感染 a surgical site infection (略: SSI). ▫ 部位別死亡率〘医〙〔がんの〕mortality rate by site.

**ブイ¹【V】** ▫ Vセール ＝優勝セール (⇒ゆうしょう). Vロード the victory road; the road to victory. ◉ 万年Bクラスだった阪神が, 今年は見事に生まれ変わって～ロード

フィールド

をひた走っている。Hanshin has always been a second-tier team, but this year they've made a splendid turnaround and are heading straight down the road to victory.

**フィールド**[1] 〘略〙フィールド・シート〘野球〙〔グラウンドに張り出した、フェンスがない客席〕the field seats. フィールド調査 a field survey; field research.

**フィールド・エミッション・ディスプレー**〘電子工学〙〔電界放出ディスプレー〕a field emission display（略: FED).

**フィヴォス**〔2004年アテネ・オリンピックのマスコット名〕Phevos.

**「V宇宙からの侵略者」**〔米国の、地球を侵略しに来た宇宙人との闘いを描くTVドラマ〕V. ▶ Vはvisitorの略.

**ブイ・エイチ・エフ**【VHF】〘略〙国際VHF〘通信〙international VHF.

**ブイ・エー**[2]【VA】〘電子工学〙〔垂直方向方式の液晶駆動方式〕VA; vertical alignment. 〘略〙VA方式 a「vertical alignment [VA] mode.

**ブイ・エー・アール**【VAR】〔付加価値再販業者〕VAR; a value-added「retailer [reseller].

**フィエステリア・ピシシーダ**〘生物〙〔渦鞭毛藻類の一種〕Pfiesteria piscicida.

**ブイ・エフ・エー**【VFA】〔米国・フィリピン間の駐留軍協定〕the VFA; the Visiting Forces Agreement.

**ブイ・エフ・エックス**【VFX】〘映〙〔ミニチュア撮影やコンピューター・グラフィックスなどの特殊映像効果〕VFX. ▶ visual effects の略.

**ブイ・エル・ビー・アイ**【VLBI】〘天〙〔超長基線電波干渉法〕VLBI; very long baseline interferometry;〔超長基線電波干渉計〕a VLBI; a very long baseline interferometer.

**ブイ・オー・アイ・ピー**【VoIP】〘通信〙〔データ通信と音声通話を同時送受信できる技術〕VoIP. ▶ voice over Internet protocol の略.

**ブイ・オー・シー**【VOC】〘化〙VOC. ▶ volatile organic compound〔揮発性有機化合物〕の略. 〘略〙VOC対策〔住宅建材などの〕VOC measures. ◐~対策建材 a low-VOC building material.

**「フィオナの海」**〘映〙The Secret of Roan Inish.

**フィオレンティーノ** Fiorentino, Linda (1960-    ；米国の映画女優).

**フィカス・プミラ**〘植〙＝おおイタビ.

**フィギス**＝フィッギス.

**ブイ・シー**【VC】〔ベンチャー・キャピタル〕〘略〙VCファンド a venture capital fund（略: VCF).

**フィスチュラ**〘医〙〔瘻孔〕a fistula（pl.〜s, -lae). 〘略〙産科フィスチュラ〔難産のため膣と、膀胱や直腸との間に穴が開通すること〕(an) obstetric fistula.

**フィツォ** Fico, Róbert (1964-    ；スロヴァキアの政治家；首相 2006-    ).

**フィッギス** Figgis, Mike (1948-    ；英国の映画監督).

**フィッシャー** Fischer, Heinz (1938-    ；オーストリアの政治家；大統領 2004-    ).

**フィッシャーしょうこうぐん**【-症候群】〘医〙(Miller) Fisher syndrome.

**フィッシュバーン** Fishburne, Laurence (1961-    ；米国の映画俳優；本名 Lawrence Fishburne III).

**フィッシュ・ロンダリング**〔獲ったマグロなどの魚種、漁場、捕獲船名等の付け替え〕fish laundering.

**フィッシング**[2] 〘略〙〔金融機関などからの正規のメールやウェブサイトを装ってクレジットカード番号や暗証番号を詐取する行為〕phishing. 〘略〙フィッシング攻撃 a phishing attack. フィッシング詐欺 a phishing scam. フィッシング・メール (a) phishing mail.

**ふいっち**【不一致】〘略〙性的不一致 sexual incompatibility.

**フィット** 〘略〙フィット性〔be〕a《good》fit.

**フィットネス** 〘略〙フィットネス器具 fitness equipment. フィットネス・ボール ＝バランス・ボール. フィットネス・マシン a fitness machine. フィットネス・ルーム a fitness room.

**フィップス**【FIPS】〔米国の連邦情報処理規格〕FIPS; the Federal Information Processing Standard.

**ブイ・ディー・エス**【VDS】〔自動車耐久品質調査〕the VDS; the Vehicle Dependability Study. ▶ 米国のコンサルティング会社 J.D. Power and Associates 社が発表する.

**ブイ・ディー・シー**【VDC】〘自動車〙〔車体の安定性を制御する装置〕VDC; vehicle dynamic control.

**フィナンシャル・アドバイザー** ＝ファイナンシャル・アドバイザー.

**フィナンシャル・エンジニアリング** ＝ファイナンシャル・エンジニアリング.

**「フィナンシャル・タイムズ」**〔英国の経済紙〕The Financial Times.

**ブイ・ピー・エヌ**【VPN】〘電算〙〔仮想閉域網〕a VPN; a virtual private network. 〘略〙VPNサービス《provide》a VPN service.

**「フィフス・エレメント」**〘映〙The Fifth Element.

**「15ミニッツ」**〘映〙15 Minutes.

**フィブラートけいやくざい**【-系薬剤】〘薬〙〔高脂血症などの治療薬〕fibrates.

**フィブリノ(ー)ゲン** 〘略〙フィブリノゲン製剤〘薬〙a fibrinogen product.

**フィラー 1**〔パテ〕putty; filler. **2**〘放送〙〔放送時間が余った時や放送時間帯終了後に穴埋め的に放送される映像〕(a) filler.

**フィラデルフィアれんぎんせいぞうぎょうけいき**〔けいきょう〕しすう〔-連銀製造業景気[景況]指数〕〘経〙the Federal Reserve Bank of Philadelphia Business Outlook Survey; the Philadelphia Fed Index.

**フィリグリー**〔銀線細工〕filigree.

**フィリックス**〔米国のアニメの主人公の利口な黒猫〕Felix (the Cat).

**フィリップ** Phillippe, Ryan (1974-    ；米国の映画俳優；本名 Matthew Ryan Phillippe).

**フィリフェラ・オーレア**〘植〙〔ヒヨクヒバの園芸品種〕(a) filifera aurea; Chamaecyparis pisifera 'Filifera Aurea'.

**フィルター** 〘略〙ハイパス・フィルター〔高域通過濾波器〕a high-pass filter（略: HPF). ローパス・フィルター〔低域通過濾波器〕a low-pass filter（略: LPF).

**フィルタリング** 〘電算〙〔インターネット上の特定のサイトの閲覧を制限すること〕Web filtering; content filtering. 〘略〙フィルタリング機能 a《spam, junk mail》filtering function; a filter. フィルタリング・ソフト filtering software.

**フィルドスひろば**【-広場】〔イラク、バグダッドの〕Firdos Square.

**フィルム** 〘略〙フィルム基板〘電子工学〙a film substrate. フィルム包装 film「wrapping [packaging]. ◐プラスチック~ plastic film「wrapping [packaging] / ~包装 (a) film wrap.

**フィロゾーマ, フィロソーマ**〘動〙〔イセエビ類の幼生〕phyllosoma.

**フィロデンドロン・セローム**〘植〙＝セローム.

**フィンチャー** Fincher, David (1962-    ；米国の映画監督).

**プーアールちゃ**【普洱茶】pu-er(h) tea.

**フーイェン**〔ベトナム中南部の省〕Phu Yen.

**ふうえいてきせいかほう**【風営適正化法】〘法〙the Law Regulating Adult Entertainment Businesses. ▶ 正式名称は「風俗営業等の規制及び業務の適正化等に関する法律」；1984年、旧「風俗営業等取締法」が改正された新法.

**ふうきょう**[3]【風況】〔風の状態〕wind conditions. 〘略〙風況調査 an anemometric survey; a wind condition survey; a survey of wind conditions. 風況マップ a wind condition map; a map of wind conditions.

**フークア** Fuqua, Antoine (1966-    ；米国の映画監督).

**ブーグロー** Bouguereau, Adolphe-William (1825-1905；フランスの画家).

フークワ =フークア.
プーケット〔タイ南部の県；その県都〕Phuket.
フーコック〔ベトナム南部，カンボジアとの国境沖合の島；"富国"島〕Phu Quoc (Island).
ふうさ【封鎖】▫️地域封鎖《impose, lift》an area blockade；〔流行病発生などに際しての〕《impose, lift》an area [a regional] quarantine. ▫️▫️封鎖解除 (the)「removal [lifting] of a blockade.
ふうし[5]【封止】sealing; a seal. 〜する seal off; close off; make [keep] airtight. ▫️▫️気密封止 hermetic sealing; a hermetic [an airtight] seal. 真空封止 vacuum sealing; a vacuum seal. ▫️▫️封止剤 (a) sealant.
プーシー〔ラオス，ルアンプラバンの丘〕Phusi.
プーシェフル =プシェール.
プーシキンひろば【-広場】〔モスクワの〕Pushkin Square.
ふうじこめ【封じ込め】▫️▫️早期封じ込め early containment (of an influenza pandemic).
ふうしゃ【風車】▫️発電用風車 a wind (power) generator; a windmill generator.
ふうしょうち【風衝地】an exposed [a wind-exposed] area; an area exposed to the wind.
ブースター ▫️▫️ブースター効果〖医〗〔免疫増強効果〕a booster effect.
ふうせい[1]【風成】▫️▫️風成循環〖海洋〗(the) wind-driven circulation.
フーゼスターン〔イラン南西部の州〕Khuzestan.
ふうせつ[2]【風説】▫️▫️風説被害 damage caused by rumors.
ふうせん【風船】▫️▫️風船療法〖医〗=経皮的冠動脈形成術 (⇨けい[2]), バルーン血管形成術 (⇨バルーン).
ふうそく【風速】▫️▫️回転開始風速 =起動風速. 起動[始動]風速〖電〗〔発電用風車の回転翼が回りはじめる風速〕(the) minimum wind velocity required to turn the blades of a wind turbine. 定格風速〖電〗〔定格出力を得られる風速〕a rated wind velocity. 発電開始風速〖電〗〔風力発電機の〕a cut-in (wind) velocity.（発電）停止風速〖電〗〔風力発電機の〕a cut-out (wind) velocity. 風速計算 calculation of wind velocity; wind velocity calculation.
ふうぞくえいぎょうてきせいかほう【風俗営業適正化法】〖法〗=ふうえいてきせいほう.
ふうぞくえいぎょうほう【風俗営業法】〖法〗=ふうえいてきせいほう.
ぶー（っ）〔クラクションの音〕beep; honk;〔ブザーの音〕buzz.
ブーツ ▫️▫️ニー・ブーツ (a pair of) knee-high boots.
ふうてきほう【風適法】〖法〗=ふうえいてきせいほう.
ブーテフリカ Bouteflika, Abdelaziz (1937- ；アルジェリアの政治家；大統領〔1999- 〕).
フート[2]〔ベトナム北東部の省〕Phu Tho.
フード[2] ▫️▫️フード・ガイド〔食生活上の指針〕a guide to healthy eating; a dietary guide. フード・ガイド・ピラミッド〔米農務省が作成した食事指導の三角図〕a [The] Food Guide Pyramid. フード・システム〔食料生産から消費までの諸産業の連鎖関係〕a food system. フード・テーマパーク a "restaurant [food]" theme park; an amusement center based around restaurants. フード・ファイター〔早食い・大食いコンテストの選手〕a contestant in an eating competition；*《口》a food fighter. フード・マイレージ〔マイル〕〔食料の輸送距離に輸送量を加味した環境負荷の指標〕food mileage [a food mile].
ブードゥーけいざいがく【-経済学】〔魅力的に見えるがいずれ破綻する経済政策〕voodoo economics. ▶ 減税による経済活性化で財政赤字削減が可能としたレーガノミックスを 1980 年の米国大統領選でブッシュ (George Bush) が評したことば.
フード・ファディズム〔特定の食物や栄養が健康や病気に与える影響を過大に評価したり信じたりすること〕food faddism.
フートン【胡同】〔主に中国北京市の旧城内に点在する細い

横丁〕a hutong.
プーノ〔ペルー南部，チチカカ湖畔の町〕Puno.
フーバーきゅうじょ【-研究所】〔米国第 31 代大統領 H. Hoover が 1919 年にスタンフォード大学内に設立〕the Hoover Institution.
ふうふ【夫婦】▫️▫️同性夫婦 a same-sex couple. ▫️▫️夫婦家族〖社会〗〔夫婦とその子からなる家族〕a conjugal family. 夫婦間感染〔性病などの〕infection from *one's* spouse. 夫婦不和 marital「strife [discord, disharmony]; a「marital [matrimonial] quarrel.
ブーメラン ▫️▫️ブーメラン・キッズ〔いったん独立したのちさまざまな理由でふたたび親元に戻った子供〕a boomerang kid.
ブーラ〔ギリシャ，アテネ近郊の都市〕Voula.
フーリー〔ベトナム北部，ハナム省の省都〕Phu Ly.
ふうりゅう【風流】▫️▫️風流心 ◐ 私には歌を詠むといった〜心はありません. I have no sense of the aesthetic refinement it takes to compose tanka.
ふうりょう【風量】(an) airflow volume. ▫️▫️最大風量 the maximum airflow. 大風量 (a) high airflow.
ふうりょく【風力】▫️▫️風力資源 wind-power resources. 風力タービン a wind turbine; a windmill.
フールースー【葫蘆絲】〖楽器〗〔ひょうたんと竹を組み合わせた中国の管楽器〕a hulusi.
フールー, フウルウ【腐乳】〖食品〗furu. [⇨ふにゅう[2]]
フーローてながざる【-手長猿】〖動〗a hoolock gibbon; *Hylobates hoolock*.
フェアウェー ▫️▫️フェアウェー・キープ fairways hit. ◐ 〜率 percentage of fairways hit.
フェアトレード〔途上国の産品を公正な価格で取引する貿易〕Fairtrade. ▫️▫️フェアトレード商品 a Fairtrade product.
フェイ・ウォン Faye Wong (1969- ；中国の映画女優；中国名姜 王菲 Wang Fei).
フェイキック・アイ・オー・エル【-IOL】〖眼科〗〔有水晶体眼内レンズ〕a phakic「IOL [intraocular lens].
「フェイク」〖映画〗Donnie Brasco.
フェイシャル ▫️▫️フェイシャル・マッサージ〔顔のマッサージ〕《give》a「facial [face] massage；《口》a facial.
「フェイス／オフ」〖映画〗Face/Off.
フェイディピデス Pheidippides (490 BC ごろのギリシャ，アテネの伝令；マラソン競技誕生のきっかけになったとされる人物).
フェース ▫️▫️フェース・シート〔アンケート回答者などの性別・年齢・職業などや個人属性に関する調査表〕a face sheet.
フェース・ツー・フェース〔対面での〕face-to-face. ◐ 〜・ツー・フェースで相談する have a face-to-face consultation《with *sb*》; consult《with *sb*》「face-to-face [in person].
フェース・マッサージ =フェイシャル・マッサージ (⇨フェイシャル).
フェード ▫️▫️フェード現象〖自動車〗〔ブレーキの〕(brake) fade. フェードボール〖ゴルフ〗〔ボールが落下する際ゆるく右に曲がるショット〕a fade (ball) [shot].
フェーベ〖天〗〔土星の衛星〕Phoebe.
フェキソフェナジン〖商標・薬〗〔塩酸フェキソフェナジンの商品名〕Fexofenadine.
フェズ[2]〔モロッコ北部の都市〕Fez.
フェスピックれんめい【-連盟】〔極東・南太平洋身体障害者スポーツ連盟〕the FESPIC Federation. ▶ FESPIC is Far East and South Pacific Games for the Disabled の略；2006 年, アジアパラリンピック委員会に発展的解消.
フェタ・チーズ〔ギリシャ産の白色のチーズ〕feta (cheese).
フェデックス〔米国の宅配便会社〕FedEx. ▶ Federal Express の略.
フェデラー Federer, Roger (1981- ；スイスのテニス選手).
フエテン〔フィリピン独特の数字選択式の違法賭博〕jueteng.
フェニックス[1] Phoenix, Joaquin (1974- ；米国の映画俳優；本名 Joaquin Raphael Phoenix; 2[1]の弟).

**2** Phoenix, River (1970-93; 米国の映画俳優; 本名 River Jude Phoenix; 1の兄).

**フェニックス・ロベレニー**〘植〙〔ヤシ科の常緑低木〕a pygmy date palm; *Phoenix roebelenii*.

**フェニルエチルアミン**〘化〙phenylethylamine.

**フェネックぎつね**【-狐】〘動〙〔北アフリカ、アラビア産の小型のキツネ〕a fennec fox; *Fennecus zerda*.

**フェミニズム** ▭ フェミニズム法学 (a) feminist jurisprudence.

**フェムト-** ▭ フェムト秒化学 femtosecond chemistry; femtochemistry.

**フェリ** Ferri, Alessandra (1963– ; イタリアのバレリーナ).

**フェリカ**〘商標〙〔非接触型ICカード技術〕FeliCa.

**「フェリックスの冒険」**〔米国の、利口な猫の勧善懲悪TVアニメ〕Felix the Cat.

**フェルール**〘機〙〔光ファイバー同士を接続する器具など〕ferrule.

**ブエルタ・ア・エスパーニャ**〔スペインの自転車レース; ヨーロッパ3大レースの1つ〕Vuelta a España; the Tour of Spain.

**プエルタ・デル・ソル**〔スペイン、マドリード中心部の広場〕the Puerta del Sol.

**フェルデン**〔オーストリアの町〕Velden.

**フェルトン** Felton, Tom (1987– ; 英国生まれの映画俳優).

**フェルナンデス** Fernández, Leonel (1953– ; ドミニカ共和国の政治家; 大統領〔1996-2000, 2004– 〕).

**フェルビナク**〘薬〙〔消炎鎮痛剤〕felbinac.

**フェルホフスタット** Verhofstadt, Guy (1953– ; ベルギーの政治家; 首相〔1999-2008〕).

**フェルミけんきゅうじょ**【-研究所】〔米国、シカゴ近郊にある国立加速器研究所〕Fermilab. ▶ 正式名称は フェルミ国立加速器研究所 (the Fermi National Accelerator Laboratory).

**フェルミこくりつかそくきけんきゅうじょ**【-国立加速器研究所】⇨ フェルミけんきゅうじょ.

**フェルラさん**【-酸】〘化〙ferulic acid.

**フェレルじゅんかん**【-循環】〘気象〙〔大気大循環の一種〕the Ferrel cell.

**フェレロ** Ferrero, Carlos (1941– ; ペルーの政治家; 首相〔2003-05〕).

**フェロー** ▭ アソシエイト・フェロー an associate fellow. シニア・フェロー = 上席フェロー. 上席〔上級〕フェロー〔研究機関などの〕a senior「fellow [researcher]《at the ABC Institute》.

**フェローシップ** ▭ フェローシップ制度〔日本学術振興会の外国人特別研究員制度〕the 「JSPS [Japan Society for the Promotion of Science] Postdoctoral Fellowship Program.

**フェロタングステン**〔タングステンを加えた高硬度・抗高温の鋼〕ferro-tungsten.

**フェロマンガン**〘冶〙〔マンガン鉄〕ferromanganese. ▭ 高炭素フェロマンガン high-carbon ferromanganese.

**フェンウェイ・パーク**〔米国マサチューセッツ州ボストンにある野球場〕Fenway Park.

**フェンサー**〔フェンシング選手〕a fencer.

**フェンス** ▭ フェンスオーバー〔(hit a ball) over the fence. ▶ 〜オーバーする〔ホームランを打つ〕clear the fences. フェンス際〔野球〕彼は〜際の打球を見事にキャッチした。He made a magnificent catch right at the fence line. / 彼は速球を〜際まで運んだ。He hit a fastball right to the fence (line). フェンス直撃〔野球〕〜直撃の二塁打 a double to the「wall [fence].

**フェンタニ(ー)ル**〘薬〙〔麻酔薬〕fentanyl.

**フェンチオン**〘化〙〔有機リン系殺虫剤〕fenthion.

**フェンディ**〘商標〙〔イタリアの服飾ブランド〕Fendi.

**フェンフルラミン**〘薬〙〔食欲減退剤〕fenfluramine. ▭ N-ニトロソ-フェンフルラミン N-nitroso-fenfluramine.

**フェンプロパトリン**〘化〙〔ピレスロイド系殺虫剤〕fenpropathrin.

**フォアぞく**【-族】〔パプアニューギニア東部の高地に住む民族〕the Fore; 〔1人〕a Fore《*pl.* ~, ~s》.

**フォアマン** Forman, Milos (1932– ; チェコスロヴァキア生まれの米国の映画監督; 本名 Tomas Jan Milos Formanova).

**フォー**[3]〘料理〙〔米からつくられるベトナムの麺〕pho.

**「フォーエバー・ヤング/時を越えた告白」**〔映画〕Forever Young.

**「フォー・ザ・ボーイズ」**〔映画〕For the Boys.

**フォーティーナイナーきゅう**【49er 級】〘ヨット〙the 49er class.

**フォート・キャンベル**〔米国ケンタッキー州南西部の軍事施設〕Fort Campbell.

**フォート・グリーリー**〔アラスカの米軍基地〕Fort Greely.

**フォート・コリンズ**〔米国コロラド州の都市〕Fort Collins.

**フォート・ベニング**〔米国ジョージア州にある、米陸軍歩兵学校練センターが置かれている基地〕Fort Benning.

**フォート・マイヤーズ**〔米国フロリダ州南西部の都市〕Fort Myers.

**フォート・ユーコン**〔米国アラスカ州のユーコン川沿いの村〕Fort Yukon.

**フォート・ローダーデール**〔米国フロリダ州南東部の都市〕Fort Lauderdale.

**フォー・バック**〘サッカー〙〔ディフェンダー4人を配置する戦術〕a「four-back [four-defender] formation.

**フォーマ**【FOMA】〘通信〙〔NTTドコモが提供する携帯電話サービスの1つ〕FOMA; Freedom of Mobile Multimedia Access.

**フォーマット** ▭ フォーマット権〘テレビ〙〔番組構成やセットのデザインなど番組制作のアイデアを利用できる権利〕format rights. フォーマット販売〘テレビ〙〔番組そのものでなく、構成やセットのデザインなど番組制作のアイデアを販売すること〕the sale of format rights.

**フォーマル** ▭ フォーマル・ケア〔公的なケアサービス〕《provide》formal care.

**フォーラムきこうのきき**【-気候の危機】〔NPO 組織〕the Kiko Forum.

**フォーリー** Foley, James (1953– ; 米国の映画監督).

**「フォーリン・ポリシー」**〔米国の外交誌〕Foreign Policy.

**フォール・イーグル**〔米軍と韓国軍の、野外機動演習の別称〕Foal Eagle.

**「フォーン・ブース」**〔映画〕Phone Booth.

**フォクシー**〔幻覚剤の一種〕Foxy; 5-MeO-DIPT.

**フォ・ジェンチイ**【霍建起】Huo Jianqi (1958– ; 中国の映画監督).

**フォックス**[2]

**5** Fox (Quesada), Vicente (1942– ; メキシコの政治家; 大統領〔2000-06〕).

**フォックス・ピー・トゥー**【FOXP2】〘遺伝〙〔言語に関わる遺伝子〕the FOXP2 gene. ▶ FOXP2 は、"*forkhead box*" + P(サブクラス名)+ 2(二番目のメンバー)の略.

**フォッシー** Fosse, Bob (1927-87; 米国の振付師・映画監督; 本名 Robert Louis Fosse).

**フォッセー** Fossey, Brigitte (1946– ; フランスの映画女優).

**フォト**[1] ▭ フォト・エッセー a photo(graphic) essay. フォト・サーバー〘電算〙〔画像データ保存用のインターネット上のサーバー〕a photo server. フォト・フレーム a photo(graph) frame. フォトマスク基板〘電子工学〙a photomask substrate.

**フォト・アイ・シー・ダイオード**【-IC -】〘電子工学〙a photo IC diode.

**フォトセラピー**〔写真療法〕phototherapy.

**フォトニック**〘光の〙photonic. ▭ フォトニック結晶〘物〙a photonic crystal. フォトニック・ネットワーク〘通〙a photonic network.

**フォトフリン**〘商標〙〔腫瘍親和性を持つ光感受性物質; 放射線治療に使う〕Photofrin.

フォホ〔ブラジルのダンス音楽〕forró.
フォボス〖ギ神話〗Phobos;〖天〗〔火星の衛星〕Phobos.
フォラーニ Forlani, Claire (1972- ；英国生まれの映画女優).
フォラステロ〖植〗〔カカオの一品種〕forastero.
フォルテシ(ッ)シモ〖It〗〖音楽〗〔演奏記号の1つ〕fortissimo (略: *fff*).
フォルテ(ッ)シモ〖It〗〖音楽〗〔演奏記号の1つ〕fortissimo (略: *ff*).
「フォレスト・ガンプ/一期一会」〔映画〕Forrest Gump.
フォレックス〔外国為替；外国為替保証金取引〕forex. ▶ foreign exchange, foreign exchange margin trading の略.
フォワード ▫ スモール・フォワード〖バスケット〗a small forward. パワー・フォワード〖バスケット〗a power forward.
フォントー〔ベトナム北部，ライチャウ省の省都〕Phong Tho.
ふか³【付加】▫ 付加価値比率 the value-added ratio; the proportion of ˹value added [added value]. 付加機能使用料〔電話などの〕(pay) an additional ˹charge [fee] for extra services; a ˹supplementary [special] services charge.
ふか⁸【孵化】▫ 自然孵化 natural incubation 《of eggs》.
ふか⁹【賦課】▫ 賦課方式〔年金財源調達の一方式〕a current disbursement method; a ˹pay-as-you-go [PAYG] system.
ふか¹¹【富化】enrichment. ▫ 酸素富化空気 oxygen-enriched air.
ふかいり²【深煎り】〔コーヒー豆の〕dark roast
ふかくさん【不拡散】▫ 不拡散体制〔核の〕a [the] nuclear nonproliferation regime.
ふかしづり【ふかし釣り】〔釣り〕=ふかせづり.
ふかしぼり【深絞り】〖金属加工〗deep drawing. ▷ deep-draw *v*.
ふかせづり【ふかせ釣り】〔釣り〕floating fishing.
ふかぞり【深剃り】a close shave.
～する give 《*sb*, *one*self》 a close shave.
ふかつか【不活化】▫ 不活化ポリオワクチン (an) inactivated polio vaccine (略: IPV).
ふかむし【深蒸し】deep steaming. ▫ 深蒸し茶 deep-steamed tea.
プカロンガン〔インドネシア，ジャワ島北岸の町〕Pekalongan.
ふかん²【不感】▫ 不感領域〔センサーなどの機器の〕a blind area.
ぶき【武器】▫ 武器査察 (a) weapons inspection. ▫ ～査察団 a weapons inspection team / ～査察官 a weapons inspector. 武器使用基準〔警官・自衛官などの〕rules on the use of firearms.
ブギーピアノ〖音楽〗〔ジャズ音楽の一形式〕boogie-woogie; boogie.
ふきかえ¹【吹き替え】▫ 吹き替え版 a dubbed version 《of a movie》.
ふきガラス【吹き-】〔管を口で吹いてガラスを膨らませて加工する工芸〕glassblowing;〔製品〕blown glass. ▷ glass-blower *n*.
ふきさい【不記載】not entering [failure to enter]《a transaction》in a report. ▶ あの議員は政治資金収支報告書への～で政治資金規正法違反に問われている. There are questions over whether the Diet member contravened the Political Funds Control Law by failing to enter donations in the political funding report.
ふきそ【不起訴】▫ 不起訴相当〖法〗〔検察審査会での議決の1つ〕a determination that prosecution is appropriate. 不起訴不当〖法〗〔検察審査会での議決の1つ〕a determination that nonprosecution is inappropriate.
ふきそく【不規則】▫ 不規則抗体〖医〗an ˹unexpected [irregular, atypical] antibody. ▫ ～抗体スクリーニング a screening test for unexpected antibodies.
ふきぬけ【吹き抜け】▫ 吹き抜け骨折〖医〗〔眼窩底骨折〕a blowout fracture.
ふきゅう⁴【普及】▫ 普及品 a product of average ˹grade [quality]; a mass market product.
ふきゅうのじゆうさくせん【不朽の自由作戦】〔2001年の同時多発テロ事件に対する報復として米英軍が国際テロ組織アルカイダおよびその支援組織に対して開始した一連の軍事作戦〕Operation Enduring Freedom (略: OEF).
ふきょう¹【不況】▫ 政治不況 a politically induced depression; (a) recession due to political mismanagement. ▫ 不況風 the 《cold, chill, icy》 wind of recession.
ふくいん³【復員】▫ 復員命令〔復員令〕demobilization orders.
ふくいん⁴【福音】▫ 福音派〈集合的に〉evangelicals; 〔1人〕an evangelical. ▫ ～派プロテスタント〈集合的に〉evangelical Protestants;〔1人〕an evangelical Protestant.
ふくいんかん【副印鑑】a seal impression in a passbook.
ふぐう【不遇】▫ 不遇感 a feeling that ˹one is unlucky [the world is against one].
ふくおうきん【腹横筋】〖解〗the ˹transversus abdominis [transverse abdominal] muscle.
ふくおうらん【複黄卵】〔1つの卵に卵黄が複数入っているもの〕a multi(ple)-yolk(ed) egg. 〔⇨におうらん, さんおうらん〕
ふくおかけんせいほうおきじしん【福岡県西方沖地震】〔2005年3月の〕the (2005) earthquake off (the western coast of) Fukuoka.
ふくげん【復元・復原】▫ 復元可能な reconstructable; reconstitutable; capable of being ˹reconstructed [reconstituted]. ▫ ～可能なデータ reconstructable [reconstitutable] data. 復元像〔破損した物体の〕a ˹reconstructed [reconstituted] image.
ふくごう³【複合】▫ 複合映画館 a cinema complex; a cineplex; a multiplex. 複合加工機〖機〗a multitasking machine. 複合型 ▫ ～型の compound; complex / ～型映画館 = 複合映画館. 複合商業施設 a commercial complex. 複合カフェ〔インターネット・漫画など飲食以外の多様なサービスを提供するカフェ〕a complex cafe; a cafe providing Internet and other services. 複合機〔複写機・スキャナー・プリンター・ファックスなどの機能を併せ持つ機器〕an all-in-one [a multifunction(al)] printer [machine, device]. ▫ カラー～機 a color ˹multifunction printer [MFP]. 複合検索〖電算〗a complex search (facility). 複合剤〖薬〗a compound (agent [drug]). 複合災害 a ˹compound [multiple] disaster. 複合的理学療法〖医〗complex physical therapy (略: CPT). 複合毒性 mixture toxicity; combined toxicity. 複合ビル ˹multipurpose [multifunction, multi-use] building. 複合不動産〔土地と建物一体と見なす不動産評価〕real estate including both land and building. 複合リゾート an integrated resort.
ふくし⁶【福祉】▫ 福祉移送サービス a welfare ˹transportation [transport] service. 福祉機器 welfare equipment. 福祉社会学 welfare sociology. 福祉車両 a welfare vehicle; a wheelchair-accessible [an accessible] vehicle; a mobility vehicle. 福祉住環境コーディネーター a ˹housing [(welfare) living] environment coordinator.
ふくしいりょうきこう【福祉医療機構】the Welfare and Medical Service Agency (略: WAM). ▶ 2003年に社会福祉・医療事業団より移行.
ふくしゅ⁵【輻射】▫ 輻射冷暖房 radiant [panel] heating and cooling.
ふくしゅう²【復讐】▫ 復讐禁止令〖日本史〗〔1873年(明治6年)の〕the prohibition of (private) redress.
ふくしゅと【副首都】a ˹subsidiary [secondary, alterna-

ふくしょく tive, substitute] capital.
ふくしょく¹【服飾】 ►◊ 服飾雑貨 haberdashery; hosiery. 服飾評論家 a clothing and accessory commentator.
ふくじんはくしつジストロフィー【副腎白質−】〖医〗adrenoleukodystrophy（略: ALD）.
ふくすい¹【復水】 ►◊ 復水(配)管〖原子力〗a cooling pipe; a condensate pipe.
ふくすう【複数】 ►◊ 複数区〖定員が2人以上の選挙区〗a multi-seat constituency. ◊ ~区では各党が独自候補を擁立した。In multi-seat constituencies, each of the parties backed its own candidate. 複数個別誘導再突入体〖軍〗〖各弾頭に誘導装置が付いている多弾頭ミサイル〗a multiple independently「targeted [targeted]reentry vehicle（略: MIRV）. ► 個別誘導複数目標弾頭 ともいう. 複数犯行 a crime committed by「several people [more than one person].
ふくせん³【複線】 ►◊ 複線型人事制度〖経営〗〖雇用形態の選択を従業員に認める制度〗a dual-ladder system.
ふくそう⁶【輻輳・輻湊】 ►◊ 企画型輻輳〖チケット予約などが殺到したときの電話回線混雑〗business-related telephone-network congestion. 災害型輻輳〖大災害発生時の電話回線混雑〗disaster-related telephone-network congestion. ►◊ 輻輳海域 crowded [congested] sea lanes.
ふくばこ【福箱】a「mystery [surprise] box.
ふくびくう【副鼻腔】〖解〗a (paranasal) sinus. ►◊ 副鼻腔炎〖医〗(paranasal) sinusitis.
ふくぶ【腹部】 ►◊ 腹部エコー〖医〗=腹部超音波検査. 腹部大動脈破裂〖医〗(a) rupture of the abdominal aorta; (an) abdominal aortic rupture. 腹部大動脈瘤〖医〗(an) abdominal aortic aneurysm（略: AAA）. 腹部超音波検査〖診断〗〖医〗(an) abdominal ultrasonography.
ふくふくせん【複々線】 ►◊ 複々線化 quadruple-tracking. ◊ ~化する quadruple-track《a railway line》.
ふくへき²【腹壁】 ►◊ 腹壁瘢痕ヘルニア〖医〗(an) (abdominal) incisional hernia. 腹壁ヘルニア〖医〗(a) ventral [(an) abdominal] hernia.
ふくまく【腹膜】 ►◊ 腹膜播種〖医〗〖がん〗peritoneal dissemination.
ふくみ【含み】 ►◊ 含み経営 management through the use of hidden assets. 含み損益 unrealized profits and losses.
ふくめん【覆面】 ►◊ 覆面捜査 an undercover investigation.
ふくろありくい【袋蟻喰】〖動〗a numbat; a banded anteater; *Myrmecobius fasciatus*.
ブグロー=ブーグロー.
ふくろしまりす【袋縞栗鼠】〖動〗a striped possum; *Dactylopsila trivirgata*.
ぶけ【武家】 ►◊ 武家町〖町人町・寺町などに対して〗the samurai quarter.
ぶけい【武警】=ちゅうごくじんみんぶそうけいさつ.
ふけいたい【不携帯】nonpossession. ►◊ 旅券不携帯 nonpossession of one's passport. 免許証不携帯 ◊ 免許証~で車を運転する drive a vehicle without having one's license「with [on] one.
プケコ〖鳥〗〖クイナ科の鳥；ニュージーランドの固有種〗a pukeko; a purple swamphen; *Porphyrio porphyrio*.
ふけまちづき【更待月】〖陰暦20日の夜の月〗the moon of the 20th day of the lunar month.
ふけんぜん【不健全】 ►◊ 不健全図書 unwholesome「publications [books, literature].
ふこうきさいばい【不耕起栽培】〖農〗〖田畑を耕さずに作物を栽培する農法〗no-tillage [natural] farming.
ふこうし【不行使】 ►◊ 武力不行使 nonuse of military force.

ふさい⁴【負債】 ►◊ 負債(自己)資本比率[倍率]〖経〗a debt-(to-)equity ratio; a debt/equity ratio; a D/E ratio.
ふさいさん【不採算】 ►◊ 不採算地各 a「non-profit-making [loss-making] district; a district which doesn't pay. 不採算店 an unprofitable [a loss-making] store. 不採算路線〖高速道路・鉄道・バス・航空便などの〗an unprofitable [a loss-making, an uneconomic] route.
フサイバ〖イラク北西部の町〗Husaybah.
ふさくい【不作為】 ►◊ 不作為義務〖特定の行為が法によって禁じられている場合に人が負う義務〗a duty of omission; a negative duty.
プサントレン〖インドネシアのイスラム教寄宿学校〗a (pondok) pesantren《*pl.* ~(s)》.
ふし⁵【父子】 ►◊ 父子鑑定 a paternity test; paternity testing.
ふじいろぼうしいんこ【藤色帽子鸚哥】〖鳥〗a lilac-crowned Amazon; *Amazona finschi*. ► 国際希少野生動植物種.
ブシェーミ=ブシェミ.
ブシェール〖イラン南部、ペルシャ湾沿岸の州；その州都〗Bushehr. ► 英語では Bushire とも綴られる. 〖⇒バンダル・ブシェール〗
ブシェミ Buscemi, Steve（1957– ）〖米国の映画俳優〗.
ふしか【不死化】〖生物〗〖細胞の〗immortalization. ▷ immortalize *v.*
ふしかんせん【父子感染】〖医〗father-to-child infection; paternal infection. ~する〖子が〗be infected by one's father;〖病気が〗pass from father to child.
ふしぎちゃん【不思議ちゃん】〖何を考えているのかわからない、一風変わった少女〗an eccentric [a strange, a spacey] girl; Little Miss Spacey.
ふしじ【不支持】nonsupport; disapproval. ◊ 昨年4月の内閣発足以来初めて~が支持を上回った。The disapproval rate exceeded the approval rate [Opposition outpaced support] for the first time since the cabinet was formed last April. ◊ 首相の~の理由でいちばん多かったのが指導力の欠如だった。The most frequently stated reason for not supporting the prime minister was his lack of leadership. ►◊ 不支持率 a《high》disapproval「rating [rate].
ふじつ²【不実】 ►◊ 不実(の)告知〖契約の重要事項について事実と異なることを告げること〗misrepresentation; false representation.
プシッタコサウルス〖古生物〗〖植物食恐竜〗a psittacosaurus; a psittacosaur.
フジッリ〖らせん状にねじれたパスタ〗fusilli.
ふしめ²【節目】 ►◊ 節目健診 a medical checkup taken at five-[ten-]yearly intervals after the age of 40.
ぶじゅつ【武術】 ►◊ 古武術 classical [ancient] martial arts. 中国武術 Chinese martial arts.
ふじょ³【婦女】 ►◊ 婦女暴行 ◊ 準~罪 (a) sexual assault against a person who cannot offer resistance (due to sleep, inebriation, etc.).
ふしょう⁸【負傷】 ►◊ 負傷降板〖野球〗◊ ~降板する leave the mound due to injury.
ふじょう³【浮上】 ►◊ 浮上走行〖リニアモーターカーなどの〗levitated [suspended, maglev] travel [motion].
ふしようしょうしょ【不使用証明書】〖有害化学物質の〗a certificate of non-use《of a banned material》.
ふしん²【不振】 ►◊ 不振企業[店] a failing「company [store]; a「company [store] in trouble [which is not doing well]. 不振産業 a troubled industry; a depressed industry.
ふしん³【不審】 ►◊ 不審死 a「suspicious [doubtful] death. ◊ 最近日本各地で野鳥の~死が相次いでいる。In Japan there has recently been a succession of「unexplained [mysterious] bird deaths. | Birds have

recently been dying 「mysteriously [from unknown causes] all over Japan. 不審死体 a suspicious corpse; the body of a person who dies in suspicious circumstances. 不審者(出没)情報 information on suspicious characters. 不審車両 a suspicious-looking vehicle.

ふじん[6]【婦人】▶婦人雑貨 women's 「goods [items]. 婦人保護施設 a「shelter [sanctuary] for women; a women's shelter.

ふじんかあくせいしゅようかがくりょうほうけんきゅうきこう【婦人科悪性腫瘍化学療法研究機構】[NPO法人] the Japanese Gynecologic Oncology Group (略: JGOG).

ふじんかいはつききん【婦人開発基金】[国連の]⇒こくれんふじんかいはつききん.

ふしんにん【不信任】▶不信任決議 a resolution of no-confidence; a no-confidence resolution.

ふずい【付随】▶付随的違憲審査[法] incidental 「constitutional [judicial] review. 付随的任務〔自衛隊などの〕incidental [auxiliary] duties.

ブスコパン〔商標・薬〕〔胃腸鎮痛鎮痙薬〕Buscopan.
フスハ(ー)〔標準アラビア語〕(al-)fusha.

ふせい[1]【不正】▶不正還付 an illegal refund. ◆税金の～還付を受ける receive an illegal tax refund. 不正支出 unwarranted use [unjustifiable disbursement] 《of public funds》. 不正受交付罪[法]〔偽造[変造]旅券などの入手・所持・提供〕the crime of receiving, carrying or providing「counterfeit [forged] passports. 不正取水 (an) illegal water intake. ◆～取水する draw water illegally《from a river》. 不正請求 improper billing; an illegal charge. 不正送金〔銀行口座などから の〕(an) illegal transfer《from another person's bank account》. 不正操作〔帳簿・価格・データなどの〕manipulating [*cooking]《「the books [stocks, data, etc.]》. 不正摘発 an exposure of sth 「illegal [(an) illegality]. ◆公共事業の受注に関する～摘発を行う expose illegalities concerning the reception of orders for public works. 不正引き出し〔銀行口座などからの〕(an) illegal withdrawal《from sb's account》. 不正乱視〔眼科〕irregular astigmatism.

ふせい[2]【不斉・不整】▶不整地形 an irregular shaped lot.

ふせい[3]【父性】▶父性(の)欠如 (a) lack of paternal influence. ◆彼女は～欠如の家庭に育った. She was brought up in a family without much paternal influence. | Her father didn't play much of a role in her upbringing. 父性原理〔心理〕the paternal principle.

ふせいき【不正規】▶不正規戦 unconventional warfare (略: UW); an unconventional war.

ふせいみゃく【不整脈】▶不整脈原性右室心筋異形成症[異形成]症 arrhythmogenic right ventricular dysplasia (略: ARVD).

フゼスタン ＝フーゼスターン.

ふせん[2]【不戦】▶不戦共同体 a community that has renounced war; an antiwar community.

ふぜん[1]【不全】▶人間関係[対人関係]不全〔心理〕failure in human relationships; (an) inability to form relationships. ▶不全感 a 「sense [feeling] of 「incompleteness [insufficiency]. ◆彼は漠然とした自己～感を持ち続けて生きてきた. All through his life he has had a vague sense of being incomplete in himself.

プソイドエフェドリン[薬] pseudoephedrine.

ぶそう[2]【武装】▶武装工作船 an armed spy ship. 武装組織[グループ] an armed 「organization [group].

ぶそう・どういん・かいじょ・しゃかいふっき【武装解除・動員解除・社会復帰】〔内戦が終結した国で元兵士に対して行われるプログラム〕Disarmament, Demobilization and Reintegration (略: DDR).

ぶぞく[1]【部族】▶部族指導者 the《religious》leader of a tribe. 部族長 the chief of a tribe; a tribal 「chief [chieftan]; the 「head [chief] of a clan.

ふぞくしょこく【附属書Ⅰ国】〔環境〕〔気候変動枠組条約の附属書Ⅰに記載されている国; 温室効果ガス削減を義務づけられている国〕an Annex Ⅰ 「country [party].

ふそついっとっけん【不訴追特権】[法]〔国務大臣の〕immunity from prosecution during《one's》term of office.

フソバクテリウム〔菌〕〔腸内細菌の1つ〕a fusobacterium.

ふぞん【賦存】〔天然資源の〕presence《of oil deposits》. ～する be present《underground》. ▶賦存量 (amount of)《mineral》reserves.

ふそんざい【不存在】nonexistence; absence; (a) lack 《of …》. ◆相続人が～の場合には… [法] in the absence of an heir…; lacking an heir…. / 市役所に文書公開を請求したが, ～のため不開示となった. We requested the document's disclosure by the city office, but it was not released as it did not exist. ▶メーカー等《義務者》不存在パソコン〔自作品や倒産したメーカーの品など, リサイクル回収義務者がいないパソコン〕a personal computer with no extant manufacturer or other responsible party.

ふたい[1]【付帯】▶付帯意見 an incidental [a collateral] opinion; an obiter dictum《pl. obiter dicta》. 付帯私訴[法]〔刑事裁判中に被告に対して起こす民事訴訟〕an incidental private 「action [lawsuit]. 付帯私訴制度[法]〔刑事裁判中に被告に対する民事訴訟を提起しうる制度〕(a system permitting) a 「parallel [simultaneous] civil action against a defendant in a criminal case. 付帯的損害〔事故・戦闘などに付随して起こる副次的な被害〕collateral damage.

ふたい[2]【浮体】▶浮体空港 a floating airport.《海上》浮体構造物 a floating structure. ▶超大型～構造物 a very large floating structure; a megafloat. 浮体工法〔土木〕〔海上空港などを造るための〕a [the] floating method.

ぶたい[1]【部隊】▶初動部隊〔災害出動などの〕a 「first-response [first-responder] team. ▶部隊行動基準 (the) rules of engagement (略: ROE).

ぶたいえんしゅつ【舞台演出】stage direction. ◆～する direct a stage 「production [performance]. ▶舞台演出家 a stage director.

ぶたけた【二桁】▶二桁安打〔野球〕double-digit hits; hits in the double digits. 二桁勝利 double-digit 「wins [victories]. ◆～勝投手〔野球〕a 「double-digit [double-figure] winner [winning pitcher]. 二桁成長 double-digit《economic》growth. 二桁増益 double-digit profit 「growth [increase]. 二桁奪三振〔野球〕double-digit strikeouts. 二桁得点 double-digit scoring; scoring in the double digits.

ふたご【双子・双生児】▶双子地震 twin earthquakes; an earthquake chain.

ふだしょ【札所】▶札所巡り a 「tour [pilgrimage] around holy temples.

ぶたせいしょくきこきゅうきしょうこうぐん【豚生殖器呼吸症候群】[獣医]⇒ぶたはんしょく・きゅうしょうがい・しょうこうぐん.

ふたつ[3]【不達】nondelivery. ◆メールアドレスが間違っていて～になった. The address was wrong, so the e-mail 「wasn't delivered [didn't get through]. ▶不達メール (an) undelivered e-mail;〔送信者に返ってきた〕(a) 「returned [bounced] e-mail. 不達通知メール an e-mail nondelivery 「report [notice].

ふたつめ【二つ目】▶〔落語家格の1つ〕a futatsume; a second-rank rakugo performer.

ぶたどん【豚丼】a bowl of steamed rice topped with thinly sliced stewed pork; a pork bowl.

ぶたはんしょく・きゅうしょうがい・しょうこうぐん【豚繁殖・呼吸障害症候群】[獣医] porcine reproductive and respiratory syndrome (略: PRRS).

ふたほしてんとう【二星天道】〘昆〙*Hyperaspis japonica*.
ふたもんてんとう【二紋天道】〘昆〙〔ヨーロッパ産のテントウムシ〕a two-spot ladybird; *Adalia bipunctata*.
「ふたりの男とひとりの女」〔映画〕Me, Myself & Irene.
フタルさん【-酸】▫▫ フタル酸ジエチルヘキシル diethylhexyl phthalate (略: DEHP).
ふたん【負担】▫▫ 応益負担〔受けるサービスの量で料金が決まる方式〕payment according to benefit received. 応能負担〔サービスを受ける人の支払い能力によって料金が決まる方式〕payment according to ability to pay. 窓口負担 ⇨まどぐち. ▫▫ 負担増 an increased「burden [cost]; a cost increase. ◆医療費制度の改革で, 患者に は～増が強いられることになった. The reform of the medical fee system forced higher costs onto patients. 負担割合 a「one's」share of 《the costs》. ◆医療費の個人～割合 the patient's (percentage) share of medical expenses; the patient's copayment (percentage) for medical expenses.
ふだん²【普段】
▫▫ 普段使い〔日常使用〕regular [everyday, day-to-day] use. ◆～使いの焼き物 china for everyday use; everyday china.
ふたんかん【負担感】〔重荷であるという気持ち〕a「burdened [burdensome] feeling. ◆介護の～の高い世代 a generation that feels especially burdened by caregiving. ◆子育ての～が大きいことが未婚の一因となっている. One reason people aren't getting married is the heavy load of child rearing.
プチかぶ【-株】=株式ミニ投資 (⇨かぶしき).
プチぎれ【-切れ】〔少しかっとする[切れる]こと〕《throw》a little fit;《have》a little (temper) tantrum.
プチせいけい【-整形】〔美容〕minor「cosmetic [plastic] surgery; a minor cosmetic (surgical) procedure.
プチだんじき【-断食】a mini fast; a mini-fast.
ぶちハイエナ【斑-】〘動〙〔ハイエナ科の動物〕a spotted hyena; *Crocuta crocuta*.
プチはんざい【-犯罪】petty crime; a「petty [minor] crime [offense, violation]; a peccadillo 《*pl.* ~es, ~s》.
プチボラ〔ささやかなボランティア活動〕《do》a little (bit of) volunteer work.
プチムゲ〔料理〕〔韓国風のお好み焼き〕buchimgae (pancakes).
ふちょう¹【不調】▫▫ 不調物件〔競売などで応札がない物件〕a property on which there were no valid bids.
ふつう²【普通】▫▫ 普通地域〔国立公園内などの保護区分の一つ〕an ordinary zone. 普通配〘株〙an ordinary [a common] dividend.
「普通じゃない」〔映画〕A Life Less Ordinary.
ぶっか²【物価】▫▫ 物価下落 a (commodity) price fall; a fall in (commodity) prices. ◆～下落率 the (a) rate of「price fall [fall in prices].
ブッカルファット〔頬の脂肪〕buccal fat.
ぶつがん【仏龕】a miniature shrine with doors, for the safekeeping of Buddha images, relics or sutra scrolls.
ふっき【復帰】▫▫ 大関[関脇など]復帰〔相撲〕a return to the rank of *ōzeki* [*sekiwake*, etc]. 完全復帰〔職場など〕a return [returning] to full duty. ◆大臣の体調は順調に回復しつつあるが, 完全～へ向けてなお療養が必要です. The Minister is on the mend, but will need further treatment before he can return to full duty.
ぶづきまい【分搗き米】〔精米時に糠層や胚芽を残したもの〕rice which retains some of the bran and germ; semibrown rice; partly polished rice. ▫▫ 三分[五分, 七分]搗き米 rice from which「thirty percent [fifty percent, seventy percent] of the bran has been removed; thirty percent [fifty percent, seventy percent] polished rice.
ふっきゅう²【復旧】▫▫ 全面復旧 (a)「complete [full] recovery.
フック¹ ▫▫ S字フック an "S" hook.
ブック¹〔特定のテーマの本について系統立てて紹介すること〕a book talk.
「フック」〔映画〕Hook.
ブックスタート〔乳幼児に絵本を贈る運動〕Bookstart.
フックせんちょう【-船長】〔児童読み物・アニメなどの, ピーター・パンに敵対する, 片腕が鉤()の海賊〕Captain Hook.
ふっけん²【福建】▫▫ 福建語 Hokkien; Fukien.
ぶっけん¹【物件】▫▫ 新築物件 a「new [newly built] property. 中古物件 a「secondhand [previously owned] property.
ふっこう⁵【復興】▫▫ 復興区画整理 reconstruction and rezoning《of a disaster site》. 復興支援[援助] reconstruction assistance. 復興組織 a reconstruction organization.
ふっこうじんどうしえんきょく[しつ]【復興人道支援局[室]】〔米国国家安全保障会議の一機関〕the Office of Reconstruction and Humanitarian Assistance (略: ORHA). ▶後に, 連合国暫定当局 (CPA) に統合.
「不都合な真実」〔ドキュメンタリー映画〕An Inconvenient Truth.
ぶっこみ(うどん)【-込み(饂飩)】ぶっ込み(饂飩) boiled「*udon* [noodles] in a thick meat and vegetable broth.
ぶっしつ【物質】▫▫ 物質循環システム a material(s) recycling system.
ぶっしつ・ざいりょうけんきゅうきこう【物質・材料研究機構】the National Institute for Materials Science (略: NIMS).
プッシュ ▫▫ プッシュ回線〔電話〕a touch-tone line.
プッシュせんりゃく【-戦略】〘商〙〔小売り・流通業者に働きかけて消費者の需要を創出する販売戦略〕a push strategy.
プッシュ・ツー・トーク〔押すと相手と話せる携帯電話機能〕push-to-talk (略: PTT).
ブッシュ・ドクトリン〔米国ブッシュ大統領(第43代)の国家安全保障戦略〕the Bush Doctrine.
「ブッシュ・ド・ノエル」〔映画〕La Buche.
ふっそ【弗素】▫▫ 弗素〔年代測定〕法〔考古〕fluorine [fluoride, fluorine absorption] dating.
ぶっちゃけ〔「ぶっちゃけた話」の略で副詞的に;正直に言うと〕to tell you the truth…; let me give it to you straight.
ふっとうすいがた(げんし)ろ【沸騰水型(原子)炉】
▫▫ 改良型沸騰水型(原子)炉 an advanced boiling water reactor (略: ABWR).
フット・スイッチ〔足踏みで ON/OFF の操作を行うスイッチ〕a foot switch.
プットニョス〔ハンガリー, トカイ産貴腐ワインの糖度の尺度〕puttonyos. ◆このトカイは6～です. It is a 6 puttonyos「Tokay [Tokaji].
フット・マッサージ《give *sb*, get》a foot massage.
フットレスト〔足置き台〕a footrest.
ぶっぱん【物販】〔物品販売〕merchandise sales. ▫▫ 物販業者 a merchandise distributor. 物販店 a merchandise outlet.
ぶっぴん【物品】▫▫ 物品販売 merchandise sales. [⇨ぶっぱん]
ぶつり¹【物理】▫▫ 物理蒸着(法)〘物・化〙physical vapor deposition (略: PVD). [=物理気相成長法] 物理気相成長法〘物・化〙physical vapor deposition (略: PVD).
ぶつりゅう【物流】▫▫ 物流効率 distribution [logistics] efficiency. 物流事業 a「distribution [logistics] business. ◆国際～事業 an international「distribution [logistics] business. 物流倉庫 a distribution warehouse. 物流台車 a distribution trolley. 物流特区 a special distribution zone. ◆国際～特区 an international distribution zone. 物流網 a distribution network.
ふで【筆】▫▫ 面相筆 a fine-tipped brush for painting

details; a detail brush.
ふていき【不定期】□□ 不定期航空会社 a nonscheduled airline; *「口」a nonsked.
ふていじほう【不定時法】〔季節や場所によって時刻の長さが変わる日本独特の時間区分法〕the 《pre-Meiji》 irregular time(-measuring) system. ⇨「ていじほう」
ふてきせい【不適正】〜な inappropriate; illegitimate; unacceptable; unfair. ◐〜な取引行為〔事業者の消費者に対する〕an inappropriate trading practice; unacceptable sales behavior ◐個人情報の〜な取り扱い inappropriate「use [handling] of private information. ◐余った予算を使い切ったように会計処理するのは〜だ. In the treatment of accounts it is「not acceptable [illegitimate] to treat remaining funds as if they had been used up.
不適正に inappropriately; illegitimately; unacceptably; unfairly. ◐当校では個人情報が〜に利用されないよう厳重に管理しています. At this「school [university] we take the greatest care to ensure that no inappropriate use is made of private information. ◐不適正支出 inappropriate [unacceptable, illegitimate] expenditure. 不適正処理〔産業廃棄物などの〕illegitimate disposal 《of industrial waste》; dealing 《with a problem》 in an unacceptable way. 不適正表示〔行為〕inappropriate [unsatisfactory, misleading] labelling; describing 《a product》 misleadingly;〔ラベル〕an inappropriate [an unsatisfactory, a misleading] label.
ふてきせつ【不適切】□□ 不適切管理〔機密情報・公金・危険物質などの〕inappropriate management.
ふでさばき【筆捌き】one's handling of a 《writing》 brush; one's brushwork.
ふとう¹【不当】□□ 不当請求 unfair billing; an unjustified charge. 不当逮捕 an unjustified [a wrongful, an unlawful] arrest. 不当要求 an「exorbitant [unreasonable, unjustified] demand.
ふどう²【不動】□□ 不動車〔動かなくなった自動車〕an unusable「vehicle [car].
ぶとう¹【武闘】□□ 武闘派〔政治上の〕an armed insurgent group. ◐〜派ების policy of armed insurgency. 武闘家〔格闘技の〕a martial artist.
ぶどう³【葡萄】□□ 葡萄狩り grape picking.
ふどうかぶしすう【浮動株指数】〔証券〕a free-float index.
ふとうこう²【不登校】□□ 不登校傾向 《have》 a tendency to「be absent from [stay away from, miss] school.
ふどうさん【不動産】□□ 企業不動産 corporate real estate (略: CRE). 担保不動産 real estate「offered [held] as「collateral [security]; real estate「collateral [security]. □□ 不動産 real estate revitalization. 不動産指定流通機構 a designated real estate distribution organization. 不動産証券化 real estate securitization. 不動産担保ローン〔融資〕a loan secured by real property. 不動産投資会社 a real estate investment「company [firm]. 不動産投資ファンド a real estate investment fund. 不動産売買契約書 a contract for real estate transaction. 不動産ファンド a real estate fund. 不動産マネー real estate money. 不動産《流通》市場 the real estate market. 不動産譲渡《所得》税 (a) real estate transfer tax. 不動産投信〔不動産投資信託〕a real estate investment trust (略: REIT). 不動産流通税 (a) real estate transfer tax.
ふどうさんきょうかい【不動産協会】the Real Estate Companies Association of Japan.
ふどうさんしょうけんかきょうかい【不動産証券化協会】the Association for Real Estate Securitization (略: ARES).
ふどうさんりゅうつうけいえいきょうかい【不動産流通経営協会】the Association of Real Estate Agents of Japan. ▶略称は日本語のローマ字表記の頭文字からFRK.
ふどうてん【不動点】□□ 不動点定理 〖数〗 the fixed-point theorem.
ぶどうとう【葡萄糖】□□ ぶどう糖果糖液糖 high fructose corn syrup (略: HFCS).
ぶどうまく【葡萄膜】□□ ぶどう膜欠損《症》〖眼科〗 uveal coloboma.
プトラジャヤ〔マレーシアの新行政首都〕Putrajaya. ▶2010年完成予定.
ふなけん【舟券】□□ 舟券(売り)場 a betting booth [window] 《at a speedboat race》; a ticket「window [office]. ◐場外〔〜売り〕場 a speedboat race betting shop where tickets can be purchased before a race.
ふなずし【鮒寿司・鮒鮨】〖料理〗 funazushi; a kind of preserved and fermented sushi made with crucian carp caught in Lake Biwa, rice and salt.
ふなづり【船釣り】〔船上からの魚釣り〕fishing from a boat.
ふなのりこみ【船乗り込み】〖歌舞伎〗〔役者たちが乗って興行地への到着をお披露目する伝統行事〕funanorikomi; a traditional summer ceremony in which kabuki actors sit atop a ceremonial boat and float downriver.
ブニア〖コンゴ民主共和国北東部の町〗Bunia.
ぷにぷに〔柔らかい弾力がある感じ〕◐〜した springy; bouncy / 赤ちゃんの肌は〜して気持ちがいい. I like the way a baby's skin is soft but resilient. /グミの〜した食感が好きだ. I like the rubbery texture of gummi candy.
ふにゅう²【腐乳】〔中国の調味料, 豆腐に香辛料を加え塩水の中で醗酵させたもの〕furu; fermented flavored tofu.
ブニョル〖スペイン・バレンシア地方の町〗Buñol. ▶トマトを投げ合う祭(La Tomatina)で有名.
ブヌンぞく【〜族】〖台湾の先住民族〗the Bunun;〔1人〕a Bunun《pl. 〜》.
ふねんか【不燃化】〔木材・家屋などの〕fireproofing; rendering [making] 《urban areas》 fireproof. ◐《都市の》〜を進める further fireproofing《in urban areas》; make progress in fireproofing《a town》. ◐不燃化促進 promotion of fireproofing. ◐〜促進事業 a fireproofing project.
ふねん(せい)¹【不稔(性)】□□ 不稔障害〔稲などの〕《cold-induced》 sterility《in rice》.
フノラン〖化〗funoran.
ふはい²【腐敗】□□ 腐敗体質〔企業・官庁などの〕《display》 a predisposition to corruption; a culture of corruption.
ふはいぼうしじょうやく【腐敗防止条約】=こくれんふはいぼうしじょうやく.
ブバスティス〖エジプトの古都〗Bubastis.
ふばらい【不払い】□□ 賃金不払い nonpayment of wages. 不当不払い〔保険金などの〕illegal nonpayment《of insurance claims》.
プブりょうほう【―療法】〖医〗〔ソラレン誘導体を内服あるいは塗布したあと長波長紫外線を皮膚に照射する光線療法〕PUVA treatment; psoralen-ultraviolet A therapy. ▶ PUVA は psoralen-ultraviolet A の略.
ぶひん【部品】□□ アフター部品 =アフターパーツ. 有寿命部品 parts with limited life expectancy; limited-life parts. □□ 部品交換 parts [part] replacement; replacement of「parts [a part]. ◐〜交換を行う replace a part. 部品サプライヤー a parts supplier. 部品調達 parts procurement; procurement of「parts [components]. ◐海外からの〜調達 overseas parts procurement; overseas procurement of「parts [components]. 部品納入業者 a parts supplier《to the car industry》. 部品保存〔保管〕期間〔修理〔交換〕用部品の〕a spare parts stocking period; the period during which a maker guarantees to stock parts for replacement or

repair.

ぶぶん【部分】 ▫️ 部分酸化法〚化〛the partial oxidation method. 部分(出産)中絶 (a) partial birth abortion. 部分提携〚企業同士などの〛〚form〛a partial tie-up. 部分肉 cut meat; meat parts.

ぶぶんはんけつせいど【部分判決制度】〚法〛〚複数の犯罪を犯した被告に対する〛a system of partial 「judgment [sentencing].

ふぶんめい【不分明】～な ambiguous; unclear; difficult to distinguish. 〚絵の世界ではプロとアマの境が～だ. With pictures it is difficult to draw a line between the professional and the amateur. / 医薬品と食品の区別が～化している. The difference between drugs and foods is growing less clear. | It is becoming more difficult to draw a line between a drug and a foodstuff.

ぶべつ[1]【侮蔑】 ▫️ 侮蔑語 an insulting [a contemptuous] word.

ふへんすいていりょう【不偏推定量】〚統計〛an unbiased estimator.

ふほ【付保】 ▫️ 保険付保 insuring. ▫️ 付保証明書 a certificate of insurance. 付保預金 an insured deposit.

ふほう[1]【不法】 ▫️ 不法在留 residence by an illegal entrant. 不法 a resident illegal entrant. 不法操業 (engage in) illegal (fishing) operations. [⇨違法操業 (⇨いほう[3])]

「不法侵入」〚映画〛Unlawful Entry.

ふまん【不満】 ▫️ 不満意見 a dissatisfied opinion 《with regard to「a product [a resolution]》. 不満の冬〚英国労働党政府の賃上げ抑制政策により労働組合のストライキが頻発した1978-79年の冬〛the Winter of Discontent.

ふみこう【文香】〚手紙に入れるシート状の香〛a「scented [perfumed] insert.

ふみだい【踏み台】 ▫️ 踏み台昇降〚健康体操の1つ〛step (box [stool]) exercise;〚医〛〚心肺機能検査のための〛a step test.

ふみのひ【文の日】〚毎月23日〛Letter-Writing Day.

ブミラ ＝おおイタビ.

ふみんしょう【不眠症】 ▫️ 致死性家族性不眠症〚医〛fatal familial insomnia (略：FFI).

ふめい【不明】 ▫️ 不明水〚水道〛water of unknown origin.

ふめいよ【不名誉】 ▫️ 不名誉除隊 a dishonorable discharge (from the military).

プヤライモンディ〚植〛〚パイナップル科の巨大高山植物〛Puya raimondii; *Puya raimondii.*

ふゆ[1]【冬】 ▫️ 冬掛け〚寝具〛winter bedding; a heavy blanket for winter. 冬太り winter's waist. ▶️ ～太りする put on weight in the winter.

ふゆう[3]【浮遊・浮游】 ▫️ 浮遊カビ菌 floating mold spores. 浮遊感 a feeling of floating. ▶️ 降りしきる雪を窓からながめていると不思議な～に襲われることがある. As I watch the snow falling thickly outside the window I am sometimes overcome by a strange feeling of floating. 浮遊ごみ floating「garbage [waste].

ふゆう[3]【富裕】 ▫️ 富裕国 a 「rich [wealthy] country [nation]. 富裕層 the moneyed class(es); the「wealthy [affluent] class(es).

ふゆうがき【富有柿】〚植〛〚カキの1品種；岐阜県原産〛a Fuyu persimmon.

フューワクー ＝フークア.

「フューネラル」〚映画〛The Funeral.

「冬のソナタ」〚韓国のテレビドラマ〛Winter Sonata; Winter Song Of Love.

ふよう[4]【扶養】 ▫️ 金銭扶養 (provide) financial support 《to「one's elderly parents》. 引き取り扶養 taking in and supporting《「one's elderly parents》.

ふよう[7]【浮葉】 ▫️ 浮葉植物 a floating plant.

ぶよう[2]【舞踊】 ▫️ 現代舞踊 contemporary dance.

ふようせい【不溶性】 ▫️ 不溶性グルカン〚生化〛insoluble glucan. 不溶性食物繊維 insoluble dietary fiber.

ブラーガ Braga, Gaetano (1829-1907;イタリア出身のチェロ奏者・作曲家).

プラーク ▫️ アテローム[粥状]プラーク〚医〛(an) atheromatous plaque.

プライス Pryce, Jonathan (1947- ；英国生まれの映画俳優).

ブライダル ▫️ ブライダル・ファッション bridal fashion. ▶️ ～・ファッション・デザイナー a bridal fashion designer. ブライダル・プランナー〚結婚式の企画立案担当者〛a「bridal [wedding] planner.

フライト ▫️ フライト情報[インフォメーション]システム a flight information system (略：FIS). フライト・スケジュール a flight schedule.

ブライトマン Brightman, Sarah (1960- ；英国出身の歌手).

ブライトンせんげん【～宣言】〚1994年、世界女性スポーツ会議での〛the Brighton Declaration on Women and Sport.

プライバシー ▫️ プライバシー・マーク〚個人情報保護の認定事業者マーク〛the Privacy Mark; an insignia identifying businesses that enact measures to protect personal privacy.

プライベート ▫️ プライベート・エクイティー・ファンド〚金融〛〚未公開株式を対象とする投資ファンド〛a private equity fund.

プライマリー・バランス〚国債費関連を除いた基礎的財政収支〛primary balance (略：PB).

プライムレート ▫️ 短期[長期]プライムレート a「long-term [short-term] prime rate.

フライヤー[4]〚ライト兄弟が作った人類初の飛行機名〛the Flyer.

フライヤー[5]〚商〛〚広告用のビラ、ちらし〛a「flyer [flier].

フライング・ドクター〚飛行機で往診する医師〛a flying doctor.

ブラインド・カーボン・コピー〚電算〛〚受信者に他の人に転送されたことが通知されない電子メール〛blind carbon copy (略：bcc, BCC).

ブラインド・ゴルフ〚視覚障害者のためのゴルフ〛blind golf. ブラインド・パッケージ〚中身を見せないで売る商品箱〛a「*grab-bag [*lucky-dip] package [item].

ブラウザー ▫️ ブラウザー・クラッシャー〚電算〛〚ブラウザーの動作を狂わせるためにホームページ上に仕込まれた悪質な仕掛け〛a browser crasher.

ブラウス ▫️ ヴィクトリアン・ブラウス〚ヴィクトリア朝風に装飾の多い〛a Victorian(-style) blouse.

ブラウラー〚米軍〛〚電子戦支援機EA-6の愛称〛a Prowler.

ブラウン Brown, Gordon (1951- ；英国の政治家；首相〚2007- 〛).

ブラウン・アノール〚動〛〚キューバ原産のトカゲ〛a brown anole; *Anolis sagrei.*

ブラウンかん【～管】 ▫️ 平面ブラウン管〚テレビなどの〛a flat picture tube; a flat-screen CRT. ▶️ CRTは cathode-ray tube (陰極線管) の略.

ブラウンきつねざる【～狐猿】〚動〛a brown lemur; *Eulemur fulvus.*

ブラウンパッチ〚植物病理〛〚西洋シバ葉腐れ病〛brown patch.

ふらく【不落】 ▫️ 不落物件〚競売などで落札されない物件〛a property unsold at auction.

フラクタル ▫️ フラクタル理論〚数〛(a) fractal theory.

「プラクティカル・マジック」〚映画〛Practical Magic.

フラグメント ▫️ フラグメント・アナライザー〚DNA自動分析装置〛a (DNA) fragment analyzer.

ブラクラ〚電算〛＝ブラウザー・クラッシャー.

「ブラザーズ・グリム」〚映画〛The Brothers Grimm.

「ブラザーフッド」〚映画〛Tae Guk Gi;〚英語タイトル〛

The Brotherhood of War.
「ブラザー・ベア」〔アニメ映画〕Brother Bear.
ぶらさがりかいけん[インタビュー]【ぶら下がり会見[-]】a walking interview《with…》.
ぶらさがりしゅざい【ぶら下がり取材】an on-the-move interview《with…》.
プラジェラート〔イタリア北西部,ピエモンテ州の町〕Pragelato.
ブラシノライド〔生化〕〔植物ホルモンの一種〕brassinolide.
ブラジャー ▭▷ 寄せて上げるブラジャー a push-up bra.
ブラジルちどめぐさ【-血止め草】〔植〕〔南アメリカ原産のセリ科の多年草〕a floating (marsh) pennywort; a water pennywort; *Hydrocotyle ranunculoides*.
ブラシレス・モーター〔電・機〕a brushless motor.
ブラス Brass, Tinto (1933- ; イタリアの映画監督).
プラス[1] ▭▷ プラス材料 a plus. ◐ 昨今の円安は日本の輸出にとって大きなプラスとなっている。The recent fall in the yen is「a plus [good news] for Japanese exports.」Japanese exports will benefit from the recent fall in the yen. プラス評価 a positive evaluation. ◐ ～評価する evaluate《an applicant's job history》positively; add points《for volunteer work》.
「ブラス!」〔映画〕Brassed Off.
プラスチック ▭▷ グリーン・プラスチック a "green" plastic; 〔生分解性プラスチック〕(a) biodegradable plastic. 植物系プラスチック plant-derived plastics. ▭▷ プラスチック・エレクトロニクス〔導電性高分子を扱うエレクトロニクス〕plastic(s) electronics. プラスチック磁石 a plastic magnet.
プラストミック〖解〗〔プラスティネーション〕plastination. ▭▷ プラストミック標本 a plastinated specimen.
プラズマ ▭▷ プラズマアドレス液晶 plasma-addressed liquid crystal (略: PALC). プラズマ・ガス (a) plasma gas. プラズマ・テレビ a plasma TV. プラズマ・パネル a plasma display panel (略: PDP). プラズマ溶接 plasma welding.
プラスミノ(ー)ゲン ▭▷ プラスミノ(ー)ゲン・アクチベーター・インヒビター 1〔血栓の溶解を阻害する物質〕plasminogen activator inhibitor-1 (略: PAI-1). 組織プラスミノ(ー)ゲン活性化因子 a tissue plasminogen activator (略: t-PA).
プラセンタ ▭▷ プラセンタ注射 (a) placenta(l) injection.
プラダー・ウィリーしょうこうぐん【-症候群】〔医〕〔遺伝子病の1つ〕Prader-Willi syndrome (略: PWS).
プラタイア〔ギリシャの古代都市〕Plataea.
プラタイアのたたかい【-の戦い】〔479 BCにペルシャ戦争でギリシャ連合軍がペルシャ軍を破った戦い〕the Battle of Plataea.
「プラダを着た悪魔」〔映画〕The Devil Wears Prada.
プラチナ ▭▷ プラチナ・チケット〔人気沸騰のため入手がきわめて困難な入場券〕a「hard-to-find [hard-to-get]」ticket.
プラチナこがね【-黄金】〔昆〕〔金属光沢のあるコガネムシ科の昆虫の総称〕a golden beetle; *Plusiotis batesi*, *Plusiotis gloriosa*, *Plusiotis optima*, *Plusiotis chrysargirea* など.
プラチュアップ・キリ・カ(ー)ン〔タイ中南部の県; その県都〕Prachuap Khiri Khan.
プラチンブリ〔タイ中部の県; その県都〕Prachinburi.
ふらつき 1〖医〗instability; giddiness; unsteadiness; being [feeling] unsteady on one's feet;《口》(get, have) the staggers.
2〖自動車〗〔車体の〕wander; wandering;〔蛇行運転〕erratic driving; weaving. ◐ この車は高速走行中の～が大きい。This car wanders a lot during high-speed driving. ◐ 彼は～運転で停止させられた。He was stopped by a patrol car for erratic driving.
ブラック[1] ▭▷ ブラック情報〔融資返済延滞・破産・失踪など個人信用に関する事故情報〕negative credit information.〔⇨ホワイト情報 (⇨ホワイト[1])〕
フラッグシップ ▭▷ フラッグシップ・ショップ〔旗艦店〕a flagship「store [shop]. フラッグシップ・モデル[機]〔企業の代表的製品〕a flagship model.
フラッグスタッフ〔米国アリゾナ州中部の都市〕Flagstaff.
ブラックタイガー〔動〕〔クルマエビの近縁種〕a (black, giant) tiger「shrimp [prawn]; *Penaeus monodon*.
「ブラック・ダイヤモンド」〔映画〕Cradle 2 the Grave.
「ブラックホーク・ダウン」〔映画〕Black Hawk Down.
ブラック・ホール ▭▷ 大質量ブラックホール a massive black hole (略: MBH). 中質量ブラックホール an intermediate-mass black hole (略: IMBH). 超大質量ブラックホール a supermassive black hole (略: SMBH).
ブラック・ボックス ▭▷ ブラック・ボックス化〔知識や技術などを外部に公開しないこと〕implementation of "black box" confidentiality; prevention of the disclosure of proprietary information.
ブラッザ・モンキー〔動〕〔オナガザル科のサル〕a De Brazza's monkey; *Cercopithecus neglectus*.
フラッシュ・メモリー ▭▷ データ格納型フラッシュメモリー data storage(-type) flash memory.
フラッシュ・モブ〔インターネットによる呼びかけに応じて公共の場に突然集合し, あらかじめ申し合わせた行動をとったあと即座に解散する不特定多数の人間〕a flash mob;〔その行為〕flash mobbing.
ブラッティ Blatty, William Peter (1928- ; 米国の小説家・脚本家・映画監督).
フラット ▭▷ フラット・シート〔背を倒すと平らになる座席〕a flat reclining seat; a lie-flat seat. ◐ フル～シート a「full [180-degree] lie-flat [reclining] seat.
ブラット Bratt, Benjamin (1963- ; 米国の映画俳優).
プラット Platt, Oliver (1960- ; 米国の映画俳優).
プラット・アンド・ホイットニー〔米国の航空機エンジンメーカー〕Pratt & Whitney (略: P&W).
フラットか【-化】〔平らにすること〕flattening; leveling; streamlining;〔屋内外の段差の除去〕removal of steps; replacement of steps《with「ramps [level access routes]》;〔格差をなくして公平な状態にすること; 機会の均等化〕leveling; flattening; equalization;〔組織などの〕flattening. ◐ テレビ(画面)の～は「switch [transition] to flat-screen televisions / 税率の～ a flattening [a leveling, an equalization] of tax rates / 組織の～ organizational flattening; the flattening of an organization.
フラットコーテッド・レトリ(ー)バー〔犬〕a flat-coated retriever.
ブラッド・パッチ〖医〗〔硬膜外自家血注入法〕an epidural blood patch (略: EBP).
ブラッドフィールドすいせい【-彗星】〔天〕Comet Bradfield.
ブラッドフィン・テトラ〔魚〕a bloodfin tetra; *Aphyocharax anisitsi*.
プラットフォーマー〔ハードウェア製造元〕a platformer.
プラットフォーム ▭▷ プラットフォーム・ソフト〔電算〕〔基盤となるソフト〕platform software.
フラットランド〔平らな場所で競うモトクロス用自転車またはスケートボードの曲乗り競技〕flatland.
「ブラッド・ワーク」〔映画〕Blood Work.
プラティニ Platini, Michel (1955- ; フランスのサッカー選手).
フラトコフ Fradkov, Mikhail E(fimovich) (1950- ; ロシアの政治家; 首相〔2004-07〕).
フラナリー Flanery, Sean Patrick (1965- ; 米国の映画俳優).
プラネトイド〖天〗〔小惑星〕a planetoid.
プラノ〔米国テキサス州北東部の都市〕Plano.
フラノクマリン〖化〗〔グレープフルーツに含まれる誘導体; 消化管内の薬剤の代謝を阻害する物質〕furanocoumarin.
フラノン〖化〗furanone.
ブラハラ〖<「ブラッドタイプ(血液型)」+「ハラスメント」〗discriminating against people on the basis of their blood

プラばん

**プラばん**【-板】a plastic board.
**フラバンジェノール**〘商標・化〙〔松樹皮ポリフェノール〕Flavangenol.
**フラビウイルス**〘医〙〔フラビウイルス科のウイルスの総称〕a flavivirus. ► フラビウイルス科 Flaviviridae.
**ブラヒミ** Brahimi, Lakhdar (1934–  ；アルジェリア出身の国連事務官).
**ぶらぶらやまい**【ぶらぶら病】a long-term malaise of uncertain origin; chronic ill health.
**プラマー** Plummer, Christopher (1927–  ；カナダ生まれの俳優; 本名 Arthur Christopher Orme Plummer).
**フラメンコ** ► フラメンコ・カスタネット flamenco castanets.
**フラワー** ► フラワー・チルドレン〔反戦の象徴として花を身に着けていた1960-70年代のヒッピーたち〕flower children (*sing.* flower child). フラワー・ホール〘服飾〙〔背広の襟(えり)に開けてある穴; 本来花を一輪挿した〕a boutonniere hole; a lapel buttonhole.
**ブランク** ► ブランク・メール = 空メール (⇨から¹).
**ブラン・クジュレン**〔インドネシア, アチェ州, ガヨ・ルス県の県都〕Blang Keujeren; Blangkeujeren.
**フランク・ミュラー**〘商標〙〔スイス製の腕時計〕Franck Muller.
**フランクリン** Franklin, Carl (1949–  ；米国の映画監督).
**プランゲぶんこ**【-文庫】〔第2次大戦後の占領期の日本語資料〕the Gordon W. Prange Collection.
**フランコ** Franco, Jorge (1962–  ；コロンビアの作家).
**プラン・コロンビア**〔コロンビア麻薬撲滅対策への援助計画〕Plan Colombia.
**ブランシェット** Blanchett, Cate (1969–  ；オーストラリア生まれの映画女優).
**フランス¹** ► フランス国家最優秀職人 a *Meilleur Ouvrier de France* (=Best Craftsman of France) 《pl. *Meilleurs Ouvriers de France*》 (略: MOF).
**フランスがも**【-鴨】(a) Barbary duck.
**フランスこうくうちゅうこうぎょうかい**【-航空宇宙工業会】the French Aerospace Industries Association (略: GIFAS). ► GIFAS は *Groupement des Industries Françaises Aéronautiques et Spatiales* の略.
**フランスこくえいこくさいほうそう**【-国営国際放送】Radio France Internationale (略: RFI).
**フランスこくりつうちゅうけんきゅうセンター**【-国立宇宙研究-】the Centre National d'Etudes Spatiales (略: CNES).
**フランス・ソワール**〔フランスの大衆紙〕France-Soir.
**フランスでんりょくこうしゃ**【-電力公社】Electricité de France (略: EDF).
**ブランチ・デュボア**〔テネシー・ウィリアムズ作の戯曲『欲望という名の電車』の女主人公〕Blanche DuBois.
**ブランディング**〘広告〙branding.
**ブランド¹** ► 企業ブランド a corporate brand. ► ブランド管理〘広告〙brand management. ブランド競争力 brand competitiveness. ブランド化粧品 brand-name cosmetics. ブランド財布 a designer wallet. ブランドショップ[店] a「brand-name [designer] goods store. ブランド信仰 (a)「(blind) faith in [(an) obsession with] name brands [brand names]. ブランド時計[ウォッチ] a designer (wrist)watch. ブランドバッグ a designer (hand)bag. ブランド・パワー[力] brand「power [strength]. ブランド服 designer clothes.
**ブラントびょう**【-病】〘医〙Blount('s) disease.
**ブランピディ**〔インドネシア, アチェ州, 西南アチェ県の県都〕Blangpidie.
**フリアーズ** Frears, Stephen (1941–  ；英国生まれの映画監督).
**プリア・カ(ー)ン**〔カンボジア中部の遺跡〕Preah Khan.
**フリー** ► フリー・アクセス・フロア〔床下の空間に電気・電話・コンピューターの配線をめぐらし, どこからでも自由にコンセントを取ることができるように工夫された床〕an access floor (system). フリー・アドレス・オフィス〔自分専用の机がなく, あいている机を自由に利用する方式のオフィス〕a free-address office; a nonterritorial office. フリー(の)演技〘スポーツ〙〔体操・フィギュアスケートなどの〕a free-style performance. フリー・カメラマン a freelance photographer. フリー記者 a freelance reporter. フリー競技〘スキー〙〔クロスカントリーの〕a freestyle race. フリーゲージ・トレイン〘鉄道〙〔レール幅が異なる路線を走る電車; 軌間可変列車〕a free-gauge train. フリー・ジャーナリスト a freelance journalist. フリー・ステート = じゆうしゅう. フリー走行〔自動車レース〕free practice. フリー走法〘スキー〙freestyle skiing. フリー・マガジン〔無料配付雑誌〕a free magazine. フリー・ルーティン〔シンクロナイズド・スイミングの〕a free routine.
**「フリー・ウィリー」**〔映画〕Free Willy. ► 続編は「フリー・ウィリー2」(Free Willy 2: The Adventure Home), 「フリー・ウィリー3」(Free Willy 3: The Rescue).
**プリーストリー** Priestley, Jason (1969–  ；カナダ生まれの俳優; 本名 Jason Bradford Priestley).
**フリーター** ► 年長フリーター〔25歳以上のフリーター〕workers of 25 years old and over with only part-time jobs.
**フリーダム・タワー**〔9.11のテロで破壊された世界貿易センター跡地に建築予定の高層ビル〕the Freedom Tower.
**フリーダムハウス**〔国際的に活動する人権尊重の促進をめざす NGO〕the Freedom House.
**プリーツ** ► (すそ)消しプリーツ〘服飾〙〔プリーツスカートの下半分または裾のプリーツを消したもの〕vanishing pleats.
**フリート²**〘保険〙► フリート契約〔自動車保険で契約者が10台以上の車を所有する場合の契約〕a fleet contract.
**ブリーフィング** ► ブリーフィング・ルーム〔事前説明などを行う部屋〕a briefing room.
**フリーモント**〔カリフォルニア州西部の市〕Fremont.
**ブリーラム**〔タイ東北部の県; 同県の県都〕Buriram.
**ふりおくれ**【振り遅れ】〘野球・ゴルフ〙a late swing. ► ~で ファウルになる hit a foul on a late swing; swing late and hit a foul.
**ふりおくれる**【振り遅れる】〘野球・ゴルフ〙swing late. ► 速球に振り遅れた. He swung late on the fastball.
**プリオンせんもんちょうさかい**【-専門調査会】〔内閣府, 食品安全委員会〕the Prions Expert Committee; the Special Committee on Prions.
**ふりかえ**【振替】► 振替授業 a replacement「class [lecture] (on a different day).
**プリカほう**【-法】〘法〙= プリペイドカード(きせい)ほう.
**ブリガム・ヤングだいがく**【-大学】〔米国ユタ州にある私立大学〕Brigham Young University (略: BYU).
**ブリガンガがわ**【-川】〔バングラデシュ, ダッカ近郊の川〕the Buriganga River; the Buringanga.
**フリクション** ► フリクション・モディファイヤー〔摩擦調整剤〕a friction modifier.
**プリクトラン**〘商標・農薬〙Plictran. ► シヘキサチン (cyhexatin) の商品名.
**プリクラ** ► プリクラ切手 = 写真付き切手 (⇨しゃしん¹).
**プリクラッシュ・セーフティー**〘自動車〙〔衝突予防安全技術〕precrash「sensing [safety] (systems); an anticipatory safety system.
**プリケー**〔プリペイド(式)携帯電話〕a prepaid「mobile [cellular] phone.
**ふりこ**【振り子】► 回転振り子 a rotary pendulum.
**ふりこみ**【振り込み】► 振り込み口座 a direct deposit account.
**ふりこめさぎ**【振り込め詐欺】〔電話や手紙でだましたり恐喝したりして現金を銀行口座に振り込ませようとする詐欺; オレオレ詐欺など〕a fraud in which the victim is「deceived [threatened] into remitting money to a bank account; a remittance scam.
**ふりさばく**【振り捌く】shake open. ► 洗濯が終わったら振りさばいてしわを伸ばしましょう. When you've finished

the washing,「shake it open [give it a (good) shake] and get rid of the wrinkles.
「ブリジット・ジョーンズの日記」〔映画〕Bridget Jones's Diary.
「ブリジット・ジョーンズの日記 きれそうなわたしの12か月」〔映画〕Bridget Jones: The Edge of Reason.
「プリズナー No. 6」〔元外務省職員が謎の村に閉じこめられ、英国の不条理劇風 TV ドラマ〕The Prisoner.
プリズム 〖プリズム眼鏡〗《眼科》〔斜視などの矯正用〕prism(atic) 〖glasses [spectacles]〗.
プリズン・フェローシップ・インターナショナル〔犯罪者の更生支援、再犯防止、被害者と家族の救援を目的とする国際的組織〕Prison Fellowship International (略: PFI).
ふりそでやなぎ【振袖柳】〖植〗〔ヤナギ科の落葉低木〕Salix × leucopithecia.
ブリックス〔新たな経済成長国としてのブラジル・ロシア・インド・中国〕the BRICs. ► BRIC is Brazil, Russia, India, China をさす.
ブリック・テスト《医》〔アレルギーテストの一種〕a (skin) prick test; (skin) prick testing.
ブリッジス 1 Bridges, Beau (1941- ; 米国の映画俳優; 3の子; 本名 Lloyd Vernet Bridges III).
2 Bridges, Jeff (1949- ; 米国の映画俳優; 3の子; 本名 Jeffrey Leon Bridges).
3 Bridges, Lloyd (1913-98; 米国の映画俳優; 1と2の父; 本名 Lloyd Vernet Bridges, Jr.).
ブリッスルコーン・パイン〖植〗〔マツ科の中高木; 米国西部原産〕a bristlecone pine; *Pinus longaeva*; *Pinus aristata*.
ブリッピング〔エンジンの空吹かし〕blipping.
「プリティ・プリンセス」〔映画〕The Princess Diaries.
「プリティ・リーグ」〔映画〕A League of Their Own.
プリナップ ＝プレナップ.
ブリニ〔< Russ.〕〖ロシア料理〗〔そば粉のパンケーキ〕blini; bliny; blinis.
ブリヌイ〖ロシア料理〗＝ブリニ.
ふりはば【振り幅】〔揺れ動きの幅〕the length of 《a pendulum's》 swing. / 〔振り子の〕 the length of a pendulum's swing. ◆〜が大きい vary widely / 価格変動の〜が大きい株は要注意だ. Caution is necessary with stocks「that vary widely in price [with wide price swings]. / あの選手は出来・不出来の〜が大きい. There's little difference between that player's best and worst performance. ◆〜の大きい相場が続いている. Large swings in stock prices are continuing. / 僕は彼女の感情の〜の大きさに翻弄されていた. I was at the mercy of her wildly swinging emotions. / その映画はコメディーといって、泣けて笑える〜の大きい映画だった. The movie may be a comedy, but it had a wide emotional range: you laugh, you cry. ◆ 速い球を打つにはバットを短く持って〜を小さくするのがコツだ. The key to hitting fast pitches is to choke up on the bat and shorten your swing.
プリブミ〔インドネシアの原住民〕a pribumi.
プリペイド〔前払いの〕prepaid. ◆ プリペイド・カード a prepaid card. プリペイド〔式〕携帯電話 a prepaid cellular phone.
プリペイドカード（きせい）ほう【―規制法】《法》〔前払式証票の規制等に関する法律〕the Prepaid Card Law.
フリマ ◆ フリマボックス〖商標〗〔常設のレンタルスペースで、収集品や手作り作品を並べて売る、透明アクリル製のロッカー式商品展示ケース〕a rental display box.
プリムラ・ポリアンサ〖植〗〔サクラソウ科の多年草〕*Primula polyantha*.
ブリヤ・カ（―）ン ＝ブリア・カ（―）ン.
ブリュッセル・グリフォン〔犬〕a Brussels griffon;〔異称〕a Belgian griffon.
ふりょうさいけん【不良債権】◆ 不良債権処理費 the 'expense [cost] of 「covering [making up, writing off] bad debt. 不良債権比率 a nonperforming loan ratio; a bad 「debt [loan] ratio.
ぶりょく【武力】◆ 武力攻撃事態 an armed attack situation. ◆ 〜攻撃事態が発生した場合、何をなすべきかを決めておかねばならぬ. We must decide what to do in case of an armed attack. 武力弾圧 an armed 「suppression [crackdown]. 武力鎮圧 armed 「subjugation [suppression]; suppression by force. ◆ プーチン政権はチェチェンの分離独立運動を〜鎮圧する方針である. The Putin regime's policy is to 「put down [suppress] the Chechen independence movement by force.
プリラム ＝ブーラム.
ふりん【不倫】◆ ダブル不倫 an (extra-marital) affair between a married man and a married woman.
ブリンクマンしすう【―指数】〔喫煙年数×1日の喫煙本数〕the 「one's] Brinkman index (略: BI).
プリンシパル・インベストメント〔自己資金投資〕a principal investment.
プリンシパルとうし【―投資】＝プリンシパル・インベストメント.
プリンズ ＝プリンゼ.
「プリンス・オブ・エジプト」〔アニメ映画〕The Prince of Egypt.
プリンゼ Prinze, Freddie Jr. (1976- ; 米国の映画俳優).
プリンター ◆ 高速プリンター a high-speed printer.
プリント ◆ アイロンプリント〔アイロンで熱を加えながら型紙の模様を布に転写する〕iron-on (transfer) printing;〔転写した模様〕an iron-on (transfer) print; an iron-on. 転写プリント〔転写紙に鏡面印刷した模様を高温プレス機で再転写する〕image transfer printing (with a high-temperature press);〔転写した模様〕an image-transfer print. ◆ プリント柄〖生地の〗a printed pattern. プリントシール a photo sticker. プリントシール機 a photo sticker machine. プリント・タイ〖服飾〗a print(ed) tie.
ぷりんぷりん〔弾力があって充実した様子〕plump; bouncy. ◆ 彼女の〜と揺れるヒップがたまらない. I just love the way her bottom jiggles. / 〜とした煮こごりが出来た. The broth has jelled nice and bouncy.
フル ◆ フル代表〖サッカー〗〔年齢制限などのない、国を代表するチーム〕a full national team;〔その選手〕a full national team player.
ふるいいれる【篩い入れる】sift 《flour》 into 《a bowl》.
フルイタフォソール〖古生物〗〔ジュラ紀の哺乳類〕*Fruitafossor windscheffeli*.
ブルー ◆ ブルー・ステーツ ＝青い州（⇨しゅう2）.
ブルー Proulx, (Edna) Annie (1935- ; 米国の作家).
ブルーウォーター・ネイビー ＝外洋［大洋］海軍（⇨かいぐん）.
ブルー・オーシャン〖経営〗〔「青い海」; 競争のない、未開拓の市場空間〕a blue ocean. ◆ ブルーオーシャン戦略 a [the] blue ocean strategy.
「ブルーサンダー」1〔映画〕Blue Thunder.
2〔米国の、ヘリコプター・アクション TV ドラマ〕Blue Thunder.
ブルーシート〖防水・防護用〗(a) blue tarpaulin; *〈口〉* (a) blue tarp.
ブルース Bluth, Don (1938- ; 米国の映画監督).
ブルースしょう【―賞】〔太平洋天文学会が天文学の発展に貢献した人に贈る賞〕the Bruce Medal.
「ブルー・ストリーク」〔映画〕Blue Streak.
フルーツ ◆ フルーツ・カービング〖料理〗〔ナイフで果物に草花・小鳥などを彫り込んで食卓を彩る芸術〕fruit carving. フルーツ牛乳 fruit-flavored milk. フルーツ酸 (a) fruit acid. フルーツ・シュガー〖果肉〗(a) fructose; (a) fruit sugar. フルーツ・ティー (a) fruit tea. フルーツ・トマト a fruit tomato;〔果肉〕suppression by force, a tomato with reduced water content, suitable for eating as fruit. フルーツ・バスケット〔鬼ごっこと席取りゲームを兼ねたもの〕《play》 fruit basket (up-

set [turnover]).
「ブルートで朝食を」〔映画〕Breakfast on Pluto.
ブルーナ Bruna, Dick (1927- ；オランダの絵本作家；ミッフィー (Miffy) というウサギのキャラクターで有名).
ブルー・バック〔映〕〔青い背景を利用した画像合成〕(a) blue「background [screen]; blue screening.
「ブルーフ・オブ・マイ・ライフ」〔映画〕Proof.
「ブルーフ・オブ・ライフ」〔映画〕Proof of Life.
ブルー・プラーク〔イギリスの保護建物章〕a Blue Plaque.
ブルーベリー〔ブルーベリー・ソース〕blueberry sauce.
ブルー・マット〔映〕blue matte.
ブルーム 1 Bloom, Claire (1931- ；英国の女優).
2 Bloom, Orlando (1977- ；英国生まれの映画俳優).
ブルー・ムーン〔ひと月のうちに満月が2回あるときの2回目の満月〕a blue moon.
ブルームバーグ〔米国の金融情報会社〕Bloomberg.
ブルーレイ・ディスク〔商標・電業〕〔青紫色のレーザーを使った次世代の光ディスク〕(a) Blu-ray Disc (略: BD). ▷ ブルーレイディスク・レコーダー a Blu-ray Disc recorder.
ブルーン〔ドライ・プルーン〕a prune.
フルオーダー(メード) 〜の custom-made; order-made; made-to-order. ▷ フルオーダー家具 custom-made furniture. フルオーダー・ドレス custom-made [order-made] dress.
フルオキセチン〔薬〕〔抗鬱剤〕fluoxetine.
フルオラスかごうぶつ【－化合物】〔化〕〔高度にフッ素で置換えられた有機物の総称〕fluorous compounds.
フルオロデオキシグルコース〔生化〕fluorodeoxyglucose (略: FDG); 2-fluoro-2-deoxy-D-glucose.
ブルガダしょうこうぐん【－症候群】〔医〕the Brugada syndrome.
フルかつよう【－活用】full [complete] use [utilization]. 〜する use 'fully [completely, to the fullest]; make full use (of…); take full advantage (of…). ▷ 彼は大学の OB 人脈を〜して現在の職を得た. He got his current job by making the most of his contacts among older alumni from his university.
プルキンエ〔プルキンエ細胞〕〔解〕a Purkinje cell.
ふるくぎ【古釘】an old [a rusty old] nail. ▷〜を踏むと治りが遅い. Your recovery is slow when you step on a rusty old nail.
フルコース・コーション〔自動車レース、オートバイレースなどで〕a full-course caution.
フル・コーラス〔一曲全部〕an entire song. ▷ 彼は「イエスタデー」を〜を歌った. He sang "Yesterday" all the way through.
ブルサット〔カンボジア西部の州；同州の州都〕Pursat.
ふるさと ▷ ふるさと創生基金〔資金〕〔旧竹下内閣の〕a "Hometown Revival" fund; funding for the "Hometown Revival" program.
フルしゅつじょう【－出場】playing [appearing in] a full [an entire, a complete] game [match]. 〜する play a 'full [entire, complete] game [match]. ▷ 先発フル出場〔サッカーなど〕playing from start to finish.
フルス〔楽器〕＝フールース.
フル・セット〔フルセット勝ち[負け]〕a full set 'win [loss]. ▷〜勝ち[負け] win [lose] (a game, a match) in full sets.
ブルセラ[1] ▷ ブルセラ・ショップ a "burusera" shop; a shop that sells underwear and uniforms of school-girls.
プルせんりゃく【－戦略】〔商〕〔消費者に直接働きかけて需要を創出する販売戦略〕a pull strategy.
ふるそうび【－装備】(a) full [complete] provision [supply, furnishing, accouterment]. 〜する ▷ 武器を〜した兵士たち soldiers fully equipped with weapons; fully armed soldiers. ▷ この車はカーナビから高級オーディオまで〜だ. This car is equipped with everything from car navigation to high-grade audio.

フルタイム ▷ フルタイムパート〔就労実態が正社員と変わらないパート労働者〕a "full-time part-timer"; an employee who works regular hours but whose working conditions are those of a part-timer as regards pay, promotion, etc.
フルタミド〔薬〕〔抗男性ホルモン剤・抗腫瘍薬〕flutamide.
フルタミナ〔インドネシアの石油・ガス公社〕Pertamina.
プルチネ(ッ)ラ〔イタリア喜劇の登場人物〕Pulcinella.
フルチョーク〔＝全絞り〔⇨しぼり〕.
ブルッキングズけんきゅうじょ【－研究所】〔米国ワシントン DC にある民間研究機関〕the Brookings Institution.
ブルックス Brooks, James L. (1940- ；米国の映画監督).
プルトニウム ▷ プルトニウム型〔核の〕a 'plutonium-based [plutonium-fueled] 'nuclear bomb'.
プルバック〔おもちゃの車を走らせるぜんまい動力；いったん後ろに引き下げて手を離すと走りだす〕a pull-back spring. ▷ プルバック・ミニカー a mini pull-back car.
フル・パワー full power; (at) full throttle. ▷ 原子炉を〜で運転中だ. The reactor is running at full power.
フルベぞく【－族】〔アフリカの半農半牧民〕the Fulbe (pl. 〜(s)).
ブルペン ▷ ブルペン入り ▷〜入りする〔投手が〕move [be sent] to the bullpen. ブルペン捕手 a bullpen catcher.
フル・ボディー〔ワインの、濃厚な味わい〕a full body. ▷ full-bodied adj.
フル・ボリューム〔音量〕(play the radio at) full volume.
ブルマスチフ〔犬〕a bullmastiff.
プルマン Pullman, Bill (1953- ；米国の映画俳優；本名 William Pullman).
フルム・ダンベール〔フランス産のチーズ〕Fourme d'Ambert (cheese).
フルメンテナンスけいやく【－契約】〔機器や装置の点検・給油・調整・修理から部品交換・機器の取替えまでを含む保守業務の契約〕a full maintenance contract. 〔⇨ピー・オー・ジーけいやく〕
「フル・モンティ」〔映画〕The Full Monty.
フルライン〔完成品までの一貫生産〕full-line 《production facilities》；〔すべての製品を取りそろえていること〕a 'complete [full] line (of products). ▷ フルライン化〔完成品までの一貫生産体制にすること〕implementation [adoption] of full-line production;〔すべての製品を取りそろえること〕provision of a 'complete [full] line. フルライン投資 full-line investment.
フル・ラインアップ a full line (of computers). ▷ 当社は大型建設機械を〜に取りそろえております. We offer a full 'line [selection] of large construction machinery.
ブルワース〔映画〕Bulworth.
ふれあい【触れ合い】▷ 触れ合い体験 a hands-on experience;〔動物園での〕a petting zoo experience.
「ブレア・ウィッチ・プロジェクト」〔映画〕The Blair Witch Project.
プレア・ヴィヒア〔カンボジア北部の州〕Preah Vihear.
プレア・シアヌーク〔カンボジア南部の都市（特別市）〕Preah Sihanouk. ► コンポン・ソム (Kompong Som), シアヌークヴィル (Sihanoukville), Preah Seihanu ともいう.
フレア・バーテンディング〔ボトルやグラスを華麗に操って客を楽しませながらカクテルを作る技〕flair bartending.
プレア・ビヒア〔＝プレア・ヴィヒア.
プレイ・ヴェン〔カンボジア南部の州；同州の州都〕Prey Veng.
ぶれいうち【無礼討ち】the killing by sword of a commoner who has offended a samurai.
フレイクス Frakes, Jonathan (1952- ；米国の映画俳優・監督).
フレイザー Fraser, Brendan (1968- ；米国の映画俳優；本名 Brendan James Fraser).
プレイステーション ▷ プレイステーション2〔商標〕

PlayStation 2〔略: PS2〕．プレイステーション・ポータブル『商標』PlayStation Portable（略: PSP）．
「**ブレイブハート**」〔映画〕Braveheart．
**ブレイ・ベン** ＝ブレイ・ヴェン．
**フレイム** Frame, Janet (1924–2004; ニュージーランドの作家）．
**プレヴァル** Préval, René Garcia (1943–　; ハイチの政治家; 大統領〔1996–2001, 2006–　〕）．
**プレー**[3]〔タイ北部の県; その県都〕Phrae．
**ブレーキ** 〇▷ ブレーキ跡 ＝ブレーキ痕．ブレーキ痕 brake [skid] marks．ブレーキ・ホース〔自動車などの〕(a) brake hose．◐ステンメッシュ・～ホース〔自動車などの〕(a) stainless steel brake hose．ブレーキ・ライニング〔機〕a brake lining．
「**ブレーキ・ダウン**」〔映画〕Breakdown．
**ブレーキング**[1]〔自動車〕〔ブレーキペダルを踏むこと〕braking．◐～が遅れたためカーブで曲がりきれなかった． He braked too late and couldn't make the curve．〇▷ ブレーキング・ポイント〔自動車レースで，ブレーキペダルを踏むタイミングの地点〕a braking point．
**ブレーキング**[2]〔ストリートダンスの一ジャンル; 1980年代中期より流行〕breaking; break dancing．
**フレーバー・ティー**〔風味を付けた紅茶〕flavored tea．
**フレーミング**[1] 〇▷ フレーミング効果〔社会〕a [the] framing effect．
**フレームエンゼル（フィッシュ）**〔魚〕〔熱帯魚の一種〕a flame angel; *Centropyge loricula*．
**プレオーダー**〔一般発売に先んじて受け付ける予約〕a preorder; an advance order．
**プレカット** 〇▷ プレカット工場〔建築木材の〕a cutting mill; a 「mill [factory] where timber is sawn up for later assembly at a construction site．
**プレカリアート**〔不安定階級〕the "precariat."▶ *pre-cari*ous と proletar*iat* の合成語．
**フレキシブル** 〇▷ フレキシブル基板〔集積回路の〕a flexible circuit．フレキシブル・スクール a school with a flexible curriculum; a free school; a flexible school．フレキシブルプリント基板〔集積回路の〕a flexible printed circuit（略: FPC）．
**プレキャスト・ブロック**〔建〕〔コンクリートブロック〕a precast concrete block．
**プレクリアランス**〔出発地空港で到着国の係官が行う事前入国審査〕preclearance．
**プレザントン**〔カリフォルニア州西部の都市〕Pleasanton．
**プレシーズン・ゲーム**〔野球など〕〔開幕前の公式戦〕a preseason game．
**プレジスタ**〔商標・薬〕〔エイズ治療薬〕Prezista．▶ 成分名はダルナビル．
**プレジデント** 〇▷ プレジデント・ジュリー〔競技〕a jury president．
**プレシン** Blethyn, Brenda (1946–　; 英国の映画女優）．
**プレス** 〇▷ プレス成形 press「forming [molding]．
**プレストン** Preston, Kelly (1962–　; 米国の映画女優; 本名 Kelly Smith）．
**プレセール**〔一般発売に先んじて行う販売〕a presale; an advance sale．
**プレセツクしゃじょう**〔-射場〕〔ロシアのロケット発射場〕the Plesetsk Space Center; the Plesetsk Cosmodrome．
**プレセニリン**〔生化〕〔たんぱく質〕家族性アルツハイマー症原因遺伝子〕presenilin（略: PS）．
**プレゼンス** 〇▷ 軍事プレゼンス〔軍事展開〕⇨ぐんじ．
**プレゼンテーション** 〇▷ プレゼンテーション・ソフト〔電算〕presentation software．プレゼンテーション能力〔自分の考えをまとめて表現する能力〕presentation ability．
**フレダー** Fleder, Gary (1965–　; 米国の映画監督）．
**プレたいかい**〔-大会〕a preliminary「meet(ing) [contest, tournament]；〔オリンピックの〕the Pre-Olympics; the Pre-Olympic Games．

「**プレタポルテ**」〔映画〕Ready to Wear；〔原題〕Pret-a-Porter．
**ブレッカー** Brecker, Michael (1949–2007; 米国のテナーサックス奏者）．
**フレックス・カー** ＝フレックスねんりょうしゃ．
**フレックスしゃ**〔-車〕〔自動車〕＝フレックスねんりょうしゃ．
**フレックスねんりょうしゃ**〔-燃料車〕〔自動車〕〔アルコールとガソリンの併用車〕a flex-fuel vehicle（略: FFV）; a flex-fuel car．
**フレッド・ペリー**〔商標〕〔月桂樹のマークの英国ブランド衣料品〕Fred Perry．
「**ブレッド＆ローズ**」〔映画〕Bread and Roses．
**ブレディニン**〔商標・薬〕〔免疫抑制剤〕Bredinin．
**フレディマック**〔米国の連邦住宅貸付担保公社の通称〕Freddie Mac．
**プレデター**〔米軍〕〔無人偵察機〕a Predator．
**プレドニン**〔商標・薬〕〔合成副腎皮質ホルモン剤〕Predonin．
**プレナップ**〔結婚後の双方の義務・資産・離婚条件などに関する結婚前の取り決め〕〔口〕a prenup; a prenuptial agreement．
**プレバイオティクス**〔腸内有用菌の増殖を助け，健康増進に役立つ物質〕prebiotics．
**プレバル** ＝プレヴァル．
**プレフィルド**〔医〕〔あらかじめ注射器内に入れてある〕pre-filled《diluent》．〇▷ プレフィルド・シリンジ a prefilled syringe．◐～シリンジ製剤 a prefilled syringe product．
**ブレマー** Bremer, L. Paul (1941–　; 米国の外交官）．
**プレミアム** 〇▷ プレミアム価格 a premium price．プレミアム・ビール〔普通品より高品質・高価格のビール〕(a) premium beer．
**プレミア・リーグ**〔英国サッカーの上位20チームによるリーグ戦〕the Premier League．
**プレミックス**〔前もって混ぜ合わせたもの〕(a) premix．
**フレミング** Flemyng, Jason (1966–　; 英国生まれの映画俳優）．
**プレム** Prem Tinsulanonda (1920–　; タイの政治家; 首相〔1980–88〕）．
**フレモント** ＝フリーモント．
**ふれんぞく**〔不連続〕〇▷ 不連続性 discontinuity．
**ブレンダー** 〇▷ ブレンダー食 ＝ミキサー食（⇨ミキサー）．
**フレンチ** 〇▷ フレンチ・パラドックス〔ワインを多く飲むフランス人に心臓病が少ないという不思議〕the French paradox．
**フレンチ・オープン**〔テニス〕＝ぜんふつオープン．
**フレンチ・クオーター**〔米国ニューオーリンズの歴史的風致保存地区〕the French Quarter．
**フレンチ・ブルドッグ**〔犬〕a French bulldog．
**ブレンナー** Brenner, Sydney (1927–　; 英国の分子生物学者）．
**ふろ**[1]〔風呂〕〇▷ 男〔女〕風呂 the 「men's [women's]」bath．牛乳風呂 a milk bath．自家風呂 a bathroom in one's house．檜風呂 a Japanese cypress bath(tub)．蜜柑風呂 a mandarin orange bath．〇▷ 風呂嫌い hating to take a bath；〔人〕a person who hates to take a bath．風呂好き liking to take a bath；〔人〕a person who likes to take a bath．◐彼は無類の～好きで，1日3回入る日もある． He's crazy about baths, sometimes he'll take three in one day．
**プロ** 〇▷ プロ・スキーヤー a professional skier．プロ・スケーター a professional skater; a pro skater．プロ・ダイバー a professional diver．プロ・ボウラー a professional bowler; a pro bowler．
**フロア** 〇▷ フロア・ホッケー〔スポーツ〕〔体育館などの床の上で行うアイスホッケーに似た競技〕floor hockey．
**プロアマ**〔プロフェッショナルとアマチュア〕pro-am《tournament》．
**プロアントシアニジン**〔化〕proanthocyanidin．
**プロイスラー** Preussler, Otfried (1923–　; ドイツの児童文学作家）．

プロヴァンス・アルプ・コートダジュール〔フランス南東部の地域〕Provence-Alpes-Côte d'Azur.
プロヴィンスタウン〔米国マサチューセッツ州南東部、ケープ・コッド先端の町〕Provincetown.
フロー ▫▫ フロー型経営《経営》flow-type「business operations [management].
ブローカ ▫▫ ブローカ野, ブローカ中枢《解》〔大脳の〕Broca's area.
「ブロークダウン・パレス」〔映画〕Brokedown Palace.
「ブロークバック・マウンテン」〔映画〕Brokeback Mountain.
「ブロークン・アロー」〔映画〕Broken Arrow.
ブロークン・ウインドウ(ズ)りろん〔-理論〕=われまどりろん.
ブローディ Prodi, Romano (1939- ；イタリアの政治家；首相〔1996-98, 2006-08〕).
ブロードこうげき〔-攻撃〕《バレーボール》〔移動攻撃〕a moving attack.
ブロードシート〔英国の、大判の(高級)新聞〕a broadsheet. ▶ タブロイド紙に対して用いる.
「フローレス」〔映画〕Flawless.
ブロガー〔ウェブログの主催者〕a blogger；〔ウェブログ作成用ソフト〕a blogger.
プロキシー・ファイト《証券》〔株主総会などの委任状争奪戦〕a proxy fight.
ブログ =ウェブログ. ▫▫ ブログ炎上〔ブログの内容に対する批判の書き込みが集中すること〕(blog) flaming; flaming on a blog.
プロクシー・ファイト《証券》=プロキシー・ファイト.
フロクマリン《化》furocoumarin.[=フラノクマリン]
プログラフ《商標・薬》《免疫抑制剤》Prograf.
プロゲリア《医》=プロジェリア.
プロジェクト ▫▫ プロジェクト・アドベンチャー《商標》〔体験学習プログラムの1つ〕Project Adventure.
プロジェリア《医》〔早老(症)〕progeria;〔Hutchinson-Gilford progeria syndrome〕（略：HGPS）.
ブロスナン Brosnan, Pierce (1953- ；アイルランド生まれの映画俳優；本名 Brendan Brosnan).
「プロ・スパイ」⇨「スパイのライセンス」.
プロセキソール《商標・薬》〔女性ホルモン剤・抗腫瘍薬〕Prosexol.
プロダクション ▫▫ プロダクション・カー "a production car. ♦ ~カー世界ラリー選手権 the Production Car World Rally Championship（略：PCWRC）.
プロダクト ▫▫ プロダクト・アウト《経営》〔製品指向型の〕product-oriented《view》; product-out《approach》. プロダクト・デザイナー〔工業製品のデザイナー〕a product designer. プロダクト・ライフサイクル・マネージメント〔製品ライフサイクル管理〕product lifecycle management（略：PLM）.
ブロチゾラム《薬》〔催眠・鎮静剤〕brotizolam.
ブロッカー《球技》a blocker.
ブロッガー =ブロガー.
フロッグ【FROG】《軍》〔旧ソ連製の無誘導ロケットに対するNATOの呼称〕a FROG. ▶ Free Rocket Over Groundの略.
ブロック Bullock, Sandra (1964- ；米国の映画女優；本名 Sandra Annette Bullock).
ブロック[1] ▫▫ 視力障害者誘導用ブロック raised paving blocks for the visually impaired. ▫▫ ブロック選択制〔公立学校の〕a system in which students may seek to enroll in any school in their designated subdistrict.
ブロック[2] ▫▫ 通貨ブロック a currency block.
フロックハート Flockhart, Calista (1964- ；米国の女優).
ブロックバスター[2]〔米国のビデオレンタル・チェーン〕Blockbuster.
プロップ[2]〔映画・演劇用の小道具〕a prop.
プロテアーゼ ▫▫ プロテアーゼ複合体 a protease complex.
プロテアス〔2004年アテネ・パラリンピックのマスコット名〕Proteas.
ブロディ〔ウクライナ西部の都市〕Brody.
プロテオグリカン《生化》proteoglycan.
プロテクト ▫▫ プロテクト選手《野球》a protected player. プロテクト枠《野球》a protected player「list [roster].
プロデュース ▫▫ プロデュース料 a production fee.
ブロデリック Broderick, Matthew (1962- ；米国の映画俳優).
プロトコル ▫▫ インターネット・プロトコル ▫▫ インターネット〜バージョン・シックス the Internet protocol version 6; IPv6.
フロド・バギンズ〔J・R・R・トールキン原作の『指輪物語』の主人公の若者〕Frodo Baggins.
プロトピックなんこう〔-軟膏〕《商標・薬》〔免疫抑制剤タクロリムスの外用薬〕Protopic Ointment.
プロバイオティクス《菌》〔生菌を利用して腸内バランスを改善して抵抗力や免疫力をつける方法；それに用いられる菌〕probiotics.
プロバイダーせきにんほう〔-責任法〕《法》the Internet Service Provider Responsibility Law. ▶ 正式名称は、「特定電気通信役務提供者の損害賠償責任の制限及び発信者情報の開示に関する法律」(the Law Providing for the Disclosure of Information on the Sender and Limitations of Damages for Providers of Specified Electronic Communications).
プロビンスタウン =プロヴィンスタウン.
プロフ《電算》〔プロフィールの略〕a profile；〔インターネット上の自己紹介サイト〕a profile site.
プロフィットロール《菓子》〔シュー皮をチョコレートで覆ったもの〕a profiterole.
プロフェッショナル・エンジニア〔米国の技術士資格〕a professional engineer（略：PE）.
ブロブディンナグ〔スウィフト作の『ガリヴァー旅行記』に出てくる巨人国〕Brobdingnag. ▷ Brobdingnagian adj.
ブロプレス《商標・薬》〔高血圧症治療薬〕Blopress.
プロペラ・シャフト《機》a propeller shaft.
プロポフォール《薬》〔麻酔・鎮静薬〕propofol.
プロポリス〔ミツバチの巣から採れる樹脂状物質；健康食品〕propolis.
プロホルモン《生化》〔ホルモンの前駆体〕a prohormone.
プロマック《商標・薬》〔胃潰瘍治療薬〕Promac.
プロミス・キーパーズ〔米国で創設された男性のみのキリスト教組織〕Promise Keepers.
「フロム・ダスク・ティル・ドーン」〔映画〕From Dusk Till Dawn.
「フロム・ヘル」〔映画〕From Hell.
ブロメリン《生化》bromelin.
ブロモクリプチン《薬》=メシル酸ブロモクリプチン（⇨メシルさん）.
ブロモさん〔-山〕〔インドネシア、ジャワ島の火山〕Mount Bromo.
プロやきゅう〔-野球〕 ▫▫ プロ野球評論家 a (professional) baseball commentator.
プロやきゅうオーナーかいぎ〔-野球-会議〕a meeting of professional baseball club owners.
プロラクチノーマ《医》〔プロラクチン産生下垂体腺腫〕prolactinoma.
フロリダ・パンサー《動》a Florida panther; Puma concolor coryi.
プロレス ▫▫ プロレス技 a professional wrestling move. ♦ ~技をかける make a professional wrestling move (on sb); tackle sb with a professional wrestling move.
「ブロンコ」〔南北戦争で孤児となった若者が悪と闘うTV西部劇〕Bronco.
フロントフリップ〔フリースタイルスキーで〕a forward flip. ♦ ~を決める do [complete, turn] a (successful) forward flip.

フロント・プロジェクション 1〚映〛〔俳優の背後に置いたスクリーンに前方から風景などの映像を投射する技法〕front projection. 2〔ホームシアターで，スクリーンに前方から映像を投射する方式〕front projection. ◘▶ フロント・プロジェクション・エフェクト〚映〛a front-projection effect. フロント・プロジェクションテレビ〔前面投射型テレビ〕a front-projection 'television [TV].

フンイエン〔ベトナム北部ホン河デルタ地帯の省；その省都〕Hung Yen.

ぶんえん²【分煙】 ◘▶ 完全分煙 complete [total] separation of smoking and nonsmoking areas. 不完全分煙 semi-separation [incomplete separation] of smoking and nonsmoking areas. ◘ この店は不完全~だ。The place doesn't separate smoking and nonsmoking areas 'completely [thoroughly, properly]. ◘▶ 分煙化 ◘ ~化を推進する promote the 'division [separation] of 《public spaces》 into smoking and nonsmoking areas.

ふんか²【噴火】 ◘▶ 山頂噴火 a summit eruption. ストロンボリ式噴火 a Strombolian eruption. ハワイ式噴火 a Hawaiian eruption. ブルカノ式噴火 a Vulcanian eruption. 割れ目噴火 a fissure eruption.

ぶんか¹【分化】 ◘▶ 高[低]分化〔がんなどの〕high [low] differentiation. ◘ 高~がん〔'well [highly] differentiated 'carcinoma [cancer] / 低~がん (a) poorly differentiated 'carcinoma [cancer]. ◘▶ 分化能〚生物〕〔幹細胞などの〕the ability to differentiate; differentiation ability. ◘ 再~能 the ability to redifferentiate; redifferentiation ability.

ぶんか²【文化】 ◘▶ 文化協力 cultural cooperation. 文化交流特使 a cultural exchange ambassador. 文化コンテンツ an item with cultural content; a cultural item. 文化財団 a cultural foundation. 文化産業 a [the] culture industry. 文化商品 a cultural commodity; cultural merchandise. 文化侵略 (a) cultural invasion. 文化創造国家 a culture-creating country. 文化干し〔冷風乾燥機を使用して作った魚の干物〕fish dried with cool-air fans. 文化力 cultural power; the power of a culture.

ふんがい²【糞害】 problems with [damage from] 《bird》 droppings.

ぶんかい³【分解】 ◘▶ 分解性ポリマー a degradable polymer. 分解保管〔銃の〕disassembly and storage.

ぶんかいさんこくさいきょうりょくセンター【文化遺産国際協力~】the Japan Center for International Cooperation in Conservation.

ぶんかいさんほごこくさいきょうりょくすいしんほう【文化遺産保護国際協力推進法】〚法〛the Law for the Promotion of International Cooperation on Protection of Cultural Heritage Abroad.

ぶんがく【文学】 ◘▶ 文学碑 a stone monument inscribed with a text from literature; a literary monument.

ぶんかざい【文化財】 ◘▶ 重要無形民俗文化財 an important intangible folk-culture asset; a folk [an ethnic] tradition or activity registered as being an important cultural treasure. 重要有形民俗文化財 an important tangible folk-culture asset; a building or structure registered as being an important ethnic cultural treasure. 無形民俗文化財 a folk [an ethnic] tradition or activity registered as being a cultural treasure. 文化財科学 cultural heritage science(s).

ぶんかざいけんぞうぶつほぞんぎじゅつきょうかい【文化財建造物保存技術協会】the Japanese Association for Conservation of Architectural Monuments (略: JACAM).

ぶんかざいほごしんぎかい【文化財保護審議会】the Council for the Protection of Cultural Properties.

ぶんかじん【文化人】 ◘▶ 文化人切手〈集合的に〉cultural leaders commemorative stamps.

ぶんかしんぎかい【文化審議会】〔文部科学省の〕the Council for Cultural Affairs.

ぶんかつ¹【分割】 ◘▶ 地域分割 regional 'partition [break-up] 《of the national railways》. ◘▶ 分割照射〚医〕〔放射線の〕fractionated irradiation. 分割発注〔工事などの〕a split order.

ぶんかてき【文化的】 ◘▶ 文化的遺伝子 a cultural gene; 〔ミーム〕⇨ミーム. 文化的公共財 cultural public goods; public cultural goods; common cultural 'property [assets]. 文化的自由 cultural freedom.

ぶんきさアミノさん【分岐鎖-酸】〚化〛a branched-chain amino acid (略: BCAA).

ぶんきょう【文教】 ◘▶ 文教費 the total national expenditure on education.

ぶんぐ【文具】 ◘▶ 文具雑貨 《sundry items [various kinds] of》 stationery. 文具店 a stationery 'shop [store]; a stationer's.

プンゲリ【豊渓里】〔北朝鮮，咸鏡北道(ハムギョンプクド)の一地域〕Punggye-ri; Punggye Village.

ぶんけん⁵【文献】 ◘▶ 文献調査 a document study;〔過去の地質調査のデータをもとに高レベル放射性廃棄物の最終処分地としての適否を決めるための文部科学省原子力発電環境整備機構による調査〕a "document study"; a suitability study by the Nuclear Waste Management Organization of Japan, used as the first stage in the selection process, to establish whether a site would be safe for a high-level radio-active waste dump. ▶ 文献調査の後，概要調査 (a rough outline study), 精密調査 (a detailed study) と進む.

ぶんげん¹【分限】 ◘▶ 分限免職〔公務員に対する〕dismissal on the ground(s) of unsuitability.

ぶんこう¹【分光】 ◘▶ 分光技術 a spectroscopic technique. レーザー~技術 a laser spectroscopic technique. 分光曲線 a spectral curve.

ふんこつ【粉骨】〔散骨のため，焼いた骨を粉状にすること〕bone grinding.

ふんさい【粉砕】 ◘▶ 粉砕痕〔列車の車輪が石などを砕いた時にできるレールの傷〕track scarring [a rail mark] caused by pulverization (of stones placed on the track). 粉砕療法〔治療〕〚医〕⇨破砕療法〔治療〕(⇨はさい).

ぶんさんサービスぼうがい【分散-妨害】〚電算〛〔不正アクセスの一種〕a 'distributed denial-of-service [DDoS] attack.

ぶんし¹【分子】 ◘▶ 分子イメージング〔生体内の分子の量や働きを画像として捉える技術〕molecular imaging. 分子化学 molecular chemistry. 分子カスケード a molecular cascade. 分子生化学 molecular biochemistry. 分子生理学 molecular physiology. 分子腫瘍学 molecular oncology. 分子プローブ〚医・生物〕a molecular probe. 分子料理法〔料理を物理・化学式で表し，新しい味覚を"発明"する〕molecular gastronomy.

ぶんししんけいがく【分子神経学】molecular neurology.

ぶんせいごうせいしんいがく【分子整合精神医学】〚医〛orthomolecular psychiatry.

ぶんしのうかがく【分子脳科学】molecular neuroscience.

ぶんしゅうりんとくべつそちほう【分収林特別措置法】〚法〛the Profit-Sharing Afforestation Special Measures Law.

ぶんしょ³【文書】 ◘▶ 紙文書〔電子文書に対して〕paper documents. 成果文書〔首脳会合などで採択される〕an outcome document. 内部文書 an internal document. ◘▶ 文書鑑識 forensic document examination. 文書管理 document management. ◘ ~管理システム a document management system. 文書訓告処

ぶんしょう

分〔公務員等に対する〕 ▷～訓告処分にする[を受ける] issue [receive] a written 'warning [reprimand]. 文書掲示違反〔公職選挙法の〕 an infringement of the rules governing the distribution of campaign literature, display of election posters, etc. 文書(作成)処理〔電算〕word processing. 文書通信交通滞在費〔国会議員に支払われる〕postage, communication, transport(ation) and accommodation expenses. 文書図画(s)〔法〕writing and 'illustrations [graphic materials]. 文書(による)厳重注意 《give sb》a 'stern [strong, strict] written warning [warning in writing]. 文書(による)注意 a written warning; a warning in writing. 文書頒布違反〔公職選挙法の〕an infringement of the rules governing the mass distribution of leaflets, etc. for election campaigning purposes. 文書保存 the 'retention [keeping] of documents. ▷～保存期間 a (time) period for the 'retention [keeping] of documents; a retention period for documents.

**ぶんしょう**[3]【文章】 ▣▷ 文章完成法(テスト)〔心理〕a sentence completion test (略: SCT).

**ぶんじょう**[3]【分譲】 ▣▷ 分譲価格 a lot price. 分譲部分〔マンションの賃貸部分に対して〕the 'condominium [privately owned] units.

**ぶんしょか**【文書化】putting into 'writing [written form]. ▷～する put (a plan) into writing; write out 《one's ideas》. ▷ 合意事項を～する set down the agreed items in writing.

**ふんしょく**[3]【糞食】〔昆虫・鳥・動物が糞を食とすること〕coprophagy. ▣▷ 糞食性の coprophagous.

**ふんじん**[1]【粉塵】 ▣▷ 粉塵計 a dust counter. 粉塵暴露《occupational》exposure to《mineral》'dust [particles].

**フンシンペックとう**【-党】〔カンボジアの政党〕the Funcinpec Party.

**ぶんせき**[1]【分析】 ▣▷ 分析記事〔新聞・雑誌などの〕an analytical article; an article of analysis.

**フン・セン** Hun Sen (1951?-　;カンボジアの政治家; 首相〔1985-93, 1998- 　〕).

**ふんそう**[2]【紛争】 ▣▷ 紛争管理 dispute management. 紛争地域 a 'conflict [troubled] area. 紛争当事国 a 'country [nation] involved in a conflict; a conflict 'country [nation].

**フンタウ**〔ベトナム南部, バリアブンタウ省の省都〕Vung Tau.

**ぶんだん**[2]【分断】 ▣▷ 分断社会 a 'divided [divisive] society.

**ぶんちゃか**〔(安っぽい)楽隊の音〕oompah; oompah-pah. ▷ 音楽隊が～と演奏を開始し, パレードが動きはじめた. As the band started to oompah, the parade began.

**ふんとう**[3]【奮闘】 ▣▷ 奮闘記 a record of 'one's struggles [what one has been through]. 奮闘劇 the drama of one's struggles; a dramatic account of what one has 'suffered [been through]. ▷ そのブログには子育てや姑との確執に苦しみながらも明るく生きる主婦の～劇が綴られている. The blog 'tells the story [recounts the dramas] of a cheerful wife's painful struggles with child-raising and conflict with her mother-in-law.

**ブンニャン** Bounnhang Vorachith (1937-　;ラオスの政治家; 首相〔2001-06〕).

**ふんにょう**【糞尿】 ▣▷ 糞尿被害〔犬猫などの〕《have, suffer from》problems with animal excrement; problems with cats and dogs 'doing their business [shitting and peeing] 《in one's garden》.

**ふんぬ**【憤怒】 ▣▷ 憤怒痙攣〔医〕〔泣き入りひきつけ〕breath-holding spells.

**ぶんぱい**【分配】 ▣▷ 分配ドラフト〔野球〕〔球団合併の際, 合併される球団の選手を他の球団と分け合うためのドラフト〕a distribution draft.

**ぶんぷ**【分布】 ▣▷ 分布表 a distribution 'chart [diagram].

**ぶんぶつ**【文物】 ▣▷ 文物鑑定 (antique [art, artifact]) appraisal. ▷～鑑定家 an (antique [art, artifact]) appraiser.

**ぶんべつ**【分別】 ▣▷ 分別管理〔顧客からの預かり資産と証券会社の資産を分けて管理すること〕separate management of 'client and brokerage assets [assets owned by a securities company and those entrusted to it by its customers]. 分別保管 ＝分別管理.

**ぶんべん**【糞便】〔医〕 ▣▷ 糞便検査〔医〕a 'stool [fecal] examination [test]; scatoscopy.

**ぶんべん**【分娩】 ▣▷ 分娩(時)事故 a birthing accident. 分娩(時)骨折〔医〕〔新生児の〕a birth fracture.

**ぶんぼう**【分房】 ▣▷ 分房(時)〔乳房の〕a (mammary) gland; 〔牛の乳房の〕a quarter; 〔ヤギの乳房の〕a half.

「**文明の衝突**」〔S・P・ハンチントンの著作〕The Clash of Civilizations and the Remaking of World Order.

**ぶんり**[2]【分離】 ▣▷ 分離独立 separation and independence; hiving off; 〔国の一部などの〕secession. ▷～独立する separate (and become independent); 〔国の一部などが〕secede (from Canada). 分離不安〔心理〕ふあん. 分離フェンス ＝分離壁. 分離壁〔イスラエルとヨルダン川西岸パレスチナ地区との間の〕the 'separation [security] wall [barrier, fence]. 分離膜〔化〕a separation membrane.

**ぶんり**[3]【文理】 ▣▷ 文理融合〔学問の〕integration of the humanities and sciences.

**ぶんれつ**[2]【分裂】 ▣▷ 分裂活動〔台湾の中国本土からの独立運動〕"separatist activities" (vis-à-vis mainland China). 分裂行動〔組織の団結[統一]を妨害する行動〕divisive 'activities [behavior]. 分裂酵母 fission yeast. 分裂選挙 a split election. ▷ 自民～選挙〔党が2つに割れた状態で臨む選挙〕an election with a split party ticket for the LDP; 〔小選挙区で候補者を一本化できずに臨む選挙〕a single-member election in which two LDP candidates compete with each other / 保守～選挙〔複数の保守政党が分裂した状態で臨む選挙〕an election in which candidates from several conservative parties compete against each other; 〔複数の保守政党が候補者を一本化できずに臨む選挙〕a single-member election in which candidates from several conservative parties compete against each other (because they have failed to resolve their differences).

**ぶんわいほう**【文匯報】〔香港の中国系日刊紙〕the Wen Wei Po.

## へ

**ペア** ▣▷ ペア鑑賞券[チケット, 入場券]〔劇場, コンサートの〕a two-person (theater, concert) ticket. ペアシート〔電車・レストランなどの〕a two-person seat; a double seat; 〔映画館などの〕a love seat.

**ヘア・アイロン**〔髪用の電気ごて〕a curling iron. ▣▷ ストレート・ヘア・アイロン a hair straightener.

**ヘア・クラック**〔金属などの細いひび割れ〕a hair crack.

**ペアレンティング**〔親業〕being a parent; parenting.

**ベイ** Bay, Michael (1965-　;米国の映画監督; 本名 Michael Benjamin Bay).

**べいえいがげいじゅつかがくアカデミー**【米映画芸術科学-】＝えいがげいじゅつかがくアカデミー.

へいかい【閉会】 ▯ 閉会中審査 deliberation(s) during an adjournment of the Diet.
べいかがくアカデミー【米科学-】=べいこくかがくアカデミー.
へいかつきん【平滑筋】 ▯ 平滑筋肉腫《医》(a) leiomyosarcoma 《pl. ~s, -mata》.
べいかん【米韓】 ▯ 米韓定例安保協議 the《37th》「Republic of Korea-United States [ROK-US] Security Consultative Meeting (略: SCM).
へいきょく【平曲】〔平家物語を平家琵琶を弾きながら語るもの〕chanting the *Heike-monogatari* to the accompaniment of a Heike *biwa*.
へいきん[1]【平均】 ▯ 平均健康寿命 ⇨けんこう[4].
へいきんがお【平均顔】〔コンピューターを使って合成した〕an averaged face.
ヘイグル Heigl, Katherine (1978- ; 米国の映画女優; 本名 Katherine Marie Heigl).
べいぐんさいへん(とくそ)ほう【米軍再編(特措)法】〔法〕the Law Concerning Special Measures to Facilitate the Reorganization of US Forces Stationed in Japan. ▶ 正式名称は「駐留軍等の再編の円滑な実施に関する特別措置法」.
へいこう[1]【平行】 ▯ 平行性 parallelness. ◐~性のよいビーム《物》a well-collimated beam; a highly parallel beam.
へいこう[3]【並行】 ▯ 並行協議 parallel「talks [negotiations, conferences]. 並行陣《テニス》《ダブルスで》a tandem formation; a「both-up [both-back] formation.
べいこくいしかい【米国医師会】=アメリカいしかい.
べいこくうんゆほあんきょく【米国運輸保安局】⇨うんゆほあんきょく.
べいこくえいがきょうかい【米国映画協会】1 the Motion Picture Association of America (略: MPAA). ▶ 1922年 the Motion Picture Producers and Distributors of America 米国映画製作者配給者協会 (略: MPPDA) として発足; 著作権者の権利擁護, 映画のレーティングなどの業務を行う. 2 the American Film Institute (略: AFI). ▶ 1967年設立.
べいこくえいがげいじゅつかがくアカデミー【米国映画芸術科学-】=えいがげいじゅつかがくアカデミー.
べいこくかいけいきじゅん【米国会計基準】〔財務会計基準審議会 (FASB) が設定する〕a Statement of Financial Accounting Standards (略: SFAS).
べいこくかがくアカデミー【米国科学-】the National Academy of Sciences (略: NAS).
べいこくきかくきょうかい【米国規格協会】the American National Standards Institute (略: ANSI).
べいこくこうくううちゅうがっかい【米国航空宇宙会】the American Institute of Aeronautics and Astronautics (略: AIAA).
べい(こく)こうくうゆそうきょうかい【米(国)航空輸送協会】the Air Transport Association of America (略: ATA).
べいこくこうしゅうえいせいきょうかい【米国公衆衛生協会】=アメリカこうしゅうえいせいきょうかい.
べいこくこくさいかいはつちょう【米国国際開発庁】⇨こくさいかいはつちょう.
べいこくざいたいきょうかい【米国在台協会】〔台湾における米国大使館の代替的存在〕the American Institute in Taiwan (略: AIT).
べいこくさんひょうじゅんゆしゅ【米国産標準油種】West Texas Intermediate (略: WTI).
べいこくしんぶんきょうかい【米国新聞協会】the Newspaper Association of America (略: NAA).
べいこくすいしつきょうかい【米国水質協会】the Water Quality Association (略: WQA).
べいこくせいしんいがくかい【米国精神医学会】the American Psychiatric Association (略: APA).

べいこくせきゆきょうかい【米国石油協会】the American Petroleum Institute (略: API).
べい(こく)ちしつちょうさじょ【米(国)地質調査所】the US Geological Survey (略: USGS).
べいこくちりがくきょうかい【米国地理学協会】=ナショナル・ジオグラフィックきょうかい.
べいこくでんきでんしぎじゅつしゃきょうかい【米国電気電子技術者協会】the Institute of Electrical and Electronic Engineers (略: IEEE).
べいこくはんドーピングきかん【米国反-機関】the United States Anti-Doping Agency (略: USADA).
べいこくびょういんきょうかい【米国病院協会】the American Hospital Association (略: AHA).
べいこくファッションデザイナーきょうかい【米国-協議会】the Council of Fashion Designers of America (略: CFDA).
べいこくりんしょうびょうりいきょうかい【米国臨床病理医協会】the College of American Pathologists (略: CAP).
へいさ【閉鎖】 ▯ 閉鎖型生態系実験施設 a closed ecology experiment facility (略: CEEF); a biosphere. 閉鎖空間 an enclosed space. 閉鎖手術《医》a closure operation; (an) operative「closure [occlusion]. 半閉鎖手術《医》a semiclosure (operation). 閉鎖生態系〔生態〕a closed「ecosystem [ecological system]. ◐~生態系生命維持システム〔生態〕a controlled ecological life support system (略: CELSS) / ~生態系循環式養殖システム〔水産〕a closed ecological recirculating aquaculture system (略: CERAS). 閉鎖病棟〔患者の自由な出入りを制限する〕a closed ward. 閉鎖不全《医》〔心臓弁〕valve「insufficiency [incompetence]. ◐大動脈弁~不全(症) aortic valve「insufficiency [incompetence] / 僧帽弁~不全(症) mitral valve「insufficiency [incompetence].
へいさつ【併殺】 ▯ 併殺打《hit》a double-play ball. ◐~に倒れる〔打者が〕hit into a double play / ~打に仕留め get《the batter, a runner》out on a double play; make [pull off] a double play.
へいさてき【閉鎖的】closed; closed off; cut off; exclusive; cloistered; self-contained; impenetrable; exclusionist;〔組織などが〕closed;〔雰囲気が〕closed; exclusive. ◐~な経済 a closed economy / ~な日本市場への参入は難しい. It is difficult to find entry into the tight Japanese market. ◐日本の農産物市場は決して~ではない. The Japanese market for agricultural products is certainly not「a closed one [closed to other countries]. ▯ 半閉鎖的 partially closed; half-closed; semi-closed《ecosystems》. ▯ 閉鎖的海域〔水域〕closed waters.
べいサプライマネジメントきょうかい【米-協会】=ぜんべいきょうかんりきょうかい.
ヘイジ =バイジ.
ヘイシャ(ー)ズとう【-島】=こくかつしとう.
べいしゅうじゆうぼうえきけん【米州自由貿易圏】=べいしゅうじゆうぼうえきちいき.
べいしゅうじゆうぼうえきちいき【米州自由貿易地域】the Free Trade Area of the Americas (略: FTAA).
ベイシンガー Basinger, Kim (1953- ; 米国の映画女優; 本名 Kimila Ann Basinger).
へいせい[1]【平成】 ▯ 平成の大合併 the great Heisei merger; the large-scale consolidation of municipalities in Japan in the early twenty-first century.
へいせいききそかがくざいだん【平成基礎科学財団】the Heisei Foundation for Basic Science.
べいせいぞうぎょうぼうえきこうどうれんごう【米製造業貿易行動連合】the American Manufacturing Trade Action Coalition (略: AMTAC).
へいそう[2]【並走・併走】running [driving, riding] side by side. ◐~する run [drive, ride] side by side. ◐ナ

「ペイチェック 消された記憶」ペイチェックけされたきおく

ンバーを付けていないバイクを発見した警官が、〜しながら窓越しに停止を呼びかけたが、バイクは加速して逃走した．The police officer in the patrol car who noticed the motorcycle without a license plate drove alongside it and called through the window for the rider to stop, but the motorcycle shot ahead and escaped.

「ペイチェック 消された記憶」〔映画〕Paycheck.

べいちゅうごうどうしょうぎょうぼうえきいいんかい【米中合同商業貿易委員会】the US-China Joint Commission on Commerce and Trade (略：JCCT).

べいちゅうせんりゃくけいざいたいわ【米中戦略経済対話】the US-China Strategic Economic Dialogue.

べいちょうわくぐみごうい【米朝枠組み合意】〔北朝鮮の核開発放棄に関する米国と北朝鮮との合意；1994 年〕the (1994) US-North Korea Framework Agreement.

ベイツ 1 Bates, Alan (1934-2003；英国の映画俳優；本名 Alan Arthur Bates).
2 Bates, Kathy (1948- ；米国の映画女優；本名 Kathleen Doyle-Bates).

ベイツ・モーテル〔A・ヒッチコックの映画『サイコ』の舞台となったモーテル〕the Bates Motel.

ヘイデンほう【-法】〔米法〕〔ナチスや大日本帝国時代の企業などによる戦時強制労働による賃金請求やその被害への補償を訴えることを認めたカリフォルニア州の州法〕the Hayden Act.

へいとう【屏東】⇒ピントン．

ベイト・ハヌ（ー）ン〔パレスチナ，ガザ地区北部の町〕Beit Hanoun.

べいにくぎゅうせいさんしゃきょうかい【米肉牛生産者協会】⇒ぜんべいにくぎゅうせいさんしゃきょうかい．

「ペイバック」〔映画〕Payback.

「ベイブ」〔映画〕Babe. ▶続編は「ベイブ／都会へ行く」(Babe: Pig in the City).

「ベイ・フォワード 可能の王国」〔映画〕Pay It Forward.

ベイブレード〔商標〕〔べいごまに似た遊具〕a Beyblade.

ベイブロウ〔略〕〔米空軍特殊作戦軍団 (AFSOC) の特殊侵攻作戦用ヘリコプター MH-53 の愛称〕a Pave Low.

べいべつ【袂別】a parting; a split; a breakup. 〜する part; split; break up.

べいほけんトラスト【米保健-】〔米国の NPO 団体〕(the) Trust for America's Health (略：TFAH).

へいめん【平面】〔〕平面アンテナ a flat(-panel) antenna; a planar antenna.

へいよう【併用】〔〕併用検診〔検査〕a combined 'test [examination]《for genetic defects》; combined testing 《for syphilis and HIV》. 併用療法 (a) combined therapy.

ベイラーいかだいがく【-医科大学】〔米国テキサス州ヒューストンにある大学〕Baylor College of Medicine.

べいりくぐんせんそうだいがく【米陸軍戦争大学】＝りくぐんせんそうだいがく．

へいりょく【兵力】〔〕兵力引き離し (a) disengagement.

ベイル ＝ベール．

ベイルートせんげん【-宣言】〔2002 年のアラブ連盟首脳会議で採択された〕the Beirut Declaration.

べいれんぽうこうかいしじょういいんかい【米連邦公開市場委員会】the Federal (Reserve) Open Market Committee (略：FOMC).

へいわ【平和】〔〕平和祈念館 a hall dedicated to prayers for peace; a "peace prayer hall." 平和祈念像 a statue dedicated to prayers for peace. 平和教育 peace education; education for peace. 平和構築 peace building. ◎国際〜構築 international peace building／〜構築委員会 ⇒こくれんへいわこうちくいいんかい／〜構築活動 peace-building operations (略：PBO). 平和時 a time of peace; peacetime. 平和親善大使 a goodwill ambassador for peace; a goodwill

peace ambassador.

へいわきねんじぎょうとくべつききん【平和祈念事業特別基金】〔独立行政法人の 1 つ〕the Special Fund for Peace Promotion Projects.

へいわしちょうかいぎ【平和市長会議】Mayors for Peace.

ヘインズ Haynes, Todd (1961- ；米国の映画監督).

ペインティング 〔〕ペインティング・ナイフ a painting knife.

ペイント 〔〕ペイントボール〔塗料が入った球状ゼラチンカプセル；サバイバルゲーム用の弾丸とされる〕a paintball；〔それで撃ち合うスポーツ〕paintball; a paintball game.

ベーカー 1 Baker, Carroll (1931- ；米国の女優).
2 Baker, Diane (1938- ；米国の女優).
3 Baker, Kathy (1950- ；米国の映画女優；本名 Kathy Whitton Baker).

ベーカーズフィールド〔米国カリフォルニア州南部の都市〕Bakersfield.

ベーカリー 〔〕ベーカリー・カフェ a bakery café.

ベーコン Bacon, Kevin (1958- ；米国の映画俳優).

ペ（-）ザロ，ペサロ〔イタリア中東部の港市〕Pesaro.

ページ 〔〕ページ・ビュー〔電算〕〔インターネットのページの閲覧(回数)〕a page view. ◎そのサイトは 1 日に 5 万〜ビューを記録した．That site logged 50,000 page views per day.

ベース[1] 〔〕ベース・カバー〔野球〕covering a base; covering《first》base. ◎〜カバーに入る〔野手が〕cover a base; cover《first》base.

ヘースタース Heesters, Johannes (1903- ；オランダの俳優).

ベース・ダウン〔基本給の減額〕a decrease of the basic wage rate; a cut in base pay.

ベースライン 〔〕ベースライン・プレー〔テニス〕baseline play. ベースライン・プレーヤー〔テニス〕a baseline player.

ベースライン・アンド・クレジット〔環境〕〔温室効果ガスの排出量取引方式〕baseline and credit; a baseline-and-credit system.

ベータ 〔〕ベータ・アゴニスト〔薬〕〔喘息などの治療薬〕a beta-[β-]agonist. ◎〜2[3]アゴニスト a beta2-[beta3-]agonist; a β2-[β3-]agonist. ベータ刺激薬〔剤〕〔薬〕〔気管支拡張薬〕a beta-[β-]stimulator. ベータ遮断薬〔薬〕〔交感神経β遮断薬〕a beta-[β-]sympatholytic agent. ベータ3 アドレナリン受容体遺伝子 the beta3-[β3-]adrenergic receptor gene. ベータ・ヘキソサミニダーゼ〔生化〕〔酵素の一種〕beta-[β-]hexosaminidase.

ベーターゼン Petersen, Wolfgang (1941- ；ドイツ生まれの映画監督).

ベータリポたんぱくしつ【-蛋白質】〔生化〕beta-lipoprotein.

ペーパー 〔〕ペーパー車検〔車体の点検も整備もしないで車検を通してしまう違法行為〕(an illegal) vehicle inspection [MOT test] conducted [done, made] without necessary maintenance work. ペーパー・レフェリー ＝書面審査員 (⇨しょめん).

ペーパーレス 〔〕ペーパーレス化 elimination of paper 《documents》. ◎インターネットの普及により行政手続きの〜化が進んでいる．Due to the spread of the Internet, more and more paperless administrative procedures are being adopted [paper is being steadily eliminated from administrative procedures].

ベール Bale, Christian (1974- ；英国の映画俳優；本名 Christian Morgan Bale).

ベール・エール〔ビールの種類〕pale ale.

ベール・ラシェーズぼち【-墓地】〔フランス，パリの〕Père-Lachaise Cemetery;〔フランス語〕Cimetière du Père-Lachaise.

ベカーこうげん【-高原】〔レバノン東部の高原〕the "Beqa'a [Bekaa] Valley.

ヘカトンケイル〔ギ神話〕〔巨人族〕the Hecatonchires; [1

人〕a Hecatonchire.
**へきしん**【壁芯】▫️ 壁芯面積〔建物などの〕the area enclosed by the center lines of the walls; the gross floor area.
**ヘキソーゲン**〔化〕〔爆薬〕hexogen. [⇨アール・ディー・エックス].
**へきち**【僻地】▫️ 僻地手当 a "remote duty allowance"; an allowance [a bonus] paid for working in a remote and inconvenient area.
**へきめん**【壁面】▫️ 壁面後退〔building〕setback 《requirements, line》. ◐ 建物は道路から1メートル以上〜後退すること. Buildings should be set back at least one meter from the street. | The building setback from the street must be at least one meter. 壁面収納家具 wall (storage) furniture; wall units; modular wall furniture. 壁面緑化 wall greening.
**ペキンせいねんほう**〔北京青年報〕〔中国の日刊紙〕the Beijing Youth Daily.
「**北京のふたり**」〔映画〕Red Corner.
**ペグインターフェロン**〔生化・薬〕peginterferon〔略：PEG-IFN〕.
**ペグイントロン**〔商標・薬〕＝ペグインターフェロン.
**ヘクシャー・オリーン・モデル**〔経〕the Heckscher-Ohlin model; the H-O model. ▶ 国際的分業構造の枠組みをいう; スウェーデンの経済学者エリ・ヘクシャー (Eli F. Heckscher: 1897–1952) とベルティル・オリーン (Bertil G. Ohlin: 1899–1979) の名にちなむ.
**ベクミックス, ベクティビックス**〔商標・薬〕〔転移性大腸がんの治療薬パニツムマブの商品名〕Vectibix.
**ベクテート・リアーゼ**〔生化〕pectate lyase.
**ベゴニア**▫️ 木立(性)ベゴニア cane-stemmed [erect-stemmed] begonia.
**ペシ** Pesci, Joe (1943– ; 米国の映画俳優; 本名 Joseph Pesci).
**ベジタブル**▫️ ベジタブル・カービング〔料理〕〔ナイフで野菜や草花・小鳥などを彫り込んで食卓を彩る芸術〕vegetable carving.
**ベジタリアン**▫️ オボ・ベジタリアン〔卵は食べる菜食主義者, 卵食菜食主義者〕an ovo-vegetarian. ラクト・ベジタリアン〔乳製品は食べる菜食主義者, 乳製品菜食主義者〕a lacto-vegetarian; a lactarian. ラクト・オボ・ベジタリアン〔乳製品と卵も食べる菜食主義者, 乳卵菜食主義者〕a lacto-ovo-vegetarian; an ovo-lactarian.
**ヘジャ(ー)ブ**〔イスラム教徒の女性が着用するスカーフ〕《wear》the hijab; the hejab.
**ベシルさんアムロジピン**【-酸-】〔薬〕〔カルシウム拮抗薬・降圧薬〕amlodipine besilate.
**ペスカトーレ**〔＜It *pescatore* ＝fisherman〕〔料理〕〔魚介類の(パスタなど)〕《pasta, risotto》pescatore.
**ベスト**³ Best, George (1946–2005; 北アイルランド出身のサッカー選手).
**ベストイレブン**〔サッカー〕an all-star eleven; an all-star ¹*soccer [¹¹football] team.
**ベストエフォートがたサービス**【-型-】〔通信など〕〔回線スピードなど, 必ずしも最大値などを保証しないサービス〕a best-effort service.
**ベスト・オブ・スリー**〔3戦中先に2勝した方を勝者とする方式〕best-of-three.
**ベスト・オブ・セブン**〔7戦中先に4勝した方を勝者とする方式〕best-of-seven.
**ベスト・オブ・ファイブ**〔5戦中先に3勝した方を勝者とする方式〕best-of-five.
**ベストグロスしょう**〔-賞〕〔ゴルフ〕a prize for the best gross (score).
**ベスト・ジーニスト**〔ジーンズが似合う有名人〕a best-dressed jeans wearer;〔その賞〕the Best-Dressed Jeans Wearer Prize.
**ベスト・ターンド・アウトしょう**〔-賞〕〔競馬〕〔最も美しく仕上げられた馬とその厩務員に与えられる〕《win》a [the] "best turned out" award.
**ベスト・ドレッサー**▫️ ベストドレッサー賞 a [the] "Best-Dressed ¹Man [Woman]" award.
**ベストナイン**〔野球〕the nine players voted best of the year in their respective positions; the all-star nine; 〔日本プロ野球の〕the Best Nine. ◐ 〜に選ばれる be voted into 《(口) make》the ¹all-star nine [Best Nine].
「**ベスト・フレンズ・ウェディング**」〔映画〕My Best Friend's Wedding.
**ベスラン**〔ロシア, 北オセチア共和国の町〕Beslan.
**ベゼル**〔指輪の宝石をはめる所, 時計のガラスがはまる溝縁など〕a bezel
**へそ**¹【臍】▫️ へそ出しルック a (bare-)midriff look.
**べた**▫️ 黒べた『印刷』(an area of) solid black; a solid area of black.
**ペタ** ⇨きょうどぼうえいぐん.
**ペタつうしん**〔-通信〕〔セルビア・モンテネグロの通信社〕the Beta News Agency.
**べたつく** 1〔粘りつく〕be [feel] (soft and) sticky; be [feel] tacky [clammy]; be [feel] gummy [gooey]; be [feel] viscous [viscid]. ◐ このシャツは汗をかいてもべたつかない. This shirt doesn't ¹stick to you [get sticky] when you perspire. / 私は脂性で肌がべたつきやすい. I have an oily skin and I tend to get sticky.
2〔甘えてまつわりつく〕cling 《to *sb*》; be all over 《*sb*》. ◐ あの二人はいつもべたついている. Those two are always ¹cuddling (each other) [fondling each other, smooching, necking]. | Those two! They can never leave each other alone.
**ペタフロップス**〔電算〕petaflops.
**べたゆき**〔べた雪〕〔水分を多く含んだ雪〕sticky snow; wet [heavy] snow. ◐ 今日は気温が低くないから〜だ. The snow is sticky today because the temperature is not that low.
**ペタライト**〔鉱〕〔葉長石〕petalite.
**へたり**▫️ へたり牛〔病気・けがなどで歩行できない牛〕a downer (cow).
**へたれ** worthlessness; laziness; weakness; incompetence; wimpiness. 〜な worthless; lazy; weak; incompetent; wimpy. ◐ 〜技術者 a poor excuse for an engineer / 〜監督 an incompetent director / 〜っぷりを¹show [display] of one's worthlessness / 〜な私の〜な一日を書いた日記 a diary entry describing a do-nothing day spent by do-nothing me / 私の〜な性格, 大学入っても直りません. My loser personality won't change even if I do get into college.
**ベタレイン**〔化〕〔植物色素〕betalain.
**へたれる** 1〔だらしない状態である〕be sloppy [lazy, no good]. ◐ 彼はへたれた生活を反省することもない. His slacker lifestyle doesn't bother him at all. / うちの犬はいつもへたれている. Our dog lies around all the time and is no good for anything.
2〔へたばる〕◐ 暑い夏に早くもへたれている私です. I'm already worn out by this hot summer. / 強烈な向かい風に 10キロ地点ですでに彼女はへたれた. The strong headwind sapped all her energy as early as the 10-kilometer point.
3〔本来の性能を失う; へたる〕◐ 彼女はへたれた毛並みのウサギのぬいぐるみを大事に抱えていた. She was earnestly hugging a stuffed rabbit doll that had most of its fur worn off. / 私は10年前のへたれたパソコンを使っています. I use a beat-up 10-year-old computer.
**へちま**〔糸瓜〕▫️ ヘチマ水 a natural liquid cosmetic made from loofah extract.
**ペチャブリ**〔タイの地名ペッブリ(-)の別称〕Phetchaburi; Petchaburi.
**ベッカー** Becker, Harold (1950– ; 米国の映画監督).
**ベッカーこうげん**〔-高原〕＝ベカーこうげん.
**ヘッカリング** Heckerling, Amy (1954– ; 米国の映画監

督).
ベッキンセイル =ベッキンセール.
ベッキンセール Beckinsale, Kate (1973- ; 英国生まれの映画女優).
ヘックス〔ボードゲームの六角形のます〕a hex. ◐1 ~移動する move one hex. ◐1~は10kmである. One hex is 10 km. / 歩兵は2~離れた敵に射撃を行なえます. Infantry can shoot at an enemy two hexes away.
べっこうとんぼ【鼈甲蜻蛉】〔昆〕Libellula angelina.
べっしつ【別室】□◉夫婦別室　うちは夫婦~だ. We [My husband and I] have separate bedrooms. □◉別室受験 an examination in a separate room.
ヘッジ・ファンド　□◉海外ヘッジファンド a foreign [an overseas] hedge fund.
ヘッシュ Heche, Anne (1969- ; 米国の映画女優; 本名 Anne Celeste Heche).
べったい【別体】〔異なる形態〕a different 「form [shape, model], 〔標準以外の字体〕a nonstandard character; 〔附属品などが本体から離れていること〕separate 《speakers)》.
べつだん【別段】□◉別段預金〔金融〕〔銀行業務に該当しないお金を一時的に保管しておくための便宜的預金科目〕a special deposit.
ペッチャブーン〔タイ北部の県; その県都〕Phetchabun.
ペッチャブリ =ペチャブリ.
ベッド　□◉介護用ベッド a (home-)care bed. □◉ベッド・テクニック bedroom skills; sexual techniques.
ペット　□◉ペット・キャリア〔ペット運搬用のかばん・かご〕a pet carrier. ペット業界 the pet industry. ペット業者 a pet dealer. ペット条例 a pet ordinance. ペット植物 a pet plant. ペット美容室 a pet beauty salon. ペット服〔ペット用の衣類〕〔an item of〕 pet 「clothing [apparel]. ペット保険 ⇨しるし[1]. ペット療法〔医〕pet-assisted therapy.
ペット[2]【PET】〔医〕〔陽電子放射断層撮影(法)〕PET; positron emission tomography.
ペット・アーキテクチャー〔建〕〔きわめて狭いいびつな形状の土地に建てられた建築〕pet architecture.
ヘッドアップ・ディスプレー〔空〕〔パイロットの視界前方に情報を投影する装置〕a head(s)-up display; an HUD.
ヘッドウインド〔向かい風〕a headwind; an opposing wind.
ベッドサイド　□◉ベッドサイド・モニター〔機器〕a bedside monitor.
ヘッド・スピード『ゴルフ・野球など』『クラブ・バットなどの』《club [bat]》head speed.
ヘッドハンティング　□◉ヘッドハンティング会社 a head-hunting company.
ヘッドボード〔ベッドの〕a headboard.
ペットボトル　□◉ペットボトル・ロケット a plastic bottle rocket; a water rocket made from a plastic bottle.
ペッパー Pepper, Barry (1970- ; カナダ生まれの映画俳優; 本名 Barry Robert Pepper).
ペプリ(ー)〔タイ, バンコク市内の通りの名〕Phetburi;〔タイ中部の県; その県都〕Phet Buri. ▶ 別称 ペ(ッ)チャブリ (Phetchaburi).
ヘディキウム〔植〕〔ショウガ科ヘディキウム属の総称〕a hedychium.
ペティ・クラークのほうそく【-の法則】〔経〕〔経済発展に伴う産業構造移行の法則〕Petty-Clark's law.
「ベティ・サイズモア」〔映画〕Nurse Betty.
ベティ・ブープ〔米国製アニメの女主人公〕Betty Boop.
ベテラン　□◉ベテラン議員 a veteran [an experienced] Diet member [legislator].
ベテランズ・スタジアム〔米国, フィラデルフィアにある野球場〕Veterans Stadium.
「ヘドウィグ・アンド・アングリーインチ」〔映画〕Hedwig and The Angry Inch.
ベトナム　□◉ベトナム症候群〔米国, 敗戦の記憶〕the Vietnam syndrome. ポスト・ベトナム症候群〔医〕〔ベトナム戦争帰還兵の〕post-Vietnam syndrome.
ベドモスチ〔ロシアの日刊経済紙〕Vedomosti.
ペトルチアーニ Petrucciani, Michel (1962-99; フランス出身のジャズピアニスト).
ヘドレン Hedren, Tippi (1935?- ; 米国の映画女優; 本名 Nathalie Hedren).
ペトロチャイナ〔中国の国営石油会社, 中国石油天然気の略称〕PetroChina.
ペトロパブロフスク・カムチャツキー〔ロシア極東, カムチャツカ州の州都〕Petropavlovsk-Kamchatsky.
ヘナ〔植物性天然染料〕henna.
ペナルティー　□◉ペナルティー・コーナー〔ホッケー・サッカーなど〕a penalty corner. ペナルティー・ボックス『アイスホッケー・サッカーなど』the penalty box.
ペナンブラ 1〔天〕〔半影〕a penumbra《pl. -brae, ~s》. ▷ penumbral adj.
2〔医〕〔脳梗塞の病巣周辺部〕a penumbra《pl. -brae, ~s》. ▷ penumbral adj.
ベニーニ Benigni, Roberto (1952- ; イタリアの映画俳優・脚本家・監督).
べにいも【紅芋】〔植〕〔サツマイモの一種〕a red sweet potato.
べにがく【紅額】〔植〕〔ユキノシタ科の落葉低木〕Hydrangea macrophylla f. rosalba.
べにがくあじさい【紅額紫陽花】〔植〕=べにがく.
べにくらげ【紅水母】〔動〕Turritopsis nutricula.
べにこぶし【紅辛夷】〔植〕〔モクレン科の落葉小高木〕Magnolia stellata var. keiskei.
「ベニスで恋して」〔映画〕Bread and Tulips;〔原題〕Pane e Tulipani.
べにずわいがに【紅ずわい蟹】〔動〕〔クモガニ科のカニ〕a red snow crab; a red queen crab; Chionoecetes japonicus.
べにばなとちのき【紅花栃】〔植〕〔トチノキ科の落葉高木〕a red (horse) chestnut; Aesculus × carnea.
ベニヤぞく【紅-族】〔中国南部の山岳地帯に住む民族〕the Red Yao;〔1人〕a Red Yao《pl. ~s》.
ベニング Bening, Annette (1958- ; 米国の映画女優).
ベネックス Beineix, Jean-Jacques (1946- ; フランスの映画監督・脚本家).
ベネットあかくびワラビー【-赤首-】〔動〕=あかくびワラビー.
ベネディクト【~16世】Benedict XVI (1927- ; ドイツ生まれのローマ教皇〔2005- 〕; 本名 Joseph Ratzinger).
ベネル・ムリア〔インドネシア, アチェ州の県〕Bener Meriah.
ヘバーデンけっせつ【-結節】〔医〕(a) Heberden's node.
ペパード Peppard, George (1928-94; 米国の映画俳優).
ベバシズマブ〔薬〕〔血管新生阻害薬〕〔がん治療薬〕bevacizumab.
ヘパリン　□◉ヘパリン生理食塩水 heparinized physiological 「saline [salt] solution.
ペパローニ〔香辛料の強いイタリアソーセージ〕pepperoni.
ヘび【蛇】□◉ヘビ柄 a snakeskin pattern.
ベビー　□◉ベビー・サイン〔赤ちゃん手話〕baby sign (language). ベビーラッシュ =出産ラッシュ《⇨ラッシュ[1]》. ベビー・リーフ〔早摘みの葉野菜〕baby leaves.
ヘビー・ユーザー〔機器などを徹底的に利用する人〕a heavy user.
ペプチド　□◉ペプチド免疫療法 peptide immunotherapy. ペプチド・ワクチン (a) peptide vaccine. ◐癌~ワクチン (a) cancer peptide vaccine.
ペプリ(ー)=ペプリ(ー).
ヘブン・アーティスト a licensed street performer.
ペペロンチーノ《<It peperoncino =chile pepper》〔料理〕〔オリーブオイル・にんにく・トウガラシだけで作るパスタ〕spaghetti aglio, olio e peperoncino (=spaghetti with garlic, oil and chilli).
ペポかぼちゃ【-南瓜】〔植〕〔ウリ科〕食材・観賞植物; 種子は健康食品〕a summer squash; "a marrow; Cucurbita pepo.

ヘマグルチニン〖生化〗〔たんぱく質〕hemagglutinin（略：HA）．
ヘマぞく【-族】〔アフリカ中部の民族〕the Hema；〔1人〕a Hema《pl. ~, ~s》．
ヘマトコッカス〖植〗〔緑藻類〕Haematococcus.
ヘミシンク〖商標〗〔特定の周波数の音を組み合わせることによって人の意識状態のコントロールを可能にする音響技術〕Hemi-Sync.
ヘム[1] 🔲 非ヘム鉄 non-heme iron.
ベムス【BEMS】〖ビルエネルギーマネジメントシステム〗BEMS; a building energy management system.
ペメトレキセド〖薬〗〔悪性胸膜中皮腫治療薬〕pemetrexed.
ヘモグロビン 🔲 還元ヘモグロビン ＝デオキシヘモグロビン．
へや【部屋】🔲 部屋頭〖相撲〗a stable master.
ペ・ヨンジュン【裴勇俊】Bae「Yong-jun [Yong-joon]（1972-　；韓国の俳優．
ヘラ 🔲 ヘラ神殿 a Temple of Hera.
へら[1]〔紙などの薄いもの1枚〕a thin sheet of paper．
[2]〔200字詰め原稿用紙・半ぺらの略〕200-character writing paper.
ペラ[1]〔マレーシア北西部, マラッカ海峡に臨む州〕Perak.
ペラ[2]〔プロペラの略〕a propeller． 🔲 三枚ペラ a three-bladed propeller.
ベライゾン・コミュニケーションズ〔米国の電気通信会社〕Verizon Communications Inc.
ヘラクレス 🔲 ヘラクレス指数〖証券〗〔ヘラクレス上場銘柄を対象とする, 大阪証券取引所の株価指数〕the Hercules index (of the Osaka Stock Exchange).
ヘラクレスおおかぶとむし【-大兜虫】〖昆〗〔コガネムシ科の昆虫；熱帯アメリカ原産〕a Hercules beetle; *Dynastes hercules*.
ヘラざお【-竿】〔釣り〕〔紀州で作られる高級和竿〕a *hera* carp fishing rod．〔⇒わざお〕
へらしぼり【へら絞り】〖金属加工〗spinning.
ペラルゴニジン〖化〗〔植物色素〕pelargonidin.
ヘリ 🔲 攻撃ヘリ〖軍〗an attack「helicopter [chopper, copter].　偵察ヘリ〖軍〗a「surveillance [spy, reconnaissance] helicopter [chopper, copter].
ペリア〖ゴルフ〗 🔲 ペリア方式〔ハンディキャップ算出法の1つ；6ホール抜粋出〕the peoria system. ◆ 新ペリア方式 ＝ダブル・ペリア方式〔⇒ダブル・ペリア〕.
ヘリアンサス〖植〗〔キク科ヒマワリ属の総称〕a helianthus.
ベリー Berry, Halle (1966-　；米国の映画女優).
「ベリー・コモ・ショー」〔米国の, 音楽ショー TV 番組〕The Perry Como Show.
ペリウィンクル〖植〗〔キョウチクトウ科のつる性多年草〕a periwinkle; *Vinca minor*.
「ペリカン文書」〔映画〕The Pelican Brief.
ヘリクタイト〖岩石〗〔ねじれた形の鍾乳石〕a helictite.
ヘリコニア〖植〗〔熱帯産バショウ科の多年草〕(a) heliconia; *Heliconia rostrata, Heliconia psittacorum* など．
ヘリコプター 🔲 消防防災ヘリコプター a fire-fighting disaster-relief helicopter.
ベリシャ Berisha, Sali (1945-　；アルバニアの政治家；大統領 [1992-97]; 首相 [2005-　]).
ヘリセノン〖化〗〔ホルモンなどの〕hericenone.
ペリツェウス・メルツバッヘル[メルツバッハー]びょう【-病】〖医〗〔進行性小児の中枢神経疾患〕Pelizaeus-Merzbacher disease（略：PMD）．
ペリトモレノひょうが【-氷河】〔アルゼンチン南部の氷河〕the Perito Moreno Glacier.
へりとりごけ【縁取り苔】〖植〗〔ヘリトリゴケ科の固着地衣〕a boulder lichen; *Porpidia albocaerulescens*.
ベリブ〔＜F *vélo libre*（＝free bicycle）；*vélo liberte*（＝bicycle freedom）〕〔パリの自転車レンタル制度〕Velib; Velib'; the (Paris) rental pushbike scheme.
ペリメニ〖料理〗〔ロシアの餃子〕pelmeni.
ベリル〖鉱〗〔緑柱石〕beryl.

ヘリング Haring, Keith (1958-90；米国の画家).
ペリントン Pellington, Mark (1962-　；米国の映画監督).
ベリンバウ〖楽器〗=ビリンバウ.
ベルカ Belka, Marek (1952-　；ポーランドの政治家；首相 [2004-05]).
ヘルゲランド Helgeland, Brian (1961-　；米国の映画監督・脚本家).
ベルゲンだいがく【-大学】〔ノルウェーの大学〕the University of Bergen.
ベルサウス〔米国の電話持株会社〕BellSouth Corp.
ヘルシーしんりんほう【-森林法】〖米法〗the Healthy Forest Restoration Act.
ベルシェ Berger, Oscar (1946-　；グアテマラの政治家；大統領 [2004-08]).
ヘルス 🔲 ヘルス・サプリメント〔健康を維持するための栄養補助食品〕a health supplement.
ベルチェこうか【-効果】〖物〗〔熱電効果の1つ〕the Peltier effect.
ベルチェそし【-素子】〖電子工〗a Peltier element.
ベルッチ Bellucci, Monica (1968-　；イタリア生まれの映画女優).
ベルディムハメドフ =ベルドイムハメドフ.
ベルテスびょう【-病】〖医〗〖獣医〗〔大腿骨頭への血行が途絶える小児, 小型犬に見られる疾患〕Perthes disease; Legg-Calvé-Perthes disease.
ベルト 🔲〔スーツ〕ケースベルト a luggage「strap [belt]; a suitcase「strap [belt].
ベルドイムハメドフ Berdymukhamedov, Gurbanguli (1957-　；トルクメニスタンの政治家；大統領 [2007-　]).
ベルナマつうしん【-通信】〔マレーシアの国営通信社〕Bernama.
ベルナンブコざい【-材】〔弦楽器の弓に用いられる〕pernambuco wood.
ヘルニア 🔲 還納性[非還納性]ヘルニア (a) reducible [(an) irreducible] hernia. 瘢痕ヘルニア (an) incisional hernia. 臍ヘルニア exomphalos.
ベルニエール Bernières, Louis de (1954-　；英国の小説家).
ヘルパー・ステーション〔訪問介護事業所〕a visiting care service center; a "Helper Station."
ヘルファイア〖米軍〗〔ヘリコプター搭載の対戦車ミサイル AGM-114 の愛称〕Hellfire. ▶ helicopter-launched, fire-and-forget〔ヘリコプター発射, 撃ちっ放し〕と hellfire〔地獄の炎〕をかけたもの.
ヘルプしょうこうぐん【HELLP 症候群】〖医〗〔妊娠中毒症の一種〕HELLP syndrome. ▶ HELLP は hemolysis〔溶血〕, elevated liver enzymes〔肝臓酵素の上昇〕, low platelet count〔血小板減少〕の略.
「ベルベット・ゴールドマイン」〔映画〕Velvet Goldmine.
ベルベル 🔲 ベルベル文化 Berber culture.
ベル・マーク〔学校備品を購入するためのマーク〕a Bell Mark. ◆ ～を集める collect Bell Marks.
ベルマークきょういくじょせいざいだん【-教育助成財団】the Bell Mark Foundation.
ヘルマン[2]〖ホテルなどの〗a bellhop; a bellboy.
ヘルマンド〔アフガニスタン南部の州〕Helmand.
ヘルメット 🔲 ヘルメット収納スペース〔バイクなどの〕(a) helmet storage space.
ペルメトリン〖薬〗〖農薬〗permethrin.
ベルリッツ〔米国に本社がある語学教育会社〕Berlitz.
ベルリンばん【-判】〔タブロイド判よりやや大きく細長い, 新聞のサイズ〕the Berliner format.
ヘレク Herek, Stephen (1958-　；米国の映画監督).
ベレスフォード Beresford, Bruce (1940-　；オーストラリアの映画監督).
ヘレナ・ルビンスタイン〖商標〗〔米国の化粧品ブランド〕Helena Rubinstein.

ヘレフォードシャー〔イングランド西部の州〕Hereford-shire.
ベレンジャー Berenger, Tom (1949/50–  ; 米国の映画俳優; 本名 Thomas Michael Moore).
ヘレンド〔商標〕〔ハンガリーの陶磁器ブランド〕Herend.
ベロー・シファカ〔動〕〔マダガスカル産のキツネザルの一種〕a Verreaux's sifaka; *Propithecus verreauxi*.
ペロシ Pelosi, Nancy (1940–  ; 米国の政治家; 下院議長〔2006–  〕).
ベロタクシー〔商標〕〔自転車タクシー〕a Velotaxi. ▶ 一般名 pedicab.
ペロブスカイト ▣ ペロブスカイト型酸化物〔化〕a perovskite-type oxide.
べん² 【弁・瓣】 弁形成術〔医〕(heart) valve plastic surgery; valvoplasty.
ペン Penn, Sean (1960–  ; 米国の映画俳優; 本名 Sean Justin Penn).
へんあつき【変圧器】▣ 変圧器室 a transformer room.
ベン・アリ Ben Ali, Zine El Abidine (1936–  ; チュニジアの政治家; 大統領〔1987–  〕).
へんい³【変異】▣ 変異株〔生物〕a mutant strain. 変異細胞〔生物〕a mutant cell.
へんか²【変化】▣ 変化咲き ＝かわりざき.
へんがお【変顔】〔カメラなどの前でわざとして見せる変な顔〕《make》a (funny) face.
へんかく¹【変革】▣ 変革期 a time of great change; an era of 'reform [transformation]. ▣ 自動車業界は今、〜期を迎えている. The automobile industry is now entering a period of transformation.
へんがくせいめいほけん【変額生命保険】variable life insurance.
へんがくねんきんほけん【変額年金保険】variable annuity insurance.
ベンガルールー〔インド南部の都市〕Bengalooru. ▶ 旧名 バンガロール.
ベンガルしょうのがん【小野雁】〔鳥〕a Bengal florican; *Houbaropsis bengalensis*.
ベンガルわんたぶんやぎじゅつけいざいきょうりょくこうそう【〜湾多分野技術経済協力構想】the Bay of Bengal Initiative for Multi-Sectoral Technical and Economic Cooperation《略：BIMSTEC》.
へんきゃく【返却】▣ 返却(予定)日〔図書館で借りた書籍・レンタルビデオなどの〕the return date; 《past》the (due) date of return.
べんきょう【勉強】▣ 勉強漬け constantly studying; being immersed in study. ▣ 〜漬けの毎日にはもううんざりだ. I am fed up with doing nothing but studying every day.
へんけい²【変型】〔紙・書籍のサイズの〕non-standard ('size [sized]). ▣ 変型判〔サイズ〕〔紙の〕a slightly non-standard size; a size which deviates slightly from the norm. ▣ B5[A4]〜判 a non-standard variety of 'B5 [A4]' paper; a sheet of slightly different size to standard 'B5 [A4]'.
ベンゲット〔フィリピン, ルソン島北部の州〕Benguet.
べんご【弁護】▣ 弁護側冒頭陳述 an [the] opening statement by the defense; the defense's [a defense] opening statement.
へんこう³【偏光】▣ 偏光板保護フィルム a polarizer protection film. 偏光膜 a polarizing film.
べんごし【弁護士】▣ 居候弁護士 ＝イソベン. 経営者弁護士 ＝ボスベン. 弁護士会照会〔弁護士が弁護に必要な情報の提供を弁護士会を通じて行政機関・企業等に求めること〕a request by a defense lawyer for confidential information concerning litigation via his or her bar association. 弁護士白書 a white paper on 'attorneys [the bar].
べんごしちざいネット【弁護士知財ネット】the Intellectual Property Lawyers Network.
へんこつ【返骨】〔ペット火葬場からの〕return of the cremated remains of a pet to the owner.
べんざ【便座】▣ 便座カバー〔布製などの〕a toilet seat cover; 〔(使い捨ての)紙製の〕a 'paper [disposable]' toilet seat cover. 便座除菌 paper toilet seat covers. 便座除菌クリーナー toilet seat disinfectant cleaner.
へんさい²【返済】▣ 返済額〔返済すべき〕an [the] amount to be repaid; the sum repayable; 〔返済済みの〕an [the] amount of money repaid; a [the] sum repaid. 返済期間 a [the] period of repayment. 返済免除 exemption from repayment. 返済猶予 (a) deferment of repayment.
へんじ²【返事】▣ 返事待ち awaiting reply. ▣ その件についてはまだ先方の〜待ちだ. As to that matter, we are still waiting for an answer from the other side.
ベンジャミン Benjamin, Richard (1937–  ; 米国の映画監督).
ベンジャミン・フランクリンしょう【〜賞】a Benjamin Franklin Medal《in Chemistry》.
へんしゅう³【編集】▣ 編集協力 editorial assistance. ▣ 〜協力費 a fee [payment] for editorial assistance. 編集ソフト(ウェア)〔電算〕editing [editor] software. ▣ 画像〜ソフト(ウェア) image editing software. 編集プロダクション a subcontractor for a publishing firm; an outsourcing bureau (for a publisher).
へんしょく²【偏食】▣ 偏食児童 a child with an unbalanced diet; 〔口〕a 'picky [fussy]' eater.
ペンシル ▣ ペンシル・ロケット a pencil rocket.
へんしん¹【返信】▣ 返信メール〔電算〕an [one's] e-mail reply.
ヘンストリッジ Henstridge, Natasha (1974–  ; カナダ生まれの米国の映画女優).
へんせい²【変声】▣ 変声器〔ボイスチェンジャー〕a voice changer.
へんせい⁴【編成・編制】▣ 編成記者〔新聞社の〕a lay-out editor.
へんそく¹【片側】▣ 片側麻痺 hemiplegia. ▷ hemiplegic an 〔精神安定剤〕benzodiazepine.
ベンゾジアゼピン〔薬〕〔精神安定剤〕benzodiazepine.
ヘンダーソン Henderson, Joe (1937-2001; 米国のジャズミュージシャン; テナーサックス奏者).
へんたい²【変体】▣ 変体紋〔蹄状紋・渦状紋・弓状紋のいずれにも属さない指紋〕an accidental (fingerprint 'pattern [type]').
へんたい³【編隊】▣ 編隊灯〔軍用機の〕a formation light.
ペンタサ〔商標・薬〕〔潰瘍性大腸炎治療薬〕Pentasa. ▶ 一般名 は メサラジン (mesalazine).
ペンタス〔植〕〔アカネ科の多年草〕an Egyptian star cluster; *Pentas lanceolata*.
ベンチ ▣ ベンチスタート〔野球などの試合で先発メンバーからはずれること〕starting (a game) on the bench. ▣ 彼はシーズン初戦じ〜スタートだった. He spent the season opener on the bench. ベンチ・レポーター〔スポーツ中継などの〕a bench reporter; 〔野球で〕a dugout reporter. ▣ 三塁側〜レポーター〔野球試合で〕a third-base dugout reporter. ベンチワーク〔スポーツ〕〔監督・コーチの作戦指揮〕《good》coaching from the bench.
ベンチェ〔ベトナム南部, メコンデルタ地帯の省; その省都〕Ben Tre.
ベンチャー ▣ ベンチャー投資 (a) venture investment. ベンチャー・ファンド a venture fund.
べんちゅう²【便柱】〔医〕a column of feces. ▣ 便柱細少 stringy stools.
ベンチュリこうか【〜効果】〔流体力学〕the [a] Venturi [venturi] effect.
べんつう【便通】▣ 便通異常 (a) bowel irregularity; irregular bowels; an irregular bowel movement.

へんとう²【扁桃】 ▭ 扁桃体〚解〛the amygdala《pl. -lae》; the amygdaloid「complex [nucleus, body]. 扁桃病巣感染症〚医〛(a) tonsillar focal infection.
へんどう【変動】 ▭ 利率変動型(の)〔保険商品など〕interest-sensitive. ♦利率～型終身保険 interest-sensitive whole-life insurance. ♦変動型(金融)商品 an interest-sensitive product. 変動金利(型)ローン a variable interest rate loan. 変動金利定期預金 a variable interest rate deposit. 変動相場制 a floating exchange rate system. ♦～相場にする float《the yen》. 変動リスク〚金融〛(a) fluctuation risk. ♦為替～リスク (an) exchange rate fluctuation risk.
べんとう【弁当】 ▭ 弁当箱ダイエット a lunch-box diet (based on packing a lunch box with three parts rice, one part main dish and two parts vegetables).
ベントン Benton, Robert (1932– ; 米国の映画監督).
へんにゅうがく【編入学】admission(s) and placement(s). ～する be admitted and allotted to a class

of an appropriate level.
べんぴ【便秘】 ▭ 器質性[機能性]便秘 organic [functional] constipation. ♦便秘薬 a laxative.
へんぴん【返品】 ▭ 返品調整引当金 an allowance for sales return; a reserve for「returned goods [loss on goods unsold]. ♦返品リスク the [a] risk that《items》will be returned. 返品率 a rate of returned goods. 返品量 a「number [volume] of returned goods.
へんむ【片務】 ▭ 片務性 the unilateral nature《of an agreement》
ベン・メリア〔カンボジアの遺跡〕Beng Mealea.
べんもうモーター【鞭毛-】〚生物〛a flagellar motor.
べんりしほう【弁理士法】〚法〛the Patent Attorney Law.
へんれい²【返戻】 ▭ 返戻率〚保険〛a [the] rate to maturity.
へんろ【遍路】 ▭ お遍路さん a (Buddhist) pilgrim. 遍路姿 a (white Buddhist) pilgrim's dress.

# ほ

ボア² ▭ ボア径〔ライフル銃の〕a bore diameter. [＝やまけい]
ボアオ【博鰲】＝はくごう².
ホアヒン〔タイ南部の保養地〕Hua Hin.
ホアビン〔ベトナム北西部の省; その省都〕Hoa Binh.
ホアルー〔ベトナム北部, ニンビン省にある古都〕Hoa Lu.
ほあん【保安】 ▭ 保安監査 a safety「inspection [check]. 保安基準適合品 a safety-standard compliant product. 保安検査〔石油コンビナートなどの〕a safety inspection;〔テロ対策などの〕a security check. ♦～検査場〔空港の〕a security checkpoint. 保安検査員〔空港など〕a security「inspector [guard].
ほあんりん【保安林】 ▭ 魚つき保安林 a fish-breeding forest. 干害防備保安林 a drought prevention forest. 航行目標保安林 a navigation landmark forest. 水害防備保安林 a flood damage prevention forest. 水源涵養(かんよう)保安林 a headwater conservation forest. 潮害防備保安林 a tide and salty wind prevention forest. 土砂崩壊防備保安林 a landslide prevention forest. 土砂流出防備保安林 a soil run-off prevention forest. なだれ防止保安林 a snow avalanche prevention forest. 飛砂防備保安林 a shifting-sand prevention forest. 風致保安林 a scenery conservation forest. 保健保安林 a public health forest. 防火保安林 a fire prevention forest. 防雪保安林 a snow drift prevention forest. 防風保安林 a windbreak forest. 防霧保安林 a fog inflow prevention forest. 落石防止保安林 a falling-rock prevention forest.
ホイアン〔ベトナム中部, クアンナム省の都市〕Hoi An.
ほいく¹【保育】 ▭ 保育学 early child and care education; infant care and education. 保育施設 a (day) nursery; an infant care facility.
ほいくじょ【保育所】 ▭ 院内保育所〔病院内の〕a hospital day care center.
ボイス ▭ ボイス・チェンジャー a voice changer. ボイス・ブログ〔電算〕〔インターネット上の音声形式のブログ〕a voice blog.
ボイス・オーバー・アイ・ピー [-IP]〚通信〛＝ブイ・オー・アイ・ピー.
ほいでる〔ぽいと捨てる〕throw away.
ポイズン・ピル〔証券〕〔企業買収の防衛策の1つ〕a poison pill.
ボイセイえんじん【-猿人】〚人類〛〔東アフリカで発掘された強い顎と歯を持つ猿人〕Paranthropus boisei.
ボイップ【VoIP】〚通信〛＝ブイ・オー・アイ・ピー.

ボイト＝ヴォイト.
ホイヘンス²〔米国の土星探査機カッシーニから発射された着陸機; 2005年, 土星の衛星タイタンに着陸〕Huygens; the Huygens probe.
ほいほい(と) ♦彼は妻のどんなわがままな注文にも～応じた. He readily went right along with anything his wife asked for, no matter how selfish it was. ／誘われたからといってどこにでも～ついて行くな. Don't be so willing to go tagging along everywhere behind someone just because they invited you.
ホイリゲ〔当年産のワインを供するウィーンの居酒屋〕a Heurige(r)《pl. Heurigen》;〔そのワイン〕(a) Heurige(r).
ボイル 1 Boyle, Danny (1956– ; 英国生まれの映画監督).
2 Boyle, Peter (1935-2006; 米国の映画俳優).
ポイント ▭ 好ポイント ♦釣りの好～ a hot fishing spot. ▭ ポイント・ガード〔バスケットボール〕〔攻撃の指示を行う選手〕a point guard (略: PG). ポイント・カラー＝さしいろ. ポイント故障〔鉄道の〕a points failure. ポイント還元〚商〛a rebate in points. ♦〔広告で〕今なら10％～還元. Buy now and get a 10% rebate in points. ／～還元率 rebate rate [the rate of rebate] in points. ポイント単価〔年金・退職金などの支給額算定に利用される〕a《pension》point (conversion) value. ポイント・ラリー〔ポイントカードで点数を集める, 商店街などの企画〕a (loyalty card) point-scoring campaign.
ほう²【法】 ▭ 法教育 law-related education. 法整備(necessary) legal adjustment(s); adjustments to the relevant laws, (legal) provision(s). ♦移植医療の急速な進歩に～整備が追いつけないのが実情である. The truth is that「the law is [legal provisions are] unable to keep up with the rapid developments in medical transplants. 法体制 ♦早急に～体制を確立する必要がある. A legal system needs to be established immediately.
ぼう²【坊】 ▭ 子坊〔寺の本坊に対して〕living quarters for monks other than the chief priest; attached living quarters. 本坊〔寺の住職の住居〕the chief priest's living quarters;〔宗派の本山〕the head temple. 次[三]男坊 one's number「two [three] son.
ぼう⁶【棒】 ▭ 棒体操 (single) stick「exercise [fitness].
ほうい¹【方位】 ▭ 方位学 divination based on eight directions around a location; the study of directions.
ぼうえい【防衛】 ▭ 防衛参与官 a director general. 防衛装備品 defense equipment. 防衛大臣 the Min-

ぼうえいしょう

ister of Defense; the Defense Minister. 防衛駐在官 a defense attaché. 防衛本能 a「defensive [defense]」instinct.

**ぼうえいしょう**[1]【防衛省】the Ministry of Defense (略: MOD); the Defense Ministry. ► 2007年防衛庁から昇格.

**ぼうえいしょう**[2]【防衛相】the Minister of Defense; the Defense Minister.

**ぼうえいちょうせっちほう**【防衛庁設置法】〖法〗the Defense Agency Establishment Law.

**ぼうえいほうがっかい**【防衛法学会】the Japan Society of Defense Law.

**ぼうえき**[1]【防疫】☐▣ 防疫措置 quarantine measures. ◐〜措置を取る[強化する] take [step up, strengthen, heighten] quarantine measures; impose [strengthen] a quarantine. 防疫服 a biohazard suit.

**ぼうえき**[2]【貿易】☐▣ 貿易赤字相手国 a nation with which (Japan) has a trade deficit. 貿易関連技術支援 trade-related technical assistance (略: TRTA). 貿易黒字相手国 a nation with which (Japan) has a trade surplus. 貿易再保険 trade reinsurance. 貿易障壁報告 ＝がいこくぼうえきしょうへきほうこく. 貿易総額 the total「value [amount] of trade. 貿易停止 《impose》a trade embargo. 貿易立国 a national commitment to (international) trade; national development based on (international) trade.

**ぼうえききねんび**【貿易記念日】〔6月28日〕(International) Trade Day.

**ぼうえきのぎじゅつてきしょうがいにかんするきょうてい**〔貿易の技術的障害に関する協定〕〔世界貿易機関(WTO) 加盟国間の〕the Agreement(s) on Technical Barriers to Trade; the TBT Agreement(s).

**ぼうえんきょう**[1]【望遠鏡】☐▣ 望遠鏡衛星〔宇宙〕a telescope satellite. ◐X線〜衛星 an X-ray telescope satellite / 赤外線〜衛星 an infrared telescope satellite / 電波〜衛星 a radio telescope satellite.

**ぼうおん**[1]【防音】☐▣ 防音カーペット a soundproof carpet. 防音車輪〖鉄道〗noise-reducing wheels.

**ぼうか**[4]【放火】☐▣ 放火事件 an incident [a case] of arson; an arson attack. 放火致死罪〖法〗(an) arson resulting in death; (a) fatal arson. 放火予備罪〖法〗《be accused of》preparation to commit arson.

**ぼうか**【防火】
☐▣ 防火戸[扉] a fire door; a fire shutter. 防火服 a「fireproof [fire-resistant] suit; fireproof [fire-resistant] clothing;〔消防士の〕turnout gear; bunker gear.

**ぼうかい**[3]【崩壊】☐▣ 崩壊実験〖物〗a decay experiment.

**ぼうがい**[1]【妨害】☐▣ 捜査妨害 obstruction of an investigation.

**ぼうかつ**【包括】☐▣ 包括対話〔あらゆる問題を対象とする二者間の協議〕comprehensive「talks [negotiations], discussion(s) on all topics. ◐両国は和平進展のための〜対話を続けることで合意した. The two countries agreed to continue comprehensive peace negotiations. 包括提携《企業間での》(form, enter into) a comprehensive tie-up (with…). ◐彼の会社はフランスの会社と〜提携した. His company「formed [entered into] a comprehensive tie-up with a French firm. 包括払い〔病名・治療内容によって定額の医療費を支払う方式〕a system of paying medical expenses based on「diagnosis-related groups [DRGs];〔日本の医療制度で〕diagnosis procedure combination (略: DPC);〔米国の医療制度で〕prospective payment.

**ぼうかつてき**【包括的】☐▣ 包括的協議＝包括提携⇨ほうかつ).

**ぼうかん**[3]【防寒】☐▣ 防寒肌着 insulated underwear.

**ぼうかんしゃ**【傍観者】☐▣ 傍観者効果〖心理〗the bystander effect; bystander apathy.

**ほうき**[4]【放棄】☐▣ 放棄田 an abandoned [a disused, an uncultivated] rice field.

**ほうぎ**【謀議】☐▣ 事前謀議 plotting in advance.

**ぼうぎ**[2]【防蟻】termite prevention. ☐▣ 防蟻剤 (a) termiticide; an antitermite chemical. 防蟻処理 antitermite treatment. 防蟻対策 antitermite measures.

**ぼうきゅう**【防球】☐▣ 防球ネット a ball net. 防球フェンス a ball fence.

**ぼうぎょりつ**【防御率】☐▣ 最優秀防御率 the「best [lowest] earned run average; the「best [lowest] ERA. ◐最優秀〜投手 the pitcher with the「best [lowest] earned run average [ERA]; the ERA leader. ☐▣ チーム防御率 a team「earned run average [ERA].

**ほうぐんほうかいしょうこうぐん**【蜂群崩壊症候群】〔ミツバチの群れが巣箱から突然消え失せる現象〕colony collapse disorder (略: CCD).

**ぼうゲラ**【棒—】〔印刷〕a galley (proof).

**ほうげん**[1]【方言】☐▣ 方言文学 (a) dialect(al) literature.

**ほうげん**[2]【放言】☐▣ 放言癖 a tendency to speak「inappropriately [out of turn]; a habit of saying the wrong thing in the wrong place [letting inappropriate things slip out].

**ぼうけん**[1]【冒険】☐▣ 冒険観光 adventure tourism. 冒険教育 adventure(-based) education.

**ほうけんじょうり**【放権譲利】〔中国の地方分権化政策〕ceding authority to the regions.

「**冒険野郎マクガイバー**」〔米国の, 豊富な科学知識と身近な物を利用して苦境を脱する男の TVドラマ〕MacGyver.

**ぼうご**【防護】☐▣ 防護基準〔有毒物質を扱う職場などの〕a protection standard;《set》standards of protection 《against ionizing radiation》. 防護服 a protective suit; a「hazmat [Hazmat] suit. ► hazmat は hazardous material (危険物質) の略. ◐化学[放射線]〜服 ⇨がく[2], ほうしゃせん[1]. 防護無線〖鉄道〗〔緊急時に列車から特殊な電波を発信して付近を走行する列車の二次事故を防止する装置〕train-protection radio equipment.

**ほうこう**[1]【方向】☐▣ 方向幕〔列車・バスなどの〕a destination「indicator [display].

**ほうこう**[3]【芳香】☐▣ 芳香植物 an aromatic plant; an aromatic. 芳香心理学 aromachology; the psychology of aromas. 芳香浴 an「aromatic [aroma] bath; aromatic [aroma] bathing.

**ぼうこう**[11]【宝鋼】〔上海宝鋼集団の略称〕Baosteel. [⇨しゃんはいほうこうしゅうだん]

**ぼうこう**[2]【膀胱】☐▣ 新膀胱〖医〗〔小腸の一部を切り取って尿をためる機能を持たせたもの〕a neobladder. 膀胱温存療法〖医〗〖膀胱がんの〕bladder「conservation [conserving] therapy. 膀胱脱〖医〗(a) prolapse of the (urinary) bladder.

**ほうこうしゃ**【包交車】〖医〗〔包帯交換のための道具や薬品を載せる手押しワゴン〕a dressing cart.

**ほうこく**[2]【報告】☐▣ 報告基準 standards [standard procedures] for reporting. 報告義務 a duty [an obligation] to report《an accident》. 報告漏れ (a) failure to report《an accident》. ◐その病院は医療事故について5件の〜漏れがあった. The hospital failed to report accidents during treatment on five occasions.

**ほうこく**[1]【亡国】☐▣ 亡国病 a disease fatal to the nation; a nationally ruinous disease.

**ぼうこんシート**【防痕—】a root barrier.

**ぼうさい**【防災】☐▣ 防災ガラス safety glass for protection against disasters; disaster safety glass. 防災環境保全林 a forest preserved to protect its ecology and to prevent damage by natural disasters. 防災基金 a disaster (prevention) fund. 防災教育 disaster mitiga-

ほうせい

tion「training [education]. 防災行政無線 government emergency radio; an official radio system for disaster prevention and relief. 防災協定 a disaster damage prevention agreement. 防災協力イニシアチブ〔2005年, 日本政府が国連防災世界会議で提唱した〕Initiative for Disaster Reduction (through ODA). 防災工学 disaster prevention engineering. 防災弱者 ＝ 災害弱者 (⇒さいがい¹). 防災頭巾 a protective padded hood; a safety hood. 防災船〔災害時に出動する〕a disaster prevention ship. 防災先進県 a prefecture with advance disaster-prevention capabilities. 防災体制 a disaster-relief system. 防災倉庫 an emergency supply「storage shed [warehouse]. 防災地理学 geography applied to disaster prevention. 防災白書 a white paper on disaster management;〔内閣府の〕the White Paper on Disaster Management《2005》. 防災服 an emergency outfit. 防災ベッド a canopy bed built to withstand natural disasters. 防災ヘリ a disaster-relief [an emergency] helicopter. 防災マーク a disaster prevention「mark [seal]. 防災ラジオ a「portable [wind-up] radio for use in disasters; a disaster radio. 防災ロボット a disaster [an accident] recovery robot.

**ぼうさいかがくぎじゅつけんきゅうじょ**【防災科学技術研究所】the National Research Institute for Earth Science and Disaster Prevention（略：NIED）.

**ぼうさいシステムけんきゅうじょ**【防災―研究所】the Disaster Prevention System Institute.

**ぼうさいせかいかいぎ**【防災世界会議】⇒こくれんぼうさいせかいかいぎ.

**ほうさく²**【豊作】▫▪ 豊作祈願《offer》a prayer for a good harvest.

**ぼうさつ²**【謀殺】▫▪ 謀殺罪〔日本の旧刑法の用語で, 計画的殺人の罪〕premeditated [deliberate, wilful, *wilful] murder.

**ほうしつ**【放湿】moisture release. 〜する release moisture. 〜性 moisture release characteristics;〔布地, 衣類などの〕wicking「properties [ability, characteristics].

**ほうしっこう**【法執行】law enforcement; enforcement of a law. ▫▪ 法執行機関 a law enforcement agency（略：LEA）. 法執行当局〔総称的に〕the law enforcement authorities;〔個々の〕a law enforcement agency. 法執行能力 (a) law enforcement capability.

**ほうしゃ⁵**【房舎】〔刑務所の〕a criminal ward.

**ほうしゃがめ**【放射亀】【動】〔リクガメ科のカメ〕a radiated tortoise; *Geochelone radiata*.

**ほうしゃせん¹**【放射線】▫▪ 放射線化学療法 chemoradiotherapy. 放射線過剰照射 excessive irradiation; over-irradiation. 放射線カプセル【医】a radioactive「seed [capsule, pellet]. 放射線外科【医】radiosurgery; radiation surgery; stereotactic external beam irradiation. 放射線検知器 a radiation detector. 放射線誤照射 mistaken exposure to irradiation;【医】misirradiation. 放射線殺菌〔食物などの〕radiation sterilization. 放射線照射 irradiation; exposure to radiation; radiation exposure. 放射線照射量 the amount of irradiation; (the degree of)「exposure to radiation [radiation exposure]; (an) irradiation《of 1200 roentgens》. 放射線診断【医】radiodiagnosis. 放射線診断医 a diagnostic radiologist. 放射線防護学 radiation protection science. 放射線防護服 a radiation protection suit. 放射線レベル a radiation level; a level of radiation.

**ほうしゃせんのえいきょうにかんするこくれんかがくいいんかい**【放射線の影響に関する国連科学委員会】⇒げんしほうしゃせんのえいきょうにかんするかがくいいんかい.

**ほうしゃのう**【放射能】▫▪ 放射能レベル a「radioactivity [radiation] level; a level of「radioactivity [radia-

tion].

**ほうしゅう**【報酬】▫▪ 報酬委員会〔委員会等設置会社の〕a remuneration committee.

**ほうじゅう³**【放獣】〔捕獲した動物などを自然に帰すこと〕releasing《captured bears》back into the wild; release into the wild; wild release. 〜する release《captured bears》(back) into the wild. ◉ 住民たちは捕獲した熊の〜に反対している. The residents oppose the release of captured bears into the wild. ▫▪ 学習放獣 release of captured《bears》back into the wild after conditioning them to fear humans and human settlements.

**ぼうしゅう**【防臭】▫▪ 防臭加工 antiodor [deodorizing] treatment [processing]. 防臭繊維 a deodorant fiber.

**ぼうじゅう**【防獣】animal-proofing; protection against wild animals; keeping「out [off] wild animals. ▫▪ 防獣ネット「網」an animal net;〈集合的に〉animal netting.

**ほうしゅつ¹**【放出】▫▪ 放出品 goods disposed of《by the government》; surplus《army》goods.

**ほうじょ**【幇助】▫▪ 幇助自殺〔医師の助けを借りた自殺〕(an) assisted suicide.

**ほうしょう⁸**【報償】▫▪ 報償費 remuneration expenses; a remuneration fund. ◉《犯罪》捜査〜費 (a) payment to citizens [remuneration to members of the public] who cooperate in an criminal enquiry.

**ほうじょう³**【放生】▫▪ 放生池 a ceremonial release pond.

**ほうしょ**（がみ）【奉書（紙）】fine-quality white Japanese paper (for ceremonial use).

**ほうしょく¹**【宝飾】▫▪ 宝飾デザイナー a jewelry designer.

**ほうじょせいがく**【法女性学】feminist jurisprudence.

**ほうしん¹**【方針】▫▪ 方針転換 a policy「switch [change]. ◉ 〜する switch [change] one's policy / 180度の〜転換 a 180 degree policy change; a (complete) policy「turnabout [about-face] / 〜転換に踏み切る embark on a「policy change [change of course].

**ほうじん¹**【邦人】▫▪ 邦人テロ対策室〔外務省領事移住部の〕the Terrorism Prevention Division. 邦人保護 protection of Japanese nationals.

**ほうじん³**【法人】▫▪ 法人企業景気予測調査〔財務省の〕the Business Outlook Survey (published by the Japanese Ministry of Finance). 法人企業統計調査〔財務省の〕the Financial Statements Statistics of Corporations by Industry. 法人二税〔法人住民税と法人事業税〕the two corporate taxes.

**ぼうじん³**【防刃】knife-proof. ▫▪ 防刃グローブ「手袋」a「stab-proof [knife-proof] glove. 防刃ベスト「チョッキ, 衣」a「stab-proof [knife-proof] vest; stab-proof [knife-proof] clothing.

**ほうじんぜいほう**【法人税法】【法】the Corporation Tax Law. ▫▪ 法人税法違反 (a) violation of the Corporation Tax Law. ◉ 〜違反で起訴される be prosecuted for a violation of the Corporation Tax Law.

**ぼうず**【坊主】▫▪ 坊主タイヤ〔溝のすり減ったタイヤ〕a bald tire.

**ほうすい³**【放水】▫▪ 放水銃「砲, 機」(a) water cannon.

**ぼうすい¹**【防水】▫▪ 防水シート a waterproof sheet; (a) tarpaulin; *〈口〉(a) tarp. 防水性 waterproofness; waterproof qualities. 防水透湿加工 permeable waterproofing.

**ほうせい²**【法制】▫▪ 法制化 legislation; giving《proposals》legal force; passage《of a bill》into law. ◉ 〜化する give《a proposal》legal force; pass《a bill》into law / 党はこの歌を国家として〜化することを望んでいるが, 私個人は反対だ. The party wants to give this song legal force as the national anthem, but I personally am opposed to that.

ほうせい⁵【縫製】▸ 縫製技術者 a (professional [trained, qualified]) sewer. 縫製工場 a sewing factory.

ほうせい⁶【放精】〔魚などの精子の放出〕(a) discharge [release] of sperm.

ほうせいししょう【乏精子症】【医】〔精子減少症〕oligospermia; oligozoospermia.

ほうせいしんぎかい【法制審議会】▸ 法制審議会人名用漢字部会 the Legislative Council's Subcommittee on Kanji for Personal Names.

ほうせつ²【抱摂】【動】amplexus.

ほうそ²【硼素】▸ 硼素化合物 a boron compound.

ほうそ³【作】＝はهて.

ほうそう¹【包装】▸ 個[個別]包装 individual [separate] packaging [wrapping]. ◯ 個[個別]～の individually [separately] packaged [wrapped] 《tea bags》.

ほうそう⁴【放送】▸ 命令放送 〔政府が NHK にさせる〕ordered broadcasting; broadcasting undertaken on the instructions of the Minister of Internal Affairs and Communications; 〔1 回〕an ordered broadcast. ▸ 放送作家 a broadcast writer. 放送時間帯 broadcasting time(s); time on air; the time during which 《news》broadcasting takes place. 放送ジャーナリスト a broadcast journalist. 放送受信料 a (broadcast) 「license [subscription, viewing] fee. 放送評論家 a broadcast(ing) critic. 放送プロデューサー a broadcast producer. 放送免許 （apply for）a broadcast(ing) license. ◯ ～免許制度 a broadcast licensing system.

ほうそう⁵【法曹】▸ 法曹資格 judicial qualifications.

ほうそう⁸【砲創】a shell wound.

ほうそう²【暴走】▸ 暴走行為 speeding; reckless [dangerous] driving; hot-rodding. 暴走車 〔無謀運転の〕a 「dangerously [recklessly] driven 「car [vehicle]; a 「car [vehicle] driven by a reckless driver; a speeding 「car [vehicle]; 〔故障などによる〕an out-of-control 「car [vehicle]; a runaway 「car [vehicle].

ほうそう³【防霜】frost protection; protection against frost damage. ▸ 防霜ファン〔霜害から農作物を守るための送風機〕a frost protection fan.

ほうそうきねんび【放送記念日】〔3 月 22 日〕Broadcasting (Commemoration) Day.

ほうそうげもん【宝相[法相]華文】〔様々な植物文様を唐草風に組み合わせたもの〕an imaginary [a fanciful] arabesque (pattern, design) of many types of plants.

ほうそうとじんけんとうけんりにかんするいいんかい【放送と人権等人権等権利に関する委員会】〔放送と人権等権利に関する委員会機構 (BRO) が運営する〕the Broadcast and Human Rights/Other Related Rights Committee（略: BRC）.

ほうそうとじんけんとうけんりにかんするいいんかいきこう【放送と人権等権利に関する委員会機構】the Broadcast and Human Rights/Other Related Rights Organization（略: BRO）. ◯ ～の〕2001 年、NHK と日本民間放送連盟が共同で設立した苦情処理機関.

ほうそうとせいしょうねんにかんするいいんかい【放送と青少年に関する委員会】〔放送倫理・番組向上機構 (BPO) の〕the Broadcasters Council for Youth Programs.

「暴走特急」〔映画〕Under Siege 2: Dark Territory.

ほうそうばんぐみこうじょういいんかい【放送番組向上委員会】〔放送倫理・番組向上機構 (BPO) の〕the Broadcasters Council for Quality Programming.

ほうそうりんけんしょういいんかい【放送倫理検証委員会】〔放送倫理・番組向上機構 (BPO) 内の〕the Broadcasting Ethics Verification Committee.

ほうそうりんり・ばんぐみこうじょうきこう【放送倫理・番組向上機構】the Broadcasting Ethics & Program Improvement Organization（略: BPO）.

ほうたい¹【包帯】▸ 弾性[弾力]包帯 an elastic bandage.

ほうたい⁵【包袋】【特許】a file wrapper.

ほうだに【防だに】tick [mite] control. ▸ 防ダニ加工 tick-[mite-]control treatment; antitick [antimite] treatment.

ほうだん【防弾】▸ 防弾ボディー〔自動車などの〕a bulletproof body.

ほうち¹【放置】▸ 放置虐待 abuse through neglect; neglectful abuse. 放置車両 an illegally parked vehicle. 放置車両確認標章 a ticket for an illegally parked vehicle; a parking ticket.

ほうちゅう²【防虫】▸ 防虫スプレー an insect repellent spray.

ほうちょう²【放鳥】▸ 自然放鳥 releasing (artificially-raised) birds into the wild. 標識放鳥 release of a tagged bird.

ほうちょう⁴【膨張・膨張】▸ 膨張試験 an expansion test (of concrete). 膨張主義〔領土・国威・経済活動などに関して〕expansionism.

ほうちょう⁵【防鳥】birdproofing; protection from birds; keeping 「out [off] birds. ▸ 防鳥ネット[網] a bird net; 〈集合的に〉bird netting.

ぼうついセンター【暴追ー】⇒ぼうりょくついほう（うんどう）すいしんセンター.

ほうてい²【法廷】▸ 法廷漁り〔自分に有利な判決を出してくれそうな裁判所の管轄区を選んで訴訟を起こすこと〕forum shopping. 法廷外紛争解決 ＝さいばんがいふんそうかいけつ. 法廷供述 testimony in 「court [a court of law]; court testimony. 法廷参加〔犯罪被害者などの〕participation （by crime victims or their families）in (criminal) trials. 法廷尋問 prosecutorial questioning （of a defendant）. 法廷地国 〔その裁判が行われている国〕the [a] country of jurisdiction.

ほうてい⁴【法定】▸ 法定貸出金利【金融】〔中国で、企業などへの貸出金利〕the 「statutory [legal] lending rate [interest rate on loans]. 法定限度 a legal limit. ◯ 金融機関が破綻した場合、普通預金は～限度額まで保護されます. If a financial institution fails, ordinary deposits are protected up to the legal limit. 法定公告〔法令により公告掲載が義務づけられている事項を利害関係者に知らせること〕a legal public notice; 〔その公告文〕a legal public announcement. 法定後見(人)制度 a 「legal [statutory] guardianship system. 法定証拠主義〔裁判官の恣意的な判断を防止するため判断基準を法で定める考え方〕the principle of legal restraint on judicial evidentiary judgments. 法定耐用年数 a statutory useful life (of three years).

ほうてき²【法的】▸ 法的係争 a legal dispute. 法的効果 (legal) validity. ◯ 「式式がきちんと守られていない遺言書では～効果[効力]がありません. If your will is not completed properly, it will 「be (legally) invalid [lack (legal) validity]. 法的整理 ⇒せいり². 法的責任 (a) legal responsibility. 法的効～ある be legally responsible. 法的地位 「a [sb's] legal status. 法的リスク (a) legal risk.

ほうテラス【法ー】＝にほんしほうしえんセンター.

ほうでん²【放電】▸ 高圧放電 (a) 「high-intensity [high-voltage] discharge. ◯ 高圧～ランプ a high-intensity discharge lamp; an HID lamp.

ぼうと²【暴徒】▸ 暴徒化〔デモ隊の一部が〕～化し、大使館を包囲して投石をはじめた. Some of the demonstrators 「went on the rampage [got out of control], surrounded the Embassy, and started throwing stones.

ほうどう²【報道】▸ 報道規制 regulation of [control over] the 「mass media [press]; a regulation governing the media; controls [restrictions] on the press. 報道検閲 news censorship. 報道自粛 voluntary restraint [self-censorship] by the press. 報道資料 a press kit. 報道制限 restrictions on 「news reporting [journalism〕. 報道被害 victimization by the media; suffering caused by the media. ◐被害者家族に〜被害が及んでいる. The victim's family are being caused extra suffering as a result of media victimization. | The media are aggravating the sufferings of the victim's family. / 〜被害救済弁護士 a lawyer who specializes in media victimization cases / 〜被害相談窓口 an advice bureau for victims of the media. 報道被害者 a victim of (reporting by) the media. 報道ヘリ a media helicopter.

ぼうとう²【冒頭】 ◻◻ 冒頭演説 《give, deliver》an opening speech.

ぼうとう⁴【暴騰】 ◻◻ 暴騰暴落 sharp increases and sudden declines《in prices》.

ほうにち【訪日】 ◻◻ 訪日外国人 a foreign visitor to Japan. ◐2006年の〜外国人の数 the number of foreign visitors to Japan in 2006 / 〜外国人旅行者 a foreign traveler visiting Japan.

ほうのう²【奉納】 ◻◻ 奉納太鼓 drumming in the precincts of a Shinto shrine 《on the day of a festival》. 奉納土俵入り 〔相撲〕a ceremonial display by sumo wrestlers in their brocaded aprons, held as an offering at a shrine.

ほうのひ【法の日】〔10月1日〕Law Day.

ぼうはいじょうこう【暴排条項】＝暴力団排除条項 (⇨ぼうりょくだん).

ぼうばく【防爆】explosion protection; ex protection. ◐〜の explosion-protected; ex-protected. 防爆機器 explosion-protected equipment; ex-protected equipment; ex equipment. 防爆構造 explosion-protected construction. 防爆スーツ ＝対爆スーツ.

ぼうはん¹【防犯】 ◻◻ 防犯委員 a member of a local crime prevention「committee [group, squad]. 防犯意識 crime (prevention) awareness; awareness of (the need to prevent) crime; crime prevention preparedness. ◐地域住民の〜意識を高める increase crime awareness among local residents; make local residents more aware of crime. 防犯ガラス security glass. 防犯環境設計 crime prevention through environmental design (略: CPTED). 防犯監視システム a crime prevention surveillance system; a surveillance system for crime prevention. 防犯機能 an「anti theft [antitheft]」function [feature] 《of a surveillance camera》. 防犯教室 a crime prevention class. ◐子供を犯罪から守るため, 警察官が小中学校で〜教室を開催しています. To protect children from crime, police are holding "crime prevention" classes in primary and secondary schools. 防犯スプレー (a) self-defense spray; (a) pepper spray. 防犯センサー a burglar detector; a burglar sensor. 防犯体制 a system for crime prevention; a crime prevention 「system [set-up]. 防犯タグ 〔万引き防止の〕＝万引き防止装置〔タグ〕(⇨まんびき). 防犯登録 〔自転車などの〕theft prevention registration. ◐〜登録証 a 《bicycle》 theft prevention registration「tag [label]. 防犯ビデオ 〔カメラ〕a (video) surveillance camera; 〔録画テープ/ディスク〕a video surveillance 「tape [disk]. ◐犯人が被害者の銀行口座から1,500万円を引き出したことがその支店の〜ビデオで確認された. The fact that the suspect withdrew fifteen million yen from the victim's account has been corroborated by the branch's surveillance「camera [video tape]. 防犯フィルム 〔窓ガラス用の〕(a) shatter-resistant window film. 防犯ホイッスル a 「crime-prevention [safety]」whistle. 防犯マップ a crime-prevention map. 防犯マニュアル a crime prevention manual. 防犯窓 a 「burglarproof [security]」window.

ぼうひ³【防匪】〔法を悪用する法律家の蔑称〕a pettifogger; a legal manipulator.

ぼうふう¹【防風】 ◻◻ 防風性 windproofness; wind-proof qualities. 防風ネット windbreak netting; a windbreak net.

ほうふく²【報復】 ◻◻ 報復合戦 tit-for-tat 「retaliation [fighting]. 報復行動 《take》 retaliatory action 《against…》. 報復声明 a statement 「of [claiming, taking]」responsibility for a retaliatory attack. ◐〜声明を出す issue a statement of [claim] responsibility for a retaliatory attack. 報復宣言 a retaliatory declaration 《of war》; a declaration of revenge.

ほうむ【法務】 ◻◻ 法務死 〔史〕〔極東国際軍事裁判有罪者の刑死および獄中死〕the death of a defendant, found guilty by the International Military Tribunal for the Far East, by execution or in jail (recognized by the Japanese authorities as having occurred during tenure of office).

ほうめん【放免】 ◻◻ 仮放免 〔入管施設からの〕(a) temporary release.

ほうもん⁵【訪問】 ◻◻ 訪問歯科 〔歯の出張治療〕a visiting dental service; visiting dental care. 訪問診療 visiting medical 「examination and treatment [care]. 訪問リハビリ home-visit rehabilitation; rehabilitative home-care.

ほうもんかいご【訪問介護】home-visit (nursing) care; (a) visiting care service. ◻◻ 夜間対応型訪問介護 (the type of) home-visit (nursing) care available at night. 予防訪問介護 preventive home-visiting; a preventive home visit (program). ▶「訪問介護」の新しい名称. 訪問介護員 a home 「help(er) [carer]; *a caregiver. 訪問介護事業所 a visiting care 「service center.

ほうもんかんご【訪問看護】 ◻◻ 訪問看護ステーション a visiting 「nurse [nursing] station.

ほうもんはんばい【訪問販売】 ◻◻ 訪問販売員 a 「door-to-door [house-to-house] salesperson [salesman, saleswoman]. 訪問販売業者 a door-to-door sales company.

ほうらん²【放卵】〔魚・カニなどの卵の放出〕spawning; (a) 「discharge [release] of eggs; 〔鳥の〕laying eggs; egg-laying.

ぼうりゃく【謀略】 ◻◻ 謀略機関 a 「disinformation [deception] organization. 謀略放送 subversive broadcasting; a subversive broadcast; broadcasting 《a broadcast》designed to 「trouble the enemy [damage enemy morale].

ほうりゅう【放流】 ◻◻ 再放流 〔釣った魚の〕catch and release (fishing). ◐再〜する catch and release 《fish》. 自然放流 〔ダムの〕natural 「discharge [overflow]. 事前放流 〔大雨が予想される場合のダムからの放水〕(a) predicted discharge. ◻◻ 放流警報 〔ダムの〕a dam 「release [discharge] warning; a warning to people downstream of a dam that water is going to be discharged. 放流施設 〔ダムの〕dam discharge facilities.

ぼうりょくだん【暴力団】 ◻◻ 暴力団周辺者 ＝暴力団準構成員 (⇨ぼうりょくだん). 暴力団準構成員 a yakuza affiliate. 暴力団排除条項 〔集合住宅の賃貸契約上の〕a clause (in a residents' contract) providing explicitly for the 「removal [exclusion] of 「gangsters [yakuza].

ぼうりょくついほう(うんどう)すいしんセンター【暴力追放(運動)推進〜】a Prefectural Center for the Elimination of Boryokudan; a prefectural branch of the Center for the Elimination of Boryokudan.

「ボウリング・フォー・コロンバイン」〔映画〕Bowling for Columbine.

ほうりんだいほうがっかい【法輪大法学会】〔法輪功の団体〕FalunDafa (in Japan).

ほうれい¹【法令】 ◻◻ 下位法令 (a) subsidiary 「regulation [law]; subsidiary legislation. 関係法令 《enactment of》relevant [related] laws and regulations. 上

位法令 (a) principal「regulation [law]; principal legislation.　□ 法令適用〘法〙the application of a law.　法令適用事前確認手続 the procedure for prior confirmation of the application of a law.
**ほうれいせん**【法令線】＝びしんこう.
**ほうろう**³【琺瑯】　□ ほうろう看板 an enamel sign.
**ぼうろさく**【防鹿柵】a deer fence;〈集合的に〉deer fencing.
**ホエイ**〘乳清〙whey.　□ ホエイ・ペプチド〘化〙whey peptide.
**ボーイスカウトにほんれんめい**【−日本連盟】the Scout Association of Japan (略: SAJ).
**「ボーイズ・ドント・クライ」**〘映画〙Boys Don't Cry.
**ボーイズリーグ**〔日本少年野球連盟の通称〕the (Japan [Japanese]) Boys League.
**ホーウィット** Howitt, Peter (1957-　; 英国生まれの映画監督).
**ポーカー・マシン**〔トランプのポーカーを模した賭博機〕a poker machine.
**ホーガン** Hogan, P.J. (1962-　; オーストラリア生まれの米国の映画監督).
**ホーク** Hawke, Ethan (1970-　; 米国の映画俳優; 本名 Ethan Green Hawke).
**ホークアイ**〘米軍〙〔早期警戒機 E-2 の愛称〕a Hawkeye.
**ポーサット**〔カンボジアの地名プルサットの別表記〕Pousa(t).
**ホーズ**〘長靴下〙(a pair of) hose; hosiery.
**ホース・セラピー**〘乗馬療法〙hippotherapy; horse therapy; therapeutic (horse) riding.
**ボーダー・コリー**〘犬〙a border collie.
**ポーターしょう**【−賞】〔業界内での競争力・企業戦略の観点から日本の企業に贈られる〕the Porter Prize.
**ボーダフォン**〘商標〙〔英国の移動電話システム; その電話機〕Vodafone.
**ポータブル**〘商標〙　□ ポータブル・トイレ〔携帯用トイレ〕a portable toilet;〘商標〙a Porta Potti.
**ポーティサット**〔カンボジアの地名プルサットの別表記〕Pouthisat.
**ボーテックス・ジェネレーター**〘流体力学・空〙〔渦流発生装置〕a vortex generator.
**ポート・アクセスほう**【−法】〘医〙〔低侵襲性の心臓手術法の1つ〕a port access procedure.
**ポートフォリオ**　□ ポートフォリオ・バランス〘金融〙(a) portfolio balance; portfolio balancing.　ポートフォリオ・リバランス〘金融〙portfolio rebalancing.　◯〜リバランス効果 the「effects [benefits] of「portfolio rebalancing [rebalancing a portfolio].
**ポートマン** Portman, Natalie (1981-　; イスラエル生まれの映画女優; 本名 Natalie Hershlag).
**ボーナス**　□ ボーナス映像〔特典映像〕a feature [clip, video].　ボーナス〔増資の際に株主に割り当てる株〕a bonus share.　ボーナス曲〔トラック〕〔特典曲〕a bonus「track [piece].
**ほおひげこうもり**【頬髭蝙蝠】〘動〙a whiskered bat; *Myotis mystacinus*.
**ホープ・エックス**【HOPE-X】〔宇宙開発事業団が計画中の宇宙往還機〕HOPE-X.　▶ H-II Orbiting Plane-Experimental の略.
**ホープけいかく**【HOPE 計画】〔国土交通省による地域に根ざした住まい・街作り計画〕the「HOPE [Housing with a Proper Environment] Project.
**ホーブラ**〘動〙〔雄ウマと雌シマウマ一代雑種〕a horbra.　▶ horse と zebra の合成語.
**ホーボー**〔米国の渡り労働者・浮浪者〕a hobo《*pl.* 〜es, 〜s》.
**ホーム**¹　□ ホーム・エネルギー・マネ(ー)ジメント・システム〔省エネルギーのための、家庭での電力管理システム〕a home energy management system (略: HEMS).　ホーム・オートメーション〔エレクトロニクス機器などの導入により住宅の利便性や快適性を高めること〕home automation (略:

HA).　ホーム・シェアリング〘福祉〙〔特別養護老人ホームの部屋を交代で定期利用すること〕rotating occupancy (of a room at an old people's home).　ホーム・ランドリー〔洗濯乾燥機〕a washing/drying machine; a (combination) washer/dryer.　ホーム・ロイヤー〔かかりつけ弁護士〕a personal lawyer; a family lawyer.
**ホーム**² 　□ 相対式ホーム〘鉄道〙〔上下線の線路をはさんで向かい合う形の 2 本のプラットホーム〕side platforms.　島式ホーム〘鉄道〙an island platform.　単式ホーム〘鉄道〙a one-side platform.　ホームゲート〘乗客の安全のためにプラットホームに設置された可動式の柵でホームドアよりもやや低いもの〕an automatic platform gate (略: APG).　ホーム〘鉄道〙a platform gate.　□ ホームドア〘鉄道〙〔乗客の安全のためにプラットホームに設置された可動式の柵〕a platform screen door (略: PSD); a platform door.
**ホーム・エクイティ・ローン**〘金融〙〔米国の, 不動産担保融資の 1 つ〕a home equity loan.
**ホームカミング・デー**〔卒業生を母校で歓待する日〕homecoming day.
**ホームズ** Holmes, Katie (1978-　; 米国の映画女優; 本名 Katherine Noelle Holmes).
**ホームスクール**〔米国の在宅教育制度〕*home-schooling; (a) home(-based) education.
**ホームストレート**〘競技〙〔競争路で, ゴール地点のある側の直線走路〕the「homestretch [「home straight].
**ホームラン**　□ ホームラン競争〘野球〙〔試合前のエキジビションとして行われる〕a home run derby.　ホームラン性〜性のファウル a foul ball that could have been a home run; a foul ball with home-run distance.
**ホームランド**〔南アフリカ共和国に 1994 年まで存在した黒人強制居住区〕a homeland.
**ホームランド・セキュリティー**〘国土安全保障〙homeland security.
**ホームレス**　□ ホームレス襲撃事件 an attack on a homeless person; a homeless attack.　ホームレス宿泊所〔宿泊施設〕a homeless shelter.　ホームレス対策 an anti-homeless(ness)「measure [policy].
**ホームレスしえんほう**【−支援法】〘法〙＝ホームレスじりつしえんほう.
**ホームレスじりつしえんほう**【−自立支援法】〘法〙the Law for the Support of Self-Reliance by the Homeless.
**ホーラマバード**〔イラン西部, ロレスターン州の州都〕Khorramabad; Khoramabad; Khoram Abad.
**ホーランド・ロップ**〘動〙〔ウサギの交配種〕a Holland Lop.
**ホーリー**² Hory, Elmyr de (1906-76?; ハンガリーの贋作画家).
**ホーリー**³〘魚〙〔中南米原産の肉食淡水魚〕a wolf fish; *Hoplias malabaricus*.
**ボーリング**¹　□ ボーリング船 an ocean drilling vessel.　ボーリング調査 exploratory drilling.
**ホール** Hall, Stuart (1932-　; 英国の社会学者; カルチュラルスタディーズの草分け).
**ボール**¹　□ 飛ぶボール〘野球〙a lively ball; a rabbit ball.　飛ばないボール〘野球〙a dead ball.　ボール気味〘彼は〜気味の球には手を出さず, 真ん中に球が来るまで待って打った. Refusing to swing at anything that looked like a ball, he waited for a pitch coming down the middle before hitting.　ボール支配率〘サッカー・バスケットなど〙ball possession.　ボール投げ〔体力測定としての〕ball throwing; a ball throw.
**ホールガーメント**〘商標・服飾〙〔無縫製ニット〕Wholegarment.
**ポール・スミス**〘商標〙〔英国の服飾ブランド〕Paul Smith.
**ホールド**　□ ホールド・ポイント〘野球〙〔ホールド数＋救援勝利数〕the total number of holds and relief victories;「hold points.
**ボールドウィン** Baldwin, Alec (1958-　; 米国の映画俳

優; 本名 Alexander Rae Baldwin III).
ボールにしきへび【-錦蛇】〖動〗a ball python; a royal python; *Python regius*.
ボール・パイソン【動】＝ボールにしきへび.
ボーロ　▫︎ 衛生ボーロ　＝卵ボーロ．蕎麦ボーロ a crunchy soba「"cookie["biscuit].　卵ボーロ　a small crunchy egg「"cookie["biscuit].
ほおん【保温】　▫︎ 保温機能 thermal [heat-retention] function.　保温シート　an [a thermal] insulation sheet.　保温弁当箱　a thermos lunch box.
「ボーン・アイデンティティー」〔映画〕The Bourne Identity.
「ボーン・アルティメイタム」〔映画〕The Bourne Ultimatum.
「ボーン・コレクター」〔映画〕The Bone Collector.
「ボーン・スプレマシー」〔映画〕The Bourne Supremacy.
「ホーンテッドマンション」〔映画〕The Haunted Mansion.
ぼか【簿価】　▫︎ 簿価ベース　〈on〉a book value basis.
ぼがい【簿外】　▫︎ 簿外管理 off-the-books management.　簿外口座 an off-the-books account.
ぼかしごえ【ぼかし肥】〖農〗(a) *bokashi* compost; (a) nutrient-rich organic composted fertilizer that acts as both a long-term and a short-term soil fertilizer and improves the soil.
ポカよけ foolproofing; mistake-proofing; failsafe design; *poka-yoke*.
ボカ・ラトン〔米国フロリダ州南東部の都市〕Boca Raton.
ポカラン〔インド、ラージャスターン州の村; 核実験場がある〕Pokhran.
ボカリーズ〖音楽〗＝ヴォカリーズ.
ほかん²【補完】　▫︎ 補完医療〖医〗complementary medicine.　補完関係 a (mutually) complementary relationship.　補完効果 a mutually complementary effect; mutual complementation; a complementary effect on each other.　補完代替医療〖医〗complementary and alternative medicine.
ほきゅう³【補給】　▫︎ 洋上補給〖軍〗underway replenishment; replenishment at sea.　▶ 洋上～艦　＝補給艦.　▫︎ 補給艦 a supply vessel; a replenishment ship; an underway replenishment ship.　補給廠(しょう)〖軍〗a depot.　▶ 総合～廠　a general depot.
ボクサー¹　▫︎ ボクサー・ショーツ〔トランクス型の男性用下着〕(a pair of)「boxer shorts [〖口〗boxers].
ぼくさいが【墨彩画】a colored「*sumi* [India-ink] painting;〖画法〗color「*sumi* [India-ink] painting.
ぼくさく【牧柵】a「pasture [grazing, cattle] fence; pasture fencing.
ぼくしょ【墨書】　▫︎ 墨書土器〖考古〗pottery inscribed with *sumi* writings and designs.
ほくせいしゅう【北西州】〔南アフリカ共和国の州〕North-West; North West; (アフリカーンス語名) Noordwes; Noord-Wes.　▶ 州都はマバトならびにマフィケング.
ほくせいたいへいようつなみじょうほうセンター【北西太平洋津波情報-】〔気象庁の〕the Northwest Pacific Tsunami Advisory Center: NWPTAC.
ほくせいへんきょうしゅう【北西辺境州】〔パキスタンの州〕(the) North-West Frontier Province (略: NWFP).　▶ 州都はペシャワル.
ぼくそう【牧草】　▫︎ 牧草肥育〖畜産〗grass feeding.　－ 肥育牛〖牛肉〗grass-fed「cattle [beef].
「僕たちのアナ・バナナ」〔映画〕Keeping the Faith.
ほくとうアジアあんぜんほしょうかいぎ【北東-安全保障会議】the Conference on Northeast Asian Security.
ほくとうアジアきょうりょくたいわ【北東-協力対話】the North East Asia Cooperation Dialogue (略: NEACD).

「僕の彼女を紹介します」〔映画〕Windstruck.
「ぼくのバラ色の人生」〔映画〕Ma Vie en Rose (=My Life in Pink).
ほくぶこっきょうしゅう【北部国境州】〔サウジアラビアの州〕the Northern「Border [Frontier]; (現地語名) Al Hudud ash Shamaliyah.
ほくべいアイスホッケーリーグ【北米-】the National Hockey League (略: NHL).
ホグマネイ〔スコットランドの大晦日(おおみそか)と元日にかけての祝い行事〕Hogmanay.
ボグリボース〖薬〗〔糖尿病治療薬〕voglibose.
「ぼくを葬(おく)る」〔映画〕Time To Leave;〔フランス語タイトル〕Le Temps Qui Reste.
ぼけ²【惚け・呆け】ぼけ防止[封じ] preventing [the prevention of] senility.　▫︎ ～防止 to「prevent [stave off] senility; to stop *one*self going senile
ポケット　▫︎ 尻[後ろ]ポケット a「hip [back] pocket.　▫︎ ポケット菓子 a pocket-sized snack.
ポケットモンスター〖商標〗＝ポケモン.
ポケモン〖商標〗Pokémon.
ぼけろうじんをかかえるかぞくのかい【呆け老人をかかえる家族の会】＝にんちしょうのひととかぞくのかい.
ほけん¹【保険】　▫︎ カード付帯保険 credit card (travel) insurance.　海外出張保険 overseas business travel insurance.　海外駐在保険 expatriate insurance; insurance for expatriates.　(海外)留学保険 overseas student insurance; insurance for people studying in another country.　所得補償保険 income protection insurance.　スポーツ安全保険〔スポーツ安全協会の〕insurance against accidents, damages, etc. organized by the Sports Safety Association.　生活総合保険 comprehensive household insurance.　団地[マンション]保険 apartment dwellers(') [condominium] insurance.　ペット保険 pet insurance.　　▫︎ 保険外診療 (medical) treatment not covered by health insurance.　保険外料金 payment [charges] for (medical) treatment not covered by health insurance.　保険使用 use of 《health》insurance 《for …; to do …》.　保険適用 application of 《health》insurance 《to the use of unapproved drugs》;〔適用を可能にすること〕making it possible for insurance to cover 《treatment with unapproved drugs》.　保険点数 insurance points; units of payment by medical insurance organizations to medical service providers.
ほけん²【保健】　▫︎ 保健教員 a school nurse.　保健手帳 a health handbook 《for a patient with a pollution-related disease》.　保健福祉動向調査 a survey of trends in health and welfare.
ほけんきんだて【保険金建て】〖保険〗〔保険金額に応じて保険料を定める方法〕flexible-premium fixed-return insurance.
ほけんりょう【保険料】　▫︎ 保険料積立金〔保険会社が将来の保険金支払いのために用意する〕an insurance reserve.
ほけんりょうだて【保険料建て】〖保険〗〔保険料に応じて保険金額を定める方法〕fixed-premium flexible-return insurance.
ほご²【保護】　▫︎ 保護犬〔保健所に保護された犬〕a rescued dog.　保護責任者遺棄致死(罪)〖法〗aggravated abandonment resulting in death.　保護房 a cell for solitary confinement.
ほこう¹【歩行】　▫︎ 歩行訓練士 a certified mobility trainer.　歩行困難牛　＝へたり牛 (⇒ふ).　歩行(補助)器〔幼児用〕a (baby) walker;〔患者・老人用〕a walking frame.
ほごう【補剛】〖建〗stiffening.　▫︎ 補剛材 (a) stiffening material; (a) stiffener.
ほこうしゃ【歩行者】　▫︎ 歩行者傷害軽減ボディー〔自動車〕a body designed to reduce injury to pedestrians.

歩行者頭部保護基準〘自動車〙pedestrian head protection standards. 歩行者頭部保護性能試験〘自動車〙〔自動車アセスメントの〕a pedestrian head protection performance test.
**ボゴールせんげん**【—宣言】〔貿易・投資の自由化についてのAPECの宣言；1994年〕the Bogor Declaration.
**ボゴールもくひょう**【—目標】〔1994年のボゴール宣言で合意された目標〕the Bogor Goals.
**ほかんさつ**【保護観察】☐☐ 保護観察処分 a sentence of probation. ○〜処分を受ける be sentenced to probation. 保護観察付き執行猶予《be given》a suspended sentence with probation.
**ほごしほう**【保護司法】〘法〙the Volunteer Probation Officer Law.
**ほさい**【補彩】＝補修彩色（⇨さいしき2）.
**ほさき**【穂先】☐☐ 穂先筍 a tip of a young bamboo stalk.
**ほし**【星】☐☐ 星勘定 a counting of「wins [victories]」.
**ぼし**[1]【母子】☐☐ 母子加算〔生活保護費への〕a welfare supplement for children of single parents and for orphans. 母子鑑定 a maternity test; maternity testing. 母子福祉資金 a (low interest) welfare loan for single mothers. 母子密着 excessive bonding between mother and child.
**ぼしかふふくしほう**【母子寡婦福祉法】〘法〙the Mother, Child and Widow's Welfare Law.
**ほしごい**【星五位】〘鳥〙〔ゴイサギの幼鳥〕a night-heron chick.
**ぼしシー・エムかんせつしょう**【母指[拇指]CM関節症】〘医〙rhizarthrosis.
**ポジション** ☐☐ ポジション争い a「fight [struggle, competition] for position.
**ボジヌルド** ＝ボジュヌールド.
**ホ・ジノ**【許秦豪】Heo [Hur] Jin-ho (1963– ；韓国の映画監督).
**ほしのまち**【星の街】〔ロシアのモスクワ北東にある、宇宙飛行士訓練施設のある地域の通称〕Star City.
**「星降る夜のリストランテ」**〔映画〕La Cena.
**ポジャギ**〔朝鮮の風呂敷〕a pojagi.
**ほしゅ**[1]【保守】☐☐ 保守管理〔保守業務の意味〕maintenance management;〔保守と管理〕maintenance and management. 保守車両〘鉄道〙a railway maintenance vehicle.
**ほしゅ**[2]【捕手】☐☐ 正捕手 a [the] starting catcher. 控え捕手 a backup catcher.
**ほしゅう**[4]【補習】☐☐ 補習教室〔学校内での補習授業〕supplementary「classes [lessons]」;〔学習塾〕a (private)「tutoring [preparatory] school; an after-school study center; a privately run school that children attend outside normal school hours to supplement school learning or prepare for entrance exams;《口》a cram school.
**ほじゅう**【補充】☐☐ 欠員補充 filling [supplying] a vacancy. 補充裁判員 an alternate [a supplementary] lay [citizen] judge. 補充授業《give, receive》supplementary lessons; remedial「teaching [work]」.
**ぼしゅう**[1]【募集】☐☐ 再募集 a second recruitment. ☐☐ 募集期間 the period for application. ○〜期間：5月30日（水曜）正午まで。Applications accepted until noon, Wednesday, May 30th.
**ほしんとう**【保守新党】the New Conservative Party. ▶ 2003年11月、自由民主党に合併.
**ボジュヌールド**〔イラン北東部、北ホラサン州の州都〕Bojnourd.
**ほじょ**【補助】☐☐ 補助療法〘医〙adjuvant [complementary] therapy.
**ほしょう**[2]【保証】☐☐ 保証年金 a guaranteed pension. 保証引き受け〔住宅ローンなどの〕a standing guarantee for《sb's housing loan》. 保証利回り〔生命保険の〕= 予定利率（⇨りりつ）.
**ほしょう**[8]【舗床】〘建〙paving. ☐☐ 舗床ガラス a glass paving block. 舗床材 paving materials.
**ほしょうそちきょうてい**【保障措置協定】〔原子力を平和利用にとどめるなどと保障する国際機関（IAEA）と当該国間の協定〕a nuclear safeguards agreement.
**ほしょうにん**【保証人】☐☐ 保証人制度 a guarantor system.
**ほじょきゃく**【補助脚】〔器具などの〕an auxiliary「leg [support]」.
**ほじょきん**【補助金】☐☐ 奨励的補助金 an incentive subsidy.
**ほじょきんてきせいかほう**【補助金適正化法】〘法〙the Law for the Normalization of Subsidies.
**ほしょく**[1]【捕食】☐☐ 捕食行動 predatory behavior.
**ほじょじょう**【補助錠】an auxiliary [a second] lock.
**ほすい**[2]【保水】☐☐ water retention; moisture retention. 保水機能 (a)「water [moisture] retention function. 保水性 water [moisture] retentivity [retention]. 保水性舗装 water-retentive「paving [pavement]」. 保水力 the「water [moisture] retaining ability《of a forest》.
**ホスキンス** Hoskins, Bob (1942– ；英国の映画俳優；本名 Robert William Hoskins).
**ポスコ**〔韓国の大手鉄鋼メーカー〕Posco.
**ポスター** ☐☐ ポスター掲示場〔選挙立候補者の〕a board for displaying campaign posters of electoral candidates. ポスター・サイズ〔用紙などの一般〕poster size. ポスター貼り putting up posters; postering; placarding.
**ポスティング**〔店の宣伝ちらしなどを各戸の郵便受けに投函すること〕putting《flyers》into home「*mailboxes [ⁿletter boxes]」; leafleting.
**ポスティング・システム**〔日本人選手の獲得を望む大リーグ球団が所属球団への移籍金の入札により交渉権を得る制度〕the posting system.
**ホステス** ☐☐ ホステスプロ〘ゴルフ〙〔自分が参戦するトーナメントのスポンサー企業と契約関係にある女子プロゴルファー〕a lady golf pro sponsored by the tournament host; a host-sponsored lady pro (golfer). [⇨ホストプロ（⇨ホスト）]
**ホスト** ☐☐ ホスト国〔国際的な行事などの主催国〕a host country. ホスト・テイスティング〔開栓したばかりのワインをその場のホスト役が味見をすること〕the「host's [hostess's]」tasting of the wine. ホストプロ〘ゴルフ〙〔自分が参戦するトーナメントのスポンサー企業と契約関係にある男子プロゴルファー〕a golf pro sponsored by the tournament host; a host-sponsored pro (golfer). [⇨ホステスプロ（ホステス）]
**ホスト**[2]〔アフガニスタン東部の州・都市〕Khost.
**ポスト-** ☐☐ ポスト工業化 postindustrialization. ○〜工業化社会 (a) postindustrial society.
**ポストゲノム**〘生物〙〔ヒトゲノム解読以後の〕postgenomic; postgenome.〔ポストゲノム研究 postgenomic [postgenome] research. ポストゲノム時代 the「postgenomic [postgenome] era.
**ポスト・プレー**〘サッカー〙getting the ball to the playmaker when attacking;〘バスケットボール〙(a) postplay.
**ポストプロダクション**〔すべてのシーンを撮り終えた後、フィルムを編集したり音などを入れたりするなど、全体の体裁を整える作業〕postproduction.
**ポスト・ペロブスカイト**〘鉱〙post-perovskite.
**ポストベンション**〔自殺者遺族への心理的支援〕(suicide) postvention.
**ポストポリオしょうこうぐん**【—症候群】〘医〙〔幼少時に脊髄性小児まひにかかった患者が治癒したのち中高年になってから筋力の低下や萎縮・関節の痛みなど起こるもの〕post-polio syndrome (略: PPS).
**ボストン・グローブ**〔米国ボストンで発行されている日刊紙〕the Boston Globe.
**ボストン・ヘラルド**〔米国マサチューセッツ州ボストン市で発行

される朝刊紙〕The Boston Herald.
**ボスニアック**〔ボスニアのイスラム教徒〕a Bosniak.
**ボスニアないせん**【-内戦】=ボスニアふんそう.
**ボスニアふんそう**【-紛争】〔1992-95年〕the Bosnian 「War [Conflict].
**ホスピス** ▫ ホスピス医 a hospice doctor.
**ホスピタル** ▫ ホスピタル・クラウン 【医】a hospital clown. [=臨床道化師 (⇨りんしょう²)]
**ホスファチジルエタノールアミン** 【生化】〔リン脂質〕phosphatidylethanolamine.
**ボスべん**【-弁】〔独立して自分の事務所を持っている弁護士〕a "boss lawyer"; an independent lawyer; a lawyer with his own practice.
**ポスルスウェイト** Postlethwaite, Pete (1945- ; 英国の俳優.
**ほせい**【補正】 ▫ 自動補正 automatic「compensation [correction]. ▫ 補正曲線 a correction curve. 補正下着 =補整下着 (⇨ほせい²) 補正型紙 〔洋裁の型紙の〕an adjustment [a pattern adjustment] line.
**ほせい²**【補整】 ▫ 補整下着 【服飾】corrective underwear.
**ほぜい**【保税】 ▫ 保税蔵置場 a bonded「warehouse [store]. 指定保税地域 a designated bonded area. 総合保税地域 a general bonded area. 保税展示場 a bonded exhibition area.
**ぼせい¹**【母性】 ▫ 母性原理 【心理】the maternal principle. 母性社会 a maternal society; a society where motherhood「rules [is honored]. 母性剥奪症候群 【医】maternal deprivation syndrome.
**ほせん¹**【保線】 ▫ 保線作業車 =保線車両. 保線車両 a track inspection「car [vehicle]; 〔無蓋で手動の〕a handcar.
**ほぜん**【保全】 ▫ 保全抗告 【法】an appeal for a temporary injunction. 保全林 a forest preserve; a preserved forest. ◯ 生活環境～林 a forest preserved to protect the living environment; a community forest preserve / 水土～林 a forest preserved for water and soil protection.
**ボセンタン** 【化】bosentan. ▫ ボセンタン水和物 【化】bosentan hydrate.
**ポソ** 〔インドネシア, スラウェシ州中部の地域〕Poso.
**ほそぬたうなぎ**【細沼田鰻】【魚】a hagfish; a hag; Myxine garmani.
**ほぞん**【保存】 ▫ 保存会 a conservation society; a society for the preservation 《of the coastline》. 保存期間 〔公文書などの〕a retention period 《for documents》. 保存版 ⇨ほぞんばん.
**ほぞんばん**【保存版】a version for「preservation [keeping]; a collector's version; 〔口〕a keeper. ▫ 永久保存版 a version for permanent preservation; a permanent collector's version. 完全保存版 a complete version for preservation; a complete collector's version.
**ぼたい¹**【母体】 ▫ 母体血清(マーカー)検査 【医】〔胎児がダウン症などの先天異常を持つ確率の検査〕a maternal serum (marker) screening. 母体・胎児集中治療室 【医】a maternal-fetal intensive care unit (略: MFICU).
**ぼたいほごほう**【母体保護法】 ▫ 母体保護法指定医 a designated gynecologist who is qualified to perform sterilization and abortion.
**ぼたっと** ◯ トーストに塗ろうとしていたジャムが床に～落ちた. The jam I was about to spread on the toast dropped with a plop onto the floor.
**ほたる**【蛍】 ▫ ホタル観賞 firefly「watching [viewing].
**ほたるスイッチ**【蛍-】【電】〔暗闇でもその位置がわかるようにオフのときに小さな明かりが点灯するスイッチ〕a glow-in-the-dark switch.
**ボチェッリ** Bocelli, Andrea (1958- ; イタリアのテノール歌手).
**ぼちまいそうほう**【墓地埋葬法】【法】the Grave and Burial Law. ▶ 正式名称は「墓地, 埋葬等に関する法律」.

**ほちょうき**【補聴器】 ▫ デジタル補聴器 a digital hearing aid. 箱型補聴器 a box-shaped hearing aid.
**ほちょうこうどういいんかい**【保釣行動委員会】〔尖閣諸島が中国領であると主張する香港の民間団体〕the Action Committee for Defending the Diaoyu Islands.
**ほっかいどうのげんゆ**【北海道の原油】〔北海道の北東海岸, イングランドの北東海岸沖合いの北海で採掘される原油〕North Sea Oil.
**ほっかいどうかいはつどぼくけんきゅうじょ**【北海道開発土木研究所】〔独立行政法人〕the Civil Engineering Research Institute of Hokkaido (略: CERI).
**ほっかいどうなんせいおきじしん**【北海道南西沖地震】〔1993年7月の〕the Southwest Hokkaidō Earthquake (of 1993).
**ほっかいブレント(げんゆ)**【北海-(原油)】〔原油価格の世界的指標の1つ〕North Sea Brent (crude). ▫ 北海ブレント先物 North Sea Brent futures.
**ほっかんたいしょうひ**【北関大捷碑】【史】〔1709年, 豊臣秀吉の朝鮮出兵に抗戦した地元義勇軍の勝利を記念して建てられた石碑〕the Bukgwandaecheopbi monument; the Bukgwan Victory Monument; a stone monument erected to mark the victories of a Korean volunteer army against Japanese invaders in the late 16th century.
**ほっきこう**【北帰行】〔渡り鳥の〕the return north.
**ほっきょく**【北極】 ▫ 北極振動 【気象】the Arctic Oscillation (略: AO).
**ほっきょくきこうえいきょうひょうか**【北極気候影響評価】〔北極評議会の委託による調査報告書〕Arctic Climate Impact Assessment (略: ACIA).
**ほっきょくけん(こくりつ)やせいせいぶつほごく**【北極圏(国立)野生生物保護区】〔米国アラスカ州の〕the Arctic National Wildlife Refuge (略: ANWR).
**ほっきょくひょうぎかい**【北極評議会】〔米・ロ・北欧諸国など8か国・6先住民団体で構成する〕the Arctic Council.
**ボック** 〔体操〕〔鞍馬の練習用具〕a training mushroom 《for the pommel horse》. [=えんぱ]
**ボックス¹** ▫ DVDボックス a DVD box set. ▫ ボックス・シルエット【服飾】〔a jacket with〕a boxy silhouette. ボックス・セット 〔DVDなどの箱入りセット〕a box set.
**ボックス・カー** 〔長崎に原爆を投下した米軍爆撃機の通称〕Bockscar; Bock's Car.
**ボックスけん**【-圏】〔相場〕〔株価の変動範囲〕a box. ▫ ボックス圏相場 〔株価が一定の価格帯内で上下を繰り返す状態〕a box market.
**ボッグ・セージ**【植】〔シソ科の植物〕a bog sage; Salvia uliginosa.
**ほっこり** 1 〔暖かくやわらかい感じ〕soft [fluffy] and warm. ◯ 昼間干したふとんは～と寝心地よかった. The futon that I had aired out during the day was fluffy and nice to sleep on.
2 〔調理したての食べ物がやわらかくほぐれる感じ〕hot and flaky (acorn squash); fluffy (pie crust); soft and crumbly (sweet potatoes), fresh from the oven.
**ほっこり²** ▫ ほっこり腹 a pot belly.
**ぼっしゅう**【没収】 ▫ 没収保全命令 【法】〔財産処分禁止の〕a confiscation and preservation order.
**ポッター** 1 Potter, Monica (1971- ; 米国の映画女優).
2 Potter, Sally (1949- ; 英国の映画監督・脚本家).
**ボッチェリ** =ボチェッリ.
**ボッチャ** 〔スポーツ〕〔パラリンピックの種目の1つ〕boccia.
**ホット** ▫ ホット・エア 【環境】〔温室効果ガスの排出余剰分〕"hot air" (reductions).
**ボット** 【電算】〔オンラインゲームの自動操作プログラム〕a bot. ▶ robotの略.
2 【電算】〔スパイウェアの1つ〕a bot (virus).
**ポッドキャスティング** 〔ウェブサイト上で音楽・画像データファイルなどを配信・聴取[視聴]する方法の1つ〕podcast-

ポッドキャスト

ing. ► アップルコンピューター社の携帯音楽プレーヤー iPod と broadcasting (放送) を組み合わせた造語．
**ポッドキャスト** a podcast. [⇨ポッドキャスティング]
**ホット・シュー**〔写真〕a hot shoe.
**ホット・スポット** ホットスポット・サービス a wireless LAN hotspot service.
**ホッパー** Hopper, Dennis (1936– ；米国の映画俳優).
**ホッピー**〔発泡酒の一種〕a low-malt beer flavored with hops.
**ボッビオ** Bobbio, Norberto (1909–2004；イタリアの政治哲学者).
**ポッピング**〔ストリートダンスの一ジャンル；1980年代前半より流行〕popping.
**ポップアップ** ポップアップ絵本〔飛び出す絵本〕a pop-up (picture) book. ポップアップ広告〔インターネットの〕a pop-up ad. ポップアップ・ブロック〔インターネット閲覧ソフトの〕pop-up blocking.
**ホップ・ポリフェノール**〔ビールの苦みとなる原料〕hop polyphenols.
**ほっぽう**【北方】 北方限界線〔朝鮮半島西部海域上の，韓国が主張する北朝鮮との軍事境界線〕the Northern Limit Line (略：NLL).
**ほっぽうよんとうぎょぎょうきょうてい**【北方四漁業協定】〔1998年の〕the Framework Agreement Concerning the Operations of Japanese Fishing Vessels in the Waters around the Four Northern Islands.
**ほっぽうりょうどのひ**【北方領土の日】〔2月7日〕Northern Territories Day.
**ほっぽうりょうどもんだいたいさくきょうかい**【北方領土問題対策協会】the Northern Territories Issue Association.
**ホッラマ(ー)バード, ホッラム(・)アーバード** =ホーラマバード．
**ボディー** ボディーサーフィン〔ボードを用いない〕body-surfing. ▷ bodysurfer *n.*; bodysurf *v.* ボディー・シェイプ〔体形〕one's figure；〔プレーする時の体の向き・姿勢〕one's body shape; one's posture. ボディー・ソープ body soap. ボディー・トリートメント (a) body treatment. ボディー・カラー〔自動車などの〕a body color.
**ほていうお**【布袋魚】〔ダンゴウオ科の海産魚；腹鰭が変形して吸盤になっているのが特徴〕a smooth lumpsucker; *Aptocyclus ventricosus*.
**ほていしめじ**【布袋占地】〔菌〕〔アルコール類と一緒に食べると中毒する白色のキノコ〕a fat-footed clitocybe; *Clitocybe clavipes*.
**ホテイチ**〔ホテルの1階にあるホテルオリジナルの持ち帰り惣菜店，デパ地下にならった造語〕hotel-brand delicatessen on the first floor of a hotel; a first-floor hotel take-out shop.
**「ボディ・バンク」**〔映画〕Extreme Measures.
**ホテル** ホテル・コスト〔介護施設利用者の居住費や食費〕hotel costs《for people in residential care homes》.
**ポテンテ** Potente, Franka (1974– ；ドイツ生まれの映画女優).
**ほとう**[2]【補糖】〔ワインのアルコール濃度を高めるため，発酵前または発酵中のブドウ果汁に砂糖を加えること〕sugaring, chaptalization. ▷ chaptalize *v.*
**ボトックス**〔顔のしわを取ったりする簡単な整形用のたんぱく質；元来は眼科・神経内科で眼瞼・顔面痙攣などの治療に使用〕botulinum toxin A；〔商標〕Botox.
**ほとほと**[2]〔戸などを静かに叩く音〕knocking; a quiet 「knocking [rapping] sound.  真夜中，雨戸を〜たく音が聞こえた．In the middle of the night I could hear the quiet knocking sound of the shutters.
**ほどほど**【程々】  お酒は〜でやっておいたほうが良いよ．You should stop drinking sake before you've had too much. / 勉強は〜でいい．たくさん遊びなさい．It's best to study in moderation. Have a lot of fun.  〜の ところで妥協することにした．We settled

on a reasonable compromise.
**ボドランドみんぞくみんしゅせんせん**【-民族民主戦線】〔インドのボド族の武装組織〕the National Democratic Front of Bodoland (略：NDFB).
**ホドルコフスキー** Khodorkovsky, Mikhail (1966– ；ロシアの実業家；石油大手ユコスの元社長).
**ボナノッテ** Bonanotte, Cecco (1942– ；イタリアの彫刻家).
**ぼにゅう**[1]【母乳】 母乳育児 breast-feeding; raising a child on breast milk. 母乳栄養 =母乳育児.  〜栄養児 a breast-fed baby. 母乳外来〔attend〕an outpatient breast-feeding clinic. 母乳中(の)ダイオキシン類濃度 dioxin concentration(s) in breast milk.
**「ボネット」**〔映画〕Ponette.
**ほねぶと**【骨太】 骨太の方針 the "Big-Boned Policy."▶「経済財政運営と構造改革に関する基本方針」の通称．
**ボノ** Bono (1960– ；アイルランドのロックバンド U2 のボーカリスト；本名 Paul Hewson).
**ほのみえる**【仄見える】〔ほのかに見える〕appear faintly; be faintly 「visible [recognizable]；〔うすうす察せられる〕appear vaguely; be vaguely understood.  朝もやの向こうに〜山々 the mountains faintly visible through the morning mist / 彼女の親切めかした言葉の裏に優越感がほの見えた．There was a (vague) hint of a sense of superiority behind her seemingly friendly words.
**ぼば**【牡馬】a stallion.
**ぼはん**[1]【母斑】 ウンナ母斑 an Unna's nevus. 色素性母斑 a pigmented「nevus [mole]. 扁平母斑 a nevus spilus; a speckled lentiginous nevus. ポートワイン母斑 a port-wine stain; an angioma simplex.
**ポハンバ** Pohamba, Hifikepunye (1935– ；ナミビアの政治家；大統領〔2005– 〕).
**「ポピュラー・サイエンス」**〔米国の月刊科学雑誌〕Popular Science.
**ポピュリズム**〔大衆迎合主義〕populism.
**ホフ** Hoff, Sydney (1912–2004；米国の絵本作家).
**ポブラ(ー)ノ**〔植〕〔メキシコ産の唐辛子の一品種〕(a) poblano (pepper).
**ホブリット** Hoblit, Gregory (1944– ；米国の映画監督).
**ポペスク・タリチェアヌ** Popescu-Tariceanu, Calin (1952– ；ルーマニアの政治家；首相〔2004– 〕).
**ボベスパしすう**【-指数】〔証券〕〔ブラジルの株価指数〕the Bovespa index.
**ボボズ**〔米国の新上流階級〕the bobos；〔その1人〕a bobo. ▶ bourgeois bohemian の略．
**ポボス**〔ギ神話〕=フォボス．
**ポメラート**〔商標〕〔イタリアの宝飾品ブランド〕Pomellato.
**ホモシスチン**〔化〕homocystine. ホモシスチン尿症〔医〕homocystinuria.
**ホモシステイン**〔生化〕homocysteine.
**ホモ・ハイデルベルゲンシス**〔人類〕*Homo heidelbergensis*.
**ホモ・フロ(ー)レシエンシス**〔人類〕〔インドネシアのフロレス島で見つかった小柄な人類とされる化石〕*Homo floresiensis*; a "hobbit" fossil.
**ほゆう**【保有】 保有株式比率 =持ち株比率〔⇨もちかぶ〕. 保有期間〔不動産・権利・免許などの〕a period of ownership; a《license》holding period. 保有権 ownership rights; rights of「ownership [possession]；〔契約選手の所属に関してチームが有する権利〕reserve rights. 保有床 owned floor space; floor space《in a shopping mall》owned《by the developer》. 農家〔自家〕保有米 rice retained by a farmer for personal consumption.
**ホラーサーン・ラザヴィ**〔イラン東部の州〕Khorasan Razavi. ▶ 以前のホラーサーン州が 2004 年に分割されて誕生した 3 州のうちの 1 つ．他の 2 州 (North/South Khorasan) と対比的に Razavi Khorasan と表記されることもある．州都はマシュハド．

ボラーニョス Bolaños, Enrique (1928– ；ニカラグアの政治家；大統領〔2002–07〕；フルネーム Enrique Jóse Bolaños Geyer).
ボラカイとう【–島】〔フィリピン中部の島〕Boracay Island.
ボラプレジンク【薬】〔胃潰瘍治療薬〕polaprezinc.
ボランタリズム〔自主・自立・自発を志向する態度〕voluntarism.
ボランティア □■ 無償ボランティア unpaid [uncompensated] volunteer「work [services]；〔人〕an「unpaid [uncompensated] volunteer. 有給ボランティア＝有償ボランティア；〔有給休暇を取って行うボランティア〕volunteer work conducted during paid leave；〔人〕a volunteer on paid leave (from his or her regular job). 有償ボランティア paid [compensated] volunteer「work [services]；〔人〕a「paid [compensated] volunteer. □■ ボランティア・ガイド a volunteer guide. ボランティア・コーディネーション〔ボランティア活動を有効化するための調整・連絡〕volunteer coordination. ボランティア出動 working voluntarily without (extra) pay; voluntary unpaid work. [＝サービス出勤(⇨サービス)] ボランティア体験 volunteer experience; experience as a volunteer.
ホランド 1 Holland, Agnieszka (1948– ；ポーランド生まれの映画監督・脚本家).
2 Holland, Tom (1943– ；米国の映画監督・脚本家).
ポリアセチレン【化】polyacetylene.
ポリアリレート【化】polyarylate (略: PAR). □■ ポリアリレート樹脂 (a) polyarylate resin. ポリアリレート繊維 (a) polyarylate fiber.
ポリープ □■ 有茎(性)[無茎(性)]ポリープ a「pedunculated [sessile] polyp.
ポリイミド □■ ポリイミド・フィルム polyimide film.
ボリウッド 〔＜*Bombay*（ムンバイの英語名）＋*Hollywood*〕〔インドのムンバイを中心としたインド映画産業〕Bollywood.
ポリウレタン □■ ポリウレタン樹脂 (a) polyurethane resin. ポリウレタン繊維 (a) polyurethane fiber.
ポリカーボネート □■ ポリカーボネート・シート a polycarbonate sheet; polycarbonate sheeting. ポリカーボネート樹脂 polycarbonate [PC] resin.
ポリグルタミンさん【–酸】【化】polyglutamic acid.
ポリゴン □■ ポリゴン・ミラー【光】a polygon mirror.
ポリしゅうかジフェニルエーテル【–臭化–】【化】polybrominated diphenyl ether (略: PBDE).
ポリしゅうかビフェニル【–臭化–】【化】polybrominated biphenyl (略: PBB).
ボリショイとう【–島】〔中国とロシアの国境の島〕Bolshoi Island. ▶ アバガイト島とも呼ぶ.
ポリスチレン □■ ポリスチレン樹脂 polystyrene resin.
ほりたて【掘り立て】◐〜のジャガイモ freshly dug potatoes.
ほりつける【彫り付ける】engrave [carve, cut]《a figure》(in relief) on 《a piece of wood》; engrave 《a plate with a name》.
ポリティカリー・コレクト〔政治的に公正な〕politically correct; PC.
ホリデー[1] □■ ホリデー・チップ〔米国で、クリスマスなどの休暇前に郵便配達人・ドアマン・駐車場係などに渡すチップ〕a holiday tip；〔チップを渡すこと〕holiday tipping.
ポリテトラフルオロエチレン【化】polytetrafluoroethylene (略: PTFE).
ポリトコフスカヤ Politkovskaya, Anna (1958–2006; ロシアのジャーナリスト; 暗殺された).
ポリトリメチレン・テレフタレート【化】〔合成繊維原料樹脂〕polytrimethylene terephthalate (略: PTT).
ボリバルかくめい【–革命】〔ベネズエラのチャベス大統領が推進する〕the Bolivarian Revolution.
ポリブタジエン【化】polybutadiene.
ポリプロピレン □■ ポリプロピレン・シート (a) polypropylene sheet. ポリプロピレン・バンド〔梱包用の〕a propopylene band.

ポリベンゾイミダゾール【化】polybenzimidazole (略: PBI).
ポリマー □■ ポリマー電池 a polymer battery.
ポリメラーゼ □■ ポリメラーゼ連鎖反応【生化】a polymerase chain reaction (略: PCR).
ほりゅう[1]【保留】□■ 保留床〔再開発事業によって建設されたビルの〕(land and) floor space not allocated to the original landowner; reserved space. [⇨権利床(⇨けん)]
ボルキア Bolkiah Mu'izzaddin Waddaulah, Haji Hassanal (1946– ；ブルネイ国王〔1967– 〕).
「ボルケーノ」〔映画〕Volcano.
ホルステン〔ドイツのビールメーカー〕Holsten-Brauerei.
ポルチーニたけ【–茸】【菌】〔イタリア産の食用キノコ〕a porcino 《pl. -cini》; *Boletus edulis*.
ボルネオしらおながも【–白髪尾長】〔鳥〕〔カラス科の鳥〕a Bornean treepie; *Dendrocitta cinerascens*.
ボルネオ・ピグミーぞう【–象】【動】a Borneo pygmy elephant; *Elephas maximus* (*borneensis*).
ボルバキア【菌】〔昆虫の細胞内共生細菌の一属〕*Wolbachia*.
ポル・ポト □■ ポルポト派 the Pol Pot「group [wing].
ホルミシス □■ ホルミシス効果 a hormetic effect.
ホルム Holm, Ian (1931– ；英国生まれの映画俳優；本名 Ian Holm Cuthbert).
ホルモズガ(ー)ン〔イラン南部、ペルシャ湾沿岸の州〕Hormozgan. ▶ 州都はバンダル・アッバース.
ホルモン □■ ホルモン障害 a hormonal disorder. ホルモン注射 a human growth hormone [an HGH] injection. ホルモン年齢 a [*one's*] hormonal age. ホルモン・バランス (a) hormone balance. ◐ 〜バランスの乱れ (a) disruption in hormone balance; (a) hormone imbalance.
ポロイダル □■ ポロイダル磁場コイル a poloidal field coil (略: PFC).
ホロー・ポイント【銃砲】〔先端を凹ませた弾頭；殺傷力が増す〕a hollow point. □■ ホロー・ポイント弾 a hollow-point bullet.
ホログラム □■ ホログラム・シール a hologram seal.
ポロクワネ〔南アフリカ共和国北部、リンポポ州の州都〕Polokwane. ▶ 旧称 ピーターズバーグ (Pietersburg).
ホロコースト □■ ホロコースト記念日〔アウシュヴィッツ強制収容所が解放された1月27日を記念する日〕(the) Holocaust Memorial Day.
ホロコーストはくぶつかん【–博物館】a Holocaust museum;〔米国ワシントン DC の〕the United States Holocaust Memorial Museum.
ぼろっちい dilapidated 《school building》; run-down 《house》; shabby 《coat》; rattletrap 《bus》; rickety 《desk》.
ホロとう【–島】〔フィリピン南部の島〕Jolo Island.
ボロネーゼせいほう【–製法】〔イタリアのボローニャ地方の伝統的な製靴技法〕the traditional Bologna method of shoe-making.
「幌馬車隊」〔米大陸を横断する幌馬車隊の苦闘を描く TV 西部劇〕Wagon Train.
ほろほろ 4〔もろくずれる感じ〕◐ この和菓子は〜した食感です. These Japanese sweets have a crumbly texture. / この豚肉はよく煮込んであるので口の中に入れると〜と崩れる. This pork has been thoroughly boiled, so it breaks apart easily when you put it in your mouth.
ポロン〔商標〕〔高密度ウレタンフォームの商品名〕PORON.
ホワイト[1] □■ ホワイト情報〔氏名・生年月日・住所・電話番号・職業、銀行融資・不動産売買に関する個人情報〕positive credit information. [⇨ブラック情報(⇨ブラック)] ホワイト・バンド〔貧困問題解決を訴える運動のシンボルとしての白い腕輪〕a white band.
ホワイトカラー・エグゼンプション, ホワイトカラー・イ

ホワイトテリア

グゼンプション〔一定以上の収入があるホワイトカラー労働者に対して使用者が超過勤務手当を支給しなくてもよいとする制度〕a white-collar exemption.
ホワイト・テリア《犬》a white terrier.
ホワイト・ナイト 1《経》〔白馬の騎士；企業乗っ取りを防ぐ救世主〕a white knight.
2〔白夜〕a white night.
ホワイト・バス《魚》〔魚食性の淡水魚〕a white bass; *Morone chrysops*.
ホワイト・プリマス・ロック(しゅ)【-(種)】《畜》〔米国産の鶏の品種〕a White Plymouth Rock.
ホワイト・レディ〔カクテル〕a white lady.
「ポワゾン」〔映画〕Original Sin.
「ホワット・ライズ・ビニース」〔映画〕What Lies Beneath.
ポワトゥー・シャラント〔フランス中西部の地域〕Poitou-Charentes.
ポワレ Poiret, Paul (1879–1944; フランスの服飾デザイナー).
ぼん³【盆】⇨ 盆飾り a *Bon* Festival decoration (placed in front of a household altar).
ボンエルフ〔＜Du〕〔自動車の速度を落としたり通行量を減らすように工夫された住宅区域内の道路〕a woonerf.
ホンカー【紅客】〔中国の愛国主義的ハッカー〕a red hacker; a honker.
ぼんがく【梵学】〔梵語の研究〕Sanskrit studies;〔仏教学〕Buddhist studies.
ほんかくかどう【本格稼働】the start of full-capacity operation; beginning to operate at full capacity. ～する start to operate「at full capacity [fully]. ◐ 工場が4月1日から～します. The factory will start operating at full capacity on April 1st.
ポンがし【-菓子】〔米などの穀物に圧力をかけ膨らませて作る駄菓子の一種〕puffed「cereals [grains].
ボン・キュッ・ボン〔バストがあり、ウエストが引き締まって、ヒップが大きい体型〕◐ 彼女は～で抜群のプロポーションだ. She has fine proportions and an hourglass figure. | She is voluptuous and wasp-waisted. | She is a perfect 36-24-36.
ほんきょち【本拠地】⇨ 本拠地球場 a home ballpark.
ボンごうい【-合意】〔2001年7月の京都議定書に関する政治合意〕the Bonn Agreement;〔2001年12月のアフガニスタンの和平プロセスに関する合意〕the Bonn Agreement.
ボンゴレ ⇨ ボンゴレ・ビアンコ〔アサリの白ワイン入りソース〕《It》*vongole bianco* (► *bianco* は白ワインの「白」の意); white clam sauce. ボンゴレ・ロッソ〔ボンゴレビアンコにトマトを加えたソース〕《It》*vongole rosso* (► *rosso* はトマトの「赤」の意); red [tomato] clam sauce.
ぼんゴロ【凡-】〔野球〕an easy grounder.
ホンコン【香港】⇨ 香港H株〔香港市場上場の中国本土銘柄〕an H-share.
ホンコンとう【香港島】〔中国広東省南岸、九竜半島対岸の島〕Hong Kong Island.
ホンコン・ハンセンしすう【香港-指数】《略》Hong Kong's [the Hong Kong] Hang Seng index.
ほんしゃ【本社】⇨ 本社機能 head-office [headquarters] functions [operations]. ◐ その証券会社は、海外業務に関する～機能を東京の本社からニューヨークに移動した. That securities company moved its head-office functions for its overseas operations from its Tokyo headquarters to New York.
ほんしゅうしこくれんらくきょうだんほう【本州四国連絡橋公団法】《法》the Honshu-Shikoku Bridge Authority Law.
ほんしゅうしこくれんらくこうそくどうろかぶしきがいしゃ【本州四国連絡高速道路株式会社】the Honshu-Shikoku Bridge Expressway Company Limited. ► 2005年の本州四国連絡橋公団の民営化に伴い設立.
ポン・ジュノ【奉俊昊】Bong Joon-ho (1969– ; 韓国の映画監督).

ボンじょうやく【-条約】〔国際自然保護連合が、1979年ボンで採択した条約（発効は1983年）の通称〕the Bonn Convention. ► 正式名称は「移動性野生動物種の保存に関する条約」(the Convention on the Conservation of Migratory Species of Wild Animals).
ほんせいいんこ【本青鸚哥】《鳥》〔インコ科の鳥〕a rose-ringed parakeet; *Psittacula krameri*.
ポンセ・デ・レオン Ponce de León, Juan (1460–1521; スペインの探検家).
ほんたいせい【本態性】⇨ 本態性血小板血症 essential thrombocythemia (略：ET). 本態性低血圧症 essential hypotension.
ボンデヴィック ＝ボンネヴィーク.
ポンデケージョ〔ブラジルのチーズパン〕《Port》pão de queijo.
ほんど【本土】⇨ 本土化〔台湾の非中国化〕(Taiwanese) localization; Taiwanization. 本土復帰〔1972年の沖縄の〕the「restoration [return] (of Okinawa) to Japan.
「ほんとうのジャクリーヌ・デュ・プレ」〔映画〕Hilary and Jackie.
「本当の話」〔ルキアノスの著作〕True History.
ボンド・ガール〔007シリーズでジェームズ・ボンドの相手役をつとめる女優〕a Bond girl.
ほんにん【本人】⇨ 本人拒否率〔生体認証機器などの〕a false-rejection rate.
ほんにんかくにんほう【本人確認法】《法》the Customer Identification Law. ► 正式名称は「金融機関等による顧客等の本人確認等及び預金口座等の不正な利用の防止に関する法律」(the Law on Customer Identification and Retention of Records by Financial Institutions, and Prevention of Fraudulent Use of Deposit Accounts).
ボンネヴィーク Bondevik, Kjell Magne (1947– ; ノルウェーの政治家；首相〔1997–2000, 2001–05〕).
ボンペびょう【-病】《医》〔糖原病II型〕Pompe('s) disease.
ほんぽう¹【本邦】⇨ 本邦株式《証券》domestic [Japanese] stocks [equity].
ほんめい²【本命】⇨ 本命視 ◐ ～視する regard 《*sb*》as the favorite／来〈きた〉る学長選で～視されていた福田氏が愛人問題で脱落したのには関係者一同驚いた. Everyone involved was surprised that Fukuda, who had been「regarded as the favorite [expected] to be chosen as the next chancellor, dropped out of the competition because of an affair.
ほんもの【本物】⇨ 本物志向 a desire for the real thing.
ほんやく³【翻訳】⇨ 翻訳会社 a translation agency. 翻訳劇 a translated play; a play in translation. 翻訳詩 a translated poem; a poem in translation;〈集合的に〉poetry in translation.
ほんやくけん【翻訳権】◐ ～の十年留保〔1971年の著作権法が施行される前の著作物について〕the expiration of translation rights for a work if no translation has appeared within 10 years after its publication (applicable to works published before the Copyright Law of 1971 took effect).
ほんやたいしょう【本屋大賞】the (Japan) Booksellers' Prize. ► 正式名称は「全国書店員が選んだいちばん! 売りたい本」.
ほんらい【本来】⇨ 本来任務〔自衛隊などの〕primary duties; *one's* primary mission.
ほんりょう【本領】⇨ 本領発揮 ◐ 雪道でこそ四輪駆動車の～発揮だ. It is on snowy roads that the four-wheel drive vehicle really「comes into its own [shows its stuff].
ほんるいだ【本塁打】⇨ チーム本塁打 a team's home runs;《set a record for》team home runs. ⇨ 本塁打王 a home-run「king [leader]. 本塁打性 ＝ホームラン性 (⇨ホームラン).

# ま

**マーカンダヤ** Markandaya, Kamala (1924–2004; インド生まれで英国に住んだ小説家; 本名 Kamala Purnaiya Taylor).
**「マーキュリー・ライジング」**〔映画〕Mercury Rising.
**マーケット** ▫▫ マーケット・イン〔経営〕market-oriented《research》; market-in《approach》. マーケット・ガバナンス〔市場統治〕market governance.
**マーケティング** ▫▫ マーケティング活動[キャンペーン] marketing activities; a marketing campaign.
**マーサ・スチュアート**〔米国の生活用品会社〕Martha Stewart Living Omnimedia.（略: MSO）.
**マーザンダラーン** =マーザンダラン.
**マーザンデラーン** =マーザンダラン.
**マーシャル 1** Marshall, Barry J. (1951- ; オーストラリアの医師; ピロリ菌の発見者の一人).
**2** Marshall, E(verett) G(unnar) (1910–98; 米国の映画俳優).
**3** Marshall, Garry (1934- ; 米国の映画監督・俳優).
**4** Marshall, Penny (1942- ; 米国の映画女優・監督).
**「マーシャル・ロー」**〔映画〕The Siege.
**マージャン**【麻雀】▫▫ 麻雀牌 a mah-jongg 「tile [piece].
**マージン** ▫▫ 中間マージン an intermediary('s) margin; a 「distribution [distributor] margin. 流通マージン a distribution margin.
**マース** Maas, Dick (1951- ; オランダの映画監督・製作者・脚本家).
**「マーズ・アタック」**〔映画〕Mars Attacks!
**マーズ・エクスプロレーション・ローバー**〔宇宙〕=マーズ・ローバー.
**マーズ・パスファインダー**〔米国の火星探査機〕(the) Mars Pathfinder.
**マーズ・ローバー**〔宇宙〕〔米国 NASA の火星探査車〕a Mars Exploration Rover; a Mars Rover.
**マーダーボール**〔車いすラグビーの別名〕murder ball.
**マータイ** Maathai, Wangari Muta (1940- ; ケニアの環境活動家でグリーンベルト運動創始者).
**マータラ**〔スリランカ南部の都市〕Matara.
**マーチ・マッドネス**〔バスケット〕〔全米大学バスケットボールトーナメント大会の通称〕March Madness.
**マーティン 1** Martin, Paul (1938- ; カナダの政治家; 首相〔2003–06〕).
**2** Martin, Steve (1945- ; 米国の映画俳優).
**マート**[3]【MAAT】〔大阪府警の特殊犯捜査係〕MAAT. ▶ Martial Arts Attack Team の略.
**マーベリック**〔米軍〕=マヴェリック.
**マーゆ**【-油】〔にんにく油〕garlic oil (obtained by frying garlic in oil).
**マーラ**〔動〕〔南米産テンジクネズミ科の哺乳類〕a mara; a Patagonian cavy; *Dolichotis patagonum*.
**マーリー** Marley, Bob (1945–81; ジャマイカのレゲエ音楽家; 本名 Robert Nesta Marley).
**マーリブ**〔イスラエルの日刊紙〕Ma'ariv.
**マールブルグ[マールブルク]・ウイルス**〔医〕(the) Marburg virus.
**マールブルグ[マールブルク]しゅっけつねつ**【-出血熱】〔医〕Marburg haemorrhagic fever.
**マーレ・アドミム**〔エルサレム東郊のユダヤ人入植地〕Maale Adumim.
**マーレー** Murray, Bill (1950- ; 米国の映画俳優; 本名 William James Murray).
**マイアミ・ヘラルド**〔米国フロリダ州マイアミ市で発行される朝刊紙〕The Miami Herald.

**マイカー** ▫▫ マイカー族〔1 人〕a car owner; a person who 「drives everywhere [uses his or her car rather than public transport];《口》a car person;〈集合的に〉car owners (who 「drive everywhere [use their cars rather than public transport]);《口》car people. マイカー・ブーム a boom in private car ownership. マイカー利用《cut down on》the use of private cars.
**マイクロ-** ▫▫ マイクロサージャリー〔医〕〔顕微手術〕microsurgery.
**マイクロアレイ**〔生化〕=DNA マイクロアレイ (⇨ディー・エヌ・エー).
**マイクロ・シー・ティー**【-CT】〔医〕〔顕微鏡的に観察するための X 線 CT〕micro-CT; microcomputed tomography.
**マイクロタービン**〔電〕〔小型ガスタービン発電機〕a microturbine (generator).
**マイクロドット**〔微粒麻薬〕a microdot 《of LSD》.
**マイクロは**【-波】▫▫ マイクロ波凝固療法〔医〕microwave coagulation therapy (略: MCT). マイクロ波発振器〔電子工学〕a microwave generator. マイクロ波誘電分光 microwave dielectric spectroscopy.
**マイクロバブル**〔微細な気泡〕a microbubble.
**マイクロビサイド**〔殺菌剤〕a microbicide.
**マイクロもじ**【-文字】〔紙幣に用いられる〕microprinting;《printed in》micro-letters[-characters].
**マイクロリアクター**〔化〕a microreactor.
**マイクロレンズ**〔写〕a microlens.
**「マイケル・コリンズ」**〔映画〕Michael Collins.
**まいご**【迷子】▫▫ 迷子紐 a child leash.
**マイコプラズマ** マイコプラズマ様微生物〔生物〕a mycoplasma-like organism (略: MLO). ▶ 現在はファイトプラズマという.
**マイコン** ▫▫ 内蔵マイコン〔電気器具などの〕a built-in microprocessor.
**マイサーン** =マイサン.
**マイサン**〔イラク南東部の州〕Maysan. ▶ 州都 アマラ.
**「マイスウィートガイズ」**〔映画〕Play It to the Bone.
**マイスリー**〔商標・薬〕〔睡眠薬〕Myslee. ▶ 一般名 酒石酸ゾルピデム (zolpidem tartrate).
**マイタイ**〔ラムベースのカクテル〕a mai tai.
**マイダン・シャル**〔アフガニスタン中部, ワルダック州の州都〕Maidan Shahr; Maidan Shah; Meydan Shahr.
**まいつきんろうとうけいちょうさ**【毎月勤労統計調査】〔厚生労働省の〕the Monthly Labor Survey.
**「マイティ・ジョー」**〔映画〕Mighty Joe Young.
**「マイティ・ハーキュリー」**〔米国の, ギリシャ時代の英雄が主人公の TV アニメ〕The Mighty Hercules.
**「マイティマウス」**〔米国の, スーパーマンのようなネズミを主人公とした TV アニメ〕Mighty Mouse.
**マイドゥーム**〔コンピュータウイルスの 1 つ〕Mydoom.
**マイナー** ▫▫ マイナー契約〔野球など〕a minor-league contract.
**マイナー**[2] Miner, Steve (1951- ; 米国の映画監督; 本名 Stephen C. Miner).
**マイナス** マイナス勧告〔人事院による国家公務員給与の引き下げ勧告〕a recommendation 「by [from] the National Personnel Authority to decrease salaries (for national civil service employees). マイナス評価 a negative evaluation. ○ 〜評価する evaluate《an applicant's job history》negatively; take points off《for a criminal conviction》. マイナス要素 a negative element; a weak point; a drawback.
**「マイノリティ・リポート」**〔映画〕Minority Report.

## マイハート, マイラブ

「マイ・ハート, マイ・ラブ」〔映画〕Playing By Heart.
**まいぼつ**【埋没】 ◆ 埋没遺跡〔文化財〕a buried 'ruin [cultural asset].
**マイヤー**[3]〔商標〕〔毛布などに用いられる合成繊維〕Mayer.
**マイヤーズ** 1 Meyers, Nancy (1949-　；米国の映画監督). 2 Myers, Mike (1963-　；カナダ生まれの映画俳優; 本名 Michael Myers).
**マイライン**〔電話〕the Myline 'carrier [telephone company] selection service.
**まいりばか**【参り墓・詣り墓】〔両墓制で, 墓参(ぼさん)用の墓〕a "memorial grave," where prayers and services are held for people actually buried elsewhere.
**マイルズ** Miles, Sarah (1941-　；英国の映画女優).
**マイレージ** ◆ マイレージ割引〔走行距離に応じた高速道路料金の割引〕a (high) mileage discount 《on expressway toll fees》.
**マイレックス**〔化〕〔殺虫剤に用いられる有機塩素系物質〕mirex.
**マヴェリック**〔米軍〕〔テレビ誘導による空対地爆弾 AGM-65 の愛称〕a Maverick.
**マウス** ◆ マウス症候群〔腱鞘(けんしょう)炎〕〔パソコンのマウスの使いすぎによって起こる, 手首の痛みなど体の不調〕mouse syndrome; repetitive stress wrist pain.
**マウンテンボード**〔4つの車輪を取り付けたボードで斜面を滑り下りる遊び〕mountainboarding; 〔そのボード〕a mountainboard. ▷ mountainboarder n.
**マウンド** ◆ マウンド度胸《show [have]》 tenacity 〔《口》guts〕on the mound.
**まえうり**【前売り】 ◆ 前売り入場券 an advance (admission) ticket.
**まえお**【前緒】〔下駄・草履などの〕a front thong; a short thong that connects the strap to the forepart of a geta and passes between the big toe and the second toe.
**まえしょり**【前処理】 pretreatment; preprocessing. ◆ 前処理建屋〔使用済み核燃料再処理工場の〕a pretreatment building.
**まえどり**【前撮り】〔写真の〕taking 'ceremonial [wedding, etc.] pictures before the event.
**まえばらいしきしょうひょうきせいほう**【前払式証票規制法】〔法〕＝プリペイドカードきせいほう.
**まえばらいしきしょうひょうのきせいにかんするほうりつ**【前払式証票の規制に関する法律】〔法〕〔「プリペイドカード(規制)法」の正式名称〕⇨プリペイドカード(きせい)ほう.
**まえふり**【前振り】 1 〔導入部〕〔論説の〕a preface; 〔芝居の〕a prologue; 〔番組・話などの〕an introduction; 〔口〕an intro 《pl. ～s》; 〔前座〕an opening act; an opener; a warm-up (act). ●思わせぶりな～ an introduction that leads one to expect things. ●～が長くて退屈な映画だった. It's a boring film that spends too much time setting the stage. ●ジョークの～をしてくれ. Set me up for a joke.
2 〔事前振り込み〕advance (electronic) bank transfer.
**マカーム**＝マカム.
**マカティ**〔フィリピン, マニラ首都圏の都市〕Makati.
**マカム**〔イスラム音楽の調律システム〕maqam; 〔イラクの音楽劇〕the (Iraqi) maqam.
**マカランガ**〔植〕〔東南アジア産トウダイグサ科オオバギ属の植物の総称〕(a) Macaranga.
**マカリーズ**＝マッカリーズ.
**まがりや**【曲(がり)屋】1 〔平面図で L 字型の民家〕an L-shaped house.
2 〔質屋〕a pawnbroker's (shop); a pawnshop.
3 〔相場〕〔思惑の外れた投資家〕a 'stale [weak] bull.
**マカレスター**〔米国オクラホマ州南東部の都市〕McAlester.
**マカロン**〔菓子〕a macaroon.
**マギー・チャン** Maggie Cheung (1964-　；香港の映画女優; 中国語名 張曼玉 Cheung Man-Yuk).

**まきかえ**【巻き替え】1 〔糸などの〕winding 《thread onto a new spool》.
2 〔相撲〕changing from an overarm to an underarm grip on one's opponent's belt.
**まきかえる**【巻き替える】1 〔糸などを〕wind 《thread onto a new spool》.
2 〔相撲〕change from an overarm to an underarm grip on one's opponent's belt.
**まきがみかやく**【巻き紙火薬】paper roll caps.
**まきこみ**【巻き込み】〔機械・車輪などへの〕entanglement; getting caught (in the machinery). ●〔衣類・人体などの〕～を防ぐ prevent 《clothing》 getting caught (up) 《in the wheels》; stop 《people》 getting 'drawn [dragged, pulled] 《into the machinery》. ◆ 巻き込み事故〔自動車の左折時の〕an accident in which a left-turning vehicle 'hits [catches] a motorcycle or bicycle coming from behind. 巻き込み防止ガード a catch-guard (to prevent entanglement of clothing). 左折時巻き込み防止確認〔自動車〕checking that there 'is nothing [are no bicycles or motorbikes] on the inside when turning left.
**マキシシングル**〔直径 12 センチの CD の大きさで, 3-4 曲入りのシングル CD〕a maxi-single.
**まきしば**【蒔き芝】〔園芸〕planting grass seedlings.
**まきづめ**【巻き爪】〔爪が横方向に巻いている状態〕an in-curved nail; 〔重度の〕a pincer nail; 〔陥入爪(かんにゅうそう)〕an 'ingrown [ingrowing] nail.
**マキノン** MacKinnon, Roderick (1956-　；米国の化学者).
**まきょう**[2]【魔鏡】〔日光など直線的な光を反射させると鏡面には見えない像や文字を反射映像内に浮かび上がらせる鏡〕a makyō; a (Japanese) magic mirror.
**まく**[2]【膜】 ◆ 膜分離 membrane separation. 膜分離工学 membrane separation engineering. 膜分離法 a membrane separation process.
**まくあつけい**【膜厚計】〔皮膜の厚さを測る〕a coating thickness gauge; a film thickness gauge.
**まくうちゅうろん**【膜宇宙論】〔天〕brane cosmology. ▶ホーキングが提唱する宇宙論.
**マクギリス** McGillis, Kelly (1957-　；米国の映画女優).
**マグサイサイしょう**【-賞】〔アジア地域で民主主義や社会福祉などの発展に貢献した個人・団体に授与される〕the (Ramon) Magsaysay Award.
**マクタンとう**【-島】〔フィリピン, セブ島沖の小島〕Mactan Island.
**マクティアナン** McTiernan, John (1951-　；米国の映画監督; 本名 John McTiernan Jr.).
**マクドーマンド** Mcdormand, Frances (1957-　；米国の映画女優).
**マグナム** ◆ マグナム弾 a Magnum bullet.
**マグナムぼうえんきょう**【-望遠鏡】〔東京大学がハワイのマウイ島ハレアカラ山山頂に建設した〕the MAGNUM Telescope. ▶ MAGNUM は Multicolor Active Galactic Nuclei Monitoring の略.
**マグネター**〔天〕〔超強磁場中性子星〕a magnetar.
「**マグノリア**」〔映画〕Magnolia.
**まくはりメッセ**【幕張-】〔千葉県にある国際展示場〕the Makuhari Messe; 〔正式名称〕the Nippon Convention Center.
**マクブライド** ◆ マクブライド賞〔国際平和ビューローが主催する平和賞〕the Sean MacBride (Peace) Prize.
**マクベイン** McBain, Ed (1926-2005；米国のミステリー作家; 本名 Evan Hunter).
**まくら**【枕】 ◆ 枕営業〔肉体関係を利用して仕事をする営業〕providing sexual favors to promote one's 'business [career]; 〔口〕sleeping one's way to success; 〔芸能界の〕〔俗〕the casting couch.
**まくり**[2]【捲り】〔競輪〕suddenly coming up from behind and overtaking on the outside.

**マグル**〔児童読み物『ハリー・ポッター』シリーズで、魔法を使えない普通の人間のこと〕a Muggle;〔一般人〕a muggle.

**マクレガー** McGregor, Ewan (1971- ；英国生まれの映画俳優；本名 Ewan Gordon McGregor).

**マグレブ**[2]〔磁気浮上式鉄道・リニアモーターカー〕a maglev;〔その技術〕maglev. ▶ *mag*netic *levi*tation より.

**マクロ** □■ マクロ撮影〔写真〕〔至近距離の撮影〕close-up photography; macro photography. マクロ的視点 a macroscopic point of view.

**マクロけいざい**【-経済】□■ マクロ経済指標 a macroeconomic indicator. マクロ経済スライド a macroeconomic slide. マクロ経済変数 a macroeconomic variable.

**マクロビオティック**《<F *macrobiotique*》〔穀物菜食中心の食事法〕macrobiotics. ▷ macrobiotic *adj.*

**マグワイア** Maguire, Tobey (1975- ；米国の映画俳優；本名 Tobias Vincent Maguire).

**まけこし**【負け越し】□■ 連続負け越し ◐ 阪神は4カード連続～となった.〔野球〕The Hanshin Tigers have lost four series in a row. / 彼は3場所連続～で大関から陥落した.〔相撲〕He 「lost his Ozeki status [was demoted from Ozeki] after losing in three successive tournaments.

**まげて**【曲げて・枉げて】〔無理に・何とかして〕◐ そこを～ご承諾願えませんか. Could you possibly 「make an exception [〈口〉bend a little] and let us have your consent on that point?

**まけのこり**【負け残り】〔相撲〕〔結びの一つ前の取り組みで負けた力士が土俵下に残ること〕sitting at ringside after losing the penultimate match.

**まげわっぱ**【曲げわっぱ】〔曲げ物の弁当箱〕a round lunch box made of thin wood.

**マゴット・セラピー**〔医〕〔蛆(うじ)を使う潰瘍などの治療法〕maggot therapy; maggot debridement therapy (略：MDT); larva [larval, larvae] therapy (略：LT).

**マコノヒー** McConaughey, Matthew (1969- ；米国の映画俳優；本名 Matthew David McConaughey).

**マザー・ハウス**〔インド、コルカタにある神の愛の宣教者会の本部〕the Mother House.

**マサイきりん**【-麒麟】〔動〕a masai giraffe; *Giraffa camelopardalis tippelskirchi*.

**マサカリとうほう**【-投法】〔元プロ野球選手 村田兆治氏の投球スタイルを指して使われた言葉〕*masakari* pitching; pitching as if throwing an ax in the manner of Murata Chōji.

**まさつ**【摩擦】□■ エネルギー摩擦〔エネルギーの供給・確保をめぐっての、国家間の〕friction over energy [policy [rights]]. 航空機摩擦〔米国と欧州間の〕(trade) friction between the US and Europe over the (civil) aircraft industry. □■ 摩擦調整剤 a friction modifier. 摩擦板〔機〕〔自動車のクラッチなどの〕a friction plate.

**まさど**【真砂土、マサ土】〔地質〕〔花崗岩などが風化してできた土〕decomposed granite soil.

**マザリーズ**〔母親などが幼児に話しかける時の言葉づかい〕motherese; baby [caretaker] talk; caretaker [child-directed] speech.

**マザンダラン**〔イラン北部の州〕Mazandaran. ▶ 州都はサーリー.

**マザンデラン**〔イランの州マザンダランの異表記〕Mazanderan.

**まじ**[2] □■ まじ切れ ◐ ～切れする (completely) lose control (of *one's* temper);〈俗〉get really pissed off; (totally) lose it.

**ましこやき**【益子焼】Mashiko ware; ceramics [pottery, porcelain] from Mashiko (Tochigi Pref.).

**マジソン・スクエア・ガーデン** =マディソン・スクエア・ガーデン.

**マジディ** Majidi, Majid (1959- ；イランの映画監督).

**「魔女の宅急便」**〔アニメ映画〕Kiki's Delivery Service.

**ますい**【麻酔】□■ 自家麻酔〔麻酔医に代わって執刀医が行う〕anesthesia administered by the operating surgeon. 並列麻酔〔1人の麻酔医が複数の患者に同時に麻酔処置を施すこと〕simultaneous anesthesia (of multiple patients). □■ 麻酔アレルギー an allergy to anesthesia (drugs) [anesthetics]. 麻酔スプレー (an) anesthetic spray. 麻酔導入薬 a sedative; a sedative premedicant. 麻酔標榜医 a (board) certified 「*anesthesiologist [*anaesthetist].

**ますいやく**[ざい]【麻酔薬[剤]】□■ 麻酔薬アレルギー =麻酔アレルギー (⇨ますい).

**マスオさん**〔漫画『サザエさん』でサザエの夫であるフグ田マスオから〕〔妻の実家に同居している男性〕a husband who lives with his wife in a house that belongs to her parents.

**マスカルさい**【-祭】〔エチオピアの新年行事〕the Meskel Festival.

**マスキーパイク**〔魚〕〔カワカマスの一種〕a muskellunge 《*pl.* ~(s)》; a musky; a muskie; *Esox masquinongy*.

**マスキュラックス**〔商標・薬〕〔筋弛緩剤〕Musculax.

**「マスク」** 1〔ピーター・ボグダノヴィッチ監督の映画 (1984)〕Mask. 2〔ジム・キャリー主演の映画 (1994)〕The Mask.

**マスこうこく**【-広告】mass media advertising.

**マスコット** □■ マスコット・ガール a girl who represents a commercial product; a "mascot girl." マスコット的 ◐ あのアヒルはこの公園の～的存在です. That duck is a sort of park 「mascot [icon]. マスコット人形 a mascot doll.

**マスコバドとう**【-糖】〔フィリピン、ネグロス島産の、サトウキビから作られる黒砂糖〕Negros muscavado sugar; brown sugar made from the cane of Negros Island, Philippines.

**マスコミりんりこんだんかいぜんこくきょうぎかい**【-倫理懇談会全国協議会】the National Conference of the Mass Media Ethics Council.

**マス・ストランディング**〔クジラ・イルカなどの生存複数同時漂着〕(a) mass stranding.

**「マスター・アンド・コマンダー」**〔映画〕Master and Commander: The Far Side of the World.

**マスター・コントローラー**〔鉄道〕〔列車の速度を制御する機器〕a master controller.

**マスタードしゅじゅつ**【-手術】〔医〕〔心房内の血流を転換させるための〕a Mustard operation; the Mustard procedure.

**マスター・トラスト**〔年金資金を集中管理して運用する信託会社〕a master trust.

**マスばいたい**【-媒体】mass media.

**マスハドフ** Maskhadov, Aslan Aliyevich (1951-2005；チェチェン共和国の軍人・政治家；大統領 [1997-2005]).

**マス・マーケティング**〔経〕〔大衆消費者向けマーケティング〕mass marketing.

**マスメディアしゅうちゅうはいじょげんそく**【-集中排除原則】the principle of preventing exclusive control of the mass media.

**マスりんこん**【-倫懇】=マスコミりんりこんだんかいぜんこくきょうぎかい.

**まず**〔しくじる〕◐ まずったなあ. Now I've (really) blown it!

**マゾい** masochistic; hard on *one*self.

**またあさ**【股浅】〔ズボンが〕〔ジーンズ〕low-rise (jeans).

**マタ(ー)ラ** 1〔スリランカ南部の町〕Matara. 2〔エリトリアの遺跡〕Matara.

**マタイこうか**【-効果】〔社会・経〕the Matthew effect.

**マダイン**〔イラク、バグダード郊外の町〕Madain.

**またがたきうち**【再敵討ち】〔日本の近世の〕(repeated) family revenge; (a) vendetta.

**またたび**[1]【股旅】□■ 股旅映画 movies of wandering gamblers.

マタニティー ▫ マタニティー・ヨガ〔妊婦向けのヨガ〕maternity yoga; yoga for pregnant women.
マタニティビクス〚＜maternity ＋ aero*bics*〛〖商標〗〔妊産婦のための運動〕MaternityBics; aerobics for expectant mothers.
まだらいるか【斑海豚】〖動〗a (pantropical) spotted dolphin; *Stenella attenuata*.
まちあわせ【待ち合わせ】▫ 待ち合わせ場所[時間] the ⌈place [time] fixed for ⌈meeting [waiting for each other].
まちかど【町角・街角】▫ 街角アンケート an on-street [⌈a sidewalk, ⌈a pavement] questionnaire. 街角景気 the street-level economy; economic conditions as reported by small-scale retailers and service providers. 街角景気調査 a ⌈street-level [street-corner] survey of the economy. 街角景況感〔街角景気調査の結果〕the ⌈street-level [street-corner] view of the economy. 街角調査 a street survey.
まちきん【町金】＝まちきんゆう.
まちきんゆう【町金融】〔業者〕a loan shark (company); 〔業〕loan sharking.
まちづくり【町づくり・街づくり】▫ 町づくり三法 the three ⌈urban development [town planning] laws. ▶ 中心市街地活性化法, 大規模小売店舗立地法, 都市計画法 の3つ.
まちなみ【町並・街並】▫ 町並[街並]条例 a townscape ordinance.
まちぶせ【待ち伏せ】▫ 待ち伏せ攻撃《be killed in》an ambush (attack).
まちや【町家】▫ 京町家 a traditional Kyoto tradesman's house, narrow but deep; typically divided from the front into store, living quarters and workshop or warehouse, and often including an internal garden.
マッカリース McAleese, Mary Patricia (1951– ; アイルランドの政治家; 大統領〔1997– 〕).
マッキンゼー〔米国の経営コンサルタント会社〕McKinsey & Company.
マック・ジー McG (1970?– ; 米国の映画監督; 本名 Joseph McGinty Nichol).
マックスファクター〖商標〗〔米国の化粧品ブランド〕Max Factor.
マックス・マーラ〖商標〗〔イタリアの服飾ブランド〕Max Mara.
マックホルツすいせい【-彗星】〖天〗Comet Machholz.
まつげ【睫毛】▫ 上睫毛 an upper eyelash. 下睫毛 a lower eyelash.
マッケラン McKellen, Ian (1939– ; 英国生まれの俳優; 本名 Ian Murray McKellen).
「マッコイじいさん」〔米国の農村のがんこな老人と息子夫婦の TV ホームドラマ〕The Real McCoys.
まつしたせいけいじゅく【松下政経塾】the Matsushita Institute of Government and Management (略: MIGM).
マッシュルーム ▫ マッシュルーム・スープ mushroom soup.
まっしょう[1]【末梢】▫ 末梢血単核球〖解〗a peripheral blood mononuclear cell (略: PBMC).
まっしょうせい【末梢性】▫ 末梢(性)血管疾患〖医〗(a) peripheral vascular disease (略: PVD). 末梢(性)動脈疾患〖医〗(a) peripheral arterial disease (略: PAD).
マッスラ【真っ-】〖野球〗〔高速スライダー〕a cut fastball; a cutter.
マッソスポンディルス〖古生物〗〔草食恐竜の一種〕*Massospondylus*.
マッチ[1] ▫ 硫化燐マッチ a sulphur-and-phosphorus match; a strike-anywhere match.
マッデン Madden, John (1949– ; 英国生まれの映画監督).

マッデン・ジュリアンしんどう【-振動】〖気象〗the Madden-Julian Oscillation (略: MJO).
マット[3]【MAAT】＝マート[3].
「マッド・シティ」〔映画〕Mad City.
まつば【松葉】▫ 松葉箒(ばうき) a bamboo ⌈rake [brush] for (gathering up) pine needles.
まつもとサリンじけん【松本-事件】〔1994年の〕the Matsumoto (Sarin) Incident.
まつり【祭り】▫ 祭り足袋 festival *tabi*; strong, rubber-soled footwear worn by festival participants.
マディガン Madigan, Amy (1950– ; 米国の映画女優).
マディソン・スクエア・ガーデン〔米国, ニューヨーク市マンハッタンにある大規模な屋内スポーツ競技場〕(the) Madison Square Garden (略: MSG); 〖口〗the Garden.
マテリアル ▫ マテリアル・フロー・コスト会計〔環境会計の手法の1つ〕material flow cost accounting (略: MFCA).
マテル〔米国の玩具メーカー〕Mattel, Inc. ▶ バービー人形の販売元.
まど【窓】▫ 窓越し ◐ ~越しに話す talk (to *sb*) through a window / ~越しに見える景色 the ⌈scene [view, scenery] through a window.
まとい【纏い】▫ 纏い振り the twirling of the fireman's standard at the New Year's Fire Brigade parade.
マドゥーロ Maduro, Ricardo (1946– ; ホンジュラスの政治家; 大統領〔2002-06〕).
マトゥラーナ Maturana, Humberto R. (1928– ; チリの神経生理学者).
まどぐち【窓口】▫ 窓口機関〔応募・問い合わせなどの〕a contact organization. 窓口業務〖事務〗business handled at the windows. 窓口ネットワーク〔郵政事業の〕an over-the-counter (postal services) network. 窓口負担(額)〔患者の医療費の〕the amount that the patient pays at the ⌈hospital [clinic]. 窓口役〔グループの代表として外部との交渉を引き受ける人〕a ⌈liaison [link] person; a coordinator ⌈for enquiries).
マドラサ〚イスラム〛〔高等教育施設〕a madrasa(h); a medrese.
マドリード〔スペイン中部の自治州〕Madrid.
「マトリックス」〔映画〕The Matrix. ▶ 続編は「マトリックス リローデッド」(The Matrix Reloaded),「マトリックス レボリューションズ」(The Matrix Revolutions).
マナー ▫ マナー違反 bad manners. マナー・コンサルタント an etiquette [a manners] consultant.
マニフェスト ▫ 電子マニフェスト〔産廃電子管理票〕《use》an electronic manifest 《to track waste shipments》. ◐ 電子~制度 an electronic manifest system. ▫ マニフェスト・サイクル〔選挙の際政党が作成するマニフェストの公表, 実行, 達成度の評価といった一連の順〕the process of releasing a ⌈platform [⌈manifesto], carrying out its pledges and evaluating their fulfillment; the "manifesto cycle."
マヌーこくりつこうえん【-国立公園】〔ペルー南部の国立公園; 世界遺産〕Manu National Park.
マネージメント ▫ マネージメント・エンプロイー・バイアウト〖経営〗〔会社の経営陣と従業員が一体となって会社やその事業の特定部門の経営権を株主から買い取ること〕a management (and) employee buyout (略: MEBO). マネージメント能力 management ability.
マネー・マネージメント・ファンド〖金融〗〔追加型公社債投資信託〕a money management fund.
マネー・リザーブ・ファンド〖証券〗a money reserve fund (略: MRF).
マネタリー・ベース〖金融〗〔現金と日銀当座預金残高の合計〕《Japan's》monetary base. ▫ マネタリーベース統計 monetary base statistics.
マノロ・ブラニク〖商標〗〔スペインの靴ブランド〕Manolo Blahnik.

マノン〖サッカー〗〔後ろに敵がいるぞという警告〕Man on!
マハーサ(ー)ラカ(ー)ム =マハサラカム.
マハウィル〔イラク中部, バビル州の町〕Mahawil; Mahaweel.
マハサラカム〔タイ東北部の県；同県の県都〕Mahasarakham; Maha Sarakham.
マバト〔南アフリカ共和国北部の都市, 北西州の州都〕Mmabatho.
マハトマ〔＜Skt「偉大なる魂」の意〕〔インドで, 聖者〕(a) Mahatma. ○ ~・ガンジー Mahatma Gandhi.
マハレさんかいこくりつこうえん【-山塊国立公園】〔タンザニアの〕Mahale Mountains National Park.
まひ[2]【麻痺】 □ベル麻痺〖医〗〔特発性顔面麻痺〕Bell's palsy.
マフディ(ー)ぐん【-軍】〔イラクのイスラム教シーア派のムクダ・サドル師が率いる民兵組織〕the Mahdi Army.
マフム(ー)ディ(ー)ヤ〔イラク, バグダッド南方の町〕Mahmudiya.
「マペット・ショー」〔米国の, 操り人形とタレントによるバラエティー TV 番組〕The Muppet Show.
ママ 〖略〗ママ友 a fellow「*mom["mum].
「ママが泣いた日」〔映画〕The Upside of Anger.
ママコート a "mama coat"; an extra-large coat for a baby-carrying mother.
マミー・トラック〔育児などのために出退社時刻・休暇などを弾力的に決めることのできる女性の就労形態〕〖口〗(be on) the「*mommy["mummy] track.
まみろくいな【眉白水鶏】〖鳥〗〔クイナ科の鳥〕a white-browed crake; Porzana cinerea; Poliolimnas cinereus.
まめ-【豆-】 □豆剣士〖柔道家〗a child「kendo player [jūdōka]; a little「kendoist [judoist].
まめかん【豆かん・豆羹】〖菓子〗sweetened (boiled) beans in jelly.
まめしば【豆柴】〖犬〗a midget Shiba Inu; a mameshiba.
マメンチサウルス〖古生物〗〔中生代ジュラ紀後期に中国に生息した大型草食恐竜；首が極端に長い〕Mamenchisaurus. ► Mamenchisaurus hochuanensis; Mamenchisaurus sinocanadorum など, 後者はアジアで発見された最大の恐竜.
まもう【摩耗・磨耗】 □摩耗量 (a) wear volume. 比摩耗量 a specific wear rate.
まやく【麻薬】 □麻薬探知機 a drug detector.
まやくいいんかい【麻薬委員会】〔国連の〕the Commission on Narcotic Drugs (略：CND).
マヤもじ【-文字】a Mayan glyph.
まゆメーク【眉-】eyebrow styling.
「真夜中のサバナ」〔映画〕Midnight in the Garden of Good and Evil.
マヨラー〔どんな料理にもマヨネーズをかけて食べる人〕a mayonnaise addict; somebody who puts mayonnaise on everything「he [she] eats.
マラカニアンきゅうでん【-宮殿】〔フィリピンの大統領府〕Malacañan Palace.
マラソン[1] □マラソン大会 a marathon (race). マラソン膝〖医〗=ランナー膝(⇒ランナー).
マラニック〖marathon と picnic を合わせた和製英語〗〔遠距離走ビクニック〕a "maranic"; a noncompetitive marathon with a picnic-like atmosphere.
マラバール 1〔インド南西部, アラビア海に臨む海岸〕the Malabar Coast. 2〖軍〗〔ベンガル湾周辺海域で行われる多国間海上合同訓練；米国・インドなどが参加〕Exercise Malabar.
「マリア・マリ」〔曲名〕Maria, Mari.
「マリー・アントワネットの首飾り」〔映画〕The Affair of the Necklace.
マリインスキー・オペラ〔ロシアの歌劇団〕the Mariinsky Opera.
マリインスキー・バレエ〔ロシアの舞踊団〕the Mariinsky Ballet.

マリーン・ワン〔米大統領専用ヘリコプターの呼称〕Marine One.
マリック Malick, Terrence (1946–　；米国の映画監督・脚本家).
マリナーラ〖料理〗〔ピザの一種〕marinara.
マリブ〔米国ロサンジェルス西方の海浜地・高級住宅地；サーフィンのメッカ〕Malibu.
マリボー〔デンマーク産のチーズ〕Maribo.
マリン・クロノメーター〔航海用の精密時計〕a marine chronometer.
まるあじ【丸鯵】〖魚〗a Japanese scad; an amberstripe scad; a deep-bodied round scad; Decapterus maruadsi.
マルカジー〔イラン中部の州〕Markazi.
まるがり【丸刈り】 □丸刈り頭 a close-cropped head.
マルガリーマン【丸刈りのサラリーマン】a salaryman who shaves his head (in imitation of fashionable sportsmen).
マルクしゅう【-州】〔インドネシアの州〕Maluku (Province).
マルケイ Mulcahy, Russell (1953–　；オーストラリア生まれの映画監督).
マルけいゆうし【-経融資】〔小企業等経営改善資金融資制度の通称〕the "maru-kei" system of providing capital to small businesses without security or a guarantor.
マルゲリータ〖料理〗〔ピザの一種〕margherita.
マルコヴィッチ Malkovich, John (1953–　；米国の映画俳優. Cf. John Gavin Malkovich).
「マルコヴィッチの穴」〔映画〕Being John Malkovich.
マルコビッチ =マルコヴィッチ.
マルコム X〔映画〕Malcolm X.
まるぞり【丸剃り】 □丸剃り頭 a「shaved [shaven] head.
マルチ □マルチヒット〖野球〗〔1試合で1人の打者が2本以上のヒットを打つこと〕multihit (game).
マルチクライアントちょうさ【-調査】〖広告〗a multiclient survey.
マルチパス〖通信〗〔多重通路〕multipath.
マルチビタミン〔総合ビタミン剤〕a multivitamin.
マルチブランド〔同一商品に対して複数の商標をつけること〕multibrand; multibranding. □マルチブランド戦略 a multibrand(ing) strategy.
マルチほうそう【-放送】〖テレビ〗multiprogram broadcasting.
マルチミネラル〔各種ミネラルを含んだサプリメント〕a multimineral.
マルチメディア □マルチメディア時代 a [the] multimedia age.
マルチンキエヴィチ, マルチンキエビッチ Marcinkiewicz, Kazimierz (1959–　；ポーランドの政治家；首相 [2005-06]).
マルツエキス〔乳幼児用便秘薬〕malt extract.
マルディ・グラ〔謝肉祭の最後の日 (告解火曜日) の祭り〕Mardi Gras.
「マルティナは海」〔映画〕Son De Mar (=Sound of the Sea).
マルデン Malden, Karl (1912–　；米国の映画俳優；本名 Mladen Sekulovich).
マルファンしょうこうぐん【-症候群】〖医〗Marfan('s) syndrome.
マルポールじょうやく【MARPOL 条約】〔国際海洋汚染防止条約〕the MARPOL Convention. ► MARPOL は Marine Pollution の略. [=かいようおせんぼうしじょうやく]
「マルホランド・ドライブ」〔映画〕Mulholland Dr.
「マレーナ」〔映画〕Malena.
マレーばく【-獏】〖動〗a Malayan tapir; Tapirus indicus.
マレーやまねこ【-山猫】〖動〗a flat-headed cat; Felis planiceps.

マレックびょう【-病】〖獣医〗Marek's disease (略: MD). ▫️マレック病ウイルス Marek's disease virus (略: MDV).

マレット・フィンガー〖医〗〔槌指〕 a 「mallet [hammer] finger.

まろまゆ【麻呂眉】〔平安時代の公卿のような眉〕eyebrows which have been shaved off or plucked and replaced with painted eyebrows higher on the brow.

まわしうち【回し打ち】〔麻薬などの注射器の連続使用〕needle sharing. 〜する share a needle.

まわりこむ【回り込む】go round and cut in. ◉パトカーはその車を追跡し、前方に回り込んで停車させた。The police car gave chase and cut in front of the car, forcing it to stop. / すばやく相手の横に回り込んで顎にフックをたたきこんだ。He nipped around his opponent and delivered a hook to the jaw.

マン Mann, Michael (1943- ; 米国の映画監督・脚本家・製作者).

「マン・オン・ザ・ムーン」〖映画〗Man on the Moon.

「まんが探偵局ディック・トレーシー」〖米国の、探偵 Dick Tracy とその仲間の TV アニメ〗The Dick Tracy Show.

マンガン ▫️マンガン鉱石 manganese ore.

まんき【満期】▫️満期慰労金〖保険〗a maturity bonus. 満期保有(目的)の債券〖証券〗a bond held to maturity; a held-to-maturity bond.

マンギョンボンごう【万景峰号】〔北朝鮮の貨客船〕the Man Gyong Bong.

まんくうじょうほう【満空情報】〔駐車場・ホテルなどの〕《provide real-time》 information on 《parking, room》 availability.

まんげんこ【万元戸】〔1980 年代の中国で、年収 1 万元の世帯〕 a "ten-thousand yuan household." ▶ 当初この語は裕福を意味していたが、その後裕福の基準は 10 万元戸、100 万元戸と上がっていった。

マンゴールド Mangold, James (1964- ; 米国の映画監督・脚本家).

まんざいうお【万歳魚】〔魚〕〔シマガツオ科の魚〕a rough pomfret; *Taractes asper*.

マンザナー(ル)〔米国、カリフォルニア州の砂漠地; 第 2 次大戦中の日系人強制収容所所在地〕Manzanar.

マンション ▫️定住型マンション ⇨ていじゅう. ▫️マンション管理士 a licensed 「condominium [apartment] manager [superintendent].

マンションかんりセンター【-管理-】〔財団法人〕the Condominium Management Center (略: CMC).

マンションたてかええんかつかほう【-建て替え円滑化法】〖法〗the Law Concerning the Facilitation of Reconstruction of Condominium Buildings.

マンシングウェア〖商標〗〔ペンギンのマークの米国ブランド衣料品〕Munsingwear.

マンスール〔イラク、バグダッド北東部の地区〕Mansour.

マンステール〔ドイツ、アルザス地方産のチーズ〕Muenster (cheese).

まんせい【慢性】▫️慢性活動性肝炎〖医〗chronic active hepatitis. 慢性化膿性中耳炎〖医〗chronic suppurative otitis media. 慢性骨髄炎〖医〗chronic osteomyelitis. 慢性消耗病〖獣医〗chronic wasting disease (略: CWD). 慢性鼻炎 chronic rhinitis.

まんぞく【満足】▫️満足顔 《with》 a look of satisfaction 《on one's face》.

まんぞくど【満足度】(a 「level [degree] of) satisfaction; how satisfied *sb* is 《with a product》. ▫️顧客満足度 (a 「level [degree] of) customer satisfaction (略: CS). 従業員満足度 (a 「level [degree] of) employee satisfaction (略: ES). 商品[サービス]満足度 (a 「level [degree] of) 'product (customer) service) satisfaction.

マンダきょう【-教】〔グノーシス主義の一派〕Mandaeanism; Mandaeism.

マンダヤきょう【-教】=マンダきょう.

マンダレー〔ミャンマー中北部の行政区画(管区)〕Mandalay (Division).

マンデートなんみん【-難民】〔国連難民高等弁務官事務所(UNHCR)が認定した難民〕a mandate refugee.

マンデビラ〔植〕〔キョウチクトウ科マンデビラ属のつる性植物の総称; 園芸植物〕a mandevilla.

まんとう[1]【万灯・万燈】▫️万灯流し a ceremony in which many votive lanterns are floated down a river.

マンドーキ Mandoki, Luis (1954- ; メキシコ生まれの米国の映画監督).

マントラ〖密教〗〔真理を表す秘密の言葉〕a mantra. ▷ mantric *adj*.

まんねん【万年】▫️万年氷〖地質〗永久氷 (⇨えいきゅう).

マンノオリゴとう【-糖】〖生化〗a mannan oligosaccharide (略: MOS).

「マンハッタン・ラプソディ」〖映画〗The Mirror Has Two Faces.

まんびき【万引き】▫️万引き防止ゲート a shoplifting gate; a (store) security gate. 万引き防止装置[タグ] an antishoplifting 「device [tag].

マンモグラフィーけんしんせいどかんりちゅうおういいんかい【-検診精度管理中央委員会】the Central Committee on Quality Control of Mammographic Screening.

マンモトーム〖商標・医〗〔乳房組織生検装置〕Mammotome. ▫️マンモトーム生検〖医〗《have》 a Mammotome biopsy.

# み

ミアキス〖古生物〗〔第三紀前期に北米・ヨーロッパに棲息した、ネコに似た肉食哺乳類〕*Miacis*.

ミーゴレン〖料理〗〔インドネシアの焼きそばに似た料理〕mee goreng; Indonesian fried noodles.

ミート[2] ▫️ミート・ポイント〖自動車〗〔クラッチの〕the friction point; 「球技で」the point of contact. ◉〜ポイントが手元に近づきすぎると打球はライト方向に飛ばない。〖野球〗The ball won't go toward right field if it hits the bat too close to the hands. ミート力〖ゴルフなどで〗a hitting rate. ミート力〖野球など〗contact ability. 〜力のある選手 a good contact hitter.

「ミート・ザ・ペアレンツ」〖映画〗Meet the Parents.

ミーム〔人間の脳から複製される文化的情報の伝達単位; 文化的遺伝〕a meme; a cultural gene. ▷ memetic *adj*. ▶ 英国の生物学者 リチャード・ドーキンス (Richard Dawkins) が提唱した架空の遺伝子.

ミール[2]〖食事〗a meal; 〔穀物の粉〕meal. ▫️ミール・ソリューション〔料理の煩雑さを解決する方法〕a meal solution.

みうめ【実梅】〔花梅に対し、果実を取るための梅〕a fruit *ume* (tree).

ミエリン ▫️ミエリン塩基性たんぱく質〖化〗myelin basic protein (略: MBP).

みえるか【見える化】〔問題点が常に見えるようにしておく工夫〕rendering 《a problem》 visible; 〔数値化〕digitization.

ミオクローヌスてんかん【-癲癇】〖医〗=ミオクロニーてんかん.

**ミオクロニーてんかん**【−癲癇】〔医〕myoclonic [myoclonus] epilepsy.

**みかえり**【見返り】▯▯ 見返り措置 a measure (taken) in return; a favor (done [given]) in return; (a) recompense.

**みがき**[2]【身欠き】gutting (fish).

**みかく**【味覚】▯▯ 味覚過敏〔医〕hypergeusia. 味覚調査〔食品などに関し，消費者を対象として行う調査と〕a taste survey.

**みかた**[2]【味方】▯▯ 味方打線〔野球〕one's own (team's)「batting line-up [batters]. ◐ 川野は好投を見せたが，打線の援護がなく，負け投手となった. Despite pitching well, Kawano did not get any offensive support, so he ended up being the losing pitcher.

**みがら**【身柄】▯▯ 身柄移管 handing over《a terrorist》to《the US Army authorities》. 身柄移送 moving [transferring, (the) transfer] 《of a suspect》《to a different prison》. 身柄引き渡し〔他国の司法機関への〕(the) transfer《of a suspect》《to the local authorities》; 〔国外逃亡犯人の〕(the) extradition《of a criminal》《to his home country》. 身柄引き渡し請求 an extradition request; a「request [demand] for extradition.

**ミカルディス**〔商標・薬〕〔降圧剤〕Micardis.

**みがわり**【身代り】▯▯ 身代り自首 ＝身代り出頭 (⇨ しゅっとう). 身代り受験〔替え玉受験〕an exam taken by a stand-in. 身代り出頭 ⇨しゅっとう. 身代り投票〔替え玉投票〕(corrupt) voting by (illegal) proxy.

**みかん**[4]【蜜柑】▯▯ みかん狩り mandarin orange picking.

**ミキサー**▯▯ ミキサー食 a food processor meal (prepared after showing《a patient》the ingredients).

**ミクロラプトル・グイ**〔古生物〕〔白亜紀の恐竜〕*Microraptor gui*.

**みけつ**【未決】▯▯ 未決拘禁者〔拘留中の被疑者〕a prisoner in custody awaiting trial; 〔拘留中の被告〕a defendant in custody awaiting judgment.

**みこうかい**【未公開】▯▯ 未公開シーン〔映画などの〕a previously「unshown [unscreened] scene; 〔公開版から は削除されたシーン〕a scene cut from the「released [original] version. 未公開写真 an (as yet)「unpublished [unexhibited] photograph; a photograph not previously shown.

**みこん**[1]【未婚】▯▯ 未婚化 a tendency「not to marry [to remain single]; a declining marriage rate. ◐ わが国は晩婚化と一化が急速に進行している. Our country is experiencing a rapid trend toward people getting married later or not at all. | In our country, more and more people are delaying marriage or staying single altogether. 未婚率 the unmarried rate. ◐ 35 歳の男女，女性の～率はどれぐらいだろう. I wonder what the unmarried rate is for men and women 35 years old.

**ミサ**【弥撒】▯▯ 就任ミサ〔ローマ教皇などの〕an inaugural Mass. 野外ミサ an outdoor [a field] mass.

**ミサイル**▯▯ 海上配備型ミサイル a sea-based missile. 海上配備型迎撃ミサイル a sea-based interceptor missile. ▯▯ ミサイル観測艦 a missile range instrumentation ship. ミサイル迎撃能力 missile interception capability. ミサイル追跡用レーダー missile tracking radar. ミサイル発射実験 a missile (launch) test; a test missile launch.

**ミサイルぼうえいきょく**【−防衛局】〔米国国防省の〕the Missile Defense Agency (略: MDA).

**ミシェル・リー** Michelle Reis (1970– ; 香港の映画女優; 中国語名 李嘉欣) Lee Ka-Yan).

**ミシシッピあかみみがめ**【−赤耳亀】〔動〕a red-eared slider (turtle); *Trachemys scripta elegans*.

**みしまばいかも**【三島梅花藻】〔植〕〔キンポウゲ科の水生多年草〕*Ranunculus nipponicus* var. *japonicus*.

**みじゅくじ**【未熟児】▯▯ 極小未熟児〔出生体重が 1,500g 未満の〕a very low birth weight「infant [baby] with a birth weight less than 1,500g. 超未熟児〔出生体重が 1,000g 未満の〕an extremely low birth weight「infant [baby] with a birth weight less than 1,000g.

**みしょうにん**【未承認】▯▯ unapproved (drugs). ◐ この避妊薬は日本では～である. This contraceptive has not been approved in Japan. ▯▯ 未承認国〔外交上の〕an unrecognized country. 未承認薬 an unapproved drug. 未承認ワクチン an unapproved vaccine.

**みしょうりば**【未勝利馬】〔競馬〕a novice; a maiden.

**みしょぶん**【未処分】▯▯ 未処分剰余金 an unappropriated surplus.

**ミシン** ▯▯ 工業用ミシン an industrial sewing machine. 家庭用ミシン a「home [domestic, household] sewing machine.

**ミジンウキマイマイ**〔動〕〔浮遊性の巻貝; クリオネの餌になる〕*Limacina helicina*.

**みず**【水】▯▯ 水恐怖症 a pathological fear of water; aquaphobia; 〔飲み水恐怖症の〕a fear of drinking water; hydrophobia. 水チャネル[チャンネル]〔医〕a water channel. 水中毒〔医〕〔過剰な水分摂取による〕water「intoxication [poisoning]; hyperhydration. 水治癒, 水療法〔医〕water cure; hydrotherapy; hydrotherapeutics; hydriatrics. 水分解〔化〕water splitting. 水分子 a water molecule; a molecule of water.

**ミス**[1] ▯▯ 印字ミス a printing「mistake [error]. 修理ミス an error (made) during repair(s). タイプミス a typing「mistake [error]; a typo《*pl.* 〜s》. 表記ミス a clerical error; a misprint; a typographical error; a typo《*pl.* 〜s》.

**みずあおい**【水葵】〔植〕〔ミズアオイ科の水草; 絶滅危惧種〕a water hyacinth; *Monochoria korsakowii*. ミズアオイ科 Pontederiaceae.

**みずおじぎそう**【水含羞草】〔植〕〔マメ科の水生植物〕*Neptunia oleracea*.

**みずき**【水着】▯▯ 競泳用水着 a competition swimsuit.

**みずきり**【水切り】▯▯ 水切り袋〔流しの〕a strainer bag.

**みすぎる**【見過ぎる】 ◐ テレビを〜と目によくない. Watching too much TV is bad for your eyes. / 彼は球を見すぎてカウントを悪くすることが多い.〔野球で〕He often pays focuses too much on the pitch and falls behind in the count. / 彼はいつもまわりの様子を見すぎて対応が遅れる. He's always slow to respond because he spends too much time watching what's going on around him.

**みずぎわ**【水際】▯▯ 水際対策〔密輸・疫病などに対する〕a「water's edge [threshold] policy.

**みずさき**【水先】▯▯ 水先区 a pilotage district. ◐ 強制〜区〔免許をもった水先人の乗船が義務付けられている水域〕a compulsory pilotage district.

**みずさきにん**【水先人】〔免許をもった水先案内人〕a licensed pilot.

**みずさきほう**【水先法】〔法〕the Pilot Law.

**みずしげん**【水資源】▯▯ 水資源開発 water resources development.

**みずしげんかいはつこうだん**【水資源開発公団】the Water Resources Development Public Corporation (略: WARDEC).

**みずしげんきこう**【水資源機構】(略: JWA) the Japan Water Agency (略: JWA).

「**Mr. & Mrs. スミス**」〔映画〕*Mr. and Mrs. Smith*.

「**Mr. インクレディブル**」〔アニメ映画〕*The Incredibles*.

「**ミスター・エド**」〔米国の, 主人と会話できる馬 Ed の TV ホームコメディ〕*Mister Ed*.

「**ミスター・ノバック**」〔米国の TV 学園ドラマ〕*Mr. Novak*.

**ミスチーフかんしょう**【−環礁】〔南沙諸島の〕Mischief Reef.

「ミスティック・リバー」〔米国の作家デニス・ルヘイン(Dennis Lehane; 1966- )作の小説; その映画化〕Mystic River.
ミステリー ▯ ミステリー小説 a mystery; a mystery novel.
「ミステリー」⇨「ミステリーゾーン」.
「ミステリーゾーン」〔米国の、一話完結の SF アンソロジーTV ドラマ〕The Twilight Zone. ▶「ミステリー」「未知の世界」の邦題でも放映.
ミストラルきゅう【―級】〔ヨットレース〕the Mistral class.
みずねこのお【水猫の尾】〔植〕〔シソ科の水草; 絶滅危惧種〕Eusteralis stellata; Eusteralis verticillata.
みずばち【水鉢】a water basin.
みずひまわり【水向日葵】〔植〕〔キク科の水生植物〕a Senegal tea plant; a temple plant; Gymnocoronis spilanthoides.
みずまし【水増し】▯ 水増し領収書 a padded receipt.
みずむけ【水向け】〔霊前に水を手向けること〕making an offering of water before a grave.
ミスる [ミス(を)する] ● ミスった! Oops!
みせいた【見せ板】〔取引〕〔取引が活発であると見せかけるためや価格操作のために、買う[売る]気がないのに買い[売り]注文を大量に出すこと〕(criminal) stock price manipulation carried out by making large-scale purchase or sell orders and cancelling them immediately.
みせパン【見せ―】〔服飾〕show-off panties; fancy panties.
みせブラ【見せ―】〔服飾〕a show-off bra; a fashion bra.
「魅せられて」〔映画〕Stealing Beauty.
みそ【味噌】▯ 合わせ味噌 a「blend [mixture] of different varieties of miso. ▯ 味噌カツ breaded pork cutlets pasted with miso. 味噌まんじゅう a miso-flavored bean-jam bun.
みそかごと【密事】〔秘密のこと〕a secret; a private「matter [affair]〕;〔密通〕a secret「affair [liaison].
ミソプロストール〔薬〕〔潰瘍治療薬〕misoprostol.
ミゾリビン〔薬〕〔免疫抑制剤〕mizoribin.
みたま【御霊】▯ 御霊祭り a festival of ancestral worship.
ミタル・スチール =ミッタル(・スチール).
みちなかば【道半ば】halfway (through); midway; in the middle (of…); mid-career《retirement》; in the course of《one's work》; during《the process》. ● ―にして病に倒れる fall ill「along the way [halfway through] / ～にして倒れる die「while still in one's prime [in the midst of one's career] / ～にして倒れた被害者の無念さは察するに余りある. The victim's feelings of resentment, with「his [her] ambitions crushed「before their accomplishment [uncompleted, midway], can be imagined. ● 日本における福祉社会の建設はいまだ～の感がある. The creation of a welfare society in Japan seems still incomplete. | We still seem only part way toward building a welfare society in Japan. ● 経済再生はいまだ～であり、財政再建も待ったなしの重要課題である. The economy is still on the route to recovery [has still not fully recovered] and financial reconstruction is a major issue which must not be postponed.
「未知の世界」⇨「ミステリーゾーン」.
みちのひ【道の日】〔8月10日; 旧建設省(現国土交通省)が1986年に制定〕Road Day.
みちわる【道悪】〔競馬〕muddy [sloppy, wet, "off"] (track) conditions. ▯ 道悪競馬 horseracing under「muddy [sloppy, wet, "off"] (track) conditions; racing in the mud. 道悪巧者 a horse that races well in「heavy ["off"] going; a (good) mudder.
みつ²【蜜】▯ 蜜入りリンゴ an apple with a sweetish glassy interior; a watercore apple.
みつおびアルマジロ【三つ帯―】〔動〕a three-banded armadillo; an apar; *Tolypeutes tricinctus*.
「ミッキーマウス・クラブ」〔ディズニーのバラエティーTV番組〕The Mickey Mouse Club.
ミックス ▯ シーフード・ミックス〔さまざまな魚介類を混ぜ合わせて冷凍した食材〕《frozen》seafood mix. ▯ ミックス犬 a mixed-breed dog. ミックスゾーン〔競技場に設けられた取材用の場所〕a (media)「mix zone [mix-zone].
みつくりえながちょうちんあんこう【箕作柄長提灯鮟鱇】〔魚〕a triplewart seadevil; *Cryptopsaras couesii*.
みつげつ【蜜月】▯ 蜜月関係 a honeymoon relationship. ● 両国間の～関係は終焉を迎えようとしていた. The honeymoon relationship between the two countries was「reaching an end [almost over].
みっこく【密告】▯ 密告社会 an「informer [informant] society; a society of「informers [informants].
ミッシェル・ヨー Michelle Yeoh (1962- ; マレーシア生まれの映画女優; 中国語名 楊紫瓊 Yeoh Chu-Kheng).
「ミッション:インポッシブル」〔映画〕Mission: Impossible.
「ミッション・トゥ・マーズ」〔映画〕Mission to Mars.
みつぞう¹【密造】▯ 密造拳銃 an illegally manufactured handgun.
ミッタル(・スチール)〔オランダに本社を置く世界最大の鉄鋼メーカー〕Mittal Steel Company.
ミッチェル 1 Michell, Roger (1957- ; 南アフリカ生まれの映画監督).
2 Mitchell, John Cameron (1963- ; 米国の映画俳優・監督).
「ミッチと歌おう」〔米国の指揮者ミッチ・ミラー (Mitch Miller) と男声合唱団のTV番組〕Sing Along with Mitch.
みっちゃく【密着】▯ 密着レポート〔取材方法〕intimate [close-up] reporting;〔その報告〕an intimate [a close-up] report. ● 今夜の番組では夜間救急医療の現場を～レポートします. On tonight's program, we're showing a report that examines close-up nighttime emergency medical services.
みっぺい【密閉】▯ 密閉空間 an「unventilated [enclosed] space. 密閉状態 airtight [hermetically sealed] conditions. ● ～状態に保つ keep《furs》in「airtight [hermetically sealed] conditions. 密閉バケツ〔生ゴミの発酵処理用の〕a compost「bucket [container].
みつほうりゅう【密放流】releasing《black bass》illegally;〔その「an] illegal release《of fish》. ● ～する release《a species into a lake》illegally.
み(つ)ゆびなまけもの【三指樹懶】〔動〕a three-toed sloth; *Bradypus tridactylus*.
ミティ【MITI】〔日本の旧通商産業省の通称〕MITI. ▶ the Ministry of International Trade and Industry の略.
ミドラー Midler, Bette (1945- ; 米国の歌手・映画女優; 本名 Bette Davis Midler).
みとり【看取り】〔病人の世話をすること〕caring for a sick person;〔人の死に立ち会うこと〕attendance at sb's deathbed.
みどり【緑】▯ 緑ナンバー〔事業用自動車のナンバープレート〕a green license plate《for commercial vehicles》.
みどりしげんきこう【緑資源機構】the Japan Green Resources Agency (略: J-Green). ▶ 2003年に緑資源公団より移行.
みどりしげんこうだん【緑資源公団】the Japan Green Resources Corporation (略: JGRC). ▶ 2003年に緑資源機構となる.
みどりのダム【緑の―】〔森林の保水機能をさす言葉〕the "green dam" effect.
みどりぼん【緑本】〔ミシュラン・ガイドの、観光案内版〕the (Michelin) Green Guide.
みどりまい【緑米】〔古代米の一種〕green rice.
ミドル・エイジ ▯ ミドルエイジ・クライシス〔心理〕〔中年の危機〕a midlife crisis.
ミトロビツァ〔セルビア、コソヴォ北部の都市〕Mitrovica.

みなし-【見做し-】 ▶ みなし額面〔株式の〕deemed face value. みなし控除〔税の〕tax deemed deducted. みなし公務員 a quasi-*public servant [*civil servant]; a public official who is bound by public service regulations but does not benefit from the same working rights as full *public servants [*civil servants]. みなし仕入れ率〔簡易課税方式における〕a deemed rate of purchases. みなし弁済〔利息制限法を上回る利息に借り手が合意しそれを支払うこと〕a high-interest loan repayment deemed legal because the debtor paid the interest voluntarily; a "voluntary" high-interest repayment to a loan shark.

みなまたびょう【水俣病】 ▶ 先天性水俣病〔医〕congenital Minamata disease. 胎児性水俣病〔医〕fetal Minamata disease.

みなみアジアじゆうぼうえきけん【南-自由貿易圏】the South Asian Free Trade Area(略: SAFTA).

みなみアチェ【南-】〔インドネシア, アチェ州の県, アチェ・セラタン〕スラタン〕Aceh Selatan.

みなみおおがしら【南大頭】〔動〕〔オーストラリア・ニューギニア原産の毒蛇〕an (eastern) brown tree snake; a night tiger; *Boiga irregularis*.

みなみオセチア【南-】〔グルジア北部の自治州〕South Ossetia.

みなみカリフォルニアだいがく【南-大学】the University of Southern California (略: USC).

みなみがわ【南側】the south side. ▶ ～に on the south side (of …). ▶ うちの～の窓 the windows on the south side of my house.

みなみしろさい【南白犀】〔動〕a southern white rhinoceros; *Ceratotherium simum simum*.

みなみたいへいようかいせん【南太平洋海戦】〔史〕〔1942年10月26日, 南太平洋のサンタクルーズ諸島沖で行われた日米海戦〕the Battle of the South Pacific. ▶ 米国では一般的に the Battle of the Santa Cruz Islands(サンタクルーズ諸島海戦)と呼ばれる.

みなみドイツしんぶん【南-新聞】〔ドイツの日刊紙〕Söeddeutsche Zeitung.

みなみホラサ(ー)ン【南-】〔イラン東部の州〕South Khorasan; 〔ペルシャ語名の音訳〕Khorasan-e「Jonubi [Jonoobi].

みなみまぐろほぞんいいんかい【みなみまぐろ保存委員会】〔漁業〕the Commission for the Conservation of Southern Bluefin Tuna (略: CCSBT).

ミニいしょく【-移植】〔医〕a minitransplant.

ミニゲーム 1〔パソコンでできる簡単な一人用のゲーム〕a "mini" computer game (for one player); a (simple) one-person computer game. 2〔スポーツ〕〔人数・時間などを縮小して行う練習試合〕(a) game-style practice; a practice game (with a reduced number of players).

ミニサッカー〔スポーツ〕〔通常よりも狭いコート・少ない人数で行うサッカー〕(a) mini-soccer.

ミニチュア・シュナウザー〔犬〕a miniature schnauzer.

ミニチュア・ダックスフント〔犬〕a miniature dachshund.

ミニチュア・プードル〔犬〕a miniature poodle.

ミニッツ・リピーター〔ボタンを押すと何時何分かを音で知らせる機能〕a minute repeater.

ミニにっけいへいきんさきもの【-日経平均先物】Mini Nikkei 225 futures.

ミニバス(ケ) = ミニバスケットボール.

ミニバスケットボール mini-basketball; mini basketball.

ミニパト〔駐車違反取り締まりなどに使われる小型のパトカー〕a mini *patrol [police] car.

ミニマックス ▶ ミニマックス原理〔ゲーム理論の〕the minimax principle. ミニマックス戦略〔ゲーム理論の〕a [the] minimax strategy.

ミニマムきゅう【-級】〔ボクシング〕minimumweight. ▶ ～のボクサー a 「minimumweight [strawweight] (boxer).

ミニマムそう【-創】〔医〕=しょうせっかい².

みにゅうりょく【未入力】 ▶ ～の not 「input(ted) [entered] / 必須項目が～の場合は~ません. If the requisite *sections [fields] are not *input(ted) [entered], registration will not be possible.

ミニラボ〔写真〕 ▶ ミニラボ機〔現像用の機械〕a 《digital》minilab (machine). ミニラボ店〔小規模の〕現像店〕a minilab.

ミニレッキス〔動〕〔ウサギの品種の1つ〕a Mini Rex (rabbit).

ミネストローネ ▶ ミネストローネ・スープ minestrone soup.

ミネリ Minnelli, Vincente (1903-86; 米国の映画監督; 本名 Lester Anthony Minnelli).

みのう【未納】 ▶ 未納率〔国民年金などの〕a [the] rate of nonpayment 《of national pension premiums》.

ミノー〔釣り〕〔小魚〕a minnow. ▶ フローティング・ミノー〔疑似餌を〕a floating minnow. ▶ ミノータイプ〔疑似餌の〕minnow-type 《lures》. ミノープラグ〔疑似餌の〕a minnow plug.

みのがし【見逃し】 ▶ 見逃し率〔天気予報などの〕a miss rate.

「身代金」〔映画〕Ransom.

みのやき【美濃焼】Mino ware; ceramics [pottery, porcelain] from the province of Mino region (now part of Gifu Pref.).

みはいび【未配備】 ▶ ～の最新型ミサイル a new type of missile (that is) not yet deployed; a new nondeployed missile.

みはっしょう【未発症】〔医〕 ▶ 未発症感染者 an infected carrier. 未発症者[患者] a carrier. ▶ 長期～者 a long-term carrier; [HIV の] a long-term nonprogressor (略: LTNP).

みはつばい【未発売】 ▶ ～の not yet on 「sale [the market]. ▶ 未発売商品 an 「item [article] not yet on 「sale [the market].

みはっぴょう【未発表】 ▶ 未発表作品 an unpublished work; 〔文学作品など〕a work not yet published; 〔絵画など〕an unexhibited work; 《a drawing》never before exhibited; 〔曲など〕an unperformed work; 《a piece》never before performed.

みひつせきにん【未必責任】〔法〕〔偶発債務〕contingent liability.

みびょう【未病】〔発症には至っていない不健康状態〕 ▶ ～のうちに治す cure 《an illness》before symptoms appear. ▶ 未病状態 a presymptomatic 「state [condition].

ミフ【MIF】〔米州開発銀行の〕多数国間投資基金〕the MIF; the Multilateral Investment Fund.

ミフェプリストン〔薬〕mifepristone. 〔⇒アール・ユー-よんはちろく〕

「ミフネ」〔映画〕Mifune's Last Song.

ミプロ【MIPRO】〔対日貿易投資交流促進協会〕MIPRO; the Manufactured Imports and Investment Promotion Organization.

みぶん【身分】 ▶ 身分照会〔スポーツ〕〔外国人選手獲得のための〕a status check (for a foreign player). 身分なき共犯〔法〕an accessory to a criminal act carried out by another person who is liable to punishment (for such crimes) because of his or her 「occupation [status, position]. 身分犯〔法〕a criminal act in which the status of the criminal establishes the criminal's liability to punishment (for such crimes).

「未亡人の一年」〔ジョン・アーヴィング作の小説〕A Widow for One Year.

みまもり【見守り】watching; monitoring. ▶ ～が必要

なひとり暮らしの高齢者 an elderly person living alone who needs to be「watched [monitored, checked up on]」. ▯ 地域見守り運動 a「local [neighborhood] watch program. 独居高齢者見守りボランティア a volunteer monitor for solitary elderly people.
**ミミガー**【料理】【豚の耳の皮；沖縄の食材】*mimiga*; Okinawan vinegared pigs' ears.
**みみざわり**[2]【耳触り】〜のよい音[言葉] a「sound [word] that sounds good; a「satisfying [pleasing] sound [word].
**みみながバンディクート**【耳長-】【動】a greater bilby; a rabbit(-eared) bandicoot; *Macrotis lagotis*.
「耳に残るは君の歌声」【映画】The Man Who Cried.
**みみのひ**【耳の日】【3月3日】Ear Day.
**ミメシス**【模倣】mimesis. ▯ ミメシス理論 mimetic theory.
**みもと**【身元】▯ 身元確認 identity confirmation. ●死体の〜確認の，歯の治療痕が調べられた。The body was examined for signs of dental treatment in order to determine its identity. / 電子商取引では〜確認をどう行うかが問題となる。How to confirm people's identities has become an issue in e-commerce. 身元照合 verification [establishment] of *sb's* identity. 身元調査 an investigation of *sb's*「antecedents [birth and parentage, family background]; a (「family [social]) background check. 身元不明死体 an unidentified body. 身元不明者 an unidentified person;【死体】an unidentified body;【引き取り手のない】an unclaimed body.
**みもも**【実桃】【花桃に対し，果実を取るための桃】a fruit peach (tree).
**ミャウリンガル**【商標】【猫語翻訳機】Meowlingual.
**ミャオリー**【苗栗】【台湾北西部の都市・県】Miaoli.
**みやぎけんおきじしん**【宮城県沖地震】【2003年5月】the (2003) earthquake off the coast of Miyagi.
**みやぎけんほくぶじしん**【宮城県北部地震】【2003年7月】the Northern Miyagi earthquake (of 2003).
**みやぎのはぎ**【宮城野萩】【植】【マメ科の落葉亜低木】a pink bush clover; *Lespedeza thunbergii*.
**みゃくは**【脈波】▯ 脈波(伝播)速度【医】pulse wave velocity (略: PWV).
**みやじまとんぼ**【宮島蜻蛉】【昆】*Orthetrum poecilops miyajimaensis*.
**みやましろちょう**【深山白蝶】【昆】【シロチョウ科のチョウ】*Aporia hippia*.
**ミャンマーこくみんみんしゅれんめい**【-国民民主連盟】⇨ こくみんしゅれんめい.
**ミャンマーのあたらしいひ**【-の新しい灯】【ミャンマーの国営日刊紙】The New Light of Myanmar.
「ミュージック・オブ・ハート」【映画】Music of the Heart.
**ミュータンスきん**【-菌】【菌】【虫歯菌の1つ】(Streptococcus) mutans bacteria; Streptococcus [Strep, S] mutans.
**ミュー・チップ**【μ-】【電子工学】a mu-chip; a μ-chip.
**ミューレン**【スイスの村，アルプス登山の起点の1つ】Mörren.
**ミューレンベッキア**【植】【タデ科のつる性常緑低木；ニュージーランド原産】a maidenhair vine; *Muehlenbeckia complexa*.
**みゆきぞく**【みゆき族】【昭和39年の】young men and women with a distinctive fashion who frequented Miyuki Street, Ginza, in the summer of 1964.
**みゆびしぎ**【三趾鷸】【鳥】【シギ科の鳥】a sanderling; *Crocethia alba*.
**みょうが**[2]【茗荷】▯ 茗荷竹【筍】【ミョウガの若い茎の部分】(a)「*myōga*【*Zingiber myioga*】shoot. 茗荷の子 ＝なみょうが2.
**みょうごう**【名号】▯ 六字(の)名号 the six (written) characters of Buddha's name (used in prayer); *na-mu-a-mi-da-butsu*.

**ミョンソンファンフ**【明成皇后】(the) Empress Myeongseong; Queen Min (1851-95; 朝鮮王朝の高宗の妃).
**ミラー**[1] ▯ ミラー・ニューロン【解】a mirror neuron.
**ミラー**[2] 1 Miller, George (1945-  ; オーストラリア生まれの映画監督・脚本家・製作者).
2 ⇨ シンプソン・ミラー.
**ミラー・サイクル**【機】【内燃機関の一種】the Miller cycle. ▯ ミラーサイクル・エンジン a Miller-cycle engine.
**ミ・ライ**【ベトナム南部，ソン・ミ村内の部落】My Lai. ▶ ベトナム戦争中の1968年，米軍による大虐殺 (the My Lai massacre) が行われた.
**ミラクリン**【生化】【ミラクルフルーツに含まれる糖たんぱく；酸味を甘味に感じさせる】miraculin.
**ミラクルフルーツ**【植】【実を食べると酸っぱい食べ物が甘く感じられる果物，その木；アカテツ科】a「miraculous [miracle] fruit; a miraculous berry; *Synsepalum dulcificum*.
**ミラノ・コレクション**【服飾】【ミラノの新作発表会】the Milan Collection.
**ミラマックス**【米国の映画会社】Miramax.
**ミランダけいこく**【-警告】【米】(give) a Miranda warning. ▷ Mirandize *vt*. ▶ 被疑者の身柄拘束時に警察[捜査]官が述べる「黙秘する権利がある，発言は法廷で不利に使われうる，弁護士をつける権利がある」といった内容の一連の言葉.
**ミランダはんけつ**【-判決】【米法】【1966年米国連邦最高裁判所が弁護人の立会なしに被疑者の取り調べはできないと判決】the Miranda「decision [ruling]. ▶ この裁判の被告人の名前から.【⇨ミランダけいこく】
**ミリアス** Milius, John (1944-  ; 米国の映画監督・脚本家).
**ミリオネーゼ**【女性富豪】a wealthy woman with a luxurious lifestyle.
「ミリオンダラー・ベイビー」【映画】Million Dollar Baby.
「ミリオンダラー・ホテル」【映画】The Million Dollar Hotel.
**ミルク**[1] ▯ ミルク・パン【牛乳を少量温めたりする小鍋】a milk pan.
**ミルグラム** Milgram, Stanley (1933-84; 米国の社会心理学者).
**ミレニアム** ▯ ミレニアム開発目標【2000年9月 国連首脳会議で宣言された】the Millennium Development Goals (略: MDGs). ミレニアム婚【西暦2000年に結婚式をあげたこと】a millennium wedding. ミレニアム総会【西暦の2000年の】the (United Nations) Millennium General Assembly. ミレニアム・プロジェクト【国連の】the UN Millennium Project.
**ミル** Miller, Leszek (1946-  ; ポーランドの政治家；首相 [2001-2004]).
**ミレン** Mirren, Helen (1945-  ; 英国の女優; 本名 Ilyena Lydia Mironoff).
**ミロシェヴィッチ** Milošević, Slobodan (1941-2006; セルビアの政治家; セルビア大統領[1989-97]; ユーゴスラヴィア大統領[1997-2000]).
**ミロシェビッチ** ＝ミロシェヴィッチ.
**ミワれ**【実割れ】【過度に生育した果実】fruit cracking.
**みんえいか**【民営化】▯ 民営化委員会 a《postal services》 privatization committee. 民営化推進委員会 どうろみんえいかこうだんみんえいかすいしんいんかい.
**みんかいきょう**【民介協】「民間事業者の質を高める」全国介護事業者協議会の略称】⇨ ぜんこくかいごじぎょうしゃきょうかい.
**みんかん**【民間】▯ 民間宇宙船 a civilian spacecraft. 民間援助 civilian [non-government(al)] assistance; civil(ian) support. 民間議員【政府の諮問会議などの】a civilian member of a committee. 民間企業資本ストック《the「quarterly [annual] report [bulletin] on》the Gross Capital Stock of Private Enterprises (略:

GCSPE). 民間企業設備投資 private capital investment. 民間救急車 a ｢private [privately run] ambulance. 民間金融機関 a private [an independent, non-government] financial institution. 民間軍事会社 a private military company (略: PMC); a private military firm. 民間警備会社 a private security firm; a private security ｢company [contractor] (略: PSC); 〔国外に武装警備員を派遣する〕⇨民間軍事会社. 民間検査機関 a private testing organization. 民間交流 non-governmental ｢exchange [contact(s)]; 〔草の根交流〕grassroots exchange; grassroots contact(s). 民間最終消費支出 private final consumption expenditure. 民間車検 a vehicle inspection carried out by a private garage. 民間借款 a private [non-government] loan; private credit; loans from independent financial institutions. 民間習俗 ⇨しゅうぞく. 民間主導 ◯次世代インターネットの開発は～主導で進められるべきだ. The development of the next-generation Internet should be led by the private sector. 民間モニター a civilian monitor; 〔ODAの〕=ODA 民間モニター (⇨オー・ディー・エー).

みんかんかつりょくかいはつきこう【民間活力開発機構】the Organization for the Development of Private Participation in Public Projects.

「みんかんじぎょうしゃのしつをたかめる」ぜんこくかいごじぎょうしゃきょうぎかい【「民間事業者の質を高める」全国介護事業者協議会】=ぜんこくかいごじぎょうしゃきょうぎかい.

みんかんとしかいはつすいしんきこう【民間都市開発推進機構】the Organization for Promoting Urban Development.

みんきゅう【明級】〔軍〕〔中国の潜水艦のクラス〕the Ming class. ◯明級潜水艦 a Ming-class submarine.

みんぐんきょうりょく【民軍協力】〔平和活動・人道支援のために民間機関と軍が連携すること〕civil-military cooperation (略: CIMIC).

ミンゲラ Minghella, Anthony (1954-2008; 英国生まれの映画監督・脚本家).

みんこう【民工】〔中国の出稼ぎ農民〕a (rural) migrant worker.

ミンコフ Minkoff, Rob (1962- ; 米国の映画監督).

みんじ【民事】◯民事告訴 a civil action; a charge [an action, a case, a prosecution] brought by ｢an individual [a private citizen]. 民事再生 《file for》 civil rehabilitation. ◯～再生手続き《commence》 civil rehabilitation proceedings. 民事調停 civil mediation. 民事手続法 〘法〙civil procedure law. 民事罰 a fine payable to the wronged party.

みんしゅう[2]【民衆】◯民衆訴訟〘法〙a popular action; a citizen's lawsuit; an action filed by private citizens against an administration (to ensure democratic control). みんしゅううんどうれんごう【民衆運動連合】=こくみんうんどうれんごう.

みんしゅか【民主化】◯民主化ドミノ a democracy domino effect. 民主化プロセス the [a] process of democratization; a [the] democratizing process. 民主化要求 《increased》 demand for ｢democracy [democratization]. ◯～要求デモ demonstrations for ｢democracy [democratization]. 民主化路線 《pursue》 a [the] ｢road [route] to ｢democracy [democratization].

みんしゅしゅぎとけいざいはってんのためのジー・ユー・エー・エム【民主主義と経済発展のためのGUAM】ODED-GUAM; the Organization for Democracy and Economic Development-GUAM. ▶ GUAM は Georgia, Ukraine, Azerbaijan, Moldova の略.

みんしゅてきせんたくきょうどうたい【民主的選択共同体】〔ウクライナ, グルジア, モルドヴァに加えバルト3国, 東欧のルーマニア, スロヴェニア, マケドニアの9か国から成る地域フォーラム〕the Community of Democratic Choice (略: CDC).

みんしゅとう【民主党】◯民主党大会〔米国の〕the Democratic National Convention.

みんしんとう【民進党】〔台湾の政党〕the Democratic Progressive Party (略: DPP).

みんせい[1]【民生】◯民生委員協議会 a welfare commission. 民生支援〔活動〕〔軍隊などが行う〕civilian support (activities). 民生品 a [the] consumer [commercial] product. 民生用核施設 a civilian nuclear facility.

みんせいいいんほう【民生委員法】〘法〙the Commissioned Welfare Volunteers Law.

みんせつ【民設】◯民設民営 privately built and ｢operated [managed].

みんぞく[2]【民族】◯民族解放闘争 a national liberation struggle; a struggle for national liberation. 民族楽器 a folk [an ethnic] (music(al)) instrument. 民族協調 ethnic [inter-ethnic] harmony [cooperation]. 民族心 a sense of ethnicity; a feeling ｢for one's people [of ethnic identity].

みんぞくぎゆうだん【民族義勇団】〔インドのヒンズー至上主義組織〕the National Volunteer Union (略: RSS). ▶ RSS は ヒンディー語 Rashtriya Swayamsevak Sangh の略.

みんちょうたい【明朝体】〔活字〕Ming(-style) type; Minchō typeface.

ミント[2]〔切手・貨幣などが未使用・未開封で〕mint《stamps》; 《stamps, coins》in mint condition.

ミントン〔商標〕〔英国の陶磁器ブランド〕Minton.

「みんな元気」〔映画〕Everybody's Fine; 〔原題〕Stanno Tutti Bene.

みんよう【民謡】◯日本民謡 a Japanese folk song.

# む

ムアン・サイ〔ラオスの地名〕Muang Xai. [=ウドムサイ]
ムーア 1 Moore, Dudley (1935-2002; 英国生まれの映画俳優).
2 Moore, Julianne (1960- ; 米国の映画女優; 本名 Julie Anne Smith).
3 Moore, Michael (1954- ; 米国のジャーナリスト・映画監督).
4 Moore, Roger (1927- ; 英国の映画俳優; 本名 Roger George Moore).

ムーアのほうそく【−の法則】〔マイクロプロセッサーのスピードが18か月ごとに2倍になるなど, コンピューター技術の進歩の速さに関する経験則〕Moore's Law.

ムーケ Mouquet, Jules (1867-1946; フランスの作曲家).

ムース[1] ◯ムース食 〔咀嚼(そしゃく)・嚥下(えんげ)が困難な人のための〕(a) semi-solid food produced with a mixer.

ムータヒダみんぞくうんどう【−民族運動】〔パキスタンのムシャラフ大統領派の政党〕the Muttahida Qaumi Movement (略: MQM).

ム（−）ダン【巫堂】〔朝鮮の霊媒〕a mudang; a Korean shaman priestess.

ムービー ◯ムービー画像 a movie image.

ムーブ・オン〔米国のリベラル系政治団体〕MoveOn.org.

「ムーラン・ルージュ」〔映画〕Moulin Rouge!

むえん[2]【無煙】◯無煙環境〔たばこの煙のない〕a ｢smoke-

むえん

free [smokeless] environment. 無煙環境 smokeless combustion. 無煙灰皿 a smokeless ashtray.

**むえん**[6]【無炎】 ～の flameless. ▶□ 無炎燃焼 flameless combustion.

**ムオ** Mouhot, Henri (1826–61；フランスの博物学者・探検家).

**むがい**[1]【無害】 ▶□ 無害化 making [rendering] sth harmless; neutralization《of a poison》. ◆有害物質を～化する技術を開発する develop a technique for「rendering harmful materials harmless [neutralizing harmful materials].

**むかいとう**【無回答】〔アンケートなどへの〕(a) nonresponse; no response; no answer. ◆残る14人は～だった. The remaining 14 people「did not respond [did not answer, left the answer blank].

**むかいとう**[2]【無解答】〔試験問題などへの〕 ◆〔試験で〕論述問題が～の生徒が多い. There are a lot of students who leave essay questions unanswered. | Many students don't「answer [attempt] essay questions.

**むかえづゆ**【迎え梅雨】a「period [spell] of rain just before the rainy season.

**むかく**[2]【無核】 ～の anucleate; anuclear;〔種なしの〕seedless;〔非核の〕nonnuclear;〔核兵器のない〕nuclear-free; denuclearized. ◆～の単細胞生物 an「anucleate [anuclear] unicellular organism.

**むかごとんぼ**【零余子蜻蛉】〔植〕〔ラン科の多年草〕Habenaria flagellifera.

**むかしつ**【無過失】 ▶□ 無過失補償制度〔医療事故についての〕a no-fault compensation system.

**むかふんすぎ**【無花粉杉】a pollen-free (Japanese) cedar (tree).

**ムガベ** Mugabe, Robert Gabriel (1924– ；ジンバブエの政治家；首相〔1980–87〕; 大統領〔1987– 〕).

**むかんしん**【無関心】 ▶□ 無関心層《politically》 'apathetic [unconcerned] people「not interested [with no interest]《in politics》.

**むき**[3]【無季】 ▶□ 無季俳句 a haiku with no season word.

**むき**[6]【無機】 ▶□ 無機 EL〔電子工学〕inorganic electroluminescence. ◆～ EL ディスプレー an inorganic electroluminescent display. 無機砒素〔薬〕inorganic arsenic.

**むきこう**【無寄港】 ▶□ 無寄港世界一周 a non-stop「voyage around the world [around-the-world voyage]. ◆彼はヨットで西回りの単独～世界一周に成功した. He succeeded in sailing a yacht single-handed around the world, non-stop from east to west.

**むきどう**【無軌道】 ▶□ 無軌道電車〔トロリーバス〕a trackless tram; a trolleybus.

**ムキムキ**〔男性の〕筋肉質の muscularity; brawniness. ◆彼は筋肉～の体が自慢だ. He's proud of his「muscular [brawny] body.

**むきゅうゆ**【無給油】 without refueling. ▶□ 無給油飛行 a non-refueling flight; a《nonstop, around-the-world》flight without refuelling.

**むきょうそう**【無競争】 ▶□ 無競争入札 non-competitive bidding; a non-competitive bid; uncontested bidding; an uncontested bid.

**むきょか**【無許可】 ▶□ 無許可デモ an unauthorized demonstration.

**むきりょく**【無気力】 ▶□ 無気力相撲 spiritless sumo; a sumo bout in which fighting spirit is notably lacking.

**ムクダハン**〔タイ東北部の県・県都, ラオスとの国境の町〕Mukdahan.

**むげ**[2]【無碍】 freedom (from all obstacles).

**むけいぶんかいさんじょうやく**【無形文化遺産条約】＝むけいぶんかいさんほごじょうやく.

**むけいぶんかいさんほごじょうやく**【無形文化遺産保護条約】〔2003年, ユネスコの〕the International Convention for the Safeguarding of the Intangible Cultural Heritage.

**むげっけい**【無月経】 ▶□ 原発性無月経 primary amenorrhea. 続発性無月経 secondary amenorrhea.

**むけっせいばいち**【無血清培地】〔生物〕a serum-free medium (略: SFM).

**むげんせきにん**【無限責任】 ▶□ 無限責任中間法人 an unlimited liability intermediate corporation.

**むこうしんぱん**【無効審判】〔特許の〕a trial for invalidation; an invalidation trial. ▶□ 無効審判請求書《file》a request for an invalidation trial.

**むこうづち**【向こう鎚】〔小鎚を使う鍛冶師に向かってふるう大鎚〕a large (sledge)hammer (used by a smith's assistant);〔その使い手〕a smith's assistant; an assistant who hammers with a sledgehammer in response to the master smith's signal.

**むこがね**【婿がね】〔(親が)娘の夫とすることに決めている人〕a [one's] chosen son-in-law.

**むこせき**【無戸籍】 non-registration [not being registered, not appearing] on a family register. ▶□ 無戸籍児 a child not registered on a family register.

**ムコソルバン**《商標・薬》〔塩酸アンブロキソールの商品名; 去痰薬〕Mucosolvan.

**ムコたとう**【-多糖】 ▶□ 複合ムコ多糖 a complex mucopolysaccharide. ▶□ ムコ多糖類 mucopolysaccharides.

**むざい**【無罪】 ▶□ 無罪(の)答弁〔申し立て〕〔法〕a "not guilty" [an innocent] plea; a plea of "not guilty" [innocent]; pleading "not guilty" [innocent]. 無罪論告〔法〕a summation by the prosecution in which the innocence of the accused is affirmed.

**ムサイブ**〔イラク中部の都市〕Musayyib.

**むさくい**【無作為】 ▶□ 無作為化(比較)試験〔医〕＝ランダム化比較試験(⇨ランダム). 無作為比較試験〔医〕＝ランダム化比較試験(⇨ランダム).

**ムザッファラ(ー)バード** ＝ムザファラバード.

**ムザファラバード**〔パキスタン, カシミール地方の中心都市〕Muzaffarabad.

**ムサンナ**〔イラク南部の州〕al-Muthanna.

**むし**[1]【虫】 ▶□ 虫恐怖症 a fear of「bugs [insects, caterpillars, worms, etc.];〔昆虫恐怖症〕entomophobia; a fear of insects.

**むしかく**【無資格】 ▶□ 無資格施術 unlicensed practice《of chiropractic》. 無資格助産行為 unlicensed midwifery (practice).

**むしどり**【蒸し鶏】《料理》steamed chicken.

**むしにゅうこけいぶん**【無脂乳固形分】(a) nonfat milk solid content.

**むしば**【虫歯】 ▶□ 虫歯菌 cavity-causing [decay-causing] bacteria. ▶ Streptococcus mutans など.

**むしぶろ**【蒸し風呂】 ▶□ 砂蒸し風呂 a (hot) sand bath.

**むしゃ**【武者】 ▶□ 武者幟 a traditional flag or banner depicting a heroic warrior.

**むしゃじけん**【霧社事件】《史》〔1930年, 台湾先住民による抗日蜂起事件〕the Wushe Uprising.

**ムジャヒディン・ハルク**〔イランの過激派組織〕the Mujahedin-e Khalq Organization (略: MEK, MKO).

**ムシャラフ** Musharraf, Pervez (1943– ；パキスタンの軍人・政治家; 大統領〔2001– 〕).

**むしゅうきょう**【無宗教】 ▶□ 無宗教追悼施設 (a site for) a secular《war》memorial; a memorial site (for the war dead) which is not affiliated with any particular religion.

**むじゅうりょく**【無重力】 ▶□ 無重力体験 experiencing「weightlessness [zero gravity].

**むしょう**[1]【無償】 ▶□ 無償供与 provision《of supplies》free of charge. ◆医療資材を～供与する provide [furnish] medical equipment「free of charge [at

no cost, at no charge]. 無償交換 exchange [replacement] free of [at no] charge. ◐ 商品開梱(かいこん)時に商品が破損していた場合は～交換いたします. If the product is found to be damaged when the「box [packaging] is opened, we will replace it free of charge. 無償資金協力 free fund-raising「assistance [cooperation]. ◐ 政府は地震被災地域に約600万ドルの緊急～資金協力を行うことを発表した. The government announced it would provide approximately 6 million dollars' worth of free emergency fund-raising assistance to the earthquake-affected region. 無償修理 free repair(s); repair(s) free of charge. 無償ソフト 【電算】 free software; freeware. 無償労働 unpaid work.
むしょうこうせい【無症候性】 ◐◑ 無症候性キャリア an asymptomatic carrier; a healthy carrier. 無症候性血尿 asymptomatic hematuria. 無症候性未破裂脳動脈瘤 (an) asymptomatic unruptured cerebral aneurysm.
むしょうしんりょうじょ【無床診療所】 a clinic with no beds.
むしょうそちほう【無償措置法】〖法〗 the Law Concerning Free Textbooks in Compulsory Education Schools. ▶ 正式名称は「義務教育諸学校の教科用図書の無償措置に関する法律」.
むじん[1]【無人】 ◐◑ 無人市場 ＝無人販売所. 無人受付 an unmanned reception「desk [area]. ◐ ～受付コーナー〔消費者金融などの〕an「automatic [automated] customer service area. 無人 ATM an unmanned ATM. 無人式速度取締装置 an automatic「speed camera; an automatic speed detector. 無人深海探査機 an unmanned deep-sea probe. 無人操業 unattended operation. 無人走行 driverless [autonomous, unmanned] travel [transit]. ◐ ～走行する travel「autonomously [without a driver]. 無人探査車 an unmanned「rover [roving vehicle]. ◐ 火星～探査車 an unmanned Mars「rover [roving vehicle]. 無人地上車両 an unmanned ground vehicle (略: UGV). 無人店〔自動販売機などによる〕an automated「shop [cafeteria];〔銀行などの〕an automated bank. 無人灯台 an unmanned lighthouse. 無人バス an autonomous, an unmanned「bus. 無人販売所 an unmanned《vegetable》stand. 無人レジ〔セルフ・レジ〔⇒セルフ〕〕self-checkout;〔機械〕a self-checkout「machine [unit];〔口〕a self-checkout.
ムスカリ〖植〗〔ユリ科ムスカリ属の総称〕a muscari; a grape hyacinth.
「息子の部屋」〖映画〗The Son's Room;〔原題〕La Stanza del figlio.
ムスダン〔北朝鮮の中距離弾道ミサイルに米国が付けた呼称〕a Musudan (missile). ▶ 北朝鮮のミサイル基地名 ムスダンリ(舞水端里)からの命名.
ムスダンリ, ムスタンリ〖舞水端里〗〔北朝鮮, 咸鏡北道(ハムギョンプクド)にあるミサイル基地名〕Musudan-ri. ▶ 旧名 テポドン.
むすびきり【結び切り】〔水引の結び方の1つで, 固結び〕a hard knot.
むすびことば【結び言葉】〔手紙を終えることを示す言葉〕a concluding word or phrase in a letter; a closing.
むすぼれ【結ぼれ】an (emotional) entanglement; a knot (of emotion). ◐ 彼女の手紙を読み, 私は長年の～が解けてゆく思いであった. Reading her letter, I felt as if a long-standing knot of emotion were being untied.
むずむずあしょうこうぐん【むずむず脚症候群】〖医〗 restless leg(s) syndrome (略: RLS).
ムセヴェニ Museveni, Yoweri Kaguta (1944– ; ウガンダの政治家; 大統領〔1986– 〕).
ムセベニ ＝ムセヴェニ.
むせん【無線】 ◐◑ 無線 IC タグ a wireless「IC [electronic] tag. 無線 IP 電話〔技術〕wireless IP telephony;〔電話機〕a wireless IP (tele)phone. 無線インター

ネット wireless Internet. 無線インターネット接続 wireless Internet access; (a) wireless Internet connection. 無線交信 wireless [radio] communication(s). ◐ ～交信する communicate「wirelessly [by radio]. 無線接続〖電算〗 wireless access; (a) wireless connection. ◐ ～接続ポイント〔拠点〕a wireless access point (略: WAP). 無線長〔船舶などの〕a chief radio operator. 無線誘導装置 a radio guidance system. 無線 LAN ルーター〖電算〗 a wireless LAN router.
むせんつうしん【無線通信】 ◐◑ 無線通信会社 a wireless communications carrier.
むだ【無駄】 ◐◑ ムダ, ムラ, ムリ〔製造〔作業〕工程などで排除すべき3つの事柄〕the "three Ms"(, referring respectively to wastefulness, uneven operation and overburdening of equipment or workers to be avoided in production; "Muda, Mura, Muri."
むだぼえ【無駄吠え】〔飼い犬の〕unwanted barking.
むだん[2]【無断】 ◐◑ 無断換金 unauthorized cashing 《of checks》. 無断掲載 unauthorized publication 《of an article in a magazine》; printing 《an article》 without permission. 無断コピー〔コピーすること〕unauthorized copying [pirating]《of copyrighted software》;〔コピーしたもの〕an unauthorized [a pirated] copy. 無断使用 unauthorized use《of a photograph》. 無断駐車 unauthorized parking; parking without permission. 無断駐車禁止. 〖掲示〗No Unauthorized Parking. | Parking by Permit Only. 無断転載 unauthorized republication《of an article》; reprinting《a photograph》without permission. 無断流用 unauthorized diversion [misappropriation]《of funds》.
むちゃ【無茶】 ◐◑ 無茶食い (just) eating and eating; gross overeating.
むちゃくしょく【無着色】 ◐◑ ～の uncolored; unpigmented; free of artificial color. ◐ このシャンプーは～無香料です. This shampoo is「uncolored and unscented [free of artificial color and fragrance].
ムチン ◐◑ ムチン層〖解〗〔角膜表面の涙液の〕a「mucin [mucous, mucus] layer.
むつう【無痛】 ◐◑ 無痛針〖医〗a painless needle. 無痛治療 a「painless [pain-free] treatment.
むつうむかんしょう【無痛無汗症】〖医〗congenital insensitivity to pain with anhidrosis (略: CIPA).
「ムッシュ・カステラの恋」〖映画〗The Taste of Others;〔原題〕Le Gout Des Autres.
「ムッソリーニとお茶を」〖映画〗Tea With Mussolini.
ムッラー〔イスラム教〕＝ムラー.
むていこう【無抵抗】 ◐◑ 無抵抗平和主義 nonresistant pacifism.
むてんか【無添加】 ◐◑ 無添加石鹸 (an) additive-free soap. 無添加パン additive-free bread.
「ムトゥ踊るマハラジャ」〖映画〗Muthu.
むとうやく【無投薬】nonuse of drugs. ◐◑ 無投薬ウナギ drug-free eel. 無投薬治療 (a) nondrug treatment.
むとろく【無登録】 ◐◑ ～の unregistered; unauthorized. ◐ 無登録営業 unregistered business. 無登録業者 ⇒ぎょうしゃ. 無登録農薬 ⇒のうやく.
むにんか【無認可】 ◐◑ 無認可共済 an unregulated「mutual aid (insurance) cooperative [kyosai].
むにんのぼたん【無人野牡丹】〖植〗〔ノボタン科の常緑低木〕Melastoma tetramerum.
むねつづき【棟続き】 ～の〔一つ屋根の下の〕《be》under the same roof;〔接して建てられた〕《be》built close by. ◐ 彼は宿舎とは～の作業所で働いている. He works in a factory built close by the company housing. ◐ 彼女の住居は店舗と～だ. Her residence is under the same roof as her store.
むねんきん【無年金】 ～の without「a pension [pension coverage]; pensionless. ◐ ～になる become pensionless; do not get a pension / 保険料を納めないと将来ム

むのうしょう

になってしまう. If the insurance premiums are not paid, then, in the future, you will not get a pension ▫️ 無年金者 a pensionless person; a person without a pension. 無年金障害者 a disabled person without pension coverage. ▶学生～障害者 a disabled person without pension coverage because of nonparticipation in the National Pension System while a student. 無年金状態 (the situation of being) without a pension; a pensionless condition. 無年金訴訟 a suit (by a pensionless person) to obtain a pension; litigation in protest against failure to provide a pension.

むのうしょう【無脳症】▫️ 無脳(症)児 an anencephalic baby; a brain-absent baby.

ムハラート =ムハバラト.

ムハバラト〔イラクの旧フセイン政権下の情報機関〕the Mukhabarat; the Iraqi Intelligence Service (略: IIS).

むはんざいしょうめいしょ【無犯罪証明書】a certificate of a clean criminal record; a police clearance certificate; a certificate of good conduct. 〔⇨犯罪歴証明書(⇨はんざい)〕

ムフティー〔イスラム教の法学者〕a mufti.

ムプマランガ〔南アフリカ共和国東部の州〕Mpumalanga.

ムベキ Mbeki, Thabo (1942-  ; 南アフリカの政治家; 大統領〔1999-  〕).

むへんしゅう【無編集】▶～の unedited. ▫️ 無編集動画〔ビデオ〕(an) unedited video; unedited video footage.

むほうそう【無包装】〔まったく包装されていない状態〕unwrapped; without (a) wrapping; without packaging; (in) an 'unwrapped [unpacked] state; loose (vegetables); 〔上包みのない状態〕without 'an outer [(an) additional] wrapping.

むほけんしゃ【無保険車】〔保険に入っていない自動車〕an uninsured 'automobile [car]. ▫️ 無保険車傷害特約 a policy covering accidents with uninsured automobiles; an uninsured motorist insurance policy. 無保険車傷害保険 uninsured motorist insurance.

むほけんせん【無保険船】an uninsured 'vessel [ship].

ムマバト =マバト.

むゆう¹【無釉】【製陶】(firing) without 'glazing [(a) glaze]; 〔その製品〕unglazed ware.

むゆう²【夢遊】【医】 ▫️ 夢遊症 somnambulism; somnambulance; sleepwalking. 夢遊症状 a 'somnambulistic [somnambulic] state.

むよう¹【無用】▫️ 無用論 ▶学歴～論 an argument 'that educational credentials are unnecessary [against the need for educational credentials]／参議院～論 an argument against the House of Councillors; opposition to the existence of the House of Councillors.

ムラー《イスラム教》〔イスラム教指導者〕a mullah.

むらいと【斑糸】〔ふぞろいの織り糸〕rough [natural] thread [yarn].

むらぐい【むら食い】irregular eating (habits).

むらさきいも【紫芋】〖植〗〔サツマイモの一種〕a purple sweet potato.

むらさきさぎ【紫鷺】〖鳥〗〔サギ科の鳥〕a purple heron; *Ardea purpurea.*

むらたじゅう【村田銃】〔明治維新期の国産銃〕a Murata rifle.

ムラピさん【―山】〔インドネシア, ジャワ島中部の活火山〕Mount Merapi; (インドネシア語名) Gunung Merapi.

ムラボ(―)〔インドネシア, アチェ州の都市, 西アチェ県の県都〕Meulaboh.

ムリキ【動】〔ブラジル産のクモザル〕a muriqui. [=ウーリークモザル].

むりょう¹【無料】▫️ 無料(インターネット)接続《offer》free Internet access. 無料開放〔施設などの〕opening [letting people use]《a facility》free of charge; free 'admission [access]《to a facility》. ▶7, 8月中は市のプールを～開放しています. We are opening the city pool to the public free of charge during July and August. ／高速道路の～開放をめざす aim to make the expressways toll-free; aim for toll-free expressway access／この店では無線 LAN を～開放している. 【電算】At this store we 'provide [offer] free wireless LAN access. 無料紙 a free paper. 無料招待 (a) free invitation. ▶～招待券 a 'complimentary [free] ticket／抽選で 500 名を本コンサートに～招待します. We will present complimentary tickets to this concert to 500 people chosen by lottery. 無料商法 a giveaway sales scam; a marketing scheme that offers free or low-priced goods or services as a come-on. 無料情報誌 a free information magazine. 無料診断〔病気・経営状態などの〕(a) free diagnosis; 〔設備などの〕a free test; free testing. 無料送迎 ▶～送迎バス a courtesy bus／空港・ホテル間～送迎付《宣伝》Courtesy Shuttle Service between the Airport and the Hotel. 無料ソフト【電算】free software; freeware. 無料体験 a free trial. ▶ダイエット体験 a free trial diet／ダイエット～体験者大募集!〔宣伝文句〕Dieters needed for free trial! 無料体験版〔商品・ソフトなどの〕a free trial version.

ムルシア〔スペイン南東部の自治州〕Murcia.

むれほうかいしょうこうぐん【群れ崩壊症候群】=ほうかいしょうこうぐん.

ムング〖植〗〔マメ科の1年草; インド原産〕a 'mung [moong] (bean); moong [mung] dal; *Vigna radiata*;〔旧分類名〕*Phaseolus aureus*.

ムンバイしすう【―指数】〖証券〗〔インドの株価指数〕the 'Mumbai [Bombay] index.

# め

メイ May, Billy (1916-2004; 米国の作曲家・トランペット奏者).

めいがざ【名画座】a revival 'movie theater ['cinema].

めいがら【銘柄】▫️ 関連銘柄〖証券〗a related 'issue [stock]. ▶輸出[IT]関連～ an 'export-related [IT-related] issue [stock].

めいかん【名鑑】▫️ 選手名鑑 a player roster. ▶プロ野球選手～ a roster of professional baseball players.

めいぎ³【名義】▫️ 名義偽装株 shares [stock] (registered) under a fictitious name. 名義料 a fee for using 'a [*sb's*] name.

めいきゅうかい【名球会】〔日本プロ野球名球会〕the Golden Players Club. ▫️ 名球会入り ▶～入りする join [〖口〗make] the Golden Players Club.

「名犬ラッシー」〔米国の, 少年とコリー犬の TV ドラマ〕Lassie.

「名犬リンチンチン」〔米国の, 騎兵隊の砦に暮らす少年とシェパード犬の TV ドラマ〕The Adventures of Rin Tin Tin.

「名犬ロンドン物語」〔カナダ製作の, 放浪するシェパード犬の TV ドラマ〕The Littlest Hobo.

めいさい¹【明細】▫️ 明細付請求書 an itemized bill. ▷ itemized billing *n*.

めいさい²【迷彩】▫️ 迷彩塗装 camouflage [dazzle] paint [painting].

めいしつ【明室】〖写真〗〔暗室に対して〕a daylight room.

▣ 明室処理 a daylight process.
めいしょうぶ【名勝負】a great [a celebrated, a memorable, an historic] game. ◐球史に残る〜 one of history's most「famous [celebrated] baseball games」; a game that「has gone [will go] down in baseball history.
メイス Mace, Ronald L. [Ron] (1941-98; 米国の建築家).
めいせいこうごう【明成皇后】=ミョンソンファンフ.
めいせき³【明晰】▣ 明晰夢〔心理〕a lucid dream.
めいせき³【銘仙】▣ 銘仙判〔座布団のサイズ〕◐〜判の座布団 a medium-size (floor) cushion (55×59cm).
「名探偵コナン」〔日本製アニメ〕Detective Conan.
メイド ▣ メイド喫茶[カフェ]〔女店員がアニメキャラの格好で給姿をしている喫茶店〕a maid cafe.
メイナード・スミス Maynard Smith, John (1920-2004; 英国の進化生物学者).
めいばく【名瀑】a「famous [celebrated] waterfall.
「名馬フューリー」〔西部の少年と愛馬の冒険を描くTVドラマ〕Fury.
めいばめん【名場面】▣ 感動名場面 striking [thrilling] highlights 《from the Olympics》.
メイベリン〔商標〕〔米国の化粧品ブランド〕Maybelline.
メイベル・チャン Mabel Cheung (1950-  ; 香港の映画監督; 中国語名 張婉婷 Cheung Yuen-Ting).
めいぼ【名簿】▣ 名簿業者 =名簿屋. 名簿屋 a mailing list dealer.
めいもく¹【名目】▣ 名目為替レート a nominal exchange rate. 名目尺度〔統計〕a nominal scale. 名目長期金利〔経〕a nominal long-term interest rate. 名目賃金上昇率 the rate of a rise in nominal wages; a nominal wage-rate rise 《of 2%》.
めいもん【名門】▣ 名門企業 a「prestigious [renowned] corporation.
めいよ【名誉】▣ 名誉(の)殺人〔家族の名誉を汚したとされる女性を身内の人間が殺すこと〕(an) honor killing. 名誉負傷章〔米軍〕a Purple Heart (Medal).
めいよだいえいくんしょう【名誉大英勲章】〔英国の〕the Order of the British Empire. ▶第一位 (Knight [Dame] Grand Cross (略: GBE), 第二位 Knight [Dame] Commander (略: K[D]BE), 第三位 Commander (略: CBE), 第四位 Officer (略: OBE), 第五位 Member (略: MBE) がある.
めいれい【命令】▣ 命令下達 the communication of orders to subordinates.
めいろ²【迷路】▣ 巨大迷路〔遊園地などの〕a labyrinth; a large (walk-through) maze; a walking maze.
メイ・ロン〔古生物〕〔小型肉食恐竜〕(a) Mei long. ▶中国語で「ぐっすり寝ている竜」の意.
めいわく【迷惑】▣ 迷惑顔 an annoyed(-looking)「face [expression]. ◐電車内でわめきちらす酔っ払いに皆〜顔だった. Everyone in the train looked annoyed at the drunk shouting (abuse) at all around him. 迷惑メール対策ソフト anti-spam software; anti-junk mail software. 迷惑料 nuisance money.
めいわくメールぼうしほう【迷惑=防止法】〔法〕the Anti-Spam Law. ▶正式名称は「特定電子メールの送信の適正化等に関する法律」(the Law on Regulation of Transmission of Specified Electronic Mail).
メウラボ =ムラボ(ー).
メーコン〔米国ジョージア州中部の市〕Macon.
メータル・ラム〔アフガニスタン東部, ラグマン州の州都〕Mehtar Lam; Mehtarlam.
メートルほうこうふきねんび【-法公布記念日】〔4月11日〕Metric System Day; the day commemorating the proclamation of the metric system.
メー・ホ(ー)ン・ソ(ー)ン〔タイ北部の県; その県都〕Mae Hong Son.
メール ▣ メール相手 one's e-mail correspondent(s);〔メル友〕《口》an e-pal. メール交換 an exchange of e-mail. ◐彼女とは毎日〜交換している. I「exchange [trade] e-mail with her every day. / 5年ぶりで会ったのがきっかけで彼との〜交換が始まった. I began to exchange e-mail with him when we met for the first time in five years. メール私語〔授業中に携帯でメールのやりとりをすること〕e-mailing secretly [sending secret e-mails] during class. メール配信 e-mail distribution. ◐〜配信サービス an e-mail distribution service. メール爆弾〔大量のメールやコンピューターウイルスを送りつけるもの〕an e-mail bomb. ▷ mail-bomb v. メール便 mail delivered by a parcel delivery service.

メーン- ▣ メーンストレート〔競技〕=ホームストレート. メーン・ボーカル the main vocal. メーン寄せ〔金融〕〔企業が破綻したとき, その再生のための支援負担をメーン銀行に集中させること〕concentration of the burden of reviving a bankrupt company onto the company's main bank.
めおし【目押し】〔スロットマシンでの〕(a) skill stop. 〜する stop 《a reel at a symbol》 intentionally. ◐7を〜する stop a reel at 7; make a reel stop turning at 7.
メガ・アライ〔米国にとっての"特上同盟国"〕mega allies. ▶英国, オーストラリア, 日本など.
メガきょうかい【-教会】=メガチャーチ.
めかくし【目隠し】▣ 目隠しシール〔個人情報保護のため葉書などに貼る〕a privacy-protection sticker; a sticker to「cover up [black out] personal information. 目隠し体験〔盲人体験〕a blindfold experience; blindfold training.
メガスタディ〔医・薬〕〔大規模臨床試験〕a large-scale clinical「trial [test].
メガストア〔取り扱い商品を絞った大型専門店〕a mega-store.
メガチャーチ〔米国のプロテスタント系の巨大教会〕a megachurch.
めがね【眼鏡】▣ めがね職人 a spectacles maker; a craftsman who specializes in making spectacles.
めがねもちのうお【眼鏡持乃魚】〔魚〕〔ベラ科モチノウオ属の〕a humphead wrasse; a Napoleon「wrasse [fish]; *Cheilinus undulatus*.
メガバンク〔巨大銀行〕a megabank.
メガピクセル〔CCDなどの画素数が100万を超えた状態〕megapixel (camera).
めかぶ²【和布蕪・芽株】〔ワカメの茎にできる成実葉; 食用〕thick *wakame* leaves (near the stalk).
メガマウス〔魚〕〔深海にすむ珍種のサメ〕a megamouth shark; *Megachasma pelagios*.
メガワティ Megawati Sukarnoputri (1947-  ; インドネシアの政治家; 大統領 [2001-04]).
メキシカン・ヘアレス・ドッグ〔犬〕a Mexican hairless (dog); a Xoloitzcuintli; a Xolo.
「めぐりあう時間たち」〔映画〕The Hours.
「めぐり逢えたら」〔映画〕Sleepless in Seattle.
メコンがわりゅういきかいはつけいかく【-川流域開発計画】the Greater Mekong Subregion Development Plan 《略: GMS》.
メサ² Mesa, Carlos (1953-  ; ボリビアの政治家; 大統領 [2003-05]).
メサ³〔米国アリゾナ州中南部の都市〕Mesa.
メザニン 1【建】〔中二階〕a mezzanine. 2【金融】〔中リスクの〕mezzanine. ▣ メザニン・ファイナンス【金融】mezzanine financing. メザニン・ローン【金融】a mezzanine loan.
メサラジン【薬】〔潰瘍性大腸炎治療薬〕mesalazine; mesalamine. ▶商品名は ペンタサ (Pentasa).
めしまこぶ【和布島瘤】〔菌〕〔キコブダケ科のキノコ〕*Phellinus linteus*. ▣ メシマコブ菌糸体 *Phellinus linteus* mycelia.
メジャー² ▣ メジャーデビュー〔音楽〕one's major-label debut;〔野球〕one's Major League debut;〔ゴルフ〕one's first (appearance in a) Major. ◐デモCDがレコード会

社に認められて昨年～デビューした。Their demo CD caught the fancy of a record company, and last year they「made their major-label debut [released their first record through a major label]」. 桑田はパイレーツで念願の～デビューを果たした。Kuwata made his long-wished-for Major League debut with the Pirates. / 国内～デビュー戦で石川は苦戦した。Ishikawa struggled in his first appearance in a domestic Major.

**メシルさん**【-酸】⇨ メシル酸ブロモクリプチン【薬】〔抗パーキンソン剤〕bromocriptine「mesylate [mesilate]」.

**めすか**【雌化】⇨ メス化現象 feminization; demasculinization.

**メソニクス**〖古生物〗〔第三紀前期にアジア・ヨーロッパ・北米に棲息した、カバに似た肉食哺乳類〗 Mesonyx.

**メソポタミアしつげん**【-湿原】〔イラク南東部、チグリス川とユーフラテス川の合流地付近の湿地〗 the Mesopotamian marshes.

**メソミル**【薬】〔農薬〗methomyl.

**めぞろえ**【目ぞろえ】〔農産物の出荷前の等級分け〕grading; ranking; classification.

**メゾン**〖<F maison〗〔家、建物〕a house. ◯～田中〔集合住宅の名称として〕Tanaka「Apartments [Mansions, "Flats]」.

**メタセシス**⇨ メタセシス反応 a metathesis reaction.

**メタノール**⇨ メタノール・クロスオーバー【化】《reduce》methanol crossover. メタノール水溶液(a)「methanol-water [water-methanol] solution.

**メタボリックしょうこうぐん**【-症候群】= メタボリック・シンドローム.

**メタボリック・シンドローム**【医】〔代謝異常症候群〕metabolic syndrome.

**めだま**【目玉】◯ 目玉候補〔選挙に〕a star candidate. 目玉政策 a centerpiece «of Abe cabinet policy».

**メタミドホス**【薬】〔農薬・殺虫剤として用いられる有機リン化合物〕methamidophos.

**めぢから**【目力】〔目元の印象力〕eyes that convey a strong sense of purpose.

**メチコバール**〖商標・薬〗〔末梢神経治療薬〗Methycobal.

**メチル**⇨ メチル・イソブチル・ケトン【化】(a) methyl isobutyl ketone. メチル化カテキン【化】methylated catechin. メチルスルフォニルメタン【化】〔有機イオウ；重要栄養素の1つ〕methylsulfonylmethane (略: MSM). メチル・ターシャリーブチル・エーテル【化】〔オクタン価向上剤〕methyl tertiary-butyl ether (略: MTBE).

**メチルホスホンさん**【-酸】【化】methylphosphonic acid. ⇨ メチルホスホン酸ジイソプロピル diisopropyl methylphosphonate (略: DIMP). ▶ サリンの副生成物. メチルホスホン酸モノイソプロピル isopropyl methylphosphonate. ▶ サリンの第一次分解物.

**メチルりゅうさんネオスチグミン**【-硫酸-】【化】〔眼筋の調節機能を改善する目薬の成分〕neostigmine methylsulfate.

**メッカコーラ**〖商標〗〔清涼飲料〗Mecca-Cola.

**めっきあじ**【めっき鯵】〔魚〕the young of trevallies, a member of the mackerel family.

**「メッセージ・イン・ア・ボトル」**〔映画〕Message in a Bottle.

**メッセネ**〖ギリシャ、ペロポネソス半島の古代都市〗Messene.

**メッセンジャー[2]**〖米国の水星探査機〗Messenger.

**メット**〔ヘルメット〕⇨ メット入れ ＝ヘルメット収納スペース《⇨ヘルメット》.

**メディア[1]**⇨ 多メディア時代 a [the] multimedia age. ⇨ メディア・アーティスト a media artist. メディア・アート〔新しい媒体を利用した芸術(表現)〕(new) media art. メディア企業 a media corporation. メディア研究 media studies. メディアコンテンツ media content. ◯～コンテンツ事業 a media-content project. メディア社会学 media sociology. ▷ media sociologist n. メディア・バイイング〔広告〕〔テレビ・新聞などの広告枠の購入〕media buying;〔1回の〕a media buy.

**メディアジャック**〔広告スペースやテレビ・ラジオの公告時間帯に対し一社独占〕single-sponsor advertising; advertising by only one company «on a train». ▶「メディアジャック」は和製英語.

**メディカル**⇨ メディカル・コントロール【医】〔医師が救急救命士に対し医療行為についての指示を与え、その質を保証すること〕medical control (略: MC). ◯ オンライン[直接的]～コントロール〔救急患者を搬送中の救命救急士に医師が電話・無線などによって医療行為に関する指示を与えること〕medical control / オフライン[間接的]～コントロール〔医師が救命救急士に対し手引き書を作成したり教育指導を行うなど事前・事後的な指示を与えること〕on-line [direct] medical control / off-line [indirect] medical control.

**メディカル・コスメ**〔開発に専門医が参加している基礎化粧品〕medical cosmetics.

**メティス**〖天〗〔木星の衛星〗Metis.

**メディック**〖自衛隊〗〔航空自衛隊の航空救難隊の通称〕an air rescue group;〔その救難員〕a member of an air rescue group.

**メドゥサン・デュ・モンド**〔医療分野の国際 NGO；世界の医師団〕Médecins du Monde (略: MDM); Doctors of the World.

**メトセラ・マウスしょう**【-賞】〔マウスの長寿を競う賞〕the Methuselah Mouse Prize.

**めどめ[2]**【芽止め】〔農・園芸〕sprout inhibiting. ⇨ 芽止め剤 a sprout inhibitor.

**メドレセ**〖イスラム神学校〗a madrasa(h); a medrese.

**メニュー**⇨ 別メニュー〔トレーニング項目などの〕a different «training»「schedule [regimen]」. ◯ 他の選手とは別～で調整する follow a different training schedule from other players.

**めのあいごデー**【目の愛護-】〔10月10日〕Eye Day.

**めばち**(まぐろ)【眼鉢(鮪)・目撥(鮪)】〔魚〕〔サバ科の海産魚〕a bigeye tuna; *Thunnus obesus*.

**メバロチン**〖商標・薬〗〔高脂血症治療薬〕Mevalotin.

**メヘルつうしん**【-通信】〔イランの通信社〕Mehr News Agency.

**メ・ホン・ソン**＝メー・ホ(ー)ン・ソ(ー)ン.

**めまい**【目眩・眩暈】◯ めまい症【医】vertigo. ◯ 良性発作性頭位(ぶ)～症 benign paroxysmal positional vertigo (略: BPPV).

**メモリアル**⇨ メモリアル・ギフト a「memorial [commemorative]」gift.

**メモリアル[2]**〖ロシアの人権擁護団体〗Memorial.

**メモリー**⇨ 外部[内部, 内蔵]メモリー〖電算〗external [internal, built-in] memory. メモリー・カード・スロット a memory card slot. メモリー・スティック〖商標・電算〗(a) Memory Stick. メモリー・ブロッカー〖電算〗a memory blocker.

**メラニン**⇨ メラニン沈着〖生理〗melanism.

**メラノイジン**【化】melanoidin.

**「メリーに首ったけ」**〔映画〕There's Something About Mary.

**メリケン・サック**〔喧嘩のとき指関節にはめる金属片〕brass knuckles.

**メリディアニ・プレヌム**〖天〗〔火星の赤道近くの平原〕Meridiani Planum.

**メルク**〖米国の医薬品会社〗Merck & Co., Inc.

**メルケル** Merkel, Angela (1954- ;ドイツの政治家；首相〔2005- 〕).

**メルテミ**〔夏のギリシャに吹く北寄りの局地風〕the Meltemi (winds); the Etesian winds.

**メルル** Merle, Robert (1908-2004;フランスの作家).

**メレス** Meles Zenawi (1955- ;エチオピアの政治家；大統領〔1991-95〕；首相〔1995- 〕).

**メロせん**【-先】＝きょくせん[3].

**めん[5]**【麺】⇨ ストレート麺〔中華めん〕straight noodles. 卵麺〔中華めん〕egg noodles. 縮れ麺 curly

noodles. 平打ち麺 flat noodles.
「メン・イン・ブラック」〔映画〕Men in Black.
めんえき² 【免疫】 □▶ 終生免疫 lifelong [lifetime] immunity. □▶ 免疫蛍光法 〔医〕 immunofluorescence. 免疫細胞療法 (an) immune cell therapy. 免疫病 (an) immune [immunological, immunologic] disease. 免疫(力)増強 increase in immunity; 〔医〕immunopotentiation. ◎ ～増強効果[作用] immunopotentiating「effect(s)[action]. 免疫(力)増強剤〔薬〕an immunopotentiator. 免疫組織化学〔生化〕immunohistochemistry (略: IHC). ▷ immunohistochemical adj. 免疫組織化学的検査〔生化〕an immunohistochemical test. 免疫組織化学法〔生化〕an immunohistochemical method. 免疫毒性〔医〕immunotoxicity.
めんえきがく 【免疫学】 □▶ 移植免疫学 transplant(ation) immunology.
めんえきグロブリン【免疫—】□▶ ヒト免疫グロブリン (a) human immunoglobulin.
めんかいしゃぜつ 【面会謝絶】〔掲示〕No visitors (allowed). ◎ ドアの外側に「～」の札を下げる put a sign saying "No Visitors" outside the door; hang out a "No Visitors" sign. ◎ 病人は重態で～です. The patient's condition is so critical that no one is allowed to see him. / 就業時間中～. 〔掲示〕Interviews declined during working hours.
めんきょ 【免許】 □▶ 大型(自動車)免許 a license to drive a large vehicle. 普通(自動車)免許 an ordinary「*driver's license["driving license]; a license to drive an ordinary car. □▶ 免許合宿＝合宿教習 ⇨きょうしゅう²). 免許更新[書き換え]〔運転免許の〕renewal《of a driver's license》; a license renewal; 〔試験を必要とする〕recertification《of a hunting license》. 免許写真 a 《driver's》license「picture [photo].
めんきょしょう 【免許証】 □▶ 免許証写真 a《driver's》 license「picture [photo].

めんごうし【面格子】〔建〕〔窓に外から取り付ける格子〕a window「grate [grating].
めんせき¹ 【免責】 □▶ 免責期間 〔保険などの〕an exemption [a deductible] period. 免責規定 an「immunity [exemption] provision.
めんせき³ 【面積】 □▶ 総床面積 the total area of the floor; a total floor「area [space]. □▶ 面積カバー率 an area coverage rate; the rate of coverage 《for Switzerland》. [⇒エリア・カバー率, ⇨エリア・カバー (⇨エリア)].
めんせつ 【面接】 □▶ 構造化面接〔心理〕a structured interview. 半構造化面接〔心理〕a semistructured interview. 非構造化面接〔心理〕an unstructured interview. □▶ 面接法〔心理〕an「interview [interviewing] method.
めんそう 【面相】 □▶ 面相筆 ⇨ふで.
メンター □▶ メンター制度〔先輩社員が後輩に指導・心理的支援などを行う制度〕a mentoring system.
めんだし 【面出し】〔出版〕〔書店の書棚で書籍の表紙が見えるように陳列する方法〕displaying [placing] 《a book》 face-out.
メンタル □▶ メンタルヘルス・ケア mental health care. メンタルヘルス指針〔厚生労働省が定めた〕guidelines for mental health care (in the workplace).
メンチ² □▶ ～を切る〔眼をつける〕stare at [fasten one's eyes on] sb (with sinister motives).
めんちん 【面陳】〔出版〕＝めんだし.
めんつゆ 【麺汁】 □▶ noodle broth. ◎ この～は同量の水で薄めて使ってください. 〔注意書き〕Mix one part noodle broth with one part water before use.
めんてき 【面的】 □▶ areal. □▶ 面的汚染〔環境〕wide-area [areal] pollution.
メンデレーエフかいれい 【—海嶺】〔地質〕〔北極圏の海底の〕the「Mendeleev [Mendeleyev] Ridge.
「メンフィス・ベル」〔映画〕Memphis Belle.
メンマ 【麺麻】 pickled bamboo shoots.

# も

モイシウ Moisiu, Alfred (1929- ；アルバニアの政治家；大統領〔2002-07〕).
モイスチャー □▶ モイスチャー・クリーム moisturizing cream. モイスチャー・ローション moisturizing lotion
モイヤー Moyer, Jack (Thomson) (1929-2004；米国出身の三宅島の海洋生物研究者).
もうきのふぼく 【盲亀の浮木】〔きわめて珍しい機会に遭遇することのたとえ〕a rare「coincidence [accomplishment, feat].
もうきゅう 【毛球】 □▶ 毛球症〔獣医〕〔毛をなめる動物が, 胃に飲み込んだ毛を詰まらせる病気〕《suffer from》 hair balls.
もうこりた 【忘己利他】〔仏教〕〔己を忘れて他を利すること；最澄の言葉〕forgetting oneself and serving others; selfless devotion to the service of others.
もうこん 【毛根】 □▶ 毛根細胞 a hair「root [bulb] cell.
もうさいかん 【毛細管】 □▶ 毛細管現象 a capillary phenomenon; 《by》 capillarity.
「孟子」〔孟子の語録；四書の 1 つ〕The Mencius; Mengzi; Meng-tzu.
もうしょ 【猛暑】 □▶ 猛暑効果 ◎ ～効果でビールの売り上げが前年同期より 20% も上がった. The fierce heat resulted in beer sales 20% higher than for the same period last year. 猛暑日〔気象〕〔最高気温 35℃ 以上の日〕a day on which the maximum temperature is 35 degrees or more.
もうじん 【盲人】 □▶ 盲人マラソン a marathon for the blind; a blind marathon.

もうそう² 【妄想】 □▶ 物盗られ妄想〔認知症の 1 症状〕delusion of theft (in patients with dementia).
もうチャージ【猛—】〔スポーツなどで〕a「huge [big, tremendous] charge [attack]. ◎ ～をかける make a「huge [big, tremendous] charge [attack] 《against sb》; attack 《the other team》fiercely.
もうちょい, もうちょっと just a「tiny bit [fraction] more [further]. ◎ ～右に寄ってください. Just a tiny bit further to the right, please. / ～でオリンピックに出られた. The tiniest bit more would have got him into the Olympics. | He was「within an ace of [as close as close could be to] getting into the Olympics.
もうどう¹【妄動・盲動】 □▶ 盲動主義 reckless [blind] adventurism; irrational recklessness.
もうどうけん 【盲導犬】 □▶ 盲導犬訓練士 a guide dog trainer.
もうにゅうとう 【毛乳頭】〔解〕a hair papilla; a dermal papilla. □▶ 毛乳頭細胞 a「hair [dermal] papilla cell.
もうはんぱつ 【猛反発】 fierce opposition; a vehement「protest [backlash]. ～する fiercely [strongly] oppose; vehemently protest. ◎ 首相の発言に野党は～した. The opposition furiously protested the Prime Minister's statement. ◎ その法案は世論の～にあい, 立ち消えになった. The bill met with fierce public opposition, and nothing came of it. ◎ その提案は住民の～を受けた[浴びた]. That proposal「aroused [evoked a shower of] vehement opposition from the residents. / 大統領決定は国際社会の～を招いた. The president's

もうほう decision provoked a furious outcry from the international community.

もうほう【毛包】 □■ 毛包細胞〘解〙a「follicle [follicular] cell.

もうぼさいぼう【毛母細胞】〘解〙a hair matrix cell; a trichocyte.

もうまく【網膜】 □■ 網膜上膜〘医〙epiretinal membrane (略: ERM); macular pucker; cellophane maculopathy. 網膜静脈分枝閉塞症〘眼科〙(a) branch retinal vein occlusion (略: BRVO). 網膜震盪〘医〙concussion of the retina; commotio retinae. 網膜中心静脈〘解〙the central retinal vein. ◆～中心静脈閉塞症〘眼科〙(a) central retinal vein occlusion (略: CRVO). 網膜中心動脈〘解〙the central retinal artery. ◆～中心動脈閉塞症〘眼科〙(a) central retinal artery occlusion (略: CRAO). 網膜電(位)図〘眼科〙an electroretinogram (略: ERG). 網膜裂孔〘眼科〙a retinal「tear [break].

もえ¹【萌え】 □■ 萌えブーム the 《maid cafe》"moe" boom. 萌え系【萌黄箱亀】"moe"-type 《anime characters》.

もえぎはこがめ【萌黄箱亀】〘カメ科のハコガメの一種〙a flowerback box turtle; *Cuora galbinifrons*; *Cistoclemmys galbinifrons*.

「燃えよ!カンフー」〘西部をさすらうカンフーの達人のTVドラマ〙Kung Fu.

もえるこおり【燃える氷】〘メタン・ハイドレートの通称〙"burning ice."

「モーガン警部」〘アリゾナの片田舎Cochiseが舞台の, 現代の保安官のTVドラマ〙The Sheriff of Cochise; (続編) U.S. Marshal.

モーグル □■ デュアル・モーグル〘二人同時に滑降して競う〙(men's, women's) dual moguls.

モーゲージ □■ モーゲージ・ブローカー〘住宅ローン希望者と金融機関を仲介する業者〙a mortgage broker.

モース Morse, David (1953–  ; 米国の映画俳優).

モーソンきち【-基地】〘オーストラリアの南極基地〙Mawson Station.

「モーターサイクル・ダイアリーズ」〘映画〙The Motorcycle Diaries.

モーテンセン Mortensen, Viggo (1958–  ; 米国の映画俳優; 本名 Viggo Peter Mortensen).

-モード〘…(な)状態〙(a) mode; 〘…(な)気分〙a mood; a frame of mind; a「mental [psychological] state; 〘…の雰囲気・様子〙an impression; a mood; an atmosphere. □■ お疲れモード ◆連日の残業ですっかりお疲れ～だよ. Working overtime day after day I'm in a state of exhaustion. / 彼はどうやらお疲れ～だ. He seems to be in a state of exhaustion. 仕事モード ◆通訳をしているので, 外国人へのインタビュー番組はつい仕事～で見てしまう. Since I'm an interpreter, I can't help going into working mode when I see interviews with people from abroad on TV [I always find myself watching TV interviews with people from abroad in a professional frame of mind]. / 仕事～になる go into working mode; get [put *one*self] into a working frame of mind / 休日出勤が続き, 常に頭が仕事～になっている. With repeated holiday shifts, I feel in working mode all the time. / 連休が終わって今日から会社だ. 仕事～に切り替えなきゃ. Now the long weekend is over it's back to work at the company today. I must get back into working mode. 本気モード ◆チームは初戦から本気～で戦った. They played really seriously from the very first game.

モートンびょう【-病】〘医〙〘足底神経腫〙Morton's neuroma; Morton's metatarsalgia; interdigital neuroma; intermetatarsal neuroma.

モーブッサン〘商標〙〘フランスの宝飾品ブランド〙Mauboussin.

モーメンタム〘勢い・はずみ〙momentum. □■ モーメンタム・ホイール〘宇宙〙〘人工衛星などの姿勢制御に使われる回転輪〙a momentum wheel.

モール² 〘モール攻撃 an attacking maul. モール・トライ a try from a maul; a「(driving [rolling]) maul try.

もぎ【模擬】 □■ 模擬患者〘医〙a simulated patient (略: SP). 模擬授業《have》a mock class. 模擬体験 a simulated experience 《of an earthquake》; a mock practice; a simulation. 模擬弾 a dummy shell. 模擬刀 ＝模造刀 (⇨もぞう). 模擬燃料〘原子力〙simulant fuel. 模擬ミサイル a dummy missile.

もくげき¹【目撃】 □■ 目撃情報 eyewitness information; an eyewitness report. ◆その県ではUFOの～情報が年間200件ほどある. There are annually around 200 eyewitness reports of UFOs in the prefecture. / 警察は現場から走り去った車の～情報を求めている. The police are appealing for eyewitness information on the vehicle that fled from the scene.

「目撃」〘映画〙Absolute Power.

もくし【目視】 □■ 目視確認〘状況〙establishing 《of the state of a battle》;「visually [with the naked eye]; 〘存在〙a sighting 《of a new species》. ◆～確認する〘状況〙establish 《the state of preservation of a mummy》;「visually [with the naked eye]; 〘存在を〙sight [make a (visual) sighting of] 《a rare species》. 目視点検《do, make》a visual「examination [check, inspection] 《of the products》.

もくしつ【木質】 □■ 木質感〘プラスチック製品などの〙a wood-like feel. 木質(系)セメント板 wood cement board. 木質系廃棄物 wood [woody] waste. 木質(系)バイオマス wood [woody] biomass. 木質パネル工法〘建〙wood panel construction.

もくじゅう【木銃】a wooden gun.

もくぞう¹【木造】 □■ 木造軸組工法〘建〙timber [wood] frame construction.

もくたいきょう【木耐協】＝にほんもくぞうじゅうたくたいしんほきょうじぎょうしゃきょうどうくみあい.

もくたん【木炭】 □■ 木炭アイロン a charcoal iron. 木炭車 a charcoal-powered「car [bus, truck]; 〘木炭列車〙a charcoal-powered train. 木炭自動車 a charcoal-burning「automobile [vehicle, car].

もくちょう¹【木彫】 □■ 木彫仏 a carved wooden Buddha (image).

もくちょう²【木調】 ◆～家具 wood-finish furniture / ～仕上げの壁材 wood-pattern wall finishing material.

もくちんアパート【木賃-】a wooden house with rooms to let.

もくてき【目的】 □■ 目的買い planned buying; purposeful purchasing. 目的(·)効果基準〘法〙〘政教分離原則への適合性を判断する司法審査基準〙the "purpose and effect"「standard(s) [principle(s)]. 目的合理性 purposive rationality. 目的合理的 purposively rational 《action》.

もくてきがい【目的外】 unintended 《purposes》. □■ 目的外支出 an「unbudgeted [unauthorized] expenditure. 目的外使用〘利用〙(an) unintended use 《of a community hall》.

もくはい²【木灰】wood ash.

もくひけん【黙秘権】 □■ 黙秘権(の)告知〘法〙notification of「the [(a suspect's)] right to remain silence.

もくひょう²【目標】 □■ 義務的目標 a mandatory target; a mandated goal. 自主的目標 an independent target. 設定目標 a set「goal [target]. 誘導目標〘経〙a target; a guidepost. 目標設定 setting [the setting of] a「goal [target]; establishing the establishment of a「goal [target]. ◆何事を成し遂げようとするなら明確な～設定をすることが重要だ. If you want to achieve anything, it is important to set yourself a clear goal. 目標相場圏〘為替相場などの〙a target zone. 目標タイム a [*one*'s] target time. ◆ハーフマラソンの～タ

イムを80分に設定する　set「a target time of 80 minutes [one's target time at 80 minutes, 80 minutes as one's target time] in a half marathon; aim to run a half marathon in 80 minutes.

**もくめ【木目】**▶木目(調)パネル〔自動車部品・建築・家具などに用いられる〕a wood-grain panel; wood-grain paneling.

**もくろみ**▶もくろみはずれ being「frustrated [balked]《in one's plans》; frustration《of a plan》.

**もじ【文字】**▶文字起こし〔音声を文字にする作業〕transcription. 文字化＝文字起こし. 文字記録 a written record; a record in writing. 文字情報 textual information. 文字資料 textual materials; textual data.

**もじ・かつじぶんかしんこうほう【文字・活字文化振興法】**〔法〕〔2005年施行〕the Law to Promote the Culture of the Written Word.

**モジュール**▶モジュール化 modularization. ▶〜化する modularize《components, a system》.

**モジュラー**▶モジュラー車いす〔利用者の身体の寸法に合わせて調節できる〕a modular wheelchair.

**モス** Moss, Carrie-Anne (1967-　; カナダ生まれの映画女優).

**モスクワこくさいかんけいだいがく【—国際関係大学】** the Moscow State Institute of International Relations.

**モスクワじょうやく【—条約】**⇨せんりゃくこうげきせんりょくさくげんじょうやく.

**モスクワせんげん【—宣言】**〔1998年, 日間の平和条約締結に関する〕the Moscow Declaration. ▶正式名称は「日本国とロシア連邦の間の創造的パートナーシップ構築に関するモスクワ宣言」(the Moscow Declaration on「Building [Establishing] a Creative Partnership between Japan and the Russian Federation.

**モスタール**＝モスタル.

**モスタル**〔ボスニア・ヘルツェゴヴィナの歴史都市〕Mostar.

**モストウ** Mostow, Jonathan (1961-　; 米国の映画監督).

**モスフィルム**〔ロシアの国営映画製作所〕Mosfilm.

**もぞう【模造】**▶模造刀 an imitation [a model] sword.

**モダシン**〔商標・薬〕〔抗生物質; セフタジジムの商品名〕Modacin.

**モダフィニール**〔薬〕〔興奮・覚醒剤・ナルコレプシー治療薬〕modafinil.

**モダリティ(—)**〔農業自由化に向けてWTO加盟国に適用される大枠のルール〕modalities.

**もちあい【持ち合い・保ち合い】**▶三角持ち合い, 三角持ち合い〔株式〕〔多数の会社が相互に株式を持ち合うこと〕cross-holding of stock by three or more companies;〔株価の上がり下がりが日を追って小さくなり, 値動きのグラフが一点に収束していく局面〕a pennant chart pattern. ▶持ち合い解消〔株〕の〜解消売りの sale of「cross-held shares [stakes in one another's business].

**もちかえり【持ち帰り】**▶持ち帰り票 an election ballot that is taken home (instead of being cast). 持ち帰り弁当 a take-out meal in a box. ▶〜弁当 a store selling take-out meals in boxes.

**もちかぶ【持ち株】**▶持ち株比率 a「shareholding [stockholding] ratio; a ratio of「shareholding [stockholding]. ▶外国人〜比率 the foreign「shareholding [stockholding] ratio; the percentage《of stock》owned by foreign investors.

**もちこみ【持ち込み】**▶持ち込み企画 an outside proposal《to a company》「to publish a book]; a proposal from an outsider《to film a story》.

**もちのり【餅海苔】**(a) glue made from mochi.

**もちひょう【持ち票】**a vote (assigned to a《country》). ▶持ち票制度 [EUの閣僚理事会での投票方式] a vote-

assignment system; a system for assigning the number of votes for each member country.

**もちぶんほう【持分法】**▶持分法投資損益 (an) equity method gain/loss. 持分法投資利益 an equity method investment gain. 持分法適用会社 an equity method company.

**もちゅう【喪中】**▶喪中はがき a postal card informing friends and acquaintances that one is in mourning and will not send a New Year's card this year; a mourning-notification card.

**もつ¹**▶もつ鍋 a「hot pot [stew] containing entrails.

**モックス【MOX】**▶フル MOX 炉 a 100% MOX-fuelled reactor.

**もったり**〔泡立ちの程度〕▶卵の白身を掻き立て, 〜してきたら砂糖を加えてさらに少し掻き立てます. Beat the egg whites until「thick (and foamy) [soft peaks form], add the sugar, and beat a little more. ∕ この石けんの泡は〜と柔らかい. This soap forms thick soft suds.

**もっちり**▶〜した puffy; springy ∕ 外はパリッとして, 中は〜感のあるパン bread crispy on the outside and「spongy [soft] on the inside.

**モディオダール**〔商標・薬〕〔興奮・覚醒剤・ナルコレプシー治療薬〕Modiodal. ▶一般名は モダフィニル.

**モディリアーニ・ミラーりろん[てい]り]【—理論[定理]】**〔経〕〔経営理論の1つ〕the Modigliani-Miller theory [theorem]. ▶米国の経済学者 Franco Modigliani と Merton Miller より. [=エム・エムりろん[てい]り]]

**モデル**▶モデル法廷〔裁判員制度などに〕a mock court. モデル料〔代〕〔絵画・写真などの〕a「modelling [model('s)] fee.

**もと-【元-】**〔かつての・過去の〕former; ex-; one-time;《文》erstwhile; sometime. ▶〜茨城県知事 the ex-Governor of Ibaraki Prefecture ∕ 〜京都大学教授吉村博士 Dr. Yoshimura, a former professor at Kyoto University ∕ 〜代議士 a former member of the Diet ∕ 〜総理 a「one-time [former] Prime Minister.

**もとおっと【元夫】**one's former husband; one's ex-husband;《口》one's ex.

**もとづま【元妻】**one's former wife; one's ex-wife;《口》one's ex.

**もとネタ【元—】**the「source [inspiration]《for…》; the origin(al)《of…》. ▶黒澤の映画『隠し砦の三悪人』に登場する農民コンビが『スター・ウォーズ』のロボットコンビの〜であるのは有名な話だ. It is well known that the two farmers who appear in Kurosawa's movie "The Hidden Fortress" inspired the two robots in "Star Wars."

**モナスティール**〔チュニジア, 地中海沿岸の町〕Monastir.

**モナスティラ(—)キひろば【—広場】**〔ギリシャ, アテネの〕Monastiraki Square.

**モナッシュだいがく【—大学】**〔オーストラリア, メルボルンにある大学〕Monash University.

**モニター**▶モニター画面〔電算〕a monitor (screen). モニター制御装置〔鉄道〕an event recorder.

**モノコック**▶モノコック構造 a monocoque structure. ▶セミ〜構造〔縦通材と外皮とを組み合わせた構造〕a semimonocoque structure.

**モノソミー**〔医〕〔2本で対となるべき染色体の片方が欠けること〕monosomy.

**ものづくり【物作り】**▶ものづくり白書 a white paper on manufacturing infrastructure;〔経済産業省・厚生労働省・文部科学省共同作成の〕the《2004》White Paper on Manufacturing Infrastructure.

**ものつくりだいがく【—大学】**the Institute of Technologists.

**ものども【者共】**▶〜, かかれ! Go at him, lads!

**ものなり【物生り】**a harvest; a crop; the fruit(s) of the earth.

**「もののけ姫」**〔アニメ映画〕Princess Mononoke.

モノリンガル〔一言語使用〕monolingualism. ➪〜の monolingual /〜の人 a monolingual (person).
ものわすれ〔物忘れ〕 ▫▫ 物忘れ検診[検査]〘医〙a forgetfulness examination.
モバイル ▫▫ モバイル勤務〔決められた場所に出勤するのではなく，情報通信手段を活用してさまざまな場所で業務を行う勤務形態〕mobile(-based) working; a mobile「working [job]」system. モバイル決済 payment by mobile phone; mobile payment. モバイル・コマース〔移動体通信を利用した電子商取引〕mobile commerce; m-commerce. モバイル・サービス〔通信会社の〕《offer》a mobile service. モバイル・サイト〔携帯電話からアクセスすることができるように最適化されたウェブサイト〕a mobile Web site. モバイル情報端末 a mobile data terminal(略: MDT). モバイル・フード〔いつどこでも片手で手軽に食べられる携帯性に優れた食べ物〕mobile [portable, easy-to-carry, one-handed] food. モバイル放送 mobile broadcasting.
モバイルけっさいすいしんきょうぎかい【−決済推進協議会】the Mobile Payment Promotion Association(略: MOPPA).
「モハメド・アリ かけがえのない日々」〔映画〕When We Were Kings.
モヒカン〔髪型〕 ▫▫ a *mohawk [''mohican''] (haircut); 〔モヒカンの人〕a ((person)) with 《his》hair in a *mohawk [''mohican'']; 「a mohican.
もふく【喪服】 ▫▫ 正喪服 ((wear, be in)) deep [full] mourning. 半[略]喪服 half mourning.  ▫▫ 喪服美人 a mourning beauty; a woman who looks beautiful in mourning clothes.
もみだま【揉み玉】〔マッサージ用の〕a massage head.
もみで【揉み手】 ▫▫ 揉み手外交 (a) sycophantic diplomacy.
モムチャン《<Kor. mom(体)+jjang(「最高」といった意の語)》〔理想的な体型を指す韓国語〕((an actor with)) a nice body. ▫▫ モムチャンダイエット a "nice-body" diet.
もめん【木綿】 ▫▫ 木綿判〔座布団のサイズ〕〜判の座布団 a medium-size (floor) cushion (51×55cm).
ももぶとはむし【腿太羽虫】〘昆〙〔大きな後ろ脚をもつ, マレー半島産の大型で極彩色の羽虫〕a frog beetle; Sagra buqueti.
ももやまとう【桃山陶】Momoyama ware.
モモルデシン〔化〕〔ニガウリの苦み成分〕momordicine.
モヨロじん【−人】〔5-10世紀の北海道先住民族〕the Moyoro; (1人) a Moyoro ((pl. ~)).
モラール ▫▫ モラールアップ〔士気を高めること〕raising [improving] the morale ((of employees)); raising morale; 〔士気が高まること〕a rise [an improvement] in morale; a rise in the morale ((of the troops)). モラールダウン〔士気を落とすこと〕lowering [reducing] the morale ((of employees)); 〔士気が落ちること〕a「decline [drop] in morale; a decline in the morale ((of the troops)).
モラーレス ＝モラレス.
モラエス ＝モラエス.
モラエス Moraesu, Wenceslau José de Sousa de (1854-1929; ポルトガル人の日本文化研究家).
モラハラ ＝モラル・ハラスメント.
モラル・ハラスメント〔精神的虐待〕moral harassment; psychological [mental] abuse [harassment].
モラレス Morales, Evo (1959-  ; ボリビアの政治家; 大統領〔2006-  〕); フル表記 Juan Evo Morales Ayma.
もりこみ【盛り込み】〔盛り込むこと〕incorporation; inclusion; 〔料理の〕piling ((a selection of food)) on one plate. ▫▫ 盛り込み料理 a plate of several kinds of food; a「varied [mixed] plate [platter]; a thali.
モリター Molitor, Paul (1956-  ; 米国の野球選手).
もりたりょうほう【森田療法】〘精神医〙Morita therapy. ▶ 精神科医 森田正馬(1874-1938)にちなむ.
モルガン・スタンレー〔米国の投資銀行〕Morgan Stanley.

モルゲンロート《<G Morgenrot》〔朝焼け〕(the flush of) dawn.
モルト[1] ▫▫ モルト・エキス malt extract. モルト・フィード〔麦芽のしぼりかす〕malt feed.
モルトンびょう【−病】〘医〙＝モートンびょう.
モルホリノ〔化〕morpholino.
もれ【漏れ】 ▫▫ 後ろ漏れ〔生理用ナプキンの〕back leakage. 横漏れ〔おむつなどの〕⇒よこもれ.
もろ〔もろに〕➪ 彼女の親父が乗り込んでくるって？〜やばいよ. Her old man is coming after me? 「That totally sucks [I'm completely screwed].
もろ-〔あらわに見せたり出したりするさま〕➪ 水着の肩ひもが外れて乳房が〜見えになった. The shoulder straps on her swimsuit slipped down and exposed her breasts completely. / 彼は下半身〜出しのままトイレから出てきた. He came out of the restroom with his private parts「in full view [completely exposed].
モロ・イスラムかいほうせんせん【−解放戦線】〔フィリピン, ミンダナオ島を本拠とするゲリラ組織〕the Moro Islamic Liberation Front (略: MILF).
もろだし【諸出し】➪ もろ出し.
モロッコ・イスラムせんとうだん【−戦闘団】the Moroccan Islamic Combatant Group (略: GICM). ▶ 略称はフランス語名 le Groupe Islamique Combattant Marocain に由来.
モロトフ・リッベントロップきょうてい【−協定】〔史〕〔独ソ不可侵条約の別称〕the Molotov-Ribbentrop Pact. ▶ 署名した両外務大臣の名前から.
もろみえ【もろ見え】➪ もろ-.
もわっと〔暖かく湿った空気がこもっている様子〕⇒もわんと. ➪ ドアを開けたとたんにこもっていた生ぬるい空気が〜きて思わず足が止まった. When I opened the door, I was stopped in my tracks by a blast of lukewarm muggy air from inside.
もわもわ〔やわらかく盛り上がった様子〕fluffily; in puffs; in billows. ➪ クリスマスツリーに綿の雪を〜と載せる put fluffy cotton snow on a Christmas tree.
もわんと〔暖かく湿った空気がたちのぼっている様子〕⇒もわっと. ➪ 浴室には湯気が〜たちこめていて中がよく見えなかった. The bathroom was filled with billowing steam, so I couldn't see inside very well. / おむつをはずすとうんちの臭いが〜立ちのぼった. The stench of poop rose up when I removed the diaper.
もん[5]【紋】 ▫▫ 紋切り(遊び)〔紙切り遊びの一種〕folded-paper [origami] cutting; monkiri.
モンキーターン〔競艇で, 全速の旋回〕cornering at full speed.
モンキーのり【−乗り】〔競馬〕〔騎乗法の１つ〕the monkey crouch.
モンク・ストラップ〔甲の部分にバックル付きの幅広ストラップを渡した靴〕a monk (shoe).
モングラ〔バングラデシュの港湾都市〕Mongla.
モンケン【建】〔杭打ち用の鉄の錘〕a drop hammer; an earth auger; a monkey. ▶ モンケンは「モンキー」がなまったもの.
もんごん【文言】 ▫▫ 文言修正 (a) correction in the wording ((of a resolution)). 文言調整〔条約文などを作成する際の〕(an) adjustment to the wording ((of a resolution)).
モンサント〔米国の総合化学メーカー〕Monsanto Co.; 〘商標〙Monsanto.
もんじん[2]【問訊】〘仏教〙a (Buddhist monk's) salutation; a bow with (the palms of one's) hands together.
「モンスーン・ウェディング」〔映画〕Monsoon Wedding.
もんすずめばち【紋雀蜂】〘昆〙〔スズメバチ科のハチ〕a (European) hornet; Vespa crabro.
「モンスターズ・インク」〔アニメ映画〕Monsters, Inc.
もんせき【問責】 ▫▫ 問責制〔中国の国内政治の制度〕an

accountability system.
**もんだい**【問題】 ▢□ 問題教師 a problem(atic) teacher. 問題作成委員 a member of a test preparation committee; a test preparer. ▷〜作成委員会 a test preparation committee. 問題設定 deciding「the issues for discussion [what needs to be discussed]. 問題設定力 an ability to identify problems.
「**モンタナの風に抱かれて**」〔映画〕The Horse Whisperer.
**モンタルバン** Montalban, Ricardo (1920- ; メキシコ出身の映画俳優).
**モントブレチア** 〔植〕＝ひめひおうぎずいせん.
**もんどりうつ**【もんどり打つ】turn a somersault; throw a somerset; tumble head over heels. ▷ もんどり打って倒れる keel over; fall「head over heels [heels over head]《on the ground》/ (自動車・動物などが)もんどり打って転がる tumble end over end.
**モンドル・キリ**〔カンボジア東部の州〕Mondol Kiri.
**モントレーこくさいもんだいけんきゅうじょ**【-国際問題研究所】〔米国の〕the Monterey Institute of International Studies (略: MIIS).
**もんぶかがく**【文部科学】▢□ 文部科学白書〔文部科学省の〕the White Paper on Science and Technology.
**もんぺ** ▢□ もんぺ姿 ▷〜姿の《a woman》in [wearing] monpe.

# や

**ヤーコン**【植】〔南米アンデス高原原産のキク科の根菜〕yacón; *Polymnia sonchifolia*; *Smallanthus sonchifolius*.

**ヤースージ(ュ)**〔イラン南部、コフギールーイェ・ブーイェルアフマド州の州都〕Yasuj.

**やあな**【矢穴】〔大きな石材を切断するために開ける穴〕an "arrow hole"; an oblong wedge hole carved into a stone to aid in splitting.

**ヤーバー**〔タイなど東南アジアに出回っている錠剤型の覚醒剤〕yaba. ► タイ語で「狂気の薬」の意.

**ヤーン**　◻︎　スリット・ヤーン〔ポリエステルフィルムを金属メッキし糸状に裂いたもの〕slit yarn.

**やいかがし**【焼嗅】〔節分を前に、焼いたイワシの頭をヒイラギの枝に刺し、それを戸口や窓の外に挿して厄払いをする風習〕a custom in which grilled sardine heads impaled on holly twigs are stuck onto the outside of doors and windows to drive away evil spirits on the night of setsubun.

**やえやまこきくがしらこうもり**【八重山小菊頭蝙蝠】〖動〗〔キクガシラコウモリ科のコウモリ〕*Rhinolophus perditus*.

**ヤオ・ミン**【姚明】Yao Ming (1980–　; 中国出身のバスケットボール選手).

**やがい**【野外】　◻︎　野外球場 an outdoor stadium《for「baseball [football, soccer]》. 野外手術システム【自衛隊】a field surgery system. 野外生活者 a person who lives outdoors; a homeless person. 野外放出〔外来生物などを放つこと〕release《of non-native species》into the wild.

**ヤカオラン**〔アフガニスタン、バーミヤン州の一地方〕Yakaolang.

**やかん[1]**【夜間】　◻︎　夜間救急 emergency (medical) treatment in the evening [at night]. 夜間養護事業〔トワイライトステイ事業〕evening [childcare ["childminding].

**やきかた**【焼き方】〔焼く方法〕a method of 「roasting [broiling]; 〔焼き加減〕extent of roasting or broiling; how well《meat》is done. ◉～はどうなさいますか.〔ステーキについて〕How would you like your steak?

**やきすぎ**【焼き杉】〔杉材の表面を焼いて炭化させてから磨る、木目を浮き出させたもの〕(decorative) charred cedar.

**やきにく**【焼き肉】　◻︎　焼肉器 a grill.

**やきむら**【焼き斑】〖窯〗uneven firing. ◉たくさんのれんがを一つの窯(釜)で一度に焼くと、窯の中の位置によってどうしても～が出る. When many bricks are fired together in the same kiln, color variations depending on the position in the kiln are unavoidable. ◉～のある壺 a pot that has been fired unevenly.

**やきやぶり**【焼き破り】〔押し込み強盗の手口〕breaking and entering by heating window glass so that it can be broken quietly.

**やきゅう**【野球】　◻︎　野球解説者 a baseball commentator. 野球肩〔投球時に肩が痛む症状〕baseball shoulder. 野球教室〔学校〕a baseball school; a school that teaches baseball;〔授業〕a baseball 「class [course]; 〔個人〕baseball lessons; lessons [a course, a class] in baseball. 野球拳〔二人が向かい合わせに歌い踊ってじゃんけんをし、負けたほうが着ているものを一枚ずつ脱いでいく遊び〕a game in which two persons sing a short song and pantomime playing baseball followed by a round of rock-paper-scissors, with the loser removing one piece of clothing; strip baseball. 野球肘〔関節炎〕baseball elbow.

**やきゅうきょうやく**【野球協約】〔日本プロフェッショナル野球協約〕the Japanese Professional Baseball Agreement.

**やくがい**【薬害】　◻︎　薬害ヤコブ病 drug-induced Creutzfeldt-Jakob disease.

**やくざい**【薬剤】　◻︎　薬剤イベント・モニタリング〖薬〗〔医薬品の効果・副作用に関する情報収集方法の１つ〕drug event monitoring（略：DEM). 薬剤情報提供料 a charge for information on the efficacy and side-effects of prescription drugs. 薬剤排出トランスポーター〔耐性菌が持つ〕a drug efflux transporter.

**やくじ**【薬事】　◻︎　薬事監視証明書 ＝やっかんしょうめい. 薬事承認 ◉～承認を取得する obtain a drug approval《of a new medicine》; obtain approval for a (new) drug《from the Ministry of Health, Labour and Welfare》.

**やくしょく**【役職】　◻︎　役職任期制 a system by which the future deployment of managerial staff is reconsidered after a fixed period, depending on results.

**やくすぎ**【屋久杉】【植】〔鹿児島県屋久島に自生するスギのうち、特に樹齢1000年を越えるスギ〕a Yaku「sugi [cedar]; a「sugi [cedar] native to Yaku Island, Kagoshima Prefecture, often more than 1000 years old.

**やくぜん**【薬膳】　◻︎　薬膳料理 herbal medicine「cuisine [cooking].

**やくそう[2]**【薬草】　◻︎　薬草風呂 a medicinal herb bath.

**やくぶつ**【薬物】　◻︎　薬物汚染〔麻薬乱用の弊害〕contamination by drugs; drug「contamination [impairment]. ◉未成年者に～汚染がじわじわ広がっている. The numbers of young people badly affected by drugs are gradually rising. 薬物常用者 a drug user;〔静脈注射による〕an intravenous drug user（略：IDU). 薬物探知機 ＝麻薬探知機（⇨まやく). 薬物統制 drug control. 薬物不法所持〖法〗◉被逮捕される for）illegal possession of drugs. 薬物乱用〔濫用〕者 a drug abuser. 薬物乱用頭痛〖医〗(a) medication-overuse headache（略：MOH).

**やくみ**【薬味】　◻︎　薬味ねぎ〔薬味専用のねぎ〕a variety of *negi* used as a herb or spice;〔細かく刻んだねぎ〕chopped *negi*.

**やくむ**【薬務】　◻︎　薬務局〔厚生労働省の〕the Pharmaceutical Affairs Bureau.

**やくもち**【役持ち】a「post [position] holder; an officer.

**やくよう**【薬用】　◻︎　薬用成分 a medicinal ingredient. 薬用入浴剤 medicated bath salts.

**やくりゲノミクス**【薬理-】〖医〗＝やくりゲノムがく.

**やくりゲノムがく**【薬理-学】〖医〗pharmacogenomics. ► pharmacology (薬理学) と genomics (ゲノム学) からの造語.

**やくわり**【役割】　◻︎　役割葛藤〖心理〗role conflict; a conflict of roles. 役割期待〖社会〗role expectation. 役割給 a「position-based [job-based] salary. 役割固定 role fixation; the fixing of a role. 役割達成度〔人事評価の方法の１つ〕one's degree of role fulfillment.

**やけい**【夜景】　◻︎　夜景スポット a night view spot; a「spot [place] with a (good) night view.

**やこう[1]**【夜光】　◻︎　夜光テープ luminous [phosphorescent, glow-in-the-dark] tape.

**やこうか**【夜香花】【植】〔ナス科の常緑低木；夜間に開花して高い香りを放つ〕(a) night (blooming [scented]) 「jasmine [jessamine]; *Cestrum nocturnum*.

**やこうじゅ**【夜香樹】【植】＝やこうか.

**やこうぼく**【夜香木】【植】＝やこうか.

**ヤコブスハンひょうが**【-氷河】〔グリーンランド西部の氷河〕

the Jakobshavn Glacier; Jakobshavn Isbræ.
**やさい**【野菜】 ▢▪ 有機野菜 organically grown [organic] vegetables. ▢▪ 野菜飲料 a vegetable drink. 野菜室〔冷蔵庫の〕a crisper;〔引き出し式の〕a crisper drawer. 野菜直売所 a direct sales「outlet [depot, store] for vegetables.
**ヤジ(ー)ディー**〔イラクを中心とする少数宗教〕Yazdanism;〔その信者〕the Yazidi; the Yezidi.
**やしおおおさぞうむし**【椰子大象虫】〔昆〕〔ヤシ類の害虫〕(a) red palm weevil; *Rhynchophorus ferrugineus*.
**やしき**【屋敷】 ▢▪ 屋敷墓〔住居の敷地内に造られた墓〕a grave within the grounds (of a house).
**やしょく**²【夜食】 ▢▪ 夜食症候群 night eating syndrome (略: NES).
**ヤシン** Yassin, Ahmed (1938?-2004; イスラム原理主義組織ハマスの創設者・精神的指導者).
**やすくにじんじゃ**【靖国神社】the Yasukuni Shrine. ▢▪ 靖国神社参拝問題 the issue of《the prime minister's》visit to the Yasukuni Shrine.
**やすでま**【安手間】low [poor,《口》lousy] pay [wages].
**ヤズド**〔イラン中部の州; その州都〕Yazd.
**やすね**【安値】 ▢▪ 安値圏〔株価などの〕a zone of low prices; a [the] low price zone;《near》the bottom.
**やせ**【痩せ】 ▢▪ 痩せ願望 a desire to slim; an obsession with slimming.
**やせい**¹【野生】 ▢▪ 野生株〔生物〕a wild-type strain. 野生種 a wild species (of…). 野生鳥獣管理学 ＝野生動物管理学. 野生動物管理学 wildlife [wild animal] management (studies). 野生復帰 return [restoration]《of an animal》to the wild.
**やせいか**【野生化】 ▢▪ 野生化訓練〔人工飼育した動物・捕獲などの〕training for「returning [reintroducing]《captive pandas》to the wild; reintroduction training.
**やせたいしょうこうぐん**【痩せたい症候群】a pathological desire to「slim [lose weight].
「**痩せゆく男**」〔映画〕Thinner.
**ヤソート(ー)**〔タイ東北部の県; 同県の県都〕Yasothon.
**ヤタイやし**〔-椰子〕〔植〕〔ヤシ科の高木性ヤシ〕a yatay palm; *Butia yatay*.
**やっか**【薬価】 ▢▪ 公定薬価 the official price of pharmaceuticals.
**やっかんしょうめい**【薬監証明】〔薬・法〕〔医薬品を個人輸入する場合に必要な, 厚生労働省発行の許可証明〕a pharmaceutical inspector's certificate.
**やっこう**【薬効】 ▢▪ 薬効成分 the effective ingredient(s)《of a drug》. 薬効発現〔医〕the pharmacological effect《of a drug》; (an) expression of drug efficacy.
**やつだ**【谷津田】〔谷間の湿地にある田〕a rice paddy in「valley wetlands [a marshy valley].
**やってられない, やってらんない** ◐日本なら5分で済む交渉にこの国では5日かかる。…ま, まったく。A negotiation that would be finished in five minutes in Japan takes five days in this country.「I can't handle it anymore. [I'm completely fed up with it.] / こんなに臭くて汚い仕事で月給15万じゃ～よ。No way I can keep doing this dirty, smelly work for just 150,000 yen a month.
**やといどめ**【雇い止め】〔労働〕〔長期継続してきたアルバイトや派遣社員などの不当労働行為的な契約解除〕unfair termination of (an employment) contract; unfair termination.
**ヤトロファ**〔植〕＝ジャトロファ.
**やな**【簗】 ▢▪ 簗漁 weir fishing.
**やなぎばひまわり**【柳葉向日葵】〔植〕〔キク科の多年草; 北米原産〕a willow-leaf sunflower; *Helianthus salicifolius*.
**ヤヌコヴィッチ** Yanukovych, Viktor Fedorovych (1950- ; ウクライナの政治家; 首相 [2006-07]).

**やね**【屋根】 ▢▪ 屋根職人 a roofer.
**やねがわらほうしき**【屋根瓦方式】〔医〕〔先輩研修医が後輩を指導する方式〕the "roof-tile" training system; the system by which senior interns train their juniors.
**やぶいぬ**【藪犬】〔犬〕〔中南米産の原始的な犬; 絶滅危惧種〕a bush dog; *Speothos venaticus*.
**やぶれべにたけ**【破れ紅茸】〔菌〕〔担子菌類ベニタケ科のキノコ〕*Russula lepida*.
**やぶれまどりろん**【破れ窓理論】＝われまどりろん.
**やまあじさい**【山紫陽花】〔植〕〔ユキノシタ科の落葉低木〕*Hydrangea serrata*.
**やまあらし**【山荒し・豪猪】 ▢▪ ヤマアラシのジレンマ〔心理〕the "porcupine('s) [hedgehog('s)] dilemma.
**やまがたこくさいドキュメンタリーえいがさい**【山形国際一映画祭】the Yamagata International Documentary Film Festival (略: YIDFF).
**やまぎり**【山切り】〔歯ブラシのブラシ部分などのギザギザのカット〕serration. ▢▪ 山切りブラシ a brush with serrated bristles.
**やまけい**【山径】〔ライフル銃の口径の一〕a bore diameter.
**やまこうもり**【山蝙蝠】〔動〕〔ヒナコウモリ科のコウモリ〕*Nyctalus aviator*.
**ヤマサクラ**〔陸上自衛隊と米陸軍共同で行われるコンピューターなどを使った図上演習; 日本有事や周辺事態を想定したもので, 1982年より年2回日米で交互に行われている〕Yamasakura [Yama Sakura] (略: YS). ▶ 正式名称は, 日米共同方面隊指揮所演習.
**やまたに**【山谷】〔経〕cyclical peaks and troughs《of the economy》.
**やまとたまむし**【大和玉虫】〔昆〕〔タマムシ科の昆虫〕a Japanese jewel beetle; *Chrysochroa fulgidissima fulgidissima*.
**やまどりやし**【山鳥椰子】〔植〕〔ヤシ科の常緑中低木〕a yellow butterfly palm; an areca palm; *Chrysalidocarpus lutescens*.
「**山の郵便配達**」〔映画〕Postmen in the Mountains.
**やまひたちおび**〔動〕〔カタツムリの一種〕a Florida rosy「wolf snail [rumina]; *Euglandina rosea*.
**やみ**【闇】 ▢▪ 闇改修〔国交省にリコールを届け出ずにメーカーがこっそり行う自動車などの欠陥改修〕carrying out a recall without reporting the problem to the Ministry of Land, Infrastructure and Transport (as required by law); an undercover recall. 闇サイト〔インターネット上の, 犯罪・自殺・中傷など反社会的目的のサイト〕an「undesirable [objectionable, unsavory] site; a clandestine site. 闇商売《run》「a shady [an illegal, a black-market, an underground] business.
**やみきん**【闇金】〔闇金融〕illegal [black-market] loaning; *口》loan-sharking.
**やみしじょう**【闇市場】a black market. ◐核の～ a nuclear black market; a black market in nuclear「material(s) [technology, weapons, etc.].
**やみれん**【闇練】〔こっそりと練習すること; 個人的に練習すること〕practicing「privately [by *one*self]. ～する practice「privately [by *one*self].
**ヤム・ビーン** ＝くずいも.
**ヤメはん**【べんごし】【-判(弁護士)】〔もと判事だった弁護士〕a judge-turned-lawyer.
**ヤラー** 1〔タイ南部の県〕Yala.
2〔タイ南部の都市, ヤラー県の県都〕Yala.
**やらせ** ▢▪ やらせ質問〔公聴会などでの〕a「scripted [staged, planted, prearranged] question.
**ヤラピン**〔サツマイモなどに含まれる樹脂成分〕jalapin.
**ヤンエグ**〔若くして管理職に就いたり自ら会社を立ち上げた青年実業家〕a young「entrepreneur [manager]; an entrepreneurial [a managerial] kid.
**ヤンキー・スタジアム**〔ニューヨーク市ブロンクスにある野球場〕Yankee Stadium.
**ヤングジョブスポット**〔若年者の就労を支援する公的施設〕

ヤングハローワーク a "Young Job Spot"; a job center [an employment agency] for 「young people [the under-30s].
ヤングハローワーク〔若年者向けの公共職業安定所〕a "Youth Hellowork"; a government 「employment office [agency] for 「young people [the under-30s].
ヤング・リポート〔米国の, 政府への政策提言報告書の通称〕the Young Report. ▶ 1985 年,「世界的競争・新しい現実」(*Global Competition: The New Reality*) というタイトルでまとめられた提言; 委員長 John A. Young の名から.

ヤンセン Janssen, Famke (1964/65- ; オランダ生まれの映画女優).
ヤンチン【揚琴】〖楽器〗=ようきん[6].
ヤンブー〔サウジアラビアの紅海沿岸の都市〕Yanbu.
やんややんや 一座の人々は～と彼女の歌をほめそやした. All over the room a babble of praise went up for her singing. | The whole room erupted in praise of her singing.

# ゆ

ゆあつ【油圧】 ▫□ 油圧クラッチ 〖機〗a hydraulic clutch. 油圧ショベル 〖機〗a hydraulic shovel.
ゆいのう【結納】 ▫□ 結納飾り (a set of) decorated betrothal gifts.
ゆうあい【友愛】 ▫□ 友愛数〖数〗amicable numbers. ◯ 準〜数 quasi-amicable numbers.
ゆうい[4]【優位】 ▫□ 優位脳〖解〗=優位半球. 優位半球〖解〗〔右脳と左脳のうち, 言語中枢がある側〕a dominant hemisphere.
ゆういみ【有意味】 ▫□ 有意味音 a meaningful sound. 有意味言語学習〖教育〗meaningful verbal learning. 有意味受容学習〖教育〗meaningful reception learning.
ユーイングにくしゅ【-肉腫】〖医〗(a) Ewing('s) sarcoma; (a) small round cell sarcoma.
ゆうえい【遊泳】 ▫□ 空中遊泳〔スカイダイビング・パラグライダーなどによる〕sky swimming;〔シミュレーターによる宇宙遊泳の疑似体験〕simulated space walking. ▫□ 遊泳禁止区域 a region where swimming is prohibited;〔掲示〕Swimming Prohibited.
ユー・エイチ・エフ【UHF】 ▫□ **UHF 帯** the UHF band.
ユー・エー・イー【UAE】〔アラブ首長国連邦〕the UAE; the United Arab Emirates.
ユー・エー・ブイ【UAV】〖軍〗〔無人機〕UAV. ▶ unmanned 「aerial [air] vehicle の略.
ユー・エス・エー・トゥデー【USA -】〔米国の朝刊紙〕USA Today.
ユー・エス・エー・ライスれんごうかい【USA-連合会】〔米国産米の業界団体〕the USA Rice Federation.
「US ニューズ・アンド・ワールド・リポート」〔米国のニュース週刊誌〕*U.S. News & World Report*.
ユー・エス・ビー【USB】 ▫□ **USB** メモリー USB memory. **USB** メモリー・スティック a USB memory stick.
ユー・エス・ビジット【US-VISIT】〔米国の外国人入国管理プログラム〕US-VISIT. ▶ US Visitor and Immigrant Status Indicator Technology の略.
ゆうえつ【優越】 ▫□ 優越的地位の濫用〔独占禁止法が禁じる〕abuse of (a) dominant bargaining position.
ユー・エヌ・イー・ピー・エフ・アイ【UNEP-FI】〔国連環境計画金融イニシアティブ〕the UNEP FI; the UNEP Finance Initiatives.
ユー・エフ・ティー【UFT】〔商標・薬〕〔抗がん剤〕UFT. ▶ 一般名 テガフール・ウラシル (tegafur uracil).
ユー・エフ・ろく【UF6】〖化〗〔6 弗化ウラン〕UF6; uranium hexafluoride.
「U.M.A. レイク・プラシッド」〔映画〕*Lake Placid*.
ゆうかい[3]【誘拐】 ▫□ 未成年者誘拐 kidnapping of a minor. わいせつ目的誘拐〖法〗kidnapping for immoral purposes.
ゆうがい[1]【有害】 ▫□ 有害活動〔他の国家・組織などに対する〕(a) harmful [deleterious] activity; activities harmful to〔Japan〕. 有害重金属 a 「harmful [hazardous] heavy metal. 有害鳥獣 harmful birds and animals; bird and animal pests. ◯ ～鳥獣駆除 harmful bird and animal control; pest control.
ゆうかしょうけん【有価証券】 ▫□ 代用有価証券 substitute securities 《for guarantee deposit》. 投資有価証券 investment securities. 有価証券届出書 a security registration statement. 有価証券評価益[損]a 「profit [loss] from securities revaluation. 有価証券報告書虚偽記載〖法〗a false securities report; a false entry in a statement of securities.
「ユー・ガット・メール」〔映画〕*You've Got Mail*.
ゆうき[1]【有期】 ▫□ 有期雇用者[労働者]a fixed-term employee.
ゆうき[2]【有機】 ▫□ 有機エレクトロニクス organic electronics; plastic electronics. 有機食品 organic food(s). 有機スズ〖化〗an organotin (compound). 有機農産物加工食品 processed food(s) from organic agricultural products. 有機発光ダイオード【LED】〖電子工学〗an organic light-emitting diode (略: OLED); an organic LED. ◯ アクティブマトリックス式[型]〜発光ダイオード【LED】an active-matrix organic light-emitting diode (略: AMOLED); an active-matrix OLED. 有機砒素化合物〖化〗an organic arsenic compound. 有機米 organic rice; organically grown rice. 有機無農薬栽培 organic cultivation without 「insecticides [pesticides]. ◯ ～無農薬栽培米 organic rice produced without 「insecticides [pesticides].
ゆうぎ[3]【遊戯】 ▫□ 遊戯銃 a toy gun.
ゆうきつむぎ【結城紬】Yūki pongee.
ゆうきゅう[3]【遊休】 ▫□ 遊休農地 idle [unused] farmland; farmland lying fallow.
ゆうぎょ[2]【遊漁】 ▫□ 遊漁税 a sportfishing tax.
ユーきょく【U 局】〔UHF 局〕a UHF station.
ゆうきょくさいぼう【有棘細胞】 ▫□ 有棘細胞がん〖医〗(a) spinocellular carcinoma. 有棘細胞層〖解〗=ゆうきょくそう.
ゆうきょくそう【有棘層】〖解〗〔皮膚の上皮の〕the stratum spinosum; the spinous layer; the prickle cell layer.
ゆうきりん【有機燐】 ▫□ 有機燐系殺虫剤 (an) 「organophosphate [organophosphorus] insecticide.
ゆうぐ【遊具】 ▫□ 総合遊具 a combination of jungle gym, climbing frames, slides and other equipment (made of natural materials); a (wooden) playground combination.
ゆうぐう【優遇】 ▫□ 最優遇貸出金利〖経〗〔プライムレート〕the prime (lending) rate.
ゆうぐれ【夕暮れ】 ▫□ 夕暮れ症候群〔認知症の症状の 1 つ〕sundown syndrome; sundowning.
ゆうけんしゃ【有権者】 ▫□ 有権者登録 registration 「as an elector [of voters, of electors]; voter [electors, electoral] registration.
ゆうげんせきにん【有限責任】 ▫□ 有限責任中間法人 a limited liability intermediate corporation.
ゆうげんせきにんじぎょうくみあい【有限責任事業組合】a limited liability partnership; (略: LLP).

**ゆうげんせきにんじぎょうくみあい(けいやく)ほう**【有限責任事業組合(契約)法】 the Limited Liability Partnership Law. ▶ 正式名称は「有限責任事業組合契約に関する法律」(the Law Concerning Limited Liability Partnership Contracts).

**ゆうこう**[1]【友好】 ▫ 友好促進 (the) promotion of friendly relations. ◐ この団体が目標としているのは世界の国々の〜促進である. The aim of the organization is to promote「friendly international relations [further the development of a good relationship between the countries of the world]. 友好提携都市 friendship [sister, "twin"] cities. 友好的買収 a friendly takeover.

**ゆうこう**[8]【有効】 ▫ 有効回答〔アンケートなどの〕a valid response. ◐ 無作為抽出した成人 3,000 人を対象に郵送でアンケートを行い, 1,796 人分の〜を得た. We conducted a survey by mail, targeting 3,000 adults who were selected at random, and received 1,796 valid responses. 有効回答率〔アンケートなどの〕a proportion of valid responses. ◐ 調査は全国の成人男女 1 万人を対象に行われ, 〜回答率は 76.1 ％だった. The poll was conducted among 10,000 adults throughout the country, both men and women, and the valid-response rate was 76.1%. 有効画素数〔電子工学〕〔デジタルカメラなどの〕the number (of) valid pixels. 有効活用 effective use 《of spare equipment》. ◐ 余暇の〜活用 《make》effective use of one's spare time. 有効求職者数 the number of registered「job-seekers [job applicants]; (the) effective labor supply. 有効求人数 the number of registered job「openings [offers]; (the) effective labor demand. 有効電力〔電〕effective [real, active] power. 有効投票 a valid ballot. 有効得票率 a proportion of valid votes (received). [＝相対得票率⇨そうたい[3]〕有効率〔治療法・薬剤などの〕an efficacy rate.

**ゆうざい**[1]【有罪】 ▫ 有罪(の)答弁[申し立て]〔法〕a guilty plea; a plea of guilty; pleading guilty. 有罪率〔裁判での〕a 《high》rate of convictions.

**ユーザビリティーひょうか**【〜評価】〔使い勝手がよいかどうかの評価〕(a) usability assessment.

**ゆうし**[12]【融資】 ▫ 押し付け融資 credit [a loan] forced on 《a customer》; a loan taken out under pressure 《from a bank》. 融資額 (the) loan amount; (the) amount financed. 融資債権 (a) loan credit. 融資条件 conditions for「credit [a loan]; conditionality. [＝コンディショナリティー] 融資審査 loan screening. 融資保証 a loan guarantee. 融資保証金詐欺 a low-interest loan fraud. [⇨かしまさぎ] 融資保証制度〔中小企業に融資する銀行に企業倒産の場合融資額の 70％の支払いを政府が保証する制度〕the Loan Guarantee System. ▶ 1980 年導入.

**ゆうじ**【有事】 ▫ 有事(関連)三法〔武力攻撃事態処理法, 改正安全保障会議設置法, 改正自衛隊法の 3 法〕the three national-emergency laws.

**ユーシェンコ** Yushchenko, Viktor Andriyovych (1954- ; ウクライナの政治家; 大統領〔2005- 〕).

**ユーじこう**【U 字溝】a U-shaped drainage「ditch [channel, trench].

**ゆうしょう**[4]【優勝】 ▫ 優勝記念セール ＝優勝セール. 優勝祝賀会 a victory「party [celebration]. 優勝賞金 a (monetary) prize for a first prize of money. ◐ 〜賞金 2,000 万円を獲得する win a first prize of ￥20,000,000. 優勝セール〔プロ野球チームなどの〕a「victory [championship] sale. 優勝戦線 the front「running [runners]. ◐ 〜戦線から脱落する drop out of the front running; drop away from the front runners. 優勝報告 a victory report. ◐ 高倉選手は市役所を訪問し〜報告をした. Takakura visited the city hall to report officially on his victory. /〜報告会 a victory celebration. 優勝ライン〔野球などで〕the number of victories thought to be needed for a championship. ◐ 今年の〜ラインは 80 勝だ. The team with 80 wins should take the championship this year.

**ゆうしょうしんりょうじょ**【有床診療所】a clinic with beds.

**ゆうしょく**[3]【有職】 ▫ 有職率 the ratio of 《women, nurses, licensed practitioners》「in gainful employment [with jobs].

**ゆうじん**[2]【有人】 ▫ 有人宇宙計画 a manned space program. 有人観測 manned observation; a manned survey. 有人深海探査船 a manned deep-sea「exploration [exploratory] vessel. 有人走行 manned「travel [transit]. ◐ 〜走行する be operated by a driver; be driver-operated; be driven. 有人探査船 a manned (space) probe.

**ゆうすいしょうたいがんないレンズ**【有水晶体眼内〜】〔眼科〕a phakic「IOL [intraocular lens]. [＝フェイキック・アイ・オー・エル]

**ゆうずう**【融通】 ▫ 相互融通〔資金などの〕mutual financing;〔技術・資材・製品などの〕mutual accommodation.

**ゆうせい**[3]【郵政】 ▫ 郵政民営化〔郵政事業民営化〕postal (services) privatization; (the) privatization of postal services; privatization of the post office. ◐ 〜民営化準備室 a preparation room for privatization of the postal service. 郵政民営化担当大臣 the Minister of State for Privatization of the Postal Services.

**ゆうせい**[6]【優生】 ▫ 優生思想 eugenic thought; the idea of eugenics.

**ゆうぜい**[4]【遊説】 ▫ 遊説先 a stop on a speaking tour;〔選挙での〕a campaign stop.

**ゆうせいみんえいかいいんかい**【郵政民営化委員会】〔郵政民営化の進捗状況を検証する委員会; 2006 年発足〕the Postal Privatization Committee.

**ゆうせき**【有責】 ▫ 有責性 culpability. 有責度 (a) degree of culpability; relative culpability.

**ゆうせつ**[5]【融雪】 ▫ 融雪剤 (a) snow-melting agent. 融雪災害 a snowmelt disaster; a disaster due to melting snow. 融雪注意報 a snow melting advisory. 融雪道路 a snow-melting road. 融雪屋根 a snow-melting roof.

**ゆうせん**[1]【優先】 ▫ 優先監視国〔米国の知的財産権保護に関する対外制裁条項で, 3 段階中 2 番目のレベルの〕the Priority Watch List. 優先国〔米国の知的財産権保護に関する対外制裁条項で, 3 段階中最も重いレベルの〕a Priority Foreign Country (略: PFC).

**ゆうせん**[7]【遊山】＝ユソン[2].

**ゆうぜん(ぞめ)**【友禅(染)】 ▫ 加賀[京]友禅 Kaga [Kyoto] yūzen; Kaga [Kyoto] printed「silk [muslin]. ◐ 京〜の着物 a kimono of Kyoto yūzen; a Kyoto printed「silk [muslin] kimono.

**ゆうたい**[5]【幽体】an astral body. ▫ 幽体離脱 astral projection; the projection of the astral body; astral travel. ◐ 〜離体験 an out-of-body experience (略: OBE).

**ゆうたいけん**[2]【遊体験】a hands-on experience. ▫ 遊体験施設 a hands-on facility.

**ゆうちょ**【郵貯】＝ゆうびんちょきん.

**ゆうちょぎんこう**【ゆうちょ銀行】Japan Post Bank Co., Ltd (略: JP Bank).

**ユー・ツー**【U2】〔アイルランドのロックバンド〕U2.

**ユー・ティー・エム・エス**【UTMS】〔警察庁開発の新交通管理システム〕UTMS; the Universal Traffic Management System.

**ユーティリティー** ▫ ユーティリティー・プレーヤー〔野球・サッカーなど〕〔いろいろなポジションをこなせる選手〕a utility player; a utility man.

**ゆうでんたい**【誘電体】 ▫ 誘電体層 a dielectric layer.

ゆうどう【誘導】▶□□ 誘導金利 a target interest rate. 誘導質問【心理】a leading question. 誘導水準〔金利などの〕a [the] target level 《for the uncollateralized overnight call rate》. 誘導灯〔交通誘導員が手に持つ〕an illuminated traffic control baton;〔空港滑走路に設置された〕a runway light;〔非常口などを示すために建物内に設けられた〕an emergency exit light; an exit sign. 誘導爆弾 a guided bomb. 誘導(用)ブロック a「leading [corduroy] block. 誘導雷〔直撃雷に対し、落雷時に発生する磁場による電磁誘導で発生する雷サージの一種などから電気機器に伝わる〕indirect lightning.
ユーノス【UNOS】〔全米臓器分配ネットワーク〕UNOS; the United Network for Organ Sharing.
ゆうパック【商標】〔一般小包郵便物配送サービスの愛称〕the "Yu-Pack" parcel delivery service.
ユー・ピー・オー・ブイ【UPOV】〔植物新品種保護国際同盟〕UPOV; the International Union for the Protection of New Varieties of Plants. ▶ UPOV はフランス語の Union internationale pour la protection des obtentions végétales の略. ▶□ UPOV 条約 the UPOV Treaty.
ゆうびん【郵便】▶□ 郵便受取代行(業)a mail-receiving service.〔＝私設私書箱(⇨しせつ1)〕郵便調査〔俗〕(conduct) a mail survey. 郵便証巳 a carrier for contents-certified mail. 郵便保険〔郵政事業の〕postal [post office] (life) insurance.
ゆうびんきょく【郵便局】▶□ 集配郵便局 a collection-and-delivery post office. 集配特定(郵便)局 a「special [privately-run] collection-and-delivery post office. 無集配郵便局 a non-collection-and-delivery post office. 無集配特定(郵便)局 a「special [privately-run] non-collection-and-delivery post office.
ゆうびんきょくかぶしきがいしゃ【郵便局株式会社】Japan Post Network Co., Ltd 《略: JP Network》.
ゆうびんじぎょうかぶしきがいしゃ【郵便事業株式会社】Japan Post Service Co., Ltd 《略: JP Post》.
ゆうびんちょきん【郵便貯金】▶□ 郵便貯金カード a「post office [postal] savings card.
ユー・ブイ²【UV】〔無人ビークル〕an unmanned vehicle.
ユーフォー【UFO】▶□ UFOキャッチャー〔ゲームセンターなどのクレーンゲームの一種〕a UFO catcher. ▶～キャッチャーの景品[人形]a UFO catcher「prize [doll].
ユーマ【UMA】〔未確認動物〕a mystery animal; a hidden animal. ▶ UMA は an unidentified mysterious animal の略とされるが、和製英語.
ゆうめい【有名】▶□ 有名どころ ▶□ 田舎から友人が上京したので都内の～ところを案内した. A friend of mine came up from the country, so I「took her around to the famous places in Tokyo [showed her the sights of Tokyo]. / クラシックはベートーヴェンやモーツァルトなど～どこしか知らない. The only classical music I know is「well-known pieces [standards] by the likes of Beethoven and Mozart.
ゆうめいむじつ【有名無実】▶□ 有名無実化 ▶□～化する become devoid of substance; come to exist in name only.
ゆうもん¹【幽門】▶□ 幽門閉鎖(症)【医】pyloric atresia. 幽門保存胃切除術【医】(a) pylorus-preserving gastrectomy 《略: PPG》.
ゆうよう¹【有用】▶□ 有用度 a「(high) degree of「usefulness [utility]; the「usefulness [utility]《of sth》.
ユーラシアかわうそ【─川獺】【動】a「European [Eurasian] (river) otter; Lutra lutra.
ゆうらん【遊覧】▶□ 遊覧コース an excursion route; a sightseeing course.
ゆうり¹【有利】▶□ 有利誤認(表示)〔景品表示法違反〕misrepresentation of《a product's》value. 有利発行【株】the「issue [issuing](of stock) at a discount from market price.

ゆうり⁴【遊離】▶□ 遊離骨【医】a「floating [free] bone. ▶～骨移植 a free bone graft; implantation of a floating bone /～骨弁 a「floating [free] bone flap. 遊離炭酸【化】free carbon dioxide.
ゆうりょう¹【有料】▶□ 有料サイト〔インターネットの〕a pay (Web) site.
ゆうりょう³【優良】▶□ 優良誤認(表示)〔景品表示法違反〕misrepresentation of《a product's》quality. ▶□ 有力馬〔競馬〕a favorite.
ゆうりょくかがくしゃどうめい[れんめい]【憂慮する科学者同盟[連盟]】〔米国の民間団体〕the Union of Concerned Scientists《略: UCS》.
ユーリンチー【油淋鶏】〔料理〕〔揚げ鶏に甘酢にからめた中華料理〕fried chicken「with [in] sweet-and-sour sauce.
ユーレップ・ギャップ【EUREPGAP】〔欧州小売業組合適正農業規範〕EUREPGAP. ▶ EUREP は Euro-Retailer Produce Working Group, GAP は Good Agricultural Practice の略.
ユーロネクスト〔ヨーロッパの証券取引所運営会社〕Euronext. ▶ パリ・アムステルダム・ブリュッセルの各証券取引所の合併によって設立.
ユーロビジョンおんがくさい【─音楽祭】the Eurovision Song Contest.
ユーロファイターにせん【─2000】〔英国・ドイツ・イタリア・スペイン共同開発の戦闘機〕a EuroFighter 2000.
ユーロポール〔欧州(刑事)警察機構〕Europol; the European Police Office.
ゆうわ²【融和】▶□ 融和姿勢 a「reconciliatory [conciliatory] attitude.
ゆえい【輸贏】gain or loss; victory or defeat. ▶～を争う contend《with each other》for「victory [supremacy].
ゆえん²【油煙】▶□ 油煙墨 inkstick made from burned-oil powder mixed with glue.
ユエン・ウーピン【袁和平】Yuen Woo-Ping (1945-  ; 中国生まれの映画監督).
ゆか¹【床】▶□ 床衝撃音【建】floor-impact sound. ▶ 軽量─衝撃音 a「light floor-impact sound /「重量─衝撃音 a heavy floor-impact sound. 床本〔太夫が見台の上に置く浄瑠璃の台本〕a jōruri text used by the narrator during a performance.
「ゆかいなブレディー家」〔米国の、子供向け TV ホームコメディー〕The Brady Bunch.
ゆかした【床下】▶□ 床下換気扇 an underfloor fan.
ゆがれ【湯枯れ】the drying up of a hot spring. ▶ 温泉ブームによる過剰な源泉掘削で、各地の温泉で～が起きている. Overdrilling of hot groundwater due to the spa boom has caused hot springs throughout the country to go dry.
ゆきどり【雪鳥】〔鳥〕〔ミズナギドリ科の海鳥〕a snow petrel; Pagodroma nivea.
ゆきれいぼう【雪冷房】snow cooling.
ゆけつ【輸血】▶□ 輸血医療 blood transfusion medicine. 輸血関連急性肺障害【医】transfusion-related acute lung injury《略: TRALI》. 輸血用血液 blood for transfusion. 輸血(用)ポンプ an infusion pump. 輸血療法 blood transfusion therapy. 輸血療法委員会〔各医療機関に設置されている〕a blood transfusion therapy committee.
ユコス【ロシアの石油会社】the Yukos Oil Company.
ゆさぶられ(っこ)しょうこうぐん【揺さぶられ(っ子)症候群】【医】shaken baby syndrome《略: SBS》.
ユシチェンコ ＝ユーシェンコ.
ゆしゅ【油種】a crude oil type; crude oil species.
ゆしゅつ【輸出】▶□ 輸出圧力 ▶□ 国内景気が悪くなると輸入が減少し、～圧力が強まる. When the domestic economy is doing badly, there is a tendency for exports to increase. / 途上国は農産物の対日～圧力を強めている. Developing countries are going to put in-

creasing pressure on Japan to import more agricultural products. 輸出競争力 export competitiveness. 輸出先 《a country》 to which 《corn》 is exported.
ゆしゅつそくしんしつ【輸出促進室】〔2004年に農水省に設置〕the Export Promotion Office.
ゆず【柚・柚子】▪️ 柚子酢 *yuzu* vinegar. ゆず大根【料理】*daikon* marinaded overnight in a sauce of *yuzu* juice, chopped *yuzu* peel, soy sauce, vinegar, sugar and sesame oil. ゆず茶 *yuzu* tea. ゆず風呂 a *yuzu* bath; a bath in which *yuzu* have been placed (to warm the body and prevent colds). 柚子湯 (a) *yuzu* bath.
ユスフ Yusuf, Abdullahi Ahmed (1934– ; ソマリアの政治家; 暫定政府大統領〔2004– 〕).
ゆせい¹【油井】▪️ 油井管 an oil well pipe
ゆせん¹【湯煎】▪️ 湯煎鍋 a water bath; a bain-marie.
ゆそう⁴【輸送】▪️ 輸送能力〔輸送力〕(build up) transportation [transport, carrying]; carrying [transit] power. 輸送袋 a (shipping) sack. 輸送ヘリ a「transportation [freight] helicopter.
ユソン¹【儒城】〔韓国, 大田市の行政区・温泉街〕Yusong.
ユソン²【遊仙】〔北朝鮮, 咸鏡北道の都市〕Yuson.
ゆだくじこたいさくきょうりょくじょうやく【油濁事故対策協力条約】the International Convention on Oil Pollution Preparedness, Response and Co-operation; the OPRC convention.
ゆだくそんがいばいしょうほしょうほう【油濁損害賠償保障法】〔法〕=せんぱくゆだくそんがいばいしょうほう.
ゆだくほう【油濁法】〔法〕=せんぱくゆだくそんがいばいしょうほしょうほう.
ユダヤじん【-人】▪️ ユダヤ人狩り〔ナチスドイツによる〕Jew hunting; a Jew hunt. ユダヤ人入植地 a Jewish settlement.
ゆっくりすべり【ゆっくり滑り】【地質】〔地殻変動の一種〕slow slippage; a slow slip.
ゆでん【油田】▪️ 油田やぐら an oil derrick; a derrick.
ユドヨノ Yudhoyono, Susilo Bambang (1949– ; インドネシアの政治家; 大統領〔2004– 〕).
ゆとり ▪️ ゆとり教育〔ゆとりのある教育〕education free from pressure; pressure-free education.
ユニオン Union, Gabrielle (1973– ; 米国の映画女優).
ユニタール【UNITAR】UNITAR. [⇨こくれんくんれんちょうさけんきゅうじょ]
ユニット ▪️ ユニット・ケア【福祉】〔老人ホームなどでの小グループ単位の介護方法〕unit care; care in small groups.
ユニバーサル ▪️ ユニバーサル・サービス〔郵便事業などの全国均質サービス〕《offer》「universal [nationwide] service. ユニバーサル社会 a society for「everyone [all people]. ユニバーサル・プレイジング〔だれもが楽しめる玩具〕a toy for「everyone [people of all ages].
ユニファイドきょうぎ【-競技】〔知的発達障害のある人がいない者が組んで行う競技〕Unified Sports; a Unified Sports event.
ユニファイド・メッセージング〔情報〕=統合メッセージング(⇨とうごう³).
ゆにゅう【輸入】▪️ 輸入解禁 lifting an import ban (on beef). 輸入価格 an import price. 輸入先 《a country》 from which 《petroleum》 is imported. 輸入証明書 (apply for) an import certificate; a proof of importation. 輸入浸透率 〔輸入と国内生産を合わせた供給全体に占める輸入の割合〕an import penetration ratio. 輸入数量指数 an import volume index. 輸入停止 (a) suspension of imports. ◐ 米国からの鶏肉の〜止に踏み切る take the step of halting the import of chicken meat from the United States. 輸入元 《a company》 that imports 《French wine》.
ユヌス Yunus, Muhammad (1940– ; バングラデシュの経済学者; グラミン銀行の設立者).

ユネスコ・アジアぶんかセンター【-文化-】〔財団法人〕the Asia/Pacific Cultural Centre for UNESCO (略: ACCU).
ユネスコせいふかんかいようがくいいんかい【-政府間海洋学委員会】the Intergovernmental Oceanographic Commission (略: IOC).
ユノカル〔米国の石油会社〕Unocal Corporation.
ゆばいほう【油賠法】〔法〕=せんぱくゆだくそんがいばいしょうほしょうほう.
ゆびえだはまさんご【指枝浜珊瑚】【動】〔沖縄以南に分布するハマサンゴ科のサンゴ〕*Porites cylindrica*.
ユビキタス ▪️ ユビキタス端末 a ubiquitous terminal.
ユビキチン ▪️ ubiquitin. ユビキチン化 ubiquitination. ユビキチン・プロテアソーム系 the ubiquitin-proteasome system.
ゆびさし【指差し】▪️ 指差し呼称〔喚呼〕pointing and calling.
ゆびまがりしょう【指曲がり症】【医】=ヘバーデンけっせつ.
ゆびもじ【指文字】〔手話の五十音〕the Japanese finger syllabary.
ゆぶん【油分】(an) oil content. ▪️ 無油分ファンデーション oil-free foundation.
ゆまく【油膜】▪️ 油膜取り〔用具・薬剤など〕an oil (film) remover; an oil skimmer; 〔行為〕oil (film) removal.
「ユマニテ」〔映画〕L'Humanite.
ゆめ¹【夢】▪️ 夢舞台 a "dream stage"; the「stage [venue] of one's dreams. ◐ 高校球児あこがれの〜舞台, 甲子園球場 Kōshien Stadium, the dream stage on which high school baseball players long to perform.
ゆめおち【夢落ち】〔物語の最後に至ってそれまでのすべては夢だったと判明する手法〕an "it was all a dream" ending; the ending of a story in which all turns out to have been a dream.
ゆめかさご【夢笠子】【魚】〔フサカサゴ科の海産魚〕a rockfish; *Helicolenus hilgendorfi*.
「夢の旅路」〔映画〕Animals.
ゆもみ【湯揉み】〔温泉の湯の温度を下げるため縦長の板でかき回すこと〕stirring hot spring bath water with a long wooden board to cool it.
「ゆりかごを揺らす手」〔映画〕The Hand That Rocks the Cradle.
ゆりもどす【揺り戻す】swing back. ◐ 右傾化している社会情勢を〜必要がある. Society needs to「recover from its current movement towards [swing back from] the right.
ユン Hung, Tran Anh (1962– ; ベトナム生まれのフランスの映画監督).
ユンカー² Juncker, Jean-Claude (1954– ; ルクセンブルクの政治家; 首相〔1995– 〕).
ユン・チアン〔張戎〕Jung Chang (1952– ; 中国生まれの英国の女性作家).
ユン・ピョウ【元彪】Yuen Biao (1957– ; 香港の映画俳優).
ユンリン【雲林】〔台湾中部の都市・県〕Yunlin.

# よ

**よう[4]【要】** ▭ 要援護者〔災害時の〕= 災害時要援護者（⇨さいがい[1]）.

**よういく【養育】** ▭ 養育家庭 a foster home; a household with foster children. 養育義務 an obligation [a duty] to provide childcare. ◐ ～義務放棄〔児童虐待の一種としての〕child neglect. 養育里親 a foster parent. 養育能力《lack》the「ability [competence]」to raise「a child [children]」 養育放棄〔児童虐待の一種としての〕child neglect.

**ようかいご【要介護】** ▭ 準要介護 some assistance required. 要介護1[5] required care level「1 [5]」 a required care level of「1 [5]」 要介護者 a person who requires nursing care. 要介護状態 a condition which requires nursing care. 要介護認定者 a person certified as requiring nursing care.

**ようがし【洋菓子】** ▭ 洋菓子職人 a pastry「chef [cook]」; a patissier.

**「八日目」**〔映画〕The Eighth Day;〔原題〕Le Huitieme jour.

**ようがん[2]【溶岩】** ▭ 溶岩浴 a "lava bath"; a "bedrock bath"; a health and beauty treatment for which people lie on heated rock slabs.

**ようぎしゃ【容疑者】** ▭ 容疑者不詳【死亡】 ◐ ～不詳［死亡］のまま書類送検する send the papers relating to a case to the Prosecutors Office even though the suspect is「unidentified [dead]」

**ようきほうそう【容器包装】**containers and packaging. ▭ 紙製容器包装 paper containers and packaging. プラスチック製容器包装 plastic containers and packaging. ▭ 容器包装ゴミ container and packaging「waste [garbage]」 容器包装プラスチック plastic for the「packing [packaging, wrapping]」of containers.

**ようきん[0]【楊琴】**〔中国の打弦楽器〕a yangqin.

**ようざい[2]【溶剤】** ▭ 水系溶剤 an aqueous solvent. 非水系溶剤 a nonaqueous solvent. 有機溶剤 an organic solvent.

**ようし[7]【陽子】** ▭ 陽子加速器 a proton accelerator. ◐ 大強度～加速器 a high-intensity proton accelerator. 陽子数 a proton number. 陽子線 a proton beam. ◐ ～線治療【医】proton beam therapy.

**ようし[9]【養子】** ▭ 海外養子 a child adopted (from) overseas. 芸養子〔歌舞伎など〕an adopted protégé. 両養子 ◐ 彼は両～を迎えて店をまかせた. He adopted a young man and woman, married them and left the management of the shop to them.

**ようじ[1]【幼児】** ▭ 幼児体形[体型] a「childish [prepubescent]」figure. 幼児用補助椅子〔自動車の〕an auxiliary seat (for a child).

**ようしえん【要支援】**requiring assistance. ▭ 要支援者 a person requiring assistance.

**ようしゃ【溶射】**metallizing; thermal spraying. ～する metallize; thermal-spray.

**ようじょう[1]【洋上】** ▭ 洋上給油 refueling [fuelling] at sea; marine refuelling. 洋上投票 voting (while) at sea; (on-)ship voting. ◐ 彼はインド洋上からファックスで～投票を行った. He cast his vote while at sea, by fax from the Indian Ocean.

**ようじょう[2]【葉状】** ▭ 葉状腫瘍【医】a phyllodes tumor.

**ようじょうばんぽう【羊城晩報】**〔中国・広州の夕刊紙〕the Yangcheng Evening News.

**ようしょく[5]【養殖】** ▭ 完全養殖〔魚介類の世代循環の全過程を人工管理下で行うこと〕complete aquaculture; producing《fish》by carrying out the entire life cycle artificially. ▭ 養殖いかだ a culture raft.

**ようすい[2]【羊水】** ▭ 人工羊水 artificial amniotic fluid.

**ようすこうかわいるか【揚子江河海豚】**【動】a Chinese river dolphin;（中国語名 バイジー）a baiji; *Lipotes vexillifer*. ▶ 絶滅が推定される種.

**ようすばんぽう【揚子晩報】**〔中国, 南京の夕刊紙〕the Yangtse Evening Post.

**ようせい[6]【陽性】** ▭ 陽性馬[鶏]【獣医】〔インフルエンザなどの〕an infected「horse [chicken]」; a「horse [bird]」 which tests positive for《horse [bird] flu》. 陽性率【医】〔感染症検査・がん検診などの〕a positive rate.

**ようせいぶ【楊成武】**Yang Chengwu (1914–2004; 中国の軍人).

**ようせつ[3]【溶接】** ▭ 溶接工学 welding (technology [engineering]). 溶接線 a「weld [welding] line [seam]」

**ようせん【陽線】**〔株式〕〔ローソク足チャートで, 上げ相場を示す白抜き四角〕a white body.

**ようそ[1]【沃素】** ▭ 沃素125 iodine-125.

**ようそ[2]【要素】** ▭ 要素所得〔経〕a factor income.

**ようそさんそ【溶存酸素】** ▭ 溶存酸素濃度 a dissolved oxygen concentration《of 5 ppm》. 溶存酸素飽和度 the proportion of dissolved oxygen. 溶存酸素量 the amount of dissolved oxygen.

**ようたい[5]【要胎】**〔四生児〕quadruplets;〔四生児の妊娠〕= 要胎妊娠. ▭ 要胎妊娠【医】(a) quadruplet pregnancy.

**ようだい[1]【容体・容態】** ▭ 容体悪化 a turn for the worse; (a) deterioration (in *sb's* condition). 容体急変 a sudden「turn [change]」for the worse; a sudden deterioration (in *sb's* condition).

**ようち[1]【用地】** ▭ 用地交渉 negotiations for site acquisition and compensation.

**ようちょうせき【葉長石】**【鉱】petalite.

**ようつい【腰椎】** ▭ 腰椎分離症【医】lumbar「spondylolisthesis [spondylolysis]」

**ようと[1]【用途】** ▭ 用途規制〔土地・建物などに対する〕restrictions [limitations] on the use of《land, etc.》.

**ようど[3]【揚土】**〔掘った土砂を上方に移すこと〕raising (excavated) earth and sand. 揚土機【機】a soil elevator. 揚土船 an unloader barge. 揚土ポンプ【機】a dredging pump.

**ようとちいき【用途地域】** ▭ 用途地域規制【都市計画】a zoning「regulation [restriction, control]」

**ようとん【養豚】** ▭ 養豚農家 a pig farmer.

**ようにん[2]【容認】** ▭ ドル安容認 acceptance of a weak dollar. ◐ 米財務長官はドル安～の発言を行った. The US Secretary of the Treasury said in a statement that「he [she]」would not intervene to protect the dollar. ▭ 容認可能性【文法】acceptability. 容認度【文法】acceptability; an acceptability rating. ◐ ～度の低い文 a sentence with low acceptability.

**ようほいちげんか【幼保一元（化）】** ▭ 保育一元・幼保一元特区 a special integrated-preschool district; a special district with integrated kindergartens and「daycare [day nurseries]」

**ようぼう[2]【容貌】** ▭ 容貌障害 (a) facial「disfigurement [deformity, difference]」

**ようほえん【幼保園】**a (combined) day nursery and kindergarten; a combined facility for infants of any age between birth and school entrance.

**ようやく[1]【要約】** ▭ 要約筆記奉仕員 a volunteer

「transcriber [notetaker].
ようゆう【溶融】 ▭ 溶融スラグ (a) vitreous slag; (a) glass slag.
ようり³【養鯉】 ▭ 養鯉業 carp farming. 養鯉業者 a carp farmer. 養鯉池 a carp culture pond.
ようりい【楊利偉】Yang Liwei (1965- ; 中国の宇宙飛行士).
ようりょう³【容量】 ▭ 容量オーバー〔電気回線などの〕an electrical overload;〔一般に, 許容量を上回ること〕an overload; an overflow; oversaturation; (an) excess.
ようりょく【揚力】 ▭ 高揚力装置《空》〔航空機の〕a high-lift device.
ようれん【溶錬】〔溶解・精錬〕smelting.
ヨー ⇨ ミッシェル・ヨー.
ヨーク York, Susannah (1941- ; 英国の映画女優; 本名 Susannah Yolande Fletcher).
ヨーダ〔映画『スター・ウォーズ』の登場人物〕Yoda.
ヨード ▭ ヨード樹脂【化】iodine resin.
ヨーロッパおおらいちょう【大雷鳥】〔鳥〕a (Western) capercaillie; *Tetrao urogallus*.
ヨーロッパきゅう【一級】《ヨットレース》the Europe class.
ヨーロッパなんてんてんもんだい【南天天文台】〔天〕the European Southern Observatory (略: ESO). ▶ ヨーロッパ 8 か国がチリに建設した南天観測施設.
ヨーロッパふうりょくエネルギーきょうかい【-風力-協会】=おうしゅうふうりょくエネルギーきょうかい.
ヨーロッパみなみてんもんだい【南天文台】〔天〕=ヨーロッパなんてんてんもんだい.
ヨーロッパやきゅうれんめい【野球連盟】〔国際野球連盟の加盟組織〕the Confederation of European Baseball (略: CEB).
ヨーロピアン・パーチ〔魚〕〔魚食性の淡水魚〕a「Eurasian [European] perch; *Perca fluviatilis*.
よき²【予期】 ▭ 予期不安《精神医》⇨ふあん.
よきん【預金】 ▭ 預金獲得 attracting deposits. ● ～獲得競争 competition to attract deposits. 預金流失〔金融機関からの〕a deposit drain; a drain「on [of] deposits.
よきんしゃほごほう【預金者保護法】《法》the Depositor Protection Law.
よくがん【浴玩】〔固めた入浴剤が湯の中で溶けると中から出てくる小型玩具; 風呂で遊ぶ玩具一般〕a bath(tub) toy.
よくげん【翼弦】《空》=げんちょう³.
よくさん【翼賛】翼賛選挙《日本史》〔1942 年の〕the "supported" general election (of 1942 in which voters were pressured into electing government-supported candidates).
よくしつ【浴室】 浴室玩具 a bath toy. 浴室乾燥機 a bathroom dryer. 浴室暖房 bathroom heating;〔器具〕a bathroom heater. ● ～暖房乾燥機 a bathroom heater (and) dryer.
よくじつ【翌日】 ▭ 翌日物《金融》〔翌日には返済する超短期貸し付け〕an overnight call. ● ～物金利 an overnight interest rate / ～物コールレート an overnight call rate.
よくじょう⁵【翼状】 ▭ 翼状片《眼科》a pterygium《*pl.* ～s, -ia》. ▷ pterygial *adj*.
ヨクト ‐[$10^{24}$ 分の 1] yocto- (略: y). ▭ ヨクト秒 a yoctosecond (略: ys).
よくどう【欲動】《心理》(a) drive.
よけん²【予見】 ▭ 予見可能性 predictability. 予見義務 a [the] duty of anticipation.
よこあつ【横圧】=おうあつ.
よこうけ【横請け】〔元請けが受注した注文を同業他社に回すこと〕a practice whereby a firm, having been contracted to do a job, contracts another firm in the same industry to perform the work.
よこく²【予告】 ▭ 予告先発投手《野球》an announced starting pitcher. 予告電話 an warning phone call.

● スタジアムを爆破するという～電話が各新聞社にあった. Newspapers received calls warning that a bomb would go off in the stadium.
よこぐわえ【横銜え】〔口の端にくわえること; 横にしてくわえること〕● 彼はたばこを～にしてキーボードをたたいていた. He was banging on the keyboard with a cigarette sticking out of the side of his mouth. ● カワセミが大きな魚を～にして枝にとまっていた. A kingfisher was perched on a branch with a big fish held sideways in its mouth.
よごし【汚し】1〔古さを出すために〕汚すこと〕making *sth* look「dirty [old, weathered]; aging; weathering. ● ～をかける〔古く見えるように加工[塗装]する〕treat *sth* to make *it* look old; apply「aging [weathering] treatment《to…》.
2《日本料理》〔和(え)物〕 ▭ 胡麻よごし《vegetables》dressed with ground sesame (seeds).
よごしとそう【汚し塗装】〔模型などの〕weathering;《give a model》a weathered effect.
よこすべり【横滑り】 ▭ 横滑り防止装置[機構]《自動車》electronic stability control (略: ESC). ▶ 自動車会社によってさまざまな名称で呼ばれている.
よこたくういき【横田空域】〔横田基地の管理下にある空域〕Yokota airspace.
よこだし【横出し】 ▭ 横出し条例 a broader regulation; an extension [a wider application] of the rules.
よこならび【横並び】 ▭ 横並び一線 ● ～一線だった上位 3 チームが, シーズン後半に入ってばらけはじめた. The top three teams, who were neck and neck, began to draw apart in the second half. 横並び社会 a conformist society.
よこばい【横ばい】 ▭ 低位[高位]横ばい〔価格・販売量などの〕levelling off《of prices》at a「low [high] level.
よこもれ【横漏れ】〔おむつ・生理用品などの〕leaking (a leak) at the edge(s); side leakage. ～する leak at the edge(s). ● このおむつは～を防ぐ工夫がしてある. These「diapers ["nappies] are designed to prevent leaking from the edges.
よさん【予算】 ▭ 修正予算〔補正後の予算〕a revised budget ● 予算化 budgeting《for…》. ● 警官の増員を～化する budget for an increase in police officers. 予算削減 budget cuts; cuts「in [to] a budget; a budget reduction; a reduction「in [of] appropriations; a reduced「budget [appropriation]《for capital equipment》. 予算執行 budget「implementation [execution]; implementation [execution] of a budget. ● ～執行権 the right to implement the budget / ～執行調査《財務省による》a budget execution survey. 予算分担金《国連》the《Japanese》assessment to the UN;《America's》assessed contribution to the UN budget.
よしきゅう【与四球】《野球》〔投手の〕walks given up.
よしだドクトリン【吉田-】《日本史》〔吉田茂首相が志向した戦後復興路線〕the Yoshida doctrine.
よしつねはっそうとび【義経八艘飛び】⇨はっそうとび.
よしゅく【予祝】〔民俗〕an advance blessing《of crops》. ▭ 予祝儀礼 an advance blessing ceremony《to ensure a good harvest》.
よじょう¹【余剰】 ▭ 余剰電力 surplus「electricity [power]. 余剰博士 a "surplus" PhD; a person with a doctorate who can't find a job.
よしん⁵【与信】 ▭ 与信供与 offering credit; an offer of credit. 与信行為 giving [granting] credit. 与信審査〔融資に先立っての〕a credit「check [review, screening].
よせ【寄席】 ▭ 寄席興行 a「vaudeville [variety] performance.
よせば【寄せ場】〔日雇い労働を希望する者が集まって仕事を斡旋してもらう場所〕an open-air (day) labor market.
よせばし【寄せ箸】pulling [moving] a plate with *one*'s

よそう

chopsticks.

**よそう¹【予想】** 〘名〙 予想インフレ率 an [the] anticipated rate of inflation. 予想進路〔台風などの〕the「expected [predicted, forecast] path《of a typhoon》. ► 進路図〔台風などの〕a forecast path map《for a typhoon》; a map of the「forecast [expected, predicted] path《of a typhoon》. 予想図 a forecast (image [drawing, diagram]).

**よそく【予測】** 〘名〙 予測精度 prediction accuracy. 予測得票数《a candidate's, a party's》forecast [predicted] share of the vote.

**よたく²【預託】** 〘名〙 預託株式 a「depositary [depository] share. ► 米国〜株式 American「Depositary [Depository] Shares ⇒ ADS」.

**よち¹【予知】** 〘名〙 短期予知〔数日から数週間以内に起こりうる地震などの〕(a) short-term《earthquake》prediction. 中期予知〔数年以内に起こりうる地震などの〕(a) medium-term《earthquake》prediction. 長期予知〔数十年から百年以内に起こりうる大規模地震などの〕(a) long-term《earthquake》prediction. 直前予知〔地震の〕(a) short-term prediction. 予知因子〔医〕a predictive factor《for breast cancer》.

**よっきゅう【欲求】** 〘名〙 欲求(5)段階説〔心理〕〔米国の心理学者 A・マズローの〕Maslow's hierarchy of needs.

**よっしゃ【承諾を表す間投詞】** Gotcha.; Got it.; Okay.

**よつだま【四つ玉】**〔キャロムビリヤードのゲームの一種〕four-ball.

**ヨット** ► ヨットウーマン a yachtswoman. ヨットマン a yachtsman.

**よつばマーク【四つ葉-】**〔車の前後に付ける身体障害者運転標識〕a "handicapped driver" sticker in the shape of a white four-leaf clover on a blue background attached to a car.

**よてい【予定】** 〘名〙 予定死亡率〔生命保険〕〔過去の死亡統計から将来の死亡者数を予測した値〕an expected mortality rate.

**よとう¹【与党】** 〘名〙 与党化 transformation (from the attitudes of an opposition party) to the ruling party. ► 総[オール]〜化は議会政治の健全な姿ではない。It is not healthy for parliamentary politics if all parties begin to act as if they are in power.

**よとうねんきんせいどかいかくきょうぎかい【与党年金制度改革協議会】**the Commission of the Ruling Parties on Pension System Reform.

**よなげや【淘げ屋】**a person who scours river garbage to recover metal (as a job).

**「世にも不思議な物語」**〔米国の，不可思議な出来事の一話完結の TV ドラマ〕One Step Beyond.

**よねつ²【余熱】** 〘名〙 余熱除去〔原子炉などの〕residual heat removal (略: RHR). ► 〜除去系統〔原子炉などの〕a residual heat removal system (略: RHRS) / 〜除去系配管〔原子炉などの〕residual heat removal piping / 〜除去ポンプ〔原子炉などの〕a residual heat removal pump.

**ヨハンソン** Johansson, Scarlett (1984- ; 米国の映画女優).

**よび【予備】** 〘名〙 予備自衛官 a member of the「SDF [Self-Defense Forces] reserve; SDF reserve personnel. 予備日〔予定がスケジュールどおりに運ばなかった場合のための〕an alternative date《for a「cancelled [rescheduled] event》; 〔野外行事が雨で流れた場合の〕a rain date.

**よびかけ【呼掛け】** 〘名〙 呼び掛け人 a personal making「an appeal [a proposal, a call]《for action》; a proposer.

**よほう【予報】** 〘名〙 1[3]か月予報 a「one-[three-]month (weather) forecast.

**よぼう¹【予防】** 〘名〙 一次［二次，三次］予防 ⇒いちじ², さんじ¹. 予防因子 a preventive factor. 予防給付〔介護の必要度がまだ比較的低い人を対象とする給付〕

《pay, receive》a preventive benefit. 予防効果 a「preventive [prophylactic] effect. 予防サービス〔介護の〕= 介護予防サービス (⇒かいご¹). 予防通所介護 ⇒つうしょ. 予防(的)投与[投薬]〔薬剤の〕preventive [prophylactic, preventative] medication; preventive administration《of a medication》. 予防訪問介護 ⇒ほうもんかいご. 予防ワクチン a preventive vaccine《against HIV》.

**よぼうせっしゅ【予防接種】** 〘名〙 任意予防接種 (a) voluntary vaccination.

**よみかき【読み書き】** 〘名〙 読み書き障害〔医〕reading and writing disorder.

**よむ²【読む】** 〘名〙 読む事典［辞典］a dictionary for perusing [browsing (in)]; a dictionary「you don't use merely as [which is more than simply] a reference tool.

**よめい【余命】** 〘名〙 余命告知 telling [informing] a patient how「long he is likely to live [how much time he has left].

**よやく【予約】** 〘名〙 予約サイト〔インターネット上の〕a reservation (Web) site. ► 旅行[宿泊]〜サイト a「travel [lodging] reservation [booking] (Web) site.

**よやとう【与野党】** 〘名〙 与野党逆転 a reversal (of power) between the ruling and opposition parties. 与野党協議 discussions [consultations] between the ruling and opposition parties.

**よゆう【余裕】** 〘名〙 余裕時分〔鉄道〕〔列車運行の遅れを吸収するために設定されている時間〕margin(s) [leeway] for delays.

**よりしろ【依代・憑代】**an object or animal occupied by a *kami*.

**よりょく【余力】** 〘名〙 生産余力 spare production capacity.

**「夜になるまえに」**〔映画〕Before Night Falls.

**よろく²【余録】**〔正式な文書には記載されなかった記録〕sth off the record; an off-(the-)record remark.

**よろん¹【世論】** 〘名〙 世論喚起 an awakening [arousal] of public opinion. 世論誘導 diversion of public opinion.

**よろんちょうさ【世論調査】** 〘名〙 討論[審議, 討議]型世論調査 a deliberative (opinion) poll.

**よわぶくむ【弱含む】**〔取引〕show bearish tendencies.

**「弱虫クルッパー」**〔米国の, 臆病なグレートデーン犬 Scooby-Doo とその飼い主たちによるミステリーものの TV ギャグアニメ〕Scooby-Doo, Where Are You!

**ヨンギ【燕岐】**〔韓国西部, 忠清南道の郡〕Yeongi.

**ヨンサン【龍山・竜山】**〔韓国, ソウル市内の地域〕Yongsan.

**「40歳の童貞男」**〔映画〕The 40-Year-Old Virgin.

**よんしゃくだま【四尺玉】**〔花火〕a (firework) shell「four *shaku* [about 120cm] in diameter. ► 〜の花火 a ball-shaped firework (with a shell four *shaku* in diameter).

**よんしんほう【四進法】** a「base-4 [quaternary] (numbering) system; base-4 [quaternary] numbering.

**よんたいりく【四大陸】** 〘名〙 the four continents. 〘名〙 四大陸選手権大会 the Four Continents Championship.

**よんふっかエチレンじゅし【四弗化-樹脂】**〔化〕polytetrafluoroethylene. [= ポリテトラフルオロエチレン]

**よんまるいちケー【401k】**〔給与天引き式確定拠出型年金; 米国内国歳入法 401 条の k 項から〕401 k (plan).

**よんろくつうたつ【四・六通達】**〔労働〕〔2001 年 4 月 6 日厚生労働省労働基準局長名で出された, 使用者の労働時間管理責任に関する通達〕a notification issued by the Ministry of Health, Labour and Welfare on April 6, 2001, concerning measures that employers should take to accurately ascertain employee working hours. [= サービスざんぎょうこんぜつ(の)つうたつ]

# ら

**ラージボールたっきゅう**【-卓球】〔大きな球で行う卓球〕large ball table tennis; a type of table tennis designed for older people, played with larger than normal balls.
**ラージャパクサ** =ラジャパクセ.
**ラーダ**〔ウクライナの議会〕the Rada. ◨ **中央[最高]ラーダ**〔国会〕the Central [Supreme] Rada; the Verkhovna Rada.
**ラート**[2]〖＜G〗〔2本の平行な鉄製の輪でできた運動器具を使って行うドイツ発祥のスポーツ〕rhönrad.
**ラービグ**〔サウジアラビアの紅海沿岸の都市〕Rabig.
**ラー・ブリ**(一)〔タイの地名ラチャブリの別称〕Rat Buri.
**ラーマン** Luhrmann, Baz (1962– ; オーストラリア生まれの映画監督).
**ラームカムヘンおうひぶん**【-王碑文】〔タイ，スコタイ王朝の〕King Ramkhamhaeng's inscription.
**ラーメン**[1]【拉麵】◨ **ラーメン・ライス**〔食堂の品目〕ramen served with rice; ramen and rice.
**ラーモア** Larmor, Joseph (1857–1942; アイルランドの物理学者).
**ラーモアしゅうはすう**[しんどうすう]【-周波数[振動数]】〔電〕the Larmor frequency.
**ライ**[3]〔釣り〕ライ角 the lie angle.
**らいえん**[3]【来園】a visit 《to a park》. ◨ **〜者** a visitor. **〜者数** the number of visitors.
**らいがい**[1]【来街】a visit 《to a shopping district》. **〜する** visit [come shopping at] 《a mall》. ◨ **来街者** a visitor; a shopper. **〜者数** the number of 「visitors [shoppers].
**らいがい**[2]【雷害】lightning damage.
**らいしょ**【来所】a visit 《to a laboratory》. ◨ **来所者** a visitor. **〜者数** the number of visitors.
**ライス**[2] **1** Rice, Anne (1941– ; 米国の小説家). **2** Rice, Condoleezza (1954– ; 米国の政治家; 大統領補佐官〔2001-05〕, 国務長官〔2005– 〕).
**ライズ**〔釣り〕〔魚がえさに食いつこうとして水面に浮いてくること〕a rise.
**ライセンシング**〔経営〕〔技術・ブランド・流通経路などの有償供与〕licensing.
**ライセンス** ◨ **ライセンス業務** licensing (services). **ライセンス供与**〔著作権・販売権などの〕licensing.
**ライゾール**〔商標・化〕〔殺菌消毒薬〕Lysol.
**ライソゾーム** ◨ **ライソゾーム**〔蓄積〕**病**〔医〕lysosomal (storage) disease.
**ライタ**〔インド風ヨーグルトサラダ〕raita.
**ライター**[2] ◨ **ターボ・ライター**〔火力の強いガスライター〕a turbo lighter; a windproof gas lighter.
**ライダー** ◨ **ライダーズ・ジャケット** a motorcycle jacket.
**ライダー**[2] Ryder, Winona (1971– ; 米国の映画俳優; 本名 Winona Laura Horowitz).
**ライダー・カップ**〔ゴルフ〕〔米国と欧州のチーム対抗戦〕the Ryder Cup.
**ライチャウ**〔ベトナム北西部の省〕Lai Chau.
**ライツプラン**〔株式〕〔新株予約権を利用した敵対的買収防衛策の仕組み〕a「shareholder [stockholder] rights plan. ◨ **事前警告型ライツプラン** a rights plan requiring prior notification to shareholders of large acquisition plans; a "poison pill" rights plan.
**ライト**[1] ◨ **ライト線**〔野球〕the right-field line. **〜線に見事なヒットを放った.** He pounded a solid hit「down [along] the left-field line.
**ライトノベル**〔主として少年少女向きの小説〕a novel for young adults; 〈集合的に〉young adult 「fiction [literature].
**ライト・ペン** Wright Penn, Robin (1966– ; 米国の映画女優).
**ライトマン** Reitman, Ivan (1946– ; チェコスロバキア生まれの米国の映画製作者・監督).
**ライナー 1** Reiner, Carl (1922– ; 米国の映画監督; 2の父). **2** Reiner, Rob (1945– ; 米国の映画監督・俳優; 本名 Robert Reiner; 1の子).
**ライナー**[1] ◨ **ライナー性** **〜性の打球[当たり]**〔野球〕a ball hit on a line; a liner; a line drive.
**ライノウイルス**〔医〕a rhinovirus.
**ライバル** ◨ **ライバル視** **彼は事あるごとに私を〜視する.** He looks upon me as his rival in everything.
**ライフ** ◨ **ライフ・イベント**〔結婚・出産・定年など人生の節目となる出来事〕a life event. **ライフ・スキル**〔日常生活上の諸問題に適切に対処する能力; 生きる力〕life skills; a life skill. **ライフ・タスク**〔生涯課題〕a [one's] life task; one's life's work. 「**ライフ・イズ・ビューティフル**」〔映画〕Life Is Beautiful; 〔原題〕La Vita e Bella. 「**ライフ・オブ・デビッド・ゲイル**」〔映画〕The Life of David Gale.
**ライフ・マスク**〔生者の面型〕a life mask.
**ライブリー・ボール**〔野球〕〔よく飛ぶボール〕a lively ball; a rabbit ball.
**ライフリンク** =じさつたいさくしえんセンター・ライフリンク.
**ライフリング**〔銃砲〕〔弾丸に回転を与えるため銃身内に刻まれた何本かの螺旋(らせん)状の溝; その溝を付ける作業; 施条(しじょう)〕rifling. ◨ **ライフリング・マーク**〔発射された銃弾に残る施条痕〕a rifling mark.
**ライフル** ◨ **ライフルマーク**〔発射された銃弾に残る施条痕〕a rifling mark.
「**ライフルマン**」〔勧善懲悪と父子の愛情をテーマにしたTV西部劇〕The Rifleman. ▶ 主演 チャック・コナーズ (Chuck Connors).
**ライヘ** Reiche, Maria (1903-98; ドイツ人の, ペルーのナスカ地上絵の研究家).
**ライミ** Raimi, Sam (1959– ; 米国の映画監督; 本名 Samuel M. Raimi).
**ライミス** Ramis, Harold (1944– ; 米国の映画監督・俳優).
**らいゆう**【来遊】◨ **来遊量**〔数〕〔漁業〕〔回遊魚の〕the number of 《fish》 migrating back to 《local waters》. **〜シラスウナギの〜量は減少の一途だ.** The number of elvers migrating back (to Japanese waters) is decreasing steadily.
**らいよぼうほう**【らい予防法】〔法〕the Leprosy Prevention Law. ▶ 1996年廃止.
「**ライラの冒険**」〔英国作家 フィリップ・プルマン (Philip Pullman) 作の児童読み物〕His Dark Materials. ▶「**黄金の羅針盤**」(The Golden Compass), 「**神秘の短剣**」(The Subtle Knife), 「**琥珀の望遠鏡**」(The Amber Spyglass) の全3巻.
「**ライラの冒険 黄金の羅針盤**」〔映画〕The Golden Compass.
**ライン** Lyne, Adrian (1941– ; 英国生まれの映画監督).
**ライン**[1] ◨ **ライン際**〔スポーツで〕the edge of the line; the line's edge. **〜の鋭いショットを**〔テニス〕hit a hard shot down the edge of the line / **〜際の打球をダイビングキャッチする**〔野球〕make a diving catch 「dive and catch a hit] on the baseline / **〜際をドリブルで上がる**〔サッカー〕dribble upfield along the line.

**ラインアップ**　□① ラインアップ表〔野球〕〔スターティングメンバーのリスト〕a lineup card.
**ラインフェルト**　Reinfeldt, John Fredrik (1965– ；スウェーデンの政治家；首相 [2006– ]).
**ラヴ**　Love, Courtney (1965– ；米国の映画女優).
**ラヴァリエール**　**1** Louise de La Vallière (1644–1710; フランス王ルイ 14 世の愛人).
　**2** ＝ラバリエール.
**ラヴァルマナナ**　Ravalomanana, Marc (1949– ；マダガスカルの政治家；大統領 [2002– ]).
「**ラヴェンダーの咲く庭で**」〔映画〕Ladies in Lavender.
**ラウターバー**　Lauterbur, Paul (1929–2007; 米国の化学者).
**ラウレンティス**　Laurentiis, Dino De (1919– ；イタリア出身の映画製作者).
**ラウンド**
　**2**〖ゴルフ〗a round. 〜する play a round. ◐ 1 日に 2 〜する play two rounds a day. ◐ 〜中は水分を摂(と)るように心がけましょう. Be careful that you take enough fluid 「while you are playing [on the course, during the round].
　**3**〔多角的な通商交渉〕a round (of 「talks [negotiations]」).
　□■ 練習ラウンド〖ゴルフ〗a 「practice [warm-up] round. □■ ラウンドガール〔ボクシングなどの試合でラウンドの合間に次のラウンド数を示したカードを掲げてリング上を回るマスコットガール〕a round card girl; a ring girl. ラウンド・レポーター〖ゴルフ〗an on-site golf-round reporter.
**ラオバオ**　〔ベトナム中部, ラオスとの国境の町〕Lao Bao.
**らかんか**〔羅漢果〕〔植〕〔中国原産, ウリ科の多年草〕a luo han guo; *Siraitia grosvenorii*.
**らくさつ**〔落札〕□① 落札額〔落札価格〕a 「contract [bid-winning] price; the amount of a successful tender; a 「winning [successful] bid price. 落札業者 a successful bidder. 落札者キャンセル詐欺〔インターネットオークションなどでの〕a "canceled-bid scam"; "Internet auction fraud by which an unsuccessful bidder is tricked into making immediate payment because the winning bidder is said to have withdrawn. 落札予定業者〔談合による〕a company selected, through collusion, to succeed in a bidding competition. 落札率〔予定価格に対する実際の落札価格の割合〕a bid ratio; the ratio of the winning bid to the scheduled price. ◐ 〜率が 98% を超えるなんて, 談合があったとしか思えない. A bid ratio of over 98% can mean only one thing: bid-rigging. 落札利回り〔国債などの〕a contract yield (of government bonds). ◐ 最高〜利回り / 平均〜利回り an average contract yield / an average maximum contract yield.
**らくせつ**[2]〔落雪〕□■ 落雪屋根 a steep roof (in a snowy region).
**ラクトスクロース**〖生化〗〔乳化オリゴ糖〕lactosucrose.
**ラクトトリペプチド**〖生化〗lactotripeptide (略: LTP).
**ラクナ**〖医〗ラクナ梗塞(こうそく) (a) lacunar infarction.
**ラグナ**〔フィリピン, ルソン島にある州〕Laguna.
**ラグマン**〔アフガニスタン東部の州〕Laghman.
**らくらい**〔落雷〕□■ 落雷死 death by lightning; being 「getting」 killed by lightning. ◐ 先月〜死が 4 件あった. There were four deaths from 「Four people were killed by」 lightning last month.
**ラコステ**〔商標〕〔ワニのマークの衣料品・香水など〕Lacoste.
**ラザリあん**〔〜案〕〔国連安全保障理事会の改革案の 1 つ〕the Razali 「Plan [plan, proposals]. ▶ マレーシアのラザリ (Razali Ismail) 国連大使が 1997 年提案した改革案. 常任理事国を 5 か国, 非常任理事国を 4 か国増やし, 24 か国に拡大するというもの.
**ラジオ**　□■ ラジオネーム〔視聴者がラジオに出した投書を読むなどの際の筆名〕a pseudonym used when 「writing (in) [calling in] to a radio program. ラジオ波〖医〗a radio-frequency wave (略: RF). ◐ 〜波焼灼療法〔凝固治〕〖医〗radio-frequency ablation (略: RFA) / 〜波治療〖医〗＝ラジオ波焼灼療法.
**ラジオじゆうアジア**【〜自由〜】〔米国の政府系放送局〕Radio Free Asia (略: RFA).
**ラジオ・フリー・アジア**　＝ラジオじゆうアジア.
**ラジャー**〖通信〗〔了解〕roger.
**ラジャパクサ**　＝ラジャパクセ.
**ラジャパクセ**　Rajapakse, Mahinda (1945– ；スリランカの政治家；大統領 [2005– ]).
**ラシカル・ガー**〔アフガニスタン南部, ヘルマンド州の州都〕Lashkar Gah.
**ラシュカレトイバ, ラシュカレタイバ**〔パキスタンのイスラム過激派組織〕the Lashkar-e-Toiba; the Lashkar-e-Taiba (略: LeT).
**ラシュト**〔イラン北西部, ギラン州の州都〕Rasht.
**ラスカーしょう**〔〜賞〕〔米国の医学研究賞〕a Lasker Award; 〔個々の賞をさして〕the Lasker Awards.
**ラス・スルタン**〔エジプト, シナイ半島東部のリゾート地〕Rasu Sultan.
**ラスタファリアニズム**〔ジャマイカで生まれた宗教・社会運動〕Rastafarianism; Rasta. ◐ 〜の信者 a Rastafarian (*pl.* 〜s; -fari).
**ラスタファリズム**　＝ラスタファリアニズム.
**ラ・スタンパ**〔イタリアの日刊紙〕La Stampa.
**ラスティー・クレイフィッシュ**〔動〕〔ザリガニの一種〕a rusty crayfish; *Orconectes rusticus*.
**ラステリしゅじゅつ**〔〜手術〕〖医〗〔心臓血管手術の 1 つ〕the Rastelli procedure.
「**ラストキング・オブ・スコットランド**」〔映画〕The Last King of Scotland.
「**ラスト, コーション**」〔映画〕Lust, Caution; 〔中国語タイトル〕色, 戒.
「**ラストサマー**」〔映画〕I Know What You Did Last Summer. ▶ 続編は「ラストサマー2」(I Still Know What You Did Last Summer).
「**ラストサムライ**」〔映画〕The Last Samurai.
**ラストほう**〔RAST 法〕〖医〗〔放射性アレルギー源吸収試験〕RAST; a radioallergosorbent test.
「**ラストマン・スタンディング**」〔映画〕Last Man Standing.
**ラスムセン**　**1** Rasmussen, Anders Fogh (1953– ；デンマークの政治家；首相 [2001– ]).
　**2** Rasmussen, Knud Johan Victor (1879–1933; デンマークの北極探検家・民族学者).
　**3** Rasmussen, 「Poul [Paul] Nyrup (1943– ；デンマークの政治家；首相 [1993–2001]).
**らぞく**〔裸族〕a naked tribe.
**ラダー・レース**〔はしご状の編み目のレース〕ladder lace.
**ラタナ・キリ**〔カンボジア北東部の州〕Ratana Kiri.
**らち**[2]〔拉致〕拉致議連 the Parliamentary League for Early Repatriation of Japanese Citizens Kidnapped by North Korea. ▶ 正式名称は「北朝鮮による拉致された日本人を早期に救出するために行動する議員連盟」. 拉致疑惑 the suspicion of 「abducting [kidnapping]」(Japanese citizens); 「(a case of) suspected 「abduction [kidnapping]. 拉致認定 (official) identification as a victim of abduction; (officially) listing *sb* as having been 「abducted [kidnapped].
**ラチェット**　□■ ラチェット死亡保障〔保険〕〔生命保険の〕a ratchet benefit.
**ラジオプレス**〔日本の通信社〕the Radio Press (略: RP).
**らちひがいしゃかぞくれんらくかい**【拉致被害者家族連絡会】＝きたちょうせんによるらちひがいしゃぞくれんらくかい.
**らちひがいしゃしえんほう**〔拉致被害者支援法〕〔法〕the Law for the Provision of Support to Victims of Abduction.
**ラチャブリ**　**1**〔タイ中部の県〕Ratchaburi.

2 〔タイ中部の都市, ラチャブリ県の県都〕 Ratchburi.
**ラチャン** Racan, Ivica (1944-2007; クロアチアの政治家; 首相〔2000-2003〕).
**らっか**¹【落下】▫️ 落下塔【物】〔人工的に無重力状態を現出するための設備〕a drop「tower [tube].
**らっかん**²【楽観】▫️ 楽観ムード an optimistic mood. ❶人質の1人が解放され, 捜査本部に事件解決に向けての〜ムードが広がっている. With one of the hostages released, optimism for a resolution of the incident has been growing at the investigation center.
**ラッキー** ▫️ ラッキー・アイテム a [one's] good-luck charm. ラッキー・カラー one's lucky color. ラッキー・パンチ〔ボクシング〕《(land)》a lucky punch.
「**ラッキー・ブレイク**」〔映画〕Lucky Break.
**らっきょう**²【落橋】a bridge collapse; the collapse of a bridge; 〔落ちた橋〕a collapsed bridge. 〜する collapse. ▫️ 落橋防止装置 a bridge collapse prevention unit.
**ラックザー**〔ベトナム南部, キエンザン省の省都〕Rach Gia.
**ラッシュ** Rush, Geoffrey (1951- ; オーストラリア生まれの映画俳優).
**ラッシュ**¹ ▫️ 結婚ラッシュ a「rush [spate] of marriages. ❶去年から有名芸能人の結婚〜が続いている. Since last year there has been a spate of marriages among showbiz celebrities. ゴールドラッシュ a「rush [flood, deluge, spate] of goals. ❶チームは後半, 怒濤のゴール〜で逆転勝ちした. With a tremendous flood of goals in the second half, our team came from behind to win the game. 出産ラッシュ a「spate [flood, rush] of births; a baby boom. ❶動物園では出産〜を迎えています. Our zoo is facing a baby boom. /最近, 私のまわりでは出産〜だ. Recently there has been a spate of new babies around me. 忘年会ラッシュ the end-of-year party rush; a「rush [spate] of year-end parties. ❶12月に入ってから忘年会〜だ. Once into December, it's the end-of-year party rush. メダルラッシュ a「flood [deluge, rush, spate] of medals. ❶メダル〜に日本中が沸いている. 〔オリンピックなどで〕The whole country is seething with excitement at Japan's deluge of medals.
**ラッセル** 1 Russell, Jay (1960- ; 米国の映画監督).
2 Russell, Kurt (1951- ; 米国の映画俳優; 本名 Kurt Vogel Russell).
**ラッセン** Lassen, Christian Riese (1956- ; 米国の画家・イラストレーター).
「**ラッチョ・ドローム**」〔映画〕Latcho Drom.
「**ラット・パトロール**」〔アフリカ戦線における米陸軍警邏(けいら)隊のTVドラマ〕Rat Patrol. ▶「砂漠鬼部隊」の邦題でも放映.
「**ラットレース**」〔映画〕Rat Race.
**ラップこうざ**【-口座】〔金融資産の運用・管理を一括提供するサービス〕a wrap account; a separately managed account (略: SMA).
**ラップリ(一)** =ラ〜ブリ(一).
**ラッフルズ・ホテル**〔シンガポール最古のホテル〕The Raffles Hotel.
**らっぽくしゃ**【拉北者】a South Korean abductee; an abducted South Korean; a South Korean abducted to North Korea.
**らっぽくしゃかぞくのかい**【拉北者家族の会】〔韓国の北朝鮮による拉致被害者家族の会〕the Coalition of South Korean Families of Abductees.
**ラティフィヤ**〔イラク, バグダッド南方の町〕Latifiyah.
**ラテらん**【-欄】〔新聞のラジオとテレビの番組表のページ〕the TV and radio listings.
**ラドクリフ** Radcliffe, Daniel (1989- ; 英国生まれの映画俳優).
**ラトナー** Ratner, Brett (1970- ; 米国の映画監督).
**ラドフォード** Radford, Michael (1946- ; インド生まれの映画監督・脚本家).

**ラトルチュ** Latortue, Gérard (1934- ; ハイチの政治家; 首相〔2004-06〕).
**ラノーン**〔タイ南部の県; その県都〕Ranong.
**ラノン** =ラノーン.
**ラバー**² ▫️ ラバー・カップ〔長柄の付いた半球形ゴムカップ; 排水管詰まり除去器具〕a plunger; a plumber's helper.
**らはつ**【螺髪】=らほつ.
**ラバリエール**〔Y字型のネックレス〕a lavaliere. [➡ラヴァリエール]
**ラヒーミー** Rahimi, Atiq (1962- ; アフガニスタン出身の作家).
**ラヒーモフ** Rakhimov, Murtaza (1934- ; バシコルトスタンの政治家; 大統領〔1993- 〕).
**ラピタ** ▫️ ラピタ人〔人類史上初めて遠洋航海を実践し太平洋の島々に住み着いたと思われる民族〕〈集合的に〉the Lapita (people). ラピタ文化 (the) Lapita culture.
**ラビット** 1〔ウサギ〕a rabbit.
2〔長距離競技で先導役をつとめるペースメーカー〕a rabbit.
**ラピュータ**〔スウィフト作の『ガリヴァー旅行記』に出てくる空飛ぶ島〕Laputa. ▷ Laputan adj., n.
**ラピュタ** =ラピュータ.
**ラヒリ** Lahiri, Jhumpa (1967- ; 英国生まれの作家).
**ラファ**〔ガザ地区南部の町〕Rafah.
「**ラブ・アクチュアリー**」〔映画〕Love Actually.
**ラファラン** Raffarin, Jean-Pierre (1948- ; フランスの政治家; 首相〔2002-05〕).
「**ラブ・アンド・ウォー**」〔映画〕In Love and War.
**ラフード** Lahoud, Emile (1936- ; レバノンの政治家; 大統領〔1998-2007〕).
**ラフェルソン** Rafelson, Bob (1934- ; 米国の映画監督).
**ラ・フォル・ジュルネ**〔フランス北西部の港町ナントで, 1995年に誕生したクラシック音楽祭〕La Folle Journee 《(au Japon)》.
**ラブカナルじけん**【-事件】〔1978年の米国での土壌汚染事件〕the Love Canal incident.
**ラブコメ**〔ラブコメディー〕(a) romantic comedy. ❶〜の女王 the [a] queen of (the) romantic comedy; the [a] Queen of (the) Romantic Comedy; a「romantic comedy queen [Romantic Comedy Queen].
**ラフテー**〔料理〕〔沖縄の豚の角煮〕rafute; Okinawan stewed pork cubes.
**ラフト** Rafto, Thoroff (1922-86; ノルウェーの経済学者・人権活動家).
**ラフトじんけんしょう**【-人権賞】the Professor Thoroff Rafto Memorial Prize; the Rafto Human Rights Prize.
**ラブ・ドラッグ**〔合成麻薬MDAの通称〕the love drug. [➡エム・ディー・エー]
**ラプラプ**〔フィリピン, マクタン島の都市〕Lapu-Lapu.
**ラブリ(一)** ▫️ ラブリー(理)【理】〔社会〕labeling theory.
**ラブロック** Lovelock, James Ephraim (1919- ; 英国の科学者; 「ガイア仮説」の提唱者).
**ラベリング(理)**【理】〔社会〕labeling theory.
**ラベロマナナ** =ラヴァルマナナ.
**らほつ**【螺髪】〔仏像の頭部の髪型〕rahotsu; rahatsu; a spiral curl, symbolic of enlightenment, on the head of a Buddhist statue.
**ラボック**〔米国テキサス州北西部の都市〕Lubbock.
**ラマディ**〔イラク, バグダッド西方の都市〕Ramadi.
**ラマラ**〔ヨルダン川西岸のパレスチナ自治区の市〕Ramallah.
**ラミナリア・コラリナ**〔ティモール海にある油田・ガス田〕Laminaria-Corallina.
**ラミン**¹【生化】lamin.
**ラミン**²【植】〔ジンチョウゲ科の広葉樹; 東南アジア原産〕(a) ramin; *Gonystylus bancanus*; ❶ラミン材 ramin (wood).
**ラム**⁶【LAM】【医】=エル・エー・エム.
**ラムサールしょう**【-賞】〔国際的に重要な湿地の保全に貢献した個人・団体に贈られる賞〕the Ramsar Award.

ラムズフェルド Rumsfeld, Donald H. (1932- ；米国の政治家；国防長官〔1975-77, 2001-06〕).
ラムドン〔ベトナム南部の省〕Lam Dong.
ラムネ ▫️ ラムネ菓子 semihard tart ["candy ["sweets].
ラムノ(一)〔インドネシア, アチェ州の町〕Lamno.
ラムバ(一)ン ＝ランバーン.
ラムブ(一)ン ＝ランブーン.
ラメ¹ ▫️ ラメ・ツイード (a) lamé tweed.
ラヨ(一)ン〔タイ中部の県；その県都〕Rayong.
「ララミー牧場」〔孤児の兄弟とガンマンが悪徳地主たちと闘うTV 西部劇〕Laramie. ▶ 主演 ロバート・フラー (Robert Fuller).
ラリアート《プロレス》〔腕の内側で相手の頸部を打つ技〕a lariat.
「ラリー・フリント」〔映画〕The People vs. Larry Flynt.
ラ・リオハ〔スペイン北部の自治州〕La Rioja; the Rioja.
ラレード ＝ラレド.
ラレド〔米国テキサス州南部の都市〕Laredo.
ラ・レプブリカ〔イタリアの日刊紙〕La Repubblica.
ラロニダーゼ〔薬〕〔ムコ多糖症治療薬〕laronidase.
ラン¹【LAN】 ▫️ 校内〔学内〕LAN a school [an in-school] LAN; an internal LAN in a [school [college]. ▫️ LAN カード a LAN card. LAN ボード a LAN board.
らんおう〔卵黄〕 ▫️ 卵黄コリン〔生化〕egg yolk phosphatidylcholine (略：EYPC).
ラン・カーブ《鉄道》〔運転曲線(図)〕a speed profile; a speed-distance diagram.
ランカウイとう〔-島〕〔マレーシア西海岸の島〕Langkawi Island.
らんかく²〔卵殻〕 ▫️ 卵殻カルシウム eggshell calcium. 卵殻手(で)〔極薄の陶器〕eggshell china. 卵殻膜 (an) eggshell membrane.
らんかん¹〔卵管〕 ▫️ 卵管鏡〔医〕a falloposcope. ▫️ 〜鏡検査 a falloposcopic examination. 卵管通水(法)〔医〕(a) hydrotubation.
ランギタイキがわ〔-川〕〔ニュージーランド北島の川〕the Rangitaiki River; the Rangitaiki.
「乱気流 タービュランス」〔映画〕Turbulence.
ランギロアとう〔-島〕〔フランス領ポリネシアの環礁〕Rangiroa Atoll.
ランキン Rankin, Ian (1960- ；英国の小説家).
ラングホブデ〔南極大陸の露岩地帯の1つ〕Langhovde.
ラングレン Lundgren, Dolph (1959- ；スウェーデン生まれの映画俳優；本名 Hans Lundgren).
ランコム〔商標〕〔フランスの化粧品ブランド〕Lancôme.
ランサ〔インドネシア, アチェ州の都市, 東アチェ州の県都〕Langsa.
ランジェリー ▫️ ランジェリー・パブ a lingerie pub; a bar where the hostesses dress in lingerie.
らんしゅうひ〔乱収費〕〔中国〕〔地方自治体などによる法的根拠のない料金徴収〕arbitrary collection of fees and charges (by local officials).
ランスウッド〔植〕〔ニュージーランド原産のウコギ科の落葉樹〕a lancewood; *Pseudopanax crassifolius*.
ランズベリー Lansbury, Angela (1925- ；英国生まれの映画女優).
「ランセット」〔英国の医学雑誌〕The Lancet.
らんそう【卵巣】 ▫️ 卵巣欠落(症状)〔医〕ovarian failure; anovulation.
ランダム ▫️ ランダム化(比較)試験〔医〕〔複数の治療法・薬剤などの〕a randomized controlled trial (略：RCT).
ランダム・スティープ・アプローチ〔空〕〔急角度で旋回する特殊な離着陸方法〕a random steep approach.
「ランダム・ハーツ」〔映画〕Random Hearts.
ランダムプレー《野球》＝挟殺プレー(⇨きょうさつ).
ランチ² ▫️ ランチ難民 ＝昼食難民 (⇨ちゅうしょく). ランチメイト症候群〔会社員などが昼食を一人でとることに対して抱く不安感〕the (loss-of-)lunch-mate(s) syndrome; a psychological condition attributed to the strain of being deprived of the company of *one's* customary lunchtime companions.
ランツゲマインデ〔スイスの州民集会；青空議会〕a Landsgemeinde 《*pl.* -den》.
ランティシ Rantisi, Abdel Aziz (1947-2004)；イスラム原理主義組織ハマスの創設者の一人；精神的指導者).
ランディス Landis, John (1950- ；米国の映画俳優・監督).
ランデブー ▫️ ランデブー技術〔宇宙〕(autonomous) rendezvous technology.
らんとう¹〔乱闘〕 ▫️ 乱闘手当〔国会開会中, 勤労の強度が著しい事務に従事した国会職員に対して支給する手当〕a "scuffle allowance"; an allowance paid to Diet staff for dangerous work during periods of political tension. 乱闘服〔機動隊員の〕(a) riot uniform; riot wear.
ランドー Landau, Martin (1931- ；米国の映画俳優).
ランドリー ▫️ ホームランドリー ＝洗濯乾燥機 (⇨せんたく).
ランドルトかん〔-環〕〔眼科〕〔視力検査用の C の環〕the Landolt "ring [C].
ランドルフ Randolph, John (1915-2004)；米国の俳優).
ランドンゆでん〔-油田〕〔ベトナムの海上油田〕the Rang Dong oilfield.
ランナー ▫️ ランナー膝〔医〕runner's knee; chondromalacia.
ランニング ▫️ ランニング・ターゲット〔射撃〕〔移動する標的〕a running target;〔種目〕the 《10 meter》running target.
ランネート〔商標・薬〕〔農薬〕Lannate. ▶ 一般名 メソミル.
ランバー・サポート〔自動車〕〔シート背もたれに設けた腰部疲労軽減のための支持部〕a lumbar support.
ランバート Lambert, Christopher (1957- ；米国の映画俳優；本名 Christophe Guy Dénis Lambert).
ランパン〔タイ北部の県；その県都〕Lampang.
ランパブ ＝ランジェリー・パブ (⇨ランジェリー).
ランパン ＝ランバーン.
ランファルシーきじゅん〔-基準〕〔金融〕the Lamfalussy standards.
ランプーン²〔タイ北部の県；その県都〕Lamphun.
ランプス〔スポーツ〕〔パラリンピック競技のボッチャで使用される投球補助具〕a ramp.
ランプフィッシュ〔魚〕〔北大西洋産の硬骨魚〕a lumpfish; a lumpsucker; *Cyclopterus lumpus*.
ランプリング Rampling, Charlotte (1945- ；イギリス出身の映画女優).
ランブルべんもうちゅうしょう〔-鞭毛虫症〕〔医〕＝ジアルジアしょう.
ランプン ＝ランプーン.
ランベオサウルス〔古生物〕〔頭部のとさか状突起が特徴のハドロサウルス科の草食恐竜〕a lambeosaurus;〔亜科名〕*Lambeosaurus*.
らんほう〔卵胞〕 ▫️ 卵胞刺激ホルモン〔生化〕(a) follicle-stimulating hormone (略：FSH).
らんぼう〔乱暴〕 ▫️ 乱暴行為《スポーツ》〔サッカーなどでの〕(an act of) violence.
蘭方医〔江戸時代の, オランダ流医学を学んだ医者〕an Edo-period doctor "whose treatment was based on [trained in] Dutch medicine.
ランボルギーニ〔商標〕〔イタリアの高性能スポーツカー〕Lamborghini.
らんゆ〔卵油〕egg-yolk oil.
らんよう〔濫用・乱用〕 ▫️ 乱用的買収 an abusive takeover. 乱用的買収者 an abusive acquirer.

# り

リアクション ▢ リアクション・ホイール 〖宇宙〗〔人工衛星などの姿勢制御に使われる回転輪〕a reaction wheel.
リア・フォグランプ 〖自動車〗〔後部用のフォグ・ランプ〕a rear fog「light [lamp]」.
リアプロ =リア・プロジェクションテレビ (⇨リア・プロジェクション).
リア・プロジェクション 1 〖映〗〔俳優の背後に置いたスクリーンに後ろ側から風景などの映像を投射する技法〕rear projection.
2 〔ホームシアターで, スクリーンに後ろ側から映像を投射する方式〕rear projection. ▢ リア・プロジェクション・エフェクト 〖映〗a rear-projection effect. リア・プロジェクションテレビ〔背面投射型テレビ〕a rear-projection「television [TV]」.
リアルタイム ▢ リアルタイム地震情報システム a real-time earthquake information system. リアルタイム防災 real-time disaster prevention.
リアル・マネー・トレード〔仮想ゲーム内の物品を現実の貨幣で売り買いすること〕real money trading; real money trade; a real money transaction; RMT.
リー 1 Lee, Spike (1957- ; 米国の映画監督; 本名 Shelton Jackson Lee).
2 Leigh, Janet (1927-2004; 米国の映画女優).
3 Leigh, Jennifer Jason (1962- ; 米国の映画女優; 本名 Jennifer Lee Morrow).
4 Leigh, Mike (1943- ; 英国の映画監督).
リーヴス Reeves, Keanu (1964- ; レバノン生まれカナダ育ちの映画俳優; 本名 Keanu Charles Reeves).
リーグ ▢ リーグ優勝 a league「victory [championship, pennant]」. ▢ ~優勝を果たす clinch the league championship.
「リーグ・オブ・レジェンド／時空を超えた戦い」〖映画〗 The League of Extraordinary Gentlemen.
リー・シェンロン【李顕龍】Lee Hsien Loong (1952- ; シンガポールの政治家; リー・クアン・ユーの子; 首相〔2004- ]).
リージョナル ▢ リージョナル空港 a regional airport. リージョナル航空 regional aviation.
リース[1] ▢ リース債権 (a) lease credit.
リーダー[2] ▢ リーダー格〔リーダー的な立場〕a leadership role; a position as「a [the] leader」;〔その立場の人〕a person in a leadership role; a leader-like person. ◎ 中堅・若手議員の〜格である加藤氏 Mr Katō, who「has a leadership role among [is seen as a leader by] middle-ranking and younger Diet members.
リーダー[3] 〖印刷〗〔点線 (...)〕leaders.
リーダーシップ ▢ 自由放任的リーダーシップ 〖心理〗laissez-faire [hands-off, bottom-up] leadership. 専制的リーダーシップ 〖心理〗autocratic [hands-on, top-down] leadership. 民主的リーダーシップ 〖心理〗democratic leadership.
リー・チーガイ【李志毅】Lee Chi-Ngai (1949- ; 香港の映画監督).
リーチマン Leachman, Cloris (1926- ; 米国の映画女優).
リーデル〔オーストリアのワイングラスメーカー〕Riedel.
リート[2]【REIT】〔不動産投資信託〕a REIT; a real estate investment trust.
リード 1 Reed, Peyton (1964- ; 米国の映画監督).
2 Reid, Tara (1975- ; 米国の映画女優).
リードバック 〖動〗〔アフリカ産レイヨウ〕a reedbuck 《pl. ~, ~s》.
リードフレーム 〖電子工学〗a leadframe. ▢ IC リードフレーム an IC leadframe. 半導体リードフレーム a semiconductor leadframe. ▢ リードフレーム材 (a) leadframe material.
リーブス =リーヴス.
リウマチせい【-性】 ▢ リウマチ性多発筋痛症 polymyalgia rheumatica (略: PMR).
リウマトレックス(カプセル)〖商標・薬〗〔リウマチ治療薬〕Rheumatrex.
りえき【利益】 ▢ 未分配利益 〖会計〗undistributed profits. ▢ 利益確定売り〖相場〗〔利食い売り〕a profit-taking sale. 利益還元〔株主への〕returning [(a [the]) return of] profits《to shareholders》. 利益成長率 a profit growth rate《of 3%》. 利益相反 a conflict of interest(s). ◎ ~相反取引 a conflict of interest transaction. 利益第一主義 a profit-first policy. 利益目標 a profit [an earnings] target; a profit「goal [objective]」; a targeted return《of 5.6%》.
リエンジニアリング〖経営〗〔業務再構築〕reengineering.
リオッタ Liotta, Ray (1955- ; 米国の映画俳優).
リオ・ティント〔多国籍の資源・鉱業大手〕Rio Tinto.
リオドセ〔ブラジルの資源最大手〕Companhia Vale Do Rio Doce S.A. (略: CVRD).
リカード ▢ リカードの等価定理〖経〗the Ricardian equivalence theorem.
りがい[1]【利害】 ▢ 利害誘導罪 〖法〗〖公職選挙法の〗(the「crime [offense]」of) inducing voters or election campaigners to vote for *one* by directly furthering their interests.
りかがくけんきゅうじょいでんしたけいけんきゅうセンター【理化学研究所遺伝子多型研究-】the RIKEN SNP Research Center.
りがく【理学】 ▢ 応用理学 applied physical science;〔応用物理学〕applied physics. 生命理学 the life sciences. 物質理学 material science.
リカステ〖植〗〔ラン科リカステ属 (*Lycaste*) の植物の総称〕a lycaste.
リカちゃん〖商標〗〔日本製の着せ替え人形〕Licca-chan. ▢ リカちゃん人形 a Licca doll; a type of Japanese doll which can be dressed in different clothes.
リカベトス〔ギリシャ, アテネ北東部の丘〕Lycabettus.
リカンベント〔座席に寝そべるようにすわり足を前に投げ出すようにしてペダルを漕ぐ自転車〕a recumbent「bicycle [bike]」.
リキシャ〔インドなどの三輪タクシー〕an auto rickshaw.
リギタンとう【-島】〔セレベス海の島〕Ligitan Island.
リキャップ 〜する〔ペットボトル飲料など, 飲み残しをキャップを締めて保存する〕recap; reclose. ▢ リキャップ缶 a「recappable [reclosable] can.
りきゅうばい【利休梅】〖植〗〔バラ科の落葉低木; 中国原産〕a common pearlbush; *Exochorda racemosa*.
りきりつ【力率】 ▢ 力率改善回路 power factor correction (略: PFC).
リグ ▢ リグ・カウント〔油田掘削装置の稼働数; 油田開発の先行指標〕a「high, low」rig count.
りくいきかんきょうがく【陸域環境学】terrestrial environmental studies; study of the terrestrial environment.
りくいきかんそくえいせい【陸域観測衛星】=りくいきかんそくぎじゅつえいせい.
りくいきかんそくぎじゅつえいせい【陸域観測技術衛星】the Advanced Land Observing Satellite (略: ALOS).
りくイグアナ【陸-】〖動〗a (Galapagos) land iguana;

リクード〔イスラエルの政党〕the Likud Party. Conolophus subcristatus.
リクープ〔回収〕～する recoup 《one's investment》.
りくぐんじょうほうぶ【陸軍情報部】〖軍〗〔米国の〕the Military Intelligence Service (略: MIS).
りくぐんせんそうだいがく【陸軍戦争大学】〔米国ペンシルヴェニア州にある〕the US Army War College.
リクシャ(ー)＝リキシャ.
りくじょう【陸上】▫️ 陸上特殊無線技師 a special on-ground radio operator,《category I, category II, category III》. ▶ 第一級から第三級まである.
リグニン ▫️ 水溶性リグニン water soluble lignin.
リクライニング ▫️ リクライニング・ベッド a reclining bed.
リクルーティングがいしゃ【～会社】〔人材紹介会社〕a recruiting company.
リクルート ▫️ リクルート会社〔人材紹介会社〕a recruiting company.
リクルートじけん【～事件】〔1988年の〕the Recruit scandal.
りけん【利権】▫️ 利権構造 a structure of interests; a concessionary structure.
りげん[3]【利源】〔保険〕a profit source.
リコイル〔銃砲〕〔発砲直後の遊底の後退〕recoil.
りこうし【李洪志】Li Hongzhi (1952- ; 法輪功の創始者).
リコッタ〔イタリア産のフレッシュチーズ〕ricotta.
「利己的な遺伝子」〔リチャード・ドーキンスの著作〕The Selfish Gene.
リコピン〔生化〕〔カロチンの一種〕lycopene.
リコメンド＝レコメンド.
りこん【離婚】▫️ 無過失離婚〔どちらかが望むことによって成立する離婚〕a no-fault divorce. ▫️ 離婚協議 divorce proceedings. ▫️ ～協議書 a (written) divorce agreement. ▫️ 離婚母子〔父子〕家庭 a (divorced)「single-mother [single-father] household.
りさい【罹災】▫️ 罹災証明(書) a (disaster) damage certificate; a disaster victim certificate.
りざい【理財】▫️ 理財局〔地方自治体などの〕the Financial Bureau.
リサイクル ▫️ リサイクル市(いち)〔〕=「recycled-goods [second-hand] market [bazaar]. リサイクル型社会 a recycling-oriented society. リサイクル効率 recycling efficiency.
りさいとしゃくちしゃっかりんじしょりほう【罹災都市借地借家臨時処理法】〖法〗the Law for Provisional Measures Concerning Land Lease and Rental Property Rights in Disaster-Stricken Cities. ▶ 1946年, 戦災処理のために作られた法律. 現在は自然災害に適用.
りさいとしほう【罹災都市法】〖法〗＝りさいとしゃくちしゃっかりんじしょりほう.
りさそん【利差損】〔生命保険〕〔予定利率と実際の利率の差によって生じる, 保険会社にとっての損〕investment losses.
りさそんえき【利差損益】〔生命保険〕〔予定利率と実際の利率の差によって生じる, 保険会社にとっての損益〕investment profits or losses.
りさん【離散】▫️ 離散家族 a dispersed family. ▫️ 南北～家族〔韓国・北朝鮮の〕families divided by the Korean War. ▫️ 離散家族再会事業〔韓国・北朝鮮の〕the inter-Korean family reunion「project [program].
リシテア〔天〕〔木星の衛星〕Lysithea.
りしょう[2]【離床】▫️ 離床センサー〔ベッドに取り付ける〕a bed sensor pad. ▫️ 離床促進 encouraging《bedridden patients》to leave bed.
りしょく[1]【利殖】▫️ 利殖商法 an investment scam.
りしりひなげし【利尻雛罌粟】〖植〗Papaver fauriei.
りしわり【利子割】the prefectural share of taxes on bank deposit interest. ▫️ 利子割県民税 money allocated for prefectural use from the prefectural share of taxes on bank deposit interest. 利子割交付金 money allocated to local governments from the prefectural share of taxes on bank deposit interest.
リスク[1] ▫️ 在庫リスク ▫️ ざいこ. ゼロ・リスク ＝リスク・ゼロ. 返品リスク ▫️ へんぴん. リスク・アセッサー〔リスク評価者〕a risk assessor. リスク許容度 risk tolerance. リスク・コミュニケーション〔リスクに関する情報交換〕risk communication. リスク・コンサルタント a risk consultant. リスク・シェアリング〔危険分担〕risk sharing. リスク情報 risk information. リスク心理学 risk psychology. リスク・ゼロ〔リスクがゼロ; 百パーセント安全〕zero risk. リスク・バッファー〔経〕〔損失を吸収するためのクッションとしての自己資本など〕a risk buffer. リスク・フリー〔リスクのないこと〕risk free. ▫️ ～フリー金利 a risk-free interest rate／～フリーレート a risk-free「(interest) rate [yield]. リスク分散 risk diversification. リスク分析〔オアナリシス〕(a) risk analysis. リスク・マネー〔ハイリスクの投資に投入される資金〕risk money. リスク・マネージャー〔病院・金融機関などの危機管理者〕a《hospital, financial》risk manager. リスク・モデル a risk model《for venture capital funds, for obesity》.
リスゴー Lithgow, John (1945- ; 米国の映画俳優; 本名 John Arthur Lithgow).
りすざる【栗鼠猿】〖動〗〔中米・南米産; オマキザル科リスザル属の小型軽量のサル〕a squirrel monkey; Saimiri sciureus.
リスティングこうこく【～広告】〔電算〕〔検索エンジンのキーワードに対応した広告〕search (engine) advertising;〔1件の〕a search (engine) ad.
リスト[2] ▫️ リストカッティング ＝リストカット. リストカット〔手首を刃物などで切る自傷行為〕wrist-cutting. ▫️ ～カットする cut [slash] one's「wrist(s). リストカット症候群〖医〗〔手首自傷症候群〕wrist-cutting syndrome.
リストラ ▫️ リストラ効果〔the〕restructuring「results [effect]. ▫️ わが社は～効果が現れて増益に転じた. Restructuring results at our company appear in the shift to increased profitability. リストラ損失 a restructuring loss; a loss 「in [due to] restructuring.
リスパダール〔商標・薬〕〔向精神薬; リスペリドンの商品名〕Risperdal.
リスベラトロール〔生化〕〔ブドウの皮や種に含まれるポリフェノール成分〕reseveratrol.
リスペリドン〔薬〕〔向精神薬〕risperidone.
リズム ▫️ リズム・ボックス ＝ドラム・マシン(⇨ドラム).
リセドロンさんナトリウム【～酸～】〔化〕risedronate sodium. ▫️ 商品名は アクトネル (Actonel).
「理想の恋人.com」〔映画〕Must Love Dogs.
リゾート ▫️ リゾート気分 ▫️ ～気分を味わう enjoy the feeling of being at a resort. リゾート婚 a destination wedding. リゾート施設 a resort facility. リゾート・ブーム《give rise to》a resort boom.
リソグラフィー ▫️ EUV[極(端)紫外線]リソグラフィー〔電子工学〕EUV [extreme ultraviolet] lithography (略: EUVL). DUV[深紫外線]リソグラフィー〔電子工学〕DUV [deep ultraviolet] lithography. 光リソグラフィー〔電子工学〕photolithography.
リゾホスファチジンさん【～酸】〔生化〕lysophosphatidic acid (略: LPA).
リタイアメント〔定年〕退職 retirement. ▫️ リタイアメント・ビザ〔定年退職者向けの海外居住ビザ〕a retirement visa.
リタニがわ【～川】〔ベカー高原に発しレバノン南部を流れ地中海に注ぐ川〕the Litani River; the Litani.
リチウム ▫️ リチウム長石〖鉱〗petalite. リチウムポリマー電池 a lithium polymer battery; a「lipo [Lipo, LiPo] battery;〔単体の〕a lithium polymer cell; a「lipo [Lipo, LiPo] cell.
リチャーズ Richards, Denise (1972- ; 米国の映画女

優).
リチャード・ジノリ〖商標〗〔イタリアの陶磁器ブランド〕Richard Ginori.
リチャードソン Richardson, Joely (1965- ; 英国の映画女優; ヴァネッサ・レッドグレーヴの娘).
リちゃくりく【離着陸】▭ 離着陸訓練 take-off and landing practice. ▶連続〜訓練 touch-and-go practice / 夜間(連続)〜訓練 night landing practice (略: NLP).
りちょうせい【李肇星】Li Zhaoxing (1940- ; 中国の政治家).
りつき【利付き】▭ 利付き債 an interest-bearing bond.
リツキサン〖商標・薬〗〔悪性リンパ腫治療薬リツキシマブの商品名〕Rituxan.
リツキシマブ〖薬〗〔悪性リンパ腫治療薬〕rituximab.
リックマン Rickman, Alan (1946- ; 英国生まれの映画俳優; 本名 Alan Sidney Patrick Rickman).
りっけん[1]【立件】▭ 立件対象 an object of prosecution.
りっこう[1]【力行】▭ 力行ハンドル〖鉄道〗= 主幹制御器 (⇨しゅかん[1]).
りっこう[3]【立項】〔項目を立てること〕adding; listing; inclusion. 〜する add 《an entry to a dictionary》; list [include] 《a reference in a bibliography》.
りっこうほ【立候補】▭ 立候補表明[宣言] announcing [declaring] one's「candidacy [''candidature''] 《for ...》.
りっしょう[1]【立哨】keeping watch; standing guard. 〜する keep watch; stand guard. ▭ 交通(安全)立哨 doing safety patrol. 校門立哨 keeping watch at the school gate.
りっしょうこうせいかい【立正佼成会】Rissho Kosei-Kai, a Buddhistic religious organization of Japanese origin.
りっしょく【立食】▭ 立食パーティー a buffet party; a buffet-style party.
りったい【立体】▭ 立体画像〔3 次元画像; 3D 画像〕a 3-D image. 立体像 a stereo image.
りったいか【立体化】〜する make 《an intersection》「two-level [multilevel];〖高架にする〗elevate. ▶すべての踏切を〜する make all crossings multilevel;〖線路を高架にして踏切を廃止する〗eliminate surface crossings / 交差点を〜する elevate an intersection; make an intersection into an overpass. ▭ 立体化工事《road》elevation work.
りったいこうさ【立体交差】▭ 鉄道高架式立体交差 an elevated railway overpass. 掘割式立体交差 a culvert underpass. 連続立体交差 continuous grade separations.
りっち【立地】▭ 立地交渉 negotiations 《with local residents》 over the siting 《of a nuclear plant》; siting「discussions [negotiations]. 立地調査 a location (suitability)「investigation [survey]; an investigation into the suitability of a site 《for a power station》.
リッチ Ricci, Christina (1980- ; 米国の映画女優).
リッチー Ritchie, Guy (1968- ; 英国生まれの映画監督; 本名 Guy Stuart Ritchie).
りっちゅうしき【立柱式】〔建造物の最初の柱を立てるときに行う儀式〕the ceremonial setting up of the first pillar; a [the] ceremony to mark the start of building.
リッツ[2] Ritts, Herb (1952- 2002; 米国の写真家).
リッピング〔パソコンを利用した音楽データなどの取り込み〕ripping. 〜する rip.▭ CD[DVD]を〜する rip a「CD [DVD]. ▭ アンチ・リッピング CD = コピーコントロール・シー・ディー.
リップ・カレント〔離岸流〕a rip current.
リップグロス〖化粧〗〔唇に光沢を与える塗布剤〕lip gloss.
りっぽう[2]【立法】▭ 立法事務費〔国会議員に支給される経費〕a legislative allowance. 立法(の)不作為〖法〗(a) legislative omission.
リテイク〖映〗〔同じシーンの撮り直し〕a retake. 〜する retake《a scene》. ▶そのシーンは〜になった. The scene had to be reshot.
リテール▭ リテール業務〔個人客向けの銀行・証券業務〕retail「business [activities].
りとう[2]【離党】▭ 離党勧告 advice to「leave [withdraw from] a party. 離党届 a notice of resignation from a party. ▶〜届を提出する submit one's formal resignation from a party.
リトビネンコ Litvinenko, Alexander (1962–2006; ロシアの元軍人; ロンドンで暗殺された).
「リトル・ダンサー」〖映画〗Billy Elliot.
リナリア〖植〗〔ゴマノハグサ科ウンラン属の総称〕a linaria.
リニアすいせい【-彗星】〖天〗a LINEAR comet.
リニー Linney, Laura (1964- ; 米国の映画女優).
リニューアル ▭ リニューアル・オープン〔店内を改装して営業を再開すること〕reopening after remodeling. ▶〜オープンする reopen [open again] after remodeling.
リノベーション〔住宅などの改修〕renovation(s).
リハーサル ▭ リハーサル・スタジオ a rehearsal studio.
「リバース」〖映画〗Retroactive.
リバーダンス〔アイルランドの舞踊団〕Riverdance.
リバー・トレッキング river trekking. [= かわあるき]
リバーブギ〔ボードにつかまって川を下るスポーツ〕riverboarding;〔そのボード〕a riverboard. ▷ riverboarder n.
「リバー・ランズ・スルー・イット」〖映画〗A River Runs Through It.
リパック 1〔商品を別の箱に詰め替えて産地・賞味期限などを偽装すること〕fraudulent repackaging (to disguise the origin or date of goods).
2〔癒着を起こして開かなくなるのを防ぐためにパラシュートを定期的に畳み直すこと〕parachute repacking.
リハビリテーション ▭ リハビリテーション医学 rehabilitation medicine.
リバビリン〖生化〗ribavirin.
リビアやまねこ【-山猫】an African wildcat; a desert cat; Felis silvestris「lybica [libyca].
リピーター ▭ リピーター医師 a physician who has made multiple mistakes; an error-prone doctor. リピーター率 a「repeat [return]《(customer)》rate.
リピート ▭ リピート客 a repeat「customer [visitor]; a regular「customer [visitor]. リピート率 a「repeat [return]《(visitor)》rate.
リヒター Richter, Charles Francis (1900–85; 米国の地震学者; リヒター震度階の提案者).
リピド〖生化〗〔脂質〕a lipid; a lipide.
リフォーム ▭ リフォーム詐欺〖商法〗a fraudulent renovation sales method.
リフティング 1〖美容整形〗《(breast)》lifting surgery.
2〖サッカー〗〔足・胸・頭などだけ使ってボールを地面に落ちないよう蹴り続けること〕keepie uppie.
リフトアップ〔持ち上げること〕▭ リフトアップ・シート〖自動車〗〔体の不自由な人などが乗降しやすいように座席が電動で向きを変え外に降りてくる仕掛けになっているもの〕a lift-up seat. リフトアップ手術〖美容〗facelift surgery; a facelift operation. リフトアップ・ブラ(ジャー) a lift-up bra. リフトアップ・ローション[ジェル] a facial lotion; a facelift lotion.
リフトカー〔障害者が車いすのまま乗車できるようにリフトが付いた自動車〕a wheelchair (lift) van; a lift van; a handicapped van.
リフトバレーねつ【-熱】〖医〗〔人畜共通感染症の1つ〕Rift Valley fever (略: RVF).
「リプリー」〖映画〗The Talented Mr. Ripley.
「リプレイスメント」〖映画〗The Replacements.
「リプレイスメント・キラー」〖映画〗The Replacement Killers.
リフレーミング〔ある事態・状況を解釈し意味づける際の準

リプロダクティブヘルス

拠枠を組み替えること〕reframing.
**リプロダクティブ・ヘルス**〔性と生殖に関する健康〕reproductive health.
**リプロダクティブ・ライツ**〔性と生殖に関する女性の決定権〕reproductive rights.
**リペア**〔修理・修繕すること〕repair. 〜する repair.
**リベット・ジョイント**《米軍》〔電波情報収集機 RC-135 の愛称〕a Rivet Joint.
**リベラシオン**〔フランスの日刊紙〕Libération.
**リベリアわかいみんしゅれんごう**〔＝和解民主連合〕〔リベリアの反政府勢力〕the Liberians United for Democracy and Reconciliation (略: LURD).
**リベンジ**〔復讐〕revenge. 〜する〔復讐する〕revenge oneself [get one's revenge] (on [against] sb); 〔スポーツなどの世界で, 雪辱する〕win a rematch (against sb).
**リポソーム**〔化〕liposome. ▷ liposomal adj.
**リポたんぱく(しつ)**【－蛋白(質)】 □ リポ蛋白分画精密測定〔医〕lipoprotein fractionation.
**リポでんち**【－電池】〔リチウムポリマー電池〕a lithium polymer battery; 〜しipo [Lipo, LiPo] battery; 〔単体の〕a lithium polymer cell; a しipo [Lipo, LiPo] cell.
**リポポリサッカライド**〔生化〕〔歯周病菌が出す毒素; リポ多糖〕a lipopolysaccharide (略: LPS).
**リマスター**〔音質や画質の改善のために新たに作り直した録音や映画の原版〕a remaster. 〜する remaster. □ リマスター版 a remastered version.
**リまわり**【利回り】 □ 実質利回り an effective「yield [rate]. 表面回りのクーポン「yield [rate]. 利回り保証〔証券〕a guarantee of interest; an interest guarantee.
**リミッター**〔自動車〕〔速度制限装置〕＝スピード・リミッター; 〔電〕〔振幅制限回路〕a limiter. 〜をはずす[解除する] remove [disconnect] the limiter. □ スピード・リミッター〔速度抑制[制限]装置〕a speed limiter; a speed-limiting device; an overspeed limiter.
**リミテッド・パートナー**《米経営》〔リミテッド・パートナーシップにおける投資家〕a limited partner (略: LP).
**リミテッド・パートナーシップ**《米経営》〔共同出資形態の〕(a) limited partnership (略: LP).
**リム・ショット**〔ドラムの縁をたたく奏法〕a rim shot.
**リムジン** □ リムジン・バス〔空港や駅などの送迎用バス〕a limousine [an airport] bus; an airport limousine.
**リムセ**〔アイヌの伝承歌舞〕(a) rimse; a kind of traditional Ainu song and dance.
**リムポポ** ⇒リンポポ.
**リメディアル**〔修正の〕remedial. □ リメディアル教育〔学習の遅れた生徒・誤った学習習慣を持った学生に対する教育〕remedial education.
**リモコン** □ リモコン・ドアロック a remote-controlled door lock; a keyless door lock; 〔自動車の〕a remote door lock.
**りゃくしゅ**【略取】 □ 成年者略取 abduction of an adult. わいせつ目的略取 abduction for immoral purposes. □ 略取罪〔法〕kidnap(p)ing; abduction by force or threat.
**りゃくだつ**【略奪・掠奪】 □ 略奪愛 stealing another person's「partner [lover, spouse].
**リヤドロ**〔商標〕〔スペインの陶磁器ブランド〕Lladró.
**リュイテリ**＝リューテル.
**リュー** Liu, Lucy (1968– ; 米国の映画女優; 本名 Lucy Alexis Liu).
**リュウ**＝リュー.
**りゅうかい**²【粒界】〔粒界割れ[破壊]〔金属〕〔結晶粒界に沿って発生する金属のひび割れ〕an intergranular fracture; a grain boundary fracture.
**りゅうがく**【留学】 □ 親子留学 a parent-and-child study trip abroad. サッカー〔野球, 相撲(など)〕留学 leaving one's school in order to learn「soccer [baseball, sumo, etc.] somewhere better. □ 野球〜生 a stu-

dent who has moved to a school which is strong at baseball (in order to improve his skills). 山村留学 spending a year or more in a school in an underpopulated rural area (in order to combine school education with experience working in a rural environment); 《spend》at least a year at a school in the country. 社費留学 company-paid study abroad; study abroad financed by one's company. □ 留学先 the「country [place] where one「is going [went] to study; one's「study destination [study-destination country]. □ 息子さんの〜先は決まりましたか. Has your son decided where he is going to study abroad? 留学仲介業者 an overseas study agency. 留学熱 enthusiasm「for study abroad [to study overseas].
**りゅうきゅうからすばと**【琉球烏鳩】〔鳥〕〔ハト科の鳥〕a Ryukyu wood pigeon; a silver-banded black pigeon; Columba jouyi.
**りゅうきゅうつつじ**【琉球躑躅】〔植〕〔ツツジ科の半落葉低木〕Rhododendron mucronatum.
**りゅうきゅうながこうもり**【琉球指長蝙蝠】〔動〕〔ヒナコウモリ科のコウモリ〕a Southeast Asian long-fingered bat; Miniopterus fuscus.
**りゅうきん**【琉金】〔魚〕a ryukin goldfish; Carassius auratus.
**りゅうけつ**【流血】 □ 流血沙汰 bloodshed; violence. ▷ 〜沙汰になる lead to「bloodshed [violence].
**りゅうこう**【流行】 □ 流行もの ＝はやりもの (⇒はやり).
**りゅうこうせい**【流行性】 □ 流行性角結膜炎〔医〕epidemic keratoconjunctivitis (略: EKC).
**りゅうさん**【硫酸】 □ 硫酸イオン a sulfide ion. 硫酸ストレプトマイシン〔薬〕streptomycin sulfate. 硫酸スラッジ acid sludge.
**りゅうさん**²【龍山・竜山】＝ヨンサン.
**りゅうざん**⁴【龍山・竜山】＝ヨンサン.
**りゅうしゅつ**¹【流出】 □ 流出情報 leaked information. 流出経路 the route of a leak; how《information》(was) leaked (out). ▷ その顧客リストの〜経路はまだ特定できていない. It has not yet been determined how the list of clients was leaked out. 流出路〔自動車道路から一般道路に出るための〕*an off-ramp; *an exit ramp; ⁱⁱa slip road.
**りゅうせい**¹【流星】 □ 流星物質 a meteoroid.
**りゅうせい**³【龍井】〔中国吉林省の都市〕Longjing.
**りゅうせつこう**【流雪溝】a snow「flowing [drainage] gutter.
**りゅうせん**¹【竜川】1〔中国広東省北東部の県〕Longchuan.
2 ＝リョンチョン.
**りゅうせん**²【龍川】＝リョンチョン.
**りゅうたい**¹【流体】 □ 流体潤滑〔物〕hydrodynamic [full-film, fluid] lubrication. 流体制御 fluid control. ▷ 〜制御機器 fluid control equipment. 流体動圧軸受〔機〕a fluid-dynamic bearing (略: FDB). [⇒エフ・ディー・ビー].
**りゅうち**【留置】 □ 留置針〔医〕a catheter needle; an indwelling needle. 留置線〔鉄道〕a storage track.
**りゅうつう**【流通】 □ 流通株 a negotiable「share [stock]. ▷ 非〜株 a nonnegotiable「share [stock]. 流通株式 negotiable「shares [stock]. ▷ 非〜株式 non-negotiable「shares [stock]. 流通管理 distribution management. 流通業者 a distributor. 流通コンサルタント a distribution consultant. 流通利回り〔債券の〕the yield on bonds traded among financial institutions. 流通履歴 a distribution「history [record]; the distribution history《of a product》.
**りゅうつうシステムかいはつセンター**〔流通－開発－〕the Distribution Systems Research Institute (略: DSRI).
**りゅうてき**【竜笛】〔楽器〕〔雅楽に用いる管楽器〕a species

of bark-covered bamboo flute used in "gagaku."
リューテル Rüütel, Arnold (1928-  ; エストニアの政治家; 大統領 [2001-06]).
りゅうどうせい【流動性】 ●□ 流動性供給入札〔国債の〕an "enhanced liquidity" auction. 流動性知能[知性] fluid intelligence.
りゅうにゅう【流入】 ●□ 流入路〔一般道路から自動車道路に入るための〕*an on-ramp; *an entrance ramp; "a slip road.
りゅうひょう【流氷】 ●□ 流氷群 (an) ice flow; (free-) floating pack ice.
りゅうひんがん【劉賓雁】 Liu Binyan; Liu Pin-yen (1925-2005; 中国のジャーナリスト・作家).
りゅうよう【流用】 ●□ 私的流用 misappropriation ((of public funds) for personal use; pocketing ((of) public funds)). ●□ 流用疑惑 suspicion of misappropriation ((of government funds)). ▷ 秘書給与～疑惑 alleged [suspected] misappropriation of a secretary's salary.
りゅうれん【流連】 =いつづけ.
リュ・シウォン【柳時元】 Ryu Si-won (1972-  ; 韓国の俳優).
りょう²【両】
3〔列車の車両〕*a car; "a carriage; a coach. ▷ 列車の2～目 the second「*car["carriage] of a train
りよう¹【利用】 ●□ 利用客 a user; a customer. 利用権 the right of use; the right to use ((a facility)); user rights; ((product)) use rights; usufruct. 利用限度額〔クレジットカード・ATM などの〕a [one's] credit [withdrawal] limit. ●□ 限度額を超過する exceed one's「credit [withdrawal] limit. 利用明細書〔クレジットカードなどの〕a (monthly) (billing) statement.
りょういき【領域】 ●□ 領域管理〔インドネシア政府による社会監視制度〕area control; territorial surveillance. 領域保全 preservation [protection] of territorial integrity.
りょういく【療育】 ●□ 療育手帳〔知的障害児[者]が各種福祉サービスを受けるために交付される〕a handbook for the mentally「disabled [handicapped].
りょういん【両院】 ●□ 両院合同会議 a joint「meeting [session] of the「two Houses [Upper and Lower Houses]((of the Diet).
りょううち【両打ち】〔野球〕〔右打席でも左打席でも打てること〕switch-hitting;〔その選手〕a switch-hitter.
りょうか⁴【両価】〔心理〕〔両価性〕ambivalence. ▷ ambivalent adj.
りょうがん¹【両岸】 ●□ 両岸関係〔中国・台湾の〕cross-strait relations between (the People's Republic of) China and Taiwan; relations between China and Taiwan.
りょうぎ²【両義】〔人類・心理〕〔矛盾する2つの感情・価値などの共存〕ambivalence [⇨りょうか⁴].
「猟奇的な彼女」〔映画〕My Sassy Girl; Bizarre Girl.
りょうぎゃく【凌虐・陵虐】 humiliation; indignity; an affront.
りょうけ¹【両家】 ●□ 両家墓〔一つの墓で夫側と妻側の両家を祀るもの〕a grave for the families of husband and wife; a grave for two families.
りょうけい⁴【量刑】 ●□ 量刑基準 a standard for (determining) a punishment; a sentencing guideline. 量刑判断 (the) determination of「(a) [an appropriate] punishment; sentencing.
りょうけつ【良血】〔競馬〕good blood. ●□ 良血馬 a blood horse; a horse of superior breeding; a thoroughbred.
りょうさん【量産】 ●□ 量産化 a「shift [move] to mass production. ●□ ～化する shift [move, ramp up] to mass production; begin mass-producing ((a new product)).

りょうし⁵【量子】 ●□ 量子暗号装置 a quantum encryption system. 量子暗号通信 quantum communication. 量子通信〔物〕quantum communication. 量子テレポーテーション〔物〕quantum teleportation. 量子トンネル効果, 量子トンネリング〔物〕quantum tunneling. 量子ビット〔物〕a quantum bit; a qubit. 量子飛躍 a quantum「leap [jump];〔思考などの非連続的な飛躍〕(make) a quantum leap. 量子もつれ[もつれあい], エンタングルメント〔物〕quantum entanglement. 量子流体〔物〕a quantum fluid.
りょうし⁶【漁師】 ●□ 漁師の指輪〔ローマ法王のシンボル〕the Fisherman's Ring; the Ring of the Fisherman.
りょうしょ²【猟書・漁書】 book hunting. ～する hunt for books. ●□ 猟書家 a book hunter; a bibliomaniac. 猟書癖 a book hunting habit;〔病的な〕bibliomania.
りょうしょうし【廖承志】Liao Chengzhi (1908-83; 中国の政治家; 中日友好協会会長).
りょうしょく²【糧食】 ●□ 糧食費 food expenses.
りょうしん²【良心】 ●□ 良心犯 a criminal of conscience.
りょうて【両手】 ●□ 両手打ち〔テニス〕double handed (play);〔携帯メールを打つときの〕texting with both hands. ●□ ～打ちのバックハンド[フォアハンド]((hit) a「two-handed [double-handed] backhand [forehand].
りょうてい¹【料亭】 ●□ 料亭政治 politics conducted through「secret [unofficial, backroom] deals [dealing].
りょうどう³【領導】 governing and leading. ～する govern and lead ((the people)). ●□ 領導者 a ruler and leader.
りょうにらみ【両睨み】〔二様の可能性に備えること〕▷ 財政再建と景気の～で政策を考える必要がある. Both financial reconstruction and economic conditions must be taken into account when considering policies. ▷ 和戦～の姿勢を見せても show readiness [be prepared] for either peace or war
りょうはん【量販】 ●□ 量販価格帯〔ボリュームゾーン〕the main price range.
りょうばん【良番】〔電話や自動車のナンバープレートなどの良い番号〕a「good [lucky, memorable] number; (自動車の) a vanity plate.
りょうぼ²【陵墓】 ●□ 陵墓参考地〔歴代の天皇や皇族の墓の可能性がある古墳〕potential sites for imperial「mausoleums [tombs].
りょうぼせい【両墓制】〔死者を埋めた埋め墓と, 詣でるための参り墓を別々に作った土葬時代の風習〕the「double-grave [double-tomb] system; the use of two "graves," one for the physical remains of the dead and a separate one for prayers and memorial services.
りょうゆう³【猟友】 ●□ 猟友会「hunters' [hunting] association.
りょうよう⁵【療養】 ●□ 療養泉 a therapeutic spa. 療養病床入院 (a) convalescent hospitalization. 療養病棟 a long-stay ward; a (long-stay)「convalescent [rehabilitation] ward.
りょうり【料理】 ●□ お薦め料理 a recommended「dish [item on the menu]. ▷ 本日のお薦め～ the dish of the day / シェフのお薦め～ the chef's「choice [recommendation]. 得意料理 one is particularly good at; one's specialty. ●□ 料理研究家 a student of「cuisine [cooking]; a「food [culinary] researcher; a「food [cooking] expert. 料理自慢 pride in one's skill at cooking. ▷ 自慢の宿 an inn that boasts (of) good food. 料理評論家 a「food [cooking, culinary] critic.
りょうりいんしょくとうしょうひぜい【料理飲食等消費税】a local government consumption tax on meals, drinks and accomodation, etc. ► 1988 年, 特別地方消費税と改称.

りょうる

**りょうる**【料る】cook 《meat [vegetables]》; dress 《(a) fish》.
**りょくち**【緑地】⇨ 緑地率《都市計画》＝りょくひりつ.
**りょくちゃ**【緑茶】⇨ 緑茶飲料 a (green-)tea drink; a (green-)tea-based「beverage [drink]; green tea. 緑茶ポリフェノール a green tea polyphenol; epigallocachetin (略: EGC).
**りょくのうきん**【緑膿菌】⇨ 多剤耐性緑膿菌 multi-drug-resistant pseudomonas.
**りょくばん**【緑礬】⇨ 緑礬泉 a copperas spring.
**りょくひりつ**【緑被率】《都市計画》a green coverage ratio; a ratio of green space (to total area).
**りょけん**【旅券】⇨ IC 旅券 an electronic passport; an e-passport. 一般旅券 an ordinary passport. 外交旅券 a diplomatic passport. 機械読み取り式旅券 a machine-readable passport. 公用旅券 an official passport. ⇨ 旅券返納命令 an order to return *one's* passport.
**りょこう**【旅行】⇨ 組み立て旅行〔個人旅行商品の１つ〕a dynamic package. ⇨ 旅行記者 a travel「correspondent [reporter]. 旅行業務取扱管理者 a certified travel services manager. ▶「旅行業務取扱主任者」から改称. ⇨ 国内〜業務取扱管理者 a certified domestic travel services manager / 総合〜業務取扱管理者 a certified general travel services manager. 旅行券 a「travel [holiday] voucher. 旅行作家 a travel writer. 旅行貯金 旅行するたびに旅先の郵便局で出入金を行って押印を受け、各地の局の印を貯める趣味》collecting stamps (in *one's* passbook) from post offices around the country. 旅行番記 ＝たびばんぐみ. 旅行命令書〔公務員の〕an (official) order to travel.
**リヨセル**【商標】〔木材パルプを原料とするセルロース繊維〕Lyocell.
**りょてい**【旅程】⇨ 旅程保証〔パッケージツアーの〕itinerary insurance.
**りょひ**【旅費】⇨ 旅費請求書 an invoice for travel expenses; a travel expenses invoice.
**リョンチョン**【龍川】〔北朝鮮, 平安北道の町; 2004年４月爆発事故があった〕Ryongchon.
**リラックス** ⇨ リラックス効果《have》a relaxing effect 《on…》.
**リリース** ⇨ リリース・ポイント〔ボール・ダーツなどを投げる際の〕a release point.
**リリー・セント・シア** Lili St. Cyr (1918-99; 米国のバーレスク・ダンサー; 本名 Willis Marie Van Schaack).
**リリーフ** ⇨ リリーフ・エース a relief ace. リリーフ登板 ⇨ 登板 pitch [come on, appear, take the mound] in relief; make a relief appearance. リリーフ・ポイント【野球】relief points.
**リリウオカラニ** (Queen) Liliuokalani (1838-1917; ハワイ王国女王 [1891-93]).
**りりく**【離陸】⇨ 離陸滑走距離 (a) runway takeoff「length [distance]. 離陸能力【航空機】an aircraft that「is just taking off [has just taken off].
**りりつ**【利率】⇨ 利率保証契約《保険》a guaranteed interest contract (略: GIC). ⇨ 予定利率 an expected interest rate;《生命保険の》an assumed interest rate.
**リルートきのう**【-機能】〔カーナビシステムのルート再検索機能〕a reroute function; rerouting.
**リレー** ⇨ リレー衛星 a relay satellite.
**リレーションシップ・バンキング**〔顧客との長期継続的関係を重視した銀行業務〕relationship banking.
**りろん**【理論】⇨ 理論原価 the theoretical cost. 理論派 a theorist; a theoretician; a thinker. ⇨ 彼は党内きっての〜派で, 若手の信望も厚い. He is the party's top thinker, and enjoys prestige among younger members.
**りん**[4]【燐】⇨ 燐鉱石 phosphorus ore.

**リン** Lynn, Jonathan (1943- ; 英国生まれの映画監督).
**りんあつ**[2]【輪圧】＝りんじゅう[2].
**りんが**【臨画】〔手本を見ながら絵を習うこと〕freehand copying (as a means of learning to draw);〔その絵〕a copied drawing; a drawn copy.
**りんかい**[2]【臨界】⇨ 即発臨界〔原子炉の〕prompt criticality. 遅発臨界〔原子炉の〕delayed criticality. ⇨ 臨界期【心理】〔言語習得などについての〕a critical period. 臨界点《物》a critical point.
**りんかん**[3]【林冠】《植》a tree canopy; a canopy of trees.
**リンギ**〔マレーシアの通貨単位〕＝リンギット.
**リンギット**〔マレーシアの通貨単位〕a ringgit 《*pl.* 〜, 〜s》.
**りんぎょう**【林業】⇨ 林業公社 a forestry corporation.
**リンク**[3] Link, Caroline (1964- ; ドイツの映画監督).
**リング**[1] ⇨ リング・ピロー〔結婚式で指輪交換の際に指輪を乗せておくクッション〕a ring pillow.
**リングイネ**〔平打ちのパスタ〕linguine; linguini.
**りんくうとし**【臨空都市】〔空港に隣接した都市〕an airport city; a city near an airport.
**リンクレイター** Linklater, Richard (1960- ; 米国の映画監督).
**りんご**【林檎】⇨ リンゴ狩り apple-picking; picking apples.
**りんこう**[7]【輪行】〔自転車を分解したり畳んだりしてバッグに入れて鉄道や飛行機で運ぶこと〕traveling with a「disassembled [folded-up] bicycle in a bag; taking a bagged bicycle onto (a train). ⇨ 輪行袋〔分解したり畳んだりした自転車を電車や飛行機に持ち込んで運ぶときの布製大型バッグ〕a bicycle bag.
**リンゴ・ラム** Ringo Lam (1954/55- ; 香港の映画監督; 中国語名 林嶺東 Lam Ling-Tung).
**りんさん**【燐酸】⇨ 燐酸オセルタミビル〔インフルエンザ治療薬〕oseltamivir phosphate. ▶ 薬品名 タミフル. 燐酸型燃料電池 a phosphoric acid fuel cell (略: PAFC).
**りんじ**[2]【臨時】⇨ 臨時雇用［採用］temporary [provisional] employment (of workers); employing (labor) on a temporary basis. ⇨ 臨時採用する employ 《*sb*》temporarily (as a part-time worker). 臨時財政対策債 ＝特例地方債 (⇨とくれい[1]). 臨時診療所 a temporary clinic.
**りんし**き【臨死期】a state of near death.
**りんじちょうさかい**【臨時調査会】a provisional [a temporary, an extraordinary] commission 《for [on]…》; the Provisional Commission 《for [on]…》.
**りんじゅう**[2]【輪重】《鉄道》〔車輪にかかる垂直方向の荷重〕a wheel load.
**りんしょう**[2]【臨床】⇨ 臨床がん〔診断の結果でがんと確定した症例〕(a) clinical cancer. 臨床研修病院 a clinical training hospital (as designated by the Ministry of Health, Labour and Welfare); a hospital for clinical training. 臨床腫瘍医 a clinical oncologist. 臨床腫瘍科 a clinical oncology department. 臨床腫瘍学 clinical oncology. 臨床所見《医》a clinical「opinion [diagnosis]. 臨床心理学 clinical psychology. ⇨ 〜心理学者 a clinical psychologist. 臨床医化師《医》〔長期入院している子供の病室に定期的に出向き, 遊びやゲームなど心のケアをする専門家; クリニクラウン〕a clown doctor; a hospital clown.〔⇨ケアリング・クラウン〕臨床動作法 clinical kinesiology. 臨床動作法 clinical motor action training; clinical *dōsa* training. 臨床能力〔医師などの〕clinical competence. 臨床発達心理士 a clinical developmental psychologist. 臨床福祉 clinical social work. ⇨ 〜福祉士 a「licensed [qualified] clinical social worker.
**りんしょう**[3]【林床】〔林の地表面〕the forest floor. ⇨ 林床植生 forest floor「vegetation [cover]. 林床植物 a forest floor plant.
**りんじょう**[1]【輪状】⇨ 輪状靱帯《解》the annular liga-

「隣人は静かに笑う」〔映画〕Arlington Road.
**りんち**[1]【林地】 ▫ 林地残材 forest-thinning waste.
**りんちょう**【臨調】〔臨時調査会の略〕⇨りんじちょうさかい.
**りんと**【凛と】 ○ ～した dignified; stately; imposing /～して with dignity; in a stately manner /～して運命を受け止める accept one's fate in a dignified way.
**リンドウズ**〔電算〕〔リナックスをパソコン向けに改良した OS〕Lindows.
**リンドグレーンきねんぶんがくしょう**【－記念文学賞】the Astrid Lindgren Memorial Award for Literature.

**リンネきょうかい**【－協会】the Linnean Society of London.
**りんぱ**【琳派】〔日本画の一派〕the Kōrin school (of Japanese painting).
**リンパきゅう**【淋巴球】 ▫ リンパ球性白血病〚医〛lymphocytic leukemia. リンパ球性脈絡髄膜炎〚医〛lymphocytic choriomeningitis (略: LCM). リンパ球治療〚医〛lymphocyte treatment.
**リンパせつ**【淋巴節】 ▫ 前哨〔見張り〕リンパ節〚解〛＝センチネル・リンパせつ. ▫ リンパ節郭清〔術〕lymphadenectomy; (a) lymphoidectomy.
**リンポポ**〔南アフリカ共和国北部の州〕Limpopo.

# る

**ルアンナムター**〔ラオス北部の県〕Luangnamtha.
**ルアン・プラバン**〔ラオス北西部の県〕Luang Prabang.
**ルイ・ヴィトン・モエ・ヘネシー**〔フランスの各種ブランド企業グループ〕LVMH Moët Hennessy Louis Vuitton.
**るいえき**【涙液】 ▫ 人工涙液〚薬〛artificial tears.
**るいじ**【類似】 ▫ 類似商号 a similar trade name.
**るいしょうかん**【涙小管】〚解〛a lacrimal canaliculus《pl. -culi》.
**ルイス** 1 Lewis, Jerry (1926- ; 米国の喜劇俳優; 本名 Joseph Levitch).
2 Lewis, Juliette (1973- ; 米国の映画女優).
**るいせき**【累積】 ▫ 累積警告〔サッカー〕《a player's》「accumulated [total] cautions. 累積走行距離 the 「total [cumulative] mileage [distance covered]. ○ 愛車の～走行距離が今月15万キロを超えた. My trusty car's total mileage went over 150,000 kilometers this month. 累積損失 (an)「accumulated [cumulative] loss. 累積 DI〚経〛〔累積景気動向指数〕a cumulative diffusion index of 「economic indicators [business conditions].
**るいそん**【累損】 ▫ 累損解消 elimination [cancellation, writing off] of accumulated losses.
**るいとう** ＝株式累積投資（⇨かぶしき）.
**るいはん**【累犯】 ▫ 累犯加重 increased [enhanced] punishment [sentencing] for recidivists.
**ルイユ**〔料理〕〔フランス, プロヴァンス地方の赤トウガラシの入ったソース; ブイヤベースに使う〕rouille.
**ルーイ**〔タイ東北部の県; 同県の県都〕Loei.
**ルーキー**〔ルーキー・イヤー〔新人としての最初の1年〕one's rookie year.
**ル（ー）クオイル**〔ロシアの石油会社〕LUKoil.
**ルーク・スカイウォーカー**〔映画『スター・ウォーズ』のエピソード4-6の主人公〕Luke Skywalker.
「**ルーシー・ショー**」〔米国の TV ホームコメディー〕The Lucy Show. ▶ 主演 ルシール・ボール (Lucille Ball).
**ルーシュ** Rouch, Jean (1917-2004; フランスの映画監督・人類学者).
**ルート**[1] ▫ ルート営業〚商〛〔ルートセールス〕route sales.
**ルート**[2] ▫ ルート・サーバー〚電算〛〔インターネットの最上位の階層にあるサーバー〕a root server.
「**ルート66**」〔車で米国中を旅する青年2人の TV ドラマ〕Route 66.
「**ルーニー・テューンズ**」〔悪者の猫・ロードランナー・ヒヨコなどが登場する米国のアニメ〕Looney Tunes.
**ループ** ▫ ループ・シュート〔サッカー〕a loop shot. ループレック〔録画スタートボタンを押した時点からさかのぼって映像・音声を記録できるビデオカメラの機能〕(a) loop recording.
**ルーブリック**〚教育〛〔教育機関での評価判断基準を文章で明確に示す表〕a rubric.
**ルーマン** Luhmann, Niklas (1927-98; ドイツの社会学者).
**ルーム** ▫ ルームシェア〔アパートなどを他人と共同で借りて住むこと〕room sharing. ○ ～をシェアする share a「room [*apartment, "flat"]《with sb》; room《with sb》; have a roommate.
**ルーラ** Lula da Silva, Luisz Inácio (1945- ; ブラジルの政治家; 大統領〔2003- 〕).
**ルール** ▫ ルール化 ○ ～化する〔ルールにする〕institute [introduce] rules [regulations, a rule system]; move to a rule system; regulate; 〔ルールになる〕be subject to 「rules [regulations, a rule system]; be regulated. / マナーが守られないのであれば, ～化するしかない. If people can't maintain good manners, we will have no option but to institute rules. / 慣例を～化する move from 「conventions [customary procedure] to a rule system / 閣僚の資産公開はすでに～化している. The disclosure of cabinet members' personal assets is already 「regulated [subject to regulation]. ルール作り rule-making; rule-setting. ○ 遺伝子研究を進める上での～作りが必要だ. Rules must be established for conducting genetic research.
**ルーレット** ▫ ルーレット族〔深夜に環状道路をサーキットに見立てて走り回るドライバー〕a group of people who regularly gather at night to drive repeatedly around a highway loop, usually at high speed.
**ルカシェンコ** Lukashenko, Aleksandr Grigoryevich (1954- ; ベラルーシの政治家; 大統領〔1994- 〕).
**ルコイル** ＝ル（ー）クオイル.
**ルサール**〔ロシアのアルミニウム製造会社〕Russar.
**ルスアル** ＝ルサール.
**ルスネフチ**〔ロシアの石油会社〕RussNeft.
**るすばん**【留守番】 ▫ 留守番〔電話〕サービス an answering [a telephone answering] service.
**るすろく**【留守録】 ▫ 簡易留守録 simple automatic recording.
**ルッソ** Russo, Rene (1954- ; 米国の映画女優; 本名 Rene Marie Russo).
**ルドゥテ** Redouté, Pierre-Joseph (1759-1840; フランスの画家).
**ルドワイヤン** Ledoyen, Virginie (1976- ; フランス生まれの映画女優).
**ルビジウム** ▫ ルビジウム原子時計 a rubidium atomic clock.
**ルフナ** 1〔スリランカ南部の地方〕Ruhuna.
2〔紅茶〕Ruhuna (tea).
**ル・ペン** Le Pen, Jean-Marie (1928- ; フランスの政治家).
**ルマナ**〔イラク西部の村〕Rumana.
**ルメイラゆでん**【－油田】〔イラク南部の油田〕the Rumaila oil field.
「**ル・モンド・ディプロマティーク**」〔フランスの月刊誌〕Le Monde diplomatique.
**ルラ**〚人名〛＝ルーラ.
**ルリスタン** ＝ロレスタ（ー）ン.
「**ルル・オン・ザ・ブリッジ**」〔映画〕Lulu on the Bridge.

ルワンダぎゃくさつ【-虐殺】〔1994年の〕the (1994) Rwanda Massacre.
ルワンダないせん【-内戦】〔1990年代の〕the Rwandan civil war.
ルンダ・ノルテ〔アンゴラ北東部の州；ダイヤモンドの産地〕Lunda Norte.

# れ

レア¹ ▫ レアアース磁石 ＝希土類磁石（⇨きどるい）．
レイ³ Rea, Stephen (1946-　；北アイルランド出身の映画俳優．
「レイ／**Ray**」〔映画〕Ray.
れいえんこうはん【冷延鋼板】(a) cold-rolled steel sheet.
れいおんぷうせん【冷温風扇】a [an electric] fan with warm and cool air functions.
れいがい²【例外】▫ 例外規定 provision(s) for exceptional cases; (an) exception provision.
れいかん²【冷間】▫ 冷間鍛造〔冶金〕cold forging.
れいかん⁴【冷感】▫ 冷感刺激 cool tingling; the cool tingle《of menthol》.
れいきゃく【冷却】▫ 冷却下着〔宇宙服の〕a liquid cooling and ventilation garment（略：LCVG）．
れいげん³【霊験】霊験所 a「temple [shrine] said to have miraculous powers.
れいこう⁴【麗江】〔中国雲南省西北部の県〕Lijiang.
れいこくひどう【冷酷非道】〜な cruel and inhuman. ▪ 〜な犯罪 a cruel and inhuman crime.
レイサム Latham, Mark (1961-　；オーストラリアの政治家；労働党党首〔2003-05〕．
れいし⁶【霊視】▫ 前世霊視 reading [a reading of] sb's past life; (a) past life reading.
れいしょう⁴【霊障】〔超自然的な霊的要因によるとされる支障・災い〕psychic interference.
れいじょう¹【令状】▫ 令状請求 a request for a warrant. 令状請求書 a (written) request [a request in writing] for a《search》warrant.
れいすい¹【冷水】▫ 冷水病〔アユなどの細菌性疾患〕(bacterial) cold-water disease.
れいたい²【霊体】the spiritual body; the causal body.
れいたいさい【例大祭】▫ 春〔秋〕季例大祭 an annual [a regular] spring [autumn, *fall] festival 《of a「shrine [temple]》．
れいだんぼう【冷暖房】▫ 冷暖房機《器具》〔冷暖房装置〕an air conditioner (and heater). 冷暖房費 heating and「cooling [air conditioning] costs.
れいちょうるいけんきゅうじょ【霊長類研究所】〔京都大学の〕the Primate Research Institute(, Kyoto University)（略：PRI）．
レイテンシー〔電算〕〔データを転送する命令を出してから転送が開始されるまでの待ち時間〕(a) latency.
れいとう¹【冷凍】▫ 冷凍イチゴ〔バナナ，みかんなど〕a frozen「strawberry [banana, mandarin, etc.]．冷凍食材 frozen [deep-frozen] food [foodstuff, ingredients]. 冷凍睡眠《SFなどで》cold [frozen, cryogenic] sleep.
レイドヴォ〔択捉(エトロフ)島の村，別飛(ベトブ)のロシア語名〕Reidovo.
レイドボ ＝レイドヴォ．
レイノルズ Reynolds, Kevin (1954-　；米国の映画監督）．
れいばい²【霊媒】▫ 霊媒師 a spiritualist; a medium; a necromancer.
れいひょう²【霊標】〔墓誌〕an inscribed「grave marker [memorial stone, gravestone].
れいふう¹【冷風】▫ 冷風扇 a cool air fan.
れいふう²【零封】▫ 零封勝ち〔野球〕a shutout「win [victory]．零封負け〔野球〕a shutout「loss [defeat]．
レイム・ダック〔選挙のあと後任の人と交替するまでの任期満了前の議員・大統領など〕a lame duck.
レイヤー ▫ レイヤー・カット〔髪型の〕a layered「cut [haircut, hairstyle]．レイヤー・ブレーク〔電算〕〔DVDの記録ущий の切り替え〕layer break. ▪ 〜ブレーク・ポイント〔電算〕a layer break point.
れいゆうかい【霊友会】Reiyukai, a Buddhistic religious organization of Japanese origin.
レイン Lane, Diane (1965-　；米国の映画女優）．
レインズ²【REINS】〔不動産情報ネットワーク〕REINS. ＝ Real Estate Information Network System の略．
「レインディア・ゲーム」〔映画〕Reindeer Games.
「レインメーカー」〔映画〕The Rainmaker.
レヴァント² Levant, Brian (1952-　；米国の映画監督）．
レヴィーしょうたいがたにんちしょう【-小体型認知症】〔医〕＝レビーshōtaigata ninchishō．
レヴィンソン Levinson, Barry (1942-　；米国の映画監督・脚本家・製作者）．
レーガン・ナショナルくうこう【-空港】〔米国ワシントンDCにある国内線空港〕Ronald Reagan Washington National Airport.
レーザー ▫ レーザー加工機 a laser beam machine. レーザー伸縮計《機》a laser extensometer. レーザー濃縮装置〔原子力〕laser enrichment equipment. レーザー法〔原子力〕〔ウラン濃縮法の1つ〕laser uranium enrichment.
レーザー溶接 laser welding. ▪ 〜溶接装置 laser welding equipment.
レーザーきゅう【-級】〔ヨットレース〕the Laser class.
レーシック〔眼科〕〔生体内レーザー角膜切開術；近視矯正手術の1つ〕LASIK. ＝ laser-assisted in-situ keratomileusis の略．
レーシング・スクール a racing school.
レース¹ ▫ レース・アップ lace-up《boots》．
レース² ▫ レース・オフィサー〔役員〕〔競技などの〕a race officer. レース勘 race sense; a feeling for the race. ▪ 一度〜勘を失うとそのあと数レースはそれを取り戻せない。Once you lose your race sense, you can't get it back for the next few races.
レーダー¹ ▫ レーダー衛星 a radar satellite. レーダー進入管制〔空〕Radar Approach Control（略：RAPCON）. レーダー探査〔地中などの〕《carry out》a radar survey. レーダー探知機 a radar detector. ▪ 車載《用》〜探知機 a radar detector for vehicles.
レーティング²〔映画やゲームソフトの内容による対象年齢の設定〕(a) rating. ▫ レーティング制度 a《movie》rating system.
レーブナーしょう【-賞】〔電算〕〔米国の対話ソフトコンテストの賞〕the Loebner Prize. ▶ 賞の設定者 Hugh Loebner に因む．
レーン¹ ▫ 自転車《専用》レーン a (bi)cycle lane. バス《専用》レーン a bus lane.
レオーニ Leoni, Téa (1966-　；米国の映画女優；本名 Elizabeth Téa Pantaleoni）．
レオーネ Leone, Sergio (1929-89；イタリアの映画監督；マカロニ・ウエスタンの生みの親）．
レガシー〔遺産；過去から引き継いだもの〕a legacy. ▫ レガシー・コスト〔経営〕〔負の遺産として生じるコスト〕legacy cost. レガシー・システム〔電算〕〔過去のコンピューターシステムやアプリケーションソフトなど〕a legacy system.
れきし²【歴史】▫ 歴史愛好家 a person who loves history; a history lover. 歴史カード〔外交上のカードとし

て自国に有利な歴史上の事実］a history card. ◎外交政策に～カードを切る play the history card as a diplomatic strategy; use history as a diplomatic (bargaining) chip. 歴史教育 history teaching;《give students》[(an) education in history [(a) historical education]. 歴史能力検定 a history proficiency「test [examination]. 歴史漫画 a historical「comic book [*manga*]. 歴史問題〔未解決な歴史上の問題〕a historical「problem [controversy]; a「question of [controversy about] what really happened. ◎日中間の歴史となっている過去の～問題 controversies about the past [historical controversies] which are an impediment in Sino-Japanese relations.

**れきしきょうどうけんきゅう**【歴史共同研究】⇨にっかんれきしきょうどうけんきゅう, にっちゅうれきしきょうどうけんきゅう.

**れきしてき**【歴史的】 ▫ 歴史的和解 a historical「reconciliation [compromise, settlement].

**れきだん**【轢断】 ▫ 死後轢断 being cut in two (by a train) after death. 生体轢断 death by being cut in two (by a train).

**れきねん**[1]【暦年】 ▫ 暦年課税 calendar-year gift and inheritance taxation.

**レギュラー** ▫ レギュラー争い jostling [competition] among players for a regular position (on a team). レギュラー定着〔野球などのチームでの〕becoming a fixture in the starting lineup. ◎5人の外野手が～定着を目指して競り合っている. Five outfielders are competing「for regular places in the starting lineup [to become regular starters].

**レグイザモ** Leguizamo, John (1964– ;コロンビア生まれの映画俳優).

**レゲット** Leggett, Anthony J. (1938– ;米国の物理学者).

**レゴ** ▫ レゴ・ブロック a Lego「block [brick].

**レコメンド**〔推薦〕(a) recommendation. **～する** recommend. ▫ レコメンドシステム a「recommendation [recommender] system.

「**レザボアドッグス**」〔映画〕Reservoir Dogs.

**レシーブ**〔バレーボール・テニスなど〕 ▫ レシーブ・ミスの失敗〕a「receive [reception] error.

**レジスチン**〔生化〕〔血糖を下げるインスリンの働きを妨げるホルモン〕resistin. ▫ レジスチン遺伝子〔遺伝〕〔糖尿病の中核的原因遺伝子〕a resistin gene.

**レジデンシャルぶっけん**【-物件】〔住宅物件〕a residential property.

**レジデンス** ▫ アーチスト・イン・レジデンス〔芸術〕〔芸術家が一定期間滞在し, 創作活動を行える施設や機関の名称〕an institution which hosts an artist-in-residence program; 〔その事業〕an artist-in-residence program.

**レジャー** ▫ レジャー関連産業 leisure-related industries. レジャー白書 a white paper on leisure.

**レジャー**[2] Ledger, Heath (1979-2008;オーストラリア生まれの映画俳優;本名 Heathcliff Andrew Ledger).

**レジューム** ▫ レジューム機能〔電算〕resume function.

**レジン**〔樹脂〕resin. ▫ 固形[粉末, 液状]レジン (a)「hard [powdered, liquid] resin.

**レスキュー** ▫ レスキューカー〔救助車両〕a rescue vehicle; 〔折りたたみ式救護車〕a collapsible gurney. レスキュー犬 a rescue dog.

**レストレス・レッグスしょうこうぐん**【-症候群】〔医〕= むずむずあししょうこうぐん.

**レスポンデント**〔心理〕〔応答的・反応的〕respondent. ▫ レスポンデント学習 respondent learning. レスポンデント行動 respondent behavior.

**レスリー・チャン** Leslie Cheung (1956-2003;香港の映画俳優;中国語名 張國榮 Cheung Kwok-Wing).

**レセプター** ▫ レセプター病〔医〕〔受容体病〕a receptor disease.

**レダー** Leder, Mimi (1957– ;米国の映画監督).

**れつい**【劣位】 ▫ 劣位脳〔解〕=劣位半球. 劣位半球〔解〕〔右脳と左脳のうち, 言語中枢があない側〕a minor hemisphere; a nondominant hemisphere.

**れっか**[3]【裂果】〔植〕〔熟した果実が裂けて種子を散らすこと〕fruit「cracking [dehiscence]; 〔その果実; 裂開果(れっかいか)〕a dehiscent fruit. **～する** dehisce; crack.

**レッキス**〔手触りのよい毛皮のウサギ〕a rex; 〔その毛皮〕rex (fur).

**レック**〔生物〕〔集団求愛場〕a lek.

**レッグ・プレス**〔脚力を鍛えるためのトレーニングマシン〕a leg press (machine).

**レックリングハウゼンびょう**【-病】〔医〕〔神経線維腫症〕Recklinghausen's disease.

**レッグレスト**〔ふくらはぎを支える脚置き〕a legrest.

**レッサー・パンダ** ▫ シセン・レッサーパンダ a Chinese red panda; *Ailurus fulgens styani*. ニシ[ネパール]・レッサーパンダ a Western lesser panda; *Ailurus fulgens fulgens*.

**れっしゃ**[1]【列車】 ▫ 列車ホテル〔事故などによる列車不通時にホテル代わりに使用される鉄道車両〕a railroad car used for sleeping in (when services are hindered).

**レッド** ▫ レッド・ステーツ =赤い州 (⇨しゅう[2]). レッド・チップ〔中国系の香港企業；またその香港市場上場銘柄〕a red chip.

**レッド・オーシャン**〔経営〕「赤い海」；企業同士が激しく競争する(既存の)市場空間〕a red ocean.

**レッド・ドーンさくせん**【-作戦】=あかいよあけさくせん.

「**レッド・プラネット**」〔映画〕Red Planet.

**レッド・レーク**〔米国ミネソタ州北部の先住民居留地〕Red Lake.

**れつり**【裂離】〔医〕avulsion. ▫ 裂離骨折〔医〕an avulsion [a sprain] fracture.

**レディース・コミック**〔出版〕〔女性向き漫画〕a women's comic.

**レディース・デー**〔映画館などの女性優待日〕(a) ladies' day.

**レディコミ** =レディース・コミック.

**レドックス** ▫ レドックス・フロー電池 a redox flow battery.

**レトルト** ▫ レトルト・パック a retort pouch.

**レトロ** ▫ レトロ・ゲーム〔電算〕〔古いタイプのゲーム機で動作する古いビデオゲーム〕a retro game.

**レトログラード**〔時計の針が回転せず扇状に動き, 一定の時間で元の位置に戻り再び表示を開始する機構〕a retrograde (type of watch dial).

**レトロネクチン**〔商標・生化〕〔遺伝子治療用たんぱく質〕RetroNectin. ▫ レトロネクチン法〔医〕RetroNectin technology.

**レナート・ニルソンしょう**【-賞】 the Lennart Nilsson Award. ▶科学写真のノーベル賞と呼ばれる.

**レノックスしょうこうぐん**【-症候群】〔医〕Lennox syndrome.

**レノボ**〔中国最大のコンピューターメーカー〕Lenovo Group Ltd. ▶漢字社名は 聯想集団有限公司.

**レバー**[2] ▫ レバー式(の) lever-operated《brake》.

**ればたら** =たられば.

**レバノンないせん**【-内戦】〔1975-90年の〕the Lebanon Civil War.

**レバラン**〔インドネシアでのイスラムの断食明けの祭り〕Lebaran. [⇨イドゥル・フィトリ]

**レバレッジド・リース**〔経〕leveraged leasing; 〔その契約〕a leveraged lease.

**レビーしょうたいがたにんちしょう**【-小体型認知症】〔医〕dementia with Lewy bodies (略: DLB); Lewy dementia (略: LBD).

**レビトラ**〔商標・薬〕〔勃起不全治療薬〕Levitra.

**レビンソン** =レヴィンソン.

**レフォルマ**〔メキシコの日刊紙〕Reforma.

**レフカダとう**【-島】〔ギリシャ西部, イオニア海の島〕Lefkada

Island.
レプチン【生化】[脂肪細胞から分泌されるホルモン] leptin.
レフティー [左利きの] a left-handed 「person [player]; a left-hander; *《口》a lefty; (サッカーなど) a left-footed player; a left-footer. □▷ レフティー・ゴルファー a left-handed golfer; 《口》a lefty golfer.
レフト □▷ レフト線【野球】the left-field line. ▷ ～線に見事なヒットを放った. She pounded a solid hit「down [along] the left-field line.
レプブリカ =ラ・レプブリカ.
レフラーしょうこうぐん【—症候群】【医】Loeffler's syndrome.
レフルノミド【薬】[抗リウマチ薬] leflunomide.
レベトール【商標】[リバビリンの商品名] Rebetol.
レベニュー・シェア(リング)【経営】[収入分配制度の1つ] a [the] revenue sharing system.
レペノマムス【古生物】[白亜紀の哺乳類] Repenomamus.
レベル □▷ レベル・メーター [さまざまな分野のレベル測定器] a level meter.
レボワ・クゴモ [南アフリカ共和国北部, リンポポ州の州都] Lebowa-Kgomo.
レミケード【商標・薬】[インフリキシマブ; 関節リウマチ治療薬] Remicade. [⇨インフリキシマブ]
レムチャバン [タイ, シャム湾の港] Laem Chabang.
レムナント・リポたんぱく【—蛋白】【化】remnant lipoprotein (略: RLP).
「レリック」【映画】The Relic.
れんあい【恋愛】 □▷ 恋愛占い うらない. 恋愛運 one's romantic fate; one's luck at love.
「恋愛小説家」【映画】As Good As It Gets.
「恋愛適齢期」【映画】Something's Gotta Give.
れんが【煉瓦】 □▷ れんが割り [空手の演技の] brick breaking.
れんぎん2【連銀】 □▷ ニューヨーク連銀 the Federal Reserve Bank of New York.
レンク【RENK】[救え!北朝鮮の民衆/緊急ネットワーク] RENK. ▶ Rescue the North Korean People! Urgent Action Network の略.
れんけい1【連係】 □▷ 連係ミス【スポーツ】[選手間の] a 「failed [missed] pass; a failure to connect.
れんけつ1【連結】 □▷ 連結 ROE【経】a consolidated ROE. 連結 ROA【経】a consolidated ROA. 連結営業利益【経】a consolidated operating profit; consolidated operating profits. 連結業績 a consolidated results; a consolidated result. 連結業績見通し《revise its》consolidated earnings forecast; a forecast of consolidated business results《for the financial year ending in March》. 連結最終赤字 a consolidated net loss《of…》; consolidated net losses. 連結最終損益【経】a consolidated bottom line. 連結債務 (a) consolidated debt; consolidated 「debts [liabilities]. 連結配当性向【経】a consolidated (dividend) payout ratio. 連結バス =連接バス(⇨れんせつ). 連結付加税 a consolidated surtax.
れんごう1【連合】 □▷ 連合戦時増援演習 [米軍と韓国軍合同の] Reception, Staging, Onward movement & Integration (略: RSOI).
れんごうこく【連合国】 □▷ 連合国戦争犯罪委員会 [第二次大戦時の枢軸国の戦争犯罪を取り扱った; 1943年発足] the United Nations War Crimes Commission (略: UNWCC).
れんごうニュース【聯合—】[韓国の通信社] the Yonhap News Agency.
れんごうほう【聯合報】[台湾の日刊紙] the United Daily News.
れんさ【連鎖】 □▷ 連鎖地図【遺伝】a linkage map. 連鎖方式【経】[国内企業物価指数算定の] a [the] chain-linking method.
れんざ【連座】 □▷ 拡大連座制 the extended guilt-by-complicity system; [公職選挙法の] the provision, under the Public Office Election Law, extended in 1994, that a candidate is disqualified from taking office if his campaign manager, finance officer, secretary etc. has violated the Law to help him win.
レンジ・ファインダー【写真】[距離計; 測距儀] a range finder. □▷ レンジ・ファインダー式カメラ a rangefinder camera.
れんしゃ2【連写】【写真】《high-speed》consecutive 「shooting [shots]. ～する take (a series of) consecutive shots.
れんしゅう2【練習】 □▷ 練習環境 a training 「environment [situation]. ▷ ～環境に恵まれている have a good training environment. 練習拠点 a training camp. ▷ 高橋はマラソン～拠点の米コロラド州ボルダーで合宿を開始した. Takahashi has started at the marathon training camp at Boulder, Colorado. 練習走行 [自動車レースなどの] a 「practice [warm-up] run. 練習漬け《six months of》「solid [nonstop] practice. ▷ 甲子園をめざし, 高校3年間は～漬けの毎日だった. With his mind set on playing at Kōshien, he practiced day in day out during his three years at high school. 練習パートナー a 「practice [training] partner. 練習メニュー a training 「program [schedule].
れんしゅうだい【練習台】1 [練習相手] a practice partner. ▷ 美容師のカットの～になる be practiced on by a beautician / フランスからの留学生にフランス語会話の～になってもらった. A student from France let me practice my conversational French on her.
2 [ドラムの] a practice (drum) 「kit [set]; (打面) a practice pad.
れんしょう【連勝】 □▷ 連勝記録 a record for consecutive wins. ▷ 彼は自分の～記録を30に伸ばした. He set a new personal record of 30 consecutive wins.
レンズ □▷ レンズ効果【光学・海洋】[光線・津波の] a lens effect. ▷ 重力～効果【天文】a gravitational lens effect / 熱～効果【光学】a thermal lens effect.
レンズまめ【—豆】【植】a lentil; a (red) dhal; a split pea; Lens culinaris; Lens esculenta.
れんせつ【連接】 □▷ 連接バス an articulated 「a jointed, an accordion, a concertina, 《口》a bendy] bus.
れんせつバス【連節—】=連接バス(⇨れんせつ).
れんせん3【連戦】[ピンイン表記] Lian Zhan (1936－ ; 台湾の政治家; 国民党主席).
れんそうしゅうだん【聯想集団】⇨レノボ.
れんぞく【連続】 □▷ 連続再生 continuous playback. 連続試合安打【野球】《the record for》 hits in consecutive games. ▷ 12～試合安打《get》hits in 12 consecutive games. 連続試合出場記録 a record for the number of consecutive games played. 連続試合フルイニング出場【野球】《a player's》 full-game appearances in consecutive games. 連続出塁【野球】an on-base streak. ▷ 32試合～出塁を達成する extend one's consecutive on-base streak to 32 games; get on base in 32 straight games. 連続使用 [注射針などの] continued [repeated] reuse《of a syringe》. 連続放火 serial arson; a series of arson attacks. ▷ ～放火犯(人) a serial arsonist. 連続ボギー【ゴルフ】consecutive bogeys. ▷ 彼女は16, 17番で～ボギーをたたいた. She made consecutive bogeys at the sixteenth and seventeenth (holes). 連続無失点試合 consecutive shutouts. 連続粒界結晶シリコン【電子工学】CG silicon; continuous-grain silicon. 連続録音 continuous (audio) recording. 連続録画 continuous (video) recording. 連続技 [柔道・レスリングなどで] renzokuwaza; a series of techniques.
れんたい2【連帯】 □▷ 世代間連帯 intergenerational solidarity; 《form》strong ties between generations.
れんたいせきにん【連帯責任】 □▷ 無限[有限]連帯責任

unlimited [limited] joint liability.
れんだこ【連凧】a string of kites.
レンタル ▷ レンタル移籍〘スポーツ〙〔選手を一定期間有償で他チームに貸し出すこと〕the loan of a player 《to…》. レンタル家電〘業〙home-appliance rental; 〔家電製品〕a home appliance available for rent. レンタル犬〔犬〕a rental dog; 〔商売〕dog rental. レンタル・ブティック〔貸衣装店〕a rental boutique. レンタル・ポスト〔私設私書箱〕a rental post box.
れんたん【練炭・煉炭】 ▷ 練炭自殺 (a) charcoal-burning suicide.
れんどう【連動】 ▷ 連動性 interconnection; linkage. ◐ 日本経済と米国経済の〜性が一段と強まっている. The interconnection between the Japanese and US economies is becoming even stronger.
レンドゥぞく【-族】〔アフリカ中部の民族〕the Lendu; 〔1人〕a Lendu (*pl.* ~, ~s).
レントゲニウム〘化〙Roentgenium. ▶ 原子番号 111, 元素記号 Rg.
レンドルミン〘商標・薬〙〔催眠・鎮静剤〕Lendormin. ▶ 一般名はブロチゾラム (brotizolam).
レンノックスしょうこうぐん【-症候群】〘医〙＝レノックスしょうこうぐん.
れんぱ²【連覇】 ▷ 連覇記録 a record for「successive [consecutive]」victories. ◐ 〜記録を6に伸ばす extend「the [*one's*] successive [consecutive] victory record to 6.
レンフロ Renfro, Brad (1982-2008; 米国の映画俳優; 本名 Brad Barron Renfro).
れんぽう¹【連邦】 ▷ 連邦管区〔ロシアの〕a federal district. ▶ 以下の 7 管区. ◐ 中央〜管区 the Central Federal District / 北西〜管区 the Northwestern Federal District / 南部〜管区 the Southern Federal District / 沿ヴォルガ〜管区 the Volga Federal District / ウラル〜管区 the Urals Federal District / シベリア〜管区 the Siberian Federal District / 極東〜管区 the Far Eastern Federal District.
れんぽうエネルギーきせいいいんかい【連邦-規制委員会】〔米国の〕the Federal Energy Regulatory Commission (略: FERC).
れんぽうこうくうきょく【連邦航空局】〔米国の〕the Federal Aviation Administration (略: FAA).
れんぽうじゅうたくかしつけていとうこうしゃ【連邦住宅貸付抵当公社】〔米国の〕the Federal Home Loan Mortgage Corporation (略: FHLMC).
れんぽうじゅうたくこうしゃかんとくきょく【連邦住宅公社監督局】〔米国の〕the Office of Federal Housing Enterprise Oversight (略: OFHEO).
れんぽうじゅうたくていとうきんこ【連邦住宅抵当金庫】〔米国の〕the Federal National Mortgage Association (略: FNMA).
れんぽうじゅうたくていとうこうしゃ【連邦住宅抵当公社】＝れんぽうじゅうたくていとうきんこ.
れんぽうじゅんかいこうそさいばんしょ【連邦巡回控訴裁判所】〔米国の〕the (United States) Court of Appeals for the Federal Circuit (略: CAFC).
れんぽうじょうほうしょりきかく【基準】〔米国の〕the Federal Information Processing Standard (略: FIPS).
れんぽうだんけつはったんきょうかい【連邦団結発展協会】〔ミャンマーの軍政支援組織〕the Union Solidarity and Development Association (略: USDA).
れんぽうとっきょさいばんしょ【連邦特許裁判所】〔ドイツの〕the Federal Patents Court; 〔ドイツ語〕*Bundespatentgericht* (略: BPatG).
れんぽうはさんほう【連邦破産法】〘米法〙the Federal Bankruptcy Act. ▷ 連邦破産法 11 条 Chapter「11 [Eleven, XI] (of the Federal Bankruptcy Act). ▶ 日本の会社更生法に相当する. ◐ 〜第 11 条の適用を申請する file (under [for]) Chapter「11 [Eleven, XI].
れんぽうほしょうほう【連邦補償法】〘ドイツ法〙the Federal Law for the Compensation of the Victims of National Socialist Persecution; 〔ドイツ語〕*Bundesentschadigungsgesetz* (略: BEG). ▶ 1956 年制定の, ナチス迫害犠牲者の補償に関する連邦法.
れんぽうよきんほけんこうしゃ【連邦預金保険公社】〔米国の〕the Federal Deposit Insurance Corporation (略: FDIC).
れんらく【連絡】 ▷ 連絡先不明者 a person whose contact「address is [details are]」unknown. 連絡調整 liaison and coordination 《between…》. 連絡調整役 a「liaison coordinator [liaison/coordinator]」《between …》. 連絡役 a「liaison [contact]」man.
れんりつ【連立】 ▷ 大連立 a grand coalition (between the SDP and the CDU). ▷ 連立協議 inter-party talks on the formation of a coalition cabinet.

# ろ

ろあくか【露悪家】a [the sort of] person who likes to make a display of *his*「faults [weaknesses]」; a self-deprecating sort of person.
ロイ・エット〔タイ東北部の県; 同県の県都〕Roi Et.
ロイ・カトぉ(ー)ン〔タイの灯籠流し祭〕Loi Krathong; the Loi Krathong festival.
ロイコボリン〘薬〙〔抗がん剤〕leucovorin.
ロイター・ジェフリーズ・シー・アール・ビーしすう【-CRB 指数】〔国際的な商品指数〕the Reuters/Jefferies CRB Index.
ロイド Lloyd, Christopher (1938- ; 米国の映画俳優).
ロイヤリティー², ロイヤルティー ▷ ロイヤリティー率 a royalty rate.
ロイヤル・インディアンナイフ〘魚〙〔ナギナタナマズ科の淡水魚〕a royal knifefish; *Chitala branchi*.
ロイヤル・スコットランドぎんこう【-銀行】〔スコットランドの銀行〕the Royal Bank of Scotland (略: RBS).
ロイヤル・メール〔英国公社の郵便部門〕the Royal Mail (略: RM).
ろう⁷【蠟】 ▷ 蠟受け, 蠟皿〔燭台の〕a bobeche; a candle drip protector.
ロウ Law, Jude (1972- ; 英国生まれの映画俳優).
ロヴァニエミ〔フィンランド北部, ラップランドの市〕Rovaniemi. ▶ 近くにサンタクロース村 (Santa Claus' Village) がある.
ろうえい²【漏洩】 ▷ 内部漏洩 leakage 《of information》 (by insiders); leaking 《confidential》 information; 〔1 回の〕an [an internal] leak.
ろうさい²【労災】 ▷ 労災遺族年金 compensation [a pension] for the (bereaved) family of a work-related accident victim; a death-in-service pension. 労災医療費 work-related medical expenses. 労災事故 a work-related [an on-the-job] accident; an accident recognized as work-related. ◐ 〜事故調査報告書 an investigative report of work-related accidents. 労災認定 recognition as a work-related accident. ◐ 〜認定基準 a standard for recognizing 《an injury》 as a work-related accident / 〜認定を申請する[受ける] apply for [receive] recognition 《of *one's* condition》 as a work-related accident. 労災年金 a work-related「ac-

ろうし

cident [disability] pension.
**ろうし**[5]【労使】▷ 労使慣行 labor-management practices. 労使折半〔年金保険料負担の〕《be paid in》equal shares by employer and employee; splitting [dividing]《a premium》equally between employer and employee.
**ろうしん**[3]【老親】▷ 老親介護 the care of [caring for] one's 「elderly [aged] parent(s).
**ろうじん**【老人】▷ 老人語〔老人特有の語彙〕old 「people's [man's] language; words used by old people. 老人骨折 an age-related fracture. 老人保健拠出金〔各種保険組合が老人保健の財源として支出している金銭〕contributions [payments] for health care for the elderly.
**ろうじんいりょう**【老人医療】▷ 老人医療費〔高齢者が個々に負担する医療費〕medical 「expenses [costs] for the elderly; 〔国民医療費のうち高齢者に充てられる費用の総額〕expenditure on [the cost of (providing)] medical care for the elderly.
**ろうじんせい**【老人性】▷ 老人性認知症 senile dementia.
**ろうすい**[2]【漏水】▷ 漏水率〔上水道などの〕(the) rate of leakage.
**ろうそうせい**【老壮青】〔老年, 壮年, 青年の3世代を合わせた言い方〕(three generations of) age, maturity and youth.
**ロウたいウェイドはんけつ**【─対─判決】《法》〔1973年, 米国で中絶を合法化した最高裁判決〕the Roe 「v. [vs.] Wade 「case [decision]; (the case of) Roe 「v. [vs.] Wade.
**ろうたけた**【﨟長けた】graceful; noble-looking; refined; elegant; ladylike. ▷ ~貴婦人 an elegant aristocratic lady.
**ろうどう**[1]【労働】▷ 労働移動支援助成金 a subsidy to help people changing jobs; financial support for people seeking new employment. 労働英雄〔共産主義国などの〕a "labor hero." 労働着 work clothes. 労働矯正＝労働教養. 労働教養〔中国で政治犯などに対して課せられる労働刑〕reeducation through labor. ▷ ~教養所 a 「Reeducation Through Labor [reeducation-through-labor, reeducation through labor] camp. ▷ ~労働刑 penal labor. 労働経済動向調査 a survey of trends in employment in the (Japanese) labor market; the "survey on labor economy trends." 労働経済白書〔厚生労働省の〕the White Paper on the Labour Economy《2005》. 労働集約財 labor-intensive 「goods [products]. 労働集約的 labor-intensive (industries). 労働審判 labor tribunal. 労働審判委員会〔労働審判の〕an industrial tribunal commission. 労働審判員〔労働審判制度で使われから選ばれる〕a labor relations referee. 労働審判官〔労働審判制度における裁判官〕an industrial tribunal judge. 労働審判制度 industrial tribunal system. 労働戦線統一《労》unity 「within the labor movement [among the workers]. 労働相談 labor counseling. 労働訴訟 labor [work] litigation; a labor case. 労働投入量 (a) labor input. 労働白書 a white paper on labor; 〔旧労働省の〕《1999》White Paper on Labour. ▶ 現在は労働経済白書という. 労働負荷 a 〔sb's〕workload. 労働争議 a labor dispute. ▷ 個別~紛争 an individual labor dispute. 労働保険特別会計 a labor insurance special account; the Japanese Ministry of Health, Labour and Welfare's special account for insurance for workers. 労働保険法〔労災保険法と雇用保険法の併称〕labor insurance law. 労働模範〔中国の模範的な労働者に与えられる称号〕a model worker.
**ろうどうえいせいちょうさぶんせきセンター**【労働衛生調査分析~】the Occupational Health Research and Development Center.

**ろうどうきょく**【労働局】〔都道府県の〕a labor bureau.
**ろうどうきんこほう**【労働金庫法】《法》the Law for Workers' Credit Unions.
**ろうどうじかん**【労働時間】▷ 労働時間規制除外制度＝ホワイトカラー・エグゼンプション. 労働時間自由裁量制＝ホワイトカラー・エグゼンプション.
**ろうどうじかんたんしゅくそくしんほう**【労働時間短縮促進法】《法》the Shorter Working Hours Law. ▶ 正式名称は「労働時間の短縮の促進に関する臨時措置法」.
**ろうどうしゃ**【労働者】▷ 期間労働者 a fixed-term employee. 常用労働者 a regular employee; 〈集合的に〉a regular workforce. ▷ 労働者死傷病報告 notification of the death, injury or sickness of a worker. 労働者福祉 workers' welfare.
**ろうどうしゃけんこうふくしきこう**【労働者健康福祉機構】the Japan Labour Health and Welfare Organization.
**ろうどうしんぱんほう**【労働審判法】《法》the Labor Adjudication Law.
**ろうどうしんぶん**【労働新聞】〔北朝鮮の日刊紙〕Rodong Sinmun.
**ろうどうせいさくけんきゅう・けんしゅうきこう**【労働政策研究・研修機構】the Japan Institute for Labour Policy and Training.
**ろうどうせいさくしんぎかい**【労働政策審議会】〔厚生労働省の〕the Labour Policy Council.
**ろうどうほけんちょうしゅうほう**【労働保険徴収法】《法》the Law for Collection of Premiums on Labor Insurance.
**ろうどうりょく**【労働力】▷ 縁辺(えんぺん)労働力〔労働市場からの流出とそこへの再流入を繰り返す労働力〕a marginal 「workforce [labor force, labor market]; marginal labor. ▷ 労働力移動 《international》labor 「migration [movement].
**ろうどく**【朗読】▷ 対面朗読〔視覚障害者のための〕face-to-face reading. 朗読劇 a 「read-aloud [recitation] play. 朗読図書館〔図書館の朗読室でボランティアの人が視覚障害者に対して行うサービス〕a face-to-face reading service. 朗読奉仕 volunteer reading《for the blind》. 朗読ボランティア〔人〕a volunteer reader; 〔行為〕volunteer reading《for the blind》. 朗読録音〔視覚障害者のための〕(a) a recording of a reading《for the blind》; recording a reading; recording《a book for the blind》; 〔録音したもの〕(a) recorded reading; recorded reading materials. ▷ ~録音奉仕者 a volunteer reader for recording; a volunteer who will record《a book》.
**ろうにん**【浪人】▷ 合格浪人 a high-school graduate who has passed the entrance exam for one university but is attempting to pass the exam for another.
**ろうねん**【老年】▷ 老年社会学 social gerontology; geriatric sociology.
**ろうむ**【労務】▷ 労務職員 a labor employee; a laborer; 〈集合的に〉the labor workforce.
**ろうむぎょうせいけんきゅうじょ**【労務行政研究所】〔財団法人〕the Institute of Labor Administration.
**ろうるい**【蠟涙】candle drips.
**ろうれい**【老齢】▷ 老齢加算〔生活保護費への〕a welfare supplement for the elderly.
**ローイ・エット**＝ロイ・エット.
**ロー・ウェイ**【羅維】Lo Wei (1918–96; 香港の映画監督).
**ローカル**▷ ローカル・パーティー〔地域政党〕a local political party.
**ローケン, Kristanna** (1979– ; 米国の女優; 本名 Kristanna Sommer Loken).
「**ローサのぬくもり**」〔映画〕Solas.
**ロース**▷ 肩ロース (a) chuck roast; (a) shoulder roast. ▷ 牛肩~ (a) beef「chuck [shoulder] roast / 豚肩~ (a)

pork shoulder roast; (a) shoulder of pork; (a) butt roast; (a) Boston butt. 牛ロース (a) beef roast; (a) beef「chuck [sirloin, shoulder] roast. 豚ロース (a) pork roast; (a) pork loin (roast). ラムロース (a) lamb roast.

ローズ・ウォーター [バラの花びらの蒸留水; バラ水; 美肌用・飲用] rose water.

ローズしょうがくきん【—奨学金】[オックスフォード大学の奨学金制度] the Rhodes Scholarships.

ローズしょうがくせい【—奨学生】[オックスフォード大学の奨学金制度受給者] a Rhodes scholar.

ローズしれい【RoHS 指令】[環境][EU の, 電気・電子機器への特定有害物質の使用を規制する指令] the RoHS Directive. ► RoHS は Restriction of the use of the certain Hazardous Substances in electrical and electronic equipment の意.

ローズすい【—水】=ローズ・ウォーター.

ロー・スタイル [床・地面に近い, 低い目線で暮らす生活様式]「low style」; low-level 《living》. ◐ 〜のテーブル a "low style" table; a low table.

ローズ・ヒップ [植][ドッグローズの実] a rose hip. ◉◑ ローズヒップ・オイル, ローズヒップ油 rose hip oil. ローズヒップ・ティー rose hip tea.

ロータリーよねやまきねんしょうがくかい【—米山記念奨学会】the Rotary Yoneyama Memorial Foundation.

ローテーション ◉◑ 裏ローテーション [野球] a backup rotation. 先発ローテーション [野球][投手の] a starting rotation. ◉◑ ローテーション入り [野球] ◐ 〜入りする [投手が] join [be put into] the (starting) rotation. ローテーション制 a rotation system. ◐ 当社の休日は〜制で, 月に 9 日ある. Our company has nine days holiday a month, on a rotation system. ローテーション投手 [野球] a pitcher in the starting rotation; a rotation pitcher.

ローデシアン・リッジバック [犬] a Rhodesian ridgeback; a lion dog; an African lion hound.

ロード¹ ◉◑ ロード・サービス [保険][車両トラブルの際の] (emergency) road service.

「ロード・オブ・ウォー」[映画] Lord of War.

「ロード・オブ・ザ・リング」[映画] The Lord of the Rings. ► 第 1 作「旅の仲間」(The Fellowship of the Ring), 第 2 作「二つの塔」(The Two Towers), 第 3 作「王の帰還」(The Return of the King) の 3 部作.

ロードサイド [都市郊外の幹線道路沿いの] roadside. ◉◑ ロードサイド【型】ホテル a roadside hotel. ロードサイド店 [舗] a roadside「shop [store].

ロード・タイム・トライアル [自転車競技] a road time trial. ◐ 男子個人〜 a men's individual road time trial.

「ロード・トゥ・パーディション」[映画] Road to Perdition.

ロードレースせかいせんしゅけん【—世界選手権】the Road Racing World Championship Grand Prix (略: WGP).

ローナ・ジェーン [商標][オーストラリアのスポーツブランド] Lorna Jane.

「ローハイド」[旅をするカウボーイたちの苦闘を描いた TV 西部劇] Rawhide. ► クリント・イーストウッド (Clint Eastwood) の出世作.

ロー・バジェット [低予算] (a) low budget.

ロハス【LOHAS】=ロハス².

ロービジョン [医][低視力] low vision. ◉◑ ロービジョン・ケア low vision care.

ロープ ◉◑ ロープ・スキッピング [縄跳び] (rope) skipping;
*jump rope; rope jumping.

ローマきてい【—規程】=国際刑事裁判所設立条約 (ろくさいけいじさいばんしょ).

ローミング ◉◑ 国際[海外]ローミング international [overseas, global] roaming.

ローラーぐつ【—靴】rolling shoes; shoes with rollers. ►

Heelys の商標で知られる.

ローラン・ギャロス [テニス][全仏オープンが開催されるフランスのテニススタジアム] Roland Garros; the Roland Garros tennis stadium; [全仏オープン] Roland Garros (⇒ぜんふつオープン).

ローリング¹ ◉◑ ローリング方式 [経営][状況に対応して年度ごとに事業計画を見直す方式] a rolling plan; [レース][自動車レースなどのスタート時の] a rolling start.

ロール
2 [円筒形に巻くこと; 巻いたもの] a roll.
3 [回転] a roll; [空][横転飛行] (a) roll motion. ◉◑ ロール剛性 [自動車] roll stiffness.

ロール・モデル [手本となる人物] a role model.

ロール・レタリング [心理][役割交換書簡法] role play using letter-writing.

ローレンス Lawrence, Martin (1965– ; ドイツ生まれの映画俳優).

ローレンス・リバモアこくりつけんきゅうじょ【—国立研究所】[米国の核研究施設] (the) Lawrence Livermore National Laboratory (略: LLNL).

ローン¹ ◉◑ 割賦ローン =分割ローン. 分割ローン an installment loan. ◉◑ ローン担保証券 [証券] a collateralized loan obligation (略: CLO).

ローン⁴ 1 [インドネシア, アチェ州, 大アチェ県の郡] Lhoong. 2 [ラオス, ルアンナムター県の郡] Long.

ローン・スター・グループ [米国の投資組合] the Lone Star Funds.

ローン・カスタマー [航空機メーカーなどに対して新機種の受注目標に到達する機数を発注しその生産開始に踏み切らせる航空会社など] a launch customer 《for…》; the [first [initial] user 《of the Boeing 787》.

「ローン・レンジャー」[黒マスク, 二挺拳銃で仇討ちのために闘う男の TV 西部劇] The Lone Ranger.

ろか² 【濾過】 ◉◑ 濾過フィルター a (purification) filter.

ろかた【路肩】 ◉◑ 路肩崩落 [崩壊] collapse of a (road) shoulder; (road) shoulder collapse.

ろくおん【録音】 ◉◑ 録音図書 [視覚障害者用の] a「recorded book [recording of a book] (for the visually impaired).

ろくが【録画】 ◉◑ 長時間録画 extended recording time. 録画時間 [映像録画機器などの] recording time. 録画出演 《make》a「recorded [video] appearance.

ろくさいき【録再機】[録音録画も再生もできる機器] a record/playback device.

ろくさいにち【六斎日】[仏教][毎月の精進日] the six days of abstinence. ► 8 日・14 日・15 日・23 日・29 日・30 日の 6 日.

ロクスマウェ [インドネシア, アチェ州の都市, 北アチェ県の県都] Lhokseumawe.

ろくそく【六速】[自動車][変速機の前進第 6 段] sixth; sixth gear. ◐ ギヤを〜に入れる put the car into sixth / 〜にシフトアップする shift up to sixth (gear). ◉◑ 六速自動変速機 a「six-speed [6-speed] automatic transmission.

ろくふっかいおう【六弗化硫黄】【化】sulfur hexafluoride (略: $SF_6$).

ろくふっかウラン【六弗化—】【化】uranium hexafluoride.

ろくぼうせい【六芒星】a hexagram.

ロクンガ =ロックガ.

ロケ ◉◑ ロケ弁 a lunch provided to a film crew on location.

ロゲ Rogge, Jacques (1942– ; ベルギーの整形外科医; IOC 会長《2001– 》).

ロケーションフリー [商標][無線 LAN を搭載したテレビシステム] LocationFree.

「ロケッティア」[映画] The Rocketeer.

ロケット¹ ◉◑ ロケット花火 a firework rocket; a rocket firework. ロケット理論 rocket theory.

ロケット・スタート〖自動車レース・競技〗〔高速スタート〕《(get (off to))》a rocket start. ◑Vを目指して開幕6連勝の〜を切った巨人だったが、5月に入ると失速してしまった。With victory in their sights, the Giants got a rocket start with six successive wins, but in May they began to run out of steam.

ロケフリ ＝ロケーションフリー．

ロゴ[1] □● ロゴ入り bearing [imprinted with] a「logo [insignia]. ◑〜入り封筒[Tシャツ] an envelope [a T-shirt] imprinted with a logo.

ろこう【露光】 □● 長時間露光 long(-duration) exposure.

ロコト〖植〗〔ペルー産の唐辛子〕(a) rocoto (pepper); (a) locoto (pepper); Capsicum pubescens.

ロサンジェルス・タイムズ〔米国ロサンジェルス発行の朝刊紙〕The Los Angeles Times.

「ロザンナのために」〖映画〗 Roseanna's Grave;〔別タイトル〕For Roseanna.

ろじ[1]【路地】 □● 路地状敷地〔道路から細い通路でしか入れない敷地〕a flag lot.

ろじ[2]【露地】 □● 露地物 field(-grown) vegetables; outdoor(-grown) vegetables.

ロジア〖建〗〔戸外吹き抜け空間・屋根付きベランダ〕a loggia.

ロシアかがくアカデミー【〜科学〜】the Russian Academy of Sciences.

ロシアじゆうみんしゅとう【〜自由民主党】〔ロシアの政党〕the Liberal Democratic Party of Russia（略：LDPR）.

ロシアつうしん【〜通信】＝ロシア・ノーボスチ通信．

ロシア・ノーボスチつうしん【〜通信】〔ロシアの国営通信社〕the Russian Information Agency Novosti（略：RIAN）.

ロシアれんぽうぐんさんぼうほんぶじょうほうそうきょく【〜連邦軍参謀本部情報総局】the Main Intelligence Directorate（略：GRU）. ▶ GRUはロシア語のGlavnoye Razvedyvatelnoye Upravlenieから．

ロジたん【〜担】〔外交活動に伴うロジスティクスを担当する外務省官吏〕a diplomat in charge of logistics; a logistics manager.

ロジャー・ラビット〔米国のアニメの主人公のウサギ〕Roger Rabbit.

ロシュ〔スイスの医薬品会社〕Roche.

ろしゅつ[2]【露出】 □● 露出値〔写真〕〔カメラの〕an exposure value; EV;〔マスコミなどへの〕《(media)》exposure;〔肌の〕(a) degree of undress.

ろじょう[1]【路上】 □● 路上禁煙〔路上での喫煙禁止〕prohibition of smoking on the street; an outdoor smoking ban;〔路上での喫煙をやめること〕cessation of [stopping] smoking on the street;〔掲示〕No Smoking on the Street. ◑〜禁止条例〔路上喫煙禁止条例〕an ordinance against smoking「on [in] the street /〜禁止地区 an area where smoking is prohibited on the street. 路上シンガー a street singer. 路上販売 street「vending [selling].

ろじょうライブ【路上〜】a street「concert [performance].

ろしん【炉心】 □● 炉心崩壊〔原子炉の〕core destruction（略：CD）.

ロス[1] □● ロス・シェアリング〖金融〗〔損失分担〕loss sharing.

ロス[3] 1 ⇨キューブラ=ロス．

　2 Ross, Herbert (1927-2001; 米国の映画監督).
　3 Roth, Joe (1948-　; 米国の映画監督・製作者).
　4 Roth, Tim (1961-　; 英国生まれの映画俳優).

ロスアトム〔ロシア原子力庁〕Rosatom; the Federal Nuclear Energy Agency.

ロス・アラモスこくりつけんきゅうじょ【〜国立研究所】〔米国の核研究施設〕(the) Los Alamos National Laboratory（略：LANL）.

「ロズウェル 星の恋人たち」〔米国の、ロマンチックSFサスペンスのTVドラマ〕Roswell. ▶ Roswellはニューメキシコ州南東部の農業・酪農業が盛んな土地だが、1947年に起きたUFO墜落疑惑事件で知られる．

ロスオボロンエクスポルト〔ロシアの国営武器輸出公社〕Rosoboroneksport.

ロスしゅじゅつ【〜手術】〖医〗〔自己肺動脈弁を用いる心臓大動脈弁置換手術〕the [a] Ross「procedure [operation]. ▶ 名称はこの方式を開発した英国の心臓外科医Donald Rossから．

「ロスト・イン・トランスレーション」〖映画〗 Lost In Translation.

「ロスト・サン」〖映画〗 The Lost Son.

「ロスト・ハイウェイ」〖映画〗 Lost Highway.

ロスト・バゲージ〔飛行機に預けた手荷物が紛失または所在不明になること〕lost「baggage [luggage].

ロストラータ 1〖植〗〔熱帯産バショウ科の多年草〕Heliconia rostrata.
　2〖植〗〔リュウゼツラン科，耐寒性に優れた細葉の観葉植物〕Yucca rostrata.

ロストワックスほう【〜法】〖金属加工〗〔蝋型鋳造法〕lost wax casting; a lost wax「method [technique]; cire perdue.

ロスネフチ〔ロシア最大の国営石油企業〕Rosneft.

ロスマウェ ＝ロクスマウェ．

ロゼッタ[2]〖宇宙〗〔欧州宇宙機関の彗星探査機〕Rosetta.

ロセフィン〖商標・薬〗〔抗生物質〕Rocephin. ▶ 一般名はセフトリアキソン・ナトリウム．

ロゼレム〖商標・薬〗〔不眠症治療薬〕Rozerem.

ろせん【路線】 □● 協調路線 a「joint [cooperative] line. ◑同業他社との協調〜を打ち出す work out a joint policy with other companies in the same line. 対決路線 a confrontational line; a policy of opposition (to…). □● 路線継承 continuance of [carrying on]《(a predecessor's)》policy. 路線変更〔バスの〕a change in a bus route;〔方針の〕a change in policy; a policy change. 路線論争 a (party) policy debate; a discussion on future policy.

ろちょう[2]【露頂】〖軍〗〔潜水艦の潜望鏡や通信用アンテナが海面上に出る状態への深度変更〕rising [coming] to periscope depth.

ロッカー[2]〔ロック歌手〕a rock singer; a rocker.

ろっかこくきょうぎ【六か国協議】〔北朝鮮の核開発問題について話し合う協議; 2003年8月より〕the「six-party [six-nation] talks.

ロッキング〔ストリートダンスのジャンル; 1980年代半ばより流行〕

ロックアップ〖証券〗〔ある株式の公開後、その株の売買を一定期間凍結する制度〕(a) lock-up. □● ロックアップ期間 a lock-up period.

ロックガ〔インドネシア, スマトラ島北端にある町〕Lhoknga.

ロック・クローリング〔アメリカ発祥のモータースポーツ〕rock crawling; rockcrawling.

「ロック, ストック&トゥー・スモーキング・バレルズ」〖映画〗 Lock, Stock & Two Smoking Barrels.

ロックスマウェ ＝ロクスマウェ．

「ロックフォード氏の事件メモ」〔米国の、探偵もののTVドラマ〕The Rockford Files.

ロックンガ ＝ロックガ．

ロッテルダムじょうやく【〜条約】the Rotterdam Convention. ▶「国際貿易の対象となる特定の有害な化学物質及び駆除剤についての事前のかつ情報に基づく同意の手続に関するロッテルダム条約」(the Rotterdam Convention on the Prior Informed Consent Procedure for Certain Hazardous Chemicals and Pesticides in International Trade) の略称．

ロット[1] □● 生産ロット a production lot.

ロットワイラー〖犬〗a rottweiler; a rottie.

「600万ドルの男」〔米国の、600万ドルでサイボーグとなった秘密機関員の活躍TVドラマ〕The Six Million Dollar

Man. ▶「サイボーグ危機一髪!!」の邦題でも放映.
**ロップイヤー**〖動〗〔耳の垂れたウサギの種類〕a lop-eared rabbit.
**ロップリー 1**〔タイ中部のリゾート地〕Lopburi; Lop Buri. **2**〔タイ中部の県;その県都〕Lopburi; Lop Buri.
**ロディック** Roddick, Anita (1942-2007;英国の実業家;環境保護志向の商品作りで急成長した化粧品チェーン Body Shop の創業者).
**ロト**〔数字選択式宝くじ〕a lotto; a numbers lottery. ◐〜6 a six-digit lotto;〔日本などの〕Lotto 6.
**ロドリゲス** Rodriguez, Robert (1968- ;米国の映画監督).
**ロナウド** Ronaldo (1976- ;ブラジルのサッカー選手;本名 Ronaldo Luiz Nazario de Lima).
**ロニー・ユー** Ronny Yu (1950- ;香港生まれの映画監督;中国語名 千仁泰 Yu Yan-Tai).
**ロハス²** 〖LOHAS〗〔健康と環境を大切にする生活様式〕LOHAS. ▶ Lifestyles of Health and Sustainability の略.
**ロバニエミ** ＝ロヴァニエミ.
**ろばん**〖路盤〗 □□ 路盤陥没 roadbed subsidence. 路盤材 roadbed material.
**ロヒプノール**〖商標・薬〗〔催眠・鎮静薬;局所麻酔時の鎮静用〕Rohypnol. ▶ 一般名はフルニトラゼパム (flunitrazepam).
**ロビンス** Robbins, Tim (1958- ;米国の映画俳優;本名 Timothy Francis Robbins).
**ロビンソン** Robinson, Phil Alden (1950- ;米国の映画監督).
**ロブスター・クロウ**〖植〗〔熱帯産バショウ科の多年草〕(a) lobster claw; *Heliconia bihai*.
**ロフト** □□ ロフト角〖ゴルフ〗the loft angle. ロフト収納 loft storage.
**ろぶね**〖艪舟〗a boat propelled by a single scull; a sculling boat; a Japanese gondola.
**ロベルト・クレメンテしょう**〔-賞〕〖野球〗〔慈善活動を行っているメジャーリーグ選手に贈られる賞〕the Roberto Clemente Award.
**ろほう**〖濾胞〗 □□ 濾胞がん〖医〗(a) follicular ｢cancer [carcinoma].
**ロボット** □□ アーム・ロボット an arm robot. 案内ロボット a ｢guidance [direction] robot; a robot for giving directions. 犬型ロボット a robot(ic) dog; a dog(-shaped) robot. 医療(用)ロボット a medical robot. お掃除ロボット a vacuuming robot. お手伝いロボット a helper robot; a robot ｢helper [assistant]. 介助ロボット a home care robot. 会話ロボット a conversational robot. 看護ロボット a nursing robot; a robot nurse. 危険物処理ロボット an explosives [an explosive ordnance, a bomb] disposal robot. 軍事ロボット a military robot. 警備ロボット a security robot; a security guard robot. 災害救助ロボット a rescue robot. 作業ロボット a ｢working [worker, work] robot. ◐深海作業〜 a robot for deep-sea operation. 産業用ロボット an industrial robot; a steel-collar worker. 自走式ロボット a self-propelled robot. 手術支援ロボット a ｢surgical [surgery] robot. 消防ロボット a firefighting robot. 人体装着型ロボット a wearable robot; a robot suit. 寿司ロボット a sushi(-making) robot. 接客ロボット a receptionist robot; a "hospitality" robot. 戦闘用ロボット a combat robot; a robot for use in combat. 双腕ロボット a dual-arm robot. 対人追従[人間追従,お供]ロボット a robot ｢attendant [companion]. 搭乗歩行型ロボット a mountable walking robot. 二足歩行ロボット a biped robot. パートナー・ロボット〔人と関わりを持ち,その活動を支援するロボット〕a partner robot. 搬送ロボット a transfer robot. 人型ロボット,ヒト型ロボット a ｢humanoid [human-type] (robot). 防災ロボット a disaster [an accident] recovery robot. 溶接ロボット a welding robot.

留守番ロボット a house-sitter robot. レスキュー・ロボ(ット) a rescue robot.
□□ ロボット介在活動《therapeutic, entertainment》activities employing a robot. ロボット介在療法 robot therapy; robot-assisted therapy (略: RAT). ロボット産業 the robot industry.
**ろまえかかく**〖炉前価格〗〖商〗〔鉄鋼・金属の取引で,売り手が運送コストを負担する場合の価格〕a delivered price.
**ロマンシュご**〔-語〕〔スイスの公用語の1つ〕the Romansh language.
**ロマン・ノワール**〔暗黒街などを舞台にした陰鬱な小説;暗黒小説〕(ジャンル) noir fiction; hardboiled fiction; (作品) a (roman) noir; a hardboiled novel; a "black [dark] novel."
**「ロミオ・マスト・ダイ」**〔映画〕Romeo Must Die.
**ロム**〖ROM〗 □□ 不正[裏]ROM〔公安委員会の検定を経ていないパチンコやパチスロの ROM 〕a ROM chip used illicitly in a pachinko or slot machine to control the winning percentage; (an) ｢unauthorized [illegal] ROM.
**ロムる**〖電算〗〔掲示板などで,発言せずに読むだけにする〕lurk 《on a BBS》.
**ロメイン・レタス**〖植〗Romaine lettuce.
**ロメロ 1** Romero, Cesar (1907-94; 米国の俳優;本名 Cesar Julio Romero Jr.). **2** Romero, George A(ndrew) (1940- ;米国の映画監督・脚本家・製作者).
**ろめん**〖路面〗 □□ 路面温度 (the) road surface temperature (略: RST). 路面陥没 road subsidence; subsidence ｢in [of] a road; road cave-in;〔1箇所の〕a depression in the road; a pothole. 路面状況 road surface conditions. 路面性状測定車 a road inspection vehicle. 路面損傷 road surface damage.
**ロモノソフかいれい**〔-海嶺〕〖地質〗〔北極圏の海底の〕the Lomonosov Ridge.
**ロヤ・ジルガ**〔アフガニスタンの国民大会議〕a [the] loya jirga.
**ロリコン** □□ ロリコン系 *lolicon*;《artwork》portraying children in an erotic style. 〜系雑誌 a *lolicon* magazine; a ｢magazine [comic book] portraying children in an erotic style.
**ロレアル**〔フランスに本社がある化粧品会社〕L'Oréal.
**ロレスタ(-)ン**〔イラン西部の州〕Lorestan; Luristan.
**ロン³**〔インドネシア・ラオスの地名〕⇨ローン⁴.
**ロンアン**〔ベトナム南部,メコンデルタ地帯の省〕Long An.
**ロング** □□ ロング缶〔ビールなどの〕a long can. ロング・パスタ〖料理〗〔スパゲッティなど,長いイタリア麺類〕long pasta.
**「ロング・キス・グッドナイト」**〔映画〕The Long Kiss Goodnight.
**ロングシート** a longitudinal seat.
**ロング・ステイ**〔短期の旅行に対して,長期の滞在〕a long [an extended] stay 《in a foreign country》.
**ロング・スロー**〖サッカー〗〔飛距離の長いスローイン〕a long throw-in.
**ロング・テール**〔統計上で,現れる頻度のごく少ない項目が非常に多数並んだ範囲〕the Long Tail. ▶ 項目を頻度の多い順に横軸に並べ,縦軸に頻度をとって線グラフ化すると長い尾が横に伸びたように見えることから. □□ ロングテール現象〔ネット通販に顕著に見られる〕the long-tail phenomenon. ロングテール理論〖商〗〔個々には売れ行きの鈍い商品も数多くそろえて常に頻度を上げれば累積的な利益につながるとする考え方〕the long-tail theory.
**ロング・ボール**〖サッカー〗〔長いパス〕a long ball ◐〜を多用 play [hit, kick] a lot of long balls /〜を放り込む fire [put] a long ball (into the penalty box).
**ロンゲラップかんしょう**〔-環礁〕〔マーシャル諸島にある環礁〕Rongelap Atoll.
**ロンゲラップとう**〖-島〗〔マーシャル諸島中の島〕Rongelap Island.

ろんじゅつ【論述】 ▭ 論述問題〔試験の〕an essay question.

ロンスエン〔ベトナム南部, アンジャン省の省都〕Long Xuyen.

ろんせつ【論説】 ▭ 論説広告 advocacy advertising.

ロン・ティボーこくさいおんがくコンクール【国際音楽-】〔パリで開催されるピアニストとバイオリニストのための国際音楽コンクール〕the Long-Thibaud International Competition. ▶ フランスのピアノ奏者 ロン (Marguerite Long) とバイオリン奏者 ティボー (Jacques Thibaud) が1943年に創設。

ろんてん【論点】 ▭ 論点整理 summarizing the points under discussion; putting the various arguments in「order [shape].

ロンドン[1] ▭ ロンドン・ブーツ 《a pair of》「"London" [flashy high-heeled] boots.

ロンドンこくさいせきゆとりひきじょ【-国際石油取引所】the International Petroleum Exchange (略：IPE).

ロンドン・コレクション 《服飾》〔ロンドンの新作発表会〕the London Collection.

ロンドン・コロシアム〔ロンドンの大劇場〕the London Coliseum.

ロンドンどうじたはつ[どうじばくは]テロ【-同時多発[同時爆破]-】＝ロンドンどうじテロ.

ロンドンどうじテロ【-同時-】〔2005年7月7日の〕the London terror(ist) bombings (of 7 July 2005); seven-seven [7-7].

ロンバート[ロンバード]がたかしだしせいど【-型貸出制度】《金融》Lombard lending.

ろんぶん【論文】 ▭ 論文博士 a person with a thesis-based Ph.D.

ろんり【論理】 ▭ 論理構成 a logical「layout [construction]. 論理構造 a logical structure.

ろんりてき【論理的】 ▭ 論理的思考 logical thinking; thinking logically. ◐ ～思考法 a means of logical thinking; how to think logically／～思考力 a capacity「for logical thinking [to think logically].

-わ³ **1**〔軽い主張・決意・詠嘆などを表す女性語〕◐ それは私じゃない〜。Now that wasn't me. / 彼はもう帰った〜。Oh, he's already left. / さあ, 行こう〜よ。We're going! Come on! / これ, あなたにあげる〜。I want to give this to you.
**2**〔文末で感動を表現〕◐ 今時手書きなんてよくやる〜, ほんとに。Wow, that's really something, to write by hand these days. / 釣れる〜, 釣れる〜, 1時間でざっと50匹に。They kept biting and biting, and in an hour I caught around 50 fish.
**3**〔並べたてて感動を強調〕◐ 歌は歌う〜, すごいね, あの女優は。She can sing, she can dance—that actress is amazing. / 財布はすられる〜, 石段で転んで捻挫する〜, 大変な旅行だったよ。My wallet was picked, I sprained myself falling down a stone staircase—the trip was just one disaster after another.

**ワーカーズ・コープ**〔労働者協同組合〕a workers' co-op.

**ワーキング・グループ**〔作業部会〕a task force; a working group [party].

**ワーキング・プア(ー)**〔フルタイムで働いても生活保護水準以下の収入しか得られない就業者〕〈集合的に〉the working poor.

**ワークフロー**〔業務・作業の処理手順〕workflow.

**ワーク・ライフ・バランス**〔仕事と生活の調和〕(a)「work/life [work-life] balance.

**ワーシト** =ワシ(ッ)ト。

**ワーファリン**〔商標・薬〕〔血液抗凝固薬〕Warfarin.

**ワーム²** ◐▷ ワーム型ウイルス〔電算〕〔ネットワークを通じて他のコンピューターに感染し自己増殖を繰り返すウイルス〕a worm virus; a worm-type virus.

**ワールド** ◐▷ ワールド・タイマー〔時計の〕a world timer; a global timepiece.

**ワールドウォッチけんきゅうじょ**〔-研究所〕〔環境問題を扱う米国の研究機関〕the Worldwatch Institute (略: WWI).

**ワールド・カップ** ◐▷ ワールド・カップ組織委員会 the Organizing Committee for the 《2006 FIFA》World Cup.

**ワールド・サイバー・ゲームズ**〔コンピューターゲーム世界選手権大会〕the World Cyber Games (略: WCG).

**ワールドスケール・レート**〔石油タンカーなどの運賃の指標〕the Worldscale rate. ▶ 正式名称は the New Worldwide Tanker Nominal Freight Scale.

**ワールド・ビジョン**〔国際NGO〕World Vision.

**ワールド・ベースボール・クラシック**〔野球〕〔国別対抗戦〕the World Baseball Classic (略: WBC).

**ワイ**【Y】◐▷ Y理論〔経営〕Theory Y.

**ワイアー・フォックス・テリア**〔犬〕a wire fox terrier.

**ワイ・イー・エス**【YES】〔金融〕〔円・ユーロ・ドルの3通貨〕YES. ▶ Y は日本円, E はユーロ (euro), S は米ドル($). ◐▷ **YES 債(券)** a YES bond. **YES 債券市場** the YES bond market. **YES 基金** a YES fund.

**ワイ・イー・オー**【YEO】〔世界青年起業家機構の略〕YEO; the Young Entrepreneurs' Organization.

**わいしょう**【矮小】◐▷ **矮小銀河**〔超コンパクト〜銀河〕an ultracompact dwarf (galaxy) (略: UCD).

**ワイズ** Weisz, Rachel (1971- ;〔英国生まれの映画女優〕.

**わいせつ**【猥褻】◐▷ **猥褻行為**〔commit〕an act of obscenity;《make》an obscene move《toward…》; an indecent [a lewd] act.

**ワイドスパン**〔建〕〔マンションなどで採光や風通しを重視しバルコニー側の開口部を広くする間取り〕a wide floor plan.

**ワイブロ**【WiBro】〔<wireless + broadband〕〔電算〕〔韓国のブロードバンド無線インターネット接続規格〕WiBro.

**ワイマラナー**〔犬〕a Weimaraner.

**ワイヤー・ゲージ**〔線番〕a wire gauge. ◐▷ アメリカン [米式]・ワイヤ(ー)ゲージ the American standard wire gauge (略: AWG). バーミンガム・ワイヤ(ー)ゲージ the Birmingham wire gauge (略: BWG). 標準ワイヤ(ー)ゲージ the standard wire gauge (略: SWG). ミリメータ・ワイヤ(ー)ゲージ the millimeter wire gauge.

**ワイヤー・プランツ**〔植〕a wire plant; a wire vine. [= ミューレンベッキア]

**ワイヤレス** ◐▷ **ワイヤレス接続**〔電算〕wireless access; (a) wireless connection. **ワイヤレス・ドアロック** a wireless door lock. [= リモコン・ドアロック (⇒リモコン)] **ワイヤレス・ブロードバンド**〔電算〕wireless broadband.

「**ワイルドシングス**」〔映画〕Wild Things.

「**ワイルド・ワイルド・ウエスト**」〔映画〕Wild Wild West.

**ワインドアップ** ◐▷ **ノーワインドアップ**〔投手が腕をふりかぶらずに投球すること〕a no-windup delivery. ◐ ノー〜で投げる work out of the stretch.

**ワインむし**〔-蒸し〕〔料理〕steaming in wine. ◐ 若鶏の白〜 young chicken steamed in white wine.

**わかい¹**【和解】◐▷ **刑事和解** an out-of-court settlement recorded in a criminal court (and having the same legal force as a court-mediated settlement). **全面和解**〔法〕a 「comprehensive [complete] settlement.

**わかいしゃかい**【和諧社会】〔中国の胡錦濤政権のスローガン〕a harmonious society.

**わかがえり**【若返り】◐▷ **若返り人事** staff rejuvenation; a personnel shakeup to bring in new blood.

**わかけほんせいいんこ**【輪掛本青鸚哥】〔鳥〕〔インコ科の鳥, ホンセイインコの亜種〕an Indian ring-necked parakeet; *Psittacula krameri manillensis*.

**わかしお**【若潮】the tide between neap and spring tide; tides with growing amplitude.

**わかて**【若手】◐▷ **若手議員** a young 「Diet member [legislator].

**わがら**【和柄】a (traditional) Japanese 「pattern [design]. ◐ 〜のバッグ a bag with a (traditional) Japanese pattern on it.

**わかれさせや**【別れさせ屋】a couple buster; an agency that tricks a spouse into divorce or separation.

**わきばら**【脇腹】(a) pain in one's side.

**わきゅう**【和弓】〔弓〕a Japanese-style bow;〔術〕Japanese-style archery.

**わくせい**【惑星】◐▷ **巨大惑星** a major planet. **巨大ガス惑星** a gas giant. **巨大氷惑星** an ice giant. **準惑星** a dwarf planet. **矮小惑星** a dwarf planet. ◐▷ **惑星科学** planetary science(s). **惑星ハンター**〔新惑星の発見に熱中する人〕a planet hunter.

**ワクチン** ◐▷ **ウイルス・ベクター・ワクチン** (a) 「viral [virus] vector vaccine. **新三種混合ワクチン**〔はしか・おたふくかぜ・風疹予防の〕(a [the]) MMR vaccine. ▶ MMR は, measles, mumps, rubella の略。**新二種混合ワクチン**〔はしか・風疹予防の〕(a [the]) MR vaccine. ▶ MR は, measles, rubella の略。**単抗原ワクチン** a single-antigen vaccine. **DNA ワクチン** (a) DNA vaccine. ◐▷ **ワクチン関連麻痺**〔医〕〔ポリオワクチンによる〕vaccine-associated paralytic poliomyelitis (略: VAPP). **ワクチン・ソフト**〔電算〕〔ウイルスに対する〕antivirus software. **ワクチン・プログラム**〔電算〕〔ウイルスに対する〕an antivirus program.

**ワクチンとよぼうせっしゅのためのせかいどうめい**【-と

予防接種のための世界同盟」the Global Alliance for Vaccines and Immunization (略: GAVI).

**わくねりせいほう**【枠練り製法】〔石けんの製造法の１つ〕the *wakuneri* method (of soap manufacture); a natural, slow-drying method of soap manufacture.

**わくものがたり**【枠物語】《文学》〔一つの話の枠内に本筋から独立した（しばしば複数の）話を含む物語形式〕『千一夜物語』『デカメロン』など〕a frame「story「tale, narrative」.

**わくわく** 🔲 わくわく感 a feeling of excited anticipation.

**ワぐん**【ワ軍】＝ワしゅうれんごうぐん.

**ワゴム**【輪－】🔲 輪ゴム結紮療法〔医〕〔痔(ぢ)の〕(a) rubber [(an) elastic] band ligation.

**わこもの**【和小物】accessories for Japanese clothing; kimono accessories.

**わさい**【和裁】🔲 和裁技能士 a certified skilled kimono-maker.

**わざお**【和竿】〔釣り〕〔漆で仕上げた竹製の釣り竿〕a Japanese lacquered bamboo fishing rod. 🔲 江戸和竿〔釣り〕〔異なる竹を何本か継ぎ合わせた和竿〕Edo-style lacquered bamboo fishing rod.

**わし**[2]【和紙】🔲 和紙人形 a doll made out of Japanese paper; a *washi*「doll [*ningyō*]」.

**ワシ(ッ)ト**〔イラク中東部の州〕Wasit. ▶ 州都 クート (Kut).

**わしゃ**【話者】🔲 話者認識 speaker「recognition [authentication, verification]」.

**ワしゅうれんごうぐん**【ワ州連合軍】〔ミャンマーの少数民族武装組織〕the United Wa State Army (略: UWSA).

**ワジリスタン**〔パキスタン西部、アフガニスタン国境の山岳地帯〕Waziristan.

**ワシントン** Washington, Denzel (1954–    ; 米国の映画俳優).

**ワシントン・カーネギーきょうかい**[けんきゅうじょ]【－協会[研究所]】〔米国の〕the Carnegie Institution of Washington.

**ワスカランこくりつこうえん**【－国立公園】〔ペルー中部の国立公園；世界遺産〕Huascarán National Park.

**わせ**[2]【早稲】an early-ripening (variety of) rice plant. 🔹 ～田〔早稲を植えた田〕early rice fields.

**わせい**[2]【和製】🔲 和製ロック Japanese rock (music);《俗》J-rock.

**わそく**[2]【話速】rate of speech. 🔲 話速変換〔テレビ・ラジオ等の音声をゆっくり聞こえるようにする技術〕rate of speech conversion.

**わだい**【話題】🔲 話題作 a「much-discussed [《口》hot]」《movie》; a《book》that everyone is talking about. 話題作り providing (an) interesting topic; thinking up something interesting to「talk about [discuss]」 彼のこの提案は単なる～作りが目的だろう. He probably only proposed this as a way of getting people talking. ｜ I guess his only motive in bringing this up was to encourage discussion. ／主演女優の来日은その映画の公開を控えてまたとない～作りになった. The visit to Japan of the female lead was the perfect opportunity to build buzz for the movie launch.

**わたおうさぎ**【綿尾兎】《動》a cottontail (rabbit).

**わたくしあめ**【私雨】very localized rainfall; isolated showers.

**わたくしてき**【私的】＝わたしてき.

**わだこ**【和凧】a Japanese kite.

**わたし**[2]【渡し】🔲 現地渡し〔チケット・商品などの〕🔹 スタジアムの入場券は郵送か現地～になります. Admission tickets can be sent to you or collected at the stadium. 🔲 渡し板 a (crossing) plank.

「**私が愛したギャングスター**」〔映画〕Ordinary Decent Criminal.

**わたしてき**【私的】🔹 ～には〔私としては〕as for me; as far as I'm concerned; for my part.

「**私の愛情の対象**」〔映画〕The Object of My Affection.

「**私の頭の中の消しゴム**」〔映画〕A Moment to Remember.

**わたしばし**【渡し箸】〔食事中に箸を食器の縁に横にわたして置くこと〕placing *one's* chopsticks across the rim of a dish before finishing a meal, which is a breach of etiquette.

**わたぼうしタマリン**【綿帽子－】《動》〔マーモセット科のサル〕a cotton-top tamarin; *Saguinus oedipus*.

**ワッツ** Watts, Naomi (1968–    ; 英国生まれの映画女優).

**ワッド** Wade, Abdoulaye (1926–    ; セネガルの政治家; 大統領《2000–    》).

**ワット・プー**〔ラオス南部のクメール遺跡〕Wat Phou.

**わっぱ**【輪－っぱ】🔲 わっぱ飯 rice with other ingredients on it, steamed in a *wappa*.

**わて**〔関西での一人称〕I; me.

**わどうかいちん**[**かいほう**]【和同開珎】《日本史》a Wadō「Kaichin [Kaihō]」; a copper or silver coin minted in Japan in the eighth century.

**ワトソン 1** Watson, Emily (1967–    ; 英国の映画女優).
**2** Watson, Emma (1990–    ; 英国の映画女優).

**ワナ**〔パキスタン北西部の都市〕Wana.

**わにがめ**【鰐亀】《動》〔北米産のカミツキガメ科のカメ〕an alligator snapping turtle; *Macroclemys temminckii*.

**わばさみ**【和鋏】〔握りばさみ〕traditional Japanese scissors.

**わふう**【和風】🔲 和風ファーストフード (a) Japanese(-style) fast food.

**ワフドとう**【－党】🔲 新ワフド党〔1983 年に再建された民族主義政党〕the New Wafd (Party).

**わぶん**[2]【和分】《統》〔数列の累積和をつくること; 差分の逆〕integration; summation. 〔⇨きょうわぶん〕

**わへい**【和平】🔲 和平会議 a peace conference.

**わへい**[2]【話柄】a「topic [subject]」of conversation.

**わへいえんぺん**【和平演変】〔中国における共産党支配体制の平和的転覆〕the peaceful overthrow of Chinese communism.

**ワヤン(・クリット)**〔インドネシア伝統芸能の影絵芝居〕Wayang (Kulit).

**わらしべ**【藁稭】〔わらくず〕straw waste; pieces [scraps] of straw; 〔稲の穂の芯〕the central stalk of a dried rice plant.

**ワラス**〔ペルー中部の町〕Huaraz.

**ワランデイ**〔ロシア北西部、バレンツ海沿岸の港町〕Varandei.

**ワラント** 🔲 カバード・ワラント a covered warrant. コール・ワラント a call warrant. プット・ワラント a put warrant.

**わりこみ**【割り込み】🔲 割り込み乗車 cutting in line to board a《train, bus, etc.》. 割り込み電話〔キャッチホン〕call waiting;〔キャッチホン式の電話機〕a telephone with call waiting;〔通話中にかかってくる別の人からの電話〕a call-waiting call.

**わりだか**【割高】🔲 割高株《株》an overvalued stock. 割高感 a sense that something is expensive. 🔹 安くなってきた海外旅行と比べると国内旅行は～感がある. Domestic travel seems expensive compared with overseas trips, which have become cheaper. ／現在の株価には～感がある. Stock prices these days are rather high.

**わりびき**【割引】🔲 大幅割引 a「major [massive, substantial] discount [rebate]. 会員割引《かいいん》[1]. 季節割引〔旅館などの〕a seasonal discount. 深夜割引〔高速道路料金・電気料金などの〕a late night discount. 🔲 割引キャッシュフロー ＝割引現在価値. 割引現在価値《会計》discounted cash flow (略: DCF). 割引短期国債 a

treasury bill 〔略: TB〕.
**わりやす**【割安】 ◫ 割安株〔株式〕a bargain stock; an undervalued stock. 割安株ファンド a bargain stock fund; an undervalued fund. 割安感 a sense that something is「inexpensive [cheap]. ▶国内旅行は, 宿泊料金の値下がりで～感が出てきたため, 復調の兆しが見え始めている. Domestic travel is beginning to show signs of recovery because lower hotel charges have made it seem less expensive. / 最近の電力株は～感がある. Shares in electronic power seem to be a bargain recently.

**ワルカ**〔イラク南部の村〕Warka.

「**ワルキューレの騎行**」〔ワーグナーの歌劇中の一曲〕the Ride of the Valkyries.

**ワルソーじょうやく**【-条約】〔航空運輸〕the Warsaw Convention; 〔正式名称〕the Convention for the Unification of Certain Rules Relating to International Carriage by Air.

**ワルダク** =ワルダック.

**ワルダック**〔アフガニスタン中部の州〕Wardak.

**ワルベルク** Wallberg, Heinz (1923–2004; ドイツの音楽指揮者).

**われまどりろん**【割れ窓理論】〔割れた窓ガラスを放置しておくと次々と他の窓ガラスが割られ, 建物全体が崩壊するという理論〕the Broken-Window(s) Theory.

**われわれ**【我々】 ◫ われわれ意識〔社会〕(a) "we-consciousness." われわれ感情〔社会〕(a) "we-feeling."

**ワンぎり**【-切り】〔電話をかけて 1 コールで切ること〕a one-ring hang-up call; 〔それを用いた犯罪〕a one-ring call-back scam.

**ワンぎりぼうしほう**【-切り防止法】〔法〕the Law Against One-Ring Hang-up Calls.

**ワンクリック**【電算】〔クリック 1 回〕one click. ～する click once《on a link》. ◫ ワンクリック詐欺〔詐欺サイトにつなげようとするアドレスをクリックさせ, 架空の利用料金を支払わせようとする詐欺〕a "one-click" scam; a fraud in which victims who click on online links are deceived into paying for services they have not requested. ワンクリック(詐欺)サイト a "one-click" scam site. ワンクリック特許 a one-click patent; a patent for a one-click purchasing method. ワンクリック募金〔クリックによる募金⇒クリック〕. ワンクリック(料金)請求 =ワンクリック詐欺.

**ワンコイン** one coin; a single coin. ▶500 円均一のお弁当は～で買える手軽さが受けて人気だ. 500-yen fixed-price lunch-boxes are popular because they are easy to buy with a single coin. ◫ ワンコイン・バス a 100-yen flat-rate bus.

**わんさ**〔わんさガールの略; 端役の女優や踊り子〕female extras.

「**ワンス・アンド・フォーエバー**」〔映画〕We Were Soldiers.

**ワンスルー**〔原子力〕〔使用済み核燃料を再処理・再利用せずに最終処分する方式〕a once-through system.

**ワンストップ** ◫ ワンストップ・サービスセンター =ジョブカフェ. ワンストップ・ショップ〔多様な商品やサービスを揃えた総合店舗など〕a one-stop shop. ワンストップ・ソリューション〔多種多様なサービスを一括して提供するシステム〕a one-stop solution.

**ワン・スルー**〔ウランなどの資源を 1 回だけの使用ののちに廃棄すること〕a one-through「system [(fuel) cycle]; the one-through use《of uranium fuel》.

**ワンセグ** =ワンセグメントほうそう.

**ワンセグほうそう**【1 -放送】=ワンセグメントほうそう.

**ワンセグメントほうそう**【1 -放送】〔地上デジタル放送を利用して携帯電話などの移動体に向けて行われる放送〕one-segment broadcasting.

「**ワンダー・ボーイズ**」〔映画〕Wonder Boys.

「**ワンダーランド駅で**」〔映画〕Next Stop Wonderland.

**ワンタッチ** ◫ ワンタッチ・プレー〔サッカー〕one-touch play.

**ワンダリング**〔自動車〕〔車体がふらつくこと〕wandering; wander.

**ワンチャンス** one chance; the only「chance [opportunity]. ▶～をものにする seize *one's* only「chance [opportunity]. ▶人生は～だ. You get only one chance in life.

**ワンチュク** 1 Wangchuk, Jigme Khesar Namgyal (1980–; ブータンの国王〔2006– ; 2 の子〕. 2 Wangchuk, Jigme Singye (1955– ; ブータンの国王〔1972–2006〕).

**ワンツー** =ワンツー・フィニッシュ a one-two finish. ▶マラソンで日本勢が～フィニッシュを飾った. Japanese runners「finished one-two [grabbed the top two spots] in the marathon.

**ワン・ツー・ワン・マーケティング**〔消費者ひとりひとりに合わせて個別に展開される販売活動〕one-to-one marketing.

**ワントップ**〔サッカー〕〔前線にフォワード 1 人を配置する攻撃態勢〕a「one-forward [one-striker] attack [formation].

「**わんぱくデニス**」〔米国の TV ホームコメディー; 原作は漫画〕Dennis the Menace.

「**わんぱくフリッパー**」〔米国の, イルカと少年たちの TV ドラマ〕Flipper.

**ワンハンドフード**〔片手に持って気軽に食べられる食品〕one-handed food.

**ワンプライス・ショップ**〔100 円ショップのように全商品が同一価格の店〕a one-price store.

**ワンプライスはんばい**【-販売】〔新車販売で, 値引きをしない販売方法〕one-price selling; fixed-price selling.

**ワンフロア**〔1 つの階〕one floor; a single floor. ▶ホテルの～を借り切る rent an entire floor at a hotel.

**ワンマン** ◫ ワンマン運転〔バス・電車などの〕one-man「operation [operating].

**ワンミン**【網民】〔中国で, インターネット利用者〕a Chinese Internet user.

**ワン・ワールド**〔空〕〔世界的な航空企業連合の 1 つ〕one-world.

# ん

**ンゲマ** Nguema Mbasogo, Teodoro Obiang (1942– ; 赤道ギニアの政治家; 大統領〔1979– 〕).

**ンゴロンゴロ**〔タンザニア北部の巨大クレーター〕Ngorongoro. ◫ ンゴロンゴロ自然保護区 (the) Ngorongoro Conservation Area.

## 付属 CD-ROM について

■ 付属の CD-ROM を利用して，登録サイトにアクセスし，シリアル番号をご登録いただくことで，「研究社オンラインディクショナリー (KOD)」を無料でご利用いただけるようになります．個人情報の登録は不要です．
1. 有効期間は，登録後，登録月をのぞく 90 日間です．
2. KOD に同時にログイン（＝アクセス）できる数は 1 です．1 回のログインは，手動でのログアウトを行なわない限り，無操作の状態が 1 時間に達するまで継続します．
3. ご利用いただける辞典は，KOD に搭載されている全 15 辞典です．(2008 年 7 月現在；一部特別な契約が必要な辞典は対象外となります)
4. 以下の手順にしたがって作成した「お気に入り」あるいは「ブックマーク」からアクセスしていただくことで，通常必要な ID，パスワードの入力なしで，KOD にログインし，機能を利用することができます．
   ※ 本 CD-ROM を用いた登録は，個人情報をお預かりしない方式のため，ID，パスワードは発行いたしません．
5. 本 CD-ROM による登録は，本書をご購入されたお客様ご自身が使用される場合に限り，複数のコンピューターで行なっていただくことができます．その際の有効期間は初回の登録時が基準となります．同時ログイン数は 1 で変わりありませんので，複数のコンピューター（またはブラウザ）から同時にアクセスすることはできません．

■ 本 CD-ROM, 登録サイト，KOD をご利用いただくには以下が必要です．
1. 使用許諾契約書にご同意ください．
2. CD-ROM 本体と同封のシリアル番号．
3. CD ドライブつきで，インターネットに接続可能なコンピューター．
4. 「インターネットエクスプローラ」などのインターネットブラウザ．
5. インターネットブラウザで JavaScript および SSL が有効に設定されていて，Cookie の上書きが許可されていること．

## 付属 CD-ROM を利用した登録の仕方

1. コンピューターに CD-ROM をセットし，Windows ならエクスプローラまたはマイコンピューター，Mac OS X ならデスクトップあるいは Finder から CD-ROM を開きます．
   ※ Windows の場合にはオートランの設定が有効であれば CD-ROM を挿入すると，自動的にファイルが開きます．

2. CD-ROM 内にある KOD.html というファイルをダブルクリックします．既定のブラウザが開き，「KOD アソシエイトパッケージ」というページが表示されますので，「登録はこちらから」とある画像をクリックしてください．
3. 「アソシエイト会員登録手続き ― ご利用約款への同意」のページにジャンプします．会員規約をお読みいただき，ページの一番下にある「同意する」を押すと次の手続きへ進みます．
4. 続いて開いたページで，お手許のシリアル番号を入力してください．入力後「決定」を押すと登録が完了し，「お気に入り」または「ブックマーク」作成用のページに移動します．
5. 「お気に入り」「ブックマーク」の作成・登録はご利用のブラウザによって方法が異なりますので以下をご注意ください．

 (**1**) Internet Explorer (Windows) の場合．
  ※ Macintosh は，下の (3) の方法をご利用ください．
 「登録方法 1」の「お気に入りに登録」ボタンを押し，「お気に入りの追加」の窓が出たら「OK」を押してください．

 (**2**) FireFox の場合．
  ※ FireFox では下の (3) の方法も利用できます．
 「登録方法 2」の「ブックマークに登録」ボタンを押し，「ブックマークに追加」の窓が出たら「追加」を押してください．このあと以下の操作を行なってください．
  ◆メニューのブックマークをクリック．
  ◆ブックマークのリストから「研究社 Online Dictionary」にマウスを当てて右クリック (Mac の場合 Ctrl+クリック) し，出てきたメニューから「プロパティ」を選択．
  ◆下の窓が出たら「このブックマークはサイドバーに読み込む」の横のチェックをはずす．
  ◆最後に「変更を保存」を押すと，完了します．

 (**3**) その他のブラウザ (Opera, Safari など) の場合．
 「登録方法 3」の最後に赤字で「右のリンクを登録してください」とある横の [**研究社 Online Dictionary**] にマウスを当てて，右クリック (Macintosh の場合 Ctrl+クリック) し，ブックマークに追加してください．
  ◆Opera の場合：「ブックマークに追加」を選択．
  ◆Safari の場合：「リンク先をブックマークに追加」を選択．
  ◆FireFox の場合：「ブックマークに追加」を選択．
  ◆Internet Explorer (Macintosh) の場合：「リンク先をブックマークに追加」を選択．

## 付属 CD-ROM 使用許諾契約書

付属 CD-ROM をご使用になる前に，以下をよくお読みいただき，内容を十分ご確認ください．

本使用許諾契約（以下「本契約」といいます）は，株式会社研究社（以下「弊社」といいます）発行の『新和英大辞典・プラス』に付属する CD-ROM（以下「本製品」といいます）に関し，本製品をご使用いただくお客様と弊社との間で締結される契約です．お客様は本契約にご同意いただいた場合のみ本製品を使用することができます．このお客様の同意をもって，本契約は成立し，効力を生じます．

第 1 条　（使用条件）
1. 本製品を使用して KOD にご登録されたお客様は「アソシエイト会員」として登録され，KOD へのアクセス権を取得します．「アソシエイト会員」とは個人情報等を登録することなく KOD を利用できる会員種別です．
2. アクセス権の有効期間は，登録を行ったその月を除く 90 日間です．登録後の利用頻度にはよりません．
3. KOD 利用の際の同時ログイン数（＝同時アクセス数）は 1 とします．1 回のログインは，手動でのログアウトを行わない限り，無操作の状態が 1 時間に達するまで継続します．
4. 本製品またはそれによって得たアクセス権は，本書籍を購入されたお客様ご自身のみが使用することができます．
5. 本製品またはそれによって得たアクセス権は，お客様ご自身がおひとりで使用される場合に限り，複数のコンピューター，ブラウザ上で使用できます．この形態で使用を行うには登録を複数回行う必要がありますが，これに際しての前 2 項，前 3 項の扱いは以下のようになります．
(1) 有効期間は初回の登録時が基準となります．
(2) KOD への同時アクセス数は 1 のままとなります．

第 2 条　（禁止事項）
お客様は，弊社の許諾がある場合を除き，以下の行為をしないものとします．
(1) 本製品またはそれによって得たアクセス権を，複製，配布，販売，譲渡，貸与したり，また第三者に有償で使用させたりすること
(2) 上記のほか，弊社ないし第三者の信用を毀損し，あるいは損害をもたらす行為をすること

第 3 条　（保証範囲及び免責事項）
1. 弊社は，お客様及びその他の第三者に対して，本製品に関連して直接的または間接的に生じる損害または損失について，いかなる場合も一切の責任を負わず，かつお客様はこれに対して弊社を免責するものとします．いかなる場合も，本契約に基づく弊社の責任は，お客様が支払った本製品の購入金額を限度とします．
2. 弊社が不可抗力により KOD のサービスの提供を継続することが不可能となり，本書籍のご購入時にすでにサービスの提供が中止されている場合であっても，これを理由とした返品，返金等の補償は行わないものとします．

第 4 条　（裁判管轄，準拠法）
1. 本契約に関して当事者間に紛争が生じた場合には，東京地方裁判所を第一審の専属管轄裁判所とします．
2. 本契約は日本法に準ずるものとします．

# Kenkyusha's New Japanese-English Dictionary PLUS
# 新和英大辞典・プラス

初版　第1刷　2008年7月

---

編者
渡邉敏郎　　Stephen Boyd

発行者
関戸雅男

発行所
株式会社　研　究　社

〒102-8152　東京都千代田区富士見 2-11-3
電話　営業 03-3288-7777　編集 03-3288-7711
振替　00150-9-26710
http://www.kenkyusha.co.jp/

印刷所
研究社印刷株式会社

装丁
目崎智子

© Kenkyusha Co., Ltd. 2008

ISBN978-4-7674-2027-1　C0582　Printed in Japan